the Next EXIT®

Congratulations...

on your purchase of the 2010 edition of the
most complete
interstate highway services guide ever printed! ®

the Next EXIT®

will save time, money and frustration.
This travel tool will help you find services along the
USA Interstate Highways
like nothing you have ever used.

PO Box 888
Garden City, UT 84028

www.theNextEXIT.com

Olympia
WASHINGTON
Salem
OREGON
MONTANA
Helena
IDAHO
Boise
NORTH DAKOTA
Bismarck
MINNESOTA
WISCONSIN
Pierre
SOUTH DAKOTA
St. Paul
WYOMING
NEBRASKA
Carson City
Sacramento
NEVADA
Salt Lake City
Cheyenne
Des Moines
Madison
Lansing
MICHIGAN
IOWA
ILLINOIS
INDIANA
Lincoln
Denver
UTAH
CALIFORNIA
Topeka
KC
Springfield
Indianapolis
Columbus
OHIO
COLORADO
KANSAS
Jefferson City
MISSOURI
Frankfort
KENTUCKY
WEST VIRGINIA
ARIZONA
Santa Fe
Oklahoma City
Nashville
TENNESSEE
ARKANSAS
NEW MEXICO
Phoenix
San Diego
OKLAHOMA
Little Rock
Atlanta
MISSISSIPPI
LOUISIANA
Montgomery
GEORGIA
Jackson
ALABAMA
TEXAS
Austin
Baton Rouge
Tallahassee
FLORIDA
MAINE
Augusta
VERMONT
Montpelier
Concord
NEW YORK
NEW HAMPSHIRE
Albany
Boston
MASSACHUSETTS
Hartford
Providence
PENNSYLVANIA
Trenton
NEW JERSEY
Harrisburg
Dover
Annapolis
DELAWARE
MARYLAND
Charleston
Richmond
VIRGINIA
Raleigh
NORTH CAROLINA
SOUTH CAROLINA
Columbia

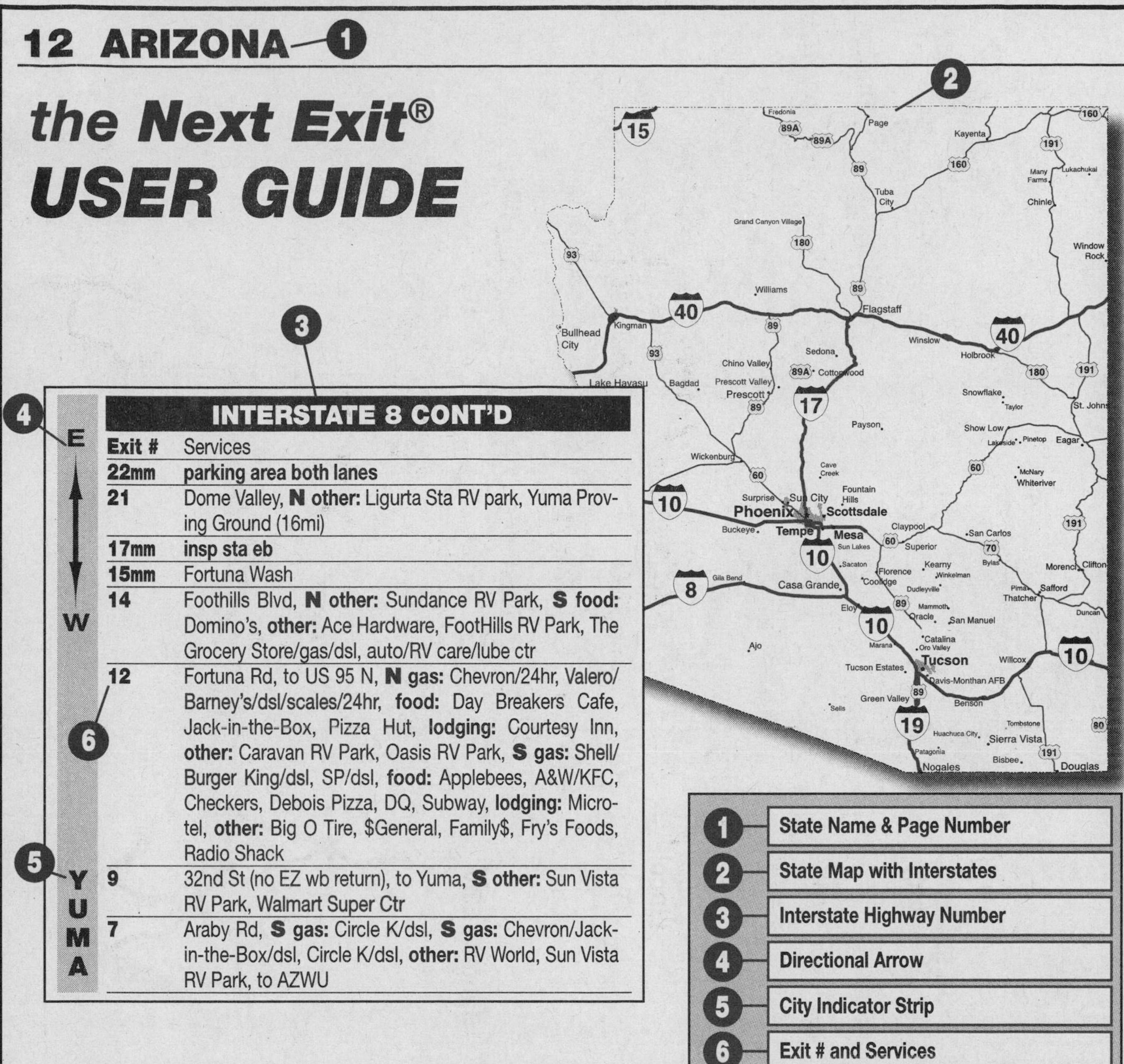

the Next Exit® USER GUIDE

INTERSTATE 8 CONT'D

E ↕ W

Exit #	Services
22mm	**parking area both lanes**
21	Dome Valley, **N other:** Ligurta Sta RV park, Yuma Proving Ground (16mi)
17mm	**insp sta eb**
15mm	Fortuna Wash
14	Foothills Blvd, **N other:** Sundance RV Park, **S food:** Domino's, **other:** Ace Hardware, FootHills RV Park, The Grocery Store/gas/dsl, auto/RV care/lube ctr
12	Fortuna Rd, to US 95 N, **N gas:** Chevron/24hr, Valero/Barney's/dsl/scales/24hr, **food:** Day Breakers Cafe, Jack-in-the-Box, Pizza Hut, **lodging:** Courtesy Inn, **other:** Caravan RV Park, Oasis RV Park, **S gas:** Shell/Burger King/dsl, SP/dsl, **food:** Applebees, A&W/KFC, Checkers, Debois Pizza, DQ, Subway, **lodging:** Microtel, **other:** Big O Tire, $General, Family$, Fry's Foods, Radio Shack
9	32nd St (no EZ wb return), to Yuma, **S other:** Sun Vista RV Park, Walmart Super Ctr
7	Araby Rd, **S gas:** Circle K/dsl, **S gas:** Chevron/Jack-in-the-Box/dsl, Circle K/dsl, **other:** RV World, Sun Vista RV Park, to AZWU

YUMA

1. State Name & Page Number
2. State Map with Interstates
3. Interstate Highway Number
4. Directional Arrow
5. City Indicator Strip
6. Exit # and Services

Exit

Most states number exits by the nearest mile marker(mm). A few states use consecutive numbers, in which case mile markers are given in ( ). Mile markers are the little green vertical signs beside the interstate at one mile intervals which indicate distance from the southern or western border of a state. Odd numbered interstates run north/south, even numbered run east/west.

Services

Services are listed alphabetically by category...**gas, food, lodging, other** services including camping. "H" indicates an exit from which a hospital may be accessed, but it may not be close to the exit. Services located away from the exit may be referred to by "access to," or "to...," and a distance may be given. A directional notation is also given, such as **N**, **S**, **E** or **W**

Directional Arrows

Follow exits DOWN the page if traveling from North to South or East to West, UP the page if traveling South to North or West to East.

Additional copies may be ordered by using the form supplied in the back of this book, or by visiting online at: ***www.theNextExit.com***
the Next EXIT, inc. makes no warranty regarding the accuracy of the information contained in this publication. This information is subject to change without notice.

TABLE OF CONTENTS

Abbreviations & Symbols used in *the Next EXIT*®

AFB .... Air Force Base	NP .... National Park
B&B .... Bed&Breakfast	NRA .... Nat Rec Area
Bfd .... Battlefield	pk .... park
Ctr .... Center	pkwy.... parkway
Coll .... College	rest. .... restaurant
Cyn .... canyon	nb .... northbound
dsl .... diesel	sb .... southbound
$ .... Dollar	eb .... eastbound
Mem.... Memorial	wb .... westbound
Mkt .... Market	SP .... state park
Mtn .... Mountain	SF .... state forest
mm .... mile marker	Sprs .... springs
N .... north side of exit	st .... street, state
S .... south side of exit	sta .... station
E .... east side of exit	TPK .... Turnpike
W .... west side of exit	USPO... Post Office
NM .... National Monument	vet .... veterinarian
NHS .... Nat Hist Site	whse.... warehouse
NWR.... Nat Wildlife Reserve	@ .... truckstop (full service)
NF .... National Forest	red print. RV accessible
H .... Hospital	♿ .... Handicapped accessible
✈ .... Airport	☎ .... Telephone
⛱ .... Picnic Tables	

For Trans Canada Highway (TCH) information and more, please visit us on the web at ***www.thenextexit.com***

TABLE OF CONTENTS

The Road to Bethune

by Mark Watson - Winter 2010

The interstate highways originated to help travelers avoid obstacles such as rivers, swamps and crossroads. Concrete and steel bridges allow travel to be virtually unstoppable, barring construction or misfortune, and you may exit when you like. What if life was that way? What if you could get from here to anywhere non-stop, with no brief barrier to require reflection on where you had been and where you were going? Just as important, what if you never had to figure out how to negotiate the cross traffic?

Last summer our daughter and her husband loaded up a moving van and headed east for graduate school. Never having lived very far away from home, they displayed a hint of apprehension as their departure neared. Their farewells were brief and no backward glances encumbered their resolve. We detected an attitude of 'we are going to do this!' that folks must adopt if they intend to succeed. We understood. There comes a time in everyone's experience when, while stopped and watching the oncoming traffic, several things come to light: turning right or left will not get you where you want to go, and turning around is something you simply cannot do. There is only one option, and that is to continue forward. For us, that moment occurred when we crossed the road to Bethune.

In the spring of 1971, the Vietnam War ended for Debby and me. A grateful nation flew me home to South Carolina for 30 days of leave to be reunited with family and friends. While I had been off wading through rice paddies and hacking through the jungle, Debby had given birth to our first son and was staying with her parents, a manageable if not ideal arrangement. They lived with each other while I lived with the second platoon. After I came home, we partied, entertained, went to the beach and enjoyed the blessings of liberty in the USA. Mostly, we acquainted ourselves with the reality that there were now three of us. Learning to be the adult in a family takes time, so we spent much of that homecoming month easing into that role, living in someone else's home, eating meals prepared by them and putting off any major decisions that would affect our future. We were twenty.

We left well before the thorns began to show, courtesy of the US Army's requirement that I serve in Kansas for another six months. One morning we stowed all our possessions in

the corner of a small trailer, filled the Falcon station wagon with our son and his equipment, said goodbye and headed west, out of town. Turning left on the old two lane road, Debby asked in bright-eyed innocence, "So, how do we get to Kansas?" Much of the next 15 miles was occupied with my reassurances that of course we could find our way to Kansas and if we really needed to eat or stay in a motel sometime during the trip we could do that as well. Oh and by the way, it shouldn't take too long to actually find a place to live once we got there. We drove through the Lynches River swamp, slowed for the approaching stop sign, rolled to a halt, and sat there in silence. To the right a few miles lay the little town of Bethune and to the left a few more miles was another little town. The only direction that was of any use to us was the way the car was already pointed.

There was no one behind us and no one coming from either way as we found ourselves at that intersection absolutely, positively, and totally alone. In that instant it occurred to me that life was different for us now. No longer was either of us singly or separately able to go our own way. For better or worse we now had a family and everything that came with it. Furthermore, these other two people in the car were now looking at me and asking not only "How do we get to Kansas?" but "where are we going to get supper tonight?" In that moment I clearly understood that obtaining food, clothing, shelter, all of life's necessities, and any of the luxuries that we might eventually want, was all on me. Of a sudden, the rigors of Southeast Asia seemed to pale.

How long we sat there, I cannot say. How many ugly doubts streaked by right then, I do not remember. We had neither family nor friends toward either town, so turning would have gotten us nowhere. Everybody and everything we knew was in the rearview mirror, but we had already said goodbye. Kansas, the army, the future, and the unknown lay straight ahead on the other side of that intersection, down a two lane asphalt road, and I could only see to the first curve. After making sure the way was clear I put my foot on the gas pedal and the car rolled forward.

Nearly 40 years later we have passed that place often, taking that road on purpose though the interstate highway is faster. During this time, we have sent our own children out into the world wondering whether they were ready for the challenge. We give them advice, counsel them from experience, and pray for their success. We caution them to slow down for curves, watch for cross traffic, to drive defensively, and with courtesy. We also encourage them to stop at all intersections. There is nothing like sitting still at a crossroads to help someone see what is coming.

INTERSTATE 10

E ↕ W

Exit #	Services
66.5mm	Alabama/Florida state line
66mm	**Welcome Ctr full [handicapped] facilities, [phone], vending, [picnic], litter barrels, petwalk**
53	rd 64, Wilcox Rd, **N gas:** BP/Oasis/Stuckeys/Subway/Chester's/dsl/scales/24hr/@, **other:** Styx RV Park, fireworks, **S gas:** Chevron/dsl, Outpost/dsl, **other:** Hilltop RV Park (1.5 mi), Wilderness RV Park, fireworks
44	AL 59, Loxley, **N gas:** Loves/Arby's/dsl/scales/24hr, S **gas:** Chevron/dsl, Exxon/DQ/dsl, RaceWay, **food:** Hardee's, McDonald's, Waffle House, **lodging:** Bay Inn, Loxley Motel (3mi), WindChase Inn, **other:** to Gulf SP
38	AL 181, Malbis, **N food:** Chick-fil-A, Cracker Barrel, Logan's Roadhouse, McDonald's, Moe's SW Grill, Olive Garden, Panera Bread, Ruby Tuesday, Russo's Rest., Ryan's, Starbucks, Stix Asian, Wendy's, **lodging:** Comfort Suites, Country Inn&Suites, Holiday Inn Express, La Quinta, **other:** Barnes&Noble, Belk, Best Buy, Dillards, $Tree, Goodyear/auto, Michael's, Old Navy, PetsMart, Ross, Tuesday Morning, Walgreens, World Mkt, **S gas:** Chevron/dsl, Shell/LA Subs, Texaco/dsl, **food:** Burger King, Don Carlos, **lodging:** Malbis Motel (1mi), **other:** Honda, Lowes Whse, Sam's Club, Toyota/Scion
35	US 90, US 98, **N gas:** Shell, Summit, **food:** Beef O'Brady's, China Fun, **lodging:** Fairfield Inn, **other:** Bass Pro Shop, JC Penney, Kohl's, Rite Aid, USPO, **S gas:** Exxon/dsl, Shell, **food:** Arby's, Burger King, Checker's, Dolive Bay, Domino's, El Rancho Mexican, Firehouse Subs, Grand Buffet, Hooters, IHOP, Krystal, Longhorn Steaks, McAlister's Deli, McDonald's, O'Charley's, Papa John's, Pizza Hut, S China Rest., Starbucks, Subway, Taco Bell, Waffle House, Wendy's, Zaxby's, **lodging:** Comfort Suites, Eastern Shore Motel, Hampton Inn, Hilton Garden, Homewood Suites, Microtel, **other:** [H], BooksAMillion, GNC, Home Depot, Office Depot, SteinMart, TJ Maxx
30	US 90/98, Battleship Pkwy, same as 27
29mm	tunnel begins wb
28mm	tunnel begins eb
27	US 90/98, Battleship Pkwy, Gov't St, **S food:** Capt's Table Seafood, Felix's Fish Camp, Oysterella's Rest., **lodging:** Best Western, **other:** to USS Alabama
26b	Water St, Mobile, downtown, **N lodging:** Hampton Inn, Radisson, Ramada, Renaissance, to Visitors Ctr
26a	Canal St (from eb), same as 26b
25b	Virginia St, Mobile, **N gas:** Shell/dsl
25a	Texas St (from wb, no return)

MOBILE

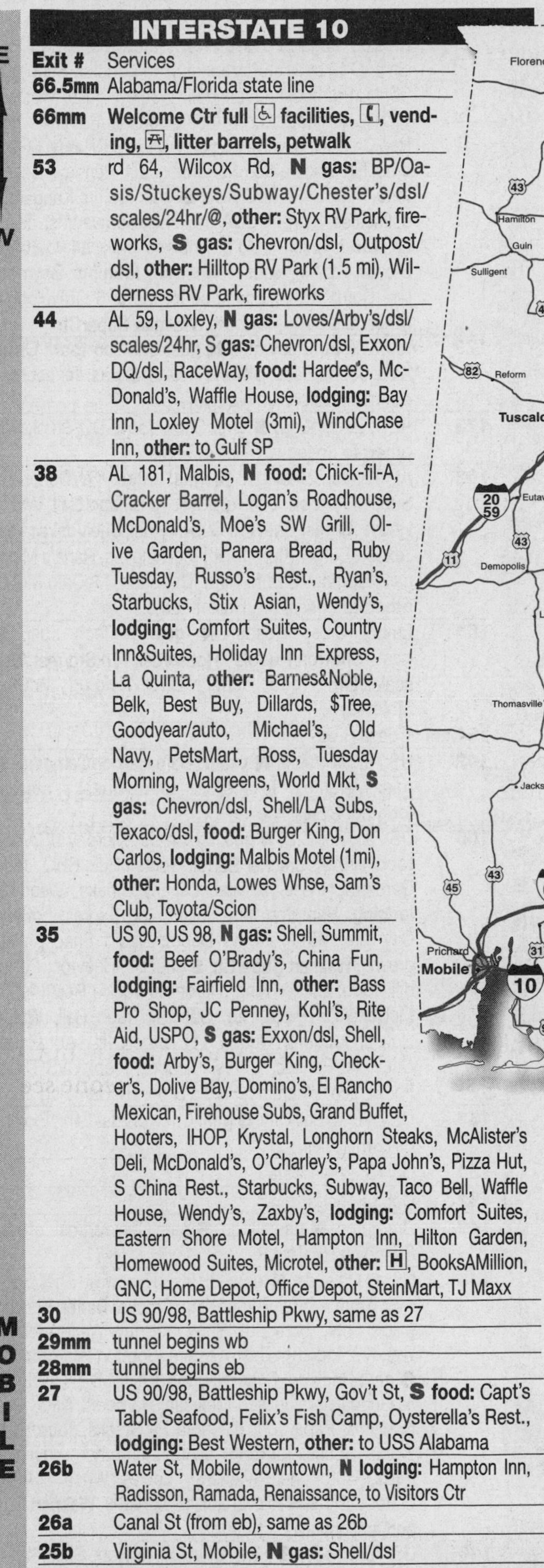

Exit #	Services
24	Broad St, to Duval St, Mobile, **N gas:** Chevron
23	Michigan Ave, **N gas:** Exxon, **other:** $General
22b a	AL 163, Dauphin Island Pkwy, **N gas:** BP, **lodging:** Port City Inn, **other:** Family$, **S gas:** Circle K/dsl, Exxon/Subway/24hr, Shell/dsl, **food:** Checker's, Gone Fishin Rest., Kim's Palace, Waffle House, **other:** $General
20	I-65 N, to Montgomery
17	AL 193, Tillmans Corner, to Dauphin Island, **N gas:** Chevron/24hr, **food:** Boiling Pot, Firehouse Subs, Golden Corral, IHOP, Ruby Tuesday, Ryan's, Zaxby's, other: [H], Big 10 Tire, Deep South RV Ctr, Lowes Whse, Radio Shack, Walmart SuperCtr/Subway
15b a	US 90, Tillmans Corner, to Mobile, **N gas:** Chevron/24hr, RaceWay, Shell, **food:** Arby's, Azteca's Mexican, Burger King, Checker's, CiCi's, Domino's, El Toro Mexican, Hooters, KFC, King's Super Buffet, McDonald's, Papa John's, Pizza Hut, Popeye's, Russell's BBQ, Sonny's BBQ, Subway, Taco Bell, Waffle House, **lodging:** Baymont
	US 90, Tillmans Corner, to Mobile, **N gas:** Inn, Best Value Inn, Comfort Suites, Day's Inn, Econolodge, Hampton Inn, Holiday Inn, InTown Suites, La Quinta, Motel 6, Quality Inn, Red Roof Inn, Rodeway Inn, Super 8, Wingate Inn, **other:** AutoZone, Big Lots,

INTERSTATE 10 CONT'D

Exit #	Services
15b a	Continued $General, $Tree, Family$, Firestone/auto, Mike's Transmissions, O'Reilly Parts, Rite Aid, Sears Essentials, Walgreens, Winn-Dixie, Vet, **S gas:** Chevron/24hr, RaceWay/dsl, Shell/dsl/24hr, **food:** Hardee's, JP's Southern Heritage Rest., Waffle House, **other:** B&R RV Ctr, Johnnys RV Ctr, Peterbilt, auto repair, tires, transmissions, USPO
13	to Theodore, **N gas:** BP, Citgo, Pilot/Wendy's/dsl/24hr, Shell/Subway, Texaco/McDonald's, **food:** Church's, Waffle House, **other:** Advance Parts, Family$, Food World, Greyhound Prk, Johnny's RV Resort, Rite Aid, **S gas:** Chevron/dsl, **other:** I-10 Kamping, Paynes RV Park (4mi), Bellingraf Gardens
10	rd 39, Bayou La Batre, Dawes, **N other:** Kenworth/Volvo
4	AL 188 E, to Grand Bay, **N gas:** Energize/Blimpie, Shell/Stuckey's/Subway, TA/BP/Buckhorn Rest./dsl/scales/24hr/@, Texaco/dsl, **food:** Arby's, McDonald's, Waffle House, **S gas:** Chevron/24hr, **food:** Hardee's, other: Trav-L-Kamp
1mm	**Welcome Ctr eb, full ♿ facilities, info, ☎, picnic, litter barrels, petwalk, RV dump**
0mm	Alabama/Mississippi state line

INTERSTATE 20

Exit #	Services
215mm	Alabama/Georgia state line, Central/Eastern time zone
213mm	**Welcome Ctr wb, full ♿ facilities, info, ☎, vending, picnic, litter barrels, petwalk, RV dump, 24hr security**
210	AL 49, Abernathy, **N** fireworks, **S** fireworks
209mm	Tallapoosa River
208mm	**weigh sta wb**
205	AL 46, to Heflin, **N gas:** BP/dsl/rest., **food:** 205 Cafe, **other:** RV Camping, tires, **S gas:** Shell/dsl/24hr, **other:** Truck Repair
199	AL 9, Heflin, **N gas:** Texaco/Subway/dsl/24hr, **food:** Hardee's, Pop's Charburgers, **lodging:** Howard Johnson, **other:** Ford, USPO, **S gas:** Chevron, SuperMart, **food:** Huddle House
198mm	Talladega Nat Forest eastern boundary
191	US 431, to US 78
188	to US 78, to Anniston, **N gas:** Shell/KFC, Texaco/Subway, **food:** Cracker Barrel, IHOP, LoneStar Steaks, Los Mexicano, Sonny's BBQ, Waffle House, Wendy's, Zaxby's, **lodging:** Country Inn&Suites, Hampton Inn, Holiday Inn Express, Jameson Inn, Sleep Inn, Wingate Inn, **other:** Camping World RV Ctr, Harley-Davidson, Honda, Lowes Whse, Nissan, O'Reilly Parts, **S food:** Arby's, Longhorn Steaks, Mexico Lindo Grill, Olive Garden, **other:**Best Buy, Home Depot, Kohl's, Old Navy, PetsMart, Ross, Target, TJ Maxx
185	AL 21, to Anniston, **N gas:** BP/dsl, Chevron/24hr, Shell, **food:** Applebee's, Arby's, Burger King, Capt D's, CiCi's, China Luck, Domino's, Garfield's Rest., HappyStar Buffet, Hardee's, Jack's Rest.,
185	Continued Krystal, Logan's Roadhouse, McAlister's, McDonald's, O'Charley's, Pizza Hut, Red Lobster, Shoney's, Sonic, Starbucks, Taco Bell, Waffle House, Western Sizzlin, **lodging:** Day's Inn, Liberty Inn, Oxford Inn, Red Carpet Inn, **other:** BooksAMillion, Dillards, $General, Firestone/auto, FoodMax, JC Penney, Sears/auto, mall, to Ft McClellan, **S gas:** Exxon, Kangaroo/dsl/scales, Murphy USA/dsl, Shell/Subway/dsl, Texaco, **food:** Chick-fil-A, El Poblano Mexican, Outback Steaks, Waffle House, Wendy's, **lodging:** Baymont Inn, Comfort Inn, Econolodge, Motel 6, Travelodge, **other:** [H], Goodyear/auto, Walmart SuperCtr
179	to Munford, Coldwater, **N gas:** Chevron **food:** China King, Jack's Rest., **other:** Rite Aid, **S gas:** Texaco/dsl, **other:** Anniston Army Depot
173	AL 5, Eastaboga, **S gas:** Shell, **food:** DQ/Stuckey's, **other:** to Speedway/Hall of Fame
168	AL 77, to Talladega, **N gas:** Citgo, QV/Domino's, Super 77, **food:** Jack's Rest., KFC/Taco Bell, Waffle House, **S gas:** Chevron/Subway/dsl, Shell/dsl/scales, Texaco/Burger King, **food:** McDonald's, Rana's Mexican, **lodging:** Comfort Inn, Day's Inn, McCaig Motel, **other:** to Speedway, Hall of Fame
165	Embry Cross Roads, **N gas:** Hi-Tech Fuel, **S gas:** Chevron/Huddle House/dsl, TrkStp/rest./dsl/scales/24hr, **food:** Carter's BBQ, **lodging:** McCaig Motel/rest.
164mm	Coosa River
162	US 78, Riverside, **N other:** Safe Harbor Camping, **S gas:** Marathon, Texaco/dsl, **food:** Budsy's Steaks, **lodging:** Best Value Inn
158	US 231, Pell City, **N gas:** Exxon/dsl, Murphy USA/dsl, **food:** Arby's, Cracker Barrel, Golden Rule BBQ, Jade Garden Chinese, Krystal, Legacy Steaks, Wendy's, **lodging:** Hampton Inn, Holiday Inn Express, **other:** City Tire, $Tree, Home Depot, Radio Shack, Walgreens, Walmart SuperCtr, **S gas:** BP, Chevron, Putts/dsl, **food:** Burger King, Hardee's, Jack's Rest., KFC, McDonald's, Pizza Hut, Subway, Taco Bell, Waffle House, **lodging:** Quality Inn, **other:** [H], AutoZone, Chevrolet/Pontiac, Chrysler/Dodge/Jeep, CVS Drug, Ford/Lincoln/Mercury, Fred's Drug, RV Camping
156	US 78 E, to Pell City, **S gas:** Chevron/dsl/24hr, Exxon/dsl/24hr, Shell
153	US 78, Chula Vista
152	Cook Springs
147	Brompton, **N gas:** Citgo, **S gas:** Chevron/dsl, **other:** Suncoast RV Ctr/LP
144	US 411, Leeds, **N gas:** BP/dsl, Raceway, Shell/Subway, **food:** Arby's, Burger King, Cracker Barrel, Krystal, Milo's Café, Pizza Hut, Ruby Tuesday, Waffle House, Wendy's, **lodging:** Best Western, Comfort Inn, **other:** **S gas:** Chevron, RaceWay, **food:** Capt D's, Chick-fil-A, Guadalajara Jalisco Mexican, Hardee's, KFC, McDonald's, Papa John's, Santa Fe Steaks, Taco Bell, Waffle House, **lodging:** Day's Inn, other: Advance Parts, AutoZone, $General, Lowes Whse, NAPA, O'Reilly Parts, Radio Shack, Walgreens, Walmart SuperCtr/Subway
140	US 78, Leeds, **S gas:** Chevron, Exxon, Shell (1mi), **lodging:** Best Value Inn, **other:** Bass Pro Shop

INTERSTATE 20 CONT'D

E ↕ W

Exit #	Services
139mm	Cahaba River
136	I-459 S, to Montgomery, Tuscaloosa
135	US 78, Old Leeds Rd, **N other:** B'ham Racetrack
133	US 78, to Kilgore Memorial Dr, (wb return at 132), **N gas:** Chevron, Exxon/dsl/24hr, **food:** Golden Rule BBQ, Hamburger Heaven, Jack's Rest., Krystal, Waffle House, **lodging:** Comfort Inn, Eastwood Hotel, Siesta, same as 132, **S gas:** BP, **food:** Arby's, China Buffet, El Mexicano, Gus' Hotdogs, McDonald's, Subway, **lodging:** Best Western, Hampton Inn, Holiday Inn Express, Quality Inn, **other:** $Tree, Ford, Graham Tire, Sam's Club/gas, **Walmart**
132b a	US 78, Crestwood Blvd, **N gas:** Exxon, **food:** Barnhill's Buffet, Krystal, Villa Fiesta, Waffle House, **other:** Chevrolet, O'Reilly Parts, SuperPetz, **S gas:** BP, Crown/24hr, Shell/24hr, **food:** Arby's, Capt D's, China Garden, Denny's, Emperor House, Hooters, IHOP, KFC, LJ Silver/Taco Bell, Logan's Roadhouse, McDonald's, New China Buffet, Olive Garden, Pizza Hut, Red Lobster, Ryan's, Wendy's, **lodging:** Comfort Inn, Delux Inn, Economy Lodge, Park Inn, USA Lodge, **other:** H, Home Depot, K-Mart, Office Depot, Radio Shack, Sears/auto, TJ Maxx, Waldenbooks, mall
130b	US 11, 1st Ave, **N gas:** BP, Chevron/24hr, Conoco/dsl, Crown, **lodging:** Bama Motel, **other:** AutoZone, Southern Foods, **S food:** McDonald's, Pacific Seafood, **lodging:** Relax Inn, Sky Inn
130a	I-59 N, to Gadsden
I-59 S and I-20 W run together from B'ham to Meridian, MS	
129	Airport Blvd, **N lodging:** Sheraton, **other:** ✈, **S gas:** BP, Shell, **food:** Hardee's, Mexican Rest., **lodging:** Best Inn, Holiday Inn
128	AL 79, Tallapoosa St, **N gas:** **Kangaroo/Subway/dsl**, Exxon/dsl
126b	31st St, **N gas:** Citgo, Shell, **food:** McDonald's
126a	US 31, US 280, 26th St, Carraway Blvd, **N gas:** Phillips 66, **food:** Church's, KFC, Rally's
125b	22nd St, **N lodging:** Sheraton
125a	17th St, Civic Ctr
124b a	I-65, S to Montgomery, N to Nashville
123	US 78, Arkadelphia Rd, **N gas:** Chevron/24hr, Jet-Pep, **Pilot/Wendy's/dsl/24hr**, Shell, **food:** Popeye's, **lodging:** Day's Inn, **other:** transmissions, **S other:** H, to Legion Field
121	Bush Blvd (from wb, no return), Ensley, **N gas:** BP, Exxon, **food:** Wings&Waffles
120	AL 269, 20th St, Ensley Ave, **N food:** KFC, **other:** GMC/Pontiac, Breeze RV, **S gas:** BP, **other:** H, Chevrolet, Chrysler/Jeep, Hyundai, Toyota
119b	Ave I (from wb)
119a	Scrushy Pkwy, Gary Ave, **N gas:** BP, Chevron/dsl, **food:** Burger King, Fairfield Seafood, McDonald's, Seafood Express, Subway, Taco Bell, **other:** Family$, Food Fair, **S gas:** Mobil, Texaco, **food:** Omelet Shoppe, **other:** H
118	AL 56, Valley Rd, Fairfield, **N** other: NAPA, **S food:** Papa John's, **lodging:** Inn At Fairfield, **other:** Home Depot, Radio Shack, Sears, Winn-Dixie

BIRMINGHAM

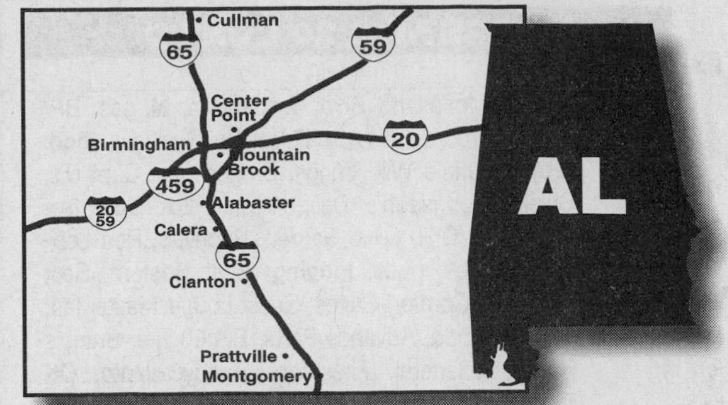

Exit #	Services
115	Allison-Bonnett Memorial Dr, **N gas:** BP/dsl, Phillips 66, RaceWay, **Shell/dsl**, **food:** Church's, Guadalajara Grill, Hardee's, Subway, **other:** Advance Parts, O'Reilly Parts
113	18th Ave, to Hueytown, **S gas:** **Chevron/dsl**, **food:** McDonald's
112	18th St, 19th St, Bessemer, **N gas:** Citgo, RaceWay, Shell, **food:** Jack's Rest., **other:** OK Tire/repair, **S gas:** Chevron, **food:** Arby's, Burger King, Krystal, McDonald's, **other:** Lowe's Whse
110	AL Adventure Pkwy
108	US 11, AL 5 N, Academy Dr, **N gas:** Exxon, **food:** Applebee's, **Cracker Barrel**, Golden Rule BBQ, Santa Fe Steaks, Waffle House, **lodging:** Best Western, Comfort Inn, Country Inn&Suites, Courtyard, Fairfield Inn, Holiday Inn Express, Jameson Inn, **other:** Chevrolet, Chrysler/Jeep/Dodge, **S gas:** BP, Citgo/Church's/dsl, **food:** Burger King, Little Caesar's, McDonald's, Milo's Burgers, Ruby Tuesday, Sonic, Wendy's, Zaxby's, **lodging:** Days Inn, Hampton Inn, Scottish Inn, **other:** H, Big 10 Tire, $Tree, Ford, Radio Shack, **Walmart SuperCtr**, Winn-Dixie, to civic ctr
106	I-459 N, to Montgomery
104	Rock Mt Lake, **S gas:** ***FLYING J*/Conoco/dsl/LP/rest./24hr**
100	to Abernant, **N gas:** Citgo, **other:** McCalla Camping, **S gas:** BP, Exxon, **Petro/Chevron/dsl/rest./scales/24hr/@**, **other:** $General, Tannehill SP (3mi)
97	US 11 S, AL 5 S, to W Blocton, **S gas:** **BP/KFC/dsl**, **Exxon/Subway/dsl**, **Shell/dsl**, **food:** Jack's Rest.
89	Mercedes Dr, **N lodging:** Baymont Inn, **S other:** Mercedes Auto Plant
86	Vance, to Brookwood, **N gas:** BP/dsl, **Shell/dsl/rest./24hr**
85mm	**rest area both lanes, full ♿ facilities, ☎, vending, picnic, litter barrels, petwalk, RV dump**
79	US 11, University Blvd, Coaling, **S gas:** Chevron/dsl
77	Cottondale, **N gas:** Chevron/McDonald's, **TA/BP/Subway/Taco Bell/dsl/@**, **Wilco/Wendy's/dsl/scales/24hr**, **food:** Arby's, Pizza Hut, Ruby Tuesday, **lodging:** Hampton Inn, Microtel, **other:** Blue Beacon, SpeedCo, USPO, **S** Chevrolet
76	US 11, E Tuscaloosa, Cottondale, **N gas:** Citgo, Exxon, Shell/dsl, **food:** Burger King, **Cracker Barrel**, Waffle House, **lodging:** Comfort Inn, Howard Johnson, Western Motel, **other:** transmissions, **S gas:** **Pilot/Subway/dsl/scales/24hr**, Texaco/dsl, **lodging:** Sleep Inn

BESSEMER

AL

INTERSTATE 20 CONT'D

E ↔ W

TUSCALOOSA

Exit #	Services
73	US 82, McFarland Blvd, Tuscaloosa, **N gas:** BP/dsl, Chevron/dsl, Exxon, RaceWay, Shell/dsl, **food:** Arby's, Buffalo Wild Wings, Burger King, Capt D's, Chick-fil-A, Jason's Deli, Krystal, Los Calientes, Moe's SW Grill, Olive Garden, Popeye's, Red Lobster, Waffle House, **lodging:** Best Western, Best Value Inn, Comfort Suites, Guest Lodge, Master Inn, **other:** Aamco, Advance Parts, Big 10 Tire, Bruno's Foods, $General, Firestone, Goodyear/auto, OK Tire, Old Navy, SteinMart, U-Haul, mall, **S gas:** Exxon, Shell, **food:** Checker's, Chili's, Grand Buffet, Guthries, Hardees, KFC, Logan's Roadhouse, McDonald's, Pizza Hut, Sonic, Subway, Taco Bell, Taco Casa, Wendy's, **lodging:** Country Inn&Suites, Days Inn, Econolodge, La Quinta, Motel 6, Quality Inn, Ramada Inn, Super 8, **other:** BooksAMillion, Chrysler/Dodge/Jeep, Dillard's, $Tree, FoodWorld, Michael's, NAPA, Office Depot, Rite Aid, Sam's Club/gas, TJ Maxx, Walmart SuperCtr
71b	I-359, Al 69 N, to Tuscaloosa, **N other:** H, U of AL, to Stillman Coll
71a	AL 69 S, to Moundville, **S gas:** Chevron, MapCo, Parade, Shell/dsl, **food:** Arby's, Hooters, IHOP, LoneStar Steaks, OutBack Steaks, Pizza Hut, Ryan's, Waffle House, Wendy's, Zaxby's, **lodging:** Courtyard, Fairfield Inn, Hilton Garden, Jameson Inn, **other:** Advance Parts, Goodyear/auto, K-Mart, Lowes Whse, Mazda/VW, O'Reilly Parts, to Mound SM
68	Northfort-Tuscaloosa Western Bypass
64mm	Black Warrior River
62	Fosters, **N gas:** BP, Chevron/dsl
52	US 11, US 43, Knoxville, **N gas:** Exxon/dsl, **other:** Knox Hill Camping
45	AL 37, Union, **S gas:** BP/dsl/rest./24hr, Chevron/Subway, **food:** Hardee's, **other:** Greene Co Greyhound Park
40	AL 14, Eutaw, **N other:** to Tom Bevill Lock/Dam, **S gas:** BP, H
39mm	**rest area wb, full ♿ facilities, ☎, vending, picnic, litter barrels, petwalk, RV dump**
38mm	**rest area wb, full ♿ facilities, ☎, vending, picnic, litter barrels, petwalk, RV dump**
32	Boligee, **N gas:** BP/dsl/rest./24hr, **S gas:** Chevron/Subway/24hr
27mm	Tombigbee River, Tenn-Tom Waterway
23	Epes, to Gainesville
17	AL 28, Livingston, **S gas:** BP/dsl/24hr, Chevron/Subway/24hr, Shell/dsl, **food:** Burger King, Pizza Hut, **lodging:** Comfort Inn, Western Inn, **other:** repair/24hr
8	AL 17, York, **S gas:** BP/dsl/rest./scales/@, **lodging:** Day's Inn/Briar Patch Rest.
1	to US 80 E, Cuba, **N gas:** Rocking Chair Trkstp/Rest./dsl/, S **gas:** Chevron, Dixie
.5mm	**Welcome Ctr eb, full ♿ facilities, ☎, vending, picnic, litter barrels, petwalk, RV dump**
I-20 E and I-59 N run together from Meridian, MS to B'ham	
0mm	Alabama/Mississippi state line

INTERSTATE 22 (FUTURE)

E ↔ W

Exit #	Services
85	US 78 (I-22 future continues eb, local traffic only)
81	rd 45, W Jefferson
78	Dora, Sumiton
72	rd 61, Cordova
70	rd 22, Cordova, Parish
65	Bevill Ind Pkwy, Jasper, **N** H, Chevrolet, to Walker Co Lake
63	AlL 269, Jasper, Parish, **N gas:** Chevron/deli/dsl
61	AL 69, Jasper, Tuscaloosa, **N gas:** 69 Superstop (1mi)
57	AL 118 E, Jasper, **S gas:** Chevron, Exxon, **food:** BBQ
52	AL 118, Carbon Hill, **S lodging:** Shadowbrook Inn
46	rd 11, Carbon Hill, Nauvoo, **S gas:** Shell
39	AL 13, Natural Bridge, Eldridge
34	AL 233, Glen Allen, Natural Bridge
30	AL 129, Brilliant, Winfield, **S gas:** Shell/deli/dsl, Texaco/deli/dsl
26	AL 44, Brilliant, Guin, **S** H
22	rd 45
16	US 43, US 278, Hamilton, Guin, **S gas:** Shell/deli/dsl
14	Hamilton, **N gas:** Woco/dsl, **food:** Huddle House, **lodging:** Keywest Inn
11	AL 17, Hamilton, Sulligent, **N gas:** Citgo/dsl, **other:** H
7	Hamilton, Weston, **N** H
3	rd 3
0mm	Alabama/Mississippi State Line

INTERSTATE 59

N ↔ S

FT PAYNE

Exit #	Services
241.5mm	Alabama/Georgia state line, Central/Eastern time zone
241mm	**Welcome Ctr sb, full ♿ facilities, ☎, vending, picnic, litter barrels, petwalk, RV dump**
239	to US 11, Sulphur Springs Rd, **E other:** Sequoyah Caverns Camping (4mi)
231	AL 40, AL 117, Hammondville, Valley Head, **E other:** Sequoyah Caverns Camping (5mi), **W gas:** Victory Fuel
222	US 11, to Ft Payne, **E gas:** Shell, **other:** Chevrolet, **1 mi E food:** Arby's, Hardee's, Jack's Rest., KFC, Krystal, Pizza Hut, Subway, Western Sizzlin, **lodging:** Rodeway Inn, **other:** $General, Foodland/gas, **W gas:** JetPep/dsl, **food:** Waffle King
218	AL 35, Ft Payne, **E food:** Asian Palace, Capt D's, Catfish 1, Fillin Station, Golden Rule BBQ, McDonald's, New China, Papa John's, Quizno's, Taco Bell, Wendy's, Zaxby's, **other:** Advance Parts, AutoZone, Big Lots, Buick/Pontiac/GMC, Chrysler/Dodge, Curves, $General, O'Reilly Parts, **W gas:** Chevron, Kangaroo/dsl, Murphy USA/dsl, Victory Fuel, **food:** Burger King, Cracker Barrel, Domino's, Hardee's, Ryan's, Ruby Tuesday, Santa Fe Steaks, Subway, Waffle House, **lodging:** Day's Inn, Econolodge, Hampton Inn, Holiday Inn Express, **other:** H, $Tree, Ford/Lincoln/Mercury, GNC, Kia, K-Mart, Lowes Whse, Radio Shack, Walgreens, Walmart SuperCtr

INTERSTATE 59 CONT'D

Exit #	Services
205	AL 68, Collinsville, **E gas:** Chevron, **food:** Jack's Rest., Smokin' Joe's Rest., **lodging:** Howard Johnson, **other:** to Little River Canyon, Weiss Lake, **W gas:** BP/dsl, Shell
188	AL 211, to US 11, Gadsden, **E gas:** Jet-Pep, **other:** Noccalula Falls RV Park, **W gas:** Jet-Pep/dsl
183	US 431, US 278, Gadsden, **E gas:** Jet-Pep/dsl, Shell, Texaco, **food:** Waffle House, Wendy's, **lodging:** Days Inn, Econolodge, Rodeway Inn, **other:** st police, **W gas:** Chevron/24hr, Exxon, Jet-Pep, **food:** KFC/Taco Bell, Krystal, Jumbo Buffet, McDonald's, Pizza Hut, Subway, **lodging:** Super Value
182	I-759, to Gadsden
181	AL 77, Rainbow City, to Gadsden, **E gas:** Petro/rest./dsl/scales/24hr/@, **food:** Austin's Rest., **lodging:** Day's Inn, **W gas:** Citgo, Kangaroo/dsl, Pure/dsl, Texaco, **food:** Arby's, Cracker Barrel, DQ, Hardee's, Los Arcos, Ruby Tuesday, Santa Fe Grill, Subway, Waffle House, **lodging:** Best Western, Comfort Suites, Fairfield Inn, Holiday Inn Express, **other:** $General, $Tree, O'Reilly Parts, Radio Shack, Walmart SuperCtr
174	to Steele, **W gas:** Clean Fuels/dsl, JetPep/dsl
168mm	**rest area sb, full ♿ facilities, ☎, vending, picnic, litter barrels, petwalk, RV dump**
166	US 231, Whitney, to Ashville, **E gas:** Chevron/dsl, Discount/gas, **W gas:** Texaco/dsl, **food:** Jack's Rest., Huddle House, Subway
165mm	**rest area nb, full ♿ facilities, ☎, vending, picnic, litter barrels, petwalk, RV dump**
156	AL 23, to US 11, Springville, to St Clair Springs, **W gas:** Horizon, **food:** Azteca's Mexican, China Stix, Waffle House, **other:** Walmart SuperCtr/Subway
154	AL 174, Springville, to Odenville, **W gas:** Chevron/24hr, Exxon, Shell/dsl, Texaco/Subway/Dominos, **food:** Jack's Rest., McDonald's, Seafood Mkt Rest, Smokin BBQ
148	to US 11, Argo, **E gas:** BP
143	Mt Olive Church Rd, Deerfoot Pkwy
141	to Trussville, Pinson, **E gas:** BP/dsl, Shell/Subway/dsl, Texaco/dsl, **food:** Applebee's, Arby's, Cracker Barrel, LoneStar Steaks, McDonald's, Papa Johns, Pizza Hut, Taco Bell, Waffle House, Wendy's, **lodging:** Comfort Inn, Holiday Inn Express, Jameson Inn, **other:** Curves, Harley-Davidson, **W gas:** Chevron/24hr, Shell, **food:** Arby's, Buffalo Wild Wings, Burger King, Chick-fil-A, Costa's BBQ, Costa's Italian, DQ, East Buffet, Frontera Grill Mexican, Krystal, Milo's Burgers, Moe's SW Grill, Palace Chinese, Ruby Tuesday, Whataburger, Zaxby's, **other:** Aldi Foods, CVS Drug, $Tree, GNC, K-Mart, Kohl's, Marshall's, Office Depot, PetsMart, Radio Shack, Sam's Club/gas, Walgreens, Walmart SuperCtr, Vet
137	I-459 S, to Montgomery, Tuscaloosa
134	to AL 75, Roebuck Pkwy, **W gas:** Chevron, Exxon, Mobil, Murphy USA/dsl, Shell, **food:** Arby's, Azteca Mexican, Burger King, Chick-fil-A, Krystal, McDonald's, Milo's Burgers, O'Brien's Seafood, O'Charley's,

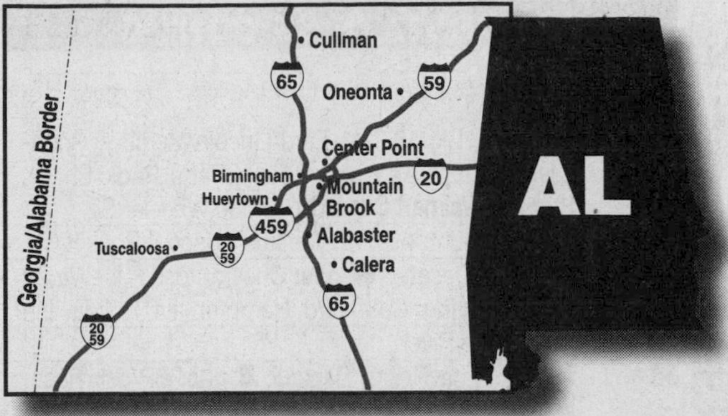

Exit #	Services
134	Continued Rally's, Ruby Tuesday, Starbucks, Steak&Ale, Subway, Taco Bell, Waffle House, Yoshiko Japanese, **other:** (H), Aldi Foods, CVS Drug, Dodge, Firestone/auto, Ford, Goodyear/auto, Honda, Hyundai, Jo-Ann Fabrics, Lincoln/Mercury, NTB, O'Reilly Parts, VW, Walgreens, Walmart SuperCtr
133	4th St, to US 11 (from nb), **W food:** Papa John's, **other:** $General, Food World, Rite Aid, Suzuki, USPO, same as 134
132	US 11 N, 1st Ave, **E** same as 131, **W gas:** Chevron/24hr, Shell, **food:** Krispy Kreme, **other:** Westwood Parts, **other:** city park
131	77th Ave (from nb), **E gas:** Exxon, **food:** Church's, **other:** CVS Drug, O'Reilly Parts, U-Haul, same as 132, **W gas:** Texaco
130	I-20, E to Atlanta, W to Tuscaloosa

I-59 S and I-20 W run together from B'ham to Mississippi
See Alabama Interstate 20.

INTERSTATE 65

Exit #	Services
366mm	Alabama/Tennessee state line
365	AL 53, to Ardmore, **E gas:** William's Service, **lodging:** Budget Inn
364mm	**Welcome Ctr sb, full ♿ facilities, info, ☎, vending, picnic, litter barrels, petwalk, RV dump**
361	Elkmont, **W gas:** BP/dsl/rest., HQ/dsl/rest., William's Service/dsl/rest., **food:** Sonny G's BBQ, **other:** antiques, repair
354	US 31 S, to Athens, **W gas:** Chevron, Texaco/dsl, **food:** Capt. D's, China Dragon, Jack's Rest., Little Caesars, McDonald's, Subway, **lodging:** Budget Inn, Mark Hotel, **other:** (H), Advance Parts, CVS Drug, $General, K-Mart, Northgate RV Park, Piggly Wiggly, Rite Aid, Walgreens
351	US 72, to Athens, Huntsville, **E gas:** Exxon, RaceWay, Shell/Subway, Texaco/dsl, **food:** Burger King, Clark's Rest., Cracker Barrel, Lawler's BBQ, McDonald's, Waffle House, Wendy's, **lodging:** Comfort Inn, Country Hearth Inn, Hampton Inn, Quality Inn, **other:** Russell Stover, Vet, **W gas:** BP, Chevron/24hr, Murphy USA, **food:** Applebee's, Arby's, Bojangles, Burger King, Catfish Cabin, Casa Blanca Mexican, Chick-fil-A, Hardee's, Krystal, Logan's Roadhouse, Papa John's, Pizza Hut, Ruby Tuesday, Shoney's, Sonic, Starbucks, Taco Bell, Zaxby's, **lodging:** Best Western, Day's Inn, Holiday Inn Express, Sleep Inn, Super 8, **other:** (H), Chevrolet, Chrysler/Jeep,

AL

INTERSTATE 65 CONT'D

N ↕ S

DECATUR / CULLMAN / BIRMINGHAM

Exit #	Services
351	Continued $General, Big 10 Tire, Ford/Lincoln/Mercury, Goodyear/auto, Lowe's Whse, O'Reilly Parts, Radio Shack, Staples, **Walmart SuperCtr**, to Joe Wheeler SP
340b	I-565, to Huntsville, to Alabama Space & Rocket Ctr
340a	AL 20, to Decatur, **W gas:** Chevron/dsl, RaceWay, **2 mi W lodging:** Courtyard, Hampton Inn, Holiday Inn
337mm	Tennessee River
334	AL 67, Priceville, to Decatur, **E gas:** BP/dsl, RaceWay/dsl, **food:** JW's Steaks, **lodging:** Day's Inn, Super 8, **other:** $General, **W gas:** Chevron, **Pilot/Subway/Wendy's/dsl/scales/24hr**, **food:** Burger King, DQ, Hardee's, Krystal, Libby's Diner, McDonalds/playplace, Smokehouse BBQ, Waffle House, **lodging:** Comfort Inn, **other:** H, Andy's RV Ctr (1mi), Hood RV Ctr
328	AL 36, Hartselle, **W gas:** BP, Cowboys/dsl, Shell, **food:** Huddle House, **lodging:** Country Hearth Inn
325	Thompson Rd, to Hartselle
322	AL 55, to US 31, to Falkville, Eva, **E gas: BP/dsl/rest.**, **W gas:** Chevron, **Loves/McDonald's/Subway/scales/dsl/24hr**, **other:** $General
318	US 31, to Lacon, **E gas:** BP/DQ/Stuckey's, **lodging:** Lacon Motel
310	AL 157, Cullman, West Point, **E gas:** BP, Chevron, Conoco/Subway/dsl, Exxon, **Shell/dsl/24hr**, Texaco/Wendy's/dsl, **food:** Arby's, Backyard Burger, Baxter's Steaks, Burger King, **Cracker Barrel**, Denny's, KFC, LJ Silver/Taco Bell, McDonald's, Ruby Tuesday, Waffle House, **lodging:** Best Western, Comfort Inn, Hampton Inn, Holiday Inn Express, Sleep Inn, **other:** H, Ford/Lincoln/Mercury, Pontiac/Buick/GMC, **W gas:** BP, Exxon/dsl, **lodging:** Super 8, **other:** Cullman Camping (2mi)
308	US 278, Cullman, **E lodging:** Day's Inn, **W gas:** Chevron/24hr, **other:** flea mkt
304	AL 69 N, Good Hope, to Cullman, **E gas:** Chevron/dsl, **Exxon/dsl**, **Shell/dsl/rest/scales**, Texaco/dsl, **food:** Hardee's, Jack's Rest., Waffle House, **lodging:** Econolodge, **other:** H, Good Hope Camping, dsl repair, **W gas:** JetPep/dsl, to Smith Lake, **other:** $General
301mm	**rest area both lanes, full ♿ facilities, ☎, vending, picnic, litter barrels, petwalk, RV dump**
299	AL 69 S, to Jasper, **E other:** Millican RV Ctr, **W gas:** BP/dsl, **Dodge City/Conoco/dsl/rest./scales/24hr**, Texaco/dsl, **Shell/McDonald's/dsl**, **food:** Jack's Rest., **other:** CarQuest, $General, repair/tires
291	AL 91, to Arkadelphia, **E gas:** Conoco/dsl, **food:** Nan's Cafe, **other:** Country View RV Park (1mi), **W gas: Shell/dsl/rest./24hr/@**, **food:** Southern Sunrise Cafe
291mm	Warrior River
289	to Blount Springs, **W gas:** BP/DQ/Stuckey's, **other:** to Rickwood Caverns SP
287	US 31 N, to Blount Springs, **E gas:** Citgo/dsl, Conoco/dsl
284	US 31 S, AL 160 E, Hayden, Corner, **E gas:** Conoco/dsl, Shell/dsl, **W** tires
282	AL 140, Warrior, **E gas:** Chevron/Subway/24hr, Exxon/McDonald's, FuelZ/dsl, **food:** Hardee's, Pizza Hut, Taco Bell, **W gas:** BP/dsl
281	US 31, to Warrior, **E other:** Chevrolet
280	to US 31, to Warrior, **E other:** Chevrolet
279mm	Warrior River
275	to US 31, Morris
272	Mt Olive Rd, **W gas:** Chevron/24hr, Shell, Texaco/dsl, **food:** Jack's Rest., **other:** $General
271	Fieldstown Rd, **E gas:** BP/Circle K, Chevron/24hr, Murphy USA/dsl, RaceWay, Shell, **food:** Arby's, Buffet Garden, Chick-fil-A, DQ, Guthrie's Diner, Habenero's Mexican, Jim'n Nick's BBQ, KFC, Little Caesar's, LJ Silver/Taco Bell, McDonald's, Milo's Burgers, Pasquales Pizza, Pizza Hut, Ruby Tuesday, Ryan's, Shoney's, Subway, Waffle House, Wendy's, Zaxby's, **lodging:** Microtel, **other:** Advance Parts, AutoZone, $Tree, Kia/Subaru, NAPA, Walgreens, **Walmart SuperCtr**, **W gas:** Shell, **food: Cracker Barrel**, **lodging:** Best Western
267	Walkers Chapel Rd, to Fultondale, **E gas:** Chevron/dsl, JetPep, Shell/Subway/dsl, **food:** Burger King, Chilli's, China One, Domino's, Fullmoon BBQ, Jack's Rest., Logan's Roadhouse, O'Charley's, Outback Steaks, Taco Bell, Waffle House, Whataburger, Zaxby's, **lodging:** Comfort Suites, Fairfield Inn, Hampton Inn, Holiday Inn Express, La Quinta, **other:** AAA, Best Buy, BooksAMillion, CVS Drug, $General, JC Penney, Lowe's Whse, O'Reilly Parts, Rite Aid, Ross, Target, Volvo Trucks, Winn-Dixie, USPO, **W gas:** Chevron/dsl
266	US 31, Fultondale, **E gas:** Chevron/24hr, **lodging:** Day's Inn, Super 8
264	41st Ave, **W gas:** ***FLYING J*/CountryMkt/dsl/LP/scales/24hr**
263	33rd Ave, **E gas:** Chevron/dsl, **lodging:** Apex Motel, **W gas:** Exxon, **other:** Colonial RV Ctr
262b a	16th St, Finley Ave, **E gas:** Bama/dsl, BP, **Shell/dsl/scales**, **W gas:** Chevron/24hr, Citgo/dsl/24hr, **Conoco/scales/dsl**, **food:** Capt D's, McDonald's, Popeye's
261b a	I-20/59, E to Gadsden, W to Tuscaloosa
260b a	3th Ave N, **E gas:** BP, Shell, Texaco, **food:** Mrs Winner's, **lodging:** Tourway Inn, **other:** Buick, Chevrolet, Chrysler/Jeep, Nissan, **W gas:** Chevron, **other:** to Legion Field
259b a	University Blvd, 4th Ave, 5th Ave, **E gas:** Chevron/dsl, **food:** Waffle House, **other:** H, **W gas:** Chevron, **other:** Goodyear
258	Green Springs Ave, **E gas:** Chevron, Shell, **food:** Exotic Wings
256b a	Oxmoor Rd, **E gas:** Exxon, Mobil/dsl, Shell, **food:** Acapulco Grill, Burger King, Capt. D's, Domino's, KFC, Krystal, Lovoy's Italian, McDonald's, Purple Onion, Qdoba Mexican, Rally's, Zaxby's, **lodging:** Howard Johnson, **other:** Aldi Foods, AutoZone, CVS Drug, $Tree, Firestone/auto, Food World, Goodyear/auto, K-Mart, Office Depot, Publix, Walmart Mkt, **W gas:** Chevron/24hr, Texaco/dsl, **food:** Hamburger Heaven, Hardee's, Jim'n Nick's BBQ, **lodging:** Econolodge, Comfort Inn, Country Hearth Inn, Microtel, Motel 6, Quality Inn, Super 8, **other:** Batteries+, Vet
255	Lakeshore Dr, **E gas:** BP/Circle K, **other:** H, to Samford U, **W gas:** Chevron, **food:** Alladdin's Grill,

INTERSTATE 65 CONT'D

N ↕ S

Exit #	Services
255	Continued Arby's, Capt D's, Chili's, Chick-fil-A, Costas BBQ, Dragon Chinese, Hooters, IHOP, Landry's Seafood, Loco's Deli, LoneStar Steaks, McAlister's Deli, Milo's Burger, Moe's SW Grill, Mr Wang's, O'Charley's, Outback Steaks, Subway, Taco Bell, Taco Casa, Wendy's, **lodging:** Best Western, Drury Inn, Hampton Inn, Hilton Garden, Holiday Inn, La Quinta, Residence Inn, Studio+, TownePlace Suites, **other:** BooksAMillion, Bruno's Foods, $Tree, IHOP, Lowe's Whse, Old Navy, Radio Shack, Sam's Club/gas, SuperPetz, Walmart SuperCtr, mall
254	Alford Ave, Shades Crest Rd, **E gas:** Chevron, **other:** vet, **W gas:** BP, Shell
252	US 31, Montgomery Hwy, **E gas:** BP, Chevron, Shell, Texaco/dsl, **food:** Arby's, Backyard Burger, Bruster's, Capt D's, ChuckeCheese, Hardee's, Milo's, Sol Azteca Mexican, **lodging:** Baymont Inn, Quality Inn, Vestavia Hotel, **other:** H, Aamco, Big 10 Tire, GMC, Lincoln/Mercury, Tuesday Morning, NAPA, Volvo, vet, **W gas:** BP, Chevron, Exxon, Shell, **food:** Burger King, Chick-fil-A, Full Moon BBQ, Golden Rule BBQ, Habanero's Mexican, Krispy Kreme, Krystal, McAlister's Deli, McDonald's, Outback Steaks, Papa John's, Salvatori's Pizza, Schlotsky's, Starbucks, Steakout, Subway, Waffle House, **lodging:** Day's Inn, **other:** Acura, Advance Parts, BooksAMillion, Bruno's Food, Buick, Chevrolet, Chrysler/Jeep, $Tree, Firestone, Goodyear/auto, Honda, Mr Transmissions, Nissan, Pontiac, Publix, Rite Aid, Staples, TJ Maxx
250	I-459, to US 280
247	Al 17, Valleydale Rd, **E gas:** BP, **W gas:** Citgo, Mobil, RaceWay, Shell, **food:** Arby's, IHOP, Milo's Burgers, Papa John's, RagTime Café, Sonic, Subway, Waffle House, Zapata's Mexican, **lodging:** Comfort Suites, La Quinta, Oaktree Lodge, **other:** O'Reilly Parts, Rite Aid, Publix, Walgreens, Vet
246	AL 119, Cahaba Valley Rd, **E other:** to Oak Mtn SP, **W gas:** BP/dsl, Kangaroo/Subway/dsl, Murphy USA/dsl, RaceWay, Shell, **food:** Applebee's, Arby's, Capt D's, Chick-fil-A, Cracker Barrel, DQ, Golden Corral, Hooters, KFC, Krystal, Margarita Grill, McDonald's, McAlister's Deli, Mkt Cafe, O'Charley's, Pizza Hut, Purple Onion, Ruby Tuesday, Shoney's, Sonic, Taco Bell, Two Pesos Mexican, TX Roadhouse, Waffle House, Wendy's, Whataburger, **lodging:** Best Western, Comfort Inn, Hampton Inn, Holiday Inn Express, Quality Inn, Ramada Ltd, Sleep Inn, Travelodge, ValuePlace, **other:** H, Advance Parts, Curves, Ezell's Fishcamp, Firestone/auto, Harley-Davidson, Mazda, Walmart SuperCtr
242	Pelham, **E gas:** Chevron/dsl/24hr, Exxon/dsl, Shell, **other:** CVS Drug, Publix, **W lodging:** Shelby Motel (2mi), **other:** Good Sam Camping (1mi)
238	US 31, Alabaster, Saginaw, **E gas:** Murphy USA/dsl, **food:** Arby's, Buffalo Wild Wings, Chick-fil-A, Coldstone Creamery, DQ, Full Moon Cafe, Habanero's Mexican, Jim'n Nick's BBQ, Longhorn Steaks, Moe's SW Grill, O'Charley's, Olive Garden, Quizno's, Ruby Tuesday, Salsarita's Mexican, Starbucks,

BIRMINGHAM

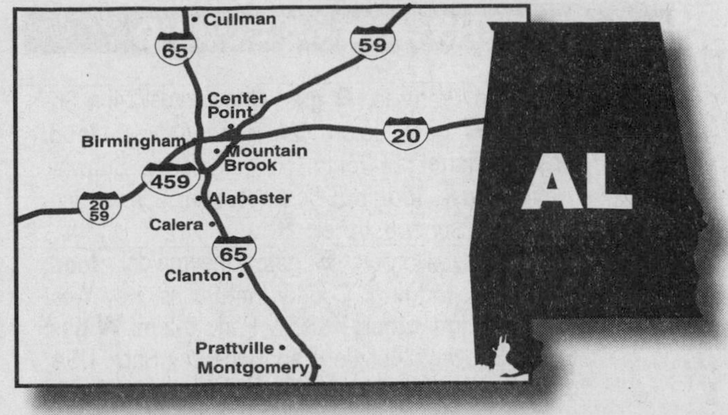

Exit #	Services
238	Continued Subway, Taco Bell, **lodging:** Candlewood Suites, **other:** Belk, Best Buy, BooksAMillion, GNC, JC Penney, Lowes Whse, Old Navy, PetsMart, Radio Shack, Ross, Target, TJ Maxx, Walmart SuperCtr, **W gas:** Cannon, Chevron/dsl, Shell/dsl, **food:** Waffle House, Whataburger, **2 mi W lodging:** Shelby Motel, **other:** H
234	**E gas:** BP/Subway/dsl, **W gas:** Chevron/dsl/24hr, Shell/dsl, **other:** GMC/Pontiac, Cahaba RV Ctr
231	US 31, Saginaw, **E gas:** BP/dsl, GasBoy, Murphy USA/dsl, Shell, **food:** Capt D's, Cracker Barrel, Fish Mkt, Golden Rule BBQ, Los Potrillos Mexican, McDonald's, Taco Bell, Waffle House, Yoe Wok Chinese, **lodging:** Hampton Inn, Holiday Inn Express, **other:** Burton RV Ctr, $Tree, Radio Shack, Rolling Hills RV Park, Walmart SuperCtr/Subway, **W food:** Donna's Café
228	AL 25, to Calera, **E gas:** Citgo/dsl, Shell/dsl, **lodging:** Best Value Inn, Day's Inn, **W gas:** Chevron/dsl, **food:** Hardee's (1mi), **other:** $General, to Brierfield Works SP
227mm	Buxahatchie Creek
219	Union Grove, Thorsby, **E gas:** Chevron/dsl/24hr, Exxon/Subway/dsl, **food:** Peach Queen Camping, **W gas:** Shell, **food:** Jack's Rest., Smokey Hollow Rest.
213mm	**rest area both lanes, full ♿ facilities, ☎, vending, picnic, litter barrels, petwalk, RV dump**
212	AL 145, Clanton, **E gas:** Chevron/dsl, **other:** Toyota/Scion, **W gas:** Texaco/Subway, Headco/dsl, **other:** H, One Big Peach
208	Clanton, **E gas:** Love's/Arby's/dsl/24hr **W gas:** Exxon/dsl/24hr, **food:** Shoney's, **lodging:** Guesthouse Inn, **other:** Heaton Pecans
205	US 31, AL 22, to Clanton, **E gas:** BP, Shell/dsl, Texaco/dsl, **food:** McDonald's, Waffle House, Whataburger, **lodging:** Best Western, Day's Inn, Holiday Inn Exress, Scottish Inn, **other:** Peach Park, to Confed Mem Park, **0-2 mi W gas:** BP/dsl, Chevron/dsl/24hr, Murphy USA/dsl, **food:** Boomerang's Grill, Burger King, Capt D's, Hardee's, KFC, New China Buffet, San Marcos Mexican, Subway, Taco Bell, Wendy's, Zaxby's, **lodging:** Key West Inn, **other:** $General, Durbin Farms Mkt, Walmart SuperCtr
200	to Verbena, **E gas:** Texaco/dsl, **W gas:** Shell/DQ/Stuckey's/dsl, **other:** RV camping
195	Worlds Largest Confederate Flag
186	US 31, Pine Level, **E other:** Confederate Mem Park (13mi), **W gas:** BP/dsl, Chevron/24hr, Citgo, Conoco/Subway/dsl, **lodging:** Pine Motel, **other:** H

CLANTON

AL

INTERSTATE 65 CONT'D

N ↕ S

Exit #	Services
181	AL 14, to Prattville, **E gas:** Chevron/dsl/24hr, Entec/dsl, **W gas:** Exxon, QV, Texaco/DQ/dsl, **food:** Cracker Barrel, El Torito, Ruby Tuesday, Subway, Waffle House, **lodging:** Best Western, Comfort Inn, La Quinta, Super 8, **other:** (H)
179	US 82 W, Millbrook, **E gas:** Chevron/dsl, **food:** Asian Grill, **lodging:** County Inn&Suites, Key West Inn, Sleep Inn, **other:** K&K RV Park, **0-2 mi W gas:** Exxon/Subway/24hr, Jet-Pep, RaceWay, Shell, USA/dsl, **food:** A&W/KFC, Applebee's, Bruster's, Burger King, Capt. D's, Casitas Mexican, Chick-fil-A, Cobbs Ford Grill, Hardee's, Jim'n Nick's BBQ, Krystal, Logan's Roadhouse, Longhorn Steaks, Lowe's, McAlister's Deli, McDonald's, Mexico Topico, Moe's SW Grill, O'Charley's, Outback Steaks, Ryan's, Sonic, Steak'n Shake, Yellow Mushroom, Waffle House, **lodging:** Courtyard, Days Inn, Econolodge, Hampton Inn, Holiday Inn, Jameson Inn, **other:** AutoZone, Bass Pro Shops, Belk, Best Buy, BigLots, Big 10 Tire, BooksAmillion, Chevrolet, CVS Drug, $General, $Tree, Ford, GNC, Home Depot, JC Penney, Lowe's Whse, Michael's, Office Depot, Ross, Target, Target, TJ Maxx, Walmart SuperCtr, Vet
176	AL 143 N (from nb, no return), Millbrook, Coosada
173	AL 152, North Blvd, to US 231
172mm	Alabama River
172	Clay St, Herron St, **E lodging:** Embassy Suites, **W gas:** Chevron/dsl
171	I-85 N, Day St
170	Fairview Ave, **E gas:** Citgo/Subway, Gas Depot, **food:** Church's, McDonald's, Wing Master, **other:** Advance Parts, AutoZone, CVS Drug, NAPA Care, O'Reilly Parts, Piggly Wiggly, Rite Aid, farmers mkt, **W gas:** Exxon, **other:** Calhoun Foods, Family$
169	Edgemont Ave (from sb), **E gas:** Liberty
168	US 80 E, US 82, South Blvd, **E gas:** BP/dsl, Entec/dsl, Kangaroo/dsl, TA/dsl/rest./24hr/@, **food:** Arby's, Capt D's, KFC, McDonald's, Popeye's, Pizza Hut, Taco Bell, Waffle House, **lodging:** Best Inn, Travel Inn, other: (H), Family$, The Woods RV Park, **W gas:** Chevron/dsl, RaceWay, Shell/Subway/dsl, Speedy/dsl, **food:** DQ, Hardee's, Wendy's, **lodging:** Best Value Inn, Candlelight Inn, Comfort Inn, Days Inn, Econolodge, Howard Johnson, Rodeway Inn
167	US 80 W, to Selma
164	US 31, Hope Hull, **E gas:** BP/24hr, Petro+, Saveway/dsl/scales/24hr, **other:** MC RV Park, auto repair, **W gas:** BP/Burger King, Chevron/24hr, Liberty/Subway, **food:** Waffle House, **lodging:** Best Western, Comfort Suites, Hampton Inn, Holiday Inn Express, Motel 6, **other:** auto repair
158	to US 31, **E gas:** BP/DQ/Stuckey's, Marathon/dsl, **other:** RV Park, **W gas:** ***FLYING J***/CountryMkt/dsl/scales/24hr
151	AL 97, to Letohatchee, **W gas:** BP, PaceCar/dsl
142	AL 185, to Ft Deposit, **E gas:** Shell/dsl/24hr, USA/dsl, **food:** Priester's Pecans, Subway, **other:** auto parts, **W gas:** Chevron/24hr
133mm	**rest areas both lanes, full ♿ facilities, ☎, vending, picnic, litter barrels, petwalk, RV dump**
130	AL10 E, AL 185, to Greenville, **E gas:** Chevron/dsl/24hr, Shell/24hr, USA/dsl, **food:** Arby's, Capt D's, China Town Rest., Hardee's, KFC, McDonald's, Old Mexico, Pizza Hut, Waffle House, Wendy's, **lodging:** Day's Inn, Greenville Inn, **other:** Advance Parts, CVS Drug, $General, Russell Stover, Super Foods, Walgreens, to Sherling Lake Park, **W gas:** Murphy USA/dsl, Phillips 66/Subway/dsl, QV, Texaco/dsl, **food:** Bates Turkey Rest., Burger King, Cracker Barrel, El Rodeo Mexican, Jelanie's Diner, Krystal, Ruby Tuesday, Shoney's, Sonic, Subway, Taco Bell, The Border, **lodging:** Best Western, Comfort Inn, Hampton Inn, Holiday Inn Express, Jameson Inn, **other:** Chevrolet, Chrysler/Dodge/Jeep, Walmart SuperCtr/Subway
128	AL 10, to Greenville, **E gas:** Shell/Smokehouse/dsl, **other:** (H), **W gas:** BP
114	AL 106, to Georgiana, **W gas:** BP, Chevron/24hr, **other:** auto repair
107	rd 7, to Garland
101	to Owassa, **E gas:** BP/dsl, **W gas:** Exxon/dsl, **other:** Owassa RV Park, dsl repair
96	AL 83, to Evergreen, **E gas:** Chevron/24hr, Shell, **food:** Burger King, Hardee's, KFC/Taco Bell, McDonald's, **other:** (H), **W gas:** Citgo/Subway/dsl, **food:** Black Angus Rest., Pizza Hut, Waffle House, **lodging:** Best Value Inn, Comfort Inn, Day's Inn
93	US 84, to Evergreen, **E gas:** USA/dsl, **W gas:** BP/dsl
89mm	**rest area sb, full ♿ facilities, ☎, vending, picnic, litter barrels, petwalk, RV dump**
85mm	**rest area nb, full ♿ facilities, ☎, vending, picnic, litter barrels, petwalk, RV dump**
83	AL 6, to Lenox, **E gas:** Exxon/dsl/LP, **other:** RV Park (4mi)
77	AL 41, to Range, Brewton, Repton, **E gas:** BP, **W gas:** Citgo/dsl, Shell/Stuckey's/dsl
69	AL 113, to Flomaton, **E gas:** BP/Subway/dsl, Chevron/dsl, Shell/dsl/scales/24hr, **other:** dsl repair, **W gas:** Minute Stop/dsl/24hr, **food:** Huddle House
57	AL 21, to Atmore, **E gas:** Exxon/dsl, **food:** Creek Family Rest., Hardee's, **lodging:** Holiday Inn Express, Muskogee Inn, **other:** Wind Creek Indian Gaming, **W gas:** BP/dsl, **other:** to Kelley SP
54	Escambia Cty Rd 1, **E gas:** BP/Subway/dsl, Citgo/dsl, **other:** to Creek Indian Res
45	to Perdido, **W gas:** Chevron/dsl
37	AL 287, Gulf Shores Pkwy, to Bay Minette, **E gas:** BP
34	to AL 59, to Bay Minette, Stockton
31	AL 225, to Stockton, **E other:** to Blakeley SP, Confederate Mem Bfd, **W gas:** Shell/dsl, **other:** Landing RV Park (2mi)
29mm	Tensaw River
28mm	Middle River
25mm	Mobile River
22	Creola, **E** marine ctr, RV Park, truck repair
19	US 43, to Satsuma, **E gas:** Chevron/dsl/24hr, Pilot/Arby's/dsl/scales/24hr, **food:** McDonald's, Pintoli's Italian (2mi), Waffle House, **lodging:** La Quinta, **W gas:** Chevron/dsl, Shell, **other:** I-65 RV Park (1.5mi)
15	AL 41, **E gas:** Chevron, **food:** China Chef, Church's, Godfather's Pizza, Kevin's Rest., **other:** Family$, Food World, O'Reilly Parts, Rite Aid, Walgreens, **W gas:** Circle K/gas, Shell/Subway/dsl, **other:** $General

MILLBROOK · MONTGOMERY · GREENVILLE · EVERGREEN · ATMORE

INTERSTATE 65 CONT'D

N ↕ S — MOBILE

Exit #	Services
13	AL 158, AL 213, to Saraland, **E gas:** Murphy USA/dsl, Shell/dsl/24hr, **food:** Krystal, Ruby Tuesday, Waffle House, Wintzell's Oyster House, **lodging:** Best Western, Comfort Suites, Day's Inn, Econolodge, Microtel, Quality Inn, **other:** Walmart SuperCtr, **W gas:** Exxon/Subway, **lodging:** Hampton Inn, Holiday Inn Express, **other:** to Chickasabogue Campground
10	W Lee St, **E gas:** Minute Stop, Parade/dsl, Shell/Subway, **lodging:** Best Inn
9	I-165 S, to Mobile, to I-10 E
8b a	US 45, to Prichard, **E gas:** Chevron/24hr, Shell/dsl, Texaco, **food:** Church's, **other:** Family$, **W gas:** BP/24hr, Conoco/dsl, 1st Stop, Pride Trkstp/dsl/scales, Texaco/dsl, **food:** Burger King, Domino's, Golden Egg Café, McDonald's, **other:** Vet
5b	US 98, Moffett Rd, **E gas:** Exxon/dsl, Texaco/dsl, **food:** Burger King, Church's, DQ, McDonald's, Saucy Q BBQ, **other:** Big 10 Tire, **W gas:** Citgo, Texaco/dsl, **food:** Hardee's, **lodging:** Super 8, auto repair
5a	Spring Hill Ave, **E gas:** Shell/dsl, **food:** KFC, McDonald's, **other:** [H], AutoZone, Big 10 Tire, Tiger Foods, **W gas:** Chevron, Shell/dsl, **food:** Guthrie's, Starbucks, Waffle House, Zaxby's, **lodging:** Extended Stay America, Wingate Inn
4	Dauphin St, **E gas:** BP/Circle K/dsl, Shell, Summit Gas, **food:** Baskin-Robbins, Checker's, Chick-fil-A, Cracker Barrel, Hong Kong Rest., Krystal, McDonald's, Popeye's, Subway, Taco Bell, TCBY, Waffle House, Wendy's, **lodging:** Comfort Inn, Comfort Suites, Red Roof Inn, Rodeway Inn, **other:** Buick/Pontiac/GMC, $General, FoodWorld, Hyundai, Lowe's Whse, Mercedes, Rite Aid, Subaru, Tuesday Morning, Walmart SuperCtr, Vet, same as 3 & 5a, **W other:** [H]
3	Airport Blvd, **E gas:** BP, **food:** Burger King, Cane's, Logan's Roadhouse, Macaroni Grill, Morrison's Cafeteria, Piccadilly's, Sammy's Grill, Starbucks, Wendy's, **lodging:** Marriott, ValuePlace Hotel, **other:** [H], Acura/Jaguar/Infiniti, Barnes&Noble, Belk, Best Buy, BooksAMillion, Cadillac, Dillard's, $Tree, Firestone/auto, Ford, Goodyear/auto, Harley-Davidson, JC Penney, Land Rover, Nissan, Old Navy, Saab, Sam's Club/gas, Sears/auto, Staples, mall, **W gas:** Mystik/dsl, Shell, **food:** Arby's, Boiling Pot, Burger King, Carrabba's, China Doll, China Super Buffet, ChuckeCheese, Denny's, El Chico, Firehouse Subs, Honeybaked Ham, Hooters, IHOP, Lenny's Subs, LoneStar Steaks, Marble Slab, McDonald's, Moe's SW Grill, Newk's Rest., O'Charley's, Olive Garden, Panera Bread, Pizza Hut, Popeye's, Quizno's, Red Lobster, Ruby Tuesday, S China Seafood, Starbucks, Subway, Taco Bell, Waffle House, Wings Grille, **lodging:** Airport Inn, Ashberry Suites, Baymont Inn, Best Inn, Courtyard, Days Inn, Drury Inn, Econolodge, Fairfield Inn, Family Inn, Hampton Inn, Hilton Garden, InTowne Suites, La Quinta, Motel 6, Quality Inn, Residence Inn, **other:** BooksAMillion, $General, Fresh Mkt Foods, Home Depot, Jo-Ann Fabrics, Marshalls, Michael's, Office Depot, PepBoys, PetsMart, Radio Shack, Ross, SteinMart, TJ Maxx, U-Haul, Walgreens, to USAL

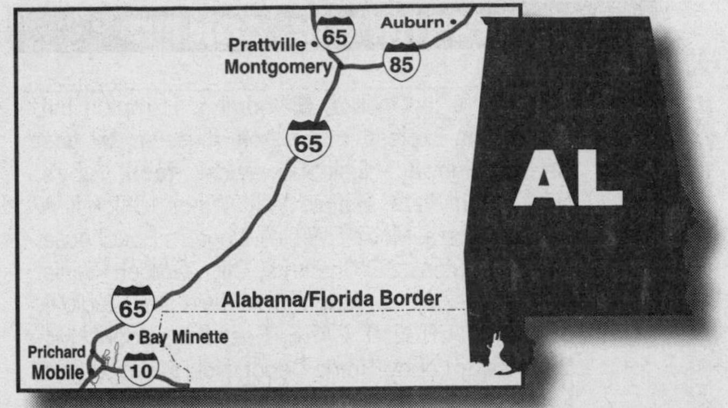

Exit #	Services
1b a	US 90, Government Blvd, **E gas:** BP, Raceway/dsl, **food:** McAlister's Deli, Steak'n Shake, **lodging:** Howard Johnson, **other:** Audi/VW, BMW, Buick/Volvo, Chevrolet, Chrysler/Jeep, Dodge, Family&, Honda, Kia, Lexus, Lincoln/Mercury, Mazda, Toyota, transmissions, **W gas:** Shell/dsl, **food:** Waffle House, **lodging:** Rest Inn
0mm	I-10, E to Pensacola, W to New Orleans, I-65 begins/ends on I-10, exit 20.

INTERSTATE 85

LANETT N ↕ S OPELIKA

Exit #	Services
80mm	Alabama/Georgia state line, Chattahoochee River
79	US 29, to Lanett, **E gas:** Big Cat/dsl, Murphy USA, **food:** Arby's, Burger King, Capt D's, Chuck's BBQ, JK House Korean, KFC, Krystal, McDonald's, Pizza Hut, San Marcos Mexican, Subway, Taco Bell, Waffle House/24hr, Wendy's, **other:** [H], Advance Parts, $General, $Tree, Walmart SuperCtr, transmissions, to West Point Lake, **W gas:** JetPep, QV, **food:** Domino's, Sonic, **lodging:** Day's Inn, Econolodge, **other:** AutoZone, CVS Drug, Kroger, O'Reilly Parts, Vet
78.5mm	**Welcome Ctr sb, full [handicapped] facilities, [phone], vending, [picnic], litter barrels, petwalk**
77	AL 208, to Huguley, **E gas:** Circle K, Jet Pep/dsl, **food:** Church's, Waffle House, **lodging:** Hampton Inn, Holiday Inn Express, **other:** Chevrolet, Chrysler/Dodge/Ford/Lincoln/Mercury, **W** fireworks
76mm	Eastern/Central time zone
70	AL 388, to Cusseta, **E gas:** BP, Perlis Trvl Plaza/Shell/Country Pride/scales/24hr/dsl/@, **W lodging:** Hampton Inn, fireworks
66	Andrews Rd, to US 29
64	US 29, to Opelika, **E gas:** BP, **lodging:** Guesthouse Inn, **W gas:** Tiger/dsl
62	US 280/431, to Opelika, **E gas:** Chevron/dsl, Eagle/dsl, Liberty Gas, Shell/Circle K/Church's/dsl, **food:** Burger King, Durango Mexican, McDonald's, Subway, Wok'n Roll Rest., Yang's Buffet, **lodging:** Day's Inn, Econolodge, GuestHouse Inn, Knight's Inn, Motel 6, Quality Inn, **other:** Lakeside RV Park (4.5mi), transmissions, **W gas:** Jet Pep, Shell, **food:** Capt. D's, Cracker Barrel, Sizzlin Steaks, Waffle House, **lodging:** Comfort Inn, Travelodge, **other:** Chevrolet, Chrysler/Dodge, Ford, H&W Tire, Harley Davidson, Jeep, USA Stores/famous brands
60	AL 51, AL 169, to Opelika, **E gas:** RaceWay, **food:** Hardee's, **other:** $General, **W food:** Tyler's Rest., Wendy's (1.5 mi), **other:** [H], auto repair

INTERSTATE 85 CONT'D

N ↕ S

Exit #	Services
58	US 280 W, to Opelika, **E lodging:** Hampton Inn, Holiday Inn Express, **other:** golf, museum, **W gas:** Chevron/Subway, Shell/Subway/dsl, **food:** Arby's, Brick Oven Pizza, Buffalo Wild Wings, Chick-fil-A, DQ, Jim Bob's, Moe's SW Grill, Logan's Roadhouse, Longhorn Steaks, O'Charley's, Olive Garden, Sonic, Starbucks, Zaxby's, **lodging:** Fairfield Inn, Studio 6, **other:** H, URGENT CARE, Best Buy, BooksAMillion, Hobby Lobby, Home Depot, Kohl's, Kroger/gas, Lowe's Whse, Office Depot, Old Navy, PetCo, Ross, Target, TJ Maxx, World Mkt, **1 mi W gas:** Liberty Gas, Dominos, Golden Corral, Honey Baked Ham, Outback Steaks, Papa John's, Taco Bell, Quizno's, **lodging:** Best Western
57	Glenn Ave, **W gas:** Exxon, QV, **food:** Provino's Italian, Shakey's Pizza, Waffle House, Wendy's, **lodging:** Hilton Garden, University Motel, **other:** Sam's Club/gas
51	US 29, to Auburn, **E lodging:** Hampton Inn, **other:** Leisure Time RV Park/Camping, Nissan, Toyota/Scion, to Chewacla SP, **W gas:** Chevron/Subway, Murphy USA, RaceWay, **food:** Ahi's Asian, Arby's, Burger King, Firehouse Subs, Hong Kong Buffet, Krystal, Little Caesar's, McDonald's, Philly Connection, Pizza Hut, Ruby Tuesday, Santa Fe Steaks, Sonic, Taco Bell, Waffle House, Wendy's, Zaxby's, **lodging:** Comfort Inn, Econolodge, Holiday Inn Express, Microtel, Sleep Inn, **other:** URGENT CARE, Advance Parts, Curves, Ford/Lincoln/Mercury, Walmart SuperCtr, Winn-Dixie, to Auburn U, tires/repair, Vet
44mm	**rest area both lanes, full facilities, phone, vending, picnic tables, litter barrels, petwalk, RV dump, 24hr security**
42	US 80, AL 186 E, Wire Rd, **E other:** to Tuskegee NF, dsl repair/tires, **W gas:** Torch 85/rest./dsl/24hr
38	AL 81, to Tuskegee, **E** to Tuskegee NHS, Tuskegee University
32	AL 49 N, to Tuskegee, **E gas:** BP/dsl
26	AL 229 N, to Tallassee, **E gas:** Shell/Guthrie's/dsl, W H
22	US 80, to Shorter, **E gas:** BP/dsl, Chevron/Petro/dsl/rest., Exxon/dsl, **lodging:** Day's Inn, **other:** to Macon Co Greyhound Pk, Windrift RV Park
16	Waugh, to Cecil, **E gas:** BP/Subway/dsl, **other:** auto repair
11	US 80, to Mt Meigs, **E gas:** Exxon/Subway/dsl, Liberty/dsl, **food:** Burger King, Cracker Barrel, Jose's Grill, McDonald's, Sommer's Grill, Thai Gratiem, Top China, Waffle House, **lodging:** Candlewood Suites, Comfort Inn, Country Inn & Suites, Holiday Inn Express, Sleep Inn, **other:** Home Depot, Walmart SuperCtr, **W gas:** Chevron/dsl/24hr
9	AL 271, to AL 110, to Auburn U/Montgomery, **E food:** Arby's, BoneFish Grill, Chick-fil-A, Chili's, Five Guys Burgers, Guthrie's, Mimi's Cafe, Moe's SW Grill, Panera Bread, Red Robin, Ruby Tuesday, Sonic, Starbucks, Texas Roadhouse, Wendy's, Whataburger, Zoe's Kitchen, **lodging:** Hampton Inn, Staybridge Suites, **other:** BooksAMillion, Costco/gas, Dillard's, Kohl's, Michaels, Old Navy, PetsMart, Radio Shack, Ross, Target, World Mkt, **W** H
6	US 80, US 231, AL 21, East Blvd, **0-2 mi E gas:** Chevron/24hr, Exxon/dsl/24hr, RaceWay, Shell, **food:** Arby's, Burger King, Carrabba's, Chick-fil-A, Golden Corral, Hardees, Hooters, Jason's Deli, KFC, Longhorn Steaks, Los Cabos, McDonald's, Ming's Chinese, O'Charley's, Olive Garden, Panera Bread, Piccadilly's, Popeye's, Ruby Tuesday, Schlotsky's, Starbucks, Subway, Taco Bell, Waffle House, Wendy's, Wings Grill, Zaxby's, **lodging:** Best Inn, Comfort Inn, Country Inn&Suites, Courtyard, Extended Stay America, La Quinta, Quality Inn, Red Roof Inn, Residence Inn, Sleep Inn, SpringHill Suites, Studio+, ValuePlace, Wingate Inn, **other:** Acura, Best Buy, BooksAMillion, $General, Ford, Fresh Mkt Foods, Home Depot, Honda, Hyundai, Lowe's Whse, Marshall's, Office Depot, PetCo, TJ Maxx, Walmart SuperCtr, Winn-Dixie, USPO, Vet, **W gas:** BP, Liberty Gas, Shell, Texaco, **food:** Buffet City, Capt D's, Hardee's, IHOP, Krispy Kreme, Krystal, LoneStar Steaks, McDonald's, Outback Steaks, Shoney's, Stevi B's Pizza, Taco Bell, Waffle House, **lodging:** Baymont Inn, Budgetel, Comfort Suites, Drury Inn, Econolodge, Express Inn, Hotel Montgomery, Lexington Hotel, Motel 6, **other:** BMW, Cadillac/Buick, Chevrolet, Chrysler/Jeep, $General, Firestone/auto, JC Penney, Kia, Lexus, Mercedes, Mitsubishi, Nissan, Sam's Club/gas, Sears/auto, Toyota/Scion, VW/Audi, mall, to Gunter AFB
4	Perry Hill Rd, **E food:** Chappy's Deli, **W gas:** Cannon Gas, Chevron/24hr, **food:** Hardee's, Subway, **lodging:** Hilton Garden, Homewood Suites, **other:** $General, Express Oil Change, vet
3	Ann St, **E gas:** BP/dsl, Chevron, **food:** Arby's, Capt D's, Country's BBQ, Domino's, Down the St Cafe, KFC, Krystal, McDonald's, Taco Bell, Waffle House, Wendy's, Zaxby's, **lodging:** Day's Inn, **other:** Big 10 Tire, **W gas:** Entec, Murphy USA/dsl, PaceCar, Ztec, **lodging:** Stay Lodge, **food:** Chick-fil-A, CiCi's Pizza, Hardees, Popeye's, Subway, **other:** $Tree, Office Depot, Radio Shack, Ross, Walmart SuperCtr
2	Forest Ave, **E** CVS Drug, **W** H
1	Court St, Union St, downtown, **E gas:** BP/dsl, Exxon, **W** to Ala St U
0mm	I-85 begins/ends on I-65, exit 171 in Montgomery

AUBURN · MONTGOMERY · MONTGOMERY

INTERSTATE 459 (BIRMINGHAM)

N ↕ S

Exit #	Services
33b a	I-59, N to Gadsden, S to Birmingham
32	US 11, Trussville, **N gas:** BP/24hr, **lodging:** Best Inn (3mi), **S gas:** Chevron/dsl/24hr, RaceWay/24hr, Shell/Wendy's/dsl, **food:** A&W/KFC, Arby's, Beef'o Brady's, Chili's, Coldstone Creamery, Habanero's Rest., Hooters, Jack's Rest., Jim'n Nick's BBQ, John's City Diner, Logan's Roadhouse, McDonald's, Quizno's, Red Robin, Starbucks, Waffle House, **lodging:** Courtyard, Hampton Inn, **other:** Belk, Best Buy, Big 10 Tires, BooksAMillion, Buick/GMC/Pontiac, Harley-Davidson, Home Depot, JC Penney, Lowes Whse, Mazda, Michael's, Old Navy, Staples, Target, TJ Maxx
31	Derby Parkway, **W other:** B'ham Race Course
29	I-20, E to Atlanta, W to Birmingham
27	Grants Mill Rd, **S gas:** Exxon/dsl, **other:** BMW/Lexus, Cadillac

AL AZ

INTERSTATE 459 CONT'D (BIRMINGHAM)

N ↕ S — BIRMINGHAM

23 Liberty Parkway, **S food:** Billy's Grill, DQ, **lodging:** Hilton Garden

19 US 280, Mt Brook, Childersburg, **N gas:** Chevron, **food:** Flemings Rest., Village Tavern, **other:** Barnes&Noble, **0-3 mi S gas:** BP/Circle K, Exxon, **food:** Arby's, Buffalo Wild Wings, Burger King, Carrabba's, Chili's, Cracker Barrel, Edgar's Rest., Full Moon BBQ, Hooters, IHOP, Jason's Deli, Joe's Crabshack, Japanese, Logan's Roadhouse, LongHorn Steaks, McDonald's, Outback Steaks, Papa John's, Pizza Hut, Ralph&Kacoos, Ruby Tuesday, Schlotzky's, Shogun Japanese, Taco Bell, TGIFriday, Wendy's, **lodging:** Candlewood Suites, Courtyard, Drury Inn, Fairfield Inn, Hampton Inn, Hilton, Holiday Inn Express, Homestead Suites, Homewood Suites, Hyatt Place, La Quinta, Marriott, Residence Inn, Sheraton, Studio Inn, Wingate, **other:** Best Buy, Fresh Mkt Foods, Home Depot, Kohl's, Michael's, NTB, PetCo, Ross, Walmart SuperCtr

17 Acton Rd, **N gas:** Shell/dsl/24hr, **food:** Krystal, McDonald's

15b a I-65, N to Birmingham, S to Montgomery

13 US 31, Hoover, Pelham, **N gas:** BP, Chevron, Exxon, Shell, **food:** Burger King, Chick-fil-A, Fish Mkt Rest., Full Moon Cafe, Golden Rule BBQ, Habanero's, Krispy Kreme, Krystal, McDonald's, Outback Steaks, Quizno's, Starbucks, Subway, **lodging:** Day's Inn, **other:** Acura/Honda, BooksAMillion, Buick, Cadillac,

13 Continued
Chevrolet, Chrysler/Jeep, $Tree, Firestone, Goodyear, Kia, Mitsubishi, Nissan, Pontiac, Rite Aid, Staples, TJ Maxx, Toyota, Vet, **S gas:** Jet-Pep, Shell/dsl/24hr, **food:** CA Pizza Kitchen, Chipotle Mexican, China Buffet, Guthrie's, Jim'n Nicks BBQ, McDonald's, Moe's SW Grill, Olive Garden, Pizza Hut, Taco Bell, Ted's MT Grill, Top China, Wendy's, **lodging:** Best Western, Courtyard, Hyatt Place, Hotel, **other:** Belk, Best Buy, Bruno's Foods, Costco/gas, CVS Drug, Hancock Fabrics, Home Depot, Infiniti, JC Penney, Macy's, Marshall's, Mercedes, Michael's, NTB, Office Depot, PetsMart, Sam's Club, Sears, Tuesday Morning, Walmart (1mi), mall

10 AL 150, Waverly, **N gas:** Chevron (1mi), Shell (1mi), **lodging:** Renaissance Motel (6mi), **S gas:** BP/dsl/24hr, Exxon, **food:** Hyatt Place, Mei China, **other:** Ford, GNC, Walgreens, Publix/deli

BESSEMER

6 AL 52, to Bessemer, **N gas:** BP/dsl, **S gas:** BP, Shell, Texaco/Taco Bell, **food:** Arby's, China Wok, Domino's, McDonald's, Pizza Hut, Quizno's, San Antonio Grill, Subway, Waffle House, Wendy's, **lodging:** Sleep Inn, **other:** Cherokee Beach RV Park, $General, CVS Drug, TrueValue, Winn-Dixie

1 AL 18, Bessemer, **N gas:** Exxon, Shell/dsl, **other:** Target, **S gas:** BP/dsl, **food:** China King, McDonald's, Momma's Rest., Subway, **other:** Advance Parts, CVS Drug, FoodWorld/drug, to Tannehill SP

0mm I-459 begins/ends on I-20/59, exit 106

ARIZONA

INTERSTATE 8

E ↕ W

Exit #	Services
178b a	I-10, I-8 begins/ends on I-10, exit 199, E to Tucson, W to Phoenix
174	Trekell Rd, to Casa Grande, **2-4 mi N other:** [H], gas, food, lodging
172	Thornton Rd, to Casa Grande, **2-4 mi N** gas, food, lodging, **S other:** Francisco Grande Resort
171mm	Santa Cruz River
169	Bianco Rd
167	Montgomery Rd, **S** Francisco Grande Golf Club
163mm	Santa Rosa Wash
161	Stanfield Rd
151	AZ 84 E, Maricopa Rd, to Stanfield, **S** Harrah's Casino (14mi), **S gas:** Gas'n Go, Pullman Trkstp/dsl, **other:** Saguaro RV Park
150mm	**picnic area wb, [picnic], litter barrels**
149mm	**picnic area eb, [picnic], litter barrels**
144	Vekol Rd
140	Freeman Rd
119	Butterfield Trail, to AZ 85, I-10, Gila Bend, **N gas:** Shell/dsl/scales/RV Park/24hr, **food:** American/Mexican Rest., **lodging:** America's Choice Inn, **other:** Augie's RV camping, **3 mi N gas:** Shell/Subway/Noble Roman's/dsl, **food:** DQ, Little Italy, Space Age Rest., **lodging:** Best Western, Travelodge, Yucca Motel
117mm	Sand Tank Wash
115	AZ 85, to Gila Bend, **1-2 mi N gas:** Loves/Taco

GILA BEND

115	Continued Bell/dsl/scales/24hr, Circle K/gas, Texaco/dsl, **food:** Burger King, McDonald's, **lodging:** Best Western, El Coronado Motel, Yucca Motel, **other:** [H], Goodyear/auto, NAPA, Wheel Inn RV park
111	Citrus Valley Rd
106	Paloma Rd
102	Painted Rock Rd
87	Sentinel, Hyder, **N gas:** Sentinel Gen Store/dsl
85mm	**rest area wb, full [handicapped] facilities, [phone], [picnic], litter barrels, vending, petwalk**
84mm	**rest area eb, full [handicapped] facilities, [phone], [picnic], litter barrels, vending, petwalk**
78	Spot Rd
73	Aztec, **4 mi S** Oasis RV Park/dump
67	Dateland, **S gas:** Exxon/24hr, **other:** Oasis RV Park/dump
56mm	**rest area both lanes, full [handicapped] facilities, [phone], [picnic], litter barrels, vending, petwalk**
54	Ave 52 E, Mohawk Valley
42	Ave 40 E, to Tacna, **N gas:** Chevron/dsl/24hr, **lodging:** Chaparral Motel
37	Ave 36 E, to Roll
30	Ave 29 E, Wellton, **N gas:** Circle K/gas, **other:** Tier Drop RV Park, **S gas:** Chevron, **food:** Jack-in-the-Box, Shooter's Cantina, **lodging:** Microtel, **other:** Coyote Wash Foods
24mm	Ligurta Wash
23mm	Red Top Wash

WELLTON

AZ

INTERSTATE 8 CONT'D

Exit #	Services
22mm	**parking area both lanes**
21	Dome Valley, **N other:** Ligurta Sta RV park, Yuma Proving Ground (16mi)
17mm	**insp sta eb**
15mm	Fortuna Wash
14	Foothills Blvd, **N other:** Sundance RV Park, **S food:** Domino's, **other:** Ace Hardware, FootHills RV Park, The Grocery Store/gas/dsl, auto/RV care/lube ctr
12	Fortuna Rd, to US 95 N, **N gas:** Chevron/24hr, Valero/Barney's/dsl/scales/24hr, **food:** Day Breakers Cafe, Jack-in-the-Box, Pizza Hut, **lodging:** Courtesy Inn, **other:** Caravan RV Park, Oasis RV Park, **S gas:** Shell/Burger King/dsl, SP/dsl, **food:** Applebees, A&W/KFC, Checkers, Debois Pizza, DQ, Subway, **lodging:** Microtel, **other:** Big O Tire, $General, Family$, Fry's Foods, Radio Shack
9	32nd St (no EZ wb return), to Yuma, **S other:** Sun Vista RV Park, Walmart Super Ctr
7	Araby Rd, **S gas:** Circle K/dsl, **S gas:** Chevron/Jack-in-the-Box/dsl, Circle K/dsl, **other:** RV World, Sun Vista RV Park, to AZWU
3	AZ 280 S, Ave 3E, **S gas:** Loves/Chester's/Subway/dsl/scales/24hr, **lodging:** Candlewood Suites, Holiday Inn Express, **other:** Harley-Davidson, to Marine Corp Air Sta
2	US 95, 16th St, Yuma, **N gas:** 76/Circle K, **food:** Arnie's Cafe, Chili's, ChuckeCheese, Cracker Barrel, Del Taco, Denny's, Famous Dave's BBQ, In-n-Out, Jamba Juice, Logans Roadhouse, Mimi's Cafe, Panda Express, Red Lobster, Subway, **lodging:** Best Western, Day's Inn, Fairfield Inn, Hampton Inn, Holiday Inn, La Fuente Inn, Holiday Inn, Motel 6, OakTree Inn, Shilo Inn/rest., SpringHill Suites, TownePlace Suites, Wingate Inn, **other:** Best Buy, Dillards, JC Penney, JoAnn Fabrics, Kohl's, Old Navy, PetsMart, Ross, Sam's Club/gas, Target, auto/tire repair, **2 mi S on Pacific Ave...food:** Mr. Lu's Chinese, Peter Piper Pizza, Subway, Wienerschnitzel, **other:** Big O Tire, NAPA, Kia, Walmart SuperCtr/24hr/gas, **S gas:** Arco/dsl/24hr, Chevron/Blimpie/dsl, Shell, Valero, **food:** Applebee's, Burger King, Carl's Jr, Chretin's Mexican, IHOP, Jack-in-the-Box, McDonald's, Golden Corral, Outback Steaks, Texas Roadhouse, Wendy's, Village Inn Pizza, **lodging:** Comfort Inn, Interstate 8 Inn, Motel 6, Super 8, **other:** H, BigLots, Big O Tires, Family$, Home Depot, KIA, Radio Shack, Staples, U-Haul
1.5mm	**weigh sta both lanes**
1	Giss Pkwy, Yuma, **N other:** to Yuma Terr Prison SP, **S** on 4th Ave **gas:** Chevron, Circle K/gas, **food:** Jack-in-the-Box, Yuma Landing Rest., **lodging:** Best Western
0mm	Arizona/California state line, Colorado River, Mountain/Pacific time zone

INTERSTATE 10

Exit #	Services
391mm	Arizona/New Mexico state line
390	Cavot Rd
389mm	**rest area both lanes, full [handicapped] facilities, [phone], [picnic], litter barrels, vending, petwalk**
383mm	**weigh sta eb, weigh/insp sta wb**
382	Portal Rd, San Simon
381mm	San Simon River
378	Lp 10, San Simon, **N gas:** 4K Trkstp/Noble Romans/Quizno's/dsl/scales/24hrs/@, **other:** auto/dsl/RV repair
366	Lp 10, Bowie Rd, **N gas:** Shell/dsl/24hr, **food:** Mama Cimino's Pizza, **S other:** Alaskan RV park
362	Lp 10, Bowie Rd, **N** gas, lodging, camping, **S** to Ft Bowie NHS
355	US 191 N, to Safford, **N** to Roper Lake SP
352	US 191 N, to Safford, same as 355
344	Lp 10, to Willcox, **N other:** Lifestyle RV Resort
340	AZ 186, to Rex Allen Dr, **N gas:** TA/Shell/Popeye's/Subway/dsl/scales/24hr/@, **lodging:** Holiday Inn Express, Super 8, **other:** Magic Circle RV Park, Stout's CiderMill, **S gas:** Circle K, Doc's/dsl, Texaco/dsl, **food:** Burger King, KFC/Taco Bell, McDonald's, Pizza Hut, Plaza Rest., **lodging:** Best Western, Day's Inn, Motel 6, **other:** H, Ace Hardware, Alco, Autozone, Beall's, Family$, Food City, $General, Radio Shack, Safeway, Grande Vista RV Park, to Chiricahua NM
336	AZ 186, Willcox, **S gas:** Chevron/dsl/LP, **1-3 mi S lodging:** Desert Inn Motel, **other:** Ft Willcox RV Park
331	US 191 S, to Sunsites, Douglas, **S other:** to Cochise Stronghold
322	Johnson Rd, **S gas:** Shell/DQ/dsl/gifts
320mm	**rest area both lanes, full [handicapped] facilities, [phone], [picnic], litter barrels, vending, petwalk**
318	Triangle T Rd, to Dragoon, **S** lodging, camping
312	Sibyl Rd
309mm	Adams Peak Wash
306	AZ 80, Pomerene Rd, Benson, **1-2 mi S gas:** Circle K, Mobil, **food:** G&F Pizza Palace, **other:** Pato Blanco RV Park, San Pedro RV Park
305mm	San Pedro River
304	Ocotillo St, Benson, **N food:** Denny's, Jack-in-the-Box, **lodging:** Day's Inn, Super 8, **other:** Benson RV Park, KOA, **S gas:** Chevron, Texaco, **food:** Apple Farm Rest., Magaly's Mexican, Palatianos Rest, Quizno's, Ruiz's Rest., Subway, Wendy's, **lodging:** Best Western, QuarterHorse Inn, **other:** H, Ace Hardware, Butterfield RV Park, Dillon RV Ctr, $General, Family$, NAPA, Pardner's RV Park, Radio Shack, Safeway, Walmart SuperCtr
303	US 80 (eb only), to Tombstone, Bisbee, **1 mi S gas: food:** Reb's Rest., Ruiz Mexican, Wendy's, **other:** NAPA, Safeway, auto/dsl/repair, to Douglas NHL
302	AZ 90 S, to Ft Huachuca, Benson, **S gas:** Gas City/A&W/Pizza Express/TCBY/dsl, Shell/Subway/dsl, **food:** KFC/Taco Bell, McDonald's, **lodging:** Holiday Inn Express, Motel 6, **other:** Cochise Terrace RV Park, Ft Huachuca NHS, Walmart SuperCtr
301	ranch exit eb
299	Skyline Rd
297	Mescal Rd, J-6 Ranch Rd, **N gas:** QuickPic/dsl/deli/24hr
292	Empirita Rd
289	Marsh Station Rd
288mm	Cienega Creek
281	AZ 83 S, to Patagonia
279	Vail/Wentworth Rd, **0-1 mi N gas:** QuikMart/gas, **food:** DQ, Quizno's, Montgomery's Grill, **other:** Curves, USPO, to Colossal Caves

INTERSTATE 10 CONT'D

E ↕ W

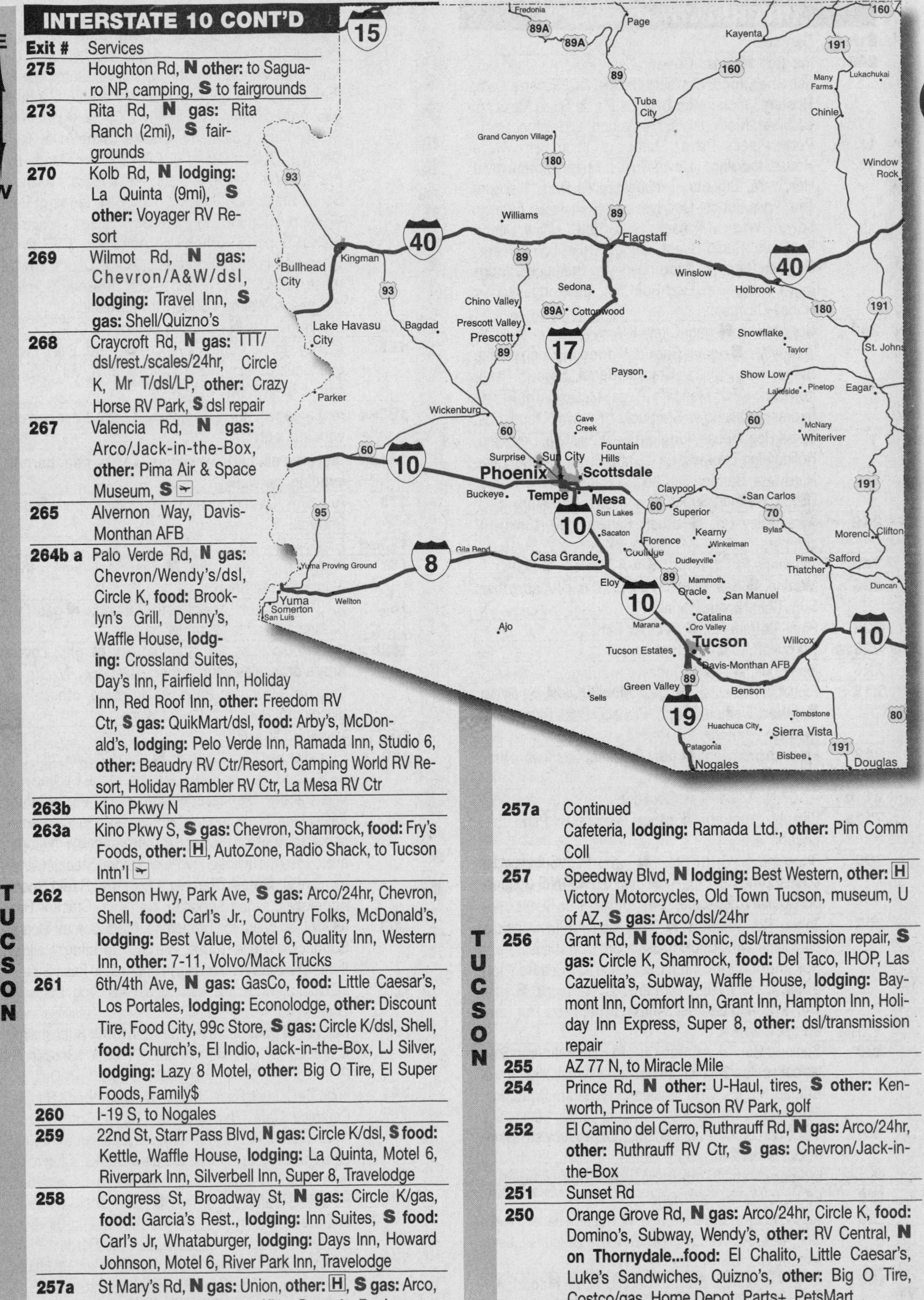

Exit #	Services
275	Houghton Rd, **N other:** to Saguaro NP, camping, **S** to fairgrounds
273	Rita Rd, **N gas:** Rita Ranch (2mi), **S** fairgrounds
270	Kolb Rd, **N lodging:** La Quinta (9mi), **S other:** Voyager RV Resort
269	Wilmot Rd, **N gas:** Chevron/A&W/dsl, **lodging:** Travel Inn, **S gas:** Shell/Quizno's
268	Craycroft Rd, **N gas:** TTT/dsl/rest./scales/24hr, Circle K, Mr T/dsl/LP, **other:** Crazy Horse RV Park, **S** dsl repair
267	Valencia Rd, **N gas:** Arco/Jack-in-the-Box, **other:** Pima Air & Space Museum, **S** ✈
265	Alvernon Way, Davis-Monthan AFB
264b a	Palo Verde Rd, **N gas:** Chevron/Wendy's/dsl, Circle K, **food:** Brooklyn's Grill, Denny's, Waffle House, **lodging:** Crossland Suites, Day's Inn, Fairfield Inn, Holiday Inn, Red Roof Inn, **other:** Freedom RV Ctr, **S gas:** QuikMart/dsl, **food:** Arby's, McDonald's, **lodging:** Pelo Verde Inn, Ramada Inn, Studio 6, **other:** Beaudry RV Ctr/Resort, Camping World RV Resort, Holiday Rambler RV Ctr, La Mesa RV Ctr
263b	Kino Pkwy N
263a	Kino Pkwy S, **S gas:** Chevron, Shamrock, **food:** Fry's Foods, **other:** H, AutoZone, Radio Shack, to Tucson Intn'l ✈
262	Benson Hwy, Park Ave, **S gas:** Arco/24hr, Chevron, Shell, **food:** Carl's Jr., Country Folks, McDonald's, **lodging:** Best Value, Motel 6, Quality Inn, Western Inn, **other:** 7-11, Volvo/Mack Trucks
261	6th/4th Ave, **N gas:** GasCo, **food:** Little Caesar's, Los Portales, **lodging:** Econolodge, **other:** Discount Tire, Food City, 99c Store, **S gas:** Circle K/dsl, Shell, **food:** Church's, El Indio, Jack-in-the-Box, LJ Silver, **lodging:** Lazy 8 Motel, **other:** Big O Tire, El Super Foods, Family$
260	I-19 S, to Nogales
259	22nd St, Starr Pass Blvd, **N gas:** Circle K/dsl, **S food:** Kettle, Waffle House, **lodging:** La Quinta, Motel 6, Riverpark Inn, Silverbell Inn, Super 8, Travelodge
258	Congress St, Broadway St, **N gas:** Circle K/gas, **food:** Garcia's Rest., **lodging:** Inn Suites, **S food:** Carl's Jr, Whataburger, **lodging:** Days Inn, Howard Johnson, Motel 6, River Park Inn, Travelodge
257a	St Mary's Rd, **N gas:** Union, **other:** H, **S gas:** Arco, Shell/24hr, **food:** Burger King, Denny's, Furr's

TUCSON

Exit #	Services
257a	Continued Cafeteria, **lodging:** Ramada Ltd., **other:** Pim Comm Coll
257	Speedway Blvd, **N lodging:** Best Western, **other:** H Victory Motorcycles, Old Town Tucson, museum, U of AZ, **S gas:** Arco/dsl/24hr
256	Grant Rd, **N food:** Sonic, dsl/transmission repair, **S gas:** Circle K, Shamrock, **food:** Del Taco, IHOP, Las Cazuelita's, Subway, Waffle House, **lodging:** Baymont Inn, Comfort Inn, Grant Inn, Hampton Inn, Holiday Inn Express, Super 8, **other:** dsl/transmission repair
255	AZ 77 N, to Miracle Mile
254	Prince Rd, **N other:** U-Haul, tires, **S other:** Kenworth, Prince of Tucson RV Park, golf
252	El Camino del Cerro, Ruthrauff Rd, **N gas:** Arco/24hr, **other:** Ruthrauff RV Ctr, **S gas:** Chevron/Jack-in-the-Box
251	Sunset Rd
250	Orange Grove Rd, **N gas:** Arco/24hr, Circle K, **food:** Domino's, Subway, Wendy's, **other:** RV Central, **N on Thornydale...food:** El Chalito, Little Caesar's, Luke's Sandwiches, Quizno's, **other:** Big O Tire, Costco/gas, Home Depot, Parts+, PetsMart

TUCSON

INTERSTATE 10 CONT'D

E ↕ W

TUCSON

Exit #	Services
248	Ina Rd, **N gas:** Chevron/dsl, Circle K, QuikMart/dsl, Shell, **food:** Carl's Jr, Chuy's, DQ, Eegee's Cafe, Hooters, Jack-in-the-Box, La Parilla Suiza Mexican, LJ Silver, McDonald's, Ms Saigon, Old Father Rest., Peter Piper's Pizza, Starbucks, Taco Bell, Waffle House, **lodging:** InTown Suites, Motel 6, **other:** Ace Hardware, BigLots, CarQuest, CVS Drug, Discount Tire, Fry's Foods, Goodyear/auto, Hancock Fabrics, Lowe's Whse, Michael's, 99c Store, Office Depot, PepBoys, Radio Shack, Target, U-Haul, Walgreens, **S gas:** Circle K, **food:** Denny's, Starbucks, **lodging:** Comfort Inn, Red Roof Inn, Travelodge, **other:** Harley-Davidson
246	Cortaro Rd, **N gas:** Circle K/Arby's/dsl, **food:** IHOP, Wendy's, **S gas:** Shell/dsl, **food:** Boston's Mkt, Burger King, Chili's, Cracker Barrel, Eegee's Rest., In-n-Out, KFC, Magpie's Pizza, McDonald's, Panda Express, Quizno's, Starbucks, Subway, Taco Bell, Texas Roadhouse, **lodging:** Best Western, Day's Inn, Holiday Inn Express, La Quinta, Super 8, **other:** Ace Hardware, Batteries+, Checker Parts, Curves, Kohl's, USPO, Walmart SuperCtr, access to RV camping
242	Avra Valley Rd, **S other:** Saguaro NP (13mi), RV camping, ✈
240	Tangerine Rd, to Rillito, **S** A-A RV Park, **S** USPO
236	Marana, **S gas:** Chevron/dsl/LP, Circle K/gas, **other:** Sun RV Park, auto repair
232	Pinal Air Park Rd, **S** Pinal Air Park
228mm	wb pulloff, to frontage rd
226	Red Rock, **S** USPO
219	Picacho Peak Rd, **N gas:** Mobil/DQ/dsl, Shell/dsl, **S other:** Ostrich Ranch, Pichaco Peak RV Park, to Picacho Peak SP
212	Picacho (from wb), **N gas:** Premium Gas/tires, **other:** USPO **S** Picacho Camping
211b	AZ 87 N, AZ 84 W, to Coolidge
211a	Picacho (from eb), **S other:** Picacho RV Park, state prison
208	Sunshine Blvd, to Eloy, **N gas:** Pilot/Subway/dsl/scales/24hr, dsl repair, **S gas:** ***FLYING J***/Conoco/Cookery/dsl/scales/24hr, **other:** Blue Beacon
203	Toltec Rd, to Eloy, **N gas:** Chevron/McDonald's/playplace/24hr, Circle K/dsl, **food:** Carl's Jr, El Zarape Rojo Mexican, **lodging:** Best Value Inn, Red Roof Inn, **other:** Desert Valley RV Park, dsl/tire repair, **S gas:** TA/A&W/Taco Bell/dsl/24hr/@, **food:** Pizza Hut, **other:** truckwash
200	Sunland Gin Rd, Arizona City, **N gas:** Petro/Iron Skillet/dsl/scales/24hr/@, Pride/Subway/dsl/24hr, **food:** Burger King, Eva's Mexican, **lodging:** Day's Inn, Travelodge, **other:** Blue Beacon, Eagle Truckwash, Las Colinas RV Park, **S gas:** Loves/Arby's/Baskin-Robbins/dsl/24hr, **food:** Golden 9 Rest., Starbucks, **lodging:** Motel 6, **other:** Speedco Lube
199	I-8 W, to Yuma, San Diego
198	AZ 84, to Eloy, Casa Grande, **N** Robson Ranch Rest./Golf, **S food:** Wendy's, **other:** Casa Grande Outlets/famous brands, Buena Tierra RV Pk
194	AZ 287, Florence Blvd, to Casa Grande, **N food:** Ah-So Steaks, In-n-Out, Mimi's Cafe, Olive Garden,

CASA GRANDE

Exit #	Services
194	Continued Red Brick Pizza, Rubio's, Subway, **other:** Best Buy, Dillards, JC Penney, Kohl's, Marshalls, Michaels, Old Navy, PetsMart, Radio Shack, Staples, Sunscape RV Park (7mi), Target, Walgreens, World Mkt, **0-2 mi S gas:** Arco/dsl/24hr, Chevron/DQ, Circle K/gas, **food:** Burger King, Coldstone, Cracker Barrel, Del Taco, Denny's, Golden Corral, IHOP, LJ Silver, Panda Express, Papa Murphy's, Peter Piper Pizza, Quizno's, Sonic, Starbucks, Subway, Taco Bell, **lodging:** Best Western, Comfort Inn, Legacy Suites, Mainstay Suites, Super 8, **other:** [H], AutoZone, CVS Drug, Discount Tire, Fry's Food/drug, Home Depot, Lowe's Whse, Palm Creek RV/golf Resort, Tuesday Morning, Walgreens, Walmart SuperCtr/McDonalds
190	McCartney Rd, **N other:** to Central AZ Coll
185	AZ 387, to Coolidge, Florence, **S food:** Eva's Mexican (6mi), **other:** Fry's Food/gas (6mi), Val Vista RV camping (3mi), hwy patrol
183mm	**rest area wb, full ♿ facilities, ☎, picnic, litter barrels, vending, petwalk**
181mm	**rest area eb, full ♿ facilities, ☎, picnic, litter barrels, vending, petwalk**
175	AZ 587 N, Casa Blanca Rd, Chandler, Gilbert, **S gas:** Shell/dsl
173mm	Gila River
167	Riggs Rd, to Sun Lake, **N gas:** Shell (3mi), **other:** Akimel Smoke Shop
164	AZ 347 S, Queen Creek Rd, to Maricopa, **N gas:** Mobil (3mi), **other:** to Chandler ✈
162b a	Wild Horse Pass Rd, Sundust Rd, **N gas:** Loves/Arby's/dsl/scales/24hr, **other:** Beaudry RV Ctr, **S lodging:** Wildhorse Pass Hotel/Casino, **other:** Firebird Sports Park, Gila River Casino
161	Pecos Rd, lp 202 E

CHANDLER

Exit #	Services
160	Chandler Blvd, to Chandler, **N gas:** Chevron/dsl, Circle K, **food:** Burger King, Denny's, Marie Callender's, Villa Pandos Mexican, Whataburger/24hr, **lodging:** Faifield Inn, Hampton Inn, Homewood Suites, Radisson, Red Roof Inn, Super 8, **other:** Aamco, Firestone/auto, Harley-Davidson, to Compadre Stadium, Williams AFB, **S gas:** Chevron, Circle K/dsl, 7-11, **food:** Applebees, Arriba Mexican, Carl's Jr, Cracker Barrel, Del Taco, Dunkin Donuts, Hooters, Jersey Mike's, Starbucks, Waffle House, Wendy's, **lodging:** Holiday Inn Express, Extended Stay America, InTown Suites, La Quinta, **other:** [H], AutoZone, CVS Drug, Discount Tire, Kohl's
159	Ray Rd, **N gas:** Circle K, Shell/dsl, **food:** Buca Italian, Carrabba's, Charleston's Rest., Chipotle Mexican, El Pollo Loco, 5&Diner, Fleming's Steaks, In-n-Out, Jasons Deli, Jilly's Rest., McDonald's, Outback Steaks, Paradise Cafe, Red Lobster, Roy's Cafe, Rumbi Grill, Starbucks, Tejas, Tomaso's Italian, **lodging:** Courtyard, **other:** BMW, Borders Books, Chevrolet, Ford, Home Depot, Lexus, Lowe's Whse, Mercedes, PetsMart, Sam's Club/gas, **S gas:** Shell, Circle K/dsl, **food:** Boston Mkt, IHOP/24hr, Jack-in-the-Box, Macaroni Grill, Mimi's Café, On-the-Border, Peter Piper Pizza, Pizza Hut, Rock Bottom Rest., Rubio's, Sweet Tomatoes, Wendy's, **lodging:** Extended Stay America, **other:** URGENT CARE, Barnes&Noble,

INTERSTATE 10 CONT'D

E ↕ W

Exit #	Services
159	Continued Best Buy, CVS Drug, JC Penney, Jo-Ann Fabrics, Michael's, Old Navy, PetCo, Ross, SteinMart, Target
158	Warner Rd, **N** **gas:** Circle K/dsl, QT, **food:** Port of Subs, **S** **gas:** Arco/24hr, Circle K/dsl, **food:** Burger King, ChuckeCheese, DQ, Macayo's Mexican, Malaya Mexican, McDonald's, Nello's Pizza, Panda Garden, Quizno's, Ruffino's Italian, **other:** Ace Hardware, Basha's Foods, Big 10 Tire, Goodyear/auto, vet
157	Elliot Rd, **N** **gas:** Chevron, Shell/Circle K, **food:** Applebee's, Arby's, Baja Fresh, Burger King, Coco's, Crackers Cafe, Crazy W Buffet, Dayton's Place, HoneyBear's BBQ, Kabab Palace, Kobe Japanese, Moe's SW Grill, Olive Garden, Panda Express, Quizno's, Red Robin Rest., Sooper Salad, Sonic, Starbucks, Subway, Taco Bell, The Groves, Wendy's, YC Mongolian Grill, Yupha's Kitchen, **lodging:** Country Inn&Suites, **other:** URGENT CARE, Acura, Cadillac/GMC, Costco/gas, Discount Tire, Dodge, $Tree, Ford/Lincoln/Mercury, Honda, Nissan, PetsMart, Pontiac/Buick, Savers, Staples, Toyota/Scion, Walmart, **S** **gas:** Shell/Circle K, **food:** Baskin-Robbins, Cactus Jack's, KFC, Mesquite Broiler, McDonald's, Sub Factory, **lodging:** Clarion, Grace Inn, **other:** Checker Parts, Safeway, Walgreens
155	Baseline Rd, Guadalupe, **N** **gas:** Shell/Circle K/Popeye's/dsl, **food:** Carl's Jr, ClaimJumper, 5& Diner, Joe's Crabshack, KFC, McDonald's, Poliberto's Tacos, Popeye's, Rainforest Cafe, Waffle House, Wendy's, **lodging:** Best Western, Candlewood Studios, Holiday Inn Express, InnSuites, Ramada, Residence Inn, SpringHill Suites, TownePlace Suites, **other:** AutoZone, AZ Mills/Famous Brands, CVS Drug, Food City, Home Depot, JC Penney Outlet, Marshall's, Pro Auto Parts, Ross, Walgreens, **S** **gas:** Arco, QT, 7-11, **lodging:** Homestead Suites, **food:** Aunt Chilada's Mexican, China Town, Denny's, Sonic, Subway, **other:** Fry's Electronics, Fry's Foods
154	US 60 E, AZ 360, Superstition Frwy, to Mesa, N **other:** to Camping World (off Mesa Dr)
153b	Broadway Rd E, **N** **gas:** Circle K/gas, **food:** Denny's, **lodging:** Comfort Suites, Courtyard, Fairfield Inn, Hilton, Homestead Suites, La Quinta, Quality Inn, Red Roof Inn, Sheraton, Sleep Inn, **other:** to Diablo Stadium, **S** **gas:** Chevron, Shell/Circle K/Del Taco/24hr, **food:** Panda Express, Papa John's, Pizza Hut, Port of Subs, Taco Bell, Whataburger, **lodging:** Hampton Inn, Homewood Suites, **other:** Staples
153a	AZ 143 N, **N** **food:** Denny's, **lodging:** Courtyard, Fairfield Inn, Hilton, La Quinta, Quality Inn, Sheraton, Sleep Inn, **other:** to Diablo Stadium, **S** same as 153b
152	40th St, **N** **gas:** Shell/dsl, **other:** U Phoenix, **S** **gas:** Shell/Circle K, **food:** Burger King
151mm	Salt River
151b a	28th St, 32nd St, University Ave, **N** **food:** Waffle House, **lodging:** Extended Stay America, Hilton Garden, Holiday Inn Express, Radisson, **other:** AZSU, U Phoenix, **S** **gas:** Circle K, **food:** McDonald's

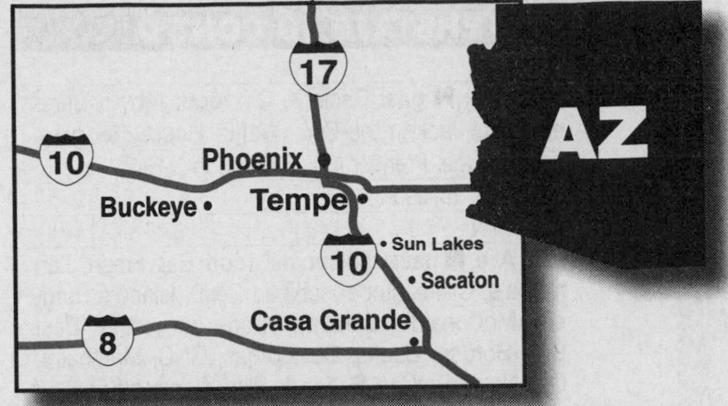

Exit #	Services
150b	24th St E (from wb), **N** Air Nat Guard, **lodging:** Motel 6, **S** **lodging:** Best Western/rest.
150a	I-17 N, to Flagstaff
149	Buckeye Rd, **N** **other:** Sky Harbor ✈
148	Washington St, Jefferson St, **N** **gas:** Chevron, Shell, Tiemco/dsl, **food:** Carl's Jr, Mandy's Fish'n Chips, McDonald's, Rally's, **lodging:** Motel 6, Sterling Hotel, **other:** to Sky Harbor Airport, **S** **gas:** Circle K, **other:** H
147b a	AZ 51 N, AZ 202 E, to Squaw Peak Pkwy
146	16th St, **N** **gas:** Circle K/Shell, **food:** KFC, **S** **gas:** Circle K, **food:** Antonio's Rest., Church's, Tradicione's, **other:** Ranch Mkt
145	7th St, **N** **food:** McDonald's, **other:** Safeway Foods, Walgreens, **S** **gas:** Circle K, Shell, **other:** H, to America West Arena
144	7th Ave, Amtrak, central bus dist
143c	19th Ave, US 60
143b a	I-17, N to Flagstaff, S to Phoenix
142	27th Ave (from eb, no return), **N** **lodging:** Comfort Inn
141	35th Ave, **N** **food:** Jack-in-the-Box, Rita's Mexican, **S** **gas:** Shell/Circle K
140	43rd Ave, **N** **gas:** Circle K/dsl, 7-11, Shell, **food:** Filberto's Mexican, Pizza Hut, Salsita's Mexican, Subway, **other:** AutoZone, Fry's Foods, 99c Store, Radio Shack, Walgreens
139	51st Ave, **N** **gas:** Chevron/dsl, Circle K, **food:** Burger King, Domino's, El Pollo Loco, McDonald's, Sonic, Waffle House, **lodging:** Budget Inn, CrossLand Suites, Day's Inn, Holiday Inn, InTowne Suites, La Quinta, Motel 6, Red Roof Inn, Travelodge, **other:** Discount Tire, Food City, 7-11, **S** **gas:** DZ/dsl, QT/dsl/scales, **food:** Carl's Jr, IHOP, Taco Bell, **lodging:** Hampton Inn, Phoenix West Inn, Super 8, Travelers Inn
138	59th Ave, **N** **gas:** Circle K, Shamrock, **food:** Armando's Mexican/24hr, Subway, **other:** AutoZone, Checker Parts, Family$, 7-11, Walgreens, **S** **gas:** Liberty/Wendy's/dsl/24hr, **food:** Waffle House, Whataburger/24hr, **other:** Blue Beacon/scales
137	67th Ave, **N** **gas:** QT, Circle K/dsl, Shell/dsl, **food:** Church's, **S** **gas:** ***FLYING J***/Conoco/CountryMkt/dsl/LP/24hr
136	75th Ave, **N** **gas:** Chevron, Circle K/gas, **food:** A&W, Del Taco, Denny's, Starbucks, Whataburger, Taco Bell/Pizza Hut, Taco Del Mar, Texas Roadhouse, Whataburger, **other:** Ford, Home Depot, Lowe's Whse, PetsMart, Staples, Walmart SuperCtr, **S** **gas:** Arco/24hr

PHOENIX

AZ

INTERSTATE 10 CONT'D

E ↕ W

PHOENIX

Exit #	Services
135	83rd Ave, **N gas:** Circle K, QT, **food:** Arby's, Burger King, Jack-in-the-Box, Waffle House, **lodging:** Econolodge, Premier Inn, **other:** Sam's Club
134	91st Ave, Tolleson
133b	Lp 101 N
133a	99th Ave, **N gas:** Chevron/dsl, **food:** Baja Fresh, Carrabba's, ClaimJumper, Ichiban Rest., Island's Burgers, McDonald's, Subway, Village Inn, **other:** Best Buy, Borders Books, Costco/gas, GNC, Marshall's, Old Navy, PetCo, **S food:** Pilot/Wendy's/Subway/dsl/scales/24hr/@, **other:** CarMax
132	107th Ave (from eb), **N other:** Walgreens, **S other:** Earnhardt RV Ctr, Dodge, Hyundai, Kia, Mazda, Mitsubishi, Nissan, Subaru
131	Avondale Blvd., to Cashion, **N gas:** Mobil, **S lodging:** Hilton Garden, Homewood Suites, **other:** to Phoenix International Raceway
129	Dysart Rd, to Avondale, **N gas:** Chevron, Shell/Circle K/dsl, **food:** Big Apple Rest., Carino's Italian, Chick-fil-A, In-n-Out, Jack-in-the-Box/24hr, Mimi's Cafe, NY Pizza, Panda Express, Papa Murphy's, Quizno's, Taco Bell, **lodging:** Wingate Inn, **other:** AutoZone, Discount Tire, $Tree, Jo-Ann Fabrics, Fry's Foods, Kohl's, Lowe's Whse, PetsMart, Walmart SuperCtr/24hr, **S gas:** QT, **food:** A&W/LJ Silver, Black Bear Diner, Del Taco, Gandolfo's, Golden Corral, KFC, McDonald's, Peter Piper Pizza, Subway, Waffle House, Whataburger, **lodging:** Best Value Inn, Super 8, **other:** Brakemasters, Chevrolet, Chrysler/Dodge/Jeep, Food City, Home Depot, Sam's Club, Suzuki, Walgreens
128	Litchfield Rd, **N gas:** Mobil/Blimpie/dsl, **food:** Applebee's, Black Angus Steaks, Carl's Jr, Chili's, Chipotle Mexican, Cracker Barrel, Denny's, El Paso BBQ, Fazoli's, Macaroni Grill, Macavo's Mexican, McDonald's, McGrath's Fishouse, On the Border, Starbucks, Subway, TGIFriday, Wendy's, **lodging:** Hampton Inn, Holiday Inn Express, Residence Inn, **other:** H, Barnes&Noble, Best Buy, Michael's, Ross, Target, Wigwam Resort/rest (3mi), to Luke AFB, **S gas:** Mobil, **food:** Arby's, Burger King, JB's, Schlotsky's, Taco Bell, **lodging:** Best Western, **other:** AutoZone, Fry's Food/drug, Goodyear/auto, 99c Store, Osco Drug, Pontiac/GMC, Radio Shack
126	PebbleCreek Pkwy, to Estrella Park, **S food:** Bro's Pizza, Its a Grind, Jack-in-the-Box, Subway, **lodging:** Comfort Suites, **other:** Safeway Foods/gas, Walgreens, Walmart SuperCtr/24hr
125mm	Roosevelt Canal
124	Cotton Lane, to AZ 303, **N** st prison, **S other:** Pheonix RV Park
121	Jackrabbit Trail, **N gas:** Chevron/dsl, **S gas:** Circle K
120	Verrado Way
117	Watson Rd, **S food:** Jack-in-the-Box, Palermo's Pizza, Peter Piper Pizza, Subway, Wendy's, **other:** Fry's Foods/gas, Lowes Whse, PetsMart, Walgreens, Walmart SuperCtr, Vet
114	Miller Rd, to Buckeye, **S gas:** Loves/Chester Fried/Subway/dsl/scales/24hr, **food:** Burger King, **lodging:** Day's Inn, **other:** Leaf Verde RV Park

TONOPAH

QUARTZSITE

Exit #	Services
112	AZ 85, to I-8, Gila Bend, **S** Subway (3mi)
109	Sun Valley Pkwy, Palo Verde Rd
104mm	Hassayampa River
103	339th Ave, **S gas:** TA/Shell/Subway/dsl/LP/scales/24hr/@, **food:** Country Fair Rest. **other:** truckwash
98	Wintersburg Rd
97mm	Coyote Wash
95.5mm	Old Camp Wash
94	411th Ave, Tonopah, **S gas:** Chevron/dsl, Mobil/dsl, Shell/Chester's/Noble Roman's/Subway/dsl/LP/24hr, **food:** Tonopah Joe's Rest., **lodging:** Mineral Wells Motel, **other:** USPO, tires/repair, Saddle Mtn RV Park, playground
86mm	**rest area both lanes, full facilities, , , litter barrels, petwalk, vending**
81	Salome Rd, Harquahala Valley Rd
69	Ave 75E
53	Hovatter Rd
52mm	**rest area both lanes, full facilities, , vending, , litter barrels, petwalk**
45	Vicksburg Rd, **N gas:** Zip TC/HotStuff/dsl/24hr, **S gas:** Valero/dsl/rest./scales/24hr, **other:** Jobski's dsl Repair/towing, RV Park, tires, wildlife refuge
31	US 60 E, to Wickenburg, **12 mi N other:** food, camping
26	Gold Nugget Rd
19	Quartzsite, to US 95, Yuma, **N gas:** Chevron/dsl, Park Place TC/subs/dsl, Shell/dsl, **food:** Taco Mio, **other:** Beall's, CarQuest, Family$, Radio Shack, Roadrunner Foods, RV camping
18mm	Tyson Wash
17	US 95, AZ 95, Quartzsite, **N gas:** Mobil/Burger King/LP, Pilot/DQ/Subway/dsl/scales/24hr, **food:** Best Mexican, Carl's Jr, McDonald's, Quarter Yacht Grill, **other:** RV camping, tires/repair, **S gas:** Loves/Chester's/Subway/dsl/24hr, **lodging:** Super 8, **other:** Desert Gardens RV Park
11	Dome Rock Rd
5	Tom Wells Rd, **N gas:** Texaco/SunMart/Quizno's/dsl
4.5mm	**rest area both lanes, full facilities, , vending, , litter barrels, petwalk**
3.5mm	eb AZ Port of Entry, **wb weigh sta**
1	Ehrenberg, to Parker, **N other:** River Breeze RV Resort, **S gas:** ***FLYING J***/Wendy's/Cookery/dsl/LP/scales24hr/@, **lodging:** Best Western
0mm	Arizona/California state line, Colorado River, Mountain/Pacific time zone

INTERSTATE 15

N ↕ S

Exit #	Services
29.5mm	Arizona/Utah state line
27	Black Rock Rd
21mm	turnout sb
18	Cedar Pocket, **S other:** Virgin River Canyon RA/camping, parking area
16mm	**truck parking both lanes**
15mm	**truck parking nb**
14mm	**truck parking nb**
10mm	**truck parking nb**
9	Desert Springs
8.5mm	Virgin River

INTERSTATE 15 CONT'D

Exit #	Services
8	Littlefield, Beaver Dam, **E other:** RV park, **1 mi W** gas/dsl, food, lodging, camping
0mm	Arizona/Nevada state line, Pacific/Mountain time zone

INTERSTATE 17

N ↕ S

FLAGSTAFF

Exit #	Services
341	McConnell Dr, I-17 begins/ends, **N gas:** Chevron/dsl, Conoco/dsl, Flag, Gasser/dsl, Giant/dsl, Mobil, Circle K, Shell, Texaco/Wendy's/dsl, **food:** Arby's, August Moon Chinese, Baskin-Robbins, Buffalo Wild Wings, Burger King, Buster's Rest., Carl's Jr, Casa Bonita, Chili's, China Garden, Coco's, Coldstone, DQ, Del Taco, Denny's, Domino's, Fazoli's, Garcia's Mexican, IHOP, Jack-in-the-Box, KFC, Mandarin Buffet, McDonald's, Olive Garden, Papa John's, Picazzo's Pizza, Peter Piper Pizza, Pizza Hut, Quizno's, Red Lobster, Roma Pizza, Szechuan Chinese, Sizzler, Starbucks, Strombolli's, Subway, Taco Bell, **lodging:** AZ Motel, Budget Inn, Canyon Inn, Comfort Inn, Courtyard, Day's Inn, Drury Inn, Econolodge, Embassy Suites, Fairfield Inn, Hampton Inn, Highland Country Inn, Hilton Garden, Knights Inn, La Quinta, Motel 6, Quality Inn, Ramada Ltd, Rodeway Inn, Sleep Inn, SpringHill Suites, Super 8, **other:** [H], Barnes&Noble, Basha's Foods, Discount Tire, Hastings Books, Jo-Ann Crafts, Kohl's, Michael's, Ross, Safeway, Staples, Target, Walgreens, Walmart, auto/RV repair
340b a	I-40, E to Gallup, W to Kingman
339	Lake Mary Rd (from nb), Mormon Lake, **E gas:** Circle K/dsl, **lodging:** AZ Mtn Inn, access to same as 341
337	AZ 89A S, to Sedona, Ft Tuthill RA, **W food:** camping
333	Kachina Blvd, Mountainaire Rd, **E food:** Mountainaire Rest. (1mi), **lodging:** Sled Dog B&B, **W gas:** Conoco/Subway/dsl
331	Kelly Canyon Rd
328	Newman Park Rd
326	Willard Springs Rd
322	Pinewood Rd, to Munds Park, **E gas:** Shell, Woody's/dsl, **food:** Lone Pine Rest., **other:** Motel in the Pines/RV camp, USPO, golf, **W other:** Munds RV Park, auto/RV repair
322mm	Munds Canyon
320	Schnebly Hill Rd
317	Fox Ranch Rd
316mm	Woods Canyon
315	Rocky Park Rd
313mm	scenic view sb, litter barrels
306	Stoneman Lake Rd
300mm	runaway truck ramp sb
298	AZ 179, to Sedona, Oak Creek Canyon, **7-15 mi W food:** Burger King, Cowboy Club Rest., Joey's Bistro, **lodging:** Belrock Inn, Hilton, La Quinta, Radisson/cafe, Wildflower Inn, **other:** Rancho Sedona RV Park
297mm	**rest area both lanes, full [handicapped] facilities, [phone], [picnic], litter barrels, vending, petwalk**
293mm	Dry Beaver Creek
293	Cornville Rd, McGuireville Rd, to Rimrock, **E gas:** ExpressFuel, **W gas:** Beaver Hollow/dsl/RV Park, 76/dsl, **food:** Crusty's Cafe, Las Margaritas Mexican

SEDONA

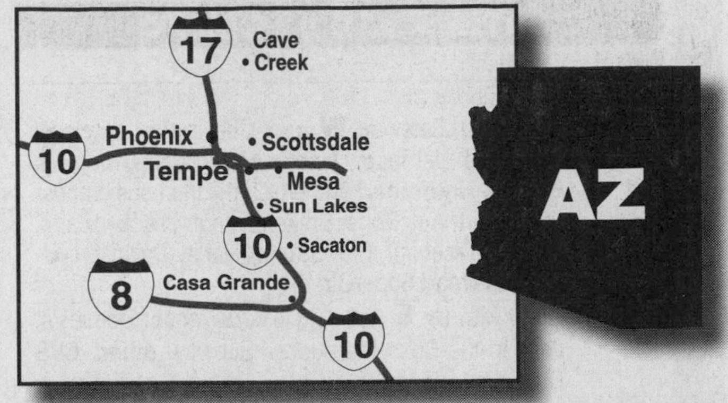

CAMP VERDE

Exit #	Services
289	Middle Verde Rd, Camp Verde, **E gas:** Mobil/dsl, **food:** Sonic, The Gathering Rest., **lodging:** Cliff Castle Lodge/casino/rest., **other:** to Montezuma Castle NM, **W other:** Distant Drums RV Park
288mm	Verde River
287	AZ 260, to AZ 89A, Cottonwood, Payson, **E gas:** Arco, Chevron, Shell/Noble Roman's/Subway/dsl/RV dump/LP/24hr, **food:** A&W/KFC, Burger King, DQ, Denny's, Los Betos Mexican, McDonald's, Quizno's, Starbucks, Taco Bell, **lodging:** Comfort Inn, Day's Inn, Super 8, **other:** Territorial RV Park (1mi), Trails End RV Park, Zane Grane RV Park, **W gas:** Chevron/Wendy's/dsl/24hr, **other:** to Jerome SP, RV camping
285	Camp Verde, Gen Crook Tr, **3 mi E food:** Rio Verde Mexican, **lodging:** Territorial Town Inn, **other:** Zane Gray RV Park (9mi), Trail End RV Park, to Ft Verde SP
281mm	safety pullout area nb
278	AZ 169, Cherry Rd, to Prescott
269mm	Ash Creek
268	Dugas Rd, Orme Rd
265.5mm	Agua Fria River
262b a	AZ 69 N, Cordes Jct Rd, to Prescott, **E gas:** Chevron/24hr, Shell/Subway/Noble Roman's/dsl/24hr, **food:** CJ's Diner, McDonald's, **lodging:** Cordes Jct Motel/RV Park
262mm	Big Bug Creek
259	Bloody Basin Rd, to Crown King, Horsethief Basin RA
256	Badger Springs Rd
252	**Sunset Point, W scenic view/rest area both lanes, full [handicapped] facilities, [phone], [picnic], litter barrels, vending**
248	Bumble Bee, **W other:** Horsethief Basin RA
244	Squaw Valley Rd, Black Canyon City, **E food:** Kid Chileean BBQ/Steaks, **other:** KOA, **W** gas
243.5mm	Agua Fria River
242	Rock Springs, Black Canyon City, **E** KOA (1mi), **W gas:** Chevron/dsl/24hr, Shell, **food:** Byler's Kitchen, Rock Springs Café, **lodging:** Bradshaw Mtn RV Resort, Mtn Breeze Motel
239.5mm	Little Squaw Creek
239mm	Moore's Gulch
236	Table Mesa Rd
232	New River, **E food:** RoadRunner Rest., **other:** Curves, Vet
231.5mm	New River
229	Anthem Way, Desert Hills Rd, **E gas:** Circle K/gas, **food:** Asiana, McDonald's, Native NewYorker Rest., Pizza Hut, Quizno's, Rosati's Pizza, Starbucks, Subway, Taco Bell, Taco Del Mar, **other:** Ace Hardware,

INTERSTATE 17 CONT'D

Exit #	Services
229	Continued CVS Drug, Safeway, **W gas:** Chevron/dsl, Circle K/gas, **food:** Del Taco, Denny's, Papa John's, **lodging:** Hampton Inn, **other:** Anthem Outlets/famous brands/food court, AutoZone, BrakeMasters, Checker Parts, Curves, Discount Tire, $Store, Harley-Davidson, U-Haul, Walmart SuperCtr, Vet
227	Daisy Mtn Dr, E **gas:** Circle K/dsl, **food:** Domino's, Jack-in-the-Box, Starbucks, Subway, **other:** CVS Drug, Fry's Foods
227mm	Dead Man Wash
225	Pioneer Rd, **W other:** Pioneer RV Park, museum
223	AZ 74, Carefree Hwy, to Wickenburg, **E gas:** Chevron, **food:** AZool Grill, Chili's, Denny's, Good Egg Cafe, In-n-Out, Krispy Kreme, McDonald's, Subway, **other:** Albertson's/Osco, Home Depot, Kohl's, Staples, **W other:** Lake Pleasant Park, camping
220	Dixileta
219	Jomax Rd
218	Happy Valley Rd, **E gas:** Shell, **food:** Applebees, Bajio, Carl's Jr, Chipotle Mexican, Coldstone Creamery, Dickey's BBQ, Jack-in-the-Box, Joey's Hotdogs, Johnny Rocket's, Logan's Roadhouse, L&L Hawaiian BBQ, Olive Garden, Panda Express, PF Chang's, Quizno's, Rays Pizza, Red Robin, Shane's Ribshack, Starbucks, Streets of NY Deli, Subway, TGIFriday's, Tilly's Grill, **lodging:** Courtyard, Hampton Inn, Homewood Suites, Residence Inn, **other:** Barnes&Noble, Best Buy, Checker Parts, Lowe's Whse, Old Navy, PetCo, Staples, TJ Maxx, Walmart SuperCtr, World Mkt
217	Pinnacle Peak Rd, **E** Phoenix RV Park
215a	Rose Garden Ln, same as 215b
215b	Deer Valley Rd, **E gas:** Circle K, Shamrock, **food:** Arby's, Armando's Mexican, Culvers, Jack-in-the-Box, McDonald's, Sonic, Taco Bell, Wendy's, **other:** Little Dealer RV Ctr, **W gas:** Arco, Circle K, **food:** Cracker Barrel, Denny's, Times Square Italian, Waffle House, **lodging:** Days Inn, Country Inn&Suites, Extended Stay America, **other:** H, NAPA, Pinnacle Peak RV Ctr, U-Haul
214c	AZ 101 loop
214b	Yorkshire Dr, **W food:** In-n-Out, Jack-in-the-Box, **lodging:** Budget Suites, **other:** H, Costco/gas, **W on 27th Ave...gas:** 7-11, **food:** El Patron Mexican, 5&Diner, Pizza Hut, Wendy's, **other:** Michael's, PetsMart, Ross, Target
214a	Union Hills Dr, **E gas:** Circle K/dsl, Valero, **W gas:** Arco, **lodging:** Comfort Inn, Sleep Inn, Studio 6
212b a	Bell Rd, Scottsdale, to Sun City, **E gas:** Chevron/dsl, Circle K/gas, QT, **food:** Big Apple Rest., Black Bear Diner, Burger Mania, Caramba Mexican, IHOP/24hr, Jack-in-the-Box, Lamar's Doughnuts, LJ Silver, McDonald's, Quizno's, Schlotzky's, Waffle House, **lodging:** Bell Hotel, Comfort Inn, Fairfield Inn, Motel 6, **other:** Big O Tire, Checker Parts, Chevrolet, Chrysler/Jeep/Dodge, Ford, Kohl's, Lincoln/Mercury, Nissan/Infiniti, Pontiac/Buick/GMC, Sam's Club/gas, Toyota, U-Haul, Walmart SuperCtr, **W gas:** Chevron, **food:** Applebee's, Denny's, Good Egg Rest., HomeTown Buffet, Hooters, Kyoto Bowl, **lodging:** Red Roof Inn, **other:** Fry's Foods
211	Greenway Rd, **E lodging:** Embassy Suites, La Quinta, **other:** 7-11
210	Thunderbird Rd, **E gas:** Arco, Circle K/dsl, Valero, **food:** Asian Cafe, Barro's Pizza, Big Tortas, DQ, Jack-in-the-Box, Macayo's Mexican, Pizza Hut/Taco Bell, Subway, Wendy's, **other:** CVS Drug, Home Depot, Jiffy Lube, Osco Drug, Walgreens, **W gas:** QT, **food:** Jamba Juice, McDonald's, Quizno's, **other:** Best Buy, Fry's Electronics, Lowe's Whse
209	Cactus Rd, **W gas:** Chevron/24hr, 7-11, **food:** Cousins Subs, China Harvest, Don Pedro's Mexican, **lodging:** Ramada Inn, **other:** Food City
208	Peoria Ave, **E food:** Fajita's, LoneStar Steaks, Pappadeaux, TGIFriday, **lodging:** Candlewood Suites, Comfort Suites, Crowne Plaza, Extended Stay America, Homewood Suites, Hyatt Place, **W food:** Black Angus, Burger King, Chili's, China Chan, Chipotle Mexican, Coldstone, Culvers, El Torito, Mimi's Cafe, Old Country Buffet, Olive Garden, Peter Piper Pizza, Red Lobster, Samurai Sam's, Sizzler, Souper Salad, Starbucks, Swenson's Ice Cream, Subway, Wendy's, Whataburger, **lodging:** Premier Inn, **other:** Barnes&Noble, Dillard's, $Tree, Firestone/auto, Macy's, Michael's, Old Navy, PetCo, PetsMart, Ross, Sears/auto, Staples, mall
208.5mm	Arizona Canal
207	Dunlap Ave, **E gas:** Circle K/gas, Shell/dsl, **food:** Big Burrito, Blimpie, Fajitas, Fuddrucker's, Lonestar Steaks, Outback Steaks, Steak'n Burger, Sweet Tomato, **lodging:** Budget Lodge, Comfort Suites, Courtyard, Homestead Suites, Mainstay Suites, Sheraton, SpringHill Suites, TownPlace Suites, **other:** URGENT CARE, Aamco, CVS Drug, Firestone, Sun City RV Ctr, mall, **W gas:** Chevron, **food:** Denny's, Schlotsky's, Subway, **lodging:** ValuePlace, **other:** U-Haul, repair
206	Northern Ave, **E gas:** Circle K, Shell/dsl, **food:** Big Burrito, Boston Mkt, Burger King, Del Taco, Denny's/24hr, Dunkin Donuts, El Pollo Loco, Los Compadres Mexican, Marie Callender's, McDonald's, Mr. Sushi, Papa John's, Pizza Hut, Subway, **lodging:** Best Western, **other:** Albertson's, Checker Parts, Osco, USPO, Walgreens, **W gas:** Arco, QT, **food:** DQ, Village Inn Rest., **lodging:** Motel 6, Residence Inn, Super 8, **other:** $General, K-Mart, 99 Cent Store, Vet
205	Glendale Ave, **E gas:** QT, **other:** Ace Hardware, Circle K, auto repair, transmissions, Vet, **W gas:** Circle K/dsl, **food:** Jack-in-the-Box, **other:** Checker Parts, 7-11, Walgreens, to Luke AFB
204	Bethany Home Rd, **E gas:** Arco/24hr, Shell/Church's/dsl, **food:** Dunkin Donuts, McDonald's, Subway, Samauri Sam's, Whataburger, **other:** H, URGENT CARE, BigLots, Circle K, Vet, **W gas:** Shell, Valero, **food:** Burger King, Great Dragon, **other:** Food City, Jiffy Lube, 99 Cent Store, Savers
203	Camelback Rd, **E food:** Blimpie, Buffet Cactus Jack's, Cubano, Church's, Country Boy's Rest., **other:** Chrysler/Jeep/Dodge, Discount Tire, Frys' Foods, Hyundai, Kia, **W gas:** QT, **food:** DQ, Jack-in-the-Box, McDonald's, TacoMex, **lodging:** Comfort Inn, **other:** AutoZone, Chevrolet, Circle K, to Grand Canyon U
202	Indian School Rd, **E gas:** Arco/24hr, **food:** Domino's, Federico's Mexican, Pizza Hut, Subway, **other:**

N ↕ S — SCOTTSDALE — PHOENIX — PHOENIX

INTERSTATE 17 CONT'D

Exit #	Services
202	Continued Ace Hardware, CVS Drug, Family$, Food City, Skyline RV Ctr, **W gas:** Circle K, Red Dog/dsl/LP, Shell, Valero/dsl, **food:** Subway, Wendy's, **lodging:** Motel 6, **other:** 7-11, Wide World of Maps, auto repair
201	Thomas Rd, **E gas:** Chevron/McDonald's/playplace, **food:** Arby's, Denny's, Dunkin Donuts, Jack-in-the-Box, Roman's Pizza, Starbucks, **lodging:** Day's Inn, La Quinta, **other:** Circle K, **W gas:** QT, **food:** Carl's Jr, Subway, Taco Factory, **other:** NAPA
200b	McDowell Rd, Van Buren, **E other:** Purcell's Tire, **W lodging:** Travelodge
200a	I-10, W to LA, E to Phoenix
199b	Jefferson St (from sb), Adams St (from nb), Van Buren St (from nb), **E gas:** Circle K/gas, **food:** Jack-in-the-Box, **other:** to st capitol, **W gas:** Circle K/gas, **food:** La Canasta Mexican, Salsita's Mexican, **other:** Penny Pincher Parts, PepBoys
199a	Grant St
198	Buckeye Rd (from nb)
197	US 60, 19th Ave, Durango St, **E food:** Jack-in-the-Box, Whataburger/24hr, to St Capitol
196	7th St, Central Ave, **W gas:** DZ/dsl
195b	7th St, Central Ave, **E gas:** Big Tiger/dsl, Circle K/dsl, **food:** Jack-in-the-Box, McDonald's, Taco Bell, **lodging:** EZ 8 Motel/rest., **other:** [H], NAPA Care
195a	16th St (from sb, no EZ return), **E food:** Burger King, **other:** Food City, to Sky Harbor Airport
194	I-10 W to AZ 151, to Sky Harbor Airport

I-17 begins/ends on I-10, exit 150a

INTERSTATE 19

Exit #	Services
	I-19 uses kilometers (km)
101b a	I-10, E to El Paso, W to Phoenix, I-19 begins/ends on I-10, exit 260
99	AZ 86, Ajo Way, **E gas:** Circle K, **food:** Eegee's Cafe, Hamburger Stand, Peter Piper Pizza, Subway, Taco Bell, **other:** Fry's Foods, GNC, Goodyear/auto, U-Haul, Walgreens, auto repair, Vet, **W gas:** Circle K, Gas City/dsl, Shell, **food:** Burger King, Church's, Domino's, Little Caesars, **other:** [H], URGENT CARE, Family$, Food City, 99 Cent Store, Jiffy Lube, to Old Tucson, museum
98	Irvington Rd, **E other:** Fry's Foods/drug/dsl, **W gas:** Chevron, Circle K, **food:** Buffalo Wild Wings, China Olive Buffet, McDonald's, Olive Garden, Panda Express, Peter Piper Pizza, Starbucks, Subway, **other:** Best Buy, Family$, Food City, Home Depot, JC Penney, Marshall's, Michael's, Office Depot, Old Navy, PetsMart, Ross, Target
95b a	Valencia Rd, **E food:** Church's, Donut Wheel, Eegee's Cafe, Jack-in-the-Box, McDonald's, Peter Piper Pizza, Sonic, Viva Burrito, Whataburger, Yokohama RiceBowl, **other:** Aamco, AutoZone, Brake Masters, Checker Parts, $Tree, Food City, Family$, Jiffy Lube, USPO, Walgreens, To Airport, **W gas:** Chevron/dsl, Circle K, **food:** Applebee's, Arby's, Burger King, Carl's Jr, Chili's, Chuey's Cafe, Denny's, Dunkin Donuts/Baskin-Robbins, El Taco Tote, Golden Corral,

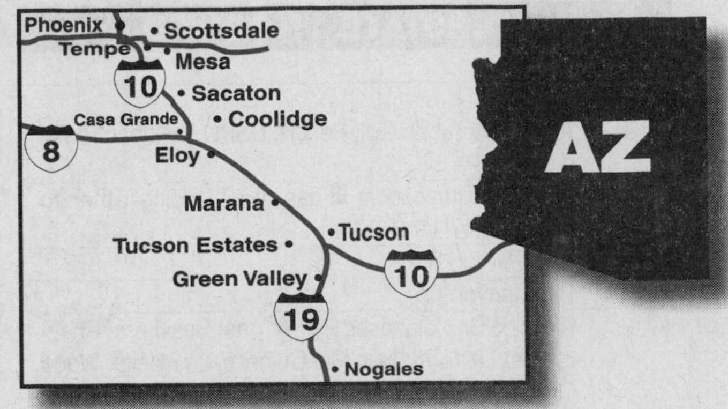

Exit #	Services
95b a	Continued Grand Buffet, Hamburger Stand, IHOP, Little Caesars, Papa John's, Papa Murphy's, Pizza Hut, Subway, Taco Bell, Wendy's, **other:** Big O Tire, CVS Drug, Lowe's Whse, 99c Store, Radio Shack, Walgreens, Walmart SuperCtr, repair, transmissions
92	San Xavier Rd, **W other:** to San Xavier Mission
91.5km	Santa Cruz River
87	Papago Rd
80	Pima Mine Rd, **E food:** Agave Rest., Diamond Casino
75	Helmut Peak Rd, to Sahuarita, **E gas:** Shell, **other:** Jerrybob's Rest., McDonald's, Sertino's Cofee/Ice Cream, Starbucks, Subway, **other:** Fry's Foods/drug, USPO
69	US 89 N, Duval Mine Rd., Green Valley, **E food:** Carl's Jr., Denny's, Pollo Feliz, Pizza Hut, Quizno's, Subway, **other:** Basha's Food, Fletcher's Repair, 99 Cent Store, Radio Shack, Walgreens, Walmart SuperCtr/24hr, **W gas:** Circle K/gas, Texaco/dsl, **food:** Burger King, Domino's, DQ, Manuel's Rest., Rigoberto's Mexican, Starbucks, Taco Bell/TCBY, **lodging:** Holiday Inn Express, **other:** Big O Tire, Curves, Ford/Lincoln/Mercury/Hyundai, Green Valley RV Resort, Safeway/gas, Titan Missile Museum, USPO, Vet
65	Esperanza Blvd, to Green Valley, **E gas:** Shell/repair/dsl, **W gas:** Texaco/dsl, **food:** AZ Family Rest., Dona's Rest., La Placita Mexican, **lodging:** Comfort Inn, Quality Inn, **other:** Ace Hardware, Family$, Walgreens
63	Continental Rd, Green Valley, **E food:** Quail Valley Rest., **other:** golf, USPO, **2 mi E other:** San Ignacio Golf Club/rest., **W gas:** Chevron, **food:** China Vic, HotStuff Pizza, KFC, Mama's Kitchen, McDonald's, Trivettie's Rest., **other:** CVS Drug, Safeway, TrueValue, Walgreens, tires/repair, to Madera Cyn RA
56	Canoa Rd, **W lodging:** San Ignacio Inn
54km	**rest area both lanes, full [handicapped] facilities, [phone], [picnic], litter barrels, vending, petwalk**
48	Arivaca Rd, Amado, **2-3 mi E lodging:** Amado Inn, **other:** Mtn View RV Park, Rex Ranch Resort, **W gas:** Amado Plaza, **food:** Cow Palace Rest., Longhorn Grill, **other:** Amado Mkt, Jim's Auto Repair
42	Agua Linda Rd, to Amado, **E other:** Mtn View RV Park
40	Chavez Siding Rd, Tubac, **E food:** Nob Hill Rest. (3mi), **other:** Tubac Golf Resort
34	Tubac, **E gas:** Nob Hill Mkt/dsl, **food:** Artists Palate, Cafe Prisidio, Chef's Table, Elvira's Cafe, **other:**

AZ

INTERSTATE 19 CONT'D

N ↕ S — NOGALES

Exit #	Services
34	Continued Anza Mkt, Tubac Golf Resort, USPO, to Tubac Presidio SP
29	Carmen, Tumacacori, **E** gas, food, lodging, **other:** to Tumacacori Nat Hist Park
25	Palo Parado Rd
22	Pec Canyon Rd
17	Rio Rico Dr, Calabasas Rd, **W gas:** Gas4Less, Chevron/dsl/LP, **food:** Hua Mei Chinese, La Placita, Wood Oven Pizza, **lodging:** Esplendor Resort, **other:** IGA Foods, JC Auto Repair/Lube, USPO, vet
12	AZ 289, to Ruby Rd, **E gas:** Pilot/Wendy's/dsl/scales/24hr, W **other:** to Pena Blanca Lake RA
8	US 89, AZ 82 (exits left from sb, no return), Nogales, **0-3 mi E gas:** Chevron, Circle K/gas, MinniMart, Pronto Fuel/dsl, **food:** 7 Mares Seafood, **other:** H, Mi Casa RV Park
4	AZ 189 S, Mariposa Rd, Nogales, **E gas:** Chevron, FasTrip, Jumpin' Jack Gas, 76, **food:** Bella Mia Rest., China Buffet, ChinaStar, Denny's, DQ, Jack-in-the-Box, KFC, Little Caesars, McDonald's, Quizno's, Subway, Taco Bell, Yokohama Rest., **lodging:** Motel 6, Super 8, **other:** AutoZone, Batteries+, BigLots, Chevrolet/Cadillac, Buick/Pontiac/GMC, $Tree, Ford/Lincoln/Mercury, GNC, Home Depot, JC Penney, K-Mart, Mexico Insurance, NAPA, Pontiac/Buick/GMC, Radio Shack, Ross, Safeway, Walgreens, Walmart SuperCtr (N Grand Ave), **W gas:** Valero/dsl, **food:** Carl's Jr, IHOP, **lodging:** Best Western, Candlewood Suites, Holiday Inn Express, **other:** Chrysler/Dodge/Jeep
1b	Western Ave, Nogales
1a	International St
0km	I-19 begins/ends in Nogales, Arizona/Mexico Border, **1/2 mi gas:** Circle K/gas, Jr.s Fuel Depot/dsl, Puchi's Gas, **food:** Burger King, Church's, Domino's, Jack-in-the-Box, McDonald's, Peter Piper Pizza, Pizza Hut, Subway, **other:** AutoZone, CarQuest, Checker Parts, Family$, Food City, NAPA, Parts+, PepBoys, museum

INTERSTATE 40

E ↕ W — CHAMBERS — HOLBROOK

Exit #	Services
359.5mm	Arizona/New Mexico state line
359	Grants Rd, to Lupton, **N Welcome Ctr/rest area both lanes, full ♿ facilities, ☎, picnic tables, litter barrels, petwalk, gas:** Speedy's/dsl/rest./24hr, **other:** Tee Pee Trading Post/rest., YellowHorse Indian Gifts
357	AZ 12 N, Lupton, to Window Rock, **N other:** USPO, **S other:** Scotty's RV/dsl Repair
354	Hawthorne Rd
351	Allentown Rd, **N other:** Chee's Indian Store, Indian City Gifts
348	St Anselm Rd, Houck, **N other:** Ft Courage Food/gifts
347.5mm	Black Creek
346	Pine Springs Rd
345mm	Box Canyon
344mm	Querino Wash
343	Querino Rd
341	Ortega Rd, Cedar Point, **N gas:** Armco/gas/gifts
340.5mm	**insp/weigh sta both lanes**
339	US 191 S, to St Johns, **S gas:** Conoco/dsl, **other:** Family$, RV Park, USPO
333	US 191 N, Chambers, **N gas:** Rte 66 Gas/dsl, **other:** to Hubbell Trading Post NHS, USPO, **S gas:** Mobil/dsl, **lodging:** Chieftain Inn/rest.
330	McCarrell Rd
325	Navajo, **S gas:** Shell/Subway/Navajo Trading Post/dsl/24hr
323mm	Crazy Creek
320	Pinta Rd
316mm	Dead River
311	Painted Desert, **N gas:** Chevron, **other:** Petrified Forest NP, Painted Desert
303	Adamana Rd, **N other:** Stewarts/gifts, **S other:** Painted Desert Indian Ctr
302.5mm	Big Lithodendron Wash
301mm	Little Lithodendron Wash
300	Goodwater
299mm	Twin Wash
294	Sun Valley Rd, **N** Root 66 RV camping, **S other:** Knife City
292	AZ 77 N, to Keams Canyon, **N gas:** Conoco/Burger King/dsl/24hr, **other:** dsl repair
289	Lp 40, Holbrook, **N gas:** Chevron/dsl, Hatch's/dsl, **food:** Denny's, Jerry's Rest., Mesa Rest., **lodging:** Best Inn, Best Western, Comfort Inn, Day's Inn, Econolodge, Motel 6, Ramada Ltd, Sahara Inn, Travelodge, **other:** Future Tire/Lube
286	Navajo Blvd, Holbrook, **N gas:** Chevron/dsl, Circle K, **food:** Aliberto's Mexican, Asian Pacific, Burger King, Hilltop Cafe, KFC, McDonald's, Pizza Hut, Taco Bell, **lodging:** Holiday Inn Express, Super 8, 66 Motel, **other:** Alco, $General, KOA, OK RV Park, **S gas:** Chevron/dsl, Heward/dsl/repair, Jack's/LP, MiniMart/gas, Speedy Dsl, **food:** DQ, Rte 66 Cafe, **lodging:** Best Value, El Rancho Motel/rest., Knight's Inn, **other:** H, Ford/Lincoln/Mercury, Jeep/Dodge, Scotty & Son Repair, SW Transmissions, museum, rockshops
285	US 180 E, AZ 77 S, Holbrook, **1 mi S gas:** Giant/dsl, **food:** Butterfield Steaks, Wayside Mexican, **lodging:** Best Western, Star Inn, Wigwam Motel, **other:** Family$, Safeway, RV repair, rest area/picnic tables/litter barrels, to Petrified Forest NP
284mm	Leroux Wash
283	Perkins Valley Rd, Golf Course Rd, **S gas:** Texaco/Country Host Rest./dsl/24hr/@
280	Hunt Rd, Geronimo Rd, **N other:** Geronimo Trading Post
277	Lp 40, Joseph City, **N gas:** Love's/Chester's/Subway/scales/dsl/24hr, **S other:** to Cholla Lake CP, RV camping
274	Lp 40, Joseph City, **N** gas, food, lodging, RV camping
269	Jackrabbit Rd, **S other:** Jackrabbit Trading Post
264	Hibbard Rd
257	AZ 87 N, to Second Mesa, **N other:** to Homolovi Ruins SP, camping, **S other:** trading post
256.5mm	Little Colorado River
255	Lp 40, Winslow, **N gas:** Winslow Fuel/dsl, **other:** Mi Pueblo Mexican, **lodging:** Holiday Inn Express, **other:** Freddy's RV Park/gas, **S gas:** ***FLYING J***

E W WINSLOW FLAGSTAFF

INTERSTATE 40 CONT'D

Exit #	Services
255	Continued /CountryMkt/dsl/LP/scales/RV Dump/24hr, **food:** Sonic, **other:** Chevrolet, Chrysler/Jeep, Nissan
253	N Park Dr, Winslow, **N gas:** Chevron, **food:** Arby's, Capt Tony's Pizza, Denny's, Pizza Hut, **other:** Checker Parts, $General, Ford, Walmart SuperCtr/Subway, tires/lube, truckwash, **S food:** Alfonso's Mexican, Dominos, KFC, McDonald's, Subway, Taco Bell/LJ Silver, **lodging:** Econolodge, Motel 6, **other:** H, Basha's Foods, Family$, NAPA, Safeway
252	AZ 87 S, Winslow, **S gas:** Shell/dsl, **food:** Entre Chinese, **lodging:** Best Value, Rest Inn, Super 8, The Lodge, **other:** NAPACare
245	AZ 99, Leupp
239	Meteor City Rd, Red Gap Ranch Rd, **S other:** Meteor City Trading Post, to Meteor Crater
235mm	**rest area both lanes, full facilities, info, phone, litter barrels, petwalk**
233	Meteor Crater Rd, **S gas:** Mobil/Hole Enchilada/Meteor Crater RV Park, **other:** to Meteor Crater NL
230	Two Guns
229.5mm	Canyon Diablo
225	Buffalo Range Rd
219	Twin Arrows
218.5mm	Padre Canyon
211	Winona, **N gas:** Shell/dsl/repair
207	Cosnino Rd
204	to Walnut Canyon NM
201	US 89, Flagstaff, to Page, **N gas:** Chevron, Conoco/dsl, Express/dsl, Shell, **food:** Arby's, Burger King, Del Taco, Jack-in-the-Box, Los Altos Mexican, McDonald's, Pizza Hut, Quizno's, Ruby Tuesday, Sizzler, Taco Bell/LJ Silver, Wendy's, Village Inn Rest., **lodging:** Best Western, Day's Inn, Hampton Inn, Howard Johnson, Luxury Inn, Super 8, Travelodge, **other:** H, Big O Tire, Checker's Parts, CVS Drug, Dillard's, Family$, Flagstaff RV Ctr/LP, Goodyear/auto, Home Depot, JC Penney, KOA, Marshall's, Old Navy, PetCo, PitStop Lube, Safeway/gas, Sears/auto, Toyota, World Mkt, auto repair, mall, **S gas:** Mobil/dsl, **lodging:** Residence Inn
198	Butler Ave, Flagstaff, **N gas:** Chevron, Conoco/dsl, Shell, Mustang Gas, **food:** Burger King, Country Host Rest., Cracker Barrel, Denny's, Hogs Rest., McDonald's, Outback Steaks, Sonic, Taco Bell, **lodging:** Econolodge, Holiday Inn Express, Howard Johnson, Motel 6, Quality Inn, Ramada Ltd, Super 8, Travelodge, **other:** NAPA, Sam's Club, **1 mi N on Rte 66... gas:** Carter/dsl, **food:** China Star, Dog Haus Cafe, KFC, Starbucks, Subway, **lodging:** Best Value, Inn Suites, King's House Hotel, Red Rose Inn, Relax Inn, 66 Motel, **other:** Albertson's, Auto Value Parts, AutoZone, Fry's Foods/dsl, U-Haul, **S gas:** Mobil, Sinclair/Little America/dsl/motel/@, **food:** Black Bart's Steaks/RV Park
197.5mm	Rio de Flag
195b	US 89A N, McConnell Dr, Flagstaff, **N gas:** Chevron/dsl, Conoco/dsl, Flag, Gasser/dsl, Giant/dsl, Mobil, Circle K, Shell, Texaco/Wendy's/dsl, **food:** Arby's, August Moon Chinese, Baskin-Robbins, Buffalo

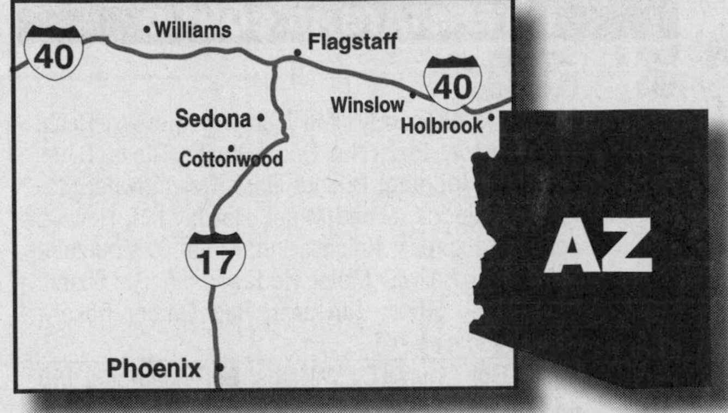

AZ

FLAGSTAFF

Exit #	Services
195b	Continued Wild Wings, Burger King, Buster's Rest., Carl's Jr, Casa Bonita, Chili's, China Garden, Coco's, Coldstone, DQ, Del Taco, Denny's, Domino's, Fazoli's, Garcia's Mexican, IHOP, Jack-in-the-Box, KFC, Mandarin Buffet, McDonald's, Olive Garden, Papa John's, Picazzo's Pizza, Peter Piper Pizza, Pizza Hut, Quizno's, Red Lobster, Roma Pizza, Szechuan Chinese, Sizzler, Starbucks, Strombolli's, Subway, Taco Bell, **lodging:** AZ Motel, Budget Inn, Canyon Inn, Comfort Inn, Courtyard, Day's Inn, Drury Inn, Econolodge, Embassy Suites, Fairfield Inn, Hampton Inn, Highland Country Inn, Hilton Garden, Knights Inn, La Quinta, Motel 6, Quality Inn, Ramada Ltd, Rodeway Inn, Sleep Inn, SpringHill Suites, Super 8, **other:** H, Barnes&Noble, Basha's Foods, Discount Tire, Hastings Books, Jo-Ann Crafts, Kohl's, Michael's, Ross, Safeway, Staples, Target, Walgreens, Walmart, auto/RV repair
195a	I-17 S, AZ 89A S, to Phoenix
192	Flagstaff Ranch Rd
191	Lp 40, to Grand Canyon, Flagstaff, **5 mi N gas:** Chevron, Maverik, Whistle Stop/dsl, **food:** Galaxy Diner, **lodging:** Best Value, Budget Host, Comfort Inn, Day's Inn, Econolodge, Radisson, Super 8, Travelodge, Travel Inn, **other:** CarQuest, Checker Parts, Chevrolet/Cadillac, Home Depot, Kia, Kit Carson RV Park, vet, Woody Mtn Camping
190	A-1 Mountain Rd
189.5mm	Arizona Divide, elevation 7335
185	Transwestern Rd, Bellemont, **N gas:** Pilot/McDonald's/Subway/dsl/scales/24hr/@, **lodging:** Motel 6, **S other:** Camping World RV Ctr, Harley-Davidson/Roadside Grill
183mm	**rest area wb, full facilities, litter barrels, vending, weather info, petwalk**
182mm	**rest area eb, full facilities, phone, litter barrels, vending, weather info, petwalk**
178	Parks Rd, **N food:** Mustang/dsl/24hr
171	Pittman Valley Rd, Deer Farm Rd, **S lodging:** Quality Inn/grill
167	Garland Prairie Rd, Circle Pines Rd, **N other:** KOA
165	AZ 64, to Williams, Grand Canyon, **N gas:** Texaco (8mi), Shell/dsl (4mi), **other:** KOA (4mi), **S lodging:** Super 8 (1mi)
163	Williams, **N gas:** Chevron/Subway/dsl, **lodging:** Fairfield Inn, **other:** Canyon Gateway RV Park, to Grand Canyon, **S gas:** Mobil/dsl, Mustang/dsl, Conoco, **food:** Jack-in-the-Box, KFC, McDonald's,

AZ

INTERSTATE 40 CONT'D

E ↕ W

WILLIAMS

Exit #	Services
163	Continued Pancho McGillicuddy's Mexican, Pine Country Rest., Pizza Factory, Pizza Hut, Rod's Steaks, Rte 66 Diner, Taco Bell, **lodging:** Budget Host, Downtowner Motel, Econolodge, Grand Motel, Holiday Inn, Howard Johnson Express, Knight's Inn, Motel 6, Mountainside Motel, Railway Motel, Rodeway Inn, Rte 66 Inn, Travelodge, **other:** CarQuest, Red Garder Bakery, USPO, same as 161
161	Lp 40, Golf Course Dr, Williams, **N** RV camping, **0-3 mi S gas:** Circle K, Conoco/dsl, Shell, **food:** Buffalo Pointe Rest., Cruiser's Cafe 66, DQ, Denny's, Jessica's Rest., Old Smoky's Pancakes, Pizza Factory, Rolando's Mexican, **lodging:** AZ Motel, Best Western, Best Value, Budget Host, Canyon Country Inn, Day's Inn, Highlander Motel, Motel 6, Westerner Motel, **other:** [H], Family$, Safeway, Railside RV Ranch, to Grand Canyon Railway
157	Devil Dog Rd
155.5mm	safety pullout wb, litter barrels
151	Welch Rd
149	Monte Carlo Rd, **N other:** Monte Carlo Truck Repair
148	County Line Rd
146	AZ 89, to Prescott, Ash Fork, **N gas:** Mobil/dsl, Mustang, **food:** Ranch House Cafe, **lodging:** Ash Fork Inn
144	Ash Fork, **N lodging:** Ash Fork Inn, **other:** Grand Canyon RV Park, USPO, **S gas:** Chevron/Piccadilly's/dsl, Texaco/dsl/RV Park, **other:** auto repair
139	Crookton Rd, to Rte 66
123	Lp 40, to Rte 66, Seligman, **N gas:** Shell, **1 mi N gas:** Chevron/A&W, Mustang/dsl, **food:** Copper Cafe, Lilo's Rest., **lodging:** Canyon Lodge, Stagecoach 66 Motel/pizza, Supai Motel,**other:** KOA (1mi), to Grand Canyon Caverns, USPO, repair, (same as 121), **S gas:** Chevron/Subway/dsl/24hr
121	Lp 40, to Rte 66, Seligman, **1 mi N gas:** Chevron/A&W, Mustang/dsl, **food:** Copper Cafe, Lilo's Rest., **lodging:** Canyon Lodge, Stagecoach 66 Motel/pizza, Supai Motel, **other:** KOA (1mi), to Grand Canyon Caverns, USPO, repair (same as 123)
109	Anvil Rock Rd
108mm	Markham Wash
103	Jolly Rd
96	Cross Mountain Rd
91	Fort Rock Rd
87	Willows Ranch Rd
86mm	Willow Creek
79	Silver Springs Rd
75.5mm	Big Sandy Wash
73.5mm	Peacock Wash
71	US 93 S, to Wickenburg, Phoenix
66	Blake Ranch Rd, **N gas:** Petro/Mobil/Iron Skillet/dsl/rest./scales/24hr/@, **other:** Blake Ranch RV Park, Blue Beacon, SpeedCo Lube
60mm	Frees Wash
59	DW Ranch Rd, Hualapai Mtn Rd, **N gas:** Love's/Chester Fried/Subway/dsl/24hr, **other:** truckwash
57mm	Rattlesnake Wash
53	AZ 66, Andy Devine Ave, to Kingman, **N gas:** Chevron, ***FLYING J***/dsl/LP/scales/24hr, Terrible's/dsl, Texaco, **food:** Arby's, Burger King, Denny's,

KINGMAN

YUCCA

Exit #	Services
53	Continued Jack-in-the-Box, McDonald's, Pizza Hut, Taco Bell, **lodging:** Day's Inn, Econolodge, First Value Inn, Motel 6, Silver Queen Motel, Super 8, Travelodge, **other:** Basha's Foods, Goodyear/auto, Harley-Davidson, K-Mart, KOA (1mi), Outdoorsman RV Ctr/Service, TireWorld, dsl/tire repair, **S gas:** Mobil, Shell/repair, **food:** JB's, Lo's Chinese, Oyster's Mexican, Sonic, **lodging:** Best Value Inn, Best Western, Comfort Inn, Day's Inn, High Desert Inn, Holiday Inn Express, Lido Motel, Rodeway Inn, Rte 66 Motel, SpringHill Suites, **other:** Kia, NAPA, Uptown Drug
51	Stockton Hill Rd, Kingman, **N gas:** Arco/24hr, Chevron, Circle K, **food:** Chili's, Cracker Barrel, Del Taco, Golden Corral, Hunan Chinese, IHOP, In-n-Out, KFC, Panda Express, Papa John's, Papa Murphy, Sonic, Starbucks, Subway, Taco Bell/24hr, **lodging:** Hampton Inn, **other:** [H], AutoZone, Big Lots, BrakeMasters, Checker Parts, Chevrolet/Buick/Pontiac/Cadillac, CVS Drug, $General, $Tree, Ford/Lincoln/Mercury, Home Depot, Honda, Hyundai, Oil Can Henry's, PetCo, Ross, Safeway/gas, Smith's Foods/dsl, Staples, Superior Tire, TrueValue, vet, Walgreens, Walmart SuperCtr, **S gas:** Circle K, **food:** Alfonso's Mexican, Kingman Co Steaks, Little Caesars, Pizza Hut, **other:** CarQuest, Family$, Hastings Books, JC Penney, Radio Shack, Safeway/gas, Sears
48	US 93 N, Beale St, Kingman, **N gas:** Chevron/dsl, Express Stop, Fill Smart, Mobil/dsl, 93 Fuel, USA/Subway/dsl/24hr, Shell/dsl/24hr, TA/Country Pride/Popeye's/dsl/scales/24hr/@, Woody's, **food:** Chan Chinese, Lotta Lou's Cafe, Wendy's, **lodging:** Budget Inn, Economy Inn, Knights Inn, **other:** Best Tire, auto/RV repair, truckwash, **S gas:** Chevron/Quizno's/dsl/24hr, **food:** Calico's Rest., Carl's Jr, Quizno's, **lodging:** AZ Inn, Motel 6, **other:** Ft Beale RV Park, museum
46.5mm	Holy Moses Wash
44	AZ 66, Oatman Hwy, McConnico, to Rte 66, **S gas:** Crazy Fred's Fuel/dsl/café, **other:** Canyon West RV Camping (3mi), truckwash
40.5mm	Griffith Wash
37	Griffith Rd
35mm	Black Rock Wash
32mm	Walnut Creek
28	Old Trails Rd
26	Proving Ground Rd, **S other:** AZ Proving Grounds
25	Alamo Rd, to Yucca, **N gas:** Micromart/dsl/diner, **food:** Jr Grill, **other:** USPO, **S** auto repair, towing
23mm	**rest area both lanes, full ♿ facilities, ☎, [picnic], litter barrels, vending, petwalk**
21mm	Flat Top Wash
20	Santa Fe Ranch Rd
18.5mm	Illavar Wash
15mm	Buck Mtn Wash
13.5mm	Franconia Wash
13	Franconia Rd
9	AZ 95 S, to Lake Havasu City, Parker, London Br, **S gas:** Chevron/Burger King/dsl, Love's/Carl's Jr/dsl/scales, Pilot/Wendy's/dsl/scales, **other:** Prospectors RV Resort
4mm	**weigh sta both lanes**
2	Needle Mtn Rd
1	Topock Rd, to Bullhead City, Oatman, **N** gas, food, camping, to Havasu NWR
0mm	Arizona/California state line, Colorado River, Mountain/Pacific time zone

INTERSTATE 30

Exit #	Services
143b a	I-40, E to Memphis, W to Ft Smith, I-30 begins/ends on I-40, exit 153b
142	15th St, **S gas:** Super Stop/dsl
141b	US 70, Broadway St, downtown, **N gas:** Exxon, US Fuel/dsl, **other:** Verizon Arena, U-Haul, **S gas:** Citgo, Valero/dsl, **food:** KFC/LJ Silver, McDonald's, Popeye's, Taco Bell, Wendy's
141mm	Arkansas River
141a	AR 10, Cantrell Rd, Markham St, wb only, to downtown
140	9th St, 6th St, downtown, **N gas:** Exxon, Phillips 66, Shell, **food:** Pizza Hut, **lodging:** Holiday Inn, **other:** USPO, **S gas:** SuperStop, **lodging:** Comfort Inn
139b	I-630, downtown
139a	AR 365, Roosevelt Rd, **N gas:** Exxon, **other:** AutoZone, **S gas:** Shell, **other:** Family$, Kroger, NAPA
138b	I-530 S, US 167 S, US 65 S, to Pine Bluff
138a	I-440 E, to Memphis, ✈
135	W 65th St, **N gas:** Exxon/dsl, MapCo, Shell/dsl, **lodging:** Executive Inn, **S lodging:** Rodeway Inn
134	Scott Hamilton Dr, **S gas:** Exxon/dsl, **food:** Waffle House, **lodging:** Best Value Inn, Motel 6
133	Geyer Springs Rd, **N gas:** Exxon, Hess, **food:** Church's, Sonic, Subway, **S gas:** Exxon, Phillips 66, Shell, **food:** Arby's, Burger King, El Chico, KFC, Little Caesars, McDonald's, Panda Chinese, Rallys, Shark's Rest., Taco Bell, Waffle House, Wendy's, **lodging:** Baymont Inn, Best Western, Comfort Inn, Rest Inn, **other:** Advance Parts, Family$, Goodyear/auto, Kroger/gas, Radio Shack, Walgreens
132	US 70b, University Ave, **N gas:** RaceWay/dsl, SuperStop, Valero, **lodging:** Best Value Inn, **other:** Chevrolet, **S food:** Luigi's Pizza
131	McDaniel Dr, **N other:** U-Haul, **S lodging:** Knight's Inn, Super 7 Inn, **other:** Crain RV Ctr, Firestone
130	AR 338, Baseline Rd, Mabelvale, **N gas:** MapCo/dsl, **food:** FatBoys Diner, **lodging:** Best Value Inn, **other:** Harley-Davidson, **S gas:** Phillips 66, Shell/Popeye's, **food:** Applebee's, China Buffet, Dixie Cafe, McDonald's, Sonic, Taco Bueno, Wendy's, **other:** AT&T, $Tree, GNC, Home Depot, Walmart SuperCtr/Subway
129	I-430 N
128	Otter Creek Rd, Mabelvale West, **S gas:** Exxon, **lodging:** La Quinta, **other:** H, Goodyear
126	AR 111, County Line Rd, Alexander, **N gas:** Phillips 66/dsl, Shell/dsl, **S gas:** Citgo
123	AR 183, Reynolds Rd, to Bryant, Bauxite, **N gas:** Murphy USA, Shell, SuperStop, **food:** Arby's, Backyard Burgers, Burger King, Catfish Barn, Cracker Barrel, D-Light Chinese, Domino's, Firehouse Subs, IHOP, KFC, Papa Murphy's, Pizza Hut, Quizno's, Ruby Tuesday, Subway, TaMolly's, Waffle House, **lodging:** Best Value Inn, Comfort Inn, Hampton Inn, Holiday Inn Express, Hometown Hotel, La Quinta, Vista Inn, **other:** AT&T, AutoZone, $Tree, Radio Shack, Walgreens, Walmart SuperCtr/Subway, **S gas:** Conoco/dsl, Exxon/dsl, **food:** Chick-fil-A, Little Caesar's, McDonald's, Mi Ranchito, Sonic, Taco Bell, Wendy's, Zaxby's, **lodging:** Super 8, **other:** $General, Lowe's Whse, O'Reilly Parts, USPO
121	Alcoa Rd, **N gas:** Citgo, Pilot/Subway/dsl/scales/24hr/@, **food:** McDonald's, **other:** Chrysler/Dodge/Jeep, Firestone, **S food:** Chili's, McAlister's Deli, Moe's SW Grill, Sakura Japanese, Starbucks, Subway, **other:** At&T, Best Buy, Buick/GMC/Pontiac, GNC, Kohls, Old Navy, PetCo, Target
118	Congo Rd, **N food:** Applebee's, Brown's Rest, CiCi's, Dixie Café, Santa Fe Grill, **other:** Chevrolet/Hummer, Curves, Home Depot, Williams Tire, **S gas:** Exxon, **food:** Burger King, **lodging:** Days Inn, Ramada Inn, **other:** Ford/Lincoln/Mercury, RV City, USPO
117	US 64, AR 5, AR 35, **N gas:** Shell, **food:** Denny's, IHOP, Papa John's, Pizza Hut, Waffle House, **lodging:** Best Inn, Best Western, Econolodge, **S gas:** Exxon, Fina, Murphy USA, Shell, **food:** Arby's, Backyard Burger, Burger King, Capt D's, Colton's Steaks, IHOP, La Hacienda Mexican, McDonald's, Popeye's, Quizno's, Rib Crib, Sonic, Subway, Taco Bell, Wendy's, Western Sizzlin, **lodging:** Days Inn, **other:** H, Advance Parts, AutoZone, $Tree, Firestone, GNC, Hastings Books,

E ↕ W

LITTLE ROCK

AR

INTERSTATE 30 CONT'D

E ↕ W

MALVERN

ARKADELPHIA

Exit #	Services
117	Continued Kroger, Office Depot, O'Reilly Parts, Radio Shack, TireTown, Tuesday Morning, Walmart SuperCtr, USPO
116	Sevier St, **N gas:** Citgo/dsl, Shell/dsl, **lodging:** Troutt Motel, **S gas:** Citgo, **lodging:** Capri Inn
114	US 67 S, Benton, **S gas:** Valero/McDonald's/dsl, **food:** Sonic
113mm	**insp sta both lanes**
111	US 70 W, Hot Springs, **N other:** Cloud 9 RV Park, to Hot Springs NP
106	Old Military Rd, **N gas:** Fina/JJ's Rest./dsl/scales/@, **S other:** JB'S RV Park
99	US 270 E, Malvern, **N** [H]
98b a	US 270, Malvern, Hot Springs, **N lodging:** Super 8, **S gas:** Fina/dsl, Murphy USA, Shell/dsl, Valero, **food:** Baskin-Robbins, Burger King, Chile Peppers, El Parian, Great Wall Buffet, Larry's Pizza, McDonald's, Pizza Hut, Pizza Pro, Sonic, Subway, Taco Bell, Waffle House, Wendy's, Western Sizzlin, **lodging:** Best Value Inn, Comfort Inn, Holiday Inn Express, **other:** [H], AutoZone, Buick/GMC/Pontiac, Chevrolet, Chrysler/Dodge/Jeep, $General, $Tree, Ford, O'Reilly Parts, Radio Shack, Verizon, Walmart SuperCtr/Subway, USPO
97	AR 84, AR 171, **N other:** Lake Catherine SP, RV camping
93mm	**rest area (both lanes exit left), full [handicapped] facilities, [phone], [picnic], litter barrels, vending, petwalk**
91	AR 84, Social Hill
83	AR 283, Friendship, **S gas:** Shell/dsl
78	AR 7, Caddo Valley, **N gas:** Fina/dsl/24hr, Valero/dsl, Shell/dsl, **food:** Cracker Barrel, **other:** Arkadelphia RV Park, to Hot Springs NP, **S gas:** Exxon/Subway/dsl, Phillips 66/Stuckey's, Shell/dsl, **food:** McDonald's, Taco Bell, TaMolly's Mexican, Waffle House, Wendy's, **lodging:** Best Value Inn, Best Western, Comfort Inn, Days Inn, Hampton Inn, Motel 6, Quality Inn, Super 8, **other:** De Gray SP
73	AR 8, AR 26, AR 51, Arkadelphia, **N gas:** Citgo/dsl, Shell/Stuckey's, **food:** Chicken Express, Domino's, Great Wall Buffet, McDonald's, Western Sizzlin, **other:** AT&T, $Tree, Radio Shack, Verizon, Walmart SuperCtr/Subway, to Crater of Diamond SP, **S gas:** Exxon/dsl, Shell, **food:** Andy's Rest., Burger King, Mazzio's, Pizza Shack, Subway, Taco Tico, **other:** [H], Ace Hardware, AutoZone, Brookshire Foods, $General, Fred's, O'Reilly Parts, USPO, Walgreens, tires/repair, Vet
69	AR 26 E, Gum Springs
63	AR 53, Gurdon, **N gas:** Citgo/dsl/rest., **lodging:** Best Value Inn, **S gas:** Shell/dsl/rest., **other:** to White Oak Lake SP
56mm	**rest area both lanes, full [handicapped] facilities, vending, [picnic], litter barrels, vending, petwalk**
54	AR 51, Gurdon, Okolona
46	AR 19, Prescott, **N gas:** Fina/dsl, Horizon/cafe/dsl/24hr, **other:** Crater of Diamonds SP (31mi), **S gas:** Love's/Hardee's/dsl/scales/24hr, **other:** dsl/tires/repair
44	AR 24, Prescott, **N gas:** TA/Country Fare/Subway/Taco Bell/dsl/scales/24hr/@, **S gas:** Norman's 44 Trkstp/dsl/rest./scales/@, **lodging:** Best Value Inn, **other:** [H], truckwash, to **S** Ark U
36	AR 299, to Emmett
31	AR 29, Hope, **N gas:** Shell/dsl, **food:** Uncle Henry's BBQ, **lodging:** Relax Inn, Village Inn/RV park, **other:** st police, **S gas:** Exxon/dsl, Valero/dsl, **food:** KFC, **lodging:** Best Value Inn, **other:** [H]
30	AR 4, Hope, **N gas:** Murphy USA, Valero, **food:** Dos Loco Gringos, **lodging:** Best Western, Holiday Inn Express, Super 8, **other:** Walmart SuperCtr, Millwood SP, Old Washington SP, **S gas:** Exxon/Baskin-Robbins/Wendy's, Shell, **food:** Amigo Juan Mexican, Burger King, McDonald's, Panda Chinese, Pizza Hut, Sonic, Subway, Taco Bell, **lodging:** Days Inn, **other:** [H], AT&T, AutoZone, Buick/Chevrolet/GMC/Pontiac, Bumper Parts, $Tree, Fred's, Ford, O'Reilly Parts, Super 1 Foods/gas, Verizon, Walgreens, Old Washington Hist SP
26mm	**weigh sta both lanes**
18	rd 355, Fulton
17mm	Red River
12	US 67 (from EB), Fulton
7mm	**Welcome Ctr eb, full [handicapped] facilities, info, [phone], [picnic], litter barrels, vending, petwalk**
7	AR 108, Mandeville, **N gas:** *FLYING J*/Conoco/Cookery/dsl/LP/24hr, **food:** J&R BBQ, **lodging:** Sunrise RV Park, **other:** truckwash
2	US 67, AR 245, Texarkana, **N gas:** Circle K/dsl, RoadRunner/dsl, **S gas:** Camp I-30 Auto TruckStop/dsl, **food:** T-Town Diner, **other:** Nick's RV Ctr
1	US 71, Jefferson Ave, Texarkana, **N other:** KOA, **S lodging:** Country Host Inn
0mm	Arkansas/Texas state line

HOPE

INTERSTATE 40

E ↕ W

WEST MEMPHIS

Exit #	Services
285mm	Arkansas/Tennessee state line, Mississippi River
284mm	**weigh sta wb**
281	AR 131, **S** to Mound City
280	Club Rd, Southland Dr, **N gas:** Pilot/Subway/Wendy's/scales/dsl, **S gas:** *FLYING J*/LP/dsl/rest., Petro/Iron Skillet/dsl/rest./24hr/@, Pilot/Subway/dsl/@, **food:** KFC/Taco Bell, McDonald's, Waffle House, **lodging:** Best Western, Deluxe Inn, Express Inn, Super 8, **other:** Blue Beacon, SpeedCo Lube
279b	I-55 S (from eb)
279a	Ingram Blvd, **N food:** Margaritas Mexican, **lodging:** Comfort Inn, Day's Inn, Homegate Inn, Red Roof Inn, Rodeway Inn, **other:** Ford, Greyhound Park, Southland Park Racetrack/casino, U-Haul, **S gas:** Citgo/dsl, **food:** Cupboard Rest., Waffle House, **lodging:** Best Value, Econolodge, Hampshire Inn, Holiday Inn, Motel 6, Ramada, Relax Inn, same as 280
278	AR 77, 7th St, Missouri St, **N gas:** Citgo/24hr, **S on 7th St food:** BBQ, Cracker Barrel, KFC, Pizza Inn, **lodging:** Quality Inn, **other:** [H], Sawyers RV Park, Sears, **S on Missouri St gas:** Exxon, Mapco, Phillips 66/dsl, Shell, **food:** Bonanza, Burger King, Domino's, Mrs Winner's, Popeye's, Subway, Taco Bell, Wendy's, **lodging:** Comfort Suites, Quality Inn, **other:** $Tree, Goodyear/auto, Walgreens

INTERSTATE 40 CONT'D

E ↕ W

Exit #	Services
277	I-55 N, to Jonesboro
276	AR 77, Rich Rd, to Missouri St (from eb only), **S gas:** Citgo, Exxon, MapCo, Phillips 66/dsl, **food:** Applebee's, Bonanza, Burger King, Krystal, Mrs. Winners, Pizza Inn, Popeye's, Shoney's, Wendy's, **lodging:** Howard Johnson, **other:** Goodyear/auto, Kroger, Walmart SuperCtr/McDonald's, same as 278
275	AR 118, Airport Rd, **S gas:** Horizon/DQ, **food:** Huddle House, **other:** URGENT CARE, city park
275mm	**Welcome Ctr wb, full facilities, info, , litter barrels, petwalk**
274mm	**weigh sta eb**
271	AR 147, to Blue Lake, **S gas:** BP/dsl, Exxon/Chester Fried, **other:** to Horseshoe Lake, RV camping
265	US 79, AR 218, to Hughes
260	AR 149, to Earle, **N gas:** Citgo/Subway/Dairy King, TA/BP/Country Pride/Burger King/Taco Bell/dsl/scales/24hr/@, Valero/dsl, **lodging:** Super 8, **other:** Shell Lake Camping, **S gas:** Shell, **other:** dsl repair
256	AR 75, to Parkin, **N gas:** MapCo/Stuckey's/dsl/rest., **other:** to Parkin SP (12mi)
247	AR 38 E, to Widener
245mm	St Francis River
243mm	**rest area wb, full facilities, , vending, , litter barrels, petwalk**
242	AR 284, Crowley's Ridge Rd, **N other:** to Village Creek SP, camping, H
241b a	AR 1, Forrest City, **N gas:** BP/dsl, Phillips 66/Popeye's/dsl, **food:** HoHo Chinese, Wendy's, **lodging:** Best Value Inn, Comfort Suites, Day's Inn, Hampton Inn, Hillside Inn, Holiday Inn, Luxury Inn, Super 8, **other:** Buick/Chevrolet/Pontiac, st police, **S gas:** Citgo, Exxon, Murphy USA/dsl, Shell, **food:** Ameca Mexican, Bonanza, Burger King, Dragon China, KFC, McDonald's, Mrs Winners, Pizza Hut, Sawmill Cafe, Subway, Taco Bell, Waffle House, **lodging:** Best Western, **other:** Advance Parts, $Tree, Food Giant, Fred's Drug, O'Reilly Parts, Sav-A-Lot, Walmart SuperCtr, Walgreens
239	to Wynne, Marianna
235mm	**rest area eb, full facilities, , vending, , litter barrels, petwalk**
234mm	L'Anguille River
233	AR 261, Palestine, **N gas:** Love's/Chester's/Subway/dsl/scales/24hr, **lodging:** Rest Inn, **S gas:** BP/BBQ/dsl, **food:** Head's Cafe
221	AR 78, Wheatley, **N gas:** gas/dsl, **lodging:** Super 8, **S gas:** BP/dsl, MapCo/Subway/dsl
216	US 49, AR 17, Brinkley, **N gas:** Citgo, Shell/dsl, **other:** KFC/Taco Bell, Los Piños Mexican, **lodging:** Baymont Inn, Best Inn, Day's Inn/RV park, Econolodge, **other:** dsl repair, **S gas:** Exxon/dsl, MapCo/dsl/24hr, Phillips 66, **food:** Gene's BBQ, McDonald's, New China, Pizza Hut, Sonic, Subway, Waffle House, **lodging:** Heritage Inn/RV Park, **other:** $General, Family$, Kroger, O'Reilly Parts
205mm	Cache River
202	AR 33, to Biscoe
200mm	White River

FORREST CITY

BRINKLEY

AR

Exit #	Services
199mm	**rest areas both lanes, full facilities, vending, , litter barrels, no phones**
193	AR 11, to Hazen, **N gas:** Exxon/Chester Fried, **S gas:** Citgo/dsl, Shell/dsl/24hr, T-rix/dsl/RV Park, **lodging:** Super 8, Travel Inn
183	AR 13, Carlisle, **S gas:** Citgo, Conoco/dsl, Exxon/dsl, Phillips 66/dsl, **food:** Nick's BBQ, Pizza 'N More, Sonic, **lodging:** Best Value, Budget Inn, **other:** $General, NAPACare
175	AR 31, Lonoke, **N gas:** Phillips 66, Valero/dsl, **food:** McDonald's, **lodging:** Day's Inn, Economy Inn, Holiday Inn Express, Super 8, **other:** Walmart SuperCtr, **S gas:** Shell/Subway, **food:** KFC/Taco Bell, Pizza Hut, Sonic, **lodging:** El Dorado Mexican, Perry's Motel/rest., **other:** Chevrolet, City Mkt Foods, Goodyear/auto
169	AR 15, Remington Rd
165	Kerr Rd
161	AR 391, Galloway, **N gas:** Love's/Chester's/dsl/24hr, **other:** Camping World RV Ctr, **S gas:** Petro/Mobil/Iron Skillet/dsl/scales/24hr/@, Pilot/Subway/Chester's/dsl/scales/24hr/@, IA-80 TruckOMat/dsl/scales, **lodging:** Galloway Inn, **other:** Blue Beacon, Freightliner
159	I-440 W, to , **S**
157	AR 161, to US 70, **N gas:** Exxon/dsl, **S gas:** Citgo, Hess, Super **S** Stop/dsl, Shell/dsl, **food:** Burger King, KFC/Taco Bell, McDonald's, Sonic, Subway, Waffle House, **lodging:** Best Value Inn, Comfort Inn, Day's Inn, Econolodge, Red Roof Inn, Super 8
156	Springhill Dr, **N gas:** Phillips 66, **food:** Burger King, Cracker Barrel, Red Lobster, **lodging:** Fairfield Inn, Holiday Inn Express, Residence Inn
155	US 67 N, US 167, to Jacksonville (exits left from eb), Little Rock AFB, **1 mi N on US 167/McCain Blvd...gas:** Murphy USA/dsl, Phillips 66, Shell, **food:** Applebee's, Arby's, Burger King, Cactus Jacks, Carino's Italian, Chili's, ChuckeCheese, CiCi's Pizza, Dixie Cafe, El Porton Mexican, Golden Corral, Hooters, IHOP, Jason's Deli, Kanpai Japanese, McDonald's, Luby's, Outback Steaks, Pizza Hut, Rally's, Red Lobster, Sonic, Shorty's BBQ, Subway, Taco Bell, TGIFriday, TX Roadhouse, Wendy's, Whole Hog Cafe, **lodging:** Comfort Inn, Hampton Inn, Hilton Garden, Holiday Inn Express, La Quinta, Super 8, **other:** Aamco, Barnes&Noble, Best Buy, BooksAMillion, Chevrolet, Chrysler/Dodge, Dillard's, $Tree, Firestone/auto, Ford/Lincoln/Mercury, Gander Mtn, Harley-Davidson, Home Depot, Honda, JC Penney,

LONOKE

LITTLE ROCK

INTERSTATE 40 CONT'D

E ↕ W

AR

Exit #	Services
155	Continued Kia, Lowe's Whse, Mazda, Michael's, Office Depot, PepBoys, PetsMart, Sam's Club/gas, Sears/auto, SteinMart, Target, TJ Maxx, Toyota/Scion, Walmart SuperCtr, mall, Vet
154	to Lakewood (from eb)
153b	I-30 W, US 65 S, to Little Rock
153a	AR 107 N, JFK Blvd, **N gas:** Exxon, Mapco, Shell, **food:** Schlotsky's, **lodging:** Travelodge, **S gas:** Exxon, **food:** Royal Buffet, Waffle House, **lodging:** Best Western, Country Inn Suites, Hampton Inn, Holiday Inn, Howard Johnson, Motel 6, **other:** H, USPO
152	AR 365, AR 176, Camp Pike Rd, Levy, **N on Camp Robinson Rd...gas:** Exxon, EZ Mart, Phillips 66, Shell, **food:** Burger King, KFC/Taco Bell, Little Caesars, Mexico Chiquito, McDonald's, Pizza Hut, Rally's, Sonic, Subway, US Pizza, Wendy's, **other:** AutoZone, Fred's, Kroger/gas, O'Reilly Parts, **S gas:** Phillips 66, **food:** Chicken King, **other:** H, Family$, Kroger, Radio Shack, Sav-A-Lot
150	AR 176, Burns Park, Camp Robinson, **S other:** info, camping
148	AR 100, Crystal Hill Rd, **N gas:** Shell, **S** KOA
147	I-430 S, to Texarkana
142	AR 365, to Morgan, **N gas:** Phillips 66, Valero/dsl, **food:** Morgan Cafe, **lodging:** Day's Inn, **other:** Auto Value Parts, Trails End RV Park, **S gas:** Shell/dsl, **food:** KFC/Taco Bell, McDonald's, Razorback Pizza, Smokeshack BBQ, Subway, Waffle House, **lodging:** Best Value, Comfort Suites, **other:** antiques
135	AR 365, AR 89, Mayflower, **N gas:** Hess/dsl, **other:** Mayflower RV Ctr (1mi), **S gas:** Exxon/dsl, Valero, **food:** Glory B's Rest., Sonic, Stroud's Country Diner, Tampico Mexican, **other:** Big Star Food/Drug, $General
134mm	**truck parking both lanes**
129	US 65B, AR 286, Conway, **S gas:** Citgo/dsl, Exxon, MapCo, **food:** Arby's, Smitty's BBQ, Subway, **lodging:** Budget Inn, Continental Motel, **other:** H, Chrysler/Dodge/Jeep, Honda, Toyota/Scion, st police, to Toad Suck SP
127	US 64, Conway, **N gas:** Exxon, Satterfield, Shell, **food:** Annie's Rest, Arby's, Chick-fil-A, Chili's, Denny's, Logan's Roadhouse, San Francisco Bread, Sonic, Starbucks, TGIFriday, Subway, Waffle House, **lodging:** Best Value, Best Western, Country Inn&Suites, Comfort Suites, Day's Inn, Economy Inn, Hampton Inn, Hilton Garden, **other:** Belk, Best Buy, Chevrolet, $General, Firestone/auto, Ford/Mercury, GMC/Buick/Pontiac, Goodyear/auto, Home Depot, Hyundai, Kohl's, Moix RV Ctr, NAPA, Nissan, Old Navy, O'Reilly Parts, PetsMart, Radio Shack, Staples, Target, TJ Maxx, repair/transmissions, to Lester Flatt Park, **Vet**, **S gas:** RaceWay, Shell/dsl, Valero/dsl, **food:** Burger King, Church's, Colton's Steaks, El Charrito Mexican, Hardee's, LJ Silver, McDonald's, Pizza Inn, Quizno's, Rally's, Shipley Doughnuts, Taco Bell, Tokyo Japanese, Wendy's, Western Sizzlin, **lodging:** Kings Inn, **other:** AutoZone, BigLots, Family$, Fred's Drugs, Goodyear/auto, Hancock Fabrics, Hobby Lobby, Kroger/gas, Sav-a-Lot Foods, Walgreens, tires
125	US 65, Conway, **N gas:** Conoco/dsl, Exxon/Subway/dsl, Phillips 66/dsl, Shell/dsl/24hr, **food:** Acapulco Mexican, China Town, Cracker Barrel, El Chico, La Hacienda Mexican, MktPlace Grill, McDonald's, **lodging:** Quality Inn, **other:** JC Penney, Office Depot, Sears, **S gas:** Citgo, Mobil/dsl, Murphy USA, **food:** Backyard Burger, Burger King, CiCi's, Dixie Cafe, Hart's Seafood, IHOP, Los 3 Potrellos Mexican, McAlister's Deli, New China, Outback Steaks, Ruby Tuesday, Ryan's, Sonic, Starbucks, Subway, Waffle House, Wendy's, **lodging:** Candlewood Suites, Fairfield Inn, Holiday Inn Express, Howard Johnson, La Quinta, Motel 6, Stacy Motel, Super 8, **other:** H, Advance Parts, $General, $Tree, Hastings Books, Lowes Whse, Tuesday Morning, Walmart SuperCtr, tires
124	AR 25 N, to Conway, **S gas:** Shell/dsl, **food:** DQ, KFC, Mazzio's, Popeye's, **other:** H, U-Haul
120mm	Cadron River
117	to Menifee
112	AR 92, Plumerville, **N gas:** Exxon/dsl, **S gas:** Country Store/dsl, **other:** USPO
108	AR 9, Morrilton, **S gas:** Phillips 66/24hr, Murphy USA, Shell/dsl/24hr, Valero, **food:** Blue Diamond Cafe, Bonanza, KFC, Chop Stix, McDonald's, Ortega's Mexican, Pizza Hut, Pizza Pro, Sonic, Subway, Taco Bell, Waffle House, Wendy's, **lodging:** Super 8, **other:** H, Ace Hardware, Buick/Chevrolet/Pontiac, Curves, $General, Goodyear, GMC, Kroger, NAPA, Walmart SuperCtr, to Petit Jean SP (21mi), RV camping, Vet
107	AR 95, Morrilton, **N gas:** Shell/dsl, **lodging:** Scottish Inn, KOA, **S gas:** Love's/Subway/dsl/scales/24hr, Shell, **food:** Mom&Pop's Waffles, Morrilton Drive Inn, Wendy's (2 mi), **lodging:** Day's Inn, **other:** CarQuest
101	Blackwell, **N gas:** Blackwell TrkStp/Valero/dsl/diner/scales/24hr, **other:** Utility Trailer Sales
94	AR 105, Atkins, **N gas:** Exxon/dsl/24hr, Shell/McDonald's/dsl, **food:** Berky's Diner, El Parian Mexican, KFC/Taco Bell, Pizza Meister, Sonic, **other:** $General, repair, **S** Saxton Foods
88	Pottsville, **S food:** Pottsville Country Cafe, **other:** truck repair/wash
84	US 64, AR 331, Russellville, **N gas:** ***FLYING J***/Conoco/Country Mkt/dsl/LP/24hr, Shell/dsl, **other:** Ivys Cove RV Retreat, trucklube, **S gas:** Phillips 66, Pilot/Subway/Wendy's/dsl/24hr/scales, **food:** CiCi's, Hardee's, Hunan Chinese, McDonald's, Sonic, Waffle House, **lodging:** Comfort Inn, Quality Inn, **other:** H AutoZone, Belk, Chevrolet/Buick/GMC, Chrysler/Dodge/Jeep, $Tree, Firestone, JC Penney, Hobby Lobby, K-Mart, Lowes Whse, Nissan, Staples, Toyota, USPO
83	AK 326, Weir Rd, **S gas:** Murphy USA, Phillips 66, **food:** DQ, Popeye's, Ryan's, Starbucks, Subway, Taco Bueno, **lodging:** Comfort Inn, **other:** AutoZone, Curves, $General, Walmart SuperCtr
81	AR 7, Russellville, **N gas:** SuperStop/dsl, **food:** Burger Boy, **lodging:** Days Inn, Motel 6, **other:** Outdoor RV Ctr/Park, **S gas:** Exxon/dsl/24hr, Phillips 66/dsl/24hr, Shell/24hr, **food:** Arby's, Burger King, Colton's Steaks, Cracker Barrel, Dixie Café, Dos Rios, IHOP, La Huerta Mexican, New China, Ruby

CONWAY · MORRILTON · RUSSELLVILLE

INTERSTATE 40 CONT'D

Exit #	Services
81	Continued Tuesday, Subway, Waffle House, **lodging:** Best Value, Best Western, Day's Inn, Economy Inn, Fairfield Inn, Hampton Inn, Holiday Inn, La Quinta, Super 8, **other:** antiques, Russell RV Ctr, to Lake Dardanelle SP, RV camping
80mm	Dardanelle Reservoir
78	US 64, Russellville, **S food:** Fat Daddy's BBQ, **other:** Darrell's Mkt, Mission RV Park, to Lake Dardanelle SP
74	AR 333, London
72mm	**rest area wb, full ♿ facilities, ☎, picnic, litter barrels, vending, petwalk**
70mm	overlook wb lane, litter barrels
68mm	**rest area eb, full ♿ facilities, ☎, picnic, litter barrels, vending, petwalk**
67	AR 315, Knoxville, **S gas:** Citgo, Knoxville Mkt, **other:** USPO
64	US 64, Clarksville, Lamar, **S** Dad's Dream RV Park
58	AR 21, AR 103, Clarksville, **N gas:** Shell/dsl, Valero, **food:** Emerald Dragon Chinese, KFC, Larry's Pizza, McDonald's, Pasta Grill, Pizza Hut, Sonic, Taco Bell, Waffle House, Wendy's, **lodging:** Best Western, Comfort Inn, Economy Inn, Super 8, **other:** H, Chevrolet/Pontiac/GMC, Curves, $General, **S gas:** Murphy USA/dsl, **food:** Arby's, South Park Rest., **other:** Chrysler/Dodge/Jeep, $Tree, Ford/Mercury, Walmart SuperCtr
57	AR 109, Clarksville, **N gas:** Fuel Stop/dsl, **food:** Subway, **other:** Family$, Harvest Foods/drug, **S gas:** Shell/pizza/subs/dsl, **other:** auto repair
55	US 64, AR 109, Clarksville, **N food:** Hardee's, Kountry Kitchen, **lodging:** Day's Inn, Hampton Inn, Holiday Inn Express, **S gas:** Exxon/dsl, **food:** Western Sizzlin, **other:** st police
47	AR 164, Coal Hill
41	AR 186, Altus, **S food:** Wiederkehr Rest., **other:** Pine Ridge RV Park, winery
37	AR 219, Ozark, **S gas:** Love's/Subway/dsl/scales/24hr, Shell/McDonald's/dsl, **food:** KFC/Taco Bell, **lodging:** Day's Inn, **other:** H
36mm	**rest area both lanes, full ♿ facilities, ☎, picnic, litter barrels, petwalk**
35	AR 23, Ozark, **3 mi S gas:** 23 One Stop, **food:** Hardee's, Subway, **lodging:** Ozark Inn, Oxford Inn, **other:** H, Aux Arc Park (5mi), to Mt Magazine SP (20 mi)
24	AR 215, Mulberry, **S** Vine Prairie Park
20	Dyer, **N gas:** Conoco/dsl, **other:** Freightliner/Western Star, **S gas:** Phillips 66/dsl, Shell/dsl, **lodging:** Mill Creek Inn
13	US 71 N, to Fayetteville, **N gas:** Phillips 66/dsl, Shell, **food:** Burger King, Catfish Hole, China Fun, Cracker Barrel, KFC, La Fiesta Mexican, Mazzio's, Pizza Parlor, Subway, Taco Bell, **lodging:** Comfort Inn, Meadors Inn, **other:** Crabtree RV Ctr/Park, Curves, $General, KOA (2mi), O'Reilly Parts, to U of AR, Lake Ft Smith SP, **S gas:** Murphy USA/dsl, Shamrock, Valero/dsl, **food:** Braum's, Geno's Pizza, McDonald's, Sonic, **lodging:** Day's Inn, **other:** C&H Tires, CV's Foods, Harp's Foods, Walgreens, Walmart SuperCtr

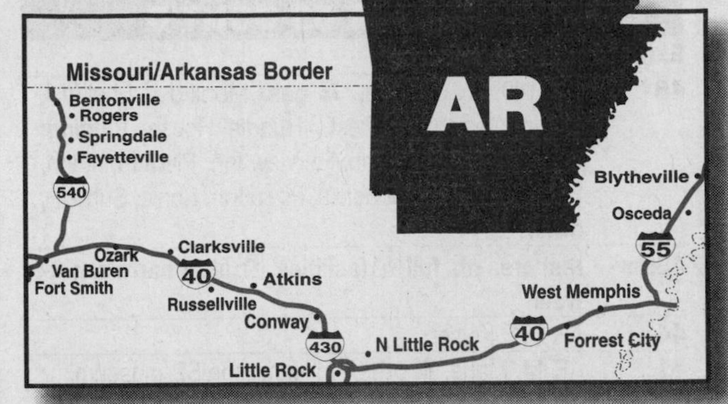

Exit #	Services
12	I-540 N, to Fayetteville, **N other:** to Lake Ft Smith SP
9mm	**weigh sta both lanes**
7	I-540 S, US 71 S, to Ft Smith, Van Buren, **S** H
5	AR 59, Van Buren, **N gas:** Citgo, Murphy USA, Phillips 66, **food:** Arby's, Burger King, Chili's, China Buffet, Domino's, Firehouse Subs, Frank's Italian, La Fiesta Mexican, McDonald's, Popeye's, Zaxby's, **lodging:** Best Western, Hampton Inn, **other:** Advance Parts, Cooley's Tire, $Tree, Radio Shack, Lowe's Whse, NAPA, Walmart SuperCtr, USPO, tires, **S gas:** Shell/dsl/24hr, **food:** Braum's, Big Jake's Steaks, El Torrito Mexican, Gino's Burgers, Geno's Pizza, KFC/Taco Bell, Rick's Rib House, Sonic, Subway, Waffle House, Wendy's, **lodging:** Holiday Inn Express, Motel 6, Sleep Inn, Super 8, **other:** CV's Foods, Grizzle Tire, Overland RV Park, Outdoor RV Ctr, Walgreens, dsl repair, truckwash
3	Lee Creek Rd, **N gas:** Shell, **other:** Park Ridge Camping
2.5mm	**Welcome Ctr eb, full ♿ facilities, ☎, picnic, litter barrels, vending, petwalk**
1	to Ft Smith (from wb), Dora
0mm	Arkansas/Oklahoma state line

INTERSTATE 55

Exit #	Services
72mm	Arkansas/Missouri state line
72	State Line Rd, **weigh sta sb**
71	AR 150, Yarbro
68mm	**Welcome Ctr sb, full ♿ facilities, ☎, picnic, litter barrels, petwalk**
67	AR 18, Blytheville, **E gas:** Phillips 66/dsl, **food:** Burger King, Capt D's, Skinny's Diner, Zaxby's, **lodging:** Day's Inn, Travelodge, **other:** $Tree, Lowe's Whse, Walmart SuperCtr, **W gas:** BP/dsl, Citgo/dsl, Shell, **food:** El Acapulco Mexican, GreatWall Chinese, Grecian Steaks, Hardee's, La Cabana, Mazzio's, McDonald's, Olympia Steaks, Pizza Inn, Red Apple Rest., Sonic, Starbucks, Subway, Taco Bell, Wendy's, **lodging:** Comfort Inn, Hampton Inn, Holiday Inn, Super 8, **other:** H, Advance Parts, AutoZone, Family$, Ford/Lincoln/Mercury, Fred's Drug, JC Penney
63	US 61, to Blytheville, **E gas:** BP/dsl, **other:** Shearins RV Park (2mi), **W gas:** Dodge's Store/dsl, Exxon/Chester Fried/dsl, Shell/McDonald's/dsl/24hr, **lodging:** Best Western, Garden Inn, Relax Inn, Royal Inn (2mi), **other:** Chevrolet, Nissan
57	AR 148, Burdette, **E other:** NE AR Coll
53	AR 158, Victoria, Luxora

INTERSTATE 55 CONT'D

Exit #	Services
48	AR 140, to Osceola, **E gas:** Mobil/dsl, Shell/dsl, **other:** Cotton Inn Rest., Huddle House, **lodging:** Days Inn, Deerfield Inn, Fairview Inn, Plum Point Inn, **3 mi E food:** McDonald's, Pizza Inn, Sonic, Subway, **other:** [H]
45mm	**rest area nb, full [handicapped] facilities, [picnic],litter barrels, petwalk**
44	AR 181, Keiser
41	AR 14, Marie, **E other:** to Hampson SP/museum
36	AR 181, to Wilson, Bassett
35mm	**rest area sb, full [handicapped] facilities, [phone], [picnic], litter barrels, petwalk**
34	AR 118, Joiner
23b a	US 63, AR 77, to Marked Tree, Jonesboro, ASU, **E gas:** Citgo/chicken/pizza
21	AR 42, Turrell, **W gas:** Exxon/rest./dsl/scales/24hr
17	AR 50, to Jericho
14	rd 4, to Jericho, **E gas:** Citgo/scales/dsl/24hr, **other:** flea market, **W gas:** Citgo/Stuckey's, **other:** Chevrolet, KOA
10	US 64 W, Marion, **E gas:** Citgo/Subway/scales, Mapco/dsl, Shell/McDonald's/dsl, **food:** KFC/Taco Bell, Tops BBQ, **lodging:** Hallmarc Inn, **other:** $General, Market Place Foods, **W gas:** BP/dsl, JP Mkt, Shell, **food:** Colton's Grill, Wendy's, Zaxby's, **lodging:** Best Western, Journey Inn, **other:** AutoZone, to Parkin SP (23mi)
9mm	**weigh sta/truck parking both lanes**
8	I-40 W, to Little Rock
278	AR 77, 7th St, Missouri St, **E gas:** Citgo/24hr, **W on 7th St...food:** BBQ, Cracker Barrel, KFC, Pizza Inn, **lodging:** Quality Inn, **other:** [H], Sawyers RV Park, Sears, **W on Missouri St...gas:** Exxon, Mapco, Phillips 66/dsl, Shell, **food:** Bonanza, Burger King, Domino's, Mrs Winner's, Popeye's, Subway, Taco Bell, Wendy's, **lodging:** Comfort Suites, Quality Inn, **other:** $Tree, Goodyear/auto, Walgreens
279b	I-40 E, to Memphis
279a	Ingram Blvd, **E food:** Margaritas Mexican, **lodging:** Comfort Inn, Day's Inn, Homegate Inn, Red Roof Inn, Rodeway Inn, **other:** Ford, Greyhound Park, Southland Racetrack, U-Haul, **W gas:** Citgo/dsl, **food:** Cupboard Rest., Waffle House, **lodging:** Best Value, Econolodge, Hampshire Inn, Holiday Inn, Motel 6, Ramada, Relax Inn
4	King Dr, Southland Dr, **E gas:** *FLYING J*/Conoco/LP/scales/RV dump/dsl/rest., Petro/Iron Skillet/dsl/rest./24hr/@, Pilot/Subway/dsl/scales/@, **food:** KFC/Taco Bell, McDonald's, Waffle House, **lodging:** Best Western, Deluxe Inn, Express Inn, Super 8, **other:** Blue Beacon, SpeedCo Lube, **W gas:** Citgo, **food:** Poncho's Mexican, **lodging:** Sunset Inn, **other:** Goodyear
3b a	US 70, Broadway Blvd, AR 131, Mound City Rd (exits left from nb), **W lodging:** Budget Inn
2mm	**weigh sta nb**
1	Bridgeport Rd
0mm	Arkansas/Tennessee state line, Mississippi River

N ↕ S — MARION — WEST MEMPHIS

INTERSTATE 430 (LITTLE ROCK)

Exit #	Services
13b a	I-40. I-430 begins/ends on I-40, exit 147.
12	AR 100, Maumelle, **W gas:** Citgo, **other:** O'Reilly Parts, NAPA, Vet
10mm	Arkansas River
9	AR 10, Cantrell Rd., **W** Maumelle Park, Pinnacle Mtn SP
8	Rodney Parham Rd, **E gas:** Conoco, Shell, **food:** Arby's, Baskin-Robbins, El Chico, Firehouse Subs, KFC, McAlister's Grill, McDonald's, Mt Fuji Japanese, New China Buffet, Sonic, Starbucks, Subway, Taco Bell, Terri Lynn's BBQ, US Pizza, **lodging:** La Quinta, **other:** Advance Parts, AutoZone, $Days, $General, Drug Emporium, Kroger, Walgreens, **W gas:** Exxon, **food:** Burger King, Chili's, Chizi's Pizza, ChuckeCheese, Dixie Cafe, Dominos, Franke's Café, Heavenly Ham, LoneStar Steaks, Olive Garden, Shorty Small's Ribs, Wendy's, **lodging:** Best Western, **other:** Firestone/auto, GNC, K-Mart, Radio Shack, USA Drug, Whole Foods Mkt, Vet
6	I-630, Kanis Rd, Markham St, to downtown, **E food:** McDonald's, **lodging:** Candlewood Suites, Comfort Inn, Motel 6, SpringHill Suites, **W gas:** Exxon, **food:** Cozymel's Grill, Denny's, Famous Dave's BBQ, IHOP, Jason's Deli, Kobe Japanese, Lenny's Subs, Macaroni Grill, McAlister's Deli, Mimi's Cafe, On-the-Border, PF Chang's, Shotgun Dan's Pizza, Starbucks, Taco Bell, Waffle House, Wendy's, **lodging:** Courtyard, Crowne Plaza, Embassy Suites, Extended Stay America, Jameson Inn, La Quinta, Ramada Ltd, **other:** AT&T, Barnes&Noble, Best Buy, PetsMart, Wal-Mart
5	Kanis Rd, Shackleford Rd, **E food:** Cracker Barrel, Panda Garden, Samurai Steaks, TX Roadhouse, **lodging:** Candlewood Suites, Comfort Inn, Motel 6, SpringHill Suites, Towneplace Suites, **other:** Gordman's, JC Penney, **W gas:** Shell, **food:** Krispy Kreme, **lodging:** Hampton Inn, Holiday Inn Select, La Quinta, Residence Inn, Studio+, Wingate Inn, **other:** [H], Lexus
4	AR 300, Col Glenn Rd, **E food:** Subway, Wendy's, **lodging:** Holiday Inn Express, ValuePlace Hotel, **other:** Toyota/Scion, **W gas:** Valero/Burger King/dsl, **other:** Honda, Hyundai, Jaguar, Land Rover, Mazda, Mercedes, Nissan
1	AR 5, Stagecoach Rd, **E food:** Our Place Grill, **W gas:** Phillips 66, Valero, **food:** Grandpa's Catfish, Jordan's BBQ, Subway, **other:** Tires
0mm	I-30. I-430 begins/ends on I-30, exit 129.

N ↕ S — LITTLE ROCK

INTERSTATE 440 (LITTLE ROCK)

Exit #	Services
11	I-40 begins ends on I-440 exit 59
10	US 70, **W other:** Peterbilt
8	Faulkner Lake Rd, **W gas:** Pioneer/dsl
7	US 165, to England, **S** Agricultural Museum, Toltec Mounds SP, Willow Beach SP
6mm	Arkansas River
5	Fourche Dam Pike, LR Riverport, **N gas:** Exxon, Shell/Subway, **food:** McDonald's, **lodging:** Travelodge, **other:** Kenworth, **S gas:** Phillips 66/dsl, Valero/dsl
4	Lindsey Rd
3	Bankhead Dr, **N lodging:** Comfort Inn, **other:** LR [airport] **S gas:** Valero, **food:** Boston's Rest., Waffle House, **lodging:** Days Inn, Holiday Inn, Holiday Inn Express
1	AR 365, Springer Blvd, **S** Little Rock Ntl Cemetery
0mm	I-440 begins/ends on I-30, exit 138.

N ↕ S

INTERSTATE 540 (FAYETTEVILLE)

Exit #	Services
93	US 71B, Bentonville, I-540 begins/ends on US 71 N.
88	AR 72, Bentonville, Pea Ridge, **E gas:** Conoco, **food:** River Grille, **lodging:** Courtyard, Simmon's Suites, **W gas:** Shell, **food:** Hot Dog Alley, Smokin' Joe's Ribs
86	US 62, AR 102, Bentonville, Rogers, **E lodging:** TownePlace Suites, **other:** Harley-Davidson, Sam's Club/gas, Walmart Mkt/gas, Pea Ridge NMP, **W gas:** Phillips 66/McDonald's/dsl, Shell/dsl, **food:** Arby's, Sonic, Subway, Taco Bell, **lodging:** Value Place Inn, **other:** Buick/GMC/Pontiac, Walmart Visitor Ctr
85	US 71B, AR 12, Bentonville, Rogers, **E gas:** BP/dsl, Citgo/dsl, **food:** Abuelo's, Applebee's, Arby's, Atlanta Bread, Carino's Italian, Chick-fil-A, Chili's, CiCi's, Colton's Steaks, Copeland's Rest., Dixie Café, Famous Dave's, IHOP, KFC, King Buffet, McDonald's, O'Charley's, Oscar's Rest., On-the-Border, Outback Steaks, Quizno's, Red Robin, Sonic, Starbucks, **lodging:** Candlewood Suites, Country Inn&Suites, Fairfield Inn, Hampton Inn, Hartland Lodge, Homewood Suites, Hyatt Place, Mainstay Suites, Regency Inn, Residence Inn, **other:** Barnes&Noble, Belk, Firestone/auto, Honda, Kohl's, Lowe's Whse, Office Depot, Old Navy, PetCo, Staples, Beaver Lake SP, Prairie Creek SP, **W gas:** Exxon, Phillips 66, **food:** Bojangles, Braum's, Brioso Brazilian, Denny's, Krispy Kreme, Lin's Chinese, Mama Fu's Asian, McAlister's Deli, Moe's Grill, Simon's Pancakes, Shogun Japanese, Taco Bueno, Village Inn, Waffle House, Zaxby's, **lodging:** Best Western, Clarion, Comfort Inn, Comfort Suites, Day's Inn, Hilton Garden, Holiday Inn Express, La Quinta (1mi), Sleep Inn, SpringHill Suites, Super 8, **other:** H, Buick/GMC/Pontiac, Honda, Hyundai, Nissan, Toyota/Scion
83	AR 94 E, Pinnacle Hills Pkway, **E food:** Hillbilly Smokehouse, Rib House, **lodging:** Best Value (3mi), Ramada Inn (3mi), **other:** H, Best Buy, Dillards, Home Depot, Horse Shoe Bend Park, **W food:** Plaza Rest., Subway, **lodging:** Embassy Suites, Holiday Inn, Staybridge Suites
81	Pleasant Grove Rd, **E food:** Backyard Burger, Chick-fil-A, Golden Corral, Mad Pizza, McDonald's, Starbucks, Subway, Taco Bueno, **lodging:** Super 8, **other:** Curves, Sportsman's Whse, Walgreens, Walmart SuperCtr/gas, **W** Green Country RV Park
78	AR 264, Lowell, Cave Sprgs, Rogers, **E gas:** Kum&Go, Phillips 66/dsl, **food:** Arby's, Domino's, DQ, KFC, Mazzio's Pizza, McDonald's, Sonic, Starbucks, Subway, Taco Bell, **other:** Ramada, **other:** New Hope RV Ctr
76	Wagon Wheel Rd, **E** to Hickory Creek Park
73	Elm Springs Rd, **E gas:** Kum&Go, Valero/dsl, **food:** AQ Chicken House (3mi), Eureka Pizza, Western Sizzlin (2mi), **lodging:** Magnolia Gardens Inn (3mi), Value Place Inn, **other:** Chevrolet, Goodyear
72mm	**weigh sta nb**
72	US 412, Springdale, Siloam Springs, **E gas:** Citgo, Exxon, Phillips 66/Subway, **food:** Applebee's, Armadillo Grill, Braum's, Chilis, Denny's, Maria's Mexican, McDonald's, Sizzler, Sonic, Taco Bell, Waffle House, Wendy's, **lodging:** Best Western, Comfort Inn, Day's Inn, DoubleTree Hotel, Executive Inn, Extended Stay America, Fairfield Inn, Hampton Inn, Hartland Inn,

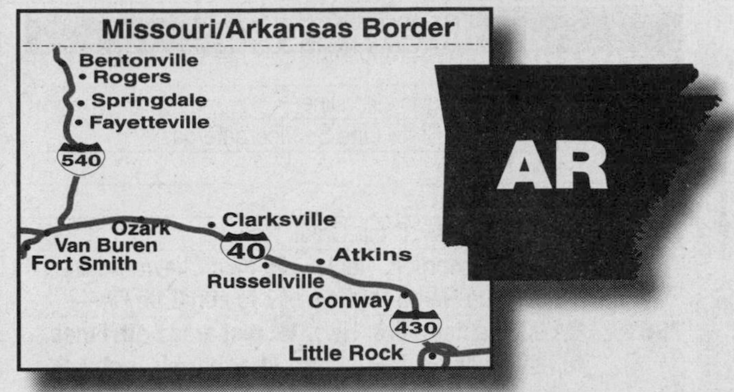

Exit #	Services
72	Continued Holiday Inn, La Quinta, Residence Inn, Sleep Inn, Springdale Motel, Super 8, **other:** Kenworth/Volvo Trucks, Lowe's Whse, Office Depot, **W gas:** Pilot/Burger King/dsl/24hr/scales/@, **food:** Cracker Barrel, Jose's Mexican, KFC, **other:** Big Lots, Buick/Pontiac/GMC/Jeep, Fred's$, Layman's Hardware, Melon RV Ctr
71mm	**weigh sta sb**
69	Johnson, **1-2 mi E food:** Chick-fil-A, Eureka Pizza, Fire Mtn Grill, Hooter's, Inn at the Mill Rest, James Rest, Shogun Japanese, **lodging:** Inn at the Mill, **W** H
67	US 71B, Fayetteville, **E** H
66	AR 112, **E gas:** BP/dsl, **lodging:** Day's Inn (2mi), **W** Acura/Chevrolet/Hummer/Honda/Toyota
65	Porter Rd
64	AR 16 W, AR 112 E, Wedington Dr, **E food:** AQ Chicken House (3mi), Eureka Pizza (2mi), **W gas:** Citgo/McDonald's/dsl, Phillips 66, **food:** Boar's Nest BBQ, Guido's Pizza, IHOP, Sonic, Subway, Taco Bell, **lodging:** Country Inn Suites, Holiday Inn Express, Quality Inn, **other:** Harp's Food/gas, **Vet**
62	US 62, AR 180, Farmington, **E gas:** Conoco, Shell, **food:** Arby's, Braum's, Burger King, Charlie's Chicken, Hardee's, JD China, KFC, McDonald's, Mexico Viejo, Sonic, Taco Bell, Taiwan Chinese, Waffle House, Wendy's, **lodging:** Best Western, Red Roof Inn, **other:** USA Drug, **W food:** Braum's, Denny's, Firehouse Subs, Papa Murphy's, Pavilion Buffet, Ruby Tuesday, **lodging:** Clarion, Comfort Inn, Hampton Inn, Quality Inn, Regency 7 Motel, Super 8, Value Place Inn, **other:** AutoZone, $Tree, Lowes Whse, Walmart SuperCtr/gas
61	US 71, to Boston Mtn Scenic Lp, sb only
60	AR 112, AR 265, Razorback Rd, **E** to U of AR
58	Greenland, **W gas:** Phillips 66/McDonalds/dsl/scales, **food:** Sonic
56	**E gas:** BP, **W other:** Acura, Chevrolet, Honda, Sam's Club/gas, Toyota
53	AR 170, West Fork, **E other:** Winn Creek RV Resort (4mi), **W** to Devils Den SP
45	AR 74, Winslow, **W** to Devils Den SP
41mm	Bobby Hopper Tunnel
34	AR 282, to US 71, Chester, **W** Chester Mercantile/gas, USPO
29	AR 282, to US 71, Mountainburg, **1 mi E gas:** BP/dsl/rest/scales, **other:** to Lake Ft Smith SP
24	AR 282, to US 71, Rudy, **E gas:** Shell/dsl, **food:** Red Hog BBQ, **other:** KOA, Boston Mtns Scenic Lp
21	Collum Ln
20	to US 71, **E gas:** Shell, **food:** KFC, Taco Bell, **lodging:** Comfort Inn, Day's Inn

I-540 N begins/ends on I-40, exit 12.

CA

INTERSTATE 5

N ↕ S

Exit #	Services
797mm	California/Oregon state line
796	Hilt, **W gas:** State Line Service/café/gas
793	Bailey Hill Rd
791mm	**inspection sta sb**
790	Hornbrook Hwy, Ditch Creek Rd
789	A28, to Hornbrook, Henley, **E gas:** Chevron/dsl/LP, **other:** Blue Heron RV Park, [phone], to Iron Gate RA
786	CA 96, Klamath River Hwy, **W rest area both lanes, full [handicapped] facilities, info, [phone], [picnic], litter barrels, petwalk,** to Klamath River RA
782mm	Anderson Summit, elev 3067
780mm	vista point sb
779mm	Shasta River
776	Yreka, Montague, **E lodging:** Holiday Inn Express, **other:** Yreka RV Park, **W gas:** USA/dsl, **food:** Casa Ramos Mexican, Ket Rest., Puerto Vallarta, **lodging:** Mtn View Motel, Super 8, **other:** Curves, Goodyear, Ray's Foods
775	Miner St, Central Yreka, **W gas:** Chevron/24hr, Texaco/dsl, Valero/dsl, **food:** China Dragon, Denny's, Grandma's House, KFC, RoundTable Pizza, **lodging:** Best Western, Budget Inn, Econolodge, Klamath Motel, Relax Inn, Rodeway Inn, Yreka Motel, **other:** [H] CarQuest, Chevrolet/Cadillac/Pontiac, Clayton Tire, Honda, PriceLess Foods, Radio Shack, Rite Aid, USPO, museum
773	CA 3, to Ft Jones, Etna, **E gas:** CFN/dsl, **other:** Schwab Tire, Trailer Haven RV Park, **W gas:** Shell/dsl, **food:** BlackBear Diner, Burger King, Carl's Jr, Jeanne's Seafood, Linda's Cafe, McDonald's, Papa Murphy's, Subway, Taco Bell, **lodging:** Baymont Inn, Comfort Inn, Motel 6, **other:** [H], $Tree, Ford/Lincoln/Mercury, JC Penney, NAPA, Raley's Foods, Schuck's Parts, Walmart, CHP, **1 mi W gas:** Valero, **food:** BBQ Express, KFC, Yreka Pizza, **lodging:** Relax Inn, **other:** PriceLess Foods, Rite Aid, transmissions
770	Shamrock Rd, Easy St, **W gas:** Beacon, Fuel 24/7/dsl, **other:** RV camping
766	A12, to Gazelle, Grenada, **E gas:** 76/dsl, **W gas:** Texaco/dsl, **other:** RV camping
759	Louie Rd
753	Weed Airport Rd, **W rest area both lanes, full [handicapped] facilities, [picnic], litter barrels, [phone], petwalk**
751	Stewart Springs Rd, Edgewood, **E lodging:** Lake Shasta RA/RV camp (2mi), **W other:** RV camp (7mi)
748	to US 97, to Klamath Falls, Weed, **E gas:** Chevron/24hr, Shell/dsl, Spirit/dsl, **food:** Ellie's Espresso, Pizza Factory, Sabor Latino, **lodging:** Hi-Lo Motel/rest., Motel 6, Summit Inn, Townhouse Motel, **other:** NAPA, Ray's Foods, golf, RV camping, Weed Repair
747	Central Weed, **E** same as 748, **other:** auto repair, **W** Coll of Siskiyou
745	S Weed Blvd, **E gas:** CFN, Chevron/dsl/24hr, Shell/dsl/24hr, Travel Plaza/Subway/dsl/scales/24hr, **food:** Burger King, Dos Amigos Mexican, McDonald's, Silva's Rest., Taco Bell, **lodging:** Comfort Inn, Quality Inn, Sis-Q Inn, **other:** Friendly RV Park
743	Summit Dr, Truck Village Dr, **E gas:** CFN/dsl

YREKA

WEED

Exit #	Services
742mm	Black Butte Summit, elev 3912
741	Abrams Lake Rd, **E other:** Schwab Tire, **W lodging:** Abrams Lake RV Park
740	Mt Shasta City (from sb), **E gas:** Pacific Pride/dsl/LP, **lodging:** Cold Creek Inn
738	Central Mt Shasta, **E gas:** 76/dsl, Chevron/dsl, Shell/dsl/LP, Spirit/dsl, **food:** BlackBear Diner, Burger King, KFC/Taco Bell, RoundTable Pizza, Subway, **lodging:** Best Western/Treehouse Rest., Travel Inn, **other:** [H], Do It Hardware, NAPA, Ray's Foods, Rite Aid, Schuck's Parts, USPO, visitors info, **W lodging:** Mt Shasta Resort/rest., Lake Siskiyou RV Park
737	Mt Shasta City (from nb), same as 738
736	CA 89, to McCloud, to Reno, **E food:** Casa Ramos, Jade Garden, Lilly's Rest, **lodging:** Strawberry Inn, Swiss Holiday Lodge, **other:** McCloud RV Park
735mm	**weigh sta sb**
734	Mott Rd, to Dunsmuir
732	Dunsmuir Ave, Siskiyou Ave, **E food:** Penny's Diner, **lodging:** Best Choice Inn, Oak Tree Inn, **W gas:** Chevron/Subway/dsl, **lodging:** Acorn Inn, Cedar Lodge
730	Central Dunsmuir, **E food:** Brown Trout Cafe, Burger Barn, Cave Springs Lodge, Cornerstone Cafe, Pizza Factory, Hot Dog Depot, **lodging:** Travelodge, **other:** NAPA, USPO, **W gas:** Chevron/Subway/dsl/LP, **lodging:** Cave Springs Motel, **other:** city park
729	Dunsmuir (from nb), **E gas:** Manfredi's/deli/dsl, **food:** Burger Barn, Cornerstone, Pizza Factory, **lodging:** Dunsmuir Lodge
728	Crag View Dr, Dunsmuir, Railroad Park Rd, **W other:** Railroad Park Motel/RV Park
727	(from nb) Crag View Dr
726	Soda Creek Rd, to Pacific Crest Trail
724	Castella, **W gas:** Chevron/dsl, **other:** RV camping, Castle Crags SP
723mm	vista point nb
723	Sweetbrier Ave
721	Conant Rd
720	Flume Creek Rd
718	Sims Rd, **W other:** RV camping
714	Gibson Rd
712	Pollard Flat, **E gas:** Exxon/dsl/LP/24hr, **food:** Pollard Flat USA Rest.
710	Slate Creek Rd, La Moine
707	Delta Rd, Dog Creek Rd, to Vollmers
705mm	**rest area sb, full [handicapped] facilities, [phone], litter barrels, [picnic]**
704	Riverview Dr, **E food:** Klondike Diner, **lodging:** Lakehead Camping
702	Antlers Rd, Lakeshore Dr, to Lakehead, **E gas:** Shell/Subway/dsl/24hr, **lodging:** Antlers RV Park, Lakehead Camping, Neu Lodge Motel, **other:** USPO, auto repair, **W food:** Bass Hole Rest., **lodging:** Shasta Lake Motel/RV, Lakeshore Villa RV Park
698	Salt Creek Rd, Gilman Rd, **W lodging:** Salt Creek Lodge/RV Park, Trail In RV Park
695	Shasta Caverns Rd, to O'Brien, **W** O'brien Mtn Lodge & Camping
694mm	**rest area nb, full [handicapped] facilities, [phone], [picnic], litter barrels, petwalk**
693	(from sb)Packers Bay Rd
692	Turntable Bay Rd

MT SHASTA

DUNSMUIR

LAKEHEAD

CA

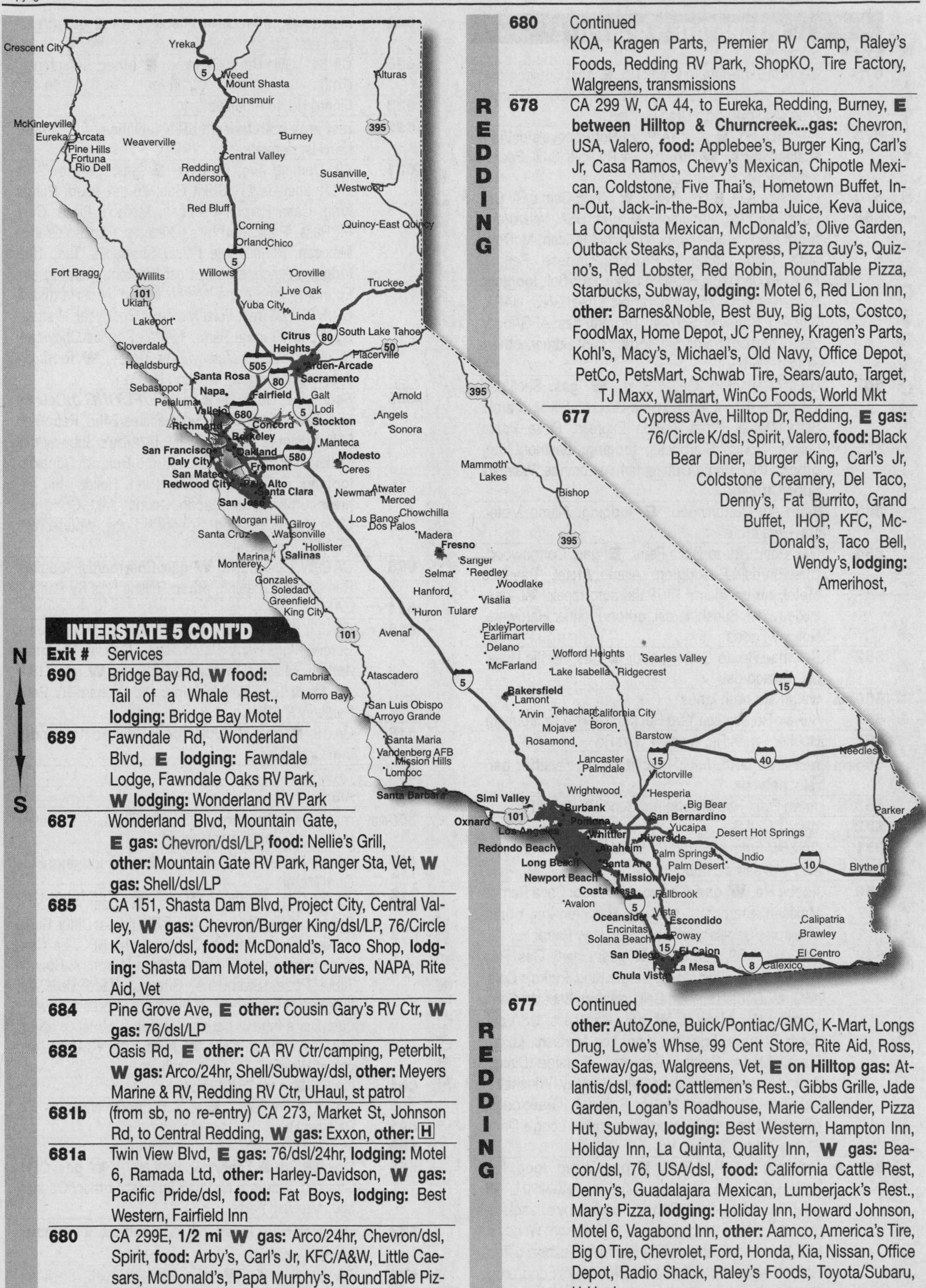

INTERSTATE 5 CONT'D

N ↕ S

Exit #	Services
690	Bridge Bay Rd, **W food:** Tail of a Whale Rest., **lodging:** Bridge Bay Motel
689	Fawndale Rd, Wonderland Blvd, **E lodging:** Fawndale Lodge, Fawndale Oaks RV Park, **W lodging:** Wonderland RV Park
687	Wonderland Blvd, Mountain Gate, **E gas:** Chevron/dsl/LP, **food:** Nellie's Grill, **other:** Mountain Gate RV Park, Ranger Sta, Vet, **W gas:** Shell/dsl/LP
685	CA 151, Shasta Dam Blvd, Project City, Central Valley, **W gas:** Chevron/Burger King/dsl/LP, 76/Circle K, Valero/dsl, **food:** McDonald's, Taco Shop, **lodging:** Shasta Dam Motel, **other:** Curves, NAPA, Rite Aid, Vet
684	Pine Grove Ave, **E other:** Cousin Gary's RV Ctr, **W gas:** 76/dsl/LP
682	Oasis Rd, **E other:** CA RV Ctr/camping, Peterbilt, **W gas:** Arco/24hr, Shell/Subway/dsl, **other:** Meyers Marine & RV, Redding RV Ctr, UHaul, st patrol
681b	(from sb, no re-entry) CA 273, Market St, Johnson Rd, to Central Redding, **W gas:** Exxon, **other:** H
681a	Twin View Blvd, **E gas:** 76/dsl/24hr, **lodging:** Motel 6, Ramada Ltd, **other:** Harley-Davidson, **W gas:** Pacific Pride/dsl, **food:** Fat Boys, **lodging:** Best Western, Fairfield Inn
680	CA 299E, **1/2 mi W gas:** Arco/24hr, Chevron/dsl, Spirit, **food:** Arby's, Carl's Jr, KFC/A&W, Little Caesars, McDonald's, Papa Murphy's, RoundTable Pizza, Starbucks, Subway, **other:** AutoZone, $Tree,
680	Continued KOA, Kragen Parts, Premier RV Camp, Raley's Foods, Redding RV Park, ShopKO, Tire Factory, Walgreens, transmissions
678	CA 299 W, CA 44, to Eureka, Redding, Burney, **E between Hilltop & Churncreek...gas:** Chevron, USA, Valero, **food:** Applebee's, Burger King, Carl's Jr, Casa Ramos, Chevy's Mexican, Chipotle Mexican, Coldstone, Five Thai's, Hometown Buffet, In-n-Out, Jack-in-the-Box, Jamba Juice, Keva Juice, La Conquista Mexican, McDonald's, Olive Garden, Outback Steaks, Panda Express, Pizza Guy's, Quizno's, Red Lobster, Red Robin, RoundTable Pizza, Starbucks, Subway, **lodging:** Motel 6, Red Lion Inn, **other:** Barnes&Noble, Best Buy, Big Lots, Costco, FoodMax, Home Depot, JC Penney, Kragen's Parts, Kohl's, Macy's, Michael's, Old Navy, Office Depot, PetCo, PetsMart, Schwab Tire, Sears/auto, Target, TJ Maxx, Walmart, WinCo Foods, World Mkt
677	Cypress Ave, Hilltop Dr, Redding, **E gas:** 76/Circle K/dsl, Spirit, Valero, **food:** Black Bear Diner, Burger King, Carl's Jr, Coldstone Creamery, Del Taco, Denny's, Fat Burrito, Grand Buffet, IHOP, KFC, McDonald's, Taco Bell, Wendy's, **lodging:** Amerihost,
677	Continued **other:** AutoZone, Buick/Pontiac/GMC, K-Mart, Longs Drug, Lowe's Whse, 99 Cent Store, Rite Aid, Ross, Safeway/gas, Walgreens, Vet, **E on Hilltop gas:** Atlantis/dsl, **food:** Cattlemen's Rest., Gibbs Grille, Jade Garden, Logan's Roadhouse, Marie Callender, Pizza Hut, Subway, **lodging:** Best Western, Hampton Inn, Holiday Inn, La Quinta, Quality Inn, **W gas:** Beacon/dsl, 76, USA/dsl, **food:** California Cattle Rest, Denny's, Guadalajara Mexican, Lumberjack's Rest., Mary's Pizza, **lodging:** Holiday Inn, Howard Johnson, Motel 6, Vagabond Inn, **other:** Aamco, America's Tire, Big O Tire, Chevrolet, Ford, Honda, Kia, Nissan, Office Depot, Radio Shack, Raley's Foods, Toyota/Subaru, U-Haul

REDDING

REDDING

INTERSTATE 5 CONT'D

N ↕ S

ANDERSON

Exit #	Services
675	Bechelli Lane, Churn Creek Rd, **E gas:** Chevron/dsl, Valero, **lodging:** Super 8, **W gas:** Texaco/Burger King/dsl, **lodging:** Hilton Garden
673	Knighton Rd, **E gas:** TA/Pizza Hut/Popeye's/dsl/LP/scales/24hr/@, **W other:** JGW RV Park (3mi), Sacramento River RV Park (3mi)
670	Riverside Ave, **E** Gaia Hotel, **W other:** Gamel RV Ctr
668	Balls Ferry Rd, Anderson, **E gas:** USA, Valero/dsl, **food:** A&W, Burger King, Mariachi Mexican, McDonald's, Papa Murphy's, Peacock Chinese, Perko's Rest., RoundTable Pizza, Subway, Taco Bell, **lodging:** Best Western, Valley Inn, **other:** $Tree, GNC, NAPA, Rite Aid, Safeway, Schwab Tire, **W gas:** AFG/food/gas, Chevron, Sarco/dsl, **food:** Giant Burger, **other:** Kragen Parts
667	CA 273, Factory Outlet Blvd, **W gas:** Shell/dsl/LP, **food:** Arby's, Jack-in-the-Box, LJ Silver, Marble Slab, Mary's Pizza, Panda Express, Pizza Pasta Luigi's, Sonic, Starbucks, **lodging:** Baymont Inn, **other:** GNC, Prime Outlets/famous brands, Walmart SuperCtr/24hr
665	(from sb) Cottonwood, **E lodging:** Alamo Motel, Travelers Motel
664	Gas Point Rd, to Balls Ferry, **E gas:** Cottonwood, Chevron/dsl/LP, **lodging:** Alamo Motel, Travelers Motel, **other:** Alamo RV Park, auto repair, **W gas:** Holiday/dsl, Sunshine/dsl, **other:** Frontier Hardware, Holiday Foods
662	Bowman Rd, to Cottonwood, **E gas:** Pacific Pride/dsl, Texaco/dsl
660mm	**weigh sta both lanes**
659	Snively Rd, Auction Yard Rd, (Sunset Hills Dr. from nb)
657	Hooker Creek Rd, Auction Yard Rd
656mm	**rest area both, full facilities, , , litter barrels, petwalk**
653	Jellys Ferry Rd, **E lodging:** Bend RV Park/LP
652	Wilcox Golf Rd
651	CA 36W (from sb), Red Bluff, **W gas:** Chevron, **other:** Ford, same as 650
650	Adobe Rd, **W gas:** Chevron/dsl, **food:** Casa Ramos Mexican, Starbucks, **lodging:** Hampton Inn, **other:** Chevrolet/Cadillac, Home Depot, Hwy Patrol
649	CA 33, CA 99, Red Bluff, **E gas:** Liberty Gas, Red Bluff Gas, Shell/dsl, **food:** Burger King, Perko's Cafe, KFC, McDonald's, Taco Bell, **lodging:** Best Western, Comfort Inn, Motel 6, **W gas:** Gas4Less, USA/dsl, **food:** Denny's, Egg Roll King, Los Mariachi, Luigi's Pizza, Maple Garden Chinese, Riverside Dining, RoundTable Pizza, Shari's/24hr, Subway, Winchell's, **lodging:** Cinderella Motel, Super 8, Travelodge, **other:** Durango RV Resort, Foodmaxx, Long's Drug, River's Edge RV Park, Vet
647a b	Diamond Ave, Red Bluff, **E gas:** Valero, **food:** Las Palmas Mexican, **lodging:** Day's Inn, **other:** H, **W gas:** Arco/dsl/24hr, USA/dsl, **food:** Arby's, Jack-in-the-Box, Pizza Hut, Starbucks, Subway, Wendy's, **lodging:** American Inn, Triangle Motel, **other:** $Tree, GNC, Kragen Parts, Radio Shack, Raley's Food/drug, Staples, Walgreens, Walmart/auto

RED BLUFF

CORNING

Exit #	Services
642	Flores Ave, to Proberta, Gerber, **1 mi E other:** Walmart Dist Ctr
636	CA 811, Gyle Rd, to Tehama, **E other:** RV camping (7mi)
633	Finnell Rd, to Richfield
632mm	**rest area both lanes, full facilities, , , litter barrels, petwalk**
631	A9, Corning Ave, Corning, **E gas:** Chevron/24hr, 7-11, Shell/dsl/LP, Spirit Gas, 76/dsl, **food:** Burger King, Casa Ramos Mexican, Marco's Pizza, Olive Pit Rest., Papa Murphy's, Quizno's, Rancho Grande Mexican, RoundTable Pizza, Starbucks, Taco Bell, **lodging:** American Inn, Best Western, Comfort Inn, Economy Inn, 7 Inn Motel, **other:** Ace Hardware, Clark Drug, $Tree, Ford/Mercury, Goodyear, Heritage RV Park, Kragen Parts, NAPA, Pontiac/Chevrolet/Buick, Rite Aid, Safeway/24hr, Tires+, **W food:** Giant Burger, **lodging:** Corning RV Park
630	South Ave, Corning, **E gas:** ***FLYING J***/Country Mkt Rest./dsl/LP/RV dump/scales/24hr, Petro/Iron Skillet/dsl/rest./scales/@, TA/Arby's/Subway/dsl/scales/24hr/@, **food:** Jack-in-the-Box, McDonald's, **lodging:** California Inn, Day's Inn, Holiday Inn Express, **other:** Blue Beacon, Country Mkt, Goodyear, Olive Hut/RV Parking, SpeedCo Lube, Woodson Br SRA/RV Park (6mi)
628	CA 99W, Liberal Ave, **W gas:** Chevron/dsl, **lodging:** Ramada/rest./casino, **other:** Rolling Hills RV Park
621	CA 7
619	CA 32, Orland, **E gas:** 76/dsl, Shell/dsl, **food:** Burger King, Berry Patch Rest., Subway, **lodging:** Amberlight Motel, **other:** Longs Drug, **W gas:** USA/dsl, **food:** Taco Bell, **lodging:** Old Orchard RV Park, Parkway RV Park
618	CA 16, **E gas:** USA/dsl, **food:** Pizza Factory, **lodging:** Orland Inn
614	CA 27
610	Artois
608mm	**rest area both lanes, full facilities, , , litter barrels, petwalk, RV dump**
607	CA 39, Blue Gum Rd, Bayliss, **2 mi E lodging:** Blue Gum Motel
603	CA 162, to Oroville, Willows, **E gas:** Arco/24hr, Chevron/24hr, Shell/dsl, **food:** BlackBear Diner, Burger King, Casa Ramos, Denny's/24hr, KFC, La Cascada Mexican, McDonald's, Papa Murphy's, RoundTable Pizza, Starbucks, Subway, Taco Bell/24hr, **lodging:** Baymont Inn, Holiday Inn Express, Travelodge, Day's Inn/RV parking, Super 8, Motel 6, **other:** H, Radio Shack, CHP, **W food:** Nancy's Café/24hr, **other:** Walmart, RV Park (8mi),
601	CA 57, **E gas:** 76/CFN/dsl
595	Rd 68, to Princeton, **E** to Sacramento NWR
591	Delevan Rd
588	Maxwell (from sb), access to camping
586	Maxwell Rd, **E other:** Delavan NWR, **W gas:** CFN, Chevron, **lodging:** Maxwell Inn/rest., **other:** Country Mkt, Maxwell Parts
583	**rest area both lanes, full facilities, , , litter barrels, petwalk**
578	CA 20, Colusa, **W gas:** Orv's/dsl/rest., Shell/dsl, **other:** H, hwy patrol

OROVILLE

INTERSTATE 5 CONT'D

Exit #	Services
577	Williams, E gas: Shell/Baskin-Robbins/Togo's/dsl/24hr, food: Carl's Jr, Straw Hat Pizza, Subway, Taco Bell, lodging: Holiday Inn Express, W gas: CFN/dsl, Chevron/dsl/24hr, 76, Shell/dsl, food: Burger King, Casa Lupe Mexican, Denny's, Granzella's Rest., McDonald's/RV parking, Williams Chinese Rest., lodging: Comfort Inn, Granzella's Inn, Motel 6, StageStop Motel, other: H, NAPA, U-Haul, USPO, ValuRite Drug, camping, hwy patrol
575	Husted Rd, to Williams
569	Hahn Rd, to Grimes
567	frontage rd (from nb), to Arbuckle, E food: El Jaliscience Mexican, W gas: CFN, Chevron/dsl
566	to College City, Arbuckle, E gas: Shell/dsl, other: Ace Hardware, USPO, W gas: J&J/grill/dsl
559	Yolo/Colusa County Line Rd
557mm	**rest area both lanes, full ♿ facilities, ☎, picnic, litter barrels, petwalk**
556	E4, Dunnigan, E gas: Chevron/dsl/24hr, Valero/dsl/LP, food: Bill&Kathy's Rest., Jack-in-the-Box, lodging: Best Value Inn, Best Western, other: USPO, W gas: Shell, lodging: Camper's RV Park/golf (1mi)
554	rd 8, E gas: Pilot/Wendy's/scales/dsl/24hr, other: Oasis Grill, lodging: Hacienda Motel, other: HappyTime RV Park, W gas: United/dsl
553	I-505 (from sb), to San Francisco, callboxes begin sb
548	Zamora, E gas: Shell/dsl
542	Yolo, 1 mi E gas
541	CA 16W, Woodland, 3 mi W other: H
540	West St, W food: Denny's
538	CA 113 N, E St, Woodland, W gas: Chevron/dsl, food: Denny's, lodging: Best Western, other: Woodland Opera House (1mi)
537	CA 113 S, Main St, to Davis, E other: Chevrolet/Buick/Pontiac, same as 536, W gas: Valero, food: Denny's, McDonald's, Rafael's Rest., Sonic, Taco Bell, Wendy's, lodging: Day's Inn, Motel 6, Quality Inn, other: Food 4 Less
536	rd 102, E on Main St...gas: Arco, Shell, food: Applebee's, Burger King, Coldstone Creamery, Jack-in-the-Box, RoundTable Pizza, Quizno's, Subway, lodging: Hampton Inn, Holiday Inn Express, other: America's Tire, Home Depot, Main St Mkt, Staples, Walmart, museum, same as 537, W gas: Chevron, food: In-n-Out, other: Best Buy, Costco/gas, Michaels, Target
531	rd 22, W Sacramento
530mm	Sacramento River
529mm	**rest area sb, full ♿ facilities, ☎, picnic, litter barrels, petwalk**
528	Airport Rd, E gas: Arco, other: ✈, food, lodging
525b	CA 99, to CA 70, to Marysville, Yuba City
525a	Del Paso Rd, E gas: Chevron, food: A&W/KFC, IHOP, In-n-Out, Jack-in-the-box, Jamba Juice, Malabar Rest., Panera Bread, Panda Express, Sizzler, Starbucks, Taco Bell, Wienerschnitzel, lodging: Hampton Inn, Holiday Inn Express, Homewood Suites, other: Rite Aid, Safeway/gas, W food: Subway, lodging: Sheraton, other: Walgreens

N ↕ S — DUNNIGAN — DAVIS

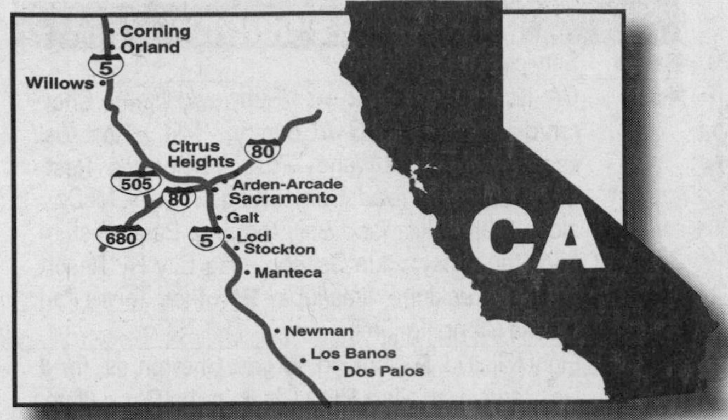

SACRAMENTO

Exit #	Services
524	Arena Blvd, E other: Arco Arena, W food: Round Table Pizza, Starbucks, other: Bel-Air Food&Drug/gas
522	I-80, E to Reno, W to San Francisco
521b a	Garden Hwy, West El Camino, W gas: Shell/dsl, food: Baja Fresh, Carl's Jr, Jack-in-the-Box, Starbucks, Subway, Togo's, lodging: Courtyard, Hilton Garden, Homestead Village, Residence Inn, Spring-Hill Suites
520	Richards Blvd, E gas: Chevron/dsl/24hr, food: Memphis BBQ, McDonald's, Monterey Rest., Stonebrooks Rest., lodging: Governor's Inn, Hawthorn Suites, Ramada Ltd, Super 8, W gas: Shell, Valero, food: Coyote Jct Mexican, lodging: Best Western/rest., Comfort Suites, Days Inn, La Quinta, Motel 6, Super 8
519b	J St, Old Sacramento, E food: Denny's, lodging: Holiday Inn, Vagabond Inn, W lodging: Embassy Suites, other: Railroad Museum
519a	Q St , downtown, Sacramento, W lodging: Embassy Suites, to st capitol
518	US 50, CA 99, Broadway, E services downtown
516	Sutterville Rd, E gas: Land Park/dsl, 76/dsl, other: Prime Foods, Wm Land Park, zoo
515	Fruitridge Rd, Seamas Rd
514	43rd Ave, Riverside Blvd (from sb), E gas: 76/repair
513	Florin Rd, E gas: Arco/24hr, Chevron/24hr, Shell/repair, food: Rosalinda's Mexican, RoundTable Pizza, Sizzling Wok, other: Bel Air Foods, Kragen Parts, Longs Drug, W food: Burger King, JimBoy's Tacos, Shari's, Starbucks, Subway, Wings Stop, other: Marshall's, Nugget Foods, Radio Shack, Rite Aid
512	CA 160, Pocket Rd, Meadowview Rd, to Freeport, E gas: Shell/dsl/24hr, Valero/dsl, food: IHOP, KFC, LJ Silver, McDonald's, Starbucks, Togo's, Wendy's, other: Home Depot, Staples
508	Laguna Blvd, E gas: Chevron/McDonald's/dsl, 76/Circle K/dsl/LP, Shell, food: A&W/KFC, Starbucks, Subway, Wendy's, lodging: Extended Stay America, Hampton Inn, other: Jiffy Lube, Laguna Tire/Wheel
506	Elk Grove Blvd, E gas: Arco/dsl, Chevron/dsl, Shell, food: Carl's Jr, Lyla's Mexican, Pete's Grill, Quizno's, Stone Lake Mexican, lodging: Comfort Suites
504	Hood Franklin Rd
498	Twin Cities Rd, to Walnut Grove
493	Walnut Grove Rd, Thornton, E gas: CFN/dsl, Chevron/Subway/dsl
490	Peltier Rd
487	Turner Rd

INTERSTATE 5 CONT'D

Exit #	Services
485	CA 12, Lodi, **E gas:** Arco/Subway/dsl/24hr, Chevron/dsl, ***FLYING J***/Country Mkt Rest./dsl/scales/24hr, Shell/Wendy's/dsl, 76/Rocky's Rest./dsl/scales/24hr, **food:** Burger King, Carl's Jr, McDonald's, Starbucks, Taco Bell, **lodging:** Best Western, Microtel, **other:** Blue Beacon, Flag City RV Resort, Profleet Trucklube, tires/lube, **W other:** Tower Park Marina Camping (5mi)
481	Eight Mile Rd, **E** camping, **W gas:** Chevron/dsl, **food:** Del Taco, Hawaiian BBQ, Jack-in-the-Box, Jamba Juice, MooMoo's Burgers, Panda Express, Panera Bread, Qdoba Mexican, RoundTable Pizza, Sonic, Starbucks, Strings Italian, Subway, Wendy's, **other:** AAA, Borders Books, Jo-Ann Fabrics, KOA, Kohl's, Lowe's Whse, Office Depot, Petsmart, Ross, Target
478	Hammer Lane, Stockton, **E gas:** Arco/24hr, 76/Circle K/dsl, **food:** Adalberto's Mexican, Carl's Jr, KFC, Little Caesar's, Shirasoni Japanese, Subway, **other:** AutoZone, Radio Shack, SMart Foods, Vet, **W gas:** Chevron/dsl, QuikStop, **food:** Jack-in-the-Box, Mexico Lindo, Taco Bell
477	Benjamin Holt Dr, Stockton, **E gas:** Arco, Chevron/dsl/24hr, **food:** Pizza Guys, **lodging:** Motel 6, **other:** Quikstop, **W food:** Fon Wong Chinese, McDonald's, Lyon's/24hr, Subway/TCBY, **other:** Ace Hardware, Marina Foods, 7-11, Vet
476	March Lane, Stockton, **E gas:** 7-11, **food:** Applebee's, Arroyo's Mexican, Black Angus, Carl's Jr, Denny's, El Torito, Jack-in-the-Box, John's Incredible Pizza, McDonald's, Marie Callender's, Olive Garden, Red Lobster, StrawHat Pizza, Taco Bell, Toot Sweets Bakery, Wendy's, **lodging:** Comfort Inn, Hilton, **other:** Longs Drug, Marshall's, SMart Foods, **1/2 mi E food:** Baskin-Robbins, Burger King, Outback Steaks, Quizno's, Subway, Wienerschnitzel, **other:** Dillard's, $Tree, 99c Store, Office Depot, Target, World Mkt, **W gas:** 76/dsl/24hr, **food:** Carrow's Rest., In-n-Out, Italian Cuisine, Jamba Juice, RoundTable Pizza, Old Spaghetti Factory, Starbucks, Subway, Wong's Chinese, **lodging:** Courtyard, Extended Stay America, La Quinta, Quality Inn, Residence Inn, **other:** Home Depot
475	Alpine Ave, Country Club Blvd, same as 474 b
474b	Country Club Blvd (from nb), **E gas:** 76/dsl, **W gas:** 7-11, USA/Subway/dsl, Safeway/gas, **other:** BigLots
474a	Monte Diablo Ave, **W other:** Aamco
473	Pershing Ave (from nb), **W gas:** Arco, **lodging:** Red Roof Inn
472	CA 4 E, to CA 99, Fresno Ave, downtown
471	CA 4 W, Charter Way, **E gas:** Chevron/24hr, Shell/24hr, **food:** Burger King, Denny's, Little Ceasar's, McDonald's, Quizno's, **lodging:** Days Inn, Motel 6, **other:** Kragen Parts, transmissions, **W gas:** 76/dsl/rest./scales/24hr, Valero, **food:** Jack-in-the-Box, Taco Bell, **lodging:** Motel 6, **other:** truck repair
470	8th St, Stockton, **W gas:** CA Stop/dsl, Shell/Subway/dsl, **lodging:** I-5 Inn
469	Downing Ave, **W food:** China Express, Jalapeños Mexican, Mtn Mike's Pizza, Subway, **other:** Curves, Food4Less/gas
468	French Camp, **E gas:** 76/Togo's/dsl, **other:** Pan Pacific RV Ctr, **W other:** H
467b	Mathews Rd, **E gas:** Exxon/CFN/dsl, **other:** RV Ctr, tires/repair, **W other:** H
467a	El Dorado St (from nb)
465	Roth Rd, Sharpe Depot, **E other:** Freightliner, Kenworth, truck/rv repair
463	Lathrop Rd, **E gas:** Chevron/dsl/24hr, Joe's Trkstp/Subway/dsl/scales, TowerMart/dsl, Valero/dsl, **food:** Country Kitchen, Little Ceasar's, Starbucks, **lodging:** Best Western, Comfort Inn, Days Inn, **other:** Harley-Davidson, SaveMart Foods, Walgreens, **W other:** Dos Reis CP, RV camping
462	Louise Ave, **E gas:** Arco/24hr, 76, Shell, **food:** A&W/KFC, Carl's Jr, Denny's, Jack-in-the-Box, McDonald's, Mtn Mike's Pizza, Quizno's, Taco Bell, Valarta Mexican, **lodging:** Hampton Inn, Holiday Inn Express, **other:** Mossdale CP, **W other:** Target
461	CA 120, to Sonora, Manteca, **E other:** Oakwood Lake Resort Camping, to Yosemite
460	Mossdale Rd, **E gas:** Arco/dsl, **W food:** fruit stand/deli
458b	I-205, to Oakland (from sb, no return)
458a	11th St, to Tracy, Defense Depot, **2 mi W gas:** gas/dsl/food
457	Kasson Rd, to Tracy, **W gas:** Valley Pacific/dsl
452	CA 33 S, Vernalis
449b a	CA 132, to Modesto, **E other:** The Orchard Campground
446	I-580 (from nb, exits left, no return)
445mm	**Westley Rest Area both lanes, full ♿ facilities, picnic, litter barrels, phone, RV dump, petwalk**
441	Ingram Creek, Howard Rd, Westley, **E gas:** Chevron/dsl/24hr, Joe's Trvl Plaza/Perko's/Quizno's/dsl/scales, 76, Stars/dsl Westley TruckStp/dsl, **food:** Antojito's Mexican, Carl's Jr, McDonald's, Subway, **lodging:** Best Value Inn, Days Inn, Econolodge, Holiday Inn Express, **W gas:** Shell/dsl/24hr, **food:** Ingram Creek Rest., fruits, **other:** truck repair
434	Sperry Ave, Del Puerto, Patterson, **E gas:** Chevron, 76/Subway/dsl, **food:** A&W/KFC, Carl's Jr, Denny's, El Rosal Mexican, Golden Lion Chinese, Jack-in-the-Box, Lamp Post Pizza, Nik's BBQ, Quizno's, Starbucks, **lodging:** Best Western, **other:** Kit Fox RV Park
430mm	vista point nb
428	Fink Rd, Crow's Landing
423	Stuhr Rd, Newman, **5 mi E** food, lodging, **other:** H, RV camping
422mm	vista point sb
418	CA 140E, Gustine, **E gas:** 76/dsl, Shell/dsl
409	**weigh sta both lanes**
407	CA 33, Santa Nella, **E gas:** Arco/24hr, Pilot/Del Taco/Wendy's/dsl/24hr, TA/76/Popeye's/dsl/rest./24hr/@, **food:** Carl's Jr, Andersen's Rest, Subway, Wendy's, **lodging:** Best Western/Andersen's, Holiday Inn Express, **W gas:** Chevron/24hr, Rotten Robbie/dsl/scales, Shell/Jack-in-the-Box/dsl, Valero/dsl, **food:** Denny's, McDonald's, Quizno's, Starbucks, Taco Bell, **lodging:** Motel 6, Ramada Inn, **other:** Santa Nella RV Park
403b a	CA 152, Los Banos, **6 mi E other:** H, **W gas:** Petro/dsl/24hr (1mi), **other:** San Luis RV Park

INTERSTATE 5 CONT'D

Exit #	Services
391	CA 165N, Mercy Springs Rd, **E** H, **W gas:** Shell
388mm	vista point (from nb)
386mm	**rest area both lanes, full facilities, phone, picnic, litter barrels, petwalk**
385	Nees Ave, to Firebaugh, **W gas:** Chevron/CFN/Subway/dsl/scales
379	Shields Ave, to Mendota
372	Russell Ave
368	Panoche Rd, **W gas:** Chevron/McDonald's, Mobil/Taco Bell/dsl, 76/dsl, Shell/dsl, **food:** Apricot Tree Rest., Fosters Freeze, **lodging:** Best Western/Apricot Inn, **other:** Palms Mkt
365	Manning Ave, to San Joaquin
357	Kamm Ave
349	CA 33 N, Derrick Ave
337	CA 33 S, CA 145 N, to Coalinga
334	CA 198, to Lemoore, Huron, **E gas:** Shell/Subway/dsl/24hr, **lodging:** Harris Ranch Inn/rest., **W gas:** Chevron, Mobil/dsl, 76/Circle K, **food:** Burger King, Carl's Jr, Cazuela's Mexican, Denny's, McDonald's, Oriental Express Chinese, Red Robin, Taco Bell, **lodging:** Best Western, Motel 6, Travelodge, **other:** H
325	Jayne Ave, to Coalinga, **W gas:** Arco/24hr, Shell/dsl, **lodging:** RV Park, **other:** H
320mm	**rest area both lanes, full facilities, phone, picnic, litter barrels, petwalk**
319	CA 269, Lassen Ave, to Avenal, **W gas:** Hillcrest TP/76/dsl/scales/rest.
309	CA 41, Kettleman City, **E gas:** CFN/dsl, Chevron/McDonald's, Exxon/Subway/dsl, Mobil/Starbucks/dsl/24hr, KwikServ/Quizno's/dsl, Shell/dsl, Valero/dsl, **food:** Carl's Jr, In-N-Out, Jack-in-the-Box, Mike's Roadhouse Café, Pizza Hut/Taco Bell, **lodging:** Best Western, Super 8, **other:** Travelers RV Park
305	Utica Ave
288	Twisselman Rd
278	CA 46, Lost Hills, **E gas:** Buford Star Mart/dsl, **other:** to Kern NWR, **W gas:** Arco/24hr, Chevron/dsl/24hr, Loves/Arby's/dsl, Mobil/McDonald's/, Pilot/Wendy's/dsl/scales/24hr, 76/Quizno's/24hr, Valero/dsl, **food:** Carl's Jr, Denny's, Jack-in-the-Box, McDonald's, **lodging:** Days Inn, Motel 6, **other:** Lost Hills RV Park
268	Lerdo Hwy, to Shafter
262	7th Standard Rd, Rowlee Rd, to Buttonwillow
259mm	**Buttonwillow Rest Area both lanes, full facilities, phone, picnic, litter barrels, petwalk**
257	CA 58, to Bakersfield, Buttonwillow, **E gas:** Arco/dsl/24hr, Bruce's/dsl/wash, Chevron/dsl/24hr, TA/Pizza Hut/Taco Bell/dsl/scales/24hr/@, Shell/dsl, **food:** Carl's Jr, Denny's, McDonald's, Starbucks, Subway, Taste of India, Tita's Mexican, Willow Ranch BBQ, **lodging:** Homeland Inn, Motel 6, Red Roof Inn, Super 8, **other:** Castro's Tire/Truckwash, **W gas:** Valero/dsl
253	Stockdale Hwy, **E gas:** Shell/dsl/24hr, **food:** IHOP, Jack-in-the-Box, **lodging:** Best Western, Rodeway Inn, **W other:** Tule Elk St Reserve
246	CA 43, to Taft, Maricopa, **other:** to Buena Vista RA

N ↕ S

BUTTONWILLOW

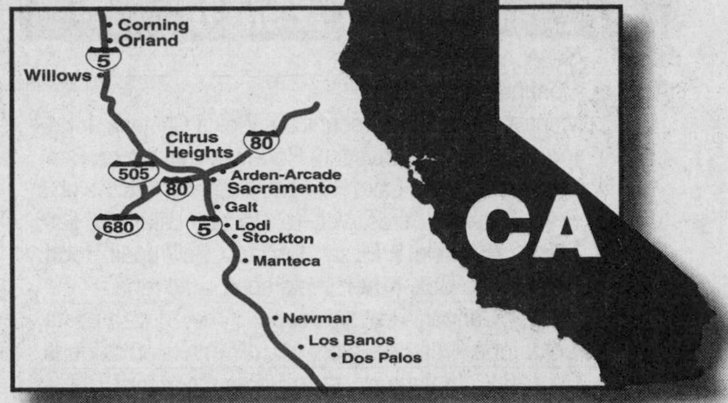

CA

Exit #	Services
244	CA 119, to Pumpkin Center, **E gas:** Mobil/dsl, **W gas:** Chevron/dsl/LP
239	CA 223, Bear Mtn Blvd, to Arvin, **E other:** Bear Mtn. RV Resort, **W other:** to Buena Vista RA, RV camping
234	Old River Rd
228	Copus Rd, **E** Murray Farms Mkt
225	CA 166, to Mettler, **2-3 mi E** gas/dsl, food
221	I-5 and CA 99 (from nb, exits left, no return)
219b a	Laval Rd, Wheeler Ridge, **E gas:** Chevron/Subway, TA/dsl/rest./scales/@, **food:** Burger King, Pizza Hut, Taco Bell, **other:** Blue Beacon, repair, **W gas:** Chevron, Petro/Mobil/Iron Skillet/Subway/dsl/scales/24hr/@, **food:** In-N-Out, McDonald's, Panda Express, Starbucks, Wendy's, **lodging:** Best Western
218	**truck weigh sta sb**
215	Grapevine, **E gas:** Mobil, **food:** Denny's, Jack-in-the-Box, **W gas:** 76/dsl, Shell/dsl, **food:** Don Perico Cantina, **lodging:** Ramda Ltd.
210	Ft Tejon Rd, **W other:** to Ft Tejon Hist SP, towing/repair
209mm	**brake check area nb**
207	Lebec Rd, **W other:** USPO, CHP, antiques, towing
206mm	**rest areas both lanes, full facilities, phone, vending, picnic litter barrels, petwalk**
205	Frazier Mtn Park Rd, **W gas:** Arco, Chevron/Subway/dsl/24hr, ***FLYING J***/dsl/LP/rest./24hr, Shell/Quizno's/dsl, **food:** Jack-in-the-Box, Los Pinos Mexican, **lodging:** BestRest Inn, Holiday Inn Select, **other:** Auto Parts+, towing/repair/radiators/transmissions, to Mt Pinos RA
204	Tejon Pass, elev 4144, **truck brake insp sb**
202	Gorman Rd, to Hungry Valley, **E gas:** Chevron/dsl/LP, 76/dsl, **food:** Carl's Jr, El Grullense, **lodging:** EconoLodge, **W gas:** Valero, **food:** McDonald's, **other:** auto repair
199	CA 138 E (from sb), Lancaster Rd, to Palmdale
198b a	Quail Lake Rd, CA 138 E (from nb)
195	Smokey Bear Rd, Pyramid Lake, **W other:** Pyramid Lake RV Park
191	Vista del Lago Rd, **W other:** visitors ctr
186mm	**brake inspection area sb**, motorist callboxes begin sb
183	Templin Hwy, **W other:** Ranger Sta, RV camping
176b a	Lake Hughes Rd, Parker Rd, Castaic, **E gas:** 7-11, Castaic Trkstp/dsl/rest./24hr, Pilot/Wendy's/dsl/24hr/scales, Shell, **food:** Baskin-Robbins, Burger King, Mike's Diner, Carl's Jr, Casa Lupa Mexican, Denny's, Domino's, El Pollo Loco, Fosters Freeze, Jersey Mikes, McDonald's, Pizza Factory, Popeye's, Quizno's, Starbucks, Subway, Telly's Drive-in,

FT TEJON

CASTAIC

CA

N ↕ S

SANTA CLARITA

SYLMAR

ARLETA

SUN VALLEY

LOS ANGELES AREA

INTERSTATE 5 CONT'D

Exit #	Services
176b a	Continued Vinny's Pizza, Wienerschnitzel, Wok's Chinese, **lodging:** Castaic Inn, Days Inn, Rodeway Inn, **other:** Benny's Tire, Castaic Lake RV Park, Kragen Parts, Ralph's Food, Rite Aid, tires, Vet, to Castaic Lake, **W gas:** Mobil, 76/Circle K/Pizza Hut/Taco Bell/repair, **food:** Jack-in-the-Box, **other:** Walgreens, auto repair
173	Hasley Canyon Rd, **W food:** Ameci Pizza/pasta, Coldstone Creamery, Subway, **other:** Ralph's Foods
172	CA 126 W, to Ventura, **E lodging:** Courtyard
171mm	**weigh sta nb**
171	Rye Canyon Rd (from sb), **W gas:** Chevron, Shell, **food:** Del Taco, Jack-in-the-Box, Jimmy Deans, Starbucks, Subway, Tommy's Burgers, **other:** 6 Flags
170	CA 126 E, Magic Mtn Pkwy, Saugus, **E food:** Denny's, Pastamichi Italian, Quizno's, Red Brick Pizza, Starbucks, **lodging:** Best Western/rest., Holiday Inn Express, **W gas:** Chevron, **food:** El Torito, Hamburger Hamlet, Marie Callender's, Red Lobster, Rio Rio Grill, Wendy's, **lodging:** Hilton Garden, **other:** Six Flags of CA
169	Valencia Blvd, **W food:** La Salsa, Nick'n Willy's Pizza, Panda Express, Starbucks, Subway, **other:** Albertson's, SavOn
168	McBean Pkwy, **E other:** [H], **W food:** Baskin-Robbins, Cabo Cabana, Chili's, ChuckeCheese, ClaimJumper Rest., Jamba Juice, Macaroni Grill, Mamma Mia Italian, Pick up Stix, Starbucks, Subway, Wood Ranch BBQ, **other:** Marshall's, Michael's, Old Navy, Staples, Vons Foods, WorldMkt
167	Lyons Ave, Pico Canyon Rd, **E gas:** Chevron/24hr, 76/Circle K, Shell/dsl, **food:** Burger King, Wendy's, **W gas:** Arco/24hr, Mobil, Shell/dsl, **food:** Carl's Jr, Chuy's Chinese, Coco's, Del Taco, Denny's, El Pollo Loco, Fortune Express Chinese, IHOP, In-N-Out, Jack-in-the-Box, McDonald's, Outback Steaks, Spumoni Italian, Taco Bell, Yamato Japanese, **lodging:** Comfort Suites, Extended Stay America, Fairfield Inn, Hampton Inn, La Quinta, Residence Inn, **other:** Camping World RV Ctr, GNC, Jiffy Lube, PetsMart, Ralph's Foods, SteinMart, Walmart
166	Calgrove Blvd
162	CA 14 N, to Palmdale
161b	Balboa Blvd (from sb)
160a	I-210, to San Fernando, Pasadena
159	Roxford St, Sylmar, **E gas:** Chevron/dsl, Mobil/dsl, **food:** Denny's/24hr, McDonald's, **lodging:** Good Nite Inn, Motel 6
158	I-405 S (from sb, no return)
157b a	SF Mission Blvd, Brand Blvd, **E gas:** Chevron, Mobil/dsl, 76, **food:** Carl's Jr, Carnita's Mexican, In-N-Out, Pollo Gordo, Popeye's, Winchell's, **other:** [H], AutoZone, Rite Aid
156b	CA 118
156a	Paxton St, Brand Ave (from nb), **E gas:** Shell/dsl/24hr
155b	Van Nuys Blvd (no EZ nb return), **E gas:** Vale, **food:** Jack-in-the-Box, KFC/LJ Silver, McDonald's, Pizza Hut, Popeye's, **other:** AutoZone, USPO, **W food:** Domino's, **other:** auto repair
155a	Terra Bella St (from nb), **E gas:** Thrifty
154	Osborne St, to Arleta, **E gas:** Arco/24hr, Chevron/dsl, 76, **food:** El Pollo Loco, Papa's Tacos, Peter Piper Pizza, **other:** BigLots, Food4Less, Target, **W gas:** Mobil/Burger King, **other:** 7-11
153b	CA 170 (from sb), to Hollywood
152a	Sheldon St, **E food:** Big Jim's Rest., **other:** Big O Parts, [H], auto repair
152	Lankershim Blvd, Tuxford, **E gas:** Superfine/dsl/scales
151	Penrose St
150b	Sunland Blvd, Sun Valley, **E gas:** Mobil, 76, **food:** Acapulco Rest., Carl's Jr, El Pollo Loco, Good Fortune Chinese, Quizno's, Subway, Taco Bell, Town Café, **lodging:** Economy Inn, **other:** Ralph's Foods, 7-11, **W gas:** Exxon, Shell, **food:** Dimion's Rest., McDonald's
150a	GlenOaks Blvd (from nb), **E gas:** Superior/dsl, **lodging:** Willows Motel
149	Hollywood Way, **W gas:** Shell/dsl, **other:** U-Haul, ✈
148	Buena Vista St, **W gas:** Exxon/dsl, **food:** Jack-in-the-Box, **lodging:** Quality Inn, Ramada Inn
147	Scott Rd, to Burbank, **E gas:** Sevan/dsl, **W food:** Krispy Kreme, Outback Steaks, Panda Express, Starbucks, Wendy's, **lodging:** Courtyard, Extended Stay America, **other:** Best Buy, Lowe's Whse, Marshall's, Michael's, Staples, Target
146b	Burbank Blvd, **E gas:** 76/repair, **food:** Carl's Jr, ChuckeCheese, El Pollo Loco, Harry's Rest., Hooters, IHOP, In-N-Out, Marie Callender, McDonald's, Popeye's, Pizza Hut, Quizno's, Shakey's Pizza, Starbuck's, Subway, Taco Bell, Tommy's Burgers, Wienerschnitzel, Yoshinoya, **lodging:** Holiday Inn, **other:** Barnes&Noble, CVS Drug, K-Mart, Macy's, Office Depot, Old Navy, Ralph's Foods, Ross, Sears, Von's Foods, **W gas:** Chevron, **food:** Subway
146a	Olive Ave, Verdugo, **E food:** Black Angus, Brewhouse Rest., **lodging:** Holiday Inn, **other:** Radio Shack, Sears, USPO, **W other:** Chevrolet, 7-11, [H]
145b	Alameda Ave, **E gas:** Chevron, **food:** Starbucks, Togo's/Baskin-Robbins, **other:** CarMax, CVS Drug, Home Depot, Ralph's Foods, Walgreen, **W gas:** Arco, Shell, **lodging:** Burbank Inn, **other:** U-Haul
145a	Western Ave, **W other:** Gene Autrey Museum
144b a	CA 134, Ventura Fwy, Glendale, Pasadena
142	Colorado St
141a	Los Feliz Blvd, **E other:** [H], **W other:** Griffith Park, zoo
140b	Glendale Blvd, **E gas:** GasMart, 76, **food:** Starbucks, Subway, **other:** auto repair, **W gas:** Valero
140a	Fletcher Dr (from sb)
139b a	CA 2, Glendale Fwy
138	Stadium Way, Figueroa St, **E food:** IHOP, McDonald's, **other:** Home Depot, **W other:** to Dodger Stadium
137b a	CA 2, Glendale Fwy
136b	Broadway St (from sb), **W gas:** 76
136a	Main St, **E gas:** Chevron/24hr, 76, **food:** Chinatown Express, Jack-in-the-Box, McDonald's, Mr Pizza, **other:** [H], Parts+
135c	I-10 W (from nb), Mission Rd (from sb), **E gas:** 76, **food:** McDonald's, **lodging:** Howard Johnson, **other:** [H]
135b	Cesar Chavez Ave, **W other:** [H]
135a	4th St, Soto St

INTERSTATE 5 CONT'D

N ↕ S

LOS ANGELES AREA

Exit #	Services
134b	Ca 60 E (from sb), Soto St (from nb)
134a	CA 60 W, Santa Monica Fwy
133	Euclid Ave (from sb), Grand Vista (from nb), **E gas:** Arco, USA/dsl, **W gas:** Mobil, Shell, **other:** [H]
132	Calzona St, Indiana St, **E gas:** Arco/dsl
131b	Indiana St (from nb), **E gas:** Arco/dsl, Valero/dsl
131a	Olympic Blvd, **E food:** McDonald's, **W food:** Jack-in-the-Box, King Taco, **other:** [H]
130c b	I-710, to Long Beach, Eastern Ave, **E food:** McDonald's
130a	Triggs St (from sb), **E other:** outlet mall, **W food:** Denny's/24hr, **lodging:** Destiny Inn
129	Atlantic Blvd N, Eastern Ave (from sb), **E food:** Carl's Jr, Starbucks, **lodging:** Wyndham Garden, **other:** Hyundai, outlet mall/famous brands, **W food:** Denny's, Steven's Steaks
128b	Washington Blvd, Commerce, **E gas:** Chevron/dsl/repair/24hr, **food:** McDonald's, **lodging:** Crowne Plaza Hotel/casino, Wyndham Hotel, **other:** Firestone, Office Depot, Old Navy, mall, **W gas:** Arco, **food:** Starbucks
128a	Garfield Blvd, **E lodging:** Commerce/Hotel/casino, **other:** Home Depot, Office Depot, **W gas:** 76
126b	Slauson Ave, Montebello, **E gas:** Shell, Valero/dsl, **food:** Burger King, Ozzie's Diner, Quizno's, Starbucks, **lodging:** Best Star Inn, Best Western, Super 8, **W gas:** Arco, **food:** Denny's, **lodging:** Best Value, Ramada Inn
126a	Paramount Blvd, Downey, **E gas:** Shell/Jack-in-the-Box/dsl
125	CA 19 S, Lakewood Blvd, Rosemead Blvd, **E gas:** Mobil, Thrifty, **food:** Foster's Freeze, Sam's Burgers, Starbucks, Taco Bell, **W food:** McDonald's, China Wok, Chris & Pitt's BBQ, Subway, **other:** Ford/Lincoln/Mercury, Ralph's Foods
124	I-605
123	Florence Ave, to Downey, **E gas:** Mobil, **W other:** Chevrolet, Honda, auto repair
122	Imperial Hwy, Pioneer Blvd, **E gas:** Chevron, **food:** Cold Stone Creamery, IHOP, Jack-in-the-Box, King Buffet, McDonald's, Plum Wok Rest, Subway, To-go's, Wendy's, **lodging:** Best Western, **other:** Audi/Porsche, BMW, Firestone/auto, Payless Foods, Rite Aid, Target, **W gas:** 7-11, Shell, **food:** Denny's, HongKong Express, Panda King, Rally's, Sizzler, Tacos Mexico, Wienerschnitzel, **lodging:** Comfort Inn, Keystone Motel, Rodeway Inn, Vistaland Motel, **other:** Ford, Walmart
121	San Antonio Dr, to Norwalk Blvd, **E food:** IHOP, McDonald's, Outback Steaks, Starbucks, **lodging:** Marriott, **W gas:** 76, **other:** auto repair
120b	Firestone Blvd (exits left from nb)
120a	Rosecrans Ave, **E gas:** Valero/dsl, **food:** Burger King, Casa Adelita Mexican, Jim's Burgers, KFC, Pizza Hut/Taco Bell, Taco Joe, **other:** [H], BigSaver Foods, **W gas:** Arco/24hr, **food:** El Pollo Loco, **lodging:** Saddleback Inn, **other:** El Monte RV Ctr, Nissan, Stier's RV Ctr, Tuneup Masters
119	Carmenita Rd, Buena Park, **E gas:** 76/dsl, **food:** Jack-in-the-Box, **lodging:** Motel 6, **other:** Ford Trucks, Lowe's Whse, **W gas:** Arco/24hr,

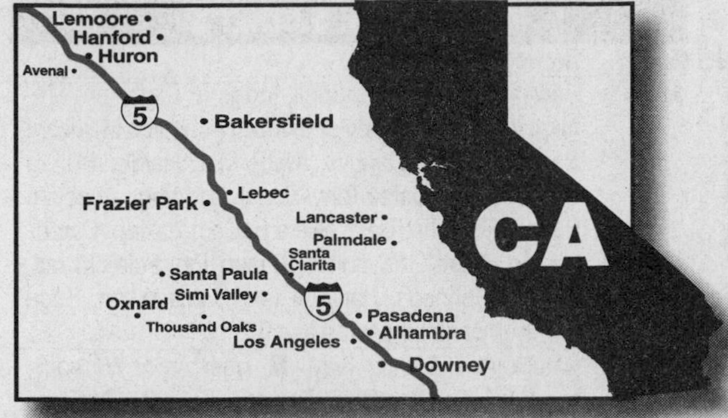

CA

LOS ANGELES AREA

Exit #	Services
119	Continued **food:** Carl's Jr, **lodging:** Budget Inn, Dynasty Suites
118	Valley View Blvd, **E gas:** Arco/dsl/24hr, **food:** Carl's Jr, Elephant Bar Rest, In-n-Out, Northwoods Rest, Red Robin, Subway, **lodging:** Extended Stay America, Holiday Inn Select, Residence Inn, **other:** Staples, **W gas:** Chevron, **food:** Denny's, El Pollo Loco, Four Seasons Buffet, Starbucks, **other:** Thompson's RV Ctr, to Camping World
117	Artesia Blvd, Knott Ave, **E gas:** 76/24hr, Shell/Subway/dsl/24hr, **lodging:** Extended Stay America, **other:** CarMax, **W gas:** Cardlock/dsl, **other:** Chevrolet, Chrysler, Knotts Berry Farm, to Camping World RV Ctr
116	CA 39, Beach Blvd, **E gas:** Chevron, **other:** [H], Acura, BMW, Buick/Pontiac/GMC, CarMax, Honda, Hyundai, Nissan, Toyota, VW, **W gas:** Chevron, Valero, **food:** Arby's, Black Angus, Denny's, Fuddruckers, Karuta Japanese, KFC, Outback Steaks, Pizza Hut, Subway, Wendy's, **lodging:** Hampton Inn, Holiday Inn, Red Roof Inn, **other:** Sater Bros, Target, to Knotts Berry Farm
115	Manchester (from nb)
114b	CA 91 E, Riverside Fwy, **W** to ✈
114a	Magnolia Ave, Orangethorpe Ave, **E gas:** Mobil/dsl, **food:** Burger King, Burger Town, Taco Bell, **other:** Harley-Davidson
113c	CA 91 W (from nb)
113b a	Brookhurst St, LaPalma, **E gas:** Chevron/24hr, **food:** Subway, **W gas:** Mobil/dsl, **food:** Carl's Jr., Quizno's, **other:** Home Depot, Staples
112	Euclid St, **E gas:** Mobil, 7-11, **food:** Chris&Pitt's BBQ, Marie Callender's, McDonald's, Subway, **other:** Kings Drug, Old Navy, Ross, Walmart, **W gas:** Arco, 76, **food:** Arby's, Burger King, Denny's, **other:** Chevrolet, Radio Shack, SavOn Drug
111	Lincoln Ave, to Anaheim, **E gas:** Shell/dsl, **food:** El Triunfo Mexican, La Casa Garcia Mexican, Starbucks, Subway, **other:** Vet, **W other:** Discount Auto Repair, Ford
110b	Ball Rd (from sb), **E gas:** Arco, Chevron/dsl, 7-11, Shell, **food:** Big's Pizza, Burger King, El Pollo Loco, McDonald's, Shakey's Pizza, Taco Bell, Subway, **lodging:** Anaheim Motel, Astoria Inn, Best Inn, Courtesy Lodge, Day's Inn, Holiday Inn, Traveler's World RV Park, **other:** laundry, **W gas:** Arco/24hr, Shell/dsl, **food:** Paris Rest., Spaghetti Sta, **lodging:** Best Western, Budget Inn, Day's Inn, Rodeway Inn, Sheraton, Super 8, **other:** Camping World RV Ctr

INTERSTATE 5 CONT'D

N ↕ S — LOS ANGELES AREA

Exit #	Services
110a	Harbor Blvd, **E** **gas:** Shell, **lodging:** Day's Inn, Menage Inn, **W** to Disneyland, **food:** Acapulco Mexican, Captain Kidd's, Dennys, IHOP, McDonald's, Millie's Rest., Mimi's Cafe, Tony Roma, **lodging:** Anaheim Resort, Best Inn, Best Western, Camelot Inn, Carousel Inn, Castle Inn Suites, Desert Inn, Fairfield Inn, Howard Johnson, ParkVue Inn, Ramada Inn, Saga Inn, Tropicana Inn, same as 109
109	Katella Ave, Disney Way, **E** **gas:** Arco, 76/repair, **food:** CA Country Café, Denny's, El Torito, McDonald's, Ming Delight, Mr Stox Dining, **lodging:** Angel Inn, Ramada Inn, Travelodge, **W** **gas:** 7-11, **food:** Del Taco, Flakey Jake's, Subway, Thai&Thai, **lodging:** Arena Inn, Comfort Inn, Desert Palms Suites, Extended Stay America, Hilton, Holiday Inn Express, Marriott, Peacock Suites, Portofino Inn, Radisson, Red Roof Inn, Residence Inn, Staybridge Suites, Super 8, to Disneyland
107c	St Coll Blvd, City Drive, **E** **lodging:** Hilton Suites, **W** **lodging:** Doubletree Hotel
107b a	CA 57 N, Chapman Ave, **E** **gas:** Mobil, **food:** Burger King, Del Taco, Denny's, **lodging:** Hilton Suites, Motel 6, Ramada Inn, **other:** [H], to Edison Field, **W** **food:** Krispy Kreme, Wendy's, **lodging:** Ayer's Inn, Country Inn/café, DoubleTree, **other:** [H], Best Buy
106	CA 22 W (from nb), Garden Grove Fwy, Bristol St
105b	N Broadway, Main St, **E** **gas:** 76, **food:** Carl's Jr, FoodCourt, Jamba Juice, Polly's Café, Rubio's Grill, Starbucks, **lodging:** Red Roof Inn, **other:** Barnes&Noble, BMW, Macy's, Nordstrom's, SavOn Drug, Bowers Museum, mall, **W** **lodging:** Golden West Motel, Travel Inn
105a	17th St, **E** **gas:** 76/dsl/24hr, **food:** Hometown Buffet, IHOP, McDonald's, **lodging:** Grand Courtyard Inn, **other:** Chevrolet, CVS Drug, Food4Less, same as 104b, **W** **gas:** B&L Gas, Chevron, **food:** Marisco's Seafood, Norm's Rest., YumYum Doughnuts, **other:** 7-11
104b	Santa Ana Blvd, Grand Ave, **E** **on Grand food:** Denny's, Hawaiian BBQ, Marie Callender, McDonald's, Popeye's, RoundTable Pizza, Starbucks, Subway, Taco Bell/Pizza Hut, Tacos Mexico, **other:** Big O Tire, CVS Drug, $Tree, Food4Less, Goodyear, Target, Vet, **W** **other:** KIA
104a	(103c from nb), 4th St, 1st St, to CA 55 N, **E** **gas:** Chevron, Shell, **food:** Del Taco
103b	CA 55 S, to Newport Beach
103a	CA 55 N (from nb), to Riverside
102	Newport Ave (from sb), **W** **gas:** Arco
101b	Red Hill Ave, **E** **gas:** Mobil/dsl, Shell/repair, **food:** Del Taco, Denny's, Starbucks, Subway, Wendy's, **lodging:** Key Inn, **other:** Drug Emporium/24hr, U-Haul, **W** **gas:** Arco/24hr, Chevron/24hr, Valero/dsl, **food:** Burger King, Pizza Shack, Roderick's, Taco Bell, **other:** Goodyear, 7-11, Stater Bros Foods
101a	Tustin Ranch Rd, **E** **food:** McDonald's, **other:** Acura, Buick, Cadillac, Chevrolet, Costco, Dodge, Ford/Lincoln/Mercury, Infiniti, Lexus, Mazda, Nissan, Pontiac, Sears Essentials, Toyota
100	Jamboree Rd, **E** **gas:** Shell, **food:** Black Angus, Buca Italian, Burger King, CA Pizza, Chick-fil-A, El Pollo Loco, In-n-Out, Macaroni Grill, On the Border, Panda Express, Pick-up Stix, Quizno's, Red Robin, Taco Rosa, **other:** AAA, Barnes&Noble, Best Buy, Costco, Loehmann's, Lowe's Whse, Old Navy, PetsMart, Ralph's Foods, Rite Aid, Ross, Target
99	Culver Dr, **E** **gas:** Shell/24hr, **other:** Vet
97	Jeffrey Rd, **E** **gas:** Arco, **food:** Baskin-Robbins, Daphne's Greek, Fatburger, Juice-it-Up, Quizno's, Starbucks, **other:** Albertson's, Kohl's, **W** **other:** Ranch Mkt Foods
96	Sand Canyon Ave, Old Towne, **W** **gas:** 76/Circle K, **food:** Denny's, Jack-in-the-Box, Knollwood Burgers, Tiajuana's Rest., **lodging:** La Quinta, **other:** [H], Traveland USA RV Park, Irvine RV Ctr
95	CA 133, Laguna Fwy, N to Riverside, S Laguna Beach
94b	Alton Pkwy, **E** **gas:** Shell/Subway, **food:** Carl's Jr, Quizno's, Starbucks, Taco Bell, **food:** Homestead Suites, **W** **food:** Cheesecake Factory, Corner Bakery, Dave&Buster's, Ling&Louie's, Panda Express, PF Chang's, Wahoo's, Yardhouse Grill, **lodging:** DoubleTree, **other:** Barnes&Noble, Macy's, Nordstroms, Target
94a	I-405 N (from nb)
92b	Bake Pkwy, same as 92a
92a	Lake Forest Dr, Laguna Hills, **E** **gas:** Chevron/24hr, Shell/dsl, **food:** Black Angus, Burger King, Del Taco, Jack-in-the-Box, McDonald's, Mimi's Café, Panera Bread, Pit BBQ, Pizza Hut, RoundTable Pizza, Subway, Taco Bell, The Hat, **lodging:** Best Western, **other:** America's Tire, Audi/Jeep, Chevrolet, Ford/Lincoln/Mercury, GMC/Kia, Honda, Isuzu, Jaguar, Mazda, Mercedes/Suzuki, PepBoys, Staples, Subaru, Toyota, VW, **W** **gas:** Chevron/24hr, Shell, **food:** Carl's Jr, Coco's, Del Taco, McDonald's, Quizno's, **lodging:** Comfort Inn, Courtyard, Quality Suites, Travelodge, **other:** AZ Leather, Best Buy, BMW/Mini, Books Etc, JC Penney
91	El Toro Rd, **E** **gas:** Chevron/dsl, Shell/dsl, USA, **food:** Arby's, Asia Buffet, Bakers Square, Carino's Italian, Carl's Jr, Coldstone Creamery, Denny's, Flamebroiler, Fuddrucker's, Jack-in-the-Box, Jamba Juice, Johnny Rockets, KFC, McDonald's, MegaBurger, Oeeshi Japanese, Quizno's, Red Lobster, Scarantino's Rest., Sizzler, Starbucks, Subway, Wendy's, **other:** CVS Drug, Home Depot, House of Fabrics, K-Mart, 99c Store, Office Depot, PetCo, Ralph's Foods, SavOn Drug, Staples, **W** **gas:** Chevron/dsl/24hr, Shell/24hr, 76/Circle K, **food:** BJ's Rest., CA Pizza, Carrows, El Torito, In-n-Out, Island Burgers, Kings FishHouse, KooRooRoo Kitchen, LoneStar Steaks, Nami Seafood Buffet, Pizza Hut, **other:** [H], Dalton's Books, Firestone/auto, JC Penney, Longs Drugs, Macy's, Marshall's, Sears/auto, Trader Joe's, Walgreens, USPO, mall
90	Alicia Pkwy, Mission Viejo, **E** **gas:** Chevron/24hr, 76/dsl, **food:** Carl's Jr, Del Taco, Denny's, Little Caesar's, Subway, Wendy's, Winchell's, **other:** Albertson's, America's Tire, Buick/Pontiac/Mazda, CVS Drug, Kragen Parts, Target, **W** **gas:** Chevron, 76/dsl, **food:** Carl's Jr, It's a Grind, Manhattan Grill, Togo's, Wendy's, **other:** AAA, Big Lots, Buick/Pontiac, Mazda

LAGUNA HILLS

INTERSTATE 5 CONT'D

MISSION VIEJO

N ↕ S

Exit #	Services
89	La Paz Rd, Mission Viejo, **E gas:** Arco/24hr, UltraMar, **food:** KFC/Pizza Hut, Starbucks, Taco Bell, **other:** Albertson's, **W gas:** 76, **food:** Claim Jumper Rest., DQ, Hot Off the Grill, Jack-in-the-Box, Krispy Kreme, La Salsa, McDonald's, Outback Steaks, Quizno's, Spasso's Italian, Wienerschnitzel, Yamato Japanese, **lodging:** Holiday Inn, **other:** Best Buy, Borders Books&Café, Curves, Goodyear/auto, Jo-Ann Fabrics, Just Tires, PetCo, 7-11, to Laguna Niguel Pk
87	Oso Pkwy, Pacific Park Dr, **E gas:** Chevron/repair, 76/repair, **food:** Carl's Jr, Starbucks, Subway, **lodging:** Fairfield Inn
86	Crown Valley Pkwy, **E gas:** Arco, Chevron, 76, **food:** Coco's, El Torito, Islands Grill, Versachee Italian, **other:** [H], Macy's, mall, Vet, **W gas:** Chevron/dsl, **other:** Aamco, Costco
85b	Avery Pkwy, **E gas:** Shell/dsl, **food:** Carrow's, Del Taco, Jack-in-the-Box, Mongolian BBQ, Quizno's, Starbucks, **other:** Acura, America's Tire/auto, Infiniti/Audi, Land Rover/Jaguar, Lexus, Parts+, Saab, World Mkt, **W gas:** Mobil, Shell/dsl/24hr, **food:** A's Burgers, Carl's Jr, In-n-Out, **lodging:** Best Value Laguna Inn, **other:** Costco, Firestone/auto, GMC/Cadillac, Hyundai, Mercedes
85a	CA 73 N (toll)
83	Junipero Serra Rd, to San Juan Capistrano, **W gas:** Shell, Spirit/dsl
82	CA 74, Ortego Hwy, **E gas:** Chevron/dsl, 76, **food:** Bravo Burgers, Denny's, **lodging:** Best Western, **other: W gas:** Chevron/24hr, **food:** Arby's, Carl's Jr, Del Taco, Jack-in-the-Box, Marie Callender's, McDonald's, Sizzler, Subway, Taco Bell, Walnut Grove Rest., **lodging:** Mission Inn, **other:** Ralph's Foods, TrueValue, San Juan Capistrano
81	Camino Capistrano, **E other:** Peugeot/VW, **W gas:** Chevron, **food:** Baskin-Robbins, Domino's, El Adobe Rest., Eng's Chinese, Harry's Rest., KFC, Pick-up-Stix, Pizza Hut, Ricardo's Mexican, Ruby's Cafe, Starbucks, **other:** Goodyear, Harley-Davidson, PetCo, Radio Shack, Rite Aid, San Juan Capistrano (1mi), SP
79	CA 1, Pacific Coast Hwy, Capistrano Bch, Capistrano, **1 mi W gas:** Arco/24hr, 76, **food:** A's Burgers, Cario's Mexican, Carl's Jr, Del Taco, Denny's, Jack-in-the-Box, JuiceStop, McDonald's, Subway, **lodging:** Dana Point Inn, DoubleTree, Harbor Inn, Holiday Inn Express, **other:** Chevrolet, Chrysler/Jeep, Honda, Nissan, Toyota, USPO, Vet
78	Camino de Estrella, San Clemente, **E gas:** 76/dsl, **food:** Bakers Square, Carl's Jr, China Well, Coldstone Creamery, JuiceStop, Melting Pot, RoundTable Pizza, Rubio's Grill, Subway, Wahoo's Fish Taco, **other:** [H], CVS Drug, Ralph's Foods, Stater Bros Foods, Trader Joe's, **W gas:** Arco/dsl, **food:** Las Golondrienas, **other:** Big Lots, Kragen Parts, Sears Essentials
77	Ave Vista Hermosa
76	Ave Pico, **E gas:** Mobil, **food:** Buono Pizza, Carrow's, Golden Spoon, Juice it Up, McDonald's, **other:** Albertson's, GNC, **W gas:** Chevron, Shell/dsl,

CAPISTRANO

SAN CLEMENTE

CA

Exit #	Services
76	Continued **food:** BurgerStop, Del Taco, Denny's/24hr, Pick-up-Stix, Pizza Hut, Subway, Waffle Lady, **lodging:** Country Plaza Inn, **other:** Curves, 99c Store, Staples, Tuesday Morning, USPO, tires/repair
75	Ave Palizada, Ave Presidio, **W gas:** Arco, Valero, **food:** Antoine's Café, Baskin-Robbins, Coffee Bean, KFC, Mr. Pete's Burgers, Ricardo's Mexican, Subway, Starbucks, **lodging:** Holiday Inn, **other:** Albertson's, Ford
74	El Camino Real, **E gas:** Chevron/dsl/24hr, **food:** El Mariachi Rest., **lodging:** San Clemente Inn, Shorehouse Landing, same as 75, **W gas:** Exxon, 76, **food:** FatBurger, KFC, LoveBurger, Pizza Hut/Taco Bell, Taste Of China, Tommy's Rest./24hr, **other:** Kragen Parts, Radio Shack, Ralph's Foods, 7-11
73	Ave Calafia, Ave Magdalena, **E gas:** Chevron, 76, Shell, **food:** El Mariachi Rest., Jack-in-the-Box, Molly Bloom's Cafe, Pipes Cafe, Sugar Shack Cafe, **lodging:** Budget Inn, Calafia Beach Motel, C-Vu Inn, Hampton Inn, LaVista Inn, San Clemente Motel, Travelodge, **other:** San-O Tire, 7-11, **W** to San Clemente SP
72	Cristianitios Ave, **E food:** Carl's Jr., **lodging:** Comfort Suites, Carmelo Motel, **other:** San Mateo RV Park/dump, **W other:** to San Clemente SP
71	Basilone Rd, **W other:** San Onofre St Beach
67mm	**weigh sta both lanes**
66mm	viewpoint sb
62	Las Pulgas Rd
59mm	**Aliso Creek rest area both lanes, full [handicapped] facilities, [phone], vending, [picnic], litter barrels, petwalk, RV dump**
54c	Oceanside Harbor Dr, **W gas:** Chevron, Mobil, **food:** Burger King (1mi), Del Taco, Denny's/24hr, **lodging:** Comfort Inn, Sandman Hotel, Travelodge, The Bridge Motel, **other:** to Camp Pendleton
54b	Hill St (from sb), to Oceanside, **W gas:** Mobil, **food:** Carrow's Rest., **lodging:** Comfort Inn
54a	CA 76 E, Coast Hwy
53	Mission Ave, Oceanside, **E gas:** Arco/24hr, Mobil/dsl, 76/LP, **food:** Arby's, Armando's Tacos, Burger King, China Star, El Charrito Mexican, Jack-in-the-Box, KFC, McDonald's, Mission Donuts, Pizza Hut, **lodging:** Econolodge, Quality Inn, Ramada Ltd, **other:** CarQuest, NAPA, PepBoys, Valu+ Foods, **W food:** Panda Express, Wendy's, **other:** 99c Store, Office Depot
52	Oceanside Blvd, **E gas:** Arco, **food:** Alberto's Mexican, Cosina Italiana, Domino's, IHOP, McDonald's, Papa John's, Pizza Hut, Rosarita's Café, Starbucks,

OCEANSIDE

CA

INTERSTATE 5 CONT'D

N ↕ S

Exit #	Services
52	Continued Subway, Taco Bell, Wienerschnitzel, **other:** Boney's Foods, CVS Drug, Longs Drug, Ralph's Food, Von's Food, CHP, **W lodging:** Oceanside Inn
51c	Cassidy St (from sb), **W gas:** 7-11, Mobil, 76, **other:** H
51b	CA 78, Vista Way, Escondido, **E gas:** Chevron/dsl/24hr, 76, Shell, **food:** Applebee's, Boston Mkt, Burger King, Chili's, ChuckeCheese, Finnigan's Grill, Fuddrucker's, Golden Taipei, Hooters, Macaroni Grill, McDonald's, Mimi's Café, Olive Garden, QuikWok, Rubio's, Spoon's Grill, Starbucks, Wendy's, West Buffet, **lodging:** Holiday Inn Express, **other:** Best Buy, CVS Drug, $Tree, JC Penney, Macy's, Marshall's, Michael's, PetCo, Sears/auto, Staples, Stater Bros Foods, SteinMart, Target, Tuesday Morning, Walmart/auto, World Mkt, **W food:** Hunter Steaks
51a	Las Flores Dr
50	Elm Ave, Carlsbad Village Dr, **E gas:** Shell/24hr, **food:** Lotus Thai Bistro, **W gas:** Carlsbad/LP, Chevron/repair/24hr, 76, Valero, **food:** Al's Cafe, Carl's Jr, Denny's/24hr, Jack-in-the-Box, KFC/Taco Bell, Mikko Japanese, **lodging:** Motel 6, **other:** Albertson's
49	Tamarack Ave, **E gas:** Chevron/24hr, Exxon/dsl, **food:** Village Kitchen, **lodging:** Carlsbad Lodge, Super 8, Travel Inn, **other:** GNC, Rite Aid, Von's Foods, **W gas:** Arco, 76/repair/24hr
48	Cannon Rd, Car Country Carlsbad, **E other:** Acura, Buick, Chevrolet/Cadillac, Ford, Honda, Isuzu, Lexus, Lincoln/Mercury, Mazda, Mercedes, Toyota, VW
47	Carlsbad Blvd, Palomar Airport Rd, **E gas:** Chevron, Mobil/dsl, 7-11, **food:** Carl's Jr, Islands Burgers, Panda Express, Pat&Oscar's Rest., Subway, Strauss Brewery Rest., Taco Bell, TGIFriday, **lodging:** Holiday Inn, Motel 6, **other:** Costco, Flower Fields/Carlsbad Ranch, Ford, Jiffy Lube, outlet mall, **W gas:** Shell/dsl, **food:** ClaimJumper Rest., In-n-Out, Marie Callender's, McDonald's, Sammy's Pizza, **lodging:** Hilton Garden, **other:** S Carlsbad St Bch
45	Poinsettia Lane, **W gas:** Chevron, **food:** Benihana, El Pollo Loco, Golden Spoon, Jack-in-the-Box, Pick-Up Sticks, Starbucks, Subway, **lodging:** La Quinta, Motel 6, Quality Inn, Ramada, **other:** Ralph's Foods, Rite Aid, Volvo/Porsche
44	La Costa Ave, **E** vista point, **W gas:** Chevron/dsl
43	Leucadia Blvd, **E lodging:** Howard Johnson, **W gas:** Shell/service
41b	Encinitas Blvd, **E gas:** Chevron, Exxon, O'Brien Sta., **food:** Coco's, Del Taco, Oggi's Pizza, **other:** Albertson's, CVS Drug, NAPA, to Quail Botanical Gardens, Vet, **W gas:** Shell, **food:** Denny's, Wendy's, **lodging:** Best Western/rest., Day's Inn, **other:** PetCo
41a	Santa Fe Dr, to Encinitas, **E gas:** Shell, **food:** Carl's Jr, El Nopalito, Papa Tonie's Pizza, **other:** 7-11, **W food:** Today's Pizza, **other:** H, Rite Aid, Von's Foods, Vet
40	Birmingham Dr, **E gas:** Chevron, Valero, **food:** Mandarin City, **lodging:** Comfort Inn, **W gas:** Arco/24hr
39mm	viewpoint sb
39	Manchester Ave, **E gas:** 76, **other:** to MiraCosta College
37	Lomas Santa Fe Dr, Solana Bch, **E food:** Baskin-Robbins, Pizza Nova, Samurai Rest., **other:** Ross, Von's Foods, We-R-Fabrics, **W gas:** Arco, Mobil, **food:** Carl's Jr, Denny's, Jamba Juice, Panda Express, Panera Bread, RoundTable Pizza, Starbucks, Togo's, **other:** CVS Drug, Discount Tire, Henry's Foods, Marshall's, Staples
36	Via de La Valle, Del Mar, **E gas:** Chevron, Mobil, **food:** Aliya Bistro, Burger King, Chevy's Mexican, Coffee Bean, McDonald's, Milton's Deli, Paradise Grill, Pasta Pronto, Papachino's Italian, Silver Skillet, Taste of Thai, **other:** Albertson's/SavOn, PetCo, Radio Shack, **W gas:** Arco/24hr, Shell/dsl, **food:** Denny's, FishMkt Rest., Red Tracton's Rest., **lodging:** Hilton, **other:** racetrack
34	Del Mar Heights Rd, **E gas:** Shell/dsl, **W gas:** 7-11, **food:** Elijah's Rest., Jack-in-the-Box, Mexican Grill, **other:** Longs Drug, Von's Foods
33	Carmel Mtn Rd, **E gas:** Arco, Shell/repair, **food:** Taco Bell, Tio Leo's Mexican, **lodging:** DoubleTree Hotel, Hampton Inn, Marriott
32	CA 56 E, Carmel Valley Rd
31	I-805 (from sb)
29	Genesee Ave, **E other:** H
28b	La Jolla Village Dr, **E food:** Italian Bistro, **lodging:** Embassy Suites, Hyatt, Marriott, **other:** H, to LDS Temple, **W gas:** Mobil/dsl, **food:** BJ's Grill, CA Pizza, Coldstone Creamery, Domino's, Elijah's Deli, El Torito, Flame Broiler, Islands Burgers, RockBottom Café, Rubio's Grill, TGIFriday, Trader Joe's, **lodging:** Sheraton, **other:** H, CVS Drug, Marshall's, PetsMart, Radio Shack, Ralph's Foods, Ross, Whole Foods
28a	Nobel Dr (from nb), **E lodging:** Hyatt, **other:** LDS Temple, **W** same as 28b
27	Gilman Dr, La Jolla Colony Dr
26b	CA 52 E, Ardath Rd (from nb)
26a	Ardath Rd (from nb)
23b	CA 274, Balboa Ave, **1 mi E gas:** Shell, **food:** Del Taco, **other:** Albertson's, **W gas:** Mobil, 76/repair, 7-11, **food:** McDonald's, In-n-Out, Rubio's Grill, Wienerschnitzel, **lodging:** Days Inn, Holiday Inn Express, Mission Bay Inn, San Diego Motel, **other:** H, Discount Tire, Express Tire, Ford, Nissan, Toyota, Mission Bay Pk
23a	Grand Ave, Garnet Ave, **W other:** Cadillac
22	Clairemont Dr, Mission Bay Dr, **E gas:** Arco, Shell, **food:** Carl's Jr, HomeTown Buffet, Jack-in-the-Box, KFC, McDonald's, Subway, **lodging:** Best Western, **other:** Chevrolet/VW, Rite Aid, **W** to Sea World Dr
21	Sea World Dr, Tecolote Dr, **E gas:** Shell, **lodging:** Seaside Motel, **other:** Circle K, Firestone, PetCo, **W lodging:** Hilton, **other:** Old Town SP, Seaworld
20	I-8, W to Nimitz Blvd, E to El Centro, CA 209 S (from sb), to Rosecrans St
19	Old Town Ave, **E gas:** Arco/24hr, Shell, **lodging:** Courtyard, La Quinta
18b	Washington St, **E lodging:** Comfort Inn
18a	Pacific Hwy Viaduct, Kettner St
17b	India St, Front St, Sassafras St, **E gas:** Mobil, Rte 66 Gas, **W other:** ✈, civic ctr
17a	Hawthorn St, Front St, **W gas:** Exxon/dsl, **lodging:** Holiday Inn, Motel 6, Radisson, **other:** H

ESCONDIDO · CARLSBAD · ENCINITAS · SAN DIEGO AREA

INTERSTATE 5 CONT'D

N ↕ S — SAN DIEGO AREA

Exit #	Services
16b	6th Ave, downtown
16a	CA 163 N, 10th St, **E other:** AeroSpace Museum, **W gas:** Shell, **food:** Del Taco, Jack-in-the-Box, McDonald's, **lodging:** Days Inn, Downtown Lodge, El Cortez Motel, Holiday Inn, Marriott, **other:** H
15c b	CA 94 E (from nb), Pershing Dr, B St, civic ctr
15a	CA 94 E, J St, Imperial Ave (from sb),
14b	Cesar Chavez Pkwy
14a	CA 75, to Coronado, **W** toll rd to Coronado
13b	National Ave SD, 28th St, **E food:** Little Caesar's, Starbucks, Subway, **other:** AutoZone, **W gas:** Shell, **food:** Burger King, Del Taco, El Pollo Loco
13a	CA 15 N, to Riverside
12	Main St, National City
11b	8th St, National City, **E gas:** Arco, Shell/24hr, **food:** Jack-in-the-Box, **lodging:** Holiday Inn, Howard Johnson, Ramada Inn, Super 8, Value Inn, **W gas:** Chevron/dsl
11a	Harbor Dr, Civic Center Dr
10	Bay Marina, 24th St, Mile of Cars Way, **1/2 mi E food:** Denny's, In-n-Out
9	CA 54 E
8b	E St, Chula Vista, **E lodging:** Motel 6, **W food:** Anthony's Fish Grotto, **lodging:** GoodNite Inn
8a	H St
7b	J St (from sb)
7a	L St, **E gas:** 7-11, 76, Shell/dsl, **food:** Mandarin Chinese, **lodging:** Best Western, **other:** AutoZone, NAPA, Parts+, Office Depot
6	Palomar St, **E gas:** Arco, **food:** China King, Del Taco, DQ, HomeTown Buffet, KFC, Little Caesar's, McDonald's, Subway, **lodging:** Palomar Inn, **other:** Food4Less, Office Depot, 7-11, E on Broadway... **food:** Jack-in-the-Box, KFC, Panda Express, Quizno's, Yoshinoya, **other:** Costco/gas, Michael's, Ross, Target, Walmart
5b	Main St, to Imperial Beach, **E gas:** Arco, **food:** AZ Chinese
5a	CA 75 (from sb), Palm Ave, to Imperial Beach, **E gas:** Arco, **food:** Armando's Mexican, Papa John's, Wahshing Chinese, **other:** Discount Tire, 7-11, Soto's Transmissions, **W gas:** Arco, 7-11, Shell/repair/24hr, Thrifty, **food:** Boll Weevil Diner, Burger King, Carl's Jr, Carrow's, Coldstone Creamery, El Chile Mexican, Los Pancho's Tacos, McDonald's, Rally's, Red Hawk Steaks, Roberto's Mexican, Subway, Taco Bell, Wienerschnitzel, **lodging:** Super 8, Travelodge, **other:** AutoZone, CVS Drug, Home Depot, Jiffy Lube, 99c Store, Von's Foods
4	Coronado Ave (from sb), **E gas:** Chevron/service, Shell/service, **food:** Denny's, Taco Bell, **lodging:** EZ 8 Motel, **other:** 7-11, **W gas:** Shell/dsl, **lodging:** Day's Inn, **other:** to Border Field SP
3	CA 905, Tocayo Ave, **W gas:** 7-11
2	Dairy Mart Rd, **E gas:** Arco/24hr, Circle K, **food:** Burger King, Carl's Jr, Coco's, KFC, McDonald's, Roberto's Mexican, **lodging:** Americana Inn, Best Value, Super 8, Valli-Hi Motel, **other:** CarQuest, Radio Shack, Pacifica RV Resort
1b	Via de San Ysidro, **E gas:** Chevron, Exxon, Mobil, 76, **other:** Max's Foods, NAPA, **W gas:** Chevron, **food:** Denny's, KFC, **lodging:** Economy Inn, Knights/RV park, Motel 6
1a	I-805 N (from nb), Camino de la Plaza (from sb), **E food:** Burger King, El Pollo Loco, Jack-in-the-Box, KFC, McDonald's, Subway, **lodging:** Flamingo Motel, Gateway Inn, Holiday Motel, Travelodge, **other:** AutoZone, **W food:** Achiato Mexican, Gingling House Chinese, IHOP, Iron Wok, McDonald's, Pizza Hut/Taco Bell, Sunrise Buffet, **other:** Baja Duty-Free, K-Mart, Ross, Marshall's, factory outlet, border parking
0	US/Mexico Border, California state line, customs, I-5 begins/ends

INTERSTATE 8

Y U M A — E ↕ W

Exit #	Services
172.5mm	California/Arizona state line, Colorado River, Pacific/Mountain time zone
172	4th Ave, Yuma, **N** Ft Yuma Casino, **S gas:** Chevron, Circle K, **food:** Jack-in-the-Box, Yuma Landing Rest., **lodging:** Best Western, **other:** Rivers Edge RV Park, to Yuma SP
170	Winterhaven Dr, **S** Rivers Edge RV Park
166	CA 186, Algodones Rd, Andrade, **S** to Mexico
165mm	**CA Insp/weigh Sta**
164	Sidewinder Rd, **N** st patrol, **S gas:** Shell/LP, **other:** Pilot Knob RV Park
159	CA 34, Ogilby Rd, to Blythe
156	Grays Well Rd, **N** Imperial Dunes RA
155mm	**rest area both lanes (exits left), portapotties, ⛱, litter barrels, petwalk**
151	Gordons Well
146	Brock Research Ctr Rd
143	CA 98, to Calexico, Midway Well
131	CA 115, VanDerLinden Rd, to Holtville, **5 mi N** gas, food, lodging, RV camping
128	Bonds Corner Rd
125	Orchard Rd, Holtville, **4 mi N** gas/dsl, food
120	Bowker Rd
118b a	CA 111, to Calexico, **1 mi N gas:** Shell/dsl/café/scales, **other:** RV park, tires/truckwash
116	Dogwood Rd, **S food:** Arby's, Carino's, Chili's, ChuckeCheese, Denny's, Famous Dave's BBQ, Jack-in-the-Box, Starbucks, Taco Bell, **lodging:** Fairfield Inn, **other:** Best Buy, Dillard's, JC Penney, Macy's, Marshall's, Old Navy, Ross, Sears/auto, Staples, mall

INTERSTATE 8 CONT'D

E ↕ W

EL CENTRO

Exit #	Services
115	CA 86, 4th St, El Centro, **N gas:** Arco/24hr, Chevron, 7-11/dsl, Shell/dsl, **food:** Carl's Jr, China Express, Exotic Thai, Jack-in-the-Box, Mexicali Taco, McDonald's, **lodging:** Holiday Inn Express, Motel 6, **other:** El Sol Foods, Firestone/auto, Goodyear/auto, Ford/Lincoln/Mercury, U-Haul, radiators, **S gas:** On the Go/Subway, **food:** Dudley's, IHOP, In-N-Out, Millie's Kitchen, Taco Bell, **lodging:** Best Western, Comfort Inn, Rodeway Inn, **other:** AutoZone, Buick/Cadillac/Pontiac, Chevrolet, Chrysler/Dodge/Jeep, Home Depot, Honda, Lucky Foods, Desert Trails RV Park
114	Imperial Ave, El Centro, **N gas:** Chevron/service, 7-11/dsl, Shell, USA/dsl, **food:** Del Taco, Denny's, Domino's, KFC, McDonald's, Pizza Hut, Scribble's Rest, TasteeFreez Burgers, **lodging:** Howard Johnson, Laguna Inn, Ramada Inn, Vacation Inn/RV Park, **other:** Kragen Parts, st patrol, **1-3 mi N gas:** Arco/24hr, **food:** Applebee's, Burger King, Carl's Jr, Carrow's, Church's, Domino's, El Pollo Loco, Farmer Boys, Golden Corral, Jack-in-the-Box, Little Caesars, Papa John's, Pizza Hut, Popeye's, Quizno's, Rally's, Sizzler, Sonic, Starbucks, Subway, Taco Bell, Wendy's, **lodging:** Day's Inn, Super Star Inn, **other:** Aamco, America's Tire, BigLots, Costco/gas, Food-4Less, Goodyear/auto, K-Mart, Kragen Parts, Lowe's Whse, PepBoys, Rite Aid, Sears/auto, Staples, Target, Toyota, Von's Foods, Walgreens, Walmart SuperCtr, Winston Tire
111	Forrester Rd, to Westmorland
108mm	**Sunbeam Rest Area both lanes, full ♿ facilities, ☎, picnic, litter barrels, petwalk, RV dump**
107	Drew Rd, Seeley, **N** Sunbeam RV Park, **S** Rio Bend RV Park
101	Dunaway Rd, Imperial Valley, elev 0 ft, **N** st prison
89	Imperial Hwy, CA 98, Ocotillo, **N food:** Old Hwy Cafe, USPO, **S gas:** Texaco/dsl, **food:** Desert Kitchen, **other:** auto repair, RV camping, museum
87	CA 98 (from eb), to Calexico
81mm	runaway truck ramp, eb
80	Mountain Springs Rd
77	**N** ☎, towing
75mm	**brake insp area eb,** ☎
73	Jacumba, **S gas:** Shell/Subway/dsl/towing/24hr, Valero/dsl, **other:** RV camping
65	CA 94, Boulevard, to Campo, **S gas:** MtnTop/dsl, **food:** Salsa Linda, **lodging:** Lux Inn, **other:** auto repair, to McCain Valley RA
63mm	Tecate Divide, elev 4140 ft
62mm	Crestwood Summit, elev 4190 ft
61	Crestwood Rd, Live Oak Springs, **S gas:** Golden Acorn Trkstp/casino/dsl, **food:** Country Broiler Rest., **lodging:** Live Oak Sprs Country Inn, **other:** Outdoor World RV Camp, info
54	Kitchen Creek Rd, Cameron Station, **S** food, RV camping
51	rd 1, Buckman Spgs Rd, to Lake Morena, **S** gas/dsl/LP, food, lodging, RV camping, Lake Morena CP (7mi), Potrero CP (19mi), **rest area both lanes, full ♿ facilities, ☎, picnic, litter barrels, petwalk, RV dump**
48	**inp sta, wb**
47	rd 1, Sunrise Hwy, Laguna Summit, elev 4055 ft, **N** to Laguna Mtn RA
45	Pine Valley, Julian, **N food:** Frosty Burger, Major's Diner, El Rancho Grande Diner, **lodging:** Pine Valley Inn, **other:** Curves, Mtn SuperMkt, to Cuyamaca Rancho SP, Vet
44mm	Pine Valley Creek
42mm	elev 4000 ft
40	CA 79, Japatul Rd, Descanso, **N food:** Descanso Rest., **other:** to Cuyamaca Rancho SP
37mm	vista point eb, elev 3000 ft
36	E Willows, **N** Alpine Sprs RV Park, Viejas Indian Res, casino
33	W Willows Rd, to Alpine, **N** Alpine Sprs RV Park, Viejas Outlets/famous brands, casino, same as 36, **S** ranger sta
31mm	elev 2000 ft
30	Tavern Rd, to Alpine, **N gas:** Chevron/dsl, Valero, **S gas:** 76/Circle K, Shell, **food:** Breadbasket Rest., Carl's Jr, China Flavor, La Carreta Mexican, Mediterranean Grill, Subway, **lodging:** Ayer's Inn, **other:** Alpine Mkt Foods, Radio Shack, Rite Aid, TrueValue, city park
27	Dunbar Lane, Harbison Canyon, **N other:** RV camping, Flinn Sprgs CP
25mm	elev 1000 ft
24mm	☎
23	Lake Jennings Pk Rd, Lakeside, **N gas:** Arco/Jack-in-the-Box/dsl/24hr, to Lake Jennings CP, **other:** RV camping, **S gas:** 7-11, **food:** Burger King, Karla's Mexican, Marechiaro's Pizza
22	Los Coches Rd, Lakeside, **N gas:** Eagle/dsl/LP, 7-11, Valero, **food:** Laposta Mexican, Las Cazuela's, Pizza Pan, **other:** RV camping/dump, **S gas:** Shell/dsl, **food:** Denny's, Giant Pizza, McDonald's, Panda Express, Subway, Taco Bell, **other:** Radio Shack, Von's Foods, Walmart
20b	Greenfield Dr, to Crest, **N gas:** Chevron/dsl, Exxon/dsl/24hr, **food:** Jack-in-the-Box, Janet's Café, McDonald's, Panchos Taco, **other:** H, Albertson's, Curves, Ford, 99c Store, RV camping, 7-11, auto repair, st patrol, **S gas:** Mobil/LP
20a	E Main St (from wb, no EZ return), **N lodging:** Embasadora Motel, Fabulous 7 Motel, HP Inn, **other:** Ford, Vacationer RV Park, **S gas:** Arco, **other:** Cadillac
19	2nd St, CA 54, El Cajon, **N gas:** Arco/24hr, Chevron, Exxon/dsl, **food:** Mariachio's Pizza, Rosanna Grilled Panini, **other:** CVS Drug, Parts+, Von's Foods, **S gas:** 76, Gas Depot, Shell, **food:** A&W/KFC, Arby's, Boll Weevil Rest., Burger King, Carl's Jr, DQ, Estrada's Mexican, IHOP, Jack-in-the-Box, KFC, McDonald's, Pizza Hut, Subway, Taco Bell, Taco Shop/24hr, Tyler's Rest., **other:** Firestone/auto, Jiffy Lube, PetCo, Ralph's Foods, Radio Shack, Rite Aid, Walgreens
18	Mollison Ave, El Cajon, **N gas:** Chevron, **food:** Denny's, **lodging:** Best Western, Days Inn, **S gas:** Arco/24hr, KwikTrip/dsl, **food:** Taco Bell, **lodging:** Super 8, Valley Motel
17c	Magnolia Ave, CA 67 (from wb), to Santee, **N food:** Del Taco, Jack-in-the-Box, LJ Silver, Panda Express, **other:** Arco, Food4Less, Target, mall, **S gas:** Shell/service, **food:** Red Brick Pizza, Wienerschnitzel, **lodging:** Motel 6, Northgate Motel, Rodeway Inn, **other:** Nudo's Drug

EL CAJON

INTERSTATE 8 CONT'D

E ↕ W

EL CAJON / SAN DIEGO AREA

Exit #	Services
17b	CA 67 (from eb), same as 17 a&c
17a	Johnson Ave (from eb), **N food:** Applebee's, Boston Mkt, Burger King, Jamba Juice, KFC, LJ Silver, On the Border, Rubio's, Sizzler, Subway, **other:** Albertson's, Best Buy, Border's Books, Chevrolet, $Tree, Home Depot, Honda, JC Penney, K-Mart, Long Drug, Macy's, Marshall's, Michael's, Office Depot, PetsMart, Rite Aid, Sears/auto, Walmart, mall, **S other:** Aamco, Isuzu
16	Main St, **N gas:** Arco/24hr, **food:** Denny's/24hr, 7-11, Sombrero Mexican, **lodging:** Relax Inn, **S gas:** 76/RV Dump, Chevron, **other:** Nissan, brakes/transmissions
15	El Cajon Blvd (from eb), **N lodging:** Quality Inn, **S gas:** Mobil/dsl, Shell, **food:** BBQ, **other:** Chrysler
14c	Severin Dr, Fuerte Dr (from wb), **N gas:** Arco/24hr, Mobil, **food:** Anthony's Fish Rest., Charcoal House Rest., La Casa Blanca, **lodging:** Holiday Inn Express, **S food:** Brigantine Seafood Rest.
14b a	CA 125, to CA 94
13b	Jackson Dr, Grossmont Blvd, **N gas:** Chevron, **food:** Arby's, BJ's Grill, Casa de Pico, Chili's, ClaimJumper, Fuddrucker's, Jamba Juice, McDonald's, Panda Express, Panera Bread, Red Lobster, Rubio's, **other:** Barnes&Noble, Chrysler/Jeep/Dodge, Dodge, Kragen Parts, Long's Drug, Macy's, 7-11, Staples, Target, Walmart, mall, **S food:** Honeybaked Ham, Jack-in-the-Box, **other:** Discount Tire, Firestone/auto, Ford, Hyundai, Ralph's Foods, Ross, VW
13a	Spring St (from eb), El Cajon Blvd (from wb), **N other:** Dodge/Kia, Jeep, **S food:** La Salsa Mexican, **lodging:** La Mesa Lodge, **other:** 99c Store
12	Fletcher Pkwy, to La Mesa, **N gas:** Shell, **food:** Baker's Square, Carl's Jr., Chipotle Mexican, McDonald's, **lodging:** EZ 8 Motel, Holiday Inn, **other:** Costco, 7-11, **S food:** La Salsa Mexican, **lodging:** Motel 6, **other:** Chevrolet, San Diego RV Resort
11	70th St, Lake Murray Blvd, **N gas:** Shell, **food:** Subway, **other:** truck/RV repair, **S gas:** Shell/dsl/repair, **food:** Aiken's Deli, Denny's, Marie Callender's, **other:** H
10	College Ave, **N gas:** Chevron/dsl, **other:** Windmill Farms Mkt, **S other:** H, to San Diego St U
9	Waring Rd, **N food:** Nicolosi's Italian, **lodging:** Days Inn, Quality Inn
8	Fairmont Ave (7 from eb), to Mission Gorge Rd, **N gas:** Arco/24hr, Mobil/dsl, Valero/dsl, **food:** Arby's, Burger King, Carl's Jr, Chili's, El Pollo Loco, Jack-in-the-Box, El Pollo Loco, KFC, McDonald's, Rally's, Starbucks, Subway, Szechuan Chinese, **lodging:** Super 8, **other:** H, Aamco, Discount Tire, Home Depot, Honda, Longs Drugs, NAPA, Radio Shack, Rite Aid, Toyota, Tuesday Morning, Von's Foods
7b a	I-15 N, CA 15 S, to 40th St
6b	I-805, N to LA, S to Chula Vista
6a	Texas St, Qualcomm Way, **N food:** Dave&Buster's, same as 5
5	Mission Ctr Rd, **N gas:** Chevron, **food:** Bennigan's, Chevy's Mexican, Fuddrucker's, Hooters, In-N-Out, King's Fishouse, Mimi's Cafe, On The Border, Outback Steaks, Pick-Up Stix, Taco Bell, **lodging:** Marriott, **other:** Best Buy, Borders Books&Café, Chevrolet,

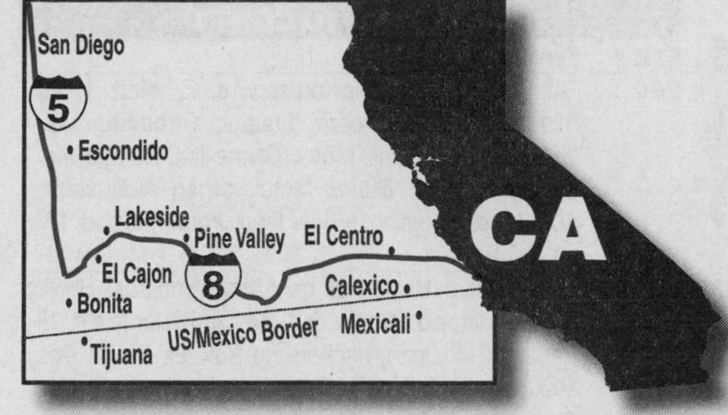

CA

SAN DIEGO AREA

Exit #	Services
5	Continued Ford, Lincoln/Mercury, Macy's, Marshall's, Michael's, Nordstrom Rack, Old Navy, Macy's, Staples, Target, mall, **S gas:** Arco/24hr, **food:** Benihana, Denny's, El Torito, Fugi Japanese Steaks, Todai Rest., Wendy's, **lodging:** Comfort Inn, Hilton, La Quinta, Radisson, Ramada Ltd, Red Lion Inn, Sheraton, **other:** Chrysler, Dodge, GMC/Pontiac, Hummer, Mazda, Subaru
4c b	CA 163, Cabrillo Frwy, **S** to downtown, zoo
4a	Hotel Circle Dr (from eb), CA 163 (from wb)
3a	Hotel Circle, Taylor St, **N gas:** Chevron, **food:** DW Ranch Rest., Hunter Steaks, Kelly's Steaks, **lodging:** Comfort Suites, Crowne Plaza, Handlery Hotel, Motel 6, Town&Country Motel, **other:** AAA, cinema, golf, **S gas:** Chevron, **food:** Adam's Cafe, Albie's Rest., Ricky's Rest., Tickled Trout, Valley Kitchen, **lodging:** Best Western, Comfort Inn, Days Inn, DoubleTree Inn, Extended Stay America, Hawthorn Suites, Hilton, Holiday Inn, Howard Johnson, King's Inn/rest., Mission Valley Hotel, Quality Resort, Ramada Inn, Residence Inn, Super 8, Travelodge, Vagabond Inn
2c	Morena Blvd (from wb)
2b	I-5, N to LA, S to San Diego
2a	Rosecrans St (from wb), CA 209, **S gas:** Chevron, **food:** Burger King, Del Taco, In-N-Out, McDonald's, Perry's Café, Rally's, **lodging:** Best Western, Day's Inn, Holiday Inn, Howard Johnson, Quality Inn, Super 8, **other:** Chrysler/Jeep, Goodyear/auto, House of Fabrics, Staples, SaveOn Drug
1	W Mission Bay Blvd, Sports Arena Blvd (from wb), **N** to SeaWorld, **S gas:** Arco, **food:** Arby's, Denny's, Jack-in-the-Box, McDonald's, Souplantation, Taco Shop, Wendy's, **lodging:** Holiday Inn Express, Premier Inn, **other:** Curves, Home Depot, U-Haul
0mm	I-8 begins/ends on Sunset Cliffs Blvd, **N** Mission Bay Park, **1/4 mi W gas:** Exxon, Shell, **food:** Jack-in-the-Box, Kaiserhof Cafe

INTERSTATE 10

E ↕ W

Exit #	Services
245mm	California/Arizona state line, Colorado River, Pacific/Mountain time zone
244mm	**inspection sta wb**
243	Riviera Dr, **S other:** Riviera RV Camp
241	US 95, Intake Blvd, Blythe, **N gas:** Mobil/dsl, **food:** Lalo's Mexican, Steaks'n Cakes Rest., Sunset Grille, **lodging:** Best Western, Days Inn, Desert Winds Motel, Travelers Inn Express, **other:** Burton's RV Park, auto/RV repair/24hr, to Needles, **S** McIntyre Park

E ↕ W

CA

BLYTHE

INTERSTATE 10 CONT'D

Exit #	Services
240	7th St, **N** **gas:** Chevron/service, EZ Mart, **food:** Blimpie, Foster's Freeze, Starbucks, **lodging:** Astro Motel, Blue Line Motel, Blythe Inn, Budget Inn, Comfort Suites, Dunes Motel, **other:** Albertson's, AutoZone, Chrysler/Dodge/Jeep, Ford, Rite Aid, RV repair/LP
239	Lovekin Blvd, Blythe, **N** **gas:** Mobil/Subs/dsl, Shell/Quizno's, **food:** Carl's Jr, Del Taco, Domino's, El Ranchito Mexican, Jack-in-the-Box, La Casita Dos Mexican, McDonald's, Pizza Hut, Popeye's, Sizzler, Starbucks, **lodging:** Best Value Inn, Best Western, Budget Host, Hampton Inn, Regency Inn, **other:** H, Ace Hardware, Big K Mart, CarQuest, Checker Parts, $Tree, Goodyear/auto, Radio Shack, **S** **gas:** Arco/dsl/24hr, Chevron/dsl/24hr, 76/dsl, Shell/DQ/dsl, Valero, **food:** Burger King, Denny's, KFC, Taco Bell, **lodging:** Holiday Inn Express, Motel 6, Super 8, **other:** Chevrolet/Pontiac/Buick/Cadillac, city park/RV dump
236	CA 78, Neighbours Blvd, to Ripley, **N** **gas:** Valero/service, **S** to Cibola NWR
232	Mesa Dr, **N** **gas:** 76/dsl/rest./24hr/@, Valero/dsl
231	**weigh sta wb**
222mm	**Wileys Well Rd, N rest area both lanes, full ♿ facilities, ☎, 🛆, litter barrels, petwalk, S** to st prison
217	Ford Dry Lake Rd
201	Corn Springs Rd
192	CA 177, Rice Rd, to Lake Tamarisk, **N** **gas:** gas/repair/24hr, **food:** Desert Ctr Cafe, **other:** camping
189	Eagle Mtn Rd
182	Red Cloud Rd
177	Hayfield Rd
173	Chiriaco Summit, **N** **gas:** Chevron/Foster's Freez/dsl/24hr, **food:** Chiriaco Rest, **other:** Patton Museum, truck/tire repair
168	to Twentynine Palms, to Mecca, Joshua Tree NM
162	frontage rd
159mm	**Cactus City Rest Area both lanes, full ♿ facilities, 🛆, litter barrels, petwalk**
147mm	0 ft elevation
146	Dillon Rd, to CA 86, to CA 111 S, Coachella, **N** **gas:** Chevron/24hr, Loves/Carl's Jr/dsl/24hr/@, **S** **gas:** TA/Arby's/Arco/Taco Bell/dsl/24hr/@, Shell/Jack-in-the-Box, **other:** Spotlight Casino
145	(from eb), CA 86 S
144	CA 111 N, CA 86 S, Indio, **N** **food:** Nuevo Paraiso Rest., **lodging:** Holiday Inn Express, **other:** Classic RV Park, Fantasy Sprgs Casino/Hotel/Cafe
143	Jackson St, Indio, **N** RV Park, **S** Circle K
142	Monroe St, Central Indio, **N** **other:** RV camping, **S** **gas:** Circle K, 76, Shell/dsl/LP, **food:** Marisco's Mexican, Mexicali Cafe, **lodging:** Quality Inn
139	Jefferson St, Indio Blvd, **N** **other:** Shadow Hills RV Resort, hwy patrol
137	Washington St, Country Club Dr, to Indian Wells, **N** **gas:** Arco/24hr, Chevron, **food:** Burger King, Burger Time, Coco's, Del Taco, Mario's Italian, Starbucks, **lodging:** Comfort Suites, Motel 6, **other:** Buick/Pontiac/GMC, Ford/Lincoln/Mercury, Giant RV Ctr,

INDIO

PALM SPRINGS

Exit #	Services
137	Continued Honda, Toyota/Scion, Rite Aid, Stater Bro's, Walgreens, **S** **gas:** Mobil/dsl, 76/Circle K, **food:** Carl's Jr, China Wok, La Tacita Mexican, Lili's Chinese, Pizza Hut, Quizno's, Subway, Togo's, Wendy's, **lodging:** Embassy Suites, **other:** Goodyear/auto
134	Cook St, to Indian Wells, **S** **gas:** Arco, Mobil, **food:** Applebees, Jack-in-the-Box, Starbucks, **lodging:** Courtyard, Hampton Inn, Hilton/Homewood Suites, Residence Inn
131	Monterey Ave, Thousand Palms, **N** **gas:** Arco/24hr, **food:** Jack-in-the-Box, **S** **food:** Del Taco, El Pollo Loco, IHOP, McDonald's, Panda Express, Quizno's, Starbucks, Subway, Taco Bell, **other:** America's Tire, Costco/gas, Home Depot, PetsMart, Sam's Club/gas, Walmart SuperCtr
130	Ramon Rd, Bob Hope Dr, **N** **gas:** Chevron/24hr, ***FLYING J***/dsl/LP/rest./24hr, Mobil/dsl, Valero, **food:** Carl's Jr, Casa de Pasta, Del Taco, Denny's, Guerro Mexican, In-n-Out, McDonald's, **lodging:** Red Roof Inn, **other:** truckwash, **S** **food:** Sage Grill, Steak House, **other:** H, Agua Caliente Casino/rest.
126	Date Palm Dr, Rancho Mirage, **S** **gas:** Arco/24hr, Mobil, Valero, **food:** Domino's
123	Gene Autry Tr, Palm Dr, to Desert Hot Sprgs, **N** **gas:** Arco, Chevron/Jack-in-the-Box, **other:** Caliente Springs Camping, **3 mi S** to Gene Autry Trail
120	Indian Ave, to N Palm Sprgs, **N** **gas:** 76/Circle K, Shell, **food:** Denny's, **lodging:** Motel 6, **S** **gas:** Chevron, Pilot/DQ/Wendy's/dsl/24hr, **food:** Jack-in-the-Box, **other:** H, Bud's Tire
117	CA 62, to Yucca Valley, Twentynine Palms, to Joshua Tree NM
114	Whitewater, many windmills
113mm	**rest area both lanes, full ♿ facilities, ☎, 🛆, litter barrels**
112	CA 111 (from eb), to Palm Springs
110	Hugeen-Lehmann
106	Main St, to Cabazon, **N** **gas:** Shell/dsl, **food:** Burger King, Spanky's BBQ, Wheel Inn Rest., **S** **gas:** Arco/dsl/24hr
104	Cabazon, same as 103
103	Fields Rd, **N** **gas:** Chevron, TC/A&W/dsl, **food:** McDonald's, Ruby's Diner, **other:** Hadley Fruit Orchards, Premium Outlets/famous brands, Morongo Reservation/casino
102.5mm	**Banning weigh sta both lanes**
102	Ramsey St (from wb)
101	Hargrave St, Banning, **N** **gas:** 76/Church's, Shell/dsl/LP, Valero, **lodging:** Country Inn, **other:** tires
100	CA 243, 8th St, Banning, **N** **gas:** Chevron, **food:** Ahloo Chinese, IHOP, Jack-in-the-Box, **other:** Rite Aid, **S** **other:** RV camping
99	22nd St, to Ramsey St, **N** **gas:** Arco/24hr, Shell, **food:** Carl's Jr, Carrow's, Chelo's Tacos, Del Taco, KFC, McDonald's, Pepe's Mexican, Pizza Hut, Sizzler, Starbucks, Subway, Wall Chinese, **lodging:** Day's Inn, Super 8, Travelodge, **other:** Chrysler/Jeep/Dodge, Ford, Goodyear/auto
98	Sunset Ave, Banning, **N** **gas:** Chevron/dsl, **food:** Domino's, Gramma's Kitchen, Gus Jr #7 Burger, **other:** Ace Hardware, AutoZone, BigLots, Chevrolet/Buick/Pontiac/GMC, Radio Shack, Ray's RV Ctr, Rio Ranch Mkt, Rite Aid, Vet

BANNING

INTERSTATE 10 CONT'D

E ↕ W

BEAUMONT

Exit #	Services
96	Highland Springs Ave, **N gas:** Arco/24hr, Chevron, Valero/dsl, **food:** Applebee's, Burger King, Denny's, Farmhouse Rest., Jack-in-the-Box, Orchid, Papa John's, Pizza Run, Subway, Wendy's, **lodging:** Hampton Inn, **other:** [H], Ace Hardware, Food4Less, Kragen Parts, NAPA, Radio Shack, Stater Bros Foods, Walgreens, **S gas:** Mobil, **food:** Baskin-Robbins, Carl's Jr, Chili's, McDonald's, **other:** Albertson's, Best Buy, BK RV Ctr, Home Depot, K-Mart, Kohls, Rite Aid, Ross, Staples, Walmart SuperCtr, hwy patrol
95	Pennsylvania Ave, Beaumont, **N gas:** Circle K, **food:** ABC Rest., Rusty Lantern Rest., **lodging:** Windsor Motel, **other:** Miller RV Ctr, Tom's RV Ctr
94	CA 79, Beaumont, **N gas:** 76, Thrifty Gas, **food:** Baker's DriveThru, McDonald's, El Rancho Steaks, Popeye's, YumYum Donuts/24hr, **lodging:** Best Western, Best Value Inn, **other:** Auto Value, NAPA, **S food:** Del Taco, Denny's, **other:** RV camping
93	CA 60 W, to Riverside
92	San Timoteo Canyon Rd, Oak Valley Pkwy, **N lodging:** Holiday Inn Express, **other:** Rite Aid, golf, **S** golf
91mm	**rest area wb, full [handicapped] facilities, [phone], [picnic], litter barrels, petwalk**
90	Cherry Valley Blvd, truck/tire repair
89	Singleton Rd (from wb), to Calimesa
88	Calimesa Blvd, **N gas:** Arco/24hr, Chevron/dsl, Shell, **food:** Best Wok, Burger King, McDonald's, Subway, Taco Bell, **lodging:** Calimesa Inn, **other:** Stater Bros Foods, bank, **S food:** Big Boy, Jack-in-the-Box
87	County Line Rd, to Yucaipa, **N gas:** FasTrip/gas, Shell/dsl, **food:** Baker's DriveThru, Del Taco, **other:** auto repair/tires
86mm	**Wildwood Rest Area eb, full [handicapped] facilities, [phone], [picnic], litter barrels, petwalk**
85	Live Oak Canyon Rd, Oak Glen
83	Yucaipa Blvd, **N gas:** Arco/dsl/24hr, Chevron, **food:** Baker's DriveThru
82	Wabash Ave (from wb)
81	Redlands Blvd, Ford St, **S gas:** 76
80	Cypress Ave, University St, **N** [H], to U of Redlands
79b a	CA 38, 6th St, Orange St, Redlands, **N gas:** Chevron, **food:** Redland Rest., **lodging:** Budget Inn, Stardust Motel, **other:** Goodyear, Stater Bros Foods, **S gas:** 76, Shell, **food:** Chipotle Mexican, Denny's, Open Kitchen Chinese, Rubio's, Togo's, Trader Joe's, Starbucks, **other:** Albertson's, Buick/GMC, Kragen Parts, Lincoln/Mercury, NAPA, Office Depot, Von's Foods
77c	(77b from wb) Tennessee St, **N food:** Shakey's Pizza, **other:** Home Depot, **S gas:** Shell, **food:** Arby's, Bakers DriveThru, Burger King, Carl's Jr, Coco's, El Pollo Loco, Papa John's, Subway, Taco Bell, **lodging:** Best Western, Comfort Suites, Dynasty Suites, **other:** Ford, Tri-City Mall, USPO
77b	(77c from wb) CA 30, to Highlands, **S** to Tri-City Mall
77a	Alabama St, **N food:** Chili's, Chick-fil-A, Denny's, Famous Dave's BBQ, Hawaiian BBQ, Jamba Juice,

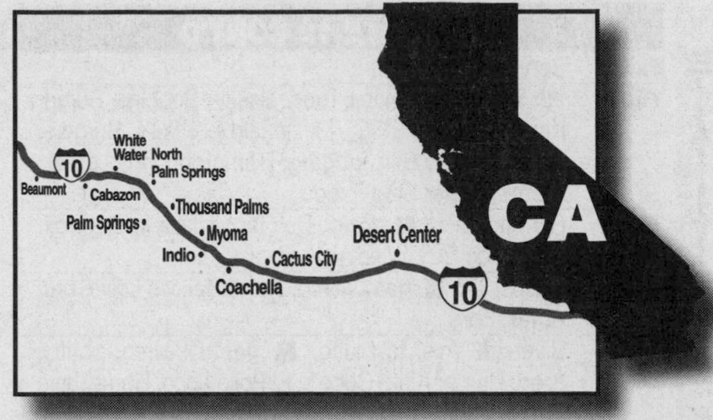

SAN BERNARDINO

Exit #	Services
77a	Continued Macaroni Grill, Mr. Tortilla, Red Robin, Starbucks, **lodging:** Courtyard, Red Lands Motel, Super 8, TownePlace Suites, **other:** Barnes&Noble, Ford, JC Penney, Jo-Ann Superstore, Marshall's, Michael's, PetCo, Target, VW, U-Haul, **S gas:** Arco, Chevron, Flagg, Shell, **food:** Comfort Suites, Del Taco, IHOP, McDonald's, Nick's Burgers, Quizno's, Slim's BBQ, Starbucks, Zabella's Mexican, **lodging:** Best Western, Country Inn&Suites, GoodNite Inn, **other:** Aamco, Chief Parts, Chevrolet, Goodyear/auto, Hyundai, K-Mart, Longs Drug, Nissan, PepBoys, Pic'n Sav Foods, Ross, Toyota, Tri-City Mall
76	California St, **N other:** funpark, museum, **S gas:** Arco/24hr, Shell/LP/24hr, **food:** Applebee's, Jack-in-the-Box, Jose's Mexican, Panda Express, Subway, Weinerschnitzel, Wendy's, **other:** Food4Less, Just Tires, Radio Shack, Walmart/auto, RV camping
75	Mountain View Ave, Loma Linda, **N gas:** Valero/dsl, **S food:** Domino's, FarmerBoys Burgers, Lupe's Mexican, Subway
74	Tippecanoe Ave, Anderson St, **N gas:** Thrifty Gas, **food:** Chipotle Mexican, Denny's, Elephant Bar Rest., El Pollo Loco, In-n-Out, Jack-in-the-Box, Jamba Juice, Pick-Up Stix, Starbucks, Wendy's, **lodging:** American Inn, Fairfield Inn, Residence Inn, **other:** Costco/gas, Sam's Club, Staples, **S gas:** 76/dsl, **food:** Baker's DriveThru, Del Taco, HomeTown Buffet, KFC, Napoli Italian, Taco Bell, Wienerschnitzel, **other:** Audi, Harley-Davidson, Honda, Jaguar, Porsche, Saab, transmissions, to Loma Linda U
73b a	Waterman Ave, **N gas:** 76, Shell/dsl/24hr, **food:** Baja Fresh, Black Angus, Chili's, ChuckeCheese, ClaimJumper, Coco's, Crabby Bob's, El Torito, Guadala-Harry's Diner, IHOP/24hr, King Buffet, Lotus Garden Chinese, Mimi's Café, Olive Garden, Outback Steaks, Panda Express, Pat&Oscar's, Red Lobster, Sizzler, Starbucks, TGIFriday, Togo's, Yamazato Japanese, **lodging:** Best Western, Comfort Inn, Hilton, La Quinta, Quality Inn, Super 8, **other:** Best Buy, Home Depot, Office Depot, PetsMart, **S gas:** Arco/24hr, Beacon/dsl/rest., **food:** Baker's Driv-Thru, Burger King, Gus Jr Burger #8, McDonald's, Popeye's, Starbucks, Taco Bell, **lodging:** Motel 6, **other:** Camping World RV Service/supplies, La Mesa RV Ctr
72	I-215, CA 91
71	Mt Vernon Ave, Sperry Ave, **N gas:** Arco/24hr, **food:** Peppersteak Rest., **lodging:** Colony Inn, **other:** brake/muffler, repair

E ↕ W

SAN BERNARDINO

INTERSTATE 10 CONT'D

Exit #	Services
70b	9th St, **N gas:** Mobil, **food:** Baskin-Robbins, Burger King, Denny's, KFC, McDonald's, P&G's Burgers, Subway, Taco Bell, **lodging:** Hampton Inn, **other:** Parts+, Stater Bros Foods
70a	Rancho Ave, **N food:** Del Taco, Jack-in-the-Box, KFC/Taco Bell, Wienerschnitzel
69	Pepper Dr, **N gas:** Valero, **food:** Baker's DriveThru, **other:** Ford
68	Riverside Ave, to Rialto, **N gas:** Chevron, Thrifty, **food:** Burger King, Coco's, El Pollo Loco, HomeTown Buffet, Jack-in-the-Box, McDonald's, Starbucks, Subway, Taco Joe's, **lodging:** American Inn, Best Western, Rialto Motel, **other:** Walmart, dsl repair, **S gas:** 76/Circle K
66	Cedar Ave, to Bloomington, **N gas:** Arco/24hr, **food:** Baker's DriveThru, Burger King, DQ, FarmerBoys Burgers, Pizza Hut/Taco Bell, **other:** USPO, **S gas:** 7-11
64	Sierra Ave, to Fontana, **N gas:** Arco/24hr, Mobil, Texaco, **food:** Applebee's, Arby's, Billy J's Rest., Burger King, ChuckeyCheese, DQ, Denny's, Del Taco, El Giro Mexican, In-n-Out, Jack-in-the-Box, KFC, McDonald's, Millie's Kitchen, Papa John's, Pizza Hut/Taco Bell, Popeye's, Sizzler, Subway, 3 Hermanos, Wendy's, Wienerschnitzel, **lodging:** Comfort Inn, Econolodge, Guest House Inn, Motel 6, **other:** H, Aamco, Albertson's, BigLots, Chevrolet, $Tree, Food4Less, Goodyear/auto, Honda/GMC, Kia, KidsRUs, K-Mart, Kragen Parts, Mazda, Nissan, PepBoys, Pic'n Sav Foods, Radio Shack, Rite Aid, SavOn Drug, Stater Bros Foods, Winston Tire, **S food:** China Buffet, Circle K/24hr, Fosters Freeze, Nogales Burgers, **other:** Ross, Target
63	Citrus Ave, **N gas:** Beacon/gas, 76, **food:** Baker's DriveThru, Taqueria Mexican, **other:** Ford
61	Cherry Ave, **N gas:** Arco/24hr, Chevron/Taco Bell/dsl, Trucktown Trkstp/dsl/24hr/@, **food:** Carl's Jr, **lodging:** Circle Inn Motel, **other:** Ford Trucks, **S gas:** North American Trkstp/dsl, 3 Sisters Trkstp/dsl/@, 76/Circle K, **food:** Farmer Boy's Rest., Mariscos Mexican, **other:** Peterbilt
59	Etiwanda Ave, Valley Blvd
58b a	I-15, N to Barstow, S to San Diego
57	Milliken Ave, **N gas:** Arco/24hr, Mobil/Subway/dsl, 76/dsl, Shell, **food:** Applebee's, Arby's, BJ's Rest., Boston's, Burger King, Cali Grill, Carl's Jr, Chevy's Mexican, Chipotle, Coldstone Creamery, Dave&Buster's, Del Taco, El Pollo Loco, Famous Dave's BBQ, Fat Burger, Fazoli's, Fuddruckers, HoneyBaked Ham, Krispy Kreme, McDonald's, NY Grill, Olive Garden, Outback Steaks, Quizno's, Rain Forest Cafe, Red Brick Pizza, Red Lobster, Rubio's, Starbucks, Subway, TokyoWako, Wendy's, Wienerschnitzel, Wing Place, **lodging:** Ayre's Suites, Country Inn&Suites, Courtyard, Hampton Inn, Hilton Garden, Holiday Inn, Homewood Suites, Hyatt, TownePlace Suites, **other:** America's Tire, Best Buy, Big O Tire, Costco/gas, JC Penney, Jo-Ann Fabrics, Kohl's, Ontario Mills Mall, Petsmart, Sam's Club/gas, Staples, Steve&Barry's, Target, **S gas:** TA/76/Subway/Taco Bell/dsl/rest./24hr/@, **other:** RV Ctr
56	Haven Ave, Rancho Cucamonga, **N gas:** Mobil, Benihana, **food:** Black Angus, Crabby Bob's Seafood, El Torito, Quizno's, Tony Roma, **lodging:** Best Western, Extended Stay America, Hilton, Holiday Inn, La Quinta, **S food:** Panda Chinese, TGIFriday, **lodging:** Fairfield Inn
55b a	Holt Blvd, to Archibald Ave, **N gas:** Arco, Mobil/dsl, **food:** Baker's Drive-thru, Weinerschnitzel
54	Vineyard Ave, **N gas:** 76/Circle K, Shell, **food:** Del Taco, Carl's Jr., One-Dollar Chinese, Pizza Hut/Taco Bell, Popeye's, Quizno's, Rocky's Foods, Sizzler, **other:** AutoZone, Chief Parts, Ralph's Foods, Rite Aid, Stater Bros Foods, **S gas:** Arco/24hr, Mobil, Shell, USA Gas, **food:** Circle K, Cowboy Bugers, Denny's, In-n-Out, Marie Callender, Michael J's Rest., Rosa's Italian, Spires Rest., Yoshinoya Japanese, Wendy's, **lodging:** Ayers Suites, Best Western, Comfort Inn, Country Suites, Countryside Suites, DoubleTree Inn, Express Inn, GoodNite Inn, Ramada Ltd, Red Roof Inn, Residence Inn, Sheraton, Super 8, **other:** Chevrolet/Cadillac
53	San Bernardino Ave, 4th St, to Ontario, **N gas:** Arco, Chevron, Circle K, Shell, **food:** Baskin-Robbins, Burger King, Carl's Jr, Del Taco, Jack-in-the-Box, Popeye's, Sizzler, Taco Bell/24hr, **lodging:** Motel 6, Quality Inn, **other:** Chief Parts, K-Mart, Radio Shack, Ralph's Foods, Rite Aid, **S gas:** Arco/24hr, 76, **food:** Alfredo's Mexican, Denny's, KFC, McDonald's, Pizza Hut, YumYum Donuts, **lodging:** CA Inn, Travelodge, West Coast Inn
51	CA 83, Euclid Ave, to Ontario, Upland, **N food:** Coco's Rest., **other:** H
50	Mountain Ave, to Mt Baldy, **N gas:** Arco, Chevron, Mobil, Shell/dsl, **food:** BBQ, Carrow's, Denny's, El Burrito, El Torito, Green Burrito, Happy Wok Chinese, Mimi's Café, Mi Taco, Subway, Trader Joe's, Wendy's, **lodging:** Super 8, **other:** Home Depot, Longs Drug of CA, Staples, **S gas:** 76/dsl, **food:** Baskin-Robbins, Carl's Jr, Cold Stone Creamery, El Gran Burrito, Mary's Mexican, Quizno's, **other:** Rite Aid, USPO
49	Central Ave, to Montclair, **N gas:** Chevron, Mobil, Shell/24hr, 7-11, **food:** Burger King, Carl's Jr., El Pollo Loco, Incredible Pizza, Island Burger, KFC, McDonald's, Quizno's, Subway, Tom's Burgers, **other:** Best Buy, Borders Books, Firestone/auto, Goodyear/auto, Hi-Lo Auto Supply, JC Penney, Just Tires, Macy's, Office Depot, PepBoys, Ross, Sears/auto, mall, same as 48, **S gas:** 76, **food:** Jack-in-the-Box, LJ Silver, Subway, Wienerschnitzel, **other:** Acura, Costco/gas, Honda, Infiniti, K-Mart, Macy's, Nissan, Target
48	Monte Vista, **N gas:** Shell, **food:** Acapulco Mexican, Applebee's, Chilis, Black Angus, Elephant Rest., Olive Garden, Red Lobster, Tony Roma, **other:** H, Lens Crafters, Nordstrom's, Macy's, mall, same as 49
47	Indian Hill Blvd, to Claremont, **N gas:** Mobil, **food:** Bakers Square, **lodging:** Claremont Lodge, Howard Johnson, **S gas:** Chevron/McDonald's, 76/dsl, **food:** Burger King, Carl's Jr, Charo Chicken, Denny's, In-n-Out, RoundTable Pizza, 7-11, Starbucks, Wienerschnitzel, **lodging:** Ramada Inn, **other:** Albertson's, America's Tire, AutoZone, Ford, Kia, Radio Shack, Toyota

E ↕ W

INTERSTATE 10 CONT'D

Exit #	Services
46	Towne Ave, **N gas:** 7-11, Puma/Subway/dsl, **food:** Jack-in-the-Box, Subway
45b	Garey Ave, to Pomona, **N gas:** Delta, **other:** H, Vet, **S gas:** Chevron, Shell/dsl, **food:** Del Taco
45	White Ave, Garey Ave, to Pomona
44	(43 from eb) Dudley St, Fairplex Dr, **N gas:** Arco/dsl, **food:** Coppacabana Rest., Denny's, **lodging:** LemonTree Motel, Sheraton, **S gas:** Chevron/24hr, **food:** McDonald's
42b	CA 71 S (from eb), to Corona
42a	I-210 W, CA 57 S
41	Kellogg Dr, **S** to Cal Poly Inst
40	Via Verde
38b	Holt Ave, to Covina, **N food:** Blake's Steaks/seafood, **lodging:** Embassy Suites
38a	Grand Ave, **N gas:** Arco/dsl, **food:** Baily's Rest, Denny's, Japanese/Mongolian/Thai Rest., **lodging:** Best Western
37b	Barranca St, Grand Ave, **N gas:** Shell/repair, **food:** BJ's Rest., Chili's, Dockside Grill, El Torito, Hooters, Marie Callender, Mariposa Mexican, Woodpit BBQ, **lodging:** Best Western, Hampton Inn, Holiday Inn, **other:** Old Navy, Target, **S food:** In-n-Out, McDonald's, **lodging:** Courtyard, 5 Star Inn
37a	Citrus Ave, to Covina, **N gas:** Chevron, **food:** Burger King, Carl's Jr, Del Taco, IHOP, Jack-in-the-Box, TGIFriday, Winchell's, **other:** Acura, Buick, GMC, Honda, Lincoln/Mercury, Longs Drug, Marshall's, Mazda, Office Depot, Old Navy, Ralph's Foods, Ross, Target, Volvo/VW, **S gas:** 76/autocare, **food:** Classic Burger, Trader Joe's, **other:** H, Cadillac
36	CA 39, Azusa Ave, to Covina, **N gas:** Arco/24hr, 76, **food:** Black Angus, Brazillian BBQ, Imperio Rest., McDonald's, Papa John's, Quizno's, Red Lobster, Subway, **lodging:** El Dorado Motel, **other:** Chrysler/Jeep/Dodge, Stater Bro's, **S gas:** Mobil, Shell, **food:** Carrow's, **other:** Honda, Hummer, Toyota
35	Vincent Ave, Glendora Ave, **N gas:** Chevron/24hr, **food:** KFC, Pizza Hut, Wienerschnitzel, **S gas:** 76, **food:** Applebee's, Baja Fresh, Chevy's Mexican, Elephant Rest., Grand Buffet, Pizza Hut, Quizno's, Red Robin, Sakura Japanese, Starbucks, Subway, Weinerschnitzel, **other:** Barnes&Noble, Best Buy, Big O Tire, JC Penney, Macy's, Sears/auto, mall
34	Pacific Ave, **N gas:** 76, **S gas:** Mobil, Shell, **food:** La Posada Mexican, **other:** H, Discount Tire, K-Mart, Goodyear/auto, JC Penney, Jo-Ann Fabrics, Sears, mall, same as 35
33	Puente Ave, **N gas:** Chevron, **food:** A&W/LJ Silver, China Palace, Denny's, Farmer Boy's, Guadalajara Grill, McDonald's, Panda Express, Quizno's, Sizzler, Starbucks, **lodging:** Courtyard, Motel 6, **other:** Home Depot, Staples, Walmart, **S gas:** Valero/dsl, **lodging:** Regency Inn, **food:** Jack-in-the-Box, **other:** Harley-Davidson, U-Haul
32b	Francisquito Ave, to La Puente, **N gas:** V&G, **food:** Papa John's, **other:** hwy patrol, **S gas:** Chevron, **food:** Carl's Jr, In-n-Out, Wienerschnitzel, **lodging:** Grand Park Inn

LOS ANGELES AREA

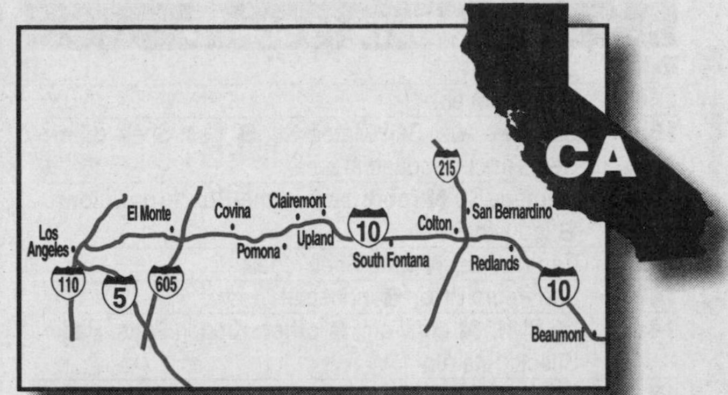

CA

Exit #	Services
32a	Baldwin Pk Blvd, **N gas:** Arco, Chevron/McDonald's, Shell, USA, **food:** Burger King, IHOP, Jack-in-the-Box, Pizza Hut/Taco Bell, Seven Mares Rest., **other:** H, CVS Drug, Food4Less, Target, **S food:** In-n-Out, **other:** Altman's RV Ctr
31c	(31b from wb) Frazier St, **N food:** 7-11, **lodging:** Angel Motel
31b a	(31a from wb) I-605 N/S, to Long Beach
30	Garvey Ave, **S** Prena Gas
29b	Valley Blvd, Peck Rd, **N gas:** Chevron, **food:** Burger King, Carl's Jr., Denny's, KFC, Shakey's Pizza, Yoshinoya, **lodging:** Motel 6, **other:** Ford, Dodge, Goodyear/auto, Honda, K-Mart, Nissan, Toyota/Scion/Lexus, **S gas:** 76/dsl, Shell, **food:** Christina'a Seafood, Del Taco, **other:** Pontiac/GMC
29a	S Peck Rd (from eb)
28	Santa Anita Ave, to El Monte, **N other:** Chevrolet, Hyundai, **S gas:** 76, **food:** 7-11
27	Baldwin Avenue, Temple City Blvd, **S gas:** Arco/24hr, **food:** Denny's, Edward's Steaks, same as 27b a
26b	CA 19, Rosemead Blvd, Pasadena, **N food:** Denny's, IHOP, Subway, **lodging:** Ramona Inn, Rosemead Inn, **other:** Goodyear/auto, Office Depot, Radio Shack, Target, **S food:** Jack-in-the-Box, Quizno's, Starbucks
26a	Walnut Grove Ave
25b	San Gabriel Blvd, **N gas:** Arco, Mobil, Shell/autocare, **food:** Carl's Jr, Popeye's, Taco Bell/Pizza Hut, Wienerschnitzel, **lodging:** Budget Inn, **other:** AutoZone, San Gabriel Foods, **S gas:** 7-11
25a	Del Mar Ave, to San Gabriel, **N gas:** 76, **other:** auto repair, **S gas:** Arco, Chevron/dsl, **lodging:** Best Value
24	New Ave, to Monterey Park, **N gas:** Mobil, to Mission San Gabriel
23b	Garfield Ave, to Alhambra, **S gas:** Shell/dsl, SoCal, **lodging:** Grand Inn, **other:** H
23a	Atlantic Blvd, Monterey Park, **N gas:** Mobil, **food:** Del Taco, Pizza Hut, Popeye's, **other:** H, **S lodging:** Best Western, **other:** Ralph's Foods, auto repair
22	Fremont Ave, **N** H, tuneup, **S** 7-11
21	I-710, Long Beach Fwy, Eastern Ave (from wb)
20b a	Eastern Ave, City Terrace Dr, **S gas:** Chevron/service, Mobil, **food:** Burger King, McDonald's
19c	Soto St (from wb), **N gas:** Shell, Soto Gas, **food:** Burger King, **other:** H, **S gas:** Mobil, Pronto
19b	I-5 (from wb), US 101 S, **N** to Burbank, **S** to San Diego
19a	State St, **N** H
17	I-5 N

LOS ANGELES AREA

INTERSTATE 10 CONT'D

Exit #	Services
16b	I-5 S (from eb)
16a	Santa Fe Ave, San Mateo St, **S gas:** Shell, **other:** Hertz Trucks, industrial area
15b	Alameda St, **N food:** Jack-in-the-Box, to downtown, **S** industrial area
15a	Central Ave, **N gas:** Shell/repair
14b	San Pedro Blvd, **S** industrial
14a	LA Blvd, **N** conv ctr, **S other:** Kragen Parts, Radio Shack, Rite Aid
13	I-110, Harbor Fwy
12	Hoover St, Vermont Ave, **N gas:** Mobil, Texaco, **food:** Burger King, King Donuts, McDonald's, **other:** Honda, PepBoys, Thrifty Drug, Toyota, **S gas:** Amin's Oil/dsl Chevron, Valero/dieses, **food:** Jack-in-the-Box, **other:** Office Depot, Staples
10	Arlington Ave, **N gas:** Chevron, 76, **S** Chevron
9	Crenshaw Blvd, **S gas:** Chevron, Shell, Thrifty, **food:** McDonald's, **other:** U-Haul
8	La Brea Ave, **N gas:** Chevron, Shell/dsl/repair, **other:** Walgreen, transmissions, **S gas:** Chevron, **other:** AutoZone
7b	Washington Blvd, Fairfax Ave, **S gas:** Mobil, same as 8
7a	La Cienega Blvd, Venice Ave (from wb), **N gas:** Chevron/24h, Mobil, **food:** Carl's Jr., Del Taco, **other:** Firestone/auto, **S food:** Subway, **other:** Aamco
6	Robertson Blvd, Culver City, **N gas:** Chevron, Mobil, **food:** Domino's, Taco Bell, **other:** EZ Lube, Goodyear, museum, **S food:** Del Taco, Albertson's, **other:** Ross, SavOn Drug, Ross
5	National Blvd, **N gas:** 76, United Oil, **food:** Papa John's, Starbucks, Subway, **other:** Rite Aid, Von's Foods, **S gas:** Arco, **food:** KFC
4	Overland Ave, **S gas:** Mobil, **food:** Winchell's
3b a	I-405, N to Sacramento, S to Long Beach
2c b	Bundy Dr, **N gas:** Chevron, Shell/dsl, **food:** Eddy's Café, Pizza Hut, Taco Bell, **other:** U-haul
2a	Centinela Ave, to Santa Monica, **N food:** Taco Bell, **S food:** McDonald's, Trader Joe's, **lodging:** Santa Monica Hotel
1c	20th St (from wb), Cloverfield Blvd, 26th St (from wb), **N gas:** Arco, Shell/repair, **other:** [H]
1b	Lincoln Blvd, CA 1 S, **N food:** Denny's, **food:** Norm's Rest., **lodging:** Holiday Inn, **other:** Brake Masters, Jo-Ann Fabrics, Macy's, Sears, Vons Foods, auto repair, transmissions, **S gas:** Chevron/24hr, Exxon, **food:** Jack-in-the-Box, **other:** EZ Lube, Firestone/auto, U-Haul
1a	4th, 5th, (from wb), **N other:** Macy's, Sears, mall
0	Santa Monica Blvd, to beaches, I-10 begins/ends on CA 1.

E ↕ W — LOS ANGELES AREA

INTERSTATE 15

Exit #	Services
298	California/Nevada state line, facilities located at state line, Nevada side
291	Yates Well Rd
286	Nipton Rd, **E** E Mojave Nat Scenic Area, to Searchlight
281	Bailey Rd
276mm	brake check area for trucks, nb
272	Cima Rd, **E gas:** Shell/cafe/dsl/towing
270mm	**Valley Wells Rest Area both lanes, full [handicapped] facilities, [phone], [picnic], litter barrels, petwalk**
265	Halloran Summit Rd
259	Halloran Springs Rd
248	to Baker (from sb), same as 246
246	CA 127, Kel-Baker Rd, Baker, to Death Valley, **W gas:** Arco, Chevron, 76/dsl, Shell/Jack-in-the-Box/dsl, Valero/A&W/Pizza Hut/Subway/TCBY, Valero/DQ/Quizno's/dsl, **food:** Alien Fresh Jerky, Arby's, Big Boy Rest., Burger King, Coco's Rest., Del Taco, Mad Greek Café, Pancake House, **lodging:** BunBoy Motel, Microtel, Will's Fargo Motel, **other:** Baker Mkt Foods, Country Store, World's Largest Thermometer, USPO, repair
245	to Baker (from nb), same as 246
239	Zzyzx Rd
233	Rasor Rd, **E gas:** Rasor Rest Sta/dsl/towing/24hr
230	Basin Rd
221	Afton Rd, to Dunn
217mm	**rest area both lanes, full [handicapped] facilities, [phone], [picnic], litter barrels, petwalk**
213	Field Rd
206	Harvard Rd, to Newberry Springs
198	Minneola Rd, **W** gas/dsl
197mm	**agricultural insp sta sb**
196	Yermo Rd, Yermo
194	Calico Rd
191	Ghost Town Rd, **E gas:** Arco/24hr, Mohsen Oil Trkstp/dsl/24hr, **food:** Jack-in-the-Box, Peggy Sue's 50s Diner, Penny's Diner, **lodging:** OakTree Inn, **W gas:** Shell/dsl/24hr, 76, **other:** Calico GhostTown (3mi), KOA
189	Ft Irwin Rd
186	CA 58 W, to Bakersfield, **W food:** Idle Spur Steaks
184	E Main, Barstow, Montera Rd (from eb), to I-40, **E gas:** 76, **food:** Doughnut Star Chinese, McDonald's, Panda Express, Popeye's, Quizno's, Starbucks, Straw Hat Pizza, Tom's Burgers, **lodging:** Best Western, Travelodge, **S of I-40...gas:** Arco/24hr, **food:** McDonald's, **other:** Walmart/auto/gas, **W gas:** Chevron, Circle K, Shell/dsl, Thrifty Gas, Valero, **food:** Burger King, Carl's Jr, Carrow's Rest., Coco's, Del Taco, Denny's, Firehouse Eatery, Gallardo's Mexican, IHOP, Jack-in-the-Box, KFC, LJ Silver, Los Domingo's, Sizzler, Taco Bell, Wienerschnitzel, **lodging:** Best Motel, Budget Inn, California Inn, Days Inn, Desert Inn, Econolodge, Economy Inn, Motel 6, Quality Inn, Ramada Inn, Rodeway Inn, Stardust Inn, Super 8, **other:** AutoZone, $Tree, Goodyear, Kragen Parts, 99c Store, Radio Shack, U-Haul/LP, Von's Foods, Vet
184a	I-40 E (from nb), I-40 begins/ends
183	CA 247, Barstow Rd, **E gas:** Circle K, Valero/gas, **food:** Pizza Hut, Jimenez Mexican, **other:** Rite Aid, **W gas:** Chevron/24hr, **other:** [H], Food4Less, TrueValue, Mojave River Valley Museum, st patrol,
181	L St, W Main, Barstow, **W gas:** Chevron, Thrifty, Valero/Mrs. B's Diner/dsl, **food:** BunBoy Rest., **lodging:** Best Value Inn, Holiday Inn Express, **other:** Home Depot, NAPA, tires/towing
179	CA 58, to Bakersfield

N ↕ S — BAKER — BARSTOW

CA

INTERSTATE 15 CONT'D

N ↕ S

Exit #	Services
178	Lenwood, to Barstow, **E gas:** Arco/dsl, Chevron/dsl, ***FLYING J***/CountryMkt/dsl/24hr, Shell/24hr, 76/dsl, Valero, **food:** Arby's, Baja Fresh, Big Boy, Burger King, Carl's Jr, Chili's, Coldstone Creamery, Del Taco, Denny's, El Pollo Loco, Food Ct, In-n-Out, Jack-in-the-Box, KFC, Panda Express, Quigley's, Starbucks, Subway, Taco Bell, Tommy's Burgers, **lodging:** Comfort Suites, Country Inn&Suites, Hampton Inn, Holiday Inn Express, **other:** Blue Beacon, Old Navy, Tanger Outlet/famous brands, **W gas:** Loves/dsl, Pilot/Subway/dsl/scales/24hr, 76/dsl/RV dump, TA/Subway/dsl/truckwash/scales/24hr/@, **food:** McDonald's, **lodging:** Days Inn, **other:** Zippy Lube, repair, truckwash
175	Outlet Ctr Dr, Sidewinder Rd, **4 mi E other:** factory outlets
169	Hodge Rd
165	Wild Wash Rd
161	Dale Evans Pkwy, to Apple Valley
157	Stoddard Wells Rd, to Bell Mtn
154	Stoddard Wells Rd, to Bell Mtn, **E other:** Shady Oasis Camping/LP, **W gas:** Mobil, 76, **lodging:** Howard Johnson, Motel 6, Queens Motel
153.5mm	Mojave River
153b	E St
153a	CA 18 E, D St, to Apple Valley, **E gas:** Arco, **other:** H, Cooper Tire, **W gas:** Arco/24hr
151b	Mojave Dr, Victorville, **E gas:** Gasmart/dsl/24hr, **lodging:** Budget Inn, **W gas:** Valero, **lodging:** Economy Inn, Sunset Inn, **other:** transmissions
151a	La Paz Dr, Roy Rogers Dr, **E gas:** Chevron, Shell/dsl, USA/dsl, **food:** Bravo Burgers, Carl's Jr, DQ, HomeTown Buffet, IHOP, Jack-in-the-Box, McDonald's, Wendy's, **other:** Asian Mkt, BigLots, Costco/gas, $Tree, Food4Less, Goodyear/auto, Grocery Outlet, Harley-Davidson, Jo-Ann Fabrics, 99c Store, Rite Aid, Toyota/Scion, same as 144, **W gas:** Arco/24hr, **food:** Carl's Jr, Dominos, Farmer Boys, Hawaiian BBQ, Papa Johns, Starbucks, Subway, **other:** Americas Tire, Chrysler/Dodge/Jeep, Curves, GMC/Nissan/Pontiac, Home Depot, Honda, Kia, Stater Bros, Winco Foods
150	CA 18 W, Palmdale Rd, Victorville, **E food:** Baker's Drive-Thru, Burger King, Denny's, KFC, Richie's Diner, Starbucks, **lodging:** Quality Inn/Greentree, Red Roof Inn, **W gas:** Arco, Shell, Valero, **food:** Coco's, Del Taco, McDonald's, Pizza Hut, Starbucks, Subway, Taco Bell, Tom's Rest., **lodging:** Ambassador Inn, Budget Inn, Days Inn, **other:** H, Aamco, AutoZone, Ford/Lincoln/Mercury, Hyundai, Kamper's Korner RV, Target, Town&Country Tire, Vet
147	Bear Valley Rd, to Lucerne Valley, **E gas:** Arco/24hr, Chevron, Mobil, 76/Circle K, **food:** A&W, Arby's, Baker's Drive-Thru, Blimpie, Burger King, Carl's Jr, Del Taco, Dragon Express, John's Pizza, KFC, Los Toritos Mexican, Marie Callender's, McDonald's, Panda Express, Pizza Palace, Popeye's, Red Robin, Starbucks, Steer'n Stein, TNT Café, Wienerschnitzel, Winchell's, **lodging:** Comfort Suites, Econolodge, Extended Studio Hotel, Hilton Garden, La Quinta,

VICTORVILLE

VICTORVILLE

Exit #	Services
147	Continued Super 8, Travelodge, **other:** Affordable RV Ctr, AutoZone, EZ Lube, Firestone/auto, Home Depot, Kragen Parts, Michael's, Range RV, Staples, Tire Depot, Vallarta Foods, Walmart/auto, Vet, **W gas:** Arco, Chevron, 76/Circle K, Valero, **food:** Applebee's, Archibald's Drive-Thru, Baja Fresh, Baskin-Robbins, Carino's, Chili's, ChuckeCheese, Cold Stone Creamery, El Pollo Loco, El Tio Pepe Mexican, Farmer Boy's Rest., Jack-in-the-Box, Jake's BBQ, Little Caesar's, Maan Fu Chinese, Mimi's Cafe, Olive Garden, Outback Steaks, Red Lobster, RoadHouse Grill, Sonic, Starbucks, Subway, Wendy's, **lodging:** Hawthorn Suites, **other:** Albertson's, Barnes&Noble, Best Buy, CVS Drug, JC Penney, Kohl's, Lowe's Whse, 99c Store, Petsmart, Range RV Ctr, Rite Aid, Sears/auto, Stater Bro's, Walgreens, World Mkt, mall
143	Main St, to Hesperia, Phelan, **E gas:** Chevron, Shell/Popeye's/dsl, Valero/Alberto's/DQ/pizza, **food:** Arby's, Burger King, Denny's, IHOP, In-n-Out, Jack-in-the-Box, Starbucks, **lodging:** Courtyard, SpringHill Suites, **W gas:** Arco/dsl/24hr, 76/Big Boy/dsl, **food:** Baker's Drive-thru, **lodging:** Holiday Inn Express, Motel 6, **other:** SuperTarget, RV camping
141	US 395, Joshua St, Adelanto, **W gas:** Pilot/Wendy's/dsl/scales/24hr, **food:** Newt's Outpost Café, **other:** Goodyear, Zippy Lube, repair, truck/RV wash
138	Oak Hill Rd, **E gas:** Shell/dsl, **food:** Summit Inn/café, **W other:** RV camping, LP
132	Cajon Summit, elevation 4260, **brake check sb**
131	CA 138, to Palmdale, Silverwood Lake, **E gas:** Chevron/McDonald's/24hr, **W gas:** 76/Circle K/Del Taco/LP, Shell/Subway/dsl, **lodging:** Best Western
131mm	**weigh sta both lanes**, elevation 3000
129	Cleghorn Rd
124	Kenwood Ave
123	I-215 S, to San Bernardino, **E gas:** Arco/24hr, to Glen Helen Park
122	Glen Helen Parkway
119	Sierra Ave, **W gas:** Arco/Jack-in-the-Box/dsl/24hr, Chevron/McDonald's/dsl, Shell/Del Taco/dsl, Valero/dsl, **other:** to Lytle Creek RA
116	Summit Ave, **E gas:** Chevron, 7-11, **food:** Chili's, Del Taco, El Ranchero, Hawaiian BBQ, Jack-in-the-Box, Paisano Ristorante, Panera Bread, Quizno's, Roundtable Pizza, Starbucks, Subway, Taco Bell, Wendy's, **other:** CVS Drug, GNC, Kohl's, Marshall's, Michael's, PetsMart, Ross, Staples, Stater Bro's, Target
115b a	CA 210, Highland Ave, **E** to Lake Arrowhead

CA

INTERSTATE 15 CONT'D

N ↕ S

Exit #	Services
113	Base Line Rd, **E gas:** USA, **food:** Denny's, Jack-in-the-Box, Logans Roadhouse, Pizza Hut, Rosa Maria's, Starbucks, **lodging:** Comfort Inn
112	CA 66, Foothill Blvd, **E gas:** Chevron, **food:** Arby's, ClaimJumper Rest., Golden Spoon, In-n-Out, Panda Buffet, Panda Express, Pizza Hut, Wienerschnitzel, **other:** Food4Less, Walmart/auto, **1-2 mi W gas:** Chevron/dsl, 76/dsl/Subway, **food:** Buffalo Wild Wings, Carino's, Cheesecake Factory, Chick-fil-A, Del Taco, Denny's, El Pollo Loco, El Torito, Harry's Grill, Jack-in-the-Box, Joe's Crab Shack, Old Spagetti Factory, Omaha Jack's Steaks, PF Chang's, Popeyes, Red Robin, Starbucks, TGIFriday, Wendy's, **lodging:** 4 Points, **other:** AutoZone, Bass Pro Shops, Border's Books, Macy's, Home Depot, JC Penney, Office Depot, Sears Grand, See's Candy
110	4th St, **E gas:** Arco/dsl, **food:** Baker's Drive-Thru, Subway, **W gas:** Arco/24hr, Mobil/Subway/dsl, 76/dsl, Shell, **food:** Applebee's, Arby's, BJ's Rest., Boston's, Burger King, Cali Grill, Carl's Jr, Chevy's Mexican, Chipotle, Coldstone Creamery, Dave&Buster's, Del Taco, El Pollo Loco, Famous Dave's BBQ, Fat Burger, Fazoli's, Fuddruckers, HoneyBaked Ham, Krispy Kreme, McDonald's, NY Grill, Olive Garden, Outback Steaks, Quizno's, Rain Forest Cafe, Red Brick Pizza, Red Lobster, Rubio's, Starbucks, Subway, TokyoWako, Wendy's, Wienerschnitzel, Wing Place, **lodging:** Ayre's Suites, Country Inn&Suites, Courtyard, Hampton Inn, Hilton Garden, Holiday Inn, Homewood Suites, Hyatt, TownePlace Suites, **other:** America's Tire, Best Buy, Big O Tire, Costco/gas, JC Penney, Jo-Ann Fabrics, Kohl's, Ontario Mills Mall, Petsmart, Sam's Club/gas, Staples, Steve&Barry's, Target
109b a	I-10, E to San Bernardino, W to LA
108	Jurupa St, **E gas:** Chevron, **food:** Del Taco, Starbucks, **other:** Affordable RV, BMW, Chrysler/Dodge/Jeep, Honda, Hyuandai, Lexus, Mazda, Nissan, Toyota/Scion, Volvo, VW, **W gas:** Arco/24hr, **food:** Carl's Jr, **other:** Ford, Kia, Lincoln/Mercury, Scandia funpark
106	CA 60, E to Riverside, W to LA
105	Cantu-Galleano Ranch Rd
103	Limonite Ave, **E food:** Carl's Jr, Charro Chicken, Del Taco, Denny's, Hawaiian BBQ, Jamba Juice, **other:** Lowe's Whse, Michael's, PetCo, Ross, **W food:** Applebee's, Carino's, Coldstone Creamery, El Grande Burrito, Farmer Boys, On-the-Border, Quizno's, Red Brick Pizza, Starbucks, Subway, Wendy's, **other:** Best Buy, Border's Books, Curves, GNC, Home Depot, Kohl's, PetsMart, Ralph's Foods/gas, Staples, Target, TJ Maxx, Vons Foods/gas
100	6th St, Norco Dr, Old Town Norco, **E gas:** Chevron/24hr, Exxon/dsl, **food:** Jack-in-the-Box, McDonald's, **other:** Rite Aid, **W gas:** Arco/24hr, Valero, **food:** Big Boy, Izzy's Mexican, Norco's Burgers, Starbucks, Wienerschnitzel, **lodging:** Guesthouse Inn, **other:** Brake Masters, Jiffy Lube, USPO, Vet

ONTARIO

Exit #	Services
98	2nd St, **W gas:** 76/dsl, Shell/dsl, Thrifty, **food:** Arby's, Burger King, Del Taco, Domino's, In-n-Out, Magic Wok, Pizza Hut, Polly's Cafe, Sizzler, **lodging:** Hampton Inn, Howard Johnson Express, **other:** America's Tire, Chrysler/Dodge/Jeep, Ford, Mazda, Mitsubishi, Norco RV, 7-11, Stater Bro's
97	Yuma Dr, Hidden Valley Pkwy, **E gas:** 7-11, **food:** Baja Fresh, Chick-fil-A, Fat Burger, **other:** Kohl's, Stater Bro's, **W gas:** Chevron, 76/dsl, Shell/dsl, **food:** Alberto's Mexican, Burger City Grill, Carl's Jr, Chipotle, Denny's, Hickory Joe's BBQ, Jamba Juice, Jack-in-the-Box, KFC, McDonald's, Miguel's, Papa John's, Pizza Hut, Quizno's, Rodrigo's Mexican, Round Table Pizza, Rubio's, Starbucks, Taco Bell, **other:** Albertson's, AutoZone, Big Lots, GNC, Kragen Parts, Radio Shack, Sears Essentials, Staples, Target, Walgreens
96b a	CA 91, to Riverside, beaches
95	Magnolia Ave, **E gas:** Chevron/dsl, **food:** Blackwoods Grill, Chui's Rest., Islands Grill, Jack-in-the-Box, Lonestar Steaks, **lodging:** Residence Inn, **other:** Lowe's Whse, Office Depot, **W gas:** Mobil, Shell, **food:** A&W/LJ Silver, Burger King, Carl's Jr, Coco's, McDonald's, Pizza Palace, Sizzler, Subway, Zendejas Mexican, **lodging:** Holiday Inn Express, **other:** CVS Drug, $Tree, El Tapatio, Kragen Parts, Rite Aid, Stater Bros Foods
93	Ontario Ave, to El Cerrito, **E gas:** Shell, **food:** Starbucks, **W gas:** Arco/24hr, Chevron/24hr, 76, **food:** Chopstix, Denny's, Eatza Pizza, Hawaiian BBQ, In-n-Out, Jack-in-the-Box, KFC, Magic Wok, McDonald's, Miguel's Mexican, Quizno's, Rubio's, Taco Bell, Tommy's Burgers, Wienerschnitzel, **food:** SpringHill Suites, **other:** Albertson's/Starbucks, Home Depot, Long's Drug, Radio Shack, Sam's Club/gas, USPO, Walmart/auto, Vet
92	El Cerrito Rd
91	Cajalco Rd, **E food:** BJ's Grill, Chick-fil-A, Chili's, Jamba Juice, King's Fish House, Macaroni Grill, Miguel's, On-the-Border, Panera Bread, Rosine's Grill, Starbucks, Wendy's, **other:** Barnes&Noble, Best Buy, Kohl's, Marshall's, Michael's, Old Navy, PetCo, Ross, See's Candies, Staples, Target, World Mkt, **W gas:** Mobil/dsl, **food:** Golden Spoon, Jack-in-the-Box, NY Pizza, Subway, **other:** Stater Bros
90	Weirick Rd, Dos Lagos Dr, **E food:** Citrus City Grill, Marble Slab Creamery, Miguel's, Starbucks, Tap's Rest., TGIFriday, Wood Ranch BBQ, **other:** 7 Oaks Gen Store
88	Temescal Cyn Rd, Glen Ivy, **E gas:** Shell, **W gas:** Arco/dsl/24hr, **food:** Carl's Jr, Tom's Farms/BBQ
85	Indian Truck Trail, **W food:** Starbucks, Subway, **other:** Von's Foods/gas, CVS Drug
81	Lake St
78	Nichols Rd, **W gas:** Arco/24hr, **other:** Outlets/famous brands
77	CA 74, Central Ave, Lake Elsinore, **E gas:** Arco/24hr, Chevron, Mobil/dsl, **food:** Archibald's, Burger King, Chili's, Coffee Bean, Coldstone Creamery, Del Taco, Douglas Burgers, Hawaiian BBQ, Panda Express, Submarina, Taco Del Mar, Wendy's, **other:** Costco/gas, $Tree, EZ Lube, Lowes Whse, PetsMart, Staples, **W food:** El Pollo Loco, Farmer Boys, IHOP,

EL CERRITO

INTERSTATE 15 CONT'D

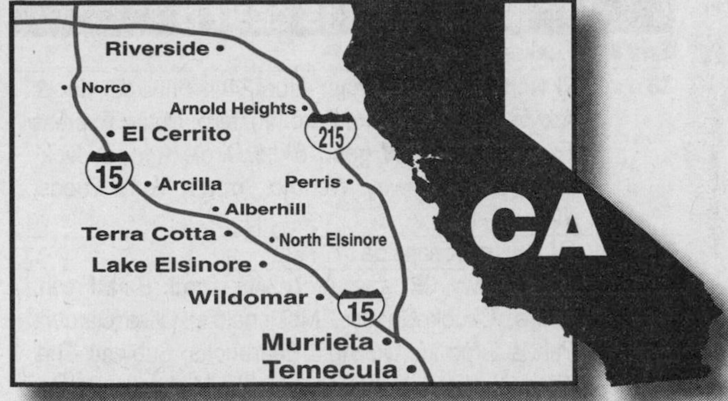

Exit #	Services
77	Continued McDonald's, **other:** Home Depot, 99c Store, PetCo, Target, Walgreens
75	Main St, Lake Elsinore, **W gas:** 76, **lodging:** Elsinore Motel, **other:** Circle K, tires/repair
73	Railroad Cyn Rd, to Lake Elsinore, **E gas:** Shell/Circle K, 76/Circle K, **food:** Denny's, El Pollo Loco, In-n-Out, KFC, Peony Chinese, Quizno's, Starbucks, **lodging:** Holiday Inn Express, **other:** GNC, Jiffy Lube, Kragen Parts, Von's Foods, Walmart/auto, **W gas:** Arco, Chevron, Mobil/dsl, **food:** Cafe China, Carl's Jr, Coco's, Del Taco, Don Jose's Mexican, Don Ruben's Mexican, McDonald's, Pizza Hut, Sizzler, Subway, Taco Bell, **lodging:** Best Western Lake View, Quality Inn, Travel Inn, **other:** Albertson's, AutoZone, BigLots, BrakeMasters, Buick/GMC/Pontiac, Chevrolet, CVS Drug, Do-It Hardware, Express Tire/auto, Ford, NAPA, Radio Shack, Rite Aid, SavOn Drug, 7-11, Vet
71	Bundy Cyn Rd, **W gas:** Arco/24hr, **food:** Jack-in-the-Box
69	Baxter Rd, **E food:** Pizza Factory
68	Clinton Keith Rd, **E gas:** Chevron/dsl, USA, **food:** Arby's, Denny's, Golden Spoon, La Cresta Mexican, McDonald's, Panda Express, Starbucks, Subway, **other:** H, Ace Hardware, Albertsons/Sav-on, **W gas:** Arco, 7-11, **food:** Charro Chicken, China Panda, Del Taco, Jack-in-the-Box, Olivera's Rest., Starbucks, **other:** Stater Bro's
65	California Oaks Rd, Kalmia St, **E gas:** Chevron, Mobil/dsl, 76/Circle K, Shell/dsl, **food:** Burger King, Cal Oaks Burger, Carl's Jr, Chili's, DQ, Jimenez Mexican, KFC, Little Caesar's, Papa John's, Starbucks, **lodging:** Comfort Inn, **other:** Albertson's/Sav-On, AutoZone, Big O Tire, Express Tire, $Tree, Kragen Parts, Radio Shack, Rite Aid, Ross, Target, Tuesday Morning, Walgreens, Vet, **W gas:** Arco/24hr, Chevron, **food:** Applebee's, Carrow's, Chick-fil-A, Farmer Boys, Jack-in-the-Box, RJ's Grill, Stix Rest., **other:** America's Tire, Giant RV Ctr, Kohl's, Lowe's Whse, Office Depot, PetCo, fun ctr
64	Murrieta Hot Springs Rd, to I-215, **E gas:** 7-11, Shell/dsl, **food:** Alberto's Mexican, Baja Grill, Buffalo Wild Wings, Carl's Jr, El Pollo Loco, Gourmet Italian, Richie's Diner, Rubio's, Seafood Grill, Sizzler, Starbucks, Wendy's, **other:** Ralph's Foods, Rite Aid, Ross, Sam's Club/gas, Walgreens, **W gas:** 7-11, Shell/Popeyes/dsl, **food:** Alberto's Mexican, Arby's, Chuy's, Coldstone Creamery, Denny's, IHOP, McDonald's, MegaToms, Panda Express, Quizno's, Starbucks, Subway, Wienerschnitzel, **other:** Best Buy, Big Lots, Home Depot, 99c Store, PetsMart, Staples, Walmart/auto
63	I-215 N (from nb), to Riverside
61	CA 79 N, Winchester Rd, **E gas:** Chevron, 76/dsl, **food:** Alberto's Mexican, Baja Fresh, Baskin-Robbins/Togo's, Bj's Rest., Burger King, Carino's, Carl's Jr, Coldstone Creamery, Del Taco, El Torito, Harry's Grill, Jamba Juice, La Salsa, Lucille's BBQ, Macaroni Grill, McDonald's, Olive Garden, On-the-Border, Outback Steaks, Panda Express, PF Chang's,
61	Continued Red Lobster, Roadhouse Grill, Ruby's Diner, Shogun Chinese, Souplantation, Starbucks, Subway, Taco Bell, TGIFriday, Togo's, Yellow Basket Hamburgers, **other:** America's Tire, AutoZone, Barnes&Noble, Big O Tire, Costco/gas, Food4Less, Express Tire, JC Penney, Jo-Ann Fabrics, K-Mart, Kragen Parts, Longs Drug, Lowe's Whse, Macy's, Office Depot, PepBoys, PetCo, Sears/auto, See's Candies, TJ Maxx, VW, WinCo Foods, World Mkt, **W gas:** Arco/24hr, Chevron/dsl, **food:** Arby's, Banzai Japanese, Big Boy, Del Taco, El Pollo Loco, Farmer Boys, Hungry Hunter, In-n-Out, Jack-in-the-Box, Sizzler, Starbucks, Subway, Super China, Wendy's, **lodging:** Best Western, Extended Stay America, Fairfield Inn, Holiday Inn Express, La Quinta, Quality Inn, **other:** Hyundai, NAPA, Richardson's RV Ctr, st patrol, tires/repair
59	Rancho California Rd, **E gas:** Arco, Mobil/dsl, Shell/dsl, Valero, **food:** Black Angus, Chili's, ClaimJumper, Del Taco, Daphne's Greek, Marie Callender's, Pat & Oscar's Rest., Pizza Hut, RoundTable Pizza, Rubio's, Texas Loosey's, Starbucks, Subway, **lodging:** Embassy Suites, **other:** Big Lots, CVS Drug, Michael's, Target, Von's Foods, Vet, **W gas:** Chevron, 76/Circle K/dsl, **food:** Denny's, KFC, McDonald's, Mexico Chiquito's, Penfold's Cafe, Rosa's Café, **lodging:** Hampton Inn, Motel 6, Rancho California Inn, Rodeway Inn, SpringHill Suites, **other:** USPO
58	CA 79 S, to Indio, Temecula, **E gas:** Mobil/dsl, Valero/Circle K/dsl, **food:** Carl's Jr, Del Taco, Domino's, In-n-Out, Starbucks, other, Ace Hardware, America's Tire, EZ Lube, Longs Drug, 7-11, **W gas:** Arco, Shell/dsl/24hr, **food:** 7 Mares Grill, Western Burrito, Wienerschnitzel, **lodging:** Ramada Inn, **other:** Express Tire, Harley-Davidson
55mm	**check sta nb**
54	Rainbow Valley Blvd, **2 mi E** gas, food, **W CA Insp Sta**
51	Mission Rd, to Fallbrook, **W** H
46	CA 76, to Oceanside, Pala, **E other:** RV camp, **W gas:** Mobil, **lodging:** Comfort Inn
44mm	San Luis Rey River
43	Old Hwy 395
41	Gopher Canyon Rd, Old Castle Rd, **1 mi E lodging:** Welk Resort, **other:** RV camping, gas
37	Deer Springs Rd, Mountain Meadow Rd, **W gas:** Arco/24hr
34	Centre City Pkwy (from sb)

INTERSTATE 15 CONT'D

N ↕ S ESCONDIDO

Exit #	Services
33	El Norte Pkwy, **E gas:** Arco/24hr, Shell/dsl, **food:** Arby's, IHOP, **lodging:** Best Western, **other:** Express Tire, RV Resort, **W gas:** 76/dsl, Circle K, **food:** Jack-in-the-Box, Subway, Wendy's, **other:** Von's Foods, Vet
32	CA 78, to Oceanside
31	Valley Pkwy, **E gas:** Arco/24hr, **food:** Baja Fresh, Chili's, ChuckeCheese, McDonald's, Olive Garden, Panda Express, Quizno's, Starbucks, Subway, Thai Kitchen, **other:** [H], Barnes&Noble, Michael's, PetCo, mall, **W gas:** Express, **food:** Applebee's, Burger King, Carl's Jr, Coco's, Del Taco, Jamba Juice, La Salsa Grill, Panera Bread, Wendy's, **lodging:** Comfort Inn, Holiday Inn Express, **other:** Albertson's, Big Lots, Dodge, Home Depot, Long's Drug, 7-11, Staples, Target, TJ Maxx, World Mkt
30	9th Ave, Auto Parkway, **E other:** Infiniti, Mercedes, same as 31
29	Felicita Rd
28	Centre City Pkwy (from nb, no return), **E food:** Center City Café, **lodging:** Palms Inn
27	Via Rancho Pkwy, to Escondido, **E gas:** Chevron/24hr, Shell, **food:** Macaroni Grill, On-the-Border, Onami Grill, Panera Bread, Red Robin, **other:** JC Penney, Macy's, Nordstrom's, Sears/auto, San Diego Animal Park, mall, **W gas:** Shell/Subway/dsl, **food:** McDonald's, Starbucks
26	W Bernardo Dr, to Highland Valley Rd, Palmerado Rd
24	Rancho Bernardo Rd, to Lake Poway, **E gas:** Arco/24hr, Mobil, **food:** Domino's, Soup Plantatino, Stirfresh, **lodging:** Hilton Garden, **other:** Barons, Von's Foods, **W gas:** 76/Circle K, Shell/repair, **food:** Elephant Bar Rest., Hooters, Starbucks, **lodging:** Holiday Inn, Rodeway Inn
23	Bernardo Ctr Dr, **E gas:** Chevron, **food:** Burger King, Carl's Jr, Coco's, Denny's, El Torito, Rubio's Grill, **other:** CVS Drug, Express Tire/auto, Firestone/auto, Vet
22	Camino del Norte
21	Carmel Mtn Rd, **E gas:** Chevron, Shell, **food:** Baskin-Robbins, Boston Mkt, CA Pizza Kitchen, Carl's Jr, Cheeburger Cheeburger, Chevy's Mexican, ClaimJumper, El Pollo Loco, In-n-Out, Islands Burgers, JambaJuice, Joey's BBQ, Marie Callender's, McDonald's, Olive Garden, Quizno's, Panera Bread, Rubio's Grill, Subway, Taco Bell, TGIFriday, Thigo Rest., Wendy's, **lodging:** Residence Inn, **other:** Barnes&Noble, Borders Books, Costco, EZ Lube, GNC, Home Depot, Marshall's, Michael's, PetCo, Ralph's Foods, Rite Aid, Ross, Sears Essentials, Staples, Trader Joes, USPO, **W gas:** Chevron, **food:** Jack-in-the-Box, Starbucks, **other:** Albertson's, Big O Tire, Office Depot, 7-11
19	CA 56 W, Ted Williams Pkwy
18	Rancho Penasquitos Blvd, Poway Rd, **E gas:** Arco/24hr, **W gas:** Exxon/dsl, Mobil/dsl, 76/dsl, **food:** IHOP, McDonald's, Mi Ranchito Mexican, NY Pizza, Starbucks, Subway, **lodging:** La Quinta, **other:** 7-11

SAN DIEGO AREA

Exit #	Services
17	Mercy Rd, Scripps Poway Pkwy, **E gas:** USA/dsl, **food:** Chili's, Fish Grille, Wendy's, **lodging:** Residence Inn, Springhill Suites, **W gas:** Chevron, **food:** KFC, Starbucks
16	Mira Mesa Blvd, to Lake Miramar, **E food:** Denny's, Filippi's Pizza, Golden Crown Chinese, Lucio's Mexican, Pizza Hut, Shozen BBQ, **lodging:** Holiday Inn Express, Quality Suites, **other:** Curves, USPO, **W gas:** Arco/24hr, Shell, **food:** Applebee's, Arby's, Buca Italian, Café China, Coldstone Creamery, In-n-Out, Islands Burgers, Jack-in-the-Box, Jamba Juice, McDonald's, Mimi's Café, On the Border, Pat & Oscar's Rest., Panera Bread, Pick Up Stix, Popeye's, Rubio's, Santana's Mexican, Starbucks, Togo's, **other:** Albertson's, AutoZone, Barnes&Noble, Best Buy, Big Lots, Home Depot, Long's Drug, Old Navy, Ralph's Foods, Rite Aid, Ross, USPO
15	Carroll Canyon Rd, to Miramar College, **E food:** Carl's Jr
14	Pomerado Rd, Miramar Rd, **W gas:** Arco/dsl, Chevron/dsl, Mobil, Shell/24hr, **food:** Carl's Jr, Chin's Rest., Keith's Rest., Subway, **lodging:** Best Western, Budget Inn, Holiday Inn, **other:** Audi/Porsche/VW, Land Rover, Vet
13	Miramar Way, US Naval Air Station
12	CA 163 S (from sb), to San Diego
11	to CA 52
10	Clairemont Mesa Blvd, **W food:** Boll Weevil Rest., Carl's Jr, Giovanni's Pizza, Jack-in-the-Box, La Salsa, McDonald's, Mr. Chick's Rest., Panda Express, Rubio's, Spice House Cafe, Starbucks, Subway, Sunny Donuts, Taco Bell, Togo's, Wendy's, **other:** 7-11
9	CA 274, Balboa Ave
8	Aero Dr, **W gas:** Arco/24hr, 7-11, Shell, **food:** Baja Fresh, Baskin Robbins, Jack-in-the-Box, McDonald's, Papa John's, Pick Up Stix, Sizzler, Starbucks, Submarina, Taco Bell, **lodging:** Holiday Inn, **other:** $Tree, Express Tire/auto, Fry's Electronics, PetSmart, Radio Shack, Von's Foods, Walmart/auto
7b	Friars Rd W, **W food:** Coldstone Creamery, Dragon Chinese, IHOP, Islands Burgers, Little Fish Mkt, McDonald's, Mondo's Mexican, Oggi's Pizza, Starbucks, Subway, **other:** Costco/gas, Lowes Whse, San Diego Stadium
7a	Friars Rd E
6b	I-8, E to El Centro, W to beaches
6a	Adams Ave, downtown
5b	El Cajon Blvd, **E gas:** Pearson, **food:** Subway, **other:** Carquest, **W gas:** Chevron/dsl, **other:** Pep Boys
5a	University Ave, **E gas:** Chevron/dsl, **food:** Burger King, Jack-in-the-Box, **other:** USPO
3	I-805, N to I-5, S to San Ysidro
2b	(2c from nb) CA 94 W, downtown
2a	Market St, downtown
1c	National Ave, Ocean View Blvd
1b	(from sb) I-5 S, to Chula Vista
1a	(from sb) I-5 N. I-15 begins/ends on I-5

INTERSTATE 40

Exit #	Services
155	California/Arizona state line, Colorado River, Pacific/Mountain time zone
153	Park Moabi Rd, to Rte 66, **N** boating, camping

INTERSTATE 40 CONT'D

Exit #	Services
149mm	**insp both lanes**
148	5 Mile Rd, to Topock, Rte 66 (from eb)
144	US 95 S, E Broadway, Needles, **N gas:** Chevron/dsl, Mobil, Shell/dsl, **food:** Domino's, **other:** Basha's Foods, Laundry, Rite Aid, **S lodging:** Best Value, **other:** $Tree, tires/repair
142	J St, Needles, **N gas:** 76/24hr, Valero, **food:** Jack-in-the-Box, McDonald's, **lodging:** Travelers Inn, **other:** NAPA, **S food:** Denny's, **lodging:** Day's Inn, Motel 6, **other:** [H], st patrol
141	W Broadway, River Rd, Needles, **N food:** KFC, **lodging:** Best Motel, Desert Mirage Inn, River Valley Motel, **S gas:** Arco/24hr, Chevron/dsl/24hr, Mobil/dsl, Shell/DQ/24hr, **food:** Carl's Jr, China Garden, River Cafe, Taco Bell, **lodging:** Best Western, Budget Inn, Needles Inn, Relax Inn, **other:** Chevrolet/Cadillac/Buick/GMC, auto/RV/tire/repair
139	River Rd Cutoff (from eb), **N** rec area, Hist Rte 66, **other:** KOA, Desert View RV Park
133	US 95 N, to Searchlight, to Rte 66
120	Water Rd
115	Mountain Springs RdMountain Springs Rd, High Springs Summit, elev 2770
107	Goffs Rd, **N** gas/dsl/food, Hist Rte 66
106mm	**rest area both lanes, full ♿ facilities, ☎, ⛱, litter barrels, petwalk**
100	Essex Rd, Essex, **N** to Providence Mtn SP, Mitchell Caverns
78	Kelbaker Rd, to Amboy, E Mojave Nat Preserve, Kelso, **S** Hist Rte 66, **other:** RV camping (14mi)
50	Ludlow, **N gas:** 76/DQ/24hr, **S gas:** Chevron, **food:** Coffee Shop, **lodging:** Ludlow Motel
33	Hector Rd, to Hist Rte 66
28mm	**rest area both lanes, full ♿ facilities, ☎, ⛱, litter barrels, petwalk**
23	Ft Cady Rd, **N gas:** Texaco/dsl/24hr, **S lodging:** Newberry Mtn RV Park
18	Newberry Springs, **N other:** Calico/dsl, **S gas:** Chevron/Kelly's Grill/LP
12	Barstow-Daggett ✈, **N** ✈
7	Daggett, **N other:** RV camping (2mi), to Calico Ghost Town
5	Nebo St (from eb), to Hist Rte 66
2	USMC Logistics Base, **N lodging:** Pennywise Inn
1	E Main St, Montara Rd, Barstow, **N gas:** 76, **food:** Doughnut Star Chinese, McDonald's, Panda Express, Popeye's, Quizno's, Starbucks, Straw Hat Pizza, Tom's Burgers, **lodging:** Best Western, Travelodge, **1 mi N gas:** Arco/24hr, Chevron, 76/Circle K/Subway/TCBY, Shell, **food:** Arby's, Burger King, Carl's Jr, Carrow's Rest., China Gourmet, Coco's, Del Taco, Denny's, FireHouse Italian, Golden Dragon, IHOP, Jack-in-the-Box, KFC, LJ Silver, Sizzler, Taco Bell, **lodging:** AstroBudget Motel, Best Motel, Budget Inn, Comfort Inn, Day's Inn, Desert Inn, Econolodge, Economy Inn, Executive Inn, Quality Inn, Ramada Inn, Super 8, **other:** AutoZone, Kragen Parts, Radio Shack, U-Haul/LP, Von's Foods, **S gas:** Arco/24hr, **other:** Walmart/McDonald's/auto/gas
0mm	I-40 begins/ends on I-15 in Barstow

INTERSTATE 80

Exit #	Services
208	California/Nevada state line
201	Farad
199	Floristan
194	Hirschdale Rd, **N** to Boca Dam, Stampede Dam
191mm	**(from wb), weigh sta., inspection sta.**
190	Overland Trail
188	CA 89 N, CA 267, to N Shore Lake Tahoe, **N other:** USFS, **S** same as 186
186	Central Truckee (no eb return), **S gas:** Beacon, 76, **food:** Burger Mee, Casa Baeza Mexican, El Toro Bravo Mexican, Wagontrain Café, **lodging:** Hilltop Lodge, Truckee Hotel
185	CA 89 S, to N Lake Tahoe, **N food:** DQ, Jiffy's Pizza, Nick'n Willy's Pizza, Panda Express, Port of Subs, RoundTable Pizza, Starbucks, Zano's Pizza, **other:** [H], URGENT CARE, Ace Hardware, GNC, NAPA, New Moon Natural Foods, Radio Shack, Rite Aid, Safeway, 7-11, hwy patrol, **S gas:** Shell/dsl, **food:** Cheesesteak, KFC, McDonald's, Mongolian BBQ, Pizzaria, Subway, **other:** Longs Drugs, Savemart Foods, auto repair, to Squaw Valley, RV camping
184	Donner Pass Rd, Truckee, **N gas:** Shell/dsl, **food:** La bamba Mexican, Pizza Shack, Smokey's Kitchen, **lodging:** Sunset Inn, **other:** factory outlet/famous brands, **S gas:** Chevron/dsl/24hr, 76, **food:** Taco Bell, **lodging:** Holiday Inn Express, **other:** chain service, to Donner SP, RV camp/dump
181mm	vista point both lanes
180	Donner Lake (from wb), **S lodging:** Donner Lake Village Resort
177mm	**Donner Summit, elev 7239, rest area both lanes, full ♿ facilities, view area, ☎, ⛱, litter barrels, petwalk**
176	Castle Park, Boreal Ridge Rd, **S lodging:** Boreal Inn/rest., **other:** Pacific Crest Trailhead, skiing
174	Soda Springs, Norden, **S gas:** Beacon/LP/dsl, **food:** Summit Rest., **lodging:** Donner Summit Lodge, **other:** chain services
171	Kingvale, **S gas:** Shell
168	Rainbow Rd, to Big Bend, **S lodging:** Rainbow Lodge/rest., **other:** RV camping
166	Big Bend (from eb)
165	Cisco Grove, **N other:** RV camp/dump, skiing, snowmobiling, **S gas:** Valero/24hr, **other:** chain services
164	Eagle Lakes Rd

CA

INTERSTATE 80 CONT'D

E ↕ W

Exit #	Services
161	CA 20 W, to Nevada City, Grass Valley
160	Yuba Gap, **S other:** snowpark, ☎, ⛱, boating, camping, skiing
158	Laing Rd, **S lodging:** Rancho Sierra Inn/café
157mm	brake check area, wb
158a	Emigrant Gap (from eb), **S lodging:** Rancho Sierra Inn/café
156	Nyack Rd, Emigrant Gap, **S gas:** Shell/Burger King/dsl, **food:** Nyack Café
156mm	**brake check area**
155	Blue Canyon
150	Drum Forebay
148b	Baxter, **N other:** RV camping, chainup services, food, ☎
148a	Crystal Springs
146	Alta
145	Dutch Flat, **N food:** Monte Vista Rest., **S gas:** Tesoro/dsl, **other:** RV camping, chainup services, hwy patrol
144	Gold Run (from wb), **N** gas/dsl, food, ☎, chainup
143mm	**rest area both lanes, full ♿ facilities, ☎, ⛱, litter barrels, petwalk**
143	Magra Rd, Gold Run, **N** chainup services
140	Magra Rd, Rollins Lake Rd, Secret Town Rd
139	Rollins Lake Road (from wb), RV camping

COLFAX

Exit #	Services
135	CA 174, to Grass Valley, Colfax, **N gas:** 76/dsl, **food:** McDonald's, Pizza Factory, Starbucks, Taco Bell, TJ's Roadhouse, **lodging:** Colfax Motel, **other:** Best Harware, Curves, One Buck Store, Sierra Mkt Foods, NAPA, **S gas:** Chevron/dsl, Valero/dsl, **food:** Drooling Dog BBQ, Shang Garden Chinese, Subway
133	Canyon Way, to Colfax, **S other:** Chevrolet, Plaza Tire
131	Cross Rd, to Weimar
130	W Paoli Lane, to Weimar, **S gas:** Weimar Store/dsl
129	Heather Glen, elev 2000 ft
128	Applegate, **N gas:** Applegate Gas/dsl/LP, **other:** chainup services
125	Clipper Gap, Meadow Vista
124	Dry Creek Rd
123	Bell Rd

AUBURN

Exit #	Services
122	Foresthill Rd, Ravine Rd, Bowman, **N other:** RV camping/dump, **S food:** Burger King, La Ponte's Rest., Sizzler, Starbucks, Subway, TioPepe Mexican, **lodging:** Best Western, Country Squire Inn/rest., Quality Inn, same as 121
121	(from eb) Lincolnway, Auburn, **N gas:** Arco, Flyers Gas/dsl, Valero, **food:** Denny's, JimBoy's Tacos, Pizza Hut/Taco Bell/24hr, Popeye's, Wienerschnitzel, **lodging:** Comfort Inn, Foothills Motel, Motel 6, Super 8, **S gas:** Beacon, Chevron/dsl/24hr, 76, Shell, **food:** Baskin-Robbins, Burger King, Burrito Shop, Carl's Jr, Ikeda's Burgers, Jack-in-the-Box, KFC, LaBonte's Rest., McDonald's, Pete's Cafe, Sierra Grill, Sizzler, Smoothie King, Starbucks, Subway, TioPepe Mexican, **lodging:** Best Western, Quality Inn, **other:** Raley's Foods
120	Russell Ave (from wb), to lincolway from eb, same as 121
119c	Elm Ave, Auburn, **N gas:** 76/dsl, Shell, **food:** Foster's, **lodging:** Holiday Inn, **other:** Grocery Outlet, Longs Drug, Rite Aid, SaveMart Foods, Staples
119b	CA 49, to Grass Valley, Auburn, **N gas:** 76, Shell, **food:** In-n-Out, Marie Callender's, **lodging:** Holiday Inn, **other:** Staples
119a	Maple St, Nevada St, Old Town Auburn, **S gas:** Valero, **food:** Mary Belle's, Tiopete Mexican

NEWCASTLE

Exit #	Services
118	Ophir Rd (from wb)
116	CA 193, to Lincoln, **S other:** truck repair
115	Indian Hill Rd, Newcastle, **N other:** transmissions, **S gas:** Arco, Flyers/dsl, **food:** Denny's, CHP
112	Penryn, **N gas:** 76/dsl/LP, Valero/Subway/dsl, **food:** Houston's Steaks, L'Omelet Cafe
110	Horseshoe Bar Rd, to Loomis, **N food:** Burger King, Quizno's, RoundTable Pizza, Starbucks, Taco Bell, **other:** Raley's Food
109	Sierra College Blvd, **N gas:** Chevron/McDonald's/dsl, 7-11, **food:** Carl's Jr, **other:** Camping World RV Service/supplies, Gamel RV Ctr, Harley Davidson, antiques
108	Rocklin Rd, **N gas:** Rocklin Gas, **food:** A&W/KFC, Arby's, Baskin-Robbins, China Gourmet, Denny's, Golden Dragon, Jack-in-the-Box, Jamba Juice, KFC, Papa Murphy's, RoundTable Pizza, Starbucks, Subway, Taco Bell, **lodging:** Days Inn, Heritage Inn, Howard Johnson, **other:** GNC, Land Rover, Longs Drug, Porsche, Radio Shack, Safeway, **S gas:** Arco/24hr, **food:** Casa Bella, **lodging:** Rocklin Park Hotel
106	CA 65, to Lincoln, Marysville, **1 mi N on Stanford Ranch Rd...gas:** Shell, **food:** Applebee's, Buca Italian, Carl's Jr, Cheesecake Factory, IHOP, Jack-in-the-Box, McDonald's, On-the-Border, Red Robin, Subway, **lodging:** Comfort Suites, **other:** AutoZone, Barnes&Noble, Best Buy, Costco, JC Penney, Macy's, Marshall's, Nordstrom's, Old Navy, Ross
105b	Taylor Rd, to Rocklin (from eb), **N food:** Cattlemen's Rest., **other:** Albertson's (1mi), **S gas:** Chevron, 76/Burger King, **food:** Islands Burgers, Paradise Grill, Sierra Mtn Dining, Tahoe Joe's, **lodging:** Courtyard, Fairfield Inn, Hilton Garden, Holiday Inn Express, Larkspur Suites, Residence Inn, **other:** H, Save-Mart

CITRUS HEIGHTS

Exit #	Services
105a	Atlantic St, Eureka Rd, **S gas:** Joe's Mkt/Sonic, 76, Shell/Circle K, **food:** Brookfield's Rest., Black Angus, Carver's Steaks, In-n-Out, Panda Express, Supermex Rest., Taco Bell, Tahoe Joe's, Wendy's, **lodging:** Marriott, **other:** America'sTire, Buick/GMC, Carmax, Chevrolet, Ford, Home Depot, Hyundai, Lexus, Nissan, PetsMart, Sam's Club, Subaru, Toyota/scion, VW, Walmart, mall
103b a	Douglas Blvd, **N gas:** Arco/24hr, Chevron, 76, **food:** Burger King, Carolina's Mexican, Jack-in-the-Box, McDonald's, Starbucks, **lodging:** Best Western, Extended Stay America, Heritage Inn, Residence Inn, **other:** H, Ace Hardware, BigLots, Big O Tire, BrakeMasters, $Tree, Firestone, Goodyear, Kragen Parts, Radio Shack, Trader Joe's, **S gas:** Shell, **food:** Carl's Jr, Carrow's, Del Taco, Denny's, Outback Steaks, Subway, Togo's, **lodging:** Hampton Inn, Orchid Suites, **other:** Lincoln/Mercury, Office Depot, Rite Aid, Ross, Target

INTERSTATE 80 CONT'D

E ↕ W

Exit #	Services
102	Riverside Ave, Auburn Blvd, to Roseville, **N gas:** Arco/24hr, Chevron/dsl, **food:** Starbucks, Subway, **other:** Vet, **S gas:** 76, Shell, Tower, Valero/dsl, **food:** Asiana China, Back 40 Rest., Baskin-Robbins, Big Joe's BBQ, CA Burgers, Charlie's Rest., DQ, Jack-in-the-Box, **other:** AutoZone, BMW Motorcycles, $World, K-Mart, NAPA, Schwab Tire, Village RV Ctr, transmissions
100	Antelope Rd, to Citrus Heights, **N gas:** 76, **food:** Carl's Jr, Giant Pizza, KFC, McDonald's, Popeye's, Round Table Pizza, Subway, Taco Bell, Wendy's, **other:** $Tree, Raley's Foods, Rite Aid, 7-11, Vet
100mm	**weigh sta both lanes**
98	Greenback Lane, Elkhorn Blvd, Orangevale, Citrus Heights, **N gas:** 76/service, **food:** Carl's Jr, McDonald's, Pizza Hut, Subway, Taco Bell, **other:** Longs Drug, Radio Shack, Safeway
96	Madison Ave, **N gas:** Chevron, Valero, **food:** Brookfield's Rest., Denny's, El Zarape Mexican, Jack-in-the-Box, Starbucks, **lodging:** Motel 6, Super 8, **other:** funpark, to McClellan AFB, **S gas:** Arco/24hr, 76, Shell/repair, **food:** Boston Mkt, Burger King, Chipotle Mexican, El Pollo Loco, IHOP, In-N-Out, Jack-in-the-Box, McDonald's, Panda Express, Starbucks, Subway, **lodging:** Holiday Inn, La Quinta, **other:** Acura, Chevrolet, Ford/Isuzu, Office Depot, PepBoys, Schwab Tire, 7-11, Target, Walgreens
95	CA 99 S
94b	Auburn Blvd
94a	Watt Ave, **N gas:** 76, **lodging:** Day's Inn, Mote 6, **other:** Firestone, McClellan AFB, **S gas:** Arco/24hr, Chevron, Shell, **food:** CheeseSteak, China Taste, Denny's, Jimboy's Tacos, Quizno's, Starbucks, Subway, Wendy's, **lodging:** Great Western Inn
93	Longview Dr
92	Winters St
91	Raley Blvd, Marysville Blvd, to Rio Linda, **N gas:** Arco/24hr, Chevron/dsl/24hr, **S other:** Mkt Basket Foods, Valley Tires, USPO
90	Norwood Ave, **N gas:** Arco/Jack-in-the-Box/24hr, Valero, **food:** McDonald's, Quizno's, RoundTable Pizza, Starbucks, Subway, **other:** Rite Aid, Viva Foods
89	Northgate Blvd, Sacramento, **N other:** Fry's Electronics, **S gas:** Arco, Circle K/gas, Shell, **food:** Carl's Jr, Classic Burgers, Domino's, El Pollo Loco, IHOP, KFC, LJ Silver, McDonald's/playplace, Subway, Taco Bell, **lodging:** Extended Stay America, Quality Inn, **other:** BigLots, $Tree, Foodsco Foods, Goodyear/auto, Kragen Parts, PepBoys, Schwab Tire
88	Truxel Rd, **N gas:** Chevron, Shell/dsl, **food:** Applebee's, BJ's Rest, Carino's Italian, Chili's, Chipotle Mexican, Del Taco, Famous BBQ, Hooters, In-n-Out, Just Juice, Logan's Roadhouse, Mimi's Cafe, On the Border, Panera Bread, Pei Wei asian diner, Qdoba, Quizno's, Sonic, Starbucks, TGI Friday's, **lodging:** Staybridge Suites, **other:** Arco Arena, Barnes&Noble, Best Buy, BevMo, Home Depot, Michael's, Old Navy, PetsMart, Raley's Depot, Ross, Sam's Club/gas, Staples, Target, Walmart, World Mkt, mall
86	I-5, N to Redding, S to Sacramento, to CA 99 N

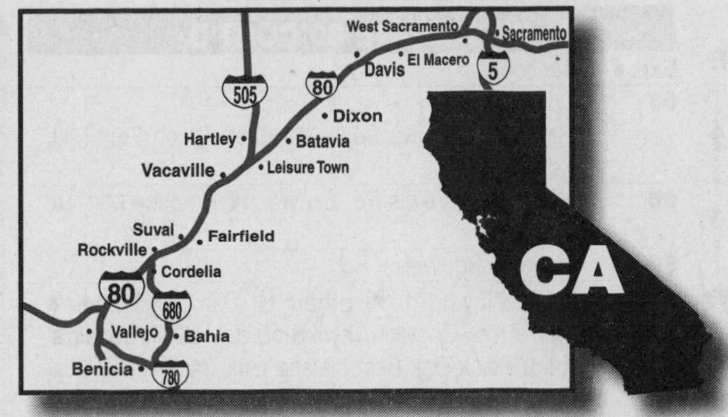

CA

SACRAMENTO

Exit #	Services
85	W El Camino, **N gas:** Chevron/Subway/dsl/24hr, 49er Trkstp/Silver Skillet/dsl/scales/24hr/@, **food:** Burger King, **lodging:** Fairfield Inn, Super 8
83	Reed Ave, **N gas:** 76/dsl, **food:** Hawaiian BBQ, Jack-in-the-Box, Los Amigo's, Quizno's, Panda Express, Starbucks, Subway, **lodging:** Extended Stay America, Hampton Inn, **other:** dsl repair, **S gas:** Arco/24hr, Shell/McDonald's/dsl, **food:** In-n-Out, Taco Bell, **other:** Home Depot, Walmart Super Ctr
82	US 50 E, W Sacramento
81	Enterprise Blvd, W Capitol Ave, W Sacramento, **N gas:** Chevron/dsl/24hr, Valero/dsl, **food:** Eppie's Rest/24hr, **lodging:** Granada Inn, **S gas:** 7-11, **food:** Denny's, JR's BBQ, Starbucks, Subway, **other:** KOA
78	Rd 32A, E Chiles Rd, **S** Fruit Stand
75	Mace Blvd, **N gas:** Arco, **S gas:** Chevron/24hr, Valero/dsl, **food:** Burger King, Cindy's Rest., McDonald's, Mtn Mike's Pizza, Subway, Taco Bell/24hr, **lodging:** Howard Johnson, Motel 6, **other:** Chevrolet, Chrysler/Dodge/Jeep, Ford, Honda, Nissan, Nugget Mkt Foods, Schwab Tire, Toyota/Scion, Tuesday Morning, to Mace Ranch
73	Olive Dr (from wb, no EZ return)
72b a	Richards Blvd, Davis, **N gas:** Shell/24hr, **food:** Caffe Italia, In-n-Out, Redrum Burger, **lodging:** University Park Inn, **other:** NAPA, **S gas:** Chevron, **food:** Applebee's, Del Taco, IHOP, KFC, Wendy's, **lodging:** Comfort Suites, Hotel Davis, **other:** Jiffy Lube, Kragen Parts
71	to UC Davis
70	CA 113 N, to Woodland, **N** H
69	Kidwell Rd
67	Pedrick Rd, **N gas:** Chevron/dsl, 76/LP, **other:** produce
66b	Milk Farm Rd (from wb)
66a	CA 113 S, Currey Rd, to Dixon, **S gas:** Arco, CFN/dsl, Shell/dsl, Valero/Popeye's/dsl, **food:** Cattlemen's Rest., Jack-in-the-Box, Papa Murphy's, Subway, Taco Del Mar, Wendy's, **lodging:** Comfort Suites, **other:** Walmart SuperCtr
64	Pitt School Rd, to Dixon, **S gas:** Chevron/24hr, Valero/24hr, **food:** Arby's, Asian Garden, Burger King, Chevy's Mexican, Denny's, IHOP, Little Ceasar's, Maria's Mexican, Mary's Pizza, McDonald's, Pizza Guys, Quizno's, Solano Bakery, Starbucks, Subway, Taco Bell, **lodging:** Best Western, Microtel, **other:** Curves, Ford, Kragen Parts, Safeway/dsl
63	Dixon Ave, Midway Rd, **N gas:** Truck Stp/dsl, **S gas:** Chevron/LP/lube, USA/24hr, **food:** Carl's Jr,

DAVIS

E ↕ W

CA

VACAVILLE

INTERSTATE 80 CONT'D

Exit #	Services
63	Continued Mr Taco, **lodging:** Super 8, **other:** Dixon Fruit Mkt, RV Dump
60	Midway Rd, Lewis Rd, Elmyra, **N** Produce Mkt, RV camping
59	Meridian Rd, Weber Rd
57	Leisure Town Rd, **N** **other:** [H], Camping World, **S** **gas:** Arco, Chevron, KwikStop/dsl, 76/McDonald's, **food:** Black Oak Rest., Island Grill, Jack-in-the-Box, King's Buffet, Omlette Bistro, Popeye's, Quizno's, **lodging:** Best Value, Extended Stay America, Fairfield Inn, Holiday Inn Express, Motel 6, Quality Inn, Residence Inn, **other:** Buick/GMC/Pontiac, Chevrolet, Chrysler/Dodge/Jeep, Harley-Davidson, Home Depot, Honda, Kohl's, Nissan, Toyota, VW
56	I-505 N, to Winters,
55	Nut Tree Pkwy, Monte Vista Dr, Allison Dr, **N** **gas:** 7-11, 76/Circle K, Valero, **food:** Amici Pizza, Arby's, Burger King, Denny's, Elephant Bar Rest., Hisui Japanese, IHOP, Jamba Juice, McDonald's, Murillo's Mexican, Nations Burger, Panera Bread, Pelayo's Mexican, Rubio's, Subway, Taco Bell, Wendy's, **lodging:** Best Value Inn, Best Western, Super 8, **other:** [H], America's Tire, Best Buy, Big O Tire, Borders Books, Firestone/auto, Lowe's Whse, Nugget Foods, Old Navy, Petsmart, See's Candies, U-Haul, transmissions, **S** **gas:** Arco/24hr, Chevron/24hr, **food:** Applebee's, Baja Fresh, BJ's Grill, Black Oak Rest., Carl's Jr, Chevy's Mexican, Chili's, Coldstone Creamery, Fresh Choice Rest., In-n-Out, Jack-in-the-Box, Jamba Juice, KFC, Mel's Diner, Olive Garden, Omlette Bistro, Popeye's, Quizno's, Starbucks, String's Italian, Tahoe Joe's Steaks, TGIFriday, Togo's, **lodging:** Comfort Suites, Courtyard, Fairfield Inn, Holiday Inn Express, Motel 6, Residence Inn, **other:** GNC, Jo-Ann Fabrics, Marshall's, Michael's, PetCo, Pontiac/GMC, Radio Shack, Ross, Safeway, Sam's Club, Staples, Target, Vacaville Stores/famous brands, Walmart/auto
54b	Mason St, Peabody Rd, **N** **gas:** Chevron, Valero, **food:** A&W/LJ Silver, **lodging:** Hampton Inn, **other:** NAPA, Schwab Tire, **S** **gas:** USA, **food:** Domino's, Starbucks, Subway, **other:** Costco/gas, 7-11
54a	Davis St, **N** **gas:** Chevron/McDonald's, **food:** Outback Steaks, **lodging:** Hampton Inn **S** **gas:** QuikStop, **other:** WinCo Foods, repair
53	Merchant St, Alamo Dr, **N** **gas:** Chevron, Shell/dsl, Valero, **food:** Bakers Square, Baldo's Mexican, Baskin-Robbins, Lyon's/24hr, RoundTable Pizza, Subway, Tin Tin Buffet, **lodging:** Alamo Inn, **other:** BigLots, Vet, **S** **gas:** 76/dsl, **food:** Jack-in-the-Box, KFC, McDonald's, Pizza Hut, Starbucks, **other:** Radio Shack
52	Cherry Glen Rd (from wb)
51b	Pena Adobe Rd, **S** **lodging:** Ranch Hotel
51a	Lagoon Valley Rd, Cherry Glen
48	N Texas St, Fairfield, **S** **gas:** Arco/24hr, Chevron, Shell, **food:** El Pollo Loco, Jim Boy's Tacos, RoundTable Pizza, Panda Express, Starbucks, Subway, Texas Roadhouse, **other:** Longs Drugs, Raley's Foods
47	Waterman Blvd, **N** **food:** Dynasty Chinese, Loard's Icecream, RoundTable Pizza, Starbucks, Strings Italian, **other:** Chevrolet/Cadillac, Safeway, to Austin's Place, **S** to Travis AFB, museum
45	Travis Blvd, Fairfield, **N** **gas:** Arco/24hr, Chevron/24hr, **food:** Baskin-Robbins, Burger King, Denny's, In-n-Out, McDonald's, Peking Rest., Subway, Taco Bell, **lodging:** Courtyard, Motel 6, **other:** Raley's Foods, Harley-Davidson, Ford, Hyundai, Nissan, PetCo, CHP, **S** **food:** BizWiz Tasty Burgers, Carino's Italian, Chevy's Mexican, Chipotle Mexican, Coldstone Creamery, FreshChoice Rest., Marie Callender's, Mimi's Café, Panda Express, Quizno's, Redbrick Pizza, Red Lobster, Starbucks, **lodging:** Hilton Garden, **other:** [H], Barnes&Noble, Best Buy, Cost+, JC Penney, Macy's, Michael's, Ross, Sears/auto, Trader Joe's, World Mkt, mall
44	W Texas St, same as 46, Fairfield, **N** **gas:** Shell/dsl, Valero/dsl, **food:** ChuckeCheese, Gordito's Mexican, Starbucks, **lodging:** Extended Stay America, **other:** Staples, **S** **gas:** Valero, **food:** Baldo's Mexican, McDonald's, Paleyo's Mexican, Scenario's Pizza, **other:** Acura/Honda, Chrysler/Jeep/Dodge, FoodMaxx, Home Depot, Hyundai, Infiniti, Mitsubishi, Nissan, Target, Toyota, Volvo, Walgreens
43	CA 12 E, Abernathy Rd, Suisun City, **S** **other:** Budweiser Plant, Walmart
4mm	**weigh sta both lanes, [phone]**
41	Suisan Valley Rd, **N** **lodging:** Homewood Suites, Staybridge Suites, **S** **gas:** Arco/24hr, Chevron, 76/dsl/24hr, Shell/dsl, Valero, **food:** Arby's, Bravo's Pizza, Burger King, Carl's Jr, Denny's, Green Bamboo, Jack-in-the-Box, McDonald's, Starbucks, Subway, Taco Bell, Wendy's, **lodging:** Best Western, Comfort Inn, Days Inn, Fairfield Inn, Holiday Inn Express, **other:** Ray's RV Ctr, Scandia FunCtr
40	I-680 (from wb)
39b	Green Valley Rd, I-680 (from eb), **N** **food:** Hawaiian BBQ, Peloyas Mexican, RoundTable Pizza, Starbucks, Sticky Rice Bistro, Subway, **lodging:** Homewood Suites, Staybridge Suites, **other:** Costco/gas, Longs Drug, Safeway, TJ Maxx, **S** **gas:** Arco
39a	Red Top Rd, **N** **gas:** 76/Circle K/24hr, **food:** Jack-in-the-Box
36	American Canyon Rd
34mm	**rest area wb, full [handicapped] facilities, info, [phone], [picnic], litter barrels, petwalk, vista parking**
33b a	CA 37, to San Rafael, Columbus Pkwy, **N** **gas:** Chevron/dsl, **food:** Baskin-Robbins, Carl's Jr., **lodging:** Best Western, Courtyard, **other:** funpark, **S** same as 32 .
32	Redwood St, to Vallejo, **N** **gas:** 76, **food:** Denny's, Panda Garden, **lodging:** Best Inn, Motel 6, **other:** [H], **S** **gas:** Arco, BonFair, Shell, **food:** Applebee's, Black Angus, Chevy's Mexican, Coldstone Creamery, IHOP, Jamba Juice, Lyon's Rest., McDonald's, Mtn. Mike's Pizza, Olive Garden, Panda Express, Red Lobster, Rubio's, Starbucks, Subway, Taco Bell, Wendy's, **lodging:** Comfort Inn, Ramada Inn, **other:** AutoZone, Best Buy, Cadillac/Chevrolet, Costco/gas, Hancock Fabrics, Home Depot, Honda, Hyundai, Longs Drug, Marshall's, Mazda, Michael's, Old Navy, PepBoys, PetCo, Radio Shack, Ross, Safeway, Toyota

FAIRFIELD

VALLEJO

INTERSTATE 80 CONT'D

E ↔ W

VALLEJO

Exit #	Services
31b	Tennessee St, to Vallejo, **S gas:** Valero/dsl, **food:** Jack-in-the-Box, Pacifica Pizza, Pizza Guys, **lodging:** Great Western Inn, Quality Inn, **other:** Grocery Outlet
31a	Solano Ave, Springs Rd, **N food:** Burger King, Church's, El Rey Mexican, Taco Bell, **lodging:** Deluxe Inn, Relax Inn, **other:** Rite Aid, U-Haul, **S gas:** Chemco, Chevron, Grand Gas, QuikStop, **food:** DQ, Domino's, Pizza Hut, Starbucks, Subway, Wok, **lodging:** Islander Motel, **other:** Island Pacific Foods, Kragen Parts
30c	Georgia St, Central Vallejo, **N gas:** Safeway/gas, **S gas:** Shell/Starbucks/dsl, **food:** McDonald's, **lodging:** California Motel
30b	Benicia Rd (from wb), **S gas:** Shell/dsl, **food:** McDonald's, Starbucks
30a	I-780, to Martinez
29b	Magazine St, Vallejo, **N gas:** BPG, **food:** Starbucks, Subway, **lodging:** Budget Inn, El Rancho, 7 Motel, **other:** Tradewinds RV Park, **S food:** McDonald's, **lodging:** Travel Inn, **other:** 7-11
29a	CA 29, Maritime Academy Dr, Vallejo, **N gas:** Chevron/dsl/24hr, 5 Star Gas, **food:** Subway, **lodging:** Motel 6, Vallejo Inn
28mm	toll plaza, pay toll from eb
27	Pomona Rd, Crockett, **N food:** Dead Fish Seafood, vista point
26	Cummings Skyway, to CA 4 (from wb), to Martinez
24	Willow Ave, to Rodeo, **N food:** Straw Hat Pizza, Subway, **other:** Safeway/24hr, USPO, **S gas:** 76/Circle K/dsl, **food:** Burger King, Mazatlan, Starbucks, Willow Garden Chinese
23	CA 4, to Stockton, Hercules, **N gas:** Shell, **food:** Extreme Pizza, Jack-in-the-Box, Starbucks, **other:** Radio Shack, **S food:** McDonald's, RoundTable Pizza, Subway, Taco Bell, **other:** BigLots, Curves, Home Depot, Lucky Foods, Rite Aid, USPO
22	Pinole Valley Rd, **S gas:** Arco/24hr, Chevron/dsl, **food:** Jack-in-the-Box, Jamba Juice, NY Pizza, Red Onion Rest., Subway, **other:** 7-11, Trader Joe's, Walgreens
21	Appian Way, **N gas:** Pinole Express, **food:** China Delite, McDonald's, Pizza Hut, **other:** Kragen Parts, Longs Drug, Safeway, **S gas:** Valero/dsl, **food:** Burger King, Carl's Jr, Coldstone Creamery, Hawaiian BBQ, HomeTown Buffet, HotDog Sta, KFC, Krispy Kreme, In-n-Out, Panda Express, Papa Murphy's, RoundTable Pizza, Sizzler, Starbucks, Subway, Taco Bell, Wendy's, Wing Stop, **lodging:** Days Inn, Motel 6, **other:** AutoZone, Best Buy, $Tree, K-Mart, Lucky Foods, Radio Shack
20	Richmond Pkwy, to I-580 W, **N gas:** Chevron, **food:** Ground Round Rest., IHOP, McDonald's, Me&Ed's Pizza, Subway, **other:** Barnes&Noble, Chrysler/Dodge/Jeep, Ford, 99c Store, Petsmart, Ross, **S gas:** Chevron, Shell/dsl, **food:** Applebee's, Chuck Steak, In-n-Out, Krispy Kreme, Outback Steaks, Panda Express, RoundTable Pizza, **other:** FoodMaxx, Kragen Parts, Old Navy, Michael's, Staples, Target

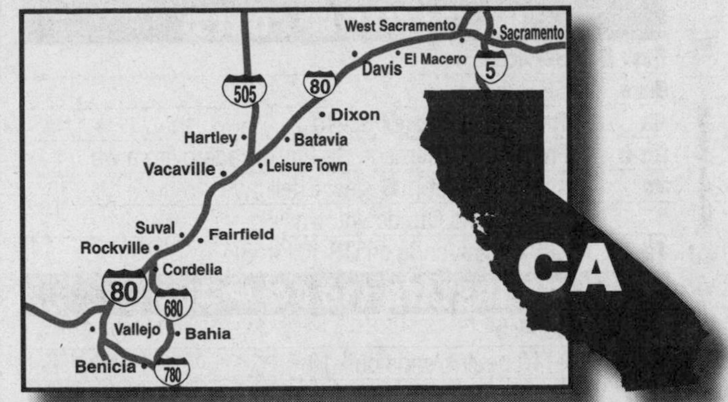

CA

RICHMOND

19b	Hilltop Dr, to Richmond, **N gas:** Chevron, **food:** Chevy's Mexican, Olive Garden, Red Lobster, Tokyo Rest., **lodging:** Courtyard, Extended Stay America, **other:** Firestone, JC Penney, Jo-Ann Fabrics, Macy's, Nissan, Sears/auto, Walmart, mall, **S gas:** Hilltop Fuel/dsl
19a	El Portal Dr, to San Pablo, **S gas:** SMP, **food:** McDonalds, Mtn. Mike's Pizza, KFC, Subway, **other:** Raley's Foods, Walgreens
18	San Pablo Dam Rd, **N gas:** Chevron, **food:** Burger King, Denny's, El Pollo Loco, Empire Buffet, Jack-in-the-Box, Jamba Juice, Nations Burgers, Popeye's, RoundTable Pizza, Starbucks, Subway, Taco Bell, **lodging:** Holiday Inn Express, **other:** H, AutoZone, $Tree, FoodMaxx, Lucky Foods, Walgreens, **S other:** CamperLand RV Ctr
17	Macdonald Ave (from eb), McBryde Ave (from wb), Richmond, **N gas:** Arco/24hr, **food:** Burger King, Church's, **S gas:** Chevron/24hr, **food:** Wendy's, **other:** Safeway, auto repair
16	San Pablo Ave, to Richmond, San Pablo, **S gas:** Chevron, **food:** KFC, LJ Silver, Subway, Wendy's, **other:** Safeway
15	Cutting Blvd, Potrero St, to I-580 Br (from wb), to El Cerrito, **N gas:** Arco, **food:** Panda Express, **other:** Target, **S gas:** Chevron, **food:** Carrow's Rest., Church's, Denny's, IHOP, Jack-in-the-Box, Little Ceasar's, McDonald's, Starbucks, **other:** $Tree, Home Depot, Honda, Staples, Walgreens
14b	Carlson Blvd, El Cerrito, **N gas:** 76, **lodging:** 40 Flags Motel, **S lodging:** Best Value Inn
14a	Central Ave, El Cerrito, **S gas:** 76, Valero, **food:** Burger King, KFC, Nations Burgers
13	to I-580 (from eb), Albany
12	Gilman St, to Berkeley, **N** Golden Gate Fields Racetrack, **S other:** Target
11	University Ave, to Berkeley, **S gas:** 76, University Gas, **lodging:** La Quinta, **other:** to UC Berkeley
10	CA 13, to Ashby Ave
9	Powell St, Emeryville, **N gas:** Shell, **food:** Chevy's Mexican, **lodging:** Hilton Garden, **S gas:** 76, **food:** Burger King, CA Pizza Kitchen, Denny's, Elephant Bar/Grill, Jamba Juice, PF Chang's, Starbucks, To-go's, **lodging:** Courtyard, Sheraton, Woodfin Suites, **other:** Barnes&Noble, Borders Books, Old Navy, Ross, Trader Joe's
8c b	Oakland, to I-880, I-580
8a	W Grand Ave, Maritime St
7mm	toll plaza wb

BERKELEY

INTERSTATE 80 CONT'D

Exit #	Services
5mm	SF Bay
4a	Treasure Island (exits left)
2c b	Fremont St, Harrison St, Embarcadero (from wb)
2a	4th st (from eb), **S gas:** Shell
1	9th st, Civic Ctr, downtown SF
1b a	I-80 begins/ends on US 101 In SF

INTERSTATE 110 (LOS ANGELES)

Exit #	Services
21	I-110 begins/ends on I-10.
20c	Adams Blvd, **E other:** Chevron, Nissan, Office Depot, LA Convention Ctr.
20b	37th St, Exposition Blvd, **E** repair, **W gas:** Chevron/McDonald's, **lodging:** Radisson
20a	MLK Blvd, Expo Park, **W gas:** Chevron, **food:** McDonald's, Subway
19b	Vernon Ave, **E gas:** Mobil, **W gas:** 76/24hr, Shell, **food:** Burger King, Jack-in-the-Box, **other:** Ralph's Foods
18b	Slauson Ave, **E gas:** Mobil, **W gas:** 76
18a	Gage Blvd, **E gas:** Arco, **food:** Church's
17	Florence Ave, **E gas:** Mobil, **food:** Jack-in-the-Box, **W gas:** Arco, Chevron, Shell/24hr, **food:** Burger King, McDonald's, Pizza Hut
16	Manchester Ave, **E gas:** Arco, **food:** McDonald's, **other:** AutoZone, **W gas:** 76/Circle K, **food:** Church's, Jack-in-the-Box, Tom's Burgers, Popeye's, **other:** Ralph's Foods
15	Century Blvd, **E gas:** Arco, Shell/Subway, **food:** Burger King, **W gas:** 76
14b	Imperial Hwy, **W gas:** Petro Zone, **food:** McDonald's, Jack-in-the-Box
14a	I-105
13	El Segundo Blvd, **E food:** Pizza Hut, Taco Bell, **W food:** Denny's
12	Rosecrans Ave, **E gas:** Arco/24hr, Prena, SC Fuels, **W gas:** Chevron/McDonald's, Mobil, **food:** Jack-in-the-Box, KFC, Popeye's, Subway, **other:** Chief Parts, 7-11
11	Redondo Beach Blvd, **E food:** McDonald's, **W gas:** Mobil, **other:** H
10b a	CA 91, 190th St, **W food:** Carl's Jr, Jack-in-the-Box, Krispy Kreme, McDonald's, Taco Bell/Pizza Hut, **other:** Albertson's, Food4Less, Sam's Club
9	I-405, San Diego Fwy
8	Torrance Blvd, Del Amo, **E food:** Baskin-Robbins, Burger King, Chile Verde, Panda Bowl, **other:** K-mart, **W gas:** Mobil, Shell/dsl
7b	Carson St, **E food:** KFC, **lodging:** Cali Inn, **W gas:** Mobil, Shell, **food:** Bakers Square, Hong Kong Garden, In-n-Out, Jack-in-the-Box, **other:** H, Carson Drug, Kragen Parts, Radio Shack
5	Sepulveda Blvd, **E food:** McDonald's, **other:** Albertson's, Home Depot, Staples, Target, **W gas:** Arco/24hr, Chevron, Mobil, Shell, **food:** Burger King, Carl's Jr, Golden Ox Burger, McDonald's, Pizza Hut/Taco Bell, Popeye's, **lodging:** Motel 6, **other:** $Tree, Food4Less, K-Mart, Rite Aid, Von's Foods
4	CA 1, Pacific Coast Hwy, **E gas:** Shell, **food:** Jack-in-the-Box, **W gas:** Chevron, Mobil/dsl, **food:** Denny's, El Pollo Loco, EZ Burger, **lodging:** Best West
4	Continued Western, **other:** H, Discount Parts, Honda, Pep-Boys
3b	Anaheim St, **E gas:** Shell
3a	C St, **E gas:** Shell/dsl, **other:** radiators, **W gas:** 76 Refinery
1b	Channel St
1a	CA 47, Gaffey Ave
0mm	I-110 begins/ends

INTERSTATE 205 (TRACY)

Exit #	Services
12	I-205 begins wb, ends eb, accesses I-5 nb
9	MacArthur Dr, Tracy, **S** gas Chevron/Jack-in-the-Box/Subway/dsl, **other:** Prime Outlet Ctr/famous brands
8	Tracy Blvd, Tracy, **N gas:** Chevron, Shell/dsl, Tracy Trkstp/Mean Gene's Burger/dsl/24hr, **food:** Denny's/24hr, **lodging:** Holiday Inn Express, Motel 6, **S gas:** Arco/24hr, **food:** American Diner, Arby's, Burger King, In-n-Out, McDonald's, Nations Burgers, Subway, Tracy Buffet, Wendy's, **lodging:** Best Western, Microtel, Quality Inn, **other:** H, FoodMaxx, Kragen Parts, Longs Drugs, Walgreens, CHP
6	Grant Line Rd, Antioch, **N gas:** Chevron, **food:** Applebee's, Burger King, Chevy's Mexican, Golden Corral, Hometown Buffet, IHOP, Jamba Juice, Olive Garden, Panda Express, Quizno's, Sonic, Starbucks, Strings Italian, Taco Bell, Texas Roadhouse, Wienerschnitzel/TasteeFreeze, **lodging:** Extended Stay America, Fairfield Inn, Hampton Inn, **other:** America's Tire, Barnes&Noble, Chevrolet, Costco/gas, Ford, Home Depot, Hyundai, JC Penney, Michael's, Nissan, Ross, Schwab Tire, Sears/auto, Staples, Target, Toyota, Walmart/McDonald's/auto, World Mkt, mall, **S gas:** Arco/24hr, 7-11, Shell/dsl, Valero, **food:** Carl's Jr, Chili's, Hawaiian BBQ, KFC/A&W, Mtn Mike's Pizza, NYPD Pizza, Orchard Rest., Taco Del Mar, **other:** Cadillac/Pontiac/GMC, Rite Aid, Tracy Marine
4	11th St (from eb), to Tracy, Defense Depot
2	Mtn House Pkwy, to I-580 E
0mm	I-205 begins eb/ends wb, accesses I-580 wb

INTERSTATE 210 (PASADENA)

Exit #	Services
74	I-215 N to Barstow S to San Bernardino
73	St. Street, University Pkwy, **N gas:** Thrifty, Valero
71	Riverside Ave, **N food:** Carl's Jr, Del Taco, Starbucks, Subway, **other:** Fresh&Easy, Ralph's Foods, Rite Aid, Walgreens, **S gas:** Arco, **food:** Jack-in-the-Box, **other:** 7-11
70	Ayala Dr, **S other:** Target
68	Alder Ave
67	Sierra Ave, **N food:** Applebee's, Carl's Jr, Dickie's BBQ, El Pollo Loco, Hawaiian BBQ, Jamba Juice, Mimi's Cafe, Panda Express, Pizza Hut, Teo's Mexican, Subway, **other:** Costco/gas, $Tree, Lowe's Whse, **S other:** Chevrolet, Nissan
66	Citrus Ave, **N food:** El Gran Burrito, FarmerBoys Rest., Marble Slab Creamery, Pick Up Stix, Quizno's, Red Brick Pizza, Wienerschnitzel, **other:** Home Depot, Ralph's Foods, Walgreens

INTERSTATE 210 CONT'D (PASADENA)

E ↕ W

Exit #	Services
64	Cherry Ave
63	I-15 N to Barstow, S to San Diego
62	Day Creek Blvd, **S gas:** Arco/dsl, Shell, **food:** Chinese Food, Jack-in-the-Box, Marble Slab Creamery, Pizza Factory, Starbucks, Wendy's, **other:** Ralph's Foods
60	Milliken Ave, **S gas:** Mobil, **food:** Taco Bell, **other:** Albertsons, CVS Drug, Kragen Parts
59	Haven Ave, **N gas:** Mobil, 76, 7-11, **food:** Del Taco, Domino's, Jack-in-the-Box, McDonald's, Subway, Teo's Mexican, **other:** Trader Joe's, Vons Foods, Walgreens
58	Archibald Ave, **S food:** Blimpie, Barboni's Pizza, Carl's Jr, **other:** Stater Bros, Vet
57	Carnelion St, **S gas:** 76, **food:** Baskin-Robbins, Del Taco, El Ranchero Mexican, Papa John's, Starbucks, **other:** Radio Shack, Rite Aid, Vons Foods, Walgreens
56	Campus Ave, **S food:** Carl's Jr, Chick-fil-A, Golden Spoon Yogurt, Hawaiian BBQ, IHOP, Jamba Juice, Magic Wok, Qdoba Mexican, Quizno's, Starbucks, Subway, **other:** Albertsons, Goodyear, Home Depot, Kohl's, Office Depot, Petsmart, Target
54	Mtn Ave, Mount Balde
52	Baseline Rd
50	Towne Ave
48	Fruit St, LaVerne, **S gas:** Shell, **food:** El Pollo Loco, Magic Wok, McDonald's, Myiabi, Panda Express, Pizza Hut, Quizno's, Round Table Pizza, Rubio's, Subway, **other:** Kohl's, Marshall's, Office Depot, Pet Depot, Vons Foods, U of LaVerne, Vet
47	Foothill Blvd, LaVerne, **N gas:** Mobil/Taco Bell, **food:** Denny's, **S gas:** Chevron/dsl, Shell, **food:** IHOP, Starbucks, Togo's, **other:** GNC, Radio Shack
46	San Dimas Ave, **N** San Dimas Canyon CP
45	CA 57 S
44	Lone Hill Ave, Santa Ana, **S gas:** Chevron, **food:** Baja Fresh, Chili's, Coco's, In-n-Out, Subway, Wendy's, **other:** Barnes&Noble, Best Buy, Chevrolet, Chrysler/Dodge/Jeep, Ford, Home Depot, Hyundai, Kohl's, Old Navy, Petsmart, Sam's Club/gas, Staples, Toyota, Walmart/auto
43	Sunflower Ave
42	Grand Ave, to Glendora, **N gas:** 76, Valero/dsl, **food:** Denny's, **other:** H
41	Citrus Ave, to Covina
40	Ca 39, Azusa Ave, **N gas:** Arco/24hr, Chevron, Mobil, Shell/Del Taco, **food:** Jack-in-the-Box, **lodging:** Rodeway Inn, Super 8, **S gas:** Chevron, Valero, **food:** Baskin-Robbins, In-n-Out, Marquez Mexican, **lodging:** Best Value, **other:** Rite Aid, 7-11
39	Vernon Ave (from wb), same as 38
38	Irwindale, **N gas:** Arco, **food:** Carl's Jr, Denny's, FarmerBoys Rest., McDonald's, Shanghai Buffet, Taco Bell, **other:** Costco/gas, NAPA
36b	Mt Olive Dr
36a	I-605 S
35b a	Mountain Ave, **N gas:** Arco, Chevron **food:** Denny's, Old Spaghetti Factory, Tommy's Hamburgers, Wienerschnitzel, **lodging:** Oak Park Motel, **other:**

SAN DIMAS

Exit #	Services
35b a	Continued Best Buy, BMW/Mini, CarMax, Buick/Chevrolet, Ford, Honda, Infiniti, Nissan, Staples, Subaru, Target, Walgreens, **S food:** IHOP, Panda Express, Roasty Toasty Chicken, Senor Fish, Subway, **other:** Home Depot, Ross, Walmart
34	Myrtle Ave, **S gas:** Chevron, 76, **food:** Jack-in-the-Box
33	Huntington Dr, Monrovia, **N gas:** Shell/dsl, **food:** Acapulco Rest., Applebee's, Black Angus, Burger King, Chili's, ChuckeCheese, Domino's, LeRoy's Rest., McDonald's, Mimi's Cafe, Panda Express, Popeye's, Quizno's, RoundTable Pizza, Rubio's, Starbucks, **lodging:** Courtyard, **other:** GNC, King Ranch Foods, Marshall's, Office Depot, Pepboy's, Radio Shack, Rite Aid, Trader Joe's, **S gas:** Chevron, **food:** Baja Fresh, BJ's Grill, Capistrano's, ClaimJumper, Daphne's Rest., Derby Rest., Fusion Grill, Golden Dragon, Macaroni Grill, Olive Garden, Outback Steaks, Red Lobster, Sesame Grill, Soup Plantation, Starbucks, Subway, Taisho Rest., Togo's, Tokyo Wako, **lodging:** Double Tree, Embassy Suites, Extended Stay America, Hampton Inn, Hilton Garden, Homestead Suites, OakTree Inn, Residence Inn, SpringHill Suites
32	Santa Anita Ave, Arcadia, **N gas:** Arco, 76, **food:** KFC, McDonald's, Pizza Hut, Subway, **other:** Ralph's Foods, Rite Aid, **S gas:** Chevron/dsl, **food:** In-n-Out, **other:** carwash
31	Baldwin Ave, to Sierra Madre
30b a	Rosemead Blvd, **N gas:** Arco, 76/dsl, **food:** Boston Mkt, ChuckeCheese, Jamba Juice, Starbucks, **other:** CVS Drug, EZ Lube, Marshall's, Ralph's Foods, Rite Aid, Sears/auto, Whole Foods Mkt, **S gas:** 76, **food:** Coco's, Jack-in-the-Box, **lodging:** Days Inn, **other:** Big O Tires
29b a	San Gabriel Blvd, Madre St, **N gas:** 76, **food:** Chipotle Mexican, El Torito, Starbucks, Togo's, **other:** Best Buy, Old Navy, Petsmart, Ross, **S gas:** 76, **food:** Jack-in-the-Box, **lodging:** Best Western, Holiday Inn Express, Quality Inn, **other:** Buick/Chevrolet/Pontiac/GMC, Cadillac, Hyundai, Jiffy Lube, Land Rover, Saab, Staples, Target, Toyota
28	Altadena Dr, Sierra Madre, **S gas:** Chevron, Mobil, **other:** Just Tires
27 b	Allen
27 a	Hill Ave
26	Lake Ave, **N gas:** Mobil, **other:** Jo-Ann Fabrics
25b	CA 134, to Ventura
25a	Del Mar Blvd, CA Blvd, CO Blvd (exits left from eb)

MONROVIA

PASADENA

CA

INTERSTATE 210 CONT'D (PASADENA)

E ↕ W

Exit #	Services
24	Mountain St
23	Lincoln Ave, **S lodging:** Lincoln Motel, **other:** auto repair
22b	Arroyo Blvd, **N food:** Jack-in-the-Box, **S** to Rose Bowl
22a	Berkshire Ave, Oak Grove Dr
21	Gould Ave, **S gas:** Arco, **food:** Dominos, McDonald's, RoundTable Pizza, Trader Joes, **other:** Firestone, Just Tires, Ralph's Foods
20	CA 2, Angeles Crest Hwy
19	CA 2, Glendale Fwy, **S other:** H
18	Ocean View Blvd, to Montrose
17b a	Pennsylvania Ave, La Crescenta, **N gas:** 76, Shell, Valero, **food:** Baja Fresh, Burger King, Domino's, Starbucks, Subway, Togo's, Wienerschnitzel, **other:** GNC, Nissan, Office Depot, Ralph's Foods, Rite Aid, Toyota, Vons Foods, Walgreens, USPO, **S other:** Gardenia Mks/deli, 7-11
16	Lowell Ave
14	La Tuna Cyn Rd
11	Sunland Blvd, Tujunga, **N gas:** Mobil, 76, Shell, **food:** Coco's, Jack-in-the-Box, KFC, Sizzler, Yum Yum Donuts, **other:** Ralph's Foods, Rite Aid, 7-11, city park
9	Wheatland Ave
8	Osborne St, Lakeview Terrace, **N food:** Ranch Side Cafe, **other:** 7-11
6a	Paxton St
6b	CA 118
5	Maclay St, to San Fernando, **S gas:** Chevron, 76/dsl, **food:** El Pollo Loco, KFC, McDonald's, Quizno's, Subway, Taco Bell, **other:** Home Depot, Office Depot, Radio Shack, Sam's Club
4	Hubbard St, **N gas:** Chevron, **food:** Denny's, Yum Yum Donuts, **other:** AutoZone, Radio Shack, Rite Aid, Valley Foods, **S gas:** Mobil/dsl, Shell, **food:** El Caporal Mexican, Jack-in-the-Box, Shakey's Pizza, Subway, **other:** Vons Foods
3	Polk St, **S gas:** Arco, Chevron/24hr, **food:** KFC, **other:** H, 7-11
2	Roxford St, **N gas:** Arco/dsl, **food:** Topia Pizza/Subs, **other:** H, Jiffy Lube, **S lodging:** Country Side Inn
1c	Yarnell St
1b a	I-210 begins/ends on I-5, exit 160.

SAN FERNANDO

INTERSTATE 215 (RIVERSIDE)

N ↕ S

Exit #	Services
55	I-215 begins/ends on I-15.
54	Devore, **E gas:** Arco/dsl, Shell, **W food:** Tony's Diner
50	Palm Ave, Kendall Dr, **E gas:** Arco, 7-11/gas, **food:** Burger King, Mico Cina Mexican,. Popeye's, Starbucks, Subway, **W food:** Denny's
48	University Pkwy, **E gas:** Chevron, 76/Circle K, **food:** Alberto's, Baskin Robbins/Togo's, Carl's Jr, Del Taco, Domino's, IHOP, KFC, Little Ceasars, McDonald's, Papa John's, Starbucks, Wienerschnitzel, **other:** Curves, EZ Lube, Jiffy Lube, Ralph's Foods, Staples, **W gas:** Arco/24hr, Shell/dsl/LP, **food:** Jack-in-the-Box, Pizza Hut/Taco Bell, Zendejas Mexican,
48	Continued **lodging:** Day's Inn, Motel 6, **other:** Lowe's Whse, Walmart/Subway
46c b	27th St, **E** golf, **W** golf
46a	CA 210 W, Highland Ave
45b	Musciape Dr, **E gas:** Shell/dsl, Thrifty, **food:** Jack-in-the-Box, **other:** Chevrolet, Home Depot, SavOn Foods, Stater Bros
45a	CA 210 E, Highlands
44b	Baseline Rd
44a	CA 66 W, 5th St, **E lodging:** Best Value, Econolodge
43	2nd St, Civic Ctr, **E gas:** Arco, Chevron/dsl, **food:** China Hut, Del Taco, In-n-Out, McDonald's, Pizza Hut/Taco Bell, Starbucks, **lodging:** Best Value, **other:** Ford, Food4Less, Marshall's
42b	Mill St, **E food:** Carl's Jr, Del Taco, Jack-in-the-Box, McDonald's, **other:** AutoZone, **W gas:** Shell, **food:** Yum-yum Donuts
42a	Inland Ctr Dr, **E gas:** Chevron/dsl, **food:** Carl's Jr, Jack-in-the-Box, Wienerschnitzel, **other:** AutoZone, Gottschalk's, Kragen Parts, Macy's, Sears/auto, mall
41	Orange Show Rd, **E gas:** Arco, Chevron, Exxon, **food:** Denny's, Pancho Villa Mexican, Subway, **lodging:** Knight's Inn, Travelodge, **other:** BigLots, Chrysler/Dodge/Jeep, Firestone/auto, Kelly Tire, Radio Shack, 99c Store, Target, **W other:** Hyundai, Isuzu, Kia, Mazda, Mitsubishi, Nissan, Scion, Suzuki, Toyota
40b a	I-10, E to Palm Springs, W to LA
39	Washington St, Mt Vernon Ave, **E gas:** Arco/24hr, 5 Points, 76, **food:** Arby's, Baker's Drive-Thru, China Town, DQ, Siquios Mexican, Taco Joe's, Starbucks, **lodging:** Colton Inn, **other:** BigLots, $Tree, Goodyear/auto, Jiffy Lube, **W food:** Burger King, Carl's Jr, Del Taco, Denny's, El Pollo Loco, Jack-in-the-Box, McDonald's, Quizno's, Starbucks, Subway, Taco Bell, Zendejas Mexican, **lodging:** Red Tile Inn, **other:** GNC, 99c Store, Radio Shack, Ross, Walmart/auto, multiple RV dealers
38	Barton Rd, **E gas:** Arco, Shell/Circle K, **food:** Quizno's, **other:** AutoZone, **W food:** Demetri's Burgers
37	La Cadena Dr, **E gas:** Shell/dsl/24hr, **food:** Jack-in-the-Box, YumYum Rest., **lodging:** Holiday Inn Express
36	Center St, to Highgrove, **W gas:** Valero/dsl
35	Columbia Ave, **E gas:** Arco, **W other:** Circle K
34b a	CA 91, CA 60, Main St, Riverside, to beach cities
33	Blaine St, 3rd St, **E gas:** 76, Shell, Valero, **food:** Baker's Drive-Thru, Jack-in-the-Box, Starbucks, **other:** EZ Lube, K-Mart
32	University Ave, Riverside, **W gas:** Mobil/dsl, Shell, Thrifty, **food:** Carl's Jr, Coco's, Del Taco, Denny's, Gus Jr, IHOP, Jack-in-the-Box, Little Ceasars, Mediterranean Palace Cafe, Mongolian BBQ, Pizza Hut, Quizno's, Rubio's, Santana's Mexican, Starbucks, Super Buffet, Subway, Taco Bell, Wienerschnitzel, **lodging:** Comfort Inn, Courtyard, Dynasty Suites, Motel 6, **other:** Food4Less, Kragen Parts, Radio Shack, Rite Aid
31	MLK Blvd, El Cerrito
30b	Central Ave, Watkins Dr

SAN BERNARDINO

RIVERSIDE

INTERSTATE 215 CONT'D (RIVERSIDE)

N ↕ S

Exit #	Services
30a	Fair Isle Dr, Box Springs, **W gas:** 76, **food:** Jack-in-the-Box, **other:** Ford
29	CA 60 E, to Indio, **E on Day St gas:** Shell/dsl, **food:** Applebees, Baker's Drive-Thru, Carl's Jr, Chick-fil-A, El Pollo Loco, Golden Chop Stix, Hawaiian BBQ, Home Town Buffet, Hooters, Jamba Juice, Jason's Deli, McDonald's, Mimi's Cafe, Olive Garden, Outback Steaks, Panda Express, Portillo's Hot Dogs, Qdoba Mexican, Quizno's, Red Robin, Starbucks, Subway, Wendy's, Wienerschnitzel, **lodging:** Hampton Inn, **other:** Best Buy, Costco/gas, $Tree, Home Depot, JC Penney, Jo-Ann Fabrics, Lowe's Whse, Macy's, Marshall's, Michael's, Old Navy, PetSmart, Sears/auto, Staples, Target, Walmart, WinCo Foods, mall
28	Eucalyptus Ave, Eastridge Ave, **E food:** Bravo Burgers, Hooters, **other:** Sam's Club/gas, Target, Walmart, same as 29
27b	Alessandro Blvd, **E gas:** Arco/24hr, 76/Circle K/dsl, **other:** Big O Tire, auto repair, **W gas:** Chevron, **food:** Farmer Boys
27a	Cactus Ave to March ARB, **E gas:** Chevron, 76/Circle K/dsl, **food:** Carl's Jr, Richie's Burgers
25	Van Buren Blvd, **E other:** March Field Museum, **W other:** Riverside Nat Cen.
23	Harley Knox Blvd, **E other:** auto repair
22	Ramona Expswy, **1 mi E on Perris Blvd...gas:** Chevron, Mobil, Shell, **food:** Old Chicago Pizza, Subway, **W gas:** Arco/dsl/scales/24hr, 76/Circle K/dsl/LP, **food:** Jack-in-the-Box
19	Nuevo Rd, **E gas:** Arco/24hr, Chevron, Mobil, **food:** Baskin Robbins, Burger King, Carl's Jr, China Palace, Del Taco, El Pollo Loco, IHOP, Jenny's Rest., McDonald's, Pizza Hut, Round Table Pizza, Sizzler, Starbucks, Subway, **other:** AutoZone, Big Lots, Food-4Less, GNC, Kragen Parts, Radio Shack, Rite Aid, Stater Bros Foods, Walmart
17	CA 74 W, 4th St, to Perris, Lake Elsinore, **E gas:** Shell/24hr, Thrifty, **W gas:** Chevron, **food:** Del Taco, Denny's, Jack-in-the-Box, Jimenez Mexican, Nick's Burgers, Popeye's, **lodging:** Holiday Inn Express, **other:** AutoZone, CarQuest, Chrysler/Dodge/Jeep/Kia, $Mart, Vet
15	CA 74 E, Hemet, **E lodging:** Sun Leisure Motel
14	Ethanac Rd, **E food:** KFC/Taco Bell, **other:** Richardson's RV, **W gas:** Circle K, Exxon/dsl, **food:** Carl's Jr, Del Taco, Hawaiian BBQ, Subway, **other:** Just Tires, Home Depot, WinCo Foods
12	McCall Blvd, Sun City, **E gas:** Valero/dsl, **food:** Wendy's, **lodging:** Best Value, Super 8, **other:** H, **W gas:** Chevron/dsl, Valero, **food:** Coco's, Domino's, McDonald's, Rong's Chinese, Santana's Mexican, Subway, **other:** Rite Aid, Stater Bros Foods, Von's Foods, Walgreens
10	Newport Rd, Quail Valley, **E gas:** Shell/Del Taco/dsl, **food:** Cathay Chinese, Coldstone Creamery, Jack-in-the-Box, Papa John's, Subway, Taco Bell, **other:** AutoZone, GNC, Ralph's Foods, Ross, **W gas:** Arco/24hr, 76/Circle K/dsl, **food:** Chipotle, In-n-Out, Panda Express, Red Robin, Starbucks, Yellow Basket Cafe, **other:** Best Buy, Kohl's, Lowes Whse,

PERRIS

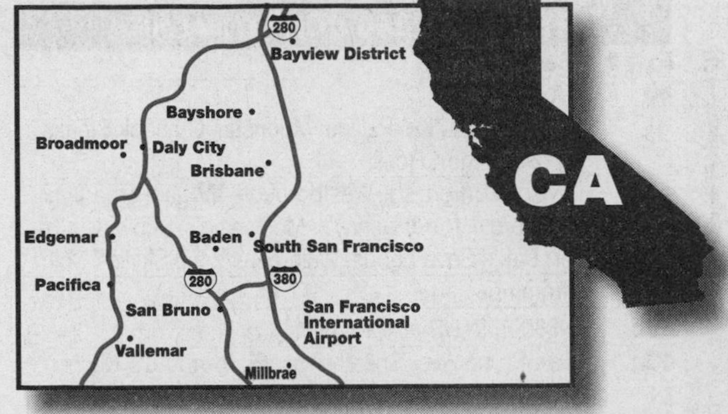

CA

Exit #	Services
10	Continued Old Navy, PetCo, Staples, SuperTarget
7	Scott Rd, **E gas:** Arco/dsl, 7-11, **food:** Carl's Jr, Del Taco, Jack-in-the-Box, Subway, **other:** Albertson's/SavOn
4	Clinton Keith Rd, **W food:** Juice It Up, Subway, **other:** Marshall's, Target
2	Los Alamos, **E gas:** Shell, **food:** Board'z Grill, In-n-Out, Mama Rose's Pizza, Peony Chinese, Taco Bell, **other:** USPO, **W gas:** Mobil/McDonald's, **food:** ChuckeCheese, City Deli/bakery, Jack-in-the-Box, Pizza Hut, Starbucks, Subway, TJ's Pizza, **other:** CVS Drug, Stater Bros Foods
1	Murrieta Hot Springs, **E gas:** 7-11, Shell/dsl, **food:** Alberto's Mexican, Baja Grill, Buffalo Wild Wings, Carl's Jr, El Pollo Loco, Gourmet Italian, Richie's Diner, Rubio's, Seafood Grill, Sizzler, Starbucks, Wendy's, **other:** Ralph's Foods, Rite Aid, Ross, Sam's Club/gas, Walgreens
0mm	I-215 begins/ends on I-15.

INTERSTATE 280 (BAY AREA)

E ↕ W

Exit #	Services
58	4th St, I-280 begins/ends, **N other:** Whole Foods Mkt, **S gas:** Shell
57	7th St, to I-80, downtown
56	Mariposa St, downtown
55	Army St, Port of SF
54	US 101 S, Alemany Blvd, Mission St, **E gas:** Shell
52	San Jose Ave, Bosworth St (from nb, no return)
51	Geneva Ave
50	CA 1, 19th Ave, **W gas:** Chevron, **other:** to Bay Bridge, SFSU
49	Daly City, **E gas:** 76/dsl/LP, **other:** Toyota, Walgreens, **W gas:** Arco, **food:** Carl's Jr, Domino's, IHOP, In-n-Out, Krispy Kreme, McDonald's, Val's Rest., **lodging:** Hampton Inn
47a	Serramonte Blvd, Daly City (from sb), **E gas:** Silver Gas, **other:** Cadillac, Chevrolet, Ford, Home Depot, Honda, Nissan, Target, **W gas:** Olympian, 76, **food:** Boston Mkt, Elephant Bar Rest., McDonald's, Sizzler, Starbucks, **other:** Macy's, Longs Drugs, Office Depot, PetsMart, Ross, Target
47b	CA 1, Mission St (from nb), Pacifica, **E food:** Hawaiian BBQ, RoundTable Pizza, Sizzler, **other:** H, Chrysler/Jeep/Dodge, Drug Barn, Fresh Choice Foods, Home Depot, Infiniti, Isuzu, Jo-Ann Fabrics, Lexus, Mitsubishi, Nordstrom's, PetCo, Target, mall
46	Hickey Blvd, Colma, **E gas:** Chevron/dsl/24hr, Shell, **W gas:** Shell/dsl/24hr, **food:** Boston Mkt,

SAN FRANCISCO

INTERSTATE 280 CONT'D (BAY AREA)

E ↕ W

Exit #	Services
46	Continued Celia's Rest., Koi Palace, Moonstar, Outback Steaks, Sizzler, **other:** Ross, 7-11
45	Avalon Dr (from sb), Westborough, **W gas:** Arco/24hr, Valero/dsl, **food:** Denny's, McDonald's, Subway, **other:** Pak'n Save Foods, Walgreens/24hr, Skyline Coll
44	(from nb)
43b	I-380 E, to US 101, to SF ✈
43a	San Bruno Ave, Sneath Ave, **E food:** Au's Kitchen, Baskin-Robbins, Carl's Jr, Jamba Juice, Quizno's, Starbucks, Taco Bell, **other:** GNC, Longs Drugs, Mollie Stones Mkt, Radio Shack, **W gas:** Chevron, 76, **food:** Baker's Square, **other:** 7-11
42	Crystal Springs (from sb), county park
41	CA 35 N, Skyline Blvd (from wb, no EZ return), to Pacifica, 1 mi **W gas:** Chevron
40	Millbrae Ave, Millbrae, **E gas:** Chevron
39	Trousdale Dr, to Burlingame, **E** H
36	Black Mtn Rd, Hayne Rd, **W** golf, vista point
36mm	**Crystal Springs rest area wb, full ♿ facilities, ☎, picnic table, litter barrels, petwalk**
35	CA 35, CA 92W (from eb), to Half Moon Bay
34	Bunker Hill Dr
33	CA 92, to Half Moon Bay, San Mateo
32mm	vista point both lanes
29	Edgewood Rd, Canada Rd, to San Carlos, **E other:** H
27	Farm Hill Blvd, **E other:** Cañada Coll, ☎
25	CA 84, Woodside Rd, Redwood City, **1 mi W gas:** Chevron/dsl, **food:** John Bentley's Rest., Buck's Rest., **other:** Robert's Mkt, USPO
24	Sand Hill Rd, Menlo Park, **1 mi E gas:** Shell, **food:** Starbucks, **other:** Longs Drug, Safeway
22	Alpine Rd, Portola Valley, **E other:** H, **W gas:** Shell/autocare, **food:** Red Lotus Cafe, RoundTable Pizza, **other:** Curves
20	Page Mill Rd, to Palo Alto, **E** H, to Stanford U
16	El Monte Rd, Moody Rd
15	Magdalena Ave
13	Foothill Expswy, Grant Rd, **E gas:** Chevron/24hr, **food:** Starbucks, Woodpecker Grill, **other:** Rite Aid, Trader Joe's, **W other:** to Rancho San Antonio CP
12b a	CA 85, N to Mtn View, S to Gilroy
11	Saratoga, Cupertino, Sunnyvale, **E gas:** Chevron, **food:** Carl's Jr, Quizno's, **lodging:** Cupertino Inn, **other:** Goodyear, Michael's, Rite Aid, TJ Maxx, repair, **W gas:** Chevron, Dianza Gas, 76, USA, **food:** BJ's Rest., Outback Steaks, **lodging:** Cypress Hotel, **other:** Apple Computer HQ, PetsMart
10	Wolfe Rd, **E gas:** Arco/24hr, **food:** Teppan Steaks, Starbucks, **lodging:** Courtyard, Hilton Garden, **other:** Ranch Mkt, **W gas:** 76, **food:** Alexander Steaks, Benihana, Vallco Dynasty Chinese, **other:** Fresh-Choice Foods, JC Penney, Jiffy Lube, Sears/auto, Vallco Fashion Park
9	Lawrence Expswy, Stevens Creek Blvd (from eb), **N food:** El Pollo Loco, McDonalds, Mtn Mikes Pizza, Panda Express, Quizno's, Starbucks, **other:** Safeway, Marshalls, **other:** Land Rover, Nissan,

SAN JOSE

Exit #	Services
9	Continued **S gas:** Rotten Robbie, 76, **food:** IHOP, Subway, **lodging:** 7-11, Woodcrest Hotel
7	Saratoga Ave, **N gas:** Arco/24hr, Chevron/24hr, **food:** Black Angus, Burger King, Garden City Rest., Happi House, Lion Rest., McDonald's, Taco Bell, **other:** Cadillac, Chevrolet, Ford, Goodyear, Jiffy Lube, PepBoys, 7-11, **S gas:** 76, Shell, Valero, **food:** Applebee's, Tony Roma's, **lodging:** MoorPark Hotel
5c	Winchester Blvd, Campbell Ave (from eb)
5b	CA 17 S, to Santa Cruz, I-880 N, to San Jose
5a	Leigh Ave, Bascom Ave
4	Meridian St (from eb), **N gas:** 76, **other:** Big O Tire, FoodMaxx, **S gas:** Chevron, **food:** KFC, Subway, Wienerschnitzel, **other:** 7-11
3b	Bird Ave, Race St
3a	CA 87, **N lodging:** Hilton, Holiday Inn, Hotel Sainte Claire, Marriott
2	7th St, to CA 82, **N** conv ctr
1	10th St, 11th St, **N other:** 7-11, **other:** to San Jose St U
0mm	I-280 begins/ends on US 101.

INTERSTATE 405 (LOS ANGELES)

N ↕ S

LOS ANGELES AREA

Exit #	Services
73	I-5, N to Sacramento, I-5, S to LA
72	Rinaldi St, Sepulveda, **E gas:** Chevron, 76, **food:** Arby's, Presidente McDonald's, Mexican, Subway, **other:** H, Toyota, **W gas:** Shell, **lodging:** Best Value
71	CA 118 W, Simi Valley
70	Devonshire St, Granada Hills, **E gas:** Arco, Mobil, 76, **food:** Holiday Burger, Millie's Rest., Papa John's, Quizno's, Safari Room Rest, Starbucks, Subway, **other:** Discount Tire, Kwik Serve, Nissan, Ralph's Foods, Rite Aid, Von's Foods, USPO
69	Nordhoff St, **E gas:** Mobil/dsl, **other:** 7-11/24hr, Vallarta Foods, Walgreen, **W gas:** Arco, 76, **food:** Jack-in-the-Box, Pizza Hut
68	Roscoe Blvd, to Panorama City, **E gas:** Exxon, 76, **food:** Burger King, Denny's, Jack-in-the-Box, McDonald's, Panda Express, Quizno's, Taco Bell, Yoshinoya, **lodging:** Holiday Inn Express, **other:** AutoZone, Ford/Lincoln/Mercury/Jaguar/Starbucks, **W gas:** Chevron/dsl, Shell/dsl, **food:** Tommy's Burgers, **lodging:** Motel 6
66	Sherman Blvd, Reseda, **E gas:** Chevron, Mobil/LP, **food:** Ameci Pizza, KFC, McDonald's, Starbucks, **other:** BigLots, CVS Drug, Jon's Foods, **W gas:** 76/dsl/24hr, **food:** Taco Bell, **other:** H, USPO
65	Victory Blvd, Van Nuys, **E on Sepulveda food:** Carl's Jr, El Pollo Loco, Jack-in-the-Box, Subway, Wendy's, **other:** CVS Drug, El Monte RV Ctr, Costco/gas, Office Depot, PepBoys, Staples, **W on Victory gas:** Arco/24hr, **other:** H
64	Burbank Blvd, **E gas:** Chevron, Shell, **food:** Denny's, **lodging:** Best Western, **other:** Target
63b	US 101, Ventura Fwy
63a	Ventura Blvd (from nb), **E gas:** Mobil, **food:** Denny's, El Pollo Loco, **other:** Food Mkt, mall, **W gas:** Chevron, 76, **food:** Corner Bakery Cafe, IHOP, McDonald's, **lodging:** Best West Inn, Courtyard, **other:** Rite Aid

INTERSTATE 405 CONT'D (LOS ANGELES)

N ↕ S

Exit #	Services
63a	Valley Vista Blvd (from sb)
61	Mulholland Dr
59	Sepulveda Blvd, **W** to Getty Ctr
57	Sunset Blvd, Morega Dr, **E gas:** Chevron/24hr, 76/dsl, **other:** to UCLA, **W lodging:** Luxe Hotel
56	Waterford St, Montana Ave (from nb)
55c b	Wilshire Blvd, **E** downtown, **W gas:** Mobil, **other:** H, 7-11
55a	CA 2, Santa Monica Blvd, **E gas:** Chevron, Mobil, Thrifty, **food:** Chinese Cuisine, Jack-in-the-Box, Jamba Juice, Quizno's, Starbucks, Winchell's, Yoshinoya, Zankau Chicken, **lodging:** Travelodge, **other:** Firestone, 7-11, LDS Temple, Staples, Vet, **W gas:** Chevron, 76/24hr, **food:** Subway, **lodging:** Holiday Inn
54	Olympic Blvd, Peco Blvd (from sb), **E food:** Pazzo Pizzaria, Subway, **other:** 7-11, **W food:** Panda Express, Starbucks, **other:** Best Buy, Marshall's, **other:** USPO
53	I-10, Santa Monica Fwy
52	Venice Blvd, **E gas:** Chevron/service, Shell/dsl, **food:** Carl's Jr, Subway, **lodging:** Ramada, **other:** 7-11, **W gas:** SP/dsl, **food:** FatBurger, **other:** services on Sepulveda
51	Culver Blvd, Washington Blvd, **E food:** Dear John's Café, Taco Bell, **other:** Chevrolet, **W gas:** 76/repair
50b	CA 90, Slauson Ave, to Marina del Rey, **E gas:** Arco/24hr, **food:** Del Taco, Shakey's Pizza, **other:** Firestone/auto, Goodyear/auto, JC Penney, Office Depot, Old Navy, Macy's, Pic'n Sav Foods, transmissions, **W gas:** 76, **food:** Denny's, **other:** Albertson's
50a	Jefferson Blvd (from sb), **E food:** Coco's, Jack-in-the-Box, **other:** Rite Aid, **W** to LA ✈
49	Howard Hughes Pkwy, to Centinela Ave, **E gas:** Mobil/dsl, **food:** Sizzler, **lodging:** Ramada Inn, Sheraton, **other:** Ford, JC Penney, Macy's, mall, **W gas:** Chevron, **food:** Dinah's Rest., Islands Burgers, On the Border, Subway, **lodging:** Extended Stay America, Radisson, **other:** CVS Drug, Howard Hughes Ctr, mall
48	La Tijera Blvd, **E gas:** Mobil, **food:** Burger King, ChuckeCheese, El Pollo Loco, Jamba Juice, KFC, McDonald's, Subway, TGIFriday, **lodging:** Best Western, **other:** CVS Drug, EZ Lube, 99c Store, Ross, Von's Foods, **W gas:** Chevron/dsl/24hr, 76/Circle K, **food:** Buggy Whip Rest., Subway, Wendy's, **other:** USPO
47	CA 42, Manchester Ave, to Inglewood, **E gas:** 76/Circle K/dsl/24hr, **food:** Carl's Jr, Subway, **lodging:** Best Western, Economy Inn, **other:** 7-11, **W gas:** Arco, Mobil, Shell, 76, **food:** Arby's, Burger King, Jack-in-the-Box, Louis Burgers, **lodging:** Day's Inn, **other:** CarMax, Chrysler/Jeep/Dodge, Home Depot, Hyundai
46	Century Blvd, **E gas:** 76, **food:** Burger King, Casa Gamino Mexican, Flower Drum Chinese, Rally's, Subway, **lodging:** Best Western, Comfort Inn, Motel 6, Tiboli Hotel, **other:** AutoZone, **W gas:** Arco/24hr, Chevron/dsl, 76/Circle K, Shell, **food:** Carl's Jr, Denny's, McDonald's, Taco Bell, **lodging:** Hampton Inn, Hilton, Holiday Inn, Marriott, Quality Hotel, Travelodge, Westin Hotel

HAWTHORNE

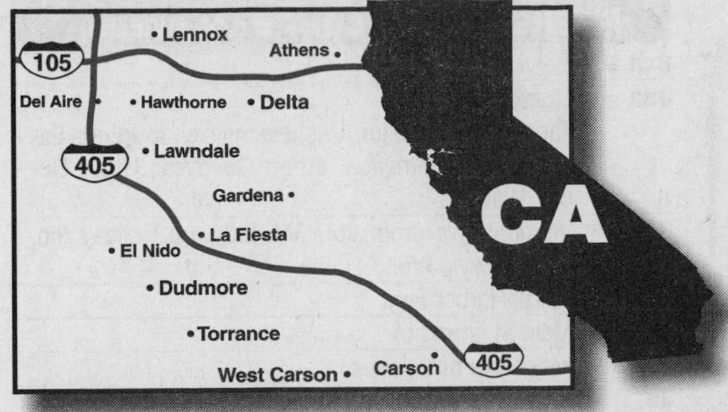

CA

Exit #	Services
45	I-105, Imperial Hwy, **E gas:** Arco, Mobil/dsl, Shell, **food:** BBQ, El Pollo Loco, El Tarasco Mexican, Jack-in-the-Box, McDonald's, **other:** J&S Trasmissions, **W food:** Proud Bird Rest. (1mi)
44	El Segundo Blvd, to El Segundo, **E gas:** Chevron/24hr, Thrifty, **food:** Burger King, Christy's Donuts, Jack-in-the-Box, Jase Burgers, Rally's, Subway, **lodging:** El Segundo Inn, **W food:** Denny's, Chappie's Rest, **lodging:** Ramada Inn
43b a	Rosecrans Ave, to Manhattan Beach, **E gas:** 76, Mobil/dsl, Shell, **food:** Del Taco, Denny's, El Pollo Loco, Pizza Hut, Starbucks, Subway, **other:** Albertson's, Best Buy, CVS Drug, Food4Less, Ford, Home Depot, Marshall's, Michael's, Office Depot, Ross, **W gas:** Thrifty, **food:** Carl's Jr, China Chef, Chipotle Mexican, Luigi's Rest., McDonald's, Qdoba Mexican, Robeks Juice, Sansai Japanese, Starbucks, **lodging:** Ayres Hotel, **other:** Chevrolet/Pontiac/GMC, Costco/gas, Staples, VW
42b	Inglewood Ave, **E gas:** Arco, **food:** Del Taco, Denny's, Domino's, Hong Kong Express, In-N-Out, Quizno's, Wok Wok Chinese, Yoshinoya, **other:** CVS Drug, Marshall's, PetCo, Von's Foods, **W gas:** Arco, 76, Shell/dsl/24hr, **food:** La Salsa Mexican, Leo's Mexican, **other:** Drug Emporium, Goodyear/auto
42a	CA 107, Hawthorne Blvd, **E food:** Jack-in-the-Box, Little Caesars, McDonald's, Panda Express, Papa John's, Spires Rest, Taco Bell, Wienerschnitzel, Wendy's, **lodging:** Best Western, Day's Inn, Holiday Inn, **other:** CVS Drug, Kragen Parts, 99c Store, Radio Shack, Vet, **W gas:** Arco/24hr, Chevron/dsl, Thrifty, **food:** Boston Mkt, Marie Callendar's, Sizzler, Subway, Taco Bell, Yoshinoya, **other:** AutoZone, Macy's
40b	Redondo Beach Blvd (no EZ sb return), Hermosa Beach, **E gas:** Arco/24hr, Prena, Thrifty, **food:** ChuckeCheese, Jack-in-the-Box, **other:** golf, **W food:** Boston Mkt, Pizza Hut, **other:** CVS Drug, Nordstrom's, U-Haul
40a	CA 91 E, Artesia Blvd, to Torrance, **W gas:** Chevron, **other:** Carl's Jr., Starbucks, **other:** Winchell's
39	Crenshaw Blvd, to Torrance, **E gas:** Arco/24hr, **food:** Burger King, McDonald's, **other:** Ralph's Foods, **W gas:** Mobil/dsl, Shell/Subway/dsl, **other:** Jiffy Lube
38b	Western Ave, to Torrance, **E gas:** Arco, Chevron, 76/dsl, **food:** Del Taco, Denny's, Papa John's, Starbucks, Wendy's, Yorgo's Burgers, **lodging:** Dynasty Inn, **other:** Albertson's, GNC, Toyota, **W gas:** Mobil, **food:** Mill's Rest., **lodging:** Courtyard, **other:** Lexus
38a	Normandie Ave, to Gardena, **E lodging:** Comfort Inn, **W gas:** Shell/dsl, **food:** Carl's Jr, Chile Verde Mexican, Quizno's, Starbucks, Subway,

TORRANCE

INTERSTATE 405 CONT'D (LOS ANGELES)

N ↕ S

Exit #	Services
38a	Continued Taco Bell/Pizza Hut, Wienerschnitzel, **lodging:** Extended Stay America, **other:** Goodyear, Office Depot, Walmart
37b	Vermont Ave (from sb), **W lodging:** Holiday Inn, **other:** hwy patrol
37a	I-110, Harbor Fwy
36	Main St (from nb)
36mm	**weigh sta both lanes**
35	Avalon Blvd, to Carson, **E gas:** Arco/24hr, Chevron, Mobil, Shell, **food:** Chili's, ChuckeCheese, Denny's, FoodCourt, Jack-in-the-Box, McDonald's, Pizza Hut, Quizno's, Shakey's Pizza, Sizzler, Subway, Tony Roma, **lodging:** Quality Inn, **other:** America's Tire, Firestone, Goodyear/auto, Ikea, JC Penney, PepBoys, Sears/auto, mall, **W gas:** Arco/24hr, Mobil, Shell, **food:** Carl's Jr, El Charro, IHOP, **other:** Chrysler/Dodge/Jeep, Ford/Lincoln/Mercury, Isuzu, Kia, Ralph's Foods, USPO
34	Carson St, to Carson, **E food:** Del Taco, **lodging:** Comfort Inn, **W gas:** Mobil, 76/dsl/24hr, **food:** Carl's Jr, El Charro, IHOP, Jack-in-the-Box, Subway, **lodging:** Hilton
33b	Wilmington Ave, **E gas:** Arco/service, **food:** Carson Burgers, **W gas:** Chevron/repair/24hr, Shell/Subway/Taco Bell/dsl, **food:** Del Taco, **other:** Chevrolet/Hyundai, Toyota
33a	Alameda St
32d	Santa Fe Ave (from nb), **E gas:** Arco/24hr, **W gas:** Chevron/24hr, Shell
32c b	I-710, Long Beach Fwy
32a	Pacific Ave (from sb)
30b	Long Beach Blvd, **E gas:** 76, **W gas:** Mobil, **other:** H, Toyota
30a	Atlantic Blvd, **E gas:** Chevron/dsl, Shell/Subway/dsl, **food:** Arby's, Black Angus, Denny's/24hr, El Patio, El Torito, Jack-in-the-Box, **other:** Mercedes, Staples, Target, Walgreen, **W other:** H, Chrysler/Jeep, Nissan
29c	Orange Ave (from sb), **W other:** Dodge/Pontiac/GMC
29b a	Cherry Ave, to Signal Hill, **E gas:** Mobil/dsl, **food:** Fantastic Burgers, **other:** Ford, auto repair, **W food:** John's Burgers, Charley Brown's Steaks/Lobster, Rib Café, **other:** BMW, Dodge, Firestone, Nissan
27	CA 19, Lakewood Blvd, **E lodging:** Marriott, **W gas:** Chevron, Shell/24hr, **food:** Spires Rest., Taco Bell, **lodging:** Holiday Inn, Residence Inn, **other:** H, Ford, Goodyear/auto, Kia
26b	Bellflower Blvd, **E gas:** Chevron, 76, **food:** Burger King, Carl's Jr, KFC, **other:** Chevrolet, Ford, K-Mart, Lowe's Whse, **W gas:** Mobil/dsl, 76, **food:** FishTale Rest., Hof's Rest., McDonald's, Quizno's, Wendy's, **other:** H, Borders Books, Goodyear/auto, Rite Aid/24hr, SavOn Drug, Sears, Target
26a	Woodruff Ave (from nb)
25	Palo Verde Ave, **W gas:** 76, **food:** Del Taco, Dr Wi Donuts, Pizza Hut/Taco Bell, Subway
24b	Studebaker Rd
24a	I-605 N
23	CA 22 W, 7th St, to Long Beach
22	Seal Beach Blvd, Los Alamitos Blvd, **E gas:** Chevron/repair/24hr, Mobil, 76, **food:** Carl's Jr, KFC, Panda Chinese, Spagatini Grill, Winchell's, **other:** Albertson's, Goodyear/auto, Ralph's Foods, Rite Aid, Target, Winston Tire
21	CA 22 E, Garden Grove Fwy, Valley View St, **E gas:** Mobil, Shell/dsl, **food:** Coco's, DQ, Maxwell's Seafood Rest., Sizzler, **other:** Chevrolet, Ford, Rite Aid, Von's Foods
19	Westminster Ave, to Springdale St, **E gas:** Arco/24hr, Chevron/dsl, 76/Circle K, Thrifty, 7-11/24hr, **food:** Café Westminster, Carl's Jr, In-N-Out, KFC, La Casa Brita, McDonald's, Taco Bell, Yoshinoya, **lodging:** Motel 6, Travelodge, **other:** Albertson's, America's Tire, Home Depot, Kragen Parts, Radio Shack, Rite Aid, **W gas:** Chevron/dsl/24hr, Shell/dsl/24hr, **food:** Pizza Hut, Subway, **lodging:** Best Western, Day's Inn
18	Bolsa Ave, Golden West St, **E food:** Pizza Hut, Popeye's, **W gas:** Chevron, Mobil, 76, Shell, **food:** Coco's, El Torito, IHOP, Jack-in-the-Box, **other:** Best Buy, JC Penney, Jo-Ann Fabrics, Jon's Foods, Macy's, Sears/auto, mall
16	CA 39, Beach Blvd, to Huntington Bch, **E gas:** Shell, **food:** Hof's Rest., Jack-in-the-Box, Mei's Chinese, **lodging:** BeachWest Inn, Princess Inn, Super 8, Westminster Inn, **other:** H, Buick/Pontiac/GMC, K-Mart, PepBoys, Toyota, **W gas:** Arco, Mobil/service, 76, **food:** Arby's, Burger King, Diedrich's Coffee, El Torito, Jack-in-the-Box, Macaroni Grill, Marie Callender's, Popeye's, Starbucks, **lodging:** Holiday Inn, **other:** Barnes&Noble, Chevrolet, Chrysler/Jeep, Dodge, Ford/Lincoln/Mercury, Just Tires, Marshall's, Mitsubishi, Subaru, Target, VW
15b a	Magnolia St, Warner Ave, **E gas:** Shell, **food:** Del Taco, Sizzler, **other: W gas:** Chevron, Mobil, **food:** Bullwinkle's Rest., Carrow's, Magnolia Café, Tommy's Burgers, **lodging:** Ramada Inn, **other:** IGA Foods, SavOn Drug
14	Brookhurst Ave, Fountain Valley, **E gas:** Arco/24hr, Chevron, Thrifty, **food:** Alberto's Mexican, Coco's, Del Taco, **lodging:** Courtyard, Residence Inn, **other:** Thompson's RV Ctr, **W gas:** Chevron/service/24hr, Shell/dsl, **food:** Black Angus, Stix Chinese, Wendy's, **other:** Albertson's, Office Depot
12	Euclid Ave, **E food:** CA Noodle Factory, Cancun Fresh, Carl's Jr, Cofee Bean, George's Burgers, Panda Express, Pita Fresh Grill, Quizno's, Starbuck's, Souplantation, Taco Bell, Z Pizza, **other:** H, Costco/gas, Fry's Electronics, Office Depot, PetsMart, Staples, Tire Whse
11b	Harbor Blvd, to Costa Mesa, **E food:** Hooters, **lodging:** La Quinta, **W gas:** Arco, Chevron, Mobil, Shell/dsl, 7-11, **food:** Burger King, Denny's, Domino's, El Pollo Loco, IHOP, Jack-in-the-Box, KFC, LJ Silver, McDonald's, Subway, **lodging:** Costa Mesa Inn, Motel 6, Super 8, Vagabond Inn, **other:** Albertson's, Big O Tire, Cadillac, Chevrolet, Dodge/Acura, Ford/Lincoln/Mercury, Honda, Infiniti, JustTires, Mazda, Pontiac/Buick, Radio Shack, Rite Aid, Target, Von's Foods, Winchell's

CARSON

COSTA MESA

INTERSTATE 405 CONT'D (LOS ANGELES)

N ↕ S

Exit #	Services
11a	Fairview Rd, **E other:** Barnes&Noble, Best Buy, Marshall's, Nordstrom's, Old Navy, **W gas:** Chevron, 76, Shell, **food:** Del Taco, Jack-in-the-Box, Round Table Pizza, Taco Bell, **other:** CVS Drug, Kragen Parts, Stater Bro's
10	CA 73, to CA 55 S (from sb), Corona del Mar, Newport Beach
9b	Bristol St, **E gas:** Chevron/dsl, Shell/24hr, **food:** Bloomingdale's, Blue Water Grill, Carrow's, Chicago Pizza, Chick-fil-A, China Olive, Chipotle Mexican, Claim Jumper Rest, Clubhouse Cafe, Greek Island Grill, In-N-Out, Jack-in-the-Box, Macaroni Grill, Maggiano's Rest., Magic Wok, McDonald's, Morton's Steaks, Pat & Oscar's, Pizza Hut, Red Robin, Scott Seafood, South Coast Rest, Starbucks, Ztejas Rest, **lodging:** Marriott Suites, Westin Hotel, **other:** BigLots, CVS Drug, Firestone/auto, Goodyear/auto, Macy's, Michael's, Nordstrom's, Office Depot, PetCo, Radio Shack, Rite Aid, Ross, Target, Sears/auto, Staples, Target, TJ Maxx, Von's Foods, World Mkt, mall, **W gas:** Chevron, 76/dsl, **food:** Del Taco/24hr, El Pollo Loco, McDonald's, Subway, Wahoo Taco, **lodging:** Hilton, Holiday Inn, **other:** PepBoys, 7-11, Vet
9a	CA 55, Costa Mesa Fwy, to Newport Bch, Riverside
8	MacArthur Blvd, **E gas:** Chevron, Mobil/Subway, **food:** Agora Rest, Carl's Jr, Juice it Up, McDonald's, Quizno's, Russel's Seafood, Starbucks, Taco Factory, **lodging:** Crowne Plaza Hotel, Holiday Inn, **other: W gas:** Chevron, **food:** El Torito, Gulliver's Ribs, IHOP, **lodging:** Atrium Hotel, Hilton, to ✈
7	Jamboree Rd, Irvine, **E lodging:** Courtyard, Hyatt, Residence Inn, **food:** Soup Plantation, **E on Main St gas:** Shell, **food:** Burger King, JambaJuice, **other:** Jiffy Lube, Ralph's Foods, **W food:** CA Pizza Kitchen, El Torito, Daily Grill, FatBurger, Gulliver's, Houston's, IHOP, Inka Grill, Jack Shrimp, Melting Pot Rest, Ruth's Chris Steaks, Subway, Taleo Mexico, Wahoo's Taco, **lodging:** Marriott
5	Culver Dr, **W gas:** Alfie's Gas, Chevron/dsl, **food:** Carl's Jr, Subway, **other:** Ace Hardware, Rite Aid, Wholesome foods Mkt
4	Jeffrey Rd, University Dr, **E gas:** Chevron, Circle K/gas, **food:** Baja Fresh, Coffee Bean, El Cholo Cantina, El Pollo Loco, Golden Spoon, Juice It Up, McDonald's, NY Pizza, Pei Wei Asian, Pomodoro Italian, Starbucks, Stix Chinese, Togo's, **other:** Ace Hardware, CVS Drug, Gelson's Mkt, Office Depot, Ralph's Foods, SavOn Drug, H, **W gas:** Mobil/dsl, **food:** IHOP, Korean BBQ, **other:** Ralph's Foods, Vet
3	Sand Canyon Ave, **E** H, **W gas:** Arco/dsl, **lodging:** Juice It Up, Lucca Cafe, Red Brick Pizza, **other:** Albertson's, Starbucks, CVS Drug
2	CA 133, to Laguna Beach, **E other:** DoubleTree Inn
1c	Irvine Center Dr, **E food:** Dave & Buster's, PF Chang's, **other:** Barnes&Noble, **W food:** Burger King
1b	Bake Pkwy, **W** Toyota
1a	Lake Forest
0mm	I-405 begins/ends on I-5, exit 132.

IRVINE

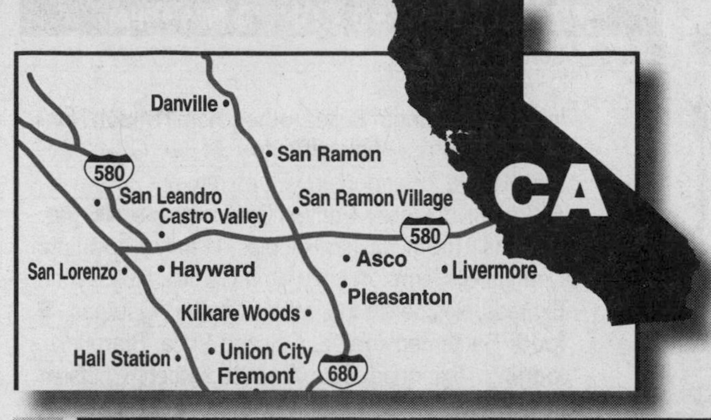

CA

INTERSTATE 505 (WINTERS)

N ↕ S

Exit #	Services
33	I-5. I-505 begins/ends on I-5.
31	CA 12A
28	CA 14, Zamora
24	CA 19
21	CA 16, to Esparto, Woodland, **W gas:** Guy's Food/fuel, **food:** La Plazita
17	CA 27
15	CA 29A
11	CA 128 W, Russell Blvd, **W gas:** Chevron/24hr, Interstate/dsl, **food:** RoundTable Pizza, Subway, **other:** Lorenzo's Mkt, Vet
10	Putah Creek Rd, **no crossover** same as 11
6	Allendale Rd
3	Midway Rd, **E other:** RV camping
1c	Vaca Valley Pkwy
1b	I-80 E. I-505 begins/ends on I-80.

INTERSTATE 580 (BAY AREA)

E ↕ W

Exit #	Services
79	I-580 begins/ends, accesses I-5 sb.
76b a	CA 132, Chrisman Rd, to Modesto, **E gas:** 76/dsl, **other:** RV camping (5mi)
72	Corral Hollow Rd
67	Patterson Pass Rd, **W gas:** 76/dsl/24hr
65	I-205 (from eb), to Tracy
63	Grant Line Rd, to Byron
59	N Flynn Rd, Altamont Pass, elev 1009, **S** Brake Check Area, many wind-turbines
57	N Greenville Rd, Laughlin Rd, Altamont Pass Rd, to Livermore Lab, **S gas:** Chevron/Subway/dsl, **lodging:** Best Western, La Quinta, **other:** Harley-Davidson
56mm	**weigh sta both lanes**
55	Vasco Rd, to Brentwood, **N gas:** Arco, Chevron, QuikStop/dsl, 76, Shell/dsl/deli, **food:** A&W/KFC, McDonald's, **S gas:** 7-11, Valero/dsl, **food:** Blimpie, Jack-in-the-Box, Taco Bell, **lodging:** Quality Inn
54	CA 84, 1st St, Springtown Blvd, Livermore, **N gas:** Chevron, **lodging:** DoubleTree Hotel, Holiday Inn, Motel 6, Springtown Inn, **other:** 7-11, **S gas:** Shell, 76/24hr, Valero/Circle K, **food:** Applebee's, Arby's, Burger King, Chevy's Mexican, Chili's, Crazy Buffet, IHOP, Italian Express, McDonald's, Panda Express, Starbucks, Subway, Taco Bell, Togo's, **other:** America's Tire, Longs Drug, Lowe's Whse, Office Depot, Radio Shack, Ross, Safeway/gas, Target
52	N Livermore Ave, **S gas:** Chevron/Jack-in-the-Box, 7-11, **food:** Baja Fresh, Coldstone Creamery, In-n-Out, Popeye's, Quizno's, String's Italian,

LIVERMORE

INTERSTATE 580 CONT'D (BAY AREA)

Exit #	Services
52	Continued **lodging:** Hawthorn Suites, **other:** Home Depot, Honda, Schwab Tire, Walmart/auto
51	Portola Ave, Livermore (no EZ eb return)
50	Airway Blvd, Collier Canyon Rd, Livermore, **N gas:** Shell/dsl, **food:** Baskin-Robbins, Wendy's, **lodging:** Courtyard, Hampton Inn, Hilton Garden, Holiday Inn Express, Residence Inn, **other:** Costco Whse/gas, **S food:** Cattlemen's Rest., Chicago Pizza, Starbucks, **lodging:** Extended Stay America, **other:** Chrysler/Jeep, Ford/Lincoln/Mercury, Mazda, 7-11
48	El Charro Rd, O'Fallon Rd
47	Santa Rita Rd, Tassajara Rd, **N other:** Buick/Pontiac/GMC, Saab, Safeway Foods, **S gas:** Shell, **food:** Bakers Square, Korea Garden, McDonald's, Quizno's, Subway, Taco Bell, TGI Friday, Thai Quisine, **other:** Acura, BMW, Cadillac, GMC, Hummer, Infiniti, Lexus, Long's Drug, MiniCooper, Mitsubishi, Rose Pavilion, Saab, Trader Joe's, Volvo
46	Hacienda Dr, Pleasanton, **N gas:** Shell, **food:** Applebee's, Black Angus, Fuddruckers, Macaroni Grill, Mimi's Cafe, On-the-Border, Papa John's, Woks Up, **lodging:** AmeriSuites, **other:** Barnes&Noble, Best Buy, Ford, Old Navy, TJ Maxx, **S food:** Red Robin, **other:** [H], Borders Books, Kohl's, Staples, Walmart/auto
45	Hopyard Rd, Pleasanton, **N gas:** 76/Circle K, Minimart, Shell/dsl, **lodging:** Hilton, Holiday Inn Express, **other:** America's Tire, Dodge, El Monte RV Ctr, Goodyear, Honda, Nissan, Office Depot, Pak'n Sav, RV Ctr, U-Haul, Toyota, **S gas:** Chevron, Shell/dsl, **food:** Arby's, Burger King, Chef India, Chevy's Mexican, Chili's, Denny's, El Balazo, In-n-Out, Nations Burgers, Pleasant Asian, Starbucks, Taco Bell, **lodging:** Candlewood Suites, Courtyard, Hilton, Larkspur Landing, Marriott, Motel 6, Sheraton, Super 8, **other:** Home Depot, Mercedes
44b	I-680, N to San Ramon, S to San Jose
44a	Foothills Rd, San Ramon Rd, **N gas:** CA Fuel, Chevron, Shell, Valero, **food:** Burger King, Casa Orozco, China Wall, Chipotle Mexican, ChuckeCheese, Country Waffles, Elephant Bar, Frankie's Johnny's & Luigi's Too, Hooters, Korean BBQ, Outback Steaks, Panera Bread, Popeye's, RoundTable Pizza, Starbucks, **lodging:** Radisson, **other:** Big Lots, Curves, $Tree, Kragen Parts, Long's Drug, Marshall's, Michael's, PetCo, PetsMart, Ranch Mkt Foods, Ross, Target, **S food:** Cheesecake Factory, PF Chang's, **lodging:** Marriott, Residence Inn, Sheraton, **other:** JC Penney, Macy's, Nordstrom's, Sears, mall
39	Eden Canyon Rd, Palomares Rd, **S other:** rodeo park
37	Center St, Crow Canyon Rd, same as 35, **S gas:** Arco/24hr, Chevron/dsl/, 76/dsl, Quikstop, **food:** McDonald's, Starbucks, Subway
35	Redwood Rd (from eb), Castro Valley, **N gas:** Chevron, 76/dsl, Shell/dsl, **food:** Baker's Square, Chipotle Mexican, KFC, McDonald's, Quizno's, RoundTable Pizza, Sizzler, Taco Bell, Wendy's, **other:** Comfort Suites, Holiday Inn Express, **other:** Goodyear, Longs Drug, Lucky Foods, NAPA, Radio Shack, Rite Aid, Safeway, Walgreens
34	I-238 W, to I-880, CA 238, **W off I-238...food:** McDonald's, Jack-in-the Box, **other:** Chrysler/Jeep, 99c Store
33	164th Ave, Miramar Ave, **E gas:** Chevron/dsl, Valero, **lodging:** Fairmont Inn
32	150th Ave, Fairmont, **E other:** [H], **W gas:** Shell, 76/dsl, **food:** Arby's, Burger King, Carrows, Chili's, Denny's, McDonald's, RoundTable Pizza, Starbucks, Tito's Cafe, **other:** Goodyear, Kohl's, Long's Drug, Macy's, Pepboys, Staples, Target
31	Grand Ave (from sb), Dutton Ave, **W gas:** Coast, **other:** Rite Aid
30	106th Ave, Foothill Blvd, MacArthur Blvd, **W gas:** Arco, **food:** Church's
29	98th Ave, Golf Links Rd, **E gas:** Shell, **other:** Oakland Zoo, **W gas:** 76, Valero
27b	Keller Ave, Mtn Blvd, **E** repair
27a	Edwards Ave (from sb, no EZ return), **E** US Naval [H]
26a	CA 13, Warren Fwy, to Berkeley (from eb)
26b	Seminary Rd, **E** Observatory/Planetarium, **W gas:** Arco/24hr
25b a	High St, to MacArthur Blvd, **E gas:** 76, **food:** Subway, Razzo's Pizza, **other:** Kragen Parts, Lucky Foods, USPO, **W gas:** 76, **other:** Walgreens
24	35th Ave (no EZ sb return), **E gas:** 76, **food:** Taco Bell, **W gas:** Chevron, QuikStop, 76
23	Coolidge Ave, Fruitvale, **E gas:** Shell/24hr, **food:** China Gourmet, McDonald's, Subway, **other:** Longs Drug, Farmer Joe's, Radio Shack
22	Park Blvd, **E gas:** Shell, **W gas:** Arco, Quikstop, **other:** [H]
21b	Grand Ave, Lake Shore, **E gas:** Chevron/dsl, 76/24hr, **food:** KFC, Subway, **other:** Long's Drug, Trader Joe's, Walgreens, USPO, **W gas:** Chevron/dsl/24hr
21a	Harrison St, Oakland Ave, **E gas:** Quikstop, **W other:** Honda
19d c	CA 24 E, I-980 W, to Oakland
19b	West St, San Pablo Ave, **E lodging:** Extended Stay America, **other:** Best Buy, Home Depot, Jo-Ann Fabrics, Michael's, Office Depot
19a	I-80 W
18c	Market St, to San Pablo Ave, downtown
18b	Powell St, Emeryville, **E gas:** 76, **food:** Burger King, CA Pizza Kitchen, Denny's, Elephant Bar/Grill, Jamba Juice, PF Chang's, Starbucks, Togo's, **lodging:** Courtyard, Sheraton, Woodfin Suites, **other:** Barnes&Noble, Borders, Old Navy, Ross, Trader Joe's, **W gas:** Shell, **food:** Chevy's Mexican, **lodging:** Hilton Garden
18a	CA 13, Ashby Ave, Bay St, same as 18b
17	University Ave, Berkeley, **E gas:** 76, University Gas, **lodging:** La Quinta, **other:** to UC Berkeley
16	Gilman St, **E other:** Golden Gate Fields Race Track, **W other:** Target
13	Albany St, Buchanan St (from eb)
12	Central Ave (from eb), El Cerrito, **E gas:** Shell, Valero, **W other:** Costco/gas
11	Bayview Ave, Carlson Blvd, **E gas:** 76
10b	Regatta Blvd, **E gas:** Golden Gate/dsl
10a	S 23rd St, Marina Bay Pkwy, **E gas:** Stop and Save/dsl, **food:** Subway, **W food:** Cafe Tiatro,

E ↕ W

CA

PLEASANTON

OAKLAND AREA

E ↕ W

INTERSTATE 580 CONT'D (BAY AREA)

Exit #	Services
10a	Continued El Molchaete, Quizno's, Wing Stop, **other:** Longs Drugs
9	Harbour Way, Cutting Blvd, **E gas:** Arco, **W food:** Burger King
8	Canal Blvd, Garrard Blvd, **W gas:** Chevron/dsl, **lodging:** Days Inn
7b	Castro St, to I-80 E, Point Richmond, downtown industrial
7a	Western Drive (from wb), Point Molate
5mm	Richmond-San Rafael Toll Bridge
2a	Francis Drake Blvd, to US 101 S, **E lodging:** Extended Stay Deluxe, **other:** BMW/Saab, Home Depot
1b	Francisco Blvd, San Rafael, **E gas:** Beacon, Circle K, Francisco, **food:** Burger King, La Croissant, **lodging:** Motel 6, Travelodge, **other:** Mazda, tires, U-Haul, **W food:** Subway, Wendy's, **other:** Office Depot, USPO, to San Quentin
1a	US 101 N to San Rafael, I-580 begins/ends on US 101.

INTERSTATE 605 (LOS ANGELES)

N ↕ S — LOS ANGELES AREA

Exit #	Services
25	Huntington Dr. I-605 begins/ends.
24	I-210
23	Live Oak Ave, Arrow Hwy, **E** Santa Fe Dam, **W** Irwindale Speedway
22	Lower Azusa Rd, LA St
21	Ramona Blvd, **E gas:** Mobil, **food:** Del Taco/24hr
20	I-10, E to San Bernardino, W to LA
19	Valley Blvd, to Industry, **E gas:** Chevron/Subway, 76, **food:** McDonald's, Taco King, **lodging:** Valley Inn
18	CA 60, Pamona Fwy
17	Peck Rd, **E gas:** Shell, **W other:** Ford Trucks
16	Beverly Blvd, RoseHills Rd
15	Whittier Blvd, **E gas:** Arco, 76, **food:** Carl's Jr, Taco Bell, **lodging:** GoodNite Inn, **other:** 7-11, **W gas:** Chevron, **other:** Buick, Chrysler/Dodge, Ford, GMC, Honda, Isuzu, Jeep, Kia, Pontiac, Toyota, Volvo
14	Washington Blvd, to Pico Rivera, **E other:** Firestone/auto
13	Slauson Ave, **E gas:** Arco, Mobil, **food:** Denny's, **lodging:** Motel 6, **other:** Jeep, Kia, Nissan, **W** H
12	Telegraph Rd, to Santa Fe Springs, **E gas:** Chevron, **food:** Del Taco, Jack-in-the-Box, KFC, Taco Bell, **other:** st patrol, **W gas:** Arco/dsl
11	I-5
10	Florence Ave, to Downey, **E gas:** Mobil, **other:** Cadillac, Chevrolet, Honda
9	Firestone Blvd, **E gas:** 76, **food:** ChuckeCheese, KFC, McDonald's, Norm's Burgers, Sam's Burgers, **lodging:** Best Western, **other:** BMW, Costco, Food-4Less, Staples, VW/Audi, **W gas:** Arco, Chevron/repair, 76/dsl, **food:** Starbucks, **other:** Dodge, Office Depot, Target
8	I-105, Imperial Hwy, **E gas:** 76, **food:** KFC, McDonald's, Pizza Hut/Taco Bell, **other:** Food4Less, SavOn Drug, **W gas:** Arco
7	Rosecrans Ave, to Norwalk, **E gas:** Chevron, Mobil, **food:** Del Taco, McDonald's, **W food:** Carrow's Rest, **lodging:** Motel 6

Exit #	Services
6	Alondra Blvd, **E gas:** 7-11, Chevron, **food:** A&W, Alondra's Mexican, KFC, **lodging:** Spires Rest., **other:** Home Depot, SavOn Drug, Staples, **W gas:** Shell/Subway/24hr
5	CA 91
4	South St, **E other:** Macy's, Nordstrom's, Sears/auto, mall, **W gas:** Shell/service, UltraMar, **other:** Buick/GMC/Pontiac, Chrysler, Dodge, Ford, Honda, Hyundai, Infiniti, Isuzu, Toyota, Volvo
3	Del Amo Blvd, to Cerritos, **E food:** Del Taco, Duke's Burgers, **other:** Ralph's Foods, **W gas:** Mobil
2	Carson St, **E gas:** Arco, 76, Shell, **food:** Jack-in-the-Box, KFC, Little Caesar's, McDonald's, Popeye's, Sky Burgers, Spike's Rest., Taco Bell/Pizza Hut, Wienerschnitzel, **lodging:** Lakewood Inn, **other:** Chief Parts, Kragen Parts, **W gas:** Chevron/dsl, Mobil/Subway/dsl, **food:** Denny's, Del Taco, El Pollo Loco, El Torito, FoodCourt, In-n-Out, Jack-in-the-Box, Leucille's BBQ, Roadhouse Grill, Starbucks, TGIFriday, Zen's Buffet, **other:** America's Tire, Barnes&Noble, GNC, Lowe's Whse, Michael's, Old Navy, Radio Shack, Ross, Staples, Sam's Club/gas, Walmart/auto
1	Katella Ave, Willow St, **E gas:** Shell, **food:** Burger King, McDonald's, **other:** H
0mm	I-605 begins/ends on I-405.

INTERSTATE 680 (BAY AREA)

N ↕ S — CONCORD

Exit #	Services
71b a	I-80 E, to Sacramento, W to Oakland, I-680 begins/ends on I-80.
70	Green Valley Rd (from eb), Cordelia, **N gas:** Arco am/pm, **other:** Costco/gas, Longs Drug, Safeway
69	Gold Hill Rd, **W gas:** TowerMart/dsl
65	Marshview Rd
63	Parish Rd
61	Lake Herman Rd, **E gas:** Arco/Jack-in-the-Box/dsl, **W gas:** Gas City/dsl, Shell/Carl's Jr/dsl/24hr, **other:** vista point
60	Bayshore Rd, industrial park
58	I-780, to Benicia, toll plaza
56	Marina Vista, to Martinez
55mm	Martinez-Benicia Toll Br
54	Pacheco Blvd, Arthur Rd, Concord, **W gas:** 76, Shell/dsl
53	CA 4 E to Pittsburg, W to Richmond,
52	CA 4 E, Concord, Pacheco, **E food:** Hometown Buffet, Marie Callender's, Starbucks, Taco Bell, **lodging:** Crowne Plaza, Holiday Inn, **other:** Chevrolet, Ford, Hyundai, Infiniti/VW, Sam's Club, Toyota, Trader Joe's, USPO, **W gas:** Grand Gas, Shell/24hr, 76,

INTERSTATE 680 CONT'D (BAY AREA)

N ↕ S

CONCORD

Exit #	Services
52	Continued **food:** Denny's, McDonald's, Wendy's, **other:** AutoZone, Barnes&Noble, Firestone, K-Mart, Kragen Parts, Pepboys, Safeway Foods, Schwab Tire, Target, Toyota
51	Willow Pass Rd, Taylor Blvd, **E food:** Benihana Rest., Buffet City, Claim Jumper, Denny's, Elephant Bar Rest., El Torito, Fuddruckers, Grissini Italian, Jamba Juice, Panera Bread, Quizno's, Sizzler, **lodging:** Hilton, **other:** Cost+, Old Navy, Willows Shopping Ctr, **W food:** Baja Fresh, Red Robin, **other:** JC Penney, Macy's, Sears/auto
50	CA 242 (from nb), to Concord
49b	Monument Blvd, Gregory Lane (from sb), **E gas:** Valero/dsl, **food:** Country Waffles, Panda Express, Rubio's, Starbucks, **other:** Kohl's, Marshall's, **W gas:** Chevron, **food:** Boston Mkt, Jack-in-the-Box, McDonald's, Nations Burgers, Pizza Hut, Red Brick Pizza, Taco Bell, **lodging:** Courtyard, Hyatt, **other:** Big O Tire, Borders, Grocery Outlet, Lucky Foods, Michael's, Radio Shack, Rite Aid, Ross, Safeway Foods, Staples, Tuesday Morning
49a	Contra Costa Blvd (from nb)
48	Treat Blvd, Geary Rd, **E gas:** Chevron, **food:** Back 40 BBQ, Heavenly Cafe, Subway, **lodging:** Embassy Suites, Extended Stay America, **other:** Best Buy, Office Depot, 7-11, **W gas:** Chevron, Shell, **food:** Black Angus, Primavera Pasta, Quizno's, Starbucks, Wendy's, Yan's China Bistro, **other:** Walgreens
47	N Main St, to Walnut Creek, **E gas:** Chevron, **food:** Fuddrucker's, Jack-in-the-Box, Taco Bell, **lodging:** Marriott, Motel 6, Walnut Cr Motel, **other:** Cadillac, Chevrolet, Chrysler/Dodge/Jeep, Harley-Davidson, Honda, Jaguar, Land Rover, Mercedes, Nissan, Target, **W gas:** 76/7-11/dsl/24hr, **food:** Domino's, **other:** NAPA, Porsche
46b	Ygnacio Valley Rd
46a	SR-24 W
45b	Olympic Blvd, Oakland
45a	S Main St, Walnut Creek, **E** H
44	Rudgear (from nb)
43	Livorna Rd
42b a	Stone Valley Rd, Alamo, **W gas:** Chevron, Shell/dsl, **food:** Papa Murphy's, Starbucks, Subway, Taco Bell, Xenia's, **other:** Curves, Longs Drugs, Rite Aid, Safeway, 7-11, Vet
41	El Pintado Rd, Danville
40	El Cerro Blvd
39	Diablo Rd, Danville, **E gas:** 76/24hr, **food:** Chinese Cuisine, Taco Bell, **other:** Walgreens, Mt Diablo SP (12mi), **W gas:** Diablo
38	Sycamore Valley Rd, **E gas:** Shell, **food:** Denny's, **lodging:** Best Western, **W gas:** 76/dsl, Valero/dsl
36	Crow Canyon Rd, San Ramon, **E gas:** Shell, **food:** Burger King, Carl's Jr, Chili's, Cheesesteak, El Ballazo, Jamba Juice, Max's Diner, O'Zachary's Rest., Starbucks, Subway, **lodging:** Extended Stay America, **other:** H, Big O Tire, Costco, Lucky Foods, Marshall's, Office Depot, PetCo, Rite Aid, Sea's Candies, USPO, **W gas:** Chevron/repair/24hr, 76, Shell/

SAN RAMON

Exit #	Services
36	Continued autocare, Valero, **food:** Chipotle Mexican, Giuseppe's Italian, In-n-Out, McDonald's, Nation's Burger's, Quizno's, Subway, Taco Bell, Togo's, **lodging:** Hotel Sierra, **other:** Home Depot, Jo-Ann Fabrics, Longs Drug, Safeway, 7-11, Staples, repair/tires, Vet
34	Bollinger Canyon Rd, **E gas:** Valero, **food:** Baja Fresh, El Ballazo, Izzy's Steaks, Subway, **lodging:** Marriott, Residence Inn, **other:** Borders Books, Long's Drug, Target, Whole Foods, **W gas:** Chevron, **food:** Applebee's, Chevy's Mexican, Marie Callender's, **lodging:** Courtyard, Homestead Village
31	Alcosta Blvd, to Dublin, **E gas:** 76/7-11, **W gas:** Chevron, Shell/dsl, **food:** DQ, Mtn Mike's Pizza, McDonalds, Papa John's, Rulu's Cafe, Subway, Taco Bell, **other:** Lucky Foods, Walgreens
30	I-580, W to Oakland, E to Tracy
29	Stoneridge, Dublin, **E lodging:** Hilton, **W food:** Cheesecake Factory, PF Chang's, Taco Bell, **other:** JC Penney, Macy's, Nordstrom's, Sears, mall
26	Bernal Ave, Pleasanton, **E gas:** Shell/Jack-in-the-Box, **food:** Lindo's Mexican
25	Sunol Blvd, Pleasanton
21b a	CA 84, Calvaras Rd, Sunol, W to Dumbarton Bridge

FREMONT

Exit #	Services
20	Andrade Rd, Sheridan Rd (from sb), **E gas:** Sunol Super Stp/dsl
19mm	**weigh sta nb**
19	Sheridan Rd (from nb)
18	Vargas Rd
16	CA 238, Mission Blvd, to Hayward, **E gas:** Shell, **food:** McDonald's, **W** H
15	Washington Blvd, Irvington Dist, **E gas:** QuikStop
14	Durham Rd, to Auto Mall Pkwy, **W gas:** 76/Circle K/Subway/24hr, Shell/Jack-in-the-Box, **other:** Fry's Electronics, Home Depot, Walmart
12	CA 262, Mission Blvd, to I-880, Warm Springs Dist, **W gas:** 76, Valero, **food:** Burger King, Carl's Jr, Denny's, KFC, RoundTable Pizza, Starbucks, Subway, Taco Bell, **lodging:** Extended Stay America, **other:** GNC, Longs Drug, Radio Shack, Ross, Safeway, 7-11, Walgreens
10	Scott Creek Rd

SAN JOSE

Exit #	Services
9	Jacklin Rd, **E other:** Bonfare Mkt, **W gas:** Shell
8	CA 237, Calaveras Blvd, Milpitas, **E gas:** Shell/repair, 76, **food:** Domino's, Flames CoffeeShop, RoadTable Pizza, Sizzler, Subway, **lodging:** Exectuive Inn, **other:** Oceans SuperMkt, 7-11, **W gas:** Shell, **food:** El Torito, Giorgio's Italian, It's a Grind, Lyon's Rest., McDonald's, Red Lobster, **lodging:** Embassy Suites, Extended Stay America, **other:** Longs Drug, Lucky Foods, Safeway, Staples
6	Landess Ave, Montague Expswy, **E gas:** Arco, Chevron, 76, **food:** Burger King, Jack-in-the-Box, McDonald's, Taco Bell, Togo's, Wienerschnitzel, **other:** Firestone, Lucky Foods, Radio Shack, Rite Aid, Target, Walgreens
5	Capitol Ave, Hostetter Ave, **E gas:** Shell, **food:** Carl's Jr, Popeye's, **other:** SaveMart Foods, **W gas:** Valero, **other:** Jiffy Lube
4	Berryessa Rd, **E gas:** Arco/24hr, USA, Valero/repair, **food:** Denny's, Lee's Sandwiches, McDonald's, Taco Bell, **other:** AutoZone, Longs Drug, Safeway

CA

INTERSTATE 680 CONT'D (BAY AREA)

N ↕ S

Exit #	Services
2b	McKee Rd, **E gas:** 76, Chevron, Shell, **food:** Burger King, HomeTown Buffet, Pizza Hut, Quizno's, Starbucks, Togo's, Wienerschnitzel, **other:** $Tree, Pakn-Save Foods, Ross, Target, Walgreens, **W gas:** World Gas, **food:** Baskin-Robbins, Foster's Freeze, Lee's Sandwiches, McDonald's, RoundTable Pizza, Yum Yum Doughnut, Wendy's, **other:** H, Kohl's
2a	Alum Rock Ave, **E gas:** Shell/dsl/24hr, **food:** Jack-in-the-Box, Taco Bell, **W gas:** Chevron, 76/24hr, **food:** Carl's Jr
1d	Capitol Expswy
1c	King Rd, Jackson Ave (from nb), **E gas:** L&D Gas, Shell, **food:** El Gallo Giro, Jamba Juice, Kings Burger, Panda Express, Starbucks, Super Buffet, Taco Bell, **other:** Target, Walgreens
1b	US 101, to LA, SF
1a	(exits left from sb) I-680 begins/ends on I-280.

INTERSTATE 710 (LOS ANGELES)

E ↕ W — LOS ANGELES AREA

Exit #	Services
23	I-710 begins/ends on Valley Blvd, **E gas:** Arco
22b a	I-10
20c	Chavez Ave
20b	CA 60, Pamona Fwy, **W gas:** Shell, **E food:** King Taco, Monterrey Hill Rest.
20a	3rd St
19	Whittier Blvd, Olympic Blvd, **W gas:** Shell, **food:** McDonald's
17b	Washington Blvd, Commerce, **W gas:** Commerce Trkstp/dsl/rest.
17a	Bandini Blvd, Atlantic Blvd, industrial
15	Florence Ave, **E food:** IHOP, KFC, McDonald's, Taco Bell, **other:** Food4Less, Ralph's Foods, Rite Aid, Kragen Parts, **W** truck repair
13	CA 42, Firestone Blvd, **E gas:** Arco, **food:** Burger King, Denny's, Krispy Kreme, McDonald's, Panda Express, Starbucks, Subway, **lodging:** Guesthouse Inn, **other:** El Super Foods, Ford, Jeep, Kia, Nissan, Radio Shack, Sam's Club, Target
12b a	Imperial Hwy, **E gas:** Shell/Subway/dsl, **food:** Carl's Jr., El Pollo Loco, Tacos Mexico, **W gas:** Chevron/dsl, 76, Shell, **food:** Casa Corona, LJ Silver/KFC, Panda Express, Starbucks, Subway, Taco Bell/Pizza Hut, Winchell's, Wienerschnitzel, **other:** AutoZone, Manny's Tires, Radio Shack, Walgreen
11b a	I-105
10	Rosecrans Ave
9b a	Alondra Ave, **E** Home Depot
8b a	CA 91
7b a	Long Beach Blvd, **E gas:** Mobil/repair, 76, **food:** El Ranchito Mexican, McDonald's, Taco Bell, **W gas:** Arco/24hr, **food:** Chano's Mexican, Jack-in-the-Box, Quizno's, **lodging:** Day's Inn, Luxury Inn
6	Del Amo Blvd
4	I-405, San Diego Freeway
3b a	Willow St, **E gas:** Chevron, **food:** Baskin-Robbins, Chee Chinese, Dominos, Pizza Hut, **other:** Walgreen, **W gas:** Arco, Mobil, 76, **food:** KFC, Popeye's, **other:** AutoZone, Ralph's Foods

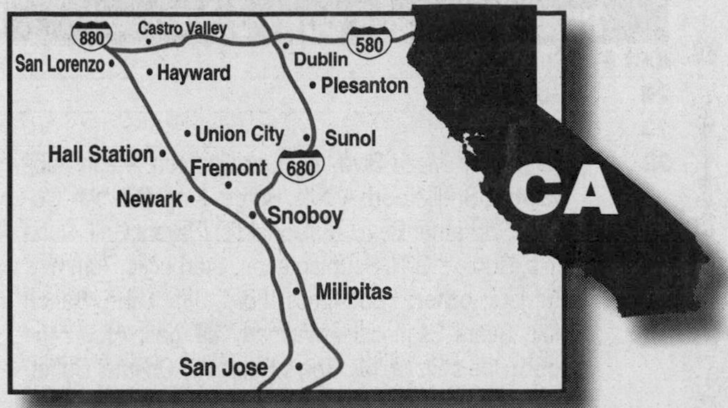

Exit #	Services
2	CA 1, Pacific Coast Hwy, **E gas:** Arco/mart, Chevron, LB Fuel, Valero/dsl, **food:** Burger Express, Hong Kong Empress, **other:** auto repair, **W gas:** 76/service, Shell/Carl's Jr/dsl, PCH Trkstp/dsl, Xpress Minimart, **food:** Golden Star Rest., Jack-in-the-Box, McDonald's, Tom's Burgers, Winchell's, **lodging:** Hyland Motel, SeaBreeze Motel
1d	Anaheim St, **W gas:** Speedy Fuel, **other:** dsl repair
1c	Ahjoreline Dr, Piers B, C, D, E, Pico Ave
1b	Pico Ave, Piers F-J, Queen Mary
1a	Harbor Scenic Dr, Piers S, T, Terminal Island, **E lodging:** Hilton
0mm	I-710 begins/ends in Long Beach

INTERSTATE 780 (VALLEJO)

E ↕ W — BENICIA

Exit #	Services
7	I-780 begins/ends on I-680.
6	E 5th St, Benicia, **N gas:** Fast&Easy, **S gas:** 7-11, Valero/dsl, **food:** China Garden, **other:** Big O Tire, repair, Vet
5	E 2nd St, Central Benicia, **N gas:** Valero, **lodging:** Best Western, **S food:** McDonald's, Pappa's Rest.
4	Southampton Rd, Benicia, **N food:** Asian Bistro, Burger King, Coldstone Creamery, Country Waffles, Jamba Juice, Rickshaw Express, RoundTable Pizza, Starbucks, Subway, **other:** Ace Hardware, Radio Shack, Raley's Foods, Vet
3b	Military West
3a	Columbus Pkwy, **N gas:** Shell, **food:** Burger King, Napoli Pizza, Subway, **other:** Jiffy Lube, Longs Drugs, **S** to Benicia RA
1d	Glen Cove Pkwy, **N** Hwy Patrol, **S food:** Baskin-Robbins, Subway, Taco Bell, **other:** Safeway
1c	Cedar St
1b a	I-780 begins/ends on I-80.

INTERSTATE 805 (SAN DIEGO)

N ↕ S

Exit #	Services
28mm	I-5 (from nb). I-805 begins/ends on I-5.
27.5	CA 56 E (from nb)
27	Sorrento Valley Rd, Mira Mesa Blvd
26	Vista Sorrento Pkwy, **E gas:** Mobil/dsl, Shell, **food:** Chili's, Jamba Juice, McDonald's, Starbucks, **lodging:** Country Inn, Courtyard, Holiday Inn Express, **other:** Staples
25b a	La Jolla Village Dr, Miramar Rd, **1 mi E gas:** 76/dsl, **other:** Discount Tire, Firestone, **W food:** Coast Cafe, Cozymel's Cantina, Donovan's Grill, Harry's Grill, Miami Grill, PF Chang's, **lodging:** Embassy Suites, Marriott, **other:** H, Macy's, Nordstom's, Sears, mall

INTERSTATE 805 CONT'D (SAN DIEGO)

N ↕ S — SAN DIEGO AREA

Exit #	Services
24	Governor Dr
23	CA 52
22	Clairemont Mesa Blvd, **E gas:** Chevron, Mega/Subway/dsl, Shell, **food:** Arby's, Burger King, Carl's Jr, Coco's, Godfather Rest., McDonald's, Players Grill, Quizno's, Rubio's Grill, Souplantation, Starbucks, Tommy's Burgers, **other:** Food4Less, Ford, Jiffy Lube, Ranch Mkt, Sears Essentials, Walmart, **W gas:** Arco/24hr, **food:** Joe's Pizza, Mr. Bon's Rest, VIP Oriental Buffet, **lodging:** Best Western, CA Suites, Motel 6
21	CA 274, Balboa Ave, **E gas:** Arco, Chevron, Exxon/dsl, 76, Shell, **food:** Applebee's, Islands Burger, Jack-in-the-Box, **other:** Albertson's/SavOn, Balboa AutoCare, Chevrolet, Dodge
20	CA 163 N, to Escondido
20a	Mesa College Dr, Kearney Villa Rd, **W** [H]
18	Murray Ridge Rd, to Phyllis Place
17b	I-8, E to El Centro, W to beaches
16	El Cajon Blvd, **E gas:** Arco/24hr, Ultra, **food: other:** Pancho Villa Mkt, **W gas:** North Park Gas, 76, **food:** Carl's Jr, Jack-in-the-Box, Starbucks, Subway, Wendy's
15	University Ave, **E gas:** Chevron, **food:** Subway, **other:** Radio Shack, **W gas:** Exxon, Thrifty/dsl, **food:** Starbucks, **other:** CVS Drug, Walgreens
14	CA 15 N, 40th St, to I-15
13b	Home Ave, MLK Ave
13a	CA 94
12b	Market St
12a	Imperial Ave, **E gas:** Exxon, Homeland Gas/dsl, **W food:** Domino's, KFC/LJ Silver, Sizzler, Starbucks, **other:** Home Depot, 99c Store
11b	47th St
11a	43rd St, **W food:** Giant Pizza, Jack-in-the-Box, **other:** AutoZone, CVS Drug, Northgate Mkt
10	Plaza Blvd, National City, **E food:** Chow King, DQ, Dragon Garden Chinese, McDonald's, Pizza Hut, Popeye's, Starbucks, Winchell's, **other:** [H], AutoZone, Firestone/auto, Ralph's Foods, Walgreens, Well's Drug, Vet, **W gas:** Thrifty Gas, **food:** Family House Rest., IHOP, Sizzler, **lodging:** Comfort Inn, Stardust Inn, **other:** Big Lots, CVS Drug, Discount Tire, Jo-Ann Fabrics
9	Sweetwater Rd, **E food:** Applebee's, Outback Steaks, **other:** JC Penney, 7-11, **W gas:** Chevron/dsl, **food:** Ben's Rest., Carl's Jr, Denny's, Hanaoka Japanese, La Placita Mexican, L&L BBQ, Pizza Hut, Starbucks, Subway, Taco Bell, **other:** Curves, Goodyear, Longs Drug, Staples
8	CA 54
7c	E St, Bonita Rd, **E on Bonita Plaza Rd...food:** Applebee's, **food:** Outback Steaks, Pat&Oscar's Rest., **other:** JC Penney, Macy's, mall, **W gas:** Chevron, Shell, **food:** Burger King, Denny's, Love's Rest., **lodging:** La Quinta, Ramada Inn, **other:** RV Park
7b a	H St, **E gas:** Carmalor Gas, **food:** China China, Coldstone Creamery, Jack-in-the-Box, Subway, Taco Bell, **other:** Longs Drug, Marshall's, Vons Foods, mall, RV camping
6	L St, Telegraph Canyon Rd, **E gas:** Canyon Fuel/dsl, **food:** Mandarin Canyon, McDonald's, Starbucks, Subway, **other:** [H], Rite Aid, Olympic Training Ctr, RV camping, **W gas:** Thrifty, **other:** 7-11
4	Orange Ave, **E** Olympic Training Ctr
3	Main St, Otay Valley Rd, **E gas:** Shell, **food:** Panda Express, Souplantation, **other:** Chevrolet, Chrysler/Jeep/Dodge, Ford, Kohl's, PetsMart, Scion, Staples, Toyota, **W lodging:** Holiday Inn Express
2	Palm Ave, **E gas:** Arco/24hr, Chevron/24hr, **food:** Carl's Jr, Hometown Buffet, Starbucks, Subway, Taco Bell, **other:** Big O Tires, Home Depot, Radio Shack, USPO, Von's Foods, Walmart, **W gas:** 76/dsl, **food:** KFC, McDonald's
1b	CA 905, **E** Brown Field ✈, Otay Mesa Border Crossing
1a	San Ysidro Blvd, **E gas:** Arco, Shell, **lodging:** Travelodge, Factory2U, Kragen Parts, Longs Drug, 99c Store, U-Haul, **W gas:** Chevron, Exxon, Mobil, 76, **food:** Denny's, McDonald's, Si Senor Mexican, **lodging:** Motel 6

I-805 begins/ends on I-5.

INTERSTATE 880 (BAY AREA)

N ↕ S — OAKLAND AREA

Exit #	Services
46b a	I-80 W (exits left). I-80 E/580 W.
44	7th St, Grand Ave, downtown
42b a	Broadway St, **E food:** KFC, **lodging:** Marriott, **W lodging:** Jack London Inn, **other:** to Jack London Square
41a	Oak St, Lakeside Dr, downtown
40	5th Ave, Embarcadero, **E food:** Burger King, **W food:** Quizno's, Starbucks, **lodging:** Executive Inn, Homewood Suites, Motel 6
39b a	29th Ave, 23rd Ave, to Fruitvale, **E gas:** Shell, **food:** Boston Mkt, Burger King, DonutStar, Popeye's, Starbucks, **other:** AutoZone, Lucky Foods, Office Depot, Radio Shack, **W gas:** 7-11
38	High St, to Alameda, **E lodging:** Bay Breeze Inn, Coliseum Motel, **other:** El Monte RV Ctr, **W gas:** Shell/dsl, **food:** McDonald's, **other:** Home Depot
37	66th Ave, Zhone Way, **E** coliseum
36	Hegenberger Rd, **E gas:** Arco/24hr, Shell/dsl, **food:** Burger King, Chubby Freeze, Denny's, Jack-in-the-Box/24hr, McDonald's, Taco Bell, **lodging:** Day's Hotel, Fairfield Inn, La Quinta, Motel 6, Quality Inn, **other:** Pak'n Save Foods, GMC/Volvo, Freightliner, **W gas:** 76/Circle K/dsl, Shell, **food:** Carrows Rest., Francesco's Rest., Hegen Burger, In-n-Out, Jamba Juice, Panda Express, Quizno's, Red Barn Pizza, Starbucks, Subway, Wing Stop, **lodging:** Best Western, Courtyard, Econolodge, Hilton, Holiday Inn, Holiday Inn Express, Marriott, Park Plaza Motel, **other:** Harley-Davidson, Infiniti, Lexus, Walmart/auto, to Oakland ✈
35	98th Ave, **W** ✈
34	Davis St, **W gas:** Shell/Burger King, **food:** Hawaiian BBQ, Jamba Juice, Starbucks, Togo's, **other:** Costco/gas, Home Depot, Office Depot, See's Candy, Walmart/McDonald's
33b a	Marina Blvd, **E gas:** Valero, **food:** Jack-in-the-Box, La Salsa Mexican, Panda Express, Starbucks, Taco Bell, **other:** Buick/GMC/Pontiac, Chevrolet,

INTERSTATE 880 CONT'D (BAY AREA)

N ↕ S

Exit #	Services
33b a	Continued Ford, Honda, Hyundai, Kia, Marshall's, Nissan, Nordstrom's, Radio Shack, Volvo, **W gas:** Flyers/dsl, **food:** A&W/KFC, DairyBelle, Denny's
32	Washington Ave (from nb), Lewelling Blvd (from sb), **W gas:** Arco, 76, TechCo, **food:** Hometown Buffet, Jack-in-the-Box, McDonald's, Papa Murphy's, Subway, **lodging:** Nimitz Motel, **other:** Big Lots, Big O Tire, Food Maxx, GNC, Home Depot, Longs Drugs, 99c Store, Radio Shack, Safeway/24hr, Walgreens/24hr, same as 30
31	I-238 (from sb), to I-580, Castro Valley
30	Hesperian Blvd, **E gas:** 76, **food:** KFC, In-n-Out, Quizno's, Starbucks, **other:** Kragen Parts, Walmart, Wheelworks Repair, **W gas:** Arco, Chevron, 76, **food:** Black Angus, Hometown Buffet, **lodging:** Hilton Garden, Nimitz Inn, **other:** BigLots, Food Maxx, Longs Drugs, Lucky Foods, 99c Store, Radio Shack, USPO, Vet, same as 32
29	A St, San Lorenzo, **E gas:** 76/Circle K, **food:** McDonald's, **lodging:** Best Western, **other:** Costco, tires/repair, **W gas:** KB/dsl, 76/Circle K, Valero, **food:** Burger King, Carrow's, Chef Ming, Hawaiian BBQ, Jamba Juice, Pizza Hut, Starbucks, Subway, **lodging:** Days Inn, Heritage Inn, La Quinta, MainStay Suites, Phoenix Lodge, **other:** $Tree, Home Depot, Mi Pueblo Foods, Target
28	Winton Ave, **W gas:** Chevron, Valero/dsl, **food:** Applebee's, Coldstone Creamery, Elephant Bar/Grill, Hawaiian BBQ, Hometown Buffet, Marie Callendar's, Mimi's Cafe, Olive Garden, Panda Express, Panera Bread, Sizzler, Subway, **other:** Firestone/auto, Goodyear/auto, JC Penney, Kragen Parts, Macy's, Ross, Sears/auto, mall
27	CA 92, Jackson St, **E gas:** Beacon, 76, Valero/24hr, **food:** Asian Wok, Baskin-Robbins, Hawaiian BBQ, Mnt Mike's Pizza, Nations Burgers, Papa Murphy's, Popeye's, Starbucks, Subway, Taco Bell, **other:** Grocery Outlet, Longs Drug, Lucky Foods, Radio Shack, Safeway, 7-11, Walgreens, **W** San Mateo Br
26	Tennyson Rd, **E gas:** All American/dsl, 76, **food:** Jack-in-the-Box, KFC, RoundTable Pizza, **other:** Kragen Parts, Walgreens, **W gas:** 76, **other:** H
25	Industrial Pkwy (from sb), **E gas:** Industrial/dsl, **food:** Lite Wok, Quizno's, Starbucks, **W lodging:** Pheonix Lodge
24	Whipple Rd, Dyer St, **E gas:** Chevron/dsl/24hr, 76, **food:** Country Waffles, Del Taco, Denny's, McDonald's, Panda Express, Taco Bell, Wing Stop, **lodging:** Best Value Inn, Motel 6, **other:** FoodMaxx, Home Depot, PepBoys, Target, **W gas:** Shell, **food:** Applebee's, Baskin-Robbins, Burger King, Chili's, FreshChoice, Fuddrucker's, In-n-Out, IHOP, Jamba Juice, Jollibee, Krispy Kreme, La Salsa Mexican, Pasta Pormadora, Starbucks, Texas Roadhouse, TGIFriday, Togo's, Tony Roma's, **lodging:** Extended Stay America, Holiday Inn Express, **other:** Best Buy, Borders Books, Lowe's Whse, Lucky Foods, Michael's, PetCo, Radio Shack, Walmart/auto

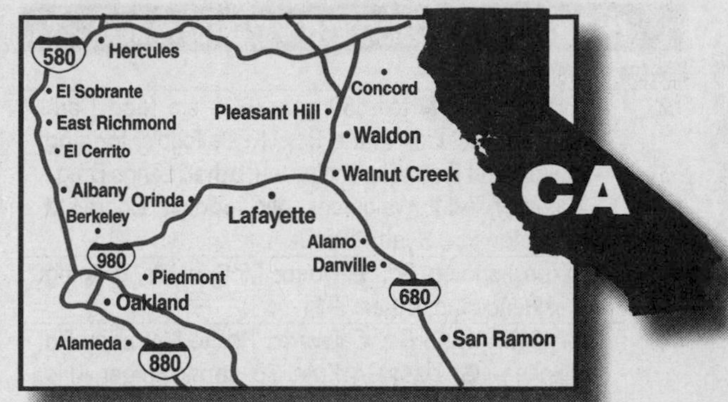

FREMONT

Exit #	Services
23	Alvarado-Niles Rd, (same as 24) **E gas:** Shell, **lodging:** Crowne Plaza, **other:** 7-11, **W gas:** Shell, **other:** Walmart/auto
22	Alvarado Blvd, Fremont Blvd, **E food:** Phoenix Garden Chinese, Subway, **lodging:** Motel 6, **other:** Lucky Foods
21	CA 84 W, Decoto Rd to Dumbarton Br, **E gas:** 7-11, **food:** McDonald's, **other:** Walgreens
19	CA 84 E, Thornton Ave, Newark, **E other:** U-Haul, **W gas:** Chevron/dsl/24hr, Shell, **food:** Carl's Jr, KFC, Mtn Mike's Pizza, Taco Bell, **other:** BigLots, Home Depot, 7-11
17	Mowry Ave, Fremont, **E gas:** Chevron/dsl, QuikStop, 76/Circle K, Valero, **food:** Applebee's, Burger King, Chinese Buffet, Denny's, HoneyBaked Ham, KFC, Olive Garden, Starbucks, Subway, T&D Sandwiches, **lodging:** Best Western, Extended Stay Deluxe, Residence Inn, **other:** H, Lucky Foods, **W gas:** 76, **food:** Arby's, BJ's Rest., Bombay Garden, El Burro Mexican, Jack-in-the-Box, McDonald's, Red Robin, Subway, Taco Bell, TK Noodles, **lodging:** Chase Suites, Comfort Inn, EZ 8 Motel, Homewood Suites, Motel 6, Towneplace Suites, **other:** Firestone, Goodyear/auto, JC Penney, Jiffy Lube, Lion Mkt., Macy's, Mazda, Sears/auto, Target, TJ Maxx, mall
16	Stevenson Blvd, **E gas:** Arco/dsl, Shell, **food:** Jack-in-the-Box, Outback Steaks, **W gas:** Chevron, **food:** Chevy's Mexican, ChuckeCheese, Palm Gardens Rest., Starbucks, Togo's, **lodging:** Hilton, **other:** FoodMaxx, Ford, Harley-Davidson, Nissan, Tuesday Morning, Walmart
15	Auto Mall Pkwy, **E gas:** Arco, Chevron, **food:** Subway, **W gas:** Shell/dsl, **food:** Applebee's, Asian Pearl, Carino's, Chipotle Mexican, ClaimJumper, Coldstone Creamery, Dickey's BBQ, Hawaiian BBQ, In-n-Out, Jamba Juice, Panda Express, Panera Bread, PF Chang's, Quizno's, Rubio's, Starbucks, Subway, Tandoori Grill, Wendy's, Wing Stop, **other:** BMW, Chrysler/Dodge/Jeep, Costco/gas, Honda, Jo-Ann Fabrics, Jaguar, Kia, Kohl's, Land Rover, Lexus, Lowes Whse, Mercedes, Office Depot, Old Navy, Porsche, Radio Shack, Staples, Toyota, Volvo
14mm	**weigh sta both lanes**
13	Fremont Blvd, Irving Dist, **W gas:** Valero/Subway, **food:** McDonald's, SmartBrew, **lodging:** GoodNite Inn, Homestead Suites, La Quinta, Marriott
13a	Gateway Blvd (from nb), **E lodging:** Holiday Inn Express

CA

INTERSTATE 880 CONT'D (BAY AREA)

Exit #	Services
12	Mission Blvd, **E** to I-680, **gas:** 76, Valero, **food:** Carl's Jr, Denny's, Jack-in-the-Box, KFC, Togo's, **lodging:** Holiday Inn Express, Quality Inn, **other:** Longs Drugs, Safeway, 7-11, Walgreens, **W lodging:** Courtyard, Hampton Inn, Hyatt Place
10	Dixon Landing Rd, **E food:** McDonald's, **lodging:** Residence Inn, **other:** 7-11
8b	CA 237, Alviso Rd, Calaveras Rd, to McCarthy Rd, Milpitas, **E gas:** CA Fuel, 76, **food:** Burger King, Carl's Jr, Chili Palace, Denny's, Lee's Sandwiches, Marie Callender's, **lodging:** Best Western, Days Inn, Travelodge, **other:** BigLots, Kragen Parts, Save-Mart Foods, 7-11, Walgreens, Vet, **W on McCarthy Rd...gas:** Chevron, **food:** Applebee's, Black Angus, HomeTown Buffet, Happi House, In-n-Out, Jamba Juice, Macaroni Grill, McDonald's, On the Border, Pasta Pomodoro, RedBrick Pizza, Starbucks, Subway, Taco Bell, **lodging:** Crowne Plaza, Hampton Inn, Hilton Garden, Homestead Suites, Larkspur Landing Hotel, Staybridge Suites, **other:** Best Buy, Borders Books, GNC, Michael's, Petsmart, RanchMkt Foods, Ross, Walmart/McDonald's/auto
8a	Great Mall Parkway, Tasman Dr, **E other:** Toyota
7	Montague Expswy, **E gas:** Shell/dsl, Valero, **food:** Jack-in-the-Box, **lodging:** Sleep Inn, **other:** U-Haul, **W gas:** Chevron/dsl, **food:** Dave&Buster's, **lodging:** Beverly Heritage Hotel, Sheraton
5	Brokaw Rd, **E other:** Lowe's Whse, **W other:** Ford Trucks, Fry's Electronics, CHP
4d	Gish Rd (nb only), **W other:** auto/dsl repair/transmissions
4c b	US 101, N to San Francisco, S to LA
4a	1st St, **E gas:** 76, Shell/repair, **food:** Subway, **W gas:** 76, **food:** Cathay Chinese, Denny's/24hr, Empire Buffet, Genji Japanese, **lodging:** Clarion, Comfort Suites, Days Inn, Executive Inn, EZ 8 Motel, Holiday Inn Express, Homestead Suites, Radisson, Red Roof Inn, Vagabond Inn, Wyndham Garden, **other:** 7-11
3	Coleman St, **E gas:** Valero/dsl, **food:** Quizno's, **W** [airport]
2	CA 82, The Alameda, **W gas:** Shell/repair, **food:** Starbucks, Subway, Taco Bell, **lodging:** Best Western, Santa Clara Inn, St. Francis Hotel, Sterling Motel, Valley Inn, **other:** Safeway, Santa Clara U
1d	Bascom Ave, to Santa Clara, **W gas:** Rotten Robbie/dsl, Valero, **food:** Burger King
1c	Stevens Creek Blvd, San Carlos St, **E gas:** Valero/dsl, Valley/dsl, **lodging:** Valley Park Hotel, **other:** [H], **W gas:** 76, **food:** Arby's, CheeseCake Factory, Jack-in-the-Box, RoundTable Pizza, **other:** Audi/VW, Best Buy, Ford, Goodyear/auto, Lexus, Longs Drugs, Macy's, Nordstrom's, Old Navy, Safeway, 7-11, Subaru, mall
1b	I-280. I-880 begins/ends on I-280
1a	Ca 17 to Santa Cruz.

COLORADO

INTERSTATE 25

Exit #	Services
299	Colorado/Wyoming state line
296	point of interest both lanes
293	to Carr, Norfolk
288	Buckeye Rd
281	Owl Canyon Rd, **E** KOA Campground
278	CO 1 S, to Wellington, **W gas:** Kum&Go, Loaf'N Jug/Blimpie, Shell, **food:** Burger King, Subway, Taco Bell, **lodging:** Days Inn, **other:** Main St Mkt/drugs, USPO
271	Mountain Vista Dr, **W** Budweiser Brewery
269b a	CO 14, to US 87, Ft Collins, **E food:** Gambler's Steaks, McDonald's, **lodging:** Mulberry Inn, **W gas:** Conoco, Phillips 66/dsl, **food:** Denny's, Waffle House, **lodging:** Comfort Inn, Day's Inn, Econolodge, La Quinta, Motel 6, Plaza Inn, Ramada Inn, Sleep Inn, Super 8, **other:** RV Service, U-Haul, truck repair, Vet, to CO St U, 2mi **W gas:** Shamrock, **food:** DQ, Papa John's, Qdoba Mexican, **other:** Home Depot, Radio Shack, Walmart SuperCtr
268	Prospect Rd, to Ft Collins, **W other:** [H], **Welcome Ctr, rest area both lanes, full handicapped facilities, litter barrels,** [picnic], **petwalk**
267mm	**weigh sta both lanes**
266mm	st patrol
265	CO 68 W, Timnath, **E** Walmart SuperCtr, **W gas:** Shell/dsl, 2-3 mi **W food:** Austin's Grill, Carrabba's, Golden Corral, Hunan Chinese, IHOP, Macaroni Grill, Outback Steaks, Papa John's, Quizno's, Subway,
265	Continued Texas Roadhouse, Village Inn Rest., **lodging:** Courtyard, Hampton Inn, Marriott, Residence Inn, Safeway/gas, Sam's Club
262	CO 392 E, to Windsor, **E gas:** Conoco/dsl, Phillips 66/Subway/dsl, **food:** Arby's, GoodTimes Burgers, Taco John's, **lodging:** AmericInn, Super 8, **W other:** Powder River RV Ctr
259	Crossroads Blvd, **E gas:** Phillips 66/dsl, **food:** Carl's Jr, Qdoba Mexican, Subway, **lodging:** Candlewood Suites, Embassy Suites, Holiday Inn Express, **W food:** Hooters, **other:** BMW, Chevrolet, Chrysler/Dodge/Jeep, GMC/Pontiac, Harley-Davidson, Subaru, to [airport]
257b a	US 34, to Loveland, **E gas:** gas/deli, **food:** Biaggi Italian, BoneFish Grill, Costa Vida, Culver's, On-the-Border, PF Chang's, Red Robin, Rock Bottom Rest., Spicy Pickle, Starbucks, **other:** Barnes&Noble, Best Buy, Macy's, **W gas:** Conoco/dsl, **food:** Arby's (2mi), Blackeyed Pea, Carino's Italian, Chick-fil-A, Chili's, Chipotle Mexican, Cracker Barrel, Hooters, IHOP, KFC/Taco Bell, LoneStar Steaks, McDonald's, Mimi's Cafe, Noodles&Co, Old Chicago, Panera Bread, Quizno's, Subway, Taco John's, Waffle House, Wendy's, **lodging:** Best Western, Comfort Inn, Fairfield Inn, Hampton Inn, Holiday Inn Express, Residence Inn, Super 8 (2mi), **other:** [H], JoAnn Fabrics, Loveland Outlets/famous brands, Marshall's, PetsMart, Ross, Sportsman's Whse, Staples, Target, RV camping, museum, to Rocky Mtn NP

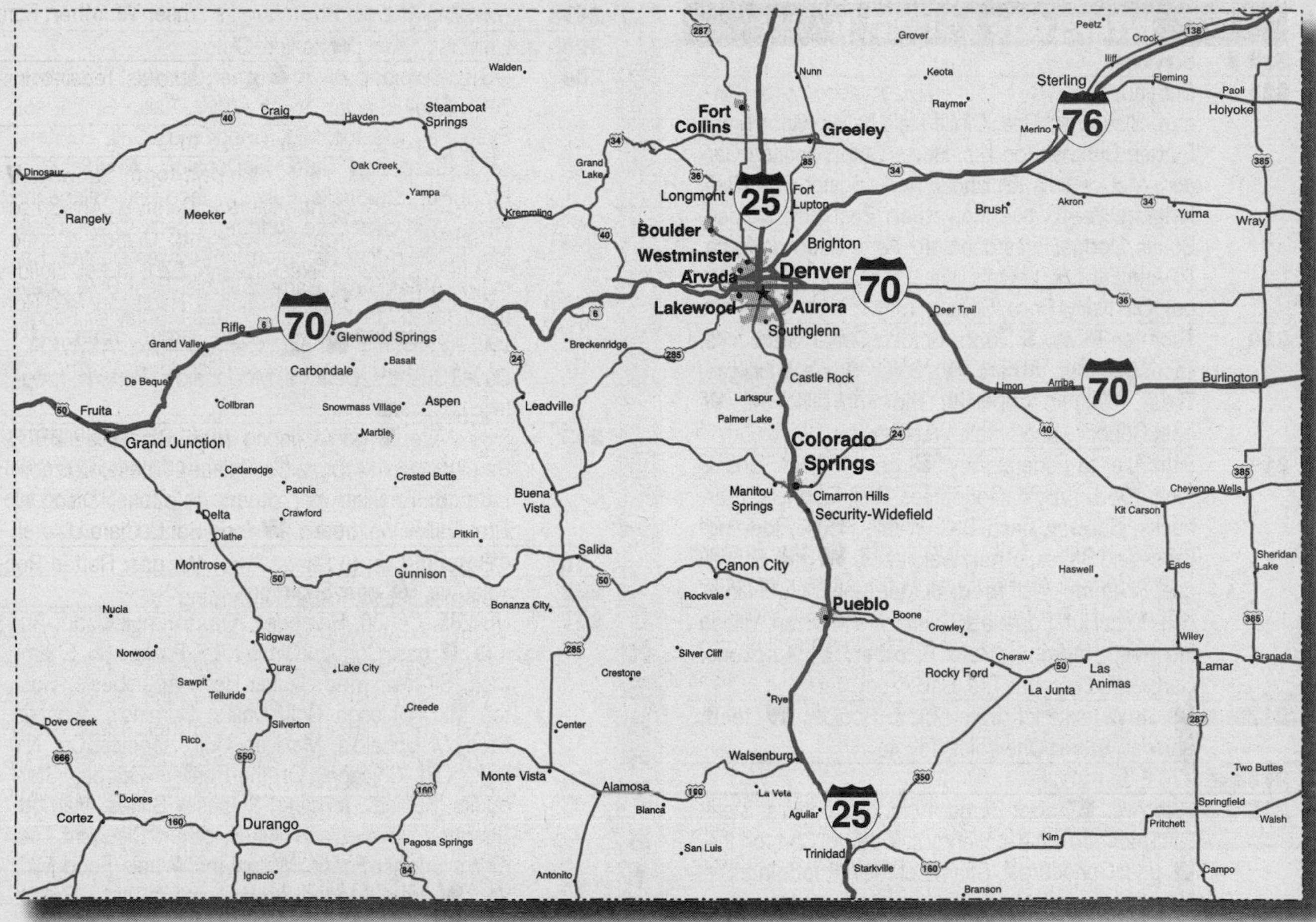

INTERSTATE 25 CONT'D

N ↕ S

Exit #	Services
255	CO 402 W, to Loveland
254	to CO 60 W, to Campion, **E gas:** Johnson's Corner/Sinclair/dsl/café/motel/24hr, **lodging:** Budget Host, **other:** RV camping/service
252	CO 60 E, to Johnstown, Milliken, **W gas:** Loaf'n Jug/Subway
250	CO 56 W, to Berthoud, **W** Berthoud B&B, to Carter Lake
245	to Mead
243	CO 66, to Longmont, Platteville, **E gas:** Conoco/dsl, Boulder Gas/Gyros/dsl, **food:** Red Rooster Rest., **other:** Big John's RV Ctr, Camping World/K&C RV Ctr, tires, **W** to Rocky Mtn NP, to Estes Park
241mm	St Vrain River
240	CO 119, to Longmont, **E gas:** Phillips 66/dsl, **food:** Carl's Jr, Del Taco, Qdoba, Quizno's, Starbucks, Wendy's, **lodging:** Best Western, Value Place Inn, **other:** Kia, Lexus, Toyota/Scion, **W gas:** Conoco/Subway/dsl/scales/24hr, Shell/dsl, **food:** Arby's, Burger King, McDonald's, Taco Bell, Waffle House, **lodging:** Best Value Inn, Comfort Inn, Day's Inn, 1st Inn, Super 8, **other:** H, Del Camino RV Ctr, Valley Camper RV Ctr, museum, to Barbour Ponds SP
237	new exit
235	CO 52, Dacono, **E other:** Ford, **W gas:** Conoco/McDonald's/dsl/LP, **food:** Pepper Jacks, **other:** Harley-Davidson, to Eldora Ski Area
232	to Erie
229	CO 7, to Lafayette, Brighton, **E food:** Chick-fil-A, Famous Dave's BBQ, Goodtimes Burgers, Gunther Toody's, Heidi's, La Fogata, Starbucks, Village Inn,

LONGMONT

Exit #	Services
229	Continued **other:** Costco/gas, Home Depot, PetsMart, Sears Grand
228	E-470, tollway, to Limon
226	**W food:** Mimi's Cafe, Red Robin, Starbucks, **other:** JC Penney, Macy's, SuperTarget
225	136th Ave, **W food:** Big Burrito, Carl's Jr, Starbucks, Subway, **other:** Lowes Whse, Walmart SuperCtr/McDonald's
223	CO 128, 120th Ave, to Broomfield, **E gas:** Conoco, Shamrock/dsl, **food:** Applebee's, Burger King, Chipotle Mexican, Chick-fil-A, Coldstone Creamery, Damon's, Fazoli's, Fuddrucker's, Krispy Kreme, LoneStar Steaks, McDonald's, Panda Express, Pizza Hut, Olive Garden, Outback Steaks, Sonic, TGI Friday, **lodging:** Hampton Inn, Radisson, Ramada Inn, Sleep Inn, **other:** Albertson's, Barnes&Noble, Big Lots, Big O Tire, Brakes+, CarQuest, Checker's Parts, Discount Tire, GNC, Michael's, PetCo, SuperTarget, Tires+, Walgreens, Vet, **W gas:** Conoco/dsl, Shell/Circle K/Popeye's/dsl, Shamrock, **food:** Chili's, Cracker Barrel, DQ, Hooters, Jade City Chinese, Laguna's Mexican, Perkins, Starbucks, Subway, Village Inn Rest., Wendy's, **lodging:** Comfort Suites, Extended Stay America, Fairfield Inn, La Quinta, Savannah Suites, Super 8
221	104th Ave, to Northglenn, **E gas:** Conoco, Phillips 66, **food:** Burger King, DQ, Denny's, IHOP, Old Chicago, Sonic, Subway, Taco Bell/Pizza Hut, Texas Roadhouse, **other:** H, AutoZone, Gander Mtn, Gordman's, Home Depot, King's Soopers, **W gas:** Conoco, 7-11, Shell/dsl, **food:** Applebee's, Bennig

BROOMFIELD

INTERSTATE 25 CONT'D

N ↕ S THORNTON

Exit #	Services
221	Continued an's, Blackeyed Pea, Cinzinetti's Italian, GoodTimes Burger, Gunther Toody's, Hop's Grill, Mandarin Garden, McDonald's, Quizno's, Red Lobster, Taco Bell, **lodging:** Best Value Inn, **other:** Best Buy, Borders Books, Dodge, Firestone/auto, Ford, Goodyear/auto, Jo-Ann Fabrics, Lowe's Whse, Marshall's, Office Depot, Old Navy, Ross, Subaru, mall
220	Thornton Pkwy, **E food:** Golden Corral, Starbucks, Taco Del Mar, **other:** H, GNC, Sam's Club/gas, Tires+, Walmart SuperCtr, Thornton Civic Ctr, **W gas:** Conoco, Shamrock, Western/gas
219	84th Ave, to Federal Way, **E gas:** Conoco, Shamrock, **food:** Arby's, Goodtimes Grill, Quizno's, Starbucks, Subway, Taco Bell, Waffle House, **lodging:** Crossland Suites, **other:** Walgreens, **W gas:** Econogas, Shamrock/dsl, **food:** Burger King, DQ, El Jimador, Pizza Hut, Popeye's, Santiago's Mexican, Village Inn Rest., **lodging:** Motel 6, **other:** H, AutoZone, CarQuest, Discount Tire, Sav-A-Lot, Vet
217	US 36 W (exits left from nb), to Boulder, **W food:** Subway, **other:** Chevrolet, Toyota
216b a	I-76 E, to I-270 E
215	58th Ave, **E food:** Burger King, McDonald's, Steak Escape, Taco John's, Wendy's, **lodging:** Comfort Inn, **W gas:** Conoco/dsl, Shamrock/dsl/LP, **lodging:** Super 8
214c	48th Ave, **E** coliseum, ✈, **W food:** Village Inn Rest., **lodging:** Holiday Inn, Quality Inn
214b a	I-70, E to Limon, W to Grand Junction
213	Park Ave, W 38th Ave, 23rd St, downtown, **E gas:** Conoco, 7-11, Shell, **food:** Denny's, Domino's, McDonald's, Starbucks, Quizno's, **lodging:** La Quinta, **other:** Goodyear, **W lodging:** Regency Inn, Town&Country Motel
212c	20th St, downtown, Denver, **W food:** Pagliacci's Italian
212b a	Speer Blvd, **E** downtown, museum, **W gas:** Conoco, Shell, **lodging:** Ramada Inn, Residence Inn, Super 8, Travel Inn
211	23rd Ave, **E** funpark
210c	CO 33 (from nb)
210b	US 40 W, Colfax Ave, **W food:** Denny's, KFC, **lodging:** Ramada Inn/rest., Red Lion Inn, **other:** Mile High Stadium
210a	US 40 E, Colfax Ave, **E** civic center, downtown, U-Haul
209c	8th Ave, **E lodging:** Motel 7, **other:** Bob's Auto Parts
209b	6th Ave W, US 6, **W lodging:** Day's Inn
209a	6th Ave E, downtown, Denver
208	CO 26, Alameda Ave (from sb), **E gas:** Shamrock/dsl, **food:** Burger King, Denny's, **other:** Home Depot, same as 207b **E gas:** Conoco
207b	US 85 S, Santa Fe Dr, same as 208
207 a	Broadway, Lincoln St, **E food:** Griff's Burgers, **other:** USPO
206b	Washington St, Emerson St, **E other:** WildOats Mkt/café, **W other:** H

DENVER AREA

Exit #	Services
206a	Downing St (from nb)
205b a	University Blvd, **W** to U of Denver
204	CO 2, Colorado Blvd, **E gas:** Conoco, Shamrock, 7-11, Shell, Sinclair, **food:** Arby's, Asian Grill, Black Eyed Pea, Boston Mkt, GoodTimes Grill, Hooters, KFC, Lazy Dog Café, McDonald's, Noodles&Co, Pizza Hut, Starbucks, Subway, Taco Bell, Village Inn Rest., Wild Oats Cafe, **lodging:** Cherry Creek, Day's Inn, Fairfield Inn, Hampton Inn, Lowes Denver, Ramada, **other:** AAA, Barnes&Noble, Best Buy, Chevrolet/Buick, Mercedes/BMW, Ross, Safeway Foods, VW, Walgreens, **W gas:** Conoco, **food:** A&W/KFC, Dave&Buster's, Denny's, McDonald's, Perkins, **lodging:** La Quinta
203	Evans Ave, **E gas:** Conoco, **food:** Big Papa's BBQ, Breakfast Inn, McDonald's, Palace Chinese, Quiznos, **lodging:** Rockies Inn, **other:** AutoZone, Discount Tire, NAPA, Walgreens, **W lodging:** Cameron Motel, **other:** Ford
202	Yale Ave, **W gas:** Shamrock

CHERRY HILLS

Exit #	Services
201	US 285, CO 30, Hampden Ave, to Englewood, Aurora, **E gas:** Conoco/Circle K/LP, Phillips 66, Shamrock, Sinclair, **food:** Ajuuai Rest, Applebee's, Boston Mkt, Chicago Grill, Chili's, Domino's, Einstein Bros, McDonald's, Mexican Grill, Noodles&Co, NY Deli, Old Chicago, On-the-Border, Qdoba, Starbucks, Subway, **lodging:** Embassy Suites, Marriott, Sheraton, TownePlace Suites, **other:** Discount Tire, King's Sooper Foods, Walgreens, Whole Food Mkt, Vet, **W gas:** Conoco, **food:** Aurelio's Pizza, Burger King, Starbucks, **other:** Safeway
200	I-225 N, to I-70
199	CO 88, Belleview Ave, to Littleton, **E gas:** Sinclair, **food:** Chipotle Mexican, Harvest Rest., Off Belleview Grill, Pancake House, Panera Bread, Sandwiches+, Starbucks, Tosh's Hacienda Rest., Wendy's, **lodging:** Hyatt Place, Hyatt Regency, Marriott, Wyndham, **W gas:** Conoco, Shamrock, **food:** McDonald's, Pappadeaux Café, Paradise Valley Grill, Pizza Hut, Taco Bell, **lodging:** Day's Inn, Extended Stay America, Holiday Inn Express, HomeStead Village, Ramada, Super 8
198	Orchard Rd, **E food:** Del Frisco's Steaks, Shepler's, **W gas:** Shell/Circle K, **food:** Quizno's, **lodging:** Hotel Denver Tech, **other:** H
197	Arapahoe Blvd, **E gas:** Conoco, Shell/Circle K, **food:** A&W, Arby's, Bro's BBQ, Burger King, Carlos Miguel's, Del Taco, Dickie's BBQ, El Parral, Gunther Toody's Rest., Hoong's Palace, KFC, Mr. Panda, Outback Steaks, Pat's Cheesesteak, Pizza Hut, Sonic, Subway, Wendy's, **lodging:** Candlewood Suites, Courtyard, Homestead Suites, Sleep Inn, **other:** Big A Parts, Buick, Cadillac, Chrysler, Discount Tire, Ford, GMC, Home Depot, Honda, Hyundai, Jeep, Lowe's Whse, Mazda, Nissan, Pontiac, Scion, Subaru, Target, Toyota, USPO, Walmart SuperCtr, **W gas:** Phillips 66, Shamrock, Shell, **food:** Arby's, Blackeyed Pea, Boston Mkt, Chipotle Mexican, DQ, Einstein Bro's, Elephant Bar Rest., Jamba Juice, KFC, Macaroni Grill, McDonald's, Mongolian BBQ, Papa John's, Qdoba, Quizno's, Red Robin, Souper Salad, Sushi Moon, Taco Bell, **lodging:** Residence Inn, Wingate Inn, **other:** Albertson's, Barnes&Noble, Brakes+, Curves, Firestone/auto, Goodyear/auto, Office Depot, Sav-On

INTERSTATE 25 CONT'D

N ↕ S

Exit #	Services
196	Dry Creek Rd, **E food:** IHOP, Landry's Seafood, Maggiano's Italian, Trail Dust Steaks, **lodging:** Best Western, Bradford Suites, Country Inn Suites, Days Inn, Holiday Inn Express, Homestead Suites, La Quinta, Quality Inn, Ramada Ltd, Studio+, **W lodging:** Drury Inn
195	County Line Rd, **E lodging:** Courtyard, Residence Inn, **W gas:** Conoco, **food:** Buffalo Wild Wings, Burger King, California Pizza Kitchen, Champ's Rest., Chick-fil-A, Fleming's Rest., PF Changs, Red Robin, Rock Bottom Brewery/Cafe, Starbucks, Thai Basil, **lodging:** Hyatt Place, **other:** Barnes&Noble, Best Buy, Borders, Costco/gas, Dillard's, Home Depot, JC Penney, JoAnn Fabrics, Michaels, Nordstrom's, PetsMart
194	CO 470 W, CO 470 E (tollway), **1 exit W on Quebec...food:** Arby's, ClaimJumper, Country Buffet, LoneStar Steaks, McDonald's, TGIFriday, **lodging:** Comfort Suites, Fairfield Inn, Hyatt Place, **other:** Barnes&Noble, Firestone, Home Depot, PepBoys, Sam's Club, Walmart/gas
193	Lincoln Ave, to Parker, **E gas:** Shamrock, **food:** Carraba's, PanAsia Bistro, Hacienda Colorado, **lodging:** Candlewood Suites, Extended Stay America, Hilton Garden, **W gas:** Conoco/dsl, **food:** Chipotle Grill, Chili's, Heidi's, McDonald's, Pizza Hut/Taco Bell, Starbucks, Subway, **lodging:** Marriott, **other:** H, Discount Tire, Safeway
192	no services
191	no services
190	Surrey Ridge
188	Castle Pines Pkwy, **W gas:** Conoco, Shell/Circle K/Popeye's/24hr, **food:** Cafe De France, La Dolce Vita, Little Italy, Starbucks, Subway, Wendy's, **other:** Big O Tires, Discount Tire, King's Sooper/dsl, Safeway, Vet
187	Happy Canyon Rd, **services 2 mi W**
184	Founders Pkwy, Meadows Pkwy, to Castle Rock, **E gas:** Conoco/dsl, Shell/dsl, **food:** A&W/KFC, Applebee's, Carl's Jr., Chipotle Mexican, Goodtimes Grill, Qdoba, Quizno's, Outback Steaks, Red Robin, Sonic, Starbucks, Subway, Taco Bell, Wendy's, **other:** Discount Tire, GNC, Goodyear, Grease Monkey, Home Depot, King's Sooper/24hr, Kohl's, Office Depot, PetsMart, Radio Shack, Target, Walgreens, Walmart SuperCtr/24hr, **W gas:** Conoco/Blimpie/Loaf'N Jug/dsl, **food:** Arby's, Blackeyed Pea, Chili's, Food Court, IHOP, McDonald's, Rockyard Café, **lodging:** Best Western, Comfort Suites, Day's Inn, Hampton Inn, **other:** Castle Rock Outlet/famous brands, Lowes Whse, Midas
183	US 85 N (from nb), Sedalia, Littleton
182	CO 86, Castle Rock, Franktown, **E gas:** Conoco, Phillips 66/dsl, Western, **food:** El Meson Mexican, Little Caesar's, Sapporo Japanese, **other:** st patrol, **W gas:** Shamrock, Shell/dsl, **food:** Burger King, KFC, Margarita's Mexican, McDonald's, Shari's/24hr, Taco Bell, Village Inn Rest., Waffle House, Wendy's, **lodging:** Comfort Inn, Holiday Inn Express, Quality Inn, Super 8, **other:** Chrysler/Dodge/Jeep, NAPA

CASTLE ROCK

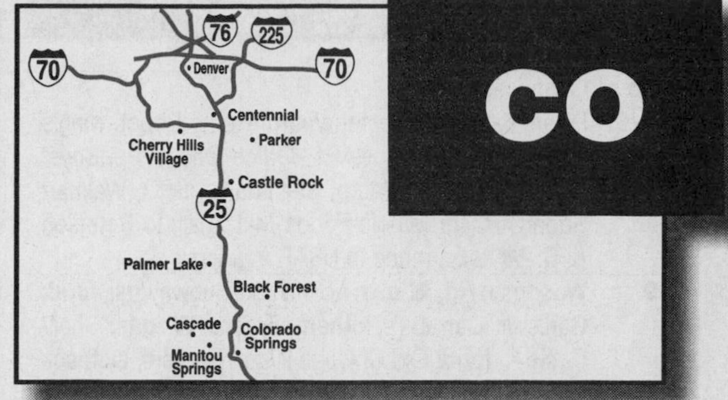

CO

Exit #	Services
181	CO 86, Wilcox St, Plum Creek Pkwy, Castle Rock, **E gas:** Conoco, 7-11, Valero, Western/dsl, **food:** DQ, Duke's Steaks, El Porral, Pizza Hut, Subway, **lodging:** Castle Rock Motel, **other:** Autozone, Big O Tire, Buick/GMC, Chevrolet, Chrysler/Dodge/Jeep, Ford/Lincoln/Mercury, Hummer, Safeway/gas, Walgreens, USPO
174	Tomah Rd, **W other:** Castle Rock RV Park
173	Larkspur (from sb, no return), **1 mi W gas:** Conoco/Larkspur Cafe/dsl/phone
172	South Lake Gulch Rd, Larkspur, **2 mi W gas:** Conoco/dsl/phone, **food:** Larkspur Pizza Cafe
167	Greenland
163	County Line Rd
162.5mm	Monument Hill, elev 7352
162mm	**weigh sta both lanes**
161	CO 105, Woodmoor Dr, **E gas:** Conoco, **food:** Margarita's Mexican, **other:** Vet, **W gas:** Conoco/Circle K/dsl, 7-11, **food:** Arby's, Casa Viejo, Domino's, McDonald's, Pizza Hut, Rosie's Diner, Starbucks, Subway, Taco Bell, Village Inn Rest., **other:** Big O Tire, Curves, Radio Shack, Safeway, USPO
158	Baptist Rd, **E gas:** Shell/Circle K/Popeye's/dsl/24hr, **food:** Asian Garden, Carl's Jr, Chili's, Jackson Creek Chinese, Nick&Willy's, Papa Murphy's, Rotelli's, Subway, Texas Roadhouse, **other:** Checker Parts, Home Depot, King's Sooper/24hr, Kohl's, PetsMart, Staples, Walmart SuperCtr, **W gas:** Shamrock/dsl/scales
156b	N Entrance to USAF Academy, **W visitors center**
156a	Gleneagle Dr, **E** mining museum
153	InterQuest Pkwy, **E lodging:** Hampton Inn, Residence Inn
152	scenic overlook on sb
151	Briargate Pkwy, **E gas:** Conoco, **food:** Biaggi's, California Pizza Kitchen, Champp's, Colorado Steaks, Panera Bread, PF Changs, Qdoba, Starbucks, Ted's MT Grill, **lodging:** Hilton Garden, Homewood Suites, **other:** to Black Forest
150b a	CO 83, Academy Blvd, **E gas:** Conoco, Shamrock/dsl, Shell/dsl, **food:** Applebee's, Blimpie, Boston Mkt, Buca Italian, Buffalo Wild Wings, Burger King, Chipotle Mexican, Country Buffet, Cracker Barrel, Denny's, Egg&I Café, Elephant Bar Rest., Extreme Pizza, Famous Daves, Fat Burger, Fazoli's, IHOP, Jason's Deli, KFC, McDonald's, Mimi's Café, Olive Garden, On-the-Border, Panera Bread, Pizza Hut, Qdoba, Quizno's, Salt Grass Steaks, Schlotsky's Starbucks, Subway, Village Inn Rest., Wendy's, **lodging:** Best Western, Comfort Suites, Day's Inn, Drury Inn, Sleep Inn, Super 8, **other:** Advance Parts, Barnes&Noble, Best Buy, Big O Tire, Borders Books, Checker Parts,

LARKSPUR

INTERSTATE 25 CONT'D

N ↕ S

Exit #	Services
150b a	Continued Dillard's, $Tree, Firestone/auto, Home Depot, King's Sooper, Marshall's, NAPA, Office Depot, PepBoys, Sam's Club, Sears/auto, Steinmart, USPO, Walmart SuperCtr/24hr, Whole Foods Mkt, mall, to Peterson AFB, **W** S Entrance to USAF Academy
149	Woodmen Rd, **E gas:** Loaf'n Jug/Subway/dsl, **food:** Carl's Jr, Carraba's, **other:** Nissan, **W gas:** Shell/ Circle K, **food:** Old Chicago Pizza, Hooters, Outback Steaks, TGIFriday, Zio's Italian, **lodging:** Comfort Inn, Embassy Suites, Fairfield Inn, Hampton Inn, Holiday Inn Express, Microtel, Staybridge Suites
148b a	Corporate Ctr Dr (exits left from sb), Nevada Ave, **E other:** Harley-Davidson, K&C RV Ctr, **W food:** New South Wales Rest. **lodging:** Bradford Suites, Extended Stay America, Marriott
147	Rockrimmon Blvd, **W gas:** Shell, **lodging:** Wyndham, to Rodeo Hall of Fame
146	Garden of the Gods Rd, **E gas:** Conoco, Shell/ dsl, **food:** Carl's Jr, Denny's, McDonald's, **lodging:** Econolodge, La Quinta, **other:** Aamco, **W gas:** Conoco, Phillips 66, 7-11, Shamrock, **food:** Applebee's, Arby's, Blackeyed Pea, Del Taco, Quizno's, Ranch Steaks, Souper Salad, Sonic, Starbucks, Subway, Taco Bell, Village Inn Rest., Wendy's, **lodging:** AmeriSuites, Day's Inn, Hyatt Place, Quality Inn, Super 8, **other:** Curves, Discount Tire, to Garden of Gods
145	CO 38 E, Fillmore St, **E gas:** 7-11, Shamrock, **food:** Burger King, DQ, **lodging:** Budget Host, **other:** H, Advance Parts, Firestone, **W gas:** Conoco/dsl, Loaf'n Jug, Shell/Circle K/dsl, **food:** Howard's BBQ, Waffle House, **lodging:** Best Western, Central Inn, Motel 6
144	Fontanero St
143	Uintah St, **E gas:** 7-11, **other:** Uintah Fine Arts Ctr
142	Bijou St, Bus Dist, **E other:** Firestone/auto, **W gas:** 7-11, **food:** Denny's, **lodging:** Clarion
141	US 24 W, Cimarron St, to Manitou Springs, **W gas:** Conoco, Phillips 66, **food:** Arby's, Burger King, Capt D's, La Castia Mexican, McDonald's, Papa John's, Popeye's, Sonic, Subway, Taco John's, Texas Roadhouse, Waffle House, **lodging:** Express Inn, Holiday Inn Express, **other:** Acura, AutoZone, Brakes+, Buick/GMC/Pontiac, Chevrolet, Chrysler, Discount Tire, Dodge, Ford, Gateway RV Ctr, Grease Monkey, Hyundai, Just Brakes, Infiniti, Isuzu, Lexus, Lincoln/ Mercury, Mazda, Mercedes, NAPA, Nissan, Office Depot, Porsche, Radio Shack, Subaru/Saab/VW, Suzuki, Toyota, Volvo, Walmart, to Pikes Peak,
140b	US 85 S, Tejon St, **E other:** Tires 4 Less, **W gas:** Conoco, **other:** Chrysler/Jeep, access to same as 141
140a	Nevada Ave, **E lodging:** Chateau Motel, Howard Johnson, Nevada Motel, Samaritan's Inn, **other:** Tire King, **W gas:** BP, 7-11, Shamrock, **food:** Burger King, China Kitchen, KFC, McDonald's, Subway, Taco Bell, Taco Express, Wendy's, **lodging:** Chief Motel, Cheyenne Motel, Econolodge, **other:** Big O Tire, Checker Parts, Sears, USPO, Walgreens, access to auto dealers at 141
139	US 24 E, to Lyman, Peterson AFB
138	CO 29, Circle Dr, **E gas:** Conoco, Shell/Circle K/dsl, **food:** McDonald's, **lodging:** Crowne Plaza, Day's Inn, Super 8, **other:** Kohl's, ✈, zoo, **W gas:** 7-11, **food:** Arby's, Burger King, Carrabba's, Carl's Jr, Chili's, ChuckeCheese, Denny's, Fazoli's, Outback Steaks, Papa John's, Village Inn Rest., Subway, **lodging:** Best Western, Comfort Inn, DoubleTree Hotel, Fairfield Inn, Hampton Inn, Holiday Inn, La Quinta, Residence Inn, Wingate Inn, **other:** Batteries+, GNC, PetCo, Radio Shack, Target
135	CO 83, Academy Blvd, **E** to Cheyenne Mtn SP, to ✈ **W** Ft Carson
132	CO 16, Wide Field Security, **E gas:** Loves/Subway/ dsl, **other:** Camping World RV SuperCtr, KOA
128	to US 85 N, Fountain, Security, **E gas:** Loaf'n Jug/ Subway/dsl, 7-11, Texaco, **food:** Grand China, **lodging:** Ute Motel, **other:** USPO, **W gas:** Tomahawk/ Shell/dsl/rest./24hr/@, **lodging:** Fountain Inn, Super 8
125	Ray Nixon Rd
123	no services
122	to Pikes Peak Meadows, **W** Pikes Peak Intn'l Raceway
119	Midway
116	county line rd
115mm	**rest area nb, full ♿ facilities, ⛺, litter barrels, petwalk**
114	Young Hollow
112mm	**rest area sb, full ♿ facilities, ⛺, litter barrels, petwalk**
110	Pinon, **W gas:** Sinclair/dsl/repair, **lodging:** Pinon Tree Inn
108	Bragdon, **E gas:** racetrack, **W** KOA
106	Porter Draw
104	Eden, **W food:** Chili's
102	Eagleridge Blvd, **E gas:** Loaf'n Jug, **food:** Burger King, TX Roadhouse, **lodging:** Holiday Inn, **other:** Big O Tire, Home Depot, Sam's Club/gas, **W gas:** Shell/Blimpie/dsl, **food:** Bellissimo Rest., Buffalo Wild Wings, Cactus Flower Mexican, Carino's, Cracker Barrel, IHOP, Starbucks, Village Inn Rest., **lodging:** Comfort Inn, Econolodge, La Quinta, Ramada, Wingate Inn, **other:** Best Buy, Kohl's, PetCo Tires+, Harley-Davidson, frontage rds access 101
101	US 50 W, Pueblo, **E gas:** Conoco, **food:** Capt D's, Denny's, 3 Margarita's Mexican, Souper Salad, Ruby Tuesday, **lodging:** Sleep Inn, **other:** Barnes&Noble, Dillards, JC Penney, Ross, Sears/auto, Target, Walmart SuperCtr, U-Haul, mall, **W gas:** Loaf'n Jug, Phillips 66, 7-11, Shamrock/dsl, **food:** Angelo's Pizza, Applebee's, Arby's, Blackeyed Pea, Boston Mkt, Burger King, Carl's Jr, Coldstone Creamery, Country Kitchen, DQ, Domino's, Fazoli's, Giacomo's Rest., Golden Corral, McDonald's, Olive Garden, Papa John's, Papa Murphy's, Popeye's, Quizno's, Red Lobster, Starbucks, Subway, SW Grill, Taco Bell, Wendy's, **lodging:** Days Inn, Motel 6, Pueblo Hotel, Quality Inn, Super 8, **other:** Aamco, Advance Parts, Albertson's/gas, AutoZone, Batteries+, Brakes+, Checker Parts, Chevrolet, Discount Tire, Dodge, Ford, Goodyear/auto, Honda, KIA, K-Mart, Lincoln/

COLORADO SPRINGS

PUEBLO

INTERSTATE 25 CONT'D

N ↕ S

Exit #	Services
101	Continued Mercury, Lowe's Whse, PetsMart, Staples, Toyota, Walgreens, frontage rds access 102
100b	29th St, Pueblo, **E food:** Country Buffet, KFC, Mongolian Grill, Panda Buffet, **other:** $Tree, King's Sooper Foods, Peerless Tires, mall, **W gas:** Phillips 66/dsl, **food:** Sonic, **lodging:** USA Motel, **other:** Grease Monkey, Safeway
100a	US 50 E, to La Junta, **E gas:** Loaf'n Jug, Phillips 66, **food:** KFC, McDonald's, Wendy's, **lodging:** Value Stay Inn, **other:** Big R Foods, Goodyear, Walgreens
99b a	Santa Fe Ave, 13th St, downtown, **W food:** Taco Bell, Wendy's, **lodging:** Guesthouse Inn, Travelers Motel, **other:** [H], Chevrolet, Chrysler/Jeep, Ford/Subaru, Honda, Mazda, Nissan, Pontiac, VW
98b	CO 96, 1st St, Union Ave Hist Dist, Pueblo, **W gas:** Loaf'n Jug, **food:** Carl's Jr, **lodging:** Marriott
98a	US 50E bus, to La Junta, **W gas:** Phillips 66/dsl, **food:** Sonic
97b	Abriendo Ave, **W gas:** Texaco
97a	Central Ave, **W gas:** Shamrock
96	Indiana Ave, **W other:** [H], Cobra Automotive
95	Illinois Ave (from sb), **W** to dogtrack
94	CO 45 N, Pueblo Blvd, **W gas:** Loaf'n Jug, Western/dsl, **food:** Pizza Hut/Taco Bell, **lodging:** Hampton Inn, Microtel, **other:** Lowes Whse, RV camping, fairgrounds/racetrack, to Lake Pueblo SP
91	Stem Beach
88	Burnt Mill Rd
87	Verde Rd
83	no services
77	Hatchet Ranch Rd, Cedarwood
74	CO 165 W, Colo City, **E gas:** Shamrock/deli/dsl/24hr, **other:** KOA, **W gas:** Shell/Subway/Noble Roman's/dsl, **food:** Los Cuervos, Max's Rest., **lodging:** Days Inn/rest., **rest area both lanes, full ♿ facilities, ☎, vending, [picnic], litter barrels, petwalk**
71	Graneros Rd, access to Columbia House
67	to Apache
64	Lascar Rd
60	Huerfano
59	Butte Rd
56	Redrock Rd
55	Airport Rd
52	CO 69 W, to Alamosa, Walsenburg, **W gas:** Phillips 66/A&W/dsl/24hr, Western Gas, **food:** Andy's BBQ, Alpine Rose Café (2mi), Carl's Jr (2mi), George's Rest., Pizza Hut, Rambler Rest., Subway (2mi), **lodging:** Best Western, Budget Host, Country Host RV Park, to Great Sand Dunes NM, San Luis Valley
50	CO 10 E, to La Junta, **W** [H], tourist info
49	Lp 25, to US 160 W, Walsenburg, **1 mi W gas:** Loaf'n Jug, **food:** Carl's Jr. **lodging:** Knight's Inn (4mi), Lathrop SP, to Cuchara Ski Valley
42	Rouse Rd, to Pryor
41	Rugby Rd
34	Aguilar, **E gas:** Cenex/dsl/rest.
30	Aguilar Rd, **W** truck/tire repair
27	Ludlow, **W** Ludlow Memorial

WALSENBURG

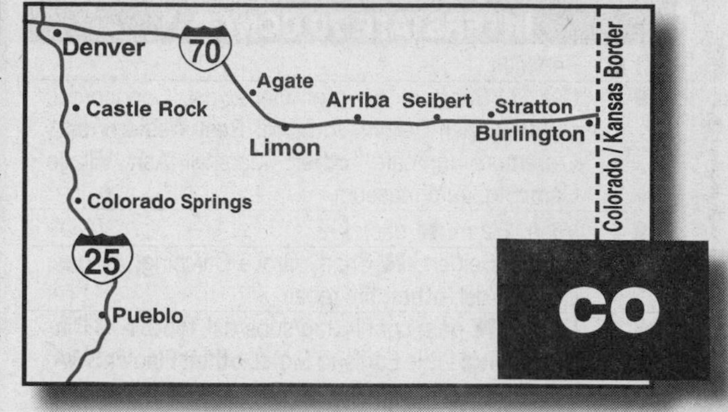

Exit #	Services
23	Hoehne Rd
18	El Moro Rd, **W rest area both lanes, full ♿ facilities, [picnic], litter barrels, petwalk**
15	US 350 E, Goddard Ave, **E food:** Burger King, **lodging:** Super 8, **other:** [H], Big R Ranch Store, Family$, **W gas:** Shell, **food:** B Lee's Café, **lodging:** Frontier Motel/café
14b a	CO 12 W, Trinidad, **E CO Welcome Ctr, gas:** Shell/Subway, **food:** KFC/Taco Bell, McDonald's, **other:** Safeway Foods, **W gas:** Shamrock, **food:** Domino's, DQ, El Captan, **lodging:** Prospect Plaza Motel, **other:** Parts+, TrueValue, RV camping, to Trinidad Lake, Monument Lake
13b	Main St, Trinidad, **E gas:** Shell, **food:** McDonald's, Sonic, **lodging:** Trinidad Hotel, **other:** CarQuest, Safeway
13a	Santa Fe Trail, Trinidad, **E lodging:** Best Western, **other:** RV camping
11	Starkville, **E gas:** Shell/Wendy's/dsl/24hr, **weigh/check sta, food:** Bob & Earl's Rest, Taquila's Mexican, **lodging:** Budget Host, Budget Summit Inn/RV Park, Holiday Inn, **other:** Bigg's RV Park, to Santa Fe Trail, **W gas:** Miristar, **food:** Country Kitchen, **lodging:** La Quinta, Quality Inn, **other:** Big O Tire, Checker Parts, Grease Monkey, Walmart SuperCtr
8	Springcreek
6	Gallinas
2	Wootten
1mm	scenic area pulloff nb
0mm	Colorado/New Mexico state line, Raton Pass, elev 7834, **weigh sta sb**

TRINIDAD

INTERSTATE 70

E ↕ W

Exit #	Services
450mm	Colorado/Kansas state line
438	US 24, Rose Ave, Burlington, **N gas:** Conoco/dsl, Phillips 66, **lodging:** Sloan's Motel, **other:** [H], Buick/GMC/Pontiac, CarQuest, Chevrolet, Family$, Ford/Lincoln/Mercury, NAPA, Safeway Foods, **S gas:** Shell/Reynaldo's Mexican/dsl/24hr, **other:** Bonny SRA, RV Camping, truck repair
437.5mm	**Welcome Ctr wb, full ♿ facilities, info, ☎, [picnic], litter barrels, petwalk, historical site**
437	US 385, Burlington, **N gas:** Conoco/dsl/24hr, Western/dsl, **food:** Arby's, Burger King, McDonald's, Pizza Hut, Route Steaks, Subway, **lodging:** Best Value Inn, Burlington Inn, Chaparral Motel, Comfort Inn, Western Motel, **other:** [H], Alco, to Bonny St RA
429	Bethune

INTERSTATE 70 CONT'D

Exit #	Services
419	CO 57, Stratton, **N gas:** Cenex/dsl, Conoco/dsl, **food:** Burger Delight, **lodging:** Best Western/rest., Claremont Inn/café, **other:** Marshall Ash Village Camping, auto museum
412	Vona, **1/2 mi N** gas, ☎
405	CO 59, Seibert, **N** Shady Grove Camping, **S gas:** Conoco/dsl, **other:** tire repair
395	Flagler, **N gas:** Loaf'N Jug/subs/dsl, **food:** I-70 Diner, **lodging:** Little England Motel, **other:** Flagler SWA, NAPA, RV camping, **S gas:** Cenex/dsl **other:** golf
383	Arriba, **N gas:** DJ/dsl/café, motel, **S rest area both lanes full ♿ facilities, [picnic], litter barrels, point of interest, petwalk, RV camping**
376	Bovina
371	Genoa, **N** point of interest, gas, food, ☎, **S** H
363	US 24, US 40, US 287, to CO 71, to Hugo, Limon, **13 mi S** H
361	CO 71, Limon, **N other:** Ace Hardware, Chrysler/Dodge/Jeep, **S gas:** Conoco/dsl/24hr, Phillips 66/Wendy's/dsl/24hr, **food:** Golden China, Pizza Hut, **lodging:** 1st Inn Gold, Travel Inn, **other:** Alco, KOA, st patrol, RV camping
360.5mm	**weigh/check sta both lanes**
359	to US 24, CO 71, Limon, **N gas:** *FLYING J*/dsl/Country Mkt/scales/LP/24hr, **other:** dsl repair, RV camping, **S gas:** Phillips 66, Qwest, TA/Shell/Subway/Country Fair/dsl/scales/24hr/@, **food:** Arby's, Denny's, McDonald's, Oscar's Grill, **lodging:** Comfort Inn, Econolodge, Holiday Inn Express, Limon Inn, Super 8, TS Inn, **other:** camping
354	no services
352	CO 86 W, to Kiowa
348	to Cedar Point
340	Agate, **1/4 mi S** gas/dsl, ☎
336	to Lowland
332mm	**rest area wb, full ♿ facilities, info, ☎, [picnic], litter barrels, vending, petwalk**
328	to Deer Trail, **N gas:** Phillips/dsl, **S gas:** Shell/dsl, **other:** USPO
325mm	East Bijou Creek
323.5mm	Middle Bijou Creek
322	to Peoria
316	US 36 E, Byers, **N gas:** Sinclair, **food:** Longhorn rest., **lodging:** Budget Host, **other:** Thriftway Foods/Drug, **S gas:** Tri Valley/gas, **food:** Country Burger Rest., **lodging:** Lazy 8 Motel (1mi), **other:** USPO
310	Strasburg, **N gas:** Conoco/dsl/24hr, Ray's gas/24hr, **food:** Corona Mexican, Pizza Shop, **lodging:** Strasburg Inn, **other:** KOA, NAPA, Parts+, Western Hardware, repair, RV camping, USPO
306mm	Kiowa , Bennett, **N rest area both lanes, full ♿ facilities, ☎, [picnic], litter barrels, petwalk**
305	Kiowa (from eb)
304	CO 79 N, Bennett, **N gas:** Conoco/Hotstuff Pizza/dsl **food:** China Kitchen, Subway, **other:** Kings Sooper Foods/dsl, USPO, **N other:** Ace Hardware
299	CO 36, Manila Rd
295	Lp 70, Watkins, **N gas:** Shell/Tomahawk/dsl/rest./24hr/@, **food:** Biscuit's Cafe, Lulu's Steak

Exit #	Services
295	Continued house, **lodging:** Country Manor Motel, **other:** USPO
292	CO 36, Airpark Rd
289	E-470 Tollway, 120th Ave, CO Springs
288	US 287, US 40, Lp 70, Colfax Ave (exits left from wb)
286	CO 32, Tower Rd, **N food:** Chili's, Chipotle Mexican, Del Taco, Starbucks, Wendy's, **other:** Best Buy, Checker Parts, Brakes+, Home Depot, Office Depot, PetCo, Walmart Super Ctr/Subway
285	Airport Blvd, **N** Denver Int ✈, **S gas:** *FLYING J*/Conoco/dsl/rest./24hr, Texaco/McDonald's/dsl, **lodging:** Comfort Inn, Crystal Inn, **other:** Harley-Davidson
284	I-225 N (from eb)
283	Chambers Rd, **N gas:** Conoco, Shell/Circle K, **food:** A&W/KFC, Applebees, Cantina Margarita, Chicago Grill, Montana Grill, Outback Steaks, Pizza Hut, Qdoba, Quizno's, Sonic, Subway, Taco Bell/LJ Silver, Ted's MT Grill, Wendy's, **lodging:** Cambria Suites, Country Inn&Suites, Crowne Plaza, Hilton Garden, Homewood Suites, Hyatt Place, Marriott, Residence Inn, Sleep Inn, Stonebridge Suites, **other:** Tires+, U-haul, **S gas:** Shamrock, **food:** Burger King, **lodging:** Crossland Suites, **other:** America East RV Ctr
282	I-225 S, to Colorado Springs
281	Peoria St, **N gas:** Conoco, Phillips 66, 7-11, **food:** Burger King, Del Taco, Domino's, GoodTimes Burgers, McDonald's, Peoria Grill, Pizza Patron, Quizno's, Subway, **lodging:** Drury Inn, Timbers Motel, **other:** Big O Tire, Family$, **S gas:** Conoco/dsl, Shamrock/dsl, **food:** Bennett's BBQ, Chester's Grill, Church's, Denny's, KFC, Old Santa Fe Grill, Pizza Hut/Taco Bell, Real Mina's Mexican, Subway, Waffle House, Wendy's, **lodging:** Motel 6, Quality Inn, Star Motel, Stay Inn, **other:** Curves, Goodyear/auto, auto/RV repair, Vet
280	Havana St, **N lodging:** Embassy Suites
279	I-270 W, US 36 W (from wb), to Ft Collins, Boulder
278	CO 35, Quebec St, **N gas:** Sapp Bros/Sinclair/Subway/dsl/@, TA/dsl/rest./24hr/@, **food:** Del Taco, Jim'n Nick's BBQ, Olive Garden, Qdoba, Red Lobster, TGIFriday, Wahoo's, **lodging:** Comfort Inn, Studio Suites, **other:** Bass Pro Shops, Border's Books, JC Penney, Macys, Old Navy, Super Target, mall, **S food:** Arby's, Country Buffet, Mariposa Mexican, McDonald's, IHOP, Panda Express, Panera Bread, Sonic, Subway, **lodging:** Courtyard, DoubleTree Hotel, Guesthouse Inn, Red Lion Inn, Renaissance Inn, **other:** GNC, Home Depot, Office Depot, Radio Shack, Ross, Sam's Club, Walmart/gas
277	to Dahlia St, Holly St, Monaco St, frontage rd
276b	US 6 E, US 85 N, CO 2, Colorado Blvd, **S gas:** Conoco/Subway/dsl, **food:** Carl's Jr, KT'S BBQ, Potrillo's Mexican, Starbucks
276a	Vasquez Ave, **N gas:** Pilot/Wendy's/dsl/scales/24hr, **lodging:** Colonial Motel, Western Inn, **other:** Blue Beacon, Ford/Mack Trucks, **S gas:** 7-11, **food:** Burger King
275c	York St (from eb), **N lodging:** Colonial Motel
275b	CO 265, Brighton Blvd, Coliseum, **N gas:** 7-11
275a	Washington St, **N food:** Pizza Hut, **S gas:** Conoco, **food:** McDonald's, Quizno's, Subway
274b a	I-25, N to Cheyenne, S to Colorado Springs

INTERSTATE 70 CONT'D

E ↕ W

Exit #	Services
273	Pecos St, **N other:** Family$, Safeway Foods, True Value, **S gas:** 7-11, **food:** Quizno's, **other:** transmissions
272	US 287, Federal Blvd, **N gas:** Conoco, Sinclair, **food:** Burger King, Goodtimes Burgers, Little Caesar's, McCoy's Rest., McDonald's, Pizza Hut, Subway, Taco Bell, Village Inn, Wendy's, **lodging:** Motel 6, **other:** Advance Parts, $Tree, tires, **S gas:** Conoco/Circle K, **food:** Popeye's, Starbucks, **lodging:** Howard Johnson, **other:** 7-11
271b	Lowell Blvd, Tennyson St (from wb)
271a	CO 95, **S** Wild Chipmunk Amusement Park
270	Sheridan Blvd, **S gas:** Phillips 66, **food:** El Paraiso Mexican, Tennessee BBQ, **other:** Family$, Firestone/auto, Radio Shack, fun park
269b	I-76 E (from eb), to Ft Morgan, Ft Collins
269a	CO 121, Wadsworth Blvd, **N gas:** Conoco, Phillips 66, 7-11, **food:** Alamos Verdes Mexican, Applebee's, Bennet's BBQ, Burger King, Chipotle Mexican, Coldstone Creamery, Fazoli's, Gunther Toody's Diner, IHOP, Koro Japanese, LoneStar Steaks, McDonald's/playplace, Red Robin, Ruby Tuesday, Starbucks, Subway, Taco Bell, **other:** Advance Parts, Brakes+, Costco/gas, Discount Tire, $Tree, Goodyear/auto, Home Depot, Lowe's Whse, Office Depot, PetsMart, Radio Shack, Sam's Club, Tires+, mall

WHEAT RIDGE

Exit #	Services
267	CO 391, Kipling St, Wheat Ridge, **N gas:** Conoco, Shell/Carl's Jr/Circle K/dsl, **food:** Amadeo's Italian, Burger King, Denny's, Einstein Bros, Furr's Dining, Jack-in-the-Box, Panda Express, Qdoba, Quizno's, Starbucks, Subway, **lodging:** American Inn, Motel 6, **other:** Cadillac/Chevrolet, Chrysler/Jeep, GNC, NAPA, 7-11, Target, Vet, **S gas:** Conoco/Circle K, Phillips 66, **food:** Pizza Hut/Taco Bell, Smokin' Joe's Grill, Village Inn, **lodging:** Affordable Inn, Comfort Inn, Holiday Inn Express, Interstate Inn, La Piazza, Ramada, **other:** Ketelesen RV Ctr
266	CO 72, W 44th Ave, Ward Rd, Wheat Ridge, **N gas:** Conoco/dsl, Phillips 66/dsl, **other:** transmissions, Vet, **S gas:** Shamrock/dsl, TA/rest./scales/dsl/24hr/@, **lodging:** Howard Johnson
265	CO 58 W (from wb), to Golden, Central City
264	Youngfield St, W 32nd Ave, **N gas:** Conoco/Circle K, **food:** GoodTimes Burgers, Marie's Country Cafe, **lodging:** La Quinta, **S food:** Abrusci's Italian, Chili's, DQ, McDonald's, Old Chicago Pizza, Pizza Hut/Taco Bell, Qdoba, Smash Burger, Starbucks, Subway, **other:** Camping World RV Ctr, Casey's RV Ctr, King's Sooper/24hr, PetsMart, Radio Shack, Walgreens, Walmart
263	Denver West Blvd, **N lodging:** Marriott/rest., **S food:** Keg Steaks, Macaroni Grill, McGrath's Fishouse, Qdoba, **other:** Barnes&Noble, Best Buy, Office Depot, Whole Foods Mkt, same as 262
262	US 40 E, W Colfax, Lakewood, **N gas:** Sinclair, **food:** El Senor Mexican, Jack-in-the-Box, **lodging:** Hampton Inn, **other:** Buick/Pontiac/GMC, Chrysler/Jeep, Dodge, Home Depot, Honda, Hyundai, Kohl's, NAPA, PetCo, Staples, Subaru, U-Haul,

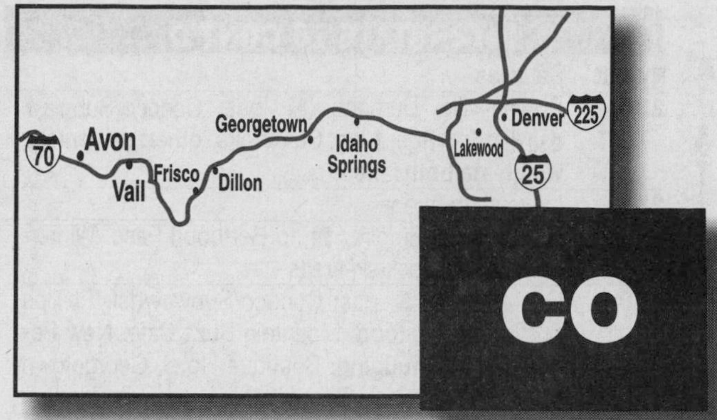

CO

LAKEWOOD

Exit #	Services
262	Continued transmissions, Vet, **S gas:** Shell/Circle K/dsl/LP, **food:** Chipotle Mexican, Coldstone Creamery, Hops Brewery, Jamba Juice, Keg Steaks, Macaroni Grill, McGrath's Fishouse, Mimi's Cafe, On-the-Border, Outback Steaks, Pei Wei Asian, Qdoba, Quizno's, Wendy's, **lodging:** Courtyard, Days Inn/rest., Holiday Inn, Residence Inn, **other:** Barnes&Noble, Best Buy, Borders Books, Chevrolet, Lexus, Old Navy, Target, Toyota, Whole Foods Mkt, mall, same as 263
261	US 6 E (from eb), W 6th Ave, to Denver
260	CO 470, to Colo Springs
259	CO 26, Golden, **N gas:** Conoco, **lodging:** Hampton Inn (2mi), **other:** Heritage Sq Funpark, **S** Music Hall, to Red Rocks SP
257mm	runaway truck ramp eb
256	Lookout Mtn, **N** to Buffalo Bill's Grave
254	Genesee, Lookout Mtn, **N** to Buffalo Bill's Grave, **S gas:** Conoco/Genesee Store, LP, **food:** Chart House Rest., Christie's Rest., Genesee Towne Cafe, Guido's Pizza, **other:** Vet
253	Chief Hosa, **S** RV Camping, (phone)
252	(251 from eb), CO 74, Evergreen Pkwy, **S gas:** Conoco, **food:** Burger King, El Rancho Rest., McDonald's, Qdoba, Smiling Moose Deli, Starbucks, Subway, **lodging:** Quality Suites, **other:** Big O Tire, Home Depot, Jiffy Lube, King's Sooper/deli, Walmart SuperCtr
248	(247 from eb), Beaver Brook, Floyd Hill, **S** antiques
244	US 6, to CO 119, to Golden, Central City, Eldora Ski Area
243	Hidden Valley
242mm	tunnel

IDAHO SPRINGS

Exit #	Services
241b a	rd 314, Idaho Springs West, **N gas:** Conoco/McDonald's/dsl, Sinclair, Shell/dsl, Western, **food:** Cherry Blossom Chinese, King's Derby Rest., Marion's Rest., Quizno's, Smokin' Yards BBQ, Starbucks, Subway, Wildfire Rest., **lodging:** Columbine Inn, H&H Motel, Heritage Inn, Idaho Springs Hotel, JC Motel, Marion's Rest., Peorina Motel, 6&40 Motel/rest., The Lodge, Tops Motel, **other:** CarQuest, Radio Shack, Safeway Foods/Drug, USPO
240	CO 103, Mt Evans, **N gas:** Shell, Sinclair/dsl, **food:** Beaujo's Pizza, Buffalo Rest., Cafe Aimee, Picci Pizza, Jiggie's Cafe, Tommy Knocker Grill, 2 Bros Deli, same as 241, **S** to Mt Evans
239	Idaho Springs, **S other:** camping
238	Fall River Rd, to St Mary's Glacier
235	Dumont (from wb)

INTERSTATE 70 CONT'D

E ↕ W

Exit #	Services
234	Downeyville, Dumont, **N gas:** Conoco/Subway/dsl, **food:** Burger King, Starbucks, **other:** ski rentals, **weigh sta both lanes**
233	Lawson (from eb)
232	US 40 W, to Empire, **N** to Berthoud Pass, Winterpark/Silver Creek ski areas
228	Georgetown, **S gas:** Conoco/Subway/dsl, Phillips 66/dsl, Valero, **food:** Mountain Buzz Cafe, New Peking Garden, **lodging:** Boutique Hotel, Georgetown Inn, Super 8, **other:** visitors ctr
226.5mm	scenic overlook eb
226	Georgetown, Silver Plume Hist Dist, **N other:** Buckley Bros Mkt, repair
221	Bakerville
220mm	Arapahoe NF eastern boundary
219mm	**parking area (eb only)**
218	no services
216	US 6 W, Loveland Valley, Loveland Basin, ski areas
214mm	Eisenhower/Johnson Tunnel, elev 11013
213mm	**parking area eb**
205	US 6 E, CO 9 N, Dillon, Silverthorne, **N gas:** Conoco/dsl, 7-11, Sav-O-Mat, Shell/7-11/dsl, **food:** Asian Oven, China Gourmet, Chipotle Mexican, Domino's, Mtn Lyon Café, Murphy's Cafe, Old Dillon Inn, Quizno's, Village Inn, Wendy's, **lodging:** Days Inn, 1st Interstate Inn, La Quinta, Luxury Suites, Quality Inn, Silver Inn, **other:** Cadillac/Chevrolet/Buick/GMC/Pontiac, CarQuest, Chrysler/Dodge/Jeep, Ford/Mercury, Old Navy, Silverthorne Outlets/famous brands, Subaru, Target, True Value, **S gas:** Phillips 66, Shamrock, **food:** Arby's, Bamboo Garden, Blue Moon Deli, Burger King, Dam Brewery/Rest., DQ, Fiesta Mexican, JJ Chinese, McDonald's, Nick'n Willy's Pizza, Pizza Hut, Qdoba, Red Mtn Grill, Ruby Tuesday, Smash Burger, Starbucks, Subway, Sunshine Cafe, **lodging:** Comfort Suites, Dillon Inn, Super 8, **other:** Borders Books, City Mkt Foods/gas, Silverthorne Outlets/famous brands, Natural Grocery, Walgreens, Vet
203.5mm	scenic overlook both lanes, ☎s
203	CO 9 S, to Breckenridge, Frisco, **S gas:** Conoco/Wendy's/dsl, Shell, Valero/dsl, **food:** A&W, Back Country Brewery/rest., KFC, Carlos Miguel's Mexican, Pizza Hut, Q4U BBQ, Smiling Moose Deli, Starbucks, Subway, Szechuan Chinese, Taco Bell, **lodging:** Best Western, Holiday Inn, Ramada Ltd, Summit Inn, **other:** Big O Tire, NAPA, Radio Shack, Safeway Foods, 7-11, Walmart/McDonald's, Vet, to Breckenridge Ski Area, Tiger Run RV Resort (6mi)
201	Main St, Frisco, **S gas:** Conoco, Loaf N' Jug, **food:** Alpine Deli, Back Country Brew Pub, Butterhorn Cafe, **lodging:** Bighorn Reservations, Frisco Lodge, Hotel Frisco, Snowshoe Motel, **other:** RV camping, museum/visitor info, USPO, to Breckenridge Ski Area
198	Officers Gulch, emergency callbox
196mm	scenic area (wb only)
195	CO 91 S, to Leadville, **1 mi S gas:** Conoco/dsl, **food:** Quizno's, Starbucks, Tucker's Tavern, **lodging:** Copper Lodging, **other:** to Copper Mtn Ski Resort
190	**S rest area both lanes, full ♿ facilities,** ☎, **picnic tables, litter barrels**
189mm	Vail Pass Summit, elev 10662 ft, parking area both lanes
180	Vail East Entrance, ☎, services **3-4 mi S**
176	Vail, **S other:** [H], ski info/lodging
173	Vail Ski Area, **N gas:** Phillips 66, Shell/dsl, **food:** DQ, Domino's, Gohanya Chinese, McDonald's, Mizabba Cafe, Subway, Taco Bell, Wendy's, **lodging:** Holiday Inn, **other:** Ace Hardware, City Mkt Foods/deli, Safeway Food/Drug, 7-11, **S gas:** Conoco/dsl/LP, **lodging:** Black Bear Inn, Marriott/Streamside Hotel, The Roost Lodge
171	US 6 W, US 24 E, to Minturn, Leadville, **N food:** Leadville Café, **other:** Ski Cooper ski area, **2.5 mi S gas:** Phillips 66, **food:** Chiliwilly's Steaks, Minturn Steaks, **lodging:** Minturn Inn, **other:** RV Camping
169	Eaglevale, from wb, no return
168	William J. Post Blvd, **S food:** McDonald's, Zaccaza Cafe, **other:** Home Depot, Walmart SuperCtr
167	Avon, **N gas:** Conoco/7-11/dsl, Phillips 66, **food:** Pizza Hut, **other:** Goodyear, Vet, **S food:** Burger King, China Garden, Denny's, Domino's, Fiesta Mexican, Golden Oven Pizza, Outback Steaks, Panda City, Quizno's, Starbucks, Subway, **lodging:** Avon Ctr Lodge, Christie Lodge, Comfort Inn, Seasons Hotel, Sheraton, Westin, **other:** City Mkt/drugs, GNC, Office Depot, Radio Shack, to Beaver Creek/Arrowhead Ski, ski info, USPO
163	Edwards, **S rest area both lanes, full ♿ facilities,** ☎, **picnic tables, litter barrel, RV dump, gas:** Conoco/dsl, Shell/Wendy's/dsl, **food:** Fiesta Cantina, Gashouse Rest., Gore Range Brewery, Marble Slab Creamery, Marko's Pizza, Moe's SW Grill, Smiling Moose, Subway, Starbucks, Woody's Grill, **lodging:** Riverwalk Inn, **other:** to Arrowhead Ski Area, USPO
162mm	scenic area both lanes
159mm	Eagle River
157	CO 131 N, Wolcott, **N** to gas, ☎, to Steamboat Ski Area
147	Eagle, **N gas:** Shamrock/dsl, **food:** Burger King, Domino's, Mi Pueblo Mexican, **lodging:** AmericInn, Comfort Inn, Holiday Inn Express, **other:** City Mkt Foods, **S gas:** Conoco/pizza, Sinclair/dsl, **food:** Back Bowl Cafe, Eagle Diner, Fiesta Jalisco, Pazzo's Pizzaria, Subway, Taco Bell, Wendy's, Gourmet China, **lodging:** Best Western, Silverleaf Suites, **other:** Costco/gas (3mi), Curves, USPO, rest area both lanes, full ♿ facilities, info
140	Gypsum, **S gas:** Conoco, Phillips 66/dsl, **food:** Columbine Mkt Deli, Salsa's Mexican, **other:** auto/truck repair, ✈, USPO, **3 mi S** River Dance Resort camping
134mm	Colorado River
133	Dotsero, **N other:** River Dance RV Camping (3mi)
129	Bair Ranch, **S rest area both lanes, full ♿ facilities, picnic tables, litter barrels, petwalk**
128.5mm	**parking area eb**
127mm	tunnel wb
125mm	tunnel
125	to Hanging Lake (no return eb)
123	Shoshone (no return eb)
122.5mm	exit to river (no return eb)

FRISCO · VAIL · AVON · EAGLE

INTERSTATE 70 CONT'D

E ↕ W

GLENWOOD SPRINGS

Exit #	Services
121	to Hanging Lake, Grizzly Creek, **S** rest area both lanes, full ♿ facilities, [picnic], litter barrels,
119	No Name, **rest area both lanes, full ♿ facilities, RV camping, rafting**
118mm	tunnel
116	CO 82 E, to Aspen, Glenwood Springs, **N gas:** Conoco/dsl, Shell/dsl, **food:** Chomp's Rest., Fiesta Guadalajara, KFC, Qdoba, Subway, Tequila Rest., Village Inn, **lodging:** AmericInn, Best Western, Glenwood Inn, Hampton Inn, Holiday Inn Express, Hotel Colorado, Ramada Inn, Silver Spruce Motel, Starlight Motel, **other:** Land Rover, NAPA, Toyota, Hot Springs Bath, funpark, **0-2 mi S gas:** Conoco, Phillips 66/dsl, Shamrock, Shell, Sinclair, **food:** Arby's, China Town, Domino's, Little Ceasar's, McDonald's, Pizza Hut, Starbucks, Subway, Taco Bell, Taipei Japanese, Wendy's, **lodging:** Caravan Inn, Cedar Lodge, Frontier Lodge, Hotel Denver, **other:** [H], Alpine Tire, City Mkt Foods, Honda, NAPA, Office Depot, Rite Aid, Safeway Foods, 7-11, Subaru/Nissan, Walmart, USPO, city park, to Ski Sunlight
115mm	**rest area eb, full ♿ facilities, [picnic], litter barrels**
114	W Glenwood Springs, **N gas:** Phillips 66/dsl, 7-11, Shell, **food:** Burger King, CharBurger, Dos Hombres Mexican, Jilbirtito's Mexican, Rancho Antigua Mexican, **lodging:** Affordable Inn, Best Value Inn, Ponderosa Motel, Red Mtn Inn, Rodeway Inn, **other:** Big O Tire, CarQuest, Checker Parts, Chevrolet, Chrysler/Dodge, Ford, JC Penney, K-Mart, Radio Shack, Staples, mall, **S gas:** Conoco/DQ/dsl, **food:** Chili's, Moe's Grill, Quizno's, Russo's Pizza, Starbucks, **lodging:** Glenwood Suites, Quality Inn, **other:** Audi/VW, Harley-Davidson, Lowe's Whse, PetCo, Target
111	South Canyon
109	Canyon Creek
108mm	**parking area both lanes**
105	New Castle, **N gas:** Conoco/dsl, Kum&Go/dsl, **food:** New Castle Diner, Subway, **lodging:** Rodeway Inn, **other:** City Mkt Foods/deli, Elk Creek Campground (4mi), **S other:** Best Hardware
97	Silt, **N gas:** Conoco/dsl/24hr, Kum&Go, Phillips 66/dsl, **lodging:** Red River Inn, **other:** auto repair, to Harvey Gap SP, **S lodging:** Holiday Inn Express, Ruby River Cabins, **other:** Heron's Nest RV Park
94	Garfield County Airport Rd
90	CO 13 N, Rifle, **N rest area both lanes, full ♿ facilities, ☎, [picnic], litter barrels, RV dump,** NF Info, **gas:** Conoco/dsl, Kum&Go/gas, Phillips 66/dsl, Shell, **lodging:** Winchester Motel (1mi), **other:** [H], USPO, Rifle Gap SP, **S gas:** Kum&Go, Phillips 66/dsl, **food:** Burger King, Domino's, Little Caesar's, McDonald's/playplace, Rib City Grill, Sonic, Starbucks, Subway, Taco Bell/LJ Silver, **lodging:** Comfort Suites, Hampton Inn, La Quinta, Red River Inn/rest., Rusty Cannon Motel, Super 8 **other:** [H], Checker Parts, Radio Shack, Walmart SuperCtr
87	to CO 13, West Rifle
81	Rulison

RIFLE

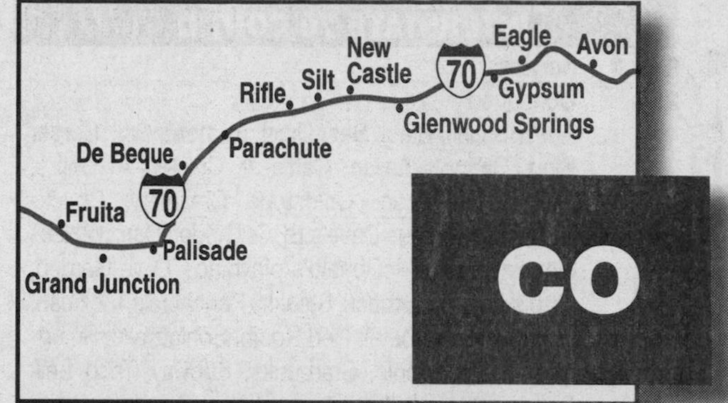

CO

PARACHUTE

Exit #	Services
75	Parachute, **N rest area both lanes, full ♿ facilities, info, ☎, [picnic], litter barrels, petwalk, gas:** Sinclair/dsl, Shell/dsl/24hr, **food:** El Tapatio Mexican, Hong's Garden Chinese, Outlaws Rest., Subway, **lodging:** Super 8, **other:** NAPA, Radio Shack, USPO, Vet, **S gas:** Conoco/Wendy's/dsl, Phillips 66/Domino's/dsl, **lodging:** Candlewood Suites, Holiday Inn Express, **other:** Family$, RV Park (4mi), True Value
63mm	Colorado River
62	De Beque, **N gas:** CFN Fuel, **other:** food, ☎, auto repair
50mm	**parking area eastbound**, Colorado River, tunnel begins eastbound
49mm	Plateau Creek
49	CO 65 S, to CO 330 E, to Grand Mesa, Powderhorn Ski Area
47	Island Acres St RA, **N** CO River SP, RV camping, **S gas:** Conoco/rest./dsl
46	Cameo
44	Lp 70 W, to Palisade, **3 mi S** gas, food, lodging
43.5mm	Colorado River
42	US 6, Palisade, **1 mi S** Fruitstand/store, gas, **lodging:** Wine Country Inn, **other:** wineries
37	to US 6, to US 50 S, Clifton, Grand Jct, **0-1 mi S gas:** Conoco/dsl, Shamrock/dsl, Sinclair, **food:** Burger King, Chin Chin Chinese, Dos Hombres Mexican, KFC, Little Caesar's, McDonald's/playplace, Papa Murphy's, Pizza Hut, Qdoba, Sonic, Starbucks, Subway, Taco Bell, The Diner, Wendy's, **lodging:** Best Western, **other:** Ace Hardware, AutoZone, Checker Parts, City Mkt Food/gas, Family$, Murdoch's Store, USPO, Walgreens, Walmart SuperCtr (2mi), repair
31	Horizon Dr, Grand Jct, **N gas:** Shamrock, Shell/dsl, **food:** Coco's, Diorio's Pizza, Pepper's Rest., Village Inn, Wendy's, **lodging:** Best Value Inn, Comfort Inn, Courtyard, Grand Vista Hotel, Holiday Inn, La Quinta, Motel 6, Ramada Inn, Residence Inn, **other:** Harley-Davidson, NAPA, USPO, Zarlingo's Repair, ✈, **S gas:** Conoco/Subway/dsl, Phillips 66/dsl, **food:** Applebee's, Burger King/playland, Denny's, Good Pastures Rest., Nick'n Willy's Pizza, Pizza Hut, Starbucks, Taco Bell, **lodging:** Affordable Inn, Best Western, Country Inn, Doubletree Hotel, Mesa Inn, Quality Inn, Super 8, **other:** [H], Safeway Food/drug/gas, golf, visitors ctr, to Mesa St Coll, CO NM
28	Redlands Pkwy, 24 Rd, **N** Kenworth, **0-2 mi S** city park, same as 26
26	US 6, US 50, Grand Jct, **N other:** Hyundai, Jct W RV Park, **0-4 mi S gas:** Conoco/A&W/dsl **food:**

GRAND JUNCTION

INTERSTATE 70 CONT'D

E ↕ W

Exit #	Services
26	Continued Austin's Grill, Black Bear Diner, Boston's Grill, Burger King, Carino's Italian, Carl's Jr, Chick-fil-A, Chili's, Chipotle Mexican, Coldstone Creamery, Chuck-eCheese, Famous Dave's BBQ, Golden Corral, IHOP, Jimmy John's, McDonald's/playplace, Olive Garden, Otto's Rest., Outback Steaks, Panchero's Mexican, Qdoba, Red Lobster, Red Robin, Schlotzky's, Smuggler's Rest., Sonic, Starbucks, Subway, Taco Bell, **lodging:** Holiday Inn Express, West Gate Inn, **other:** AutoZone, Barnes&Noble, Best Buy, Big O Tire, Borders Books, Buick/Chevrolet/Pontiac, Cameron's RV Ctr, Chrysler/Dodge/Jeep, $Tree, Firestone/auto, Ford/Lincoln/Merury, Freightliner, Home Depot, Honda, JC Penney, Kohl's, Lowe's Whse, Michael's, Mobile City RV Park, Nissan, Office Depot, Old Navy, PetCo, Petsmart, Rite Aid, Ross, Sam's Club/gas, Scott RV Ctr, Sears/auto, Subaru, Target, Toyota, Walmart SuperCtr, mall
19	US 6, CO 340, Fruita, **N gas:** Conoco/dsl, **food:** Burger King, Munchie's Burgers/Pizza, **lodging:** Balanced Rock Motel, **other:** H, City Mkt Foods/deli/24hr, NAPA, USPO, Walgreens, **S Welcome Ctr both lanes, full ♿ facilities, ☎, picnic, litter barrels, RV dump, petwalk, gas:** Conoco/Subway/dsl/24hr, Shell/Wendy's/dsl/24hr, **food:** El Tipatio Mexican, McDonald's/playplace, Rib City Grill, Taco Bell, **lodging:** Comfort Inn, La Quinta, Super 8, **other:** Monument RV Park, Peterbilt, dinosaur museum, to CO NM, Vet
17mm	Colorado River
15	CO 139 N, to Loma, Rangely, **N** to Highline Lake SP, gas/dsl, ☎
14.5mm	**weigh/check sta both lanes,** ☎
11	Mack, **2-3 mi N** gas/dsl, food
2	Rabbit Valley, to Dinosaur Quarry Trail
0mm	Colorado/Utah state line

FRUITA

INTERSTATE 76

E ↕ W

Exit #	Services
184mm	Colorado/Nebraska state line
180	US 385, Julesburg, **N gas:** *FLYING J*/dsl/LP/rest./24hr, Shell, **food:** Subway, **lodging:** Budget Host, **other:** H, Welcome Ctr/rest area both lanes, full ♿ facilities, info, RV dump, **S gas:** Conoco/dsl
172	Ovid, **2 mi N** gas, food
165	CO 59, to Haxtun, Sedgwick, **N** Lucy's Cafe/gas
155	Red Lion Rd
149	CO 55, to Fleming, Crook, **S gas:** Sinclair/dsl/café
141	Proctor
134	Iliff
125	US 6, Sterling, **N gas:** Cenex/dsl, **lodging:** Best Western, 1st Interstate Inn, **other:** H, N Sterling SP, museum, st patrol, **rest area both lanes full ♿ facilities, picnic, litter barrels, petwalk, vending, RV dump, 0-3 mi N gas:** Sinclair, **food:** Arby's, Burger King, KFC, McDonald's, Pizza Hut, Sonic, Taco John's, Village Inn, Wendy's, **other:** Chrysler/Jeep/Dodge, Checker Parts, $Tree, Home Depot, NAPA,
125	Continued Walgreens, Walmart SuperCtr/gas/24hr, tires **S gas:** Phillips 66/Quizno's/dsl, **food:** Country Kitchen, **lodging:** Comfort Inn, Ramada Inn, Super 8, Travelodge, **other:** Jellystone Camping
115	CO 63, Atwood, **N gas:** Sinclair/dsl, **other:** H, **S food:** Steakhouse
102	Merino
95	Hillrose
92	to US 6 E, to US 34, CO 71 S
90b a	CO 71 N, to US 34, Brush, **N gas:** Tomahawk Trkstp/Shell/rest./dsl/24hr, **food:** China Buffet, Pizza Hut, Wendy's, **lodging:** Econolodge, **S gas:** Conoco/dsl, **food:** McDonald's, Subway, **lodging:** Microtel
89	H Rd, **S** H, golf
86	Dodd Bridge Rd
82	Barlow Rd, **N gas:** Conoco/dsl, **food:** Maverick's Grill, **lodging:** Comfort Inn, Rodeway Inn, **S gas:** Phillips 66/dsl/scales, **food:** Burger King, Quizno's, **other:** $Tree, Walmart SuperCtr/Subway/dsl/24hr
80	CO 52, Ft Morgan, **N other:** City Park, Golf, RV Camping, **S gas:** Conoco/dsl/24hr, Shell/dsl, **food:** Arby's, DQ, McDonald's, Sonic, Subway, Taco John's, **lodging:** Best Western/rest., Central Motel, Day's Inn, Super 8, **other:** H, AutoZone, Rite Aid
79	CO 144, to Weldona, no WB return
75	US 34 E, to Ft Morgan, st patrol
74.5mm	**weigh sta both lanes**
73	Long Bridge Rd
66b	US 34 W (from wb), to Greeley
66a	CO 39, CO 52, to Goodrich, **N gas:** Phillips 66, **other:** to Jackson Lake SP, **S gas:** Sinclair/cafe/dsl, **other: rest area both lanes, full ♿ facilities, picnic, litter barrels, petwalk, ☎, vending**
64	Wiggins (from eb)
60	to CO 144 E, to Orchard
57	rd 91
49	Painter Rd (from wb)
48	to Roggen, **N gas:** Phillips 66/dsl, **S other:** USPO
39	Keenesburg, **S gas:** Phillips 66/dsl, **food:** Rooster's Rest., **lodging:** Keene Motel
34	Kersey Rd
31	CO 52, Hudson, **N gas:** Love's/Subway/Carls Jr/scales/24hr/dsl, **S gas:** Conoco/dsl, Phillips 66/dsl, **food:** El Faro Mexican, Pepper Pod Rest., **other:** RV camping, USPO
25	CO 7, Lochbuie, **N gas:** Shell/dsl
22	Bromley Lane, **N gas:** Shamrock/dsl, **food:** Wendy's, **other:** Kohl's, Home Depot, Lowe's Whse, Target, **other:** H, **2-4 mi N food:** Applebee's, Arby's, Kings Sooper/gas, Starbucks, Village Inn, **lodging:** Brighton Inn, Comfort Inn, **S** Barr Lake SP
21	144th Ave, **N food:** Chili's, Heidi's Deli, Quizno's, Taco Bell, **other:** $Tree, GNC, Home Depot, Kohl's, PetsMart, Super Target
20	136th Ave, **N** Barr Lake RV Park, same as 21
18	E-470 tollway, to Limon (from wb)
16	CO 2 W, Sable Blvd, Commerce City, **N gas:** Shell/Tomahawk Trkstp/Blimpie/dsl/24hr/@, to Denver ✈
12	US 85 N, to Brighton, Greeley
11	96th Ave, **N** dsl repair, **S** GMC Trucks
10	88th Ave, **N gas:** Phillips 66/Blimpie/dsl, **lodging:**

STERLING

FORT MORGAN

E ↕ W

INTERSTATE 76 CONT'D

Exit #	Services
10	Continued Holiday Inn Express, Super 8, **S** flea mkt
9	US 6 W, US 85 S (wb returns st 10), Commerce City, **S gas:** Shell/dsl, **other:** GMC/Freightliner, transmissions, st patrol
8	CO 224, 74th Ave (no EZ eb return), **1 mi N** NAPA, **S gas:** Shamrock/dsl
6b a	I-270 E, to Limon, to ✈, to I-25 N, to ✈
5	I-25, N to Ft Collins, S to Colo Springs
4	Pecos St
3	US 287, Federal Blvd, **N gas:** Shamrock/dsl, **S food:** Taco House
1b	CO 95, Sheridan Blvd
1a	CO 121, Wadsworth Blvd, **N gas:** Conoco, Phillips 66, 7-11/gas, **food:** Alamos Verdes Mexican, Applebee's, Bennet's BBQ, Burger King, Chipotle Mexican, Coldstone Creamery, Fazoli's, Gunther Toody's Diner, IHOP, Koro Japanese, LoneStar Steaks, McDonald's/playplace, Red Robin, Ruby Tuesday, Starbucks, Subway, Taco Bell, **other:** Advance Parts, Brakes+, Costco/gas, Discount Tire, $Tree, Goodyear/auto, Home Depot, Lowe's Whse, Office Depot, Petsmart, Radio Shack, Sam's Club, Tires+, mall
0mm	I-76 begins/ends on I-70, exit 269b.

INTERSTATE 225 (DENVER)

N ↕ S

Exit #	Services
12b a	I-70, W to Denver, E to Limon
10	US 40, US 287, Colfax Ave, **E gas:** Conoco/dsl, Phillips 66, 7-11, Shell, Sinclair, **food:** Arby's, Burger King, Del Taco, DQ, KFC, McDonald's, Pizza Hut/Taco Bell, Popeye's, Starbucks, Subway, Wendy's, Village Inn, **other:** Aamco, Advance Parts, Chevrolet, Family$, King's Sooper/gas, K-Mart, NAPA, RV camping, Walgreens, **W gas:** Conoco/dsl, **food:** Anthony's, Caribou Coffee, Chipotle Mexican, Noodles&Co, Spicy Pickle, **other:** H, Curves, U-Haul
9	Co 30, 6th Ave, **E gas:** Conoco/dsl, **food:** Denny's, **lodging:** Super 8, ValuePlace Inn, **other:** Hobby Lobby, **W gas:** Phillips 66/dsl, **other:** H
8	Alameda Ave, **E gas:** Conoco, Shamrock, **food:** Atlanta Bread, Baja Fresh, Benny's Cafe, BJ's Rest., Chili's, FatBurger, Jamba Juice, L&L BBQ, Macaroni Grill, Mimi's Cafe, Panda Express, Starbucks, TGIFriday, Wingstop, **other:** Barnes&Noble, Dillards, Gordman's, JC Penney, Macys, Old Navy, Petsmart, Ross, Sears/auto, Super Target, **W gas:** Conoco/dsl, Shell/Circle K, **other:** $Tree
7	Mississippi Ave, Alameda Ave, **E food:** Arby's, Bono's BBQ, Burger King, CiCi's, Chubby's Mexican, ChuckeCheese, Fazoli's, Guadalajara Mexican, Schlotsky's, Sonic, Subway, Village Inn, **lodging:** Best Western, Holiday Inn Express, La Quinta, **other:** Best Buy, Burlington Coats, Home Depot, JoAnn Fabrics, Sam's Club/gas, Tires +, Walmart, **W food:** IHOP, McDonald's, Senor Ric's, Waffle House, **other:** AutoZone, 7-11, Office Depot, Pepboys, PetCo
5	Iliff Ave, **E gas:** 7-11, **food:** Applebee's, Boston Mkt, Carrabba's, Fuddrucker's, Hibachi Japanese, Joe's

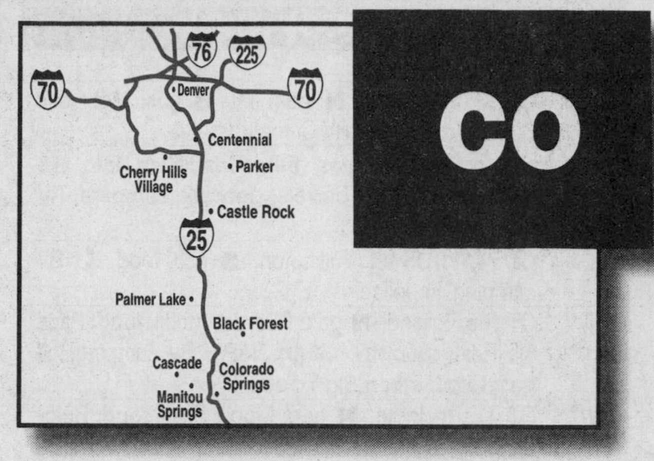

Exit #	Services
5	Continued Crabshack, Outback Steaks, Rosie's Diner, Ruby Tuesday, Sweet Tomatoes, TX Roadhouse, **lodging:** Comfort Inn, Crestwood Suites, Extended Stay Deluxe, Fairfield Inn, Homestead Suites, Motel 6, **W gas:** Phillips 66, **food:** Dragon's Boat, Subway, **lodging:** DoubleTree
4	CO 83, Parker Rd, **E lodging:** Red Lion, **other:** Cherry Creek SP, **W gas:** Phillips 66/dsl, **food:** Big Burrito, Bent Noodle, DQ, Little Caesars, Popeyes, Starbucks, Subway, Table Steaks, Taco Bell, Wendy's, **other:** $Tree, Firestone/auto, King Sooper/dsl, 7-11
2b	no services
2	DTC Blvd, Tamarac St, **W gas:** Conoco, **food:** La Fogata Mexican, Quizno's, Sonic, **other:** Curves, Goodyear, 7-11, Vet
1b a	I-25, I-225 begins/ends on I-25, exit 200

INTERSTATE 270 (DENVER)

Exit #	Services
4	I-70
3	**N gas:** TA/Burger King/Country Pride/Popeye's/Pizza Hut/dsl/24hr/@, **S gas:** Sapp Bros/Sinclair/Subway/dsl/@
2b a	US 85, CO 2, Vasquez Ave, **N food:** Arby's, Carls Jr, Chipotle Mexican, GoodTimes Grill, KFC/LJ Silver, McDonald's, Taco John's, Wendy's **other:** TDS, Walgreens, Walmart SuperCtr
1b	York St
1a	I-76 E, to Ft Morgan
1c	I-25 S, to Denver

CONNECTICUT

INTERSTATE 84

E ↕ W

Exit #	Services
98mm	Connecticut/Massachusetts state line
74 (97)	CT 171, Holland, **S food:** Traveler's Book Rest., **other:** RV camping
95mm	**weigh sta wb**
73 (95)	CT 190, Stafford Springs, **N other:** camping (seasonal), motor speedway, st police
72 (93)	CT 89, Westford, **N lodging:** Ashford Motel, camping (seasonal), ☎
71 (88)	Ruby Rd, **N** Citgo, **S gas:** TA/Shell/Burger King/Country Fried/dsl/scales/24hr/@, **lodging:** Econolodge

CO CT

INTERSTATE 84 CONT'D

Exit #	Services
70 (86)	CT 32, Willington, **N gas:** [H], **S gas:** Mobil/dsl, Sunoco/dsl, **other:** RV Camping
85mm	**rest area both lanes, full [handicapped] facilities, info, [phone], vending, [picnic], litter barrels, petwalk, campers, RV dump**
69 (83)	CT 74, to US 44, Willington, **S** gas, food, [phone], RV camping, st police
68 (81)	CT 195, Tolland, **N gas:** Gulf/dsl, Mobil, **food:** Papa T's Rest., Subway, **other:** NAPA, RV camping, **S gas:** Citgo, **other:** Big Y Foods,
67 (77)	CT 31, Rockville, **N gas:** Mobil, Shell, **food:** Burger King, China Taste, McDonald's, Subway, Theo's Rest., Tim Horton, **other:** [H], **S** Nathan Hale Mon
66 (76)	Tunnel Rd, Vernon
65 (75)	CT 30, Vernon Ctr, **N gas:** Mobil/24hr, Shell, **food:** ChowderTown, KFC, Vernon Diner, **lodging:** Comfort Inn, Howard Johnson Express, **other:** CarQuest, Vernon Drug
64 (74)	Vernon Ctr, **N gas:** Mobil/24hr, Sunoco, **food:** Acqua Oyster Bar, Angellino's Italian, Anthony's Pizza, D'Angelo's, Denny's, Dunkin Donuts, Friendly's, McDonald's, 99 Rest., Taco Bell, **lodging:** Holiday Inn Express, **other:** Advance Parts, AutoZone, CVS Drug, Firestone, GNC, Goodyear/auto, K-Mart, PriceChopper, Radio Shack, Staples, Stop&Shop, TJ Maxx, TownFair Tire, **S lodging:** Quality Inn
63 (72)	CT 30, CT 83, Manchester, S Windsor, **N gas:** Shell, **food:** Macaroni Grill, McDonald's, HomeTown Buffet, Outback Steaks, TGIFriday, Uno Pizzaria, **lodging:** Courtyard, **other:** Barnes&Noble, Best Buy, JC Penney, Michael's, Office Depot, Sears/auto, Walgreens, Walmart, same as 62, **S gas:** Getty, Gulf, Shell/24hr, Xtra, **food:** Century Buffet, Panera Bread, Roy Roger's, **lodging:** Best Value Inn, Extended Stay America, Super 8, **other:** [H], Big Y Mkt, Chrysler, Ford/Kia, Kohl's, Lincoln/Mercury/Mazda, Rite Aid, Subaru, Toyota
62 (71)	Buckland St, **N gas:** Exxon/dsl/24hr, **food:** Boston Mkt, Bugaboo Creek Steaks, Chili's, Friendly's, Hooters, John Harvard's Brewhouse, Olive Garden, Taco Bell, **other:** Borders Books, Firestone/auto, Home Depot, Jo-Ann Fabrics, Lowes Whse, Sam's Club, mall, same as 63, **S gas:** Citgo/dsl, Xtra, **food:** Burger King, Carraba's, ChuckeCheese, Dunkin Donuts, Golden Dragon, McDonald's, Subway, Wendy's, **other:** Buick, Honda, USPO
61 (70)	I-291 W, to Windsor
60 (69)	US 6, US 44, Burnside Ave (from eb)
59 (68)	I-384 E, Manchester
58 (67)	Roberts St, Burnside Ave, **N food:** Margarita's Grill, **lodging:** Days Inn, Holiday Inn, **S other:** Vet
57 (66)	CT 15 S, to I-91 S, Charter Oak Br
56 (65)	Governor St, E Hartford, **S** [airport]
55 (64)	CT 2 E, New London, downtown
54 (63)	Old State House, **N other:** Ford/Isuzu, Lincoln/Mercury, **S lodging:** Marriott, Sheraton
53 (62)	CT Blvd (from eb)
52 (61)	W Main St (from eb), downtown
51 (60)	I-91 N, to Springfield
50 (59.8)	to I-91 S (from wb)
48 (59.5)	Asylum St, downtown, **N lodging:** Crowne Plaza, **S lodging:** Hilton, Holiday Inn Express, Residence Inn, **other:** [H]
47 (59)	Sigourney St, downtown, **N** Hartford Seminary, Mark Twain House
46 (58)	Sisson St, downtown, UConn Law School
45 (57)	Flatbush Ave (exits left from wb), **N** Shaw's Foods
44 (56.5)	Prospect Ave, **N gas:** Exxon, Shell, **food:** Burger King, D'angelo's, Gold Roc Diner/24hr, HomeTown Buffet, McDonald's, **other:** Shaw's Foods/Osco Drug
43 (56)	Park Rd, W Hartford, **N** to St Joseph Coll
42 (55)	Trout Brk Dr (exits left from wb), to Elmwood
41 (54)	S Main St, American School for the Deaf
40 (53)	CT 71, New Britain Ave, **S gas:** Shell, Sunoco, **food:** California Pizza, Dunkin Donuts, Olive Garden, Red Robin, Starbucks, Wendy's, **lodging:** Courtyard, **other:** Barnes&Noble, Best Buy, Borders, JC Penney, Office Depot, Old Navy, Radio Shack, Sears/auto, Target, mall
39a (52)	CT 9 S, to New Britain, Newington, **S** [H]
39 (51.5)	CT 4, Farmington, **N** [H]
38 (51)	US 6 W (from wb), Bristol, **N gas:** Shell
37 (50)	Fienemann Rd, to US 6 W, **N gas:** Shell, **food:** Subway, **lodging:** Marriott
36 (49)	Slater Rd (exits left from eb), **S** [H]
35 (48)	CT 72, to CT 9 (exits left from wb), New Britain, **S** [H]
34 (47)	CT 372, Crooked St, **N gas:** Citgo, Sunoco, **food:** Applebee's, Friendly's, Imperial Buffet, LJ Silver/Taco Bell, McDonald's, Starbucks, Wendy's, **lodging:** Plainville Inn, **other:** Big Y Mkt, Ford, Kohl's, Lowe's Whse, Old Navy, VW
33 (46)	CT 72 W, to Bristol
32 (45)	Ct 10, Queen St, Southington, **N gas:** Cumberland Farms, Exxon, Shell/dsl, **food:** Bertucci's, Burger King, Chili's, D'angelo's, Denny's, Dunkin Donuts, JD's Rest., KFC, McDonald's, Outback Steaks, Puerto Valarta, Randy's Pizza, Ruby Tuesday, Starbucks, Subway, Taco Bell, **lodging:** Motel 6, **other:** [H], CVS Drug, $Tree, Shaw's Foods, Staples, TJ Maxx, TownFair Tire, **S gas:** Hess, Mobil, Sunoco, **food:** Blimpie, Brannigan's Ribs, Friendly's, Ponderosa, Subway, Wendy's, Wood'n Tap Grill, **lodging:** Holiday Inn Express, Howard Johnson, Travelers Inn, **other:** Chevrolet, Jaguar, Firestone, PriceChopper Foods, Walmart
31 (44)	CT 229, West St, **N gas:** Mobil, Sunoco/dsl/24hr, **S gas:** Citgo, Gulf, **food:** Dunkin Donuts, Giovanni's Pizza, Subway, Valendino's Pizzaria, **lodging:** Residence Inn
30 (43)	Marion Ave, W Main, Southington, **N** ski area, **S gas:** Mobil/repair, **other:** [H]
29 (42)	CT 10, Milldale (exits left from wb)
41.5mm	**rest area eb, full [handicapped] facilities, info, [phone], [picnic], litter barrels, petwalk**
28 (41)	CT 322, Marion, **S gas:** Mobil, Sams Gas, TA/Pizza Hut/Popeye's/dsl/scales/24hr/@, **food:** Blimpie, Burger King, DQ, Dunkin Donuts, Manor Inn Rest., Milldale Diner, **lodging:** Comfort Suites, Milldale Inn, **other:** Home Depot, radiators, USPO
27 (40)	I-691 E, to Meriden
26 (38)	CT 70, to Cheshire, **N food:** Silver Diner, **lodging:** CT Grand Hotel

E ↕ W

VERNON CTR · WINDSOR · HARTFORD · SOUTHINGTON · MARION

CT

INTERSTATE 84 CONT'D

E ↕ W

Exit #	Services
25a (37)	Austin Rd (from eb), **N lodging:** CT Grand Hotel, **other:** Costco/gas
25 (36)	Scott Rd, E Main St, **N gas:** Exxon, Gulf/dsl, **food:** Dunkin Donuts, **S gas:** Mobil, **food:** Burger King, Friendly's, McDonald's, Nino's Rest., **lodging:** Ramada Inn, Super 8, **other:** BJ's Whse, Cadillac, Chevrolet, CVS Drug, Super Stop&Shop
24	Harper's Ferry (from eb), **S gas:** Gulf, Shell/24hr
24	Harper's Ferry (from eb), Gulf, Shell/24hr
23 (33.5)	CT 69, Hamilton Ave, **N gas:** Citgo, **food:** Bertucci's, Chili's, HomeTown Buffet, McDonald's, Ruby Tuedsay, TGIFriday's, **other:** H, Barnes&Noble, JC Penney, Macy's, Sears/auto, Shaw's Foods, Walgreens, mall, **S gas:** Shell, **food:** Dunkin Donuts
22 (33)	Baldwin St, Waterbury, **N gas:** McDonald's, **lodging:** Courtyard, **other:** H, same as 23
21 (33)	Meadow St, Banks St, **N gas:** Citgo, **other:** 7-11, Shaw's Foods, **S gas:** Sunoco/dsl/24hr, **other:** Home Depot, PetsMart
20 (32)	CT 8 N (exits left from eb), to Torrington, **N gas:** Shell, **food:** Burger King, McDonald's
19 (32)	CT 8 S (exits left from wb), to Bridgeport
18 (32)	W Main, Highland Ave, **N food:** Lena's Deli, **lodging:** Hampton Inn, **other:** H, CVS Drug
17 (30)	CT 63, CT 64, to Watertown, Naugatuck, **N food:** Maggie McFly's Rest., **S gas:** Mobil/dsl, **food:** Maples Rest.
16 (25)	CT 188, to Middlebury, **N gas:** Mobil, **food:** Patty's Pantry Deli, **lodging:** Crowne Plaza
15 (22)	US 6 E, CT 67, Southbury, **gas:** Shell, **food:** Dunkin Donuts, Friendly's, McDonald's, **lodging:** Heritage

SOUTHBURY

Exit #	Services
15 (22)	Continued Inn, **other:** K-Mart, Stop&Shop, to Kettletown SP, Mobil
14 (20)	CT 172, to S Britain, **N gas:** Mobil/24hr, **food:** Maggie McFly's, Miranda's Pizza, **other:** st police
20mm	motorist callboxes begin eb, end wb
13 (19)	River Rd (from eb), to Southbury
11 (16)	CT 34, to New Haven
10 (15)	US 6 W, Newtown, **S gas:** Mobil/dsl, Shell/24hr, **food:** Blue Colony Diner/24hr, Pizza Palace, **other:** H
9 (11)	CT 25, to Hawleyville, **S lodging:** Best Western, Hillside Inn, Microtel
8 (8)	Newtown Rd, **N gas:** Global, Mobil/dsl, **food:** Outback Steaks, **other:** Lowes Whse, **lodging:** Wellesley Inn, **S gas:** BP, Shell, Sunoco, **food:** Bertucci's Italian, Boston Mkt, Burger King, Chili's, Denny's, Dunkin Donuts, Friendly's, Ichiro Steaks, McDonald's, Subway, Taco Bell, Union Buffet, **lodging:** Best Western, Hampton Inn, Holiday Inn/rest., Quality Inn, **other:** Buick/Pontiac, Chrysler/Jeep/Kia, Goodyear/auto, Marshall's, Radio Shack, Staples, Stop&Shop, Target, Walmart
7 (7)	US 7N/202E, to Brookfield, (exits left from eb), New Milford, **1 exit N on Federal Rd...food:** Applebee's, **lodging:** Best Inn, **other:** Borders Books, Ford, Harley-Davidson, Home Depot, mall
6 (6)	CT 37 (from wb), New Fairfield, **E gas:** Bob's, Flash, **food:** KFC, Los Compadres, **lodging:** Budget Inn, **other:** same as 63a, **W food:** Pit Stop BBQ
5 (5)	CT 37, CT 39, CT 53, Danbury, **N gas:** Exxon, Shell, **lodging:** Best Value Inn, **S gas:** Mobil, **food:** Dunkin Donuts, Taco Bell, **other:** H, to Putnam SP
4 (4)	US 6 W/202 W, Lake Ave, **N gas:** Gulf/dsl, Shell/dsl, Xtra, **food:** Dunkin Donuts, McDonald's, **lodging:** Ethan Allen Hotel, Maron Hotel, Super 8, **other:** CVS Drug, Goodyear/auto, Stop&Shop, **S gas:** Sunoco, **food:** Chuck's Steaks, **lodging:** Residence Inn, to mall
3 (3)	US 7 S (exits left from wb), to Norwalk, **S gas:** Exxon, **food:** Coldstone Creamery, Olive Garden, Red Lobster, **other:** Barnes&Noble, JC Penney, Macy's, Sears/auto, mall

E ↕ W

INTERSTATE 84 CONT'D

Exit #	Services
2b a (1)	US 6, US 202, Mill Plain Rd, **N gas:** Exxon/dsl, **food:** Desert Moon Café, Starbucks, **lodging:** Comfort Suites, Hilton Garden, **other:** , Staples, **S Welcome Ctr/weigh sta, full ♿ facilities, info, ⛰, litter barrels, petwalk, to Old Ridgebury, lodging:** Sheraton
1 (0)	Saw Mill Rd, **N lodging:** Comfort Suites (2mi), Danbury Motel, Hilton Garden
0mm	Connecticut/New York state line

N ↕ S

INTERSTATE 91

Exit #	Services
58mm	Connecticut/Massachusetts state line
49 (57)	US 5, to Longmeadow, MA, **E gas:** Pride, Valero, **food:** Friendly's, McDonald's, **lodging:** Crowne Plaza, **other:** Acme Auto Repair, **W food:** Cloverleaf Café
48 (56)	CT 220, Elm St, **E gas:** Mobil, **food:** Arby's, Burger King, Denny's, Dunkin Donuts, Friendly's, McDonald's, Oyama Japanese, Outback Steaks, Panera Bread, Ruby Tuesday, TGIFriday, Wendy's, **other:** AutoZone, Best Buy, Costco/gas, $Tree, JC Penney, Macy's, Home Depot, Honda, Kohl's, Nissan, Radio Shack, Sears/auto, Target, same as 47
47 (55)	CT 190, to Hazardville, **E gas:** Mobil, **food:** Bickford's, D'angelo, Domino's, Dunkin Donuts, Hazard Grille, KFC, McDonald's, 99 Rest., Olive Garden, Pizza Hut, Quizno's, Red Robin, Starbucks, Taco Bell, **lodging:** Hampton Inn, Motel 6, Red Roof Inn, **other:** H, Advance Parts, AutoZone, Barnes&Noble, Big Y Foods, CVS Drug, $Tree, Ford, Marshall's, Michael's, NAPA, Office Depot, PetCo, Rite Aid, Shaw's Foods, Staples, Stop&Shop Foods, Walgreen, mall, same as 48
46 (53)	US 5, King St, to Enfield, **E gas:** Mobil, **food:** Astro's Rest., **W lodging:** Super 8
45 (51)	CT 140, Warehouse Point, **E gas:** Shell/Dunkin Donuts, **food:** Blimpie, Burger King, Cracker Barrel, Friendly's, Green Tea China, Sofia's Pizza, Starbucks, **lodging:** Comfort Inn, **other:** Big Y Foods, Walmart, to Trolley Museum, **W gas:** Sunoco/dsl/24hr, **lodging:** Clarion, **other:** Advance Parts
44 (50)	US 5 S, to E Windsor, **E gas:** Sunoco/dsl, **food:** Dunkin Donuts, E Windsor Rest., KFC, Wendy's, Taco Bell, **lodging:** Holiday Inn Express
49mm	Connecticut River
42 (48)	CT 159, Windsor Locks, **E** Longview RV Ctr, **W** same as 41
41 (47)	Center St (exits with 39), **W food:** Ad Pizzaria, **lodging:** Beverly Hills Suites
40 (46.5)	CT 20, **W** Old New-Gate Prison, ✈
39 (46)	Kennedy Rd (exits with 41), Community Rd, **W gas:** Shell/dsl/24hr, **food:** Chili's, **other:** $Tree, GNC, PetCo, Radio Shack, Stop&Shop Foods, Target
38 (45)	CT 75, to Poquonock, Windsor Area, **E gas:** Mobil/dsl, **food:** Buffalo Wild Wings, China Sea, Domino's, Dunkin Donuts, Quizno's, Subway, **other:** to Ellsworth Homestead, Price Chopper Foods, **W lodging:** Courtyard, Hilton Garden, Marriott
37 (44)	CT 305, Bloomfield Ave, Windsor Ctr, **E gas:** Mobil/dsl, **food:** McDonald's, **W gas:** Sunoco, **lodging:** Residence Inn
36 (43)	CT 178, Park Ave, to W Hartford
35b (41)	CT 218, to Bloomfield, to S Windsor, **E** gas/dsl, food
35a	I-291 E, to Manchester
34 (40)	CT 159, Windsor Ave, **E gas:** Shell/dsl, **W gas:** Citgo/dsl, **lodging:** Flamingo Inn, **other:** H
33 (39)	Jennings Rd, Weston St, **E other:** Buick/Pontiac/GMC, repair, **W gas:** Mobil/Subway, Sunoco/dsl, **food:** Burger King, Dunkin Donuts, McDonald's, Quizno's, **lodging:** Motel 6, Super 8, **other:** Cadillac, CarMax, Honda, Hyundai, Jaguar, Nissan, Subaru, Toyota/Scion
32b (38)	Trumbull St (exits left from nb), **W** to downtown, **lodging:** Crowne Plaza, Hilton, **other:** H, Goodyear
32a	(exit 30 from sb), I-84 W
29b	(37)I-84 E, Hartford
29a	(36.5)US 5 N, CT 15 N (exits left from nb), **W** downtown, **other:** H, capitol, civic ctr
28 (36)	US 5, CT 15 S (from nb), **W food:** Burger King, Wendy's
27 (35)	Brainerd Rd, Airport Rd, **E gas:** Mercury/Dunkin Donuts/Subway/dsl, Shell/dsl, **food:** McDonald's, **lodging:** Day's Inn, Holiday Inn Express, **other:** Ford Trucks, to Regional Mkt
26 (33.5)	Marsh St, **E** Silas Deane House, Webb House, CT MVD
25 (33)	CT 3, Glastonbury, Wethersfield
24 (32)	CT 99, Rocky Hill, Wethersfield, **E gas:** Phillips 66, Sunoco, **food:** Chuck's Steaks, Dakota Steaks, Dunkin Donuts, McDonald's, On-the-Border, Rockyhill Pizza, Subway, Tim Horton, **lodging:** Hampton Inn, Howard Johnson, **other:** Aldi Foods, Kohl's, **W gas:** Mobil, Shell, Valero/dsl, **food:** Burger King, D'angelo's, Denny's, Dunkin Donuts, Friendly's, Giovanni's Pizza, HomeTown Buffet, Humphrey's Grill, McDonald's, Mihng Chinese, Quizno's, Red Lobster, Saki Japanese, Sapporro Japanese, Starbucks, Townline Diner, Wendy's, Wood-n-Tap Grill, **lodging:** Best Western, Motel 6, **other:** Curves, CVS Drug, $Tree, Goodyear/auto, Marshalls, Office Depot, Radio Shack, Stop&Shop, TJMaxx, TownFair Tire, True Value, Walgreens, Walmart/Subway
23 (29)	to CT 3, West St, Rocky Hill, Vet Home, **E lodging:** Marriott, **other:** H, to Dinosaur SP, **W gas:** Citgo/dsl, Mobil, **food:** Angelo's Pizza, D'angelo's, Dunkin Donuts, Subway, **lodging:** Residence Inn, **other:** IGA Foods
22 (27)	CT 9, to New Britain, Middletown
21 (26)	CT 372, to Berlin, Cromwell, **E gas:** Sunoco/dsl/repair, Wooster St Pizza, **lodging:** Comfort Inn, Crowne Plaza, **other:** Krauszer's Foods, **W gas:** Citgo/Subway/dsl, Mobil/dsl, **food:** Blimpie, Burger King, Chili's, Cromwell Diner/24hr, Dunkin Donuts, McDonald's, Oyama Japanese, Slice Heaven Pizza, **lodging:** Courtyard, Holiday Inn, Super 8, **other:** A&P, Curves, Firestone/auto, Price Rite Foods, Walmart/drug
20 (23)	Country Club Rd, Middle St
22mm	**rest area/weigh sta nb, full ♿ facilities, info, ☎, ⛰, litter barrels, vending, RV dump, petwalk**
19 (21)	Baldwin Ave (from sb)
18 (20.5)	I-691 W, to Marion, access to same as 16 & 17, ski area
17 (20)	CT 15 N (from sb), to I-691, CT 66 E, Meriden, **W gas:** BP, **food:** Getty, **lodging:** Best Western, Extended Stay America, Residence Inn
16 (19)	CT 15, E Main St, **E gas:** Gulf/dsl, Mobil, Valero, **food:** American Steaks, Gianni's Rest., NY Pizza, Olympos Diner, Subway, Zorba's Rest., **lodging:** Candlewood Suites, Hampton Inn, Sheraton, The Meridan Inn, **other:** Family$, Ford, Lowe's Whse,

HAZARDVILLE

WINDSOR AREA

ROCKY HILL

CT

INTERSTATE 91 CONT'D

Exit #	Services
16 (19)	Continued Volvo, **W gas:** BP/dsl, Getty/dsl, Gulf/repair, **food:** Boston Mkt, Burger King, Dominos, Dunkin Donuts, Friendly's, Great Wall Chinese, KFC, McDonald's, Subway, Taco Bell, Tim Horton, Wendy's, **lodging:** Comfort Inn, **other:** [H], CarQuest, CVS Drug, Hancock's Drug, Walgreens
15 (16)	CT 68, to Durham, **E** golf, **W lodging:** Courtyard, Fairfield Inn, Homewood Suites
15mm	**rest area sb, full [handicapped] facilities, info, [phone], [picnic], litter barrels, petwalk**
14 (12)	CT 150 (no EZ return), Woodhouse Ave, Wallingford
13 (10)	US 5 (exits left from nb), Wallingford, **2 mi W on US 5** services, to Wharton Brook SP
12 (9)	US 5, Washington Ave, **E gas:** Shell, Sunoco, Valero, **food:** Boston Mkt, Burger King, D'angelo, Dunkin Donuts, Friendly's, Jade City Chinese, McDonald's, Quizno's, Rustic Oak Rest., Starbucks, Subway, Wendy's, **other:** CVS Drug, Stop&Shop Food, Walgreens, **W gas:** Getty, Gulf/dsl, Mobil, **food:** Arby's, Athena II Diner, Blimpie, Greatwall Chinese, Outback Steaks, Thai Cuisine, **lodging:** Holiday Inn/Harry's Grill, **other:** BigY Foods/drug, CarQuest, Vet
11 (7)	CT 22 (from nb), North Haven, same as 12
10 (6)	CT 40, to Cheshire, Hamden
9 (5)	Montowese Ave, **W gas:** Berkshire/dsl, Sunoco, **food:** Coldstone Creamery, Dunkin Donuts, Friendly's, McDonald's, Panera Bread, Subway, **other:** Barnes&Noble, BJ's Whse/gas, Home Depot, Michael's, PetCo, PetsMart, Staples, Target, TJMaxx
8 (4)	CT 17, CT 80, Middletown Ave, **E gas:** Citgo, Global/dsl, 7-11/gas, Shell, Splash/dsl, Sunoco/24hr, **food:** Burger King, Dominos, Dunkin Donuts, Exit 8 Diner, KFC, McDonald's, Taco Bell/Pizza Hut, **lodging:** Day's Inn, **other:** Advance Parts, Lowe's Whse, Walgreens, Vet, Walmart SuperCtr/Subway, **W gas:** Mobil/dsl, Splash/dsl
7 (3)	Ferry St (from sb), Fair Haven, **W gas:** Hess
6 (2.5)	Willow St (exits left from nb), Blatchley Ave, **E gas:** New Star Diner
5 (2)	US 5 (from nb), State St, Fair Haven, **E food:** New Star Diner
4 (1.5)	State St (from sb), downtown
3 (1)	Trumbull St, downtown, **W** Peabody Museum
2 (.5)	Hamilton St, downtown, New Haven
1 (.3)	CT 34W (from sb), New Haven, **W** [H], downtown
0mm	I-91 begins/ends on I-95, exit 48.

INTERSTATE 95

Exit #	Services
112mm	Connecticut/Rhode Island state line
106mm	**Welcome Ctr/rest area sb, full [handicapped] facilities, [phone], [picnic], litter barrels, petwalk, vending**
100mm	scenic overlook nb
94.5mm	Thames River
93 (111)	CT 216, Clarks Falls, **E gas:** Shell/repair, to Burlingame SP, **W gas:** Mobil/dsl, Shell/Stuckey's/Roy Rogers/dsl/scales/24hr, Republic/Citgo/dsl/rest./@, **food:** McDonald's, Tim Horton, **lodging:** Stardust Motel
92 (107)	CT 2, CT 49 (no EZ nb return), Pawcatuck, **E gas:** Shell, **other:** [H], **W lodging:** Cedar Park Suites, **other:** FoxWoods (8mi), KOA

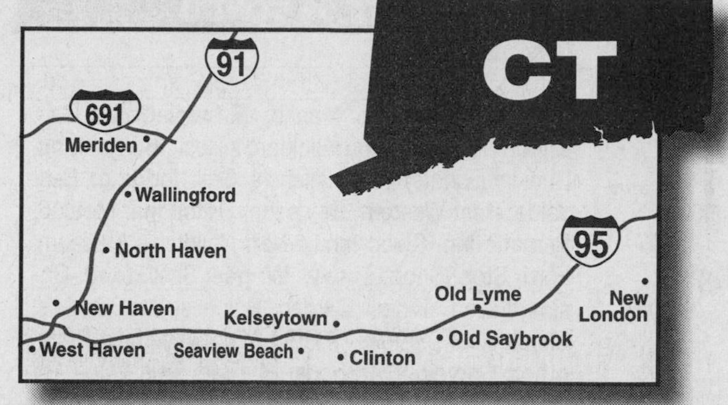

Exit #	Services
92 (107)	Continued
91 (103)	CT 234, N Main St, to Stonington, **E other:** [H]
90 (101)	CT 27, Mystic, **E gas:** Mobil/Domino's/dsl, **food:** Bickford's, Friendly's, GoFish Rest., Jamm's Seafood, McDonald's, Peking Tokyo, Quizno's, Starbucks, Steak Loft, **lodging:** Econolodge, Hilton, Holiday Inn Express, Howard Johnson, Hyatt Place, **other:** Curves, Mystic Outlet Shops, aquarium, **W gas:** Shell/Subway/Dunkin Donuts/dsl, **food:** Ground Round, Pizza Grille, Starbucks, **lodging:** Best Western, Comfort Inn, Day's Inn, Hampton Inn, Residence Inn, **other:** Chevrolet, Chrysler/Dodge, Ford, RV camping, True Value
89 (99)	CT 215, Allyn St, **W** camping (seasonal)
89mm	**weigh sta both lanes**
88 (98)	CT 117, to Noank, **E** [airport], **W food:** Octagon Steaks, Starbucks, Tim Horton, **lodging:** Marriott
87 (97)	Sharp Hwy (exits left from sb), Groton, **E lodging:** Hampton Inn, **other:** to Griswold SP, [airport]
86 (96)	rd 184 (exits left from nb), Groton, **E food:** Applebees, 99 Rest., **lodging:** Hampton Inn, Knight's Inn, Quality Inn, **W gas:** Cory's Gas, Hess, Mobil, Shell/dsl, **food:** Chinese Kitchen, Domino's, Dunkin Donuts, Flanagan's Diner, Groton Rest., KFC, Taco Bell, **lodging:** Best Western, Super 8, **other:** Advance Parts, $Tree, Honda, Kohl's, Mitsubishi, Stop'n Shop, to US Sub Base
85 (95)	US 1 N, Groton, downtown, **E gas:** Citgo/dsl, **other:** NAPA
84 (94)	CT 32 (from sb), New London, downtown
83 (92)	CT 32, New London, **E** to Long Island Ferry
82a (90.5)	frontage rd, New London, **E food:** Pizza Hut, **other:** AutoZone, Goodyear, Staples, TownFair Tire, Town-Town Foods, same as 82, **W food:** Chili's, Chucke-Cheese, Outback Steaks, Subway, **lodging:** Holiday Inn, SpringHill Suites, **other:** Marshall's, ShopRite Foods, same as 82
82 (90)	New London, **W gas:** Mobil, **food:** Charley's Rest., Coldstone Creamery, FoodCourt, Olive Garden, Panera Bread, Ruby Tuesday, Subway, Wendy's, **lodging:** Fairfield Suites, Holiday Inn, **other:** Best Buy, Borders Books, Home Depot, JC Penney, Macy's, Marshall's, Michael's, PetCo, Sears/auto, Target, mall
81 (89.5)	Cross Road, **W lodging:** Rodeway Inn, **other:** BJ's Whse/gas, Lowes Whse, Walmart SuperCtr/McDonald's
80 (89.3)	Oil Mill Rd (from sb), **W lodging:** Rodeway Inn
78mm	Connecticut River
76 (89)	I-395 N (from nb), to Norwich

CT

INTERSTATE 95 CONT'D

N ↕ S

Exit #	Services
75 (88)	US 1, to Waterford
74 (87)	rd 161, to Flanders, Niantic, **E gas:** Cory's Gas, Citgo/dsl, Mobil, **food:** Bickford's Rest., Burger King, Dunkin Donuts, KFC, Illiano's Grill, **lodging:** Best Value, Best Western, Day's Inn, Hilltop Inn, Motel 6, Ramada Inn, Sleep Inn, **other:** Children's Museum, Ford, Stop&Shop, Tires+, **W gas:** Shell, **food:** Cusina Italian, Kings Garden Chinese, McDonald's, Shack Rest., Smokey's BBQ, Yummy yummy Pizza, **other:** Curves, IGA Foods, Rite Aid, True Value, RV camping, Vet
74mm	**rest area sb, full [handicapped] facilities, st police**
73 (86)	Society Rd
72 (84)	to Rocky Neck SP, **2 mi E** food, lodging, RV camping, to Rocky Neck SP
71 (83)	4 Mile Rd, River Rd, to Rocky Neck SP, beaches, **1 mi E** camping (seasonal)
70 (80)	US 1, CT 156, Old Lyme, **W gas:** Shell/dsl, **lodging:** Bee & Thistle Inn, Old Lyme Inn/dining, Subway, **other:** A&P, Old Lyme Drug, Griswold Museum
69 (77)	US 1, CT 9 N, to Hartford, **W food:** Saybrook Fish House, Vinnie's Fishouse, **lodging:** Comfort Inn
	OLD SAYBROOK
68 (76.5)	US 1 S, Old Saybrook, **E gas:** Citgo/dsl, Mobil, **food:** Cloud 9 Deli, Bellasera Italian, Pat's Country Kitchen, Subway, **other:** Ford, **W lodging:** Liberty Inn, **other:** Chevrolet/Nissan, Kia, NAPA, Pontiac/Buick/GMC, Toyota/Scion, antiques
67 (76)	CT 154, Elm St (no EZ sb return), Old Saybrook, **E food:** Pasta Vita Itaian, same as 68
66mm	**service area both lanes**, Mobil/dsl, McDonald's, atm
66 (75)	to US 1, Spencer Plain Rd, **E gas:** Citgo/dsl/24hr, **food:** Aleia's Rest, Atlantic Seafood, Blue Crab Steaks, Brick Oven Pizza, Cuckoo's Mexican, DQ, Dunkin Donuts, Luigi's Italian, Sal's Pizza, Stella D'Oro Italian, **lodging:** Day's Inn, Heritage Inn, Sandpiper Motel, Sabrook Motel, Super 8, **other:** Benny's Mkt, transmissions, Vet
65 (73)	rd 153, Westbrook, **E gas:** Mobil, Valero, **food:** Denny's, Fiore's Pizza, Subway, Westbook Deli, **lodging:** Sandpiper Hotel, **other:** Honda, Old Navy, Tanger Factory Stores/famous brands, Walgreens
64 (70)	rd 145, Horse Hill Rd, Clinton
63 (68)	CT 81, Clinton, **E gas:** Shell, **1 mi E on US 1...gas:** Shell/dsl/LP, Sunoco/dsl, **food:** Chips Rest., Friendly's, McDonald's, **other:** CVS Drug, Vet, **W food:** Coldstone Creamery, Dunkin Dounits, **other:** Clinton Crossing Premium Outlets/famous brands, PetCo
62 (67)	**E** to Hammonasset SP, RV camping, beaches
	MADISON
61 (64)	CT 79, Madison, **E gas:** Gulf, Shell, Sunoco, **food:** Cafe Allegre, Starbucks, Subway, Village Pizza, **other:** CVS Drug, Stop&Shop, USPO
61mm	East River
60 (63.5)	Mungertown Rd (from sb, no return), **E** food, lodging
59 (60)	rd 146, Goose Lane, Guilford, **E gas:** Citgo, Mobil/24hr, Shell/DQ/dsl, **food:** Dunkin Donuts, First & Last Rest., First Garden Chinese, Nick & Tony's Pizza, McDonald's, Pasta Avest Pizza, Shoreline Diner, The Whole Enchilada, Wendy's, **lodging:** Comfort Inn, Tower Motel, **other:** Chevrolet/Pontiac, NAPA, **W** URGENT CARE, st police
58 (59)	CT 77, Guilford, on US 1 **E food:** Getty, Hess, Mobil, Sunoco, **other:** CVS Drug, to Whitfield Museum, **W** st police
57 (58)	US 1, Guilford, **W other:** Land Rover, Saab
56 (55)	rd 146, to Stony Creek, **E lodging:** Rodeway Inn, **W gas:** Mobil, TA/Popeye's/Starbucks/Subway/dsl/rest./24hr/scales/@, Sunoco, **food:** Dunkin Donuts, Friendly's, Humphrey's Rest., USS Chowderpot, **lodging:** Best Western, Best Value, **other:** Freightliner, Stop&Shop Foods
	BRANFORD
55 (54)	US 1, **E gas:** Branford, Global, Thornton/dsl, **food:** Campania Ristorante, D'amato's Seafood, Lynn's Rest, Marco Pizzaria, Rita's Custard, Hole in the wall Deli, **lodging:** Holiday Inn Express, Motel 6, **other:** Ford, Walgreens, Vet, **W gas:** Exxon/dsl, Mobil/Dunkin Donuts/dsl, **food:** Brother's Deli, Chuck's Margarita Grill, Gourmet Wok, Parthenon Diner/24hr, Su Casa Mexican, **lodging:** Day's Inn
54 (53)	Cedar St, Branford, **E gas:** Citgo/repair, Mobil, **food:** Branford Townhouse Rest., Dragon East Chinese, Dunkin Donuts, La Luna Ristorante, **other:** Hyundai, Staples, Subaru, **W** Krauszer's Foods
52mm	**service area both lanes**, Mobil/dsl/24hr, McDonald's, atm
52 (50)	rd 100, North High St, **E other:** to Trolley Museum, **W** st police
51 (49.5)	US 1, Easthaven, **E gas:** Shell, Sunoco, **food:** Boston Mkt, Chili's, Friendly's, KFC, McDonald's, **lodging:** Quality Inn, **other:** Chevrolet, Lexus, Rite Aid, TJ Maxx, **W food:** Dunkin Donuts, King China, Wendy's, **other:** AutoZone, CarMax, Home Depot, USPO
50 (49)	Woodward Ave (from nb), **E other:** US Naval/Marine Reserve, Ft Nathan Hale
49 (48.5)	Stiles St (from nb)
48 (48)	I-91 N, to Hartford
	NEW HAVEN
47 (47.5)	CT 34, New Haven, **W gas:** Mobil/dsl, **lodging:** Omni Hotel, **other:** [H]
46 (47)	Long Wharf Dr, Sargent Dr, **E food:** Leon's Rest., **W gas:** Mobil/dsl, **food:** Brazi Italian, Dunkin Donuts, **lodging:** La Quinta
45 (46.5)	CT 10 (from sb), Blvd, same as 44, **W gas:** Getty, **food:** DQ, Dunkin Donuts, McDonald's
44 (46)	CT 10 (from nb), Kimberly Ave, **E lodging:** Super 8, **W gas:** Getty, **food:** DQ, Dunkin Donuts, McDonald's, Wendy's, same as 45
43 (45)	CT 122, 1st Ave (no EZ return), West Haven, **W gas:** First Fuel/dsl, **food:** China Sea, **other:** [H], to U of New Haven
42 (44)	CT 162, Saw Mill Rd, **E gas:** Mobil, **food:** Pizza Hut, **lodging:** Econolodge, **W gas:** Shell, Mobil, 7-11, **food:** American Steaks, D'angelo's, Denny's, Dunkin Donuts, Friendly's, Pizza Hut, Subway, TX Roadhouse, **lodging:** Best Western, Hampton Inn, **other:** Staples, Walmart
41 (42)	Marsh Hill Rd, to Orange
41mm	**service area both lanes, gas:** Mobil/dsl, **food:** McDonald's
40 (40)	Old Gate Lane, Woodmont Rd, **E gas:** Citgo/dsl, Pilot/Wendy's/dsl/scales/24hr, Shell, Sunoco, **food:** Bennigan's, Cracker Barrel, D'angelo's, Duchess Rest., Dunkin Donuts, Gipper's Rest., **lodging:** Hilton Garden, Hyatt Place, Mayflower Hotel, Milford Inn, Quality Inn, **other:** Blue Beacon, Lowe's Whse

INTERSTATE 95 CONT'D

Exit #	Services
39 (39)	US 1, to Milford, **E gas:** Cumberland Farms/dsl, **food:** Athenian Diner, Chicago Grill, Friendly's, Hooters, **lodging:** Howard Johnson, Super 8, **other:** Firestone/auto, Mazda/Volvo, Walgreens, **W on US 1... gas:** Mobil, **food:** Arby's, Boston Mkt, Buffalo Wild Wings, Burger King, Chili's, Dunkin Donuts, HoneyBaked Ham, KFC, Krispy Kreme, Moe's SW Grill, McDonald's, Starbucks, Subway, Taco Bell, Wendy's, **other:** Acura, Barnes & Noble, Borders Books, Chrysler/Jeep, Macy's, JC Penney, Jo-Anne Fabrics, Macy's, Marshall's, Michael's, Old Navy, PetCo, Rite Aid, Sears/auto, Staples, Stop&Shop Food, Target, TownFair Tire, USPO, Walmart, mall
38 (38)	CT 15, Merritt Pkwy, Cross Pkwy
37 (37.5)	High St (from nb), **E gas:** Gulf, Sunoco, USA Fuel, **food:** Kimberly Diner, **other:** 7-11, Toyota/Scion
36	Plains Rd, **E gas:** Mobil, **lodging:** Hampton Inn
35 (37)	Bic Dr, School House Rd, **E gas:** Citgo, **food:** Armellino's Italian, McDonald's, Pizza Hut, Subway, Taco Bell, Wendy's, **lodging:** Fairfield Inn, **other:** AutoZone, Buick, Chevrolet, Chrysler/Jeep, Dennis Parts, Dodge, Ford/Lincoln/Mercury, Honda, Kia, K-Mart, Land Rover, Pontiac/Nissan, Stop&Shop Foods, Subaru, Walgreens, **W lodging:** Red Roof Inn, SpringHill Suites
34 (34)	US 1, Milford, **E food:** Dunkin Donuts, McDonald's, Pizza Hut, Taco Bell, **lodging:** Devon Motel
33 (33.5)	US 1 (from nb, no EZ return), CT 110, Ferry Blvd, **E gas:** Shell/dsl, Sunoco, **food:** Harborside Grill, Margarita Grill, **other:** BJ's Whse, PetCo, Staples, **W food:** McDonalds, 99 Rest., Pepino's Italian, Subway, **other:** Home Depot, Marshall's, Shaw's Foods, Stop&Shop Foods, Walmart
32 (33)	W Broad St, Stratford, **E gas:** Mobil, **food:** Subway, **W gas:** Gulf, **food:** Dunkin Donuts
31 (32)	South Ave, Honeyspot Rd, **E gas:** Gulf/Dunkin Donuts, **lodging:** Comfort Suites, **W gas:** Citgo/dsl, **other:** NAPA, TownFair Tire
30 (31.5)	Lordship Blvd, Surf Ave, **E gas:** Shell/24hr, **food:** Dunkin Donuts, **lodging:** Ramada/rest., **other:** Harley-Davidson, **W gas:** Massey/dsl
29 (31)	rd 130, Stratford Ave, Seaview Ave, **W** H
28 (30)	CT 113, E Main St, Pembrook St
27 (29.5)	Lafayette Blvd, downtown, **W food:** Dunkin Donuts, Subway, **other:** H, Barnum Museum
27a (29)	CT 25, CT 8, to Waterbury
26 (28)	Wordin Ave, downtown
25 (27)	CT 130 (from sb, no EZ return), State St, Commerce Dr, Fairfield Ave, **E gas:** Getty/dsl, **other:** Stop&Shop, USPO, **W gas:** Gulf, **food:** McDonald's, **other:** transmissions
24 (26.5)	Black Rock Tpk, **E food:** Blackrock Oyster Bar, D'Angelo, Starbucks, Subway, **lodging:** Best Western, **other:** Audi, Lexus, Mercedes, Pontiac, Porsche, Staples, **other:** BJ's Whse, Staples, USPO, **W gas:** Getty, Gulf, **other:** Firestone/Auto, Ford/Nissan
23 (26)	US 1, Kings Hwy, **E gas:** Sunoco/dsl, **food:** Ziggy's Grill, **other:** Home Depot
22 (24)	Round Hill Rd, N Benson Rd
23.5mm	**service area both lanes, gas:** Mobil/dsl, **food:** FoodCourt (sb), McDonald's/24

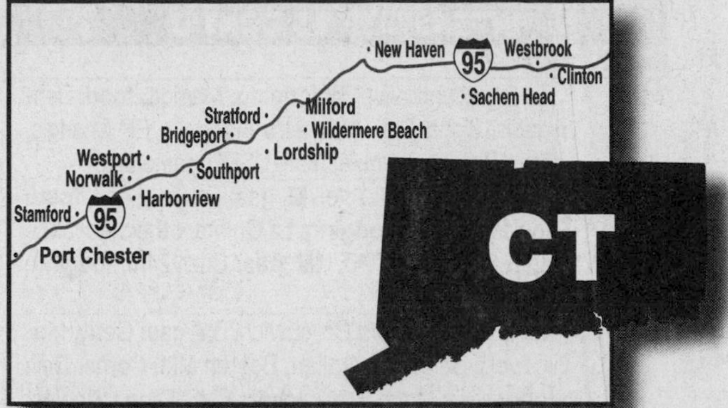

Exit #	Services
21 (23)	Mill Plain Rd, **E gas:** Citgo, Mobil, Shell, Sunoco, **food:** Avellino's Italian, DQ, Domino's, Starbucks, Subway, Wilson's BBQ, **other:** Borders Books, Hemlock Hardware, Rite Aid
20 (22)	Bronson Rd (from sb)
19 (21)	US 1, Center St, **E** Southport Brewing/rest., **W gas:** Getty, Shell/Dunkin Donuts/dsl, **food:** Athena Diner, Friendly's, **other:** TownFair Tire, Walgreens
18 (20)	to Westport, **E** Sherwood Island SP, beaches, **1 mi on US 1 W gas:** Citgo, Exxon, Gulf, Mobil, **food:** Arbys, Bertucci's Italian, Carvel Ice Cream, Cedar Brook Café, Chef's Table, McDonald's, Sakura Japanese, Sherwood Diner, Starbucks, Swanky Frank's Sandwiches, Subway, Westport Pancakes, **other:** Barnes & Noble, Cadillac/Pontiac/GMC, Toyota/Scion, Shaw's Foods, Volvo, Walgreens, st police, Vet
17 (18)	CT 33, rd 136, Westport, **W other:** FastStop Mart
16 (17)	E Norwalk, **E gas:** Citgo, Mobil, Shell/dsl, Sunoco, **food:** Baskin-Robbins/Dunkin Donuts, Eastside Café, Penny's Diner, Subway, **other:** Rite Aid
15 (16)	US 7, to Danbury, Norwalk, **E gas:** Shell, **W gas:** Getty
14 (15)	US 1, CT Ave, S Norwalk, **E** st police, **W gas:** BP/dsl, C Gas, Shell, Sunoco, **food:** Angela Mia's Café, Burger King, Dunkin Donuts, Post Road Diner, Silver Star Diner, **other:** H, Barnes&Noble, Best Buy, Home Depot, Kohl's, Old Navy, Radio Shack, ShopRite Foods, Shoprite Foods, Stop&Shop, TJ Maxx, TownFair Tire, same as 13
13 (13)	US 1 (no EZ return), Post Rd, Norwalk, **W gas:** Exxon, Mobil, Shell/24hr, **food:** American Steaks, Bertucci's, Burger King, Driftwood Diner, Duchess Rest., Dunkin Donuts, Friendly's, KFC, Matsuri Japanese, McDonald's, Pasta Fair Rest., Wendy's, **lodging:** DoubleTree Hotel, **other:** Costco, Home Depot, Kohl's, Land Rover, Old Navy, PetsMart, Radio Shack, ShopRite Foods, Staples, TownFair Tire, Walmart, Vet, same as 14
12.5mm	**service area nb**, Mobil/dsl, McDonald's
12 (12)	rd 136, Tokeneke Rd (from nb, no return), **W food:** deli
11 (11)	US 1, Darien, **E gas:** BP, **lodging:** Chuck's Steaks, **other:** Chevrolet, Jaguar, Nissan, Vet, **W gas:** Exxon, **lodging:** Howard Johnson, **other:** BMW
10 (10)	Noroton, **W gas:** Getty, Shell
9.5mm	**service area sb, gas:** Mobil/dsl, **food:** McDonald's
9 (9)	US 1, rd 106, Glenbrook, **W gas:** Gulf, **food:** Dunkin Donuts, McDonald's, **other:** Aamco, AutoZone, Firestone, Toyota, cat Vet
8 (8)	Atlantic Ave, Elm St, **E** Uhaul, **W gas:** Sunoco, **lodging:** Marriott, **other:** H

INTERSTATE 95 CONT'D

Exit #	Services
7 (7)	CT 137, Atlantic Ave, **W lodging:** Marriott, **food:** Bennigan's, Kona Grill, Mitchell's Fish mkt, PF Chang's, **other:** Barnes & Noble, mall, USPO, same as 8
6 (6)	Harvard Ave, West Ave, **E gas:** Exxon, Shell, **food:** City Limits Diner, **lodging:** La Quinta, **other:** Advance Parts, Subaru, USPO, **W gas:** Shell/24hr, **lodging:** Super 8, **other:** H
5 (5)	US 1, Riverside, Old Greenwich, **W gas:** Getty, Mobil, **food:** Balducci's Italian, Boston Mkt, Corner Deli, McDonald's, Taco Bell, **other:** CVS Drug, Staples, Walgreens, tires
4 (4)	Indian Field Rd, Cos Cob, **W other:** Bush-Holley House Museum
3 (3)	Arch St, Greenwich, **E** Bruce Museum, **W gas:** Mobil, **other:** H, Lexus, Saab
2mm	**weigh sta nb**
2 (1)	Delavan Ave, Byram
0mm	Connecticut/New York state line

INTERSTATE 395

Exit #	Services
55.5mm	Connecticut/Massachusetts state line
100 (54)	E Thompson, to Wilsonville
99 (50)	rd 200, N Grosvenor Dale, **E** W Thompson Lake Camping (seasonal)
98 (49)	to CT 12 (from nb, exits left), Grosvenor Dale, same as 99
97 (47)	US 44, to E Putnam, **E food:** Dunkin Donuts, Empire Buffet, McDonald's/playplace, Subway, Wendy's, **other:** Advance Parts, $Tree, GNC, Radio Shack, Sears Essentials, Stop&Shop Foods/gas, TJ Maxx, **W gas:** Shell/dsl/repair/24hr, Sunoco, **other:** Walmart
96 (46)	to CT 12, Putnam, **W lodging:** King's Inn, **other:** H
95 (45)	Kennedy Dr, to Putnam, **E** Ford/Mercury, **W** H
94 (43)	Ballouville, **W food:** Gold Eagle Rest., **lodging:** Holiday Inn Express
93 (41)	CT 101, to Dayville, **E gas:** Shell/dsl, **food:** Burger King, China Garden, Dunkin Donuts, Subway, Zip's Diner, **other:** Wibberley Tire, **W gas:** Xtra/dsl/24hr, **food:** Dunkin Donuts, McDonald's, Mozzarella's Grill, **other:** Lowe's Whse, Michael's, Target, Staples, Super Stop & Shop, city park
92 (39)	to S Killingly, **W food:** Giant Pizza, **other:** Bonneville Drug, st police
91 (38)	US 6 W, to Danielson, to Quinebaug Valley Coll
90 (36)	to US 6 E (from nb), to Providence
35mm	**rest area both lanes, full** ♿ **facilities, gas: Mobil/dsl**
89 (32)	CT 14, to Sterling, Central Village, **E gas:** Gulf, **other:** Chevrolet/Dodge/Jeep, RV camping, **W gas:** 7-11/dsl, Shell/Dunkin Donuts/dsl, **food:** Music Lady Cafe, Subway, **lodging:** Plainfield Motel, **other:** transmissions
88 (30)	CT 14A to Plainfield, **E** RV camping (seasonal), **W gas:** Mobil
87 (28)	Lathrop Rd, to Plainfield, **E gas:** Shell/Tim Horton's/Domino's/dsl, **food:** Dunkin Donuts, HongKong Star Chinese, Subway, Wendy's, **lodging:** Holiday Inn Express, Quality Inn, **other:** Big Y Foods, Ford, Hyundai, Mazda, Radio Shack, **W gas:** Citgo, Sunoco/dsl, **food:** Bakers Dozen Cafe, McDonald's, O'Connor's
87 (28)	Continued Steaks/Pizza, Paradise Rest., **other:** Advance Parts, CVS Drug
86 (24)	rd 201, Hopeville, **E** Hopeville Pond SP, RV camping
85 (23)	CT 164, CT 138, to Pachaug, Preston, **E other:** Curves, $Tree, RV camping, **W lodging:** AmericInn
84 (21)	CT 12, Jewett City, **E food:** Ruby Tuesday, **other:** Ford, Home Depot, Kohl's, Walmart SuperCtr, **W gas:** Gulf/dsl, Mobil/dsl, Shell/dsl, **food:** McDonald's, **other:** Val-U Foods
83a (20)	CT 169 (from nb), Lisbon, **E** RV camping
83 (18)	rd 97, Taftville, **E gas:** Getty/dsl, **other:** camping, repair, **W gas:** 7-11/gas
82 (14)	to CT 2 W, CT 32 N, Norwichtown, **E food:** Friendly's, **other:** tires, **W gas:** Chucky's/dsl, Citgo/dsl, Lukoil/Dunkin Donutsdsl, Shell/dsl, **food:** Illiano's Grill, McDonald's, Mona Lisa's Rest., Subway, **lodging:** Courtyard, Rosemont Suites, **other:** Ace Hardware
81 (14)	CT 2 E, CT 32 S, Norwich, **E** H, to Mohegan Coll
80 (12)	CT 82, Norwich, **E gas:** Mobil, Shell, Xtra, **food:** Burger King, Chinese Buffet, Dominic's Pizza, Dunkin Donuts, Friendly's, KFC/Taco Bell, McDonald's, 99 Rest., Papa Gino's, Subway, Tim Horton, Wendy's, **other:** Brooks Drug, Jo-Ann Fabrics, Radio Shack, ShopRite Foods, Staples, TownFair Tire, **W lodging:** Hampton Inn, Holiday Inn, **other:** Big Y Foods, Walmart
79a (10)	CT 2A E, to Ledyard, **E** to Pequot Res
8.5mm	nb st police, ☎, sb Mobil/dsl, **rest area, full facilities**
79 (6)	rd 163, to Uncasville, Montville, **1 mi E gas:** Mobil/dsl, **food:** Dunkin Donuts, Friendly Pizza, McDonald's, Subway, **other:** Beit Bro's Foods, Rite Aid, auto repair
78 (5)	CT 32 (from sb, exits left), to New London, RI Beaches
77 (2)	CT 85, to I-95 N, Colchester, **1/2 mi E gas:** Shell/dsl, Dunkin Donuts, **lodging:** Oakdell Motel
0mm	I-95. I-395 begins/ends on I-95, exit 76.

INTERSTATE 691

Exit #	Services
I-69	1 begins/ends on I-91
12 (12)	Preston Ave
11 (11)	I-91 N, to Hartford
10 (11)	I-91 S, to New Haven, CT 15 S, W Cross Pkwy
8 (10)	US 5, Broad St, **N gas:** Citgo, Cumberland, Shell/dsl, **food:** Broad St Pizza, Chinese Gourmet, DQ
7 (9)	downtown, Meriden (from wb), **S gas:** Citgo
6 (8)	Lewis Ave (from wb, no EZ return), to CT 71, **N food:** Ruby Tuesday, **other:** H, Best Buy, Borders Books, Macy's, JC Penney, Macy's, Sears/auto, Target, mall, **S** 7-11/gas
5 (7)	CT 71, to Chamberlain Hill (from eb, no EZ return), **N other:** H, Best Buy, Target, mall, **S gas:** 7-11/gas, **food:** McDonald's, Subway
4 (4)	CT 322, W Main St (no re-entry from eb), **1 mi N gas:** Exxon, **food:** Arbys, Dominique's Pizza, McDonald's, Subway, **N gas:** Sunoco, **food:** Dunkin Donuts, **other:** H
3mm	Quinnipiac River
3 (1)	CT 10, to Cheshire, Southington, **N gas:** Sunoco, **food:** Sam's Clams Rest.
2 (0)	I-84 E, to Hartford
1 (0)	I-84 W, to Waterbury
I-69	1 begins/ends on I-84

INTERSTATE 95

Exit #	Services
23mm	Delaware/Pennsylvania state line, motorist callboxes for 23 miles sb
11 (22)	I-495 S, DE 92, Naamans Rd, **E food:** China Star, **other:** Burlington Coats, $General, Goodyear/auto, Jo-Ann Fabrics, K-Mart, Sav-A-lot Foods, WaWa, **W gas:** Gulf/dsl, **food:** Crossroads Rest, KFC/Taco Bell, Quizno's, **lodging:** Holiday Inn Select, **other:** Home Depot, Radio Shack, Rite Aid
10 (21)	Harvey Rd (no nb return)
9 (19)	DE 3, to Marsh Rd, **E** to Bellevue SP, st police, **W food:** Lamberti's Cafe, Starbucks, **other:** museum
8b a (17)	US 202, Concord Pike, to Wilmington, **E other:** Home Depot, **W gas:** Cumberland Farms, **food:** Arby's, Dunkin Donuts, 5 Guys Burgers, Golden Castle Diner, McDonald's, Taco Bell, **lodging:** Best Western, Quality Inn, **other:** H
7b a (16)	DE 52, Delaware Ave
6 (15)	DE 4, MLK Blvd, **E food:** McDonald's, **other:** Fresh Grocer Foods, Rite Aid, **W gas:** BP
5c (12)	I-495 N, to Wilmington, to DE Mem Bridge
5b a (11)	DE 141, to US 202, to New Castle, Newport, **E lodging:** Quality Inn
4b a (8)	DE 1, DE 7, to Christiana, **E food:** Don Pablo, Food-Court, Houlihan's, Ruby Tuesday, **other:** Costco, JC Penney, Macy's, Michael's, Nordstrom's, mall, **W food:** Applebees, Bugaboo Steaks, Cheeseburger Paradise, Chili's, Dunkin Donuts, Michael's Rest., Old Country Buffet, Olive Garden, Quizno's, Red Lobster, **lodging:** Country Inn&Suites, Courtyard, Day's Inn, Fairfield Inn, Hilton, Red Roof Inn, **other:** H, Best Buy, Borders Books, Home Depot, Office Depot, PetsMart, TJ Maxx, casino/racetrack
3b a (6)	DE 273, to Newark, Dover, **E gas:** BP/24hr, Exxon/dsl, **food:** Bertucci's, Bob Evans, Boston Mkt, Famous Dave's BBQ, Red Robin, Olive Grill Italian, Shell Hammer's Grille, Wendy's, **lodging:** Ramada Inn, Residence Inn, Staybridge Suites, TownePlace Suites, **other:** Acme Foods, Boscov's, Jo-Ann Fabrics, Old Navy, Staples, **W gas:** Getty, Shell, **food:** Denny's, Dunkin Donuts, Pizza Hut, **lodging:** Econolodge, Hampton Inn, Holiday Inn Express, **other:** 7-11
5mm	**service area both lanes (exits left from both lanes), info, gas:** Sunoco, **food:** Big Boy, Roy Rogers, Sbarro's, Starbucks
1b a (3)	DE 896, to Newark, to U of DE, Middletown, **W gas:** Exxon, Gulf/dsl, Shell/dsl/24hr, Sunoco, **food:** Boston Mkt, College Town Cafe, China Garden, Dunkin Donuts, Friendly's, Mario's Pizza, Matilda's Rest, McDonald's, TGIFriday, **lodging:** Courtyard (3mi), Embassy Suites, Homewood Suites, Howard Johnson, Quality Inn, Sleep Inn
1mm	toll booth, st police
0mm	Delaware/Maryland state line, motorist callboxes for 23 miles nb

INTERSTATE 295 (WILMINGTON)

Exit #	Services
15mm	Delaware/New Jersey state line, Delaware River, Delaware Memorial Bridge
14.5mm	toll plaza
14	DE 9, New Castle Ave, to Wilmington, **E gas:** BP/24hr, Citgo, **food:** Giovanni's Cafe, **other:**

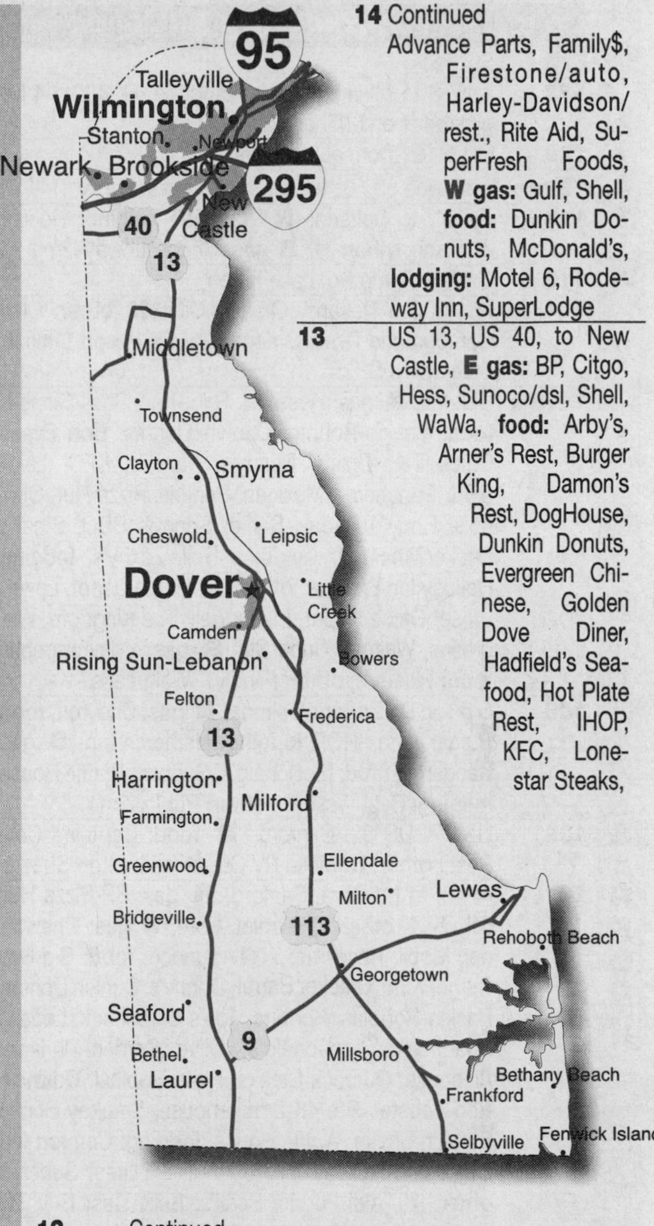

Exit #	Services
14	Continued Advance Parts, Family$, Firestone/auto, Harley-Davidson/rest., Rite Aid, SuperFresh Foods, **W gas:** Gulf, Shell, **food:** Dunkin Donuts, McDonald's, **lodging:** Motel 6, Rodeway Inn, SuperLodge
13	US 13, US 40, to New Castle, **E gas:** BP, Citgo, Hess, Sunoco/dsl, Shell, WaWa, **food:** Arby's, Arner's Rest, Burger King, Damon's Rest, DogHouse, Dunkin Donuts, Evergreen Chinese, Golden Dove Diner, Hadfield's Seafood, Hot Plate Rest, IHOP, KFC, Lonestar Steaks,
13	Continued McDonald's, Pizza Hut, Popeye's, Rascal's Seafood, Season's Pizza, Subway, Taco Bell, TGIFriday, Wendy's, **lodging:** Quality Inn, **other:** AutoZone, BJ's Whse, Chevrolet, Cottman Transmissions, $Tree, Happy Harry's Drugs, Home Depot, Hyundai, Kia, Mazda, Nissan, PathMark Foods, PepBoys, Radio Shack, Ross, Sav-A-Lot, 7-11, Staples, Toyota/Scion, repair, **W gas:** Shell, WaWa, **food:** Dunkin Donuts, **lodging:** Clarion, **other:** Ford Trucks, Lowes Whse
12	I-495, US 202, N to Wilmington

I-295 begins/ends on I-95

INTERSTATE 495

Exit #	Services
11mm	I-95 N I-495 begins/ends on I-95.
5 (10)	US 13, Phila Pike, Claymont, **W gas:** Sunoco, **food:** Arby's, Boston Mkt, Claymont Steaks, Jake's, McDonald's,
4 (5)	US 13, rd 3, Edgemoor Rd, to Fox Point Park
3 (4)	12th St
2 (3)	rd 9A, Terminal Ave, Port of Wilmington
1 (1)	US 13, **E gas:** Shell, WaWa, **food:** Dunkin Donuts, **lodging:** Clarion, **other:** Ford Trucks, Kia, Lowes Whse
0mm	I-95 S. I-495 begins/ends on I-95.

E ↕ W

INTERSTATE 4

Exit #	Services
132	I-95, S to Miami, N to Jacksonville, FL 400. I-4 begins/ends on I-95, exit 260b
129	to US 92 (from eb, exits left)
126mm	**rest area eb, [picnic], litter barrels, no security**
118	FL 44, to DeLand, **N gas:** BP, **lodging:** Howard Johnson, **other:** [H], **S gas:** Citgo/Subway (2mi)
116	Orange Camp Rd, Lake Helen
114	FL 472, to DeLand, Orange City, **N other:** Clark Campground (1mi), Orange City RV Resort (1mi), to Blue Sprgs SP
111b a	Deltona, **N gas:** Hess/dsl, RaceTrac, Shell/Circle K, **food:** Baskin-Robbins/Dunkin Donuts, Bob Evans, Chick-fil-A, Chili's, Denny's, Fazoli's, KFC, Lelo's BBQ, Panchero's Mexican, Perkins, Pizza Hut, Quizno's, Ruby Tuesday, Sonic, Sonny's BBQ, Steak'n Shake/24hr, Subway, Taco Bell, Zaxby's, **lodging:** Holiday Inn Express, **other:** [H], Home Depot, Lowe's Whse, Office Depot, Publix/deli, Tire Kingdom, Walgreens, Walmart SuperCtr, **S gas:** Chevron/repair, **food:** Wendy's, **other:** Family$, Walgreens
108	Dirksen Dr, DeBary, Deltona, **N gas:** Chevron, **food:** Burger King, IHOP, **lodging:** Hampton Inn, **S gas:** Kangaroo, **food:** McDonald's, Subway, Waffle House, **lodging:** Best Western, **other:** Publix (2mi)
104	US 17, US 92, Sanford, **N food:** Captains Cove Rest., **other:** La Mesa RV Ctr, **S gas:** Citgo/Subway
101c	rd 46, to Mt Dora, Sanford, **N gas:** BP/Pizza Hut/dsl, 7-11, **other:** Chevrolet, Ford, **S gas:** Chevron/dsl, Mobil, RaceTrac, 7-11, Sunoco, **food:** Big Boy, Burger King, Cracker Barrel, Denny's, Dunkin Donuts/Baskin-Robbins, Hooters, Joe's Crabshack, Logan's Roadhouse, McDonald's, Olive Garden, Orlando Alehouse, Outback Steaks, Pollo Tropical, Quizno's, Red Lobster, Rte 46 Smokehouse, Smokey Bones, Steak'n Shake, Waffle House, **lodging:** Comfort Inn, Day's Inn, Holiday Inn, SpringHill Suites, Super 8, **other:** [H], Aldi Foods, Beall's, Belk, Best Buy, Big 10 Tire, BJ's Whse/gas, Books-A-Million, Carmax, Dillards, Dillard's, $Tree, CVS Drug, JC Penney, Jo-Anne, Macy's, Marshall's, Michael's, Old Navy, Ross, Sears/auto, Target, Tire Kingdom, Toyota/Scion, Walmart SuperCtr, World Mkt, mall
101a b	rd 46a, FL 417 (toll), FL 46, Sanford, Heathrow, **N food:** Applebees, Crisper's, FishBones, Moes SW Grill, Ruth's Chris Steaks, **lodging:** Hampton Inn, Marriott, **other:** Chevrolet, Walgreens, **S gas:** Chevron, Sunoco, **food:** Olive Garden, Cracker Barrel, McDonald's, Outback Steaks, Red Lobster, Waffle House, **lodging:** Comfort Inn, Days Inn, Super 8, **other:** Acura, Books-A-Million, Dillards, Harley-Davidson, Honda, JC Penney, Macy's, Sam's Club/gas, Sears, Toyota
98	Lake Mary Blvd, Heathrow, **N gas:** Shell, **food:** Mario's Pizza, Panera Bread, Stonewood Grill, **lodging:** Courtyard, Hyatt Place, **other:** CVS Drug, Walgreens, Winn-Dixie, **S gas:** BP/24hr, Chevron/24hr, Citgo, Mobil/dsl, 7-11, **food:** Arby's, Bob Evans, Boston Mkt, Burger King, Checkers, Chick-fil-A, Chili's, Chipotle Mexican, Chop Stix, Cuban Cafe, Dunkin Donuts/Baskin-Robbins, Firehouse Subs, Frank&Naomi's,
98	Continued KFC, Krystal, Longhorn Steaks, Macaroni Grill, McDonald's, Papa John's, Papa Joe's Pizza, Pizza Hut, Quizno's, Starbucks, Steak'n Shake, Subway, Taco Bell, Taste of China, TGIFriday, Tropical Smoothie, Uno, Wendy's, WingZone, **lodging:** Candlewood Suites, Extended Stay America, Hilton Garden, Homestead Suites, Homewood Suites, La Quinta, **other:** Advance Parts, Albertson's, Gander Mtn, Goodyear, Home Depot, K-Mart, PestMart, Publix, Staples, Target, Tires+, TJ Maxx, USPO, mall, Vet
95mm	**rest areas both lanes, full [handicapped] facilities, [phone], vending, [picnic], litter barrels, petwalk, 24hr security**
94	FL 434, to Winter Springs, Longwood, **N gas:** Hess/dsl, Mobil, 7-11, **food:** Burger King, Imperial Dynasty, Kobe Japanese, Melting Pot Rest., Miami Subs, Panera Bread, Papa Joe's Pizza, Quizno's, Starbucks, Wendy's, **lodging:** Comfort Inn, **other:** CVS Drug, **S food:** Bonefish Grill, Boston Mkt, Calipso Grill, Carmela's Rest., Crisper's, **lodging:** Candlewood Suites, **other:** [H], 7-11
92	FL 436, Altamonte Springs, **N gas:** Medallion, 7-11, Shell/Circle K/dsl, **food:** Boston Mkt, Checker's, Chick-fil-A, Chipotle Mexican, ChuckeCheese, Cracker Barrel, Dominos, Golden City Chinese, Kobe Japanese, LongHorn Steaks, McDonald's, Olive Garden, Perkins, Pollo Tropical, Popeye's, Red Lobster, Steak&Ale, Sweet Tomatoes, Taco Bell, TGIFriday, WingHouse, **lodging:** Day's Inn, Hampton Inn, Hotel Altamonte, Quality Suites, Ramada, SpringHill Suites, **other:** Best Buy, CVS Drug, Family$, Firestone/auto, Goodyear/auto, Tire Kingdom, U-Haul, Walgreens, **S gas:** BP, Citgo, Hess, Mobil, **food:** Bahama Breeze, Burger King, Chili's, Denny's, Dunkin Donuts, Elephant Bar, Five Guys Burgers, Moe's SW Grill, Jason's Deli, Mimi's Cafe, Orlando Alehouse, Panda Express, Pizza Hut, Shane's Ribshack, Straud's Seafood, Chili's, Denny's, Steak'n Shake, Subway, **lodging:** Embassy Suites, Hilton, Homestead Suites, **other:** [H], Advance Parts, Albertsons, Barnes & Noble, CVS Drug, Dillards, JC Penney, Marshall's, Michael's, Office Depot, PetCo, Publix, Ross, Sears/auto, TJ-Maxx, Vet
90b a	FL 414, Maitland Blvd, **N gas:** 7-11/gas, **food:** Applebee's, Chick-fil-A, Oak Grill, Wendy's, **lodging:** Extended Stay, Extended Stay Deluxe, Courtyard, Sheraton, **S** Maitland Art Ctr
88	FL 423, Lee Rd, **N gas:** 7-11/gas, Texaco, **food:** Arby's, Burger King, China One, Del Frisco, IHOP, Little Caesars, LJ Silver/Taco Bell, McDonald's, Quizno's, Shell's Seafood, Taco Bell, **lodging:** Comfort Inn, Countryside Inn, InTown Inn, La Quinta, Motel 6, **other:** Aamco, Firestone, Home Depot, Infinity, Land Rover, Tires+, VW, **S gas:** Chevron/dsl, Mobil/dsl, Sunoco, **food:** Denny's, **other:** BMW
87	FL 426, Fairbanks Ave (no eb re-entry), **N gas:** Hess/Blimpie/Godfather's/dsl, **1mi S gas:** Chevron, **food:** Burger King, Steak'n Shake, Subway, Wendy's
86	Par Ave (from eb, no re-entry), **S gas:** Shell/Circle K
85	Princeton St, **S gas:** Chevron, 7-11, **other:** [H]
84	FL 50, Colonial Dr (from wb), Ivanhoe Blvd, **N lodging:** Crowne Plaza, **S lodging:** Sheraton

SANFORD

HEATHROW

ALTAMONTE SPRINGS

FL

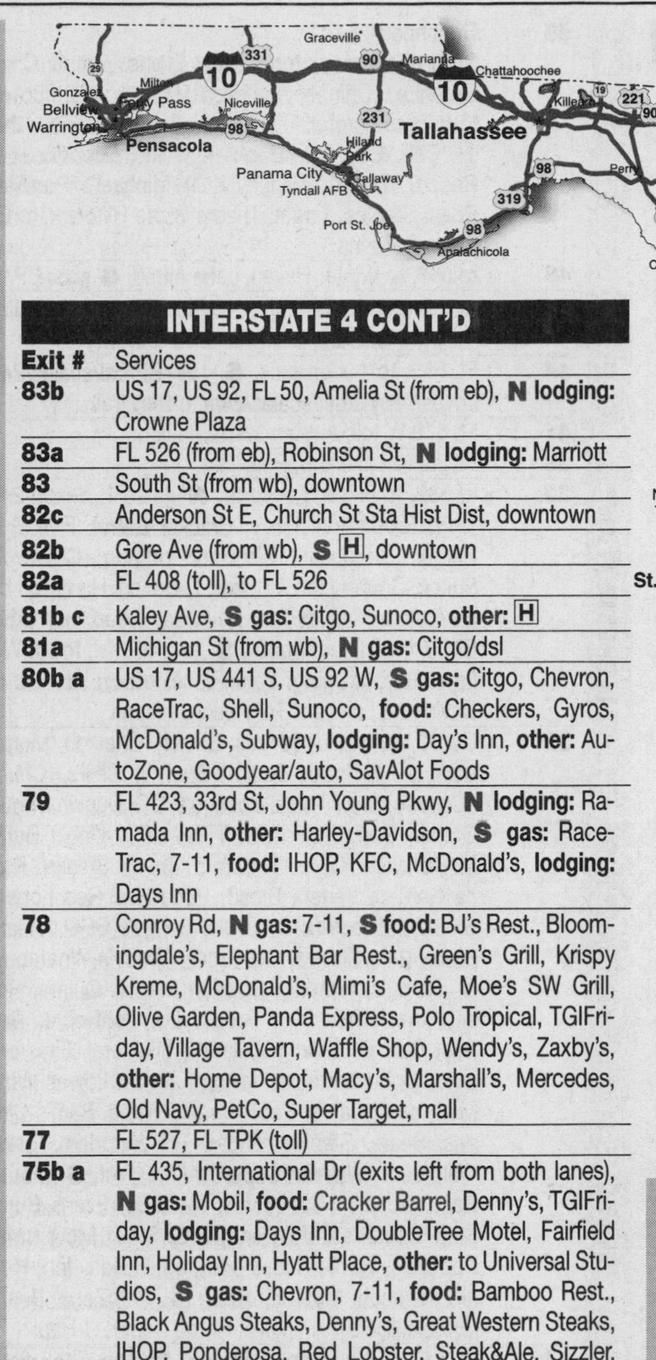

INTERSTATE 4 CONT'D

Exit #	Services
83b	US 17, US 92, FL 50, Amelia St (from eb), **N lodging:** Crowne Plaza
83a	FL 526 (from eb), Robinson St, **N lodging:** Marriott
83	South St (from wb), downtown
82c	Anderson St E, Church St Sta Hist Dist, downtown
82b	Gore Ave (from wb), **S** [H], downtown
82a	FL 408 (toll), to FL 526
81b c	Kaley Ave, **S gas:** Citgo, Sunoco, **other:** [H]
81a	Michigan St (from wb), **N gas:** Citgo/dsl
80b a	US 17, US 441 S, US 92 W, **S gas:** Citgo, Chevron, RaceTrac, Shell, Sunoco, **food:** Checkers, Gyros, McDonald's, Subway, **lodging:** Day's Inn, **other:** AutoZone, Goodyear/auto, SavAlot Foods
79	FL 423, 33rd St, John Young Pkwy, **N lodging:** Ramada Inn, **other:** Harley-Davidson, **S gas:** RaceTrac, 7-11, **food:** IHOP, KFC, McDonald's, **lodging:** Days Inn
78	Conroy Rd, **N gas:** 7-11, **S food:** BJ's Rest., Bloomingdale's, Elephant Bar Rest., Green's Grill, Krispy Kreme, McDonald's, Mimi's Cafe, Moe's SW Grill, Olive Garden, Panda Express, Polo Tropical, TGIFriday, Village Tavern, Waffle Shop, Wendy's, Zaxby's, **other:** Home Depot, Macy's, Marshall's, Mercedes, Old Navy, PetCo, Super Target, mall
77	FL 527, FL TPK (toll)
75b a	FL 435, International Dr (exits left from both lanes), **N gas:** Mobil, **food:** Cracker Barrel, Denny's, TGIFriday, **lodging:** Days Inn, DoubleTree Motel, Fairfield Inn, Holiday Inn, Hyatt Place, **other:** to Universal Studios, **S gas:** Chevron, 7-11, **food:** Bamboo Rest., Black Angus Steaks, Denny's, Great Western Steaks, IHOP, Ponderosa, Red Lobster, Steak&Ale, Sizzler, **lodging:** Best Western, Clarion, Court of Flags Hotel, Econolodge, Hampton Inn, Hilton Garden, Holiday Inn Express, Homewood Suites, Howard Johnson, International Gateway Inn, Knight's Inn, Lakefront Inn, Las Palmas Hotel, Motel 6, Rodeway Inn, Sheraton, Super 8, multiple hotels & resorts, **other:** Bass Pro Shops, Belz Outlet/famous Brands, Books A Million, Office Depot, Walgreens
74b	Universal Studios (from wb)
74a	FL 482, Sand Lake Rd, **N gas:** Chevron, 7-11, **food:** Alexander's Rest., Chick-fil-A, McDonald's, Timpano Italian, Wendy's, multiple restaurants, **lodging:** Comfort Suites, **other:** K-Mart, Publix, Whole Food Mkt, Walgreens, Walmart SuperCtr, **S gas:** BP, Chevron, Mobil, 7-11, Shell/Circle K, **food:** Buffalo Wild Wings, Burger King, Cattleman's Steaks, Charley's Steaks, Checker's, Chili's, Cici's, Denny's, Don Pablos, Friendly's, Golden Corral, IHOP, Italianni's, Kobe Japanese, Lobster Feast, McDonald's, Olive Garden,
74a	Continued Perkins, Pizza Hut, Ponderosa, Popeye's, TGIFriday, Tony Roma, Uno, Vito's Chophouse, Wendy's, Wild Bean Cafe, **lodging:** Best Western, Castle Hotel, Courtyard, Comfort Inn, Crowne Plaza, Econolodge, Embassy Suites, Fairfield Inn, Fishbones, Hampton Inn, Holiday Inn, Howard Johnson, Hyatt Place, Knights Inn, La Quinta, Marriott, Masters Inn, Microtel, Peabody Hotel, Quality Inn, Radisson Inn, Ramada Inn, Red Roof Inn, Residence Inn, Rodeway Inn, Staybridge Suites, Wyndham Garden, **other:** [H], Harley-Davidson, Ripley's Believe-it-or-not!, Stouffer Resort, Walgreens, RV Park
72	FL 528 E (toll, no eb re-entry), to Cape Canaveral, **S** to ✈
71	Central FL Pkwy (from eb no re-entry), **S gas:** Chevron, **food:** Wendy's, **lodging:** Hilton Garden, Renaissance Resort, Residence Inn, to SeaWorld
68	FL 535, Lake Buena Vista, **N gas:** Chevron/24hr, 7-11, Shell/Circle K/dsl, **food:** AleHouse, Black Angus Steaks, Buffalo Wild Wings, Burger King, Cici's, Chevy's Mexican, Chili's, China Buffet, Crossroads Dining, Denny's, Domino's, Dragon Buffet, Flipper's Pizzaria, Fortune Chinese, Fuddrucker's, Giordano's, Havana's Cuisine, Hooters, IHOP, Joe's Crabshack,

E ↕ W ORLANDO

INTERSTATE 4 CONT'D

Exit #	Services
68	Continued Jonnie's Rest., Kobe Japanese, Macaroni Grill, McDonald's, Olive Garden, Perkins, Pizza Hut, Qdoba Mexican, Quizno's, Red Lobster, Shoney's, Sizzler, Steak'n Shake, Subway, Taco Bell, TGIFriday, Uno, Vallarta Mexican, Willy's Rest., **lodging:** Comfort Inn, Country Inn&Suites, Courtyard, Doubletree, Embassy Suites, Extended Stay Deluxe, Hampton Inn, Hawthorn Suites, Hilton, Holiday Inn Express, Homewood Suites, Hotel Orlando, Hyatt Hotel, Quality Inn, Radisson, Residence Inn, Sheraton, SpringHill Suites, StayBridge Suites, **other:** Gooding's Foods, USPO, Walgreens, **S gas:** Chevron, 7-11, Shell, **food:** Bahama Breeze, Carrabba's, Chick-fil-A, Cici's Pizza, Dunkin Donuts, Golden Corral, Landry's Seafood, LoneStar Steaks, Panera Bread, Starbucks, Wendy's, **lodging:** Blue Heron Resort, Buena Vista Suites, Courtyard, Fairfield Inn, Holiday Inn Resort, Marriott Village, Residence Inn, Sheraton, SpringHill Suites, **other:** CVS Drug, Orlando Premium Outlets, Super Mkt Foods, Walgreens
67	Fl 536, to Epcot (wb only), **N** DisneyWorld, **1 mi S gas:** 7-11, **food:** Ponderosa, **lodging:** Buena Vista, Marriott, **other:** CVS Drug, Prime Outlet, to ✈, multiple resorts
65	Osceola Pkwy, to FL 417 (toll), **N** to DisneyWorld, Epcot, Animal Kingdom, and Wide World of Sports
64b a	US 192, FL 536, to FL 417 (toll), to Kissimmee, **N gas:** 7-11, to DisneyWorld, MGM, **S gas:** Mobil/dsl, RaceTrac, 7-11, **food:** Arbys, Bob Evans, Boston Lobster Feast, Burger King, Cattleman's Steakhouse, Charlie's Rest., Chili's, Chinese Buffet, Cici's Pizza, Cracker Barrel, Denny's, Domino's, Golden Corral, IHOP, Joe's Crabshack, Kabuki Japanese, KFC, Kobe Japanese, Logans Roadhouse, Longhorn Steaks, Macaroni Grill, McDonald's, Nemo's Steaks, Ocean 11 Rest., Olive Garden, Orange World, Pacino's Italian, Papa John's, Perkins, Pizza Hut, Ponderosa, Quizno's, Red Lobster, Ruby Tuesday, Shoney's, Sizzlin Grill, Starbucks, Subway, Taco Bell, TGIFriday, Uno Pizzaria, Waffle House, Wendy's, **lodging:** Comfort Suites, Days Inn, Econolodge, Holiday Inn, Howard Johnson, Masters Inn, Mona Lisa Motel, Motel 6, Old Towne Suites, Orlando Resort, Parkway Resort, Quality Suites, Radisson, Red Roof Inn, Rodeway Inn, Sun Inn, Super 8, Seralago Hotel, Travelodge, **other:** Ace Hardware, Camping World RV Service/supplies (3mi), CVS Drug, Harley-Davidson, Publix, Walgreens, USPO, factory outlet/famous brands
62	FL 417 (toll, from eb), World Dr, **N** to DisneyWorld, **S** Celebration, to ✈
60	Fl 429 N (toll), Apopka
58	FL 532, to Kissimmee, **N gas:** BP, 7-11, **food:** Chili's, China One, McDonald's, Pizzaria, Subway, **other:** Publix, Walgreens, **S** Dunkin Donuts (1mi)
55	US 27, to Haines City, **N gas:** 7-11, Sunoco, **food:** Burger King, Cracker Barrel, Denny's, McDonald's, Waffle House, Wendy's, **lodging:** Fairfield Inn, Hampton Inn, Super 8, **other:** Ford, FL CampInn (5mi), **S gas:** BP/dsl, Exxon, Marathon, RaceWay/24hr, 7-11,

LAKELAND

Exit #	Services
55	Continued Shell/dsl/service, **food:** Bob Evans, Grand China, GreenLeaf Chinese, Perkins/24hr, Quizno's, Subway, **lodging:** Microtel, Quality Inn, Southgate Inn, **other:** H, Belk, Best Buy, Books A Million, Deer Creek RV Resort, $Tree, JC Penney, KOA, Michael's, PetsMart, Ross, Staples, Target, Theme World RV Park, to Cypress Gardens
48	rd 557, to Winter Haven, Lake Alfred, **S gas:** BP/dsl
46mm	**rest area both lanes, full ♿ facilities, ☎, vending, picnic, litter barrels, petwalk, 24hr security**
44	FL 559, to Auburndale, **S gas:** BP/dsl/scales/24hr, Loves/Arby's/dsl/scales/24hr, **other:** fruit
41	FL 570 W toll, Auburndale, Lakeland
38	FL 33, to Lakeland, Polk City
33	rd 582, to FL 33, Lakeland, **N gas:** BP, Exxon/24hr, 7-11, **food:** Applebee's, Cracker Barrel, Five Guys Burger, Starbucks, Wendy's, **lodging:** Crestwood Suites, Country Inn & Suites, Days Inn, Hampton Inn, La Quinta, Quality Inn, Ramada, Sleep Inn, **other:** BMW, CVS Drug, Publix, **S gas:** BP/dsl, **food:** Waffle House, **lodging:** ValuePlace, **other:** H, Harley-Davidson, Lakeland RV Resort, Nissan
32	US 98, Lakeland, **N gas:** BP/dsl, Chevron, Murphy USA, 7-11, **food:** Beef O'Brady's, Chili's, ChuckeCheese, Cici's Pizza, Domino's, DQ, Dunkin Donuts, Golden Corral, Hooters, IHOP, KFC, Ling's Buffet, McDonald's, Olive Garden, Outback Steaks, Palaca Garden, Panera Bread, Pizza Hut, Red Lobster, Smokey Bones BBQ, Sonic, Sonny's BBQ, Steak'n Shake/24hr, Subway, TGIFriday, Wendy's, Whataburger, Zaxby's, **lodging:** Comfort Inn, La Quinta, Royalty Inn, **other:** Aldi Foods, Barnes&Noble, Belk, Best Buy, CVS Drug, Dillard's, $General, Firestone/auto, Goodyear/auto, JoAnn Fabrics, Lowes Whse, Macy's, Michael's, PepBoys, RV World, Sam's Club/gas, Sears, Staples, Target, Tire Kingdom, Tires+, Walgreens, Walmart SuperCtr (2mi), Vet, **S gas:** BP, RaceTrac, 7-11, Sunoco/dsl, **food:** Bob Evans, Burger King, Cassie's Cafe, Denny's, LJ Silver, McDonald's, Popeye's, Waffle House, **lodging:** Holiday Inn, Howard Johnson, Motel 6, **other:** H, AutoZone, Beall's, Chrysler/Dodge, Family$, Home Depot, U-Haul
31	FL 539, to Kathleen, Lakeland, **N gas:** Shell, **food:** Romeo's Pizza, Wendy's, **other:** Publix, **S** hist dist
28	FL 546, to US 92, Memorial Blvd, Lakeland
27	FL 570 E toll, Lakeland
25	County Line Rd, **S gas:** Citgo/dsl, Shell/Circle K/Subway, **food:** McDonald's, Wendy's, **lodging:** Fairfield Inn, **other:** FL Air Museum
22	FL 553, Park Rd, Plant City, **N other:** Chevrolet, **S gas:** Shell/Circle K/Subway, **food:** Arby's, Burger King, Denny's, Popeye's, **lodging:** Comfort Inn, Holiday Inn Express, **other:** RV Sales
21	FL 39, Alexander St, to Zephyrhills, Plant City, **S gas:** BP/dsl, Citgo, Shell, **lodging:** Day's Inn, Red Rose Inn/rest.
19	FL 566, to Thonotosassa, **N gas:** BP, **S gas:** RaceTrac, **food:** Applebee's, BuddyFreddy's Rest., Carraba's, Lin's Express, Little Caesars, McDonald's, Mi Casa, OutBack Steaks, Sonny's BBQ, Starbucks, Subway, Waffle House, **other:** H, $General, Publix

INTERSTATE 4 CONT'D

E ↔ W

Exit #	Services
17	Branch Forbes Rd, **N gas:** Marathon, Sunoco, **other:** Dinosaur World, **S gas:** BP, Citgo, Shell/Circle K/Subway/dsl, **other:** Advance Parts, AutoZone
14	McIntosh Rd, **N gas:** BP/dsl, **other:** Longview RV Ctr, Windward RV Park (2mi), **S gas:** 7-11/dsl, **food:** Burger King, McDonald's/playplace, **other:** Bates RV Ctr, East Tampa RV Park
12mm	**weigh sta, both lanes**
10	rd 579, Mango, Thonotosassa, **N gas:** *FLYING J*/CountryMkt/dsl/LP/scales/24hr, Sunoco, TA/Arby's/Popeye's/dsl/scales/24hr/@, **food:** Bob Evans, Cracker Barrel, **lodging:** Country Inn Suites, Hampton Inn, **other:** Camping World RV Service/supplies, Ford/Lincoln/Mercury, Hillsboro River SP, Lazy Day's RV Ctr, Rally RV Park, **S gas:** Shell/Circle K/dsl, **food:** Hardee's, Subway, Wendy's, **lodging:** Masters Inn
9	I-75, N to Ocala, S to Naples
7	US 92W, to US 301, Hillsborough Ave, **N on US 92 gas:** Citgo/rest./scales/dsl, **food:** Waffle House, **other:** Motel 6, **other:** Hard Rock Hotel/casino, **S gas:** BP, Citgo, Hess, **food:** WingHouse, **lodging:** Holiday Inn Express, La Quinta, Red Roof Inn, **other:** FL Expo Fair
6	Orient Rd (from eb)
5	FL 574, MLK Blvd, **N food:** McDonald's, **S gas:** BP, Sunoco, **food:** Subway, Wendy's, **lodging:** Holiday Inn Express, Masters Inn, **other:** Kenworth
3	US 41, 50th St, Columbus Dr (exits left from eb), **N gas:** Shell, **lodging:** Day's Inn, Motel 29, **other:** Busch Gardens, **S gas:** Marathon, Sunoco/dsl, **food:** Checker's, Church's, KFC, McDonald's, Salem's Subs, Subway, Taco Bell, **lodging:** Howard Johnson, **other:** Advance Parts, Family$
1	FL 585, 22nd, 21st St, Port of Tampa, **S gas:** BP/24hr, **food:** Burger King, Columbia Rest., McDonald's, **other:** museum
0mm	I-4 begins/ends on I-275, exit 45b.

MANGO · TAMPA

INTERSTATE 10

E ↔ W

Exit #	Services
363mm	I-10 begins/ends on I-95, exit 351b.
362	Stockton St, to Riverside, **S gas:** BP, Gate, **other:** H
361	US 17 S (from wb), downtown
360	FL 129, McDuff Ave, **S gas:** BP, Chevron, **food:** Popeye's
359	Lenox Ave, Edgewood Ave (from wb)
358	FL 111, Cassat Ave, **N gas:** Hess/Blimpie/dsl, Shell/Subway/dsl, **food:** Burger King, McDonald's, Wendy's, **other:** AutoZone, **S gas:** BP, RaceWay/24hr, **food:** Domino's, Dunkin Donuts, Taco Bell, **other:** Advance Parts, Discount Tire, Lowes Whse, Walgreens
357	FL 103, Lane Ave, **N gas:** Hess/dsl, **food:** Andy's Sandwiches, **lodging:** Day's Inn, Ramada Ltd, **S gas:** BP, Shell/dsl, **food:** Applebee's, Bono's BBQ, Cross Creek Steaks, Hardee's, KFC, Lee's Drive-In, Linda's Seafood, McDonald's, Piccadilly's, **lodging:** Budget Inn, Diamond Inn, **other:** Home Depot, Office Depot, Pep Boys
356	I-295, N to Savannah, S to St Augustine

JACKSONVILLE

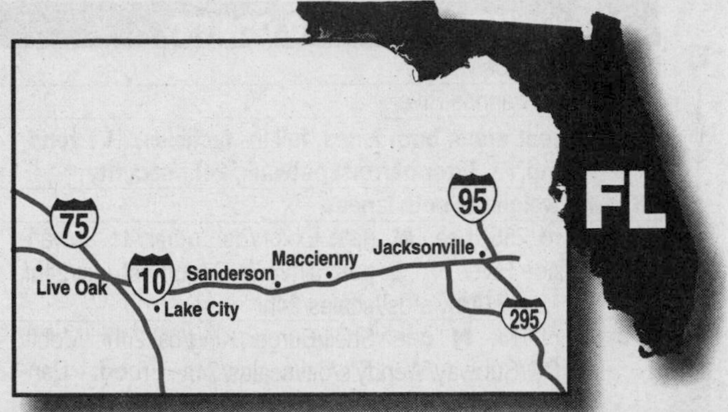

Exit #	Services
355	Marietta, **N gas:** Gate/dsl/24hr, Exxon, **S gas:** Hess/Blimpie/dsl, Shell/dsl
351	FL 115, Chaffee Rd, to Cecil Fields, **N gas:** Kangaroo/dsl/24hr, **other:** Rivers RV Ctr, **S gas:** Chevron, KwikChek/gas, Shell/Subway/dsl/24hr, **food:** Cracker Barrel, Fastboys Wings, King Wok, McDonald's, Quizno's, Wendy's, **lodging:** Best Western, Hampton Inn, Holiday Inn Express, **other:** Family$, Winn-Dixie
349	new exit
343	US 301, to Starke, Baldwin, **S gas:** BP, Chevron, Pilot/Subway/dsl/scales/24hr/@, TA/Shell/Arby's/dsl/scales/rest./24hr/@, **food:** Burger King, McDonald's, Waffle House, **lodging:** Best Western, **other:** NAPA
336	FL 228, to Maxville, Macclenny, **N food:** Starbucks, **other:** H, Walmart SuperCtr/Subway/24hr, fireworks
335	FL 121, to Lake Butler, Macclenny, **N gas:** BP/dsl, Citgo, **food:** China Dragon, Domino's, Hardee's, KFC, McDonald's, Pier 6, Pizza Hut, Subway, Taco Bell, Waffle House, Wendy's, Woody's BBQ, Zaxby's, **lodging:** American Inn, **other:** H, Advance Parts, AutoZone, Curves, $General, $Tree, Food Lion, Radio Shack, Walgreens, Winn-Dixie, **S gas:** RaceWay, Exxon/dsl, **food:** Burger King, China Buffet, Down Home Cafe, **lodging:** Econolodge, Travelodge
333	rd 125, Glen Saint Mary, **N gas:** Citgo/dsl/24hr
327	rd 229, to Raiford, Sanderson, **1 mi N** gas
324	US 90, to Olustee, Sanderson, **S gas:** Citgo/dsl, to Olustee Bfd
318mm	**rest area both lanes, full facilities, vending, litter barrels, petwalk, 24hr security**
303	US 441, to Fargo, Lake City, **N gas:** Chevron/dsl/24hr, **other:** Lake City Camping (1mi), Oaks'n Pines RV Park, **S gas:** SuperTest/dsl, Shell/dsl, **food:** Huddle House, **lodging:** Day's Inn, **other:** H
301	US 41, to Lake City, **N gas:** Exxon/dsl, **other:** Kelly's RV Park (6mi), to Stephen Foster Ctr, **S other:** H
296b a	I-75, N to Valdosta, S to Tampa
294mm	**rest area both lanes, full facilities, vending, litter barrels, petwalk, 24hr security**
292	rd 137, to Wellborn
283	US 129, to Live Oak, **N gas:** Penn/dsl, to Boys Ranch, **S gas:** BP, Chevron, Shell/dsl, Texaco, **food:** China Buffet, Huddle House, Krystal, McDonald's, Subway, Taco Bell, Waffle House, Wendy's, **lodging:** Best Western, Econolodge, Holiday Inn Express, **other:** H, $Tree, Lowe's Whse, Walmart SuperCtr/gas/24hr
275	US 90, Live Oak, **N** to Suwannee River SP, **S other:** H
271mm	**weigh sta both lanes**

INTERSTATE 10 CONT'D

Exit #	Services
269mm	Suwannee River
265mm	**rest areas both lanes, full ♿ facilities, ☎, vending, picnic, litter barrels, petwalk, 24hr security**
264mm	**weigh sta both lanes**
262	rd 255, Lee, **N gas:** Exxon/dsl, **other:** to Suwannee River SP, **S gas:** Jimmy's/Citgo/Rest./dsl/24hr, Love's/Arby's/dsl/scales/24hr
258	FL 53, **N gas:** Shell/Burger King/dsl/24hr, Mobil/DQ/Subway/Wendy's/dsl/scales/24hr, **food:** Denny's, Waffle House, **lodging:** Day's Inn, Holiday Inn Express, Super 8, **other:** H, **S lodging:** Deerwood Inn, **other:** Jellystone Camping, Madison Camping
251	FL 14, to Madison, **N gas:** Mobil/Arby's/24hr, **other:** H
241	US 221, Greenville, **N gas:** Mobil/DQ
234mm	**rest area both lanes, full ♿ facilities, ☎, picnic, litter barrels, petwalk, 24hr security**
233	rd 257, Aucilla, **N gas:** Shell/dsl
225	US 19, to Monticello, **S gas:** BP, Chevron/McDonald's, Exxon/Wendy's, Mobil/Arby's/dsl, **food:** Huddle House, **lodging:** Day's Inn, Super 8, **other:** KOA, dogtrack
217	FL 59, Lloyd, **S gas:** BP/dsl/rest./scales/24hr, Shell/Subway/dsl, **lodging:** Quality Inn
209b a	US 90, Tallahassee, **S gas:** Circle K/dsl, Shell/Subway/dsl, **food:** Cross Creek Grill, Paulina's Pizza, Waffle House, **lodging:** Best Western, Country Inn&Suites, **other:** Publix, Tallahassee RV Park, car museum
203	FL 61, US 319, Tallahassee, **N gas:** BP/dsl, Shell/Circle K, USA Gas, **food:** Applebee's, Bonefish Grill, Firehouse Subs, Great Wall Chinese, Hungry Howie's, KFC, McDonald's, Moe's SW Grill Popeye's, Starbucks, Subway, Taco Bell, TCBY, Waffle House, Wendy's, **lodging:** Motel 6, **other:** Albertson's, BooksAMillion, CVS Drug, Discount Tire, Fresh Mkt Foods, GNC, Publix, Radio Shack, Sav-On, SteinMart, SuperLube, TJ Maxx, Walgreens, Walmart SuperCtr/24hr (3mi), **S gas:** Citgo, **food:** Boston Mkt, Carraba's, Chick-fil-A, Osaka Japanese, Outback Steaks, Quizno's, Steak'n Shake, Ted's MT Grill, TGIFriday, Village Inn, Zaxby's, **lodging:** Cabot Lodge, Courtyard, Hampton Inn, Hilton Garden, Residence Inn, Studio+, **other:** H, Advance Parts, Home Depot, Infiniti, Office Depot, PetsMart, Vet
199	US 27, Tallahassee, **N gas:** BP/dsl, Chevron/dsl, McKenzie/dsl, **food:** Burger King, Dominos, Pizza Hut, Taco Bell, Waffle House, **lodging:** Comfort Inn, Country Inn&Suites, Days Inn, Fairfield Inn, Holiday Inn, Microtel, Quality Inn, Sunshine State Inn, **other:** Big Oak RV Park (2mi), **S gas:** BP/24hr, Chevron/dsl, Shell, USA, **food:** Arby's, Boston Mkt, Burger King, Chick-fil-A, China Buffet, ChuckeCheese, Cracker Barrel, Crystal River Seafood, DQ, Firehouse Subs, Golden Corral, Hooters, Julie's Rest., KFC, Krispy Kreme, Longhorn Steaks, Los Compadres Mexican, McDonald's, On-the-Border, Papa John's, Qdoba Mexican, Quizno's, Red Lobster, Shoney's, Sonny's BBQ, Starbucks, Subway, TCBY, Whataburger, Wendy's, Zaxby's, **lodging:** Best Value Inn, Cabot Lodge, Econolodge, Howard Johnson, La Quinta,
199	Continued Ramada Inn, Red Roof Inn, Rodeway Inn, Super 8, Wingate Inn, **other:** Albertson's/Sav-On, AutoZone, Barnes&Noble, Big 10 Tire, CVS Drug, $Tree, Old Navy, Publix, Ross, Staples, Sun Tire, Tire Kingdom, Tuffy Auto, Walgreens, mall, Vet
196	FL 263, Tallahassee, **S gas:** BP, Chevron/dsl, Shell/dsl, Stop'n Save Gas, **food:** Applebee's, Firehouse Subs, KFC, Sonic, Steak'n Shake, Subway, Waffle House, Wendy's, Zaxby's, **lodging:** Sleep Inn, **other:** Aamco, Chrysler/Jeep/Dodge, Harley-Davidson, Home Depot, Lowe's Whse, Mazda, Walgreens, Walmart SuperCtr
194mm	**rest area both lanes, full ♿ facilities, ☎, vending, picnic, litter barrels, petwalk, 24hr security**
192	US 90, to Tallahassee, Quincy, **N gas:** BP, ***FLYING J***/Conoco/dsl/LP/scales/24hr, **lodging:** Comfort Inn, Howard Johnson, **S gas:** Pilot/Subway/dsl/scales/24hr, **food:** Waffle House, **lodging:** Best Western, **other:** Lakeside RV Park (4mi)
181	FL 267, Quincy, **N other:** H, Walmart Super Ctr/gas/24hr, **S gas:** BP/dsl, Pure, **lodging:** Hampton Inn, Holiday Inn Express, Parkway Inn, to Lake Talquin SP
174	FL 12, to Greensboro, **N gas:** BP, Shell/Burger King/dsl, **other:** Beaver Lake RV Park
166	rd 270A, Chattahoochee, **N** to Lake Seminole, to Torreya SP, **S gas:** Shell/dsl, **other:** KOA (1mi)
161mm	**rest area both lanes, full ♿ facilities, ☎, vending, picnic, litter barrels, petwalk, 24hr security**
160mm	Apalachicola River, central/eastern time zone
158	rd 286, Sneads, **N** Lake Seminole, to Three Rivers SP
155mm	**weigh sta both lanes**
152	FL 69, to Grand Ridge, **N gas:** BP, Exxon, **lodging:** Durdens Inn
142	FL 71, to Marianna, Oakdale, **N gas:** Pilot/Arby's/dsl/scales/24hr, **food:** Burger King, Firehouse Subs, KFC/LJ Silver, Pizza Hut, PoFolks, Ruby Tuesday, San Marco's Mexican, Sonny's BBQ, Waffle House, **lodging:** Comfort Inn, Country Inn&Suites, Hampton Inn, Holiday Inn Express, Microtel, Quality Inn, Super 8, **other:** H, $Tree, Lowes Whse, Radio Shack, Walmart SuperCtr/dsl/24hr, to FL Caverns SP (8mi), **S gas:** Chevron/dsl, Sunoco/dsl, TA/BP/dsl/rest./scales/24hr/@, **food:** McDonald's, **lodging:** Best Value Inn, **other:** camping
136	FL 276, to Marianna, **N other:** to FL Caverns SP (8mi)
133mm	**rest area both lanes, full ♿ facilities, ☎, picnic, litter barrels, petwalk, 24hr security**
130	US 231, Cottondale, **N gas:** BP/dsl, Chevron, **food:** Hardee's, Subway, **other:** Big Rig RV Park, **S gas:** RaceWay
120	FL 77, to Panama City, Chipley, **N gas:** BP/dsl, Exxon/Burger King, Petro/Domino's, **food:** Arby's, Hardee's, JJ's Kitchen, KFC, New Star Chinese, McDonald's, Pizza Hut, Sonic, Taco Bell, Waffle House, Wendy's, **lodging:** Comfort Inn, Day's Inn/rest., Executive Inn, Holiday Inn Express, Super 8, **other:** H, CVS Drug, $Tree, Save-a-Lot Foods, Walmart SuperCtr/gas/24hr, **S** Falling Water SRA
112	FL 79, Bonifay, **N gas:** Chevron, Exxon/dsl, Tom Thumb/dsl, **food:** Blitch's Rest., Burger King,

INTERSTATE 10 CONT'D

E ↕ W

Exit #	Services
112	Continued Hardee's, McDonald's, Pizza Hut, Simbo's Rest, Subway, Waffle House, **lodging:** Bonifay Inn, Economy Inn, Tivoli Inn, **other:** H, Fred's Drug
104	rd 279, Caryville
96	FL 81, Ponce de Leon, **N** to Ponce de Leon SRA, Vortex Spring Camping, **S gas:** BP/dsl/24hr, 87 Depot/Subway/dsl, Exxon/dsl, **other:** Ponce de Leon Motel, **rest area both lanes, full ♿ facilities, phone, picnic, litter barrels, petwalk, 24hr security**
85	US 331, De Funiak Springs, **N gas:** Chevron/24hr, **food:** Arby's, Beef O'Brady's, Burger King, LaRumba Mexican, McLain's Steaks, Pizza Hut, Sonic, Subway, Waffle House, **lodging:** Best Value Inn, Sundown Inn, Super 8, Travelodge, **other:** H, $General, Lowes Whse, Walgreens, Walmart SuperCtr/gas/24hr, Winn-Dixie, winery, **S gas:** BP, 87 Depot/dsl, Emerald Express/dsl, **food:** KFC, McDonald's, Whataburger, **lodging:** Best Western, **other:** H
70	FL 285, to Ft Walton Bch, Eglin AFB, **N gas:** RaceWay, **S other:** repair
60mm	**rest area both lanes, full ♿ facilities, phone, vending, picnic, litter barrels, petwalk, 24hr security**
56	FL 85, Crestview , Eglin AFB, **N gas:** BP/dsl, Mobil, Shell/dsl, **food:** Applebee's, Asian Garden, Beef O'Brady's, Burger King, Capt D's, Firehouse Subs, Lee's Chicken, McDonald's, Ryan's, Sonic, Starbucks, Taco Bell, **lodging:** Country Inn&Suites, Econolodge, **other:** H, Advance Parts, AutoZone, Big Lots, $General, Lowes Whse, Publix, Walgreens, Walmart SuperCtr/24hr, **S gas:** Exxon, Tom Thumb/dsl, **food:** Arby's, Coach-n-Four Steaks, Cracker Barrel, Hardee's, Hooters, LaRumba Mexican, Tokyo Rest., Waffle House, Wendy's, Whataburger, **lodging:** Comfort Inn, Day's Inn, Hampton Inn, Holiday Inn Express, Jameson Inn, Quality Inn, Super 8, **other:** Buick/Pontiac/GMC, Chrysler/Dodge/Jeep, Ford/Mercury, museum, RV camping
45	rd 189, to US 90, Holt, **N gas:** Chevron (1mi), **other:** to Blackwater River SP, Cozy Corner RV Park, Eagle's Landing RV Park, **S** River's Edge RV Park (1mi)
31	FL 87, to Ft Walton Beach, Milton, **N gas:** Exxon/Quizno's/dsl/24hr, **food:** Waffle House, **lodging:** Holiday Inn Express, **other:** Blackwater River SP, Gulf Pines Camping, KOA, **S gas:** BP, Shell/dsl, **lodging:** Comfort Inn, Red Carpet Inn
31mm	**rest area both lanes, full ♿ facilities, phone, picnic, litter barrels, petwalk, 24hr security**
28	rd 89, Milton, **N** H, **S** Cedar Lakes RV Camping (2mi)
27mm	Blackwater River
26	rd 191, Bagdad, Milton, **N gas:** Shell/Circle K/dsl, **other:** H, **S gas:** Chevron/DQ/Stuckey's, **other:** Pelican Palms RV Park
22	N FL 281, Avalon Blvd, **N gas:** BP/dsl, Tom Thumb, **food:** McDonald's, Oval Office Cafe, **S gas:** Shell/Subway/dsl, **food:** Waffle House, **lodging:** Red Roof Inn, **other:** By the Bay RV Park (3mi)
18mm	Escambia Bay

CRESTVIEW

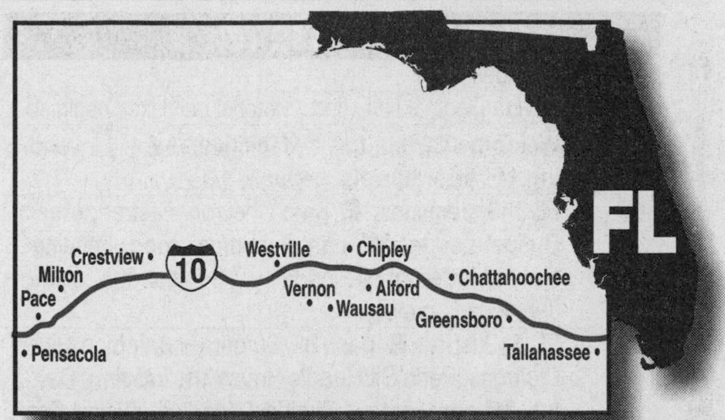

PENSACOLA

Exit #	Services
17	US 90, Pensacola, **N gas:** BP/dsl, **S gas:** Exxon, **food:** DQ, **lodging:** Ramada Inn/rest.
14mm	**truck inspection sta**
13	FL 291, to US 90, Pensacola, **N gas:** BP, Exxon, Shell/dsl, **food:** Arby's, Barnhill's Buffet, Capt D's, Denny's, La Hacienda Mexican, McDonald's, Starbucks, Subway, Taco Bell, Waffle House, **lodging:** Best Value Inn, Comfort Inn, Holiday Inn, La Quinta, Motel 6, Villager Inn, **other:** CVS Drug, Food World/24hr, Walgreens, **S food:** Bennigan's, ChuckeCheese, Fazoli's, Honeybaked Ham, Los Rancheros Mexican, O'Charley's, Steak&Ale, Waffle House, Wendy's, Whataburger, **lodging:** Clarion, Courtyard, Extended Stay America, Fairfield Inn, Hampton Inn, Motel 6, Red Roof Inn, Residence Inn, TownePlace Suites, **other:** H, Belk, Big 10 Tire, BooksaMillion, $General, Firestone/auto, JC Penney, Jo-Ann Fabrics, Pepboys, PetsMart, Sears/auto, TJ Maxx, Tuesday Morning, U-Haul, mall
12	I-110, to Pensacola, Hist Dist, Islands Nat Seashore
10b a	US 29, Pensacola, **N gas:** BP, Fleet/dsl/scales, **food:** Church's, Hardee's, Ryan's, Sonic, Waffle House, **other:** Advance Parts, AutoZone, Carpenter's RV Ctr, $Tree, GNC, Office Depot, O'Reilly Parts, Radio Shack, Tires+, Walmart SuperCtr/gas/24hr, **S gas:** RaceWay, Shell, **food:** Burger King, Capt D's, Founaris Bro's Rest., IHOP, Las Palma's Mexican, McDonald's, Ruby Tuesday, Smokey's BBQ, Wendy's, Whataburger, **lodging:** Best Value Inn, Day's Inn, Econolodge, Executive Inn, Howard Johnson, Hity Inn, Luxury Suites, Motel 6, Palm Court, Ramada Inn, Travelodge, **other:** Chevrolet, Ford, Harley-Davidson, Jeep, KIA, Leisure Tyme RV Ctr, Lincoln/Mercury, NAPA, Suzuki/Toyota
7b a	Fl 297, Pine Forest Rd, **N gas:** Chevron, **food:** Beef O'Brady's, Starbucks, Wendy's, **lodging:** Best Western, Comfort Inn, Garden Inn, Value Place, **other:** Albertson's/gas, Tall Oaks Camping, **S gas:** BP, Citgo, **food:** Burger King, Carnley's Diner, Cracker Barrel, Hardee's, McDonald's, Ruby Tuesday, Sonny's BBQ, Subway, Waffle House, **lodging:** Country Inn&Suites, Holiday Inn Express, Microtel, Quality Inn, Sleep Inn, **other:** Food World/24hr, Big Lagoon SRA (12mi), museum
5	US 90 A, **N gas:** BP, Fleet/Shell/Subway/dsl, **other:** Albertson's/gas, Walgreens, **S** Leisure Lakes Camping
4mm	**Welcome Ctr eb, full ♿ facilities, info, phone, vending, picnic, litter barrels, petwalk, 24hr security**
3mm	**weigh sta both lanes**
1mm	**inspection sta eb**
0mm	Florida/Alabama state line, Perdido River

PENSACOLA

INTERSTATE 75

Exit #	Services
471mm	Florida/Georgia state line., Motorist callboxes begin sb.
469mm	**Welcome Ctr sb, full ♿ facilities, info, ☎, vending, 🅿, litter barrels, petwalk**
467	FL 143, Jennings, **E gas:** Chevron, Fastrac, **other:** Budget Lodge, **W gas:** Exxon/dsl, **food:** Jennings House, **lodging:** N Florida Inn, Scottish Inn, **other:** Jennings Camping
460	FL 6, Jasper, **E gas:** BP/Burger King, Indian River Fruit/gas, Penn Oil/Huddle House/dsl, **lodging:** Day's Inn, **W gas:** Fastrac, Shell/dsl, **food:** Sheffield's Catfish, **lodging:** Scottish Inn, **other:** Suwanee River SP
451	US 129, Jasper, Live Oak, **E gas:** Mobil/DQ/Subway/dsl, **W gas:** BP/Cowboys BBQ/dsl, **other:** Suwanee Music Park (4mi), to FL Boys Ranch
448mm	**weigh sta both lanes**
446mm	**insp sta both lanes**
443mm	Historic Suwanee River
439	to FL 136, White Springs, Live Oak, **E gas:** Fastrac, Gate/dsl, Shell/dsl, **food:** Kitchen, McDonald's, **lodging:** Scottish Inn, **other:** Kelly RV Park (5mi), Lee's Camping (3mi), Suwanee RV Camping (4mi), to S Foster Ctr, **W lodging:** Best Value Inn
435	I-10, E to Jacksonville, W to Tallahassee
427	US 90, to Live Oak, Lake City, **E gas:** BP, Chevron/dsl/24hr, Exxon, Gas'n Go/Subway, Murphy USA, Shell, **food:** Applebee's, Arby's, Burger King, Cazbor's Grille, Cedar River Seafood, Coolwater Grille, Cracker Barrel, Domino's, Elliano's Coffee, El Potro, Hardee's, IHOP, Ken's BBQ, KFC, Krystal, McDonald's, Moe's SW Grill, Ole Times Buffet, Pizza Hut, Red Lobster, Ruby Tuesday, Sonny's BBQ, Starbucks, Steak&Shake, Subway, Taco Bell, TX Roadhouse, Waffle House, Wendy's, Zaxby's, **lodging:** Best Inn, Cypress Inn, Day's Inn, Driftwood Inn, Holiday Inn, Howard Johnson, Jameson Inn, Knight's Inn, Piney Woods Motel, Ramada Ltd, Rodeway Inn, Scottish Inn, **other:** H, Advance Parts, AutoZone, Belk, CVS Drug, Ford/Lincoln/Mercury, , Home Depot, JC Penney, Lowe's Whse, Publix, Radio Shack, Tire Kingdom, Walgreens, Walmart SuperCtr/24hr, In&Out RV Park, mall, **W gas:** BP, Chevron, Citgo, Shell, **food:** Bob Evans, Shoney's, Subway, Waffle House, **lodging:** Best Western, Comfort Suites, Country Inn&Suites, Econolodge, Fairfield Inn, Gateway Inn, Hampton Inn, Motel 6, Quality Inn, Red Roof Inn, Travelodge, White Swan Inn, **other:** Chevrolet/Mazda, Chrysler/Dodge, Vet
423	FL 47, to Ft White, Lake City, **E gas:** Shell/dsl, **other:** Mack Trucks/Volvo, **W gas:** BP/dsl, Exxon/dsl, **food:** Little Caesar's, Subway, **lodging:** Motel 8, Super 8, **other:** Casey Jones Camping, Freightliner, Never Dunn (6mi), USPO
414	US 41, US 441, to Lake City, High Springs, **E gas:** Chevron/dsl/24hr, Pitstop/gas, Texaco, **lodging:** Traveler's Inn, Travelodge, **W gas:** BP/dsl, Shell/dsl, **food:** Huddle House, Subway, **lodging:** Econolodge, **other:** antiques, tires, to O'Leno SP
413mm	**rest areas both lanes, full ♿ facilities, ☎, vending, 🅿, litter barrels, petwalk**
409mm	Santa Fe River
404	rd 236, to High Springs, **E gas:** Chevron/fruits/gifts, Citgo/dsl, Sunoco, **W** High Sprs Camping
399	US 441, to High Sprs, Alachua, **E gas:** BP, **food:** Dominos, McDonald's, Moe's SW Grill, Pizza Hut, Sonny's BBQ, Subway, Waffle House, **lodging:** Econolodge, Quality Inn, **other:** Advance Parts, Family$, FoodLion, Hitchcock's Foods, Traveler's Campground (1mi), **W gas:** Chevron, Citgo/Taco Bell/dsl, Exxon/Wendy's, **food:** Kazbor's Grille, KFC, **lodging:** Day's Inn, Royal Inn
390	FL 222, to Gainesville, **E gas:** Chevron/dsl, Exxon/McDonald's/dsl, Kangaroo/dsl, **food:** Burger King, La Fiesta Mexican, Pomodoro Cafe, Sonnys BBQ, Wendy's, **other:** Publix, Walgreens, **W gas:** BP/DQ/dsl, **lodging:** Best Western, **other:** Harley-Davidson, Jeep/Mercedes, auto repair, Vet
387	FL 26, to Newberry, Gainesville, **E gas:** BP, Chevron, Sunoco, Shell/dsl, **food:** Bono's BBQ, Boston Mkt, Buffet City, Burger King, Dunkin Donuts, FoodCourt, LJ Silver, Macaroni Grill, McAlister's Deli, McDonald's, Perkins, Red Lobster, Ruby Tuesday, Starbucks, Subway, Wendy's, **lodging:** La Quinta, **other:** H, Belk, BooksAMillion, Borders Books, Dillard's, JC Penney, Macy's, Office Depot, PetCo, Sears/auto, Steinmart, to UFL, mall, **W gas:** BP, Chevron/dsl, Exxon/dsl, Mobil/dsl/LP, **food:** El Nortino's Mexican, KFC, Krystal, Macaroni Grill, Moe's SW Grill, Napolatanos Rest., Taco Bell, Waffle House, Whataburger, **lodging:** Clarion, Day's Inn, Econolodge, Fairfield Inn, **other:** Advance Parts, $Tree, Goodyear/auto, Home Depot, JoAnn Fabrics, K-Mart, PepBoys, Publix, TJ Maxx, Walgreens, Winn-Dixie, tires/repair, Vet
384	FL 24, to Archer, Gainesville, **E gas:** BP, Chevron/dsl/24hr, Citgo, Exxon/dsl, Shell, **food:** Arby's, Atlanta Bread, BoneFish Grill, Burger King, Capt D's, Checker's, Chick-fil-A, Chili's, Chipotle Mexican, Ci-Ci's Pizza, Coldstone Creamery, DQ, Firehouse Subs, Gainesville Alehouse, Hooters, KFC, McAlister's Deli, McDonald's, Moe's SW Grill, Olive Garden, On-the-Border, OutBack Steaks, Panera Bread, Papa John's, Pizza Hut, Shoney's, Sonny's BBQ, Starbucks, Steak'n Shake, Subway, Taco Bell, TX Roadhouse, TGIFriday, Zaxby's, **lodging:** Cabot Lodge, Comfort Inn, Courtyard, Extended Stay America, Hampton Inn, Motel 6, Red Roof Inn, Sleep Inn, SpringHill Suites, Super 8, **other:** Albertson's, Barnes&Noble, Best Buy, CarQuest, CVS Drug, Firestone/auto, GNC, Kohls, Lowe's Whse, Michael's, Old Navy, PetsMart, Publix, Radio Shack, Ross, Target, Walmart, **W gas:** Mobil/dsl, **food:** Cracker Barrel, **lodging:** Country Inn&Suites, Holiday Inn Express, **other:** Sunshine RV Park, to Bear Museum
382	FL 121, to Williston, Gainesville, **E gas:** Citgo/dsl/24hr, Mobil/dsl, **food:** First Wok, McDonalds, Subway, **lodging:** Travelodge, **other:** Publix, **W gas:** BP/dsl, Chevron/dsl/24hr, Kangaroo/dsl, **food:** 43rd St Deli, **lodging:** Quality Inn, Rodeway Inn, **other:** Fred Bear Museum
381mm	**rest areas both lanes, full ♿ facilities, ☎, vending, 🅿, litter barrels, petwalk, 24hr security**
374	rd 234, Micanopy, **E gas:** BP, Chevron/dsl, **other:** antiques, fruit, to Paynes Prairie SP, **W gas:** Micanopy/repair, Texaco, **lodging:** Knight's Inn

N ↕ S

SILVER SPRINGS OCALA

INTERSTATE 75 CONT'D

Exit #	Services
368	rd 318, Orange Lake, **E gas:** Chevron, Jim's/BBQ, Petro/Mobil/dsl/scales/24hr/@, **food:** Wendy's, **other:** Grand Lake RV Park (3mi), **W** Ocala N RV Camping
358	FL 326, **E gas:** BP/FL Citrus Ctr/dsl, Mobil/McDonald's/dsl, Pilot/Arby's/dsl/scales/24hr, Pilot/Wendy's/dsl/24hr, **other:** Freightliner, auto/truck repair, **W gas:** Chevron/dsl, **food:** DQ
354	US 27, to Silver Springs, Ocala, **E gas:** BP/24hr, RaceTrac, **food:** Burger King, Rascal's BBQ, **lodging:** Golden Palms Inn, **W gas:** BP/dsl, Chevron, Texaco, **food:** Barbazon's Grill, Blanca's Cafe, Waffle House, **lodging:** Budget Host, Comfort Suites, Day's Inn, Howard Johnson, Ramada, **other:** Ace Hardware, $General, Nelson's Trailers, Oaktree Village Camping, Publix, Walgreens, Winn-Dixie
352	FL 40, to Silver Springs, Ocala, **E gas:** BP/dsl, Chevron, Citgo, RaceTrac/24hr, **food:** Dunkin Donuts, McDonald's, Pizza Hut/Taco Bell, Subway, Wendy's, Whataburger/24hr, **lodging:** Day's Inn/café, Economy Inn, GS RV Park, Motor Inn/RV, Quality Inn, **other:** park, fruits, **W gas:** Shell/dsl, Texaco, **food:** Denny's, Golden Coast Buffet, Waffle House, **lodging:** Red Roof Inn, Super 8, Travelodge, **other:** Gander Mtn, Holiday Trav-L Park, Vet
350	FL 200 , to Hernando, Ocala, **E gas:** BP, Chevron, Citgo/repair, Kangaroo, RaceWay, Texaco/dsl, **food:** Applebee's, Arby's, Backyard Burger, Bob Evans, Boston Mkt, Burger King, Carrabba's, Checkers, Chick-fil-A, Chili's, ChuckeCheese, Cici's Pizza, Crisper's, Coldstone Creamery, Domino's, El Toreo Mexican, Fazoli's, Firehouse Subs, Flipside Cafe, Golden Corral, Grand Buffet, Hooters, Krystal, Lee's Chicken, Little Caesars, Logan's Roadhouse, McDonald's, Olive Garden, Outback Steaks, Papa John's, Panera Bread, Perkins, PetsMart, Pizza Hut, Red Lobster, Roadhouse Grill, Ruby Tuesday, Smoothie King, Starbucks, Sonic, Sonny's BBQ, Subway, Taco Bell, Wendy's, Whataburger, Zaxby's, **lodging:** Country Inn Suites, Hampton Inn, Hilton, La Quinta, **other:** H, Acura, Advance Parts, Aldi Foods, Belk, Best Buy, Buick, Chevrolet/Nissan, CVS Drug, Discount Tire, Dodge, $General, Goodyear/auto, Home Depot, JC Penney, JoAnn Fabrics, Kia, K-Mart, Kohl's, Lowe's Whse, Macy's, Michael's, Office Depot, Pep-Boys, PetsMart, Publix, Ross, Sears, Staples, Steinmart, Suzuki, Target, Tire Kingdom, TJ Maxx, Toyota, Walgreens, Walmart SuperCtr/24hr, fruits, mall, **W gas:** BP/24hr, Chevron/24hr, Shell, **food:** Bonefish Grill, Burger King, Cracker Barrel, Dunkin Donuts, KFC, Mimi's Cafe, Panera Bread, Stabucks, Steak'n Shake/24hr, Waffle House, **lodging:** Best Western, Courtyard, Fairfield Inn, Holiday Inn, Homewood Suites, Residence Inn, **other:** Barnes&Noble, BMW/posrche, Cadillac, Camper Village RV Park, Dillards, Kohl's, Ocala RV Park, Old Navy, PetCo, Pontiac, Sam's Club/gas, Tires+, Walgreens, Vet
346mm	**rest area both lanes, full ♿ facilities, ☎, vending, picnic, litter barrels, petwalk, 24hr security**
341	FL 484, to Belleview, **E gas:** Chevron/fruit/24hr, Citgo/Dunkin Donuts, Exxon/dsl, Shell, **food:** Cracker Barrel, Sonny's BBQ, Zaxby's, **lodging:** Microtel,

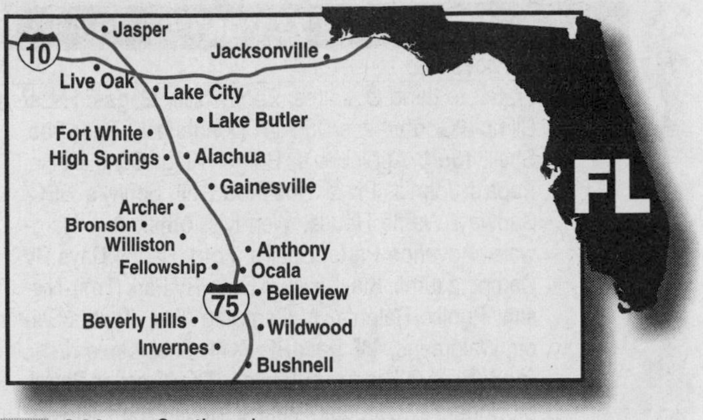

INVERNESS

DADE CITY

Exit #	Services
341	Continued Sleep Inn, **other:** FL Citrus Ctr, museums, **W gas:** BP/repair, Pilot/Arby's/DQ/dsl/scales/24hr, **food:** McDonald's, Waffle House, **other:** Ocala Ranch RV Park, outlets
338mm	**weigh sta both lanes**
329	FL 44, to Inverness, Wildwood, **E gas:** Gate/Steak'n Shake/dsl, Mobil/dsl, Sunoco, **food:** Burger King, Denny's, DQ, McDonald's, Waffle House, Wendy's, **other: other:** FL Citrus Ctr, Three Flags RV Resort (1mi), KOA, **W gas:** Citgo/dsl/repair/24hr, Pilot/dsl/24hr/scales, TA/BP/Pizza Hut/Subway/Popeye's/scales/dsl/24hr/@, **food:** IHOP, KFC, **lodging:** Day's Inn/rest., Economy Inn, Super 8, Wildwood Inn, **other:** truckwash, truck repair
328	FL TPK (from sb), to Orlando
321	rd 470, to Sumterville, Lake Panasoffkee, **E gas:** Spirit/deli/scales/dsl/rest./24hr, **other:** Coleman Correctional, **W gas:** BP/Hardee's/Subway/dsl, Chevron/7-11, **other:** Countryside RV Park (1mi), Turtleback RV Resort (1mi)
314	FL 48, to Bushnell, **E gas:** BP/dsl, Citgo, Murphy USA, Shell/Circle K/Subway, **food:** Four-Season Chinese, KFC/Taco Bell, Little Caesars, McDonald's, Wendy's, **lodging:** Rodeway Inn, **other:** BlueBerry Hill RV Camp, Red Barn RV Camp, The Oaks Camp (1mi), Walmart SuperCtr, to Dade Bfd HS, **W gas:** Shell/dsl, Sunoco/dsl, **food:** Beef O'Brady's, Sonny's BBQ, Waffle House, **lodging:** Microtel, **other:** Flagship RV Ctr
309	rd 476, to Webster, **E** Breezy Oaks RV Park (1mi), Sumter Oaks RV Park (1mi)
307mm	**rest areas both lanes, full ♿ facilities, ☎, coffee, vending, picnic, litter barrels, petwalk, 24hr security**
301	US 98, FL 50, to Dade City, **E gas:** BP, RaceTrac, Sunoco, **food:** Arbys, Beef O'Brady's, Cracker Barrel, Denny's, McDonald's, Quinzo's, Waffle House, Wendy's, **lodging:** Day's Inn, Holiday Inn Express, **other:** H (10mi), Advance Parts, Curves, $General, Tall Pines RV Park, Winn-Dixie, USPO, **W gas:** Chevron/Subway/dsl, **food:** Burger King, **lodging:** Best Western, Hampton Inn, Microtel
293	rd 41, to Dade City, **E gas:** Citgo (2mi), **other:** to Sertoma Youth Ranch, **W other:** Travelers Rest Resort RV Park
285	FL 52, to Dade City, New Port Richey, **E gas:** ***FLYING J***/Country Mkt/dsl/LP/scales/24hr, **other:** H, **W gas:** Citgo/dsl/scales/24hr, **food:** Waffle House

FL

INTERSTATE 75 CONT'D

N ↕ S

Exit #	Services
279	FL 54, to Land O' Lakes, Zephyrhills, **E gas:** Hess/Blimpie/Godfather's/Dunkin Donuts/dsl, RaceTrac, Shell, **food:** Applebee's, Burger King, Gona China, Papa's John's, Pizza Hut/Taco Bell, Sonny's BBQ, Subway, Waffle House, Wendy's, **other:** Ace Hardware, Advance Parts, Beall's, Ford, Happy Days RV Camping (9mi), Kia, Leasure Days RV Park (7mi), Nissan, Publix, Ralph's RV Camping (7mi), Toyota/Scion, Walgreens, **W gas:** BP, 7-11, Shell/Circle K/dsl, **food:** Beef O'Brady's, Buffalo's, DQ, Cracker Barrel, McDonald's, Outback Steaks, Remington's Steaks, Shanghai Chinese, SW Cafe, **lodging:** Best Western, Comfort Inn, Holiday Inn Express, Sleep Inn, **other:** Best Buy, CVS Drug, $Tree, Encore RV Camping, Goodyear/auto, Honda, Hyundai, Mazda, Michael's, PetsMart, Quail Run RV Camping, Ross, SweetBay Foods, TJ Maxx, USPO
278mm	**rest areas both lanes, full [handicapped] facilities, [phone], vending, [picnic], litter barrels, petwalk, 24hr security**
275	FL 56
274	I-275 (from sb), to Tampa, St Petersburg
270	rd 581, Bruce B Downs Blvd, **E gas:** Citgo/7-11, Hess/Blimpie/Godfather's/dsl, Mobil, Shell/Taco Bell/dsl, **food:** Bennigan's, Boston Mkt, Burger King, Chick-fil-A, Chili's, Coldstone Creamery, DQ, Golden China, KFC, Liang's Asian Bistro, Macaroni Grill, McDonald's, Moe's SW Grill, Panera Bread, Papa John's, Quizno's, Ruby Tuesday, Selmon's Cafe, Starbucks, Subway, **lodging:** Holiday Inn Express, Wingate Inn, **other:** Home Depot, Kauffman's Tire, Michael's, Panera Bread, Publix, Walgreens, **W gas:** Citgo/7-11, **food:** McDonald's, Olive Garden, Red Lobster, Stonewood Grill, **other:** BJ's Whse, Lowe's Whse
266	rd 582A, Fletcher Ave, **W gas:** Shell/Circle K/dsl, **food:** Baskin Robbins/Dunkin Donuts, Bob Evans, Lenny's Subs, Starbucks, Wendy's, **lodging:** Courtyard, Extended Stay America, Fairfield Inn, Hampton Inn, Hilton Garden, La Quinta, Residence Inn, Sleep Inn, **other:** [H]
265	FL 582, Fowler Ave, Temple Terrace, **E other:** Happy Traveler RV Park, flea mkt, **W gas:** BP, Chevron/dsl, **food:** IHOP, **lodging:** Ramada Inn, **other:** NAPA Auto Care, UHaul
261	I-4, W to Tampa, E to Orlando
260b a	FL 574, to Mango, Tampa, **E gas:** Chevron/24hr, Citgo, Shell/Circle K/Subway/24hr, **food:** Dunkin Donuts/Baskin-Robbins, China Wok, Quizno's, Waffle House, **other:** SweetBay Foods, Walgreens, **W gas:** BP, Mystik, **lodging:** Crowne Plaza Hotel, Hilton Garden, Residence Inn
257	FL 60, Brandon, **E gas:** Citgo, Mobil, **food:** Arby's, Brandon Ale House, Boston Mkt, Buddy Freddy, Cheescake Factory, Chili's, China Buffet, Chuck-eCheese, Cody's Roadhouse, Denny's, DQ, Dunkin Donuts, Firehouse Subs, Fuego Steaks, Hungry Howie's, Kabuki Japanese, Macaroni Grill, Moe's SW Grill, Olive Garden, Outback Steaks, Panda Express, Panera Bread, Papa John's, Picadilly's, Red Lobster, Smokey Bones BBQ, Subway, Village Inn, Waffle House, Wendy's, **lodging:** Holiday Inn Express, HomeStead Suites, La Quinta, **other:** [H], Aamco,
257	Continued Advance Parts, Barnes&Noble, Best Buy, Books A Million, Curves, CVS Drug, Dillard's, $General, Firestone/auto, JC Penney, Jo-Ann Fabrics, Kia, Kohl's, K-Mart, Macy's, Marshall's, Michael's, Office Depot, PepBoys, PetCo, Radio Shack, Ross, Sam's Club, Sears/auto, Staples, Target, Tires+, TJ Maxx, Tuffy Auto, Uhaul, mall, **E on Causeway Blvd...gas:** Hess, **food:** Buca Italian, Longhorn Steaks, McDonald's, Quizno's, Starbucks, Steak'n Shake, **other:** Cadillac, Costco/gas, JoAnne, Kohl's, PetsMart, Publix, Walmart SuperCtr, **W gas:** Citgo, Marathon, Shell, **food:** Beef O'Brady's, Bob Evans, Burger King, Hooters, McDonald's, Sonny's BBQ, Subway, Sweet Tomatoes, Wendy's, **lodging:** Best Western, Comfort Inn, Country Inn & Suites, Courtyard, Day's Inn, Embassy Suites, Fairfield Inn, Homewood Suites, La Quinta, Red Roof Inn, **other:** Buick/Pontiac/GMC, Chevrolet, Chrysler/Dodge/Jeep, Harley-Davidson, Home Depot, Honda, KIA, Mazda, Mitsubishi/Hyundai/Suzuki, Nissan, Office Depot, Toyota/Scion, VW
256	FL 618 W (toll), to Tampa
254	US 301, Riverview, **S gas:** RaceTrac, **food:** Steak'n Shake, **other:** CVS Drug, Home Depot, Super Target, **W gas:** Circle K, 7-11/dsl, Shell, **food:** Subway, **lodging:** Hilton Garden
250	Gibsonton Dr, Riverview, **E gas:** RaceWay, 7-11, **food:** Burger King, DQ, Little Caesars, McDonald's, New China, Pizza Hut, Quizno's, Ruby Tuesday, Subway, Taco Bell, Wendy's, **other:** Alafia River RV Resort, Beall's, CVS Drug, Family$, Hidden River RV Resort (4mi), Lowe's Whse, Winn-Dixie, USPO, **W gas:** BP, Murphy USA, **other:** Walmart SuperCtr
246	FL 672, Big Bend Rd, Apollo Bch, **E gas:** Hess/dsl, 7-11, **food:** Applebees, Beef O'Brady's, Buffalo Wild Wings, China Taste, CiCi's Pizza, East Coast Pizza, Five Guys Burgers, Little Caesars, McDonald's, Panera Bread, Papa John's, Sonic, Starbucks, Subway, Qdoba, Quizno's, Village Inn Rest., Vocelli, **other:** Ace Hardware, Advance Parts, Beall's, Goodyear/auto, Publix, Sweetbay Foods, **W gas:** Chevron, 7-11
240b a	FL 674, Sun City Ctr, Ruskin, **E Visitors Ctr, gas:** Shell, **food:** Beef O' Brady's, Bob Evans, Burger King, Checker's, Denny's, King Buffet, Pizza Hut, Sonny's BBQ, Taco Bell, Wendy's, **lodging:** Comfort Inn, **other:** [H], Beall's, GNC, Home Depot, Radio Shack, SweetBay Foods, SunLake RV Resort (1mi), to Little Manatee River SP, **W gas:** Circle K/dsl, Hess/dsl, RaceTrac, **food:** China Wok, Domino's, KFC, McDonald's, Ozzie's Buffet, Subway, **lodging:** Holiday Inn Express, **other:** CVS Drug, NAPA, auto repair
237mm	**rest area both lanes, full [handicapped] facilities, [phone], vending, [picnic], litter barrels, petwalk, 24hr security**
229	rd 683, Moccasin Wallow Rd, to Parrish, **E** Little Manatee Sprs SRA (10mi), **W other:** Circle K, Fiesta Grove RV Park (3mi), Frog Creek RV Park (3mi), Terra Ceia RV Village (2mi), Winterset RV Park (3mi)
228	I-275 N, to St Petersburg
224	US 301, to Bradenton, Ellenton, **E gas:** BP, Chevron/24hr, RaceWay, Shell/dsl, **food:** Applebee's, Checker's, Kings Wok, Hungry Howie's, McDonald's, Ruby Tuesday, Sonic, Wendy's, Woody's River Grill, **lodging:** Hampton Inn, Sleep Inn, **other:** Ace

INTERSTATE 75 CONT'D

N ↕ S

BRADENTON

Exit #	Services
224	Continued Hardware, Beall's, $Tree, Just Brakes, K-Mart, Publix, Walgreens, USPO, Prime Outlets/famous brands, **W gas:** Pilot/dsl, **food:** Anna Maria's, Crabtrap Seafood, Waffle House, **lodging:** GuestHouse Inn, Ramada Ltd
220b a	FL 64, to Zolfo Springs, Bradenton, **E** Lake Manatee SRA, **W gas:** BP/dsl, Citgo/dsl/24hr, RaceTrac, Shell/Circle K/dsl, **food:** Burger King, Cracker Barrel, Dunkin Donuts, Friendly's, KFC/LJ Silver, McDonald's, Sonny's BBQ, Subway, Waffle House, Wendy's, **lodging:** Budget Inn, Comfort Inn, Day's Inn, Econolodge, Holiday Inn Express, Motel 6, **other:** H, Dream RV Ctr, Encore RV Resort (1mi), Harley-Davidson, Walmart SuperCtr
217b a	FL 70, to Arcadia, **E gas:** Hess/Blimpie/Godfather's/dsl/24hr, **food:** Crisper's Salads, **other:** Goodyear/auto, Sweetbay Foods, **W gas:** BP/dsl/LP, Circle K, 7-11/dsl, Shell/Circle K, **food:** Applebee's, Arby's, Bob Evans, Chick-fil-A, Hungry Howie's, LJ Silver, McDonald's, Papa John's, Starbucks, Subway, Taco Bell, **other:** Beall's, CVS Drug, Lowe's Whse, Macy's, Publix, Tire Kingdom, Tires+, HorseShoe RV Park, Pleasant Lake RV Resort, Publix, Vet
213	University Parkway, to Sarasota, **E gas:** Mobil/dsl, **food:** Broken Egg Rest., Chili's, Monty's Pizza, Pizza Hut, **lodging:** Fairfield Inn, Holiday Inn, **other:** GNC, Publix, Walgreens, **W food:** Altanta Bread, Bellacino's, BoneFish Grill, Carrabba's, Five Guys Burgers, Moe's SW Grill, Ruby Tuesday, Starbucks, Stonewood Grill, Wendy's, **lodging:** Comfort Suites, **other:** Beall's, Best Buy, BJ's Whse, CVS Drug, Fresh Mkt Foods, Home Depot, Kohl's, Michael's, Ringling Museum, Staples, Super Target
210	FL 780, Fruitville Rd, Sarasota, **1 mi E other:** Sun'n Fun RV Park (1mi), **W gas:** BP/dsl/LP, Mobil/dsl, RaceTrac, Shell, **food:** Applebee's, Bob Evans, Burger King, Checker's, Chick-fil-A, Dunkin Donuts, Rest, KFC, Longhorn Steaks, McDonald's, Perkins, Quizno's, Subway, Taco Bell, Wings'n Weenies, **lodging:** AmericInn, Homewood Suites (2mi), **other:** Advance Parts, $Tree, Curves, CVS Drug, GNC, Lowe's Whse, Publix, Radio Shack, Sam's Club, Target, Winn-Dixie
207	FL 758, Sarasota, **W gas:** BP, Shell/Subway, **food:** Arby's, Chili's, Bella Cucina Italian, Grand China Buffet, Grand China, Italian Buffet, MadFish Grill, McDonald's, Panera Bread, Pizza Hut, Sarasota Alehouse, Steak'n Shake, Sugar&Spice, Taco Bell, Tuesday Morning, **lodging:** Hampton Inn, **other:** H, Beall's, $Tree, Goodyear/auto, Home Depot, Publix, Selby Botanical Gardens (8mi), Tuesday Morning, Walgreens, Walmart, Vet
205	FL 72, to Arcadia, Sarasota, **E** Myakka River SP (9mi), **W gas:** BP/dsl, Exxon/dsl, Mobil, 7-11/dsl, **food:** Applebee's, Burger King, Chick-fil-A, Dunkin Donuts, Firehouse Subs, Gecko's Grill, McDonald's, Quizno's, Starbucks, Subway, Waffle House, Wendy's, Wings & Weenies, **lodging:** Comfort Inn, Country Inn & Suites, Days Inn, **other:** Beall's, BMW, CVS Drug, Jaguar, Land Rover, Lexus, Mercedes, Publix, Tire Kingdom, USPO, Walgreens, Windward Isle RV Park, Vet

SARASOTA

SARASOTA

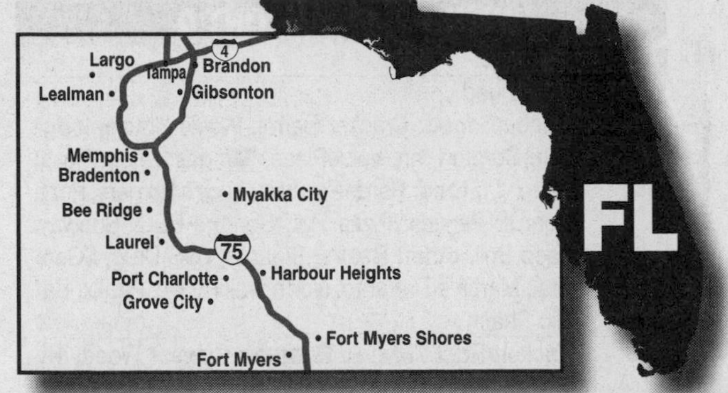

VENICE

Exit #	Services
200	FL 681 S (from sb), to Venice, Osprey, Gulf Bchs
195	Laurel Rd, Nokomis, **E gas:** BP/dsl, **other:** Stay'n Play RV Park (1mi), USPO, **W other:** Encore RV Park (2mi), Scherer SP (6mi)
193	Jaracanda Blvd, Venice, **W gas:** Citgo/Subway/dsl/24hr, Hess/Blimpie/Godfather's/dsl, RaceTrac, **food:** Cracker Barrel, McDonald's, Ping's Chinese, Waffle House, **lodging:** Best Western, Holiday Inn Express, **other:** H, CVS Drug, Publix
191	rd 777, Venice Rd, to Inglewood, **W other:** Encore RV Park (3mi), Venice Campground (1mi), to Myakka SF (9mi)
182	Sumter Blvd, to North Port, **2mi W gas:** Hess/Quizno's, **other:** Publix
179	Toledo Blade Blvd, North Port, **1-2 mi W gas:** Shell, **food:** Quizno's, **other:** Publix
170	rd 769, to Arcadia, Port Charlotte, **E gas:** Murphy USA, RaceTrac, 7-11/dsl, **food:** Applebees, **lodging:** Hampton Inn, Holiday Inn Express, **other:** Lettuce Lake Camping (7mi), Riverside Camping (5mi), Walmart SuperCtr, **W gas:** Hess/dsl, Chevron/dsl, 7-11/Subway/DQ/dsl, Shell/Circle K, **food:** Brick House Pizza, Burger King, Cracker Barrel, Domino's, DQ, McDonald's, Quizno's, Taco Bell/Pizza Hut, Waffle House, Wendy's, **lodging:** Country Inn & Suites, La Quinta, **other:** H, Ace Hardware, Advance Parts, Beall's, Curves, CVS Drug, $General, GNC, Publix, USPO, Walgreens, Winn-Dixie
167	rd 776, Port Charlotte
164	US 17, Punta Gorda, Arcadia, **E gas:** Chevron/dsl, RaceWay, Shell/dsl/24hr, **food:** King House Chinese, Subway, **other:** $General, KOA (2mi), Winn-Dixie, **W gas:** Shell/Circle K, **food:** Fisherman's Village Rest. (2mi), **lodging:** Best Western (2mi), **other:** H, Vet
161	FL 768, Punta Gorda, **E rest area both lanes, full facilities, vending, litter barrels, petwalk, 24hr security,** Waters Edge RV Park (2mi), **W gas:** BP/DQ/Subway/dsl, Murphy USA, Pilot/Arby's/dsl/scales/24hr, Sunoco/Quizno's, **food:** Burger King, McDonald's, Paradise Cafe, Pizza Hut, Waffle House, Wendy's, **lodging:** Day's Inn, Motel 6, **other:** Encore RV Park (2mi), Walmart SuperCtr
160mm	**weigh sta both lanes**
158	rd 762, **E** Babcock-Wells Wildlife Mgt Area, **W** Tamiami RV Camping (12mi)
143	FL 78, to Cape Coral, N Ft Myers, **E gas:** Marathon/dsl, **W gas:** RaceTrac/dsl/24hr, **food:** AZ Pizza, **lodging:** Encore RV Camping
141	FL 80, Palm Bch Blvd, Ft Myers, **E gas:** Citgo,

PUNTA GORDA

FL

INTERSTATE 75 CONT'D

N ↕ S

Exit #	Services
141	Continued Sunoco, **food:** Cracker Barrel, Waffle House, **lodging:** Comfort Inn, ValuePlace, **W gas:** Citgo, Hess/dsl, 7-11, **food:** Hardee's, Juicy Lucy's Burgers, Papa John's, Perkins, Pizza Hut, Sonny's BBQ, Subway, Taco Bell, **other:** Beall's, BigLots, CVS Drug, $General, Martin's Tire/auto, North Trail RV Ctr, Publix, Radio Shack
139	Luckett Rd, Ft Myers, **E other:** Cypress Woods RV Resort, Mark's RV Ctr, **W gas:** Pilot/Subway/dsl/scales/24hr/@, **other:** Camping World RV Service/supplies, Lazy J's RV Park
138	FL 82, to Lehigh Acres, Ft Myers, **E food:** Subway, **W gas:** Citgo/dsl, Sunoco
136	FL 884, Colonial Blvd, Ft Myers, **E lodging:** Candlewood Suites, **food:** Five Guys Burgers, Starbucks, **other:** Best Buy, Books-A-Million, Home Depot, PetCo, Ross, Staples, Target, **W gas:** BP, Marathon/Subway, Murphy USA, Shell/Circle K/dsl, **food:** Applebees, Bob Evans, Chick-fil-A, Golden Corral, McDonald's, Steak'n Shake, **other:** H, Beall's, Honda, Kohl's, Lowe's Whse, Tire Choice/auto, Walmart SuperCtr
131	Daniels Pkwy, to Cape Coral, **E rest area both lanes, full ♿ facilities, ☎, vending, picnic, litter barrels, petwalk, 24hr security, gas:** BP/Subway/dsl, **food:** Cracker Barrel, Starbucks, **lodging:** AmericInn, Comfort Inn, WynStar Inn, ✈, **W gas:** Chevron/dsl, Hess/Krispy Kreme/dsl, RaceTrac/24hr, 7-11/24hr, Shell/Circle K/24hr, **food:** Arby's, Bella Rica Italian, Burger King, DQ, Denny's, J. Daniels Grill, McDonald's, New China, Taco Bell, Uno Pizzaria, Waffle House, Wendy's, **lodging:** Best Western, Comfort Suites, Country Inn Suites, Econolodge, Hampton Inn, La Quinta, SpringHill Suites, **other:** H, American RV Ctr, CVS Drug, Publix, Tire Choice/auto
128	Alico Rd, San Carlos Park, **E gas:** 7-11, **food:** Chick-fil-A, Firepit Grill, Gators Grill, Miller's Alehouse, McDonald's, Moe's SW Grill, Outback Steaks, Red Robin, **lodging:** Courtyard, Hilton Garden, Holiday Inn, Homewood Suites, Residence Inn, **other:** Bass Pro Shop, Belk, Best Buy, Borders, Costco/gas, $Tree, JC Penney, JoAnn, Marshall's, PetCo, Ross, Staples, Super Target, **W gas:** Hess/Dunkin Donuts/dsl, Site/Subway/dsl
123	rd 850, Corkscrew Rd, Estero, **E gas:** BP/dsl, Chevron/dsl, **food:** McDonald's, Perkins, Subway, **other:** CVS Drug, Germaine Arena, Johnson Tire/auto, Miramar Outlet/famous brands, Publix, **W gas:** 7-11, Shell, Sunoco/Subway/Dunkin Donuts, **food:** Applebee's, Arby's, Arizona Pizza, Ruby Tuesday, **lodging:** Embassy Suites, Hampton Inn, **other:** Chevrolet, Lowe's Whse, Tire Choice/auto, Koreshan St HS (2mi), Woodsmoke RV Park (4mi)
116	Bonita Bch Rd, Bonita Springs, **E gas:** Chevron/dsl, Mobil, **other:** Publix, Tire Choice, **W gas:** BP/McDonald's/24hr, Hess/Blimpie/dsl/24hr, **food:** Subway, Waffle House, **lodging:** Best Western, **other:** Advance Parts, Albertson's/gas, CVS Drug, Home Depot, Imperial Bonita RV Park, Publix, Tire Choice/auto, Walgreens
111	rd 846, Immokalee Rd, Naples Park, **E gas:** 7-11, **food:** Bob Evans, Chili's, Panera Bread, Pizza Hut, Starbucks, **lodging:** Hampton Inn, **other:** Staples, Super Target, World Mkt, **W gas:** Shell/Circle K/dsl, **food:** CiCi's Pizza, Jasons Deli, McDonald's, **other:** H, Publix, TrueValue, Walmart SuperCtr, to Delnor-Wiggins SP
107	rd 896, Pinebridge Rd, Naples, **E gas:** BP/McDonald's/dsl/24hr, **food:** China Garden, Clubhouse Cafe, Coldstone Creamery, Giovanni Ristorante, Starbucks, Subway, **other:** H, Publix, Walgreens, Vet, **W gas:** Chevron/dsl24hr, RaceTrac, Shell/dsl/24hr, **food:** Bajio Grill, Burger King, Figaro's Pizza, Five Guys Burgers, Hooters, IHOP, Perkins, Roman Oven, Waffle House, **lodging:** Best Western, Hawthorn Suites, Spinnaker Inn, **other:** Goodyear/auto, Harley-Davidson, Johnson Tire/auto, Nissan, Vet
105	rd 886, to Golden Gate Pkwy, Golden Gate, **E food:** Subway, **W gas:** to ✈, zoo
101	rd 951, to FL 84, to Naples, **E gas:** BP/Subway, **lodging:** Fairfield Inn, Springhill Suites, **W gas:** BP/Cafe/dsl, Circle K, Shell/dsl/24hr, **food:** Cracker Barrel, McDonald's, Mr V's, Subway, Taco Bell, Waffle House, **lodging:** Comfort Inn, Holiday Inn Express, La Quinta, Super 8, **other:** Club Naples RV Ctr, Endless Summer RV Park (3mi), KOA
100mm	toll plaza from eb
80	FL 29, to Everglade City, Immokalee, **W other:** Big Cypress NR, Everglades NP, Smallwoods Store
71mm	Big Cypress Nat Preserve, hiking, no security
63mm	**W rest area both lanes, full ♿ facilities, ☎, vending, picnic, litter barrels, petwalk, 24hr security**
49	Gov't Rd, Snake Rd, Big Cypress Indian Reservation, **E gas:** Miccosukee Service Plaza/deli/dsl, **other:** museum, swamp safari
41mm	**rec area eb, picnic, litter barrels**
38mm	**rec area wb, picnic, litter barrels**
35mm	**W rest area both lanes, full ♿ facilities, ☎, vending, picnic, litter barrels, petwalk, 24hr security**
32mm	**rec area both lanes, picnic, litter barrels**
26mm	toll plaza wb, motorist callboxes begin/end
23	Us 27, FL 25, Miami, South Bay
22	NW 196th, Glades Pkwy, **W other:** Publix, same as 21
21	FL 84 W (from nb), Indian Trace, **W gas:** Chevron (1mi), Citgo/dsl, **food:** Mamma Nostra, Papa John's
19	I-595 E, FL 869 (toll), Sawgrass Expswy
15	Royal Palm Blvd, Weston, Bonaventure, **W gas:** Exxon, Mobil, **food:** Flanigan's Rest, Iltoscano Rest., La Granja, Lucille's Cafe, Offerdahl's Grill, Pollo Tropical, Ristorante, Quizno's, Subway, The Catch Rest., Wendy's, **lodging:** Courtyard, Hawthorn Suites, Residence Inn, **other:** H, Tires+, USPO
13b a	Griffin Rd, **E gas:** Shell/dsl, **food:** Burger King, Outback Steaks, Waffle House/24hr, **other:** Goodyear/auto, Infiniti, Publix, **W gas:** 7-11, Tom Thumb/gas, **food:** Chili's, Mayer's Rest., McDonald's, Ultimate Burrito, **other:** Home Depot, Honda, Hyundai, Nissan/Volvo, Office Depot, Publix, Toyota/Scion, Walgreens
11b a	Sheridan St, **E gas:** Chevron, **food:** Cracker Barrel, Wendy's, **lodging:** Hampton Inn, Holiday Inn Express, **other:** H (3mi), BMW, Lincoln/Mercury, **W gas:** Shell, **food:** Applebees, Bistro 555, China One,

FT MYERS · CAPE CORAL · ESTERO · NAPLES · WESTON

FL

INTERSTATE 75 CONT'D

Exit #	Services
11b a	Continued Coldstone Creamery, El Mariachi, Little Caesars, McDonald's, Original Pancake House, Roasters'n Toasters, Rotelli Cafe, Starbucks, Subway, TGIFriday, Original Pancake House, **other:** GNC, Lowe's Whse, Publix, Walgreens
9b a	FL 820, Pine Blvd, Hollywood Blvd, **E gas:** BP, Shell, **food:** Boston Mkt, Brio Italian, Brimstone Woodfire Grill, Chili's, Jason's Deli, Latin-American Grill, Macaroni Grill, McDonald's, Starbucks, Village Tavern, Wendys, **other:** Barnes&Noble, BJ's Whse/gas, Dodge, JC Penney, Macy's, Mercedes, Walgreens, USPO, **W gas:** BP, Exxon, Shell, **food:** KFC/Taco Bell, Las Vegas Cuban, McDonald's, Panda Express, Quizno's, Starbucks, Sweet Tomatoes, **other:** Acura, Advance Parts, Buick, Costco/gas, Lexus, Pontiac/GMC, Publix, Staples, Tires+, USPO, Walgreens, Winn-Dixie
7b a	Miramar Pkwy, **E gas:** Chevron, **food:** Brushetta Italian, Dunkin Donuts, La Carreta, McDonald's, Pollo Tropical, Sal's Italian, Subway, Wendy's, **lodging:** Courtyard, Hilton Garden, Residence Inn, Wingate Inn, **other:** Publix, Walgreens, USPO, **W gas:** Shell, **food:** Chick-fil-A, Chili's, McDonald's, Panera Bread, Quizno's, Starbucks, **other:** H, CVS Drug, Home Depot, Marshall's, Office Depot, Ross, SuperTarget, Walgreens, Winn-Dixie
5	to FL 821 (from sb), FL TPK (toll)
4	FL 860, NW 186th, Miami Gardens Dr, **E gas:** BP/24hr, Chevron/24hr, **food:** Carrabba's, McDonald's, Subway, **other:** CVS Drug, GNC, Publix/deli, Sedenos Foods
2	NW 138th, Graham Dairy Rd, **W gas:** Mobil/dsl, Shell, **food:** China Casa, Little Caesars, McDonald's, Starbucks, Subway, Wendy's, **other:** H, GNC, Publix, Walgreens
1b a	I-75 begins/ends on FL 826, Palmetto Expswy, multiple services on FL 826.

INTERSTATE 95

Exit #	Services
382mm	Florida/Georgia state line, St Marys River, motorist callboxes begin/end.
381mm	**inspection sta both lanes**
380	US 17, to Yulee, Kingsland, **E** Osprey RV Park, **W gas:** Shell/24hr, **lodging:** Day's Inn
378mm	**Welcome Ctr sb, full facilities, phone, vending, picnic, litter barrels, petwalk, 24hr security**
376mm	**weigh sta both lanes**
373	FL 200, FL A1A, to Yulee, Callahan, Fernandina Bch, **E gas:** Flash/Krystal, Sunoco, **food:** Burger King, KFC/Pizza Hut, DQ, McDonald's, Wendy's, **lodging:** Comfort Inn, Country Inn&Suites, Hampton Inn (3mi), Nassau Holiday Motel (3mi), **other:** Lofton Creek Camping (3mi), to Ft Clinch SP (16mi), **W gas:** BP/Domino's/Subway/dsl, Exxon/dsl
366	Pecan Park Rd, **W** Flea&Farmer's Mkt, Pecan Park RV Camping
363b a	Duval Rd, **E gas:** Mobil, **food:** Arby's, Boston's, Chick-fil-A, Chili's, Coldstone Creamery, Cracker

Exit #	Services
363b a	Continued Barrel, 5 Guys Burgers, Green Papaya, Hardee's, Jasmine's Bistro, McDonald's, Panda Express, Panera Bread, Red Lobster, Starbucks, Sticky Fingers, **other:** Best Buy, Discount Tire, $Tree, Gander Mtn, GNC, Goodyear/auto, Lowes Whse, Michael's, Old Navy, PetsMart, Ross, Walmart SuperCtr/24hr, **W gas:** BP, Exxon, Shell/dsl, Sunoco/Subway, **food:** Denny's, Longhorn Steaks, Millhouse Steaks, Ruby Tuesday, Waffle House, Wendy's, Zaxby's, **lodging:** Airport Inn, Best Western, Comfort Suites, Country Hearth Inn, Fairfield Inn, Hampton Inn, Hilton Garden, Holiday Inn, Microtel, Red Roof Inn, Residence Inn, Rodeway Inn, Springhill Suites, Travelodge, Wingate Inn, **other:** RV Ctr
362b a	I-295 S, FL 9A, to Blount Island, Jacksonville
360	FL 104, Dunn Ave, Busch Dr, **E gas:** Gate/dsl, **food:** Applebee's, Hardee's, Waffle House, **lodging:** Executive Inn, **other:** Sam's Club/gas, USPO, **W gas:** BP, Hess, Shell, **food:** Arby's, Bono's BBQ, Burger King, Capt D's, Chan's Chinese, Checker's, CiCi's, KFC, Krystal, McDonald's, New Century Buffet, New China, Pizza Hut, Popeye's, Shoney's, Sonny's BBQ, Subway, Taco Bell, Wendy's, **lodging:** Best Value Inn, Best Western, La Quinta, Motel 6, **other:** Aamco, Advance Parts, BigLots, CVS Drug, $Tree, Family$, Office Depot, PepBoys, Publix, Radio Shack, Tire Kingdom, Tires+, Walgreens
358b a	FL 105, Broward Rd, Heckscher Dr, **E** zoo, **W lodging:** USA Inn
357mm	Trout River
357	FL 111, Edgewood Ave, **W gas:** BP/repair, Gas Express
356b a	FL 115, Lem Turner Rd, **E food:** Hardee's, **W gas:** BP/24hr, Hess, Shell/repair, **food:** Burger King, Checker's, Golden EggRoll, Krystal, Popeye's, Taco Bell, **other:** Advance Parts, Foods, Tires+, Walgreens, flea mkt
355	Golfair Blvd, **E gas:** BP, Shell, **W gas:** Chevron/dsl, RaceWay
354b a	US 1, 20th St, to Jacksonville, to AmTrak, MLK Pkwy
353d	FL 114, to 8th St, **E food:** McDonald's, **other:** H, Walgreens
353c	US 23 N, Kings Rd, downtown
353b	US 90A, Union St, Sports Complex, downtown
353a	Church St, Myrtle Ave, Forsythe St, downtown
352c	Monroe St (from nb), downtown
352b a	Myrtle Ave (from nb), downtown

INTERSTATE 95 CONT'D

N ↕ S — JACKSONVILLE

Exit #	Services
351d	Stockton St, H, downtown
351c	Margaret St, downtown
351b	I-10 W, to Tallahassee
351a	Park St, College St, H, to downtown
351mm	St Johns River
350b	FL 13, San Marco Blvd, **E** H
350a	Prudential Dr, Main St, Riverside Ave (from nb), to downtown, **E gas:** BP, **lodging:** Extended Stay America, Hampton Inn, Wyndham, **W food:** Panera Bread, **lodging:** Hilton Garden
349	US 90 E (from sb), to beaches, downtown, **W lodging:** Super 8
348	US 1 S (from sb), Philips Hwy, **W lodging:** Scottish Inn, Super 8, **other:** Volvo
347	US 1A, FL 126, Emerson St, **E gas:** Chevron, Shell, **food:** Hot Wok, **other:** Advance Parts, Family$, O'Reilly Parts, **W gas:** BP/dsl, Gate/dsl, Hess/dsl, **food:** McDonald's, Taco Bell, **lodging:** Emerson Inn, **other:** Chevrolet, Goodyear/auto
346b a	FL 109, University Blvd, **E gas:** BP, Exxon/dsl, Hess/dsl, Shell, **food:** Capt D's, Checkers, DQ, El Potro Mexican, Family$, Firehouse Subs, Happy Garden Chinese, Huddle House, Korean BBQ, Krystal, Mi Tierra, Papa John's, Pizza Hut, Subway, Ying's Chinese, **other:** H, Ace Hardware, CVS Drug, Firestone/auto, NAPA, Tire Kingdom, Tires+, Sun Tire, Winn-Dixie, **W gas:** BP/dsl, Chevron, RaceTrac, **food:** Arby's, Burger King, Dunkin Donuts/Baskin Robbins, KFC, McDonald's, Sonny's BBQ, Taco Bell, Wendy's, **lodging:** Comfort Lodge, Day's Inn, Ramada Inn, **other:** U-Haul, auto repair
345	FL 109, University Blvd (from nb), **E gas:** Chevron, Gate/dsl/24hr, Hess/Blimpie/Godfather's Pizza/dsl, **food:** Bono's BBQ, Schnitzel House, **other:** H
344	FL 202, Butler Blvd, **E gas:** Gate, **food:** Dave&Buster's, **lodging:** Best Western, Candlewood Suites, Econolodge, Holiday Inn Express, Homestead Suites, Howard Johnson, Marriott, Radisson, **other:** H, USPO, **W gas:** BP/dsl, Shell, **food:** Applebee's, Chick-fil-A, Cracker Barrel, Dunkin Donuts, Hardee's, Latin Cuisine, McDonald's, Quizno's, Sonic, Starbucks, Waffle House, Wendy's, Whataburger/24hr, Zaxby's, **lodging:** Courtyard, Extended Stay America, Fairfield Inn, Jameson Inn, La Quinta, Microtel, Red Roof Inn, Wingate Inn
341	FL 152, Baymeadows Rd, **E gas:** BP/dsl, Gate/dsl, Shell/dsl, **food:** Arby's, Buffalo Wild Wings, Chili's, Hardee's, Omaha Steaks, Quizno's, Starbucks, Waffle House, **lodging:** Comfort Suites, Embassy Suites, Holiday Inn, HomeStead Suites, **other:** Publix, Tires+, Winn-Dixie, **W gas:** Exxon/dsl, Gate, Kangaroo, **food:** Burger King, Chicago Pizzaria, Denny's, Firehouse Subs, Gator's Seafood, IHOP, KFC, Larry's Subs, McDonald's, Red Chilies, Red Lobster, Starbucks, Steak-Out, Taco Bell, Wendy's, Woody's BBQ, **lodging:** Best Inn, Homewood Suites, La Quinta, Quality Inn, Residence Inn, Sheraton, Studio 6, Sun Suites, **other:** BJ's Whse/gas, Discount Tire, $Tree, Harley-Davidson, Lowe's Whse, Office Depot
340	FL 115, Southside Blvd (from nb), **E on FL 115...gas:** Kangaroo/dsl, **food:** Five Guys Burgers, Longhorn Steaks, **other:** Borders, Home Depot, Michael's, PetsMart, Target, same as 339
339	US 1, Philips Hwy, **E gas:** Kangaroo/dsl, **food:** Arby's, Bono's BBQ, Buca Italian, Burger King, Chick-fil-A, McDonald's, Olive Garden, Ruby Tuesday, Starbucks, Taco Bell, Waffle House, **other:** Belk, Best Buy, Chevrolet, Dillard's, Ford, JC Penney, Kia, Sears/auto, Tire Kingdom, Toyota, mall, **W gas:** BP/dsl, **food:** Steak&Shake
337	I-295 N, to rd 9a, Orange Park, Jax Beaches
335	Old St Augustine Rd, **E gas:** Chevron, Gate/dsl, Shell, **food:** Applebees, McDonald's, Panera Bread, Starbucks, **lodging:** Courtyard, Hampton Inn, **other:** H, Walgreens, Kohl's, Publix
331mm	**rest area both lanes, full ♿ facilities, ☎, vending, picnic, litter barrels, petwalk, 24hr security**
329	rd 210, **E gas:** Pilot/McDonald's/dsl/scales/24hr, Sunoco/fruit, TA/Shell/Subway/dsl/rest./scales/@, **food:** Waffle House, **W gas:** BP/Subway/dsl, Mobil/dsl, Shell, **food:** Burger King, Cherry's Grill, China Wok, Domino's, Firehouse Subs, Jenk's Pizza, Larry's Subs, Starbucks, Subway, Tropical Smoothie, **other:** CVS Drug, Winn-Dixie, USPO, fireworks
323	International Golf Pkwy, **E gas:** BP/Sbarro's/dsl, Shell/Subway/dsl, **lodging:** Comfort Suites, **W food:** Cino's Pizza, King Wok, Village Grill/Subs, **lodging:** Renaissance Resort, **other:** Publix, World Golf Village, Vet

ST AUGUSTINE

Exit #	Services
318	FL 16, Green Cove Sprgs, St Augustine, **E gas:** BP/DQ, Gate/dsl/fruit, Kangaroo/dsl, Shell, **food:** Burger King, McDonald's, Huddle House, Subway, **lodging:** Comfort Inn, Econolodge, Ford, Quality Inn, **other:** Camping World RV Ctr, Cadillac, Gander Mtn, Lincoln/Mercury, Prime Outlets, **W gas:** Exxon, RaceTrac, **food:** Cracker Barrel, Denny's, IHOP, KFC, Ruby Tuesday, Shoney's, Sonny's BBQ, Taco Bell, Wendy's, **lodging:** Best Western, Day's Inn, Hampton Inn, Ramada Ltd, Scottish Inn, Super 8, Wingate Inn, **other:** Harley-Davidson, St Augustine Premium Outlets Ctr, Premium Outlets/Famous Brands, RV camping, funpark
311	FL 207, St Augustine, **E gas:** BP/dsl, Chevron/24hr, Hess/Subway/dsl, Indian River Fruit/gas, **other:** H Indian Forest RV Park (2mi), KOA (7mi), St Johns RV Park, flea mkt, to Anastasia SP, fruit/fireworks, **W gas:** Mobil/dsl, **lodging:** Quality Inn
305	FL 206, to Hastings, Crescent Beach, **E gas:** ***FLYING J***/Country Mkt/dsl/scales/LP/24hr, **other:** Gore RV Ctr, to Ft Matanzas NM, truck repair
302mm	**rest areas both lanes, full ♿ facilities, ☎, vending, picnic, litter barrels, petwalk, 24hr security**
298	US 1, to St Augustine, **E gas:** BP/dsl, Indian River Fruit/gas, Sunoco, **other:** to Faver-Dykes SP, **W gas:** Mobil/DQ/dsl, Sunrise/gas, **food:** Waffle House
289	to FL A1A (toll br), to Palm Coast, **E gas:** Kangaroo/dsl, RaceTrac, Shell, **food:** Beef o' Brady's, Cracker Barrel, Denny's, Grand Hong Kong, KFC, Lucky Buffet, Chinese, McDonald's, Pizza Hut, Starbucks, Taco Bell, Wendy's, **lodging:** Best Western, Courtyard, Microtel, Sleep Inn, **other:** CVS Drug, Publix, Staples, Walgreens, **W gas:** Chevron, Shell, Kangaroo,

INTERSTATE 95 CONT'D

N ↕ S

Exit #	Services
289	Continued **food:** Baskin-Robbins/Dunkin Donuts, Bob Evans, Brusters, Golden Corral, Honey Baked Ham, Outback Steaks, Perkins, Ruby Tuesday, Sonny's BBQ, Steak'n Shake/24hr, Taco Bell, **other:** Advance Parts, Beall's, Belk, CVS Drug, Ford, Home Depot, Lowe's Whse, Tire Kingdom, Walgreens, Walmart SuperCtr, Winn-Dixie, USPO
286mm	**weigh sta both lanes,** ☎
284	FL 100, to Bunnell, Flagler Beach, **E gas:** Chevron/dsl/24hr, Citgo, Shell, **food:** Burger King, Domino's, McDonald's, Oriental Garden, Subway, Woody's BBQ, **lodging:** Hampton Inn, Holiday Inn Express, **other:** Ace Hardware, Russell Stover's, Winn-Dixie, Vet, **W gas:** BP/dsl, **lodging:** Hilton Garden, **other:** H, Chevrolet, Chrysler/Dodge/Jeep
278	Old Dixie Hwy, **E gas:** 7-11, **other:** Publix, Bulow RV Park (3mi), to Tomoka SP, **W gas:** BP/dsl, **food:** Luigi's Pizza, Rodeo Mexican, **lodging:** Country Hearth Inn, **other:** Holiday Travel Park
273	US 1, **E gas:** Chevron, Mobil/Wendy's/dsl, RaceTrac, **food:** McDonald's, Saddle Jack's Grill, Waffle House, **lodging:** Comfort Suites, Econolodge, **other:** fruit/fireworks, RV Ctr, **W gas:** Exxon/Burger King, Loves/Arby's/dsl/scales/24hr, **food:** DQ, Houligan's, **lodging:** Days Inn, Daytona Hotel, Ormond Inn, Scottish Inn, Super 8, **other:** Encore RV Park, Harley-Davidson
268	FL 40, Ormond Beach, **E gas:** Chevron/dsl, Shell, **food:** Applebee's, Boston Mkt, Chili's, Chick-fil-A, Denny's/24hr, Dustin's BBQ, Krispy Kreme, Papa John's, Quizno's, Royal Dynasty, Starbucks, Steak'n Shake, Subway, Taco Bell, Takeya Japanese, Waffle House, Wendy's, Wok&Roll, **lodging:** Sleep Inn, **other:** H, Beall's, Discount Tire, K-Mart, Lowe's Whse, Publix, Ross, Pomok SP, USPO, Vet, Walmart SuperCtr, **W gas:** BP, Mobil/dsl, 7-11/gas, Texaco, **food:** Cracker Barrel, Domino's, Legends Grill, McDonald's, **lodging:** Hampton Inn, Jameson Inn, **other:** Walgreens
265	LPGA Blvd,, Holly Hill, Daytona Beach, **E gas:** 7-11, Shell/dsl, **food:** Wendy's, Subway (2mi), **other:** CVS Drug, **W lodging:** Hampton Inn, **other:** Chrysler/Dodge, Ford, Kia, Mazda, Nissan
261b a	US 92, to DeLand, Daytona Bch, **E gas:** Hess/Blimpie/dsl, Mobil, RaceWay/24hr, 7-11/gas, Shell/dsl, **food:** Bob Evans, Buca Italian, Burger King, Cancun Rest., Carrabba's, Checker's, Chick-fil-A, Chilli's, China Buffet, Chipotle Mexican, Cracker Barrel, Daytona Ale House, Denny's, Fazoli's, Friendly's, Honey Baked Ham, Hooters, Jimmy John's, KFC, Krystal, Longhorn Steaks, McDonald's, Olive Garden, Panera Bread, Picadilly, Pizzaria Uno, Quizno's, Red Lobster, Ruby Tuesday, Sonny's BBQ, Smoothie King, Sonny's BBQ, Sorrento's, Subway, Taco Bell, Tijuana Flats, Tuesday Morning, Waffle House, Winghouse, **lodging:** Comfort Suites, Courtyard, Hampton Inn, Hilton Garden, Holiday Inn Express, Homewood Suites, La Quinta, Quality Inn, Ramada Inn, Residence Inn,

ORMOND BEACH

DAYTONA BEACH

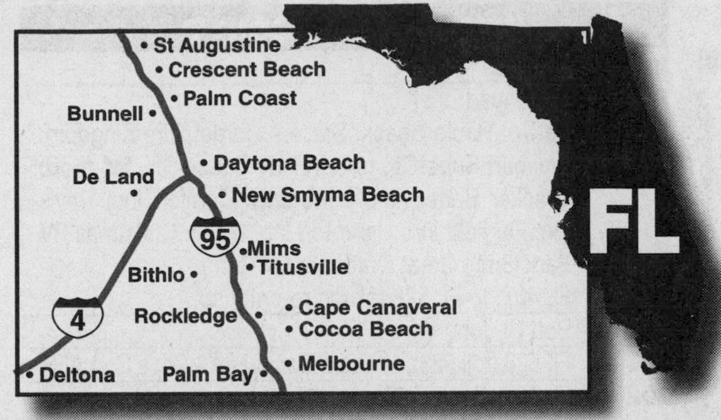

DAYTONA BEACH

Exit #	Services
261b a	Continued **other:** H, Barnes&Noble, Beall's, Best Buy, Dillard's, Firestone/auto, Home Depot, JC Penney, Jo-Anne Fabrics, K-Mart, Macy's, Marshall's, Michael's, Office Depot, Old Navy, PepBoys, PetCo, PestMart, Ross, Sears/auto, Staples, SteinMart, Target, TJMaxx, World Mkt, mall, to Daytona Racetrack, **W gas:** BP/dsl, Sunoco, **food:** IHOP, McDonald's, **lodging:** Day's Inn, Super 8, **other:** KOA, RV camping, flea mkt
260b a	I-4, to Orlando, FL 400 E, to S Daytona, **E gas:** Chevron/dsl
256	FL 421, to Port Orange, **E gas:** BP, Circle K/gas, Shell, **food:** Applebee's, Bob Evans, Chick-fil-A, Chili's, Denny's/24hr, Dustin's BBQ, Firehouse Subs, Marble Slab Creamery, Monterey Grill, Panera Bread, Papa John's, Quizno's, Smoothie King, Sonny's BBQ, Tijuana Flats, Tropical Smoothie, **lodging:** Country Inn & Suites, Day's Inn, La Quinta, **other:** Holiday Camp RV Park, Home Depot, Lowe's Whse, Super Target, Walgreens, Walmart SuperCtr (1mi), Vet, **W gas:** 7-11, Hess, Texaco, **food:** McDonald's, Subway, Wendy's, **other:** Kohls, Publix, Walgreens
249b a	FL 44, to De Land, New Smyrna Beach, **E gas:** Shell/dsl/fruit, **other:** New Smyrna RV Camp (3mi), **W gas:** Chevron/dsl
244	FL 442, to Edgewater, **E gas:** BP/dsl/24hr, **other:** truck repair
231	rd 5A, Scottsmoor, **E gas:** BP/Stuckey's/dsl, **other:** Crystal Lake RV Park
227mm	**rest area sb, full ♿ facilities, ☎, vending, picnic, litter barrels, petwalk, 24hr security**
225mm	**rest area nb, full ♿ facilities, ☎, vending, picnic, litter barrels, petwalk, 24hr security**
223	FL 46, Mims, **E gas:** Chevron (2mi), **food:** McDonald's, **other:** Willow Lakes Camping, **W gas:** BP, Shell, **other:** KOA/LP, Seasons RV Camp
220	FL 406, Titusville, **E gas:** BP/dsl, Shell/dsl, **food:** Beef 'O' Brady's, 1st Wok, Kelsey's Pizzaria, McDonald's, Rodeo Mexican, Subway, Wendy's, **lodging:** Super 8, **other:** H, Advance Parts, Beall's, Belk, $General, Publix, Tires+, Walgreens, to Canaveral Nt'l Seashore, **W gas:** Chevron/dsl
215	FL 50, to Orlando, Titusville, **E gas:** BP/KFC/Pizza Hut/dsl, Circle K/gas, Murphy USA, Shell/DQ/dsl, **food:** Burger King, Denny's, Durango Steaks, McDonald's, Panda Express, Quizno's, Sonny's BBQ, Taco Bell, Waffle House, Wendy's, Whistle Jct, **lodging:** Best Western, Ramada Inn, **other:** Aldi Foods, Ford/Mercury, GNC, Hame Depot, Lowe's Whse,

INTERSTATE 95 CONT'D

N ↕ S

Exit #	Services
215	Continued PetCo, Radio Shack, Staples, Target, Tire Kingdom, Walmart SuperCtr, to Kennedy Space Ctr, **W food:** Cracker Barrel, IHOP, **lodging:** Comfort Inn, Day's Inn, Fairfield Inn, Hampton Inn, **other:** Christmas RV Park (8mi), Great Outdoors RV Camp
212	FL 407, to FL 528 toll (no re-entry sb)
208	Port St John
205	FL 528 (toll 528), to Cape Canaveral & Cape Port AFS
202	FL 524, Cocoa, **E gas:** Shell/dsl, **other:** Museum of History & Science, **W gas:** BP/dsl, **lodging:** Day's Inn, Ramada Inn/rest., Super 8
201	FL 520, to Cocoa Bch, Cocoa, **E gas:** BP/dsl, Chevron, Pilot/Subway/scales/dsl/24hr, **food:** IHOP, Waffle House, **lodging:** Best Western, Motel 6, **other:** H, Sams Club/gas, fireworks, **W gas:** Chevron/dsl, Shell/Burger King, Sunoco/dsl, **food:** McDonald's, **lodging:** Holiday Inn Express, **other:** Sun Coast RV Ctr
195	FL 519, Fiske Blvd, **E gas:** 7-11, Shell/dsl (1mi), fod: Ruby Tuesday, **lodging:** Swiss Inn, **other:** H, Lowe's Whse, Space Coast RV Park
191	rd 509, to Satellite Beach, **E gas:** BP, Citgo/7-11, Hess/dsl, **food:** Bob Evans, Denny's, McDonald's, Perkins, Sonny's BBQ, Tropical Smoothie, Uno, Wendy's, **lodging:** Hampton Inn, Holiday Inn, **other:** CVS Drug, Goodyear/auto, UHaul, to Patrick AFB, **W gas:** Chevron/dsl, Murphy USA, **food:** Asian Wok, Burger King, Chili's, Cracker Barrel, Longhorn Steaks, Mimi's Cafe, Starbucks, Steak&Shake, Subway, **lodging:** La Quinta, **other:** Belk, $Tree, Kohl's, Office Depot, PetCo, Ross, SuperTarget, Walmart SuperCtr/McDonald's, World Mkt
183	FL 518, Melbourne, Indian Harbour Beach, **E gas:** BP, Chevron/Baskin Robbins/Dunkin Donuts/dsl, RaceTrac/24hr, 7-11, **other:** art museum, **W** Flea Mkt
180	US 192, to Melbourne, **E gas:** BP/dsl, Circle K/gas, Mobil/dsl, 7-11/gas, Sunoco/dsl, **food:** Denny's, IHOP, Waffle House, **lodging:** Budget Inn, Days Inn, Fairfield Inn, Hampton Inn, Holiday Inn Express, Howard Johnson, York Inn, **other:** H, Sam's Club/gas, Vet
176	rd 516, to Palm Bay, **E gas:** BP/dsl, Murphy USA, 7-11/gas, **food:** Baskin Robbins/Dunkin Donuts, Bob Evans, Chick-fil-A, Cracker Barrel, Denny's, Golden Corral, Starbucks, **lodging:** Jameson Inn, **other:** Aldi Foods, BJ's Whse/gas, Chevrolet, $Tree, GNC, Harley-Davidson, Office Depot, Walmart SuperCtr, Walgreens, **W gas:** 7-11/gas, Shell, **food:** Ranchero's Mexican, Subway, Wendy's, **other:** Curves, CVS Drug, Publix, Walgreens
173	FL 514, to Palm Bay, **E gas:** Shell/dsl, Sunoco/dsl, **other:** H, Ford, Subaru, truck/RV repair, **W gas:** BP/dsl, Hess, Shell, **food:** Arby's, Baskin-Robbins, Burger King, IHOP, McDonald's/playplace, Panda Express, Sonny's BBQ, Subway, Taco Bell, TX Roadhouse, Waffle House, Wendy's, Woody's BBQ, **lodging:** Comfort Suites, Motel 6, **other:** Advance Parts, BigLots, CVS Drug, $General, Gatto's Tire/repair, Home Depot, Lowe's, Publix, Tire Kingdom, USPO, Walgreens, Walmart SuperCtr
168mm	**rest areas both lanes, full ♿ facilities, ☎, vending, picnic, litter barrels, petwalk, 24hr security**
156	rd 512, to Sebastian, Fellsmere, **E gas:** BP/DQ/Stuckey's/dsl, Chevron/McDonald's, **other:** H, Encore RV Park, Sebastian Inlet SRA, Vero Bch RV Park (8mi), **W other:** Marsh Landing Camping, St Sebastian SP
147	FL 60, Osceola Blvd, **E gas:** Citgo/dsl/24hr, Mobil/dsl, Sunoco, Texaco, TA/BP/Popeye's/Subway/dsl/24hr/scales/@, 7-11/gas, Valero/dsl, **food:** IHOP, Mrs. B's Rest., Quizno's, Sloane's Rest., Waffle House, Wendy's, **lodging:** Best Western, Days Inn, Howard Johnson, Travelodge, **other:** H, NAPA, USPO, Vet, **W food:** Cracker Barrel, McDonald's, Steak'n Shake, **lodging:** Country Inn&Suites, Hampton Inn, Holiday Inn Express, **other:** Vero Bch Outlets/famous brands
138	FL 614, Indrio Rd, **3 mi E other:** Oceanographic Institute
133mm	**rest areas both lanes, full ♿ facilities, ☎, vending, picnic, litter barrels, petwalk, 24hr security**
131b a	FL 68, Orange Ave, **E** to Ft Pierce SP, **W gas:** ***FLYING J***/CountryMkt/dsl/LP/scales/24hr, **other:** Blue Beacon
129	FL 70, to Okeechobee, **E gas:** Hess/dsl, Mystik/dsl, Murphy USA, RaceTrac, Sunoco/dsl, **food:** Applebee's, Sonic, Gator's Rest., Golden Corral, Waffle House, **other:** H, Advance Parts, $General, $Tree, Firestone/auto, Home Depot, Radio Shack, Walgreens, Walmart SuperCtr, truck tires, **W gas:** Chevron, Citgo/scales/dsl, Exxon, Mobil/Dunkin Donuts/Subway, Pilot/Arby's/dsl/24hr/@, Pilot/McDonald's/dsl/scales/24hr, Shell/dsl, **food:** Burger King, Cracker Barrel, LJ Silver, KFC, McDonald's, Mi Rancho Mexican, Red Lobster, Steak'n Shake, Waffle House, Wendy's, **lodging:** Best Western, Comfort Suites, Day's Inn, Fairfield Inn, Hampton Inn, Holiday Inn Express, La Quinta, Motel 6, Quality Inn, Rodeway Inn, Sleep Inn, Treasure Coast Inn, **other:** Treasure Coast RV Park, to FL TPK, UF R&E Ctr
126	rd 712, Midway Rd, **services 3-5 mi E**
121	St Lucie West Blvd, **E gas:** BP/Dunkin Donuts, Chevron/24hr, Murphy USA, 7-11/gas, Shell/Subway/dsl, **food:** Arbys, Bob Evans, Burger King, Chili's, Coldstone, Crisper's Rest., Duffy's Grill, Friendly's, McDonald's, Morelli's, Outback Steaks, Quizno's, Red Ginger Asian, Ruby Tuesday, TGI Friday, Wendy's, **lodging:** Hampton Inn, Holiday Inn Express, Residence Inn, SpringHill Suites, **other:** Curves, Outdoor Resorts Camping (2mi), PetCo, Publix/deli, Steinmart, Radio Shack, Tires+, Tire Kingdom, USPO, Walgreens, Walmart SuperCtr, **W gas:** Mobil/dsl, **lodging:** Hilton Garden, MainStay Suites, Sheraton, **other:** PGA Village
120	new exit
118	Gatlin Blvd, to Port St Lucie, **E gas:** BP/dsl/LP, Chevron/dsl, Sunoco, **food:** Dunkin Donuts, Subway, **other:** Home Depot, Sam's Club/gas, Walgreens, Walmart SuperCtr, **W food:** Longhorn Steaks, McDonald's, Olive Garden, **other:** Michaels, Old Navy, PetsMart, Publix, Target, TJ Maxx
113mm	new exit

MELBOURNE

PALM BAY

OKEECHOBEE

INTERSTATE 95 CONT'D

N ↕ S

Exit #	Services
110	FL 714, to Stuart, Palm City, **E** H
106mm	**rest areas both lanes, full facilities, phone, vending, picnic, litter barrels, petwalk, 24hr security**
102	FL 713, to Stuart, Palm City
101	FL 76, to Stuart, Indiantown, **E gas:** Chevron/24hr, Sunoco/dsl, **food:** Baskin-Robbins/Dunkin Donuts, Cracker Barrel, McDonald's, Wendy's, **lodging:** Courtyard, Holiday Inn Express, **other:** H, RV camping, **W gas:** Shell/DQ/Stuckey's/deli/dsl, food:
96	rd 708, to Hobe Sound, **E** Dickinson SP (11mi), RV camping
87b a	FL 706, to Okeechobee, Jupiter, **E gas:** Citgo, Mobil, Shell, **food:** Applebee's, Cheeseburgers & More, China Dragon, Duffy's Rest., Dunkin Donuts, Gator's Rest, IHOP, KFC, McDonald's, Pollo Tropical, Sonny's BBQ, Starbucks, Subway, Taco Bell, Tomato Pie, **lodging:** Comfort Inn, Fairfield Inn, **other:** H, URGENT CARE, Advance Parts, Books-A-Million, Dodge/Mazda, GNC, Home Depot, PepBoys, Publix, Tire Kingdom, Walgreens, Winn-Dixie, to Dickinson SP, hist sites, museum, Vet, **W gas:** Sunoco, **other:** info, RV camping, to FL TPK
83	Donald Ross Rd, **E gas:** Shell, **lodging:** Homewood Suites, **other:** stadium
79c	FL 809 S (from sb), **W** to FL TPK, same services as 79b
79a b	FL 786, PGA Blvd, **E gas:** Shell, **food:** Chili's, TGIFriday, **lodging:** Hampton Inn, Marriott, **other:** H, Best Buy, Michael's, Publix, **W gas:** Shell/dsl/24hr, **food:** Abbey Rd Grill, Cantina Laredo, Field Of Greens Cafe, Outback Steaks, **lodging:** DoubleTree Hotel, Embassy Suites, **other:** Publix

W PALM BEACH

Exit #	Services
77	Northlake Blvd, to W Palm Bch, **E gas:** Hess, Shell/dsl, Texaco, **food:** Applebee's, Arby's, Burger King, Checker's, Chick-fil-A, McDonald's, Panera Bread, Pollo Tropical, Quarter Deck Rest., Starbucks, Taco Bell, **other:** H, Buick/Pontiac/GMC, Chevrolet, Chrysler/Jeep/Dodge, Costco, CVS Drug, $Tree, Ford, Gander Mtn, Home Depot, Hyundai, K-Mart, Lincoln/Mercury, Lowe's Whse, PepBoys, Ross, Staples, Subaru, Target, VW, Walgreens, **W gas:** BP, Chevron, Mobil/dsl, Shell, Sunoco, **food:** Duffy's Grill, Gator's Rest., Papa John's, Pizza Hut, Wendy's, **lodging:** Inn of America, **other:** Advance Parts, Albertson's, CVS Drug, Radio Shack, Publix, Winn-Dixie
76	FL 708, Blue Heron Blvd, **E gas:** BP/dsl, Shell/dsl, **food:** Wendy's, **lodging:** Travelodge, **other:** Honda, Kia, Nissan, Walgreens, **W gas:** BP, Cumberland Farms, RaceTrac, Texaco/dsl, **food:** Burger King, Denny's, McDonald's, Quizno's, **lodging:** Super 8
74	FL 702, 45th St, **E food:** Burger King, Hong Kong Cafe, IHOP, **lodging:** Day's Inn, **other:** H, Cadillac, Walgreens, **W gas:** RaceTrac, Sunoco, **food:** Cracker Barrel, McDonald's, Pollo Tropical, Subway, Taco Bell, Wendy's, **lodging:** Courtyard, Extended Stay Deluxe, Holiday Inn Express, Homewood Suites, Inn Town Suites, Red Roof Inn, Residence Inn, Springhill Suites, **other:** Curves, Goodyear, Harley-Davidson, Palm Beach RV Ctr, Sams Club/gas, Goodyear/auto, Walmart SuperCtr

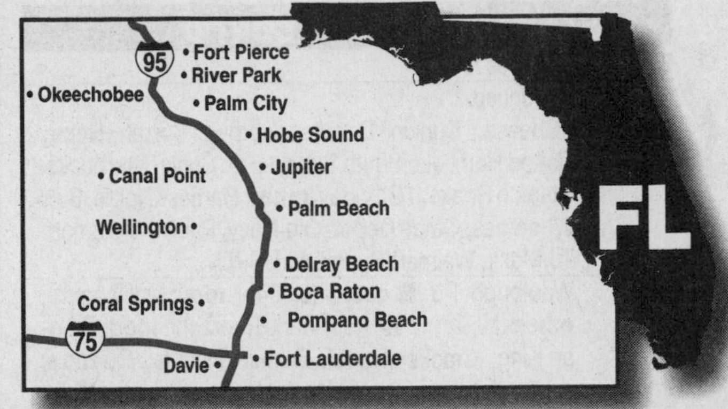

PALM BEACH

Exit #	Services
71	Lake Blvd, Palm Beach, **E gas:** BP, **food:** McDonald's, **lodging:** Best Western, Hawthorn Suites, **other:** H, Best Buy, Dillard's, Firestone/auto, JC Penney, Macy's, Sears/auto, Target, mall, **W gas:** Texaco/dsl, **food:** Carrabba's, Chick-fil-A, Chipotle Mexican, Hooters, Manzo Italian, PA BBQ, Picadilly's, Rain Dancer Steaks, Red Lobster, Sweet Tomatoes, **lodging:** Comfort Inn, La Quinta, **other:** Walgreens, Vet
70b a	FL 704, Okeechobee Blvd, **E gas:** Exxon, **lodging:** Marriott, **other:** museum, **W gas:** Chevron/dsl, Exxon/dsl, Hess, Shell, Texaco, **food:** Checkers, McDonald's, Nick's Diner, Pizza Hut, Pollo Tropical, Shell's Rest., **other:** BMW, Chevrolet, Lincoln/Mercury, Old Navy, PetsMart, Staples
69	Belvedere Rd, **W on Australian Ave...gas:** BP, Shell, **food:** Burger King, Denny's, IHOP, Wendy's, **lodging:** Best Western, Courtyard, Crowne Plaza, Doubletree, Hampton Inn, Hilton Garden, Holiday Inn/rest., Motel 6, Studio 6, **other:** to airport
68	US 98, Southern Blvd, **E gas:** Texaco, **other:** CVS Drug, Publix, **W lodging:** Hilton
66	Forest Hill Blvd, **E** Havana Cafe, **W gas:** Sunoco, **food:** Amigo's Mexican, Palm Spring Pizza,
64	10th Ave N, **W gas:** Citgo, Shell/dsl/24hr, **food:** China Empire, Dunkin Donuts, Flanigans Grill, McDonald's, Wendy's, **other:** CarQuest, $General, Family$, Ford, Goodyear, President Foods, Urgent Care, Vet
63	6th Ave S, **W** H
61	FL 812, Lantana Rd, **E gas:** Shell, **food:** Dominos, KFC, McDonald's, Quizno's, Reggin's Crabhouse, Subway, **lodging:** Motel 6, **other:** Ace Hardware, Beall's, CVS Drug, $General, Publix, 7-11, **W food:** Rosalita's Café, **other:** H, Costco/gas
60	Hypoluxo Rd, **E gas:** BP, Mobil/dsl, Shell/dsl, **food:** Popeye's, Taco Bell, Wendy's, **lodging:** Best Western, Comfort Inn, Super 8, **other:** Sam's Club, Tires+, Tire Kingdom, **W gas:** Chevron/dsl, **other:** Advance Parts
59	Gateway Blvd, **W gas:** Mobil/Blimpie/dsl, **food:** Bonefish Grill, Carrabba's, Chili's, Firehouse Subs, Friendlys, McDonald's, Original Pancake House, Starbucks, Tropical Smoothie, **lodging:** Hampton Inn, **other:** CarMax, CVS Drug, Kohl's, Publix, Tuesday Morning, Vet
57	FL 804, Boynton Bch Blvd, **E gas:** Majestic Gas, **food:** KFC, **lodging:** Holiday Inn Express, **other:** H, USPO, **W gas:** Texaco, **food:** Checker's, Subway, Waffle House, Wendy's, **other:** Radio Shack, 7-11, **1mi W gas:** Shell, **food:** Applebee's, Burger King, Chick-Fil-A, Chuck

INTERSTATE 95 CONT'D

N S

Exit #	Services
57	Continued eCheese, Dunkin Donuts, Golden Corral, Honey Baked Ham, Jim Smith Subs, KFC, Sonic, Starbucks, Steak'n Shake, TGIFriday, **other:** Barnes&Noble, BJ's Whse/gas, Office Depot, Old Navy, Publix, Steinmart, TJ Maxx, Walmart SuperCtr, USPO
56	Woolbright Rd, **E gas:** Shell/24hr, **food:** McDonald's, **other:** H, 7-11, **W gas:** RaceTrac/24hr, **food:** Burger King, Cracker Barrel, Dunkin Donuts, Quizno's, **other:** Advance Parts, Home Depot, Lowe's Whse, Staples
52b a	FL 806, Atlantic Ave, **W gas:** Chevron, Shell/dsl, **food:** Burger King, McDonald's, Sandwich Man, **other:** H, Aamco, Publix, Tires+, Walgreens, Vet
51	rd 782, Linton Blvd, **E gas:** Shell, **food:** Applebees, Arby's, Chipotle Mexican, DQ, KFC, Lucille's BBQ, McDonald's, Outback Steaks, Pollo Tropical, Steak'n Shake, Subway, Taco Bell, Wendy's, **other:** Chevrolet, Ford, Home Depot, Mercedes, Nissan, PetsMart, Publix, Ross, Staples, Target, Tire Kingdom, **W gas:** Shell, **other:** H, Family$, Winn-Dixie, auto repair
50	Congress Ave, **W gas:** NeXStore/gas, **lodging:** Hilton Garden, Homestead Motel
48b a	FL 794, Yamato Rd, **E gas:** Mobil, **food:** Panera Bread, **other:** CVS Drug, Vet, **W gas:** Chevron/dsl, **food:** Blue Fin, Dunkin Donuts, Jimmy John's, McDonald's, Quizno's, Sal's Italian, Starbucks, Subway, Wendy's, **lodging:** DoubleTree, Embassy Suites, Hampton Inn, SpringHill Suites, TownePlace Suites
45	FL 808, Glades Rd, **E food:** Alexander's Rest, Jamba Juice, McCormick and Schmick's, Mon Ami Cafe, Subway, **lodging:** Fairfield Inn, **other:** Barnes&Noble, Jamba Juice, PF Chang's, Whole-Foods Mkt, museum, **W gas:** BP, **food:** Abe&Louie's, Brewzzi Cafe, Cheesecake Factory, Chili's, Chipotle Mexican, Houston Rest., Maggiano's Italian, Mario's Italian, Moe's SW Grill, Quizno's, Starbucks, **lodging:** Courtyard, Holiday Inn, Marriott, Renaissance/grill, **other:** Macy's, Nordstrom, Sears/auto
44	Palmetto Park Rd, **E gas:** Sunoco, **food:** Denny's, Dunkin Donuts, Red's BBQ, Subway, Tomasso's Pizza, **other:** K-Mart, Publix, museums, **W food:** McDonald's (2mi)
42b a	FL 810, Hillsboro Blvd, **E gas:** BP, Shell/dsl, **food:** McDonald's, Popeye's, Wendy's, **lodging:** Hampton Inn, Hilton, La Quinta, **other:** Advance Parts, **W gas:** Chevron, Mobil/dsl, **food:** Boston Mkt, Checker's, Denny's, **lodging:** La Quinta, **other:** CVS Drug, Home Depot, Walgreens
41	FL 869 (toll), SW 10th, to I-75, **E gas:** Mobil, **food:** Cracker Barrel, **lodging:** Extended Stay America, **W lodging:** Best Western, Comfort Suites,
39	FL 834, Sample Rd, **E gas:** BP, Hess, Marathon, Shell/dsl, **other:** H, 7-11, UHaul, **W gas:** Chevron, Mobil/dsl, Sunoco/dsl, **food:** Arby's, Checker's, IHOP, McDonald's, Miami Subs, Subway, **other:** CarMax, Costco/gas, CVS Drug, Family$, Seabra Foods, 7-11, Vet
38b a	Copans Rd, **E food:** McDonald's, Subway, **other:** Land Rover, Mercedes, PepBoys, Porche/Audi,

POMPANO BEACH

Exit #	Services
38b a	Continued Walmart, **W gas:** BP, Chevron, **other:** Harley-Davidson, Home Depot, NAPA
36b a	FL 814, Atlantic Blvd, to Pompano Beach, **E gas:** RaceTrac, **food:** KFC/Pizza Hut/Taco Bell, Miami Subs, **1 mi W gas:** BP, Mobil/dsl, Murphy USA, **food:** Burger King, Dunkin Donuts, Golden Corral, KFC/LJ Silver, McDonald's, Pollo Tropical, Popeye's, Wendy's, **other:** Advance Parts, Chevrolet, CVS Drug, $Tree Radio Shack, Walmart SuperCtr, Winn-Dixie, USPO, to FL TPK, Power Line Rd has multiple services
33b a	Cypress Creek Rd, **E gas:** BP, Hess, **lodging:** Extended Stay America, Hampton Inn, Westin Hotel, **W gas:** Hess, Shell/repair, **food:** Arby's, Burger King, Chili's, Hooters, Jamba Juice, Longhorn Steaks, McDonald's, Moonlite Diner, Quizno's, Steak&Ale, Subway, Sweet Tomatoes, Wendy's, **lodging:** Courtyard, Extended Stay Deluxe, La Quinta, Marriott, Sheraton Suites, **other:** GNC, Jaguar, Office Depot, Tires+
32	FL 870, Commercial Blvd, Lauderdale by the Sea, Lauderhill, **E food:** Subway, **W gas:** BP, Circle K, Mobil, Shell, Sunoco/dsl, **food:** Burger King, Dunkin Donuts, KFC, McDonald's, Miami Subs, Waffle House, **lodging:** El Palacio, Red Roof Inn, University Inn, **other:** Advance Parts, BJ's Whse, Larrys Tires/Repair

FT LAUDERDALE

Exit #	Services
31b a	FL 816, Oakland Park Blvd, **E gas:** Chevron, Mobil/24hr, **food:** Burger King, CC's Fishcamp, Denny's, Dunkin Donuts, Little Caesars, McDonald's, Miami Subs, Subway, Wendy's, **other:** K-Mart, Lowe's Whse, Publix, Radio Shack, Walgreens, **W gas:** BP/dsl, Citgo, RaceTrac, Shell, Texaco, **food:** Burger King, Dunkin Donuts/Baskin-Robbins, IHOP, KFC, **lodging:** Day's Inn, **other:** $General, Home Depot, Toyota, USPO, Vet
29b a	FL 838, Sunrise Blvd, **E gas:** Shell, Sunoco/dsl, **food:** Burger King, Popeye's, **other:** Advance Parts, Family$, Winn-Dixie, **W gas:** Citgo, Shell, Sunoco, **food:** Capt Crabs, Church's, McDonald's, Subway, **other:** H, Walgreens
27	FL 842, Broward Blvd, Ft Lauderdale, **E** H
26	I-595 (from sb), FL 736, Davie Blvd, **W** to ✈
25	FL 84, **E gas:** Marathon, RaceTrac/24hr, 7-11, Shell/dsl, Sunoco, Texaco, Valero, **food:** Dunkin Donuts, Li'l Red's BBQ, McDonald's, Subway, Wendy's, **lodging:** Best Western, Candlewood Suites, Hampton Inn, Holiday Inn Express, Motel 6, Sky Motel, **other:** BigLots, Firestone/auto, Radio Shack, U-Haul, Winn-Dixie, **W lodging:** Ramada Inn, Red Carpet Inn, Rodeway Inn, **other:** Ford Trucks
24	I-595 (from nb), to I-75, **E** to ✈
23	FL 818, Griffin Rd, **E lodging:** Hilton, Sheraton, **W gas:** BP, Citgo/dsl, **food:** Subway, Tropical Acres, **lodging:** Courtyard, **other:** Bass Pro Shops
22	FL 848, Stirling Rd, Cooper City, **E gas:** Mobil, **food:** AleHouse Grill, Burger King, Dave&Buster's, Quizno's, McDonald's, Moonlite Diner, Quizno's, Red Lobster, Sweet Tomatoes, Taco Bell, TGIFriday, Wendy's, **lodging:** Comfort Inn, Hampton Inn, Hilton Garden, La Quinta, SpringHill Suites, **other:** Advance Parts, Barnes&Noble, BigLots, BJ's Whse, CVS Drug,

FL

INTERSTATE 95 CONT'D

Exit #	Services
22	Continued GNC, Home Depot, K-Mart, Marshall's, Michael's, Old Navy, PetsMart, Ross, to Lloyd SP, **W food:** Las Vegas Cuban, Mr M's Sandwiches, Subway, **lodging:** Best Western, **other:** Circle K, CVS Drug, PepBoys, Tire Kingdom, Walgreens
21	FL 822, Sheridan St, **E gas:** BP, Citgo, Cumberland Farms/gas, same as 22, **W gas:** Shell, **food:** Denny's, **lodging:** Day's Inn, Holiday Inn
20	FL 820, Hollywood Blvd, **E gas:** Shell, **food:** IHOP, Miami Subs, **lodging:** Hollywood Gateway Inn, **other:** Goodyear/auto, Office Depot, Vet, **W gas:** BP, Chevron, **food:** Boston Mkt, Dunkin Donuts, Firehouse Subs, McDonald's, Offerdahl's Grill, Quizno's, Taco Bell, Starbucks, Subway, Wendy's, **other:** [H], Publix, Target, Walgreens
19	FL 824, Pembroke Rd, **E gas:** Shell, **W gas:** Shell
18	FL 858, Hallandale Bch Blvd, **E gas:** Exxon, 7-11, Shell, Ugas/E85, **food:** Burger King, Denny's, Dunkin Donuts, Fat Lou's, IHOP, KFC, Little Caesar's, McDonald's, Miami Subs, Pollo Tropical, Subway, Wendy's, Won Ton Garden, **lodging:** Best Western, **other:** [H], Family$, Goodyear/auto, Office Depot, Tire Kingdom, Walgreens, Winn-Dixie, Vet, **W gas:** BP, RaceTrac, **other:** Advance Parts
16	Ives Dairy Rd, **E** [H], mall, **W gas:** BP, **food:** Subway
14	FL 860, Miami Gardens Dr, N Miami Beach, **E** [H], Oleta River SRA, **W gas:** BP, Chevron, Citgo, Marathon/dsl, **food:** Subway
12c	US 441, FL 826, FL TPK, FL 9, **E gas:** BP, Chevron, Hess, 7-11, Ugas/dsl, Valero, **food:** Burger King, Dunkin Donuts/Baskin-Robbins, Wendy's **lodging:** Holiday Inn, **other:** [H]
12b	US 441 (from nb), same as 12c
12a	FL 868 (from nb), FL TPK N
11	NW 151st (from nb), **W gas:** Sunoco, **food:** McDonald's, **other:** Advance Parts, Winn-Dixie, services on US 441 N
10b	FL 916, NW 135th, Opa-Locka Blvd, **W gas:** Chevron, Liberty, Mobil, **food:** Checker's, Subway
10a	NW 125th, N Miami, Bal Harbour, **W gas:** Shell, **food:** Wendy's
9	NW 119th (from nb), **W gas:** BP/McDonald's, **food:** KFC, **other:** AutoZone, Family$, Walgreens, Winn-Dixie
8b	FL 932, NW 103rd, **E gas:** Shell, Texaco, **other:** 7-11, **W gas:** Chevron, Marathon, Sunoco, **food:** Baskin-Robbins/Dunkin Donuts, Bravo Foods
8a	NW 95th, **E gas:** BP, **W gas:** Mobil, **food:** McDonald's, **other:** [H], Advance Parts, Walgreens
7	FL 934, NW 81st, NW 79th, **E gas:** Chevron/dsl, Citgo/dsl, **W gas:** Texaco, **food:** Cafe China, Checker's, **other:** Lincoln/Mercury
6b	NW 69th (from sb)
6a	FL 944, NW 62nd, NW 54th, **W food:** McDonald's, Subway, **other:** Family$, Jorge&Jerry's Foods, Walgreens
4b a	I-195 E, FL 112 W (toll), Miami Beach, **E** downtown, **W** [airport]

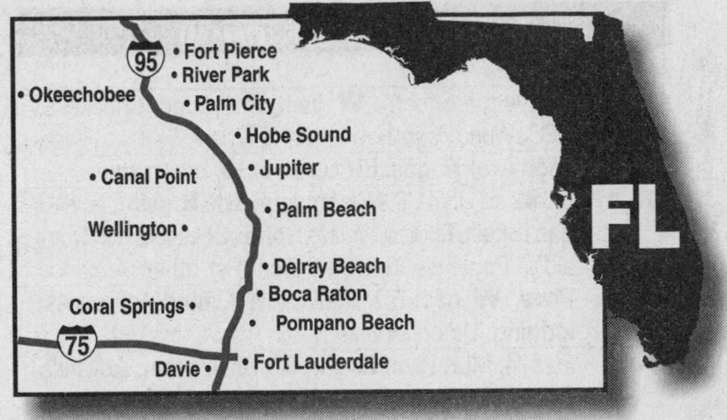

Exit #	Services
3b	NW 8th St (from sb)
3a	FL 836 W (toll) (exits left from nb), **W** [H], to [airport]
2d	I-395 E (exits left from sb), to Miami Beach
2c	NW 8th, NW 14th (from sb), Miami Ave, **E** Port of Miami
2b	NW 2nd (from nb), downtown Miami
2a	US 1 (exits left from sb), Biscayne Blvd, downtown Miami
1b	US 41, SW 7th, SW 8th, Brickell Ave, **E gas:** Chevron, Citgo, **food:** McDonald's, Subway, **lodging:** Extended Stay America, Hampton Inn, Holiday Inn Express, **other:** CVS Drug, GNC, Publix, **W gas:** Shell, **food:** Papa John's
1a	SW 25th (from sb), downtown, to Rickenbacker Causeway, **E lodging:** Hampton Inn, **other:** museum, to Baggs SRA
0mm	I-95 begins/ends on US 1., **1 mi S gas:** Citgo, **food:** Quizno's

INTERSTATE 275 (TAMPA)

Exit #	Services
59mm	I-275 begins/ends on I-75, exit 274.
53	Bearss Ave, **E gas:** Citgo/dsl, **other:** Carmax, **W gas:** BP, CC's/dsl, Chevron/dsl, RaceTrac, Shell, **food:** Burger King, McDonald's, Perkins, Quizno's, Subway, **lodging:** Quality Inn, **other:** BigLots, CVS Drug, GNC, Ross
52	Fletcher Ave, **E gas:** BP, Citgo, Hess, RaceTrac, Sunoco, Texaco, **food:** Arby's, DQ, Golden Dynasty, Hoho, Krystal, Little Caesars, McDonald's, Popeye's, **lodging:** Day's Inn, **other:** [H], Tire Kingdom, Toyota, auto repair, **W gas:** BP, Chevron, Citgo, **lodging:** Super 8, **other:** Beall's, Cadillac, Family$, Jaguar, Sweetbay Foods
51	FL 582, Fowler Ave, **E gas:** Citgo/dsl, GK, Shell/Circle K, **food:** A&W/LJ Silver, Burger King, Chili's, China Buffet, Chipotle Mexican, City Mkt, Denny's, Dunkin Donuts, Jason's Deli, Longhorn Steaks, McDonald's, Pizza Hut, Quizno's, Steak'n Shake, Subway, Taco Bell, TGIFriday's, Waffle House, Wendy's, **lodging:** Clarion, Howard Johnson, **other:** Advance parts, CarQuest, CVS Drug, Dillards, Family$, Macy's, Office Depot, Sears/auto, Walgreens, **W lodging:** Economy Inn, Motel 6, Rodeway Inn, **other:** BMW
50	FL 580, Busch Blvd, **E gas:** BP, Chevron, Citgo, **food:** Sonny's BBQ, **lodging:** Comfort Inn, Econolodge, **other:** AutoZone, Busch Gardens, Famliy$, Walgreens, **W gas:** Citgo, **food:** Burger King, KFC, Pizza Hut, **other:** CVS Drug, Firestone/auto, Goodyear/auto, Home Depot, Radio Shack, Walmart Mkt/drug

INTERSTATE 275 (TAMPA)

N ↕ S — TAMPA

Exit #	Services
49	Bird Ave (from nb), **W gas:** Shell, **food:** Checker's, KFC, Wendy's, **other:** K-Mart
48	Sligh Ave, **E gas:** BP, Sunoco, **W other:** zoo
47b a	US 92, to US 41 S, Hillsborough Ave, **E gas:** Circle K/gas, Shell, Texaco, Valero, **food:** Checkers, McDonald's, Popeye's, Subway, Wendy's, **other:** Advance Parts, **W gas:** BP, Shell/Circle K, **food:** Starbucks, **lodging:** Dutch Motel
46b	FL 574, MLK Blvd, **E gas:** BP, Shell, **other:** Advance Parts, Sweetbay Foods, Walgreens, **W gas:** Marathon, **food:** McDonald's, **other:** [H]
46a	Floribraska Ave
45b	I-4 E, to Orlando, I-75
45a	Jefferson St, downtown E
44	Ashley Dr, Tampa St, downtown W
42	Howard Ave, Armenia Ave, **W gas:** Texaco/dsl, **food:** Popeye's
41c	Himes Ave (from sb), **W** RJ Stadium
41b a	US 92, Dale Mabry Blvd, **E gas:** BP, Marathon, Mobil/dsl, Shell/Circle K, **food:** Alexander's Rest., Burger King, Carrabba's, Chick-Fil-A, Don Pan Cuban, Donatello Italian, Giordano's Italian, Honey Baked Ham, IHOP, PeiWei Asian, Perkins, Pizza Hut, Ruby Tuesday, Shells Rest., Starbucks, Village Inn, **lodging:** Best Western, Courtyard, **other:** Barnes & Noble, Borders, CVS Drug, Office Depot, PetsMartto MacDill AFB, **W gas:** BP, **food:** Burger King, Chili's, China 1, Crazy Buffet, Denny's, Longhorn Steaks, Macaroni Grill, McDonald's, Quizno's, Smoothie King, Sonic, Sonny's BBQ, Subway, Sweet Tomatoes, Tia's TexMex, Tijuana Iguana, Wendy's, **lodging:** Day's Inn, Howard Johnson, **other:** Best Buy, Dodge/Chrysler/Jeep, Home Depot, K-Mart, PetsMart, Staples, SweetBay Foods, Target, Walmart, Whole Foods Mkt
40b	Lois Ave, **W gas:** Marathon, **food:** Charlies Rest., **lodging:** DoubleTree Hotel, Sheraton
40a	FL 587, Westshore Blvd, **E gas:** Chevron, Citgo, Shell, **food:** Chipotle Mexican, Maggiano's Rest., Panera Bread, PF Chang's, Starbucks, Steak&Ale, Taco Bell, Waffle House, **lodging:** Embassy Suites, Ramada Inn, Wyndam, **other:** Goodyear, JC Penney, Macy's, Old Navy, PetCo, Sears/auto, Walgreens, **W gas:** Shell/Subway, **food:** West Shore Rest., **lodging:** Marriott, Quorum Hotel, SpringHill Suites
39b a	FL 60 W, **W food:** Outback Steaks, **other:** to ✈
32	Fl 687 S, 4th St N, to US 92 (no sb reentry)
31b a	9th St N, MLK St N (exits left from sb), info, ✈
30	FL 686, Roosevelt Blvd, **2mi W food:** Quaker Steak & Lube, **lodging:** Wingate Inn
28	FL 694 W, Gandy Blvd, Indian Shores, **0-2mi W food:** Bob Evans, Godfather's Pizza, **lodging:** La Quinta, **other:** Robert's RV Resort
26b a	54th Ave N, **E gas:** Cracker Barrel, **lodging:** Comfort Inn, Holiday Inn Express, **W gas:** Citgo, RaceTrac, **food:** Waffle House, **lodging:** Day's Inn, **other:** [H], Harley-Davidson, NAPA
253	8th Ave N, to beaches, **E food:** McDonald's, **W gas:** Citgo/dsl, **food:** Burger King, Hardee's

ST PETERSBURG

Exit #	Services
24	22nd Ave N, **E gas:** Mobil, 7-11, **other:** Sunken Garden, **W gas:** Citgo/dsl, RaceTrac, **other:** Home Depot, Lowe's Whse
23b	FL 595, 5th Ave N, **E** [H]
23a	I-375, **E** The Pier, Waterfront, downtown
22	I-175 E, Tropicana Fields, **W** [H]
21	28th St S, downtown
20	31st Ave (from nb), downtown
19	22nd Ave S, Gulfport, **W gas:** Chevron, Citgo, Shell, **food:** Church's, Cici's Pizza, KFC, Quizno's, **other:** Family$, PriceBuster Foods
182	6th Ave S (from nb)
17	FL 682 W, 54th Ave S, Pinellas Bayway, **services W on US 19 (34th St)...gas:** 7-11, Sunoco, **food:** Bob Evans, Burger King, Denny's, McDonald's, Papa John's, Pizza Hut, Ponderosa, Subway, Taco Bell, Wendy's, **lodging:** Bayway Inn, Crystal Inn, **other:** Beall's, CVS Drug, GNC, K-Mart, Publix, to Ft DeSoto Pk, St Pete Beach
16	Pinellas Point Dr, Skyway Lane, to Maximo Park, **E lodging:** Holiday Inn resort, **W** marina
16mm	toll plaza sb
13mm	N Skyway Fishing Pier, **W rest area both lanes, full ♿ facilities, ☎, vending, picnic tables, litter barrels, petwalk**
10mm	Tampa Bay
7mm	S Skyway Fishing Pier, **E rest area both lanes, full ♿ facilities, ☎, vending, picnic tables, litter barrels, petwalk**
6mm	toll plaza nb
5	US 19, Palmetto, Bradenton
2	US 41 last nb exit before toll, Palmetto, Bradenton, **E other:** Terra Ceia Village Campground, Circle K, Fiesta Grove RV Resort, Frog Creek Campground, Winterset RV Resort, **W gas:** BP/DQ/Subway/dsl
0mm	I-275 begins/ends on I-75, exit 228.

INTERSTATE 295 (JACKSONVILLE)

N ↕ S — JACKSONVILLE

Exit #	Services
35b a	I-95, S to Jacksonville, N to Savannah. I-295 begins/ends on I-95, exit 362b.
33	Duval Rd, **W** ✈
32	FL 115, Lem Turner Rd, **E food:** China Wok, Cross Creek Steak, Larry's Subs, McDonald's (1mi), Subway, Wendy's, **other:** Home Depot, Radio Shack, Walmart SuperCtr, **W other:** Flamingo Lake RV Resort, Lakeside Cabins/RV Park
30	FL 104, Dunn Ave, **E gas:** Gate/dsl, Shell/24hr (1mi), **food:** McDonald's (1mi), **W other:** Big Tree RV Park
28b a	US 1, US 23, to Callahan, Jacksonville, **E gas:** Kangaroo/gas, **W gas:** BP/DQ/dsl, Chevron/Subway/dsl, RaceTrac/24hr, auto repair
25	Pritchard Rd, **W gas:** Kangaroo/Subway/dsl/deli/24hr
22	Commonwealth Ave, **E gas:** Sprint/dsl, **food:** Burger King, Hardee's, Waffle House, **lodging:** Holiday Inn, **other:** dogtrack, **W food:** Wendy's, **lodging:** Comfort Suites, Country Inn & Suites
21b a	I-10, W to Tallahassee, E to Jacksonville
19	FL 228, Normandy Blvd, **E gas:** BP/dsl/24hr, Murphy USA, **food:** Arby's, Burger King, El Potro, Firehouse Subs, Golden Corral, Hot Wok, McDonald's,

INTERSTATE 295 CONT'D (JACKSONVILLE)

N ↕ S JACKSONVILLE

Exit #	Services
19	Continued Papa John's, Sonic, Wendy's, **other:** CVS Drug, $Tree, Food Lion, Radio Shack, Walgreens, Walmart SuperCtr, st patrol, **W gas:** BP, Hess/dsl, QuickStop, RaceTrac, Shell, **food:** China Wok, Famous Amos, Golden China, Hardee's, Hungry Howie's Pizza, KFC/A&W, McDonald's, Pizza Hut, Popeye's, Subway, Whataburger, **other:** Advance Parts, Curves, CVS Drug, Family$, K-Mart, Publix, Winn-Dixie
17	FL 208, Wilson Blvd, **E gas:** BP/Subway/dsl, Hess/dsl, **food:** China Wok, Hardee's, McDonald's (1mi), **other:** Advance Parts, $General, Food Lion, **W gas:** Kangaroo
16	FL 134, 103rd St, Cecil Field, **E gas:** BP, Gate/dsl, Hess, **food:** Applebee's, Arby's, Capt D's, Firehouse Subs, McDonald's, Papa John's, Popeye's, Red Apple Asian, Shoney's, Sonic, Wendy's, Ying's Chinese, **lodging:** Hospitality Inn, **other:** Advance Parts, $General, GNC, NAPA, Tires+, Walmart SuperCtr/24hr, **W gas:** BP, Chevron, Exxon/dsl, Hess, Kangaroo, Shell, **food:** Burger King, DQ, Dragon Garden Chinese, El Chaparral Mexican, Mexican, Hot Wok, IHOP, KFC, McDonald's, Mi Toro Mexican, Pizza Hut, Subway, Taco Bell, **other:** Aamco, AutoZone, Family$, Food Lion, Goodyear/auto, Publix, SavRite Foods, Sun Tires, Walgreens, Vet
12	FL 21, Blanding Blvd, **E gas:** BP, RaceWay, Texaco, **food:** Burger King, Larry's Subs, McDonald's, Pizza Hut, Subway, Sunrise Cafe, **other:** Acura, Best Buy, Buick/Pontiac, Cadillac, CVS Drug, $General, Dodge, Ford, Honda, Office Depot, PetsMart, U-Haul, **W gas:** BP, Kangaroo/dsl, Shell, **food:** Applebee's, Arby's, Buffalo's, Burger King, Carrabba's, Chick-fil-A, Chili's, China Buffet, ChuckeCheese, Denny's, El Potro, Honey Baked Ham, Hooters, Ichiro Japanese, KFC, Kyodai Steaks, Longhorn Steaks, Maggie Moo's, Olive Garden, Outback Steaks, Panera Bread, Papa John's, Quizno's, Red Lobster, Ruby Tuesday, Smokey Bones, Sonic, Starbucks, Steak&Shake, Subway, Taco Bell, Ted's MT Grill, TGIFriday, Thai Garden, **lodging:** Country Inn, Hampton Inn, La Quinta, Motel 6, Red Roof Inn, Suburban Lodge, Super 8, **other:** H, Belk, Books A Million, Dillard's, Discount Tire, $Tree, Food Lion, Goodyear/auto, Home Depot, JC Penney, JoAnn Fabrics, Michael's, Old Navy, O'Reilly Parts, Publix, Sam's Club/gas, Sears/auto, Target, TJMaxx, Toyota, Walgreens, mall
10	US 17, FL 15, Roosevelt Blvd, Orange Park, **E lodging:** Best Western, **W gas:** BP, Chevron/dsl/24hr, Hess, RaceWay, **food:** Aaron's Pizza, Cracker Barrel, Krystal, McDonald's, Sam's Seafood, Ramirez Rest., Subway, Waffle House, Wendy's, **lodging:** Comfort Inn, Courtyard, Day's Inn, Econolodge, Fairfield Inn, Hilton Garden, Holiday Inn, Howard Johnson, Rodeway Inn, **other:** H, Chrysler/Jeep, $General, Harley-Davidson, Honda, Nissan, Sun Tire, VW
7mm	St Johns River, Buckman Br
5b a	FL 13, San Jose Blvd, **E gas:** Chevron/DQ/dsl, Hess, **food:** Arby's, Bob Evans, Bono's BBQ, Boston Mkt, Carrabba's, Domino's, Famous Amos, Fastboy's

Bruing
West Park
Del Rio
4
Plant City
275
Tampa
Brandon
75
Lealman
St Petersburg
Apollo Beach
Ruskin
Fort Lonely
Memphis
Bradenton
FL

JACKSONVILLE

5b a	Continued Wings, Firehouse Subs, Krystal, Mi Torro Mexican, Outback Steaks, Popeye's, Smoothie King, Starbucks, St. John's Seafood, Steak'n Shake, Subway, Tijuana Flats, Village Inn, Wendy's, Woody's BBQ, **lodging:** La Quinta, Ramada Inn, **other:** Aamco, Ace Hardware, Advance Parts, CVS Drug, Firestone/auto, Goodyear/auto, K-Mart, Office Depot, PepBoys, Publix, Sun Tire, Target, Tire Kingdom, Walgreens, auto repair, **W gas:** BP, Citgo, Shell (1mi), **food:** Brooklyn Pizza, Bruster's, Chili's, Chipotle Mexican, Golden China, Golden Corral, Hardees, Kan-Ki Japanese, Krispy Kreme, Lee's Chicken, Mamafu's, McDonald's, Moe's SW Grill, Osaka Grill, Panera Bread, Papa John's, Pizza Hut, Subway, Taco Bell, **other:** Ace Hardware, Advance Parts, Barnes&Noble, BooksAMillion, Fresh Mkt, Friendly$, Goodyear/auto, Marshall's, Michael's, NAPA, PetCo, Publix, Radio Shack, Staples, SteinMart, Tire Kingdom, TJMaxx, U-Haul, Walmart SuperCtr, Winn-Dixie, World Mkt
3	Old St Augustine Rd, **E gas:** BP, Shell, **food:** Burger King, China Garden, Little Caesars, Little China, McDonald's, Pizza Hut, Taco Bell, Wendy's, **lodging:** Holiday Inn Express, **other:** CVS Drug, $General, Family$, Food Lion, Publix/deli, Winn-Dixie, **W gas:** Gate/dsl, Kangaroo/dsl, **food:** Firehouse Subs, KFC/Pizza Hut, Rosy's Mexican, Subway, **other:** Lowe's Whse, Walgreens, Vet
61 a b	I-295 begins/ends on I-95, exit 337.

GEORGIA

INTERSTATE 16

E ↕ W

Exit #	Services
167b a	W Broad, Montgomery St, Savannah, **0-1 mi N gas:** Chevron, Enmark, Parker's, **lodging:** Doubletree, Country Inn Suites, Courtyard, Hampton Inn, Hilton Garden, Quality Inn, Residence Inn, Sheraton, **other: S food:** Burger King, Popeye's, Wendy's, I-16 begins/ends in Savannah.
166	US 17, Gwinnet St, Savannah, **Savannah Visitors Ctr**
165	GA 204, 37th St (from eb), to Ft Pulaski NM, Savannah College
164b a	I-516, US 80, US 17, GA 21
162	Chatham Pkwy, **S gas:** Shell/dsl, **food:** Kan Pai Japanese, Larry's Subs, Sunrise Rest., **other:** Kia, Lexus, Toyota
160	GA 307, Dean Forest Rd, **N gas:** Shell/dsl, Pilot/Subway/dsl/scales, **food:** Ronnie's Rest., Waffle House

INTERSTATE 16 CONT'D

E ↕ W

Exit #	Services
157b a	I-95, S to Jacksonville, N to Florence
155	Pooler Pkwy, **S gas:** BP/dsl, to ✈
152	GA 17, to Bloomingdale
148	Old River Rd, to US 80
144mm	**weigh sta both lanes**
143	US 280, to US 80, **S gas:** El Cheapo/dsl/café, Zip'N Go/Subway
137	GA 119, to Pembroke, Ft Stewart
132	Ash Branch Church Rd
127	GA 67, to Pembroke, Ft Stewart, **N gas:** El Cheapo/dsl, Shell/dsl, **food:** Morgan Creek Rest., **other:** antiques, **S gas:** Chevron/dsl/24hr
116	US 25/301, to Statesboro, **N gas:** Chevron/dsl/rest/scales/24hr, **food:** Magnolia Springs SP (45 mi), to GA S U, **S gas:** Sunoco/dsl, **lodging:** Scottish Inn
111	Pulaski-Excelsior Rd, **S gas:** Citgo/Grady's Grill/dsl, **other:** tires/repair
104	GA 22, GA 121, Metter, **N gas:** BP/dsl/scales/24hr, Chevron/dsl, Exxon, Pure, Shell/dsl, **food:** Bevrick's Grill, Burger King, Crabby Joes, DQ, Hardee's, Huddle House, Jomax BBQ, KFC/Taco Bell, Krispy Chic, McDonald's, Señor Luis, Subway, Village Pizza, Waffle House, Zaxby's, **lodging:** American Inn, Econolodge, Scottish Inn, Holiday Inn Express, **other:** H, Chevrolet, Rite Aid, to Smith SP, RV camping, **S gas:** Marathon/dsl, Phillips 66/dsl, **other:** Ford
101mm	Canoochee River
98	GA 57, to Stillmore, **S gas:** BP/dsl/24hr, Chevron/dsl, **other:** to Altahama SP
90	US 1, to Swainsboro, **N gas:** Marathon/dsl, **other:** tires
88mm	Ohoopee River
84	GA 297, to Vidalia, **N** truck sales
78	US 221, GA 56, to Swainsboro, **N gas:** BP/dsl (1mi)
71	GA 15, GA 78, to Soperton, **N gas:** Chevron/dsl
67	GA 29, to Soperton, **S gas:** Chevron/dsl, Marathon/dsl, **food:** Huddle House
58	GA 199, Old River Rd, East Dublin
56mm	Oconee River
54	GA 19, to Dublin, **S gas:** Chevron
51	US 441, US 319, to Dublin, **N gas:** BP/Stuckey's/Subway/dsl, Flash/gas, Neighbor's/dsl, Pilot/dsl/scales, Shell/24hr, **food:** Arby's, Buffalo's Café, Burger King, KFC, McDonald's, Ruby Tuesday, Shoney's, Taco Bell, Waffle House/24hr, Wendy's, **lodging:** Comfort Inn, Day's Inn, Econolodge, Hampton Inn, Holiday Inn Express, Jameson Inn, Super 8, Travelodge, **other:** H, Ace Hardware, Chrysler/Jeep/Dodge, Steve's RV, **S gas:** Chevron, **food:** Cracker Barrel, Longhorn Steaks, Zaxby's, **lodging:** La Quinta, **other:** Pinetucky Camping (2mi), to Little Ocmulgee SP
49	GA 257, to Dublin, Dexter, **N gas:** Chevron, **other:** H, **S gas:** Love's/Subway/dsl/scales/24hr, **other:** auto/dsl repair
46mm	**rest area wb, full ♿ facilities, ☎, 🛒, litter barrels, vending, petwalk, RV dump**
44mm	**rest area eb, full ♿ facilities, ☎, 🛒, litter barrels, vending, petwalk, RV dump**
42	GA 338, to Dudley
39	GA 26, to Cochran, Montrose
32	GA 112, Allentown, **S gas:** Chevron/dsl
27	GA 358, to Danville
24	GA 96, to Jeffersonville, **N gas:** Marathon/dsl, **S gas:** BP/dsl/24hr, **food:** Huddle House/24hr, **lodging:** Best Value, **other:** to Robins AFB, museum
18	Bullard Rd, to Jeffersonville, Bullard
12	Sgoda Rd, Huber, **N gas:** Marathon/dsl
6	US 23, US 129A, East Blvd, Ocmulgee, **N gas:** BP/Circle K/DQ, **lodging:** Day's Inn (2mi), **other:** to ✈, GA Forestry Ctr, **S gas:** Chevron/Huddle House/dsl, Friendly Gus, **food:** Subway
2	US 80, GA 87, MLK Jr Blvd, **N other:** H, Ocmulgee NM, conv ctr, **S gas:** Marathon/dsl, **other:** to Hist Dist
1b	GA 22, to US 129, GA 49, 2nd St (from wb), **N other:** coliseum, **S lodging:** Ramada, **other:** H
1a	US 23, Gray Hwy (from eb), **N gas:** BP, Citgo, Flash/dsl, Marathon, Shell, **food:** Arby's, Burger King, Chen's Wok, DQ, El Sombrero Mexican, Fincher's BBQ, Krispy Kreme, Krystal, Little Caesars, McDonald's, Papa John's, Subway, Taco Bell, Wendy's, **other:** H, Kroger, O'Reilly Parts, Radio Shack, Tire Planet, U-Haul, Walgreens, transmissions, **S gas:** Exxon, Spectrum, **food:** Burger King, Checker's, Krystal, Pizza Hut, Waffle House, Zaxby's, **lodging:** Ramada, Scottish Inn
0mm	I-75, S to Valdosta, N to Atlanta. I-16 begins/ends on I-75, exit 165 in Macon.

METTER · DUBLIN · OCMULGEE

INTERSTATE 20

E ↕ W

Exit #	Services
202mm	Georgia/South Carolina state line, Savannah River
201mm	**Welcome Ctr wb, full ♿ facilities, ☎, vending, 🛒, litter barrels, petwalk**
200	GA 104, Riverwatch Pkwy, Augusta, **N gas:** Pilot/Wendy's/dsl/24hr, **food:** Waffle House, **lodging:** Baymont Inn, Candlewood Suites, Comfort Suites, Jameson Inn, Microtel, Sleep Inn, Value Place
199	GA 28, Washington Rd, Augusta, **N gas:** BP, Raceway/24hr, Shell/Circle K, Sprint Gas, **food:** Applebees, Baskin-Robbins, Burger King, CA Dreaming, Capt D's, Checker's, Chick-fil-A, DQ, Dominos, Denny's, Dunkin Donuts, Fujiyama Japanese, KFC, Kobe Japanese, Krystal, Longhorn Steaks, McDonald's, Mi Rancho Mexican, Omakase Japanese, Piccadilly, Pizza Hut, Quizno's, Rhinehart's Seafood, Starbucks, Subway, Waffle House, Wife Saver Cafe, Wild Wing Cafe, **lodging:** Best Value Inn, Clarion, Courtyard, Days Inn, Hampton Inn, Hilton Garden, Homewood Suites, La Quinta, Masters Inn, Scottish Inn, Sunset Inn, Travelodge, **other:** AutoZone, Buick/GMC/Pontiac, Chrysler/Jeep, Chevrolet, CVS Drug, Goodyear/auto, Hancock Fabrics, Hyundai, Infiniti, Lexus, Mercedes, NAPA, Nissan, Toyota/Scion, Tuesday Morning, **S gas:** BP, 76/Circle K, Shell/Circle K/dsl, **food:** Arby's, BoneFish Grill, Carrabba's, Church's, Famous Dave's BBQ, Five Guys Burgers, Hooters, Krispy Kreme, Little Caesars, McDonald's, Moe's SW Grill, New Peking, Olive Garden, Outback Steaks, Peking Chinese, Quizno's, Red Lobster, Shangri-La Chinese, Subway, Taco Bell, T-Bonz Steaks, TGIFriday, Thai Jong Rest., Vallarta Mexican, Waffle House,

AUGUSTA

GA

INTERSTATE 20 CONT'D

E ↕ W

AUGUSTA

Exit #	Services
199	Continued Wendy's, **lodging:** Best Western, Country Inn&Suites, Knight's Inn, Parkway Inn, Ramada Inn, Staybridge Suites, Super 8, Westbank Inn, **other:** Aamco, BooksAMillion, $Tree, Firestone, Fred's Drug, Fresh Mkt Foods, Goodyear/auto, Kroger/gas, PepBoys, Publix, Rite Aid, Shangri La, SteinMart, Tire Kingdom, Walgreens
196b	GA 232 W, **N gas:** Enmark, Raceway, **food:** Arby's, Bojangles, Burger King, Checker's, Golden Corral, Krystal, Ruby Tuesday, Ryan's, Salsa's Grill, Waffle House, Wendy's, **lodging:** Travel Inn, **other:** $Tree, GNC, Home Depot, Lowes Whse, O'Reilly Parts, Sam's Club, Tire Kingdom, Tires+, Walgreens, Walmart SuperCtr/24hr
196a	I-520, Bobby Jones Fwy, **S gas:** BP, **food:** Backyard Burger, Chili's, Logan's Roadhouse, Macaroni Grill, O'Charley's, Sticky Fingers, Waffle House, **lodging:** DoubleTree Hotel, **other:** H, Best Buy, Border's, Office Depot, Target, Tires+, to ✈
195	Wheeler Rd, **N gas:** Sprint Gas, **0-2 mi S gas:** BP/dsl, Shell/Circle K/Blimpie/24hr, **food:** Chili's, O'Charley's, Sonic, Waffle House, **lodging:** Candlewood Suites, Day's Inn, **other:** H, Harley-Davidson, Rite Aid
194	GA 383, Belair Rd, to Evans, **N gas:** Citgo, Shell/Circle K/Blimpie/dsl, Sprint Gas, **food:** Burger King, Popeye's, Sun Kwong Chinese, Waffle House, Wendy's, **lodging:** GA Inn, **other:** Food Lion, Funsville Park, **S gas:** BP/DQ/Stuckey's/dsl, Pilot/Subway/dsl/24hr, **food:** A&W/KFC, Cracker Barrel, Huddle House, Waffle House, **lodging:** Best Suites, Best Value Inn, Best Western, Comfort Inn, Econolodge, Hampton Inn, Holiday Inn, Motel 6, Quality Inn, Red Roof Inn, Super 8, Wingate Inn, **other:** Goodyear/auto
190	GA 388, to Grovetown, **N gas:** BP/dsl, **food:** Waffle House, **2 mi S gas:** Shell, **food:** KFC, McDonald's, Subway
189mm	**weigh sta both lanes**
183	US 221, to Harlem, Appling, **N gas:** Shell (2mi), **other:** Travel Country RV Ctr, **S gas:** BP/dsl
182mm	**rest area both lanes, full ♿ facilities, ☎, vending, picnic, litter barrels, RV dump, petwalk**

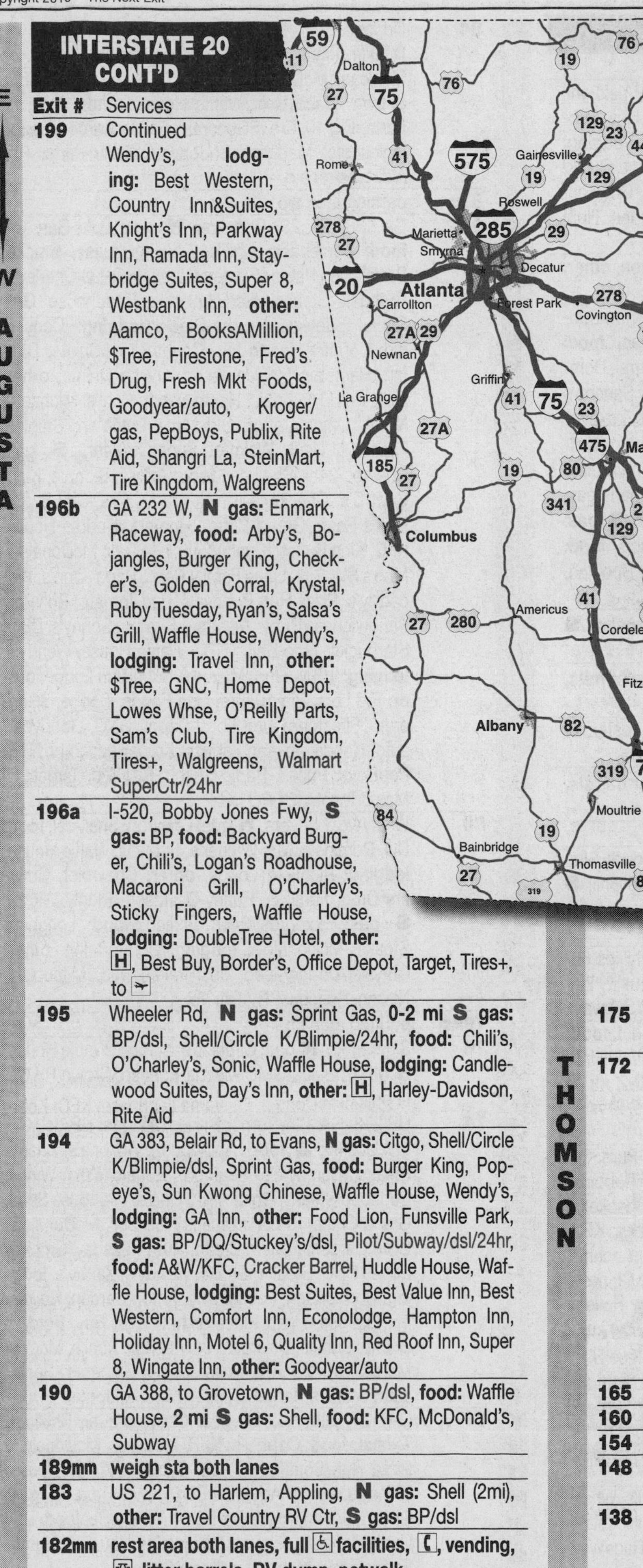

THOMSON

Exit #	Services
175	GA 150, **N gas:** Chevron/USA Trkstp/dsl/rest./24hr, **lodging:** Day's Inn, **other:** to Mistletoe SP
172	US 78, GA 17, Thomson, **N gas:** Chevron/dsl, Loves/Subway/dsl/scales/24hr, **food:** Waffle House, **other:** Chrysler/Dodge/Jeep, Ford/Mercury, GMC/Pontiac, **S gas:** BP/DQ/dsl/24hr, M&A, Raceway/dsl, 76/Blimpie/Circle K, Shell, **food:** Amigo's Mexican, Arby's, Burger King, Checker's, Domino's, Krystal, LJ Silver, Lucky Rest., McDonald's, Mingwah Chinese, Pappa's BBQ, Pizza Hut, Taco Bell, Waffle House, Wendy's, Zaxby's, **lodging:** Best Western, Econolodge, Holiday Inn Express, Scottish Inn, **other:** H, Advance Parts, AutoZone, Buick/Cadillac/Chevrolet, CVS Drug, Family$, Food Lion, K-Mart, Lowes Whse, Walmart SuperCtr/gas (2mi)
165	GA 80, Camak
160	E Cadley Rd, Norwood
154	US 278, GA 12, Barnett
148	GA 22, Crawfordville, **N gas:** BP/dsl, **other:** to Stephens SP, **S gas:** Pure/rest./dsl
138	GA 77, GA 15, Siloam, **N gas:** ⊘***FLYING J***/Country Mkt/dsl/LP/scales/24hr, **S gas:** BP/dsl, Metro/dsl, **other:** H

INTERSTATE 20 CONT'D

E ↕ W

Exit #	Services
130	GA 44, Greensboro, **weigh sta**, **N gas:** BP/dsl/24hr, Exxon/Subway, **food:** McDonald's, Pizza Hut, Subway, Waffle House, Wendy's, Zaxby's, **lodging:** Jameson Inn, Microtel, Thrift Court, **other:** H, Buick/Chevrolet/Pontiac, $General, **S gas:** Chevron/dsl/24hr, **food:** Arby's, **lodging:** Hampton Inn, Holiday Inn Express, **other:** Home Depot
121	to Lake Oconee, Buckhead, **S gas:** Chevron, **other:** Museum of Art (3mi)
114	US 441, US 129, to Madison, **N gas:** Chevron/Subway, Citgo, Pilot/dsl/scales/24hr, RaceTrac, **food:** Arby's, Burger King, Chick-fil-A, Cracker Barrel, Domino's, KFC, Krystal, McDonald's, Pizza Hut, Sancho's Mexican, Starbucks, Waffle House, Wendy's, Zaxby's, **lodging:** Comfort Inn, Day's Inn, Hampton Inn, Holiday Inn, **other:** H, Advance Parts, AutoZone, Buick/Chevrolet/GMC/Pontiac, $General, Ingles Foods/gas, Lowes Whse, Rite Aid, Walmart SuperCtr, **S gas:** Flash, TA/BP/Popeye's/dsl/@, Shell, Texaco, **food:** Waffle House, **lodging:** Best Value Inn, Red Roof Inn, Super 8, Wingate Inn, **other:** RV camping
113	GA 83, Madison, **N gas:** BP, **other:** H, st patrol, **S gas:** Liberty/gas
108mm	**rest area wb, full ♿ facilities, ☎, 🛆, litter barrels, vending, RV dump, petwalk**
105	Rutledge, Newborn, **N gas:** BP/dsl, **food:** Yesterday Café, **other:** Hard Labor Creek SP
103mm	**rest area eb, full ♿ facilities, ☎, 🛆, litter barrels, vending, RV dump, petwalk**
101	US 278
98	GA 11, to Monroe, Monticello, **4 mi N food:** Blue Willow Inn/rest., Log Cabin Rest., Sycamore Grill, **S gas:** BP/Blimpie/dsl, Chevron/dsl, Citgo
95mm	Alcovy River
93	GA 142, Hazelbrand Rd, **S gas:** Citgo, Phillips 66/dsl, **food:** Sonic, Waffle House, **lodging:** Quality Inn, **other:** H, Ingles Foods, Walmart SuperCtr/Subway
92	Alcovy Rd, **N gas:** Chevron/dsl, Circle K/dsl, **food:** Waffle House, **lodging:** Baymont Inn, Best Value Inn, Cornerstone Lodge, Day's Inn, Super 8, **0-2 mi S gas:** Shell, **food:** Chick-fil-A, Dunkin Donuts, Krystal, McDonald's, Pizza Hut, Wendy's, **other:** H
90	US 278, GA 81, Covington, **S gas:** Citgo, Pure, QT, Raceway, **food:** Applebees, Arby's, Baskin-Robbins/Dunkin Donuts, Bojangles, Capt D's, Checker's, Chick-fil-A, Church's, DQ, Hong Kong Buffet, KFC, Longhorn Steaks, Nagano Japanese, Papa John's, Pizza Hut/Taco Bell, Popeye's, Royal Palace Chinese, Sunset Grill, Waffle House, Zaxby's, **lodging:** Holiday Inn Express, **other:** Aamco, Advance Parts, Big Lots, Chevrolet, $General, Food Depot, Ingles Foods, K-Mart, Kroger/gas, O'Reilly Parts, Rite Aid
88	Almon Rd, to Porterdale, **N gas:** Chevron/dsl, **S gas:** BP/Blimpie, Liberty, **food:** McDonald's, Subway (2mi), **other:** Riverside Estates RV Camp, transmissions/repair
84	GA 162, Salem Rd, to Pace, **N gas:** BJ's Whse/gas, QuickSpot/dsl, **other:** Suzuki, Turning Wheel RV Ctr, **S gas:** Chevron/24hr, Phillips 66, QT, RaceWay, **food:** Baskin-Robbins, Burger King, Chick-fil-A,
84	Continued Dunkin Donuts, Hardee's, House Of Min, Los Bravos Mexican, McDonald's, Quizno's, Rib Tickling BBQ, Subway, Taco Bell, Waffle House, **other:** Advance Parts, Big 10 Tire, $General, , Family$, Food Depot, Ingles/gas, Medicine Shoppe, O'Reilly Parts, Rite Aid, tires/repair
83mm	**parking area wb**
82	GA 138, GA 20, Conyers, **N gas:** BJ's Gas, QT, **food:** Applebees, Chili's, ChuckeCheese, Cracker Barrel, Don Pablo, Golden Corral, IHOP, O'Charley's, Outback Steaks, Red Lobster, Roadhouse Grill, Sonic, Subway, Up-the-Creek, **lodging:** Conyers Inn, Country Hearth Inn, Country Inn&Suites, Days Inn, Hampton Inn, Jameson Inn, La Quinta, **other:** Belk, Ford/Hyundai, , Home Depot, Kohl's, Michael's, NAPA, Office Depot, Old Navy, PetsMart, Staples, Tires+, U-Haul, Walmart SuperCtr/24hr, **S gas:** Chevron/24hr, Shell/dsl, **food:** Arby's, Blimpie, King, Capt D's, Checker's, Chick-fil-A, CiCi's, City Buffet, Folk's Rest., Grand Buffet, Hooters, Huddle House, KFC, King Buffet, Krystal/24hr, LJ Silver, McDonald's, Moe's SW Grill, Oaks Family Rest., Papa John's, Piccadilly's, Pizza Hut, Popeye's, Red Tomato, RolyPoly Sandwiches, Ruby Tuesday, Ryan's, Sonny's BBQ, Starbucks, Taco Bell, TCBY, Waffle House, Wendy's, **lodging:** InTown Inn, Microtel, Suburban Lodge, **other:** Big Lots, Big 10 Tire, Cub Foods, Dodge, $General, , Firestone/auto, Food Depot, GNC, Goodyear/auto, Honda, Jo-Ann Fabrics, Kroger/gas/24hr, NTB, PepBoys, Publix, Radio Shack, Rite Aid, Target, TJ Maxx, Toyota, USPO, mall
80	West Ave, Conyers, **N gas:** Chevron, Shell/dsl, **food:** DQ, Domino's, Mrs Winner's, Subway, Waffle House, **lodging:** Richfield Lodge, **other:** Chevrolet, Conyers Drug, Family$, Harley-Davidson, Piggly Wiggly, **S gas:** Exxon/dsl/24hr, Texaco, **food:** Longhorn Steaks, McDonald's, **lodging:** Comfort Inn, **other:** Chrysler/Dodge/Jeep, JustBrakes, Kia, Mitsubishi, Nissan, Suncoast RV Ctr, Vet
79mm	**parking area eb**
78	Sigman Rd, **N gas:** Circle K/gas, **food:** Waffle House, **S other:** Buick/GMC/Mazda/Pontiac, Crown RV Ctr, st police
75	US 278, GA 124, Turner Hill Rd, **N gas:** BP/dsl, Citgo/dsl/24hr, **S food:** Applebee's, Arizona's, Atlanta Steaks, Barnacle's Seafood, Buffalo Wild Wings, Bugaboo Steaks, Chick-fil-A, Chili's, Firehouse Subs, Grand China, KFC/Pizza Hut/Taco Bell, McDonald's, Olive Garden, Panera Bread, Ruby Tuesday, Smokey Bones BBQ, Steak n'Shake, Wendy's, Zaxby's, **lodging:** Comfort Inn, Fairfield Inn, Hilton Garden, Holiday Inn Express, Hyatt Place, **other:** Best Buy, Borders Books, Curves, Dillard's, , JC Penney, Kohl's, Macy's, Marshall's, Rite Aid, Ross, Sam's Club/gas, Sears/auto, Staples, Target, Tires+, World Mkt, mall
74	GA 124, Lithonia, **N gas:** Chevron/24hr, Shell/24, Texaco, **food:** Capt D's, KFC/Taco Bell, McDonald's, Pizza Hut, SoulFood Rest., Subway, Waffle House, Wendy's, **other:** Advance Parts, CVS Drug, **S gas:** Citgo/dsl/24hr, **food:** Da-Bomb Wings/Seafood, DQ, Dudley's Rest., Krystal/24hr, Waffle House, **lodging:** Econolodge, Microtel, **other:** $General

MADISON

COVINGTON

CONYERS

LITHONIA

GA

E ↕ W

LITHONIA

ATLANTA AREA

INTERSTATE 20 CONT'D

Exit #	Services
71	Hillandale Dr, Farrington Rd, Panola Rd, **N gas:** QT/dsl, **food:** Burger King, Checker's, KFC, McDonald's, Mrs. Winner's, Popeye's, Waffle House, **lodging:** Holiday Inn Express, Motel 6, Super 8, **other:** Family$, **S gas:** BP/dsl/24hr, Citgo, Shell, **food:** IHOP, New China, Popeye's, Ruby Tuesday, Starbucks, Subway, Taco Bell/LJ Silver, Wendy's, **lodging:** Red Roof Inn, **other:** Lowes Whse, NAPA, Publix, Radio Shack, Walgreens, Walmart SuperCtr/gas/24hr
68	Wesley Chapel Rd, Snapfinger Rd, **N food:** Blimpie, Capt D's, Checker's, Chick-fil-A, China Buffet, Church's, KFC, Popeye's, Subway, Taco Bell, Waffle House, Wendy's, **lodging:** Economy Inn, **other:** CVS Drug, Ford, Home Depot, Kroger, NTB, **S gas:** Chevron/dsl/24hr, Mobil, Shell/dsl, Texaco, **food:** Dragon Chinese, JJ's Fish& Chicken, McDonald's, Popeye's, **lodging:** Super Inn
67b a	I-285, S to Macon, N to Greenville
66	Columbia Dr (from eb, no return), **N gas:** Chevron
65	GA 155, Candler Rd, to Decatur, **N gas:** BP/24hr, Chevron, Citgo, Marathon, **food:** Pizza Hut, Popeye's, Red Lobster, Supreme Fish Delight, Wendy's, **lodging:** Econolodge, Motel 6, **other:** CVS Drug, U-Haul, **S gas:** BP, Chevron/24hr, Marathon, Shell/dsl, Stop&Go, **food:** Baskin-Robbins/Dunkin Donuts, Burger King, Checker's, China Café, Church's, DQ, Homebox Rest., KFC/Pizza Hut, McDonald's, Picadilly's, Taco Bell, **lodging:** Sunset Lodge, **other:** Big Lots, Firestone/auto, Kroger, Macy's, mall
63	Gresham Rd, **N gas:** Chevron, Citgo/dsl, **other:** Walmart SuperCtr/Subway, **S gas:** BP/24hr/dsl, Citgo, Phillips 66, Shell, **food:** Church's, **other:** auto repair
62	Flat Shoals Rd (from eb, no return), **N gas:** Exxon
61b	GA 260, Glenwood Ave, **N gas:** BP, Chevron, Texaco/dsl, **food:** KFC, Wild Bean Cafe
61a	Maynard Terrace (from eb, no return)
60b a	US 23, Moreland Ave, **N gas:** Exxon, **lodging:** Atlanta Motel, **S gas:** Phillips 66/dsl, Shell, **food:** Checker's, Krystal, LJ Silver, McDonald's, Mrs Winner's, Wendy's
59b	Memorial Dr, Glenwood Ave (from eb)
59a	Cyclorama, **N gas:** Chevron/dsl, Shell **food: other:** Confederate Ave Complex, MLK Site, **S gas:** BP
58b	Hill St (from wb, no return), **N gas:** Shell, **food:** Mrs. Winners
58a	Capitol St (from wb, no return), downtown, **N** to GA Dome, **S** Holiday Inn
57	I-75/85
56b	Windsor St (from eb), to Turner Field
56a	US 19, US 29, McDaniel St (eb only), **N gas:** Chevron
55b	Lee St (from wb), Ft McPherson, **S gas:** BP, **food:** Church's, Popeye's, Taco Bell
55a	Ashby St, **S gas:** BP, Exxon/dsl, **food:** Church's, Popeye's, Stop 1 Food Court, Taco Bell, **other:** CVS Drug, Family$, Sav-a-Lot Foods, Sears, mall
54	Langhorn St (from wb), to Cascade Rd
53	MLK Dr, to GA 139, **N gas:** Chevron/24hr, Shell/dsl/24hr, **S gas:** BP, Right Stuf Gas, **other:** auto repair

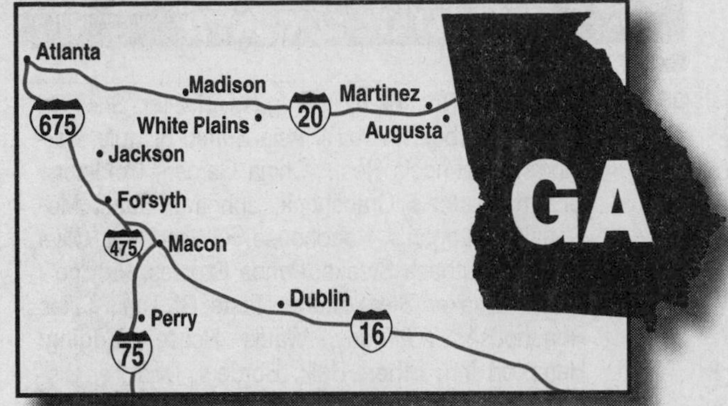

ATLANTA AREA

DOUGLASVILLE

Exit #	Services
52b a	GA 280, Holmes Dr, High Tower Rd, **S gas:** Chevron, Exxon/dsl, **food:** Church's, McDonald's, Wendy's, **other:** AutoZone, CVS Drug
51b a	I-285, S to Montgomery, N to Chattanooga
49	GA 70, Fulton Ind Blvd, **N gas:** Citgo/dsl/24hr, Shell, **food:** Capt D's, DQ, Subway, Wendy's, **lodging:** Best Value Inn, Fulton Inn, In Home Suites, Moseley Motel, **S gas:** BP/dsl, Chevron, Citgo/dsl, Shell, **food:** Grand Buffet, McDonald's, Waffle House, **lodging:** Super 8, Travelodge
48mm	Chattahoochee River
47	Six Flags Pkwy (from wb), **N gas:** BP, **lodging:** Royal Inn, **S lodging:** Howard Johnson, Sleep Inn, Wingate Inn, **other:** Six Flags Funpark
46b a	Riverside Parkway, **N gas:** Citgo/Church's, Marathon, QT, **food:** Hong Kong Buffet, Waffle House, **lodging:** Baymont Inn, **S gas:** Pure, **food:** Wendy's, **lodging:** Howard Johnson, Sleep Inn, Wingate Inn, **other:** Six Flags Funpark
44	GA 6, Thornton Rd, to Lithia Springs, **N gas:** BP/24hr, QT, RaceTrac, Shell, **food:** Burger King, Chick-fil-A, El Pollo Loco, Golden Dragon Chinese, IHOP, KFC, Krystal, McDonald's, Ruby Tuesday, Shoney's, Sonic, Subway, Taco Bell, Waffle House, Wendy's, Zaxby's, **lodging:** Budget Inn, Comfort Inn, $General, Knight's Inn, Suburban Lodge, **other:** [H], Carmax, Chevrolet, Ford, Harley-Davidson, Home Depot, Honda, Kroger/gas, Mazda, Nissan, Office Depot, Tires+, VW, Walgreens, **S food:** Cracker Barrel, La Fiesta Mexican, Wendy's, **lodging:** Country Inn&Suites, Courtyard, Fairfield Inn, Hampton Inn, Hilton Garden, Motel 6, SpringHill Suites, **other:** Buick/GMC, Chrysler/Jeep, Dodge, Toyota, Walmart SuperCtr/24hr, to Sweetwater Creek SP
42mm	**weigh sta eb**
41	Lee Rd, to Lithia Springs, **N gas:** Citgo/dsl, **other:** transmissions, **S gas:** Chevron/dsl, Shell/Blimpie/dsl, **food:** Waffle House
37	GA 92, to Douglasville, **N gas:** Marathon, RaceTrac, Shell/dsl/24hr, **food:** Checker's, Chick-fil-A, Church's, Cracker Barrel, DQ, Dunkin Donuts, Kenny's Rest., KFC, Krystal, Longhorn Steaks, McDonald's, Monterrey Mexican, Mrs Winner's, Papa John's, Pizza Hut, Subway, Waffle House, Wendy's, **lodging:** Best Western, Comfort Inn, Day's Inn, Holiday Inn Express, Ramada Ltd, Royal Inn, Super 8, **other:** [H], Advance Parts, AutoZone, Big Lots, CVS Drug, Family$, Fred's Drug, Kroger/24hr, NAPA, O'Reilly Parts, Tires+, Walgreens, **S gas:** QT, Waffle House, **other:** Aamco

E ↔ W

DOUGLASVILLE

VILLA RICA

GA

INTERSTATE 20 CONT'D

Exit #	Services
36	Chapel Hill Rd, **N** [H], **S** **gas:** QT/24hr, Shell/dsl **food:** Applebee's, Arby's, Asia Buffet, Blimpie, Carraba's, Chaunce's Rest., China Garden, Coldstone Creamery, Joe's Crabshack, Johnny's Subs, McDonald's, Logan's Roadhouse, O'Charley's, Olive Garden, Outback Steaks, Panda Express, Provino's Italian, Quaker Steak&Lube, Taste Of Thai, Texas Roadhouse, TGIFriday, Waffle House, **lodging:** Hampton Inn, **other:** Belk, Borders, Dillard's, Discount Tire, Firestone/auto, JC Penney, Kohl's, Macy's, Marshall's, Michael's, Old Navy, PetsMart, Rite Aid, Ross, Sears/auto, Target, mall
34	GA 5, to Douglasville, **N** **gas:** RaceTrac, Texaco, **food:** Hooters, Ryan's, Waffle House, Williamson Bro's BBQ, Zaxby's, **lodging:** Holiday Inn Express, La Quinta, Sleep Inn, **other:** $Tree, Honda/Isuzu, Sam's Club, Walmart SuperCtr/24hr, **S** **gas:** Chevron/24hr, Circle K, Shell, **food:** Applebee's, Atlanta Bread, Bruster's, Buffalo Wild Wings, Burger King, Chili's, Chick-fil-A, ChuckeCheese, CiCi's, DQ, Dunkin Donuts, El Rodeo Mexican, Fiesta Mexican, Folk's Rest., Golden Buddah, Golden Corral, IHOP, KFC, Krystal, LJ Silver, McDonald's, Moe's SW Grill, Papa John's, Pizza Hut, Quizno's, Red Lobster, Ruby Tuesday, Seabreeze Seafood, Sonic, Sonny's BBQ, Subway, Taco Bell, Taco Mac, Waffle House, Wendy's, **lodging:** InTown Suites, **other:** Advance Parts, Best Buy, Big 10 Tire, , GNC, Goodyear/auto, Home Depot, Jo-Ann Crafts, K-Mart, Kroger, Lowes Whse, Office Depot, PetCo, Publix, Radio Shack, Tuesday Morning, U-Haul, USPO, Walgreens
30	Post Rd, **S** **gas:** Shell/dsl
26	Liberty Rd, Villa Rica, **N** **gas:** Shell/dsl, Swifty/dsl, **food:** China Wok, Mex-Grill, Subway, Waffle House, **other:** [H], Publix, Walgreens, **S** **gas:** Chevron, Wilco/Hess/Subway/Godfather's Pizza/dsl/scales/24hr/@, **lodging:** American Inn
24	GA 101, GA 61, Villa Rica, **N** **gas:** Citgo, RaceTrac, Shell/dsl, **food:** Arby's, Chick-fil-A, Hardee's, KFC/Taco Bell, Krystal, McDonald's, Pizza Hut, Romero's Mexican, Subway, Waffle House, Wendy's, **lodging:** Comfort Inn, Days Inn, Hometowne Lodge, Super 8, **other:** [H], AutoZone, CVS Drug, Ingles Foods, Piggly Wiggly, Rite Aid, **S** **gas:** QT, Shell/dsl, **food:** Burger King, Capt D's, Domino's, El Ranchito Mexican, O'Charley's, Papa John's, Philly Connection, Waffle House, Zaxby's, **other:** Chevrolet, $Tree, Home Depot, GNC, Walmart SuperCtr/Subway/24hr, to W GA Coll
21mm	Little Tallapoosa River
19	GA 113, Temple, **N** **gas:** ***FLYING J***/Conoco/Country Mkt/dsl/24hr, Pilot/Subway/Wendy's/dsl/24hr/@, Texaco, **food:** Fortune Star Chinese, Hardee's, McDonald's, Waffle House, **other:** Truck-o-Mat/scales
15mm	**weigh sta wb**
11	US 27, Bremen, Bowdon, **N** **gas:** Bremen Express/dsl, SuperMart/dsl, Texaco, **food:** Arby's, Capt D's, Checker's, Chopsticks Chinese, Cracker Barrel, Juanito's, KFC, McDonald's, Papa John's, Pizza Hut, Quizno's, Subway, Waffle House, Wendy's, Zaxby's, **lodging:** Day's Inn, Holiday Inn Express, Hampton
11	Continued Inn, Quality Inn, **other:** [H], Advance Parts, $General, Ford, Ingles Foods, Walmart SuperCtr/24hr/gas (1mi), **S** **gas:** BP/dsl, Kangaroo, **food:** Waffle House, John Tanner SP
9	Waco Rd, **N** Love's/Subway/dsl
5	GA 100, Tallapoosa, **N** **gas:** Citgo/dsl/24hr, Exxon/dsl/24hr, **food:** Waffle House **other:** Big Oak RV park, **S** **gas:** Noble TrkStp/dsl/24hr/@, Pilot/KFC/Taco Bell/dsl/scales/24hr, Shell/Subway, **food:** DQ, Huddle House, Janet's Diner, **lodging:** Comfort Inn, **other:** to John Tanner SP
1mm	**Welcome Ctr eb, full [handicapped] facilities, [phone], vending, [picnic], litter barrels, petwalk**
0mm	Georgia/Alabama state line, Eastern/Central time zone

INTERSTATE 59

N ↔ S

TRENTON

Exit #	Services
	I-59 begins/ends on I-24, exit 167. For I-24, turn to Tennessee Interstate 24.
20mm	I-24, W to Nashville, E to Chattanooga
17	Slygo Rd, to New England, **W** **gas:** Midnite/dsl, **other:** KOA (2mi)
11	GA 136, Trenton, **E** **gas:** Chevron/dsl, Exxon/dsl, Kangaroo, **food:** Asian Garden, Hardee's, McDonald's, Pizza Hut, Subway, **lodging:** Days Inn, **other:** Advance Parts, CVS Drug, Family$, Ingles, O'Reilly Parts, to Cloudland Canyon SP, **W** **gas:** BP, Citgo, **food:** Huddle House, Krystal, Little Caesar's, Taco Bell, Wendy's, **other:** BiLo, $General, Food Lion
4	Rising Fawn, **E** **gas:** Citgo/24hr, **W** **gas:** BP/dsl/24hr, Pilot/Chester Fried/Subway/dsl/24hr, **other:** camping
0mm	Georgia/Alabama state line, eastern/central time zone

INTERSTATE 75

N ↔ S

Exit #	Services
355mm	Georgia/Tennessee state line
354mm	Chickamauga Creek
353	GA 146, Rossville, **E** **gas:** BP/24hr, **lodging:** Cloud Springs Lodge, **W** **gas:** BP/Subway/dsl, Shell, **other:** antiques
352mm	**Welcome Ctr sb, full [handicapped] facilities, info, [phone], vending, [picnic], litter barrels, petwalk**
350	GA 2, Bfd Pkwy, to Ft Oglethorpe, **E** **gas:** BP/dsl, Kangaroo, **lodging:** Hampton Inn, Hometown Inn, **W** **gas:** Murphy USA, RaceTrac/dsl/24hr, Shell, **food:** BBQ Corral, **other:** [H], KOA, **1-4 mi W food:** Fazoli's, O'Charly's, Panera Bread, Taco Bell, Zaxby's, **other:** Walmart SuperCtr/24hr, to Chickamauga NP
348	GA 151, Ringgold, **E** **gas:** BP/dsl, Shell/dsl, **food:** Cracker Barrel, Hardee's, Krystal/24hr, KFC, McDonald's, Pizza Hut, Ruby Tuesday, Subway, Taco Bell, Waffle House, **lodging:** Day's Inn, Holiday Inn Express, Red Roof Inn, Super 8, **other:** Advance Parts, Curves, CVS Drug, Chevrolet, Chrysler/Jeep, Family$, Ingles, RV camping, Walgreens, **W** **gas:** BP, Exxon, Shell, **food:** Domino's, New China, Wendy's, **lodging:** Comfort Inn, **other:** Food Lion, Peterbilt
345	US 41, US 76, Ringgold, **E** **gas:** BP, **W** **gas:** Chevron, Cochran's/Midnite/rest./scales/dsl/24hr/@, Kangaroo/Subway/scales/dsl, **food:** Waffle House

INTERSTATE 75 CONT'D

N ↕ S

DALTON

Exit #	Services
343mm	**weigh sta both lanes**
341	GA 201, to Varnell, Tunnel Hill, **W gas:** Chevron, Shell, **other:** carpet outlets
336	US 41, US 76, Dalton, Rocky Face, **E gas:** Murphy USA, RaceTrac, Shell, **food:** Waffle House, **lodging:** Econolodge, Stay Lodge, **other:** [H], Checker Parts, Ford/Lincoln/Mercury, Home Depot, Walmart SuperCtr/24hr, **W gas:** BP/dsl, Exxon, **food:** Bryson's Grill, Cornerstone Grill, Tijuana's Mexican, Wendy's, **lodging:** Best Western, Guest Inn, Motel 6, Staylodge, Super 8, carpet outlets
333	GA 52, Dalton, **E gas:** BP/dsl, Citgo, Exxon/dsl, RaceTrac/dsl, **food:** Amici's Italian, Applebee's, Burger King, Capt D's, Chick-fil-A, CiCi's, Cracker Barrel, DQ, Five Guys Burgers, Fuji Japanese, IHOP, KFC, Los Pablos Mexican, LJ Silver, Longhorn Steaks, McDonald's, O'Charley's, Outback Steaks, Panera Bread, Pizza Hut, Schlotsky's, Shoney's, Sonic, Starbucks, Steak'n Shake, Taco Bell, Waffle House, Wendy's, **lodging:** Best Inn, Days Inn, Hampton Inn, Travelodge, **other:** BigLots, Chevrolet, Chrysler/Jeep, Harley-Davidson, Isuzu, K-Mart, Kroger/gas, Tanger Outlets/famous brands, TJ Maxx, Walgreens, **W food:** Chili's, Red Lobster, **lodging:** Comfort Inn, Courtyard, Country Inn Suites, Holiday Inn, Jameson Inn, La Quinta, Quality Inn, Ramada, **other:** NW GA Trade/Conv Ctr
328	GA 3, to US 41, **E gas:** BP/dsl, Pilot/Arby's/dsl/scales/24hr, **food:** Waffle House, Wendy's, **lodging:** Super Motel, **W** carpet outlets
326	Carbondale Rd, **E gas:** Chevron/dsl, Pilot/McDonalds/Subway/dsl/scales, **W gas:** BP, Exxon
320	GA 136, to Lafayette, Resaca, **E gas:** ***FLYING J*** /Cookery/dsl/LP/rest./24hr, **other:** truckwash, truck repair/parts
319mm	Oostanaula River, **rest area sb, full [handicapped] facilities, [phone], vending, [picnic], litter barrels, petwalk**
318	US 41, Resaca, **E gas:** Hess/Wilco/DQ/Wendy's/scales/dsl/24hr, **food:** Hardee's, **lodging:** Relax Inn, **W gas:** Pure, Shell/dsl, **food:** Chuckwagon Rest., **lodging:** Best Inn, Super 8
317	GA 225, to Chatsworth, **E** New Echota HS, Vann House HS, **W gas:** BP (1mi), **lodging:** Express Inn
315	GA 156, Redbud Rd, to Calhoun, **E gas:** Citgo/dsl, Kangaroo, **food:** Waffle House, **lodging:** Oglethorpe Inn, **other:** Food Lion, KOA (2mi), **W gas:** BP/dsl, Liberty/Subway/dsl, Shell, **food:** Arby's, Shoney's, **lodging:** Ramada Ltd, **other:** [H], Rite Aid
312	GA 53, to Calhoun, **E gas:** Shell/dsl, **food:** Cracker Barrel, Longhorn Steaks, **lodging:** Budget Host, Days Inn, Country Inn, La Quinta, **other:** Prime Outlets/famous brands, **W gas:** BP/Arby's, Chevron/dsl, Kangaroo, Murphy USA, **food:** Big John's Rest., Bojangles, Burger King, Capt D's, Checker's, Chick-fil-A, China Palace, DQ, Domino's, Eastern Cafe, El Nopal Mexican, Gondolier Pizza, Huddle House, IHOP, KFC, Krystal/24hr, Little Caesar's, Los Reyes Mexican, LJ Silver, McDonald's, Papa's Pizza, Pizza Hut, Ryan's, Ruby Tuesday, Starbucks, Subway, Taco Bell, Tokyo Steaks, Wendy's, Zaxby's, **lodging:**

RESACA

CALHOUN

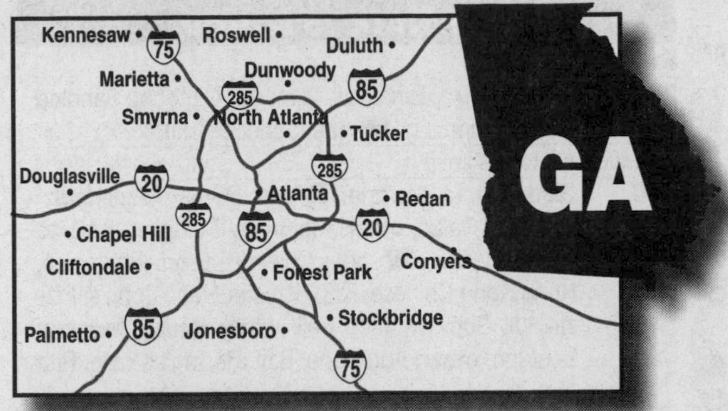

ADAIRSVILLE

Exit #	Services
312	Continued Guest Inn, Hampton Inn, Holiday Inn Express, Jameson Inn, Motel 6, Royal Inn, **other:** Advance Parts, AutoZone, $General, GNC, Goodyear/auto, Home Depot, Ingles, Kroger/gas, Office Depot, Walmart SuperCtr/24hr, Vet
308mm	**rest area nb, full [handicapped] facilities, [phone], [picnic], litter barrels, vending, petwalk**
306	GA 140, Adairsville, **E gas:** Cowboy's/dsl, Patty's/Citgo/dsl/24hr/@, QT/dsl/scales/24hrs, Shell, **food:** Cracker Barrel, Huddle House, Wendy's, **W gas:** All American/dsl/scales, BP/dsl, Chevron, Exxon/dsl, **food:** Burger King, Hardee's, McDonald's, Taco Bell, Waffle House, Zaxby's, **lodging:** Best Western, Comfort Inn, Ramada Ltd, **other:** Harvest Moon RV Park
296	Cassville-White Rd, **E gas:** Pilot/McDonald's/Subway/dsl/scales, Pure, TA/Exxon/Burger King/Pizza Hut/Popeye's/Taco Bell/dsl/scales/24hr/@, Texaco/24hr, **lodging:** Sleep Inn, **other:** truckwash, **W gas:** Chevron, Citgo/dsl, Shell, **food:** Second Half Grill, **lodging:** Best Inn, Budget Host/rest., Howard Johnson, Red Carpet Inn, **other:** KOA
293	US 411, to White, **E gas:** BP/dsl, Sunoco/dsl, **lodging:** Quality Inn, **W gas:** Chevron/dsl, Citgo/dsl/24hr, **food:** AJ's Cafe, Waffle House, **lodging:** Courtesy Inn, Holiday Inn, **other:** Harley-Davidson, RV camping, mineral museum, st patrol
290	GA 20, to Rome, **E gas:** Chevron/Subway/dsl, Exxon/dsl, Kangaroo/dsl, **food:** Arby's, Fruit Jar Cafe, McDonald's, Wendy's, **lodging:** Best Western, Country Inn Suites, Econolodge, Motel 6, Ramada Ltd, Red Roof Inn, Super 8, **W gas:** BP, Murphy USA (1.5mi), Shell, **food:** Cracker Barrel, Michael's BBQ, Pruitt's BBQ, Shoney's, Waffle House, **lodging:** Day's Inn, Hampton Inn, **other:** [H], RV camping (7mi), Walmart SuperCtr (1.5mi)
288	GA 113, Cartersville, **0-2 mi W gas:** BP/dsl, Exxon/Subway/dsl, **food:** Applebee's, Burger King, Chick-Fil-A, Chili's, Gondolier Pizza, IHOP, KFC, Krystal/24hr, Las Palmas Mexican, Longhorn Steaks, McDonald's, Moe's SW Grill, Mrs Winner's, Pizza Hut, Publix, Red Lobster, Starbucks, Taco Bell, Waffle House, Wing Moon, **lodging:** Fairfield Inn, Knight's Inn, Quality Inn, **other:** Belk, Chrysler/Jeep/Dodge, K-Mart, Kohl's, Kroger, Rite Aid, Staples, Target, to Etowah Indian Mounds (6mi)
286mm	Etowah River
285	Emerson, **E gas:** Texaco/24hr, **lodging:** Red Top Mtn Lodge, **other:** to Allatoona Dam, to Red Top Mtn SP

INTERSTATE 75 CONT'D

N ↕ S

Exit #	Services
283	Allatoona Rd, Emerson, **2 mi E** Allatoona Landing Resort, camping, **W gas:** Sunoco (1mi)
280mm	Allatoona Lake
278	Glade Rd, to Acworth, **E gas:** BP/dsl, Shell, **lodging:** Best Value, **other:** McKinney Camping (3mi), to Glade Marina, **W gas:** Chevron, **food:** Bojangles, Hong Kong Chinese, KFC, Krystal, Papa John's, Pizza Hut, Subway, Taco Bell, Waffle House, **lodging:** Best Inn, **other:** AutoZone, BigLots, Ingles/cafe, Rite Aid
277	GA 92, Acworth, **E gas:** BP, RaceTrac, **food:** Hardee's, Shoney's, Waffle House, **lodging:** Comfort Suites, La Quinta, Ramada Ltd, **W gas:** Chevron/dsl, Shell/DQ/dsl, **food:** Bamboo Garden, China Chef, Domino's, McDonald's, Ricardo's Mexican, Sonic, Subway, Taco 2 Go, Waffle House, Wendy's, Zaxby's, **lodging:** Best Western, Day's Inn, Econolodge, Motel 6, Super 8, **other:** Advance Parts, CVS Drug, Goodyear/auto, Publix, Walgreens
273	Wade Green Rd, **E gas:** BP, Pure, RaceTrac, **food:** Arby's, Burger King, Dunkin Donuts, Las Palmas Mexican, McDonald's, Mrs Winners, Papa John's, Pizza Hut/Taco Bell, Subway, Waffle House, **lodging:** Sleep Inn, Travelodge, **other:** BigLots, , GNC, Goodyear/auto, Publix, Rite Aid, **W gas:** Shell, Texaco/dsl, **food:** BBQ Street, Coldstone Creamery, Johnny's Pizza/Subs, Quizno's, Starbucks, Wendy's, Wing Zone, **other:** Home Depot, Kroger/gas, Walgreens
271	Chastain Rd, to I-575 N, **E gas:** Chevron, **food:** CA Dreaming, Brewsters, Chick-Fil-A, Chilito's Mexican, Cracker Barrel, Dunkin Donuts, Firehouse Subs, Five Guys Burgers, Kayson's Grill, Little Zio, Los Reyes, McAlister's Deli, O'Charley's, Panda Express, Panera Bread, Sidelines Grille, Starbucks, Taco Mac, ToGo's/Baskin Robbins, Zaxby's, Zucca Pizza, **lodging:** Best Western, Comfort Inn, Embassy Suites, Extended Stay America, Fairfield Inn, La Quinta, Residence Inn, Suburban Lodge, Super 8, **other:** Goodyear/auto, Outlets Ltd Mall, **W gas:** Citgo, Swifty Save Gas/Blimpie, Shell/dsl, **food:** Arby's, Mrs Winners, Waffle House/24hr, Wendy's, **lodging:** Country Inn Suites, SpringHill Suites, Sun Suites, **other:** museum
269	to US 41, to Marietta, **E gas:** Chevron/24hr, Shell, Texaco/dsl, **food:** Applebee's, Burger King, Fuddrucker's, Highlands Grill, Honey Baked Ham, Longhorn Steaks, McDonald's, New China, Olive Garden, Pizza Hut, Provino's, Red Lobster, Shogun Japanese, Smoothie King, Smokey Bones, Starbucks, Subway, Twisted Taco, Waffle House, **lodging:** Comfort Inn, Econolodge, Holiday Inn Express, La Quinta, Red Roof Inn, Super 8, **other:** Barnes&Noble, Big 10 Tire, Firestone/auto, Home Depot, JC Penney, Macy's, Marshall's, Publix, Sears/auto, TJ Maxx, mall, **W gas:** BP, Exxon, **food:** Bahama Breeze, Bailey's Grill, Bugaboo, Carrabbas, Copelands Grill, Creek Steaks, Chick-fil-A, Chili's, ChuckeCheese, Coldstone, Golden Corral, Joe's Crabshack, Macaroni Grill, On-the-Border, Outback Steaks, Rafferty's, Starbucks, Steak'n Shake, Sweet Tomato, TGIFriday, Willy's Mexican, **lodging:** Day's Inn, Hampton Inn, Hilton
269	Continued Garden, Quality Inn, Wingate Inn, **other:** Best Buy, Borders, Buick/Pontiac/GMC, CarMax, Chevrolet, Costco/gas, Ford/Lincoln/Mercury, Goodyear/auto, Jo-Anne Fabrics, Kia/Toyota, Nissan, Mitsubishi, NTB, Office Depot, Old Navy, PetsMart, Target, mall, to Kennesaw Mtn NP
268	I-575 N, GA 5 N, to Canton
267b a	GA 5 N, to US 41, Marietta
265	GA120, N Marietta Pkwy, **W gas:** Chevron, Shell/dsl, **food:** Arbys, Bojangles, Chick-fil-A, KFC, **lodging:** Days Inn, Sun Inn, Suburban Lodge, Travelers Motel
263	GA 120, to Roswell, **E gas:** Chevron/dsl/24hr, QT, Texaco/24hr, **W gas:** Exxon/dsl, RaceTrac, **food:** Applebee's, Capt D's, China Kitchen, DQ, Hardee's, Haveli Rest., Piccadilly's, Subway, **lodging:** Best Western, Crowne Plaza, Fairfield Inn, Hampton Inn, Marietta Motel, Ramada Ltd, Regency Inn, Super 8, Wyndham Garden, **other:** U-Haul, Atl-Marietta RV Resort
261	GA 280, Delk Rd, to Dobbins AFB, **E gas:** Exxon, RaceTrac, Shell/McDonald's/24hr, **food:** CC Cafeteria, China Wok, Hardee's, KFC/Taco Bell, Murphy's Deli, Ruby Tuesday, Spaghetti Whse, **lodging:** Budget Inn, Courtyard, Drury Inn, Motel 6, Scottish Inn, Sleep Inn, Super 8, Travelers Inn, **other:** Publix, **W gas:** BP, Chevron/24hr, **food:** Cracker Barrel, D&B Rest., Waffle House, **lodging:** Best Inn, Comfort Inn, Days Inn, Fairfield Inn, Holiday Inn, La Quinta, Quality Inn, Wingate Inn
260	Windy Hill Rd, to Smyrna, **E gas:** BP, **food:** Boston Mkt, Famous Dave's, Fuddrucker's, Houston's Rest., Jersey Mike's Subs, NY Pizza, Pappasito's Cantina, Pappadeaux Seafood, Philly Cafe, Salgrosso Brazilian, , Schlotsky's, Starbucks, Subway, TGIFriday, **lodging:** Econolodge, Extended Stay Deluxe, Hilton Garden, Hyatt, Marriott, Studio Lodge, **other:** CVS Drug, **W gas:** Chevron, Citgo, Shell, **food:** Arby's, Chick-fil-A, Fatburger, Halftime Grill, McDonald's, Panda Express, Popeye's, Starbucks, Waffle House, Wendy's, **lodging:** Best Western, Country Inn Suites, Courtyard, Day's Inn, DoubleTree, Hilton, Masters Inn, Red Roof Inn, **other:** H, Target
259b a	I-285, W to Birmingham, E to Greenville, Montgomery
258	Cumberland Pkwy, **W food:** Doc Green's Rest., Hooters, Moe's SW Grill, Shane's Ribshack, Subway
257mm	Chattahoochee River
256	to US 41, Northside Pkwy
255	US 41, W Paces Ferry Rd, **E gas:** Chevron, Shell/dsl, **food:** Blue Ridge Grill, Caribou Coffee, Chick-fil-A, Houston's Rest., McDonald's/playplace, OK Café/24hr, Pero's Pizza, Starbucks, Steak'n Shake, Taco Bell, Willy's Rest., **other:** H, Ace Hardware, CVS Drug, Publix, **W gas:** Exxon/24hr
254	Moores Mill Rd
252b	Howell Mill Rd, **E gas:** Shell, **food:** Chick-fil-A, Domino's, McDonald's, Willy's Grill, **other:** Goodyear, Publix, Rite Aid, USPO, **W gas:** Shell, **food:** Arby's, Arthur's Italian, Chin Chin Chinese, Einstein Bro's, Kayson's, KFC/Pizza Hut, Mexican, Rest., Piccadilly, Sensational Subs, Starbucks, Subway, Taco Bell, US BBQ, Waffle House, Wendy's, **lodging:** Budget Inn, Holiday Inn, **other:** Ace Hardware, Firestrone/auto,

ACWORTH / MARIETTA / SMYRNA

INTERSTATE 75 CONT'D

N ↕ S

Exit #	Services
252b	Continued GNC, Just Brakes, Kroger, Office Depot, PetsMart, Ross, TJ Maxx, Walmart Super Ctr/24hr
252a	US 41, Northside Dr, **E gas:** [H], **W gas:** Shell, **food:** Krystal/24hr, Little Zio's, McDonald's, Waffle House, **lodging:** Day's Inn
251	I-85 N, to Greenville
250	Techwood Dr (from sb), 10th St, 14th St, **E lodging:** Travelodge
249d	10th St, Spring St (from nb), **E gas:** BP, Chevron/24hr, **food:** Checker's, Domino's, Pizza Hut, The Varsity, **lodging:** Fairfield Inn, Regency Suites, Renaissance Hotel, Residence Inn, **W food:** McDonald's, **lodging:** Courtyard, Comfort Inn, **other:** [H], to GA Tech
249c	Williams St (from sb), downtown, to GA Dome
249b	Pine St, Peachtree St (from nb), downtown, **W lodging:** Hilton, Marriott
249a	Courtland St (from sb), downtown, **W lodging:** Hilton, Marriott, **other:** GA St U
248d	Piedmont Ave, Butler St (from sb), downtown, **W lodging:** Courtyard, Fairfield Inn, Radisson, **other:** [H], Ford, MLK NHS
248c	GA 10 E, Intn'l Blvd, downtown, **W lodging:** Hilton, Holiday Inn, Marriott Marquis, Radisson
248b	Edgewood Ave (from nb), **W other:** [H], downtown, hotels
248a	MLK Dr (from sb), **W** st capitol, to Underground Atlanta
247	I-20, E to Augusta, W to Birmingham
246	Georgia Ave, Fulton St, **E lodging:** Comfort Inn, Country Inn& Suites, Holiday Inn, **other:** stadium, **W gas:** BP, **food:** KFC, **other:** to Coliseum, GSU
245	Ormond St, Abernathy Blvd, **E lodging:** Comfort Inn, Country Inn& Suites, **other:** stadium, **W** st capitol
244	University Ave, **E gas:** Chevron, Exxon, **other:** NAPA, **W food:** Mrs Winner's
243	GA 166, Lakewood Fwy, to East Point
242	I-85 S, to ✈
241	Cleveland Ave, **E gas:** BP, Chevron, **food:** Checker's, Church's, McDonald's, Subway, **lodging:** Palace Inn, **other:** Advance Parts, K-Mart, **W gas:** Shell, Marathon, Phillips 66, Texaco, **food:** Blimpie, Burger King, Krystal/24hr, Mrs Winners, **lodging:** American Inn, Day's Inn, **other:** CVS Drug, Kroger
239	US 19, US 41, **E gas:** Chevron/dsl, **food:** Waffle House, **other:** USPO, **W gas:** Texaco, **food:** IHOP, McDonald's, Wendy's, **lodging:** Best Western, to ✈
238b a	I-285 around Atlanta
237a	GA 85 S (from sb), **W food:** Denny's, **lodging:** Burger King, McDonald's, Waffle House, **lodging:** Day's Inn, Day's Lodge
237	GA 331, Forest Parkway, **E gas:** BP, Chevron/dsl, Shell/McDonald's, **food:** Burger King, Mr Taco, Subway, Waffle House, **lodging:** Econolodge, **other:** Farmer's Mkt, **W gas:** BP, **food:** Denny's, **lodging:** Day's Inn, Ramada Ltd
235	US 19, US 41, GA 3, Jonesboro, **E gas:** Chevron/dsl, Exxon/Subway/dsl, Phillips 66, Valero, **food:**

ATLANTA AREA

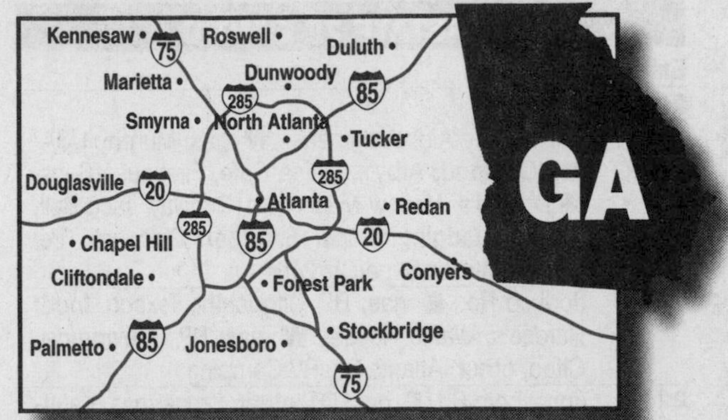

Exit #	Services
235	Continued Waffle House, **lodging:** Travelodge, **W gas:** BP, Shell, Texaco/dsl, **food:** Applebee's, Burger King, Checker's, ChuckeCheese, Dunkin Donuts, Folk's Rest., Hooters, Krystal, Popeye's, Red Lobster, Tokyo Buffet, Waffle House, Zaxby's, **lodging:** Best Value, Econolodge, Holiday Inn, Motel 6, **other:** [H], Office Depot, O'Reilly Parts
233	GA 54, Morrow, **E gas:** BP, Citgo, Marathon, **food:** Cracker Barrel, IHOP, Krystal/24hr, Mrs Winner's, Papa Buffet, Taco Bell, Waffle House, Wendy's, **lodging:** Best Western, Days Inn, Drury Inn, Red Roof Inn, **other:** Walmart SuperCtr, **W gas:** Circle K, Exxon/24hr, **food:** China Café, KFC, Lenny's Subs, McDonald's, Quizno's, Subway, Waffle House, **lodging:** Hampton Inn, Quality Inn, **other:** Acura, Best Buy, Costco/gas, Harley-Davidson, Macy's, Nissan, TJ Maxx, Toyota, Tuesday Morning
231	Mt Zion Blvd, **E gas:** QT, **other:** Chrysler/Dodge/Jeep, Ford/Lincoln/Mercury, Honda, **W gas:** Chevron, Exxon/dsl, Texaco/dsl, **food:** Arby's, Boston's Rest., Brewster's, Burger Shack, Burger King, Chick-fil-A, Chili's, Joe's Crabshack, Longhorn Steaks, McDonald's, Mo-Joe's, Panda Express, Papa John's, Pizza Hut, Steak'n Shake, Subway, Truett's Rest., Waffle House, Wendy's, Wok Asian, **lodging:** Country Inn&Suites, Extended Stay America, Sleep Inn, Sun Suites, **other:** Barnes & Noble, Best Buy, Home Depot, Michael's, NTB, Old Navy, PetsMart, Publix, Ross, Target
228	GA 54, GA 138, Jonesboro, **E gas:** Exxon, Raceway/24hr, **food:** Applebee's, Arby's, Broadway Diner, Burger King, Chick-fil-A, ChinChin Chinese, CiCi's, DQ, Frontera Mexican, Golden Corral, Honeybaked Ham, IHOP, KFC, Krystal, McDonald's, O'Charlie's, Piccadilly's, Subway, Taco Mac, Tokyo Seafood, Waffle House, Wendy's, **lodging:** Best Western, Day's Inn, Comfort Inn, Holiday Inn, Howard Johnson, La Quinta, Hampton Inn, Holiday Inn, Motel 6, Red Roof Inn, **other:** [H], GNC, Goodyear, K-Mart, Kroger/dsl, Lowes Whse, Office Depot, Tires+, **W gas:** BP/24hr, Marathon, Sunoco/Wendy's, **food:** Dragon Garden Chinese, Ranchero's Mexican, **other:** CarMax, CVS Drug, Kohl's
227	I-675 N, to I-285 E (from nb)
224	Hudson Bridge Rd, **E gas:** Shell, Texaco/dsl, **food:** Chick-fil-A, China Wok, DQ, KFC, La Hacienda, Outback Steaks, Pizza Hut, Starbucks, Subway, Waffle House, Wendy's, **lodging:** Baymont Inn, **other:** [H],

MORROW

JONESBORO

GA

INTERSTATE 75 CONT'D

Exit #	Services
224	Continued Publix, Rite Aid, Walgreens, **W gas:** Murphy USA/dsl, QT, **food:** Arby's, China Cafe, Firehouse Subs, McDonald's, Mellow Mushroom, Subway, Taco Bell, Zaxby's, **lodging:** Super 8, **other:** Discount Tire, $Tree, Walmart SuperCtr/24hr
222	Jodeco Rd, **E gas:** BP, Citgo/24hr, Texaco, **food:** Hardee's, Waffle House, **W gas:** BP, Chevron/dsl, Citgo, **other:** Atlanta So. RV Camping
221	Jonesboro Rd, **E gas:** QT, **other:** Kroger/gas, Kauffman Tire, **W food:** Arby's, Burger King, Chili's, Cici's Pizza, Golden Corral, Hooter's, Logan's Roadhouse, Longhorn Steaks, Marble Slab Creamery, McDonald's, O'Charley's, Olive Garden, Quizno's, Red Lobster, Rocky's Pizza, Starbucks, Subway, Truett's Grill, Wendy's, **lodging:** Fairfield Inn, **other:** Belk, Best Buy, Books-A-Million, BJ's Whse/gas, Home Depot, Marshall's, Michael's, PetsMart, Radio Shack, Ross, Sam's Club/gas, Staples, Target
218	GA 20, GA 81, McDonough, **E gas:** BP, Murphy USA, QT, Texaco, **food:** Applebee's, Arby's, Blimpie, Burger King, China Star, Cracker Barrel, DQ, KFC, IHOP, McDonald's, Moe's SW Grill, Mrs Winner's, OB's BBQ, Pizza Hut, Quizno's, Ruby Tuesday, Taco Bell, 3 Dollar Cafe, Tokyo Japanese, Waffle House, Wendy's, Zaxby's, **lodging:** Best Inn, Best Western, Economy Inn, Hampton Inn, Motel 6, **other:** Aamco, $General, Goodyear, Lowe's Whse, Office Depot, Rite Aid, Walmart SuperCtr, **W gas:** Citgo/dsl, RaceTrac, Shell/24hr, **food:** Chick-fil-A, El Agade Mexican, Firehouse Subs, Fuddruckers, Starbucks, Subway, Waffle House, **lodging:** Comfort Inn, Econolodge, Hilton Garden, Holiday Inn Express, Super 8, **other:** JC Penney, Kohl's, Toyota
216	GA 155, McDonough, Blacksville, **E gas:** Shell, Sunoco/Backyard Burger, Texaco/dsl, **food:** Blimpie, **lodging:** Best Value, Budget Inn, Day's Inn, Roadway Inn, **other:** Chevrolet, Buick/Pontiac, Lincoln/Mercury, GMC/Pontiac, **W gas:** BP/dsl, Chevron, Citgo, Citgo/dsl/24hr, Mystik/dsl, QT, **food:** Da Vinci's Pizza, Krystal, Kuma Japanese, Legends Grill, Subway, Waffle House, **lodging:** Country Inn&Suites, Quality Inn
212	to US 23, Locust Grove, **E gas:** BP/McDonald's/dsl, Chevron/Burger King, Citgo/dsl, JP, Marathon/Subway, Shell/dsl, **food:** Capt D's, Country Steaks, Denny's, Gabino's Mexican, Huddle House, KFC/Pizza Hut/Taco Bell, Shane's Ribshack, Sunrise China, Waffle House, Wendy's, Zaxby's, **lodging:** Economy Inn, Executive Inn, La Quinta, Ramada Ltd, Red Roof Inn, **other:** Ingles/gas, NapaCare, Tanger Outlet/famous brands, **W gas:** Citgo/DQ/dsl, Exxon/dsl, **lodging:** Comfort Suites, Scottish Inn, Sundown Lodge, Super 8, **other:** Bumper Parts
205	GA 16, to Griffin, Jackson, **E gas:** BP, **W gas:** BP, Chevron/dsl, **other:** Forest Glen RV Park, auto repair
201	GA 36, to Jackson, Barnesville, **E gas:** Love's/McDonald's/dsl/grill/scales/24hr, TA/Subway/Taco Bell/dsl/scales/24hr/@, Wilco/Hess/DQ/Stuckey's/Wendy's/dsl/scales/24hr/@, **other:** Blue Beacon, **W gas:** BP/dsl, *FLYING J*/Conoco/Cookery/dsl/LP/24hr, **other:** Sagon RV Ctr, Speedco Lube, truckwash
198	Highfalls Rd, **E gas:** Exxon (1mi), **food:** High Falls BBQ, Ken's Cafe, **lodging:** High Falls Lodge, **other:** High Falls SP, **W** High Falls RV Park
193	Johnstonville Rd, **E gas:** BP
190mm	**weigh sta both lanes**
188	GA 42, **E gas:** Shell/24hr, **lodging:** Best Western, Budget Inn, **other:** to Indian Spings SP, RV camping
187	GA 83, Forsyth, **E lodging:** Econolodge, New Forsyth Inn, Regency Inn, **W gas:** BP/Circle K, Citgo/dsl, Marathon, Shell, **food:** Burger King, Capt D's, China Inn, DQ, Hardee's, McDonald's, Pizza Hut, Subway, Taco Bell, Waffle House, Wendy's, **lodging:** Day's Inn, Tradewinds Motel, **other:** Advance Parts, Freshway Foods, O'Reilly Parts, Walmart
186	Tift College Dr, Juliette Rd, Forsyth, **E** Jarrell Plantation HS (18mi), KOA, **W gas:** BP/dsl, Chevron, Marathon, **food:** Waffle House, **lodging:** Holiday Inn/rest., Holiday Inn Express, Super 8, **other:** H, CVS Drug, Ingles/Deli
185	GA 18, **E** L&D RV Park (2mi), **W gas:** BP/Circle K/24hr, Shell/dsl, **food:** Shoney's, **lodging:** Comfort Inn, **other:** Ford, repair, st patrol
181	Rumble Rd, to Smarr, **E gas:** BP/dsl/24hr, Shell/dsl/24hr
179mm	**rest area sb, full facilities, phone, vending, picnic, litter barrels, petwalk**
177	I-475 S around Macon (from sb)
175	Pate Rd, Bolingbroke (from nb, no re-entry)
172	Bass Rd, **E food:** Pig in a Pit BBQ, McDonald's, Quizno's, Zaxby's, **other:** Bass Pro Shop, **W gas:** Citgo/dsl/24hr, **food:** Magarita's Mexican, Mellow Mushroom, **food:** Homewood Suites, **other:** Publix, to Museum of Arts&Sciences
171	US 23, to GA 87, Riverside Dr, **E gas:** BP, Marathon/dsl, **food:** Bonefish Grill, Chili's, Jock&Jill's Grill, Mandarin Express, Sticky Fingers, **other:** Acura, Barnes & Noble, Belk, Dillards, KIA, Mercedes, Subaru, Volvo, **W food:** Cracker Barrel, **other:** Lexus, Toyota/Scion, same as 169 W
169	to US 23, Arkwright Dr, **E gas:** Shell/Circle K/24hr, **food:** Carrabba's, Logan's Roadhouse, Outback Steaks, Waffle House, Wager's Grill, **lodging:** Candlewood Suites, Comfort Inn, Country Inn & Suites, Courtyard, Fairfield Inn, Hampton Inn, Holiday Inn, La Quinta, Red Roof Inn, Residence Inn, Sleep Inn, Super 8, **other:** Buick/Cadillac/GMC, **W gas:** BP/dsl, Chevron/24hr, Marathon/dsl, **food:** Arby's, Burger King, Cheddar's, Cheng's Kitchen, Chick-fil-A, Corky Bells, Cracker Barrel, Dunkin Donuts, El Azteca Mexican, 5 Guys Burgers, Guiseppi's Italian, Hooters, KFC, Krystal, Longhorn Steaks, Mandarin Chinese, McDonald's, Papa John's, Papoulis' Gyros, Panera Bread, Pizza Hut, Shoki Japanese, Starbucks, Steak'n Shake, Steve B's Pizza, Subway, Taco Bell, Waffle House, **lodging:** Baymont Inn, Best Inn, Extended Stay Deluxe, Quality Inn, Travelodge, Wingate Inn, **other:** H, Ace Hardware, Chrysler/Jeep/Dodge, $Tree, Hyundai, K-Mart, Kroger, Mazda, Publix, Radio Shack, same as 167
167	GA 247, Pierce Ave, **E lodging:** Days Inn, **W gas:** BP/Circle K/dsl, Chevron, Conoco, Exxon, LoBucks Gas, Marathon/Subway/dsl, Shell, **food:** Applebee's, Loco's Grill, Pier 97 Seafood, Pizza Hut, Red Lob

N ↕ S — MC DONOUGH — FORSYTH — MACON — GA

INTERSTATE 75 CONT'D

N ↕ S

Exit #	Services
167	Continued ster, San Marcos Mexican, Shogun Japanese, Steak-Out Rest., Waffle House, **lodging:** Best Western/rest., Comfort Inn, Holiday Inn Express, Howard Johnson, Motel 6, **other:** ExperTire, Rite Aid
165	I-16 E, to Savannah
164	US 41, GA 19, Forsyth Ave, Macon, **E food:** Sid's Rest., **other:** hist dist, **W gas:** BP, Citgo, **other:** [H], museum
163	GA 74 W, Mercer U Dr, **E lodging:** Hilton Garden, **other:** to Mercer U, **W gas:** Citgo, Marathon/dsl
162	US 80, GA 22, Eisenhower Pkwy, **W gas:** BP, Chevron/24hr, Lo-lo Gas, **food:** Burger King, Capt D's, Checker's, IHOP, Krispy Kreme, Krystal, LJ Silver, McDonald's, Mrs Winners, Subway, Taco Bell, Wendy's, **other:** $Tree, Office Depot, O'Reilly Parts, PepBoys, SavAlot Foods, Walgreens
160	US 41, GA 247, Pio Nono Ave, **E gas:** Flash/dsl, RaceWay/Dunkin Donuts, **food:** Waffle House, **lodging:** Best Inn, **W gas:** BP, Enmark/dsl, **food:** Advance Parts, Arby's, DQ, KFC, King Buffet, McDonald's, Subway, Waffle House, **other:** Advance Parts, $General, Goodyear/auto, NAPA, O'Reilly Parts, Roses, USPO, same as 162
156	I-475 N around Macon (from nb)
155	Hartley Br Rd, **E gas:** BP/KFC/dsl/24hr, **food:** Wendy's, **other:** Curves, Kroger/gas, **W gas:** Citgo/dsl, Exxon, **food:** McDonald's, Subway, Waffle House, Zaxby's, **lodging:** Best Value, **other:** CVS Drug
149	GA 49, Byron, **E gas:** Chevron/dsl, Marathon/dsl, Shell/24hr, **food:** Burger King, Denny's, Krystal, McDonald's, Pizza Hut, Subway, Waffle House, Wendy's, Zaxby's, **lodging:** Best Western, Comfort Inn & Suites, Holiday Inn Express, Super 8, **other:** Campers Inn RV Ctr, Mid-State RV Ctr, Peach Stores/famous brands, antiques, **W gas:** BP, Citgo/dsl/24hr, Exxon, Flash/dsl, Marathon, RaceWay, **food:** DQ, Huddle House, Waffle House, **lodging:** Econolodge, Passport Inn, Quality Inn, **other:** Advance Parts, Camping World RV Ctr, CarQuest, Chevrolet, $General, Family$, Ford, Suncoast RV Ctr
146	GA 247, to Centerville, **E gas:** Exxon, Flash/dsl, Shell, **food:** Subway, Waffle House, **lodging:** Econolodge, Knights Inn, **other:** [H], to Robins AFB, museum, **W gas:** Pilot/Arby's/dsl/24hr
144	Russel Pkwy, **E** Robins AFB, aviation museum
142	GA 96, Housers Mill Rd, **E gas:** Chevron/dsl, **other:** Ponderosa RV Park
138	Thompson Rd, **E gas:** Texaco/Chester's/dsl, **other:** [H], **W** ✈
136	US 341, Perry, **E gas:** BP, Flash, Shell/dsl, **food:** Arby's, Burger King, Capt D's, Chick-fil-A, Hong Kong Buffet, KFC, Krystal, Longhorn Steaks, McDonald's, Pizza Hut, Red Lobster, Sonny's BBQ, Subway, Taco Bell, Waffle House, Wendy's, Zaxby's, **lodging:** Best Inn, Great Inn, Hampton Inn, Howard Johnson, Jameson Inn, Super 8, **other:** [H], Ace Hardware, Advance Parts, $Tree, GNC, Kroger, NAPA, Radio Shack, Rite Aid, Walmart SuperCtr, **W gas:** Chevron/dsl, RaceWay/24hr, **food:** Applebee's, Green

MACON · BYRON · PERRY

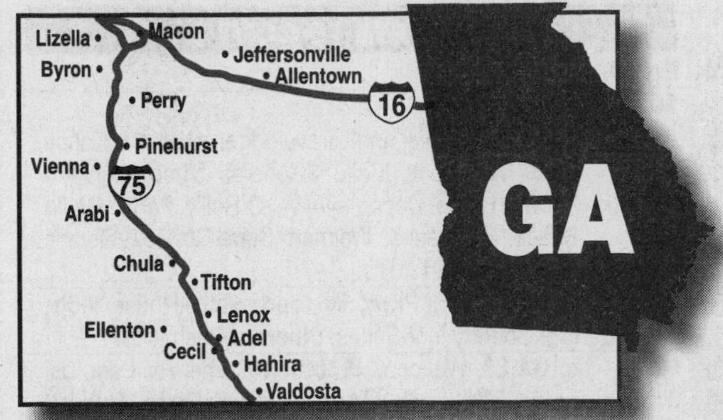

Exit #	Services
136	Continued Derby Rest., **lodging:** Ashburn Inn, Comfort Inn, Econolodge, Holiday Inn, Knight's Inn, Passport Inn, Quality Inn, **other:** Ford, Crossroads Camping
135	US 41, GA 127, Perry, **E gas:** BP/dsl, Exxon, Flash, Marathon, Shell, **food:** Cracker Barrel, Subway, Waffle House, **lodging:** Best Western, Red Carpet Inn, Relax Inn, Rodeway Inn, Travelodge, **other:** Chrysler, Jeep/Dodge, GA Nat Fair, **W other:** Fair Harbor RV Park, st Patrol
134	South Perry Pkwy, **W gas:** Texaco/dsl, **lodging:** Microtel, **other:** Chevrolet/Buick/Pontiac/GMC, Priester's Pecans
127	GA 26, Henderson, **E** Twin Oaks Camping, **W gas:** Chevron
122	GA 230, Unadilla, **E gas:** Chevron/dsl, Colonial/dsl, **other:** Chevrolet/Ford, **W lodging:** Red Carpet Inn, **other:** Bleakley RV Ctr
121	US 41, Unadilla, **E gas:** BP, Borum/repair, Flash/DQ/dsl, Shell, **food:** Country Boys BBQ, Don Ponchos Mexican, Subway, **lodging:** Economy Inn, Scottish Inn, **other:** $General, Piggly Wiggly, Southern Trails RV Resort, **W gas:** Citgo/dsl/rest./scales/24hr, **lodging:** Regency Inn
118mm	**rest area sb, full ♿ facilities, ☎, vending, picnic, litter barrels, petwalk, RV dump**
117	to US 41, Pinehurst, **W gas:** BP/Pinehurst/cafe/dsl/scales/24hr
112	GA 27, Vienna, **W gas:** BP/dsl, Marathon
109	GA 215, Vienna, **E gas:** Pilot/McDonalds/dsl/scales/24hrs, **W gas:** Citgo/dsl, El Cheapo, Shell/Subway/dsl/E85, **food:** Huddle House, **lodging:** Executive Inn, **other:** [H], antiques
108mm	**rest area nb, full ♿ facilities, ☎, vending, picnic, litter barrels, petwalk, RV dump**
104	Farmers Mkt Rd, Cordele
102	GA 257, Cordele, **W food:** Pecan House, **other:** [H]
101	US 280, GA 90, Cordele, **E gas:** Exxon/dsl, Pilot/Arby's/dsl/scales/24hr, Shell, **food:** Denny's, Golden Corral, Waffle House, **lodging:** Day's Inn, Fairfield Inn, Ramada Inn, **other:** Ford/Lincoln/Mercury, st patrol, **W gas:** BP/dsl, Danfair, Liberty, RaceWay/24hr, **food:** Bob Evans, Burger King, Capt D's, Compadres Mexican, Cracker Barrel, Cutter's Steaks, DQ, Hardee's, KFC/Pizza Hut/Taco Bell, Krystal/24hr, McDonald's, Shoney's, Sonic, Subway, Super China, Taco Bell, TJ's Rest., Wendy's, Zaxby's, **lodging:** Ashburn Inn, Athens 8 Motel, Best Western, Comfort Inn, Deluxe Inn, Econolodge, Hampton Inn, Holiday Inn

PERRY · UNADILLA · CORDELE

INTERSTATE 75 CONT'D

N ↕ S

Exit #	Services
101	Continued Express, Premier Inn, Travelodge, **other:** Advance Parts, AutoZone, Belk, $General, $Tree, Harvey's Foods, Home Depot, NAPA, O'Reilly Parts, Radio Shack, Walgreens, Walmart SuperCtr, to Veterans Mem SP, J Carter HS
99	GA 300, GA/FL Pkwy, **W food:** Waffle House, **lodging:** Country Inn&Suites, **other:** to Chehaw SP
97	to GA 33, Wenona, **E other:** Cornel RV Park, dsl repair, **W gas:** TA/BP/Popeye's/Pizza Hut/dsl/scales/24hr/@, **other:** KOA, truckwash
92	Arabi, **E gas:** Chevron/Plantation House, **W gas:** BP/dsl, **other:** Southern Gates RV Park
85mm	**rest area nb, full ♿ facilities, ☎, vending, picnic, litter barrels, petwalk**
84	GA 159, Ashburn, **E gas:** Shell/dsl, **W gas:** Chevron/dsl/24hr, **food:** DQ, Subway, **lodging:** Ashburn Inn/RV Park
82	GA 107, GA 112, Ashburn, **W gas:** BP, Shell, **food:** KFC, Huddle House/24hr, McDonald's, Pizza Hut, Shoney's, Waffle House, Zaxby's, **lodging:** Best Western, Day's Inn, Howard Johnson, Super 8, **other:** Chevrolet/Buick/Pontiac/GMC, $General, O'Reilly Parts, Rite Aid, to Chehaw SP
80	Bussey Rd, Sycamore, **E gas:** Shell, **lodging:** Budget Inn, **W gas:** Citgo, **other:** Allen's Tires
78	GA 32, Sycamore, **E** to Jefferson Davis Mem Pk (14mi)
76mm	**rest area sb, full ♿ facilities, ☎, vending, picnic, litter barrels, petwalk**
75	Inaha Rd, **W gas:** BP/Stuckey's
71	Willis Still Rd, Sunsweet, **W gas:** BP/dsl
69	Chula-Brookfield Rd, **E gas:** Phillips 66, **lodging:** Carpet Inn, **other:** antiques
66	Brighton Rd
64	US 41, Tifton, **E gas:** BP/dsl, **other:** [H], $General, Harvey's Foods, **W gas:** Petro
63b	8th St, Tifton, **E gas:** Bob's, Flash, **food:** KFC, Los Compadres, **lodging:** Budget Inn, **other:** , same as 63a, **W food:** Pit Stop BBQ
63a	2nd St, Tifton, **E gas:** BP, Chevron, **food:** Asahi Xpress, Arby's, Burger King, Checker's, El Cazador Mexican, Krystal, McDonald's, Pizza Hut, Red Lobster, Taco Bell, Waffle House, **lodging:** Econolodge, Super 8, **other:** Advance Parts, Belk, Buick/Pontiac/Cadillac/GMC, $Tree, JC Penney, **W gas:** West Side/Cafe/dsl, **food:** TX Jack's Grill, **lodging:** Quality Inn, Travelodge
62	US 82, to US 319, Tifton, **E gas:** Citgo, Flash/dsl, **food:** Applebee's, Charles Seafood, Chili's, Country Buffet, Cracker Barrel, DQ, Golden Corral, Red Lobster, Sonic, Waffle House, Zaxby's, **lodging:** Comfort Inn, Courtyard, Country Inn & Suites, Fairfield Inn, Hampton Inn, Microtel, **other:** Advance Parts, $Tree, Family$, Ford/Lincoln/Mercury, Pecan Outlet, Staples, **W gas:** BP, Chevron/Burger King, EZ Mart, Murphy USA, RaceWay/24hr, Shell/dsl, **food:** Burger King, Capt D's, Chick-fil-A, Cici's Pizza, $General, Little Caesars, Loco's Grill, Longhorn Steaks,
62	Continued McDonald's, Old Mexico, Moe's SW Grill, Quizno's, Ruby Tuesday, Shoney's, Sonny's BBQ, Subway, Starbucks, Waffle House, Wendy's, **lodging:** Day's Inn, Hilton Garden, Holiday Inn, Ramada Ltd, Rodeway Inn, **other:** Chevrolet, Chrysler/Dodge, $General, Honda, Lowe's Whse, Radio Shack, Toyota, Walmart SuperCtr
61	Omega Rd, **W gas:** Petro USA/Stuckey's/Waffle King/dsl/24hr, **lodging:** Motel 6, **other:** Harley-Davidson, Pines RV Park, **E** Nissan
60	Central Ave, Tifton, **E gas:** Chevron, **food:** Dragon 1 Chinese, **W gas:** Pilot/Subway/Steak'n Shake/dsl/scales/24hr, **other:** Amy's RV Camping, Blue Beacon
59	Southwell Blvd, to US 41, Tifton, **E gas:** Loves/Hardees/dsl/24hr
55	to Eldorado, Omega, **E gas:** Chevron/Magnolia Plantation, **W gas:** Pure/dsl
49	Kinard Br Rd, Lenox, **E gas:** Dixie/dsl, **lodging:** Knight's Inn, **W gas:** BP/dsl/24hr
47mm	**rest area both lanes, full ♿ facilities, ☎, vending, picnic, litter barrels, petwalk**
45	Barneyville Rd, **E lodging:** Relax Inn
41	Rountree Br Rd, **E gas:** Citgo, **W** to Reed Bingham SP
39	GA 37, Adel, Moultrie, **E gas:** Shell/McDonald's/dsl, Texaco, **food:** DQ, Hardee's, Subway, Waffle House, **lodging:** Budget Lodge, Scottish Inn, Super 8, **other:** Family$, Rite Aid, Winn-Dixie, **W gas:** BP, Citgo/Huddle House/dsl/@, **food:** Burger King, Capt D's, IHOP, Mama's Table, Taco Bell, Wendy's, Western Sizzlin, **lodging:** Day's Inn, Hampton Inn, **other:** Factory Stores/famous brands, to Reed Bingham SP
37	Adel
32	Old Coffee Rd, Cecil, **W gas:** Chevron
29	US 41 N, GA 122, Hahira, Sheriff's Boys Ranch, **E food:** Subway, **other:** NAPA, **W gas:** Big Foot TC/Apple Valley/dsl, BP/Blimpie/TCBY/dsl, **lodging:** Knights Inn
23mm	**weigh sta both lanes**
22	US 41 S, to Valdosta, **E gas:** BP, Shell/Subway/dsl, **food:** Waffle House, **lodging:** Hawthorn Suites, **other:** [H], Chevrolet/Mazda, Dodge/Jeep, Lincoln/Mercury, golf, **W gas:** Citgo/Burger King/DQ/Stuckey's, **lodging:** Day's Inn
18	GA 133, Valdosta, **E gas:** Big Foot/dsl, Exxon, Flash, Phillips 66, Texaco/dsl, **food:** Applebee's, Arby's, Atl. Bread Co, Beijing Cafe, Brusters, Burger King, Chick-fil-A, Chili's, Cracker Barrel, Cici's Pizza, Crystal River Seafood, Denny's, El Potro Mexican, El Toreo, Fazoli's, Hooters, KFC, Krystal, Little Caesar's, Longhorn Steaks, McCalister's Deli, McDonald's, Ole Times BBQ, Outback Steaks, Quizno's, Red Lobster, Ruby Tuesday, Sonny's BBQ, Starbucks, Steak'n Shake, Taco Bell, TX Roadhouse, Waffle House, Wendy's, **lodging:** Comfort Suites, Country Inn&Suites, Courtyard, Hampton Inn, Hilton Garden, InnTown Suites, Jameson Inn, Jolly Inn, La Quinta, Lee's Grill, Quality Inn, Rodeway Inn, **other:** Belk, Best Buy, Books A Million, $Tree, Home Depot, JC Penney, Kohl's, Lowe's Whse, Michaels, Office Depot,

WENONA · ASHBURN · TIFTON · GA · ADEL · VALDOSTA

INTERSTATE 75 CONT'D

N ↕ S VALDOSTA

Exit #	Services
18	Continued Old Navy, PetsMart, Publix, Ross, Sears/auto, Target, TJ Maxx, Walgreens, mall, **W gas:** BP/dsl, RaceWay, Shell, **lodging:** Best Western, Econolodge, Sleep Inn, **other:** RiverPark Camping, Toyota
16	US 84, US 221, GA 94, Valdosta, **E gas:** Big Foot/dsl, BP/dsl, Chevron, Citgo/Stuckey's/dsl, Danfair Express, Shell/dsl, **food:** Aligatou Japanese, Burger King, IHOP, McDonald's, Old South BBQ, Pizza Hut, Shoney's, Sonic, Waffle House, Wendy's, **lodging:** Day's Inn, Guesthouse Inn, Hampton Inn, Holiday Inn, Motel 6, New Valdosta Inn, Quality Inn, Ramada Ltd, Super 8, Wingate Inn, **other:** Sam's Club/gas, Walmart Super Ctr/Subway, to Okefenokee SP, **W gas:** Shell/Dee Dee's Rest./dsl/24hr, **food:** Austin's Steaks, **lodging:** Comfort Inn, Knight's Inn
13	Old Clyattville Rd, Valdosta, **W** Wild Adventures Park
11	GA 31, Valdosta, **E gas:** Pilot/Subway/dsl/24hr/@, Wilco/Hess/Stuckey's/dsl/scales/24hr, **food:** Waffle House, **lodging:** Travelers Inn, **W gas:** BP
5	GA 376, to Lake Park, **E gas:** Chevron, Flash/Krystal/dsl, RaceWay, Shell, **food:** Chick-fil-A, Domino's, FarmHouse Rest., Hardee's, Lin's Garden Chinese, Shoney's, Sonic, Sonny's BBQ, Subway, Waffle House, **lodging:** Guesthouse Inn, Quality Inn, **other:** Eagles Roost RV Park, Family$, Preferred Outlets/famous brands, Travel Country RV Ctr, Winn-Dixie, USPO, **W gas:** Citgo/dsl, Shell/dsl, **food:** Cracker Barrel, McDonald's, Pizza Hut, Taco Bell, Wendy's, **lodging:** Day's Inn, Hampton Inn, Super 8, Travelodge, **other:** KOA, SunCoast RV Ctr
3mm	**Welcome Ctr nb, full ♿ facilities, ☎, vending, picnic, litter barrels, petwalk**
2	Lake Park, Bellville, **E gas:** Mobil/DQ, SpeedCo, Shell/dsl, TA/BP/Arby's/dsl/rest./scales/24hr/@, **W gas:** ***FLYING J***/Conoco/dsl/LP/rest./scales/24hr, **other:** lube/tires/wash
0mm	Georgia/Florida state line

INTERSTATE 85

N ↕ S LAVONIA

Exit #	Services
179mm	Georgia/South Carolina state line, Lake Hartwell, Tugaloo River
177	GA 77 S, to Hartwell, **E gas:** BP/gifts/dsl, **food:** Dad's Grill, **other:** to Hart SP, Tugaloo SP
176mm	**Welcome Ctr sb, full ♿ facilities, info, ☎, picnic, litter barrels, vending, petwalk**
173	GA 17, to Lavonia, **E gas:** RaceTrac/24hr, **food:** Blimpie, Domino's, La Cabana Mexican, McDonald's, Subway, Taco Bell, Waffle House, **lodging:** Best Western, Sleep Inn, **other:** $General, Lavonia Foods, Rite Aid, **W gas:** Chevron/dsl, Exxon/dsl, **food:** Burger King, Hardee's, Pizza Hut, Shoney's, Wendy's, Zaxby's, **lodging:** Holiday Inn Express, Super 8, **other:** Chrysler/Dodge/Jeep, Ford, to Tugaloo SP
171mm	**weigh sta nb**
169mm	**weigh sta sb**

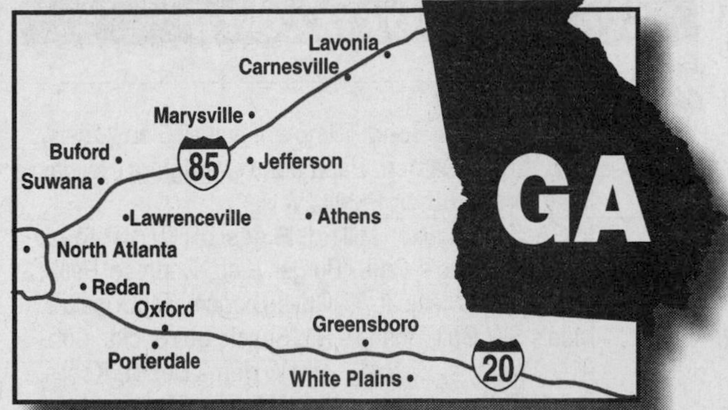

COMMERCE / JEFFERSON

Exit #	Services
166	GA 106, to Carnesville, Toccoa, **E gas:** Wilco/Hess/DQ/Wendy's/dsl/scales/24hr, **W gas:** Echo Trkstp/Chevron/Country Kitchen/dsl/rest./scales/24hr, **other:** truck repair
164	GA 320, to Carnesville, **E gas:** Citgo/dsl
160mm	**rest area nb, full ♿ facilities, ☎, vending, picnic, litter barrels, petwalk**
160	GA 51, to Homer, **E gas:** Shell/Subway/dsl/24hr, **other:** to Russell SP, Victoria Bryant SP, **W gas:** ***FLYING J***/Country Mkt/dsl/24hr, Petro/Pizza Hut/dsl/scales/24hr/@, **other:** Blue Beacon
154	GA 63, Martin Br Rd
149	US 441, GA 15, to Commerce, Homer, **E gas:** Murphy USA, Shell, TA/76/dsl/rest./24hr/@, **food:** Capt D's, Denny's, El Azteca, Grand Buffet, Longhorn Steaks, Outback Steaks, Papa John's, Pizza Hut/Taco Bell, Sonny's BBQ, Waffle House, Zaxby's, **lodging:** Dandelion Inn, Days Inn, Hampton Inn, Scottish Inn, **other:** H, $General, Funopolis, GNC, KOA, Old Navy, Radio Shack, Walmart SuperCtr, **W gas:** BP/dsl, Citgo, RaceTrac/dsl, **food:** Applebee's, Arby's, Burger King, Checker's, Chick-fil-A, Cracker Barrel, DQ, KFC, Krystal, La Fiesta, La Hacienda, McDonald's, Moore's Wing&Things, Pizza Hut, Ruby Tuesday, Ryan's, Sonic, Starbucks, Subway, Wendy's, **lodging:** Best Inn, Best Western, Comfort Inn, Comfort Suites, Holiday Inn Express, Howard Johnson, Jameson Inn, Motel 6, Super 8, **other:** Buick/GMC/Pontiac, Home Depot, Pritchett Tires, Tanger Outlet/famous brands
147	GA 98, to Commerce, **E gas:** Citgo/dsl, ***FLYING J*** cafe/dsl/24hr/, FuelMart/dsl, **other:** H **W other:** Cody's Fuel
140	GA 82, Dry Pond Rd, **E** Freightliner, **W** RV & Truck Repair
137	US 129, GA 11 to Jefferson, **E gas:** RaceTrac/dsl, Shell, **food:** Arby's, El Jinete Mexican, KFC/Taco Bell, McDonald's, Waffle House, Zaxby's, **lodging:** Comfort Inn, **other:** museum, **W gas:** QT/dsl/scales/24hr, **food:** Burger King, Waffle House, Wendy's, **other:** flea mkt
129	GA 53, to Braselton, **E gas:** Chevron/dsl, Shell/Golden Pantry/dsl, **food:** La Hacienda Mexican, Waffle House, **lodging:** Best Western, **W gas:** Pilot/McDonald's/dsl/scales/24hr, **food:** Cracker Barrel, Domino's, Stonewall's, Subway, Tea Garden Chinese, Wendy's, Zaxby's, **other:** $Store
126	GA 211, to Chestnut Mtn, **E gas:** Shell/dsl, **lodging:** Country Inn&Suites, **food:** Subway, Waffle House,

INTERSTATE 85 CONT'D

Exit #	Services
126	Continued **W gas:** BP/dsl, **food:** Blimpie, Chateau Elan Winery/rest., China Garden, Papa John's, **lodging:** Holiday Inn Express, **other:** Publix, Vet
120	to GA 124, Hamilton Mill Rd, **E gas:** BP, QT/dsl, **food:** Arby's, Buffalo's Café, Burger King, Caprese Rest., Dos Copas Mexican, 5 Guys Burgers, McDonald's, Moe's SW Grill, Shane's Rib Shack, Starbucks, Subway, Wendy's, Zaxby's, **other:** Home Depot, Kohl's, Publix/Deli, auto repair, Vet, **W gas:** Chevron, Murphy USA, Shell/Huddle House/dsl, **food:** Barbarito's, Bigby Coffee, Chick-fil-A, Chili's, Hardee's, **other:** CVS Drug, O'Reilly Parts, Tires+, Walmart SuperCtr
115	GA 20, to Buford Dam, **E gas:** QT, **W gas:** QT/dsl, **food:** Arby's, Artuzzi's Italian, Bruster's, Buffalo's Cafe, Burger King, Chick-fil-A, Chili's, ChuckeCheese, Einstein's Bagels, 5 Guy's Burgers, Kani House, Krispy Kreme, Longhorn Steaks, Liu's Buffet, Macaroni Grill, McDonald's, Mimi's Cafe, Moe's SW Grill, O'Charley's, Olive Garden, On-the-Border, Panda Express, PF Chang's, Quizno's, Red Lobster, Shogun Japanese, Starbucks, Steak n' Shake, Subway, Taxco Mexican, Ted's MT Grill, TGIFriday, Waffle House, Wendy's, **lodging:** Country Inn&Suites, Courtyard, Hampton Inn, SpringHill Suites, Wingate Inn, **other:** Belk, Best Buy, Borders Books, Costco/gas, Dillard's, $Tree, JC Penney, Lowe's Whse, Macy's, Mazda, Michael's, Nissan, Nordstrom's, PetCo, Petsmart, Ross, Sam's Club, Staples, Target, TJ Maxx, Toyota/Scion, Walmart SuperCtr/24hr, Mall of GA, to Lake Lanier Islands
113mm	**rest area (from sb)**
113	I-985 N (from nb), to Gainesville
111	GA 317, to Suwanee, **E gas:** BP, Phillips 66/dsl, Sim's, **food:** Applebee's, Arby's, Blimpie, Burger King, Checker's, Chick-fil-A, Cracker Barrel, Mrs Winner's, Oriental Garden, Outback Steaks, Philly Connection, Pizza Hut, Subway, Taco Bell/Pizza Hut, Waffle House, Wendy's, **lodging:** Admiral Benbow Inn, Best Western, Comfort Inn, Courtyard, Days Inn, Fairfield Inn, Holiday Inn, Red Roof Inn, Sun Suites, **other:** CVS Drug, GNC, Kauffman Tire, **W gas:** Chevron/dsl/24hr, Murphy USA, RaceTrac, Shell, **food:** A&W/KFC, Atlanta Bread, CiCi's Pizza, Kacey's Rest., McDonald's, Moe's SW Grill, Shane's Ribshack, Sonic, Wild Wing Cafe, **lodging:** Motel 6, Super 8, **other:** $Tree, Office Depot, Radio Shack, Tires +, Walmart SuperCtr, flea mkt
109	Old Peachtree Rd, **E gas:** QT/dsl/24hr, **food:** McDonald's, **lodging:** Hampton Inn, **other:** Bass Pro Shops, $World, Publix, **W food:** Bistro's Sandwich Cafe, Califonia Dreaming, China Delight, Magnolia Cafe, Sidelines Grille, Subway, Waffle House, **lodging:** Hilton Garden, Holiday Inn, **other:** Home Depot
108	Sugarloaf Pkwy, **E lodging:** Hampton Inn, **W food:** Chick-fil-A, **lodging:** Hilton Garden, Holiday Inn, **other:** Gwinnett Civic Ctr
107	GA 120, to GA 316 E, Athens, **E gas:** Shell, **food:** Burger King, Carino's, Jillian's, Zaxby's, **other:** Bass Pro Shops, Books-a-Million, Burlington Coats,
107	Continued Discount Tire, Food Ct, Mercedes, Nieman-Marcus, Rite Aid, Ross, Saks 5th Ave, Sears, Suburban Tire, **W gas:** BP, Chevron, **food:** Carrabba's, China Gate, McDonald's, Roadhouse Grill, Subway, **lodging:** La Quinta, Suburban Lodge
106	Boggs Rd (from sb, no return), Duluth, **W gas:** QT/dsl/24hr
104	Pleasant Hill Rd, **E gas:** Chevron/24hr, Circle K, Sim's, **food:** Bahama Breeze, Blue Marlin, Burger King, Chick-fil-A, East Pearl, GA Diner, Grand Buffet, Ida's Pizza Kitchen, Joe's Crabshack, Krispy Kreme, La Pantera Rosa, Macaroni Grill, McDonald's, Moe's SW Grill, Popeye's, Starbucks, Subway, TGIFriday, Waffle House, Wendy's, **lodging:** Candlewood Suites, Comfort Suites, Hampton Inn Suites, Holiday Inn Express, Marriott, Residence Inn, Sun Suites, **other:** Best Buy, $General, , Goodyear/auto, Home Depot, Old Time Pottery, Publix, Walgreens, **W gas:** BP/dsl, Chevron, Murphy USA/dsl, RaceTrac, **food:** Applebee's, Arby's, Bruster's, Burger King, Checker's, Chili's, Chipotle Mexican, Golden China, Hooters, IHOP, KFC, McDonald's, Olive Garden, On the Border, Panda Express, Pizza Hut, Red Lobster, Ryan's, Starbucks, Steak'n Shake, Subway, Taco Bell, Waffle House, Wendy's, **lodging:** Courtyard, Days Inn, Extended Stay America, Hyatt Place, InTown Suites, Quality Inn, Wingate Inn, **other:** Barnes&Noble, Batteries+, BMW, Chevrolet, Dodge, Firestone/auto, Ford/Lincoln/Mercury, Fry's Electronics, Goodyear/auto, Honda, Jo-Ann Fabrics, KIA, Macy's, Marshall's, Mazda/Hyundai, Mitsubishi, Nissan, PetCo, Rite Aid, Sears/auto, Staples, Target, TJ Maxx, Toyota, Walmart Super Ctr, mall
103	Steve Reynolds Blvd (from nb, no return), **W gas:** QT, Shell, **food:** Dave&Buster's, La Fiesta Mexican, Waffle House, **other:** Costco/gas, Kohl's, Sam's Club
102	GA 378, Beaver Ruin Rd, **E gas:** Shell/dsl, QT, **W gas:** Citgo
101	Lilburn Rd, **E gas:** QT/dsl, Shell/dsl/24hr, **food:** Blimpie, Bojangles, Bruster's, Burger King, Hong Kong Buffet, Manhattan Pizza, McDonald's/playplace, Quizno's, Starbucks, Krystal, KFC, Taco Bell, Waffle House, **lodging:** Guesthouse Inn, InTown Suites, **W gas:** Chevron/24hr, QT, **food:** Arby's, El Indo Mexican, El Taco Veloz, Little Caeser's, Mrs Winner's, Papa John's, Pizza Plaza, Waffle House, Wendy's, **lodging:** Knight's Inn, Red Roof Inn, **other:** CarMax, Chrysler/Jeep, CVS Drug, Little Giant Mkt, Lowe's Whse
99	GA 140, Jimmy Carter Blvd, **E gas:** Phillips 66/dsl, Shell, **food:** Checker's, Chick-fil-A, Cracker Barrel, Denny's, Don Taco, KFC, McDonald's, Papa John's, Pizza Hut/Taco Bell, Waffle House, Wendy's, **lodging:** Best Western, Comfort Inn, Courtyard, La Quinta, Motel 6, **other:** Advance Parts, Aldi Foods, CVS Drug, Family$, Goodyear, Office Depot, U-Haul, Walgreens, **W gas:** Chevron/24hr, Citgo, QT/dsl/24hr, **food:** Barnacle's Grill, Five Guys Cafe, Hong Kong Buffet, Hooters, Pappadeaux Steak/seafood, Sonic, Waffle House, Wendy's, **lodging:** Days Inn, Drury Inn, Country Inn Suites, Microtel, **other:** AutoZone,

N ↕ S

SUWANEE

DULUTH

ATLANTA AREA

ATLANTA AREA

INTERSTATE 85 CONT'D

N ↕ S

ATLANTA AREA

Exit #	Services
99	Continued Big 10 Tire, BJ's Whse/gas (3mi), CarQuest, NTB, O'Reilly Parts, PepBoys
96	Pleasantdale Rd, Northcrest Rd, **E food:** Burger King, Pleasantdale Chinese, **lodging:** Peachtree Inn, **W gas:** Exxon/dsl, QT/dsl, **food:** Waffle House, **lodging:** US Economy Lodge
95	I-285
94	Chamblee-Tucker Rd, **E gas:** Shell, Texaco, **lodging:** Masters Inn, **W gas:** QT/dsl, Shell, **food:** DQ, Waffle House, **lodging:** Motel 6, Super 8, **other:** to Mercer U
93	Shallowford Rd, to Doraville, **E gas:** Shell, **food:** Blimpie, Collard Green Cafe, El Salvador, Hop Shing Chinese, **other:** Publix, U-Haul, **W gas:** Circle K, Shell/dsl, **lodging:** Quality Inn
91	US 23, GA 155, Clairmont Rd, **E gas:** Chevron, Shell, **food:** Grand Buffet, IHOP, Mo's Pizza, Popeye's, **other:** Brakes&More/repair, IGA Foods, **W gas:** BP, **food:** Donnie's, McDonald's, Roadhouse Grill, Waffle House, **lodging:** Marriott, Wingate Inn, **other:** NTB, Sam's Club/gas
89	GA 42, N Druid Hills, **E gas:** Chevron/Subway/dsl, QT/dsl/24hr, Shell, **food:** Arby's, Boston Mkt, Burger King, Chick-fil-A, Einstein Bro's, Lettuce Souperise, McDonald's, Moe's SW Grill, Panera Bread, Picadilly's, Starbucks, Taco Bell, TCBY, **lodging:** Courtyard, Homestead Suites, **other:** $Tree, Firestone/auto, Target, **W gas:** Chevron, Exxon, Shell, **food:** Atlanta Diner, Dunkin Donuts, HoneyBaked Ham, Krystal, Waffle House, **lodging:** DoubleTree, Hampton Inn, Red Roof Inn, **other:** CVS Drug, Just Brakes, Vet
88	Lenox Rd, GA 400 N, Cheshire Br Rd (from sb), **E gas:** Shell, **lodging:** La Quinta
87	GA 400 N (from nb)
86	GA 13 S, Peachtree St, **E gas:** BP, **food:** Denny's, Wendy's, **lodging:** Intown Inn, La Quinta, **other:** Brake-O
85	I-75 N, to Marietta, Chattanooga
84	Techwood Dr, 14th St, **E gas:** BP, Shell, **food:** CheeseSteaks, La Bamba Mexican, Thai Cuisine, VVV Ristorante Italiano, **lodging:** Best Western, Hampton Inn, Marriott, Sheraton, Travelodge, **other:** Woodruff Arts Ctr, **W food:** Blimpie, **lodging:** Courtyard, Knight's Inn, **other:** CVS Drug, Dillard's, Office Depot, to Georgia Tech
249d	10th St, Spring St (from nb), **E gas:** BP, Chevron/24hr, Shell, **food:** Checker's, Domino's, Pizza Hut, Varsity Drive-In, **lodging:** Fairfield Inn, Marriott, Regency Suites, Renaissance Hotel, Residence Inn, Wyndham Hotel, **other:** Publix, to Mitchell House, **W food:** McDonald's, **lodging:** Courtyard, **other:** H, CVS Drug, to GA Tech
249c	Williams St (from sb), downtown, to GA Dome
249b	Pine St, Peachtree St (from nb), downtown, **E lodging:** Reniassance Inn, **other:** H, to midtown, **W** downtown, hotels
249a	Courtland St (from sb), downtown, **W lodging:** Hilton, Marriott, **other:** GA St U

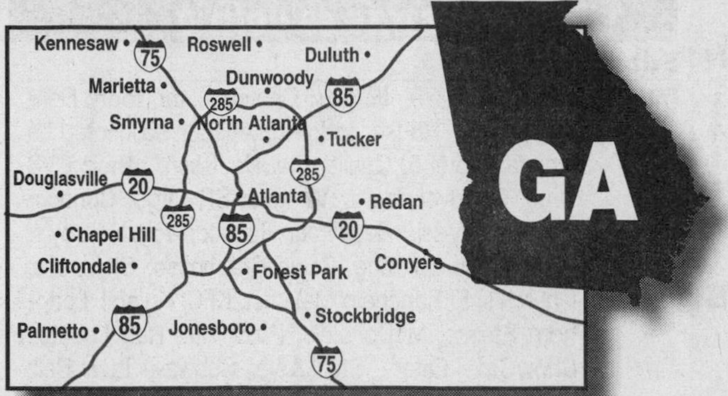

ATLANTA AREA

Exit #	Services
248d	Piedmont Ave, Butler St (from sb), downtown, **W lodging:** Courtyard, Fairfield Inn, Radisson, **other:** H, Ford, MLK NHS
248c	GA 10 E, Intn'l Blvd, downtown, **W lodging:** Hilton, Holiday Inn, Marriott Marquis, Radisson
248b	Edgewood Ave (from nb), **W other:** H, downtown, hotels
248a	MLK Dr (from sb), **W** st capitol, to Underground Atlanta
247	I-20, E to Augusta, W to Birmingham
246	Georgia Ave, Fulton St, **E lodging:** Hampton Inn, Holiday Inn Express, **other:** to Turner Stadium, **W food:** KFC, **other:** to Coliseum, GSU
245	Ormond St, Abernathy Blvd, **E lodging:** Comfort Inn, Country Inn Suites, Hampton Inn, Holiday Inn Express, **other:** Turner Stadium, **W** st capitol
244	University Ave, **E gas:** Chevron, Exxon, **food:** Wendy's, **other:** NAPA, **W gas:** Amoco, **food:** Mrs Winner's, **other:** Ford Trucks
243	GA 166, Lakewood Fwy, to East Point
77	I-75 S
76	Cleveland Ave, **E gas:** Citgo/dsl, Marathon, Phillips 66/Blimpie, **food:** Arby's, Burger King, Krystal, Mrs Winner's, McDonald's, **other:** H, BigLots, CVS Drug, $Tree, Kroger, Radio Shack, **W gas:** Shell/dsl, Texaco/dsl, **food:** Chick-fil-A, Church's, KFC, **other:** Chevrolet, CVS Drug, Honda, O'Reilly Parts
75	Sylvan Rd, **E gas:** Citgo, Phillips 66, Shell/dsl, **food:** Chick-fil-A, City Garden Chinese, IHOP, McDonald's, Wendy's, **lodging:** InnCity Suites
74	Loop Rd, Aviation Commercial Center
73b a	Virginia Ave, **E gas:** Citgo/dsl, **food:** Hambone's BBQ, Jonny's Pizza, Landmark Diner, Magnolia Grill, Malone's Grill, McDonald's, Pizza Hut, Ruby Tuesday, Schlotsky's, Spondivit's Rest., Waffle House, Wendy's, Willy's Mexican, **lodging:** Courtyard, Drury Inn, Hilton, Renaissance Hotel, Red Roof Inn, Residence Inn, **W gas:** Chevron/Subway/24hr, Shell, **food:** Arby's, Blimpie, Happy Buddah Chinese, Harsfield's Grill, KFC/A&W, La Fiesta Mexican, Steak&Ale, Waffle House, **lodging:** Comfort Inn, Crowne Plaza, DoubleTree, Econolodge, Fairfield Inn, Hampton Inn, Holiday Inn, Hyatt Place, Wellesley Inn
72	Camp Creek Pkwy
71	Riverdale Rd, Atlanta ✈, **E food:** Ruby Tuesday, **lodging:** Courtyard, Fairfield Inn, Microtel, Hampton Inn, Holiday Inn, Hyatt Place, La Quinta, Sheraton/grill, Sleep Inn, Springhill Suites, Super 8, **W gas:** Chevron, **food:** Joe's Rest., **lodging:** Day's Inn, Embassy Suites, Hilton Garden, Holiday Inn Express, Marriott, Westin Hotel

INTERSTATE 85 CONT'D

N ↕ S — ATLANTA AREA — FAIRBURN — NEWNAN — MOUNTVILLE

Exit #	Services
69	GA 14, GA 279, **E gas:** Chevron/24hr, **food:** Denny's, Waffle House, **lodging:** Atlanta So. Hotel, La Quinta, Motel 6, Quality Inn, Radisson, **other:** CVS Drug, Goodyear/auto, **W gas:** BP, Citgo, Conoco/dsl, Exxon/dsl, RaceTrac, Texaco, **food:** Arby's, Blimpie, Burger King, Cajun Crabhouse, Checker's, Church's, El Ranchero Mexican, KFC, Krystal, Longhorn Steaks, McDonald's, Pizza Hut, Red Lobster, ShowCase Eatery, Steak&Ale, Subway, Taco Bell, Wendy's, **lodging:** Baymont Inn, Day's Inn, Fairfield Inn, Red Roof Inn, **other:** Advance Parts, AutoZone, Cottman Transmissions, Family$, Kroger, Radio Shack, Target, U-Haul
68	I-285 Atlanta Perimeter
66	Flat Shoals Rd, **W gas:** BP, Chevron/dsl, Shell/Blimpie, **food:** Supreme Fish Delight, Waffle House, **lodging:** Motel 6
64	GA 138, to Union City, **E gas:** BP/dsl, RaceTrac/dsl, **food:** Waffle House, **lodging:** Econolodge, Super 8, **other:** BMW/Mini, Buick/Pontiac/GMC, Chevrolet, Chrysler/Jeep/Dodge, Ford, Honda, Infiniti, Kia/Nissan, Lexus, Lincoln/Mercury, Subaru, Toyota, VW, **W gas:** Chevron/dsl, QT, Shell, **food:** Arby's, Burger King, Capt D's, China Garden, Corner Cafe, Cracker Barrel, IHOP, KFC, Krystal, McDonald's, Papa John's, Pizza Hut, Shoney's, Sonic, Subway, Taco Bell, Wendy's, Zaxby's, **lodging:** Best Western, Comfort Inn, Country Hearth Inn, Garden Inn, La Quinta, Microtel, **other:** BigLots, $Tree, Firestone, Goodyear/auto, Kroger, Macy's, NTB, O'Reilly Parts, PepBoys, Radio Shack, Sears/auto, Walgreens, Walmart SuperCtr
61	GA 74, to Fairburn, **E gas:** BP/Huddle House/dsl/scales, RaceTrac, Shell, **food:** Chick-fil-A, Dunkin Donuts, McDonald's, Waffle House, Wendy's, Zaxby's, **lodging:** Country Inn & Suites, Hampton Inn, Holiday Inn Express, Sleep Inn, Wingate Inn, **other:** Tire Depot, Vet, **W gas:** Chevron /dsl, Citgo/dsl, Marathon, Phillips 66/Blimpie/dsl, **lodging:** Efficiency Motel
56	Collinsworth Rd, **W gas:** BP, Marathon/dsl, **food:** Frank's Rest., **other:** South Oaks Camping
51	GA 154, to Sharpsburg, **E gas:** Phillips 66/dsl, Texaco/Blimpie, **food:** Hardee's, **W gas:** Chevron/dsl, Shell/dsl, **food:** Waffle House
47	GA 34, to Newnan, **E gas:** Chevron/dsl, Marathon/Subway/dsl, QT, Shell, **food:** Applebee's, Arby's, Asian Chef, Capt. D's, Cici's Pizza, DQ, Hooters, La Hacienda, Larrys Subs, LongHorn Steaks, Moe's SW Grill, Panda Express, Red Lobster, Ruby Tuesday, Sprayberry's BBQ, Steak'n Shake, Texas Roadhouse, Waffle House, Wendy's, **lodging:** Hampton Inn, Jameson Inn, **other:** Goodyear, Hobby Lobby, Home Depot, Kauffman Tire, Kohl's, Lowe's Whse, PetsMart, Ross, Walmart SuperCtr, **W gas:** Phillips 66, RaceTrac, **food:** Bugaboo Creek Steaks, Burger King, Chick-fil-A, Coldstone, Cracker Barrel, Five Guys Burgers, Golden Corral, Honey Baked Ham, IHOP, KFC, La Parrilla Mexican, Mama Lucia's, O'Charley's, Olive Garden, Panera Bread, Red Robin, Shane's BBQ, Taco Mac, Tokyo Japanese, Zaxby's,
47	Continued **lodging:** Best Western, Comfort Inn, La Quinta, Motel 6, Ramada, **other:** [H], Belk, Best Buy, BigLots, BJ's Whse, Chevrolet, Chrysler/Jeep, Dillards, $Tree, Ford/Lincoln/Mercury, Hyundai, JC Penney, Michael's, Office Depot, Old Navy, Pontiac/Buick/GMC, Publix, Radio Shack, Target, Tires+, TJ Maxx, Toyota/Scion, Walgreens, USPO
41	US 27/29, Newnan, **E gas:** Pilot/Subway/Wendy's/dsl/scales/24hr, **other:** Roosevelt SP, **W gas:** BP/dsl/24hr, Chevron, Phillips 66/dsl, **food:** Huddle House, McDonald's, Waffle House, **lodging:** Day's Inn, Howard Johnson, Travelodge
35	US 29, to Grantville, **W gas:** BP/dsl, Phillips 66/dsl
28	GA 54, GA 100, to Hogansville, **E gas:** Shell/dsl, **W gas:** BP/dsl, Chevron/dsl, Love's/Arby's/dsl/scales/24hr, **food:** China Cafe, Intnat'l Cafe, McDonald's, Roger's BBQ, Subway, Waffle House, Wendy's, **lodging:** Garden Inn, Key West Inn, **other:** Ingles
23mm	Beech Creek
22mm	**weigh sta both lanes**
21	I-185 S, to Columbus
18	GA 109, to Mountville, **E gas:** Marathon/Dominos, **lodging:** Quality Inn, Wingate Inn, **other:** to FDR SP, Little White House HS, **W gas:** BP/dsl, Circle K/Spectrum/dsl, RaceTrac/dsl, Shell/dsl, Texaco/dsl, Summit/dsl, **food:** Applebee's, Banzai Japanese, Burger King, Conestoga Steaks, Cracker Barrel, IHOP, Juanito's Mexican, Longhorn Steaks, Los Nopales, Moe's SW Grill, Ryan's, Starbucks, Subway, Waffle House, Wendy's, Zaxby's, **lodging:** Baymont Inn, Best Western, Comfort Inn, Country Inn & Suites, Holiday Inn Express, Jameson Inn, Super 8, **other:** Belk, Chrysler/Dodge/Jeep, Ford/Lincoln/Mercury, Home Depot, Honda, JC Penney, RV Park (3mi), mall
14	US 27, to La Grange, **W gas:** BP/24hr, Pure, Shell, **lodging:** Hampton Inn
13	GA 219, to La Grange, **E gas:** Shell/dsl/scales/24hr, **food:** Waffle House, **lodging:** Day's Inn, Great Value Lodge, **W gas:** BP/dsl, Pilot/Subway/dsl/scales/24hr, **food:** Arbys, McDonald's, **other:** [H]
10mm	Long Cane Creek
6	Kia Blvd, **W** Kia Plant
2	GA 18, to West Point, **E gas:** BP, Shell/dsl/24hr, **lodging:** Travelodge, **W food:** KFC (1.5mi), Subway (1.5), **other:** to West Point Lake, camping
.5mm	**Welcome Ctr nb, full [♿] facilities, [☎], [picnic], litter barrels, vending, petwalk**
0mm	Georgia/Alabama state line, Chattahoochee River

INTERSTATE 95

N ↕ S

Exit #	Services
113mm	Georgia/South Carolina state line, Savannah River
111mm	**Welcome Ctr/weigh sta sb, full [♿] facilities, info, [☎], vending, [picnic], litter barrels, petwalk**
109	GA 21, to Savannah, Pt Wentworth, Rincon, **E gas:** Enmark/dsl, Pilot/McDonald's/Subway/dsl/scales/24hr, **food:** Waffle House, **lodging:** Country Inn&Suites, Hampton Inn, Mulberry Grove Inn, Wingate Inn, **other:** Peterbilt, **W gas:** Flash/dsl, Shell/Circle K/Quizno's/dsl, **food:** Island Grill, Sea Grill, Wendy's, Zaxby's, **lodging:** Comfort Suites, Day's

N ↕ S

INTERSTATE 95 CONT'D

Exit #	Services
109	Continued Inn, Holiday Inn Express, Quality Inn, Ramada Ltd, Sleep Inn, Super 8, **other:** CVS Drug, Family$, Food-Lion, Green Piece RV Park (5mi), Whispering Pines RV Park (3mi)
107mm	Augustine Creek
106	Jimmy DeLoach Pkwy
104	Savannah ✈, **E gas:** BP, Shell/dsl, **food:** Sneed's Tavern, Waffle House, **lodging:** Cambria Suites, Candlewood Suites, Comfort Suites, Country Inn&Suites, Fairfield Inn, Hampton Inn, Hawthorn Suites, Hilton Garden, Sheraton, Springhill Suites, Staybridge Suites, Towneplace Suites, Wingate Inn, **other:** to ✈, **W gas:** Murphy USA, Shell/Subway, **food:** Arby's, Cheddar's, Chick-fil-A, Hilliard's Rest., Lemongrass Grill, Longhorn Steaks, Ruby Tuesday, Sonic, Zaxby's Café, **lodging:** Red Roof Inn, **other:** Home Depot, Sam's Club/gas, Walmart SuperCtr/McDonald's/24hr
102	US 80, to Garden City, **E gas:** BP, Enmark/dsl, Flash/dsl, **food:** Busy Dean's, Cracker Barrel, Huddle House, KFC, Krystal, Larry's Subs, Masato Japanese, McDonald's, Okyama Japanese, Peking Chinese, Pizza Hut/Taco Bell, Quizno's, Waffle House, **lodging:** Best Western, Jameson Inn, Microtel, Ramada Ltd, Travelodge, **other:** Camping World RV Ctr, Food Lion, Family$, to Ft Pulaski NM, museum, **W gas:** BP, Gate/Subway/dsl, Shell, Texaco, **food:** Burger King, Domino's, Don's BBQ, El Potro Mexican, Hardee's, Italian Pizza, Mihn Xing Chinese, Wendy's, Western Sizzlin, **lodging:** Econolodge, Holiday Inn, La Quinta, Magnolia Inn, Quality Inn, Sleep Inn, **other:** NAPA, auto repair
99b a	I-16, W to Macon, E to Savannah
94	GA 204, to Savannah, Pembroke, **E gas:** BP/dsl, El Cheapo, Exxon, 76/Circle K, Shell/dsl, **food:** Applebees, Cracker Barrel, Denny's, Hardee's, Hooligan's, McDonald's, Perkins, Ruby Tuesday, Shoney's, Sonic, **lodging:** Baymont Inn, Best Value Inn, Best Western, Clarion, Comfort Suites, Country Inn&Suites, Day's Inn, Fairfield Inn, Hampton Inn, Holiday Inn Express, Howard Johnson, La Quinta, Quality Inn, Ramda Inn, Red Roof Inn, Rodeway Inn, Sans Boutique Hotel, Sleep Inn, SpringHill Suites, Super 8, Wingate Inn, **other:** H, Factory Stores/Famous Brands, GNC, Walmart SuperCtr/24hr/gas (2mi), **W gas:** Chevron/dsl/24hr (2mi), Shell, **food:** El Potro Mexican, Hooters, JT's Grill, Shellhouse Rest, Subway, Waffle House, **lodging:** Country Hearth Inn, Econolodge, Microtel, Travelodge, **other:** Harley-Davidson, Bellaire Woods RV Park (2mi)
91mm	Ogeechee River
90	GA 144, Old Clyde Rd, to Ft Stewart, Richmond Hill SP, **E gas:** Chevron, Exxon, **other:** Kroger/deli, **W gas:** Love's/McDonald's/dsl/scales/24hr, Shell/dsl, **other:** Gore's RV Ctr
87	US 17, to Coastal Hwy, Richmond Hill, **E gas:** BP/Subway, Chevron/dsl/24hr, Citgo, RaceWay, **food:** China 1, Denny's/24hr, Domino's, Smokehouse Grill, Southern Image Rest., Steamer's Rest., Subway,

SAVANNAH

SAVANNAH

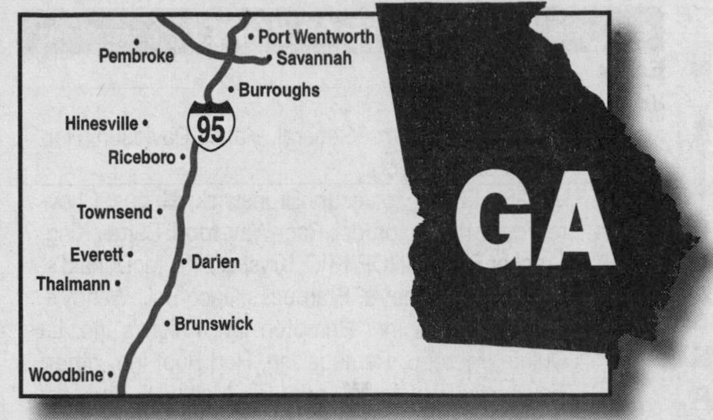

Exit #	Services
87	Continued Waffle House, **lodging:** Day's Inn, Motel 6, Royal Inn, Scottish Inn, Travelodge, **W gas:** El Cheapo, Exxon/McDonald's/dsl, TA/BP/LJSilver/Pizza Hut/Popeye's/dsl/24hr/@, Shell/dsl, **food:** Arby's, Burger King, KFC/Taco Bell, Waffle House, Wendy's, **lodging:** Best Western, Comfort Suites, Econolodge, Hampton Inn, Holiday Inn, Knight's Inn, **other:** KOA
85mm	Elbow Swamp
80mm	Jerico River
76	US 84, GA 38, to Midway, Sunbury, **E** hist sites, **W gas:** BP/dsl, El Cheapo/dsl/scales, **food:** Holton's Seafood, Huddle House, **other:** H, museum
67	US 17, Coastal Hwy, to S Newport, **E gas:** Chevron/Subway/dsl, Citgo/dsl, El Cheapo, Shell/McDonald's, **food:** Jones BBQ, **other:** Harris Neck NWR, Newport Camping (2mi), **W gas:** BP
58	GA 99, GA 57, Townsend Rd, Eulonia, **E gas:** BP/dsl, Citgo, **lodging:** Eulonia Lodge, **other:** $General, USPO, **W gas:** Chevron/dsl/24hr, Citgo, Shell/Stuckey's/dsl, **food:** Huddle House, **lodging:** Day's Inn, Knight's Inn, **other:** McIntosh Lake RV Park, Lake Harmony RV Camp
55mm	**weigh sta both lanes,** ☎
49	GA 251, to Darien, **E gas:** Chevron/dsl/24hr, Mobil/dsl, **food:** DQ, McDonald's, Waffle House, **lodging:** King George Motel, **other:** Ford, Inland Harbor RV Park, Tall Pines RV Park, **W gas:** BP, El Cheapo/Larry's Subs/dsl/scales, Shell/dsl, **food:** Burger King, Huddle House, KFC/Pizza Hut/Taco Bell, Ruby Tuesday, Smokey Joe's BBQ, TCBY, Wendy's, **lodging:** Clean Stay USA, Comfort Inn, Hampton Inn, Quality Inn, Super 8, **other:** Preferred Outlets/famous brands, flea mkt
47mm	Darien River
46.5mm	Butler River
46mm	Champney River
45mm	Altamaha River
42	GA 99, **E** to Hofwyl Plantation HS
41mm	**rest area sb, full ♿ facilities, info, ☎, vending, picnic, litter barrels, petwalk**
38	GA 25, to US 17, N Golden Isles Pkwy, Brunswick, **E gas:** RaceTrac, **food:** Millhouse Steaks, **lodging:** Country Inn&Suites, Embassy Suites (2mi), Fairfield Inn, Holiday Inn, Microtel, St James Suites, **other:** H, Nissan, **W gas:** BP, Chevron, Flash, Shell/dsl, **food:** China Town, Denny's, Huddle House/24hr, La Fuente Mexican, Waffle House, **lodging:** Courtyard, Econolodge, Guest Cottage Motel, Hampton Inn,

DARIEN

GA

INTERSTATE 95 CONT'D

N ↕ S — BRUNSWICK — ST MARYS

Exit #	Services
38	Continued Quality Inn, **other:** $General, Harley Davidson, Harvey's Foods, Toyota
36b a	US 25, US 341, to Jesup, Brunswick, **E gas:** Chevron/dsl/24hr, Exxon/dsl, RaceWay, **food:** Burger King, Cracker Barrel, IHOP, KFC, Krystal/24hr, McDonald's, Pizza Hut, Shoney's, Starbucks, Taco Bell, Wendy's, **lodging:** Day's Inn, Hampton Inn, Knight's Inn, La Quinta, Motel 6, Ramada Inn, Red Roof Inn, **other:** Newcastle RV Ctr, **W gas:** BP, Mobil/dsl, Parker's/dsl, Sunoco, **food:** Beef'o Brady's, Capt Joe's Seafood, Huddle House/24hr, Larry's Subs, Sonny's BBQ, Subway, Waffle House, **lodging:** Best Western, Clarion, Clean Stay USA, Rodeway Inn, Sleep Inn, Super 8, **other:** Advance Parts, CVS Drug, $General, Family$, Fred's Drug, Winn-Dixie
33mm	Turtle River
30mm	S Brunswick River
29	US 17, US 82, GA 520, S GA Pkwy, Brunswick, **E gas:** Citgo/Church's/dsl, Exxon, Mobil, Pilot/Steak'n Shake/Subway/dsl/scales/24hr, Sunoco/Backyard Burger, **food:** GA BBQ, Huddle House, Krystal, McDonald's, Whataburger, **other:** Blue Beacon, Speed-Co Lube, **W gas:** ***FLYING J***/Conoco/Country Mkt/dsl/LP/scales/24hr, Goasis/Burger King/Subway/dsl/24hr, Mobil, **food:** Waffle House, **lodging:** GuestHouse Inn, Microtel, Super 8, **other:** $General, Golden Isles Camping, TA Truck Service
27.5mm	Little Satilla River
26	Dover Bluff Rd, **E gas:** Mobil/Stuckey's/dsl
21mm	White Oak Creek
19mm	Canoe Swamp
15mm	Satilla River
14	GA 25, to Woodbine, **W food:** Chevron/Sunshine/dsl/rest./24hr, **food:** Jack's BBQ, **lodging:** Stardust Motel (3mi)
7	Harrietts Bluff Rd, **E gas:** Exxon/dsl, Shell/Subway, **food:** Huddle House, **W gas:** BP/dsl
6.5mm	Crooked River
6	Laurel Island Pkwy, **E gas:** Cisco/BP/Arby's/dsl/scales/24hr
3	GA 40, to St Marys, **E gas:** El Cheapo, Exxon/Krystal, Shell/Subway, **food:** Applebee's, Bonzai, Burger King, Chick-fil-A, China Wok, Hong Kong Buffet, KFC, McDonald's, Pablo's Mexican, Ruby Tuesday, Shoney's, Sonny's BBQ, Taco Bell, Waffle House, Wendy's, Zaxby's, **lodging:** Best Western, Comfort Inn, Country Inn&Suites, Day's Inn, 4Star Inn, Hampton Inn, Hawthorn Suites, Holiday Inn Express, Magnolia Inn, Microtel, Quality Inn, Sleep Inn, **other:** [H], Chevrolet/Buick, Chrysler/Dodge/Jeep, CVS Drug, $Tree, Ford/Mercury, Kia, K-Mart, Lowes Whse, Publix, Winn-Dixie, to Submarine Base, **W gas:** Citgo, Flash/dsl, Petro/Quizno's/Church's/dsl/scales/24hr/@, **food:** Cracker Barrel, IHOP, Oasis Grill, Waffle House, **lodging:** Clean Stay USA, Days Inn, Econolodge, Jameson Inn, La Quinta, Ramada Inn
1	St Marys Rd, **E Welcome Ctr nb, full [handicapped] facilities,** [phone], **vending,** [picnic], **litter barrels, petwalk, gas:** Cisco/
1	Continued Blimpie/DQ/LJ Silver/Mrs Winners/Pizza Hut/dsl, Shell/dsl, **food:** to Cumberland Is Nat Seashore, **W gas:** BP/dsl, Chevron/dsl, Wilco/Hess/Wendy's/dsl/scales, **food:** Jack's BBQ, **other:** GS RV Park, KOA
0mm	Georgia/Florida state line, St Marys River

INTERSTATE 185 (COLUMBUS)

N ↕ S — COLUMBUS

Exit #	Services
48	I-85. I-185 begins/ends on I-85.
46	Big Springs Rd, **E** BP, **W gas:** Shell/dsl, **other:** tires
42	US 27, Pine Mountain, **E gas:** BP, Shell/dsl, **food:** Waffle House, **other:** to Callaway Gardens, Little White House HS
34	GA 18, to West Point, **E gas:** Shell/dsl/24hr
30	Hopewell Church Rd, Whitesville, **W gas:** BP/dsl
25	GA 116, to Hamilton, **W** RV camping
19	GA 315, Mulberry Grove, **W gas:** Chevron/dsl/24hr
14	Smith Rd
12	Williams Rd, **W Welcome Ctr/rest rooms, gas:** BP/dsl/cafe, Shell, **lodging:** Country Inn Suites, Microtel
10	US 80, GA 22, to Phenix City, **W** Springer Opera House
8	Airport Thruway, **E food:** Blimpie, China Moon, Shoney's, **other:** $Tree, GNC, Hobby Lobby, Home Depot, Walmart/Subway, **W gas:** BP, Circle K/Spectrum, **food:** Applebee's, Buffet City, Burger King, Capt D's, Fuddruckers, Hardee's, Houlihan's, IHOP, McDonald's, Mikata Japanese, Monkey Joe's, Outback Steaks, River City Grill, Stevie B's Pizza, Subway, Taco Bell, **lodging:** Comfort Suites, Doubletree, Extended Stay America, Hampton Inn, Sleep Inn, **other:** K-Mart
7	45th St, Manchester Expswy, **E gas:** Chevron, **food:** Applebee's, Burger King, Carino's Italian, Krystal, Ruby Tuesday, **lodging:** Courtyard, La Quinta, Super 8, **other:** Best Buy, Chevrolet/Cadillac, Dillard's, JC Penney, Macy's, mall, **W gas:** BP, Chevron, Circle K/Spectrum, Texaco, **food:** Arby's, China Express, Dunkin Donuts, Golden Corral, Jimmy John's, KFC, Logan's Roadhouse, Lucky China, McDonald's, Pizza Hut, Ryan's, Sonic, Starbucks, Subway, Waffle House, Wendy's, **lodging:** Fairfield Inn, Holiday Inn, TownePlace Suites, **other:** [H], Advance Parts, Big 10 Tire, $General, Mr. Transmissions, tires, Vet
6	GA 22, Macon Rd, **E gas:** Chevron/dsl, Circle K/Spectrum/dsl, **food:** Bruster's, Burger King, DQ, KFC, Little Caesars, Sushiko Japanese, Taco Bell, Viva El Torro, Waffle House, **lodging:** Best Western, Comfort Inn, Day's Inn, **other:** Curves, $General, Ford, Kia, Nissan, Rite Aid, U-Haul, Walgreens, USPO, **W gas:** BP, Chevron, **food:** American Deli, Capt D's, ChuckeCheese, Cici's Pizza, Country BBQ, Denny's, Firehouse Subs, Jimmy John's, Longhorn Steaks, McDonald's, Subway, **lodging:** Efficiency Lodge, La Quinta, **other:** Books-A-Million, CVS Drug, $Tree, Freds Drug, GNC, Goodyear, Hancock Fabrics, K-Mart, Publix, Radio Shack
4	Buena Vista Rd, **E gas:** BP, Circle K, Solo, **food:** Burger King, Capt D's, Chef Lee Chinese, Checker's, Church's, Krystal, McDonald's, Papa John's, Pizza Hut, Subway, Taco Bell, Waffle House, Zaxby's,

N ↕ S COLUMBUS

INTERSTATE 185 CONT'D (COLUMBUS)

Exit #	Services
4	Continued **other:** AutoZone, $Tree, Firestone/auto, Goodyear/auto, Rainbow Foods, Walgreens, Walmart, Winn-Dixie, repair, USPO, Vet, **W gas:** Circle K/Spectrum/dsl
3	St Marys Rd, **E lodging:** Microtel, **food:** Dominos, **other:** Family$, **W gas:** BP, FuelTech/dsl, **food:** Hardee's, Zeb's Seafood Chicken, **other:** Ace Hardware, $General, Piggly Wiggly
1b a	US 27, US 280, Victory Dr, **0-3 mi W gas:** Chevron, Circle K, Liberty Gas, RaceWay/dsl/24hr, **food:** Arbys, Burger King, Capt D's, Checker's, Hibachi Express, Krystal, McDonald's, Papa John's, Sonic, Subway, Taco Bell, Valarta Mexican, Wendy's, **lodging:** Candlewood Suites, Colony Inn, Day's Inn, Econolodge, Holiday Inn Express, Motel 6, Suburban Lodge, **other:** Advance Parts, Autozone, $General, Family$, Mkt Place Foods, Piggly Wiggly, I-185 begins/ends.

ATLANTA AREA

INTERSTATE 285 (ATLANTA)

Exit #	Services
62	GA 279, S Fulton Hwy, Old Nat Hwy, **N gas:** Chevron, Texaco, **food:** City Cafe, **lodging:** Econolodge, **S gas:** Chevron, Exxon, Shell, **food:** Blimpie, Burger King, Checker's, China Cafeteria, Church's, El Nopal Mexican, KFC/Pizza Hut, Krystal, Longhorn Steaks, McDonald's, Mrs Winner's, Popeye's, Subway, Taco Bell, Waffle House, Wendy's, **lodging:** Clarion, Comfort Inn, Day's Inn, Howard Johnson, Motel 6, Quality Inn, **other:** AutoZone, Cottman Transmissions, Curves, Family$, NAPA, U-Haul
61	I-85, N to Atlanta, S to Montgomery, **Services 1 mi N GA I-85, exit 71. E food:** Ruby Tuesday, **lodging:** Comfort Suites, Courtyard, GA Conv Ctr, Microtel, Hampton Inn, Sheraton/grill, Sleep Inn, Sumner Suites, Super 8, Wingate Inn, **W food:** Bennigan's, **lodging:** Comfort Inn, Day's Inn, Embassy Suites, Marriott, Quality Inn, Ramada, Super 8, Travelodge, Westin Hotel
60	GA 139, Riverdale Rd, **N lodging:** Fairfield Inn (2mi), Microtel (2mi), Wingate Inn (2mi), **S gas:** Exxon, QT, Shell/dsl, **food:** Checker's, Church's, KFC/LJ Silver, McDonald's, **lodging:** Best Western, Country Inn&Suites, Day's Inn, Quality Inn, Ramada Inn, **other:** Advance Parts, Aldi Foods, $General, Family$, U-Haul
59	Clark Howell Hwy, **N** air cargo
58	I-75, N to Atlanta, S to Macon (from eb), to US 19, US 41 , to Hapeville, **S gas:** BP, Chevron/24hr, **food:** Bojangles, Philly Connection, Subway, Waffle House, Wendy's, **lodging:** Home Lodge Motel
55	GA 54, Jonesboro Rd, **N lodging:** Super 8, **S gas:** BP, Citgo/dsl, Phillips 66, Shell/dsl, **food:** Alondra's Mexican/Chinese, Capt D's, Church's, DaiLai Vietnamese, Golden Gate Chinese, LJ Silver, McDonald's, Subway, Taco Bell, **other:** Home Depot, repair
53	US 23, Moreland Ave, to Ft Gillem, **N gas:** BP, Citgo, Conoco/dsl, **S gas:** Citgo, Shell, TA/dsl/24hr/@, **food:** Popeye's, Wendy's, **lodging:** Economy Inn

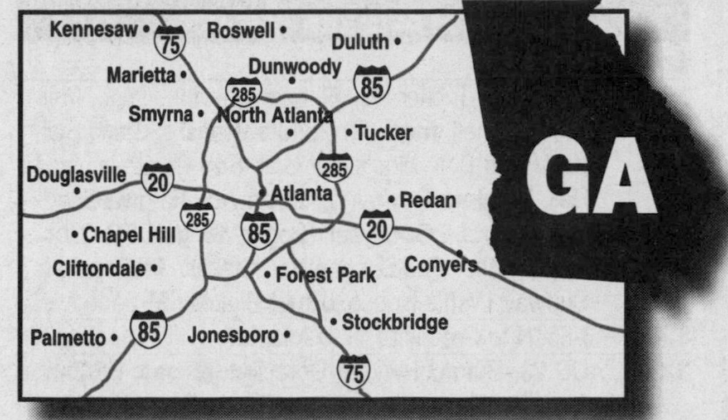

ATLANTA AREA

Exit #	Services
52	I-675, S to Macon
51	Bouldercrest Rd, **N gas:** BP, Pilot/Wendy's/dsl/24hr, **food:** A&W/LJ Silver, Hardee's, KFC/Pizza Hut, WK Wings, **lodging:** DeKalb Inn, **other:** Family$, Wayfield Foods, **S gas:** Chevron/dsl
48	GA 155, Flat Shoals Rd, Candler Rd, **N gas:** BP, Chevron, Marathon, Shell/dsl, Stop'n Go, **food:** Arby's, Burger King, Checker's, DQ, KFC/Pizza Hut, McDonald's, Subway, Taco Bell, Waffle King, WK Wings, **lodging:** Country Hearth Inn, Gulf American Inn, **other:** BigLots, Macy's, Pep Boys, **S gas:** QT, Phillips 66, **food:** Sonic
46b a	I-20, E to Augusta, W to Atlanta
44	GA 260, Glenwood Rd, **E gas:** Marathon, Super 8, **lodging:** Old English Inn, **W gas:** Citgo, Shell, **food:** Church's, Mrs Winner's, **lodging:** Glenwood Inn
43	US 278, Covington Hwy, **E gas:** Chevron/Subway/24hr, Citgo/dsl, **food:** Waffle House, **other:** U-Haul, **W gas:** BP/24hr, QT, Shell/dsl, **food:** Blimpie, Checker's, KFC/Taco Bell, Mrs Winner's, Wendy's, **lodging:** Best Inn, **other:** Advance Parts, Family$, Firestone/auto
42	(from nb), Marta Station
41	GA 10, Memorial Dr, Avondale Estates, **E gas:** Citgo, QT, Shell/dsl, **food:** Applebee's, Arby's, Burger King, Church's, DQ, McDonald's, Pancake House, Pizza Hut, Super China, Waffle House, Wendy's, **lodging:** Savannah Suites, Suburban Lodge, **other:** Advance Parts, AutoZone, Big 10 Tire, $General, Firestone/auto, Office Depot, Radio Shack, U-Haul
40	Church St, to Clarkston, **E gas:** Chevron, Shell/dsl, Texaco, **W** gas:**other:** H
39b a	US 78, to Athens, Decatu
38	US 29, Lawrenceville Hwy, **E gas:** Phillips 66, Shell, **food:** Waffle House, **lodging:** Knight's Inn, Super 8, **other:** H, **W gas:** BP, USA, **food:** Waffle House, **lodging:** Masters Inn, Motel 6
37	GA 236, to LaVista, Tucker, **E gas:** Chevron, Circle K, **food:** Checker's, Chili's, Folks Rest., IHOP, O'Charley's, Olive Garden, Picadilly's, Schlotsky's, Steak&Ale, Waffle House, **lodging:** Comfort Suites, Country Inn Suites, **other:** Firestone, Target, **W gas:** BP/repair, Citgo/dsl, Shell, **food:** Arby's, Blackeyed Pea, Blue Ribbon Grill, Capt D's, City Cafe, Domino's, DQ, Fuddrucker's, Jason's Deli, McDonald's, Panera Bread, Philly Connection, Pizza Hut, Red Lobster, Taco Bell, Wendy's, **lodging:** Courtyard, Fairfield Inn, Holiday Inn, Magnolia Motel, Quality Inn, Radisson, **other:** Best Buy, $Tree, Goodyear/auto, JC Penney, Kroger, Macy's, Michael's, Office Depot, Publix, TJ Maxx, mall

INTERSTATE 285 (ATLANTA)

Exit #	Services
34	Chamblee-Tucker Rd, **E gas:** Chevron, Citgo, Phillips 66, Shell, **food:** Arby's/Mrs Winner's, China Star, KFC/Taco Bell, Moe's SW Grill, S&S Cafeteria, Taco Bell, **lodging:** Day's Inn, **other:** Ace Hardware, Advance Parts, , Goodyear, Kroger, **W gas:** BP, Citgo, **food:** Little Cuba, LoneStar Steaks, McDonald's, Subway, Waffle House, **other:** BigLots, $Tree
33b a	I-85, N to Greenville, S to Atlanta
32	US 23, Buford Hwy, to Doraville, **E gas:** BP/24hr, **food:** Baldino's Subs, Burger King/playland, Checker's, Chick-fil-A, El Pescador, Krystal, Wendy's, **other:** Big 10 Tire, Firestone/auto, Goodyear/auto, K-Mart, 99c Store, **W gas:** Citgo, Shell, **food:** First China, McDonald's, Monterrey Mexican, Waffle House, **lodging:** Holiday Inn
31b a	GA 141, Peachtree Ind, to Chamblee, **W gas:** Citgo, Shell, Texaco, **food:** Arby's, Chick-fil-A, Dunkin Donuts, McDonald's, Piccadilly, Pizza Hut, Waffle House, Wendy's, **other:** Acura, Advance Parts, Audi/VW, Buick/Pontiac/GMC, Chevrolet, Chrysler/Jeep/Dodge, CVS Drug, Dodge, Firestone, Ford, Honda, Hyundai, Kia, Lexus, Mazda, Porsche, Saab, Toyota, VW
30	Chamblee-Dunwoody Rd, N Shallowford Rd, to N Peachtree Rd, **N gas:** BP, Chevron, **food:** Bagel&Co., Burger King, Garcia's Mexican, Guthrie's, Lucky China, Maggie's Creamery, McDonald's, Quizno's, Starbucks, Subway, Waffle House, **other:** Kroger, **S gas:** Exxon/Blimpie/Arby's, Mobil, Phillips 66/dsl, Shell, **food:** Bombay Grill, City Café, La Botana Mexican, Mad Italian Rest., Olde Mill Steaks, Papa John's, Taco Bell, Wendy's, Wild Ginger Thai, **lodging:** Holiday Inn Select, Residence Inn
29	Ashford-Dunwoody Rd, **N gas:** BP, Exxon/Subway, **food:** Applebee's, Brio Tuscan, Bloomingdale's, CA Pizza Kitchen, Denny's, Food Court, Garrison's Broiler, Goldfish, Houlihan's, Jason's Deli, J. Alexander's, Maggiano's Italian, McDonald's, McCormick & Shmick's, PF Chang's, Schlotsky's, **lodging:** Crowne Plaza, Fairfield Inn, **other:** Barnes&Noble, Best Buy, Border's, Dillard's, Firestone/auto, Goodyear/auto, Macey's, Marshall's, Old Navy, Walmart SuperCtr, USPO, mall, **S gas:** Chevron, **food:** Arby's, **lodging:** Hilton Garden
28	Peachtree-Dunwoody Rd (no EZ return wb), **N food:** Arby's, Chequer's Grill, Fuddrucker's, Sweet Tomatos, **lodging:** Comfort Suites, Courtyard, Extended Stay America, Extended Stay Deluxe, Fairfield Inn, Hampton Inn, Hilton Suites, Holiday Inn Express, Homestead Suites, La Quinta, Marriott, Microtel, Residence Inn, Westin, **other:** Costco/gas, Home Depot, PetsMart, Publix, Rite Aid, Ross, Target, TJ Maxx, mall, **S** H
27	US 19 N, GA 400, **2 mi N** LDS Temple
26	Glenridge Dr (from eb), Johnson Ferry Rd
25	US 19 S, Roswell Rd, Sandy Springs, **N gas:** BP, Chevron, Exxon, Shell/dsl, **food:** American Pie Rest., Applebee's, Arby's, Boston Mkt, Burger King, Caribbean Cafe, Chicago Pizza, Chick-fil-A, Chipotle
25	Continued Mexican, Domino's, Dunkin Donuts, El Azteca Mexican, El Toro Mexican, IHOP, KFC/Pizza Hut, Landmark Diner, La Rumba Cafe, Longhorn Steaks, Madarin House, McDonald's, Mellow Mushroom Cafe, Noodles Cafe, Panera Bread, Rumi's Kitchen, Ruth's Chris Steaks, Starbucks, Steak'n Shake, Subway, Taco Bell, Waffle House, Wendy's, **lodging:** Comfort Inn, Hampton Inn, Homestead Suites, **other:** H , CVS Drug, DeKalb Tire, $Tree, Hancock Fabrics, Marshall's, NAPA AutoCare, Office Depot, PepBoys, Publix, Target, Toyota, Whole Foods Mkt, **S gas:** Chevron/24hr, Shell, **food:** El Taco Veloz, Frankie's Grill, Kobe Steaks, Mama's Café, **lodging:** Day's Inn/rest., **other:** Kroger/gas (1.5mi)
24	Riverside Dr
22	New Northside Dr, to Powers Ferry Rd, **N gas:** Shell, **S gas:** BP, Chevron/24hr, **food:** McDonald's, Waffle House, Wendy's, **lodging:** Candlewood Suites, Crowne Plaza, Hawthorn Suites, Homestead Suites, **other:** CVS Drug
21	(from wb), **N gas:** Shell, **food:** HillTop Café, Homestead Village, **other:** BMW/Mini
20	I-75, N to Chattanooga, S to Atlanta (from wb), to US 41 N
19	US 41, Cobb Pkwy, to Dobbins AFB, **N gas:** BP, Chevron/24hr, Citgo, Shell, **food:** Arby's, BBQ, Bruster's, Carrabba's, ChuckeCheese, Denny's, Dunkin Donuts, Hardee's, IHOP, Jade Palace, Joe's Crabshack, KFC, McDonald's, Olive Garden, Papa John's, Pizza Hut, Red Lobster, Steak'n Shake, Subway, Sunny's BBQ, The Border Mexican, Waffle House, Wendy's, Wingate Inn, **lodging:** Hilton, Holiday Inn Express, **other:** Best Buy, Cadillac, Buick/Pontiac/Subaru, Chevrolet/Saab, , Honda, Hyundai, Lexus, Marshall's, Michael's, Office Depot, PetsMart, Ross, Target, Walgreen, **S gas:** Chevron/24hr, **food:** Buffalo's Café, Cheese Factory, Chipotle Mexican, Chick-fil-A, El Toro Mexican, Hooters, Jason's Deli, Johnny Rocket's, Longhorn Steaks, Maggiano's Italian, Malone's Grill, Olde Mill Steaks, PF Chang, Pizza Hut, Ruby Tuesday, Schlotsky's, **lodging:** Courtyard, Homewood Suites, Renaissance Motel, Sheraton Suites, Stouffer Waverly Hotel, Sumner Suites, **other:** A&P, Barnes&Noble, Costco/gas, JC Penney, Macy's, Sears/auto, USPO, mall
18	Paces Ferry Rd, to Vinings, **N food:** Panera Bread, **lodging:** Fairfield Inn, La Quinta, **S gas:** QT/24hr, **food:** Chick-fil-A, Subway, Willy's Grill, **lodging:** Extended Stay Deluxe, Hampton Inn, Wyndham, **other:** Goodyear/auto, Home Depot, Publix
16	S Atlanta Rd, to Smyrna, **N food:** Five Guys Burgers, Waffle House, Zio's Italian, **lodging:** Holiday Inn Express, **other:** H, **S gas:** Pilot/Wendy's/dsl/scales/24hr, Shell/dsl, Texaco, **other:** Kroger
15	GA 280, S Cobb Dr, **E lodging:** Microtel, **other:** U-Haul, **W gas:** BP/dsl, RaceTrac, Shell, **food:** Arby's/Mrs Winners, Checker's, Chick-fil-A, China Buffet, IHOP, Krystal/24hr, McDonald's, Subway, Taco Bell, Wendy's, Zaxby's, **lodging:** AmeriHost, Comfort Inn, Country Inn Suites, Knight's Inn, Sun Suites, **other:** H
14mm	Chattahoochee River

INTERSTATE 285 (ATLANTA)

ATLANTA AREA

Exit #	Services
13	Bolton Rd (from nb)
12	US 78, US 278, Bankhead Hwy, **E gas:** Citgo/dsl, Petro/Iron Skillet/dsl/rest./scales/24hr/@, Shell/dsl/24hr, **food:** Mrs Winner's, **other:** Blue Beacon, **W gas:** BP, Marathon
10b a	I-20, W to Birmingham, E to Atlanta (exits left from nb), **W** to Six Flags
9	GA 139, MLK Dr, to Adamsville, **E gas:** Phillips 66, Shell, **food:** Mrs Winner's, **other:** Family$, Wayfield Foods, **W gas:** Chevron, Shell, **food:** Checker's, Church's, Golden House Chinese, KFC/Taco Bell, McDonald's
7	Cascade Rd, **E gas:** Marathon, **food:** Papa John's, **other:** Kroger, **W gas:** BP, Phillips 66, **food:** Applebee's, China Express, KFC, McDonald's, Moe's SW Grill, Mrs Winner's, Pizza Hut, Quizno's, Starbucks, Subway, Up the Creek, Wendy's, **other:** [H], GNC, Home Depot, Publix, Radio Shack, Tires+
5b a	GA 166, Lakewood Fwy, **E gas:** Chevron, Shell, **food:** Blimpie, Burger King, Capt D's, Checker's, IHOP, KFC, Taco Bell, Wendy's, **other:** Goodyear, Firestone, Kroger, Macy's, mall, **W gas:** BP, Citgo/dsl, RaceWay, Shell/dsl/24hr, **food:** Church's, KFC, Mrs Winner's, Wendy's, **lodging:** Deluxe Inn, **other:** Vet, AutoZone, CVS Drug, Family$
2	Camp Creek Pkwy, to [airport], **E gas:** BP, Exxon, Texaco, **food:** Checker's, McDonald's, Mrs Winner's, **lodging:** Comfort Suites, **W gas: food:** American Deli, Brewster's, Carino's, Chick-fil-A, Jason's Deli, LongHorn Steaks, Panda Express, Red Lobster, Ruby Tuesday, Wendys, **other:** Barnes&Noble, BJ's Whse/gas, Lowes Whse, Marshall's, Old Navy, PetsMart, Publix, Ross, Staples, Target, Walgreens
1	Washington Rd, **E gas:** Texaco/dsl, **W gas:** Chevron, **lodging:** Regency Inn

INTERSTATE 475 (MACON)

N ↕ S MACON

Exit #	Services
16mm	I-475 begins/ends on I-75, exit 177.
15	US 41, Bolingbroke, **1 mi E gas:** Exxon/dsl/LP, Marathon/dsl
9	Zebulon Rd, **E gas:** Citgo, Shell/Pizza Hut/Taco Bell/24hr, **food:** Buffalo's Café, Chick-fil-A, Hong Kong Rest., Krystal, Margarita's Mexican, McAlister's Deli, McDonald's, NU Wiener's, Papa John's, Subway, Taki Japanese, Waffle House, Wendy's, **lodging:** Baymont Inn, Fairfield Inn, Sleep Inn, **other:** [H], GNC, Kohl's, Kroger, Krystal, Lowe's Whse, Radio Shack, Walgreens, Walmart SuperCtr/dsl, USPO, **W gas:** Marathon, Polly's Café, **other:** Advance Parts, CVS Drug
8mm	**rest area nb, full [handicapped] facilities, [phone], vending, [picnic], litter barrels, petwalk**
5	GA 74, Macon, **E gas:** RaceWay, **food:** Waffle House, **other:** Harley-Davidson/Suzuki, to Mercer U, **W gas:** Flash/Subway, Texaco/Church's/dsl, **food:** Capt D's, Wok&Roll Chinese, **lodging:** Howard Johnson, **other:** $General, Food Lion, Tires+, Vet, to Lake Tobesofkee

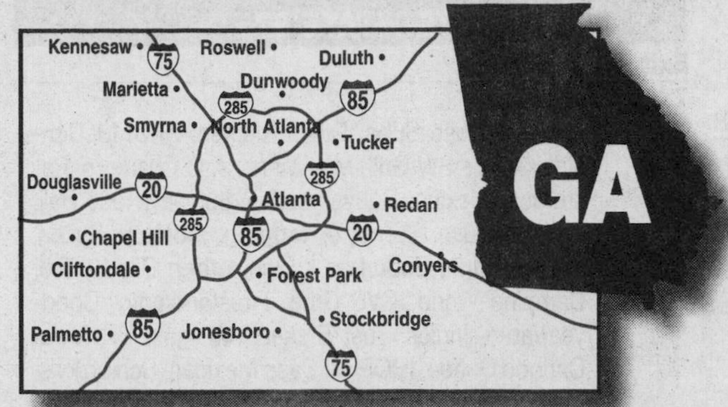

MACON

Exit #	Services
3	US 80, Macon, **E gas:** Marathon/dsl, Raceway, Spectrum/Subway, **food:** China Buffet, Cracker Barrel, JL's BBQ, McDonald's, Waffle House, **lodging:** Best Western, Comfort Inn, Day's Inn, Discovery Inn, Economy Inn, Hampton Inn, Holiday Inn, Motel 6, Quality Inn, Red Carpet Inn, Rodeway Inn, Super 8, Travelodge, Villager Inn, **other:** Walmart SuperCtr/gas/24hr, **1 mi E gas:** Stop n' Shop, **food:** Applebee's, Chick-fil-A, Cici's, DQ, Golden Corral, KFC, Krystal, Ryan's, Sonny's BBQ, Taco Bell, **other:** Best Buy, BooksAMillion, Chrysler, CVS Drug, Dillard's, Home Depot, Jo-Ann Fabrics, Kroger, Lowe's Whse, Marchall's, Michael's, Nissan, Old Navy, PetsMart, Sam's Club/gas, Target, Toyota, mall, **W gas:** Marathon/dsl, Shell, **food:** Burger King, **lodging:** Econolodge, Knight's Inn
0mm	I-475 begins/ends on I-75, exit 156.

INTERSTATE 575

N ↕ S CANTON

Exit #	Services
30mm	I-575 begins/ends on GA 5/515.
27	GA 5, Howell Br, to Ball Ground
24	Airport Dr
20	GA 5, to Canton, **E gas:** BP, **food:** Casey's rest., Chick-fil-A, Hooters, Ryan's, Stevi B's Pizza, Waffle Wouse, Wendy's, **lodging:** Comfort Inn, Homestead Inn, **other:** Chevrolet, Toyota, Walmart SuperCtr/24hr, **W gas:** Citgo, RaceTrac, **food:** Applebee's, Arby's, Cracker Barrel, Longhorn Steaks, McDonald's, O'Charley's, Outback Steaks, Panda Express, Red Lobster, Starbucks, Subway, Waffle House, Zaxby's, **lodging:** Holiday Inn Express, **other:** Belk, Home Depot, Michaels, Publix, Radio Shack, Ross
19	GA 20 E, Canton
17	GA 140, to Roswell (from sb), Canton
16	GA 20, GA 140, **E gas:** Pure, **W gas:** Citgo, Shell, **food:** BBQ, Burger King, KFC, Mandarin House, LJ Silver, Papa John's, Taco Bell, Waffle House, **other:** $General, K-Mart
14	Holly Springs, **E gas:** Citgo/dsl, **food:** Domino's, Pizza Hut, **lodging:** Pinecrest Motel, **W gas:** BP, Chevron, RaceTrac, Shell, **food:** Subway, Viva Mexico, Wendy's, Zaxby's, **other:** Kroger, Publix, Walgreens
11	Sixes Rd, **E gas:** Chevron, QT, **W gas:** Citgo
8	Towne Lake Pkwy, to Woodstock, **E gas:** Citgo, Shell, **food:** McDonald's, Waffle House, Waffle King/24hr, **other:** Ford, Hyundai, **W gas:** Phillips 66
7	GA 92, Woodstock, **E gas:** Chevron, QT, Shell, **food:** Arby's, Burger King, Capt D's, Checker's, Chick-fil-

INTERSTATE 575

Exit #	Services
7	Continued DQ, Firehouse Subs, Folk's Kitchen, KFC, McDonald's, Moe's SW Grill, Mrs Winner's, O'Charley's, Resturante Mexico, Ruby Tuesday, Subway, Taco Bell, Waffle House, Wendy's, **lodging:** Comfort Suites, Hampton Inn, Suburban Lodge, **other:** Big 10 Tire, Camping World, CVS Drug, Firestone/auto, Goodyear/auto, Ingles, Just Brakes, **W gas:** BP, **food:** Caribou Coffee, IHOP, Mi Casa Mexican, Schlotzky's, Steak'n Shake, Taco Mac, **other:** Atlanta Bread, Big Lots, BJ's Whse/gas, Discout Tire, Honda, Home Depot, Kohl's, Lowe's Whse, Office Depot, Old Navy, Target
4	Bells Ferry Rd, **W gas:** QT/24hr, Shell/dsl, **food:** Arby's, Burger King, Ralph's Grill, Subway, Waffle House, other:
3	Chastain Rd, to I-75 N, **W gas:** Chevron, Citgo, Shell, **food:** Arby's, Cracker Barrel, Mrs. Winner's, Los Reyes, O'Charley's, Panda Express, Sidelines Grill, Subway, ToGo's/Baskin Robbins, Waffle House, Wendy's, **lodging:** Best Western, Comfort Inn, Country Inn&Suites, Fairfield Inn, Residence Inn, Springhill Suites, Suburban Inn, **other:** to Kennesaw St Coll
1	Barrett Pkwy, to I-75 N, US 41, **E gas:** Chevron, Murphy USA/dsl, QT, **food:** Barnacle's Cafe, Buffalo Wild Wings, Burger King, Fuddruckers, KFC, Moe's SW Grill, Quizno's, Starbucks, Texas Roadhouse, Waffle House, Wendy's, Zaxby's, **other:** Atlanta Bread, Barnes&Noble, CVS Drug, $Tree, Firestone, Publix, Ross, SteinMart, Walmart SuperCtr/dsl, **W gas:** Shell, Texaco, **food:** Applebee's, Fuddrucker's, McDonald's, Olive Garden, Provino's Italian, Red Lobster, Smokey Bones, Starbucks, Waffle House, **lodging:** Comfort Inn, Crestwood Suites, Day's Inn, Holiday Inn Express, La Quinta, Ramada Ltd, Red Roof Inn, **other:** Big 10 Tire, Firestone/auto, Home Depot, Marshall's, Michael's, TJ Maxx, mall
0mm	I-575 begins/ends on I-75, exit 268.

INTERSTATE 675

Exit #	Services
10mm	I-285 W, to Atlanta ✈, E to Augusta. I-675 begins/ends on I-285, exit 52.
7	Anvil Block Rd, Ft Gillem, **E gas:** BP, **food:** Subway, **W gas:** Exxon
5	Forest Pkwy, **E gas:** Texaco/dsl, **W gas:** QT/dsl/scales, **food:** McDonald's, Waffle House
2	US 23, GA 42, **E gas:** BP, Texaco, **food:** Horizon/Backyard Burger, Mo-Joe's Café, **W gas:** Chevron/dsl, Citgo, **food:** Teapot Chinese, Waffle House, **other:** Family$, Food Depot, Goodyear/auto, USPO
1	GA 138, to I-75 N, Stockbridge, **E gas:** BP, Chevron/24hr, Citgo/dsl, Exxon, QT, Shell, **food:** Arby's, Burger King, Capt D's, Checker's, Church's Chicken, DQ, Dunkin Donuts, Golden Corral, Hong Kong Buffet, KFC, McDonald's, Papa John's, Pizza Hut, Popeye's, Taco Bell, Waffle House, Wendy's, Zaxby's, **lodging:** Best Value, Country Hearth Inn, Motel 6, Quality Inn, Sleep Inn, Stockbridge Inn, Suburban Lodge, **other:** Ace Hardware, Advance Parts,
1	Continued Aldi Foods, BigLots, Big10 Tire, CVS Drug, $General, $Tree, Goodyear/auto, NAPA, Radio Shack, Walmart SuperCtr/24hr/gas, USPO, **W gas:** Exxon, Raceway/24hr, **food:** Applebee's, Arby's, Broadway Diner, Burger King, Chick-fil-A, ChinChin Chinese, CiCi's, DQ, Folk's Rest., Frontera Mexican, Golden Corral, Honeybaked Ham, IHOP, KFC, Krystal, LJ Silver, McDonald's, Piccadilly's, Philly Connection, Shoney's, Subway, Taco Bell, Taco Mac, Tokyo Seafood, Waffle House, Wendy's, **lodging:** Best Western, Day's Inn, Comfort Inn, Holiday Inn, La Quinta, Hampton Inn, Motel 6, Red Roof Inn, **other:** [H], GNC, Goodyear, K-Mart, Kroger, Lowes Whse, Office Depot, Tires+
I-675	begins/ends on I-75, exit 227.

INTERSTATE 985 (GAINESVILLE)

Exit #	Services
I-985	begins/ends on US 23, 25mm.
24	to US 129 N, GA 369 W, Gainesville, **N other:** [H], GA Mtn Ctr, **S gas:** BP/Subway/dsl, Chevron/dsl, Citgo, **food:** Double B Burger, Rabbit Trail Cafe,
22	GA 11, Gainesville, **N gas:** BP/dsl, Citgo, QT/24hr, **food:** Burger King, McDonald's, **lodging:** Best Western/rest., **S gas:** Chevron, Shell/dsl, **food:** Waffle House, **lodging:** Motel 6
20	GA 60, GA 53, Gainesville, **N** gas Citgo/dsl, **food:** El Manarca, McDonald's, Mrs Winners, **lodging:** Best Value Inn, Hampton Inn, **S gas:** Kangaroo, **food:** Subway, Waffle House
16	GA 53, Oakwood, **N gas:** BP, Citgo, **food:** Arby's, Baskin-Robbins/Dunkin Donuts, Burger King, DQ, El Sombrero Mexican, Hardee's, KFC, McDonald's, Pizza Hut, Subway, Taco Bell, Waffle House, Zaxby's, **lodging:** Admiral Benbow Inn, Country Inn Suites, Jameson Inn, **other:** Chrysler/Jeep, CVS Drug, Food Lion, RV Ctr, Sam's Club, **S gas:** Citgo/dsl, QT/dsl, **food:** Checker's, Krystal, Mrs Winners, Sonny's BBQ, Waffle House, Wendy's, **lodging:** Comfort Inn, **other:** AutoZone, Goodyear/auto, Publix, Walgreens
12	Spout Springs Rd, Flowery Branch, **N gas:** Exxon/dsl, **S gas:** BP/Subway, Chevron/dsl, **food:** Burger&Shake, China Garden, CrossRoads Grill, Domino's, El Sombrero Mexican, TCBY, Thai Dish, **other:** , Publix
8	GA 347, Friendship Rd, Lake Lanier, **N gas:** BP, Chevron, Shell, Texaco, **food:** Backyard Burger, Blimpie, Burger King, China Garden, Huddle House, McDonald's, Sonia's Mexican, Subway, 3rd Coast, Waffle House, Wendy's, Vinny's NY Grill, Zaxby's, **other:** Advance parts, Publix, **S** Harley Davidson, Camper City RV Ctr
4	US 23 S, GA 20, Buford, **N gas:** QT, Shell, **food:** Arby's, Burger King, Capt D's, Checker's, Golden Buddah, Golden Corral, Huddle House, IHOP, KFC, McDonald's, Saigon Bangkok, Taco Bell, Wendy's, Zaxby's, **lodging:** Days Inn, Holiday Inn Express, **other:** Ace Hardware, Buick/Pontiac/GMC, Dodge/Jeep, Home Depot, KIA, Tuesday Morning, **S gas:** BP, Chevron, Citgo, Texaco, **food:** Ryan's, Sonny's BBQ, Waffle House, **other:** $Tree, Expert Tire, Honda, Lowes Whse, Walmart SuperCtr/24hr
0mm	I-985 begins/ends on I-85.

N ↕ S — WOODSTOCK — STOCKBRIDGE — GA — GAINESVILLE — BUFORD

INTERSTATE 15

E ↕ W

Exit #	Services
196mm	Idaho/Montana state line, Monida Pass, continental divide, elev 6870
190	Humphrey
184	Stoddard Creek Area, **E** Historical Site, RV camping, **W** Stoddard Creek Camping
180	Spencer, **E** **gas:** Opal Mtn Mine/gas, **food:** Opal Country Café, **other:** High Country Opal Store, RV Park
172	no services
167	ID 22, Dubois, **E** **gas:** Exxon/dsl/24hr, Phillips 66/dsl, **other:** Scoggins RV Park, USPO, **RV Dump, rest area both lanes, full ♿ facilities, ☎, 🛆, litter barrels, petwalk, W** to Craters NM, Nez Pearce Tr
150	Hamer, **E** **other:** Ron's Tire, USPO, Camus NWR, food, ☎
143	ID 33, ID 28, to Mud Lake, Rexburg, **W** Sacajawea Hist Bywy, **weigh sta both lanes**
142mm	roadside parking, hist site
135	ID 48, Roberts, **E** **gas:** Tesoro/dsl/LP, **other:** Roberts Mkt, **W** Western Wings RV Park
128	Osgood Area, **E** gas, camping (6mi)
119	US 20 E, to Rexburg, Idaho Falls, **E** **on Lindsay gas:** Sinclair/dsl, **food:** Chili's, Denny's, Outback Steaks, Sandpiper Rest., Smitty's Rest., **lodging:** Best Western, Comfort Inn, Day's Inn, Guesthouse Inn, LeRitz Hotel, Microtel, Motel 6, Red Lion Hotel, Shilo Inn/rest., Super 8, **other:** KOA, LDS Temple, RV Park, **W** **lodging:** Microtel
118	US 20, Broadway St, Idaho Falls, **E** **gas:** Phillips 66/dsl, **food:** Applebees, Arctic Circle, Brownstone Rest., Domino's, Jalisco Mexican, Mini's Rest., Olive Garden, Quizno's, Ruby River, Sherry's Rest., Starbucks, Wendy's, **lodging:** AmeriTel, Fairfield Inn, Hilton Garden, **other:** Ⓗ, American RV, Buick/GMC, Ford, Harley-Davidson, Subaru, LDS Temple, Walmart SuperCtr/Subway/24hr, tires, **W** **gas:** Chevron/dsl, Exxon, ***FLYING J***, Maverik, Phillips 66/dsl, **food:** Arby's, Burger King, DQ, Jack-in-the-Box, Little Caesar's, McDonald's, O'Brady's, Papa Murphy's, Pizza Hut, Subway, **lodging:** Comfort Inn, Motel 6, Motel West/rest., **other:** Albertson's, AutoZone, Checker Parts, Rite Aid, Walgreens
116	no services
113	US 26, to Idaho Falls, Jackson, **E** **gas:** Chevron/A&W/dsl, Sinclair/Dad's/dsl/24hr/@, Exxon/dsl, **other:** Ⓗ, Jack's Tires, Peterbilt, Sunnyside RV Park, Targhee RV Park
108	Shelley, Firth Area, **1 mi E other:** RV Park/dump
101mm	**rest area both lanes, full ♿ facilities, ☎, 🛆, litter barrels, petwalk, geological site**
98	Rose-Firth Area
94.5mm	Snake River
93	US 26, ID 39, Blackfoot, **E** **gas:** Chevron/24hr, ***FLYING J***/dsl/LP/24hr, Maverik, **food:** Arby's, Arctic Circle, Domino's, Homestead Rest., Italiano's, KFC, Little Caesar's, McDonald's, Papa Murphy's, Pizza Hut, Roberto's Mexican, Sonic, Subway, Taco Bell, Taco Time, Wendy's, Wingers, **lodging:** Best Western, Super 8, **other:** Albertson's, Auto Zone, Checker Parts, Chrysler/Dodge, Kesler's Foods, Radio Shack, RiteAid, Sav-On, Schwab Tire, Walmart SuperCtr/24hr, **W** Phillips 66, Riverside Boot/saddleshop (4mi)
90.5mm	Blackfoot River
89	US91, S Blackfoot, **2mi E lodging:** Y Motel
80	Ft Hall, **W** **gas:** Sinclair/dsl/rest./casino, **other:** Shoshone Bannock Tribal Museum
72	I-86 W, to Twin Falls
71	Pocatello Creek Rd, Pocatello, **E** **gas:** Chevron/Burger King, Phillips 66/dsl, Shell/dsl/24hr, **food:** Applebee's, Jack-in-the Box, Perkins, Sandpiper Rest., Subway, **lodging:** AmeriTel, Best Western, Comfort Inn, Holiday Inn, Red Lion Inn, Super 8, **other:** Ⓗ, KOA (1mi), **W** **gas:** Exxon, Maverik/dsl, **food:** Arby's, Bamboo Garden, Butterber's, Changs Garden Chinese, DQ, Golden Corral, Jamba Juice, KFC, McDonald's, Papa Kelsey's Pizza, Papa Murphy's, Pier 49 Pizza, Pizza Hut, Schlotsky's, Senor Iguana's Mexican, SF Pizza, Sizzler, Skipper's, Taco Bell, Taco Time, TCBY, Wendy's, Winger's, **other:** Albertson's, AutoZone, CarQuest, Checker Parts, Chevrolet, Ford, Fred Meyer, Grease Monkey, Harley Davidson, Honda, Jeep, JoAnn Fabrics, Radio Shack, RiteAid, Subaru, Toyota, Walgreens, WinCo Foods
69	Clark St, Pocatello, **E** **gas:** Maverik/dsl, Shell/Blimpie/dsl, Sinclair/Arctic Circle/dsl, **lodging:** Hampton Inn, TownPlace Suites, **W** **other:** Ⓗ, to ID St U, museum

DUBOIS

IDAHO FALLS

POCATELLO

ID

INTERSTATE 15 CONT'D

Exit #	Services
67	US 30/91, 5th St, Pocatello, **E gas:** Exxon/24hr, **1-2 mi W gas:** Phillips 66/dsl, Shell, Sinclair/dsl, **food:** Elmer's Dining, 5th St Bagels Deli, Jimmy John's, McDonald's, Pizza Hut, Poppa Cafe, Subway, Taco Bell, **lodging:** Best Western, Econolodge, Thunderbird Motel, **other:** [H], Albertson's, Cowboy RV Park, Old Fort Hall, info, museum, zoo
63	Portneuf Area, **W other:** to Mink Creek RA, RV camp/dump
59mm	**rest area/weigh sta both lanes, full [♿] facilities, [☎], picnic table, litter barrel, vending, petwalk, hist site**
58	Inkom (from sb), **1/2 mi W gas:** Sinclair/dsl/café, **other:** Pebble Creek Ski Area, USPO, repair
57	Inkom (from nb), same as 58
47	US 30, to Lava Hot Springs, McCammon, **E gas:** Chevron/A&W/Taco Time/dsl, ***FLYING J***/dsl/LP/RV Dump/rest./24hr, **food:** Subway, **other:** to Lava Hot Springs RA, McCammon RV Park
44	Lp 15, Jenson Rd, McCammon, **E** access to food
40	Arimo, **E gas:** Sinclair/dsl/deli, **other:** USPO
36	US 91, Virginia
31	ID 40, to Downey, Preston, **E gas:** Shell/Flags West/dsl/motel/café/24hr/@, **other:** Downata Hot Springs RV camping (6mi)
25mm	**rest area sb, full [♿] facilities, [☎], [picnic], litter barrels, petwalk**
24.5mm	Malad Summit, elev 5574
22	to Devil Creek Reservoir, **E** RV camping
17	ID 36, to Weston, to Preston
13	ID 38, Malad City, **W gas:** Chevron/Burger King, Phillips 66/dsl/café, Texaco/dsl, **food:** Me&Lou's Rest., Subway, **lodging:** Village Inn Motel, **other:** [H], 3R's Tire, TrueValue, pioneer museum, repair, RV dump
7mm	**Welcome Ctr nb, full [♿] facilities, info, [☎], [picnic], litter barrels, vending, petwalk**
3	to Samaria, Woodruff
0mm	Idaho/Utah state line

INTERSTATE 84

Exit #	Services
275mm	Idaho/Utah state line
270mm	**rest area both lanes, full [♿] facilities, geological site, [☎], [picnic], litter barrels, petwalk**
263	Juniper Rd
257mm	Sweetzer Summit, elev 5530
254	Sweetzer Rd
245	Sublett Rd, to Malta, **N gas:** Sinclair/dsl/café, **other:** camping
237	Idahome Rd
234mm	Raft River
229mm	**rest area/weigh sta both lanes, full [♿] facilities, [☎], [picnic], litter barrels, petwalk**
228	ID 81, Yale Rd, to Declo
222	I-86, US 30, E to Pocatello
216	ID 77, ID 25, to Declo, **N gas:** Phillips 66/FoodCourt/dsl, **other:** [H], Village of Trees RV Park, to Walcott SP, **S gas:** Shell/Jake's Café/dsl
215mm	Snake River
211	ID 24, Heyburn, Burley, **N gas:** Sinclair/A&W/dsl/café, **food:** Wayside Cafe, **lodging:** Tops Motel, **other:** [H], Country RV Village/park, **S gas:** Love's/Carl's Jr./dsl/scales/24hr, **other:** Riverside RV Park, truck repair
208	ID 27, Burley, **N gas:** Phillips 66/dsl, **food:** Conner's Cafe, **lodging:** Super 8, **S gas:** Chevron/Subway/dsl/24hr, Maverik/dsl, Shell/Taco Bell, Sinclair, **food:** Aguila's Mexican, Arby's, Burger King, Garibaldi Mexican, Jack-in-the-Box, JB's, Little Caesar's, McDonald's, Morey's Steaks, Perkins, Wendy's, **lodging:** Best Western, Budget Motel, Fairfield Inn, **other:** [H], Cal Store, $Tree, JC Penney, Radio Shack, Walmart SuperCtr/dsl/24hr, to Snake River RA, **1 mi S gas:** Sinclair/dsl, **food:** Guadalajara Mexican, KFC, **other:** Buick/GMC/Pontiac, CarQuest, Checker Parts, Chrysler/Dodge/Jeep, Commercial Tire, NAPA, Stoke's Foods
201	ID 25, Kasota Rd, to Paul
194	ID 25, to Hazelton, **S gas:** Sinclair/dsl/café, **other:** RV camping
188	Valley Rd, to Eden
182	ID 50, to Kimberly, Twin Falls, **N gas:** Sinclair/dsl, **other:** Gary's RV Ctr/park/dump, **S gas:** Shell/Blimpie/Taco Time/dsl/24hr/@, **lodging:** Amber Inn, **other:** [H], repair, to Shoshone Falls scenic attraction
173	US 93, Twin Falls, **N gas:** ***FLYING J***/Thad's/dsl/24hr/@, **food:** Subway, **lodging:** Day's Inn, Wingate Inn, **other:** KOA (1mi), Blue Beacon/24hr, Freightliner, to Sun Valley, **5 mi S gas:** Chevron/dsl, Exxon, Phillips 66, Shell, Sinclair, **food:** Applebee's, Arby's, Arctic Circle, Aztlan Mexican, Baskin-Robbins, Blimpie, Burger King, Cafe Rio, Carino's Italian, Chili's, Coldstone Creamery, DQ, Elmer's, Golden Corral, Idaho Joe's, IHOP, Jack-in-the-Box, KFC, La Fiesta, Mandarin Chinese, McDonald's, Olive Garden, Outback Steaks, Papa Murphy's, Pizza Hut, Quizno's, Shari's, Sizzler, Sonic, Subway, Taco Bell, Tomato's Grill, Wendy's, Wok In Grill, **lodging:** Ameritel, Best Western, Comfort Inn, Hampton Inn, Hilton Garden, Holiday Inn Express, Motel 6, Red Lion, Shilo Inn, Super 8, Weston Inn, **other:** [H], AutoZone, Barnes&Noble, Best Buy, Buick/GMC/Pontiac, Cadillac/Chevrolet, Chrysler/Dodge/Jeep, Commercial Tire, Costco/gas, Curves, $Tree, Ford, Goodyear, Hancock Fabrics, Hastings, Home Depot, Honda, Hyundai, JC Penney, Jo-Ann Fabrics, Lowe's Whse, Macy's, Mazda/VW, Michael's, Nissan, Old Navy, Petsmart, Schwab Tire, ShopKO, Sportsman's Whse, Target, TJ Maxx, Tuesday Morning, WinCo Foods, Coll of S ID, LDS Temple
171mm	**rest area/weigh sta eb, full [♿] facilities, [☎], vending, [picnic], litter barrels, petwalk**
168	ID 79, to Jerome, **N gas:** Chevron/dsl, Shell/Wendy's/dsl, Sinclair/dsl, **food:** Burger King, Little Caesar's, McDonald's, Sonic, **lodging:** Best Western, Crest Motel, **other:** AutoZone, Brockman RV Ctr, $Tree, Schwab Tire, Walmart SuperCtr/gas/24hr, **2 mi N food:** DQ, **lodging:** Holiday Motel, **other:** [H], **S food:** Subway, **other:** Chevrolet/GMC/Pontiac, ID RV Ctr/marine
165	ID 25, Jerome, **N gas:** Sinclair/dsl, **lodging:** Holiday Motel (1mi), **other:** [H], RV camping/dump

INTERSTATE 84 CONT'D

E ↕ W

Exit #	Services
157	ID 46, Wendell, **N food:** Subway, **1 mi N other:** H CarQuest, Family$, Intermountain RV Park, **S gas:** Phillips 66/dsl, **food:** Farmhouse Rest.
155	ID 46, to Wendell, **N** Intermountain RV Camp/ctr
147	to Tuttle, **S other:** to Malad Gorge SP, High Adventure RV Park/cafe
146mm	Malad River
141	US 26, to US 30, Gooding, **N** H, **S gas:** Phillips 66/dsl/café, Sinclair/dsl/24hr, **lodging:** Amber Inn, Hagerman Inn (9mi), **other:** Hagerman RV Village (8mi)
137	Lp 84, to US 30, to Pioneer Road, Bliss, **2 mi S gas:** Sinclair/Stinker/dsl/24hr, **other:** camping
133mm	**rest area both lanes, full facilities, info, litter barrels, petwalk,**
129	King Hill
128mm	Snake River
125	Paradise Valley
122mm	Snake River
121	Glenns Ferry, **1 mi S gas:** Shell/dsl, Sinclair, **lodging:** Redford Motel, **other:** Carmela Winery/rest., NAPA, tires, to 3 Island SP, Trails Break RV camp/dump
120	Glenns Ferry (from eb), same as 121
114	ID 78 (from wb), to Hammett, **1 mi S** access to gas/dsl, to Bruneau Dunes SP
112	to ID 78, Hammett, **1 mi S** gas/dsl, food, to Bruneau Dunes SP
99	ID 51, ID 67, to Mountain Home, **2 mi S lodging:** Maple Cove Motel, camping
95	US 20, Mountain Home, **N gas:** Chevron/KFC/dsl/24hr, Pilot/Arby's/dsl/scales/24hr, **food:** AJ's Rest., Jack-in-the-Box, Subway, **lodging:** Best Western, Hampton Inn, Sleep Inn, **S food:** Golden Crown Chinese, McDonald's, Wendy's, **lodging:** Hilander Motel (1mi), Towne Ctr Motel (1mi), **other:** H, Curves, $Tree, Family$, Walmart SuperCtr/gas/24hr, to Mtn Home RV Park
90	to ID 51, ID 67, W Mountain Home, **S gas:** Chevron/Burger King/dsl/24hr, **food:** McDonald's (4mi), **lodging:** to Hilander Motel (4mi), Maple Cove Motel (4mi), Towne Ctr Motel (4mi), **other:** KOA
74	Simco Rd
71	Orchard, Mayfield, **S gas:** Sinclair/dsl/StageStop Motel/rest./24hr, **other:** , truckwash
66mm	**weigh sta both lanes**
64	Blacks Creek, Kuna, historical site
62mm	**rest area both lanes, full facilities, OR Trail info, , , litter barrels, vending, petwalk**
59b a	S Eisenman Rd, Memory Rd
57	ID 21, Gowen Rd, to Idaho City, **N food:** Jack-in-the-Box, McDonald's, Perkins, Quizno's, Subway, Taco Del Mar, Tulley's Coffee, **lodging:** Best Western, **other:** Albertsons/gas, Peterbilt, to Micron, **S gas:** Chevron/24hr, **food:** Burger King, FoodCourt, **other:** Boise Stores/famous brands, ID Ice World
54	US 20/26, Broadway Ave, Boise, **N gas:** Chevron/dsl/24hr, ***FLYING J***/dsl/LP/24hr, Shell/dsl, **food:** A&W, Arby's, Chili's, Fiesta Mexican, Jack-in-the-Box, IHOP, KFC, Mongol Grill, Nick'n Willy's Pizza,

MOUNTAIN HOME

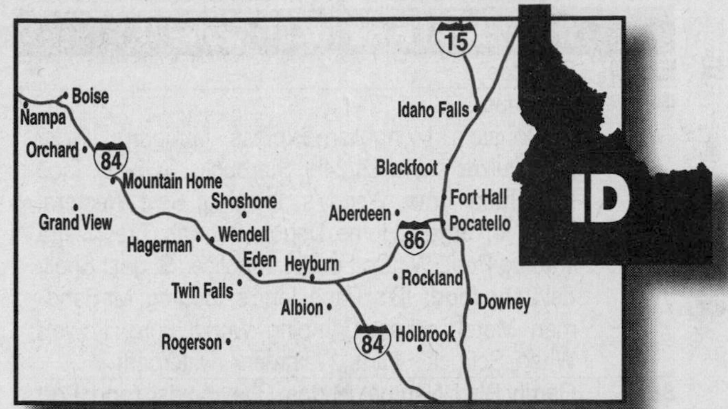

BOISE

Exit #	Services
54	Continued Port Of Subs, Subway, Wendy's, **lodging:** Courtyard (3mi), **other:** H, Big O Tire, Dowdie's Automotive, Fred Meyer, Goodyear/auto, Home Depot, Hyundai, Jo-Ann Fabrics, PetCo, Radio Shack, Ross, Shop-KO, Walgreens, Vet, to Boise St U, **S gas:** TA/Tesoro/Taco Bell/Subway/dsl/24hr/@, **lodging:** Shilo Inn, **other:** Kenworth, Mtn View RV Park
53	Vista Ave, Boise, **N gas:** Shell/dsl, Texaco/dsl, **food:** Applebee's, Pizza Hut, **lodging:** Cambria Suites, Comfort Suites, Extended Stay America, Fairfield Inn, Hampton Inn, Holiday Inn/rest., Holiday Inn Express, Super 8, **other:** museums, st capitol, st police, zoo, **S gas:** Chevron/McDonald's/24hr, **food:** Denny's, Kopper Kitchen, **lodging:** Best Western, Comfort Inn, InnAmerica, Motel 6, Sleep Inn
52	Orchard St, Boise, **N gas:** Shell/dsl/24hr, **other:** KIA, Mazda/Nissan, GMC, **1-2 mi N food:** Burger King, Jack-in-the-Box, McDonald's, Raedean's Rest., Round Table Pizza, Wendy's, **other:** Albertson's/gas, Walgreens
50b a	Cole Rd, Overland Rd, **N gas:** Chevron/24hr, Shell, Sinclair, **food:** Cancun Mexican, Eddie's Rest., Golden Spoon Yogurt, McDonald's, Outback Steaks, Pizza Hut, Subway, Taco Bell, Taco Time, **other:** LDS Temple, transmissions, **S gas:** ***FLYING J***/Conoco/dsl/24hr, Phillips 66/dsl, **food:** A&W/KFC, Bajio, Burger King, Carino's, Carl's Jr, Chappala Mexican, Chuck-a-Rama, Cracker Barrel, Fuddruckers, Goodwood BBQ, McGrath's FishHouse, Legend's Grill, Panda Express, Primo's, On the Border, Port Of Subs, Quizno's, Ruby River Steaks, Sonic, Starbucks, Tucano's, **lodging:** AmeriTel, Budget Host, Hilton Garden, Homewood Suites, Oxford Suites, **other:** Commercial Tire, Costco/gas, Dillon RV Ctr, Goodyear, Lowe's Whse, Schwab Tire, Walmart SuperCtr/24hr, Vet
49	I-184 (exits left from eb), to W Boise, **N other:** H
46	ID 55, Eagle, **N gas:** Chevron/McDonald's/dsl/24hr, Shell/dsl/24hr, **food:** Buffalo Wild Wings, Chronic Taco's, Del Taco, Los Beto's, Starbucks, Subway, **lodging:** Comfort Suites, Country Inn&Suites, Hampton Inn, Holiday Inn Express, **other:** H, Vet, **S gas:** Shell/Jack-in-the-Box/dsl, **food:** Chicago Connection, Jack-in-the-Box, Pita Pit, Qdoba, Quizno's, Sakana Japanese, Subway, Taco Bell, Tulley's Coffee, **lodging:** Candlewood Suites, Courtyard, Towneplace Suites, **other:** Harley Davidson,
44	ID 69, Meridian, **N gas:** Chevron/dsl/24hr, Sinclair, **food:** A&W/KFC, Blimpie, China Wok, DQ, El Bajio,

EAGLE

ID

INTERSTATE 84 (WEST) CONT'D

E ↕ W — NAMPA

Exit #	Services
44	Continued McDonald's, Mongolian Express, Mulligan's, Pizza Hut, Quizno's, Shari's/24hr, Starbucks, Subway, Taco Bell, Taco Time, Wendy's, **lodging:** Best Western, Motel 6, **other:** Home Depot, Schwab Tire, Sierra Trading Post, WinCo Foods, at police, **S gas:** Shell/dsl/24hr, **food:** JB's, Papa John's, **lodging:** Mr Sandman Motel, **other:** Camping World, Ford, Lowe's Whse, Schuck's Parts, Walgreens, waterpark
38	Garrity Blvd, Nampa, **N gas:** Chevron/dsl, **food:** Port of Subs, Taco Del Mar, **lodging:** Hampton Inn, **other:** Buick/GMC/Pontiac, Cadillac/Chevrolet, Chrysler/Dodge/Jeep, Ford, KIA, Nissan, Sam's Club, Swiss Village Cheese, Toyota/Scion, Walmart SuperCtr, **S gas:** Phillips 66/dsl, Shell/Taco Time/dsl/24hr, **food:** A&W, McDonald's, Pizza Hut, Subway, **lodging:** Holiday Inn Express, **other:** H, Garrity RV Park, JC Penney, Macy's, War Hawk Museum
36	Franklin Blvd, Nampa, **N gas:** Maverik, **food:** Jack-in-the-Box, Noodles Rest., **lodging:** Shilo Inn/rest., **S gas:** Chevron/dsl/24hr, Shell/dsl/RV dump/scales/4hr, **lodging:** Sleep Inn, **other:** H, Freightliner, Mason Cr RV Park, 7th Heaven RV Ctr
35	ID 55, Nampa, **S gas:** Shell/dsl, **food:** Denny's/24hr, **lodging:** Days Inn, Shilo Inn, Super 8, **1 mi S food:** Burger King, McDonald's, Pizza Hut, Taco Time, El Tanampa Mexican, **other:** H
33b a	ID 55 S, Midland Blvd, Marcine, **N food:** Gandolfo's, McDonald's, Olive Garden, Port of Subs, Qdoba Mexican, Sonic, Taco Del Mar, TGIFriday, Tulley's Coffee, Winger's, **lodging:** Fairfield Inn, **other:** Best Buy, Costco, Kohl's, Michael's, Old Navy, PetCo, Target, World Mkt, **S gas:** Maverik, Shell, **food:** Applebee's, Arby's, Baskin-Robbins, Blimpie, Carl's Jr, Coldstone Creamery, DQ, Golden Corral, IHOP, Jack-in-the-Box, Jade Garden, Outback Steaks, Primo's, Quizno's, Red Robin, Shari's Rest, Skipper's, Smokey Mtn Grill, Starbucks, Subway, Taco Bell, Wendy's, **other:** BigLots, Big O Tire, $Tree, Home Depot, Jo-Ann Fabrics, K-Mart, Lowe's Whse, Macy's, Ross, Saver's, ShopKo, Staples, U-Haul, Walgreens, WinCo Foods
29	US 20/26, Franklin Rd, Caldwell, **N gas:** *FLYING J*/Conoco/Country Mkt/dsl/LP/rest./scales/24hr, **other:** Ambassador RV camping, RV dump, **S gas:** Sage/Sinclair/cafe/dsl/24hr, **food:** Perkins/24hr, **lodging:** Best Western, La Quinta
28	10th Ave, Caldwell, **N gas:** Maverik/gas, **lodging:** I-84 Motel, **other:** city park, **S gas:** Chevron/24hr, Shell, **food:** Carl's Jr, Domino's, Fiesta Mexican, Jack-in-the-Box, KFC, Mr V's Rest., Pizza Hut, Subway, Wendy's, **lodging:** Sundowner Motel, **other:** H, AutoZone, Paul's Food/Drug, Tire Factory, Walgreens
27	ID 19, to Wilder, **1 mi S gas:** Tesoro/dsl/24hr
26.5mm	Boise River
26	US 20/26, to Notus, **N other:** Caldwell Campground, **S gas:** Sinclair/dsl
25	ID 44, Middleton, **N gas:** Shell/dsl, **food:** 44 Burgers/shakes, **S Insp sta eb**
17	Sand Hollow, **N food:** Sand Hollow Café, **other:** Country Corners RV Park
13	Black Canyon Jct, **S gas:** Sinclair/dsl/motel/rest./scales/24hr, phone
9	US 30, to New Plymouth
3	US 95, Fruitland, **N gas:** Shell/A&W/dsl, **5 mi N other:** Neat Retreat RV Park, to Hell's Cyn RA
1mm	**Welcome Ctr eb, full handicapped facilities, info, phone, picnic, litter barrels, petwalk**
0mm	Snake River, Idaho/Oregon state line

INTERSTATE 86

E ↕ W — POCATELLO

Exit #	Services
63b a	I-15, N to Butte, S to SLC. I-86 begins/ends on I-15, exit 72.
61	US 91, Yellowstone Ave, Pocatello, **N gas:** Exxon, Shell/dsl, **food:** Arby's, Arctic Circle, Burger King, Chapala Mexican, Johnny B Goode's Diner, Lei's BBQ, Papa Murphy's, Pizza Hut, Subway, Wendy's, **lodging:** Motel 6, Ramada Inn, **other:** Budget RV Park, Checker Parts, $Tree, Family$, Smith's Foods/dsl, **S gas:** *FLYING J*/dsl/24hr, Phillips 66/dsl, **food:** Bajio, Chili's, Del Taco, Denny's, Green Tea Grill, IHOP, McDonald's, Red Lobster, Starbucks, Taco John's, TX Roadhouse, **other:** Costco/gas, Dillard's, Ford, Home Depot, JC Penney, K-Mart, Lowe's Whse, Macy's, Michael's, PetCo, Ross, Schwab Tire, Sears, ShopKO, Sportsmans Whse, Staples, TJ Maxx, Walgreens, Walmart SuperCtr, dsl repair, mall
58.5mm	Portneuf River
58	US 30, W Pocatello
56	**N** Pocatello Air Terminal, **S gas:** Sinclair/dsl/24hr
52	Arbon Valley, **S gas:** Sinclair/Bannock Peak/dsl, **other:** casino
51mm	Bannock Creek
49	Rainbow Rd
44	Seagull Bay
40	ID 39, American Falls, **N gas:** Phillips 66/dsl, Sinclair, **food:** Pizza Hut, Subway, Tres Hermanos Mexican, **lodging:** American Motel, **other:** H, Alco, Jiffy Lube, King's, NAPA, Schwab Tire, to Am Falls RA, RV Park/dump, **S lodging:** Hillview Motel
36	ID 37, to Rockland, American Falls, **2 mi N gas:** Shell/dsl/24hr, **lodging:** Falls Motel, **other:** H, **2 mi S** Indian Springs RV Resort
33	Neeley Area
31mm	**rest area wb, full handicapped facilities, phone, picnic table, litter barrel, petwalk, vending, hist site**
28	**N other:** to Massacre Rock SP, Register Rock Hist Site, RV camping/dump
21	Coldwater Area
19mm	**rest area eb, full handicapped facilities, phone, picnic table, litter barrel, petwalk, vending, hist site**
15	Raft River Area
1	I-84 E, to Ogden. I-86 begins/ends on I-84, exit 222.

INTERSTATE 90

E ↕ W

Exit #	Services
74mm	Idaho/Montana state line,, Pacific/Central time zone Lookout Pass elev 4680
73mm	scenic area/hist site wb
72mm	scenic area/hist site eb
71mm	runaway truck ramp wb
70mm	runaway truck ramp wb

INTERSTATE 90 CONT'D

E ↕ W

Exit #	Services
69	Lp 90, Mullan, **N gas:** gas/dsl/24hr, **lodging:** Lookout Motel (1mi), **other:** USPO, museum
68	Lp 90 (from eb), Mullan, same as 69
67	Morning District,
66	Gold Creek (from eb)
65	Compressor District
64	Golconda District
62	ID 4, Wallace, **S gas:** Exxon, **food:** Pizza Factory, Smokehouse BBQ, **lodging:** Brooks Hotel, Stardust Motel, **other:** H, Accelerated Parts, Depot RV Park, Harvest Foods, TrueValue, museum, repair
61	Lp 90, Wallace, **S gas:** Conoco/dsl, **food:** Wallace Sta Rest./gifts, **lodging:** Brooks Hotel/rest., Molly B-Damm Inn, Wallace Inn, **other:** auto repair, info ctr, same as 62
60	Lp 90, Silverton, **S lodging:** Molly B-Damm Inn, **other:** RV camping
57	Lp 90, Osburn, **S gas:** Shell/dsl/24hr, **other:** Blue Anchor RV Park, auto repair, USPO
54	Big Creek, **N other:** Elk Creek Store/repair, hist site, rv dump
51	Lp 90, Division St, Kellogg, **N gas:** Conoco/dsl, **food:** Broken Wheel Rest., **lodging:** Trail Motel, **other:** H, Buick/Cadillac/Chevrolet/GMC/Pontiac, Chrysler/Dodge/Jeep, Schwab Tire, Stein's Foods, Sunnyside Drug, **S food:** In Cahoots Cafe, Moose Creek Grill, **other:** USPO, auto repair, museum
50	Hill St (from eb), Kellogg, **N lodging:** Trail Motel, **other:** Ace Hardware, NAPA, Stein's Foods, Sunnyside Drug, **S gas:** Conoco/dsl **other:** Gary's Drug, Silver Mtn Ski/summer resort/rec area, Yoke's Foods, museum
49	Bunker Ave, **N gas:** Conoco/dsl, **food:** McDonald's, Sam's Drive-In, Subway, **lodging:** Silverhorn Motel/rest., **other:** H, **S food:** Noah's Canteen, Silver Mtn rest., **lodging:** Baymont Inn, Morning Star Lodge, **other:** museum, RV dump
48	Smelterville, **N gas:** Silver Valley Car/trkstp/motel/café, **S food:** Boat Rest., **other:** Tire Factory, Walmart SuperCtr
45	Pinehurst, **S gas:** Chevron/dsl, Conoco/dsl/24hr, **other:** By-the-way Camping, Harvest Foods, NAPA, KOA, RV Park/dump, True Value Hardware
43	Kingston, **N gas:** Shell/dsl/24hr, **food:** Snakepit Café, **lodging:** Enaville Resort, RV camping, **S gas:** Exxon/dsl/rv dump, USPO
40	Cataldo, **N food:** Mission Inn Rest., USPO, **S** RV Park
39.5mm	Coeur d' Alene River
39	Cataldo Mission, **S other:** Old Mission SP, Nat Hist Landmark
34	ID 3, to St Maries, Rose Lake, **S gas:** Conoco/dsl, Rose Lake/dsl, **food:** Rose Lake Cafe, **other:** White Pines Scenic Rte
32mm	chainup area/**weigh sta wb**
31.5mm	Idaho Panhandle NF, eastern boundary, 4th of July Creek
28	4th of July Pass Rec. Area, elev 3069, Mullan Tree HS, ski area, snowmobile area, turnout both lanes
24mm	chainup eb, removal wb

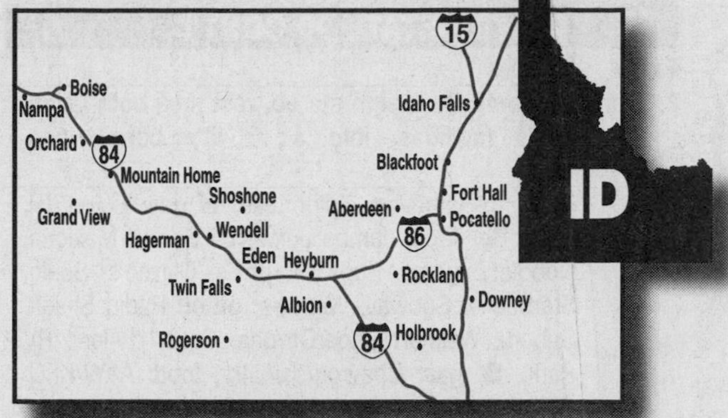

Exit #	Services
22	ID 97, to St Maries, L Coeur d' Alene Scenic ByWay, Wolf Lodge District, Harrison, **1 mi N** Wolf Lodge Campground, **S other:** A-Ok RV Park, Squaw Bay Resort (7mi)
20.5mm	Lake Coeur d' Alene
17	Mullan Trail Rd
15	Lp 90, Sherman Ave, Coeur d' Alene, **N other:** forest info, Lake Coeur D' Alene RA/HS, **S gas:** Shell, Tesoro/dsl, Texaco, **food:** Michael D's Eatery, Willie's Rest., **lodging:** Bates Motel, BudgetSaver Motel, Cedar Motel, El Rancho Motel, Holiday Motel, Japan House Suites, La Quinta, Lake Drive Motel, Monte Vista Motel, State Motel, **other:** Peterson's Foods/24hr, NAPA, tourist info
14	15th St, Coeur d' Alene, **S gas:** TAJ Mart, **other:** Jordon's Grocery
13	4th St, Coeur d' Alene, **N gas:** A&D/dsl, **food:** Baskin-Robbins, Carl's Jr, DQ, Davis Donuts, Denny's, Fiesta Mexican, Godfather's, IHOP, KFC, Little Caesar's, Panda Express, Wendy's, **lodging:** Comfort Inn, **other:** AutoZone, Big Lots, Costco/gas (1mi), Hastings Books, NAPA, Radio Shack, Schuck's Parts, Schwab Tire, Tire Factory, same as 12, **S gas:** Exxon/dsl, **food:** Subway, Thai Bamboo
12	US 95, to Sandpoint, Moscow, **N gas:** Exxon/dsl, Holiday/dsl, Mobil, **food:** Applebees, Arby's, Burger King, Cafe Chulo Mexican, Casa de Oro, Chili's, Dragon House Chinese, JB's Rest., McDonald's, Olive Garden, Panda Express, Perkins, Pizza Hut, Pizza Shoppe, Red Lobster, Skipper's, Taco Bell, **lodging:** Best Western, Guesthouse Inn, La Quinta, Motel 6, Shilo Suites, Super 8, **other:** Alton's Tires, AutoZone, Best Buy, Borders Books, Buick/Pontiac/GMC, Cadillac/Isuzu, Dodge, $Tree, Ford/Lincoln/Mercury, Fred Meyer, GNC, Grocery Outlet, Harley-Davidson, Home Depot, JC Penney, Kia, K-Mart, Kohl's, Mazda, Michael's, Office Depot, PetCo, Ross, Safeway/gas, Schuck's Parts, Sears/auto, Super 1 Foods, Target, TJ Maxx, Toyota, Tuesday Morning, U-haul, Walgreens, radiators, **S gas:** Shell, **food:** Jack-in-the-Box, Papa John's, Qdoba Mexican, Quizno's, Schlotsky's, Shari's, Starbucks, **lodging:** AmeriTel, **other:** H, Albertson's/gas, Rite Aid, ShopKO/drugs, Staples, same as 13
11	Northwest Blvd, **N gas:** Conoco/Taco Time/dsl, **other:** Lowes Whse, **S gas:** Texaco/dsl, **food:** Azteca Mexican, Cold Stone Creamery, Joey's BBQ, Outback Steaks, Pizza Smizza, Red Robin, SF Sourdough, Starbucks, Subway, **lodging:** Day's Inn, Holiday Inn Express, **other:** H, Honda, Kohl's, Riverwalk RV Park

INTERSTATE 90 CONT'D

Exit #	Services
8.5mm	**Welcome Ctr/weigh sta eb, rest area both lanes, full [handicapped] facilities, info, [phone], [picnic], litter barrels, petwalk**
7	ID 41, to Rathdrum, Spirit Lake, **N gas:** Exxon/dsl, **food:** Del Taco, Jamba Juice, La Cocina Mexican, Noodle Express, Papa Murphy's, Quizno's, Sonic, Starbucks, Subway, Wendy's, **other:** Radio Shack, Subaru, Walmart SuperCtr/gas, Couer d'Alene RV Park, **S gas:** Chevron/dsl/24hr, **food:** A&W/KFC, Capone's Grill, DQ, **lodging:** Comfort Inn, **other:** truck repair
6	Seltice Way, **N gas:** 7-11, **food:** La Cabana Mexican, Pizza Hut, **other:** AutoZone, Chevrolet, Hyundai, NAPA, Nissan, Subaru, Super 1 Foods/24hr, Walgreens, Vet, **S gas:** Conoco/dsl/LP, **food:** Arby's/Taco John's, Big Cheese Pizza, Denny's, Hot Rod Café, McDonald's, Subway, Taco Bell, Wingers, **other:** Ace Hardware, Alton's Tire, Curves, Schuck's Parts, USPO
5	Lp 90, Spokane St, Treaty Rock HS, **N gas:** Shell/dsl, **food:** Domino's, Golden Dragon Chinese, Hunter's Steaks, Rob's Seafood/burgers, WhiteHouse Grill, **other:** AutoZone, CarQuest, Mazda, Schwab Tire, Seltice RV Ctr, **S gas:** 76/dsl, **food:** MillTown Grill, **lodging:** Red Lion Inn
2	Pleasant View Rd, **N gas:** *FLYING J*/Conoco/dsl/rest./LP/scales/24hr, Shell/dsl, **food:** McDonald's, Toro Viejo Mexican, **lodging:** Howard Johnson, **other:** Suntree RV Park, **S gas:** Shell/Subway/dsl/24hr, **food:** Zip's Drive-in, **lodging:** Riverbend Inn, Sleep Inn, **other:** GNC, North Idaho Outlets/famous brands, dogtrack
0mm	Idaho/Washington state line

INTERSTATE 184 (BOISE)

Exit #	Services
6mm	I-184 begins/ends on 13th St, downtown, **gas:** Shell, **food:** PF Chang's, **lodging:** Hampton Inn, Safari Inn, **other:** Harley-Davidson, Office Depot, USPO
5	River St (from eb), **W gas:** Chevron, **food:** McDonald's, **other:** Ford/Mercury
4.5mm	Boise River
3	Fairview Ave, to US 20/26 E, **W food:** McDonald's, **lodging:** Budget Inn, DoubleTree Inn, Econolodge, **other:** Commercial Tire
2	Curtis Rd, to Garden City, **E lodging:** Rodeway Inn, other: [H]
1b a	Cole Rd, Franklin Rd, **E gas:** Chevron/Subway, **lodging:** Harrison Hotel, **other:** Acura/Honda, Buick/Pontiac, Dodge, Jaguar, Land Rover, Volvo, **W gas:** Maverik, Sinclair, **food:** Burger King, Carl's Jr, Cheesecake Factory, Chili's, Hooters, Jack-in-the-Box, LoneStar Steaks, Old Chicago Pizza, Perkins, Quizno's, Red Robin, Sizzler, Shari's, Starbucks, TGI Friday, Wendy's, Yang Sheng Chinese, **lodging:** Ameritel, Residence Inn, **other:** Best Buy, Borders, Cabela's, Dillard's, JC Penney, Macy's, Michael's, Office Depot, Old Navy, PetCo, Ross, Sears/auto, Target, TJ Maxx, mall, Vet
0mm	I-184 begins/ends on I-84, exit 49.

ILLINOIS

INTERSTATE 24

Exit #	Services
38mm	Illinois/Kentucky state line, Ohio River
37	US 45, Metropolis, **N rest area both lanes, full [handicapped] facilities, info, vending, [picnic], litter barrels, petwalk,** Citgo/dsl, **S 1-2 mi gas:** BP/Quizno's/dsl, **food:** Huddle House, KFC, McDonald's, Pizza Hut, **lodging:** Comfort Inn, Holiday Inn Express, Metropolis Inn, Super 8, **other:** [H], Buick/GMC/Pontiac, Chevrolet, Chrysler/Dodge/Jeep, O'Reilly Parts, to Riverboat Casino, Ft Massac SP, camping
27	to New Columbia, Big Bay
16	IL 146, Vienna, **N lodging:** Gambit Inn, **S gas:** BP/dsl, Citgo, Gas&Go/dsl, **food:** Dolly's Rest., DQ, Jumbo Grill, McDonald's, Newt's Pizza, Subway, **lodging:** Limited Inn
14	US 45, Vienna, **S** camping
7	to Goreville, Tunnel Hill, **N gas:** Fast Stop/dsl, **other:** winery, **S other:** to Ferne Clyffe SP, camping
1	I-57, N to Chicago, S to Memphis. I-24 begins/ends on I-57, exit 44.

INTERSTATE 39

Exit #	Services
I-39 and I-90 run together into Wisconsin. See Illinois Interstate 90.	
122b a	US 20 E, Harrison Ave, to Belvidere, **W gas:** Road Ranger/Subway, **food:** Arby's, Bergner's, Burger King, DQ, Franchesco's Rest., Taco Bell, TGIFriday, **other:** Barnes & Noble, Chevrolet, Collier RV Ctr, Harley-Davidson, Hilander Foods/gas, Macy's, Menard's, Sears/auto, Tires+, mall, last nb exit before toll rd
119	US 20 W, Alpine Rd, to Rockford
116.5mm	Kishwaukee River
115	Baxter Rd, **E gas:** Shell/dsl/scales/24hr/@
111	IL 72, to Monroe Center, **E gas:** BP/Sunrise Family Rest./dsl/24hr, Marathon (1mi)
104	IL 64, to Oregon, Sycamore, **W** Grubsteakers Rest/**truck parking** (2mi)
99	IL 38, to De Kalb, Rochelle, **0-2 mi W gas:** BP/dsl, Petro/Iron Skillet/dsl/scales/rest./RV Dump/@, Road Ranger/Pilot/Subway/scales/dsl/24hr, Shell, **food:** Arby's, Butterfly Rest, China Wok, Culver's, DQ, Little Ceasar's, McDonald's, Taco Bell, Wendy's, **lodging:** Baymont Inn, Comfort Inn, US Express, Super 8, **other:** [H], Blue Beacon, Curves, $General, Radio Shack, Sullivan's Foods, Walgreens
97b a	I-88 tollway, to Moline, Rock Island, Chicago
93	Steward
87	US 30, to Sterling, Rock Falls, **E** to Shabbona Lake SP, **W** Jellystone Camping (16mi)
84.5mm	**rest area both lanes, full [handicapped] facilities, [phone], [picnic], litter barrels, vending, petwalk**
82	Paw Paw, **3 mi E** Casey's, **W** many wind turbines
72	US 34, to Mendota, Earlville, **W gas:** BP/Buster's Buffet/scales/dsl/24hr, Road Ranger/Pilot/dsl/24hr, **food:** KFC/Taco Bell, McDonald's, Ziggie's Rest, **lodging:** Comfort Inn, Super 8/**truck parking**, **other:** [H]

INTERSTATE 39 CONT'D

N ↕ S

Exit #	Services
67.5mm	Little Vermilion River
66	US 52, Troy Grove, **E** KOA (1mi)
62.5mm	Tomahawk Creek
59b a	I-80, E to Chicago, W to Des Moines
57	US 6, to Peru, La Salle, **1-2 mi W gas:** Casey's, Shell/24hr, **food:** Hardee's, **lodging:** Daniel's Motel
56mm	Illinois River, Abraham Lincoln Mem Bridge
54	Oglesby, **E gas:** BP, Casey's, Phillips 66/dsl, Shell/24hr, **food:** Delaney's Rest., Burger King, KFC/Taco Bell, McDonald's, Mr Salsa Mexican, Root Beer Stand, Subway, **lodging:** Days Inn, Holiday Inn Express, **other:** Starved Rock SP
52	IL 251, to La Salle, Peru
51	IL 71, to Hennepin, Oglesby
48	Tonica, **E gas:** Casey's, Tonica/dsl
41	IL 18, to Streator, Henry
35	IL 17, to Wenona, Lacon, **E gas:** BP/dsl, Casey's (2mi), Shell/Burger King/Subway/dsl/RV dump, **food:** Pizza Hut, **lodging:** Super 8/**truck parking**
27	to Minonk, **E gas:** Shell/Subway/Woody's Rest./dsl/24hr, **lodging:** Motel 6, **other:** NAPA, **1 mi E gas:** Casey's
22	IL 116, to Peoria, Benson
14	US 24, to El Paso, Peoria, **E gas:** Freedom/dsl, Shell/Subway/dsl/24hr, **food:** DQ, Hardee's/24hr, McDonald's, Oriental Buffet, Woody's Family Rest., **lodging:** Days Inn, **other:** Doc's Drugs, El Paso RV Ctr, Ford, IGA Foods, NAPA, Radio Shack, **W food:** Monical's Pizza, **lodging:** Super 8, **other:** $General, Hickory Hill Camping (4mi), antiques
9mm	Mackinaw River
8	IL 251, Lake Bloomington Rd, **E** Lake Bloomington, **W other:** Evergreen Lake, to Comlara Park, RV camping
5	Hudson, **1 mi E gas:** Casey's
2	US 51 bus, Bloomington, Normal
0mm	I-39 begins/ends on I-55, exit 164., **Services located N on I-55, exit 165, E gas:** BP/Circle K/24hr, Mobil/Arby's/dsl, Qik-n-EZ, Shell/24hr, **food:** A&W/KFC, Burger King, Denny's, McDonald's, Moe's SW Grill, Pizza Hut, Steak'n Shake, Subway, Uncle Tom's Pancakes, **lodging:** Best Western, Crowne Plaza, Motel 6, Super 8, **other:** H, $General, $Tree, Schuncks Foods, Walgreens, to Ill St U, **W** dsl repair

NORMAL

INTERSTATE 55

N ↕ S

Exit #	Services
295mm	I-55 begins/ends on US 41, Lakeshore Dr, in Chicago.
293a	to Cermak Rd (from nb)
292	I-90/94, W to Chicago, E to Indiana
290	Damen Ave, Ashland Ave (no EZ nb return), **E gas:**

CHICAGO AREA

Exit #	Services
290	Continued Marathon, **food:** Burger King, Popeye's, Subway, White Castle, **other:** $Tree, Dominick's Foods, GNC, Radio Shack, Target
289	to California Ave (no EZ nb return), **E gas:** Citgo, Speedway/Subway/dsl
288	Kedzie Ave, (from sb no ez return), **E gas:** Citgo
287	Pulaski Rd, **E gas:** Mobil/dsl, Shell, **food:** Burger King, Quizno's, Subway, **other:** Advance Parts, Aldi Foods, Dodge, Honda, Pete's Mkt, Staples, Target, Walgreens
286	IL 50, Cicero Ave, **E gas:** Citgo/dsl, Marathon, Phillips 66, **food:** Burger King, Dunkin Donuts, McDonald's, Starbucks, Subway, **other:** AutoZone, Family$, U-Haul
285	Central Ave, **E gas:** BP/dsl, Citgo, Marathon, **food:** Burger King, Donald's HotDogs

IL

INTERSTATE 55 CONT'D

N ↕ S — CHICAGO AREA

Exit #	Services
283	IL 43, Harlem Ave, **E** **gas:** Shell, **food:** Arby's, Burger King, Domino's, El Pollo Loco, Subway, **other:** AT&T, Walgreens
282b a	IL 171, 1st Ave, **W** **other:** Brookfield Zoo, Mayfield Park
279b	US 12, US 20, US 45, La Grange Rd, **0-2 mi W** **gas:** BP/24hr, Mobil, Shell, **food:** Al's Beef, Arby's, Baskin-Robbins/Dunkin Donuts, Boston Mkt, Brown's Chicken, Burger King, Cocula's Rest., George's Rest., Jimmy John's, Komb's Rest., Ledo's Pizza, LJ Silver, LoneStar Steaks, Main St. Pizza, McDonald's, Nancy's Pizza, NoNo's Pizza, Old Country Buffet, Panda Express, Pizza Hut, Popeye's, Subway, Taco Bell, Taco Taco, Time Out Grill, Wendy's, White Castle, Wok'n Roll, **lodging:** Best Western, Holiday Inn, **other:** Aldi Foods, Best Buy, Buick/Cadillac/GMC/Pontiac, Chevrolet, Discount Tire, Dodge, $Tree, Firestone/auto, Ford, GNC, Home Depot, Honda, Hyundai, JoAnn Fabrics, Kohl's, Mazda, Nissan, NTB, PepBoys, PetsMart, Sam's Club/gas, Subaru, Suzuki, Target/drugs, Toyota/Scion, Verizon, VW, Walmart
279a	La Grange Rd, to I-294 toll, S to Indiana
277b	I-294 toll (from nb), S to Indiana
277a	I-294 toll, N to Wisconsin
276c	Joliet Rd (from nb)
276b a	County Line Rd, **E** **food:** Capri Rest., China King, Ciazzi's Cafe, Cooper's Hawk, Max&Erma's, Moon Dance Diner, Salerno's Pizza, Starbucks, Subway, Topaz Rest., **lodging:** Extended Stay America, Marriott, **other:** Brookhaven Mkt, **W** **lodging:** SpringHill Suites
274	IL 83, Kingery Rd, **E** **gas:** Shell/24hr, **W** **gas:** Citgo, Mobil/dsl, Phillips 66, Shell/24hr, **food:** Bakers Square, Barnelli's Pasta, Burger King, Chipotle Mexican, Denny's, Domino's, Dunkin Donuts, Jamba Juice, Jimmy John's, Papa John's, Patio BBQ, Portillo's HotDogs, Potbelly's Rest., Starbucks, Subway, Wendy's, **lodging:** Holiday Inn, La Quinta, Red Roof Inn, Super 8, **other:** AT&T, Firestone, Ford/KIA, K-Mart, Michael's, Radio Shack, Staples, Target, Verizon
273b a	Cass Ave, **W** **gas:** Shell/24hr, **food:** Cornerstone Rest., Lanottedue Rest., Rosati's Pizza, Uncle Mao's Chinese, **other:** Vet
271b a	Lemont Rd, **E** **lodging:** Extended Stay America, **W** **gas:** Shell/24hr
269	I-355 toll N, to W Suburbs
268	(from sb only), Joliet, same as 267
267	IL 53, Bolingbrook, **E** **gas:** BP, Citgo, Phillips 66/55 Trkstp/dsl/rest./scales/24hr/@, **food:** Bono's Rest., McDonald's, **lodging:** La Quinta, Ramada Ltd, Super 8, **other:** Chevrolet, **W** **gas:** Shell/Circle K, Speedway/dsl, **food:** A&W/LJ Silver, Arby's, Bucho's Mexican, Burger King, Cheddar's, Culver's, Denny's, Dunkin Donuts, El Burrito Loco, Family Square Rest., Golden Chopsticks, Golden Corral, IHOP, Little Caesar's, Popeye's, Rancho Santa Fe Mexican, Starbucks, Subway, Wendy's, White Castle, **lodging:** AmericInn, Hampton Inn, Holiday Inn, SpringHill Suites, **other:** AAA, Aldi Foods, CarQuest, $Tree, Family$, Fiesta Mkt, Food-4-Less/gas, Just Tires, Menards, Murray's Parts, NAPA, U-Haul, Walgreens, Walmart
266mm	weigh sta both lanes
263	Weber Rd, **E** **gas:** BP/dsl, GasCity/Dunkin Donuts/dsl, 7-11, **food:** Applebee's, A&W/KFC, Burger King, Burrito's, Culver's, Little China, McDonald's, Mr Taco, Popeye's, Quizno's, Rosati's Pizza, Starbucks, Subway, White Castle, **lodging:** Best Western, **other:** Ace Hardware, Discount Tire, Dominick's Food/gas, GNC, Walgreens, **W** **gas:** 7-11, Shell/24hr, **food:** Arby's, Cracker Barrel, Wendy's, **lodging:** Comfort Inn, Country Inn&Suites, Extended Stay America
261	IL 126 (from sb), to Plainfield
257	US 30, to Joliet, Aurora, **E** **gas:** Shell, **food:** Applebee's, Baskin Robbins/Dunkin Donuts, Burger King, Diamand's Rest., Hooters, KFC, LJ Silver/Taco Bell, LoneStar Steaks, McDonald's, Old Country Buffet, Outback Steaks, Panera Bread, Pizza Hut, Red Lobster, Steak'n Shake, Subway, TX Roadhouse, TGIFriday's, Wendy's, **lodging:** Comfort Inn, Fairfield Inn, Hampton Inn, Holiday Inn Express, Motel 6, Super 8, **other:** Aldi Foods, Barnes&Noble, Best Buy, Discount Tire, Gander Mtn, Home Depot, Honda, JC Penney, Macy's, NTB, Old Navy, PetsMart, Sears/auto, Target, Verizon, **W** **gas:** Marathon/dsl, Mobil/dsl, **other:** Chevrolet, Ford, Suzuki
253b a	US 52, Jefferson St, Joliet, **E** **gas:** Citgo/dsl, Mobil/dsl, Shell/24hr, **food:** KFC/Pizza Hut, McDonald's, Joe's Rest., **lodging:** Best Budget Inn, Best Western, Elk's Motel, Joliet Inn, Wingate Inn, **other:** H, Ford, Harley-Davidson, Rick's RV Ctr, ✈, **W** **gas:** BP/dsl/24hr, **food:** Baba's Rest., Burger King, DQ, Louis Rest., Rosati's Pizza, Subway (1mi), **other:** H, Chrysler/Dodge/Jeep, Jewel-Osco/gas, 7-11
251	IL 59 (from nb), to Shorewood, access to same as 253 W
250b a	I-80, W to Iowa, E to Toledo
248	US 6, Joliet, **E** **gas:** Pilot/Dunkin Donuts/Subway/dsl, Speedway/dsl, **food:** Ivo's Rest., Quizno's, Taco Burrito King, **lodging:** Manor Motel, **W** **gas:** BP/McDonald's, **food:** Lone Star Rest. (2mi), **other:** to Ill/Mich SP
247	Bluff Rd
245mm	Des Plaines River
245	Arsenal Rd, **E** **other:** Exxon/Mobil Refinery
241	to Wilmington
241mm	Kankakee River
240	Lorenzo Rd, **E** **gas:** Valero/dsl, **W** **gas:** Mobil/Subway/pizza/dsl/scales/24hr, **food:** River Rest., **lodging:** Knight's Inn
238	IL 129 S, to Wilmington (exits left from sb), Braidwood
236	IL 113, Coal City, **E** **food:** Good Table Rest., **other:** Chrysler/Dodge/Jeep, Fossil Rock Camping, **W** **gas:** Shell/DQ/dsl, **3 mi W** **gas:** BP, Mobil/dsl/24hr, **food:** Agizio's, McDonald's, Subway
233	Reed Rd, **E** **gas:** Marathon/dsl, **lodging:** Sun Motel, **W** **other:** antiques
227	IL 53, Gardner, **E** **gas:** Casey's, **food:** Gardner Haus Rest., **W** **gas:** BP/dsl/24hr
220	IL 47, Dwight, **E** **gas:** BP/Burger King/dsl/24hr, Casey's, Marathon/Circle K/dsl/24hr, **food:** Arby's,

JOLIET

IL

INTERSTATE 55 CONT'D

Exit #	Services
220	Continued Dwight Pizza, McDonald's, Pete's Rest., Subway, **lodging:** Classic Motel, Super 8
217	IL 17, Dwight, **E gas:** Casey's, Shell/50's Rest./Circle K/dsl/24hr, **food:** DQ, Rte 66 Rest., **other:** Best Hardware, Chrysler/Dodge/Jeep, Family$, NAPA
213mm	Mazon River
209	Odell, **E gas:** BP, **other:** USPO
201	IL 23, Pontiac, **2-3 mi E gas:** Marathon, **food:** DQ, **other:** 4H RV Camp (seasonal)
198mm	Vermilion River
197	IL 116, Pontiac, **E gas:** BP/dsl/24hr, Freedom, Shell, Thornton's/dsl, **food:** Arby's, Baby Bull's Rest., Burger King, Family Table Rest., KFC, LJ Silver, McDonald's, Subway, Taco Bell, Wendy's, **lodging:** Comfort Inn, Fiesta Motel (1mi), Holiday Inn Express, Super 8, **other:** [H], Aldi Foods, AT&T, AutoZone, Big R Store, Buick/Chevrolet, Cadillac/GMC/Pontiac, $Tree, K-Mart, Lincoln/Mercury/Dodge, Walmart SuperCtr, st police, **W gas:** Citgo
193mm	**rest area both lanes, full [handicapped] facilities, [phone], [picnic], litter barrels, vending, petwalk**
187	US 24, Chenoa, **E gas:** Casey's, Phillips 66/McDonald's, Shell/Subway/dsl/24hr, **food:** Chenoa Family Rest., Super 8, **other:** Chevrolet
179mm	Des Plaines River
178	Lexington, Lexington, **E gas:** BP/McDonalds/dsl, Freedom/dsl, **W** Chevrolet
178mm	Mackinaw River
171	Towanda, **E gas:** FastStop
167	Lp 55 S Veterans Pkwy, to Normal, **0-3 mi E gas:** BP/Circle K, Marathon/Circle K/dsl, Quik-n-Ez, **food:** Applebee's, Bennigan's, Blimpie, Biaggi's Ristorante, Bob Evans, Burger King, Carlos O'Kelly's, Chili's, Cold Stone, DQ, Fazoli's, Fiesta Ranchera Mexican, Godfather's Pizza, Logan's Roadhouse, Lonestar Steaks, McDonald's, Monical's Pizza, Hardee's, Olive Garden, Outback Steaks, Papa John's, Papa Murphy's, Panera Bread, Pizza Hut, Qdoba, Quizno's, Ruby Tuesday, Schlotzky's, Starbucks, Steak'n Shake, Subway, Taco Bell, Wendy's, Wild Berries Rest., **lodging:** Baymont Inn, Candlewood Suites, Chateau, Clarion, Comfort Suites, Courtyard, Days Inn, Hampton Inn, Holiday Inn Express, Signature Inn, Super8, **other:** [H], Advance Parts, Aldi Foods, AutoZone, Barnes&Noble, Best Buy, BigLots, Borders Books, CVS Drug, $Tree, Fresh Mkt, Goodyear/auto, Gordman's, Hobby Lobby, Home Depot, Honda, Jewel-Osco, K-Mart, Kroger, Macy's, Meijer/dsl, Menard's, Mitsubishi, Office Depot, PetCo, Sam's Club/gas, Schnuck's Foods, Sears/auto, Target, TJ Maxx, Von Maur, Walgreens, Walmart SuperCtr/gas, mall, to [airport]
165b a	US 51 bus, to Bloomington, **E gas:** BP/Circle K/24hr, Mobil/Arby's/dsl, Qik-n-EZ, Shell/24hr, **food:** A&W/KFC, Burger King, Denny's, McDonald's, Moe's SW Grill, Pizza Hut, Steak'n Shake, Subway, Uncle Tom's Pancakes, **lodging:** Best Western, Crowne Plaza,

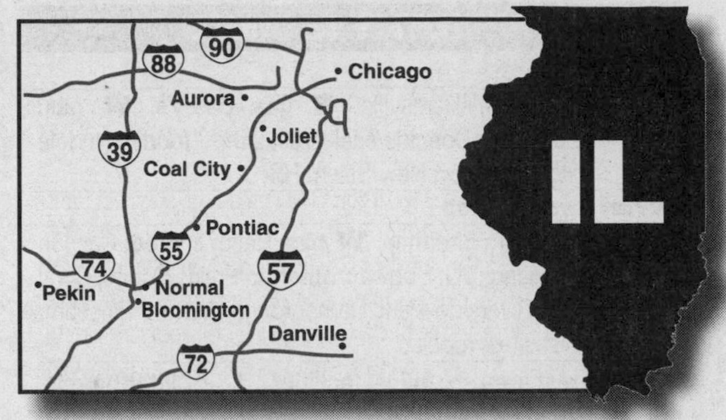

Exit #	Services
165b a	Continued Motel 6, Super 8, **other:** [H], $General, $Tree, Schuncks Foods, Walgreens, to Ill St U, **W** dsl repair
164	I-39, US 51, N to Peru
163	I-74 W, to Peoria
160b a	US 150, IL 9, Market St, Bloomington, **E gas:** BP/Circle K, Freedom/dsl, Pilot/Wendy's/dsl/scales/24hr, Shell, EnergyMart/dsl, TA/dsl/rest./scales/24hr/@, **food:** Arby's, Cracker Barrel, Culver's, KFC, La Bamba, McDonald's, Popeye's, Subway, Taco Bell, **lodging:** Best Inn, Days Inn, Econolodge, Hawthorn Suites, La Quinta, Quality Suites, **other:** [H], Advance Parts, Blue Beacon, Family$, **W gas:** Marathon/Circle K, Murphy USA, **food:** Bob Evans, Fiesta Ranchera Mexican, Greatwall Chinese, Steak'n Shake/24hr, **lodging:** Comfort Suites, Country Inn&Suites, Fairfield Inn, Hampton Inn, Holiday Inn Express, Ramada Ltd, **other:** Aldi Foods, $Tree, F&F/dsl, Radio Shack, Walmart SuperCtr/24hr
157b	Lp 55 N, Veterans Pkwy, Bloomington, **E gas:** Clark, **other:** [H], to [airport]
157a	I-74 E, to Indianapolis, US 51 to Decatur
154	Shirley
149	**W rest area both lanes, full [handicapped] facilities, [phone], [picnic], litter barrels, vending, playground, petwalk**
145	US 136, **E** RV Ctr, **W gas:** Dixie/Stuckey's/scales/dsl/rest./24hr, Shell, **food:** McDonald's, Subway, **lodging:** Super 8
140	Atlanta, **E** RV camping, **W gas:** Casey's, Faststop/dsl, **food:** Country-Aire Rest., **lodging:** Best Value Inn, **other:** NAPA
133	Lp 55, Lincoln, **2 mi E gas:** Lincoln, **lodging:** Budget Inn, **other:** [H], Camp-A-While Camping
127	I-155 N, to Peoria
126	IL 10, IL 121 S, Lincoln, **E gas:** Shell/Arby's, Thornton/dsl/scales/24hr, **food:** Burger King, Rusty's Clubhouse Cracker Barrel, Culver's, KFC/Taco Bell, LJ Silver, McDonald's, Pizza Hut, Quizno's, Steak'n Shake, Wendy's, **lodging:** Comfort Inn, Hampton Inn, Holiday Inn Express, Super 8, **other:** [H], Aldi Foods, AutoZone, Chrysler/Dodge/Jeep, $General, $Tree, Ford/Lincoln/Mercury, Kroger, Radio Shack, Russell Stover, Walmart SuperCtr/Subway
123	Lp 55, to Lincoln, **E lodging:** Lincoln Inn/**truck parking, other:** [H]
119	Broadwell
115	Elkhart

INTERSTATE 55 CONT'D

N ↕ S

Exit #	Services
109	IL 123, Williamsville, **E gas:** Casey's, **W gas:** Love's/McDonalds/scales/dsl/24hr, **food:** Huddle House, **other:** New Salem HS
107mm	**weigh sta sb**
105	Lp 55, to Sherman, **W gas:** Casey's, **food:** Cancun Mexican, DQ, Subway, **other:** to Prairie Capitol Conv Ctr, Riverside Park Campground, Military Museum, hist sites, repair
103mm	**rest area sb, full ♿ facilities, ☎, picnic, litter barrels, vending, petwalk**
102mm	Sangamon River
102mm	**rest area nb, full ♿ facilities, ☎, picnic, litter barrels, vending, petwalk**
100b	IL 54, Sangamon Ave, Springfield, **W gas:** BP/Circle K/24hr, Marathon/Circle K, Murphy USA, Shell/dsl, **food:** Arby's, Burger King, Culver's, Hickory River BBQ, International Buffet, McDonald's, Parkway Cafe, Ryan's, Sonic, Steak'n Shake, Subway, Taco Bell, Wendy's, Wings Etc, Xochimilco Mexican, **lodging:** Northfield Suites, Ramada Ltd, **other:** Harley-Davidson, Lowe's Whse, Menard's, Walmart SuperCtr/24hr, ✈, to Vet Mem
100a	Il 54, E to Clinton, **E gas:** Road Ranger/Pilot/Subway/dsl/scales/24hr, **food:** Star Cafe/24hr **other:** Kenworth/Ryder/Volvo, truckwash
98b	I-72, IL 97, Springfield, **W gas:** BP/Circle K/24hr, Shell/dsl/24hr, **food:** Arby's, Hardee's, McDonald's, Seafood House, Starbucks, Subway, Taco Bell, **lodging:** Best Rest Inn, Best Western, Parkview Motel, **other:** H, Ford Trucks, Goodyear, K-Mart, Walgreens, to Capitol Complex
98a	I-72 E, US 36 E, to Decatur
96b a	IL 29 N, S Grand Ave, Springfield, **W gas:** Road Ranger/dsl/24hr, **food:** Burger King, Godfather's, Popeye's, **lodging:** Red Roof Inn, Super 8, **other:** Advance Parts, AutoZone, Hyundai, Isuzu, JC Penney, O'Reilly Parts, Pontiac/GMC, Shop'n Save, Volvo, museum
94	Stevenson Dr, Springfield, **E** KOA (7mi), **W gas:** BP/Circle K/Quizno's, Mobil/Subway/dsl, **food:** Antonio's Pizza, Applebee's, Arby's, Bob Evans, Carlos O'Kelly's, Cheddar's, Denny's, Hardees, Hooters, IHOP, La Fiesta Mexican, LJ Silver, Maverick Steaks, McDonald's, Outback Steaks, Panera Bread, Papa John's, Red Lobster, Smokey Bones BBQ, Steak'n Shake, Taipan Chinese, **lodging:** Candlewood Suites, Comfort Suites, Crowne Plaza, Day's Inn/rest., Drury Inn, Hampton Inn, Hilton Garden, Holiday Inn Express, Microtel, PearTree Inn, Signature Inn, Stevenson Inn, **other:** BigLots, CVS Drug, $General, GNC, Jo-Ann Fabrics, Radio Shack, ShopKO, Walgreens, USPO
92b a	I-72 W, US 36 W, 6th St, Springfield, **W gas:** Road Ranger, Thornton's, **food:** Arby's, Bellacino's Rest., Burger King, DQ, Golden Corral, Jimmy John's, KFC, McDonald's, Pizza Hut, Sgt. Pepper's Cafe', Subway, Taco Bell, **lodging:** Route 66, Super 8, Travelodge/rest., **other:** H, AutoZone, Lincoln/Mazda/Mercury, Walgreens, Walmart SuperCtr

SPRINGFIELD

Exit #	Services
90	Toronto Rd, **E gas:** Qik-n-EZ/dsl, Shell/Circle K, **food:** Antonio's Pizza, Cracker Barrel, HenHouse, China Express, McDonald's, Subway, Taco Bell, Wendy's, **lodging:** Baymont Inn, Motel 6, Ramada Ltd, **other:** H
89mm	Lake Springfield
88	E Lake Dr, Chatham, **E other:** to Lincoln Mem Garden/Nature Ctr, st police, **W** KOA
83	Glenarm, **W** JJ RV Park/LP (4mi)
82	IL 104, to Pawnee, **E** to Sangchris Lake SP, **W gas:** Mobil/Auburn Trvl Ctr/Subway/scales/dsl/rest/24hr, **food:** Myra's Rest, **other:** antiques/crafts
80	Hist 66, Divernon, **W gas:** Marathon/Quizno's/dsl, **other:** antiques
72	Farmersville, **W gas:** Jumping Jimmy's/Subway/dsl/24hr, Shell/24hr, **lodging:** Art's Motel/rest.
65mm	**rest area both lanes, full ♿ facilities, ☎, picnic, litter barrels, vending, playground, petwalk**
63	IL 48, IL 127, to Raymond
60	IL 108, to Carlinville, **E other:** Kamper Kampanion RV Park, truck parts, **W gas:** Shell/dsl/LP/café, **lodging:** Best Western, **other:** antiques, to Blackburn Coll
56mm	**weigh sta nb**
52	IL 16, Hist 66, Litchfield, **E gas:** BP/24hr, Casey's, Conoco/Jack-in-the-Box/dsl, Faststop/deli/dsl/scales, Murphy USA, Shell/24hr, **food:** A&W/LJ Silver, Arby's, Ariston Café, Burger King, China Town, DQ, Denny's, Domino's, Jubelt's Rest., KFC, Maverick Steaks, McDonald's, Pizza Hut, Ponderosa, Ruby Tuesday, Subway, Taco Bell, Wendy's, **lodging:** Best Value Inn, Comfort Inn, Hampton Inn, Holiday Inn Express, Super 8, **other:** H, Aldi Foods, Cadillac/Chevrolet/GMC/Pontiac, $General, $Tree, Firestone/auto, Ford/Mercury, Goodyear/auto, IGA Foods, NAPA, Radio Shack, Walgreens, Walmart SuperCtr/24hr, camping (8mi), **W** st police
44	IL 138, to Benld, Mt Olive, **E gas:** Jumping Jimmy's Gas, **food:** Crossroads Diner, **other:** Mother Jones Mon
41	to Staunton, **W gas:** Casey's, **food:** DQ, Schweppes Rest., Subway, **lodging:** Super 8, **other:** H
37	Livingston, New Douglas, **W gas:** BP/dsl/24hr, **food:** Country Inn, Gasperoni's Café
33	IL 4, to Staunton, Worden, **W** Gas & Tires
30	IL 140, Hamel, **E** Innkeeper Motel, **W gas:** Shell, **food:** Scotty's Rest
28mm	**rest area both lanes, full ♿ facilities, ☎, picnic, litter barrels, vending, petwalk**
23	IL 143, Edwardsville, **E gas:** Phillips 66/dsl, **other:** repair, **W** Red Barn Camping (apr-oct)
20b	I-270 W, to Kansas City
20a	I-70 E, to Indianapolis
I-55 S and I-70 W run together 18 mi	
18	IL 162, to Troy, **E gas:** Phillips 66/dsl, Pilot/Arby's/dsl/scales/24hr, TA/BP/Country Pride/dsl/scales/24hr/@, Zx Gas, **food:** Burger King, China King, DQ, Domino's, Imo's Pizza, Jack-in-the-Box, Little Caesar's, McDonald's/playplace, Pizza Man, Pizza Hut, Subway, **other:** H, Ace Hardware, $General, NAPA,

LITCHFIELD

IL

INTERSTATE 55 CONT'D

N ↕ S COLLINSVILLE

Exit #	Services
18	Continued Speedco, SuperValu Foods, Walgreens, USPO, **W gas:** Phillips 66/dsl/24hr, **food:** Cracker Barrel, Taco Bell, **lodging:** Congress Motel, Holiday Inn Express, Red Roof Inn, Super 8, **other:** Freightliner
17	US 40 E, to Troy, to St Jacob
15b a	IL 159, Maryville, Collinsville, **E gas:** Phillips 66/dsl, Shell, Zx Gas, **food:** Carisillo's Mexican, KFC, Sharky's Rest, Steak-Out, **other:** Aldi Foods, $General, Ford/Lincoln/Mercury, Walgreens, Vet **W lodging:** Econolodge
14mm	**weigh sta sb**
11	IL 157, Collinsville, **E gas:** Casey's, **food:** A&W/LJ Silver, Denny's, Golden Corral, Han's Buffet, Little Caesar's, McDonald's, Penn Sta Subs, Qdoba, St Louis Bread Co, Starbucks, Waffle House, Wendy's, **lodging:** Motel 6, **other:** Home Depot, Midas, Radio Shack, Walgreens, Walmart SuperCtr, **W gas:** Motomart/dsl/24hr, **food:** Applebee's, Arby's, Bandana's BBQ, Bob Evans, Burger King, Culver's, DQ, Pizza Hut, Ponderosa, Ravanelli's Rest, Ruby Tuesday, Steak'n Shake, White Castle/24hr, Zapata's Mexican, **lodging:** Comfort Inn, Days Inn, Double Tree Inn, Drury Inn, Extended Stay Suites, Fairfield Inn, Hampton Inn, Super 8, **other:** Buick/GMC/Pontiac, Chrysler/Dodge/Jeep, st police
10	I-255, S to Memphis, N to I-270
9	Black Lane (from nb, no return), **E** Fairmount Race-Track
6	IL 111, Great River Rd, Fairmont City, **E gas:** Phillips 66, **lodging:** Indian Mound Inn, Royal Budget Inn, Cahokia Mounds SP, **W** Horseshoe SP
5mm	motorist callboxes begin at 1/2 mi intervals nb
4b a	IL 203, Granite City, **E gas:** Phillips 66/dsl/24hr, **lodging:** Western Inn, **W gas:** Pilot/Subway/Taco Bell/dsl/scales/24hr/@, **food:** Burger King, **other:** Gateway Int Raceway
3	Exchange Ave
2	I-64 E, IL 3 N, St Clair Ave
2b	3rd St
2a	M L King Bridge, to downtown E St Louis
1	IL 3, to Sauget (from sb)
I-55 N and I-70 E run together 18 mi	
0mm	Illinois/Missouri state line, Mississippi River

INTERSTATE 57

N ↕ S

Exit #	Services
358mm	I-94 E to Indiana, I-57 begins/ends on I-94, exit 63 in Chicago.
357	IL 1, Halsted St, **E gas:** BP, Mobil, **other:** auto repair, **W gas:** Clark, Shell, **food:** McDonald's, Shark's, **other:** Walgreens
355	111th St, Monterey Ave, **W gas:** Citgo
354	119th St, **W gas:** Citgo, **food:** Chili's, DQ, Panda Express, Subway, **other:** $Tree, Jewel-Osco, Marshall's, PetCo, Staples, Target
353	127th St, Burr Oak Ave, **E gas:** Citgo, Marathon, Shell, **food:** Burger King, McDonald's, Subway,

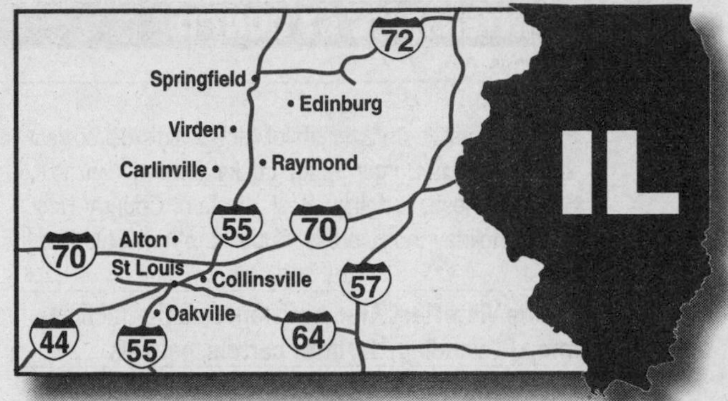

CHICAGO

Exit #	Services
353	Continued Wendy's, **lodging:** Heritage Inn, Motel 6, Plaza Inn, **other:** [H], Ace Hardware, Advance Parts, Aldi Foods, Family$, Ultra Foods, Walgreens, **W gas:** BP, Citgo/dsl, **other:** JJ Fish&Chicken
352mm	Calumet Sag Channel
350	IL 83, 147th St, Sibley Blvd, **E gas:** Marathon/dsl, **food:** Checker's, Dunkin Donuts, Harold's Chicken, McDonald's, Subway, **other:** Aldi Foods, **W other:** USPO
348	US 6, 159th St, **E gas:** Citgo/dsl, Marathon/dsl, **food:** Baskin-Robbins/Dunkin Donuts, Burger King, Harold's Chicken, McDonald's, Popeye's, Subway, Taco Bell, White Castle, **lodging:** Comfort Inn, **other:** AutoZone, BigLots, $Tree, Family$, U-Haul, Walgreens, **W gas:** Citgo/dsl, Mobil/dsl
346	167th St, Cicero Ave, to IL 50, **E gas:** BP, Citgo/dsl, **food:** Applebee's, Baskin Robbins/Dunkin Donuts, Harold's Chicken, McDonald's, Panda Express, Shark's Fish&Chicken, Sonic, Thom's BBQ, Wendy's, **lodging:** Best Western Oak Forest, **other:** Radio Shack, Walmart SuperCtr/Subway, **W gas:** Shell, **other:** 7-11
345b a	I-80, W to Iowa, E to Indiana, to I-294 N toll to Wisconsin
342a	Vollmer Rd, **E gas:** Shell/24hr, **other:** [H]
340b a	US 30, Lincoln Hwy, Matteson, **E gas:** BP/24hr, Citgo/dsl, **food:** A&W/LJ Silver, Afusion Chinese, Applebee's, Burger King, ChuckeCheese, Cracker Barrel, Culver's, Fuddrucker's, IHOP, Jimmy John's, KFC, Knock-Outs Rest., McDonald's, Michael's Grill, Nino's Pizza, Olive Garden, Panda Express, Panera Bread, Pizza Hut, Quizno's, Red Lobster, Shark's, Starbucks, Subway, Taco Bell, Wendy's, White Castle, **lodging:** Best Value Inn, Country Inn&Suites, Hampton Inn, Holiday Inn/rest., La Quinta, **other:** Aldi Foods, AT&T, Best Buy, Border's, Chrysler/Dodge/Jeep, Discount Tire, $Tree, Dominick's Foods, Firestone/auto, Home Depot, JC Penney, Marshall's, Menards, NTB, Pep Boys, Radio Shack, Sam's Club/gas, Sears/auto, Target, Walgreens, Verizon, Walmart, mall, USPO, **W other:** Buick, Cadillac, Chevrolet, Ford, GMC, Honda, Hyundai, Kia, Mitsubishi, Nissan, Pontiac, Toyota, VW
339	Sauk Trail, to Richton Park, **E gas:** Citgo/dsl, **food:** McDonald's, **other:** Walgreens
335	Monee, **E gas:** BP/Dunkin Donuts/Subway/dsl,

INTERSTATE 57 CONT'D

N ↕ S

Exit #	Services
335	Continued Petro/dsl/rest./e-85/24hr, Pilot/McDonald's/dsl/scales/24hr/@, **food:** Burger King, Lucky Burrito, Quizno's, Schoops Rest., **lodging:** Best Western, Country Host Motel, Holiday Inn Express, Super 8, **other:** Blue Beacon
332mm	**Prairie View Rest Area both lanes, full facilities, info, vending, litter barrels, petwalk**
330mm	**weigh sta both lanes**
327	to Peotone, **E gas:** Casey's, Shell/Circle K/24hr, **food:** Bierstube German, McDonald's
322	Manteno, **E gas:** BP/McDonald's/24hr, Phillips 66/Subway, **food:** Jimmy John's, KFC/Pizza Hut/Taco Bell, Monical's Pizza, Wendy's, **lodging:** Country Inn&Suites, Howard Johnson, **other:** Curves, Harley-Davidson, **W gas:** GasCity/dsl
315	IL 50, Bradley, **E gas:** Shell/Burger King/Circle K, **food:** Armenise's Rest., Buffalo Wild Wings, Cracker Barrel, LoneStar Steaks, McDonald's, Pizza Hut, Red Lobster, Ruby Tuesday, TGIFriday's, White Castle, **lodging:** Fairfield Inn, Hampton Inn, Holiday Inn Express, Lee's Inn, **other:** Barnes&Noble, Best Buy, Chrysler/Dodge/Jeep, F&F, JC Penney, Kohl's, Marshall's, Michael's, PetCo, PetsMart, Sears/auto, Staples, Target, T-Mobile, Walmart SuperCtr/Subway, mall, **W gas:** BP/dsl, Speedway/dsl, **food:** Applebee's, Arby's, Bakers Square, Coyote Canyon, Denny's, El Campesino Mexican, IHOP, LJ Silver, McDonald's, Oberweis Ice Cream, Old Country Buffet, Panda Express, Pizza Hut, Starbucks, Steak'n Shake, Subway, Taco Bell, VIP's Rest., Vito's Pizza, Wendy's, **lodging:** Motel 6, Quality Inn, Super 8, **other:** Aldi Foods, Brown RV Ctr, Buick/Nissan, Chevrolet, $Tree, Hobby Lobby, Honda, Hyundai, Jo-Ann Fabrics, KIA, K-Mart, Lowe's Whse, Menards, Verizon, Vet, to Kankakee River SP
312	IL 17, Kankakee, **E other:** Twin River's Camping, **W gas:** BP, Marathon/dsl, Shell/Circle K/24hr, **food:** McDonald's, PoorBoy Rest., **other:** [H], Advance Parts, Family$, Walgreens, auto repair
310.5mm	Kankakee River
308	US 45, US 52, to Kankakee, **E** camping (3mi), **W gas:** Gas City/Dunkin Donuts/Subway/dsl, Gas Depot, **food:** KFC/Taco Bell, **lodging:** Fairview Motel, Hilton Garden, **other:** Aldi Foods, $Tree, Walmart SuperCtr, ✈
302	Chebanse, **W** truck repair
297	Clifton, **W gas:** Phillips 66/DQ/dsl, **food:** CharGrilled Cheeseburgers
293	IL 116, Ashkum, **E gas:** BP/Subway/dsl, **W food:** Loft Rest., **other:** st police, tires
283	US 24, IL 54, Gilman, **E gas:** Apollo/Citgo/dsl/scales/24hr@, K&HTruckPlaza/BP/dsl/scales/24hr/@, Shell, **food:** Burger King, DQ, McDonald's, Monical's Pizza, **lodging:** Budget Host, Super 8, Travel Inn, **W gas:** BP/Subway/dsl, **other:** R&R RV Ctr
280	IL 54, Onarga, **E gas:** Casey's (1mi), Phillips 66, **other:** USPO (1mi), **W** other Lake Arrowhead RV camping
272	to Roberts, Buckley
268.5mm	**rest area both lanes, full facilities, vending, litter barrels, petwalk**
261	IL 9, Paxton, **E food:** Hardee's, Monical's Pizza, Pizza Hut, Subway, **other:** Buick/Chevrolet/GMC/Pontiac, Family$, TrueValue, **W gas:** BP, Marathon, **food:** Country Garden Rest., **lodging:** Paxton, Inn, **1 mi E gas:** Casey's, Phillips 66/dsl, **other:** IGA Foods, USPO
250	US 136, Rantoul, **E gas:** BP/Circle K/24hr, **food:** Arby's, Burger King, Hardee's, KFC/Taco Bell, LJ Silver, McDonald's, Red Wheel Rest., **lodging:** Best Western, Days Inn, Super 8, **other:** $General, NAPA, Walmart SuperCtr, camping, Vet, to Chanute AFB, **1 mi E gas:** Phillips 66/dsl, **food:** Baskin-Robbins/Dunkin Donuts, Hardee's, Monical's Pizza, Papa John's, Subway, **other:** Chrysler/Dodge/Jeep, Ford, Walgreens
240	Market St, **E gas:** Road Ranger/Pilot/McDonald's/dsl/scales, **other:** D&W Lake Camping, Kenworth, truck/tire repair
238	Olympian Dr, to Champaign, **W gas:** Mobil/dsl, **food:** DQ, **lodging:** Microtel, **other:** RV/dsl repair
237b a	I-74, W to Peoria, E to Urbana
235b	I-72 W, to Decatur
235a	University Ave, to Champaign, **E** [H], U of Ill
232	Curtis Rd, new exit
229	to Savoy, Monticello, **E gas:** Marathon/dsl/24hr
221.5mm	**rest area both lanes, full facilities, litter barrels, vending, petwalk**
220	US 45, Pesotum, **W gas:** Citgo, st police
212	US 36, Tuscola, **E gas:** FuelMart/dsl, **W gas:** BP/24hr, Marathon, Road Ranger/dsl/scales, **food:** Amish Buffet, Burger King, DQ, Denny's, McDonald's, Monical's Pizza, Pizza Hut, Subway, Tuscany Steaks, **lodging:** Cooper Motel, Holiday Inn Express, Super 8, **other:** Chevrolet/Pontiac/Buick/GMC, Ford, IGA Foods, Pamida, Radio Shack, Tanger Outlets/Famous Brands, camping
203	IL 133, Arcola, **E gas:** Citgo/dsl/24hr, **other:** CampALot, **W gas:** Shell/Subway/dsl/24hr, Sunrise Gas, **food:** DQ, Flower Patch B&B, Hen House, Monical's Pizza, **lodging:** Arcola Inn, Budget Inn, Comfort Inn, **other:** Country Charm Amish, $General, NAPA, Rockome Gardens, Arcola Camping
192	IL 18, new exit
190b a	IL 16, to Mattoon, **E gas:** BP/dsl, **other:** [H], to E IL U, Fox Ridge SP, **W gas:** Marathon/Subway, **food:** Alamo Steaks, Buffalo Wild Wings, Cody's Roadhouse, Cracker Barrel, Don Sol Mexican, El Vaquero Mexican, Jumbo Buffet, McDonald's/playplace, QQ Buffet, Quizno's, Stadium Grill, Steak'n Shake/24hr, Taco Bell, Wendy's, **lodging:** Baymont Inn, Budget Inn, Comfort Suites, Hampton Inn, Holiday Inn Express, Ramada Inn/rest., Super 8, **other:** Aldi Foods, Big Lots, CVS Drug, $General, Home Depot, JC Penney, Sears, Staples, Walgreen, Walmart SuperCtr/dsl, mall
184	US 45, IL 121, to Mattoon, **E gas:** Marathon/pizza/dsl, **W gas:** Marathon/dsl, Subway, **food:**

BRADLEY KANKAKEE CHAMPAIGN MATTOON

IL

INTERSTATE 57 CONT'D

N ↕ S

Exit #	Services
184	Continued McDonald's, **lodging:** Budget Inn, US Grant Motel (2mi), **other:** to Lake Shelbyville
177	US 45, Neoga, **E gas:** Depot/Subway/dsl, **W gas:** Casey's (1mi), Marathon/rest./dsl
166.5mm	**rest area both lanes, full ♿ facilities, vending, ☎, picnic, litter barrels, petwalk**
163	I-70 E, to Indianapolis
I-57 S and I-70 W run together 6 mi	
EFFINGHAM	
162	US 45, Effingham, **E gas:** Motomart, **other:** Harley-Davidson, **W gas:** Pilot/McDonald's/dsl/scales/24hr, **food:** Subway, Tuscany Steaks, **other:** Crossroads RV Ctr, Camp Lakewood (2mi), truck repair
160	IL 33, IL 32, Effingham, **E food:** Jimmy John's, LoneStar Steaks, Pizza Hut, **lodging:** Comfort Inn, Fairfield inn, Hampton Inn, **other:** (H), Aldi Foods, $General, K-Mart, Midas, Walgreens, Vet, **W gas:** BP/Quizno's, FLYING J CountryMkt/dsl/scales/24hr, Marathon, Murphy USA/dsl, TA/Popeye's/dsl/rest./@, **food:** Arby's, Buffalo Wild Wings, Burger King, Cracker Barrel, Denny's, El Rancherito Mexican, KFC, LJ Silver, McDonald's, Ryan's, Ruby Tuesday, Starbucks, Steak'n Shake, Subway, Taco Bell, TGIFriday's, Wendy's, **lodging:** Country Inn&Suites, Days Inn, Hilton Garden, Holiday Inn Express, Motel 6, Rodeway Inn, Super 8, **other:** AT&T, Blue Beacon, $Tree, Ford/Lincoln/Mercury, Kohl's, Menard's, Peterbilt, Radio Shack, SpeedCo, Walmart SuperCtr
159	US 40, Effingham, **E gas:** BP/dsl/24hr, Marathon/dsl, **food:** China Buffet, Culver's, Domino's, Hardee's/24hr, Little Caesar's, Niemerg's Rest, Papa John's, Subway, **lodging:** Comfort Suites, Crossroads Inn, Econolodge, Howard Johnson, **other:** AutoZone, Family$, O'Reilly Parts, SavALot Foods, Walgreens, tires/repair, **W gas:** Petro/Mobil/Iron Skillet/dsl/rest./24hr/@, **lodging:** Best Western, **other:** Blue Beacon, Truck-O-Mat/scales/wash
I-57	**N and I-70 E run together 6 mi**
157	I-70 W, to St Louis
151	Watson, **5 mi E** Percival Springs RV Park
150mm	Little Wabash River
145	Edgewood, **E gas:** Marathon
135	IL 185, Farina, **E gas:** BP/Subway/dsl, **other:** Ford
127	to Kinmundy, Patoka
SALEM	
116	US 50, Salem, **E gas:** Huck's, Motomart/dsl/24hr, Shell/Circle K, **food:** Burger King, Domino's, KFC, La Cabana Mexican, LJ Silver, McDonald's, Pizza Hut, Subway, Taco Bell, Village Garden, Wendy's, **other:** AutoZone, Chrysler/Dodge/Jeep, Forbes SP (17mi), NAPA, O'Reilly Parts, Pontiac/GMC, to Forbes SP, **W gas:** Marathon/dsl, **food:** Applebee's, Arby's, Denny's, **lodging:** Comfort Inn, Salem Inn, Super 8, **other:** Carlisle Lake (23mi), Chevrolet/Buick, $Tree, Ford, Salem Tires, Walmart SuperCtr/gas
114mm	**rest area both lanes, full ♿ facilities, ☎, picnic, litter barrels, vending, petwalk, playground**
109	IL 161, to Centralia, **W gas:** Biggie's General Store/cafe/dsl

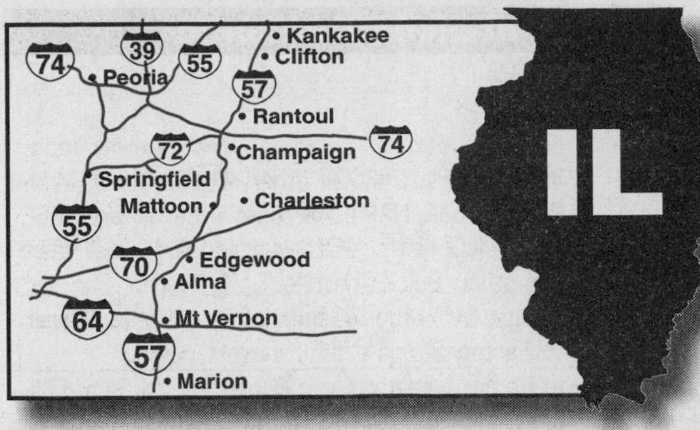

Exit #	Services
103	Dix, **E gas:** Phillips 66/dsl, **lodging:** Red Carpet Inn, **other:** camping
96	I-64 W, to St Louis
MT VERNON	
95	IL 15, Mt Vernon, **E gas:** BP/dsl/24hr, Hucks, Jimmy's/dsl, Marathon/Circle K, Phillips 66, **food:** El Rancherito Mexican, Fazoli's, Grand Buffet, Hardee's, KFC, LJ Silver, McDonald's, Papa John's, Pasta House, Pizza Hut, Steak'n Shake/24hr, Subway, Taco Bell, Wendy's, **lodging:** Best Inn, Best Value Inn, Comfort Suites, Drury Inn, Motel 6, Red Roof Inn, Super 8, Thrifty Inn, **other:** (H), Aldi Foods, AutoZone, Chevrolet, CVS Drug, $Tree, Ford, Harley-Davidson, JC Penney, K-Mart, Kroger/gas, O'Reilly Parts, Radio Shack, Sears, Walgreens, **W gas:** Hucks/dsl/scales/rest./24hr, Marathon/Circle K, Pilot/Denny's/dsl/scales/24hr, Shell/Circle K/24hr, TA/Citgo/Popeye's/dsl/24hr/@, **food:** Applebee's, Arby's, Bob Evans, Burger King, Chili's, Cracker Barrel, LoneStar Steaks, McDonald's, Quizno's, Ryan's, Sonic, Stonewolf Steakhouse, Subway, **lodging:** Days Inn, Fairfield Inn, Hampton Inn, Holiday Inn, Quality Inn, **other:** Buick/Cadillac/GMC/Pontiac, Freightliner, Lowe's Whse, NAPA, Outlet Mall, Quality Times RV Ctr/camping, Staples, Toyota, Walmart SuperCtr, truckwash
94	Veteran's Memorial Dr
92	I-64 E, to Louisville
83	Ina, **E gas:** Lakeview/dsl/deli/24hr, Love's/McDonald's/dsl/scales, **other:** Sherwood Camping (2mi), **W** to Rend Lake Coll
79mm	**rest area sb, full ♿ facilities, info, vending, ☎, picnic, litter barrels, petwalk, playground**
77	IL 154, to Whittington, **E gas:** Shell/24hr, **food:** Tambo's Rest., **other:** Whittington Woods RV Park, **W lodging:** Seasons at Rend Lake Lodge/rest., **other:** to Rend Lake, golf, Wayne Fitzgerrell SP
74mm	**rest area nb, full ♿ facilities, vending, ☎, picnic, litter barrels, petwalk, playground**
BENTON	
71	IL 14, Benton, **E gas:** Jimmy's/dsl, **food:** Arby's, Hardee's, KFC/Taco Bell, Pizza Hut, **lodging:** Day's Inn/rest., Gray Plaza Motel, Super 8, **other:** (H), AutoZone, CVS Drug, KOA (1.5mi), O'Reilly Parts, Plaza Tire, **W gas:** BP/dsl, Murphy USA, Phillips 66/dsl/24hr, **food:** Applebee's, Burger King, McDonald's, Subway, **other:** Curves, Walmart SuperCtr/24hr, to Rend Lake
65	IL 149, W Frankfort, **E gas:** Shell/dsl, W Frankfort Gas/dsl, **food:** China Star, Dixon Deli, Hardee's,

INTERSTATE 57 CONT'D

N ↕ S — MARION

Exit #	Services
65	Continued La Fiesta Mexican, LJ Silver, Sonic, Subway, **lodging:** Gray Plaza Motel, **other:** [H], CarQuest, Mad-Pricer Foods, NAPA, **W gas:** Casey's, **food:** EEE Rest, McDonald's, Pizza Hut, **lodging:** Best Value Inn, **other:** Buick/Chevrolet/GMC/Pontiac, Chrysler/Dodge, CVS Drug, $General, $Tree, K-Mart, Kroger, VF Factory Stores
59	to Herrin, Johnston City, **E gas:** BP/dsl, ROC/E85, **food:** DQ, McDonald's, Subway, **other:** $General, NAPA, camping (2mi), **W other:** [H], camping (4mi)
54b a	IL 13, Marion, **E gas:** Phillips 66/24hr, **food:** Arby's, Fazoli's, Hardee's, KFC, La Fiesta Mexican, LJ Silver, Papa John's, Pizza Hut, Quizno's, Subway, Tequila Mexican, Wendy's, Western Sizzlin, **lodging:** Day's Inn, Econolodge, **other:** Aldi Foods, Advance Parts, AutoZone, Cadillac/Chevrolet, $General, Ford/Hyundai/Lincoln/Mercury, Kroger/gas, Plaza Tire, Menards, Radio Shack, SavALot Foods, Walgreens, USPO, **W gas:** BP/dsl/rest/scales/24hr/@, Marathon, Phillips 66, **food:** Applebee's, Asian Bistro, Backyard Burger, Bob Evans, Burger King, McAlister's Deli, McDonald's, O'Charley's, Wok'n Roll Buffet, Red Lobster, Ryan's, 17th Street Grill, Sonic, Steak'n Shake, Taco Bell, **lodging:** Best Inn, Country Inn&Suites, Drury Inn, Fairfield Inn, Hampton Inn, Motel 6, Super 8, **other:** Buick/GMC/Pontiac, Chrysler/Dodge/Jeep, Dillard's, Harley-Davidson, Home Depot, Honda, Mercedes, Nissan, Sam's Club/gas, Sears, Subaru, Suzuki, Target, Toyota/Scion, Walmart SuperCtr/24hr, mall
53	Main St, Marion, **E food:** DQ, **lodging:** Motel Marion, **other:** [H], Marion Campground, NAPA, **W gas:** Motomart/24hr, **food:** Cracker Barrel, HideOut Steaks, **lodging:** Comfort Inn, Comfort Suites, Holiday Inn Express
47mm	**weigh sta both lanes**
45	IL 148, **1 mi E gas:** King Tut's Food/dsl/24hr, **lodging:** Lake Tree Inn, **other:** camping, dsl repair
44	I-24 E to Nashville
40	Goreville Rd, **E other:** Ferne Clyffe SP, camping, scenic overlook
36	Lick Creek Rd, **W other:** vineyards
32mm	**Trail of Tears Rest Area both lanes, full ♿ facilities, info, ☎, ⊞, litter barrels, vending, petwalk, playground**
30	IL 146, Anna, Vienna, **W gas:** Shell/dsl/rest./24hr, **other:** [H], auto/tire repair
25	US 51 N (from nb, exits left), to Carbondale
24	Dongola Rd, **W gas:** BP/dsl
18	Ullin Rd, **W gas:** Citgo/dsl/24hr, **food:** EEE BBQ, **lodging:** Best Western, **other:** st police
8	Mounds Rd, to Mound City, **E other:** K&K AutoTruck/dsl/repair
1	IL 3, to US 51, Cairo, **E lodging:** Belvedere Motel (2mi), Day's Inn, **other:** $General, Mound City Nat Cem (4mi), camping, **W** camping
0mm	Illinois/Missouri state line, Mississippi River

IL

INTERSTATE 64

E ↕ W — MT VERNON

Exit #	Services
131.5mm	Illinois/Indiana state line, Wabash River
131mm	**Skeeter Mtn Welcome Ctr wb, full ♿ facilities, ☎, vending, ⊞, litter barrels, petwalk**
130	IL 1, to Grayville, **N gas:** Casey's (2mi), Shell/dsl/24hr, **food:** Subway, **lodging:** Best Western/rest., Super 8, **other:** museum, Beall Woods St Park
124mm	Little Wabash River
117	Burnt Prairie, **S gas:** Marathon/dsl, **food:** ChuckWagon Charlie's Café, **other:** antiques
110	US 45, Mill Shoals
100	IL 242, to Wayne City, **N gas:** Marathon/dsl
89	to Belle Rive, Bluford
86mm	**rest area wb, full ♿ facilities, ☎, vending, ⊞, litter barrels, petwalk**
82.5mm	**rest area eb, full ♿ facilities, ☎, vending, ⊞, litter barrels, petwalk**
80	IL 37, to Mt Vernon, **2 mi N gas:** BP/Burger King/dsl/24hr, Hucks/dsl/24hr, **lodging:** Royal Inn, **other:** $General, camping
78	I-57, S to Memphis, N to Chicago
95 [I-57]	Mt Vernon, **I-64 and I-57 run together 5 mi. N gas:** BP/dsl/24hr, Hucks, Jimmy's/dsl, Marathon/Circle K, Phillips 66, **food:** El Rancherito Mexican, Fazoli's, Grand Buffet, Hardee's, KFC, LJ Silver, McDonald's, Papa John's, Pasta House, Pizza Hut, Steak'n Shake/24hr, Subway, Taco Bell, Wendy's, **lodging:** Best Inn, Best Value Inn, Comfort Suites, Drury Inn, Motel 6, Red Roof Inn, Super 8, Thrifty Inn, **other:** [H], Aldi Foods, AutoZone, Chevrolet, CVS Drug, $Tree, Ford, Harley-Davidson, JC Penney, K-Mart, Kroger/gas, O'Reilly Parts, Radio Shack, Sears, Walgreens, **S gas:** Hucks/dsl/scales/rest./24hr, Marathon/Circle K, Pilot/Denny's/dsl/scales/24hr, Shell/Circle K/24hr, TA/Citgo/Popeye's/dsl/24hr/@, **food:** Applebee's, Arby's, Bob Evans, Burger King, Chili's, Cracker Barrel, LoneStar Steaks, McDonald's, Quizno's, Ryan's, Sonic, Stonewolf Steakhouse, Subway, **lodging:** Days Inn, Fairfield Inn, Hampton Inn, Holiday Inn, Quality Inn, **other:** Buick/Cadillac/GMC/Pontiac, Freightliner, Lowe's Whse, NAPA, Outlet Mall, Quality Times RV Ctr/camping, Staples, Toyota, Walmart SuperCtr, truckwash
73	I-57, N to Chicago, S to Memphis
69	Woodlawn
61	US 51, to Centralia, Richview, **S** access to gas, food
50	IL 127, to Nashville, **N** to Carlyle Lake, **S gas:** Citgo/E-85/dsl, Little Nashville/Conoco/dsl/rest./scales/24hr, Shell/dsl/24hr, **food:** McDonald's, **lodging:** Best Western, **other:** [H]
41	IL 177, Okawville, **S gas:** Pilot/Road Ranger/dsl/24hr, **food:** Burger King, DQ, Hen House/24hr, Subway, **lodging:** Original Springs Motel, Super 8, **other:** $General, truck repair
37mm	Kaskaskia River
34	to Albers, **3 mi N gas:** Casey's
27	IL 161, New Baden, **N gas:** Shell/dsl/24hr, **food:** McDonald's, Outside Inn Rest., Subway, **other:** Chevrolet, $General

INTERSTATE 64 CONT'D

E ↕ W

Exit #	Services
25mm	**rest area both lanes, full ♿ facilities, info, ☎, vending, 🅿, litter barrels, petwalk**
23	IL 4, to Mascoutah, **N gas:** Mobil, **lodging:** La Quinta, 3mi **N food:** McDonald's, **S** ✈
19b a	US 50, IL 158, **N gas:** Motomart/24hr, **food:** Schiappa's Italian, Subway, **lodging:** South Inn, **S other:** H, to Scott AFB
18mm	**weigh sta eb**
16	to O'Fallon, Shiloh, **N food:** Sonic, **lodging:** Hilton Garden, **other:** CVS Drug, Harley-Davidson, **S gas:** Motomart, **food:** Applebee's, Arby's, Buffalo Wild Wings, Cafe Avanti, Coldstone Creamery, Cracker Barrel, 54th St. Grille, Golden Corral, Little Caesars, McAlister's Deli, McDonald's, Qdoba Mexican, Quizno's, St. Louis Bread Co., Starbucks, TX Roadhouse, **lodging:** Drury Inn, Holiday Inn Express, **other:** Dierbergs Foods, Dobb's Tire, Michael's, Radio Shack, Target, World Mkt
15mm	motorist callbox every 1/2 mile wb
14	O'Fallon, **N gas:** Circle K, QT, Shell/24hr, **food:** IHOP, Japanese Garden, Steak'n Shake/24hr, Subway, **lodging:** Baymont Inn, Country Inn&Suites, Extended Stay America, Sleep Inn, Suburban Inn, **other:** Cadillac, Chevrolet, Ford, O'Reilly Parts, **S food:** Chevy's Mexican, Culver's, DQ, Hardee's, Jack-in-the-Box, KFC, LoneStar Steaks, McDonald's, O'Charley's, Royal Bamboo, Sake Grill, Taco Bell, **lodging:** Candlewood Suites, Days Inn, Quality Inn, **other:** Aldi Foods, BMW, Chrysler/Jeep, Home Depot, Honda, Hyundai, Kia, Mazda, Mitsubishi, Nissan, Petsmart, Sam's Club/gas, Toyota/Scion, VW, Walmart SuperCtr
12	IL 159, to Collinsville, **N food:** Applebee's, Bob Evans, Ginger Buffet, Houlihan's, Joe's Crabshack, Lotawalla Creek Grill, Olive Garden, Red Lobster, TGIFriday, **lodging:** Best Western, Comfort Suites, Drury Inn, Fairfield Inn, Hampton Inn, Ramada Inn, Sheraton, Super 8, **other:** Gordman's, **S gas:** BP/24hr, Motomart/dsl/24hr, **food:** Arby's, Boston Mkt, Burger King, Capt D's, Casa Gallardo, Chili's, Chipotle Mexican, ChuckeCheese, Domino's, Fazoli's, Hometown Buffet, Honeybaked Ham, Hooters, Krispy Kreme, Logan's Roadhouse, Longhorn Steaks, LJ Silver, Maggie Lou's, McDonald's, Pizza Hut, Ponderosa, Popeye's, Quizno's, Rally's, Red Robin, Ruby Tuesday, Smokey Bones BBQ, Steak'n Shake, St. Louis Bread, Taco Bell, White Castle, **other:** Aamco, Advance Parts, Barnes&Noble, Best Buy, Borders, Dillard's, Dobb's Tire, $Tree, JC Penney, Jo-Ann Fabrics, K-Mart, Kohl's, Lowe's Whse, Macy's, Marshall's, NTB, Office Depot, Old Navy, PetCo, Russell Stover, Schnuck's Foods, Sears/auto, TJ Maxx, Walgreens, mall, USPO
9	IL 157, to Caseyville, **N gas:** BP/24hr, Phillips 66/Subway/repair, **food:** Hardee's, **lodging:** Western Inn, **S gas:** BP/dsl/repair, **food:** Cracker Barrel, DQ, Domino's, McDonald's, Pizza Hut/Taco Bell, **lodging:** Day's Inn, Econolodge, Motel 6, Quality Inn

EAST ST LOUIS

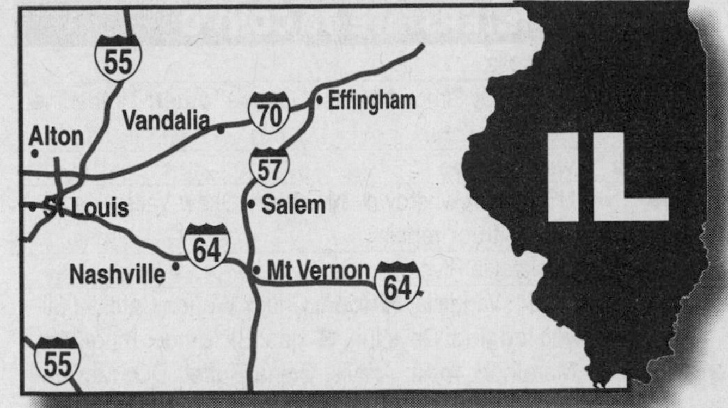

Exit #	Services
7	I-255, S to Memphis, N to Chicago
6	IL 111, Kingshighway, **N gas:** BP, Mobil/24hr, **lodging:** Econo Inn **food:** Popeye's
5.5mm	no services
5	25th St
4	15th St, Baugh
3	I-55 N, I-70 E, IL 3 N, to St Clair Ave, to stockyards
2b a	3rd St, **S** gas
1	IL 3 S, 13th St, E St Louis, **N** Casino Queen
0mm	Illinois/Missouri state line, Mississippi River

INTERSTATE 70

E ↕ W

Exit #	Services
156mm	Illinois/Indiana state line
154	US 40 W
151mm	**weigh sta wb**
149mm	**rest area wb, full ♿ facilities, info, ☎, 🅿, vending, litter barrels, petwalk**
147	IL 1, Marshall, **N gas:** Jerry's Rest., **S gas:** Casey's (1mi), Jiffy/dsl/24hr, Marathon/Arby's/dsl, **food:** Burger King, McDonald's, Pizza Hut, Sam's Steaks, Subway, Wendy's, **lodging:** Lincoln Motel (2mi), Relax Inn, Super 8, **other:** Ford, Walmart SuperCtr, Lincoln Trail SP, antiques, camping
136	to Martinsville, **S gas:** Fast Stop/dsl/24hr
134.5mm	N Fork Embarras River
129	IL 49, Casey, **N other:** RV service, KOA (seasonal), **S gas:** BP/Subway/dsl, Casey's, Fast Stop/DQ, Marathon/Circle K/dsl, **food:** Hardee's, McDonald's, Pizza Hut, **lodging:** Comfort Inn, **other:** IGA Foods
119	IL 130, Greenup, **S gas:** Casey's, Marathon/dsl, **food:** DQ, Subway, **lodging:** Budget Host, 5 Star Motel, **other:** $General, camping, hist sites
105	Montrose, **N other:** Spring Creek Camping (1mi), **S gas:** BP/dsl, Marathon/dsl/24hr, **lodging:** Fairview Inn
98	I-57, N to Chicago,
	I-70 & I-57 run together 6 mi. See Interstate 57 exits 159-162.
92	I-57, S to Mt Vernon
91mm	Little Wabash River
87mm	**rest area both lanes, full ♿ facilities, info, ☎, vending, 🅿, litter barrels, playground, petwalk, RV dump**
82	IL 128, Altamont, **N gas:** Casey's, Jumpin Jimmy's/Subway/dsl/24hr, Marathon/dsl, **food:** Dairy Bar, McDonald's, **lodging:** Altamont Motel, Knight's Inn, **other:** city park, **S food:** Longhorn Rest., **lodging:** Super 8

CASEY

INTERSTATE 70 CONT'D

E ↕ W

Exit #	Services
76	US 40, St Elmo, **N gas:** Casey's, **other:** Timberline Camping (2mi)
71mm	**weigh sta eb**
68	US 40, Brownstown, **N other:** Okaw Valley Kamping, **S** truck repair
63.5mm	Kaskaskia River
63	US 51, Vandalia, **N food:** Chuck Wagon Cafe, LJ Silver, **lodging:** Days Inn, **S gas:** BP/Burger King/24hr, Marathon, **food:** Arby's, China Buffet, DQ, McDonald's, Pizza Hut, Quizno's, Rancho Nuevo Mexican, Sonic, Subway, Wendy's, **lodging:** Jay's Inn, Travelodge, **other:** H, Aldi Foods, Harmons Foods, city park, hist site
61	US 40, Vandalia, **N gas:** Fast Stop/dsl/scales/24hr, **S gas:** Murphy USA/dsl, **food:** KFC/Taco Bell, Ponderosa, **lodging:** Holiday Inn Express, Ramada Ltd, **other:** AutoZone, Walmart SuperCtr/24hr
52	US 40, Mulberry Grove, **N gas:** Jumpin Jimmy's/dsl, **other:** Timber Trail Camp-In (2mi), tires, **S** Cedar Brook Camping (1mi)
45	IL 127, Greenville, **N gas:** Jumpin Jimmy's/Domino's/dsl, Love/rest/dsl/scales/24hr, Shell/dsl/24hr, **food:** KFC/Taco Bell, Lu-Bob's Rest., Red Apple Rest., Mabry's Rest., McDonald's, **lodging:** Budget Host, Econolodge, Super 8, 2 Acre Motel, **other:** H, Ford/Mercury, **S food:** La Hacienda Mexican, **lodging:** Sleep Inn, **other:** American Farm Heritage Museum, RV Service, to Carlyle Lake
41	US 40 E, to Greenville
36	US 40 E, Pocahontas, **S gas:** BP/dsl/24hr, Phillips 66/dsl/24hr, **lodging:** Lighthouse Lodge, Powhatan Motel/rest., Tahoe Motel, **other:** truck/tire repair
30	US 40, IL 143, to Highland, **S gas:** Shell/dsl/wifi/24hr, **food:** Blue Springs Café, **other:** H, Tomahawk RV Park (7mi)
26.5mm	**Silver Lake rest area both lanes, full ♿ facilities, ☎, picnic, litter barrels, vending, petwalk**
24	IL 143, Marine, **4 mi S food:** Ponderosa, **lodging:** Holiday Inn Express, **other:** H
21	IL 4, Lebanon
15b a	I-55, N to Chicago, S to St Louis, I-270 W to Kansas City

I-70 & I-55 run together 18 mi. See Interstate 55 exits 1-18.

0mm	Illinois/Missouri state line, Mississippi River

VANDALIA

INTERSTATE 72

E ↕ W

Exit #	Services
183mm	**1 mi E on University food:** Arby's, Asian Buffet, Burger King, Famous Dave's BBQ, La Bamba Mexican, McDonald's, Monical's Pizza, Pizza Hut, Sonic, Subway, Taco Bell, TX Roadhouse, Village Inn Pizza, **other:** Advance Parts, Aldi Foods, AutoZone, CVS Drug, County Mkt Foods, Schnuck's Foods/gas, Walgreens
182b a	I-57, N to Chicago, S to Memphis, to I-74
176	IL 47, to Mahomet
172	IL 10, Clinton
169	White Heath Rd
166	IL 105 W, Market St, **N** Ford/Mercury, **S gas:** Mobil/Subway/dsl, **food:** Red Wheel Rest., **lodging:** Best Western, Foster Inn
165mm	Sangamon River
164	Bridge St, **1 mi S gas:** Mobil/dsl, **food:** China Star, DQ, Hardee's, McDonald's, Monical's Pizza, Pizza Hut, Subway, **other:** H, Buick/Chevrolet/Pontiac, Chrysler/Dodge/Jeep, $General
156	IL 48, to Weldon, Cisco, **S** Friends Creek Camping (may-oct) (3mi)
153mm	**rest area both lanes, full ♿ facilities, ☎, picnic, litter barrels, vending, petwalk**
152mm	Friends Creek
150	Argenta
144	IL 48, Oreana, **S gas:** Pilot/McDonald's/Subway/dsl/scales/24hr, **lodging:** Sleep Inn, **other:** H, Chrysler/Dodge, Honda, Hyundai, Mitsubishi
141b a	US 51 S, Decatur, **N gas:** Shell/Circle K, **food:** Applebee's, Buffalo Wild Wings, Cheddar's, Cracker Barrel, HomeTown Buffet, McDonald's, O'Charley's, Pizza Hut, Red Lobster, Skinny's Diner, Sorento's Pizza, Steak'n Shake, Subway, Taco Bell, TX Roadhouse, **lodging:** Baymont Inn, Comfort Inn, Country Inn&Suites, Fairfield Inn, Hampton Inn, Holiday Inn Express, Homewood Suites, Ramada Ltd, **other:** Advance Parts, Bergner's, Best Buy, Buick/Cadillac/GMC/Pontiac, $Tree, Harley-Davidson, JC Penney, Menard's, Lowe's Whse, Kohl's, Menard's, PetsMart, Sears/auto, Staples, mall, **S food:** Arby's, Burger King, China Buffet, El Rodeo Mexican, Monical's Pizza, Olive Garden, Panera Bread, Papa Murphy's, Starbucks, Subway, **other:** H, Jo-Ann Fabrics, Radio Shack, Sam's Club, Target, Walgreens, Walmart SuperCtr/24hr
138	IL 121, Decatur, **S** H
133b a	US 36 E, US 51, Decatur, **S gas:** Phillips 66/Subway/dsl, **lodging:** Days Inn, Decatur Hotel/rest.
128	Niantic
122	to Mt Auburn, Illiopolis, **S gas:** Faststop
114	Buffalo, Mechanicsburg, **S gas:** Faststop
108	Riverton, Dawson
107mm	Sangamon River
104	Camp Butler, **2 mi N lodging:** Best Rest Inn, Best Western, Park View Motel, **food:** Chesapeake Seafood, Starbucks, **other:** golf
103b a	I-55, N to Chicago, S to St Louis, Il 97, to Springfield

I-72 & I-55 run together 6 mi. See Interstate 55 exits 92-98

93	IL 4, Springfield, **N gas:** Hucks, Thorntons/dsl, **food:** Applebee's, Arby's, Bakers Square, Buffet King, Burger King, Cara BBQ, Chili's, Chipotle Mexican, Denny's, Ginger Asian, LoneStar Steaks, Longhorn Steaks, Los Rancheros Mexican, McDonald's, Olive Garden, Panera Bread, Pasta House, Perkins, Popeye's, Qdoba Mexican, Sonic, Starbucks, Subway, Taco Bell, TGIFriday, TX Roadhouse, **lodging:** Comfort Inn, Courtyard, Fairfield Inn, Sleep Inn, **other:** Barnes&Noble, Best Buy, County Mkt Foods, Discount Tire, Gordman's, Hancock Fabrics, Jo-Ann Crafts, K-Mart, Kohl's, Lowe's Whse, Menard's, Michael's, Office Depot, Old Navy, PetCo, PetsMart, Sam's Club/gas, Sears/auto, ShopKO, Staples,

DECATUR

SPRINGFIELD

IL

INTERSTATE 72 CONT'D

E ↕ W

Exit #	Services
93	Continued St Fair Camping, Target, TJ Maxx, Walgreens, Walmart/auto, Vet, **S gas:** Meijer/dsl/E85, **food:** Bob Evans, Monical's Pizza, O'Charley's, Steak'n Shake, **lodging:** Hampton Inn, Staybridge Suites, **other:** Cadillac, Chevrolet, Chrysler/Jeep, Ford, Gander Mtn, Honda
91	Wabash Ave, to Springfield, **N food:** Buffalo Wild Wings, Coz's Pizza, Culver's, **other:** Dodge, Kia, Nissan, Toyota, **S** Colman RV SuperCtr
82	New Berlin, **S gas:** Phillips 66/The Plaza Rest./dsl
76	IL 123, to Ashland, Alexander
68	to IL 104, to Jacksonville, **2 mi N gas:** BP, **other:** H
64	US 67, to Jacksonville, **N gas:** Clark/Quizno's/dsl, **food:** Classic Diner, **lodging:** Comfort Inn, Econolodge, Holiday Inn Express, **other:** Hopper RV Ctr, **2 mi N gas:** BP/Circle K/dsl, Phillips 66, **food:** DQ, KFC, McDonald's, **other:** H, CVS Drug, $General, Walgreens
60	to US 67 N, to Jacksonville, **6 mi N** H, gas, food, lodging
52	to IL 106, Winchester, **N** golf, **2 mi S** gas, food, lodging
46	IL 100, to Bluffs
42mm	Illinois River
35	US 54, IL 107, to Pittsfield, Griggsville, **4 mi N** gas, food, lodging, **S other:** H, Pine Lakes Camping (6mi), st police
31	to Pittsfield, New Salem, **5 mi S** H, gas, food, lodging, Pine Lake Camping
20	IL 106, Barry, **S gas:** Phillips 66/dsl/24hr, Shell/dsl/24hr, **food:** Wendy's, **lodging:** Ice House Inn, **other:** antiques, winery
10	IL 96, to Payson, Hull
4a	I-172, N to Quincy
1	IL 106, to Hull
0mm	Illinois/Missouri state line, Mississippi River.
Exits 157 & 156 are in Missouri.	
157	to Hannibal, MO 179, **S gas:** Ayerco, BP, Phillips 66, Shell, **food:** Mark Twain Dinette, **lodging:** Hannibal Inn, Hotel Clemens, Super 7 Motel, Travelodge
156	US 61, New London, Palmyra. I-72 begins/ends in Hannibal, MO on US 61., **N gas:** BP, Conoco/dsl, **food:** Burger King, Country Kitchen, Golden Corral, Hardee's, Hunan Chinese, LJ Silver, McDonald's, Papa John's, Pizza Hut, Sonic, Taco Bell, **other:** Aldi Foods, BigLots, $General, $Tree, Ford, Kroger, Radio Shack, TrueValue, Walmart SuperCtr/gas/24hr, **0-2 mi S gas:** Ayerco, Shell/dsl, **food:** Cassano's Subs, DQ, Domino's, Hardee's, KFC, Loge's Rest, Wendy's, **lodging:** Comfort Inn, Days Inn, Econolodge, Hannibal Inn, Holiday Inn Express, Mark Twain Motel, Super 8, **other:** AutoZone, Buick/Chevrolet/Pontiac, County Mkt Foods, Family$, Injun Joe's RV Camp, O'Reilly Parts, Walgreens

SPRINGFIELD

INTERSTATE 74

Exit #	Services
221mm	Illinois/Indiana state line, Central/Eastern Time Zone
220	Lynch Rd, Danville, **N gas:** BP/dsl, Marathon (1mi),

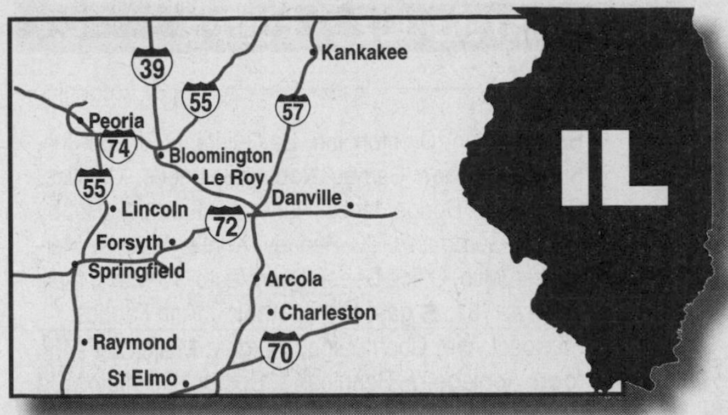

E ↕ W

DANVILLE

Exit #	Services
220	Continued **food:** Big Boy, **lodging:** Best Western, Comfort Inn, Danville Inn, Fairfield Inn, Hampton Inn, Holiday Inn Express, Sleep Inn, Super 8
216	Bowman Ave, Danville, **N gas:** Mobil/dsl/24hr, Phillips 66/dsl, **food:** Godfather's, KFC
215b a	US 150, IL 1, Gilbert St, Danville, **N gas:** Circle K, Harper/dsl, **food:** Arby's, Baskin-Robbins/Dunkin Donuts, El Toro, La Potosina, LJ Silver, McDonald's, Pizza Hut, Steak'n Shake, Subway, Taco Bell, **lodging:** Best Western, Days Inn, **other:** H, Aldi Foods, **S gas:** Casey's/dsl, Marathon/Circle K/dsl, **food:** Burger King, Green Jade Chinese, Mike's Grill, Monical's Pizza, **other:** AutoZone, Big R, Buick/Cadillac/Chevrolet/GMC/Pontiac, $General, Family$, Harley-Davidson, Forest Glen Preserve Camping (11mi), Toyota/Scion
214	G St, Tilton
210	US 150, MLK Dr, **2 mi N gas:** Marathon, **food:** Little Nugget Steaks, **other:** H, to Kickapoo SP, **S food:** PossumTrot Rest.
208mm	**Welcome Ctr wb, full ♿ facilities, info, ☎, picnic tables, litter barrels, vending, petwalk**
206	Oakwood, **S gas:** Phillips 66/Subway/dsl/scales, Casey's (1mi), **food:** McDonald's, Oaks Grill, Oakwood Rest.
200	IL 49 N, to Rankin
197	IL 49 S, Ogden, **S gas:** Phillips 66/dsl, **food:** Billy Bud's Steaks, Godfather's Pizza, **other:** city park
192	St Joseph, **S food:** DQ, Monical's Pizza, **other:** antiques
185	IL 130, University Ave
184	US 45, Cunningham Ave, Urbana, **N lodging:** Hanford Inn, **other:** Chrysler, Farm&Fleet, Honda, Hyundai, KIA, Mazda, Toyota/Scion, VW, **S gas:** Marathon/Circle K/Subway, Shell, **food:** Arby's, Cracker Barrel, Domino's, El Toro, Hickory River BBQ, McDonald's, Steak'n Shake/24hr, **lodging:** Eastland Suites, Motel 6, **other:** $General, Firestone/auto, Walgreens, Vet
183	Lincoln Ave, Urbana, **S gas:** Circle K/dsl, Marathon/Circle K/dsl, Mobil/dsl, **food:** Urbana Garden Rest., **lodging:** Comfort Suites, Holiday Inn/rest., Holiday Inn Express, Ramada Inn, Sleep Inn, Super 8, **other:** H, Harley-Davidson, to U of IL
182	Neil St, Champaign, **N food:** Alexander Steaks, Bob Evans, Chevy's Mexican, McDonald's, Olive Garden, Panera Bread, Taco Bell, Za's Italian, **lodging:**

INTERSTATE 74 CONT'D

E ↕ W — CHAMPAIGN

Exit #	Services
182	Continued Baymont Inn, Comfort Inn, La Quinta, Red Roof Inn, Super 8, **other:** Barnes&Noble, Bergner's, Cadillac/Chevrolet, Dodge/Jeep, Hancock Fabrics, Hobby Lobby, Gordman's, JC Penney, Kohl's, Macy's, Mercedes/Volvo, Office Depot, Sears/auto, TJ Maxx, mall, same as 181, **S gas:** Mobil, **other:** JoAnn Fabrics
181	Prospect Ave, Champaign, **N gas:** Meijer/dsl/24hr, **food:** Applebee's, Bennigan's, Boston's, Buffalo Wild Wings, Burger King, Cheddar's, Chili's, China Town, Culver's, Fazoli's, Panda Express, Penn Sta Subs, Quizno's, Red Lobster, Ruby Tuesday, Starbucks, Steak'n Shake/24hr, Subway, Taco Loco, Wendy's, **lodging:** Country Inn&Suites, Courtyard, Drury Inn, Extended Stay America, Fairfield Inn, Value Place Hotel, Wingate Inn, **other:** Advance Parts, Best Buy, Borders Books, $Tree, Lowe's Whse, Menard's, Michael's, Old Navy, PetsMart, Sam's Club/gas, Staples, Target, Tires+, Walmart SuperCtr/dsl, same as 182, **S gas:** Freedom/dsl, Marathon/Circle K, Mobil/Jimmy John's, **food:** Arby's, Dos Reales Mexican, Dunkin Donuts, KFC, LJ Silver, **lodging:** Days Inn, Econolodge, **other:** CarX, $General, Home Depot, NAPA, Tire Barn, RV/dsl repair, Walgreens
179b a	I-57, N to Chicago, S to Memphis
174	Lake of the Woods Rd, Prairieview Rd, **N gas:** BP/dsl, Casey's, Mobil/dsl, **food:** Hideaway Woods Cafe, **other:** Lake of the Woods SP, repair, **S gas:** Marathon/Subway/dsl, **food:** McDonald's
172	IL 47, Mahomet, **N other:** R&S RV Sales, **S gas:** BP, Mobil/dsl, Shell/Domino's/dsl, **food:** Azteca, Arby's, DQ, HenHouse Rest., Los Zarapes, Mahomet Pancake House, Monical's Pizza, Peking House, Subway, The Wok, **lodging:** Heritage Inn, **other:** Ace Hardware, Curves, CVS Drug, IGA Foods, NAPA, R&S RV Sales, Walgreens, Vet
166	Mansfield, **S gas:** BP, **other:** Mansfield Gen. Store/Rest.
159	IL 54, Farmer City, **S gas:** Casey's, Huck's/Quizno's/dsl, **food:** Family Rest., **lodging:** Budget Motel, Days Inn, **other:** NAPA, USPO, to Clinton Lake RA
156mm	**rest area both lanes, full ♿ facilities, ☎, picnic, litter larrels, vending, playground, petwalk**
152	US 136, to Heyworth
149	Le Roy, **N gas:** BP, Freedom, Love's/Arby's/dsl/scales/24hr, **food:** Jack's Cafe, KFC, McDonald's, Roma Ralph's Pizza, Subway, **lodging:** Holiday Inn Express, **other:** Doc's Drug, $General, IGA Foods, NAPA, True Value, to Moraine View SP, **S gas:** Shell/Woody's Rest./dsl/scales/24hr, **lodging:** Super 8, **other:** Clinton Lake, camping
142	Downs, **N gas:** BP/Pizza/Subs/dsl/24hr, **other:** USPO
135	US 51, Bloomington, **E gas:** BP/Circle K, EnergyMart/dsl, Freedom/dsl, Huck's, Mobil, Pilot/Wendy's/dsl/scales/24hr, Shell, TA/dsl/rest./scales/24hr/@, **food:** Arby's, Cracker Barrel, Culver's, KFC, La Bamba, McDonald's, Popeye's, Subway, Taco Bell, **lodging:** Best Inn, Days Inn, Econolodge, Hawthorn

BLOOMINGTON

Exit #	Services
135	Continued Suites, La Quinta, Quality Suites, **other:** H, Advance Parts, Blue Beacon, Family$, **W gas:** Marathon/Circle K, Murphy USA, **food:** Bob Evans, Fiesta Ranchera Mexican, Greatwall Chinese, Steak'n Shake/24hr, **lodging:** Comfort Suites, Country Inn&Suites, Fairfield Inn, Hampton Inn, Holiday Inn Express, Ramada Ltd, **other:** Aldi Foods, $Tree, F&F/dsl, Radio Shack, Walmart SuperCtr/24hr
134b	Veterans Pkwy, Bloomington, **N gas:** Clark, **other:** H, to ✈
134a	I-55, N to Chicago, S to St Louis, I-74 E
160ba [I-55]	**I-74 and I-55 run together 6 mi. N gas:** BP/Circle K, Freedom/dsl, Pilot/Wendy's/dsl/scales/24hr, Shell, EnergyMart/dsl, TA/dsl/rest./scales/24hr/@, **food:** Arby's, Burger King, Cracker Barrel, Culver's, KFC, McDonald's/playplace, Popeye's, Subway, Taco Bell, **lodging:** Best Inn, Comfort Inn, Days Inn, Econolodge, Hawthorn Suites, La Quinta, Quality Suites, **other:** H, Advance Parts, Blue Beacon, Family$, Morforless Foods, **S gas:** Marathon/Circle K, **food:** Bob Evan's, Greatwall Chinese, Steak'n Shake/24hr, **lodging:** Comfort Suites, Country Inn&Suites, Fairfield Inn, Holiday Inn Express, Ramada Ltd, **other:** Aldi Foods, $tree, F&F/dsl, Radio Shack, Walmart SuperCtr/gas/24hr
127[163]	I-55, N to Chicago, S to St Louis, I-74 W to Peoria
125	US 150, to Bloomington, Mitsubishi Motorway
123mm	**weigh sta wb**
122mm	**weigh sta eb**
120	Carlock, **N gas:** BP/dsl/repair, **S** Kamp Komfort Camping (Apr-Oct)
114.5mm	**rest area both lanes, full ♿ facilities, vending, ☎, picnic, litter barrels, petwalk**
113.5mm	Mackinaw River
112	IL 117, Goodfield, **N gas:** Shell/Subway/dsl, **food:** Busy Corner Rest., **other:** to Timberline RA, Jellystone Camping (1mi), Eureka Coll, Reagan Home
102b a	Morton, **N gas:** BP/rest/dsl, Casey's, Mobil/Arby's/dsl/scales/24hr, **food:** Burger King, Pizza Ranch, Cracker Barrel, Culver's, Ruby Tuesday, Steak'n Shake, Subway, Taco Bell, **lodging:** Best Western, Comfort Inn, Day's Inn, Quality Inn, Travelodge, **other:** Freightliner, Walmart SuperCtr, **S gas:** Circle K/gas, Shell/Subway/dsl/24hr, **food:** China Dragon, KFC, La Fiesta, Lin's Buffet, McDonald's, Monical's Pizza, Quizno's, **other:** Buick/GMC, Chrysler/Dodge/Jeep, CVS Drug, $Tree, Ford, K-Mart, Kroger
101	I-155 S, to Lincoln
99	I-474 W, ✈
98	Pinecrest Dr
96	95c (from eb), US 150, IL 8, E Washington St, E Peoria, **N gas:** Fast Stop, **food:** Monical's Pizza, **lodging:** Super 8, **other:** O'Reilly Parts
95b	IL 116, to Metamora, **N gas:** Shell/dsl, **food:** Burger King, **lodging:** Hampton Inn, Paradise Hotel, **other:** casino
95a	N Main St, Peoria, **S gas:** BP/24hr, **food:** A&W/LJ Silver, Bob Evans, China Buffet, Godfather's Pizza, Hardee's, Subway, **lodging:** Holiday Inn Express, Motel 6, **other:** Aldi Foods, Advance Parts, Curves,

IL

E ↕ W

INTERSTATE 74 CONT'D

Exit #	Services
95a	Continued CVS Drug, $General, Goodyear/auto, Kohls, Kroger, Walgreens, transmissions/auto repair
94	IL 40, RiverFront Dr, **S gas:** Hucks/Godfather's/24hr, **food:** Applebee's, Arby's, Buffalo Wild Wings, Chili's, Culver's, Logan's Roadhouse, Lorena'a Mexican, Ming's Rest., Panera Bread, Papa John's, Quizno's, Shlotzky's, Steak'n Shake, Texas Roadhouse, **lodging:** Embassy Suites, **other:** Lowe's Whse, PetsMart, Radio Shack, Walmart SuperCtr
93.5mm	Illinois River
93b	US 24, IL 29, Peoria, **N gas:** BP, **S** civic ctr
93a	Jefferson St, Peoria, **S food:** Chicago Grill, **lodging:** Holiday Inn, Mark Twain Hotel, **other:** to civic ctr
92	Glendale Ave, Peoria, **S other:** [H], downtown
92a	IL 40 N, Knoxville Ave, Peoria, **S lodging:** Holiday Inn, **other:** [H]
91	University St, Peoria
90	Gale Ave, Peoria, **S gas:** Marathon, **food:** Mikey's Pizza, **other:** to Bradley U
89	US 150, War Memorial Dr, Peoria, **N on War Memorial...gas:** BP/Circle K, **food:** Arby's, Avanti's Rest., Baskin-Robbins/Dunkin Donuts, Beef O'Brady's, Bob Evans, Cheddar's, Chevy's Mexican, ChuckeCheese, Hometown Buffet, IHOP, Krispy Kreme, Lonestar Steaks, Louie's Rest., McDonald's, Perkins/24hr, Pizza Hut, Red Lobster, Ruby Tuesday, Schlotsky's, Starbucks, Steak'n Shake, Subway, Wendy's, **lodging:** Baymont Inn, Best Western, Comfort Suites, Courtyard, Extended Stay America, Heritage Inn, Ramada, Red Roof Inn, Residence Inn, Sleep Inn, Springhill Suites, Super 8, **other:** AutoZone, Barnes&Noble, Best Buy, Chevrolet, Cub Foods, $Tree, Firestone, JC Penney, Lowe's Whse, Macy's, PetsMart, Pontiac/Cadillac, Sears/auto, Target, Tires+, U-Haul, Walmart, Walgreens, mall, Vet
88	to US 50, War Memorial Dr, same as ex 89
87b a	I-474 E, IL 6, N to Chillicothe, **E** [airport]
82	Edwards Rd, Kickapoo, **N gas:** Mobil/dsl/service, Shell/Subway/dsl, **food:** Jubilee Café, **other:** craft mall, to Jubilee Coll SP, **S other:** USPO, Wildlife Prairie SP
75	Brimfield, Oak Hill, **N gas:** Casey's
71	to IL 78, to Canton, Elmwood
62mm	**rest area both lanes, full [handicapped] facilities, [phone], [picnic], litter barrels, vending, petwalk**
61.5mm	Spoon River
54	IL 97, Lewistown, **N other:** TravL Park Camping (1mi), **S gas:** Mobil/dsl (2mi)
51	Knoxville, **S gas:** BP/dsl, Phillips 66/Charlie's Subs/dsl/scales, **food:** Hardee's/24hr, McDonald's, **lodging:** Super 8
48b a	E Galesburg, Galesburg, **N lodging:** Best Western, **other:** Harley-Davidson, **S gas:** Beck's, BP/Circle K, Mobil/dsl, Phillips 66, **food:** DQ, KFC, Hardee's, Jalisco Mexican, McDonald's, Pizza Hut, Subway, Taco Bell, **lodging:** Holiday Inn Express, **other:** Econo Foods, Family$, Firestone, Goodyear,

PEORIA

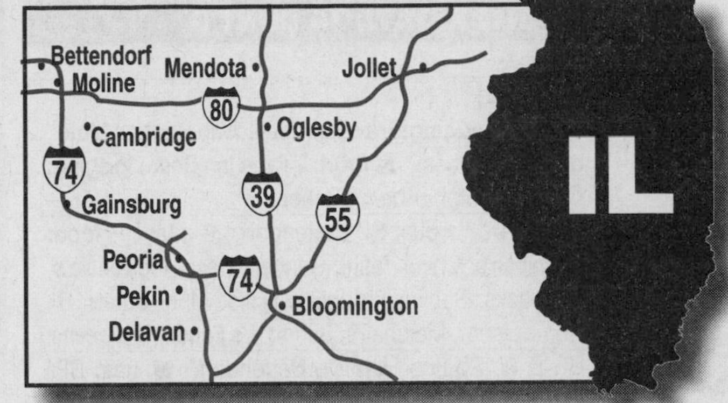

Exit #	Services
48b a	Continued HyVee Foods/gas, Save-A-Lot Foods, Walgreens, to Sandburg Birthplace, Lincoln-Douglas Debates
46b a	US 34, to Monmouth, **N other:** Nichol's dsl Service, **S other:** [H], **1 mi S food:** Buffalo Wild Wings, **other:** Menard's, Walmart SuperCtr
32	IL 17, Woodhull, **N gas:** BP/dsl, Shell/dsl/scales, **food:** Homestead Rest., Subway, **S other:** Shady Lakes Camping (8mi)
30mm	**rest area wb, full [handicapped] facilities, vending, [picnic], litter barrels, [phone], playground, petwalk, RV dump**
28mm	**rest area eb, full [handicapped] facilities, vending, [picnic], litter barrels, [phone], playground, petwalk, RV dump**
24	IL 81, Andover, **N gas:** Casey's (2mi), camping
14mm	I-80, E to Chicago, I-80/I-280 W to Des Moines
8mm	**weigh sta wb**
6mm	**weigh sta eb**
5b	US 6, Moline, **S gas:** Shell/dsl, **food:** McDonald's, MT Jack's, **lodging:** Best Inn, Country Inn&Suites, Days Inn, Econolodge, Hampton Inn, La Quinta, Quality Inn, Ramada Inn, **other:** [airport]
5a	I-280 W, US 6 W, to Des Moines
4b a	IL 5, John Deere Rd, Moline, **N gas:** BP, Phillips 66, Star Gas, **food:** Applebee's, Burger King, Carlos O'Kelly's, Culver's, Hungy Hobo, Panera Bread, Ryan's, Shoney's, Starbucks, Steak'n Shake, Subway, Wendy's, **other:** Cadillac, Curves, $Tree, Lowe's Whse, Radio Shack, Ryan's, Staples, Tires+, Toyota/Scion, Volvo, Walmart SuperCtr, **S gas:** BP, **food:** Arby's, Denny's, Dillard's, Garfield's Rest., Gordman's Rest., IHOP, Los Agaves Mexican, LJ Silver/A&W, Miss Mamie's, New Mandarin Chinese, Osaka Japanese, Taco Bell, Wendy's, **lodging:** Best Western, Comfort Inn, Fairfield Inn, Super 8, **other:** Best Buy, Chevrolet, $General, Firestone/auto, Ford/Lincoln/Mercury, Goodyear/auto, Hancock Fabrics, JC Penney, Old Navy, PetCo, Pontiac/Buick/GMC, Sears/auto, Von Maur, Walgreens, Younkers, mall
3	23rd Ave, Moline, **N lodging:** Economy Inn
2	7th Ave, Moline, **S gas:** Cenex, **other:** to civic ctr, riverfront
1	3rd Ave (from eb), Moline, **S gas:** Cenex, **lodging:** Stony Creek Inn
0mm	Illinois/Iowa state line, Mississippi River. **Exits 4-1 are in Iowa.**
4	US 67, Grant St, State St, Bettendorf, **N gas:** BP, Phillips 66/dsl, Shell, **food:** Ross' Rest./24hr,

MOLINE

IL

INTERSTATE 74 CONT'D

E ↕ W BETTENDORF

Exit #	Services
4	Continued Subway, **lodging:** Traveler Motel, Twin Bridges Motel, **other:** CarQuest, **S food:** Village Inn Rest., **lodging:** City Ctr Motel, **other:** $General
3	Middle Rd, Locust St, Bettendorf, **S gas:** BP, **food:** Bennigan's, China Taste, Grinders Rest., McDonald's, Starbucks, Subway, **lodging:** Holiday Inn, **other:** H, Home Depot, Marshall's, Schnuck's Foods, Walgreens
2	US 6 W, Spruce Hills Dr, Bettendorf, **N gas:** BP/dsl, Phillips 66, **food:** Domino's, Old Chicago Pizza, **lodging:** Courtyard, Heartland Inn, Ramada Inn, The Lodge Hotel/rest., **other:** U-Haul, **S food:** Applebee's, Burger King, Godfather's, KFC, Panera Bread, Red Lobster, Subway, **lodging:** Day's Inn, Fairfield Inn, La Quinta, **other:** Buick/Pontiac/GMC/Cadillac, Kohl's, Gander Mtn, Gordman's, Kohl's, Lowe's Whse, Sam's Club/gas, st patrol
1	53rd St, Hamilton, **N gas:** BP, **food:** Biaggi's Italian, Chili's, Granite City Rest., Red Robin, Ruby Tuesday, TX Roadhouse, **lodging:** Hampton Inn, Staybridge Suites, **other:** H, Borders Books, Harley-Davidson, HyVee Foods, Michael's, Old Navy, TJ Maxx, Walgreens, **S gas:** Phillips 66, **food:** Arby's, Azteca Mexican, China Cafe, DQ, Dynasty Buffet, El Sembrador Mexican, Golden Corral, Hungry Hobo, IHOP, Noodles & Co., Qdoba Mexican, Quizno's, Sonic, Starbucks, Steak'n Shake, Subway, TGIFriday's, Village Inn Rest., Taco Bell, Wendy's, **lodging:** Sleep Inn, **other:** Best Buy, Staples, Target, Walmart SuperCtr/gas
0mm	I-74 begins/ends on I-80, exit 298., **Exits 1-4 are in Iowa.**

INTERSTATE 80

E ↕ W — CHICAGO AREA

Exit #	Services
163mm	Illinois/Indiana state line
161	US 6, IL 83, Torrence Ave, **N gas:** BP, **food:** Burger King, Chili's, Culver's, Dixie Kitchen, Hooters, IHOP, Kenny's Ribs, Liang's Garden, New China Buffet, Oberweiss, Olive Garden, Shark's, Taco-Burrito's, Wendy's, **lodging:** Comfort Suites, Days Inn, Extended Stay America, Holiday Inn Express, Howard Johnson Express, Red Roof Inn, Sleep Inn, Super 8, **other:** Aldi Foods, AT&T, Best Buy, CarEx, Chrysler/Jeep, Curves, $General, $Tree, Dunkin Donuts, Fannie May Candies, Firestone/auto, Home Depot, Honda, JustTires, K-Mart, PepBoys, Radio Shack, Ultra Foods, Walmart SuperCtr **S gas:** Citgo, Marathon, Mobil, **food:** China Chef, Burger King, DQ, Dunkin Donuts, Jonny's K's Cafe, McDonald's/playplace, Mr Gyros, Popolono's Italian, Subway, **lodging:** Pioneer Motel, **other:** Chevrolet, PetsMart, Saab, SunRise Foods, Tuesday Morning, Walgreens, Vet
160b	I-94 W, to Chicago, tollway begins wb, ends eb
160a	IL 394 S, to Danville
159mm	Oasis, **gas:** Mobil/dsl, **food:** McDonald's, Panda Express, Starbucks, Subway
157	IL 1, Halsted St, **N gas:** Citgo/dsl, Marathon/dsl, **food:** Burger King, **lodging:** Chicago Southland
157	Continued Hotel, Clarion, Comfort Inn, Comfort Suites, EconoLodge, Regency Inn, **S gas:** Citgo, Delta Sonic, Shell, Speedway, **food:** Applebee's, Athens Gyros, Arby's, Boston Mkt, Burger King, Chili's, Dunkin Donuts, Fannie May Candies, KFC, McDonald's, Panda Express, Pizza Hut, Popeye's, Starbucks, Subway, Taco Bell, Washington Square Rest., Wendy's, White Castle, **lodging:** Homewood Hotel, Super 8, **other:** Aldi Foods, AT&T, Best Buy, Chevrolet, Discount Tire, $Tree, Fanny May Candies, Firestone/auto, Goodyear/auto, Home Depot, Jewel-Osco, Jo-Ann Fabrics, K-Mart, Kohl's, Menards, PepBoys, PetCo, Radio Shack, Target, TJ Maxx, Walgreens
156	Dixie Hwy (from eb, no return), **S gas:** Mobil, **food:** Leona's Rest., **other:** golf
155	I-294 N, Tri-State Tollway, toll plaza
154	Kedzie Ave (from eb, no return), **N gas:** Speedway, **S** H
151b a	I-57 (exits left from both directions), N to Chicago, S to Memphis
148b a	IL 43, Harlem Ave, **N gas:** Speedway/dsl, **food:** Al's Beef, Buffalo Wild Wings, Burger King, Cracker Barrel, Culver's, Dunkin Donuts, Eggi Grill, Hamada of Japan, Pop's Italian Beef, Quizno's, Taco Fresco, Tin Fish Grill, Wendy's, **lodging:** Comfort Suites, Fairfield Inn, Hampton Inn, Holiday Inn, La Quinta, Sleep Inn, Wingate Inn, **S food:** Arby's, Boston's Grill, Subway, Taco Bell, TGIFriday's, **other:** Best Buy, Carmax, Kohl's, Michael's, PetsMart, SuperTarget, ampitheater
147.5mm	**weigh sta wb**
145b a	US 45, 96th Ave, **N food:** Arby's, Arrenello's Pizza, Baskin-Robbins/Dunkin Donuts, 4K Asian, Quizno's, Tokyo Steaks, TX Roadhouse, **lodging:** Country Inn&Suites, Hilton Garden, **other:** Harley-Davidson, **0-2 mi S gas:** BP, Clark, Gas City, Shell/Circle K/dsl/24hr, **food:** A&W, Applebee's, Beggar's Pizza, DQ, Denny's, KFC, Mindy's Ribs, Nick's Rest., Rising Sun Chinese, Stoney Pt Grill, Subway, White Castle, Wendy's, **lodging:** Super 8, **other:** Brookhaven Foods, CVS Drug, Tuesday Morning, repair
143mm	**weigh sta eb**
140	SW Hwy, I 355 N Tollway, US 6 S
137	US 30, New Lenox, **N food:** Williamson's Rest., **other:** K-Mart, **S gas:** Speedway/dsl, **food:** Beggar's Pizza, Burger King, KFC, LJ Silver/Papa Joe's, McDonald's/playplace, Paisono's Pizza, Pizza Hut, Subway, Taco Bell, **other:** Ace Hardware, Goodyear/auto, Jewel-Osco/dsl, Walgreens, city park, Vet
134	Briggs St, **N gas:** Citgo, Speedway, **other:** H, **S gas:** Shell/dsl, Valero/dsl, **other:** EZ Lube, Martin Camping, US RV Ctr
133	Richards St
132b a	US 52, IL 53, Chicago St
131.5mm	Des Plaines River
131	US 6, Meadow Ave, **N** to Riverboat Casino
130b a	IL 7, Larkin Ave, **N gas:** Clark, Delta Sonic/dsl, Marathon/24hr, Mobil, Shell/24hr, Speedway, **food:** A&W/KFC, Baskin-Robbins/Dunkin Donuts, Boston Mkt, Bellagio Pizzaria, Bob Evans, Burger King,

IL

INTERSTATE 80 CONT'D

E ↕ W

Exit #	Services
130b a	Continued DQ, JJ Fish&Chicken, McDonald's, Quizno's, Steak'n Shake, Subway, Taco Bell, Wendy's, White Castle, **lodging:** Budget Inn, Comfort Inn, Holiday Inn, Motel 6, Red Roof Inn, Super 8, **other:** [H], Aldi Foods,
130b a	Continued Cadillac/Chevrolet, Discount Tire, Ford, Goodyear/auto, K-Mart, Pepboys, Radio Shack, Sam's Club/gas, 7-11, to Coll of St Francis, Vet, **S gas:** Citgo, **other:** auto repair
127	Houbolt Rd, to Joliet, **N gas:** BP/deli, 7-11, **food:** Arby's, Burger King, China Kitchen, Cracker Barrel, Dunkin Donuts, Heros Sports Grill, Jimmy John's, McDonald's, Papa&Nana's Pizza, **lodging:** Fairfield Inn, Hampton Inn, Ramada Inn, **other:** Riverboat Casino
126b a	I-55, N to Chicago, S to St Louis
125.5mm	Du Page River
122	Minooka, **N gas:** Citgo/dsl/24hr, **S gas:** BP/24hr, Pilot/Arby's/scales/dsl/24hr, **food:** Baskin-Robbins/Dunkin Donuts, Gino Angelo's Pizza, KFC/LJ Silver, McDonald's/playplace, Subway, Taco Bell, Wendy's, **other:** $General, 7-11
119mm	**rest area wb, full [handicapped] facilities, vending, [phone], [picnic], litter barrels, playground, petwalk**
117mm	**rest area eb, full [handicapped] facilities, vending, [phone], [picnic], litter barrels, playground, petwalk**
112	IL 47, Morris, **N gas:** Marathon/dsl, TA/BP/Quizno's/scales/dsl/24hr/@, **food:** Bellacino's, Chili's, IHOP, **lodging:** Comfort Inn, Days Inn, Holiday Inn Express, Quality Inn, **other:** $General, Menards, **S gas:** BP, Mobil, Phillips 66, Shell/24hr, **food:** Burger King, Culver's, DQ, Dunkin Donuts, Hong Kong Chinese, KFC/LJ Silver, Maria's Ristorante, McDonald's, Morris Diner, Pizza Hut, Rosati's Pizza, Taco Bell, Wendy's, **lodging:** Park Motel, Sherwood Oaks Motel, Super 8, **other:** Aldi Foods, AT&T, Big R Store, Buick/Cadillac/Chevrolet, Curves, Fisher Parts, Ford, GMC/Pontiac, Jewel-Osco, Morris Drug, Radio Shack, Verizon, Walgreens, Walmart SuperCtr/Subway/24hr, to Stratton SP, transmissions/repair
105	to Seneca
97	to Marseilles, **S food:** Taco Time, **other:** Four Star Camping, Glenwood Camping (4mi), to Illini SP, RV camping
93	IL 71, Ottawa, **N gas:** Mobil/24hr, Shell/dsl/24hr, **other:** Skydive Chicago RV Park (2mi), **S food:** Hank's Farm Rest., **other:** [H]
92.5mm	Fox River
90	IL 23, Ottawa, **N gas:** BP/Subway, **food:** Arby's, Cracker Barrel, Quizno's, Taco Bell, **lodging:** Hampton Inn, Holiday Inn Express, **other:** AT&T, F&F, Ford/KIA/Lincoln/Mercury, Honda, Toyota/Scion, Verizon, Walmart SuperCtr/McDonald's, **S gas:** BP/dsl/LP, Thornton's/dsl **food:** Dunkin Donuts, KFC/LJ Silver, Papa Murphy's, **lodging:** Comfort Inn, Sands Motel (2mi), Super 8, Surrey Motel, **other:** [H], Aldi Foods, $Tree, Harley-Davidson, Kroger, Radio Shack

Exit #	Services
81	IL 178, Utica, **N gas:** Loves/McDonald's/Subway/dsl/scales/24hr, **other:** Hickory Hollow Camping, KOA (2mi), **S gas:** Shell/Jimmy Johns/dsl, **food:** Duffy's Tavern (2mi), **lodging:** Starved Rock Inn, **other:** to Starved Rock SP, repair
79b a	I-39, US 51, N to Rockford, S to Bloomington
77.5mm	Little Vermilion River
77	IL 351, La Salle, **S gas:** ***FLYING J***/Country Mkt/dsl/scales/24hr, **food:** UpTown Grill (3mi), **lodging:** Daniels Motel (1mi), **other:** st police
75	IL 251, Peru, **N gas:** BP, Shell/dsl/rest./24hr, **food:** Arby's, McDonald's, Quizno's, Starbucks, Taco Bell, **lodging:** Baymont Inn, Holiday Inn Express, Kings Inn, Super 8, **other:** Kohl's, Walmart/SuperCtr/Dunkin Donuts/Subway, flea mkt, **S gas:** BP, Phillips 66, Shell, **food:** Applebee's, Burger King, Culver's, DQ, IHOP, Master Stir Fry, McDonald's, Mi Margarita, Papa John's, Pizza Hut, Red Lobster, Steak'n Shake, Subway, Wendy's, **lodging:** Fairfield Inn, La Quinta, **other:** [H], AutoZone, BigLots, Buick/Cadillac/GMC/Pontiac, Chevrolet/Mercedes/Nissan, Chrysler/Dodge/Jeep, CVS Drug, $Tree, Goodyear/auto, Hobby Lobby, Home Depot, Hyundai, HyVee Food/gas, JC Penney, Jewel Foods, K-Mart, Marshall's, Menards, Mitsubishi, Sears/auto, Staples, Target, Verizon, Walgreens
73	Plank Rd, **N gas:** Sapp Bros/Burger King/dsl/scales/@, **food:** Big Apple Rest., **other:** Kenworth, Volvo Trucks, camping
70	IL 89, to Ladd, **N gas:** Casey's, **S gas:** BP (3mi), Shell (3mi), **lodging:** Spring Valley Motel, **other:** [H]
61	I-180, to Hennepin
56	IL 26, Princeton, **N gas:** Road Ranger/Pilot/Stuckey's/scales/dsl/@, **lodging:** Super 8, **S gas:** Beck's, Shell/dsl, **food:** Big Apple Rest., Burger King, Coffee Cup Rest., Country Kitchen, Culver's, KFC, McDonald's, Wendy's, **lodging:** Americinn, Days Inn, Econolodge, Princeton Motel, **other:** [H], AutoZone, Buick/Cadillac/Chevrolet/Pontiac, $General, O'Reilly Parts, Pennzoil, Sullivan's Food/gas, Walmart SuperCtr, antiques, Vet
51mm	**rest area both lanes, full [handicapped] facilities, [phone], [picnic], litter barrels, vending, playground, petwalk, RV dump**
45	IL 40, **N other:** to Ronald Reagan Birthplace (21mi), antiques, **S other:** Hennepin Canal SP, camping
44mm	Hennepin Canal
33	IL 78, to Kewanee, Annawan, **N gas:** Shabbona RV Ctr/Camp (3mi), **S gas:** Cenex, FS/dsl/e-85,

JOLIET — OTTAWA — PERU

INTERSTATE 80 CONT'D

Exit #	Services
33	Continued Shell/dsl, **food:** Burbons Rest., **lodging:** Best Western, **other:** to Johnson-Sauk Tr SP
27	to US 6, Atkinson, **N gas:** Casey's (1mi), Mobil/dsl/24hr
19	IL 82, Geneseo, **N gas:** BP, Phillips 66/dsl/scales/24hr, **food:** Culvers, DQ, Hardee's, Happy Joe's Pizza, McDonald's, Pizza Hut, Quizno's, Sweet Pea's Grill, Subway, **lodging:** Amerihost, Super 8 (1mi), **other:** [H], $General, Ford, Verizon, Walgreens, Walmart/drugs, Vet
10	I-74, I-280, W to Moline, E to Peoria
9	US 6, to Geneseo, **N food:** Lavender Crest Winery/Cafe, **S other:** Niabi Zoo
7	Colona, **N gas:** Shell/dsl, **food:** Country Fixins Rest.
5mm	Rock River
4a	IL 5, IL 92, W to Silvis, **S other:** to Quad City Downs, Lundeen's Camping
4b	I-88, IL 92, E to Rock Falls
2mm	**weigh sta both lanes**
1.5mm	**Welcome Ctr eb, full [handicapped] facilities, info, [phone], [picnic], litter barrels, petwalk, scenic overlook**
1	IL 84, 20th St, Great River Rd, E Moline, **N gas:** BP/diesel, Git-Go, **food:** Brothers Rest., **other:** auto repair, camping, The Great River Rd, **3 mi S gas:** BP, **other:** camping
0mm	Illinois/Iowa state line, Mississippi River

INTERSTATE 88

Exit #	Services
139.5mm	I-88 begins/ends on I-290.
139	I-294, S to Indiana, N to Milwaukee
138mm	toll plaza
137	IL 83 N, Cermak Rd, **N food:** Clubhouse rest., Ditkas Rest., McDonald's, **lodging:** Marriott, Renaissance Inn, **other:** Barnes&Noble, Lord&Taylor, Macy's, Nieman-Marcus
136	IL 83 S, Midwest Rd (from eb), **N gas:** Shell/Circle K, **food:** All-Stars Rest., Burger King, Capri Ristorante, Chipotle Mexican, Denny's, Dunkin Donuts, Eggstacy, Giordano's Rest., Jamba Juice, McDonalds, Noodles&Co, Quizno's, Redstones, Starbucks, Subway, Subway, **lodging:** Holiday Inn, La Quinta, **other:** AT&T, Costco/gas, Home Depot, Nordstrom's, Old Navy, TJ Maxx, Walgreens, World Mkt
134	Highland Ave (no EZ wb return), **N food:** Baker's Square, Bennigan's, Bouna Beef, Brio Grille, Buca Italian, Burger King, Capital Grille, Champps Grill, Cheeseburger Paradise, Cici's, Claimjumper Rest., Fuddruckers, Harry Caray's, Hooters, Joe's Crabshack, Kona Grill, Kyoto, McCormick & Schmick's, Miller's Steakhouse, Olive Garden, Panera Bread, PF Chang's, Portilo's Hotdogs, Potbelly's, Qdoba, Red Lobster, Rockbottom Brewery, Ruby Tuesday, Starbucks, Subway, Taylor Brewing Co, TGIFriday's, Uncle Milio's, Weber Grill, **lodging:** Comfort Inn, Embassy Suites, Holiday Inn Express,
134	Continued Homestead Studios, Hyatt Place, Marriott, Red Roof Inn, Westin Hotel, **other:** [H], Best Buy, Firestone/auto, Home Depot, JC Penney, Kohl's, Marshall's, PetsMart, Vonmaur, mall, **S food:** Parkers Ocean Grill
132	I-355 N (from wb)
131	I-355 S (from eb)
130	IL 53 (from wb), **1 mi N gas:** BP, Mobil, **food:** McDonald's, **other:** Walmart
127	Naperville Rd, **N food:** Mullen's Grill, **lodging:** Hilton, Wyndam, **S gas:** Mobil, **food:** Buona Beef, Froots, HoneyBaked Ham, Jason's Deli, Maggiano's, McDonald's, Morton's Steaks, Pizza Hut, Subway, Taco Fresco, TGIFriday's, Wendy's, White Chocolate Grill, **lodging:** Best Western, Courtyard, Days Inn, Fairfield Inn, Hampton Inn, Holiday Inn Select, **other:** Dodge, Ford, Kia, Office Depot, Radio Shack, Subaru
125	Winfield Rd, **N gas:** BP, Mobil, **lodging:** Hamton Inn, **other:** [H], Walgreens, **S food:** Arby's, Atlanta Bread, Buffalo Wild Wings, CA Pizza Kitchen, Chipotle Mexican, Corner Bakery Cafe, GoRoma, Jamba Juice, Max&Erma's, McDonald's, Potbelly's, Red Robin, Rockbottom Brewery, Starbucks, StirCrazy Grill, **lodging:** Hilton Garden, Springhill Suites, **other:** SuperTarget
123	IL 59, **N gas:** Gas City/dsl, **food:** Omega Rest, **other:** Carmax, **S gas:** BP, Mobil/dsl, Speedway, **food:** Baskin Robbins/Dunkin Donuts, Caribou Coffee, Cracker Barrel, Danny's Grill, Jimmy John's, Lee's Garden, Oberweis, Spicy Pickle, Starbucks, Steak'n Shake, Subway, TX Roadhouse, Wendy's, **lodging:** Extended Stay America, Fairfield Inn, Red Roof Inn, Sleep Inn, SpringHill Suites, Towneplace Suites, **other:** CVS Drug, 7-11, Walgreens
119	Farnsworth Ave, **N gas:** BP, Shell, **food:** McDonald's, Millet's Grill, Papa Bear Rest., Quizno's, Sonic, Starbucks, **lodging:** Fox Valley Inn, Motel 6, **other:** Firestone/auto, Premium Outlets/Famous Brands, Walmart SuperCtr, **S gas:** Marathon, Phillips 66/dsl, Shell, Speedway, **food:** Baskin-Robbins/Dunkin Donuts, Drive-Thru, Little Caesars, McDonald's, Mike&Denise's Pizza, Subway, Taco Bell, **other:** AutoZone, Family$, Goodyear, 7-11, Walgreens
118mm	toll plaza
117	IL 31, IL 56, to Aurora, Batavia, **N gas:** Citgo/dsl, **food:** A&W, **other:** 7-11, **S gas:** Mobil, Thornton's, **food:** Arby's, Baskin-Robbins/Dunkin Donuts, Burger King, Culver's, Denny's, KFC, LJ Silver, McDonald's, Nikary's, Rest., Popeye's, Quizno's, Subway, Taco Bell, White Castle, **lodging:** Baymont Inn, **other:** [H], Ace Hardware, AutoZone, Cermak Foods, $Store, Firestone, GNC, Jewel/Osco, Murray's Parts, Radio Shack, U-Haul, Walgreens
115	Orchard Rd, **N food:** McDonald's, Subway, **other:** Best Buy, Chrysler/Dodge/Jeep, Ford/Lincoln/Mercury, Hyundai, JC Penney, Michaels, Nissan, PetCo, Subaru, Target, Woodman's/dsl, **0-2 mi S gas:** 7-11, **food:** A&W/KFC, Arby's, Buffalo Wild Wings, Chili's, Cold Stone, IHOP, Jimmy John's, Panera Bread,

INTERSTATE 88 CONT'D

Exit #	Services
115	Continued Papa Saverio's, Pizza Hut, Quizno's, Starbucks, Wendy's, **lodging:** Candlewood Suites, Hampton Inn, Holiday Inn, **other:** AT&T, CVS Drug, Discount Tire, Home Depot, Lowe's Whse, Office Depot, T-Moble
114	IL 56W, to US 30 (from wb, no EZ return), to Sugar Grove
109	IL 47 (from eb), Elburn
94	Peace Rd, to IL 38, **N** [H]
93mm	Dekalb Oasis/24hr both lanes, Dekalb Oasis/24hr both lanes, **gas:** Mobil/dsl, **food:** McDonald's, Panda Express, Subway
92	IL 38, IL 23, Annie Glidden Rd, to DeKalb, **N lodging:** Super 8, **2-3 mi N gas:** BP, Road Ranger/dsl, Marathon, Shell, **food:** Aldorado, Baskin-Robbins, Blackstone Rest, Burger King, Chipotle Mexican, El Burrito Loco, Gyro's, Happy Wok Chinese, Jct Rest., KFC, LJ Silver, Lukulo's Rest., McDonald's, Molly's Eatery, Pagliai's Pizza, Pancake Rest., Panda Express, Papa John's, Potbelly, Pizza Hut, Pizza Pros, Pizza Villa, Quizno's, Starbucks, Subway, Taco Bell, Tom&Jerry's, Topper's Pizza, Vinny's Pizza, Wendy's, **lodging:** Best Western, Magneson Inn, Travelodge, **other:** $General, Ford, Illini Tire, Schnuck's Food/Drug, Walgreens, to N IL U
86mm	toll plaza
78	I-39, US 51, S to Bloomington, N to Rockford
76	IL 251, Rochelle, **N gas:** BP, Casey's, Shell, **food:** Olive Branch Rest., **other:** [H], Ford/Mercury, GMC, tires/repair
56mm	toll plaza
54	IL 26, Dixon, **N gas:** BP/Subway/scales/dsl, Murphy USA/dsl, **food:** Panda Chinese, Pizza Hut, **lodging:** Comfort Inn, Quality Inn, Super 8, **other:** $Tree, Verizon, Walmart/Super Ctr/24hr, **1-2 mi N food:** Culver's, Hardee's, **other:** [H], to Ronald Reagan Birthplace, to John Deere HS, to St Parks
44	US 30 (last free exit eb), **N** gas, food, lodging, **other:** Leisure lake RV Ctr (2mi)
41	IL 40, to Sterling, Rock Falls, **1-2 mi N gas:** Marathon, Mobil/dsl, Shell, **food:** American Grill, Arby's, Arthur's Deli, Bennigan's, Burger King, Candlelight Rest., Culver's, El Tapatio Mexican, First Wok Chinese, Gazi's Rest., Hardee's, KFC, McDonald's/playplace, Perna's Pizza, Pizza Hut, Red Apple Rest., Subway, **lodging:** All Seasons Motel, Candlelight Inn, Country Inn&Suites, Holiday Inn, Super 8, **other:** [H], AutoZone, Country Mkt Foods, Curves, $General, Harley-Davidson, O'Reilly Parts, Sav-a-Lot, Walgreens, Walmart
36	to US 30, Rock Falls, Sterling
26	IL 78, to Prophetstown, Morrison, **N other:** to Morrison-Rockwood SP
18	to Albany, Erie
10	to Port Byron, Hillsdale, **S gas:** Phillips 66/dsl, Shell/Mama J's Rest./scales/dsl/24hr,
6	IL 92 E, to Joslin, **N food:** Jammerz Roadhouse (2mi), **S other:** Sunset Lake Camping (1mi)
2	Former IL 2
1b a	I-80, W to Des Moines, E to Chicago
0mm	I-88 begins/ends on I-80, exit 4b. IL 5, IL 92, W to Silvis, to Quad City Downs, Lundeen's Camping

DEKALB

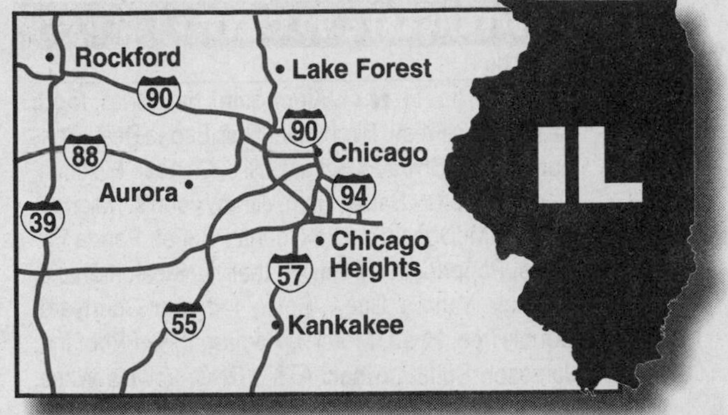

INTERSTATE 90

Exit #	Services
0mm	Illinois/Indiana state line, Chicago Skyway Toll Rd begins/ends
1mm	US 12, US 20, 106th St, Indianapolis Blvd, **N gas:** Citgo, Mobil, Shell/dsl, **other:** casino, **S food:** Burger King, KFC, McDonald's, **other:** Aldi Foods, Jewel-Osco, auto repair
2.5mm	**gas:** Skyway Oasis, **food:** McDonald's, **other:** toll plaza
3mm	87th St (from wb)
4mm	79th St, services along 79th St and Stoney Island Ave
5.5mm	73rd St (from wb)
6mm	State St (from wb), **S gas:** Citgo
7mm	I-94 N (mile markers decrease to IN state line)
I-90 E and I-94 E run together. See Interstate 94 Exits 43b - 59a.	
84	I-94 **W** Lawrence Ave, **N gas:** BP
83b a	Foster Ave (from wb), **N gas:** BP, **food:** Checker's, Dunkin Donuts, **other:** Firestone/auto, Goodyear/auto, Walgreen
82c	Austin Ave, to Foster Ave
82b	Byrn-Mawr (from wb)
82a	Nagle Ave
81b	Sayre Ave (from wb)
81a	IL 43, Harlem Ave, **S gas:** BP, Shell
80	Canfield Rd (from wb), **N other:** Walgreen
79b a	IL 171 S, Cumberland Ave, **N gas:** 7-11, Marathon, **food:** Hooters, McDonald's, Outback Steaks, Starbucks, **lodging:** Holiday Inn, Marriott, SpringHill Suites, Westin Hotel, **other:** Dominick's Foods, **S food:** Bennigan's, **lodging:** Ramada, Renaissance
0mm	River Road Plaza, **N food:** McDonald's, **lodging:** Marriott, Westin Hotel, **S** Hyatt (mile markers increase to Rockford)
1mm	I-294, I-190 W, to O'Hare [airport]
2mm	IL 72, Lee St (from wb), **N lodging:** Extended Stay America, Quality Inn, Wyndham, **S food:** McDonald's, **lodging:** Best Western, Holiday Inn Express, Holiday Inn Select, Sheraton Gateway, Studio+
5mm	**Des Plaines Oasis both lanes, gas:** Mobil/dsl/24hr, **food:** McDonald's/24hr, Panda Express, Starbucks, Subway
6mm	Elmhurst Rd (from wb), **S gas:** Shell, **food:** McDonald's, **lodging:** Best Western, Comfort Inn, Days Inn, La Quinta, Microtel, Motel 6

CHICAGO AREA

E ↕ W

CHICAGO AREA

INTERSTATE 90 CONT'D

Exit #	Services
7.5mm	Arlington Hts Rd, **N on Algonquin...gas:** Shell, **food:** Arby's, Baja Fresh, Birch River Grill, Buona Beef, Caribou Coffee, Chicago Pizza, Chili's, Chipotle Mexican, Denny's, Honey Baked Ham, Jimmy John's, Magnum Steaks, McDonald's, Old Country Buffet, Panda Express, Pappadeaux Rest., Potbelly's, Steak'n Shake, Subway, Yanni's Greek Rest., **lodging:** Courtyard, DoubleTree, Hyatt, Motel 6, Radisson, Red Roof Inn, Jameson Suites, **other:** AT&T, GNC, Lowe's Whse, Meijer, NTB, Sam's Club, Staples, Walmart, Vet, **S gas:** Mobil, Shell, **food:** Subway, **lodging:** Sheraton
11mm	I-290, IL 53, **N lodging:** Embassy Suites, Holiday Inn, Renaissance Inn, **other:** mall, **1 mi S food:** Houlihan's, Joe's Crabshack, Olive Garden, Ruby Tuesday, TGI Friday's, **lodging:** Extended Stay America, Hyatt, Residence Inn, **other:** Firestone, JC Penney, Macy's
13mm	Roselle Rd (from wb), **N other:** Medieval Times, **S gas:** Mobil, **food:** Bahama Breeze, Boston Mkt, Caribou Coffee, Denny's, Fox&Hound, Fuddrucker's, KFC, Outback Steaks, Subway, Wendy's, **lodging:** Country Inn&Suites, Extended Stay America, Homestead Suites, **other:** BMW/Mini, Carmax, Firestone, Hancock Fabrics, Lexus, Michael's, Office Depot, PetCo, 7-11, TJ Maxx
16mm	Barrington Rd (from wb), **N food:** Apple Villa Pancake House, Hunan Beijing, Jimmy John's, La Strada Ristorante, Millrose Rest., Quizno's, Subway, **lodging:** Hilton Garden, **S gas:** BP, Shell, **food:** Chili's, IHOP, McDonald's, Starbucks, Steak'n Shake, TGI Friday's, **lodging:** Comfort Inn, Hampton Inn, Hyatt Place, La Quinta, Red Roof Inn, **other:** U-Haul
19mm	IL 59, **N food:** Buffalo Wild Wings, Caribou Coffee, Chipotle Mexican, Claim Jumper Rest., Cooper's Hawk Rest., Hasta la Pasta, Jimmy John's, Moe's SW Grill, Noodles&Co, Panda Express, Potbelly's, Red Robin, Ruth's Chris Steaks, Subway, **lodging:** Marriott, **other:** AT&T, Cabela's, CVS Drug, Michael's, PetsMart, Target, TJ Maxx, to Poplar Creek Music Theatre
21mm	Beverly Rd (from wb)
22mm	IL 25, **N lodging:** Days Inn, **S gas:** BP, Citgo, Shell, Speedway/dsl, **food:** Arby's, Baker Hill Pancakes, Subway, Wendy's, **other:** [H], Advance Parts, NAPA
24mm	IL 31 N, **N gas:** BP, Speedway, **food:** Alexander's Rest., Baskin-Robbins/Dunkin Donuts, Bennigan's, **lodging:** Courtyard, Hampton Inn, Holiday Inn, Quality Inn, Super 8, TownePlace Suites
25mm	toll plaza, [phone]
27mm	Randall Rd, **N food:** Big Sammy's Hot Dogs, Burnt Toast, Cafe Roma, Froots, Henessey Rest., Jimmy John's, Jimmy's Charhouse, Panera Bread, Rookies Grill, Starbucks, Village Pizza, **lodging:** Comfort Inn, Country Inn&Suites, **other:** Honda, **S gas:** 7-11, **lodging:** Candlewood Suites, **other:** [H]
32mm	IL 47 (from wb), to Woodstock, **N other:** Prime Outlets/famous brands, Chevrolet, Ford
37mm	US 20, Marengo, **N gas:** Citgo/Arrowhead Rest/dsl/scales/24hr, Pilot/Subway/dsl/scales/24hr, TA/BP/Burger King/Popeye's/scales/dsl/24hr/@, **food:** McDonald's, Wendy's, **lodging:** Super 8, **other:** Chevrolet, Ford, museums, to Prime Outlets at exit 32 (6mi)
41mm	Marengo toll plaza (from eb)
53mm	Genoa Rd, to Belvidere, **N gas:** Murphy USA, **food:** Applebee's, Quizno's, Rosati's Pizza, Starbucks, Subway, Thai Basil, **other:** Verizon, Walmart SuperCtr, camping
55mm	**Belvidere Oasis both lanes, gas:** Mobil/dsl/24hr, **food:** Food Court, Kronos Cafe, McDonald's/24hr, Panda Express, Starbucks, Subway, Taco Bell, [phone]
56mm	toll plaza
60.5mm	Kishwaukee River
61mm	I-39 S, US 20, US 51, to Rockford, **S** funpark
63mm	US 20, State St, **N gas:** Mobil/dsl, Phillips 66/Subway/dsl, **food:** Cracker Barrel, **lodging:** Baymont Inn, Clocktower Best Western Resort, Days Inn, **S gas:** Mobile/dsl, Road Ranger/dsl, **food:** Applebee's, BD Mongolian Grill, Buffalo Wild Wings, Burger King, Cheddar's, Chili's, Culver's, Denny's, Dos Reales,Gerry's Pizza, Giovanni's Rest., Hong Kong Buffet, IHOP, Japanese Express, KFC/LJ Silver, Lino's Pizza, LoneStar Steaks, Machine Shed Rest, McDonald's, Old Chicago Grill, Old Country Buffet, Olive Garden, Outback Steaks, Panino's Drive-Thru, Perkins, Pizza Hut/Taco Bell, PotBelly, Quizno's, Red Lobster, Red Robin, Royal Dragon, Ruby Tuesday, Starbucks, Steak'n Shake, Subway, ThunderBay Grille, Tom & Jerry's, Tumbleweed Grill, TX Roadhouse, Uncle Nick's, Wendy's, **lodging:** Candlewood Suites, Comfort Inn, Courtyard, Extended Stay America, Fairfield Inn, Hampton Inn, Hilton Garden, Holiday Inn, Motel 6, Quality Suites, Radisson, Red Roof Inn, Residence Inn, Sleep Inn, Staybridge Suites, Studio+, Super 8, **other:** [H], Advance Parts, Aldi Foods, Best Buy, Borders Books, Buick/GMC/Pontiac, Discount Tire, Dodge, $Tree, Gordman's, Hancock Fabrics, Hobby Lobby, Home Depot, Jo-Ann Fabrics, K-Mart, Kohl's, Lexus, Lowe's Whse, Marshall's, Michael's, Office Depot, Old Time Pottery, Old Navy, PepBoys, PetCo, Petsmart, Radio Shack, Sam's Club/gas, Target, Toyota/Scion, Tuesday Morning, Walgreens, Walmart SuperCtr
66mm	E Riverside Blvd, Loves Park, **1-2 mi S gas:** Mobil/dsl, Phillips 66/dsl, Road Ranger/Pilot/Subway/dsl, Shell, **food:** Arby's, BeefARoo, Ciaobella, Culver's, DQ, Domino's, Happy Joe's Pizza, Japanese Express, KFC, McDonald's, Sam's Ristorante, 2nd Cousin's Grill, Singapore Grill, Subway, Waffle Shop, Wendy's, **lodging:** Holiday Inn Express, Quality Inn, **other:** Audi/Honda/Jaguar/Mercedes, Autowerks, Farm&Fleet, Walgreens, to Rock Cut SP, funpark
70mm	Il 173, **S** to Rock Cut SP
75.5mm	tollbooth, [phone] (mile markers decrease from W to E to Chicago)
3	Rockton Rd, **S gas:** Love's/Hardee's/dsl/scales/24hr
1.5mm	**Welcome Ctr/rest area eb, full [handicap] facilities, info, [picnic], litter barrels, [phone], petwalk, playground, RV dump**
1	US 51 N, IL 75 W, S Beloit, **N gas:** Road Ranger/

ROCKFORD

CHICAGO AREA

IL

INTERSTATE 90 CONT'D

E ↕ W

Exit #	Services
1	Continued McDonald's/dsl, **S gas:** Road Ranger/Pilot/Subway/scales/dsl/24hr, *FLYING J* Country Mkt/scales/dsl/24hr, **lodging:** Best Western, Knight's Inn, Ramada (2mi), **other:** Finnegan's RV Ctr, Pearl Lake camping (2mi)
0mm	Illinois/Wisconsin state line

INTERSTATE 94

E ↕ W

Exit #	Services
77mm	Illinois/Indiana state line
161	US 6, IL 83, Torrence Ave, **I-94 and I-80 run together 3 mi. N gas:** BP, **food:** Arby's, Bob Evans, Chili's, Dixie Kitchen, Hooters, IHOP, Olive Garden, On-the-Border, Oriental Palace, Wendy's, **lodging:** Comfort Suites, Day's Inn, Extended Stay America, Fairfield Inn, Red Roof Inn, Sleep Inn, Super 8, **other:** Best Buy, Chrysler/Jeep, Dominick's Foods, Firestone/auto, Home Depot, JustTires, K-Mart, PepBoys, Radio Shack, **S gas:** Gas City, Marathon, Mobil, **food:** Al's Diner, Brown's Chicken/pasta, Burger King, Dunkin Donuts, Golden Crown Rest., McDonald's, Pappy's Gyro's, **other:** Auto Clinic, Chevrolet, Saab, Sam's Club, SunRise Foods, Walgreen
I-94 and I-80 run together 3 mi. See Interstate 80 exit 161	
74b [160]	I-80/I-294 W
74a	IL 394 S to Danville
73b a	US 6,159th St, **N food:** Fuddrucker's, Outback Steaks, **other:** Chevrolet, Honda, Lincoln/Mercury, Nissan/Hyundai, Target, Tire Barn, Toyota, **S gas:** Marathon, **food:** Fannie May Candies, Subway, **lodging:** Cherry Lane Motel, **other:** Aldi Foods, Buick/Pontiac, Ford, Stanfa Tire/auto
71b a	Sibley Blvd, **N gas:** Citgo, Mobil/dsl, **food:** McDonald's, Nicky's Gyros, Popeye's, Subway, **lodging:** Baymont Inn, **other:** Dominick's Foods, **S gas:** BP, Shell, **food:** Dusty's Buffet, Wendy's, White Castle
70b a	Dolton
69	Beaubien Woods (from eb), Forest Preserve
68b a	130th St
66b	115th St, **S food:** McDonald's
66a	111th Ave, **S gas:** BP, Shell, **other:** Firestone
65	103rd Ave, Stony Island Ave
63	I-57 S
62	**N gas:** Citgo, Mobil, **food:** Subway
61b	87th St, **N gas:** BP, Shell, **food:** Burger King, McDonald's, **S other:** Best Buy, Burlington Coats, $Tree, Food-4-Less, Home Depot, Jewel-Osco, Marshall's, Murray Parts
61a	83rd St (from eb), **N gas:** Shell, **food:** Subway, **other:** st police
60c	79th St, **N gas:** BP, Mobil, Shell, **other:** Walgreens, **S gas:** Citgo/dsl, **food:** Church's
60b	76th St, **N gas:** BP, Mobil, Shell, **other:** Walgreens, **S food:** KFC, Popeye's
60a	75th St (from eb), **N gas:** BP, Mobil, Shell, **other:** Aldi Foods, **S food:** KFC, Pizza Hut, Popeye's, **other:** Walgreens

CHICAGO AREA

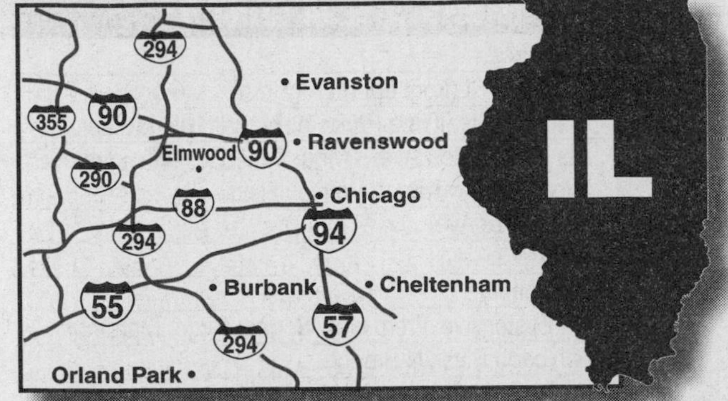

CHICAGO AREA

Exit #	Services
59c	71st St, **N gas:** BP, **S food:** McDonald's
59a	I-90 E, to Indiana Toll Rd
58b	63rd St (from eb), **N gas:** Citgo, **S gas:** Mobil
58a	I-94 divides into local and express, 59th St, **S gas:** BP
57b	Garfield Blvd, **N food:** Checker's, Popeye's, Subway, **other:** Family$, Trak Auto, Walgreens, **S gas:** Mobil, Shell/24hr, **food:** Wendy's, **other:** H
57a	51st St, **N food:** McDonald's
56b	47th St (from eb)
56a	43rd St, **S gas:** Citgo/dsl, Econo/Subway/dsl
55b	Pershing Rd
55a	35th St, **S** to New Comiskey Park
54	31st St
53c	I-55, Stevenson Pkwy, N to downtown, Lakeshore Dr
53b	I-55, Stevenson Pkwy, S to St Louis
52c	18th St, **N other:** Dominick's Foods
52b	Roosevelt Rd, Taylor St (from wb), **N gas:** Citgo
52a	Taylor St, Roosevelt Rd (from eb), **N gas:** Citgo
51h-i	I-290 W, to W Suburbs
51g	E Jackson Blvd, downtown
51f	W Adams St, downtown
51e	Monroe St (from eb), downtown, **S lodging:** Quality Inn, **other:** Walgreens
51d	Madison St (from eb), downtown, **S lodging:** Crowne Plaza, **other:** Dominick's Foods, Walgreens
51c	E Washington Blvd, downtown
51b	W Randolph St, downtown
51a	Lake St (from wb)
50b	E Ohio St, downtown, **S gas:** Marathon
50a	Ogden Ave
49b a	Augusta Blvd, Division St, **N other:** Lexus, Mercedes, **S gas:** BP, Shell, **food:** Pizza Hut
48b	IL 64, North Ave, **N gas:** BP, **other:** Home Depot, **S gas:** Valero
48a	Armitage Ave, **N other:** Best Buy, Kohl's, **S gas:** Shell, **other:** Jaguar, Land Rover, Volvo
47c b	Damen Ave, **N gas:** Citgo, car/vanwash
47a	Western Ave, Fullerton Ave, **N gas:** Citgo, **food:** Burger King, Dunkin Donuts, Popeye's, Starbucks, Subway, **other:** Costco/gas, Cub Foods, Home Depot, Jo-Ann Fabrics, Pepboys, PetsMart, Staples, Target, **S gas:** Marathon
46b a	Diversey Ave, California Ave, **N gas:** Citgo, **S food:** IHOP/24hr, Popeye's
45c	Belmont Ave, **N food:** Wendy's
45b	Kimball Ave, **N gas:** Marathon/dsl, **S gas:** Valero, **food:** Dunkin Donuts, Pizza Hut, Subway, **other:** Delray Farms Foods, Radio Shack, Walgreens

INTERSTATE 94 CONT'D

Exit #	Services
45a	Addison St (from eb)
44b	Pulaski Ave, Irving Park Rd, **N** **gas:** BP, Mobil
44a	IL 19, Keeler Ave, Irving Park Rd, **N** **gas:** BP, Shell/24hr, **other:** to Wrigley Field
43c	Montrose Ave
43b	I-90 W
43a	Wilson Ave
42	W Foster Ave (from wb), **S** **gas:** Citgo, Marathon
41mm	Chicago River, N Branch
41c	IL 50 S, to Cicero, to I-90 W
41b a	US 14, Peterson Ave, **N** **other:** Whole Foods Mkt
39b a	Touhy Ave, **N** **gas:** BP/dsl, Shell, **other:** Cassidy Tire, Toyota/Scion, **S** **gas:** BP, Citgo, Shell, **food:** Baja Fresh, Baskin-Robbins/Dunkin Donuts, Bennigan's, Buffalo Wild Wings, Burger King, Chili's, Chipotle Mexican, ChuckeCheese, Jack's Rest./24hr, McDonald's, Noodles&Co, Outback Steaks, Quizno's, Sander's Rest., Starbucks, Subway, **lodging:** Holiday Inn, **other:** Barnes&Noble, Best Buy, GNC, Jewel-Osco, Lee's Auto Parts, Nissan, Office Depot, PepBoys, PetCo, Radio Shack, Walgreens, Walmart, Vet
37b a	IL 58, Dempster St
35	Old Orchard Rd, **N** **gas:** BP, Shell, **food:** Bloomingdale's, California Pizza Kitchen, Cheese Factory, McCormick&Schmick's Seafood, **other:** H, Nissan, mall, **S** **food:** Ruby Tuesday, **lodging:** Extended Stay America, Hampton Inn
34c b	E Lake Ave, **N** **gas:** BP, **food:** Omaha Steaks, Panda Express, Starbucks, **other:** Borders Books, GNC, **S** **gas:** BP, Shell, **food:** DQ
34a	US 41 S, Skokie Rd (from eb)
33b a	Willow Rd, **S** **gas:** BP, Shell, **food:** Starbucks, **other:** Dominick's Foods, Walgreens
31	E Tower Rd, **S** **other:** BMW, Carmax, Chrysler/Dodge/Jeep, Infiniti, Mercedes, Toyota/Scion, Vet
30b a	Dundee Rd (from wb, no EZ return), **S** **gas:** Citgo, Marathon, **food:** Barnaby's Rest., Morton's Steaks, Potbelly's, Ruth's Chris Steaks, Starbucks, **lodging:** Renaissance
29	US 41, to Waukegan, to Tri-state tollway
50mm	IL 43, Waukegan Rd, **N** **gas:** BP, Shell, **food:** Baja Fresh, Old Country Buffet, **lodging:** Red Roof Inn, Embassy Suites, **other:** Best Buy, Borders Books, Home Depot, Jewel-Osco, NTB, Steinmart, TJ Maxx
53mm	I-294 S, Lake-Cook Rd (from sb), **E** **food:** J-Alexander's Rest, **lodging:** Hyatt
53.5mm	Deerfield Rd toll plaza, ☎
54mm	Deerfield Rd (from nb), **W** **gas:** Mobil, **lodging:** Marriott Suites
56mm	IL 22, Half Day Rd, **E** **lodging:** La Quinta
59mm	IL 60, Town Line Rd, **E** H, **W** **lodging:** Hilton Garden, Residence Inn
60mm	**Lake Forest Oasis both lanes**, **E** **gas:** Mobil/dsl, **food:** KFC, McDonald's, Panda Express, Starbucks, Subway, Taco Bell, **other:** info
62mm	IL 176, Rockland Rd (no nb re-entry), **E** **other:** Harley-Davidson, to Lamb's Farm
64mm	IL 137, Buckley Rd, **E** **other:** to VA H, Chicago Med School
67mm	IL 120 E, Belvidere Rd (no nb re-entry), **E** H
68mm	IL 21, Milwaukee Ave (from eb, no sb re-entry), **E** **food:** Papa John's, **other:** H, Six Flags
70mm	IL 132, Grand Ave, **E** **gas:** Speedway/dsl, **food:** Baskin-Robbins/Dunkin Donuts, Burger King, ChuckeCheese, Cracker Barrel, Culver's, Golden Corral, Ichibahn, IHOP, Joe's Crabshack, Jimmy John's, Krispy Kreme, McDonald's, Moe's SW Grill, Monkey Dish Grill, Oberweiss, Old Chicago Red Hots, Olive Garden, Outback Steaks, Subway, **lodging:** Comfort Suites, Country Inn&Suites, Grand Hotel, Extended Stay America, Hampton Inn, La Quinta, **other:** Six Flags Park, **W** **gas:** Shell, **food:** Applebee's, Bakers Square, Boston Mkt, Chicago Grill, Chili's, Denny's, LoneStar Steaks, Max&Erma's, McDonald's, Noodles&Co, Panda Express, Panera Bread, Pizza Hut, Potbelly's, Quizno's, Red Lobster, Ruby Tuesday, Starbucks, Steak'n Shake, Taco Bell, TGIFriday, Wendy's, White Castle, **lodging:** Comfort Inn, Fairfield Inn, Holiday Inn, **other:** AutoZone, Bass Pro Shops, Borders, Buick/GMC/Pontiac, Dodge, Dominick's Foods, Firestone/auto, Gurnee Mills Outlet Mall/famous brands, Home Depot, Honda, Hyundai, JC Penney, Jewel-Osco, Kohl's, Menard's, Michaels, Nissan, Old Navy, PetsMart, Radio Shack, Sam's Club, Sears/auto, Target/drugs, TJ Maxx, VW, Walgreens, Walmart/drugs, World Mkt
73mm	Waukegan toll plaza, Waukegan toll plaza, ☎
76mm	IL 173 (from nb, no return), Rosecrans Ave, **E** to IL Beach SP
1b	US 41 S, to Waukegan, **E** **other:** Sky Harbor RV Ctr
1a	Russell Rd, **W** **gas:** Citgo/dsl/scales/24hr, TA/Country Pride/dsl/scales/24hr/@, **other:** Peterbilt
0mm	Illinois/Wisconsin state line

E ↕ W — CHICAGO AREA

INTERSTATE 225 (ST LOUIS)

N ↕ S — EAST ST LOUIS

Exit #	Services
I-255 begins/ends on I-270, exit 7.	
30	I-270, W to Kansas City, E to Indianapolis
29	IL 162, to Glen Carbon, to Pontoon Beach, Granite City
26	Horseshoe Lake Rd, **E** st police
25b a	I-55/I-70, W to St Louis, E to Chicago, Indianapolis
24	Collinsville Rd, **E** **gas:** BP/24hr, **food:** Jack-in-the-Box, **other:** Shop'n Save, **W** Fairmount Racetrack
20	I-64, US 50, W to St Louis, E to Louisville, services **1 mi** **E** off I-64, exit 9.
19	State St, E St Louis, **E** **lodging:** Western Inn, **other:** Holten SP
17b a	IL 15, E St Louis, to Belleville, Centreville, **E** **gas:** ***FLYING J***/CountryMkt/dsl/scales/24hr, **W** **gas:** Phillips 66
15	Mousette Lane, **E** H, **W** **other:** Peterbilt
13	IL 157, to Cahokia, **E** **gas:** Phillips 66, **W** **gas:** BP/24hr, QT, **food:** Capt D's, China Express, Classic K Burgers, DQ, Domino's, Hardee's, Jade Garden, KFC, McDonald's, Pizza Hut, Popeye's, Rally's, Subway, **lodging:** Holiday Inn Express, **other:** Advance Parts, Aldi Foods, AutoZone, Buick/GMC/Pontiac, Cahokia RV Park, CarQuest, Curves, Dobb's Tires, Family$, $General, Schnuck's, Shop'n Save Foods, Walgreens, Walmart/drugs, Cahokia RV Parque (2mi)

INTERSTATE 225 CONT'D (ST LOUIS)

N ↕ S

Exit #	Services
10	IL 3 N, to Cahokia, E St Louis, **W gas:** ZX/Subway/dsl
9	to Dupo, **W gas:** BP
6	IL 3 S, to Columbia (exits left from sb), **E gas:** Phillips 66, Shell/dsl/24hr, **lodging:** Hampton Inn (2mi), **other:** Chevrolet
4mm	Missouri/Illinois state line, Mississippi River
3	Koch Rd,
2	MO 231, Telegraph Rd, **N gas:** Conoco, Shell/Circle K, **food:** McDonald's, Pizza Hut/Taco Bell, Steak'n Shake, Waffle House, **other:** Advance Parts, $Tree, Radio Shack, Walmart SuperCtr/24hr, Jefferson Barracks Nat Cem, **S gas:** CFM/dsl, Mobil, QT, Shell, **food:** China Wok, DQ, Imo's Pizza, **other:** Curves
1d c	US 50, US 61, US 67, Lindbergh Blvd, Lemay Ferry Rd, accesses same as I-55 exit 197 E, **N gas:** Phillips 66, **food:** Arby's, Buffalo Wild Wings, ChuckeCheese, CiCi's Pizza, Dillard's, Hometown Buffet, HoneyBaked Ham, Hooters, KFC, Krispy Kreme, Macaroni Grill, Noodles&Co, Qdoba Mexican, Quizno's, Station Subs, Steak'n Shake, St Louis Bread Co, Subway, Tucker's Place, **other:** Advance Parts, Best Buy, Border's Book, Costco/gas, Dillard's, Discount Tire, Dodge, Ford, Home Depot, JC Penney, Kia, K-Mart, Macy's, Marshall's, NTB, Sears/auto, Tuesday Morning, mall, **S gas:** Phillips 66, **food:** Jack-in-the-Box, McDonald's, Rich & Charlie's Italian, White Castle, **other:** BigLots, $General, Firestone, Old Navy, Petsmart, Sam's Club/gas, Walgreens
1b a	I-55 S to Memphis, N to St Louis. I-255 begins/ends on I-55, exit 196.

INTERSTATE 270 (ST LOUIS)

See Missouri Interstate 270 (St Louis)

INTERSTATE 294 (CHICAGO)

E ↕ W CHICAGO AREA

Exit #	Services
I-294	**begins/ends on I-94, exit 74. Numbering descends from west to east.**
I-294 & I-80 run together 5 mi. See Interstate 80 exits 155-160.	
160b	I-94 W, to Chicago, tollway begins wb, ends eb
160a	IL 394 S, to Danville
159mm	Oasis, **gas:** Mobil/dsl, **food:** Burger King, TCBY
157	IL 1, Halsted St, **N gas:** Citgo/dsl, Clark, Marathon/dsl, **food:** Burger King, Yellow Ribbon Rest., **lodging:** Best Western, Comfort Inn, Econolodge, Hilton Garden, Holiday Inn Express, Motel 6, Park Inn, **S gas:** Shell, Speedway, **food:** Applebee's, Arby's, Boston Mkt, Dunkin Donuts, Fannie May Candies, KFC, McDonald's, Popeye's, Shooter's Buffet, Subway, Taco Bell, Washington Square Rest., Wendy's, **lodging:** Rodeway Inn, Super 8, Villager Lodge, **other:** Chevrolet, $Tree, Firestone/auto, Goodyear/auto, Home Depot, Jewel-Osco, K-Mart, PepBoys, Target
156	Dixie Hwy (from eb), **S** golf
155	I-294 N, Tri-State Tollway, toll plaza
5mm	I-80 W, access to I-57
5.5mm	167th St, toll booth, [phone]
6mm	US 6, 159th St, **E gas:** BP, Citgo, Mobil, Shell, **other:** Aldi Foods, AutoZone, Walgreen, **W gas:** Citgo/dsl, Marathon/dsl, **food:** Baskin-Robbins/Dunkin

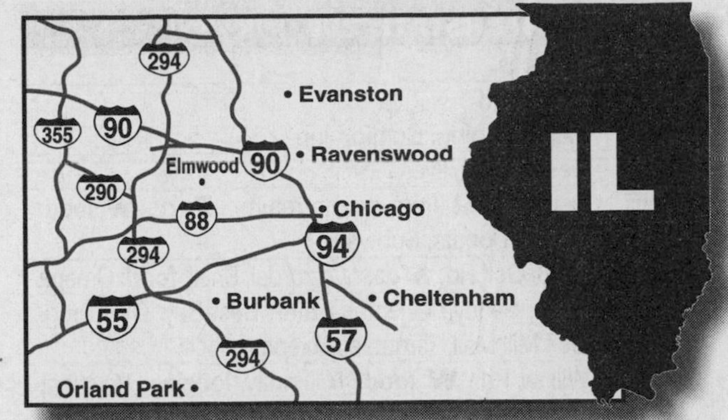

CHICAGO AREA

Exit #	Services
6mm	Continued Donuts, Burger King, Harold's Chicken, McDonald's, Popeye's, Subway, Taco Bell, White Castle, **lodging:** Comfort Inn, **other:** AutoZone, BigLots, $Tree, Family$, U-Haul, Walgreens
11mm	Cal Sag Channel
12mm	IL 50, Cicero Ave, **E gas:** Citgo/7-11, Speedway, **food:** Onion Field Rest., **W gas:** BP, Gas City/Subway/dsl/24hr, **food:** Boston Mkt, IHOP, Pizza Hut, Pizzaria Uno, Popeye's, Portillo's Dogs, Quizno's, Starbucks, **lodging:** Baymont Inn, Hampton Inn, **other:** Best Buy, Dominick's Foods, NTB, PepBoys, Sears/auto
18mm	US 12/20, 95th St, **E gas:** Clark, **food:** Bennigan's, McDonald's, Papa John's, **other:** [H], Buick, Honda, Mazda, Sears/auto, mall, **W gas:** Citgo/7-11, Shell, Speedway/dsl, **food:** Arby's, Burger King, Denny's, George's Rest., Quizno's, Schoop's Burgers, Wendy's, **lodging:** Exel Inn, **other:** [H], Jewel-Osco, Walgreen
20mm	toll booth, [phone]
22mm	75th St, Willow Springs Rd
23mm	I-55, Wolf Rd, to Hawthorne Park
25mm	**Hinsdale Oasis both lanes, gas:** Mobil/dsl, **food:** Baskin-Robbins, Wendy's/24hr
28mm	US 34, Ogden Ave, **E** zoo, **W gas:** BP, Shell/deli, **food:** Dunkin Donuts, McDonald's, Starbucks, **other:** [H], Audi/Porsche, Firestone/auto, LandRover, Maserati, Rolls-Royce/Bentley/Ferrari/Lotus, Wild Oats Mkt
28.5mm	Cermak Rd (from sb, no return)
29mm	I-88 tollway
30mm	toll booth, [phone]
31mm	IL 38, Roosevelt Rd (no EZ nb return), **E gas:** Citgo/dsl, **lodging:** Hillside Manor Motel
32mm	I-290 W, to Rockford (from nb)
34mm	I-290 (from sb), to Rockford
38mm	**O'Hare Oasis both lanes, gas:** Mobil/dsl, **food:** Burger King, TCBY
39mm	IL 19 W (from sb), Irving Park Rd, **E gas:** Clark, Marathon/dsl, **other:** 7-11, Walgreen, **1 mi E gas:** BP/repair, Clark, **food:** DQ, Dunkin Donuts, McDonald's, Subway, Wendy's, **lodging:** Comfort Suites, **other:** Aldi Foods, **W lodging:** Candlewood Suites, Day's Inn, Hampton Inn, Howard Johnson, Sheraton
40mm	I-190 W, **E services from I-90, exit 79 gas:** Mobil, **food:** McDonald's, **lodging:** Courtyard, Doubletree, Embassy Suites, Holiday Inn, Hotel Softel, Hyatt, Marriott, Radisson, Rosemont Suites, Westin
41mm	toll booth, [phone]
42mm	Touhy Ave, **W gas:** Mobil/service, **food:** Tiffany's

IL

INTERSTATE 294 (CHICAGO)

E ↕ W

Exit #	Services
42mm	Continued Rest., **lodging:** Comfort Inn
43mm	Des Plaines River
44mm	Dempster St (from nb, no return), **E** [H], **W food:** Dunkin Donuts, Subway
46mm	IL 58, Golf Rd, **E gas:** Citgo/dsl, Shell, **food:** Omega Rest., Senoya Oriental, **other:** Best Buy, CVS Drug, Golf Mill Mall, Target, auto repair
49mm	Willow Rd, **W food:** TGIFriday, **lodging:** Baymont Inn, Doubletree Suites, Courtyard, Fairfield Inn, Motel 6, **1 mi W on Milwaukee...gas:** BP, **food:** Burger King, Denny's, McDonald's, **lodging:** Wingate Inn
53mm	Lake Cook Rd (no nb re-entry), **E** Hyatt, **lodging:** Embassy Suites

I-294 begins/ends on I-94.

INTERSTATE 474 (PEORIA)

E ↕ W

Exit #	Services
15	I-74, E to Bloomington, W to Peoria
9	IL 29, E Peoria, to Pekin, **N gas:** Shell/Arby's, Thornton's, **food:** Driftwood Pizza, DQ, Pizza Hut, Taco John's, **lodging:** Ragon Motel, **other:** Riverboat Casino (6mi), **S gas:** Casey's, Shell/Subway/dsl, **food:** Denny's, KFC, McDonald's, **other:** Chrysler/Jeep/Dodge, Toyota
8mm	Illinois River
6b a	US 24, Adams St, Bartonville, **S gas:** BP/dsl, Shell/24hr, **food:** Hardee's, KFC, McDonald's, Tyroni's Café
5	Airport Rd, **S gas:** Phillips 66
3a	to IL 116, Farmington, **S** Wildlife Prairie Park
0b a	I-74, W to Moline, E to Peoria. I-474 begins/ends on I-74, exit 87.

INDIANA

INTERSTATE 64

N ↕ S

Exit #	Services
124mm	Indiana/Kentucky state line, Ohio River
123	IN 62 E, New Albany, **N gas:** BP/Circle K/24hr, Sunoco, **food:** DQ, **other:** Firestone/auto, Goodyear/auto, Sav-a-Lot Foods, **S gas:** Circle K/gas, Marathon/dsl/24hr, **food:** Lancaster's Deli, Subway, Waffle House, **lodging:** Hampton Inn, Holiday Inn Express, **other:** [H]
121	I-265 E, to I-65 (exits left from eb), **N** access to [H]
119	US 150 W, to Greenville, **1/2 mi N gas:** Marathon, **food:** Bean St Cafe, Beef'O Brady's, China Cafe, Domino's, DQ, El Nopal, Los Indios, Papa John's, Sam's Family Rest., Subway, Taco Bell, Tumbleweed Grill, **other:** Curves, Huber Winery, Rite Aid, Walgreens
118	IN 62, IN 64W, to Georgetown, **N gas:** Marathon/dsl/24hr, Shell/Circle K, **food:** Korner Kitchen, McDonald's, **lodging:** Motel 6, **other:** Mr. Hardware, Thriftway Foods, Vet, **S gas:** Marathon/dsl
115mm	**Welcome Ctr wb, full [handicapped] facilities, vending, [phone], [picnic], litter barrels**
113	to Lanesville
105	IN 135, to Corydon, **N gas:** Marathon/dsl, Shell/24hr, **food:** Big Boy, **S gas:** BP/dsl, Chevron, **food:** Arby's, Beef'O Brady's, Burger King, Cracker Barrel, Culver's, DQ, El Nopal Mexican, Hong Kong Buffet, Lee's Chicken, LJ Silver, McDonald's, O'Charley's, Papa John's, Pizza Hut, Quizno's, Ryan's, Subway, Taco Bell, Waffle House, Wendy's, White Castle, **lodging:** Baymont Inn, Hampton Inn, Holiday Inn Express, Super 8, **other:** AutoZone, BigO Tire, Chevrolet/Pontiac/Buick, CVS Drug, $Tree, Ford/Mercury, Pontiac, Radio Shack, Walgreens, Walmart SuperCtr/24hr, RV camping
100mm	Blue River
97mm	**parking area both lanes**
92	IN 66, Carefree, **N** Marengo Caves, **S gas:** Marathon/dsl/rest./24hr, Pilot/Subway/dsl/scales/24, **food:** Country Style Rest., **lodging:** Day's Inn, **other:** to
92	Continued Wyandotte Caves, Harrison Crawford SF, auto/truck repair
88mm	Hoosier Nat Forest eastern boundary
86	IN 37, to Sulphur, **N** to Patoka Lake, **S** gas, food, [phone], scenic route
79	IN 37, to Tell City, St Croix, **S** to Hoosier NF, Rec. Facilities, [phone], to OH River Br
76mm	Anderson River
72	IN 145, to Birdseye, **N** to Patoka Lake, **S** gas, [phone], St Meinrad Coll
63	IN 162, to Ferdinand, **N gas:** Sunoco/dsl, **food:** Wendy's, **lodging:** Comfort Inn, **other:** Ferdinand SF, **S** (8mi)Lake Rudolph RV Camping
58mm	**rest areas both lanes, full [handicapped] facilities, info, vending, [picnic], litter barrels, [phone]**
57	US 231, to Dale, Huntingburg, **N** [H], **S gas:** Shell/dsl/24hr, **food:** Denny's, **lodging:** Baymont Inn, Motel 6, **other:** Lincoln Boyhood Home, Lincoln SP
54	IN 161, to Holland,Tennyson
39	IN 61, Lynnville, **N gas:** Fast Fuel
32mm	Wabash & Erie Canal
29b a	I-164 S, IN 57 S, to Evansville, **N gas:** Sunoco/Sunny's Subs/dsl/24hr
25b a	US 41, to Evansville, **N gas:** ***FLYING J***/CountryMkt/dsl/24hr/scales/@, Pilot/Wendy's/dsl/24hr, Pilot/Subway/dsl/24hr, **lodging:** Quality Inn, **other:** Blue Beacon, truck repair/lube, **S gas:** BP/motel, **food:** Arby's, Denny's, McDonald's, Stoll's Rest., Triple Dragon Buffet, **lodging:** Best Western, Comfort Inn, Holiday Inn Express, Super 8, **other:** Freightliner, st police, to U S IN
18	IN 65, to Cynthiana, **S gas:** Motomart/dsl/24hr
12	IN 165, Poseyville, **S** gas, dsl, food, **other:** Chevrolet, New Harmonie Hist Area/SP
7mm	**Black River Welcome Ctr eb, full [handicapped] facilities, [phone], [picnic] litter barrels, petwalk**
5mm	Black River

IL IN

INTERSTATE 64 CONT'D

Exit #	Services
44	IN 69 S, New Harmony, Griffin, **1 mi N** gas/dsl, food, motel, antiques, USPO, **S** Harmony St Park
2mm	Big Bayou River
0mm	Indiana/Illinois state line, Wabash River

INTERSTATE 65

Exit #	Services
262	I-90, W to Chicago, E to Ohio, I-65 begins/ends on US 12, US 20.
261	15th Ave, to Gary, **E** Mack/Volvo Trucks, **W gas:** Clark
259b a	I-94/80, US 6W
258	US 6, Ridge Rd, **E gas:** Marathon/dsl, Speedway/dsl, **food:** Country Lounge Diner, Diner's Choice Rest., **W gas:** Glen Park Gas, Phillips 66
255	61st Ave, Merrillville, **E gas:** Speedway/dsl/24hr, Thornton's, **food:** Arby's, Cracker Barrel, McDonald's, Pizza Hut/Taco Bell, Wendy's, **lodging:** Comfort Inn, $Inn, Lee's Inn, **other:** Chevrolet, I-65 Repair, Menard's, Mid-West Tire, **1 mi W gas:** Shell, **food:** Burger King, Subway, **other:** H
253b	US 30 W, Merrillville, **W gas:** Mobil/dsl, Shell, Speedway/dsl, **food:** Abuelo's Mexican, America's Donut, Applebee's, Baskin-Robbins/Dunkin Donuts, Barnelli's Rest., Denny's, Gino's Rest., Golden Corral, Hooters, House of Kobe, Johnnie's Rest., KFC, La Carreta, Maloney's Grill, Max&Erma's, Old Chicago Pizza, Oriental Buffet, Outback Steaks, Panda Express, Panera Bread, Pizza Hut, Portillo's Hot Dogs, Starbucks, Steak'n Shake, Subway, TX Corral Steaks, Wendy's, White Castle, **lodging:**
253b	Continued Courtyard, Fairfield Inn, Hampton Inn, Holiday Inn Express, Radisson, Red Roof Inn, Residence Inn, **other:** H, Aldi Foods, Aamco, CarEx, CarQuest, $Tree, Discount Tire, Fanny May Candies, Ford, Goodyear/auto, Hyundai/Mitsubishi, Jo-Ann Fabrics, K-Mart, Lincoln/Mercury, Mazda, Meijer/dsl, Midas, NTB, Old Time Pottery, Staples, Subaru, U-Haul, Walgreens, Verizon, transmissions
253a	US 30 E, **E gas:** Speedway/dsl, **food:** Arby's, Bakers Square, Bennigan's, Bob Evans, Buffalo Wild Wings, Chili's, Chipotle Mexican, ChuckeCheese, Culver's,

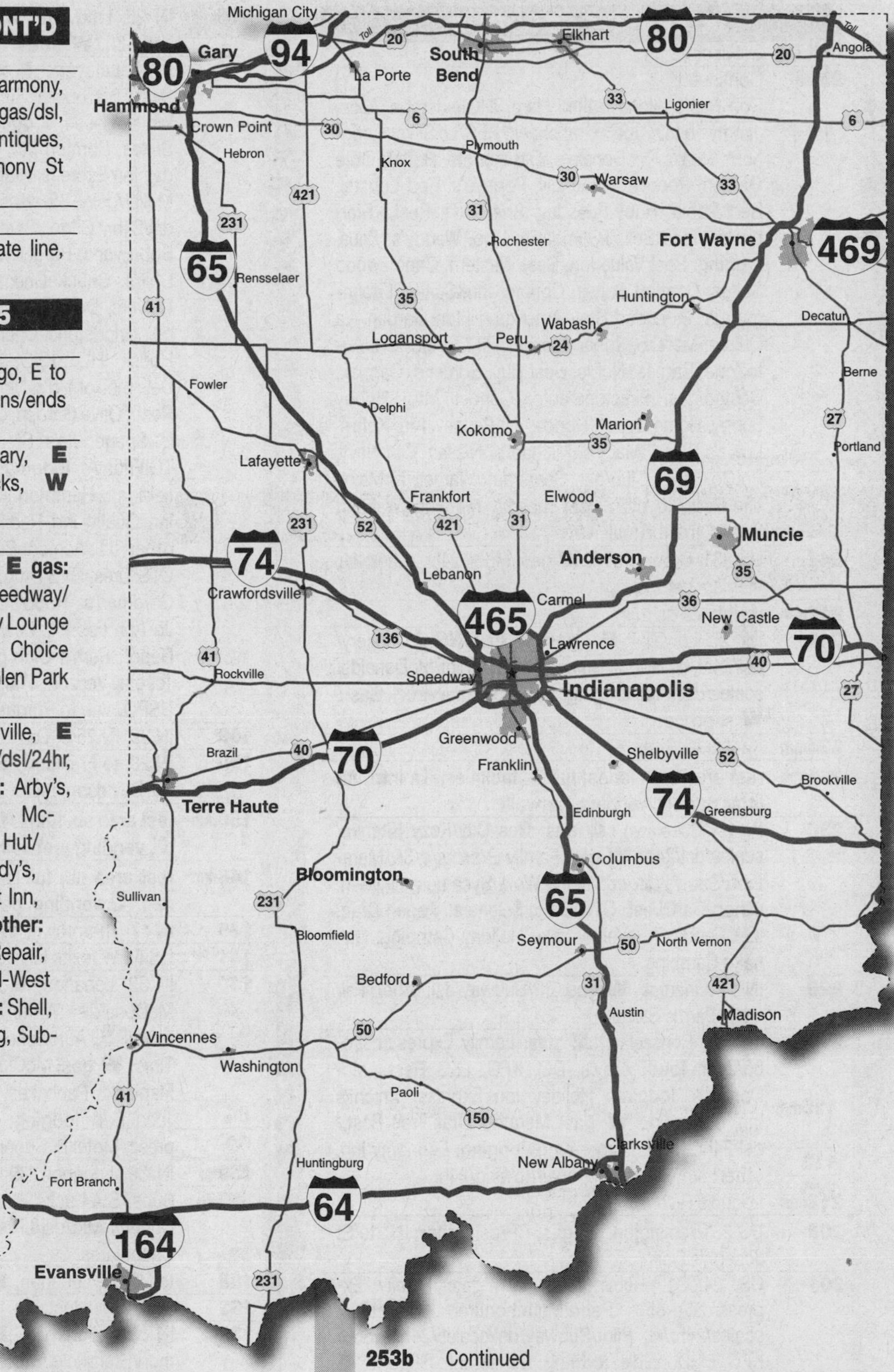

INTERSTATE 65 CONT'D

N ↕ S

Exit #	Services
253a	Continued Don Pablo, HoneyBaked Ham, IHOP, Jamba Juice, Jimmy John's, Joe's Crabshack, KFC/LJ Silver, Longhorn Steaks, McDonald's, Old Country Buffet, Olive Garden, Popeye's, Potbelly, Popeye's, Red Lobster, Red Robin, Ruby Tuesday, Sheffield's Rest., Starbucks, Taco Bell, TGIFriday's, Uno, Wendy's, Zeus, **lodging:** Best Value Inn, Best Western, Candlewood Suites, Comfort Suites, Country Inn&Suites, Economy Inn, Extended Stay America, Hilton Garden, La Quinta, Motel 6, Super 8, **other:** AT&T, Audi/VW, AutoZone, Barnes&Noble, Best Buy, Border's, Carmax, Costco/gas, Firestone/auto, Gander Mtn, Hobby Lobby, Home Depot, Honda, JC Penney, Kia, Kohl's, Lowe's Whse, Macy's, Michael's, Nissan, Old Navy, PetCo, Sam's Club/gas, Sears/auto, Target, TJ Maxx, Tire Barn, Toyota/Scion, Tuesday Morning, Walmart SuperCtr/24hr, mall, Vet
247	US 231, Crown Point, **W gas:** Mobil/24hr, **other:** H, Vietnam Vet Mem
241mm	**weigh sta sb**
240	IN 2, Lowell, **E gas:** *FLYING J*/Cookery/dsl/24hr/@, Mobil/Burger King, Pilot/McDonalds/scales/dsl/24hr, **lodging:** Super 8, **other:** truck wash, **W** st police
234mm	Kankakee River
231mm	**rest area both lanes, full ♿ facilities, ☎, info, picnic, litter barrels, vending, petwalk**
230	IN 10, Roselawn, **E gas:** Gas City/Kozy Kitchen/scales/dsl/24hr, **W gas:** Family Express/e-85, Marathon/Subway, **food:** China Wok, Sycamore Drive-In, **other:** CarQuest, CVS Drug, $General, Fagen Drug, IGA Foods, TrueValue, Lake Holiday Camping, Oak Lake Camping
220	IN 14 Winamac, **W gas:** BP/Subway/dsl, **other:** Fair Oaks Farms Store
215	IN 114, Rensselaer, **E gas:** Family Express/dsl/e-85/24hr, **food:** Arby's, DQ, KFC, L&G Rest., McDonald's, **lodging:** Holiday Inn Express, Knight's Inn, **other:** H, **W gas:** Marathon/Trail Tree Rest./dsl/24hr, **food:** Burger King, **lodging:** Economy Inn, **other:** fireworks, tires/repair/towing/24hr
212mm	Iroquois River
205	US 231Remington, **E gas:** BP/dsl, **other:** H, to St Joseph's Coll
201	US 24/231, Remington, **W gas:** Family Express/dsl/e-85, Petro/Marathon/Iron Skillet/dsl/scales/24hr/@, Pilot/Subway/dsl/scales/24hr, **food:** KFC, McDonald's, **lodging:** Sunset Inn, Super 8, **E other:** Caboose Lake RV Camping
196mm	**rest area both lanes, full ♿ facilities, vending, ☎, info, picnic, litter barrels, petwalk**
193	US 231, to Chalmers, **E gas:** BP/DQ/Stuckey's
188	IN 18, to Brookston, Fowler
178	IN 43, W Lafayette, **E gas:** GA/Taco Bell, Phillips 66/Subway/dsl, **food:** McDonald's, Wendy's, **lodging:** EconoLodge, **other:** to Tippecanoe Bfd, museum, st police, **W** to Purdue U
176mm	Wabash River

LAFAYETTE

Exit #	Services
175	IN 25, Lafayette, **E gas:** BP/dsl, Family Express/dsl/e-85, **W other:** H
172	IN 26, Lafayette, **E food:** Cracker Barrel, DQ, Rodeo Rest., Starbucks, Steak'n Shake, Subway, Taj Mahal, White Castle, **lodging:** Baymont Inn, Candlewood Suites, Comfort Inn, Comfort Suites, Days Inn, Holiday Inn Express, Motel 6, TownePlace Suites, **other:** Meijer/dsl/e-85, visitor's ctr, **W gas:** BP/Circle K/dsl/24hr, Citgo, Shell, Speedway/dsl, **food:** Arby's, Bob Evans, Burger King, Camille's Cafe, Chick-fil-A, Chili's, ChuckeCheese, Cici's Pizza, Country Cafe, Culvers, Denny's, Don Pablo, Fazoli's, Golden Corral, Grindstone Charlie's, Hour Time Rest., Hunan House, IHOP, KFC, Logan's Roadhouse, McAlister's Deli, McDonald's, Moe's SW Grill, Mt Jack's, Nanking Rest., Olive Garden, Outback Steaks, Pizza Hut, Sonic, Spageddie's, Steak'n Shake, Subway, Taco Bell, TGIFriday's, **lodging:** Best Western, Courtyard, Fairfield Inn, Hampton Inn, Homewood Suites, Knight's Inn, Quality Inn, Red Roof Inn, Signature Inn, Super 8, **other:** H, Aamco, Buick/Cadillac/Nissan, Chevrolet, CTS Tires, CVS Drug, Discount Tire, $General, $Tree, Gordman's, Hobby Lobby, Home Depot, Hyundai, Jo-Ann Fabrics, Lowe's Whse, Marsh Foods, Office Depot, Sam's Club/gas, Target, TJ Maxx, T-Moble, Toyota, Verizon, Walgreens, Walmart SuperCtr/24hr, USPO, Vet, to Purdue U
168	IN 38, IN 25 S, Dayton, **E gas:** Mobil/dsl
158	IN 28, to Frankfort, **E gas:** BP/dsl/24hr, **other:** Harley-Davidson, repair, **2 mi W other:** H, camping
150mm	**rest area sb, full ♿ facilities, info, picnic, litter barrels, ☎, vending, petwalk**
148mm	**rest area nb, full ♿ facilities, info, picnic, litter barrels, ☎, vending, petwalk**
146	IN 47, Thorntown, **W** camping
141	US 52 W (exits left from sb), Lafayette Ave, **E** H
140	IN 32, Lebanon, **E gas:** BP/repair, **food:** Denny's, McDonald's, White Castle, **lodging:** Comfort Inn, **other:** H, AutoZone, Goodyear/auto, NAPA, Pomp's Tires, **W gas:** McClure/dsl/e-85, Shell, **food:** Arby's, Flapjacks Pancakes, KFC, Steak'n Shake, Subway, Taco Bell, **lodging:** EconoLodge, Holiday Inn Express, Motel 6, Super 8, **other:** truckwash
139	IN 39, Lebanon, **E gas:** GA/dsl, **food:** Penn Sta. Subs, Starbucks, Wendy's, **W gas:** *FLYING J*/Country Mkt/dsl/LP/scales/24hr, **other:** Donaldson's Chocolates
138	to US 52, Lebanon, **E gas:** BP/dsl
133	IN 267, Whitestown
130	IN 334, Zionsville, **E gas:** CF/Subway/dsl, Marathon/Starbucks/Stuckey's/Noble Roman's/dsl/24hr, **food:** Burger King, El Rodeo Mexican, Hong Kong House, Taco Bell, **other:** CVS Drug, Lowe's Whse, **W gas:** TA/BP/Popeye's/dsl/scales/24hr/@
129	I-865 E, to I-465 E, US 52 E (from sb)
126mm	Fishback Creek
124	71st St, **1 mi E gas:** BP, **food:** Bob Evans, Steak'n Shake, **lodging:** Courtyard, Hampton Inn, Hilton Garden, Residence Inn, Wingate Inn, **W** Eagle Creek Park
123	I-465 S, S to ✈

LEBANON

IN

INTERSTATE 65 CONT'D

N ↕ S

Exit #	Services
121	Lafayette Rd, **E gas:** GA, Speedway/dsl, **lodging:** Quality Inn, **W gas:** Shell/Circle K/24hr, **food:** Applebee's, Arby's, Church's, Fazoli's, KFC, King Wok, Papa John's, Taco Bell, Wendy's, **lodging:** Best Value Inn, **other:** H, Batteries+, Chrysler/Dodge/Jeep, Discount Tire, Family$, Firestone/auto, Kia, NAPA, Nissan, PepBoys, Scion/Toyota, Tire Barn, Verizon, Walmart SuperCtr, mall, transmissions, Vet, same as 119
119	38th St (no nb return), **W gas:** Speedway, **food:** Arby's, ChuckeCheese, Cici's Pizza, Hooters, KFC/Taco Bell, McDonald's, New Taste Buffet, Penn Sta Subs, Pizza Hut, Popeye's, Red Lobster, Starbucks, Taco Bell, WTT Buffet, **other:** Aldi Foods, Best Buy, Chevrolet, Ford, Honda, Hyundai, K-Mart, NAPA, Tires+, mall, same as 121
117.5mm	White River
117	MLK St (from sb), **W gas:** Marathon/dsl
116	29th St, 30th St (from nb), Marian Coll
115	21st St, **E gas:** Shell/Circle K, **other:** H, **W** museums, zoo
114	MLK St, West St, downtown
113	US 31, IN 37, Meridian St, to downtown, **E other:** H
112a	I-70 E, to Columbus
111	Market St, Michigan St, Ohio St, **E food:** Hardee's, **W other:** City Market, to Market Square Arena, museum
110b	I-70 W, to St Louis
110a	Prospect St, Morris St, E St
109	Raymond St, **E** H, **W gas:** Speedway/dsl, **food:** Little Caesar's, White Castle, **other:** CVS Drug, Family$, Safeway
107	Keystone Ave, **E gas:** Mystik, **lodging:** Best Value Inn, **other:** H, **W gas:** Phillips 66/dsl, Speedway/dsl, Valero, **food:** Big Kahuna Pizza, Burger King, Denny's, McDonald's, Subway, Walmart Mkt, Wendy's, **lodging:** Holiday Inn Express, **other:** $General, Walmart Mkt, U of Indianapolis
106	I-465 and I-74
103	Southport Rd, **E gas:** BP/McDonald's/24hr, Shell/Circle K, **food:** Arby's, Chick-fil-A, El Puerto, Hardees, Jimmy John's, Knock-Outs Grill, Longhorn Steaks, Noble Roman's, O'Charley's, Panda Express, Panera Bread, Penn Sta. Subs, Qdoba, Quizno's, Starbucks, Taco Bell, Uno, **other:** Aldi Foods, AT&T, Firestone/auto, Harley-Davidson, Home Depot, Kohl's, Lowe's Whse, Menard's, Meijer/dsl/e-85/24hr, Radio Shack, Staples, Target, **W gas:** Citgo, Marathon/Circle K, Speedway/dsl/24hr, **food:** Beef&Brew, Bob Evans, Burger King, Carrabba's, Cheeseburger Paradise, Cracker Barrel, KFC, McDonald's, Starbucks, Steak'n Shake, TX Roadhouse, Waffle House, Wendy's, **lodging:** Best Western, Comfort Suites, Country Inn&Suites, Courtyard, Fairfield Inn, Hampton Inn, Jameson Inn, Quality Inn, **other:** H, 7-11
101	CountyLine Rd, **E food:** Candlewood Suites, **other:** H, **W gas:** Murphy USA, **food:** Buffalo Wild Wings, Fireside Rest., Tokyo Buffet, **lodging:** Hilton Garden, Holiday Inn Express, Value Place Hotel, **other:** H, AT&T, Gander Mtn, Kroger, Walmart SuperCtr/Subway

INDIANAPOLIS AREA

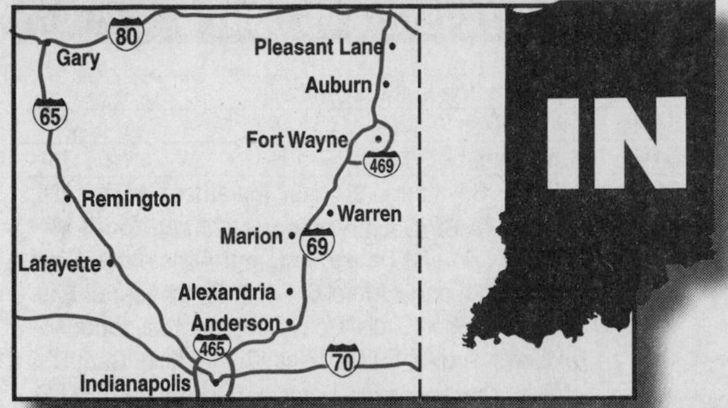

Exit #	Services
99	Greenwood, **E gas:** Road Ranger/Pilot/Subway/scales/dsl/24hr, **W gas:** Marathon, Shell/Circle K, Sunoco, **food:** Arby's, Bob Evans, Byrd's Cafeteria, Denny's, McDonald's, Noble Roman's, Starbucks, Subway, Taco Bell, Waffle House, White Castle, **lodging:** Baymont Inn, Comfort Inn, InTown Suites, Red Carpet Inn, Red Roof Inn, **other:** H, Camping World RV Ctr, Sam's Club, Vet
95	Whiteland, **E gas:** *FLYING J*/CountryMkt/scales/dsl/24hr, **other:** SpeedCo, tires, **W gas:** Pilot/Arby's/dsl/24hr, Pilot/McDonald's/dsl/scales/24hr/@, **other:** Family RV Ctr
90	IN 44, Franklin, **W gas:** Marathon/Subway, Shell/Circle K, **food:** Burger King, McDonald's, Subway, Waffle House, **lodging:** Comfort Inn, EconoLodge, Howard Johnson, Quality Inn, Super 8, **other:** H, golf
85mm	Sugar Creek
82mm	Big Blue River
80	IN 252, to Flat Rock, Edinburgh, **W gas:** Marathon/dsl, Shell/dsl
76b a	US 31, Taylorsville, **E gas:** Shell/Circle K/dsl, Speedway/dsl, **food:** A&W/KFC, Burger King, Waffle House, **lodging:** Red Roof Inn, **other:** H, Buick/Cadillac/Chevrolet/GMC/Pontiac, Toyota, **W gas:** Marathon, Thornton's/café/dsl, **food:** Arby's, Cracker Barrel, Hardee's, Max&Erma's, McDonald's, Montana Mikes, Ruby Tuesday, Snappy Tomato Pizza, Subway, Taco Bell, **lodging:** Best Western, Hampton Inn, Hilton Garden, Holiday Inn Express, **other:** Driftwood RV Camp, Goodyear, Harley-Davidson, Premium Outlets/famous brands, antiques, repair
73mm	**rest area both lanes, full facilities, phone, vending, info, picnic, litter barrels, petwalk**
68mm	Driftwood River
68	IN 46, Columbus, **E gas:** Shell/Circle K, Speedway/dsl, **food:** Buffalo Wild Wings, Burger King, Cold Stone, Culver's, Dimitri's Rest., McDonald's, Snappy Tomato Pizza, Starbucks, Subway, **lodging:** Comfort Inn&Suites, Holiday Inn/rest., Sleep Inn, Super 8, **other:** H, Menards, Sam's Club/gas, Walgreens, Walmart SuperCtr/Subway, **W gas:** BP, Swifty, **food:** Arby's, Bob Evans, Denny's, KFC, Max's Grill, Noble Roman's, Papa's Grill, Taco Bell, Wendy's, **lodging:** Courtyard, Days Inn, Knight's Inn, Motel 6, Residence Inn, **other:** CVS Drug, $General, Jay-C Foods, Tuesday Morning, to Brown Co SP
64	IN 58, Walesboro, **W gas:** Marathon/dsl, **other:** to RV camping

COLUMBUS

INTERSTATE 65 CONT'D

Exit #	Services
55	IN 11, to Jonesville, Seymour
54mm	White River
51mm	**weigh sta both lanes**
50b a	US 50, Seymour, **E gas:** Marathon/Circle K/dsl, Swifty, TA/BP/Country Pride/dsl/24hr/@, **food:** McDonald's, Waffle House, **lodging:** Allstate Inn, Days Inn, EconoLodge, Motel 6, Super 8, **W gas:** Bi-Rite, Citgo/dsl, Shell/Circle K/dsl, Speedway/dsl, **food:** Applebee's, Arby's, Buffet China, Burger King, Capt D's, Chili's, Cracker Barrel, Dominos, DQ, Hardee's, KFC, Little Caesars, LJ Silver, Max&Erma's, McDonalds, Papa John's, Pizza Hut, Rally's, Ryan's, Santa Fe Mexican, Steak'n Shake, Subway, Taco Bell, Tumbleweed Grill, Wendy's, **lodging:** Fairfield Inn, Hampton Inn, Holiday Inn Express, Knight's Inn, Quality Inn, **other:** H, Aldi Foods, AutoZone, BigLots, Buick/Chevrolet/GMC/Pontiac, Chrysler/Dodge/Jeep, CVS Drug, $General, $Tree, Ford, GNC, Home Depot, Jay-C Foods, JC Penney, O'Reilly Parts, Russell Stover Candies, Staples, Walgreens, Walmart SuperCtr, st police
41	IN 250, Uniontown, **E** tires, **W gas:** UnionTown/dsl/rest./24hr, **other:** auto/truck repair
36	US 31, Crothersville, **E gas:** Shell, **W gas:** Marathon
34a b	IN 256, Austin, **E gas:** Shell/Circle K, **other:** to Hardy Lake, Clifty Falls SP, **W gas:** Fuelmart/scales/dsl, **food:** rest.
29b a	IN 56, to Salem, Scottsburg, **E gas:** MotoMart, Speedway/dsl, **food:** Burger King, Cracker Barrel, KFC, Papa John's, Ponderosa, Sonic, Subway, Taco Bell, **lodging:** Holiday Inn Express, Mariann Motel/rest., **other:** H, Ace Hardware, Advance Parts, AutoZone, CVS Drug, Family$, **W gas:** Marathon, Murphy USA/dsl, Shell/Circle K, **food:** Arby's, Domino's, LJ Silver, McDonald's, Pizza Hut, Roadhouse USA, Waffle House, Wendy's, **lodging:** Hampton Inn, Super 8, Quality Inn, **other:** Big O Tire, Jellystone Camping (4mi), Walmart SuperCtr
22mm	**rest area both lanes, full facilities, info, litter barrels, vending, petwalk**
19	IN 160, Henryville, **E gas:** Shell/Circle K/24hr, Sprint/Subway/dsl, **food:** Schuler's Rest.
16	Memphis Rd, Memphis, **E gas:** Love's/Subway/McDonald's/dsl/scales/24hr, **food:** Fill'n Station Cafe, **W gas:** Pilot/Arby's/scales/dsl/24hr/@, **other:** Customers 1st RV Ctr.
9	IN 311, to New Albany, Sellersburg, **E gas:** BP, Five Star Gas, Shell/Circle K, Swifty, **food:** Arby's, Cracker Barrel, DQ, Quizno's, Waffle House, **lodging:** Ramada Inn, **other:** Carmerica/repair, Ford, O'Reilly Parts, st police, **W gas:** Marathon/Circle K, **food:** Burger King, McDonald's, Taco Bell, **lodging:** Comfort Inn, **other:** city park
7	IN 60, Hamburg, **E gas:** Clark/dsl, **W food:** Cricket's Cafe, KFC/Pizza Hut, **lodging:** Days Inn
6b a	I-265 W, to I-64 W, IN 265 E, New Albany
5	Veterans Parkway, **E gas:** H, **W food:** Asian Buffet, Buffalo Wild Wings, Cheddars, Chick-fil-A, DQ, Famous Dave's BBQ, IHOP, Kansai Japanese, Longhorn Steaks, McAlisters Deli, Moe's SW Grill, Olive Garden, Panera Bread, Papa Murphy's, Pizza Hut, Ruben's Mexican, Ruby Tuesday, Sonic, Subway, Taco Bell, **other:** AT&T, Bass Pro Shops, Best Buy, Chevrolet, Lowe's Whse, Old Navy, PetsMart, Sam's Club, Staples, Target, Tuesday Morning, Verizon, Walmart SuperCtr/Subway/gas
4	US 31 N, IN 131 S, Clarksville, New Albany, **E gas:** Thorntons/Dunkin Donuts/dsl, **food:** White Castle, **lodging:** Value Place Inn, **other:** Raben Tire, **W gas:** Speedway/dsl, **food:** Applebee's, Arby's, Bob Evans, Burger King, Capt D's, ChuckeCheese, Denny's, Don Pablo, El Caporal, Fazoli's, Frisch's, Golden Corral, Hooters, Iguana Rest., Logan's Roadhouse, LJ Silver, McDonald's, Mr Gatti's, O'Charley's, Outback Steaks, Papa John's, Rally's, Red Lobster, Steak'n Shake/24hr, Wendy's, **lodging:** Best Western, Candlewood Suites, Hampton Inn, Suburban Lodge, **other:** AT&T, AutoZone, BigLots, Buick/GMC/Pontiac, Dillard's, $Tree, Firestone/auto, Ford, Goodyear, Hancock Fabrics, Hobby Lobby, Home Depot, Honda, JC Penney, Kia, Kroger/gas, Office Depot, O'Reilly Parts, PepBoys, Sears/auto, Toyota/Scion, Tuesday Morning, USPO, Walgreens, mall
2	Eastern Blvd, Clarksville, **E lodging:** Comfort Suites, Days Inn, Motel 6, Super 8, **other:** H, U-Haul, **W gas:** Shell/Circle K, **lodging:** Best Inn
1	US 31 S, IN 62, Stansifer Ave, **E gas:** Thorntons, **food:** DQ, **other:** H, Advance Parts, Walgreens, info ctr, **W lodging:** Holiday Inn, **other:** Stinnett RV Ctr
0	Jeffersonville, **E gas:** Thornton, **food:** Hardee's, McDonald's, Waffle House, **other:** H, Chrysler/Jeep, Hyundai, Nissan, Walgreens, to Falls of OH SP, **W food:** Hooters, **lodging:** Sheraton
0mm	Indiana/Kentucky state line, Ohio River

Side labels: SEYMOUR, SCOTTSBURG, CLARKSVILLE; N ↕ S

INTERSTATE 69

Exit #	Services
158mm	Indiana/Michigan state line
157	Lake George Rd, to IN 120, Fremont, Lake James, **E gas:** Petro/Mobil/dsl/24hr/@, **lodging:** Lake George Inn, **other:** Freightliner, **W gas:** Pilot/Wendy's/dsl/scales/24hr, Shell/Subway/dsl/24hr, **food:** McDonald's, Red Arrow Rest., **other:** Jellystone Camping (5mi), Outlet Shops/Famous Brands, fireworks
156	I-80/90 Toll Rd, E to Toledo, W to Chicago
154	IN 127, to IN 120, IN 727, Fremont, Orland, **E food:** Applebee's (2mi), Bennigans (2mi), Ruby Tuesday, **lodging:** Hampton Inn, Super 8, Travelers Inn, **other:** Oak Hill RV camp, golf, **W gas:** Marathon/dsl, **lodging:** Budgeteer Motel, Holiday Inn Express, **other:** Prime Outlets/Famous Brands, to Pokagon SP, Jellystone Camping (4mi)
150	rd 200 W, to Lake James, Crooked Lake, **E gas:** BP/dsl, **W gas:** Marathon, Shell, **other:** Marine Ctr
148	GA, Speedway/dsl, **food:** McDonald's, Wendy's (1mi), **other:** H, **other:** Circle B RV Prk
145mm	Pigeon Creek
144mm	**rest area sb, full facilities, info, litter barrels, vending, petwalk**
140	IN 4, to Hamilton, Ashley, Hudson, **1 mi W gas:** BP/Ashley Deli/dsl

IN

INTERSTATE 69 CONT'D

N ↕ S

AUBURN

Exit #	Services
134	US 6, to Waterloo, Kendallville, **W gas:** BP/dsl, Marathon/dsl/24hr, **food:** Morning Star Rest
129	IN 8, to Garrett, Auburn, **E gas:** Citgo, GA, Lassus, Marathon/dsl/24hr, Speedway/dsl, **food:** Applebee's, Arby's/24hr, Ard's Rest., Bob Evans, Burger King, DQ, Fazoli's, KFC, McDonald's, Papa Murphy's, Pizza Hut, Ponderosa, Starbucks, Steak'n Shake, Subway, Taco Bell, TCBY, Wendy's, Zesto Drive-In, **lodging:** Best Western, Comfort Suites, Days Inn, Holiday Inn Express, La Quinta, Super 8, **other:** H, Ace Hardware, Advance Parts, AutoZone, Chevrolet/Pontiac/Buick/RV Ctr, Chrysler/Jeep/Dodge, CVS Drug, Davis RV Ctr, $General, $Tree, Ford, GMC, Kroger, Radio Shack, Staples, Walmart SuperCtr/24hr, museum, **W gas:** Marathon, **food:** Buffalo Wild Wings, Cracker Barrel, FireMtn Grill, Sonic, **other:** Home Depot
126	IN 11-A, to Garrett, Auburn, **E** Kruse Auction Park, **W** KOA
116	IN 1 N, Dupont Rd, **E gas:** Citgo/Burger King, **food:** Arby's, Culver's, **lodging:** Comfort Suites, **other:** H, **W gas:** Lassus/Elmo's Pizza, Speedway/dsl, **food:** Bandito's Mexican, Bob Evans, Ground Level Coffee, Laguna Grill, Mancino's Grinders, RolyPoly, Trolley Grill, **lodging:** AmericInn, Sleep Inn, **other:** H
115	I-469, US 30 E
112b a	Coldwater Rd, **E gas:** BP/dsl/24hr, Marathon, Sunoco, **food:** Arby's,'s, Carlos O'Kelly's, Chili's, DeBrand's Chocolate, Hall's Factory Rest., Hunan Chinese, IHOP, LoneStar Steaks, Papa John's, Ponderosa, Quizno's, Rally's, Red Lobster, Red River Steaks, Steak'n Shake, Taco Bell, Wendy's, **lodging:** Hyatt Place, Marriott, **other:** Hyundai, Jo-Ann Fabrics, NAPA, U-Haul, Walmart SuperCtr/24hr, **W** DQ (1mi)
111b a	US 27 S, IN 3 N, **E gas:** Shell, **food:** Arby's, Cap'n Cork, ChuckeCheese, Don Pablo, DQ, Fazoli's, Golden Corral, Hall's Rest., **lodging:** Candlewood Suites, Residence Inn, **other:** Discount Tire, Ford, Honda, Infiniti, Nissan, Pontiac/GMC, Toyota, **W gas:** Lassus/dsl, Marathon, Meijer/dsl/24hr, **food:** Applebee's, Burger King, Cracker Barrel, IHOP, KFC, Logan's Roadhouse, McDonald's, Mega Wraps, O'Charley's, Quizno's, Starbucks, Subway, Taco Bell, Teriyaki Express, Texas Roadhouse, **lodging:** Baymont Inn, Best Value Inn, Courtyard, County Inn&Suites, Day's Inn, Guesthouse Motel, Hampton Inn, Signature Inn, Studio+, **other:** CVS Drug, Gander Mtn, Home Depot, Lowe's Whse, Sam's Club/gas, VW
109b a	US 33, Goshen Rd, Ft Wayne, **E gas:** BP, Citgo/Subway/dsl/scales, Marathon, **food:** McDonald's, Pointe Rest., **lodging:** Best Inn, Country Hearth Inn, Knight's Inn, Motel 6, Quality Inn, Red Roof Inn, Travel Inn, **other:** H, Blue Beacon, NAPA, to Children's Zoo
105b a	IN 14 W, Ft Wayne, **E gas:** Lassus, Shell/Subway/dsl, Speedway/LP, **food:** Arby's, Bob Evans, Chick-fil-A, El Patron Mexican, Flat Top Grill, Great Wall Buffet, Krispy Kreme, Logan's Roadhouse, O'Charley's, Papa Murphy's, Smokey Bones BBQ, Starbucks, Steak'n Shake, Wendy's, **lodging:** Klopfenstein Suites, **other:** H, Acura, Audi/Porsche, Barnes&Noble, Best Buy, Big Lots, BMW, Cadillac,

FT WAYNE

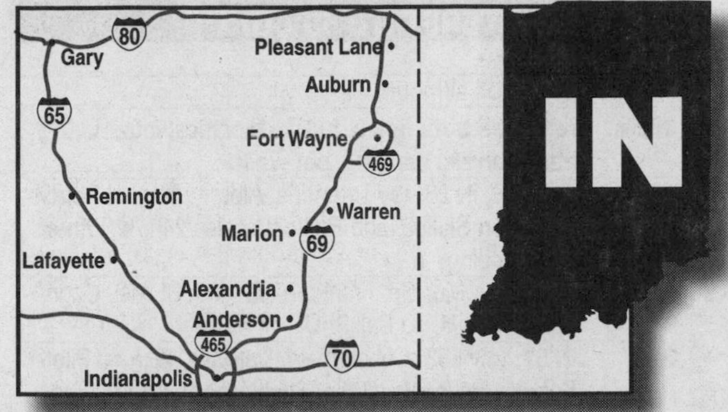

Exit #	Services
105b a	Continued Chevrolet, Chrysler/Jeep, Dodge, Harley-Davidson, Hummer, KIA, Kohl's, Lexus, Lowe's Whse, Mazda, Meijer/dsl/24hr, NAPA, Old Navy, PetsMart, Pontiac/Buick/GMC, Saab, Staples, Subaru, Toyota/Scion, Tuesday Morning, Volvo, Walmart SuperCtr/gas/24hr, to St Francis U, **W food:** Bandito's, **other:** Corvette Museum
102	US 24, to Jefferson Blvd, Ft Wayne, **E food:** Subway (1mi), Taco Bell (1mi), **lodging:** Extended Stay America, Hampton Inn, **other:** H, to In Wesleyan U, **W gas:** Lassus, Marathon, **food:** Antigua Grill, Applebee's, Arby's, Bob Evans, Carlos O'Kelly's, Coventry Tavern Rest., McDonald's, Outback Steaks, Pizza Hut, Sara's Rest., Starbucks, Wendy's, Zesto Drive-In, **lodging:** Comfort Suites, Hilton Garden, Holiday Inn Express, Luxbury Inn, Staybridge Suites, **other:** Kroger, Scott's Foods, Walgreen, st police
99	Lower Huntington Rd
96b a	I-469, US 24 E, US 33 S, **E** to ✈
93mm	**rest area sb, full ♿ facilities, info, ☎, vending, picnic, litter barrels, pet walk**
89mm	**rest area nb, full ♿ facilities, info, ☎, vending, picnic, litter barrels, pet walk**
86	US 224, to Huntington, Markle, **E gas:** Marathon/24hr (1mi), Sunoco/Subway, **food:** DQ, Huddle House, Vinatelli's, **lodging:** Guesthouse Inn, Super 8, **other:** H, **W** repair/tires, to Huntington Reservoir
80mm	**weigh sta sb/parking area nb**
78	IN 5, to Warren, Huntington, **E gas:** Sunoco/dsl, **lodging:** Huggy Bear Motel, **W gas:** Crazy D's/dsl/24hr, Marathon/Subway/dsl/24hr, **food:** McDonald's, Ugalde's Rest., **lodging:** Comfort Inn, Motel 6, **other:** H RV Camping, fireworks, to Salmonie Reservoir
76mm	Salamonie River
73	IN 218, to Warren
64	IN 18, to Marion, Montpelier, **W gas:** BP/Subway/dsl, Marathon/dsl, **food:** Arby's, **lodging:** Days Inn, **other:** H, Harley-Davidson, Jeep/Chrysler, **E gas:** Love's/McDonalds/dsl/scales/24hr
60mm	Walnut Creek
59	US 35 N, IN 22, to Upland, **E gas:** Valero/Subway, **food:** Burger King, China 1, Cracker Barrel, E Chicago Pizza, Taste of Texas, **lodging:** B&B, Best Western, Super 8, **other:** Mar-Brook Camping, Taylor U, **W gas:** Marathon/dsl/24hr, McClure Trkstp/dsl/24hr, Shell/dsl, **food:** KFC/Taco Bell, Starbucks, **lodging:** Holiday Inn Express, **other:** Smitty's Truckwash, to IN Wesleyan

IN

INTERSTATE 69 CONT'D

Exit #	Services
55	IN 26, to Fairmount
50mm	**rest area both lanes, full [handicapped] facilities, info, [phone], [picnic], litter barrels, vending, pet walk**
45	US 35 S, IN 28, to Alexandria, Albany, **E gas:** Petro/Shell/Iron Skillet/Taco Bell/dsl/scales/24hr/@, **other:** RV Camping
41	IN 332, to Muncie, Frankton, **E gas:** BP/dsl, Citgo/dsl, **other:** [H], to Ball St U
34	IN 67, to IN 32, Chesterfield, Daleville, **E gas:** Pilot/Subway/dsl/scales/24hr, Shell, **food:** Arby's, Taco Bell, White Castle, **lodging:** Budget Inn, **other:** [H], **W gas:** GA/dsl, Pilot/Cafe/dsl/24hr, **food:** McDonald's, Subway, 3rd Generation Pizza, Wendy's, **lodging:** Best Value Inn, **other:** flea mkt
26	IN 9, IN 109, to Anderson, **E gas:** Meijer/dsl/24hr, **food:** Culver's, KFC/A&W, Ryan's, **lodging:** Deluxe Inn, Hampton Inn, Quality Inn, **other: W gas:** BP, GA, Marathon, Speedway, **food:** Applebee's, Arby's, Bob Evans, Burger King, China Buffet, Cracker Barrel, Fazoli's, Great Wall Chinese, IHOP, La Charreada Mexican, LoneStar Steaks, McDonald's, Noble Roman's, Panera Bread, Penn Sta. Subs, Perkins, Pizza Hut, Olive Garden, Red Lobster, Ritter's, Ruby Tuesday, Starbucks, Steak'n Shake, Subway, Taco Bell, Waffle House, Wendy's, White Castle, Wings Etc., **lodging:** Baymont Inn, Best Inn, Comfort Inn, Days Inn, Fairfield Inn, Garden Inn, Lee's Inn, Motel 6, Rose Carpet Inn, **other:** [H], Aldi Foods, Cadillac/GMC, Curves, Freightliner, Kohl's, Old Navy, O'Rielly Parts, Payless Foods, Radio Shack, Target, Tire Barn, Toyota, Walmart SuperCtr, to Anderson U, to Mounds SP
22	IN 9, IN 67, to Anderson, **W gas:** GA, **food:** Skyline Chili, **lodging:** Anderson Country Inn (1mi), **other:** [H] st police
19	IN 38, Pendleton, **E gas:** Marathon, **food:** Burger King, McDonald's, Subway
14	IN 13, to Lapel, **E gas:** BP, **W gas:** Pilot/Subway/dsl/scales/24hr, **other:** camping
10	IN 238, to Noblesville, Fortville, **W other:** JC Penney
5	IN 37 N, 116th St, to Noblesville, Fishers, **E gas:** BP/Wild Bean Cafe, **W gas:** Shell/autocare, Speedway, **food:** A&W/KFC, Greek Pizzaria, Handel's Ice Cream, Hawg Wild BBQ, McAlister's Deli, McDonald's, O'Charley's, Qdoba Mexican, Quizno's, Starbucks, Station Rest., Steak'n Shake, Subway, Wendy's, **lodging:** Hampton Inn, **other:** Target
3	96th St, **E gas:** Meijer/dsl/24hr, Shell, VP/dsl, **food:** Applebee's, Bennigan's, Cracker Barrel, Donato's Pizza, Golden Wok Chinese, McDonald's, New China, Noble Roman's, Panera Bread, Pizza Shop, Qdoba Mexican, Ruby Tuesday, Steak'n Shake, **lodging:** Hilton Garden, Holiday Inn, Holiday Inn Express, Hotel Indigo, Studio 6, **other:** Kohl's, Marsh Food/gas, PepBoys, PetCo, Radio Shack, Staples, Tuesday morning, Walmart SuperCtr/gas/24hr, **W gas:** Marathon, **food:** Arby's, Bob Evans, Burger King, Cheeseburger Paradise, Culver's, Journey Rest., Panda Express, Peterson's Steaks/seafood, Quizno's, Starbucks, Taco Bell, **lodging:** Comfort Suites,
3	Continued Residence Inn, SpringHill Suites, Staybridge Suites, **other:** Aldi Foods, $Tree, Home Depot, NAPA, Sam's Club/gas
1	82nd St, Castleton, **E food:** Pizza Hut, **lodging:** Country Inn&Suites, Drury Inn, Extended Stay America, Hilton, Super 8, **other:** [H], Lowe's Whse, **W gas:** Speedway, **food:** Applebee's, Arby's, Burger King, Cancun Mexican, Charleston's Rest., Denny's, Fazoli's, Hooters, IHOP, KFC/A&W, Loonlake Lodge Rest., McDonald's, Olive Garden, Penn Sta. Subs, Rally's, Red Lobster, Skyline Chili, Starbucks, Steak'n Shake, Taco Bell, Tuscany Grill, Wendy's, **lodging:** Best Western, Candlewood Suites, Day's Inn, Hampton Inn, Red Roof Inn, **other:** Aamco, Best Buy, Discount Tire, $Tree, Goodyear/auto, Indy Tires, Sears/auto, Tire Barn, mall
0mm	I-465 around Indianapolis. I-69 begins/ends on I-465, exit 37, at Indianapolis.

INTERSTATE 70

Exit #	Services
156.5mm	Indiana/Ohio state line, **weigh sta**
156b a	US 40 E, Richmond, **N gas:** Petro/Marathon/Pizza Hut/dsl/rest./24hr/@, Swifty, **lodging:** Fairfield Inn, **other:** Blue Beacon, **S gas:** BP/White Castle, Shell, Speedway/dsl, **food:** A&W/LJ Silver, Applebee's, Arby's, Big Boy, Bob Evans, Buffalo Wings Cafe, Burger King, Chili's, Cici's Pizza, Cracker Barrel, Domino's, Fazoli's, Golden Corral, Hacienda Mexican, IHOP, Jade House Chinese, KFC, McDonald's, MCL Cafeteria, O'Charley's, Pizza Hut, Red Lobster, Ritter's Custard, Ryan's, Starbucks, Steak'n Shake, Subway, Super China, Taco Bell, TX Roadhouse, **lodging:** Best Western, Days Inn, Hampton Inn, Holiday Inn, Lee's Inn, Motel 6, **other:** AAA, Aamco, Advance Parts, Aldi Foods, AT&T, BigLots, Buick/GMC/Pontiac, Cadillac/Chevrolet, Carquest, Chrysler/Jeep, Curves, Dillards, $General, Expert Tire, Ford, Goodyear/auto, Hastings Books, Hobby Lobby, JC Penney, Jo-Ann Fabrics, Kohl's, Kroger, Lowes Whse, Menards, Sav-a-Lot Foods, Sears/auto, Target, Tires+, Toyota/Scion, Tuffy, U-Haul, Walgreens, Walmart SuperCtr/gas/24hr, Vet
153	IN 227, to Whitewater, Richmond, **2 mi N** Grandpa's Farm RV Park (seasonal)
151b a	US 27, to Chester, Richmond, **N food:** Fricker's Rest., **other:** Dodge, Honda, KOA, **S gas:** Shell, **food:** Bob Evans, Burger King, Carver's Rest., China Buffet, McDonald's, Pizza Hut, Rally's, Subway, Taco Bell, Wendy's, **lodging:** Comfort Inn, Super 8, **other:** [H], Harley-Davidson, Meijer food/gas
149b a	US 35, IN 38, to Muncie, **N** Love's/Hardee's/dsl/scales/24hr, **S gas:** Shell/Quizno's/dsl, **other:** Raper RV Ctr
148mm	**weigh sta wb**
145	Centerville, **N gas:** BP/DQ/Stuckey's, **lodging:** Super 8, **other:** Goodyear/truck repair, **S** Warm Glow Candles
145mm	Nolands Fork Creek
144mm	**rest area both lanes, full [handicapped] facilities, info, vending, [phone], [picnic], litter barrels, petwalk**

INTERSTATE 70 CONT'D

E ↕ W

Exit #	Services
141mm	Greens Fork River
137	IN 1, to Hagerstown, Connersville, **N** Amish Cheese, **S gas:** GA/24hr, Gas City/dsl/rest./24hr, Shell/24hr, **food:** Burger King, McDonald's
131	Wilbur Wright Rd, New Lisbon, **S gas:** Marathon/ KFC/Taco Bell/dsl/scales/24hr/@, **other:** New Lisbon RV park
126mm	Flatrock River
123	IN 3, to New Castle, Spiceland, **N lodging:** All American Inn (3mi), Best Value Inn, Best Western (3mi), Holiday Inn Express (3mi), **other:** H, Irwin RV Park (1mi), **S gas:** *FLYING J*/CountyMkt/dsl/scales/ LP/24hr, **other:** tires/repair
117mm	Big Blue River
115	IN 109, to Knightstown, Wilkinson, **N gas:** GA/Gas Grill/dsl/scales/24hr, **food:** Burger King, **other:** Jellystone Camping
107mm	**rest area both lanes, full ♿ facilities, vending, ☎, picnic, litter barrels, petwalk**
104	IN 9, Greenfield, Maxwell, **N gas:** GA, **S gas:** GA, Murphy USA, Shell/Circle K, Sunoco/dsl, Swifty, **food:** Applebee's, Arby's, Bamboo Garden, Bob Evans, Burger King, China Inn, Cracker Barrel, Culver's, Dunkin Donuts, El Rodeo Mexican, Hardee's, KFC, McDonald's, Mi Casa Mexican, MT Mike's Steaks, Mozzie's Pizza, O'Charley's, Papa John's, Papa Murphy's, Penn Sta. Subs, Pizza Hut, Ponderosa, Quizno's, Ritter's Custard, Starbucks, Steak'n Shake, Subway, Taco Bell, Wendy's, White Castle, **lodging:** Comfort Inn, $Inn, Hampton Inn, Holiday Inn Express, Quality Inn, Super 8, **other:** H, Advance Parts, Aldi Foods, AutoZone, Big Lots, Big O Tire, CVS Drug, $General, $Tree, GNC, Home Depot, Kroger, Marsh Foods, Radio Shack, Walgreens, Walmart SuperCtr/24hr
96	Mt Comfort Rd, **N gas:** GA/Subway/mart, Pilot/ Pizza Hut/dsl/scales/24hr, **food:** Burger King, El Napal, Wendy's, **other:** Heartland RV Park (2mi), **S gas:** Shell/Circle K, **food:** McDonald's, **other:** KOA (seasonal), Mt Comfort RV Ctr
91	Post Rd, to Ft Harrison, **N gas:** 7-11, **food:** Cracker Barrel, Denny's, Joe's Crabshack, Outback Steaks, Steak'n Shake, Wendy's, **lodging:** InTown Suites, La Quinta, **other:** Lowe's Whse, st police, **S gas:** Admiral, BP/mart, Shell/mart, Speedway, **food:** Hardee's, KFC/Taco Bell, Waffle House, **lodging:** Country Hearth Inn, Days Inn, Super 8, **other:** CVS Drug, Family$, Home Depot, Marsh Foods
90	I-465 (from wb)
89	Shadeland Ave, I-465 (from eb), **N gas:** Marathon/ dsl, **food:** Bob Evans, **lodging:** Comfort Inn, Comfort Suites, Hampton Inn, Motel 6, **other:** Toyota, U-Haul, **S gas:** Admiral/dsl, Circle K, Marathon, Shell/24hr, Speedway/dsl, **food:** Arby's, Burger King, Blimpie, El Dorado Mexican, 4Seasons Diner, Lincoln's Rest., McDonald's, Noble Roman's, Papa John's, Quizno's, Rally's, Red Lobster, Ryan's, Starbucks, Subway, Taco Bell, TX Roadhouse, Wendy's, **lodging:** Always Inn, Best Value Inn, Fairfield Inn, Holiday Inn/Damon's, Knight's Inn, La Quinta, Marriott, Quality Inn,

INDIANAPOLIS AREA

Exit #	Services
89	Continued **other:** Aamco, Buick, CVS Drug, Chevrolet, Dodge, Honda, Kia, Kroger, Nissan
87	Emerson Ave, **N gas:** BP/McDonald's, Speedway, **S gas:** Shell, **other:** H
85b a	Rural St, Keystone Ave, **N** fairgrounds
83b (112)	I-65 N, to Chicago
83a (111)	Michigan St, Market St, downtown, **S food:** Hardee's
80 (110a)	I-65 S, to Louisville
79b	Illinois St, McCarty St, downtown
79a	West St, **N gas:** Speedway/dsl, **lodging:** Comfort Inn, Holiday Inn Express, Hyatt, Staybridge Suites, **other:** H, to Union Sta, Govt Ctr, Lucas Oil Stadium, RCA Dome, zoo
78	Harding St, to downtown, **S gas:** Marathon, **food:** Wendy's
77	Holt Rd, **N food:** Steak'n Shake, **S gas:** Shell, **food:** McDonald's, **other:** Ford Trucks
75	Airport Expswy, to Raymond St (no EZ wb return), **N gas:** Marathon, Speedway/dsl, **food:** Denny's, Indy's Rest., Library Rest, Waffle House, **lodging:** Adam's Mark, Candlewood Suites, Courtyard, Econolodge, Extended Stay Deluxe, Fairfield Inn, Hyatt Place, La Quinta, Quality Inn, Ramada, Residence Inn, **other:** NAPA, to ✈
73b a	I-465 N/S, I-74 E/W
69	(only from eb)to I-74 E, to I-465 S
68	Six Points Rd, **N lodging:** Hampton Inn, Hilton Garden, **other:** ✈
66	IN 267, to Plainfield, Mooresville, **N gas:** BP/24hr, Shell/Circle K, Speedway/dsl, Thornton's/dsl, **food:** Arby's, Bob Evans, Burger King, Coachman Rest., Cracker Barrel, Denny's, Golden Corral, Hog Heaven BBQ, McDonald's, Quizno's, Steak'n Shake, Subway, White Castle, Wood Fire Grill, **lodging:** Baymont Inn, Best Western, Budget Inn, Cambria Suites, Comfort Inn, Days Inn, Hampton Inn, Holiday Inn Express, Homewood Suites, Motel 6, Staybridge Suites, Super 8, ValuePlace Inn, Wingate Inn, **other:** Chateau Thomas Winery, Harley-Davidson
65mm	**rest area both lanes, full ♿ facilities, info, vending, ☎, picnic, litter barrels, petwalk**
59	IN 39, to Belleville, **N other:** H, **S gas:** TA/Country Pride/rest/dsl/scales/24hr/@, truckwash
51	rd 1100W, **S gas:** Koger's/Sunoco/dsl/rest/24hr, **other:** repair/towing/24hr
41	US 231, to Greencastle, Cloverdale, **S gas:** BP/dsl, Casey's (2mi), Marathon/Subway/dsl/scales/24hr,

INTERSTATE 70 CONT'D

Exit #	Services
41	Continued **food:** Arby's, Chicago's Pizza, KFC, McDonald's, Taco Bell, Wendy's, **lodging:** Days Inn, Econolodge, Holiday Inn Express, Motel 6, Super 8, **other:** H, Bill's Hardware, Discount Tire, Value Mkt Foods, to Lieber SRA
37	IN 243, to Putnamville, **S gas:** Marathon/dsl, **food:** Wilderness Cafe, **other:** Misty Morning Campgrd (4mi), to Lieber SRA
23	IN 59, to Brazil, **N gas:** Pilot/McDonald's/Subway/dsl/scales/mart/24hr, **other:** H, **S gas:** AM Best/Brazil Grill/dsl/scales/24hr/@, BP/Rally's/dsl/mart, Road Ranger/Pilot/Subway/dsl/scales, **food:** Burger King, Family Table Rest, **lodging:** Howard Johnson Express
15mm	Honey Creek
11	IN 46, Terre Haute, **N gas:** Pilot/Arby's/scales/dsl/mart/24hr, Thornton/dsl, **food:** Burger King, McDonald's, **other:** ✈, **S** KOA
7	US 41, US 150, Terre Haute, **N gas:** Marathon/dsl, Thornton's/dsl, **food:** Applebee's, Beef o'Brady's, Bob Evans, Cracker Barrel, China Buffet, Fazoli's, IHOP, LoneStar Steaks, Pasta House, Pizza Hut, Quizno's, Real Hacienda Mexican, Sam's Steaks, Starbucks, Steak'n Shake, TX Roadhouse, Tumbleweed SW Grill, **lodging:** Best Western, Comfort Suites, Days Inn, Drury Inn, Econolodge, Fairfield Inn, PearTree Inn, Super 8, **other:** AutoZone, Kia, **S gas:** Speedway/dsl, Thornton's/mart, **food:** Arby's, Baskin-Robbins, Buffalo Wild Wings, Burger King, Cheeseburger Paradise, Crazy Buffet, DQ, Denny's, Garfield's Rest., Golden Corral, Hardee's, Ichiban Japanese, KFC, Little Caesar's, Los Tres Caminos, LJ Silver, McDonald's, Olive Garden, Outback Steaks, Panera Bread, Papa John's, Penn Sta. Subs, Rally's, Red Lobster, Ruby Tuesday, Ryan's, Starbucks, Subway, Taco Bell, TGIFriday's, Wendy's, White Castle, **lodging:** Hampton Inn, Holiday Inn, Knight's Inn, SpringHill Suites, **other:** H, Aldi Foods, AT&T, BigLots, BooksAMillion, Buick/Cadillac/GMC/Pontiac, Burlington Coats, Chevrolet/Hyundai/Nissan, Dodge, $Tree, Gander Mtn., Goodyear/auto, Harley-Davidson, Hobby Lobby, Jo-Ann Fabrics, K-Mart/gas, Kohl's, Kroger/gas, Lowe's Whse, Macy's, NAPA, Old Navy, PetCo, Petsmart, Sam's Club/gas, Sears/auto, Staples, Tire Barn, TJ Maxx, Tuesday Morning, Walgreens, Walmart SuperCtr
5.5mm	Wabash River
3	Darwin Rd, W Terre Haute, **N** to St Mary of-the-Woods Coll
1.5mm	**Welcome Ctr eb, full ♿ facilities, info, picnic, litter barrels, phone, vending, petwalk**
1	US 40 E (from eb, exits left), to Terre Haute, W Terre Haute
.5mm	**weigh sta, eb only**
0mm	Indiana/Illinois state line

INTERSTATE 74

Exit #	Services
171.5mm	Indiana/Ohio state line
171mm	**weigh sta wb**
169	US 52 W, to Brookville
168.5mm	Whitewater River
164	IN 1, St Leon, **N gas:** Exxon/Noble Romans, Shell/dsl, **S gas:** BP/Blimpie/dsl
156	IN 101, to Sunman, Milan, **S gas:** Exxon/dsl
152mm	**rest area both lanes, full ♿ facilities, phone, picnic, litter barrels, vending, petwalk**
149	IN 229, to Oldenburg, Batesville, **N gas:** Shell/dsl/24hr, Sunoco, **food:** Acapulco Mexican, China Wok, McDonald's, Subway, Wendy's, **lodging:** Hampton Inn, **other:** Advance Parts, $General, Kroger/gas, Pamida, **S gas:** BP, **food:** Arby's, DQ, KFC/Taco Bell, La Rosa's Pizza, Skyline Chili, **lodging:** Comfort Inn, **other:** H, CVS Drug
143	to IN 46, New Point, **N gas:** Petro/Marathon/Iron Skillet/dsl/scales/24hr/@, **S gas:** BP
134b a	IN 3, to Rushville, Greensburg, **S gas:** BP/dsl, Marathon/DQ/Subway, Shell/24hr, Speedway/dsl, **food:** A&W, Acupulco Mexican, Arby's, Big Boy, Burger King, Chili's, El Reparo Mexican, Great Wall Buffet, KFC, LJ Silver, McDonald's, Papa John's, Papa Murphy's, Subway, Taco Bell, Waffle House, Wendy's, **lodging:** Fairfield Inn, Lee's Inn, Holiday Inn Express, **other:** Advance Parts, Aldi Foods, AutoZone, Cadillac/Chevrolet, Chrysler/Dodge/Jeep, CVS Drug, $General, $Tree, Ford/Mercury, Marsh Foods, NTB, Radio Shack, Staples, Walmart SuperCtr/24hr, Walgreens
132	US 421, to Greensburg, **S gas:** BP, **lodging:** Hampton Inn
130mm	Clifty Creek
123	Saint Paul, **S** camping
119	IN 244 E, to Milroy
116	IN 44, to Shelbyville, Rushville, **N gas:** Bigfoot/dsl, **S gas:** Marathon, Murphy USA, Shell/24hr, Swifty, **food:** Applebee's, Arby's, Bellacino's, Bob Evans, Burger King, China Buffet, China Inn, Cholula Mexican, Denny's, DQ, King Buffet, LJ Silver, McDonald's, Papa Muprhy's, Pizza Hut, Rally's, Starbucks, Subway, Taco Bell, Wendy's, **lodging:** Lee's Inn, **other:** H, Ace Hardware, Advance Parts, Aldi Foods, Big Lots, Chevrolet, Curves, $General, $Tree, Ford/Lincoln/Mercury, GNC, Kroger/gas, Marsh Foods, Radio Shack, Walgreens, Walmart SuperCtr/24hr
115mm	Little Blue River
113mm	Big Blue River
113	IN 9, to Shelbyville, **N gas:** GA/dsl, **food:** Cracker Barrel, Santa Fe Steaks, Wendy's, **S gas:** CF/Subway/dsl, Gas USA, **food:** El Emparador Mexican, McDonald's, Waffle House, **lodging:** Best Value Inn, Comfort Inn, Hampton Inn, Knight's Inn, Super 8, **other:** H
109	Fairland Rd, **N gas:** Pilot/McDonald's/dsl/scales/24hr, **other:** Indiana Downs/casino, **S other:** Brownie's Marine
103	London Rd, to Boggstown
102mm	Big Sugar Creek
101	Pleasant View Rd, **N gas:** Country Mark/dsl/repair
99	Acton Rd
96	Post Rd, **N gas:** Marathon/Subway/dsl/24hr, **food:** McDonald's, **S gas:** Shell/Circle K/dsl, **food:** Cholula Mexican, Wendy's, **other:** Chevrolet
94b a	I-465/I-74 W, I-465 N, US 421 N

TERRE HAUTE

SHELBYVILLE

INTERSTATE 74 CONT'D

Exit #	Services
I-74 & I-465 run together 21 miles. See I-465, exits 2-16, and 52-53	
73b	I-465 N, access to same services as 16a on I-465
73a	I-465 S, I-74 E
71mm	Eagle Creek
68	Ronald Reagan Pkwy
66	IN 267, Brownsburg, N gas: Citgo/dsl, Shell, food: Applebee's, Asia Wok, Dunkin Donuts, Hardee's, Steak'n Shake, Subway, lodging: Hampton Inn, Holiday Inn Express, other: Big O Tire, S gas: BP/dsl, Speedway/dsl, food: Arby's, Blimpie, Bob Evans, Burger King, China's Best, Howah Chinese, Jimmy John's, KFC, Los Toros Mexican, McDonald's, Papa Murphy's, Quizno's, Starbucks, Taco Bell, Wendy's, White Castle, Wings Etc., lodging: Comfort Suites, Super 8, other: Curves, $Tree, Ford, Kohl's, Kroger/gas, K-Mart, Lowe's Whse, Radio Shack, Walmart SuperCtr/24hr
61	to Pittsboro, S gas: Loves/Godfathers/Subway/dsl/scales/24hr
58	IN 39, to Lebanon, Lizton, S H
57mm	**rest area both lanes, full ♿ facilities, phone, picnic, litter barrels, vending, petwalk**
52	IN 75, to Advance, Jamestown, 2 mi S gas, food, camping
39	IN 32, to Crawfordsville, S gas: Pilot/Subway/dsl/scales/24hr
34	US 231, to Linden, S gas: BP/Circle K, CTP/dsl/scales/24hr, GA, Marathon/dsl, food: Burger King, McDonald's, Subway, lodging: Candlewood Suites, Comfort Inn, Days Inn, Hampton Inn, Holiday Inn Express, Quality Inn, Ramada Ltd., Super 8, other: H, Buick/GMC/Pontiac, KOA (1mi), Sugar Creek Campground (4mi)
25	IN 25, to Wingate, Waynetown
22mm	**rest area both lanes, full ♿ facilities, phone, picnic, litter barrels, vending, petwalk**
19mm	**weigh sta eb/parking area wb**
15	US 41, to Attica, Veedersburg, 1/2 mi S gas: Marathon/Subway/dsl, food: Apple Tree Diner, other: to Turkey Run SP, camping
8	Covington, N food: Maple Corner Rest. (1mi), Overpass Pizza, other: Ford, fireworks
7mm	Wabash River
4	IN 63, to Newport, N gas: Pilot/Arby's/dsl/scales/24hr, food: Beefhouse Rest., Wendy's
1mm	**Welcome Ctr eb, full ♿ facilities, info, phone, picnic, litter barrels, vending, petwalk**
0mm	Indiana/Illinois state line, Eastern/Central Time Zone

INTERSTATE 80/90

Exit #	Services
157mm	Indiana/Ohio state line
153mm	toll plaza, litter barrels
146mm	TP both lanes, Mobil/dsl, DQ, McDonald's, playground
144	I-69, US 27, Angola, Ft Wayne, N gas: Petro/Mobil/dsl/LP/@, Pilot/Wendy's/dsl/scales, Shell/Subway/dsl, food: McDonald's, Red Arrow Rest., lodging: Redwood Lodge, Lake George Inn, other: Freightliner/Western Star/truck repair, S gas: Marathon/dsl/24hr, lodging: Holiday Inn Express, other: Outlet Shops/famous brands, services on IN 120 E lodging: Hampton Inn, Super 8, Traveler's Inn, other: golf/rest, W to Pokagon SP, Jellystone Camping (5mi)
131.5mm	Fawn River
126mm	TP both lanes, Mobil/dsl, Fazoli's, Hardee's, gifts, RV dump
121	IN 9, to Lagrange, Howe, N gas: Golden Buddha, lodging: Best Value Inn, Best Western, Hampton Inn, Travel Inn, other: H (4mi), 2 mi N gas: Speedway/dsl, food: Applebee's, Burger King KFC, King Dragon, Little Caesar's, McDonald's, Pizza Hut, Savory Rest., Subway, Taco Bell, Wendy's, lodging: Regency Inn, other: $Tree, Ford, GNC, K-Mart, Kroger, Radio Shack, Walgreens, Walmart SuperCtr/gas, S gas: Valero, lodging: Holiday Inn Express, Super 8, other: H (8mi)
120mm	Fawn River
108mm	**trucks only rest area both lanes**
107	US 131, IN 13, to Middlebury, Constantine, N gas: Marathon/dsl, food: Country Table Rest. (2mi), lodging: Patchwork Quilt B&B, Plaza Motel, 1 mi S gas: BP/Blimpie/dsl, food: Yup's DairyLand, other: Eby's Pines RV Park, KOA (apr-nov)
101	IN 15, to Goshen, Bristol, 1 mi S gas: Speedway/dsl, food: River Inn Rest., other: Eby's Pines Camping (3mi)
96	rd 1, E Elkhart, 2 mi S gas: BP/dsl, Marathon, 7-11, food: Arby's, China Star, DQ, McDonald's, Subway, other: Ace Hardware
92	IN 19, to Elkhart, N gas: Marathon, Phillips 66/Subway/dsl, 7-11, food: Applebee's, Cracker Barrel, Perkins, Steak'n Shake, lodging: Best Western, Candlewood Suites, Comfort Suites, Country Inn&Suites, Diplomat Motel, Econolodge, Fairway Inn, Hampton Inn, Hilton Garden, Holiday Inn Express, Knight's Inn, Quality Inn, Sleep Inn, Turnpike Motel, other: Aldi Foods, CVS Drug, Elkhart Campground (1mi), GNC, K-Mart, Martin's Foods, Tiara RV Ctr, tires, transmissions, 0-2 mi S gas: Marathon/dsl, Shell, food: Arby's, Bennigan's, Blimpie, Bob Evans, Burger King, Callahan's Rest., Chicago Grill, CiCi's Pizza, Culver's, Da Vinci's Pizza, DQ, KFC, LJ Silver, Matterhorn Rest., McDonald's, North Garden Buffet, Olive Garden, Pizza Hut, Red Lobster, Ryan's, Taco Bell, Texas Roadhouse, Wendy's, Wings Etc., lodging: Budget Inn, Day's Inn, Jameson Inn, Ramada Inn, Red Roof Inn, Super 8, other: H, Ace Hardware,

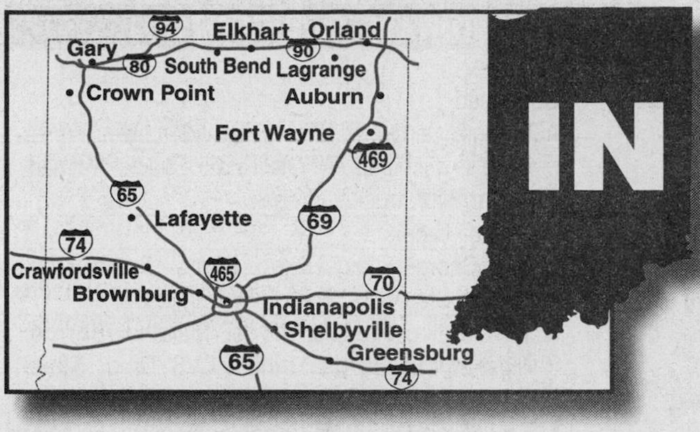

E ↕ W BROWNSBURG

E ↕ W ELKHART

Gary, Elkhart, Orland, South Bend, Lagrange, Crown Point, Auburn, Fort Wayne, Lafayette, Crawfordsville, Brownburg, Indianapolis, Shelbyville, Greensburg — 94, 80, 90, 469, 65, 69, 74, 465, 70, 65, 74

IN

IN

INTERSTATE 80/90 CONT'D

E ↔ W — SOUTH BEND

Exit #	Services
92	Continued AutoZone, CarQuest, $Tree, Family$, Lowes Whse, Menard's, Michiana RV Ctr, Radio Shack, Walmart SuperCtr/24hr, truck/RV repair
91mm	Christiana Creek
90mm	TP eb, George Craig TP wb, BP/dsl, Burger King, Pizza Hut, Starbucks, Z Mkt, RV Dump, USPO
83	to Mishawaka, **N gas:** BP/dsl, Marathon/Blimpie, Phillips 66/Subway/dsl, **other:** CVS Drug, $Tree, Marshall's, Martin's Foods/gas, Menard's, Walgreens, **1-2 mi N on IN 23 W food:** Applebee's, Famous Dave's BBQ, King's Buffet, Olive Garden, Pizza Hut, Quizno's, Wendy's, **lodging:** Country Inn&Suites, Fairfield Inn, Hampton Inn, Holiday Inn Express, Super 8, **other:** Best Buy, JC Penney, Kroger, Macy's, Michael's, Sears/auto, Target, KOA (mar-nov), mall, **2 mi S on Grape Rd & Main St (off IN 23W)... gas:** Meijer/dsl/24hr, **food:** Arby's, Bob Evans, Buffalo Wild Wings, Burger King, Carraba's, Chick-fil-A, Chili's, Chipotle Mexican, Del Taco, Houlihan's, Hooters, Jimmy John's, Krispy Kreme, Logan's Roadhouse, Mancino's Pizza, Max&Erma's, McDonald's, Outback Steaks, Panera Bread, Papa Vino's Italian, Red Lobster, Ryan's, Starbucks, Steak'n Shake, Subway, Taste of Asia, Texas L&C, TGIFriday, **lodging:** Comfort Inn, Courtyard, Extended Stay America, Hyatt Place Hotel, Residence Inn, SpringHill Suites, Studio+, **other:** Aldi Foods, Barnes&Noble, Borders, Buick/GMC/Pontiac, Chrysler, Discount Tire, Home Depot, Honda, Hyundai, Jo-Ann Fabrics, Kohl's, Lexus, Lowes Whse, Mercedes, Nissan, Old Navy, Sam's Club, TJ Maxx, Walmart SuperCtr/24hr
77	US 33, US 31B, IN 933, South Bend, **N gas:** Admiral, Mobil/dsl, **food:** Arby's, Burger King, DQ, Eleni's Rest., Fazoli's, J-Willy's Grill, KFC, Marco's Pizza, McDonald's, Papa John's, Ponderosa, Starbucks, Steak&Ale, Steak&Shake, Subway, **lodging:** Comfort Suites, Day's Inn, Hampton Inn, Motel 6, Waterford Lodge, **other:** AutoZone, BMW, Mazda, NAPA, O'Reilly Parts, Radio Shack, TrueValue, Walgreens, **2 mi N on frtge rd...gas:** Meijer/dsl/24hr, Phillips 66, **food:** Applebees, Burger King, McDonald's, Sonic, **other:** Aldi Foods, $Tree, Walmart SuperCtr, **S gas:** Marathon, Phillips 66/dsl, **food:** Bob Evans, Denny's, King Gyro's, Mikados Japanese, Pancake House, Perkins, Taco Bell, Wendy's, **lodging:** Best Value Inn, Hilton Garden, Holiday Inn Express, Howard Johnson, Jameson Inn, Knight's Inn, Quality Inn, St Marys Inn, **other:** [H], Vet, to Notre Dame
76mm	St Joseph River
72	US 31, to Niles, South Bend, **N gas:** Pilot/Subway/dsl/scales/24hr, Speedway/Subway/dsl, **lodging:** Super 8, **2 mi S on US 20...food:** 4 Seasons Rest., McDonald's, Ponderosa, Taco Bell, Wendy's, **lodging:** Day's Inn, Quality Inn, **other:** RV Ctr, to Potato Creek SP (20mi), [airport], st police
62mm	Eastern Time Zone/Central Time Zone
56mm	**Rockne travel plaza both lanes**, BP/dsl, DQ, McDonald's, [phone], RV dump, litter barrel
49	IN 39, to La Porte, **N lodging:** Hampton Inn, **S lodging:** Best Value Inn, Cassidy Inn & RV, **3 mi S gas:** Mobil/dsl, **lodging:** Blue Heron Motel, Holiday Inn Express, Super 8
39	US 421, to Michigan City, Westville, **5 mi N lodging:** Hampton Inn, Holiday Inn, Knight's Inn, **other:** Premium Outlets/famous brands, **S** Purdue U North Cent
38mm	**trucks only rest area both lanes, litter barrels**
31	IN 49, to Chesterton, Valparaiso, **N lodging:** Best Western, Hilton Garden, Super 8 (3mi), **other:** Sand Creek RV Park (4mi, Apr-Oct), to IN Dunes Nat Lakeshore, **S lodging:** Hampton Inn (8mi), **other:** Yellow Brick Rd Museum/gifts
24mm	toll plaza
23	Portage, Port of Indiana, **0-2 mi N gas:** Marathon, Shell, **food:** Mark's Grill, **lodging:** Day's Inn, Comfort Inn, Country Inn&Suites, Holiday Inn Express, $Inn, Ramada Inn, Super 8, **S gas:** BP, Clark, Marathon, **food:** Burger King, Cici's Pizza, Dunkin Donuts, DQ, First Wok Chinese, Jimmy John's, KFC, McDonald's, Starbucks, Subway, Wendy's, **other:** Advance Parts, Ace Hardware, $General, Family$, GNC, Town&Country Mkt/24hr, USPO, Walgreens
22mm	TP both lanes, info, **gas:** BP/dsl, **food:** Fazoli's, Hardee's, **other:** playground, scales
21mm	**I-90 and I-80 run together eb, separate wb. I-80 runs with I-94 wb. For I-80 exits 1 through 15, see Indiana Interstate 94.**
21	I-94 E to Detroit, I-80/94 W, US 6, IN 51, Lake Station, **S gas:** *FLYING J*/Cookery/dsl/scales/24hr/@, Road Ranger/Subway/dsl/scales, TA/BP/Popeye's/dsl/scales/24hr/@, **food:** McDonald's, **other:** Blue Beacon
17	I-65 S, US 12, US 20, Dunes Hwy, to Indianapolis
14b	IN 53, to Gary, Broadway, **S gas:** Citgo, **food:** Bennigan's
14a	Grant St, to Gary, **S** [H]
10	IN 912, Cline Ave, to Gary, **N** [airport], casino
5	US 41, Calumet Ave, to Hammond, **S gas:** Nice'n Easy, RaceCo, Speedway/dsl, **food:** Arby's, Aurelio's Pizza, Dunkin Donuts, Johnel's Rest., KFC, McDonald's, Subway, Taco Bell, White Castle, **lodging:** Quality Inn, Ramada Inn, Super 8, **other:** Aldi Foods, AutoZone, Murray's Parts, Walgreens
3	IN 912, Cline Ave, to Hammond, to Gary Reg [airport], **S gas:** BP
1.5mm	toll plaza
1mm	US 12, US 20, 106th St, Indianapolis Blvd, **N gas:** Citgo, Mobil, Shell/dsl, **other:** casino, **S food:** Burger King, KFC, McDonald's, **other:** Aldi Foods, Jewel-Osco, auto repair
0mm	Indiana/Illinois state line

PORTAGE — GARY AREA

INTERSTATE 94

E ↔ W

Exit #	Services
46mm	Indiana/Michigan state line
43mm	**Welcome Ctr wb, full [handicapped] facilities, info, [phone], [picnic], litter barrels, vending, petwalk**
40b a	US 20, US 35, to Michigan City, **N food:** McDonald's (3mi), **other:** [H], **S gas:** Speedway/dsl

IN

INTERSTATE 94 CONT'D

E ↕ W

Exit #	Services
34b a	US 421, to Michigan City, **N gas:** BP/dsl, Citgo/dsl, Meijer/dsl/24hr, Speedway/White Castle/dsl, Xpress/gas, **food:** Applebee's, Arby's, Baker's Square, Bob Evans, Buffalo Wings, Burger King, Chili's, Culver's, Denny's, El Bracero Mexican, IHOP, KFC, LJ Silver, McDonald's, New China, Pizza Hut/Taco Bell, Popeye's, Quizno's, Red Lobster, Ryan's, Schoop's Rest., Starbucks, Steak'n Shake, Subway, Texas Corral, Wendy's, **lodging:** Comfort Inn, Country Inn Suites, Hampton Inn, Holiday Inn, Knight's Inn, Milan Inn, Red Roof Inn, Super 8, **other:** H, Aldi Foods, AutoZone, BigLots, $Tree, Fanny May Candies, Ford/Lincoln/Mercury, JC Penney, Jo-Ann Fabrics, Lowe's Whse, Meijer, Parts+, Radio Shack, Sears/auto, Walgreens, Walmart/auto, **S gas:** Gas City/Subway, **other:** Buick/Pontiac/GMC, Harley-Davidson
29mm	**weigh sta both lanes**
26b a	IN 49, Chesterton, **N** to IN Dunes SP, **S gas:** BP/White Castle, Shell/24hr, Speedway/dsl, **food:** Applebee's, A&W/KFC, Arby's, Burger King, China Chef, Cold Stone Creamery, Dunkin Donuts, El Salto Mexican, LJ Silver, McDonald's, Pizza Hut, Quizno's, Schoops Rest., Subway, Sunrise Rest., Taco Bell, Wendy's, **lodging:** Best Western, Econolodge, Hilton Garden (3mi), Super 8, **other:** Advance Parts, Curves, Jewel-Osco, K-Mart, Sand Cr Camping (5mi), Walgreens, to Valparaiso
22b a	US 20, Burns Harbor, **N gas:** Steel City Express/scales/dsl, TA/Subway/Buckhorn Rest./scales/dsl/rest./24hr/@, **other:** Blue Beacon, **S gas:** Mobil, Pilot/McDonald's/Subway/dsl/scales/24hr, **other:** Camp-Land RV Ctr, Chevrolet, Chrysler/Dodge/Jeep, Ford/Mercury, Toyota/Scion, fireworks
19	IN 249, to Port of IN, Portage, **N gas:** Family Express/dsl, **food:** Hooters, Longhorn Steaks, **lodging:** Country Inn Suites, **other:** Bass Pro Shops, **S gas:** Marathon/24hr, Shell, **food:** Denny's, Ryan's Rest., **lodging:** Best Value, Day's Inn, Dollar Inn, Hampton Inn, Super 8, **2 mi S food:** Burger King, Subway, Wendy's
16	access to I-80/90 toll road E, I-90 toll road W, IN 51N, Ripley St, same as 15b&a
I-94/I-80 run together wb	
15b	US 6W, IN 51, **N gas:** BP, ***FLYING J***/Cookery/dsl/scales/24hr/@, Road Ranger/Subway/dsl/scales/24hr, TA/BP/Popeye's/dsl/scales/24hr/@, **food:** McDonald's, **other:** Blue Beacon, **N on US 20 gas:** Dunes/scales/dsl repair, Marathon, **food:** Bayside Grill, Ponderosa, **other:** Parts+
15a	US 6E, IN 51S, to US 20, **S gas:** Mobil/dsl, Road Ranger/Subway/scales/dsl, Shell, **food:** Burger King, DQ, Papa John's, LJ Silver, Reuben's Café, Wendy's, **other:** Ace Hardware, Walgreens
13	Central Ave (from eb)
12b	I-65 N, to Gary and toll road
12a	I-65 S (from wb), to Indianapolis
11	I-65 S (from eb)
10b a	IN 53, Broadway, **N gas:** Citgo, Gas for Less, **food:** JJ Fish, **S gas:** Mobil, **food:** DQ, Rally's

PORTAGE

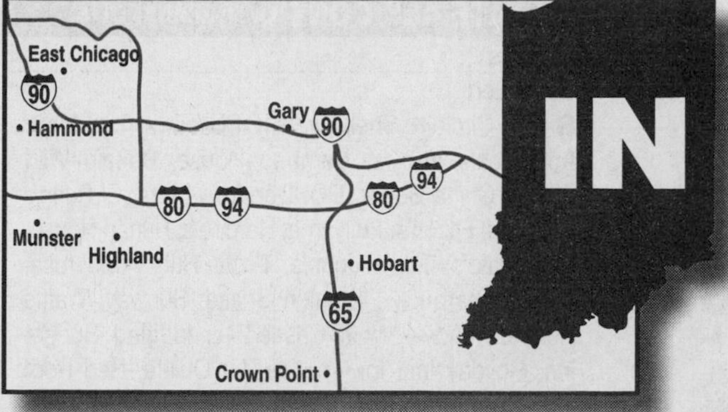

GARY AREA

Exit #	Services
9	Grant St, **N gas:** Clark, **food:** Chicago Hotdogs, **other:** County Mkt Foods, Sav-a-Lot Foods, Walgreens, **S gas:** Citgo, ***FLYING J***/Cookery/scales/dsl/LP/24hr/@, Steel City/dsl/scales/rest./24hr, **food:** A&W/KFC, Burger King, Church's, Dunkin Donuts, J&J Fish, McDonald's, Subway, **other:** Aldi Foods, AutoZone, CarEx, $Tree, Fagen Drug, Firestone/auto, Midas
6	Burr St, **N gas:** Pilot/Subway/dsl/scales/24hr/@, TA/Chester's/Pizza Hut/Taco Bell/dsl/scales/24hr/@, **food:** J&J Fish & Chicken, Philly Steaks, Rico's Pizza, **other:** SpeedCo, **S gas:** Citgo/dsl/24hr
5	IN 912, Cline Ave, **S gas:** BP, Clark, Marathon, Speedway, **food:** Arby's, DQ, Jedi's Garden Rest., KFC, McDonald's, Pizza Hut, Popeye's, Taco Bell, Wendy's, White Castle, **lodging:** Best Western, Hometowne Lodge, Motel 6, Super 8, **other:** $Tree, Fannie May Candies, K-Mart, Radio Shack
3	Kennedy Ave, **N gas:** Clark, Mobil/dsl, Speedway, **food:** Burger King, Domino's, McDonald's, **other:** Walgreens, repair, **S gas:** Citgo, **food:** Cholie's Pizza, Cracker Barrel, Squigi's Pizza, Subway, Wendy's, **lodging:** Courtyard, Fairfield Inn, Residence Inn, **other:** IN Welcome Ctr, USPO
2	US 41S, IN 152N, Indianapolis Blvd, **N gas:** GoLo, Luke, SavAStop, **food:** Arby's, Dunkin Donuts, House Of Pizza, La Rosa, Papa John's, Pizza Hut, Popeye's, Rally's, Schoop's Burgers, Taco Bell, Wheel Rest., Woodmar Rest., **other:** CarEx, Goodyear, Midas, Vet, **S gas:** Pilot/scales/dsl/24hr, **lodging:** Hammond Inn, **other:** Aldi Foods, Cabela's
1	US 41N, Calumet Ave, **N gas:** BP/dsl, Gas City, **food:** Barton's Pizza, Baskin-Robbins/Dunkin Donuts, Subway, **other:** Walgreens, **S gas:** BP, Mobil/dsl, Marathon, Shell, **food:** Arby's, Baskin-Robbins/Dunkin Donuts, Boston Mkt, Burger King, Canton House Chinese, Edwardo's Pizza, Fortune House, Munster Gyros, Subway, Taco Bell, Wendy's, **other:** $Jct, Jewel-Osco, Radio Shack, Staples, Target, Vet
0mm	Indiana/Illinois state line

INTERSTATE 465 (INDIANAPOLIS)

Exit #	Services
I-465 loops around Indianapolis. Exit numbers begin/end on I-65, exit 108.	
53b a	I-65 N to Indianapolis, S to Louisville
52	Emerson Ave, **N gas:** Marathon, Shell/Circle K, Speedway, **food:** Asian Spice, Burger King, Denny's, Domino's, KFC, LJ Silver, Subway, Taco Bell, Wendy's, **lodging:** Motel 6, **other:** H, $General, Family$,

INTERSTATE 465 CONT'D (INDIANAPOLIS)

INDIANAPOLIS AREA

Exit #	Services
52	Continued **S gas:** Circle K, Shell/Circle K, Speedway/dsl, **food:** Applebee's, Arby's, Bamboo House, Buffalo Wild Wings, China Buffet, DQ, Donato's Pizza, El Puerto Mexican, Fazoli's, Fujiyama, Hardee's, Hunan House, McDonald's, Papa John's, Pizza Hut, Ponderosa, Rally's, Starbucks, Steak'n Shake, Subway, Waffle House, Wendy's, White Castle/24hr, **lodging:** Budget Inn, Holiday Inn, InnAmerica, La Quinta, Red Roof Inn, **other:** Advance Parts, AutoZone, Curves, $Tree, GNC, Goodyear/auto, K-Mart, Kroger, Lowe's Whse, Marsh Foods, NAPA, Radio Shack, Walgreens, Walmart SuperCtr, Vet

I-74 W and I-465 S run together around S Indianapolis 21 miles

Exit #	Services
16b	I-74 W, to Peoria
16a	US 136, to Speedway, **E gas:** Circle K, Shell/Circle K, Thornton's/dsl, **food:** Applebee's, Arby's, Buffalo Wild Wings, Denny's, Hardee's, KFC, LJ Silver, McDonald's, Quizno's, Papa Murphy's, Pizza Hut, Subway, Taco Bell, Wendy's, **lodging:** Budget Inn, $Inn, Motel 6, Red Roof Inn, **other:** CVS Drug, $General, $Tree, Firestone/auto, Goodyear/auto, Kroger, Marsh Foods, PetCo, Radio Shack, **W lodging:** Clarion
14b a	10th St, **E food:** Peking Chinese, Penn Sta, Pizza Hut, Wendy's, **other:** H, Lowe's Whse, **W gas:** GA/Subway, Shell/Circle K, Speedway/24hr, **food:** Arby's, Fazoli's, Hardee's, McDonald's, Rally's, Starbucks, Taco Bell, **other:** CVS Drug
13b a	US 36, Rockville Rd, **E gas:** Marathon, **lodging:** Comfort Inn, Microtel, Sleep Inn, Wingate Inn, **other:** Sam's Club, **W gas:** Speedway/dsl/24hr, **food:** Bob Evans, **lodging:** Best Western
12b a	US 40 E, Washington St, **E food:** Burger King, China Buffet, Church's, Fazoli's, McDonald's, Papa John's, Pizza Hut, Taco Bell, Wendy's, White Castle, **other:** Ace Hardware, Advance Parts, AutoZone, CVS Drug, $Tree, Family$, Kroger/gas, Speedway Parts, U-Haul, Walgreens, repair, **W gas:** Marathon/Circle K, Phillips 66/Noble Roman's/dsl, Thornton's/24hr, **food:** Arby's, Hardee's, KFC, LJ Silver, McDonald's, Pizza Hut, Steak'n Shake, Subway, **lodging:** $Inn, **other:** Aamco, Goodyear, K-Mart, TireBarn
11b a	Sam Jones Expwy, **E gas:** Marathon, **food:** Denny's, Indy's Rest., Schlotzky's, Waffle House, **lodging:** Adam's Mark Hotel, Candlewood Suites, Courtyard, Day's Hotel, Econolodge, Extended Stay America, Extended Stay Deluxe, Fairfield Inn, Hyatt Place, La Quinta, Quality Inn, Ramada Inn, Residence Inn, **W lodging:** Crowne Plaza, Radisson
9b a	I-70, E to Indianapolis, W to Terre Haute
8	IN 67 S, Kentucky Ave, **E** H, **W gas:** BP/McDonald's/dsl, Swifty, Speedway/dsl, Shell, Subway, **food:** Burger King, Culver's, Damon's, Denny's, KFC, **lodging:** Country Inn&Suites
7	Mann Rd (from wb), **E** H
4	IN 37 S, Harding St, **N gas:** Mr Fuel/dsl/scales, Pilot/Subway/dsl/scales/24hr, **food:** Omelette Shoppe,
4	Continued **lodging:** Best Inn, Quality Inn, **other:** H, Blue Beacon, **S gas:** *FLYING J*/Conoco/dsl/LP/rest./scales/24hr/@, Marathon, **food:** Hardee's, McDonald's, Taco Bell, White Castle, **lodging:** Knight's Inn, **other:** Freightliner, SpeedCo, TruckoMat/scales
2b a	US 31, IN 37, **E gas:** BP/24hr, **food:** Arby's, China Garden, CiCi's, Domino's, DQ, El Azabache, KFC, King Gyros, LJ Silver, MCL Cafeteria, Old Country Buffet, Penn Sta, Pizza Hut, Steak'n Shake, White Castle, **other:** Advance Parts, Aldi Foods, AutoZone, Chrysler/Jeep, $General, $Tree, Family$, Firestone, GNC, Goodyear, Jiffy Lube, Kroger/gas, Lincoln/Mercury, Office Depot, Radio Shack, Save-A-Lot, U-Haul, **W gas:** Speedway, **food:** Bob Evans, Denny's, 8Lucky Buffet, McDonald's, Red Lobster, Subway, Taco Bell, Wendy's, **lodging:** Best Value Inn, Comfort Inn, Holiday Inn Express, Ramada, Super 8, Travelers Inn, Travelodge, **other:** CVS Drug, Walgreens
53b a	I-65 N to Indianapolis, S to Louisville

I-465 loops around Indianapolis. Exit numbers begin/end on I-65, exit 108.

INTERSTATE 469 (FORT WAYNE)

N ↕ S FT WAYNE

Exit #	Services
31c b a	I-69, US 27 S., Auburn Road. I-469 begins/ends.
29.15mm	St Joseph River
29b a	Maplecrest Rd, **W gas:** BP/DQ/Subway/dsl, **food:** Mozzarelli's Pizza, Sonic, **other:** Marsh Foods
25	IN 37, to Ft Wayne, **W gas:** Meijer/dsl/24hr, **food:** Antonio's Pizza, Applebee's, Bob Evans, Buffalo Wild Wings, Cracker Barrel, Golden Corral, HoneyBee Chinese, McDonald's, Steak'n Shake, Subway, Wendy's, Uno Pizzaria, **other:** Discount Tire, Kohls, Marshall's, Office Depot, Walgreens, Walmart SuperCtr/gas/24hr
21	US 24 E
19b a	US 30 E, to Ft Wayne, **E gas:** Sunoco/Taco Bell/dsl, **other:** truck/tire repair, **W gas:** Citgo/dsl/mart, **food:** Garno's Italian, Golden Gate Chinese, Mancino's Grinders, Richard's Rest., Zesto Drive-In, **lodging:** Holiday Inn Express, **other:** Curves, $General
17	Minnich Rd
15	Tillman Rd
13	Marion Center Rd
11	US 27, US 33 S, to Decatur, Ft Wayne, **E gas:** BP/Subway/dsl
10.5mm	St Marys River
9	Winchester Rd
6	IN 1, to Bluffton, Ft Wayne, **W** to ✈
2	Indianapolis Rd, **W** to ✈
1	Lafayette Ctr Rd

IOWA

INTERSTATE 29

N ↕ S

Exit #	Services
152mm	Iowa/South Dakota state line, Big Sioux River
151	IA 12 N, Riverside Blvd, **E gas:** Casey's, **other:** $General, Fareway Foods, Riverside Prk, to Stone SP, Pecaut Nature Ctr
149	Hamilton Blvd, **E gas:** Conoco, **food:** Horizon Rest, **lodging:** Rodeway Inn, **other:** JiffyLube, tires, to Briar Cliff Coll, **W** Iowa Welcome Ctr sb, full facilities, **lodging:** Hilton Garden Inn, **other:** Riverboat Museum

IN IA

INTERSTATE 29 CONT'D

N ↕ S

Exit #	Services
148	US 77 S, to S Sioux City, Nebraska, **W gas:** Casey's, Conoco/dsl, Sam's, **food:** DQ, Kahill's Rest., La Fiesta Mexican, McDonald's, Pizza Hut, Taco Bell, Wendy's, **lodging:** Budget Host, Marina Inn, Regency Inn, **other:** Advance Parts, Curves, O'Reilly Parts
147b	US 20 bus, Sioux City, **E gas:** Heritage Gas, **food:** Arby's, Burger King, Chili's, Famous Dave's, Hardee's, IHOP, Perkins/24hr, **lodging:** City Center Hotel, Holiday Inn, Ramada, **other:** [H], Chevrolet, Staples, USPO, Walgreens
147a	Floyd Blvd, **E other:** Home Depot, **W** to Riverboat Casino
146.5mm	Floyd River
144b	I-129 W, US 20 W, US 75 S
144a	US 20 E, US 75 N, to Ft Dodge, **1 mi E on Lakeport Rd...gas:** Casey's, Shell, **food:** Applebee's, Buffalo Wild Wings, Burger King, Carlos'o Kelly's, ChuckeCheese, Golden Corral, Hardee's, HuHot Chinese, Jimmy John's, LJ Silver/A&W, McDonald's, Olive Garden, Outback Steaks, Red Lobster, Red Robin, Starbucks, Taco Del Mar, TX Roadhouse, **lodging:** Comfort Inn, Fairfield Inn, Hampton Inn, Holiday Inn Express, **other:** URGENT CARE, Barnes&Noble, Best Buy, Buick/Honda/Isuzu, Gordman's, Hobby Lobby, Hy-Vee Foods/gas/24hr, JC Penney, Jiffy Lube, Kohls, Lowe's Whse, Michael's, Old Navy, PetsMart, Sears/auto, Target, Younkers, mall
143	US 75 N, Singing Hills Blvd, **E gas:** Cenex/dsl, Murphy USA, Shell/dsl/café/24hr/@, **food:** China Buffet, Culver's, KFC, McDonald's, Pizza Hut, Quizno's, Taco John's, **lodging:** AmericInn, Baymont Inn, Days Inn, Haven Motel, **other:** Urgent Care, Cadillac/Pontiac/GMC, $Tree, KIA, Nissan, Sam's Club/gas, Toyota/Scion, Walmart SuperCtr/24hr, Sgt Floyd Mon, **W gas:** BP/dsl/motel/café/24hr/@, **food:** Wendy's, **lodging:** Super 8, **other:** Kenworth/Peterbilt, truckwash/repair
141	D38, Sioux Gateway ✈, **E gas:** Phillips 66/dsl, Shell/dsl, **food:** Aggies Rest., China Wok, Godfather's, Pizza Ranch, Subway, **lodging:** Econolodge, **other:** Curves, **W lodging:** Motel 6, **other:** ✈, museum
139mm	**rest area both lanes, full facilities, phone, info, picnic, litter barrels, RV dump, wireless internet**
135	Port Neal Landing
134	Salix, **W** camping
132mm	**weigh sta sb, rest area nb, picnic, litter barrels, parking only**
127	IA 141, Sloan, **E gas:** Casey's, Kum&Go/Subway/dsl, Shell/dsl, **lodging:** Rip Van Winkle Motel, WinnaVegas Inn, **other:** RV Park, **3 mi W gas:** Heritage Express, **other:** to Winnebago Indian Res/casino
120	to Whiting, **W** camping
112	IA 175, Onawa, **E gas:** Conoco/Subway/dsl, Phillips 66/dsl, **food:** Bamboo Village Chinese, DQ, McDonald's, Michael's Rest., Pizza Hut, **lodging:** Super 8, **other:** [H], NAPA, On-Ur-Wa RV Park, Pamida, **2 mi W other:** KOA, Lewis&Clark SP, Keel Boat Exhibit
110mm	**rest area both lanes, full facilities, phone, info, picnic, litter barrels, petwalk, RV dump, wireless internet**
105	E60, Blencoe
96mm	Little Sioux River
95	F 20, Little Sioux, **E** gas, **other:** Loess Hills SF (9mi), **W** Woodland RV Park
92mm	Soldier River
91.5mm	**rest area both lanes, litter barrels, parking only**
89	IA 127, Mondamin, **1 mi E gas:** Jiffy Mart/dsl
82F	50, Modale, **1 mi W gas:** Cenex/dsl
79mm	**rest area both lanes, full facilities, info, phone, picnic, litter barrels, RV dump, wireless internet**
75	US 30, Missouri Valley, **E** Iowa Welcome Ctr (5mi), **gas:** Shell/dsl/24hr, **food:** Arby's, Bluegrass cafe, McDonald's, Subway, **lodging:** Oaktree Inn, **other:** [H] (2mi), to Steamboat Exhibit, **W gas:** BP/dsl,

IA

INTERSTATE 29 CONT'D

N ↕ S

Exit #	Services
75	Continued Phillips 66/rest/dsl, **food:** Burger King, Taco John's, **lodging:** Days Inn, Rath Inn, Super 8, **other:** Buick/ Chevrolet/Pontiac
73.5mm	**weigh sta nb**
72.5mm	Boyer River
72	IA 362, Loveland, **E gas:** Phillips 66/dsl, **W** to Wilson Island SP (6mi)
71	I-680 E, to Des Moines, **I-29 S & I-680 W run together 10 mi.**
66	Honey Creek, **W** RV Camping,
61b	I-680 W, to N Omaha, **I-29 N & I-680 E run together 10 mi, W** Mormon Trail Ctr
61a	IA 988, to Crescent, **E gas:** Phillips 66/dsl, **other:** to ski area
56	IA 192 S (sb only, exits left), Council Bluffs, **E lodging:** Super 7 Inn, **other:** [H]
55	N 25th, Council Bluffs, **E gas:** Pump'n Munch/dsl, Sinclair/24hr
54b	N 35th St (from nb), Council Bluffs
54a	G Ave (from sb), Council Bluffs
53b	I-480 W, US 6, to Omaha
53a	9th Ave, S 37th Ave, Council Bluffs, **E gas:** Shell, Valero, **food:** Red Onion Cafe, **lodging:** Days Inn, **W other:** Harrah's Casino/hotel, RiverBoat Casino, camping
52	Nebraska Ave, **E gas:** Phillips 66/dsl, **food:** Quaker Steak, Ruby Tuesday, **lodging:** Comfort Suites, Microtel, SpringHill Suites, ValuePlace Inn, **other:** Bass Pro Shops, **W lodging:** AmeriStar Hotel/casino, Hampton Inn, Holiday Inn, **other:** RiverBoat Casino
51	I-80 W, to Omaha
I-29 and I-80 run together 3 miles.	
1b [I-80]	S 24th St, Council Bluffs, **N gas:** BP, Pilot/Arby's/ scales/dsl/24hr, Sapp Bros/Shell/Burger King/dsl/ rest., **food:** Famous Dave's BBQ, Hooters, Islamorada Fish Co, Quaker Steak, Ruby Tuesday, **lodging:** American Inn, Best Western, Country Inn&Suites, Hilton Garden, Microtel, Sleep Inn, SpringHill Suites, Super 8, **other:** Bass Pro Shop, Blue Beacon, Camping World RV Ctr, Horseshoe RV Park, Peterbilt, SpeedCo, casino, **S Welcome Ctr, full facilities, other:** JC Penney, PetCo, ShopKO
3	IA 192 N, Council Bluffs, **E** to Hist Dodge House, **W gas:** Phillips 66/dsl, Shell/dsl, TA/dsl/24hr/scales/@, **food:** Applebee's, Burger King, Cracker Barrel, DQ, Fazoli's, Golden Corral, Hardee's, Huhot Mongolian, La Mesa Mexican, LJ Silver, McDonald's, Old River Pizza, Perkins, Red Lobster, Subway, Taco Bell, **lodging:** Days Inn, Fairfield Inn, Motel 6, Settle Inn, **other:** Advance Parts, Aldi Foods, Best Buy, Buick/Pontiac, Chrysler/Jeep/Suzuki, Ford, Freightliner, Gordman's, Home Depot, Kia, Menards, Nissan, Outdoor Recreation RV, Sam's Club/gas, Subaru/Hyundai, U-Haul, Walmart SuperCtr, truck/dsl repair
48	I-80 E (from nb), to Des Moines, **E** [H]
47	US 275, IA 92, Lake Manawa, **E gas:** Phillips 66, **other:** Iowa School for the Deaf, **W food:** Buffalo Wild Wings, **other:** $Tree, Hobby Lobby, Kohls, PetsMart, Radio Shack, Target
42	IA 370, to Bellevue, **W other:** K&B Saddlery, to Offutt AFB, camping, truck parts
38mm	**rest area both lanes, full [handicap] facilities, [phone], info, [picnic], litter barrels, RV dump, petwalk, wireless internet**
35	US 34 E, to Glenwood, **E food:** McDonalds (4mi), **lodging:** Western Inn (4mi), **other:** RV Park, **W gas:** BP/dsl, **lodging:** Bluff View Motel, **other:** Harley-Davidson
32	US 34 W, Pacific Jct, to Plattsmouth
24	L31, to Tabor, Bartlett
20	IA 145, Thurman
15	J26, Percival, **1-2 mi E** gas/dsl
11.5mm	**weigh sta nb**
10	IA 2, to Nebraska City, Sidney, **E** to Waubonsie SP (5mi), **W gas:** BP/Sapp/rest./dsl/scales/24hr, Phillips 66/dsl, Shell/Subway/Crossroads Cafe/dsl/scales/24hr, **food:** Wendy's, **lodging:** Best Value Inn, Super 8, **other:** to Arbor Lodge SP, antiques, tire repair
1	IA 333, Hamburg, **1 mi E gas:** Casey's/dsl, **food:** Pizza Hut, **lodging:** Hamburg Motel, **other:** [H], Soda Fountain
0mm	Iowa/Missouri state line

INTERSTATE 35

N ↕ S

Exit #	Services
219mm	Iowa/Minnesota state line
214	rd 105, to Northwood, Lake Mills, **E lodging:** Royal Motel (7mi), **W Welcome Ctr both lanes, full [handicap] facilities, [picnic], litter barrels, vending, petwalk, RV dump, wireless internet, gas:** BP/Burger King/dsl, **lodging:** Country Inn&Suites, **other:** casino
212mm	**weigh sta sb, rest area nb, [picnic], litter barrels**
208	rd A38, to Joice, Kensett, windmills
203	IA 9, to Manly, Forest City, to Pilot Knob SP
202mm	Winnebago River
197	rd B20, **8 mi E** Lime Creek Nature Ctr
196mm	**rest area both lanes, litter barrels, parking only**
194	US 18, to Mason City, Clear Lake, **E gas:** Ruby's/ dsl, **other:** [H] (8mi), Chevrolet, Freightliner, truck repair, **W gas:** Casey's, Pilot/Subway/dsl/scales, Kum&Go, Shell/Wendy's/dsl, **food:** Arby's, Bennigan's, Cancun mexican, Culver's, Denny's, DQ, KFC/ Taco Bell, McDonald's, Perkins/24hr, Pizza Hut, Rice House Chinese, Subway, **lodging:** AmericInn, Best Western/rest., Budget Inn, Microtel
193	rd B35, to Mason City, Emery, **E gas:** Kum&Go/Taco John's/dsl/e-85, **lodging:** Super 8, **other:** truckwash, **W other:** Ford, to Clear Lake SP
190	US 18, rd 27 E, to Mason City
188	rd B43, to Burchinal
182	rd B60, to Rockwell, Swaledale
180	rd B65, to Thornton, **W gas:** Cenex (2mi), **other:** camping
176	rd C13, to Sheffield, Belmond
170	rd C25, to Alexander
165	IA 3, **E gas:** Shell/dsl/rest., **lodging:** AmericInn (9mi), Hampton Motel (9mi), **other:** [H] (7mi)
159	rd C47, Dows, **W rest area both lanes, full [handicap] facilities info, [phone], [picnic], litter barrels, petwalk, vending, RV dump, wireless internet**, Shell/Arby's/Godfather's/dsl/24hr
155mm	Iowa River
151	rd R75, to Woolstock
147	rd D20, to US 20 E
144	rd D25, Williams, **E gas:** Boondocks Trkstp/cafe/dsl, **lodging:** Best Western, Boondocks Motel, **other:** RV camping, **W gas:** *FLYING J*/Trump's Rest/dsl/scales/24hr

COUNCIL BLUFFS

IA

INTERSTATE 35 CONT'D

N ↕ S

Exit #	Services
142b a	US 20, to Webster City, Ft Dodge
139	rd D41, to Kamrar
133	IA 175, to Jewell, Eldora, **W gas:** Kum&Go/Subway/dsl, Prarie Land
128	rd D65, to Stanhope, Randall, **5 mi W** Little Wall Lake Pk
124	rd 115, Story City, **W gas:** Casey's, Kum&Go/dsl/24hr, **food:** DQ, Happy Chef/24hr, McDonald's, Old Hamburg Rest, Pizza Ranch, Subway, **lodging:** Comfort Inn, Super 8, Viking Motel/rest, **other:** Ford, Story City RV Ctr, VF Factory Stores/famous brands, Whispering Oaks Camping
123	rd E18, to Roland, McCallsburg
120mm	**rest area nb, full facilities, info, litter barrels, vending, wireless internet, RV dump/scenic prairie area sb**
119mm	**rest area sb, full facilities, litter barrels, vending, wireless internet, RV dump**
116	rd E29, to Story, **2 mi W** Story Co Conservation Ctr
113	13th St, Ames, **W gas:** Kum&Go/Burger King/dsl, Phillips 66/Arby's, **food:** Pizza Ranch, **lodging:** Holiday Inn Express, Quality Inn, **other:** H, Harley-Davidson, to USDA Vet Labs, ISU
111b a	US 30, to Nevada, Ames, **E** Twin Acres Campground (11mi), **W gas:** Kum&Go/DQ/Subway/dsl, **food:** Azteca Mexican, **lodging:** AmericInn, Comfort Inn, Country Inn&Suites, Fairfield Inn, Hampton Inn, Heartland Inn, Microtel, Super 8, **other:** to IA St U
109mm	S Skunk River
106mm	**weigh sta both lanes**
102	IA 210, to Slater, **3 mi W food:** DQ, Subway
96	to Elkhart, **W** to Big Creek SP (11mi), Saylorville Lake
94mm	**rest area both lanes, full facilities, info, litter barrels, vending, petwalk, wireless internet**
92	1st St, Ankeny, **W gas:** Kum&Go, QT, **food:** Ankeny Diner, Applebee's, Arby's, Burger King, Cazador Mexican, Fazoli's, Guadalajara Mexican, KFC, Quizno's, Subway, Village Inn, **lodging:** Best Western/rest., Days Inn, Fairfield Inn, Heartland Inn, Super 8, **other:** H, Goodyear/auto, O'Reilly Parts, Staples, Tires+, auto repair
90	IA 160, Ankeny, **E food:** Chip's Diner, Outback Steaks, **lodging:** AmericInn, Comfort Inn, Country Inn&Suites, Holiday Inn Express, **other:** Buick/GMC/Pontiac, **W gas:** Casey's/dsl, Phillips 66, **food:** B-bops Rest., Buffalo Wild Wings, Burger King, Chili's, China Buffet, Culver's, El Charro, IHOP, Jimmy John's, Marble Slab, McDonald's, Old Chicago, Panchero's Mexican, Panera Bread, Starbucks, Wendy's, **other:** Best Buy, Big O Tires, Chevrolet, Dodge/Jeep, Ford, GNC, Home Depot, Kohl's, Menard's, Michael's, Petsmart, Radio Shack, Target, TJ Maxx, Tuesday Morning, Tuffy Auto, Walgreens, Walmart SuperCtr, Vet, to Saylorville Lake (5mi)
89	Corporate Woods Dr, **E lodging:** Hampton Inn, **W lodging:** ValuePlace
87b a	I-235, I-35 and I-80
I-35 and	**I-80 run together 14 mi around NW Des Moines. See Iowa Interstate 80, Exits 124-136.**
72c	University Ave, **E gas:** Kum&Go/Burger King, QT,

AMES

ANKENY

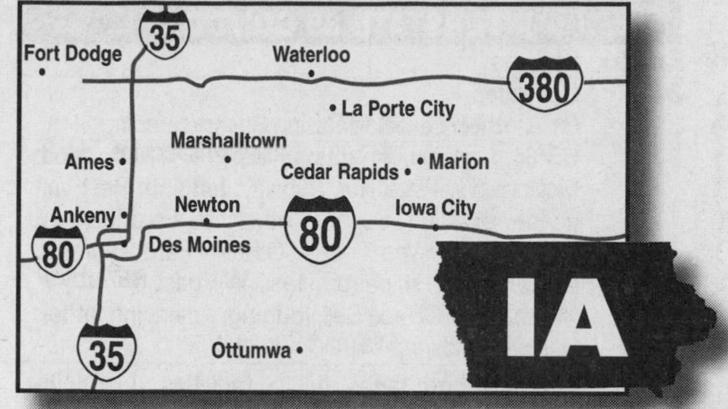

Exit #	Services
72c	Continued **food:** Biaggi's Rest, Boston's, Caribou Coffee, Cracker Barrel, El Rodeo Mexican, Wendy's, **lodging:** Best Western, Country Inn&Suites, La Quinta, **other:** H HOSPITAL, Granite City Food, Walgreens, **W gas:** BP/MaidRite, **food:** Applebee's, Bakers Square, Cheddar's, Chili's, Huhot Mongaolian, Jason's Deli, Macaroni Grill, McDonald's, Mi Mexico, Outback Steaks, Qdoba Mexican, RockBottom Rest./brewery, **lodging:** Chase Suites, Courtyard, Heartland Inn, Ramada Inn, Sheraton, Wildwood Lodge, **other:** Barnes&Noble, Best Buy, Borders, K-Mart, Kohl's, Lowe's Whse, Marshall's, Office Depot, PetsMart, SteinMart, Target, World Mkt
72b	I-80 W
72a	I-235 E, to Des Moines
70	Civic Pkwy, Mills, **E gas:** Kum&Go/McDonald's, **food:** Fire Creek Grill, Legend's Grill, Quizno's, **other:** Hy-Vee Foods/gas, Walgreens, **W gas:** Casey's/MaidRite/dsl, **food:** Applebee's, BoneFish Grill, Buffalo Wild Wings, Caribou Coffee, Champp's Grill, Cheesecake Factory, Cusina Italiana, Fleming's Rest., Fuddruckers, Iron Wok, Joe's Crabshack, Johnny's Italian Steaks, Joseph's Steaks, Mimi's Cafe, O'Charly's, On-the-Border, Panera Bread, PF Chang's, Quizno's, Red Robin, Starbucks, **lodging:** Courtyard, Drury Inn, Hilton Garden, Holiday Inn, Residence Inn, **other:** H, Barnes&Noble, Best Buy, Costco/gas, Dillards, Kohl's, Lowe's Whse, Old Navy, PetCo, Scheel's Sports, Target, TJ Maxx, Walmart SuperCtr
69b a	Grand Ave, W Des Moines
68.5mm	Racoon River
68	IA 5, **7 mi E** to ✈, to Walnut Woods SP
65	G14, to Norwalk, Cumming, **14 mi W** John Wayne Birthplace, Madison Co Museum
61mm	North River
56	IA 92, to Indianola, Winterset, **W gas:** Kum&Go/cafe/dsl, Shamrock/dsl, **food:** Hitchin Post Grill, **other:** Diamond Trail RV Ctr
56mm	Middle River
53mm	**rest area nb, litter barrels**
52	G50, St Charles, St Marys, **W gas:** Kum&Go, other, **14 mi:** John Wayne Birthplace, museum
51mm	**rest area sb, litter barrels, parking only**
47	rd G64, to Truro, **W gas:** Kum&Go (1mi)
45.5mm	South River
43	rd 207, New Virginia, **E gas:** Kum&Go/Subway/dsl
36	rd 152, to US 69, **3 mi E lodging:** Blue Haven Motel, Evergreen Inn, **W** st patrol
34	Clay St, Osceola, **W gas:** Terrible, **food:** Maid-Rite

DES MOINES

INTERSTATE 35 CONT'D

N ↕ S

Exit #	Services
34	Continued Cafe, **other:** Lakeside Casino Resort/camping
33	US 34, Osceola, **E** **gas:** Casey's/dsl/scales, **food:** McDonald's, Pizza Hut, Subway, **lodging:** Best Value Inn, Days Inn, Super 8, **other:** H, Ford/Mercury, Goodyear, Hy-Vee Foods, O'Reilly Parts, Pamida, Radio Shack, st patrol, tires, **W** **gas:** BP/Arby's/dsl, **food:** KFC/Taco Bell, **lodging:** AmericInn, **other:** Harley-Davidson, Walmart SuperCtr
32mm	**rest area both lanes, full ♿ facilities, ☎, picnic, litter barrels, vending, petwalk, RV dump, wireless internet**
31mm	**weigh sta nb, parking area sb**
29	rd H45
22	rd J14, Van Wert
18	rd J20, to Grand River
12	rd 2, Decatur City, Leon, **E** **gas:** Shell/dsl/rest, **food:** Country Corner Rest., **5 mi** **E** **lodging:** Little River Motel, **other:** H
7.5mm	Grand River
7mm	**Welcome Ctr nb/rest area sb, full ♿ facilities, info, ☎, picnic, litter barrels, vending, petwalk, RV dump, wireless internet**
4	US 69, to Davis City, Lamoni, **E** to 9 Eagles SP (10mi), **W** **gas:** Casey's (2mi), Kum&Go/dsl, **food:** Maid-Rite Cafe, Pizza Hut (2mi), QC Rest, Subway (2mi), **lodging:** Chief Lamoni Motel, Super 8, **other:** CarQuest, auto/truck repair, IA Welcome Ctr
0mm	Iowa/Missouri state line

INTERSTATE 80

E ↕ W

DAVENPORT

Exit #	Services
307mm	Iowa/Illinois state line, Mississippi River
306	US 67, to Le Claire, **N** **Welcome Ctr wb (no trucks), full ♿ facilities, picnic, litter barrels, ☎, petwalk, gas:** Phillips 66/dsl, **food:** McDonald's, Subway, **lodging:** Comfort Inn, Holiday Inn Express, Super 8, **other:** Slagles Foods, **1 mi** **N** **gas:** BP, **food:** A&W (2mi), **other:** Buffalo Bill Museum, **S** **gas:** BP (2mi)
301	Middle Rd, to Bettendorf
300mm	**rest area both lanes, full ♿ facilities, ☎, picnic, litter barrels, vending, petwalk, RV dump**
298	I-74 E, to Peoria, **S** **other:** to H, st patrol
295b a	US 61, Brady St, to Davenport, **N** **gas:** BP, **other:** Hummer, to Scott CP, **0-2 mi** **S** **gas:** BP, Phillips 66, Shell, **food:** Burger King, Cracker Barrel, Happy Joe's, Hardee's, McDonald's, Royal Wok, Thunder-Bay Grille, Village Inn Rest., **lodging:** AmericInn, Best Western/rest., Baymont Inn, Casa Loma Suites, Clarion, Country Inn&Suites, Day's Inn, Heartland Inn, Motel 6, Residence Inn, Super 8, Travelodge, **other:** AutoZone, CarQuest, Meneards, Radio Shack, Sears/auto, Toyota, US Adventures RV Ctr, Von Mar, mall, Vet
292	IA 130 W, Northwest Blvd, **N** **gas:** *FLYING J*/Phillips 66/Cookery/dsl/LP/rest./scales/24hr, **lodging:** Comfort Inn, **other:** Interstate RV Park (1mi), Farm&Fleet, Peterbilt, truckwash, **S** **gas:** BP/McDonald's, Sinclair, **food:** Machine Shed Rest., **lodging:** Econolodge
290	I-280 E, to Rock Island
284	Y40, to Walcott, **N** **gas:** Pilot/Arby's/dsl/24hr/scales, TA/IA 80/BP/DQ/Wendy's/dsl/scales/24hr/@, **food:** Gramma's Rest., **lodging:** Comfort Inn, Walcott Motel, **other:** Blue Beacon, IA 80 Trucking Museum, SpeedCo Lube, tires, **S** **gas:** Pilot/Subway/dsl/24hr, **food:** McDonald's, **lodging:** Day's Inn, **other:** Cheyenne RV Ctr, Walcott CB
280	Y30, to Stockton, New Liberty
277	Durant, **2 mi** **S** food
271	US 6 W, IA 38 S, to Wilton
270mm	**rest area both lanes, full ♿ facilities, info, ☎, picnic, litter barrels, vending, petwalk, RV dump, wireless internet**
268mm	**parking areas**
267	IA 38 N, to Tipton, **N** **gas:** Kum&Go, **other:** Cedar River Camping
266mm	Cedar River
265	to Atalissa, **S** **gas:** Diesel Depot/Blues BBQ/Chesterfried/dsl/scales/24hr
259	to West Liberty, Springdale, **S** **gas:** BP/dsl/24hr, **lodging:** Econolodge, **other:** KOA
254	X30, West Branch, **N** **gas:** BP/Quizno's, Casey's, **other:** Jack&Jill Foods, USPO, Hoover NHS, **S** **gas:** Kum&Go, **food:** McDonald's, **lodging:** Presidential Inn, **other:** Chrysler/Dodge/Jeep
249	Herbert Hoover Hwy, **N** winery (2mi), **S** golf
246	IA 1, Dodge St, **N** **gas:** BP/A&W/Subway/dsl, **lodging:** Quality Inn, **S** **gas:** Sinclair, **food:** Bob's Pizza, **lodging:** Travelodge
244	Dubuque St, Iowa City, **N** Coralville Lake, **S** H, to Old Capitol, museum
242	to Coralville, **N** **food:** River City Grille, **lodging:** Hampton Inn, Holiday Inn, **S** **gas:** BP, Conoco, Kum&Go, **food:** Arby's, Big Tenn, Burger King, Cancun Mexican, Edge Rest., Hardee's, IA Riverpower Rest., KFC, LJ Silver, LoneStar Steaks, McDonald's, Milio's Sandwiches, Mondo's Cafe, Old Chicago Grill, Papa John's, Peking Buffet, Perkins/24hr, Slugger's Grill, Sonic, Taco Bell, Taco John's, **lodging:** Baymont Inn, Best Western, Comfort Inn, Days Inn, Fairfield Inn, Marriott, Motel 6, Super 8, **other:** H, Walgreens, Vet
240	IA 965, to US 6, Coralville, N Liberty, **N** **gas:** Phillips 66/dsl, **food:** Buffalo Wild Wings, Culver's, McDonald's, Steak'n Shake, TX Roadhouse, Village Inn Rest., Wendy's, **lodging:** AmericInn, Country Inn&Suites, Suburban Lodge, **other:** Colony Country Camping (3mi), Harley-Davidson, Kohl's, Walmart SuperCtr/Subway, **S** **gas:** BP, Casey's/Blimpie, **food:** Applebee's (1mi), Bennigan's, Boston's Pizza, Caribou Coffee, Chili's, Coldstone Creamery, DQ (1mi), Huhot Mongolian, Outback Steaks, Olive Garden, Outback Steaks, Panchero's Mexican, Papa Murphy's, Pizza Hut, Ranchero's Mexican, Red Lobster, Starbucks, **lodging:** Comfort Suites, Holiday Inn Express, **other:** Ace Hardware, Barnes&Noble, Best Buy, Dillard's, HyVee Foods/gas, JC Penney, Lowe's Whse, Radio Shack, Scheel's Sports, Sears/auto, Target, Tires+, U-Haul, Younkers, mall
239b	I-380 N, US 218 N, to Cedar Rapids
239a	US 218 S
237	Tiffin, **1 mi** **N** **food:** Jon's Rest., L&J BBQ

IOWA CITY

IA

INTERSTATE 80 CONT'D

E ↕ W

Exit #	Services
236mm	**rest area both lanes, full ♿ facilities, ☎, ⛱, litter barrels, vending, RV dump, petwalk, wireless internet**
230	W38, to Oxford, **N other:** Sleepy Hollow Camping, Kalona Museum
225	US 151 N, W21 S, **N** to Amana Colonies, **lodging:** Heritage Inn, **S** Welcome Ctr, **gas:** BP, Casey's, **food:** Colony Village Rest., MaidRite Cafe, Little Amana Rest./Winery, 7 Villages Rest., Ox Yoke Rest., **lodging:** Econolodge, Holiday Inn, Super 8
220	IA 149 S, V77 N, to Williamsburg, **N gas:** BP, Casey's/dsl, **food:** Arby's, McDonald's, Subway, **lodging:** Best Western, Crest Motel, Super 8, **other:** GNC, Old Navy, factory outlets/famous brands, **S lodging:** Day's Inn
216	to Marengo, **N gas:** Kum&Go/Subway/dsl, **lodging:** Sudbury Court Motel (7mi), **other:** H
211	to Ladora, Millersburg, **S** Lake IA Park (5mi)
208mm	**rest area both lanes, full ♿ facilities, ☎, vending, ⛱, litter barrels, petwalk, wireless internet, RV dump**
205	to Victor
201	IA 21, to Deep River, **N gas:** Phillips 66/SS/dsl/24hr, **food:** Nick's Rest., **lodging:** Sleep Inn, **S gas:** Kwik-Star/Pinecone Rest./dsl/scales/24hr/@, truck repair
197	to Brooklyn, **N gas:** BP/diner/dsl, **other:** RV camping
191	US 63, to Montezuma, **N gas:** Sinclair/dsl, **S** to Fun Valley Ski Area (13mi)
182	IA 146, to Grinnell, **N gas:** Casey's (1mi), Kum&Go/Subway/dsl, **food:** KFC, Taco Bell, **lodging:** Best Western, Comfort Inn, Country Inn, Day's Inn, Super 8, **other:** H (4mi), Chrysler/Dodge/Jeep (1mi), $General, Hyvee Foods, Walmart SuperCtr/24hr (1mi), Vet, **S** Fun Valley Ski Area (16mi)
180mm	**rest area both lanes, full ♿ facilities, ☎, vending, weather info, ⛱, litter barrels, petwalk, playground, RV dump (eb) wireless internet**
179	IA 124, to Oakland Acres, Lynnville
175mm	N Skunk River
173	IA 224, Kellogg, **N gas:** Phillips 66/Best Burger/dsl/rest./24hr, **other:** Kellogg RV Park, Rock Creek SP (9mi), **S** Lake Pla-mor Camping, Pella Museum **other:** camping
168	SE Beltline Dr, to Newton, **1 mi N gas:** Casey's/dsl, **food:** Arby's, Taco John's, **lodging:** Mid-Iowa Motel, **other:** $Tree, Chrysler/Jeep/Dodge, Radio Shack, Rolling Acres Camping, Walmart SuperCtr/gas/24hr, **S gas:** Cenex/dsl, Love's/McDonald's/scales/dsl, **lodging:** AmericInn, **other:** Iowa Speedway
164	US 6, IA 14, Newton, **N gas:** Casey's, Phillips 66/Subway/dsl, **food:** Country Kitchen, Culver's, KFC/Taco Bell, Okoboji Grill, Perkins/24hr, Pizza Ranch, Senor Tequila Mexican, **lodging:** Day's Inn, Econolodge, Quality Inn, Super 8, **other:** H, museum, **S lodging:** Newton Inn/rest., **other:** Chevrolet/Cadillac, Ford/Lincoln/Mercury, to Lake Red Rock
159	F48, to Jasper, Baxter
155	IA 117, Colfax, **N gas:** BP/McDonald's, **lodging:**

Exit #	Services
155	Continued Comfort Inn, Microtel, **other:** Pitstop RV Camping, truck repair, **S gas:** Casey's, Kum&Go/Subway/dsl/24hr
153mm	S Skunk River
151	**weigh sta wb**
149	Mitchellville
148mm	**rest area both lanes, full ♿ facilities, ☎, ⛱, litter barrels, petwalk, vending, RV dump, wireless internet**
143	Altoona, Bondurant, **N food:** Quizno's (1mi), **S gas:** Casey's, **lodging:** Holiday Inn Express, **other:** HyVee Foods (2mi)
142b a	US 65, Hubble Ave, Des Moines, **S gas:** BP, Bosselman/Pilot/Sinclair/dsl/rest./24hr/@, Git'n Go, **food:** Big Steer Rest., Burger King, Culver's, Godfather's, KFC/Taco Bell, McDonald's/playpalce, Pizza Hut, Subway, Taco John's, **lodging:** Adventureland Inn, Heartland Inn, Motel 6, Regency Inn, Settle Inn, **other:** Blue Beacon, Freightliner, Peterbilt, camping, casino
141	US 6 W, US 65 S, Pleasant Hill, Des Moines
137b a	I-35 N, I-235 S, to Des Moines

I-80 W and I-35 S run together 14 mi.

Exit #	Services
136	US 69, E 14th St, Camp Sunnyside, **N gas:** BP/dsl, Casey's, **food:** Bonanza Steaks, Country Kitchen, **lodging:** Budget Inn, Motel 6, Red Roof Inn, Rodeway Inn, **other:** Volvo/GMC, antiques, **0-1 mi S gas:** Casey's/dsl, Star Gas, QT/Burger King/scales/24hr, **food:** Arby's, Fazoli's, KFC, McDonald's, Papa Murphy's, Pueblo Viejo Mexican, Subway, Taco Bell, Taco John's, Village Inn, **lodging:** Baymont Inn, Travelodge, **other:** Advance Parts, Aldi Foods, CarQuest, $General, Family$, O'Reilly Parts, Tires+, TruckLube
135	IA 415, 2nd Ave, Polk City, **N other:** Harley-Davidson, Rider Trucks, antiques, **S gas:** Git'n Go, QT, Shell, **other:** H, Earl's Tire, NAPA, USPO (2mi), st patrol
133mm	Des Moines River
131	IA 28 S, NW 58th St, **N gas:** Casey's, QT, **food:** Bandit Burrito, Chopsticks, DQ, El Mariachi Mexican, Greenbriar Rest., Pagliai's Pizza, Panera Bread, Quizno's, Sonic, Subway, VanDee's Icecream/Sandwiches, **lodging:** Best Inn, **other:** Ace Hardware, Acura, Audi/VW, Goodyear/auto, Hy-Vee Food, USPO, Vet, **S gas:** BP/dsl/24hr, Casey's, QT, **food:** Applebee's, Arby's, Bennigan's, Carlos O'Kelly's, Cici's Pizza, Daytona's Rest, Famous Dave's BBQ, Fazoli's, KFC, McDonald's, Old Chicago, Perkins, Popeye's, Quiz

INTERSTATE 80 CONT'D

E ↕ W

Exit #	Services
131	Continued no's, Shangrila Buffet, Starbucks, Wendy's, **lodging:** Days Inn, Econolodge, Holiday Inn, Quality Inn, Ramada, Super 8, **other:** [H], Advance Parts, Best Buy, BigLots, Chevrolet, Dahl's Food/Fuel, $Tree, Ford, Goodyear, Hobby Lobby, Kohl's, NAPA, Nissan, Office Depot, Old Navy, Scion/Toyota, Sears/auto, Staples, Target, mall, Vet
129	NW 86th St, Camp Dodge, **N gas:** Kum&Go, **food:** Burger King, Coldstone Creamery, Legends Grill, MaidRite Cafe, McDonald's, Okoboji Grill, Panchero's Mexican, Planet Sub, Starbucks, TX Roadhouse, Village Inn, **lodging:** Hilton Garden, Stoney Creek Inn, TownePlace Suites, **other:** Dahl's Foods, **S gas:** BP, Casey's, **food:** Arby's, B-Bops Burgers, Culver's, Friedrich's Coffee, Happy Joe's Pizza, Overtime Grill, Ruby Tuesday, **lodging:** Microtel, **other:** Walgreens
127	IA 141 W, Grimes, **N gas:** BP/dsl, Phillips 66/dsl, **food:** MaidRite Cafe, McCoy's Grill, Subway, **lodging:** AmericInn (3mi), **other:** Kia/Saab/Suzuki, to Saylorville Lake, **S food:** Quizno's, **other:** Home Depot, Target
126	Douglas Ave, Urbandale, **N gas:** Pilot/Grandma Max's/Subway/dsl/24hr/scales/@, **food:** Jimmy's Pizza, Maverick Grill, **S food:** Dragon House, **lodging:** Best Value Inn, Extended Stay America, Villa Lodge
125	US 6, Hickman Rd, **N gas:** ***FLYING J***/Cookery/dsl/LP/24hr, **other:** Dodge/Jeep, Menard's, to Living History Farms, **S food:** IA Machine Shed Rest., **lodging:** Clive Hotel, Comfort Suites, Sleep Inn, **other:** Goodyear, Honda, Hyundai
124	(72c from I-35 nb), University Ave, **N gas:** Kum&Go/Burger King, QT, **food:** Biaggi's Rest, Boston's, Caribou Coffee, Cracker Barrel, El Rodeo Mexican, Red Rossa Pizza, Shane's Rib Shack, Wendy's, Z'Marik's Cafe, **lodging:** Best Western, Country Inn&Suites, La Quinta, **other:** [H], Granite City Food, Walgreens, **S gas:** BP/MaidRite, **food:** Applebee's, Bakers Square, Bandana's BBQ, Cheddar's, Chili's, Huhot Mongolian, Jason's Deli, KFC, Macaroni Grill, McDonald's, Mi Mexico, Outback Steaks, Qdoba Mexican, RockBottom Rest./brewery, TCBY, **lodging:** Chase Suites, Courtyard, Heartland Inn, Ramada Inn, Sheraton, Wildwood Lodge, **other:** AT&T, Barnes&Noble, Best Buy, Borders, Home Depot, K-Mart, Kohl's, Marshall's, Office Depot, Petsmart, Target, Verizon, World Mkt.
I-80 E and I-35 N run together 14 mi.	
123b a	I-80/I-35 N, I-35 S to Kansas City, I-235 to Des Moines
122	(from eb) 60th St, W Des Moines
121	74th St, W Des Moines, **N food:** Biaggi's Rest., Panera Bread, **lodging:** Hampton Inn, Staybridge Suites, **other:** Granite City Foods, HyVee Food/gas, Walgreens, **S gas:** Kum&Go/Subway, **food:** Arby's, Burger King, CK's, Culver's, McDonald's, Perkins, Quizno's, Taco John's, **lodging:** Candlewood Suites, Fairfield Inn, Marriott, Motel 6, SpringHill Suites, Vet
119mm	**rest area both lanes, full [handicapped] facilities, info, vending, [phone], [picnic], petwalk, RV dump, Wireless Internet**
117	R22, Booneville, Waukee, **N food:** Organic Farm Rest., **other:** Timberline Camping (2mi), **S gas:** Kum&Go/24hr, **food:** Rube's Steaks, Waveland Rest. (2mi)
115mm	**weigh sta eb**
113	R16, Van Meter, **1 mi S gas:** Casey's, **other:** Feller Museum, Veteran's Cemetary
112mm	N Racoon River
111mm	Middle Racoon River
110	US 169, to Adel, DeSoto, **N** Aircraft Supermkt, John Wayne Birthplace, camping (6mi), **S gas:** Casey's, Kum&Go/dsl, **lodging:** Countryside Inn, Edgetowner Motel
106	F90, P58
104	P57, Earlham, **S gas:** Casey's (2mi), **food:** Master Griller (2mi)
100	US 6, to Redfield, Dexter
97	P48, to Dexter, **N gas:** Casey's (2mi), camping
93	P28, Stuart, **N gas:** BP/dsl/24hr, Casey's/dsl/scales, Kum&Go, **food:** Burger King, McDonald's/playplace, Subway, **lodging:** AmericInn, Super 8, **other:** Chevrolet, $General, Hometown Foods, **S gas:** Phillips 66/dsl, **food:** Country Kitchen, **lodging:** Edgetowner Motel, **other:** NAPA
88	P20, Menlo
86	IA 25, to Greenfield, Guthrie Ctr, **S other:** [H] (13mi), to Preston/Spring Brook SP
85mm	Middle River
83	N77, Casey, **1 mi N gas:** Kum&Go, **other:** camping
80.5mm	**rest area both lanes, full [handicapped] facilities, [phone], [picnic], litter barrels, vending, petwalk, RV dump, wireless internet**
76	IA 925, N54, Adair, **N gas:** Casey's/dsl, Kum&Go/Subway/dsl, **food:** Happy Chef, Smiley's Steaks, **lodging:** Adair Budget Inn, Super 8, **other:** camping
75	G30, to Adair
70	IA 148 S, Anita, **S** to Lake Anita SP (6mi)
64	N28, to Wiota
61mm	E Nishnabotna River
60	US 6, US 71, to Atlantic, Lorah, **S gas:** Phillips 66/Country Cafe/dsl/24hr, **lodging:** Day's Inn
57	N16, to Atlantic, **S** [H] (7mi)
54	IA 173, to Elk Horn, **6 mi N Welcome Ctr/Wireless Internet**, **lodging:** AmericInn, **other:** Windmill Museum, gas, food (7mi)
51	M56, to Marne
46	M47, Walnut, **N gas:** BP/McDonald's/24hr, **food:** Villager Buffet, **lodging:** Super 8, to Prairie Rose SP (8mi), **S gas:** Kum&Go/dsl/24hr, **food:** Aunt B's Kitchen, **lodging:** Red Carpet Inn, repair
44mm	**weigh sta, wb/parking area eb**
40	US 59, to Harlan, Avoca, **N gas:** Phillip 66/Taco John's/Maidrite/dsl/24hr/scales, **food:** Subway, **lodging:** Motel 6, **other:** [H] (12mi), truckwash, **S gas:** Shell/dsl (1mi), **food:** Embers Rest., **lodging:** Avoca Motel, Capri Motel (1mi), **other:** Avoca Foods, Nishna Museum
39.5mm	W Nishnabotna River
34	M16, Shelby, **N gas:** Shell/Cornstalk Cafe/dsl, **food:** DQ, **lodging:** Shelby Country Inn/RV Park, **S other:** dsl/tire repair

INTERSTATE 80 CONT'D

E ↕ W — COUNCIL BLUFFS

Exit #	Services
32mm	**rest area both lanes, parking only**
29	L66, to Minden, **S gas:** Phillips 66/A&W, **lodging:** Mid-Town Motel (2mi), **other:** winery (4mi)
27	I-680 W, to N Omaha
23	IA 244, L55, Neola, **S gas:** Kum&Go/dsl, **other:** to Arrowhead Park, camping
20mm	**Welcome Ctr eb/rest area wb, full ♿ facilities, ☎, picnic table, litter barrels, vending, petwalk, RV dump, Wireless Internet**
17	G30, Underwood, **N gas:** Phillips 66/Subway/dsl/24hr, **lodging:** Underwood Motel, **other:** truck/tire repair
8	US 6, Council Bluffs, **N gas:** Phillips 66/dsl (1mi)
5	Madison Ave, Council Bluffs, **N gas:** BP, **food:** Burger King, FoodCourt, Great Wall Chinese, KFC, McDonald's, Panera Bread, Pizza Hut, Skeeter Barn's Steaks, Subway, **lodging:** Heartland Inn, **other:** Barnes&Noble, Dillard's, HyVee Food/drug, JC Penney, Old Navy, Sears/auto, Target, Walgreens, mall, **S gas:** Cenex/dsl, Phillips 66, **food:** DQ, Valentino's Rest., Village Inn Rest., **lodging:** Western Inn, **other:** TruValue
4	I-29 S, to Kansas City
3	IA 192 N, Council Bluffs, **N** to Hist Dodge House, **S gas:** Phillips 66/dsl, Shell/dsl, /dsl/24hr/scales/@, **food:** Applebee's, Burger King, Cracker Barrel, DQ, Fazoli's, Golden Corral, Hardee's, Huhot Mongolian, La Mesa Mexican, LJ Silver, McDonald's, Old River Pizza, Perkins, Red Lobster, Subway, Taco Bell, **lodging:** Days Inn, Fairfield Inn, Motel 6, Settle Inn, **other:** Advance Parts, Aldi Foods, Best Buy, Buick/Pontiac, Chrysler/Jeep/Suzuki, Ford, Freightliner, Gordman's, Home Depot, Kia, Menards, Nissan, Outdoor Recreation RV, Sam's Club/gas, Subaru/Hyundai, U-Haul, Walmart SuperCtr, truck/dsl repair
1b	S 24th St, Council Bluffs, **N gas:** BP, Pilot/Arby's/scales/dsl/24hr, Sapp Bros/Shell/Burger King/dsl/rest., **food:** Famous Dave's BBQ, Hooters, Islamorada Fish Co, Quaker Steak, Ruby Tuesday, **lodging:** American Inn, Best Western, Country Inn&Suites, Hilton Garden, Microtel, Sleep Inn, SpringHill Suites, Super 8, **other:** Bass Pro Shop, Blue Beacon, Camping World RV Ctr, Horseshoe RV Park, Peterbilt, SpeedCo, casino, **S Welcome Ctr, full facilities, other:** JC Penney, PetCo, ShopKO
1a	I-29 N, to Sioux City
0mm	Iowa/Nebraska state line, Missouri River

INTERSTATE 235 (DES MOINES)

N ↕ S

Exit #	Services
15	I-80, E to Davenport
13	US 6, E Euclid Ave, **E gas:** Casey's, **food:** Burger King, Dragon House Chinese, Papa John's, Perkins, **other:** $Tree, Hancock Fabrics, HyVee Foods/drug, Walgreen, **W gas:** QT, **other:** Great Outdoor RV Ctr, NAPA
11	Guthrie Ave, **W other:** CarQuest
10a b	IA 163 W, E University Ave, Easton Dr
9	US 65/69, E 14th, E 15th, **N other:** Walgreen, **S food:** McDonald's, Quizno's, **other:** [H], st capitol, zoo

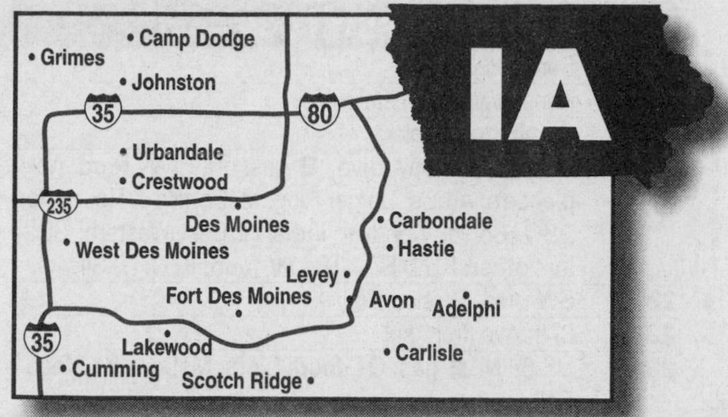

DES MOINES

Exit #	Services
8b	E 6th St, Penn Ave (from wb), **N** [H]
8a	3rd St, 5th Ave, **N lodging:** Holiday Inn, **other:** [H] **S lodging:** Embassy Suites, Marriott, Quality Inn, **other:** Conv Ctr
7	Keo Way
6	MLK Blvd/31st St, Drake U, Governor's Mansion, **S** [✈]
5b	42nd St, Science & Art Ctr, **N gas:** Git'n Go, **food:** Papa John's, **other:** Curves
5a	56th St (from wb), **N** golf
4	IA 28, 63rd St, to Windsor Heights, **S** Hist Valley Jct, zoo
3	8th St, W Des Moines, **N gas:** Kum&Go, **food:** B-Bop's Café, Burger King, **other:** HyVee Foods, PetCo, Sam's Club/gas, Sears AutoCtr, Walmart SuperCtr/24hr, **S gas:** BP, Kum&Go, **food:** Coach's Corner Grill, Garcia's Mexican, Jimmy's American Café, **lodging:** Best Western
2	22nd St, 24th St, W Des Moines, **N gas:** BP, Phillips 66/dsl, **food:** ChuckeCheese, Culver's, Famous Dave's BBQ, Gordman's, Hardee's, Hooters, LoneStar Steaks, McDonald's, Old Country Buffet, Taco Bell, Village Inn Rest., Zachary's Grill, **lodging:** Studio+, **other:** Firestone/auto, Goodyear/auto, Gordman's, Hancock Fabrics, Michael's, Office Depot, Walgreen
1b	Valley West Dr,, W Des Moines, **N gas:** BP/dsl, **food:** Olive Garden, Red Lobster, TGI Friday's, **other:** HyVee Foods, JC Penney, SteinMart, Target, Younker's, mall
0mm	I-235 begins/ends on I-80, exit 123.

INTERSTATE 280 (DAVENPORT)

E ↕ W

Exit #	Services
18b a	I-74, US 6, Moline, **S gas:** Shell/dsl, **food:** McDonald's, MT Jack's, **lodging:** Best Inn, Country Inn&Suites, Days Inn, Econolodge, Hampton Inn, La Quinta, Quality Inn, Ramada Inn, **other:** [✈]
15	Airport Rd, Milan, **N food:** (1mi) MaidRite Café, Subway, **other:** Buick/Chevrolet, Firestone
11b a	IL 92, to Andalusia, Rock Island, **S** KOA Camping
9.5mm	Iowa/Illinois state line, Mississippi River
8	rd 22, Rockingham Rd, to Buffalo
6	US 61, W River Dr, to Muscatine, **W** gas, camping
4	Locust St, rd F65, 160th St, **E** [H], to Palmer Coll, St Ambrose U, **W gas:** Star Gas/Subway/dsl
1	US 6 E, IA 927, Kimberly Rd, to Walcott, **E** lodging, transmissions
0mm	I-280 begins/ends on I-80, exit 290.

INTERSTATE 35

N ↕ S

KANSAS CITY AREA

OLATHE

OTTAWA

Exit #	Services
235mm	Kansas/Missouri state line
235	Cambridge Circle
234b a	US 169, Rainbow Blvd, **E gas:** QT, Shell, **food:** Applebee's, Arby's, Burger King, McDonald's, Rosedale BBQ, Sonic, Wendy's, **lodging:** Best Western, Sun Inn, **other:** KU MED CTR, **W food:** KFC, LJ Silver
233a	SW Blvd, Mission Rd
233b	37th Ave (from sb)
232b	US 69 N, **E gas:** QT, **food:** Cici's, McDonald's, Taco Bell
232a	Lamar Ave, **E gas:** QT, **lodging:** ValuePlace Inn
231b a	I-635 (exits left from sb)
230	Antioch Rd (from sb), **E gas:** QT
229	Johnson Dr, **E gas:** Phillips 66, **food:** Arby's, Bob Evans, Chili's, Chipotle Mexican, McDonald's, Papa John's, Starbucks, **other:** GNC, Hen House Mkt, Home Depot, Marshall's, Old Navy, Petsmart, Walgreens, **W gas:** Cenex/dsl
228b	US 56 E, US 69, Shawnee Mission Pkwy, **E gas:** Shell, **food:** Caribou Coffee, Denny's, IHOP, Krispy Kreme, Pizza Hut, Taco Bell, **lodging:** Drury Inn, Homestead Suites, Winsteads Suites, **other:** BMW/Mini, Sears Grand, **W gas:** Valero, **food:** A&W, LJ Silver, Panera Bread, Pizza Hut, Subway, Wendy's, **other:** Cotman's Transmissions, Firestone, Ford, Goodyear/auto, Jo-Ann Fabrics, Office Depot, O'Reilly Parts, Russell Stover, Walgreens
228a	67th St, **E lodging:** Quality Inn, **other:** CarMax, **W gas:** Phillips 66/Circle K/dsl, **other:** Jaguar, Land Rover, Maserati, Mercedes, Porsche, Saab, Smart
227	75th St, **E food:** McDonald's, **lodging:** Extended Stay America, **other:** [H], Acura, Walmart, Vet, **W gas:** QT/dsl, **food:** Domino's, Sonic, Subway, Taco Bell, 2 Amigos Mexican, Wendy's, **lodging:** Hampton Inn, **other:** Hyundai
225b	US 69 S (from sb), Overland Pkwy
225a	87th St, **E gas:** Phillips 66, **food:** Green Mill Rest, **lodging:** Holiday Inn, **W gas:** Phillips 66/Circle K/dsl, **food:** Taco Bell, Zarda BBQ, **other:** auto repair
224	95th St, **E gas:** Phillips 66/Circle K, Shell, **food:** Applebee's, BD Mongolian BBQ, Burger King, Chick-fil-A, Chipotle Mexican, Denny's, Houlihan's, KFC, McDonald's, Mimi's Café, On-the-Border, Outback Steaks, Panda Express, Subway, Taco Bell, TGIFriday, Winstead's Cafe, **lodging:** Comfort Inn, Crowne Plaza, Days Inn, Extended Stay America, Knight's Inn, La Quinta, Motel 6, Super 8, **other:** [H], Advance Parts, Barnes&Noble, Best Buy, Dillard's, Firestone/auto, Hy-Vee Foods, JC Penney, Kohl's, Macy's, Nordstrom's, Office Depot, PetCo, Sam's Club/gas, Target, mall, **W gas:** Phillips 66, **food:** Mi Ranchito, **other:** Costco/gas, O'Reilly Parts, U-Haul
222b a	I-435 W & E
220	119th St, **E gas:** Phillips 66/Circle K, Shell, **food:** A&W, Burger King, Chick-fil-A, Chipotle Mexican, Coldstone Creamery, Cracker Barrel, 5 Guys Burgers, Granite City Cafe, Haru's Steak, Honey Baked Cafe, Hooters, IHOP, Jimmy John's, Joe's BBQ, Joe's Crabshack, LJ Silver, McDonald's, Noodles&Co, OK Joe's BBQ, Old Chicago, Olive Garden, On-the-Border
220	Continued Panda Express, Panera Bread, Pei Wei, Planet Sub, Popeye's, Ruby Tuesday, Schlotsky's, Starbucks, Steak'n Shake, Subway, TX Roadhouse, Wendy's, Zio's Italian, **lodging:** Best Western, Comfort Suites, Fairfield Inn, Hampton Inn, Residence Inn, SpringHill Suites, ValuePlace Inn, **other:** Aamco, Best Buy, Borders Books, Chrysler/Dodge/Jeep, GNC, Goodyear/auto, Home Depot, Honda, Marshall's, Mazda, Michael's, NTB, Old Navy, Petsmart, Radio Shack, Target, U-Haul, transmissions, **W** Bass Pro Shop
218	135th, Santa Fe St, Olathe, **E gas:** Phillips 66, **food:** Applebee's, Ari's Greek Rest, Buffalo Wild Wings, Burger King, Chapala Mexican, China Buffet, China Star, Church's, Corona Garden Mexican, Garozzo's Italian, Other Place Grill, Papa John's, Perkins, Pizza St, Quizno's, Sheridan's Custard, Taco World, **other:** Ace Hardware, Aldi Foods, AutoZone, BigLots, CVS Drug, $General, $Tree, GNC, Hobby Lobby, Hy-Vee Foods, K-Mart, Kohl's, Office Depot, PriceChopper Foods, Tuesday Morning, Vet, **W gas:** QT, **food:** A&W, Domino's, KFC, La Hacienda Mexican, LJ Silver, McDonald's, New Fortune Chinese, Taco Bell, Waffle House, Wendy's, **lodging:** Days Inn, **other:** Advance Parts, Buick/GMC/Pontiac, Car-X, Chevrolet, Cottman Transmissions, Harley-Davidson, Hyundai, Kia, O'Reilly Parts, Radio Shack, Scion/Toyota
217	Old Hwy 56 (from sb), same as 215
215	US 169 S, KS 7, Olathe, **E gas:** Phillips 66/dsl, QT/dsl, **food:** China Inn, Chipotle Mexican, IHOP, Outback Steaks, Panera Bread, Red Robin, Ryan's, **lodging:** Candlewood Suites, Comfort Inn, **other:** Aldi Foods, AT&T, Home Depot, NTB, Target, **W gas:** Presto, Shell/dsl/scales/24hr, **food:** Applebee's, Burger King, Chili's, 54th St Grill, FoodCourt, Red Lobster, McDonald's, Taco Bell, Waffle House, Wendy's, **lodging:** Best Western, Econolodge, Holiday Inn, La Quinta, Microtel, Sleep Inn, **other:** [H], Mazda, mall
214	no services
213mm	**weigh sta both lanes**
210	US 56 W, Gardner, **W gas:** Phillips 66/Circle K/dsl, **food:** Arby's, KFC, McDonald's, Mr Goodcents Subs, Pizza Hut, Subway, Taco Bell, Waffle House, **lodging:** Super 8, **other:** NAPA, Walmart SuperCtr
207	US 56 E, Gardner Rd, **E** Olathe RV Ctr, **W gas:** Gas City/dsl, Shell/dsl
202	Edgerton
198	KS 33, to Wellsville, **W** gas/dsl
193	Tennessee Rd, Baldwin
187	KS 68, Ottawa, **W gas:** Zarco/dsl/e-85, **other:** Buick/Cadillac/Chevrolet/Pontiac, Crist RV Ctr
185	15th St, Ottawa
183	US 59, Ottawa, **W gas:** BP, Conoco/dsl, Ottawa Gas/dsl, **food:** Applebee's, Burger King, KFC, McDonald's, Old 56 Rest, Pizza Hut, Sirloin Stockade, Subway, Taco Bell, Wendy's, **lodging:** Best Western, Comfort Inn, Econolodge, Super 8, Travelodge, **other:** [H], Advance Parts, CountryMart Foods, $General, $Tree, Walmart SuperCtr/gas
182b a	US 50, Eisenhower Rd, Ottawa
176	Homewood, **W** RV camping
175mm	**rest area both lanes, full [handicapped] facilities, [phone], [picnic], litter barrels, vending, petwalk, RV dump, wireless internet**

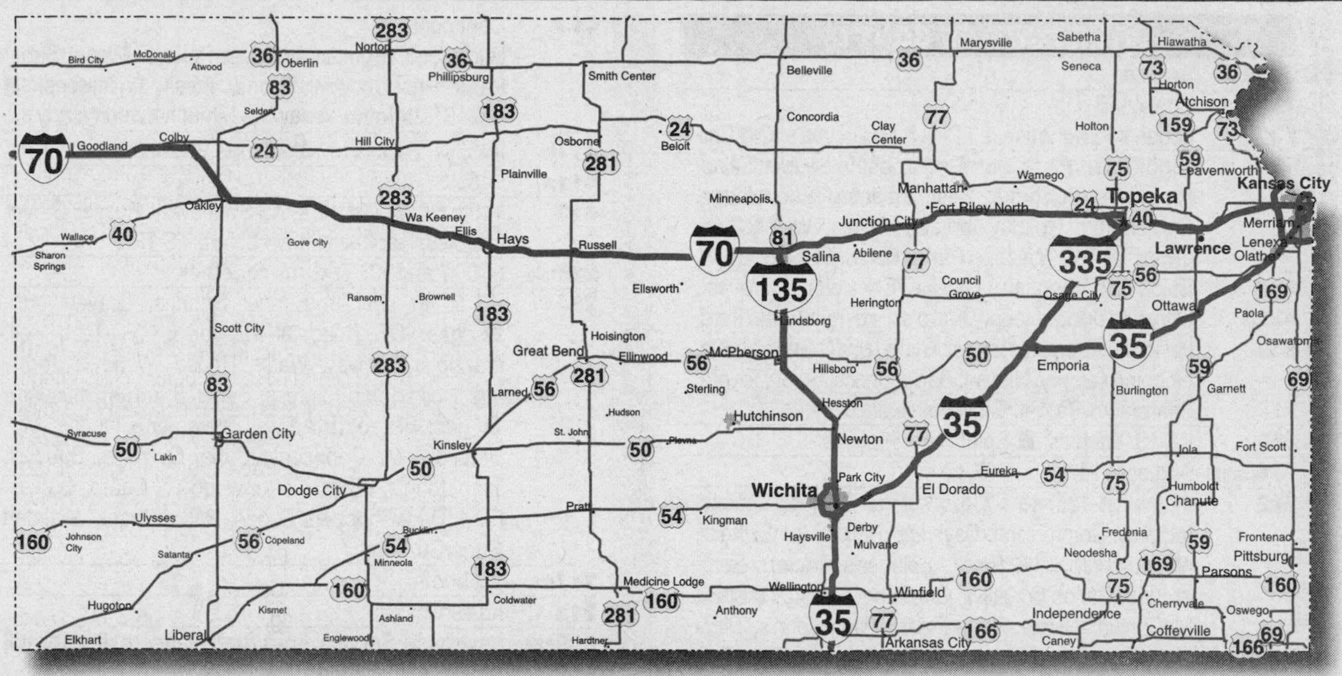

N ↕ S

EMPORIA

INTERSTATE 35 CONT'D

Exit #	Services
170	KS 273, Williamsburg, **W** **gas:** Sinclair/café/dsl
162	KS 31 S, Waverly
160	KS 31 N, Melvern
155	US 75, Burlington, Melvern Lake, **E** **gas:** BP/Subway/dsl, TA/Shell/Wendy's/dsl/scales/24hr/@, **food:** Beto Jct Rest., **lodging:** Wyatt Earp Inn, **other:** dsl repair
148	KS 131, Lebo, **E** **gas:** Casey's, Cenex/dsl, **food:** Lebo Diner, **lodging:** Universal Inn, **W** to Melvern Lake
141	KS 130, Neosho Rapids, **E** NWR (8mi)
138	County Rd U
135	County Rd R1, **W** RV camping/
133	US 50 W, 6th Ave, Emporia, **1-3 mi E** **gas:** Casey's, **food:** McDonald's, Pizza Hut, **lodging:** Budget Host
131	KS 57, KS 99, Burlingame Rd, **E** **gas:** Conoco/dsl, **food:** Hardee's, Mr Goodcents Subs, **other:** Dillon's Food, repair, tires
130	KS 99, Merchant St, **E** **gas:** Phillips 66/dsl, **food:** Subway, **other:** Emporia St U, Lyon Co Museum
128	Industrial Rd, **E** **gas:** Conoco, FL, **food:** Arby's, Bruff's Steaks, Burger King, Centinela Mexican, China Buffet, Cobern's Drive Inn, Gambino's Pizza, Subway, **lodging:** Econolodge, GuestHouse Inn, Motel 6, **other:** H, Aldi Foods, CarQuest, $General, Family$, Goodyear/auto, Hastings Book, JC Penney, Walgreens, **W** **gas:** Phillips 66/Wendy's/dsl, **food:** Applebee's, Golden Corral, KFC, McDonald's, MT Mike's Steaks, Papa Murphy's, Pizza Hut, Pizza Ranch, Planet Sub, Starbucks, Taco Bell, Village Inn, **lodging:** Candlewood Suites, Comfort Inn, Fairfield Inn, Holiday Inn Express, **other:** Medicine Shoppe, Radio Shack, Staples, Walmart SuperCtr/24hr
127c	KS Tpk, I-335 N, to Topeka
127b a	US 50, KS 57, Newton, **E** **gas:** *FLYING J*/Conoco/Country Mkt/dsl/scales/rest./24hr, Shell, **food:** Arby's, China Buffet, Papa John's, **lodging:** Best Value Inn, Best Western/rest., Days Inn, Rodeway Inn, **other:** Buick/Chevrolet/Pontiac, Chrysler/Dodge/Jeep/Toyota, Ford/Lincoln/Mercury/Nissan, Napa,
127b a	Continued PriceChopper Foods, Tires4Less, dsl repair, **W** Emporia RV Park
127mm	I-35 and I-335 KS Tpk, toll plaza,
	I-35 S and KS Tpk S run together.
125mm	Cottonwood River
111	Cattle Pens
97.5mm	**Matfield Green Service Area (both lanes exit left)**, Phillips 66/dsl, McDonald's
92	KS 177, Cassoday, **E** **gas:** Fuel'n Service,
76	US 77, El Dorado N, **E** El Dorado SP, **3 mi E** **gas:** Casey's, **food:** Pizza Hut, Taco Bell, **other:** Ace Hardware, Dillon's Foods/gas, $General, Walgreens, city park
71	KS 254, KS 196, El Dorado, **E** **gas:** Conoco/dsl, Phillips 66/dsl, QT, **food:** Arbys, Braum's, Burger King, China Star Buffet, DD Family Rest, Freddy's Frozen Custard, Gambino's Pizza, KFC, Kountry Kettle, LJ Silver, McDonald's, Papa Murphy's, Pizza Hut, Playa Azul Mexican, Sonic, Spangles, Subway, Taco Tico, **lodging:** Best Western, Heritage Inn, Holiday Inn Express, Sunset Inn, Super 8, **other:** H, Buick/Cadillac/Pontiac, Bumper Parts, Deer Grove RV Park, $General, KS Oil Museum, O'Reilly Parts, Radio Shack, Walmart SuperCtr
65mm	**Towanda Service Area (both lanes exit left)**, Phillips 66/dsl, McDonald's
62mm	Whitewater River
57	21st St, Andover, **W** golf,
53	KS 96, Wichita, **1 mi W on Kellogg** Phillips 66
50	US 54, Kellogg Ave, **E** McConnell AFB, **W** **lodging:** Comfort Inn, Fairfield Inn, GuestHouse Inn, Hampton Inn, Hawthorn Suites, Marriott, Motel 6, Studio+, Super 8, **E on Kellogg Ave...gas:** Conoco/Wendy's/dsl, **food:** Burger King, Golden Corral, IHOP, McDonald's, Pizza Hut, Sonic, Subway, Taco Bell, **other:** Acura, AT&T, Buick/Infiniti, CarMax, Jaguar/Porsche, Lowe's Whse, Mazda, Michael's, PepBoys, VW, Walmart SuperCtr/24hr, **W on Kellogg Ave...food:** Arby's, Chipotle Mexican, Denny's, Green Mill Rest.,

WICHITA

KS

INTERSTATE 35 CONT'D

N ↕ S — WICHITA

Exit #	Services
50	Continued Logan's Roadhouse, LJ Silver, McDonald's, Old Chicago Pizza, Pizza Hut, Red Lobster, Souper Salad, Steak&Ale, **lodging:** Best Western, Econolodge, Garden Inn, Holiday Inn, La Quinta, Wichita Inn, **other:** VA [H], Advance Parts, Barnes&Noble, BMW, Buick/GMC/Pontiac, Cadillac/Chevrolet, Carquest, Chrysler/Dodge/Jeep, Dillard's, Firestone/auto, Ford, Hancock Fabrics, Honda, Hyundai, JC Penney, Kia, Lincoln/Mercury, Nissan, Radio Shack, Scion/Toyota, Sears/auto, Target, TJ Maxx, mall
45	KS 15, Wichita, **E** Spirit Aero Systems
44.5mm	Arkansas River
42	47th St, I-135, to I-235, Wichita, **E gas:** Conoco, **lodging:** Comfort Inn, Days Inn, Holiday Inn Express, **W gas:** Phillips 66, **food:** Applebee's, Braum's, Burger King, Carlos O'Kelly's, Godfather's, KFC, LJ Silver, McDonald's, New China Rest., Papa John's, Pizza Hut, Quizno's, Spangles Rest., Subway, Taco Bell, Taco Tico, **lodging:** Best Western, Heritage Inn, Red Carpet Inn, Value Place, **other:** Checker's Foods, Dillon's Foods/dsl, K-Mart, O'Reilly Parts, Radio Shack
39	US 81, Haysville, **W lodging:** Haysville Inn
33	KS 53, Mulvane, **E** Mulvane Hist Museum, **W** Wyldewood Winery
26mm	**Belle Plaine Service Area (both lanes exit left), gas:** Phillips 66/dsl, **food:** McDonald's
19	US 160, Wellington, **3 mi W food:** KFC, Penny's Diner, **lodging:** OakTree Inn, Sunshine Inn, **other:** RV camping
17mm	toll plaza
I-35 N and KS TPK N run together.	
4	US 166, to US 81, South Haven, **E lodging:** Economy Inn/cafe, **W** Oasis RV Park
1.5mm	**weigh sta nb**
0mm	Kansas/Oklahoma state line

KS

INTERSTATE 70

E ↕ W — KANSAS CITY / TOPEKA

Exit #	Services
423b	3rd St, James St
423a	5th St
422d c	Central Ave, service rd
422b a	US 69 N, US 169 S
421b	I-670
421a	**S** railroad yard
420b a	US 69 S, 18th St Expswy, **N** SunFresh Foods
419	38th St, Park Dr, access to 10 motels
418b	I-635 N (eb only)
418a	I-635 S
417	57th St
415a	KS 32 E (from eb)
415b	to US 24 W, State Ave, Kansas City, **N on US 24... gas:** Concordia, Phillips 66/dsl, **food:** Papa John's, Taco Bell, **lodging:** Gables Motel, **other:** Chrysler/Jeep, Ford, Lowe's Whse, Mazda, Toyota, Walmart/auto
414mm	**vehicle insp sta wb, parking area both lanes,** [phone]
414	78th St, **N gas:** QT, **food:** Wendy's, **lodging:** Days Inn, **N on US 40...gas:** Phillips 66, **food:** Arby's, Burger King, DQ, Lucky Chinese, McDonald's, Papa John's, Sonic, Subway, **other:** [H], Advance Parts,
414	Continued Buick/GMC/Pontiac, Goodyear/auto, K-Mart, O'Reilly Parts, PriceChopper Foods, Tires+, Walgreens, **S gas:** BP, **lodging:** American Motel, Comfort Inn
411b	I-435 N, access to Woodlands Racetrack, to KCI [airport]
411a	I-435 S
410	110th St, **N** Cabela's, KS Speedway, Russell Stover Candies, last free exit wb before KS TPK
225mm	**I-70 W and KS TPK run together**
224	KS 7, to US 73, Bonner Springs, Leavenworth, **N gas:** QT, Roadstar/dsl, **food:** KFC/Taco Bell, Mazzio's, Subway, Waffle House, Wendy's, **lodging:** Holiday Inn Express, Super 8, **other:** museum, **S gas:** BP, **food:** Arby's, Evergreen Chinese, McDonald's, Mr Goodcents Subs, Quizno's, Subway, Taco John's, **other:** Cottonwood RV Camp, Curves, Ford, PriceChoppers Foods, Radio Shack, Walmart SuperCtr/24hr
217mm	toll booth
212	no services
209mm	**Lawrence Service Area (both lanes exit left), full facilities,** Conoco/dsl, McDonald's
204	US 24, US 59, to E Lawrence, **S gas:** Presto/dsl, Woody's/dsl, **food:** Burger King, Sonic, **lodging:** Motel 6, SpringHill Suites (1mi), **other:** Harley-Davidson, O'Reilly Parts
203mm	Kansas River
202	US 59 S, to W Lawrence, **S on US 40...gas:** BP, Conoco/dsl, Phillips 66/dsl, **food:** Burger King, Domino's, McDonald's, Panda Garden, Sonic, Spangles, Subway, Taco Bell, Taco John's, Wendy's, **lodging:** Baymont Inn, Best Value Inn, Days Inn, Econolodge, Hampton Inn, Holiday Inn, Quality Inn, Rodeway Inn, Virginia Inn, **other:** [H], Advance Parts, CarQuest, Dillon's Foods/gas, $General, to Clinton Lake SP, to U of KS
197	KS 10, Lecompton, Lawrence, **N** Perry Lake SP, **S** Clinton Lake SP
188mm	**Topeka Service Area, full** [handicap] **facilities,** Conoco/dsl, Taco Bueno, Hardee's
183	I-70 W (from wb), to Denver
367mm	toll plaza
366	I-470 W, to Wichita, **I-70 E and KS TPK E run together**
365	21st St, Rice Rd, access to Shawnee Lake RA
364b	US 40 E, Carnahan Ave, to Lake Shawnee
364a	California Ave, **0-1 mi S gas:** BP/dsl, Phillips 66/dsl, **food:** Arby's, Baskin-Robbins, Burger King, Domino's, McDonald's, Pizza Hut, Subway, Tacos De Mexicano, **other:** Ace Hardware, Advance Parts, AutoZone, Dillon's Food/gas, $General, Family$, O'Reilly Parts, TrueValue, Walgreens, auto repair
363	Adams St, downtown
362c	10th Ave (from wb), **N lodging:** Ramada Inn, Red Carpet Inn, **S other:** St capitol
362b a	to 8th Ave, downtown, **N lodging:** Ramada Inn, Red Carpet Inn, **S other:** to St Capitol
361b	3rd St, Monroe St
361a	1st Ave, **S** Ryder
359	MacVicar Ave
358b a	Gage Blvd, **S** [H]
357b a	Fairlawn Rd, 6th Ave, **S gas:** Conoco/dsl, Phillips 66, **food:** Casa Ramos, **lodging:** Best Western, Holiday Inn/rest., Motel 6, **other:** $General, repair, zoo-

INTERSTATE 70 CONT'D

E ↕ W

Exit #	Services
357b a	Continued rain forest, Vet
356b a	Wanamaker Rd, **N food:** Carino's, Red Robin, **lodging:** Hyatt Place, **other:** KS Museum of History, **S gas:** BP, Conoco, Phillips 66/dsl, **food:** Applebee's, Arby's, Boston Mkt, Buffalo Wild Wings, Burger King, Chili's, Chipotle Mexican, ChuckeCheese, CiCi's Pizza, Coldstone Creamery, Coyote Canyon Café, Cracker Barrel, Denny's, Freddy's Custard, Golden Corral, Hardee's, Hooters, Huhot Chinese, IHOP, Jason's Deli, Jimmy John's, Longhorn Steaks, McDonald's, Mike's Subs, Mr Goodcents, Old Chicago, Olive Garden, On the Border, Panda Buffet, Panera Bread, Papa John's, Perkins, Pizza Hut, Qdoba, Red Lobster, Rib Crib, Ruby Tuesday, Sonic, Spangles, Starbucks, Steak'n Shake, Taco Bell, Taco John's, TX Roadhouse, Timberline Steaks, Wendy's, **lodging:** Baymont Inn, Candlewood Suites, Clubhouse Inn, Comfort Inn, Country Inn&Suites, Courtyard, Days Inn, Fairfield Inn, Hampton Inn, Holiday Inn Express, Motel 6, Quality Inn, Residence Inn, Sleep Inn, Super 8, ValuePlace, **other:** Barnes&Noble, Best Buy, Dillard's, Goodyear/auto, Hobby Lobby, Home Depot, JC Penney, K-Mart, Kohl's, Lowe's Whse, Macy's, Michael's, Office Depot, Old Navy, PetCo, Radio Shack, Sam's Club, Sears/auto, Suzuki, Target, TJ Maxx, Tuesday Morning, Walmart SuperCtr/24hr, mall

TOPEKA

Exit #	Services
355	I-470 E, to VA Med Ctr, Topeka, air museum, **1 mi S** same as 356
353	KS 4, to Auburn Rd
351	frontage rd (from eb), Mission Creek
350	Valencia Rd
347	West Union Rd
346	Carlson Rd, to Rossville, Willard
343	Ranch Rd
342	Eskridge Rd, Keene Rd, access to Lake Wabaunsee
341	KS 30, Maple Hill, **S gas:** 24-7/dsl/café
338	Vera Rd
336mm	**rest area (exits left from both lanes), full ♿ facilities, ☎, ⛱, litter barrels, RV dump, wireless internet, petwalk**
335	Snokomo Rd, Paxico, Skyline Mill Creek Scenic Drive
333	KS 138, Paxico, **N** Mill Creek RV Park, winery
332	Spring Creek Rd
330	KS 185, to McFarland
329mm	**weigh sta both lanes**
328	KS 99, to Alma, **S** Wabaunsee Co Museum
324	Wabaunsee Rd, **N** Grandma Horners Store & Factory
322	Tallgrass Rd
318	frontage rd
316	Deep Creek Rd
313	KS 177, to Manhattan, **8 mi N gas:** Phillips 66, **food:** Applebee's, Chili's, McDonald's, Village Inn Rest., **lodging:** Best Western, Comfort Inn, Fairfield Inn, Hampton Inn, Motel 6, Super 8, **other:** Jeep, Nissan, Sears/auto, to KSU
311	Moritz Rd

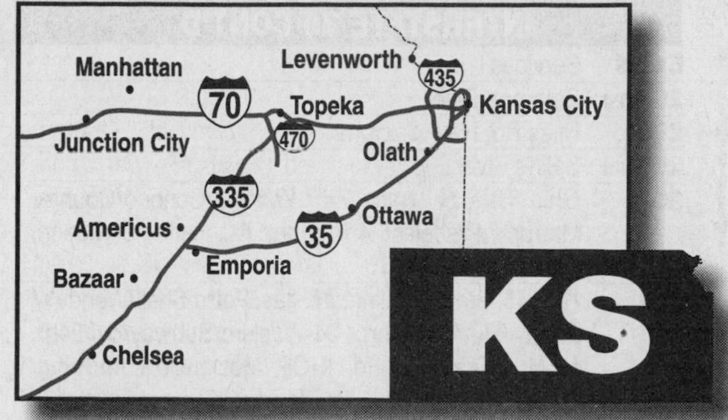

JCT CITY

Exit #	Services
310mm	**rest area both lanes, full ♿ facilities, ☎, ⛱, litter barrels, petwalk**
307	McDowell Creek Rd, scenic river rd to Manhattan
304	Humboldt Creek Rd
303	KS 18 E, to Ogden, Manhattan, **N other:** to KSU
301	Marshall Field, **N other:** Cavalry Museum, Custer's House, KS Terr Capitol, to Ft Riley
300	US 40, KS 57, Council Grove, **N lodging:** Dreamland Motel, **S** hist church
299	Flinthills Blvd, to Jct City, Ft Riley, **N gas:** Phillips 66/dsl, **food:** Stacy's Rest., **lodging:** Econolodge, Great Western Inn, Red Carpet Inn, Super 8
298	Chestnut St, to Jct City, Ft Riley, **N gas:** Shell/Burger King/dsl/24hr, **food:** Arby's, Cracker Barrel, Family Buffet, Mr Goodcents Subs, Taco Bell, **lodging:** Best Western, Candlewood Suites, Courtyard, Holiday Inn Express, Quality Inn, **other:** Curves, $General, $Tree, Walmart SuperCtr/24hr
296	US 40, Washington St, Junction City, **N gas:** Casey's, Cenex/dsl, Phillips 66, Shell/dsl/24hr, **food:** Denny's, McDonald's, Peking Chinese, Pizza Hut, Sirloin Stockade, Sonic, Subway, **lodging:** Budget Host, Days Inn, Howard Johnson, Ramada Ltd, ValuePlace Hotel, **other:** Cadillac, Chevrolet, Haas Tire, Harley-Davidson, Jeep, Pontiac
295	US 77, KS 18 W, Marysville, to Milford Lake, **N gas:** Phillips 66/Sapp Bro's/A&W/dsl/24hr, **lodging:** Motel 6, **other:** [H], truckwash, **S** RV Ctr, truckwash
294mm	**rest area both lanes, full ♿ facilities, ☎, ⛱, litter barrels, RV dump, petwalk**
290	Milford Lake Rd
286	KS 206, Chapman, **S gas:** Cenex/dsl, **other:** KS Auto Racing Museum, **1 mi S gas:** Casey's
281	KS 43, to Enterprise, **N gas:** Shell/dsl, **other:** 4 Seasons RV Ctr/Park
277	Jeep Rd

ABILENE

Exit #	Services
275	KS 15, to Clay Ctr, Abilene, **N food:** DQ, **lodging:** Brookville Hotel/rest., Holiday Inn Express, **S gas:** Phillips 66, 24-7/dsl, **food:** Burger King, Joe Snuffy's Grill, Kuntz's Drive Inn, M&R Grill, McDonald's, Pizza Hut, Sonic, Subway, **lodging:** Best Value Inn, Budget Inn, Super 8, **other:** [H], Alco/gas, AutoZone, Buick/Cadillac/Chevrolet/Pontiac, Chrysler/Dodge/Jeep, CountryMart Foods, $General, Ford, O'Reilly Parts, Radio Shack, Ricco Drug, to Eisenhower Museum
272	Fair Rd, to Talmage, **S** Russell Stover Candies
266	KS 221, Solomon
265mm	**rest area both lanes, full ♿ facilities, ☎, ⛱, litter barrels, vending, petwalk, RV dump**

INTERSTATE 70 CONT'D

Exit #	Services
264mm	Solomon River
260	Niles Rd, New Cambria
253mm	Saline River
253	Ohio St, **S gas:** *FLYING J*/Conoco/Country Mkt/dsl/LP/scales/24hr, **other:** H, Harley-Davidson, Kenworth
252	KS 143, 9th St, Salina, **N gas:** Petro/Shell/Wendy's/Pizza Hut/dsl/24hr, 24-7/Valero/Subway/dsl/24hr, **food:** Bayard's Café, IHOP, McDonald's, **lodging:** Best Inn, Days Inn, Holiday Inn Express, Motel 6, Super 8, **other:** Blue Beacon, Freightliner, KOA, dsl repair, **S gas:** Bosselman/Pilot/Sinclair/rest./scales/dsl/24hr/@, **lodging:** Best Western, Econolodge
250b a	I-135, US 81, N to Concordia, S to Wichita
249	Halstead Rd, to Trenton
244	Hedville, **N** Sundowner West RV Park, **S gas:** Cenex/dsl, **other:** Rolling Hills Park
238	to Brookville, Glendale, Tescott
233	to Beverly, Carnerio
225	KS 156, to Ellsworth, **S gas:** Elkhorn Corner/pizza/dsl, **other:** Ft Harker Museum, Ft Larned HS
224mm	**rest area both lanes, full ♿ facilities, ☎, picnic, litter barrels, petwalk, RV dump**
221	KS 14 N, to Lincoln
219	KS 14 S, to Ellsworth, **S gas:** Conoco/dsl
216	to Vesper
209	to Sylvan Grove
206	KS 232, Wilson, **N gas:** Travel Shoppe/rest., **other:** RV Park, Wilson Lake (6mi), winery
199	Dorrance, **N** to Wilson Lake, **S gas:** Agco/dsl/food
193	Bunker Hill Rd, **N gas:** Conoco/Quizno's/dsl/rest/24hr, to Wilson Lake WA
189	US 40 bus, Pioneer Rd, Russell
187mm	**rest area both lanes, full ♿ facilities, ☎, picnic, litter barrels, RV dump, petwalk**
184	US 281, Russell, **N gas:** Phillips 66/Mesquite Grill/dsl, 24-7/dsl, **food:** A&W, Meridy's Rest., McDonald's, Pizza Hut, Sonic, Subway, **lodging:** AmericInn, Days Inn, Russell's Inn, Super 8, **other:** H, Alco, CarQuest, $General, JJJ RV Park, Fossil Creek RV Park, st patrol, Vet
180	Balta Rd, to Russell
175	Gorham, **1 mi N gas:** Co-Op, food, ☎
172	Walker Ave
168	KS 255, to Victoria, **S gas:** Ampride/dsl, to Cathedral of the Plains
163	Toulon Ave
161	Commerce Parkway
159	US 183, Hays, **N gas:** Qwest/dsl, **food:** Applebee's, Carlos O'Kelly's, Golden Corral, IHOP, Subway, **lodging:** Best Western Butterfield, Comfort Inn, Fairfield Inn, Hampton Inn, Sleep Inn, **other:** Chrysler/Dodge/Jeep, Ford/Lincoln/Mercury, Harley-Davidson, Home Depot, Radio Shack, Toyota, Walmart SuperCtr/24hr, **S gas:** BP/24hr, Conoco/dsl/24hr, Love's, Phillips 66/dsl, 24-7/dsl, **food:** Arby's, Burger King, China Garden, Jimmy John's, KFC, LJ Silver, Lucky Buffet, McDonald's, MT Mike's Steaks, Pizza Hut, Sonic, Subway, Taco Bell, Taco Grande, Vagabond Rest., Village Inn, Wendy's, Whiskey Creek Grill, **lodging:**
159	Continued Baymont Inn, Best Value Inn, Days Inn, Econolodge, Motel 6, Quality Inn, Ramada Inn, Super 8, **other:** H Ace Hardware, Advance Parts, Chevrolet, Dillon's Foods/gas, Firestone/auto, Hastings Books, JC Penney, NAPA, Tires 4 Less, Walgreens, mall, st patrol
157	US 183 S byp, to Hays, **S other:** museum, tourist info, to Ft Hays St U
153	Yocemento Ave
145	KS 247 S, Ellis, **S gas:** Casey's, Phillips 66/DQ/Subway/dsl/24hr, **other:** to Chrysler Museum, Railroad Museum, RV camping, USPO
140	Riga Rd
135	KS 147, Ogallah, **N gas:** Frontier/dsl/24hr, **S** to Cedar Bluff SP (13mi)
132mm	**rest area both lanes, full ♿ facilities, picnic, litter barrels, petwalk, RV dump**
128	US 283 N, WaKeeney, **N gas:** Sinclair/dsl/24hr, **lodging:** Budget Host, Super 8, **other:** H
127	US 283 S, WaKeeney, **N food:** Jade Garden Rest., McDonald's, Pizza Hut, **lodging:** Best Western, KS Kountry Inn, **other:** $General, **S gas:** Conoco/Subway/dsl, 24-7/Real Country Cafe/dsl/24hr, **lodging:** Econolodge, **other:** KOA, antiques, auto repair
120	Voda Rd
115	KS 198 N, Banner Rd, Collyer
107	KS 212, Castle Rock Rd, Quinter, **N gas:** Sinclair/dsl, **lodging:** Budget Host/rest., **other:** H, auto repair, **S gas:** Conoco/dsl/24hr, **food:** DQ, Pizza Station
99	KS 211, Park, **1 mi N gas:** Sinclair/dsl
97mm	**rest area both lanes, full ♿ facilities, picnic, litter barrels, vending, petwalk, RV dump**
95	KS 23 N, to Hoxie
93	KS 23, Grainfield, **N gas:** Sinclair/dsl/24hr
85	KS 216, Grinnell, **N** gas (.5 mi)
79	Campus Rd
76	US 40, to Oakley, **S gas:** TA/Shell/Subway/Buckhorn Rest./scales/dsl/E-85/24hr/@, **lodging:** Econolodge (2mi), 1st Interstate Inn, Sleep Inn, **other:** H, Blue Beacon, Fick Museum
70	US 83, to Oakley, **N lodging:** Free Breakfast Inn, **S gas:** Phillips 66/dsl, **food:** Colonial Steaks, **other:** H, High-Plains RV Park, Prairie Dog Town, Fick Museum
62	rd K, Mingo, **S gas:** gas/dsl/☎
54	Country Club Dr, Colby, **N gas:** Bosselman's/Pilot/Wendy's/dsl/scales/24hr, **other:** H, truck repair
53	KS 25, Colby, **N gas:** Conoco/DQ/dsl, 24-7/dsl, **food:** Arby's, Burger King, China Buffet, McDonald's, MT Mike's Steaks, Pizza Hut, Sonic, Subway, Taco John's, **lodging:** Days Inn, Country Club Motel, Holiday Inn Express, Motel 6, Quality Inn, Super 8, **other:** H, Dillon's Foods/gas, $General, Ford/Lincoln/Mercury, Haas Tire, Prairie Art Museum, Quilt Cabin, Radio Shack, Walmart Super Ctr/24hr, dsl repair, trucklube/wash, **S gas:** Petro/Phillips 66/scales/dsl/@, **food:** Baskin-Robbins, Chester's, City Limits Grill, Quizno's, Starbucks, Village Inn, **lodging:** Comfort Inn, Crown Inn, **other:** Buick/Cadillac/Chevrolet/Pontiac, truck wash
48.5mm	**rest area both lanes, full ♿ facilities, ☎, picnic, litter barrels, RV park/dump, vending, petwalk**

E ↕ W SALINA HAYS COLBY KS

INTERSTATE 70 CONT'D

GOODLAND

Exit #	Services
45	US 24 E, Levant
36	KS 184, Brewster, **N gas:** Fuel Depot/dsl/24hr
35.5mm	Mountain/Central time zone
27	KS 253, Edson
19	US 24, Goodland, **N food:** Pizza Hut, **lodging:** Motel 7, **other:** $General, KOA, High Plains Museum
17	US 24, KS 27, Goodland, **N gas:** Cenex, Conoco, Phillips 66/dsl, **food:** DQ, El Reynaldo's, McDonald's, Mexico #3, Subway, Taco John's, Wendy's, Wonderful House Chinese, **lodging:** Best Value Inn, Comfort Inn, Howard Johnson, Motel 6, Super 8, **other:** [H], CarQuest/Firestone, Buick/Chevrolet, Cadillac/GMC/Pontiac, Walmart SuperCtr/24hr, **S gas:** Valero/deli/scales/dsl, **lodging:** Holiday Inn Express, **other:** Mid-America Camping
12	rd 14, Caruso
9	rd 11, Ruleton
7.5mm	**Welcome Ctr eb/rest area wb, full ♿ facilities, info, ☎, picnic, litter barrels, petwalk, vending, wireless internet, RV dump**
1	KS 267, Kanorado, **N** gas, food
.5mm	**weigh sta eb**
0mm	Kansas/Colorado State Line

INTERSTATE 135 (WICHITA)

Exit #	Services
95b a	I-70, E to KS City, W to Denver. **I-135 begins/ends on I-70, exit 250. US 81 continues nb.**
93	KS 140, State St, Salina
92	Crawford St, **E gas:** KwikShop, Phillips 66/dsl, Shell, Sinclair, 24-7/dsl, **food:** Arby's, Braum's, Guiterra's Rest., McDonald's, Russell's Rest., Spangles, Taco Bell, Subway, Western Sizzlin, **lodging:** Best Western, Comfort Inn, Fairfield Inn, Holiday Inn, Rodeway Inn, **other:** Advance Parts, Dillan's Foods, O'Reilly Parts, Radio Shack, Walgreens, **W gas:** Cenex/dsl, **lodging:** Quality Inn
90	Magnolia Rd, **E gas:** Phillips 66/dsl, Shell/24hr, **food:** Carlos O'Kelly's, Chili's, Cici's, Coyote Canyon Café, Domino's, Fazoli's, Hong Kong Buffet, IHOP, McDonald's, Mr Goodcents Subs, Papa Murphy's, Potrillo's Mexican, Quizno's, Schlotsky's, Sonic, Subway, Taco Tico, **lodging:** Best Value Inn, Candlewood Suites, **other:** Advance Parts, AutoZone, Buick/Subaru, Dillard's, Dillon's Foods/dsl, $General, $Tree, Honda, JC Penney, Jo-Ann Fabrics, Old Navy, O'Reilly Parts, PetCo, Sears, Toyota, Tuesday Morning, mall, **W gas:** Cenex/dsl
89	Schilling Rd, **E gas:** KwikShop/dsl, **food:** Applebee's, Burger King, Pizza Hut, Popeye's, Red Lobster, Taco Bueno, Tucson's Steaks, Wendy's, **lodging:** Country Inn&Suites, Courtyard, Hampton Inn, **other:** Cadillac/Chevrolet, Lowe's Whse, Sam's Club/gas, Target, Walmart SuperCtr/24hr, **W gas:** Casey's, **lodging:** Baymont Inn, Comfort Inn, Super 8
88	Waterwell RD, **E other:** Ford/Lincoln/Mercury, Nissan
86	KS 104, Mentor, Smolan
82	KS 4, Falun Rd, Assaria, **E other:** RV Camping
78	KS 4 W, Lindsborg, **E other:** Sandz Gallery/Museum
72	US 81, Lindsborg, **4 mi E other:** McPherson St

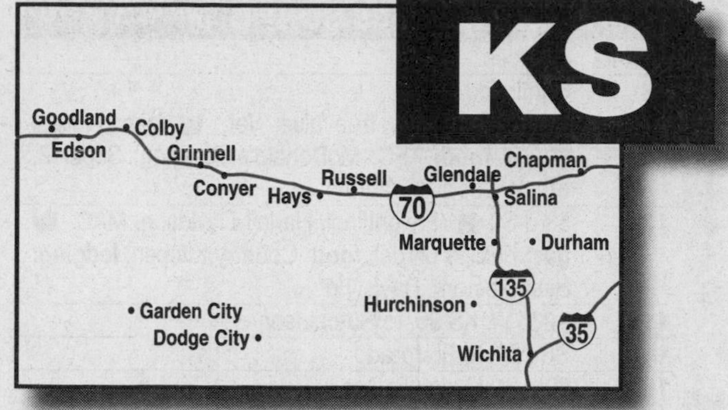

MCPHERSON

Exit #	Services
72	Continued Fishing Lake, Maxwell WR, **W other:** [H], gas, food, lodging, ☎, camping, museum
68mm	**rest areas (both lanes exit left), full ♿ facilities, ☎, picnic, litter barrels petwalk, RV dump**
65	Pawnee Rd
60	US 56, McPherson, Marion, **W gas:** Midway/dsl, **food:** Applebee's, Arby's, Braum's, Golden Dragon Chinse, KFC/LJ Silver, Krehbiels BBQ, La Fiesta Mexican, McDonald's, MT Mike's, Pizza Hut, Subway, Taco Bell, Taco Tico, **lodging:** Best Value Inn, Best Western, Days Inn, Holiday Inn Express, Red Coach Inn, **other:** [H], AutoZone, Chrysler/Dodge/Jeep, $General, Walmart SuperCtr/24hr
58	US 81, KS 61, to Hutchinson, McPherson
54	Elyria
48	KS 260 E, Moundridge, **2 mi W** gas, food, ☎
46	KS 260 W, Moundridge, **2 mi W** gas, food, ☎
40	Lincoln Blvd, Hesston, **E food:** Aggie Grill, **lodging:** AmericInn, **W gas:** Cenex/dsl, **food:** El Sarito Grill, Lincoln Perk Coffee, Pizza Hut, Sonic, Subway, **lodging:** Best Value Inn
34	N Newton, Avalene, KS 15, **E other:** RV camping, **W food:** Subway, **other:** Kaufman Museum
33	US 50 E, to Peabody (from nb)
31	1st St, Broadway St, **E gas:** Cenex, Conoco/dsl, Shamrock, **food:** Applebee's, CJ's Rest., KFC, **lodging:** Best Value Inn, Day's Inn, 1st Inn, **other:** Chevrolet/Cadillac, Chrysler/Dodge/Jeep, Ford/Lincoln/Mercury, **W food:** Braum's, MT Mike's, **lodging:** Best Western/rest.
30	US 50 W, KS 15 (exits left from nb), to Hutchinson, Newton, **W gas:** Cenex, KwikShop/dsl, **food:** Arby's, Papa Murphy's, Pizza Hut, Quizno's, Sonic, Subway, **other:** [H], AutoZone, Dillon's Foods, $Tree, Walmart SuperCtr/24hr
28	SE 36th St, **W gas:** Shell, **food:** Burger King, **other:** Chisholm Trail Outlets/famous brands
25	KS 196, to Whitewater, El Dorado
23mm	**rest areas both lanes, full ♿ facilities, ☎, picnic, litter barrels, vending, petwalk, RV dump**
22	125th St
19	101st St, **W other:** RV camping
17	85th St, **E** Valley Ctr, KS Coliseum
16	77th St, **E lodging:** Sleep Inn, **other:** Wichita Greyhound Park
14	61st St, **E gas:** QT/dsl, Valero, **food:** Applebee's, Chopstix, Cracker Barrel, Pizza Hut, Spangles Rest., Subway, Taco Bell, Wendy's, **lodging:** Comfort Inn,

NEWTON

INTERSTATE 135 CONT'D (WICHITA)

N ↕ S — WICHITA

Exit #	Services
14	Continued **other:** Chevrolet, TrueValue, Vet, **W gas:** Phillips 66/dsl, **food:** KFC, McDonald's, **lodging:** Super 8, **other:** Goodyear/auto
13	53rd St, **E** Freightliner, Harley-Davidson, MAC, **W gas:** Phillips 66/dsl, **food:** Country Kitchen, **lodging:** Best Western, Day's Inn
11b	I-235 W, KS 96, to Hutchinson
11a	KS 254, to El Dorado
10b	29th St, Hydraulic Ave
10a	KS 96 E
9	21st St, **E food:** Sonic, **other:** Wichita St U
8	13th St
7a	downtown
7b	8th St, 9th St, Central Ave., **E** School of Medicine
6b	1st St, 2nd St, **E** AutoZone, **W** Chevrolet, Chrysler/Jeep
5b	US 54, US 400, Kellogg Ave, **E gas:** QT, Valero, **food:** Chipotle Meixcan, McDonald's, Spangles, Subway
5a	Lincoln St, **E food:** DQ, **W gas:** QT
4	Harry St, **1 mi E gas:** QT, **food:** Church's, Denny's, McDonald's, Spangles Rest., Subway, Wendy's, **W gas:** Don's/dsl
3	Pawnee Ave, **E gas:** QT, **W gas:** Phillips 66, Shell, **food:** Burger King, Church's, Papa John's, Pizza Hut, Spangles, **lodging:** Pawnee Inn, **other:** AutoZone, Checker's Foods, $General
2	Hydraulic Ave, **E gas:** QT, **W food:** McDonald's, Subway
2mm	Arkansas River
1c	I-235 N, **2 mi W** Hilton
1b a	US 81 S, 47th St, **E gas:** Conoco, **lodging:** Comfort Inn, Day's Inn, Holiday Inn Express, **W gas:** Phillips 66, **food:** Applebee's, Braum's, Burger King, Carlos O'Kelly's, Godfather's, Hog Wild BBQ, KFC, LJ Silver, McDonald's, New China Buffet, Papa John's, Pizza Hut, Quizno's, Spangles Rest., Subway, Taco Bell, Taco Tico, **lodging:** Best Western, Heritage Inn, Red Carpet Inn, Value Place, **other:** Checker's Foods, Curves, Dillon's Foods/dsl, $General, Home Depot, K-Mart, O'Reilly's Parts, Radio Shack
0mm	I-135 begins/ends on I-35, exit 42.

KENTUCKY

INTERSTATE 24

E ↕ W — PADUCAH

Exit #	Services
93.5mm	Kentucky/Tennessee state line
93mm	**Welcome Ctr wb, full ♿ facilities, ☎, 🛆, litter barrels, vending, petwalk**
91.5mm	Big West Fork Red River
89	KY 115, to Oak Grove, **N** to Jeff Davis Mon St HS, **S gas:** Pilot/McDonald's/dsl/scales/24hr, Shell/dsl
86	US 41A, to Ft Campbell, Pennyrile Pkwy, Hopkinsville, **N gas:** Chevron/Chester Fried/dsl/scales/24hr, **S gas:** BP/dsl/24hr, *FLYING J*/Country Mkt/dsl/LP/scales/24hr, Pilot/Subway/Wendy's/dsl/scales/24hr, **food:** McDonald's, Waffle House, **lodging:** Day's Inn, Holiday Inn Express, Quality Inn, **other:** H
79mm	Little River
73	KY 117, to Gracey, Newstead
65	US 68, KY 80, to Cadiz, **S gas:** BP/dsl, Chevron/dsl, Shell/dsl/24hr, **food:** Cracker Barrel, KFC, McDonald's, Taco Bell, Wendy's, **lodging:** Broadbent Inn, Knight's Inn, Super 7 Inn, Super 8, **other:** H, Candy's RV Ctr, Chevrolet, golf, to NRA
56	KY 139, to Cadiz, Princeton, **S gas:** Chevron/dsl, **other:** KOA (9mi), NRA
47mm	Lake Barkley
45	KY 293, to Princeton, Saratoga, **N other:** classic car museum, **S gas:** Chevron/dsl, **other:** Mineral Mound SP, RV Camping, to KY St Penitentiary
42	to W KY Pkwy, Elizabethtown
40	US 62, US 641, Kuttawa, Eddyville, **N lodging:** Regency Inn, Relax Inn, **other:** camping, **S gas:** BP/Wendy's/dsl/24hr, Huck's/Quizno's/dsl/scales/24hr, **food:** Huddle House, SW Grill, **lodging:** Day's Inn, Hampton Inn, **other:** to Lake Barkley, KY Lake Rec Areas, camping
36mm	**weigh sta both lanes, ☎**
34mm	Cumberland River
31	KY 453, to Grand Rivers, Smithland, **N gas:** BP/dsl, **lodging:** Patti's Inn, **S gas:** Exxon/dsl, **food:** Miss Scarlett's, **lodging:** Barkley Lakes Inn, Grand Rivers Resort (3mi), Lighthouse Landing Resort, **other:** Exit 31 RV Park, NRA
29mm	Tennessee River
27	US 62, to KY Dam, Calvert City, **N gas:** BP, Marathon/dsl, **food:** Cracker Barrel, DQ, McDonald's, KFC, Waffle House, Willow Pond Rest., **lodging:** Days Inn, KY Dam Motel, Super 8, **other:** Cypress Lakes Camp, Freightliner, KOA, Vet, **S gas:** Love's/Arby's/dsl/scales/24hr, **food:** Subway, **other:** truck repair
25b a	to Calvert City, Carroll/Purchase Pkwy, services **1 mi** N, **S** KY Lake RA
16	US 68, to Paducah, **S gas:** BP/Southern Pride/Subway/dsl/scales/24hr, **other:** antiques, flea mkt
11	rd 1954, Husband Rd, to Paducah, **N gas:** Exxon/dsl, **lodging:** Best Western, **other:** Duck Creek RV Park, **S other:** Harley-Davidson
7	US 45, US 62, to Paducah, **N gas:** BP/dsl, **food:** Burger King, Taco Bell, **other:** H, **S Welcome Ctr both lanes, full ♿ facilities, ☎, vending, 🛆, litter barrels, petwalk, gas:** BP, Marathon/dsl, **food:** Arby's, Backyard Burger, Chong's Chinese, KFC, Los Amigo's Mexican, McDonald's, Pizza Hut, Popeye's, Sonic, Waffle House, **lodging:** Denton Motel, **other:** K-Mart, O'Reilly Parts, SuperValu Foods/gas
4	US 60, to Paducah, **N gas:** BP, **food:** Applebee's, Bob Evans, Burger King, McDonald's, O'Charley's, Outback Steaks, Rafferty's, **lodging:** Candlewood Suites, Courtyard, Day's Inn, Drury Inn, Hampton Inn, Holiday Inn Express, Residence Inn, **other:** Hancock Fabrics, Toyota/Scion, **S gas:** BP, **food:** Arby's, Backwoods BBQ, Capt D's, Chong's Chinese, Chuck

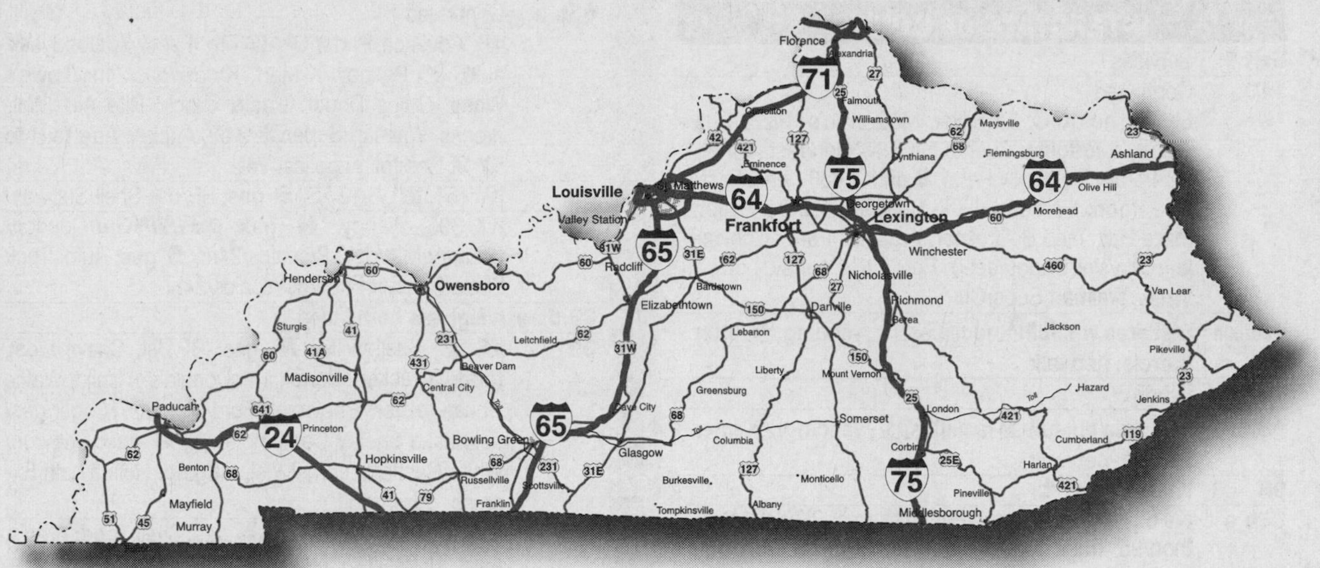

INTERSTATE 24 CONT'D

E ↕ W — PADUCAH

Exit #	Services
4	Continued eCheese, Cracker Barrel, Dominos, El Chico's, Fazoli's, Hardee's/24hr, IHOP, Logan's Roadhouse, Los Amigos, McAlister's Deli, Olive Garden, Penn Sta. Subs, Pizza Hut, Red Lobster, Ryan's, Sonic, Steak'n Shake, Subway, Taco Bell, TX Roadhouse, TGIFriday, Wendy's, **lodging:** Comfort Suites, Country Inn&Suites, Drury Suites, Motel 6, Paducah Inn, PearTree Inn, Thrifty Inn, **other:** AAA, Advance Parts, Aldi Foods, Best Buy, BooksAMillion, Dillard's, Gander Mtn, Goodyear, Home Depot, JC Penney, Kohl's, Lowe's Whse, Michael's, Office Depot, Old Navy, Petsmart, Sam's Club/gas, Sears/auto, TJ Maxx, Walmart SuperCtr/gas/24hr, mall
3	KY 305, to Paducah, **N gas:** BP/dsl/scales, **lodging:** Best Value Inn, Comfort Inn/rest., Econolodge, **S gas:** Cheers/dsl, Pilot/Subway/dsl/scales/24hr, **food:** Yu's Kitchen, Waffle Hut, **lodging:** Baymont Inn, **other:** Fern Lake Camping
0mm	Kentucky/Illinois state line, Ohio River

INTERSTATE 64

E ↕ W — GRAYSON

Exit #	Services
192mm	Kentucky/West Virginia state line, Big Sandy River
191	US 23, to Ashland, **1-2 mi N gas:** Exxon, GoMart, Marathon/Subway/dsl, Speedway, **food:** Arby's, McDonald's, Waffle House, Wendy's, **lodging:** Ramada Ltd, **other:** [H], Rite Aid, Foodland Foods
185	KY 180, Cannonsburg, **1-3 mi N gas:** BP/dsl, Chevron/McDonald's, **food:** Arby's, Bob Evan's, Burger King, DQ, Subway, Wendy's, **lodging:** Day's Inn, Fairfield Inn, Hampton Inn, Holiday Inn Express, Knight's Inn, **other:** st police, **S gas:** ***FLYING J***/CountryMkt/dsl/LP/scales/24hr, **other:** Hidden Valley Camping
181	181 US 60, to Princess, **N gas:** BP/dsl, **S gas:** Marathon
179	rd 67, Industrial Parkway
174mm	**rest areas wb, full ♿ facilities, ☎, vending, picnic, litter barrels, petwalk**
173mm	**rest areas wb, full ♿ facilities, ☎, vending, picnic, litter barrels, petwalk**
172	rd 1, rd 7, Grayson, **N gas:** Texaco/dsl/24hr, Superquik/dsl/24hr, **food:** A&W/LJ Silver, Huddle House, KFC, LJ Silver, Pizza Hut, Shoney's, Subway, **lodging:** Day's Inn, Holiday Inn Express, Quality Inn, **other:** Chrysler/Jeep, $General, $Tree, Ford, K-Mart, SaveALot Foods, **S gas:** BP, Chevron/Quizno's, Exxon/Hardees, Marathon, Speedway, Pilot/Wendy's/dsl/24hr, Speedway, **food:** Arby's, Biscuit World, China House, DQ, Little Caesar's, McDonald's, Papa John's, Taco Bell, **lodging:** Super 8, **other:** Advance Parts, AutoZone, $General, Family$, Rite Aid
161	US 60, to Olive Hill, **N gas:** BP, **other:** to Carter Caves SP, camping, **S gas:** Marathon/dsl/24hr, **lodging:** Spanish Manor Motel
156	rd 2, to KY 59, to Olive Hill, **S gas:** BP, **food:** DQ
148mm	**weigh sta both lanes**
141mm	**rest areas both lanes, full ♿ facilities, ☎, vending, picnic, litter barrels, petwalk**
137	KY 32, to Morehead, **N gas:** BP/DQ/dsl, **food:** CiCi's Pizza, Huddle House, Reno's Roadhouse, **other:** Big Lots, Curves, Kroger/dsl, Lowes Whse, Walmart SuperCtr, **S gas:** BP, Chevron/McDonald's/dsl/24hr, Marathon, **food:** China Buffet, Domino's, Hardee's, KFC, Lee's Chicken, McDonald's, Ponderosa, Shoney's, **lodging:** Day's Inn, Hampton Inn, Holiday Inn Express, Knights Inn, Mtn Lodge Motel, Quality Inn, Super 8, **other:** [H], Ace Hardware, Buick/Pontiac, $General, Food Lion, Radio Shack, st police
133	rd 801, to Sharkey, Farmers, **S gas:** BP/Subway/dsl, **lodging:** Comfort Inn
123	US 60, to Salt Lick, Owingsville, **N gas:** Chevron/dsl
121	KY 36, to Owingsville, **N gas:** BP/dsl, Exxon, Marathon, Marathon/dsl, **food:** DQ, McDonald's, Subway, **lodging:** Super 8, **other:** $General, Family$
113	US 60, to Mt Sterling, **N gas:** Chevron/dsl, **S gas:** Pilot/McDonald's/Subway/scales/dsl/24hr
110	US 460, KY 11, Mt Sterling, **N gas:** Chevron/dsl/24hr, Shell/Krystal/dsl, **food:** Cracker Barrel, **lodging:** Fairfield Inn, Ramada Ltd, **other:** golf, **S gas:** BP/dsl, Exxon/Subway, Marathon/Huddle House, Speedway/dsl, **food:** Applebee's, Arby's, Burger King,

E ↕ W

INTERSTATE 64 CONT'D

Exit #	Services
110	Continued El Camino, KFC, LJ Silver, McDonald's, Pizza Hut, Wendy's, **lodging:** Budget Inn, Day's Inn/rest., **other:** [H], Family$, O'Reilly Parts, **S on KY 686...gas:** Fastlane, **food:** Hardee's, Little Caesar's, Peking Buffet, Pizza Hut, Taco Bell, **other:** Advance Parts, Chevrolet, Chrysler/Dodge/Jeep, Ford, JC Penney, Lowe's Whse, Walmart SuperCtr
108mm	**rest area wb, full [♿] facilities, [phone], vending, [picnic], litter barrels, petwalk**
101	US 60
98.5mm	**rest area eb, full [♿] facilities, [phone], vending, [picnic], litter barrels, petwalk**
98	KY 402 (from eb)
96b a	KY 627, to Winchester, Paris, **N gas:** BP/dsl, Marathon/96 Truck Plaza/dsl/rest./scales/, **S lodging:** Day's Inn, Hampton Inn, Quality Inn, **other:** Chevrolet/Buick/Pontiac
94	KY 1958, Van Meter Rd, Winchester, **N gas:** Chevron/dsl/24hr, Shell/scales/dsl, **lodging:** Best Value Inn, Holiday Inn Express, **other:** flea mkt, **S gas:** BP/dsl, Chevron, Shell, Speedway/dsl, **food:** Applebee's, Arby's, Cantuckee Diner, Capt D's, Domino's, DQ, El Camino, Fazoli's, Golden Corral, Great Wall Chinese, Hardee's, Jade Garden Chinese, KFC, Little Caesar's, McDonald's, Mi Finca Mexican, Papa John's, Pizza Hut, Quizno's, Rally's, Sonic, Subway, Taco Bell, Taste Of China, Waffle House, Wendy's, **lodging:** Best Western, **other:** [H], Advance Parts, AutoZone, Chrysler/Dodge/Jeep, $General, Ford/Mercury, K-Mart, Lowe's Whse, Office Depot, O'Reilly Parts, Radio Shack, Rite Aid, SaveAlot Foods, Walgreens, Walmart SuperCtr, to Ft Boonesborough Camping
87	KY 859, Blue Grass Sta
81	I-75 S, to Knoxville
I-64 and I-75 run together 7 mi. See Kentucky Interstate exits 113-115.	
75	I-75 N, to Cincinnati, access to KY Horse Park
69	US 62 E, to Georgetown, **N** antiques (mi), **S** Equus Run Vineyards (2mi)
65	US 421, Midway, **S** antiques
60mm	**rest area both lanes, full [♿] facilities, litter barrels, petwalk, vending**
58	**N gas:** Chevron/dsl, Marathon, Shell, Speedway, **food:** Arby's, Capt. D's, Cattleman's Roadhouse, KFC, McDonald's, Waffle House, White Castle, **lodging:** Best Western, Bluegrass Inn, Fairfield Inn, **other:** Chevrolet/Cadillac/Nissan, Chrysler/Jeep/Dodge, $General, $Tree, Ford/Lincoln/Mercury, Honda, Kohl's, Kroger, Pontiac, Toyota/Scion, to KY St Capitol, KYSU, to Viet Vets Mem, transmissions
55mm	Kentucky River
53b a	US 127, Frankfort, **N gas:** Chevron/24hr, Marathon, Shell/24hr, Speedway, **food:** A&W/LJ Silver, Applebee's, Beef O'Brady's, Big Boy, Burger King, Capt D's, Carino's Italian, Chili's, DQ, Fazoli's, Hardee's, KFC, Longhorn Steaks, McDonald's, O'Charley's, Panera Bread, Pizza Hut, Qdoba Mexican, Rio Grande Mexican, Shoney's, Starbucks, Steak'n Shake, Subway, Taco Bell, Taco John's, Wendy's, **lodging:** Best Value Inn, Hampton Inn, Holiday Inn Express, **other:**
53b a	Continued [H], Advance Parts, Big-O Tire, Family$, Goodyear/auto, JC Penney, K-Mart, Kroger/gas/24hr, Lowe's Whse, Office Depot, Radio Shack, Rite Aid, Walgreens, Walmart SuperCtr/24hr, Ancient Age Tour, to KY St Capitol, st police, Vet
48	KY 151, to US 127 S, **S gas:** BP/dsl, Shell/Subway
43	KY 395, Waddy, **N gas:** *FLYING J*/Conoco/Country Mkt/dsl/LP/scales/24hr, **S gas:** Auto/Truck Plaza/Chester Fried/dsl/scales/24hr
38.5mm	**weigh sta both lanes**
35	KY 53, Shelbyville, **N gas:** BP/dsl, Chevron/dsl, **food:** Cracker Barrel, McDonald's (1mi), Waffle House, **other:** Chevrolet, Ford/Mercury, Kroger/gas/deli, Lake Shelby Camping (3mi), **S gas:** Chevron/White Castle/dsl, Shell/dsl, **lodging:** Holiday Inn Express, **other:** golf
32b a	KY 55, Shelbyville, **1-3 mi N gas:** Shell, **food:** Arby's, Asian Buffet, DQ, Finefresh BBQ, KFC, McDonald's, Quizno's, Subway, Waffle House, Wendy's, **lodging:** Country Hearth Inn, Day's Inn, **other:** [H], AutoZone, Buick/Pontiac/GMC, $Tree, Lowes Whse, Rolling Hills Camping (16mi), Walgreens, Walmart SuperCtr/gas, **S food:** Cattleman's Roadhouse, **lodging:** Ramada, **other:** Taylorsville Lake SP
28mm	**rest area eb, full [♿] facilities, info, [phone], [picnic], litter barrels, vending, petwalk**
28	KY 1848, Veechdale Rd, Simpsonville, **N gas:** Pilot/Wendy's/dsl/scales/24hr, **food:** DQ, **other:** golf, **S gas:** Chevron/dsl
19b a	I-265, Gene Snyder Fwy, **N** to Tom Sawyer SP
17	S Blankenbaker, **N gas:** Circle K/gas, **lodging:** Staybridge Suites, **other:** Harley-Davidson, **S gas:** BP/Subway, Chevron, Marathon, Thornton's/dsl, **food:** Arby's, BackYard Burger, Burger King, Cracker Barrel, HomeTown Buffet, KFC/A&W, King Buffet, Kingfish Rest., McDonald's, Penn Sta., Ruby Tuesday, Taco Bell/LJ Silver, Waffle House, Wendy's, **lodging:** Candlewood Suites, Comfort Suites, Country Inn&Suites, Hampton Inn, Hilton Garden, Holiday Inn Express, Homestead Suites, Jameson Inn, Microtel, Sleep Inn, Super 8, Wingate Inn, **other:** Lexus, Sam's Club/gas
15	Hurstbourne Pkwy, Louisville, **N gas:** Shell/Circle K/dsl, Speedway, Thorton's/dsl, **food:** Amerigo Italian, Arby's, Bob Evans, Bonefish Grill, Carrabba's, Chili's, Fazoli's, Great Harvest, Jimmy John's, Macaroni Grill, McDonald's, Mimi's Cafe, Olive Garden, Panera Bread, Papa John's, PF Changs, Qdoba, Sichuan Garden, Starbucks, Skyline Chili, Subway, TGIFriday, Waffle House, **lodging:** Baymont Inn, Courtyard, Days Inn, Drury Inn, Holiday Inn, Hyatt, Red Roof Inn, **other:** Barnes&Noble, Kroger/gas, Lowe's Whse, Walgreens, **S gas:** Marathon, Meijer/dsl/24hr, **food:** Applebee's, BD BBQ, Buca Rest., Burger King, China Star, ChuckeCheese, Coldstone Creamery, DQ, Famous Daves, Home Run Burgers, Jumbo Grill, Longhorn Steaks, Lonestar Steaks, McAlister's Deli, Mercedes Grill, Moe's SW Grill, O'Charley's, Old Chicago, Picadilly, Qdoba, Quizno's, Smokey Bones BBQ, Starbucks, Steak'n Shake, Taco Bell, Tumbleweeds Mexican, Wendy's, White Castle, **lodging:** Clarion, Marriott, Red Carpet Inn, **other:** Autozone,

WINCHESTER

SHELBYVILLE

LOUISVILLE

INTERSTATE 64 CONT'D

E ↕ W

Exit #	Services
15	Continued Borders, Cadillac, Carmax, Chevrolet/Subaru, $Tree, Home Depot, Hancock Fabrics, Honda, Infiniti, Kroger/gas, Michael's, Office Depot, Pontiac/GMC, Radio Shack, Staples, Subaru, Target, VW, Walgreens, Walmart/drugs
12b	I-264 E, Watterson Expswy, **1 exit N on US 60...gas:** Chevron, **food:** Alexander's Rest., Arby's, Big Boy, BJ's Rest., CA Pizza, Cheesecake Factory, Cosina Italian, Fox&Hound, Jay Alexandar's, Logan's Roadhouse, McDonald's, Outback Steaks, Panera Bread, Taco Bell, Wendy's, **other:** Acura, Best Buy, Dillard's, Ford/Lincoln/Mercury, Goodyear/auto, JC Penney, Kia, Kohl's, Macy's, Staples, SteinMart, Towery's AutoCare, Vonmaur, Whole Foods Mkt, mall
12a	I-264 W, access to [H]
10	Cannons Lane
8	Grinstead Dr, Louisville, **S** gas, **food:** KT Cafe, Jim Porter's Rest.
7	US 42, US 62, Mellwood Ave, Story Ave
6	I-71 N (from eb), to Cincinnati
5a	I-65, S to Nashville, N to Indianapolis
5b	3rd St, Louisville, **N food:** Joe's CrabShack, McDonald's, **S lodging:** Galt House Hotel, Marriott, **food:** Kingfish Rest., **other:** [H]
4	9th St, Roy Wilkins Ave, **S** KY Art Ctr, science museum, downtown
3	US 150 E, to 22nd St, **S gas:** BP/Circle K, Chevron, **food:** DQ, McDonald's, Subway, other:
1	I-264 E, to Shively, **S** [airport], zoo
0mm	Kentucky/Indiana state line, Ohio River

INTERSTATE 65

N ↕ S LOUISVILLE

Exit #	Services
138mm	Kentucky/Indiana state line, Ohio River
137	I-64 W, I-71 N, I-64 E, **W** to Galt House, downtown
136c	Jefferson St, Louisville, **E other:** [H], Walgreens, **W gas:** Shell, **food:** McDonald's, Subway, White Castle, **lodging:** Courtyard, Fairfield Inn, Hampton Inn, Hyatt, Marriott, Springhill Suites, **other:** Tires+
136b	Broadway St, Chestnut St (from nb), **E other:** [H], NAPA, Walgreens, **W gas:** Shell, Thornton's, **food:** McDonald's, Rally's, Subway, White Castle, **lodging:** Courtyard, Fairfield Inn, Hampton Inn, Hyatt, Marriott, Springhill Suites, **other:** Tires+, same as 136c
135	W St Catherine, **E gas:** Shell
134b a	KY 61, Jackson St, Woodbine St, **W gas:** BP/Circle K, **lodging:** Day's Inn, Quality Inn, **other:** Harley-Davidson
133b	US 60A, Eastern Pkwy, Taylor Blvd, **E food:** Denny's, Papa John's, Pizza Mia, Snappy Tomato Pizza, Subway, **W gas:** Shell, **food:** Cracker Barrel, McDonald's, **lodging:** Country Hearth Inn, **other:** U of Louisville, Churchill Downs, museum
133b	Crittenden Dr (132 from sb), **W food:** Arby's, Burger King, Cracker Barrel, Hall of Fame Cafe', **lodging:** Country Inn& Suites, Hilton Garden, Holiday Inn, Ramada Inn, Super 8 **E food:** Denny's, same as 133
131b a	I-264, Watterson Expswy, **W** Cardinal Stadium, Expo Center, [airport]

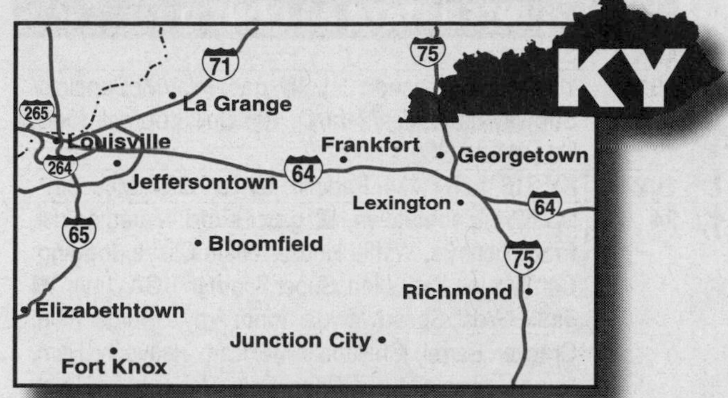

Exit #	Services
130	KY 61, Preston Hwy, **E on Ky 61...gas:** BP/Circle K, Speedway/dsl, Thornton, **food:** Blimpie, Bob Evans, Burger King, Domino's, Fazoli's, KFC, Little Caesar's, McDonald's, Papa John's, Popeyes, Rally's, Royal Garden Buffet, Subway, Taco Bell, Waffle House, Wendy's, **lodging:** Econolodge, Red Roof Inn, Super 8, **other:** Aamco, Ace Hardware, AutoZone, Big O Tire, BigLots, Chevrolet/KIA, Chrysler, Cox Drug, $General, Dodge, Ford, O'Reilly Parts, PepBoys, Radio Shack, Sav-A-lot Foods, Staples, Tires+, U-Haul
128	KY 1631, Fern Valley Rd, **E gas:** FiveStar, Marathon/Circle K, Thornton/dsl, **food:** Arby's, Big Boy, El Nopal Mexican, Hardee's, Indi's Rest., McDonald's, Outback Steaks, Shoney's, Subway, Taco Bell, Waffle House, White Castle, Wendy's, **lodging:** Comfort Suites, Days Inn, Holiday Inn, InTown Suites, Jameson Inn, **other:** Cottman Transmissions, Lincoln/Mercury, NAPA Care, Sam's Club/gas, Walgreens, **W** UPS Depot
127	KY 1065, outer loop, **E** TX Roadhouse, **W food:** McDonald's, to Motor Speedway,
125b a	I-265 E, KY 841, Gene Snyder Fwy
121	KY 1526, Brooks Rd, **E gas:** BP, Marathon, **food:** Arby's, Burger King, Cracker Barrel, McDonald's, Tumbleweed Grill, **lodging:** Fairfield Inn, Holiday Inn Express, Ramada, **other:** [H], Tinker's RV Ctr, **W gas:** BP/dsl, Pilot/Subway/Taco Bell/dsl/24hr/scales, Shell/dsl, **food:** Waffle House, **lodging:** Baymont Inn, Comfort Inn, Econolodge, Hampton Inn, Quality Inn
117	KY 44, Shepherdsville, **E gas:** Shell/dsl, **food:** Denny's, Kitchen Rest., **lodging:** Best Western/rest., Day's Inn, **other:** KOA (2mi), **W gas:** Marathon, Speedway/dsl, **food:** Arby's, China Buffet, DQ, El Nopal, Fazoli's, LJ Silver, KFC, McDonald's/playplace, Mr Gatti's, Papa John's, Quizno's, Rio's Steaks, Sonic, Subway, Taco Bell, Waffle House, Wendy's, White Castle, **lodging:** Country Inn&Suites, Motel 6, Sleep Inn, Super 8, **other:** Ace Hardware, Advance Parts, BigLots, $General, Family$, Kroger/gas, Lowe's Whse, NAPA Autocare, Radio Shack, Rite Aid, Sav-a-Lot
116.5mm	Salt River
116	KY 480, KY 61, **E gas:** Love's/Subway/Chester's/dsl/scales/24hr, Shell/dsl, **other:** House of Quilts, **W gas:** Chevron/dsl, **other:** Grandma's RV Park
114mm	**rest area sb, full [handicapped] facilities, [phone], vending, [picnic], litter barrels, petwalk**
112	KY 245, Clermont, **E gas:** Shell/dsl, **other:** Jim Beam Outpost, Bernheim Forest, to My Old Kentucky Home SP

KY

INTERSTATE 65 CONT'D

N ↕ S

Exit #	Services
105	105 KY 61, Lebanon Jct, **W gas:** Pilot/McDonald's/Subway/dsl/scales/24hr/@, 105 QuikStop/dsl, **food:** Hog-Wild BBQ
102	KY 313, to KY 434, Radcliff, **W** to Patton Museum
94	US 62, Elizabethtown, **E gas:** BP/dsl, Marathon/dsl, **food:** Denny's, Waffle House, White Castle, **lodging:** Comfort Inn, Day's Inn, Super 8, **other:** KOA (1mi), **W gas:** BP/dsl, Speedway/dsl, **food:** Arby's, Burger King, Cracker Barrel, Chalupa's Mexican, Heavenly Ham, Hungry Howie's, KFC/Taco Bell, McDonald's, Ruby Tuesday, Ryan's, Shoney's, Stone Hearth, Subway, TX Outlaw Steaks, TX Roadhouse, Wendy's, **lodging:** Baymont Inn, Best Western, Comfort Inn, Country Hearth Inn, Fairfield Inn, Hampton Inn, Holiday Inn Express, Fairfield Inn, La Quinta, Motel 6, Ramada Inn, **other:** H, Advance Parts, AutoZone, Curves, $General, $Tree, Family$, Kroger/gas, Skagg's RV Ctr, True Value, Walgreens, USPO, st police
93	to Bardstown, to BG Pky, **E** to My Old KY Home SP, Maker's Mark Distillery
91	US 31 W, KY 61, WK Pkwy, Elizabethtown, **E gas:** Marathon/dsl, **food:** LJ Silver, **lodging:** Bluegrass Inn, Budget Motel, Commonwealth Lodge, **other:** to Lincoln B'Place, **W gas:** Doug's/dsl, **food:** Jerry's Rest./24hr, **lodging:** KY Cardinal Inn, Roadside Inn, **other:** H
90mm	**weigh sta both lanes**
86	KY 222, Glendale, **E gas:** Pilot/McDonalds/dsl/scales/24hr, **other:** Glendale Camping, **W gas:** Petro/dsl/rest./scales/24hr/@, **lodging:** Economy Inn, Glendale Inn, **other:** Blue Beacon
83mm	Nolin River
81	KY 84, Sonora, **E gas:** BP, Marathon/dsl, Pilot/Subway/dsl/scales/24hr, **other:** Blue Beacon, to Lincoln B'Place, **W gas:** Shell
76	KY 224, Upton, **E gas:** Chevron/dsl, **W** to Nolin Lake
75mm	eastern/central time zone
71	KY 728, Bonnieville
65	US 31 W, Munfordville, **E gas:** BP/Subway/dsl, Killman/dsl, **food:** DQ, King Buffet, Pizza Hut, McDonald's, Sonic, **lodging:** Super 8, **other:** Advance Parts, $General, Family$, Pamida, **W gas:** Chevron/dsl/24hr, Shell, **food:** Mazatlan Mexican, to Nolin Lake
61mm	**rest area both lanes, full ♿ facilities, info, ☎, 🛆, litter barrels, vending, petwalk Green River**
58	KY 218, Horse Cave, **E gas:** Love's/McDonald's/dsl/scale/24hr, **other:** H, **W gas:** Chevron/Pizza/dsl, Marathon/dsl/repair, **food:** Aunt Bee's Rest./24hr, **lodging:** Country Hearth Inn, Hampton Inn, **other:** KOA, to Mammoth Cave NP
53	KY 70, KY 90, Cave City, **E gas:** BP/dsl, JR's, Marathon/dsl, Chevron, Shell, **food:** Cracker Barrel, El Mazatlan Mexican, KFC, LJ Silver/A&W, McDonald's, Pizza Hut/Taco Bell, Subway, Wendy's, **lodging:** Best Western, Comfort Inn, Day's Inn/rest., Econolodge, Knight's Inn, Masters Inn, Super 8, **other:** H, Barren River Lake SP (24mi), **W gas:** Marathon/dsl, **food:** Watermill Rest., **other:** Onyx Cave, Mammoth Cave NP, Jellystone Camping, Singing Hills Camping
48	KY 255, Park City, **E gas:** Shell/dsl/24hr, **other:** Park Mammoth Resort (1 1/2mi), tire repair, **W** Diamond Caverns Resort, to Mammoth Cave NP
43	Nunn Cumberland Pky, to Barren River Lake SP
39mm	**rest area nb, full ♿ facilities, ☎, vending, 🛆, litter barrels, petwalk**
38	KY 101, Smiths Grove, **W gas:** BP/scales/dsl, Bestway Pizza, Marathon/Subway/dsl, Shell, **food:** McDonald's, Wendy's, **lodging:** Bryce Motel, **other:** $General, IGA Foods, 7 Springs Park, antiques
36	US 68, KY 80, Oakland, no nb return
30mm	**rest area sb, full ♿ facilities, ☎, vending, 🛆, litter barrels, petwalk**
28	rd 446, to US 31 W, Bowling Green, **W gas:** BP, Shell/24hr, **food:** Hardee's, Jerry's Rest., Wendy's, **lodging:** Continental Inn, Country Hearth Inn, Super 8, Value Lodge, **other:** H, Corvette Museum, **3 mi W** to WKYU
26	rd 234, Bowling Green
22	US 231, Bowling Green, **E gas:** Keystop Gas, Scott/dsl, Shell, **food:** Cracker Barrel, Culver's, Denny's, Domino's, Godfather's, Hardee's, Ryan's, Sonic, Subway, Waffle House, Zaxby's, **lodging:** Best Value, Comfort Inn, Day's Inn, Econolodge, Fairfield Inn, Hometowne Suites, La Quinta, Microtel, Quality Inn, Ramada/rest., Sleep Inn, **other:** URGENT CARE, Camping World RV Supply, $General, Gander Mtn, Harley-Davidson, IGA Foods, USPO, **W gas:** Chevron/dsl, Marathon, RaceWay, Shell/dsl, Speedway/dsl, **food:** Applebee's, Arby's, Baymont Inn, Beijing Chinese, Bob Evans, Bruster's, Buffalo Wild Wings, Burger King, Capt D's, ChuckeCheese, Chick-fil-A, Double-Dog's Chowhouse, KFC, Krystal, Kyoto Steaks, Logan's Roadhouse, LoneStar Steaks, Longhorn Steaks, McDonald's, Moe's SW Grill, MT Grille, O'Charley's, Outback Steaks, Panera Bread, Pizza Hut, Rafferty's, Red Lobster, Ruby Tuesday, Santa Fe Steaks, Shogun Japanese, Shoney's, Smokey Bones BBQ, Sonic, Starbucks, Steak'n Shake, Subway, Taco Bell, TGIFriday, Toots Rest., Waffle House, Wendy's, White Castle, **lodging:** Candlewood Suites, Courtyard, Drury Inn, Hampton Inn, Hilton Garden, Holiday Inn, Motel 6, News Inn, Red Roof Inn, Rodeway Inn, **other:** H, Advance Parts, Barnes&Noble, Best Buy, Buick/GMC, BMW/Mercedes, Cadillac, Chevrolet, Chrysler/Jeep, Curves, CVS Drug, Dillard's, $General, Ford/Lincoln/Mercury, Goodyear, Home Depot, Honda, Hyundai, JC Penney, K-Mart, KOA, KIA, Kohls, Kroger/gas/24hr, Lowe's, Nissan, Office Depot, Old Navy, PetCo, Pontiac, Sam's Club/gas, Scotty's Parts, Sears, Target, Toyota, U-Haul, Walmart SuperCtr/24hr, mall, Vet
20	WH Natcher Toll Rd, to Bowling Green, access to W KY U, KY st police
6	KY 100, Franklin, **E gas:** BP/dsl/24hr, Shell/dsl/24hr/@, **W gas:** Pilot/Subway/dsl/scales/24hr/, Pilot/Wendy's/dsl/scales/24hr/, **lodging:** Budget Inn, Day's Inn, **other:** H, Bluegrass RV Park, Petrolube, SpeedCo, truck & tires/repair, truckwash
4mm	**weigh sta nb**
2	US 31 W, to Franklin, **E gas:** ***FLYING J***/Conoco/Country Mkt/dsl/LP/rest./24hr, Keystop/Marathon/Burger King/dsl/24hr, **W gas:** BP/dsl, **food:** Cracker Barrel, McDonald's, Waffle House, **lodging:** Best

ELIZABETHTOWN · BOWLING GREEN · FRANKLIN

KY

INTERSTATE 65 CONT'D

Exit #	Services
2	Continued Western, Comfort Inn, Econolodge, Hampton Inn, Holiday Inn Express, Super 8, **other:** [H]
1mm	**Welcome Ctr nb, full ♿ facilities, ☎, vending, picnic tables, litter barrels, petwalk**
0mm	Kentucky/Tennessee state line

INTERSTATE 71

Exit #	Services
	Kentucky/Ohio state line, Ohio River
	I-71 and I-75 run together 19 miles. See Kentucky Interstate 75, exits 175-192.
77 [173]	I-75 S, to Lexington
75mm	**weigh sta sb**
72	KY 14, to Verona, **E gas:** BP/dsl, Chevron/dsl, **other:** Oak Creek Camping (5mi)
62	US 127, to Glencoe, **E gas:** 62 TrkPlaza/rest./dsl, **W gas:** BP/dsl/rest., **lodging:** 127 Motel
57	KY 35, to Sparta, **E gas:** Marathon/dsl, **other:** Eagle Valley Camping (10mi), Sparta RV Park (3mi), **W gas:** BP/dsl, **lodging:** Ramada Ltd, **other:** KY Speedway
55	KY 1039, **W gas:** Love's/McDonald's/Subway/dsl/scales/24hr, **other:** KY Speedway
44	KY 227, to Indian Hills, **W gas:** BP/dsl, Chevron/dsl/24hr, Marathon, Shell, Murphy USA/dsl, **food:** Arby's, Burger King, El Nopal, Hometown Pizza, KFC, LJ Silver, McDonald's, New China, Sonic, Subway, Taco Bell, Waffle House, **lodging:** Best Western, Comfort Inn, Econolodge, Hampton Inn, Holiday Inn Express, Super 8, **other:** [H], AutoZone, Chevrolet, Do-It Hardware, $General, Ford, Kroger/dsl, Radio Shack, Sav-a-Lot Foods, Walmart SuperCtr/24hr, Carroll Butler SP, flea mkt
43.5mm	Kentucky River
43	KY 389, to KY 55, English
34	US 421, Campbellsburg, **W gas:** BP/Subway/dsl, Marathon/dsl, **other:** st police
28	KY 153, KY 146, to US 42, Pendleton, **E gas:** BP/dsl, Marathon/dsl, **food:** Taylor's Cafe, Pilot/Subway/dsl/scales/24hr/@, **W gas:** Pilot/McDonald's/scales/dsl/24hr, **other:** SpeedCo
22	KY 53, La Grange, **E gas:** BP/dsl, Speedway/Rally's/dsl, **food:** Applebee's, Beef O'Brady's, Burger King, Jumbo Buffet, Papa John's, Ponderosa, Sonic, Subway, Waffle House, Wendy's, **lodging:** Best Western-Ashbury, Holiday Inn Express, **other:** [H], AT&T, Big-O Tire, $General, Kroger/gas, Radio Shack, Walgreens, Walmart SuperCtr/24hr, **W gas:** Chevron/dsl/24hr, Swifty, **food:** Arby's, Cracker Barrel, Domino's, DQ, El Nopal, KFC, LJ Silver, McDonald's, Taco Bell, **lodging:** Comfort Suites, Super 8, **other:** Advance Parts, Buick/Chevrolet/Pontiac, Curves, Lee Tires, NAPA, Rite Aid, Sav-a-Lot, tires, flea mkt, USPO, Vet
18	KY 393, Buckner, **W gas:** Marathon/dsl, **food:** Subway
17	KY 146, Buckner, **E other:** Ford, **W gas:** Shell/dsl, Thornton's/dsl/24hr, **other:** USPO, st police
14	KY 329, Crestwood, Pewee Valley, Brownsboro, **E gas:** BP/dsl, Shell, **food:** Starbucks, **2 mi E food:** DQ, Hometown Pizza, McDonald's, Sonic, Subway

Exit #	Services
13mm	**rest area both lanes, full ♿ facilities, ☎, vending, picnic tables, litter barrels, petwalk**
9b a	I-265, KY 841, Gene Snyder Fwy, **E** to Sawyer SP
5	I-264, Watterson Expswy (exits left from sb), **E** to Sawyer SP
2	Zorn Ave, **E** VA [H], **W gas:** BP, Chevron, **food:** KingFish Rest., **lodging:** Ramada Inn, **other:** WaterTower Art Museum
1b	I-65, S to Nashville, N to Indianapolis

INTERSTATE 75

Exit #	Services
193mm	Kentucky/Ohio state line, Ohio River
192	5th St (from nb), Covington, **E gas:** BP, Shell, Speedway, **food:** Big Boy, Burger King, GoldStar Chili, McDonald's, Skyline Chili, Subway, Taco Bell, Waffle House, White Castle, **lodging:** Courtyard, Extended Stay America, Holiday Inn, Radisson, **other:** Lexus, Subaru/VW, Toyota, Riverboat Casino, **W lodging:** Hampton Inn
191	12th St, Covington, **E other:** [H], museum, same as 192
189	KY 1072 (from sb), Kyles Lane, **W gas:** BP/dsl, Marathon/dsl, Shell/dsl, Speedway, **food:** Big Boy, Reality Coffeehouse, Skyline Chili, Substation II Subs, **lodging:** Days Inn, Rodeway Inn, same as 188
188	US 25, US 42, Dixe Hwy, **E gas:** Sunoco, **food:** Subway, **other:** GNC, Kroger, Tuesday Morning, **W food:** Pizza Hut, **lodging:** Days Inn, Rodeway Inn, USA Hotel, **other:** $Tree, SteinMart, Walgreens, same as 189
186	KY 371, Buttermilk Pike, Covington, **E gas:** BP/dsl, Marathon, Texco/DQ, **food:** Graeter's Ice Cream, Montgomery Inn, Oriental Wok, Papa John's, **lodging:** Drawbridge Inn/rest., Super 8, **W gas:** BP, Shell, Sunoco/dsl, **food:** Arby's, Bonefish Grill, Burger King, Chipotle Mexican, Domino's, Dunkin Donuts/Baskin-Robbins, Empire Buffet, GoldStar Chili, La Rosa's Pizza, LJ Silver, McDonald's, Outback Steaks, Pizza Hut, Rema's Diner, Skyline Chili, Subway, **other:** Home Depot, Remke Foods, Staples, Walgreens
185	I-275 E and W, **W** to ✈
184	KY 236, Donaldson Rd, to Erlanger, **E gas:** BP/deli, Marathon, **food:** Double Dragon Chinese, **W gas:** Marathon, Speedway/dsl, Sunoco/Subway/dsl, **food:** Southern Kitchen Rest., Waffle House, **lodging:** Airport Inn, Comfort Inn, Days Inn, Econolodge, **other:** Goodyear/auto
182	KY 1017, Turfway Rd, **E gas:** BP, Shell, **food:** Big Boy, Lee's Chicken, McDonald's, New Wok, Ryan's,

INTERSTATE 75 CONT'D

N ↕ S

Exit #	Services
182	Continued 3 Amigo's Mexican, **lodging:** Comfort Inn, Courtyard, Ivy Inn, Rodeway Inn, **other:** Big Lots, Office Depot, Remke Foods, funpark, **W gas:** Meijer/dsl/24hr, **food:** Applebee's, CiCi's Pizza, Cracker Barrel, Dynasty Buffet, Famous Dave's BBQ, Karlo's Italian, Longhorn Steaks, O'Charley's, Rafferty's, Steak'n Shake, Tumbleweeds Grill, Wendy's, **lodging:** Extended Stay America, Hampton Inn, Hilton, Hyatt Place, La Quinta, Red Roof Inn, Studio+, **other:** H, Best Buy, Biggs Foods, Home Depot, Kohl's, Lowe's Whse, Michaels, PetsMart, Sam's Club, Target, Turfway Park Racing
181	KY 18, Florence, **E gas:** Speedway, TA/Sunoco/Pizza Hut/Popeye's/dsl/rest./24hr/@, **food:** Goodfellow's Dining, Waffle House, **lodging:** Best Value Inn, Best Western, **other:** Chevrolet, **W gas:** BP/dsl, Chevron, Shell, Speedway, **food:** Cheddars, Hooters, IHOP, Fazoli's, Hooters, La Rosa's, Logan's Roadhouse, LoneStar Steaks, Macaroni Grill, MiYoshi, Panera Bread, Quizno's, **lodging:** Microtel, Stay Lodge, **other:** URGENT CARE, Buick, Chrysler/Jeep, $Tree, Dodge, Ford, Honda, JC Penney, K-Mart, Lincoln/Mercury, Mazda, Nissan, Sears/auto, Staples, Tire Discounters, Toyota/Scion, TJ Maxx, Walmart SuperCtr, Vet
180a	Mall Rd (from sb), **W food:** Asian Buffet, Chipotle Mexican, ChuckeCheese, Coldstone Creamery, GoldStar Chili, Hardee's, HoneyBaked Ham, Lonestar Steaks, Qdoba, Olive Garden, Pizza Hut, Quizno's, Skyline Chili, Smokey Bones BBQ, Starbucks, Subway, Taco Bell, **other:** AAA, Barnes&Noble, $General, $Tree, Hobby Lobby, Jo-Ann Fabrics, Kroger/24hr, Macy's, Michael's, Nissan, Old Navy, PepBoys, Sears/auto, Staples, TJ Maxx, mall, same as 180
180	US 42, US 127, Florence, Union, **E gas:** BP/dsl, Shell, Speedway/dsl, **food:** Big Boy, Bob Evans, Burger King, Camino Real, Capt D's, Dragon Buffet, Dunkin Donuts, Mai Thai, McDonald's, Penn Sta, Pizza Hut, Rally's, Red Lobster, Subway, Wendy's, **lodging:** Knight's Inn, Motel 6, Quality Inn, Super 8, **other:** Cadillac, funpark, **W gas:** Shell/dsl/24hr, Speedway, Thornton's, **food:** Acapulco Mexican, Arby's, Burger King, DQ, KFC, LJ Silver, Perkins/24hr, Ponderosa, Waffle House, White Castle, **lodging:** Ramada Inn, Travelodge, **other:** Kroger/deli, Midas, PepBoys, Tire Discounters, Walgreens
178	KY 536, Mt Zion Rd, **E gas:** BP/Rally's/dsl, Mobil, Shell/dsl, Sunoco/dsl, **food:** GoldStar Chili, Hometown Pizza, Jersey Mike's Subs, Margarita's Mexican, Steak'n Shake, Subway, **other:** Goodyear/auto, Kroger
177mm	**Welcome Ctr sb/rest area nb, full ♿ facilities, 📞, vending, 🅿, litter barrels, RV dump**
175	KY 338, Richwood, **E gas:** TA/BP/Country Pride/Taco Bell/dsl/rest./@, Pilot/Subway/dsl/@, **food:** Arby's, Burger King, White Castle/24hr, **lodging:** Comfort Inn, **other:** RV Park, **W gas:** BP, Pilot/Subway/dsl/scales/24hr, Shell/dsl, **food:** GoldStar Chili, McDonald's, Penn Sta Subs, Skyline Chili, Waffle House, Wendy's, **lodging:** Econolodge, Holiday Inn Express, Ivy Lodge, **other:** to Big Bone Lick SP
173	I-71 S, to Louisville
171	KY 14, KY 16, to Verona, Walton, **E gas:** Marathon/dsl, Texaco/DQ, **food:** China Moon, McDonald's, Starbucks, Waffle House, **other:** Kohl's, Kroger/gas, Walton Drug, **W gas:** *FLYING J*/dsl/rest/scales/24hr **other:** Blue Beacon, Delightful Days RV Ctr, Oak Creek Camping (1mi), to Big Bone Lick SP
168mm	**weigh sta/rest haven sb**
166	KY 491, Crittenden, **E gas:** EZ Stop, Marathon, Sunoco/dsl, **food:** McDonald's, **other:** Chrysler/Dodge/Jeep, Cincinnati S Camping (2mi), **W gas:** Chevron, Shell/Burger King/dsl, **food:** Subway, Wendy's, **other:** Curves, General
159	KY 22, to Owenton, Dry Ridge, **E gas:** BP, Marathon/DQ, Shell/dsl, **food:** Arby's/24hr, Burger King, Happy Dragon Chinese, KFC/Taco Bell, LJ Silver, McDonald's, Pizza Hut, Skyline Chili, Subway, Waffle House, Wendy's, **lodging:** Best Rate Hotel, Microtel, Super 8, **other:** H, $General, Radio Shack, Walmart SuperCtr/24hr, **W gas:** Speedway/dsl, Sunoco/dsl, **food:** Cracker Barrel, **lodging:** Hampton Inn, Holiday Inn Express, **other:** Camper Village, Dry Ridge Outlets/famous brands, Sav-A-Lot, Toyota, Tire Discounters
156	Barnes Rd, **E other:** H
154	KY 36, Williamstown, **E gas:** Chevron, Texaco/dsl, **food:** Red Carpet Rest., **other:** H, to Kincaid Lake SP, **W gas:** Marathon/dsl, **food:** El Jalisco Mexican, **lodging:** Best Value Inn, Days Inn
144	KY 330, to Owenton, Corinth, **E gas:** Marathon/dsl, Noble's Trk Plaza/dsl/rest., **W gas:** BP, **food:** Bob&Lois' Diner, **lodging:** 3 Springs Motel/Camping
136	KY 32, to Sadieville, **W gas:** Marathon
130.5mm	**weigh sta nb**
129	KY 620, Cherry Blossom Wy, **E gas:** Pilot/Wendy's/dsl/scales/24hr/@, **food:** Waffle House, **lodging:** Days Inn, Motel 6, **W gas:** Pilot/McDonald's/dsl/scales/24hr, Shell/24hr
127mm	**rest area both lanes, full ♿ facilities, 📞, vending, 🅿, litter barrels, petwalk**
126	US 62, to US 460, Georgetown, **E gas:** Murphy USA/dsl, Standard, **food:** Applebee's, Asian Royal Buffet, Big Boy, CiCi's, Golden Corral, Gold Star Chili, McDonald's, Mi Mexico, O'Charley's, Papa John's, Quizno's, Subway, **lodging:** Holiday Inn, **other:** Kohl's, Lowe's Whse, Tire Discounters, Valvoline, Walmart SuperCtr/24hr, **W gas:** BP, Marathon, Shell/Subway/24hr, Speedway/dsl, **food:** Cracker Barrel, Fazoli's, KFC, Ruby Tuesday, Waffle House, **lodging:** Best Western, Comfort Suites, Country Inn&Suites, Econolodge, Fairfield Inn, Hampton Inn, Hilton Garden, Microtel, Quality Inn, Super 8, **other:** H, Buick/Chevrolet/Pontiac, Chrysler/Dodge/Jeep, Ford, to Georgetown Coll, same as 125
125	US 460 (from nb), Georgetown, **E gas:** Shell, Texaco, **food:** FatKats Pizza, **lodging:** Econolodge, **W gas:** Chevron/dsl, Swifty, **food:** Arby's, DQ, LJ Silver, Taco Bell, Wendy's, **other:** Advance Parts, Big Lots, K-Mart, Radio Shack, Outlets/Famous Brands, same as 126
120	rd 1973, to Ironworks Pike, KY Horse Park, **E** KY Horse Park Camping, **W gas:** Chevron/AM Best/dsl

FLORENCE

GEORGETOWN

KY

INTERSTATE 75 CONT'D

N ↕ S

LEXINGTON

Exit #	Services
118	I-64 W, to Frankfort, Louisville
115	KY 922, Lexington, **E gas:** Shell/Subway/24hr, **food:** Cracker Barrel, McDonald's, Waffle House, **lodging:** Fairfield Inn, Knight's Inn, La Quinta, Sheraton, **other:** SaddleHorse Museum (4mi), **W gas:** Chevron/dsl, **food:** Denny's, Happy Dragon Chinese, **lodging:** Embassy Suites, Holiday Inn, Marriott/rest., **other:** museum
113	US 27, US 68, to Paris, Lexington, **E gas:** Marathon, Speedway, **food:** Waffle House, **lodging:** Ramada Inn, **0-1 mi W gas:** Chevron/dsl/24hr, Shell, **food:** Burger King, Capt D's, Fazoli's, Hardee's, McDonald's, Penn Sta, Taco Bell, **lodging:** Catalina Motel, Days Inn, Red Roof Inn, **other:** Advance Parts, Bluegrass RV Ctr, Chevrolet, Chrysler/Jeep, Kroger/deli, Northside RV Ctr, O'Reilly Parts, Walmart SuperCtr, to UKY, Rupp Arena
111	I-64 E, to Huntington, WV
110	US 60, Lexington, **W gas:** Murphy USA, Shell, Speedway/dsl, Thorntons/24hr, **food:** Arby's, Bajio, Bob Evans, Calistoga Rest, Cane's Chicken, Cracker Barrel, McDonald's, Starbucks, Subway, Waffle House, Wendy's, **lodging:** Baymont Inn, Best Western, Comfort Inn, Country Inn&Suites, Hampton Inn, Holiday Inn Express, Microtel, Motel 6, Ramada Ltd, Super 8, **other:** Lowe's Whse, Rite Aid, Walmart SuperCtr
108	Man O War Blvd, **E gas:** Chevron, **W gas:** Marathon, Meijer/dsl/24hr, Shell/KFC/Wendy's/24hr, **food:** Applebee's, Arby's, Backyard Burger, BD Mongolian Grill, BoneFish Grill, Carino's, Carrabba's, Cheddar's, Chick-fil-A, Coldstone Creamery, Domino's, Fazoli's, GoldStar Chili, IChing Asian, Logan's Roadhouse, Malone's, Max&Erma's, McDonald's, Old Chicago, Outback Steaks, Pizza Hut, Qdoba, Rafferty's, Ruby Tuesday, Starbucks, Steak'n Shake, Taco Bell, TGIFriday, Waffle House, **lodging:** Courtyard, Hilton Garden, Homewood Suites, Hyatt Place, Sleep Inn, **other:** H, Audi, Barnes&Noble, Best Buy, GNC, Harley-Davidson, Kohl's, Old Navy, Porsche, Radio Shack, Staples, Target, Tire Discounters, Walgreens
104	KY 418, Lexington, **E gas:** Exxon/Arby's/dsl/24hr, Shell/Hardee's, **food:** Waffle House, **lodging:** Best Western, Comfort Inn, Days Inn, Econolodge, Red Roof Inn, **W gas:** Chevron, Speedway/Subway, **food:** Wendy's, **other:** H
99	US 25 N, US 421 N, Clays Ferry
98mm	Kentucky River
97	US 25 S, US 421 S, **E gas:** Marathon/Huddle House/dsl/scales/24hr
95	KY 627, to Boonesboro, Winchester, **E gas:** BP/dsl, Love's/Arby's/dsl/scales/24hr, **food:** McDonald's, **other:** Ft Boonesborough SP, camping, **W gas:** Shell/dsl/24hr
90	US 25, US 421, Richmond, **E gas:** Shell, **food:** Cracker Barrel, **lodging:** Knight's Inn, La Quinta, Motel 6, Red Roof Inn, **W gas:** BP, Exxon/Arby's/dsl, Marathon, Shell, Thoroughbred, **food:** Big Boy, DQ, Hardee's, Pizza Hut, Subway, Waffle House, Wendy's, **lodging:** Days Inn, Super 8, **other:** Aamco, $General, NTB, USPO

RICHMOND

Exit #	Services
87	KY 876, Richmond, **E gas:** BP/dsl, Chevron/24hr, Marathon, Shell/dsl/24hr, Speedway/dsl, Texaco, **food:** Arby's, Casa Fiesta Mexican, Domino's, Fazoli's, Fong's Chinese, Hardee's, Hooters, King Buffet, Krystal/24hr, Little Caesar's, LJ Silver/A&W, McDonald's, Papa John's, Penn Sta, Pizza Hut, Qdoba, Rally's, Subway, Taco Bell, Waffle House, Wendy's, **lodging:** Best Western, Econolodge, Quality Quarters Inn, **other:** H, Ace Hardware, Big Lots, $General, Goodyear/auto, Rite Aid, Suzuki, to EKU, **W gas:** BP/dsl, Marathon/Circle K, **food:** Bob Evans, Burger King, Culver's, Logan's Roadhouse, Ryan's, Starbucks, Steak'n Shake/24hr, **lodging:** Comfort Suites, Hampton Inn, Holiday Inn Express, Jameson Inn, **other:** Belk, Hastings Books, JC Penney, TJ Maxx
83	US 25 Rd 2872, Duncannon Ln, Richmond, **E other:** Bluegrass Army Depot
77	KY 595, Berea, **E other:** H, KY Artisan Ctr/Cafe/Travelers Ctr, to Berea Coll, **W gas:** BP/Subway/24hr, Shell, **food:** Huddle House, La Casa Real, Smokehouse Grill, **lodging:** Country Inn&Suites, Days Inn
76	KY 21, Berea, **E gas:** BP, Marathon/Circle K, Shell/Burger King, Speedway/dsl, **food:** A&W/LJ Silver, Arby's, Burger King, Cracker Barrel, Dinner Bell Rest., Hong Kong Buffet, KFC, Little Caesar's, Mariachi Mexican, Mario's Pizza, McDonald's, Papa John's, Pizza Hut, Subway, Taco Bell, WanPen Chinese/Thai, Wendy's, **lodging:** Holiday Motel, Knight's Inn, Super 8, **other:** H, $General, Radio Shack, Walmart SuperCtr, tires, **W gas:** BP, Chevron/24hr, Marathon/dsl, Shell/dsl, **food:** Lee's Chicken, **lodging:** Comfort Inn, Econolodge, Fairfield Inn, **other:** Oh! Kentucky Camping, Walnut Meadow Camping
62	US 25, to KY 461, Renfro Valley, **E gas:** Derby City/rest./dsl, Shell/24hr, **food:** Hardee's, **lodging:** Heritage Inn, **other:** KOA (2mi), Renfro Valley RV Park/rest, **W gas:** BP/Blimpie/24hr, Chevron/Wendy's/24hr, Marathon/Taco Tico, Shell/24hr, **food:** Arby's, Denny's, Godfather's/Subway, KFC, McDonald's, **lodging:** Days Inn, Econolodge, **other:** H, Rite Aid, to Big South Fork NRA, Lake Cumberland
59	US 25, to Livingston, Mt Vernon, **E gas:** BP, Shell/dsl, TravelCtr/dsl, **food:** El Cazador Mexican, Jean's Rest., Pizza Hut, **lodging:** Kastle Inn, **W gas:** BP, **food:** Mt Vernon Pizza, **lodging:** Mtn View Inn
51mm	Rockcastle River
49	KY 909, to US 25, Livingston, **E other:** Camp Wildcat BFD, **W gas:** 49er/dsl/24hr, **other:** RV Park, truck/tire repair

BEREA

KY

INTERSTATE 75 CONT'D

Exit #	Services
41	KY 80, to Somerset, London, **E** **gas:** Speedway, **food:** Arby's, Azteca Mexican, Burger King, DQ, KFC, McDonald's, Sonic, White Castle, **lodging:** Days Inn, Econolodge, Quality Inn, Red Roof Inn, Sleep Inn, Super 8, **other:** H, Advance Parts, AutoZone, CVS Drug, $General, Kroger/deli, Parsley's Tire/repair, st police, **W** **gas:** BP/dsl/rest/24hr, Chevron/McDonald's, Clark/dsl, Marathon, Shell/24hr, **food:** Chuckle's Cafe, Cracker Barrel, LJ Silver, Shiloh Roadhouse, Subway, Taco Bell, Waffle House, **lodging:** Budget Host, Hampton Inn, **other:** Curves, Dog Patch Ctr, Westgate RV Camping
38	KY 192, London, **E** **gas:** BP/dsl, Marathon, Shell/Quizno's/dsl, Speedway/dsl, **food:** Asian Bistro, Big Boy, Burger King, Capt D's, Dino's Italian, Domino's, El Azteca Mexican, El Dorado Mexican, Fazoli's, Golden Corral, Great Wall Chinese, Hardee's, Huddle House, Krystal, Pizza Hut, Ruby Tuesday, Starbucks, Steak'n Shake, Taco Bell, **lodging:** Comfort Suites, Country Inn&Suites, Hampton Inn, Heritage Inn, Holiday Inn Express, **other:** H, Advance Parts, E Kentucky RV Ctr, K-Mart, Kroger/gas, Lowe's Whse, Nissan, Office Depot, Peterbilt, Radio Shack, USPO, Walgreens, Walmart SuperCtr/24hr, airport, camping, toll rd to Manchester/Hazard, to Levi Jackson SP, **W** to Laurel River Lake RA
34mm	**weigh sta both lanes, truck haven**
30.5mm	Laurel River
29	US 25, US 25E, Corbin, **E** **gas:** BP, Marathon/Waffle King/dsl/scales/24hr, Murphy USA, Pilot/McDonald's/Subway/dsl/scales/24hr, **food:** Burger King, David's Steaks, Fiesta Mexican, Huddle House, Shoney's, Taco Bell, **lodging:** Super 8, **other:** Aldi Foods, Blue Beacon, Lowe's Whse, Radio Shack, Walmart SuperCtr/24hr, flea mkt, to Cumberland Gap NP, **W** **gas:** BP/Krystal/dsl, Love's/Hardee's/dsl, Marathon, Shell/dsl/24hr, **food:** Cracker Barrel, Sonny's BBQ, **lodging:** Baymont Inn, Comfort Suites, Fairfield Inn, Hampton Inn, Knight's Inn, **other:** KOA, tires/repair, to Laurel River Lake RA
25	US 25W, Corbin, **E** **gas:** Speedway/dsl, **food:** Applebee's, Buckner's Grill, Burger King, McDonald's, O'Mally's, Wendy's, **lodging:** Country Inn&Suites, Days Inn, Holiday Inn Express, Landmark Inn, **other:** H, auto repair/tires, **W** **gas:** Shell/24hr, **food:** Arby's, El Dorado Mexican, Jade China Buffet, Subway, Waffle House, **lodging:** Best Western, Mtn View Lodge, **other:** to Cumberland Falls SP
15	US 25W, to Williamsburg, Goldbug, **W** **gas:** Shell, Xpress/dsl, **other:** Cumberland Falls SP
14.5mm	Cumberland River
11	KY 92, Williamsburg, **E** **gas:** BP/dsl, Exxon/dsl, Shell, **food:** Arby's, El Dorado Mexican, Hardee's, KFC, Little Caesar's, McDonald's, Pizza Hut, Sonic, Subway, Taco Bell, **lodging:** Cumberland Inn, Scottish Inn, Super 8, **other:** Advance Parts, AutoZone, $General, Family$, Ford, NAPA, Sav-a-Lot, museum, **W** **gas:** Shell/dsl, Pilot/Wendy's/dsl/scales, **food:** Burger King, Huddle House, Krystal, LJ Silver, **lodging:** Williamsburg Motel/RV Park, **other:** Walmart SuperCtr/24hr, to Big South Fork NRA
1.5mm	**Welcome Ctr nb, full handicapped facilities, phone, vending, picnic, litter barrels, petwalk**
0mm	Kentucky/Tennesee state line

INTERSTATE 275 (CINCINNATI)

Exit #	Services
0mm	Kentucky/Tennesee state line
84	Louisville, I-75, I-71, N to Cincinnati, S to Lexington
83	US 25, US 42, US 127, **S** **gas:** Shell, Speedway, **food:** Carrabba's, Max&Erma's, Panera Bread, TGIFriday, Wendy's, **other:** Dillards
82	rd1303, Turkeyfoot Rd, **S** H
80	KY 17, Independence, **N** **gas:** Mobil, Speedway, **food:** Big Boy, Bob Evans, Burger King, Snappy Pizza, Texas Roadhouse, Wendy's, **other:** Tire Discounters, Walmart SuperCtr/24hr
78	KY 16, Taylor Mill Rd, **N** **gas:** Speedway, **other:** Kroger/gas, **S** **gas:** BP/dsl, **food:** McDonald's, KFC, Taco Bell
77	KY 9, Maysville, Wilder, **S** **gas:** Mobil, Shell, **food:** DQ, Waffle House
74a	Alexandria, to US 27, (exits left from sb)
74b	I-471 N, Newport, Cincinnati, **N** H
73mm	OH/KY state line, OH River
72	Kelogg Ave, **S** **gas:** Marathon, airport
71	US 52
69	5 mile rd, **W** **gas:** BP/dsl, **food:** Big Boy, IHOP, La Rosa Mexican, McDonald's, TGIFriday, Wendy's, **other:** H
65	OH 125, Beechmont Ave, Amelia, **E** **gas:** Marathon, Shell, Sunoco, **food:** Arby's, China Bistro, Hooters, Red Lobster, Wendy's, **lodging:** Motel 6, **other:** Ford, Lowe's Whse, Walgreen, **W** **gas:** BP, Speedway, Marathon, **food:** Big Boy, McDonald's, Best Western, Bob Evans, Tony Roma, **lodging:** Best Western, Days Inn, Red Roof Inn, **other:** Home Depot
63b a	OH 32, Betavia, Newtown, **E** **gas:** BP, Meijer, Shell, Thornton's, **food:** Cheeseburger Paradise, Bob Evans, Burger King, Fazolie's, Max & Erma's, McDonalds, Perkins, Pizza Hut, **lodging:** Comfort Inn, Fairfield Inn, Holiday Inn, **other:** Best Buy, Big's Foods, Dillards, Kohl's, Sears/auto, **W** **gas:** Speedway, **food:** Big Boy, La Rosa Mexican, Roy Rogers, **lodging:** Comfort Inn, Fairfield Inn, Hampton Inn, Holiday Inn
59	Milford Pkwy, **S** **gas:** Mobil, **food:** Buffalo Wings, Cracker Barrel, Goldstar Chili, Red Robin, Ruby Texas Roadhouse, Tuesday, Wendy's, **lodging:** Homewood Suites, **other:** Chryler/Jeep, Office Depot, Target
57	OH 14 W, Forbes Rd, Broadway Ave, **N** **gas:** Meijer (1mi), **food:** Arby's, Burger King, Dunkin Donuts, IHOP, Taco Bell, White Castle, **other:** K-Mart, Lowe's Whse, **S** **gas:** BP, Exxon, **food:** Bob Evans, Cazadora Mexican, Charlie Basil's, **lodging:** Holiday Inn Express, Roadhouse Grill, **other:** H, Kroger
54	Wards Corner Rd, **N** **gas:** BP, Mobil, **food:** Perkins, **lodging:** Hilton Garden, **other:** Lowe's Whse, **S** **gas:** Mobil, **food:** Big Boy, Dominos, Hilton, Subway
53mm	Little Miami River
52	Loveland, Indian Hill, **1 mi** **N** **gas:** Circle K, Marathon, Shell, Speedway, **food:** Arby's, Burger King, Taco Bell, Skyline Chili, Starbucks, Wendy's
50	US 22, OH 3, Montgomery, **N** **food:** Chili's, DQ, Pizzaria, Starbucks, **S** **gas:** BP/dsl, Shell, **food:** Goldstar Chili, La Rosa's, McDonald's, Skyline Chili, Wendy's, **other:** H

INTERSTATE 275 (CINCINNATI)

N ↕ S

Exit #	Services
49	I-71 N to Columbus, S to Cincinnati
47	Reed Hartman Hwy, Blue Ash, **S food:** Goldstar Chili, McDonald's, Starbucks, **lodging:** Amerisuites, Comfort Suites, Doubletree
46	US 42, Mason, **N gas:** BP, **food:** Perkins, McDonald's, Taco Bell, Wendy's, White Castle, **lodging:** Holiday Inn, Motel 6, **other:** CVS Drug, **S gas:** Marathon, Shell, Speedway, **food:** Arby's, Schezwan House, Waffle House, **lodging:** Days Inn, **other:** Goodyear, Tire Discounters
44	Mosteller Rd, **S lodging:** Homewood Suites
43b a	I-75, N to Dayton, S to Cincinnati
42	OH 747, Springdale, Glendale
41	OH 4, Springfield Pk, **N gas:** Shell, Sunoco, **food:** Bahama Breeze, Carlo's Bistro, Pappadeaux, **lodging:** Baymont Inn, Ramada Inn, **S gas:** BP, Shell, **food:** Applebee's, Big Boy, DQ, Penn Station Subs, Perkins, Ponderosa, Rosita's Mexican, White Castle, Wok'n Roll, **lodging:** Extended Stay, Howard Johnson, Super 8, Holiday Inn Express, **other:** Dillard's, Sears
39	Winton Rd, Winton Woods, **N gas:** BP, **food:** Bob Evans, Chipotle Mexican, Golden Corral, IHOP, McDonald's, Old Spagetti Factory, Panera Bread, Red Lobster, Roadhouse Grill, Ruby Tuesday, Ryan's, Steak'n Shake, **lodging:** Hampton Inn, **other:** Bass Pro Shops, Biggs Foods, Home Depot, K-Mart, Kohl's, Meijer, Outdoor World, **S gas:** Marathon, Mobil, Shell, **food:** Big Boy, Cracker Barrel, Fiesta Brava Mexican, Fuddrucker's, Popeye's, Skyline Chili, Subway, Wendy's, **lodging:** AmeriSuites, Lee's Inn, **other:** Goodyear, Jo-Ann Fabrics, Kroger/gas, Tires+, Walmart SuperCtr/24hr
36	US 127, Hamilton, Mt Healthy, **N gas:** Citgo, Speedway, **food:** Skyline Chili, Wendy's, **S gas:** Sunoco, **food:** Arby's, Big Boy, La Rosa's Pizza, McDonald's, Pizza Hut/Taco Bell, Subway, **other:** Advance Parts, $General
33	US 27, US 126, Colerain Ave, **N gas:** BP, Speedway, **food:** Burger King, Skyline Chili, Steak'n Shake, Wendy's, **other:** Colerain RV Ctr, Walmart, **S gas:** Shell, **food:** Arby's, Big Boy, Bob Evans, Cici's Pizza, KFC,

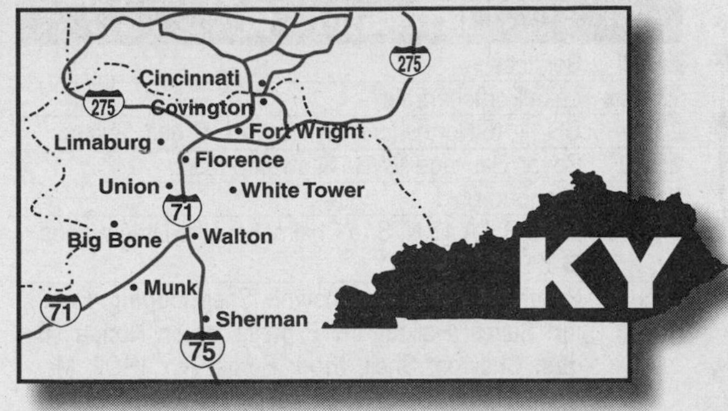

Exit #	Services
33	Continued LJ Silver, McDonald's, Olive Garden, Outback Steaks, Pizza Hut, Red Lobster, TGIFriday, White Castle, **lodging:** Red Carpet Inn, **other:** Isuzu, Kia, Macy's, Walgreens
31	Ronald Reagan Hwy, Blue Rock Rd
28	I-74, US 52, E to Cincinnati, W to Indianapolis
21	Kilby Rd
16	US 50, Greendale, Lawrenceburg, **W gas:** Ameristop/dsl, Marathon/dsl, Shell/Circle K/Subway, **food:** Buffalo's, Burger King, McDonald's, **lodging:** Comfort Inn, Holiday Inn Express, Quality Inn, Riverside Inn, **other:** Chevrolet/Pontiac/GMC, Chrysler/Dodge/Jeep, Tire Discounters, Walgreens
14mm	Ohio River, Kentucky/Indiana state line
11	to KY 20, Petersburg
8b a	KY 237, Hebron, **N gas:** BP/DQ/dsl, Mobil/dsl, **food:** Arby's, El Mariachi, Nicky's Pizzaria, Wendy's, **S gas:** Marathon, Mobil/dsl, Shell/Subway, **food:** Burger King, Goldstar Chili, McDonald's, Waffle House
4a b	KY 212, KY 20, **N gas:** ValAir Gas, **lodging:** Country Inn&Suites, Hampton Inn, Marriott, Sheraton, **S** [H], [airport]
2	Mineola Pike, **N gas:** Mobil/dsl, **food:** Subway, **lodging:** Baymont Inn, Holiday Inn, **S lodging:** Courtyard Inn, Residence Inn

LOUISIANA

INTERSTATE 10

E ↕ W — SLIDELL

Exit #	Services
274mm	Louisiana/Mississippi state line, Pearl River
272mm	West Pearl River
270mm	**Welcome Ctr wb, full [handicapped] facilities, info, [phone], [picnic], litter barrels, petwalk, RV dump**
267b	I-12 W, to Baton Rouge
267a	I-59 N, to Meridian
266	US 190, Slidell, **N gas:** Jubilee Express, Magnolia/dsl, TA/dsl/rest./scales/24hr/@, **food:** Arby's, Baskin-Robbins, Cane's Rest., Carreta's Mexican, Copeland's Rest., Crawfish Paradise, Golden Dragon Chinese, KFC, Los Tres Amigos, McDonald's, Pizza Hut, Quizno's, Shoney's, Sonic, Steakout, Taco Bell, Wendy's, **lodging:** Best Value Inn, Best Western, Deluxe Motel, Motel 6, **other:** [H], Firestone/auto, Harley-Davidson, Hobby Lobby, Office Depot, O'Reilly Parts, PepBoys, Radio Shack, Rouses Mkt, U-Haul, **S gas:** Chevron/Subway/dsl/24hr, Murphy USA, RaceTrac,

SLIDELL

Exit #	Services
266	Continued **food:** Applebee's, Big Easy Diner, Cracker Barrel, McAlister's, Deli, Osaka Grill, Outback Steaks, Ruby Tuesday, Sonic, Starbucks, Texas Roadhouse, Waffle House, **lodging:** La Quinta, Regency Inn, Value Inn, **other:** [H], Home Depot, Lowes Whse, Walmart SuperCtr, auto repair/transmissions, casino, Vet
265	US 190, Fremaux Ave
263	LA 433, Slidell, **N gas:** Eagle, Exxon, Shell, **food:** China Buffet, Waffle House, **lodging:** Hampton Inn, Super 8, **other:** Hyundai, auto repair, **S gas:** Fleet/Subway/scales/dsl, Texaco/dsl, **food:** McDonald's, Wendy's, **lodging:** Holiday Inn, **other:** Pinecrest RV Park, Chevrolet/Cadillac, Chrysler/Dodge/Jeep, Ford/Lincoln/Mercury, Honda, Nissan, Pontiac/Buick/GMC, Toyota, Slidell Factory Outlet/famous brands, KOA (1mi)
261	Oak Harbor Blvd, Eden Isles, **N gas:** Exxon/dsl, **food:** Waffle House, **lodging:** Sleep Inn, **S gas:** Shell/Subway/dsl, **other:** Bayou Country Store

INTERSTATE 10

Exit #	Services
255mm	Lake Pontchartrain
254	US 11, to Northshore, Irish Bayou, **S gas:** Texaco
251	Bayou Sauvage NWR, **S** swamp tours
248	Michoud Blvd
246b a	I-510 S, LA 47 N, S to Chalmette, N to Little Woods, **S** 6 Flags of NO
245	Bullard Ave, **N gas:** Chevron, Shell, **lodging:** Comfort Suites, Holiday Inn Express, **other:** Honda, **S gas:** Chevron, Shell, **food:** Burger Kin, IHOP, McDonald's, Super Cajun Seafood, **lodging:** La Quinta, Motel 6, **other:** Chrysler/Jeep/Dodge, Ford, Home Depot, Nissan, PepBoys, Rite Aid, Tire Kingdom, Toyota/Scion, Walgreens
244	Read Blvd, **N food:** McDonald's, **S gas:** EZ Stop/dsl, **food:** Popeye's, **lodging:** Best Western, Best Value Inn, **other:** Lowe's Whse, URGENT CARE, H
242	Crowder Blvd, **N gas:** Chevron **S gas:** Crowder Ctr, **lodging:** Quality Inn, **other:** Walgreens
241	Morrison Rd, **N gas:** EZ Mart/dsl
240b a	US 90 E, Chef Hwy, Downman Rd, **N gas:** Sporeco/dsl, **lodging:** Super 8, **other:** Chevrolet, U-Haul, USPO, **S gas:** Chevron/dsl, DZ
239b a	Louisa St, Almonaster Blvd, **N gas:** Chevron/dsl, FuelZone, **food:** Burger King, McDonald's, Popeyes, Rally's, Subway, **lodging:** Econolodge, **other:** Family$, Goodyear/auto, Home Depot, Walgreens, Winn-Dixie, **S gas:** Day&Night/dsl
238b	I-610 W (from wb)
237	Elysian Fields Ave, **N other:** Lowe's Whse
236c	St. Bernard Ave
236b	LA 39, N Claiborne Ave
236a	Esplanade Ave, downtown
235a	Orleans Ave, to Vieux Carre, French Qtr, **S gas:** Chevron, **lodging:** Clarion, Marriott, Sheraton
235b	Poydras St, **N** H, **S** to Superdome, downtown
234a	US 90A, Claiborne Ave, to Westbank, Superdome
232	US 61, Airline Hwy, Tulane Ave, **N food:** Burger King, **S on Carolton gas:** Exxon, Shell, **food:** KFC, McDonald's, Popeye's, Rallys, **other:** Family$, Pepboys, USPO, Vet, to Xavier U
231b	Florida Blvd, WestEnd
231a	Metairie Rd
230	I-610 E (from eb), to Slidell
229	Bonnabel Blvd
228	Causeway Blvd, **N gas:** Exxon, Shell, **food:** PF Chang's, **lodging:** Best Western, Hampton Inn, Ramada Ltd, **other:** Borders Books, Dillard's, Macy's, Old Navy, **S gas:** DZ, Exxon, **food:** IHOP, **lodging:** Courtyard, Days Inn, Extended Stay America, La Quinta, Quality Hotel, Residence Inn, Sheraton
226	Clearview Pkwy, Huey Long Br, **N gas:** Chevron, Exxon, **food:** Cafe Dumonde, Chili's, Copeland's Cheesecake Bistro, Corky's BBQ, Don's Seafood Hut, Hooters, Popeyes, Quizno's, Semolina, Taco Bell, Taco Tico, **lodging:** Sleep Inn, **other:** Cadillac, Lincoln/Mercury, Sears/auto, Target, Tire Kingdom, **S gas:** Chevron, Danny&Clyde, **food:** Beijing Chinese, Burger King, Piccadilly, Shoney's, Smoothie King, Subway, **lodging:** Sun Suites, Super 8, **other:** H, Buick/GMC/Pontiac, Firestone/auto
225	Veterans Blvd, **N gas:** Chevron, DZ, Shell, **food:** Burger King, Cuco's Mexican, Denny's, McDonald's, Subway, **lodging:** La Quinta, **other:** CVS Drug, Honda, Radio Shack, Rite Aid, Rouses Mkt, **S gas:** DZ, Shell, **food:** Casa Garcia, Louisiana Purchase Kitchen, New Orleans Burgers, O'Henry's, Piccadilly's, Popeyes, Rally's, Tiffin Pancakes, Wendy's, **lodging:** Evergreen Hotel, Sheraton, **other:** Acura, Best Buy, BigLots, BMW, Chevrolet, $General, Home Depot, Hyundai, Jo-Anne Fabrics, KIA, K-Mart, Lexus, Nissan, Office Depot, PepBoys, PetsMart, TJ Maxx, Toyota, VW, Walgreens, Walmart/auto, Vet
224	Power Blvd (from wb)
223b a	LA 49, Williams Blvd, **N gas:** DZ/dsl, Exxon, Shell, **food:** Baskin-Robbins, Cane's Chicken, Casa Tequilla, Fisherman's Cove, Hibachi House, IHOP, Jumbo Buffet, Papa's Pizza, Popeye's, Rally's, Smitty's Seafood, Subway, Taco Bell, Taqueria Jalisco, Wendy's, **lodging:** Fairfield Inn, **other:** AutoZone, $Tree, Family$, Ford, Office Depot, PetCo, Rite Aid, True Value Hardware, Tuesday Morning, Walmart Mkt, **S gas:** Exxon/dsl, Shell, **food:** Brick Oven, Fat Hen Grill, Iron Pot Grill, KFC/LJ Silver, McDonald's, Quizno's, Sonic, Subway, **lodging:** Best Inn, Comfort Inn, Contempra Inn, Country Inn & Suites, Crowne Plaza, Extended Stay America, La Quinta, Radisson, Travelodge, **other:** CVS Drug, $General, Firestone/auto, Goodyear/auto, NAPA, Radio Shack, U-Haul, mall
221	Loyola Dr, **N gas:** Circle K, Exxon/dsl, Loyola, Shell/dsl, **food:** Church's, McDonald's, Popeye's, Rally's, Taco Bell, **other:** Advance Parts, Sam's Club/gas, **S gas:** DZ, **food:** Cuban-American Rest., Wendys, **lodging:** Motel 6, **other:** Family$, ✈, info
220	I-310 S, to Houma
214mm	Lake Pontchartrain
210	I-55N (from wb)
209	I-55 N, US 51, to Jackson, LaPlace, Hammond, **N gas:** Shell/Huddle House/casino/dsl, **lodging:** Suburban Lodge, **S gas:** Circle K/dsl, Pilot/Subway/dsl/24hr/scales, Shell/dsl, **food:** Bully's Seafood, Burger King, McDonald's, Shoney's, Waffle House, Wendy's, **lodging:** Best Western, Day's Inn, Hampton Inn, Holiday Inn Express, Quality Inn
207mm	**weigh sta both lanes**
206	LA 3188 S, La Place, **S gas:** Shell/dsl, Texaco/dsl, **other:** H, Chrysler/Dodge/Jeep, Ford, Goodyear/auto
194	LA 641 S, to Gramercy, **3-5 mi S gas:** Chevron, Taylors/dsl, **food:** Golden Grove Rest, Popeye's, **other:** H, **11-15 mi S** plantations
187	US 61, N to Sorrento, S to Gramercy
182	LA 22, Sorrento, **N gas:** Chevron/Popeye's/dsl, Texaco/dsl, **S gas:** Chevron/scales/dsl, SJ/dsl, **food:** Lafitte's Café, McDonald's, Subway, Waffle House
179	LA 44, Gonzales, **N gas:** Exxon, **1 mi N other:** Buick/Pontiac/GMC, $General, Fred's Store, Walgreens, **3 mi S food:** Cabin Fine Cajun Food, Pelican Point Café, **other:** Vesta RV Park (5mi)
177	LA 30, Gonzales, **N gas:** Freedom/dsl, Shell, **food:** Burger King, Jack-in-the-Box, McDonald's, Outback Steaks, Shoney's, Taco Bell, Waffle House, **lodging:** Best Western, Budget Inn, Highland Inn, Holiday

E ↕ W SLIDELL — NEW ORLEANS AREA — GONZALES

LA

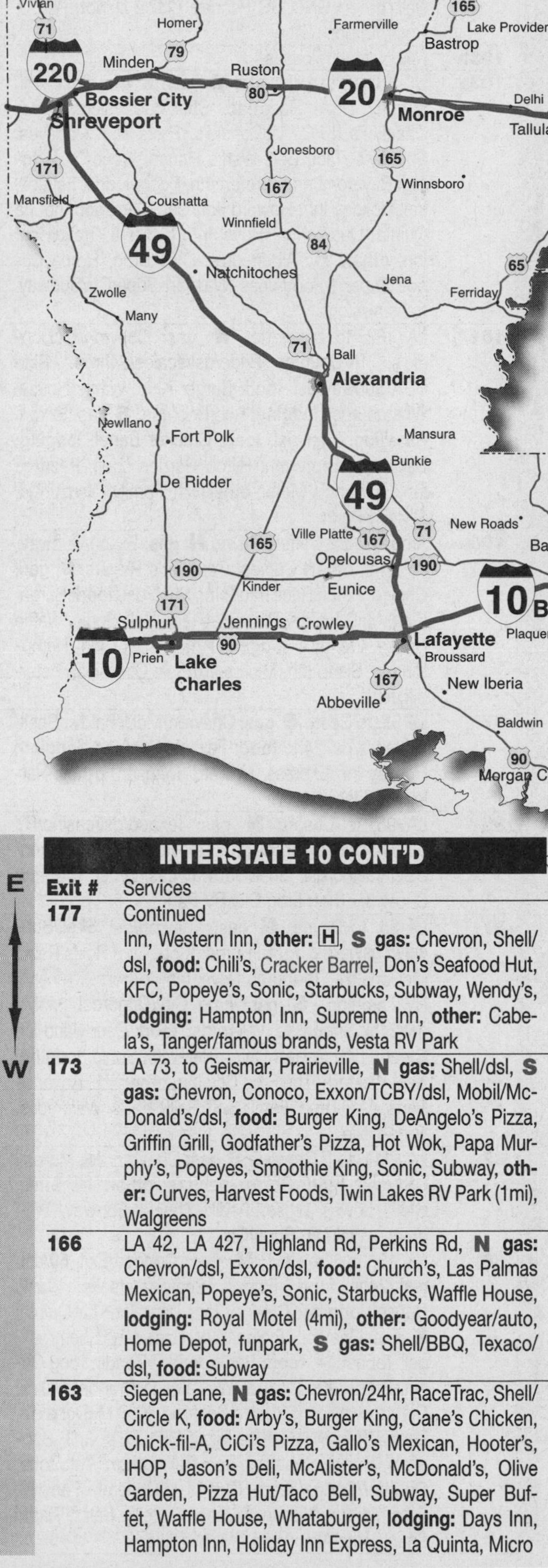

INTERSTATE 10 CONT'D

E ↕ W

Exit #	Services
177	Continued Inn, Western Inn, **other:** [H], **S gas:** Chevron, Shell/dsl, **food:** Chili's, Cracker Barrel, Don's Seafood Hut, KFC, Popeye's, Sonic, Starbucks, Subway, Wendy's, **lodging:** Hampton Inn, Supreme Inn, **other:** Cabela's, Tanger/famous brands, Vesta RV Park
173	LA 73, to Geismar, Prairieville, **N gas:** Shell/dsl, **S gas:** Chevron, Conoco, Exxon/TCBY/dsl, Mobil/McDonald's/dsl, **food:** Burger King, DeAngelo's Pizza, Griffin Grill, Godfather's Pizza, Hot Wok, Papa Murphy's, Popeyes, Smoothie King, Sonic, Subway, **other:** Curves, Harvest Foods, Twin Lakes RV Park (1mi), Walgreens
166	LA 42, LA 427, Highland Rd, Perkins Rd, **N gas:** Chevron/dsl, Exxon/dsl, **food:** Church's, Las Palmas Mexican, Popeye's, Sonic, Starbucks, Waffle House, **lodging:** Royal Motel (4mi), **other:** Goodyear/auto, Home Depot, funpark, **S gas:** Shell/BBQ, Texaco/dsl, **food:** Subway
163	Siegen Lane, **N gas:** Chevron/24hr, RaceTrac, Shell/Circle K, **food:** Arby's, Burger King, Cane's Chicken, Chick-fil-A, CiCi's Pizza, Gallo's Mexican, Hooter's, IHOP, Jason's Deli, McAlister's, McDonald's, Olive Garden, Pizza Hut/Taco Bell, Subway, Super Buffet, Waffle House, Whataburger, **lodging:** Days Inn, Hampton Inn, Holiday Inn Express, La Quinta, Micro
163	Continued tel, Motel 6, Super 8, **other:** Advance Parts, BigLots, $Tree, Firestone/auto, Harley-Davidson, Honda, Hummer, Kia, Office Depot, PetCo, Radio Shack, Ross, Saab, Target, **S food:** Backyard Burger, Chili's, ChuckeCheese, Honeybaked Ham, Joe's Crabshack, Sicily's, Texas Roadhouse, Wendy's, **lodging:** Courtyard, Residence Inn, **other:** BooksAMillion, Kohl's, Lowe's Whse, Old Navy, PetsMart, Sam's Club/gas, Old Navy, TJ Maxx, Walmart SuperCtr/Subway
162	Bluebonnet Rd, **N gas:** Chevron/dsl, **food:** Cadillac Cafe, Primo's Italian, **lodging:** Quality Suites, **other:** Vet, **S gas:** RaceWay, **food:** BJ's Brewhouse, Bravo Italiano, Burger King, Copeland's Cheesecake Bistro, J Alexander's, King Buffet, Logan's Roadhouse, Ralph&Kacoo's, Sake Cafe, Shenanigans, **lodging:** Hyatt Place, **other:** Best Buy, Borders, Dillard's, JC Penney, Macy's, Sears/auto, Mall of LA, mall, World Mkt, [H]
160	LA 3064, Essen Lane, **S gas:** Exxon, RaceTrac, Valero, **food:** Burger King, Copeland's Bistro, Domino's, McDonald's, Gatti's Pizza, Piccadilly, Popeye's, Quizno's, Sakura Hibachi, Subway, Taco Bell, Time's Grill, Wendy's, **lodging:** Drury Inn, Fairfield Inn, Springhill Suites, **other:** Albertson's, $General, Firestone, O'Reilly Parts, Rite Aid, Tire Kingdom, Walgreens, [H]
159	I-12 E, to Hammond
158	College Dr, Baton Rouge, **N gas:** USA/dsl, **food:** Alabasha Café, Cane's Chicken, CiCi's, Fox&Hound Grill, Hooters, Izzo's Grill, Jason's Deli, Macaroni Grill, Mansurs Rest., Marble Slab Creamery, Melting Pot, On-the-Border, Ruby Tuesday, Subway, Waffle House, Wendy's, **lodging:** Best Western, Chase Suites, Extended Stay America, Homewood Suites, Marriott, **other:** [H], Barnes&Noble, **S gas:** Chevron/24hr, Exxon, Shell/Circle K, **food:** Casa Maria Mexican, Chili's, China Wall, Great Wall Chinese, IHOP, McDonald's, Ninfa's Mexican, Quizno's, Ruth's Chris Steaks, Sarrita's Mexican, Starbucks, Taco Bell, **lodging:** Cambria Suites, Comfort Inn, Crowne Plaza, Embassy Suites, Hampton Inn,

INTERSTATE 10 CONT'D

E ↕ W

Exit #	Services
158	Continued Holiday Inn Express, Holiday Inn Select, **other:** Albertson's/Sav-On, AutoZone, $Tree, Hobby Lobby, Office Depot, Radio Shack, Rite Aid, Walgreens, Walmart SuperCtr/24hr
157b	Acadian Thwy, **N gas:** Chevron, Shell/Circle K, **food:** Mestizo's Grill, Rib's Rest., **lodging:** La Quinta, Red Lion Inn, **other:** H, **S gas:** Shell/Circle K, **food:** Acme Oyster House, Outback Steaks, **lodging:** Courtyard, **other:** CVS Drug, Tuesday Morning
157a	Perkins Rd (from eb), same as 157b
156b	Dalrymple Dr, **S** to LSU
156a	Washington St
155c	Louise St (from wb)
155b	I-110 N, to Baton Rouge bus dist, ✈
155a	LA 30, Nicholson Dr, Baton Rouge, **N** Sheraton, **S** to LSU
154mm	Mississippi River
153	LA 1, Port Allen, **N gas:** Chevron, Shell/Circle K, **food:** Church's, **other:** AutoZone, Family$, Kenworth, NAPA Care, **S gas:** Chevron, LA 1S Truck Plaza/Exxon/Casino/dsl/24hr, RaceTrac, **food:** Quizno's, Smoothie King, Waffle House, **other:** $Tree, Walmart SuperCtr/Subway
151	LA 415, to US 190, **N gas:** Cash's Trk Plaza/dsl/scales, Chevron, Exxon/dsl, Gold Mine/casino/dsl, Nino's Trkstp/casino, Shell/Blimpie/dsl, **food:** Burger King, Chinese Inn, Domino's, KFC/Taco Bell, LA Steakhouse, McDonald's, Popeyes, Waffle House, **lodging:** Best Western, Comfort Inn, Hampton Inn, Holiday Inn Express, Quality Inn, West Inn, **S gas:** Love's/Arby's/dsl/scales/24hr, Shell/dsl/24hr, **lodging:** Audubon Inn, Motel 6, Super 8, **other:** truck repair
139	LA 77, Grosse Tete, **N gas:** Shell/Subway/dsl, **other:** Chevrolet, casino, **S gas:** Tiger/Conoco/dsl/rest./@
135	LA 3000, to Ramah
127	LA 975, to Whiskey Bay
126.5mm	Pilot Channel of Whiskey Bay
122mm	Atchafalaya River
121	Butte La Rose, **visitors ctr/rest area, both lanes, full facilities, ⛱, litter barrels, vending, petwalk, tourist info, , S food:** Lazy Cajun Grill (2mi), **other:** Frenchman's Wilderness Camground (.5mi)
115	LA 347, to Cecilia, Henderson, **N gas:** Exxon/dsl/24hr, Texaco/dsl, **food:** Boudin's Rest., Landry's Seafood, **lodging:** Holiday Inn Express, **other:** casinos, **S gas:** Chevron/dsl, Citgo/dsl, Exxon/Subway/dsl, Shell/McDonald's, Valero, **food:** Popeye's, Waffle House
109	LA 328, to Breaux Bridge, **N gas:** Shell/dsl, Texaco/grill/dsl/24hr, **lodging:** Microtel, **other:** Campers Unlimited, casino, **S gas:** Chevron/Popeyes, Mapco, Mobil/Domino's/dsl, Pilot/Arby's/dsl/scales/24hr, **food:** Burger King, Crazy Bout Cajun, McDonald's, Pizza Hut, Taco Bell, Waffle House, Wendy's, Zapote Mexican, **lodging:** Sona Inn, Super 8, **other:** AutoZone, Chevrolet, $General, Family$, Walgreens, Walmart SuperCtr, Winn-Dixie
108mm	**weigh sta both lanes**

LAFAYETTE

Exit #	Services
104	Louisiana Ave, **S food:** Chick-fil-A, Subway, Taco Bell, **other:** GNC, JC Penney, Office Depot, PetCo, Ross, Target,
103b	I-49 N, to Opelousas
103a	US 167 S, to Lafayette, **S gas:** Chevron/dsl/24hr, Murphy USA, RaceTrac, Shell/dsl, Valero, **food:** Checker's, KFC, McDonald's, Pizza Hut, Popeyes, Shoney's, Taco Bell, Waffle House, Wendy's, **lodging:** Baymont Inn, Comfort Inn, Econolodge, Fairfield Inn, Holiday Inn, Howard Johnson, Jameson Inn, La Quinta, Quality Inn, Royal Inn, Super 8, TravelHost Inn, **other:** H, Albertson's, CVS Drug, Home Depot, Super 1 Foods/gas, Walmart SuperCtr/Subway, transmissions
101	LA 182, to Lafayette, **N gas:** Chevron/McDonald's, TA/Country Pride/dsl/scales/24hr/@, Ride USA/Subway/dsl, **food:** Burger King, Waffle House, Whataburger, **lodging:** Red Roof Inn, **S gas:** Exxon, RaceTrac, Shell/dsl, **food:** Cracker Barrel, **lodging:** Day's Inn, Drury Inn, Hilton Garden (2mi), Peartree Inn, St Francis Motel, **other:** H, Family$, Isuzu/Kia, O'Reilly Parts
100	Ambassador Caffery Pkwy, **N gas:** Exxon/Subway/dsl/24hr, **other:** Curves, Gauthier's RV Ctr, **S gas:** Chevron/24hr, RaceTrac/24hr, Shell/dsl, **food:** Burger King, McDonald's, Pizza Hut/Taco Bell, Sonic, Waffle House, Wendy's, **lodging:** Ambassador Inn, Hampton Inn, Sleep Inn, Microtel, **other:** Goodyear, Peterbilt, H
97	LA 93, to Scott, **S gas:** Chevron/McDonald's, Shell/Church's/dsl/24hr, **food:** Fezzo's Seafood, **lodging:** Holiday Inn Express, Howard Johnson, **other:** Harley-Davidson, KOA
92	LA 95, to Duson, **N gas:** Texaco/dsl/casino/RV dump/scales/24hr, **S gas:** Chevron/dsl, X92/Exxon/BBQ/casino/dsl, Shell/Subway/casino/dsl, **lodging:** Super 8, **other:** Frog City RV Park
87	LA 35, to Rayne, **N gas:** Chevron/dsl, Shell/Subway/casino/dsl, **food:** Burger King, Chef Roy's Rest., McDonald's, **lodging:** Days Inn, **other:** $General, RV camping, **S gas:** Frog City/Citgo/dsl, Mobil/dsl/24hr, Shop Rite, Valero/dsl, **food:** Candyland Ice Cream, DQ, Gabe's Café, Popeye's, Sonic, **lodging:** Best Western, The Frog City Inn, **other:** H, Advance Parts, CVS Drug, Family$, O'Reilly Parts, Walgreens, Winn-Dixie

CROWLEY

Exit #	Services
82	LA 1111, to E Crowley, **S gas:** Chevron/dsl, Murphy USA/gas, **food:** Chili's, Wendy's, **other:** H, $Tree, GNC, Lowes Whse, Radio Shack, Subway, Walgreens, Walmart SuperCtr
80	LA 13, to Crowley, **N gas:** Conoco/Exit 80/dsl/rest./24hr, **food:** Fezzo's Seafood/steaks, Waffle House, **lodging:** Crowley Inn, Days Inn, La Quinta, **S gas:** Chevron, Exxon/24hr, RaceWay, Shamrock/dsl, Tobacco+, **food:** Bamboo Inn, Boudin King Cajun, Burger King, Cajun Way, China Dragon, DQ, El Dorado Mexican, Golden Seafood, KFC McDonald's, Lucky Wok, Mr Gatti's, Pizza Hut, PJ's Grill, Popeye's, Sonic, Subway, Taco Bell, **other:** AutoZone, Chrysler/Dodge/Jeep, Curves, $General, Family$, Ford/Mercury/Nissan, Nissan, O'Reilly Parts, Radio Shack, Rite Aid, U-Haul, Winn-Dixie

INTERSTATE 10 CONT'D

E ↕ W

Exit #	Services
76	LA 91, to Iota, **S gas:** Petro/Mobil/Subway/dsl/scales/24hr
72	Egan, **N food:** Cajun Haven RV Park
67.5mm	**rest areas both lanes full ♿ facilities, ☎, picnic, litter barrels, petwalk, RV dump**
65	LA 97, to Jennings, **N gas:** Spur/dsl (1.5mi), **S gas:** Shell/dsl/casino, **lodging:** Day's Inn, **other:** to SW LA St School
64	LA 26, to Jennings, **N** Boudreaux Inn, **other:** RV Park, **S gas:** Chevron, Exxon/dsl, EZ Mart, Murphy USA, Jennings Trvl Ctr/dsl, Valero, **food:** Burger King, General Wok Chinese, McDonald's, Mr Gatti's, Pizza Hut, Popeye's, Shoney's, Sonic, Subway, Taco Bell, Waffle House, Walker's Cajun Rest., Wendy's, **lodging:** Hampton Inn, Holiday Inn, Quality Inn, **other:** H AutoZone, Chrysler/Jeep/Dodge, $General, O'Reilly Parts, Rite Aid, Walgreens, Walmart SuperCtr
59	LA 395, to Roanoke
54	LA 99, Welsh, **S gas:** Circle R/Perky's Pizza, Cajun Lunch/dsl, Exxon/dsl/24hr, **food:** Cajun Tales Seafood, DQ
48	LA 101, Lacassine, **S gas:** Exxon
44	US 165, to Alexandria, **N other:** Quiet Oaks RV Park (10mi), **S food:** Rabideaux's Cajun, **other:** RV Park
43	LA 383, to Iowa, **N gas:** Exxon/Pit Grill/dsl/24hr, Loves/Hardee's/dsl/scales/24hr, **food:** Burger King, **lodging:** Howard Johnson Express, La Quinta, **other:** United RV Ctr, **S gas:** Citgo/dsl, Conoco/dsl, Valero,, **food:** Fausta's Rest., McDonald's, Subway, **other:** $General, I-10 Outlet/famous brands, Mkt Basket Foods, RV park
36	LA 397, to Creole, Cameron, **N** Jean Lafitte RV Park (2mi), I-10 RV Camping, Jellystone Camping, **S gas:** Chevron/dsl, Fuel Stop 36/dsl/RV Dump, **lodging:** Red Roof Inn, **other:** casino, RV Camping
34	I-210 W, to Lake Charles
33	US 171 N, **N gas:** Citgo, Exxon/dsl, Murphy USA, Tobacco Stop, **food:** Burger King, Church's, Pink Pig BBQ, Subway, Taco Bell, **lodging:** Baymont Inn, Best Western, Comfort Suites, Econolodge, La Quinta, **other:** AutoZone, $General, Family$, O'Reilly Parts, Walgreens, Wal-Mart SuperCtr/McDonalds, to Sam Houston Jones SP, **S lodging:** Holiday Inn Express, Motel 6, Treasure Inn
32	Opelousas St, **N gas:** Exxon, **S lodging:** Holiday Inn Express, Motel 6, Treasure Inn
31b	US 90 E, Shattuck St, to LA 14, **N gas:** Shell/cafe/dsl/casino, **S gas:** PakCo Gas
31a	US 90 bus, Enterprise Blvd, **S food:** Popeye's
30b	downtown
30a	LA 385, N Lakeshore Dr, Ryan St, **N gas:** Exxon, **food:** Steamboat Bill's Rest., Waffle House, **lodging:** Days Inn, Oasis Inn, **S gas:** Citgo, **food:** Wendy's, **lodging:** Best Suites
29	LA 385 (from eb), same as 30a
28mm	Calcasieu Bayou, Lake Charles
27	LA 378, to Westlake, **N gas:** Conoco/dsl, Shell, Valero, **food:** Burger King, McDonald's, Popeye's, Sonic, Subway, **other:** Bumper Parts, $General, O'Reilly Parts, to Sam Houston Jones SP, **S lodging:** Inn at the Isle, **other:** Riverboat Casinos

JENNINGS

LAKE CHARLES

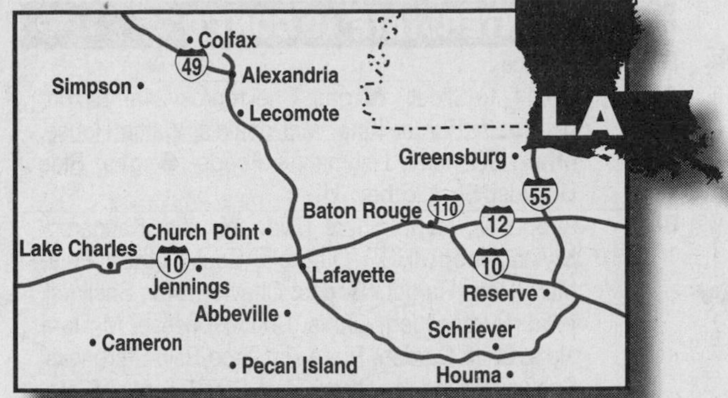

SULPHUR

Exit #	Services
26	US 90 W, Southern Rd, Columbia, **N gas:** Circle K/gas
25	I-210 E, to Lake Charles
23	LA 108, to Sulphur, **N gas:** Circle K/gas, Citgo, Exxon, Murphy USA, **food:** Burger King, Chili's, China Wok, McDonald's, Popeye's, Subway, Taco Bell, Wendy's, **lodging:** Quality Inn, **other:** Bumper Parts, $General, Lowe's Whse, Radio Shack, Walgreens, Walmart SuperCtr, **S gas:** Cash Magic/dsl, Chevron/Jack-in-the-Box/dsl, **food:** Cracker Barrel, Waffle House, **lodging:** Best Western, Days Inn, Comfort Suites, Crossland Suites, Holiday Inn Express, Super 8, **other:** casino, tires
21	LA 3077, Arizona St, **N gas:** Conoco/dsl, Shell, **food:** Boiling Point Cajun, China Taste, KFC, Papa John's, **other:** CVS Drug, $General, Ford, GNC, Kroger/gas, NAPA, Walgreens, Vet, **S gas:** Chevron/dsl, Valero/dsl/casino, **other:** H, Hidden Ponds RV Park
20	LA 27, to Sulphur, **N gas:** Chevron, Circle K, Citgo, Conoco, **food:** Bonanza, Burger King, Casa Ole Mexican, Cajun Charlie's, Checker's, Gatti's Pizza, Gudalajara Rest., Hollier's Cajun, Hong Kong Chinese, Joe's Pizza/Pasta, McDonald's, Pitt Grill Cajun, Popeye's, Subway, Taco Bell, Wendy's, **lodging:** Econolodge, Hampton Inn, Sulphur Inn, **other:** Brookshire Foods/gas, Family$, Firestone/auto, Goodyear/auto, Jiffy Lube, **S gas:** Pilot/dsl, Shell/dsl, **food:** Navroskey's Burgers, Pizza Hut, Sonic, Waffle House, **lodging:** Baymont Inn, Candlewood Suites, Fairfield Inn, Holiday Inn, La Quinta, Microtel, Wingate Inn, **other:** H, casino, to Creole Nature Trail
8	LA 108, Vinton, **N gas:** Chevron/dsl, Exxon/dsl, **food:** Cajun Cowboy's Rest., **other:** V RV Park
7	LA 3063, Vinton, **N gas:** Exxon/dsl, **food:** Burger King, Sonic, Subway, Taco Rico, **other:** $General, casino, tires/repair, **S gas:** Loves/Arby's/dsl/scales/24hr
4	US 90, LA 109, Toomey, **N gas:** Cash Magic/dsl/grill/casino, Chevron/dsl/casino, **other:** truck repair, **S gas:** Exxon/dsl, Shell/dsl/rest, **food:** TX Pelican Rest., Subway, **other:** RV Park, casinos
2.5mm	**weigh sta both lanes**
1.5mm	**Welcome Ctr eb, full ♿ facilities, ☎, picnic, litter barrels, petwalk**
1	(from wb), Sabine River Turnaround
0mm	Louisiana/Texas state line, Sabine River

INTERSTATE 12

Exit #	Services
85c	I-10 E, to Biloxi. I-12 begins/ends on I-10, exit 267.
85b	I-59 N, to Hattiesburg
85a	I-10 W, to New Orleans

INTERSTATE 12 CONT'D

E ↕ W

Exit #	Services
83	US 11, to Slidell, **N gas:** Chevron/dsl/24hr, Exxon/dsl, **food:** Burger King, McDonald's, Waffle House, **other:** $General, Lishmann's Foods, **S gas:** Ride USA/dsl, Shell, **other:** H
80	Airport Dr, North Shore Blvd, **N gas:** Kangaroo/Krystal, **food:** IHOP, Quizno's, Sonic, **other:** PetsMart, Ross, Target, **S gas:** Chevron/24hr, Shell/dsl, **food:** Burger King, Chili's, ChuckeCheese, McDonald's, Olive Garden, Pizza Hut/Taco Bell, Starbucks, Subway, Wendy's, **other:** Best Buy, Dillard's, $Tree, Goodyear/auto, Home Depot, JC Penney, Marshall's, Office Depot, Sam's Club/gas, Sears/auto, Walmart SuperCtr/24hr, mall
74	LA 434, to Lacombe, **N gas:** Chevron/Subway/dsl, **other:** H, **S** Big Branch Marsh NWR
65	LA 59, to Mandeville, **N gas:** Chevron/dsl, Danny&Clyde's/cafe, Shell, **food:** Sonic, Waffle House, **S gas:** Kangaroo/Burger King/dsl, Texaco/Domino's/dsl, **other:** Winn-Dixie, to Fontainebleau SP, camping, USPO, Vet
63b a	US 190, Covington, Mandeville, **N gas:** Chevron, Exxon, RaceTrac, Shell/Circle K, **food:** Acme Oyster House, Applebee's, Burger King, Cane's Rest., Chick-fil-A, Copeland's Grill, 4 Seasons Chinese, Honeybaked Ham, IHOP, KFC, McAlister's Deli, Osake Japanese, Outback Steaks, Piccadilly's, Quizno's, Sonic, Starbucks, Subway, TGIFriday, Waffle House, Wendy's, **lodging:** Best Western, Comfort Inn, Courtyard, Hampton Inn, Holiday Inn, Super 8, **other:** Albertson's, BooksAMillion, Chevrolet, GNC, Home Depot, Hyundai, Lowes Whse, Nissan, Office Depot, Toyota, Walmart SuperCtr/24hr, **S other:** H, Chrysler, st police, to New Orleans via toll causeway
60mm	**rest area both lanes, full ♿ facilities, ⛱ litter barrels, vending, petwalk**
59	LA 21, to Covington, Madisonville, **N gas:** Chevron/dsl, Kangaroo, Shell, **food:** Bistro Italia, Coldstone Creamery, Isabella's Pizza, McDonald's, Subway, Wow Cafe, **lodging:** La Quinta, **other:** H, Walgreens, **S gas:** Texaco, **food:** Chick-fil-A, Domino's, Longhorn Steaks, Moe's SW Grill, Quizno's, Taco Bell, Wendy's **other:** Belk, Best Buy, JC Penney, Marshall's, Ross, Target, World Mkt, Fairview Riverside SP
57	LA 1077, to Goodbee, Madisonville, **S** Family RV Park, to Fairview Riverside SP
47	LA 445, to Robert, **1-3 mi N other:** Jellystone Camping, to Global Wildlife Ctr
42	LA 3158, to ✈, **N gas:** Chevron/dsl/24hr, **lodging:** Friendly Inn, **other:** Truckwash, **S other:** H, Berryland RV Ctr
40	US 51, to Hammond, **N gas:** RaceTrac, Shell/Circle K/24hr, **food:** Burger King, China Garden, Church's, Coldstone Creamery, IHOP, McDonald's, Pizza Hut, Quizno's, Ryan's, Taco Bell, Wendy's, **lodging:** Best Western, Supreme Inn, **other:** Dillard's, Harley Davidson, Rite Aid, Sears/auto, U-Haul, Walgreens, mall, **S gas:** Petro/Mobil/Subway/dsl/scales/24hr/@, Pilot/Arby's/dsl/scales/24hr, Shell, **food:** Waffle House, **lodging:** Colonial Inn, Days Inn, **other:** H, Blue Beacon, $General, KOA, SpeedCo
38b a	I-55, N to Jackson, S to New Orleans
37mm	**weigh sta both lanes**
35	Pumpkin Ctr, Baptist, **N gas:** Exxon/dsl, **other:** Camping World RV Service/Supplies, Dixie RV Ctr, Punkin RV Park (2mi), **S gas:** Chevron/24hr
32	LA 43, to Albany, **N gas:** Chevron/Subway, Exxon/dsl, **S gas:** Citgo/dsl, **other:** to Tickfaw SP
29	LA 441, to Holden, **N** gas/dsl, **other:** Berryland Campers, RV RestStop (1mi), st police
22	LA 63, to Frost, Livingston, **N gas:** Chevron/dsl, Conoco/dsl, Mobil, **food:** Subway, Wayne's BBQ, **other:** Family$, **S other:** Lakeside RV Park (1mi)
19	to Satsuma
15	LA 447, to Walker, **N gas:** Murphy Express, Shell/Subway/24hr, Texaco, **food:** Burger King, Domino's, Jack-in-the-Box, La Fleur's Seafood, McDonald's, Popeye's, Sherwood PoBoy's, Sonic, Taco Bell, Waffle House, Wendy's, **lodging:** La Quinta, **other:** AutoZone, $Tree, Walmart SuperCtr/24hr, Winn-Dixie, Vet, **S gas:** Chevron/dsl, **other:** Family RV Ctr
12	LA 1036, Juban Rd
10	LA 3002, to Denham Springs, **N gas:** Chevron, Circle K, RaceTrac, Shell/Circle K/dsl, **food:** Arby's, Burger King, Cactus Café, Cane's Rest., Chili's, Chinese Inn, Crawford's Cajun, Don's Rest., Fernando's Mexican, IHOP, McDonald's, Popeye's, Ryan's, Sonic, Starbucks, Subway, Waffle House, Wendy's, **lodging:** Best Western, Hampton Inn, HomeGate Inn, **other:** Advance Parts, $General, Home Depot, PetCo, Radio Shack, Rite Aid, Tire Kingdom, Walmart SuperCtr, **S gas:** Pilot/Subway/dsl/scales/24hr, Shell, **food:** Backyard Burger, Fish Co Rest., Piccadilly's, Shoney's, **lodging:** Day's Inn, Highland Inn, **other:** Bass Pro Shop, Dodge/Isuzu, Ford, KOA
8.5mm	Amite River
7	O'Neal Lane, **N gas:** Mobil, **lodging:** Comfort Suites, **other:** H, Night's RV Park, Office Depot, Toyota/Scion, **S gas:** BP, Chevron/24hr, RaceTrac, **food:** Burger King, Las Palmas Mexican, LoneStar Steaks, McDonald's, Pizza Hut/Taco Bell, Popeye's, Sonic, Subway, Waffle House, Wendy's, **other:** H, AutoZone, $Tree, Radio Shack, Walgreens, Walmart SuperCtr/24hr
6	Millerville Rd, **N gas:** Chevron/dsl/24hr, **food:** Chick-fil-A, Chili's, **other:** Best Buy, Lowes Whse, Office Depot, PetsMart, Super Target, **S gas:** Texaco/dsl, **other:** Ace Hardware
4	Sherwood Forest Blvd, **N gas:** Exxon, Shell/dsl, **food:** Burger King, Jack-in-the-Box, McDonald's, Popeye's, Sonic, Subway, Taco Bell, Waffle House, **lodging:** Crossland Suites, Red Roof Inn, Super 8, **other:** Goodyear/auto, Rite Aid, **S gas:** RaceTrac, Shell/24hr, **food:** Cane's Rest., Picadilly's, Pizza Hut, Podnuh's BBQ, Schlotzky's, Sherwood PoBoys, **lodging:** Calloway Inn, **other:** Harley-Davidson
2b	US 61 N, **N gas:** B-Quik, Chevron, **food:** Applebee's, Cracker Barrel, McDonald's, Pizza Hut/Taco Bell, Shoney's, Subway, Taste of China, **lodging:** Days Inn, Holiday Inn, Microtel, Motel 6, Ramada Inn, Sleep Inn, **other:** Albertson's/gas, Dodge, Ford/Lincoln/Mercury, Hyundai, Marshall's, Michael's, Nissan, PepBoys, SteinMart, Toyota, Walgreens, WalMart Mkt, transmissions

COVINGTON

HAMMOND

BATON ROUGE

LA

E ↕ W

INTERSTATE 12 CONT'D

Exit #	Services
2a	US 61 S, **S gas:** Chevron, Circle K/gas, Exxon/dsl, **food:** McDonald's, Waffle House, **lodging:** Deluxe Inn, **other:** Cadillac/Volvo, Home Depot, Jubilee/dsl, Mitsubishi
1b	LA 1068, to LA 73, Essen Lane, **N gas:** Shell/Circle K/dsl, **food:** Cane's Rest., McDonald's, **other:** H, Family$, Hancock Fabrics, Hi-Nabor Foods, Radio Shack
1a	**I-10 (from wb). I-12 begins/ends on I-10, exit 159 in Baton Rouge**

E ↕ W

TALLULAH

RAYVILLE

INTERSTATE 20

Exit #	Services
189mm	Louisiana/Mississippi state line, Mississippi River
187mm	**weigh sta both lanes**
186	US 80, Delta, **S gas:** Chevron/Subway/dsl/24hr
184mm	**rest area both lanes, full facilities, , , litter barrels, petwalk, RV dump**
182	LA 602, Mound
173	LA 602, Richmond, **S other:** Ford
171	US 65, Tallulah, **N gas:** Chevron/Subway/dsl, Kangaroo/dsl, Shell/dsl, **food:** KFC, McDonald's, Wendy's, **lodging:** Day's Inn, Super 8, **other:** H, **S gas:** Conoco/dsl/scales, Love's/Arby's/dsl/scales/24hr, TA/dsl/rest./scales/24hr/@, Texaco
164mm	Tensas River
157	LA 577, Waverly, **N gas:** Tiger Trkstp/dsl/rest./24hr, to Tensas River NWR, **S** Chevron/Subway/dsl/24hr, Shell/dsl
155mm	Bayou Macon
153	LA 17, Delhi, **N gas:** Chevron/Subway/dsl, Texaco/dsl, **food:** Burger King, Boomer's rest., China Garden, DQ, Pizza Hut, Sonic, **other:** H, Brookshire's Foods, $General, Fred's Drugs, **S gas:** Valero/dsl, **lodging:** Best Western, Executive Inn
148	LA 609, Dunn
145	LA 183, rd 202, Holly Ridge
141	LA 583, Bee Bayou Rd
138	LA 137, Rayville, **N gas:** BP, Pilot/Wendy's/dsl/scales/24hr, **food:** Dragon Buffet, McDonald's, Sonic, **lodging:** Day's Inn, **other:** H, AutoZone, Chevrolet/Pontiac/Buick, $General, Family$, Firestone, Walmart SuperCtr, **S gas:** Chevron/Subway/dsl/24hr, Exxon/Circle K/dsl, RaceWay, **food:** Big John's Rest., Popeye's, Waffle House, **lodging:** Super 8
135mm	Beouf River
132	LA 133, Start, **N gas:** Exxon/dsl
128mm	Lafourche Bayou
124	LA 594, Millhaven, **N gas:** EZ Mart/dsl, **other:** st police, to Arsage Wildlife Area
120	Garrett Rd, Pecanland Mall Dr, **N gas:** Chevron/dsl, Shell, **food:** Applebee's, Copeland's Rest., Eastern Empire Chinese, Hawg Wild BBQ, IHOP, McAlister's, O'Charleys, Olive Garden, Red Lobster, Sonic, Subway, **lodging:** Courtyard, Residence Inn, **other:** Belk, Dillard's, Firestone/auto, Home Depot, JC Penney, Kohl's, PetCo, Ross, Sears/auto, Target, mall, **S gas:** Kangaroo/dsl, **lodging:** Best Western, Day's Inn, **other:** Freightliner, Harley-Davidson, Hope's RV Ctr, Lowes Whse, Pecanland RV Park, Sam's Club/gas, Shilo RV Camp

MONROE

Exit #	Services
118b a	US 165, **N lodging:** Holiday Inn, La Quinta, **other:** Chrysler/Dodge, Goodyear, Home Depot, KIA, Nissan, to NE LA U, **S gas:** Chevron, Exxon, Shell/Circle K, **food:** Burger King, Capt D's, Church's, KFC, McDonald's, Popeye's, Sonic, Subway, Wendy's, **lodging:** Comfort Suites, Hampton Inn, Motel 6, Ramada Ltd
117b	LA 594, Texas Ave, **N** gas/dsl
117a	Hall St, Monroe, **N** H, Civic Ctr, **S food:** Popeye's
116b	US 165 bus, LA 15, Jackson St, **N** H
116a	5th St, Monroe
115	LA 34, Mill St, **N gas:** Chevron, **S other:** Clay's RV Service
114	LA 617, Thomas Rd, **N gas:** Raceway, **food:** Bennigan's, Burger King, Cane's BBQ, Capt D's, Chick-fil-A, El Chico, Grandy's, KFC, McAlister's Deli, McDonald's, Pizza Hut, Popeye's, Subway, Taco Bell, TCBY, Wendy's, **lodging:** Shoney's Inn/rest., Super 8, Wingate Inn, **other:** H, Big Lots, Office Depot, Walgreens, Walmart SuperCtr/gas/24hr, **S gas:** Chevron, Exxon/Circle K/dsl, **food:** Chili's, China Garden, Cracker Barrel, Hooters, Logan's Roadhouse, LoneStar Steaks, Mohawk Seafood, Nicky's Mexican, Outback Steaks, Peking Chinese, Pizza Hut, Sonic, Waffle House, **lodging:** Best Western, Fairfield Inn, Jameson Inn, Red Roof Inn, **other:** Firestone, Radio Shack
113	Downing Pines Rd, **N lodging:** Hilton Garden, Holiday Inn Express, **other:** Chrysler/Dodge/Jeep
112	Well Rd, **N gas:** Conoco, Shell/Circle K/dsl/24hr, Texaco/dsl, **food:** Domino's, McDonald's, Sonic, Taco Bell, Waffle House, **other:** Walgreens, **S gas:** Pilot/Subway/Wendy's/dsl/scales/24hr, **other:** Pavilion RV Park
108	LA 546, to US 80, Cheniere, **N gas:** Shell/dsl
107	Camp Rd, rd 25, Cheniere, **N** RV Park
103	US 80, Calhoun, **N gas:** Chevron/dsl/rest., **food:** Johnny's Pizza (1mi), **lodging:** Avant Motel
101	LA 151, to Calhoun, **S gas:** Citgo/Subway/dsl, Exxon, **food:** Huddle House/24hr, Sonic
97mm	**rest area wb, full facilities, , , litter barrels, petwalk, RV dump**
95mm	**rest area eb, full facilities, , , litter barrels, petwalk, RV dump**
93	LA 145, Choudrant, **S gas:** Chevron, **other:** Jimmy Davis St Park, camping
86	LA 33, Ruston, **N gas:** RaceWay, Shell/Circle K/Quizno's/dsl, **food:** Cajun Cafe, Cane's Chicken, Chili's, Hot Rod BBQ, Log Cabin Grill, Ryan's, Sonic,

INTERSTATE 20 CONT'D

E ↔ W

Exit #	Services
86	Continued Z Buffet, **lodging:** Comfort Inn, Day's Inn, **other:** Buick/GMC, Cadillac/Chevrolet/Pontiac, Chrysler/Dodge/Jeep, Firestone, Ford/Lincoln/Mercury, Fred's Drug, Lowes Whse, Toyota, Walmart SuperCtr/gas/24hr, **S gas:** gas/dsl, **lodging:** Fairfield Inn, Holiday Inn Express
85	US 167, Ruston, **N gas:** Chevron/Subway, Exxon, Shell/Circle K, **food:** Applebees, Burger King, Capt D's, Huddle House, McDonald's, Peking Chinese, Wendy's, **lodging:** Budget Lodge, Hampton Inn, Howard Johnson, Relax Inn, **other:** $General, Office Depot, Radio Shack, Super 1 Foods, TrueValue, **S gas:** BP/dsl, Valero/dsl, **food:** Pizza Hut, **lodging:** Best Value Inn, Sleep Inn, **other:** H, Advance Parts
84	LA 544, Ruston, **N gas:** Mobil/dsl, **S gas:** Chevron, Exxon, **food:** Domino's, Johnny's Pizza, Pizza Inn, Quizno's, Sam Miguel Cantina, Starbucks, Subway, TCBY, Waffle House, **lodging:** Super 8, Travel Inn, **other:** Curves
81	LA 141, Grambling, **S gas:** Chevron/Church's/dsl/24hr, Exxon, **other:** to Grambling St U
78	LA 563, Industry, **S gas:** Texaco/dsl
77	LA 507, Simsboro
69	LA 151, Arcadia, **S gas:** BP/dsl, Citgo, Exxon, Shell, **food:** Country Cottage Rest., McDonald's, Sonic, Subway, **lodging:** Day's Inn, **other:** Bonnie& Clyde RV Park, Brookshire Foods, $General, Factory Stores/famous brands, Fred's Drugs
67	LA 9, Arcadia, **N** to Lake Claiborne SP, **S gas:** Shell/dsl
61	LA 154, Gibsland, **N** to Lake Claibourne SP
55	US 80, Ada, Taylor
52	LA 532, to US 80, Dubberly, **N gas:** Exxon/Mom's Diner/dsl/scales/24hr, Valero/dsl, **S gas:** Clark/dsl
49	LA 531, Minden, **N gas:** Loves/Arby's/dsl/scales/24hr, Minden TrkStp/Shell/dsl/rest./24hr/@, QuickDraw/Subway/dsl, **food:** Pizza Hut (3mi), Taco Bell (3mi), **other:** Walmart SuperCtr/gas/24hr (3mi)
47	US 371 S, LA 159 N, Minden, **N gas:** Chevron/dsl, Citgo/dsl, Mobil/dsl, **food:** Golden Biscuit, **lodging:** Best Western, Exacta Inn/rest., Holiday Inn Express, Southern Inn, **other:** H, **S** B&B, to Lake Bistineau SP, camping
44	US 371 N, Cotton Valley, **N gas:** Chevron, Exxon/Huddle House/dsl, **food:** Crawfish Hole #2, Nicky's Cantina, **lodging:** Minden Motel (2mi), **other:** Family$
38	Goodwill Rd, Ammo Plant, **S gas:** BP/Rainbow Diner/dsl/24hr, **other:** Interstate RV Park
33	LA 157, Fillmore, **N gas:** Texaco, **other:** Hilltop Camping (2mi), Johnny's Rest., (6mi), **S gas:** Exxon, Pilot/Arby's/dsl/scales/24hr, **food:** Waffle House, **other:** $General, Family$, USPO, Lake Bistineau SP
26	I-220, Shreveport, **1 mi N gas:** Raceway, **other:** Casino
23	Industrial Dr, **N gas:** Exxon/Subway, Shell/Circle K, Texaco/Popeye's/24hr, **food:** Barnhill's Buffet, Burger King, McDonald's, Sue's Country Kitchen, Taco Bell, Wendy's **lodging:** Ramada Inn, **other:** O'Reilly Parts, st police, **S gas:** Chevron/dsl, Mobil/dsl, **lodging:** Econolodge, **other:** Southern RV Ctr
22	Airline Dr, **N gas:** Chevron/McDonald's/dsl, Citgo/dsl, Shell/Circle K, **food:** Applebee's, Arby's, Backyard Burger, Burger King, Chili's, ChuckeCheese, DQ, IHOP, Little Caesar's, Luby's, Pizza Hut, Popeye's, Red Lobster, Sonic, Starbucks, Taco Bell, Waffle House, **lodging:** Best Western, Crossland Suites, Rodeway Inn, Super 8, **other:** Albertson's/gas, Big Lots, Books-A-Million, CVS Drug, Dillard's, Firestone/auto, Goodyear/auto, JC Penney, K-Mart, Michael's, Office Depot, Old Navy, PepBoys, Sears/auto, Walgreens, mall, **S gas:** Exxon/dsl, Texaco/dsl/24hr, **food:** Capt John's, Church's, Darrell's Rest., Outback Steaks, Quizno's, **lodging:** Microtel, Quality Inn, Red Carpet Inn, Super 8, **other:** H, AutoZone, Super1 Foods, to Barksdale AFB
21	LA 72, to US 71 S, Old Minden Rd, **N gas:** Circle K, Exxon, Valero, **food:** Burger King, El Chico, McDonald's, Podnah's BBQ, Ralph&Kacoo's, RJ's Rest., Shoney's, Subway, Texas Roadhouse, Whataburger, **lodging:** Budgetel, Hampton Inn, Holiday Inn, La Quinta, Residence Inn, **other:** Audi/Mazda, Advance Parts, AutoZone, $General, O'Reilly Parts, VW, USPO, **S gas:** RaceWay, **food:** Waffle House, Wendy's, **lodging:** Day's Inn, Motel 6
20c	(from wb), to US 71 S, to Barksdale Blvd
20b	LA 3, Benton Rd, same as 21
20a	Hamilton Rd, Isle of Capri Blvd, **N gas:** Circle K, Texaco/24hr, **lodging:** Comfort Inn, **S gas:** Exxon, **lodging:** Best Value Inn, **other:** casino
19b	Traffic St, Shreveport, downtown, **N other:** Bass Pro Shop, Chevrolet, casino
19a	US 71 N, LA 1 N, Spring St, Shreveport, **N food:** Don's Seafood, **lodging:** Best Western, Hilton, Holiday Inn
18b-d	Fairfield Ave (from wb), downtown Shreveport, **S** H
18a	Line Ave, Common St (from eb), downtown, **S gas:** Citgo, **other:** H
17b	I-49 S, to Alexandria
17a	Lakeshore Dr, Linwood Ave
16b	US 79/80, Greenwood Rd, **N** H, **S gas:** Citgo/dsl, **food:** El Chico, **lodging:** Travelodge
16a	US 171, Hearne Ave, **N gas:** Citgo/dsl, **food:** Subway, **other:** H, **S gas:** Raceway, Texaco/dsl, **food:** KFC, **lodging:** Cajun Inn
14	Jewella Ave, Shreveport, **N gas:** Citgo/dsl, Texaco/dsl/24hr, Valero, **food:** Burger King, China Hat, Church's, McDonald's, Popeye's, Subway, Sonic, Whataburger, **other:** Advance Parts, AutoZone, County Mkt Foods, Family$, O'Reilly Parts, Rite Aid, Super 1 Foods, Walgreens
13	Monkhouse Dr, Shreveport, **N food:** Bro's Cafe, **lodging:** Best Value Inn, Day's Inn, Guesthouse Inn, Residence Inn, **S gas:** Chevron, Citgo, Exxon/Subway/dsl, **food:** Waffle House, **lodging:** Best Western, Candlewood Suites, Hampton Inn, Holiday Inn Express, Regency Inn, Super 8, **other:** to ✈
11	I-220 E, LA 3132 E, to I-49 S
10	Pines Rd, **N gas:** BP/dsl, **food:** DQ, Pizza Hut, Popeye's, Subway, **S gas:** Exxon/dsl, Shell/Quizno's, **food:** Becca's Cafe, Burger King, CiCi's Pizza, Cracker Barrel, Domino's, Dragon Chinese, Grandy's, IHOP, KFC, Nicky's Cantina, Sonic, Starbucks, Subway, Taco Bell, Waffle House, Wendy's, Whataburg

RUSTON · MINDEN · SHREVEPORT

INTERSTATE 20 CONT'D

E ↕ W

Exit #	Services
10	Continued er, **lodging:** Comfort Suites, Courtyard, Fairfield Inn, La Quinta, Hilton Garden, Holiday Inn, Jameson Inn, **other:** Chrysler/Dodge, CVS, $Tree, $General, Family$, GNC, Home Depot, KOA, Kroger, O'Reilly Parts, Radio Shack, Rite Aid, USPO, Walgreens, Walmart SuperCtr/gas/24hr
8	US 80, LA 526 E, **N lodging:** Motel 6, **other:** Freightliner, **S gas:** Chevron/dsl, Citgo/dsl, Petro/Mobil/dsl/rest./scales/@, **food:** Wendy's, **other:** Blue Beacon, Camper's RV Ctr/park
5	US 79 N, US 80, to Greenwood, **N gas:** TA/Country Fried/Subway/dsl/scales/24hr/@, Texaco/dsl, **lodging:** Country Inn, Mid Continent Motel
3	US 79 S, LA 169, Mooringsport, **S gas:** *FLYING J* /Conoco/dsl/LP/rest./scales/24hr, Love's/Arby's/dsl/scales/24hr, **food:** Sonic, **other:** SpeedCo
2mm	**Welcome Ctr eb, full handicapped facilities, phone, picnic, litter barrels, petwalk, RV dump**
1mm	**weigh sta both lanes**
0mm	Louisiana/Texas state line

INTERSTATE 49

N ↕ S

Exit #	Services
I-49 begins/ends in Shreveport on I-20, exit 17.	
206	I-20, E to Monroe, W to Dallas
205	King's Hwy, **E food:** Cane's, McDonald's, Piccadilly's, **other:** Dillard's, Sears/auto, mall, **W gas:** Valero/dsl, **food:** Burger King, LJ Silver, Subway, Taco Bell, **other:** H
203	Hollywood Ave, Pierremont Rd
202	LA 511, E 70th St, **E gas:** RaceWay, **W gas:** Circle K, **food:** SC Chicken
201	LA 3132, to Dallas, Texarkana
199	LA 526, Bert Kouns Loop, **E gas:** Chevron/Arby's/dsl/24hr, Exxon/Circle K, **food:** Burger King, KFC, Taco Bell, Wendy's, **lodging:** Comfort Inn, **other:** Home Depot, **W gas:** RaceWay, Shell/dsl, **food:** McDonald's, Sonic, Starbucks, **other:** Brookshire Foods
196	Southern Loop
196mm	Bayou Pierre
191	LA 16, LA 3276, to Stonewall
186	LA 175, to Frierson, Kingston, **W gas:** Relay Sta./Exxon/rest./casino/dsl/scales
177	LA 509, to Carmel, **E gas:** Texaco/Eagles Trkstp/casino/dsl/rest.
172	US 84, to Grand Bayou, Mansfield, **W** New Rockdale RV Prk, Civil War Site
169	Asseff Rd
162	US 371, LA 177, to Evelyn, Pleasant Hill
155	LA 174, to Ajax, Lake End, **W gas:** Spaulding/dsl, **other:** Country Livin' RV Pk
148	LA 485, Powhatan, Allen
142	LA 547, Posey Rd
138	LA 6, to Natchitoches, **E gas:** Exxon/Subway, French Mkt Express, RaceWay, **food:** Popeye's, Shoney's, Wendy's, **lodging:** Best Western, Holiday Inn Express, Super 8 (5mi), Travel Express Inn, **other:** H, Walmart SuperCtr/24hr (5mi), **W gas:** Chevron/

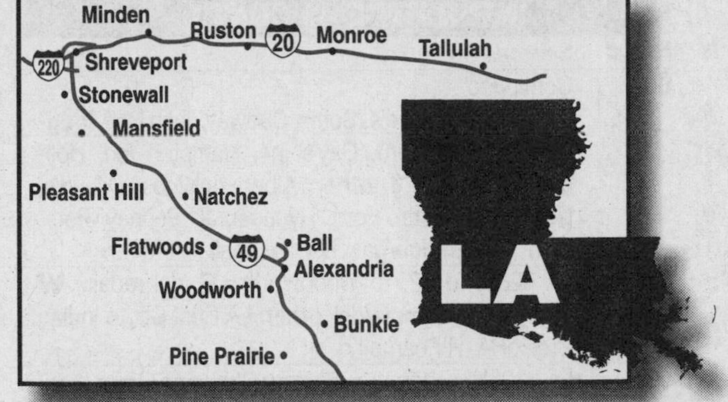

NATCHITOCHES

Exit #	Services
138	Continued dsl, Exxon, Texaco/dsl, **food:** Burger King, El Giro, Huddle House, McDonald's, **lodging:** Country Hearth Inn, Econolodge, Hampton Inn, **other:** Nakatosh RV Park, to Kisatchie NF
132	LA 478, rd 620
127	LA 120, to Cypress, Flora, **E gas:** Texaco, **other:** to Cane River Plantations
119	LA 119, to Derry, Cloutierville, **E** to Cane River Plantations
113	LA 490, to Chopin
107	to Lena, **E** USPO
103	LA 8 W, to Flatwoods, **E gas:** Shell/dsl, **other:** to Cotile Lake, RV camping
99	LA 8, LA 1200, to Boyce, Colfax, **6 mi W** Cotile Lake RV camping
98	LA 1 (from nb), to Boyce
94	rd 23, to Rapides Sta Rd, **E gas:** Rapides/dsl, **W** LA Welcome Ctr, full handicapped facilities, litter barrels, petwalk, picnic, vending, **other:** I-49 RV Ctr
90	LA 498, Air Base Rd, **W gas:** Chevron/dsl/24hr, Exxon/dsl, Mobil/dsl, Texaco/BBQ/dsl, **food:** Burger King, Cracker Barrel, McDonald's, **lodging:** La Quinta, Super 8, Travel Express Inn
86	US 71, US 165, MacArthur Dr, **0-2 mi W gas:** Chevron, Conoco/dsl, Exxon, Mobil, Shell/Circle K, Texaco, **food:** Applebee's, Arby's, Burger King, Cane's, Cajun Landing Rest., Church's, DQ, Fire Mtn Grill, Little Caesar's, Outlaw's BBQ, Popeye's, Schlotzky's, Shoney's, Sonic, Subway, Taco Bell, **lodging:** Alexandria Inn, Best Western, Comfort Inn, Days Inn, Econolodge, Guesthouse Inn, Holiday Inn Express, Motel 6, Quality Inn, Ramada Ltd, Sai Hotel, Super 8, Value Place Inn, **other:** Advance Parts, AutoZone, BigLots, Checker's, $General, Family$, Kroger, O'Reilly Parts, Rite Aid, Super 1 Foods
85b	Monroe St, Medical Ctr Dr (from nb), **E** H
85a	LA 1, 10th St, MLK Dr, downtown
84	US 167 N, LA 28, LA 1, Pineville Expswy (, no ez return nb
83	Broadway Ave, **E** gas, **1 mi W food:** Wendy's, **other:** BooksAMillion, Harley-Davidson, Lowe's Whse, Sam's Club/gas, Target, Walmart SuperCtr/24hr
81	US 71 N, LA 3250, Sugarhouse Rd, MacArthur Dr (from sb), **W** same as 80 and 83
80	US 71 S, US 167, MacArthur Dr, Alexandria, **0-3 mi W gas:** Chevron/dsl, Exxon, Mobil, Shell, **food:** Burger King, Capt D's, Carino's Italian, Chili's, KFC, Logan's Roadhouse, McDonald's, Outback Steaks,

INTERSTATE 49 CONT'D

Exit #	Services
80	Continued Pizza Hut, Popeye's, Sonic, Subway, Taco Bell, **lodging:** Best Western, Day's Inn, Hampton Inn, Holiday Inn, Super 8, **other:** Albertson's/gas, Dillard's, Dodge, $General, Ford, Hyundai, JC Penney, PetsMart, Sam's Club/gas, U-Haul, mall
73	LA 3265, rd 22, to Woodworth, **E** dsl repair, **W gas:** Exxon/Blimpie/dsl, **other:** LA Conf Ctr, to Indian Creek RA, RV camping
66	LA 112, to Lecompte, **E gas:** Chevron/Burger King/dsl, **food:** Lea's Lunch, **W gas:** Exxon/dsl, **other:** museum
61	US 167, to Meeker, Turkey Creek, **E** to Loyd Hall Plantation (3mi)
56	LA 181, Cheneyville
53	LA 115, to Bunkie, **E gas:** Sammy's/Chevron/dsl/casino/24hr
46	LA 106, to St Landry, **W** to Chicot SP
40	LA 29, to Ville Platte, **E gas:** Exxon/Cafe Mangeur/casino/dsl
35mm	**E rest area/rec area both lanes, full ♿ facilities, picnic, litter barrels, vending, petwalk, RV dump**
27	LA 10, to Lebeau
25	LA 103, to Washington, Port Barre, **W gas:** Citgo, Mobil, **other:** Family$
23	US 167 N, LA 744, to Ville Platte, **E gas:** Chevron/Subway/Stuckey's/dsl, Texaco/dsl/casino
19b a	US 190, to Opelousas, **E** Evangeline Downs Racetrack, **W gas:** Exxon/dsl, Mobil, RaceTrac/dsl, **other:** H, Lowes Whse, USPO
18	LA 31, to Cresswell Lane, **E food:** Casa Ole's, **lodging:** Holiday Inn, **other:** Chrysler/Dodge/Jeep/Isuzu, $Tree, Home Depot, Little Caesar's, Radio Shack, Walmart SuperCtr/dsl/24hr, **W gas:** Chevron/dsl/24hr, Shell, Valero, **food:** Burger King, Cresswell Lane, Domino's, Hacienda Mexican, King Buffet, McDonald's, Mr Gatti's, Pizza Hut, Popeye's, Subway, Taco Bell, Wendy's, **lodging:** Day's Inn, **other:** Buick/Cadillac/GMC/Pontiac, CVS Drug, Family$, Nissan, Piggly Wiggly, Walgreens, repair
17	Judson Walsh Dr, **E gas:** Texaco/dsl, **W other:** Goodyear/auto
15	LA 3233, Harry Guilbeau Rd, **W lodging:** Best Value Inn, **other:** H, Toyota, RV Ctr
11	LA 93, to Grand Coteau, Sunset, **E gas:** Citgo/rest./dsl/24hr, Exxon/Popeye's/dsl, **food:** Beau Chere Rest., **W food:** Subway, **other:** $General, Family$, Janise's Foods
7	LA 182, **W** Primeaux RV Ctr
4	LA 726, Carencro, **W gas:** Chevron/Popeye's/dsl, Texaco/Subway/dsl, **food:** Burger King, McDonald's, **lodging:** Economy Inn, **other:** Mack, Kenworth
2	LA 98, Gloria Switch Rd, **E gas:** Chevron/dsl/deli, **food:** Chili's, IHOP, Prejean's Rest., Wendy's, **other:** Stevens RV Ctr, Lowes Whse, **W gas:** Shell/Church's/dsl, **food:** Domino's, Picante Mexican, Subway
1b	Pont Des Mouton Rd, **E gas:** Exxon/dsl, Texaco/Subway/dsl, **food:** Burger King, **lodging:** Motel 6, Plantation Inn, **other:** st police, **W** Ford
1a	I-10, W to Lake Charles, E to Baton Rouge, US 167 **S gas:** Chevron/dsl/24hr, RaceTrac, Shell/dsl, **food:** Checker's, KFC, McDonald's, Pizza Hut, Popeye's, Shoney's, Subway, Taco Bell, Waffle House, Wendy's, **lodging:** Baymont Inn, Econolodge, Fairfield Inn, Hawthorn Suites, Holiday Inn, Howard Johnson, Jameson Inn, La Quinta, Quality Inn, Royal Inn, Super 8, TravelHost Inn, **other:** H, Albertson's/gas, CVS Drug, Home Depot, Rite Aid, Super 1 Foods/gas, Walmart SuperCtr/gas/24hr, transmissions

I-49 begins/ends on I-10, exit 103.

INTERSTATE 55

Exit #	Services
66mm	Louisiana/Mississippi state line
65mm	**Welcome Ctr sb, full ♿ facilities, tourist info, phone, picnic, litter barrels, petwalk**
64mm	**weigh sta nb**
61	LA 38, Kentwood, **E gas:** BP/dsl, Chevron/dsl, Texaco, **food:** Jam Chicken, Kentwood Seafood Rest., Popeye's, Sonic, **other:** H, AutoZone, Brown Drug, $General, Family$, Ford/Mercury, IGA Foods, Super$, **W gas:** Exxon/Subway/dsl, Kangaroo/dsl, **other:** Chevrolet, Chrysler/Jeep/Dodge
58.5mm	**weigh sta sb**
57	LA 440, Tangipahoa, **E** to Camp Moore Confederate Site
53	LA 10, to Greensburg, Fluker, **W** H
50	LA 1048, Roseland, **E gas:** Chevron/dsl/24hr
46	LA 16, Amite, **E gas:** Exxon/dsl, RaceTrac/dsl, Shell, **food:** Burger King, Domino's, Hot Wok, KFC, McDonald's, Popeye's, Sonic, Subway, Waffle House, Wendy's, **lodging:** Comfort Inn, **other:** H, AutoZone, Fred's Drugs, O'Reilly Parts, Walmart SuperCtr/dsl, Winn-Dixie, **W gas:** Amite Trkstp/rest./dsl (2mi), **food:** Ardillo's, **lodging:** Colonial Inn, **other:** Ford, RV Camping
40	LA 40, Independence, **E gas:** Conoco, **other:** H, Sweetwater Camping (7mi), **W** Indian Cr Camping (2mi)
36	LA 442, Tickfaw, **E gas:** Chevron/dsl/24hr, **other:** camping, to Global Wildlife Ctr (15mi)
32	LA 3234, Wardline Rd, **E gas:** Kangaroo/dsl, **food:** Burger King, McDonald's, Sonic, Subway, Wendy's, **lodging:** Best Western, **other:** Tony's Tire
31	US 190, Hammond, **E gas:** Chevron/dsl, Exxon/dsl, Shell/dsl/scales/24hr, **food:** Adobe's Mexican, Applebee's, Buffalo Wild Wings, Burger King, Cane's, Casa Garcia, Chili's, China One, Cici's, Cracker Barrel, KFC, McDonald's, Picadilly's, Pizza Hut, Quizno's, Sonic, Subway, Taco Bell, Waffle House, Wendy's, **lodging:** Comfort Inn, Hampton Inn, Super 8, The Inn, **other:** H, Advance Parts, Albertson's, AutoZone, Big Lots, BooksAMillion, Chrysler/Jeep/Buick/Dodge, CVS Drug, $General, $Tree, Family$, Lowe's Whse, Office Depot, Radio Shack, Sav-A-Lot Foods, Tuesday Morning, Walgreens/24hr, Walmart SuperCtr/gas, Winn-Dixie, transmissions/repair
29b a	I-12, W to Baton Rouge, E to Slidell
28	US 51 N, Hammond, **E gas:** Exxon, RaceTrac, **food:** Don's Seafood Rest., **lodging:** Landmark Inn/park, Quality Inn, Rockwood Inn, **other:** H, Mitchell RV Ctr, Toyota/Scion, dsl repair

N S CARENCRO AMITE HAMMOND LA

INTERSTATE 55 CONT'D

N ↕ S

Exit #	Services
26	LA 22, to Springfield, Ponchatoula, **E gas:** Chevron/dsl, Exxon/dsl, Shell, **food:** Burger King, China King, KFC, McDonald's/playplace, Popeye's, Sonic, Subway, Waffle House, Wendy's, **lodging:** Microtel, **other:** AutoZone, Curves, CVS Drug, $General, Family$, Ford, O'Reilly Parts, Walgreens, Winn-Dixie, **W gas:** Exxon/Domino's/dsl, **other:** Tickfaw SP
23	US 51, Ponchatoula
22	frontage rd (from sb)
15	Manchac, **E food:** Middendorf Café, **other:** [phone], swamp tours
7	Ruddock
1	US 51, to I-10, Baton Rouge, La Place, **S gas:** Circle K/dsl, Pilot/Subway/dsl/24hr/scales/@, Shell/dsl, **food:** Bully's Seafood, McDonald's, Shoney's, Waffle House, Wendy's, **lodging:** Best Western, Day's Inn, Hampton Inn, Quality Inn

I-55 begins/ends on I-10, exit 209.

INTERSTATE 59

N ↕ S

Exit #	Services
11	Pearl River Turnaround. Callboxes begin sb.
5b	Honey Island Swamp
5a	LA 41, Pearl River, **E gas:** Chevron/gifts
3	US 11 S, LA 1090, Pearl River, **W gas:** Shell/Subway/dsl, **1 mi W** Chevron/dsl/24hr, **food:** D&K Rest.
1.5mm	**Welcome Ctr sb, full [handicapped] facilities, info, [phone], [picnic], litter barrels, petwalk, RV dump**
1c b	I-10, E to Bay St Louis, W to New Orleans
1a	I-12 W, to Hammond. I-59 begins/ends on I-10/I-12.

INTERSTATE 220 (SHREVEPORT)

E ↕ W — SHREVEPORT

Exit #	Services
	I-220 begins/ends on I-20, exit 26.
17b	I-20, W to Shreveport, E to Monroe
17a	US 79, US 80, **N gas:** RaceWay, Shell/Circle K, **food:** Waffle House, **lodging:** SpringHill Suites, **other:** LA Downs Racetrack/casino, **S gas:** Chevron/Huddle House/dsl, **food:** 1 Eyed Jack's
15	Shed Rd
13	Swan Lake Rd
12	LA 3105, Airline Dr, **N gas:** Shell/Circle K, **food:** Chick-fil-A, Domino's, McAlister's Deli, Quizno's, Starbucks, Subway, **other:** [H], Belk, Best Buy, PetsMart, Ross, Target, Walgreens, **S gas:** Exxon/dsl, Shell/Circle K/Subway, Valero/dsl, **food:** Applebee's, Burger King, Capt D's, CiCi's, McDonald's, Moe's SW Grill, Nicky's Rest., Ruby Tuesday, Ryan's, Sonic, Taco Bell, Trejo's Mexican, Wendy's, **lodging:** Best Western, **other:** $Tree, Home Depot, Lowes Whse, Radio Shack, Walmart SuperCtr/gas/24hr
11	LA 3, Bossier City, **N other:** [H], Buick/GMC/Pontiac, Ford, Lexus/Toyota, Maplewood RV Park (3mi), Suzuki, **S gas:** Chevron/dsl/24hr, **other:** Chrysler/Dodge/Jeep, Nissan
7b a	US 71, LA 1, Shreveport, **N gas:** Citgo, Exxon/dsl, **food:** Domino's, Sonic, Subway, Whataburger/24hr, **other:** Brookshire Foods/gas, Curves, $General, Walgreens, **S gas:** Chevron/24hr, RaceWay, Texaco/dsl/24hr, **food:** Burger King, Church's, KFC, McDonald's, Podnuh's BBQ, Popeye's, Sammy's Rest.,

Minden
Shreveport
Monroe
Bawcomville
Stonewall
Mansfield
Coushatta
Pleasant Hill
Natchitoches
Provencal
Colfax
Flatwoods
Alexandria
Woodworth
Lecompte
LA
Pine Prairie
Opelousas
Baton Rouge
Lake Charles
Lafayette
20
220
49
10
12

Exit #	Services
7b a	Continued Taco Bell, Wendy's, **other:** Advance Parts, AutoZone, CVS Drug, Family$, O'Reilly Parts, Radio Shack, Rite Aid, repair/transmissions
5	LA 173, Blanchard Rd, **S gas:** Citgo
2	Lakeshore Dr
1a	Jefferson Paige Rd, **S lodging:** Best Value Inn, Best Western, Day's Inn, Residence Inn, Super 8
1b c	**I-20, E to Shreveport, W to Dallas. I-220 begins/ends on I-20, exit 11.**

INTERSTATE 610 (NEW ORLEANS)

E ↕ W

Exit #	Services
	I-610 begins/ends on I-10
4	Franklin Ave (from eb)
3	Elysian fields, **N** [H], **S gas:** B Express, Shell, **food:** Burger King, McDonald's, **other:** Lowe's Whse
2b	US 90, N Broad St, New Orleans St (from wb)
2c	Paris Ave (from wb, no return), **S gas:** Shell/24hr, Spur, **food:** Popeye's
2a	St Bernard Ave (from eb), to LSU School of Dentistry, auto racetrack
1a	Canal Blvd
1b	I-10, to New Orleans
	I-610 begins/ends on I-10

MAINE

INTERSTATE 95

N ↕ S — HOULTON

Exit #	Services
305mm	US/Canada border, Maine state line, US Customs. I-95 begins/ends., US Customs
305	US 2, to Houlton, **E other:** Houlton [airport], DFA Duty Free Shop
303mm	Meduxnekeag River
302	US 1, Houlton, **E gas:** Irving/dsl/24hr, **food:** Burger King, KFC, McDonald's, Pizza Hut, Tang's Chinese, **other:** [H], IGA Foods, Rite Aid, **W rest area both lanes, full [handicapped] facilities, [phone], [picnic], litter barrels, petwalk, gas:** Citgo/Subway/dsl, Exxon/dsl/LP, Irving/dsl/scales/@, **food:** Tim Horton, York's DairyBar, **lodging:** Ivey's Motel, Shiretown Motel/rest., **other:** Chevrolet/Pontiac/Buick, Family$, Ford/Lincoln/Mercury, Shop'n Save, Walmart
301mm	B Stream
291	US 2, to Smyrna, **E lodging:** Brookside Motel/rest.
286	Oakfield Rd, to ME 11, Eagle Lake, Ashland, **W gas:** Irving/dsl, Valero/dsl, **food:** A Place To Eat, **other:** UPSO
277mm	Mattawamkeag River, W Branch

LA
ME

N ↕ S

INTERSTATE 95 CONT'D

Exit #	Services
276	ME 159, Island Falls, **E gas:** Porter's/rest., Dysarts Fuel, **other:** Bishop's Mkt, **W** to Baxter SP (N entrance), RV camping
264	to ME 11, Sherman, **E gas:** Shell/dsl/LP/rest., **W gas:** Irving/dsl, **lodging:** Katahdin Valley Motel, **other:** to Baxter SP (N entrance)
259	Benedicta (from nb, no re-entry)
252mm	scenic view Mt Katahdin, nb
247mm	Salmon Stream
244	ME 157, to Medway, E Millinocket, **W gas:** Irving/dsl, **lodging:** Gateway Inn, **other:** H, Pine Grove Camping (4mi), USPO, Vet, to Baxter SP (S entrance), city park
244mm	Penobscot River
243mm	**rest area both lanes, full ♿ facilities, ☎, ⛺, litter barrels, petwalk**
227	to US 2, ME 6, Lincoln, **4 mi E** H, gas, food, lodging, RV camping
219mm	Piscataquis River
217	ME 6, Howland, **E gas:** Irving/95 Diner/dsl, **food:** Jim & Jill's Grill, **other:** 95er Towing/repair, LP, camping
201mm	Birch Stream
199	ME 16 (no nb re-entry), to LaGrange
199mm	**weigh sta both lanes**
197	ME 43, to Old Town, **E** gas/dsl
196mm	Pushaw Stream
193	Stillwater Ave, to Old Town, **E gas:** Citgo/dsl, Irving/dsl, Mobil/dsl, **food:** Burger King, Dunkin Donuts, Governor's Rest., McDonald's/playplace, Subway, Wendy's, **lodging:** Best Western, **other:** $Tree, IGA Foods, mall
191	Kelly Rd, to Orono, **2-3 mi E** gas, food, lodging, camping
187	Hogan Rd, Bangor Mall Blvd, to Bangor, **E gas:** Citgo, **food:** Denny's, **lodging:** Courtyard, Hilton Garden, **other:** H, Audi/VW, Chevrolet/Cadillac, Chrysler/Dodge, Firestone/auto, Ford, GMC/Isuzu, Honda/Nissan/Volvo, Jeep, Mitsubishi/Hyundai/Mercedes/Saab/Subaru, Sam's Club/gas, **W gas:** Citgo/dsl, Exxon/dsl, **food:** Applebee's, Arby's, Bugaboo Creek Café, Burger King, Chicago Grill, Chili's, China Wall, Happy China, House of Pizza, KFC, McDonald's, Miguel's Mexican, 99 Rest., Olive Garden, Oriental Buffet, Pizza Hut, Starbucks, Subway, TX Roadhouse, **lodging:** Bangor Motel, Comfort Inn, Country Inn, Hampton Inn, **other:** Advance Parts, Best Buy, Borders Books, $Tree, Goodyear/auto, Harley-Davidson, Hannaford Foods, Home Depot, JC Penney, Jo-Ann Fabrics, K-Mart, Kohl's, Lincoln/Mercury/Kia, LL Bean, Macy's, Mr. Quick's Lube, Office Depot, Old Navy, PetCo, Sears/auto, Shaw's Foods, Staples, Target, VIP Parts, Walmart, mall
186	Stillwater Ave, same as 187
185	ME 15, to Broadway, Bangor, **E gas:** Irving, **food:** Tri-City Pizza, **other:** H, **W gas:** Exxon, Mobil, **food:** Amato's, BoBo Chinese, China Light, DQ, Governor's Rest., KFC, McDonald's, Pizza Hut, Starbucks, Subway, Tim Horton, **other:** Hannaford Foods, Rite Aid, TJ Maxx, Walgreens
184	ME 222, Union St, to Ohio St, Bangor, **E gas:** Citgo, Exxon, **other:** Rite Aid, **W gas:** Exxon, Gulf, Mobil/dsl, **food:** Burger King, Capt Nick's Rest., Dunkin Donuts, McDonald's, Nicky's Rest., Quizno's, Wendy's, **lodging:** Sheraton, **other:** Hannaford Foods, Marshall's, Staples
183	US 2, ME 2, Hammond St, Bangor, **E gas:** Exxon, **food:** Papa Gambino's Pizza, **other:** Corner Store, NAPA, TrueValue, **W** ✈
182b	US 2, ME 100 W, **W gas:** Irving/Subway/dsl, Mobil/dsl, **food:** Dunkin Donuts, Ground Round, **lodging:** Day's Inn, Econolodge, Fairfield Inn, Holiday Inn, Howard Johnson, Motel 6, Ramada Inn, Super 8, Travelodge, **other:** RV camping, VIP Parts/service
182a	I-395, to US 2, US 1A, Bangor, downtown
180	Cold Brook Rd, to Hampden, **E** Citgo, **W gas:** Citgo/dsl/24hr/@, **lodging:** Best Western, **other:** dsl repair
178mm	**rest area sb, full ♿ facilities, info, ☎, vending, ⛺, litter barrels, petwalk**
177mm	Soudabscook Stream
176mm	**rest area nb, full ♿ facilities, info, ☎, vending, ⛺, litter barrels, petwalk**
174	ME 69, to Carmel, **E gas:** Citgo/dsl, **W** RV camping
167	ME 69, ME 143, to Etna
161	ME 7, to E Newport, Plymouth, **E** LP, **W** RV camping
159	Ridge Rd (from sb), to Plymouth, Newport
157	to US 2, ME 7, ME 11, Newport, **E** H, **W gas:** Irving/dsl/24hr, Mobil/dsl, **food:** Burger King, China Way, Dunkin Donuts, McDonald's, Pando Italian, Pizza House, Quizno's, Sawyers Dairybar, Subway, Tim Horton, **lodging:** Lovley's Motel, **other:** Auto Value Parts, CarQuest, Chrysler/Jeep, GMC, NAPA, Radio Shack, Rite Aid, Shop'n Save, Walmart SuperCtr
151mm	Sebasticook River
150	Somerset Ave, Pittsfield, **E gas:** Mobil, **food:** Subway, **lodging:** Pittsfield Motel, **other:** H, CarQuest, Chevrolet, Family$, Rite Aid, Shop'n Save Foods
147mm	**rest area both lanes, full ♿ facilities, ☎, ⛺, litter barrels, petwalk**
138	Hinckley Rd, Clinton, **W gas:** ME Country Store/dsl
134mm	Kennebec River
133	US 201, Fairfield, **E food:** Purple Cow Pancakes
132	ME 139, Fairfield, **E gas:** Gene's/deli, **W gas:** Irving/Subway/dsl/scales/24hr/@
130	ME 104, Main St, Waterville, **E gas:** Mobil, **food:** Arby's, Friendly's, Governor's Rest., McDonald's, Ruby Tuesday, Starbucks, Subway, Tim Horton, Wendy's, **lodging:** Best Western, Comfort Inn, Holiday Inn, **other:** H, Advance Parts, Audi/VW, Hannaford Foods, Home Depot, JC Penney, K-Mart, Mazda, Mr Paperback, Radio Shack, Staples, VIP Parts/service, Walmart SuperCtr/24hr
129mm	Messalonskee Stream
127	ME 11, ME 137, Waterville, Oakland, **E gas:** Citgo/Burger King, Irving/dsl/24hr, Mobil, Xpress Stop, **food:** Applebee's, DQ, Dunkin Donuts, Grand Asian Buffet, McDonald's, Papa John's, Pizza Hut, Quizno's, Subway, Weathervane Seafood, **lodging:** Budget Host, Econolodge, Hampton Inn, **other:** H, Buick/Chevrolet/Pontiac, Chrysler/Dodge/Jeep, Marden's, Shaw's Foods/Osco Drug, Toyota/Scion, **W gas:**

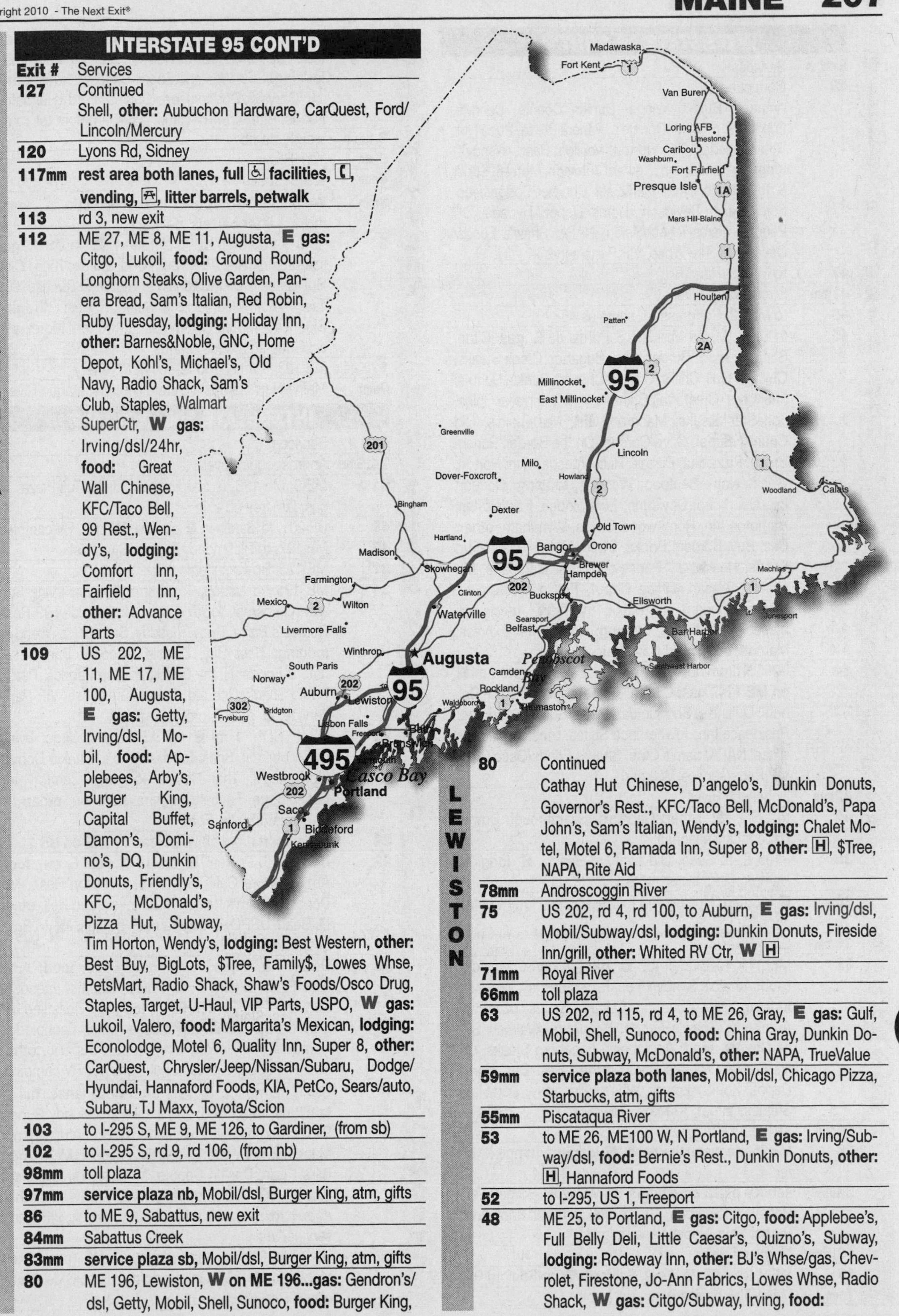

N ↕ S

INTERSTATE 95 CONT'D

Exit #	Services
127	Continued Shell, **other:** Aubuchon Hardware, CarQuest, Ford/Lincoln/Mercury
120	Lyons Rd, Sidney
117mm	**rest area both lanes, full ♿ facilities, ☎, vending, 🅿, litter barrels, petwalk**
113	rd 3, new exit
112	ME 27, ME 8, ME 11, Augusta, **E gas:** Citgo, Lukoil, **food:** Ground Round, Longhorn Steaks, Olive Garden, Panera Bread, Sam's Italian, Red Robin, Ruby Tuesday, **lodging:** Holiday Inn, **other:** Barnes&Noble, GNC, Home Depot, Kohl's, Michael's, Old Navy, Radio Shack, Sam's Club, Staples, Walmart SuperCtr, **W gas:** Irving/dsl/24hr, **food:** Great Wall Chinese, KFC/Taco Bell, 99 Rest., Wendy's, **lodging:** Comfort Inn, Fairfield Inn, **other:** Advance Parts
109	US 202, ME 11, ME 17, ME 100, Augusta, **E gas:** Getty, Irving/dsl, Mobil, **food:** Applebees, Arby's, Burger King, Capital Buffet, Damon's, Domino's, DQ, Dunkin Donuts, Friendly's, KFC, McDonald's, Pizza Hut, Subway, Tim Horton, Wendy's, **lodging:** Best Western, **other:** Best Buy, BigLots, $Tree, Family$, Lowes Whse, PetsMart, Radio Shack, Shaw's Foods/Osco Drug, Staples, Target, U-Haul, VIP Parts, USPO, **W gas:** Lukoil, Valero, **food:** Margarita's Mexican, **lodging:** Econolodge, Motel 6, Quality Inn, Super 8, **other:** CarQuest, Chrysler/Jeep/Nissan/Subaru, Dodge/Hyundai, Hannaford Foods, KIA, PetCo, Sears/auto, Subaru, TJ Maxx, Toyota/Scion
103	to I-295 S, ME 9, ME 126, to Gardiner, (from sb)
102	to I-295 S, rd 9, rd 106, (from nb)
98mm	toll plaza
97mm	**service plaza nb,** Mobil/dsl, Burger King, atm, gifts
86	to ME 9, Sabattus, new exit
84mm	Sabattus Creek
83mm	**service plaza sb,** Mobil/dsl, Burger King, atm, gifts
80	ME 196, Lewiston, **W on ME 196...gas:** Gendron's/dsl, Getty, Mobil, Shell, Sunoco, **food:** Burger King,

AUGUSTA

LEWISTON

Exit #	Services
80	Continued Cathay Hut Chinese, D'angelo's, Dunkin Donuts, Governor's Rest., KFC/Taco Bell, McDonald's, Papa John's, Sam's Italian, Wendy's, **lodging:** Chalet Motel, Motel 6, Ramada Inn, Super 8, **other:** H, $Tree, NAPA, Rite Aid
78mm	Androscoggin River
75	US 202, rd 4, rd 100, to Auburn, **E gas:** Irving/dsl, Mobil/Subway/dsl, **lodging:** Dunkin Donuts, Fireside Inn/grill, **other:** Whited RV Ctr, **W** H
71mm	Royal River
66mm	toll plaza
63	US 202, rd 115, rd 4, to ME 26, Gray, **E gas:** Gulf, Mobil, Shell, Sunoco, **food:** China Gray, Dunkin Donuts, Subway, McDonald's, **other:** NAPA, TrueValue
59mm	**service plaza both lanes,** Mobil/dsl, Chicago Pizza, Starbucks, atm, gifts
55mm	Piscataqua River
53	to ME 26, ME100 W, N Portland, **E gas:** Irving/Subway/dsl, **food:** Bernie's Rest., Dunkin Donuts, **other:** H, Hannaford Foods
52	to I-295, US 1, Freeport
48	ME 25, to Portland, **E gas:** Citgo, **food:** Applebee's, Full Belly Deli, Little Caesar's, Quizno's, Subway, **lodging:** Rodeway Inn, **other:** BJ's Whse/gas, Chevrolet, Firestone, Jo-Ann Fabrics, Lowes Whse, Radio Shack, **W gas:** Citgo/Subway, Irving, **food:**

INTERSTATE 95 CONT'D

N ↕ S

Exit #	Services
48	Continued Amato's, Buffalo Wings, Dunkin Donuts, Denny's, Friendly's, KFC, McDonald's, Panera Bread, Pizza Hut, Ruby Tuesday, Tim Horton, Verillo's Rest., Wendy's, **lodging:** Holiday Inn, Howard Johnson, Motel 6, Super 8, Travelodge, **other:** CarQuest, Chrysler/Dodge/Jeep, Ford, Harley-Davidson, Home Depot, Hyundai, JC Penney, Lexus/Toyota/Scion, NAPA, Shaw's Foods/Osco Drug, Tire Whse, VIP Parts/service
47	to ME 25, Rand Rd
47mm	Stroudwater River
46	to ME 22, Congress St, same as 45
45	to US 1, Maine Mall Rd, S Portland, **E gas:** Citgo, Sunoco, **food:** Burger King, Bugaboo Creek Steaks, Chicago Grill, Chili's, ChuckeCheese, Dunkin Donuts, Friendly's, Great Wall Chinese, IHOP, Imperial China, LoneStar Steaks, Macaroni Grill, McDonald's, Old Country Buffet, Olive Garden, On the Border, Panera Bread, Pizza Hut, Pizza+, Ruby Tuesday, Tim Horton, Weathervane Seafood, Wendy's, **lodging:** Comfort Inn, Courtyard, Day's Inn, Econolodge, Fairfield Inn, Hampton Inn, Homewood Suites, Wyndham, **other:** Best Buy, Borders Books, $Tree, Macy's, Hannaford Foods, Honda, JC Penney, Macy's, Marshall's, Michael's, Nissan, Office Depot, PetCo, Sears/auto, Staples, Subaru, TJ Maxx, mall, **W food:** Applebee's, Starbucks, **lodging:** Holiday Inn Express, Marriott, **other:** Old Navy, Target
44	I-295 N (from nb), to S Portland, Scarborough, **1 mi E on ME 114...gas:** Citgo/Domino's, **food:** Dunkin Donuts, Quizno's, Shogun Japanese, Subway, **lodging:** Residence Inn, TownePlace Suites, **other:** [H] Lowes Whse, NAPA, Sam's Club, Shaw's Foods/Osco Drug, VIP Parts/service, Walmart
42mm	Nonesuch River
42	to US 1, **E other:** Cabela's, Scarborough Downs Racetrack (seasonal)
36	I-195 E, to Saco, Old Orchard Beach, **E lodging:** Hampton Inn, **other:** KOA
35mm	**E lodging:** Holiday Inn Express/Saco Hotel Conference Ctr
33mm	Saco River
32	ME 111, to Biddeford, **E gas:** Irving/Subway/dsl, **food:** Amato's Sandwiches, Ruby Tuesday, Wendy's, **lodging:** Best Value Inn, Comfort Suites, **other:** [H] AutoZone, Shaw's Foods, VIP Parts, Walmart SuperCtr, **W food:** Applebees, Longhorn Steaks, Olive Garden, Panera Bread, **other:** Best Buy, Home Depot, Kohl's, Lowes Whse, Old Navy, PetsMart, Staples, Target, TJ Maxx, Townfair Tire
25mm	Kennebunk River
25	ME 35, Kennebunk Beach, **E lodging:** Turnpike Motel
24mm	**service plaza both lanes,** sb Mobil/dsl, Burger King, Popeye's, Sbarro's, Starbucks, gifts, nb Mobil/dsl, Burger King, Popeye's, atm, gifts
19.5mm	Merriland River
19	ME 9, ME 109, to Wells, Sanford, **W** to Sanford RA
7mm	Maine Tpk begins/ends, toll booth
7	ME 91, to US 1, The Yorks, **E gas:** Gulf, Irving/dsl, Mobil/dsl, Shell, **food:** Ruby's Pizza, Wildcat Pizza, **lodging:** Best Western, Econolodge, Microtel, **other:** [H], Chrysler/Dodge/Jeep, Curves, Ford, Hannaford Foods, Rite Aid, TrueValue, last exit before toll rd nb
5.5mm	**weigh sta nb**
5mm	York River
4mm	**weigh sta sb**
3mm	**Welcome Ctr nb, full [handicapped] facilities, info, [phone], vending, [picnic], litter barrels, petwalk**
2	(2 & 3 from nb), US 1, to Kittery, **E on US 1...gas:** Irving/dsl/scales, 7-11/dsl, **food:** Burger King, Clam Hut Diner, DQ, McDonald's, Subway, Sunrise Grill, Tasty Thai, Weathervane Seafood Rest., **lodging:** Blue Roof Motel, Coachman Inn, Kittery Motel, **other:** Outlets/Famous Brands
1	ME 103 (from nb, no re-entry), to Kittery
0mm	Maine/New Hampshire state line, Piscataqua River

PORTLAND · BIDDEFORD · KITTERY

INTERSTATE 295 (PORTLAND)

N ↕ S

Exit #	Services
74.5mm	Androscoggin River
51	ME 9, ME 126, to Gardiner, Litchfield, Toll Plaza, **W** gas, last free nb exit
49	US 201, to Gardiner, **E** gas/dsl, **W** gas, RV camping
43	ME 197, to Richmond, **E gas:** Citgo/dsl
37	ME 125, Bowdoinham
31	ME 196, to Lisbon, Topsham, **E gas:** Irving/Subway, Gibbs/dsl, **food:** Arby's, McDonald's, 99 Rest., Romeo's Pizza, Ruby Tuesday, Starbuck's, Wendy's, **lodging:** Best Buy, Double Discount Parts, Hannaford Foods, Home Depot, Jo-Ann Fabrics, PetCo, Radio Shack, Rite Aid, Target, Tire Whse, VIP Parts/service, **E gas:** Express Stop
28	US 1, Bath, **1 mi E on US 1...gas:** Citgo, Irving/dsl, Mobil/dsl, Shell, **food:** Amato's, Dunkin Donuts, McDonald's, Thai House, **lodging:** Comfort Inn, Econolodge, Fairfield Inn, Travelers Inn, **other:** [H], Chevrolet/Mazda, Ford
24	to Freeport (from nb), **services 1 mi E on US 1**
22	ME 125, to Pownal, **E on US 1...gas:** Exxon, **food:** Arby's, Azure Cafe, Friendly's, Jameson Rest., McDonald's, Sam's Italian, Starbucks, Taco Bell, **other:** LL Bean, USPO, outlets/famous brands, **W** to Bradbury Mtn SP
20	Desert Rd, Freeport, **E gas:** Citgo, **food:** Antonia's Pizza, Buck's BBQ, Dunkin Donuts, Friendly's, Subway, Thai Garden Rest., **lodging:** Coastline Inn, Comfort Inn, Dutch Lighthouse Motel, Econolodge, Hampton Inn, Holiday Inn Express, Super 8, **other:** Shaw's Foods, outlets/famous brands, RV camping
17	US 1, Yarmouth, **E rest area both lanes, full [handicapped] facilities, info, food:** Day's Takeout, Muddy Rudder Rest., **lodging:** Best Western, **other:** Ford, Delorme Mapping, **W gas:** Citgo/dsl, Clipper Mart, **food:** Bill's Pizza, Dunkin Donuts, McDonald's, Old World Pizza, Pat's Pizza, **lodging:** Casco Bay Inn, **other:** Ace Hardware, Hannaford Foods, NAPA, VIP Parts/service, Vet
15	US 1, to Cumberland, Yarmouth, **W gas:** Exxon, Mobil, **food:** 233 Grill, **lodging:** Brookside Motel, **other:** Rite Aid

BATH · YARMOUTH

ME

INTERSTATE 295 CONT'D (PORTLAND)

N ↕ S — PORTLAND

Exit #	Services
11	to I-95, ME Tpk
I-295 begins/ends on I-95, exit 103.	
10	US 1, to Falmouth, **E gas:** Exxon/dsl, Gulf/dsl, **food:** Dunkin Donuts, Finches Rest., McDonald's, Yummy Pizza, Subway, **other:** Audi/VW, Mazda, Radio Shack, Rite Aid, Saab, Shaw's Foods, Walmart
9mm	Presumpscot River
9	US 1 S, ME 26, to Baxter Blvd
8	ME 26 S, Washington Ave, **E other:** U-Haul
7	US 1A, Franklin St, **E other:** AAA, CarQuest, NAPA
6b a	US 1, Forest Ave, **E gas:** Mobil, **other:** H, Firestone/auto, USPO, **W food:** Arby's, Burger King, Leonardo's Pizza, Pizza Hut, Stavro's Pizza, Subway, **other:** CVS Drug, Hannaford Foods
5b a	ME 22, Congress St, **E food:** Amato Cafe, Denny's, D'Angelo Sandwiches, McDonald's, Subway, **lodging:** La Quinta, **other:** H, Sullivan Tire, **W gas:** Citgo/Dunkin Donuts, Mobil/dsl, **food:** Ananias Italian, **lodging:** Clarion
3mm	Fore River
4	US 1 S, to Main St, to S Portland, US 1 S, **E** services on US 1
3	ME 9, to Westbrook St, no sb return, **W gas:** Irving/dsl, Mobil/dsl, **food:** Costa Vida Mexican, Eggspectation, Olive Garden, Outback Steaks, Ricetta's Pizza, Subway, Wild Willy's Burger, **other:** Chevrolet, Home Depot
2	to US 1 S, S Portland, **services E on US 1...gas:** Irving/dsl, Mobil, 7-11/gas, **food:** Dunkin Donuts, Governor's Rest., Mexico Lindo, Tony Roma's, Yankee Grill, **lodging:** Best Western, Howard Johnson, Knight's Inn, Quality Inn, **other:** Discount Tire
1	to I-95, to US 1, multiple services E on US 1, same as 2
I-295 begins/ends on I-95, exit 44.	

Howland, Bradford, 95, Newport, Bangor, Norridgewock, Waterville, Winthrop, Augusta, Lewiston, 95, 295, Brunswick, Standish, Portland, Alfred, Biddeford, 95, York Beach, ME

MARYLAND

INTERSTATE 68

E ↕ W

Exit #	Services
82c	I-70 W, to Breezewood. **I-68 begins/ends on I-70, exit 1.**
82b	I-70 E, US 40 E, to Hagerstown
82a	US 522, Hancock, **N** Chevrolet, Chrysler/Dodge/Jeep, **S gas:** Sheetz/24hr, **food:** Hardee's, Pizza Hut, Park'n Dine, Subway, Weaver's Rest., **lodging:** Best Value Inn, Super 8, **other:** $General, Happy Hills Camping, Sav-a-Lot Foods
77	US 40, MD 144, Woodmont Rd, **S** RV camping
75mm	runaway truck ramp eb
74mm	**Sideling Hill rest area/exhibit both lanes, full ♿ facilities, vending, 1269 ft**
74	US 40, Mountain Rd (no return from eb)
73mm	Sideling Hill Creek
72mm	truck ramp wb
72	US 40, High Germany Rd, Swain Rd, **S gas:** BP/dsl
68	Orleans Rd, **N gas:** Exxon/dsl
67mm	Town Hill, Town Hill, elevation 940 ft
64	MV Smith Rd, **S** to Green Ridge SF HQ, scenic overlook, ☎, 1040 ft
62	US 40, 15 Mile Creek Rd, **N** Billmeyer Wildlife Mgt Area
58.7mm	Polish Mtn, elevation 1246 ft
57mm	Town Creek
56mm	Flintstone Creek
56	MD 144, National Pike, Flintstone, **S gas:** Flintstone Petroleum
52	MD 144, Pleasant Valley Rd, National Pike
50	Pleasant Valley Rd, **N food:** Lakeside Grill, Signature's Grill, **lodging:** Rocky Gap Lodge/golf/rest., **other:** to Rocky Gap SP
47	US 220 N, MD 144, Dehaven Rd (from wb), Old National Pike, Bedford, same as 46
46	US 220 N, Dehaven Rd, Baltimore Pike, Naves Crossroads, **N lodging:** Cumberland Motel, **other:** Advance Parts, Foodland, Vet, **S food:** Puccini's Rest.
45	Hillcrest Dr, **S gas:** BP/dsl
45	Hillcrest Dr, **S gas:** BP/dsl
44	US 40A, Baltimore Ave, Willow Brook Rd, to Allegany Comm Coll, to Allegany Comm Coll
43d	Maryland Ave (from eb), **N** H, USPO, **S gas:** Liberty/dsl, **food:** Chick-fil-A, Papa John's, Quizno's, Thai-Chai Quisine, **other:** AutoZone, Martin's Foods/gas
43c	(from wb), same as 43b
43b	Maryland Ave, **N food:** McDonald's, **lodging:** Holiday Inn, **S gas:** Citgo/dsl, **food:** Pizza Hut/Taco Bell, Roy Rogers, Wendy's, **other:** AutoZone
43a	to WV 28A, Beall St, Industrial Blvd, to Cumberland, **N gas:** Sheetz
42	42 US 220 S, Greene St, Ridgedale
41	Seton Dr (from wb)
41mm	Haystack Mtn, elev 1240 ft
40	US 220 S, to US 40A, Vocke Rd, La Vale, **N gas:** BP/dsl, Exxon/repair, Sunoco, **food:** Arby's, Asian Garden, Bob Evans, Burger King, D'Atri Rest., DQ, Denny's, Gehaufe's Rest., KFC, LJ Silver, McDonald's, Pizza Hut, Ruby Tuesday, Subway, Texas Grill, Wendy's, **lodging:** Comfort Inn, Slumberland Motel, Super 8, **other:** H, Advance Parts, CVS Drug, $General, Ford, Harley-Davidson, Jo-Ann Fabrics, Lowes Whse, Mr Tire, Staples, st police, **S food:** Applebees, Dragon China Buffet, CiCi's Pizza, LaVale Diner, Ponderosa, **lodging:** Red Roof Inn, **other:** BonTon, $Tree, JC Penney, Kohl's, Martin's Foods/gas, Sears/auto, Walmart SuperCtr, mall

INTERSTATE 68 CONT'D

E ↕ W

Exit #	Services
39	US 40A (from wb), same as 40
34	MD 36, to Westernport, Frostburg, **N gas:** BP, Sheetz, **food:** Burger King, Fox's Pizza, McDonald's, Peking House, Pizza Hut, Subway, Taco Del Mar, **lodging:** Day's Inn, Hampton Inn, **other:** H, CarQuest, $General, Family$, Food Lion, Rite Aid, **S** to Dans Mtn SP
33	Midlothian Rd, to Frostburg, **N** H, **S** to Dans Mt SP
31mm	**weigh sta eb**
30mm	Big Savage Mtn, elevation 2800 ft
29	MD 546, Finzel, **N food:** Hen House Rest., **other:** Mason-Dixon Camping (4mi/seasonal), **S** Savage River Lodge Rest.
25.8mm	eastern continental divide, elevation 2610 ft
24	Lower New Germany Rd, to US 40A, **S** to New Germany SP, to Savage River SF
23mm	Meadow Mtn, elevation 2780 ft
22	US 219 N, to Meyersdale, **N gas:** BP/dsl/24hr, Pilot/Arby's/dsl/scales/24hr, **food:** Burger King, Penn Alps Rest., Subway, **lodging:** Elliott House Inn, **other:** $Discount, $General, Foodland, TrueValue Hardware, Hilltop Fruit Mkt, NAPA, Rite Aid, **S gas:** BP/dsl, **lodging:** Comfort Inn, **other:** New Germany SP, Savage River SF
20mm	Casselman River
19	MD 495, to US 40A, Grantsville, **N gas:** Exxon/dsl, Sunoco/dsl, **food:** Parkside Grill, **lodging:** Casselman Motel/rest., **other:** Beachy's Drug, CarQuest, Chevrolet, USPO
15mm	Mt Negro, elevation 2740 ft
14mm	Keyser's Ridge, elevation 2880 ft
14b a	US 219, US 40 W, Oakland, **N gas:** Citgo/dsl, BP/Ridge/dsl/rest., **food:** McDonald's, repair
6mm	**Welcome Ctr eb, full ♿ facilities, info, ☎, picnic, litter barrels, vending, petwalk**
4.5mm	Bear Creek
4mm	Youghiogheny River
4	MD 42, Friendsville, **N gas:** BP/dsl, Citgo/dsl, **food:** Jubilee Junction Rest., Old Mill Rest., **lodging:** Yough Valley Motel, **other:** S&S Mkt, USPO, **S lodging:** Sunset Inn, **other:** to Deep Creek Lake SP, camping
0mm	Maryland/West Virginia state line

INTERSTATE 70

E ↕ W

Exit #	Services
	I-70 begins/ends in Baltimore at Cooks Lane.
94	Security Blvd N, **S gas:** Shell
91b a	I-695, **N off exit 17...gas:** Exxon, Sunoco, **food:** Burger King, 5 Guys Burgers, McDonald's, Panera Bread, Popeye's, Quizno's, **lodging:** Best Western, **other:** Best Buy, Ford, Macy's, Old Navy, Sears/auto, SuperFresh Foods, mall, **S gas:** BP/repair, Shell, **food:** Dunkin Donuts, Subway, Wendy's, **lodging:** Day's Inn, Motel 6, Quality Inn, **other:** Chevrolet, Mitsubishi, Nissan,
87b a	US 29 (exits left from wb)to MD 99, Columbia, **2 mi S on US 40...gas:** BP/dsl, Shell, Sunoco, Texaco, **food:** Boston Mkt, Burger King, Checker's, Crab Shanty, Domino's, Dunkin Donuts, Jerry's Subs, McDonald's, Oriental Rest., Papa John's, Qdoba Mexican, Quiz
87b a	Continued no's, Subway, **other:** Acura/Infiniti, Advance Parts, Cadillac/Chevrolet, Carmax, Curves, Ford, Giant Foods, Home Depot, Honda, Mar's Foods, Mr Tire, NAPA, Nissan, Rite Aid, Safeway Foods, 7-11, SuperFresh Food, Walmart
83	US 40, Marriottsville (no EZ wb return), **2 mi S lodging:** Turf Valley Hotel/Country Club/rest.
82	US 40 E (from eb), same as 83
80	MD 32, Sykesville, **N** golf, **S gas:** Citgo, **food:** Subway
79mm	**weigh/insp sta wb,** ☎
76	MD 97, Olney, **S gas:** Citgo
73	MD 94, Woodbine, **N gas:** Shell, **food:** Baskin Robbins, China Yee, Dunkin Donuts, Harvest Chicken, McDonald's, Pizza Hut, Subway, **other:** $Tree, Food Lion, Ramblin Pines RV Park (6mi), **S gas:** BP/dsl, Citgo
68	MD 27, Mt Airy, **N gas:** BP/Blimpie/dsl/24hr, 7-11, Shell, **food:** Arby's, Burger King, China Taste, Domino's, KFC/Taco Bell, Ledo's Pizza, McDonald's, Papa John's, Pizza Hut, Subway, TCBY, **other:** Ace Hardware, Food Lion, Goodyear, Mr Tire, Radio Shack, Rite Aid, Safeway, SuperFresh Foods, Walmart/auto, Vet, **S gas:** Exxon/dsl/24hr, Shell, **food:** 4 Seasons Rest., **lodging:** Budget Inn
66mm	**truckers parking area eb**
64mm	**weigh/insp sta eb**
62	MD 75, Libertytown, **N gas:** Shell, **food:** Baskin Robbins, Domino's, Dunkin Donuts, McDonald's, Morgan's Grill, **other:** Food Lion, Vet, New Market Hist Dist
59	MD 144
57mm	Monocacy River
56	MD 144, **N gas:** Citgo, Sheetz, **food:** Beijing, Burger King, JR's Pizza, McDonald's, Roy Rogers, Taco Bell, Waffle House, Wendy's, **other:** $General, **to Hist Dist S other:** Triangle RV Ctr,
55	South St, **1 mi N gas:** Citgo, Pacific Pride, Sheetz
54	Market St, to I-270, **N gas:** Costco/gas, **lodging:** Travelodge, **S gas:** Exxon/dsl, Lowest Price, 7-11, Sheetz/24hr, Shell/24hr, SouStates/dsl, **food:** Arby's, Bob Evans, Burger King, Checker's, Cracker Barrel, El Paso Cantina, Jerry's Rest., KFC, Longhorn Steaks, McDonald's, Papa John's, Peking Gourmet, Popeye's, Roy Rogers, Ruby Tuesday, Subway, Waffle House, Wendy's, **lodging:** Days Inn, Econolodge, Fairfield Inn, Hampton Inn, Holiday Inn Express, Sleep Inn, **other:** Aamco, Audi, Best Buy, Buick, Chrysler, CVS Drug, Ford/Lincoln/Mercury/Isuzu, Home Depot, Honda, Hyundai, JC Penney, Kohl's, Lowes Whse, Michael's, Nissan, Ross, Sam's Club, Sears/auto, Staples, Tires+, Volvo, Walmart SuperCtr, mall
53b a	I-270 S, US 15 N, US 40 W, to Frederick
52b a	US 15 S, US 340 W, Leesburg
49	US 40A (no EZ wb return), Braddock Heights, **N on US 40...gas:** Chevron, Citgo/dsl, Exxon/dsl, Freestate/dsl, GetGo, Shell, Sunoco, **food:** Arby's, Bob Evans, Boston Mkt, Burger King, Casarico Mexican, Denny's, Fritchie's Rest., Ground Round, Hunter's Rest., McDonald's, Miyako Japanese, Mtn View Diner, Outback Steaks, Pizza Hut, Popeye's, Red Horse Rest., Red Lobster, Roy Rogers, Starbucks, Subway, Taco Bell, Wendy's, **lodging:** Comfort Inn, Holiday Inn,

BALTIMORE

FREDERICK

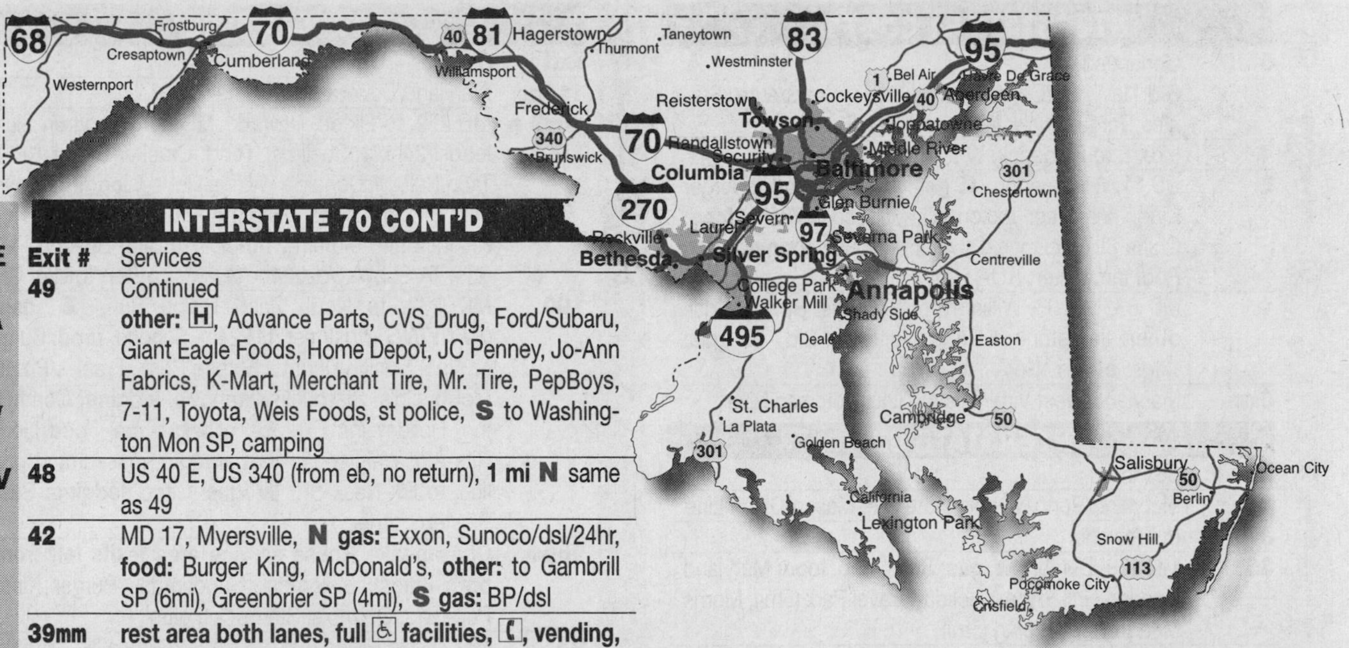

INTERSTATE 70 CONT'D

Exit #	Services
49	Continued **other:** [H], Advance Parts, CVS Drug, Ford/Subaru, Giant Eagle Foods, Home Depot, JC Penney, Jo-Ann Fabrics, K-Mart, Merchant Tire, Mr. Tire, PepBoys, 7-11, Toyota, Weis Foods, st police, **S** to Washington Mon SP, camping
48	US 40 E, US 340 (from eb, no return), **1 mi N** same as 49
42	MD 17, Myersville, **N gas:** Exxon, Sunoco/dsl/24hr, **food:** Burger King, McDonald's, **other:** to Gambrill SP (6mi), Greenbrier SP (4mi), **S gas:** BP/dsl
39mm	**rest area both lanes, full [handicapped] facilities, [phone], vending, [picnic], litter barrels, petwalk**
35	MD 66, to Boonsboro, **S gas:** Sheetz (1mi), **other:** to Greenbrier SP, camping
32b a	US 40, Hagerstown, **1-3 mi N gas:** BP/Blimpie, Exxon/24hr, 7-11, Sunoco, **food:** Bob Evans, Cancun Cantina, Denny's, DQ, Dunkin Donuts, Hong Kong Chinese, Ledo's Pizza, McDonald's, Pacific Ocean Buffet, Pizza Hut, Popeye's, Quizno's, Subway, Super Buffet, TX Roadhouse, **lodging:** Clarion, Comfort Suites, Day's Inn, Hampton Inn, Holiday Inn/rest., Sheraton, Super 8, **other:** [H], Chevrolet/Cadillac, Chrysler/Dodge, CVS Drug, $Tree, Goodyear/auto, Martin's Foods, Mercedes, Nissan, Subaru, Suzuki, Toyota/Scion, Weis Foods, **S other:** Buick/GMC/Pontiac, Honda, Kia, VW
29b a	MD 65, to Sharpsburg, **N gas:** Exxon/dsl/24hr, Sheetz/24hr, Sunoco/dsl/24hr, Shell, **food:** FoodCourt, Longhorn Steaks, Pizza Hut, Starbucks, Subway, TCBY, **other:** [H], Prime Outlets/famous brands, st police, **S gas:** Shell/Blimpie/dsl/24hr, **food:** Burger King, Cracker Barrel, McDonald's, Waffle House, Wendy's, **lodging:** Sleep Inn, **other:** Safari Camping, to Antietam Bfd
28	MD 632, Hagerstown, **2 mi N gas:** Shell, **food:** Bob Evan's, Burger King, Chick-fil-A, Domino's, Fazoli's, Pizza Hut, Roy Rogers, Shoney's, Western Sizzlin, **lodging:** Country Inn&Suites, **other:** Advance Parts, AutoZone, Food Lion, **S** Jellystone Camping
26	I-81, N to Harrisburg, S to Martinsburg
24	MD 63, Huyett, **N gas:** Pilot/Subway/dsl/24hr, Sheetz (2mi), **S other:** KOA (2mi), C&O Canal
18	MD 68 E, Clear Spring, **N gas:** BP, Chevron, **food:** McDonald's, **S gas:** Exxon/dsl, **food:** Wendy Hill Café
12	MD 56, Indian Springs, **S gas:** Exxon/dsl, **other:** Ft Frederick SP
9	US 40 E (from eb, exits left), Indian Springs
5	MD 615 (no immediate wb return), **N** Log Cabin Rest. (2mi)
3	MD 144, Hancock (exits left from wb), **S gas:** ACT/Exxon/dsl, BP/dsl/rest./24hr, **food:** Hardee's, Park'n Dine, Pizza Hut, Subway, Weaver's Rest., **lodging:** Best Value Inn, Hilltop Inn, Super 8, **other:** Ford, NAPA, repair
1b	US 522 (exits left from eb), Hancock, **N** Chevrolet, Chrysler/Dodge/Jeep, **gas:** Citgo/dsl, PitStop, Sheetz/dsl, **food:** Hardee's, Lockhouse Rest., Pizza Hut, Subway, Weaver's Rest., **lodging:** Best Value Inn, Super 8, **other:** $General, Sav-a-Lot Foods, Happy Hills Camp, NAPA
1a	I-68 W, US 40, W to Cumberland
0mm	Maryland/Pennsylvania state line, Mason-Dixon Line

INTERSTATE 81

Exit #	Services
12mm	Maryland/Pennsylvania state line
10b a	Showalter Rd, **E** to [airport]
9	Maugans Ave, **E gas:** BP, Sheetz, Shell/Domino's/dsl, **food:** McDonald's, Pizza Hut, Taco Bell, Waffle House, **lodging:** Hampton Inn, **other:** AutoZone, Curves, CVS Drug, $General, Martin's Foods/gas **W food:** Burger King, **lodging:** Microtel, **other:** GMC Trucks, Kenworth, U-haul, Volvo
7b a	MD 58, Hagerstown, same as 6
6b a	US 40, Hagerstown, **E gas:** Liberty, Shell, **lodging:** Days Inn, Quality Inn, **other:** [H], **W food:** Arby's, Chipotle Mexican, IHOP, KFC, McDonald's, Panera Bread, Uno, Ryan's, Starbucks, Subway, TGIFriday, Wendy's, **other:** Best Buy, Borders Books, $Tree, Home Depot, Marshall's, PetsMart, Walmart SuperCtr
5	Halfway Blvd, **E gas:** AC&T/dsl/rest., **food:** Bob Evans, Bonton Rest., Boston Mkt., Buffalo Wild Wings, Burger King, Chick-fil-A, ChuckeCheese, CiCi's Pizza, Denny's, Garfield's Rest., McDonald's, Olive Garden, Orchid Garden, Outback Steaks, Popeye's, Red Lobster, Roy Rogers, Ruby Tuesday, Sakura Steaks, Shoney's, Taco Bell, Wendy's, **lodging:** Country Inn&Suites, Holiday Inn Express, Homewood Suites, Motel 6, Plaza Hotel, SpringHill Suites, **other:** Bon-Ton, CVS Drug, $Tree, Ford/Lincoln/Mercury, Hyundai, JC Penney, K-Mart, Kohl's, Lowes Whse, Macy's, Martin's Foods/gas, Michael's, Office Depot,

INTERSTATE 81 CONT'D

5	Continued Old Navy, PetCo, Sam's Club/gas, Sears/auto, Staples, Target, mall, **W gas:** AC&T, Exxon
4	I-70, E to Frederick, W to Hancock, to I-68
2	US 11, Williamsport, **E gas:** AC&T/dsl, **food:** Burger King, **W gas:** Exxon/dsl, Sunoco/dsl/24hr, **food:** China 88, McDonald's, Waffle House, **lodging:** Red Roof Inn, **other:** KOA (4mi)
1	MD 63, MD 68, Williamsport, **E gas:** Bowman/dsl, **other:** Jellystone, KOA, to Antietam Bfd, **W gas:** Citgo, **other:** NAPA
0mm	Maryland/West Virginia state line, Potomac River

INTERSTATE 83

Exit #	Services
38mm	Maryland/Pennsylvania state line, Mason-Dixon Line
37	to Freeland
36	MD 439, Bel Air, **W gas:** Sub-Shop, **food:** Maryland Line Inn Grill, **other:** Holiday Travel Park (5mi), Morris Meadows Camping (5mi)
35mm	**weigh/insp sta sb**
33	MD 45, Parkton, **E** USPO
31	Middletown Rd, to Parkton, golf
27	MD 137, Mt Carmel, Hereford, **E gas:** Exxon/dsl, **food:** Subway, **other:** Graul's Foods, Hereford Drug, Mt Carmel Drug, NAPA, USPO, Vet
24	Belfast Rd, to Butler, Sparks
20	Shawan Rd, Hunt Valley, **E gas:** BP, Exxon/dsl, **food:** Burger King, Caribou Coffee, Carmine's Pizza, Carrabba's, Chipotle Mexican, McDonald's, Noodles&Co, Outback Steaks, Quizno's, Panera Bread, Subway, Wendy's, Wong's Kitchen, **lodging:** Chase Suites, Courtyard, Embassy Suites, Hampton Inn, Hunt Valley Marriott, Ramada Ltd, **other:** Giant Foods, Goodyear/auto, Sears/auto, 7-11, Wegman's Foods, mall, Vet
18	Warren Rd (from nb, no return), Cockeysville, **E gas:** Exxon, **lodging:** Residence Inn, multiple services **E** on York Rd
17	Padonia Rd, Deereco Rd, **E gas:** BP/dsl, Hess, Shell, Texaco, **food:** Applebees, Bob Evans, Chili's, Macaroni Grill, Wendy's, **lodging:** Day's Hotel, Extended Stay America, **other:** Audi/VW, Chevrolet, Goodyear/auto, Mar's Foods, Mr Tire, Porsche, Shopper's Foods, Subaru, Target, USPO, multiple services E on York Rd
16b a	Timonium Rd, **E gas:** BP, Petro/Subway, Sunoco/dsl, **food:** Baja Fresh, McDonald's, Steak&Ale, **lodging:** Crowne Plaza, Red Roof Inn, **other:** Infiniti/Nissan, Rite Aid
14	I-695 N
13	I-695 S, Falls Rd, H, st police
12	Ruxton Rd (from nb, no return)
10b a	Northern Parkway, **E gas:** Exxon, Shell, **other:** H
9b a	Cold Spring Lane
8	MD 25 N (from nb), Falls Rd
7b a	28th St, **E** H, **W** Baltimore Zoo
6	US 1, US 40T, North Ave, downtown
5	MD Ave (from sb), downtown
3	Chase St, Gilford St, downtown
2	Pleasant St (from sb), downtown
1	Fayette St, I-83 begins/ends, downtown Baltimore

BALTIMORE

MD

INTERSTATE 95

Exit #	Services
110mm	Maryland/Delaware state line
109b a	MD 279, to Elkton, Newark, **E gas:** Petro/Iron Skillet/dsl/24hr/@, Shell/dsl, **food:** Cracker Barrel, KFC/Taco Bell, McDonald's, Waffle House, **lodging:** Days Inn, Elkton Lodge, Hampton Inn, Hawthorn Inn, Knight's Inn, Motel 6, **other:** H, Blue Beacon, **W gas:** TA/Subway/dsl/24hr/@, 7-11, **other:** to U of DE
100	MD 272, to North East, Rising Sun, **E gas:** ***FLYING J***/dsl/rest./LP/24hr, Sunoco, **food:** Burger King, Dunkin Donuts, Empire Rest., Frank's Pizza, McDonald's, Starbucks, Wendy's, **lodging:** Comfort Inn, Holiday Inn Express, **other:** $Tree, Food Lion, Rite Aid, Walgreens, Walmart/auto, museum, st police, to Elk Neck SP, **W gas:** Citgo, **lodging:** Best Western, **other:** zoo
96mm	**Chesapeake House service area (exits left from both lanes)**, Exxon/dsl, Sunoco/dsl, Burger King, Popeye's, Quizno's, Starbucks, gifts
93	MD 275, to Rising Sun, US 222, to Perryville, **E gas:** Exxon/dsl, Pilot/Subway/dsl/scales/24hr, **food:** Denny's, KFC/Taco Bell, **lodging:** Ramada Inn, **other:** H, Perryville Outlets/famous brands, Riverview Camping
92mm	**weigh sta/toll booth**
91.5mm	Susquehanna River
89	MD 155, to Havre de Grace (last nb exit before toll), **1-3 mi E food:** Burger King, McDonald's, MacGregor's Rest., Waffle House, **lodging:** Best Budget Inn, Super 8, Van Divers B&B, **other:** H, **W** to Susquehanna SP
85	MD 22, to Aberdeen, **E gas:** BP/dsl, 7-11, Royal Farms, **food:** Applebees, Arby's, Bob Evans, Burger King, Durango's, Dunkin Donuts, Family Buffet, Fast Eddie's, Japan House, KFC, Little Caesar's, Mamie's Cafe, McDonald's, Olive Tree Italian, Papa John's, Pizza Hut, Quizno's, Rita's Ice Cream, Subway, Taco Bell, Wendy's, **lodging:** Clarion, Day's Inn, Holiday Inn, La Quinta, Red Roof Inn, Super 8, Travelodge, **other:** Cadillac/GMC/Pontiac, $Express, $General, $Tree, GNC, Home Depot, Klein's Foods, Mars Foods, Radio Shack, Rite Aid, Target, Walgreens, museum
81mm	**MD House service area (exits left from both lanes)**, Exxon/dsl, Sunoco/dsl, Big Boy, Phillips Seafood, Roy Rogers, Sbarro's, Starbucks, TCBY, gifts
80	MD 543, to Riverside, Churchville, **E gas:** BP/Burger King, 7-11, Sunoco, Texaco/dsl, **food:** Arby's, China Moon, Cracker Barrel, Don's Crabs, McDonald's, Pizza Hut, Riverside Pizzaria, Ruby Tuesday, Waffle House, **lodging:** Country Inn&Suites, Extended Stay America, SpringHill Suites, Wingate Inn, **other:** Bar Harbor RV Park (4mi), Klein's Foods, Rite Aid
77b a	MD 24, to Edgewood, Bel Air, **E gas:** Citgo/dsl, Exxon/dsl, Royal Farms/dsl, **food:** Burger King, Charlie's Subs, Denny's/24hr, Giovanni's Rest., McDonald's, My 3 Sons Rest., Vitali's Rest., Waffle House, **lodging:** Best Western, Day's Inn, Hampton Inn, Holiday Inn Express, La Quinta, Ramada Inn, Sleep Inn, **W gas:** Exxon/dsl, Wawa, **food:** Chick-fil-A, KFC/Taco Bell, McDonald's, Subway, **other:** H, BJ's Whse, Lowes Whse, Target, Walmart/drugs, Weis Foods

ABERDEEN

INTERSTATE 95 CONT'D

N ↕ S

Exit #	Services
74	MD 152, Joppatowne, **E gas:** BP/dsl, Citgo/dsl, Exxon/dsl, Sheetz, **food:** Friendly's, KFC, Venitian Palace, Wendy's, **lodging:** Edgewood Motel, Super 8, **other:** [H], Toyota (1mi), **W gas:** Royal Farms
70mm	Big Gunpowder Falls
67b a	MD 43, to White Marsh Blvd, US 1, US 40, **E on MD 7...gas:** BP/dsl, Shell, Texaco, **food:** Chick-fil-A, 5 Guys Burgers, McDonald's, Noodles&Co, Panera Bread, Qdoba Mexian, Starbucks, Subway, **other:** Best Buy, Carmax, Chevrolet, Lowes Whse, Nissan, Target, **W on White Marsh Blvd...gas:** Exxon/dsl, 7-11, **food:** Bertucci's, Boscoe's, Buffalo Wild Wings, Chili's, Don Pablo, Fuddrucker's, Lin's Chinese, McDonald's, Olive Garden, PF Chang's, Red Brick Sta., Ruby Tuesday, Taco Bell, TGIFriday, Wendy's, **lodging:** Fairfield Inn, Hampton Inn, Hilton Garden, Residence Inn, **other:** Barnes&Noble, Giant Foods, GNC, Macy's, JC Penney, Macy's, Old Navy, Sears/auto, Staples, USPO, mall, to Gunpowder SP
64b a	I-695 (exits left), E to Essex, W to Towson
62	to I-895 (from sb)
61	US 40, Pulaski Hwy, **E gas:** BP, Shell/dsl, **food:** McDonald's
60	Moravia Rd, **E gas:** Citgo/dsl, Shell, **food:** Burger King, **other:** GMC/Pontiac, KIA, K-Mart, Suzuki
59	Eastern Ave, **W gas:** BP/dsl/24hr, Enroy Gas/dsl, Exxon, Royal Farms, **food:** Broadway Diner, Subway, Wendy's, **other:** [H], Home Depot, Shopper's Foods
58	Dundalk Ave, (from nb), **E gas:** Citgo, Sunoco/dsl
57	O'Donnell St, Boston St, **E gas:** TA/Buckhorn/Subway/dsl/scales/@, **food:** A&W, McDonald's, KFC, Sbarro's, **lodging:** Best Western, Rodeway Inn
56	Keith Ave
56mm	McHenry Tunnel, toll plaza (north side of tunnel)
55	Key Hwy, to Ft McHenry NM, last nb exit before toll
54	MD 2 S, to Hanover St, **W** downtown, [H]
53	I-395 N, to MLK, **W** downtown, Oriole Park
52	Russell St N, **W** [H]
51	Washington Blvd
50.5mm	**inspection sta nb**
50	Caton Ave, **E gas:** Citgo, Hess/dsl, Shell/24hr, Texaco, **food:** Caton House, McDonald's, **lodging:** Quality Inn, **other:** Aldi Foods, Toyota/Scion, **W** [H]
49b a	I-695, E to Key Bridge, Glen Burnie, W to Towson, to I-70, to I-83
47b a	I-195, to MD 166, to BWI ✈, to Baltimore
46	I-895, to Harbor Tunnel Thruway
43	MD 100, to Glen Burnie, **1 mi E on US 1...gas:** Exxon/Wendy's, **lodging:** Best Western
41b a	MD 175, to Columbia, **E gas:** Exxon/dsl, Shell, **food:** Arby's, Burger King, Frank's Diner, McDonald's, Panda Express, Starbucks, **lodging:** Comfort Suites, Fairfield Inn, Holiday Inn, Red Roof Inn, Super 8, **W gas:** Crown Gas, Exxon, **food:** Applebees, Bob Evans, Fat Burger, Houlihan's, McDonald's, Mimi's Cafe, Olive Garden, On the Border, TGIFriday, **lodging:** Homewood Suites, Studio+, **other:** [H], Best Buy, Costco/gas, Lowes Whse, Office Depot, Royal Farms, to Johns Hopkins U, Loyola U

BALTIMORE

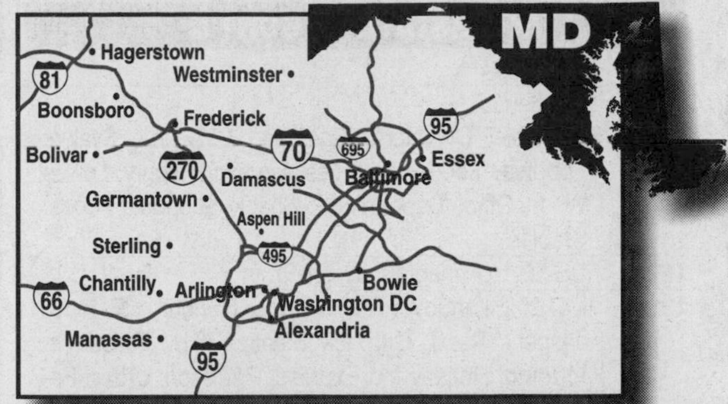

Exit #	Services
38b a	MD 32, to Ft Meade, **2 mi E on US 1...gas:** BP, Royal Farms, **food:** Burger King, McDonald's, Taco Bell, **lodging:** Comfort Inn, Extended Stay America, **other:** to BWI ✈, **E other:** [H]
37mm	**Welcome Ctr both lanes, full ♿ facilities, info, ☎, vending, picnic tables, litter barrels, petwalk, RV Dump**
35b a	MD 216, to Laurel, **E gas:** Exxon, Shell/dsl, **food:** McDonald's, Red Hot&Blue BBQ, Subway, **lodging:** Quality Inn, **other:** Weis Food/drug
34mm	Patuxent River
33b a	MD 198, to Laurel, **E gas:** Exxon, **other:** [H], **W gas:** Exxon/Blimpie, Shell, **food:** McDonald's, Outback Steaks, Starbucks, **lodging:** Holiday Inn
29	MD 212, to Beltsville, **W gas:** Exxon/Blimpie/dsl, **food:** Baskin-Robbins, Danny's Subs, KFC, McDonald's, Taco Bell, Wendy's, **lodging:** Fairfield Inn, Sheraton, **other:** Cherry Hill Park, CVS Drug, Giant Foods
27	I-495 S around Washington
25b a	US 1, Baltimore Ave, to Laurel, College Park, **E gas:** BP, Chevron, Exxon/dsl, 7-11, Shell/24hr, **food:** Arby's, Burger King, Dickey's BBQ, Domino's, El Mexicano, Jerry's Subs, KFC, McDonald's, Papa John's, Pizza Hut, Potbelly's, Quizno's, Taco Bell, 3 Bro's Rest., Wendy's, **lodging:** Holiday Inn, **other:** Advance Parts, Costco, Cottman Transmissions, CVS Drug, PetCo, Radio Shack, Rite Aid, US Agri Library, **W gas:** BP/24hr, Shell, **food:** Dunkin Donuts, China Buffet, College Park Diner, IHOP, Pizza Hut, Yung's Express, **lodging:** Comfort Inn, Day's Inn, Econolodge, Hampton Inn, Howard Johnson, Ramada Ltd, Super 8, **other:** Dick's RV Ctr, GNC, Home Depot, Honda, Hyundai, Shoppers Foods, VW, Vet, to U of MD
23	MD 201, Kenilworth Ave, **E food:** Starbucks, **lodging:** Marriott/rest., **1 mi W on Greenbelt...gas:** Shell, **food:** Atlanta Bread, Bennigan's, Boston Mkt, Checker's, Chipotle Mexican, KFC, McDonald's, Popeye's, Silver Diner, TGIFriday's, Wendy's, **lodging:** Courtyard, Hilton Garden, Residence Inn, **other:** Cadillac, CVS Drug, Giant Food/drug, Jo-Ann Fabrics, Marshall's, Staples, Target
22	Baltimore-Washington Pkwy, **E** to NASA
20b a	MD 450, Annapolis Rd, Lanham, **E gas:** Sunoco, **food:** Burger King, Jerry's Rest., McDonald's, Pizza Hut, Red Lobster, **lodging:** Best Western, Day's Inn/rest., Red Roof Inn, **other:** Ford/Kia, **W gas:** BP, Chevron/dsl, Liberty, 7-11, Shell, Sunoco/24hr, Texaco, **food:** Bojangles, Dunkin Donuts, KFC, Pap Pohn's, Popeye's, Quizno's, Wendy's, **lodging:** Sheraton, **other:** [H], Aamco, Advance Parts,

INTERSTATE 95 CONT'D

N ↕ S — WASHINGTON DC AREA

Exit #	Services
20b a	Continued Chevrolet, Chrysler/Dodge/Jeep, CVS Drug, $Value, Foodway Foods, JustTires, Lincoln/Mercury, Lowes Whse, Office Depot, Radio Shack, Shoppers Foods, Staples
19b a	US 50, to Annapolis, Washington
17	MD 202, Landover Rd, to Upper Marlboro, **E food:** Jasper's Rest., Outback Steaks, Ruby Tuesday's, **lodging:** Holiday Inn Express, Radisson, **other:** FedEx Center, **W other:** Sears/auto
16	Arena Dr, **W** to Arena
15	MD 214, Central Ave, **E lodging:** Extended Stay America, Hampton Inn/rest., **food:** ChuckeCheese, Golden Corral, **other:** FedEx Center, to Six Flags, **W gas:** Exxon/dsl, Liberty, Shell, Texaco, **food:** A&W/LJ Silver, Checker's, KFC, IHOP, Jerry's Subs, McDonald's, Panda Express, Pizza Hut, Taco Bell, Wendy's, **lodging:** Comfort Inn, **other:** Family$, Goodyear, Home Depot, NTB, U-Haul
13	Ritchie-Marlboro Rd, Capitol Hgts, **W food:** Chick-fil-A
11	MD 4, Pennsylvania Ave, to Upper Marlboro, **W gas:** BP, Exxon, Sunoco, **food:** Applebees, Arby's, 5 Guy's Burgers, IHOP, Ledo's Pizza, LJ Silver, Old Country Buffet, Pizza Hut, Starbucks, Subway, Taco Bell, Wendy's, **other:** CVS Drug, $Tree, Hancock Fabrics, JC Penney, Marshall's, PetCo, Shopper's Foods, Staples, Target, st police
9	MD 337, to Allentown Rd, **E gas:** Shell/repair, Texaco, **food:** Arby's, Bojangle's, Checker's, Dunkin Donuts, McDonald's, Popeye's, **lodging:** Days Inn, Quality Inn, Ramada Inn, Super 8, **other:** H, Advance Parts, Family$, U-Haul, to Andrews AFB
7	MD 5, Branch Ave, to Silver Hill, **E gas:** Exxon, Getty, Sunoco, **food:** Wendy's, **lodging:** Motel 6, **W gas:** Shell/Subway/dsl, **other:** H, Buick/GMC/Pontiac, Dodge, Ford, KIA, Lincoln/Mercury, Nissan, VW
4b a	MD 414, St Barnabas Rd, Marlow Hgts, **E gas:** Citgo/dsl, Exxon, Shell, Sunoco, **food:** Bojangles, Burger King, Checker's, KFC, McDonald's, Outback Steaks, Pizza Hut, Starbucks, Wendy's, loding: Red Roof Inn, **other:** Aldi Foods, $Tree, Home Depot, K-Mart, Old Navy, PetsMart, Safeway, 7-11, Staples, **W gas:** Exxon/dsl, Shell/autocare, **food:** McDonald's, Subway, **other:** Family$
3b a	MD 210, Indian Head Hwy, to Forest Hgts, **E gas:** Chevron, Shell, **food:** Danny's Burgers, Dunkin Donuts, La Hacienda, Pizza Hut, Ranch House Rest., Taco Bell, **lodging:** Comfort Inn, Lexington Hotel, **other:** Advance Parts, Aldi Foods, Shopper's Foods, USPO, **W gas:** BP/dsl/24hr, Exxon, Lowest Price, Shell, Texaco, **food:** Burger King, McDonald's, Papa John's, Popeye's, Subway, **food:** CVS Drug, Family$, Giant Foods, Goodyear/auto, Radio Shack, Rite Aid, 7-11
2b a	I-295, N to Washington
0mm	Maryland/Virginia state line, Potomac River, Woodrow Wilson Bridge

INTERSTATE 97

N ↕ S

Exit #	Services
17	I-695. I-97 begins/ends on I-695.
16	MD 648, Ferndale, Glen Burnie, **E gas:** BP, Shell, **food:** Hong Kong Cafe, KFC, McDonald's, Quizno's, Rita's Ice Cream, Wendy's, **other:** $General, Giant Foods, **W gas:** Citgo
15b a	MD 176 W, Dorsey Rd, Aviation Blvd, **E gas:** BP, Shell, **food:** KFC, Wendy's, **W gas:** Royal Farms/dsl, 7-11, **other:** to BWI, st police
14b a	MD 100, Ellicott City, Gibson Island
13b a	MD 174, Quarterfield Rd, **E gas:** AP/dsl, 7-11, Texaco, **food:** The Grill, **other:** WaWa, **W gas:** Shell/dsl, **food:** Chick-fil-A, Quizno's, **other:** Kohl's, Lowes Whse, Rite Aid, Sam's Club/gas, Shoppers Foods, Walmart SuperCtr
12	MD 3, New Cut Rd, Glen Burnie, **E on Veterans Hwy...gas:** WaWa, **food:** Domino's, KFC/Taco Bell, McDonald's, Wendy's, **other:** CVS Drug, Vet, **E gas:** Exxon/24hr, Sunoco, **food:** Burger King, Fortune Cooky, Pizza Hut, **other:** H, Ace Hardware, Giant Foods, Goodyear/auto, Target, Walgreens
10b a	Benfield Blvd, Severna Park, **E gas:** Citgo, Exxon/dsl, Royal Farms, **food:** Baskin-Robbins/Dunkin Donuts, Hella's Rest., **lodging:** White Gables Motel, **other:** KOA, access to same as 12
7	MD 3, MD 32, Bowie, Odenton, **E** motel
5	MD 178 (no EZ sb return), Crownsville
0mm	I-97 begins/ends on US 50/301.

INTERSTATE 270 (ROCKVILLE)

E ↕ W — FREDERICK

Exit #	Services
32	I-270 begins/ends on I-70, exit 53.
31b a	MD 85, **N gas:** Exxon/dsl, Lowest Price, 7-11, Sheetz/24hr, Shell/24hr, SouStates/dsl, **food:** Arby's, Bob Evans, Burger King, Checker's, Cracker Barrel, El Paso Cantina, Jerry's Rest., KFC, Longhorn Steaks, McDonald's, Papa John's, Peking Gourmet, Popeye's, Roy Rogers, Ruby Tuesday, Subway, Waffle House, Wendy's, **lodging:** Days Inn, Econolodge, Fairfield Inn, Hampton Inn, Holiday Inn Express, Sleep Inn, **other:** Aamco, Audi, Best Buy, Buick, Chrysler, CVS Drug, Ford/Lincoln/Mercury/Isuzu, Home Depot, Hyundai, JC Penney, Kohl's, Lowes Whse, Michael's, Nissan, Ross, Sam's Club, Sears/auto, Staples, Tires+, Volvo, Walmart SuperCtr, mall, **S gas:** BP/Blimpie, **food:** Chipotle Mexican, Cracker Barrel, IHOP, Macaroni Grill, McDonald's, Mediterranean Grill, Panda Express, Quizno's, Smoothie King, Starbucks, TGIFriday, **lodging:** Comfort Inn, Courtyard, Extended Stay America, Fairfield Inn, Hampton Inn, Hilton Garden, MainStay Suites, Residence Inn, **other:** Honda, Toyota
30mm	Monocacy River
28mm	viewpoint wb
26	MD 80, Urbana, **N gas:** Exxon, 7-11, **food:** Dunkin Donuts, Foster's Grill, Mangia Ebevi, McDonald's, Waffle House
22	MD 109, to Barnesville, Hyattstown, **S food:** Hyattstown Deli, **other:** Food+
21mm	**weigh/insp sta both lanes**
18	MD 121, to Clarksburg, Boyds, **N** Little Bennett Pk, camping, gas, **S** Blackhill Pk

INTERSTATE 270 CONT'D (ROCKVILLE)

E ↕ W

Exit #	Services
16	MD 27, Father Hurley Blvd, to Damascus, **N gas:** Exxon, Free State, Sunoco, W Express/dsl, **food:** Applebees, Bob Evans, Burger King, McDonald's, Starbucks, Subway, **lodging:** Extended Stay America, Hampton Inn, **other:** Best Buy, Borders Books, Giant Foods, Home Depot, Kohl's, Michael's, PepBoys, TJ Maxx, Target, Walmart, World Mkt, **S gas:** BP, Exxon, 7-11, **food:** Baja Fresh, Burger King, CA Tortilla, Carrabba's, Chick-fil-A, Coldstone Creamery, 5 Guys Burgers, IHOP, McDonald's, Red Robin, Longhorn Steaks, Panera Bread, Pizza Hut, Ruby Tuesday, Subway, Taco Bell, Wendy's, **lodging:** Fairfield Inn, **other:** Giant Foods, NAPA, Office Depot, PetCo, Rite Aid, same as 15
15b a	MD 118, to MD 355, **S other:** Honda, same as 16
13b a	Middlebrook Rd (from wb)
11b a	MD 124, Quince Orchard Rd, **N gas:** Exxon, **food:** Boston Mkt, Panera Bread, Starbucks, Subway, **lodging:** Hilton, Holiday Inn, TownePlace Suites, Wyndham Garden, **other:** Acura, Costco, CVS Drugs, Ford, Hyundai, JC Penney, Lord&Taylor, Macy's, Mazda, NAPA, Nissan, Sam's Club, Sears/auto, Tires+, Toyota, mall, **S gas:** Shell/dsl, **food:** Chevy's Mexican, CiCi's Pizza, Jerry's Subs, Mangaire Italian, Rita's Ice Cream, Starbucks, **lodging:** Motel 6, **other:** Advance Parts, Chevrolet, Giant Foods, Jo-Ann Fabrics, McGruder's Foods, Rite Aid, Staples, Seneca Creek SP
10	MD 117, Clopper Rd (from wb), same as 11
9b a	I-370, to Gaithersburg, Sam Eig Hwy, **S on Washington Blvd...gas:** Chevron, **food:** Joe's Crabshack, Macaroni Grill, Pizza Hut, Red Rock Grill, Subway, Uncle Julio's, **lodging:** Courtyard, **other:** Barnes&Noble, Kohl's, Target, Weis Mkt
8	Shady Grove Rd, **N lodging:** Chase Suite Hotel, Sheraton, **S lodging:** Marriott, Quality Suites, Residence Inn, Sleep Inn, SpringHill Suites, **other:** H
6b a	MD 28, W Montgomery Ave, **N other:** H, **S lodging:** Best Western
5b a	MD 189, Falls Rd
4b a	Montrose Rd, **N** gas, **S other:** Harris Teeter, st police
2	I-270/I-270 spur diverges eb, converges wb
1	MD 187, Old Georgetown Rd, **S gas:** Exxon, **food:** Hamburger Hamlet, **other:** H, Giant Foods, GNC
1b a	(I-270 spur) Democracy Blvd, **E lodging:** Marriott, **W gas:** Exxon/Shell/dsl, **other:** Macy's, Nordstrom's, Sears, mall
0mm	I-270 begins/ends on I-495, exit 35.

INTERSTATE 495 (DC)

See Virginia Interstate 495 (DC)

INTERSTATE 695 (BALTIMORE)

N ↕ S

BALTIMORE

Exit #	Services
48mm	Patapsco River, Francis Scott Key Br
44	MD 695 (from nb)
43mm	toll plaza
42	MD 151 S, Sparrows Point (last exit before toll sb), **E gas:** Citgo/dsl, **other:** North Point SP

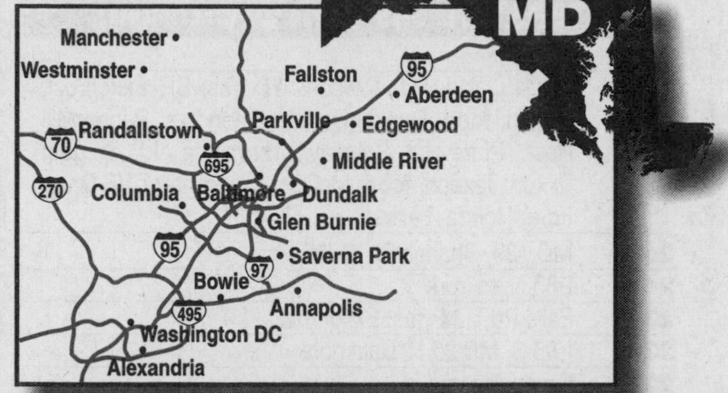

Exit #	Services
41	MD 20, Cove Rd, **W gas:** Royal Farms, WaWa, **food:** McDonald's
40	MD 150, MD 151, North Point Blvd, (nb only)
39	Merritt Blvd, **W gas:** BP, **food:** McDonald's, **other:** Aldi Foods, $Tree, Ford, JC Penney, Mr Tire, Sears/auto, 7-11, Suzuki, Walmart
38b a	MD 150, Eastern Blvd, to Baltimore, **E gas:** Royal Farms, **W food:** Applebees, Burger King, Checker's, Dunkin Donuts, **other:** Chevrolet/Nissan, Sears/auto, Staples, Walgreens, mall
36	MD 702 S (exits left from sb), Essex
35	US 40, **N gas:** WaWa/gas, Sunoco, **food:** Arby's, Bennigan's, DQ, Dunkin Donuts, Grand Buffet, Longhorn Steaks, Panda Express, Panera Bread, **other:** Aldi Foods, Best Buy, Harley-Davidson, Home Depot, NTB, Office Depot, PetCo, Sam's Club/gas, U-Haul, Walmart, same as 34
34	MD 7, Philadelphia Rd, **N food:** McDonald's, Quizno's, Wendy's, **lodging:** La Quinta, **other:** H, $General, $Tree, Giant Foods, Goodyear/auto, Marshall's, **S gas:** Exxon, **other:** Walgreens, same as 35
33b a	I-95, N to Philadelphia, S to Baltimore
32b a	US 1, Bel Air, **N gas:** Exxon, **food:** Arby's, Bob Evan's, Burger King, Denny's, Golden Corral, IHOP, McDonald's, Taco Bell, **other:** BJ's Whse, Curves, Giant Foods, GMC/Pontiac, K-Mart, Mr Tire/auto, 7-11, Toyota/Scion, Vet, **S gas:** Getty, Texaco, **food:** Carrabba's, Dunkin Donuts, McDonald's, Mr Crab, Subway, Szechuan Taste, **other:** Goodyear/auto
31c	MD 43 E (from eb)
31b a	MD 147, Harford Rd, **N gas:** BP/24hr, Carroll, 7-11, Shell/dsl, **food:** Dunkin Donuts, Wendy's, **other:** CVS Drug, Chrysler/Jeep, Honda, Mar's Foods, VW, Walgreens
30b a	MD 41, Perring Pkwy, **N gas:** Shell, **food:** Burger King, Checker's, Chick-fil-A, McDonald's, Popeye's, Quizno's, **other:** Chevrolet, Ford, Giant Foods, Home Depot, Jo-Ann Fabrics, K-Mart, NTB, Office Depot, Ross, Safeway Foods, Shopper's Foods
29b	MD 542, Loch Raven Blvd, **S gas:** BP, Hess, Royal Farms, Texaco, **food:** Bel-Loch Diner, Hooters, Pizza Hut, Subway, **lodging:** Comfort Inn, Ramada Inn, Welcome Inn
29a	Cromwell Bridge Rd, **S lodging:** Holiday Inn
28	Providence Rd, **S gas:** Citgo, **other:** Royal Farms
27b a	MD 146, Dulaney Valley Rd, **N** Hampton NHS, **S gas:** Exxon, **food:** Bahama Breeze, Burger King, Rainforest Cafe, **lodging:** Sheraton, **other:** Barnes&Noble, Macy's, SuperFresh Food, mall

INTERSTATE 695 CONT'D (BALTIMORE)

N ↕ S

Exit #	Services
26b a	MD 45, York Rd, Towson, **N gas:** BP, Exxon/dsl, Ocean, **food:** Dunkin Donuts, Friendly's, PepperMill Rest., Pizza Hut, Subway, **other:** Rite Aid, **S gas:** Exxon, Texaco, **food:** McDonald's, **other:** CVS Drug, Ford, Honda, Lexus
25	MD 139, Charles St, **S** H
24	I-83 N, to York
23b	Falls Rd, , **N gas:** Exxon/dsl
23a	I-83 S, MD 25 N, Baltimore
22	Greenspring Ave
21	to Stevenson Rd, Park Hghts Rd
20	MD 140, Reisterstown Rd, Pikesville, **N gas:** Exxon/7-11/dsl, **other:** Barnes&Noble, **S gas:** BP, Shell, Sunoco/Subway, **food:** McDonald's, Olive Branch Italian, **lodging:** Hilton, Ramada Inn, **other:** Target
19	I-795, NW Expswy
18b a	MD 26, Randallstown, Lochearn, **E gas:** Texaco, **W gas:** BP, Exxon/dsl Shell, **food:** Burger King, Dunkin Donuts, Subway, Taco Bell, **other:** H, Firestone/auto, Giant Foods, 7-11, Walgreens
17	MD 122, Security Blvd, **E gas:** BP/repair, Shell, **food:** Dunkin Donuts, Subway, Wendy's, **lodging:** Day's Inn, Motel 6, Quality Inn, **other:** Chevrolet, Mitsubishi, Nissan, **W gas:** Exxon, Sunoco, **food:** Burger King, 5 Guys Burgers, McDonald's, Panera Bread, Popeye's, Quizno's, **lodging:** Best Western, **other:** Best Buy, Ford, Macy's, Old Navy, Sears/auto, SuperFresh Foods, mall
16b a	I-70, E to Baltimore, W to Frederick
15b a	US 40, Ellicott City, Baltimore, **E gas:** BP, **food:** Burger King, Checker's, Chick-fil-A, ChuckeCheese, KFC, IHOP, McDonald's, Panda Express, Quizno's, **lodging:** Day's Inn, Comfort Inn, **other:** CVS Drug, Dodge, $Tree, Lowes Whse, Rite Aid, Ross, Safeway Foods/gas, Sam's Club/gas, U-Haul, Walgreens, **W**
15b a	Continued **gas:** BP/dsl, Exxon, Shell, Texaco, **food:** Bob Evan's, McDonald's, Popeye's, Taco Bell, TT Diner, **other:** Firestone/auto, Giant Foods, Goodyear, Home Depot, NTB, Staples, Toyota/Scion, Walmart
14	Edmondson Ave, **E gas:** Sunoco, **other:** Royal Farms, **W gas:** CF, **food:** Papa John's
13	MD 144, Frederick Rd, Catonsville, **W gas:** BP, Cisco, Texaco, **food:** Dunkin Donuts, McDonald's/24hr, Subway, **other:** 7-11
12c b	MD 372 E, Wilkens, **E** H
11b a	I-95, N to Baltimore, S to Washington
10	US 1Washington Blvd (from wb only), **E gas:** Royal Farms, **food:** 3 Bro's Pizza, Quizno's, Wendy's, **lodging:** Beltway Motel/rest., **other:** Goodyear/auto, Home Depot, Office Depot, PetCo, Walmart SuperCtr **W gas:** Exxon, **food:** Burger King
9	Hollins Ferry Rd, Lansdowne, **E gas:** BP, Sunoco/dsl, **other:** Royal Farms
8	MD 168, Nursery Rd, **N gas:** Exxon, Shell, **food:** Burger King, KFC, McDonald's, Taco Bell, Wendy's, **lodging:** Motel 6, **S gas:** BP, Citgo, **food:** Snyder's Rest.
7b a	MD 295, **N** to Baltimore, **S** BWI ✈
6b a	Camp Mead Rd (from nb)
5	MD 648, Ferndale, gas, food, lodging
4b a	I-97 S, to Annapolis
3b a	MD 2 N, Brooklyn Park, **S gas:** Exxon, Hess, Shell, **food:** Bennigan's, Bob Evan's, BoneFish Grill, Checker's, Chick-fil-A, ChuckeCheese, Denny's, Hunan Rest., KFC, Krispy Kreme, McDonald's, Panera Bread, Pizza Hut, Qdoba, Quizno's, Starbucks, Subway, Taco Bell, **lodging:** Day's Inn, Hampton Inn, Holiday Inn, **other:** Advance Parts, Aldi Foods, Best Buy, $Tree, Giant Foods, Just Tires, K-Mart, Lowes Whse, Mar's Foods, Office Depot, PetCo, Target, Walgreens
2	MD 10, Glen Burnie
1	MD 174, Hawkins Point Rd, **S gas:** Citgo/deli/dsl

MASSACHUSETTS

INTERSTATE 84 EAST

E ↕ W — STURBRIDGE

Exit #	Services
4 (11)	I-84 begins/ends on I-90, Exit 9.
3b a (9)	US 20, Sturbridge, **E gas:** BeeVee, Citgo, **food:** Applebees, Cracker Barrel, Pizzaria Uno, Subway, Wendy's, **lodging:** Comfort Inn, Publick House, **other:** Marshall's, Old Navy, Staples, Stop&Shop, Walmart **W gas:** Citgo, Cumberland Farms, Mobil/dsl, **food:** Burger King, Friendly's, McDonald's, Piccadilly's, Sturbridge Pizza House, **lodging:** Best Value Inn, Best Western, Econolodge, Hampton Inn, Holiday Inn Express, Sturbridge Host Motel, Super 8, **other:** H, USPO, st police
2 (5)	MA 131, to Old Sturbridge Village, Sturbridge, **S** Day's Inn, RV camping
4mm	picnic area wb, litter barrels
1 (2.5)	Mashapaug Rd, to Southbridge, **E gas:** Mobil/dsl/24hr, Pilot/deli/dsl/rest./scales/24hr/@, Shell/dsl/24hr, **food:** Boston Pizza, Roy Rogers, Sbarro's, **lodging:** Quality Inn
2mm	**weigh sta wb**
.5mm	**picnic area eb**
0mm	Massachusetts/Connecticut state line

INTERSTATE 90

E ↕ W

Exit #	Services
137mm	I-90 begins/ends on I-93, exit 20 in Boston.
25	to I-93, to downtown Boston
24	to I-93, to downtown Boston
22 (134)	Presidential Ctr, downtown
20 (132)	MA 28, Alston, Brighton, Cambridge, **N lodging:** Courtyard, Doubletree Inn, **other:** H, **S gas:** Sunoco
131mm	toll plaza
19 (130)	MA Ave (from eb), **N food:** IHOP, McDonald's, **lodging:** Day's Inn
17 (128)	Centre St, Newton, **N lodging:** Sheraton, **other:** Cadillac, Chevrolet, Honda, Nissan
16 (125)	MA 16, W Newton, **S gas:** Mobil/repair
15 (124)	I-95, **N gas:** Marriott
123mm	toll plaza
14 (122)	MA 30, Weston
117mm	**Natick Travel Plaza eb**, Gulf/dsl, McDonald's, Dunkin Donuts, info

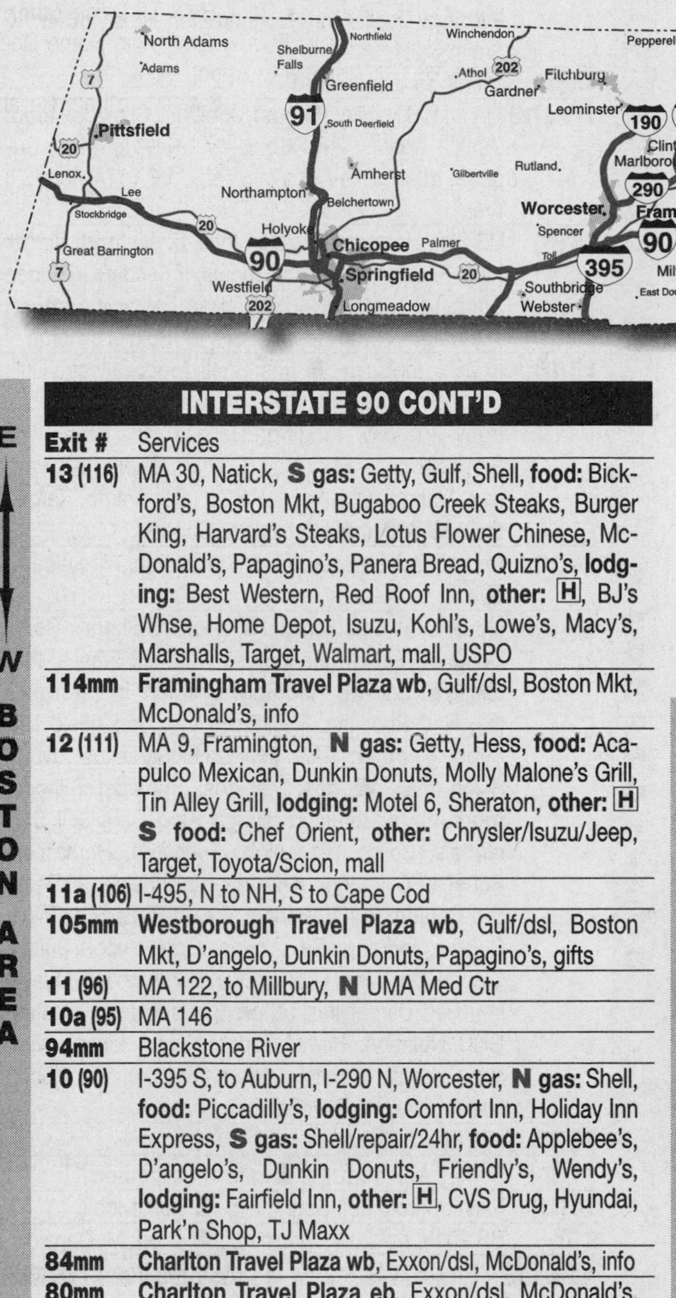

E ↕ W

BOSTON AREA

INTERSTATE 90 CONT'D

Exit #	Services
13 (116)	MA 30, Natick, **S gas:** Getty, Gulf, Shell, **food:** Bickford's, Boston Mkt, Bugaboo Creek Steaks, Burger King, Harvard's Steaks, Lotus Flower Chinese, McDonald's, Papagino's, Panera Bread, Quizno's, **lodging:** Best Western, Red Roof Inn, **other:** H, BJ's Whse, Home Depot, Isuzu, Kohl's, Lowe's, Macy's, Marshalls, Target, Walmart, mall, USPO
114mm	**Framingham Travel Plaza wb**, Gulf/dsl, Boston Mkt, McDonald's, info
12 (111)	MA 9, Framington, **N gas:** Getty, Hess, **food:** Acapulco Mexican, Dunkin Donuts, Molly Malone's Grill, Tin Alley Grill, **lodging:** Motel 6, Sheraton, **other:** H **S food:** Chef Orient, **other:** Chrysler/Isuzu/Jeep, Target, Toyota/Scion, mall
11a (106)	I-495, N to NH, S to Cape Cod
105mm	**Westborough Travel Plaza wb**, Gulf/dsl, Boston Mkt, D'angelo, Dunkin Donuts, Papagino's, gifts
11 (96)	MA 122, to Millbury, **N** UMA Med Ctr
10a (95)	MA 146
94mm	Blackstone River
10 (90)	I-395 S, to Auburn, I-290 N, Worcester, **N gas:** Shell, **food:** Piccadilly's, **lodging:** Comfort Inn, Holiday Inn Express, **S gas:** Shell/repair/24hr, **food:** Applebee's, D'angelo's, Dunkin Donuts, Friendly's, Wendy's, **lodging:** Fairfield Inn, **other:** H, CVS Drug, Hyundai, Park'n Shop, TJ Maxx
84mm	**Charlton Travel Plaza wb**, Exxon/dsl, McDonald's, info
80mm	**Charlton Travel Plaza eb**, Exxon/dsl, McDonald's, info, st police
79mm	toll plaza
9mm (78)	I-84, to Hartford, NYC, Sturbridge, access to H
67mm	Quaboag River
8 (62)	MA 32, to US 20, Palmer, **S on MA 32...gas:** Citgo, Getty, Shell/dsl, **food:** McDonald's, Oriental Express, Subway, **other:** H, Big Y Foods, Brooks Drug, Buick/Chevrolet/Pontiac, repair/transmissions
58mm	Chicopee River
56mm	**Ludlow Travel Plaza wb**, Exxon/dsl, Boston Mkt, D'angelo's
55mm	**Ludlow Travel Plaza eb**, Exxon/dsl, McDonald's
7 (54)	MA 21, to Ludlow, **N gas:** Gulf, Mobil, Sunoco, **food:** Burger King, Dunkin Donuts, Friendly's, Joy's Pizzaria, McDonald's, Subway, Wendy's, **other:** H Ace Hardware, Big Y Foods, CVS Drug, Jo-Ann Fabrics, NAPA, **N gas:** Pride, Shell, **food:** Domino's, Wendy's, **lodging:** Comfort Inn

SPRINGFIELD

Exit #	Services
6 (51)	I-291, to Springfield, Hartford CT, **N gas:** Pride/Subway/dsl, **food:** Dragon House Chinese, McDonald's, **lodging:** Econolodge, Motel 6, Plantation Inn, **other:** H, to Bradley Int ✈, Basketball Hall of Fame
5 (49)	MA 33, to Chicopee, Westover AFB, **N food:** Applebee's, Arby's, Burger King, Denny's, Dunkin Donuts, Friendly's, 99 Rest., Pizza Hut, Royal Buffet, Starbucks, Subway, Wendy's, **lodging:** Days Inn, Hampton Inn, Quality Inn, **other:** BJ's Whse/gas, Big Y Foods, Chevrolet/Cadillac, Dodge, Home Depot, Honda/Subaru, Marshall's, Staples, Stop&Shop Food/gas, TownFair Tire, U-Haul, Walmart, mall, **S gas:** Pride/Subway/dsl, **other:** Buick/Pontiac/GMC, Ford
46mm	Connecticut River
4 (46)	I-91, US 5, to Holyoke, W Springfield, **US 5 N gas:** Shell, **food:** Dunkin Donuts, **lodging:** Welcome Inn, **US 5 S food:** B'Shara's Rest., Dougnut Dip, On the Border, Outback Steaks, Piccadilly's, Subway, **lodging:** Comfort Inn, Knight's Inn, Red Roof Inn, Residence Inn, Springfield Inn, Super 8, **other:** AAA, BMW, Honda/Lexus/Toyota/Scion, mall
41mm	st police wb
3 (40)	US 202, to Westfield, **N gas:** Mobil, **food:** Cafe Santorini, NE Pizza, **lodging:** Country Court Motel, **S gas:** Citgo/Subway/dsl, Shell, **food:** Friendly's, Whip City Brewery/rest., Wendy's, **lodging:** Econolodge, **other:** H, repair
36mm	Westfield River
35.5mm	runaway truck ramp eb
29mm	**Blandford Travel Plaza both lane S** Exxon/dsl, McDonalds, gifts, info, vending
20mm	1724 ft, highest point on MA Tpk
14.5mm	Appalachian Trail
12mm	**parking area both lanes, litter barrels**
2 (11)	US 20, to Lee, Pittsfield, **N gas:** Citgo, Shell/dsl/24hr, Sunoco/repair, **food:** Arizona Pizza, Athena's Rest., Dunkin Donuts, Friendly's, McDonald's, Red Apple

INTERSTATE 90 CONT'D

Exit #	Services
2 (11)	Continued Chinese, **lodging:** Pilgrim Inn, Sunset Motel, Super 8, **other:** Brooks Drug, PriceChopper Foods, **S gas:** Lee/dsl, JFS, **food:** Orient Taste, Subway, Villa Pizza, **other:** Prime Outlets/famous brands
10.5mm	Hoosatonic River
8mm	**Lee Travel Plaza both lanes,** Exxon/dsl, McDonald's, TCBY, atm, bank, info, vending
4mm	toll booth,
1 (2)	MA 41 (from wb, no return), to MA 102, W Stockbridge, the Berkshires, **N lodging:** Pleasant Valley Motel, **other:** to Bousquet Ski Area
0mm	Massachusetts/New York state line

INTERSTATE 91

Exit #	Services
55mm	Massachusetts/Vermont state line, callboxes begin/end
54mm	**parking area both lanes,**
28 (51)	US 5, MA 10, Bernardston, **E food:** Bella Notte Ristorante, **lodging:** Fox Inn, **W gas:** Sunoco, **food:** Antonio's Ristorante, Four-leaf Clover Rest., **other:** Country Corner Store, RV camping, USPO
27 (45)	MA 2 E, Greenfield, **US 5 E gas:** Gulf, Magic Fuel, Sunoco, **food:** Burger King, Denny's Pantry, Friendly's, McDonald's, Subway, **other:** H, AutoZone, Bond Parts, Buick/Pontiac/GMC, CVS Drug, Honda
26 (43)	MA 2 W, MA 2A E, Greenfield, **E gas:** Planet/dsl, Shell/dsl, **food:** Applebee's, China Gourmet, Dunkin Donuts, Herm's, **lodging:** GreenField Inn, Hampton Inn, **other:** H, Chevrolet, Ford/Lincoln/Mercury, **W gas:** Exxon/24hr, Irving, **food:** Bickford's, Friendly's, KFC/Taco Bell/Pizza Hut, McDonald's, 99 Rest., **lodging:** Hampton Inn, Super 8, **other:** Big Y Foods, BJ's Whse, $Tree, Family$, Home Depot, Hyundai, Staples, to Mohawk Tr
39mm	Deerfield River
37mm	**weigh sta both lanes**
25 (36)	MA 116 (from sb), S Deerfield, hist dist, camping, same as 24
24 (35)	US 5, MA 10, MA 116, Deerfield (no EZ return), **E gas:** Irving/Subway/Dunkin Donuts, **food:** Chandler's Rest., New Golden China, Wolfy's Rest., **lodging:** Red Roof Inn, **other:** Yankee Candle Co, **W gas:** Exxon/diner/dsl, **food:** 24hr Diner, **lodging:** Whatley Inn
34.5mm	**parking area nb**
23 (34)	US 5 (from sb), **E other:** Rainbow Motel/camping
22 (30)	US 5, MA 10 (from nb), N Hatfield, **W** Diamond RV Ctr
21 (28)	US 5, MA 10, Hatfield, **W gas:** Sunoco, **food:** Subway, **lodging:** Scottish Inn, **other:** Long View RV Ctr, st police
20 (26)	US 5, MA 9, MA 10 (from sb), Northampton, **W gas:** Hess/dsl, Pride/Dunkin Donuts, **food:** Bickford's, Burger King, D'angelo's, McDonald's, Papagino's Italian, **other:** H, Chevrolet/VW, CVS Drug, Firestone/auto, Ford, Honda, NAPA, Pontiac/GMC/Cadillac, Radio Shack, Stop&Shop, Subaru, Toyota/Scion, Townfair Tire, VW, Walmart/Subway
19 (25)	MA 9, to Amherst, Northampton, **E gas:** Getty, Shell, **food:** Butterfly Asian, **lodging:** Comfort Inn, Hampton Inn, Holiday Inn, **other:** H, to Elwell SP
18 (22)	US 5, Northampton, **E food:** Montana Steaks, **lodging:** Clarion, **W gas:** Shell/Dunkin Donuts/24hr, **lodging:** Quality Inn, Northampton Hotel, **other:** to Smith Coll
18mm	scenic area both lanes
17b a (16)	MA 141, S Hadley, **E gas:** Mobil/dsl, Shell/dsl, **food:** Dunkin Donuts, Real China, Subway, **lodging:** Super 8, **other:** Rite Aid, Walgreens, **W** to Mt Tom Ski Area
16 (14)	US 202, Holyoke, **E gas:** Mobil, Shell, **food:** Burger King, Denny's, Dunkin Donuts, Friendly's, Golden Chopsticks, McDonald's, Yankee Pedlar Inn, **other:** H, Walgreens, to Heritage SP, **W** Soldier's Home
15 (12)	to US 5, Ingleside, **E gas:** Shell, **food:** Chicago Grill, Cracker Barrel, Friendly's, McDonald's, Red Robin, Ruby Tuesday, **lodging:** Holiday Inn, **other:** H, Barnes&Noble, Best Buy, Borders Books, JC Penney, Macy's, Old Navy, PetCo, Sears/auto, Target, mall, **W lodging:** Homewood Suites
14 (11)	to US 5, to I-90 (Mass Tpk), E to Boston, W to Albany, **E** H
13b a (9)	US 5 N, W Springfield, **E food:** B'Shara's Rest., Dougnut Dip, On the Border, Outback Steaks, Piccadilly's, Subway, **lodging:** Comfort Inn, Knight's Inn, Red Roof Inn, Residence Inn, Springfield Inn, Super 8, **other:** AAA, BMW, Honda/Lexus/Toyota/Scion, mall, **W gas:** Mobil/dsl, Pride/dsl, Sunoco, **food:** Arby's, Bertucci's, Burger King, Cal's Grill, Carrabba's, Chili's, D'angelo's, Friendly's, HomeTown Buffet, KFC, Longhorn Steaks, McDonald's, 99 Rest., Old Country Buffet, Panera Bread, Pizza Hut, Tokyo Cuisine, **lodging:** Bel Air Inn, Candlewood Suites, Clarion, Day's Inn, Econolodge, Hampton Inn, Quality Inn, Red Carpet Inn, **other:** Chrysler/Jeep, Costco, GNC Nutrition, Home Depot, Kohl's, Lincoln/Mercury, Mazda, Michael's, Nissan/Subaru, Stop&Shop Foods, Staples, TownFair Tire
12 (8.5)	I-391 N, to Chicopee
11 (8)	Burney Ave (from sb), **E gas:** Mobil, **other:** H
10 (7.5)	Main St (from nb), Springfield, **E gas:** Mobil
9 (7)	US 20 W, MA 20A E (from nb), **E food:** McDonald's
8 (6.5)	I-291, US 20 E, to I-90, **E** downtown, **food:** Hooters, **lodging:** Holiday Inn, **other:** H,
7 (6)	Columbus Ave (from sb), **E lodging:** Marriott, Sheraton, **W gas:** Pride/Subway/dsl, **other:** to Basketball Hall of Fame
6 (5.5)	Springfield Ctr (from nb), **W gas:** Pride/Dunkin Donuts/Subway/dsl
5 (5)	Broad St, **E gas:** Mobil/dsl, Shell/dsl, **W gas:** Sunoco/dsl, **food:** Chicago Grill, **lodging:** Hilton Garden, **other:** Buick/GMC, same as 4
4 (4.5)	MA 83, Broad St, Main St, **E other:** Hyundai, **W food:** Chicago Grill, **lodging:** Hilton Garden, same as 5
3 (4)	US 5 N, to MA 57, Columbus Ave, W Springfield, **E gas:** Sunoco, **other:** Cadillac, **W** Chevrolet
2 (3.5)	MA 83 S (from nb), to E Longmeadow, **E food:** Friendly's
1 (3)	US 5 S (from sb)
0mm	Massachusetts/Connecticut state line, callboxes begin/end

E ↕ W

N ↕ S

GREENFIELD

SPRINGFIELD

INTERSTATE 93 CONT'D

N ↕ S

Exit #	Services
47mm	Massachusetts/New Hampshire state line, callboxes begin/end
48 (46)	MA 213 E, to Methuen, **E** [H]
47 (45)	Pelham St, Methuen, **E gas:** Sunoco/24hr, **food:** Dunkin Donuts, McDonald's, Outback Steaks, **W gas:** Getty, **food:** Fireside Rest., **lodging:** Day's Hotel/rest., Guesthouse Inn, **other:** Chrysler/Jeep
46 (44)	MA 110, MA 113, to Lawrence, **E gas:** Getty, Mobil, Shell, **food:** Burger King, Dunkin Donuts, McDonald's/24hr, PapaGino's, Pizza Hut/KFC, Mkt-Basket Foods, Taco Bell, **other:** [H], $Tree, Rite Aid, **W gas:** Citgo/dsl, Global, **food:** Dunkin Donuts, Jackson's Rest., Millhouse Rest.
45 (43)	Andover St, River Rd, to Lawrence, **E lodging:** Comfort Suites, Courtyard, Wyndham, **W gas:** Mobil/Dunkin Donuts, **food:** Chateu Italian, Chili's, **lodging:** La Quinta, Residence Inn, Springhill Suites
44b a (40)	I-495, to Lowell, Lawrence, **E** [H]
43 (39)	MA 133, N Tewksbury, **E gas:** Mobil/Dunkin Donuts/24hr
42 (38)	Dascomb Rd, East St, Tewksbury
41 (35)	MA 125, Andover, st police
40 (34)	MA 62, Wilmington
39 (33)	Concord St, **E** Shriners Auditorium
38 (31)	MA 129, Reading, **W gas:** Mobil/Dunkin Donuts/dsl, **food:** Burger King, 99 Rest.
37c (30)	Commerce Way, Atlantic Ave, **W food:** Starbucks, **lodging:** Red Roof, Residence Inn, **other:** PetCo, Target
37b a (29)	I-95, S to Waltham, N to Peabody
36 (28)	Montvale Ave, **E gas:** Mobil, **lodging:** Courtyard, **W gas:** Citgo/dsl, Exxon/24hr, Lukoil, **food:** Bickford's/24hr, Dunkin Donuts, McDonald's, Polcari's Italian, Spud's Rest., Wendy's, **lodging:** Best Western, Comfort Inn, **other:** [H]
35 (27)	Winchester Highlands, Melrose, **E** [H] (no EZ return to sb)
34 (26)	MA 28 N (from nb, no EZ return), Stoneham, **E gas:** Mobil, **food:** Friendly's, **other:** [H]
33 (25)	MA 28, Fellsway West, Winchester, **E** [H]
32 (23)	MA 60, Salem Ave, Medford Square, **W lodging:** AmeriSuites, **other:** [H], to Tufts U
31 (22)	MA 16 E, to Revere (no EZ return sb), **E gas:** Shell, **food:** Bertucci's, Friendly's, McDonald's, Subway, **lodging:** Howard Johnson Rest., **other:** CVS Drug, Lincoln/Mercury, Marshall's, Kohl's, Shaw's Foods, Stop&Shop Foods, mall, st police, **W gas:** Fred's Gas, Mr. C/dsl, **food:** Avellino's Italian, Burger King, Dunkin Donuts, Pizza Hut, **other:** AutoZone, KIA, Mitsubishi, Staples
30 (21)	MA 28, MA 38, Mystic Ave, Somerville, **W gas:** Mr. C's Gas, **food:** Burger King, **other:** AutoZone, Lincoln/Mercury
29 (20)	MA 28 (from nb), Somerville, **E food:** Dunkin Donuts, 99 Rest., **lodging:** La Quinta, **other:** Home Depot, K-Mart, Staples, TJ Maxx, mall, **W** same as 30, **gas:** Gulf, Hess, **lodging:** Holiday Inn, **other:** Radio Shack, Stop&Shop
28 (19)	Sullivans Square, Charles Town, downtown

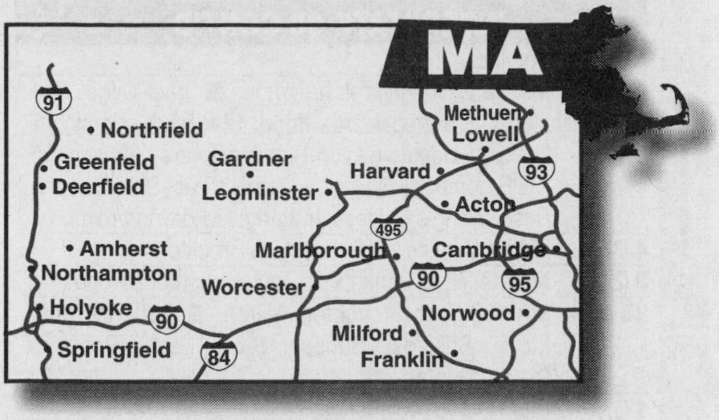

BOSTON AREA

MA
Methuen
Lowell
Northfield
Greenfield
Deerfield
Gardner
Leominster
Harvard
Acton
Amherst
Northampton
Marlborough
Cambridge
Worcester
Holyoke
Springfield
Norwood
Milford
Franklin
91
93
495
90
95
84

Exit #	Services
27	US 1 N (from nb)
26 (18.5)	MA 28 N, Storrow Dr, North Sta, downtown
25	Haymarket Sq, Gov't Center
24 (18)	Callahan Tunnel, **E** [airport]
23 (17.5)	High St, Congress St, **W lodging:** Marriott
22 (17)	Atlantic Ave, Northern Ave, South Sta, Boston World Trade Ctr
21 (16.5)	Kneeland St, ChinaTown
20 (16)	I-90 W, to Mass Tpk
19 (15.5)	Albany St (from sb), **W gas:** Mobil/dsl, **other:** [H]
18 (15)	Mass Ave, to Roxbury, **W** [H]
17 (14.5)	E Berkeley (from nb), **E** New Boston Food Mkt
16 (14)	S Hampton St, Andrew Square, **W gas:** Shell/24hr, **food:** Bickford's, **lodging:** Holiday Inn Express, **other:** Home Depot, K-Mart/Little Caesar's, Marshall's, Old Navy
15 (13)	Columbia Rd, Everett Square, **E lodging:** DoubleTree Motel, **other:** JFK Library, to UMA, **W gas:** Shell
14 (12.5)	Morissey Blvd, **E** JFK Library, **W gas:** Shell, **food:** D'angelo's, **lodging:** Howard Johnson, Ramada Inn, **other:** Stop&Shop Foods
13 (12)	Freeport St, to Dorchester, **W gas:** Citgo/7-11, **food:** Boston Mkt, **other:** CVS Drug, Dodge, Toyota
12 (11.5)	MA 3A S (from sb, no EZ return), Quincy, **E gas:** Shell, **food:** Café Pacific, Domino's, **lodging:** Best Western, **W gas:** Boston Mkt, Citgo/7-11, Exxon, Shell, Sunoco, **food:** Arby's, Bickford's, Ground Round, PapaGino's, Wendy's, **other:** AutoZone, CVS Drug, Ford/Lincoln/Mercury, Pontiac/GMC, Staples, Walgreen
11b a (11)	to MA 203, Granite Ave, Ashmont, **W food:** McDonald's
10 (10)	Squantum Ave (from sb), Milton, **W** [H]
9 (9)	Adams St, Bryant Ave, to N Quincy, **W gas:** Shell/repair
8 (8)	Brook Pkwy, to Quincy, Furnace, **E gas:** Global, Gulf/dsl, Mobil, **other:** Home Depot
7 (7)	MA 3 S, to Cape Cod (exits left from sb), Braintree, **E lodging:** Marriott
6 (6)	MA 37, to Holbrook, Braintree, **E gas:** Mobil/24hr, **food:** Boardwalk Café, D'angelo's, Pizzaria Uno, TGI Friday, **lodging:** Sheraton/café, **other:** Firestone/auto, Lord&Taylor, Macy's, Sears/auto, mall, **W gas:** Sunoco, **food:** Ascari Café, **lodging:** Candlewood Suites, Extended Stay America, Hampton Inn, Holiday Inn Express, **other:** Barnes&Noble, Ford, Nissan, VW

BOSTON AREA

INTERSTATE 93 CONT'D

Exit #	Services
5b a (4)	MA 28 S, to Randolph, Milton, **E gas:** Citgo, Mobil/dsl, Shell/repair/24hr, **food:** D'angelo's, Domino's, Dunkin Donuts/Baskin-Robbins/Togo's, Friendly's, IHOP, Lombardo's Rest., Picadilly's Pub, Sal's Calzone Rest., Wong's Chinese, **lodging:** Holiday Inn/rest.
4 (3)	MA 24 S (exits left from sb), to Brockton
3 (2)	MA 138 N, to Ponkapoag Trail, Houghtons Pond
2b a (1)	MA 138 S, to Stoughton, Milton, **E** golf, **W gas:** Mobil, Shell/dsl, Sunoco, **food:** Baskin-Robbins, Dunkin Donuts
1 (0)	I-95 N, S to Providence.

I-93 begins/ends on I-95, exit 12.

INTERSTATE 95

Exit #	Services
89.5mm	Massachusetts/New Hampshire state line, **Welcome Ctr/rest area sb, full (handicapped) facilities, [picnic], litter barrels**
60 (89)	MA 286, to Salisbury, beaches, **E gas:** Mobil/dsl, **food:** Capt. Hook's, Dunkin Donuts, Lena's Seafood Rest., **other:** camping (seasonal)
59 (88)	I-495 S (from sb)
58b a (78)	rd 110, to I-495 S, to Amesbury, Salisbury, **E gas:** Sunoco/Subway/dsl, **food:** China Buffet, Niko's Place, Sylvan St Grille, Winner's Circle Rest., **other:** Chrylser/Jeep/Dodge, U-Haul, radiators, **W gas:** Best Choice/Domino's/dsl, Irving Gas, Mobil, **food:** Acapulco's Mexican, Burger King, Dunkin Donuts, Friendly's, McDonald's, PapaGino's, **lodging:** Fairfield Inn, **other:** Chevrolet/VW, Stop&Shop Foods
86mm	Merrimac River
57 (85)	MA 113, to W Newbury, **E gas:** Mobil/24hr, Shell/repair/24hr, Sunoco, **food:** China One, d'Angelo's, Dunkin Donuts, Giuseppe's Italian, McDonald's, PapaGino's, Wendy's, White Hen Pantry/deli, **other:** [H] Brook's Drug, GNC, K-Mart, Marshall's, MktBasket Foods, Radio Shack, Shaw's Foods, Walgreens
56 (78)	Scotland Rd, to Newbury, **E** st police
55 (77)	Central St, to Byfield, **E food:** Gen Store Eatery, Village Diner, **W gas:** Prime/dsl/repair
54b a (76)	MA 133, E to Rowley, W to Groveland
75mm	**weigh sta both lanes**
53b a (74)	MA 97, S to Topsfield, N to Georgetown
52 (73)	Topsfield Rd, to Topsfield, Boxford
51 (72)	Endicott Rd, to Topsfield, Middleton
50 (71)	US 1, to MA 62, Topsfield, **E gas:** Exxon/24hr, Mobil/24hr, **other:** Honda, **W food:** Quizno's, **lodging:** Sheraton, **other:** CVS Drug, Hyundai, Staples, Stop&Shop, st police
49 (70)	MA 62 (from nb), Danvers, Middleton, **W** same as 50
48 (69)	Hobart St (from sb), **W food:** Italian Rest., **lodging:** Comfort Inn, Extended Stay America, Motel 6, **other:** Home Depot, Honda, KIA
47b a (68)	MA 114, to Middleton, Peabody, **E gas:** Gulf, Sunoco, **food:** Dunkin Donuts, McDonald's, Outback, PapaGino's, Quizno's, **other:** Chevrolet/Buick/Pontiac, Dodge, Infiniti, Lexus, Lowe's Whse, Mazda, Mitsubishi, NTB, PetsMart, Quizno's, Subaru, Toyota/Scion, Walmart, **W gas:** Hess, **food:** Chili's, TGIFriday, **lodging:** Motel 6, Residence Inn, TownePlace Suites, **other:** BigLots, Costco, Dodge, Home Depot, LandRover, Mini, NAPA, Pontiac/Hyundai
46 (67)	to US 1, **W gas:** Best, Gulf/dsl, Shell, Sunoco, **food:** Burger King, **other:** Auto Parts+
45 (66)	MA 128 N, to Peabody
44b a (65)	US 1 N, MA 129, **E gas:** Shell, **W gas:** Best/gas, Citgo, Gulf, Sunoco, **food:** Bennigan's, Bertucci's, Burger King, Carrabba's, Dunkin Donuts, Wendy's, **lodging:** Carriage House Hotel, Hampton Inn, Homewood Suites, SpringHill Suites, **other:** [H]
43 (63)	Walnut St, Lynnfield, **E** to Saugus Iron Works NHS (3mi), **W lodging:** Sheraton, **other:** golf
42 (62)	Salem St, Montrose, **E gas:** Prime, Sunoco, **food:** Sub Stop, **W lodging:** Sheraton
41 (60)	Main St, Lynnfield Ctr, **E gas:** Shell
40 (59)	MA 129, Wakefield Ctr, N Reading, **E gas:** Exxon, **food:** HoneyDew Doughnuts, **other:** Vet, **W gas:** Gulf, **other:** Chevrolet, dsl repair
39 (58)	North Ave, Reading, **E gas:** Citgo, **lodging:** Best Western, **other:** Curves, Mazda/Isuzu/Volvo/Saab, **W gas:** Shell/dsl/24hr, **food:** BearRock Cafe, Chili's, Fuddrucker's, Macaroni Grill, Starbucks, **other:** [H], Ford, Home Depot, Staples
38b a (57)	MA 28, to Reading, **E gas:** Gulf, Hess/dsl, **food:** Baja Fresh, Boston Mkt, Burger King, China Moon, d'Angelo's/PapaGino's, Dunkin Donuts, 99 Rest., Subway, **other:** AutoZone, CVS Drug, Ford, GNC, Marshalls, Radio Shack, Shaw's Foods, Walgreens, **W gas:** Exxon, Mobil, Shell, Sunoco, **food:** Burger King, Domino's, Dunkin Donuts, Harrow's Rest., McDonald's, Starbucks
37b a (56)	I-93, N to Manchester, S to Boston
36 (55)	Washington St, to Winchester, **E gas:** Lukoil, **food:** Dunkin Donuts, FarEast Chinese, The Bistro, **lodging:** Woburn Plaza Motel, **other:** BJ's Whse, Buick/Pontiac/GMC, Hogan Tire, Jaguar, Mitsubishi, Nissan, Staples, Toyota, **W gas:** Mobil, Sunoco, **food:** China Pearl, d'Angelo's, Joe's Grill, McDonald's, 99 Rest., On the Border, Panera Bread, PapaGino's, Pizza Hut, Pizzaria Uno, TGIFriday, McDonald's, **lodging:** Courtyard, Fairfield Inn, Hampton Inn, Red Roof Inn, **other:** CVS Drug, Kohl's, Lowe's Whse, Mkt Basket Foods, NTB, Office Depot, TJ Maxx, USPO, mall
35 (54)	MA 38, to Woburn, **E lodging:** Holiday Inn, **other:** [H], **W gas:** Mobil/dsl, **food:** Applebee's, Dunkin Donuts, **lodging:** Extended Stay Deluxe, **other:** Stop&Shop Foods
34 (53)	Winn St, Woburn
33b a (52)	US 3 S, MA 3A N, to Winchester, **E food:** Bickford's Grille, Café Escadrille, ChuckeCheese, Outback Steaks, Panera Bread, Paparazzi's, **other:** [H], CVS Drug, Honda, Marshalls, Michael's, Roach Bro's Foods, **W gas:** Citgo, Hess, **lodging:** Marriott, **other:** [H], Audi/Porsche, repair
32b a (51)	US 3 N, MA 2A S, to Lowell, **E gas:** Shell, **lodging:** Hilton Garden, **other: W food:** Boston Mkt, Burger King, Cheesecake Factory, Chili's, d'Angelo's, Macaroni Grill, McDonald's, Pizzaria Uno, TCBY, **lodging:** Candlewood Suites, Homestead Suites, **other:** Barnes&Noble, Dodge, Kohl's, Macy's, Sears/auto, Staples, mall
31b a (48)	MA 4, MA 225, Lexington, **E gas:** Gulf, Mobil/repair, Shell, **food:** Alexander's Pizza, Starbucks, **other:** Walgreens, **W gas:** Exxon/24hr, Shell/24hr, **food:** d'Angelo's, Friendly's, Lexington Cafe, McDonald's, **lodging:** Bedford Motel, Best Western, Quality Inn, **other:** Vet, Curves, Staples

N ↕ S

AMESBURY

PEABODY

READING

LEXINGTON

INTERSTATE 95 CONT'D

Exit # Services

30b a (47) MA 2A, Lexington, **E gas:** Shell, **other:** [H], **W lodging:** Sheraton, **other:** to MinuteMan NP, Hanscom AFB

46.5mm travel plaza nb, Mobil/dsl/24hr, HoneyDew Doughnuts, McDonald's, gifts

29b a (46) MA 2 W, Cambridge

28b a (45) Trapelo Rd, Belmont, **E gas:** Exxon/dsl, Mobil/dsl, Shell, **food:** Boston Mkt, Dunkin Donuts, Friendly's, McDonald's, Panera Bread, PapaGino's, **other:** Osco Drugs, Shaw's Foods

27b a (44) Totten Pond Rd, Waltham, **E gas:** Shell, **food:** Naked Fish Rest., **lodging:** Best Western, Courtyard, Hilton Garden, Holiday Inn Express, Homestead Suites, Westin Hotel, **W food:** Bertucci's Rest., Pizzaria Uno, **lodging:** DoubleTree/rest., **other:** Costco, Home Depot

26 (43) US 20, to MA 117, to Waltham, **E gas:** Sunoco/dsl, **W gas:** Mobil

25 (42) I-90, MA Tpk

24 (41) MA 30, Newton, Wayland, **E gas:** Mobil, **lodging:** Marriott

23 (40) Recreation Rd (from nb), to MA Tpk

22b a (39) Grove St, **E lodging:** Holiday Inn Express, **other:** golf

38.5mm travel plaza sb, Mobil/dsl, McDonald's, gifts

21b a (38) MA 16, Newton, Wellesley, **E** [H], **W gas:** Sunoco, **food:** Paparazzi, Starbucks

20b a (36) MA 9, Brookline, Framingham

19 (35) Highland Ave, Newton, Needham, **E gas:** Gulf, Hess, **food:** d'Angelo's, Dunkin Donuts, Ground Round, Mandarin Cuisine, McDonald's, Mighty Subs, **lodging:** Sheraton/rest., **other:** PetCo, Staples, **W food:** Bickford's, **other:** Chevrolet, Ford

18 (34) Great Plain Ave, W Roxbury

33.5mm parking area sb, litter barrels

17 (33) MA 135, Needham, Wellesley

32mm truck turnout sb

16b a (31) MA 109, High St, Dedham, **W gas:** Mobil/dsl

15b a (29) US 1, MA 128, **E gas:** Gulf, **food:** Bickford's, Bugaboo Steaks, Chili's, Joe's Grill, Krispy Kreme, Panera Bread, PapaGino's, TGIFriday, Vinny T's Rest., **lodging:** Comfort Inn, Fairfield Inn, Holiday Inn, Residence Inn, **other:** Vet, Best Buy, BJ's Whse, CVS Drug, Lincoln/Mercury, Nissan, NTB, PepBoys, Speedy Repair, Star Foods, Volvo, **W gas:** Shell/dsl/24hr, **food:** Burger King, Dunkin Donuts, Jade Chinese, McDonald's, **lodging:** Budget Motel, **other:** Aamco, Audi, Buick, Chrysler/Jeep, Hyundai, Mercedes, Pontiac

14 (28) East St, Canton St, **E lodging:** Hilton

27mm rest area sb, full facilities, litter barrels

13 (26.5) University Ave

12 (26) I-93 N, to Braintree, Boston, motorist callboxes end nb

11b a (23) Neponset St, to Canton, **E gas:** Citgo/repair, Sunoco/repair, **food:** Dunkin Donuts

22.5mm Neponset River

10 (20) Coney St (from sb, no EZ return), to US 1, Sharon, Walpole, **1 mi W on US 1...gas:** Citgo, Mobil, **food:** Caldo's Rest., Dunkin Donuts, Friendly's, IHOP, McDonald's, 99 Rest., Old Country Buffet, Out

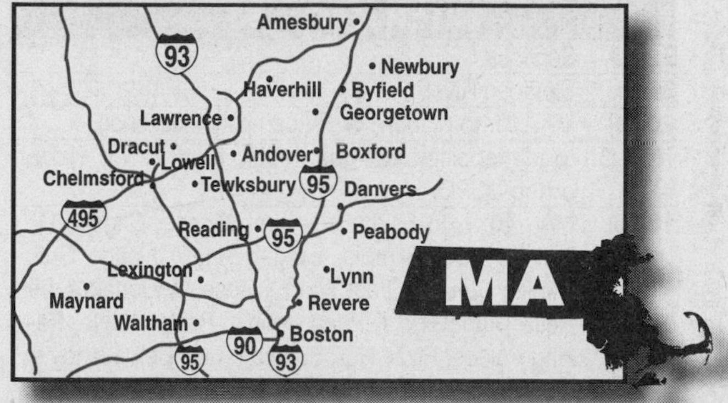

10 (20) Continued
back Steaks, PapaGino's, Pizza Hut, Starbucks, Taco Bell, TGIFriday, **lodging:** Courtyard, Residence Inn, Sheraton, **other:** Acura, Advance Parts, Barnes&Noble, Brook's Drug, CVS Drug, Home Depot, Kohl's, Lexus, Old Navy, Staples, Stop&Shop Foods, VW, Walgreens, mall

9 (19) US 1, to MA 27, Walpole, **W gas:** Mobil, **food:** Applebee's, Bickford's, Boston View, Clyde's Roadhouse, Dunkin Donuts, **lodging:** Econolodge, Holiday Inn Express, **other:** BigY Food/drug, Walmart, same as 10

8 (16) S Main St, Sharon, **E food:** Dunkin Donuts, **other:** Brook's Drug, Shaw's Foods, whaling museum

7b a (13) MA 140, to Mansfield, **E food:** Domino's, 99 Rest., Piccadilly's, **lodging:** Comfort Inn, Courtyard, Holiday Inn, Red Roof Inn, Residence Inn. **W gas:** Shell, **food:** PapaGino's, **other:** Radio Shack

6b a (12) I-495, S to Cape Cod, N to NH

10mm Welcome Ctr/rest area nb, full facilities, info, litter barrels, petwalk

9mm truck parking area sb

5 (7) MA 152, Attleboro, **E** [H], **W gas:** Gulf/dsl, **food:** Bill's Pizza, Piccadilly Rest., Wendy's, **other:** Radio Shack, Shaw's Foods/Osco Drug

4 (6) I-295 S, to Woonsocket

3 (4) MA 123, to Attleboro, **E gas:** Shell/dsl, **other:** [H], zoo

2.5mm parking area/weigh sta both lanes, no restrooms, litter barrels, motorist callboxes

2b a (1) US 1A, Newport Ave, Attleboro, **E gas:** Mobil/dsl, Shell, Sunoco, **food:** Honeydew Doughnuts, McDonald's, Olive Garden, Spumoni's Italian, **other:** Home Depot, K-Mart, Shaw's Foods, **W gas:** Getty/dsl

1 (.5) US 1 (from sb), **E lodging:** Day's Inn, **other:** Brooks Drug, Volvo

0mm Massachusetts/Rhode Island state line

INTERSTATE 195

Exit # Services

22 (41) I-495 N, MA 25 S, to Cape Cod.

I-195 begins/ends on I-495, exit 1.

21 (39) MA 28, to Wareham, **N gas:** Maxi/dsl/24hr, **food:** Longhorn Steaks, Pomodore's Italian, Qdoba Mexican, Red Robin, **other:** Best Buy, Borders Books, JC Penney, LL Bean, Lowe's Whse, Michaels, Old Navy, PetCo, Staples, Target, **S gas:** Gateway Gas/dsl, Mobil, **other:** [H], **other:** NAPA, repair

37mm rest area eb, info, litter barrels, petwalk, boat ramp

INTERSTATE 195

N ↕ S

Exit #	Services
36mm	Sippican River
20 (35)	MA 105, to Marion, **S** RV camping (seasonal)
19b a (31)	to Mattapoisett, **S gas:** Mobil, **food:** Nick's Pizza, **other:** USPO
18 (26)	MA 240 S, to Fairhaven, **1 mi S gas:** Citgo/7-11, Lukoil, **food:** Blimpie, Burger King, Chicago Grill, Dunkin Donuts, Great Wall Chinese, McDonald's, 99 Rest., PapaGino's, Papa John's, Pasta House, Peking Palace, Pizza Hut, Subway, Taco Bell, Wendy's, **lodging:** Hampton Inn, **other:** AutoZone, Curves, $Tree, GMC/Buick/Pontiac, GNC, K-Mart, Marshalls, Mazda, Radio Shack, Shaw's Foods, Staples, Stop$Shop, TownFair Tire, Walgreens, Walmart
25.5mm	Acushnet River
17 (24)	Coggeshall St, New Bedford, **N gas:** Petro, 7-11/gas, Sunoco, **food:** Dunkin Donuts, EndZone Café, McDonald's, same as 16
16 (23)	Washburn St (from eb), **N gas:** Sunoco, **food:** McDonald's, Papa John's
15 (22)	MA 18 S, New Bedford, **S** Whaling Museum, hist dist, to downtown,
14 (21)	Penniman St (from eb), New Bedford, downtown
13b a (20)	MA 140, **N** [airport], **S gas:** Buttonwood/dsl, Sunoco, **food:** Dunkin Donuts, Quizno's, **other:** [H], Buttonwood Park/zoo, CVS Drug, Honda, Shaw's Foods, Walgreens, VW
12b a (19)	N Dartmouth, **S gas:** Hess, Mobil/dsl, **food:** Burger King, D'angelo's, Dunkin Donuts, Friendly's, IHOP, McDonald's, 99 Rest., Old Country Buffet, Olive Garden, Panera Bread, PapaGino's, Peking Garden, Quizno's, Ruby Tuesday, Subway, Taco Bell, TX Roadhouse, Wendy's, **lodging:** Comfort Inn, Residence Inn, **other:** Barnes&Noble, Best Buy, BJ's Whse, Chevrolet, Curves, Firestone/auto, JC Penney, Kohl's, Lowe's Whse, Macy's, Old Navy, Sears/auto, Stop&Shop Food/gas, TJ Maxx, TownFair Tire, Toyota/Scion, Walmart, USPO, mall, st police
11b a (17)	Reed Rd, to Dartmouth, **2 mi S gas:** Shell/24hr
10 (16)	MA 88 S, to US 6, Westport, **S gas:** Irving, Rte 6 Gas, Valero/dsl, **lodging:** Hampton Inn
9 (15.5)	MA 24 N (from nb), Stanford Rd, Westport, **S gas:** Rte 6 Gas, **food:** LePage's Seafood, White's Rest., **lodging:** Hampton Inn
8b a (15)	MA 24 S, Fall River, Westport, **N gas:** Crosson Gas, **food:** Papa John's, **S food:** Dunkin Donuts, Subway
7 (14)	MA 81 S, Plymouth Ave, Fall River, **N gas:** Getty, Hess, **food:** Boston Mkt, Burger King, D'angelo's Rest., Dunkin Donuts, Honeydew Doughnuts, KFC, 99 Rest., Subway, Wendy's, **other:** [H], Buick/Pontiac, CVS Drug, **S gas:** Shell, **food:** Applebee's, McDonald's, **other:** Goodyear/auto, Walgreens
6 (13.5)	Pleasant St, Fall River, downtown
5 (13)	MA 79, MA 138, to Taunton, **S gas:** Exxon, Lukoil, **food:** Honeydew Doughnuts, Papa John's, **lodging:** Day's Inn
12mm	Assonet Bay
4b a (10)	MA 103, to Swansea, Somerset, **N gas:** Getty, **food:** Rogers Rest., **other:** auto repair, **S gas:** Shell/24hr, **food:** Jillian's Cafe, **lodging:** Quality Inn, Swansea Motel
3 (8)	US 6, to MA 118, Swansea, Rehoboth, **N gas:** Citgo/dsl, Hess, **food:** Burger King, Dunkin Donuts, Friendly's, McDonald's, Ponderosa, Thai Taste, Tim Horton, Wendy's, **other:** BigLots, CarQuest, $Tree, Firestone/auto, Jo-Anne, Macy's, Marshall's, NAPA, Old Navy, Price Rite Foods, Seabra Foods, Sears/auto, mall, **S gas:** Gulf/24hr, **food:** Anthony's Seafood, **lodging:** Swansea Motel
6mm	**rest area eb, full [handicapped] facilities, [phone], [picnic], litter barrels, petwalk**
5.5mm	**parking area wb**
2 (5)	MA 136, to Newport, **S gas:** Mobil/24hr, Shell/24hr, **food:** Cathay Pearl Chinese, Dunkin Donuts, McDonald's, Michael's Rest., Subway
3mm	**weigh sta both lanes**
1 (1)	MA 114A, to Seekonk, **N gas:** Citgo, Exxon/dsl, Shell/24hr, **food:** Dunkin Donuts, Honeydew Doughnuts, Newport Creamery, 99 Rest., Tony's Pizza, **lodging:** Motel 6, **other:** Vet, **S gas:** Hess, Mobil/24hr, Sunoco/dsl, **food:** Applebee's, BigLots, Bugaboo Creek Steaks, Burger King, Chili's, Darling's Rest., Dunkin Donuts, Friendly's, McDonald's, Old Country Buffet, Outback Steaks, Panera Bread, PapaGino's, Subway, Taco Bell, TGIFriday, Tuesday Morning, Wendy's, Vinny T's Rest., **lodging:** Best Western, Comfort Inn, Extended Stay America, Hampton Inn, Knight's Inn, Mary's Motel, Ramada Inn/rest., Town'n Country Motel, **other:** Acura, Best Buy, BigLots, Bob's Stores, $Tree, Firestone/Auto, GNC, Home Depot, Jiffy Lube, Kohl's, Lowe's Whse, Michael's, PepBoys, PetCo, Sam's Club, Staples, Stop&Shop Foods, Target, TJMaxx, TownFair Tire, Volvo, Walmart/drug
0mm	**I-95 begins/ends on I-95, exit 20 in Providence, RI, Exits 1-8 are in RI**

FALL RIVER

INTERSTATE 290

E ↕ W

Exit #	Services
26b a (20)	I-495. I-290 begins/ends on I-495, exit 25.
25b a (17)	Solomon Pond Mall Rd, to Berlin, **N food:** Bertucci's, TGIFriday, **food:** Olive Garden, **lodging:** Comfort Inn, Residence Inn, **other:** Best Buy, Borders Books, JC Penney, Sears/auto, Target, mall, **S** Solomon Pond Grill
24 (15)	Church St, Northborough
23b a (13)	MA 140, Boylston, **N gas:** Citgo/dsl, Mobil, **food:** Dunkin Donuts, Other Place Rest.
22 (11)	Main St, Worchester, **N gas:** Exxon/24hr, Shell, **food:** Bickford's, Friendly's, McDonald's, Wendy's, **other:** [H]
21 (10)	Plantation St (from eb), **N lodging:** Best Western, **other:** Lowe's Whse, Staples, Stop&Shop, Target
20 (8)	MA 70, Lincoln St, Burncoat St, **N gas:** Charter/24hr, Exxon/Subway/24hr, Shell, Sunoco, **food:** Bickford's, Denny's, Dunkin Donuts, Friendly's, McDonald's, Papa Gino's, Taco Bell, Wendy's, **lodging:** Day's Inn, Econolodge, Holiday Inn, **other:** Auto Palace, CVS Drug, Radio Shack, Shaw's Food/24hr, Walgreen
19 (7)	I-190 N, MA 12
18	MA 9, Framington, Ware, Worcester [airport], **N** [H]
16	Central St, Worcester, **N food:** 99 Rest., **lodging:** Crowne Plaza, Hampton Inn, mall

WORCESTER

MA

INTERSTATE 290 CONT'D

E ↕ W

Exit #	Services
14	MA 122, Barre, Worcester, downtown
13	MA 122A, Vernon St, Worcester, downtown
12	MA 146 S, to Millbury
11	Southbridge St, College Square, **N gas:** Shell/dsl, **food:** Wendy's, **S gas:** Getty
10	MA 12 N (from wb), Hope Ave
9	Auburn St, to Auburn, **E gas:** Shell, **food:** Arby's, Bickford's, Wendy's, McDonald's, **lodging:** Baymont Inn, Comfort Inn, Holiday Inn Express, **other:** Acura, AutoZone, Firestone, Sears/auto, Shaw's Foods, Staples, mall
8	MA 12 S (from sb), Webster, **W gas:** Shell, **lodging:** Best Western
7	I-90, E to Boston, W to Springfield.

I-290 begins/ends on I-90.

INTERSTATE 395

N ↕ S

Exit #	Services
	I-395 begins/ends on I-90, exit 10.
7 (12)	to I-90 (MA Tpk), MA 12, **E gas:** Shell, **food:** Piccadilly's, **lodging:** Comfort Inn, Holday Inn Express
6b a (11)	US 20, **E gas:** Gulf, **food:** Dunkin Donuts, KFC, **other:** Honda, Saab/VW, TCI Tires, truck repair, **W gas:** Shell, **food:** Chuck's Steakhouse, Friendly's, **lodging:** Fairfield Inn, Hampton Inn, **other:** BJ's Whse, Buick/Pontiac/GMC/Cadillac, Ford/Mercury, Home Depot, Mitsubishi, Nissan, TJ Maxx, transmissions
5 (8)	Depot Rd, N Oxford
4b a (6)	Sutton Ave, to Oxford, **W gas:** Mobil/24hr, **food:** Dunkin Donuts, McDonald's, NE Pizza, Subway, **other:** Cahill's Tire/Repair, Cumberland Farms, CVS Drug
3 (4)	Cudworth Rd, to N Webster, S Oxford
2 (3)	MA 16, to Webster, **E** Subaru, **W gas:** Exxon/24hr, Getty, Hi-Lo Gas, Sunoco, **food:** Burger King, D'angelo, Dunkin Donuts, Empire Wok, Friendly's, Honey Dew Donuts, KFC/Taco Bell, McDonald's, Papa Gino's, **other:** H, Advance Parts, Auto Repair, Consumer Parts, CVS Drug, Ford, PriceChopper Foods, Rite Aid, Walgreen
1 (1)	MA 193, to Webster, **E** H, **W gas:** Citgo/dsl, **food:** Golden Greek Rest., Wind Tiki Chinese, **other:** Goodyear/auto
0mm	Massachusetts/Connecticut state line

INTERSTATE 495

N ↕ S

Exit #	Services
	I-495 begins/ends on I-95, exit 59.
55 (119)	MA 110 (from nb, no return), to I-95 S, **E gas:** Best Choice/Domino's/dsl, Irving, **food:** Acupulco Mexican, Burger King, Dunkin Donuts, Friendly's, McDonald's, **lodging:** Fairfield Inn, **other:** Chevrolet/VW, Stop&Shop, **W gas:** Gulf, **food:** Amesbury Pizza, **other:** Curves, NAPA
54 (118)	MA 150, to Amesbury, **W** RV camping
53 (115)	Broad St, Merrimac, **W gas:** Gulf, **food:** Dunkin Donuts
114mm	parking area sb, phone, restrooms, picnic, litter barrels (6AM-8PM)
52 (111)	MA 110, to Haverhill, **E** H, **W gas:** Lukoil, Mobil/dsl, **food:** Dunkin Donuts, King's Roast Beef

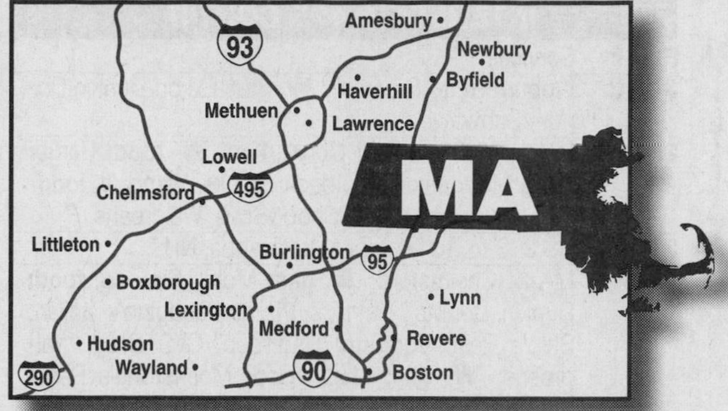

HAVERHILL

Exit #	Services
110mm	**parking area nb, phone, picnic, litter barrels**
51 (109)	MA 125, to Haverhill, **E gas:** Citgo, Mobil, **food:** Bros Pizza, China King, **other:** H, Family$, **W food:** Dunkin Donuts, Friendly's, Longhorn Steaks, Lucky Corner Chinese, McDonald's, Starbucks, Wendy's
50 (107)	MA 97, to Haverhill, **E** H, **W** Ford, Lowe's Whse, Target
49 (106)	MA 110, to Haverhill, **E gas:** Gulf, Sunoco/24hr, **food:** A1 Deli, Athens Pizza, Dunkin Donuts, McDonald's, Oriental Garden, 99 Rest., PapaGino's, **lodging:** Best Western, Comfort Inn, **other:** Chevrolet/Pontiac/Buick, CVS Drug, MktBasket Foods, Walgreens
105.8mm	Merrimac River
48 (105.5)	MA 125, to Bradford, **E gas:** BJ's Whse/gas
47 (105)	MA 213, to Methuen, **1-2 mi W food:** Applebees, Bugaboo Steaks, Burger King, ChuckeCheese, McDonald's, Starbucks, TGIFriday, Wendy's, **other:** Borders Books, Home Depot, Marshalls, Old Navy, Walmart, Methuen Mall, Stop&Shop Foods, Target
46 (104)	MA 110, **E gas:** Pleasant Valley Gas, Sunoco/24hr, **gas:** Capalini's Italian, **other:** Lincoln/Mercury, **W** H
45 (103)	Marston St, to Lawrence, **W other:** Chevrolet, Honda, Kia
44 (102)	Merrimac St, to Lawrence
43 (101)	Mass Ave
42 (100)	MA 114, **E gas:** Exxon, Gulf, Mobil, **food:** Boston Mkt, Dunkin Donuts, Friendly's, Lee Chin Cninese, Pizza Hut, **lodging:** Holiday Inn Express, **other:** MktBasket Foods, PetCo, Walgreens, **W gas:** Gas-N-Go, **food:** Denny's, Dunkin Donuts, Pizza Hut, Subway, Taco Bell, Wendy's, **other:** H, Rite Aid, Save-A-Lot Foods, VIP Parts/service
41 (99)	MA 28, to Andover, **E food:** Dunkin Donuts, **other:** Chevrolet
40b a (98)	I-93, N to Methuen, S to Boston
39 (94)	MA 133, to Dracut, **E gas:** Hess, **food:** Longhorn Steaks, McDonald's, **lodging:** Extended Stay America, **W gas:** Mobil/dsl, **food:** Cracker Barrel, Wendy's, **lodging:** Fairfield Inn, Holiday Inn/rest., Residence Inn
38 (93)	MA 38, to Lowell, **E gas:** Shell/dsl, **food:** Applebee's, Burger King, Dunkin Donuts, El Pollo Loco, IHOP, Jade East, 99 Rest., Waffle House, **lodging:** Motel 6, **other:** Home Depot, Honda/VW, Walmart, **W gas:** Citgo, Mobil, Sunoco, USA/dsl, **food:** Dunkin Donuts, Milan Pizza, McDonald's, Wendy's, **other:** Chevrolet/Pontiac/Buick/GMC, CVS Drug, Hannaford Foods, Marshalls, Sears Essentials, Staples

INTERSTATE 495 CONT'D

N ↕ S

Exit #	Services
37 (91)	Woburn St, to S Lowell, **W gas:** Exxon/Dunkin Donuts/Subway
35c (90)	to Lowell SP, Lowell ConX, **1 mi W food:** Burger King, McDonald's, Outback Steaks, Wendy's, **lodging:** Courtyard, **other:** Shop&Save, Walgreens
35b a (89)	US 3, S to Burlington, N to Nashua, NH
34 (88)	MA 4, Chelmsford, **E gas:** Mobil, Sunoco, **food:** Dunkin Donuts, Jimmy's Pizza, Papagino's Italian, Skip's Rest., **lodging:** Radisson, CVS Drug, Walgreens, **W gas:** Shell, **food:** Moonstone's Rest., **lodging:** Best Western
33	MA 4, N Chelmsford (from nb)
88mm	motorist aid call boxes begin sb
87mm	**rest area both lanes, full facilities, litter barrels, vending, petwalk, (8AM-8PM)**
32 (83)	Boston Rd, to MA 225, **E gas:** Exxon/24hr, Gulf/service, Mobil/24hr, **food:** Applebee's, Burger King, Chili's, D'angelo's, Dunkin Donuts, McDonald's, Starbucks, Westford Grill, **lodging:** Hampton Inn, Residence Inn, **other:** CVS Drug, MktBasket Foods, Radio Shack, Rite Aid, Walgreens, to Nashoba Valley Ski Area
31 (80)	MA 119, to Groton, **E gas:** Gulf, Mobil/dsl/24hr, Shell, **food:** Dunkin Donuts, Ken's Café, **other:** CVS Drug, Vet
30 (78)	MA 110, to Littleton, **1 mi E gas:** Shell, **food:** USPO, **W gas:** Citgo/dsl, Shell, Sunoco/dsl, **other:** H, RV camping, Vet
29b a (77)	MA 2, to Leominster, **E** to Walden Pond St Reserve
28 (75)	MA 111, to Boxborough, Harvard, **E gas:** Exxon/Dunkin Donuts, **lodging:** Holiday Inn
27 (70)	MA 117, to Bolton, **E gas:** Mobil/dsl, **food:** Subway, **W food:** Bolton Pizza, **other:** Curves, Vet
26 (68)	MA 62, to Berlin, **E gas:** Exxon/Dunkin Donuts, **lodging:** Holiday Inn Express, **W gas:** Shell/dsl, **other:** Berlin Farms Cafe
66mm	Assabet River
25b (64)	I-290, to Worchester
25a	to MA 85, Marlboro, **1 mi E gas:** Gulf, Mobil/dsl, **food:** Burger King, Checkerboards Rest., D'angelo's, Domino's, Honeydew Donuts, 99 Rest., Piccadilly's, **other:** CVS Drug, Family$, GMC, Hannaford Foods, Stop&Shop, TJ Maxx, Walgreens
24b a (63)	US 20, to Northboro, Marlboro, **E gas:** Gulf/repair, Mobil, **food:** Allora Rest., D'angelo's, Dunkin Donuts, Lake Williams Pizza, **lodging:** Holiday Inn, **W gas:** Exxon, Shell, **food:** Boston Mkt, China Taste, Longhorn Steaks, McDonald's/playplace, 99 Rest., Panera Bread, PapaGino's, Quizno's, Starbucks, Subway, Tandoori Grill, Wendy's, **lodging:** Best Western, Courtyard, Embassy Suites, Hampton Inn, Homestead Suites, **other:** $Tree, GNC, Hannaford Foods
23c (60)	Simrano Dr, Marlboro
23b a (59)	MA 9, to Shrewsbury, Framingham, **E gas:** Exxon/dsl, Gulf, **food:** Wendy's, **lodging:** Red Roof Inn, **W gas:** Mobil/dsl/24hr, Shell, **food:** Bertucci's, Burger King, Chateau Rest., D'angelo's, Dunkin Donuts, Friendly's, McDonald's, Piccadilly's, Ruby Tuesday, **lodging:** Doubletree Inn, Extended Stay America, Extended Stay Deluxe, Residence Inn, **other:** H, Chrysler/Jeep, Marshall's, Mitsubishi, Pontiac/Buick/GMC, Staples, Stop&Shop, VW
22 (58)	I-90, MA TPK, E to Boston, W to Albany
21b a (54)	MA 135, to Hopkinton, Upton, **E gas:** Gulf, Mobil, **food:** Dino's Pizza, Dynasty Chinese, Golden Spoon Rest.
20 (50)	MA 85, to Milford, **W gas:** Gulf/dsl/LP, Mobil/dsl, **food:** 99 Rest., Pizza 85/deli, TGIFriday, Wendy's, **lodging:** Baymont Inn, Comfort Inn, Courtyard/rest, Day's Inn, Fairfield Inn, Holiday Inn Express, **other:** H, Best Buy, Lowe's Whse, Staples, Stop&Shop, Target, TJ Maxx
19 (48)	MA 109, to Milford, **W gas:** Mobil/dsl/24hr, Shell, **food:** Alamo Mexican, Applebee's, Bugaboo Cr Steaks, Burger King, D'angelo, Dunkin Donuts, Friendly's, KFC/Pizza Hut, Maria Italian, McDonald's/playplace, PapaGino's, Subway, **lodging:** La Quinta, Sheraton, **other:** AutoZone, CVS Drug, Hannaford Foods, Jo-Ann Fabrics, K-Mart, Kohl's, Radio Shack, Rite Aid
18 (46)	MA 126, to Bellingham, **E food:** Chili's, Coldstone Creamery, McDonald's, **other:** Barnes&Noble, Mkt-Basket Foods, Old Navy, Staples, Walmart/Subway, Whole Foods Mkt, **W gas:** Hess, Mobil/24hr, Sunoco/dsl, **food:** DQ, Dunkin Donuts, Outback Steaks, Pizzaria Uno, **other:** Home Depot, PetsMart
17 (44)	MA 140, to Franklin, Bellingham, **E gas:** Mobil/dsl, Shell, Sunoco, **food:** Applebee's, Asian Cuisine, Burger King, D'angelo's, Dunkin Donuts, KFC, Longhorn Steaks, Panera Bread, PapaGino's, Subway, Taco Bell, **other:** AutoZone, Buick/GMC, Curves, CVS Drug, GNC, Marshalls, Radio Shack, Stop&Shop, **W** H, BJ's Whse/gas, **food:** 99 Rest., Piccadilly's, **lodging:** Residence Inn
16 (42)	King St, to Franklin, **E gas:** Sunoco/24hr, **food:** Dunkin Donuts, Franklin Deli, Joe's Grill, King St Cafe, McDonald's, **lodging:** Hampton Inn, **other:** Spruce Pond Creamery, **W lodging:** Hawthorn Inn
15 (39)	MA 1A, to Plainville, Wrentham, **E gas:** Mobil, **other:** H, **W gas:** Mobil/dsl, **food:** Chicago Grill, Cracker Barrel, Dunkin Donuts, Friendly's, Ruby Tuesday, Uno Pizzaria, **other:** Premium Outlets/famous brands
14b a (37)	US 1, to N Attleboro, **E gas:** Interstate/D'angelo's/PapaGino's/dsl, **food:** Luciano's Rest., **lodging:** Arbor Motel, **other:** Bass Pro Shops (4mi), **W gas:** Mobil, **food:** Chili's, Dunkin Donuts, Panera Bread, **other:** Macdonald's RV Ctr, Stop&Shop, Lowe's, NTB, Target, TJ Maxx, Vet
13 (32)	I-95, N to Boston, S to Providence, access to H
12 (30)	MA 140, to Mansfield, **E food:** Bertucci's Italian, Honeydew Doughnuts, Longhorn Steaks, Qdoba Mexican, TGIFriday, Wendy's, **other:** Best Buy, Borders Books, Home Depot, LL Bean, Michael's, PetCo, Kohl's, Shaw's Foods, Staples, Wildharvest Food
11 (29)	MA 140 S (from sb, no EZ return), **1 mi W gas:** Gulf, **food:** Dunkin Donuts, Mandarin Chinese, McDonald's, Subway, **other:** $Tree
10 (26)	MA 123, to Norton, **E food:** Dunkin Donuts, **other:** QuickStop, **W** H
9 (24)	Bay St, to Taunton, **E food:** Chateau Rest., **W food:** Dunkin Donuts, Jaybo Cafe, Quizno's, Ruby Tuesday's, Wendy's, **lodging:** Holiday Inn, **other:** BJ's Whse

MARLBORO

INTERSTATE 495 CONT'D

N ↕ S — MIDDLEBORO

Exit #	Services
8 (22)	MA 138, to Raynham, **E gas:** Hess, Mobil/dsl, **food:** Honeydew Donuts, Yummyhouse Rest., **W gas:** Citgo/dsl, Exxon/dsl, Irving/dsl, Shell/dsl/repair, **food:** Cape Cod Cafe, China Garden, D'angelo, Dunkin Doughnuts, Honeydew Donuts, La Casa Mia Rest., Lucky Corner Chinese, McDonald's, Pepperoni's Pizza, Quizno's, Subway, **other:** H, CVS Drug, Mkt Basket Foods, USPO, Vet
7b a (19)	MA 24, to Fall River, Boston, **1/2 mi E food:** Burger King
18mm	**weigh sta both lanes**
17.5mm	Taunton River
6 (15)	US 44, to Middleboro, **E gas:** Super/dsl, **food:** Burger King, Dunkin Donuts, Fireside Grille, Friendly's, Hong Kong Taste, PapaGino's, Subway, **W gas:** Mobil/dsl, **lodging:** Dunkin Donuts, Fairfield Inn, Holiday Inn Express, **other:** Crossroads RV Ctr
5 (14)	MA 18, to Lakeville, **E food:** Burger King, Dunkin Donuts, Fireside Grille, Friendly's, PapaGino's, **other:** CVS Drug, Kelly's Tire, Stop&Shop Food, **W other:** Massasoit SP, RV camping (seasonal)
4 (12)	MA 105, to Middleboro, **E gas:** Exxon/dsl/24hr, Shell/24hr, Sunoco/24hr, **food:** DQ, Dunkin Donuts,

Exit #	Services
4 (12)	Continued McDonald's, **lodging:** Day's Inn, **other:** AutoZone, Chevrolet, Rite Aid
10.5mm	**parking area eb**
10mm	**parking area both lanes**
3 (8)	MA 28, to Rock Village, S Middleboro, **E gas:** Citgo/dsl, **other:** Buds RV's, Fred's Repair, **W gas:** Mobil/Dunkin Donuts/Subway/dsl, **food:** Chicken House Rest
2 (3)	MA 58, W Wareham, **E other:** to Myles Standish SF, **W gas:** 7-11/gas
2mm	Weweantic River
1 (0)	I-495 begins/ends on I-195, MA 25 S.

MICHIGAN

INTERSTATE 69

N ↕ S — PORT HURON

Exit #	Services
199	Lp 69 (from eb, no return), to Port Huron, **S gas:** Mobil/dsl, **other:** AutoZone, K-Mart, Sam's Club/gas
I-69 E and I-94 E run together into Port Huron. See Michigan 94 Exits 274-275mm.	
198	I-94, to Detroit and Canada
196	Wadhams Rd, **N gas:** BP, Marathon, Speedy Q/dsl, Shell/Wendy's, **food:** Hungry Howie's, McDonald's, Peking Kitchen, Subway, **other:** Carter's Foods, Wadham's Drugs, KOA (1mi), **S** golf
194	Taylor Rd, **N** Good L's CP, RV camping
189	Wales Center Rd, to Goodells, **S** golf
184	MI 19, to Emmett, **N gas:** Citgo/dsl/scales/rest./24hr, **other:** repair, **S gas:** Marathon/dsl/24hr
180	Riley Center Rd, **N** KOA
176	Capac Rd, **N gas:** BP/McDonald's/dsl, **food:** Subway (2mi)
174mm	**rest area wb, full facilities, phone, picnic, litter barrels, vending, petwalk**
168	MI 53, Imlay City, **N gas:** BP/dsl/24hr, Speedway/dsl, **food:** Big Boy, Big Joe's Pizza, Burger King, DQ, Hungry Howie's, Jet's Pizza, Little Caesar's, Lucky's Steaks, McDonald's, New China, Taco Bell, Wah Wong Chinese, Wendy's/Tim Horton, **lodging:** Day's Inn, M53 Motel, **other:** AutoZone, Chevrolet/Pontiac, Chrysler/Dodge/Jeep, Discount Drug, $Discount, Ford, GNC, IGA Foods, Kroger, NAPA, Pamida, Radio Shack, **S** camping
163	Lake Pleasant Rd, to Attica
160mm	**rest area eb, full facilities, phone, picnic, litter barrels,**

LAPEER

Exit #	Services
160mm	Continued **vending, petwalk**
159	Wilder Rd
158mm	Flint River
155	MI 24, Lapeer, **1 mi N gas:** BP, Clark/dsl, FS, Meijer/dsl/24hr, Speedy Q, **food:** Apple Tree Rest., Arby's, Blind Fish Rest., Brian's Rest., Burger King, Coffee Tree Cafe, DQ, Farmhouse Rest., Hot'n Now, Jet's Pizza, KFC, Little Caesar's, McDonald's, Mr Pita, Nick's Rest., Subway, Taco Bell, Tim Horton, Wah Wong Chinese, Wendy's, **lodging:** Best Western, Fairfield Inn, **other:** H, AutoZone, Curves, $Tree, Home Depot, K-Mart, Kroger, Murray's Parts, Office Depot, Radio Shack, SavALot, st police, Vet, **S gas:** Mobil/dsl, **other:** Buick/Pontiac
153	Lake Nepessing Rd, **S** to Thumb Correctional, camping, golf
149	Elba Rd, **S other:** Country Mkt, Torzwski CP, RV/truck repair
145	MI 15, Davison, **N gas:** Marathon, Shell/dsl, Speedway, **food:** Apollo Rest., Applebee's, Arby's, Big Boy, Big John's Rest., Burger King, Chee Kong Chinese, Country Sun Rest., Hungry Howie's, Italia Gardens, KFC, Little Caesar's, McDonald's, Senor Lucky, Subway, Taco Bell, Tim Horton, **lodging:** Comfort Inn, **other:** AutoValue Parts, GNC, Pontiac/Buick/GMC, Radio Shack, Rite Aid/24hr, Walgreens, repair, **S gas:** Mobil/dsl
143	Irish Rd, **N gas:** Speedway/dsl, **S gas:** Meijer/dsl, Shell/McDonald's/24hr, **other:** Meijer, 7-11
141	Belsay Rd, Flint, **N gas:** 1 stop, Shell/Wendy's/dsl/24hr, **food:** Country Kitchen, Dominos,

INTERSTATE 69 CONT'D

N ↕ S

FLINT

Exit #	Services
145	Continued McDonald's, Taco Bell, **other:** Harley-Davidson, K-Mart, Kroger, Walmart SuperCtr/Subway/auto, **S gas:** Sunoco/A&W/LJ Silver/dsl
139	Center Rd, Flint, **N gas:** Speedway/dsl, **food:** Applebee's, Boston Mkt, Coney Island, Cottage Pizza, Empire Wok, Halo Burger, Moykong Chinese, Old Country Buffet, Ponderosa, Quizno's, Starbucks, Subway, Tim Horton, **lodging:** Best Inn, **other:** Aldi Foods, Discount Tire, Family$, Home Depot, JC Penney, Jo-Ann Fabrics, Lowe's Whse, Old Navy, Staples, VG Foods, mall, **S gas:** Meijer/dsl/24hr, **food:** Bob Evans, Coney Island, DQ, Firkin & Fox Rest., McDonald's, Mancino's/SaLoupes, Subway, Walli's Rest., **lodging:** Super 8, **other:** Belle Tire, $Tree, Hungry Howies, Meijer, Office Depot, Saab, Target, TJ Maxx, Vet
138	MI 54, Dort Hwy, **N gas:** BP/24hr, Speedway/dsl, Sunoco/dsl, **food:** Big John's Rest., KFC, Little Caesar's, YaYa's Chicken, **other:** H, $General, KanRock Tires, Rite Aid, Walgreens, **S gas:** Marathon, Speedway, Sunoco, **food:** Arby's, Big John's Steaks, Burger King, Carl's BBQ, China Empress, Coney Island, El Potrero, KFC, McDonald's, Subway, Taco Bell, **lodging:** Genessee Inn, Travel Inn, **other:** Aamco, Advance Parts, AutoZone, BigLots, Cadillac/Pontiac, $General, Family$, Goodyear, K-Mart, Rite Aid, 7-11, U-Haul, Walgreen
137	I-475, UAW Fwy, to Detroit, Saginaw
136	Saginaw St, Flint, **N gas:** Sunoco, **other:** H, U MI at Flint, **S other:** ExpertTire, GMC
135	Hammerberg Rd, industrial area
133b a	I-75, S to Detroit, N to Saginaw, US 23 S to Ann Arbor
131	MI 121, to Bristol Rd, **1/2 mi N on Miller Rd...gas:** Speedway, **food:** Chili's, ChuckeCheese, Golden Moon Chinese, Halo Burger, LJ Silver, Logan's Roadhouse, Old Country Buffet, Outback Steaks, Ruby Tuesday, Subway, Taco Bell, Valley Diner, **other:** Best Buy, BigLots, Borders Books, Discount Tire, $Tree, Firestone/auto, Gander Mtn, JC Penney, Jo-Ann Fabrics, Macy's, Michael's, Sears/auto, TJ Maxx, mall
129	Miller Rd, **S gas:** Marathon, **food:** Arby's, Burger King, McDonald's, Wendy's, **other:** Kroger/gas
128	Morrish Rd, **S gas:** Admiral/24hr, BP/dsl/24hr, **other:** Sports Creek Horse Racing
126mm	**rest area eb, full ♿ facilities, info, ☎, picnic, litter barrels, petwalk**
123	MI 13, to Saginaw, Lennon, **N gas:** Speedway/dsl
118	MI 71, to Corunna, Durand, **N** st police, **S gas:** Shell/dsl, Sunoco, **food:** McDonald's, Subway, Wendy's, **lodging:** Quality Inn, Sunset Motel (1.5), **other:** Ace Hardware, Carter's Foods, Chevrolet/Pontiac, Family$, Rite Aid, golf
115mm	Shiawassee River
113	Bancroft, **S gas:** BP/dsl, **other:** RV camping
105	MI 52, to Owosso, Perry, **S gas:** Citgo, Mobil, 7-11/

LANSING

Exit #	Services
105	Continued gas, Sunoco/Subway/dsl, **food:** Burger King, Café Sports, McDonald's, Taco Bell, **lodging:** Heb's Inn, **other:** Family$, Ford, IGA Foods, Rite Aid, RV camping, truck repair (1mi)
101mm	**rest area wb, full ♿ facilities, ☎, picnic, litter barrels, petwalk**
98.5mm	Looking Glass River
98	Woodbury Rd, to Laingsburg, Shaftsburg, **S** RV camping
95	I-496, to Lansing
94	Lp 69, Marsh Rd, to E Lansing, Okemos, **S gas:** Admiral/dsl, Speedway/DQ/dsl, **food:** McDonald's, **other:** Gillett RV Ctr, SavALot
93b a	MI 43, Lp 69, Saginaw Hwy, to Grand Ledge, **E gas:** Meijer/dsl/24hr, **food:** Bennigan's, Burger King, Denny's, McDonald's, North Pine Grill, TGIFriday, **lodging:** Best Western, Fairfield Inn, Hampton Inn, Holiday Inn, Motel 6, Quality Suites, Red Roof Inn, Residence Inn, **other:** H, **1 mi E gas:** Shell, Speedway/dsl, **food:** Carrabba's, Outback Steaks, **other:** Chrysler/Jeep, Kroger, **W gas:** BP/24hr, QD, Sunoco/McDonald's, **food:** Arby's, Bob Evans, Cracker Barrel, Steak'n Shake, Subway, **other:** Belle Tire, Discount Tire, GMC/Mazda, Lowe's Whse, Michael's, Walmart/auto
92	Webster Rd, Bath
91	I-96, W to Lansing, I-69/US 27 N to Flint
89	US 127 S, to E Lansing
87	Old US 27, to Clare, Lansing, **N gas:** Marathon, Meijer/dsl, Speedway/dsl, **food:** Arby's, Bob Evans, Burger King, China Gourmet, FlapJack's Rest., Little Ceasars, McDonald's, Subway, **lodging:** Sleep Inn, **other:** Annie Rae RV Ctr, Chevrolet, L&L Foods, Meijer, True Value, Vet, **S gas:** Speedway/dsl, **lodging:** AmeriHost
85	DeWitt Rd, to DeWitt
84	Airport Rd
81	I-96 (from sb), W to Grand Rapids, Grand River Ave, Frances Rd, **W gas:** ***FLYING J***/Country Mkt/dsl/24hr, **food:** Pepperoni's Rest.
72	I-96, E to Detroit, W to Grand Rapids
70	Lansing Rd, **1 mi E gas:** Citgo/dsl/rest./24hr, **food:** Coyote Creek Grille, Wendy's, **lodging:** Amerihost, **other:** st police
68mm	**rest area nb, full ♿ facilities, ☎, picnic, litter barrels, vending, petwalk**
66	MI 100, to Grand Ledge, Potterville, **W gas:** BP, Shell/Subway, **food:** McDonald's, to Fox Co Park
61	Lansing Rd, **E food:** Applebee's, **lodging:** Comfort Inn, Crestview Motel, **other:** AutoZone, Chevrolet/Buick/Pontiac/GMC, Chrysler/Jeep/Dodge, $Tree, Walmart SuperCtr/Subway/24hr, **W gas:** Speedway, QD, **food:** Arby's, Big Boy, Blimpie, Burger King, KFC, Little Caesar's, McDonald's, Pizza Hut, Taco Bell, Top Chinese, Wendy's, **other:** H Advance Parts, CarQuest, Family$, Ford/Mercury, Geldhof Tire/auto, Jo-Ann Fabrics, Radio Shack, TrueValue

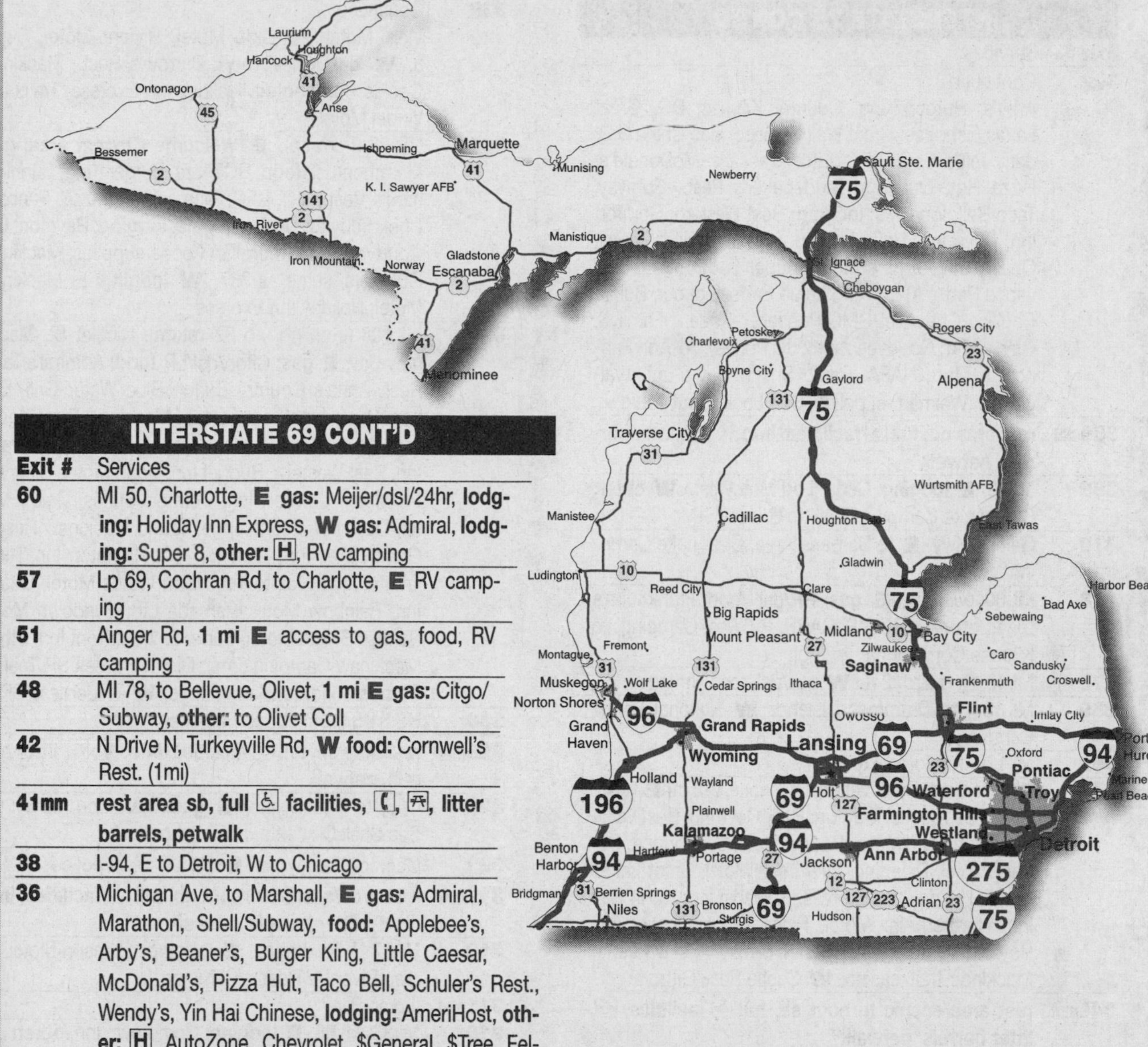

INTERSTATE 69 CONT'D

N ↕ S

MARSHALL

Exit #	Services
60	MI 50, Charlotte, **E gas:** Meijer/dsl/24hr, **lodging:** Holiday Inn Express, **W gas:** Admiral, **lodging:** Super 8, **other:** [H], RV camping
57	Lp 69, Cochran Rd, to Charlotte, **E** RV camping
51	Ainger Rd, **1 mi E** access to gas, food, RV camping
48	MI 78, to Bellevue, Olivet, **1 mi E gas:** Citgo/Subway, **other:** to Olivet Coll
42	N Drive N, Turkeyville Rd, **W food:** Cornwell's Rest. (1mi)
41mm	**rest area sb, full ♿ facilities, ☎, 🛆, litter barrels, petwalk**
38	I-94, E to Detroit, W to Chicago
36	Michigan Ave, to Marshall, **E gas:** Admiral, Marathon, Shell/Subway, **food:** Applebee's, Arby's, Beaner's, Burger King, Little Caesar, McDonald's, Pizza Hut, Taco Bell, Schuler's Rest., Wendy's, Yin Hai Chinese, **lodging:** AmeriHost, **other:** [H], AutoZone, Chevrolet, $General, $Tree, Felpausch Foods, GNC, K-Mart, NAPA, Radio Shack, Rite Aid, Sav-a-Lot Foods, **W lodging:** Arbor Inn, **other:** Chrysler/Dodge/Jeep
32	F Drive S, **E gas:** Shell (3/4 mi), **food:** Moonraker Rest. (3mi), **W other:** RV Camping
25	MI 60, to Three Rivers, Jackson, **E gas:** BP/dsl, Citgo/Te-Kon/Norma's/dsl/scales/24hr, Sunoco/dsl, **food:** McDonald's, **other:** NAPA Truck Care, RV camping
23	Tekonsha, **E gas:** Citgo, **W** access to RV camping
16	Jonesville Rd, **W** Waffle Farm Camping (2mi)
13	US 12, to Quincy, Coldwater, **E gas:** Meijer/dsl/24hr, Speedway/dsl, **food:** Applebee's, Bob Evans, Grand Buffet, Subway, **lodging:** Hampton Inn, Red Roof Inn, **other:** Aldi Foods, AutoZone, Big-Lots, Chevrolet/Cadillac, $Tree, GNC, Home Depot, N Country RV Ctr, Radio Shack, SavALot, Walmart SuperCtr/24hr, **W gas:** BP/24hr, Citgo, Speedway/dsl, **food:** Arby's, Benedict's Steaks, Big Boy, Burger King, Coldwater Garden Rest., KFC, Little Caesar's, McDonald's, Pizza Hut, Ponderosa, Subway, Taco Bell, Wendy's, **lodging:** Cadet Motel, Comfort Inn,
13	Continued Holiday Inn Express, Super 8, **other:** [H], Advance Parts, Ford/Lincoln/Mercury, Rite Aid, Walgreens, st police
10	Lp 69, Fenn Rd, to Coldwater
8mm	**weigh sta nb**
6mm	**Welcome Ctr nb, full ♿ facilities, ☎, 🛆, litter barrels, vending, petwalk**
3	Copeland Rd, Kinderhook, **W gas:** BP, **food:** camping
0mm	Michigan/Indiana state line

INTERSTATE 75

N ↕ S

Exit #	Services
395mm	US/Canada Border, Michigan state line, I-75 begins/ends at toll bridge to Canada
394	Easterday Ave, **E gas:** Citgo/dsl, **food:** McDonald's, **lodging:** Holiday Inn Express, **other:** [H], to Lake Superior St U, **W** Welcome Ctr/rest area, info, **gas:** Admiral/dsl, Holiday/dsl/currency exchange, **food:** Freighter's Rest (2mi), **lodging:** Ramada Inn (2mi)
392	3 Mile Rd, Sault Ste Marie, **E gas:** Admiral/dsl, BP/dsl, Holiday/dsl, Marathon, Shell, **food:** Applebee's,

INTERSTATE 75 CONT'D

N ↕ S

Exit #	Services
392	Continued Arby's, Burger King, Country Kitchen, DQ, Great Lakes Fishouse, Great Wall Chinese, Indo China Garden, Jeff's Café, KFC, Little Caesar's, McDonald's, Pizza Hut, Quizno's, Studebaker's Rest., Subway, Taco Bell, Wendy's, **lodging:** Best Western, Comfort Inn, Days Inn, Hampton Inn, Park Inn, Plaza Motel, Quality Inn, Skyline Motel, Super 8, **other:** H, Advance Parts, AT&T, Auto Value Parts, BigLots, Buick/Cadillac/Chevrolet/GMC/Pontiac, $Tree, Family$, Glen's Mkt, Goodyear/auto, JC Penney, Jo-Ann Fabrics, K-Mart, NAPA, Radio Shack, Sav-a-Lot, Walgreens, Walmart, st police, Soo Locks Boat Tours
389mm	**rest area nb, full ♿ facilities, info, ☎, picnic, litter barrels, petwalk**
386	MI 28, **E lodging:** Cedar Log Motel/rest., **W other:** Clear Lake Camping (5mi), to Brimley SP
379	Gaines Hwy, **E** to Barbeau Area, Clear Lake Camping
378	MI 80, Kinross, **E gas:** BP/dsl, **food:** Frank&Jim's Diner, **other:** URGENT CARE, RV West Camping, to Kinross Correctional, ✈, golf
373	MI 48, Rudyard, **2 mi W** gas/dsl, food, lodging
359	MI 134, to Drummond Island, **W** National Forest Camping
352	MI 123, to Moran, Newberry
348	H63, to Sault Reservation, St Ignace, **0-2 mi E food:** Dockside Steaks, **lodging:** Bear Cove Inn, Best Value Inn, Birchwood Motel, Budget Host, Comfort Inn, Cedars Motel, Days Inn, Evergreen Motel, Great Lakes Motel, Holiday Inn Express, Kewadin Inn, North Bay Inn, NorthernAire Motel, Pines Motel, Quality Inn, Royale Inn, Tradewinds Motel, **other:** ✈, st police, to Mackinac Trail, casino, **W** Castle Rock Gifts
346mm	**rest area/scenic turnout sb, full ♿ facilities, picnic, litter barrels, petwalk**
345	Portage St (from sb), St Ignace
344b	US 2 W, **W gas:** BP/dsl/rest./24hr, Holiday/dsl, Shell/dsl/24hr, **food:** Big Boy, Burger King, Clyde's Drive-In McDonald's, Subway, Suzy's Pasties, Up North Rest, **lodging:** 4 Star Motel, Quality Inn, Sunset Motel, Super 8, **other:** Ford, Lakeshore RV Park
344a	Lp 75, St Ignace, **0-2 mi E gas:** Shell, **food:** BC Pizza, Driftwood Rest, Flame Rest., Galley Rest., Mackinac Grille, Marina Rest., Northern Lights Rest., Subway, **lodging:** Aurora Borealis Motel, Best Value Inn, Best Western, Boardwalk Inn, Budget Host, Colonial House, Comfort Inn, Days Inn, Econolodge, Getaway Inn, Holiday Inn Express, Huron Motel, K Royale Motel, Moran Bay Motel, Normandy Motel, Quality Inn, Sunbar Motel, Thunderbird Motel, Village Inn/rest., Vitek's Motel, Voyager Motel, **other:** H, Ace Hardware, Bay Drug, Family$, Glen's Mkt, Radio Shack, TrueValue, USPO, to Island Ferrys, Straits SP, KOA, public marina, st police, **E** KOA
343mm	**toll booth to toll bridge, E Welcome Ctr nb, full ♿ facilities, ☎, picnic, litter barrels, W museum**
341mm	toll bridge, Lake Huron, Lake Michigan
339	US 23, Jamet St, **E food:** Audie's Rest., **lodging:** Budget Host, Days Inn, Econolodge, LightHouse View Motel, Parkside Motel, Riviera Motel, Super 8, **W gas:** Shell, **food:** Darrow's Rest., Mackinaw Cookie Co, **lodging:** Holiday Inn Express, Trails Inn, Vindel Motel,
338	US 23 (from sb), **E Welcome Ctr/rest area, gas:** Marathon/dsl, **food:** BC Pizza, Burger King, Cunningham's Rest., DQ, KFC, Mama Mia's Pizza, Pancake Chef, Subway, Up North Cafe, **lodging:** Baymont Inn, Courtyard Inn, **other:** IGA Foods/supplies, Mackinaw Outfitters, same as 337, **W lodging:** Ft Mackinaw Motel, Holiday Inn Express
337	MI 108 (from nb, no EZ return), Nicolet St, Mackinaw City, **E gas:** Citgo/dsl/LP, **food:** Admiral's Table Rest, Anna's Country Buffet, Blue Water Grill, Embers Rest., Lighthouse Rest., Mancino's Pizza, **lodging:** Anchor Inn, BeachComber Motel, Best Value Inn, Best Western, Budget Inn, Capri Motel, Clearwater Motel, Comfort Inn, Comfort Suites, Dale's Motel, Days Inn, Econolodge, Grand Mackinaw Resort, Great Lakes Inn, Hamilton Inn, Hampton Inn, Nicolet Inn, NorthPointe Inn, North Winds Motel, Quality Inn, Rainbow Motel, Ramada Ltd, Sundown Motel, Sunrise Beach Motel, Super 8, Waterfront Inn, **other:** Mackinaw Camping (2mi), Old Mill Creek SP, TeePee Campground, to Island Ferrys, **W** Wilderness SP
336	US 31 S (from sb), to Petoskey
328mm	**rest area sb, full ♿ facilities, info, ☎, picnic, litter barrels, petwalk**
326	C66, to Cheboygan, **E gas:** Marathon, **other:** H, Sea Shell City/gifts, **other:** st police
322	C64, to Cheboygan, **E** H, LP, ✈, st police
317mm	**rest area/scenic turnout nb, full ♿ facilities, info, ☎, picnic, litter barrels, petwalk**
313	MI 27 N, Topinabee, **E lodging:** Johnson Motel, Indian River RV Resort/Camping
311mm	Indian River
310	MI 33, MI 68, **E lodging:** Hometown Inn, **other:** Jellystone Park (3mi), **W gas:** BP/dsl, Ken's Gas, Shell/McDonald's/24hr, **food:** Burger King, DQ, Paula's Cafe, Subway, **lodging:** Coach House Motel, **other:** Family$, Ken's Mkt, Village Mkt/Drug, to Indian River Trading Post/RV Resort, to Burt Lake SP
301	C58, Wolverine, **E gas:** Marathon/dsl, **food:** Whistle Stop Rest., **other:** Elkwood Campground (5mi), **W other:** Sturgin River Campground (3mi)
297mm	Sturgeon River
290	Vanderbilt, **E gas:** BP/dsl/LP/RV dump, Spirit, **other:** Village Mkt Foods, USPO, **W gas:** Mobil/dsl
287mm	**rest area sb, full ♿ facilities, info, ☎, picnic, litter barrels**
282	MI 32, Gaylord, **E gas:** BP, Clark, Holiday/24hr, Marathon/dsl, Speedway/dsl, **food:** Alpine Oven, Arby's, Big Buck Steaks, Burger King, DQ, KFC, La Senorita Mexican, McDonald's, Quizno's, Subway, Wendy's, **lodging:** Alpine Lodge, Baymont Inn, Quality Inn/Gino's Italian, Royal Crest Motel, **other:** H, Advance Parts, AutoZone, Ben Franklin, Glen's Foods, Harley-Davidson, Johnson Tires, K-Mart, NAPA, Rite Aid, st police, **W gas:** BP/dsl, Citgo/dsl, Marathon/dsl, Mobil/dsl, Shell/dsl, **food:** Applebee's, BC Pizza, Big Boy, Bob Evans, China 1, Culver's, Little Caesar's,

SAULT STE MARIE · MACKINAW CITY · GAYLORD

N ↕ S

INTERSTATE 75 CONT'D

Exit #	Services
282	Continued Mancino's Pizza, Ponderosa, Ruby Tuesday, Spicy Bob's, Taco Bell, **lodging:** Hampton Inn, Holiday Inn Express, Timberly Motel, **other:** URGENT CARE, AT&T, BigLots, Chrysler/Dodge/Jeep, Dayton Tire, $General, $Tree, GNC, Home Depot, Lowe's Whse, Radio Shack, Save-A-Lot Foods, Walgreens, Walmart SuperCtr/Subway/24hr, RV camping, transmissions, tires
279mm	45th Parallel halfway between the equator & north pole
279	Old US 27, Gaylord, **E gas:** Marathon/Subway/dsl, Mobil/dsl, Shell, **food:** Burger King, Mama Leone's, **lodging:** Best Value Inn, **other:** Ace Hardware, Buick/GMC/Pontiac, Chevrolet, Ford/Lincoln/Mercury, st police, **W food:** Bennethums Rest, Stampede Saloon, **lodging:** Marsh Ridge Motel (2mi), KOA (3mi)
277mm	**rest area nb, full ♿ facilities, info, ☎, picnic, litter barrels, petwalk**
270	Waters, **E gas:** BP/dsl, **food:** Hilltop Rest., **W** lodging, Waters Inn, **other:** IGA Food/gas, RV repair, Waters RV Ctr, USPO, to Otsego Lake SP
264	Lewiston, Frederic, **W** access to food, camping
262mm	**rest area sb, full ♿ facilities, ☎, picnic, litter barrels, petwalk**
259	MI 93, **E** Hartwick Pines SP, **2-4 mi W lodging:** Fay's Motel, North Country Lodge, Pointe North Motel, River Country Motel, Woodland Motel, **other:** Buick/Cadillac/Chevrolet/Pontiac, Chrysler/Dodge/Jeep, Curves, auto/rv repair, rv camping
256	(from sb), to MI 72, Grayling, access to same as 254
254	MI 72 (exits left from nb, no return), Grayling, **1 mi W gas:** Admiral/dsl, Citgo, 7-11, Clark, Speedway, Valero, **food:** Big Boy, Burger King, Canadian Steaks, DQ, McDonald's, Pizza Hut, Subway, Taco Bell, Wendy's, **lodging:** Days Inn, Ramada, **other:** H Ace Hardware, $General, Family$, Ford/Mercury, Glen's Foods/24hr, K-Mart, NAPA, Rite Aid, Save-A-Lot Foods, Walgreens
251mm	**rest area nb, full ♿ facilities, info, ☎, picnic, litter barrels, petwalk, vending**
251	4 Mile Rd, **E** Jellystone RV Park (5mi), skiing, **W gas:** Marathon/Arby's/dsl/scales/RV Dump/24hr, **lodging:** Super 8
249	US 127 S (from sb), to Clare
244	MI 18, Roscommon, **3 mi E food:** McDonald's, **W gas:** Valero/dsl, **other:** KOA (1mi), Higgins Lake SP, museum
239	MI 18, Roscommon, S Higgins Lake SP, **3 mi E gas:** Marathon/McDonald's/dsl, **other:** camping, **W** Higgins Lake SP, camping
235mm	**rest area sb, full ♿ facilities, ☎, info, picnic, litter barrels, petwalk, vending**
227	MI 55 W, rd F97, to Houghton Lake, **5 mi W** food
222	Old 76, to St Helen, **5 mi E** food, lodging, camping
215	MI 55 E, West Branch, **E gas:** Citgo/dsl, **food:** Carver's Rest., Willow Tree Rest. (2mi), **other:** H
212	MI 55, West Branch, **E gas:** Murphy USA/dsl, 7-11, Shell/Subway, **food:** Applebee's, Arby's, Big Boy, Burger King, KFC, Lumberjack Rest., McDonald's, Ponderosa, Taco Bell, Wendy's, **lodging:** Quality Inn,

GRAYLING

Sault Ste. Marie
Seney
Brimley
Rudyard
Barbeau
Pickford
75
Moran
Cedarville
Mackinaw City
Mackinac Island
Levering
Mullett Lake
Indian River
Wolverine
Posen
Leland
Elmira
Gaylord
Frederic
Curran
Traverse City
Grayling
MI

Exit #	Services
212	Continued Super 8, **other:** H, Home Depot, Tanger Outlet/famous brands, Walmart SuperCtr/Subway, st police, **W gas:** BP/dsl
210mm	**rest area nb, full ♿ facilities, info, ☎, picnic, litter barrels, petwalk, vending**
202	MI 33, to Rose City, Alger, **E gas:** BP/Narski's Mkt/jerky (1/2mi), Mobil/jerky outlet/dsl, Shell/Subway, **other:** camping
201mm	**rest area sb, full ♿ facilities, ☎, picnic, litter barrels, petwalk, vending**
195	Sterling Rd, to Sterling, **6 mi E** gas, Riverview Camping (seasonal)
190	MI 61, to Standish, **E other:** H, Standish Correctional, **W gas:** Marathon, Mobil/jerky
188	US 23, to Standish, **2-3 mi E** gas, food, camping
181	Pinconning Rd, **E gas:** Mobil, Shell/McDonald's, **food:** Cheesehouse Diner, **lodging:** Pinconning Inn (2mi), **other:** Pinconning Camping, **W gas:** Sunoco/pizza/dsl/24hr
175mm	**rest area nb, full ♿ facilities, ☎, picnic, litter barrels, petwalk, vending**
173	Linwood Rd, to Linwood, **E gas:** Mobil/dsl/jerky
171mm	Kawkawlin River
168	Beaver Rd, to Willard, **E other:** to Bay City SP, **W gas:** Mobil/jerky
166mm	Kawkawlin River
164	to MI 13, Wilder Rd, to Kawkawlin, **E food:** Applebee's, Cracker Barrel, Lucky Steaks, McDonald's, Ponderosa, Tim Horton, Uno, **lodging:** AmericInn, Fairfield Inn (3mi), Holiday Inn Express, **other:** Kan-Rock Tire, Meijer/dsl, Menards
162b a	US 10, MI 25, to Midland, **E** H
160	MI 84, Delta, **E gas:** Mobil/Subway, Shell, **W gas:** 7-11, Speedway, **food:** Berger's Rest., Burger King, KFC/Taco Bell, McDonald's, **lodging:** Econolodge, **other:** RV World Super Ctr, to Saginaw Valley Coll
158mm	**rest area sb, full ♿ facilities, ☎, picnic, litter barrels, vending, petwalk**
155	I-675 S, to downtown Saginaw, **4 mi W food:** Outback Steaks, **lodging:** Hampton Inn, Super 8
154	to Zilwaukee
153mm	Saginaw River
153	MI 13 E Bay City Rd, Saginaw, **2-3 mi W** lodging
151	MI 81, to Reese, Caro, **E gas:** Sunoco/McDonald's/dsl, **other:** GMC/Volvo Trucks, **W gas:** *FLYING J* Wendy's/dsl/LP/24hr
150	I-675 N, to downtown Saginaw, **6 mi W food:** Outback Steaks, **lodging:** Hampton Inn, Super 8

SAGINAW

INTERSTATE 75 CONT'D

N ↕ S

Exit #	Services
149b a	MI 46, Holland Ave, to Saginaw, **W gas:** Admiral, Marathon, Speedway/dsl, Sunoco, **food:** Arby's, Big John's Steaks, Burger King, McDonald's, Subway, Taco Bell, Texan Rest., **lodging:** Best Value Inn, Motel 6, Super 7 Inn, **other:** H, Advance Parts, Sav-a-Lot Foods, USPO
144b a	Bridgeport, **E gas:** Marathon/dsl, Speedway/dsl/24hr, **other:** Jellystone Camping (9mi), **W gas:** Mobil/dsl/e-85, TA/Country Pride/dsl/scales/24hr/@, **food:** Arby's, Big Boy, Cracker Barrel, Hungry Howie's, Little Caesar's, McDonald's, Peking City, Subway, Taco Bell, Wendy's, **lodging:** Baymont Inn, Knight's Inn, **other:** Kroger/gas, Rite Aid, st police
143mm	Cass River
138mm	pull off both lanes
136	MI 54, MI 83, Birch Run, **E gas:** Mobil/dsl/24hr, **food:** Exit Rest., Halo Burger, KFC, Subway, **lodging:** Best Western, Comfort Inn, Hampton Inn, Holiday Inn Express, Super 8, **other:** CarQuest, General RV Ctr, Mejier/dsl, Totten Tires, **W gas:** Marathon, 7-11, Sunoco/dsl, **food:** A&W, Arby's, Applebee's, Big Boy, Bob Evans, Culver's, DQ, Little Caesar's, McDonald's, Quizno's, Sonic, Starbucks, Taco Bell, Tony's Rest., Uno, Victor&Merek's Pizza, Wendy's, **lodging:** Country Inn&Suites, **other:** Buick/Chevrolet, GNC, Harley-Davidson, Old Navy, Prime Outlet/famous brands
131	MI 57, to Montrose, **E gas:** Shell, Sunoco, **food:** Arby's, Big John's Steaks, Burger King, DQ, KFC, McDonald's, Oriental Express, Subway, Taco Bell, Twins Pizza, Tim Horton, Wendy's, **other:** AutoZone, Chevrolet, Chrysler/Dodge/Jeep, Ford, KanRock Tire, K-Mart, **W gas:** Mobil/Rally's/dsl, Murphy USA/dsl, **food:** Big Boy, Lucky Steaks, Quizno's, **other:** Menards, Walmart SuperCtr/Subway
129mm	**rest area both lanes, full ♿ facilities, ☎, picnic, litter barrels, vending, petwalk**
126	to Mt Morris, **E gas:** B&B/Burger King/dsl/24hr, **W gas:** BP/dsl, carwash
125	I-475 S, UAW Fwy, to Flint
122	Pierson Rd, to Flint, **E gas:** BP, Marathon/dsl, **food:** McDonald's, Papa's Coney's, Subway, **lodging:** Econolodge, **other:** Kroger/gas, Murray's Parts, NW Tire, Tuffy Auto, **W gas:** Citgo, Shell/dsl, **food:** A&W/KFC, Applebee's, Arby's, Big John's Steaks, Bob Evans, Burger King, Cottage Inn Pizza, Cracker Barrel, Denny's, Halo Burger, LJ Silver, Red Lobster, Taco Bell, Tim Horton, Wendy's, YaYa Chicken, **lodging:** Baymont Inn, Great Western Inn, **other:** Aldi Foods, AT&T, Discount Tire, $Tree, Home Depot, Meijer/dsl
118	MI 21, Corunna Rd, **E gas:** Sunoco, **food:** Atlas Coney Island, Badawest Lebanese, Big John's Steaks, Burger King, Halo Burger, Hollywood Diner, Hungry Howie's, Little Caesar's, Taco Bell, Wing Fong Chinese, YaYa Chicken, **other:** H, CarQuest, $Zone, Family$, Kroger/gas, Rite Aid, **W gas:** BP/dsl, Mobil, Shell/Wendy's, Speedway, Valero, **food:** A&W/KFC, Blue Collar Grill, Burger King, Fazoli's, Happy Valley Rest., McDonald's, Mega Diner, Tim Horton, White Castle, **lodging:** Economy Motel, **other:** Aldi

FLINT

Exit #	Services
118	Continued Foods, AutoZone, Buick, Chevrolet, $General, GMC, Home Depot, KanRock Tire, Kroger/gas, Lowe's Whse, Rite Aid, Sam's Club/gas, VG's Foods, Walgreens, Walmart SuperCtr/auto, st police
117b	Miller Rd, to Flint, **E gas:** Speedway/dsl, Sunoco/dsl, **food:** Applebee's, Arby's, Bennigan's, Cottage Inn, Pizza, Don Pablo, Fuddrucker's, KFC, LoneStar Steaks, McDonald's, Qdoba, Sonic, Subway, West Side Diner, **lodging:** Comfort Inn, Motel 6, Sleep Inn, **other:** URGENT CARE, Belle Tire, K-Mart, Tuffy Auto, **W gas:** BP, Marathon, **food:** BD's BBQ, Big Boy, Bob Evans, Chili's, ChuckeCheese, Famous Dave's BBQ, Fire Mtn Grill, Happy's Pizza, HoneyBaked Ham, Hooters, Italia Garden, Logan's Roadhouse, Old Country Buffet, Olive Garden, Outback Steaks, Pizza Hut, Rib City, Quizno's, Red Robin, Salvatori's Ristorante, Starbucks, Subway, Taco Bell, Telly's Coney Island, Valley Rest., **lodging:** Hometown Inn, Red Roof Inn, Super 8, **other:** AT&T, Barnes&Noble, Best Buy, Borders Books, Dale's Foods, Discount Tire, Dodge, Gander Mtn, Goodyear, Hobby Lobby, JC Penney, Jo-Ann Fabrics, Macy's, Michael's, Office Depot, Old Navy, PetCo, Radio Shack, Sears/auto, Target, U-Haul, Valley Tire, mall, Vet
117a	I-69, E to Lansing, W to Port Huron
116	MI 121, Bristol Rd, **E gas:** Citgo, Speedway/dsl, **food:** Capitol Coney Island, KFC, McDonald's, **lodging:** Days Inn, Rodeway Inn, **other:** AutoZone, **W gas:** Mobil/dsl, **other:** ✈
115	US 23 (from sb), **W on Hill Rd...gas:** Citgo, Meijer/dsl/24hr, Mobil, **food:** Hill St Grill, Maxie's Rest., McDonald's, Redwood Lodge, Turkey Farm Deli, **lodging:** AmericInn, Courtyard, Holiday Inn, Residence Inn
111	I-475 N (from nb), UAW Fwy, to Flint
109	MI 54, Dort Hwy (no EZ return to sb)
108	Holly Rd, to Grand Blanc, **E gas:** Sunoco/dsl, **food:** Big Apple Bagels, Buffalo Wild Wings, Da Edoardo Ristorante, Quizno's, Taco Bell, **lodging:** Comfort Inn, Holiday Inn Express, **other:** URGENT CARE, BMW/Mercedes/Toyota, **W gas:** BP/McDonald's/dsl, **food:** Arby's, **other:** H
106	Dixie Hwy (exits left from sb, no nb return), Saginaw Rd, to Grand Blanc
101	Grange Hall Rd, Ortonville, **E other:** Holly RA, KOA, st police, **W gas:** Mobil/dsl, **other:** to Seven Lakes/Groveland Oaks SP, RV camping
98	E Holly Rd, **E gas:** Mobil/Subway/dsl/24hr, **other:** Ford, golf
96mm	**rest area nb, full ♿ facilities, picnic, litter barrels, info, ☎, vending, petwalk**
95mm	**rest area sb, full ♿ facilities, picnic, litter barrels, info, ☎, vending, petwalk**
93	US 24, Dixie Hwy, Waterford, **E gas:** BP/dsl, **other:** Dodge, Kroger/gas (2mi), **1-3 mi W gas:** Speedway, **food:** Big Boy, McDonald's, Subway, Taco Bell, Wendy's, **other:** Chrysler/Jeep, Walgreens, to Pontiac Lake RA
91	MI 15, Davison, Clarkston, **E gas:** Sunoco/dsl, **food:** Bullfrog's (5mi), Subway (5mi), **other:** camping, **W gas:** Shell/dsl, **food:** Brioni Grill, Mesquite Creek Café, **other:** H

N ↕ S

INTERSTATE 75 CONT'D

Exit #	Services
89	Sashabaw Rd, **E gas:** Shell/dsl, **food:** Culvers, Ruby Tuesday, Tropical Smoothie Cafe, **other:** county park, **W gas:** BP/24hr, Citgo, **food:** Caribou Coffee, Chicken Shack, Dunkin Donuts, E Ocean Chinese, Guido's Pizza, Hong Kong Chinese, Hungry Howie's, Leo's Coney Island, Little Caesars, McDonald's, Quizno's, Rio Wraps, Subway, Tim Horton, Wendy's, **other:** CVS Drug, $Tree, Kroger, Vet
86mm	weigh sta sb, parking area nb
84b a	Baldwin Ave, **E gas:** Shell/24hr, **food:** Arby's, Big Boy, Joe's Crabshack, Longhorn Steaks, Wendy's, **other:** Best Buy, Costco/gas, Discount Tire, $Castle, Kohl's, Michael's, Old Navy, PetCo, Staples, **W gas:** Mobil/24hr, **food:** Chili's, Jimmy John's, Kerry's Coney Island, Max&Erma's, McDonald's, On-the-Border, Oriental Forest, Quizno's, Rainforest Cafe, Starbucks, Steak'n Shake/24hr, Subway, **other:** Holiday Inn Express, **other:** AT&T, Bass Pro Shops, Borders Books, Great Lakes Crossing Outlet/famous brands, Marshall's, TJ Maxx, Vitamin Shoppe, USPO
83b a	Joslyn Rd, **E gas: food:** Applebee's, Olive Garden, **other:** Belle Tire, Home Depot, Jo-Ann Fabrics, Meijer/dsl, Sam's Club/gas, Target, **W gas:** Sunoco
81	MI 24, Pontiac (no EZ return), **E** The Palace Arena
79	University Dr, **E gas:** BP, **food:** Jimmy John's, Rio Wraps, Spargo Coney Island, Subway, Taste of Thailand, **W gas:** Mobil, Speedway/dsl, **food:** A&W/KFC, Burger King, Lelli's Steaks, McDonald's, Taco Bell, Wendy's/Tim Horton, **lodging:** Candlewood Suites, Comfort Suites, Courtyard, Crowne Plaza, Extended Stay America, Extended Stay Deluxe, Fairfield Inn, Hampton Inn, Hilton, Holiday Inn, Hyatt, Motel 6, Staybridge Suites, Wingate Inn, **other:** H, GM, Jakes Auto
78	Chrysler Dr, **E other:** Chrysler, Chrysler Museum, Oakland Tech Ctr
77b a	MI 59, to Pontiac, **2 mi on Adams E food:** 5 Guys Burgers, Panera Bread, **other:** Meijer/dsl, PetsMart, Walmart/auto, **1 mi W on Opdyk E gas:** Fastrack/Tubby's/dsl
75	Square Lake Rd (exits left from nb), to Pontiac, **W** H St Mary's Coll
74	Adams Rd
72	Crooks Rd, to Troy, **W food:** Charlie's Crabs, Kerby's Coney Island, Loccino Italian, Quizno's, Red Robin, Starbucks, **lodging:** Embassy Suites, Ramada Inn
69	Big Beaver Rd, **E food:** Champp's Grill, Kona Grill, Shula's Steaks, TGIFriday's, **lodging:** Drury Inn, Marriott, **other: W gas:** BP, **food:** Benihana, Chipotle Mexican, Maggiano's Italian, Melting Pot Rest., Morton's Steaks, Noodles&Co, Potbelly's, Ruth's Chris Steaks, Starbucks, **other:** mall
67	Rochester Rd, to Stevenson Hwy, **E gas:** BP, Marathon, Shell, **food:** Arby's, Bahama Breeze, Burger King, Caribou Coffee, Hooter's, Hungry Howies, Jimmy John's, Mr Pita, Ntl Coney Island, Orchid Rest., Panera Bread, Papa John's, Peiwei, Qdoba, Ram's Horn Rest., Rio Wraps, Subway, Taco Bell, Troy Deli, **other:** Discount Tire, Nordstrom's, Office Depot, PetsMart, Radio Shack, transmissions, **W lodging:** Holiday Inn, Red Roof Inn, **other:** tires/repair

DETROIT AREA

Exit #	Services
65b a	14 Mile Rd, Madison Heights, **E gas:** Marathon/dsl, Mobil, **food:** Azteca Mexican, Bob Evans, Burger King, Chili's, Krispy Kreme, Logan's Roadhouse, McCool's Grill, McDonald's, Panera Bread, Pizza Papalis, Starbucks, Steak'n Shake, Taco Bell, Wendy's, **lodging:** Motel 6, Red Roof Inn, **other:** AT&T, Barnes&Noble, Belle Tire, Best Buy, Borders Books, Dodge, Firestone, Ford, Home Depot, JC Penney, Kohl's, Lowe's Whse, Macy's, NAPA, Office Depot, Radio Shack, Sam's Club, Sears/auto, Target, TJ Maxx, mall, **W gas:** Mobil, Valero, **food:** Applebee's, Bennigan's, Big Fish Seafood, Caribou Coffee, Dolly's Pizza, McDonald's, NY Coney Island, Outback Steaks, Quizno's, **lodging:** Best Western, Courtyard, Econolodge, Extended Stay America, Fairfield Inn, Hampton Inn, Residence Inn, **other:** Chevrolet, Costco/gas, Value Ctr Foods
63	12 Mile Rd, **E gas:** Marathon, **food:** Blimpie, Green Lantern Rest., Marinelli's Pizza, McDonald's, Red Lobster, Sero's Rest., Starbucks, TX Roadhouse, Tim Horton, **other:** Curves, Home Depot, K-Mart/foods, Lowe's Whse, Radio Shack, Uncle Ed's Oil, auto repair, Vet, **W gas:** Marathon/Dunkin Donuts, Speedway, **food:** Col's Rest., **other:** Chevrolet, Costco/gas
62	11 Mile Rd, **E gas:** Mobil, **food:** Boodles Rest., Cottage Pizza, Jets Pizza, **other:** Advance Parts, CVS Drug, Sav-a-Lot, 7-11, Tuffy Auto, Walgreens, repair/tires, Vet, **W gas:** BP, Marathon/dsl, Mobil, **food:** KFC, Taco Bell, Tim Horton, Tubby's Subs, **other:** Belle Tire
61	I-696 E, to Port Huron, W to Lansing, to Hazel Park Raceway
60	9 Mile Rd, John R St, **E food:** Checkers, China 1 Buffet, DQ, Hardee's, McDonald's, Subway, Wendy's, **other:** $Store, Kroger, USPO, **W gas:** Exxon, Mobil, **food:** Tubby's Subs, Wendy's, **other:** Hasting's Parts, repair
59	MI 102, 8 Mile Rd, **3 mi W** st fairgrounds
58	7 Mile Rd, **W gas:** BP/dsl
57	McNichols Rd, **E gas:** Shell/dsl, **food:** KFC, LA Coney Island, Taco Bell, **other:** Auto Parts/Repair
56b a	Davison Fwy
55	Holbrook Ave, Caniff St, **E gas:** Mobil/dsl, **W food:** Grandy's Coney Island
54	E Grand Blvd, Clay Ave, **W gas:** BP/dsl, **food:** Super Coney Island
53b	I-94, Ford Fwy, to Port Huron, Chicago
53a	Warren Ave, **E gas:** Mobil, **W gas:** BP
52	Mack Ave, **E gas:** Shell, **food:** McDonald's

INTERSTATE 75 CONT'D

N ↕ S

Exit #	Services
51c	I-375 to civic center, tunnel to Canada, downtown
51b	MI 3 (exits left from nb), Gratiot Ave, downtown
50	Grand River Ave, downtown
49b	MI 10, Lodge Fwy, downtown
49a	Rosa Parks Blvd, **E** Tiger Stadium, **W gas:** Mobil, **other:** Firestone
48	I-96 begins/ends
47b	Porter St, **E** bridge to Canada, DutyFree/24hr
47a	MI 3, Clark Ave, **E gas:** Mobil, Sunoco, **W gas:** Marathon
46	Livernois Ave, to Hist Ft Wayne, **E gas:** Marathon, **food:** Coney Island, KFC/Taco Bell
45	Fort St, Springwells Ave, **E gas:** BP/dsl, Pure Petro/dsl, **W gas:** Mobil, **food:** McDonald's
44	Deerborn St (from nb)
43b a	MI 85, Fort St, to Schaefer Hwy, **E gas:** BP, **W gas:** Marathon Refinery, **other:** to River Rouge Ford Plant
42	Outer Dr, **E gas:** Marathon, **food:** Happy's Pizza, **other:** URGENT CARE, **W gas:** BP/Subway/dsl, **other:** Family$, truck tires
41	MI 39, Southfield Rd, to Lincoln Park, **E food:** A&W, Bill's Place Rest., Tim Horton, White Castle, **other:** Aldi Foods, Family$, Murray Parts, Walgreens, **W gas:** Shell/Tim Horton, **food:** Big Boy, Starbucks, Wendy's, **lodging:** Sleep Inn, **other:** AT&T, Kroger/gas, Rite Aid, Walgreens
40	Dix Hwy, **E gas:** Marathon/A&W/dsl, Welcome, **food:** Baskin-Robbins/Dunkin Donuts, Coney Island Diner, **other:** URGENT CARE, CVS Drug, Meijer, 7-11, repair, **W gas:** Marathon, Mobil, **food:** Big Boy, Burger King, Checker's, DQ, LJ Silver, McDonald's, Pizza Hut, Quizno's, Taco Bell, **other:** AT&T, Belle Tire, Family$, Kroger, Rite Aid, Sav-a-Lot, Sears/auto, Walgreens
37	Allen Rd, North Line Rd, to Wyandotte, **E gas:** BP, Shell/Tim Horton, **lodging:** Holiday Inn, **other:** H Sam's Club/gas, **W gas:** Mobil, Sunoco, **food:** Arby's, Burger King, Mallie's Grill, McDonald's, Wendy's, **lodging:** Comfort Suites, La Quinta, Motel 6
36	Eureka Rd, **E gas:** BP, **food:** Bob Evans, Denny's, Fire Mtn Grill, Orleans Steaks, **lodging:** Ramada Inn, Super 8, **other:** Vet, **W gas: food:** American Thai Grill, Big Boy, Coldstone Creamery, Culver's, HoneyBaked Ham, Hooters, Jimmy John's, Little Daddy's Rest., McDonald's, Ruby Tuesday, Starbucks, Subway, TX Roadhouse, Wendy's, **lodging:** Red Roof Inn, **other:** AT&T, Belle Tire, Best Buy, Borders Books, Discount Tire, Home Depot, JC Penney, Kohl's, Macy's, Meijer/dsl, PetsMart, mall
35	US 24, Telegraph Rd, (from nb, exits left)
34b	Sibley Rd, Riverview, **W gas:** Sunoco/Baskin-Robbins/Dunkin Donuts/Subway, **other:** RV Ctr
34a	to US 24 (from sb), Telegraph Rd
32	West Rd, to Trenton, Woodhaven, **E gas:** Detroiter/Sunoco/dsl/rest./scales/24hr/@, Speedway/dsl, **food:** Applebee's, Baskin-Robbins/Dunkin Donuts, Bellacino's Italian, Blue Margarita Mexican, Bob Evans, Burger King, Christoff's Rest., Grand Buffet, Ground Round, IHOP, Jersey Subs, Panera Bread, Pizza Hut, Quizno's, Steak'n Shake, Subway, Taco Bell, Tim Horton, Wendy's, White Castle, **other:**
32	Continued Chevrolet, Discount Tire, Firestone/auto, Ford, GNC, Home Depot, K-Mart, Kohl's, Kroger, Lowe's Whse, Meijer/dsl, Michael's, Murray Parts, Office Depot, PetsMart, Radio Shack, Target, Walmart/auto, **W gas:** BP/Tim Horton/24hr, Shell, **food:** Amigo's Mexican, Andy's Pizza, Domino's, McDonald's, Ram's Horn Rest., Sunday's Ice Cream, **lodging:** Best Western/rest., Holiday Inn Express, Westwood Inn, **other:** SavOn Drug
29	Gilbralter Rd, to Flat Rock, Lake Erie Metropark, **E gas:** FasTrack/dsl, **food:** Chinese Food, Cottage Inn Pizza, McDonald's, Subway, Wendy's, **other:** H, Curves, GNC, Kroger, **W gas:** Marathon/dsl, **lodging:** Sleep Inn, **other:** Ford, st police
28	rd 85 (from nb), Fort St, **E** H
27	N Huron River Dr, to Rockwood, **E gas:** Marathon/Subway/dsl, **food:** Benito's Pizza, Famous Coney Island, Huron River Rest., Ocean Duck Chinese, **other:** Curves, FoodTown Foods, Rite Aid, **W gas:** Speedway/dsl, **food:** Riverfront Rest.
26	S Huron River Dr, to S Rockwood, **E gas:** Sunoco/dsl, **food:** Dixie Cafe, Drift Inn, **other:** USPO
21	Newport Rd, to Newport, **E gas:** BP/Subway/dsl, **other:** repair, **W gas:** Marathon/Burger King/dsl/24hr
20	I-275 N, to Flint
18	Nadeau Rd, **W gas:** Pilot/Arby's/dsl/scales/24hr, **other:** H, RV camping
15	MI 50, Dixie Hwy, to Monroe, **E gas:** Shell, **food:** Bob Evans, Burger King, Red Lobster, **lodging:** Best Value Inn, Best Western, Hampton Inn, Motel 6, **other:** to Sterling SP, **W gas:** Pilot/Subway/dsl/scales/24hr, TA/BP/Country Pride/Pizza Hut/Popeye's/Tim Horton/dsl/scales/24hr/@, **food:** Big Boy, Cracker Barrel, Denny's, El Maguey, McDonald's, Wendy's, **lodging:** Holiday Inn Express, Knight's Inn, **other:** H, to Viet Vet Mem
14	Elm Ave, to Monroe
13	Front St, Monroe
11	La Plaisance Rd, to Bolles Harbor, **W gas:** Marathon/Taco Bell/dsl, Speedway, **food:** Burger King, McDonald's, Wendy's, **lodging:** Baymont Inn, Comfort Inn, Harbor Town RV Resort, **other:** Outlet Mall/famous brands, st police
10mm	**Welcome Ctr nb, full services, info, litter barrels, vending, petwalk**
9	S Otter Creek Rd, to La Salle, **W** antiques
7mm	**weigh sta both lanes**
6	Luna Pier, **E gas:** Sunoco/dsl, **food:** Beef Jerky Ultd. Ganders Rest., Roma's Pizza, **lodging:** Super 8, **W** st police
5	to Erie, Temperance
2	Summit St
0mm	Michigan/Ohio state line

MONROE

INTERSTATE 94

E ↕ W

Exit #	Services
275mm	I-69/I-94 begin/end on MI 25, Pinegrove Ave in Port Huro **N gas:** BP/24hr, Citgo, Speedway, **food:** Chicken Shack, Jet's Pizza, McDonald's, Tim Horton, Wendy's, White Castle, **lodging:** Day's Inn, Holiday Inn Express, **other:** Buick/Pontiac, Can-Am Duty

INTERSTATE 94 CONT'D

E ↕ W

Exit #	Services
275mm	Continued Free, Family$, Ford, Honda, Rite Aid, tollbridge to Canada
274.5mm	Black River
274	Water St, Port Huron, **N Welcome Ctr/rest area, full facilities (only from wb), food:** Cracker Barrel, **lodging:** Best Western, **S gas:** SpeedyQ/dsl, Speedway/dsl, **food:** Bob Evans, **lodging:** Comfort Inn, Fairfield Inn, Hampton Inn, **other:** Lake Port SP, RV camping
271	**I-69 E and I-94 E run together eb, Lp I-69, S gas:** Mobil, **food:** Arby's, McDonalds, KFC, Quay St Grill, Wendy's, **other:** Kroger/gas, K-Mart, Sam's Club, to Port Huron
269	Dove St, Range Rd, **N gas:** Speedway/dsl/24hr, **lodging:** AmeriHost
266	Gratiot Rd, Marysville, **S gas:** Admiral, BP/dsl/scales/24hr, Marathon/scales/dsl, Meijer, Speedway, **food:** Arby's, Big Boy, Burger King, KFC, 4 Star Rest., Little Caesars Mancino's Pizza, McDonald's, Mr Pita, Pelican Café, Pizza Hut, Taco Bell, Tim Horton, **lodging:** Super 8, **other:** [H], AutoZone, Curves, Rite Aid, Wally's Foods
262	Wadhams Rd, **N** camping, **S gas:** Marathon/dsl/showers/24hr, Mobil/dsl
257	St Clair, Richmond, **S gas:** BP/dsl, **other:** st police
255mm	**rest area eb, full [handicapped] facilities, [phone], info, [picnic], litter barrels, petwalk**
251mm	**rest area wb, full [handicapped] facilities, [phone], info, [picnic], litter barrels, petwalk**
248	26 Mile Rd, to Marine City, **N food:** McDonald's (2mi), **S gas:** Mejier, 7-11/gas, Speedy Q (1mi)
247mm	Salt River
247	MI 19 (no eb return), New Haven
243	MI 29, MI 3, Utica, New Baltimore, **N gas:** BP, Marathon/dsl, Meijer/dsl/24hr, Sunoco/dsl, **food:** Applebee's, Arby's, Burger King, Chophouse, Cold Stone, Coney Island, Dimitri's Rest., Empire Buffet, Gus Coney Island, McDonald's, Outback Steaks, Panera Bread, Papa Romano's Pizza, Ruby Tuesday, Subway, Starbucks, TX Roadhouse, Wendy's, White Castle, **lodging:** Chesterfield Motel, **other:** Belle Tire, Best Buy, Discount Tire, GNC, Home Depot, Jo-Ann Fabrics, K-Mart, Kohl's, Lowe's Whse, Michael's, PetCo, Radio Shack, Rite Aid, Staples, Target, TJ Maxx, Walgreen, **S gas:** Marathon/dsl/24hr, 7-11/gas, Speedway/dsl/24hr, **food:** Big Boy, Buscemis Pizza, Hot'n Now Burgers, Taco Bell, **lodging:** LodgeKeeper, **other:** Chevrolet
241	21 Mile Rd, Selfridge, **N gas:** Marathon/dsl, Shell, **food:** China King, Hungry Howie's, Quizno's, Subway, **other:** Advance Parts, CVS Drug, same as 240
240	to MI 59, **N gas:** 7-11/gas, Marathon, Speedway, **food:** Arby's, Bob Evans, Coney Island, McDonald's, O'Charley's, Taco Bell, Tim Horton, **lodging:** Best Western, **other:** $General, Ford, Walmart SuperCtr
237	N River Rd, Mt Clemens, **N gas:** BP/dsl, Mobil/Subway/dsl, **food:** McDonald's, **lodging:** Quality Inn, **other:** [H], General RV Ctr, Gibralter Trade Ctr
236.5mm	Clinton River

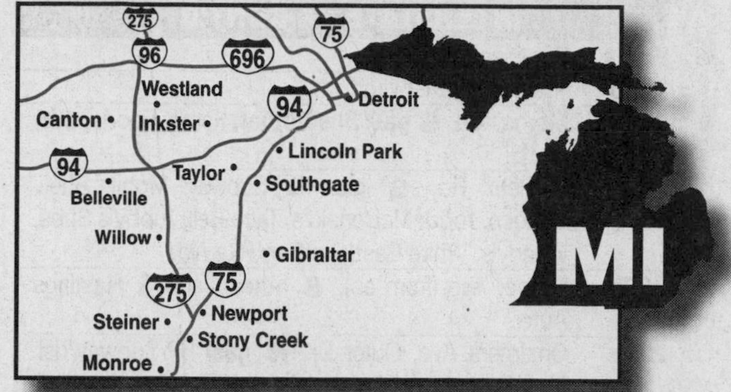

DETROIT AREA

Exit #	Services
236	Metro Parkway, **S food:** Big Apple Bagels, Little Caesars, McDonald's, Subway, **other:** [H], Curves, CVS Drug, GNC, Kroger
235	Shook Rd (from wb)
234b a	Harper Rd, 15 Mile Rd, **N gas:** BP/McDonald's, Marathon/dsl, SpeedyQ, Sunoco/dsl/24hr, **food:** Sorrento Pizza, **other:** Vet, **S gas:** FL Gas, **food:** China Moon, Subway, Winners Grill
232	Little Mack Ave (from wb only), **N gas:** Marathon, 7-11/gas, Sunoco, **food:** Arby's, Burger King, Chili's, Cold Stone, Del Taco, Denny's, Hooters, Longhorn Steaks, McDonald's, Panera Bread, Pizza Hut, Red Robin, Sea Breeze Diner, Tim Horton, Woody's Grill, **lodging:** Days Inn, Eastin Hotel, Holiday Inn Express, Red Roof Inn, Super 8, Victory Inn, **other:** Belle Tire, Firestone, JC Penney, Sam's Club, Sears/Auto, Staples, **S gas:** Marathon, Meijer/dsl/24hr, Speedway/dsl, **food:** Cracker Barrel, IHOP, **lodging:** Baymont Inn, Gelato Roama Pizza, **other:** Family$, Home Depot, Jo-Ann Fabrics, PetsMart, same as 231
231	(from eb), MI 3, Gratiot Ave, **N gas:** Shell, Speedway, Sunoco, **food:** Applebee's, Arby's, Big Boy, Bob Evans, ChuckeCheese, Denny's, Famous Dave's, Logan's Raodhouse, McDonald's, Pizza Hut, Starbucks, TX Roadhouse, **lodging:** Best Western, Day's Inn, Econolodge, Extended Stay America, Microtel, **other:** Best Buy, Discount Tire, Firestone/auto, Honda/Acura, Kia, Nissan, Sam's Club/gas, Target, Toyota, U-Haul, mall
230	12 Mile Rd, **N gas:** American Gas, Mobil/dsl, **food:** BD's Mongolian, Burger King, Jimmy John's, Krispy Kreme, Outback Steaks, **other:** CVS Drug, $Tree, Hyundai/Suzuki, Lincoln/Mercury, Marshall's, Mitsubishi, NAPA, Walmart/Subway, mall, **S gas:** Marathon
229	I-696 W, Reuther Fwy, to 11 Mile Rd, **N gas:** BP, **S gas:** BP/dsl, Speedway, **other:** 7-11
228	10 Mile Rd, **N gas:** BP/24hr, Mobil, Shell, **food:** Eastwind Chinese, Coney Island, Jet's Pizza, **other:** CVS Drug
227	9 Mile Rd, **N gas:** Mobil/dsl, Speedway/dsl, Sunoco, **food:** McDonald's, Papa John's, Subway, Taco Bell/Pizza Hut, Wendy's, **other:** Aldi Foods, CVS $Tree, Drug, Fresh Choice Foods, Office Depot, Pete & Franks Mkt, True Value, **S gas:** Mobil/dsl, **lodging:** Shore Pointe Motel, **other:** BMW, Cadillac, Mercedes
225	MI 102, Vernier Rd, 8 Mile Rd, **S gas:** BP/Subway, Mobil, Sunoco/dsl, **food:** Coney Island, KFC, Taco Bell, Wendy's, **other:** Kroger, Walgreen

DETROIT AREA

INTERSTATE 94 CONT'D

E ↕ W

DETROIT AREA

Exit #	Services
224b	Allard Ave, Eastwood Ave
224a	Moross Rd, **S gas:** Shell, **other:** Family Foods, **other:** H
223	Cadieux Rd, **S gas:** BP/Subway, Mobil, Shell, Sunoco, **food:** McDonald's, Taco Bell, Tubby's Subs, Wendy's, White Castle, **other:** Rite Aid
222b	Harper Ave (from eb), **S other:** Family$, Hastings Auto
222a	Chalmers Ave, Outer Dr, **N gas:** BP/Subway/dsl, Marathon, **food:** Coney Island, KFC, Little Caesars, White Castle, **other:** Family$
220b	Conner Ave, **N gas:** BP, Sunoco
220a	French Rd, **S gas:** Marathon
219	MI 3, Gratiot Ave, **N gas:** Marathon/Subway, Speedy, **food:** Coney Island, KFC, McDonald's, **other:** Family$, **S gas:** GasMart, **food:** Burger King
218	MI 53, Van Dyke Ave, **N gas:** BP, Mobil/dsl
217b	Mt Elliott Ave, **S gas:** Marathon, Sunoco/dsl, **food:** Young's BBQ
217a	E Grand Blvd, Chene St, **S gas:** Marathon
216b	Russell St (from eb), to downtown
216a	I-75, Chrysler Fwy, to tunnel to Canada
215c	MI 1, Woodward Ave, John R St
215b	MI 10 N, Lodge Fwy
215a	MI 10 S, tunnel to Canada, downtown
214b	Trumbull Ave, to Ford H
214a	(from wb)Grand River Ave
213b	I-96 W to Lansing, E to Canada, bridge to Canada, to Tiger Stadium
213a	W Grand (exits left from eb)
212b	Warren Ave (from eb)
212a	Livernois Ave, **S gas:** Marathon/Subway/dsl, Sunoco
211b	Cecil Ave (from wb), Central Ave
211a	Lonyo Rd, **S** Ford
210	US 12, Michigan Ave, Wyoming Ave, **N gas:** Mobil, **S gas:** BP/dsl, Citgo/dsl, Sunoco/dsl, **food:** YumYum Donuts
209	Rotunda Dr (from wb)
208	Greenfield Rd, Schaefer Rd, **N gas:** Mobil, **other:** 7-11, **S** River Rouge Ford Plant
207mm	Rouge River
206	Oakwood Blvd, Melvindale, **N gas:** Marathon, **food:** Applebee's, Carino's, Coney Island, Chili's, Cold Stone, Little Caesars, Longhorn Steaks, Moe's SW Grill, On-the-Border, Panera Bread, Starbucks, Subway, **other:** Best Buy, Ford Plant, GNC, Home Depot, Jo-Ann Fabrics, Lowe's Whse, Meijer, Michaels, Old Navy, PetCo, Staples, Target, TJ Maxx, UPS, World Mkt, Greenfield Village Museum, **S gas:** BP, **food:** Burger King, Coney Island, McDonald's, O'Henry's, Sabina's, Subway, **lodging:** Best Western, Holiday Inn Express, **other:** Belle Tire, Big A Parts, Curves, CVS Drug, $General, Rite Aid, 7-11
205mm	Largest Uniroyal Tire in the World
204b a	MI 39, Southfield Fwy, Pelham Rd, **N gas:** Marathon, Mobil, Valero/dsl, **food:** Ponderosa Steaks, **other:** 7-11, to Greenfield Village, **S gas:** Marathon, **other:** Walgreen
202b a	US 24, Telegraph Rd, **N gas:** Clark, Shell, Sunoco, **food:** Burger King, Checkers, Dunkin Donuts, Jet's Pizza, KFC, McDonald's, Pizza Hut, Ram's Horn Rest., Subway, Taco Bell, Wendy's, **lodging:** Casa Bianca Motel, **other:** Advance Parts, Aldi Foods, Rite Aid, Walgreen, **S gas:** BP, Citgo, Marathon/dsl, **food:** Burger King, Hungry Howie's, Leon's Rest., Marina's Pizza, Old Country Buffet, Pizza Hut, Popeye's, Quizno's, Subway, Super China, Yum Yum Donuts, **lodging:** Comfort Inn, **other:** AutoZone, Curves, Family$, Radio Shack, Rite Aid, U-Haul, Walgreens, Walmart, st police
200	Ecorse Rd, (no ez eb return), to Taylor, **N gas:** Marathon/scales/dsl, **S gas:** Rich, Speedy/dsl, **food:** Danny's Pizza, Norms Subs
199	Middle Belt Rd, **S gas:** BP/dsl/24hr, **food:** Denny's, McDonald's, Wendy's, **lodging:** Day's Inn, Howard Johnson, Super 8
198	Merriman Rd, **N food:** Bob Evans, **lodging:** Baymont Inn, Best Value, Best Western, Clarion, Comfort Inn, Courtyard, Crowne Plaza Hotel, Doubletree Inn, Econolodge, Extended Stay America, Fairfield Inn, Hampton Inn, Hilton Garden, Holiday Inn, Howard Johnson, Marriott, Metropolitan Motel, Motel 6, PearTree Inn, Ramada Inn, Sheraton, **S** Wayne Co ✈
197	Vining Rd
196	Wayne Rd, Romulus, **N gas:** Shell, **food:** McDonald's, **S gas:** Mobil/dsl, **food:** Burger King, Subway
194b a	I-275, N to Flint, S to Toledo
192	Haggerty Rd, **N gas:** BP, Mobil/24hr, Travel&Truck Plaza/dsl (2mi), **food:** Burger King (2mi), Subway, **S** Lower Huron Metro Park
190	Belleville Rd, to Belleville, **N gas:** BP/24hr, Meijer/dsl/24hr, Marathon, **food:** Applebee's, Arby's, Big Boy, Cracker Barrel, McDonald's, O'Charley's, Quizno's, Taco Bell, Tim Horton, Wendy's, **lodging:** Hampton Inn, Holiday Inn Express, Red Roof Inn, **other:** Camping World RV Service/supplies, CVS Drug, $Tree, Firestone/auto, Ford, Meijer, Michal's RV Ctr, U-Haul, Walgreens, Walmart, **S gas:** Shell, **food:** Burger King, China City, Dimitri's Kitchen, Dos Pesos Mexican, Subway, **lodging:** Comfort Inn, Super 8, **other:** USPO
189mm	**rest area wb, full ♿ facilities, info, ☎, picnic, litter barrels, vending, petwalk**
187	Rawsonville Rd, **S gas:** Mobil/dsl, Speedway/dsl, **food:** Burger King, Denny's, KFC, Little Caesar's, LoneStar Steaks, Maria's Pizza, McDonald's, Pizza Hut, Tim Horton, Wendy's, **other:** $General, $Tree, GNC, K-Mart, KOA (3mi), Radio Shack
185	US 12, Michigan Ave (from eb, exits left, no return), to frontage rds, ✈
184mm	Ford Lake
183	US 12, Huron St, Ypsilanti, **N gas:** Marathon/dsl, **other:** to E MI U, **S food:** Baker's Square, McDonald's, Primo Coffee, **lodging:** Marriott, **other:** H, Chevrolet/Pontiac/Buick/GMC, st police
181b a	US 12 W, Michigan Ave, Ypsilanti, **N gas:** Meijer/dsl/24hr, Rich, Speedway, **food:** Burger King, Taco Bell/Pizza Hut, Tim Horton/Wendy's, **other:** H, Aamco, BigLots, $Tree, 7-11, Sheena's Food/24hr, Radio Shack, Walmart, **S gas:** Shell, **food:** Domino's, Harvest Moon Rest., McDonald's, Subway

INTERSTATE 94 CONT'D

E ↕ W

Exit #	Services
180b a	US 23, to Toledo, Flint
177	State St, **N gas:** BP/24hr, Mobil, Shell, **food:** Bennigan's, Burger King, CA Pizza, Damon's, Graham's Steaks, Los Tres Mexican, Macaroni Grill, Max&Erma's, Olive Garden, Wendy's, **lodging:** Best Value, Crowne Plaza Hotel, Comfort Inn, Courtyard, Fairfield Inn, Hampton Inn, Hilton, Holiday Inn Express, Motel 6, Red Roof Inn, Sheraton, **other:** Firestone, JC Penney, Mitsubishi, Sears/auto, VW, World Mkt, mall, to UMI, **S gas:** Citgo/Subway, **food:** Coney Island, McDonald's, Pizza Hut/Taco Bell, **lodging:** Motel 6, **other:** U-Haul
175	Ann Arbor-Saline Rd, **N gas:** Shell, **food:** Applebee's, Coney Island, Moe's SW Grill, Old Country Buffet, Panera Bread, Subway, **lodging:** Candlewood Suites, **other:** Office Depot, mall, to UMI Stadium, **S gas:** Meijer/dsl/24hr, **food:** Big Boy, Jet's Pizza, Joe's Crabshack, McDonald's, Outback Steaks, TGIFriday, **other:** Best Buy, Jo-Ann Fabrics, Kohl's, Meijer, Target
172	Jackson Ave, to Ann Arbor, **N gas:** BP, Marathon, Shell, Sunoco, **food:** Boston Mkt, Burger King, Holiday's Rest., KFC, LJ Silver, Marathon, McDonald's, Quarter Rest., Quizno's, Starbucks, Subway, Taco Bell, Zingerman's Roadhouse, **other:** [H], CVS Drug, $Tree, Discount Tire, Goodyear, K-Mart, Kroger, Rite Aid, Staples, TJ Maxx, Walgreens, mall, **S lodging:** Best Western, Super 8, **other:** Chevrolet/Pontiac/Cadillac, Ford
171	MI 14 (from eb, exits left), to Ann Arbor, to Flint by US 23
169	Zeeb Rd, **N gas:** BP/dsl/24hr, **food:** Grand Pies Co, Metzger's Rest., McDonald's, **S gas:** Citgo/dsl, Meijer/dsl, **food:** Arby's, Burger King, Panera Bread, Pizza Hut, Subway, Taco Bell, Wendy's, Westside Grill, **other:** Harley-Davidson, Lowe's Whse, Meijer
167	Baker Rd, Dexter, **N gas:** Pilot/Subway/scales/dsl/24hr, **S gas:** Pilot/Arby's/dsl/scales/24hr, TA/BP/Popeye's/dsl/rest./scales/24hr/@, **food:** Reddeman Farms Rest. (4mi), McDonald's, **other:** Blue Beacon
162	Jackson Rd, Fletcher Rd, **S gas:** Clark/dsl/24hr, **food:** Stiver's Rest.
161mm	**rest area eb, full ♿ facilities, ☎, [picnic], litter barrels, vending, petwalk**
159	MI 52, Chelsea, **N gas:** Mobil/dsl, Rich Gas, Sunoco/dsl, **food:** Big Boy, Chelsea Grill, China Garden, Coney Island, Hungry Howie's, KFC/Taco Bell, Little Caesar's, Main St Coney Island, McDonald's, Subway, Wendy's, **lodging:** Comfort Inn, Holiday Inn Express, **other:** [H], Chelsea Drug, Chevrolet/Buick, Chrysler/Dodge/Jeep, Country Mkt Foods/drug, Curves, CVS Drug, Ford, Pamida, Travel Land RV Ctr, Vet
157	Jackson Rd, Pierce Rd, **N** Gerald Eddy Geology Ctr
156	Kalmbach Rd, **N** to Waterloo RA
153	Clear Lake Rd, **N gas:** Marathon/dsl
151.5mm	**weigh sta both lanes**
150	to Grass Lake, **S gas:** Mobil/Subway, **other:** Apple Creek Campground

ANN ARBOR

JACKSON

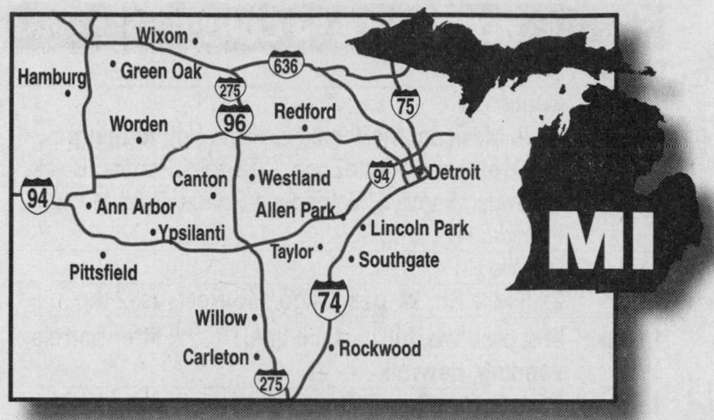

Exit #	Services
150mm	**rest area wb, full ♿ facilities, ☎, [picnic], litter barrels, vending, petwalk**
147	Race Rd, **N** Hideaway RV Camp, to Waterloo RA, camping, **S** lodging
145	Sargent Rd, **S gas:** BP/dsl, Mobil/145 Rest/dsl/scales/rest./24hr, **food:** McDonald's, Wendy's, **lodging:** Colonial Inn
144	Lp 94 (from wb), to Jackson
142	US 127 S, to Hudson, **3 mi S gas:** Meijer/dsl/24hr, Speedway, **food:** Domino's, McDonald's, Wendy's, **other:** Advance Parts, Kroger, Parts+, Rite Aid, to MI Speedway
141	Elm Rd, **N lodging:** Travelodge, **other:** Chevrolet/Dodge/Honda/Hyundai, Ford, **S**
139	MI 106, Cooper St, to Jackson, **N** st police/prison, **S gas:** Citgo/Subway, **other:** [H]
138	US 127 N, MI 50, to Lansing, Jackson, **N food:** Red Lobster, **lodging:** Baymont Inn, Comfort Inn, Fairfield Inn, Hampton Inn, Holiday Inn, Jackson Inn, **other:** Vet, **S gas:** Clark, Marathon, Rich Gas, Shell/24hr, **food:** Arby's, Big Boy, Bob Evans, Dunkin Donuts, Fazoli's, Ground Round, KFC, LJ Silver, Los Tres Amigos, McDonald's, Old Country Buffet, Outback Steaks, Panera Bread, Papa John's, Pizza Hut, Quizno's, Starbucks, Subway, **lodging:** Country Hearth Inn, Motel 6, **other:** Advance Parts, AutoZone, Best Buy, Discount Tire, Home Depot, Kohl's, Kroger, Lowe's Whse, Michael's, Sears/auto, Target, TJ Maxx, Walgreens
137	Airport Rd, **N gas:** Meijer/dsl/24hr, Shell/Taco Bell/24hr, 7-11, **food:** Burger King, Denny's, Hudson's Rest., McDonald's, Steak'n Shake/24hr, Subway, Wendy's, **other:** Bumper Parts, Meijer, **S gas:** BP/24hr, **food:** Cracker Barrel, Culvers, Olive Garden, LoneStar Steaks, **lodging:** Country Inn&Suites, **other:** K-Mart, Sam's Club/gas
136	Lp 94, MI 60, to Jackson
135mm	**rest area eb, full ♿ facilities, ☎, [picnic], litter barrels, vending, petwalk**
133	Dearing Rd, Spring Arbor, **S** to Spring Arbor U
130	Parma, **S gas:** Citgo/dsl/rest./24hr
128	Michigan Ave, **N gas:** BP/Burger King/scales/dsl/24hr, Marathon/dsl/24hr, **other:** RV camping
127	Concord Rd, **N** St Julian's Winery
124	MI 99, to Eaton Rapids, **S** lodging
121	28 Mile Rd, to Albion, **N gas:** Mobil, **food:** Arby's, **lodging:** Best Western, **S gas:** FT/dsl/24hr, Marathon, Speedway/dsl/24hr, **food:** Albion Garden, Burger King, Frosty Dan's, Full Moon Rest., KFC, La

INTERSTATE 94 CONT'D

E ↕ W

Exit #	Services
121	Continued Casa Mexican, McDonald's, Pizza Hut, **lodging:** Super 9, **other:** [H], AutoZone, Chevrolet/Pontiac/Buick, $General, Family$, Felpausch Foods, Ford/Mercury, Pamida, RV camping
119	26 Mile Rd
115	22.5 Mile Rd, **N gas:** Citgo/115 Rest./dsl/24hr
113mm	**rest area wb, full [handicap] facilities, [phone], [picnic], litter barrels, vending, petwalk**
112	Partello Rd, **S gas:** Loves/Hardee's/scales/dsl/24hr, **food:** Schuler's Rest.
110	Old US 27, Marshall, **N gas:** Shell/Subway/dsl/24hr, **food:** Country Kitchen/24hr, **S gas:** Citgo/KFC/dsl, **food:** Denny's, Pizza Hut (2mi), Schuler's Rest. (2mi), **lodging:** Hampton Inn, Holiday Inn Express, **other:** [H], sheriff
108	I-69, US 27, N to Lansing, S to Ft Wayne
104	11 Mile Rd, Michigan Ave, **N gas:** Pilot/scales/dsl/24hr, Sunoco/Te-Khi Trkstp/rest./scales/24hr/@, **S gas:** Citgo/Subway/dsl/24hr, **lodging:** Quality Inn/rest.
103	Lp 94 (from wb, no return), to Battle Creek, **N** [H]
102mm	Kalamazoo River
100	Beadle Lake Rd, **N food:** Moonraker Rest., **S gas:** Citgo/dsl, **other:** Binder Park Zoo
98b	I-194 N, to Battle Creek
98a	MI 66, to Sturgis, **S gas:** Citgo/Blimpie/dsl, Meijer/dsl/24hr, **food:** Chili's, Don Pablo, McDonald's, Ruby Tuesday, Schlotsky's, Starbucks, Steak'n Shake, **lodging:** Holiday Inn, **other:** Best Buy, Discount Tire, Kohl's, Lowe's Whse, Meijer, Michael's, PetCo, Sam's Club/gas, Staples, TJ Maxx, Walgreens, Walmart SuperCtr/24hr, same as 97
97	Capital Ave, to Battle Creek, **N gas:** BP/24hr, Marathon, **food:** Arby's, LoneStar Steaks, Lux Cafe, McDonald's, Red Lobster, **lodging:** Comfort Inn, Knight's Inn, **S gas:** Citgo, Shell/24hr, Sunoco/Subway/24hr, **food:** Applebee's, Bob Evans, Burger King, Canton Buffet, Cici's Pizza, Cocina Mexicana, Coney Island, Cracker Barrel, Denny's, Don Pablo, Fazoli's, Godfather's Pizza, Old Country Buffet, Pizza Hut, Quizno's, Taco Bell, Tuesday Morning, Wendy's, **lodging:** Baymont Inn, Best Western, Day's Inn, Fairfield Inn, Hampton Inn, Motel 6, Ramada Inn, Super 8, **other:** Apple Valley Foods, Best Buy, Borders Books, $Tree, Firestone/auto, Goodyear/auto, Harley-Davidson, JC Penney, Macy's, Marshall Fields, Sears/auto, Target, mall, Vet
96mm	**rest area eb, full [handicap] facilities, [phone], [picnic], litter barrels, vending, petwalk**
95	Helmer Rd, **N gas:** Citgo/dsl, **other:** st police, **2 mi N gas:** Meijer/dsl/24hr, **food:** Big Boy
92	Lp 94, to Battle Creek, Springfield, **N gas:** Citgo/Arlene's Trkstp/dsl/rest./24hr, Shell/24hr, **other:** RV camping, to Ft Custer RA
88	Climax, **N** Galesburg Speedway
85	35th St, Galesburg, **N gas:** Shell/Subway/dsl/24hr, **food:** McDonald's, Subway, **other:** Galesburg Speedway, to Ft Custer RA, River Oaks CP, **S other:** Colebrook CP, Scottsville CP, Winery Tours, RV camping
85mm	**rest area wb, full [handicap] facilities, [phone], [picnic], litter barrels, vending, petwalk**
81	Lp 94 (from wb), to Kalamazoo
80	Cork St, Sprinkle Rd, to Kalamazoo, **N gas:** Citgo/dsl, Double Express, Speedway/dsl, **food:** Arby's, Burger King, Chicken Coop, Denny's, Godfather's, Hana East Asian, Perkins, Taco Bell, **lodging:** Best Western, Clarion Hotel, Fairfield Inn, Holiday Inn Express, Red Roof Inn, Vet, **S gas:** BP/dsl/24hr, Speedway/dsl, **food:** Derk's Rest., Hometown Diner, Horizon Inn, McDonald's, Subway/24hr, Wendy's, **lodging:** Comfort Inn, Econolodge, Horizon Inn, Motel 6
78	Portage Rd, Kilgore Rd, **N gas:** BP/Circle K, **food:** China Hut, Cottage Pizza, Uncle Earnie Pancakes, **lodging:** Hampton Inn, **other:** [H], **S gas:** Shell/24hr, Speedway, **food:** Angelo's Italian, Bravo Rest., Brewster's, Callahan's Rest., Fat Tony's, McDonald's, Pizza King, Quizno's, Taco Bell, Theo&Stacy's Rest., Subway, **lodging:** Country Inn Suites, Lee's Inn, **other:** AutoValue Parts, museum
76b a	Westnedge Ave, **N gas:** Admiral, Meijer/dsl/24hr, Speedway/dsl, **food:** Arby's, Beaners, Bennigan's, BD BBQ, Hooters, IHOP, Kazoopie's, Lee's Chicken, Mancino's Eatery, Outback Steaks, Papa John's, Pappy's Mexican, Pizza Hut, Root Beer Stand, Steak'n Shake, Stirmax Asian, Subway, Taco Bell, Theo & Stacy's Rest., **other:** BigLots, Discount Tire, Gander Mtn, Goodyear/auto, Lowe's Whse, Meijer, Midas, Office Depot, Rite Aid, **S gas:** Shell/24hr, **food:** Antique Kitchen, Applebee's, Bilbo's Pizza, Bob Evans, Burger King, Carrabba's, Chili's, ChuckeCheese, Cold Stone, Culvers, Empire Chinese, Fazoli's, Heavenly Ham, Jimmy Johns, KFC, Krispy Kreme, Little Caesar's, LJ Silver, Logan's Roadhouse, MacKenzie's Bakery, McDonald's, Noodles & Co, Old Country Buffet, Olive Garden, Panchero's Mexican, Panera Bread, Pizza Hut, Qdoba Mexican, Red Lobster, Red Robin, Schlotsky's, Subway, Taco Bell, TX Roadhouse, Wendy's, **lodging:** Holiday Motel, **other:** AutoZone, Barnes&Noble, Belle Tire, Best Buy, Cadillac/Pontiac/Nissan, $Tree, Fannie Mae Candies, Firestone/auto, Harding's Foods, Home Depot, JC Penney, Jo-Ann Fabrics, K-Mart, Kohl's, MktPlace Foods, Michael's, Old Navy, PepBoys, Pontiac/Cadillac, Radio Shack, Sam's Club, Sears/auto, Target, Walgreens, WorldMkt, mall
75	Oakland Dr
74b a	US 131, to Kalamazoo, **N** to W MI U, Kalamazoo Coll
72	Oshtemo, **N gas:** Citgo/dsl, Speedway/dsl, **food:** Arby's, Burger King, Culver's, McDonald's, Taco Bell, Wendy's, **lodging:** Hampton Inn, **other:** NAPA, **S food:** Cracker Barrel, **lodging:** Fairfield Inn, Towne Place Suites
66	Mattawan, **N gas:** Speedway/Subway/dsl/24hr, **food:** Main St Grill, Mancino's Italian, **other:** Freightliner, Rossman Auto/towing, **S gas:** Shell
60	MI 40, Paw Paw, **N gas:** BP/24hr, Speedway/dsl/24hr, **food:** Arby's, Big Boy, Burger King, Chicken Coop, Gallagher's Eatery, McDonald's, Pizza Hut, Root Beer Stand, Subway, Taco Bell, Wendy's, **lodging:** Econolodge, Comfort Inn, Super 8, **other:** [H], Advance Parts, Chrysler/Dodge/Jeep, Curves, Felpausch Foods, St Julian Winery, Warner Winery

MARSHALL

KALAMAZOO

INTERSTATE 94 CONT'D

E ↕ W

Exit #	Services
56	MI 51, to Decatur, **N** st police, **S** **gas:** Citgo/dsl, Marathon/dsl/24hr
52	Lawrence, **N** **food:** Waffle House of America
46	Hartford, **N** **gas:** Shell/dsl/24hr, **food:** McDonald's, Panel Room Rest.
42mm	**rest area wb, full ♿ facilities, ☎, [picnic], litter barrels, vending, petwalk**
41	MI 140, to Niles, Watervliet, **N** **gas:** BP/24hr, Citgo, Marathon, Wesco, **food:** Burger King, Chicken Coop, Frosty Boy, Rookies, Subway, Taco Bell, Waffle House, **lodging:** Ramada, **other:** [H], Curves, camping
39	Millburg, Coloma, Deer Forest, **0-1 mi N** **gas:** BP/dsl, Marathon, Speedway, Westco/dsl, **food:** Diggins Rest., Friendly Grill, McDonald's, Pizza Hut, Subway, **other:** Ace hardware, Family$, Holiday RV Ctr, Krenek RV Ctr, True Value, **S** **gas:** NAPA Auto Care
36mm	**rest area eb, full ♿ facilities, ☎, [picnic], litter barrels, vending, petwalk**
34	I-196 N, US 31 N, to Holland, Grand Rapids
33	Lp I-94, to Benton Harbor, **2-4 mi N** ✈, sheriff's dept
30	Napier Ave, Benton Harbor, **N** **gas:** *FLYING J* /Wendy's/dsl/24hr/@, Shell/24hr, **food:** Hot'n'Now (1mi), **lodging:** Super 8, **other:** [H], Blue Beacon, **S** Chrysler/Dodge/Honda
29	Pipestone Rd, Benton Harbor, **N** **gas:** Meijer/dsl/24hr, **food:** Applebee's, Asian Buffet, Burger King, Hacienda Mexican, Hardee's, IHOP, McDonald's, Pizza Hut, Sophia's Pancake House, Steak'n Shake, Super Buffet, Texas Corral, **lodging:** Best Western, Courtyard, Motel 6, Red Roof Inn, **other:** Aldi Foods, Best Buy, $Tree, Home Depot, JC Penney, Lowe's Whse, Meijer, Radio Shack, Sears/auto, Staples, Walgreens, Walmart SuperCtr/Subway/24hr, **S** **gas:** Mobil/dsl/24hr, **food:** Bob Evans, **lodging:** Comfort Suites, Holiday Inn Express
28	US 31 S, MI 139 N, Scottdale Rd, to Niles, **N** **gas:** Citgo/dsl, Marathon/dsl, **food:** Bejing House, Burger King, Capozio's Pizza, Chicken Coop, Country Kitchen, DQ, Henry's Burgers, KFC, Pizza Hut, Subway, Taco Bell, **lodging:** Economy Inn, Executive Inn/rest., **other:** [H], AutoZone, BigLots, Chevrolet, $Tree, Family$, M&W Tire, Midas, NAPA, Office Depot, Old Navy, Rite Aid, Target, TJ Maxx, radiators/repair/transmissions, st police, Vet, **S** **lodging:** Best Value
27mm	St Joseph River
27	MI 63, Niles Ave, to St Joseph, **N** **gas:** BP/24hr, **food:** Nye's Apple Barn, **S** **food:** Panera Bread, **other:** Goodyear
23	Red Arrow Hwy, Stevensville, **N** **gas:** Admiral, BP, Marathon/dsl, Mobil, Shell/dsl/24hr, **food:** Big Boy, Burger King, Cracker Barrel, Culver's, DQ, Fireside Inn Rest., LJ Silver, McDonald's, Papa John's, Popeye's, Quizno's, Subway, Tony's Rest., **lodging:** Baymont Inn, Candlewood Suites, Comfort Suites, Park Inn, Ray's Motel, **other:** Curves, Walgreen, **S** **food:** Five O'Clock Grill, **lodging:** Hampton Inn
22	John Beers Rd, Stevensville, **N** to Grand Mere SP, **S** **gas:** Marathon/dsl, **food:** Pizza Hut

BENTON HARBOR

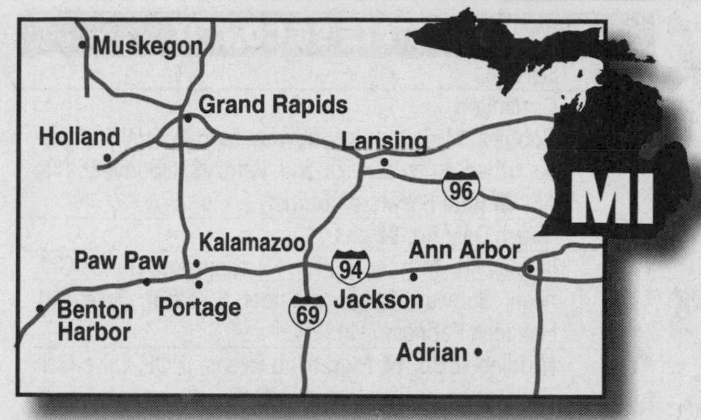

Exit #	Services
16	Bridgman, **N** **gas:** BP/A&W/dsl/24hr, **other:** to Warren Dunes SP, **S** **gas:** JR's Trvl Ctr/dsl/24hr, **food:** McDonald's, **lodging:** Bridgman Inn, **1/2 mi S** **food:** Olympus Rest., Pizza Hut, Roma Pizza, Sammies Rest., Subway, **other:** Chevrolet/Buick, Vet
12	Sawyer, **N** **gas:** Citgo/scales/dsl/rest./24hr, **food:** Chubby's Diner, **S** **gas:** TA/Burger King/Country Pride/Popeye's/Taco Bell/scales/dsl/24hr/@, **food:** Pizza Hut, **lodging:** Super 8, **other:** USPO
6	Lakeside, Union Pier, **N** **other:** St Julian's Winery, antiques, **S** RV camping
4b a	US 12, to Three Oaks, New Buffalo, **N** **food:** Pizza Hut, st police
2.5mm	**weigh sta both lanes**
1	MI 239, to Grand Beach, New Buffalo, **N** **gas:** Shell/Quizno's, **food:** Hana's Rest. (1mi), McDonald's, Wheel Inn Rest., **lodging:** Best Western, Holiday Inn Express, Rodeway Inn, **other:** $General, **S** **gas:** New Buffalo/rest./dsl/24hr, **food:** Wendy's, **lodging:** Obrien's Inn
.5mm	**Welcome Ctr eb, full ♿ facilities, info, ☎, [picnic], litter barrels, vending, petwalk**
0mm	Michigan/Indiana state line

INTERSTATE 96

E ↕ W

Exit #	Services
I-96 begins/ends on I-75, exit 48 in Detroit.	
191	I-75, N to Flint, S to Toledo, US 12, to MLK Blvd, to Michigan Ave
190b	Warren Ave, **N** **gas:** BP/dsl, **S** **gas:** Marathon
190a	I-94 E to Port Huron
189	W Grand Blvd, Tireman Rd, **N** **gas:** BP/Subway, Mobil
188b	Joy Rd, **N** **food:** Church's
188a	Livernois, **N** **gas:** Mobil, Shell, **food:** Burger King, KFC, McDonald's, Wendy's
187	Grand River Ave (from eb)
186b	Davison Ave, I-96 local and I-96 express divide, no exits from express
186a	Wyoming Ave
185	Schaefer Hwy, to Grand River Ave, **N** **gas:** BP/24hr, Mobil, **food:** Coney Island, McDonald's, **other:** CVS Drug, **S** **gas:** Sunoco
184	Greenfield Rd
183	MI 39, Southfield Fwy, exit from expswy and local
182	Evergreen Rd
180	Outer Dr, **N** **gas:** BP/dsl/lube
180mm	I-96 local/express unite/divide
179	US 24, Telegraph Rd, **N** **gas:** BP, Marathon/dsl, **food:** Arby's, China King, Dunkin Donuts/Baskin-

DETROIT AREA

INTERSTATE 96 CONT'D

E ↕ W

Exit #	Services
179	Continued Robbins, McDonald's, Subway, Taco Bell, White Castle, **other:** Chevrolet, Dodge, Family$, Goodyear, Rite Aid, **S gas:** BP, Marathon/dsl
178	Beech Daly Rd, **N** gas
177	Inkster Rd, **N gas:** BP/Tim Horton, **food:** Panda Chinese, Subway, **lodging:** Super 8, **other:** $General, Hancock Fabrics, 7-11
176	Middlebelt Rd, **N food:** Bob Evans, IHOP, Olive Garden, **lodging:** Comfort Inn, **S food:** Logan's Roadhouse, **lodging:** Crossland Studios, **other:** Costco/gas, Home Depot, Marshall's, Meijer, Michael's, Pet-Co, Target, Walgreens, Walmart SuperCtr
175	Merriman Rd, **N gas:** Mobil, Speedway/dsl, **S gas:** Sunoco, **food:** Blimpie
174	Farmington Rd, **N gas:** Mobil/dsl, Sunoco, **food:** Looney Baker, **S gas:** BP, **food:** KFC
173b	Levan Rd, **N** [H], to Madonna U
173a	Newburgh Rd
171mm	**I-275 and I-96 run together 9 miles**
170	6 Mile Rd, **N food:** Big Boy, CA Pizza Kitchen, Coney Island, Ground Round, Jimmy John's, Louie's Grill, Max&Erma's, Panera Bread, Red Robin, **lodging:** Best Western, Courtyard, Marriott, Radisson, **other:** [H] Busch's Fresh Foods, Murray Parts, Rite Aid, Walgreens, mall, **S gas:** BP, Mobil, **food:** Applebee's, Baja Fresh, Brann's Steaks, Buca Italian, Caribou Coffee, Charlie's Grill, Chi Burger, Cold Stone, Claddagh Rest., Flemings, McDonald's, Mitchell's Fishmarket, Noodles & Co, Panchero's, Papa Vino's, PF Chang, Potbelly, **lodging:** Fairfield Inn, Residence Inn, TownePlace Suites, **other:** Barnes&Noble, CVS Drug, Office Depot
169b a	7 Mile Rd, **N food:** Doc's Grill, **lodging:** Embassy Suites, **S food:** Alexander's Rest., Bahama Breeze Rest., Champp's Rest., Gaucho Steaks, Macaroni Grill, **lodging:** AmeriSuites, **other:** Home Depot
167	8 Mile Rd, to Northville, **S gas:** Meijer/dsl/24hr, Speedway/dsl, **food:** Benihana, Big Boy, Chili's, McDonald's, Koney Island, On-the-Border, Quizno's, Starbucks, Taco Bell, Uno Pizzaria, Zoup, **lodging:** Country Inn Suites, Extended Stay America, Hampton Inn, Holiday Inn Express, Sheraton, **other:** Best Buy, Costco/gas, Firestone, Home Depot, Kohl's, Meijer, Target, Trader Joe's, to Maybury SP
165	I-696, I-275, MI 5, Grand River Ave.
I-275 and I-96 run together 9 miles	
163	I-696 (from eb)
162	Novi Rd, to Walled Lake, Novi, **N gas:** BP, **food:** Buffalo Wild Wings, Carrabba's, ChuckeCheese, Denny's, Oaks Grill, Red Lobster, Subway, **lodging:** Crowne Plaza, Hotel Baronette, Residence Inn, **other:** [H] Gander Mtn, JC Penney, Jo-Ann Fabrics, Kohl's, Kroger, Michael's, PetCo, Sears/auto, WorldMkt, mall, **S gas:** Mobil, **food:** Baja Fresh, Big Boy, Bonefish Grill, Boston Mkt, Coney Island, Famous Dave's, Kim's Chinese, Melting Pot Rest., Olive Garden, Red Robin, Steve & Rocky's, TGIFriday, Wendy's, **lodging:** Courtyard, Wyndham Garden, **other:** Borders Books, Discount Tire, Old Navy, TJ Maxx, auto repair, Vet
161mm	**rest area eb, full [♿] facilities, [phone], vending, [picnic], litter barrels, petwalk**
160	Beck Rd, 12 Mile Rd, **S food:** Coney Island **other:** [H], Home Depot, Kroger, Staples, to Maybury SP
159	Wixom Rd, Walled Lake, **N gas:** Marathon/dsl, **food:** Wendy's, **lodging:** Baymont Inn, **other:** to Proud Lake RA, **S gas:** Meijer/dsl/24hr, Mobil, Shell, Valero, **food:** Arby's, Baskin-Robbins/Dunkin Donuts, Burger King, KFC/A&W, McDonald's, Stinger's Grill, Taco Bell, **lodging:** Comfort Suites, **other:** General RV Ctr, Lincoln/Mercury, Meijer
155b a	to Milford, New Hudson, **N** Ford, to RV camping, to Lion Oaks CP, **S gas:** Mobil, Sunoco, **food:** Applebee's, Arby's, Chili's, Cold Stone, Coney Island, Jet's Pizza, McDonald's, Quizno's, Starbucks, Subway, Wendy's, **other:** Chevrolet, Discount Tire, Lowe's Whse, Walmart SuperCtr/24hr
153	Kent Lake Rd, **N** Kensington Metropark, **S gas:** Mobil
151	Kensington Rd, **N** Kensington Metropark, **S** Island Lake RA, food, lodging
150	Pleasant Valley Rd (no return wb), **S** [phone]
148b a	US 23, N to Flint, S to Ann Arbor
147	Spencer Rd, **N gas:** Mobil, **other:** st police, **S** to Brighton St RA
145	Grand River Ave, to Brighton, **N gas:** BP, Shell/dsl, **food:** Arby's, Cracker Barrel, Outback Steaks, Pizza Hut, **lodging:** Courtyard, Homewood Suites, **other:** Cadillac/GMC, $General, Ford/Mercury, Honda, **S gas:** Clark/Subway/dsl, **food:** Big Boy, Burger King, Chili's, Coney Island, DQ, IHOP, KFC, Lil Chef, Little Caesar's, McDonald's, Panera Bread, Red Robin, Starbucks, Stillwater Grill, Taco Bell, Tim Horton, Wendy's, **lodging:** Holiday Inn Express, **other:** AAA, Best Buy, Bob's Tire, Borders Books, Home Depot, Honda, Jo-Ann Etc., Marshall's, Mazda, Meijer/dsl, Michael's, Radio Shack, Rite Aid, PetsMart, Sears, Staples, Target, USPO, mall, to Brighton Ski Area
141	Lp 96 (from wb, no EZ return), to Howell, **N gas:** Shell, Sunoco/dsl, **food:** Applebee's, Bob Evans, Little Caesar's, McDonald's, Mesquite Jct, TW's Italian, **lodging:** Grandview Inn, **other:** Chevrolet, Kohl's, **S gas:** Speedway, **food:** Arby's, Big Boy, Taco Bell, Wendy's
141mm	**rest area wb, full [♿] facilities, [phone], vending, [picnic], litter barrels, petwalk**
137	D19, to Pinckney, Howell, **N gas:** Mobil, Shell/dsl, Speedway/dsl, Sunoco/Blimpie/Baskin-Robbins/Dunkin Donuts/dsl, **food:** Coney Island, **lodging:** Kensington Inn, **other:** [H], Parts+, Spartan Tire, **S food:** Country Kitchen, **lodging:** Best Western
135mm	**rest area eb, full [♿] facilities, vending, [phone], [picnic], litter barrels, petwalk**
133	MI 59, Highland Rd, **N gas:** 7-11, Sunoco/McDonald's/dsl, **food:** Arby's, Castaway Cafe (1mi), HoneyTree Grille, **lodging:** Baymont, **other:** Tanger Outlets/famous brands
129	Fowlerville Rd, Fowlerville, **N gas:** BP/rest./24hr, Shell/dsl, Sunoco/dsl, **food:** A&W/KFC, Big Boy, CO Coffee, Fowlerville Rest., McDonald's, Taco Bell/Pizza Hut, Wendy's, **lodging:** Best Western, **S gas:** Mobil, **food:** Quizno's, Subway, **other:** Chysler/Dodge/Jeep, **other:** Ford

INTERSTATE 96 CONT'D

E ↕ W

Exit #	Services
126mm	**weigh sta both lanes**
122	MI 43, MI 52, Webberville, **N gas:** Mobil/dsl/24hr, **food:** Angel's Café, McDonald's, **other:** MI Brewing Co
117	to Dansville, Williamston, **0-3 mi N gas:** Admiral, Marathon/subs/dsl, **food:** Jersey's Giant Subs, Spag's Grill, **S gas:** Sunoco/dsl, **food:** Subway
111mm	**rest area wb, full ♿ facilities, 📞, 🛒, litter barrels, vending, petwalk**
110	Okemos, Mason, **N gas:** BP/Dunkin Donuts/24hr, Marathon, Sunoco, **food:** Applebee's, Arby's, Backyard BBQ, Big Boy, Big John's Steaks, Cracker Barrel, Dunkin Donuts, Gilbert&Blake's Seafood, Grand Traverse, Little Caesar's, McDonald's, Panchero's Mexican, Sheshiang Garden, Starbucks, Stillwater Grill, Subway, Taco Bell, **lodging:** Comfort Inn, Fairfield Inn, Hampton Inn, Holiday Inn Express, **other:** 7-11, to stadium
106b a	I-496, US 127, to Jackson, Lansing, **N** St Police
104	Lp 96, Cedar St, to Holt, Lansing, **N gas:** Admiral, Speedway, **food:** Aldaco's Mexican, Applebee's, Barley's Grill, Beaner's, Blimpie, Bob Evans, Boston Mkt., China King, Cici's Pizza, Coney Island, Finley's Rest., Hooters, Jet's Pizza, KFC, Legend's Grill, LJ Silver, Los Tres Amigos, Mr Taco, New China, Pizza Hut, Steak'n Shake, Texas Roadhouse, Wendy's, White Castle/Church's, Zeus Rest., **lodging:** Day's Inn, Econolodge, Governors Inn, Regent Inn, Super 8, **other:** H, Aldi Foods, Belle Tire, Cadillac, Chevrolet, Chrysler/Jeep, Discount Tire, Dodge, Family$, GMC, Harley-Davidson, Hyundai, Kia/Suzuki, Lexus, Lincoln/Mercury, Meijer/dsl/24hr, Mitsubishi, Radio Shack, Saab, Sam's Club/gas, Target, Toyota, Walgreen, **S gas:** Marathon, Speedway/24hr, **food:** Buffalo's SW Café, Burger King, China East Buffet, Dairy Dan, Flapjack's Rest., Hungry Howie, Kang's Buffet, McDonald's, Ponderosa, Sir Pizza, Subway, **lodging:** Holiday Inn, **other:** AutoZone, Budget Tire, CarQuest, Family$, Kroger, L&L Foods, Lowe's Whse
101	MI 99, MLK Blvd, to Eaton Rapids, **0-3 mi N gas:** Meijer/dsl/24hr, QD, **food:** Arby's, **S gas:** Speedway/Subway/dsl/24hr, Sunoco/dsl, **food:** Coach's Grill, McDonald's, Wendy's
98b a	Lansing Rd, to Lansing, **N food:** Arby's, Wendy's, **lodging:** AmeriHost, **S gas:** Citgo/dsl/Windmill Rest./24hr, Don's Trkstp, **food:** Coyote Creek Grill
97	I-69, US 27 S, S to Ft Wayne, N to Lansing
95	I-496, to Lansing
93b a	MI 43, Lp 69, Saginaw Hwy, to Grand Ledge, **0-1 mi N gas:** Meijer/dsl/24hr, Shell, Speedway/dsl, **food:** Bennigan's, Burger King, Carrabba's, Denny's, Dolly's Pizza, Fine China, Frank's Grill, Jet's Pizza, McDonald's, Outback Steaks, Red Robin, Roxy's Grill, TGIFriday, Subway, **lodging:** Best Western, Fairfield Inn, Hampton Inn, Holiday Inn, Motel 6, Quality Suites, Red Roof Inn, Residence Inn, **other:** H, NAPA, Kohl's, Kroger, Walgreens, **S gas:** BP/24hr, QD, Sunoco/McDonald's, **food:** Arby's, Art's Pizza, Beaner's, Bob Evans, Cracker Barrel, Steak'n Shake, Subway, **lodging:** SpringHill Suites, **other:** Belle Tire, Discount Tire, Gander Mtn, GMC/Mazda, Lowe's Whse, Michael's, Walmart/auto

LANSING

Exit #	Services
92mm	Grand River
91	I-69 N, US 27 N (from wb), to Flint, **S gas:** *FLYING J*/Country Mkt/dsl/24hr
90	Grand River Ave, to ✈
89	I-69 N, US 27 N (from eb), to Flint
87mm	**rest area eb, full ♿ facilities, 📞, 🛒, litter barrels, vending, petwalk**
86	MI 100, Wright Rd, to Grand Ledge, **S gas:** Mobil/McDonald's/dsl, Speedway/Subway/24hr
84	to Eagle, Westphalia
79mm	**rest area wb, full ♿ facilities, info, 📞, 🛒, litter barrels, vending, petwalk**
77	Lp 96, Grand River Ave, Portland, **N gas:** BP/24hr, Marathon/dsl, Shell/Burger King, Speedway/dsl, **food:** Arby's, China Star, Little Caesar's, Hungry Howie's, McDonald's, Subway, Two Rivers Rest., Wendy's, **lodging:** Best Western, **other:** Family$, Ford, Rite Aid, Tom's Foods, **S food:** Wendy's, **other:** Ford
76	Kent St, Portland
76mm	Grand River
73	to Lyons-Muir, Grand River Ave
69mm	**weigh sta both lanes**
67	MI 66, to Ionia, Battle Creek, **N gas:** Meijer/dsl/24hr (4mi), Pilot/Subway/dsl/scales/24hr, **food:** Corner Landing Grill, **lodging:** AmeriHost (6mi), Midway Motel, Super 8, **other:** H, Meijer, Walmart SuperCtr (4mi), RV camping, st police
64	to Lake Odessa, Saranac, **N** Ionia St RA, **S** I-96 Speedway
63mm	**rest area eb, full ♿ facilities, 📞, 🛒, litter barrels, petwalk, vending**
59	Clarksville
52	MI 50, to Lowell, **N gas:** Mobil/Subway/dsl, **other:** fairgrounds, **S gas:** Marathon/Noble Roman's/dsl (2mi), **other:** RV camping
46	rd 6, to rd 37
46mm	Thornapple River
44	36 St, **S** ✈
43b a	MI 11, 28th St, Cascade, **N gas:** Marathon/dsl, Meijer/dsl/24hr, **food:** Big Boy, Brann's Steaks, Burger King, Culver's, Macaroni Grill, Panera Bread, Pizza Hut, Quizno's, Sundance Grill, Subway, Wendy's, **lodging:** Baymont Inn, Best Western, Country Inn Suites, Crowne Plaza Hotel, Holiday Inn Express, Howard Johnson, **other:** Audi/Subaru/Porsche, Meijer, Mercedes/Volvo/VW, Walmart, **S gas:** BP, Citgo, Shell, Speedway/dsl, **food:** Applebee's, Arby's, Arnie's Rest., Bennigan's, Bob Evans, Burger King, Carabba's, Carlos O'Kelley's, Cantina

GRAND RAPIDS

INTERSTATE 96 CONT'D

Exit #	Services
43b a	Continued Mexican, Chili's, ChuckeCheese, Cold Stone, Denny's, Don Pablo, Grand Rapids Brewery, Honey Baked Ham, Hooters, IHOP, Jimmy Johns, Moe's SW Grill, Noodles & Co, Olive Garden, Panera Bread, Perkins, Smokey Bones, Subway, **lodging:** Comfort Inn, Days Inn, Extended Stay America, Fairfield Inn, Hampton Inn, Hilton, Holiday Inn, Homewood Suites, Knight's Inn, Motel 6, Quality Inn, Ramada, Red Roof Inn, Sleep Inn, Springhill Suites, **other:** Acura/Audi/Subaru, Barnes&Noble, Belle Tire, CarQuest, Costco/gas, $Tree, Ford, Fresh Mkt Foods, Gander Mtn, Home Depot, Jo-Ann Fabrics, Lentz Automotive, Lowe's Whse, Nissan, Old Navy, PetsMart, Sam's Club/gas, Staples, Target, TJ Maxx, U-Haul
40b a	Cascade Rd, **N gas:** Forrest Hills Fuel, Marathon/dsl, **food:** Beaners Rest., Blimpie, China Garden, Forrest Hills Rest, Little Bangkok, Subway, **other:** 7-11/24hr, Vet, **S gas:** Shell/Quizno's/dsl, Speedway/dsl, **food:** Jimmy John's, Zoup, **other:** [H], Keystone Drug
39	MI 21 (from eb), to Flint
38	E Beltline Ave, to MI 21, MI 37, MI 44, **N gas:** BP, Meijer/dsl, **food:** O'Charley's, **other:** Meijer, RV camping, **S food:** Uno Pizzaria, **lodging:** Country Inn Suites, **other:** [H]
37	I-196 (from wb, exits left), Gerald Ford Fwy, to Grand Rapids
36	Leonard St, **1-2 mi S food:** Arby's, McDonald's (24hr), **other:** sheriff's dept
33	Plainfield Ave, MI 44 Connector, **N gas:** BP, Meijer/dsl/24hr, Speedway, **food:** Arby's, Beaners, Big Apple Bagel, Blimpie, Buddy's Pizza, Cheers Grill, Fred's Pizza, Golden Dragon, KFC, Little Caesar's, Little Caesars, LJ Silver, McDonald's, Oriental Forrest., Papa Ramano's Pizza, Pizza Hut, Russ' Rest., Taco Bell, Wendy's, **lodging:** Grand Inn, Lazy T Motel, **other:** AutoZone, Belle Tire, BigLots, CarQuest, Chevrolet, Chrysler/Jeep, Discount Tire, Dodge, Firestone, Ford, Lincoln/Mercury, Lowe's, Mitsubishi, Goodyear/auto, K-Mart, Meijer, Midas, NAPA, Nissan/VW, NTB, Jeep, Radio Shack, Save-a-Lot Foods, Toyota, U-Haul, Walgreens, transmissions, Vet, **S gas:** BP/24hr, **food:** Breakfast Nook, Denny's
31mm	Grand River
31b a	US 131, N to Cadillac, S to Kalamazoo, **1 mi N gas:** BP, **food:** McDonald's
30b a	Alpine Ave, Grand Rapids, **N gas:** Marathon, 7-11/gas, **food:** Applebee's, Bennigan's, Buffalo Wild Wings, Checkers, ChuckeCheese, Cold Stone, Culvers, El Burroti Mexican, Fire Mtn Grill, First Wok, IHOP, Jimmy John's, Logan's Roadhouse, McDonald's, Old Country Buffet, Olive Garden, Outback Steaks, Panera Bread, Peppino's Pizza, Perkins, Qdoba, Quizno's, Russ' Rest., Ryan's, Starbucks, Steak'n Shake, Subway, Taco Bell, TGIFriday, Tuesday Morning, Zoup, **lodging:** Hampton Inn, SpringHill Suites, **other:** Aldi Foods, AutoZone, Belle Tire, Best Buy, CarQuest, Discount Tire, $Tree, Ford/Kia, Kohl's, Marshall's, Michael's, NAPA, PepBoys, Radio Shack, Sam's Club/gas, Schuler Books, Target, TJ
30b a	Continued Maxx, Walgreens, Walmart SuperCtr/auto, **S gas:** Admiral/dsl, Marathon, Meijer/dsl/24hr, Speedway/dsl, **food:** Arby's, Burger King, Casa De Martina, Fazoli's, KFC, LJ Silver, McDonald's, Papa John's, Pizza Hut, Ponderosa, Wendy's, **lodging:** Motel 6, **other:** Goodyear/auto, Home Depot, Jo-Ann Fabrics, Meijer, Midas, Tuffy Auto, U-Haul
28	Walker Ave, **S gas:** Meijer/dsl/24hr, **food:** Bob Evans, McDonald's, **lodging:** Baymont Inn, Quality In
26	Fruit Ridge Ave, **N gas:** Citgo/dsl, **S gas:** Citgo/deli/dsl
25mm	**rest area eb, full [handicapped] facilities, [phone], [picnic], litter barrels, petwalk**
25	8th Ave, 4Mile Rd (from wb), **S gas:** Marathon/dsl, **lodging:** Wayside Motel
24	8th Ave, 4Mile Rd (from eb), **S gas:** Marathon/dsl, **lodging:** Wayside Motel
23	Marne, **N other:** tires, **S food:** Depot Café, Rinaldi's Café, **other:** USPO, Ernie's Mkt, fairgrounds/raceway
19	Lamont, Coopersville, **N** food, **S food:** Sam's Joint Rest., **other:** LP
16	B-35, Eastmanville, **N gas:** BP/Subway/dsl, Speedway/dsl/24hr, Shell/Burger King/dsl, **food:** Arby's, Little Caesar's, McDonald's, Taco Bell, **lodging:** AmeriHost, Rodeway Inn, **other:** Chevrolet/Poniac/Buick, Curves, Family Fare, Fun 'N Sun RV Ctr, Jeep/Dodge, Rite Aid, **S gas:** Pacific Pride/dsl, **other:** RV camping
10	B-31 (exits left from eb), Nunica, **N food:** Turk's Rest., **S gas:** Marathon, **other:** RV camping, golf course/rest.
9	MI 104 (from wb, exits left), to Grand Haven, Spring Lake, **S gas:** Marathon, **other:** to Grand Haven SP
8mm	**rest area wb, full [handicapped] facilities, [phone], [picnic], litter barrels, vending, petwalk**
5	Fruitport (from wb, no return)
4	Airline Rd, **N other:** race track, **S gas:** Speedway/dsl, Wesco/dsl, **food:** Burger Crest Diner, Dairy Bar, McDonald's, Subway, Village Inn, **other:** Grover Drug, NAPA, Orchard Mkt Foods, Pleasure Island Water Park (5mi), USPO, to PJ Hoffmaster SP
1c	Hile Rd (from eb), **S other:** racetrack
1b a	US 31, to Ludington, Grand Haven, **N lodging:** Alpine Motel, Bel-aire Motel, Haven Motel, **other:** All Seasons RV Ctr, **2 mi N on Sherman Blvd...gas:** Citgo/dsl, Westco/dsl, **food:** Applebee's, Arby's, Fazoli's, McDonald's, Old Country Buffet, Pizza Ranch, Red Wok, Ruby Tuesday, Subway, Wendy's, **lodging:** Comfort Inn/rest., **other:** [H], Lowe's Whse, PetsMart, Radio Shack, Sam's Club, Staples, Target, Walmart SuperCtr/24hr/gas, **S lodging:** AmeriHost, **other:** [airport], racetrack

I-96 begins/ends on US 31 at Muskegon.

INTERSTATE 196 (GRAND RAPIDS)

Exit #	Services
81mm	**I-196 begins/ends on I-96, 37mm in E Grand Rapids.**
79	Fuller Ave, **N** sheriff, **S gas:** Shell/dsl, Speedway/dsl, **food:** Buddy's Pizza/Dogs, Checkers, Elbow Room, KFC, Subway, Taco Bell, Wendy's, **other:** HOSTIPAL, Ace Hardware, Family Foods, Walgreens
78	College Ave, **S gas:** Marathon/Circle K, **food:** McDonald's, **other:** [H], Rite Aid, ford museum

INTERSTATE 196 CONT'D (GRAND RAPIDS)

E ↕ W

Exit #	Services
77c	Ottawa Ave, downtown, **S** Gerald R Ford Museum
77b a	US 131, S to Kalamazoo, N to Cadillac
76	MI 45 E, Lane Ave, **S food:** El Ganadero Mexican, **other:** Gerald R Ford Museum, John Ball Park&Zoo, Parts Plus
75	MI 45 W, Lake Michigan Dr, **N** to Grand Valley St U
74mm	Grand River
73	Market Ave, **N** to Vanandel Arena
72	Lp 196, Chicago Dr E (from eb)
70	MI 11 (exits left from wb), Grandville, Walker, **S gas:** BP/Subway/dsl, Shell/repair, **lodging:** Day's Inn, **other:** USPO, Vet
69b a	Chicago Dr, **N gas:** Meijer/dsl/24hr, **food:** China City, Culver's, KFC, McDonald's, Papa John's, Peppino's Pizza, Perkins, Subway, Taco Bell, **other:** Aldi Foods, AutoZone, BigLots, $General, $Tree, Meijer, Radio Shack, Save-a-Lot Foods, 7-11, Target, **S gas:** Admiral, Speedway/24 hr, **food:** Adobe Mexican, Arby's, Burger King, Dunkin Donuts/Baskin-Robbins, Little Caesar's, Pizza Hut, Russ' Rest., Wendy's, **lodging:** Best Western, Holiday Inn Express, **other:** NAPA
67	44th St, **N gas:** Mobil/dsl, **food:** Burger King, Cracker Barrel, Panera Bread, Steak'n Shake, **lodging:** Comfort Suites, **other:** AAA, Honda, Walmart/auto, **S food:** Famous Dave's, Logan's Roadhouse, Quizno's, Ritter's Custard, Starbucks, Wendy's, **lodging:** Residence Inn (2mi), **other:** Discount Tire, Gander Mtn., Lowe's Whse, PetsMart, World Mkt
64	MI 6 E, to Lansing (exits left from wb)
62	32nd Ave, to Hudsonville, **N gas:** BP/dsl/24hr, Citgo/dsl, **food:** Arby's, Burger King, Maurizio's Pizza, McDonald's, Village Grill, **lodging:** Quality Inn, **other:** Chevrolet, camping, **S gas:** Mobil/Subway/dsl/24hr, **food:** Rainbow Grill, **lodging:** Super 8, **other:** Harley-Davidson, Harvest Foods
58mm	**rest area eb, full ♿ facilities, ☎, 🛆, litter barrels, vending, petwalk**
55	Byron Rd, Zeeland, **N gas:** 7-11, **food:** Blimpie, McDonald's, **other:** Curves, **3-5 mi N** H, to Holland SP
52	16th St, Adams St, **2 mi N gas:** Meijer/dsl/24hr, **food:** Wendy's, **lodging:** Best Inn, Econolodge, **other:** H, Meijer, **S gas:** Mobil/Subway/dsl, **food:** Burger King
49	MI 40, to Allegan, **N gas:** BP/McDonald's/dsl, **lodging:** Residence Inn, **S gas:** Tulip City/Marathon/dsl/scales/24hr, **food:** Rock Island Rest.
44	US 31 N (from eb), to Holland, **3-5 mi N lodging:** Country Inn, **other:** H, gas, food
43mm	**rest area wb, full ♿ facilities, info, ☎, 🛆, litter barrels, vending, petwalk**
41	rd A-2, Douglas, Saugatuck, **N gas:** Marathon/dsl, Shell/Subway/dsl, **food:** Babaloo's Pizza, Burger King, Spectators Grill, **lodging:** Best Western (1mi), Hootin Motel, Timberline Motel (3mi), **other:** $General, NAPA, Saugatuck RV Resort, to Saugatuck SP, **S food:** Ravine's Rest (1mi), **food:** Belvedere Inn, **lodging:** Shangrai-la Motel, **other:** Red Barn Gifts
38mm	Kalamazoo River
36	rd A-2, Ganges, **N gas:** Shell, **lodging:** AmericInn
34	MI 89, to Fennville, **N** to West Side CP, **S gas:** Shell/24hr, **other:** Cranes Pie Pantry (4mi, seasonal), Lyons Fruits, Winery Tours
30	rd A-2, Glenn, Ganges, **N** to Westside Cty Park
25mm	**rest area eb, full ♿ facilities, ☎, 🛆, litter barrels, vending, petwalk**
26	109th Ave, to Pullman
22	N Shore Dr, **N food:** Tello's Ristorante, **other:** to Kal Haven Trail SP, Cousin's RV Camping/rest.
20	rd A-2, Phoenix Rd, **N gas:** BP/dsl, Marathon/dsl, **food:** Arby's, Checkers, China Buffet, Taco Bell, **lodging:** SouthHaven Motel, **other:** H, AutoZone, Walgreens, st police, **S gas:** Shell, **food:** Big Boy, McDonald's, Sherman's Dairybar, Wendy's, **lodging:** Comfort Suites, Hampton Inn, Holiday Inn Express, Ramada, **other:** $General, Walmart SuperCtr/gas/dsl/24hr
18	MI 140, MI 43, to Watervliet, **0-2 mi N gas:** BP, Shell/dsl/24hr, Xpress/dsl, **food:** Burger King, 50's Drive Inn, McDonald's, Pizza Hut, **lodging:** Great Lakes Inn, LakeBluff Motel, **other:** AutoValue Parts, Buick/Pontiac/Cadillac/GMC, Chevrolet, Chrysler/Dodge/Jeep, Ford, Village Mkt Foods
13	to Covert, **N** to Van Buren SP, RV camping
7	MI 63, to Benton Harbor, **N food:** DiMaggio's Pizza, Vitale's Mkt/subs, **other:** RV camping
4	to Coloma, Riverside, **S gas:** Marathon/dsl, **other:** KOA
2mm	Paw Paw River
1	Red Arrow Hwy, **N** Ross Field ✈
0mm	I-94, E to Detroit, W to Chicago

BENTON HARBOR

I-196 begins/ends on I-94, exit 34 at Benton Harbor.

Shelby, Whitehall, Muskegon, Grand Haven, 96, Grand Rapids, 75, Holland, 196, Kentwood, 69, Lansing, 496, MI, Ganges, 96, South Haven, Kalamazoo, 94, Ann Arbor, Benton Harbor, Portage, 69, 94, Lake View

INTERSTATE 275 (LIVONIA)

N ↕ S

Exit #	Services
	I-275 and I-96 run together 9 miles. See Michigan Interstate 96 Exits 165-170.
29	I-96 E, to Detroit, MI 14 W, to Ann Arbor
28	Ann Arbor Rd, Plymouth, **E gas:** BP/Dunkin Donuts/24hr, Shell, **food:** Atlantis Rest., Denny's, Little Caesars, **lodging:** Days Inn, Red Roof Inn, **W food:** Bennigan's, Burger King, McDonald's, Steak&Ale, **lodging:** Comfort Inn, **other:** Cadillac, CVS Drug, Dodge, K-Mart, Lincoln/Mercury, Vet
25	MI 153, Ford Rd, Garden City, **W gas:** BP, Shell, Speedway, Valero, **food:** Applebee's, Arby's, BD Mongolian BBQ, Bob Evans, Boston Mkt., Bowery Grille, Buffalo Wild Wings, Carrabba's, Chili's, Chuck-eCheese, Coney Island, Dunkin Donuts/Baskin-Robbins, Hunan Empire Chinese, KFC, Little

INTERSTATE 275 (LIVONIA)

N ↕ S LIVONIA

Exit #	Services
25	Continued Caesar's, Outback Steaks, Panera Bread, Quizno's, Roman Forum Rest., Subway, TGIFriday, Tim Horton, TX Corral, Wendy's, White Castle/Church's, **lodging:** Extended Stay America, Fairfield Inn, La Quinta, Motel 6, **other:** Discount Tire, Firestone, Lowe's, PetCo, Richardson Drug, Target, Walgreens, Vet
23	**rest area nb, full facilities, , info, , litter barrels**
22	US 12, Michigan Ave, to Wayne, **E gas:** BP/24hr, Marathon, Shell, Valero/dsl, **food:** Arby's, Jonathan's Rest., McDonald's, Subway, Wendy's, **lodging:** Day's Inn, Fellows Cr Motel, Holiday Inn Express, Super 8, Willo Acres Motel, **W gas:** Marathon/dsl, 7-11, **food:** Dunkin Donuts, McDonald's
20	Ecorse Rd, to Romulus, **E gas:** 7-11, **W gas:** Mobil/Burger King/scales/dsl/24hr
17	I-94 E to Detroit, W to Ann Arbor, **E**
15	Eureka Rd, **E gas:** Shell,
13	Sibley Rd, New Boston, **W gas:** Fusion/Subway/dsl, **food:** LC's Chicken, **other:** to Lower Huron Metro Park
11	S Huron Rd, **1 mi W gas:** Sunoco/Burger King/dsl, **food:** Jacob's Rest, **other:** RV LP (1mi)
8	Will Carleton Rd, to Flat Rock
5	Carleton, South Rockwood, **W** food
4mm	**rest area sb, full facilities, , , litter barrels**
2	US 24, to Telegraph Rd, **W gas:** Marathon/dsl, lodging
0mm	I-275 begins/ends on I-75, exit 20.

INTERSTATE 475 (FLINT)

N ↕ S FLINT

Exit #	Services
17.5mm	I-475 begins/ends on I-75, exit 125.
15	Clio Rd, **W gas:** BP, **other:** Chevrolet
13	Saginaw St, **E gas:** BP, **food:** McDonald's, Papa John's, Taco Bell, **other:** Advanced Parts, Family$, Kroger/gas, **W gas:** Marathon, Sunoco, **food:** Burger King, KFC, Little Caesar's
11	Carpenter Rd
10	Pierson Rd
9	rd 54, Dort Hwy, Stewart Ave, **E gas:** Citgo, **food:** McDonald's
8mm	Flint River
8b	Davison Rd, Hamilton Ave
8a	Longway Blvd, **W food:** China 1 Buffet, **lodging:** Holiday Inn Express, **other:** H, USPO
7	rd 21, Court St, downtown Flint
6	I-69, W to Lansing, E to Port Huron
5	Atherton Rd (from sb), **E gas:** Citgo, Marathon, **other:** Curves
4	Hemphill Rd, Bristol Rd, **E gas:** Sunoco, **food:** Benitos Pizza, McDonald's, New China, **other:** Rite Aid, **W gas:** Speedway, **food:** Little Caesars, Ole Time Burgers, Tim Horton, Wendy's, **other:** Family$, Kroger/gas
2	Hill Rd, **E gas:** Speedway, **food:** Applebee's, Bob Evans, **lodging:** Wingate Inn, **other:** Ford, Vet, **W gas:** Sunoco/Tim Horton, **food:** Arby's, Bangkok
2	Continued Peppers, Blimpie, Burger St Grill, Little Caesars, Pizza Hut, Wendy's, **lodging:** Courtyard, Holiday Inn, Residence Inn, **other:** Rite Aid
0mm	I-475 begins/ends on I-75, exit 111.

INTERSTATE 696 (DETROIT)

E ↕ W DETROIT

Exit #	Services
I-696 begins/ends on I-94.	
28	I-94 E to Port Huron, W to Detroit, 11 Mile Rd, **E gas:** BP/dsl, Speedway, 7-11
27	MI 3, Gratiot Ave, **N gas:** BP, **food:** National Coney Island, **other:** Costco/gas, **S gas:** BP, Mobil/McDonald's, **food:** White Castle, **other:** Goodyear/auto
26	MI 97, Groesbeck Ave, Roseville, **N gas:** Mobil/dsl, **S gas:** Marathon, **food:** Wendy's
24	Hoover Rd, Schoenherr Rd, **N gas:** Sunoco, **food:** Burger King, KFC, **S gas:** BP, Mobil, food: Subway, Taco Bell, Tim Horton, **lodging:** Holiday Inn Express, **other:** CVS Drug, Kroger, Marshall's
23	MI 53, Van Dyke Ave, **N gas:** BP, **food:** Arby's, Coney Island, Dunkin Donuts, McDonald's, **lodging:** Baymont Inn, **other:** Cadillac/Pontiac/GMC, Dodge, Jo-Ann Fabrics, radiators, **S gas:** BP/24hr, **food:** Burger King, **other:** Chevrolet, Ford, Toyota, USPO
22	Mound Rd
20	Ryan Rd, Dequindre Rd, **N gas:** Marathon, **food:** IHOP, **lodging:** Knight's Inn, Red Roof Inn, **S food:** Bob Evans, McDonald's, **lodging:** Comfort Suites, Ramada Ltd, **other:** Rite Aid, transmissions
19	Couzens St, 10 Mile Rd, **S** Hazel Park Racetrack
18	I-75 N to Flint, S to Detroit
17	Campbell Ave, Hilton Ave, Bermuda, Mohawk, **S gas:** Marathon/dsl
16	MI 1, Woodward Ave, Main St, **N food:** Burger King, **other:** zoo
14	Coolidge Rd, 10 Mile Rd, **S gas:** Mobil, Speedway, **food:** Dunkin Donuts, **food:** Jade Palace Chinese, Little Caesar's, LJ Silver, Pizza Hut, Subway, Taco Bell, Wendy's, **other:** CVS Drug, Jo-Ann Fabrics
13	Greenfield Rd, **S gas:** Mobil, Sunoco, **food:** Dunkin Donuts, **other:** Ford
12	MI 39, Southfield Rd, 11 Mile Rd, **S gas:** Shell
11	Evergreen Rd, **S lodging:** Residence Inn
10	US 24, Telegraph Rd, **N gas:** BP, Marathon, **food:** Denny's, Seoul Garden Korean, **lodging:** Hampton Inn, Embassy Suites, **other:** Belle Tire, Best Buy, Chevrolet, Chrysler/Jeep, Dodge, $General, Farmer Jack's, Ford, Honda/Nissan/Isuzu, Hyundai, Jo-Ann Fabrics, K-Mart, Lexus, Lincoln/Mercury, Office Depot, Pontiac/Buick, USPO, mall, **S gas:** Mobil, **lodging:** Courtyard, Hilton, Holiday Inn, Marriott
8	MI 10, Lodge Fwy
5	Orchard Lake Rd, Farmington Hills, **N gas:** Marathon, Mobil, Shell, **food:** Arby's, Hong Hua Chinese, Roberto's Rest., Ruby Tuesday, Starbucks, Steak&Ale, Steamer's Seafood, Subway, Wendy's, **lodging:** Comfort Inn, **other:** Discount Tire, to St Mary's Coll
1	(from wb), I-96 W, I-275 S, to MI 5, Grand River Ave

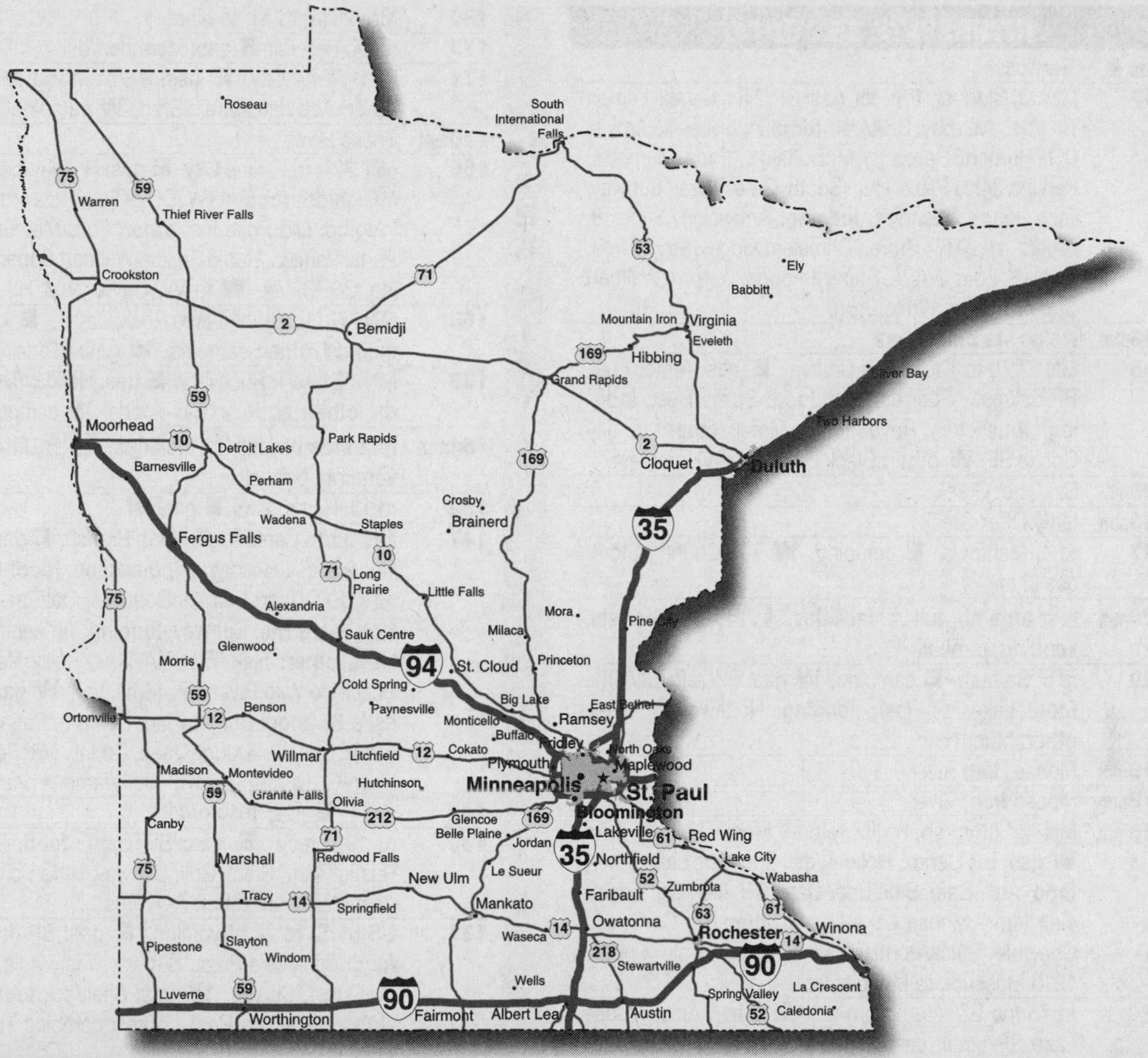

INTERSTATE 35

N ↕ S

DULUTH

Exit #	Services
260mm	I-35 begins/ends on MN 61 in Duluth.
259	MN 61, London Rd, to Two Harbors, North Shore, **W gas:** BP, Holiday/dsl, ICO/dsl, **food:** Blackwoods Grill, Burger King, KFC, McDonald's, Perkins, Pizza Hut, Subway, Taco John's, Wendy's, **lodging:** Edgewater Inn, **other:** Vet
258	21st Ave E (from nb), to U of MN at Duluth, same as 259
256b	Mesaba Ave, Superior St, **E gas:** ICO/DQ, **food:** Bellicio's, Caribou Coffee, Grandma's Grill, Famous Dave's BBQ, Greenmill Rest., Little Angie's Cantina, Old Chicago, Red Lobster, Subway, Timberlodge Steaks, Tradewinds Rest., **lodging:** Canal Park Lodge, Comfort Suites, Hampton Inn, Hawthorn Suites, Inn at Lake Superior, Suites Motel, The Inn, **W lodging:** Holiday Inn, Radisson, Sheraton
256a	Michigan St, **E** waterfront, **W** [H], downtown
255a	US 53 N (exits left from nb), downtown, mall, **W other:** Auto Value Parts, Kia
255b	I-535 spur, to Wisconsin
254	27th Ave W, **W gas:** Holiday/Burger King/dsl, Spur/dsl, **food:** Duluth Grill, Quizno's, Subway, **lodging:** Motel 6, **other:** USPO
253b	40th Ave W, **W gas:** BP/dsl/24hr, **food:** Perkins/24hr, **lodging:** Comfort Inn, Super 8
253a	US 2 E, US 53, to Wisconsin
252	Central Ave, W Duluth, **W gas:** Holiday/dsl/24hr, Little Store/dsl, **food:** Beaner's Cafe, Giant Panda, Herbert&Gerbert Subs, Jade Fountain Rest., FC, McDonald's, Pizza Hut, Sammy's Café, **other:** Advance Parts, $Tree, Falk's Drug, K-Mart, Menard's, O'Reilly Parts, Sav-a-Lot Foods, Super 1 Foods, Walgreens, Vet
251b	MN 23 S, Grand Ave, **E lodging:** Holiday Inn Express
251a	Cody St, **E lodging:** Allyndale Motel, **other:** zoo
250	US 2 W (from sb), to Grand Rapids, **1/2 mi W gas:** Holiday/dsl, Mobil/dsl/LP, **food:** Blackwoods Grill, **lodging:** AmericInn
249	Boundary Ave, Skyline Pkwy, **E gas:** Holiday/McDonald's/dsl, **lodging:** Country Inn&Suites, **other:** to ski area, **W rest area both lanes, full [handicapped] facilities, info, [phone], [picnic], litter barrels, vending, gas:** Little Store/dsl/e-85/24hr, **food:** Blackwoods Grill, **lodging:** AmericInn, Red Roof Inn
246	rd 13, Midway Rd, Nopeming, **W gas:** Armor/dsl, **food:** Dry Dock Rest.
245	rd 61, **E food:** Buffalo House Rest./camping
242	rd 1, Esko, Thomson, **E gas:** BP/dsl
239.5mm	St Louis River
239	MN 45, to Cloquet, Scanlon, **E other:** Jay Cooke SP, KOA (May-Oct), **W gas:** Holiday, **food:** Pantry Rest., Trapper Pete's Steaks, **lodging:** Golden Gate Motel, **other:** [H], Buick/Chevrolet/Pontiac, camping, dsl repair

INTERSTATE 35 CONT'D

N ↕ S

Exit #	Services
237	MN 33, Cloquet, **1 mi W gas:** BP/24hr, Cenex, Lemon Tree/dsl, Murphy USA/dsl, **food:** Applebee's, Arby's, DQ, Herbert&Gerberts, McDonald's, Papa Murphy's, Perkins/24hr, Pizza Hut, South Gate Pizza, Subway, Taco John's, Wendy's, **lodging:** AmericInn, Super 8, **other:** H, ATT Store, Chrysler/Dodge/Jeep, $Tree, Family$, Ford, NAPA, Super 1 Foods, Verizon, Walmart SuperCtr/24hr, White Drug
236mm	**weigh sta both lanes**
235	MN 210, to Cromwell, Carlton, **E gas:** Armor Fuel, BP/dsl/rest., Spur/dsl/24hr, **food:** Spirits Rest, **lodging:** AmericInn, Royal Pines Motel, **other:** to Jay Cooke SP, **W other:** Black Bear Casino/Hotel/rest.
235mm	Big Otter Creek
233mm	Little Otter Creek
227	rd 4, Mahtowa, **E** camping, **W** TJ's Country Store/gas (2 mi)
226mm	**rest area nb, full facilities, litter barrels, vending, petwalk**
220	rd 6, Barnum, **E** camping, **W gas:** BP/dsl/café/24hr, **food:** Lakeside Rest., **lodging:** Northwoods Motel, **other:** Munger Tr
219mm	Moose Horn River
218mm	Moose Horn River
216	MN 27 (from sb, no EZ return), Moose Lake, **1-2 mi W gas:** BP, Cenex, Holiday/dsl, Spur, The Little Store, **food:** Art's Café, Blue Bear Cafe, DQ, **lodging:** AmericInn (4mi), Moose Lake Motel, **other:** H, CarQuest, Chevrolet/Buick/Pontiac, Ford, Super Valu Foods, 1918 Museum, to Munger Trail
214	rd 73 (no EZ return from nb), **E other:** Alco, Moose Lake SP (2mi), camping, **W gas:** Little Store/Subway/dsl/e-85, **lodging:** AmericInn, **2 mi W lodging:** Moose Lake Motel, **other:** H, Munger Trail, Red Fox Camping
209	rd 46, Sturgeon Lake, Sturgeon Lake **E gas:** Cenex, **W lodging:** Sturgeon Lake Motel, **food:** Ernie's Rest. (seasonal), **other:** camping (3mi), quilt shop
209mm	**rest area sb, full facilities, litter barrels, vending, petwalk**
206.5mm	Willow River
205	rd 43, Willow River, **W gas:** BP/dsl/cafe, **other:** camping (2mi)
198.5mm	Kettle River
198mm	**rest area nb, full facilities, litter barrels, vending, petwalk**
195	rd 18, rd 23 E, to Askov, **E gas:** Cenex/cafe/dsl, **food:** Banning Jct Cafe, **lodging:** Best Value Inn, **other:** to Banning SP, camping, **W** camping
191	MN 23, rd 61, Sandstone, **E gas:** BP/dsl/LP, Victory/dsl, **lodging:** Sandstone 61 Motel (2mi), **other:** Thrifty White Drug
184mm	Grindstone River
183	MN 48, Hinckley, **E gas:** Holiday/Hardee's/dsl, Marathon/Tobie's Rest./dsl, **food:** Burger King, DQ, Subway, Taco Bell, **lodging:** Days Inn, Grand Northern Inn, **other:** casino, to St Croix SP (15mi), **W gas:** Little Store/White Castle/dsl, **food:** Cassidy's Rest., **lodging:** Travelodge
180	MN 23 W, rd 61, to Mora
175	rd 14, Beroun, **E gas:** Marathon/dsl
171	rd 11, Pine City, **E gas:** SA/dsl, **food:** McDonald's, **other:** Ace Hardware, $Stuff, **W** camping
170mm	Snake River
169	MN 324, rd 7, Pine City, **E gas:** Holiday/dsl, Pump-n-Munch/dsl, **food:** A&W, DQ, KFC, Pizza Hut, Subway, **lodging:** Old Poke Inn, **other:** Ford/Mercury, O'Reilly Parts, Pamida, Radio Shack, Walmart SuperCtr, camping, USPO, Vet, **W** to NW Co Fur Post HS
165	MN 70, to Grantsburg, Rock Creek, **E gas:** Marathon/dsl, **other:** camping, **W gas:** BP/dsl/café
159	MN 361, rd 1, Rush City, **E gas:** Holiday/Burger King/dsl, **other:** H, Rush City Foods, **W** camping (2mi)
154mm	**rest area nb, full facilities, litter barrels, vending, petwalk**
152	rd 10, Harris, **2 mi E** gas/dsl
147	MN 95, to Cambridge, North Branch, **E gas:** Casey's, Conoco/dsl, Holiday/dsl, Marathon, **food:** DQ, Domino's, KFC/Taco Bell, McDonald's, Oak Inn Rest, Perkins, Pizza Hut, Subway, **lodging:** AmericInn, Budget Host, **other:** Fisk Tire, NAPA, O'Reilly Parts, Radio Shack, to Wild River SP (14mi), Vet, **W gas:** Holiday/dsl/e-85, **food:** Burger King, Denny's, Papa Murphy's, **other:** Chrysler/Dodge/Jeep, County Mkt Foods, Ford, ShopKo, North Branch Outlets/famous brands, USPO
143	rd 17, **E gas:** Tesoro/dsl
139	rd 19, Stacy, **E gas:** BP, Gas+, **food:** Pizza Man, Rustic Rest., Stacy Grill, Subway, **other:** city park, **W gas:** Marathon, **other:** A-1 Tires
135	US 61 S, rd 22, Wyoming, **E gas:** BP/dsl, Casey's, **food:** DQ, Joe's Pizza, Subway, Tasty Asia, **other:** H CarQuest, Curves, **W gas:** Shell/dsl, **food:** McDonald's, Village Inn Rest., **other:** camping (10mi), golf, Vet
132	US 8 (from nb), to Taylors Falls
131	rd 2, Forest Lake, **E gas:** BP/24hr, Holiday/dsl, SA/dsl, **food:** Applebee's, Arby's, Burger King, Culvers, KFC, McDonald's, Papa John's, Perkins, Quack's Cafe, Subway, Sbarro's, Taco Bell, White Castle, **lodging:** AmericInn, **other:** H, AutoValue Parts, Kennedy Transmissions, O'Reilly Parts, Rainbow Foods/24hr, Target, Tires+, Walgreens, Walmart, RV/Auto repair, **W gas:** Holiday/dsl, **food:** Famous Dave's BBQ,JimmyJohn's, Papa Murphy's, Taco John's, Starbucks, Wendy's, **lodging:** Country Inn&Suites, **other:** AT&T, Buick/GMC/Pontiac, Cadillac/Chevrolet, Cub Foods, Ford, GNC, Home Depot, Jiffy Lube, Menards
131mm	**rest area sb, full facilities, litter barrels, vending, petwalk**
129	MN 97, rd 23, **E gas:** Kwik Trip/dsl/e-85, **other:** camping (6mi), **W gas:** BP/dsl, **other:** Coates RV Ctr, Gander Mtn., camping (1mi)
128mm	**weigh sta both lanes**
127	I-35W, S to Minneapolis. See I-35W.
123	rd 14, Centerville, **E gas:** Kwik Trip, **food:** Blue Heron Grill, Papa Murphy's, **other:** Festival Foods, Otter Lake RV Ctr, **W gas:** Mobil/dsl, Shell, **food:** DQ, WiseGuys Pizza, **other:** NAPA
120	rd J (from nb, no return)
117	rd 96, **E gas:** Marathon, SA/dsl, **food:** Burger King, Casa Lupita, **lodging:** AmericInn, **other:** Goodyear/

HINCKLEY — PINE CITY — FOREST LAKE

INTERSTATE 35 CONT'D

N ↕ S

Exit #	Services
117	Continued auto, NAPA, **W gas:** Holiday, PDQ, **food:** Applebee's, Arby's, Caribou Coffee, Culver's, Herbert&Gerbert's Subs, McDonald's, Subway, **other:** Cub Foods, Tires+, Walgreens, USPO
115	rd E, **E gas:** BP, Conoco, SA/dsl, **food:** Jimmy's Rest., Perkins, **lodging:** Country Inn&Suites, Holiday Inn Express, **W food:** Dunn Bros Coffee, KFC/Pizza Hut, Mad Jack's Cafe, McDonald's, Panera Bread, Papa Murphy's, Wendy's, **other:** Curves, Festival Foods, GNC, Panera Bread, Radio Shack, Target, Walmart/auto
114	I-694 E (exits left from sb)
113	I-694 W
112	Little Canada Rd, **E gas:** BP, **W gas:** Sinclair/dsl, **food:** Porterhouse Rest
111a/b	MN 36 E, to Stillwater/MN 36 W, to Minneapolis
110b	Roselawn Ave
110a	Wheelock Pkwy, **E gas:** BP, Oasis Mkt, **food:** Subway, **W food:** Champps Grill
109	Maryland Ave, **E gas:** SA/dsl, **food:** Taco John's, **W food:** Wendy's, **other:** K-Mart
108	Pennsylvania Ave, downtown
107c	University Ave, downtown, **E gas:** Marathon/dsl, **W other:** [H], to st capitol
107b a	I-94, W to Minneapolis, **E to St Paul. I-35 and I-94 run together.**
106c	11th St (from nb), Marion St, downtown
106b	Kellogg Blvd (from nb), downtown, **E food:** Eagle St. Grill, Subway, **lodging:** Holiday Inn, **other:** [H]
106a	Grand Ave, **E** [H]
105	St Clair Ave
104c	Victoria St, Jefferson Ave
104b	Ayd Mill Rd (from nb)
104a	Randolph Ave
103b	MN 5, W 7th St, **E food:** Burger King, **W gas:** SA/dsl, **other:** USPO
103a	Shepard Rd (from nb)
102mm	Mississippi River
102	MN 13, Sibley Hwy, **W gas:** BP, Holiday/Subway
101b a	MN 110 W, **E gas:** BP, **food:** Caribou Coffee, McDonald's, Subway, Teresa's Mexican, **other:** Tuesday Morning, **W gas:** SA
99b a	I-494 W/I-494 E
98	Lone Oak Rd, **E lodging:** Homestead Suites, Microtel, **other:** Sam's Club/gas, USPO, **W gas:** Marathon, **food:** Joe Senser's Grill, Magic Thai Café, **lodging:** Hampton Inn, Residence Inn
97b	Yankee Doodle Rd, **E food:** Applebee's, Arby's, Buffalo Wild Wings, Burger King, Coldstone Creamery, Culver's, DQ, Houlihan's, Jake's Grill,JimmyJohn's, KFC, New China Buffet, Noodles&Co, Old Chicago Pizza, Panera Bread, Papa Murphy's, Perkins, Pizza Hut, Pizza Man, Pot Bellys, Savoy Pizza, Taco Bell, **other:** At&T, Barnes&Noble, Best Buy, Byerly's Foods, Firestone, Goodyear, Home Depot, Michael's, Kohl's, Office Depot, Old Navy, PetsMart, Radio Shack, Rainbow Foods, TJ Maxx, Walgreens, Walmart, **W gas:** BP, SA/dsl, **food:** Al Baker's Rest., Dragon Palace Chinese, El Loro Mexican, Starbucks, Steak Bones

ST PAUL

ST PAUL

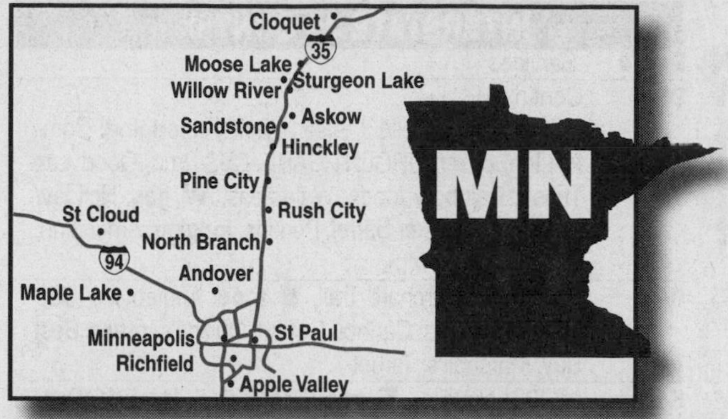

Exit #	Services
97b	Continued Grill, **lodging:** Best Western, Extended Stay America, **other:** NAPA
97a	Pilot Knob Rd, same as 97b, **E gas:** Holiday, SA, **food:** Chili's, McDonald's, Wendy's, **lodging:** SpringHill Suites, TownePlace Suites, **other:** Kohl's, Tires+, mall, **W gas:** BP, SA/dsl, **lodging:** Best Western
94	rd 30, Diffley Rd, to Eagan, **E gas:** Holiday/dsl, **other:** CVS Drug, Kowalski's Mkt/Starbucks, **W gas:** Sinclair/Goodyear
93	rd 32, Cliff Rd, **E gas:** Holiday, **food:** Bonfire Grill, Subway, **other:** Ace Hardware, **W gas:** Holiday/dsl, Marathon/dsl, **food:** Ansari's Grill, Burger King, Caribou Coffee, DQ, Dolittle's Grill, Greenmill Rest., Hong Wong Chinese, KFC, Leeann Chin's, McDonald's, Pizza Hut, Quizno's, Starbucks, Taco Bell, Wendy's, **lodging:** Hilton Garden, Holiday Inn Express, Staybridge Suites, **other:** Cub Foods, O'Reilly Parts, Target, Walgreen, USPO
92	MN 77, Cedar Ave, **E** Zoo, **1 m W** access to Cliff rd services
90	rd 11, **E gas:** KwikTrip, **food:** Subway, **other:** Valley Natural Foods, **W gas:** SA/dsl
88b	rd 42, Crystal Lake Rd, **E food:** Chianti Grill, **other:** Byerly's Foods, PetsMart, Tuesday Morning, **W gas:** Holiday/dsl, SA, **food:** Applebee's, Arby's/Sbarro's, Azteca Mexican, Buca Italian, Burger King,, Cam Aranh Bay, Champp's Grill, Chili's, Dakota County Grill, HoneyBaked Ham, IHOP,JimmyJohn's, KFC, Kings Buffet, Macaroni Grill, McDonald's, Old Country Buffet, Olive Garden, Outback Steaks, Panera Bread, Papa John's, Papa Murphy's, Qdoba Mexican, Red Lobster, Roasted Pear, Starbucks, Taco Bell/Pizza Hut, TGIFriday's, Wendy's, **lodging:** Days Inn, Fairfield Inn, Hampton Inn, Holiday Inn, InTown Suites, **other:** [H], AT&T, Barnes&Noble, Best Buy, Cadillac, Chevrolet, Cub Foods, Discount Tire, Goodyear/auto, Home Depot, JC Penney, K-Mart, Kohl's, Macy's, Michael's, PetCo, Rainbow Foods, Sears/auto, Target, Tires+, Walgreens, mall, USPO
88a	I-35W (from nb), N to Minneapolis. See I-35W.
87	Crystal Lake Rd (from nb), **W gas:** KwikTrip, **other:** Buick, Ford/Lincoln/Mercury, Honda/Nissan, Toyota, Beaver Mtn Ski Area
86	rd 46, **E gas:** KwikTrip, SA/dsl, **food:** KFC, Starbucks, **other:** Harley-Davidson, **W other:** O'Reilly Parts
85	MN 50, **E gas:** BP/24hr, F&F/dsl, SA/dsl, **food:** Burger King, Caribou Coffee, Culver's, DQ, Greenmill Rest., Jimmy John's, Nick'n Willy's Pizza, Pizza Hut,

INTERSTATE 35 CONT'D

Exit #	Services
85	Continued Subway, Taco Bell/LJ Silver, Wendy's, **lodging:** Comfort Inn, **other:** URGENT CARE, CVS Drug, Goodyear, Tires+, Rainbow foods, Walgreens, **W gas:** Holiday/dsl, **food:** Cracker Barrel, Perkins, **lodging:** AmericInn, **other:** Gander Mtn.
84	185th St W, Orchard Trail, **E food:** Applebee's, Buffalo Wild Wings, Caribou Coffee, Quizno's, **other:** Best Buy, Marshall's, Target
81	rd 70, Lakeville, **E gas:** Holiday/dsl, **food:** McDonald's, Porterhouse Rest., Subway, Tacoville, **lodging:** Holiday Inn/rest, Motel 6, **W food:** Harry's Cafe
76	rd 2, Elko, **E** gas/dsl, **W food:** Endzone Grill, **other:** Elko Speedway
76mm	**rest area sb, full [handicapped] facilities, [phone], [picnic], litter barrels, vending, petwalk**
69	MN 19, to Northfield, New Prague, **6-8 mi E gas:** KwikTrip, **food:** Applebee's, McDonald's, Subway, Taco Bell, **lodging:** AmericInn, College City Motel, Country Inn&Suites, Super 8, **other:** [H], Carleton Coll, St Olaf Coll, **W gas:** Shell/dsl/rest./scales
68mm	**rest area nb, full [handicapped] facilities, [phone], [picnic], litter barrels, vending, petwalk**
66	rd 1, to Dundas, **1 mi W food:** Boonie's Grill
59	MN 21, Faribault, **0-2 mi E gas:** BP/dsl/rest./scales/24hr, KwikTrip, SA, **food:** A&W, Arbys, Burger King, DQ, Hardee's, KFC, Pizza Hut, Taco John's, **lodging:** AmericInn, Best Value Inn, Days Inn, Galaxy Inn, Grandstay, Lyndale Motel, **other:** Aldi Foods, Chevrolet/GMC/Pontiac, Ford, O'Reilly Parts, Satakah St Trail, Vet, **W other:** Harley-Davidson, camping
56	MN 60, Faribault, same as 59 **E gas:** KwikTrip, **food:** Arby's, Burger King, Great China Buffet, Hardee's,JimmyJohn's, KFC, Perkins, Pizza Hut, Subway, Taco John's, **other:** [H], Aldi Foods, Auto Value Parts, Buick/Pontiac, Chevrolet, Chrysler/Jeep, Dodge, $Tree, Family$, Goodyear/auto, Hy-Vee Foods/gas, JC Penney, O'Reilly Parts, Radio Shack, Tires+, True Value, Walmart SuperCtr, mall, **W gas:** Petro/dsl, **food:** Country Kitchen, DQ, **lodging:** Regency Inn, **other:** Sakatah Lake SP, camping
55	rd 48, (from nb, no return), **1 mi E gas:** SA/dsl, KwikTrip, Mobil/dsl, **food:** A&W, Broaster Rest., Burger King, DQ, KFC, Pizza Hut, Southern China Cafe, Subway, Taco John's, **lodging:** AmericInn, Galaxy Inn, **other:** Ford
48	rd 12, rd 23, Medford, **W food:** McDonald's, **other:** Outlet Mall/famous brands
45	rd 9, Clinton Falls, **W gas:** KwikTrip/dsl, **food:** Caribou Coffee, Famous Dave's BBQ, Sportsman's Grille, Subway, TimberLodge Steaks, Wendy's, **lodging:** Comfort Inn, Holiday Inn, **other:** Cabela's Sporting Goods, Russell-Stover Candies, museum
43	rd 34, 26th St, Airport Rd, Owatonna, **W other:** Noble RV Ctr
42b a	US 14 W, rd 45, to Waseca, Owatonna, **E food:** Kernel Rest., **lodging:** Budget Host, **other:** AutoZone, CashWise Foods, Chrysler/Dodge/Jeep, Ford/Lincoln/Mercury, O'Reilly Parts, **W gas:** KwikTrip/dsl, **food:** Big 10 Rest., Culver's, Dunn Bros Coffee, Eastwind
42b a	Continued Buffet, McDonald's, Perkins, **lodging:** Best Budget Inn, Super 8, **other:** $Tree, GNC, Kohls, Lowe's Whse, Radio Shack, Walmart SuperCtr/Subway/24hr
41	Bridge St, Owatonna, **E gas:** BP, Holiday/dsl, **food:** Applebee's, Arby's, Burger King, DQ, KFC, Papa Murphy's, Quizno's, Starbucks, Subway, Taco Bell, **lodging:** AmericInn, Country Inn&Suites, **other:** [H], **W gas:** F&F/dsl, **lodging:** Microtel, **other:** Target
40	US 14 E, US 218, Owatonna, **1 mi E on rd 6...food:** El Tequila Mexican, Godfather's, Taco John's, **lodging:** Oakdale Motel, **other:** [H], Buick/Cadillac/Chevrolet/Pontiac, Curves, Hy-Vee Foods/24hr, TrueValue, Walgreens, WholesaleTire
38mm	Turtle Creek
35mm	**rest area both lanes, full [handicapped] facilities, [phone], [picnic], litter barrels, vending, petwalk**
34.5mm	Straight River
32	rd 4, Hope, **1/2 mi E** camping, **1 mi W** gas, food
26	MN 30, to Blooming Prairie, Ellendale, **E gas:** Cenex/dsl/rest., **W gas:** BP/pizza/dsl
22	rd 35, to Hartland, Geneva, **1 mi E** gas, food
18	MN 251, to Hollandale, Clarks Grove, **W gas:** BP/dsl/LP, **other:** camping
17mm	**weigh sta, both lanes**
13b a	I-90, W to Sioux Falls, E to Austin, **W** [H]
12	US 65 S (from sb), Lp 35, Albert Lea, same as 11
11	rd 46, Albert Lea, **E gas:** Loves/Wendy's/dsl/scales/24hr, TA/Shell/Coldstone/Pizza Hut/dsl/scales/24hr/@, **food:** McDonald's, **lodging:** Comfort Inn, **other:** KOA (may-oct/6mi), dsl repair, **W gas:** KwikTrip, Shell/dsl, **food:** Burger King, Casa Zamora Mexican, China Buffet, Domino's, Godfather's, Green Mill Rest, McDonald's, Perkins, Pizza Hut, Quizno's, Subway, Taco Bell, Taco John's, Trumble's Rest., Wok'n Roll, **lodging:** Albert Lee Inn, Best Value Inn, Country Inn&Suites, Countryside Inn, Super 8, **other:** [H], Advance Parts, Auto Value Parts, AutoZone, Buick/Cadillac/GMC/Pontiac, CarQuest, Chrysler/Dodge/Jeep, $Tree, Ford, Goodyear/auto, Home Depot, Honda, NAPA, Nissan/VW, O'Reilly Parts, Radio Shack, Walgreens, Walmart, to Myre-Big Island SP
9mm	Albert Lea Lake
8	US 65, Lp 35 US 65, Lp 35, Albert Lea, **2 mi W gas:** Freeborn City Co-op/dsl, **food:** DQ, Hardee's
5	rd 13, to Glenville, Twin Lakes, **3 mi W** camping
2	rd 5
1mm	**Welcome Ctr nb, full [handicapped] facilities, [phone], [picnic], litter barrels, vending, petwalk**
0mm	Minnesota/Iowa state line

INTERSTATE 35 - WEST

Exit #	Services
41mm	I-35W begins/ends on I-35, exit 127.
36	rd 23, **E gas:** Holiday/dsl, **lodging:** Country Inn&Suites, **W gas:** US/dsl, **food:** Caribou Coffee, DQ, McDonald's, Subway, **lodging:** Hampton Inn, **other:** Discount Tire, Kohl's, Super Target
33	rd 17, Lexington Ave, **E gas:** F&F/dsl, Holiday, **1 mi E food:** Burger King, McDonald's, **W food:** Applebee's, Arby's, Bonfire Rest., Caribou Coffee, Green Mill Rest., Quizno's, Taco Bell/LJ Silver, Wendy's, Zantigo's Mexi

INTERSTATE 35 - WEST CONT'D

N ↕ S

Exit #	Services
33	Continued can, **other:** Cub Foods, GNC, Home Depot, Michael's, Radio Shack, Walgreens, Walmart
329	5th Ave NE, to Lexington, Circle Pines, **W** Nat Sports Ctr
31b a	Lake Dr, **E gas:** Shell/dsl, **food:** Quizno's, Red Ginger Asian, Steamin Bean Coffee, **lodging:** Country Inn&Suites
30	US 10 W, MN 118, to MN 65
29	rd I
28c b	rd 10, rd H, **W gas:** BP, **food:** KFC, LJ Silver/Taco Bell, McDonald's, Mermaid Café, RJ Riches Rest., **lodging:** AmericInn, Days Inn, **other:** NAPA, carwash
28a	MN 96
27b a	I-694 E and W
26	rd E2, **W gas:** Exxon/dsl, **food:** Jimmy John's, Limu Coffee
25b	MN 88, to Roseville (no EZ return to sb), same as 25a
25a	rd D (from nb), **E gas:** BP/dsl, **food:** Blimpie, **lodging:** Courtyard, Fairfield Inn, Residence Inn, **W gas:** PDQ, SA, **food:** Barley John's, Caribou Coffee, Jake's Café, McDonald's, New Hong Kong, Perkins/24hr, Sarpino's Italian, Subway
24	rd C, **E food:** Burger King, India Palace Rest., Joe Senser's Rest., **lodging:** Days Inn, Motel 6, Radisson, **other:** USPO, **W lodging:** Holiday Inn Express, **other:** Chevrolet/GMC/Pontiac, Chrysler/Dodge/Jeep, Volvo
23b	Cleveland Ave, MN 36
23a	MN 280, Industrial Blvd (from sb)
22	MN 280, Industrial Blvd (from nb), **E lodging:** Ramada Plaza
21b a	Broadway St, Stinson Blvd, **E** Ford/Isuzu Trucks, **W food:** Baja Sol, Burger King, Caribou Coffee, Cousins Subs, Leeann Chin, McDonald's, Pizza Hut/Taco Bell, **other:** GNC, Home Depot, Old Navy, Rainbow Foods/24hr, Target
19	E Hennepin (from nb)
18	US 52, 4th St SE, University Ave, to U of MN, **E gas:** BP/repair
17c	11th St, Washington Ave, **E lodging:** Holiday Inn, **W gas:** Mobil, **other:** [H], Goodyear, to Metrodome
17b	I-94 W (from sb)
17a	MN 55, Hiawatha
16b a	I-94 (from nb), E to St Paul, W to St Cloud, to MN 65
15	31st St (from nb), Lake St, **E food:** McDonald's, Taco Bell, **other:** Auto Zone, **W** [H]
14	35th St, 36th St
13	46th St
13mm	Minnehaha Creek
12b	Diamond Lake Rd
12a	60th St (from sb), **W gas:** Mobil, **other:** Cub Foods
11b	MN 62 E, to ✈, to ✈
11a	Lyndale Ave (from sb)
10b	MN 62 W, 58th St
10a	rd 53, 66th St, **E gas:** SA
9c	76th St (from sb)
9b a	I-494, MN 5, to ✈, to ✈

MINNEAPOLIS

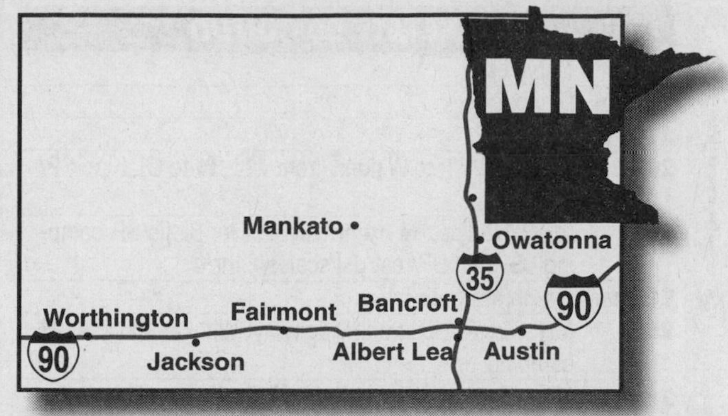

Exit #	Services
88	2nd St, **E other:** BMW, **W food:** Bennigan's, Caribou Coffee, Jimmy Johns, Red Lobster, Sonic, Timberlodge Steaks, Wendy's, **lodging:** Embassy Suites, **other:** Chevrolet, Chrysler/Dodge/Jeep, Hyundai, Infiniti, Kia, Kohl's, TJ Maxx, Walgreens
7b	90th St
7a	94th St, **E other:** Goodyear/auto, **W lodging:** Holiday Inn
6	rd 1, 98th St, **E gas:** Holiday, **food:** Applebee's, Bakers Square, Burger King, Coldstone, Domino's, Golden Wok, Jimmy John's, Leeann Chen, McDonald's, Starbucks, Wendy's, White Castle, URGENT CARE, Bloomington Drug, Festival Foods, Ford, Radio Shack, Walgreens, **W gas:** SA/dsl, **food:** Denny's
5	106th St
5mm	Minnesota River
4b	113th St, Black Dog Rd
4a	Cliff Rd, **E** Dodge, Subaru, **W** VW
3b a	MN 13, Shakopee, Canterbury Downs, **E lodging:** Select Inn
2	Burnsville Pkwy, **E gas:** BP, Marathon, **food:** Bumpers Grill, **W gas:** Holiday, **food:** Gourmet Chinese, Hooters, Perkins, TimberLodge Steaks, **lodging:** Best Value Inn, LivInn, Prime Rate Motel, Travelodge, **other:** Best Buy, Goodyear/auto, Vet
1	rd 42, Crystal Lake Rd, **E food:** Chianti Grill, **other:** Byerly's Foods, PetsMart, Tuesday Morning, **W gas:** Holiday/dsl, SA, **food:** Applebee's, Arby's/Sbarro's, Azteca Mexican, Buca Italian, Burger King,, Cam Aranh Bay, Champp's Grill, Chili's, Dakota County Grill, HoneyBaked Ham, IHOP, Jimmy John's, KFC, Kings Buffet, Macaroni Grill, McDonald's, Old Country Buffet, Olive Garden, Outback Steaks, Panera Bread, Papa John's, Papa Murphy's, Qdoba Mexican, Red Lobster, Roasted Pear, Starbucks, Taco Bell/Pizza Hut, TGIFriday's, Wendy's, **lodging:** Days Inn, Fairfield Inn, Hampton Inn, Holiday Inn, InTown Suites, **other:** [H], AT&T, Barnes&Noble, Best Buy, Cadillac, Chevrolet, Cub Foods, Discount Tire, Goodyear/auto, Home Depot, JC Penney, K-Mart, Kohl's, Macy's, Michael's, PetCo, Rainbow Foods, Sears/auto, Target, Tires+, Walgreens, mall, USPO
0mm	I-35W begins/ends on I-35, exit 88a.

INTERSTATE 90

Exit #	Services
277mm	Minnesota/Wisconsin state line, Mississippi River
275	US 14, US 61, to MN 16, La Crescent, **N Welcome Ctr wb, rest area nb, full ♿ facilities, ☎, picnic, litter barrels, vending, petwalk S gas:** Kwik Trip (1mi)

INTERSTATE 90 CONT'D

E ↕ W

Exit #	Services
272b a	Dresbach
270	Dakota
269	US 14, US 61, to Winona (from wb), **N** to OL Kipp SP/ camping
266	rd 12, Nodine, **N other:** Great River Bluffs SP, camping, **S gas:** BP/rest/dsl/scales/24hr/@
261mm	**weigh sta both lanes**
257	MN 76, to Houston, Ridgeway, Witoka, **N** gas, **S** camping
252	MN 43 N, to Winona, **7 mi N food:** Taco Bell, **lodging:** Express Inn, Holiday Inn, Holiday Inn Express, Quality Inn, **other:** [H]
249	MN 43 S, to Rushford, **N other:** Peterbilt Trucks/ repair
244mm	**rest area eb, full ♿ facilities, ☎, [picnic], litter barrels, vending, petwalk**
242	rd 29, Lewiston
233	MN 74, to Chatfield, St Charles, **N gas:** Kwik Trip/ LP/24hr (2mi), **food:** A&W (2mi), Subway (2mi), **other:** Whitewater SP, **S gas:** BP/dsl, **food:** Amish Ovens Rest./bakery, **other:** RV dump/LP
229	rd 10, Dover
224	MN 42, rd 7, Eyota, **N gas:** KwikTrip/dsl/e-85 (3mi), **food:** Country Cafe
222mm	**rest area wb, full ♿ facilities, ☎, [picnic], litter barrels, vending, petwalk**
218	US 52, to Rochester, **8 mi N food:** Old Country Buffet, **lodging:** Hampton Inn, Holiday Inn, Ramada Inn, Relax Inn, Sleep Inn, **other:** Brookside RV Park, **S gas:** BP/dsl, **other:** KOA (Mar-Oct) (1mi)
209b a	US 63, MN 30, to Rochester, Stewartville, **8-10 mi N lodging:** Comfort Inn, Econolodge, Hampton Inn, Holiday Inn, Relax Inn, **1 mi S gas:** KwikTrip, **food:** DQ, Subway, **lodging:** AmericInn
205	rd 6
202mm	**rest area eb, full ♿ facilities, ☎, [picnic], litter barrels, vending, petwalk**
193	MN 16, Dexter, **N gas:** BP/rest./dsl, **S lodging:** Windmill Motel/Rest., **other:** many wind turbines
189	rd 13, to Elkton
187	rd 20, **S** Beaver Trails Camping
183	MN 56, to Rose Creek, Brownsdale, **S gas:** Freeborn City Co-op/dsl/LP
181	28th St NE
180b a	US 218, 21st St NE, to Austin, Oakland Place, **S gas:** Shell, **lodging:** Austin Motel
179	(AUSTIN) 11th Dr NE, to Austin, **N gas:** BP/dsl/rest./24hr
178b	6th St NE, to Austin, downtown
178a	4th St NW, **N food:** Culver's, Harvest Buffet, Perkins, **lodging:** AmericInn, Day's Inn, Holiday Inn **other:** AutoValue Parts, Cadillac/Chevrolet/GMC/Pontiac, Vet, **S gas:** KwikTrip, **food:** A&W, Burger King, Subway, **other:** [H]
177	US 218 N, to Owatonna, Austin, Mapleview, **N food:** Applebee's, Arby's, China Star, KFC/LJ Silver, King Buffet, Quizno's, Subway, Wendy's, **other:** Aldi Foods, $Tree, Family$, Hy-Vee Foods/gas, K-Mart, O'Reilly Parts, Radio Shack, ShopKO, Staples, Target, Walmart SuperCtr, Younkers, mall, **S gas:** Sinclair/McDonald's/dsl, **lodging:** Super 8
175	MN 105, rd 46, to Oakland Rd, **N food:** Sportts Grill, **lodging:** Countryside Inn, **S gas:** BP, Shell/dsl, **other:** Chrysler/Dodge/Jeep, Ford/Mercury, camping, Vet
171mm	**rest area wb, full ♿ facilities, ☎, [picnic], litter barrels, vending, petwalk**
166	rd 46, Oakland Rd, **N other:** KOA/LP, golf (par3)
163	rd 26, Hayward, **S gas:** Shell (4mi), Freeborn County Co-op, **food:** Pizza Hut (4mi), Trails Rest. (4mi), **other:** Myre-Big Island SP, camping
161.5mm	**rest area eb, full ♿ facilities, ☎, [picnic], litter barrels, vending, petwalk**
159b a	I-35, N to Twin Cities, S to Des Moines
157	(ALBERT LEA) rd 22, Albert Lea, **S food:** Applebee's, Arby's, DQ, Herberger's, McDonald's, Pizza Ranch, **lodging:** AmericInn, Holiday Inn Express, **other:** [H], Ace Hardware, Chevrolet, Famliy$, GNC, Harley-Davidson, Hy-Vee Foods/gas/24hr, ShopKO, mall
154	MN 13, to US 69, to Manchester, Albert Lea, **N gas:** SA/dsl, **3 mi S lodging:** BelAire Motel
146	MN 109, to Wells, Alden, **S gas:** BP/dsl/rest., Co-Op Gas/dsl/e-85, **other:** truck/dsl repair
138	MN 22, to Wells, Kiester, **S** camping
134	MN 253, rd 21, to Bricelyn, MN Lake
128	MN 254, rd 17, Frost, Easton
119	US 169, to Winnebago, Blue Earth, **S gas:** Shell/dsl, Sinclair/dsl, **food:** Country Kitchen, DQ, McDonald's, Pizza Hut, Subway, **lodging:** AmericInn, Super 8, **other:** [H], $General, Walmart/drugs, Jolly Green Giant, camping
119mm	**rest area both lanes, full ♿ facilities, ☎, [picnic], litter barrels, petwalk, playground**
113	rd 1, Guckeen
107	MN 262, rd 53, to East Chain, Granada, **S other:** Flying Goose Camping (May-Oct) (1mi), gas/dsl
102	(FAIRMONT) MN 15, to Madelia, Fairmont, **N gas:** Walmart SuperCtr, **0-2 mi S gas:** BP, Cenex/dsl, ProFuel/dsl, SA/dsl/24hr, **food:** Arby's, Burger King, China Buffet, Green Mill Rest., McDonald's, Perkins, Pizza Ranch, Ranch Family Rest., Subway, Taco John's, **lodging:** Budget Inn, Comfort Inn, Hampton Inn, Holiday Inn, Super 8, **other:** [H], Ace Hardware, Buick/GMC/Pontiac, CarQuest, Chrysler/Dodge/Jeep, County Mkt Foods, $Tree, Freightliner, Goodyear, Hy-Vee Foods, JC Penney, NAPA, Radio Shack, Sears, ShopKO, Walgreens, USPO, camping, repair
99	rd 39, Fairmont, **services 2 mi S**
93	MN 263, rd 27, **Welcome, 1/2 mi S gas:** Cenex, camping
87	MN 4, Sherburn, **N other:** Everett Park Camping, **S gas:** Cenex, Kum&Go/Subway/dsl
80	rd 29, Alpha
73	US 71, Jackson, **N gas:** SA/dsl, **food:** Burger King, **lodging:** Econolodge, Super 8, **other:** KOA, to Kilen Woods SP, **S gas:** BP/DQ, Casey's, **food:** Embers Rest., Pizza Ranch, Subway, **lodging:** AmericInn, Budget Host, Earth Inn, Prairie Winds Motel, **other:** [H], Ace Hardware, Family$, Buick/Chevrolet/Pontiac, Chrysler/Dodge/Jeep, Sunshine Foods, to Spirit Lake
72.5mm	W Fork Des Moines River
72mm	**rest area wb, full ♿ facilities, ☎, [picnic], litter barrels, vending, petwalk**

INTERSTATE 90 CONT'D

E ↕ W

Exit #	Services
69mm	**rest area eb, full [handicapped] facilities, [phone], [picnic], litter barrels, vending, petwalk**
64	MN 86, Lakefield, **N** [H], gas/dsl, food, camping, to Kilen SP (12mi)
57	rd 9, to Heron Lake, Spafford
50	MN 264, rd 1, to Brewster, Round Lake, **S** camping
47	rd 3 (from eb), no return
46mm	**weigh sta eb**
45	MN 60, Worthington, **N gas:** BP/Blueline Cafe/dsl/scales, **S gas:** Casey's, Shell/dsl/scales/24hr, **other:** camping, truckwash
43	US 59, Worthington, **N gas:** Mobil/dsl, **lodging:** Travelodge, **S gas:** Casey's, Cenex/dsl, Shell, **food:** Arby's, Burger King, DQ, Godfather's, Ground Round, Hardee's, KFC, McDonald's, Perkins/24hr, Pizza Hut, Pizza Ranch, Subway, Taco John's, **lodging:** AmericInn, Budget Inn, Holiday Inn Express, **other:** [H], Fleet&Farm, Hy-Vee Foods, Buick/Cadillac/Chevrolet/Pontiac, $General, JC Penney, O'Reilly Parts, Radio Shack, ShopKO, Walgreens, Walmart SuperCtr/24hr
42	MN 266, rd 25, to Reading, **S lodging:** Days Inn, Super 8
33	rd 13, to Wilmont, Rushmore
26	MN 91, Adrian, **S gas:** Cenex/dsl, Kum&Go/Subway/dsl/e-85/24hr, **food:** Countryside Steaks, **other:** Adrian Camping
25mm	**rest area wb, full [handicapped] facilities, [phone], [picnic], litter barrels, petwalk**
24mm	**rest area eb, full [handicapped] facilities, [phone], [picnic], litter barrels, petwalk**
18	rd 3, Kanaranzi, Magnolia, **N** camping
12	US 75, Luverne, **N gas:** BP/dsl/e-85, Casey's, FuelTime/dsl, Shell/Subway/dsl, **food:** ChitChat's Grill, McDonald's, Taco John's, Tasty Drive-In, **lodging:** Comfort Inn, Cozy Rest Motel (1mi), Hillcrest Motel (2mi), **other:** [H], Ace Hardware, Buick/Cadillac/Chevrolet/GMC/Pontiac, Chrysler/Jeep, $General, Family$, Lewis Drugs, to Blue Mounds SP, Pipestone NM, **S food:** Magnolia Steaks, **lodging:** Super 8, **other:** Pamida
5	rd 6, Beaver Creek, **N gas:** Shell/dsl
3	rd 4 (from eb), Beaver Creek
1	MN 23, rd 17, to Jasper, **N other:** to Pipestone NM, access to gas/dsl
0mm	Minnesota/South Dakota state line, **Welcome Ctr/weigh sta eb, full [handicapped] facilities, info, [picnic], [phone], litter barrels**

WORTHINGTON

INTERSTATE 94

E ↕ W

Exit #	Services
259mm	Minnesota/Wisconsin state line, St Croix River
258	MN 95 N, to Stillwater, Hastings, Lakeland, **N food:** Bungalow Grill
257mm	**weigh sta wb, Welcome Ctr wb, full [handicapped] facilities, [phone], [picnic], litter barrels, vending, petwalk**
253	rd 15, Manning Ave, **N other:** StoneRidge Golf, **S** to Afton Alps SP, ski area
251	rd 19, Keats Ave, Woodbury Dr, **S gas:** KwikTrip, SA/dsl, **food:** Applebee's, Arby's, Boston's Rest., Burger King, Caribou Coffee, Chili's, Chipotle Mexican,
251	Continued Dino's Rest, Outback Steaks, Ray J's Grill, Subway, **lodging:** Extended Stay America, Holiday Inn Express, **other:** $Tree, Gander Mtn, Hancock Fabrics, Michael's, Sam's Club, Sportsman's Whse, Tuesday Morning, Walmart/auto, outlet mall/famous brands
250	rd 13, Radio Dr, Inwood Ave, **N food:** Buffalo Wild Wings, Caribou Coffee, Machine Shed Rest., Milio's Rest., Red Lobster, Olive Garden, **lodging:** Hilton Garden, Wild Wood Lodge, **other:** Best Buy, **S gas:** Holiday, **food:** Champp's, Quizno's, Starbucks, Sunsets Grill, Taco Bell, TGIFriday, Veitnam Rest., Wendy's, **other:** Borders Books/Café, Cub Foods, GNC, Hepner's Auto Ctr, Home Depot, JC Penney, Jo-Ann Crafts, LandsEnd Inlet, Old Navy, PetsMart, Tires+, World Mkt, Vet
249	I-694 N & I-494 S
247	MN 120, Century Ave, **N food:** Denny's, Olympus Grill, **lodging:** AmericInn, Live Inn, **other:** Harley-Davidson, **S gas:** SA, Sinclair, **food:** GreenMill Rest., **lodging:** Country Inn/rest., **other:** Chevrolet
246c b	McKnight Ave, **N** 3M
246a	Ruth St (from eb, no return), **N food:** Culvers's, Perkins, **other:** Firestone/auto, Michael's, TJ Maxx
245	White Bear Ave, **N gas:** SA/Subway, Gas4Less, **food:** Subway, **lodging:** La Quinta, Super 8, **other:** Walgreens, **S gas:** BP, Marathon, **food:** Arby's, Davanni's Pizza/subs, KFC/Pizza Hut, McDonald's, Papa John's, Sonic, Taco Bell, **other:** Byerly's Foods, Chrysler, Curves, Family$, O'Reilly Parts, Target
244	US 10 E, US 61 S, Mounds/Kellogg
243	US 61, Mounds Blvd, **S** River Centre
242d	US 52 S, MN 3, 6th St, **N gas:** Holiday, **food:** Subway
242c	7th St, **S gas:** SA
242b a	I-35E N, US 10 W, I-35E S (from eb)
241c	I-35E S (from wb)
241b	10th St, 5th St, to downtown
241a	12th St, Marion St, Kellogg Blvd, **N lodging:** Best Western Kelly Inn, **other:** Sears, **S gas:** BP, Holiday, SA, **lodging:** Savoy Inn, **other:** [H], st capitol
240	Dale Ave
239b a	Lexington Pkwy, Hamline Ave, **N gas:** BP, SA, **food:** Chevy's Mexican, Hardee's/24hr, **other:** [H], Cub Foods, K-Mart, Target, **S gas:** Holiday
238	Snelling Ave, **N food:** Applebee's, McDonald's, Perkins, **lodging:** Sheraton, **other:** CVS Drug, Jo-Ann Fabrics, Rainbow Foods, Walgreens, same as 239
237	Cretin Ave, Vandalia Ave, to downtown

ST PAUL

INTERSTATE 94 CONT'D

E ↕ W

MINNEAPOLIS

Exit #	Services
236	MN 280, University Ave, to downtown
235b	Huron Blvd
235mm	Mississippi River
235a	Riverside Ave, 25th Ave, **N gas:** Winner, **food:** Starbucks, **S food:** Perkins, Taco Bell
234c	Cedar Ave, downtown
234b a	MN 55, Hiawatha Ave, 5th St, **N lodging:** Holiday Inn, **other:** to downtown
233b	I-35W N, I-35W S (exits left from wb)
233a	11th St (from wb), **N** downtown
231b	Hennepin Ave, Lyndale Ave, to downtown
231a	I-394, US 12 W, to downtown, to downtown
230	US 52, MN 55, 4th St, 7th St, Olson Hwy, **N** Metrodome, **S** H, Int Mkt Square
229	W Broadway, Washington Ave, **N gas:** Holiday, **S gas:** Winner, **food:** Buger King, Little Caesar's, KFC, McDonald's, Subway, Taco Bell, Wendy's, **other:** Cub Foods, Walgreens
228	Dowling Ave N
226	53rd Ave N, 49th Ave N
225	I-694 E, MN 252 N, to Minneapolis
34	to MN 100, Shingle Creek Pkwy, **N food:** Barnacle Bill's, Denny's, Oak City Rest., **lodging:** AmericInn, Comfort Inn, Country Inn&Suites, Crowne Plaza, Days Inn, Extended Stay America, Motel 6, Super 8, **S food:** C1 Buffet, Familia Mexican, King Buffet, Panera Bread, **other:** Best Buy, Kohl's, PepBoys, Target, Tires+
33	rd 152, Brooklyn Blvd, **N gas:** SA, Shell, **food:** Culver's, Subway, **other:** Chevrolet, Dodge, Honda, Mazda, **S gas:** BP, **food:** Arby's, 50's Grill, Taco Bell, **other:** Family$, Sun Foods, Walgreens
31	rd 81, Lakeland Ave, **N gas:** SA, Shell, **food:** Beach House Grille, Wendy's, **lodging:** Grand Rios, Ramada Inn, **S lodging:** Best Value Inn, Budget Host
30	Boone Ave, **N lodging:** La Quinta, Northland Inn/rest., **S other:** Discount Tire, Home Depot
29b a	US 169, to Hopkins, Osseo
28	rd 61, Hemlock Lane, **N on Elm Creek...food:** Arby's/Sbarro's, Benihana, Biaggi's Italian, Boston's Grill, Champp's Grill, ChuckeCheese, Granite City Rest., Ground Round, Joe's Crabshack, Olive Garden, Panera Bread, Pittsburgh Blue, Potbelly's, Qdoba, Red Lobster, Starbucks, TimberLodge Steaks, TGI Fridays, **lodging:** Courtyard, Hampton Inn, Holiday Inn, Staybridge Suites, **other:** Best Buy, Border's, Jo-Ann Fabrics, Kohl's, Old Navy, World Mkt, **S gas:** BP, **food:** Perkins/24hr, **lodging:** Select Inn
216	I-94 W and I-494
215	rd 109, Weaver Lake Rd, **N gas:** SA/dsl, **food:** Bakers Square, Bella Sera, Broadway Pizza, Bucadibeppo, Burger King, Cattle Co Steaks, ChuckeCheese, DQ, Don Pablo, El Rodeo Mexican, Famous Dave's BBQ, Houlihan's, J Cousineau's Rest., KFC, Krispy Kreme, McDonald's, Old Country Buffet, Papa John's, Pizza Hut, Ricky Shawl's, Starbucks, Subway, Taco Bell, Timberlodge Steaks, Wendy's, **other:** Barnes&Noble, Byerly's Foods, Cub Foods, Gander Mtn, GNC, Goodyear/auto, JC Penney, K-Mart, Michael's, PetCo, Tires+, USPO, Walgreens, mall, same as 28, **S food:** Applebee's, Fuddrucker's
214mm	**rest area eb, full ♿ facilities, ☎, picnic, litter barrels**
213	rd 30, 95th Ave N, Maple Grove, **N gas:** SA/dsl, **food:** Chipotle Mexican, Subway, **other:** H, Home Depot, Target, **S gas:** Holiday/dsl, **food:** Culver's, McDonald's, Orient Buffet, Quizno's, **other:** Goodyear/auto, Menard's, Rainbow Foods, Sam's Club, Walgreens, Walmart SuperCtr/24hr, KOA (2mi)
207	MN 101, to Elk River, Rogers, **N gas:** SA/dsl, TA/dsl/scales/24hr/@, **food:** Applebee's, Arby's, Burger King, Culver's, Denny's, Domino's, DQ, Maynard's, McDonald's, Subway, Taco Bell, Wendy's, **lodging:** Hampton Inn, Super 8, **other:** Best Buy, Cabela's, Camping World, Cub Foods, Discount Tire, Goodyear/auto, Kohl's, Lowes Whse, NAPA, Target, Tires+, Walgreens, Vet, **S gas:** BP/dsl, Sinclair/dsl, Holiday, **food:** Black Bear Rest., BoBo Asia, Cottage Grill, Guadalahara Mexican, **lodging:** AmericInn, **other:** Chevrolet, Curves, CVS Drug
205.5mm	Crow River
205	MN 241, rd 36, St Michael, **S gas:** SA/dsl
202	rd 37, Albertville, **N gas:** Hacks/dsl, **S gas:** BP, Sunoco
201	rd 19 (from eb), Albertville, St Michael, **N food:** Burger King, Michael B's Grill, Perkins, **lodging:** Country Inn&Suites, **other:** Albertville Outlets/famous brands, Old Navy, **S gas:** Casey's, Mobil, **food:** Caribou Coffee, China Dragon, Culver's, Major's Cafe, Papa Murphy's, Rancho Grande Mexican, Space Aliens Grill, Subway, **other:** Ace Hardware, Coburn's Foods, Goodyear/auto
195	rd 75, Monticello, **N gas:** Cruiser's/dsl, Marathon/dsl, **food:** Caribou Coffee, **other:** H, Home Depot, Target
193	MN 25, to Buffalo, Monticello, Big Lake, **N gas:** Holiday/dsl, **food:** Burger King, Caribou Coffee, Guadalajara Mexican, KFC, Papa Murphy's, Perkins, Quizno's, Rancho Grande Mexican, Taco Bell, **lodging:** AmericInn, **other:** AutoValue Parts, Cub Foods, K-Mart, Radio Shack, USPO, **S gas:** SA/dsl, Holiday/dsl, Shell, **food:** Applebee's, Arby's, Chatter's Rest., China Buffet, Culver's, D'Angelo's Pizza, DQ, McDonald's, Subway, Taco John's, **lodging:** Best Western, Day's Inn, Select Inn, **other:** Buick/GMC/Pontiac, Checker Parts, Chevrolet, Ford/Mercury, Chrysler/Dodge/Jeep, Goodyear/auto, KIA, Suzuki, Walmart SuperCtr/24hr, Vet, Lake Maria SP
187mm	**rest area eb, full ♿ facilities, ☎, picnic, litter barrels, vending, petwalk**
183	rd 8, to Silver Creek, Hasty, Maple Lake, **S gas:** BP/dsl/rest./scales/24hr/@, **other:** to Lake Maria SP, camping
178	MN 24, to Annandale, Clearwater, **N gas:** Holiday/Petro/dsl/scales/24hr/@, **food:** DQ, Burger King, Keith's Rest., Subway, **lodging:** Best Value Inn, Best Western, **other:** KOA (1mi), Coburn's Foods, **S other:** RV Camping (1mi)
178mm	**rest area wb, full ♿ facilities, ☎, picnic, litter barrels, petwalk, vending**
173	Opportunity Dr., **N** Good Sam RV Park (May-Oct) (5mi)
171	rd 7, rd 75, St Augusta, **N gas:** Cenex, MacDaddy's, Pilot/dsl/scales/24hr, **food:** McDonald's, RJ's Grill, Subway, **lodging:** AmericInn, Holiday Inn Express, Travelodge, **other:** H, Goodyear/auto, **S other:** Pleasureland RV Ctr

INTERSTATE 94 CONT'D

E ↕ W

ST CLOUD

Exit #	Services
167b a	MN 15, to St Cloud, Kimball, **4 mi N gas:** Holiday, SA/dsl, **food:** Applebee's, Arby's, Bonanza, Buffalo Wild Wings, Burger King, Chipotle Mexican, IHOP, Little Caesar's, McDonald's, Noodles&Co, Old Chicago Pizza, Olive Garden, Panchero's Mexican, Perkins, Pizza Hut, Taco Bell, Starbucks, TGIFriday's, TimberLodge Steaks, Wendy's, **lodging:** Comfort Inn, Country Inn&Suites, Days Inn, Fairfield Inn, Hampton Inn, Holiday Inn, Homewood Suites, Super 8, **other:** [H], Barnes&Noble, Best Buy, CashWise Foods, JC Penney, Kohl's, K-Mart, Macy's, Office Depot, Old Navy, Sam's Club, Scheel's Sports, Sears/auto, ShopKO, Sportsman's Whse, Target, **S gas:** Shell/dsl (2mi)
164	MN 23, to St Cloud, Rockville, **4-6 mi N gas:** BP, **food:** Culver's, IHOP, KFC, Space Aliens Rest., Taco Bell, **lodging:** Motel 6, **other:** Gander Mtn, Hyundai, Menard's, PetsMart, Toyota/Scion
162.5mm	Sauk River
160	rd 2, to Cold Spring, St Joseph, **N gas:** Holiday, **lodging:** Super 8, **other:** Coll of St Benedict
158	rd 75 (from eb exits left), to St Cloud, **3 mi N** same as 160
156	rd 159, St Joseph, **N** St Johns U
153	rd 9, Avon, **N gas:** Shell/dsl, Tesoro/McDonald's/dsl, **food:** Subway, **lodging:** Budget Host, **other:** Dhalin's Foods, TrueValue, USPO, **S other:** El Rancho Manana Camping (10mi), auto parts
152mm	**rest area both lanes, full facilities, litter barrels, vending, petwalk**
147	MN 238, rd 10, Albany, **N gas:** Holiday/dsl/24hr, Shell/A&W/Subway/dsl, **food:** DQ, Godfather's, Hillcrest Rest., **lodging:** Country Inn&Suites, **other:** [H], Amby's Foods, **S other:** Chrysler/Dodge/Jeep
140	rd 11, Freeport, **N gas:** Cenex/dsl, Freeport/dsl, **food:** Ackie's Pioneer Rest., Charlie's Café, **other:** Corner Store Foods, USPO, Vet
137	MN 237, rd 65, New Munich
137mm	Sauk River
135	rd 13, Melrose, **N gas:** Mobil/dsl/repair, Tesoro/Subway/dsl/24hr, **food:** Burger King, Gundy's Rest., **other:** [H], Ernie's Foods, NAPA, **S gas:** Casey's/dsl, **food:** DQ, El Portal Mexican, **lodging:** Super 8, **other:** Save Foods, Vet
132.5mm	Sauk River
131	MN 4, to Paynesville, Meire Grove
128mm	Sauk River
127	US 71, MN 28, Sauk Centre, **N gas:** Casey's, Holiday/dsl, **food:** DQ, Hardee's, McDonald's, Pizza Hut, Subway, **lodging:** AmericInn, Best Value Inn, Palm's Motel, **other:** [H], Coborn's Foods, Ford/Mercury, Lewis Ctr/rest area, Walmart SuperCtr, **S gas:** BP/dsl/café/scales/24hr/@, **other:** Buick/Chevrolet/Chrysler/Dodge/Jeep/Pontiac, Freightliner
124	Sinclair Lewis Ave (from eb), Sauk Centre
119	rd 46, West Union
114	MN 127, rd 3, to Westport, Osakis, **3 mi N** gas, food, lodging
105mm	**rest area wb, full facilities, litter barrels, vending, petwalk**

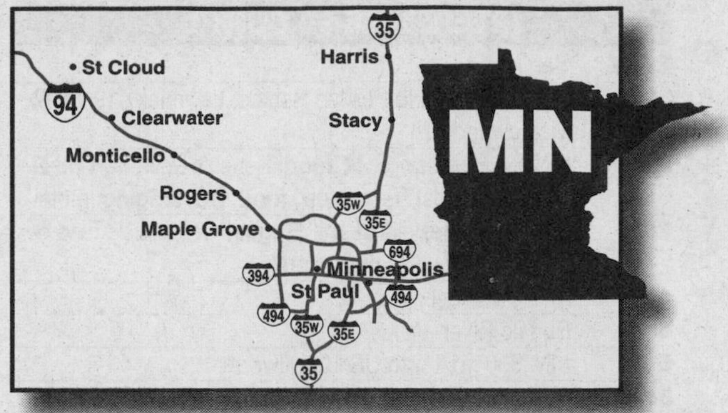

ALEXANDRIA

FERGUS FALLS

Exit #	Services
103	MN 29, to Glenwood, Alexandria, **N gas:** F&F/dsl, Holiday, Tesoro, **food:** Bennigan's, Burger King, Caribou Coffee, Country Kitchen, Culver's, Dolittle's Café, Hardee's, KFC, McDonald's, Perkins, Pizza Hut, Subway, Taco Bell, Wendy's, Whiskey Creek, **lodging:** AmericInn, Day's Inn, Super 8, **other:** [H] Cadillac/Chevrolet/Mazda, County Mkt Foods, Goodyear/auto, Jeep, K-Mart, Menard's, Target, Walmart SuperCtr/24hr, **S gas:** Holiday/dsl, **food:** Rudy's Grill, **lodging:** Country Inn&Suites, Holiday Inn, **other:** Alexandria RV Ctr, Buick/GMC/Pontiac
100	MN 27, **N lodging:** L Motel/RV Park, Skyline Motel, **other:** [H], **S** camping
100mm	Lake Latoka
99mm	**rest area eb, full facilities, litter barrels, vending, petwalk**
97	MN 114, rd 40, to Lowry, Garfield
90	rd 7, Brandon, **2-3 mi N** gas, food, **lodging:** Lake Country Motel (1mi), **S** camping, ski area
82	MN 79, rd 41, to Erdahl, Evansville, **2 mi N gas:** BP/dsl, Spur, **food:** Kramer's Rest., **S other:** [H], camping
77	MN 78, rd 10, to Barrett, Ashby, **N** gas/dsl, food, camping, **S** camping
69mm	**rest area wb, full facilities, litter barrels, petwalk, vending**
67	rd 35, Dalton, **N** camping, **S** camping
61	US 59 S, rd 82, to Elbow Lake, **N gas:** Tesoro/dsl/café/LP/24hr, **other:** [H], Pine Plaza RV Ctr, camping (4mi), **S** camping
60mm	**rest area eb, full facilities, litter barrels, petwalk, vending**
57	MN 210, rd 25, Fergus Falls, **N** [H]
55	rd 1, to Wendell, Fergus Falls
54	MN 210, Lincoln Ave, Fergus Falls, **N gas:** Cenex/dsl, F&F/dsl, Holiday, Tesoro/dsl, **food:** Applebee's, Arby's, Burger King, Burger Time, Debbie's Kitchen, Godfather's, Hunan Buffet, KFC, McDonald's, Papa Murphy's, Perkin's, Pizza Hut, Pizza Ranch, Speedway Grill, Subway, **lodging:** AmericInn, Best Western, Comfort Inn, Day's Inn, Motel 7, Super 8, **other:** [H] Advance Parts, Chrysler/Dodge/Jeep, $Tree, Ford/Lincoln/Mercury, GMC/Pontiac, Herbergers, Home Depot, K-Mart, NAPA, Parts+, Radio Shack, SunMart Foods, Target, Tires+, Toyota, mall, **S food:** Mabel Murphy's Rest., **other:** Walmart/drugs/24hr
50	rd 88, rd 52, to US 59, to Fergus Falls, Elizabeth
38	rd 88, Rothsay, **S gas:** Tesoro/dsl/café/24hr, **lodging:** Comfort Zone Inn, **other:** Tires

INTERSTATE 94 CONT'D

E ↕ W — MOORHEAD

Exit #	Services
32	MN 108, rd 30,to Pelican Rapids, Lawndale, **19 mi N** Maplewood SP
24	MN 34, Barnesville, **N food:** Renee's Drive-in, **1 mi S gas:** Cenex/dsl, Tesoro/dsl, **food:** DQ, **lodging:** motel
22	MN 9, Barnesville, **1 mi S gas:** Cenex/dsl, Tesoro/dsl, **food:** DQ, **lodging:** motel
15	rd 10, Downer
8mm	Buffalo River
6	MN 336, rd 11, to US 10, Dilworth
5mm	**Red River weigh sta eb**
2	rd 52, Moorhead, **1-2 mi N gas:** Holiday/dsl, **food:** Bennigan's, Perkins, Pizza Ranch, **lodging:** Travelodge, **other:** [H], KOA, Menard's, Target, **S other:** antiques
2mm	**Welcome Ctr eb, full [handicapped] facilities, info, [phone], [picnic], litter barrels, vending**
1b	20th St, Moorhead (from eb, no return)
1a	US 75, Moorhead, **N gas:** Clark, **food:** Blimpie, Burger King, Papa Murphy's, Qdoba Mexican, Starbucks, Village Inn, **lodging:** Courtyard, **other:** Curves, SunMart Foods, **S gas:** Bud's, Casey's, Orton's Gas, **food:** Panchero's Grill, Snapdragon Rest., Subway, **lodging:** AmericInn, Grand Inn, Super 8, **other:** CVS Drug, GMC, KIA, Loopy's $Store, TrueValue
0mm	Minnesota/North Dakota state line, Red River

INTERSTATE 494/694

E ↕ W — ST PAUL

Exit #	Services
	I-494/I-694 loops around Minneapolis/St Paul.
71	rd 31, Pilot Knob Rd, **N lodging:** Courtyard, Fairfield Inn, **S lodging:** Best Western, Crowne Plaza, **food:** LoneOak Café
70	I-35E, N to St Paul, S to Albert Lea
69	MN 149, MN 55, Dodd Rd, **N food:** Ziggy's Deli, **S food:** Caribou Coffee, McDonald's, Subway, **lodging:** Budget Host, Country Inn&Suites,
67	MN 3, Roberts St, **1 mi N gas:** BP, Mobil, Holiday, **food:** Acre's Rest., Arby's/Sbarro's, Baker's Square, Buffalo Wings, Burger King, Chipotle Mexican, ChuckeCheese, Culver's, Grand Buffet, KFC, Old Country Buffet, Pizza Hut, Taco Bell, Timber Lodge Steaks, White Castle, **other:** Aamco, Best Buy, Buick/Pontiac, Checker Parts, Chevrolet, Cub Foods, Dodge, Ford, Jo-Ann Fabrics, Kia, K-Mart, Lincoln/Mercury, Mazda, NAPA, Nissan, Rainbow Foods/24hr, Target, Tires+, Toyota, VW, Walmart, **S gas:** PDQ
66	US 52, **S gas:** SA, **food:** Old World Pizza, Outback Steaks, **lodging:** Country Inn&Suites, Microtel
65	7th Ave, 5th Ave
64b a	MN 56, Conco rd St, **N gas:** Conoco/dsl, **lodging:** Best Western Drovers, **other:** Ford Trucks, Goodyear, Peterbilt, **S gas:** EZ Stop, **other:** Chrysler/Jeep/Dodge, Parts+
63mm	Mississippi River
63c	Maxwell Ave
63b a	US 10, US 61, to St Paul, Hastings, **S gas:** BP, SA, **food:** Burger King, Subway, **lodging:** Boyd's Motel, **other:** NAPA
60	Lake Rd, **E gas:** SA/dsl, **W lodging:** Country Inn&Suites

ST PAUL

Exit #	Services
59	Valley Creek Rd, **E gas:** BP/repair, SA/dsl/LP, **food:** America's Burger, Applebees, Broadway Pizza, Chipotle Mexican, DQ, Old Country Buffet, Papa Murphy's, Perkins, Potbelly's Rest., Yang's Chinese, **lodging:** Red Roof Inn, **other:** Barnes&Noble, Kohl's, Marshall's, Office Depot, PetCo, Rainbow Foods, Target, Walgreens, USPO, **W gas:** PBQ, **food:** Bonfire Rest., Burger King, McDonald's, Pizza Hut, Subway, **lodging:** Hampton Inn, **other:** [H], Ace Hardware, Goodyear
58c	Tamarack Rd, **E food:** Paisano's Cafe, Woodbury's Cafe, **lodging:** Sheraton
58b a	I-94, E to Madison, **W** to St Paul. I-494 S begins/ends, I-694 N begins/ends
57	rd 10, 10th St N, **E gas:** SA **food:** IHOP, Quizno's, **lodging:** Wingate Inn, **W gas:** Holiday, **food:** Burger King, Hunan Buffet, KFC, **other:** $Tree, K-Mart, Rainbow Foods/24hr, mall, Vet
55	MN 5, **E other:** Target, **W gas:** Holiday/dsl, **food:** Subway, **other:** Menard's, st patrol
52b a	MN 36, N St Paul, to Stillwater, **W gas:** F&F/dsl
51	MN 120, **E gas:** BP, SA/dsl, **food:** Jethro's, Starbucks, **W gas:** Kellie's Corner/gas
50	White Bear Ave, **E gas:** SA, **other:** K-Mart, Sam's Club/gas, **W gas:** BP, Shell, **food:** Acupulco Chicken, Arby's, Bakers Square, Buffalo Wild Wings, Caribou Coffee, Chili's, Denny's, Great Moon Buffet, IHOP, Jake's Grill,JimmyJohn's, KFC, McDonald's, Noodles&Co, North China, Old Country Buffet, Outback Steaks, Peiwei Asian, Perkins/24hr, Red Lobster, Taco Bell, TGI Friday, Wendy's, **lodging:** Emerald Inn, **other:** Aamco, Best Buy, Goodyear/auto, JC Penney, Jo-Ann Fabrics, Kohl's, Macy's, Marshall's, Michael's, PetCo, Sears/auto, Tires+, Tuesday Morning, Walgreens, mall
48	US 61 (from wb), **E other:** Acura, Chrysler/Dodge/Jeep, Ford, Honda, Hyundai, Isuzu/Subaru, Lincoln/Mercury, **W food:** Chili's, Gulden's Rest., McDonald's, Olive Garden, **lodging:** Best Western, **other:** [H], Audi/Porsche, Lexus, Mercedes, Toyota, Venburg Tire, Volvo
47	I-35E, N to Duluth
46	I-35E, US 10, S to St Paul
45	rd 49, Rice St, **N gas:** Gas+, Marathon/dsl, **food:** Papa John's, Subway, Taco Bell, **other:** Checker Parts, **S gas:** Marathon/dsl, **food:** A&W, Burger King, Caribou Coffee, Taco John's, **other:** Kath Parts

MINNEAPOLIS

Exit #	Services
43b	Victoria St, **S** Bill's Foods
43a	Lexington Ave, **N food:** Greenmill Rest., Red Robin, **lodging:** Hampton Inn, Hilton Garden, **S gas:** Exxon, Sinclair, **food:** Blue Fox Grill, Burger King, Davanni's Pizza, Papa Murphy's, Perkins, Subway, Wendy's, **lodging:** Holiday Inn, Super 8, **other:** Cub Foods, Goodyear/auto, Target, transmissions
42b	US 10 W (from wb), to Anoka
42a	MN 51, Snelling Ave, **1 mi S gas:** Shell, **food:** Flaherty's Grill, Lindey's Steaks, McDonald's, **lodging:** Country Inn&Suites, Holiday Inn
41b a	I-35W, S to Minneapolis, N to Duluth
40	Long Lake Rd, 10th St NW
39	Silver Lake Rd, **N gas:** BP, **food:** Acupulco Mexican, Champps, McDonald's, Subway, **other:** Fairview Drug, Ford, U-Haul

INTERSTATE 494/694 CONT'D

E ↕ W

MINNEAPOLIS

Exit #	Services
38b a	MN 65, Central Ave, **N gas:** Holiday/dsl, **food:** Subway, **S gas:** SA, SuperStop, **food:** A&W/KFC, Applebee's, Asia Rest., Big Marina Deli, Buffalo Wild Wings, Flameburger Rest., La Casita Mexican, McDonald's, Mr BBQ, Papa John's, Ricky's, Sonic, Subway, Taco Bell, Wendy's, White Castle, **lodging:** LivInn Hotel, **other:** Advance Parts, AutoZone, $General, Discount Tire, Menards, O'Reilly Parts, PetCo, Rainbow Foods, Target, Tires+, Walgreens, Vet
37	rd 47, University Ave, **N gas:** Holiday, SA/dsl, **food:** Burger King, McDonald's, Papa Murphy's Pizza, Zantigo's Rest., **other:** Cub Foods, CVS Drug, Goodyear, Home Depot, **S gas:** Bona Bros/repair, Shell
36	E River Rd
35mm	I-494 W begins/ends, I-694 E begins/ends
35c	MN 252, **N gas:** Holiday, SA
35b a	I-94 E to Minneapolis
34to	MN 100, Shingle Creek Pkwy, **N food:** Barnacle Bill's, Denny's, Oak City Rest., **lodging:** AmericInn, Comfort Inn, Country Inn&Suites, Crowne Plaza, Days Inn, Extended Stay America, Motel 6, Super 8, **S food:** C1 Buffet, Great India, Panera Bread, Perkins, **lodging:** Embassy Suites, **other:** AT&T, Best Buy, Curves, Kohl's, PepBoys, Target, Tires+
33	rd 152, Brooklyn Blvd, **N gas:** SA, Shell, **food:** Culver's, Subway, **other:** Buick/GMC, Chevrolet, Honda, **S gas:** BP, **food:** Burger King, **other:** Cub Foods, CVS Drug, Family$, Sun Foods, Walgreens
31	rd 81, Lakeland Ave, **N gas:** SA, Shell, **food:** Beach House Grille, Chipotle Mexican, Wagner's Drive-In, Wendy's, **lodging:** Ramada Inn, **S lodging:** Best Value Inn, Budget Host
30	Boone Ave, **N lodging:** La Quinta, Northland Inn/rest., **S other:** Discount Tire, Home Depot
29b a	US 169, to Hopkins, Osseo
28	rd 61, Hemlock Lane, **N on Elm Creek...food:** Arby's/Sbarro's, Bella Sera, Benihana, Biaggi's Italian, Boston's Grill, Broadway Pizza, Buca Italian, CA Pizza Kitchen, Caribou Coffee, Champp's, Chipotle Mexican, ChuckeCheese, Coldstone, Dave&Buster's, Dickey's BBQ, Don Pablo's, El Rodeo Mexican, Famous Dave's BBQ, Granite City Rest., Herbert&Gerbert's Subs, Houlihan's, Jimmy John's, Leeann Chin, Noodles&Co, Old Country Buffet, Olive Garden, Panera Bread, Papa John's, PF Chang's, Pittsburgh Blue, Potbelly's, Qdoba, Red Lobster, Starbucks, TimberLodge Steaks, TGIFridays, **lodging:** Courtyard, Hampton Inn, Holiday Inn, Staybridge Suites, **other:** URGENT CARE, Best Buy, Border's, Byerly's Foods, Costco/gas, Cub Foods, $Tree, Jo-Ann Fabrics, Kohl's, Lowe's Whse, Marshall's, Michael's, Old Navy, PetCo, **S gas:** BP, **food:** Perkins/24hr, **lodging:** Select Inn
27	I-94 W to St Cloud, I-94/694 E to Minneapolis
26	rd 10, Bass Lake Rd, **E gas:** Freedom, **food:** Caribou Coffee, Culver's, McDonald's, Subway, **lodging:** Extended Stay America, **other:** mall, Vet, **W gas:** BP, Marathon/dsl, **food:** Dunn Bro's Cofee, Milio's Sandwiches, Pancake House, Pizza Hut, **lodging:** Hilton Garden, **other:** CVS Drug

MINNEAPOLIS

Exit #	Services
23	rd 9, Rockford Rd, **E gas:** Holiday, **food:** Chili's, Peony's Chinese, **other:** GNC, O'Reilly Parts, PetsMart, Rainbow Foods, Target, TJ Maxx, Walgreens, Vet, **W gas:** PDQ, **food:** Cousins Subs, DQ, LeAnn Chin, Panchero's, Subway
22	MN 55, **E gas:** Holiday/dsl, **food:** Broadway Pizza, Caribou Coffee, Green Mill Rest.,JimmyJohn's, McDonald's, Red Robin, Solos Pizza, Starbucks, **lodging:** Best Western Kelly, Radisson, Red Roof Inn, Residence Inn, **W gas:** Holiday/dsl, **food:** Arby's, Burger King, Davanni's Rest., Jake's Rest., Perkins, Wendy's, **lodging:** Comfort Inn, Days Inn, **other:** Goodyear/auto, Tires+
21	rd 6, **E gas:** KwikTrip, **other:** Discount Tire, Home Depot
20	Carlson Pkwy, **E gas:** Holiday/dsl, **food:** Pizza Hut, Subway, **W food:** Woody's Grill, **lodging:** Country Inn&Suites
19b a	I-394 E, US 12 W, to Minneapolis, **1 mi E off of I-394... food:** Applebee's, Wendy's, **other:** Barnes&Noble, Best Buy, Borders Books, Byerly's Foods, Ford, JC Penney, Jo-Ann Fabrics, Mazda, Mazerati, Mercedes, Sears/auto, Subaru, Target, Tires+, **1/2 mi W gas:** BP, Holiday, **food:** KFC, McDonald's, **other:** BMW, Chevrolet, Lexus, Mitsubishi, Nissan
17b a	Minnetonka Blvd, **W gas:** US Gas, **food:** Cousin's Subs, Dunn Bros Coffee
16b a	MN 7, **1 mi W gas:** Marathon, **food:** Christo's Rest., Davanni's Rest., Famous Dave's BBQ, Taco Bell, **other:** Goodyear
13	MN 62, rd 62
12	Valleyview Rd, rd 39 (from sb)
11c	MN 5 W, same as 11 a b
11b a	US 169 S, US 212 W, **N food:** Don Pablo, Subway, **lodging:** Courtyard, Fairfield Inn, Hampton Inn, Hyatt Place, Residence Inn, **S gas:** BP, Marathon, Holiday, **food:** Caribou Coffee, Davanni's Rest., Fuddruckers, Jake's Grill, Jason's Deli, KFC, Leeann Chin, Old Chicago, Panera Bread, Papa John's, Qdoba, Starbucks, **lodging:** Best Western, Discount Tire, Homestead Suites, SpringHill Suites, JC Penney, Office Depot, Sears/auto, Target, Walgreens, Walmart
10	US 169 N, to rd 18
8	rd 28 (from wb, no return), E Bush Lake Rd, same as 7 a b
7b a	MN 100, rd 34, Normandale Blvd, **N gas:** Shell/dsl, **food:** Burger King, Caribou Coffee, Chili's, DQ, Subway, TGIFriday, **lodging:** Days Inn, Sheraton, Sofatel, **S food:** Oak City Rest., **lodging:** Country Inn&Suites, Crowne Plaza, Hilton Garden, La Quinta, Staybridge Inn

INTERSTATE 494/694 CONT'D

E ↕ W — MINNEAPOLIS

Exit #	Services
6b	rd 17, France Ave, **N gas:** Mobil, **food:** Cattle Co Rest., ChuckeCheese, Fuddrucker's, Hot Wok, Macaroni Grill, McDonald's, Perkins, Quizno's, **lodging:** Best Western, Le Bourget, Park Plaza Hotel, **other:** H, Michael's, Office Depot, **S food:** Denny's, Joe Senser's Grill, Olive Garden, **lodging:** Hampton Inn, Hilton, **other:** Buick/GMC/Pontiac, Ford, Mercedes, Nissan, Toyota/Scion
6a	Penn Ave (no EZ eb return), **N lodging:** Residence Inn, **other:** Best Buy, Buick, Hyundai, Isuzu, **S food:** Applebee's, Atlantic Buffet, Bennigan's, McDonald's, Starbucks, Steak&Ale, Subway, **lodging:** Embassy Suites, **other:** Chevrolet, Chrysler/Jeep/Plymouth, Dodge, Hancock Fabrics, Herberger's, Kohl's, Rainbow Foods, Target, TJ Maxx
5b a	I-35W, S to Albert Lea, N to Minneapolis
4b	Lyndale Ave, **N food:** Boston Mkt, Chipotle Mexican, Don Pablo's, DQ, Eddie Cheng's, Papa John's, Subway, **lodging:** Candlewood Suites, Hampton Inn, Ramada Inn, other: Best Buy, Borders, Honda, Lands End, PetsMart, Tires+, **S lodging:** Extended Stay
4b	Continued America, **other:** Lincoln/Mercury, Mazda, Subaru
4a	MN 52, Nicollet Ave, **N gas:** SA/dsl, **food:** Burger King, Ember's, Rest, Jumbo Chinese, **lodging:** Candlewood Suites, **other:** Honda, Menards, **S gas:** Mobil, Shell, **food:** Culver's, Kwik Mart, Big Boy, McDonald's, **lodging:** La Quinta, Super 8, **other:** Home Depot, Sam's Club
3	Portland Ave, 12th Ave, **N gas:** Phillips 66, Sinclair, PDQ Mart, **food:** Arby's, **lodging:** AmericInn, **S gas:** BP, **food:** Denny's, Outback Steaks, Subway, **lodging:** Comfort Inn/rest., Holiday Inn Express, Microtel, Quality Inn, Residence Inn, Travelodge, **other:** Walgreens, Walmart
2c b	MN 77, **N lodging:** Motel 6, **S gas:** BP, SA, **lodging:** AmeriSuites, Best Western, Courtyard, Embassy Suites, Exel Inn, Fairfield Inn, Grand Motel, Marriott, Sheraton, **other:** Nordstrom's, Sears, Mall of America
2a	24th Ave, same as 2c b
1b	34th Ave, Nat Cemetary, **S lodging:** Embassy Suites, Hilton, Holiday Inn
1a	MN 5 E, **N** ✈
0mm	Minnesota River. I-494/I-694 loops around Minneapolis/St Paul.

MISSISSIPPI

INTERSTATE 10

E ↕ W — MOSS POINT — BILOXI — GULFPORT

Exit #	Services
77mm	Mississippi/Alabama state line, **weigh sta wb**
75	Franklin Creek Rd
75mm	**Welcome Ctr wb, full ♿ facilities, ☎, picnic, litter barrels, petwalk, RV dump, weigh sta eb**
74mm	Escatawpa River
69	MS 63, to E Moss Point, **N gas:** Texaco/Domino's/dsl/24hr, **food:** Waffle House, **lodging:** Best Value, Deluxe Inn, La Quinta, **S gas:** Chevron/dsl, Cone/dsl, Exxon/Subway/24hr, Shell, **food:** Barnhill's Buffet, Burger King, Cracker Barrel, Hardee's, KFC, McDonald's, Pizza Hut, Ruby Tuesday, San Miguel Mexican, Waffle House, Wendy's, **lodging:** Best Western, Comfort Inn, Day's Inn, Hampton Inn, Holiday Inn Express, Quality Inn, Shular Inn, **other:** H
68	MS 613, to Moss Point, Pascagoula, **N gas:** BP, Chevron/dsl, **food:** Coco Loco, Tugus Rest., **lodging:** Super 8, **S gas:** BP/dsl, **other:** H
64mm	Pascagoula River
63.5mm	**rest area both lanes, full ♿ facilities, ☎, picnic, litter barrels, petwalk, RV dump, 24hr security**
61	to Gautier, **N other:** MS Nat Golf Course, **1-3 mi S gas:** BP/dsl, **lodging:** Best Western, Suburban Lodge, **other:** Shepha rd Camping, Sandhill Crane WR
57	MS 57, to Vancleave, **N gas:** Shell/dsl, **food:** Shed BBQ, **other:** Journey's End Camping, tires, **S gas:** Exxon, **other:** H
50	MS 609 S, Ocean Springs, **N gas:** Texaco/Domino's/dsl, **food:** Waffle House, **lodging:** Best Western, Comfort Inn, Country Inn&Suites, Ramada Ltd, Red Carpet Inn, Scottish Inn, Super 8, **other:** Martin Lake Camping (1mi), **S gas:** BP/dsl, Chevron/McDonald's, Fleet/dsl/scales, **food:** Denny's, Waffle House, Wendy's, **lodging:** Comfort Inn, Day's Inn, Hampton Inn, Holiday Inn
50	Continued Express, Howard Johnson, Quality Inn, **other:** $General, Nat Seashore, Vet
46b a	I-110, MS 15 N, to Biloxi, **N gas:** Chevron, Kangaroo/dsl, **food:** Beef O'Brady's, Beijing Chinese, Chili's, CiCi's Pizza, Outback Steaks, Papa John's, Ruby Tuesday, Strami's Italian, Sonic, Subway, Toro Japanese, Waffle House, Wendy's, Whataburger, **lodging:** Regency Inn, Wingate Inn, **other:** Best Buy, Lowes Whse, Marshalls, PetsMart, Radio Shack, Target, Tire Kingdom, Walgreens, Walmart SuperCtr, **S** H, to beaches
44	Cedar Lake Rd, to Biloxi, **N gas:** Pilot/Subway/dsl/scales/24hr, **other:** Chevrolet, **S gas:** Chevron/dsl, Shell/dsl, **food:** Applebee's, El Saltillo, KFC/LJ Silver, McDonald's, Red Eye Grill, Sonic, Subway, Waffle House, Wow Cafe, **lodging:** La Quinta, **other:** H, Beauvoir, $General, Harley-Davidson, Home Depot, O'Reilly Parts, to Jeff Davis Shrine, Biloxi Nat Cem
41	MS 67 N, to Woolmarket, **N gas:** Chevron/dsl, Texaco, **other:** golf (6mi), **S** Mazalea RV Prk, Parkers Landing RV Prk, Reliable RV Ctr
39.5mm	Biloxi River
38	Lorraine-Cowan Rd, **N gas:** Exxon/Subway, Kangaroo/dsl, **food:** Capt Al's Cafe, Domino's, McDonald's, Sonic, **S gas:** Pure/dsl, **other:** H, Baywood RV Park (3mi), Foxes RV Park (8mi), to beaches
34b a	US 49, to Gulfport, **N gas:** Exxon, Kangaroo/dsl, Texaco/dsl, **food:** Azteca Mexican, Backyard Burger, Barnhill's Buffet, Beef O'Brady's, Burger King, Cane's Chicken, Chick-fil-A, Chili's, ChuckeCheese, CiCi's Pizza, Cracker Barrel, Domino's, Golden Corral, Hardee's, KFC, Logan's Roadhouse, Longhorn Steaks, O'Charley's, Papa John's, Pizza Hut, Popeye's, Smoothie King, Sonic, Starbucks, Taco Bell, TGIFriday, Waffle House, Wendy's,, Whataburger, **other:** Advance Parts , Backyard

INTERSTATE 10 CONT'D

E ↕ W — GULFPORT

Exit #	Services
34b a	Continued Burger, Barnes&Noble, Belk, Best Buy, Chevrolet/Cadillac, Chick-fil-A, CVS Drug, $General, Food Giant, Goodyear/auto, Honda, K-Mart, Office Depot, Old Navy, Panda Pallace, PetsMart, Radio Shack, Rite Aid, Ross, Sam's Club/gas, Tire Kingdom, TJ Maxx, USPO, Walgreens, Winn-Dixie, **S gas:** Chevron, Kangaroo/dsl, Murphy USA, RaceWay, Shell/dsl, **food:** Applebee's, Arby's/24hr, Burger King, Choung's Garden, IHOP, KFC/LJ Silver, Krispy Kreme, Los Tres Amigos, McAlister's Deli, McDonald's, Morelia's Mexican, Sonic, Steve's Marina, Subway, Tiffin Pancake House, Waffle House, Wendy's, Wok Express, Zaxby's, **lodging:** Best Value, Best Western, Comfort Inn, Day's Inn, Fairfieid Inn, Hampton Inn, Holiday Inn, Motel 6, Quality Inn, Ramada, Suites, Value Place, **other:** H, $World, Ford/Lincoln/Mercury, Freightliner, Home Depot, Kia, Mazda, Michael's, NAPA Care, Nissan, Prime Outlets/famous brands, Walmart SuperCtr, transmissions
31	Canal Rd, to Gulfport, **N gas:** Exxon, Love's/Arby's/dsl/scales/24hr, **other:** Bayberry RV Park, **S gas:** /FLYING J/Conoco/Cookery/dsl/LP/scales/24hr, Shell/McDonald's/dsl/24hr, **food:** Waffle House, Wendy's, **lodging:** Crystal Inn, Legacy Inn, **other:** Plantation Pines RV Prk
28	to Long Beach, **S gas:** Chevron/dsl, Shell/dsl, **other:** RV camping, tires
27mm	Wolf River
24	Menge Ave, **N gas:** Chevron/dsl/scales, **S gas:** Texaco, **other:** A1 RV Park, flea mkt, golf, to beaches
20	to De Lisle, to Pass Christian, **N gas:** Kin-Mart
16	Diamondhead, **N gas:** Chevron/24hr, Shell/Domino's, **food:** Bigge's Grill, Burger King, DQ, Five Happiness Chinese, Smoothie King, Subway, Waffle House, **lodging:** Diamondhead Resort, **other:** Ace Hardware, Rouse's Mkt, **S lodging:** Econolodge
15mm	Jourdan River
13	MS 43, MS 603, to Kiln, Bay St Louis, **N** McLeod SP, **S gas:** Chevron, Exxon/Subway/dsl, Pure, **lodging:** Traveler's Choice, **other:** H, RV Camping (8-13mi)
10mm	**weigh sta, eb**
2	MS 607, to Waveland, NASA Test Site, **S Welcome Ctr both lanes, full ♿ facilities, phone, picnic, litter barrels, RV dump, petwalk, 24hr security,** Buccaneer SP, camping, to beaches
	weigh sta, wb
	...isiana state line, Pearl River

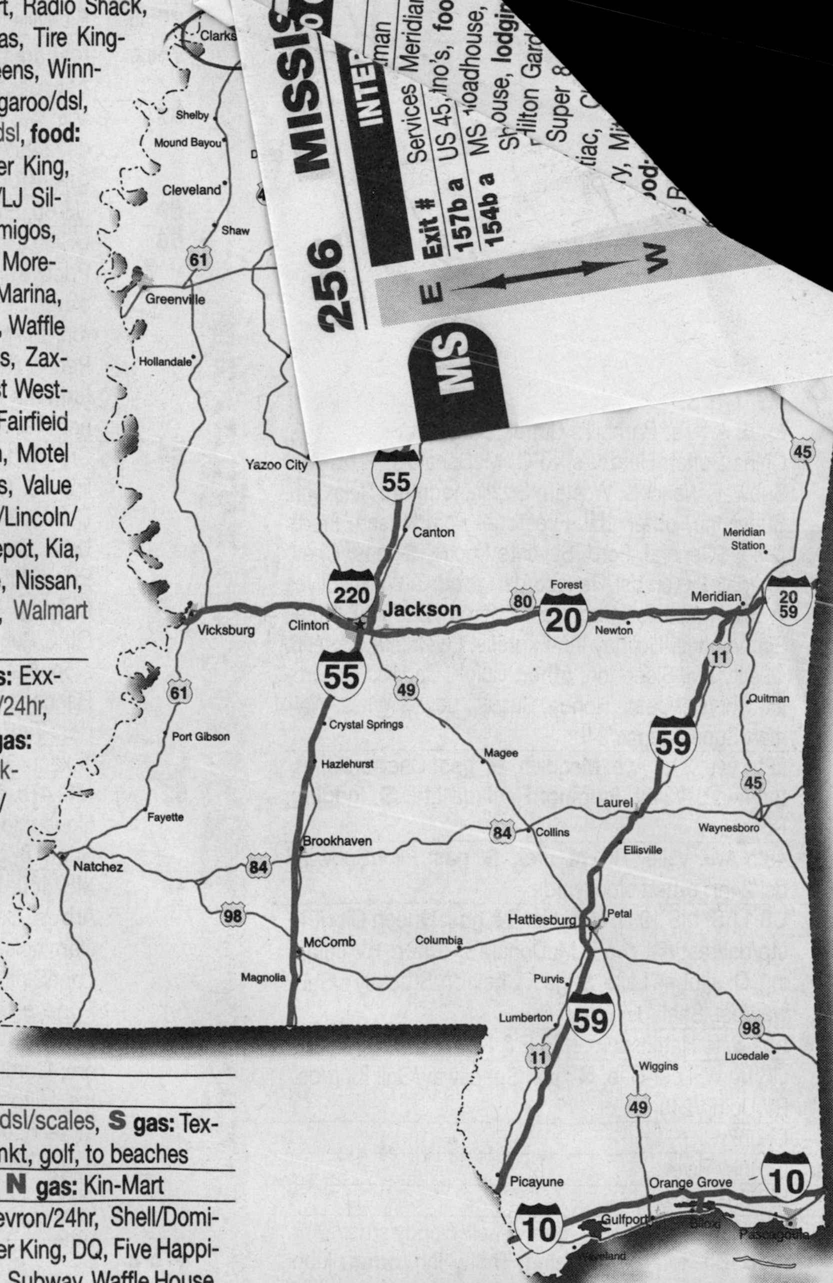

INTERSTATE 20

E ↕ W

Exit #	Services
I-20 W and I-59 S run together to Meridian.	
172mm	Mississippi/Alabama state line
170mm	**weigh sta both lanes**
169	Kewanee, **S gas:** Kewanee Trkstp/dsl
165	Toomsuba, **N gas:** Shell/Subway/24hr, Texaco/ChesterFried/dsl, **S gas:** Loves/Arby's/dsl/scales, **other:** KOA (2mi)
164mm	**Welcome Ctr wb, full ♿ facilities, phone, vending, picnic, litter barrels, petwalk, RV dump, 24hr security**
160	to Russell, **N gas: TA/BP/dsl/rest./scales/24hr/@, other:** Nanabe RV Camping (1mi), **S gas:** Shell/dsl

: BP/dsl, Pure,
pplebee's, Cracker
enn's Rest., Western
g: Day's Inn, Drury Inn,
en, Holiday Inn, Relax Inn,
other: Benchmark RV Park,
hrysler/Jeep/Kia, Hyundai, Lin-
tsubishi, U-Haul, **S gas:** Chevron,
Chick-fil-A, CiCi's, Crescent City Grill,
est., McAlister's, McDonald's, O'Charley's,
Steaks, Popeye's, Red Lobster, Ryan's, Taco
lodging: Comfort Inn, Jameson Inn, Microtel,
her: Belk, Best Buy, BooksAMillion, Dillard's, $Tree, Ethridge RV Ctr, Harley-Davidson, JC Penney, Old Navy, PetCo, Ross, Sam's Club/gas, Sears/auto, TJ Maxx, mall, same as 153

153 MS 145 S, 22nd Ave, Meridian, **N gas:** BP, Shell, **food:** Arby's, Barnhill's Buffet, Burger King, Capt D's, China Buffet, Hardee's, KFC, McDonald's, Pizza Hut, Subway, Wendy's, Western Sizzlin, **lodging:** Relax Inn, Super Inn, **other:** H, Firestone, Ford/Nissan, Fred's Drug, $General, Ford, Saverite Foods, **S gas:** Chevron/dsl, Exxon/dsl, Texaco/dsl, **food:** A&W/LJ Silver, Waffle House, **lodging:** Best Western, Budget 8 Motel, Econolodge, Holiday Inn Express, La Quinta, Motel 6, Quality Inn, Sleep Inn, **other:** Buick, Cadillac/Chevrolet, Chrysler/Jeep, Honda, Suzuki, Lowes Whse, Walmart SuperCtr/gas/24hr

152 29th Ave, 31st Ave, Meridian, **N gas:** Chevron/ChesterFried/dsl/24hr, **lodging:** Ramada Ltd, **S lodging:** Royal Inn

151 49th Ave, Valley Rd, **N** tires, **S gas:** Pilot/Subway/dsl/24hr, **other:** stockyards

150 US 11 S, MS 19 N, Meridian, **N gas:** Queen City Trkstp/dsl/rest./@, **food:** McDonald's, **other:** RV camping, Okatibbee Lake, **S gas:** Chevron/Stuckey's/Subway/dsl, Shell/dsl **other:** ✈

130[149] I-59 S, to Hattiesburg. **I-20 E & I-59 N run together.**

129 US 80 W, Lost Gap, **S gas:** Spaceway/Grill King/dsl/RV Dump/24hr

121 Chunky

119mm Chunky River

115 MS 503, Hickory

NEWTON

109 MS 15, Newton, **N gas:** Shell/Wendy's/dsl/24hr, **food:** Bo-Ro Rest., **lodging:** Thrifty Inn, **other:** lube, **S gas:** Chevron/dsl/24hr, Newton Jct/dsl, Texaco/dsl, **food:** Hardee's, KFC/Taco Bell, McDonald's, N-Hop Pancakes, Pizza Hut, Sonic, Subway, **lodging:** Day's Inn, **other:** H, Advance Parts, AutoZone, $General, Fred's Drug, Piggly Wiggly, Walmart SuperCtr/24hr

100 US 80, Lake, Lawrence, **N gas:** BP/dsl/rest.

96 Lake

95mm Bienville Nat Forest, Bienville Nat Forest, eastern boundary

90mm **rest area eb, full ♿ facilities, ☎, picnic, litter barrels, petwalk, RV dump, 24hr security**

88 MS 35, Forest, **N gas:** BP/Subway/dsl, Shell, Texaco/Domino's/dsl, **food:** KFC, McDonald's, Pizza Hut, Popeye's, Taco Bell, Wendy's, **lodging:** Best Value Inn,

88 Continued
Comfort Inn, Day's Inn, Holiday Inn Express, **other:** H Chevrolet/GMC/Pontiac, Honda, Walmart SuperCtr/gas, **S gas:** Chevron/dsl/24hr, **food:** Penn's Rest.

80 MS 481, Morton

77 MS 13, Morton, **N gas:** 77 Truck Ctr/dsl, **other:** H, dsl repair, RV camping, to Roosevelt SP

76mm Bienville NF, western boundary

75mm **rest area wb, full ♿ facilities, ☎, picnic, litter barrels, petwalk, RV dump, 24hr security**

68 MS 43, Pelahatchie, **N gas:** Chevron/Subway/dsl/24hr, Texaco/dsl/rest./24hr, **other:** RV camping, **S gas:** BP/dsl

BRANDON

59 US 80, E Brandon, **2 mi S gas:** Texaco

56 US 80, Brandon, **N food:** CiCi's, Krystal, McDonald's, Popeye's, Sonny's BBQ, Taco Bell, **lodging:** Microtel, **other:** AutoZone, O'Reilly Parts, **S gas:** BP, Chevron, Exxon, Mac's Gas, Shell/dsl, Texaco, **food:** DQ, Penn's Rest., Sonic, Subway, Waffle House, Wendy's, **lodging:** Day's Inn, Red Roof Inn, **other:** to Ross Barnett Reservoir

54 Crossgates Blvd, W Brandon, **N gas:** BP, Exxon, Phillips 66, **food:** Applebees, Burger King, China Buffet, Domino's, El Sombrero, Fernando's Mexican, KFC, Little Caesar's, Mazzio's, McDonald's, Papa John's, Pizza Hut, Popeye's, Subway, Waffle House, Wendy's, **lodging:** Ridgeland Inn, **other:** H, Big Lots, Buick/GMC/Pontiac, Chevrolet, CVS Drug, $General, , Firestone/auto, Ford, Fred's Drug, GNC, Goodyear/auto, Hancock Fabrics, Kroger, Lincoln/Mercury, Office Depot, Tire Pros, Walmart SuperCtr/gas/24hr, **S gas:** Texaco/Domino's, **other:** Home Depot, Honda

52 MS 475, **N gas:** Chevron, Texaco/dsl, **food:** Waffle House, **lodging:** Quality Inn, Ramada Ltd, Sleep Inn, Super 8, **other:** Peterbilt, to Jackson ✈

PEARL

48 MS 468, Pearl, **N gas:** BP, Shell/dsl, Texaco, **food:** Arby's, Baskin-Robbins, Burger King, Cracker Barrel, Domino's, El Charro's Mexican, Jose's Tamales, KFC, LoneStar Steaks, McDonald's, O'Charley's, Pizza Hut, Popeye's, Ruby Tuesday, Ryan's, Sonic, Starbucks, Subway, Waffle House, Wendy's, **lodging:** Best Western, Comfort Inn, Econolodge, Fairfield Inn, Hampton Inn, Hilton Garden, Holiday Inn Express, Jameson Inn, Motel 6, **other:** CarCare, transmissions, **S gas:** Chevron/dsl/24hr, Huff/dsl/24hr, **lodging:** Candlewood Suites, Country Inn&Suites, Day's Inn, La Quinta, **other:** $General

47b a US 49 S, Flowood, **N gas:** *FLYING J*/Conoco/CountryMkt/dsl/LP/24hr, Pilot/Krystal/Subway/dsl/24hr, **food:** Western Sizzlin, **lodging:** Airport Inn, Holiday Inn, **other:** Bass Pro Shop, SpeedCo, **2-3 mi S food:** DQ, Waffle House, **lodging:** Executive Inn, **other:** Freightliner, Kenworth, Truck-Man RV Center, Tires

46 I-55 N, to Memphis

45b US 51, State St, to downtown

45a Gallatin St (from wb), to downtown, **N gas:** BP, Petro/dsl/rest./24hr/@, **other:** Blue Beacon, tires/truck repair, Vet, **S gas:** Pilot/McDonald's/dsl, **lodging:** Hilltop Inn, **other:** Hyundai, Mitsubishi, Nissan

44 I-55 S (exits left from wb), to New Orleans

43b a Terry Rd, **N gas:** Exxon/dsl, Gas

INTERSTATE 20 CONT'D

E–W

Exit #	Services
42b a	Ellis Ave, Belvidere, **N gas:** BP, Shell, **food:** Capt D's, McDonald's, Pizza Hut, Popeye's, Rally's, Sonny's BBQ, Wendy's, **lodging:** Day's Inn, Econolodge, Metro Inn, Quality Inn, Ramada, Sleep Inn, Super 8, **other:** Advance Parts, AutoZone, Chrysler/Dodge, Family$, Firestone, Kia, O'Reilly Parts, Radio Shack, Sav-a-Lot Foods, U-Haul, transmissions, zoo, **S gas:** Exxon/dsl, QuickPay, **food:** DQ
41	I-220 N, US 49 N, to Jackson
40b a	MS 18 W, Robinson Rd, **N gas:** BP, Exxon/Subway, Shell/dsl, **food:** Arby's, China Buffet, Krystal, Mazzio's, Piccadilly's, Popeye's, **lodging:** Day's Inn, Sleep Inn, **other:** Metro Mall, Office Depot, Sears/auto, USPO, auto repair, **S gas:** Expressway, Mac's, **food:** IHOP, McDonald's, Waffle House, Wendy's, **lodging:** Comfort Inn, **other:** H, $Tree, GNC, Lowes Whse, Radio Shack, Walmart SuperCtr/gas/24hr
36	Springridge Rd, Clinton, **N gas:** Mac's/Burger King, Orbit Gas, Shell, **food:** Capt D's, Chick-fil-A, DQ, KFC, Little Ceasar's, Mazzio's, McAlister's, McDonald's, Sonic, Starbucks, Subway, Taco Bell, Waffle House, Wendy's, Zaxby's, **lodging:** Clinton Inn, Comfort Inn, Day's Inn, **other:** Advance Parts, Home Depot, Kroger, O'Reilly Parts, Radio Shack, Walgreens, Walmart SuperCtr/gas/24hr (2mi), **S gas:** Exxon, Texaco/dsl, **food:** Applebee's, Corky's BBQ, Frogs Head Grill, Pizza Hut, Popeye's, Salsa's Mexican, Shoney's, **lodging:** Best Western, Econolodge, Hampton Inn, Holiday Inn Express, Quality Inn, Ramada Ltd, **other:** Curves, Davis Tire, Springridge RV Park, Vet
35	US 80 E, Clinton, **N gas:** Chevron/dsl, Texaco/dsl, **food:** Backyard Burger, Chick-fil-A, McAlister's Deli, **lodging:** Ridgland Inn
34	Natchez Trace Pkwy
31	Norrell Rd
27	Bolton, **N gas:** Chevron, **S gas:** BP/dsl/24hr
19	MS 22, Edwards, Flora, **N other:** Askew Landing RV Camping (2mi), **S gas:** BP/dsl, Phillips 66
17mm	Big Black River
15	Flowers
11	Bovina, **N gas:** Texaco/Subway/dsl/24hr, **other:** RV camping
10mm	**weigh sta wb**
8mm	**weigh sta eb**
6.5mm	**parking area eb**
5b a	US 61, MS 27 S, **N gas:** Chevron, Kangaroo/dsl, **food:** Sonic, **S** same as 4a
4b a	Clay St, **N gas:** Chevron, Texaco, **food:** KFC, Pizza Hut, **lodging:** Hampton Inn, Motel 6, Quality Inn, Vicksburg Inn, **other:** H, KOA, RV Park, to Vicksburg NP, **S gas:** Texaco/Domino's/dsl, **food:** Bumper's Drive-In, China Buffet, Cracker Barrel, Pizza Inn, McAlister's, Scottish Inn, Waffle House, **lodging:** Beechwood Inn/rest., Comfort Inn, Courtyard, Holiday Inn Express, Jameson Inn, Scottish Inn, **other:** Chrysler/Jeep/Toyota, $General, Lincoln/Mercury, Outlet Mall/famous brands/deli, Toyota, same as 5
3	Indiana Ave, **N gas:** Texaco/Subway/dsl, **food:** China King, McDonald's, Waffle House, **lodging:** Best Western, Deluxe Inn, **other:** Chevrolet, Chrysler/Dodge/

CLINTON

Exit #	Services
3	Continued Jeep, Corner Mkt Foods, Ford/Lincoln/Mercury, Honda, Mazda, Rite Aid, **S gas:** BP, **food:** KFC, Goldie's BBQ, **lodging:** Best Inn, **other:** Buick/GMC/Pontiac/Subaru, Family$,
1c	Halls Ferry Rd, **N gas:** Chevron/24hr, Exxon, **food:** Burger King, Sonic, **lodging:** Econolodge, **other:** H, **S gas:** Kangaroo/dsl, **food:** Capt D's, DQ, Garfield's Rest., Goldie's BBQ, Pizza Hut, Popeye's, Ryan's, Shoney's, Subway, Taco Bell, Taco Casa, TCBY, Wendy's, Whataburger, **lodging:** Day's Inn, Fairfield Inn, Super 8, Wingate Inn, **other:** Advance Parts, Belk, Big Lots, Dillard's, Home Depot, Fred's Drug, JC Penney, Kroger, Walgreens, USPO, mall
1b	US 61 S, **S gas:** BP, Chevron/Domino's, **food:** McDonald's, **other:** Walmart SuperCtr/Subway/24hr, same as 1c
1a	Washington St, Vicksburg, **N Welcome Ctr both lanes, full ♿ facilities,** ☎, **gas:** Kangaroo/dsl, Shell/Subway/dsl, **lodging:** AmeriStar Hotel, **other:** AmeriStar RV Park, casino, **S food:** Waffle House, **lodging:** La Quinta, Ridgeland Inn
0mm	Mississippi/Louisiana state line, Mississippi River

VICKSBURG

INTERSTATE 22 (FUTURE)

E–W

Exit #	Services
118mm	I-22 (future), Alabama/Mississippi State Line
116mm	**Welcome Ctr/Rest Area wb, ⛺, litter barrels, petwalk, vending, RV dump**
113	rd 23, Tremont, Smithville
108	rd 25 N, Belmont, Iuka
107mm	**weigh sta, both lanes**
104	rd 25 S, Fulton, Amory, **N gas:** Shell/cafe/scales/dsl, Woco/dsl, **food:** Burger King, Hardees, Huddle House, McDonald's, Sonic, Subway, **lodging:** Days Inn, **other:** AutoZone, Fred's, O'Reilly Parts, RV camping, Whitten HS, **S gas:** Murphy USA/dsl, **other:** Los Compadres Mexican, Pizza Hut, Wendy's, **other:** Walmart SuperCtr
104mm	Tombigbee River/Tenn-Tom Waterway
101	rd 178, rd 363, Peppertown, Mantachie, **N gas:** Exxon, **S gas:** Dorsey Fuel/dsl (2mi)
97	Fawn Grove Rd
94	rd 371, Mantachie, Mooreville, **N gas:** Woco/dsl
90	Auburn Rd, **N gas:** BP/dsl
87	Veterans Blvd, **N gas:** Shell/Chix Rest/dsl, **food:** Huddle House, **lodging:** Wingate Inn, **other:** E. Presley Campground/Park, **S** Tombigbee SP
86	US 45 N, Corinth, **1 exit N gas:** BP, Shell, Texaco, **food:** Abner's Rest., Applebees, Burger King, Chick-fil-A, Chili's, ChuckeCheese, Cracker Barrel, Kyoto

INTERSTATE 22 (FUTURE)

CORINTH

E ↕ W

Exit #	Services
86	Continued Japanese, McDonald's, New China, O'Charley's, Olive Garden, Pizza Hut, Red Lobster, Ryan's, Sonic, Subway, Taco Bell, Wendy's, **lodging:** Baymont Inn, Best Inn, Comfort Inn, Days Inn, Holiday Inn Express, Jameson Inn, Lenny's Subs, **other:** Barnes & Noble, Belk, Best Buy, Books-a-Million, Ford/Lincoln/Mercury, Home Depot, JC Penney, Kohl's, Kroger/gas, Lowe's Whse, NAPA, Old Navy, PetsMart, Sam's Club/gas, Sears, Staples, Tuesday Morning, Walmart
85	Natchez Trace Pkwy
81	rd 178, McCullough Blvd, **S gas:** Exxon/dsl, Shell/dsl, Texaco/dsl, **food:** Old Venice Pizza, Sonic, **lodging:** Super 8, **other:** $General, USPO
76	rd 9 S, Sherman, Pontotoc, **N gas:** Wild Bill's/dsl, **other:** Sherman RV Ctr
73	rd 9 N, Blue Springs
64	rd 15, rd 30 E, Pontotoc, Ripley, **N gas:** BP, Chevron, **food:** George's Rest., **other:** tire repair, USPO, **S gas:** Pilot/Arby's/scales/dsl/24hr, Shell/dsl
63	New Albany, **N gas:** Dee's Oil/dsl, **food:** Chevrolet/Buick/Pontiac/GMC, Ford, HP
62mm	Tallahatchie River
61	rd 30 W, W New Albany, **S gas:** Express, Murphy USA, Shell, **food:** Capt. D's, Huddle House, KFC, McAlisters Deli, McDonald's/playplace, Pizza Hut, Pueblo Mexican, Subway, Taco Bell, Wendy's, Western Sizzlin, **lodging:** Comfort Inn, Hallmarc Inn, **other:** H, $Tree, Rite Aid, Walgreens, Walmart SuperCtr, to U of MS
60	Glenfield, **S** U of MS
55	Myrtle
48	rd 178, Hickory Flat, **N gas:** Dee's Oil/dsl, **S gas:** BP/rest/dsl/24hr
41	rd 346, Potts Camp, **S gas:** BP/dsl, **other:** $General, NAPA
41mm	Tippah River
37	Lake Center, **N** Chewalla Lake/RV camping
30	rd 7, rd 4, Holly Springs, Oxford, **N gas:** BP, Exxon, Shell/Chester's/BBQ, **food:** Huddle House, KFC, McDonalds, Panda Buffet, Pizza Hut, Popeye's, Sonic, Subway, Wendy's, **lodging:** Magnolia Inn, **other:** H AutoZone, $General, Walldoxey SP/RV camping, **S gas:** Exxon, **lodging:** Days Inn, Le Brooks Inn, **other:** Walmart SuperCtr
26	W Holly Springs
21	Red Banks, **N gas:** BP/dsl, Texaco/dsl
18	Victoria, E Byhalia, **N gas:** BP
14	rd 309, Byhalia, **N gas:** Exxon, Shell, **lodging:** Best Value
10	W Byhalia
6	Bethel Rd, Hacks Crossroad, **N gas:** BP, *FLYING J*/Country Mkt/dsl/scales/LP/RV dump/24hr, Horizon, **food:** JR's Grill, Tops BBQ, **lodging:** Best Western, Super 8
6mm	**parking area, both lanes**
4	rd 305, Olive Branch, Independence, **N gas:** BP/dsl, Mobil/Huddle House, Shell/Circle K, **food:** Old Style BBQ, Pizza Hut, **lodging:** Holiday Inn Express, **S gas:** BP/Quizno's
3.5mm	**weigh sta, both lanes**
2	rd 302, Olive Branch, **N food:** Abbay's Rest., Buffalo Wild Wings, Chick-fil-A, Chili's, Colton's Steaks, IHOP, Krystal, Lenny's Subs, McAlisters Deli, O'Charley's, Starbucks, Wendy's, **lodging:** Comfort Suites, **other:** $Tree, Ford, Home Depot, Lowes, Radio Shack, Walmart SuperCtr, **S gas:** Chevron/dsl, Shell/Circle K, **food:** Applebees, Backyard Burger, Burger King, Casa Mexicana, McDonald's, Subway, Taco Bell, Waffle House, Zaxby's, **lodging:** Comfort Inn, Hampton Inn, **other:** AutoZone, GNC Nutrition, Goodyear/auto, Kroger/gas
1	Craft Rd, **N lodging:** Candlewood Suites, Holiday Inn, **other:** American RV Ctr, Hyundai, Southaven RV Ctr, Suzuki
0mm	Mississippi/Tennessee state line, I-22 (future) begins/ends. US 78 continues wb.

INTERSTATE 55

N ↕ S

SOUTHAVEN

Exit #	Services
291.5mm	Mississippi/Tennessee state line
291	State Line Rd, Southaven, **E food:** Exline's Pizza, Interstate BBQ, Little Caesars, Tops BBQ, Waffle House, **lodging:** Comfort Inn, Holiday Inn Express, Quality Inn, Southern Inn, **other:** Family$, Firestone/auto, Goodyear/auto, Kroger, Southaven RV Park, Walgreens, **W food:** Capt D's, Checker's, Dales Rest, El Patron Mexican, Lucky China, Mrs Winner's, Sonic, Taco Bell, Wendy's, **other:** Big Lots, Fred's Drug, Rite Aid, Walgreens, USPO, tires
289	MS 302, to US 51, Horn Lake, **E gas:** BP/Circle K, Shell/Circle K, **food:** Backyard Burger, Burger King, Chick-fil-A, Chili's, Coldstone, Danver's, Fazoli's, Firehouse Subs, Fox&Hound, Gordman's, IHOP, Krystal, Huey's Rest., Hunan Buffet, La Hacienda, Logan's Roadhouse, Lonestar Steaks, Longhorn Steaks, McDonald's, O'Charley's, Olive Garden, On-the-Border, Outback Steaks, Qdoba Mexican, Quizno's, Red Lobster, Sonic, Starbucks, Steak'n Shake, Subway, TGIFriday, Wendy's, **lodging:** Comfort Suites, Courtyard, Fairfield Inn, Hampton Inn, Hilton Garden, Residence Inn, **other:** H, Aldi Foods, Best Buy, BooksAMillion, Chevrolet, Chrysler/Jeep, Dillards, $Tree, Ford, JC Penney, Lowe's Whse, Marshall's, Nissan, Office Depot, Old Navy, PetCo, Pontiac/Buick/GMC, Radio Shack, Sam's Club/gas, Sportsman's Whse, Tuesday Morning, Walmart SuperCtr, World Mkt, mall, **W gas:** BP/Circle K, Phillips 66/dsl, Shell/dsl, **food:** Applebee's, Arby's, Country Home Buffet, ChuckeCheese, Cracker Barrel, Hooters, KFC, McDonald's, Mrs Winner's, Papa John's, Pizza Hut, Popeye's, Quizno's, Ryan's, Sekisui Japan, Taco Bell, TX Roadhouse, Waffle House, Wendy's, Zaxby's, **lodging:** Day's Inn, Drury Inn, Motel 6, Sleep Inn, Super 8, **other:** CVS Drug, Family$, Harley Davidson, Home Depot, Kroger, Sav-A-Lot Foods, Target, Walgreens, tires
287	Church Rd, **E gas:** Citgo/dsl, **other:** AutoZone, **W gas:** Shell/DQ/dsl, **food:** Boiling Point Seafood, McDonald's, Subway, Taco Bell, Waffle House, **lodging:** Keywest Inn, Magnolia Inn, **other:** Audubon Point RV Park (1mi), El Daze RV Camping (1mi), Southaven RV Ctr
285mm	**weigh sta both lanes**

INTERSTATE 55 CONT'D

N ↕ S

Exit #	Services
284	to US 51, Nesbit Rd, **W gas:** BP, **food:** Happy Daze Dairybar, **other:** USPO
283	I-69, Tunica
280	MS 304, US 51, Hernando, **E gas:** Exxon, **food:** Arby's, Backyard Burger, Capt D's, Dominos, Guadalahara Mexican, Huddle House, KFC, Kyoto, Sonic, Steak Escape, Taco Bell, **lodging:** Day's Inn, Hampton Inn, Hernando Inn, Scottish Inn, **other:** $Tree, Walmart SuperCtr/gas, Walgreens, repair/tires, **W gas:** BP, GasMart, Shell/Circle K/dsl, **food:** Brick Oven Rest., Coleman's BBQ, La Siesta, Lenny's Subs, McDonald's, Mi Pueblo, Papa John's, Pizza Hut, Quizno's, Sonic, Wendy's, **lodging:** Super 8, **other:** AutoZone, Desoto Museum, Kroger/gas, NAPA, Memphis S Camping (2mi), to Arkabutla Lake
279mm	**Welcome Ctr sb, full ♿ facilities, ☎, ⊼, litter barrels, petwalk, RV dump, 24hr security**
276mm	**rest area nb, full ♿ facilities, ☎, ⊼, litter barrels, petwalk, RV dump, 24hr security**
273mm	Coldwater River
271	MS 306, Coldwater, **W gas:** BP, **food:** Subway, **other:** Memphis S RV Park, Lake Arkabutla
265	MS 4, Senatobia, **W gas:** BP/dsl, Exxon, Kangaroo/Stuckey's/Huddle House/dsl/scales/24 hr, Shell, **food:** Backyard Burger, Coleman's BBQ, Domino's, KFC, McDonald's/playplace, New China Buffet, Pizza Hut, Popeye's, Rio Lindo Mexican, Sonic, Subway, Taco Bell, Waffle House, Wendy's, Western Sizzlin, **lodging:** Days Inn, Motel 6, **other:** [H], Buick/Pontiac/GMC, CarQuest, City Drug, Fred's Drug, Kaye Mkt, Pontiac/Buick/GMC, USPO
263	S Senatobia, new exit
257	MS 310, Como, **E gas:** BP/dsl, **other:** N Sardis Lake, **W food:** Windy City Grille (1mi)
252	MS 315, Sardis, **E gas:** Chevron/dsl, Pure/dsl, **food:** McDonald's, Sardis Lake Cafe, **lodging:** Lake Inn, Super 8, **other:** to Kyle SP, Sardis Dam, RV camping, **W gas:** Shell/dsl, **food:** Sonic, **lodging:** Happy Days Motel, **other:** [H], $General, Fred's
246	MS 35, N Batesville, **E** to Sardis Lake, **W gas:** Mobil, **Shell/dsl**
243b a	MS 6, to Batesville, **E gas:** BP/dsl, Shell/dsl, **food:** Backyard Burger, Chili's, Mi Pueblo Mexican, Starbucks, **other:** Lowe's Whse, Walmart SuperCtr/dsl, to Sardis Lake, U of MS, **W gas:** BP, Chevron/dsl, Exxon/dsl, Phillips 66/dsl, Shell/dsl, **food:** Abner's Rest., Burger King, Cafe Ole, Capt D's, Cracker Barrel, Domino's, Hardee's, Huddle House, KFC, McDonald's, Pizza Hut, Popeye's, Quizno's, Sonic, Subway, Taco Bell, Waffle House, Wendy's, Western Sizzlin, **lodging:** Baymont Inn, Day's Inn, Hampton Inn, Holiday Inn, Ramada Ltd, **other:** [H], Advance Parts, AutoZone, $General, Factory Stores/famous brands, Family$, Fred's Drug, Kroger, O'Reilly Parts, Walgreens, USPO
240mm	**rest area both lanes, full ♿ facilities, ☎, ⊼, litter barrels, petwalk, RV dump, 24hr security**
237	to US 51, Courtland, **E gas:** Pure/dsl
233	to Enid Dam, **E** to Enid Lake, RV camping, **W gas:** Benson's/groceries

BATESVILLE

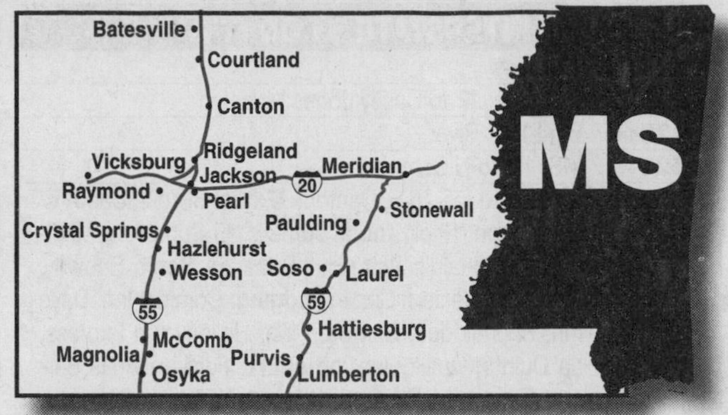

GRENADA

Exit #	Services
227	MS 32, Oakland, **E** to Cossar SP, Sunrise RV Park, **W gas:** Exxon/dsl, Shell/dsl, **food:** Subway
220	MS 330, Tillatoba, **E gas:** Conoco/rest./dsl/@
211	MS 7 N, to Coffeeville, **E** Frog Hollow RV Park, **W gas:** Shell/Chester Fried/dsl
208	Papermill Rd, **E** Grenada ✈
206	MS 8, MS 7 S, to Grenada, **E gas:** BP, Exxon/dsl, RaceWay, Shell/dsl, **food:** Burger King, China Buffet, Cosina Mexican, Domino's, Jake&Rip's Café, La Cabana Mexican, McAlister's Deli, McDonald's, Pizza Hut, Pizza Inn, RagTime Grill, Shoney's, Subway, Taco Bell, Wendy's, Western Sizzlin, **lodging:** Best Value Inn, Budget Inn, Comfort Inn, Day's Inn, Hampton Inn, Holiday Inn Express, Jameson Inn, Knights Inn, Quaity Inn, Super 8, **other:** [H], Advance Parts, AutoZone, Chrysler/Dodge, Curves, CVS Drug, $General, Ford/Lincoln/Mercury, GNC, O'Reilly Parts, Radio Shack, USPO, Walmart SuperCtr/24hr, to Grenada Lake/RV camping, **W gas:** Exxon/HuddleHouse, **food:** Waffle house, **lodging:** Country Inn&Suites, Econolodge, **other:** Nissan, Toyota/Scion
204mm	**parking area sb, ☎, litter barrels**
202mm	**parking area nb, ☎, litter barrels**
199	Trout Rd, S Grenada, **E** to camp McCain
195	MS 404, Duck Hill, **E** to camp McCain, **W gas:** Conoco/dsl
185	US 82, Winona, **E gas:** Exxon, Shell/dsl, **food:** Huddle House, KFC, McDonald's, Sonic, Subway, **lodging:** Budget Inn, Magnolia Lodge, Relax Inn, Western Inn, **other:** [H], **W gas:** Pilot/Taco Bell/dsl/24hr/scales/repair
174	MS 35, MS 430, Vaiden, **E gas:** Chevron/dsl, Down Home/dsl/scales/24hr, Shell, **lodging:** 35-55 motel, **other:** NAPA, Vaiden Camping, **W gas:** Exxon/Chesterfried/dsl, **other:** $General
173mm	**rest area sb, full ♿ facilities, ☎, ⊼, litter barrels, petwalk, RV dump, 24hr security**
164	to West, **W gas:** West Trkstp/Pure/dsl
163mm	**rest area nb, full ♿ facilities, ☎, ⊼, litter barrels, petwalk, RV dump, 24hr security**
156	MS 12, Durant, **E gas:** Shell/dsl, **lodging:** Durant Motel/rest. (3mi), Super 8, **W** [H] (7mi)
150	**E** Holmes Co SP, RV camping
146	MS 14, Goodman, **W** to Little Red Schoolhouse
144	MS 17, to Pickens, **E gas:** Texaco/HomePlace Rest./dsl/24hr, **W gas:** BP/dsl/rest./24hr, **other:** to Little Red Schoolhouse
139	MS 432, to Pickens

MS

INTERSTATE 55 CONT'D

N ↕ S — CANTON — MADISON — JACKSON

Exit #	Services
133	Vaughan, **E** to Casey Jones Museum
128mm	Big Black River
124	MS 16, to N Canton
119	MS 22, to MS 16 E, Canton, **E gas:** BP/dsl, Cappy's/dsl, Exxon, Shell, **food:** Domin's, El Sombrero Mexican, McDonald's, Pizza Hut, Popeye's, Sonic, Subway, Wendy's, Western Sizzlin, **lodging:** Comfort Inn, Days Inn, Econolodge, Hampton Inn, Holiday Inn Express, La Quinta, Quality Inn, **other:** H, Ford, to Ross Barnett Reservoir, **W gas:** Chevron/KFC/dsl, Citgo/dsl, Love's/Arby's/dsl/scales/24hr/@, Texaco/dsl, **food:** Bumpers Drive-In, 2 Rivers Steaks
118a b	Nissan Parkway, **E** to Nissan Factory
114a b	Sowell Rd
112	US 51, Gluckstadt, **E gas:** Exxon/Krystal/dsl, Kangaroo/Subway/dsl, **lodging:** Super 8, **W** Camper Corral RV Ctr
108	MS 463, Madison, **E gas:** Shell/dsl, Texaco/Domino's/dsl, **food:** Alexander's Italian, Anthony Z's, Applebees, Backyard Burger, Burger King, Chick-Fil-A, Chili's, Coldstone, El Potrillo, Haute Pig Café, Lenny's Subs, Starbucks, **other:** $Tree, Lowe's Whse, Walmart SuperCtr/24hr **W gas:** Exxon/KFC/dsl, **food:** Atlantica Grill, Beef O'brady's, BoneFish Grill, Nagoya Japanese, Papito's Grill, Pizza Inn, Wendy's, **lodging:** Hilton Garden, **other:** H, CVS Drug, Home Depot, Kroger
105b	Old Agency Rd, **E gas:** Chevron/dsl, **other:** Honda, Pontiac/Buick/GMC, **W food:** Peppers Cafe, PF Changs, Ruth's Chris Steaks, **lodging:** Hyatt Place, **other:** Barnes & Noble, Fresh Mkt Foods
105a	Natchez Trace Pkwy
104	I-220, to W Jackson
103	County Line Rd, **E gas:** BP, Chevron, Exxon/dsl, **food:** Applebee's, Barnhill's Rest., Bop's Custard, Bulldog Grill, Cane's Chicken, Chick-fil-A, Cozumel Mexican, Garfield's, Grand China, Honey Baked Ham, Huntington's Grill, Jason's Deli, KFC, King Buffet, Krispy Kreme, Macaroni Grill, Mazzio's, Moe's SW Grill, O'Charley's, Popeye's, Quizno's, Shoney's, Starbucks, Subway, Taco Bell, Wendy's, Whataburger, Zaxby's, **lodging:** Cabot Lodge, Courtyard, Day's Inn, Hilton, Quality Inn, Red Roof Inn, **other:** Acura, Barnes&Noble, Belk, Best Buy, Cadillac, Dillard's, $Tree, Goodyear, Lowe's Whse, Marshall's, Michael's, Office Depot, Old Navy, Sam's Club, TJ Maxx, Walgreens, Walmart SuperCtr, mall, to Barnett Reservoir, **W food:** Chili's, Olive Garden, Red Lobster, Logan's Roadhouse, Subway, **lodging:** Comfort Suites, Drury Inn, Motel 6, Studio 6, **other:** Fred's Drug, Home Depot, Office Depot, PetsMart, Target
102b	Beasley Rd, Adkins Blvd, **E gas:** Phillips 66, **food:** Cracker Barrel, LoneStar Steaks, OutBack Steaks, **lodging:** La Quinta, Super 8, **other:** Brookshire Food/gas, Chevrolet, Chrysler/Jeep, Ford, Lincoln/Mercury, Nissan, Toyota/Scion, **W gas:** Exxon/TCBY, **food:** McDonald's, **lodging:** Best Western, Extended Stay Deluxe, Fairfield Inn, Hampton Inn, InTown Suites, **other:** Big Lots, Carmax, Mercedes, frontage rds access 102a
102a	Briarwood, **E lodging:** La Quinta, **other:** Kroger, Office Depot, Steinmart, UHaul, **W food:** America's Diner, Capt D's, ChuckeCheese, Peking Chinese, Popeye's, **lodging:** Best Inn, Best Value Inn, Clarion, Hampton Inn, **other:** BigLots, Chevrolet, Chrysler/Jeep/Dodge, Mercedes/Porsche
100	North Side Dr W, **E gas:** BP, Chevron, **food:** Char Rest., McAlister's Deli, McDonald's, Papa John's, Piccadilly's, Pizza Hut, Starbucks, SteakOut, Steam Room Grill, Subway, Wendy's, **lodging:** Extended Stay America, **other:** Audi, BooksAMillion, CVS Drug, Jaguar/Landrover, Kroger/gas, Office Depot, Radio Shack, Steinmart, Tuesday Morning, VW, Walgreens, Vet, **W gas:** BP, Exxon/dsl, Shell, **food:** Domino's, Hooters, IHOP, Waffle House, **lodging:** Select Hotel
99	Meadowbrook Rd, Northside Dr E (from nb)
98c b	MS 25 N, Lakeland Dr, **E gas:** Shell, **lodging:** Parkside Inn, **other:** LaFleur's Bluff SP, museum, **W** H, ✈
98a	Woodrow Wilson Dr, downtown
96c	Fortification St, **E lodging:** Residence Inn, **W** H, Bellhaven College
96b	High St, Jackson, **E other:** BMW, Chevrolet, Infiniti, Lexus, **W gas:** Shell/dsl, Texaco/dsl, **food:** Arby's, Domino's, Farmers Mkt Grill, Popeye's, Shoney's, Taco Bell, Waffle House, Wendy's, Whataburger, **lodging:** Day's Inn, Best Western, Hampton Inn, Holiday Inn Express, Quality Inn, Red Roof Inn, Regency Hotel, **other:** H, Honda, Subaru/Volvo, museum, st capitol
96a	Pearl St (from nb), Jackson, **W** downtown, access to same as 96b
94	(46 from nb), I-20 E, to Meridian, US 49 S
45b [I-20]	US 51, State St, to downtown, **N gas:** Petro, **other:** Subaru, Pontiac, Volvo **S gas:** Pilot
45a	Gallatin St (from sb), **N gas:** Petro/dsl, **S gas:** Pilot/McDonald's/dsl/@, **other:** Hyundai/Mazda, Nissan, Toyota
92c	(44 from sb), I-20 W, to Vicksburg, US 49 N
92b	US 51 N, State St, Gallatin St
92a	McDowell Rd, **E gas:** Petro/dsl, Pilot/McDonald's/dsl, **lodging:** Knight's Inn, **W gas:** BP, BJ's, Dixie, Shell, **food:** Waffle House, Wendy's, **lodging:** Super S Inn, **other:** Brookshire's Food/Drug, Rite Aid
90b	Daniel Lake Blvd (from sb), **W gas:** Shell, **other:** Harley-Davidson
90a	Savanna St, **E lodging:** Save Inn, **other:** transmissions, **W gas:** BP, **food:** Bodan's Seafood, **other:** Turning Wheel RV Center
88	Elton Rd, **W gas:** Chevron, Exxon/ChesterFried/dsl
85	Byram, **E gas:** Blue Sky, HotSpot/dsl/24hr, **food:** Krystal, Mexican Grill, **lodging:** ValuPlace Hotel, **other:** Swinging Bridge RV Park, **W gas:** Byrem Gas/dsl, Chevron, Exxon/dsl, Texaco/dsl, **food:** Backya rd Burger, Capt'n D's, Mazzio's, McAlister's Deli, McDonald's, New China, Pizza Hut, Popeye's, Quizno's, Sonic, Subway, Taco Bell, Waffle House, Wendy's, **lodging:** Day's Inn, **other:** Ace Hardware, AutoZone, Country Creek RV Ctr, $General, Market Place Foods, NAPA, O'Reilly Parts, Super D Drugs, Walgreens, USPO
81	Wynndale Rd, **W gas:** Chevron/dsl
78	Terry, **E gas:** Texaco/Subway/dsl/24hr, **other:** USPO, **W gas:** Mac's, **other:** $General

INTERSTATE 55 CONT'D

N ↕ S

Exit #	Services
72	MS 27, Crystal Springs, **E gas:** Exxon/Subway/dsl, Phillips 66/dsl, **food:** McDonald's, Popeye's, **other:** Ford/Lincoln/Mercury
68	to US 51, S Crystal Springs, gas/dsl, **other:** Red Barn Produce, Vet
65	to US 51, Gallman, **E gas:** Stuckey's/gas
61	MS 28, Hazlehurst, **E gas:** BP, Exxon, Phillips 66/dsl, Pump&Save, **food:** Bumpers Drive Inn, Burger King, Country Catfish, KFC, McDonald's, Sonic, Stark's Rest., Subway, Taco Bell, Wendy's, **lodging:** Best Value, Claridge Inn, Western Inn, **other:** H, Advance Parts, CVS Drug, $General, Family$, Fred's Drugs, Piggly Wiggly, Supervalu Foods, Walmart SuperCtr
59	to S Hazlehurst
56	to Martinsville
54mm	**rest area both lanes, full ♿ facilities, ☎, picnic, litter barrels, petwalk, RV dump, vending, 24hr security**
51	to Wesson, **E other:** Lake Lincoln SP, **W gas:** Country Jct Trkstp/dsl/rest.
48	Mt Zion Rd, to Wesson
42	to US 51, N Brookhaven, **E gas:** Exxon/Subway, Shell/Kasko/scales/dsl, **other:** H, **W lodging:** Super 8
40	to MS 550, Brookhaven, **E gas:** BP/Domino's, Blue Sky, Exxon/Subway, Fleetway, Shell/dsl/24hr, **food:** Bowle BBQ, Burger King, China Buffet, Cracker Barrel, DQ, Hall's BBQ, KFC, Krystal, McDonald's, Mitchell's Steaks, Pizza Hut, Popeye's, Quizno's, Sonic, Taco Bell, Wendy's, Western Sizzlin, **lodging:** Best Value Inn, Comfort Inn, Day's Inn, Lincoln Inn, Hampton Inn, Spanish Inn, **other:** H, AutoZone, CarQuest, Chevrolet, Chrysler/Dodge/Jeep, Fred's Drugs, Honda, Nissan, O'Reilly Parts, Rite Aid, SaveALot Foods, Super D Drugs, Toyota, Walgreens, Walmart SuperCtr/gas, **W other:** Home Depot
38	US 84, S Brookhaven, **W gas:** Chevron/dsl/24hr
30	Bogue Chitto, Norfield, **E gas:** Shell/BogueChitto/dsl, **W other:** Bogue Chitto RV Park
24	Johnston Station, **E** to Lake Dixie Springs
20b a	US 98 W, to Natchez, Summit, **E gas:** BP/dsl, Shell/dsl, Stop'n Shop/dsl, **W gas:** Exxon/Subway/dsl, Phillips 66/dsl
18	MS 570, Smithdale Rd, N McComb, **E gas:** BP, **food:** Burger King, China Buffet, McDonald's, Piccadilly's, Ruby Tuesday, **lodging:** Holiday Inn Express, **other:** H, Belk, JC Penney, Kia, Lowe's Whse, Sears/auto, Walmart SuperCtr/Subway, mall, **W gas:** Chevron/Quizno's/dsl, **food:** Arby's, El Dorado Mexican, Santa Fe Grille, **lodging:** Deerfield Inn, Hampton Inn, Hawthorn Inn, **other:** Ford/Lincoln/Mercury
17	Delaware Ave, McComb, **E gas:** BP/Subway, Blue Sky Gas, Chevron/dsl, Exxon, Pump & Save, Pure, RaceWay, Shell/dsl, **food:** Backyard BBQ, Burger King, Domino's, Golden Corral, Mexican Grill, McDonald's, New China, Pizza Hut, Pizza Inn, Popeye's, Sonic, Taco Bell, Waffle House, Wendy's, **lodging:** Best Western, Comfort Inn, Executive Inn, National Inn, Super 8, **other:** H, AutoZone, CVS Drug, $General, Family$, Fred's Drug, Kroger, O'Reilly Parts, Rite Aid, **W lodging:** Day's Inn, **other:** Chrysler/Dodge/Jeep

BROOKHAVEN

MC COMB

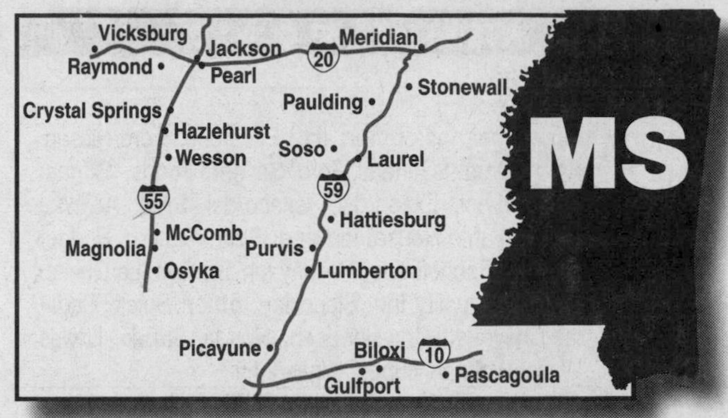

Exit #	Services
15b a	US 98 E, MS 48 W, McComb, **1 mi E gas:** Exxon/Subway, Pure, Shell, **food:** Church's, Hardee's, KFC, **lodging:** Camellian Motel, **other:** Advance Parts, $General, Family$, tires, Vet, **W gas:** BP/dsl
13	Fernwood Rd, **W gas:** Conoco/Fernwood/dsl/rest./scales/24hr/@, **lodging:** Fernwood Motel, **other:** golf, to Percy Quin SP
10	MS 48, Magnolia, **1 mi E gas:** Exxon, MTS, **food:** Subway, **other:** RV camping
8	MS 568, Magnolia, **E** Pike Co Speedway
4	Chatawa
3mm	**Welcome Ctr nb, full ♿ facilities, ☎, picnic, litter barrels, petwalk, RV dump, 24hr security**
2mm	**weigh station, nb only**
1	MS 584, Osyka, Gillsburg
0mm	Mississippi/Louisiana state line

INTERSTATE 59

N ↕ S

Exit #	Services
I-59 S and I-20 W run together to Meridian.	
172mm	Mississippi/Alabama state line
170mm	**weigh sta both lanes**
169	Kewanee, **S gas:** Kewanee Trkstp/dsl
165	Toomsuba, **N gas:** Shell/Subway/24hr, Texaco/ChesterFried/dsl, **S gas:** Loves/Arby's/dsl/scales, **other:** KOA (2mi)
164mm	**Welcome Ctr wb, full ♿ facilities, ☎, vending, picnic, litter barrels, petwalk, RV dump, 24hr security**
160	to Russell, **N gas:** TA/BP/dsl/rest./scales/24hr/@, **other:** Nanabe RV Camping (1mi), **S gas:** Shell/dsl
157b a	US 45, to Macon, Quitman
154b a	MS 19 S, MS 39 N, Meridian, **N gas:** BP/dsl, Pure, Shell, Texaco/Domino's, **food:** Applebee's, Cracker Barrel, Penn's Rest., Western Sizzlin, Waffle House, **lodging:** Day's Inn, Drury Inn, Hampton Inn, Hilton Garden, Holiday Inn, Relax Inn, Rodeway Inn, Super 8, **other:** Benchmark RV Park, Cadillac/Pontiac, Chrysler/Jeep/Kia, Hyundai, Lincoln/Mercury, Mitsubishi, U-Haul, **S gas:** Chevron, Texaco, **food:** Chick-fil-A, CiCi's, Crescent City Grill, Garfield's Rest., McAlister's, McDonald's, O'Charley's, Outback Steaks, Popeye's, Red Lobster, Ryan's, Taco Bell, **lodging:** Comfort Inn, Jameson Inn, Microtel, **other:** Belk, Best Buy, BooksA-Million, Dillard's, $Tree, Ethridge RV Ctr, Harley-Davidson, JC Penney, Old Navy, PetCo, Ross, Sam's Club/gas, Sears/auto, TJ Maxx, mall, same as 153
153	MS 145 S, 22nd Ave, Meridian, **N gas:** BP, Shell, **food:** Arby's, Barnhill's Buffet, Burger King, Capt D's, China Buffet, Hardee's, KFC, McDonald's, Pizza Hut, Subway, Wendy's, Western Sizzlin, **lodging:** Relax

MERIDIAN

MS

INTERSTATE 59 CONT'D

Exit #	Services
153	Continued Inn, Super Inn, **other:** H, Firestone, Ford/Nissan, Fred's Drug, $General, Ford, Saverite Foods, **S gas:** Chevron/dsl, Exxon/dsl, Texaco/dsl, **food:** A&W/LJ Silver, Waffle House, **lodging:** Best Western, Budget 8 Motel, Econolodge, Holiday Inn Express, La Quinta, Motel 6, Quality Inn, Sleep Inn, **other:** Buick, Cadillac/Chevrolet, Chrysler/Jeep, Honda, Suzuki, Lowes Whse, Walmart SuperCtr/gas/24hr
152	29th Ave, 31st Ave, Meridian, **N gas:** Chevron/ChesterFried/dsl/24hr, **lodging:** Ramada Ltd, **S lodging:** Royal Inn
151	49th Ave, Valley Rd, **N** tires, **S gas:** Pilot/Subway/dsl/24hr, **other:** stockyards
150	US 11 S, MS 19 N, Meridian, **N gas:** Queen City Trkstp/dsl/rest./@, **food:** McDonald's, **other:** RV camping, Okatibbee Lake, **S gas:** Chevron/Stuckey's/Subway/dsl, Shell/dsl **other:** ✈
149mm	**I-59 N and I-20 E run together 22 mi**
142to	US 11, Savoy, **W** to Dunns Falls
137	to N Enterprise, to Stonewall
134	MS 513, S Enterprise
126	MS 18, to Rose Hill, Pachuta, **E gas:** BP/dsl/24hr
118	to Vossburg, Paulding
113	MS 528, to Heidelberg, **E gas:** BP/JR's/dsl/24hr, Chevron/dsl, Exxon/Subway/dsl, Shell
109mm	**parking area sb, litter barrels, no restrooms**
106mm	**parking area nb, litter barrels, no restrooms**
104	Sandersville
99	US 11, **E lodging:** Magnolia Motel, **other:** Sleepy Hollow RV Park (1mi)
97	US 84 E, **E gas:** Exxon/dsl/scales, Kangaroo/Subway/dsl/24hr, **food:** Hardee's, Ward's Burgers, **W gas:** BP/dsl, Shell/24hr, **food:** KFC, Vic's Rest.
96b	MS 15 S, Cook Ave
96a	Masonite Rd, 4th Ave
95d	(from nb)
95c	Beacon St, Laurel, **W gas:** Pump & Save Gas, **food:** Burger King, Church's, McDonald's, Old Mexico, Popeye's, **lodging:** TownHouse Motel, **other:** Expert Tire, Family$, Grocery Depot, JC Penney, USPO, XpertTire
95b a	US 84 W, MS 15 N, 16th Ave, Laurel, **0-2 mi W gas:** Exxon/dsl, Pure, Shell, Texaco, **food:** Applebees, Buffet City, Checkers, China Town, Domino's, Fred's, Hardee's, KFC, Laredo Grill, Lenny's Subs, McDonald's, Pizza Hut, Quizno's, Shoney's, Sonic, Subway, Sweet Peppers Deli, Taco Bell, Waffle House, Ward's Burgers, Wendy's, Western Sizzlin, **lodging:** Comfort Suites, Econolodge, Hampton Inn, Holiday Inn Express, Super 8, **other:** H, Advance Parts, AutoZone, BigLots, Chevrolet/Buick/Pontiac, Chrysler/Dodge/Jeep, CVS Drug, $General, $Tree, Ford, Kroger, Lowe's Whse, Office Depot, O'Reilly Parts, Piggly Wiggly, Roses, Toyota, Walgreens, Walmart SuperCtr, Winn-Dixie
93	US 11, S Laurel, **W gas:** Exxon/Subway/dsl, Shell/dsl/24hr, Uncle Roy's/dsl, **food:** Hardee's
90	US 11, Ellisville Blvd, **E gas:** Texaco/dsl, **food:** Huddle House, **W gas:** Dixie/dsl
88	MS 588, MS 29, Ellisville, **E gas:** Chevron/dsl, Fast-Trak, **food:** Domino's, KFC, McDonald's, Pizza Hut, Subway, **other:** Ellisville Drug, Food Tiger, Family$, NAPA, **W gas:** Exxon/dsl, **lodging:** Best Western
85	MS 590, to Ellisville, **W** auto repair
80	to US 11, Moselle, **E gas:** BP/dsl
78	Sanford Rd
76	**W** Hattiesburg-Laurel Reg ✈
73	Monroe Rd, to Monroe
69	to Glendale, Eatonville Rd
67b a	US 49, Hattiesburg, **E gas:** BP, Exxon, Kangaroo/dsl, Shell, Texaco, **food:** Arby's, Burger King, Cracker Barrel, DQ, Krystal, McDonald's, Pizza Hut, Waffle House, **lodging:** Budget Inn, Comfort Inn, Econolodge, Howard Johnson, La Quinta, Motel 6, Quality Inn, Ramada, Red Carpet Inn, Regency Inn, Scottish Inn, Sleep Inn, Super 8, **other:** $General, **W gas:** BP/dsl, Chevron, MapleLeaf/dsl, Pure/dsl, Shell/Subway, Stuckey's/dsl, **food:** Sonic, Waffle House, Ward's Burgers, Wendy's, **lodging:** Best Western, Candlewood Suites, Holiday Inn
65b a	US 98 W, Hardy St, Hattiesburg, **E gas:** Exxon, Shell/dsl, Texaco, **food:** Applebee's, Bop's Custard, Buffalo Wild Wings, Cane's Checkers, Chicken, CiCi's, Domino's, IHOP, KFC, La Fiesta Brava, Lenny's Subs, McDonald's, Panino's Italian, Pizza Hut, Quizno's, Smoothie King, Starbucks, Subway, Taco Bell, Ward's Burgers, **lodging:** Courtyard, Executive Inn, Fairfield Inn, Western Motel, **other:** CarQuest, Curves, CVS Drug, Goodyear/auto, Home Depot, Roses, Walgreens, S MS U, Vet, **W gas:** BP/dsl, Exxon/Domino's, Kangaroo, Pump & $ave, Shell, **food:** Arby's, Backyard Burger, Burger King, Chick-fil-A, Chili's, China Buffet, ChuckeCheese, Coldstone, FireHouse Subs, Hardee's, Krispy Kreme, Lion's Choice, Logan's Roadhouse, LongHorn Steaks, Mazzio's, McDonald's, McCalisters Deli, Newt's Grill, O'Charley's, Olive Garden, Outback Steaks, Peking Garden, Pepper's Cafe, Pizza Hut, Popeye's, Red Lobster, Ryan's, Starbucks, Stoney's, Subway, Taco Bell, TGIFridays, Waffle House, Ward's Burgers, Wendy's, Zaxby's, **lodging:** Baymont Inn, Comfort Suites, Hampton Inn, Hilton Garden, Microtel, Sun Suites, **other:** H, Advance Parts, AutoZone, Belk, Best Buy, BooksAMillion, Dillard's, $Tree, Firestone/auto, Gander Mtn, Goodyear/auto, JC Penney, Kohl's, Lincoln/Mercury, Lowe's Whse, Michael's, Nissan, Office Depot, Old Navy, PetsMart, Radio Shack, Rite Aid, Ross, SaveRite Foods, Sam's Club/gas, Sears/auto, Target, TJ Maxx, Walgreens, Walmart SuperCtr/24hr, mall
60	US 11, S Hattiesburg, **E gas:** Shell/dsl, **W gas:** BP/dsl, Kangaroo/Subway/dsl/24hr
59	US 98 E, to US 49, Lucedale, MS Gulf Coast, no facilites
56mm	**parking area both lanes, litter barrels, no restrooms**
51	rd 589, to Purvis, **W gas:** Chevron/dsl, Pinebelt Oil/dsl, Shell/dsl (2mi), **food:** Pizza Hut (2mi), to Little Black Cr Water Park
48mm	Little Black Creek
41	MS 13, to Lumberton, **W gas:** Pure, **other:** Bass Pecan Store, $General, to Little Black Cr Water Park

N ↕ S LAUREL HATTIESBURG

INTERSTATE 59 CONT'D

Exit #	Services
35	Hillsdale Rd, **E** **gas:** Pitstop/dsl, **lodging:** to Kings Arrow Ranch, to Lake Hillside Resort
32mm	Wolf River
29	rd 26, to Poplarville, **W** **gas:** Kangaroo/dsl (2mi), Pure/dsl, **food:** Burger King (2mi), Hardee's (2mi)
27	MS 53, to Poplarville, **W** **gas:** Kangaroo/dsl (2mi), Shell/dsl, **other:** RV Camping (2mi)
19	to US 11, Millard
15	to McNeill, **W** **gas:** McNeill Trkstop/dsl/rest.
13mm	**parking area sb, litter barrels, no restrooms**
10to	US 11, Carriere, **E** **gas:** Texaco/Huddle House/dsl, **other:** Clearwater RV Camp (5mi), repair/tires
8mm	**parking area nb, litter barrels, no restrooms**
6	MS 43 N, N Picayune, **E** **food:** Marble Slab Creamery, Paul's Pastries, **W** **gas:** Chevron/dsl, **lodging:** Best Value, **other:** H, CVS Drug, Winn-Dixie, Vet
4	MS 43 S, to Picayune, **E** **gas:** RaceTrac, **food:** McDonald's, Ryan's, Wow Cafe, **other:** URGENT CARE, Chevrolet/Pontiac/Buick/Cadillac, Home Depot, Nissan, Sun Roamers RV Park, Walgreens, Walmart SuperCtr/gas, **W** **gas:** Chevron, Exxon/dsl, K&T/dsl, Shell/dsl, **food:** Burger King, Domino's, El Mariachi, Hardee's, KFC, McDonald's, Papa John's, Pizza Hut, Popeye's, Shoney's, Subway, Taco Bell, Waffle House, Wendy's, **lodging:** Comfort Inn, Day's Inn, Heritage Inn, **other:** H, Advance Parts, AutoZone, Chrysler/Dodge/Jeep, Curves, $General, Ford/Lincoln/Mercury, Fred's Drug, O'Reilly Parts, Radio Shack, Rite Aid, Winn-Dixie, Vet
3mm	**Welcome Ctr nb, full facilities, vending, litter barrels, petwalk, RV dump**
1.5mm	**weigh sta both lanes**
1	US 11, MS 607, **E** NASA, **W** **gas:** Chevron/dsl, Shell/dsl
0mm	Mississippi/Louisiana state line, Pearl River. **Exits 11-1 are in Louisiana**
11	Pearl River Turnaround. Callboxes begin sb.
5b	Honey Island Swamp
5a	LA 41, Pearl River, **E** **gas:** Chevron
3	US 11 S, LA 1090, Pearl River, **W** **gas:** Shell/dsl, **1 mi W** Chevron/dsl/24hr
1.5mm	**Welcome Ctr sb, full facilities, info, litter barrels, petwalk, RV dump**
1c b	I-10, E to Bay St Louis, W to New Orleans
1a	I-12 W, to Hammond. **I-59 begins/ends on I-10/I-12. Exits 1-11 are in Louisiana.**

Exits 1-11 are in Louisiana.

N ↕ S — PICAYUNE

INTERSTATE 220 (JACKSON)

Exit #	Services
11mm	I-220 begins/ends on I-55, exit 104.
9	Hanging Moss Rd, County Line Rd, **E** **gas:** BP
8	Watkins Dr, **E** **gas:** Shell/Chester Fried, Spur
5b a	US 49 N, Evers Blvd, to Yazoo City, **E** **gas:** BP, Pump&Save, **food:** KFC, Sonic, **lodging:** Star Motel, Family$, Food Depot, **W** **gas:** BP, Exxon/Burger King, Shell/Subway/dsl
3	Industrial Dr
2b a	Clinton Blvd, Capitol St, **E** to Jackson Zoo, **W** **gas:** RaceWay, Shell, **food:** McDonald's, Popeye's, Sonic, **other:** Family$
1b a	US 80, **E** **food:** Bumer's Drive-in, Capt D's, KFC, McDonald's, Pizza Hut, Popeye's, Sonny's BBQ, Taco Bell, Wendy's, **lodging:** Day's Inn, Econolodge, Sleep Inn, Super 8, **W** **gas:** BP, Exxon/dsl, **food:** Arby's, Krystal, **other:** Belk, Dillard's, Hyundai, Sears/auto
0mm	I-220 begins/ends on I-20, exit 41.

E ↕ W — JACKSON

MISSOURI

INTERSTATE 29

Exit #	Services
124mm	Missouri/Iowa state line
123mm	Nishnabotna River
121.5mm	**weigh sta both lanes**
116	rd A, rd B, to Watson, **W** fireworks
110	US 136, Rock Port, Phelps City, **E** **gas:** Shell/dsl, **lodging:** Rockport Inn, to NW MO St U, **W** **gas:** BP/dsl/24hr, Phillips 66/Subway/dsl/24hr, **food:** McDonald's, Trails End Rest., **lodging:** Super 8, **other:** KOA, fireworks
109.5mm	**Welcome Ctr sb, full facilities, info, litter barrels, petwalk**
107	MO 111, to Rock Port, **W** motel/RV Park
106.5mm	Rock Creek
102mm	Mill Creek
99	rd W, Corning
97mm	Tarkio River
92	US 59, to Fairfax, Craig, **W** **gas:** Sinclair/dsl
90.5mm	Little Tarkio Creek
86.5mm	Squaw Creek
84	MO 118, Mound City, **E** **gas:** Phillips 66/Subway/dsl, Shamrock/dsl, **food:** Breadeaux Pizza, McDonald's, Quacker's Steaks, **lodging:** Audrey's Motel, Super 8,
84	Continued **other:** Dodge/Jeep, $General, Mound City Foods, **W** **gas:** Shell/dsl/24hr, **other:** Big Lake SP (12mi)
82mm	**rest area both lanes, full facilities, litter barrels, vending, petwalk**
79	US 159, Rulo, **E** **gas:** Squaw Creek Trkstp/dsl/rest/RV dump/@, **W** to Big Lake SP (12mi), to Squaw Creek NWR (3mi)
78mm	Kimsey Creek
75	US 59, to Oregon
67	US 59 N, to Oregon
66.5mm	Nodaway River
65	US 59, rd RA, to Fillmore, Savannah, **E** **gas:** Conoco/dsl, **other:** antiques
60	rd K, rd CC, Amazonia, **W** **other:** Hunt's Fruit Barn, antiques
58.5mm	Hopkins Creek
56b a	I-229 S, US 71 N, US 59 N, to St Joseph, Maryville
55mm	Dillon Creek
53	US 59, US 71 bus, to St Joseph, Savannah, **E** AOK Camping, fireworks, **W** **gas:** Phillips 66/dsl
50	US 169, St Joseph, King City, **1-3 mi W on Belt Hwy...** **gas:** Conoco, Phillips 66/Domino's, Shell, **food:** Bob Evans, Cheddar's, Chili's, Chipotle Mexican, Culver's, Famous Dave's, 54th St Grill, Hardee's, LJ Silver, McDonald's, Panda Express, Ryan's, Sonic, Subway,

N ↕ S — ST JOSEPH

MO

N ↕ S

INTERSTATE 29 CONT'D

Exit #	Services
50	Continued Taco Bell, Wendy's, **other:** Advance Parts, Border's Books, Home Depot, Kohl's, Lowe's Whse, Michaels, Sam's Club, Target, Tires+, TJ Maxx, Walgreen, Walmart SuperCtr/24hr
47	MO 6, Frederick Blvd, to Clarksdale, St Joseph, **E gas:** Conoco, **food:** Bandanas BBQ, Country Kitchen, **lodging:** Day's Inn, Drury Inn, **W gas:** Sinclair, Phillips 66/dsl, **food:** Applebee's, Carlos O'Kelly's, Cracker Barrel, Denny's, Dunkin Donuts, Ground Round, Hazel's Coffee, KFC, McDonald's, Perkins/24hr, Pizza Hut, Red Lobster, Russell Stover, Sonic, Subway, Taco Bell, Whiskey Creek Steaks, Village Steaks, **lodging:** Budget Inn, Comfort Suites, Hampton Inn, Motel 6, Ramada Inn, Stoney Creek Inn, Super 8, **other:** H, BigLots, Chevrolet/Mazda, Dillard's, Ford, Firestone/auto, Goodyear/auto, PriceChopper Foods, Sears, RV camp, **1 mi W on US 169...food:** Arby's, Blimpie, Burger King, Church's, Fazoli's, Ground Round, LJ Silver, Pizza Hut, Rib Crib BBQ, Schlotsky's, Sonic, Starbucks, Taco Bell, **other:** Advance Parts, Aldi Foods, AutoZone, Buick/Pontiac/GMC, Cub Foods, CVS Drug, Food4Less/drugs/24hr, Ford/Lincoln/Mercury, Hastings Books, HyVee Foods, JC Penney, Jo-Ann Fabrics, Office Depot, Radio Shack, U-Haul, Walgreen
46b a	US 36, to Cameron, St Joseph, **1 mi W on US 169... gas:** BP/dsl, FL, Shell, **food:** Burger King, Godfather's, La Mesa Mexican, Pizza Hut, Taco John's, Wendy's, **other:** $General, Isuzu, Kia, Nissan, QwikLube, Save-a-Lot Foods, Walgreen, Walmart SuperCtr/gas/24hr, to MO W St Coll
44	US 169, to Gower, St Joseph, **E gas:** Phillips 66, Loves/Arby's/dsl/scales/24hr, **food:** Nelly's Mexican, Subway, **lodging:** Best Western, **other:** dsl repair, **W gas:** Shell/dsl/rest/24hr, **food:** DQ, McDonald's, San Jose Steaks, Taco Bell, **other:** Chrysler/Jeep/Dodge, $Tree, Goodyear, Harley-Davidson, Hyundai, Walmart SuperCtr/gas/24hr
43	I-229 N, to St Joseph
39.5mm	Pigeon Creek
35	rd DD, Faucett, **W gas:** Farris Trkstp/dsl/motel/rest/24hr/@
33.5mm	Bee Creek
30	rd Z, rd H, Dearborn, New Market, **E gas:** Conoco/Subway/dsl/24hr
29.5mm	Bee Creek
27mm	**rest area both lanes, full ♿ facilities, ☎, picnic, litter barrels, vending, petwalk**
25	rd E, rd U, to Camden Point, **E gas:** Phillips 66/dsl/rest.
24mm	**weigh sta both lanes**
20	MO 92, MO 273, to Atchison, Leavenworth, **W gas:** Phillips 66, **other:** to Weston Bend SP
19.5mm	Platte River
19	rd HH, Platte City, **E** antiques, **W gas:** Casey's, Conoco, Platte City/dsl, **food:** DQ, Red Dragon Chinese, **lodging:** Comfort Inn, Travelodge, **other:** Airport RV Park, Cash Saver Foods, CountryMart Foods, Dodge, CarQuest, USPO, same as 18
18	MO 92, Platte City, **E** Basswood RV Park (5mi), **W gas:** Casey's, Conoco/KFC, QT/dsl, **food:** Arby's, Burger King, McDonald's, Mr GoodCents Subs, Pizza Shoppe, Rancho Grande Cantina, Sonic, Subway, Taco Bell/Pizza Hut, Waffle House, **lodging:** Best Western, Comfort Inn, Super 8, **other:** Chevrolet/Pontiac/GMC, CVS Drug, Goodyear/auto, Ford, same as 19
17	I-435 S, to Topeka
15	Mexico City Ave, **W lodging:** Marriott
14	I-435 E (from sb), to St Louis
13	to I-435 E, **E lodging:** Best Western, Clarion, Comfort Suites, Extended Stay America, Fairfield Inn, Holiday Inn, Microtel, Radisson, Sheraton, **W lodging:** Marriott, **other:** KCI Airport
12	NW 112th St, **E gas:** BP, Conoco/dsl, **lodging:** Day's Inn, Extended Stay America, Day's Inn, Hampton Inn, Hilton, Holiday Inn Express, Microtel, **W lodging:** Econolodge
10	Tiffany Springs Pkwy, **E gas:** Phillips 66, Shell, **food:** Jade Garden, SmokeBox BBQ, **lodging:** Embassy Suites, Homewood Suites, **W food:** Cracker Barrel, Ruby Tuesday, Waffle House, Wendy's, **lodging:** AmeriSuites, Chase Suites, Courtyard, Drury Inn, Homeswood Suites, Howard Johnson, MainStay Suites, Ramada Inn, Residence Inn, Sleep Inn, **other:** Honda, Lexus, Nissan, Toyota, Volvo
9b a	MO 152, to Liberty, Topeka
8	MO 9, rd T, NW Barry Rd, **E gas:** Valero/dsl, **food:** Applebee's, Boston Mkt, Chili's, Chipotle Mexican, 54th St Grill, Hong's Buffet, Hooters, Kato Japanese, LoneStar Steaks, On the Border, Panda Express, Panera Bread, Pizza Hut/Taco Bell, Starbucks, Subway, Wendy's, Winstead's Rest., **other:** H, HyVee Foods, Lowe's Whse, Old Navy, SteinMart, Walmart SuperCtr/24hr, **W gas:** Phillips 66, QT/dsl, Shell, **food:** Abuelo's Mexican, Hardee's, LJ Silver/A&W, McDonald's, Mimi's Cafe, Minsky's Pizza, Outback Steaks, Rainbow Oriental, Smokehouse BBQ, Sonic, Taco Bueno, **lodging:** Motel 6, Quality Inn, Super 8, **other:** Barnes&Noble, CVS Drug, Tires+
6	NW 72nd St, Platte Woods, **E gas:** Sinclair/dsl, **W gas:** Phillips 66, **food:** KFC, Papa John's, Tasty Thai, **other:** Sears Grand
5	MO 45 N, NW 64th St, **W gas:** Shell/dsl, **food:** Goodcents Subs, IHOP, KFC, McDonald's, Nick & Jake's, O'Quigley's Grill, Papa Murphy's, Quizno's, Subway, Thai Place, **other:** CVS Drug, $General, GNC, Goodyear, Radio Shack
4	NW 56th St (from nb), **W gas:** Phillips 66, same as 5
3c	rd A (from sb), Riverside, **W gas:** QT, **food:** Argosy Café, Corner Café, MeanGreen's Cafe, Sonic, **lodging:** Skyline Inn, Super 8, **other:** USPO
3b	I-635 S
3a	Waukomis Dr, rd AA (from nb)
2b	US 169 S (from sb), to KC
2a	US 169 N (from nb), to Smithville
1e	US 69, Vivion Rd, **E gas:** Shell/dsl, **food:** McDonald's, Steak'n Shake, **other:** Chrysler/Jeep, Chevrolet/Cadillac, Home Depot, Lincoln/Mercury, Mitsubishi, PriceChopper Foods/24hr, **W gas:** Shell, **food:** McDonald's, Subway
1d	MO 283 S, Oak Tfwy (from sb), **W gas:** Phillips 66, **food:** McDonald's

ST JOSEPH

PLATTE CITY

KANSAS CITY

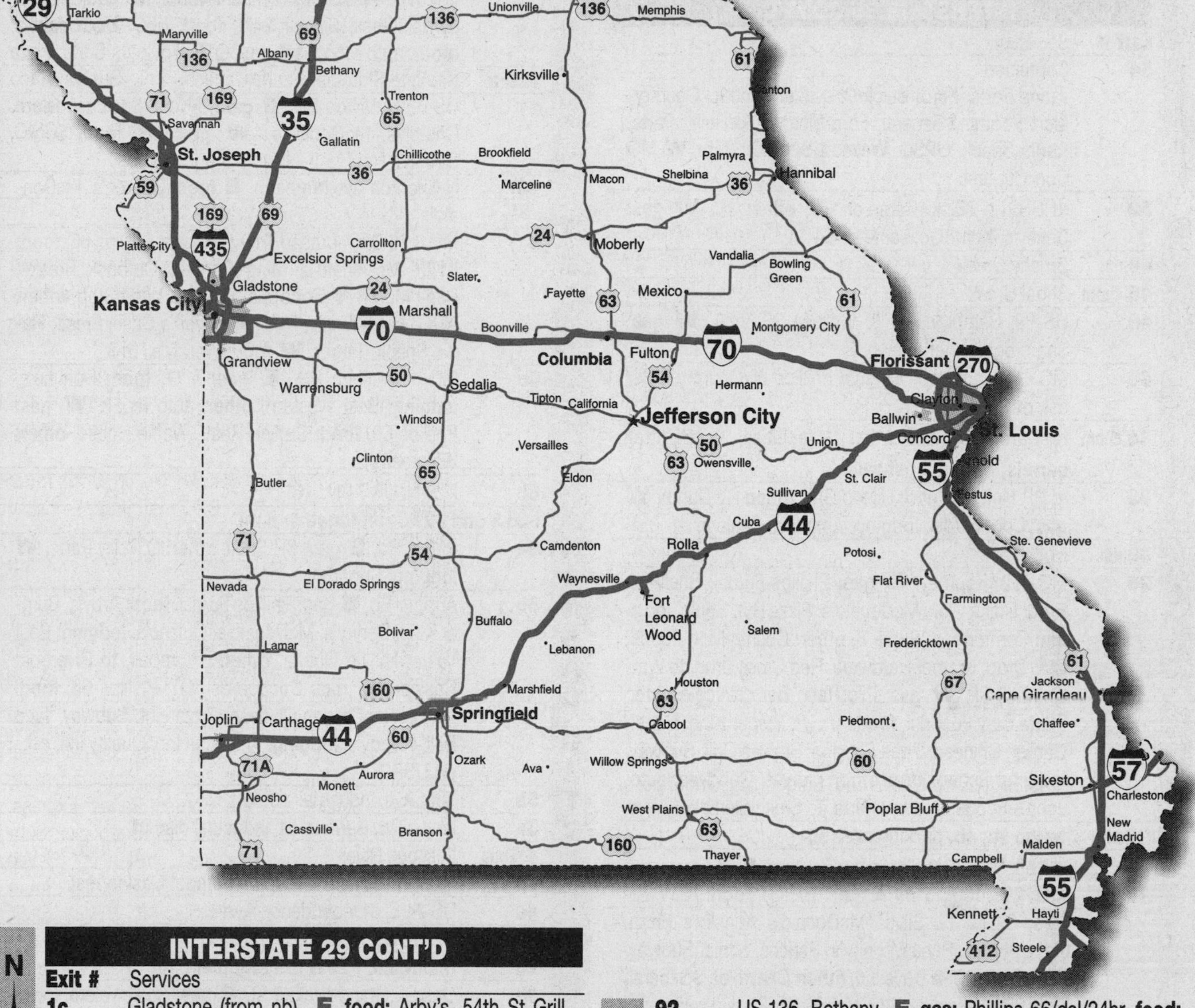

N ↕ S

INTERSTATE 29 CONT'D

Exit #	Services
1c	Gladstone (from nb), **E food:** Arby's, 54th St Grill, Perkins, Pizza St Buffet, Ryan's, Smokehouse BBQ, Tippen's Café
1b	I-35 N (from sb), to Des Moines
1a	Davidson Rd
8mm	**I-35 N. I-29 and I-35 run together 6 mi. See Missouri Interstate 35, exits 3-8a.**

N ↕ S

INTERSTATE 35

Exit #	Services
114mm	Missouri/Iowa state line
114	US 69, to Lamoni, **W gas:** Conoco/dsl/24hr, **other:** RV camping
113.5mm	Zadie Creek
112mm	**MO welcome ctr sb, full ♿ facilities, ☎, 🛈, litter barrels, petwalk, wireless internet**
110	**weigh sta both lanes**
106	rd N, Blythedale, **E gas:** Conoco/fireworks, Phillips 66/dsl/café/motel/24hr/@, **food:** DinnerBell Rest., **lodging:** Eagle's Landing Motel, **other:** dsl repair, **W gas:** Phillips 66/dsl/24hr, **other:** Eagle Ridge RV Park (2mi)
99	rd A, to Ridgeway, **5 mi W** Eagle RV Camping
94mm	E Fork Big Creek
93	US 69, Bethany, **W food:** Big Boys BBQ (1mi), Dos Chiquitas Mexican
92	US 136, Bethany, **E gas:** Phillips 66/dsl/24hr, **food:** KFC/Taco Bell, McDonald's, **lodging:** Budget Inn, **W gas:** BP/dsl, Kum&Go/Wendy's/dsl, MFA, **food:** Breadeaux Pizza, Country Kitchen, DQ, Nopal Mexican, Sonic, Subway, Taco Bell, TootToot Rest., **lodging:** Comfort Inn, Super 8, **other:** [H], Russell Stover, Walmart SuperCtr
90mm	Pole Cat Creek
88	MO 13, to Bethany, Gallatin
84	rds AA, H, to Gilman City, **E** Crowder SP (24mi)
81mm	**rest area both lanes, full ♿ facilities**
80	rds B, N, to Coffey
78	rd C, Pattonsburg, **W gas:** Phillips 66/dsl
74.5mm	Grand River
72	rd DD
68	US 69, to Pattonsburg
64	MO 6, to Maysville, Gallatin
61	US 69, Winston, Gallatin, **E gas:** Shell/dsl/rest./24hr
54	US 36, Cameron, **E gas:** Shell/Wendy's/dsl/24hr, Sinclair/dsl/scales, **food:** McDonald's, Subway, **lodging:** Best Western, Budget Inn, Comfort Inn, **other:** Crossroads RV Park, **W gas:** Valero, **food:** Burger King, Domino's, DQ, El Maguey Mexican, Ma&Pa's Kettle Rest, KFC/Taco Bell, Pizza Hut, Sonic, **lodging:** Days Inn, Econolodge, Relax Inn, Super 8, **other:** [H], Ad

BETHANY

CAMERON

MO

N ↕ S

INTERSTATE 35 CONT'D

Exit #	Services
54	Continued vance Parts, Ford, Buick/Chevrolet/Pontiac, CountryMart Foods, $General, Ford/Mercury, O'Reilly Parts, Radio Shack, UPSO, Walmart SuperCtr/24hr, **W** MO Corr Ctr, tires
52	rd BB, Lp 35, to Cameron, **E other:** [H], **W gas:** Casey's, Kum&Go, same as 54
49mm	Brushy Creek
48.5mm	Shoal Creek
48	US 69, Cameron, **E** to Wallace SP (2mi), **W gas:** Shamrock, **other:** fireworks
40	MO 116, Lathrop, **E gas:** Phillips 66/Country Café/dsl, **other:** antiques
34.5mm	**rest area both lanes, full [handicap] facilities, [phone], [picnic], litter barrels, vending, petwalk**
33	rd PP, Holt, **E food:** Hilltop Grill, **other:** RV Dump, **W gas:** Conoco/dsl, **lodging:** American Eagle Inn
30mm	Holt Creek
26	MO 92, Kearney, **E gas:** Phillips 66/dsl, Shell/dsl, **food:** China Wok, McDonald's, Pizza Hut, Sonic, **lodging:** Comfort Inn, Super 8, **other:** CountryMart Foods, CVS Drug, Kramer Hardware, Red Cross Drug, to Watkins Mill SP, **W gas:** Pilot/Taco Bell/dsl/scales/24hr, Platte Clay Fuel/dsl, **food:** Arby's, Burger King, Hunan Garden Chinese, Pizza Shoppe, Stables Grill, Subway, **lodging:** Econolodge, **other:** Curves, Goodyear/auto, John's Foods, O'Reilly Parts, to Smithville Lake
22mm	**weigh sta nb, parking area sb**
20	US 69, MO 33, to Excelsior Springs, **E** [H]
17	MO 291, rd A, **1 mi E gas:** BP, QT, **food:** A&W, Arby's, CiCi's, LJ Silver, McDonald's, Minsky's Pizza, Papa John's, Papa Murphy's, Perkins, Sonic, Subway, Taco Bell, **other:** Days Inn, **other:** Chevrolet, $General, Firestone, Lifestyle RV Ctr, O'Reilly Parts, Walgreens, same as 16, **W gas:** Phillips 66/dsl, QT, **food:** McDonald's, Sonic, Subway, **lodging:** ValuePlace Inn, **other:** KCI Airport, Price Chopper Foods
16	MO 152, Liberty, **E gas:** Phillips 66/Circle K, **food:** Baskin-Robbins, Chick-fil-A, Culver's, 5 Guys Burgers, Godfather's, Olive Garden, Pizza Hut, Planet Sub, Red Robin, Texas Roadhouse, Wendy's, **lodging:** Days Inn, Super 8, **other:** [H], Advance Parts, Chevrolet, CVS Drug, Firestone/auto, Ford, Hy-Vee Foods, Lowe's Whse, Sears Grand, Walgreens, **W gas:** Phillips 66/Circle K/dsl, **food:** Applebee's, Backyard Burger, Bob Evans, Buffalo Wild Wings, Burger King, Chili's, Cracker Barrel, 54th St Grill, Golden Corral, KFC, LongHorn Steaks, McDonald's, O'Charley's, Panera Bread, Panda Express, Quizno's, Schlotsky's, SmokeBox BBQ, Steak'n Shake, Subway, Taco Bell, Uno, Waffle House, **lodging:** Comfort Suites, Fairfield Inn, Hampton Inn, Holiday Inn Express, **other:** Aldi Foods, AT&T, Best Buy, Ford, Home Depot, JC Penney, Jiffy Lube, Kohl's, Michael's, NAPA, NTB, Office Depot, Radio Shack, Target, TJ Maxx, Walmart SuperCtr
14	US 69 (exits left from sb), Liberty Dr, to Glenaire, Pleasant Valley, **E gas:** Phillips 66, Sinclair, Shell, **other:** I-35 RV Ctr, **W gas:** QT/dsl
13	US 69 (from nb), to Pleasant Valley, **E gas:** Phillips 66/dsl, Shell, Sinclair/24hr, **food:** KFC, McDonald's, **other:** auto repair, **W gas:** QT/dsl
12b a	I-435, to St Louis
11	US 69 N, Vivion Rd, **E gas:** BP/dsl, Shell/dsl, **food:** Church's, McDonald's, **W gas:** QT, **food:** Sonic, Stroud's Rest.
10	N Brighton Ave (from nb), **E food:** Church's, McDonald's
9	MO 269 S, Chouteau Trfwy, **E gas:** Phillips 66, **food:** IHOP, McDonald's, Ming Garden, Outback Steaks, Papa Murphy's, Popeye's, Subway, Wing Stop, **other:** AT&T, Food Festival, GNC, Harrah's Casino/rest., Radio Shack, Target, **W food:** Wendy's (1mi)
8c	MO 1, Antioch Rd, **E gas:** 7-11, **food:** Domino's, **lodging:** Best Western, **other:** auto repair, **W gas:** Phillips 66, **food:** Catfish Rest., Waffle House, **other:** Walgreens
8b	I-29 N, US 71 N, KCI [airport]
I-35 S and I-29 S run together 6 mi.	
8a	Parvin Rd, **E gas:** BP, Shell, **other:** O'Reilly Parts, **W lodging:** Super Inn
6b a	Armour Rd, **E gas:** Phillips 66/dsl, **food:** Arby's, Burger King, Denny's, McDonald's, Quizno's, **lodging:** Best Value Inn, La Quinta, **other:** [H], repair, to Riverboat Casino, **W gas:** Conoco/dsl, QT, Phillips 66, **food:** DQ, Lucky Dragon Chinese, Pizza Hut, Subway, Taco Bell, Wendy's, **lodging:** American Inn, Quality Inn, **other:** USPO
5b	16th Ave, industrial district
5a	Levee Rd, Bedford St, industrial district
4.5mm	Missouri River
4b	Front St, **E** Isle of Capri Riverboat Casino/rest.
4a	US 24 E, Independence Ave
3	I-70 E, US 71 S, to St Louis
2g	**I-35 N and I-29 N run together 6 mi**
2e	Oak St, Grand-Walnut St, **E gas:** Shell, Valero, **lodging:** Marriott
2d	Main-Delaware, Wyandotte St, downtown
2a	I-70 W, to Topeka
2y	US 169, Broadway, to downtown
2w	12th St, Kemper Arena, to downtown
2v	14th St, to downtown
2u	I-70 E, to Broadway, **E food:** Denny's
1d	20th St (from sb)
1c b	27th St, SW Blvd, W Pennway (from nb), **E gas:** Phillips 66, **other:** [H]
1a	SW Trafficway (from sb)
0mm	Missouri/Kansas state line

KEARNEY · LIBERTY · KANSAS CITY

INTERSTATE 44

E ↕ W

Exit #	Services
290mm	I-44 begins/ends on I-55, exit 207 in St Louis.
290a	I-55 S, to Memphis
290c	Gravois Ave (from wb), 12th St, **S food:** McDonald's
290b	18th St (from eb), downtown
289	Jefferson Ave, St Louis, **N gas:** Phillips 66, **lodging:** Holiday Inn Express, Residence Inn, **S gas:** Conoco, **food:** Lee's Chicken, McDonald's
288	Grand Blvd, St Louis, **N gas:** BP, **lodging:** Water Tower Inn, **other:** [H], **S food:** Jack-in-the-Box, Qdoba, St Louis Bread

INTERSTATE 44 CONT'D

E ↕ W

ST LOUIS

Exit #	Services
287b a	Kingshighway, Vandeventer Ave, St Louis, **N gas:** BP, **other:** [H], Jiffy Lube, U-Haul, **S gas:** BP, **other:** Chevrolet, Walgreens, to MO Botanical Garden
286	Hampton Ave, St Louis, **N gas:** BP, Mobil, Phillips 66, Shell/Circle K, **food:** Denny's, Jack-in-the-Box, McDonald's, Steak'n Shake, Subway, Taco Bell, **S gas:** Shell/Circle K, **food:** Hardee's, **lodging:** Drury Inn, Holiday Inn, Red Roof Inn, **other:** museums, zoo
285	SW Ave (from wb, no EZ return)
284b a	Arsenal St, Jamieson St
283	Shrewsbury (from wb), some services same as 282
282	Laclede Sta Rd, Murdock Ave (from eb), St Louis, **N gas:** Phillips 66, **food:** DQ, Front Row Grill, Imo's Pizza, McDonald's, Racanelli's Pizza, Starbucks, Subway, Webster Wok Chinese, **other:** Ben Franklin Crafts, Subaru, Vet
280	Elm Ave, St Louis, **N gas:** BP/repair, **food:** Lenny's Subs, **other:** Schnuck's Food/24hr, **S gas:** BP (1mi), Circle K, **other:** Walgreens
279	(from wb), Berry Rd
278	Big Bend Rd, St Louis, **N food:** Hardee's, Sonic, **other:** [H], Sam's Club/gas, **S gas:** Mobil/dsl, QT
277b	US 67, US 61, US 50, Lindbergh Blvd, **N gas:** Shell, **food:** Arby's, Chili's, Chipotle Mexican, O'Charley's, Steak&Rice Chinese, TX Roadhouse, Uno, White Castle, **lodging:** Best Western, **other:** [H], AT&T, $Tree, Hancock Fabrics, Harley-Davidson, Hobby Lobby, Lowe's Whse, Office Depot, PetCo, Target, TJ Maxx, Verizon, Walmart SuperCtr, **S gas:** Phillips 66, Shell/Circle K, **food:** Burger King, Denny's, Fuddrucker's, Helen Fitzgerald's Grill, IHOP, Lion's Choice, Longhorn Steaks, Ruby Tuesday, Steak'n Shake, St Louis Bread, Viking Rest, **lodging:** Days Inn/rest., Hampton Inn, Holiday Inn, Quality Inn, **other:** Borders Books, Dobb's Auto/Tire, Home Depot, Marshall's, Old Navy, Petsmart, WorldMkt
277a	MO 366 E, Watson Rd, access to same as 277b S
276b a	I-270, N to Chicago, S Memphis
275	N Highway Dr (from wb), Soccer Pk Rd, **N gas:** Road Ranger/dsl/rest.
274a b	Bowles Ave, **N gas:** Road Ranger/Pilot/Subway/dsl, **S gas:** Phillips 66, QT, ZX/dsl, **food:** Bandana's BBQ, Cracker Barrel, Denny's, Jack-in-the-Box, Krispy Kreme, Mandarin Cuisine, McDonald's, Quizno's, Sonic, White Castle, **lodging:** Drury Inn, Fairfield Inn, Holiday Inn Express, Motel 6, PearTree Inn, Stratfo rd Inn, Super 8, TownePlace Inn, **other:** Goodyear
272	MO 141, Fenton, Valley Park, **N gas:** Motomart, **S gas:** Phillips 66, QT, **food:** Bob Evans, Burger King, Dickey's BBQ, Domino's, Hardee's, Imo's Pizza, Jimmy John's, McDonald's, Ruby Tuesday, Starbucks, Steak'n Shake, Subway, Taco Bell, **lodging:** Drury Inn, Hampton Inn, **other:** AT&T, Curves, Sav-A-Lot Foods
269	Antire Rd, Beaumont
266	Lewis Rd, **N other:** Rte 66 SP, golf
266mm	Meramec River
265	Williams Rd (from eb)
264	MO 109, rd W, Eureka, **N gas:** Phillips 66, **food:** Arby's, Burger King, Domino's, DQ, El Lopel Mexican, McDonald's, Pizza Hut, Ponderosa, Rich&Charlie's

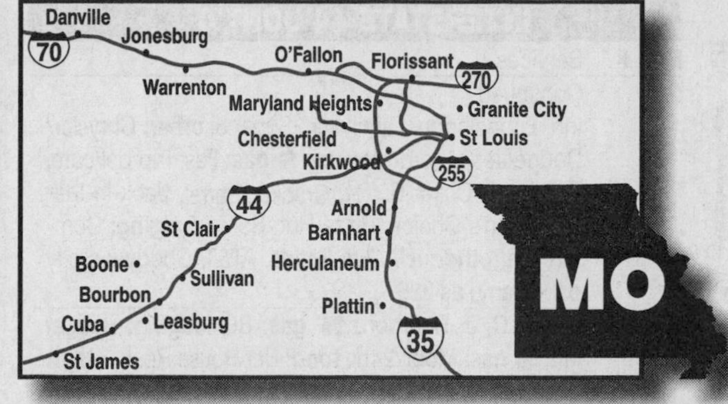

SULLIVAN

Exit #	Services
264	Continued Italian, Smokers BBQ, St Louis Bread, Subway, Taco Bell, White Castle, **lodging:** Days Inn, **other:** AT&T, AutoTire, O'Reilly Parts, Schnuck's Foods, to Babler SP, **S gas:** QT, **other:** Walgreens
261	Lp 44, to Allenton, **N gas:** Motomart/McDonald's/dsl, **food:** Applebee's, China King, Denny's, Imo's Pizza, KFC, Lion's Choice, Pizza Hut, Steak'n Shake, Taco Bell, White Castle, **lodging:** Econolodge, Holiday Inn, Super 8, **other:** AutoZone, $Tree, GNC, O'Reilly Parts, Radio Shack, Verizon, Walmart SuperCtr/24hr, to Six Flags, same as 264, **S gas:** Shell/Circle K/dsl, **other:** Ford, KOA
257	Lp 44, Pacific, **N gas:** Phillips 66, Pilot/Subway/dsl/scales/24hr, **food:** Huddle House, **lodging:** Comfort Inn, **other:** fireworks, **S gas:** BP/dsl, Mobil/dsl/24hr, Motomart/24hr, **food:** Hardee's, KFC, McDonald's, New China, Pizza Hut, Taco Bell, **lodging:** Quality Inn, **other:** Chevrolet, Chrysler/Dodge/Jeep, $General, NAPA, O'Reilly Parts, Queen's Foods
253	MO 100 E, to Gray Summit, **S gas:** Phillips 66/dsl, **lodging:** Travelodge, **other:** fireworks
251	MO 100 W, to Washington, **N gas:** BP/dsl/24hr, Mr Fuel/dsl/scales, Phillips 66/Burger King/dsl, **food:** Domino's, Subway
247	US 50 W, rd AT, rd O, to Union, **N other:** Harley-Davidson, **S** to Robertsville SP
247mm	Bourbeuse River
242	rd AH, to Hist Rte 66
240	MO 47, St Clair, **N gas:** Phillips 66/Taco Bell/dsl, **food:** Burger King, **other:** Reed RV Ctr, **S gas:** Mobil/dsl, **food:** McDonald's, Subway, **lodging:** Budget Lodge, Super 8, **other:** $General, USPO
239	MO 30, rds AB, WW, St Clair, **N** repair, **S gas:** Phillips 66/dsl
238mm	**weigh sta both lanes**
235mm	**rest area both lanes (both lanes exit left), full [handicapped] facilities, [phone], [picnic], litter barrels, vending, petwalk**
230	rds W, Stanton, **S gas:** Shell/fireworks, **other:** KOA, Meramec Caverns Camping (3mi)
226	MO 185 S, Sullivan, **N gas:** *FLYING J*/Conoco/Country Mkt/dsl/LP/scales/24hr, **S gas:** Phillips 66/Burger King, **food:** Applebee's, Arby's, Bison Grill, DQ, Hardee's, KFC, McDonald's, Steak'n Shake, Subway, Taco Bell, **other:** AutoZone, $General, Lowe's Whse, O'Reilly Parts, Walmart SuperCtr/24hr, RV Camping, to Meramec SP, same as 225
225	MO 185 N, rd D, Sullivan, **N gas:** Mobil, Phillips 66/dsl, **food:** Domino's, Dukumn Rest, **lodging:** Baymont

INTERSTATE 44 CONT'D

E ↕ W

Exit #	Services
225	Continued Inn, Econolodge, Family Inn, Super 8, **other:** Chrysler/Dodge/Jeep, Ford/Mercury, **S gas:** Fas-Trip/dsl/café, ZX, **food:** China Buffet, Cracker Barrel, Jack-in-the-Box, Lion's Choice, Pizza Hut, Sonic, **lodging:** Comfort Inn, **other:** H, Aldi Foods, AT&T, Goodyear, city park, same as 226
218	rds N, C, J, Bourbon, **N gas:** BP, **lodging:** Budget Inn, **S gas:** Mobil/24hr, **food:** HenHouse Rest., **other:** Bourban RV Ctr, Blue Sprgs Camping (6mi), Riverview Ranch Camping (8mi)
214	rd H, Leasburg, **N gas:** Mobil/dsl, **S food:** Skippy's Rest, **other:** to Onandaga Cave SP (7mi)
210	rd UU, **N other:** Meremac Valley Resort, **S food:** MO Hick BBQ (2mi), Rte 66 Roadhouse, **other:** winery
208	MO 19, Cuba, **N gas:** Phillips 66, Voss/dsl/rest./scales/24hr/@, **food:** Country Kitchen, Huddle House, Pizza Hut, **lodging:** Best Western, Super 8, **other:** Blue Beacon, **S gas:** Casey's, Delano/dsl, Mobil/24hr, **food:** Domino's, East Sun Chinese, Hardee's, Jack-in-the-Box, McDonald's, Sonic, Subway, **lodging:** Holiday Inn Express, **other:** $General, Mace Foods, O'Reilly Parts, Walmart, to Ozark Nat Scenic Riverways, Vet
203	rds F, ZZ, **N** Ladybug RV Park, **S** Rosatti Winery (2mi)
195	MO 8, MO 68, St James, Maramec Sprg Park, **N gas:** Mobil/dsl, Shell, **food:** McDonald's, Pizza Hut, Sonic, Subway, **lodging:** Days Inn, Economy Inn, **other:** Ford, NAPA, O'Reilly Parts, Ray's Tires, to Maremac Winery, **S gas:** Delano/dsl, Phillips 66/dsl, **food:** Burger King, **other:** CountryMart Foods
189	rd V, **S gas:** Loves/McDonald's/Subway/dsl/scales/24hr, **food:** Matt's Steaks
186	US 63, MO 72, Rolla, **N gas:** Sinclair, **food:** Steak'n Shake, **lodging:** Drury Inn, Hampton Inn, Sooter Inn, **other:** Big O Tire, Kia, Nissan, Lowe's Whse, Plaza Tire, **S gas:** BP, Mobil/dsl, Phillips 66, **food:** Denny's, Donut King, Lee's Chicken, **lodging:** Budget Motel, Fortune Inn, **other:** H
185	rd E, to Rolla, **S gas:** Delano, Phillips 66, **food:** Applebee's, Arby's, DQ, Hardee's, Huddle House, Kyoto Japanese, Papa John's, Subway, Taco Bell, **other:** H Ford/Lincoln/Mercury, Walgreens, UMO at Rolla, st patrol
184	US 63 S, to Rolla, **N lodging:** Comfort Suites, Holiday Inn Express, **S gas:** Delano, Gas+, MotoMart, **food:** Arby's, Burger King, Little Caesar's, LJ Silver, Lucky House Chinese, Maid-Rite, McDonald's, Pizza Hut, Pizza Inn, Shoney's, Sirloin Stockade, Waffle House, Wendy's, Zeno's Steaks, Ziggy's, **lodging:** Baymont Inn, Best Inn, Best Way Inn, Best Western, Days Inn, Econolodge, Quality Inn, Rolla Inn, Super 8, Wayfarer Inn, **other:** H, Buick/Cadillac/Chevrolet/GMC/Pontiac, Goodyear/auto, Kroger, city park
179	rds T, C, to Doolittle, Newburg, **S gas:** BP/24hr, **food:** Cookin' From Scratch Rest.
178mm	**rest area both lanes, full facilities, litter barrels, vending, petwalk**
176	Sugar Tree Rd, **N lodging:** Vernelle's Motel, **S other:** Arlington River Resort Camping (2mi)
172	rd D, Jerome, **N** camping
169	rd J
166	to Big Piney
164mm	Big Piney River
163	MO 28, to Dixon, **N gas:** Pilot/Road Ranger/Chesters/Subway/dsl/scales/24hr, **S gas:** Phillips 66/dsl, **food:** Country Café, Sweetwater BBQ, **lodging:** Best Western, Country Hearth Inn, Days Inn, **other:** RV Park
161b a	rd Y, to Ft Leonard Wood, **N gas:** Mobil/dsl, **food:** Aussie Jack's, Cracker Barrel, Domino's, Home Cookin' Diner, Kyoto Japanese, Miller's Grill, Pizza Hut, Ruby Tuesday, Ryan's, Subway, Wendy's, **lodging:** Baymont Inn, Best Value Inn, Candlewood Suites, Comfort Inn, Fairfield Inn, Hampton Inn, Mainstay Suites, Red Roof Inn, **other:** $Tree, Lowe's Whse, Scion/Toyota, Walmart SuperCtr/24hr, **S gas:** Cenex/dsl, Conoco, **food:** Arby's, China Buffet, El Sombrero, KFC, McDonald's, Mediterranean Grill, Papa John's, Subway, Taco Bell, Waffle House, **lodging:** Budget Inn, Econolodge, Holiday Inn Express, Motel 6, Ramada Inn, **other:** AutoZone, Chrysler/Dodge, $General, Family$, Ford/Lincoln/Mercury/Mazda, Goodyear/auto, NAPA, O'Reilly Parts, Radio Shack
159	Lp 44, to Waynesville, St Robert, **N gas:** Gas City/dsl, **food:** DQ, Sonic, **lodging:** Star Motel, Super 8, **other:** O'Reilly Parts, True Value, auto repair, **S gas:** BP/dsl, **food:** Pepper's Grill, **lodging:** Microtel, **other:** Big O Tire, Cadillac/GMC/Pontiac
158mm	Roubidoux Creek
156	rd H, Waynesville, **N gas:** BP, Casey's, Kum&Go/dsl, **food:** McDonald's, Subway, **other:** Buick/Chevrolet, $General, Price Cutter+, Vet
153	MO 17, to Buckhorn, **N gas:** Whitmor Farms/dsl, **lodging:** Ft Wood Inn, **S gas:** Shell/dsl, **other:** Glen Oaks RV Park
150	MO 7, rd P to Richland, **S food:** Sundown Steaks
145	MO 133, rd AB, to Richland, **N gas:** Oasis/dsl/rest./24hr, **S** camping
143mm	Gasconade River
140	rd N, to Stoutland, **S gas:** Conoco, Phillips 66
139mm	Bear Creek
135	rd F, Sleeper
130	rd MM, **N gas:** Cenex, Phillips 66, **food:** Andy's Rest, Bell Rest, **lodging:** Best Western, Budget Inn, Munger Moss Inn, **S gas:** Kum&Go, **other:** H
129	MO 5, MO 32, MO 64, to Hartville, Lebanon, **N gas:** BreakTime, Kum&Go, **food:** A&W, Applebee's, Arby's, Bamboo Garden, Burger King, Country Kitchen, DQ, KFC, LJ Silver, McDonald's, Papa John's, Shoney's, Sonic, Steak'n Shake, Subway, Taco Bell, Wendy's, Western Sizzlin, **other:** Aldi Foods, AT&T, AutoZone, Chevrolet, Ford, O'Reilly Parts, Radio Shack, Smitty's Foods, Walgreens, Walnut Bowl Factory, to Bennett Sprgs SP, **S gas:** Conoco/dsl, Phillips 66, **food:** Capt D's, Domino's, Hardee's, Pizza Hut, T's Steaks, **other:** H, $General, $Tree, FSA/Famous Brands, Goodyear, Lowe's Whse, Walmart SuperCtr/24hr, tires, Vet, to Lake of the Ozarks

CUBA ROLLA LEBANON

MO

INTERSTATE 44 CONT'D

E ↔ W

Exit #	Services
127	Lp 44, Lebanon, **N gas:** B&D/rest/dsl/scales, Sinclair/dsl, **food:** Dowd's BBQ, El Sombrero Mexican, Great Wall Chinese, Maid-Rite, Waffle House, **lodging:** Days Inn, Hampton Inn, Holiday Inn Express, Midwest Inn, Super 8, Travelers Inn, **other:** Cutlery/Walnut Bowl Outlet, Chrysler/Dodge/Jeep, tires, **S gas:** Phillips 66/dsl, **other:** Buick/Cadillac/GMC/Pontiac, Harley-Davidson, MO Cheese Outlet, Russell Stover
123	County Rd, **S other:** Happy Trails RV Ctr, KOA
118	rds C, A, Phillipsburg, **N gas:** Conoco/dsl, **S gas:** Phillips 66, **other:** antiques, tourist info
113	rds J, Y, Conway, **N gas:** Conoco/dsl, Phillips 66, **food:** Rockin Chair Café, **lodging:** Budget Inn, **other:** to Den of Metal Arts, **S gas:** Sinclair/dsl, **other:** SummerFresh Foods, USPO
111mm	**rest area both lanes, full facilities, vending, litter barrels, petwalk**
108mm	Bowen Creek
107	Sparkle Brooke Rd, Sampson Rd
106mm	Niangua River
100	MO 38, rd W, Marshfield, **N gas:** Murphy USA, Phillips 66, **food:** Subway, Tiny's Smokehouse, **other:** Big O Tires, Chevrolet, Ford, Radio Shack, Walmart SuperCtr/24hr, **S gas:** Conoco/dsl, Kum&Go/dsl, Phillips 66/dsl/24hr, **food:** DQ, El Charro, KFC/Rib Crib, La Hacienda Mexican, McDonald's, Pizza Hut, Pizza Inn, Quizno's, Sonic, Subway, Taco Bell, Ziggy's, **lodging:** Holiday Inn Express, **other:** AutoZone, $General, O'Reilly Parts, PriceCutter Foods, RV Express RV Park, Walgreens
96	rd B, Northview
89mm	**weigh sta both lanes**
88	MO 125, to Fair Grove, Strafford, **N gas:** Shell/scales, TA/CountryFried/Subway/TacoBell/dsl/scales/24hr/@, **food:** McDonald's, **other:** Camping World RV Ctr, truckwash, **S gas:** Conoco/dsl, Kum&Go, **food:** Fox's Pizza, **lodging:** Super 8, **other:** $Station, Strafford RV Park
84	MO 744, **S** Peterbilt
82b a	US 65, to Branson, Fedalia, **S gas:** Kum&Go, Phillips 66/dsl, **food:** Waffle House, **lodging:** American Inn, **other:** st patrol, to Table Rock Lake, Bull Shoals Lake
80b a	rd H to Pleasant Hope, Springfield, **N gas:** Conoco/dsl/rest./24hr, **food:** Waffle House, **lodging:** Budget Lodge, Days Inn, Super 8, **other:** to SWSU, **S gas:** Conoco/dsl, Kum&Go, Phillips 66/dsl, QT, Shell, Sinclair, **food:** Andy's Custard, Applebee's, Backyard Burger, Bob Evans, Braum's, Brueadeaux Pizza, Buckingham Smokehouse, Burger King, Chicago Gyros, Costa Mesa Mexican, Cracker Barrel, El Maguey Mexican, Fazoli's, Hardee's, Hong Kong Garden, Houlihan's, Jade East Chinese, Kyoto Japanese, Krispy Kreme, Little Tokyo, LJ Silver, McDonald's, Papa Murphy's, Pizza Hut, Rib Crib, Ruby Tuesday, Ryan's, Schlotzsky's, Shoney's, Sonic, Steak'n Shake, Subway, Taco Bell, Western Sizzlin, Ziggy's Cafe, **lodging:** Best Value Inn, Best Western, Budget Inn, Candlewood Suites, Comfort Inn, Dogwood Park Inn, Doubletree Hotel, Drury Inn, Eagles Lodge, Econolodge, Economy Inn, Flagship Motel, Hampton Inn, Holiday Inn

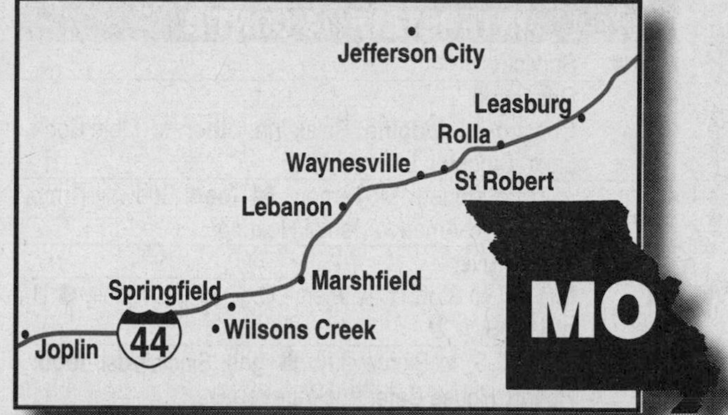

Exit #	Services
80b a	Continued Lamplighter Hotel, La Quinta, Motel 6, Ozark Inn, Plaza Inn, Quality Inn, Ramada, Rancho Motel, **other:** H, Aldi Foods, AutoZone, $General, Goodyear/auto, K-Mart, O'Reilly Parts, PriceCutter Foods, U-Haul, Walmart/auto, Vet
77	MO 13, KS Expswy, **N gas:** Kum&Go/dsl/e-85, **other:** Lowe's Whse, **S gas:** Gas+, Phillips 66/dsl, QT, **food:** Buffalo Wild Wings, Braum's, CiCi's, Golden Corral, IHOP,Jimmy John's, McAlister's Deli, McDonald's, Mr Goodcents, Panera Bread, Papa John's, Papa Murphys, Pizza Inn, Subway, Taco Bell, Waffle House, **lodging:** Econolodge, **other:** AT&T, BigLots, Dillon's Foods, $Tree, Drug Mart, GNC, Goodyear/auto, Hobby Lobby, Radio Shack, ShopKO, Staples, Walgreens, Walmart SuperCtr/24hr
75	US 160 W byp, to Willard, Stockton Lake, **S gas:** Kum&Go, **food:** Quizno's, Wendy's, **lodging:** Baymont Inn, Courtyard
72	MO 266, to Chesnut Expwy, **1-2 mi S gas:** Casey's, Cenex, Kum&Go, **food:** Alli's Rest, Arby's, Hardee's, KFC, La Hacienda Mexican, LJ Silver, McDonald's, Sonic, Subway, Taco Bell, Taco Bueno, Waffle House, **lodging:** Best Budget Inn, Ramada Ltd, Redwood Motel, **other:** AutoZone, Curves, $General, city park
70	rds MM, B, **N** antiques, fireworks, **S other:** Wilson's Creek Nat Bfd (5mi), KOA (1mi)
69	to US 60, Springfield
67	rds N, T, Bois D' Arc, to Republic, **S gas:** Shell/dsl, **lodging:** AmericInn (5mi), **other:** art glass
66mm	Pond Creek
64.6mm	Dry Branch
64.5mm	Pickerel Creek
61	rds K, PP, **N gas:** Cenex/Hoods/dsl/rest./motel/scales/24hr, Phillips 66
58	MO 96, rds O, Z, to Carthage, Halltown, **S gas:** Shell/dsl, **other:** antiques, RV/truck parts
57to	rd PP (from wb)
56.5mm	Turnback Creek
56mm	Goose Creek
52.5mm	**rest area both lanes, full facilities, litter barrels, vending, petwalk**
49	MO 174E, rd CCW, Chesapeake
46	MO 39, MO 265, Mt Vernon, Aurora, **N gas:** Casey's/dsl, Phillips 66/dsl, TA/Conoco/Country Pride/dsl/24hr/@, **food:** Bamboo Garden Chinese, KFC/LJ Silver, Mazzio's, McDonald's, Sonic, Subway, Taco Bell, **lodging:** Super 8, USA Inn, **other:** $General, Family$, Hometown Drug, O'Reilly Parts, Radio Shack, Summer Fresh Foods, True Value, **S gas:**

MO

INTERSTATE 44 CONT'D

E ↕ W

Exit #	Services
46	Continued Conoco/dsl, **lodging:** Relax Inn, **other:** to Table Rock Lake, Stockton Lake
44	rd H, to Monett, Mt Vernon, **N** **food:** Subway (1mi), **other:** Mid-America Dental/Hearing
43.5mm	Spring River
38	MO 97, to Stotts City, Pierce City, **N** gas/repair, **S** U of MO SW Ctr
33	MO 97 S, to Pierce City, **S** **gas:** Sinclair/dsl, **food:** Hungry House Cafe, truck/tire repair
29	rd U, to La Russell, Sarcoxie, **N** Ozark Village Gifts, WAC RV Park, antiques, **S** **gas:** Casey's (1mi), Conoco/rest/dsl, Kum&Go/Subway/dsl
29mm	Center Creek
26	MO 37, to Reeds, Sarcoxie, **N** Bill's Truck/trailer repair
22	rd 100 N, **N** Colaw RV Ctr
21mm	Jones Creek
18b a	US 71 N, MO 59 S, to Carthage, Neosho, **N** **other:** Big Barn Camping, Coachlight RV Ctr/Camping
15	MO 66 W, Lp 44 (from wb), Joplin, **N** **lodging:** Tara Motel
15mm	Grove Creek
14mm	Turkey Creek
11b a	US 71 S, MO 249 N, to Neosho, Ft Smith, **S** **gas:** *FLYING J*/Conoco/Country Mkt/dsl/LP/scales/24hr, Phillips 66, Speedco, **other:** Blue Beacon, Kenworth
8b a	US 71, to Neosho, Joplin, **N** **gas:** Conoco, Kum&Go/dsl, Phillips 66, **food:** Applebee's, Arby's, Backyard Burger, Bella Pepper's, Bob Evans, Braum's, Burger King, Carino's Italian, Casa Montez Mexican, Cheddar's, Chick-fil-A, CiCi's, ChuckeCheese, Denny's, Domino's, Freddy's Custard, Golden Corral, Great Wall Chinese, Hardee's, IHOP, Jim Bob's Steaks, Jimmy John's, KFC, King Palace, Logan's Roadhouse, LJ Silver, Mazzio's, McAlister's, McDonald's, Noodle&Grill, Olive Garden, Outback Steaks, Pizza Hut, Pizza Inn, Quizno's, Red Hot&Blue Grill, Red Lobster, Rib Crib, Ruby Tuesday, Ryan's, Schlotzky's, Sonic, Starbucks, Steak'n Shake, Subway, Taco Bell, Taco Hut, Waffle House, Wendy's, Whiskey Creek Steaks, **lodging:** Baymont Inn, Best Western, Candlewood Suites, Comfort Inn, Days Inn, Drury Inn, Fairfield Inn, Halmark Inn, Hampton Inn, Hilton Garden, Holiday Inn, La Quinta, Motel 6, Quality Inn, Residence Inn, Rodesite Inn, Super 8, **other:** Aldi Foods, AT&T, AutoZone, Best Buy, Books-A-Million, Chrysler/Dodge/Jeep, $Tree, Firestone, Food4Less/24hr, Ford/Lincoln/Mercury, Freightliner, Goodyear/auto, Hasting's, Hobby Lobby, Home Depot, Honda, Hyundai, JC Penney, Jo-Ann Fabrics, Kia, Kohl's, Lowe's Whse, Macy's, Michael's, Nissan, Office Depot, Old Navy, O'Reilly Parts, Petsmart, Sam's Club/gas, Scion/Toyota, Sears, Target, TJ Maxx, Verizon, Walgreens, Walmart SuperCtr/24hr, **S** **gas:** Casey's, **food:** Cracker Barrel, Fazoli's, **lodging:** Microtel, TownePlace Suites, **other:** Wheelen RV Ctr
6	MO 86, MO 43 N, to Racine, Joplin, **N** **gas:** Phillips 66, **food:** KFC (1mi), Schlotzky's (1mi), **other:** Walgreens (2mi), **S** Harley-Davidson
5.5mm	Shoal Creek
4	MO 43 to Seneca, **N** **gas:** Loves/Hardee's/dsl/24hr, **other:** Peterbilt, antiques, **S** **gas:** Conoco/Subway/dsl, Petro/Iron Skillet/dsl/scales/@, Pilot/Wendy's/dsl/scales/24hr, **food:** McDonald's, **lodging:** Sleep Inn, **other:** IA 80 Truckomat, KOA, fireworks
3mm	**weigh sta both lanes**
2mm	**Welcome Ctr eb, rest area wb, full facilities, litter barrels, , vending**
1	US 400, US 166W, to Baxter Springs, KS, **S** **other:** Sandstone Gardens
0mm	Missouri/Oklahoma state line

JOPLIN

INTERSTATE 55

N ↕ S

ST LOUIS

Exit #	Services
209mm	Missouri/Illinois state line at St. Louis, Mississippi River
209b	I-70 W to Kansas City
209a	to Arch, Busch Stadium
208	Park Ave, 7th St, **W** **gas:** BP, **food:** Rally's, Taco Bell, White Castle, **lodging:** Hilton
207c b	Truman Pkwy, **W** I-44 W, to Tulsa
207a	Gravois St (from nb), **E** **gas:** Midwest Petroleum, **W** **food:** A-1 Chinese Wok, Jack-in-the-Box
206c	Arsenal St, **E** Anheuser-Busch Tour Ctr, **W** **gas:** Shell
206b	Broadway (from nb)
206a	Potomac St (from nb)
205	Gasconade, **W** H
204	Broadway, **E** **gas:** Phillips 66/repair, **W** **gas:** Sinclair/dsl, **food:** Hardee's, McDonald's, Subway, **other:** Radio Shack, Walgreen/24hr
203	Bates St, Virginia Ave, **W** **gas:** BP, 7-11
202c	Loughborough Ave, **W** **food:** St Louis Bread Co, Starbucks, **other:** Lowe's Whse, Schnuck's Foods
202b	Germania (from sb)
202a	Carondelet (from nb)
201b	Weber Rd
201a	Bayless Ave, **E** **gas:** BP, **food:** McDonald's, **W** **gas:** Mobil, 7-11/gas, **food:** China Wok, DQ, Jack-in-the-Box, Pizza Hut/Taco Bell, Subway, Taco Bell, **other:** Walgreens, auto repair
200	Union Rd (from sb)
199	Reavis Barracks Rd, **E** **gas:** Shell, **food:** Pennie's BBQ, **other:** Hancock Fabrics
197	US 50, US 61, US 67, Lindbergh Blvd, **E** **gas:** Phillips 66, **food:** Arby's, Buffalo Wild Wings, ChuckeCheese, Dillard's, Honey Baked Ham, Hooters, KFC, Krispy Kreme, Macaroni Grill, Noodle's & Co, Qdoba Mexican, Quizno's, Station Subs, Steak'n Shake, St Louis Bread Co, Subway, Tucker's Place, **lodging:** Holiday Inn, **other:** Advance Parts, Best Buy, Border's Book, Costco/gas, Dillard's, Discount Tire, Dodge, Ford, Home Depot, JC Penney, Kia, K-Mart, Macy's, Marshall's, NTB, Sears/auto, Tuesday Morning, mall, **W** **food:** Bob Evans, Casa Gallardo's, Culvers, Denny's, Lenny's Subs, O'Charley's, Ponderosa, **lodging:** Motel 6, Oak Grove Inn, **other:** Aldi Foods, Costco/gas, Ford/Lincoln/Mercury, Honda, Hyundai, Mazda, Office Depot, Target
196b	I-270 W, to Kansas City
196a	I-255 E, to Chicago

INTERSTATE 55 CONT'D

N ↕ S

Exit #	Services
195	Butler Hill Rd, **E gas:** Phillips 66, **lodging:** Holiday Inn/rest., **other:** Advance Parts, Walgreens, **W gas:** Sinclair, **food:** Burger King, Hardee's, Pizza Hut/Taco Bell, Waffle House, **other:** Schnuck's Foods, tires/repair
193	Meramec Bottom Rd, **E gas:** Mobil, QT, **food:** Cracker Barrel, **lodging:** Best Western, **other:** Howard RV Ctr
191	MO 141, Arnold, **E gas:** QT, **food:** Applebee's, Bandana's BBQ, Cici's Pizza, Denny's, Fazoli's, 54th St Grill, Jack-in-the-Box,JimmyJohn's, LJ Silver, McDonald's/playplace, Papa John's, Pizza Hut, Steak'n Shake, Super Chinese Buffet, Taco Bell, **lodging:** Drury Inn, Ramada Ltd, **other:** Goodyear, Kohl's, Lions Choice, Napa, O'Reilly Parts, PetCo, Schnuck's Foods, Shop'n Save Foods, Walgreens, Walmart/auto, USPO, mall, **W gas:** Phillips 66/dsl, **food:** Pasta House, **other:** Dierberg's Foods, Lowe's Whse
190	Richardson Rd, **E gas:** EM/dsl, QT, Shell/dsl, **food:** Culver's, Domino's, DQ, Pizza Hut, Ponderosa, Quizno's, Roly-Poly Sandwiches, Sonic, Taco Bell, White Castle, **other:** Advance Parts, Auto Tire, Firestone, Ford, SavALot Foods, **W gas:** CFM, Phillips 66/dsl, 7-11/gas, Shell/dsl, **food:** Burger King, Happy Wok, Imo's Pizza, McDonald's/playplace, Mr. Goodcents Subs, Ruby Tuesday, Waffle House, **lodging:** Comfort Inn, **other:** Aamco, AutoZone, GNC, Home Depot, Plaza Tire, Radio Shack, Shnuck's Foods/24hr, Target, Walgreens, Vet
186	Imperial, Kimmswick, **E gas:** Mobil, Shell, **food:** Blue Owl (1mi), **other:** auto repair, **W gas:** Phillips 66/Jack-in-the-Box, **food:** Cafe Breve, China Wok, Domino's, Iggy's Mexican, O'aces Grill, Papa John's, Quizno's, Subway, **other:** USPO, to Mastodon SP
185	rd M, Barnhart, Antonia, **E gas:** EM/gas, **food:** Jenny's Kitchen, **W gas:** EM/gas, 7-11/gas, U-Gas, **other:** Walgreens, **other:** KOA
184.5mm	**weigh sta both lanes**
180	rd Z, to Hillsboro, Pevely, **E gas:** Mobil/dsl, **food:** BBQ, Burger King, Domino's, Subway, **other:** $General, Queens Foods, **W gas:** Mr Fuel, Phillips 66/McDonald's/scales/dsl, **lodging:** Super 8, **other:** KOA (2mi), auto repair
178	Herculaneum, **E gas:** QT/Wendy's/scales/dsl, Shell, **food:** Cracker Barrel, DQ, Jack-in-the-Box, **other:** Toyota/Scion, **W** Chevrolet, Ford, Pontiac/Cadillac/Buick
175	rd A, Festus, **E gas:** Mobil, Phillips 66/dsl, **food:** Arby's, Bob Evans, Burger King, Capt D's, Cici's Pizza, Fazoli's, McDonald's/playplace, Papa John's, Quizno's, Ryan's, Sonic, St. Louis Bread Co, Steak'n Shake, Subway, Taco Bell, Tanglefoot Steaks, White Castle, **lodging:** Drury Inn, Holiday Inn Express, Twin City Motel, **other:** Advance Parts, Aldi Foods, $Tree, Home Depot, Kmart, Radio Shack, Schnuck's Foods, Walgreens, Walmart SuperCtr/gas/24hr, **W gas:** Phillips 66/Domino's/dsl, 7-11/dsl, **food:** Hardee's, Ruby Tuesday, Waffle House, **lodging:** Comfort Inn, **other:** Dodge, Lowe's Whse

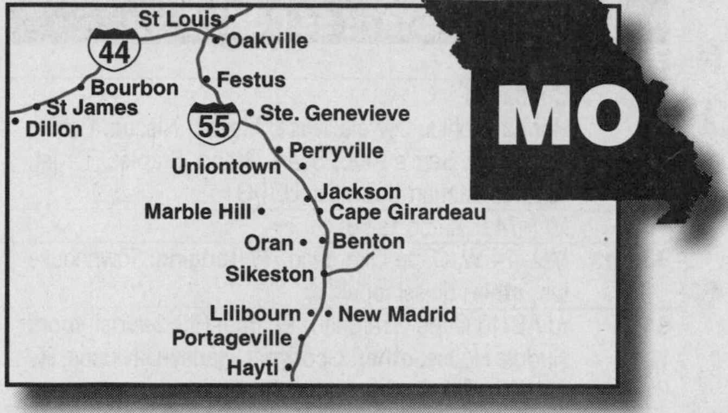

MO

PERRYVILLE

Exit #	Services
174b a	US 67, Lp 55, Festus, Crystal City, **E gas:** Phillips 66/dsl
170	US 61, **W gas:** BP/dsl/LP
162	rds DD, OO
160mm	**rest areas both lanes, full facilities, litter barrels, vending, petwalk**
157	rd Y, Bloomsdale, **E gas:** Phillips 66, **W gas:** Shell/Subway/dsl
154	rd O
150	MO 32, rds B, A, to St Genevieve, **E gas:** BP, **food:** DQ, **lodging:** Microtel (4mi), **other:** [H], Hist Site (6mi), **W gas:** Phillips 66/dsl, **other:** Hawn SP (11mi)
143	rds N, M, Ozora, **W gas:** Ozora Country Store/dsl, Shell/Subway/dsl/@, **lodging:** Budget Inn/rest.
141	rd Z, St Mary
135	rd M, Brewer, **E** propane depot
129	MO 51, to Perryville, **E gas:** MotoMart/McDonald's/dsl, Phillips 66/dsl, **food:** Burger King, KFC, Ponderosa, Taco Bell, **other:** [H], Ford, **W gas:** Rhodes/dsl, **food:** China Buffet, DQ, **lodging:** Comfort Inn, Super 8, Travelodge, **other:** Chevrolet/Pontiac/Buick, Chrysler/Dodge/Jeep, $Tree, KOA (1mi), Walmart SuperCtr/24hr
123	rd B, Biehle, **W gas:** Rhodes/dsl
119mm	Apple Creek
117	rd KK, to Appleton, **E food:** Ron's Diner
111	rd E, Oak Ridge
110mm	**rest area both lanes, full facilities, litter barrels, vending, petwalk**
105	US 61, Fruitland, **E gas:** BP/dsl, Casey's, Rhodes/dsl, **other:** Trail of Tears SP (11mi), **W gas:** D-Mart, **food:** DQ, Pizza Inn, **lodging:** Drury Inn
102	E Main St
99	US 61, MO 34, to Jackson, **E other:** Cape RV Park (1mi)
96	rd K, to Cape Girardeau, **E gas:** BP, **food:** Applebee's (1mi), Blimpie, Bob Evans, Buffalo Wild Wings, Burger King, Cedar St Cafe, Cici's Pizza, Cracker Barrel, DQ (1mi), Dexter BBQ, El Acapulco, Great Wall Chinese, Honey Baked Ham, Logan's Roadhouse, O'Charley's, Olive Garden, Panera Bread, Pizza Inn, Popeye's, Red Lobster, Ruby Tuesday, Ryan's, Starbucks, Steak'n Shake, Subway, Taco Bell, TX Roadhouse, **lodging:** Drury Lodge/rest., Holiday Inn Express, PearTree Inn, Victorian Inn, **other:** [H], Barnes&Noble, Best Buy, Big Lots, JC Penney, Macy's, Old Navy, Schnuck's Foods, mall, to SEMSU, **W gas:** Shell/24hr, **food:** McDonald's/playplace, Outback Steaks, Sonic, White Castle, **lodging:** Drury Suites, Hampton Inn, **other:** $Tree,

INTERSTATE 55 CONT'D

Exit #	Services
96	Continued Honda, Kohl's, Lowe's Whse, Mazda, Nissan, PetCo, Plaza Tire, Sam's Club, Sears Grand, Staples, Target, Toyota, Walmart SuperCtr, USPO
95	MO 74 E, same as 96
93a b	MO 74 W, Cape Girardeau, **E lodging:** Townhouse Inn, **other:** diesel repair
91	rd AB, to Cape Girardeau, **E gas:** Rhodes/dsl, **food:** Huddle House, **other:** Goodyear, Harley-Davidson, RV America, **W** Capetown RV Ctr, airport
89	US 61, rds K, M, Scott City, **E gas:** Rhodes, Store 24, **food:** Burger King, Ice Cream Corner, Las Brisas Mexican, Pizza Pro, **other:** $General, Plaza Tires, Vet
80	MO 77, Benton, **W gas:** BP/McDonald's/dsl, Express/dsl, **other:** antiques, winery (8mi)
69	rd HH, to Sikeston, Miner, **E other:** Peterbilt, **W gas:** Keller Trkstp/dsl (1mi), **other:** RV America, golf
67	US 60, US 62, Miner, **E gas:** Breaktime/dsl, Express/dsl, **lodging:** Best Western, Holiday Inn Express, Motel 6, **other:** Hinton RV Park, **0-2 mi W gas:** Cenex, Hucks, Jasper's Gas, **food:** Bo's BBQ, Burger King, China Garden, El Tapatio Mexican, Lambert's Rest., McDonald's, Pizza Hut, Pizza Inn, Ruby Tuesday, Sonic, Subway, Taco Bell, Taco John's, Wendy's, **lodging:** Comfort Inn, Country Hearth Inn, Drury Inn, PearTree Inn, Super 8, **other:** H, AutoZone, Chevrolet/Pontiac/Buick, $General, GMC/Cadillac, Family$, Food Giant, Goodyear/auto, Pennzoil, Sikeston Outlets/famo US brands, Walgreen
66b	US 60 W, to Poplar Bluff, **3 mi W on US 61/62... gas:** BP, Breaktime, Sinclair, **food:** A&W/LJ Silver, Applebee's, Arby's, China Buffet, DQ, El Bracero Mexican, Hardee's, KFC, McDonald's, Sonic, **lodging:** Day's Inn, **other:** Aldi Foods, Chrysler/Dodge/Jeep, $Tree, Ford/Lincoln/Mercury, GNC, JC Penney, Lowe's Whse, Mkt Place Foods, O'Reilly Parts, Radio Shack, Walmart SuperCtr/24hr
66a	I-57 E, to Chicago, US 60 W
59mm	St Johns Bayou
58	MO 80, Matthews, **E gas:** TA/Taco Bell/scales/dsl24hr/@, **other:** truck repair, **W gas:** *FLYING J* /Conoco/Country Pride/LP/rest./RV dump/dsl/24hr, Loves/Chester Fried/Subway/scales/dsl, **other:** truckwash
52	rd P, Kewanee, **E gas:** BP/dsl
49	US 61, US 62, New Madrid
44	US 61, US 62, Lp 55, New Madrid, **E gas:** Cenex/dsl (1mi), **other:** Relax Inn (2mi), **other:** hist site
42mm	**Welcome Ctr nb/rest area both lanes, full facilities, litter barrels, vending, petwalk**
40	rd EE, St Jude Rd, Marston, **E gas:** Pilot/Arby's/scales/dsl/24hr, **lodging:** Super 8, **W gas:** BP/dsl, **lodging:** Budget Inn
32	US 61, MO 162, Portageville, **W gas:** BP/dsl, Casey's, **food:** China King, McDonald's, **lodging:** New Orleans Inn, **other:** dsl repair
27	rds K, A, BB, to Wardell, **E other:** KOA (2mi)
19	US 412, MO 84, Hayti, **E gas:** Breaktime/dsl, Pilot/scales/dsl, **food:** McDonald's, KFC/Taco Bell, Pizza Hut, **lodging:** Comfort Inn/rest., Econolodge, **other:**
19	Continued H, KOA (6mi), **W gas:** BP/dsl, Hayti Trvl Ctr/Subway/dsl, R&P, **food:** Apple Barrel, Chubby's BBQ, Los Portales, Patty Ann's BBQ, **lodging:** Drury Inn, **other:** H, Fred's Drug, Goodyear/auto, Hay's Foods, repair
17a	I-155 E, to TN, US 412
14	rds J, H, U, to Caruthersville, Braggadocio
10mm	**weigh sta nb**
8	MO 164, Steele, **W gas:** BP/Subway/Chester Fried/scales/dsl, **lodging:** Deerfield Inn, **other:** truck repair
4	rd E, to Holland, Cooter
3mm	**rest area both lanes, full facilities, litter barrels, vending, petwalk**
1	US 61, rd O, Holland, **W gas:** Shell/dsl/24hr
0mm	Missouri/Arkansas state line

MINER · HAYTI

INTERSTATE 57

Exit #	Services
22mm	Missouri/Illinois state line, Mississippi River
18.5mm	**weigh sta both lanes**
12	US 62, MO 77, Charleston, **E gas:** Cheers/Quiznos/dsl/scales/24hr, **lodging:** Economy Motel, **W gas:** Casey's (1mi), Phillips 66/dsl, **food:** Cotton Inn Rest, **lodging:** Econolodge, **other:** Chrysler/Dodge/Jeep
10	MO 105, Charleston, **E gas:** BP/Boomland/dsl, Pilot/Subway/dsl/scales/24hr, **food:** Wally's Rest., **other:** Boomland RV Park, **W gas:** Casey's, **food:** China Buffet, DQ, McDonald's, Pizza Hut, **lodging:** Comfort Inn, **other:** Alco, CountryMart Foods, Plaza Tire
4	rd B, Bertrand
1b a	I-55, N to St Louis, S to Memphis.

I-57 begins/ends on I-55, exit 66

INTERSTATE 64

Exit #	Services
41mm	Missouri/Illinois state line, Mississippi River
40b a	Broadway St, to Stadium, to the Arch, **N lodging:** Hilton, Sheraton, stadium, **S other:** Dobb's Tire
40c	(from wb), I-44 W, I-55 S
39c	11th St (exits left), downtown
39b	14th St, downtown, **N lodging:** Sheraton, **S gas:** BP
39a	21st St, Market St (from wb), **N lodging:** Drury Inn, Hampton Inn
38d	Chestnut at 20th St, **N lodging:** Drury Inn, Hampton Inn
38c	Jefferson Ave, St Louis Union Sta, **N other:** Joplin House, **S lodging:** Residence Inn
38a	Forest Park Blvd (from wb), **N gas:** Shell
37b a	Market St, Bernard St, Grand Blvd, **N gas:** Shell, **food:** Del Taco, **lodging:** Courtyard, Hampton Inn, Hyatt, Drury Inn, Adam's Mark Hotel, Marriott
36d	Vandeventer Ave, Chouteau Ave
36b a	Kingshighway, **N other:** H, **S gas:** BP
34d c	Hampton Ave, Forest Park, **N** museums, zoo, **S gas:** BP, Mobil, Phillips 66, **food:** Courtesy Diner, Hardee's, Imo's Pizza, Jack-in-the-Box, Smokin' Al's BBQ, Steak'n Shake, Subway, Taco Bell, **lodging:** Hampton Inn
34a	Oakland Ave, **N gas:** BP, **food:** Del Taco, Subway, **other:** H
33d	McCausland Ave, **N gas:** BP, **food:** Del Taco
33c	Bellevue Ave, **N** H

ST LOUIS

INTERSTATE 64 CONT'D

E ↕ W

Exit #	Services
33b	Big Bend Blvd
32b a	Eager Rd, Hanley Rd, **S** **gas:** Shell, **food:** Lion's Choice, Macaroni Grill, McDonald's, St Louis Bread Co, Subway, **other:** Best Buy, Borders Books, Dierberg's Foods, Home Depot, Target, Whole Foods Mkt
31b a	I-170 N, **N** **gas:** Shell, **food:** Burger King, DQ, IHOP, KFC, Steak'n Shake, TGIFriday, Dillard's, **other:** mall, **S** **gas:** BP, **food:** Macaroni Grill, Subway, **other:** Borders Books, Dierberg's Foods, Goodyear, Target
30	McKnight Rd
28c	Clayton Rd (from wb)
28b a	US 67, US 61, Lindbergh Blvd, **S** **gas:** BP, **food:** Brio Grill, Fleming's Rest., Schneithouse Rest., Starbucks, **lodging:** Hilton, **other:** Honda, Shnuck's Foods, mall
27	Spoede Rd
26	rd JJ, Ballas Rd, **N** [H], **S** [H]
25	I-270, N to Chicago, S to Memphis
24	Mason Rd, **N** **lodging:** Courtyard, Marriott, **other:** LDS Temple, hwy patrol
23	Maryville Centre Dr (from wby), **N** **lodging:** Courtyard, Marriott
22	MO 141, **N** **food:** Regatta Grille, **other:** [H], **S** **food:** Pizza Hut
21	Timberlake Manor Pkwy
20	Chesterfield Pkwy (from wb), same as 19b a
19b a	MO 340, Chesterfield Pkwy, Olive Blvd, **N** **gas:** BP, Shell, **food:** Applebee's, Pizzaria Uno, Sheridan's Custard, Taco Bell, Yaya's Cafe, **lodging:** DoubleTree Hotel, Hampton Inn, Homewood Suites, Residence Inn, **other:** USPO, Dobb's Tire, Schnucks Foods, Walgreens, **S** **gas:** Mobil, **food:** Bahama Breeze Rest., Bacana Cafe, Casa Gallardo's, California Pizza Kitchen, Chili's, Houlihans, Macaroni Grill, PF Chang's, **lodging:** Drury Plaza Hotel, **other:** Borders Books, Dillard's, mall
17	Boones Crossing, Long Rd, Chesterfield Airport Rd, **1 mi** **S** **gas:** Mobil, **food:** Bob Evans, Chick-fil-A, Coldstone Creamery, Cousins Subs, East Coast Pizza, Emperor's Buffet, Fox & Hound, Golden China, Hardee's, Hometown Buffet, IHOP, IMO's Pizza, Joe's Crabshack, Kaldi's Coffe, Lion's Choice, Longhorn Steaks, Matadoe Cafe., McDonald's, Mimi's Cafe, O'Charley's, Old Country Buffet, Old Spaghetti Factory, Olive Garden, Original Pancakes, Qdoba Mexican, Quizno's, Red Lobster, Red Robin, SmokeHouse Rest., Sonic, Starbucks, Steak'n Shake, Subway, Taco Bell, **lodging:** Hampton Inn, Hilton Garden, **other:** Best Buy, Dobb's Tire, $Tree, Firestone, Ford, Home Depot, Lowe's Whse, Michael's, PetsMart, Radio Shack, Sam's Club, Target, Walmart Super Ctr/auto, WorldMkt, Vet
14	Chesterfield Airport Rd (from eb), **S** **gas:** Phillips 66, **lodging:** Comfort Inn
13mm	Missouri River
11	Research Park Ctr Dr
10	MO 94, St. Charles, **N** **gas:** Mobil, QT, Shell, **food:** Jack-in-the-Box, McDonald's, **other:** Mercedes, Busch Wildlife Area
9	rd K, O'Fallon, **N** **gas:** Mobil, QT, **food:** Cracker Barrel, Ruby Tuesday, Starbucks, **lodging:** Holiday Inn Express, Residence Inn, Staybridge Suites, **other:** Chevrolet, Honda, Volvo

MO

Exit #	Services
6	rd DD, Wing Haven Blvd, **N** **gas:** Phillips 66, **food:** Massa's Italian, Outback Steaks, Subway, **lodging:** Hilton Garden
4	rd N, **N** **gas:** PetroMart, Phillips 66, **food:** McDonald's, Qdoba Mexican, Red Robin, Steak'n Shake, St. Louis Bread Co., **other:** JC Penney, Shop'n Save, Target, **S** **gas:** Murphy USA/dsl, Phillips 66, **food:** Dragon Buffet, El Maguay, Jack-in-the-Box, McDonald's, Sonic, Starbucks, Subway, Taco Bell, Wendy's, White Castle, **other:** Aldi Foods, AutoZone, Dobb's Tire, $Tree, Firestone, GNC, Lowe's Whse, Radio Shack, Walmart SuperCtr
2	Lake St. Louis Blvd, **N** **food:** Quizno's, **other:** Old Navy, Schnuck's Foods
1	Prospect Rd, **N** **gas:** Shell
0mm	I-70 E to St Louis, W to Kansas City

INTERSTATE 70

E ↕ W

Exit #	Services
252mm	Missouri/Illinois state line, Mississippi River
251a	I-55 S, to Memphis, to I-44, to downtown/no return
250b	Memorial Dr, downtown, Stadium, **S** **gas:** Shell, **food:** McDonald's, **lodging:** Day's Inn
250a	Arch, Riverfront, **N** **other:** The Arch, **S** **lodging:** Drury Inn, Econolodge, Hampton Inn, Millineal Hotel, Renaissance, Edwa rd Jones Dome
249c	6th St (from eb)
249a	Madison St, 10th St, **N** **gas:** ZX/dsl
248b	St Louis Ave, Branch St
248a	Salisbury St, McKinley Br, **N** truck repair/24hr, **S** **gas:** BP, Phillips 66
247	Grand Ave, **N** **gas:** Phillips 66/dsl, **lodging:** Western Inn
246b	Adelaide Ave
246a	N Broadway, O'Fallon Park, **N** **gas:** Mobil/dsl, **other:** Freightliner
245b	W Florissant
245a	Shreve Ave, **S** **gas:** BP
244b	Kingshighway, **3/4 mi** **S** **food:** Burger King, McDonald's, Subway
244a	Bircher Blvd, Union Blvd
243b	(243c from eb) Bircher Blvd
243a	Riverview Blvd
243	Goodfellow Blvd, **N** **gas:** Shell
242b a	Jennings Sta Rd, **N** **gas:** Shell, **S** **lodging:** Western Inn
241b	Lucas-Hunt Rd, **N** **gas:** Shell, **3/4 mi** **S** **food:** Lee's Chicken, McDonald's
241a	Bermuda Rd, **S** **gas:** Sinclair, **other:** [H]
240b a	Florissant Rd, **N** **gas:** BP/McDonald's, **food:** DQ, Sonic, Taco Bell, **other:** Schnuck's Foods, Walgreens

MO

INTERSTATE 70 CONT'D

ST LOUIS

E ↕ W

Exit #	Services
239	N Hanley Rd, **N food:** Jack-in-the-Box, **lodging:** Hilton Garden, **S gas:** Mobil, **food:** McDonald's
238c b	I-170 N, I-170 S, no return
238a	**N** Lambert-St Louis ✈, **S lodging:** Renaissance Hotel
237	Natural Bridge Rd (from eb), **S gas:** BP, Phillips 66, Shell, **food:** Airport Diner, Arby's, Burger King, Denny's, Jack-in-the-Box, KFC, Pizza Hut, Steak'n Shake, Waffle House, Wendy's, DoubleTree, **lodging:** Best Western, Days Inn, Double Tree, Holiday Inn, Renaissance, Travelodge
236	Lambert-St Louis ✈, **S gas:** BP, **food:** BBQ, Big Boy, Coco's, Grone Cafeteria, Hardee's, Lombardo's Café Rafferty's Rest., Tiffany's Rest., **lodging:** Best Western, Day's Inn, Drury Inn/rest., Hampton Inn, Hilton Garden, Holiday Inn, Marriott, Motel 6
235c	Cypress Rd, rd B W, **N** to ✈
235b a	US 67, Lindbergh Blvd, **N gas:** Shell, **lodging:** Executive Intn'l Inn, Holiday Inn/café, Howard Johnson, **S gas:** Shell, **food:** Lion's Choice Rest., Steak'n Shake, TGIFriday, **lodging:** Congress Inn, Embassy Suites, Homestead Studios, Radisson, **other:** Chevrolet, Dillard's, Firestone, JC Penney, Sears/auto, mall
234	MO 180, St Charles Rock Rd, **N gas:** Phillips 66, Shell, **food:** Applebee's, Casa Gallardo's, Fazoli's, Hardee's, Hatfield's/McCoy's Rest., Jack-in-the-Box, LoneStar Steaks, LJ Silver, McDonald's, Old Country Buffet, Ponderosa, Quizno's, Red Lobster, Shoney's, Steak'n Shake, Taco Bell, Tony Bono's Rest., **lodging:** Economy Inn, **other:** [H], Best Buy, $Tree, GrandPa's Food/drug, Honda, K-Mart, NTB, Office Depot, Sam's Club, Target, Walgreens/24hr, **S** Isuzu
232	I-270, N to Chicago, S to Memphis
231b a	Earth City Expwy, **N gas:** Motomart, Phillips 66/Jack-in-the-Box/dsl, **food:** McDonald's, Quizno's, **lodging:** Candlewood Suites, Courtyard, Holiday Inn, Residence Inn, Studio+, **S gas:** Mobil, **food:** Burger King, Dave&Buster's, **lodging:** Holiday Inn Express, Homewood Suites, Wingate Inn, **other:** Harrah's Casino/Hotel, Riverport Ampitheatre
230mm	Missouri River
229b a	5th St, St Charles, **N gas:** BP, Mobil/dsl, **food:** Bellacino's Italian, Buffalo Wild Wings, Denny's, El Tio Pepe, Gordman's, Jack-in-the-Box, KFC, Lee's Chicken, McDonald's, Waffle House, **lodging:** Best Western, Comfort Suites, Quality Inn, **other:** Aldi Foods, Ameristar Casino, Bass Pro Shops, Walgreens/24hr, **S gas:** QT/dsl, **food:** Cracker Barrel, **lodging:** Embassy Suites, Fairfield Inn, **other:** malls
228	MO 94, to Weldon Springs, St Charles, **N gas:** Phillips 66, ZX Gas/dsl, **food:** Arby's, Chinatown Express, DQ, Imo's Pizza, Papa John's, Steak'n Shake, **other:** Advance Parts, Chevrolet, NAPA, Walgreen, Valvoline, **S gas:** QT, **food:** Chinese Express, ChuckeCheese, Fazoli's, Gingham's Rest., Grappa Grill, Outback Steaks, Pizza Hut, **lodging:** Days Inn, Intown Suites, **other:** Dobb's Tire, Vet, access to 227
227	Zumbehl Rd, **N gas:** ZX Gas, **food:** Culpepper's Grill, **lodging:** Super 8, **other:** Lowe's Whse, SavALot Foods, **S gas:** BP, Mobil, **food:** Applebee's,

ST CHARLES

Exit #	Services
227	Continued Bob Evans, Boston Mkt, Capt D's, Chevy's Mexican, Chirco's Grill, CiCi's Pizza, El Mariachi Mexican, Fazoli's, Gingham's Rest., Golden Corral, Great Wall Chinese, Hardee's, Hoho Chinese, Jack-in-the-Box, McCalister's, McDonald's, Quizno's, Subway, Taco Bell/Pizza Hut, Wiliker's Cafe, **lodging:** Days Inn, Red Roof Inn, TownePlace Suites, Travelodge, **other:** Big-Lots, Dierberg's Foods/24hr, $Tree, GNC, Jiffy Lube, Michael's, NTB, PetsMart, Radio Shack, Sam's Club/gas, Schnuck's Foods/24hr, Walmart/auto, Walgreens, Vet, access to 228
225	Truman Rd, to Cave Springs, **N gas:** BP, Casey's, Shell, ZX Gas, **lodging:** Hampton Inn, Motel 6, **other:** Buick/Pontiac, Cadillac, Kenworth, Mazda, Subaru, U-Haul, **S gas:** Conoco, Mobil, QT, **food:** Bandanas BBQ, Big Boy, Burger King, China Wok, Culver's, DQ, Denny's, El Tio Pepe, Hooters, IHOP, Jack-in-the-Box, Longhorn Steaks, Lion's Choice Rest., LJ Silver, McDonald's, O'Charley's, Pasta House, Pizza Hut, Pizza St, Ponderosa, Red Lobster, Steak'n Shake, Subway, Taco Bell, Thai Kitchen, White Castle, **lodging:** Holiday Inn Select, **other:** [H], Batteries+, Dodge, Firestone, Home Depot, Kia, Office Depot, Shop'n Save, Target, TJ Maxx
224	MO 370 E
222	Mid-Rivers Mall Dr, rd C, St Peters, **N gas:** QT/dsl/24hr, **food:** Burger King, **other:** Chevrolet, Honda, Lincoln/Mercury, Mitsubishi, Toyota/Scion, **S gas:** Mobil, ZX Gas/dsl, **food:** Arby's, Bob Evans, Chili's, China Wok, Domino's, Honeybaked Ham, Jack-in-the-Box, Joe's Crabshack, Macaroni Grill, Max & Erma's, McDonald's/playplace, Olive Garden, Pizza Hut/Taco Bell, Red Robin, Ruby Tuesday, Steak'n Shake, Subway, Wendy's, **lodging:** Drury Inn, Extended Stay America, **other:** Aldi Foods, AutoZone, Barnes&Noble, Best Buy, Big Lots, Borders Books, Costco/gas, Dillard's, Discount Tire, Hancock Fabrics, Hyundai/Nissan/VW, JC Penney, Marshall's, NTB, Sears/auto
220	MO 79, to Elsberry, **N** Cherokee Lakes Camping (7mi), hardware, **S gas:** BP, Phillips 66/dsl, 7-11/gas, **food:** Hardee's, Jack-in-the-Box, McDonald's/playplace, Quizno's, Sonic, Subway, **other:** Ramada Ltd, **other:** Curves, Dierberg's Foods/drug, O'Reilly Parts, Walgreens
219	Tru's Rd, **S gas:** QT, **lodging:** Comfort Inn
217	rds K, M, O'Fallon, **N gas:** BP, **food:** Burger King, Burger King, Jack-in-the-Box, Rally's, Piggy's BBQ, Pizza Hut/Taco Bell, Sonic, Waffle House, **other:** Firestone, Jiffy Lube, Radio Shack, **S gas:** Phillips 66/dsl, QT, ZX Gas, **food:** Applebee's, Arby's, Bob Evans, Chick-fil-A, Domino's, Fazoli's, IHOP, KFC, Krieger's Grill, Lion's Choice Rest., McDonald's/playplace, Pantera's Pizza, Papa John's, Pizza Hut, Red Robin, Stefanina's Pizza, Subway, **other:** Advance Parts, Aldi Foods, Auto Tire, AutoZone, GNC, Home Depot, K-Mart/drugs, Lowe's Whse, Schnuck's Foods, Shop'n Save Foods, TrueValue, Walgreens, Walmart, camping
216	Bryan Rd, **N lodging:** Super 8, **other:** CarQuest, Ford, Peterbilt, **S gas:** Conoco, Phillips 66/Jack-in-the-Box/dsl, QT, **food:** DQ, Cappuccino's, Mr. Goodcents

O' FALLON

E ↕ W

INTERSTATE 70 CONT'D

Exit #	Services
214	Lake St Louis, **N gas:** Q-Stop, **S gas:** Phillips 66/dsl, Shell, **food:** Denny's, El Maguey Mexican, Hardee's, Subway, **lodging:** Day's Inn, **other:** H, Wharf Drug
212	rd A, **N lodging:** Economy Inn, Relax Inn, **other:** Freedom RV Ctr, **S gas:** Mobil, **food:** Burger King, Imo's Pizza, **lodging:** Holiday Inn, **other:** Chrysler/Dodge/Jeep
210b a	US 61, US 40, to I-64 E, **S gas:** Phillips 66/dsl, Shell, **other:** H
209	rd Z, Church St, New Melle, **N food:** DQ, **S gas:** Phillips 66/dsl
208	Pearce Blvd, Wentzville Pkwy, Wentzville, **N gas:** Mobile, QT/dsl, Shell, **food:** Applebee's, Arby's, Bob Evans, Buffalo Wild Wings, Culvers, Domino's, 54th St Grill, El Maguey Mexican, Fritz's Custard, Hardee's, Imo's Pizza, Jack-in-the-Box,JimmyJohn's, KFC, Lion's Choice, McDonald's, Mr Goodcents, Papa John's, Penn Station, Pizza Hut, Pizza Pro, Qdoba, Queen Buffet, Ruby Tuesday, Starbucks, Steak'n Shake/24hr, St Louis Bread, Subway, Taco Bell, Waffle House, White Castle, **other:** H, AutoZone, Best Buy, Buick/Chevrolet, Curves, Dierberg's Foods, Dobb's Tire, $General, Family$, Home Depot, Kohl's, Lowe's Whse, Michael's, O'Reilly Parts, Petsmart, Radio Shack, Save-A-Lot Foods, Schnuck's Food, Target, Walgreens, Walmart SuperCtr/auto/24hr, Vet, **S gas:** BP, **food:** Bandana's BBQ, **lodging:** Super 8, **other:** Thomas RV Ctr
204mm	**weigh sta both lanes**
203	rds W, T, Foristell, **N gas:** TA/BP/Pizza Hut/Popeye's/Taco Bell/dsl/scales/24hr/@, Mr Fuel/dsl/scales, **lodging:** Best Western, **other:** Freightliner, **S gas:** Phillips 66/McDonald's/dsl, **other:** dsl repair
200	rds J, H, F (from wb), Wright City, **N gas:** Midwest/dsl, **food:** Ruiz Castillo's Mexican (1mi), **S gas:** Phillips 66, **food:** New China, **lodging:** Super 7 Inn
199	**N gas:** Shell/McDonald's/dsl, **other:** $General, **S lodging:** Super 7 Inn, **other:** Volvo Trucks
198mm	**rest area both lanes, full facilities, litter barrels, petwalk**
193	MO 47, Warrenton, **N gas:** Phillips 66/dsl, ZX Gas/dsl, **food:** Applebee's, Burger King, China House, Dominos, Jack-in-the-Box, Los Cantaritos Mexican, McDonald's, Pizza Hut, Subway, Waffle House, **lodging:** Days Inn, Holiday Inn Express, Super 8, **other:** Curves, Family$, Mosers Foods, Radio Shack, Walmart SuperCtr/24hr, **S gas:** BP, Conoco/dsl, Phillips 66/dsl, **food:** Denny's, Hardee's, KFC, Mkt St Grill, Taco Bell, **lodging:** Comfort Inn, **other:** Aamco, AutoZone, CarQuest, Chevrolet/Pontiac, Chrysler/Dodge/Jeep, Ford, GNC, Goodyear/auto, NAPA, Walgreens, Warrenton Outlets/famous brands
188	rds A, B, to Truxton, **S gas:** *FLYING J*/Conoco/Cookery/dsl/LP/RV Dump/scales/24hr, **lodging:** Budget Inn
183	rds E, NN, Y, Jonesburg, **1 mi N** Jonesburg Gardens Camping, **S gas:** Phillips 66/dsl, Shell/dsl, **other:** USPO
179	rd F, High Hill, **S lodging:** Budget Motel, Colonial Inn
175	MO 19, New Florence, **N gas:** BP/Hardee's/dsl, Shell/dsl/24hr, **food:** Maggie's Café, McDonald's, **lodging:**

WENTZVILLE

WARRENTON

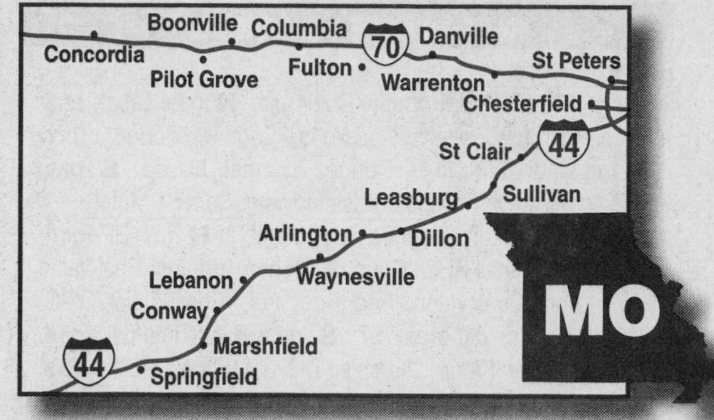

Exit #	Services
175	Continued Best Inn, Clark Plaza Hotel, Days Inn, **other:** Stone Hill Winery/gifts (15mi), auto repair
170	MO 161, rd J, Danville, **N gas:** Sinclair/dsl, **other:** to Graham Cave SP, Kan-Do RV Park, **S** Lazy Day RV Park
169.5mm	**rest area wb, full facilities, vending, litter barrels, petwalk**
168mm	Loutre River
167mm	**rest area eb, full facilities, vending, litter barrels, petwalk**
161	rds D, YY, Williamsburg, **N gas:** Cranes/mkt, **food:** Marlene's Rest, **other:** USPO, **S gas:** Conoco/dsl/24hr
155	rds A, Z, to Calwood, **N** antiques
148	US 54, Kingdom City, **N gas:** BP/dsl, Phillips 66/dsl, **food:** Taco Bell, **other:** MO Tourism Ctr, to Mark Twain Lake, **S gas:** Conoco/Subway/scales/dsl, Petro/Mobil/Iron Skillet/dsl/scales/24hr/@, Phillips 66/dsl, Shell/Gasper's/Arby's/dsl/scales/@, **food:** Denny's, McDonald's, **lodging:** Comfort Inn, Days Inn, Motel 6, Super 8, **other:** Wheeler's Truckwash
144	rds M, HH, to Hatton, **S other:** fireworks
137	rds DD, J, to Millersburg, Stephens, **S** Freightliner, antiques, to Little Dixie WA (4mi)
133	rd Z, to Centralia, **N other:** Loveall's RV
131	Lake of the Woods Rd, **N gas:** BP, Phillips 66/Subway/dsl, **food:** Georgia Salad Bar, Sonic, **lodging:** Super 8, **other:** Harley-Davidson, **S gas:** Conoco/dsl/24hr
128a	US 63, to Jefferson City, Columbia, **N gas:** BP, QT, **food:** Bob Evans, Burger King, China Garden, Cracker Barrel, Golden Corral, Hooters, KFC, Lee's Chicken, Lonestar Steaks, McDonald's/playplace, Pizza Hut, Quizno's, Ruby Tuesday, Steak'n Shake, Taco Bell, Waffle House, Wendy's, **lodging:** Comfort Inn, Fairfield Inn, Hampton Inn, Hilton Garden, Residence Inn, Super 8, **other:** Bass Pro Shop, Cottonwood's RV Park, Home Depot, Menard's, **S gas:** BreakTime/dsl, **food:** Applebees, Chili's, Chipotle Mexican, CiCi's, Culvers, Houlihan's, IHOP, Kobe Japanese, Longhorn Steaks, Sonic, Starbucks, Subway, TGI Friday, **lodging:** Best Western, Candlewood Suites, Country Inn&Suites, Holiday Inn Express, Motel 6, Ramada, Staybridge Suites, Wingate Inn, **other:** H, $Tree, Lowe's Whse, Patricia's Foods, Sam's Club, Staples, Walmart SuperCtr/24hr
128	Lp 70 (from wb), Columbia, **N food:** Hardee's, **lodging:** Super 7, **S food:** Capt D's, **lodging:** Eastwood Motel, **other:** H, Big O Tire, same as 128a

COLUMBIA

MO

INTERSTATE 70 CONT'D

E ↕ W

COLUMBIA

Exit #	Services
127	MO 763, to Moberly, Columbia, **N gas:** BreakTime/dsl, **food:** Waffle House, **lodging:** Travelodge, **other:** Cadillac/Pontiac, Dodge, Hyundai, Mazda, **S gas:** Midwest, Phillips 66/dsl, **lodging:** Super 7 Motel
126	MO 163, Providence Rd, Columbia, **N gas:** BP, **food:** Bandanas BBQ, Country Kitchen, **lodging:** Best Value Inn, Quality Inn, Red Roof Inn, **other:** Buick/GMC, Honda, same as 127, **S gas:** BreakTime/dsl, **food:** Burger King, Church's, DQ, LJ Silver, McDonald's, Pizza Hut, Sonic, Subway, Taco Bell, **other:** H, Aldi Foods, AutoZone, Chevrolet, Nissan, O'Reilly Parts
125	Lp 70, West Blvd, Columbia, **N lodging:** Comfort Suites, **S gas:** Phillips 66/dsl, Shell/dsl, **food:** Chevy's Mexican, Domino's, Fazoli's, JJ's Cafe, Kabuki Japanese, Olive Garden, Outback Steaks, **lodging:** Econolodge, **other:** Advance Parts, BMW, Chrysler/Jeep, Firestone/auto, Kia, Mosers Foods, Subaru, U-Haul, same as 124
124	MO 740, rd E, Stadium Blvd, Columbia, **N lodging:** Extended Stay America, **S gas:** BreakTime, Phillips 66, **food:** Applebee's, ChuckeCheese, Hardee's, KFC, Macaroni Grill, Panera Bread, Pizza Hut, Red Lobster, Ruby Tuesday, Steak'n Shake, Subway, Taco Bell, Wendy's, **lodging:** Days Inn, Drury Inn, Holiday Inn Select/rest., La Quinta, Motel 6, **other:** Barnes&Noble, Best Buy, Dillard's, Ford, Hobby Lobby, JC Penney, Macy's, Michael's, Old Navy, PetCo, Radio Shack, Sears/auto, Target, mall, to U of MO, Vet, same as 125
122mm	Perche Creek
121	US 40, rd UU, Midway, **N gas:** Conoco/dsl/rest., Phillips 66, **lodging:** Budget Inn, **other:** Goodyear, antiques, **S** golf
117	rds J, O, to Huntsdale
115	rd BB N, Rocheport, **N** to Katy Tr SP
114.5mm	Missouri River
111	MO 98, MO 179, to Wooldridge, Overton, **S gas:** Phillips 66/dsl/repair
106	MO 87, Bingham Rd, to Boonville, **N gas:** Cenex/dsl, **S gas:** BP
104mm	**rest area both lanes, full ♿ facilities, ☎, picnic, litter barrels, vending, petwalk**
103	rd B, Main St, Boonville, **N gas:** Breaktime, Phillips 66/dsl, **food:** Breadeaux Pisa, Happy China, KFC/LJ Silver, La Hacienda Mexican, McDonald's, Pizza Hut, Sonic, Subway, Taco Bell, **lodging:** Days Inn, Super 8, **other:** H, Daves Mkt, $General, Radio Shack, Walmart SuperCtr, to Kay Tr SP, **S gas:** Cenex/dsl, Shell/Bobber Cafe/dsl/24hr, **lodging:** QT Inn, **other:** Bobber Lake Camping
101	US 40, MO 5, to Boonville, **N gas:** Pilot/Wendy's/dsl/24hr, **food:** Arby's, **lodging:** Comfort Inn, Holiday Inn Express, **other:** Buick/Cadillac/Chevrolet/GMC/Pontiac, Ford/Lincoln/Mercury, Russell Stover Candies, **S gas:** Love's/Hardee's/scales/dsl/24hr, **other:** Chrysler/Dodge/Jeep, to Lake of the Ozarks
98	MO 41, MO 135, Arrow Rock, **N** to Arrow Rock HS (13mi), tires, **S gas:** Conoco/Dogwood Rest./dsl, Phillips 66/dsl, **other:** repair
93mm	Lamine River

BOONVILLE

Exit #	Services
89	rd K N, to Arrow Rock, **N** to Arrow Rock HS
84	rd J, **N gas:** BP/DQ/Stuckey's, truck repair
78b a	US 65, to Marshall, **N gas:** Conoco/dsl, **other:** Lazy Days RV Park, fireworks, **S gas:** Breaktime/dsl
77mm	Blackwater River
74	rd YY, **N gas:** Shell/Betty's/dsl/repair/24hr, motel/rest
71	rds EE, K, to Houstonia
66	MO 127, Sweet Springs, **N** H, **S gas:** BreakTime/dsl, Casey's/E85, **lodging:** Super 8, **other:** NAPA
65.5mm	Davis Creek
62	rds VV, Y, Emma
58	MO 23, Concordia, **N gas:** TA/Pizza Hut/Subway/dsl/scales/24hr/@, **food:** KFC/Taco Bell, McDonald's, **other:** $General, Patricia's Foods, truck wash, **S gas:** Breaktime/dsl, Casey's, Conoco/dsl, Phillips 66 **food:** Biffle's BBQ, Hardee's, Pizza Hut, Sonic, **lodging:** Budget Inn, Days Inn, Travelodge
57.5mm	**rest area both lanes, full ♿ facilities, ☎, picnic, litter barrels, vending, petwalk**
52	rd T, Aullville
49	MO 13, to Higginsville, **N gas:** BP, Pilot/McDonald's/Subway/scales/dsl/24hr, **lodging:** Camelot Inn/rest, **other:** to Whiteman AFB, to Confederate Mem, **S lodging:** Super 8, **other:** Interstate RV Park
45	rd H, to Mayview
43mm	**weigh sta both lanes**
41	rds O, M, to Lexington, Mayview
38	MO 131 (from wb), Odessa, **S gas:** BP/dsl, Shell, Sinclair, **food:** McDonald's, Pizza Hut, Sonic, Subway, Taco John's, **other:** $General, Radio Shack, camping, same as 37
37	MO 131, Odessa, **N food:** Countryside Diner, **other:** Country Gardens RV Park/dump, **S gas:** BP/dsl, Shell, Sinclair, **food:** El Camino Real, McDonald's, Pizza Hut, Sonic, Subway, Taco John's, **lodging:** Parkside Inn, **other:** Chrysler/Dodge, Ford, O'Reilly Parts, Prime Outlets/famous brands, Patricia's Foods, fireworks, same as 38
35mm	**truck parking both lanes**
31	rds D, Z, to Bates City, Napoleon, **N other:** Bates City RV Camping, **S gas:** BP/dsl, **food:** Bates City BBQ, **other:** fireworks
29.5mm	Horse Shoe Creek
28	rd HF, Oak Grove, **N gas:** TA/Conoco/Popeye's/Pizza Hut/dsl/scales/24hr/@, **lodging:** Days Inn, **other:** Blue Beacon, Freightliner, KOA, **S gas:** QT/dsl/24hr, Petro/BP/DQ/Wendy's/scales/dsl/@, **food:** Hardee's, KFC/Taco Bell, McDonald's, Pizza Hut, PJ's Rest., Subway, Waffle House, **lodging:** Econolodge, **other:** O'Reilly Parts, Speedco Lube, Walgreens, Walmart SuperCtr/24hr
24	US 40, rds AA, BB, to Buckner, **N gas:** McShop/dsl, Phillips 66/dsl, **lodging:** Comfort Inn, Travelodge, **other:** Lifestyles RV Ctr, **S gas:** Conoco/Subway/dsl/scales/24hr, **food:** Sonic, **other:** Trailside RV Park/Ctr
21	Adams Dairy Pkwy, **N lodging:** Days Inn, **other:** Nationwide RV Ctr (1mi), Target, **S gas:** Murphy USA, Phillips 66/Burger King/dsl, **food:** Panda Exress, Panera Bread, Sonic, Taco Bell, TX Roadhouse, **lodging:** Courtyard, **other:** Home Depot, NTB, Target, Walmart Super Ctr/24hr

CONCORDIA

ODESSA

MO

INTERSTATE 70 CONT'D

E ↕ W

BLUE SPRINGS

INDEPENDENCE

Exit #	Services
20	MO 7, Blue Springs, **N gas:** Phillips 66/Circle K/dsl, Valero/dsl, **food:** Backyard Burger, Bob Evans, China One, Dos Amigo's Mexican, Harley Grill, Minsky's Pizza, Papa Murphy's, Pizza St, Quizno's, Ranch Grande, Sonic, Steamin Bean, Torero's Pizza, **lodging:** Comfort Inn, Days Inn, Econolodge, Motel 6, **other:** Ace Hardware, Curves, CVS Drug, $General, O'Reilly Parts, PriceChopper Foods, Walgreens, **S gas:** BP/dsl/24hr, QT, Shell, Valero, **food:** Applebee's, Arby's, Bua Thai, Clancy's Cafe, Denny's, Godfather's, Jin's Buffet, KFC, LJ Silver, McDonald's, Original Pizza, Starbucks, Subway, Taco Bueno, Wendy's, Winsteads Cafe, Zarda's BBQ, **lodging:** Hampton Inn, Quality Inn, **other:** H, Advance Parts, AutoZone, Chevrolet, $1 Shop, Firestone/auto, Goodyear/auto, Hobby Lobby, NAPA, Office Depot
18	Woods Chapel Rd, **N gas:** BP, **lodging:** American Inn, La Quinta, Night's Inn, Super 8, **other:** Harley-Davidson, **S gas:** Conoco/dsl, Phillips 66/dsl, QT, **food:** China Kitchen, KFC/Taco Bell, Las Playas Mexican, McDonald's, Pizza Hut, Sonic, Subway, Taco John's, Waffle House, **other:** Ford, Hyundai, Nissan, same as 20
17	Little Blue Pkwy, 39th St, **N food:** Buffalo Wild Wings, Coldstone Creamery, Hereford House, Joe's Crabshack, O'Charley's, On the Border, Sonic, **lodging:** Hilton Garden, **other:** H, World Mkt, mall entrance, **S gas:** QT, **food:** Arby's, BD Mongolian, Carrabba's, Chipotle Mexican, Corner Cafe, El Maguay Mexican, Hooters, IHOP, Kobe Steaks, Outback Steaks, Red Robin, Rib Crib, Subway, Wendy's, **lodging:** Comfort Suites, Holiday Inn Express, **other:** Carmax, Costco/gas, Lowe's Whse
16mm	Little Blue River
15b	MO 291 N, Independence, **1 exit N on 39th St...gas:** QT, Phillips 66, **food:** Applebee's, Arby's, Bob Evans, Chick-fil-A, Chili's, Denny's, 54th St Grill, Fox&Hound Smokehouse, Fazoli's, Logan's Roadhouse, Longhorn Steaks, McDonald's, Quizno's, Smokehouse BBQ, TGIFriday, Zio's Italian, **lodging:** Fairfield Inn, Residence Inn, **other:** H, Barnes&Noble, Best Buy, Dillard's, JC Penney, Jo-Ann Fabrics, Kohl's, Macy's, Marshall's, NTB, Petsmart, Sam's Club/gas, Sears/auto, Target, Walmart, mall
15a	I-470 S, MO 291 S, to Lee's Summit
14	Lee's Summit Rd, **1 mi N food:** Bob Evans, Longhorn Steaks, **S food:** Cracker Barrel, Olive Garden, Ruby Tuesday, Salty Iguana Mexican, Steak'n Shake, **other:** Bass Pro Shops, CVS Drug, Home Depot
12	Noland Rd, Independence, **N gas:** Conoco, QT, Shell, **food:** ChuckeCheese, Denny's, Domino's, Hardee's, Mr Goodcents, Pizza St, Sheridan's Custard, Sonic, **lodging:** Best Western, Super 8, **other:** Advance Parts, CVS Drug, $General, Firestone/auto, Hancock Fabrics, K-Mart, Office Depot, TrueValue, Walgreens, to Truman Library, **S gas:** Phillips 66/Circle K, **food:** Arby's, Bandana's BBQ, Burger King, Fuddrucker's, KFC/Taco Bell, Krispy Kreme, Kyoto Steaks, McDonald's, Olive Garden, Pizza Hut, Quizno's, Red Lobster, Ruby Tuesday, Wendy's, **lodging:** American Inn, Best Value Inn, Crossland Inn, Motel 6, Quality Inn, **other:** $Tree, Gordman's, Hobby Lobby, HyVee Foods/gas, Meineke, Pricechopper Foods, Savers, Tires+, U-Haul

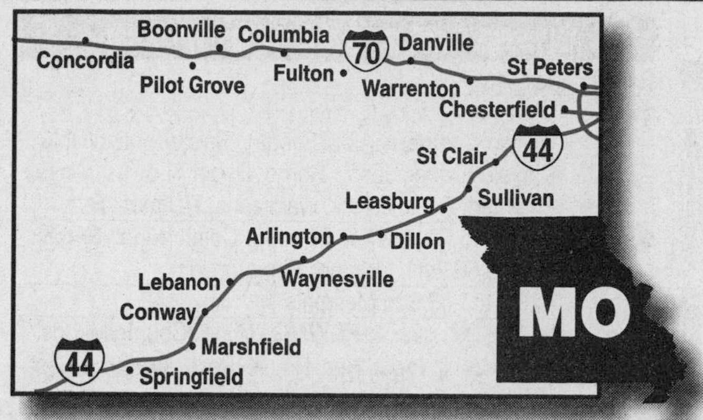

KANSAS CITY

Exit #	Services
11	US 40, Blue Ridge Blvd, Independence, **N gas:** Conoco, QT, **food:** A&W/LJ Silver, Gates BBQ, Sonic, Subway, V's Italiano, **other:** Radio Shack, **S gas:** BP, 7-11, Sinclair, **food:** Applebee's, Big Boy, Church's, East Buffet, McDonald's, Papa John's, Samurai Chef, Starbucks, Steak'n Shake, Subway, Taco Bell, **other:** Cadillac, $General, GNC, Lowe's Whse, O'Reilly Parts, Walmart SuperCtr
10	Sterling Ave (from eb), same as 11
9	Blue Ridge Cutoff, **N food:** Denny's, Wendy's, **lodging:** Drury Inn, Sheraton, Sports Stadium Motel, **other:** H, **S gas:** BP/24hr, Conoco/Subway, **food:** Taco Bell, **lodging:** Holiday Inn, **other:** Sports Complex
8b a	I-435, N to Des Moines, S to Wichita
7b	Manchester Trafficway
7mm	Blue River
7a	US 40 E, 31st St
6	Van Brunt Blvd, **N gas:** 7-11, **S gas:** BP, **food:** McDonald's, Pizza Hut, **other:** VA H, NAPA
5c	Jackson Ave (from wb)
5b	31st St (from eb)
5a	27th St (from eb)
4c	23rd Ave
4b	18th St
4a	Benton Blvd (from eb), Truman Rd, **N gas:** Super Stop/Wendy's/dsl, **other:** Advance Parts
3c	Prospect Ave, **N gas:** BP, **food:** Church's, Gates BBQ, **S food:** McDonald's
3b	Brooklyn Ave (from eb), **N food:** Gates BBQ, **S food:** Bryant's, Church's, McDonald's
3a	Paseo St, **S gas:** BP/dsl, **other:** tires
2m	US 71 S, downtown
2l	I-670, to I-35 S
2j	11th St, downtown
2g	I-29/35 N, US 71 N, to Des Moines
2h	US 24 E, downtown
2e	MO 9 N, Oak St, **S gas:** Shell, Valero, **lodging:** Marriott
2d	Main St, downtown
2c	US 169 N, Broadway, **S gas:** Shell, Valero
2b	Beardsley Rd
2a	I-35 S, to Wichita
0mm	Missouri/Kansas state line, Kansas River

INTERSTATE 270 (ST LOUIS)

N ↕ S

Exit #	Services
15b a	I-55 N to Chicago, S to St Louis. I-270 begins/ends in Illinois on I-55/I-70, exit 20.
12	IL 159, to Collinsville, **1 mi N gas:** Conoco, Phillips 66, **food:** Applebee's, China Rest., DQ, Denny's, Hardee's, Jack-in-the-Box, KFC, Papa John's, Ponderosa,

INTERSTATE 270 CONT'D (ST LOUIS)

N ↕ S

ST LOUIS

Exit #	Services
12	Continued Quizno's **other:** Aldi Foods, Buick/Pontiac/GMC, Chrysler/Dodge/Jeep, Home Depot, Lowes Whse, PetsMart, Radio Shack, Walgreens, Walmart, **S** [H]
9	IL 157, to Collinsville, **N food:** Comfort Inn, **S gas:** Phillips 66/24hr, **lodging:** Hampton Inn
7	I-255, to I-55 S to Memphis
6b a	IL 111, **N gas:** ***FLYING J***/Shell/CountryMkt/dsl/scales/24hr, **food:** Hen House Rest., **lodging:** Best Western, **other:** Blue Beacon/scales, Speedco Lube, truck/trailer repair, **S gas:** Mobil/dsl, **food:** Denny's, McDonald's/playplace, La Mexicana Rest., Taco Bell, **lodging:** Day's Inn, Holiday Inn Express, Super 8, **other:** [H], to Pontoon Beach
4	IL 203, Old Alton Rd, to Granite City
3b a	IL 3, **N** Riverboat Casino, **S gas:** Phillips 66, **food:** Hardee's, Waffle House, **lodging:** Budget Motel, Econolodge, Sun Motel, **other:** KOA, MGM Camping
2mm	Chain of Rocks Canal
0mm	Illinois/Missouri state line, Mississippi River, motorist callboxes begin eb
34	Riverview Dr, to St Louis, **N gas:** Moto Mart, **Welcome Ctr/rest area both lanes, full [handicapped] facilities, info, [picnic], litter barrels, [phone]**
33	Lilac Ave, **N** USPO, **S gas:** Phillips 66/Jack-in-the-Box/dsl, QT/dsl/scales/24hr, **food:** Hardee's
32	Bellefontaine Rd, **N gas:** Mobil, Shell, **food:** China King, McDonald's, Pizza Hut, Steak'n Shake, **lodging:** Economy Inn, Motel 6, **other:** Advance Parts, Firestone, Schnuck's Foods, **S gas:** BP/24hr, **food:** White Castle, **other:** Aldi Foods
31b a	MO 367, **N gas:** BP, QT, **food:** Jack-in-the-Box, McDonalds, Subway, **other:** [H], Chevrolet, $General, Shop'n Save Foods, U-Haul, Walgreens
30b a	Hall's Ferry Rd, rd AC, **N gas:** Mobil/dsl, Phillips 66/dsl, QT/24hr, ZX, **food:** Applebees, Capt. D's, Popeye's, Waffle House, White Castle, **lodging:** Super 8, **other:** Ford/Lincoln/Mercury, **S gas:** BP/dsl, Conoco, Phillips 66, **food:** China Wok, Church's, CiCi's Pizza, Cracker Barrel, IHOP, Steak'n Shake, Subway, **other:** AutoZone, $Buster, Family$, Home Depot, Jo-Ann Fabrics, O'Reilly Parts, Shop'n Save Foods
29	W Florissant Rd, **N food:** Jack-in-the-Box, Lion's Choice, Pasta House, **other:** Dobb's Tire/auto, $General, K-Mart, Firestone, Office Depot, **S gas:** Sinclair, **food:** Arby's, Burger King, Krispy Kreme, Malone's Grill, McDonald's, Pantera's Pizza, Sonic, **other:** Big Lots, $Tree, Mazda, NTB, Radio Shack, Sam's Club/gas, Walmart/auto, Walgreens
28	Elizabeth Ave, Washington St, **N gas:** Sinclair, **food:** Jack-in-the-Box, Jerome's Pizza, Pizza Hut/Taco Bell, Subway, **other:** Chevrolet, Schnuck's Foods/24hr, Walgreens, **S gas:** BP/24hr
27	New Florissant Rd, rd N, **N gas:** BP, Shell
26b	Graham Rd, N Hanley, **N gas:** 7-11/dsl **food:** Arby's, LJ Silver, Starbucks, **lodging:** Hampton Inn, Red Roof Inn, **other:** [H], **S food:** McDonald's, **lodging:** Day's Inn, **other:** $General, Hancock Fabrics
26a	I-170 S
25b a	US 67, Lindbergh Blvd, **N gas:** BP, Phillips 66, QT, **food:** Bandana's BBQ, Burger King, China Wok, Church's, Del Taco, IHOP, Imo's Pizza, Jack-in-the-Box, McDonald's, Outback Steaks, Papa John's, Pizza Hut/Taco Bell, Pueblo Nuevo Mexican, Quizno's, Rally's, Sonic, Starbucks, Waffle House, Wendy's, **lodging:** Comfort Inn, InTown Suites, La Quinta, Ramada Inn, **other:** AutoZone, Cadillac, Dierberg's Deli, Family$, Firestone/auto, Ford, GNC, Goodyear, NAPA, Nissan, Radio Shack, Sav-a-Lot Foods, Schnuck's Foods, Toyota, Walgreens, **S gas:** 7-11, **food:** Subway, **lodging:** Budget Inn, Econolodge, Extended Stay America, Studio+, **other:** Honda, VW, transmissions, USPO
23	McDonnell Blvd, **E food:** Denny's, Quizno's, **lodging:** La Quinta, **W gas:** BP, QT, ZX, **food:** Arby's, Jack-in-the-Box, Lion's Choice, McDonald's, Starbucks, Steak'n Shake, **other:** Buick/GMC/Pontiac
22b a	MO 370 W, to MO Bottom Rd
20c	MO 180, St Charles Rock Rd, **E gas:** BP, Phillips 66/dsl, Shell, **food:** Applebees, Casa Gallardo's, Culpepper's Grill, Hometown Buffet, Fazoli's, Jack-in-the-Box, Lonestar Steaks, McDonald's, New China, Ponderosa, Pizza Hut, Quizno's, Red Lobster, St. Louis Bread, Subway, Taco Bell, **lodging:** Economy Inn, **other:** [H] Aldi Foods, AutoZone, Best Buy, $Tree, Honda, K-Mart, Kohl's, Lowes Whse, NTB, Office Depot, PetsMart, Target, Tuesday Morning, Walgreens/24hr, **W gas:** QT, ZX, **food:** Bob Evans, Olive Garden, Waffle House, **lodging:** Econolodge, Motel 6, Red Roof Inn, Super 8
20b a	I-70, E to St Louis, W to Kansas City
17	Dorsett Rd, **E gas:** BP, QT, **food:** BBQ, Syberg's Grill, **lodging:** Best Western, Drury Inn, Hampton Inn, **W gas:** Mobil, Phillips 66, Shell, **food:** Arby's, Denny's, Fuddrucker's, McDonald's, Steak'n Shake, Subway, **lodging:** Baymont Inn
16b a	Page Ave, rd D, MO 364 W, **E gas:** BP, CFM, Citgo/7-11, QT, Sinclair, **food:** Blimpie, Copperfield's Rest., Hardee's, Hooters, Malone's Grill, McDonald's, Stazio's Café, **lodging:** Comfort Inn, Courtyard, DoubleTree, Holiday Inn, Homestead Suites, Red Roof Inn, Residence Inn, Sheraton
14	MO 340, Olive Blvd, **E gas:** BP, Mobil, **food:** Applebee's, Bristol Cafe, Denny's, Domino's, KFC, McDonald's, Lion's Choice Rest., Pasta House, Steakout, **lodging:** Courtyard, Drury Inn, **other:** [H], BMW/Land Rover/Cadillac, Borders, Chevrolet, Crysler/Jeep, Lexus, **W gas:** Schnucks, **food:** Coldstone Creamery, Culpepper's Café, House of Wong, Subway, TGI-Friday, **other:** Dierberg's Foods, Kohl's, Walgreens
13	rd AB, Ladue Rd
12b a	I-64, US 40, US 61, E to St Louis, W to Wentzville, **E** [H]
9	MO 100, Manchester Rd, **E gas:** BP, **food:** Café America, Houlihan's Rest, IHOP, Lion's Choice Rest., McDonald's, **other:** Famous Barr, Galyan's, Lord&Taylor, Nordstrom's, mall, **W gas:** Phillips 66, Shell, **food:** Applebee's, Casa Gallardo's Mexican, Olive Garden, Red Robin
8	Dougherty Ferry Rd, **S gas:** Citgo/7-11, Mobil, **food:** McDonald's, **other:** [H]

INTERSTATE 270 CONT'D (ST LOUIS)

Exit #	Services
7	Big Ben Rd, **N** H
5b a	I-44, US 50, MO 366, E to St Louis, W to Tulsa
3	MO 30, Gravois Rd, **N gas:** BP, Phillips 66, **food:** Bandana BBQ, Olive Garden, Outback Steaks, **lodging:** Days Inn, Quality Inn, **other:** Ford
2	MO 21, Tesson Ferry Rd, **N gas:** BP, **food:** El Muguey Mexican,Jimmy John's, Panda Chinese, Pizza Hut, **other:** Acura, AutoZone, Buick, Dobb's Auto, O'Reilly Parts, Scion/Toyota, Vet, **N on Lindbergh...gas:** Mobil, **food:** Burger King, Church's, 54th St Grill, Jack-in-the-Box, Olive Garden, Outback Steaks, Quizno's, Red Lobster, Subway, Taco Bell, TGIFriday's, Waffle House, White Castle, **other:** Buick/GMC/Pontiac, Honda, Schnuck's Foods, Shop'n Save, Walgreens, **S gas:** Shell/Circle K/dsl, **food:** Little Caesar's, other Dierberg's Foods
1b a	I-55 N to St Louis, S to Memphis

INTERSTATE 435 (KANSAS CITY)

Exit #	Services
83	I-35, N to KS City, S to Wichita
82	Quivira Rd, Overland Park, **N food:** Burger King, Old Chicago Pizza, Pizza Hut, Ponderosa, Taco Bell, **other:** H, CVS Drug, **S food:** McDonald's, Subway, Wendy's, **lodging:** Extended Stay America
81	US 69 S, to Ft Scott
79	US 169, Metcalf Ave., **N gas:** BP, Shell, **food:** Denny's, Dick Clark's Grill, Hooters, Tippin's Café, **lodging:** Clubhouse Inn, Embassy Suites, Hampton Inn, Red Roof Inn, Super 8, Wyndham Garden, **other:** H Chrysler/Dodge, **S food:** KC BBQ, McDonald's, **lodging:** Courtyard, Drury Inn, Marriott, PearTree Inn
77b a	Nall Ave, Roe Ave, **N gas:** BP, Shell, **food:** DQ, On-the-Border, Panera Bread, Winstead's Grill, **lodging:** Fairfield Inn, **S gas:** BP, **food:** Cactus Grill, McDonald's, Wendy's, **lodging:** AmeriSuites, Courtyard, Hilton Garden, Holiday Inn, Homestead Suites, Sheraton
75b	State Line Rd, **N gas:** BP, Conoco, **food:** Applebee's, McDonald's, Taco Bell, Waid's Rest., Wendy's, **other:** Buick/Cadillac, Ford, Goodyear, Infiniti, Lexus, Volvo, **S** H, city park
75a	Wornall Rd, **N gas:** QT, **food:** Applebees, Coach's Rest, Wendy's, **other:** Chevrolet, Honda, Toyota, VW, **S gas:** BP
74	Holmes Rd, **S gas:** Phillips 66, **food:** Burger King, Guacamole Grill, Patrikio's Mexican, Subway, **lodging:** Courtyard, Extended Stay America
73	103 rd St (from sb)
71b a	I-470, US 71 S, US 50 E
70	Bannister Rd, **E gas:** Shell, **food:** China Buffet, McDonalds, Wendy's, **other:** K-Mart, **W food:** HomeTown Buffet, KFC/Taco Bell, LJ Silver/A&W, Pizza Hut, **other:** Firestone/auto, Home Depot
698	7th St., **E food:** Subway, **lodging:** Day's Inn, Motel 6, Super 8, **other:** Suzuki, **W gas:** BP/dsl, **lodging:** Baymont Inn
67	Gregory Blvd (same as 66a b), **E gas:** Shell, **food:** Applebee's, Niece's Rest., Wendy's, **other:** Big Lots, $General, PriceChopper Foods, **W** Nature Ctr, IMAX Theatre, zoo
66a b	MO 350 E, 63rd st, **E gas:** Shell, **food:** Applebee's, Wendy's, **other:** Big Lots, $General, PriceChopper Foods, **W food:** LC's BBQ, **lodging:** Relax Inn
65	Eastwood Tfwy, **W gas:** Conoco, **food:** KFC, LC's BBQ, McDonald's, Peachtree Buffet, Pizza Hut, **lodging:** Relax Inn
63c	Raytown Rd, Stadium Dr (nb only), **E lodging:** Day's Inn, Sports Stadium Motel, Villager Lodge, **other:** Sports Complex
63b a	I-70, W to KC, E to St Louis
61	MO 78, **1 mi E** Church's Chicken
60	MO 12 E, Truman Rd, 12th St, **E gas:** BP/dsl, Shamrock, **W gas:** QT
59	US 24, Independence Ave, **E gas:** QT, **food:** Hardee's, **other:** to Truman Library, **W other:** CarQuest, Waffle House
57	Front St, **E gas:** *FLYING J*/Conoco/dsl/rest./scales/24hr, **other:** Blue Beacon, Freightliner, Kenworth, **W gas:** Phillips 66, QT, **food:** Denny's, McDonald's, Pizza Hut, Smugglers Rest, Subway, Taco Bell, Waffle House, Wendy's, **lodging:** La Quinta, Park Place Hotel
56mm	Missouri River
55b a	MO 210, **E lodging:** Ameristar Hotel/Casino, Red Roof Inn, **other:** Riverboat Casino, Ford/Volvo/GMC/Mercedes Trucks, **W food:** Arby's, Burger King, Denny's
544	8th St, Parvin Rd, **E** RV Park, **W gas:** QT, **food:** Alamo Mexican, Golden Buffet, KFC, Mama Jo's BBQ, Ponderosa, Waffle House, Wendy's, **lodging:** Comfort Inn, Crossland Suites, Day's Inn, Fairfield Inn, Hampton Inn, Holiday Inn, Super 8
52a	US 69, **E gas:** Phillips 66, Shell, Sinclair, **W gas:** Fuel Outlet, **food:** McDonald's, Pizza Hut, Subway, Taco Bell, **other:** CVS Drug, $General, Osco Drug, Sav-A-Lot Foods
52b	I-35, S to KC
51	Shoal Creek Dr
49b a	MO 152 E, to I-35 N, Liberty, **E food:** Applebee's, Bob Evans, Buffalo Wild Wings, Cracker Barrel, 54th St Grill, Longhorn Steaks, Steak'n Shake, **lodging:** Best Western, Comfort Inn, Fairfield Inn, Hampton Inn, Holiday Inn Express, Super 8
47	NE 96th St
46	NE 108th St
45	MO 291, NE Cookingham Ave, **E** to I-35 N
42	N Woodland Ave
41b a	US 169, Smithville, **N food:** Burger King, McDonald's, Sonic, **lodging:** Super 8

MO MT

INTERSTATE 435 CONT'D (KANSAS CITY)

N ↕ S

Exit #	Services
40	NW Cookingham
37	NW Skyview Ave, rd C, **N gas:** Shamrock (1mi), **S** golf (3mi)
36	to I-29 S, to KCI ✈, **N gas:** Shamrock, **S gas:** BP, **lodging:** Best Western, Clarion, Comfort Suites, Fairfield Inn, Hampton Inn, Hilton, Holiday Inn Express, Microtel, Radisson, Wyndham Garden
31mm	Prairie Creek
29	rd D, NW 120th St
24	MO 152, rd N, NW Berry Rd
22	MO 45, Weston, Parkville
20mm	Missouri/Kansas state line, Missouri River
18	KS 5 N, Wolcott Dr, **E** to Wyandotte Co Lake Park
15b a	Leavenworth Rd, **E** Woodlands Racetrack
14b a	Parallel Pkwy, **E gas:** QT, **other:** H
13b a	US 24, US 40, State Ave, **E food:** Frontier Steaks, **W other:** Cabela's Sporting Goods, KS Race Track
12b a	I-70, KS Tpk, to Topeka, St Louis

KANSAS CITY

Exit #	Services
11	Kansas Ave
9	KS 32, KS City, Bonner Springs, **W gas:** Phillips 66/dsl
8b	Woodend Rd, **E** Peterbilt
8.8mm	Kansas River
8a	Holliday Dr, to Lake Quivira
6c	Johnson Dr
6b a	Shawnee Mission Pkwy, **E gas:** BP/dsl, **food:** Sonic, **other:** museum
5	Midland Dr, Shawnee Mission Park, **E gas:** Conoco, Shell/Blimpie, **food:** Arizona's Grille, Barley's Brewhaus, Jose Pepper's Grill, Paula&Bill's Ristorante, Wendy's, **lodging:** Hampton Inn
3	87th Ave, **E gas:** BP, Phillips 66, Shell, **food:** McDonald's, **other:** NY Burrito, Panera Bread, Sonic, Zarda BBQ, K-Mart, museum
2	95th St
1b	KS 10, to Lawrence
1a	Lackman Rd, **N gas:** QT, Shell
0mm	I-435 begins/ends on I-35.

MONTANA

INTERSTATE 15

N ↕ S

SHELBY

Exit #	Services
398mm	Montana/US/Canada Border
397	**Sweetgrass, W rest area both lanes, full ♿ facilities, picnic, litter barrels, petwalk, phone, gas:** Gastrack, **other:** Duty Free
394	ranch access
389	MT 552, Sunburst, **W** gas/dsl, **food:** Big D's BBQ, **other:** Prairie Mkt foods, Sunburst RV Park
385	Swayze Rd
379	MT 215, Mt 343, to Kevin, Oilmont, **W food:** Four Corners Café
373	Potter Rd
369	Bronken Rd
366.5mm	**weigh sta sb**
364	Shelby, **E** Lewis&Clark RV Park, **W** ✈
363	US 2, to Cut Bank, Shelby, **0-1 mi E gas:** Cenex, Pilot/Exxon/Subway/dsl/scales/24hr, Sinclair/dsl, **food:** Dash Drive-In, Dixie Inn Steaks, Pizza Hut, South of the Border, The Griddle, **lodging:** Comfort Inn, Crossroads Inn, Glacier Motel, O'Haire Motel, **other:** H, Albertson's, CarQuest, Mark's Tire, Parts+, Radio Shack, TrueValue, **W other:** Pamida/drugs, to Glacier NP
361mm	**parking area nb**
358	Marias Valley Rd, to Golf Course Rd, **E** camping
357mm	Marias River
352	Bullhead Rd
348	rd 44, to Valier, **W** Lake Frances RA (15mi)
345	MT 366, Ledger Rd, **E** to Tiber Dam (42mi)
339	Conrad, **W gas:** Cenex/dsl, Dan's Gas/Tires, Exxon/Subway/dsl, MRC/dsl, **food:** A&W/KFC, Home Cafe, Keg Rest., Main Drive-In, **lodging:** Northgate Motel, Super 8, **other:** H, Buick/Chevrolet/GMC/Pontiac, IGA Foods, Olson's Drug, Radio Shack, Ford, Pondera RV Park, TrueValue, Westco RV Ctr, Vet
335	Midway Rd, Conrad, **4 mi W** H, gas, food, phone, lodging, RV camping
328	MT 365, Brady, **W gas:** Mtn View Co-op/dsl, **other:** USPO, tires

GREAT FALLS

Exit #	Services
321	Collins Rd
319mm	**Teton River, rest area both lanes, full ♿ facilities, phone, picnic, litter barrels, petwalk**
313	MT 221, MT 379, Dutton, **W gas:** Cenex/dsl, **food:** Café Dutton, **other:** USPO
302	MT 431, Power
297	Gordon
290	US 89 N, rd 200 W, to Choteau, **W gas:** Exxon/dsl, Sinclair/dsl/LP/RV dump, **other:** USPO
288mm	**parking area both lanes**
286	Manchester, **W** livestock auction, same as 290 (2mi)
282	US 87 N (from sb), **weigh sta, 2-3 mi E gas:** Conoco/dsl, Exxon/dsl, **food:** Arby's, Burger King, McDonald's, Pizza Hut, Subway, Taco Bell, Taco John's, **lodging:** Day's Inn, **other:** Albertson's/gas, Checker Parts, $Tree, K-Mart, Sam's Club/gas, ShopKO, Staples, Tire-Rama, Walmart Super Ctr/24hr
280	US 87 N, Central Ave W, Great Falls, **E gas:** Loaf 'N Jug, **food:** A&W/KFC, Arby's, Double Barrel Diner, Ford's Drive-In, Hardee's, Papa John's, **lodging:** Alberta Inn, Central Motel, Day's Inn, **other:** Freightliner, NAPA, U-Haul/LP, Whalen Tire, to Giant Sprgs SP, Vet
280mm	Sun River
278	US 89 S, rd 200 E, 10th Ave, Great Falls, **E food:** Chili's, Classic 50's Diner/casino, Golden Corral, Macaroni Grill, McDonald's Taco Del Mar, Tony Roma's, **lodging:** Hampton Inn, Hilton Garden, Holiday Inn Express, **other:** Barnes&Noble, Home Depot, Michael's, Old Navy, PetCo, Smith's Foods, **1-3 mi E gas:** Cenex/dsl, Conoco, Exxon/Subway/dsl, MRC/dsl, Sinclair/dsl, **food:** Applebee's, Arby's, Best Wok, Big Mouth BBQ, Boston's Pizza, Burger King, Burger Master, China Buffet, China Town, DQ, 4B's Rest., Fuddrucker's, Godfather's, Hardee's, Jaker's Ribs, Jalisco Mexican, JB's Rest., KFC, Ming's Chinese, Monty's Rest., Papa John's, Papa Murphy's, Pizza Hut, PrimeCut Rest., Quizno's, Starbucks, Taco Bell, Taco John's, Taco Treat, Wendy's, **lodging:** Best Western, Comfort Inn, Extended Stay America, Fairfield Inn, Holiday Inn,

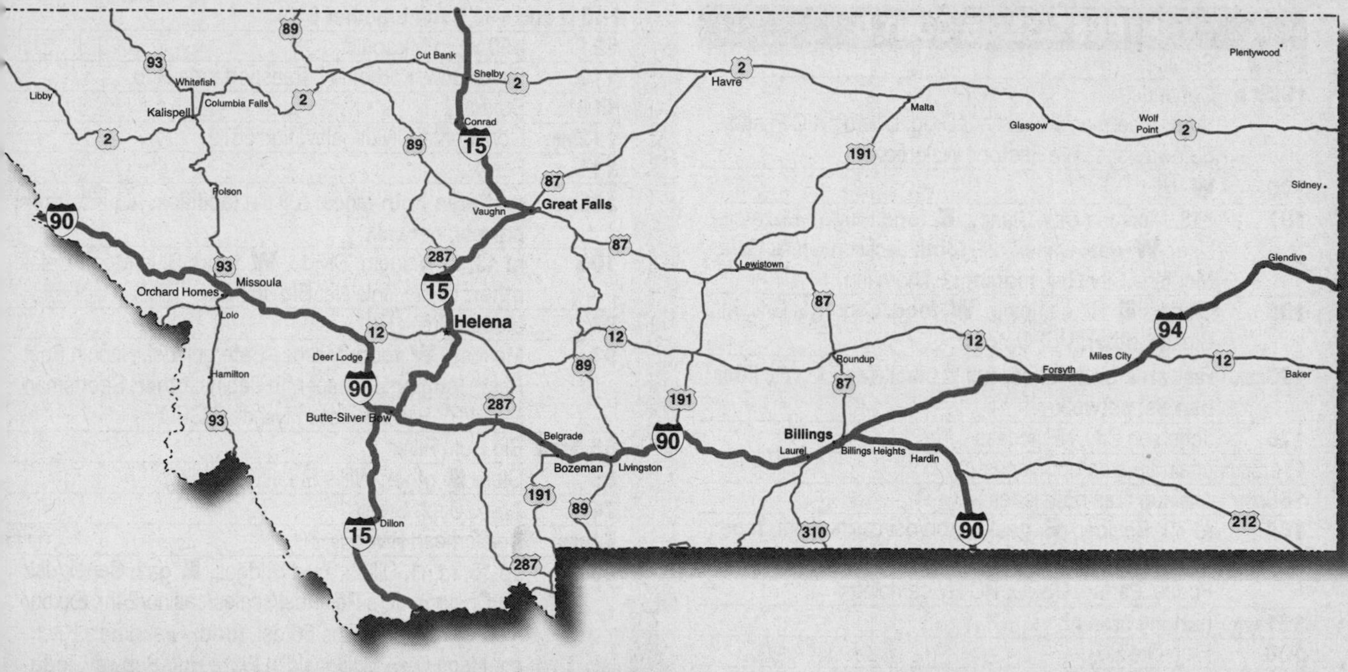

MT

INTERSTATE 15 CONT'D

N / S
GREAT FALLS

Exit #	Services
278	Continued La Quinta, Motel 6, Plaza Inn, Super 8, Townhouse Inn, Western Motel, **other:** [H] Ace Hardware, Albertson's/gas, Big-O Tire, BMW, Cadillac/Chevrolet/Toyota, Checker Parts, Chrysler/Dodge/Jeep, Dick's RV Park, Discount Drug, $Tree, Firestone/auto, Ford, Hancock Fabrics, Harley Davidson, Hastings Books, Herberger's, Honda, Hyundai, JC Penney, Jo-Ann Crafts, KOA, Lincoln/Mercury, McCollum RVs, NAPA, Nissan, Parts+, Jeep, O'Reilly Parts, Ross, Scheels Sports, Sears/auto, Target, Tire-Rama, Travel Time RV Ctr, Van's Foods, VW, Walgreens, USPO, transmissions, Vet, to Malmstrom AFB
277	Airport Rd, **E gas:** *FLYING J*/Country Mkt./dsl/24, Pilot/Conoco/Subway/dsl/café/casino/scales/24hr, **lodging:** Crystal Inn **W** [airport]
275mm	**weigh sta nb**
270	MT 330, Ulm, **E gas:** Conoco/dsl/LP, **other:** USPO, **W** to Ulm SP
256	rd 68, Cascade, **1/2 mi E gas:** Sinclair, **lodging:** Badger Motel/café, **other:** NAPA, Tom's Foods, USPO
254	rd 68, Cascade, **1/2 mi E** same as 256
250	local access
247	Hardy Creek, Hardy Creek, **W** to Tower Rock SP, food, phone, RV camping
246.5mm	Missouri River
245mm	scenic overlook sb
244	Canyon Access, **2 mi W** camping, food, RV camping, rec area
240	Dearborn, **E** RV park
239mm	**rest area both lanes, full [handicapped] facilities, [phone], [picnic], litter barrels, petwalk**
238mm	Stickney Creek
236mm	Missouri River
234	Craig, **E food:** Izaak's Cafe, Trout Shop Café/lodge, **other:** rec area, boating, camping
228	US 287 N, to Augusta

HELENA

Exit #	Services
226	MT 434, Wolf Creek, Wolf Creek, **E gas:** Exxon/dsl, **food:** Oasis Café, **other:** Mt River Outfitters/lodge/flyshop, camping, **W food:** Frenchman&Me Café, **other:** USPO
222mm	**parking area both lanes**
219	Spring Creek, Recreation Rd (from nb), boating, camping
218mm	Little Prickly Pear Creek
216	Sieben
209	**E** to Gates of the Mtns RA
205mm	turnout sb
202mm	**weigh sta sb**
200	MT 279, MT 453, Lincoln Rd, **W gas:** Sinclair/Bob's Mkt/dsl, **food:** GrubStake Rest., **other:** Helena Campground (4mi), Lincoln rd RV Park, to ski area
193	Cedar St, Helena, **E gas:** Conoco, **food:** Chili's, IHOP, Macaroni Grill, **other:** Costco, Helena RV Park (5mi), Home Depot, Whalen Tire, **W gas:** Conoco/dsl, **food:** Perkins, Wheat Montana/deli, **lodging:** Wingate Inn, **other:** NAPA, **W on Montana Ave... gas:** Cenex/dsl, Exxon/dsl, **food:** Applebee's, Arby's, DQ, Godfather's, Jade Garden Chinese, McDonald's, McKenzie River Pizza, Pizza Hut, Subway, Taco Bell, Taco Del Mar, Taco John's, **lodging:** Quality Inn, **other:** Albertson's/24hr, AutoZone, CarQuest, Checker Parts, Chevrolet, $Tree, Hastings Books, Jo-Ann Fabrics, K-Mart, Lowes Whse, Macy's, Murdock's, Office Depot, O'Reilly Parts, Ross, ShopKO, Snyder's Drugs, Target, Tire-Rama, USPO
192b a	US 12, US 287, Helena, Townsend, **E food:** Burger King, Pizza Hut, Subway, **lodging:** Hampton Inn, **other:** Buick/Cadillac/GMC, Chrysler/Dodge, D&D RV Ctr, Ford/Lincoln/Mercury, Honda, Montana RV Ctr, Toyota, Schwab Tire, Staples, Walmart SuperCtr/24hr, st patrol, **W gas:** Exxon/dsl, Sinclair/24hr, **food:** A&W/KFC, DQ, JB's Rest, L&D Chinese, McDonald's, Overland Express Rest., Papa John's, Papa Murphy's, Quizno's, Starbucks, Taco John's, Taco Treat, Wendy's, **lodging:** Comfort Inn, Day's Inn, Fairfield Inn, Guesthouse Inn, Holiday Inn Express, Jorgenson's Inn, Motel 6, Red Lion Inn, Shilo Inn, Super 8, **other:** [H],

INTERSTATE 15 CONT'D

Exit #	Services
192b a	Continued AAA, Albertson's/gas, CVS Drug, Dillard's, JC Penney, Safeway/gas, Tire Factory, Walgreens
190	W [H]
187	518, Montana City, Clancy, **E food:** Hugo's Pizza/casino, **W gas:** Cenex/dsl, **food:** Jackson Creek Cafe, Montana City Grill, **lodging:** Elkhorn Inn
182	Clancy, **E** RV camping, **W food:** Chubby's Grill, Mt Steaks, **other:** USPO, to NF,
178mm	**rest area both lanes, full [handicap] facilities, [phone], [picnic], litter barrels, petwalk**
176	Jefferson City, NF access
174.5mm	chain up area both lanes
168mm	chainup area both lanes
164	rd 69, Boulder, **E gas:** Exxon/dsl/casino/24hr, **food:** Gator's Pizza Parlour, Mtn Good Rest., **other:** L&P Foods, Parts+, USPO, RC RV camping
161mm	**parking area nb**
160	High Ore Rd
156	Basin, **E other:** Merry Widow Health Mine/RV camping, **W other:** Basin Cr Pottery, camping, USPO
154mm	Boulder River
151	to Boulder River Rd, Bernice, **W** camping, picnic area
148mm	chainup area both lanes
143.5mm	chainup area both lanes
138	Elk Park, **W other:** Sheepshead Picnic Area, wildlife viewing
134	Woodville
133mm	continental divide, elev 6368
130.5mm	scenic overlook sb
129	I-90 E, to Billings

I-15 S and I-90 W run together 8 mi

BUTTE

Exit #	Services
127	Harrison Ave, Butte, **E gas:** Conoco/dsl, Exxon/dsl/24hr, Sinclair, **food:** A&W/KFC, Arby's, Asia Gardens, Burger King, 4B's Rest., Godfather's, McDonald's, McKenzie River Pizza, Perkins, Pizza Hut, Ray's Rest., Silver Bow Pizza, Subway, Taco Bell, Wendy's, **lodging:** Best Western, Comfort Inn, Copper King, Hampton Inn, Ramada Inn, Super 8, **other:** American Car Care, Buick/GMC/Pontiac, Checker Parts, Chevrolet, Chrysler/Dodge/Jeep, Ford, Herberger's, Honda, JC Penney, Jo-Ann Crafts, K-Mart, Lincoln/Mercury, O'Reilly Parts, Staples, Subaru, Walmart SuperCtr/24hr, Whalen Tire, casinos, **W gas:** Cenex/dsl, Conoco, **food:** Denny's, Derby Steaks, Domino's, DQ, El Taco Mexican, Hanging 5 Rest., John's Rest., L&D Chinese, Papa John's, Papa Murphy's, Quizno's, Royce's Burgers, Taco John's, **lodging:** Day's Inn, Holiday Inn Express, War Bonnet Inn, **other:** Ace Hardware, Checker Parts, Hastings Books, NAPA, Nissan/Toyota, Safeway
126	Montana St, Butte, **E gas:** Conoco, Exxon/dsl, **W food:** Chef's Garden Italian, **lodging:** Eddy's Motel, **other:** [H], KOA, Safeway, Schwab Tire
124	I-115 (from eb), to Butte, City Ctr
123mm	**weigh sta wb**
122	Rocker, **E gas:** Pilot/Conoco/Arby's/McDonald's/Subway/dsl/scales/24hr, **lodging:** Motel 6, **other:** repair, **W gas:** *FLYING J*/rest./dsl/LP/24hr, **lodging:** Rocker Inn Motel, **other: weigh sta eb**, RV camping

I-15 N and I-90 E run together 8 mi

Exit #	Services
121	I-90 W, to Missoula
119	Silver Bow, Port of MT Transportation Hub
116	Buxton
112mm	Continental Divide, elevation 5879
111	Feely
109mm	**rest area both lanes, full [handicap] facilities, [phone], [picnic], litter barrels, petwalk**
102	rd 43, to Wisdom, Divide, **W food:** Blue Moon Cafe, **other:** to Big Hole Nat Bfd (62mi)
99	Moose Creek Rd
93	Melrose, **W food:** Melrose Café/grill/dsl, Hitchin Post Rest., **lodging:** Pioneer Mtn Cabins, **other:** Sportsman Motel/RV Park, Sunrise Flyshop, USPO
85.5mm	Big Hole River
85	Glen, **E other:** Willis Sta. RV camping
74	Apex, Birch Creek
64mm	Beaverhead River

DILLON

Exit #	Services
63	Lp 15, rd 41, Dillon, Twin Bridges, **E gas:** Cenex/dsl/LP, Chevron/JD's Rest./dsl/scales/casino/24hr, Exxon/KFC/dsl/24hr, Phillips 66/dsl, **food:** Grandma's Kitchen, Lions Den, McDonald's, Pizza Hut, Subway, **lodging:** Best Western/rest., Comfort Inn, GuestHouse Inn, Sundowner Motel, Super 8, **other:** [H],CarQuest, Chevrolet/Pontiac/Buick/Cadillac, Ford/Chrysler/Dodge, KOA, O'Reilly Parts, Safeway/drug/gas, Schwab Tire, museum, RV Park, W MT Coll
62	Lp 15, Dillon, **E food:** DQ, Sparky's Rest., Taco John's, **lodging:** Creston Motel, Flyshop Inn, **other:** [H], KOA, Southside RV Park, to WMT
60mm	Beaverhead River
59	MT 278, to Jackson, **W other:** Bannack SP, Countryside RV Park
56	Barretts, **E** RV camping
52	Grasshopper Creek
51	Dalys (from sb, no return)
50mm	Beaverhead River
46mm	Beaverhead River
45mm	Beaverhead River
44	MT 324, **E food:** Buffalo Lodge, **other:** Armstead RV Park, Beaverhead Flyshop, **W other:** Clark Cyn Reservoir/RA, RV camping
38.5mm	Red Rock River
37	Red Rock
34mm	**parking area both lanes, litter barrels, restrooms**
29	Kidd
23	Dell, **E gas:** Cenex/dsl, **food:** Yesterdays Cafe, **other:** USPO
16.5mm	**weigh sta both lanes**
15	Lima, **E gas:** Exxon/dsl, **food:** Jan's Café, **lodging:** Mtn View Motel/RV Park, **other:** Big Sky tire/auto, USPO, ambulance
9	Snowline
0	Monida, **E** [phone], to Red Rock Lakes
0mm	Monida Pass, elevation 6870, Montana/Idaho state line

INTERSTATE 90

Exit #	Services
559.5mm	**weigh sta both lanes**
554.5mm	Montana/Wyoming state line
549	Aberdeen
544	Wyola

E ↕ W

INTERSTATE 90 CONT'D

Exit #	Services
530	MT 463, Lodge Grass, **1 mi S gas:** gas, dsl, food, lodging, ☎
517.5mm	Little Bighorn River
514	Garryowen, **N gas:** Conoco/Subway, **other:** Custer Bfd Museum, **S other:** 7th Ranch RV camp
511.5mm	Little Bighorn River
510	US 212 E, **N gas:** Exxon/KFC/dsl/café/gifts, **food:** Crows Nest Café, **other:** H, to Little Bighorn Bfd, casino, **S other:** Little Bighorn RV Camp/dump
509.5mm	**weigh sta, both lanes exit left**
509.3mm	Little Bighorn River
509	Crow Agency, **N gas:** Conoco/24hr, **S** to Bighorn Canyon NRA
503	Dunmore
498mm	Bighorn River
497	MT 384, 3rd St, Hardin, **S** H, Bighorn Cty Museum, **2 mi S lodging:** Western Motel, **other:** Casino Rest./lounge
495	MT 47, City Ctr, Hardin, **N gas:** Shell/dsl, **food:** Purple Cow Rest., **other:** KOA, **S gas:** Cenex/dsl, Conoco/Subway/dsl/LP/24hr, Exxon/dsl, Sinclair/dsl, **food:** DQ, McDonald's, Pizza Hut, Shawna's Steaks, Taco John's, **lodging:** American Inn, Super 8, Western Motel, **other:** H, Grand View Camping/RV Park, Sunset Village RV Park, casinos
484	Toluca
478	Fly Creek Rd
477mm	**rest area both lanes, full ♿ facilities, ☎, picnic, litter barrels, petwalk**
469	Arrow Creek Rd, **N food:** Rock Shop/Cafe
462	Pryor Creek Rd
456	I-94 E, to Bismarck, ND
455	Johnson Lane, **S gas:** Exxon/A&W/Blimpie/dsl/24hr, ***FLYING J***/Conoco/Cookery/dsl/LP/rest./24hr/scales, **food:** Burger King, DQ, Subway, **lodging:** Holiday Inn Express, **other:** Tour America RV Ctr (1mi)
452	US 87 N, City Ctr, Billings, **N gas:** Conoco/Arby's/dsl/LP, Exxon/dsl, **lodging:** Best Western, **other:** American Spirit RV Ctr, Chevrolet, Metra Rv Ctr, transmissions, **2-4 mi N on US 87...gas:** Cenex/dsl, Conoco/dsl, Holiday/dsl, **food:** Applebee's, Arby's, Bugz Rest./casino, Burger King, DQ, Fuddrucker's, Godfather's Pizza, Golden Phoenix, Guadalajara Mexican, KFC, Little Caesar's, MacKenzie River Pizza, Main St Grill, McDonald's, Mongolian Grill, Papa John's, Papa Murphy's, Pizza Hut, Subway, Taco Bell, Taco John's, Wendy's, **lodging:** Country Inn&Suites, Foothills Inn, Heights Motel, **other:** Ace Hardware, Albertson's, Big Lots, CarQuest, Checkers Parts, CVS Drug, O'Reilly Parts, Office Depot, Radio Shack, Schnider's Drug, Target, U-Haul, Walgreens, Walmart SuperCtr/24hr, Western Drug, Vet, **S gas:** Cenex/dsl, **other:** RV Capming
451.5mm	Yellowstone River
450	MT 3, 27th St, Billings, **N gas:** Conoco/dsl/24hr, Sinclair, **food:** Blondy's Cafe, Pizza Hut, **lodging:** Crowne Plaza, War Bonnet Inn/rest., **other:** H, CarQuest, USPO, **S** KOA, Yellowstone River Camping
447	S Billings Blvd, **N gas:** Conoco/Subway/dsl/24hr, Holiday, **food:** Burger King, DQ, McDonald's,

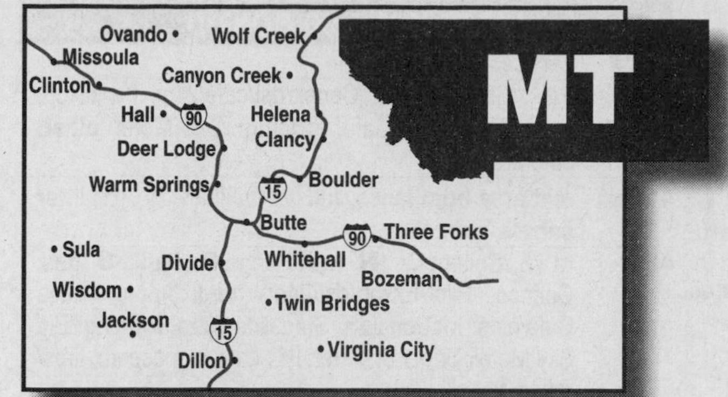

Exit #	Services
447	Continued **lodging:** Best Western/Kelly, Day's Inn, Extended Stay America, Hampton Inn, Sleep Inn, Super 8, Cabela's Sporting Goods, NAPA, **S other:** Billings RV Park (2mi), Freightliner, Kenworth, KOA (2mi), Yellowstone River Campground
446	King Ave, Billings, **N on King Ave...gas:** Exxon, Conoco/dsl, Holiday/dsl/LP/RV dump, Sinclair, **food:** Applebee's, Arbys, Burger King, Carrie's Rest., Cactus Creek Steaks, Carino's Italian, City Brew Coffee, Del Taco, Denny's, Dos Machos, Famous Dave's, Fuddrucker's, Gusicks Rest., Hot Mongolian, IHOP, Jade Palace, Olive Garden, Old Chicago, Outback Steaks, Perkins, Pizza Hut, Quizno's, Red Lobster, Taco John's, Taste Of Italy, TX Roadhouse, Wendy's, Wheat Montana, **lodging:** C'Mon Inn, Comfort Inn, Fairfield Inn, Hilton Garden, La Quinta, Quality Inn, Residence Inn, Springhill Suites, Western Executive Inn, **other:** Best Buy, Borders Books, Chevrolet, Chrysler/Jeep/Kia, Costco/gas, Dodge, Ford, Home Depot, Isuzu, Lowe's Whse, Michael's, Nissan, Office Depot, Old Navy, O'Reilly Parts, PetsMart, Ross, ShopKO, Subaru/Hyundai, Toyota, USPO, Walmart SuperCtr, World Mkt, mall, **N on 24th...gas:** Conoco/dsl, Exxon/Subway, **food:** Buffalo Wild Wings, Golden Corral, Hardee's, Little Caesar's, McDonald's, Taco Bell, Wendy's, **other:** Albertson's/Osco, Barnes&Noble, Cadillac/GMC/Pontiac, Dillards, JC Penney, K-Mart, Subaru, Tuesday Morning, **S gas:** Conoco/dsl/24hr, **food:** Cracker Barrel, Emporium Rest., **lodging:** Billings Hotel, ClubHouse Inn, Holiday Inn, Kelly Inn, Motel 6, Ramada Ltd, Red Roof Inn, **other:** Volvo/Mac Trucks, water funpark
443	Zoo Dr, to Shiloh Rd, **N gas:** Holiday/dsl, **food:** Mt Rib/Chophouse, **lodging:** Hampton Inn, Wingate Inn, **other:** Pierce RV Ctr, Sportsman's Whse, zoo, **S other:** Harley-Davidson, Vet
439mm	**weigh sta both lanes**
437	E Laurel, **S gas:** Sinclair/dsl/rest./casino/motel/RV Park/24hr
434	US 212, US 310, to Red Lodge, Laurel, **N gas:** Cenex/dsl, Conoco/dsl, Exxon/dsl/24hr, **food:** Burger King, City Brew Coffee, Hardee's, McDonald's, Pizza Hut, Subway, Taco John's, **lodging:** Best Western, Howard Johnson, **other:** Ace Hardware, Chevrolet, CVS Drug, Ford, Jan's Foods, Rapid Tire, Walmart SuperCtr, **S other:** Riverside Park/RV Camping, Vet, to Yellowstone NP
433	Lp 90 (from eb), same as 434

INTERSTATE 90 CONT'D

E ↕ W

Exit #	Services
426	Park City, **S gas:** Cenex/dsl/café/24hr, KwikStop, **food:** The Other Cafe, **lodging:** CJ's Motel, **other:** auto/tire repair
419mm	**rest area both lanes, full ♿ facilities, ☎, ⛺, litter barrels, petwalk**
408	rd 78, Columbus, **N** Mtn Range RV Park, **S gas:** Conoco, Pilot/Exxon/dsl/24hr, **food:** Apple Village Café/gifts, McDonald's, Stageline Pizza, **lodging:** Big Sky Motel, Super 8, **other:** H, casino, museum, tires/repair, to Yellowstone
400	Springtime Rd
398mm	Yellowstone River
396	ranch access
392	Reed Point, **N gas:** Sinclair/dsl, **other:** Old West RV Park, USPO
384	Bridger Creek Rd
381mm	**rest area both lanes, full ♿ facilities, ☎, ⛺, litter barrels, petwalk**
377	Greycliff, **S other:** Prairie Dog Town SP, KOA
370	US 191, Big Timber, **1 mi N gas:** Cenex, Sinclair/dsl, **food:** Frosty Freez Diner, **lodging:** Grand Hotel, Lazy J Motel, **other:** Spring Creek RV Ranch (4mi), USPO
369mm	Boulder River
367	US 191 N, Big Timber, **N gas:** Exxon/dsl, Conoco/dsl, **food:** Country Skillet, **lodging:** River Valley Inn, Super 8, **other:** CarQuest, Chevrolet, Ford, Spring Creek Camping (3mi), historic site/visitor info
362	De Hart
354	MT 563, Springdale
352	ranch access
350	East End access
340	US 89 N, to White Sulphur Sprgs, **S** ✈
343	Mission Creek Rd, **N** Ft Parker HS
337	Lp 90, to Livingston, **2 mi N** services
333mm	Yellowstone River
333	US 89 S, Livingston, **N gas:** Loaf'n Jug, **food:** Clark's Rest., DQ, Taco John's, **lodging:** Best Western, Livingston Inn, Quality Inn, Rodeway Inn, **other:** H, Ace Hardware, Ford/Lincoln/Mercury, Pamida, Radio Shack, RV Park, Town&Country Foods, Western Drug, **S gas:** Cenex/dsl, Conoco/dsl, Exxon/dsl, **food:** Arby's, Buffalo Jump Steaks, McDonald's, Subway, **lodging:** Comfort Inn, Super 8, **other:** Albertson's, Osen's RV Park, LP, Vet, to Yellowstone
330	Lp 90, Livingston, **1 mi N gas:** Yellowstone Trkstp/dsl/rest./24hr, **lodging:** Del Mar Motel
326.5mm	chainup/chain removal area both lanes
324	ranch access
323mm	chainup/chain removal area wb
322mm	Bridger Mountain Range
321mm	turnouts/hist marker both lanes
319	Jackson Creek Rd
319mm	chainup area both lanes
316	Trail Creek Rd
313	Bear Canyon Rd, **S other:** Bear Canyon Camping
309	US 191 S, Main St, Bozeman, **N other:** Subaru, Sunrise RV Park, VW, **S gas:** Cenex/dsl, Exxon, **food:** Mt AleWorks, **lodging:** Blue Sky Motel, Continental Motel, Ranch House Motel, Western Heritage Inn, **other:** H, Heeb's Foods, RV service, to Yellowstone, Vet
306	US 191, N 7th, Bozeman, **N gas:** Sinclair, **food:** McDonald's, **lodging:** Best Value Inn, Fairfield Inn, Microtel, Ramada Ltd, Super 8, TLC Inn, **other:** Whalen Tire, RV supplies, ski area, **S gas:** Conoco/Arby's/dsl, Exxon, **food:** Applebee's, Bar-3 BBQ, Dominos, DQ, Famous Dave's, McDonald's, Papa John's, Santa Fe Red's Cafe, Taco John's, **lodging:** Best Western, Bozeman/rest., Comfort Inn, Day's Inn, Hampton Inn, Holiday Inn, Royal 7 Inn, **other:** Big O Tire, CarQuest, Firestone/auto, K-Mart, U-Haul, Van's Foods, Walmart SuperCtr/24hr, Museum of the Rockies
305	MT 412, N 19th Ave, **N gas:** Exxon, **lodging:** AmericInn, **0-3 mi S food:** Bennigan's, Carino's Italian, IHOP, KFC, MacKenzie River Pizza, Old Chicago Pizza, Outback Steaks, Papa Murphy's, Pizza Hut, Subway, Wendy's, Wheat Mt Bakery, **lodging:** C'mon Inn, Hilton Garden, Residence Inn, Wingate Inn, **other:** Borders Books, Costco/gas, Ford/Lincoln/Mercury, Home Depot, Lowes Whse, Michaels, Old Navy, Office Depot, PetsMart, Target, Radio Shack, Ross, Smith's, Sportsman's Whse, Staples, UPS, World MKT, USPO, Vet, **rest area, full ♿ facilites, ⛺/litter barrels, petwalk**
298	MT 291, Mt 85, Belgrade, **N gas:** Cenex/dsl, Conoco, Exxon/Subway/dsl, **food:** Burger King, DQ, McDonald's, Pizza Hut, **other:** Albertson's/Osco, IGA Foods, NAPA, Radio Shack, Whalen Tire, **S gas:** ***FLYING J***/Conoco/dsl/scales/LP, **food:** Country Kitchen, **lodging:** Holiday Inn Express, La Quinta, Super 8, **other:** Harley-Davidson, Interwest Tire, KOA (9mi), TrueValue, truckwash, to Yellowstone NP.
292.5mm	Gallatin River
288	Manhattan, **N gas:** Conoco/dsl, **other:** RV camping
283	Logan, **S other:** Madison Buffalo Jump SP (7mi)
279mm	Madison River
278	MT 205, rd 2, Three Forks, Trident, **N** Missouri Headwaters SP, **1 mi S gas:** Conoco/dsl, Sinclair/dsl, **lodging:** Broken Spur Motel, **other:** camping, phone
277.5mm	Jefferson River
274	US 287, to Helena, Ennis, **N gas:** Sinclair/dsl, **food:** Wheat Mt Bakery/deli, lodging: Ft 3 Forks Motel, **other:** KOA (2mi), to Canyon Ferry SP, dsl repair, **S gas:** Pilot/Exxon/Subway/dsl/scales/24hr, **other:** Camp 3 Forks, Lewis&Clark Caverns SP, to Yellowstone NP
267	Milligan Canyon Rd
261.5mm	chain-up area
257mm	Boulder River
256	MT 359, Cardwell, **S gas:** Cardwell/dsl/RV Park, **other:** to Yellowstone NP, Lewis&Clark Caverns SP, RV camping
249	rd 55, to rd 69, Whitehall, **S gas:** Exxon/Subway/dsl/24hr, **food:** A&W/KFC, **lodging:** Super 8, **other:** Virginia City NHS, camping, casino
241	Pipestone
240.5mm	chainup/chain removal area both lanes
238.5mm	runaway ramp eb
237.5mm	pulloff eb
235mm	**truck parking both lanes, litter barrels, rest rooms**
233	Homestake, Continental Divide, elev 6393
230mm	chain-up area both lanes
228	MT 375, Continental Dr, **S gas:** Conoco/dsl, **other:** Harley Davidson, 3 Bears Foods
227	I-15 N, to Helena, Great Falls

LIVINGSTON · BOZEMAN · BELGRADE

INTERSTATE 90 CONT'D

E ↕ W

DEER LODGE

Exit #	Services
I-90 and I-15 run together 8 mi. See Montana Interstate 15 Exits 122-127.	
219	I-15 S, to Dillon, Idaho Falls
216	Ramsay
211	MT 441, Gregson, **3-5 mi S** food, lodging, Fairmont RV Park (Apr-Oct)
210.5mm	**parking area wb**, Pintlar Scenic route info
208	rd 1, Pintler Scenic Loop, Georgetown Lake RA, Opportunity, Anaconda, **S other:** [H], gas, food, lodging, RV camp/dump, ski area, **rest area both lanes, full ♿ facilities, 🛆, litter barrels, petwalk**
201	Warm Springs, **S** MT ST [H]
197	MT 273, Galen, **S** to MT ST [H]
195	Racetrack, **S other:** dsl repair
187	Lp 90, Deer Lodge (no wb return), **2 mi S food:** Montey's Subs, **lodging:** Downtowner Motel, Scharf's Motel/rest., **other:** [H], KOA (seasonal), Radio Shack, Valley Foods, Old MT Prison, Tow Ford Museum, same as 184
184	Deer Lodge, **0-1 mi S gas:** Exxon/dsl/casino, Conoco/dsl/casino, Sinclair/dsl, **food:** A&W, Broken Arrow Steaks, Chinese Garden, 4B's Rest., McDonald's, Pizza Hut, **lodging:** Downtowner Motel, Rodeway Inn, Western Big Sky Inn, **other:** [H], Indian Cr Camping, Keystone Drug, KOA, Safeway/deli, Schwab Tire, Grant-Kohrs Ranch NHS
179	Beck Hill Rd
175mm	Little Blackfoot River
175	US 12 E, Garrison, **N other:** RiverFront RV Park, phone, hist site
174	US 12 E (from eb), **S food:** Ranch House Cafe/RV Park, same as 175
170	Phosphate
168mm	**rest area both lanes, full ♿ facilities, ☎, 🛆, litter barrels, petwalk, hist site**
166	Gold Creek, **S other:** Camp Mak-A-Dream
162	Jens
154	to MT 1 (from wb), Drummond, **S gas:** Cenex/dsl, Conoco/dsl/24hr, Sinclair/dsl/24hr, **food:** Tastee-Freeze, Wagon Wheel Café, **lodging:** Sky Motel, **other:** Pintler Scenic Lp, Georgetown Lake RA, Goodtime RV Park (3mi)
153	MT 1 (from eb), **N other:** Garnet GhostTown, Goodtime RV Park (3mi) **S** same as 154
150.5mm	**weigh sta both lanes**
143mm	**rest area both lanes, full ♿ facilities, ☎, 🛆, litter barrels, petwalk**
138	Bearmouth Area, **N other:** Chalet Bearmouth Camp/rest., to gas, food, lodging
130	Beavertail Rd, **S other:** to Beavertail Hill SP, rec area, camping (seasonal)
128mm	**parking area both lanes, litter barrels/restrooms**
126	Rock Creek Rd, **S lodging:** Rock Creek Lodge/gas/casino, **other:** rec area
120	Clinton, **N gas:** Sinclair/dsl, **food:** Poor Henry's Café (1mi W in on frtg rd), **other:** Clinton Market, **S other:** USPO
113	Turah, **S** Turah RV Park/gas
109.5mm	Clark Fork, Clark Fork

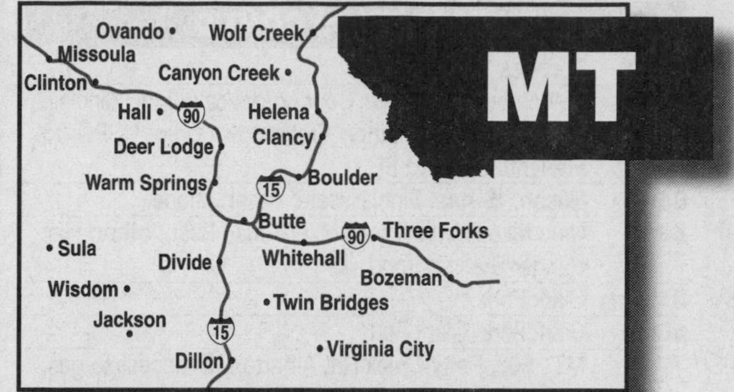

MISSOULA

Exit #	Services
109mm	Blackfoot River
109	MT 200 E, Bonner, **N gas:** Pilot/Exxon/Arby's/Subway/dsl/scales/casino/LP/24hr, Sinclair/dsl, **food:** River City Grill, **other:** USPO, banking, hist site
108.5mm	Clark Fork, Clark Fork
107	E Missoula, **N gas:** Ole's Mkt/Conoco/diner/dsl/24hr, Sinclair/24hr, **food:** Reno Cafe **lodging:** Aspen Motel, **other:** dsl repair, **2 mi S lodging:** Holiday Inn Express
105	US 12 W, Missoula, **S gas:** Cenex/dsl/24hr, Conoco/dsl/24hr, Sinclair/dsl, **food:** Burger King, Finnegan's, McDonald's, Pizza Hut, Quizno's, Subway, Taco Bell, **lodging:** Campus Inn, Creekside Inn, DoubleTree, Family Inn, Holiday Inn, Holiday Inn Express, Ponderosa Motel, Thunderbi rd Motel, **other:** Ace Hardware, Albertson's, Kingfisher Flyshop, O'Reilly Parts, U of MT, Vietnam Vet's Mem
104	Orange St, Missoula, **S gas:** Conoco/dsl, **food:** Pagoda Chinese, Subway, Taco John's **lodging:** Mountain Valley Inn, Red Lion Inn, **other:** [H], Curves, Tire-rama, to City Ctr
101	US 93 S, Reserve St, **N gas:** Conoco/dsl, **food:** Cracker Barrel, McKenzie River Pizza, Starbucks, **lodging:** Best Western, C'Mon Inn, Motel 6, **other:** ski area, **0-2 mi S gas:** Cenex/dsl/LP, Conoco/24hr, Exxon/dsl/24hr, Sinclair, **food:** Arby's, Blue Canyon Rest., Burger King, Carino's, China Bowl, Coldstone Creamery, DQ, Famous Dave's BBQ, Fuddrucker's, Hooters, McDonald's, Mt Club rest./casino, Outback Steaks, Perkins, Quizno's, Taco Bell, Taco Time/TCBY, Wendy's, **lodging:** Courtyard, Econolodge, Hampton Inn, Hilton Garden, La Quinta, Ruby's Inn/rest., Staybridge Suites, Super 8, Travelers Inn, **other:** Albertson's, Barnes&Noble, Best Buy, Bretz RV/Marine, Chevrolet, Costco/gas, Firestone/auto, Home Depot, KOA, Lowes Whse, Michael's, Old Navy, PetsMart, Radio Shack, Ross, Sportsman's Whse, Staples, Target, TJ Maxx, Walgreens, Walmart SuperCtr/24hr, casinos, dsl repair
99	Airway Blvd, **S gas:** Mobil/dsl/24hr, Sinclair/dsl, **lodging:** Hawthorn Suites, Wingate Inn, **other:** Chrysler/Dodge, Harley-Davidson, ✈
96	US 93 N, Mt 200W, Kalispell, **N gas:** Conoco/dsl/rest./scales/24hr/@, **lodging:** Day's Inn/rest., **other:** Freightliner, Peterbilt, Jellystone RV Park (1mi), Jim&Mary's RV Park (1mi), to Flathead Lake & Glacier NP, **S gas:** CrossroadsTC/Sinclair/rest/dsl/24hr, **lodging:** Redwood Lodge, **other:** Kenworth, RV repair
92.5mm	**inspection sta both lanes**

MT

INTERSTATE 90 CONT'D

E ↕ W

Exit #	Services
89	Frenchtown, **S gas:** Conoco/dsl/café/24hr, Sinclair, **food:** Alcan Grill, **other:** Frenchtown Drug, USPO, to Frenchtown Pond SP
85	Huson, **S gas:** Sinclair/café, **other:** phone
82	Nine Mile Rd, **N food:** Mile House Rest., **other:** Hist Ranger Sta/info, food, [phone]
81.5mm	Clark Fork
80mm	Clark Fork, Clark Fork
77	MT 507, Petty Creek Rd, Alberton, **S** access to gas, food, lodging, phone
75	Alberton, **S lodging:** River Edge Rest, **other:** RV camp, casino
73mm	**parking area wb, litter barrels**
72mm	**parking area eb, litter barrels**
70	Cyr
70mm	Clark Fork
66	Fish Creek Rd
66mm	Clark Fork
61	Tarkio
59mm	Clark Fork
58mm	**rest area both lanes, full [handicapped] facilities, [phone], [picnic], litter barrels, petwalk, NF camping (seasonal)**
55	Lozeau, Quartz
53.5mm	Clark Fork
49mm	Clark Fork
47	MT 257, Superior, **N gas:** Cenex/24hr, Conoco/dsl, Sinclair/Durango's Rest., **food:** Rosie's Rest., **lodging:** Budget Host, Hilltop Motel, **other:** [H], Best Hardware, Family Foods, Mineral Drug, NAPA, TrueValue, USPO, **S gas:** Pilot/Exxon/dsl/casino/24hr, **other:** Carl's Repair
45mm	Clark Fork, Clark Fork
43	Dry Creek Rd, **N** NP camping (seasonal)
37	Sloway Area
34mm	Clark Fork, Clark Fork
33	MT 135, St Regis, **N gas:** Conoco/dsl/rest./gifts, Exxon, Sinclair, **food:** Frosty Drive-In, Huckleberry Patch Rest., Jasper's Rest., OK Café/casino, Subway, **lodging:** Little River Motel, Super 8, **other:** Nugget Campground, St Regis Campground, USPO, antiques
30	Two Mile Rd, **S** fishing access
29mm	fishing access, wb
26	Ward Creek Rd (from eb)
25	Drexel
22	Camels Hump Rd, Henderson, **N other:** camping (seasonal), antiques (1mi)
18	DeBorgia, **N food:** Billy Big Riggers, O'aces Rest.
16	Haugan, **N gas:** Exxon/dsl/24hr, **lodging:** 50,000 Silver $/motel/rest./casino/RV park
15mm	**weigh sta both lanes, exits left from both lanes**
10	Saltese, **N food:** MT Grill, **lodging:** Mangold's Motel, **other:** antiques
10mm	St Regis River
5	Taft Area, access to Hiawatha Trail
4.5mm	**rest area both lanes, full [handicapped] facilities, [picnic], litter barrels, petwalk, chainup/removal**
0	Lookout Pass, **other:** access to Lookout Pass ski area/lodge, info
0mm	Montana/Idaho state line, Central/Pacific time zone, Lookout Pass elev 4680

INTERSTATE 94

E ↕ W

Exit #	Services
250mm	Montana/North Dakota state line
248	Carlyle Rd
242	MT 7 (from wb), Wibaux, **S rest area both lanes, full [handicapped] facilities, [phone], [picnic], litter barrels, gas:** Amsler's/dsl, Cenex/dsl/service, **food:** Tastee Hut, **lodging:** Beaver Creek Inn, **other:** RV camping
241	MT 261 (from eb), to MT 7, Wibaux, **S** same as 242
240mm	**weigh sta both lanes**
236	ranch access
231	Hodges Rd
224	Griffith Creek, frontage road
222.5mm	Griffith Creek
215	MT 335, Glendive, City Ctr, **N gas:** Conoco, **food:** C's Family Café, **lodging:** Comfort Inn, Day's Inn, Super 8, Yellowstone River Inn, **other:** Glendive Camping (apr-oct), TrueValue, museum, **S gas:** Exxon/dsl, Holiday/gas, Sinclair/dsl/repair, **food:** DQ, Subway, Taco John's, **lodging:** Best Western, Budget Motel, El Centro Motel, **other:** [H], to Makoshika SP
215mm	Yellowstone River
213	MT 16, to Sidney, Glendive, **N gas:** Exxon/dsl, **other:** Green Valley Camping, st patrol, truck tire/repair, **S gas:** Cenex, Conoco/dsl, Sinclair/dsl, **food:** Pizza Hut, **lodging:** Parkwood Motel, Riverside Inn, **other:** Albertson's/Osco, Ford, K-Mart, Radio Shack
211	MT 200S (from wb, no EZ return), to Circle
210	Lp 94, to rd 200S, W Glendive, **S gas:** Cenex, **other:** Buick/Chevrolet/Pontiac, Bumper Parts, Chrysler/Dodge/Jeep, Makoshika SP
206	Pleasant View Rd
204	Whoopup Creek Rd
198	Cracker Box Rd
192	Bad Route Rd, **S rest area/weigh sta both lanes, full [handicapped] facilities, weather info, [phone], [picnic], litter barrels, camping, petwalk**
187mm	Yellowstone River
185	MT 340, Fallon, **S** café, [phone]
184mm	Fallon Creek
176	MT 253, Terry, **N gas:** Conoco/dsl, **food:** Dizzy Diner, **lodging:** Diamond Motel, Kempton Hotel, **other:** [H], Terry RV Oasis
170mm	Powder River
169	Powder River Rd
159	Diamond Ring
148	Valley Access
141	US 12 E, Miles City, **N other:** RV Camping
138	MT 58, Miles City, **N gas:** Cenex/dsl/24hr, Conoco/dsl, Pilot/Exxon/dsl/24hr, **food:** Bruster's, DQ, 4B's Rest., Gallagher's Rest., KFC, Little Caesar's, McDonald's, Pizza Hut, Subway, Taco John's, Wendy's, **lodging:** Best Western, Econolodge, Motel 6, **other:** [H], Ace Hardware, Albertson's/Osco Drug, O'Reilly Parts, Radio Shack, Walmart SuperCtr, casinos, RV Park, **S food:** Hunan Chinese, **lodging:** Comfort Inn, Guesthouse Inn, Holiday Inn Express, Super 8
137mm	Tongue River
135	Lp 94, Miles City, **N other:** KOA (April-October)
128	local access
126	Moon Creek Rd
117	Hathaway

GLENDIVE

TERRY

MT
NE

INTERSTATE 94 CONT'D

E ↕ W

FORSYTH

Exit #	Services
114mm	**rest area eb, full ♿ facilities, ☎, ⛾, litter barrels, petwalk**
113mm	**rest area wb, full ♿ facilities, ☎, ⛾, litter barrels, petwalk, overlook**
106	Butte Creek Rd, to Rosebud, **N** food, ☎
103	MT 446, MT 447, Rosebud Creek Rd, **N** food, phone
98.5mm	**weigh sta both lanes**
95	Forsyth, **N gas:** Cenex, Exxon/dsl/24hr, **food:** DQ, **lodging:** Sundowner Motel, **other:** [H], Ford, Van's Foods, Yellowstone Drug, to Rosebud RA, **S** camping
93	US 12 W, Forsyth, **N gas:** Cenex, Exxon/dsl/24hr, **food:** Top That Eatery, **lodging:** Rails Inn, Restwell Inn, WestWind Motel, **other:** NAPA, repair/tires, RV camping
87	MT 39, to Colstrip
82	Reservation Creek Rd
72	MT 384, Sarpy Creek Rd
67	Hysham, **1-2 mi N** gas, phone, food, lodging
65mm	**rest area both lanes, full ♿ facilities, ☎, ⛾, litter barrels, petwalk**
63	ranch access
53	Bighorn, access to ☎
52mm	Bighorn River
49	MT 47, to Hardin, Custer, **S food:** Ft Custer Café, **other:** to Little Bighorn Bfd, camping
47	Custer, **S gas:** Custer Sta./dsl, **food:** Jct City Saloon/café, **other:** Custer Food Mkt, USPO
41.5mm	**rest area wb, full ♿ facilities, ☎, ⛾, litter barrels, petwalk**
38mm	**rest area eb, full ♿ facilities, ☎, ⛾, litter barrels, petwalk**
36	frontage rd, Waco
23	Pompeys Pillar, **N other:** Pompeys Pillar Nat Landmark
14	Ballentine, Worden, **S food:** Long Branch Café/casino
6	MT 522, Huntley, **N** gas/phone, **food:** Pryor Creek Café
0mm	I-90, E to Sheridan, W to Billings, I-94 begins/ends on I-90, exit 456.

NEBRASKA

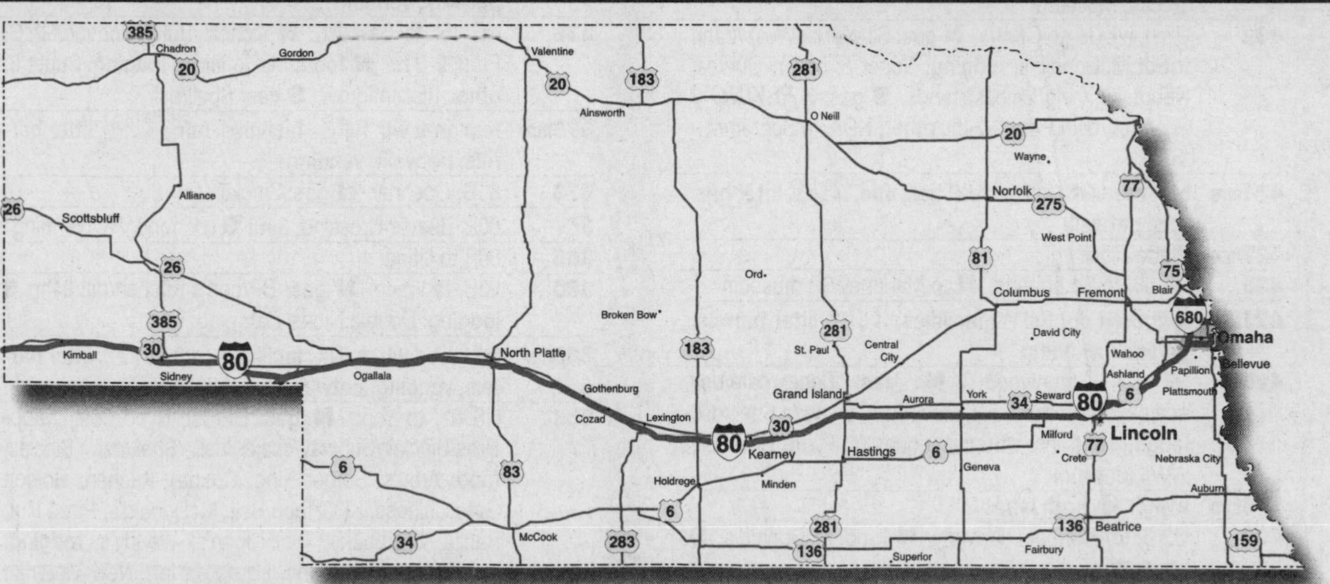

INTERSTATE 80

E ↕ W

OMAHA

Exit #	Services
455mm	Nebraska/Iowa state line, Missouri River
454	13th St, **N gas:** BP/dsl, Infinite, Valero, **food:** Big Horn BBQ, Burger King, McDonald's/playplace, **lodging:** Comfort Inn, **other:** Family$, auto repair, **S food:** King Kong Burgers, **other:** Doorly Zoo, Imax, stadium
453	24th St (from eb)
452b	I-480 N, US 75 N, to Henry Ford's Birthplace, Eppley Airfield
452a	US 75 S
451	42nd St, **N gas:** BP/dsl, **S gas:** Phillips 66, **food:** Burger King, McDonald's, Taco Bell, **other:** [H], Pitstop Lube
450	60th St, **N gas:** Phillips 66, **other:** NAPA, to U of NE Omaha, **S gas:** Omaha 66/dsl, **other:** transmissions
449	72nd St, to Ralston, **N gas:** BP, **food:** Burger King, Margarita's Mexican, Perkins, Spezia Italian, **lodging:**
449	Continued Baymont Inn, Comfort Inn, Holiday Inn/rest., Homewood Suites, Howard Johnson, Quality Inn, Super 8, Travelodge, **other:** [H], **S gas:** Cenex/dsl, **food:** Anthony's Steaks
448	84th St, **N gas:** BP, Shell, **food:** Arby's, Denny's, Farmhouse Café, Great Wall Chinese, Husker Hounds, McDonald's, Subway, Taco Bell, **lodging:** Econolodge, **other:** Advance Parts, Hancock Fabrics, Mangelson's Crafts, NAPA AutoCare, ShopKO, **S gas:** QT, Shell/dsl, **food:** Wendy's, **other:** Chevrolet, Kia
446	I-680 N, to Boystown
445	US 275, NE 92, I thru L St, **N gas:** Cenex, **food:** Austin's Steaks, Wendy's, **lodging:** Clarion, **other:** Buick/Pontiac/GMC, Home Depot, Nelsen's RV Ctr, Sam's Club/gas, Walmart SuperCtr/24hr **S food:** Village Inn Rest., **lodging:** Baymont Inn, Best Western, Carlisle Hotel, Comfort Inn, Day's Inn, Econolodge, Hawthorn

INTERSTATE 80 CONT'D

Exit #	Services
445	Continued Suites, Holiday Inn Express, Howard Johnson, La Quinta, Motel 6, Super 8, **other:** Goodyear, NE Beef Co, **S on 108th...gas:** Conoco/dsl, QT/dsl, **food:** Arby's, Burger King, China 1, Godfather's Pizza, Hong Kong Café, LJ Silver, McDonald's, Perkins, Pizza Hut/Taco Bell, Sonic, Subway, Valentino's, Wendy's, **other:** Albertson's, U-Save Drug
444	Q St, **N gas:** Cenex/dsl
442	126th St, Harrison St, **N other:** Chrysler/Jeep/Dodge, Toyota, VW, **S gas:** Phillips 66, **food:** Runza, **lodging:** Embassy Suites, Hampton Inn, ValuePlace Hotel, **other:** Cabela's
440	NE 50, to Springfield, **N gas:** Phillips 66, Shell/Sapp Bros/Subway/dsl/24hr/@, Woody's/dsl, **food:** Azteca Mexican, Cracker Barrel, Hardee's, McDonald's, Pizza Machine, Quizno's, **lodging:** Ben Franklin Motel, Comfort Inn, Countryside Suites, Days Inn, Quality Inn, Rodeway Inn, **other:** H, Ford, truckwash, **S gas:** BP/dsl, to Platte River SP
439	439 NE 370, to Gretna, **N gas:** Kum&Go/Quizno's, Phillips 66/dsl, **lodging:** Suburban Inn, **S** H, Volvo Trucks, museum
432	US 6, NE 31, to Gretna, **N gas:** Sinclair/dsl/rest./24hr, **food:** McDonald's, **lodging:** Super 8, **other:** Curves, Nebraska X-ing/famous brands, **S gas:** *FLYING J* /Conoco/dsl/LP/rest./24hr, **other:** KOA, to Schramm SP
431mm	**rest area wb, full facilities, info, , , litter barrels, petwalk**
427mm	Platte River
426	NE 66, to Southbend, **N** to Mahoney SP, museum
425.5	**rest area eb, full facilities, , , litter barrels, petwalk, vending**
420	NE 63, Greenwood, **N gas:** Cenex/cafe/dsl/scales/24hr, **other:** RV camping, **S gas:** Shell/dsl, **lodging:** Big Inn, **other:** antiques, to Platte River SP, WWII Museum
416mm	**weigh sta both lanes**
409	US 6, to E Lincoln, Waverly, **N food:** McDonald's, **S other:** H
405	US 77 N, 56th St, Lincoln, **S gas:** Phillips 66, **other:** H, Freightliner, truck parking, **1 mi S food:** Misty's Rest., **lodging:** Howard Johnson, Travelodge, **other:** antiques
403	27th St, Lincoln, **S gas:** Conoco/Wendy's/dsl, Phillips 66/Subway/dsl, **food:** Arby's, Cracker Barrel, DQ, King Kong Burger, Popeye's/Taco Inn, Quizno's, **lodging:** AmericInn, Best Western, Countryside Suites, Settle Inn, Staybridge Suites, ValuePlace Hotel, **other:** BMW, Chevrolet/Pontiac/Cadillac/GMC, Ford/Lincoln/Mercury/Mazda, Lexus, Suzuki, Toyota, **1-3 mi S gas:** Git'N Split, Mobil, Phillips 66/Subway, Shell, **food:** Applebee's, Beacon Hill Rest., Burger King, Carlos O'Kelly's, China Buffet, CiCi's Pizza, Culver's, DaVinci's Italian, Godfather's, Golden Corral, IHOP, McDonald's, Papa John's, Ruby Tuesday, Runza Rest., Schlotsky's, Sonic, Taco Bell, Taco Bueno, Taco John's, Valentino's, Village Inn, **lodging:** Comfort Suites, Country Inn&Suites, Fairfield Inn, Holiday Inn Express,
403	Continued Quinta, Microtel, Super 8, **other:** AutoZone, Curves, Dodge/Jeep, $Tree, GNC, Haas Tire, Home Depot, HyVee Foods, Menards, Michael's, PetsMart, Radio Shack, Sam's Club/gas, ShopKO, Walmart SuperCtr, to U NE, st fairpark
401b	US 34 W, **S** RV camping
401a	I-180, US 34 E, to 9th St, Lincoln
399	Lincoln, **N gas:** BP/dsl, Phillips 66, **food:** Baskin-Robbins, McDonald's, Perkins, Quizno's, **lodging:** Airport Inn, Best Value Inn, Comfort Inn, Day's Inn, Hampton Inn, Holiday Inn Express, Horizon Inn, Motel 6, Ramada Inn, Sleep Inn, Quality Inn, **other:** to airport, **S gas:** Sinclair/dsl, **lodging:** Econolodge, Economy Lodge
397	US 77 S, to Beatrice
396	US 6, West O St (from eb), **S gas:** Sinclair/dsl, **lodging:** Super 8, Travelodge, **other:** Lincoln/Mercury
395	US 6, NW 48th St, **S gas:** Shoemaker's/Shell/dsl, **lodging:** Cobbler Inn, **other:** Harley-Davidson, truck repair
388	NE 103, to Crete, Pleasant Dale
382	US 6, Milford
381mm	**rest area eb, full facilities, , , litter barrels, petwalk, vending**
379	NE 15, to Seward, **N other:** Buick/Pontiac/GMC, Ford, **2-3 mi N food:** McDonald's, **lodging:** Super 8, **other:** H, antiques, **S gas:** Shell/dsl,
375mm	**rest area wb, full facilities, info, , , litter barrels, petwalk, vending**
373	80G, Goehner, **N gas:** Sinclair
369	80E, Beaver Crossing, **3 mi S** H, food, RV camping
366	80F, to Utica
360	93B, to Waco, **N gas:** BP/Lori's Kitchen/dsl/24hr, **S lodging:** Double Nickel Camping
355mm	**rest area wb, full facilities, info, , , litter barrels, vending, petwalk**
353	US 81, to York, **N gas:** BP/dsl, Byco Fuel, Sapp-Bros/Sinclair/Subway/scales/dsl, Shell/dsl, Sinclair, **food:** Arby's, Burger King, Country Kitchen, Golden Gate Chinese, KFC/Taco Bell, McDonald's, Pizza Hut, Runza, Starbucks, Taco John's, Wendy's, **lodging:** Comfort Inn, Day's Inn, Hampton Inn, New Victorian Inn, Palmer Inn, Super 8, Yorkshire Motel, **other:** H, Buick/GMC, Chevrolet/Pontiac, Elms RV Park, Ford, Walmart SuperCtr/Subway, **S gas:** Petro/Phillips 66/Iron Skillet/Pizza Hut/dsl/24hr/@, Shell/dsl/rest./24hr, **food:** Applebee's, **lodging:** Camelot Inn, Holiday Inn, **other:** Blue Beacon, tires/wash/lube
351mm	**rest area eb, full facilities, info, , , litter barrels, petwalk, vending**
348	93E, to Bradshaw
342	93A, Henderson, **N other:** Prarie Oasis Camping, **S gas:** Fuel/dsl, **food:** Subway, **lodging:** Grace Inn, **other:** H
338	41D, to Hampton
332	NE 14, Aurora, **N gas:** Shell/dsl, **food:** McDonald's (3mi), Pizza Hut (3mi), Subway (2.5), **lodging:** Budget Host (3mi), Hamilton Motel/rest., **other:** H, to Plainsman Museum, **S gas:** Love's/Arby's/dsl/scales
324	41B, to Giltner

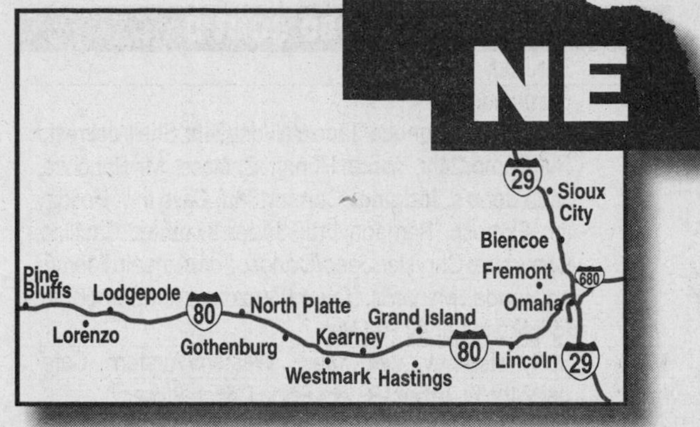

INTERSTATE 80 CONT'D

Exit #	Services
318	NE 2, to Grand Island, **S other:** KOA
317mm	**rest area wb, full ♿ facilities, info, ☎, [picnic], litter barrels, vending, petwalk**
315mm	**rest area eb, full ♿ facilities, info, ☎, [picnic], litter barrels, vending, petwalk**
314mm	Platte River
314	Locust Street, to Grand Island, (4-6mi) **N gas:** Byco, Casey's, **food:** LJ Silver, Subway, Tommy's Rest., Wendy's, **lodging:** Holiday Inn, Howard Johnson, Island Inn Motel, Rodeway Inn, Travelodge, **other:** Walmart
312	US 34/281, to Grand Island, **N gas:** Bosselman/Pilot/Sinclair/Max's/Subway/scales/dsl/24hr, Phillips 66, **lodging:** Motel 6, USA Inn/rest., **other:** [H], Mormon Island RA, to Stuhr Pioneer Museum, **S gas:** Sinclair/Arby's/dsl, **lodging:** Holiday Inn/rest., Holiday Inn Express, **other:** Peterbilt, Hastings Museum (15mi)
305	40C, to Alda, **N gas:** Sinclair/dsl/scales/24hr, TA/Country Pride/dsl/scales/24hr/@, **S other:** Crane Meadows Nature Ctr/rest area
300	NE 11, Wood River, **S gas:** Bosselman/Pilot/Sinclair/Grandma Max's/Subway/dsl/24hr/@, **lodging:** motel/RV park
291	10D, Shelton, **N other:** War Axe SRA
285	10C, Gibbon, **N gas:** Petro Oasis/dsl, **other:** Windmill SP, RV camping, **S lodging:** Country Motel
279	NE 10, to Minden, **N gas:** Shell/dsl, **S other:** Pioneer Village Camping
275mm	The Great Platte River Road Archway Monument
272	NE 44, Kearney, **N gas:** Casey's, Cenex/Subway/dsl, Gas Stop, Shell/dsl, Sinclair, Valero, **food:** Amigo's, Arby's, Burger King, Carlos O'Kelly's, DQ, Hunan's Rest., King's Buffet, LJ Silver, McDonald's, Old Chicago, Perkins/24hr, Pizza Hut, Quizno's, Red Lobster, Ruby Tuesday, Runza Rest., San Pedro Mexican, Taco Bell, Taco John's, USA Steaks, Wendy's, Whiskey Creek, **lodging:** AmericInn, Best Western, Comfort Inn, Country Inn&Suites, Days Inn, Econolodge, Hampton Inn, Holiday Inn, Microtel, Motel 6, Quality Inn, Ramada Inn/rest., Rodeway Inn, Super 8, Western Inn, Wingate Inn, **other:** [H], Big Apple Foods, Boogaart's Foods, Buick/Cadillac, Chevrolet, Chrysler/Dodge/Jeep, $General, Goodyear, NAPA, Walmart SuperCtr/24hr (3mi), to Archway Mon, U NE Kearney, Museum of NE Art, **S gas:** Qwest/dsl, **food:** Grandpa's Steaks, Skeeter's BBQ, **lodging:** Best Western, Holiday Inn Express
271mm	**rest area wb, full ♿ facilities, info, ☎, [picnic], litter barrels, vending, petwalk**
269mm	**rest area eb, full ♿ facilities, info, ☎, [picnic], litter barrels, vending, petwalk**
263	rd 10 b, Odessa, **N gas:** Sapp/Shell/dsl/rest., **other:** UP Rec Area
263	rd 10 b, Odessa, **N gas:** Sapp/Shell/dsl/rest., **other:** UP Rec Area
257	US 183, Elm Creek, **N gas:** Bosselman/Pilot/Sinclair/Subway/dsl/scales/24hr, **other:** Antique Car Museum, Nebraska Prarie Museum, Nebraska Tire, Sunny Meadows Camping
248	Overton
237	US 283, Lexington, **N gas:** Casey's, Cenex/dsl, Conoco/Baskin-Robbins/KFC/Taco Bell/dsl, Shell,
237	Continued **food:** Arby's, Burger King, DQ, Hong Kong Buffet, Little Caesar's, McDonald's, Pizza Hut, San Pedro Mexican, Sonic, Wendy's, **lodging:** Comfort Inn, Days Inn, 1st Interstate Inn, Gable View Inn, Holiday Inn Express, Minute Man Motel, **other:** [H], Advance Parts, Buick/Cadillac/Chevrolet/Pontiac, $General, Goodyear/auto, Plum Creek Foods, Walmart SuperCtr/Subway, Military Vehicle Museum, **S gas:** Sinclair/dsl/@, **food:** Kirk's Café, **lodging:** Super 8, to Johnson Lake RA
231	Darr Rd, **S** truckwash/24hr
227mm	**rest area both lanes, full ♿ facilities, info, ☎, [picnic], litter barrels, vending, petwalk**
222	NE 21, Cozad, **N gas:** Cenex/dsl, Casey's/dsl, **food:** Burger King, DQ, El Paraiso Mexican, Pizza Hut, PJ's Rest., Runza Rest., South 40 Rest., Subway, **lodging:** Best Value Inn, Rodeway Inn, **other:** [H], Alco, Firestone/auto, museum
211	NE 47, Gothenburg, **N gas:** Shell/dsl/24hr, Sinclair/rest./cafe/dsl, **food:** China Cafe, Lasso Espresso, McDonald's, Mi Ranchito Mexican, Pizza Hut, Randazzle Cafe, Runza Rest., **lodging:** Pony Express Inn, Super 8, Travel Inn, **other:** [H], Chevrolet/Buick/Pontiac, Pony Express Sta Museum (1mi), Chevrolet/Pontiac/Buick, NAPA, Pamida, truck permit sta, **S** KOA/Sinclair
199	Brady, **N gas:** Brady 1 Stop/DQ/dsl
194mm	**rest area both lanes, full ♿ facilities, ☎, [picnic], litter barrels, vending, petwalk**
190	Maxwell, **N gas:** Sinclair/dsl, **S other:** to Ft McPherson Nat Cemetary, RV camping
181mm	**weigh sta both lanes, ☎**
179	to US 30, N Platte, **N gas:** Sinclair, **lodging:** La Quinta, (1mi) Stanford Motel, **other:** RV camping, **S gas:** ***FLYING J***/Conoco/CountryMkt/dsl/LP/24hr, **other:** truck tire/lube/repair, truckwash
177	US 83, N Platte, **N gas:** Cenex/dsl, Shell/dsl, Sinclair/McDonald's/dsl, **food:** A&W, Amigo's Rest., Applebee's, Arby's, Burger King, Cold stone Creamery, DQ, Hong Kong Chinese, LJ Silver/Taco Bell, McDonald's, Perkins/24hr, Pizza Hut, Quizno's, Roger's Diner, Ruby Tuesday, Runza Rest., Sonic, Starbucks, Subway, Valentino's, Village Inn Rest., Wendy's, Whiskey Creek Steaks, **lodging:** Best Western, Blue Spruce Motel, Hampton Inn, Hospitality Inn, Motel 6, Oak Tree Inn, Quality Inn, Royal Colonial Inn, Sands Motel, **other:** [H], Advance Parts, $General, Goodyear/auto, Harley-Davidson, Holiday TravL Park, Staples, Sun-Mart Foods, U-Save Drug, Walmart SuperCtr, mall, museum, to Buffalo Bill's Ranch, Vet, **S**

INTERSTATE 80 CONT'D

Exit #	Services
177	Continued **gas:** Cenex, Conoco/Taco Bell/dsl/24hr, Shell/dsl/rest./RV Dump/24hr, **food:** Hunan Chinese, Mi Ranchito, Taco John's, **lodging:** Comfort Inn, Days Inn, Holiday Inn Express, Ramada Ltd, Super 8, **other:** Cadillac, Chevrolet, Chrysler/Jeep/Dodge, Ford/Lincoln/Mercury, Honda, Menards, Toyota/Mazda, truck permit sta, to Lake Maloney RA, Vet
164	56C, Hershey, **N** **gas:** Western/Western Cafe/dsl/24hr/@, **other:** Rivers Edge Ranch Store
160mm	**rest area both lanes, full ♿ facilities, info, ☎, ⛱, litter barrels, petwalk**
158	NE 25, Sutherland, **N** **lodging:** Park Motel (1mi), **S** **gas:** Sinclair/dsl/24hr, **other:** RV camping
149mm	Central/Mountain time zone
145	51C, Paxton, **N** **gas:** Shell/dsl/24hr, **lodging:** Days Inn, **other:** RV camping
133	51B, Roscoe
132mm	**rest area wb, full ♿ facilities, info, ☎, ⛱, litter barrels, petwalk**
126	US 26, NE 61, Ogallala, **N** **gas:** Cenex/dsl, Petro, Sapp/Shell/dsl/24hr, Sinclair, **food:** Arby's, Country Kitchen, Front Street Cafe, McDonald's, Mi Ranchito, Peking Chinese, Pizza Hut, Runza Rest., Taco John's, The Star Steak, Valentino's, **lodging:** Best Western, Days Inn, Gray Goose Lodge, Holiday Inn Express, **other:** H, Buick/Chevrolet, Cadillac/GMC/Pontiac, Chrysler/Dodge/Jeep, Ford/Lincoln/Mercury, NAPA, SunMart Foods, TrueValue, U-Save Drug, to Lake McConaughy, **S** **gas:** Conoco/Subway/dsl, TA/dsl/rest./24hr/scales/@, **food:** DQ, KFC/Taco Bell, Wendy's, **lodging:** Comfort Inn, Rodeway Inn, Super 8, **other:** $General, Corral RV Park, Countryview Camping, Pamida
124mm	**rest area eb, full ♿ facilities, info, ☎, ⛱, litter barrels, petwalk**
117	51A, Brule, **N** **gas:** Sinclair/dsl, **other:** Riverside RV camping
107	25B, Big Springs, **N** **gas:** Big Springs/dsl, Bosselman/Pilot/Sinclair/Grandma Max's/Little Caesar's/Subway/dsl/scales/@, **food:** Sam Bass' Steaks, **lodging:** Motel 6, **other:** truckwash, **S** **other:** McGreer's Camping
102	I-76 S, to Denver
102mm	S Platte River
101	US 138, to Julesburg, **S** **truck parking**
99mm	scenic turnout eb
95	NE 27, to Julesburg
88mm	**Lodgepole Creek, rest area wb, full ♿ facilities, ☎ ⛱, litter barrels, vending, petwalk**
85	25A, Chappell, **N** **gas:** Cenex/dsl, **other:** Creekside RV Park/Camping, USPO, wayside park
82.5mm	**rest area eb, full ♿ facilities, ☎, ⛱, litter barrels, vending, petwalk**
76	17F, Lodgepole, **1 mi N** gas/dsl, lodging
69	17E, to Sunol
61mm	**rest area wb, full ♿ facilities, ☎, ⛱, litter barrels, vending, petwalk**
59	US 385, 17J, Sidney, **N** **gas:** Conoco/KFC/Taco Bell/TCBY/dsl, Sapp/Shell/dsl/24hr, **food:** Arby's,
59	Continued Buffalo Paint Rest., China 1 Buffet, DQ, McDonald's, Mi Ranchito Mexican, Perkins, Pizza Hut, Runza Rest., **lodging:** AmericInn, Comfort Inn, Days Inn, Motel 6, **other:** Cabela's RV Park/Outfitter, Chrysler/Jeep/Dodge, Maddox RV Ctr, Radio Shack, Walmart SuperCtr/24hr, RV camping (2mi), golf, truck permit sta, **S** **gas:** Shamrock, **lodging:** Holiday Inn/rest., **other:** truckwash, auto tire/truck repair
55	NE 19, to Sterling, Sidney
51.5mm	**rest area/hist marker eb, full ♿ facilities, ☎, ⛱, litter barrels, vending, petwalk**
48	to Brownson
38	rd 17 b, Potter, **N** **gas:** Cenex/dsl/LP, **other:** repair
29	53A, Dix, **1/2 mi N** gas, food
25mm	**rest area wb, full ♿ facilities, ☎, ⛱, litter barrels, vending, petwalk**
22	53E, Kimball, **N** **lodging:** (1mi) Day's Inn, **other:** Kimball RV Park, golf, **2 mi N** **lodging:** Days Inn, **food:** DQ, **other:** Family$, NAPA
20	NE 71, Kimball, **N** **gas:** Sinclair, **lodging:** 1st Interstate Inn, Super 8, **other:** H, Pamida, RV Park, truck permit sta., **1 mi N** **food:** Pizza Hut, Subway, Taco John's, **lodging:** Days Inn
18mm	**parking area eb, litter barrel**
10mm	**rest area eb, full ♿ facilities, info, ☎, ⛱, litter barrels, petwalk**
8	53C, to Bushnell
1	53B, Pine Bluffs, **1 mi N** RV camping
0mm	Nebraska/Wyoming state line

INTERSTATE 680 (OMAHA)

Exit #	Services
29b a	I-80, W to Omaha, E to Des Moines. I-680 begins/ends on I-80, exit 27.
28	IA 191, to Neola, Persia
21	L34, Beebeetown
19mm	**rest area wb, full ♿ facilities, info, ☎, ⛱, litter barrels, petwalk**
16mm	**rest area eb, full ♿ facilities, info, ☎, ⛱, litter barrels, petwalk**
15mm	scenic overlook
7	1I-29 N, to Sioux City
6	6 Honey Creek, **W** **gas:** Sinclair/dsl/rest., **food:** Iowa Feed&Grain Co Rest.
3b a	(61 b a from wb) I-29, S to Council Bluffs, IA 988, to Crescent, **E** **gas:** Phillips 66, **other:** to ski area
1	County Rd
14mm	Nebraska/Iowa state line, Missouri River, Mormon Bridge
13	US 75 S, 30th St, Florence, **E** **gas:** Shell/dsl, **food:** Firehouse Pizza, Zesto Diner, **lodging:** Mormon Trail Motel, **other:** LDS Temple, Mormon Trail Ctr, **W** **gas:** Sinclair
12	US 75 N, 48th St, **E** **gas:** Phillips 66, **food:** Burger King
9	72nd St, **E** **gas:** QuikShop, (1-3 mi) **food:** Famous Dave's BBQ, IHOP, Sonic, Village Inn, **other:** H, **W** Cunningham Lake RA
6	NE 133, Irvington, **E** **gas:** Conoco/dsl, **food:** Burger King, **other:** Walmart/Subway/drugs/24hr
5	Fort St, **W** **gas:** KwikShop, Sinclair, **other:** USPO

INTERSTATE 680 CONT'D (OMAHA)

E ↕ W

Exit #	Services
4	NE 64, Maple St, **E gas:** BP, **W** Conoco/dsl, Kum&Go, **food:** Burger King, Godfather's Pizza, KFC, La Mesa Mexican, McDonald's, Perkins, Pizza Hut, Runza, Subway, Taco Bell, **lodging:** Comfort Suites, La Quinta, **other:** Bag'n Save, Champion Parts
3	US 6, Dodge St, **E food:** Macaroni Grill, Panera Bread, PF Chang's, TGIFriday, **lodging:** Hampton Inn, Marriott, **other:** AAA, BMW, Dodge, Ford, Jaguar/Land Rover, JC Penney, Mazda, Whlle Foods Mkt,
3	Continued Von Maur, mall, **W gas:** BP, Phillips 66, **food:** Boston Mkt, Burger King, China buffet, DQ, McDonald's, Starbucks, **lodging:** Best Western, Crowne Plaza Motel, Super 8, **other:** Cadillac, Chevrolet, Costco/gas, Hummer, Nissan/Hyundai, Toyota
2	Pacific St, **E gas:** BP, **lodging:** Regency Lodge
1	NE 38, W Center Rd, **E gas:** Cenex/dsl, food Blimpie, Don Carmelo's, Don&Millie's Rest., Garden Cafe, **W gas:** Phillips 66, **food:** Burger King, Ozark BBQ, Wendy's
0mm	I-680 begins/ends on I-80, exit 446

OMAHA

NE

NEVADA

NV

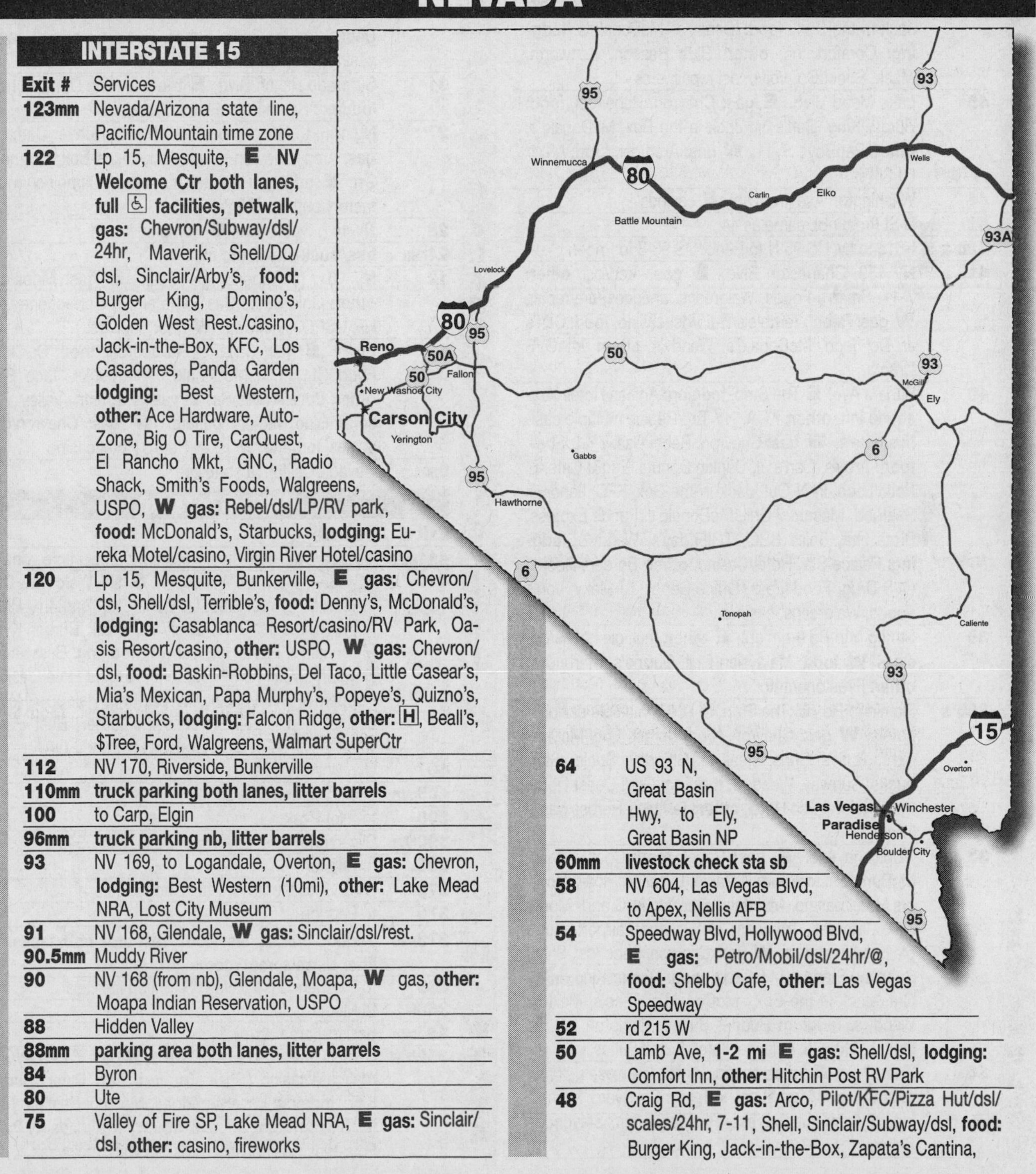

INTERSTATE 15

N ↕ S

MESQUITE

Exit #	Services
123mm	Nevada/Arizona state line, Pacific/Mountain time zone
122	Lp 15, Mesquite, **E NV Welcome Ctr both lanes, full ♿ facilities, petwalk, gas:** Chevron/Subway/dsl/24hr, Maverik, Shell/DQ/dsl, Sinclair/Arby's, **food:** Burger King, Domino's, Golden West Rest./casino, Jack-in-the-Box, KFC, Los Casadores, Panda Garden **lodging:** Best Western, **other:** Ace Hardware, AutoZone, Big O Tire, CarQuest, El Rancho Mkt, GNC, Radio Shack, Smith's Foods, Walgreens, USPO, **W gas:** Rebel/dsl/LP/RV park, **food:** McDonald's, Starbucks, **lodging:** Eureka Motel/casino, Virgin River Hotel/casino
120	Lp 15, Mesquite, Bunkerville, **E gas:** Chevron/dsl, Shell/dsl, Terrible's, **food:** Denny's, McDonald's, **lodging:** Casablanca Resort/casino/RV Park, Oasis Resort/casino, **other:** USPO, **W gas:** Chevron/dsl, **food:** Baskin-Robbins, Del Taco, Little Casear's, Mia's Mexican, Papa Murphy's, Popeye's, Quizno's, Starbucks, **lodging:** Falcon Ridge, **other:** H, Beall's, $Tree, Ford, Walgreens, Walmart SuperCtr
112	NV 170, Riverside, Bunkerville
110mm	**truck parking both lanes, litter barrels**
100	to Carp, Elgin
96mm	**truck parking nb, litter barrels**
93	NV 169, to Logandale, Overton, **E gas:** Chevron, **lodging:** Best Western (10mi), **other:** Lake Mead NRA, Lost City Museum
91	NV 168, Glendale, **W gas:** Sinclair/dsl/rest.
90.5mm	Muddy River
90	NV 168 (from nb), Glendale, Moapa, **W** gas, **other:** Moapa Indian Reservation, USPO
88	Hidden Valley
88mm	**parking area both lanes, litter barrels**
84	Byron
80	Ute
75	Valley of Fire SP, Lake Mead NRA, **E gas:** Sinclair/dsl, **other:** casino, fireworks
64	US 93 N, Great Basin Hwy, to Ely, Great Basin NP
60mm	**livestock check sta sb**
58	NV 604, Las Vegas Blvd, to Apex, Nellis AFB
54	Speedway Blvd, Hollywood Blvd, **E gas:** Petro/Mobil/dsl/24hr/@, **food:** Shelby Cafe, **other:** Las Vegas Speedway
52	rd 215 W
50	Lamb Ave, **1-2 mi E gas:** Shell/dsl, **lodging:** Comfort Inn, **other:** Hitchin Post RV Park
48	Craig Rd, **E gas:** Arco, Pilot/KFC/Pizza Hut/dsl/scales/24hr, 7-11, Shell, Sinclair/Subway/dsl, **food:** Burger King, Jack-in-the-Box, Zapata's Cantina,

INTERSTATE 15 CONT'D

Exit #	Services
48	Continued **other:** Firestone, to Nellis AFB, **W gas:** 7-11, **food:** Cannery Grill, Carl's Jr, Chipotle Mexican, Del Taco, Jamba Juice, Famous Dave's BBQ, Marble Slab, Mulligan's, Panda Express, Poppa's Grill, Quizno's, Sonic, Starbucks, Subway, **lodging:** Hampton Inn, Holiday Inn Express, **other:** Freightliner, Just Brakes, Lowe's Whse, Sam's Club/gas, dsl repair
46	Cheyenne Ave, **E gas:** Arco/24hr, **food:** CiCi's Pizza, Lucy's Grill, Marianna's Mkt, Panda Express, Starbucks, Subway, **other:** $Tree, NAPA, 7-11, Vet, **W gas:** *FLYING J*/dsl/LP/rest./24hr, 7-11, Sinclair/ Jack-in-the-Box, **food:** Denny's, McDonald's, **lodging:** Comfort Inn, **other:** Blue Beacon, Kenworth, Mack, SpeedCo, Volvo, dsl repair, tires
45	Lake Mead Blvd, **E gas:** Chevron, Rebel/dsl, **food:** Burger King, Carl's Jr., Jack-in-the-Box, McDonald's, **other:** PepBoys, 7-11, **W gas:** Arco/dsl, **food:** A&W/ LJ Silver
44	Washington Ave (from sb), **E** casinos
43	D St (from nb), same as 44
42b a	I-515 to LV, US 95 N to Reno, US 93 S to Phoenix
41b a	NV 159, Charleston Blvd, **E gas:** Arco/dsl, **other:** 7-11, Smith's Foods, Walgreens, antiques, tire/repair, **W gas:** Rebel, Terrible's/E-85/dsl/casino, **food:** Carl's Jr, Del Taco, McDonald's, Wendy's, **other:** H, CVS Drug
40	Sahara Ave, **E** The Strip, **lodging:** Artisan Hotel, Vagabond Inn, **other:** KOA, NV Tire/Repair, multiple casinos/hotels, **W gas:** Chevron, Rebel Gas, 7-11, Shell, **food:** Arby's, Carl's Jr, Dunkin Donuts, Egg&I Cafe, El Pollo Loco, In-N-Out, Jack-in-the-Box, KFC, Landry's Seafood, Macaroni Grill, McDonald's, Panda Express, Pizza Hut, Shilla BBQ, TGIFriday's, Wendy's, **lodging:** Palace Sta. Hotel/Casino, **other:** Borders Books, CVS Drug, Food4Less, Office Depot, TJ Maxx, Von's Foods, Walgreens, casinos
39	Spring Mtn Rd (from sb), **E other:** multiple hotels/casinos **W food:** Malaysian Grill, Quizno's, Starbucks, **other:** Firestone/auto
38b a	Flamingo Rd, **E** The Strip, to UNLV, multiple casinos/ hotels, **W gas:** Chevron, **food:** Burger King, McDonald's, Ruth's Chris Steaks, TGIFriday, Sonic, Starbucks, Subway, Wendy's, **lodging:** Gold Coast Hotel, Palms Hotel, Rio Hotel, **other:** Terrible's Herbst/wash/ lube
37	Tropicana Ave, **E gas:** Rebel, **food:** Coco's Rest., McDonald's, **lodging:** Bellagio, Excaliber Hotel, Hooters Hotel/casino, Mandalay Bay, MGM Grand, Monte Carlo, Motel 6, Tropicana Hotel, **other:** airport, multiple hotels/casinos, **W gas:** Chevron, Rebel/dsl, Shell/ Subway, Standard, Texaco, **food:** Burger King, In-N-Out, Jack-in-the-Box, McDonald's, Taco's Mexico, Wendy's, **lodging:** Budget Suites, Hampton Inn, La Quinta, Motel 6, Orleans Hotel, Siegel Suites
36	Russell Rd, **E other:** multiple hotels/casinos, to ✈, **W gas:** Chevron/Herbst/dsl, **lodging:** Courtyard, Fairfield Inn, Holiday Inn Express, Residence Inn, Staybridge Suites
34	to I-215 E, Las Vegas Blvd, to The Strip, McCarran ✈
33	NV 160, to Blue Diamond, Death Valley, **E gas:** Chevron, Rebel/dsl, 7-11/dsl, **food:** Bootlegger Bistro, Buffalo Wild Wings, Chili's, Cane's Rest, Chipotle Mexican, Dickey's BBQ, Dunkin Donuts, IHOP, La Cosina Mexican, McDonald's, Outback Steaks, Panda Express, Popeyes, Quizno's, Starbucks, Subway, Wienerschnitzel, **lodging:** Budget Suites, Crestwood Suites, Hilton Garden, Microtel, **other:** CVS Drug, Food4Less, Oasis RV Resort, factory outlet/famous brands, **W gas:** Chevron/dsl, TA/Burger King/Subway/TacoTime/dsl/ LP/scales/24hr/@, Shell, Sinclair, **food:** Bilbo's Grill, Del Taco, Famous Dave's, BBQ, In-N-Out, Jack-in-the-Box, Quizno's, Taco Bell, **lodging:** Silverton Hotel/ Casino, **other:** Bass ProShops, $Tree, Kohl's, Office Depot, PetCo, Radio Shack, Ross, Silverton Lodge/ casino, Target, WorldMkt
31	Silverado Ranch Blvd, **E food:** Dunkin Donuts (1mi), **lodging:** South Point Hotel/Casino
27	NV 146, to Henderson, Lake Mead, Hoover Dam, **E gas:** Arco, Chevron, **food:** Jack-in-the-Box, Quizno's, 2 mi **E lodging:** Hampton Inn, **other:** Camping World, factory outlets, **W** Vet
25	NV 161, Sloan, 1 mi **E** Camping World
24mm	**bus/truck check sta nb**
12	NV 161, to Goodsprings, Jean, **E gas:** Mobil/dsl, **other:** Gold Strike Casino/hotel, NV Correctional, NV HP, USPO, skydiving, **W gas:** Shell/dsl
1	Primm, **E gas:** Chevron, Texaco/dsl, **food:** Carl's Jr, Food Ct., KFC, McDonald's, Starbucks, Taco Bell, **other:** Buffalo Bill's Resort/casino, Primm Valley Resort/casino, factory outlets, **W gas:** Chevron/dsl/ scales, **lodging:** Whiskey Pete's Hotel/casino
0mm	Nevada/California state line

INTERSTATE 80

Exit #	Services
411mm	Nevada/Utah state line, Pacific/Mountain time zone
410	US 93A, to Ely, W Wendover, **S NV Welcome Ctr/ info, full ♿ facilities,** ☎, **gas:** Chevron/24hr, Pilot/ Arby's/dsl/scales/24hr, Shell/dsl, **food:** Burger King, McDonald's, Pizza Hut, Subway, **lodging:** Best Value, Day's Inn, Knights Inn, Motel 6, Nugget Hotel/casino, Peppermill Hotel/casino/**RV parking**, Rainbow Hotel/ casino, Red Garter Hotel/casino, **other:** Best Hardware, Smith's Foods, StateLine RV Park, KOA
407	Ola, W Wendover
405mm	pacific/central time zone
398	to Pilot Peak
390mm	Silverzone Pass, Silverzone Pass, elev 5940
387	to Shafter
378	NV 233, to Montello, Oasis, no facilites
376	to Pequop
373mm	**Pequop Summit, elev 6967, rest area both lanes,** ⛱ **litter barrels, rest rooms**
365	to Independence Valley, **N** prison facilities
360	to Moor
354mm	**parking area eb**
352b a	US 93, Great Basin Hwy, E Wells, **N gas:** *FLYING J* /dsl/café/casino, Shell, **food:** Bella's Diner, Burger King, **lodging:** LoneStar Motel, Motel 6, Rest Inn Motel, Sharon Motel, Super 8, **other:** Crossroads RV Park, Four-Way Casino/Rest., Les Schwab, tuckwash,

N ↕ S LAS VEGAS — JEAN — E ↕ W WELLS

INTERSTATE 80 CONT'D

E ↕ W

Exit #	Services
352b a	Continued **S gas:** ⊕**FLYING J**/Conoco/cookery/dsl/scales/LP/casino/RV Dump/24hr, Love's/McDonalds/dsl/scales/24hr, **other:** Great Basin NP
351	W Wells, **N gas:** Tesoro/dsl, **lodging:** Wagon Wheel Rest., **other:** Mtn Shadows RV Park, NAPA, Stuart's Foods, Well's Hardware, USPO, to Angel Lake RA, **S other:** Angel Lake RV Park
348	to Beverly Hills, **N** RV camping
343	to Welcome, Starr Valley, **N** Welcome RV Park, [phone], food
333	Deeth, Starr Valley
328	to River Ranch
321	NV 229, Halleck, Ruby Valley
318mm	N Fork Humboldt River
317	to Elburz
314	to Ryndon, Devils Gate, **N gas:** Sinclair/cafe/dsl, **S** RV camping
312mm	**check sta both lanes**
310	to Osino, **4 mi S** Valley View RV Park

ELKO

Exit #	Services
303	E Elko, **N gas:** CFN/dsl, Sinclair/Arctic Circle/dsl/24hr, **food:** Wingers, **S gas:** Chevron/24hr, Conoco/dsl, Maverik, Sinclair, Tesoro/dsl, **food:** Burger King, Chef Cheng's Chinese, DQ, JR's Grill, King Buffet, McDonald's/playplace, Monkey Sun Chinese, Pizza Barn, Pizza Hut, Ruby Sta. Rest., Subway, Taco Time, Toki Ona Diner, Wendy's, **lodging:** Budget Inn, Comfort Inn, Day's Inn, Econolodge, Elko Inn, High Desert Inn, Hilton Garden, Holiday Inn Express, Holiday Hotel, Microtel, Motel 6, Red Lion Inn/casino, Super 8, Travelodge, **other:** [H], Albertson's, Buick/Cadillac/GMC, Cal Store, Chevrolet/Pontiac, Chrysler/Jeep/Toyota/Honda, Double Dice RV Park, Ford, Gold Country RV Park, Goodyear/auto, Iron Horse RV Park, JC Penney, Lincoln/Mercury, NAPA, Radio Shack, USPO
301	NV 225, Elko, **N gas:** Maverik, **food:** Arby's, Coffee Mug Rest., Greatwall Chinese, Mattie's Grill, McDonald's/playplace, Papa Murphy's, Port of Subs, RoundTable Pizza, **lodging:** OakTree Inn, Shilo Inn Suites, **other:** GNC, Home Depot, K-Mart, Raley's Foods, True Value, Walmart SuperCtr, **S gas:** Shell, Texaco/dsl/RV park, **food:** Cimarron West Rest., Dominos, Dos Amigos, KFC, Starbucks, Taco Bell, **lodging:** American Inn, Arctic Circle, Centre Motel, Esquire Motel, Key Motel, Manor Inn, Midtown Motel, Rodeway Inn, Stampede Motel, Stockmen's Hotel/casino, Thunderbird Motel, **other:** [H], CarQuest, Checker Parts, CVS Drug, Family$, Parts+, Roy's Foods, Smith's Foods/24hr, casino/rest., [airport]
298	W Elko
292	to Hunter
285mm	tunnel
285mm	Humboldt River

CARLIN

Exit #	Services
282	NV 221, E Carlin, **N** prison area
280	NV 766, Carlin, **N other:** Desert Gold RV Park, dsl repair, **S gas:** Pilot/Subway/dsl/scales/24hr, Texaco/Burger King/dsl, **food:** Chin's Cafe, Pizza Factory, State Café/casino, **lodging:** Cavalier Motel, Comfort Inn, **other:** Ace Hardware, USPO, tires
279	NV 278 (from eb), to W Carlin, **1 mi S** gas/dsl

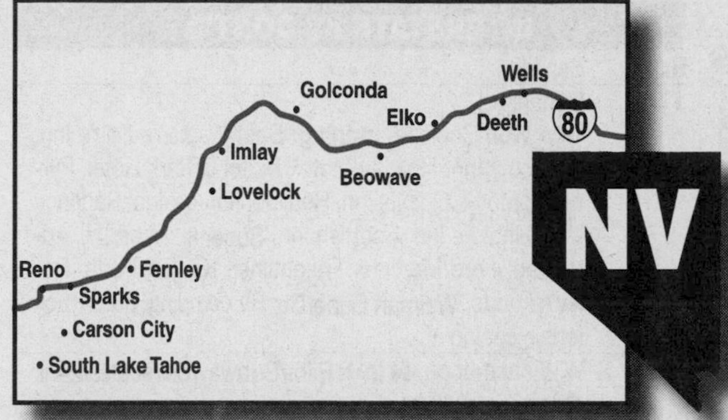

Exit #	Services
271	to Palisade
270mm	Emigrant Summit, elev 6114, **truck parking both lanes, litter barrels**
268	to Emigrant
261	NV 306, to Beowawe, Crescent Valley
258mm	**rest area both lanes, full [handicapped] facilities, [picnic], litter barrels, petwalk**
257mm	Humboldt River
254	to Dunphy
244	to Argenta

BATTLE MTN

Exit #	Services
233	NV 304, to Battle Mountain, **N gas:** Conoco/dsl/24hr, **food:** Mama's Pizza/deli, **lodging:** Comfort Inn, **other:** [H], FoodTown, Royal Harware
231	NV 305, Battle Mountain, **N gas:** Chevron/dsl/24hr, Quickmart/pizza, **food:** Hide-a-way Steaks, McDonald's, **lodging:** Super 8, **other:** CarQuest, Mills Drug, NAPA, USPO, **1 mi N gas:** ⊕**FLYING J**/Exxon/Blimpie/dsl/casino/24hr, **food:** El Aguila Mexican, Owl Rest., **lodging:** Big Chief Motel, Nevada Hotel, **other:** [H], NAPA, Tire Factory, True Value
229	NV 304, W Battle Mountain, **N gas:** ⊕**FLYING J**/Blimpie/dsl/casino/scales/24hr, Shell/dsl, **lodging:** Battle Mtn. Inn, Big Chief Motel, **other:** Colt RV camping, NAPA
222	to Mote
216	Valmy, **N gas:** Shell/USPO/dsl/24hr, **S rest area both lanes, full [handicapped] facilities, [phone], [picnic], litter barrels, petwalk, RV dump**
212	to Stonehouse
205	to Pumpernickel Valley
203	to Iron Point
200	Golconda Summit, Golconda Summit, elev 5145, **truck parking area both lanes, litter barrels**
194	Golconda, **N food:** Waterhole #1 Cafe, **other:** USPO
187	to Button Point, **N rest area both lanes, full [handicapped] facilities, [phone], [picnic], litter barrels, petwalk, RV dump**

WINNEMUCCA

Exit #	Services
180	NV 794, E Winnemucca Blvd
178	NV 289, Winnemucca Blvd, Winnemucca, **S gas:** Chevron, Maverik, Sinclair, **food:** Las Margaritas, Rte 66 Grill, **lodging:** Budget Inn, Cozy Motel, Frontier Motel, Scott Motel, Valu Motel, **other:** CarQuest, carwash
176	US 95 N, Winnemucca, **N gas:** Pacific Pride/dsl, **S gas:** Chevron/dsl/24hr, ⊕**FLYING J**/Conoco/dsl/LP/rest./RV dump/24hr, Mirastar, Shell/dsl, Texaco, **food:** A&W, Arby's, Burger King, Dos Amigos Mexican, Griddle Rest., Jack-in-the-Box, KFC, LJ Silver, McDonald's/playplace, Pizza Hut, RoundTable Pizza, San Fermin Rest., Sid's Rest., Subway, Taco Time,

NV

INTERSTATE 80 CONT'D

Exit #	Services
176	Continued Twin Wok Chinese, **lodging:** Best Western, Day's Inn, Economy Inn, Holiday Motel, Motel 6, Park Hotel, Pyrenees Motel, Quality Inn, Red Lion Inn/casino, Regency Inn, Santa Fe Inn, Scottish Inn, Super 8, **other:** H, AutoZone, Ford/Mercury, Freightliner, Kragen Parts, Raley's Foods, Walmart SuperCtr, RV camping, auto/truck repair, casino
173	W Winnemucca, **N gas:** Pilot/Subway/dsl/scales/24hr, **S**
168	to Rose Creek, **S** prison area
158	to Cosgrave, **S rest area both lanes, full facilities, litter barrels, petwalk**
151	Mill City, **N gas:** TA/Subway/Taco Bell/Fork/dsl/casino/24hr/@, **lodging:** Knight's Inn
149	NV 400, Mill City, **1 mi N gas:** TA/Subway/Taco Bell/Fork/dsl/24hr/@, **lodging:** Knights Inn, **S** Star Point Gen. Sore/RV camping
145	Imlay
138	Humboldt
129	Rye Patch Dam, **N food:** Oasis Pizza, **other:** to Rye Patch SRA, **S gas:** Rye Patch Trkstp/dsl
119	to Rochester, Oreana
112	to Coal Canyon, **S** to correctional ctr
107	E Lovelock (from wb), same as 106
106	Main St, Lovelock, **N gas:** Chevron/dsl/LP, PJ's Gas/subs/dsl, Two Stiffs, **food:** Cowpoke Cafe, McDonald's, Pizza Factory, Ricardo's BBQ, **lodging:** Cadillac Inn, Covered Wagon Motel, Royal Inn, Sturgeons Motel/rest., Super 10 Inn, **other:** H, Ace Hardware, Lazy K Camping, Safeway Foods, city park/playground/restrooms, dsl repair
105	W Lovelock (from eb), **N gas:** Shell/dsl, Shop'n Go/dsl, **food:** La Cacita Mexican, **lodging:** Lovelock Inn/rest., **other:** H, Brookwood RV Park, NAPA, museum, same as 106
93	to Toulon, **S**
83	US 95 S, to Fallon, **S rest area both lanes, full facilities, litter barrels**
78	to Jessup
65	to Hot Springs, Nightingale
48	US 50A, US 95A, to Fallon, E Fernley, **N gas:** Texaco/dsl, Truck Inn Travel Plaza/dsl/scales/24hr, **other:** RV camping, truckwash, **S gas:** Shell/dsl/24hr, Siverado/dsl, **food:** Bully's Grill, Burger King, Domino's, Jack-in-the-Box, KFC, Louie's China, McDonald's, Pizza Factory, Port Of Subs, Quizno's, Siverado Rest./casino, Starbucks, Subway, Taco Bell, **lodging:** Best Western, Super 8, **other:** AutoZone, Curves, D&D Tires, Kragen Parts, Lowe's Whse, Radio Shack, Scolari's Foods, Walmart SuperCtr, USPO, casinos, to Great Basin NP
46	US 95A, W Fernley, **N gas:** Love's/Arby's/scales/dsl, **S gas:** Pilot/DQ/Wendy's/dsl/24hr, **food:** Chukars Grill/Casino, **other:** Blue Beacon, SpeedCo
45mm	Truckee River
43	to Pyramid Lake, Wadsworth, **N gas:** Pyramid Lake gas/dsl/RV camping
42mm	**rest area wb, full facilities, litter barrels, petwalk, wireless internet, check sta eb**
40	Painted Rock
38	Orchard
36	Derby Dam
32	USA Pkwy, Tracy, Clark Station
28	NV 655, Waltham Way, Patrick
27mm	scenic view, eb
25mm	**check sta wb**
23	Mustang, **N other:** RV camping, **S** Chevron/dsl
22	Lockwood
21	Vista Blvd, Greg St, Sparks, **N gas:** Chevron/McDonald's, QwikStop, **food:** Del Taco, **lodging:** Fairfield Inn, **other:** H, **S gas:** Petro/Iron Skillet/dsl/rest./24hr/@, **lodging:** Super 8, **other:** Freightliner, truckwash
20	Sparks Blvd, Sparks, **N gas:** Shell/dsl/24hr, **food:** Best Buy, Outback Steaks, Subway, **other:** Sheel's Sports, Target, water funpark, **S gas:** Petro/dsl/rest./24hr/@, **lodging:** Super 8
19	E McCarran Blvd, Sparks, **N gas:** Chevron/dsl, TA/76/dsl/scales/rest./@, Sinclair, Texaco, **food:** Applebee's, Black Bear Diner, Burger King, El Pollo Loco, Hong Kong Kitchen, IHOP, Jack-in-the-Box, KFC, Little Caesars, McDonald's, Pollo Loco, Quizno's, Sizzler, Taco Bell, Wendy's, Wienerschnitzel, **lodging:** Aloha Inn, Sunrise Motel, Windsor Inn, **other:** BigLots, CVS Drug, $Tree, Kragen Parts, Longs Drugs, Pep Boys, Radio Shack, Savemart Foods, Victorian RV Park, **S food:** Denny's, Super Burrito, **lodging:** Holiday Inn, **other:** NAPA Autocare
18	NV 445, Pyramid Way (from eb), Sparks, **N gas:** 7-11/gas, **food:** In-N-Out, **lodging:** Nugget Courtyard, Silver Club Hotel/casino, **S lodging:** Nugget Hotel/casino
17	Rock Blvd, Nugget Ave, Sparks, **N gas:** Arco/24hr, Chevron, 76, **lodging:** Victorian Inn, Wagon Train Motel, **other:** Kragen Parts, casinos, **S lodging:** Nugget Hotel/casino
16	B St, E 4th St, Victorian Ave, **N gas:** Arco/24hr, Texaco, **lodging:** Motel 6, **other:** Rail City Casino, **S gas:** Chevron/repair
15	US 395, to Carson City, **1 mi N on McCarran Blvd... gas:** Chevron, Shell/dsl, **food:** Arby's, Burger King, Del Taco, Szechuan Chinese, Sonic, Subway, Taco Bell, TCBY, Wendy's, **other:** Home Depot, Kragen Parts, Ross, Walmart/auto, WinCo Foods, **S food:** Bally's, **lodging:** Hilton/Casino, Holiday Inn, 6 Gun Motel
14	Wells Ave, Reno, **N lodging:** Motel 6, **S gas:** Chevron, Shell, **food:** Carrow's Rest., Denny's, **lodging:** Day's Inn, Econolodge, Super 8, **other:** Goodyear
13	US 395, Virginia St, Reno, **N gas:** Shell, **food:** JimBoy's Taco's, **S gas:** Shell/dsl, **other:** H, Circus Circus, NAPA, Walgreens, to downtown hotels/casinos, to UNVReno
12	Keystone Ave, Reno, **N gas:** Arco/24hr, 76, **food:** Pizza Hut, Rose Garden Asian, Starbucks, **lodging:** Gateway Inn, Motel 6, **other:** CVS Drug, Raley's Foods, 7-11, **S gas:** Chevron, Texaco, **food:** Baskin-Robbins, Burger King, Jack-in-the-Box, KFC, McDonald's, Pizza Baron, Port of Subs, Round Table Pizza, Taco Bell, Wendy's, **other:** Kragen Parts, Meineke, Midas, Radio Shack, Savemart/drug, casinos, RV park
10	McCarran Blvd, Reno, **N gas:** Arco/24hr, 7-11, **food:** Arby's, Asian Wok, Burger King, Bully's Grill, Carl's Jr, Chili's, Del Taco, DQ, El Pollo Loco, Hacienda

INTERSTATE 80 CONT'D

E ↕ W — RENO

Exit #	Services
10	Continued Mexican, IHOP, Jack-in-the-Box, KFC, Keva Juice, McDonald's, Papa Murphy's, Pizza+, Port Of Subs, Qdoba, Quizno's, RoundTable Pizza, Starbucks, Subway, Taco Bell, The Chocolate Factory, **other:** Big O Tire, Curves, $Tree, Kohl's, Kragen Parts, PetsMart, Ross, Safeway/dsl, Savemart Foods, Tires+, Walgreens, Walmart Super Ctr/24hr, **S gas:** 7-11/gas, **other:** URGENT CARE, Home Depot, Vet
9	Robb Dr, **N gas:** Chevron/dsl, **food:** Bully's Grill, Coldstone, Dominos, Jimmy John's, Moxi's Cafe, Papa John's, Port Of Subs, Starbucks, Subway, Tahoe Burger, **other:** AAA, Longs Drug, Raley's Foods, Scolari's Foods
8	W 4th St (from eb), Robb Dr, Reno, **S** RV camping
7	Mogul
6.5mm	**truck parking**/hist marker/scenic view both lanes
5	to E Verdi (from wb), **N** Backstop Grill
4.5mm	scenic view eb
4	Garson Rd, Boomtown, **N gas:** Chevron/Boomtown Hotel/dsl/casino, **other:** Cabela's, KOA/RV dump
3.5mm	**check sta eb**
3	Verdi (from wb)
2.5mm	Truckee River
2	Lp 80, to Verdi, **N gas:** Terribles/Chevron/dsl/24hr, **food:** Jack-in-the-Box, Taco Bell, **lodging:** Gold Ranch Hotel/casino
0mm	Nevada/California state line

NEW HAMPSHIRE

INTERSTATE 89

N ↕ S — LEBANON

Exit #	Services
61mm	New Hampshire/Vermont state line, Connecticut River
20 (60)	NH 12A, W Lebanon, **E gas:** Irving, Sunoco/24hr, **food:** Benning St Grill, Brick Oven Pizza, Chili's, Domino's, Dunkin Donuts, KFC/Taco Bell, 99 Rest., Subway, Wok Chinese, **other:** GNC, Jo-Ann Fabrics, K-Mart, LL Bean, Rite Aid, Shaw's Foods, TJ Maxx, **W food:** Applebee's, Burger King, D'angelo, Friendly's, Koto Japanese, Lantern Buffet, McDonald's, Panera Bread, Pizza Hut, 7 Barrel Rest., Weathervane Seafood, Wendy's, **lodging:** Baymont Inn, Fireside Inn, **other:** Best Buy, BJ' Whse, Borders Books, CVS Drug, $Tree, Home Depot, JC Penney, PriceChopper Foods, Radio Shack, Sears, Shaw's Foods, Staples, Walgreens, Walmart
19 (58)	US 4, NH 10, W Lebanon, **E gas:** Exxon/dsl/24hr, Shell, **food:** China Station, **other:** AutoZone, Family$, Ford, Harley-Davidson, Honda, NAPA, P&C Foods, **W gas:** Sunoco
57mm	**Welcome Ctr/rest area/weigh sta sb, full facilities, phone, picnic, litter barrels, vending, petwalk, weigh sta nb**
18 (56)	NH 120, Lebanon, **E lodging:** Courtyard (3mi), Day's Inn, Residence Inn (2mi), **other:** Buick/Pontiac/GMC, Chevrolet/Cadillac/VW, Dodge/Mazda, Nissan/Jeep/Volvo, Wilson Tire/repair, to Dartmouth Coll, **W gas:** Citgo/dsl, Shell, **other:** H, U-Haul
17 (54)	US 4, to NH 4A, Enfield, **E food:** Riverside Grill, Shaker Museum, **other:** Northern States Tire
16 (52)	Eastman Hill Rd, **E gas:** Exxon/Subway/dsl/24hr, **W gas:** Mobil/Dunkin Donuts/dsl/24hr, **other:** Whaleback Ski Area
15 (50)	Montcalm
14 (47)	NH 10 (from sb), N Grantham
13 (43)	NH 10, Grantham, **E gas:** Valero/dsl/Gen Store, **W gas:** Irving/Dunkin Donuts/repair, **food:** Pizza Chef

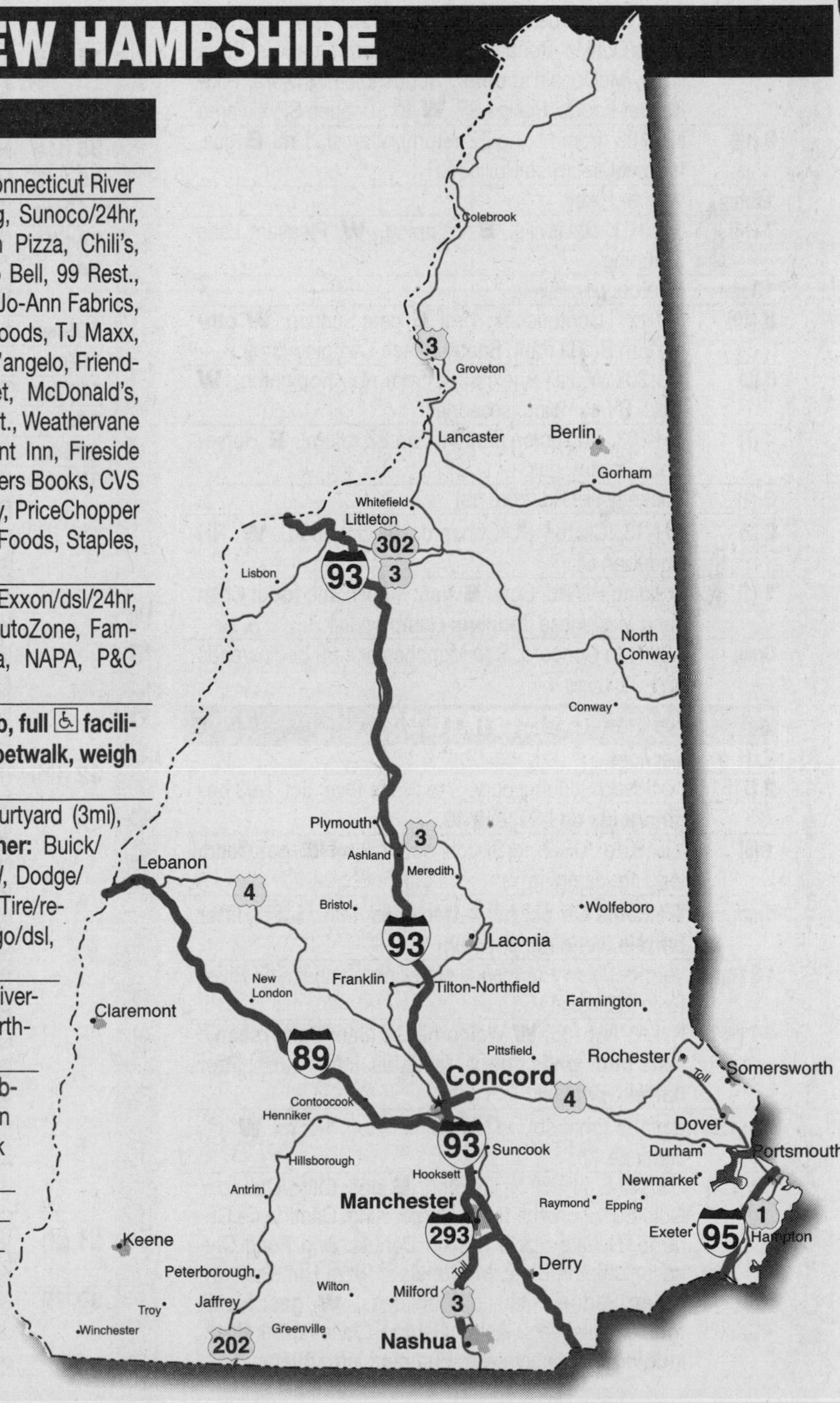

Colebrook
3
Groveton
Lancaster
Berlin
Gorham
Whitefield
Littleton
302
93
3
Lisbon
North Conway
Conway
Plymouth
3
Ashland
Meredith
Lebanon
4
Bristol
Wolfeboro
93
Laconia
New London
Franklin
Tilton-Northfield
Farmington
Claremont
89
Pittsfield
Rochester
Somersworth
Concord
4
Contoocook
Henniker
Dover
93
Suncook
Portsmouth
Hillsborough
Durham
Hooksett
Newmarket
Antrim
Manchester
Raymond
Epping
1
293
Exeter
95
Hampton
Keene
Derry
Peterborough
Wilton
Milford
Troy
Jaffrey
3
Winchester
Greenville
202
Nashua
Toll

INTERSTATE 89 CONT'D

Exit #	Services
40mm	**rest area nb, full ♿ facilities, info, ☎, picnic, litter barrels, vending, petwalk**
12A (37)	Georges Mills, **W other:** to Sunapee SP, food, phone, lodging, RV camping
12 (34)	NH 11 W, New London, **2 mi E gas:** Exxon/dsl, **food:** McKenna Rest., Peter Christian's Tavern, **lodging:** Maple Hill Country Inn, New London Inn, **other:** H
11 (31)	NH 11 E, King Hill Rd, New London, **2 mi E lodging:** Fairway Motel, ski area, food, **2 mi W lodging:** Shaker Mt House B&B
10 (27)	to NH 114, Sutton, **E** to Winslow SP, **1 mi W** lodging, to Wadleigh SB
26mm	**rest area sb, full ♿ facilities, info, ☎, picnic, litter barrels, vending, petwalk**
9 (19)	NH 103, Warner, **E gas:** Citgo/Subway/Pizza Hut, Irving/Dunkin Donuts/dsl/24hr, **food:** Charlie's Pizza (1mi), McDonald's, **other:** Aubuchon Hardware, Mkt-Basket Foods, Rollins SP, **W** to Sunapee SP, ski area
8 (17)	NH 103 (from nb, no EZ return), Warner, **1 mi E** gas, food, museum, to Rollins SP
15mm	Warner River
7 (14)	NH 103, Davisville, **E** camping, **W** Pleasant Lake Camping
12mm	Contoocook River
6 (10)	NH 127, Contoocook, **1 mi E gas:** Sunoco, **W other:** Elm Brook Park, Sandy Beach Camping (3mi)
5 (8)	US 202 W, NH 9 (exits left from nb), Hopkinton, **W** food, RV camping (seasonal)
4 (7)	NH 103, Hopkinton (from nb, no EZ return), **E** Horse-Shoe Tavern, gas
3 (4)	Stickney Hill Rd (from nb)
2 (2)	NH 13, Clinton St, Concord, **E** H, food, **W** NH Audubon Ctr
1 (1)	Logging Hill Rd, Bow, **E gas:** Mobil/24hr, **food:** Chen Yang Li Chinese, **lodging:** Hampton Inn
0mm	I-93 N to Concord, S to Manchester, I-89 begins/ends on I-93, 36mm

INTERSTATE 93

Exit #	Services
2 (11)	I-91, N to St Johnsbury, S to White River Jct. **I-93 begins/ends on I-91, exit 19.**
1 (8)	VT 18, to US 2, to St Johnsbury, **2 mi E** gas, food, lodging, camping
1mm	**Welcome Ctr nb, full ♿ facilities, info, ☎, picnic, litter barrels, vending, petwalk**
131mm	Vermont/New Hampshire state line, Connecticut River. Exits 1-2 are in VT.
44 (130)	NH 18, NH 135, **W Welcome Ctr (8am-8pm) /scenic vista both lanes, full ♿ facilities, info, ☎, picnic, litter barrels, petwalk**
43 (125)	NH 135 (from sb), to NH 18, Littleton, **1-2 mi W** H, same as 42
42 (124)	US 302 E, NH 10 N, Littleton, **E gas:** Citgo/Quizno's, Gulf, Sunoco/24hr, **food:** Burger King, Cantida de Gerardo, Deluxe Pizza, Dunkin Donuts, Jing Fong Chinese, Littleton Diner, McDonald's, Pizza Hut, Subway, **other:** Parts+, Rite Aid, Walgreens, **W gas:** Mobil, **food:** Applebee's, Asian Garden Chinese, 99 Rest., **lodging:** Continental Inn, Hampton Inn, Littleton
42 (124)	Continued Motel, **other:** Aubuchon Hardware, Bond Parts, Buick/Chevrolet/Pontiac, Chrysler/Dodge/Jeep, $Tree, Home Depot, KOA (5mi), Lowes Whse, Shaw's Foods/Osco Drug, Staples, Tire Whse, TJ Maxx, VIP Parts/repair, Walmart/drug, camping
41 (122)	US 302, NH 18, NH 116, Littleton, **E gas:** Irving/dsl/24hr, **lodging:** Eastgate Motel/rest., **W other:** NE Tire
40 (121)	US 302, NH 10 E, Bethlehem, **E lodging:** Adair Country Inn/Rest., **other:** to Mt Washington
39 (119)	NH 116, NH 18 (from sb), N Franconia, Sugar Hill, **W** lodging
38 (117)	NH 116, NH 117, NH 142, NH 18, Sugar Hill, **E food:** Shaw's Rest., **lodging:** Best Western, **W gas:** Mobil, **food:** DutchTreat Rest., Franconia Seafood Dairybar, **lodging:** Franconia Inn (2mi), **other:** Frost Museum, Mac's Mkt, TrueValue, USPO, camping, gifts, info
37 (115)	NH 142, NH 18 (from nb), Franconia, Bethlehem, **E food:** Farmhouse Rest., **lodging:** Cannon Mtn View Motel, Stonybrook Motel
36 (114)	NH 141, to US 3, S Franconia, **W** golf, food, lodging
35 (113)	US 3 N (from nb), to Twin Mtn Lake
112mm	S Franconia, Franconia Notch SP begins sb
34c (111)	NH 18, Echo Beach Ski Area, view area, info
34b	Cannon Mtn Tramway, **W other:** Boise Rock, Old Man Viewing, Lafayette Place Camping
109mm	trailhead parking
108mm	Lafayette Place Camping (from sb), trailhead parking
107mm	The Basin
34a	US 3, The Flume Gorge, info, camping (seasonal)
104mm	Franconia Notch SP begins nb
33 (103)	US 3, N Woodstock, **E gas:** Irving/dsl, **food:** Dad's Rest., Frescolones Pizza, Longhorn Palace Rest., Notchview Country Kitchen, **lodging:** Beacon Resort, Econolodge, Green Village Cottages, Mt Coolidge Motel, Pemi Motel, Profile Motel, Red Doors Motel, Woodward's Resort/Rest., **other:** Indian Head viewing, to Franconia Notch SP, waterpark, **W lodging:** Country Bumpkin Cottages/RV Park, Cozy Cabins, Mt Liberty Motel, White Mtn Motel, **other:** Clark's Trading Post, Cold Springs Camping, Tim's Repair
32 (101)	NH 112, Loon Mtn Rd, N Woodstock, **E gas:** Irving, Mobil, Shell/dsl, **food:** Bill&Bob's Roast Beef, Brittani's Cafe, Cheng Chinese, Dunkin Donuts, Elvio's Pizza, Flapjack's Pancakes, Fratello's Rest., George's Rest., GH Pizza, Gordi's Fish&Steaks, McDonald's, Mr. W's Pancakes, Mtn View Pizza, Nacho's Mexican Grill, Subway, **lodging:** Comfort Inn, Inn Season Resorts, Kancamagu's Lodge, Lincoln Sta. Lodge, Nordic Inn, River Green Hotel, **other:** Aubuchon Hardware, CarQuest, Family$, P&C Foods, Rite Aid, USPO, to North Country Art Ctr, **W gas:** Citgo, Mobil, **food:** Emperial Palace Japanese, Landmark II Rest., Lafayette Dinner Train, Peg's Café, Truant's Rest., **lodging:** Alpine Lodge, Autumn Breeze Motel, Cascade Lodge, Carriage Motel, Woodstock Inn/rest., **other:** NAPA, USPO, candy/fudge/gifts
31 (97)	to NH 175, Tripoli Rd, **E** RV camping (seasonal), **W** KOA (2mi)
30 (95)	US 3, Woodstock, **E food:** Tony's Rest., **lodging:** Jack-O-Lantern Inn/rest., **other:** golf, **W** flea mkt, RV camping (seasonal)

INTERSTATE 93 CONT'D

N ↕ S

Exit #	Services
29 (89)	US 3, Thornton, **E** Pemi River RV Park/LP, **W lodging:** Gilcrest Motel
28 (87)	NH 49, Campton, **E gas:** Citgo, Mobil, **food:** Bella Pizza, Dunkin Donuts, **other:** Handy Man Hardware, USPO, to ski area, RV camping, **W gas:** Citgo/dsl, **food:** Sunset Grill, **other:** Branch Brook Camping, Chesley's Glory Sta., Mtn Vista RV Park
27 (84)	Blair Rd, Beebe River, **E food:** Country Cow Rest., **lodging:** Day's Inn, Red Sleigh Condos
26 (83)	US 3, NH 25, NH 3A, Tenney Mtn Hwy, **W on US 3... food:** McDonald's, **lodging:** Common Man Inn, Pilgrim Inn, Red Roof Inn, **other:** H
25 (81)	NH 175 (from nb), Plymouth, **W gas:** Irving/dsl, Mobil, **food:** Bro's Pizza, HongKong Garden, Subway, Thai Smile, **other:** H, Chase St Mkt, USPO, to Holderness SchoolSt Coll
24 (76)	US 3, NH 25, Ashland, **E gas:** Gulf, Irving/dsl, Mobil/dsl, **food:** Ashland Pizza, Burger King, Common Man Diner, Dunkin Dounts, John's Cafe, Lucky Dragon Chinese, Village Grill, **lodging:** Lakes Region Inn, **other:** AutoValue Parts, Bob's Foods, Jellystone RV Camp (4mi), TrueValue, USPO, repair
23 (71)	NH 104, NH 132, to Mt Washington Valley, New Hampton, **E gas:** Citgo/dsl, Irving/dsl/24hr, **food:** Dunkin Donuts, Quizno's, Rossi Italian, Subway, **other:** New Hampton Parts, info, USPO, **W food:** Homestead Rest. (2mi), **other:** RV Park (2mi), ski area
22 (62)	NH 127, Sanbornton, **1-5 mi W other:** H, gas/dsl, food, phone
61mm	**rest area sb, full ♿ facilities, info, ☎, picnic, litter barrels, vending, petwalk**
20 (57)	US 3, NH 11, NH 132, NH 140, Tilton, **E gas:** Exxon/Subway/dsl/24hr, Irving/dsl/24hr, **food:** Applebees, Burger King, Chicago Grill, Dunkin Donuts, Green Ginger Chinese, KFC, McDonald's, 99 Rest., Pizzaria Uno, Starbucks, Thai Cuisine, Tilt'n Diner, UpperCrust Pizza, Wendy's, **lodging:** Hampton Inn, Super 8, **other:** BJ's Whse/gas, Home Depot, Tanger Outlet/famous brands, Shaw's Foods/Osco Drug, Staples, VIP Auto, **W food:** Chili's, Pizza Hut, **other:** Chrysler/Dodge/Jeep, Ford, Kohl's, Lowes Whse, MktBasket Foods, USPO, Walmart/auto
56mm	Winnipesaukee River
19 (55)	NH 132 (from nb), Franklin, **W gas:** Exxon, **other:** H NH Vet Home, antiques
51mm	**rest area nb, full ♿ facilities, ☎, info, picnic, litter barrels, vending, petwalk**
18 (49)	to NH 132, Canterbury, **E gas:** Sunoco, **other:** to Shaker Village HS
17 (46)	US 4 W, to US 3, NH 132, Boscawen, **4 mi W** gas
16 (41)	NH 132, E Concord, **E gas:** Mobil/dsl, **other:** Quality Cash Mkt
15W (40)	US 202 W, to US 3, N Main St, Concord, **W gas:** Citgo, Gulf, Hess, **food:** Domino's, Friendly's, **lodging:** Courtyard/café
15E	I-393 E, US 4 E, to Portsmouth
14 (39)	NH 9, Loudon Rd, Concord, **E gas:** Shell, **food:** Boston Mkt, Chicago Grill, Family Buffet, Outback Steaks, Panera Bread, **other:** AAA, Ace Hardware, AutoZone,

CONCORD

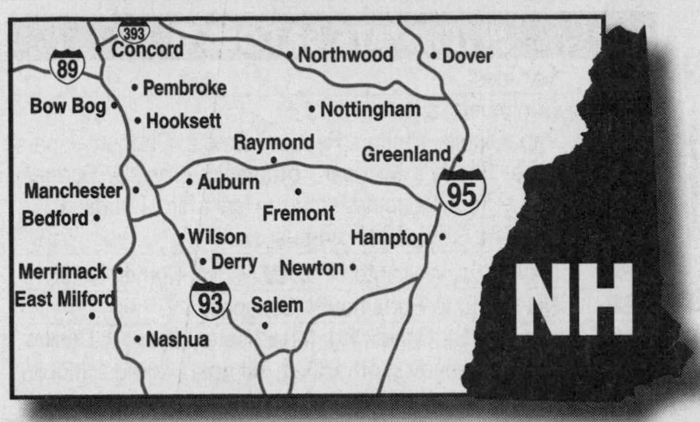

CONCORD

Exit #	Services
14 (39)	Continued Borders Books, $Tree, GNC, Hannaford Foods, LL-Bean, Mkt Basket Foods, Radio Shack, Rite Aid, Shaw Foods/24hr, Staples, TJ Maxx, USPO, **1-2 mi E on Loudon Rd...gas:** Irving/Subway, 7-11, Shell/dsl, Sunoco, **food:** Applebee's, Burger King, D'angelo, Dunkin Donuts, Friendly's, Fusion Asian, KFC, LJ Silver/Taco Bell, Longhorn Steaks, McDonald's, Newick's Lobster House, 99 Rest., Olive Garden, PapaGino, Pizza Hut, Ruby Tuesday, Starbucks, TGIFriday, Wendy's, Windmill Rest., **other:** Aamco, Advance Parts, Best Buy, BonTon, Home Depot, JC Penney, Michael's, PetsMart, Sears/auto, Shaw's Foods/Osco Drug, Target, Walgreens, Walmart SuperCtr, **W gas:** Citgo, Gulf/dsl, Hess, **food:** Domino's, Nonni's Rest., Rainbow Buffet, Tea Garden Rest., **lodging:** Holiday Inn, **other:** Pill MktPlace, to state offices, hist sites, museum
13 (38)	to US 3, Manchester St, Concord, **E gas:** Cumberland Farms, Sunoco/dsl/deli, **food:** Beefside Rest., Cat'n Fill Rest., Cityside Grille, Dunkin Donuts, Kaylen's Pizza, Red Blazer Rest., **other:** Buick/GMC/Pontiac, Chrysler, Dodge/Jeep, Ford/Lincoln, Harley-Davidson, KIA, Mitsubishi/Volvo, Outdoor RV Ctr, Saab, Subaru, **W gas:** Hess, Mobil/dsl, **food:** Burger King, Common Man Diner, D'angelo's, KFC, McDonald's, **lodging:** Best Western, Comfort Inn, Fairfield Inn, **other:** H, Aubuchan Hardware, CVS Drug, Firestone, GMC, Goodyear/auto, NAPA
12N (37)	NH 3A N, S Main, **E gas:** Gulf, Irving/Subway/dsl/24hr, **food:** Dunkin Donuts, **lodging:** Day's Inn, **other:** Ford/Mazda, Honda, Hyundai, Suzuki, Toyota/Scion, **W other:** H
12S	NH 3A S, Bow Junction
36mm	I-89 N to Lebanon, toll road begins/ends
31mm	**rest area both lanes, full ♿ facilities, info, ☎, vending**
11 (30)	NH 3A, to Hooksett, toll plaza, ☎, **4 mi E gas:** Citgo Trkstp/dsl/rest.
28mm	I-293 (from sb), Everett Tpk
10 (27)	NH 3A, Hooksett, **E gas:** Irving/Quizno's/dsl, **food:** Subway, Wendy's, **other:** BJ's Whse, Home Depot, Kohl's, Staples, Target, **W gas:** Irving/Dunkin Donuts, Supreme, **food:** Big Cheese Pizza, **other:** Lowes Whse, Walmart
26mm	Merrimac River
9N S (24)	US 3, NH 28, Manchester, **W gas:** Manchester/dsl, Sunoco/dsl/24hr, **food:** Amato's Pizza, Burger King, Cheng Du Chinese, D'Angelo's, Happy Garden Chinese, KFC, La Carreta Mexican, Lusia's Italian,

NH

INTERSTATE 93 CONT'D

Exit #	Services
9N S (24)	Continued PapaGino's, Puritan Rest., Quizno's, Shogun Japanese, Shorty's Mexican, **other:** H, Chrysler/Dodge/Jeep, Ford/Lincoln/Mercury, Hannaford Foods, KIA, Rite Aid, U-Haul, VIP Parts/service
8 (23)	to NH 28a, Wellington Rd, **W** VA H, Currier Gallery
7 (22)	NH 101 E, to Portsmouth, Seacoast
6 (21)	Hanover St, Candia Rd, Manchester, **E food:** Dunkin Donuts, Wendy's, **other:** Vet, **W gas:** Citgo/dsl, Mobil/dsl, Shell, **food:** McDonald's, **other:** Goodyear/auto
19mm	I-293 W, to Manchester, to ✈
5 (15)	NH 28, to N Londonderry, **E gas:** Sunoco/Dunkin Donuts/dsl, **food:** Poor Boy's Diner, **3 mi E gas:** Shell, **food:** Applebee's, Burger King, **other:** Dodge/Jeep, Hannaford Foods, Lincoln/Mercury, NAPA, Sullivan Tire, VIP Parts, Walmart/gas, **W gas:** Shell/dsl, **food:** Subway, **lodging:** Sleep Inn, other:
4 (12)	NH 102, Derry, **E gas:** Citgo/dsl, Lukoil, Mobil/24hr, Rte 102 Gas, Shell/24hr, Sunoco/dsl, **food:** Burger King, Cracker Barrel, Derry Rest., **other:** H, **W gas:** Exxon/dsl, Global, Hess, 7-11, **food:** Domino's, McDonald's, 99 Rest., PapaGino's, Wendy's, **other:** Curves, Ford, Hannaford Foods, Home Depot, Marshall's, Mkt Basket Foods, Radio Shack, Sears Essentials, Shaw's Foods, Staples, TJ Maxx, USPO, VIP Auto, Walgreen
8mm	**weigh sta both lanes**
3 (6)	NH 111, Windham, **E gas:** Mobil/McDonald's, **food:** House of Pizza, Windham Rest., **other:** Curves, **W food:** Capri Pizza, Clemm's Bakery, Lobster Tail (3mi), **other:** Castleton Conference Ctr, Osco Drug, Shaw's Foods, USPO
2 (3)	to NH 38, NH 97, Salem, **E lodging:** Red Roof Inn, **W food:** Dunkin Donuts, Margarita's Cafe, **lodging:** Holiday Inn, La Quinta
1 (2)	NH 28, Salem, **E gas:** Citgo/dsl, Exxon, Getty, **food:** Bickfords, Burger King, Chili's, Denny's, Friendly's, McDonald's, 99 Rest., Taco Bell, T-Bones, **lodging:** Park View Inn, **other:** Barnes&Noble, Best Buy, BJ's Whse, DeMoula's Foods, Dodge/Nissan/Toyota, Home Depot, JC Penney, Kohl's, K-Mart, Macy's, Marshall's, MktBasket Foods, NTB, PetCo, Radio Shack, Sears/auto, Shaw's Foods, Staples, Target, TJ Maxx, TownFair Tire, Walgreens, racetrack, mall, Vet
1mm	**Welcome Ctr nb, full ♿ facilities, info, ☎; 🛒, litter barrels, vending, petwalk**
0mm	New Hampshire/Massachusetts state line

INTERSTATE 95

Exit #	Services
17mm	New Hampshire/Maine state line, Piscataqua River
7 (16)	Market St, Portsmouth, Port Authority, waterfront hist sites, **E lodging:** Sheraton, **W gas:** Gulf, Lukoil, Mobil, **food:** Applebee's, Boston Mkt, Bugaboo Creek Steaks, D'Angelo's, IHOP, Panera Bread, Starbucks, Wendy's, **lodging:** Courtyard, Hampton Inn, Homewood Suites, **other:** Chevrolet, BJ's Whse/gas, K-Mart, Marshall's, MktBasket Foods, PetCo, Rite Aid, Shaw's Foods
6 (15)	Woodbury Ave (from nb), Portsmouth, **E lodging:** Anchorage Inn, Best Inn, **W** same as 7
5 (14)	US 1, US 4, NH 16, The Circle, Portsmouth, **E gas:** Citgo, Shell/dsl, **food:** Momma D's Rest., **lodging:** Anchorage Inn, Best Inn, Best Western, Fairfield Inn, Holiday Inn, Port Inn, **other:** H, Buick/Cadillac/GMC/Pontiac, Chrysler/Dodge/Toyota, U-Haul, **W gas:** Mobil, **food:** D'Angelo's, Dunkin Donuts, Longhorn Steaks, McDonald's, Pizza Hut, **lodging:** Hampton Inn, Motel 6, Residence Inn, **other:** Barnes&Noble, Best Buy, Ford, Home Depot, Kohl's, Mazda/VW, Michael's, Nissan, Old Navy
4 (13.5)	US 4 (exits left from nb), to White Mtns, Spaulding TPK, **E** H, **W** to Pease Int Trade Port
3a (13)	NH 33, Greenland
3b (12)	NH 33, to Portsmouth, **E** H, **W gas:** Sunoco/dsl, TA/dsl/rest./scales/24hr/@, **food:** McDonald's (1mi), **other:** Target, VW
6.5mm	toll plaza
2 (6)	NH 101, to Hampton
4mm	Taylor River
1 (1)	NH 107, to Seabrook, toll rd begins/ends, **E gas:** Getty, Irving/dsl, Prime, Sunoco/Subway/dsl, Xtra, **food:** Applebees, Chili's, Dunkin Donuts, KFC/Taco Bell, McDonald's, 99 rest., PapaGino's, Pizza Hut, Starbucks, Wendy's, **lodging:** Hampshire Inn, Holiday Inn Express, **other:** Ace Hardware, Advance Parts, AutoZone, CVS Drug, Home Depot, Kohl's, Lowes Whse, MktBasket Foods, NTB, Radio Shack, Shaw's Foods, Staples, TJ Maxx, TownFair Tire, Walmart, to Seacoast RA, **W gas:** Citgo, **food:** McGrath's Dining, Sal&Anthony's Pizza, **lodging:** Best Western, **other:** NAPA, Sam's Club, Seabrook Greyhound Pk
.5mm	**Welcome Ctr nb, full ♿ facilities, ☎, vending, 🛒, litter barrels, petwalk**
0mm	New Hampshire/Massachusetts state line

INTERSTATE 293 (MANCHESTER)

Exit #	Services
8 (9)	I-93, N to Concord, S to Derry. **I-293 begins/ends on I-93, 28mm**
7 (6.5)	NH 3A N, Dunbarton Rd (from nb)
6 (6)	Amoskeag Rd, Goffstown, **E gas:** Sunoco, **food:** Harts Rest., **lodging:** Clarion, **W gas:** Shell/dsl, **food:** Dunkin Donuts, **other:** H
5 (5)	Granite St, Manchester, **E lodging:** Radisson, **W gas:** Gulf, 7-11/gas, **food:** Dunkin Donuts, **other:** H, Walgreens, tires
4 (4)	US 3, NH 3A, NH 114A, Queen City Br, **E gas:** 7-11, Mobil/dsl, Sunoco, **lodging:** Emperial Kitchen, **W on US 3 gas:** Hess/dsl, Z1 Gas/dsl, **food:** Applebee's, Bickford's, Burger King, Clam King, D'angelo's, DQ, Dunkin Donuts, KC's Rib Shack, KFC, Ling Garden, Little Caesars, McDonald's, Papa John's, Taco Bell, Subway, Wendy's, **lodging:** Comfort Inn, Econolodge, **other:** Goodyear, Hannaford Foods, Radio Shack, Rite Aid, Subaru
3 (3)	NH 101, **W on US 3...food:** Carrabba's, Dunkin Donuts, Outback Steaks, Panera Bread, Papagino's, Quacker's Rest., Sparks Rest., T-Bones Steaks, **lodging:** Quality Inn, **other:** CVS Drug, House Of Cloth, Lowe's, Macy's, Marshalls, Radio Shack, Rite Aid, Stop'n Shop/gas, Staples, Target, VIP Auto, Vet, **1-2 mi W lodging:** Country Inn & Suites, Hampton Inn, **food:** Applebees, Bugaboo Creek Steaks

INTERSTATE 293 (MANCHESTER)

Exit #	Services
2.5mm	Merrimac River
2 (2)	NH 3A, Brown Ave, **S gas:** Citgo/Subway/dsl, Mobil/dsl, 7-11, **food:** Airport Diner, Dunkin Donuts, McDonald's, **lodging:** Holiday Inn, Super 8, **other:** Manchester ✈
1 (1)	NH 28, S Willow Rd, **N gas:** Citgo, Mobil/dsl, Sunoco/dsl, **food:** Bickford's, Boston Mkt, Burger King, Cactus Jack's, Chili's, Coldstone Creamery, D'angelo, Friendly's, McDonald's, Panera Bread, PapaGino's, Papa John's, Pizza Hut, Quizno's, Starbucks, Taco Bell, Wendy's, Yee Dynasty Chinese, **lodging:** Fairfield Inn, Holiday Inn Express, Sheraton, **other:** H AutoZone, Batteries+, Buick/Chevrolet, CVS Drug, $Tree, GMC,
1 (1)	Continued Harley-Davidson, Hannaford Foods, Home Depot, Michael's, Osco Drug, PepBoys, PetCo, PetsMart, Pontiac/Cadillac/Mazda, Radio Shack, Sam's Club, Shaw's Foods, Stop'n Shop, Sullivan Tire, TJ Maxx, Town Fair Tire, U-Haul, VW, Vet, **S gas:** Shell, **food:** Bertucci's, Chicago Grill, ChuckeCheese, Famous Dave's, FoodCourt, Ground Round, Longhorn Steaks, 99 Rest., Olive Garden, Ruby Tuesday, TGIFriday, **lodging:** Courtyard, TownePlace Suites, **other:** H, Barnes&Noble, Best Buy, Chrysler, Ford, Honda, Hyundai, JC Penney, Lexus, LL Bean, Lowe's, Nissan, Macy's, NTB, Sears/auto, Staples, Toyota/Scion, Walmart, mall
0mm	I-93, N to Concord, S to Derry. **I-293 begins/ends on I-93.**

NEW JERSEY

INTERSTATE 78

Exit #	Services
58b a	US 1N, US 9N, NJ Tpk
57	US 1S, US 9S, **N lodging:** Holiday Inn, Sheraton, **S lodging:** Courtyard, Fairfield Inn, SpringHill Suites, **other:** to Newark ✈
56	Clinton Ave (exits left from eb)
55	Irvington (from wb), **N gas:** Delta, **food:** Wendy's, **other:** H, Goodyear
54	Hillside, Irvington (from eb), **N gas:** Delta, **food:** Wendy's, **other:** H, Goodyear
52	Garden State Pkwy
50b a	Millburn (from wb), **N gas:** BP, Exxon, Lukoil, **food:** Manny's Wieners, **other:** Best Buy, Firestone/auto, Home Depot Superstore, Lincoln/Mercury, Target, USPO, Whole Foods Mkt.
49b	(from eb), to Maplewood, same as 50b a
48	to NJ 24, NJ 124, to I-287 N, (exits left from eb), Springfield
48mm	I-78 eb divides into express & local
45	NJ 527 (from eb), Glenside Ave, Summit
44	(from eb), to Berkeley Heights, New Providence
43	to New Providence, Berkley Heights
41	to Berkeley Heights, Scotch Plains
40	NJ 531, The Plainfields, **S gas:** Valero (1mi), **food:** Stewart's, **other:** H
36	NJ 651, to Warrenville, Basking Ridge, **N gas:** Exxon/service/24hr, **food:** Dunkin Donuts, **other:** A&P, **S gas:** Exxon
33	NJ 525, to Martinsville, Bernardsville, PGA Golf Museum, **N food:** Ciao Italian, LingLing Chinese, Starbucks, **lodging:** Courtyard, Somerset Hills Inn, **S gas:** Exxon/KwikPik, **food:** Panera Bread
32mm	scenic overlook wb
29	I-287, to US 202, US 206, I-80, to Morristown, Somerville, **S** H
26	NJ 523 spur, to North Branch, Lamington
24	NJ 523, to NJ 517, to Oldwick, Whitehouse, **2-3 mi S gas:** Exxon/dsl/24hr, Liberty, **food:** McDonald's, Readington Diner
20b a	NJ 639 (from wb), to Cokesbury, Lebanon, **S gas:** Exxon/24hr, Shell/24hr, Sunoco, **food:** Bagelsmith Deli, Dunkin Donuts, Spinning Wheel Diner, **lodging:**

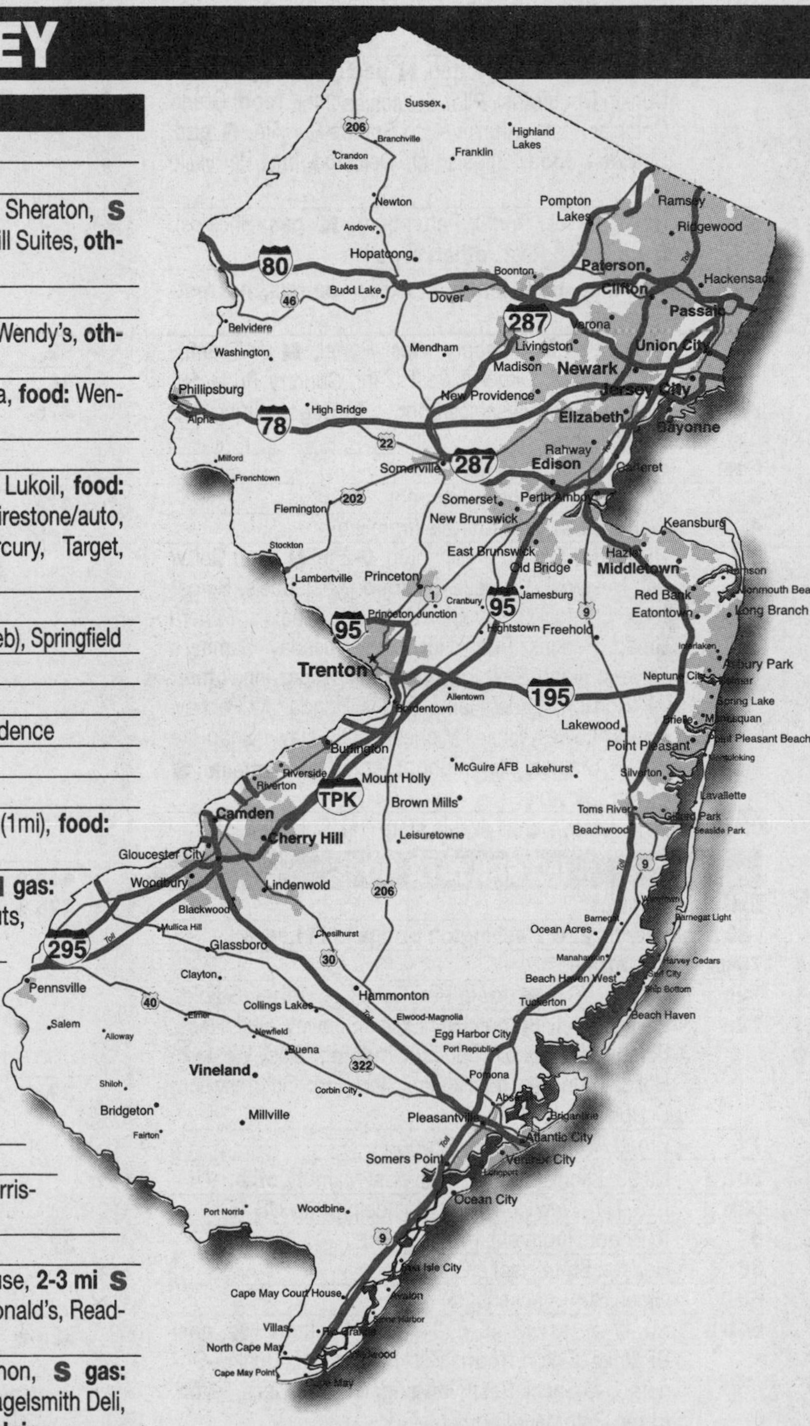

INTERSTATE 78 CONT'D

E ↔ W CLINTON

Exit #	Services
20b a	Continued Courtyard, **other:** to Round Valley RA
18	US 22 E, Annandale, Lebanon, **N** [H], same as 17, **S** Honda
17	NJ 31 S, Clinton, **N gas:** Exxon, Hess/24hr, Valero, **food:** Country Griddle, Dunkin Donuts/Baskin Robbins, Blimpie, McDonald's, **lodging:** Courtyard
16	NJ 31 N (from eb), Clinton, **N** same as 17
15	NJ 173 E, to Pittstown, Clinton, **N gas:** Exxon, Shell/dsl/24hr, **food:** Subway, **lodging:** Holiday Inn Select, **other:** museum, **S food:** Cracker Barrel, Frank's Pizza, Hunan Wok, **lodging:** Hampton Inn, **other:** [H] $Tree, ShopRite Foods, TJMaxx, Walmart/grill
13	NJ 173 W (from wb), **N food:** Clinton Sta. Diner, same as 12
12	NJ 173, to Jutland, Norton, **N gas:** Clinton/dsl, Exxon/Dunkin Donuts/dsl, Pilot/dsl/scales/24hr, **food:** Grand Colonial Rest., **other:** vet, to Spruce Run RA, **S gas:** Shell/dsl, **food:** Bagelsmith Deli, **lodging:** Perryville Inn
11	NJ 173, West Portal, Pattenburg, **N gas:** Shell/dsl, **food:** Chalet Rest., **other:** st police
8mm	**rest area both lanes, [picnic], litter barrels, no restrooms**
7	NJ 173, to Bloomsbury, West Portal, **N** RV camping, **S gas:** Citgo/dsl/rest./24hr, Country Pride/dsl, Pilot/Subway/dsl/scales/24hr, TA/Buger King/dsl/scales/24hr/@
6mm	**weigh sta both lanes**
6	Warren Glen, Asbury (from eb)
4	Warren Glen, Stewartsville (from wb)
3	US 22, NJ 173, to Phillipsburg, **0-2 mi N gas:** Getty/dsl, Hess/dsl, US/dsl/24hr, **food:** Applebee's, Burger King, Friendly's, Key City Diner, McDonald's, Panera Bread, Perkins, Pizza Hut, Ruby Tuesday, Sammy's Drive-in, Taco Bell, **lodging:** Phillipsburg Inn, **other:** [H], BonTon, $Tree, Home Depot, Honda, JC Penney, Kohl's, Lowes Whse, Michael's, Old Navy, ShopRite Foods, Staples, Stop'n Shop, Target, Walmart/auto, **S other:** Chevrolet
0mm	New Jersey/Pennsylvania state line, Delaware River

INTERSTATE 80

E ↔ W PATERSON

Exit #	Services
	I-80 begins/ends at G Washington Bridge in Ft Lee, NJ.
73mm	toll plaza eb
72b	US 1 S, US 9, **N food:** Red Oak Rest., **other:** Staples
72a	US 46, NJ 4, **N gas:** BP, Exxon/Subway, Gulf, Hess/Blimpie/dsl, Lukoil, Sunoco, **lodging:** Best Western, Holiday Inn, **S gas:** Lukoil, **lodging:** Courtesy Inn, DoubleTree Inn
71	Broad Ave, Leonia, Englewood
70b a	NJ 93, Leonia, Teaneck, **N gas:** Marriott, **other:** [H]
68b a	I-95, N to New York, S to Philadelphia, to US 46
67	to Bogota (from eb)
66	Hudson St, to Hackensack
65	Green St, S Hackensack
64b a	NJ 17 S, to US 46 E, Newark, Paramus, **S gas:** BP/24hr, Exxon, **food:** Baskin-Robbins, Dunkin Donuts, Sea Shack Rest., **lodging:** Crowne Plaza, Hilton, **other:** PathMark Foods
63	NJ 17 N, **N gas:** BP/24hr, Hess/dsl/24hr, Valero, **food:** Boston Mkt, Subway, **other:** [H], CVS Drug, Harley-Davidson, Home Depot, 7-11
62b a	GS Pkwy, to Saddle Brook, **N gas:** Shell, **lodging:** Marriott, **S lodging:** Wyndham
61	NJ 507, to Garfield, Elmwood Park, **N** Marcal Paper Co, **S gas:** Sunoco
60	NJ 20, N to Hawthorne, **N other:** [H], Lowes Whse, Michelin/Cooper Tires
59	Market St (from wb), to Paterson
58b a	Madison Ave, to Paterson, Clifton, **S** [H]
57c	Main St (from wb), to Paterson
57b a	NJ 19 S, to Clifton, downtown Paterson
56b a	Squirrelwood Rd, to Paterson, **S gas:** Lukoil
55b a	Union Blvd (from wb, no EZ return), Totowa, **N gas:** Sunoco/dsl, **S lodging:** Holiday Inn
54	Minnisink Rd, to Paterson, **S gas:** BP, **other:** Home Depot, JC Penney, Marshall's, Staples, mall
53	US 46 E, NJ 23 (no eb return), **S gas:** Exxon, Gulf, Sunoco, **food:** Applebee's, Burger King, Dunkin Donuts, Hooters, IHOP, McDonald's, Pizzaria Uno, Red Lobster, Ruby Tuesday, Steak'n Ale, TX Wieners, TGIFriday, Wendy's, **lodging:** Holiday Inn, Ramada Inn, Sheraton, **other:** Borders Books, Costco, Firestone/auto, Ford, Home Depot, Lord&Taylor, Macy's, Nissan, Old Navy, Sears/auto, Target, mall
52	US 46, the Caldwells
48	to Montville (from wb), Pine Brook
47b	US 46 W, to Montclair, **N gas:** BP, **lodging:** Holiday Inn, **S gas:** BP, Gulf, Shell, **food:** Dakota Diner/24hr, Dunkin Donuts, McDonald's, Subway
47a	I-280 E, to The Oranges, Newark
45to	US 46, Lake Hiawatha, Whippany, **N on US 46...gas:** BP, Gulf, Sunoco, **food:** Applebees, Burger King, Chili's, Coldstone Creamery, Eccola Rest., Empire Diner, 5 Guys Burgers, Franco's Pizza, IHOP, Jasper Chinese, Longhorn Steaks, Moe's SW Grill, Outback Steaks, Perkins, Red Lobster, Taco Bell, Wendy's, **lodging:** Budget Inn, Holiday Inn/rest., Howard Johnson, Ramada Ltd, Red Roof Inn, **other:** Cost Cutter Foods, $Tree, Drug Fair, Firestone, K-Mart, PathMark Foods, PepBoys, PetCo, Radio Shack, ShopRite Foods, Staples
43b a	I-287, to US 46, Boonton, Morristown
42b a	US 202, US 46, to Morris Plains, Parsippany, **N on US 46...gas:** Gulf, Hess, Shell, **food:** Fuddrucker's, McDonald's, TGIFriday, Wendy's, **lodging:** Courtyard, Day's Inn, Embassy Suites, Fairfield Inn, Hampton Inn, **other:** Chrysler/Dodge, Ford, Marshall's, Michael's, Subaru, USPO, same as 39
39	(from wb) (38 from eb), US 46 E, to NJ 53, Denville, **N on US 46...gas:** Enrite Gas, Gulf/dsl, **food:** Casa Villa Italian, Hunan Taste, Paul's Diner, Wendy's, West Side Diner, **other:** [H], BMW, Chevrolet, Discount Tire, Firestone, PathMark Foods, Vet, **S gas:** Shell
37	NJ 513, to Hibernia, Rockaway, **N gas:** Exxon/dsl, Shell/24hr, **food:** Hibernia Diner, **lodging:** Best Western, Hampton Inn, **S gas:** BP, **other:** [H]
35b a	to Dover, Mount Hope, **S gas:** Exxon/24hr, **food:** Coldstone Creamery, Dunkin Donuts, Fat Burger, La Salsa Mexican, Olive Garden, Peking Garden, Quizno's, Sizzler, **lodging:** Hilton Garden, **other:** [H],

NJ

INTERSTATE 80 CONT'D

Exit #	Services
35b a	Continued Acme Foods, Best Buy, Border's Books, FoodWorks, JC Penney, Lord&Taylor, Macy's, Michael's, Sears/ auto, mall
34b a	NJ 15, to Sparta, Wharton, **N gas:** Exxon/dsl, **food:** McDonald's, Ming Buffet, Subway, **other:** [H], Rite Aid, **S food:** Dunkin Donuts, King's Chinese, Townsquare Diner, **other:** [H], Costco, $Tree, Home Depot, Pets-Mart, ShopRite Foods, Target, Walmart
32mm	truck rest area wb
30	Howard Blvd, to Mt Arlington, **N gas:** Exxon/dsl/24hr, **food:** China City, Cracker Barrel, Davy's Hotdogs, IHOP, **lodging:** Courtyard, Holiday Inn Express, **other:** QuickChek Foods
28	NJ 10, to Ledgewood, Lake Hopatcong, **0-1 mi S gas:** Delta Gas, Sunoco, **food:** Cliff's Dairy Maid, Dunkin Donuts, KFC, McDonald's, Outback Steaks, Pizza Hut, Red Lobster, Roxbury Diner, Ruby Tuesday, Subway, Taco Bell, TGI Friday, Wendy's, White Castle, **other:** AutoZone, BJ's Whse, CVS Drug, ShopRite Foods, Toyota, Walgreens
27	US 206 S, NJ 182, to Netcong, Somerville, **N gas:** Valero/dsl, **food:** Perkins, **lodging:** Comfort Inn, Quality Inn, **other:** Ford, **S gas:** Shell/dsl/24hr, **food:** Applebees, Chili's, Longhorn Steaks, Macaroni Grill, McDonald's, Panera Bread, Subway, Wendy's, **lodging:** Extended Stay America, **other:** Lowes Whse, Michael's, Old Navy, PetsMart, Sam's Club, Staples, TJMaxx, Tuesday Morning, Walmart
26	US 46 W (from wb, no EZ return), to Budd Lake, **S gas:** Shell/dsl, same as 27
25	US 206 N, to Newton, Stanhope, **1-2 mi N gas:** Exxon/24hr, Shell/dsl, **food:** Byram Diner, DQ, Dunkin Donuts, Lockwood Tavern, McDonald's, Subway, **lodging:** Extended Stay America, Residence Inn, Wyndham Garden, **other:** CVS Drug, Nissan, Radio Shack, ShopRite Foods, STS tires/repair, to Waterloo Village, Int Trade Ctr
23.5mm	Musconetcong River
21mm	**rest area both lanes, NO TRUCKS, scenic overlook (eb), [☎], [picnic], litter barrels, petwalk**
19	NJ 517, to Hackettstown, Andover, **N gas:** Shell, **other:** RV camping, **1-2 mi S gas:** Shell, **food:** BLD's Rest., Terra Nova Pizza, **lodging:** Panther Valley Inn/ rest., **other:** [H], 7-11, USPO
12	NJ 521, to Blairstown, Hope, **N food:** Mediterranean Diner, **other:** Harley-Davidson, st police, **S gas:** US Gas, **food:** Gio's Pizza, **lodging:** Millrace Pond Inn, **other:** RV camping (5mi), Land of Make Believe, Jenny Jump SF
7mm	**rest area eb, full [♿] facilities, info, [☎], [picnic], litter barrels, vending, petwalk**
6mm	scenic overlook wb, no trailers
4c	to NJ 94 N (from eb), to Blairstown
4b	to US 46 E, to Buttzville
4a	NJ 94, to US 46 E, to Portland, Columbia, **N gas:** TA/ BP/Pizza Hut/Taco Bell/dsl/scales/24hr/@, **food:** McDonald's, **other:** RV camping, **S gas:** Shell/dsl/24hr
3.5mm	Hainesburg Rd (from wb), accesses services at 4

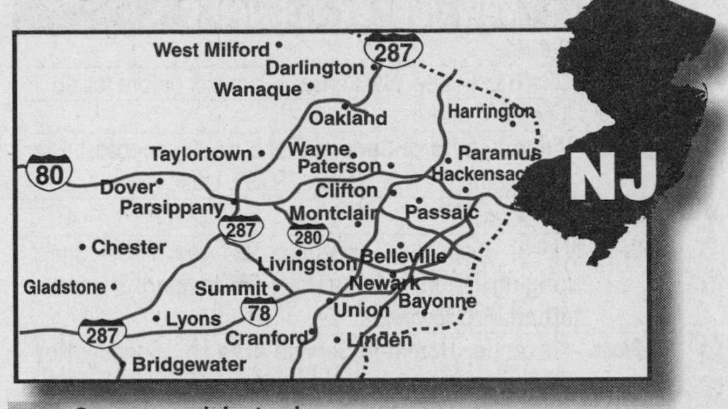

Exit #	Services
2mm	**weigh sta eb**
1mm	Worthington SF, **S rest area both lanes, restrooms, info, [picnic], litter barrels, petwalk**
1	to Millbrook (from wb), **N** Worthington SF
0mm	New Jersey/Pennsylvania state line, Delaware River

INTERSTATE 95

Exit #	Services
124mm	New Jersey/New York state line, Geo Washington Br, Hudson River
123mm	Palisades Pkwy (from sb)
72 (122)	US 1, US 9, US 46, Ft Lee, **E gas:** Mobil, Shell, **lodging:** Courtesy Motel, Hilton
71 (121)	Broad Ave, Leonia, Englewood, **E gas:** Shell, **W gas:** Gulf, **lodging:** Day's Inn, Executive Inn
70 (120)	to NJ 93, Leonia, Teaneck, **W lodging:** Marriott
69 (119)	I-80 W (from sb), to Paterson
68 (118)	US 46, Challenger Blvd, Ridgefield Park, **E gas:** Exxon, **lodging:** Hampton Inn
I-95 & NJ Turnpike run together sb. See NJ TPK, exits 7a-18	
I-95 nb becomes I-295 sb at US 1.	
67b a	US 1, to Trenton, New Brunswick, **E gas:** Shell/24hr, **food:** Michael's Diner, **lodging:** Howard Johnson, Sleepy Hollow Motel, **other:** Acura, **0-3 mi W gas:** Gulf, LukOil/dsl, **food:** Applebees, Big Fish Rest., Chevy's Mexican, Chili's, ChuckeCheese, Denny's, Dunkin Donuts, Hooters, Houlihan's Rest., Joe's Crabshack, Macaroni Grill, Olive Garden, On-the-Border, Panera Bread, PF Chang's, Princetonian Diner, Quizno's, Red Lobster, Starbucks, TGIFriday, Wendy's, **lodging:** Clarion, Comfort Inn, Extended Stay America, Hyatt Regency, Red Roof Inn, Residence Inn, **other:** Barnes&Noble, Best Buy, BMW/Mini, Border's Books, Buick/GMC/Pontiac, Chevrolet, GNC, Home Depot, JC Penney, Jo-Ann Fabrics, Kohl's, Lord&Taylor, Lowes Whse, Macy's, Marshall's, Michael's, NTB, Office Depot, Old Navy, PepBoys, PetCo, PetsMart, Porche, Ross, Sam's Club, Sears, Shop Rite Foods, Staples, Suzuki, Target, TJ Maxx, Walmart, Wegman's Foods, Whole Foods Mkt., mall
8b a	NJ 583, NJ 546, to Princeton Pike
7b a	US 206, **W gas:** LukOil, **food:** Tasty Subs, TJ's Pizza
5b a	Federal City Rd (sb only)
4b a	NJ 31, to Ewing, Pennington, **E gas:** Citgo, Exxon, **food:** Dunkin Donuts, **W gas:** LukOil, **other:** Shop-Rite Foods
3b a	Scotch Rd, **E lodging:** Courtyard
2	NJ 579, to Harbourton, **E gas:** LukOil (1mi), **food:** Red Star Pizza, **other:** 7-11, **W gas:** BP
1	NJ 29, to Trenton, **2 mi W** museum, st police
0mm	New Jersey/Pennsylvania state line, Delaware River

NEW JERSEY TURNPIKE

Exit #	Services
18 (117)	US 46 E, Ft Lee, Hackensack, last exit before toll sb
17 (116)	Lincoln Tunnel
115mm	**Vince Lombardi Service Plaza nb...**Sunoco/dsl, Big Boy, Nathan's, Roy Rogers, TCBY, gifts
114mm	toll plaza, [phone]
16W (113)	NJ 3, Secaucus, Rutherford, **E gas:** Hess, Shell, **lodging:** Hilton, M Plaza Hotel, **W lodging:** Sheraton, **other:** Meadowlands
112mm	**Alexander Hamilton Service Area sb...**Sunoco, Roy Rogers, gifts
16E (112)	NJ 3, Secaucus, **E** Lincoln Tunnel
15W (109)	I-280, Newark, The Oranges
15E (107)	US 1, US 9, Newark, Jersey City, **E** Lincoln Tunnel
14c	Holland Tunnel
14b	Jersey City
14a	Bayonne
14 (105)	I-78 W, US 1, US 9, **2 mi W lodging:** Fairfield Inn, Holiday Inn, SpringHill Suites, **other:** [airport]
102mm	**Halsey Service Area,** Sunoco, Roy Rogers, other services in Elizabeth
13a (102)	Elizabeth, **E lodging:** Courtyard, Extended Stay America, Residence Inn, **W food:** McDonald's, **lodging:** DoubleTree, Econolodge, Hilton, Sheraton, Wyndham Garden, services on US1/US9
13 (100)	I-278, to Verrazano Narrows Bridge, no
12 (96)	Carteret, Rahway, **E food:** McDonald's, **lodging:** Holiday Inn, **W food:** Radisson
93mm	**Cleveland Service Area nb...food:** Nathans, Roy Roger's, Starbucks, **T Edison Service Area sb...gas:** Sunoco/dsl, **food:** Burger King, Dunkin Donuts, Popeye's, Sbarro's, Starbucks
11 (91)	US 9, Garden State Pkwy, to Woodbridge, **E lodging:** Hampton Inn, Homestead Suites, **other:** Home Depot
10 (88)	I-287, NJ 514, to Perth Amboy, **E lodging:** Courtyard, **W gas:** Hess/dsl, **lodging:** Holiday Inn
9 (83)	US 1, NJ 18, to New Brunswick, E Brunswick, **E gas:** Gulf, Hess/dsl, **food:** Bone Fish Grill, Boston Mkt, Burger King, Carrabbas, Dunkin Donuts, Grand Buffet, KFC, Perkins, Starbucks, **lodging:** Days Inn, Motel 6, **other:** Best Buy, Goodyear/auto, Lowes Whse, Office Depot, PetsMart, Rite Aid, Sam's Club, Shopper's World Foods, Shop Rite Foods, Staples, TJ Maxx, **W gas:** Exxon, **food:** Bennigan's, Fuddrucker's, **lodging:** Hilton, Holiday Inn Express, Howard Johnson
79mm	**Kilmer Service Area nb...gas:** Sunoco/dsl, **food:** Dick Clark's Grill, Nathan's, Roy Rodgers, Starbucks
8a (74)	to Jamesburg, Cranbury, **W lodging:** Courtyard, Crowne Plaza
72mm	**Pitcher Service Area sb...gas:** Sunoco/dsl, **food:** Dick Clark's Grill, Nathan's, Roy Rogers, Starbucks
8 (67)	NJ 33, NJ 571, Hightstown, **E gas:** Exxon/dsl, Hess/dsl, Petro, Shell/Dunkin Donuts, **food:** Prestige Diner, **lodging:** Day's Inn, Holiday Inn, **other:** CVS Drug, Vet, **W lodging:** Quality Inn
7a (60)	I-195 W to Trenton, E to Neptune
59mm	**Richard Stockton Service Area sb...gas:** Sunoco/dsl, **food:** Blimpie, Burger King, Pizza Hut, Starbucks, TCBY, Woodrow Wilson Service Area nb...**gas:** Sunoco, **food:** Roy Rogers
7 (54)	US 206, to Bordentown, to Ft Dix, McGuire AFB, to I-295, **Trenton, Services W on US 206...gas:** Petro/dsl/rest./24hr/@, Pilot/Wendy's/dsl/@, Sunoco, Valero, WaWa, **food:** Burger King, Denny's, **lodging:** Best Western/rest., Comfort Inn, Day's Inn/rest., Hampton Inn, Ramada Inn, **other:** RV Ctr
6 (51)	I-276, to Pa Turnpike
5 (44)	to Mount Holly, Willingboro, **E gas:** US gas/dsl, **food:** Applebees, Cracker Barrel, **lodging:** Hampton Inn, **W gas:** BP, Exxon/dsl, Valero/dsl, **food:** Burger King, China House, ChuckeCheese, Dunkin Donuts, Subway, TGI Friday, Quizno's, **lodging:** Holiday Inn Express, **other:** $Tree, Home Depot, JC Penney, Kohl's, Macy's, Sears/auto, Target, Vet
39mm	**James Fenimore Cooper Service Area nb...gas:** Sunoco/dsl, **food:** Burger King, Cinabon, Popeye's, Roy Rogers, TCBY, **other:** gifts
4 (34)	NJ 73, to Philadelphia, Camden, **E gas:** Exxon, LukOil, **food:** Bennigan's, Chick-fil-A, Cracker Barrel, Chili's, Denny's, Macaroni Grill, McDonald's, On-the-Border, Sage Rest., TGIFriday, Wendy's, **lodging:** Candlewood Suites, Comfort Inn, Extended Stay America, Hampton Inn, Howard Johnson, Hyatt Place, Rodeway Inn, Staybridge Suites, Wingate Inn, Wyndham Hotel, **other:** BMW, Cadillac, Ford, Lexus, Rite Aid, 7-11, Whole Foods Mkt, **1-2 mi W gas:** Exxon, Gulf/dsl, Hess, LukOil/dsl, Shell, **food:** Bob Evans, Burger King, Dunkin Donuts, KFC, Pizza Hut, **lodging:** Courtyard, DoubleTree Motel, Fairfield Inn, Hampton Inn, Marriott, Motel 6, Ramada Inn/rest., Red Roof Inn, Super 8, Track&Turf Motel, **other:** Lincoln/Mercury, Mazda, transmissions, to st aquarium
30mm	Walt Whitman Service Area, **Walt Whitman Service Area sb...gas:** Sunoco, **food:** Cinnabon, Roy Rogers, Nathan's, TCBY, **other:** gifts
3 (26)	NJ 168, Atlantic City Expwy, Walt Whitman Br, Camden, Woodbury, **E gas:** Pioneer, 7-11, WaWa, **food:** Luigi's Pizza, Phily Diner, Rita's Ice Cream, Venuto's Pizza, **lodging:** Comfort Inn, Holiday Inn, **other:** Chrysler, CVS Drug, Toyota/Scion, Walgreens, **W gas:** BP, Gulf/repair, Shell/dsl, Valero/dsl, **food:** Burger King, Dunkin Donuts, Pizza Hut, Wendy's, **lodging:** Bellmawr Motel, Econolodge, Howard Johnson, Red Roof Inn, Super 8, **other:** transmissions
2 (13)	US 322, to Swedesboro, **W gas:** Shell/Dunkin Donuts/dsl
5mm	**Barton Service Area sb...gas:** Sunoco, Burger King, Nathan's, Pizza Hut, Starbucks, TCBY, **Fenwick Service Area nb...gas:** Sunoco, **food:** TCBY
1 (1.2)	Deepwater, **W gas:** Gulf, Pilot/Subway/dsl/scales/24hr/, **lodging:** Comfort Inn, Friendship Motor Inn, Holiday Inn Express, Wellesley Inn
1mm	toll road begins/ends
2 (I-295)	I-295 N divides from toll road, I-295 S converges with toll road
1 (I-295)	NJ 49, to Pennsville, **E gas:** Exxon, **food:** Burger King, McDonald's, **W lodging:** Seaview Motel
0mm	New Jersey/Delaware state line, Delaware River, Delaware Memorial Bridge

INTERSTATE 195 (NEW JERSEY)

Exit #	Services
36	Garden State Parkway N. I-195 begins/ends on GS Pkwy, exit 98.

INTERSTATE 195 CONT'D (NEW JERSEY)

E ↕ W FREEHOLD

Exit #	Services
35b a	NJ 34, to Brielle, GS Pkwy S., Pt Pleasant, **0-2 mi S gas:** Exxon/dsl/24hr, Getty, Lukoil/dsl, **food:** Legends Japanese
31b a	NJ 547, NJ 524, to Farmingdale, **N other:** Chevrolet, to Allaire SP
28b a	US 9, to Freehold, Lakewood, **N gas:** Lukoil/dsl, **food:** Ivy League Grill, Stewart's Drive-In, **S gas:** Exxon/24hr, Getty, Gulf, Lukoil, WaWa, **food:** Applebees, Arby's, Boston Mkt, Burger King, Carino's, Chick-fil-A, China Moon, Coldstone Creamery, Domino's, Dunkin Donuts, Longhorn Steaks, Luigi's Pizza, McDonald's, Panera Bread, Pizza Hut, Ruby Tuesday, Starbucks, Taco Bell, **other:** Barnes&Noble, Best Buy, Curves, $Life, Drug Fair, GNC, K-Mart, Kohl's, Lowes Whse, Michael's, Office Depot, PathMark Foods, PepBoys, Radio Shack, Staples, Stop&Shop, Target, TJ Maxx, Walgreens, Walmart, repair, USPO
22	to Jackson Mills, Georgia, **N** to Turkey Swamp Park, **2 mi S food:** McDonald's, **other:** ShopRite Foods
21	NJ 526, NJ 527, to Jackson, Siloam
16	NJ 537, to Freehold, **N gas:** Remington/dsl/LP, Sunoco, **food:** Dairy Queen, FoodCourt, Gianmarco's Pizza, Java Moon Café, **other:** H, Jackson Outlets/famous brands, **S gas:** Wawa/dsl/24hr, **food:** BellaV Pizzaria, Burger King, Chicken Holiday, Dunkin Donuts, KFC, McDonald's, Rio Grande Mexican, Tommy's Rest., Vinci's Grill, **other:** 6Flags Themepark
11	NJ 524, Imlaystown, **S** to Horse Park of NJ
8	NJ 539, Allentown, **S gas:** Shell (1mi), Valero/repair, **food:** American Hero Deli, **other:** Crosswicks HP, Vet
7	NJ 526 (no eb return), Robbinsville, Allentown, **1 mi S food:** La Piazza Ristorante
6	NJ Tpk, N to NY, S to DE Memorial Br
5b a	US 130, **N gas:** Delta/dsl, **food:** Domino's, Dunkin Donuts, Rusert's Deli, ShrimpKing Rest., **other:** AAA, Harley-Davidson, Vet, **S gas:** GS Fuel/dsl, **food:** Chick-fil-A, Chili's, China Grill, Cracker Barrel, Dairy Queen, Longhorn Steaks, McDonald's, Outback Steaks, Red Robin, Ruby Tuesday, TGI Friday, Wendy's, **lodging:** Hilton Garden, **other:** Barnes&Noble, BJ's Wholesale, GNC, Hamilton Shops/famous brands, Harry's Army Navy, Home Depot, Kohl's, Lowes Whse, Michael's, Old Navy, PetsMart, Ross, ShopRite Foods, Staples, USPO, Walmart/auto, mall, to state aquarium
3b a	Hamilton Square, Yardville, **N** H
2	US 206 S, S Broad St, Yardville, **N other:** 7-11, **S gas:** Shell, Valero, **food:** Burger King, Subway, **other:** Acme Foods, CVS Drug, Rite Aid
1b a	US 206 (eb only), **N food:** Taco Bell, **S other:** ShopRite Foods
0mm	I-295, I-195 begins/ends.

INTERSTATE 287

N ↕ S

Exit #	Services
68mm	New Jersey/New York state line
66	NJ 17 S, Mahwah, **1-3 mi E gas:** Getty, Gulf, Pilot/dsl, Royal, Sunoco, Valero/Subway/dsl, **food:** Boston Mkt, Burger King, Dunkin Donuts, McDonald's, State Line Diner, Wendy's, **lodging:** Best Western, Comfort Suites, Courtyard, Doubletree, Homewood Suites,

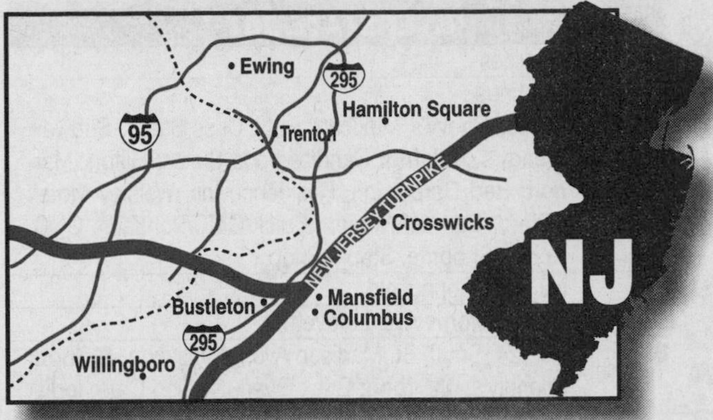

Exit #	Services
66	Continued Holiday Inn Express, Sheraton, Super 8, **other:** Aamco, Chrysler/Jeep, GMC/Pontiac, Home Depot, Hyundai, Mini
59	NJ 208 S, Franklin Lakes, **W food:** Blimpie, **other:** Super Stop'n Shop Foods
58	US 202, Oakland, **E gas:** Gulf/dsl, Lukoil, **food:** Dunkin Donuts, Mike's Doghouse, Jr's Pizza, Ruga Rest., **other:** ShopRite Foods, Walgreens, **W gas:** Exxon/24hr
57	Skyline Dr, Ringwood
55	NJ 511, Pompton Lakes, **E food:** Frank's Pizza, Quizno's, Wendy's **other:** A&P, **W gas:** Getty/dsl, **food:** Baskin-Robbins, Burger King, Dunkin Donuts, **lodging:** Holiday Inn Express, **other:** Stop'n Shop
53	NJ 511A, rd 694, Bloomingdale, Pompton Lakes, **E gas:** Sunoco, Valero, **food:** Blimpie, **other:** USPO
52b a	NJ 23, Riverdale, Wayne, Butler, **0-3 mi E gas:** BP, Lukoil, United/dsl, **food:** Baskin-Robbins, Dunkin Donuts, Friendly's, Fuddrucker's, McDonald's, Pompton Queen Diner, 23 Buffet, **lodging:** Best Western, La Quinta, **other:** H, A&P, Buick/GMC/Pontiac, Goodyear/auto, Honda, TJ Maxx, Toyota/Scion, **W gas:** Getty, Lukoil, **food:** Applebees, Chili's, Ruppert's Rest., Subway, Wendy's, **other:** BJ's Whse, Borders Books, Harley-Davidson, Home Depot, Lowes Whse, Staples, Target, Walmart SuperCtr
47	US 202, Montville, Lincoln Park, **E gas:** Exxon/24hr, **food:** Harrigan's Rest.
45	Myrtle Ave, Boonton, **W gas:** Hess, Shell, **food:** Dunkin Donuts, IHOP, McDonald's, Subway, **other:** A&P/24hr, Buick/Chevrolet, Drug Fair
43	Intervale Rd, to Mountain Lakes, **E gas:** Valero, **W** Dodge
42	US 46, US 202 (from sb only), **W gas:** Exxon, Shell, Sunoco, **food:** Applebees, Dunkin Donuts, Fuddrucker's, Longhorn Steaks, McDonald's, Subway, Wendy's, **lodging:** Courtyard, Day's Inn, Embassy Suites, Fairfield Inn, Hampton Inn, **other:** Ford, GNC, Marshall's, Michael's, Subaru, USPO
41b a	I-80, E to New York, W to Delaware Water Gap
40	NJ 511, Parsippany Rd, to Whippany, **W gas:** BP, Shell/dsl, Woroco Gas, **food:** Fuddrucker's (2mi), Marco's Pizza, Wok's Chinese, Subway, **lodging:** Embassy Suites (1mi)
39b a	NJ 10, Dover, Whippany, **E gas:** Exxon, Shell, **food:** Bensi Italian, Brookside Diner, Capriccio's Italian, Dunkin Donuts, Melting Pot, Nikko's Japanese, Pancake House, **other:** CVS Drug, PathMark Foods, Tuesday Morning, **W gas:** Lukoil, Raceway, **food:** Atlanta

INTERSTATE 287

N ↕ S

Exit #	Services
39b a	Continued Bread, Chevy's Mexican, Ruth Criss Steak, Subway, Wendy's, **lodging:** Candlewoods Suites, Hilton, Marriott, Red Carpet Inn, Residence Inn, Welsley Motel, **other:** Barnes&Noble, Buick/GMC/Pontiac, GNC, Kohl's, Shoprite, Stop'n Shop
37	NJ 24 E, Springfield
36b a	rd 510, Morris Ave, Lafayette
35	NJ 124, South St, Madison Ave, Morristown, **E food:** Friendly's, **W food:** Brick Oven, Calaloo Cafe, **lodging:** Best Western, **other:** H, Rite Aid, Walgreens
33	Harter Rd
33mm	**rest area nb, full facilities, , , litter barrels, vending, petwalk**
30b a	to US 202, N Maple Ave, Basking Ridge, **E food:** Bamboo Grill, **lodging:** Dolce Resort, **W gas:** Gulf, **food:** Burger King, Friendly's, GrainHouse Rest., **lodging:** Olde Mill Inn/rest.
26b a	rd 525 S, Mt Airy Rd, Liberty Corner, **3 mi E gas:** Exxon/24hr, **lodging:** Courtyard, Somerset Hotel, **other:** Kwik-Pik Foods
22b a	US 202, US 206, Pluckemin, Bedminster, **E gas:** Exxon, **food:** Burger King, Golden Chinese, **other:** King's Foods, **W gas:** Shell, **food:** Dunkin Donuts
21b a	I-78, E to NY, W to PA
17	US 206 (from sb), Bridgewater, **E other:** Buick, **W gas:** Exxon, Hess, **food:** Chipotle Mexican, Dunkin Donuts, Friendly's, KFC, Lonestar Steaks, Maggino's Italian, McDonald's, Red Town Diner, Starbucks, TGI-Friday, Wendy's, **lodging:** Marriott, **other:** Best Buy, Bloomingdale's, Borders Books, Lord&Taylor, Macy's, TJ Maxx, mall
14b a	US 22, to US 202/206, **E gas:** Hess/dsl, **other:** Chevrolet/Lexus, **W food:** Fuddrucker's, Houlihan's, Red Lobster, **lodging:** Day's Inn, **other:** Acura, Buick/Cadillac/Pontiac, Infiniti, Mercedes
13b a	NJ 28, Bound Brook, **E gas:** BP/24hr, Sunoco, **food:** Amazing Hot Dog, Burger King, Dunkin Donuts, Frank's Pizza, Girasole Rest., Joey's Grill, Rosinas Rest., Subway, **other:** Radio Shack, Rite Aid, 7-11, ShopRite Foods, Walgreens, **W food:** Applebees, ChuckeCheese, McDonald's, **lodging:** Hilton Garden, **other:** H, Costco, Home Depot, Marshall's, Michael's, Old Navy, PepBoys, PetsMart, Target
12	Weston Canal Rd, Manville, **E other:** ShopRite (3mi), USPO, **W food:** SportsTime Rest., **lodging:** Ramada Inn
10	NJ 527, Easton Ave, New Brunswick, **E lodging:** Crowne Plaza, **W gas:** Exxon, **food:** Burger King (2mi), Dunkin Donuts, McDonald's (2mi), Ruby Tuesday, **lodging:** Courtyard, Holiday Inn, Doubletree, Hampton Inn, Madison Suites, Quality Inn, Staybridge Suites, **other:** H, Drug Fair, Garden State Exhibit Ctr
9	NJ 514, River Rd, **W gas:** Delta, **lodging:** Embassy Suites, Radisson
8.5mm	**weigh sta nb**
8	Possumt own Rd, Highland Park
7	S Randolphville Rd, Piscataway, **E gas:** Lukoil/dsl
6	Washington Ave, Piscataway, **E gas:** Shell, **W food:** Applebees, Burger King, Friendly's, KFC, McDonald's,
6	Continued TGIFriday, Johnny Carino's, Longhorn Steaks, Panera Bread, Ray's Pizza, Red Lobster, White Castle, **other:** GNC, Lowes Whse, PetCo, ShopRite Foods, same as 5
5	NJ 529, Stelton Rd, Dunellen, **E gas:** Gulf/dsl, Lukoil, Shell, **food:** Banzai Japanese, KFC, **lodging:** Ramada Ltd., **other:** Home Depot, Stop'n Shop, **W gas:** Exxon, **food:** Baja Fresh, Bennigans, Burger King, Chicago Grill, Dunkin Donuts, Friendly's, Gianni Pizza, IHOP, Fontainbleu Diner, Gabrieles Grill, Grand Buffet, McDonald's, New York Deli, Red Lobster, Red Robin, Quiznos, Starbucks, Taco Bell, Wendy's, **lodging:** Best Western, Motel 6, Hampton Inn, Holiday Inn, **other:** Burlington Coats, $Tree, Kohl's, Lowes Whse, Macy's, Marshall's, PathMark Foods, Pep Boys, Radio Shack, Sears Essentials/auto, Staples, Target, Walmart/auto
4	Durham Ave (no EZ nb return), S Plainfield, **E gas:** Lukoil, **other:** H
3	New Durham Rd (from sb), **E gas:** Shell, **W food:** Dunkin Donuts, **lodging:** Fairfield Inn, Red Roof Inn, **other:** Walgreens
2b a	NJ 27, Metuchen, New Brunswick, **W gas:** BP, Lukoil, **food:** Dunkin Donuts, **other:** Costco, USPO, Walmart SuperCtr
1b a	US 1, **1-2 mi N on US 1...gas:** Exxon/dsl, Getty, Gulf, RaceWay/dsl, **food:** Bennigan's, Bone Fish Grill, Cheese Burger Paradise, China Cafe, Dunkin Donuts, Famous Dave's BBQ, KFC, Macaroni Grill, McDonald's, Menlo Park Diner, Panera Bread, Polo Tropical, Red Lobster, Ruby Tuesday, TGI Friday, Uno, White Castle, **lodging:** Woodbridge Hotel, **other:** A&P Foods, Best Buy, Goodyear/auto, Macy's, Marshall's, Nordstrom's, Rite Aid, Sears/auto, 7-11, mall, **S gas:** Shell, **food:** Applebees, Boston Mkt, ChuckeCheese, Grand Buffet, McDonald's, Quizno's, **lodging:** Holiday Inn Express, **other:** Astin Martin/Jaguar/Porche, BJ's Whse, BMW, Home Depot, Infiniti, Mercedes, Office Depot, PepBoys, PetCo, Staples, Stop'n Shop Foods
0mm	I-287 begins/ends on NJ 440, I-95, NJ Tpk.

BRIDGEWATER

INTERSTATE 295

N ↕ S

Exit #	Services
67b a	US 1 **I-295 nb becomes I-95 sb at US 1. See NJ I-95, exit 67b a.**
65b a	Sloan Ave, **E gas:** Exxon, **food:** Burger King, Dunkin Donuts, New China Buffet, Subway, Taco Bell, Uno, **other:** Goodyear/auto, Rizoldi's
64	NJ 535 N (from sb), to NJ 33 E, same as 63
63b a	NJ 33 W, rd 535, Mercerville, Trenton, **E gas:** Hess, Lukoil, Valero, **food:** Applebee's, Boston Mkt, Lobster Dock, McDonald's, Pizza Hut, Popeye's, Subway, Vincent's Pizza, Wendy's, **other:** CVS Drug, Ford, Rite Aid, auto repair, USPO, **W gas:** Exxon/24hr, **food:** Dunkin Donuts, Golden Gate Diner/24hr, Szechuan House, WaWa, **other:** Advance Parts, Family$
62	Olden Ave N (from sb, no return), **W gas:** Delta
61b a	Arena Dr, White Horse Ave, **W gas:** 7-11
60b a	I-195, to I-95, W to Trenton, E to Neptune
58mm	scenic overlook both lanes
57b a	US 130, US 206, **E gas:** Petro, Shell/24hr, Valero, **food:** Burger King, Denny's, McDonald's, **lodging:** Best Western, Comfort Inn, Day's Inn, Econolodge, Hampton Inn, **other:** Acme Foods, Blue Beacon, **W**

TRENTON

NJ

INTERSTATE 295

N ↕ S

Exit #	Services
57b a	Continued **lodging:** Candlewood Suites, **other:** st police
56	US 206 S (from nb, no return), to NJ Tpk, Ft Dix, McGuire AFB, **E gas:** Sunoco, **lodging:** Day's Inn, Holiday Inn Express, same as 57
52b a	rd 656, to Columbus, Florence, **E gas:** Petro/dsl/rest./24hr/@, Pilot/Wendy's/dsl/24hr
50mm	**rest area both lanes, no facilities**
47b a	NJ 541, to Mount Holly, NJ Tpk, Burlington, **E gas:** BP, Exxon/dsl/24hr, GasWay, Mobil/dsl, **food:** Applebees, Burger King, ChuckeCheese, Cracker Barrel, Dunkin Donuts, FoodCourt, McDonald's, Taco Bell, TGIFriday, **lodging:** Best Western, Econolodge, Hampton Inn, Holiday Inn Express, **other:** Home Depot, Kohl's, Macy's, Sears, Target, mall, Vet, **W gas:** Citgo, Exxon, Hess/dsl, **food:** Checker's, Friendly's, Mulligan's Ice Cream, Subway, Wedgewood Farms Rest., Wendy's, **other:** H, AutoZone, Acme Foods, Curves, Goodyear/auto, K-Mart, Marshall's, WaWa, Walmart/auto
45b a	to Mt Holly, Willingboro, **W gas:** LukOil, **other:** H, auto repair
43b a	rd 636, to Rancocas Woods, Delran, **W gas:** Exxon/24hr, **food:** Carlucci's Rest.
40b a	NJ 38, to Mount Holly, Moorestown, **W gas:** Shell/Subway/dsl/24hr, **food:** Arby's, Baja Fresh, Burger King, Chick-fil-A, Dunkin Donuts, Panera Bread, Perkin's (3mi), Starbucks, TGIFriday, **lodging:** Quality Inn (4mi), Residence Inn, **other:** H, Acme Foods/Sav-On, Costco, GNC, Jo-Ann Fabrics, PetsMart, Target, TJ Maxx, U-Haul, Wegman's
36b a	NJ 73, to NJ Tpk, Tacony Br, Berlin, **E gas:** Exxon, LukOil/dsl, **food:** Bennigan's, Bob Evans, Denny's, McDonald's, Sage Rest, Wendy's, **lodging:** Comfort Inn, Courtyard, Fairfield Inn, Hampton Inn, Howard Johnson, Marriott, Red Roof Inn, Rodeway Inn, Super 8, Wingate Inn, **W gas:** Citgo, Exxon, Shell, **food:** Boscov's, Burger King, Chick-fil-A, Chipotle Mexican, Don Pablo, Dunkin Donuts, 5 Guys Burgers, KFC/Taco Bell, McDonald's, Friendly's, Panera Bread, PeiWei Asian, Perkins, Pizza Hut, Uno, Wendy's, **lodging:** Bel-Air Motel, Crossland Suites, Crossroads Inn, Homewood Suites, Motel 6, Quality Inn, Track&Turf Motel, **other:** Acura, AutoZone, Barnes&Noble, Best Buy, Chevrolet, Chrysler, $Tree, Firestone/auto, Ford, Goodyear/auto, Home Depot, Infiniti, K-Mart, Lincoln/Mercury, Lowes Whse, Macy's, Marshall's, NTB, Old Navy, PepBoys, PetsMart, Ross, Sears/auto, ShopRite Foods, mall
34b a	NJ 70, to Camden, Cherry Hill, **E gas:** BP, Exxon/24hr, Liberty, LukOil, **food:** Big John's Steaks, Burger King, Dunkin Donuts, McDonald's, **lodging:** Extended Stay America, **other:** Curves, Jaguar/Saab, Tires+, **W gas:** Citgo, Exxon, Gulf/dsl, LukOil, **food:** Boston Pizza, Dunkin Donuts, Elephant & Castle, Famous Dave's BBQ, McDonald's, Mirabella Cafe, Pizza Hut, Ponzio's Rest, Steak&Ale, Starbucks, Subway, **lodging:** Best Value Inn, Clarion, Crowne Plaza, **other:** H, $Tree, Goodyear/auto, Rite Aid, Steinmart, WaWa, Vet
32	NJ 561, to Haddonfield, Voorhees, **3 mi E gas:** LukOil/dsl/24hr, **food:** Applebees, Fuddruckers, Olive Garden, Panera Bread, **lodging:** Hampton Inn, Wingate Inn, **other:** H, USPO, **W gas:** Pioneer/dsl,

CHERRY HILL

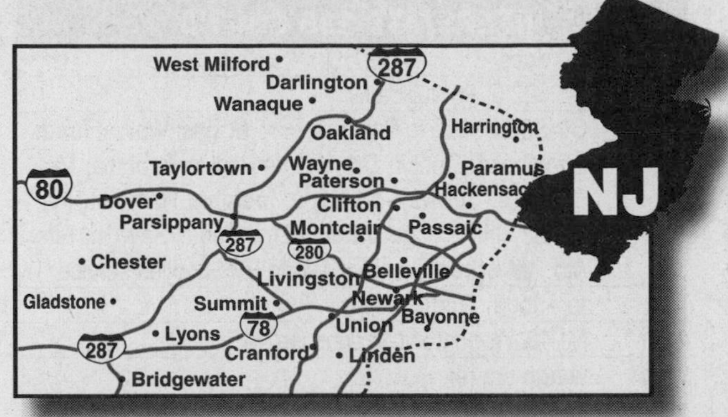

Exit #	Services
32	Continued Sunoco, **food:** Burger King, Dunkin Donuts, Quizno's, **other:** Curves, Ford, 7-11, Vet
31	Woodcrest Station
30	Warwick Rd (from sb)
29b a	US 30, to Berlin, Collingswood, **E gas:** Astro/dsl, Exxon, LukOil, **food:** Arby's, Church's, Dunkin Donuts, Popeye's, Wendy's, **other:** AutoZone, Home Depot, PathMark Foods, PetsMart, Sears Essentials
28	NJ 168, to NJ Tpk, Belmawr, Mt Ephraim, **E gas:** Citgo, Gulf/repair, Shell/dsl, Valero/dsl, **food:** Burger King, Club Diner, Dunkin Donuts, Wendy's, **lodging:** Bellmawr Motel, Comfort Inn, Econolodge, Holiday Inn, Howard Johnson, Red Roof Inn, Super 8, **other:** CVS Drug, Walgreens, transmissions, **W gas:** BP, Exxon/LP/24hr, Hess, WaWa, **food:** Black Horse Diner, Domino's, Dunkin Donuts, Golden Corral, McDonald's, Subway, **other:** AutoZone, Chrysler/Dodge, Curves, CVS Drug, Harley Davidson, Pepboys, Staples, Walgreens, Walmart
26	I-76, NJ 42, to I-676, Walt Whitman Bridge, Walt Whitman Bridge
25b a	NJ 47, to Westville, Deptford
24b a	NJ 45, NJ 551 (no EZ sb return), to Westville, **E gas:** Garden State, **other:** H, AutoZone, **W other:** Chevrolet, Family$
23	US 130 N, to National Park
22	NJ 644, to Red Bank, Woodbury, **E gas:** LukOil, **1 mi W gas:** Crown Point Trkstp/dsl/@, WaWa, **food:** Wendy's
21	NJ 44 S, Paulsboro, Woodbury, **W food:** WaWa, Wendy's, **lodging:** Westwood Motor Lodge
20	NJ 643, to NJ 660, to National Park, Thorofare, **E lodging:** Best Western, **W lodging:** Red Bank Inn
19	NJ 656, to NJ 44, Mantua
18b a	NJ 667, to NJ 678, Clarksboro, Mt Royal, **E gas:** BP/dsl, TA/Exxon/Buckhorn Rest./dsl/rest./@, **food:** Dunkin Donuts, KFC/Taco Bell, McDonald's, Wendy's, **other:** RV camping
17	NJ 680, to Mickleton, Gibbstown, **W food:** Burger King, Domino's, **lodging:** Motel 6, **other:** Advance Parts, Family$, GNC, Rite Aid, ShopRite Foods, WaWa
16b	NJ 551, to Gibbstown, Mickleton
16a	NJ 653, to Paulsboro, Swedesboro
15	NJ 607, to Gibbstown
14	NJ 684, to Repaupo
13	US 130 S, US 322 W, to Bridgeport (from sb, no return)

NJ

INTERSTATE 295 CONT'D

N ↕ S

Exit #	Services
11	US 322 E, to Mullica Hill
10	Ctr Square Rd, to Swedesboro, **E gas:** WaWa, **food:** Applebees, Dunkin Doughnuts/Baskin Robbins, McDonald's, Subway, Wendy's, **lodging:** Hampton Inn, Holiday Inn Select, **other:** Acme Foods/Sav-On, Rite Aid, **W other:** Camping World RV Supplies/service
7	to Auburn, Pedricktown
4	NJ 48, Woodstown, Penns Grove
3mm	**weigh sta nb**
2mm	**rest area nb, full ♿ facilities, info, ☎, 🛈, litter barrels, rv dump, vending**
2c	to US 130 (from sb), Deepwater, **E** same as 2b, **W gas:** All-American Plaza/Exxon/Dunkin Donuts/dsl/scales/24hr, ***FLYING J***/CountryMkt/dsl/scales/
2c	Continued LP/24hr, **other:** H
2b	US 40 E, to NJ Tpk, **E gas:** Gulf, Pilot/Subway/dsl/24hr/@, **lodging:** Comfort Inn, Econolodge, Friendship Motel, Holiday Inn Express, Quality Inn, Wellesley Inn, **W** same as 2c
2a	US 40 W (from nb), to Delaware Bridge
1c	NJ 551 S, Hook Rd, to Salem, **E lodging:** White Oaks Motel, **W** H
1b	US 130 N (from nb), Penns Grove
1a	NJ 49 E, to Pennsville, Salem, **E gas:** Exxon/dsl/repair, **food:** Applebees, Burger King, Cracker Barrel, KFC/Taco Bell, McDonald's, **lodging:** Hampton Inn, **other:** Peterbilt, **W gas:** Coastal, **lodging:** Seaview Motel
0mm	New Jersey/Delaware state line, Delaware River, Delaware Memorial Bridge

NEW MEXICO

NJ NM

INTERSTATE 10

E ↕ W

Exit #	Services
164.5mm	New Mexico/Texas state line
164mm	**Welcome Ctr wb, full ♿ facilities, ☎, 🛈, litter barrels, petwalk**
162	NM 404, Anthony, **S** RV camping
160mm	**weigh sta wb**
155	155 NM 227 W, to Vado, **N** Western Sky's RV Park, **S gas:** NTS/dsl/rest./scales/@, Texaco/rest./dsl/scales/24hr, **other:** El Camino Real HS
151	Mesquite
144	I-25 N, to Las Cruces
142	rd 188, rd 101, Valley Dr, Las Cruces, **N gas:** Chevron/dsl, **food:** Chilito's Mexican, Dick's Cafe, Whataburger/24hr, **lodging:** Best Western, Comfort Inn, Holiday Inn Express, Motel 6, Quality Inn, Ramada Inn, Super 8, Teakwood Inn, **other:** H, Chevrolet/Cadillac, Dalmont's RV Camping, Ford/Lincoln/Mercury, Honda, Hyundai, Mazda, Nissan, auto/RV repair/tires, NMSU, Vet, **S gas:** Fina, **other:** USPO
140	NM 28, to Mesilla, Las Cruces, **N gas:** Fina/dsl, **food:** Applebee's, Blake's Lotaburger, BurgerTime, Cracker Barrel, Eddie's Grill, McDonald's, Murry Express, Quizno's, Starbucks, Subway, **lodging:** Days Inn, Drury Inn, Hampton Inn, La Quinta, SpringHill Suites, **other:** Radio Shack, Walmart SuperCtr/24hr, **N on Valley Dr food:** American BBQ, Domino's, Old Town Rest., **other:** Dodge, Toyota, VW, **S food:** Gadsden Purchase Grill, **lodging:** Comfort Inn, **other:** Hacienda RV Resort, Harley-Davidson, Siesta RV Park, Sunland RV Ctr, United RV Ctr
139	NM 292, Amador Ave, Motel Blvd, Las Cruces, **N gas:** Pilot/Subway/dsl/scales/24hr, TA/Burger King/Pizza Hut/Taco Bell/dsl/rest./24hr/scales/@, **S food:** PitStop Café, **lodging:** Coachlight Inn/RV Park, **other:** NAPACare
138mm	Rio Grande River
135.5mm	**rest area eb, full ♿ facilities, 🛈, litter barrels, petwalk, scenic view, RV dump**
135	US 70 E, to W Las Cruces, Alamogordo, **1 mi N other:** KOA
132	**N** to ✈, fairgrounds, **S gas:** Love's/Subway/dsl/scales/24hr
127	Corralitos Rd, **N gas:** Exxon, **other:** Bowlin's Trading Post, to fairgrounds
120.5mm	**insp sta wb**
116	NM 549
111mm	**parking area wb, litter barrels**
102	Akela, **N gas:** Exxon/dsl/gifts
85	East Motel Dr, Deming, **S gas:** Chevron/dsl, Fina, Save Gas/dsl, **lodging:** Hampton Inn, Holiday Inn, La Quinta, Motel 6, **other:** Chrysler/Dodge/Jeep
82b	Railroad Blvd, Deming, **N gas:** Chevron/dsl, **S gas:** Fina, **food:** Burger King, China Wok, DQ, KFC, La Fonda Mexican, Wendy's, **lodging:** Day's Inn, Grand Motel, Mirador Motel, **other:** AutoZone, Big O Tire, Checker Parts, Chevrolet/Pontiac/GMC, $General, $Tree, Ford/Lincoln/Mercury, Firestone, Goodyear, K-Mart, Little Vinyard RV Park, NAPA, Roadrunner RV Park, Sunrise RV Park, Wagon Wheel RV Park, Walmart SuperCtr/Subway, to Rock Hound SP, st police
82a	US 180, NM 26, NM 11, Deming, **N gas:** Chevron, **food:** Blake's Lotaburger, **S gas:** Exxon, Phillips 66, Save Gas, Shell/dsl, **food:** Burger King, China Star, Denny's, KFC, Palma's Italian, Pizza Hut, Rancher's Grill, Si Senor, **lodging:** Butterfield Stage Motel, **other:** Budget Tire, CarQuest, Goodyear, Radio Shack, museum, tires, to Pancho Villa SP, Rockhound SP
81	NM 11, W Motel Dr, Deming, **S gas:** Chevron/24hr, Shamrock/dsl, **food:** Burger Time, McDonald's, Sonic, Subway, Taco Bell, **lodging:** Best Western, Comfort Inn, Deming Motel, Deluxe Inn, Executive Motel, Super 8, Western Motel, **other:** 81 Palms RV Park, Hitchin Post RV Park, to Pancho Villa SP, Rock Hound SP
68	NM 418, **S gas:** Savoy/dsl/rest./24hr, tires/repair
62	Gage, **S gas:** Butterfield Station/Exxon/DQ/dsl/RV Park
61mm	**rest area wb, full ♿ facilities, 🛈, litter barrels, vending, petwalk**
55	Quincy
53mm	**rest area eb, full ♿ facilities, 🛈, litter barrels, vending, petwalk**

LAS CRUCES

DEMING

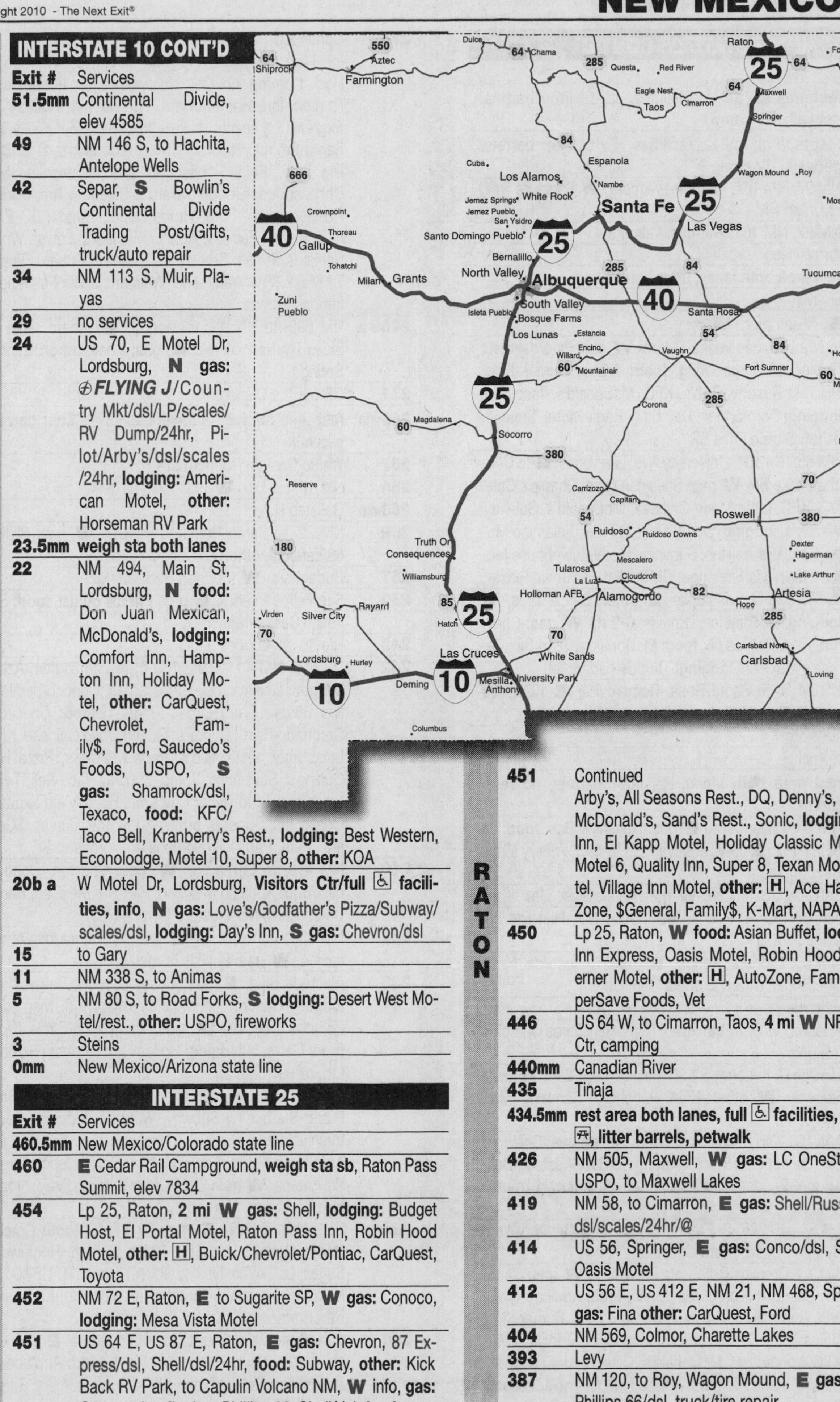

E ↕ W

INTERSTATE 10 CONT'D

Exit #	Services
51.5mm	Continental Divide, elev 4585
49	NM 146 S, to Hachita, Antelope Wells
42	Separ, **S** Bowlin's Continental Divide Trading Post/Gifts, truck/auto repair
34	NM 113 S, Muir, Playas
29	no services
24	US 70, E Motel Dr, Lordsburg, **N gas:** ⊘***FLYING J***/Country Mkt/dsl/LP/scales/RV Dump/24hr, Pilot/Arby's/dsl/scales/24hr, **lodging:** American Motel, **other:** Horseman RV Park
23.5mm	**weigh sta both lanes**
22	NM 494, Main St, Lordsburg, **N food:** Don Juan Mexican, McDonald's, **lodging:** Comfort Inn, Hampton Inn, Holiday Motel, **other:** CarQuest, Chevrolet, Family$, Ford, Saucedo's Foods, USPO, **S gas:** Shamrock/dsl, Texaco, **food:** KFC/Taco Bell, Kranberry's Rest., **lodging:** Best Western, Econolodge, Motel 10, Super 8, **other:** KOA
20b a	W Motel Dr, Lordsburg, **Visitors Ctr/full ♿ facilities, info, N gas:** Love's/Godfather's Pizza/Subway/scales/dsl, **lodging:** Day's Inn, **S gas:** Chevron/dsl
15	to Gary
11	NM 338 S, to Animas
5	NM 80 S, to Road Forks, **S lodging:** Desert West Motel/rest., **other:** USPO, fireworks
3	Steins
0mm	New Mexico/Arizona state line

INTERSTATE 25

N ↕ S

Exit #	Services
460.5mm	New Mexico/Colorado state line
460	**E** Cedar Rail Campground, **weigh sta sb**, Raton Pass Summit, elev 7834
454	Lp 25, Raton, **2 mi W gas:** Shell, **lodging:** Budget Host, El Portal Motel, Raton Pass Inn, Robin Hood Motel, **other:** [H], Buick/Chevrolet/Pontiac, CarQuest, Toyota
452	NM 72 E, Raton, **E** to Sugarite SP, **W gas:** Conoco, **lodging:** Mesa Vista Motel
451	US 64 E, US 87 E, Raton, **E gas:** Chevron, 87 Express/dsl, Shell/dsl/24hr, **food:** Subway, **other:** Kick Back RV Park, to Capulin Volcano NM, **W** info, **gas:** Conoco, Loaf'n Jug, Phillips 66, Shell/dsl, **food:**

RATON

451	Continued Arby's, All Seasons Rest., DQ, Denny's, K-Bob's, KFC, McDonald's, Sand's Rest., Sonic, **lodging:** Best Value Inn, El Kapp Motel, Holiday Classic Motel, Microtel, Motel 6, Quality Inn, Super 8, Texan Motel, Travel Motel, Village Inn Motel, **other:** [H], Ace Hardware, AutoZone, $General, Family$, K-Mart, NAPA, Visitor's Ctr
450	Lp 25, Raton, **W food:** Asian Buffet, **lodging:** Holiday Inn Express, Oasis Motel, Robin Hood Motel, Westerner Motel, **other:** [H], AutoZone, Family$, KOA, SuperSave Foods, Vet
446	US 64 W, to Cimarron, Taos, **4 mi W** NRA Whittington Ctr, camping
440mm	Canadian River
435	Tinaja
434.5mm	**rest area both lanes, full ♿ facilities, weather info, ⛱, litter barrels, petwalk**
426	NM 505, Maxwell, **W gas:** LC OneStop/dsl, **other:** USPO, to Maxwell Lakes
419	NM 58, to Cimarron, **E gas:** Shell/Russell's/Subway/dsl/scales/24hr/@
414	US 56, Springer, **E gas:** Conco/dsl, Shell, **lodging:** Oasis Motel
412	US 56 E, US 412 E, NM 21, NM 468, Springer, **1 mi E gas:** Fina **other:** CarQuest, Ford
404	NM 569, Colmor, Charette Lakes
393	Levy
387	NM 120, to Roy, Wagon Mound, **E gas:** Chevron/dsl, Phillips 66/dsl, truck/tire repair

NM

INTERSTATE 25 CONT'D

N ↕ S

Exit #	Services
376mm	**rest area sb, full ♿ facilities, ☎, 🅿, litter barrels, petwalk, RV camp**
374mm	**rest area nb, full ♿ facilities, ☎, 🅿, litter barrels, petwalk, RV camp**
366	NM 97, NM 161, Watrous, Valmora, **W** Santa Fe Trail, Ft Union NM
364	NM 97, NM 161, Watrous, Valmora
361	no services
360mm	**rest area both lanes, litter barrels**
356	Onava
352	**E** RV camping, **W** ✈
347	to NM 518, Las Vegas, **0-2 mi W gas:** Pino/dsl/rest., Phillips 66/Burger King, **food:** Arby's, Burger King, Hillcrest Rest., K-Bob's, KFC, McDonald's, Taco Bell, **lodging:** Comfort Inn, Day's Inn, Regal Motel, Super 8, **other:** Storrie Lake SP
345	NM 65, NM 104, University Ave, Las Vegas, **E** to Conchas Lake SP, **W gas:** Shell/dsl, **food:** Charlie's Cafe, DQ, KFC, Little Moon Chinese, McDonald's, Subway, Wendy's, **lodging:** Budget Inn, El Fidel, Palamino Motel, Sante Fe Trail Inn, Sunshine Motel, Townhouse Motel, **other:** [H], Firestone, GMC, Hist. Old Town Plaza
343	to NM 518 N, Las Vegas, **E other:** Garcia Tires, **W lodging:** Holiday Inn Express, **0-2 mi W gas:** Chevron, Fina, Phillips 66, **food:** McDonald's, Taco Bell, Teresa's Mexican, **lodging:** Thunderbird Motel
339	US 84 S, to Santa Rosa, Romeroville, **E** KOA, **W gas:** Phillips 66/Subway/dsl
335	Tecolote
330	Bernal
325mm	**rest area both lanes, 🅿, litter barrels, no restrooms**
323	NM 3 S, Villanueva, **E gas:** Sunshine Gas, **food:** La Risa (1mi), **E** to Villanueva SP, Madison Winery (6mi), RV camping
319	San Juan, San Jose, **W gas:** Pecos River Sta.
307	NM 63, Rowe, Pecos, **W** Pecos NM, Hist Rte 66, same as 299
299	NM 50, Glorieta, Pecos, **W gas:** Conoco/dsl (4mi), Shell (6mi), **other:** Glorieta Conf Ctr
297	Valencia
294	Apache Canyon, **W other:** KOA, Rancheros Camping (Mar-Nov)
290	US 285 S, to Lamy, S to Clines Corners, **2 mi E food:** Subway, **W other:** KOA, Rancheros Camping (Mar-Nov)
284	NM 466, Old Pecos Trail, Santa Fe, **W gas:** Chevron/dsl, Sunset Gen Store, **lodging:** to Best Western, Desert Inn, Pecos Trail Inn, The Sands, **other:** [H], museums
282	US 84, US 285, St Francis Dr, **W gas:** Conoco/Wendy's/dsl, Giant, **food:** Church's
278	NM 14, Cerrillos Rd, Santa Fe, **0-4 mi W gas:** Conoco, Giant, Phillips 66/dsl, Shell, **food:** Adelita's Mexican, Applebee's, Arby's, Blue Corn Cafe, Burger King, China Star, Denny's, Domino's, Flying Tortilla, IHOP, KFC, Lotaburger, McDonald's, Olive Garden, Outback Steaks, Panda Express, Pizza Hut, Quizno's, Lobster, Schlotsky's, Sonic, Starbucks, Taco Bell, Village
278	Continued Inn Rest., Wendy's, **lodging:** Best Western, Budget Host, Comfort Inn, Courtyard, Day's Inn, Econolodge, Fairfield Inn, Hampton Inn, Holiday Inn, Holiday Inn Express, La Quinta, Luxury Inn, Motel 6, Quality Inn, Santa Fe Inn, Super 8, **other:** Albertson's, Best Buy, Big Lots, Buick/Pontiac, Cadillac, Chevrolet/GMC, Chrysler/Jeep/Dodge, Dillard's, Discount Tire, Dodge, Firestone/auto, Ford, Home Depot, Honda, JC Penney, Jo-Ann Fabrics, Kohl's, Michael's, Lowes Whse, Sam's Club/gas, Sears/auto, Staples, Subaru, Target, TJ Maxx, VW, Walgreens, Walmart, Santa Fe Outlets/famous brands
276b a	NM 599, to NM 14, to Madrid, **E other:** Santa Fe Skies RV Park, **4 mi W gas:** Shell, **other:** Sunrise Springs
271	CR 50F, La Cienega
269mm	**rest area nb, full ♿ facilities, ☎, 🅿, litter barrels, petwalk**
267	Waldo Canyon Rd, **insp sta.**
264	NM 16, Pueblo, **W** to Cochiti Lake RA
263mm	Galisteo River
259	NM 22, to Santo Domingo Pueblo, **W gas:** Phillips 66/cafe/dsl, **other:** to Cochiti Lake RA
257	Budaghers, **W** Mormon Battalion Mon
252	San Felipe Pueblo, **E gas:** Phillips 66/dsl, **food:** San Felipe Casino/rest.
248	Rte 66, Algodones
242	US 550, NM 44 W, NM 165 E, to Farmington, Aztec, **W gas:** Chevron/dsl, Circle K/gas, Conoco/dsl, Phillips 66/dsl, Shell/Burger King/dsl, **food:** Checkers, Coronado Rest., Denny's, Guang Dong Chinese, KFC, Lotaburger, McDonald's, Papa Murphy's, Pizza Hut, Quizno's, Starbucks, Sonic, Subway, Taco Bell, Twisters, Wendy's, **lodging:** Day's Inn, Holiday Inn Express, Quality Inn, Super 8, **other:** AutoZone, Curves, $General, KOA, Parts+, Walgreens, to Coronado SP
240	NM 473, to Bernalillo, **W gas:** Chevron, Conoco/dsl, **food:** Abuelito Mexican, Pueblito Mexican, Range Café, **other:** KOA, Vet, to Coronado SP
234	NM 556, Tramway Rd, **E gas:** Shamrock/dsl, **other:** casino, **W gas:** Phillips 66/dsl
233	Alameda Blvd, **E gas:** Chevron, **food:** Burger King, **lodging:** Comfort Inn, Motel 6, **other:** Audi, Mercedes, Porsche, Toyota, **W gas:** Phillips 66/Circle K/dsl, **food:** Carl's Jr, **lodging:** Holiday Inn Express, Ramada Ltd, **other:** Carmax
232	Paseo del Norte, **E food:** China Luck, Red Brick Pizza, Starbucks, Subway, Wendy's, **lodging:** Country Inn&Suites, Howard Johnson, **other:** Aloha RV Ctr, AutoZone, Kohl's, Lowe's Whse, Office Depot, Target, Walgreens, **W gas:** Shell/Circle K, **food:** Arby's, **lodging:** Courtyard, Marriott
231	San Antonio Ave, **E gas:** Fina/7-11, **food:** Cracker Barrel, Denny's, **lodging:** Hilton Garden, Homewood Suites, La Quinta, Quality Suites, **other:** [H], USPO, **W lodging:** Crossland Suites, Hampton Inn, La Quinta, **other:** Mazda, VW
230	San Mateo Blvd, Osuna Rd, Albuquerque, **E gas:** Circle K, Giant/dsl, Phillips 66, Shell, **food:** Applebee's, Arby's, Azuma Grill, Bennigan's, Bob's Burgers, Burger King, Chili's, Furrs Buffet, Hooters, KFC,

LAS VEGAS · SANTA FE · NM

N ↕ S

ALBUQUERQUE

INTERSTATE 25 CONT'D

Exit #	Services
230	Continued LJ Silver, McDonald's, Olive Garden, Pizza Hut/Taco Bell, Schlotsky's, Sonic, Souper Salad, Starbucks, Subway, SweetTomatoes, Taco Cabana, Teriyaki Chicken, Texas Roadhouse, Village Inn Rest., Wendy's, Wienerschnitzel, **lodging:** Nativo Lodge, **other:** H, Brake Masters, Buick/Pontiac/GMC, Cadillac, Curves, Firestone/auto, Hummer, Just Brakes, Mercedes, NAPA, Nissan, PepBoys, Subaru/Isuzu, Tires-4-less, Walgreens, Wild Oats Mkt, **W gas:** Chevron, Shamrock, **food:** Cajun Kitchen, McDonald's, Oasis Cafe, Whataburger, **lodging:** Studio 6 **other:** Mini/BMW
229	Jefferson St, **E food:** Carrabba's, Landry's Seafood, Outback Steaks, **lodging:** Holiday Inn, **other:** H, same as 230, **W food:** Boston's Pizza, Chama River Rest., Coldstone Creamery, Dickey's BBQ, Food Ct., Fuddrucker's, Jersey Jack's, Mimi's Café, Pappadeaux, PF Chang's, Red Robin, Rockfish Café, Subway, Texas Land&Cattle Steaks, **lodging:** Drury Inn, Residence Inn **other:** Lexus
228	Montgomery Blvd, **E gas:** Chevron/dsl, Conoco/dsl, Fina7/11, **food:** Fiestas Cantina, Lotaburger, **lodging:** Best Western, **other:** H, Discount Tire, **W gas:** Shell, **food:** Arby's, Carls Jr., IHOP, McDonald's, Panda Express, Sonic, Starbucks, Wendy's, **lodging:** InTowne Suites, **other:** Acura, Ford, Costco/gas, Home Depot, Infiniti, Office Depot, PetsMart, Sam's Club/gas, Sportsman's Whse
227b	Comanche Rd, Griegos Rd, **E** UPS Depot
227a	Candelaria Rd, Albuquerque, **E gas:** Chevron/rest., Circle K, Fina/Subway/dsl, Shell, TA/dsl/24hr/@, **food:** IHOP, Subway, Village Inn Rest., **lodging:** Comfort Inn, Clubhouse Inn, Day's Inn, Fairfield Inn, Hilton, Holiday Inn, Rodeway Inn, Motel 6, Super 8, **W gas:** Chevron, **food:** Waffle House, **lodging:** Ambassador Inn, Red Roof Inn, **other:** Volvo
226b a	I-40, E to Amarillo, W to Flagstaff
225	Lomas Blvd, **E gas:** Chevron/7-11, **food:** JB's, **lodging:** Plaza Inn/rest., **other:** Chevrolet, Dodge, Ford **W food:** Burger King, **lodging:** Embassy Suites **other:** H
224	Lead Ave, Coal Ave, Grand Ave, Central Ave, **E lodging:** Crossroads Motel, **other:** H **W gas:** Chevron, **lodging:** Econolodge, Stardust Inn
223	Chavez Ave, **E lodging:** Motel 6, **other:** sports arena
222b a	Gibson Blvd, **E gas:** Phillips 66, **food:** Applebee's, Burger King, Fuddrucker's, Subway, Waffle House, Village Inn Rest., **lodging:** Best Western, Comfort Inn, Country Inn&Suites, Courtyard, Hampton Inn, Hawthorn Suites, Hilton Garden, La Quinta, Quality Suites, Vagabond Inn, **other:** H, Curves, Kirtland AFB, museum, **W gas:** Fina/7-11, **food:** Church's, LotaBurger
221	Sunport, **E lodging:** Holiday Inn Select, Homewood Suites, Hyatt Place, **other:** USPO, ✈
220	Rio Bravo Blvd, Mountain View, **E** golf, **2 mi W gas:** Shamrock, **food:** Burger King, Church's, McDonald's, Pizza Hut, Subway, Taco Bell, **other:** Albertson's, Family$, Walgreens

BELEN

SOCORRO

Exit #	Services
215	NM 47, **E gas:** Conoco/dsl, Phillips 66/dsl, **other:** to Isleta Lakes RA/RV Camping, casino, st police
214mm	Rio Grande
213	NM 314, Isleta Blvd, **W gas:** Chevron/Subway/dsl/24hr
209	NM 45, to Isleta Pueblo
203	NM 6, to Los Lunas, **E gas:** Chevron/dsl/24hr, Shamrock, Shell/Wendy's/dsl/24hr, **food:** Benny's, China Buffet, Del Taco, Denny's, McDonald's, Papa John's, Sonic, Starbucks, Village Inn Rest., **lodging:** Day's Inn, Las Lumas Inn, **other:** AutoZone, Big O Tire, Chevrolet, Ford, Home Depot, Walgreens, **W gas:** Phillips 66/Subway/dsl, **food:** Carl's Jr, Coldstone Creamery, Chili's, KFC, Panda Express, **lodging:** Western Skies Inn, **other:** Discount Tire, Walmart SuperCtr/24hr
195	Lp 25, Los Chavez, **1 mi E food:** KFC, McDonald's, Pizza Hut/Taco Bell, **lodging:** Hub Motel, **other:** Walmart SuperCtr/gas/24hr
191	NM 548, Belen, **1 mi E gas:** Conoco/dsl, **food:** McDonald's, **lodging:** Super 8, **other:** $General, **W food:** Rio Grande Diner, **lodging:** Holiday Inn Express, La Mirada Hotel/RV park
190	Lp 25, Belen, **1-2 mi E gas:** Akins/dsl, Conoco/dsl, Phillips 66, **food:** A&W, Arby's, Casa de Pizza, McDonald's, TJ's Mexican, **lodging:** Super 8, **other:** AutoZone, Big O Tire
175	US 60, Bernardo, **E** Salinas NM, **W other:** Kiva RV Park
174mm	Rio Puerco
169	**E** La Jolla St Game Refuge, Sevilleta NWR
167mm	**rest area both lanes, full ♿ facilities, picnic tables, litter barrels, vending, petwalk**
166mm	Rio Salado
165mm	**weigh sta/parking area both lanes**
163	San Acacia
156	Lemitar, **W** Phillis 66/dsl/24hr
152	Escondida, **W** to st police
150	US 60 W, Socorro, **W gas:** Chevron, Exxon/dsl, Phillips 66/dsl, Shamrock, **food:** Burger King, China Best, Denny's/24hr, Domino's, El Camino Rest., Healthy Heart Cafe, K-Bob's, KFC, Lotaburger, McDonald's, Pizza Hut, RoadRunner Steaks, Socorro Springs Rest., Sonic, Taco Bell, **lodging:** Best Western, Comfort Inn, Days Inn, Economy Inn, Econolodge, Holiday Inn Express, Howard Johnson, Sands Motel, San Miguel Inn, Super 8, **other:** Ace Hardware, Alco, AutoZone, Brooks Foods, CarQuest, Chevrolet/Pontiac/Buick, Chrysler/Dodge/Jeep, $General, Family$, Ford/Mercury, NAPA, Radio Shack, Smith's Foods, TrueValue, Walmart SuperCtr/24hr, to NM Tech

INTERSTATE 25 CONT'D

N ↕ S Albuquerque

Exit #	Services
147	US 60 W, Socorro, **W gas:** Chevron/dsl/RV dump, Conoco/LP, Shell/dsl, **food:** Arby's, **lodging:** Motel 6, **other:** [H], Socorro RV Park, to [airport]
139	US 380 E, to San Antonio, **E** gas/food, to Bosque Del Apache NWR
124	to San Marcial, **E other:** to Bosque del Apache NWR, Ft Craig
115	NM 107, **E gas:** Truck Plaza/dsl/rest./24hr, to Camino Real Heritage Ctr
114mm	**rest areas both lanes, full [handicapped] facilities, [picnic], litter barrels, petwalk, RV parking, vending**
107mm	Nogal Canyon
100	Red Rock
92	Mitchell Point
90mm	La Canada Alamosa, La Canada Alamosa
89	NM 181, to Cuchillo, to Monticello, **4 mi E:** Monticello RV Park
83	NM 52, NM 181, to Cuchillo, **3 mi E food:** Ivory Tusk Inn& Tavern, **lodging:** Elephant Butte Inn/rest., **other:** RV Park, Elephant Lake Butte SP
82mm	**insp sta nb**
79	Lp 25, to Truth or Consequences, **E gas:** Chevron/dsl, Circle K, Phillips 66/dsl, **food:** China Buffet, DQ, Denny's, Hilltop Café, K-Bob's, KFC/Taco Bell, La Cocina Mexican, Los Arcos Steaks, McDonald's, Pizza Hut, Sonic, Subway, **lodging:** Ace Lodge, Comfort Inn, Desert View Motel, Hot Springs Inn, Oasis Motel, Super 8, **other:** [H], AutoZone, IGA Foods, NAPA, TrueValue, USPO, Walmart SuperCtr, to Elephant Butte SP
76	(75 from nb) Lp 25, to Williamsburg, **E gas:** Chevron/24hr, Conoco/dsl, Phillips 66/dsl, Shell/dsl, **food:** Big-A-Burger, **lodging:** Rio Grande Motel, **other:** Alco, Buick/Chevrolet/GMC/Pontiac, Cielo Vista RV Park, Ford, RJ RV Park, Shady Corner RV Park, USPO, auto/tire repair, city park
71	Las Palomas
63	NM 152, to Hillsboro, Caballo, **E** Lakeview RV Park/dsl, cliff dwellings
59	rd 187, Arrey, Derry, **E** to Caballo-Percha SPs
58mm	Rio Grande
51	rd 546, to Arrey, Garfield, Derry
41	NM 26 W, Hatch, **1 mi W gas:** Fina/Subway/dsl, **food:** DQ, **lodging:** Village Plaza Motel, **other:** Franciscan RV Ctr, USPO
35	NM 140 W, Rincon
32	Upham
27mm	**scenic view nb, [picnic], litter barrels**
26mm	**insp sta nb**
23mm	**rest area both lanes, full [handicapped] facilities, [picnic], litter barrels, vending, petwalk**
19	Radium Springs, **W** Leasburg SP, Fort Selden St Mon, RV camping
9	Dona Ana, **W gas:** Circle K/dsl, Chucky's/dsl, Texaco, **food:** Alejandro's Mexican, Lakes Cafe, **other:** Family$, RV camping, USPO
6b a	US 70, to Alamogordo, Las Cruces, **E gas:** Fina/dsl, Shell, **food:** Coldstone Creamery, IHOP, New China Buffet, Outback Steaks, Papa Johns, Peter Piper Pizza, Pizzaria Uno, Ruby Tuesday, **lodging:** Fairfield Inn, Motel 6, Staybridge Suites, Towneplace Suites, **other:** [H], K-Mart, Sam's Club/gas, USPO, **W gas:** Chevron, Chucky's/dsl, Shamrock, Shell, **food:** BurgerTime, DQ, Domino's, KFC, Little Caesar's, Lotaburger, McDonald's, Sonic, Spanish Kitchen, Starbucks, Subway, Taco Bell, Whataburger/24hr, **other:** Albertson's, AutoZone, Checker Parts, $General, Family$, Kohl's, Jiffy Lube, Lowe's Whse, Radio Shack, Walgreens, golf, Vet
3	Lohman Ave, Las Cruces, **E gas:** Shell, Valero, **food:** Applebee's, Burger King, Cattle Baron Steaks, Chili's, ChuckeCheese, Farley's Grill, Fidencio's Mexican, Garduno's Mexican, Golden Corral, Jack-in-the-Box, KFC, Pizza Hut, Red Lobster, Risotto's, Sonic, Starbucks, Village Inn Rest., Whataburger, **lodging:** Hotel Encanto, **other:** Albertson's, Barnes&Noble, Dillard's, Discount Tire, Home Depot, JC Penney, Marshalls, PetCo, Ross, Sears/auto, Sportsman's Whse, Target, mall, **W gas:** Western/dsl, **food:** Arby's, Carl's Jr, Casa Luna Pizza, Furr's Buffet, McDonald's, Papa Murphy's, Quizno's, Si Senor, Subway, Taco Bell, Texas Roadhouse, Wendy's, Wienerschnitzel, **lodging:** Hampton Inn, **other:** Best Buy, Big Lots, Hastings Books, Martin Tires, NAPA, Old Navy, PepBoys, PetsMart, Staples, Walgreens, Walmart SuperCtr/24hr, Vet
1	University Ave, Las Cruces, **E other:** [H], golf, museum, st police, **W gas:** Western/dsl, **food:** Bennigan's, DQ, Lorenzo's Italian, McDonald's, **lodging:** Comfort Suites, Ramada Inn, Sleep Inn, Value Place Inn, **other:** $Tree, Jo-Ann Fabrics, NMSU
0mm	I-25 begins/ends on I-10, exit 144 at Las Cruces.

Las Cruces

INTERSTATE 40

E ↕ W Tucumcari

Exit #	Services
373.5mm	New Mexico/Texas state line, Mountain/Central time zone
373mm	**Welcome Ctr wb, full [handicapped] facilities, [phone], [picnic], litter barrels, petwalk**
369	NM 93 S, NM 392 N, to Endee, **N gas:** Russell's/cafe/dsl/24hr
361	Bard
358mm	**weigh sta both lanes**
356	NM 469, San Jon, **N gas:** Dillon/cafe/dsl/24hr, **other:** repair, to Ute Lake SP, **S gas:** Phillips 66/dsl, **lodging:** San Jon Motel, **other:** USPO, city park
343	ranch access
339	NM 278, **N** [airport]
335	Lp 40, E Tucumcari Blvd, Tucumcari, **N gas:** Conoco/dsl, Phillips 66, **food:** Denny's, **lodging:** Comfort Inn, Econolodge, Gateway Inn, Hampton Inn, Motel 6, Quality Inn, Super 8, **other:** Empty Saddle RV Park, to Conchas Lake SP, **S gas:** KOA
333	US 54 E, Tucumcari, **N gas:** ***FLYING J***/Country Mkt/dsl/LP/scales/RV Dump/24hr/@, Love's/Arbys/Chester's/Godfather's/dsl/scales, **food:** Dean's Rest., Del's Rest., **lodging:** Tucumcari Inn, **other:** Cactus RV Park, K-Mart, Mtn rd RV Park, truckwash, truck repair
332	NM 209, NM 104, 1st St, Tucumcari, **2 mi N** $General, Family$, Lowe's Foods, st police, **N gas:** Chevron/Subway/dsl/24hr/@, Phillips 66, **food:** A&W/LJ Silver, KFC, K-Bob's, McDonald's, Lotaburger, Pizza Hut,

NM

INTERSTATE 40 CONT'D

E ↔ W

Exit #	Services
332	Continued Sonic, **lodging:** Best Western, Day's Inn, Holiday Inn Express, La Quinta, Microtel, **other:** H, to Conchas Lake SP
331	Camino del Coronado, Tucumcari
329	US 54, US 66 E, W Tucumcari Ave
321	Palomas, **S gas:** Shell/DQ/Stuckey's/dsl
311	Montoya
302mm	**rest area both lanes, full ♿ facilities, ☎, ⛺, litter barrels, petwalk, RV dump**
300	NM 129, Newkirk, **N gas:** Rte 66/dsl, **other:** USPO, to Conchas Lake SP
291	to Rte 66, Cuervo, **N** Cuervo Gas/repair
284	no services
277	US 84 S, to Ft Sumner, **N gas:** Phillips 66/dsl, **food:** DQ, Denny's, Silver Moon Café, **lodging:** Baymont Inn, Best Western, Budget Inn, Comfort Inn, Hampton Inn, Holiday Inn Express, Motel 6, **other:** RV/auto repair, **S gas:** Love's/Carl's Jr/dsl/24hr, TA/Shell/Subway/dsl/24hr/@, **other:** NAPACare
275	US 54 W, Santa Rosa, **N gas:** Phillips 66, **food:** KFC/LJ Silver, McDonald's, Rte 66 Rest., Santa Fe Grill, **lodging:** Best Western, Day's Inn, La Quinta, Travelodge, **other:** Donnie's RV Park, Santa Rosa Camping, st police, **S gas:** Shell/Circle K/dsl/24hr, **food:** Joseph's Grill, Papo's Pizza, **lodging:** American Inn, Laloma Motel/Rv Park, Sun'n Sand Motel/rest., Super 8, Tower Motel, **other:** H, CarQuest, Family$, NAPA, Rte 66 Drug, USPO
273.5mm	Pecos River
273	US 54 S, Santa Rosa, **N other:** Santa Rosa Lake SP, **S gas:** Phillips 66, **other:** Budget 10 Inn, **other:** NAPACare
267	Colonias, **N gas:** Shell/Stuckey's/dsl/rest.
263	San Ignacio
256	US 84 N, NM 219, to Las Vegas
252	no services
251.5mm	**rest area both lanes, full ♿ facilities, ☎, ⛺, litter barrels, petwalk, RV dump**
243	Milagro, **N gas:** Phillips 66/dsl
239	no services
234	**N gas:** Exxon/Flying C/DQ/dsl/gifts
230	NM 3, to Encino, **N other:** to Villanueva SP
226	no services
220mm	**parking area both lanes, litter barrels**
218b a	US 285, Clines Corners, **N gas:** Shell/Subway/dsl/24hr, **food:** Clines Corners Rest., **S other:** to Carlsbad Caverns NP
208	Wagon Wheel
207mm	**rest area both lanes, full ♿ facilities, ⛺, litter barrels, petwalk**
203	**N** RV Park
197	to Rte 66, Moriarty, **S gas:** Lisa's/dsl/rest./@, **other:** auto/RV repair, **1-2 mi S** same as 194, 196
196	NM 41, Howard Cavasos Blvd, **S gas:** Phillips 66/dsl, **food:** Lotaburger, SuperChina Buffet, **lodging:** Comfort Inn, Sunset Motel, **other:** Family$, NAPA, USPO, to Salinas NM (35mi), auto repair

SANTA ROSA

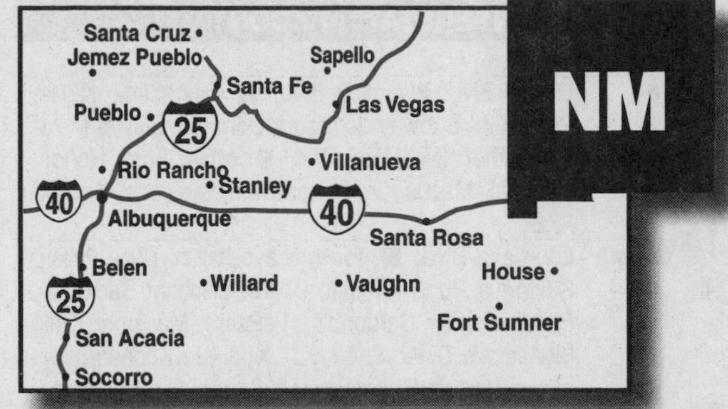

MORIARTY

Exit #	Services
194	NM 41, Moriarty, **S gas:** Conoco, Pump'n Save, TA/Pizza Hut/CF/Burger King/dsl/24hr/scales/@, **food:** Arby's, KFC/Taco Bell, McDonald's, **lodging:** Day's Inn, Holiday Inn Express, Luxury Inn, Ponderosa Motel, Super 8, **other:** Alco, Chevrolet/GMC, $General, Mike's Store, RV Ctr
187	NM 344, Edgewood, **N gas:** Conoco/DQ/dsl, **other:** Walmart SuperCtr/McDonald's, **S gas:** Phillips 66/dsl, **food:** Chili Hills Mexican, China Chef, McDonald's, Pizza Barn, Subway, **other:** AutoZone, $General, Family$, Ford, Smith's Foods/gas, Walgreens, USPO, RV Camping
181	NM 217, Sedillo, **S gas:** Phillips 66/dsl
178	Zuzax, **S gas:** Chevron/dsl, **other:** Hidden Valley RV Park
175	NM 337, NM 14, Tijeras, **N food:** Subway (2mi), **other:** to Cibola NF, Turquoise Trail RV Park
170	Carnuel, **S gas:** Chevron/24hr, **food:** Waffle House
167	Central Ave, to Tramway Blvd, **S gas:** Chevron/24hr, Phillips 66, **food:** Canana's Mexican, Carl's Jr., KFC, Lotaburger, McDonald's, Pizza Hut/Taco Bell, Starbucks, Subway, Waffle House, **lodging:** Best Value, Budget Host, Comfort Inn, Day's Inn, Deluxe Inn, Econolodge, Rodeway Inn, Travelodge, Value Place, **other:** Albertsons, $Tree, GNC, Goodyear/U-Haul/auto, Raley's Foods, Rocky Mtn RV/marine, Smith's/gas, to Kirtland AFB
166	Juan Tabo Blvd, **N gas:** Gasmax, Phillips 66/Circle K, **food:** China King, Fedrico's Mexican, Lin's Chinese, McDonald's, Olive Garden, Pizza Hut/Taco Bell, Tuesday Morning, Twisters Diner, Village Inn Rest., Weck's Rest, Wendy's, **lodging:** Best Value, Super 8, **other:** Albertson's, Big O Tire, Discount Tire, $General, Hastings Books, Hobby Lobby, Family$, Sav-On Drug, transmissions, Vet, **S food:** Sonic, Wienerschnitzel, **other:** Holiday RV Ctr, KAO, Meyer's RV Ctr, Walgreens, repair
165	Eubank Blvd, **N gas:** Chevron, Phillips 66/Circle K, **food:** Applebee's, JB's Rest., Panda Express, Sonic, **lodging:** Day's Inn, Econolodge, Guesthouse Inn, Holiday Inn Express, Quality Inn, Sandia Courtyard, **other:** Best Buy, CarQuest, PetCo, Radio Shack, Target, **S gas:** Shamrock, **food:** Bob's Burgers, Boston Mkt, Chili's, Church's, Golden Corral, Pizza Hut, Starbucks, Subway, Taco Bell, Taco Cabana, Twister's Burritos, Wendy's, **other:** Office Depot, PetsMart, Sam's Club/gas, Toyota, Walgreens, Walmart SuperCtr, auto repair/tires

NM

INTERSTATE 40 CONT'D

Exit #	Services
164	Lomas Blvd, Wyoming Blvd, **N gas:** Circle K/gas, Phillips 66/Subway/dsl, **food:** Dominos, Eloy' s Mexican, **other:** H, NAPA, Vet, **S other:** Ford, Honda, Hyundai, Mazda/Kia, Subaru, transmissions, Kirtland AFB
162b a	Louisiana Blvd, **N food:** Bravo Italian, Buca Italian, California Pizza Kitchen, Chili's, Elephant Bar Rest., Fuddrucker's, Garduno's, LePeep, Macaroni Grill, McAlister's Diner, Shoney's, Japanese Kitchen, Starbucks, **lodging:** Homewood Suites, Hilton Garden, Hyatt Place, Marriott, Sheraton, **other:** Barnes&Noble, Borders Books, Dillard's, Firestone, JC Penney, Macy's, Sears/auto, **S gas:** Shell, **food:** Burger King, **other:** atomic museum
161b a	San Mateo Blvd, Albuquerque, **N gas:** Conoco, Giant/dsl, Shell, **food:** Arby's, Bob's Burgers, Boston Mkt, Carl's Jr., Denny's, Dos Hermano's, KFC, McDonald's, Pizza Hut, Starbucks, Subway, Taco Bell, Wendy's, **lodging:** La Quinta, **other:** Office Depot, Radio Shack, **S gas:** Chevron/dsl
160	Carlisle Blvd, Albuquerque, **N gas:** Circle K/gas, Pump'n Save, Shell, **food:** Applebee's, Cheesecake Factory, China Wok, Lotaburger, McDonald's, Pizza Hut, Rudy's BBQ, Sonic, Subway, Twisters Grill, Village Inn Rest., Whataburger, **lodging:** AmeriSuites, Candlewood Suites, Day's Inn, Econolodge, Elegante Hotel, Hampton Inn, Hilton, Holiday Inn Express, La Quinta, Motel 6, Radisson, Residence Inn, Rodeway Inn, Suburban Motel, **other:** Firestone/auto, JC Penney, Smith's Foods, Walgreens, Wal-Mart SuperCtr, **S gas:** Phillips 66/Subway/dsl, **food:** Burger King, **other:** H, K-Mart, Whole Foods Mkt
159b c	I-25, S to Las Cruces, N to Santa Fe
159a	2nd St, 4th St, eb only, Albuquerque, **N gas:** Chevron/24hr, Love's/Subway/dsl, **food:** Furr's Café, **other:** $Tree, Family$, U-Haul
158	6th St, 8th St, 12th St, Albuquerque, **N gas:** Love's/Subway/dsl, **other:** U-Haul, **S gas:** Chevron, **lodging:** Quality Inn
157b	12th St (from eb), **N gas:** Fina/Arby's/dsl, **lodging:** Holiday Inn Express, **other:** Lowe's Whse, Walgreens
157a	Rio Grande Blvd, Albuquerque, **N gas:** Valero, **S gas:** Chevron/24hr, Shell, **food:** Starbucks, **lodging:** Best Western/grill, Hotel Albuquerque, **other:** auto repair
156mm	Rio Grande River
155	Coors Rd, Albuquerque, **N gas:** Chevron/Circle K, Duke City/dsl, Giant Gas/dsl, Shamrock/dsl, **food:** Applebee's, Arby's, Baskin-Robbins, Carl's Jr, Chili's, Cracker Barrel, Golden Corral, IHOP, McDonald's, Panda Express, Papa Murphy's, Quizno's, Red Brick Pizza, Sonic, Starbucks, Subway, Taco Cabana, Twisters Burritos, Wendy's, **other:** AutoZone, Brake Masters, Brook's Foods, Curves, $Tree, Goodyear/auto, Home Depot, Jiffy Lube, Radio Shack, Staples, Walgreen, Walmart SuperCtr/24hr, Vet, **S gas:** Chevron/24hr, Phillips 66/Circle K/dsl, Shell, Shamrock, **food:** Del Taco, Denny's, Furr's Diner, Lotaburger, Marisco's Mexican, McDonald's, New China, Pizza Hut/Taco Bell, Subway, Taco John's, Village Inn Rest., **lodging:**
155	Continued Comfort Inn, Day's Inn, Hampton Inn, La Quinta, Motel 6, Quality Inn, Super 8, **other:** Checker Parts, Discount Tire, U-Haul
154	Unser Blvd, **N gas:** Shamrock, **other:** to Petroglyph NM
153	98th St, **S gas:** *FLYING J*/Conoco/CountryMkt/dsl/LP/24hr, Valero, **food:** McDonald's, Subway, **lodging:** Microtel, **other:** AutoZone, $Tree, Palasades RV Park
149	Central Ave, Paseo del Volcan, **N other:** American RV Ctr/Camping World, Enchanted Trails RV Camping, Freightliner, to Shooting Range SP, **S gas:** Chevron/dsl/24hr, **other:** American RV Park, High Desert RV Park
140.5mm	Rio Puerco River, **N gas:** 66 Pit Stop
140	Rio Puerco, **S gas:** Rte 66 Trvel Ctr/Phillips 66/DQ/Road Runner Cafe/hotel/casino/dsl/rest./@
131	To'Hajiilee
126	NM 6, to Los Lunas
120mm	Rio San Jose, Rio San Jose
117	Mesita
114	NM 124, Laguna, **1/2 mi N** Conoco/dsl
113.5mm	scenic view both lanes, litter barrels
108	Casa Blanca, Paraje, **S gas:** Conoco/DQ/dsl/24hr, **other:** Ace hardware, Dancing Eagle Mkt, casino, RV park
104	Cubero, Budville
102	Sky City Rd, Acomita, **N gas:** Sky City/McDonald's/hotel/casino/dsl, **food:** Huwak'a Rest., **other:** RV Park/laundry, casino, **S rest area both lanes, full facilities, litter barrels, petwalk, H**
100	San Fidel
96	McCartys
89	NM 117, to Quemado, **N gas:** Skyway/Shell/Subway/dsl/gifts, **S** El Malpais NM
85	NM 122, NM 547, Grants, **N gas:** Chevron/dsl/24hr, Fina, Shell/dsl, **food:** Asian Buffet, Denny's, Lotaburger, Pizza Hut, Subway, Taco Bell, **lodging:** Best Western, Comfort Inn, Day's Inn, Economy Inn/rest., Holiday Inn Express, Motel 6, Sands Motel, South West Motel, Super 8, Travelodge, **other:** H, AutoZone, Checker Parts, Chevrolet/Buick, $Tree, Walmart SuperCtr/24hr, **S** Lavaland RV Park
81b a	NM 53 S, Grants, **N gas:** Phillips 66, **food:** Domino's, KFC, McDonald's, **other:** Ford/Lincoln/Mercury, NAPA, True Value, USPO, **S other:** Blue Spruce RV Park, KOA/Cibola Sands RV Park, El Malpais NM
79	NM 122, NM 605, Milan, **N gas:** Chevron/dsl, Love's/Chester's/Subway/dsl/24hr, **food:** DQ, **lodging:** Crossroads Motel, **other:** Bar-S RV Park, **S gas:** Petro/Iron Skillet/dsl/scales/24hr/@, **other:** Speedco Lube, st police
72	Bluewater Village, **N gas:** Exxon/DQ/dsl
63	NM 412, Prewitt, **S** to Bluewater SP (7mi)
53	NM 371, NM 612, Thoreau, **N gas:** Giant/Blimpie/dsl, **other:** Family$, USPO
47	Continental Divide, 7275 ft, **N gas:** Chevron, **other:** Continental Divide Trdg Post, towing/repair, **S** USPO
44	Coolidge
39	Refinery, **N gas:** Pilot/Subway/Dennys/dsl/scales/24hr/@

N ↕ S

ALBUQUERQUE

ALBUQUERQUE

GRANTS

NM

INTERSTATE 40 CONT'D

N ↕ S GALLUP

Exit #	Services
36	Iyanbito
33	NM 400, McGaffey, Ft Wingate, **N other:** to Red Rock SP, RV camping, museum
26	E 66th Ave, E Gallup, **N gas:** Plaza/Subway/dsl, **food:** Denny's/24hr, **lodging:** Comfort Inn, La Quinta, Sleep Inn, **other:** KOA, to Red Rock SP, museum, st police, **S on Rte 66...gas:** Conoco/dsl, Fina/dsl, Mustang, Shell/Ortega Gifts, **food:** Aurelie's Diner, Burger King, KFC, Lotaburger, McDonald's, Sonic, Wendy's, **lodging:** Best Western, Roadrunner Motel, **other:** H
22	Montoya Blvd, Gallup, **N rest area both lanes, full facilities, info, S on Rte 66...gas:** Mustang, Phillips 66, Texaco, **food:** Avalon Rest., Big Cheese Pizza, Burger King, Church's, Earl's Rest., El Capitan, LJ Silver, McDonald's, Papa John's, Pizza Hut, Quizno's, Subway, Taco Bell, Wendy's, **lodging:** Blue Spruce Motel, El Capitan Motel, El Rancho Motel/rest.,**other:** Albertson's, Radio Shack, Shop'n Save
20	US 491, to Shiprock, Gallup, **N gas:** Giant/dsl, Texaco, **food:** Applebee's, Arby's, Burger King, CA Chinese, Carl's Jr., Church's, Cracker Barrel, DQ, Denny's, Furr's Café, Golden Corral, KFC, King Dragon Chinese, Lotaburger, McDonald's, Pizza Hut, Sizzler,

GALLUP

Exit #	Services
20	Continued Sonic, Taco Bell, Wendy's, **lodging:** Hampton Inn, Quality Inn, Ramada Ltd, **other:** AutoZone, Checker Parts, Chrysler/Dodge/Jeep, $Tree, Family$, Home Depot, Hyundai, JC Penney, NAPA, Nissan, PepBoys, Radio Shack, Safeway, Walmart SuperCtr/24hr, mall, **S on Rte 66...gas:** Shell/dsl, **food:** El Dorado Rest., El Sombrero Mexican, Garcia's Rest., Lotaburger, Royal Holiday, Rte 66 Diner, Sonic, McDonald's, **lodging:** Ambassador Motel, Best Value Inn, Day's Inn, Desert Skies, Rodeway Inn, Super 8, **other:** H, Big O Tire, Ford/Lincoln/Mercury, RV camping
16	NM 118, W Gallup, Mentmore, **N gas:** Love's/Chester's/Subway/dsl/24hr, Navajo/dsl/24hr, TA/Country Pride/dsl/scales/24hr/@, **other:** Blue Beacon, dsl repair, **S gas:** Best Value/dsl, Conoco, Phillips 66/Allsup's, **food:** Olympic Kitchen, Ranch Kitchen, Taco Bell, **lodging:** Best Western, Budget Inn, Comfort Inn, Day's Inn, Econolodge, Gallup Inn, Hampton Inn, Microtel, Motel 6, Red Roof Inn, Travelodge, **other:** KOA, USA RV Park
12mm	**inspection/weigh sta eb**
8	to Manuelito
3mm	**Welcome Ctr eb, full ♿ facilities, ☎, picnic, litter barrels, petwalk**
0mm	New Mexico/Arizona state line

NM NY

NEW YORK

INTERSTATE 81

N ↕ S

Exit #	Services
184mm	US/Canada border, New York state line. I-81 begins/ends.
183.5mm	US Customs (sb)
52 (183)	Island Rd, to De Wolf Point, last US exit nb, **E** food
51 (180)	Island Rd, to Fineview, Islands Parks, **2-3 mi E food:** Thousand Islands Club, **lodging:** Seaway Island Resort, Torchlite Motel, **other:** Nature Ctr, camping, golf, USPO, **W gas:** Sunoco/dsl
179mm	St Lawrence River
178.5mm	Thousand Islands Toll Bridge Booth, **rest area sb, full ♿ facilities, ☎, picnic, litter barrels, petwalk**
50NS (178)	NY 12, **N** to Alexandria Bay, **gas:** Mobil/dsl, **food:** Kountry Kottage Rest., Subway, **lodging:** Bonnie Castle/rest., Green Acres River Motel, PineHurst Motel, River Edge Hotel, **other:** H, funpark (seasonal), to Thousand Island Region, **S** to Clayton, **gas:** Mobil, **lodging:** Bridgeview Motel, PJ's Motel, **other:** NY Welcome Ctr, to RV camping
174mm	**rest area nb, full ♿ facilities, ☎, vending, picnic, litter barrels, petwalk, st police**
49 (171)	NY 411, to Theresa, Indian River Lakes, **E gas:** Mobil/dsl (4mi)
168mm	**parking area sb, picnic table**
161mm	**parking area nb**
48 (158)	US 11, NY 37, **1-4 mi E gas:** Mobil/dsl, Nice'n Easy/dsl, Sunoco/dsl, **food:** Arby's, McDonald's, Longway's Diner, **lodging:** Allen's Budget Motel, Hotis Motel, Microtel, Royal Inn, **other:** st police
156.5mm	**parking area both lanes**
47 (155)	NY 12, Bradley St, Watertown, **E gas:** Nice'n Easy/Subway/dsl, **other:** H, **W lodging:** Rainbow Motel

WATERTOWN

Exit #	Services
154.5mm	Black River
46 (154)	NY 12F, Coffeen St, Watertown, **E gas:** Mobil, **food:** Cracker Barrel, Shorty's Diner, **other:** URGENT CARE, Home Depot
45 (152)	NY 3, to Arsenal St, Watertown, **E gas:** Mobil, Sunoco, **food:** Applebee's, Arby's, Buffalo Wild Wings, Burger King, China Buffet, Dunkin Donuts, Friendly's, Jreck Subs, KFC, LJ Silver, McDonald's, Panda Buffet, Ponderosa, Quizno's, Ruby Tuesday, Starbucks, Taco Bell, **lodging:** Day's Inn, Econolodge, Hampton Inn, Holiday Inn Express, The Inn, **other:** Advance Parts, Aldi Foods, AutoZone, Big Lots, Chrysler/Dodge/Jeep, $General, $Tree, Jo-Ann Fabrics, Kost Tire, Michael's, PriceChopper Foods/24hr, Radio Shack, Rite Aid, Staples, TJ Maxx, USPO, Walgreens, **W gas:** Fastrac, **food:** Bob Evans, Panera Bread, Pizza Hut, Red Lobster, Subway, Texas Roadhouse, TGI Friday, **lodging:** Ramada Inn, **other:** Best Buy, Borders Books, Ford, Gander Mtn Hannaford Foods, JC Penney, K-Mart, Kohl's, Lowes Whse, Old Navy, PetCo, Sam's Club, Sears/auto, Target, Walmart, mall, to Sackets Harbor
149mm	**parking area nb, ☎**
44 (148)	NY 232, to Watertown Ctr, **3 mi E gas:** Mobil, **lodging:** Best Western
147mm	**rest area sb, full ♿ facilities, ☎, picnic, litter barrels, vending, petwalk**
43 (146)	US 11, to Kellogg Hill
42 (144)	NY 177, Adams Center, **E gas:** Nice'n Easy/dsl, **food:** Depot Cafe, **other:** Harley-Davidson, Tucker's Camping
41 (140)	NY 178, Adams, **E gas:** Citgo/dsl, **food:** 2 Bros Pizza, McDonald's, **other:** st police
138mm	South Sandy Creek

INTERSTATE 81 CONT'D

N ↕ S — PULASKI

Exit #	Services
40 (135)	NY 193, to Ellisburg, Pierrepont Manor
134mm	**parking area/picnic tables, both lanes**
39 (133)	Mannsville
38 (131)	US 11, **E lodging:** 81-11 Motel
37 (128)	Lacona, Sandy Creek, **E food:** J&R Diner, **lodging:** Harris Lodge, Lake Effect Inn, **W gas:** Citgo, Sunoco/dsl, **food:** Sandy Creek Diner, **lodging:** Pink House Inn, Salmon River Motel, **other:** Sandy Island Beach SP, USPO
36 (121)	NY 13, Pulaski, **E gas:** Citgo, **food:** Ponderosa, **lodging:** Red Carpet Inn, Scottish Inn, **W gas:** KwikFill, Mobil/dsl, Nice'n Easy/Subway, Sunoco/dsl, **food:** Arby's, Burger King, Dunkin Donuts, Eddy's Place, McDonald's, River House Rest., Stefano's Rest., **lodging:** Super 8, **other:** Aldi Foods, Buick/Chevrolet, Family$, Kinney Drug, NAPA, P&C Foods, Radio Shack, Rite Aid, to Selkirk Shores SP, camping, fish hatchery
35 (118)	to US 11, Tinker Tavern Rd, **W** Grandpa Bob's Animal Park
34 (115)	NY 104, to Mexico, **E gas:** Sunoco/dsl/scales/24hr, **food:** Maple View Rest., **2-12 mi W gas:** Citgo, **lodging:** Cedar Creek, **other:** J&J/Salmon Country/Dowiedale/Jellystone Camping
33 (111)	NY 69, Parish, **E gas:** Sunoco/dsl/24hr, **food:** Grist Mill Rest., **lodging:** E Coast Resort (4mi), **other:** Up Country RV Park (8mi), **W gas:** Citgo, Mobil/dsl, **lodging:** Parish Motel, other:USPO
32 (103)	NY 49, to Central Square, **E gas:** Mobil/dsl, Sunoco/Subway/dsl, **food:** Golly's Rest., **other:** NAPA, **W gas:** Fastrac/gas, Quick Mart, **food:** Burger King, Dunkin Donuts, McDonald's, Quinto's NY Pizza, **lodging:** Town&Country, **other:** Advance Parts, $Tree, Ford, Rite Aid, Walmart SuperCtr, st police
101mm	**rest area sb, full ♿ facilities, ☎, picnic, litter barrels, vending, petwalk**
31 (99)	to US 11, Brewerton, **E** Oneida Shores Camping, **W gas:** Mobil/dsl, Nice'n Easy, **food:** Brickhouse Cafe, Burger King, Castaway's Cafe, Dunkin Donuts, LinLi's Chinese, Little Caesar's, McDonald's, Subway, **lodging:** BelAir Motel, Brewerton Motel, Holiday Inn Express, **other:** $General, Kinney Drugs, Vet
30 (96)	NY 31, to Cicero, **0-1 mi E gas:** Fastrac/dsl, Hess/dsl, KwikFill, **food:** Arby's, Cracker Barrel, Dunkin Donuts, Gino's&Joe's Pizza, McDonald's, **other:** Gander Mtn, Rite Aid, Walgreens, **W gas:** Citgo/dsl, Kwikfill, **food:** Cicero Pizza, Denny's, Frank's Café, Plainville Farms Rest., **other:** Bellair Motel, Brewerton Motel, **other:** RV Ctrs
29 (93)	I-481 S, NY 481, to Oswego, Syracuse, **1 mi W on US 11...gas:** Hess, Mobil/dsl, **food:** Buffalo Wild Wings, Burger King, Denny's, KFC, McDonald's, Moe's SW Grill, Panera Bread, Pizza Hut, Quizno's, Starbucks, Taco Bell, Tully's Rest., Wendy's, **lodging:** Budget Inn, **other:** Advance Parts, Audi/Porsche/VW, Buick/GMC/Pontiac, Burlington Coats, Curves, $Tree, Dunn Tire, Firestone/auto, Goodyear/auto, Home Depot, Hyundai, KIA, Lincoln/Mercury, Lowes Whse, Marshall's, Nissan, PepBoys, PriceChopper Foods, Rite Aid, Target, Toyota, Wegman's Foods, Walmart mall

SYRACUSE

Exit #	Services
28 (91)	N Syracuse, Taft Rd, **E gas:** KwikFill, Sunoco/dsl, **other:** U-Haul, **W gas:** Mobil, **other:** Auto Value Parts, USPO
27 (90)	N Syracuse, **E** ✈
26 (89)	US 11, Mattydale, **E gas:** Mobil, **food:** Asian 98 Buffet, Hofmann Rest., Pizza Hut, **lodging:** Red Carpet Inn, **other:** Big Lots, $Tree, Goodyear/auto, K-Mart, Michael's, PetCo, Rite Aid, Staples, TJ Maxx, Vet, **W gas:** Delta Sonic, **food:** Arby's, Burger King, Denny's, Dunkin Donuts, Jreck Subs, KFC, McDonald's, Ponderosa, Subway, Taco Bell, Wendy's, **lodging:** Candlewood Suites, Econolodge, Holiday Inn Express, **other:** Advance Parts, Aldi Foods, Kost Tire, P&C Foods
25a (88)	I-90, NY Thruway
25 (87.5)	7th North St, **E gas:** Pilot/McDonald's/dsl/scales/24hr, **other:** NAPA, repair, **W gas:** Mobil, **food:** Burger King, Colorado Steaks, Denny's, Dunkin Donuts, Jreck Subs, 7th North Buffet, Tully's Rest., **lodging:** Clarion, Comfort Inn, Hampton Inn, Maplewood Inn, Ramada, Super 8, United Inn
24 (86)	NY 370 W, to Liverpool, same as 23
23 (86)	NY 370 E, Hiawatha Blvd, **W gas:** Hess, **other:** Best Buy, Border's, JC Penney, Macy's, mall
22 (85)	NY 298, Court St
21 (84.5)	Spencer St, Catawba St (from sb), industrial area
20 (84)	I-690 W (from sb), Franklin St, West St
19 (84)	I-690 E, Clinton St, Salina St, to E Syracuse
18 (84)	Harrison St, Adams St, **E lodging:** ParkView Hotel, Renaissance Hotel, **other:** H, to Syracuse U, Civic Ctr
17 (82)	Brighton Ave, S Salina St, **W gas:** KwikFill, Valero/Subway
16a (81)	I-481 N, to DeWitt
16 (78)	US 11, to Nedrow, Onondaga Nation, **1-2 mi W gas:** Hess, Valero, **food:** McDonald's, Pizza Hut
15 (73)	US 20, La Fayette, **E gas:** Sunoco/dsl/deli, **food:** Old Tymes Rest., **other:** La Fayette Inn, **other:** $General, NAPA, USPO, st police, Vet, **W food:** McDonald's
71mm	**truck insp sta both lanes, ☎**
14 (67)	NY 80, Tully, **E gas:** Nice'n Easy/deli/dsl, **lodging:** Best Western, **other:** Chevrolet, Kinney Drug, **W food:** Burger King
13 (63)	NY 281, Preble, **E** to Song Mtn Ski Resort
60mm	**rest area/truck insp nb, full ♿ facilities, ☎, picnic, litter barrels, vending, petwalk**
12 (53)	US 11, NY 281, to Homer, **W gas:** Mobil/dsl/24hr, KwikFill, Valero, **food:** Applebees, Burger King, Doug's Fishfry, Fabio's Italian, Little Italy, Ponderosa, **lodging:** Budget Inn, Country Inn&Suites, **other:** H, to Fillmore Glen SP

CORTLAND

Exit #	Services
11 (52)	NY 13, Cortland, **E food:** Apple Annie's, **lodging:** Comfort Inn, Quality Inn, **W gas:** Mobil/dsl, **food:** Arby's, China Moon, Crown City Rest., Friendly's, Golden Skillet, McDonald's, Subway, Taco Bell, Wendy's, **lodging:** Hampton Inn, Ramada Inn, **other:** Advance Parts, Family$, Jo-Ann Fabrics, Kost Tire, P&C Foods/24hr, camping, museum
10 (50)	US 11, NY 41, to Cortland, McGraw, **W gas:** Citgo/Dunkin Donuts/dsl/cafe, Mobil/Subway/dsl/24hr, Sunoco/dsl, **lodging:** Cortland Motel, Day's Inn, **other:** NAPA

NY

INTERSTATE 81 CONT'D

N ↕ S

Exit #	Services
9 (38)	US 11, NY 221, **W gas:** Citgo, Sunoco/XtraMart/dsl/24hr, **food:** NY Pizzaria, **lodging:** 3 Bear Inn/rest., Greek Peak Lodge, **other:** NAPA, Country Hills Camping
33mm	**rest area sb, full ♿ facilities, 📞, 🛆, litter barrels, vending, petwalk**
8 (30)	NY 79, to US 11, NY 26, NY 206 (no EZ return), Whitney Pt, **E gas:** Hess, Kwikfill, Mobil/dsl/24hr, Sunoco, **food:** Aiello's Ristorante, Arby's, McDonald's, Subway, **lodging:** Point Motel, **other:** Chevrolet, $General, Gregg's Mkt, NAPA, Parts+, Radio Shack, Strawberry Valley Farms (3mi), USPO, to Dorchester Park
7 (21)	US 11, Castle Creek
6 (16)	US 11, to NY 12, I-88E, Chenango Bridge, **E on US 11...gas:** Citgo/dsl, Exxon, Hess/dsl, **food:** Arby's, Burger King, Denny's, Dunkin Donuts, King Buffet, Pizza Hut, Ponderosa, Subway, Wendy's, **other:** Advance Parts, Curves, CVS Drug, Giant Foods, Kost Tire, Lowes Whse, Radio Shack, Rite Aid, Staples, Vet, **W gas:** Diamond Fuel, KwikFill, **food:** Friendly's, McDonald's, Nirchi's Pizza, Spot Diner, Subway, **lodging:** Comfort Inn, Howard Johnson, Motel 6, **other:** $Bazaar, Harley-Davidson, Walgreens
15mm	I-88 begins eb
5 (14)	US 11, Front St, **1 mi W gas:** Sunoco, Valero, **food:** Applebees, Coldstone Creamery, Cracker Barrel, KFC/Taco Bell, McDonald's, Quizno's, Starbucks, **lodging:** Comfort Inn, Econolodge, Fairfield Inn, **other:** Cutler Botanical Garden
4 (13)	NY 17, Binghamton
3 (12)	Broad Ave, Binghamton, **W gas:** Valero, **food:** KFC, **other:** CVS Drug, Giant Foods
3 (10)	Industrial Park, same as 2
2 (8)	US 11, NY 17, **1-2 mi W gas:** Exxon/dsl, Pilot/Wendy's/dsl/scales/24hr/@, TA/dsl/rest./24hr/@, **food:** Arby's, Burger King, McDonald's, Subway, **lodging:** Del Motel
1 (4)	US 11, NY 7, Kirkwood, **1-2 mi W gas:** Mobil/dsl/24hr, Xtra, **lodging:** Kirkwood Motel, Wright Motel

BINGHAMTON

2mm	**Welcome ctr nb, full ♿ facilities, 📞, 🛆, litter barrels, vending, petwalk**
1mm	**weigh sta nb**
0mm	New York/Pennsylvania state line

INTERSTATE 84

E ↕ W

Exit #	Services
71.5mm	New York/Connecticut state line
21 (68)	US 6, US 202, NY 121 (from wb), N Salem, same as 20
20N (67.5)	US 6, US 202, NY 22, **N gas:** Citgo, Mobil/24hr, Valero, **food:** Bob's Diner, Burger King, McDonald's, **other:** Cadillac/Chevrolet, Curves, Ford, Honda, Subaru
20S	I-684, to NYC
20S	I-684, to NYC
19 (65)	NY 312, Carmel, **S food:** Applebee's, Dunkin Donuts, Friendly's, Gaetano's Deli, McDonald's, Sonoma Cafe, Wendy's, **other:** H, Home Depot, Kohl's, Marshall's, Michael's, st police
18 (62)	NY 311, Lake Carmel, **S** Lake Carmel Gen Store, Lakeview Pizza
17 (59)	Ludingtonville Rd, **S gas:** Hess/Blimpie/dsl/24hr, Sunoco, **food:** Cutiloo's Rest. (2mi), Gappy's Pizza, Lou's Deli
56mm	elevation 970 ft
55mm	**rest area both lanes, full ♿ facilities, 📞, vending, 🛆, litter barrels, petwalk**
16 (53)	Taconic Parkway, N to Albany, S to New York
15 (51)	Lime Kiln NY, **3 mi N gas:** Mobil/24hr, **food:** Dunkin Donuts, **lodging:** Royal Inn
13 (46)	US 9, to Poughkeepsie, **N gas:** Citgo, Gulf, Mobil/dsl, **food:** A&W/KFC, Boston Mkt, Burger King, Charlie Brown Steaks, Cracker Barrel, Denny's, Hudson

NY

INTERSTATE 84 CONT'D

Exit #	Services
13 (46)	Continued Buffet, Panera Bread, Pizza Hut, Ruby Tuesday, Sidewinder's Grill, Stanley's Eatery, Taco Bell, ViaNove Italian, Wendy's, **lodging:** Comfort Inn, Courtyard, Extended Stay America, Hampton Inn, Hilton Garden, Holiday Inn, Homestead Suites, Ramada Inn, Residence Inn, Sierra Suites, **other:** Rite Aid, Sam's Club, ShopRite Foods, Starbucks, Walmart SuperCtr, **S gas:** Hess/Blimpie/dsl/24hr, **food:** Maya Cafe, McDonald's, **other:** Home Depot
12 (45)	NY 52 E, Fishkill, **N gas:** Valero, **food:** Chan's Buffet, Friendly's, **other:** CVS Drug, $King, **S gas:** Mobil, Sunoco/dsl, **food:** Dunkin Donuts, Hometown Deli, I-84 Diner/24hr, **other:** Lincoln/Mercury
11 (42)	NY 9D, to Wappingers Falls, **1 mi N gas:** Mobil/dsl, Sunoco
41mm	toll booth wb
40mm	Hudson River
10 (39)	US 9W, NY 32, to Newburgh, **N gas:** Citgo, Mobil, Sunoco, Xtra, **food:** Alexis Diner, Andiamo Pizza, Burger King, China King, McDonald's, Pizza Hut, Subway, **lodging:** Budget Inn, Economy Inn, **other:** Advance Parts, Big Lots, $Tree, Family$, PriceChopper Foods, **S gas:** Exxon/dsl, Gulf, Sunoco/dsl, **lodging:** Travel Inn, Windsor Inn (4mi), **other:** H, Jo-Ann Fabrics
8 (37)	NY 52, to Walden, **N gas:** Citgo/dsl, Sunoco/24hr
7 (36)	NY 300, to I-87 (NY Thruway), Newburgh, **N lodging:** Hilton Garden, **S gas:** Getty, Hess/Blimpie/dsl, Mobil, Sunoco, **food:** Applebees, Burger King, Chili's, Cosimos Ristorante, Denny's, Dunkin Donuts, Gateway Diner, Ground Round, Jak Steaks, King Buffet, Longhorn Steaks, Neptune Diner, Newburgh Buffet, Old Town Buffet, Perkins, Union Sq Rest., Subway, Taco Bell, TGIFriday, Wendy's, **lodging:** Hampton Inn, Howard Johnson, Quality Inn, Ramada Inn, Super 8, **other:** Adam's Food Mkt, Aldi Foods, AutoZone, Barnes&Noble, BonTon, Cadillac/Chevrolet, Chrysler/Dodge/Jeep, Curves, $Tree, Ford/Lincoln/Mercury, Harley-Davidson, Home Depot, Honda, Lowes Whse, Mavis Tire, Michael's, Midas, Nissan, Kohl's, Office Depot, Old Navy, PetsMart, Radio Shack, Sears/auto, Stop'n Shop, Target, Walmart SuperCtr
6 (34)	NY 17K, to Newburgh, **N gas:** Mobil/24, Gulf, Pilot/Arby's/dsl/scales/24hr, **food:** Airport Diner, **lodging:** Comfort Inn, **S gas:** Exxon/dsl, **lodging:** Courtyard, **3 mi S lodging:** Days Inn, Howard Johnson, Quality Inn
33mm	new exit
5 (29)	NY 208, Maybrook, **N gas:** Exxon/24hr, Mobil, **food:** Baskin-Robbins/Dunkin Donuts, Burger King, McDonald's, **other:** , ShopRite Foods, **S gas:** Hess/Blimpie, TA/Pizza Hut/dsl/rest./@, **food:** Maybrook Diner, Renee's Deli, Roadside Rest., Subway, **lodging:** Rodeside Inn, Super 8, **other:** Blue Beacon, Winding Hills Camping
24mm	**rest area wb, full facilities, phone, vending, picnic, litter barrels, petwalk**
4 (19)	NY 17, Middletown, **N gas:** Mobil/24hr, Sunoco, **food:** Americana Diner, Applebee's, Baskin-Robbins/
4 (19)	Continued Dunkin Donuts, Boston Mkt, Cheeseburger Paradise, Cosimo's Brick Oven, Denny's, Friendly's, KFC, McDonald's, Olive Garden, Perkins, Red Lobster, Ruby Tuesday, Subway, Taco Bell, Wendy's, **lodging:** Howard Johnson, Middletown Motel, Super 8, **other:** H, Best Buy, Borders Books, Firestone/auto, Gander Mtn, Hannaford Foods, Home Depot, Honda, JC Penney, Jo-Ann Fabrics, Kohl's, Lowe's Whse, Old Navy, PetCo, PriceChopper Foods, Rite Aid, Sam's Club, Sears/auto, ShopRite Foods, Staples, Stop&Shop Foods, TJ Maxx, U-Haul, mall, Vet, Walmart SuperCtr/24hr, mall, **S gas:** Citgo/dsl, **food:** Chili's, El Bandido Mexican, Outback Steaks, TGIFriday, **lodging:** Courtyard, Hampton Inn, Holiday Inn, Microtel, **other:** st police
17mm	**rest area eb, full facilities, phone, vending, picnic, litter barrels, petwalk**
3 (15)	US 6, to Middletown, **N gas:** Citgo/dsl/24hr, Mobil, Valero, **food:** Bradley's Corner Diner, Colonial Diner, Dunkin Donuts, McDonald's, NY Buffet, Perkins, Quinzno's, Subway, Taco Bell, Wendy's, **other:** H, Acura, Buick/Pontica/GMC, Chevrolet/Isuzu, Mazda, ShopRite Foods, Subaru, **S gas:** Citgo, Sunoco/dsl, **lodging:** Day's Inn, Global Budget Inn, **other:** Chrysler/Jeep, Nissan, Kia, Suzuki, Toyota, USPO, transmissions
2 (5)	Mountain Rd, **S** Greenville's Deli
4mm	elevation 1254 ft wb, 1272 ft eb
3	**parking area both lanes**
1 (1)	US 6, NY 23, Port Jervis, **N gas:** Sunoco/dsl, **food:** Arlene&Tom's Diner, Dunkin Donuts/Baskin Robbins, **lodging:** Deerdale Motel, Painted Aprons Motel, **other:** H, 84 RV Ctr, Ford/Lincoln/Mercury/Jeep, **S gas:** Citgo/dsl, Gulf/dsl, Lukoil, Valero, **food:** Cumberland Farms, DQ, McDonald's, Village Pizza, **lodging:** Comfort Inn, **other:** H, ShopRite Foods, TJ Maxx, mall
0mm	New York/Pennsylvania state line, Delaware River

INTERSTATE 86 (NEW YORK)

Exit #	Services
I-86 begins/ends on I-87, exit 16, toll booth	
131 (379)	NY 17, **N other:** Outlets/famous brands, **S gas:** Exxon/dsl, **food:** Chicago Grill, Chili's, McDonald's, TGIFriday's, **lodging:** American Budget Inn, Hampton Inn, **other:** Home Depot, Kohls, Staples, TJMaxx,
130a (378)	US 6, Bear Mtn, to West Point (from eb), **S food:** Sonny's Pizza, Outback Steaks, **other:** Best Buy, BJ's Whse, BMW, Home Depot, PetsMart, Target, TJ Maxx, Walmart SuperCtr
130 (377)	NY 208, Monroe, Washingtonville, **N lodging:** James Motel, Lake Anne Motel, **other:** Chrysler/Dodge/Jeep, Isuzu, st police, **S gas:** Mobil/dsl, Sunoco, Valero, **food:** Burger King, Dunkin Donuts, Monroe Diner, **lodging:** American Budget Inn, **other:** Kohl's, Michael's, ShopRite Foods, Staples
129 (375)	Museum Village Rd
128 (374)	rd 51 (only from wb), Oxford Depot
127 (373)	Greycourt Rd (from wb only), Sugar Loaf, Warwick
126 (372)	NY 94 (no EZ wb return), Chester, Florida, **N gas:** Mobil, Shell, Sunoco/dsl, **food:** Chester Diner, McDonald's, Wendy's, **lodging:** Holiday Inn Express, **other:** CVS Drug, Radio Shack, Rite Aid, ShopRite Foods, USPO, **S other:** Lowes Whse

INTERSTATE 86 CONT'D (NEW YORK)

E ↕ W

Exit #	Services
125 (369)	NY 17M E, South St, **S food:** Hacienda Mexican, Pizza Deli, **other:** H
124 (368)	NY 17A, NY 207, **N gas:** Exxon/Subway/dsl, Mobil/dsl, **food:** Burger King, Friendly's, Dunkin Donuts, Pizza Hut, **other:** H, CVS Drug, **S lodging:** Comfort Inn, **other:** Chrysler/Dodge/Jeep, Hyundai
123	US 6, NY 17M (wb only), Port Jervis
122a (367)	Fletcher St, Goshen
122 (364)	rd 67, E Main St, Crystal Run Rd, **N gas:** Mobil, **food:** Chili's, El Bandido Rest., Outback Steaks, TGIFriday's, **lodging:** Courtyard, Hampton Inn, Holiday Inn, Microtel, **S gas:** Citgo/dsl
121 (363)	I-84, E to Newburgh, W to Port Jervis
120 (363)	NY 211, **N gas:** Lukoil, Mobil, Sunoco, **food:** Cosimo's Ristorante, Olive Garden, **lodging:** Howard Johnson, Middletown Motel, Super 8, **other:** Best Buy, Gander Mtn, Macy's, Hannaford's Foods, JC Penney, Rite Aid, Sam's Club, Target, **S gas:** Valero, **food:** Americana Diner, Arby's, Boston Mkt, Burger King, Cheeseburger Paradise, Denny's, Dunkin Donuts, Friendly's, KFC, Panera Bread, Pizza Hut, Red Lobster, Subway, Taco Bell, Wendy's, Youyou Chinese, **other:** Aldi Foods, AutoZone, $Tree, Home Depot, Kohl's, Lowes Whse, PriceChopper, Rite Aid, ShopRite Foods, Staples, TJ-Maxx, U-Haul, Walmart SuperCtr
119 (360)	NY 309, Pine Bush, **S gas:** Best Gas/dsl
118a (358)	NY 17M, Fair Oaks
118 (358)	Circleville, **S gas:** Exxon/dsl, Mobil, **food:** Subway
116 (355)	NY 17K, Bloomingburg, **S gas:** Citgo/dsl, **food:** Quickway Diner
114	Wurtsboro, Highview (from wb)
113 (350)	US 209, Wurtsboro, Ellenville, **N gas:** Mobil/dsl, Stewarts/gas, **food:** Giovanni's Café, Subway, **lodging:** Gold Mtn Chalet, Day's Inn, Valley Brook Motel, **other:** Spring Glen Camping, **S other:** American Family Campground
112 (347)	Masten Lake, Yankee Lake, **N food:** Potager Diner, **lodging:** Days Inn, ValleyBrook Motel, **other:** Catskill Mtn Ranch Camping, WonderWood Camping, Yankee Lake
111 (344)	(eb only), Wolf Lake
110 (343)	Lake Louise Marie, **N food:** Dodge Inn Rest, **lodging:** Rock Hill Lodge
109 (342)	Rock Hill, Woodridge, **N gas:** Exxon/dsl, **food:** Dutch's Cafe, RockHill Diner, Rock Pizza, **lodging:** Rock Hill Lodge, Rosemond Motel, **other:** Ace Harware, Hilltop Farms Camping, auto repair, **S gas:** Mobil/dsl
108 (341)	Bridgeville, same as 109
107 (340)	Thompsonville, **S food:** Hana Rest., Old Homestead Diner, **lodging:** Pines Motel, Raleigh Motel, **other:** Chevrolet, Chrysler/Dodge/Jeep, Toyota
106 (339)	(wb only), E. Broadway, **N** Ford/Lincoln/Mercury, **S gas:** Mobil/dsl, **food:** Monitcello Cafe, **lodging:** Super 8 (2 mi), Travel Inn (2mi), **other:** GMC Trucks, Hyundai, tires
105 (337)	NY 42, Monticello, **N gas:** Exxon/dsl, Mobil, Valero, **food:** Bro Bruno's, Blue Horizon Diner, Burger King, Dunkin Donuts, KFC, McDonald's, Subway, **other:** AutoZone, Home Depot, ShopRite Foods, Staples,

MIDDLETOWN

MONTICELLO

Exit #	Services
105 (337)	Continued Walmart SuperCtr, **S gas:** Citgo, Sunoco/dsl, **food:** Pizza Hut, Wendy's, **lodging:** Ramada Ltd, Super 8, **other:** Advance Parts, Family$, NAPA, Rite Aid
104 (336)	NY 17B, Raceway, Monticello, **S gas:** Citgo, Exxon/dsl, **food:** Colosseo Rest., Taco Maker, **lodging:** Best Western, Raceway Motel, Super 8 (2mi), Travel Inn, **other:** Monticello Raceway, Swinging Bridge Camp, Woodstock Camping, ✈
103	Rapp rd (wb only)
102 (332)	Harris, **S other:** H, Swan Lake Camping
101 (327)	Ferndale, Swan Lake, **S gas:** Exxon/dsl
100 (327)	NY 52 E, Liberty, **N gas:** Citgo, Mobil, Sunoco, **food:** Albert's Rest., Burger King, Dunkin Donuts, Grapevine Grill, Last Licks Cafe, McDonald's, Piccolo Italian, Pizza Hut, Subway, Taco Bell, Wendy's, **lodging:** Day's Inn, Howard Johnson, **other:** Ace Hardware, Advance Parts, Curves, ShopRite Foods, USPO, **S gas:** Exxon/dsl, Xtra, **lodging:** Lincoln Motel, **other:** Ford/Lincoln/Mercury, Pontiac/Buick, Southend Parts, Neversink River Camping, Swan Lake Camping, Yogi Bear Camping
100a	NY 52 W (no wb return), Liberty, **S food:** McCabe's Rest, **other:** st police
99 (325)	NY 52 W, to NY 55, Liberty, **S gas:** Exxon, Sunoco, **lodging:** Catskill Motel
98 (321)	Cooley, Parksville, **N gas:** Mobil, **food:** Charlie's Rest., Dari-King, I-86 Diner, **lodging:** Best Western, **other:** USPO
97 (319)	Morsston
96 (316)	Livingston Manor, **N food:** Tony's Pizza, **lodging:** Econo Motel, **other:** Covered Bridge Camping, Mongaup Pond Camping, **S food:** Tony's Pizza, Puleez Lueez, **lodging:** DeBruce Inn, OZ B&B, Willowemoc Motel
313mm	**rest area eb, full ♿ facilities, picnic tables, litter barrels, phone, vending, petwalk, truck insp. sta (eb)**
94 (311)	NY 206, Roscoe, Lew Beach, **N gas:** Exxon/dsl, Sunoco/dsl, **food:** 1910 Coffeshop, Raimondo's Diner, Roscoe Diner, **lodging:** Reynolds House Motel, Rockland House Motel, Roscoe Motel, Tennanah Lake Motel, **other:** Roscoe Camping, **S gas:** Mobil/dsl, **other:** Beaverkill St Camping (8mi)
93 (305)	to Cooks Falls (from wb)
92 (303)	Horton, Cooks Falls, Colchester, **S gas:** Sunoco/dsl, **food:** Riverside Café/lodge, **other:** Russell Brook Camping
90 (297)	NY 30, East Branch, Downsville, **N gas:** Sunoco, **other:** Beaver-Del Camping, Catskill Mtn Camping,

NY

INTERSTATE 86 CONT'D (NEW YORK)

E ↕ W

Exit #	Services
90 (297)	Continued Oxbow Camping, Peaceful Valley Camping, **S lodging:** E Branch Motel
295mm	**rest area wb, full ♿ facilities, picnic, litter barrels, phone, vending, petwalk**
89 (293)	Fishs Eddy
87a (288)	NY 268 (from wb), same as 87
87 (284)	NY 97, to NY 268, to NY 191, Hancock, Cadosia, **S gas:** Getty, Mobil/Subway, Sunoco, **food:** Bluestone Grill, Family Rest., McDonald's, **lodging:** Capra Inn, Colonial Motel, Starlight Lake Inn, **other:** Buick/Chevrolet, Grand Union Foods, NAPA, Parts+, Rite Aid
276mm	**parking area wb, litter barrels**
84 (274)	Deposit, **N gas:** Citgo/dsl/24hr, **food:** Grand Stand Rest., Pines Rest., Wendy's, **lodging:** Deposit Motel, Laurel Bank Motel, Scott's Motel, **other:** Family$, QuickWay, st police
83 (272)	Deposit, Oquaga Lake
82 (270)	NY 41, McClure, Sanford, **N other:** Kellystone Park, **S lodging:** Chestnut Inn/rest., Mountain Hollow B&B/diner, **other:** Guestward Camping (3mi)
265mm	**parking area eb, picnic, litter barrels**
81 (263)	E Bosket Rd
80 (261)	Damascus, **N gas:** Exxon/dsl, **other:** Forest Hill Lake Park Camping, auto repair
79 (259)	NY 79, Windsor, **N gas:** Citgo, Sunoco/dsl, **food:** Chip's Pizza, Subway, **other:** Big M Foods, **S food:** Golden Oak Rest., Marian's Pizza, **other:** Lakeside Camping
78 (256)	Dunbar Rd, Occanum
77 (254)	W Windsor, **N gas:** Mobil/dsl, **food:** McDonald's
76 (251)	Haskins Rd, to Foley Rd
75 (250)	I-81 S, to PA (exits left from wb), **N gas:** Exxon/dsl, **food:** Subway, **lodging:** Dell Motel
72 (244)	I-81 N, US 11, Front St, Clinton St, (no wb re-entry), **S food:** McDonald's, **other:** Advance Parts, K-Mart, antiques
71 (242)	Airport Rd, Johnson City, **S gas:** Valero
70 (241)	NY 201, Johnson City, **N gas:** Hess/Blimpie, Valero, **food:** China Buffet, Christy's Grill, Dunkin Donuts, Friendly's, Ground Round, McDonald's, Papa John's, Pizza Hut, Ponderosa, Quizno's, Ruby Tuesday, Taco Bell, **lodging:** Best Western, Hampton Inn, La Quinta, Red Roof Inn, **other:** $Tree, Gander Mtn, Giant Foods, JC Penney, Kost Tire, Macy's, PetCo, Sears/auto, Wegman's Foods, mall, Vet, **S** Home Depot
69 (239)	NY 17C
238mm	Susquehanna River
68 (237)	NY 17C, Old Vestal Rd, (from eb)
67 (236)	NY 26, NY 434, Vestal, Endicott, **S on NY 434...gas:** Hess, Stop'N Gas, Valero/dsl, **food:** A&W/LJ Silver, Arby's, Burger King, California Grill, Chicago Grill, China Wok, Dunkin Donuts, La Vita Bella, McDonald's, Old Country Buffet, Olive Garden, Outback Steaks, Quizno's, Red Lobster, Starbucks, Subway, Taco Bell, TGIFriday, **lodging:** Parkway Motel, Skylark Mote/Diner, Vestal Motel, **other:** Advance Parts, Barnes&Noble, Chevrolet, Chrysler/Jeep/Subaru, CVS Drug, $Tree, Firestone/auto, Ford/Lincoln/Mercury, Giant Foods, Jo-Ann Fabrics, Kohl's, Kost Tire, Lowe's Whse, Michael's, Nissan, Sam's Club, Subaru, Target, TJ Maxx, Volvo, Walmart SuperCtr/24hr, USPO, Vet
66 (231)	NY 434, Apalachin, **S gas:** KwikFill, Mobil/dsl, **food:** Blue Dolphin Diner, Dunkin Donuts, McDonald's, Subway, **lodging:** Econolodge, Quality Inn, **other:** Evelyn's Mkt, Red Apple
65 (225)	NY 17C, NY 434, Owego, **N gas:** Citgo, Mobil/dsl, **food:** A&W/KFC, Arbys, McDonald's, Panda Wok, Papa John's, Pizza Hut, Subway, Wendy's, **lodging:** Hampton Inn, Holiday Inn Express, Treadway Motel/rest., **other:** $General, Hickories Park Camping, Kost Tire, Medicine Shop Drug, P&C Foods, **S** st police
64 (223)	NY 96, Owego, **N other:** CVS Drug, USPO, **S gas:** Citgo, **other:** auto repair, Vet
222mm	**rest area wb, full ♿ facilities, phone, vending, picnic, litter barrels, petwalk**
63 (218)	Lounsberry, **S gas:** Valero/rest./24hr/dsl
62 (214)	NY 282, Nichols, **S gas:** Citgo/Pizza Hut/dsl, **other:** Jim's RV Ctr, Tioga Downs Race Track (2mi)
212mm	**rest area eb, full ♿ facilities, picnic, litter barrels, phone, vending, petwalk**
208mm	Susquehanna River
61 (206)	NY 34, PA 199, Waverly, Sayre, **N other:** $General, Goodyear/gas, **S gas:** Gulf/24hr, Sunoco, **food:** McDonald's, **lodging:** Best Western/rest., **other:** Chevrolet/Buick/Pontiac, Chrysler/Jeep/Dodge, Joe's RV Ctr, Nissan
60 (204)	US 220, to Sayre, Waverly, **N lodging:** O'brien's Inn, **other:** Clark's Foods, **S gas:** Citgo/dsl, Xtra/dsl, **food:** Wendy's (3mi), **lodging:** Hampton Inn, **other:** Advance Parts, Aldi Foods, K-Mart, Rite Aid, Top's Foods
59a (202)	Wilawana, **S gas:** Sunoco/Subway/dsl
59 (200)	NY 427, Chemung, **N gas:** Dandy/dsl
58 (195)	rd 2, Lowman, Wellsburg, **N food:** W Diner, **lodging:** Red Jacket Motel, **S other:** Gardiner Hill Campsites (4mi)
56 (190)	Jerusalem Hill, **S gas:** Citgo/dsl, KwikFill, Sunoco/Subway, **food:** Hilltop Rest., McDonalds, Pizza Hut, **lodging:** Coachman Motel, Holiday Inn, Mark Twain Motel
54 (186)	NY 13, to Ithaca
54	I-86 begins ends., **S gas:** Mobil, Sunoco, **food:** Burger King, Dunkin Donuts, Guiseppe's Pizza, LJ Silver, McDonald's, Subway, Wendy's, **lodging:** Motel 6, Red Carpet Inn, **other:** Advance Parts, Family$, K-Mart, Rite Aid, Sav-A-Lot Foods
53	Horseheads, same as 54
52b (184)	NY 14, to Watkins Glen, **N food:** Friendly's, **lodging:** Holiday Inn, Knight's Inn, Landmark Inn, **S food:** Denny's
52a (183)	Commerce Ctr, same as 52b
51 (182)	Chambers Rd, **N gas:** Mobil/Subway/dsl, Sunoco/dsl, **food:** Bon Ton, Chili's, Dunkin Donuts, Friendly's, McDonald's, Olive Garden, Outback Steaks, Red Lobster, Ruby Tuesday, **lodging:** Country Inn&Suites, Hilton Garden, Holiday Inn Express, Knights Inn, **other:** Firestone/auto, JC Penney, Jo-Anne Fabrics, Sears/auto, mall, **S food:** Applebee's, Charlie's Subs, Old Country Buffet, Panera Bread, Taco Bell, TGIFriday, Wendy's, **lodging:** Econolodge, **other:** Barnes&Noble, Best Buy, Buick/Pontiac/GMC, $Tree, Kohl's, Kost Tire, Lowe's Whse, Macy's, Michael's, Nissan, Old Navy, PetCo, PetsMart, Sam's Club, Staples, Subaru, Target, TJ Maxx, Toyota/Scion, Walmart SuperCtr, museum

WINDSOR · VESTAL · OWEGO · ELMIRA

NY

INTERSTATE 86 CONT'D (NEW YORK)

E ↕ W

Exit #	Services
50 (180)	Kahler Rd, **N** to [airport]
49 (178)	Olcott Rd, Canal St, Big Flats, **N** [airport], antiques, **S gas:** Sunoco, **food:** Picnic Pizza, **other:** $General
48 (171)	NY 352, E Corning, **N gas:** Citgo, **food:** Tag's Rest., **lodging:** Budget Inn, Gatehouse Motel
47 (174)	NY 352, Gibson, Corning, **N lodging:** Radisson Inn, to [H], Museum of Glass
46 (171)	NY 414, to Watkins Glen, Corning, **5mi N other:** Ferenbaugh Camping, KOA, Watkins Glen Camping, **S gas:** Citgo/dsl, **lodging:** Comfort Inn, Day's Inn, Staybridge Suites, **other:** [H], museums
45 (170)	NY 352, Corning, **N gas:** Sunoco, **food:** McDonald's, **S gas:** Fastrac, **food:** Bob Evans, Burger King, EnEn Chinese, Friendly's, Subway, Wendy's, **lodging:** Fairfield Inn, **other:** AutoZone, CarQuest, Rite Aid
44 (168)	US 15 S, NY 417 W, Gang Mills
43 (167)	NY 415, Painted Post, **N gas:** Citgo, **food:** Burger King, **other:** AutoValue Parts, $General, Firestone/auto, Jo-Ann Fabrics, **S gas:** Sunoco, **food:** Denny's, **lodging:** Hampton Inn
167mm	**parking area wb, litter barrels**
42 (165)	Coopers Plains, **N** st police
41 (161)	rd 333, Campbell, **N other:** Camp Bell Camping (1mi), **S gas:** Sunoco, **other:** Cardinal Campsites (6mi), antiques
160mm	**rest area eb, full [handicapped] facilities, [picnic], litter barrels, [phone], vending, petwalk**
40 (156)	NY 226, Savona, **N gas:** Mobil/dsl, **food:** Savona Diner, Subway, **other:** Green Acres Camping
39 (153)	NY 415, Bath, **N food:** Chat-a-Whyle Rest. (3mi), **lodging:** Holland American Country Inn, National Hotel, **S other:** Babcock Hollow Camping (2mi)
38 (150)	NY 54, to Hammondsport, Bath, **N gas:** Citgo, Kwik-Fill, Mobil, Sunoco, **food:** Arby's, Burger King, Dunkin Donuts, Ling Chinese, McDonald's/playplace, Pizza Hut, Ponderosa, Subway, **lodging:** Budget Inn, Day's Inn, Microtel, Super 8, VineHurst Inn, **other:** [H], Advance Parts, AutoValue Parts, Camping World RV Ctr, $General, Family$, Hickory Hill Camping (3mi), K-Mart, Rite Aid, Top's Foods/gas, Walgreens, museum, st police, winery, to Keuka Lake
147mm	**rest area wb, full [handicapped] facilities, [phone], [picnic], litter barrels, vending, petwalk**
37 (146)	NY 53, to Prattsburg, Kanona, **S gas:** Pilot/Subway/dsl/scales/@, Sunoco/Smokey's/dsl/scales, **food:** Tally-Ho Rest., **other:** Wagon Wheel Camping, Wilkin's RV Ctr (1mi), USPO
36 (145)	I-390 N, NY 15, to Rochester
35 (138)	Howard, **S** to Lake Demmon RA, phone
34 (130)	NY 36, Hornell, Arkport, **0-3 mi S gas:** KwikFill, Sunoco, **food:** Burger King (3mi), China King, Country Kitchen, Dunkin Donuts, Friendly's (3mi), McDonald's, Subway, **lodging:** Comfort Inn (3mi), Day's Inn, Econolodge, Sunshine Motel, **other:** Aldi, Chevrolet, Chrysler/Dodge/Jeep, $Tree, Ford, GNC, NAPA, Walmart/auto, Wegman's Foods
125mm	scenic overlook eb, litter barrels
33 (124)	NY 21, to Alfred, Almond, Andover, **S gas:** Mobil, **lodging:** Economy Inn, Saxon Inn Hotel, **other:** Lake Lodge Camping (8mi), Kanakadea Camping

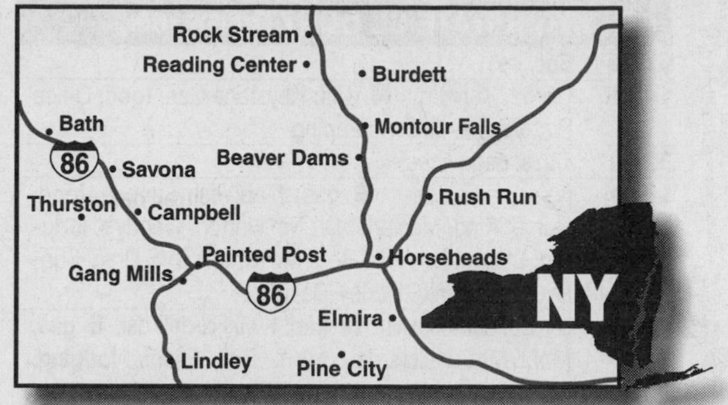

Exit #	Services
117mm	highest elevation on I-86, elev 2110 ft eb, 2080 ft wb
32 (116)	W Almond
31 (108)	Angelica, **N gas:** Citgo, **lodging:** Angelica Inn B&B
30 (104)	NY 19, Belmont, Wellsville, **N** 6-S Camping (3mi), **S gas:** American Trkstp/diner/24hr, **food:** Iron Kettle Rest., **other:** Mothers Piknchikn Camping (6mi)
101mm	**rest area eb, full [handicapped] facilities, [phone], [picnic], litter barrels, vending, petwalk**
29 (99)	NY 275, to Bolivar, Friendship, **S gas:** Mobil, Sunoco, Miller&Brandes Gas, **food:** Subway
28 (92)	NY 305, Cuba, **N food:** Moonwink's Rest., **lodging:** Econolodge, **other:** $General, Maple Lane RV Park, **S gas:** Sunoco/dsl, Valero/dsl, **food:** McDonald's, **other:** [H], Cuba Drug, Giant Foods
27 (84)	NY 16, NY 446, Hinsdale, **N** food, **S** gas, lodging
26 (79)	NY 16, Olean, **S gas:** Sunoco, **food:** Burger King, Wendy's, **other:** [H]
25 (77)	Buffalo St, Olean, **S gas:** Citgo/dsl, **other:** [H], **2 mi S on Constitution N gas:** KwikFill, **food:** Applebee's, Burger King, Dunkin Donuts, Friendly's, McDonald's, Perkins, Pizza Hut, Ponderosa, Quizno's, Tim Horton, **lodging:** Best Western, Comfort Inn, Country Inn, Knight's Inn, Microtel, **other:** Advance Parts, BJ's Whse/gas, $Tree, GNC, Home Depot, Jo-Ann Fabrics, K-Mart, NAPA, Old Navy, Radio Shack, Tops Foods/gas, Walmart, St Bonaventure U
24 (74)	NY 417, Allegany, **1mi S gas:** Mobil/dsl, **other:** to St Bonaventure U
73mm	**rest area wb, full [handicapped] facilities, [picnic], litter barrels, petwalk**
23 (68)	US 219 S, **N gas:** Allegany Jct./Subway/dsl
66mm	Allegheny River
21 (61)	US 219 N, Salamanca, **S food:** Red Garter Rest
20 (58)	NY 417, NY 353, Salamanca, **N gas:** Antone's Gas, Nafco Quickstop/Burger King/24hr, Seneca OneStop/dsl/24hr, VIP Gas, **food:** McDonald's/24hr, **lodging:** Holiday Inn Express, Westgate Motel, **other:** AutoZone, Rail Museum, Seneca-Iroquis Museum, **S** casino
19 (54)	**S other:** Allegany SP, Red House Area
18 (51)	NY 280, **S other:** Allegany SP, Quaker Run Area
17 (48)	NY 394, Steamburg, **N** gas, **other:** RV camping, **S gas:** M&M/dsl/rest., **other:** camping
16 (42)	W Main St, Randolph, **N gas:** Mobil/dsl, **food:** R&M Rest., **other:** RV camping
41mm	**rest area eb, [phone], [picnic], litter barrel**
15 (40)	School House Rd
39mm	**rest area wb, [phone], [picnic], litter barrel**

INTERSTATE 86 CONT'D (NEW YORK)

Exit #	Services
14 (36)	US 62, Kennedy, **N gas:** Keystone Gas, **food:** Office Pizza/Subs, **S** RV camping
32mm	Cassadaga Creek
13 (31)	NY 394, Falconer, **S gas:** Mobil/dsl, Sunoco, **food:** Burger King, McDonald's, Tim Horton, Wendy's, **lodging:** Budget Inn, Red Roof Inn, **other:** CVS Drug, Sugar Creek Stores, Harley-Davidson
12 (28)	NY 60, Jamestown, **N gas:** KwikFill/deli/dsl, **S gas:** Mobil/McDonald's/dsl, **food:** Bob Evans, **lodging:** Comfort Inn, Hampton Inn, **other:** H, st police
11 (25)	to NY 430, Jamestown, **S** gas, dsl, food, lodging
22mm	**welcome ctr/rest area eb, full ♿ facilities, picnic, litter barrels, petwalk, vending**
10 (21)	NY 430 W, Bemus Point
9 (20)	NY 430 E, **N gas:** Mobil, **S** gas, food, lodging
19mm	Chautauqua Lake
8 (18)	NY 394, Mayville, **N gas:** Mobil/dsl, lodging, **other:** RV camping
7 (15)	Panama
6 (9)	NY 76, Sherman, **N gas:** Keystone Gas, **food:** Village Pizzeria, **other:** NAPA, Sherman Drug, USPO
4 (1)	NY 430, Findley Lake, **N lodging:** Holiday Inn Express, Peek'n Peak Motel, **S** gas, food, lodging, **other:** RV camping, to Peek'n Peak Ski Area
0mm	New York/Pennsylvania state line. **Exits 3-1 are in PA.**
3	PA 89, North East, Wattsburg, **N** gas, food
1b a	I-90, W to Erie, E to Buffalo. **I-86 begins/ends on I-90, exit 37. I-390 begins/ends on I-86, exit 36.**

INTERSTATE 87

Exit #	Services
176mm	US/Canada Border, NY state line, I-87 begins/ends.
43 (175)	US 9, Champlain, **E** World Duty Free, **W gas:** Peterbilt Trkstp/dsl/deli/scales/24hr/@, **other:** repair
42 (174)	US 11 S, to Rouse's Point, Champlain, **E gas:** Mobil, **food:** J-reck Subs, Pizza+, Subway, **other:** Ace Hardware, Chevrolet/Pontiac (3mi), Kinney Drug, PriceChopper/24hr, Rite Aid, USPO, **W gas:** Exxon/dsl, Mobil/dsl, **food:** McDonald's
41 (167)	NY 191, Chazy, **E** st police, **W** Miner Institute
162mm	**rest area both lanes, full ♿ facilities, info, phone, picnic, litter barrels, petwalk**
40 (160)	NY 456, Beekmantown, **E gas:** Mobil/dsl, **lodging:** Pt Auroche Lodge, Stonehelm Motel/café, **W** Twin Ells Camping
39 (158)	NY 314, Moffitt Rd, Plattsburgh Bay, **E gas:** Mobil/dsl, Stewarts, **food:** A&W, Dunkin Donuts, Gus' Rest, McDonald's, **lodging:** Rip van Winkle Motel, Sundance Inn, Super 8, **other:** Plattsburgh RV Park, **W other:** Shady Oaks Camping, to Adirondacks
38 (154)	NY 22, NY 374, to Plattsburgh, **E gas:** Mobil/dsl, **food:** Kinney Drug
37 (153)	NY 3, Plattsburgh, **E gas:** Mobil, Shell, Stewarts, Sunoco, **food:** Burger King, China Buffet, Domino's, Dunkin Donuts, Jade Buffet, KFC, Legends Rest., Mangia Pizza, McDonald's, Michigan's Rest., Papa John's, Perkins, Pizza Hut, Quizno's, Starbucks, Subway, Wendy's, **lodging:** Comfort Inn, Holiday Inn, **other:** H, Aldi Foods, BigLots, Buick/Cadillac/GMC/Ponitac, Family$, Ford, Michael's, PetsMart, Radio Shack, Rite Aid,
37 (153)	Continued Sam's Club, Staples, TJ Maxx, Walmart SuperCtr/24hr, Vet, **W gas:** Exxon, Mobil, Sunoco/J-reck Subs, **food:** Anthony's Rest., Applebee's, Butcher Block Rest., Dunkin Donuts, Friendly's, Ground Round, 99 Rest., Ponderosa, **lodging:** Best Value Inn, Best Western, Day's Inn, Econolodge, La Quinta, Microtel, **other:** Advance Parts, AutoZone, Best Buy, Borders Books, Gander Mtn Harley-Davidson, Honda, JC Penney, Kinny Drug, K-Mart, Lowes Whse, 1$Store, Prays Mkt, PriceChopper Foods, Sears/auto, Suzuki, Target, Vet
151mm	Saranac River
36 (150)	NY 22, Plattsburgh ✈, **E gas:** Mobil/dsl/24hr, **other:** U-Haul, **W other:** st police
146mm	**truck insp sta nb, rest area nb full ♿ facilities, picnic, litter barrels, phone, petwalk**
35 (144)	NY 442, to Port Kent, Peru, **2-8 mi E other:** Iroquois/Ausable Pines Camping, **W gas:** Citgo, Mobil/Subway/Dunkin Donuts/dsl, **food:** Cricket's Rest., McDonald's, **other:** Auchuban Hardware, Grand Union Foods, USPO, repair
143mm	emergency phones at 2 mi intervals begin sb/end nb
34 (137)	NY 9 N, Ausable Forks, **E gas:** Sunoco/dsl, **food:** Pleasant Corner Rest., Mac's Drive-in, **other:** vet, **W other:** Prays Mkt, Ausable River RV Camping
136mm	Ausable River
33 (135)	US 9, NY 22, to Willsboro, **E** gas/dsl, food, lodging, RV camping, to Essex Ferry
125mm	N Boquet River
32 (124)	Lewis, **E other:** RV Camping, **W gas:** Lukoil/dsl, **food:** Trkstp Diner, **other:** RV Camping
123mm	**rest area sb, full ♿ facilities, info, phone, picnic, petwalk, rest area nb, no restrooms**
120mm	Boquet River
31 (117)	NY 9 N, to Elizabethtown, Westport, **E gas:** Mobil, **lodging:** HillTop Motel, **other:** RV camp/dump, **W other:** H, st police
111mm	**rest area nb only, full ♿ facilities, phone, picnic, litter barrels, vending, petwalk**
30 (104)	US 9, NY 73, Keene Valley
99mm	**rest area both lanes, full ♿ facilities, phone, picnic, litter barrels, petwalk**
29 (94)	N Hudson, **E other:** Jellystone Camping, USPO, **W** Blue Ridge Falls Camping
28 (88)	NY 74 E, to Ticonderoga, Schroon Lake, **E gas:** Getty, Sunoco/dsl, **lodging:** Maple Leaf Motel, Schroon Lake B&B, **other:** RV camp/dump, st police, services on US 9
83mm	**rest area both lanes, full ♿ facilities, phone, picnic, litter barrels, petwalk, vending**
27 (81)	US 9 (from nb, no EZ return), Schroon Lake, to gas/dsl, food, lodging
26 (78)	US 9 (no EZ return), Pottersville, Schroon Lake, **E lodging:** Lee's Corner Motel, **other:** RV Camping, **W gas:** Valero/dsl, **food:** Black Bear Rest.
25 (73)	NY 8, Chestertown, **E gas:** Crossroads Country Store, **W gas:** Mobil/dsl, **other:** RV camping
24 (67)	Bolton Landing, **E** RV camping
66mm	**parking area sb,** picnic, Schroon River
64mm	**parking area nb,** picnic

INTERSTATE 87 CONT'D

N ↕ S

Exit #	Services
23 (58)	to US 9, Diamond Point, Warrensburg, **W gas:** Citgo/dsl, Mobil, Stewarts, **food:** Dunkin Donuts, Geroge Henry's Rest., McDonald's, **lodging:** Super 8, **other:** Ford/Mercury, Central Adirondack Tr, RV Camping, ski area
22 (54)	US 9, NY 9 N, to Diamond Pt, Lake George, **E gas:** Citgo, **food:** Boardwalk Rest., KFC, Luigi's Italian, Mario's Italian, Subway, Trattoria Siciliano, **lodging:** Admiral Motel, Balmoral Motel, Blue Moon Motel, Brookside Motel, Heritage Motel, Mohawk Cottages, Oasis Motel, Windsor Lodge, multiple services, **W parking area both lanes**
21 (53)	NY 9 N, Lake Geo, Ft Wm Henry, **E on US 9...gas:** Getty Gas, Stewarts, Sunoco, Valero, **food:** Adirondack Brewery, A&W, Barnsider Smokehouse, Dining Room, Flapjack Pete's, Gino&Tony's, Guiseppe's Pizza, Jasper's Steaks, Kelly's Rest., Lobster Pot, Mama Riso's Italian, McDonald's, Mountaineer Rest., Paolini's, Pizza Hut, Prospect Mt Diner, Quizno's, Smokey Joe's Grill, Sub City, **lodging:** Best Value Inn, Best Western, Comfort Inn, Country Hearth Inn, Econolodge, Ft Henry Inn, Georgian Resort, Hampton Inn, Holiday Inn, Howard Johnson/rest., Lake Crest Hotel, Lake George Inn, Lake Haven Hotel, Lakeview Hotel, Marine Village Resort, Motel Montreal, Nordick's Motel, Park Lane Inn, Ramada Inn, Travelodge, Tiki Motel, Scottish Inn, 7 Dwarf's Motel, Sullivan's Motel, Sundowner Motel, Super 8, Surfside Motel, Villager Motel, Wingate Inn, **other:** Harley-Davidson, King Phillip/Lake George Camping (2mi), Rite Aid, USPO, multiple services, **W gas:** Mobil/dsl/LP, **lodging:** Kathy's Motel
51mm	Adirondack Park
20 (49)	NY 149, to Ft Ann, **E N on US 9...gas:** Mobil/Subway, Sunoco/dsl, **food:** CK's Eatery, Domino's, Frank's Pizza, Leo's Rest., Logjam Rest., Montcalm Rest., Old Post Grill, **lodging:** Comfort Suites, Col. Williams Resort, Day's Inn, Mohican Motel, Rodeway Inn, Rosie's Cabins, Tall Pines Motel, Whipporwill Motel/RV Park, **other:** Carquest, Chevrolet, Ledgeview RV Park (3mi), Factory Outlets/famous brands, st police, **E S on US 9...food:** Johnny Rocket's, **lodging:** Country Inn&Suites, **other:** 6 Flags Funpark
19 (47)	NY 254, Glens Falls, **E gas:** Citgo, Getty, Hess, Mobil, Sunoco, **food:** Bon Ton, Burger King, Chicago Pizza, China Town, Dunkin Donuts, Friendly's, LJ Silver, McDonald's, Mr B's Rest., 99 Rest., Olive Garden, Panera Bread, Pizza Hut, Red Lobster, Remington Grill, Silo Rest., Starbucks, Subway, Taco Bell, Wendy's, **lodging:** Alpen Haus, Budget Inn, Econolodge, Quality Inn, Red Roof Inn, Sleep Inn, **other:** Ace Hardware, AutoZone, Firestone/auto, Goodyear, Home Depot, JC Penney, Jo-Ann Fabrics, PriceChopper Foods, Radio Shack, Rite Aid, Sears, Staples, Steve&Barry's, Target, TJ Maxx, Walmart, mall, **W gas:** Mobil, Stewarts, **lodging:** Ramada/rest., st police
18 (45)	Glens Falls, **E gas:** Gulf/Subway/24hr, Hess/dsl/24hr, **food:** Carl R's Café, Dunkin Donuts, Lefty's Ice Cream, Pizza Hut, Steve's Place Rest., **lodging:** Best Inn, Queensbury Hotel, **other:** [H], CVS Drug, Hannaford Foods, Lincoln/Mercury, Toyota/Scion, U-Haul, **W gas:** Stewarts, **food:** McDonald's, **other:** Super 8

GLENS FALLS

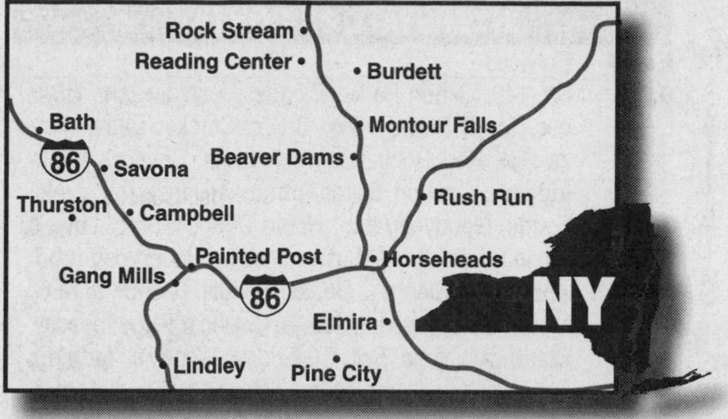

SARATOGA SPRINGS

Exit #	Services
43mm	**rest area both lanes, full [handicapped] facilities, [picnic], litter barrels, [phone], vending, petwalk**
42mm	Hudson River
17 (40)	US 9, S Glen Falls, **E gas:** Citgo/dsl, Gulf, Hess/Blimpie, Sunoco/dsl, Valero/Subway/dsl/24hr, **food:** Dunkin Donuts, Fitzgerald's Steaks, **lodging:** Budget Inn, Landmark Motel (1mi), Sara-Glen Motel, Town&Country Motel, **other:** Adirondack RV Camp, Jeep, Suzuki, auto repair, transmissions, Vet, **W** Moreau Lake SP
16 (36)	Ballard Rd, Wilton, **E other:** Coldbrook Campsites, golf, **W gas:** Mobil, Stewart's, Sunoco/Scotty's Rest./dsl/scales/24hr, **lodging:** Mt View Acres Motel, **other:** Alpin Haus RV Ctr, Ernie's Grocery
15 (30)	NY 50, NY 29, Saratoga Springs, **E gas:** Hess/dsl/24hr, Mobil, **food:** Applebees, BonTon, Burger King, Chicago Grill, Denny's, Dunkin Donuts, Food-Court, Friendly's, Giavanno's Pizza, Golden Corral, KFC/Taco Bell, McDonald's, Moe's SW Grill, 99 Rest., Panera Bread, Ruby Tuesday, Subway, TGIFriday, Uno Pizzaria, **lodging:** Comfort Inn, **other:** Barnes&Noble, Best Buy, BJ's Whse, Dodge, Ford/Mercury, Hanaford Foods, Home Depot, JC Penney, Lowes Whse, Mazda, Old Navy, PetsMart, PriceChopper Foods, Rite Aid, Sears/auto, Staples, Subaru, Target, TJ Maxx, Toyota/Scion, Walgreens, Walmart SuperCtr/24hr, mall, **W lodging:** Residence Inn, **other:** [H]
14 (38)	NY 9P, Schuylerville, **2 mi .W gas:** Citgo/repair/LP, **lodging:** Holiday Inn, **other:** HOPSITAL, museum, racetrack
13 (25)	US 9, Saratoga Springs, **E food:** Bentley's Rest., DeLucia's Deli, Saratoga Pizza Place, **lodging:** Budget Inn, Maggiore's Motel, Post Road Lodge, **other:** Nissan, Northway RV, Ballston Spa SP, **W gas:** Mobil, Stewarts, **food:** Big Apple Rest., El Mariachi, Hibachi Grill, PJ's BBQ, **lodging:** Best Western, Design Motel, Hilton Garden (4mi), Roosevelt Inn/rest., Thorobred Motel, Top Hill Hotel
12 (21)	NY 67, Malta, **E gas:** Exxon, **food:** Dunkin Donuts, KFC, Malta Diner, McDonald's, Subway, Taco Bell, Tasty Chinese, **lodging:** Cocca's Motel, Fairfield Inn, Riviera Motel, **other:** CVS Drug, GNC, PriceChopper Foods, Stewarts, Saratoga NHP, st police
11 (18)	Round Lake Rd, Round Lake, **E food:** MyWay Cafe, **W gas:** Citgo/dsl, Sunoco/dsl, **food:** Round Lake Rest., **other:** Rite Aid, Stewarts
10 (16)	Ushers Rd, **E gas:** Hess/dsl, Xtra/dsl, **food:** Ferretti's Rest., **other:** auto repair, **W other:** Stewarts
14mm	**rest area nb, full [handicapped] facilities, info, [phone], [picnic], litter barrels, vending, petwalk**

NY

INTERSTATE 87 CONT'D

N ↕ S

Exit #	Services
9 (13)	NY 146, Clifton Park, **E** **gas:** Hess/dsl/24hr, USA/gas, **food:** Burger King, Chili's, Cracker Barrel, Pizza Hut, Red Robin, Sam's Pizzaria, Snyder's Rest., **lodging:** Comfort Suites, **other:** Advance Parts, Aldi Foods, Goodyear/auto, Home Depot, Kohl's, Lowe's Whse, Michael's, **W** **gas:** Mobil, Sunoco/dsl, **food:** Applebee's, Denny's, Dunkin Donuts, Friendly's, KFC, McDonald's, Outback Steaks, Quizno's, Ruby Tuesday, Starbucks, Taco Bell, TGIFriday, Wendy's, **lodging:** Best Western, Hampton Inn, **other:** AutoZone, BordersBooks, Chevrolet, CVS Drug, Firestone, Freedom RV Ctr, Hannaford Foods, JC Penney, Jo-Ann Fabrics, K-Mart, Marshall's, PriceChopper Foods, mall, st police
8a (12)	Grooms Rd, to Waterford, **1-2 mi E on US 9...gas:** Getty, Gulf, **food:** 1/2 Moon Diner, Wendy's, **other:** Walmart SuperCtr/24hr
8 (10)	Crescent, Vischer Ferry, **E** **gas:** Hess/Blimpie/Godfather's/dsl/24hr, **food:** Krause's Rest. (3mi), McDonald's, **W** **gas:** Citgo, Sunoco/24hr, **food:** Pancho's Mexican, **other:** CVS Drug, Stewarts
8mm	Mohawk River
7 (7)	NY 7, Troy, **E on US 9... N** **gas:** Hess/dsl, **food:** Kirker's Steaks, Mr. Subb, **lodging:** Clarion, Hampton Inn, Holiday Inn Express, **other:** Acura, Buick/GMC/Pontiac, Dodge, $General, Firestone, Ford, Lincoln/Mercury, Nissan, Rite Aid, Volvo, **E on US 9...S** **gas:** Mobil, **food:** Dunkin Donuts, McDonald's, New Panda, Subway, **other:** Firestone, Marshall's
6 (6)	NY 2, to US 9, Schenectady, **E** **gas:** Getty, Mobil, **food:** Applebee's, BonTon, Boston Mkt, Chicago Grill, ChuckeCheese, Circle Diner, Dakota Steaks, Domino's, Panera Bread, Red Robin, Starbucks, Wendy's, **lodging:** Cocca's Inn, La Quinta, Travelodge, **other:** CVS Drug, Goodyear/auto, Hannaford Foods, Infiniti, JC Penney, Lowes Whse, PetsMart, PriceChopper Foods, Sam's Club, Staples, Toyota/Scion, VW, Walmart, same as 7, **W** **gas:** Mobil/24hr, **food:** Carabba's, Fillet 7, Friendly's, Kings Buffet, Ruby Tuesday, Subway, **lodging:** Fairfield Inn, Microtel, Quality Inn, Super 8, **other:** Target, TJ Maxx
5 (5)	NY 155 E, Latham, **E** **food:** DeeDee's Rest., Philly's Grill, **lodging:** Econolodge, **other:** USPO
4 (4)	NY 155 W, Wolf Rd, **E on Wolf Rd...gas:** Hess/dsl, Sunoco, **food:** Arby's, Capital Buffet, Denny's, Firkin&Fox, Macaroni Grill, Maurice's Sandwiches, McDonald's, Moe's SW Grill, 99 Rest., Old Chicago Grill, Olive Garden, Outback Steaks, Pizza Hut, Real Seafood Co, Red Lobster, Starbucks, Wings&Rings, Wolfrd Diner, **lodging:** Best Western, Courtyard, Hampton Inn, Holiday Inn, Homewood Suites, Marriott, Red Roof Inn, **other:** Chevrolet, CVS Drug, Ford/Lincoln/Mercury, Hannfords Foods, KIA, **W** **food:** Koto Japanese, **lodging:** Desmond Hotel, Hotel Indigo, **other:** to Heritage Park
2 (2)	NY 5, Central Ave, **E** **gas:** Sunoco, **food:** Wendy's, **lodging:** Cocca's Inn, Scottish Inn, Springhill Suites, **other:** Jo-Ann Fabrics, Kost Tire, Macy's, Marshalls, Lowes Whse, PetCo, Sears, Staples, Target, **E on Wolf Rd** **gas:** Mobil/Subway/dsl, Sunoco, **food:** Cheesecake Factory, Chili's, Dunkin Donuts,
2 (2)	Continued Emperor Chinese, Friendly's, Fuddruckers, Honeybaked Ham, IHOP, LJ Silver/Taco Bell, PF Chang's, **lodging:** Days Inn, Econolodge, **other:** Barnes&Noble, Borders Books, Firestone/auto, Goodyear/auto, LL Bean, Macy's, Steve&Barry's, mall, **W** **gas:** Exxon, **food:** Butcher Block Grill, Delmonico's Steaks, Domino's, Dunkin Donuts, Empress Diner, Garcia's Mexican, Mr Subb, Quizno's, Smokey Bones BBQ, Subway, Wendy's, **lodging:** Best Value Inn, Comfort Inn, Howard Johnson, Knights Inn, Quality Inn, Rodeway Inn, Super 8, **other:** Buick/GMC, Krause's Candy, Subaru
1W (1)	NY State Thruway (from sb), **I-87 S to NYC, I-90 W to Buffalo**
1E (1)	I-90 E (from sb), to Albany, Boston
1S (1)	to US 20, Western Ave, **W** **gas:** Mobil, **food:** Burger King, Chicago Grill, Dunkin Donuts, Friendly's, Hana Grill, Ichyban Japanese, McDonald's, Metro 80 Diner, Moe's SW Grill, 99 Rest., Panera Bread, Starbucks, TGIFriday, Wendy's, **lodging:** Holiday Inn Express, **other:** Best Buy, Borders Books, Home Depot, JC Penney, Macy's, Michael's, Old Navy, PetsMart, PriceChopper Foods, Walmart SuperCtr, mall, USPO, Vet
1N (1)	I-87 N (from nb), to Plattsburgh, **NY State Thruway goes west to Buffalo (I-90), S to NYC (I-87), I-87 N to Montreal**
24 (148)	I-90 and I-87 N
23 (142)	I-787, to Albany, US 9 W, **E on US 9...W** **gas:** Cumberland Farms/Dunkin Donuts/dsl, Mobil/dsl, **lodging:** Comfort Inn, Regency Inn, **other:** transmissions, to Knickerbocker Arena, **W** **gas:** Stewarts, **lodging:** Econolodge
139mm	**parking area sb, [phone], [picnic], litter barrel**
22 (135)	NY 396, to Selkirk
21a (134)	I-90 E, to MA Tpk, Boston
127mm	New Balitmore Travel Plaza both lanes, Mobil/dsl, Famous Famiglia, Quizno's, Roy Rogers, Starbucks, TCBY, atm, gifts, info, UPS
21b (124)	US 9 W, NY 81, to Coxsackie, **W** **gas:** Trvl Plaza/dsl/rest./24hr/@, Sunoco/dsl, **food:** McDonald's (5mi), **lodging:** Best Western, Budget Inn, Holiday Inn Express, Red Carpet Inn, **other:** Boat'n RV Whse, repair, Vet
21 (114)	NY 23, Catskill, **E** **gas:** Mobil, Sunoco/dsl/24hr, **lodging:** Catskill Motel/rest. (2mi), Pelokes Motel (2mi), Quality Inn, **other:** Home Depot, transmissions, to Rip van Winkle Br, **W** **food:** Anthony's Italian, LogSider Café, **lodging:** Astoria Motel, Budget Inn (3mi), Quality Inn, Rip Van Winkle Motel, **other:** to Hunter Mtn/Windham Ski Areas
103mm	**Malden Service Area nb,** Mobil/dsl, Carvel Ice Cream, Hotdogs, McDonald's, atm, gifts, [phone], **parking area sb**
20 (102)	NY 32, to Saugerties, **E** **gas:** Citgo, Mobil/dsl, Stewarts, **food:** Dunkin Donuts, Emiliani Italian, Giordano's Pizza, McDonald's, Pizza Star, Starway Café, Subway, **other:** CarQuest, Chrysler/Dodge/Jeep, Curves, CVS Drug, Family$, Grand Union Foods, PriceChopper Foods, Vet, **W** **gas:** Hess/Blimpie/dsl, Sunoco, **food:** Cafe Mezzaluna, Johnny G's Diner, Land&Sea Grill, **lodging:** Comfort Inn, Howard Johnson/rest., **other:** Blue Mtn Campground (5mi), Brookside Campground (10mi), KOA (2mi), Rip Van Winkle Campground (3mi), to Catskills

ALBANY

NY

INTERSTATE 87 CONT'D

N ↕ S

Exit #	Services
99mm	**parking area nb, ☎, 🛈, litter barrels**
96mm	**Ulster Travel Plaza sb**, Sunoco/dsl, Nathan's, Roy Rogers, Starbucks, TCBY, atm, gifts, phone
19 (91)	NY 28, Kingston, **E gas:** Mobil, **food:** Dietz Diner, Friendly's, Olympic Diner, Picnic Pizza, Savona's Pizza, **lodging:** Holiday Inn, Super 8, **other:** Advance Parts, Hannaford Foods, Radio Shack, Walgreens, **W food:** Family Diner, Lorenzo's Pizza, Roudigan's Steaks, **lodging:** Budget 19 Motel, Quality Inn, Skytop Motel/steaks, SuperLodge, **other:** Buick, Camper's Barn RV, Ford, Nissan, access to I-587, US 209
18 (76)	NY 299, to Poughkeepsie, New Paltz, **E gas:** Citgo/dsl, Mobil, **food:** Carribean Cuisine, College Diner/24hr, Village Grill, **lodging:** Econolodge, 87 Motel, Super 8 (5mi), **other:** repair, to Mid-Hudson Br, **W gas:** Sunoco/24hr, **food:** Burger King, Dunkin Donuts, McDonald's, Pasquale's Pizza, Quizno's, Subway, TCBY, **lodging:** Super 8, **other:** Advance Parts, Midas, Radio Shack, Rite Aid, ShopRite Foods, Stop'n Shop, Jellystone (9mi), KOA (10mi), Vet
66mm	**Modena service area sb...gas:** Sunoco/dsl, **food:** Arby's, Carvel's Ice Cream/bakery, Uno Pizzaria, McDonald's, **other:** atm, fax, gifts, UPS
65mm	**Plattekill Travel Plaza nb...gas:** Sunoco/dsl, **food:** Big Boy, Nathan's, Roy Rogers, **other:** atm, gifts, info
17 (60)	I-84, NY 17K, to Newburgh, **E on NY 300...gas:** Getty, Hess/Blimpie/dsl, Mobil, Sunoco, **food:** Applebees, Burger King, Chili's, Cosimos Ristorante, Denny's, Dunkin Donuts, Gateway Diner, Ground Round, Jak Steaks, King Buffet, Longhorn Steaks, Neptune Diner, Newburgh Buffet, Old Town Buffet, Perkins, Union Sq Rest., Subway, Taco Bell, TGIFriday, Wendy's, **lodging:** Hampton Inn, Howard Johnson, Quality Inn, Ramada Inn, Super 8, **other:** Adam's Food Mkt, Aldi Foods, AutoZone, Barnes&Noble, BonTon, Cadillac/Chevrolet, Chrysler/Dodge/Jeep, Curves, $Tree, Ford/Lincoln/Mercury, Harley-Davidson, Home Depot, Honda, Lowes Whse, Mavis Tire, Michael's, Midas, Nissan, Kohl's, Office Depot, Old Navy, PetsMart, Radio Shack, Sears/auto, Stop'n Shop, Target, Walmart SuperCtr, **W lodging:** Hilton Garden
16 (45)	US 6, NY 17, to West Point, Harriman, **W gas:** Exxon/dsl, **food:** TGIFriday's, **lodging:** American Budget Inn, Hampton Inn, **other:** Buick/Chevrolet, Kohl's, Staples, Walmart SuperCtr/24hr (1mi), Woodbury Outlet/famous brands, st police
34mm	**Ramapo Service Area sb...gas:** Sunoco/dsl/24hr, **food:** McDonald's, **other:** atm
33mm	**Sloatsburg Travel Plaza nb, gas:** Sunoco/dsl/24hr, **food:** Burger King, Dunkin Donuts, Quizno's, Sbarro's, **other:** atm, gifts, info
15a (31)	NY 17 N, NY 59, Sloatsburg
15 (30)	I-287 S, NY 17 S, to NJ. **I-87 S & I-287 E run together.**
14b (27)	Airmont Rd, Montebello, **E lodging:** Holiday Inn, **W gas:** Exxon/dsl, Sunoco, **food:** Airmont Diner, Applebee's, Dunkin Donuts, Friendly's, Pasta Cucina, Starbucks, Subway, Sutter's Mill Rest., Water Wheel Cafe, Wendy's, **lodging:** Howard Johnson, **other:** H DrugMart, ShopRite Foods, Walgreens, Walmart

NEWBURGH

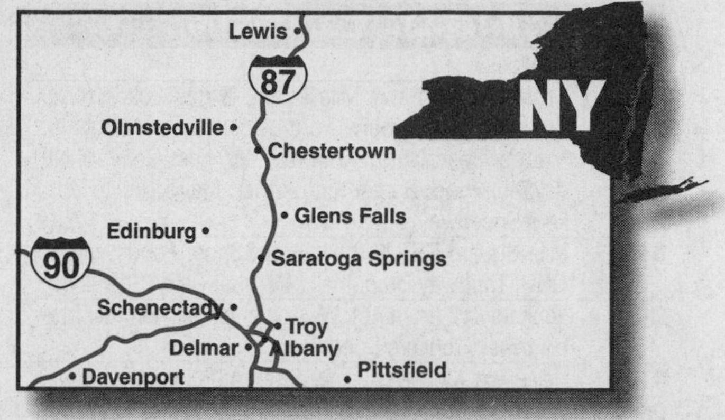

Exit #	Services
14a (23)	Garden State Pkwy, to NJ, Chestnut Ridge
14 (22)	NY 59, Spring Valley, Nanuet, **E gas:** Citgo/dsl, Mobil, Shell/dsl, Valero/dsl, **food:** Burger King, Domino's, McDonald's, Planet Wings, **lodging:** Fairfield Inn, **other:** AutoZone, BMW/Ferrari, CarQuest, Michaels, Target, TJ Maxx, **W gas:** Citgo, **food:** ChuckeCheese, Dunkin Donuts/Baskin-Robbins, Great China, KFC, Nanuet Diner, Red Lobster, Starbucks, Taco Bell, White Castle, Wendy's, **lodging:** Day's Inn, Hampton Inn, Hilton Garden, **other:** AutoZone, Barnes&Noble, $Tree, Home Depot, Hyundai, Macy's, Marshalls, PetCo, Sears/auto, Staples, Stop'n Shop Foods, mall
13 (20)	Palisades Pkwy, N to Bear Mtn, S to NJ
12 (19)	NY 303, Palisades Ctr Dr, W Nyack, **E W gas:** Mobil, **food:** Bravo Italian, Buffalo Wild Wings, Cheesecake Factory, Dunkin Donuts, **lodging:** Nyack Motel, **other:** Barnes&Noble, Best Buy, BJ's Whse, Dave&Buster's, Macy's, Home Depot, JC Penney, Lord&Taylor, Old Navy, Staples, ShopRite Foods, Target, mall
11 (18)	US 9W, to Nyack, **E gas:** Gulf, Shell, **lodging:** Best Western, **W gas:** Discount Fuel, Quality Gas, Shell/dsl, **food:** Dunkin Donuts, McDonald's, Quizno's, **lodging:** Super 8, **other:** H, J&L Repair/tire
10 (17)	Nyack (from nb), same as 11
14mm	Tappan Zee Br, Hudson River
13mm	toll plaza
9 (12)	to US 9, to Tarrytown, **E gas:** Hess, Shell/repair, **other:** Stop&Shop, **W gas:** Mobil, **food:** El Dorado West Diner, **lodging:** Hilton, **other:** Honda/Subaru, Mavis Tire
8 (11)	I-287 E, to Saw Mill Pkwy, White Plains, **E lodging:** Hampton Inn, Marriott
7a (10)	Saw Mill River Pkwy S, to Saw Mill River SP, Taconic SP
7 (8)	NY 9A (from nb), Ardsley, **W lodging:** Ardsley Acres Motel, **other:** H
6mm	**Ardsley Travel Plaza nb**, Sunoco/dsl, Burger King, Popeye's, TCBY, vending
5.5mm	toll plaza, ☎
6ba (5)	Stew Leonard Dr, to Ridge Hill, **W other:** Costco, Home Depot, Stew Leonard's Farmfresh Foods
6 (4.5)	Tuckahoe Dr, Yonkers, **E gas:** Getty/repair, **food:** Marcellino's Italian, McDonald's, Subway, **lodging:** Tuckahoe Motel, **other:** ShopRite Foods/drug, **W gas:** Gulf, Mobil, **food:** Domino's, Dunkin Donuts, Kim Wei Chinese, Quizno's, Totonno's Italian, **lodging:** Ramada Inn, Regency Hotel
5 (4.3)	NY 100 N (from nb), Central Park Ave, White Plains, **E gas:** Getty, Shell, Sunoco, **food:** Ground Round

NYACK

INTERSTATE 87 CONT'D

Exit #	Services
4 (4)	Cross Country Pkwy, Mile Sq Rd, **E gas:** Lukoil, **food:** Burger King, **other:** Ford/Lincoln/Mercury/Subaru, Macy's, Sears/auto, TJ Maxx, **W gas:** Getty, Shell/dsl/24hr, **food:** Burger King, **other:** Mavis Tire, to Yonkers Speedway
3 (3)	Mile Square Rd, **E gas:** Stop&Shop, Foods, **other:** GNC, Thriftway Drug, mall, **W gas:** Getty, Shell/24hr
2 (2)	Yonkers Ave (from nb), Westchester Fair, **E gas:** Mobil, **other:** Yonkers Speedway
1 (1)	Hall Place, McLean Ave, **E other:** A&P Foods/Subway
0mm	**New York St Thruway & I-87 N run together to Albany**
14 (11)	McLean Ave, **E gas:** Shell, **food:** Dunkin Donuts
13 (10)	E 233rd , NE Tollway, **service plaza both lanes**/Mobil
12 (9.5)	Hudson Pkwy (from nb), Sawmill Pkwy
11 (9)	Van Cortlandt Pk S
10 (8.5)	W 230th St (from sb), W 240th (from nb), **E gas:** Lukoil, **W gas:** Getty, **other:** H, Target
9 (8)	W Fordham Rd, **E gas:** BP/dsl, **other:** H, Toyota
8 (7)	W 179th (from nb), **W** Roberto Clemente SP
7 (6)	I-95, US 1, S to Trenton, NJ, N to New Haven, CT
6 (5)	E 153 rd t, River Ave, Stadium Rd, **E other:** Yankee Stadium
5 (5)	E 161st, Macombs Dam Br, **E other:** Yankee Stadium
3 (3)	E 138th St, Madison Ave Br, **E gas:** BP/dsl
2 (2)	Willis Ave, 3rd Ave Br, **E gas:** Mobil/dsl, **W food:** McDonald's
1 (1)	Brook Ave, Hunts Point, **E gas:** BP, Hess
0mm	I-87 begins/ends on I-278.

INTERSTATE 88 (NEW YORK)

Exit #	Services
25a	I-90/NY Thruway. I-88 begins/ends on I-90, exit 25a.
117mm	toll booth (to enter or exit NY Thruway)
25 (116)	NY 7, to Rotterdam, Schenectady, **S gas:** Citgo/Friendly's/Dunkin Donuts/dsl/24hr, **3 mi S gas:** Gulf, **food:** Burger King, McDonald's, Top's Diner, **lodging:** L&M Motel, Rotterdam Motel, **other:** Frosty Acres Camping
24 (112)	US 20, NY 7, to Duanesburg, **N gas:** Mobil, Stewarts, **food:** Dunkin Donuts, **other:** st police, **S food:** Duanesburg Diner, **other:** USPO
23 (101)	NY 30, to Schoharie, Central Bridge, **N lodging:** Holiday Motel, **other:** Hideaway Camping, Locust Park Camping, **S gas:** Mobil/Subway/dsl, **food:** Dunkin Donuts, **lodging:** Holiday Inn Express, Hyland House B&B (2mi), Parrott House 1870 Inn (4mi), Wedgewood B&B (2mi)
22 (95)	NY 7, NY 145, to Cobleskill, Middleburgh, **2-5 mi N gas:** Hess/dsl, Mobil, **food:** Dunkin Donuts, Pizza Hut, Subway, **lodging:** Colonial CT Motel, Holiday Inn Express, Holiday Motel, Super 8, **other:** H, Advance Parts, Buick/Chevrolet/GMC/Pontiac, Chrysler/Dodge/Jeep, $General, $Tree, Ford, Howe Caverns Camping, PriceChopper Foods, Walmart SuperCtr to Howe Caverns, **S other:** Twin Oaks Camping, st police
21 (90)	NY 7, NY 10, to Cobleskill, Warnerville, **2-3 mi N gas:** Hess, Mobil/dsl, **food:** Arby's, Burger King, Dairy Deli, KFC/Taco Bell, McDonald's, Pizza Hut, Red Apple Rest., **lodging:** Bast Western, Gables B&B, **other:** H Ace Hardware, CarQuest, PriceChopper Foods, Walmart SuperCtr/24hr
20 (87)	NY 7, NY 10, to Richmondville, **S gas:** Mobil/dsl/24hr, Sunoco, **food:** Reinhardt's Deli, Sub Express, **lodging:** Rodeway Inn, **other:** USPO
79mm	**rest area wb, full facilities, , vending, , litter barrels, petwalk**
19 (76)	to NY 7, Worcester, **N gas:** Stewarts, Sunoco/dsl
73mm	**rest area eb, full facilities, , vending, , litter barrels, petwalk**
18 (71)	to Schenevus, **N gas:** Citgo, **food:** Schenev US Rest.
17 (61)	NY 7, to NY 28 N, Colliersville, Cooperstown, **2 mi N gas:** Mobil/dsl, **food:** La Teranella, **lodging:** Amber Life Motel, Best Western (14mi), Knott's Motel, Redwood Motel, **other:** to Baseball Hall of Fame
16 (59)	NY 7, to Emmons, **N food:** Arby's, Brooks BBQ, Farmhouse Rest., Morey's Rest., Perrucci's Pizza, Pizza Hut, Sonny's Pizza, **lodging:** Rainbow Inn, **other:** PriceChopper Foods, Rite Aid
15 (56)	NY 28, NY 23, Oneonta, **N gas:** Citgo, Hess, KwikFill, **food:** Friendly's, KFC, **lodging:** Clarion, Townhouse Inn, **other:** H, Advance Parts, to Soccer Hall of Fame, **S gas:** Citgo, Hess, **food:** Applebees, Burger King, Denny's, LJ Silver/Taco Bell, McDonald's, Neptune Diner/24hr, Quizno's, Sabatini's Italian, Subway, Wendy's, **lodging:** Budget Inn, Christopher's Lodge/rest., Holiday Inn, Sun Lodge, Super 8, **other:** Aldi Foods, Beaver Spring Camping, BJ's Whse/gas, $Tree, Hannaford Foods, Home Depot, JC Penney, Kost Tire, NAPA, Steve&Barry's, Walmart SuperCtr/24hr
14 (55)	Main St (from eb), Oneonta, **N gas:** Citgo, Kwikfill, Stewarts, Sunoco, **food:** Alfresco's Italian, **other:** CVS Drug, **S food:** Denny's, McDonald's
13 (53)	NY 205, **1-2 mi N gas:** Citgo, Hess, Mobil, **food:** Burger King, China Buffet King, DQ, Dunkin Donuts, McDonald's, Ponderosa, **lodging:** Celtic Motel, Hampton Inn, Maple Terrace Motel, Oasis Motor Inn, **other:** Buick/Cadillac/GMC/Pontiac, Chevrolet, Chrysler/Jeep, Honda, Nissan, Parts+, Rite Aid, to Susquehanna Tr, Gilbert Lake SP (11mi), camping
12 (47)	NY 7, to Otego, **S gas:** Citgo/dsl/cafe, Lukoil
43mm	**rest area wb, full facilities, , , litter barrels, vending, petwalk**
11 (40)	NY 357, to Unadilla, Delhi, **N** KOA
39mm	**rest area eb, full facilities, , , litter barrels, vending, petwalk**
10 (38)	NY 7, to Unadilla, **2 mi N gas:** Apple Gas, **lodging:** Country Motel (4mi), **other:** Great American Foods, USPO, st police
9 (33)	NY 8, to Sidney, **N gas:** Citgo/QuickWay/dsl, Hess/dsl, Mobil/dsl, **food:** China Buffet, McDonald's, Pizza Hut, Subway, **lodging:** Algonkin Motel, Country Motel, Super 8, **other:** H, Advance Parts, $General, K-Mart/Little Caesar's, PriceChopper Foods, Tall Pines Camping, USPO
8 (29)	NY 206, to Bainbridge, **N gas:** Citgo, Sunoco/Taco Xtra/dsl/24hr, **food:** Bob's Family Diner, **lodging:** Algonkin Motel, **other:** Chevrolet/GMC/Pontiac, Riverside RV Park, Parts+, USPO, to Oquage Creek Park
7 (22)	NY 41, to Afton, **1-2 mi N gas:** Mobil/24hr, Sunoco/dsl, Xtra, **food:** RiverClub Rest., Vincent's Rest., **other:** Afton Golf/rest., Echo Lake Park, Kellystone Park, Smith-Hale HS

INTERSTATE 88 CONT'D (NEW YORK)

E ↕ W

Exit #	Services
6 (16)	NY 79, to NY 7, Harpursville, Ninevah, **N food:** Gramma's Country Cafe, **S gas:** Citgo/Quickway/dsl, **other:** USPO, to Nathanial Cole Park
5 (12)	Martin Hill Rd, to Belden, **N other:** Belden Manor Camping
4 (8)	NY 7, to Sanitaria Springs, **S gas:** Hess/dsl
3 (4)	NY 369, Port Crane, **N** to Chenango Valley SP, **S gas:** Fastrac/dsl, KwikFill
2 (2)	NY 12a W, to Chenango Bridge, **N gas:** Mirabito, **other:** Red&White Foods, USPO
1 (1)	NY 7 W (no wb return), to Binghamton
0mm	I-81, N to Syracuse, S to Binghamton. I-88 begins/ends on I-81.

INTERSTATE 90

E ↕ W

Exit #	Services
B24.5mm	New York/Massachusetts state line
B3 (B23)	NY 22, to Austerlitz, New Lebanon, W Stockbridge, **N gas:** Citgo/dsl/scales/24hr, **food:** Lilly's Diner, **S gas:** Sunoco/dsl, **lodging:** Berkshire Spur Motel, **other:** Woodland Hills Camp
B18mm	toll plaza, phone
B2 (B15)	NY 295, Taconic Pkwy, **1-2 mi S** gas
B1 (B7)	US 9, NY Thruway W, to I-87, toll booth, [phone]
12 (20)	US 9, to Hudson, **1-3 mi S gas:** Mobil/dsl/24hr (3mi), Sunoco/dsl (3mi), **food:** McDonald's, **lodging:** Bel Air Motel (1mi), Blue Spruce Motel (4mi), **other:** to Van Buren NHS
18.5mm	**rest area wb, full [handicapped] facilities, [phone], [picnic], litter barrels, vending, petwalk**
11 (15)	US 9, US 20, E Greenbush, Nassau, **N gas:** Citgo/dsl, Hess/dsl, **food:** BBQ, Dunkin Donuts, **other:** st police, **S gas:** Mobil (2mi), Stewarts, **food:** Burger King, Goomba's Pizza, Mercato's, My Place Rest., **lodging:** Dewitt Motel, Rodeway Inn, **other:** Chevrolet, Rite Aid, USPO, Vet
10 (10)	Miller Rd, to E Greenbush, **S gas:** Mobil/dsl, **lodging:** Comfort Inn, **1-3 mi S gas:** Stewarts, Sunoco, **food:** Dunkin Donuts, E Greenbush Diner, My Place Rest., Pizza Hut, **lodging:** Dewitt Motel
9 (9)	US 4, to Rensselaer, Troy, **N gas:** Mobil, **food:** Applebee's, Ground Round, McDonald's, OffShore Pier Rest., Panera Bread, Starbucks, Subway, **lodging:** Holiday Inn Express, Residence Inn, **other:** $Tree, Grand Union Foods, Home Depot, PetsMart, Radio Shack, Staples, Target, Walmart SuperCtr, **S gas:** Stewart's, **food:** Denny's, Cracker Barrel, **other:** Fairfield Inn, **1-2 mi S gas:** Mobil, **food:** Dunkin Donuts, Friendly's, Wendy's, **lodging:** Econolodge
8 (8)	NY 43, Defreestville
7 (7)	Washington Ave (from eb), Rensselaer
6.5mm	Hudson River
6a	I-787, to Albany
6 (4.5)	US 9, Northern Blvd, to Loudonville, **N gas:** Stewarts, **food:** Mr Subb, Siena Pizza, Ta-Ke Japanese, **lodging:** Red Carpet Inn, **other:** [H]
5a (4)	Corporate Woods Blvd
5 (3.5)	Everett Rd, to NY 5, **S gas:** Hess, **food:** Bob&Ron's Fishfry, Chinese Buffet, Friendly's, Gateway Diner, LJ Silver/Taco Bell, Lucky Garden, McDonald's,

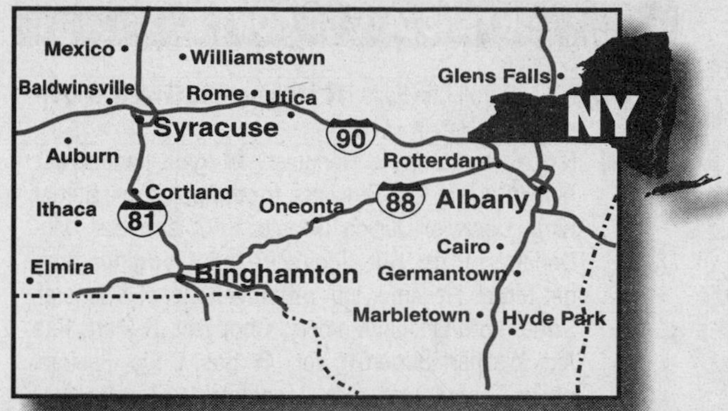

ALBANY

Exit #	Services
5 (3.5)	Continued Popeye's, Quizno's, Subway, **lodging:** Clarion, **other:** [H], Aamco, Advance Parts, AutoZone, Chevrolet, Chrysler/Jeep, CVS Drug, Dodge, $Tree, Ford, Hannaford's Foods/24hr, Home Depot, Honda/Nissan, Mazda, Nissan, PepBoys, Pontiac, PriceChopper Foods, Radio Shack, Suzuki, multiple facilities on NY 5
4 (3)	NY 85 S, to Slingerlands
3 (2.5)	State Offices
2 (2)	Fuller Rd, Washington Ave, **S gas:** Sunoco, **food:** Dunkin Donuts, **lodging:** Courtyard, CrestHill Suites, Extended Stay America, Fairfield Inn, Red Carpet Inn, TownePlace Inn same as 1S
1N (1)	I-87 N, to Montreal, to Albany [airport]
1S (1)	US 20, Western Ave, **S gas:** Mobil, **food:** Burger King, Chicago Grill, Dunkin Donuts, Friendly's, Hana Grill, Ichyban Japanese, McDonald's, Metro 80 Diner, Moe's SW Grill, 99 Rest., Panera Bread, Starbucks, TGIFriday, Wendy's, **lodging:** Holiday Inn Express, **other:** Best Buy, Borders Books, Home Depot, JC Penney, Macy's, Michael's, Old Navy, PetsMart, PriceChopper Foods, Walmart SuperCtr, mall, USPO, Vet
24 (149)	I-87 N to Albany, Montreal, S to NYC
153mm	**Guilderland Service Area eb**, Mobil/dsl, McDonald's, Mr Subb
25 (154)	I-890, NY 7, NY 146, to Schenectady
25a (159)	I-88 S, NY 7, to Binghamton
26 (162)	I-890, NY 5 S, Schenectady
168mm	**Pattersonville Service Area wb**, Mobil/dsl, Big Boy, Quizno's, Roy Rogers, Starbucks, TCBY, atm, fax, gifts, info, UPS
172mm	**Mohawk Service Area eb**, Mobil/dsl, Breyer's, Fresh Fudge, McDonald's,
27 (174)	NY 30, Amsterdam, **N gas:** Citgo, Mobil/dsl, **lodging:** Super 8/diner/24hr, Valleyview Motel, **1 mi N lodging:** Best Value Inn, **other:** Camping World RV Ctr
28 (182)	NY 30A, Fonda, **N gas:** Citgo/dsl/rest./motel/24hr, Gulf/repair, Lukoil, TA/dsl/rest/motel/scales/24hr/@, **food:** McDonald's, **lodging:** Econolodge, Riverside Motel, **other:** [H], st police, truck repair
184mm	**parking area both lanes, [phone], litter barrels**
29 (194)	NY 10, Canajoharie, **N gas:** Gulf, Stewarts, **food:** McDonald's, Pizza Hut, **other:** $General, Rite Aid, **S gas:** Lukoil/dsl, Petro USA/dsl, Sunoco, **food:** Joey D's Seafood, **other:** Chevrolet, NAPA, USPO
210mm	**Indian Castle Service area eb...gas:** Mobil/dsl, **food:** Hershey's Ice Cream, Roy Rogers, **other:** atm, gifts, UPS. **Iroquois Service Area wb...gas:** Mobil/dsl, Burger King, Dunkin Donuts, gifts, UPS

NY

INTERSTATE 90 CONT'D

Exit #	Services
29a (211)	NY 169, to Little Falls, **N lodging:** Best Western, **other:** [H], to Herkimer Home
30 (220)	NY 28, to Mohawk, Herkimer, **N gas:** Fastrac/dsl, Mobil/Subway/dsl, Stewarts, **food:** Applebees, Burger King, Denny's, Dunkin Donuts, KFC/Taco Bell, McDonald's, Pizza Hut, Tony's Pizzaria, **lodging:** Budget Motel, Herkimer Inn, **other:** AutoZone, $General, $Tree, Ford/Lincoln/Mercury, Goodyear, K-Mart, Rite Aid, Walmart SuperCtr, Vet, **S gas:** Citgo, Fastrac, **other:** Factory Depot, to Cooperstown (Baseball Hall of Fame)
227mm	**Schuyler Service Area wb**, Mobil/dsl, Breyer's, McDonald's, atm, st police
31 (233)	I-790, NY 8, NY 12, to Utica, **N gas:** Citgo/dsl, Fastrac, **food:** Burger King, Charlie's Pizza, Colozzi's Cafe, Franco's Pizza, Jreck Subs, **other:** Big Lots, BJ's Whse, $Tree, Lowes Whse, PriceChopper Foods, Rite Aid, **1 mi N on frontage rd food:** Applebees, **other:** BJ's Whse/gas, Lowes Whse, Walmart SuperCtr, **S gas:** Hess/dsl, **food:** Babe's Grill, Delmonico's Steaks, Denny's, Dunkin Donuts, Friendly's, Grand's Pizza, McDonald's, Pizza Hut, Taco Bell, Wendy's, **lodging:** Best Western, Days Inn, Hampton Inn, Happy Journey Motel, Red Roof Inn, Scottish Inn, Super 8
236mm	I-790 (from eb), to Utica
237.5mm	Erie Canal
238mm	Mohawk River
32 (243)	NY 232, Westmoreland, **N lodging:** Quality Inn, Ramada Inn, Red Carpet Inn, **S lodging:** Carriage House Motel, Pinecrest Motel, **1 mi S** gas/dsl
244mm	**Oneida Service Area eb**, Sunoco/dsl, Burger King, Sbarro's, Starbucks, atm, gifts
250mm	**parking area eb, [phone], [picnic], litter barrel**
33 (253)	NY 365, to Vernon Downs, Verona, **N gas:** SavOn Gas/dsl, **lodging:** Comfort Suites (6mi), Inn at Turning Stone, Quality Inn (9mi), Red Carpet Inn, **S gas:** SavOn Gas/LP/repair, **lodging:** Super 8 (3mi), **other:** [H], Turning Stone Casino
256mm	**parking area wb, [phone], [picnic], litter barrel**
34 (262)	NY 13, to Canastota, **S gas:** Mobil/dsl, SavOn/dsl/24hr, **food:** Dunkin Donuts, McDonald's, **lodging:** Days Inn, Graziano Motel/rest., Super 8 (7mi), **other:** Boxing Hall of Fame, Verona Beach SP Camping
266mm	**Chittenango Service Area wb**, Sunoco/dsl, Dunkin Donuts, Freshen's Treats, Sbarro's, TCBY, atm, gifts
34a (277)	I-481, to Syracuse, Chittenango
35 (279)	NY 298, The Circle, Syracuse, **S gas:** Mobil, Valero/dsl, **food:** Burger King, Denny's, Dunkin Donuts, East Wok, Green Onion Rest., Joey's Italian, Jreck Subs, Justin's Grill, McDonald's, Pronto's Pizza, Ruby Tuesday, Starbucks, **lodging:** Candlewood Suites, Comfort Inn, Courtyard, Cresthill Suites, Day's Inn, Doubletree Inn, Embassy Suites, Extended Stay America, Hampton Inn, Hilton Garden, Holiday Inn, John Milton Inn, Microtel, Motel 6, Quality Inn, Ramada Ltd, Red Roof Inn, Residence Inn, Super 8, **other:** Goodyear/auto
280mm	**Dewitt Service Area eb**, Sunoco/dsl, McDonald's, ice cream
36 (283)	I-81, N to Watertown, S to Binghamton
37 (284)	7th St, Electronics Pkwy, to Liverpool, **N lodging:** Best Western, **S gas:** Hess/Blimpie/24hr, **food:** KFC/Taco Bell, **lodging:** Holiday Inn, Knight's Inn, **other:** Kinny Drug
38 (286)	NY 57, to Liverpool, Syracuse, **N gas:** Fastrac/dsl, Hess, KwikFill, **food:** Bangkok Thai, Kirby's Rest., Pier 57 Diner, Pizza Hut, Quizno's, Salsarita's Grill, **lodging:** Hampton Inn (7mi), Super 8, **other:** Aldi Foods, $Tree, NAPA, Rite Aid
39 (290)	I-690, NY 690, Syracuse, **N lodging:** Comfort Inn/rest., **other:** Camping World RV Ctr
292mm	**Warners Service Area wb**, Mobil/dsl/rest., Boston Pizza, Edy's Ice Cream, McDonald's,
40 (304)	NY 34, to Owasco Lake, Weedsport, **N** Riverforest RV Park, **S gas:** Fastrac, KwikFill, Sunoco/dsl, **food:** Arby's, Arnold's Rest., DB's Drive-In, Lin Bo Chinese, Old Erie Diner, **lodging:** Best Western, Day's Inn, Holiday Inn (12mi), **other:** Ace Hardware, Bass Pro Shops (12mi), Big M Foods, $General, Kinney Drug, NAPA
310mm	**Port Byron Service Area eb**, Mobil/dsl/rest., Edy's ice Cream, McDonald's, Original Pizza
318mm	**parking area wb, litter barrels, phones**
41 (320)	NY 414, to Cayuga Lake, Waterloo, **S gas:** Nice'n Easy/dsl, Petro/dsl/rest./scales/24hr/@, **food:** MaGee Country Diner, **lodging:** Holiday Inn (4mi), Microtel (4mi), **other:** Cayuga Lake SP, Waterloo Outlets/famous brands (3mi)
324mm	**Junius Ponds Service Area wb**, Sunoco/dsl, Dunkin Donuts, Roy Rogers
42 (327)	NY 14, to Geneva, Lyons, **N** RV camping, **S gas:** Mobil/dsl/scales, **lodging:** Red Carpet Inn, **other:** Waterloo Outlets/famous brands (3mi), RV Camping, **6 mi S lodging:** Amherst, Best Value Inn, Hampton Inn, Motel 6, Ramada Inn
337mm	**Clifton Springs Service Area eb**, Sunoco/dsl, Roy Rogers, Sbarro's, Starbucks, atm, gifts
43 (340)	NY 21, to Palmyra, Manchester, **N** Hill Cumorah LDS HS (6mi), **S gas:** Sunoco/dsl/24hr, **food:** Lehigh Valley Rest., McDonald's, **lodging:** Roadside Inn
44 (347)	NY 332, Victor, **S gas:** Getty/Subway/dsl, Mobil/dsl, Sunoco, **food:** Di Pacific's Rest., KFC, King's Wok, McDonald's, **lodging:** Best Value Inn, Budget Inn, Comfort Inn, Econolodge, **other:** CVS Drug, KOA (4mi), casino, st police
350mm	**Seneca Service Area wb...gas:** Mobil/dsl, **food:** Fuddrucker's, Tim Horton, Villa Pizza, **other:** atm, info, phone
45 (351)	I-490, NY 96, to Rochester, **N gas:** Citgo, **food:** Belini's, Biaggi's Rest., BoneFish Grill, Bonton, Champp's Grill, Chicago Grill, King Buffet, Olive Garden, PF Chang's, TGIFriday, **lodging:** Hampton Inn, **other:** BJ's Whse, Border's Books, K-Mart, Lord&Taylor, Macy's, Michael's, Sears/auto, **S gas:** KwikFill, **food:** Burger King, Charlie's Rest., Chili's, Denny's, Wendy's, **lodging:** Best Western, Holiday Inn Express, Homewood Suites, Microtel, Royal Inn, **other:** Ballantyne RV Ctr, Chevrolet
353mm	**parking area eb, [phone], litter barrels**
46 (362)	I-390, to Rochester, **N on NY 253 W gas:** Citgo/dsl, Hess, Sunoco/dsl, **food:** McDonald's, Peppermint's Rest., Tim Horton, Wendy's, **lodging:** Country Inn&Suites, Day's Inn, Fairfield Inn, Microtel, Red Carpet Inn, Red Roof Inn, Super 8 **other:** GMC/Pontiac, Jeep

INTERSTATE 90 CONT'D

E ↕ W

Exit #	Services
366mm	**Scottsville Service Area eb...gas:** Mobil/dsl, **food:** Arby's, Tim Horton, Villa Pizza, **other:** atm, info
376mm	**Ontario Service Area wb...gas:** Sunoco/dsl, **food:** Boston Pizza, McDonald's
47 (379)	I-490, NY 19, to Rochester, **N** Timberline Camping
48 (390)	NY 98, to Batavia, **N lodging:** Comfort Inn, Hampton Inn, **S gas:** Citgo, **food:** Applebee's, Bob Evans, Peking Buffet, **lodging:** Best Western, Budget Inn, Day's Inn, Holiday Inn, Quality Inn, Ramada Ltd, Super 8, **other:** AutoZone, BJ's Whse, Home Depot, K-Mart, Lowes Whse, PetCo, Target, Walmart SuperCtr/24hr
397mm	**Pembroke Service Area eb...gas:** Sunoco/dsl, **food:** Fuddrucker's, Tim Horton, **other:** atm, gifts, ☎, UPS
48a (402)	NY 77, Pembroke, **S gas:** ***FLYING J***/dsl/LP/rest./scales/24hr, TA/dsl/rest./scales/24hr/@, **food:** Subway, **lodging:** Econolodge, 6 Flags Motel/RV Park (5mi), **other:** Sleepy Hollow Camping (8mi)
412mm	**Clarence Service Area wb, full ♿ facilities, gas:** Sunoco/dsl, **food:** Arby's, Fuddrucker's, Tim Horton, **other:** info, phone
49 (417)	NY 78, Depew, **1-3 mi N gas:** Mobil, Sunoco, **food:** Applebee's, Arby's, Atlanta Bread, Bennigan's, Bonton, Boston Mkt, Buffalo Wild Wings, Burger King, Cracker Barrel, Dave&Buster's, Denny's, Dibella's Subs, Don Pablo, DQ, Fazoli's, Golden Corral, KFC, McDonald's, Mighty Taco, Moe's SW Grill, Old Country Buffet, Panera Bread, Perkins, Picasso's Pizza, Pizza Hut, Pizza Plant, Ponderosa, Protocol Rest., Red Lobster, Roadhouse Grill, Ruby Tuesday, Spilio's Rest., Starbucks, Subway, Taco Bell, TGIFriday, Tim Horton, Tulley's Rest., Wendy's, **lodging:** Clarion, Econolodge, Fairfield Inn, Holiday Inn Express, Microtel, Ramada Ltd, **other:** VET, Acura, Barnes&Noble, Big Lots, BJ's Whse, Buick, Chevrolet, Dodge, $General, Dunn Tire, /24hr, Firestone/auto, Ford, Home Depot, Honda, JC Penney, Jo-Ann Fabrics, K-Mart, Lowes Whse, Michael's, NTB, Office Depot, Radio Shack, Sears/auto, SteinMart, Target, TJ Maxx, Top's Food/deli, Walmart SuperCtr/24hr, Wegman's Foods, mall, **S gas:** Kwikfill, Mobil, **food:** Bob Evans, John&Mary's Cafe, Salvatore's Italian, **lodging:** Garden Place Hotel, Hospitality Inn, Howard Johnson, Red Roof Inn, **other:** Aamco, CarQuest, Top's Foods
419mm	toll booth
50 (420)	I-290 to Niagara Falls
50a (421)	Cleveland Dr (from eb)
51 (422)	NY 33 E, Buffalo, **S** ✈, st police
52 (423)	Walden Ave, to Buffalo, **N food:** Applebees, Famous Dave's BBQ, McDonald's, Ruby Tuesday, Starbucks, Subway, TGIFriday, Tim Horton, **lodging:** Hampton Inn, Residence Inn, **other:** Aldi Foods, $Tree, Ford, Goodyear/auto, Home Depot, Michael's, Office Depot, PetsMart, Target, Top's Foods, Walmart, **S gas:** Delta Sonic, Jim's Trk Plaza/Sunoco/dsl/rest./scales/24hr, KwikFill, **food:** Alton's Rest., Bravo Italiano, Cheesecake Factory, Fuddrucker's, Krispy Kreme, McDonald's, Milton's Rest., Olive Garden, Pizza Hut, Smokey Bones BBQ, **lodging:** Millenium Hotel, **other:** Best Buy, Borders Books, Burlington Coats, Lord&Taylor, Macy's, JC Penney, K-Mart, Niagara Hobby, Wegman's Foods, mall

BUFFALO

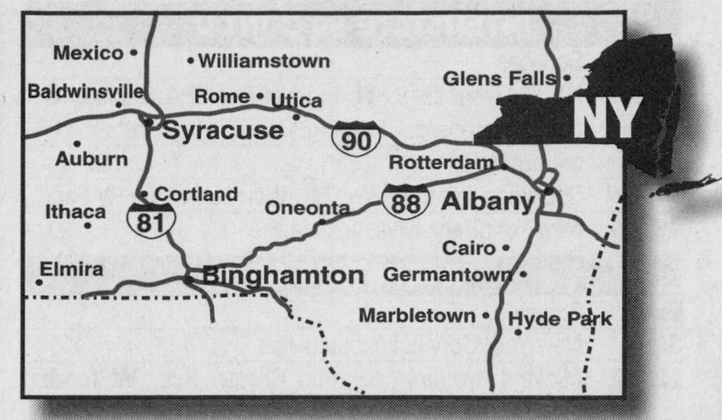

Exit #	Services
52a (424)	William St
53 (425)	I-190, to Buffalo, Niagara Falls, **N lodging:** Holiday Inn Express
54 (428)	NY 400, NY 16, to W Seneca, E Aurora
55 (430)	US 219, Ridge Rd, Orchard Park, to Rich Stadium, **S gas:** Citgo, Delta Sonic, **food:** Denny's, Ponderosa, Subway, Wendy's, **lodging:** Hampton Inn, **other:** Aldi Foods, Goodyear/auto, Home Depot, K-Mart, Lowes Whse, Tops Foods, Wegman's Foods
431mm	toll booth
56 (432)	NY 179, Mile Strip Rd, **N gas:** Choice, Citgo, Sunoco, **food:** Blasdelle Pizza, DiPallo's Rest., Odyssey Rest., Whse Grill, **lodging:** Econolodge, **other:** CarQuest, CVS Drug, repair, **S food:** Applebee's, Bonton, Boston Mkt, ChuckeCheese, Friendly's, McDonald's, Olive Garden, Outback Steaks, Panera Bread, Pizza Hut, Red Lobster, Roadhouse Grill, Ruby Tuesday, Starbucks, Subway, TGIFriday, Wendy's, **lodging:** Clarion, Red Carpet Inn, **other:** Aldi Foods, Barnes&Noble, Best Buy, BJ's Whse, $Tree, Firestone/auto, Home Depot, JC Penney, Jo-Ann Etc, Old Navy, PepBoys, Sears, TJ Maxx, Wegman's Foods, mall
57 (436)	NY 75, to Hamburg, **N gas:** Mobil/dsl, **food:** Anthony's Diner, Denny's, McDonald's, Wendy's, **lodging:** Comfort Inn, Red Roof Inn, Tallyho Motel, **other:** Chrysler/Dodge/Jeep, Ford, transmissions, **S gas:** Go Gas, Kwikfill/dsl, Stop&Gas, **food:** Arby's, Burger King, Camp Road Diner, Pizza Hut, Subway, **lodging:** Holiday Inn, **other:** AutoZone, Camping World RV Supplies/Service, $General, Goodyear/auto, USPO, Vet
442mm	**parking area both lanes, ☎, litter barrels**
57a (445)	to Eden, Angola, **2 mi N gas:** Sunoco/dsl
447mm	**Angola Service Area both lanes**, Sunoco/dsl, Denny's, Ella's Pizza, McDonald's, phone/fax, gifts
58 (456)	US 20, NY 5, to Silver Creek, Irving, **N gas:** Citgo, Kwikfill, **food:** Burger King, Millie's Rest., Primo's Rest., Subway, Sunset Grill, Tim Horton, Tom's Rest., **other:** H, to Evangola SP
59 (468)	NY 60, Fredonia, Dunkirk, **N lodging:** Dunkirk Motel (4mi), **other:** Lake Erie SP (7mi), **S gas:** Country Fair, Kwikfill/dsl, Mobil/dsl, **food:** Applebee's, Arby's, Azteca Mexican, Best Buffet, Bob Evans, Burger King, Denny's, Dunkin Donuts, KFC/Taco Bell, McDonald's, Pizza Hut, Subway, Tim Horton, Wendy's, Wing City Grill, **lodging:** Best Western, Comfort Inn, Day's Inn, **other:** Aldi Foods, AutoZone, $Tree, Ford/Lincoln/Mercury, GNC, Home Depot, NAPA, Radio Shack, Rite Aid, Tops Foods/gas, TJ Maxx, Walmart SuperCtr/24hr/gas

BUFFALO / DUNKIRK

INTERSTATE 90 CONT'D

Exit #	Services
60 (485)	NY 394, Westfield, **N** to Lake Erie SP, camping, **S gas:** Keystone/dsl, **lodging:** Holiday Motel, **other:** H
494mm	toll booth
61 (495)	Shortman Rd, to Ripley, **N other:** Lakeshore RV Park
496mm	New York/Pennsylvania state line

INTERSTATE 95

N ↕ S

Exit #	Services
32mm	New York/Connecticut state line
22 (30)	Midland Ave (from nb), Port Chester, Rye, **W food:** Subway, **other:** H, Home Depot, Staples
21 (29)	I-287 W, US 1 N, to White Plains, Port Chester, Tappan Zee
20 (28)	US 1 S (from nb), Port Chester, **E gas:** Shell, **other:** CVS Drug, Ford, Subaru
19 (27)	Playland Pkwy, Rye, Harrison
18b (25)	Mamaroneck Ave, to White Plains, **E gas:** Hess, Shell, **other:** A&P Foods
18a (24)	Fenimore Rd (from nb), Mamaroneck, **E gas:** Sunoco
17 (20)	Chatsworth Ave (from nb, no return), Larchmont
19.5mm	toll plaza
16 (19)	North Ave, Cedar St, New Rochelle, **E food:** Applebees, Buffalo Wild Wings, **lodging:** Residence Inn, **other:** Toyota, **W** H
15 (16)	US 1, New Rochelle, The Pelhams, **E gas:** Getty/dsl, PitStop/24hr, **other:** AutoZone, Cadillac, BMW/Jaguar/Lexus/Mercedes, Costco, CVS Drug, Harley-Davidson, Home Depot, NAPA, **W** auto repair
14 (15)	Hutchinson Pkwy (from sb), to Whitestone Br
13 (16)	Conner St, to Mt Vernon, **E gas:** Gulf/dsl, **lodging:** Econolodge, **W gas:** BP, **food:** McDonald's, **lodging:** Andrea Motel, **other:** H
12 (15.5)	Baychester Ave (from nb)
11 (15)	Bartow Ave, Co-op City Blvd, **E gas:** Mobil, **food:** Applebees, Burger King, Checker's, Dragon City, Little Caesar's, McDonald's, Panera Bread, Popeye's, Red Lobster, **other:** Barnes&Noble, JC Penney, K-Mart, Marshall's, Old Navy, PathMark Foods, Pay Half, Staples, **W gas:** Shell/mart, Sunoco/dsl, **food:** ChuckeCheese, Dunkin Donuts, Eastern Wok, Pizza Hut, Subway, **other:** Home Depot
10 (14.5)	Gun Hill Rd (from nb), **W lodging:** Pelham Bay Hotel/diner
9 (14)	Hutchinson Pkwy
8c (13.5)	Pelham Pkwy W
8b (13)	Orchard Beach, City Island
8a (12.5)	Westchester Ave (from sb)
7c (12)	Pelham Bay Park (from nb), Country Club Rd
7b (11.5)	E Tremont (from sb), **W other:** Super FoodTown
7a (11)	I-695 (from sb), to I-295 S, Throgs Neck Br
6b (10.5)	I-278 W (from sb), I-295 S (from nb)
6a (10)	I-678 S, Whitestone Bridge
5b (9)	Castle Hill Ave, **W gas:** Sunoco, **food:** McDonald's, **other:** GNC
5a (8.5)	Westchester Ave, White Plains Rd
4b (8)	Bronx River Pkwy, Rosedale Ave, **E gas:** BP, Getty
4a (7)	I-895 S, Sheridan Expsy
3 (6)	3rd Ave, H
2b (5)	Webster Ave, **E** H
2a (4)	Jerome Ave, to I-87
1c (3)	I-87, Deegan Expswy, to Upstate
1b (2)	Harlem River Dr
1a (1)	US 9, NY 9A, H Hudson Pkwy, 178th St, downtown
0mm	New York/New Jersey state line, Hudson River, Geo Washington Br

NEW YORK CITY AREA

INTERSTATE 190 (BUFFALO)

E ↕ W

Exit #	Services
25.5mm	US/Canada Border, US Customs
25b a	R Moses Pkwy, NY 104, NY 265, Lewiston, **E** H
24	NY 31, Witmer Rd, **E** H, st police
23	NY 182, Porter Rd, Packard Rd, **E gas:** Sunoco, **food:** Applebees, Burger King, DQ, Mighty Taco, Perkins, Subway, Tim Horton, **other:** Big Lots, CarQuest, Chrysler/Jeep, Firestone/auto, Jo-Ann Fabrics, K-Mart, NAPA, Prime Outlets/famous brands, U-Haul, **W food:** Wendy's, **other:** Aldi Foods, Sam's Club, Walmart/Subway
22	US 62, Niagara Falls Blvd, **E gas:** Sunoco, **food:** Bob Evans, Burger King, Denny's, Dunkin Donuts, KFC, McDonald's, Pizza Hut, Taco Bell, Wendy's, **lodging:** Budget Host, Caravan Motel, Holiday Motel, Howard Johnson, Knight's Inn, Pelican Motel, Quality Inn, Red Carpet Inn, Super 8, Swiss Cottage Inn, **other:** Advance Parts, Ford, Radio Shack, Rite Aid, Target, Top's Foods/gas, Toyota, **W lodging:** Econolodge, Sunrise Inn, **other:** Home Depot
21a	NY 384, Buffalo Ave, R Moses Pkwy, **W gas:** Getty, **other:** casino, to NY SP, American Falls
21	La Salle Expswy
20.5mm	Niagara River East, toll booth sb
20b a	Long Rd, **E lodging:** Budget Motel
19	Whitehaven Rd, **E gas:** Getty, Noco Gas, **food:** McDonald's, Subway, **lodging:** Chateu Motel (2mi), Holiday Inn (4mi), **other:** $Tree, Top's Foods/gas, KOA (1mi), funpark, **W other:** Chevrolet, Toyota/Scion, Vet
18b a	NY 324 W, Grand Island Blvd, **E food:** Asian Buffet, Burger King, Tim Horton, Wendy's, **lodging:** Chateu Motel, Grand Suites, **other:** NAPA, **W** Beaver Island SP
17.5mm	Niagara River East, toll booth
17	NY 266, last free exit nb
16	I-290 E, to I-90, Albany
15	NY 324, Kenmore Ave, **E gas:** 7-11, **W other:** U-Haul
14	Ontario St, **E gas:** KwikFill, **food:** McDonald's, Tim Horton, **other:** Advance Parts, Family$, **W food:** Harry's Grille
13	(from nb), same as 14
12	Amherst St, (from nb), downtown
11	NY 198, Buffalo, **E gas:** Sunoco
9	Porter Ave, to Peace Bridge, Ft Erie
8	NY 266, Niagara St, downtown, **E lodging:** Adam's Mark Hotel
7	NY 5 W, Church St, Buffalo, downtown
6	Elm St, **E** H, downtown, **W** HSBC Arena
5	Louisiana St, Buffalo, downtown
4	Smith St, Fillmore Ave, Buffalo, downtown
3	NY 16, Seneca St, from sb, **W other:** CarQuest
2	US 62, NY 354, Bailey Ave, Clinton St
1	Ogden St, **E gas:** Sunoco, **food:** Wendy's, **lodging:** Comfort Inn, Holiday Inn Express, **other:** CVS Drug, Tops Foods, Volvo/GMC Trucks

NIAGARA FALLS

NY

INTERSTATE 190 CONT'D (BUFFALO)

Exit #	Services
.5mm	toll plaza nb
0mm	I-90. I-190 begins/ends on I-90, exit 53

INTERSTATE 287 (NEW YORK CITY)

E ↕ W — NYC AREA

Exit #	Services
12	I-95, N to New Haven, **S to NYC. I-287 begins/ends on I-95, exit 21.**
11	US 1, Port Chester, Rye, **N gas:** BP, Mobil, Shell/dsl, Sunoco, **food:** Burger King, Domino's, Dunkin Donuts, Mary Anne's Mexican, McDonald's, Port Chester Diner, Subway, Wendy's, **other:** H, A&P, Goodyear/auto, Kohl's, Nissan, Staples, repair
10	Bowman Ave, Webb Ave
9	N SHutchinson Pkwy, Merritt Pkwy, to Whitestone Br
9a	I-684, Brewster
8	Westchester Ave, to White Plains, **S gas:** Getty, **other:** Nordstrom's, Westchester Mall Place
7	Taconic Pkwy (from wb), to N White Plains
6	NY 22, White Plains
5	NY 100, Hillside Ave, **S gas:** Citgo, Getty, Mobil, **food:** Applebees, Planet Pizza, **other:** Aamco, A&P, K-mart
4	NY 100A, Hartsdale, **N gas:** Shell, **other:** H, **S food:** Bamboo Garden Chinese, Burger King, **other:** BMW/Minl, Jaguar, Nissan, Staples, Volvo
3	Sprain Pkwy, to Taconic Pkwy, NYC
2	NY 9A, Elmsford, **N gas:** BP, Mobil, Shell, **food:** Dunkin Donuts, KFC/Taco Bell, Subway, **other:** Bridge Auto Parts, Sam's Club, **S gas:** Shell, **food:** Wendy's
1	NY 119, Tarrytown, **N food:** Ruth's Chris Steaks, **lodging:** Marriott, Sheraton, **S gas:** Exxon/dsl, **food:** El Dorado Diner, **lodging:** Extended Stay America, Hampton Inn

I-287 runs with I-87 N.

INTERSTATE 290 (BUFFALO)

E ↕ W

Exit #	Services
8	I-90, NY Thruway, I-290 begins/ends on I-90, exit 50.
7b a	NY 5, Main St, **N gas:** Mobil, Sunoco, **food:** La Nova Pizza/Wings, McDonald's, Pizza Plant, Subway, Tim Horton, Wendy's, **other:** Quality Mkt Foods, Walgreens, **S gas:** Valero, **food:** Sonoma Grille, **lodging:** Amherst Motel, **other:** vet
6	NY 324, NY 240, **N gas:** Getty, **lodging:** Courtyard, **S gas:** Valero, **food:** China Star, ChuckeCheese, Subway, **other:** Chrysler/Jeep, CVS Drug, Hyundai/Subaru, KIA/Mazda, Lexus, Nissan
5b a	NY 263, to Millersport, **N food:** Houlihan's, **lodging:** Comfort Inn, Marriott, Red Roof Inn, **S gas:** Mobil, **lodging:** Homewood Suites, **other:** Scion/Toyota, VW, Walgreens
4	I-990, to St U
3b a	US 62, to Niagara Falls Blvd, **N gas:** Citgo, Valero, **food:** Bob Evans, Dunkin Donuts, Just Pizza, Max's Grill, Pancake House, Ted's Hot Dogs, **lodging:** Blvd Inn, Econolodge, Extended Stay America, Holiday Inn, Knight's Inn, Red Carpet Inn, Sleep Inn, **other:** Buick/GMC/Pontiac, CarQuest, Dodge, Home Depot, Honda, Walmart/auto, Vet, **S gas:** Delta Sonic, Mobil, **food:** Applebee's, Arby's, BoneFish Grill, Burger King, Carrabba's, Chili's, Denny's, Dibella's Subs, John's Pizza,

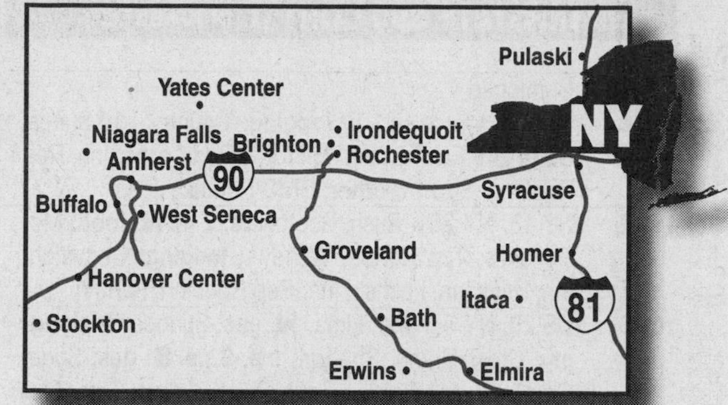

Exit #	Services
3b a	Continued McDonald's, Moe's SW Grill, Montana's Grill, Outback Steaks, Panera Bread, Pizza Hut, Starbucks, Subway, Swiss Chalet Grill, TGIFriday, Tim Horton, Tulley's, **lodging:** Days Inn, Royal Inn, **other:** Barnes&Noble, Best Buy, $Tree, Firestone, Goodyear/auto, JC Penney, Jo-Ann Fabrics, Lowes Whse, Macy's, Michael's, PetCo, PetsMart, Sears/auto, Target, mall
2	NY 425, Colvin Blvd, **N food:** Athena's Rest., KFC, McDonald's, Subway, Texas Roadhouse, Tim Horton, Wendy's, **other:** H, Big Lots, BJ's Whse/gas, Family$, Gander Mtn, Goodyear/auto, Top's Foods/gas, **S gas:** KwikFill
1b a	Elmwood Ave, NY 384, NY 265, **N gas:** KwikFill, **food:** John's Pizza/Subs, Sam's Cafe, **lodging:** Microtel, **other:** H, $Tree, NAPA, Rite Aid, **S gas:** Mobil/dsl, **food:** Arby's
0mm	I-190. I-290 begins/ends on I-190 in Buffalo.

INTERSTATE 390 (ROCHESTER)

N ↕ S — ROCHESTER

Exit #	Services
38mm	**rest area both lanes, full ♿ facilities, 🛆, litter barrels, vending, petwalk**
20a b (76)	I-490. I-390 begins/ends on I-490 in Rochester
19 (75)	NY 33a, Chili Ave, **N food:** Wishing Well Rest., **S gas:** Sunoco, **food:** Burger King, Pizza Hut, Subway, **lodging:** Motel 6, Quality Inn, **other:** $General
18a b (74)	NY 204, Brooks Ave, **N lodging:** Holiday Inn, **S lodging:** Fairfield Inn, **other:** ✈
17 (73)	NY 383, Scottsville Rd, **W gas:** Sunoco/Subway/dsl
16 (71)	NY 15a, to E Henryetta, **S food:** Basil's Rest, **lodging:** Courtyard, Hampton Inn, **other:** H
15 (70)	I-590, Rochester
14 (68)	NY 15a, NY 252, **E food:** Domino's, Gray's Cafe, McDonald's, Outback Steaks, Papa John's, Perkins, Tully's Rest., **lodging:** Extended Stay America, **other:** Staples, **W gas:** Mobil/dsl, **food:** Boston Mkt, Dunkin Donuts, Starbucks, Subway, Taco Bell, **lodging:** Best Western, DoubleTree Inn, **other:** Big Lots, Office Depot, Radio Shack, Top's Foods
13 (67)	Hylan Dr., **E food:** Cracker Barrel, **lodging:** Comfort Suites, Homewood Suites, **W gas:** Mobil, **food:** Bonton, Chicago Grill, ChuckeCheese, IHOP, McDonald's, Panera Bread, Ruby Tuesday, Tony Roma's, Wendy's, **other:** Best Buy, BJ's Whse, Border's Books, Gander Mtn, Michael's, Lowes Whse, Pep Boys, Sam's Club/gas, Target, Walmart SuperCtr/24hr, Wegman's Foods, mall
12 (66)	I-90. NY Thruway, NY 253, **W gas:** Citgo/dsl, Hess, Sunoco/dsl, **food:** McDonald's, Peppermint's Rest.,

INTERSTATE 390 CONT'D (ROCHESTER)

N ↕ S

Exit #	Services
12 (66)	Continued Tim Horton, Wendy's, **lodging:** Country Inn&Suites, Day's Inn, Fairfield Inn, Microtel, Red Carpet Inn, Red Roof Inn, Super 8 **other:** GMC/Pontiac, Jeep
11 (62)	NY 15, NY 251, Rush, Scottsville, **2 mi N food:** McDonald's, Tim Horton, Wendy's, **lodging:** Cartwright Inn, Days Inn, Fairfield Inn, Red Roof Inn, RIT Inn
10 (55)	US 20, NY 5, Avon, Lima, **N gas:** Sunoco/dsl, **lodging:** CrestHill Inn, Stratford Inn, **3 mi S gas:** Sugar Creek/dsl, **food:** Avon Cafe, Dutch Hollow Cafe, McDonald's, Tom Wahls Cafe, Subway, **lodging:** Avon Cedar Lodge, **other:** Chrysler/Dodge/Jeep, Ford, Sugar Creek Camping
9mm	scenic area wb
9 (52)	NY 15, **N gas:** Mobil/dsl, **food:** Dunkin Donuts, Fratelli's Rest., Lakeville Rest., McDonald's, Tee&Gee Cafe, **lodging:** Cones US motel, **other:** Chevrolet
8 (48)	US 20a, Geneseo, **N food:** Arby's, **lodging:** Oak Valley Inn, **other:** Cones Us Camping, **S food:** Denny's, Dunkin Donuts, KFC/Taco Bell, McDonald's, Wendy's, **lodging:** Quality Inn
7 (39)	NY 63, NY 408, Geneseo, **S gas:** Mobil, KwikFill, **food:** Brian's Diner, McDonald's, **lodging:** Alligence B&B, Country Inn, Geneseo Hotel/Rest., Greenway Motel, **other:** Ridge Camping
6 (33)	NY 36, MT Morris, Sonyea
5 (26)	NY 36, Dansville, **N gas:** KwikFill, Mobil/Subway, **food:** Arby's, Burger King, Dunkin Donuts, HoHo Chinese, McDonald's, Pizza Hut, Subway, **other:** Advance Parts, Chevrolet/Cadillac/Pontiac, CVS Drug, Radio Shack, Rite Aid, Top's Foods/gas, **S gas:** TA/Mobil/Buckhorn Rest./@, **lodging:** Day's Inn
4 (23)	NY 36, Dansville, **N gas:** Sunoco/dsl, **lodging:** Logan's Inn, **other:** H, Larocca RV Ctr, **S gas:** Skybrook Camping, Stonybrook Park Camping, Sugar Creek Camping, Sunvalley Camping
3 (17)	NY 15, NY 21, Waylend, **N food:** Farmer's Kitchen Rest., **other:** Holiday Hill Campground (7mi), st patrol
2 (11)	NY 415, Cohocton, Naples, **N gas:** Mobil, ohter: Tumble Hill Camping (2mi)
1 (2)	NY 415, I-390 begins/ends, Avoca, **N** truck/auto repair, **S gas:** Mobil, **lodging:** Caboose Motel (3mi)

INTERSTATE 495 (LONG ISLAND)

E ↕ W

LONG ISLAND

Exit #	Services
I-495 begins/ends on NY 25.	
73	rd 58, Old Country Road, to Greenport, Orient, **S gas:** Hess/dsl, Exxon, Lukoil, Mobil, **food:** Applebees, Boulder Creek Steaks, Panera Bread, TGI Friday, Taco Bell, Wendy's, **lodging:** Holiday Inn Express, **other:** Best Buy, Borders Books, Chevrolet, CVS Drug, Ford/Lincoln/Mercury, Harley-Davidson, Home Depot, Honda, Michael's, Nissan/Hyundai/Suzuki, PetCo, Tanger/famous brands, Target, Toyota, VW Subaru, Waldbaum's, Walgreens
72	NY 25, (no ez eb return), Riverhead, Calverton, **N** funpark, **S gas:** Hess, **lodging:** Best Western, **other:** Tanger/famous brands/foodcourt
71	NY 24, to Hampton Bays (no ez eb return), Calverton, **N gas:** Hess/Subway/dsl
70	NY 111, to Eastport, Manorville, **S gas:** Citgo/7-11, Mobil, **food:** McDonald's, Michelangelo's Italian, Starbucks, **other:** King Kullen Food/drug
69	Wading River Rd, Center Moriches, to Wading River
68	NY 46, to Shirley, Wading River, **S lodging:** Holiday Inn, golf
67	Yaphank Ave
66	NY 101, Sills Rd, Yaphank, **N gas:** Shell/24hr
65	Horse Block rd, **N food:** Dunkin Donuts/Baskin-Robbins, **other:** Eddy's RV Ctr
64	NY 112, to Coram, Medford, **N gas:** Getty's, Mobil, **other:** , Lowes Whse, Radio Shack, Sam's Club, 7-11, Target, **S gas:** BP, Exxon, Gulf, US/dsl, **lodging:** Comfort Inn, **other:** Aid Parts
63	NY 83, N Ocean Ave, **N gas:** Hess/dsl, Mobil, **food:** Applebees, Burger King, McDonald's, 7-11, Taco Bell, TGI Fridays, **other:** Hampton Inn, **other:** K-Mart, Stop'n Shop, **S gas:** BP, Exxon, **food:** City Grill, **lodging:** Radisson
62	rd 97, to Blue Point, Stony Brook, **N gas:** Gulf, **S food:** Charlie Brown's Steaks, Chili's, Wendy's, **lodging:** Residence Inn
61	rd 19, to Patchogue, Holbrook, **N gas:** Mobil, **S gas:** Exxon/dsl, Hess/dsl, **food:** China 4, Greek Islands Rest, Outback Steaks, Subway, **other:** CVS Drug, 7-11, Waldbaums Foods
60	Ronkonkoma Ave, **N gas:** Exxon, **S food:** Red Lobster, Smokey Bones BBQ, **lodging:** Courtyard
59	Ocean Ave, to Oakdale, Ronkonkoma, **S gas:** Citgo/7-11, Exxon, Sunoco, **lodging:** Hilton Garden (1mi)
58	Old Nichols Rd, Nesconset, **N gas:** Exxon, **food:** Hooters, **lodging:** Marriott, **other:** BJ's Whse, **S gas:** BP
57	NY 454, Vets Hwy, to Hauppauge, **N gas:** Exxon/dsl, **food:** TGIFriday, **S gas:** Citgo/dsl, Getty's, Gulf/dsl/24hr, Shell, Sunoco, **food:** Dave&Buster's, New Horizon Diner, Subway, **lodging:** Hampton Inn, **other:** Stop&Shop Foods, Radio Shack, TJ Maxx, Walmart
56	NY 111, Smithtown, Islip, **N gas:** Exxon/Subway/Domino's/dsl, Mobil, **S gas:** Mobil, **food:** Café La Strada, **lodging:** Holiday Inn Express
55	Central Islip, **N gas:** Mobil, **S gas:** Exxon/dsl
54	Wicks Rd, **N gas:** BP, **other:** Bennigan's, **lodging:** Sheraton, **S gas:** Mobil
53	Sunken Meadow Pkwy, to ocean beaches, Bayshore
52	rd 4, Commack, **N gas:** Mobil/dsl, Shell/repair, **food:** Conca d'Oro Pizza, Ground Round, **lodging:** Hampton Inn, **other:** Costco
51.5mm	**parking area both lanes, phone, litter barrels**
51	NY 231, to Northport, Babylon
50	Bagatelle Rd, to Wyandanch
49N	NY 110 N, to Huntington, **N lodging:** Marriott
49S	NY 110 S, to Amityville
48	Round Swamp Rd, Old Bethpage, **S gas:** Mobil/dsl, **food:** Old Country Pizza/deli, **lodging:** Homewood Suites, Palace Hotel, Sheraton, **other:** USPO
46	Sunnyside Blvd, Plainview, **N lodging:** Holiday Inn
45	Manetto Hill Rd, Plainview, Woodbury
44	NY 135, to Seaford, Syosset
43	S Oyster Bay Rd, to Syosset, Bethpage, **N gas:** Mobil

INTERSTATE 495 CONT'D (LONG ISLAND)

E ↕ W — LONG ISLAND

Exit #	Services
42	Northern Pkwy, rd N, Hauppauge
41	NY 106, NY 107, Hicksville, Oyster Bay, **S gas:** BP, Mobil, Sunoco, **food:** Boston Mkt, Boulder Creek Steaks, Broadway Diner, Burger King, Dunkin Donuts, McDonald's, On the Border, **other:** Goodyear/auto, Sears/auto
40	NY 25, Mineola, Syosset, **S gas:** BP, Exxon, Hess/dsl, Shell, **food:** A&W, Burger King, Friendly's, IHOP, McDonald's, Wendy's, **lodging:** Howard Johnson, **other:** Home Depot, Kohl's, 7-11, Staples
39	Glen Cove Rd, **N gas:** Mobil
38	Northern Pkwy E, Meadowbrook Pkwy, to Jones Beach
37	Willis Ave, to Roslyn, Mineola, **N gas:** Exxon, Shell, **other:** repair, **S gas:** Gulf,
36	Searingtown Rd, to Port Washington, **S** H
35	Shelter Rock Rd, Manhasset
34	New Hyde Park Rd
33	Lakeville Rd, to Great Neck, **N** H
32	Little Neck Pkwy, **N food:** pizza
31	Douglaston Pkwy, **S gas:** BP, **other:** Macy's, USPO, Waldbaum's Foods, mall
30	E Hampton Blvd, Cross Island Pkwy
29	Springfield Blvd, **S gas:** Exxon, **food:** Dunkin Donuts, McDonald's
27	I-295, Clearview Expswy, Throgs Neck, **N gas:** Gulf, 7-11, **food:** Blue Bay Diner, **other:** Rockbottom Drug
26	Francis Lewis Blvd
25	Utopia Pkwy, 188th St, **N gas:** Citgo, Gulf, Mobil, Sunoco, **S gas:** Citgo, Mobil, Sunoco, **food:** Arby's, Subway, **other:** Radio Shack, USPO
24	Kissena Blvd, **N gas:** Exxon/dsl, **food:** Baskin-Robbins, Dunkin Donuts, **S gas:** Mobil
23	Main St, **N food:** Palace Diner
22	Grand Central Pkwy, to I-678, College Pt Blvd, **N lodging:** Eden Park Hotel, Paris Suites
21	108th St, **N gas:** BP
19	NY 25, Queens Blvd, Woodhaven Blvd, to Rockaways, **N other:** JC Penney, Macy's, mall, **S gas:** BP, **food:** Applebees, **other:** Marshall's, Old Navy, Sears
18.5	69th Ave, Grand Ave (from wb)
18	Maurice St, **N gas:** Exxon **S gas:** BP, **food:** McDonald's, **other:** dsl repair
17	48th St, to I-278, **N lodging:** Holiday Inn Express
16	I-495 begins/ends in NYC.

NORTH CAROLINA

NY NC

INTERSTATE 26

E ↕ W — HENDERSONVILLE — ARDEN

Exit #	Services
71mm	North Carolina/South Carolina state line
69mm	N Pacolet River
67.5mm	**Welcome Ctr wb, full ♿ facilities, ☎, ⛱, litter barrels**
67	US 74 E, to NC 108, Columbus, Tryon, **N gas:** BP/Burger King/dsl, Texaco, **food:** Cocula Mexican, McDonald's, Subway, Waffle House, Wendy's, **other:** H Advance Parts, CVS Drug, Family$, Food Lion, **S gas:** Exxon/dsl, Shell, **food:** KFC/Taco Bell, Mtn View Deli, **lodging:** Days Inn, **other:** BiLo, $General
59	Saluda, **N lodging:** Saluda Motel, **other:** camping, **S gas:** BP/dsl/mart, Texaco/mart, **food:** Schafer's Grill, Subway, **lodging:** B&B, **other:** Vet
56mm	Green River
54	US 25, to Greenville, E Flat Rock, access to Carl Sandburg Home
53.5mm	Eastern Continental Divide, 2130 ft
53	Upward Rd, Hendersonville, **N gas:** Texaco/dsl, **food:** Waffle House, Zaxby's, **lodging:** Mtn Inn Suites, Mtn Lodge, **other:** Bloomfields Giftshop, **S gas:** Exxon/McDonald's/dsl, Shell/Pizza Inn/dsl, **food:** Cracker Barrel, Subway, **lodging:** Holiday Inn Express, **other:** RV camping, to Carl Sandburg Home
49b a	US 64, Hendersonville, **N gas:** Chevron, Shell/dsl/24hr, Texaco/dsl, **food:** Atlanta Bread Co, Baby Joe's Smokehouse, Chick-fil-A, El Paso Mexican, Golden Corral, Jack-in-the-Box, O'Charley's, Sonic, Waffle House, Zaxby's, **lodging:** Best Western, Hampton Inn, Quality Inn, Ramada Ltd, **other:** H, Advance Parts, CarQuest, $Tree, Ingles, Radio Shack, Sam's Club, Staples, Walmart SuperCtr/gas/24hr, World of Clothing, **S gas:** Exxon/dsl/LP, Shell/dsl, **food:** Applebee's, Arby's, Binion's Roadhouse, Bojangles,
49b a	Continued Burger King, China Sea, Cici's, Denny's, Fatz Café, Hardee's, Honeybaked Ham, KFC, Krispy Kreme, LJ Silver, McDonald's, Outback Steaks, Patron Mexican, Pizza Hut, Subway/TCBY, Taco Bell, Wendy's, **lodging:** Comfort Inn, Day's Inn, Red Roof Inn, **other:** H Aldi Foods, Belk, BigLots, BiLo Foods, CVS Drug, Home Depot, JC Penney, K-Mart, Lowe's Whse, mall
46mm	**weigh sta both lanes, ☎**
44	US 25, Fletcher, **N gas:** Exxon/dsl, **food:** Hardee's, Subway, **other:** H, flea mkt campground, Vet, **S gas:** Citgo/dsl, Shell/Bojangles/Stuckey's/dsl/scales/24hr, United/dsl, **food:** Burger King, Naples Diner, **other:** Todd's RV/marine, USPO, to Uncle John's
41mm	**rest area both lanes, full ♿ facilities, ☎, ⛱, litter barrels, vending**
40	NC 280, Arden, **N gas:** Exxon/dsl, Shell/Arby's/dsl, **food:** Carrabba's, Chili's, Cracker Barrel, McDonald's, Pizza Hut, Ruby Tuesday, Waffle House, **lodging:** Budget Motel, Comfort Inn, Day's Inn, Econolodge, Hampton Inn, Holiday Inn/rest., **other:** Best Buy, Honda/Acura/Kia, Lowes Whse, Marshall's, Michael's, Ross, Target, World Mkt, **S gas:** BP/dsl, **food:** J&S Cafeteria, Smokehouse BBQ, **lodging:** Fairfield Inn, **other:** Asheville ✈, BMW, Rutledg Lake Camping
37	NC 146, Skyland, **N gas:** Exxon, Shell/McDonald's/dsl/24hr, **food:** Arby's, Shoney's, Waffle House, **lodging:** Quality Inn, **other:** CVS Drug, **S food:** Riverside Grill
34mm	French Broad River
33	NC 191, Brevard Rd, **N other:** Toyota, **2 mi N other:** Asheville Farmers Mkt, Bear Creek RV Camp, **S gas:** Citgo, HotSpot/dsl, **food:** Apollo Bistro, China Garden, Garfield's, Harbor Inn Seafood, LJ Silver, McDonald's, Ryan's, Stoneridge Grill, Taco Bell, Waffle House,

INTERSTATE 26 CONT'D

Exit #	Services
33	Continued **lodging:** Comfort Suites, Country Inn&Suites, Fairfield Inn, Hampton Inn, Holiday Inn Express, Super 8, **other:** Belk, Dillard's, $Tree, KIA, K-Mart, Ingles Foods, SuperPetz, mall, to Blue Ridge Pkwy
31b a	I-40, E to Statesville, W to Knoxville
27mm	Hill St
25	rd 251, to UNCA, **S** Richmond Hill Inn (1mi)
24	Elk Mtn Rd, Woodfin
23	Merrimon Ave, N Asheville, **N gas:** BP/dsl, HotSpot, **food:** Bellagio Bistro, **lodging:** Day's Inn, **other:** Food Lion, Tuesday Morning, camping
21	New Stock Rd, **N gas:** BP, Citgo/dsl, **food:** Pizza Hut, **other:** Ingles/gas, camping
19a b	N US 25, W US 70, Marshall, **N gas:** Shell/dsl, **food:** Arby's, Bojangles, Burger King, KFC, McDonald's, Subway, Waffle House, **other:** Advance Parts, Curves, Kerr Drug, Ingles/gas, Roses, **S gas:** Shell/Huddle House/dsl, **other:** Lowes Whse, Walmart
18	Weaverville (no EZ return from eb)
17	to Flat Creek
15	rd 197, to Jupiter, Barnardsville
13	Forks of Ivy, **N gas:** BP/dsl, **S gas:** Exxon/dsl
11	rd 213, to Mars Hill, Marshall, **N** tires, **S gas:** Chevron/dsl, Exxon//Hardee's/dsl, Shell/Subway/dsl, **food:** Blazerz Steaks, Pizza Roma, Waffle House, Wagon Wheel Rest., **lodging:** Comfort Inn, **other:** Ford, NAPA, Radio Shack
9	Burnsville, Spruce Pine, to Mt Mitchell SP
7mm	scenic overlook wb, runaway truck ramp eb
6mm	**Welcome Ctr. rest area eb, full [H] facilities**
5.5mm	runaway truck ramp eb
5mm	Buckner Gap, elev. 3370
3to	US 23, Wolf Laurel, **N gas:** Exxon, **food:** Little Creek Cafe, **other:** to ski areas
2.5mm	runaway truck ramp
0mm	North Carolina/Tennessee state line

E ↕ W ASHEVILLE

INTERSTATE 40

Exit #	Services
420mm	I-40 begins/ends at Wilmington, **Facilities on US 17, N other:** Ford/Lincoln/Mercury, Land Rover, Hyundai, Home Depot, Nissan, Suzuki, Toyota/Scion, VW, **S gas:** BP, Crown/dsl/24hr, Dodge's Store/dsl, Exxon/dsl/24hr, **food:** Arby's, Bonefish Grill, Buffalo Wings, Carrabba's, Chick-fil-A, Church's Chicken, Cracker Barrel, Hardee's, Hooters, IHOP, McDonald's, O'Charley's, Old Chicago Pizza, Olive Garden, Quizno's, Ruby Tuesday, Sonic, Sticky Fingers Rest., Taco Bell, Waffle House, Whitey's Rest., **lodging:** Best Value, Comfort Suites, Day's Inn, Extended Stay America, Fairview Inn, GreenTree Inn, Holiday Inn, Howard Johnson, Innkeeper, MainStay Suites, Motel 6, Quality Inn, Ramada Inn, Red Roof, Sleep Inn, Super 8, Travelodge, Travel Inn, Wingate Inn, **other:** Advance Parts, AutoZone, BMW, Costco/gas, Food Lion, Marshall's, PetsMart, Radio Shack, Rite Aid, Saab, Target, Walmart SuperCtr/gas, **Facilities 2-4 mi S on NC 132... gas:** BP, Exxon/dsl, **food:** Applebee's, Bojangles, Burger King, Checker's, Chili's, Cici's Pizza,
420mm	Continued Domino's, Dragon Garden, Farmhouse Rest., Golden Corral, Hardee's, Honey Baked Ham, KFC, McAlister's Deli, McDonald's, Outback Steaks, Starbucks, Taco Bell, TCBY, Wendy's, **lodging:** Baymont Inn, Comfort Inn, Courtyard, Holiday Inn Express, **other:** Best Buy, Chevrolet, $Tree, Harris-Teeter/24hr, Honda/Acura, Hyundai, K-Mart, Lowe's Foods, Lowe's Whse, PetCo, Pontiac/Buick/GMC/Mercedes, Sam's Club, Staples, TJ Maxx
420b a	Gordon Rd, NC 132 N, **2 mi N gas:** Kangaroo/dsl, **food:** McDonald's, Smithfield's Chicken/BBQ, Zaxby's, **other:** KOA (4mi), **S gas:** BP/dsl, Kangaroo/dsl, **food:** Carolina BBQ, Subway, **other:** Family$, Lowe's Foods, Rite Aid
416b a	I-140, US 17, to Topsail Island, New Bern, & Myrtle Beach
414	to Brunswick Co beaches, Castle Hayne, **S gas:** BP/24hr, Kangaroo, **food:** Hardee's, **other:** CVS Drug, Piggly Wiggly, USPO
412	NE Cape Fear River
408	NC 210, **N** Mack/Volvo/International Trucks, **S gas:** CW's Trvl Ctr/cafe/dsl, Exxon/dsl, Hess/Wilco/Wendy's/dsl/24hr, Shell, **food:** Hardee's, Noble Roman's, Sub Express, **other:** Food Lion, to Moore's Creek Nat Bfd/camping
398	NC 53, Burgaw, **2 mi S food:** Andy's Rest., CW's Cafe, Hardee's, McDonald's, Subway, Wendy's, **lodging:** Burgaw Motel, **other:** [H], camping
390	to US 117, Wallace
385	NC 41, Wallace, **N gas:** Exxon, **food:** Mad Boar Rest., **lodging:** Holiday Inn Express, **other:** Lake Leamon Camping
384	NC 11, Wallace
380	Rose Hill, **S gas:** BP/dsl (1mi), Pure
373	NC 903, Magnolia, **N gas:** BP/dsl/24hr., **lodging:** B&B, **other:** [H], Cowan Museum
369	US 117, Warsaw
364	NC 24, to NC 50, Clinton, **rest area both lanes, full [H] facilities, [phone], [picnic], litter barrels, vending, petwalk, N gas:** Wilco/Hess/Arby's/Stuckey's/dsl/24hr, **S gas:** BP/dsl, Crown/24hr, Kangaroo/dsl, Marathon, Sunoco/Bojangles, **food:** KFC, McDonald's, Smithfield's BBQ, Subway, Waffle House, Wendy's, **lodging:** Day's Inn, Holiday Inn Express
355	NC 403, to US 117, to Goldsboro, Faison, **3 mi N gas:** Pure
348	Suttontown Rd
343	US 701, Newton Grove, **1 mi N gas:** Exxon/dsl, to Bentonville Bfd
341	NC 50, NC 55, to US 13, Newton Grove, **1.5 mi N gas:** Exxon/dsl, **food:** Hardee's, **S gas:** BP/McDonald's, Shell/Subway, **food:** Smithfield BBQ
334	NC 96, Meadow, **S gas:** BP/dsl (1mi)
328b a	I-95, N to Smithfield, S to Benson
325	NC 242, to US 301, to Benson, **S gas:** Citgo/dsl
324mm	**rest area both lanes, full [H] facilities, [phone], [picnic], litter barrels, vending, petwalk, no overnight parking**
319	NC 210, McGee's Crossroads, **N gas:** Citgo/DQ/Papa's Subs & Pizza/dsl, Shell/BBQ/dsl/24hr, **food:** McDonald's, **other:** [H], **S gas:** Mobil/CW's Cafe, **food:** China Star, Italian Pizza/Pasta, KFC/Taco Bell, Subway, Wendy's, **other:** AutoZone, Food Lion, $General

E ↕ W WILMINGTON

NC

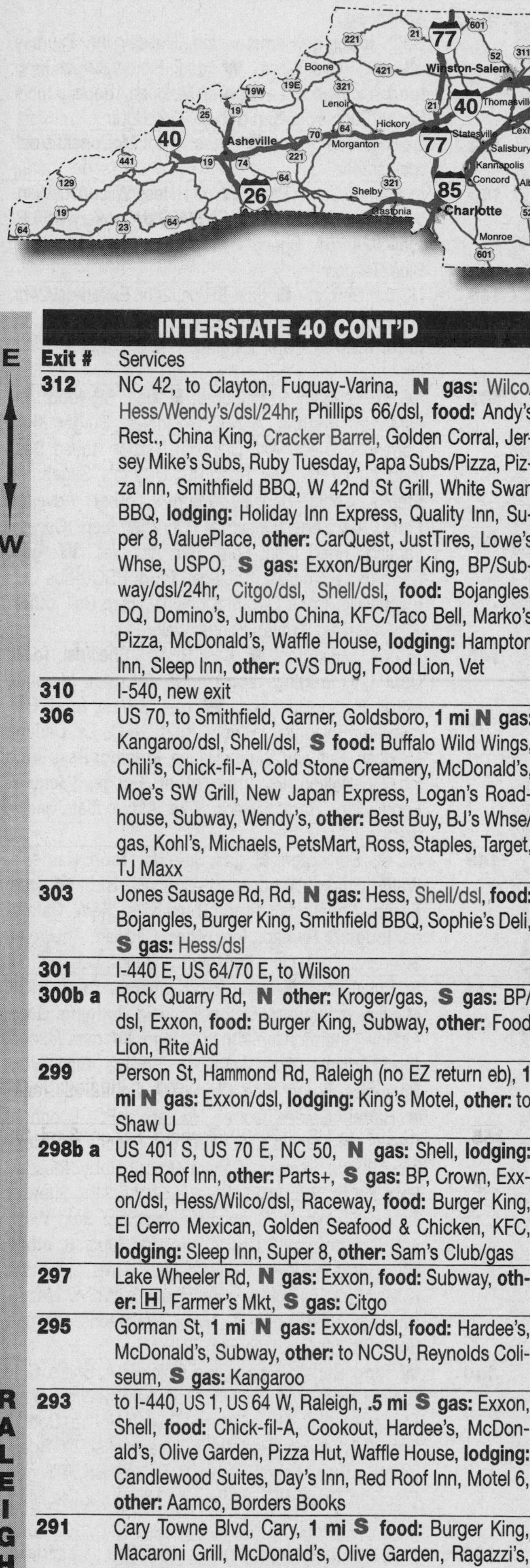

INTERSTATE 40 CONT'D

E ↕ W

Exit #	Services
312	NC 42, to Clayton, Fuquay-Varina, **N gas:** Wilco/Hess/Wendy's/dsl/24hr, Phillips 66/dsl, **food:** Andy's Rest., China King, Cracker Barrel, Golden Corral, Jersey Mike's Subs, Ruby Tuesday, Papa Subs/Pizza, Pizza Inn, Smithfield BBQ, W 42nd St Grill, White Swan BBQ, **lodging:** Holiday Inn Express, Quality Inn, Super 8, ValuePlace, **other:** CarQuest, JustTires, Lowe's Whse, USPO, **S gas:** Exxon/Burger King, BP/Subway/dsl/24hr, Citgo/dsl, Shell/dsl, **food:** Bojangles, DQ, Domino's, Jumbo China, KFC/Taco Bell, Marko's Pizza, McDonald's, Waffle House, **lodging:** Hampton Inn, Sleep Inn, **other:** CVS Drug, Food Lion, Vet
310	I-540, new exit
306	US 70, to Smithfield, Garner, Goldsboro, **1 mi N gas:** Kangaroo/dsl, Shell/dsl, **S food:** Buffalo Wild Wings, Chili's, Chick-fil-A, Cold Stone Creamery, McDonald's, Moe's SW Grill, New Japan Express, Logan's Roadhouse, Subway, Wendy's, **other:** Best Buy, BJ's Whse/gas, Kohl's, Michaels, PetsMart, Ross, Staples, Target, TJ Maxx
303	Jones Sausage Rd, Rd, **N gas:** Hess, Shell/dsl, **food:** Bojangles, Burger King, Smithfield BBQ, Sophie's Deli, **S gas:** Hess/dsl
301	I-440 E, US 64/70 E, to Wilson
300b a	Rock Quarry Rd, **N other:** Kroger/gas, **S gas:** BP/dsl, Exxon, **food:** Burger King, Subway, **other:** Food Lion, Rite Aid
299	Person St, Hammond Rd, Raleigh (no EZ return eb), **1 mi N gas:** Exxon/dsl, **lodging:** King's Motel, **other:** to Shaw U
298b a	US 401 S, US 70 E, NC 50, **N gas:** Shell, **lodging:** Red Roof Inn, **other:** Parts+, **S gas:** BP, Crown, Exxon/dsl, Hess/Wilco/dsl, Raceway, **food:** Burger King, El Cerro Mexican, Golden Seafood & Chicken, KFC, **lodging:** Sleep Inn, Super 8, **other:** Sam's Club/gas
297	Lake Wheeler Rd, **N gas:** Exxon, **food:** Subway, **other:** [H], Farmer's Mkt, **S gas:** Citgo
295	Gorman St, **1 mi N gas:** Exxon/dsl, **food:** Hardee's, McDonald's, Subway, **other:** to NCSU, Reynolds Coliseum, **S gas:** Kangaroo
293	to I-440, US 1, US 64 W, Raleigh, **.5 mi S gas:** Exxon, Shell, **food:** Chick-fil-A, Cookout, Hardee's, McDonald's, Olive Garden, Pizza Hut, Waffle House, **lodging:** Candlewood Suites, Day's Inn, Red Roof Inn, Motel 6, **other:** Aamco, Borders Books
291	Cary Towne Blvd, Cary, **1 mi S food:** Burger King, Macaroni Grill, McDonald's, Olive Garden, Ragazzi's, Taco Bell, **other:** Belk, JC Penney
290	NC 54, Cary, **1 mi N other:** Comfort Suites, **2 mi S gas:** Citgo, Exxon, Shell, **lodging:** Hampton Inn
289	to I-440, Wade Ave, to Raleigh, **N other:** [H], museum, **S** to fairgrounds
287	Harrison Ave, Cary, **N** to Wm B Umstead SP, **S gas:** BP, **food:** Bonefish Grill, Burger King, Carolina Cafe, Chick-fil-A, Maggie's Ice Cream, McDonald's, Moe's SW Grill, NY Pizza, Ruth's Chris Steaks, Starbucks, Wendy's, **lodging:** Embassy Suites, Studio+, TownePlace Suites (3mi), **other:** Colony Tire, Jiffy Lube, Sam's Club
285	Aviation Pkwy, to Morrisville, Raleigh/Durham ✈ **gas:** Sheetz/dsl, **lodging:** Hilton Garden
284	Airport Blvd, **N** to RDU ✈, **S gas:** BP/dsl, Mobil, **food:** Bojangles, Cracker Barrel, Hooters, Jersey Mike's Subs, KFC/Taco Bell, Quizno's, Schlotsky's, TX Roadhouse, Waffle House, Wendy's, **lodging:** Courtyard, Days Inn, Extended Stay America, Fairfield Inn, Hampton Inn, Holiday Inn, Holiday Inn Express, Microtel, La Quinta, Residence Inn, Sheraton, Staybridge Suites, **other:** Morrisville Outlets/famous brands/food court
283	I-540, to US 70, Aviation Pkwy
282	Page Rd, **S food:** Arby's, Bojangles, Jimmy John's, McDonald's, Starbucks, **lodging:** Comfort Suites, Hilton, Sheraton, Sleep Inn, Wingate Inn, **other:** World Trade Ctr
281	Miami Blvd, **N lodging:** Marriott, Wyndham Garden, **S gas:** BP, Shell, **food:** Arby's, Bojangles, Quizno's, Randy's Pizza, Rudino's Grill, Subway, Wendy's, Wok'n Grill, **lodging:** Extended Stay Deluxe, Holiday Inn Express, Homewood Suites, **other:** Atlantic Tire
280	Davis Dr, **N** to Research Triangle, **S lodging:** Radisson
279b a	NC 147, Durham Fwy, to Durham, **N** [H]
278	NC 55, to NC 54, World Trade Ctr, Apex, Foreign Trade Zone 93, **N gas:** Citgo, **food:** Sansui Grill, Waffle House, **lodging:** Best Value Inn, Comfort Inn, Doubletree, La Quinta, Red Roof Inn, **S gas:** Exxon/dsl, Mobil/dsl (1mi), **food:** Arby's, Backyard BBQ, Bojangles, Chick-fil-A, Cpt D's, El Dorado Mexican, Golden Corral, Hardee's, McDonald's, Oh'Brian's, Papa John's, Pizza Hut, Quizno's, Starbucks, Subway, Taco Bell, Wendy's, Zorba's Grill, **lodging:** Candlewood Suites, Courtyard, Crossland Suites, Homestead Suites,

RALEIGH

NC

E ↕ W

CHAPEL HILL

NC

INTERSTATE 40 CONT'D

Exit #	Services
278	Continued Residence Inn, **other:** Aamco, Alltune/Lube, AutoZone, BigLots, CVS Drug, $Tree, Food Lion, Jiffy Lube, tires
276	Fayetteville Rd, **N gas:** Circle K/dsl, Exxon/dsl, **food:** McDonald's, Orient Garden, Quizno's, Ruby Tuesday, Rudino's Pizza, Souper Salad, Starbucks, Waffle House, Wendy's, Wing Stop, **other:** Harris-Teeter, Kroger, Walgreens, to NC Central U, **S food:** Carino's Italian, Chili's, Cold Stone Creamery, Melting Pot, Moe's SW Grill, PF Chang's, Starbucks, Ted's Mt Grill, **lodging:** Hilton Garden, **other:** Belks, Best Buy, Macy's, JC Penney, Nordstrom's, Old Navy, Sears/auto, mall
274	NC 751, to Jordan Lake, **1-2 mi N gas:** BP, **food:** Burger King, McDonald's, Waffle House, Wendy's, **S gas:** BP, **food:** Chick-fil-A, Subway
273	NC 54, to Durham, UNC-Chapel Hill, **N gas:** Shell/dsl, **S gas:** BP, Shell/dsl, **food:** Hardee's, Nantucket Cafe, New China, **lodging:** Courtyard (2mi), Hampton Inn, Holiday Inn Express, **other:** vet
270	US 15, US 501, Chapel Hill, Durham, **N food:** Bob Evans, Carrabbas, Dickey's BBQ, Firehouse Subs, Jason's Deli, Kanki Japanese, Lonestar Steaks, Longhorn Steaks, Moes' SW Grill, Outback Steaks, Philly Steaks, Reb Robin, Starbucks, Subway, **lodging:** Comfort Inn, Homewood Suites, Springhill Suites, Staybridge Suites, **other:** H, Barnes&Noble, Best Buy, $Tree, Home Depot, Kohl's, Kroger, Marshall's, Michael's, Old Navy, Petsmart, Saab, Walmart, to Duke U, **S gas:** Exxon, **food:** Applebee's, Boston Mkt, Golden Corral, Hardee's, La Hacienda Mexican, McDonald's, Subway, Wendy's, **lodging:** Hampton Inn, Red Roof Inn, Residence Inn, Sheraton, **other:** Acura, Advance Parts, BMW, Borders Books, Chevrolet, Food Lion, Lowe's Whse, Subaru
266	NC 86, to Chapel Hill, **2 mi S gas:** BP, Exxon, Wilco/Hess/dsl, **food:** Pop's Pizza, Quizno's, Subway
263	New Hope Church Rd
261	Hillsborough, **1.5 mi N gas:** BP, Citgo/dsl, Shell, **food:** Hardee's, KFC/Taco Bell, McDonald's, Subway, Waffle House, Wendy's, **lodging:** Holiday Inn Express, Microtel
259	I-85 N, to Durham

I-40 and I-85 run together 30 mi. See Interstate 85 Exits 131-161.

Exit #	Services
161	to US 70 E, NC 86 N
160	Efland, **W gas:** Exxon/dsl
158	**weigh sta both lanes**
157	Buckhorn Rd, **E gas:** BP/dsl, Petro/Mobil/Iron Skillet/dsl/scales/24hr/@, **W gas:** PopShoppe
154	Mebane-Oaks Rd, **E gas:** Murphy USA, Shell/dsl/24hr, Sheetz/dsl, **food:** Andy's Rest., Ciao Pizza, Subway, **other:** $Tree, Walmart SuperCtr/24hr, **W gas:** BP, Hess/Wilco/dsl, Shell/dsl/24hr, **food:** Biscuitville, Bojangles, La Fiesta Mexican, McDonald's, Quizno's, Roma Pizza, Sake Japanese, Stir King, Waffle House, **lodging:** Budget Inn, **other:** Advance Parts, AutoZone, CVS Drug, Lowe's Foods, Vet
153	NC 119, Mebane, **E gas:** BP/KFC/Taco Bell/Pizza Hut, **food:** Cracker Barrel, Hibachi Rest., Jersey Mike's, Overtime Rest., Ruby Tuesday, Smithfield's

BURLINGTON

Exit #	Services
153	Continued BBQ, **lodging:** Hampton Inn, Holiday Inn Express, **other:** Lowe's Whse, **W gas:** Exxon/Burger King, **food:** Domino's, La Cocina Mexican, Papa John's, Sonic, Subway, **other:** Curves, Food Lion
152	Trollingwood Rd, **E gas:** Pilot/McDonald's/dsl/scales/24hr
150	to Roxboro, Haw River, **W gas:** Hess/Wilco/DQ/Wendy's/dsl/scales/24hr, ***FLYING J***/Cookery/dsl/LP/scales/24hr/@, SpeedCo, **lodging:** Days Inn, **other:** Blue Beacon
148	NC 54, Graham, **E gas:** BP/dsl/24hr, Exxon/dsl/24hr, QP, **food:** Waffle House, **lodging:** Comfort Suites, **W food:** MexAm Cafe, **lodging:** Ember's Motel, Travel Inn
147	NC 87, Graham, to Pittsboro, **E gas:** BP, **food:** AnnaMaria's Pizzeria, Arby's, Bojangles, Burger King, Domino's, Great Wall Chinese, Harbor House Seafood, Lucky Bamboo, Pizza Hut, Quizno's, Sagebrush Steaks, Sonic, Subway, Wendy's, **other:** Advance Parts, AutoZone, Chevrolet, Chrysler/Jeep, Curves, Family$, Food Lion, Ford, Rite Aid, Vet, **W gas:** Citgo/dsl, Exxon/dsl, Shell/dsl, **food:** BBQ&Ribs Co., Biscuitville, Cook Out, McDonald's, Taco Bell, **other:** H, CVS Drug, Lowe's Foods, Walgreens
145	NC 49, Burlington, **E gas:** BP/dsl, Shell/dsl, **food:** Capt D's, **lodging:** Econolodge, Microtel, Motel 6, **other:** Harley-Davidson, **W gas:** BP/dsl, **food:** Biscuitville, Bojangles, Burger King, KFC, La Cabana Mexican, Subway, Waffle House, **lodging:** Best Value Inn, Quality Inn, Royal Inn, **other:** Dodge, $General, Food Lion, Radio Shack, Rite Aid, outlets/famous brands
143	NC 62, Burlington, **E gas:** Sav-Way, **food:** Hardee's, Waffle House, Wendy's, to Alamance Bfd, **W gas:** Exxon, Sheetz/dsl, **food:** Biscuitville, K&W Cafeteria, **lodging:** Ramada Inn, **other:** Cadillac, Chevrolet, $General, Food Lion, Ford, Home Depot, Vet
141	to Burlington, **E gas:** BP, Kangaroo, **food:** IHOP, Mayflower Seafood, Outback Steaks, **lodging:** Comfort Inn, Hampton Inn, **other:** Nissan, **W gas:** Texaco, **food:** Amante Pizza, Applebee's, Arby's, Biscuitville, Bojangles, Burger King, Chick-fil-A, Cook Out, Cracker Barrel, Golden Corral, Hooters, KFC, Longhorn Steaks, McDonald's, O'Charley's, Panchero's Mexican, Panda Express, Panera Bread, Ruby Tuesday, Sal's Italian, Starbucks, Steak'n Shake/24hr, Subway, Taco Bell, Wholly Guacamole, **lodging:** Best Western, Country Inn&Suites, Courtyard, Super 8, **other:** H, Books-a-Million, Buick/GMC, $Tree, Hyundai, K-Mart/gas, Lincoln/Mercury, Lowe's Whse, Mazda, Rite Aid, Sears/auto, TJ Maxx, Walgreens, Walmart SuperCtr/24hr, mall, to Elon Coll
140	**W food:** Buffalo Wing Wings, Chick-fil-A, Chili's, Cold Stone Creamery, Little Italy, McDonald's, Mimi's Cafe, Moe's SW Grill, Olive Garden, Peking House, Qdoba, Red Bowl Asian, Red Robin, Starbucks, TX Roadhouse, **other:** Barnes&Noble, Belk, Best Buy, Dillard's, Discount Tire, GNC, JC Penney, Michael's, Old Navy, Petsmart, Ross, Target
139mm	**rest area both lanes, full facilities, litter barrels, vending**

INTERSTATE 40 CONT'D

E ↕ W

Exit #	Services
138	NC 61, Gibsonville, **W gas:** TA/BP/Burger King/Popeye's/dsl/scales/@
135	Rock Creek Dairy Rd, **W gas:** Citgo, Exxon, **food:** Bojangles, Ciao Pizza,China 1, Domino's, Guacamole Mexican, Jersey Mike's Subs, McDonald's, **other:** Curves, CVS Drug, $General, Food Lion, Midtown Drug, Vet
132	Mt Hope Church Rd, **E gas:** Citgo/Subway/dsl, **food:** Pascalli's Pizza, **W gas:** Shell/dsl, Hess/Wendy's/dsl/24hr, **lodging:** Hampton Inn
131to	US 70, Loop 85
129	Youngsmill Rd, **W lodging:** Holiday Inn Express (3mi)
128	Alamance Church Rd
122c b a	US 220, to Greensboro, Asheboro (from sb)
220	US 220 S, to Greensboro
219	Loop 85 N, US 29 N, US 70 E, Greensboro
218	I-85 S, US 29 S, US 70 W, High Point, Charlotte
214	Wendover Ave, **N food:** Applebee's, Arby's, Biscuitville, Bojangles, Calabash Seafood, Chick-fil-A, Chipotle Mexican, Cracker Barrel, Fuddrucker's, Golden Corral, IHOP, Imperial Gourmet, Jimmy John's, Kabuto Japanese, La Hacienda Mexican, Logan's Roadhouse, Longhorn Steaks, McDonald's, O'Charley's, Panda Express, Papa John's, Quizno's, Red Lobster, Steak'n Shake, Subway, TGIFriday, Taco Bell, Tripp's Rest., Vilarosa Italian, Wendy's, **lodging:** Best Western, Courtyard, Hyatt Place, La Quinta, Lodge America, SpringHill Suites, Suburban Lodge, Wingate Inn, **other:** Best Buy, Goodyear, Home Depot, Hummer, Kohl's, K-Mart/gas, Lowe's Whse, Macy's, Petsmart, Ross, Sam's Club/gas, Target, Walmart SuperCtr/24hr
212b a	Loop 40, US 241 S, to Bryan Blvd, **N** to ✈
211	Gallimore Dairy Rd, **N other:** Freightliner
210	NC 68, to High Point, Piedmont Triad, **N gas:** Shell, **food:** Arby's, **lodging:** Days Inn, Embassy Suites, Fairview Inn, Homewood Suites, Sleep Inn, Wyndham Garden, **other:** Ford Trucks, Kenworth, to airport, **S gas:** Exxon/dsl, **food:** Bojangles, Fatz Cafe, McDonald's, Pizza Hut/Taco Bell, Ruby Tuesday, Shoney's, Subway, Wendy's, **lodging:** Best Western, Candlewood Suites, Comfort Suites, Courtyard, Extended Stay Deluxe, Fairfield Inn, Hampton Inn, Holiday Inn Express, Motel 6, Quality Inn, Red Roof Inn, Residence Inn
208	Sandy Ridge Rd, **N gas:** Wilco/Hess/dsl, **other:** Camping World RV Ctr, **S gas:** Citgo/dsl, **other:** Farmer's Mkt, Out Of Doors Mart/Airstream
206	Lp 40 (from wb), to Kernersville, Winston-Salem, downtown
203	NC 66, to Kernersville, **N gas:** Citgo/McDonald's/dsl, Exxon/Subway, Hess/dsl, **food:** Capt Tom's Seafood, Clark's BBQ, Out West Steaks, Wendy's, **lodging:** Sleep Inn, **other:** Ford, Merchant Tire/repair, **S gas:** Shell/dsl, **lodging:** Holiday Inn Express
201	Union Cross Rd, **N gas:** BP, Citgo/dsl, QM/dsl, **food:** Blue Naples Pizza, Burger King, China Café, **other:** CVS Drug, Food Lion
196	US 311 S, to High Point

GREENSBORO

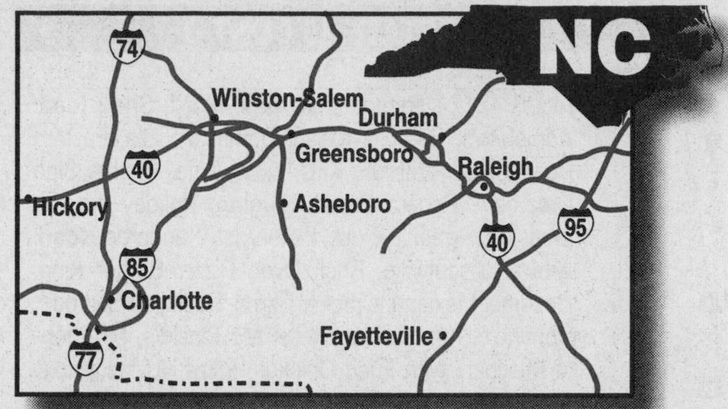

WINSTON • SALEM

Exit #	Services
195	US 311 N, NC 109, to Thomasville, **S gas:** Citgo, Wilco/Hess/dsl
193b a	US 52, NC 8, to Lexington, **S gas:** Hess/dsl, Shell, **food:** Hardee's
193c	Silas Creek Pkwy (from eb), same as 192
192	NC 150, to Peters Creek Pkwy, **N gas:** Wilco/Hess, Texaco, **food:** Bojangles, Burger King, Checker's, China Buffet, China Wok, Hong Kong Buffet, IHOP, KFC, Little Caesar's, Mayflower Seafood, Monterrey Mexican, Sonic, Subway, Taco Bell, Tokyo Japanese, **lodging:** Innkeeper, **other:** Acura/Subaru/Isuzu, Audi, AutoZone, BigLots, $General, $Tree, Ford, Hyundai, Lincoln/Mercury, Mazda, NAPA, Office Depot, Radio Shack, Rite Aid, VW, **S gas:** BP, QM, **food:** Arby's, Baskin-Robbins/Dunkin Donuts, Cook Out, McDonald's, K&W Cafeteria, Pizza Hut, Waffle House, Wendy's, **lodging:** Holiday Inn Express, **other:** Advance Parts, BMW/Mini, CVS Drug, Food Lion, Hancock Fabrics, Honda, K-Mart, Mock Tire, Toyota
190	Hanes Mall Blvd (from wb, no re-entry), **N food:** Chipotle Mexican, Jimmy John's, McDonald's, O'Charley's, Quizno's, Ruby Tuesday, TGIFriday, Tripp's Rest., **lodging:** Days Inn, Quality Inn, **other:** H, Belk, Dillard's, Firestone/auto, JC Penney, Macy's, Marshall's, Sears/auto, mall, same as 189, **S food:** ChuckeCheese, Lonestar Steaks, Outback Steaks, Starbucks, Subway, **lodging:** Comfort Suites, Microtel, **other:** Office Depot
189	US 158, Stratford Rd, Hanes Mall Blvd, **N gas:** BP, Exxon, **food:** Bojangles, Chili's, Golden Corral, Olive Garden, Red Lobster, Taco Bell, TX Roadhouse, **lodging:** Courtyard, Fairfield Inn, **other:** H, Belk, Chevrolet, Dillard's, JC Penney, Jo-Ann Fabrics, Macy's, Michael's, Sears/auto, Walgreens, mall, **S gas:** BP, Shell, **food:** Applebee's, Bleu Rest., Buffalo Wild Wings, Burger King, Chick-fil-A, Dynasty Buffet, 5 Guys Burgers, Fuddruckers, Hooters, Jason's Deli, Jimmy's Seafood, KFC/LJ Silver, Longhorn Steaks, Macaroni Grill, Moe's SW Grill, Panera Bread, Subway, TX Land&Cattle, Wild Wing Cafe, **lodging:** Extended Stay America, Hampton Inn, Hilton Garden, La Quinta, Sleep Inn, SpringHill Suites, **other:** Barnes&Noble, Best Buy, Costco/gas, CVS Drug, Discount Tire, $Tree, Food Lion, Home Depot, Kohl's, Lowe's Whse, Petsmart, Ross, Sam's Club, Target
188	US 421, to Yadkinville, to WFU (no EZ wb return), Winston-Salem, **1/2mi N off US 421 gas:** BP, Exxon, Kangaroo, Shell, **food:** Arby's, Boston Mkt, Burger King, McDonald's, Starbucks, Subway, Waffle House, Wendy's, **other:** CarMax, Mercedes, Walmart SuperCtr/24hr

NC

INTERSTATE 40 CONT'D

E ↕ W — CLEMMONS — MOCKSVILLE — STATESVILLE — HICKORY

Exit #	Services
184	to US 421, Clemmons, **N gas:** Mobil, Shell, **food:** Applebee's, Bambini Italian, Donato's Pizza, Eastern Pearl Chinese, IHOP, KFC, K&W Cafe, Marble Slab Creamery, Panera Bread, **lodging:** Holiday Inn Express, **S gas:** BP/dsl, Exxon/dsl, Kangaroo, **food:** Arby's, Biscuitville, Brick Oven Pizza, Burger King, Cozumel Mexican, Cracker Barrel, Dockside Seafood, Domino's, Kimono Japanese, McDonald's, Mi Pueblo Mexican, Mtn Fried Chicken, Pizza Hut, Quizno's, Ruby Tuesday, Sagebrush Steaks, Sonic, Starbucks, Subway, Taco Bell, Time to Eat Cafe, Waffle House, Wendy's, **lodging:** Super 8, Village Inn, **other:** Advance Parts, BigLots, CVS Drug, $Tree, K-Mart, Lowe's Foods, Merchant Tire, Parts+, Southern Mkt, Staples, TrueValue, Walgreens, USPO, Vet
182	Bermuda Run (from wb, no re-entry), Tanglewood, **S food:** Chang Thai, Lee's Chinese, Libby Hill Chicken&Seafood, Papa John's, **other:** Harris-Teeter
182mm	Yadkin River
180	NC 801, Tanglewood, **N food:** Capt's Galley Seafood, Cicciones Rest., Domino's, Saratogo Steaks, Subway, **other:** Lowe's Foods, Rite Aid, **S gas:** BP/McDonald's/dsl, Hess/dsl, **food:** Bojangles, DQ, Jimmy's Greek, Venezia Italian, View Chinese, Wendy's, **other:** Ace Hardware, CVS Drug, $General, Food Lion, Radio Shack, Walgreens, Vet
177mm	**rest areas both lanes, full [handicapped] facilities, [phone], vending, [picnic], litter barrels, petwalk**
174	Farmington Rd, **N gas:** Shell/dsl, **other:** antiques, **S other:** vineyards
170	US 601, Mocksville, **N gas:** Citgo, Murphy USA/dsl, Pure/Horn's Rest/DQ/Jersey Mike's/dsl/24hr, **food:** JinJin Chinese, La Carreta Mexican, Moe's BurgerHouse, Subway, **other:** $Tree, RV Superstore, Walmart SuperCtr, **S gas:** BP/dsl, Exxon, Shell/Taco Bell, **food:** Arby's, Bojangles, Burger King, Chile Verde, China Grill, KFC, Marco's Pizza, McDonald's, Pier 601, Pizza Hut, Sagebrush Steaks, Shiki Japanese, Wendy's, **lodging:** Comfort Inn, HighWay Inn, Quality Inn, Scottish Inn, **other:** [H], Advance Parts, $General, Ford/Mercury, Lowe's Whse, Walgreens, USPO, Vet
168	US 64, to Mocksville, **N gas:** Exxon/dsl, **other:** Lake Myers RV Resort (3mi), **S gas:** BP/dsl, **other:** [H]
162	US 64, Cool Springs, **N other:** Lake Myers RV Resort (5mi), **S gas:** Shell, **other:** KOA
161mm	S Yadkin River
154	to US 64, Old Mocksville Rd, **N** [H], **S gas:** Citgo/dsl, **food:** Jaybee's Hotdogs, **other:** repair/tires
153	US 64 (from eb), **1/2 mi S gas:** Citgo/dsl, **food:** Jaybee's Hotdogs, **other:** repair/tires
152b a	I-77, S to Charlotte, N to Elkin
151	US 21, E Statesville, **N gas:** Hess/Wilco/24hr, Texaco/dsl, **food:** Applebee's, Bojangles, Chick-fil-A, Chili's, Cook Out, Cracker Barrel, Dunkin Donuts, Golden Corral, Hooters, Jack-in-the-Box, KFC, K&W Cafeteria, Little China, Logan's Roadhouse, McDonald's, Mi Pueblo Café, Pizza Hut/Taco Bell, Quizno's, Red Lobster, Ruby Tuesday, Sagebrush Steaks, Sakura Japanese, Sorrento Pizza, Wendy's, Zaxby's, **lodging:**
151	Continued Days Inn, Sleep Inn, **other:** Advance Parts, Aldi Foods, AutoZone, BigLots, Bi-Lo, Cadillac/Chevrolet, Chrysler/Jeep, Curves, CVS Drug, $Tree, GNC, Home Depot, Lowe's Whse, Radio Shack, Russell Stover, Staples, Tire Kingdom, Walmart SuperCtr, **S gas:** Exxon, **food:** Lonestar Steaks, Ming Court, Sonic, Waffle House, **lodging:** Econolodge, Holiday Inn Express, Masters Inn, Quality Inn, **other:** URGENT CARE, $General
150	NC 115, Statesville, **N gas:** BP/dsl, Citgo, Sheetz, Shell/Subway, **food:** Amalfi's Italian, Little Caesar's, Ol'Bob's BBQ, **other:** CVS Drug, Food Lion, Fred's Drug, museum
148	US 64, NC 90, W Statesville, **N gas:** Citgo/dsl, QP, Shell, **food:** Arby's, BoxCar Grille, Burger King, McDonald's, Shiki Japanese, Subway, Village Inn Pizza, **lodging:** Economy Inn, **other:** CVS Drug, $General, Ingles Foods
146	Stamey Farm Rd
144	Old Mountain Rd, **N gas:** BP/dsl/repair, **food:** Troy's Rest., **S gas:** BP/dsl, Shell/dsl
143mm	**weigh sta both lanes**
141	Sharon School Rd, **N gas:** Citgo
140mm	Catawba River
138	Oxford School Rd, to Catawba, **N gas:** Exxon/dsl/24hr
136mm	**rest areas both lanes, full [handicapped] facilities, [phone], [picnic], vending, litter barrels, petwalk**
135	Claremont, **S gas:** Shell, **food:** BoxCar Grille, Burger King, Hannah's BBQ, Raffie's Subs, **lodging:** Super 8, **other:** Carolina Coach RV Ctr, $General, Lowe's Foods, TCS LP
133	Rock Barn Rd, **N gas:** Shell/dsl, **S gas:** Wilco/Hess/Stuckey's/Subway/Godfather's Pizza/dsl/scales/24hr
132	to NC 16, Taylorsville, **N gas:** BP, Shell/dsl, **food:** Burger King, Zaxby's, **lodging:** Holiday Inn Express, **other:** Walmart SuperCtr
130	Old US 70, **N food:** Domino's, Jack-in-the-Box, Subway, **other:** $General, K-Mart, NAPA, Vet, **S gas:** Citgo, Pure, Texaco, **other:** repair, USPO
128	US 321, Fairgrove Church Rd, Hickory, **N gas:** BP, Shell, Solo/dsl, **food:** McDonald's, Waffle House, **other:** [H], to Catawba Valley Coll, **S gas:** Citgo/dsl, **food:** Bennett's Smokehouse, Harbor Inn Seafood, Shoney's, Wendy's, **lodging:** Days Inn, Ramada Inn, **other:** Chrysler/Dodge/Jeep, GMC/Volvo
126	to US 70, NC 155, **S gas:** Citgo, Exxon, Shell, **food:** Applebee's, Bob Evans, IHOP, Libby Hill Seafood, McDonald's, O'Charley's, Olive Garden, Taco Bell, Subway, **lodging:** Holiday Inn Express, **other:** Barnes&Noble, $Tree, Hickory Furniture Mart, Lowe's Whse, Michael's, Office Depot, Sam's Club, TJ Maxx, Walmart SuperCtr/24hr
125	Hickory, **N gas:** Raceway, **food:** Bojangles, Golden Corral, Quizno's, Rancho Viejo Mexican, Starbucks, Texas Roadhouse, Tripp's Rest., Yewei Guan Chinese, **lodging:** Red Roof Inn, **other:** Advance Parts, BMW/Mercedes, **S gas:** Hess, Shell/dsl, **food:** Arby's, Atlanta Bread, Carraba's, Chick-fil-A, ChuckeCheese, CiCi's, Cracker Barrel, Firebonz Rest., Fuddrucker's, Hooters, Jack-in-the-Box, Judge's BBQ, J&S

INTERSTATE 40 CONT'D

E ↕ W

Exit #	Services
125	Continued Cafeteria, KFC, Kobe Japanese, Longhorn Steaks, Mamma's Pizza, Outback Steaks, Panda Express, Quizno's, Red Lobster, Ruby Tuesday, Waffle House, Wendy's, Zaxby's, **lodging:** Comfort Suites, Courtyard, Crowne Plaza, Fairfield Inn, Hampton Inn, Sleep Inn, **other:** Aldi Foods, Belk, Best Buy, Bottom$ Foods, Carmax, Dillards, $Tree, Ford, Hancock Fabrics, Harley-Davidson, Home Depot, Honda, JC Penney, Kohl's, Marshall's, Mazda, Mitsubishi, Office Depot, Old Navy, O'Reilly Parts, Petsmart, Porsche/VW, Scion/Toyota, Sears/auto, Suzuki, Target, Tire Kingdom, TJ Maxx, Tuesday Morning, dsl repair, mall
123	US 70/321, to NC 127, Hickory
121	Long View, **N other:** Kenworth
119b a	Hildebran, **N gas:** Shell, **food:** Bojangles, Hardee's, **other:** $General
118	Old NC 10, **N gas:** Pure, Shell/dsl
116	Icard, **S gas:** Marathon/McDonald's/dsl, **food:** Burger King, Granny's Kitchen, **lodging:** Icard Inn/rest.
113	Connelly Springs, **N gas:** Citgo, Southern Star/dsl, **food:** Subway, **other:** H, CVS Drug, Ford/Hyundai
112	Mineral Springs Mtn Rd, Valdese
111	Valdese
107	NC 114, to Drexel
106	Bethel Rd, **S gas:** Exxon/dsl, **lodging:** Economy Inn
105	NC 18, Morganton, **N gas:** Wilco/dsl, **food:** Abele's Rest., Arby's, Capt D's, Coffeehouse, Fatz Café, Harbor Inn Seafood, McDonald's, Sonic, Uptown BBQ, Wendy's, Zaxby's, Zeko's Italian, **lodging:** Hampton Inn, **other:** H, Cadillac/Chevrolet/GMC/Pontiac, **S gas:** Shell/dsl, Texaco, **food:** El Paso Mexican, Sagebrush Steaks, Waffle House, **lodging:** Holiday Inn/rest., Plaza Inn, Sleep Inn, **other:** to South Mtns SP
104	Enola Rd, **S gas:** Citgo, **food:** Chick-fil-A, Jersey Mike's Subs, **other:** Belk, BigLots, $Tree, Food Lion, Staples, st patrol
103	US 64, Morganton, **N gas:** Exxon/dsl/24hr, **food:** Allison's Rest., Village Inn Pizza, **lodging:** Days Inn, **S gas:** Marathon, RaceWay, **food:** Butch's BBQ, Checker's, Denny's, Dragon Chinese, Hardee's, KFC, Subway, Taco Bell, **lodging:** Comfort Inn, **other:** Clarks Tire, Food Lion, GNC, Ingles Foods, Lowe's Whse, Radio Shack, Walmart/drugs
100	Jamestown Rd, **N gas:** BP/dsl/24hr, **food:** Waffle Shop, **other:** Chrysler/Dodge/Jeep, Ford/Lincoln/Mercury, **2 mi N food:** KFC, Taco Bell, **lodging:** Eagle Motel
98	Causby Rd, to Glen Alpine, **S** B&B/food
96	Kathy Rd
94	Dysartsville Rd
90	Nebo, **N gas:** Country Cookin'/dsl/rest, **other:** to Lake James SP, **S gas:** BP/dsl, **other:** Springs Creek RV Ctr
86	NC 226, to Spruce Pine, Marion, **N gas:** Exxon, Love's/Subway/Godfather's/dsl/scales/24hr, **food:** Hardee's, KFC, Waffle House, **other:** Jellystone RV Park (1mi)
85	US 221, Marion, **N lodging:** Hampton Inn, **other:** to Mt Mitchell SP, **S gas:** Shell/dsl/24hr, **food:** Legends Roadhouse, **lodging:** Days Inn, Super 8

MORGANTON

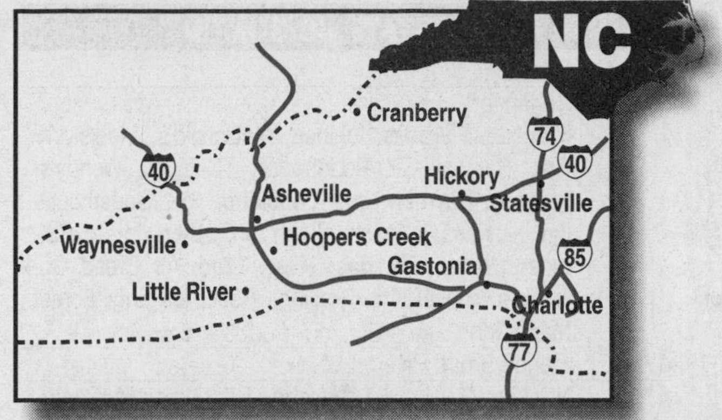

Exit #	Services
83	Ashworth Rd
82mm	**rest area both lanes, full ♿ facilities, ☎, 🛆, vending, litter barrels, petwalk**
81	81 Sugar Hill Rd, to Marion, **N gas:** BP/dsl, **other:** H Chrysler/Dodge/Jeep, **S gas:** Exxon/rest/dsl/24hr
76mm	Catawba River
75	Parker Padgett Rd, **S gas:** Exxon/Stuckey's/DQ/dsl
73	Old Fort, **N gas:** BP/dsl, **food:** Hardee's, **lodging:** B&B, **other:** Mtn Gateway Museum, NAPA, **S gas:** Super Test/dsl, **food:** McDonald's, **other:** Auto+
72	US 70 (from eb), Old Fort, **N** B&B
71mm	Pisgah Nat Forest, eastern boundary
67.5mm	**truck rest area eb**
66	Ridgecrest, **N lodging:** B&B
65	(from wb), to Black Mountain, Black Mtn Ctr
64	NC 9, Black Mountain, **N gas:** Exxon, Shell/Subway/24hr, **food:** Pizza Hut, **other:** BiLo/café, **S gas:** BP/dsl, **food:** Denny's, Huddle House, KFC, McDonald's, Phil's BBQ, Taco Bell, Wendy's, **lodging:** Comfort Inn, **other:** Ingles Foods/gas, Rite Aid
63mm	Swannanoa River
59	Swannanoa, **N gas:** BP/Subway, Exxon/dsl, **food:** Athens Pizza, Burger King, Okies Dokies Smokehouse, **other:** Ace Hardware, Harley-Davidson, Ingles Foods/gas, KOA (2mi), Miles RV Ctr/Park, to Warren Wilson Coll, USPO, **S other:** Mama Gertie's Camping
55	E Asheville, US 70, **N gas:** BP, Citgo/Subway, Mobil, **food:** Arby's, Bojangles, Cocula Mexican, Waffle House, Zaxby's, **lodging:** B&B, Days Inn, Holiday Inn, Motel 6, Quality Inn, **other:** VA H, Go Groceries, Top's RV park, to Mt Mitchell SP, Folk Art Ctr
53b a	I-240 W, US 74, to Asheville, Bat Cave, **N food:** Burger King, China Buffet, Fat Buddy's BBQ, KFC, J&S Cafeteria, McDonald's, Subway, **lodging:** Ramada Inn, **other:** Advance Parts, BiLo, CVS Drug, $General, Hamrick's, Hancock Fabrics, **1-2 mi N on US 74... gas:** BP, Citgo, Exxon/dsl, **food:** Applebee's, Burger King, Carrabba's, Chili's, Chick-fil-A, Damon's, IHOP, O'Charley's, Olive Garden, Red Lobster, Subway, Waffle House, **lodging:** Courtyard, Day's Inn, Econolodge, Extended Stay America, Hampton Inn, Ramada Ltd, **other:** Barnes& Noble, Best Buy, Dillard's, Home Depot, Ingles Foods, K-Mart, Lowes Whse, Michael's, Office Depot,, Radio Shack, Ross, Sears/auto, mall, **S gas:** BP/dsl/LP, **food:** Subway, **other:** to Blue Ridge Pkwy
51	US 25A, Sweeten Creek Rd, **S food:** Subway, **lodging:** Brookstone Lodging
50	US 25, Asheville, **N gas:** BP, CitiStop, Shell/dsl, **food:** A&W/LJ Silver, Arby's, Asaka Japanese, Chapala

ASHEVILLE

NC

INTERSTATE 40 CONT'D

Exit #	Services
50	Continued Mexican, Hardees, Ichiban, McDonald's, Moe's SW Grill, Subway, TX Roadhouse, TGIFriday, Wendy's, **lodging:** Baymont Inn, Doubletree Inn, Guesthouse Inn, Howard Johnson, Sleep Inn, **other:** [H], to Biltmore House, **S gas:** Hess, **food:** Atl Bread Co, Huddle House/24hr, Province Rest., **lodging:** Forest Manor Inn
47mm	French Broad River
47	NC 191, W Asheville, **N other:** Bear Creek RV Camping, **S food:** Moose Cafe, **other:** Farmer's Mkt, **2 mi S lodging:** Comfort Inn, Country Inn&Suites, Fairfield Inn, Hampton Inn, Holiday Inn Express, Super 8
46b a	I-26 & I-240 E, **2 mi N** multiple services from I-240
44	US 19, US 23, W Asheville, **N gas:** BP, Exxon, Hess/dsl, Shell/24hr, **food:** Applebee's, Asiana Buffet, Burger King, Country Kitchen, Cracker Barrel, El Chapala Mexican, Fatz Cafe, Hardees, IHOP, Pizza Hut, Waffle House, Wendy's, **lodging:** Comfort Inn, Country Inn&Suites, Ramada Inn, Red Roof Inn, Rodeway Inn, Sleep Inn, Whispering Pines Motel, **other:** Chevrolet, Chrysler/Jeep, Family$, Ingles Foods, Lowe's Whse, Mazda/Mercedes, **S food:** McDonald's, Shoney's, **lodging:** Budget Motel, Holiday Inn, ValuePlace Inn, **other:** BiLo Foods, CVS Drug, Home Depot
41mm	**weigh sta both lanes**
37	Candler, **N gas:** BP, TA/Buckhorn Rest./dsl/scales/24hr/@, **other:** Goodyear, tires, **S gas:** Exxon/dsl, **lodging:** Days Inn, Plantation Motel, **other:** KOA
33	Newfound Rd, to US 74, **S** gas
31	rd 215, Canton, **N food:** Sagebrush Steaks, **lodging:** Days Inn, **S gas:** BP/dsl, Chevron/DQ, Shell/dsl, **food:** Arby's, Burger King, McDonald's, Pizza Hut (2mi), Subway (1mi), Taco Bell, Waffle House, **lodging:** Comfort Inn, **other:** Ford, Ingles Foods, RV/truck repair
27	US 19/23, to Waynesville, Great Smokey Mtn Expswy, **3 mi S gas:** Shell/Burger King, **food:** Shoney's, Subway, Taco Bell, **lodging:** Super 8, **other:** [H], Food Lion, GNC, Lowe's Whse, to WCU (25mi)
24	NC 209, to Lake Junaluska, **N gas:** Pilot/Subway/dsl/scales/24hr/@, **lodging:** Midway Motel, **S gas:** Shell/cafe/dsl/24hr, **other:** [H]
20	US 276, to Maggie Valley, Lake Junaluska, **S gas:** BP/dsl, Exxon/dsl, Marathon (2mi), **other:** Creekwood RV Park, Pride RV Resort, Winngray RV Park
16mm	Pigeon River
15	Fines Creek
13mm	Pisgah NF eastern boundary
10mm	**rest area both lanes, full [handicapped] facilities, [phone], vending, [picnic], litter barrels, petwalk**
7	Harmon Den
4mm	tunnel both lanes
0mm	North Carolina/Tennessee state line

INTERSTATE 77

Exit #	Services
105mm	North Carolina/Virginia state line
105mm	**Welcome Ctr sb, full [handicapped] facilities, info, [phone], vending, [picnic], litter barrels, petwalk**
103mm	**weigh sta both lanes**
101	I-74 E, to Mt Airy, Winston-Salem, Greensboro, **E lodging:** Hampton Inn, **other:** [H] (12mi)
100	NC 89, to Mt Airy, **E gas:** BP/Brintle's/rest/dsl/scales/24hr/@, Exxon/dsl, Marathon/Subway/dsl, **food:** Wagon Wheel Rest., **lodging:** Best Western, **other:** [H] (12mi), clothing outlet
93	to Dobson, Surry, **E gas:** BP/DQ/dsl, Citgo/dsl, **lodging:** Hampton Inn, Surry Inn, **other:** camping
85	NC 118, CC Camp Rd, to Elkin, **1-3 mi W gas:** Murphy Express/dsl, Neighbor's, Shell/Blimpie/Stuckey's/dsl, Wilco/Hess/dsl, **food:** Burger King, KFC, Mazzini's Italian, McDonald's, Sonic, **lodging:** Elk Inn, Fairfield Inn, **other:** AT&T, BigLots, $Tree, Food Lion, Lowe's Whse, Rite Aid, Walmart SuperCtr/Subway
83	US 21 byp, to Sparta (from nb)
82.5mm	Yadkin River
82	NC 67, Elkin, **E gas:** BP/Backyard Burger/dsl, BP/Case Outlet/dsl, Exxon/dsl, **food:** Arby's, Cracker Barrel, Jordan's Rest., **lodging:** Holiday Inn Express, **other:** Holly Ridge Camping (8mi), **W gas:** Wilco/Hess/dsl, **food:** Bojangles, Capt Galley, McDonald's, Valentino's Pizza, Waffle House, Wendy's, **lodging:** Comfort Inn, Days Inn, Hampton Inn, Rose's Motel, **other:** AutoValue Parts, Buick/GMC/Pontiac, Curves, D-Rex Drug, Food Lion, Vet
79	US 21 S, to Arlington, **E gas:** Citgo/Subway/dsl, **lodging:** Super 8, **W gas:** BP/dsl, **food:** Glenn's BBQ, **lodging:** Best Value Inn
73b a	US 421, to Winston-Salem (20mi), **E gas:** Shell/Subway/dsl (1mi), USPO
72mm	**rest area nb, full [handicapped] facilities, [phone], vending, [picnic], litter barrels, petwalk**
65	NC 901, to Union Grove, Harmony, **E other:** Van Hoy Farms Camping, **W gas:** BP/dsl, Shell/Subway/dsl/24hr, **food:** Burger Barn, **lodging:** B&B, **other:** Ace Hardware, Fiddler's Grove Camping (2mi)
63mm	**rest area sb, full [handicapped] facilities, [phone], vending, [picnic], litter barrels, petwalk**
59	Tomlin Mill Rd, **W gas:** Citgo/dsl
56.5mm	S Yadkin River
54	US 21, to Turnersburg, **E gas:** Citgo, **W gas:** Shell/dsl, **food:** Arby's, **2mi W gas:** Chick-fil-A, CookOut, Dunkin Donuts, Golden Corral, Zaxby's
51b a	I-40, E to Winston-Salem, W to Hickory
50	E Broad St, Statesville, **E gas:** BP, Citgo, Kangaroo/dsl, Shell, **food:** Arby's, Bojangles, Burger King, Charenda Mexican, CiCi's Pizza, Domino's, Golden Dragon, IHOP, Jack-in-the-Box, Little Caesar's, McDonald's, Papa John's, Pizza Hut, Shanghai Buffet, Shoney's, Starbucks, Subway, Wendy's, **lodging:** Brookwood Inn, Red Roof Inn, **other:** URGENT CARE, Ace Hardware, AT&T, Belk, Bi-Lo, $General, $Tree, Food Lion, JC Penney, JR Outlet, K-Mart, Rite Aid, Sears/auto, USPO
49b a	US 70, G Bagnal Blvd, to Statesville, **E gas:** BP, Citgo/dsl, Kangaroo, Shell, Solo, **food:** Brewsters, KFC, Outback Steaks, Rice Fun Chinese, Subway, Waffle House, **lodging:** Baymont Inn, Best Western, Courtyard, Hampton Inn, Holiday Inn/rest., Motel 6, Super 8, **other:** Camping World RV Ctr, Chrysler/Dodge/Jeep, Ford/Lincoln/Mercury, Harley-Davidson, Honda, Nissan, Scion/Toyota, **W gas:** Citgo, Exxon, **food:** Carolina BBQ, **lodging:** Best Value Inn, Microtel

INTERSTATE 77 CONT'D

N ↕ S

MOORESVILLE

Exit #	Services
45	to Troutman, Barium Springs, **E** KOA, RV Repair, **W gas:** 4 Bros (3mi)
42	US 21, NC 115, to Troutman, Oswalt, **E gas:** Hess/Wilco/Subway/dsl/scales/24hr, **food:** McDonald's, Wendy's, **other:** Lowe's Whse, **W gas:** Citgo, **food:** Arby's, **other:** to Lake Norman SP, camping
39mm	**rest area both lanes, full facilities, litter barrels, petwalk, vending**
36	NC 150, Mooresville, **E gas:** Accel/dsl, Exxon, Shell/dsl/24hr, **food:** Applebee's, Bob Evans, CiCi's Pizza, CookOut, Denny's, FatBoy's Cafe, Jack-in-the-Box, Pizza Hut, Quizno's, Sonny's BBQ, Taco Bell, Waffle House, Wendy's, **lodging:** Days Inn, Fairfield Inn, Holiday Inn Express, Ramada Ltd, **other:** URGENT CARE, AT&T, Belk, $Tree, Gander Mtn, GNC, Kohl's, Tuesday Morning, Walmart SuperCtr/Subway/24hr, **W gas:** BJ's Whse, BP/dsl, Hess, Marathon, Shell/dsl/24hr, **food:** Arby's, Baskin-Robbins/Dunkin Donuts, Bojangles, Chick-fil-A, Chili's, Cracker Barrel, Domino's, Donato's Pizza, Duckworth's Rest, 5 Guys Burgers, Golden Corral, Hardee's, Hickery Tavern Grill, Hooters, Joe Fish Rest, KFC, Kyoto Japanese, LoneStar Steaks, McAlister's Deli, McDonald's, Monterrey Mexican, O'Charley's, Panda Express, Panera Bread, Poppa's Hotdogs, Red Robin, Sonic, Starbucks, Steak'n Shake, Subway, TX Steaks, **lodging:** Hampton Inn, Sleep Inn, Super 8, Wingate Inn, **other:** Advance Parts, AutoZone, Best Buy, Bloom Foods, CVS Drug, Discount Tire, Lowe's Whse, Michael's, Old Navy, PetCo, Petsmart, Staples, Target, Tire Kingdom, Verizon, Walgreens
33	US 21 N, **E gas:** Shell, **food:** Big League Hotdogs, China Express, DQ, Jeffrey's Rest, McDonald's, Quizno's, Showmar's Rest, Starbucks, Subway, **lodging:** Hilton Garden, SpringHill Suites, TownePlace Suites, **other:** H, AT&T, **W gas:** BP, Citgo/dsl, **food:** Arby's, Baskin-Robbins/Dunkin Donuts, Sauza's Mexican, **other:** Food Lion, Lake Norman RV Resort (13mi), Vet
31	Langtree
30	Davidson, **E gas:** Exxon/dsl, **food:** Donato's Pizza, Ming's Chinese, Subway, **lodging:** Homewood Suites, **other:** Harris-Teeter, to Davidson College, **W food:** North Harbor Rest
28	US 21 S, NC 73, Cornelius, Lake Norman, **E gas:** Cashion/dsl, Citgo/24hr, **food:** Acropolis Cafe, Gilligan's Rest, **lodging:** Days Inn, Hampton Inn, **other:** NAPA, **W gas:** Texaco, **food:** Bojangles, Domino's, Dragon Buffet, Gator's Grill, HoneyBaked Ham, Jersey Mike's, KFC, Kobe Japanese, K&W Cafeteria, Mac's Grill, McAlister's Deli, McDonald's, Pizza Hut, Starbucks, Subway, Taco Bell, Waffle House,Wendy's, **lodging:** Clarion, Comfort Inn, EconoLodge, **other:** Chrysler/Dodge/Jeep, Fresh Mkt, Goodyear/auto, Rite Aid, SteinMart, Walgreens, USPO
25	NC 73, Concord, Lake Norman, **E gas:** Shell/dsl, **food:** Buffalo Pizza, Burger King, Chick-fil-A, Chili's, Donato's Pizza, Fuddrucker's, IHOP, Longhorn Steaks, McDonald's, Moe's SW Grill, Panda Express, Panera Bread, Starbucks, Wendy's, **lodging:** Country Inn&Suites, Hawthorn Suites, Quality Inn, **other:**

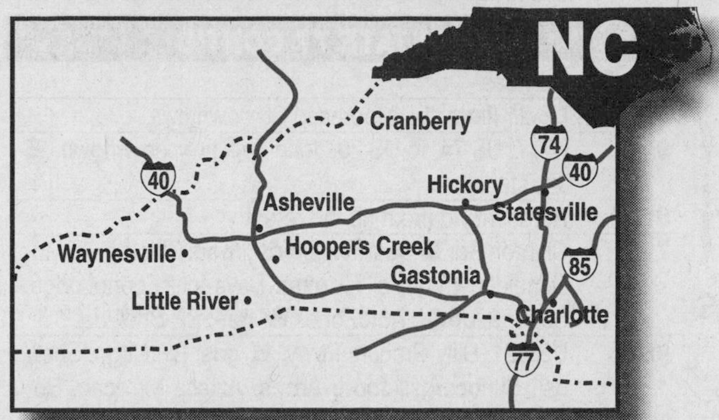

CONCORD

CHARLOTTE

Exit #	Services
25	Continued AT&T, GNC, Harris-Teeter, Kohl's, Lowe's Whse, Marshall's, PetCo, Staples, Target, Tuffy Auto, Verizon, **W gas:** Shell/dsl, **food:** Arby's, Bob Evans, Bojangles, Carrabba's, Cold Stone, DQ, Jason's Deli, Hickery Tavern Grill, Kabuto Japanese, Max&Erma's, Outback Steaks, Qdoba, Quiznos, Red Rock's Cafe, Starbucks, Subway, **lodging:** Candlewood Suites, Courtyard, Residence Inn, Sleep Inn, **other:** Barnes&Noble, Food Lion/deli, Walgreens, to Energy Explorium
23	NC 73, Huntersville, **E gas:** BP, Citgo, Shell/24hr, **food:** Baskin-Robbins/Dunkin Dounuts, Chico's Mexican, CookOut, Hardee's, Palace of China, Subway, Waffle House, Wendy's, **lodging:** Holiday Inn Express, Red Roof Inn, **other:** AutoZone, Buick/GMC/Pontiac, Food Lion, Ford, Goodyear/auto, Hancock Fabrics, Honda, O'Reilly Parts, Rite Aid, Toyota, Tuesday Morning, VW, USPO, **W gas:** Shell, **food:** CiCi's Pizza, Firehouse Subs, 5 Guys Burgers, Friendly's, Pizza Hut, Quizno's, Starbucks, Vocelli's Pizza, **other:** H, Batteries+, Bi-Lo, CVS Drug, GNC, Harris-Teeter, Walgreens
19b a	S I-485 Outer, rd 115, to Spartanburg
18	Harris Blvd, Reames Rd, **E gas:** BP/Arby's, Shell/dsl, **food:** Azteca, Bangkok Square, Bob Evans, Hickory Tavern, Jack-in-the-Box, Lin's Buffet, Pilly Connection, Quizno's, Waffle House, **lodging:** Comfort Suites, Fairfield Inn, Hilton Garden, Suburban Lodge, **other:** H, Advance Parts, Staples, to UNCC, Univ Research Park, **W food:** Bravo Italian, Chick-fil-A, Chili's, Cold Stone, Edomae Grill, Firehouse Subs, 5 Guys Burgers, Fox&Hound, Mimi's Cafe, Moe's SW Grill, Olive Garden, On-the-Border, Panera bread, PF Chang's, Red Robin, Shane's Rib Shack, TGI Friday's, Wendy's, **lodging:** Drury Inn, **other:** AT&T, Belk, Best Buy, Borders Books, Dillard's, Lowe's Whse, Macy's, Old Navy, Petsmart, Target, mall
16b a	US 21, Sunset Rd, **E gas:** 76/Circle K, Shell, **food:** Capt D's, Hardee's, KFC, McDonald's, Papa John's, Subway, Taco Bell, Wendy's, **lodging:** Days Inn, Super 8, **other:** AutoZone, NAPA, **W gas:** Citgo/dsl, Shell/dsl/scales/24hr, 76/Circle K, **food:** Baskin-Robbins/Dunkin Donuts, Bojangles, Bubba's BBQ, CookOut, Denny's, Domino's, Jack-in-the-Box, Waffle House, **lodging:** Microtel, Sleep Inn, **other:** Advance Parts, Aldi Foods, CVS Drug, Family$, Food Lion, Walgreens
13b a	I-85, S to Spartanburg, N to Greensboro
12	La Salle St, **W gas:** Shell/dsl, Texaco/dsl
11b a	I-277, Brookshire Fwy, NC 16
10b	Trade St, 5th St, **E other:** to Discovery Place, **W gas:** Texaco, **food:** Bojangles

NC

INTERSTATE 77 CONT'D

Exit #	Services
10a	US 21 (from sb), Moorhead St, downtown
9	I-277, US 74, to US 29, John Belk Fwy, downtown, **E** Ⓗ, stadium
8	Remount Rd (from nb, no re-entry)
7	Clanton Rd, **E gas:** Texaco/dsl, **food:** Chick-fil-A, McDonald's, Wendy's, **lodging:** Days Inn, EconoLodge, Super 8, **other:** AutoZone, **W gas:** BP, Shell/dsl
6b a	US 521, Billy Graham Pkwy, **E gas:** BP, Citgo, Shell/dsl, Sunoco/dsl, **food:** Arby's, Azteca Mexican, Bojangles, Capt D's, Carolina Prime Steaks, Domino's, Dragon House, Firehouse Subs, HoneyBaked Ham, IHOP, KFC, Papa John's, Waffle House, **lodging:** Best Western, Days Inn, Howard Johnson, Ramada Ltd, Sheraton, Tres Pesos, **other:** CVS Drug, Family$, Home Depot, TJ Maxx, Walgreens, to Queens Coll, **W gas:** Texaco, **food:** Omaha Steaks, **lodging:** Embassy Suites, Holiday Inn, Hyatt Place, InTown Suites, La Quinta, Sleep Inn, **other:** ✈
5	Tyvola Rd, **E gas:** Shell, Texaco, **food:** Chili's, China King, Kabuto Japanese, McDonald's, Royal Buffet, Sonny's BBQ, Subway, **lodging:** Candlewood Suites, Comfort Inn, Hilton, Marriott, Quality Inn, Residence Inn, Studio+, **other:** Aldi Foods, Costco/gas, Jaguar, Buick/GMC/Pontiac, Verizon, **services E of S blvd, W lodging:** Extended Stay America, Wingate Inn
4	Nations Ford Rd, **E gas:** Citgo, 76/Circle K/24hr, **food:** New England Seafood, **lodging:** Best Value Inn, Knights Inn, La Casa Inn, Motel 6, **W gas:** Shell/Burger King
3	Arrowood Rd, **E food:** Jack-in-the-Box, McDonald's, Sonic, Starbucks, Wendy's, **lodging:** Courtyard, Fairfield Inn, Holiday Inn Express, Hyatt Place, Mainstay Suites, Staybridge Suites, TownePlace Suites, **W food:** Ruby Tuesday, **lodging:** Hampton Inn
2	I-485
1.5mm	**Welcome Ctr nb, full ♿ facilities, info, ☎, vending, [picnic], litter barrels, petwalk**
1	Westinghouse Blvd, to I-485 (from nb), **E gas:** BP/dsl, **food:** Jack-in-the-Box, Subway, Waffle House, **lodging:** Super 8, **W gas:** Shell/dsl, **food:** Burger King
0mm	North Carolina/South Carolina state line

NC

INTERSTATE 85

Exit #	Services
234mm	North Carolina/Virginia state line
233	US 1, to Wise, **E gas:** Citgo/Wise/dsl, **food:** Budget Inn
231mm	**Welcome Ctr sb, full ♿ facilities, ☎, [picnic], litter barrels, petwalk**
229	Oine Rd, to Norlina, **E gas:** BP, **W** rec area
226	Ridgeway Rd, **W other:** to Kerr Lake, to St RA
223	Manson Rd, **E gas:** BP/dsl, **other:** camping, **W** to Kerr Dam
220	US 1, US 158, Fleming Rd, to Middleburg, **E gas:** BP/dsl, **W gas:** Exxon/dsl/scales, **lodging:** Chex Motel/rest.
218	US 1 S (from sb exits left), to Raleigh
217	Nutbush Bridge, **E** same as 215 on US 158, **W gas:** Exxon/dsl, **other:** Kerr Lake RA

HENDERSON

Exit #	Services
215	US 158 BYP E, Henderson (no EZ return from nb), **E gas:** BP, Hess, Shell, Sunoco, **food:** BBQ, Burger King, Golden China, Subway, Waffle Pancakes, **lodging:** Ambassador Inn, Budget Host, Comfort Inn, Scottish Inn, **other:** $General, Food Lion, Goodyear/auto, Roses, services on US 158
214	NC 39, Henderson, **E gas:** BP, **food:** Andy's Rest., **other:** uspo, **W gas:** BP/dsl, Shell/HotStuff Pizza
213	US 158, Dabney Dr, to Henderson, **E gas:** BP, Parade, Shell, **food:** Bamboo Garden, Bojangles, DQ, Denny's, KFC, McDonald's, Papa John's, Pizza Inn, Subway, Wendy's, **other:** CVS Drug, Family$, Food Lion, Goodyear/auto, Radio Shack, Roses, **W gas:** BP, Shell, **food:** Chick-fil-A, Golden Corral, Smithfields BBQ, Taco Bell, **lodging:** Holiday Inn Express, **other:** Chevrolet/GMC, Chrysler/Dodge, $Tree, Ford/Lincoln/Mercury, K-Mart, Lowe's Whse, Pontiac, Staples, Tires+
212	Ruin Creek Rd, **E gas:** Shell/dsl, **food:** Cracker Barrel, Mazatlan Mexican, SiLo Rest., **lodging:** Day's Inn, **W gas:** BP/Burger King, **food:** Christoper's Grill, Gary's BBQ, Golden Corral, Pizza Hut, Western Sizzlin, **lodging:** Hampton Inn, Jameson Inn, Sleep Inn, **other:** Ⓗ, Belk, JC Penney, Walmart SuperCtr/24hr, mall
209	Poplar Creek Rd, **W** Vance-Granville Comm Coll

OXFORD

Exit #	Services
206	US 158, Oxford, **E gas:** Exxon, **W gas:** BP/dsl, **food:** Tony's Rest., **other:** ✈
204	NC 96, Oxford, **E gas:** BP/dsl, **lodging:** Best Western, King's Inn, **other:** Honda, Pontiac/Buick/GMC, **W gas:** Exxon/DQ/24hr, Hess, Shell/Pizza Hut/24hr, Texaco, **food:** Burger King, Domino's, KFC, McDonald's, 96 Buffet, Subway, Taco Bell, Wendy's, **lodging:** Econolodge, **other:** Ⓗ, $Tree, GNC, Lowe's Foods, Walmart
202	US 15, Oxford, **2 mi W lodging:** Crown Motel
199mm	**rest area both lanes, full ♿ facilities, ☎, [picnic], litter barrels, petwalk**
198mm	Tar River

BUTNER

Exit #	Services
191	191 NC 56, Butner, **E gas:** BP/dsl, Hess/dsl, **food:** Bob's BBQ, Bojangles, Burger King, El Rio Mexican, KFC/Taco Bell, McDonald's, Pizza Hut, Stone Crab Landing, Subway, Wendy's, **lodging:** Comfort Inn, **other:** Ace Hardware, Advance Parts, Curves, $General, Food Lion, M&H Tires, Vet, to Falls Lake RA, **W gas:** Exxon/dsl/24hr, Shell/dsl, **food:** Hardee's, Waffle&Pancake House, **lodging:** Econolodge, Holiday Inn Express, Ramada Ltd, **other:** auto repair
189	Butner
186b a	US 15, to Creedmoor
185mm	Falls Lake
183	Redwood Rd
182	Red Mill Rd, **E gas:** Exxon/repair, **other:** Kenworth/Isuzu Trucks
180	Glenn School Rd
179	E Club Blvd, **E gas:** Exxon
178	US 70 E, to Raleigh, Falls Lake RA, Research Triangle, RDU ✈
177	Avondale Dr, NC 55, **W** gas Shell, **food:** American Hero, Arby's, Hong Kong Buffet, Los Comales, McDonalds, Pizza Village, **other:** Advance Parts, Big Lots, Jiffy Lube

INTERSTATE 85 CONT'D

N ↕ S

Exit #	Services
176b a	Gregson St, US 501 N, **E food:** Champps Grill, Tripps Rest., **other:** H, Belk, Macy's, Museum of Life&Science, Office Depot, Sears/auto, mall
175	Guess Rd, **E gas:** Citgo/dsl, **food:** Hog Heaven BBQ, **lodging:** Best Value Inn, Holiday Inn Express, Super 8, **other:** , **W gas:** BP/dsl, Pure, **food:** Bojangles, Honey's Diner/24hr, IHOP, JJ Fish &Chicken, Texas Steaks, Zero's Subs, **lodging:** Red Roof Inn, **other:** CVS Drug, Home Depot, Kroger
174a	Hillandale Rd, **W gas:** BP/dsl, **food:** El Corral, Papa's Grill, Sal's Pizza, **lodging:** Courtyard, Hampton Inn, Howard Johnson, **other:** Kerr Drug
174b	US 15 S, US 501 S (from sb), **E lodging:** Forest Inn
173	173 US 15, US 501, US 70, Colemill Rd, W Durham, **E gas:** BP, Exxon/dsl, Shell/Texaco, **food:** Arby's, BBQ, Bojangles, Burger King, Checker's, Chick-fil-a, KFC/Taco Bell, Cracker Barrel, DogHouse Rest., Domino's, Galley Seafood, Italian Garden Rest., McDonald's, Miami Subs, Subway, Taco Bell, Waffle House, Wendy's, **lodging:** Day's Inn, Holiday Inn, Innkeeper, Quality Inn, **other:** H, Autozone, Dodge/Jeep, Kroger, Rite Aid
172	NC 147 S, to US 15 S, US 501 S (from nb), Durham, from nb
170	to NC 751, to Duke U (no EZ return from nb), **E lodging:** Best Western/rest., Scottish Inn, **W** to Eno River SP
165	NC 86, to Chapel Hill, **E gas:** Pure/dsl, **food:** Papa John's, Subway, **other:** $Hut, Home Depot, Walmart SuperCtr/24hr., **W gas:** BP/dsl
164	Hillsborough, **E gas:** BP, Citgo/dsl, **food:** McDonald's, **lodging:** Holiday Inn Express, **W gas:** Exxon/dsl, Shell, **food:** Bojangles, Casa Ibarra Mexican, Domino's, Hardee's, KFC/Taco Bell, Occoneechee Steaks, Pizza Hut, Subway, Waffle House, Wendy's, **lodging:** Microtel, **other:** AutoZone, CarQuest, Chevrolet/Buick, $Tree, Food Lion, Ford, GNC, Goodyear/auto, Lowe's Foods
163	I-40 E, to Raleigh. **I-85 S and I-40 W run together 38 mi.**
161	to US 70 E, NC 86 N
160	to NC 86 N, Efland, **W gas:** Exxon/dsl
158mm	**weigh sta both lanes**
157	Buckhorn Rd, **E gas:** BP/dsl, Petro/Mobil/Iron Skillet/dsl/scales/24hr/@, **W gas:** PopShoppe
154	Mebane, Oaks Rd, **E gas:** Murphy USA, Shell/dsl/24hr, Sheetz/dsl, **food:** Andy's Rest., Ciao Pizza, Subway, **other:** $Tree, Walmart SuperCtr/24hr, **W gas:** BP, Hess/Wilco/dsl, Shell/dsl/24hr, **food:** Biscuitville, Bojangles, La Fiesta Mexican, McDonald's, Quizno's, Roma Pizza, Sake Japanese, Stir King, Waffle House, **lodging:** Budget Inn, **other:** Advance Parts, AutoZone, CVS Drug, Lowe's Foods, Vet
153	NC 119, Mebane, **E gas:** BP/KFC/Taco Bell/Pizza Hut, **food:** Cracker Barrel, Hibachi Rest., Jersey Mike's, Overtime Rest., Ruby Tuesday, Smithfield's BBQ, **lodging:** Hampton Inn, Holiday Inn Express, **other:** Lowe's Whse, **W gas:** Exxon/Burger King, **food:** Domino's, La Cocina Mexican, Papa John's, Sonic, Subway, **other:** Curves, Food Lion
152	Trollingwood Rd, **E gas:** Pilot/McDonald's/dsl/scales/24hr

DURHAM

MEBANE

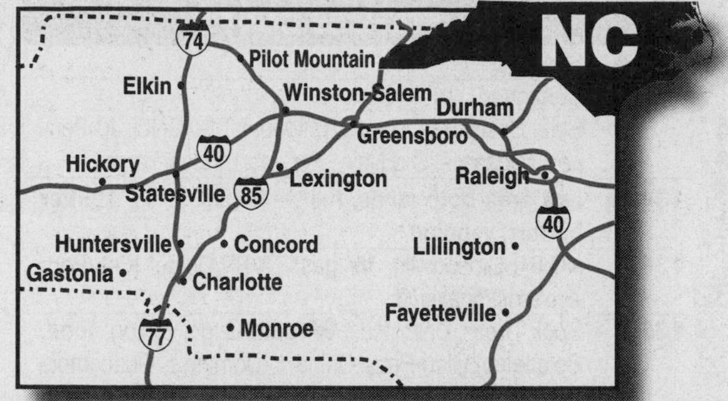

Exit #	Services
150	Haw River, to Roxboro, **W gas:** Hess/Wilco/DQ/Wendy's/dsl/scales/24hr, ***FLYING J***/Cookery/dsl/LP/scales/24hr/@, SpeedCo, **lodging:** Days Inn, **other:** Blue Beacon
148	NC 54, Graham, **E gas:** BP/dsl/24hr, Exxon/dsl/24hr, QP, **food:** Waffle House, **lodging:** Comfort Suites, **W food:** MexAm Cafe, **lodging:** Ember's Motel, Travel Inn
147	NC 87, to Pittsboro, Graham, **E gas:** BP, **food:** AnnaMaria's Pizzeria, Arby's, Bojangles, Burger King, Domino's, Great Wall Chinese, Harbor House Seafood, Lucky Bamboo, Pizza Hut, Quizno's, Sagebrush Steaks, Sonic, Subway, Wendy's, **other:** Advance Parts, AutoZone, Chevrolet, Chrysler/Jeep, Curves, Family$, Food Lion, Ford, Rite Aid, Vet, **W gas:** Citgo/dsl, Exxon/dsl, Shell/dsl, **food:** BBQ&Ribs Co., Biscuitville, Cook Out, McDonald's, Taco Bell, **other:** H, CVS Drug, Lowe's Foods, Walgreens
145	NC 49, Burlington, **E gas:** BP/dsl, Shell/dsl, **food:** Capt D's, **lodging:** Econolodge, Microtel, Motel 6, **other:** Harley-Davidson, **W gas:** BP/dsl, **food:** Biscuitville, Bojangles, Burger King, KFC, La Cabana Mexican, Subway, Waffle House, **lodging:** Best Value Inn, Quality Inn, Royal Inn, **other:** Dodge, $General, Food Lion, Radio Shack, Rite Aid, outlets/famous brands
143	NC 62, Burlington, **E gas:** Sav-Way, **food:** Hardee's, Waffle House, Wendy's, to Alamance Bfd, **W gas:** Exxon, Sheetz/dsl, **food:** Biscuitville, K&W Cafeteria, **lodging:** Ramada Inn, **other:** Cadillac, Chevrolet, $General, Food Lion, Ford, Home Depot, Vet
141	to Burlington, **E gas:** BP, Kangaroo, **food:** IHOP, Mayflower Seafood, Outback Steaks, **lodging:** Comfort Inn, Hampton Inn, **other:** Nissan, **W gas:** Texaco, **food:** Amante Pizza, Applebee's, Arby's, Biscuitville, Bojangles, Burger King, Chick-fil-A, Cook Out, Cracker Barrel, Golden Corral, Hooters, KFC, Longhorn Steaks, McDonald's, O'Charley's, Panchero's Mexican, Panda Express, Panera Bread, Ruby Tuesday, Sal's Italian, Starbucks, Steak'n Shake/24hr, Subway, Taco Bell, Wholly Guacamole, **lodging:** Best Western, Country Inn&Suites, Courtyard, Super 8, **other:** H, Books-a-Million, Buick/GMC, $Tree, Hyundai, K-Mart/gas, Lincoln/Mercury, Lowe's Whse, Mazda, Rite Aid, Sears/auto, TJ Maxx, Walgreens, Walmart SuperCtr/24hr, mall, to Elon Coll
140	University Dr, Elon, **W food:** Buffalo Wing Wings, Chick-fil-A, Chili's, Cold Stone Creamery, Little Italy, McDonald's, Mimi's Cafe, Moe's SW Grill, Olive Garden, Peking House, Qdoba, Red Bowl Asian, Red Robin, Starbucks, TX Roadhouse, **other:** Barnes&Noble,

BURLINGTON

INTERSTATE 85 CONT'D

N ↕ S

GREENSBORO

Exit #	Services
140	Continued Belk, Best Buy, Dillard's, Discount Tire, GNC, JC Penney, Michael's, Old Navy, Petsmart, Ross, Target
139mm	**rest area both lanes, full [handicapped] facilities, [phone], [picnic],litter barrels, vending**
138	NC 61, Gibsonville, **W gas:** TA/BP/Burger King/Popeye's/dsl/scales/@
135	Rock Creek Dairy Rd, **W gas:** Citgo, Exxon, **food:** Bojangles, Ciao Pizza,China 1, Domino's, Guacamole Mexican, Jersey Mike's Subs, McDonald's, **other:** Curves, CVS Drug, $General, Food Lion, Midtown Drug, Vet
132	Mt Hope Church Rd, **E gas:** Citgo/Subway/dsl, **food:** Pascalli's Pizza, **W gas:** Shell/dsl, Hess/Wendy's/dsl/24hr, **lodging:** Hampton Inn
131	to US 70, Loop 85, Loop 40
129	Youngsmill Rd, **W lodging:** Holiday Inn Express (3mi)
128	Alamance Church Rd
126b a	US 421, to Sanford, **E gas:** Exxon/dsl, Kangaroo/dsl, **other:** Hagan Stone Park Camping
124	S Elm, Eugene St, **W food:** Bojangles, Cracker Barrel, McDonald's, Starbucks, Starbuck, Subway, Wendy's, Wing Stop, **other:** Lowe's Whse, Walmart SuperCtr
122c b a	US 220, to Greensboro, Asheboro (from sb)
121	I-40 W, I-73 N, to Winston-Salem
120N	US 29, E US 70, to I-40 W
119	Groometown Rd, from nb, **W gas:** Citgo/dsl
118	US 29 S, US 70 W, to High Point, Jamestown, **W lodging:** Grandover Resort, **other:** [H]
115mm	Deep River
114mm	new exit
113	NC 62, Archdale, **E gas:** Citgo/dsl, **W gas:** BP/dsl, **lodging:** Quality Inn
111	US 311, to High Point, Archdale, **E food:** Amici Pizza, Bamboo Garden, Bojangles, Carolina Diner, Hardee's, Subway, Wendy's, **lodging:** Innkeeper, **other:** Curves, CVS Drug, $General, $City, Food Lion, Lowe's Foods/24hr, **W gas:** Circle K/dsl, Exxon/McDonald's, Marathon/dsl, Shell/dsl, **food:** Biscuitville, Kosta's Rest, Waffle House, **lodging:** Comfort Inn, Country Inn&Suites, Fairfield Inn, Hampton Inn, Holiday Inn Express, **other:** [H], O'Reilly Parts, USPO, tires
108	Hopewell Church Rd, Trinity
106	Finch Farm Rd, **E gas:** BP/dsl, **W food:** Subway (1mi)
103	NC 109, to Thomasville, **E gas:** Murphy USA/dsl, Shell, Texaco/dsl, **food:** Arby's, Chen's Kitchen, Cookout Burgers, Taco Bell, **lodging:** ValuePlace, **other:** CVS Drug, $Tree, Ingles Foods, K-Mart, Radio Shack, Walmart SuperCtr, **W gas:** Exxon/Subway/dsl, Race-Way, Hess/Wilco/dsl, Shell, **food:** BBQ Shack, Biscuitville, Bojangles, Burger King, Captain Tom's, China Garden, Denny's, Dino's Italian, Hardee's, Hunan Chinese, KFC, La Carreta Mexican, Mandarin Express, Mazatlan Mexican, McDonald's, Mr Gatti's, Papa John's, Ruby Tuesday, Sonic, Sunrise Diner, Waffle House, Wendy's, **lodging:** Country Hearts Inn, Quality Inn, **other:** Advance Parts, Aldi Foods, AutoZone, Family$, Food Lion, Merchant's Tire, Mighty$, NAPA, O'Reilly Parts, Peebles, Rite Aid, Walgreens

THOMASVILLE

NC

Exit #	Services
102	Lake Rd, **W gas:** Marathon, Sunoco, **lodging:** Days Inn/rest., Microtel, **other:** [H]
100mm	**rest area both lanes, full [handicapped] facilities, [phone], vending, [picnic], litter barrels, petwalk**
96	US 64, to Asheboro, Lexington, **E gas:** Exxon/dsl, **other:** Modern Tire, **W gas:** Citgo/dsl, Texaco/dsl, **food:** Randy's Rest., **other:** to Davidson Co Coll, NC Zoo
94	Old US 64, **E gas:** Shell, **other:** Timber Lake Gallery
91	NC 8, to Southmont, **E gas:** BP/dsl, Citgo, Shell/dsl, **food:** Biscuit King, Burger King, Christo Rest., Hunan Express, Jimmy's BBQ, KFC, Mayberry Rest., McDonald's, Ocean View Seafood, Subway, Wendy's, **lodging:** Comfort Suites, Highway 8 Motel, **other:** Food Lion, High Rock Lake Camping (7mi), Kerr Drug, Mock Tire, **W gas:** Exxon/dsl, Murphy USA/dsl, QM/dsl, **food:** Applebee's, Arby's, Burger King, Cracker Barrel, Golden Corral, King House, La Carreta Mexican, Little Caesar's, Mi Pueblo, Pizza Hut (1mi), Taco Bell, Zaxby's, **lodging:** Country Hearth Inn, Quality Inn, **other:** [H], Belk, $Tree, GNC, Lowe's Whse (1mi), Radio Shack, Walmart SuperCtr (1mi)
88	Linwood, **W gas:** Texaco/dsl, **other:** [H]
87	US 29, US 70, US 52 (from nb), High Point, **W other:** [H], [airport]
86	Belmont Rd, **W gas:** Bill's Trkstp/dsl/scales/24hr/@
85	Clark Rd, to NC 150
83	NC 150 (from nb), to Spencer
82	US 29, US 70 (from sb), to Spencer
81.5mm	Yadkin River
81	Spencer, **E gas:** Liberty, **other:** camping
79	Spencer Shops SHS, Spencer, E Spencer, **W food:** Subway (1mi)
76b a	US 52, to Albemarle, Salisbury, **E gas:** BP, Pop Shoppe, **food:** Applebee's, Capriano's, China Rainbow, Cold Stone Creamery, IHOP, LoneStar Steaks, Mr Gatti's Pizza, Pancho Villa Mexican, Top China, Zaxby's, **lodging:** Days Inn, Economy Inn, Happy Traveler Inn, Super 8, **other:** Aldi Foods, CVS Drug, $Tree, Food Lion, GNC, Harley-Davidson, Lowe's Whse, Marshall's, Old Navy, Radio Shack, Rite Aid, Staples, Tire Kingdom, Walgreens, **W gas:** Murphy Express/dsl, Shell/Circle K/dsl, Wilco/Hess/dsl, **food:** Beijing Chinese, Blue Bay Seafood, Bojangles, Burger King, Capt D's, Chick-fil-A, China Buffet, Christo's Rest., Cookout, Cracker Barrel, Hardee's, HoneyBaked Ham, Jade Express, KFC, McDonald's, O'Charley's, Outback Steaks, Papa John's, Pizza Hut, Starbucks, Subway, Taco Bell, Tokyo Express, Wendy's, **lodging:** Comfort Suites, **other:** [H]Advance Parts, AutoZone, Family$, Firestone/auto, Goodyear/auto, K-Mart, Office Depot, USPO, Walmart SuperCtr
75	US 601, Jake Alexander Blvd, **E food:** Arby's, Farmhouse Rest., **lodging:** Travelodge, **other:** NAPA, to Dan Nicholas Park, **W gas:** BP, Citgo, Shell/dsl, **food:** Casa Grande Mexian, Ichiban Japanese, Ryan's, Sagebrush Steaks, Subway, Waffle House, Wendy's, **lodging:** Hampton Inn, Holiday Inn, Quality Inn, **other:** Cadillac/Chevrolet, Chrysler/Dodge/Jeep, Ford, Honda, Kia, Magic Mart, Nissan, Toyota
74	Julian Rd, **W food:** Longhorn Steaks, Olive Garden, **other:** Kohl's

SALISBURY

INTERSTATE 85 CONT'D

N ↕ S

Exit #	Services
72	Peach Orchard Rd
71	Peeler Rd, **E gas:** Derrick TravelCtr/Shell/CW's Cafe/dsl/24hr/scales, **W gas:** Hess/Wilco/Bojangles/Subway/dsl/scales/24hr, **other:** auto/dsl repair
70	Webb Rd, **E** flea mkt, **W gas:** Mikey's, **other:** st patrol
68	US 29, US 601, to Rockwell, China Grove, **1 mi W gas:** BP, **food:** Domino's, Gary's BBQ, Hardee's, Pizza Hut, Subway, **other:** AutoZone, $General, Family$, Food Lion, Rite Aid
63	Kannapolis, **E gas:** Pilot/Subway/dsl/scales, **food:** Waffle House, **lodging:** Best Value Inn
60	Earnhardt Rd, Copperfield Blvd, **E gas:** BP, Exxon/dsl, **food:** Bob Evans, Bojangles, Cracker Barrel, **lodging:** Hampton Inn, Sleep Inn, **other:** H, Discount Tire, **W gas:** BP/dsl, **food:** Bruster's, Carino's Italian, Casa Grande Mexican, Dragon Wok, Firehouse Subs, Logan's Roadhouse, McDonald's, Ruby Tuesday, Steak'n Shake, Subway, Taco Bell, Unique Pizza, Wendy's, Yamayi Japanese, **lodging:** Holiday Inn Express, **other:** Hobby Lobby, Kohl's, Lowe's Whse, NAPA, Sam's Club/gas, Walmart SuperCtr/24hr, visitor info
59mm	**rest area both lanes, full facilities, phone, vending, picnic, litter barrels, petwalk**
58	US 29, US 601, Concord, **E gas:** BP, Shell/dsl, Texaco, **food:** Applebee's, Capt D's, Chick-fil-A, Chili's, El Vallarta Mexican, Golden Corral, Mayflower Seafood, McDonald's, Moe's SW Grill, Mr C's Rest., O'Charley's, Starbucks, Taco Bell, Wendy's, **lodging:** Best Value Inn, Howard Johnson, Mayfair Motel, **other:** H, Belk, Harris Teeter, JC Penney, Lowe's Whse, Rite Aid, Sears/auto, Staples, Tire Kingdom, U-Haul, Walgreens, mall, st patrol, **W gas:** BP, Hess, **food:** CiCi's, Domino's, Hibachi Grill, IHOP, **lodging:** Comfort Inn, Econolodge, Fairfield Inn, Microtel, **other:** $General, Ford/Lincoln/Mercury, Hancock Fabrics, Home Depot, Vet
55	NC 73, to Davidson, Concord, **E gas:** Exxon/dsl, Shell, **food:** McDonald's, Waffle House, **W gas:** Shell/Punchy's Diner, 76/Circle K/dsl, World Gas, **lodging:** Days Inn
54	Kannapolis Pkwy, George W Lyles Pkwy, **E gas:** Citgo, **food:** Backyard Burger, Bojangles, China Bowl, China Garden, Noodles & Co, Off-the-Grill, Quizno's, **other:** AutoZone, CVS Drug, Food Lion, Harris Teeter, Walgreens, Vet, **W gas:** Exxon, **food:** Arby's, Asian Cafe, Buffalo Wild Wings, Chick-fil-A, Dickey's BBQ, Fatz Cafe, McDonald's, **other:** Best Buy, $Tree, Goodyear/auto, Marshall's, Steinmart, Petsmart, Super Target
52	Poplar Tent Rd, **E gas:** Shell/dsl, Texaco/dsl, **food:** R&R BBQ, **other:** to Lowe's Speedway, museum, **W gas:** Accel/dsl, Exxon/24hr
49	Bruton Smith Blvd, Concord Mills Blvd, **E gas:** BP/McDonalds, Shell/dsl, **food:** Arby's, Bob Evans, Bojangles, Carrabbas, ChuckeCheese, Cinco de Mayo Mexican, Cookout, Cracker Barrel, Firehouse Subs, 5 Guys Burgers, Hooters, KFC/Taco Bell, Quaker Steak, Quizno's, Jack-in-the-Box, Ruby Tuesday, Sonic, Starbucks, Subway, Sonny's BBQ, Taco Bell, TX Roadhouse, Waffle House, Wendy's, Zaxby's, **lodging:** Comfort Suites, Courtyard, Embassy Suites,

CONCORD

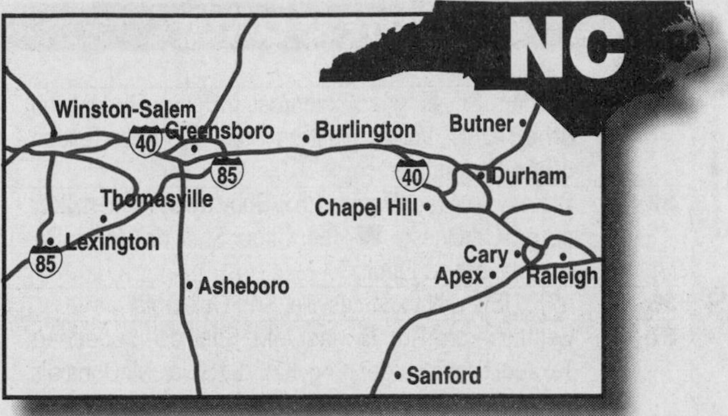

CHARLOTTE

Exit #	Services
49	Continued Hampton Inn, Hilton Garden, Holiday Inn Express, Residence Inn, Sleep Inn, SpringHill Suites, Suburban Lodge, Wingate Inn, **other:** BJ's Whse/gas, Fleetwood RV camping (1.5mi), Harley-Davidson, Honda, Scion/Toyota, Tom Johnson RV Ctr (1.5mi), to Lowe's Motor Speedway, **W gas:** Texaco, **food:** Applebee's, Burger King, Charanda Mexican, Chick-fil-A, Foster's Grille, Mayflower Seafood, McAlisters Deli, Olive Garden, On-the-Border, Panera Bread, Razzoo's Cafe, Red Lobster, Ryan's, Steak'n Shake, Sticky Fingers, TGI Friday, **other:** URGENT CARE, BassPro Shops, BooksAMillion, Discount Tire, $Tree, Concord Mills Mall, Goodyear/auto, Lowe's Whse, Old Navy, PetCo, Radio Shack, Ross, TJ Maxx, Walmart
48	I-485, to US 29, to Rockhill
46	Malla rd Creek Church Rd, **E gas:** Exxon/24hr, Texaco/dsl, **food:** China Cafe, Giacolos Pizza, Jack-in-the-Box, K&W Cafeteria, Utopia Rest, **other:** Research Park, **W gas:** Circle K/Blimpie/dsl, Texaco/dsl, **food:** Firehouse Subs, 5 Guys Burgers, Hickory Tavern, Quizno's, Rita's, Starbucks, Thai Taste, **other:** Trader Joes
45	Harris Blvd, **E food:** Applebee's, Bikini's Grill, Bojangles, Burger King, Cheddar's, Chick-fil-A, Chili's, China Palace, Ham's Rest, HoneyBaked Ham, IHOP, Jersey Mike's Subs, Max&Erma's, McDonald's, Melting Pot, Nakto's, Panda Express, Panera Bread, Papa John's, Picasso's Pizza, Qdoba, Quizno's, Shane's Rib Shack, Shoney's, Showmar's Rest, Smokey Bones, Starbucks, Taco Bell, TGIFriday, TX Land & Cattle, **lodging:** Courtyard, Drury Inn, Extended Stay America, Hampton Inn, Hilton, Holiday Inn, Homewood Suites, Residence Inn, Sleep Inn, **other:** H Best Buy, Bloom Foods, Kohl's, Michael's, Office Depot, Old Navy, Ross, Sam's Club, TJ Maxx, Walgreens, Walmart/auto, mall, to UNCC, to Miz Scarlett's, U Research Park, **0-2 mi W gas:** Citgo, Shell, **food:** Longhorn Steaks, Maccaroni Grill, Red Robin, Tony's Pizza, **lodging:** Springhill Suites, TownePlace Suites, **other:** Harris Teeter, Rite Aid
43	to City Blvd
42	US 29 (nb only)
41	Sugar Creek Rd, **E gas:** RaceWay, Shell/dsl, **food:** Bojangles, McDonald's, Taco Bell, Wendy's, **lodging:** Best Value Inn, Brookwood Inn, Continental Inn, Economy Inn, Garden Inn, Microtel, **W gas:** Shell/Circle K, **food:** Cookout, Dominic's Cafe, Sugar's Rest., Texas Ranch Steaks, **lodging:** Comfort Inn, Country Hearth Inn, Days Inn, Ramada Inn, Rodeway Inn, Super 8

INTERSTATE 85 CONT'D

Exit #	Services
40	Graham St, **E gas:** Exxon/dsl, **lodging:** Budget Inn, **other:** UPS, Volvo, Western Star, **W gas:** Texaco, **other:** Freightliner
39	Statesville Ave, **E gas:** Pilot/Subway/dsl/scales/24hr, **other:** CarQuest, **W gas:** Citgo, Shell/dsl, **food:** Bojangles, **other:** Family$
38	I-77, US 21, N to Statesville, S to Columbia
37	Beatties Ford Rd, **E gas:** MM, Shell/dsl, SuperMart, Texaco, **food:** Burger King, KFC/LJ Silver, McDonald's, Subway, **other:** Food Lion, USPO, **W gas:** BP
36	NC 16, Brookshire Blvd, **E gas:** BP/dsl, **lodging:** Brookshire Inn, **other:** H, repair, **W gas:** Hari/dsl, RaceWay, Sunoco, **food:** Burger King, Jack-in-the-Box, La Unica Mexican, Subway, **other:** Family$
35	Glenwood Dr, **E lodging:** Knight's Inn, **W gas:** Shell/dsl
34	NC 27, Freedom Dr, **E gas:** BP/dsl, 76/Circle K, Shell, Walker/gas, **food:** Beauregard's Rest, Bojangles, Capt D's, Cookout, Gilligan's Rest., KFC, McDonald's, Mr C's Rest, Pizza Hut, Showmar's, Subway, Taco Bell, Tung Hoy Chinese, Wendy's, **other:** Advance Parts, Aldi Foods, AutoZone, $Tree, Goodyear, K-Mart, Rite Aid, Walgreens, **W lodging:** Real Value Inn, **other:** JiffyLube
33	US 521, Billy Graham Pkwy, **E gas:** 76/Circle K/dsl, Shell, **food:** Bojangles, KFC/Taco Bell, McDonald's, Wendy's, **lodging:** Comfort Suites, Days Inn, Sheraton, Springhill Suites, **other:** ✈, **W gas:** Exxon/dsl, **food:** Cracker Barrel, Prime Sirloin, Waffle House/24hr, **lodging:** Best Value Inn, Econolodge, La Quinta, Microtel, Motel 6, Quality Inn, Red Roof Inn
32	Little Rock Rd, **E gas:** Shell/dsl, **lodging:** Airport Inn, Courtyard, Hampton Inn, Holiday Inn, **W gas:** Exxon/dsl, Shell/dsl, **food:** Arby's, Hardee's, Showmar's Rest., Shoney's, Subway, **lodging:** Country Inn Suites, Ramada Inn, Wingate Inn, **other:** Family$, Firestone, Food Lion, Rite Aid
30	I-485, to 1-77, Pineville
29	Sam Wilson Rd, **E gas:** BP (1mi), **other:** camping, **W gas:** Shell/dsl
28mm	**weigh sta both lanes**
27.5mm	Catawba River
27	NC 273, Mt Holly, **E gas:** Exxon/dsl, Murphy USA, **food:** KFC, Pizza Hut, Subway, Taco Bell, Waffle House, Wendy's, **other:** Chrysler/Dodge/Jeep, Family$, Food Lion, Lowe's Whse, NAPA, Rite Aid, Walgreens, Walmart SuperCtr, **W gas:** BP/dsl, **lodging:** Holiday Inn Express
26	NC 7, **E gas:** BP, Texaco, **food:** Bojangles, Grand Buffet, Happy China, Hardee's, McDonald's, New China, Papa John's, **lodging:** Hampton Inn, **other:** Advance Parts, Aldi Foods, BiLo, Curves, Ford, **W** Belmont Abbey Coll
24mm	South Fork River
23	NC 7, McAdenville, **W gas:** Exxon/dsl, Shell/Subway, **food:** Hardee's, Hillbilly's BBQ/Steaks
22	Cramerton, Lowell, **E gas:** Hess, Texaco, **food:** Applebee's, Burger King, Chick-fil-A, Gator's Rest., Hooters, Jack-in-the-Box, Moe's SW Grill, Schlotsky's, Zaxby's, **other:** BooksAMillion, Cadillac/Chevrolet/
22	Continued GMC/Pontiac, Discount Tire, Honda, Kia, K-Mart, Kohl's, Lowe's Whse, Mazda, Misubishi, Old Navy, Petsmart, Sam's Club/gas, U-Haul
21	Cox Rd, **E gas:** Exxon, Texaco, **food:** Akropolis Cafe, Chili's, ChuckeCheese, Cookout, Fuel Pizza Cafe, Golden Corral, IHOP, Krispy Kreme, La Fuente, Logan's Roadhouse, Longhorn Steaks, McAlister's Deli, McDonald's, Olive Garden, On-the-Border, Panera Bread, Peking Garden, Pizza Inn, Quizno's, Ryan's, Ruby Tuesday, Steak'n Shake, Subway, **other:** AAA, Best Buy, Chrysler/Dodge/Jeep, Discount Tire, $Tree, Ford/Lincoln/Mercury, GNC, Harley-Davidson, Harris-Teeter/24hr, Home Depot, Lowe's Whse, Mazda, Michael's, Nissan, PepBoys, Radio Shack, Ross, Ryan's, Subaru, Tire Kingdom, Walgreens, Walmart SuperCtr, mall, Vet, **W gas:** Citgo, Texaco, **food:** Arby's, IHOP, **lodging:** Super 8, **other:** H, Rite Aid
20	NC 279, New Hope Rd, **E gas:** Texaco, **food:** Capt D's, Checker's, Firehouse Subs, Hong Kong Buffet, Jackson's Cafeteria, McDonald's, O'Charley's, Pizza Hut, Red Lobster, Sake Japanese, Showmar's Rest, Taco Bell, Wendy's, **lodging:** Knight's Inn, Ramada Ltd, **other:** Advance Parts, AutoZone, Belk, Dillard's, Family$, Hobby Lobby, JC Penney, NAPA, Office Depot, Sears/auto, Target, TJ Maxx, Tuesday Morning, mall, **W food:** Bojangles, Cracker Barrel, KFC, Outback Steaks, TX Roadhouse, Waffle House, **lodging:** Best Western, Comfort Suites, Courtyard, Fairfield Inn, Hampton Inn, **other:** H, CarMax
19	NC 7, E Gastonia, **E gas:** Shell
17	US 321, Gastonia, **E gas:** Exxon/dsl/LP, **food:** Los Arcos Mexican, **lodging:** Days Inn, **other:** Family$, **W gas:** Texaco/dsl, **food:** Hardee's, **lodging:** Holiday Inn Express, Microtel, Motel 6
14	NC 274, E Bessemer, **E food:** Burger King (1mi), McDonald's (1mi), **W gas:** BP/Subway, Citgo/dsl, **food:** Bojangles, Waffle House, **lodging:** Express Inn
13	Edgewood Rd, Bessemer City, **E** to Crowders Mtn SP, **W gas:** Exxon/dsl/24hr, **lodging:** Economy Inn
10b a	US 74 W, US 29, Kings Mtn
8	NC 161, to Kings Mtn, **E lodging:** Holiday Inn Express, **other:** camping, **W gas:** BP, **food:** McDonald's, Mi Pueblito Mexican, Taco Bell, Waffle House, Wendy's, **lodging:** 1st Victory Inn, Quality Inn, **other:** H
5	Dixon School Rd, **E gas:** Citgo/Subway/dsl/24hr, **other:** truck/tire repair
4	US 29 S (from sb)
2.5mm	**Welcome Ctr nb, full ♿ facilities, info, ☎, vending, picnic, litter barrels, petwalk**
2	NC 216, Kings Mtn **E** to Kings Mtn Nat Military Park
0mm	North Carolina/South Carolina state line

N ↕ S — CHARLOTTE — GASTONIA

INTERSTATE 95

Exit #	Services
181mm	North Carolina/Virginia state line, **Welcome Ctr sb, full ♿ facilities, ☎, picnic, litter barrels, vending, petwalk**
180	NC 48, to Gaston, to Lake Gaston, Pleasant Hill, **W gas:** Pilot/Subway/dsl/scales/24hr
176	NC 46, to Garysburg, **W gas:** Shell, **food:** Aunt Sarah's, Burger King, **lodging:** Best Western

NC

N ↕ S

ROANOKE RAPIDS

WILSON

SELMA

INTERSTATE 95 CONT'D

Exit #	Services
174mm	Roanoke River
173	US 158, Roanoke Rapids, Weldon, **E** **gas:** BP/dsl, Shell/Blimpie, Texaco/dsl, **food:** Ralph's BBQ, Waffle House, **lodging:** Day's Inn, Interstate Inn/RV Park, Orchard Inn, **other:** [H], **W** **gas:** BP/dsl, Exxon/DQ/Stuckey's, Murphy USA, RaceWay, Shell, **food:** Applebee's, Arby's, Burger King, Chick-fil-A, Cici's Pizza, Cracker Barrel, Hardee's, J&L Grill, KFC, Little Caesar's, Logan's Roadhouse, Lonestar Steaks, Mayflower Seafood, McDonald's, New China, Pizza Hut, Ruby Tuesday, Ryan's, Starbucks, Subway, Super King Buffet, Texas Steaks, Waffle House, Wendy's, **lodging:** Comfort Suites, Hampton Inn, Jameson Inn, Motel 6, Sleep Inn, **other:** Advance Parts, AutoZone, Belk, Biglots, $General, $Tree, Firestone/auto, Food Lion, Harley Davidson, Lowe's Whse, Radio Shack, Rite Aid, Staples, Walgreens, Walmart SuperCtr
171	NC 125, Roanoke Rapids, **E** **food:** Olive Garden, **other:** Carolina Crossroads RV Resort, **W** **gas:** Texaco/dsl, **food:** Chick-fil-A (2mi), Ryan's (2mi), Wendy's (2mi), **lodging:** Hilton Garden, Holiday Inn Express, **other:** Parton Theater, st patrol
168	NC 903, to Halifax, **E** **gas:** Exxon/Subway/dsl, Shell/Burger King/dsl, **W** **gas:** Oasis/Dunkin Donuts/LP/dsl
160	NC 561, to Brinkleyville, **E** **gas:** Exxon/24hr, **W** **gas:** Citgo/dsl/rest.
154	NC 481, to Enfield, **1mi** **W** **other:** KOA
152mm	**weigh sta both lanes**
150	NC 33, to Whitakers, **E** golf, **W** **gas:** BP/Subway/DQ/Stuckey's/dsl
145	NC 4, to US 301, Battleboro, **E** **gas:** BP/dsl, Exxon/DQ, **food:** BBQ, Denny's, 4Seasons, Hardee's, Shoney's, Waffle House, Wendy's, **lodging:** Best Value, Best Western/rest., Budget Inn, Comfort Inn, Day's Inn, Deluxe Inn, Guesthouse Inn, Howard Johnson, Red Carpet Inn, Rodeway Inn
142mm	**rest area both lanes, full ♿ facilities, [phone], [picnic], litter barrels, vending, petwalk**
141	NC 43, Red Oak, **E** **gas:** BP/dsl, Exxon/dsl/LP, **3mi** **food:** Chick-fil-A, Ruby Tuesday, **lodging:** Days Inn (4mi), Quality Inn (4mi), **W** **lodging:** Econolodge
138	US 64, **1 mi** **E** **on Winstead...gas:** BP, Exxon, **food:** Cracker Barrel, Gardner's BBQ, Outback Steaks, Texas Steaks, **lodging:** Comfort Inn, Courtyard, Hampton Inn, Holiday Inn, Residence Inn, **other:** [H]Buick/Pontiac/GMC, Harley-Davidson, Honda, to Cape Hatteras Nat Seashore
132	to NC 58, **E** **gas:** Pitstop/dsl, **1 mi** **W** **gas:** BP/dsl
128mm	Tar River
127	NC 97, to Stanhope, **E** **gas:** BP/dsl, **other:** airport
121	US 264a, Wilson, **E** **gas:** Citgo/Subway, Eagle Gas, Kangaroo/dsl/LP, Shell, **food:** KFC/LJ Silver, Waffle House, **lodging:** Quality Inn, **other:** [H], **3-4 mi** **E** **gas:** BP, Exxon, Hess/dsl, **food:** Applebee's, Arby's, Burger King, Chick-fil-A, Chili's, CiCi's, Coldstone Creamery, Denny's, El Tapatio, Golden Corral, Hardee's, Ruby Tuesday, Sonic, Starbucks, Subway, Texas Steaks, Wendy's, **lodging:** Candlewood Suites, Comfort Inn, **other:** [H], Aldi Foods, Belk, BooksAMillion, Chrysler/Jeep/Dodge, $General, Farmfresh Foods, Harris-Teeter, Home Depot, Honda, Lowe's Whse, Marshall's, PetsMart, Ross, Staples, Target, Toyota/Scion, Walmart SuperCtr/24hr/dsl, **W** **gas:** BP/dsl, **food:** Bojangles, Burger King, Cracker Barrel, McDonald's, **lodging:** Country Inn Suites, Fairfield Inn, Hampton Inn, Holiday Inn Express, Jameson Inn, Microtel, Sleep Inn, **other:** to Country Doctor Museum
119b a	US 264, US 117
116	NC 42, to Clayton, Wilson, **E** **gas:** Shell/dsl, **other:** [H] **W** **gas:** BP/dsl, **other:** Rock Ridge Camping
107	US 301, Kenly, **E** **gas:** BP/dsl, Eagle Gas, Exxon/McDonald's/dsl, Fuel Doc, PitStop/Subway, **food:** Moore's BBQ, Nik's Pizza, Patrick's Rest., **lodging:** Budget Inn, Deluxe Inn, Econolodge, **other:** CarQuest, Food Lion, Ford, Family$, Kinley Tires, Tobacco Museum
106	Truck Stop Rd, Kenly, **E** **gas:** *FLYING J*/CountryMkt/dsl/LP/scales/24hr, **W** **gas:** Shell, TA/Wendy's/dsl/24hr/scales/@, Wilco/Hess/Arby's/dsl/scales/24hr/scales, **food:** Waffle House, **lodging:** Day's Inn, Super 8, **other:** Blue Beacon, Speedco Lube, Truck-o-Mat
105.5mm	Little River
105	Bagley Rd, Kenly, **E** **gas:** Big Boys/Shell/Pizza/dsl/scales/24hr
102	Micro, **W** **gas:** Shop'N-Go, **food:** Backdoor Cafe, **other:** USPO
101	Pittman Rd
99mm	**rest area both lanes, full ♿ facilities, vending, [phone], [picnic], litter barrels, petwalk, hist marker**
98	to Selma, **E** **other:** RVacation
97	US 70 A, to Pine Level, Selma, **E** **gas:** Citgo/dsl/24hr, Savannah's Gas/dsl, **food:** Denny's, Southern Buffet, Subway, **lodging:** Holiday Inn Express, **other:** J&R Outlet, **W** **gas:** BP/dsl, Exxon/dsl/24hr, Shell/dsl, **food:** Bojangles, Carolina Cookout, China Buffet, Golden China, KFC, McDonald's, Shoney's, Waffle House, **lodging:** Comfort Inn, Day's Inn, Hampton Inn, Masters Inn, Quality Inn, Regency Inn, Royal Inn, **other:** [H]
95	US 70, Smithfield, **E** **lodging:** Log Cabin Motel/rest., Howard Johnson Express, Village Motel, **other:** Ava Gardner Museum, **W** **gas:** Hess, Shell, Sunoco, **food:** Bob Evans, Burger King, Checker's, CiCi's Pizza, Coldstone Creamery, Cracker Barrel, El Sombrero Mexican, Outback Steaks, Ruby Tuesday, Smithfield BBQ (2mi), Texas Steaks, Waffle House, Zaxby's, **lodging:** Best Western, Jameson Inn, Sleep Inn, Super 8

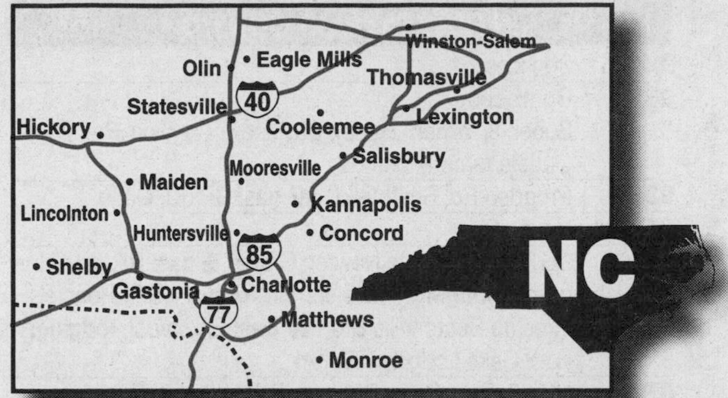

NC

N ↕ S

INTERSTATE 95 CONT'D

Exit #	Services
95	Continued Super 8, **other:** Harley-Davidson, Carolina Premium Outlets/famous brands
93	Brogden Rd, Smithfield, **W gas:** BP/dsl, Citgo
91.5mm	Neuse River
90	US 301, US 701, to Newton Grove, **E gas:** BP/dsl, Citgo/dsl, **lodging:** Travelers Inn, **other:** KOA, Ronnie's Tires, to Bentonville Bfd, **W gas:** Exxon/dsl, **lodging:** Four Oaks Lodging/RV Park
87	NC 96, Four Oaks, **W gas:** BP/dsl, **food:** Subway
81b a	I-40, E to Wilmington, W to Raleigh
79	NC 50, to NC 27, Benson, Newton Grove, **E gas:** BP/dsl, Citgo, **food:** Waffle House, **lodging:** Dutch Inn, **other:** auto repair, **W gas:** Mobil/McDonald's, Phillips 66/Burger King, Pure, **food:** Charro Mexican, China 8, Domino's, KFC, Pizza Hut, Subway, **lodging:** Day's Inn, **other:** Family$, Food Lion, Kerr Drug
77	Hodges Chapel Rd, **E gas:** Pilot/Subway/dsl/scales/24hr
75	Jonesboro Rd, **W gas:** Sadler's/Shell/DQ/Quizno's/dsl/24hr/@, Texaco/Milestone Diner
73	US 421, NC 55, to Dunn, Clinton, **E food:** Cracker Barrel, Wendy's, **other:** Chrysler/Jeep, Family$, Food Lion, **W gas:** Exxon/dsl, Hess/dsl, Shell, **food:** Bojangles, Burger King, Dairy Freeze, Sagebrush Steaks, Subway, Taco Bell, Triangle Waffle, **lodging:** Econolodge, Hampton Inn, Holiday Inn Express, Jameson Inn, Ramada Inn/rest., **other:** IGA Foods, museum
72	Pope Rd, **E lodging:** Comfort Inn, Red Carpet Inn, Royal Inn, **W gas:** BP, Pure, **food:** Brass Lantern Steaks, Prime Rib, **lodging:** Budget Inn, Express Inn, **other:** Cadillac/GMC
71	Longbranch Rd, **E gas:** Citgo/Hardee's/dsl/scales/24hr, **W** to Averasboro Bfd
70	SR 1811, **E lodging:** Relax Inn
65	NC 82, Godwin, **W** Children's Home
61	to Wade, **E gas:** Citgo/dsl, **other:** KOA (1mi), **W gas:** BP/Subway/dsl/24hr
58	US 13, to Newton Grove, I-295 to Fayetteville, **E gas:** Eastgate, Shell, **food:** Quizno's, **lodging:** Day's Inn/rest.
56	Lp 95, to US 301 (from sb), Fayetteville, **W gas:** Epco/dsl, Kangaroo/24hr, **lodging:** Budget Inn, **other:** [H], to Ft Bragg, Pope AFB
55	NC 1832, Murphy Rd, **W gas:** Epco/dsl, Kangaroo/24hr, **lodging:** Scottish Inn
52	NC 24, Fayetteville, **W other:** to Ft Bragg, Pope AFB, botanical gardens, museum
49	NC 53, NC 210, Fayetteville, **E gas:** Citgo, Exxon, Kangaroo, Mobil, **food:** Burger King, McDonald's, Pizza Hut, Taco Bell, Waffle House, **lodging:** Deluxe Inn, Motel 6, Quality Inn, **W gas:** BP/Subway/dsl, Exxon/dsl, Shell/dsl, **food:** Cracker Barrel, Fuller's BBQ, Ruby Tuesday, Shoney's, **lodging:** Best Western, Comfort Inn, Days Inn, Econolodge, Fairfield Inn, Fayetteville Hotel, Hampton Inn, Holiday Inn, Red Roof Inn, Sleep Inn, Super 8
48mm	**rest area both lanes, full [handicapped] facilities, [phone], [picnic], litter barrels, vending, petwalk**
47mm	Cape Fear River
46b a	NC 87, to Fayetteville, Elizabethtown, **W other:** [H], museum, Civic Ctr, to Agr Expo Ctr
44	Claude Lee Rd, **W other:** Lazy Acres Camping, to [airport]
41	NC 59, to Hope Mills, Parkton, **E gas:** Kangaroo/24hr, **W gas:** BP/dsl, **other:** Lake Waldo Camping, Spring Valley RV Park
40	Lp 95, to US 301 (from nb), to Fayetteville, **facilities on US 301** (5-7mi)
33	US 301, St Pauls, **E gas:** BP/dsl/repair/24hr
31	NC 20, to St Pauls, Raeford, **E gas:** BP, Mobil/McDonald's, Pit Row Gas, Shell/Huddle House/dsl/24hr, **food:** Burger King, **lodging:** Day's Inn, **other:** Volvo Trucks, **W gas:** Citgo, Exxon/dsl, **other:** FoodLion
25	US 301, **E gas:** BP/dsl
24mm	**weigh sta both lanes**
22	US 301, **E gas:** Exxon, Shell/DQ, **food:** Burger King, China Wok, Denny's, Hardee's, Huddle House, John's Rest, Outback Steaks, Quizno's, Ruby Tuesday, Ryan's, San Jose Mexican, Smithfield BBQ, Texas Steaks, Waffle House, Wendy's, Zaxby's, **lodging:** Best Western, Comfort Suites, Hampton Inn, Holiday Inn, Super 8, **other:** Black's Tire, $Tree, Lowe's Foods, Lowe's Whse, Office Depot, Walmart SuperCtr/24hr, st patrol, **W gas:** Circle B, Sun-Do/dsl, Pure/dsl, **other:** Ford/Lincoln/Mercury, Sam's Club/gas
20	NC 211, to NC 41, Lumberton, **E gas:** Citgo, Exxon/dsl, Liberty/dsl, **food:** Arby's, Bojangles, Buger King, Capt D's, Golden City Chinese, Hardee's, KFC, Little Caesar's, McDonald's, River City Grill, Shoney's, Sonic, Subway, Taco Bell, Tokyo Express, Waffle House, **lodging:** Econolodge, Howard Johnson, Quality Inn, **other:** [H], Advance Parts, Belk, CVS Drug, Food Lion/deli, JC Penney, K-Mart, Walgreens, **W gas:** Shell/dsl, Sun-do/dsl, **food:** Cracker Barrel, Fuller's BBQ Buffet, LungWah Chinese, San Jose Mexican, **lodging:** Best Value Inn, Comfort Inn, Country Inn&Suites, Day's Inn/rest., Econolodge, Fairfield Inn
19	Carthage Rd, Lumberton, **E gas:** BP/dsl, **lodging:** Travelers Inn, **W gas:** Circle B, Exxon/dsl, **lodging:** Knight's Inn, Motel 6
18mm	Lumber River
17	NC 72, **E gas:** Atkinson's/dsl, BP/dsl, Dobb's/Stuckey's/Wendy's, Go-Gas/dsl, Mobil/dsl, **food:** Burger King, Hardee's, Huddle House, McDonald's, Subway, Waffle House, **lodging:** Budget Inn, Southern Inn, **other:** Advance Parts, AutoZone, Food Lion
14	US 74, to Laurinburg, Maxton, **W gas:** BP/dsl, **other:** Sleepy Bear's RV Camp
13	US 74, to Wilmington
10	US 301, to Fairmont
7	to McDonald, Raynham
5mm	**Welcome Ctr nb, full [handicapped] facilities, [phone], [picnic], litter barrels, vending, petwalk**
2	NC 130, to NC 904, Rowland
1b a	US 301, US 501, Dillon, **E gas:** Exxon, Shell, **food:** Hot Tamale Rest., Pedro's Diner, Porky's Truckstp, **lodging:** Budget Motel, South-of-the-Border Motel, **other:** Pedro's Campground, **W gas:** Shell/dsl, Sun-Do, **food:** Waffle House, **lodging:** Day's Inn, Super 8
0mm	North Carolina/South Carolina state line

DUNN

FAYETTEVILLE

LUMBERTON

INTERSTATE 240 (ASHEVILLE)

E ↕ W — ASHEVILLE

Exit #	Services
9mm	**I-240 begins/ends on I-40, exit 53b a.**
8	Fairview Rd, **N gas:** Shell/Blimpie, **food:** Buddie's Ribs&BBQ, Burger King, J&S Cafeteria, KFC, Little Caesar's, Little Venice, McDonald's, Subway, **lodging:** Best Western, Ramada Inn, **other:** Advance Parts, Bilo Foods, CVS Drug, Hamrick's, Kohl's, PetsMart, Subaru, Walmart SuperCtr/24hr **S gas:** Citgo, **food:** Pizza Hut, Rezeals Rest., **other:** Aldi Foods, Home Depot
7.5mm	Swannanoa River
7	US 70, **N** U-Haul, **S gas:** BP, Exxon/dsl, **food:** Applebee's, Bonefish Grill, Burger King, Carraba's, Cheeseburger Paradise, Chili's, China Palace, Chuck-eCheese, Cornerstone Rest., Cracker Barrel, Don Pablo, DQ, East Buffet, Frank's Pizza, Greenery Rest., Guadalahara Mexican, Ham's Rest., Hooters, IHOP, Joe's Crabshack, Lonestar Steaks, Longhorn Steaks, Mikado, Mtn Ear Inn, O'Charley's, Olive Garden, Outback Steaks, Red Lobster, Ruby's BBQ, Subway, Taco Bell, Waffle House, **lodging:** Best Western, Country Inn&Suites, Courtyard, Day's Inn, Econolodge, Extended Stay America, Hampton Inn, Homewood Suites, In-Town Motor Inn, Royal Inn, Spring Hill Suites, **other:** Belk, Best Buy, Books-a-Million, Dillards, $Tree, Firestone, Ingles Foods, K-Mart, Lowe's Whse, Michael's, Office Depot, Radio Shack, Ross, Sears/auto, Target, TJ Maxx, Walgreens
6	Tunnel Rd (from eb), same as 7
5b	US 70 E, US 74A, Charlotte St, **N gas:** BP, Pure, **food:** Charlotte St., Fuddruckers, Starbucks, Two Guys Hogi, **lodging:** B&B, **S food:** Tripp's Rest., **lodging:** Best Western, Renaissance Motel, Civic Ctr
5a	US 25, Merrymont Ave, **N gas:** Exxon/dsl, Shell, **food:** Bojangles, La Caterina, 3 Pigs BBQ, **other:** Staples
4c	Haywood St (no EZ return to eb), Montford, **S food:** 3 Bros Rest.
4b	Patton Ave (from eb), downtown
4a	US 19 N, US 23 N, US 70 W, to Weaverville
3b	Westgate, **N food:** Jae Thai, **lodging:** Crowne Plaza, **other:** CVS Drug, EarthFare Foods, NTB, Sam's Club/gas
3a	US 19 S, US 23 S, W Asheville, **N gas:** BP, **food:** A&W/LJ Silver, Arby's, Bojangles, Denny's, Green Tea Japanese, KFC, Krispy Kreme, Little Caesar's, McDonald's, New 1 China, Nona Mia Italian, Pizza Hut, Ryan's, Subway, Taco Bell, Vera Cruz Mexican, Wendy's, **other:** Advance Parts, AutoZone, BiLo, Curves, Goodyear/auto, Ingles, Kerr Drug, K-Mart, Radio Shack, Sav-Mor Foods, Vet
2	US 19, US 23, W Asheville, **N other:** B&B Drug, **S gas:** Shell
1c	Amboy Rd (from eb)
1b	NC 191, to I-40 E, Brevard Rd, **S other:** farmers mkt, camping
1a	I-40 W, to Knoxville
0mm	I-240 begins/ends on I-40, exit 46b a.

INTERSTATE 440 (RALEIGH)

E ↕ W — RALEIGH

Exit #	Services
16	I-40
15	Poole Rd, **W gas:** BP/dsl, Citgo/dsl, **food:** Burger King, McDonald's, Subway KFC/Taco Bell

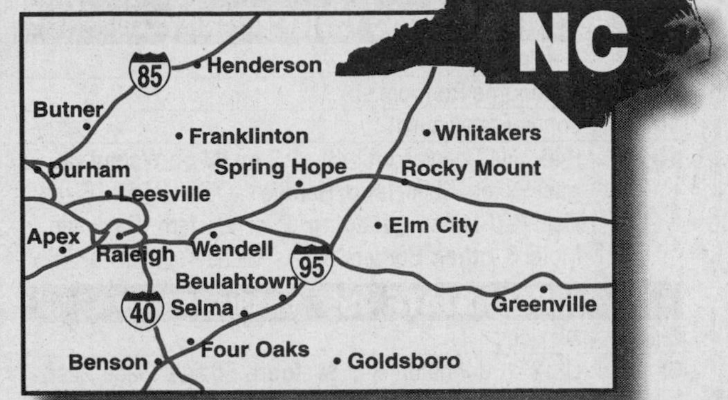

Exit #	Services
14	US 64, to Rocky Mount, limited access hwy
13b a	US 64, US 264 E, New Bern Ave, to Wilson, **2-3 mi E gas:** BP, 76/Circle K, Exxon, Phillips 66 (1mi), Shell/Texaco, Speedway, Circle K, **food:** Arby's, Burger King, Checker's, Hardee's, K&S Cafeteria, Last Catch Grill, McDonald's, Miami Subs, O'Brian's, Papa John's, Pizza Hut, Subway, Taco Bell, Waffle House, Wendy's, **lodging:** Best Western, Holiday Inn Express, Microtel, Red Roof Inn, Super 8, **other:** Firestone/auto, Ford, Hamrick's, K-Mart, Kroger, Food Lion, Radio Shack, RV Ctr, Winn-Dixie, **W** [H]
12	Yonkers Rd, Brentwood Rd
11b a	US 1, US 401, Capital Blvd N, **N gas:** BP, Citgo, Crown Gas, Kangaroo, Shell, **food:** Applebee's (1mi), BBQ, Bojangle's, Buffalo Bro.s, Burger King, Carver's Creek, Don Murray's BBQ, Dunkin Donuts, IHOP, Mayflower Seafood, McDonald's, Outback Steaks, Perkins, Subway, Taco Bell, Vallerta Mexican, Waffle House, Wendy's, **lodging:** Best Western, Comfort Inn, Country Inn, Day's Inn, Econolodge, Holiday Inn, Homestead Suites, Hotel Europa, Lodge America, Sleep Inn, Travelodge, Wingate Inn, **other:** , IGA Foods, USPO
10	10 Wake Forest Rd, **N food:** Denny's, **food:** Bajama Breze, **lodging:** AmeriSuites, Days Inn, Hilton, **other:** CVS Drug, **S gas:** BP, **food:** A&W/KFC, Applebee's, Bojangles, Jersey Mike's, Melting Pot Rest., Papa John's, Schlotzsky's, Taco Bell, **lodging:** Courtyard, Extended Stay America, Hampton Inn, Residence Inn, **other:** [H], Discount Tire, Staples
8b a	6 Forks Rd, North Hills, **N gas:** Exxon, **food:** Bonefish Grill, Panera Bread, Starbucks, **lodging:** Comfort Inn, **other:** Dillard's/JC Penney, GNC, Firestone/auto, Kerr Drug, Target, Winn-Dixie
7b a	US 70, NC 50, Glenwood Ave, Crabtree Valley, **N gas:** BP, Exxon, **food:** McDonald's, PF Chang's, Ruby Tuesday, **lodging:** Candlewood Suites, Courtyard, Crabtree Inn, Fairfield Inn, Holiday Inn, La Quinta, Marriott, Motel 6, Residence Inn, Sheraton, **other:** Barnes&Noble, Belk, Goodyear/auto, Macy's, Sears/auto, mall
6	Ridge Rd (from nb), same as 7
5	Lake Boone Tr, **W gas:** Phillips 66, **food:** McDonald's, Subway, Wendy's, **other:** [H], Food Lion
4b a	to I-40 W, Wade Ave, **W** to I-40, rd [airport]
3	NC 54, Hillsboro St, **E gas:** BP, Citgo, Crowne Gas, Exxon, **food:** Arby's, Bean Sprout Chinese, Quizno's, Snoopy's Hotdogs, Waffle House, **lodging:** Ramada Inn, **other:** to Meredith Coll, to St Mary's
2b a	Western Blvd, **E gas:** Crowne Gas, 76/Circle K, **food:** Domino's, Subway, **other:** to NCSU, Shaw U, **W** K-Mart

NC

INTERSTATE 240 CONT'D (ASHEVILLE)

Exit #	Services
1d	Melbourne Rd (from sb)
1c	Jones-Franklin Rd
1b a	I-40. I-440 begins on I-40., **1-2 mi W on Walnut St... gas:** Exxon, Shell, **food:** Hardee's, Olive Garden, Pizza Hut, Red Lobster, **lodging:** Best Western, Day's Inn, Motel 6, **other:** Borders Books Michael's, mall

INTERSTATE 485 (CHARLOTTE)

Exit #	Services
61	US 251, Johnston Rd, **N food:** Eddie's Place Rest, Global Rest, Hickory Tavern, Quizno's, Red Robin, Ruby Tuesday, Sticky Fingers, **lodging:** SpringHill Suites, **other:** Earth Fare Foods, **S gas:** Texaco/dsl, **food:** Buffalo's SW Cafe, 5 Guys Burgers, Flat Rock Grille, Moe's SW Grill, Smoothie King, Tony's Pizza, **lodging:** Ballantyne Hotel, Courtyard, Staybridge Suites, **other:** CVS Drug
64b a	rd 51, **N gas:** Exxon, Shell/Circle K, **food:** Bojangles, Donato's Pizza, KFC/Pizza Hut, McDonald's, Pier 57 Seafood, Wendy's, **lodging:** Extended Stay America, Extended Stay Deluxe, **other:** H, Bi-Lo, Firestone/auto, **S gas:** Shell, **food:** Applebee's, Buca Italian, Burger King, China Buffet, IHOP, Jason's Deli, Red Lobster, Subway, Taco Bell, Tony Roma's, **lodging:** Holiday Inn Express, Quality Inn, **other:** Belk, Dillard's, $General, Food Lion, Home Depot, JC Penney, K-Mart, Office Depot, Petsmart, Rite Aid, Sear/auto, SteinMart, TJ Maxx
65	South Blvd, **N gas:** Texaco, **food:** Chick-fil-A, Golden Corral, Hooters, McDonald's, Rafferty's, Sonny's BBQ, Steak'n Shake, TX Roadhouse, Wendy's, **other:** Advance Parts, Chevrolet, Discount Tire, $Tree, Kohl's, Nissan, Old Navy, PetCo, Ross, Target, VW, World Mkt, **S other:** Cadillac, CarMax, Pineville Tires, Vet
67	I-77, US 21, to Charlotte, Columbia, I-485 begins/ends
61b a	US 521 S, Johnston Rd, **E gas:** Exxon, **food:** Applebee's, Chick-fil-A, China Bistro, 1511 Cantina, JoJo China Bistro, Firebird's Grill, Marble Slab, Miro Spanish Grill, Noodles Rest, Pizza Inn, Starbucks, Wendy's, **lodging:** Residence Inn, **other:** Borders Books, GNC, Goodyear/auto, Harris-Teeter, Radio Shack, Target, Vet
59	Rea Rd
57	Providence Rd, rd 16, **E gas:** Texaco/Wendy's, **food:** Hickory Tavern, Penn Sta, The Wok, **other:** Curves, Harris-Teeter, USPO, **W gas:** Exxon, Shell, **food:** BBQ Shack, Cold Stone, Macaroni Grill, Red Bowl Rest, Starbucks, **other:** CVS Drug, Home Depot, Lowes Foods, Rite Aid, Staples, SteinMart, Vet
52	to Matthews
51b a	US 74, to Charlotte, Monroe, **E gas:** 76/Circle K/dsl, Shell, Sunoco/dsl, **lodging:** Country Inn&Suites, Holiday Inn Express, InTown Suites, **other:** Country Camping RV Ctr, Scion/Toyota, **W gas:** Exxon, Shell, **food:** Bojangles, Pizza Hut, Taco Bell, Wendy's, **lodging:** Courtyard, EconoLodge, Microtel, **other:** H Aamco, AutoZone, Firestone/auto, Goodyear/auto, Radio Shack, Tuesday Morning
49	Idlewild Rd, **E gas:** Exxon/dsl, **food:** China Cafe, El Maguey Mexican, Mama's Pizza, **other:** Lowe's Foods, Rite Aid
47	Lawyers Rd, **E gas:** Gate, **food:** Aladdin's, Bellacino's Pizza, Best China, Domino's, McDonald's, **other:** CVS Drug, Harris-Teeter, Vet, **2 mi W food:** Dunkin Donuts, Wendy's
44	rd 218, to Mint Hill, **W gas:** BP/dsl
43	rd 51, to Mint Hill
41	rd 24, rd 27, to Albemarle, **2 mi W food:** Chick-fil-A, Taco Bell
39	Harrisburg Rd, **W gas:** BP, **food:** China Garden, Papa John's, Wendy's, **other:** Food Lion
36	Rocky River Rd, **N gas:** Citgo/dsl, Gate, **food:** Best China, Bojangles, Capriccio's Pizza, Subway, **other:** CVS Drug, Discount Tire, Harris-Teeter, Tuffy Auto
33	rd 49, to Harrisburg, **N gas:** Hess/dsl, **food:** Cici's Pizza, **other:** Food Lion, **S gas:** BP, Exxon, 76/Circle K, Sunoco, **food:** Little Caesar's, Wendy's, **other:** Family$
32	US 29, **N other:** CVS Drug, **S gas:** Texaco, **food:** Jack-in-the-Box, **other:** H
23c	rd 115, to Huntersville, I-485 begins/ends on I-85
23b a	I-77, to Charlotte, Statesville
21	rd 24, Harris Blvd, **S food:** Bravo Italian, Chick-fil-A, Chili's, Cold Stone, Edomae Grill, Firehouse Subs, 5 Guys Burgers, Fox&Hound, Mimi's Cafe, Moe's SW Grill, Olive Garden, On-the-Border, Panera bread, PF Chang's, Red Robin, Shane's Rib Shack, TGI Friday's, Wendy's, **lodging:** Drury Inn, **other:** AT&T, Belk, Best Buy, Borders Books, Dillard's, Lowe's Whse, Macy's, Old Navy, Petsmart, Target, mall
16	rd 16, to Newton, Brookshire Blvd, **W food:** Bojangles, Bull&Barrister Rest, Chick-fil-A, CiCi's Pizza, McDonald's, Pizza Hut, Red Bowl Asian, Subway, Wendy's **other:** Harris-Teeter, Rite Aid, Walmart SuperCtr
14	rd 27, to Mt Holly Rd, **W gas:** BP (2mi)
12	Moores Chapel Rd, **E food:** Jin Jin Chinese, **other:** Advance Parts, CVS Drug, Food Lion
10	I-85, to Spartanburg, Greensboro
9	US 29, US 74, Wilkinson Blvd, **S gas:** BP
4	rd 160, to Fort Mill, **N gas:** Exxon/dsl, **other:** CVS Drug
3	Arrowood Rd, **S gas:** Quizno's
1	S Frion St, rd 49, **N gas:** Exxon, Shell, Texaco, **food:** Bojangles, Dragon Buffet, McDonald's, O'Charley's, Panera Bread, Qdoba, **other:** Bi-Lo, Lowe's Whse, Walmart SuperCtr, **S gas:** Texaco/dsl, **food:** Applebee's, Baskin-Robbins/Dunkin Donuts, Burger King, Domino's, Don Pedro Mexican, Firehouse Subs, Fortune Cookie, Hungry Howie's, McAlister's Deli, Moe's SW Grill, Pan China, Starbucks, Subway, Wild Wing Cafe, **lodging:** Hilton Garden, Yorkshire Inn, **other:** AT&T, AutoZone, Discount Tire, $Tree, Food Lion, NAPA, Office Depot, Tire Kingdom, Tuffy Auto

NORTH DAKOTA

INTERSTATE 29

Exit #	Services
218mm	North Dakota state line, US/Canada border
217mm	US Customs sb
216mm	historical site nb, tourist info sb
215	ND 59, rd 55, Pembina, **E gas:** Gastrak/DutyFree Store/dsl, Gastrak/pizza/dsl/scales/24hr, **other:** Pembina State Museum/info

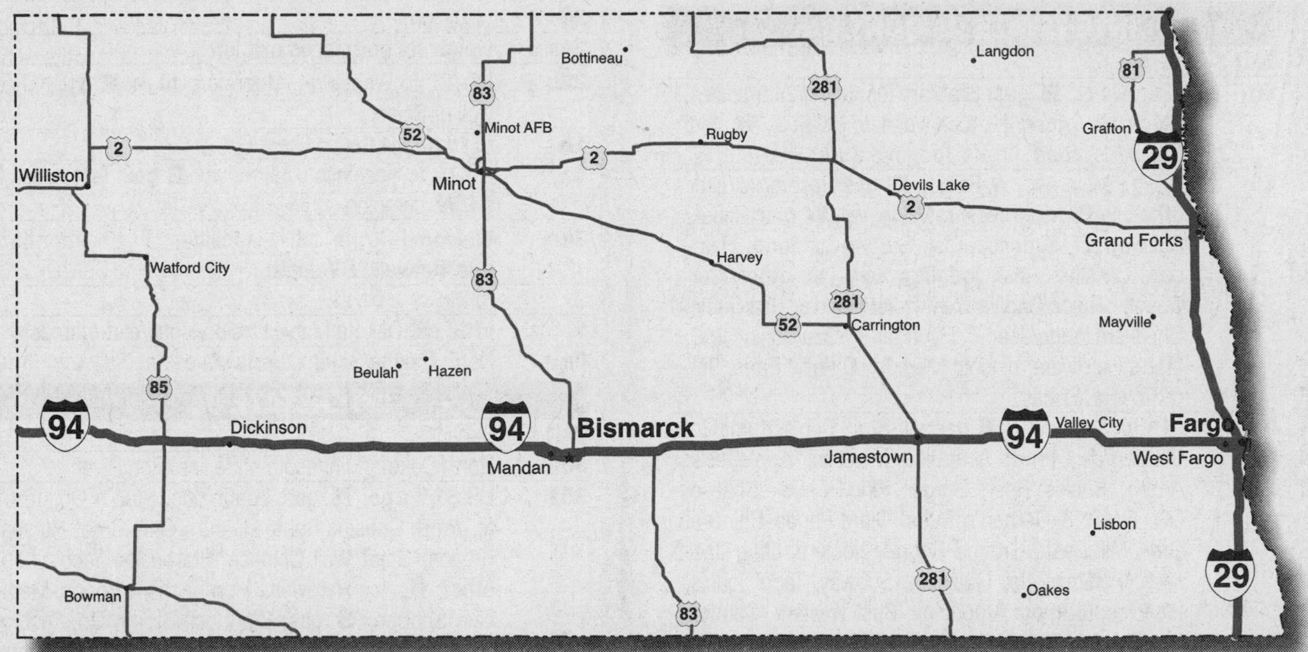

INTERSTATE 29 CONT'D

N ↕ S

Exit #	Services
212	no services
208	rd 1, to Bathgate
203	US 81, ND 5, to Hamilton, Cavalier, **W** to Icelandic SP (25 mi), **weigh sta both lanes**
200	no services
196	rd 3, Bowesmont
193	no services
191	rd 11, to St Thomas
187	ND 66, to Drayton, **E gas:** Cenex/pizza/dsl, Tesoro/dsl, **food:** Rte 44 Café, **lodging:** Motel 66, **other:** USPO, city park
184	to Drayton, **2 mi E** gas/dsl, USPO
180	rd 9
179mm	**rest area both lanes (both lanes exit left), full ♿ facilities, ☎, 🧺, litter barrels, vending, petwalk**
176	ND 17, to Grafton, **10 mi W** [H], gas, food, **lodging:** AmericInn
172	no services
168	rd 15, to Minto, Warsaw
164	no services
161	ND 54, rd 19, to Ardoch, Oslo
157	no services
152	US 81, to Gilby, Manvel, **W gas:** Manvel/dsl/food
145	US 81 bus, N Washington St, to Grand Forks
141	US 2, Gateway Dr, Grand Forks, **E gas:** Cenex, Loaf'N Jug/dsl, Stamart, Univ. Sta/dsl, **food:** Al's Grill, Burger King, Greatwall Buffet, McDonald's, **lodging:** Best Value Inn, Budget Inn, Clarion, Econolodge, Ramada Inn, Select Inn, Super 8, **other:** Ford/Lincoln/Mercury, O'Reilly Parts, transmissions, to U of ND, **1 mi E food:** DQ, Domino's, Taco John's, **other:** [H], Freightliner, U-Haul, auto repair, **W gas:** Simonson/dsl/café/24hr/@, StaMart/Tesoro/dsl/RV dump/scales/@, **food:** Emerald Grill, Perkins, **lodging:** Settle Inn, **other:** Budget RV Ctr, GMC/Volvo, **port of entry/weigh sta,** ✈, dsl repair, to AFB
140	DeMers Ave, **E gas:** Cenex, Loaf'N Jug, Valley Dairy, **food:** Red Pepper Cafe, **lodging:** Canada Inn, Hilton Garden, **other:** [H], Alerus Ctr, to U of ND
138	US 81, 32nd Ave S, **E gas:** Cenex, Holiday/dsl, **food:** Arby's, Buffalo Wild Wings, Burger King, China Garden, Coldstone Creamery, Culver's, DQ, Denny's, Golden Corral, Grizzly's Steaks, Ground Round, Jimmy John's, McDonald's, Papa Murphy's, Pizza Hut, Qdoba Mexican, Quizno's, Red Lobster, Space Alien's Rest, Starbucks, Taco Bell, Texas Roadhouse, Village Inn, Wendy's, **lodging:** C'mon Inn, Comfort Inn, Country Inn&Suites, Days Inn, Fairfield Inn, Holiday Inn Express, Lakeview Inn, Roadking Inn, SpringHill Suites, **other:** Best Buy, Chrysler, CVS Drug, $Tree, Ford/Lincoln/Mercury, Gordman's, Hugo's Foods, JC Penney, Jo-Ann Fabrics, Kohl's, Lowe's Whse, Macy's, Menard's, Michael's, Old Navy, PetCo, Sam's Club/gas, Scion/Toyota, Super 1 Foods, Target, Tires+, TJ Maxx, Walmart SuperCtr, mall, **W gas:** Sinclair/Subway/dsl, **other:** Grand Forks Camping
130	ND 15, rd 81, Thompson, **1 mi W** gas, food
123	to Reynolds, **E** to Central Valley School
119mm	no services
118	to Buxton
111	ND 200 W, to Cummings, Mayville, **W other:** Big Top Fireworks, to Mayville St U
104	Hillsboro, **E gas:** Cenex/Burger King/dsl/LP/24hr, Tesoro/Stop-n-Go/dsl/24hr, **food:** Country Hearth Rest., Pizza Ranch, Subway, **lodging:** Hillsboro Inn, **other:** [H], RV park, USPO
100	ND 200 E, ND 200A, to Blanchard, Halstad
99mm	**rest area both lanes, full ♿ facilities, ☎, 🧺, litter barrels, vending, petwalk**
92	rd 11, Grandin, **E** Co-op/dsl, **W gas:** Stop&Shop/dsl
86	Gardner
79	Argusville
74.5mm	Sheyenne River
73	rd 17, rd 22, Harwood, **E gas:** Cenex/pizza/dsl/LP/café/24hr
69	rd 20
67	US 81 bus, 19th Ave N, **E lodging:** Homewood Suites, **other:** VA [H], Hector Int ✈

GRAND FORKS

INTERSTATE 29 CONT'D

Exit #	Services
66	12th Ave N, **E gas:** StaMart/Tesoro/dsl/24hr/scales, Stop'n Go, **other:** [H], tuck wash, to ND St U, **W gas:** Cenex/dsl, **food:** Arby's, **lodging:** Super 8
65	US 10, Main Ave, W Fargo, **E gas:** Tesoro/dsl/24hr, **other:** NAPA, OK Tire, True Value, Vet, **W gas:** Cenex/Subway/dsl, Simonson/dsl, Stop-n-Go, **food:** Hardee's, O'Kelly's Rest, **lodging:** Kelly Inn, **other:** CarQuest, Buick/Cadillac/Chevrolet/Honda, CarQuest, Chrysler/Dodge/Jeep, Hyundai, Isuzu/Volvo/GMC, Mac's Hardware, Lincoln/Mercury, O'Reilly Parts, Scion/Toyota, Subaru
64	64 13th Ave, Fargo, **E gas:** All-Stop, Don's, Kum&Go, StaMart/dsl, **food:** Acapulco Mexican, Applebee's, Arby's, Buck's Rest, Burger King, ChuckeCheese, DQ, Erbert & Gerbert's Subs, Giant Panda Chinese, GreenMill Rest., Ground Round, Hooters, Little Caesar's, Perkins/24hr, Quizno's, Subway, Taco John's, Wendy's, **lodging:** AmericInn, Best Western, Comfort Inn, Comfort Suites, Country Inn&Suites, Econolodge, Grand Inn, Hampton Inn, Motel 6, Super 8, **other:** CashWise Foods/drug/24hr, CVS Drug, Family$, Goodyear/auto, O'Reilly Parts, Tires+/transmissions, White Drug, auto repair, **W gas:** All-Stop/dsl, Cenex, Tesoro, **food:** Applebee's, Arby's, Buffalo Wild Wings, Caribou Coffee, Chili's, Culver's, DQ, Denny's, Domino's, Grizzly's, Godfather's, Happy Joe's Pizza, KFC, Kroll's Diner, LoneStar Steaks, McDonald's, Olive Garden, Paradiso Mexican, Pizza Hut, Red Lobster, Ruby Tuesday, Schlotsky's, Spitfire Grill, Subway, Taco Bell, Taco John's, Texas Roadhouse, TGIFriday, TimberLodge Steaks, **lodging:** Comfort Inn, Days Inn, Fairfield Inn, Holiday Inn Express, Kelly Inn, Ramada Inn, Red River Lodge, Select Inn, **other:** Barnes&Noble, Best Buy, BigLots, Chevrolet, Chrysler/Dodge/Jeep, $Tree, GNC, Gordman's, Hancock Fabrics, Herberger's, Hobby Lobby, Honda, Hornbacher's Foods, JC Penney, Jo-Ann Fabrics, Kohl's, Lowe's Whse, Macy's, Menard's, Michael's, Office Depot, Old Navy, PetCo, Petsmart, Sam's Club/gas, Savers Foods, Sears/auto, SunMart Foods, Target, TJ Maxx, Walmart SuperCtr, Walgreens, USPO, mall
63b a	I-94, W to Bismarck, E to Minneapolis
62	32nd Ave S, Fargo, **E gas:** F&F/dsl, Holiday, Tesoro, **food:** Arby's, Country Kitchen, Culver's, KFC, Little Caesar's, Moe's SW Grill, Papa John's, Quizno's, Starbucks, Subway, Taco John's, Village Inn, **other:** [H], Buick/GMC/Pontiac, Ford, Freightliner, JiffyLube, SunMart Foods, **W gas:** ***FLYING J***/Conoco/dsl/LP/motel/24hr/@, **other:** Goodyear/auto, Peterbilt, Volvo
60	52nd Ave S, to Fargo, **W other:** Walmart SuperCtr
56	to Wild Rice, Horace
54	rd 16, to Oxbow, Davenport
50	rd 18, Hickson
48	ND 46, to Kindred
44	to Christine, **1 mi E** gas
42	rd 2, to Walcott
37	rd 4, to Abercrombie, Colfax, **E** to Ft Abercrombie HS, 3 mi **W** gas
31	rd 8, Galchutt
26	to Dwight
24mm	**weigh sta both lanes exit left**
23b a	ND 13, to Wahpeton, Mooreton, **10 mi E** [H], ND St Coll of Science
15	rd 16, to Mantador, Great Bend
8	ND 11, to Hankinson, Fairmount, **E gas:** Tesoro/dsl, **3 mi W** camping
3mm	**Welcome Ctr nb, full [handicapped] facilities, [phone], [picnic], litter barrels, petwalk, RV dump**
2	rd 22
1	rd 1E, **E** Dakota Magic Casino/Hotel/rest./gas/dsl
0mm	North Dakota/South Dakota state line

INTERSTATE 94

Exit #	Services
352mm	North Dakota/Minnesota state line, Red River
351	US 81, Fargo, **N gas:** Loaf'n Jug, Stop'n Go, Tesoro, **food:** Cousins Subs, Duane's Grill, Great Harvest Breads, Great Wall Chinese, Starbucks, Taco Shop, **other:** [H], Ace Hardware, Hornbacher's Foods, Medicine Shoppe, **S gas:** Clark/dsl, Stop'n Go, Tesoro, **food:** A&W/LJ Silver, Burger King, Gina's Pizza, Happy Joe's Pizza, KFC, McDonald's, N American Steaks, Papa Murphy's, Pepper's Café, Randy's Diner, Subway, Taco Bell, **lodging:** Prarie Rose Inn, Rodeway Inn, **other:** Hyundai/Nissan, K-Mart, USPO
350	25th St, Fargo, **N gas:** Stop'n Go, **S gas:** Cenex/dsl, Loaf'n Jug, **food:** Dolittle's Grill, Ruby Tuesday
349b a	I-29, N to Grand Forks, S to Sioux Falls, **facilities 1 mi N**, exit 64
348	45th St, **0-2 mi N Visitor Ctr/full facilities...gas:** Holiday, Petro/dsl/LP/rest./24hr/@, **food:** Bennigan's, Carino's, Culver's, Denny's, IHOP, Little Caesars, McDonald's, Pizza Hut, Qdoba Mexican, Quizno's, Papa Murphy's, Subway, Wendy's, **lodging:** Best Western, C'mon Inn, Expressway Suites, Hilton Garden, MainStay Suites, Ramada Inn, Sleep Inn, Staybridge Suites, Wingate Inn, **other:** Blue Beacon, Home Depot, Kohl's, Office Depot, NAPA, Sam's Club, Scheel's Sports, Target, Walmart SuperCtr/24hr, **S gas:** Tesoro/DQ/dsl, **food:** Famous Dave's BBQ, Golden Corral, Old Chicago Pizza, Up the Creek Grill, **lodging:** Settle Inn, **other:** Gander Mtn, Red River Zoo
346b a	to Horace, W Fargo, **S gas:** Tesoro/dsl, repair
343	US 10, Lp 94, W Fargo, **N gas:** Cenex/dsl, **food:** Speedway Steaks, **lodging:** Sunset Motel **other:** Adventure RV Ctr, Harley-Davidson, Pioneer Village
342	no services
342mm	**weigh sta wb**
340	to Kindred
338	Mapleton, **N gas:** Petro/dsl
337mm	**truck parking wb, litter barrels**
331	ND 18, to Leonard, Casselton, **N gas:** Tesoro/Subway/dsl, **food:** Capitol Rest., **lodging:** Governors Inn/RV park, **other:** NAPA
328	to Lynchburg
327mm	**truck parking eb, litter barrels**
324	Wheatland, to Chaffee
322	Absaraka
320	to Embden
317	to Ayr
314	ND 38, to Alice, Buffalo, **3 mi N** gas, food
310	no services

INTERSTATE 94 CONT'D

Exit #	Services
307	to Tower City, **N gas:** Mobil/dsl/café/RV Park/24hr, motel
304mm	**rest area both lanes (both lanes exit left), full facilities, info, , , litter barrels, vending, petwalk**
302	ND 32, to Fingal, Oriska, **1 mi N** Scotty's Grill
298	no services
296	no services
294	Lp 94, to Kathryn, Valley City, **N** H, camping
292	Valley City, **N gas:** Tesoro/dsl/café/24hr, **food:** Sabir's Rest., **lodging:** AmericInn, Super 8, Wagon Wheel Inn/rest., **other:** H, to Bald Hill Dam, camping, **S other:** Ft Ransom SP (35mi)
291	Sheyenne River
290	Lp 94, Valley City, **N gas:** Tesoro/dsl, **food:** Burger King, Kenny's Rest., Pizza Hut, Roby's Rest., Subway, **other:** H, Chrysler/Dodge/Jeep, Family$, Ford, NAPA, Pamida
288	ND 1 S, to Oakes, **S** Fort Ransom SP (36 mi)
283	ND 1 N, to Rogers
281	to Litchville, Sanborn, **1-2 mi N** gas, food, lodging
276	Eckelson, **S other:** Prairie Haven Camping/gas/dsl
275mm	continental divide, elev 1490
272	to Urbana
269	Spiritwood
262	Bloom, **N**
260	Jamestown, **N gas:** Stop'n Go, Tesoro/dsl/café/@, **lodging:** Starlite Motel, **other:** to St H, Buick/Chevrolet Dodge, camping, tires, Vet
259mm	James River
258	US 281, Jamestown, **N gas:** Super Xpress/TCBY/dsl, Tesoro/dsl, **food:** Arby's, DQ, Hardee's, Little Caesar's, McDonald's, Pizza Ranch, Subway, Taco Bell, **lodging:** Comfort Inn, Day's Inn, Holiday Inn Express, Ranch House Motel, **other:** H, Buffalo Herd/museum, Cadillac/GMC/Pontiac, Chrysler/Toyota, Firestone/auto, NW Tire, O'Reilly Parts, **S gas:** Sinclair/dsl/24hr, **food:** Applebee's, Burger King, Grizzly's Rest., Hong Kong Buffet, Paradiso Mexican, Perkins, **lodging:** Quality Inn, Super 8, **other:** Ford, Harley-Davidson, JC Penney, K-Mart, Sears, Walmart Super Ctr, mall, USPO, Vet
257	Lp 94 (from eb), to Jamestown, **N** dsl repair
256	US 52 W, US 281 N, **S other:** Wiest truck/trailer repair, **1 mi S** Jamestown Campground/RV dump
254mm	**rest area both lanes, full facilities, , , litter barrels, petwalk, vending**
251	Eldridge
248	no services
245	no services
242	Windsor, **1/4 mi N** gas
238	to Gackle, Cleveland
233	no services
230	Medina, **1 mi N gas:** Cenex/dsl/LP, **food:** DairyTreat, **other:** Medina RV Park, USPO, city park
228	ND 30 S, to Streeter
224mm	**rest area wb, full facilities, , , litter barrels, vending, petwalk, RV dump**
221	Crystal Springs
221mm	**rest area eb, full facilities, , , litter barrels, vending, petwalk, RV dump**

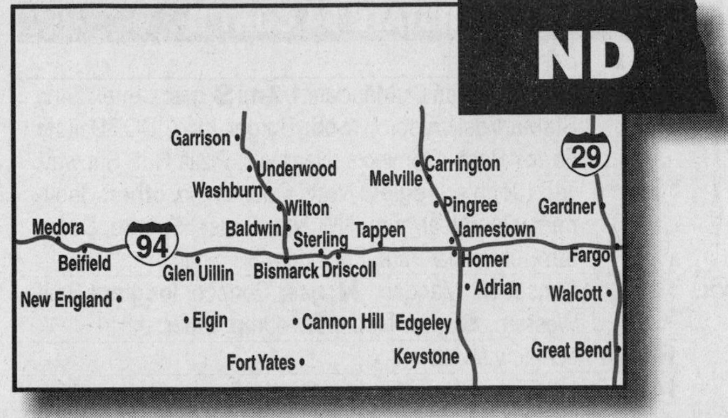

Exit #	Services
217	Pettibone
214	Tappen, **S** gas/dsl/food
208	ND 3 S, Dawson, **N** RV camping, **1/2 mi S** gas, food, to Camp Grassick, RV camping
205	Robinson
200	ND 3 N, to Tuttle, Steele, **S gas:** Cenex/dsl/24hr, **food:** Lone Steer café, **lodging:** OK Motel, **other:** truckwash
195	no services
190	Driscoll, **S** food
182	US 83 S, ND 14, to Wing, Sterling, **S gas:** Cenex/dsl/24hr, **food:** Darnell's Café, **lodging:** Top's Motel (1mi)
176	McKenzie
170	Menoken, **S** to McDowell Dam, RV Park
168mm	**rest area both lanes, full facilities, , , litter barrels, vending, petwalk**
161	Lp 94, Bismarck Expswy, Bismarck, **N gas:** Cenex/dsl/LP/RV Dump/24hr, Express, **food:** Quizno's, **other:** Dodge/Toyota, **S gas:** Tesoro/Oasis/dsl/rest./24hr, **food:** McDonald's, **lodging:** Ramada Ltd, **other:** Capital RV Ctr, Dakota Zoo, Freightliner, Kenworth, OK Tires, Volvo
159	US 83, Bismarck, **N gas:** Best Stop/dsl, Simonson/dsl, **food:** Applebee's, Arby's, Burger King, Capt Jack's Rest., China Town, Golden Corral, Hooters, KFC, Kroll's Diner, McDonald's, Paradiso Mexican, Perkins, Quizno's, Red Lobster, Ruby Tuesday, Schlotsky's, Space Alien Grill, Taco Bell, TCBY, Wendy's, **lodging:** AmericInn, Candlewood Suites, Comfort Inn, Country Suites, Fairfield Inn, Hampton Inn, Holiday Inn Express, **other:** Chevrolet, CVS Drug, Dan's Foods, Hancock Fabrics, K-Mart, Menard's, NW Tire, Sears/auto, U-Haul, Walmart Super Ctr/Subway, mall, **S gas:** Conoco/dsl, StaMart/dsl, Tesoro, **food:** DQ, Hardee's, Minerva's Rest., North American Steaks, Pizza Hut, Starbucks, Subway, Taco John's, Woodhouse Rest., **lodging:** Best Western, Day's Inn, Kelly Inn, Select Inn, Super 8, **other:** H, O'Reilly Parts
157	Divide Ave, Bismarck, **N gas:** Conoco/dsl/LP/24hr, **food:** Carino's, Cracker Barrel, Goodtimes Grill/Taco John's, McDonald's, Quizno's, Texas Roadhouse, Wendy's, **other:** Best Buy, $Tree, Kohls, Lowes Whse, PetsMart, TJ Maxx, **S gas:** Cenex/dsl/LP/RV Dump, **other:** Central Mkt Foods
156mm	Missouri River
156	I-194, Bismarck Expswy, Bismarck City Ctr, **1/2 mi S** Dakota Zoo
155	to Lp 94 (exits left from wb), Mandan, City Ctr, same as 153

INTERSTATE 94 CONT'D

E ↕ W

Exit #	Services
153	ND 6, Mandan Dr, Mandan, **1/2 mi S gas:** Cenex/24hr, StaMart/dsl, Tesoro, **food:** Burger King, DQ, Dakota Farms Rest., Domino's, Hardee's, Pizza Hut, Subway, Taco John's, **lodging:** North Country Inn, **other:** Chevrolet, Goodyear/auto, NW Tire, Parts+, Subaru, Dacotah Centennial Park, Ft Lincoln SP (5mi)
152	Sunset Dr, Mandan, **N gas:** Conoco, **lodging:** Best Western, **S gas:** Tesoro/RV dump, **other:** H
152mm	scenic view eb
147	ND 25, to ND 6, Mandan, **S gas:** Sinclair/Subway/dsl/café/24hr
140	to Crown Butte
135mm	scenic view wb, litter barrel
134	to Judson, Sweet Briar Lake
127	ND 31, to New Salem, **N** Knife River Indian Village (35mi), **S gas:** Cenex/dsl, Tesoro/dsl, **food:** Sunset Cafe, **lodging:** Arrowhead Inn/café, **other:** Farmer's/gas, Food Pride, Gaebe Drug, World's Largest Cow, Vet
123	to Almont
120	no services
119mm	**rest area both lanes, full facilities, litter barrels, petwalk**
117	no services
113	no services
110	ND 49, to Glen Ullin
108	to Glen Ullin, Lake Tschida, **3 mi S** gas, food, lodging, camping
102	Hebron, to Glen Ullin, to Lake Tschida, **3 mi S** gas, food, lodging, camping
97	Hebron, **2 mi N** gas, food, lodging
96.5mm	central/mountain time zone
90	no services
84	ND 8, Richardton, **N gas:** Cenex/dsl, **other:** H, to Assumption Abbey, Schnell RA
78	to Taylor
72	to Enchanted Hwy, Gladstone
64	Dickinson, **S gas:** Tesoro/Tiger Truckstop/dsl/rest./24hr, **food:** Dakota Diner, **other:** Ford/Lincoln/Mercury, Honda/Toyota, NW Tire, dsl repair
61	ND 22, Dickinson, **N gas:** Cenex/dsl/LP/24hr, Simonson/dsl, **food:** Applebee's, Arby's, Bonanza, Burger King, DQ, El Sombrero Mexican, Happy Joe's Pizza, Papa Murphy's, Sanford's Rest., Taco Bell, Taco John's, Wendy's, **lodging:** AmericInn, Comfort Inn, Days Inn, Holiday Inn Express, **other:** Dan's Foods, Goodyear/auto, Herberger's, JC Penney, K-Mart, NAPA, O'Reilly Parts, TrueValue, Walmart SuperCtr/Subway/24hr, White Drug, **S gas:** Cenex/dsl, Conoco/repair, Holiday/dsl/24hr, Tesoro, **food:** A&W/KFC, Country Kitchen, Domino's, King Buffet, McDonald's, Perkins, Subway, **lodging:** Quality Inn, Select Inn, Super 8, Travel Host, **other:** H, Ace Hardware, museum, visitor info
59	Lp 94, to Dickinson, **S** to Patterson Lake RA, camping, **3 mi S** services in Dickinson
51	South Heart
42	US 85, to Grassy Butte, Belfield,Williston, **N** T Roosevelt NP (52mi), **S** info, **gas:** Conoco/dsl, Tesoro/dsl/24hr, **food:** DQ, **lodging:** Trapper's Inn/rest., **other:** NAPA
36	Fryburg
32	**T Roosevelt NP, Painted Canyon Visitors Ctr, N rest area both lanes, full facilities, litter barrels, petwalk**
27	Lp 94, Historic Medora (from wb), T Roosevelt NP
24.5mm	Little Missouri Scenic River
24	Medora, Historic Medora, Chateau de Mores HS, T Roosevelt NP, **S Visitors Ctr**
23	West River rd (from wb)
22mm	scenic view eb
18	Buffalo Gap, **N** Buffalo Gap Camping (seasonal), food/lodging
10	Sentinel Butte, Camel Hump Lake, **S** gas
7	Home on the Range
1	ND 16, Beach, **N lodging:** Outpost Motel, **other:** camping, **S gas:** Cenex/dsl/LP/24hr, *FLYING J*/Country Mkt/dsl/scales/LP/24hr, **lodging:** Buckboard Inn, **other:** H, **Welcome/Visitor Ctr, full facilities, litter barrels, petwalk,**
1mm	**weigh sta both lanes, litter barrel**
0mm	North Dakota/Montana state line

OHIO

INTERSTATE 70

E ↕ W

Exit #	Services
225.5mm	Ohio/West Virginia state line, Ohio River
225	US 250 W, OH 7, Bridgeport, **N gas:** Marathon, StarFire, Sunoco/24hr, **food:** KFC, Papa John's, Pizza Hut, Wendy's (1mi), **other:** Advance Parts, AutoZone, Family$, NAPA, **S gas:** Exxon, Gulf, **food:** Domino's
220	US 40, rd 214, **N gas:** Marathon, Sunoco/dsl, **S gas:** Chevron/dsl, **lodging:** Day's Inn, **other:** vet
219	I-470 E, to Bel-Aire, Washington PA, new exit
218	Mall Rd, to US 40, to Blaine, **N gas:** BP, Exxon, **food:** Applebees, Arby's, Buffalo Wild Wings, Burger King, DeFelice Pizza, Denny's, Eat'n Park, King Buffet, Outback Steaks, Red Lobster, Steak'n Shake, Subway, Taco Bell, Undo Italian, Wendy's, W Texas Steaks, **lodging:** Best Value Inn, Econolodge, Hampton Inn,
218	Continued Holiday Inn Express, Red Roof Inn, Super 8, **other:** Aldi Foods, AutoZone, Buick/Cadillac/Chevrolet/Pontiac, $General, $Tree, Kroger, Lowes Whse, Sam's Club, Staples, Stewart's RV Ctr, Walmart SuperCtr, **S food:** Bob Evans, Bonanza, Cracker Barrel, Elder Beerman, Garfield's Rest., KFC/LJ Silver, Longhorn Steaks, McDonald's, Panera Bread, Quizno's, Starbucks, **lodging:** Fairfield Inn, **other:** CVS Drug, Jo-Ann Fabrics, K-Mart, Macy's, NTB, Sears/auto, mall
216	OH 9, St Clairsville, **N gas:** BP
215	National Rd, **N gas:** Chevron, **food:** Burger King, Domino's, WenWu Chinese, **other:** NAPA, Riesbeck's Foods, USPO
213	OH 331, Flushing, **S gas:** BP, Marathon/dsl, Sunoco/dsl, **food:** Subway, **lodging:** Twin Pines Motel

E ↕ W

INTERSTATE 70 CONT'D

Exit #	Services
211mm	**rest area both lanes, full ♿ facilities, ☎, ⛱, litter barrels, petwalk, vending**
208	OH 149, Morristown, **N gas:** BP/McDonald's/dsl, **food:** Schlepp's Rest., **lodging:** Arrowhead Motel (1mi), **other:** Cannonball Speedway, Ford/Lincoln/Mercury, **S gas:** Chevron/Quizno's/dsl, **other:** Harley-Davidson, Barkcamp SP
204	US 40 E (from eb, no return), National Rd
202	OH 800, to Barnesville, **S gas:** 202 Gas/dsl, **other:** H
198	rd 114, Fairview
193	OH 513, Middlebourne, **N gas:** BP, FuelMart/dsl, **other:** fireworks
189mm	**rest area eb, full ♿ facilities, ☎, ⛱, litter barrels, petwalk, vending**
186	US 40, OH 285, to Old Washington, **N gas:** BP, **S gas:** GoMart/dsl
180b a	I-77 N, to Cleveland, to Salt Fork SP, I-77 S, to Charleston
178	OH 209, Cambridge, **0-1 mi N gas:** BP/dsl, Sheetz/dsl, Shell, **food:** Bob Evans, China Village, Cracker Barrel, Denny's, DQ, Forum Rest, KFC, McDonald's,
178	Continued Papa John's, Pizza Hut, Ruby Tuesday, Subway, Taco Bell, USA Steaks, Wendy's, **lodging:** Best Western, Comfort Inn, Days Inn, Hampton Inn, Ramada Inn, Super 8, **other:** H, Advance Parts, AutoZone, BigLots, Buick/Cadillac/GMC/Pontiac, $General, Family$, Value-Fresh Foods, **S gas:** Murphy USA/dsl, Pilot/Subway/dsl/scales/24hr, **food:** Arby's, Burger King, Great Chinese, Little Caesar's, Talaquepaque Mexican, **lodging:** Baymont Inn, **other:** Aldi Foods, $Tree, $Zone, K-Mart/gas, Radio Shack, Spring Valley RV Park, Walmart SuperCtr/24hr
176	US 22, US 40, to Cambridge, **N gas:** Sunoco/dsl, **lodging:** Budget Inn, **other:** Western Shop, RV camping, st patrol
173mm	**weigh sta both lanes**
169	OH 83, to Cumberland, New Concord, **N gas:** BP, **other:** John & Annie Glen Historic Site, RV camping, to Muskingum Coll
164	US 22, US 40, Norwich, **N gas:** BP, **lodging:** Baker's Motel, Zane Gray Museum, **S other:** pottery
163mm	**rest area wb, full ♿ facilities, ☎, ⛱, litter barrels, petwalk, vending**

INTERSTATE 70 CONT'D

E ↕ W

ZANESVILLE

Exit #	Services
160	OH 797, [airport], **N gas:** Love's/Arby's/dsl/scales/24hr, **S gas:** BP, Exxon/Subway/dsl, **food:** Denny's, McDonald's, Wendy's, **lodging:** Best Value Inn, Best Western, Ramada Inn, **other:** [airport], st patrol
157	OH 93, Zanesville, **N gas:** BP, **S gas:** Marathon, Shell/dsl, st patrol
155	OH 60, OH 146, Underwood St, Zanesville, **N food:** Bob Evans, Olive Garden, Oriental Buffet, Red Lobster, Steak'n Shake, Tumbleweed Grill, **lodging:** Comfort Inn, Fairfield Inn, Hampton Inn, Holiday Inn Express, **other:** [H], **Visitor Info**, Pick'n Save Foods, USPO, **S gas:** Exxon/dsl, **food:** Adornetto Café, Cracker Barrel, Subway, Wendy's, **lodging:** Baymont Inn, Econolodge, Travelodge, **other:** Family$, Rite Aid
154	5th St (from eb)
153b	Maple Ave (no EZ return from wb), **N gas:** BP, **food:** Big Boy, DQ, Papa John's, Tee Jaye's Rest, **other:** [H] CVS Drug, Family$
153a	State St, **N gas:** Speedway/dsl, **other:** to Dillon SP (8mi), **S gas:** Marathon
153mm	Licking River
152	US 40, National Rd, **N gas:** Exxon/A&W/Blimpie, Starfire/dsl, **food:** McDonald's, **lodging:** Super 8
142	US 40 (from wb, no EZ return), Gratiot, **N** RV camping
141	OH 668, US 40 (from eb, no return), to Gratiot, same as 142
132	OH 13, to Thornville, Newark, **N** Dawes Arboretum (3mi), **S gas:** BP, Shell, **food:** Subway (2mi), **other:** RV camping
131mm	**rest area both lanes, full [handicapped] facilities, [phone], [picnic], litter barrels, petwalk, vending**
129b a	OH 79, to Buckeye Lake, Hebron, **N lodging:** Quality Inn (7mi), **S gas:** BP, Valero, **food:** Catfish Charley's Pizza, McDonald's, Pizza Hut/Taco Bell, Wendy's, **lodging:** Super 8, **other:** CarQuest, IGA Foods, KOA (2mi), Blue Goose Marina (2mi)
126	OH 37, to Granville, Lancaster, **N gas:** Marathon/dsl, Pilot/Chester's/Subway/dsl/scales/24hr, **S gas:** Sunoco/dsl, TA/BP/Sbarro's/Popeye's/dsl/scales/24hr/@, **lodging:** Deluxe Inn, Red Roof Inn, **other:** IOA Truckomat, KOA, camping, truckwash,
122	OH 158, to Baltimore, Kirkersville, **N lodging:** Regal Inn, **S gas:** ***FLYING J***/CountryMkt/dsl/scales/LP/24hr, **other:** fireworks
118	OH 310, to Pataskala, **N gas:** BP/McDonald's, Speedway/dsl, Sunoco, **food:** DQ, **S gas:** Duke's/Subway/dsl, **other:** RCD RV Ctr
112c	OH 204, to Blecklick rd (from eb)
112	OH 256, to Pickerington, Reynoldsburg, **N gas:** BP, Shell/McDonald's, **food:** Buffalo Joe's, Chipotle Mexican, Culver's, Dynasty Buffet, Logan's Roadhouse, Noodles&Co, O'Charley's, Olive Garden, Panera Bread, Penn Sta, Rotolo's Pizza, Smokey Bones BBQ, TGIFriday's, Tim Horton, **lodging:** Country Inn&Suites, Fairfield Inn, **other:** Best Buy, Gander Mtn Jo-Ann Fabrics, Marshall's, NTB, Radio Shack, Sam's Club/gas, Staples, Target, Tire Discounters, T-Mobile, Verizon, Walgreens, Walmart SuperCtr/Subway/gas/24hr,
112	Continued **S gas:** Speedway, **food:** Arby's, Bob Evans, Classic's Diner, Cold Stone, Cracker Barrel, Dragon Chinese, Feta Greek Cafe, KFC, LJ Silver, Longhorn Steaks, Quizno's, Steak'n Shake, Stone Creek Diner, Uno, Wendy's, **lodging:** Best Western, Hampton Inn, Holiday Inn Express, **other:** URGENT CARE, Barnes&Noble, Tuesday Morning
110	Brice Rd, to Reynoldsburg, **N gas:** Speedway, Sunoco, **food:** Arthur Treachers, Burger King, Donato's, Eastern Palace, Genji Japanese, Golden China, Max&Erma's, Popeye's, Subway, TeeJaye's Rest., Tim Horton, Waffle House, **lodging:** Days Inn, Extended Stay America, La Quinta, Red Roof Inn, Super 8, **other:** Family$, Goodyear/auto, Home Depot, O'Reilly Parts, **S gas:** BP, Speedway, **food:** Applebee's, Arby's, Asian Star, Big Boy, Boston Mkt, Burger King, Chipotle Mexican, KFC, McDonald's, Ruby Tuesday, Starbucks, Taco Bell, Waffle House, White Castle, **lodging:** Best Value Inn, Comfort Suites, Econolodge, Motel 6, **other:** Acura, Advance Parts, Aldi Foods, Discount Tire, Farber RV Ctr, Firestone/auto, GNC, Hobby Lobby, Honda, Lincoln/Mercury, Lowe's Whse, Michael's, NTB, Old Navy, Petsmart, Scion/Toyota, Walgreens
108b a	I-270 N to Cleveland, access to [H], I-270 S to Cincinnati
107b a	OH 317, Hamilton Rd, to Whitehall, **S gas:** Shell/dsl, Valero, **food:** Arby's, Bob Evans, Burger King, Capt D's, Donato's, Eastland Buffet, Ichiban Japanese, McDonald's, Olive Garden, Papa John's, Pizza Hut, Red Lobster, Steak'n Shake, Taco Bell, White Castle, **lodging:** Fort Rapids Resort, Hampton Inn, InTown Suites, Knight's Inn, **other:** AT&T, $General, Firestone/auto, Kohl's, Macy's, PepBoys, Staples
105a	to Lancaster, **2 mi N food:** Tat Italian, Wendy's
105b	US 33, James Rd, Bexley, **N food:** Tat Italian, Wendy's
103b a	Livingston Ave, to Capital University, **N gas:** BP, Exxon, Speedway/dsl, **food:** KFC, Mr Hero Subs, Peking Dynasty, Popeye's, Subway, Taco Bell, Wendy's, **other:** Kroger/gas, auto repair, **S gas:** Marathon, Shell, **food:** McDonald's, Rally's, White Castle/24hr
102	Kelton Ave, Miller Ave, **S** [H]
101a	I-71 N, to Cleveland
100b	US 23, to 4th St, downtown
99c	Rich St, Town St (exits left from eb), **N gas:** Sunoco, **other:** Ford
99b	OH 315 N, downtown
99a	I-71 S, to Cincinnati
98b	Mound St (from wb, no EZ return), **S gas:** Marathon, **food:** LJ Silver, McDonald's, Rally's
98a	US 62, OH 3, Central Ave, to Sullivant, access to same as 98b
97	US 40, W Broad St, **N gas:** Valero/dsl, **food:** Arby's, Burger King, KFC, McDonald's, Pizza Hut/Taco Bell, Subway, Tim Horton, Wendy's, White Castle, **lodging:** Knight's Inn, **other:** Aamco, CVS Drug, U-Haul, USPO
96	I-670 (exits left from eb), to [airport]
95	Hague Ave (from wb), **S gas:** Sunoco
94	Wilson Rd, **N gas:** Marathon/Circle K/Subway/dsl, Mobil, **S gas:** BP, Pilot/Wendy's/dsl/scales/24hr, Shell/24hr, Speedway/24hr, **food:** McDonald's, Waffle House, White Castle, **lodging:** Econolodge

COLUMBUS AREA

INTERSTATE 70 CONT'D

E ↔ W

Exit #	Services
93b a	I-270, N to Cleveland, S to Cincinnati
91b a	to Hilliard, New Rome, **N gas:** Get N'Go, Shell, Speedway/dsl, **food:** AA China, Applebee's, Arby's, Big Boy, Buffalo Wild Wings, Burger King, Cracker Barrel, Chick-fil-A, Chipotle Mexican, CiCi's Pizza, Cold Stone/Tim Horton, Culver's, Donato's Pizza, El Vaquero Mexican, Fazoli's, Golden Chopsticks, HoneyBaked Ham, Hooters, KFC, McDonald's, Outback Steaks, Perkins, Pizza Hut/Taco Bell, Red Robin, Ruby Tuesday, Salvi's Bistro, Skyline Chili, Smoothie King, Subway, TX Roadhouse, White Castle, Wendy's, **lodging:** Best Value Inn, Comfort Suites, Hampton Inn, Hawthorn Inn, Hilliard Inn, Holiday Inn Express, La Quinta, Motel 6, Red Roof Inn, Tanglewood Suites, **other:** Advance Parts, Discount Tire, Firestone/auto, Ford, Gander Mtn, Giant Eagle Foods/gas, GNC, Kohl's, Marshall's, Meijer/dsl, Michael's, Old Navy, Petsmart, Sam's Club/gas, Radio Shack, Target, Walmart SuperCtr/24hr/gas, **S gas:** BP/dsl, Marathon/dsl, **food:** Bob Evans, Handel's Icecream, Steak'n Shake, **lodging:** Best Western, Country Inn&Suites, Microtel
85	OH 142, to Plain City, W Jefferson, **N other:** Prairie Oaks RV Park, **S other:** Battele Darby RV Park
80	OH 29, to Mechanicsburg, **S** hwy patrol
79	US 42, to London, Plain City, **N gas:** Pilot/Arby's/dsl/scales/24hr, **food:** Waffle House, **other:** truck/auto repair, **S gas:** Speedway/Subway/dsl/24hr, Sunoco/24hr, TA/BP/Pizza Hut/Popeye's/dsl/scales/24hr/@, **food:** McDonald's, Taco Bell, Wendy's, **lodging:** Holiday Inn Express, Motel 6, **other:** [H], truckwash
72	OH 56, to London, Summerford, **N gas:** Marathon/24hr, **4 mi S** [H], lodging
71mm	**rest area both lanes, full [handicapped] facilities, [phone], [picnic], litter barrels, vending, petwalk**
66	OH 54, to Catawba, South Vienna, **S gas:** Speedway/dsl, **other:** NAPA, rv camping
62	US 40, Springfield, **N lodging:** Harmony Motel, **other:** Harmony Farm Mkt, antiques, auto repair, to Buck Creek SP, **S** Beaver Valley Camping
59	OH 41, to S Charleston, **N other:** [H], Harley-Davidson, st patrol, **S gas:** BP/dsl, Clark/dsl, antiques
54	OH 72, to Cedarville, Springfield, **N gas:** BP/dsl, Shell, Speedway/dsl, Sunoco/dsl/24hr, **food:** A&W/LJ Silver, Arby's, Bob Evans, Cassano's Pizza/subs, Cracker Barrel, Domino's, El Toro Mexican, Hardee's, Lee's Chicken, Little Caesar's, McDonald's, Panda Chinese, Rally's, Rudy's Smokehouse, Subway, Taco Bell, Wendy's, **lodging:** Comfort Suites, Days Inn, Hampton Inn, Holiday Inn, Ramada Ltd, Red Roof Inn, Super 8, **other:** [H], Advance Parts, BigLots, Family$, Kroger/deli, Rite Aid, Walgreens, **S gas:** Marathon/dsl, Swifty
52b a	US 68, to Urbana, Xenia, **S** to John Bryan SP
48	OH 4 (from wb), to Enon, Donnelsville, **N gas:** Speedway, **other:** camping
47	OH 4 (from eb), to Springfield, **N gas:** Speedway, **other:** RV Camping
44	I-675 S, Spangler Rd, to Cincinnati
43mm	Mad River

SPRINGFIELD

Exit #	Services
41b a	OH 4, OH 235, to Dayton, New Carlisle, **1 mi N gas:** BP/dsl, **food:** KFC/LJ Silver, McDonald's, Wendy's, **other:** Freightliner, Kenworth
38	OH 201, Brandt Pike, **N gas:** Marathon/dsl, **other:** Meijer/dsl/E-85, **S gas:** Mobil/dsl, Shell, **food:** Bob Evans, Sonic, Tim Horton, Waffle House, Wendy's, **lodging:** Best Value Inn, Comfort Inn, **other:** Walmart SuperCtr/McDonald's/24hr
36	OH 202, Huber Heights, **N gas:** Speedway/dsl/24hr, **food:** A&W/KFC, Applebee's, Big Boy, El Toro Grill, Fazoli's, Quizno's, Steak'n Shake, Taco Bell, Waffle House, **lodging:** Baymont Inn, **other:** URGENT CARE, Elder Beerman, Gander Mtn., GNC, Hobby Lobby, Kohl's, Lowe's Whse, Marshall's, Petsmart, Staples, Target, Verizon, Vet, **S gas:** BP/dsl, Marathon/dsl, **food:** Arby's, Bob Evans, Buffalo Wild Wings, Burger King, Cadillac Jack's Grill, CiCi's Pizza, McDonald's, Skyline Chili, Subway, TGIFriday's, TX Roadhouse, White Castle, **lodging:** Days Inn, Hampton Inn, Holiday Inn Express, **other:** $Tree, K-Mart, Kroger/gas, Tuesday Morning
33b a	I-75, N to Toledo, S to Dayton
32	Vandalia, **N** to Dayton Intn'l [airport]
29	OH 48, to Dayton, Englewood, **N gas:** BP, Speedway, Sunoco, Valero, **food:** Arby's, Big Boy, Bob Evans, Buffalo Wild Wings, KFC, Lee's Chicken, Perkins, Penn Sta. Subs, Skyline Chili, Taco Bell, Tim Horton, Tony's Italian, Wendy's, Yen Ching Chinese, **lodging:** Best Western, Hampton Inn, Holiday Inn, Motel 6, Super 8, **other:** Advance Parts, Aldi Foods, Big Lots, Family$, O'Reilly Parts, Vet, **S food:** McDonald's, Steak'n Shake, Tumbleweed SW Grill, Waffle House, **lodging:** Comfort Inn, Motel 6, **other:** [H], Meijer/dsl/e-85/24hr
26	OH 49 S, **N gas:** Murphy USA/dsl, **food:** Bob Evans, La Rosa's Pizzaria, Sonic, Subway, **other:** URGENT CARE, Radio Shack, Walmart SuperCtr/24hr, **S food:** Wendy's
24	OH 49 N, to Greenville, Clayton, **S gas:** Sunoco/dsl/24hr, **other:** KOA (seasonal)
21	rd 533, Brookville, **N gas:** GA/Subway, **S gas:** Speedway/dsl, Swifty, **food:** Arby's, Brookville Grill, DQ, Great Wall Chinese, K's Rest., KFC/Taco Bell, McDonald's, Rob's Rest., Subway, Waffle House, Wendy's, **lodging:** Days Inn, Holiday Inn Express, **other:** Brookville Parts, Chevrolet, Curves, $General, Family$, IGA Foods, Rite Aid, True Value
14	OH 503, to West Alexandria, Lewisburg, **N gas:** Marathon/Subway/dsl, **food:** Dairi Twist, **lodging:** Super Inn, **other:** IGA Foods, **S gas:** Valero/dsl

DAYTON

INTERSTATE 70 CONT'D

Exit #	Services
10	US 127, to Eaton, Greenville, **N gas:** TA/BP/Burger King/Subway/dsl/scales/24hr/@, st patrol, **S gas:** Pilot/Subway/dsl/scales/24hr, **lodging:** Budget Inn
3mm	**Welcome Ctr eb/rest area both lanes, full facilities, ☎, vending, picnic, litter barrels, petwalk**
1	US 35 E (from eb), to Eaton, New Hope
0mm	Ohio/Indiana state line, **Welcome Arch, weigh sta eb**

INTERSTATE 71

Exit	Services
247b	I-90 W, I-490 E. I-71 begins/ends on I-90, exit 170 in Cleveland.
247a	W 14th, Clark Ave
246	Denison Ave, Jennings Rd (from sb)
245	US 42, Pearl Rd, **E gas:** BP, Sunoco, **other:** H, zoo
244	W 65th, Denison Ave
242b a	W 130th, to Bellaire Rd, **W gas:** Sunoco, **food:** Burger King (1/2mi)
240	W 150th, **E gas:** Marathon, Speedway/dsl, **food:** Denny's, **lodging:** Marriott, **W gas:** BP/Subway/dsl, **food:** Burger King, MacKenzie's Grill, Somers Rest., Taco Bell, **lodging:** Holiday Inn, La Quinta
239	OH 237 S (from sb), **W** to airport
238	I-480, Toledo, Youngstown, **W** airport
237	Snow Rd, Brook Park, **E gas:** BP, Marathon, Shell, **food:** Bob Evans Cafe, KFC, McDonald's, Suwaby, **lodging:** Best Western, Holiday Inn Express, Howard Johnson, **other:** AutoZone, Top's Foods, **W** to airport
235	Bagley Rd, **E food:** Bob Evans, **W gas:** BP/dsl, Shell, Speedway, **food:** Burger King, Caribou Coffee, Chipotle Mexican, Damon's, Denny's, Friendly's, McDonald's, Olive Garden, Panera Bread, Perkins, Pizza Hut, Roadhouse Grill, Taco Bell, **lodging:** Comfort Inn, Courtyard, Motel 6, Plaza Motel, Radisson, Ramada Inn, Red Roof Inn, Studio+, TownePlace Suites, **other:** HOSPITAL, Aldi Foods, Buick, GMC, K-Mart
234	US 42, Pearl Rd, **E gas:** Sunoco/dsl, **food:** Hunan Chinese, Katherine's Rest., Wendy's, **other:** Audi/Porsche, Honda, Hyundai, **W gas:** AP/dsl, **food:** Buffalo Wild Wings, Jennifer's Rest, Mad Cactus Mexican, **lodging:** Day's Inn, Kings Inn, La Siesta Motel, Metrick's Motel, Village Motel, **other:** Circle K, Home Depot, Lowes Whse, Walmart, vet,
233	I-80 and Ohio Tpk, to Toledo, Youngstown
231	OH 82, Strongsville, **E gas:** Shell, **lodging:** Holiday Inn, Motel 6, **W gas:** BP/Subway/dsl, Marathon/dsl, Sunoco/dsl, **food:** Applebee's, Buca Italian, Demetrio's Rest., Longhorn Steaks, Macaroni Grill, Panera Bread, Red Lobster, **other:** Borders Books, Dillard's, Giant Eagle Foods, JC Penney, Kohl's, NTB, Sears/auto, Target, mall
226	OH 303, Brunswick, **E gas:** Shell/dsl/24hr, **food:** Pizza Hut, **other:** Chrysler/Jeep/Toyota, **W gas:** BP, GetGo, Marathon/dsl, Sunoco/dsl, **food:** Arby's, Bob Evans, Burger King, CiCi's Pizza, McDonald's, Starbucks, Steak'n Shake, Subway, Taco Bell, Wendy's, **lodging:** Howard Johnson, Sleep Inn, **other:** Ford, Giant Eagle Food, K-Mart
225mm	**rest area nb, full facilities, ☎, picnic, litter barrels, petwalk**
224mm	**rest area sb, full facilities, ☎, picnic, litter barrels, petwalk**
222	OH 3, **W** st patrol
220	I-271 N, (from nb) to Erie, PA
218	OH 18, to Akron, Medina, **E gas:** BP/dsl/24hr, Marathon, Shell/dsl, Sunoco/dsl, **food:** Alexandri's Rest., Blimpie, Burger King, DQ, **lodging:** Best Value, Holiday Inn Express, Super 8, Traveler's Choice, **other:** $General, GMC, KIA, Mitsubishi, **W gas:** Speedway/dsl, **food:** Arby's, Bob Evans, Buffalo Wild Wings, Denny's, McDonald's, Pizza Hut, Waffle House, Wendy's, **lodging:** Hampton Inn, Motel 6, Red Roof Inn, **other:** H Aldi Foods, Dodge, Harley-Davidson, Honda, NTB, Pontiac/Buick/Cadillac/GMC
209	I-76 E, to Akron, US 224, **W gas:** Pilot/Country Kitchen/Subway/dsl/scales/24hr, TA/Burger King/Popeye's/dsl/24hr/@, **food:** Arby's, McDonald's, Starbucks, **lodging:** Super 8, **other:** Blue Beacon, Chippewa Valley Camping(1mi), SpeedCo
204	OH 83, Burbank, **E gas:** BP/dsl, Duke/dsl, Loves/Hardees/scales/dsl/24hr, **lodging:** Plaza Motel, **W gas:** Pilot/Wendy's/dsl/scales/24hr, **food:** Bob Evans, Burger King, McDonald's, **other:** H, Buick/Chevrolet/Pontiac, Chrysler/Jeep/Dodge, Lodi Outlets/famous brands
198	OH 539, W Salem
196mm	**rest area both lanes, full facilities, ☎, vending, picnic, litter barrels, petwalk**
196	OH 301(from nb, no re-entry), W Salem, **no services**
186	US 250, Ashland, **E gas:** Marathon, **food:** Perkins, Grandpa's Village/cheese/gifts, **other:** Hickory Lakes Camping(7mi), **W gas:** Citgo, Goasis/Pizza Hut/Popeye's/Starbucks/Taco Bell/dsl/rest./24hr, **food:** Bob Evans, Buehler's Rest., Denny's, Donato's Pizza, Jake's Rest., McDonald's, Wendy's, **lodging:** AmeriHost, Day's Inn, Holiday Inn Express, Super 8, **other:** H, GNC, Home Depot, Walmart SuperCtr, st patrol, to Ashland U
176	US 30, to Mansfield, **E lodging:** Econolodge, **other:** fireworks
173	OH 39, to Mansfield
169	OH 13, Mansfield, **E gas:** Marathon/dsl, **food:** Applebee's, Cracker Barrel, HillTop Dairy Bar, Steak'n Shake, Wendy's, **other:** Walmart SuperCtr/Subway/gas/24hr, Mohican SP, **lodging:** Best Western, La Quinta, **W gas:** Marathon, **food:** Arby's, Bob Evans, Burger King, Cracker Barrel, El Compacino Mexican, Joe's Rest., McDonald's, Taco Bell, **lodging:** Hampton Inn, Super 8, Travelodge, **other:** H, st patrol
165	OH 97, to Bellville, **E gas:** BP, Speedway/dsl, Shell/dsl, **food:** Burger King, Dutch Heritage Rest., McDonald's, **lodging:** Day's Inn, Comfort Inn, Knight's Inn, Quality Inn, **other:** to Mohican SP, **W food:** Dinner Bell Rest., Wendy's
151	OH 95, to Mt Gilead, **E gas:** Duke/BP/dsl/rest./24hr/@, Marathon, **food:** Gathering Rest., McDonald's, Wendy's, **lodging:** Best Western, **other:** st patrol, **W gas:** Sunoco/dsl, Shell/dsl, **food:** Leaf Rest., **lodging:** Knight's Inn, **other:** H, Mt Gilead SP(6mi)
149mm	**truck parking both lanes**
140	OH 61, Mt Gilead, **E gas:** Pilot/Arby's/dsl/scales/24hr, **W gas:** BP/Taco Bell, Sunoco/Subway, **food:** Ole Farmstead Rest.

E–W; N–S; CLEVELAND; ASHLAND; MANSFIELD; OH

INTERSTATE 71 CONT'D

N ↕ S

Exit #	Services
131	US 36, OH 37, to Delaware, **E gas:** *FLYING J*/Cookery/dsl/LP/rest./scales/24hr, Pilot/Subway/dsl/scales/24hr, **food:** Burger King, **other:** Harley-Davidson, **W gas:** BP/dsl, Shell/Tim Horton, **food:** Arby's, Bob Evans, Cracker Barrel, KFC/LJ Silver, McDonald's, Starbucks, Taco Bell, Waffle House, Wendy's, White Castle, **lodging:** Day's Inn, Hampton Inn, Holiday Inn Express, **other:** H, Alum Cr SP, Cross Creek Camping(6mi)
129mm	**weigh sta nb**
128mm	**rest area both lanes, full facilities, phone, vending, picnic, litter barrels, petwalk**
121	Polaris Pkwy, to Gemini Pl, **E gas:** BP, Mobil/24hr, **food:** Bonefish Grill, Buffalo Wild Wings, Canes, Carfagna's, Dynasty Express, McDonald's, Pei Wei Chinese, Quizno's, Skyline Chili, Starbucks, Steak'n Shake, **lodging:** Best Western, Hampton Inn, Wingate Inn, **other:** Mr. Tire, Polaris Ampitheatre, **W gas:** BP, Shell/Circle K/Tim Horton/USPO, **food:** Applebee's, Arby's, BJ's Rest., Caribou Coffee, Carrabba's, Charley Subs, Cheese Burger Paradise, Chick-fil-A, Chipotle Mexican, City BBQ, Domino's, Fox's Pizza, Hoggy's Grille, Honey Baked Ham, Hooters, House of Japan, Krispy Kreme, Marcella's Italian, Max&Erma's, Merlot's Rest., MiMi's Cafe, Mitchell Steaks, Noodles & Co., O'Charley's, Olive Garden, Panera Bread, Papa John's, Pizza Hut/Taco Bell, Potbelly, Qdoba Mexican, Quaker Steaks, Red Lobster, Red Robin, Rudedog Grill, Shane's Ribshack, Sonic, Smokey Bones BBQ, Sonic, Starbucks, Subway, TGIFriday, TX Roadhouse, Uncle Chan, Waffle House, Wendy's, **lodging:** Cambria Suites, Candlewood Suites, Comfort Inn, Extended Stay Deluxe, Hilton, Hilton Garden,other: Barnes&Noble, Best Buy, Costco/gas, GNC, JC Penney, Jo-Ann Fabrics, Kroger/gas, Lowe's Whse, Macy's, NTB, Old Navy, Sears/auto, Target, Tire Discounters, TJ Maxx, Walmart SuperCtr/24hr (3mi), World Mkt, funpark, mall
119b a	I-270, to Indianapolis, Wheeling
117	OH 161, to Worthington, **E gas:** BP/dsl, Shell, Speedway/dsl, Sunoco, **food:** Burger King, China Dynasty, Chipotle Mexican, KFC, LJ Silver, Max&Erma's, McDonald's, Rally's, Red Lobster, Subway, Super Seafood Buffet, White Castle, **lodging:** Comfort Inn, Day's Inn, Holiday Inn Express, Knight's Inn, Motel 6, **other:** Big Bear Foods, CVS Drug, $General, Staples, Tire Discounters, Walgreens, auto repair, vet, **W gas:** Clarion, GetGo, Shell, Speedway/dsl, **food:** Bob Evans, China Jade, McDonald's, Pizza Hut, Skyline Chili, Subway, Tim Horton, Waffle House, Wendy's, **lodging:** Baymont Inn, Best Western, Clarion, Crowne Plaza, Country Inn&Suites, Extended Stay America, Family$, Rodeway Inn, Super 8, Travelodge, **other:** Advance Parts, Chevrolet, Family$, Giant Eagle/gas, Walgreens
116	Morse Rd, Sinclair Rd, **E gas:** BP, Shell, Speedway, **food:** McDonald's, Subway, **lodging:** Howard Johnson, **other:** Buick/Pontiac/GMC, CVS Drug, $General, Ford, Kia, Kohl's, Kroger, PepBoys, Save-a-Lot Foods, **W gas:** Sunoco, **food:** La Hacienda Mexican, **lodging:** Best Value Inn, Motel 6, Ramada, **other:** NTB

COLUMBUS AREA

Piqua
Urbana
Troy
Englewood
Springfield
70
Dayton
675
Yellow Springs
Kettering
Beavercreek
Jeffersonville
Centerville
71
Middletown
75
Wilmington
Fairfield
Mason
Greenfield
275
Goshen
Hillsboro
OH

Exit #	Services
115	Cooke Rd
114	N Broadway, **W gas:** Sunoco, **food:** Broadway Mkt Cafe, Subway
113	Weber Rd, **W gas:** Speedway/dsl, **other:** CarQuest, NAPA
112	Hudson St, **E gas:** Marathon, Shell, **food:** Wendy's, **lodging:** Holiday Inn Express, **W food:** Big Boy, **other:** Aldi Foods, Lowe's Whse, NTB
111	17th Ave, **W food:** McDonald's, **lodging:** Comfort Inn, Day's Inn
110b	11th Ave
110a	5th Ave, **E gas:** Sunoco, **food:** White Castle, **W gas:** Valero, **food:** Church's, KFC, Popeye's, Rally's, Wendy's, **other:** AutoZone
109a	I-670
109b	OH 3, Cleaveland Ave
109c	Spring St
108b	US 40, Broad St, downtown
108a	Main St
101a[70]	I-70 E, US 23 N, to Wheeling
100b a[70]	US 23 S, Front St, High St, downtown
106a	I-70 W, to Indianapolis
106b	OH 315 N, Dublin St, Town St
105	Greenlawn, **W gas:** Marathon, **food:** White Castle, **other:** H
104	OH 104, Frank Rd
101b a	I-270, Wheeling, Indianapolis
100	Stringtown Rd, **E gas:** BP, **food:** Bob Evans, Chick-fil-A, Chipotle Mexican, CiCi's Pizza, Coldstone Creamery, DQ, Longhorn Steaks, O'Charley's, Olive Garden, Panda Express, Red Robin, Smokey Bones BBQ, Sonic, Starbucks, Steak'n Shake, White Castle, **lodging:** Best Western, Drury Inn, Hampton Inn, Holiday Inn Express, Hilton Garden, La Quinta, Microtel, Red Roof Inn, **other:** Best Buy, Discount Tire, Home Depot, Michael's, PetsMart, Staples, Target, TJ Maxx, Walmart SuperCtr/24hr, **W gas:** GetGo, Speedway/dsl, Sunoco/Subway, **food:** Applebee's, Arby's, Burger King, China Bell, Cracker Barrel, Fazoli's, Golden Corral, KFC, Mariachi Mexican, McDonald's, Papa John's, Rally's, Ruby Tuesday, Starbucks, Taco Bell, TeeJaye's Rest., Tim Horton, Waffle House, Wendy's, **lodging:** Comfort Inn, Day's Inn, Motel 6, Saver Motel, **other:** Aldi Foods, AutoZone, CVS Drug, Giant Eagle Foods, K-Mart, Kroger/24hr, Radio Shack, Walgreens
97	OH 665, London-Groveport Rd, **E gas:** Marathon/Circle K, Meijer, Sunoco, **food:** Arby's, McDonald's, Quizno's, Tim Horton/Wendy's, **other:** URGENT CARE, Kroger/gas/E85, to Scioto Downs, **W other:** Eddie's Repair

COLUMBUS AREA

INTERSTATE 71 CONT'D

N ↕ S

Exit #	Services
94	US 62, OH 3, Orient
84	OH 56, Mt Sterling, **E gas:** BP/Subway/dsl, Sunoco, **food:** Brewster's Grill, **lodging:** Royal Inn, **other:** to Deer Creek SP (9mi)
75	OH 38, Bloomingburg, **E** fireworks, **W gas:** Sunoco/dsl
69	OH 41, OH 734, Jeffersonville, **E gas:** *FLYING J* /CountryMkt/dsl/scales/LP/24hr, **other:** H, Walnut Lake Camping, **W gas:** BP, Shell/Subway, **food:** Arby's, Wendy's, **lodging:** Quality Inn, **other:** Family$
68mm	**rest area both lanes, full ♿ facilities, ☎, vending, picnic, litter barrels, petwalk**
65	US 35, Washington CH, **E gas:** Shell, TA/BP/Pizza Hut/Popeye's/dsl/scales/24hr/@, **food:** A&W/KFC, Bob Evans, McDonald's/playplace, Taco Bell/LJ Silver, Waffle House, Wendy's, **lodging:** AmeriHost, Hampton Inn, **other:** H, Prime Outlets/famous brands, **W gas:** Loves/Hardee's/dsl/scales/24hr, **lodging:** Budget Motel, Econolodge
58	OH 72, to Sabina
54mm	**weigh sta sb**
50	US 68, to Wilmington, **E other:** H, **W gas:** Pilot/Subway/dsl/scales/24hr, Shell/dsl/24hr, **food:** Max&Erma's, McDonald's, Wendy's, **lodging:** Budget Inn, Holiday Inn, Robert Senter
49mm	**weigh sta nb**
45	OH 73, to Waynesville, **E gas:** BP, **other:** H, RV Park, **W** Caesar Creek SP (5mi), flea mkt
36	Wilmington Rd, **E** to Ft Ancient St Mem, RV camping
35mm	Little Miami River
34mm	**rest area both lanes, full ♿ facilities, scenic view, ☎, vending, picnic, litter barrels, petwalk**
32	OH 123, to Lebanon, Morrow, **E gas:** BP, Valero, **food:** Country Kitchen, **other:** Morgan's RV Park, **3 mi W food:** Bob Evans, Skyline Chili, **lodging:** Knight's Inn
28	OH 48, S Lebanon, **E lodging:** Countryside Inn (1mi), **W other:** Lebanon Raceway (6mi), hwy patrol
25	OH 741 N, Kings Mills Rd, **E gas:** Shell/Popeye's, Speedway/dsl, **food:** El Toro Mexican, McDonald's, Ruby Tuesday, Taco Bell, Outback Steaks, **lodging:** Comfort Suites, Great Wolf Lodge, Kings Island Inn, Quality Inn, **other:** Harley-Davidson, **W gas:** BP, Exxon/Subway, **food:** Arby's, Big Boy, Bob Evans, Burger King, DQ, Perkins, Pizza Hut, Skyline Chili, Waffle House, Wendy's, **lodging:** Best Western, Hampton Inn, Microtel, Super 8, **other:** Curves, CVS Drug, GNC, Kroger
24	Western Row, King's Island Dr (from nb), **E gas:** Sunoco, **lodging:** King's Island, **other:** Jellystone Camping, funpark
19	US 22, Mason-Montgomery Rd, **E gas:** Meijer/dsl/24hr, Shell, Speedway, Sunoco/24hr, **food:** Arby's, Big Boy, Bennigan's, Bob Evans, Boston Mkt, Cracker Barrel, Fazoli's, Fiesta Brava, Fushon Buffet, Golden Corral, Honey-Baked Ham, KFC, McDonald's, Olive Garden, Pizza Hut, Taco Bell, TGIFriday, Wendy's, White Castle, **lodging:** Comfort Inn, Quality Inn,

CINNCINATI AREA

Exit #	Services
19	Continued Signature Inn, **other:** AutoZone, Barnes&Noble, Best Buy, Chevrolet, Costco/gas, Firestone/auto, GMC/Buick/Pontiac, Goodyear, Kohl's, Kroger, Lincoln/Mercury, Michael's, Old Navy, Radio Shack, Sam's Club/gas, Target, Tires+, Tire Discounters, Toyota, Walgreens, Vet, **W gas:** BP/dsl, Marathon/dsl/24hr, Shell, **food:** Abuleo's, Amon's Steaks, Applebee's, Burger King, Carrabba's, Chipotle Mexican, China City, LoneStar Steaks, Macaroni Grill, McAlister's Deli, MiMi's Cafe, Noodles, O'Charley's, Palacio Azteca, Polo Grill, Qdoba Mexican, Red Robin, River City Grill, Steak'n Shake, Skyline Chili, Subway, Tumbleweed Grill, Waffle House, Wendy's, Wild Oats Mkt, **lodging:** AmeriSuites, Best Western, Day's Inn, King's Inn, La Quinta, Marriott, Ramada Ltd, Red Roof Inn, **other:** Bigg's Foods, Border's Books, Home Depot, Lowe's Whse, Staples, Subaru, Walmart Super Ctr/24hr
17b a	I-275, to I-75, OH 32
15	Pfeiffer Rd, **E** H, **W gas:** BP, Shell/dsl, Sunoco/dsl/24hr, **food:** Applebee's, Bob Evans, Buffalo Wild Wings, Subway, Watson Bro's Bistro, **lodging:** Courtyard, Crowne Plaza, Embassy Suites, Hampton Inn, Holiday Inn Express, Red Roof Inn, **other:** Office Depot
14	OH 126, Reagan Hwy, Blue Ash
12	US 22, OH 3, Montgomery Rd, **E gas:** BP/dsl, Shell/24hr, **food:** Arby's, Bob Evans, Chipotle Mexican, Ember's, Jalapeno Cafe, KFC, LJ Silver, Outback Steaks, Panera Bread, Red Lobster, Ruby Tuesday, Subway, Taco Bell, TGIFriday, Wendy's, **lodging:** Best Western, **other:** Dodge, Firestone, Goodyear, Hyundai, PepBoys, Staples, Tuesday Morning, **W gas:** Chevron, **food:** Cheesecake Factory, IHOP, KFC, Johnny Rocket's, Macaroni Grill, Max&Erma's, McDonald's, Potbelly's, Starbucks, Wendy's, **other:** H, Barnes&Noble, Dillard's, Firestone/auto, Fresh Mkt Foods, Macy's, Old Navy, Staples, mall
11	Kenwood Rd, (from nb), **W** H, same as 12
10	Stewart Rd (from nb), to Silverton, **W gas:** Marathon/dsl
9	Redbank Rd, to Fairfax, (no ez sb return), **E gas:** Mobil, Speedway, **other:** BMW
8	Kennedy Ave, Ridge Ave W, **E gas:** Meijer/dsl, **food:** IHOP, **lodging:** Motel 6, **other:** Dodge, Sam's Club/gas, Target, **W gas:** Marathon/dsl, Shell/Subway, Speedway, **food:** Denny's, Golden Corral, Gold Star Chili, KFC, LJ Silver, McDonald's, Old Country Buffet, Pizza Hut, Rally's, Taco Bell, White Castle, Wendy's, **other:** Bigg's Foods, Big Lots, Ford, Goodyear, Home Depot, Lowes Whse, Office Depot, Tire Discounter, Walmart, transmissions
7b a	OH 562, Ridge Ave E, Norwood, **E gas:** BP, **food:** Ponderosa, **other:** AutoZone
6	Edwards Rd, **E gas:** BP, Shell, Speedway, **food:** Boston Mkt, Buca Italian, Donato's, Don Pablo, Fuddrucker's, GoldStar Chili, J Alexander's Rest., Longhorn Steaks, Max&Erma's, Noodles, PF Chang's, Starbucks, **other:** GNC, SteinMart, **W gas:** Shell
5	Dana Ave, Montgomery Rd, **W other:** Xavier Univ, Zoo
3	Taft Rd (from sb), U of Cincinnati

INTERSTATE 71 CONT'D

Exit #	Services
2	US 42, Reading Rd, Gilbert ave (from sb), **W other:** H, art Museum, ballpark stadium arena, downtown
1k j	I-471 S
1d	Main St, downtown
1c b	Pete Rose Way, Fine St, stadium, downtown
1a	I-75 N, US 50, to Dayton
I-71 S and I-75 S run together	
0mm	Ohio/Kentucky state line, Ohio River

INTERSTATE 74

CINCINNATI AREA

Exit #	Services
20	I-75 (from eb), N to Dayton, S to Cincinnati, I-74 begins/ends on I-75.
19	Gilmore St, Spring Grove Ave
18	US 27 N, Colerain Ave
17	Montana Ave (from wb), **N gas:** Circle K
14	North Bend Rd, Cheviot, **N gas:** Shell, Speedway/dsl, **food:** DQ, Dunkin Donuts, McDonald's, Papa John's, Perkins, Skyline Chili, Subway, Wendy's, White Castle, **other:** Curves, Family$, Kroger, Sam's Club/gas, Tire Discounters, Walgreens, **S gas:** BP, **food:** Bob Evans, **other:** Vet
11	Rybolt Rd, Harrison Pike, **S gas:** BP, **food:** Longhorn Steaks, Marco's Pizza, McDonald's, Sakura Steaks, Skyline Chili, Wendy's, White Castle, **lodging:** Holiday Inn Express, **other:** Kohl's, Meijer/gas,
9	I-275 N, to I-75, N to Dayton, (exits left from eb)
8mm	Great Miami River
7	OH 128, to Hamilton, Cleves, **N gas:** BP/dsl, Marathon/dsl, **food:** Wendy's
5	I-275 S, to Kentucky
3	Dry Fork Rd, **N gas:** BP, **S gas:** Marathon/dsl, Shell/Dunkin Donuts/dsl
2mm	**weigh sta eb**
1	1 New Haven Rd, to Harrison, **N gas:** BP/dsl, **food:** Buffalo Wild Wings, Cracker Barrel, GoldStar Chili, O'Charley's, Subway, **lodging:** Comfort Inn, **other:** Biggs Foods, Ford, Home Depot, Staples, Tires+, **S gas:** Marathon/dsl, Shell/Circle K, Speedway/dsl, Sunoco, **food:** A&W/KFC, Arby's, Big Boy, Burger King, Domino's, DQ, Happy Garden, McDonald's, Papa John's, Penn Sta, Perkins, Pizza Hut, Skyline Chili, Taco Bell, Waffle House, Wendy's, White Castle, **lodging:** Holiday Inn Express, **other:** Advance Parts, AutoZone, Big Lots, CVS Drug, $General, Family$, Firestone, GNC, Jo-Ann Fabrics, K-Mart, Kroger, NAPA, Radio Shack, Walgreens
0mm	Ohio/Indiana state line

INTERSTATE 75

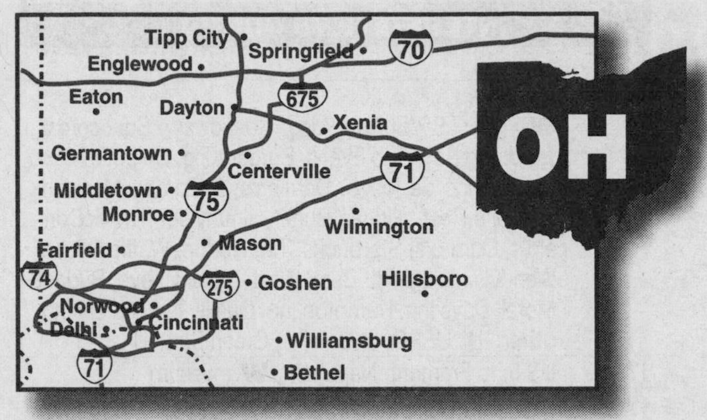

TOLEDO

Exit #	Services
211mm	Ohio/Michigan state line
210	OH 184, Alexis Rd, to Raceway Park, **W gas:** BP/dsl/24hr, Pilot/Subway/dsl/scales/24hr/@, **food:** Arby's, Bob Evans, Burger King, Ground Round, McDonald's, Taco Bell, Wendy's, **lodging:** Comfort Inn, Fairfield Inn, Hampton Inn, **other:** Ford Trucks, Meijer/dsl, Menards
210mm	Ottawa River
209	Ottawa River Rd (from nb), **E gas:** BP, Sunoco, **food:** China King, Little Caesar's, Marco's Pizza, **other:** Family$, Kroger/Starbucks/gas, Rite Aid, Vet
208	I-280 S, to I-80/90, to Cleveland
207	Stickney Ave, Lagrange St, **E gas:** BP, **food:** Arby's, McDonald's, Pizza Hut, Wendy's, **other:** Family$, K-Mart, Kroger, Rite Aid, Sav-a-Lot Foods
206	to US 24, Phillips Ave, **W** transmissions
205b	Burdan St, **E** H, **W gas:** Phillips 66, **food:** Burger King, Subway, **other:** Rite Aid
205a	to Willys Pkwy, to Jeep Pkwy
204	I-475 W, to US 23, to Maumee, Ann Arbor
203b	US 24, to Detroit Ave, **W gas:** BP/24hr, **food:** KFC, McDonald's, Rally's, Wendy's, **other:** American Petroleum, Rite Aid, Sav-A-Lot Foods, U-Haul
203a	Bancroft St, downtown
202	Washington St, Collingwood Ave (from sb, no EZ return), **E gas:** BP, **other:** H, Art Museum, **W food:** McDonald's
201b a	OH 25, Collingwood Ave, **W** Toledo Zoo
200	South Ave, Kuhlman Dr
200mm	Maumee River
199	OH 65, Miami St, to Rossford, **E lodging:** Days Inn
198	Wales Rd, Oregon Rd, to Northwood, **E gas:** Shell/Subway/dsl/24hr, Sunoco, **food:** Arby's, China Wok, Coney Is. **lodging:** Baymont Inn, Comfort Inn
197	Buck Rd, to Rossford, **E gas:** Shell/dsl, **food:** Wendy's/Tim Horton, **W gas:** BP/24hr, Sunoco/dsl, **food:** Denny's, McDonald's, **lodging:** American Inn, Knight's Inn
195	to I-80/90, OH 795, OH Tpk (toll), Perrysburg, **E gas:** BP/Subway/dsl, **lodging:** Country Inn&Suites, Courtyard, Hampton Inn, **other:** Bass Pro Shops
193	US 20, US 23 S, Perrysburg, **E gas:** BP/dsl/24hr, Get'n Go, Sunoco, **food:** Arby's, Big Boy, Bob Evans, Burger King, Chili's, China City, Coldstone Creamery, Cracker Barrel, 1st Wok, Fricker's, IHOP, KFC, Mancino's Pizza, McDonald's, Mi Hacienda, Panera Bread, Quizno's, Ralphie's, Sonic, Subway, Taco Bell, **lodging:** Candlewood Suites, Comfort Suites, Days Inn, Holiday Inn, Holiday Inn Express, Quality Inn, **other:** Belle Tire, Best Buy, Discount Tire, $Tree, Giant Eagle Foods, GNC, Home Depot, Kohl's, Kroger/gas/24hr, KOA (7mi), Lowe's Whse, Meijer/dsl, Michael's, PetsMart, Target, Tuffy, Walgreens, Walmart, **W gas:** Speedway/dsl, **lodging:** La Quinta, **other:** AutoZone, Harley-Davidson
192	I-475, US 23 N (exits left from nb), to Maumee, Ann Arbor
187	OH 582, to Luckey, Haskins
181	OH 64, OH 105, to Pemberville, Bowling Green, **E lodging:** Holiday Inn Express, **other:** Meijer/dsl/e-85,

INTERSTATE 75 CONT'D

Exit #	Services
181	Continued **W gas:** BP/Subway/dsl, Speedway, Sunoco/dsl, **food:** Big Boy, Bob Evans, Burger King, Chipotle Mexican, Cinco de Mayo, Domino's, El Zarape Mexican, Fricker's Rest., Hunan Buffet, Jimmy John's, McDonald's, Quizno's, Starbucks, Tim Horton, Waffle House, Wendy's, **lodging:** Best Western, Buckeye Budget Motel, Days Inn, Hampton Inn, Quality Inn, Victory Inn, **other:** [H], USPO, to Bowling Green State U
179	US 6, to Fremont, Napoleon, **W** museum
179mm	**rest area both lanes, full [handicap] facilities, [phone], [picnic], litter barrels, vending, petwalk**
175mm	**weigh sta nb**
171	OH 25, Cygnet
168	Eagleville Rd, Quarry Rd, **E gas:** FuelMart/dsl
167	OH 18, to Fostoria, North Baltimore, **E gas:** Petro/Mobil/Iron Skillet/dsl/scales/24hr/@, **food:** McDonald's, **other:** Blue Beacon, truck repair, **W gas:** Loves/Arby's/dsl/scales/24hr, Sunoco/dsl, **lodging:** Crown Inn, **other:** $General
165mm	Rocky Ford River
164	OH 613, to McComb, Fostoria, **E other:** RV Camping, to Van Buren SP, **W gas:** Pilot/Subway/Taco Bell/dsl/scales/24hr
162mm	**weigh sta sb, [phone]**
161	OH 99, **E gas:** Speedway/dsl, Shell/Subway, **lodging:** Comfort Suites, **other:** Ford/Lincoln/Mercury, hwy patrol **W** antiques
159	US 224, OH 15, Findlay, **E gas:** BP/dsl, Speedway/dsl, Swifty, **food:** Archie's Ice Cream, Burger King, Dakota Grill, KFC/LJ Silver, McDonald's, Ming's Great Wall, Pizza Hut, Ponderosa, Ralphie's, Spaghetti Shop, Steak'n Shake, Subway, Taco Bell, Wendy's, **lodging:** Drury Inn, Red Roof Inn, Rodeway Inn, Super 8, **other:** [H], **W gas:** Murphy USA/dsl, Shell/dsl, **food:** Bob Evans, China Garden, Coldstone Creamery, Cracker Barrel, Denny's, Jac&Do's Pizza, Landing Pad, Max&Erma's, Outback Steaks, Waffle House, **lodging:** Country Inn&Suites, Hampton Inn, Holiday Inn Express, Quality Inn, **other:** Chrysler/Dodge/Jeep, Peterbilt, Walmart SuperCtr/Subway
158	Blanchard River
157	OH 12, Findlay, **E gas:** GA/dsl, Marathon/Blimpie/Noble Roman's/dsl, **other:** Findlay Convention Ctr, **W food:** Fricker's Rest., **lodging:** Econolodge, **other:** Vet
156	US 68, OH 15, to Carey, **E** [H]
153mm	**rest area both lanes, full [handicap] facilities, [phone], [picnic], litter barrels, vending, petwalk**
145	OH 235, to Ada, Mount Cory, **E** TwinLakes Camping
142	OH 103, to Arlington, Bluffton, **E lodging:** Knight's Inn, **W gas:** BP, Marathon/Circle K/dsl, **food:** Arby's, Burger King, KFC, McDonald's, Subway, Taco Bell, **lodging:** Comfort Inn, **other:** $General, Vet, to Bluffton Coll
140	Bentley Rd, to Bluffton, **W** [H]
135	OH 696, to US 30, to Delphos, Beaverdam, **E gas:** Speedway/dsl/24hr, **W gas:** ***FLYING J***/Cookery/dsl/scales/LP/24hr, Pilot/McDonald's/Subway/dsl/24hr/@, **food:** Waffle House, **other:** Blue Beacon, NAPA Truck Repair, SpeedCo, tires, truck repair
134	Napolean Rd (no nb re-entry), to Beaverdam
130	Blue Lick Rd, **E lodging:** Best Value Inn
127b a	OH 81, to Ada, Lima, **W gas:** BP, Marathon/dsl, **food:** Subway, Waffle House, **lodging:** Comfort Inn, Days Inn/rest., Econolodge
126mm	Ottawa River
125	OH 309, OH 117, Lima, **E gas:** BP/dsl, Murphy USA/dsl, Speedway/dsl, **food:** Applebee's, Arby's, Bob Evans, Burger King, Capt D's, China Buffet, Cracker Barrel, Hunan Garden, McDonald's, Olive Garden, Panera Bread, Pizza Hut, Ralphie's, Red Lobster, Skyline Chili, Subway, Taco Bell, TX Roadhouse, Tumbleweed Grill, Wendy's, **lodging:** Courtyard, Motel 6, **other:** Ford, K-Mart, Ray's Foods, Sam's Club/gas, Walgreens, Walmart SuperCtr/24hr, **W gas:** Shell, **food:** Kewpee Hamburger's, Season Grill, **lodging:** Country Inn&Suites, Holiday Inn, Travelodge, **other:** [H], Curves, $General, Rite Aid, Sav-A-Lot Foods
124	4th St, **E** hwy patrol
122	OH 65, Lima, **E gas:** Speedway/dsl, **W gas:** Marathon/dsl, Shell/dsl, **other:** Freightliner, GMC, Mack, Volvo, Vet
120	Breese Rd, Ft Shawnee, **W** Harley-Davidson
118	to Cridersville, **W gas:** Fuelmart/Subway/dsl, Speedway/dsl, **food:** Dixie Ley Diner, **other:** $General
114mm	**truck parking both directions**
113	OH 67, to Uniopolis, Wapakoneta
111	Bellefontaine St, Wapakoneta, **E gas:** TA/Marathon/rest./dsl/scales/@, **food:** Country Charm Rest., **lodging:** Knight's Inn, **other:** KOA, **W gas:** BP/dsl, Murphy USA/dsl, Shell, **food:** Arby's, Bob Evans, Burger King, Capt D's, Comfort Zone, DQ, El Azteca, King Buffet, Lucky Steer Rest., McDonald's, Pizza Hut, Taco Bell, Waffle House, Wendy's, **lodging:** Comfort Inn, Holiday Inn Express, Super 8, Western Inn, **other:** Advance Parts, Aldi Foods, CVS Drug, Lowe's Whse, Neil Armstrong Museum, O'Reilly Parts, Radio Shack, Walmart SuperCtr/24hr, st patrol
110	US 33, to St Marys, Bellefontaine, **E** KOA, hwy patrol
104	OH 219, **W gas:** Marathon/dsl, Shell/Subway/dsl, **food:** Wrecker's Grill, **lodging:** Budget Host
102	OH 274, to Jackson Ctr, New Breman, **E** bicycle museum, **W** air stream tours
99	OH 119, to Minster, Anna, **E gas:** 99/dsl, **W gas:** GA/Taco Bell, Marathon, **food:** Subway, Wendy's, **other:** lube/wash/repair
94	rd 25A, Sidney, **E gas:** Marathon
93	OH 29, to St Marys, Sidney, **W** Lake Loramie SP, RV camping
92	OH 47, to Versailles, Sidney, **E gas:** Shell, Speedway/dsl, **food:** Arby's, China Garden, Coldstone Creamery, Subway, Time Horton, Wendy's, **other:** [H], AutoZone, CVS Drug, $General, DM, NAPA, Sav-AL-ot Foods, Walgreens, **W gas:** Murphy USA, Sunoco/dsl, Valero, **food:** A&W/LJ Silver, Applebee's, Bob Evans, Buffalo Wild Wings, Burger King, Cazadores Mexican, Culver's, Highmarks Rest., KFC, McDonald's, Perkins, Pizza Hut, Quizno's, Taco Bell, Waffle House, **lodging:** Comfort Inn, Country Hearth Inn, Days Inn, Quality Inn, **other:** Aldi Foods, AT&T, Best 1 Tires/repair, BigLots, Buick/GMC/Pontiac, Chevrolet, Chrysler/Dodge/Jeep, Curves, $Tree, Ford/Lincoln/Mercury, Kroger, Lowe's Whse, Menard's, Radio Shack, Staples, Walmart SuperCtr/24hr

INTERSTATE 75 CONT'D

N ↕ S

Exit #	Services
90	Fair Rd, to Sidney, **E gas:** Sunoco, **W gas:** Marathon/DQ/dsl, **lodging:** Hampton Inn
88mm	Great Miami River
83	rd 25A, Piqua, **W gas:** Marathon/MaidRite Cafe/ Noble Roman's/dsl, **lodging:** Red Carpet Inn, **other:** Chevrolet, Chrysler/Dodge/Jeep, Sherry RV Ctr, to Piqua Hist Area
82	US 36, to Urbana, Piqua, **E gas:** Murphy USA/dsl, Valero, **food:** A&W/LJ Silver, Arby's, China East, China Garden, DQ, El Sombrero Mexican, KFC, Pizza Hut/ Taco Bell, Subway, Waffle House, Wendy's, **other:** Aldi Foods, BigLots, Home Depot, Jo-Ann Fabrics, Radio Shack, Walmart SuperCtr, st patrol, Vet, **W gas:** Speedway, **food:** Bob Evans, Cracker Barrel, Elder Beerman, El Tapatio Mexican, McDonald's, Red Lobster, **lodging:** Comfort Inn, Knight's Inn, La Quinta, **other:** JC Penney, Sears/auto, mall
81mm	**rest area both lanes, full facilities, , , litter barrels, vending**
78	rd 25A, **E** H
74	OH 41, to Covington, Troy, **E gas:** BP/dsl, **food:** Al's Pizza, China Garden, Donato's Pizza, Fox's Pizza, McDonald's, Pizza Hut, Subway, Taco Bell, **other:** H, Radio Shack, Sav-A-Lot Foods, Super Petz, to Hobart Arena, **W gas:** Shell, Speedway/dsl, **food:** Applebee's, Big Boy, Bob Evans, Buffalo Wild Wings, Burger King, Culver's, El Rancho Grande, Fazoli's, Friendly's, KFC, Outback Steaks, Panera Bread, Penn Sta. Subs, Ruby Tuesday, Sakai Japanese, Skyline Chili, Sonic, Steak'n Shake, **lodging:** Best Inn, Comfort Suites, Fairfield Inn, Hampton Inn, Holiday Inn Express, Residence Inn, **other:** AutoZone, Curves, $Tree, GNC, Goodyear, Kohl's, Lowe's Whse, Meijer/ dsl/24hr, Staples, Tire Discounters, Verizon, Walmart SuperCtr/24hr
73	OH 55, to Ludlow Falls, Troy, **E gas:** BP, Shell, **food:** Boston Stoker Coffee House, Lincoln Sq Rest., Papa John's, Subway, Waffle House, Wendy's, **lodging:** Quality Inn, Super 8, **other:** H, $General, Kroger/gas
69	rd 25A, **E gas:** BP/Circle K/Subway, Starfire/dsl, **other:** Arbogast RV Ctr, Buick/GMC/Pontiac, Chrysler/ Dodge/Jeep, Ford, Suzuki
68	OH 571, to West Milton, Tipp City, **E gas:** BP/dsl, Shell, Speedway/dsl, **food:** Burger King, Cassano's Pizza, Domino's, Hickory River Rest., McDonald's, Subway, Taco Bell, **other:** Do-It Hardware, CarQuest, CVS Drug, Family$, FoodTown, Goodyear, Honda, **W gas:** Speedway/dsl, Valero, **food:** Arby's, Big Boy, Bob Evans, Tipp' O the Town Rest., Wendy's, **lodging:** Holiday Inn Express, La Quinta, **other:** Main St Parts, Menards
64	Northwoods Blvd, **E food:** El Toro Mexican, Quizno's, **other:** $Tree, Kroger/dsl
63	US 40, to Donnelsville, Vandalia, **E gas:** Speedway/ dsl, **food:** Bunker's Grill, Dragon China, Fricker's, **other:** repair, **W gas:** BP/dsl, Shell, Speedway, **food:** Arby's, Burger King, Domino's, KFC/LJ Silver, McDonald's, Pizza Hut, Rib House, Subway, Taco Bell, Waffle House, Wendy's, **lodging:** Best Value Inn (2mi), Super 8, **other:** Goodyear/auto, Rexall Drug, Rite Aid

TROY

Exit #	Services
61b a	I-70, E to Columbus, W to Indianapolis, to Dayton Int
59	Wyse Rd, Benchwood Rd, **E food:** El Rancho Grande Mexican, Little York Pizza, Mr. Lee's, **lodging:** Dayton Inn, Hawthorn Suites, **other:** BMW/Volvo/VW, Discount Tire, **W gas:** Speedway/dsl, **food:** Arby's, Asian Buffet, Bob Evans, Cassano's Pizza, Chick-fil-A, Chipotle Mexican, Coldstone Creamery, Cracker Barrel, Fricker's, Golden Corral, Hooter's, LoneStar Steaks, Max&Erma's, McDonald's, O'Charley's, Olive Garden, Outback Steaks, Panera Bread, Pop's Diner, Red Lobster, Ruby Tuesday, Sake Japanese, Skyline Chili, SmokeyBones BBQ, Steak'n Shake, Subway, Tim Horton, **lodging:** Comfort Inn, Country Inn&Suites, Courtyard, Days Inn, Drury Inn, Extended Stay America, Fairfield Inn, Hampton Inn, Knight's Inn, Motel 6, Red Roof Inn, Residence Inn, Rodeway Inn, Towneplace Suites, Villager Lodge, **other:** Batteries+, Office Depot, Radio Shack, Sam's Club/gas, Walmart SuperCtr
58	Needmore Rd, to Dayton, **E gas:** BP/dsl, Shell/McDonald's, **food:** Hardee's, **lodging:** Dayton Executive Hotel, **other:** Goodyear/auto, to AF Museum, **W gas:** Clark, Marathon/dsl, Speedway/dsl, Sunoco/dsl, Swifty, **food:** A&W/LJ Silver, Church's, Domino's, New Peking, Subway, Tim Horton, Waffle House, Wendy's, **other:** Advance Parts, AutoZone, $Tree, Kroger/gas, O'Reilly Parts, Walgreens, USPO, repair/transmissions
57b	Wagner Ford Rd, Siebenthaler Rd, Dayton, **E gas:** Sunoco, **lodging:** Holiday Inn
57a	Neva Rd
56	Stanley Ave, Dayton, **E gas:** Shell, **W gas:** Clark, **food:** Dragon City Chinese, Gold Star Chili, McDonald's, Rally's, **lodging:** Dayton Motel, **other:** truck repair
55b a	Keowee St, Dayton, downtown
54c	OH 4 N, Webster St, to Springfield, downtown
54mm	Great Miami River
54b	OH 48, Main St, Dayton, **E gas:** Cadillac, Honda, **W gas:** BP, **other:** H
54a	Grand Ave (from sb), Dayton, downtown
53b	OH 49, 1st St, Salem Ave, Dayton, downtown
53a	OH 49, 3 rd St, downtown
52b a	US 35, E to Dayton, W to Eaton
51	Edwin C Moses Blvd, Nicholas Rd, **E lodging:** Courtyard, **other:** H, to U of Dayton, **W gas:** BP/dsl, **food:** McDonald's, Wendy's, **lodging:** Econolodge, **other:** SunWatch Indian Village

DAYTON

OH

N ↕ S

INTERSTATE 75 CONT'D

Exit #	Services
50b a	OH 741, Kettering St, Dryden Rd, **E** [H], Vet, **W gas:** Marathon/dsl, **lodging:** Holiday Inn, Super 8, **other:** U-Haul
47	Dixie Dr, Kettering, Moraine, **E gas:** Shamrock, Sunoco, **food:** Big Boy, Waffle House, **other:** auto repair, transmissions, **W gas:** BP, Speedway, **food:** Ele Cafe, KFC, McDonald's, Pizza Hut, Sonic, Taco Bell, Wendy's, **other:** $General, USPO
44	OH 725, to Centerville, Miamisburg, **E gas:** BP/dsl, Shell, Speedway, **food:** Applebee's, Big Boy, Bone Fish Grill, Bravo Italiana, Buffalo Wild Wings, Burger King, Capt D's, Friendly's, Golden Corral, Hardee's, Jimmy John's, KFC, Lonestar Steaks, Max&Erma's, McDonald's, O'Charley's, Olive Garden, Panera Bread, PF Chang's, Red Lobster, Rooster's Grill, Rusty Bucket Grill, Skyline Chili, Starbucks, Steak'n Shake, Subway, Taco Bell, TGIFriday's, Waffle House, Wendy's, **lodging:** Comfort Suites, Courtyard, Doubletree Suites, Holiday Inn, Homewood Suites, SpringHill Suites, Studio 6, **other:** [H], Aldi Foods, Barnes&Noble, Best Buy, Borders Books, Cub Foods, $Tree, Elder Beerman, Goodyear/auto, Hobby Lobby, Home Depot, Honda/Nissan/Mazda, JC Penney, Jo-Ann Fabrics, Kia, Lowe's Whse, Macy's, Michael's, Mitsubishi, NTB, Office Depot, PepBoys, Petsmart, Pontiac, Sears/auto, Super Petz, Target, Tire Discounters, TJ Maxx, Toyota, Verizon, Walmart/SuperCtr, mall, **W gas:** BP, Chevron, Marathon, Shell, **food:** Bob Evans, LJ Silver, Perkins, Tim Horton, **lodging:** Knight's Inn, Quality Inn, Red Roof Inn, Super 8, **other:** [H], Aamco, CarMax, $General, Ford, NAPA
43	I-675 N, to Columbus
41	new exit
38	OH 73, Springboro, Franklin, **E gas:** Shell, Speedway, **food:** Applebee's, Arby's, Bob Evans, Burger King, China Wok, Chipotle Mexican, KFC/Taco Bell, LJ Silver, McDonald's, Papa John's, Pizza Hut, Royal Wok, Skyline Chili, Subway, Tim Horton, Wendy's, **lodging:** Hampton Inn, Springboro Inn, **other:** K-Mart, Kroger, Radio Shack, Tire Discounters, Vet, **W gas:** Circle K, Murphy USA/dsl, Road Ranger, Shell, Swifty, **food:** A&G Pizza, Big Boy, Cazadore's Mexican, Domino's, Gold Star Chili, Lee's Chicken, McDonald's, **lodging:** Econolodge, Holiday Inn Express, Knight's Inn, **other:** AutoZone, Clark's Drug, $General, $Tree, Kimper Auto, Marsh Foods, NAPA, Walgreens, Walmart SuperCtr, USPO, repair/tires
36	OH 123, to Lebanon, Franklin, **E gas:** BP, Exxon/Wendy's/dsl/24hr, Pilot/Subway/Pizza Hut/dsl/scales/24hr/@, **food:** McDonald's, Waffle House, **lodging:** Quality Inn, **W gas:** Marathon/White Castle/dsl, Sunoco
32	OH 122, Middletown, **E food:** McDonald's, **lodging:** Best Value, Days Inn, Super 8, Ramada Inn, **other:** [H] CVS Drug, **W gas:** Murphy USA, **food:** Applebee's, Big Boy, Bob Evans, Cracker Barrel, Golden Corral, Golden Dragon, Gold Star Chili, KFC, LoneStar Steaks, O'Charley's, Olive Garden, Schlotzsky's, Sonic, Steak'n Shake, Wendy's, **lodging:** Best Western, Country Hearth Inn, Drury Inn, Fairfield Inn, Holiday Inn Express, **other:** URGENT CARE, Buick/GMC/Pontiac,
32	Continued Elder Beerman, Kohl's, Kroger, Lowe's Whse, Meijer/dsl/24hr, Sears/auto, Staples, Super Petz, Target, Tire Discounters, Walmart, mall
29	OH 63, to Hamilton, Monroe, **E gas:** Shell/Popeye's/dsl, Stony Ridge/dsl, **food:** Burger King, Gold Star Chili, Tim Horton/Wendy's, Waffle House, **lodging:** Comfort Inn, **other:** Premium Outlets/Famous Brands, **W gas:** Shell/dsl, Speedway/dsl, **food:** Froggy Blue's, McDonald's, Richard's Pizza, Sara Jane's Rest., Subway, **lodging:** Hampton Inn, Howard Johnson, **other:** flea mkt
27.5mm	**rest area both lanes, full [handicapped] facilities, info, [phone], [picnic], litter barrels, vending, petwalk**
24	OH 129 W, to Hamilton, **W** Cinncinati Gardens
22	Tylersville Rd, to Mason, Hamilton, **E gas:** Sunoco, Thornton's/dsl, **food:** Arby's, Bob Evans, BoneFish Grill, Burger King, Caribou Coffee, Chick-fil-A, Chipotle Mexican, Chopsticks, City BBQ, GoldStar Chili, IHOP, KFC, LJ Silver, Longhorn Steaks, McAlister's Deli, McDonald's, Noodles&Co, Panera Bread, Perkins, Qdoba, Ruby Tuesday, Skyline Chili, Soho Japanese, Starbucks, Subway, Taco Bell, TGIFriday's, Twin Dragon, Waffle House, Wendy's, **lodging:** Econolodge, **other:** [H], AT&T, BigLots, Firestone, GNC, Goodyear/auto, Home Depot, Kohl's, Kroger, Michael's, Office Depot, Petsmart, Radio Shack, Target, Tires+, TJ Maxx, Walgreens, **W gas:** Shell, Speedway/dsl/24hr, **food:** O'Charley's, **lodging:** Wingate Inn, **other:** Aldi Foods, CarX, Lowe's Whse, Meijer/dsl/24hr, Tire Discounters
21	Cin-Day Rd, **E food:** Big Boy, **lodging:** Holiday Inn Express, **W gas:** Marathon, Mobil/Subway/dsl, Speedway/dsl, **food:** Arby's, Casa Tequila Mexican, Domino's, Gunther's Steaks, La Rosa's Pizza, Little Caesar's, Papa John's, Waffle House, Wendy's, **other:** Ace Hardware, Curves, Pet Mart, Verizon, Walgreens, Walmart SuperCtr/24hr
19	Union Centre Blvd, to Fairfield, **E food:** Bravo Italian, Champps Rest., Cucina Italian, Mitchell's Fish Mkt, Original Pancakes, Panera Bread, PF Chang's, Red Robin, Smokey Bones BBQ, Steak'n Shake, **other:** Barnes&Noble, **W gas:** BP/Subway/dsl, Marathon/Circle K, Shell, **food:** Aladdin's Eatery, Applebee's, Bob Evans, Buffalo Wild Wings, Burger King, Chipotle Mexican, El Rancho Grande, Jag's Steaks, Max&Erma's, McDonald's, Quizno's, Rafferty's, River City Grille, Skyline Chili, Smoothie King, Starbucks, Tazza Mia, Uno, Wendy's, **lodging:** Comfort Inn, Courtyard, Hampton Inn, Marriott, Residence Inn, Staybridge Suites, **other:** Mercedes, Volvo
16	I-275 to I-71, to I-74
15	Sharon Rd, to Sharonville, Glendale, **E gas:** Sunoco, Thornton's/dsl, **food:** Big Boy, Bob Evans, Burbanks BBQ, Cracker Barrel, Jim Dandy BBQ, Ruby Tuesday, Skyline Chili, Subway, Waffle House, **lodging:** Baymont Inn, Best Value Inn, Country Inn&Suites, Drury Inn, Hilton Garden, Holiday Inn Express, La Quinta, Red Roof Inn, Travelodge, **W on Kimper... gas:** Sunoco, **food:** Arby's, Burger King, Chick-fil-A, Chili's, ChuckeCheese, Dos Amigos, IHOP, Macaroni Grill, McDonald's, Penn Sta, Pizza Hut, Taco Bell, Subway, Tokyo Japanese, Vincenzo's, Wendy's, **lodging:** Econolodge, Extended Stay Deluxe, Extended Stay

OH

MIDDLETOWN

INTERSTATE 75 CONT'D

N ↕ S — CINCINNATI AREA

Exit #	Services
15	Continued America, Fairfield Inn, LivInn Suites, Residence Inn, Sheraton, **other:** Best Buy, Costco/gas, Nissan, Sam's Club, Target
14	OH 126, to Woodlawn, Evendale, **E** GE Plant, **lodging:** Wingate Inn (3mi), **W gas:** Swifty
13	Shepherd Lane, to Lincoln Heights, **E** GE Plant, **W food:** Taco Bell, Wendy's, **other:** Advance Parts
12	Wyoming Ave, Cooper Ave, to Lockland, **W gas:** Marathon, **food:** DQ, Subway
10a	OH 126, Ronald Reagan Hwy
10b	Galbraith Rd (exits left from nb), Arlington Heights
9	OH 4, OH 561, Paddock Rd, Seymour Ave, **E** to Cincinnati Gardens, **W** fairgrounds
8	Towne St, Elmwood Pl (from nb)
7	OH 562, to I-71, Norwood, Cincinnati Gardens
6	Mitchell Ave, St Bernard, **E gas:** Marathon, Shell, Sunoco, **food:** White Castle, **lodging:** Holiday Inn Express, **other:** Walgreens, to Cincinnati Zoo, to Xavier U, **W gas:** BP/Subway/dsl, **food:** McDonald's, Rally's, **other:** Advance Parts, Chevrolet, Family$, Ford, Honda, Hyundai, Kroger, Tires+
4	I-74 W, US 52, US 27 N, to Indianapolis
3	to US 27 S, US 127 S, Hopple St, U of Cincinnati, **E gas:** BP/Subway/dsl, **food:** Camp Washington Chili, Isador Italian, White Castle, **other:** [H], Family$, **W gas:** Shell, **food:** Wendy's
2b	Harrison Ave, industrial district, **W gas:** BP, **food:** McDonald's
2a	Western Ave, Liberty St (from sb)
1g	Ezzard Charles Dr, **W lodging:** Ramada Inn
1f	US 50W, Freeman Ave, **W gas:** Sunoco, **food:** Big Boy, Pizza Hut/Taco Bell, Wendy's, White Castle, **lodging:** Ramada Inn, **other:** Ford, NAPA, Pontiac/GMC, USPO
1e	7th St (from sb), downtown, downtown
1c	5th St, downtown, **E lodging:** Crowne Plaza, Hyatt, Millenial Hotel, Sheraton, **other:** Macy's, to Duke Energy Center
1a	I-71 N, to Cincinnati, downtown, to stadium
0mm	Ohio/Kentucky state line, Ohio River

INTERSTATE 76

E ↕ W

Exit #	Services
	Ohio/Pennsylvania state line Exits 232-235 are on the Ohio Turnpike.
235	I-680 (from wb), to Youngstown
232	OH 7, to Boardman, Youngstown, **N food:** DQ, Smaldino's Family Rest., **lodging:** Budget Inn, Day's Inn, Econolodge, Microtel, North Lima Inn, Super 8, **S gas:** Shell/dsl, Speedway/dsl, **food:** Road House Diner, **lodging:** Davis Motel, Rodeway Inn, **other:** truck repair
60mm	I-76 eb joins Ohio TPK (toll)
57	to OH 45, Bailey Rd, to Warren
54	OH 534, to Newton Falls, Lake Milton, **N** RV camping, **S gas:** BP, **other:** to Berlin Lake, camping
52mm	Lake Milton
48	OH 225, to Alliance, **N** to W Branch SP, camping, **S** to Berlin Lake

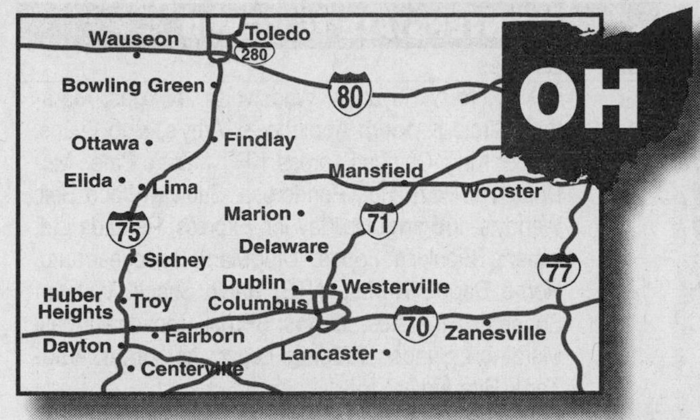

AKRON

Exit #	Services
45.5mm	**rest area both lanes, full [handicap] facilities, [phone], [picnic], litter barrels, petwalk**
43	OH 14, to Alliance, Ravenna, **N** to W Branch SP, **S gas:** Marathon/dsl, **other:** fireworks
38b a	OH 5, OH 44, to Ravenna, **N gas:** BP, Speedway/dsl, **food:** Acupulco Mexican, Arby's, McDonald's, Wendy's, **other:** [H], **S gas:** Marathon/Circle K/Subway, **food:** Cracker Barrel, **other:** $General, Giant Eagle Foods/drug, auto repair, RV camping
33	OH 43, to Hartville, Kent, **N gas:** BP/dsl, Sunoco, **food:** Salsita's Mexican, **lodging:** Comfort Inn, Day's Inn, Econolodge, Hampton Inn, Holiday Inn Express, Ramada Inn, Super 8, **other:** to Kent St U, **S gas:** Speedway/dsl, **food:** Giomino's Italian, McDonald's, Wendy's, **other:** RV camping, Vet
31	rd 18, Tallmadge, **N food:** Applebee's, Arabica Cafe, Beef O'Brady's, Quizno's, Strickland's Cafe, **other:** $Tree, Lowe's, Walmart SuperCtr/Subway
29	OH 532, Tallmadge, Mogadore
27	OH 91, Canton Rd, Gilchrist Rd, **N food:** Bob Evans, **S gas:** Marathon/Subway/dsl, **food:** Hardee's, **lodging:** Best Western, NAPA Truck Parts
26	OH 18, E Market St, Mogadore Rd, **N gas:** Circle K/dsl, Marathon/dsl, **other:** Goodyear/auto, **S food:** Arby's, McDonald's, Subway, Wendy's, **other:** $General
25b a	Martha Ave, General St, Brittain, **N gas:** Citgo, **other:** Goodyear World Hdqtrs, Mercedes, Toyota/Scion
24	Arlington St, Kelly Ave, **N** Goodyear World Hdqtrs
23b	OH 8, Buchtell Ave, to Cuyahoga, to U of Akron
23a	I-77 S, to Canton
22b	Wolf Ledges, Akron, downtown, **S gas:** BP, **food:** McDonald's
22a	Main St, Broadway, downtown
21c	OH 59 E, Dart Ave, **N** [H]
21b	Lakeshore St, Bowery St (from eb)
21a	East Ave (from wb)
20	I-77 N (from eb), to Cleveland
19	Battles Ave, Kenmore Blvd
18	I-277, US 224 E, to Canton, Barberton, interchange
17b a	OH 619, Wooster Rd, State St, to Barberton, **S gas:** Sunoco/dsl, **other:** [H], NAPA, tires/repair
16	Barber Rd, **S gas:** Rocky's Gas, **food:** Tomaso's Italian, **other:** Chrysler/Jeep/Suzuki
14	Cleve-Mass Rd, to Norton, **S gas:** BP, **food:** Charlie's Rest.
13b a	OH 21, N to Cleveland, S to Massillon
11	OH 261, Wadsworth, **N gas:** Speedway, **S gas:** GNC Nutrition, Kohl's, Lowe's Whse, MC Sports, PetCo, Target

INTERSTATE 76 CONT'D

Exit #	Services
9	OH 94, to N Royalton, Wadsworth, **N gas:** Marathon/Circle K, **food:** Applebee's, Arby's, Bob Evans, Burger King, Chinda Express, KFC, Marie's Cafe., McDonald's, Pizza Hut, Ponderosa, Subway, Taco Bell, Wendy's, **lodging:** Holiday Inn Express, Ramada Ltd, **other:** Buehler's Foods, DrugMart, Goodyear/auto, Home Depot, K-Mart, NTB, Radio Shack, Walmart SuperCtr/24hr, tires, **S gas:** BP/dsl, Convenient/gas, Marathon, Sunoco, **lodging:** Legacy Inn, **other:** AutoZone, Rite Aid
7	OH 57, to Rittman, Medina, **N gas:** Marathon/dsl, **other:** [H], ✈
6mm	**weigh sta both lanes**
2	OH 3, to Medina, Seville, **N gas:** Marathon/Circle K, **food:** DQ, Hardee's, Huddle House, Subway, **lodging:** Comfort Inn, Hawthorn Suites, **other:** Maple Lakes Camping (seasonal), **S gas:** Petro US/dsl, Sunoco, **food:** Acorn Rest., **other:** Curves, Ritzman Drug
1	I-76 E, to Akron, US 224, **W on US 224...gas:** Pilot/Country Kitchen/Subway/dsl/scales/24hr, TA/Burger King/Popeye's/dsl/24hr/@, **food:** Arby's, McDonald's, **lodging:** Super 8, **other:** Blue Beacon, SpeedCo, Chippewa Valley Camping (1mi), SpeedCo
0mm	I-76 begins/ends on I-71, exit 209.

INTERSTATE 77

Exit #	Services
	I-77 begins/ends on I-90 exit 172, in Cleveland.
163c	I-90, E to Erie, W to Toledo
163b	E 9th St, Tower City
162b	E 22nd St, E 14th St (from nb)
162a	E 30th St, Woodland Ave, Broadway St (from nb), **W** USPO
161b	I-490 W, to I-71, E 55th, **E** [H]
161a	OH 14 (from nb), Broadway St
160	Pershing Ave (from nb), **W** [H]
159b	Fleet Ave, **E gas:** BP/Subway/dsl
159a	Harvard Ave, Newburgh Heights, **W gas:** BP/Subway/dsl/24hr, Marathon
158	Grant Ave, Cuyahoga Heights
157	OH 21, OH 17 (from sb), Brecksville Rd
156	I-480, to Youngstown, Toledo
155	Rockside Rd, to Independence, **E gas:** Shell, Sunoco, **food:** Bob Evans, Bonefish Grill, Chester's, Chipotle Mexican, Del Monico's Steaks, Denny's, McDonald's, Outback Steaks, Red Robin, Shula's Steaks, Wendy's, Zoup, **lodging:** Comfort Inn, Doubletree, Embassy Suites, Holiday Inn, La Quinta, Red Roof Inn, **other:** Lincoln/Mercury, Walgreens, **W gas:** BP/dsl, **food:** Applebee's, Damon's, Longhorn Steaks, **lodging:** Courtyard, Hampton Inn, Hyatt Place, Residence Inn, Sheraton
153	Pleasant Valley Rd, to Independence, 7 Hills
151	Wallings Rd
149	OH 82, to Broadview Heights, Brecksville, **1 mi E gas:** BP, Shell, **food:** McDonald's, Panera Bread, Simons Cafe, Starbucks, **other:** Walgreens, **W gas:** BP, **food:** Coco's, Domino's, Mr. Hero, **lodging:** Tallyho Motel, **other:** Curves
147	to OH 21, Miller Rd (from sb)
146	I-80/Ohio Tpk, to Youngstown, Toledo
145	OH 21 (from nb), **E gas:** Pilot/Wendy's/dsl/scales, **food:** DQ, Memories Rest., Richfield Rest., Subway, **lodging:** Hampton Inn, Holiday Inn Express, Howard Johnson, Quality Inn, Super 8
144	I-271 N, to Erie
143	OH 176, to I-271 S, **E** to Coliseum, **W gas:** Sunoco, **food:** Arabica Café, McDonald's, Panda Chinese, Subway, Teresa's Pizza, **other:** Curves
141mm	**rest area both lanes, full ♿ facilities, ☎, picnic, litter barrels, vending, petwalk**
138	Ghent Rd, **2 mi E lodging:** Hilton, Sheraton, **W gas:** Circle K/dsl, **food:** Lanning's Rest., Vaccaro's Italian
137b a	OH 18, to Fairlawn, Medina, **E gas:** BP, Circle K, Get-Go, Shell, Speedway, **food:** A Wok, Applebee's, Bob Evans, Boston Mkt, Chili's, Chipotle Mexican, Cracker Barrel, Donato's Pizza, Dynasty Chinese, Fleming's Steaks, Friendly's, Honeybaked Ham, Hyde Park Grill, KFC, LoneStar Steaks, Macaroni Grill, Max&Erma's, McDonald's, Olive Garden, Pad Thai, Quizno's, Red Lobster, Ruby Tuesday, Starbucks, Steak'n Shake, Taco Bell, Wendy's, **lodging:** Courtyard, Hampton Inn, Hilton, Holiday Inn, Quality Inn, Motel 6, Super 8, **other:** Acme Foods, Barnes&Noble, Best Buy, Borders Books, Ford, Dillard's, $Tree, Giant Eagle Foods, Home Depot, Jo-Ann Fabrics, Lowes Whse, Macy's, Michael's, Mr. Tire, Old Navy, PetsMart, Sam's Club, Staples, TJ Maxx, Walmart, World Mkt, **W gas:** Sunoco/dsl, **food:** Bennigan's, Burger King, Don Pablo, Longhorn Steaks, Outback Steaks, TGIFriday, Tres Patrilios, Wasabi Grill, **lodging:** Best Western, Comfort Inn, Extended Stay America, Radisson, Residence Inn, Studio+
136	OH 21S, to Massillon
135	Cleveland-Massillon Rd (from nb)
133	Ridgewood Rd, Miller Rd, **E gas:** Circle K/dsl, **food:** Wendy's
132	White Pond Dr, Mull Ave, **E** Rosarita Cantina, golf
131	OH 162, Copley Rd, **E gas:** Circle K, **other:** SavALot Foods, Walgreens, USPO, **W gas:** BP/dsl/24hr, **food:** McDonald's, Pizza Hut
130	OH 261, Wooster Ave, **E gas:** Circle K, Valero, **food:** Ann's Place, Burger King, Church's, New China, Rally's, Subway, White Castle, **other:** Acme Foods, Advance Parts, AutoZone, Family$, **W food:** KFC, **other:** Chevrolet, Toyota/Scion, U-Haul
129	I-76 W, to I-277, to Kenmore Blvd, Barberton
21a	East Ave (from nb), **I-77 S and I-76 E run together**
21b	Lakeshore (from sb), to Bowery St
21c	OH 59 E, Dart Ave, downtown, **E** [H]
22a	Main St, Broadway St, downtown, **W** auto parts
22b	Grant St, Wolf Ledges, **W gas:** BP, **food:** McDonald's, **other:** Family$
125b	I-76 E, to Youngstown, I-77 and I-76 run together
125a	OH 8 N, to Cuyahoga Falls, U of Akron
124b	Lover's Lane, Cole Ave
124a	Archwood Ave, Firestone Blvd
123b	OH 764, Wilbeth Rd, **E** to ✈
123a	Waterloo Rd, **W gas:** Marathon, **other:** Acme Foods
122b a	I-277, US 224 E, to Barberton, Mogadore
120	Arlington Rd, to Green, **E gas:** Speedway/dsl, **food:** Applebee's, Church's, Denny's, Friendly's, Golden

INTERSTATE 77 CONT'D

E ↕ W

Exit #	Services
120	Continued Corral, IHOP, Pizza Hut, Ryan's, Starbucks, Waffle House, White Castle, **lodging:** Comfort Inn, Quality Inn, Red Roof Inn, **other:** $General, Home Depot, Kohl's, Staples, Walmart/auto, **W gas:** BP, Speedway, **food:** Bob Evans, Burger King, Lion Garden, Mariachi Mexican, McDonald's, Subway, Taco Bell, TGIFriday, Wendy's, **lodging:** Fairfield Inn, Hampton Inn, **other:** Buick/Pontiac/GMC, Chevrolet, Goodyear/auto, Honda/Mazda, Hyundai, Lexus, Lowes Whse, Nissan, Sirpilla RV Ctr/Camping World, Target
118	OH 241, to OH 619, Massillon, **E gas:** Sheetz, Speedway/dsl, **food:** Gionino's Pizza, Subway, **W gas:** BP/Circle K, GetGo, **food:** Arby's, Belgrade Gardens, McDonald's, Menche's Rest., Pancho's Mexican, Quizno's, **lodging:** Cambria Suites, Super 8, **other:** H
113	Akron-Canton ✈, **2 mi W lodging:** Hilton Garden, **other:** Clay's RV
112	new exit
111	Portage St, N Canton, **E gas:** Circle K, Marathon, Speedway, Sunoco/dsl, TA/Country Pride/dsl/scales/24hr/@, **food:** Burger King, Cheing's Express, Giesen Haus, KFC, Palambo's Italian, Subway, Sylvester's Italian, **other:** TrueValue, **W gas:** BP/dsl, **food:** Carrabba's, ChuckeCheese, Coldstone Creamery, Cracker Barrel, Donato's Pizza, Don Pablo, Dunkin Donuts/Baskin-Robbins, Hungry Howie's, IHOP, Longhorn Steaks, Lucky Star Chinese, McDonald's, Pizza Hut, Quizno's, Red Robin, Rockne's Cafe, Samantha's, Starbucks, Taco Bell, Wendy's, **lodging:** Best Western, Microtel, Motel 6, **other:** Best Buy, BJ's Whse, Borders Books, Chevrolet, DrugMart, Gander Mtn, Giant Eagle Foods, GNC, Goodyear/auto, Harley-Davidson, Home Depot, Lowes Whse, Marshall's, Old Navy, Sam's Club/gas, Walmart/Subway/auto
109b a	Everhard Rd, Whipple Ave, **E gas:** Citgo/Subway, Speedway/dsl, **food:** Burger King, Denny's, Fazoli's, McDonald's, Taco Bell, **lodging:** Comfort Inn, Fairfield Inn, Hampton Inn, Residence Inn, **other:** Ford, **W gas:** Marathon, **food:** Applebee's, Arby's, Bennigan's, Bob Evans, Bravo Italian, Buffalo Wild Wings, Buffet Dynasty, Chick-fil-A, Chipotle Mexican, Cheeseburger Paradise, CiCi's Pizza, Damon's, Friendly's, HomeTown Buffet, HoneyBaked Ham, Hong Kong Buffet, Logan's Roadhouse, LoneStar Steaks, Macaroni Grill, Manchu Café, Max&Erma's, Mulligan's, Olive Garden, Outback Steaks, Panera Bread, Panini's Grill, Papa Bear's, Penn Sta. Subs, Ponderosa, Red Lobster, Ricky Ly's Chinese, Robek's Grill, Ruby Tuesday, Sahara Grill, Starbucks, Steak'n Shake, TGIFriday, Wendy's, **lodging:** Courtyard, Day's Inn, Holiday Inn, Parke Suites, Red Roof Inn, **other:** Advance Parts, Best Buy, Dillard's, $Tree, Firestone/auto, Goodyear/auto, Jo-Ann Crafts, Kohl's, Macy's, Marc's Foods, Michael's, PetsMart, Radio Shack, Sears/auto, Target, TJ Maxx, World Mkt, mall
107b a	US 62, OH 687, Fulton Rd, to Alliance, **E** City Park, **W gas:** Circle K, **other:** Pro Football Hall of Fame
106	13th St NW, **E** H
105b	OH 172, Tuscarawas St, downtown

CANTON

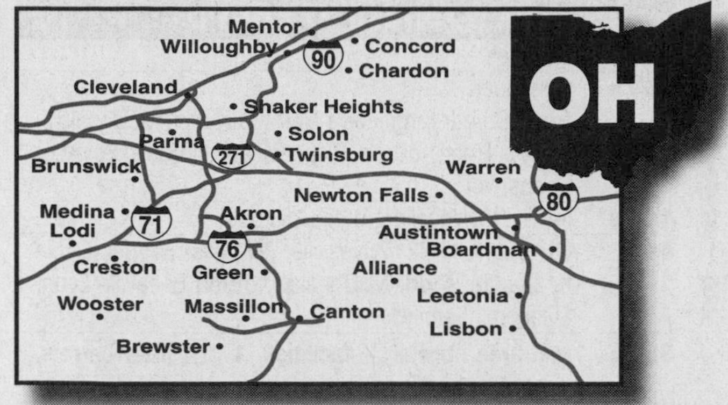

Exit #	Services
105a	6th St SW (no EZ return from sb), **W food:** Subway, **other:** H, AutoZone
104	US 30, US 62, to E Liverpool, Massillon
103	OH 800 S, **E gas:** Marathon/Subway, Speedway, **food:** Arby's, Taco Bell, Waffle House, **other:** Advance Parts, Firestone
101	OH 627, to Faircrest St, **E gas:** Gulliver's Trvl Plaza/dsl/rest./scales, Speedway/McDonald's, **food:** Wendy's
99	Fohl Rd, to Navarre, **W gas:** Sunoco, KOA (4mi)
93	OH 212, to Zoar, Bolivar, **E gas:** Speedway/Subway, **food:** McDonald's, Pizza Hut, Wendy's, **lodging:** Sleep Inn, **other:** $General, Giant Eagle Foods, NAPA, Zoar Tavern (3mi), Vet, to Lake Atwood Region, **W gas:** Marathon/DQ, **other:** KOA
92mm	**weigh sta both lanes**
87	US 250W, to Strasburg, **3 mi E food:** Arby's, **W gas:** Marathon/Quizno's/dsl, **food:** Creekside Cafe, Damon's Pizza, Hardee's, Manor Rest., McDonald's, Subway, **lodging:** Ramada Ltd, Twins Motel
85mm	**rest areas both lanes, full ♿ facilities, info, ☎, picnic tables, litter barrels, petwalk**
83	OH 39, OH 211, to Sugarcreek, Dover, **E gas:** BP, Speedway/Subway/dsl, **food:** Bob Evans, KFC, McDonald's, Shoney's, Wendy's, **lodging:** Hity Inn, **other:** H, Ford/Chrysler/Dodge/Jeep, Lincoln/Mercury/Nissan, tires, **W gas:** Marathon/DQ, **lodging:** Comfort Inn
81	US 250, to Uhrichsville, OH 39, New Philadelphia, **E gas:** Marathon, Sheetz/dsl, Speedway, **food:** Burger King, Denny's, El San Jose Mexican, Hog Heaven, LJ Silver, McDonald's, Pizza Hut, Quizno's, Taco Bell, Texas Roadhouse, **lodging:** Hampton Inn, Holiday Inn, Knight's Inn, Motel 6, Schoenbrunn Inn, Super 8, **other:** Advance Parts, Aldi Foods, Big Lots, $General, Walmart SuperCtr/24hr, **W gas:** Eagle/dsl/rest./24hr, **other:** Harley-Davidson
73	OH 751, to rd 21, Stone Creek, **W gas:** Marathon
65	US 36, Port Washington, Newcomerstown, **W gas:** BP, Duke/dsl/rest., Speedway/Wendy's/24hr, **food:** McDonald's, **lodging:** Hampton Inn, Super 8
64mm	Tuscarawas River
54	OH 541, rd 831, to Plainfield, Kimbolton, **W gas:** BP, **food:** Jackie's Rest.
47	US 22, to Cadiz, Cambridge, **E** to Salt Fork SP (6mi), lodging, RV camping, **W gas:** BP/repair, **other:** H, to Glass Museum, info
46b a	US 40, to Old Washington, Cambridge, **W gas:** BP/24hr, Exxon/Wendy's/dsl, Speedway/dsl/24hr,

INTERSTATE 77 CONT'D

Exit #	Services
46b a	Continued **food:** Burger King, Lee's Rest., LJ Silver, McDonald's, Wally's Pizza, **other:** Riesbeck's Food/deli, SavALot Foods, Vet
44b a	I-70, E to Wheeling, W to Columbus
41	OH 209, OH 821, Byesville, **W gas:** BP/dsl, Circle K, Starfire, **food:** McDonald's, **other:** Byesville Drug, $General, Family$
39mm	**rest area nb, full facilities, phone, picnic, litter barrels, petwalk, vending**
37	OH 313, Buffalo, **E gas:** BP, Duke, **food:** Coutos Pizza, Subway, **other:** truck repair, to Senecaville Lake, UPSO
36mm	**rest area sb, full facilities, phone, picnic, litter barrels, petwalk, vending**
28	OH 821, Belle Valley, **E gas:** Sunoco/dsl, **other:** USPO, to Wolf Run SP, RV camping
25	OH 78, Caldwel, **E gas:** BP, Pilot/Arby's/dsl/scales/24hr, Sunoco/Subway/dsl, **food:** DQ, Lori's Rest., McDonald's, **lodging:** Best Western, **other:** Buick/Chevrolet/Pontiac
16	OH 821, Macksburg, **E** food, **other:** antiques
6	OH 821, to Devola, **E gas:** Exxon, **W gas:** BP/dsl/LP, **other:** H, RV camping
3mm	**rest area nb, full facilities, info, phone, vending, picnic litter barrels, petwalk**
1	OH 7, to OH 26, Marietta, **E gas:** GoMart/dsl/24hr, **food:** CiCi's, DQ, River City Grill, Ryan's, Subway, **lodging:** Comfort Inn, Econolodge, Holiday Inn, **other:** Aldi Foods, Buick/GMC/Pontiac, Cadillac/Chevrolet, Chrysler/Jeep, Dodge, Ford/Lincoln/Mercury, Harley-Davidson, Lowes Whse, Toyota/Scion, Walmart SuperCtr/24hr, **W gas:** BP/dsl, Duke/dsl, GetGo, Marathon/dsl, Speedway/dsl, **food:** Applebees, Arby's, Bob Evan's, Bruster's, Bob Evans, Burger King, Capt D's, China Fun, E Chicago Pizza, Empire Buffet, LJ Silver, McDonald's, Napoli's Pizza, Papa John's, Pizza Hut, Quizno's, Shoney's, Subway, Taco Bell, Tim Horton, Wendy's, **lodging:** Hampton Inn, Microtel, Super 8, **other:** AutoZone, $General, Food4Less, Jo-Ann Crafts, K-Mart, Kroger/24hr, Sav-a-Lot Foods, TrueValue, Walgreens, museum, st patrol
0mm	Ohio/West Virginia state line, Ohio River

INTERSTATE 80

Exit #	Services
237mm	Ohio/Pennsylvania state line
237mm	**Welcome Ctr wb, full facilities, info, phone, picnic, litter barrels, vending, petwalk**
234b a	US 62, OH 7, to Sharon, PA, Hubbard, **N gas:** ***FLYING J***/Country Mkt/Magic Dragon Chinese/dsl/scales/24hr/LP, Shell/dsl/rest./motel/24hr/@, **food:** Arby's, Burger King, McDonald's, Waffle House, **lodging:** Best Western, **other:** Blue Beacon, Homestead RV Ctr., RV camping (2mi), tire/dsl repair, **S gas:** Love's/Chester's/Subway/dls/scales/24hr, other Chevrolet
232mm	**weigh sta wb**
229	OH 193, Belmont Ave, to Youngstown, **N gas:** GetGo, Speedway/dsl, **food:** Fortune Garden Chinese, Handel's Ice Cream, Knight's Inn, Rotelli Italian, Subway,
229	Continued **lodging:** Hampton Inn, Metroplex Hotel, Super 8, TallyHo-tel, Travel Inn, **other:** Giant Eagle Foods, **S gas:** BP, Shell, **food:** Arby's, Antone's Italian, Bob Evans, Charley's Subs, Cancun Mexican, Denny's, Golden Hunan Chinese, Ianazone's Pizza, Inner Circle Pizza, Jimmy's Italian, KFC, LJ Silver, McDonald's, Papa John's, Pizza Hut, Subway, Taco Bell, Treacher's, Yougtown Crab Co, Wendy's, Westfork Roadhouse, **lodging:** Days Inn, Quality Inn, **other:** Advance Parts, Aldi Foods, AutoZone, BigLots, Family$, Firestone, Goodyear/auto, Rite Aid, Sav-A-Lot Foods, Walgreens
228	OH 11, to Warren (exits left from eb), Ashtabula
227	US 422, Girard, Youngstown, **N gas:** Shell/dsl/24hr, **food:** Burger King, DQ, JibJab Hotdogs, Subway
226	Salt Springs Rd, to I-680 (from wb), **N gas:** BP/Dunkin Donuts/dsl, Sheetz/24hr, **food:** McDonald's, Waffle House, **other:** vet, **S gas:** Mr Fuel/Piccadilly/dsl/24hr, Petro/dsl/rest./scales/24hr/@, Pilot/Arby's/scales/dsl/24hr, **other:** Blue Beacon, SpeedCo, dsl repair
224b	I-680 (from eb), to Youngstown
224a	OH 11 S, to Canfield
223	OH 46, to Niles, **N gas:** Country Fair, Pilot/McDonald's/scales/dsl/24hr, **food:** Bob Evans, Burger King, IceHouse Rest., Salsita's Mexican, **lodging:** Comfort Inn, Economy Inn, **S gas:** BP/dsl, FuelMart/dsl, Sunoco/Subway, TA/Counry Pride/dsl/rest./scales/24hr/@, **food:** Arby's, Brudders Grill, Cracker Barrel, DQ, LJ Quaker Steak & Lube, Silver/Taco Bell, Perkins, Starbucks, Wendy's, **lodging:** Best Western, Country Inn & Suites, Econolodge, Fairfield Inn, Hampton Inn, Knight's Inn, Sleep Inn, Super 8, **other:** Blue Beacon, Freightliner/24hr, Harley-Davidson
221mm	Meander Reservoir
219mm	I-80 wb joins Ohio Tpk (toll)

For I-80 exits 2-218, see Ohio Turnpike.

INTERSTATE 90

Exit #	Services
244mm	Ohio/Pennsylvania state line
242mm	**Welcome Ctr/weigh sta wb, full facilities, info, phone, picnic, litter barrels, petwalk**
241	OH 7, to Andover, Conneaut, **N food:** Burger King, McDonald's (2mi), **lodging:** Day's Inn, **other:** H, AutoZone, CVS Drug, Evergreen RV Park, K-Mart, **S food:** Beef&Beer Café
235	OH 84, OH 193, to Youngstown, N Kingsville, **N gas:** Grab&Go/gas, Marathon/Circle K, **lodging:** Dav-Ed Motel, **other:** Village Green Camping (2mi), **S gas:** Circle K/Subway/dsl, TA/BP/Burger King/dsl/scales/24hr/@, **food:** Kay's Place Diner, **lodging:** Kingsville Motel, **other:** tire repair
228	OH 11, to Ashtabula, Youngstown, **N** H (4mi)
223	OH 45, to Ashtabula, **N gas:** ***FLYING J***/Shell/Country Mkt/dsl/LP/scales/24hr, **food:** Mr C's Rest., **lodging:** Best Value Inn, Comfort Inn, Holiday Inn Express, Sleep Inn, **other:** Buccaneer Camping, **S gas:** BP, Pilot/Subway/dsl/scales/24hr, SpeedCo, **food:** Burger King, McDonald's, Waffle House, **lodging:** Hampton Inn
218	OH 534, Geneva, **N gas:** BP, GetGo, **food:** Best Friend's Grill, Chop's Grille, McDonald's, Pizza Hut,

INTERSTATE 90 CONT'D

E ↕ W

Exit #	Services
218	Continued Wendy's, **lodging:** Howard Johnson, **other:** H, Goodyear/repair, Indian Creek Camping (8mi), to Geneva SP, **S gas:** KwikFil/dsl/rest./scales/24hr, **food:** Quizno's, **other:** Kenisse's Camping
212	OH 528, to Thompson, Madison, **N food:** McDonald's, **other:** Mentor RV Ctr, **S gas:** Marathon/dsl, **food:** Medvec's Grill, **other:** Heritage Hills Camping (4mi), radiators
205	Vrooman Rd, **0-1 mi S gas:** BP/dsl, Marathon/dsl, **food:** Capps Eatery, Subway
200	OH 44, to Painesville, Chardon, **S gas:** BP/Subway/dsl, Sunoco/dsl, **food:** Bellacino's, McDonald's, Palmer's Bistro, Red Hawk Grille, Teresa's Pizzaria, Waffle House, **lodging:** Baymont Inn, Renaissance, **other:** H, Curves, Reider's Foods, hwy patrol
198mm	**rest area both lanes, full ♿ facilities, phone, picnic, litter barrels, vending, petwalk**
195	OH 615, Center St, Kirtland Hills, Mentor, **1-2 mi N gas:** BP, **food:** El Rodeo Mexican, Yours Truly Rest., **lodging:** Best Western
193	OH 306, to Mentor, Kirtland, **N gas:** BP/Subway, **food:** McDonald's, **lodging:** Motel 6, **S gas:** Marathon, **food:** Burger King, Dino's Rest., Texas Cattle Co, **lodging:** Day's Inn/café, Red Roof Inn, **other:** H Kirtland Temple LDS Historic Site
190	Express Lane to I-271 (from wb)
189	OH 91, to Willoughby, Willoughby Hills, **N gas:** BP/dsl, Shell/24hr, **food:** Bob Evans, Café Europa, Cracker Barrel, Damon's, Eat 'n Park, Peking Chef, Subway, Texas Roadhouse, Wendy's, **lodging:** Courtyard, Motel 6, Travelodge, **other:** H, CVS Drug, Walgreens, **N other:** Lexus
188	I-271 S, to Akron
187	OH 84, Bishop Rd, to Wickliffe, Willoughby, **S gas:** BP/dsl, Shell, **food:** Baker's Square, Burger King, China King, Manhattan Deli, Mazzio's, McDonald's, Quizno's, Subway, **lodging:** Holiday Inn, **other:** H Curves, CVS Drug, Chevrolet, Giant Eagle Foods, Marc's Foods, Mazda/VW, NTB, Sam's Club, Vet
186	US 20, Euclid Ave, **N gas:** Sunoco, **food:** Grand Rodeo Mexican, McDonald's, **lodging:** Comfort Inn, **other:** Dodge/Subaru, Ford, Isuzu, radiators, **S gas:** Shell, **food:** Arby's, KFC, Pizza Hut, Popeye's, R-Ribs, Sidewalk Cafe, Taco Bell, **other:** Advance Parts, $General, Firestone/auto, NAPA, SaveAlot Foods
185	OH 2 E (exits left from eb), to Painesville
184b	OH 175, E 260th St, **N gas:** Shell/autocare, **S other:** NTB, Ruff's RV Ctr, transmissions, Vet
184a	Babbitt Rd, same as 183
183	E 222nd St, **N other:** GMC, **S gas:** BP, Sunoco/dsl/24hr
182b a	185 St, 200 St, **N food:** Muldoon's Eatery, **other:** Home Depot, Honda, Hyundai, **S other:** Marathon/dsl, Shell, Speedway
181b a	E 156th St, **S gas:** BP/24hr
180b a	E 140th St, E 152nd St
179	OH 283 E, to Lake Shore Blvd
178	Eddy Rd, to Bratenahl

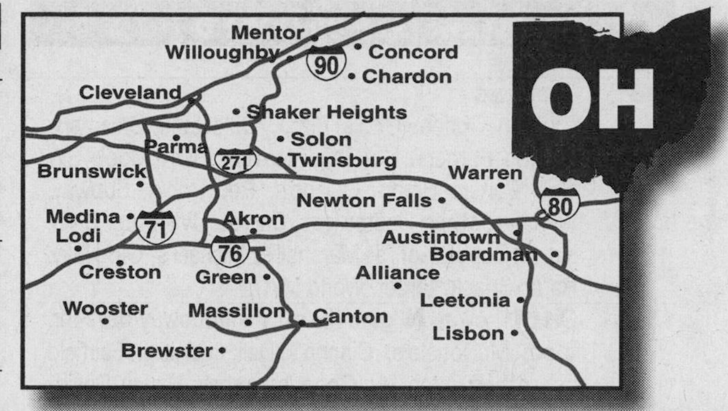

CLEVELAND

Exit #	Services
177	University Circle, MLK Dr, **N other:** Cleveland Lake SP, **S other:** H, Rockefeller Park
176	E 72nd St
175	E 55th St, Marginal Rds
174b	OH 2 W, to Lakewood, downtown, Rock&Roll Hall of Fame, Browns Stadium
174a	Lakeside Ave
173c	Superior Ave, St Clair Ave, downtown, **N gas:** BP
173b	Chester Ave, **S gas:** BP
173a	Prospect Ave (from wb), downtown
172d	Carnegie Ave, downtown, **S food:** Burger King, **other:** Cadillac
172c b	E 9th St, **S other:** H, to Cleveland St U
172a	I-77 S, to Akron
171b a	US 422, OH 14, Broadway St, Ontario St, **N lodging:** Hilton Garden, **other:** to Browns Stadium
170c b	I-71 S, to I-490
170a	US 42, W 25th St, **S** gas
169	W 44th St, W 41st St, **N** H
167b a	OH 10, West Blvd, 98th St, to Lorain Ave, **N** H, **S gas:** BP/dsl, **other:** CVS Drug
166	W 117th St, **N gas:** BP/dsl, Get Go, Shell, **food:** KFC, Penn Sta. Subs, **other:** Advance Parts, Home Depot, Staples, Target, **S food:** Church's/White Castle
165	W 140th St, Bunts Rd, Warren Rd, **N other:** H
164	McKinley Ave, to Lakewood
162	Hilliard Blvd (from wb), to Westway Blvd, Rocky River, **S gas:** BP, Shell
161	OH 2, OH 254 (from eb, no EZ return), Detroit Rd, Rocky River
160	Clague Rd (from wb), **S other:** H, same as 159
159	OH 252, Columbia Rd, **N gas:** Speedway, **food:** Carrabba's, Clubhouse Grill, Dave&Buster's, Key West Cafe, Outback Steaks, **lodging:** Courtyard, TownePlace Suites, Super 8, **S gas:** BP, **food:** Houlihan's, KFC, McDonald's, Taco Bell, **other:** Chevrolet, NTB, Rico's Mkt
156	Crocker Rd, Bassett Rd, Westlake, Bay Village, **N gas:** BP, Shell, **lodging:** Extended Stay Deluxe, Holiday Inn, Red Roof Inn, Residence Inn, **S gas:** Marathon/dsl, **food:** Applebee's, Blake's Seafood, Bob Evans, Cheesecake Factory, Max&Erma's, McDonald's, Subway, TGIFriday, Wendy's, **lodging:** Hampton Inn, **other:** H, Borders Books, CVS Drug, Giant Eagle, GNC, K-Mart, Marc's Foods, Radio Shack, mall
153	OH 83, Avon Lake, **N gas:** GetGo/dsl, Marathon/Circle K, Speedway, **food:** Bubba's BBQ, Buffalo Wild Wings, Perkins, **other:** Best Buy, Walmart/auto/gas, **S food:** Applebees, Bob Evans, Burger King,

INTERSTATE 90 CONT'D

E ↕ W

Exit #	Services
153	Continued Caribou Coffee, CiCi's Pizza, Coldstone Creamery, 5 Guys Burgers, Hot Dog Heaven, IHOP, Moe's SW Grill, Panera Bread, Quizno's, Red Robin, Subway, Wendy's, **other:** Costco/gas, Curves, CVS Drug, GNC, Home Depot, Kohl's, Marshall's, Michael's, Old Navy, Radio Shack, Target, World Mkt
151	OH 611, Avon, **N gas:** BP/dsl, Pilot/Subway/dsl/24hr, **food:** McDonald's, Dianna's Deli, **lodging:** Fairfield Inn, **other:** Avon RV, Goodyear/repair, Harley Davidson, **S gas:** BJ's Whse/gas, **food:** Mulligan's Grille
148	OH 254, Sheffield, Avon, **N food:** Quaker Steak, **other:** Dodge, Ford, KIA, Mazda, Mitsubishi, Nissan, **S gas:** BP, GetGo, Speedway, **food:** Arby's, Burger King, Cracker Barrel, Donato's Pizza, KFC, McDonald's, Pizza Hut, Quizno's, Ruby Tuesday, Sedona Grill, Steak'n Shake, Subway, Taco Bell, Wendy's, **other:** Aldi Foods, CVS Drug, $General, Drug Mart, Gander Mtn Giant Eagle, NTB, Sam's Club/gas
147mm	Black River
145	OH 57, to Lorain, I-80/Ohio Tpk E, Elyria, **N food:** Burger King, George's Rest., KFC, **other:** H, U-Haul, **S gas:** BP/McDonald's/dsl, Shell, Speedway **food:** Applebee's, Arby's, Bennigan's, Bob Evans, Buffalo Wild Wings, Denny's, Eat'n Park, Fazoli's, Golden Corral, Harry Buffalo, Jumbo Buffet, Olive Garden, Qdoba Mexican, Red Lobster, Subway, TGIFriday's, Tokyo Steaks, Wendy's, **lodging:** Best Western, Comfort Inn, Country Inn&Suites, Econolodge, Holiday Inn, Howard Johnson, Red Roof Inn, Super 8, **other:** Best Buy, Curves, $Tree, Firestone/auto, Home Depot, Honda/Hyundai, JC Penney, Jo-Ann Fabrics, Marc's Foods, Michael's, Lowe's Whse, Macy's, NTB, PetsMart, Radio Shack, Sears/auto, Staples, Target, Walmart/auto
144	OH 2 W (from wb, no return), to Sandusky, **1 mi N on Broadway Ave E gas:** Marathon, Shell/24hr, **food:** McDonald's, **other:** H
143	I-90 wb joins Ohio Tpk
WB exits to Ohio/Indiana state line are on Ohio Turnpike. See Ohio Turnpike Exits 142-0.	
142	I-90 (from eb), OH 2, to W Cleveland
139mm	**Middle Ridge Service Plaza wb, Vermilion Service Plaza eb,** Sunoco/dsl/24hr, FoodCourt, gifts, ☎, **RV parking**
135	rd 51, Baumhart Rd, to Vermillion
132mm	Vermilion River
118	US 250, to Norwalk, Sandusky, **N gas:** DM/dsl, Marathon, Speedway, **food:** 4Monks Italian, McDonald's, Subway, **lodging:** Comfort Inn, Day's Inn, Hampton Inn, Motel 6, Ramada Ltd, Super 8, **other:** Oulet/famous brands, **5 mi N food:** Perkins, Roadhouse Grill, **lodging:** Econolodge, Fairfield Inn, Red Roof Inn, **S lodging:** Colonial Inn, Homestead Inn/rest., **food:** Race Café, **other:** Chevrolet, to Edison's Birthplace
110	OH 4
100mm	**Erie Islands Service Plaza wb, Commodore Perry Service Plaza eb, gas:** Sunoco/dsl/24hr, **food:** Burger King, Cinnabon, Max&Erma's, Sbarro's, Starbucks, **other:** ☎
93mm	Sandusky River
91	OH 53, to Fremont, Port Clinton, **N food:** Z's Diner, **lodging:** Best Budget Inn, Day's Inn, **S gas:** Shell/dsl/24hr, **food:** Applebee's (2mi), **lodging:** Fremont Tpk Motel, Holiday Inn, **other:** H
81	OH 51, Elmore, Woodville, Gibsonburg
80.5mm	Portage River
77mm	**Blue Heron Service Plaza wb, Wyandot Service Plaza eb,** Sunoco/dsl/24hr, Hardee's/chicken, ☎
71	I-280, OH 420, to Stony Ridge, Toledo, **N gas:** Petro/Mobil/dsl/rest./24hr/@, ***FLYING J***/Conoco/dsl/rest./24hr/LP/@, **food:** Charter House Rest., Country Diner, **lodging:** Howard Johnson, Pizza Hut, Knight's Inn, Ramada Ltd, Stony Ridge Inn/truck plaza/dsl/@, **other:** Blue Beacon, **S gas:** FuelMart/dsl/@, Pilot/dsl/24hr/@, TA/BP/Burger King/Taco Bell/dsl/24hr/@, **food:** McDonald's, Wendy's, **other:** truckwash
64	I-75 N, to Toledo, Perrysburg
63mm	Maumee River
59	US 20, to I-475, Maumee, Toledo, **N gas:** Amoco, BP/dsl, Speedway/dsl, **food:** Arby's, Bob Evans, China Gate Rest., Church's, Dominic's Italian, Indian Cuisine, Max's Diner, McDonald's, Pizza Hut, **lodging:** Budget Inn, Econolodge, Holiday Inn, Motel 6, Quality Inn, **other:** Advance Parts, Goodyear/auto, Jo-Ann Fabrics, K-Mart/Little Caesar's, NAPA, Radio Shack, Savers Foods, Sears/auto, to Toledo Stadium, **S gas:** Meijer/dsl/24hr, Speedway, **food:** Big Boy,'s, Fazoli's, Fricker's, Friendly's, Ralphie's Burgers, Red Lobster, Schlotsky's, Taco Bell, **lodging:** Best Western, Comfort Inn, Cross Country Inn, Day's Inn, Hampton Inn, Red Roof Inn, Super 8, **other:** Ames, Chevrolet, Ford/Lincoln/Mercury, Honda, Toyota
52	OH 2, to Toledo, **S lodging:** Days Inn, Quality Inn (6mi), Super 8, **other:** RV/truck repair
49mm	**service plaza both lanes,** Valero/dsl/24hr, gifts/ice cream
39	OH 109, Delta, **N gas:** Valero, **food:** Country Lion's
34	OH 108, to Wauseon, **S gas:** Shell/Subway/dsl/24hr, **food:** Smith's Rest., **lodging:** Arrowhead Motel, Best Western, Holiday Inn Express, Super 8, **other:** H, Toledo RV Ctr, Woods Trucking/repair (1mi), **2 mi S on US 20A...gas:** BP/Circle K, **food:** Burger King, DQ, McDonald's, Pizza Hut, Taco Bell, Wendy's, **other:** Ace Hardware, Rite Aid, Walmart SuperCtr/dsl
25	OH 66, Burlington, **3 mi S other:** Sauder Village Museum
24.5mm	Tiffin River
13	OH 15, to Bryan, Montpelier, **S gas:** Marathon/Subway/dsl, Sunoco, **food:** Country Fair Rest., **lodging:** Econolodge, Holiday Inn Express, Rainbow Motel, Ramada Inn, **other:** Hutch's dsl Repair
11.5mm	St Joseph River
3mm	toll plaza, ☎
20	H 49, to US 20, **N food:** Burger King, **other:** tire repair
0mm	Ohio/Indiana state line

INTERSTATE 270 (COLUMBUS)

Exit #	Services
55	**I-71, to Columbus, Cincinnati**
52b a	US 23, High St, Circleville, **N gas:** Marathon/Circle K, Speedway/dsl, **food:** A&W/KFC, Arby's, Bob Evans, Burger King, China Town, LJ Silver, Los Campero's,

OH

INTERSTATE 270 CONT'D (COLUMBUS)

E ↕ W

Exit #	Services
52b a	Continued McDonald's, Pizza Hut, Ponderosa, Roadhouse Grill, Skyline Chili, Subway, Taco Bell, Tim Horton, Waffle House, Wendy's, White Castle, **lodging:** Kozy Inn, **other:** AutoZone, Curves, $General, Firestone, Kroger/gas, Lowe's, Walgreens, Walmart, **S gas:** BP/dsl, **lodging:** Budget Inn, **other:** Kioto Downs
49	Alum Creek Dr, **N gas:** Duke/dsl, Sunoco/dsl, **food:** Donato's Pizza, KFC/LJ Silver, Subway, **S gas:** BP/dsl, **food:** Arby's, McDonald's, Taco Bell, Wendy's, **lodging:** Comfort Inn, Sleep Inn
46b a	US 33, Bexley, Lancaster
43b a	I-70, E to Cambridge, W to Columbus
41b a	US 40, **E gas:** BP, Shell, **food:** Bob Evans, Boston Mkt, Hooters, McDonald's, Outback Steaks, Rally's, Steak'n Shake, Texas Roadhouse, **other:** Walgreens, **W gas:** Mobil, Shell, Speedway, **food:** Fuddruckers, Golden Corral, Hunan Chinese, LoneStar Steaks
39	OH 16, Broad St, **E gas:** Meijer/dsl, Speedway/dsl, **food:** Arby's, Chipotle Grill, Church's, Quizno's, Waffle House, White Castle, **lodging:** Country Inn&Suites, **other:** H, **W gas:** Shell, **food:** Applebee's, **lodging:** Ramada Inn
37	OH 317, Hamilton Rd, **E gas:** BP/dsl, Marathon, Speedway/dsl, **food:** Big Boy, Bob Evans, Burger King, Chinese Express, Damon's, Donato's Pizza, Hickory House, KFC, Pizza Hut/Taco Bell, Starbucks, **lodging:** Holiday Inn Express, SpringHill Suites, **other:** Firestone, GNC, Kroger, **2 mi W lodging:** Comfort Suites, Hampton Inn, Hilton Garden
35b a	I-670W, US 62, **E gas:** Speedway/dsl, **food:** City BBQ, Donato's Pizza, McDonald's, Tim Horton, **other:** CVS Drug, **W** I-670
33	no services
32	Morse Rd, **E gas:** Marathon/DM, Speedway/dsl, **food:** Donato's Pizza, **other:** Mazda, Toyota, **W gas:** BP, Mobil/dsl, Shell/Subway, **food:** Applebee's, Champp's Grill, HomeTown Buffet, Kobe Japanese, Logan's Roadhouse, McDonald's, On-the-Border, Pizza Hut/Taco Bell, Steak'n Shake, Wendy's, **lodging:** Extended Stay America, Hampton Inn, **other:** Best Buy, BMW, Cadillac, Carmax, Discount Tire, Jo-Ann Fabrics, Lexus, Lowe's Whse, Macy's, Mercedes, Nordstrom's, NTB, Sam's Club, Target, Walmart SuperCtr/24hr, mall
30	OH 161 E to New Albany, W to Worthington
29	OH 3, Westerville, **N gas:** BP/dsl, Shell, **food:** Applebee's, Arby's, Chipotle Mexican, McDonald's, Fazoli's, Pizza Hut, Tim Horton, **lodging:** Baymont Inn, Knight's Inn, **other:** CarQuest, Firestone/auto, Kroger, **S gas:** Speedway/dsl, Sunoco/dsl, **food:** Carsoni's Italian, China House, Domino's, Subway, **other:** Aldi Foods, Family$, Midas
27	OH 710, Cleveland Ave, **N gas:** Speedway, **food:** Subway, Tim Horton, Wendy's, **lodging:** Quality Inn, Ramada Inn, Signature Inn, **other:** CVS Drug, NAPA, Tuffy, **S food:** Bob Evans, McDonald's, O'Charley's, Steak'n Shake, **lodging:** Embassy Suites, **other:** Home Depot
26	I-71, S to Columbus, N to Cleveland

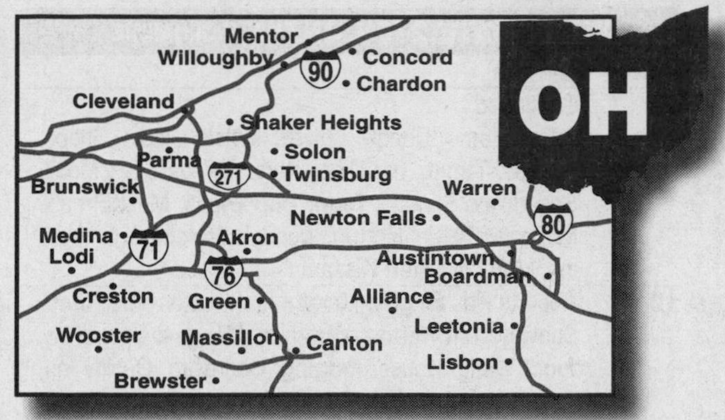

COLUMBUS

Exit #	Services
23	US 23, Worthington, **N food:** Alexander's, Amazon Grill, Bob Evans, Bravo Italian, Buffalo Wild Wings, Champp's Grill, Chipotle Mexican, Columbus Fish Mkt, El Acapulco, Gilbert's Steaks, Lotus Grill, Mitchell's Steaks, Panera Bread, Quizno's, Ruth's Chris Steaks, Starbucks, Sushiko Japanese, Tutt's Italian, **lodging:** AmeriSuites, Courtyard, Days Inn, DoubleTree, Extended Stay America, Motel 6, Homewood Suites, Red Roof Inn, Residence Inn, Sheraton, **S gas:** BP, **food:** Buca Italian, Cosi Grill, Jimmy John's, McDonald's, **lodging:** Econolodge, Holiday Inn
22	OH 315, **N gas:** Marathon/dsl
20	Sawmill Rd, **N gas:** BP, Marathon/dsl, **food:** Burger King, McDonald's, Olive Garden, Subway, Taco Bell, Wendy's, **other:** Buick/Pontiac/GMC, CVS Drug, Ford, Hyundai, Lincoln-Mercury, Mazda, NTB, Subaru, Tire Kingdom, **S gas:** Meijer, Shell, Speedway, **food:** Applebee's, Asian Star, Arby's, BajaFresh, Bob Evans, Boston Mkt, Burger King, Charlie's Subs, Chili's, Chipotle Mexican, Cosi Grill, Don Pablo, Golden Corral, HoneyBaked Cafe, Joe's Crabshack, KFC, Krispy Kreme, McDonald's, Mongolian BBQ, Steak'n Shake, Red Lobster, Ruby Tuesday, Ted's Mt Grill, **lodging:** Hampton Inn, Quality Inn, Woodfin Suites, **other:** Barnes&Noble, Big Lots, Borders Books, Cadillac/Honda, Discount Tire, $Tree, Firestone, Jo-Ann Fabrics, Kohl's, Lowe's Whse, PetCo, Sam's Club, Staples, SteinMart, Target, Toyota/Scion, Trader Joe's
17b a	US 33, Dublin-Granville Rd, **E gas:** Marathon, Sunoco, **food:** Bob Evans, Donato's, Max&Erma's, McDonald's, Subway, **lodging:** Best Value Inn, Courtyard, Crowne Plaza, Embassy Suites, Hilton Garden, Red Roof Inn, Residence Inn, **other:** BMW/Mini, CVS Drug, Kroger, Mitsubishi, Mr Tire, USPO
15	Tuttle Crossing Blvd, **E gas:** BP, Mobil, **food:** Bob Evans, Boston Mkt, Chipotle Mexican, Cozymel's, Longhorn Steaks, Macaroni Grill, McDonald's, PF Chang's, Pizza Hut/Taco Bell, River City Grill, TGIFriday, Wendy's, **lodging:** Drury Inn, Homewood Suites, Hyatt Place, La Quinta, Marriott, **other:** JC Penney, Macy's, Sears/auto, mall, **W gas:** Exxon/Subway/dsl, Shell, **food:** Quizno's, Steak'n Shake, Uno Pizzaria, **lodging:** Staybridge Suites, **other:** Best Buy, NTB, Walmart/auto, World Mkt
13	Cemetery Rd, Fishinger Rd, **E gas:** Shell/Subway, Speedway, **food:** Burger King, CheeseBurger Paradise, Chili's, Chiotle Mexican, Damon's, Dave&Buster's, Donato's Pizza, KFC, Panera Bread, Quizno's, Skyline Chili, Spaghetti's, TGIFriday, Tropical Bistro, **lodging:** Comfort Suites, Homewood Suites, **other:** CVS

INTERSTATE 270 CONT'D (COLUMBUS)

E ↕ W

Exit #	Services
13	Continued Drug, Home Depot, Lowe's Whse, Radio Shack, Staples, Target, Tire Dicounters, **W gas:** BP, Mobil, Speedway, Sunoco, **food:** Bob Evans, Max&Erma's, McDonald's, Tim Horton, Wendy's, **lodging:** Hampton Inn, Motel 6, **other:** Nissan
10	Roberts Rd, **E gas:** Marathon, Thornton's/dsl, **food:** Subway, Tim Horton, Wendy's, **W gas:** Speedway, **food:** Waffle House, **lodging:** Courtyard, Quality Inn, Royal Inn, **other:** Kroger/gas
8	I-70, E to Columbus, W to Indianapolis
7	US 40, Broad St, **E gas:** BP, Speedway, **food:** Bob Evans, Boston Mkt, Burger King, McDonald's, Popeye's, TeeJay's, Wendy's, White Castle, **other:** Buick/Pontiac/GMC, Chevrolet, Chrysler/Jeep, Family$, Firestone/auto, Kohl's, NTB, Pepboys, Sears/auto, Staples, Suzuki, Target, Tuffy, **W gas:** GetGo, Speedway/dsl, Thornton's, **food:** A&W/LJ Silver, Arby's, Big Boy, KFC, Papa John's, Waffle House, **lodging:** Holiday Inn Express, Hometown Inn, **other:** H, CVS Drug, Giant Eagle Foods, Goodyear, Home Depot, Jo-Ann Fabrics
5	Georgesville, **E gas:** Marathon, Mobil, Sunoco/dsl, **other:** Walmart SuperCtr, **W food:** Applebee's, Arby's, Bob Evans, Buffalo Wild Wings, Chipotle Mexican, DQ, Fazoli's, Fiesta Mariachi, KFC/LJ Silver, LoneStar Steaks, McDonald's, O'Charley's, Red Lobster, Steak'n Shake, Subway, Wendy's, White Castle, **other:** Advance Parts, GNC, Hyundai/Isuzu/Subaru, KIA, Kroger/gas, Lowe's Whse, NTB, Toyota/Scion, VW
2	US 62, OH 3, Grove City, **N gas:** BP, **S gas:** Shell, Speedway, Sunoco, **food:** Big Boy, Brewster's, Burger King, Domino's, Donato's Pizza, McDonald's, Quizno's, Subway, Tim Horton/Wendy's, Waffle House, lodging: Knight's Inn
0mm	I-71

OH

INTERSTATE 271 (CLEVELAND)

N ↕ S

CLEVELAND

MACEDONIA

Exit #	Services
39mm	I-271 begins/ends on I-90, exit 188
38mm	I-271/I-480, Express Lanes
36	Wilson Mills Rd, Highland Hts, Mayfield, **E lodging:** Hilton Garden, **W gas:** BP, Marathon/dsl, **food:** Denny's, Wellington's Rest., **other:** Home Depot, Kohl's, Tuesday Morning
34	US 322, Mayfield Rd, **E gas:** BP, **food:** TGI Friday, **lodging:** Holiday Inn, **other:** NTB, Walgreens, **W gas:** Shell, Speedway, **food:** Bob Evans, Buca Italian, Burger King, Caribou Coffee, Fat Burger, McDonald's, Panini's Grill, Starbucks, **lodging:** Baymont Inn, **other:** H Best Buy, Costco/gas, CVS Drug, Ford, Giant Eagle Foods, Lincoln/Mercury, Marshall's, Midas, Murray's Parts, Old Navy, PetsMart, World Mkt, Walmart, Vet
32	32 Braine rd Rd, Cedar Rd, **E** H
29	US 422 W, OH 87, Chagrin Blvd, Harvard Rd, **E gas:** Marathon, Shell, Sunoco, **food:** Bahama Breeze, Bob Evan's, Corky&Lenny's Rest., McDonald's, Olive Garden, Pizza Hut, Red Lobster, Starbucks, Uno Café, Wendy's, **lodging:** Courtyard, Extended Stay America, Fairfield Inn, Hampton Inn, Homestead Suites, Super 8, **other:** TJ Maxx, Wild Oats Mkt, **W gas:** BP/Subway, Shell, **food:** PF Chang's, Your's Truly, **lodging:** Clarion, Embassy Suites, Hilton, Homewood Suites, **other:** Cadillac, Chrysler/Jeep, NTB
28b	Harvard Rd, **E food:** Red Robin, **W food:** Abuelo's, Chipotle Mexican, DiBella's Subs, River City Grille, Robek's Cafe, **lodging:** Marriott, **other:** H
28a	OH 175, Richmond Rd, Emery Rd, **E gas:** BP, GetGo, Marathon/Circle K/Subway, **food:** Baskin Robbins/Dunkin Donuts, Marianne's Bakery, McDonald's, Quizno's, **W food:** BJ's Whse
27b	I-480 W
26	Rockside Rd, **E gas:** Sunoco, **food:** City Diner, **lodging:** Red Roof Inn, **other:** Lowe's Whse
23	OH 14 W, Forbes Rd, Broadway Ave, **E gas:** Sunoco, **food:** Double Dragon Chinese, McDonald's,Subway, Wendy's, **lodging:** Holiday Inn Express, **other:** Sam's Club/gas, **W gas:** BP, Marathon/Circle K, **other:** H
21	I-480 E, OH 14 E (from sb), to Youngstown
19	OH 82, Macedonia, **E gas:** Speedway, **food:** Papa John's, **W gas:** Sunoco, **food:** Applebee's, Arby's, Caribou Coffee, Chili's, Chipotle Mexican, Golden Corral, KFC, Outback Steaks, Panera Bread, Pizza Hut, Qdoba, Steak'n Shake, Taco Bell, Wendy's, **other:** Best Buy, CVS Drug, $Tree, Giant Eagle Foods, GNC, Home Depot, Kohl's, Lowes Whse, NTB, PetCo, Radio Shack, Target, Walgreens, Walmart/auto
18	OH 8, Boston Hts, to Akron, **E gas:** BP/Subway/dsl, Speedway, **food:** Bob Evans, Denny's, **lodging:** Country Inn&Suites, Days Inn, Knight's Inn, La Quinta, Motel 6, **W** same as 19
12	OH 303, Richfield, Peninsula
10	I-77, to I-80, OH Tpk (from nb), to Akron, Cleveland
9	I-77 S, OH 176 (from nb), to Richfield
8mm	**rest area both lanes, full ♿ facilities, ☎, picnic, litter barrels, petwalk**
3	OH 94, to I-71 N, Wadsworth, N Royalton, **W gas:** Marathon
0mm	I-271 begins/ends on I-71, exit 220.

INTERSTATE 275 (CINCINNATI)

See Kentucky Interstate 275

INTERSTATE 280 (TOLEDO)

E ↕ W

Exit #	Services
13	I-280 begins/ends on exit 13 I-75
12	Manhattan Blvd, **E gas:** Sunoco, **W gas:** Sunoco, **food:** Arby's, McDonald's
11	OH 25 S, Eerie St, **W other:** Convention Ctr, Eerie St Mkt
10mm	Maumee River
9	OH 65, Front St, **E gas:** Sunoco, **W gas:** Sunoco
8	Star Ave, (from sb only)
7	OH 2, Oregon, **E gas:** Sunoco, **food:** Arby's, Tim Horton, **other:** H, Ford, K-Mart
6	OH 51, Woodville rd, Curtice, **E gas:** BP/dsl, **food:** Bob Evan's, Burger King, **other:** H, Menard's, **W gas:** Meijer, Speedway/dsl, **food:** Applebees, Arby's, Big Boy, Gino's Pizza, McDonald's, Subway, Taco Bell, **lodging:** Sleep Inn, **other:** Advance Parts, Aldi Foods, $General, $Tree, Jo-Ann Fabrics, Rite Aid, Tires+
4	Walbridge

INTERSTATE 280 CONT'D (TOLEDO)

E ↕ W

Exit #	Services
2	OH 795, Perrysburg, **W gas:** Sunoco/Subway/dsl
1b	Hanley Rd, Latcha Rd, **E gas:** *FLYING J*/Cookery/dsl/LP/scales/24hr, **lodging:** Crown Inn, Vista Inn, **W gas:** Petro/Mobil/Iron Skillet/dsl/scales/24hr/@, **lodging:** Howard Johnson, Super 8, **other:** Blue Beacon, Speedco
1a	I-280 begins/ends on Ohio Tpk

INTERSTATE 475 (TOLEDO)

N ↕ S TOLEDO

Exit #	Services
20	I-75. I-475 begins/ends on I-75, exit 204.
19	Jackman Rd, Central Ave, **S gas:** Shell, **other:** H
18b	Douglas Rd (from wb)
18a	OH 51 W, Monroe St
17	Secor Rd, **N gas:** BP, Shell/dsl, **food:** Applebee's, Bob Evans, Boston Mkt, Burger King, China 1 Buffet, Famous Dave's BBQ, Hooters, KFC, Penn Sta. Subs, Red Lobster, Red Robin, Rudy's Hot Dogs, Tim Horton, **other:** Best Buy, Kroger, Murray's Parts, PharmX Drug, Walgreens, **S gas:** BP, **food:** Big Boy, El Vaquero, McDonald's, Original Pancakes, Pizza Hut, Ponderosa, Popeye's, Taco Bell, Uncle John's Pancakes, **lodging:** Clarion Hotel, Comfort Inn, Red Roof Inn, **other:** Costco/gas, Home Depot, Radio Shack, Sears/auto, Steinmart, U of Toledo
16	Talmadge Rd (from wb, no return), **N gas:** BP/dsl, Speedway, **food:** Arby's, Panera Bread, **other:** JC Penney, mall
15	Corey Rd (from eb, no return)
14	US 23 N, to Ann Arbor
13	US 20, OH 120, Central Ave, **E gas:** Speedway, Sunoco, **food:** Big Boy, Bob Evans, Magic Wok, McDonald's, Rally's, Wendy's, **other:** BMW, Cadillac, Chrysler/Jeep, Ford, Honda, Kia, Mitsubishi, Nissan, Subaru, Toyota/Scion, **W gas:** BP, Shell, Speedway, **other:** Lowes Whse
8b a	OH 2, **E gas:** BP/dsl, **food:** Don Pablo, Texas Roadhouse, **lodging:** Extended Stay America, Knight's Inn, Red Roof Inn, Residence Inn, **other:** H, Home Depot, Kohl's, Old Navy, to OH Med Coll, **W gas:** BP, Speedway, Sunoco/dsl, **food:** Arby's, Big Boy, Bob Evans, Boston Mkt, Brewhouse Rest., Burger King, Chili's, Empire Chinese, Little Caesar's, Mancino's Pizza, McDonald's, Rally's, Subway, Wendy's, **lodging:** Courtyard, Econolodge, Quality Inn, **other:** Best Buy, Big Lots, Firestone/auto, Kroger, PetsMart, Rite Aid, Sam's Club/gas, Target, Walmart SuperCtr
6	Dussel Dr, Salisbury Rd, to I-80-90/tpk, **E gas:** Barney's/BP, Speedway, **food:** Applebee's, Arby's, Bankok Kitchen, Bluewater Grill, Buffalo Wild Wings, Burger King, Coldstone Creamery, Cracker Barrel, Gino's Pizza, Ground Round, Jimmy John's, Longhorn Steaks, Marie's Diner, Max&Erma's, McDonald's, Panera Bread, Wendy's, Subway, Yoko Japanese, **lodging:** Country Inn&Suites, Courtyard, Fairfield Inn, Homewood Suites, Residence Inn, Studio+, Super 8, **W gas:** BP, **food:** Abuelo's, Bob Evans, Briarfield Café, Carraba's, Fox's Pizza, Ground Round, Mancino's Pizza, **lodging:** Baymont Inn, **other:** Churchill's Foods, Vet

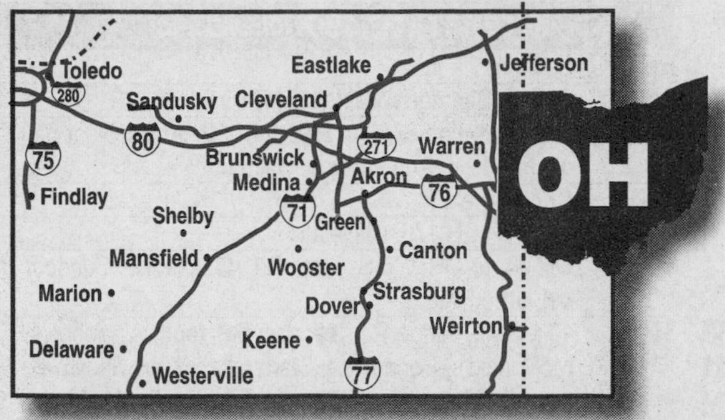

Exit #	Services
4	US 24, to Maumee, Napolean, **N other:** H, Toledo Zoo
3mm	Maumee River
2	OH 25, to Bowling Green, Perrysburg, **N gas:** BP/dsl, Circle K, Shell, **food:** Arby's, Buffalo Wild Wings, Beaner's Coffee, Café Marie, Charlie's Rest., El Vaquero, Gino's Pizza, Hungry Howie, Marco's Pizza, McDonald's, Papa John's, Subway, Wendy's, **other:** Bassett's Mkt Foods, Compounding, Goodyear/auto, Pontiac/GMC, Saab/VW, Toms Tire/repair, Volvo, Young's RV Ctr, **S gas:** Speedway/dsl, **food:** Biaggi's, Bob Evans, Chicago Pizza, Johnny Rockets, Louie's Grill, Maggi's Rest., Max&Erma's, Starbucks, TeaTree Asian, Waffle House, **lodging:** Economy Inn, **other:** Books-a-Million, Tire Man, Vet
0mm	I-475 begins/ends on I-75, exit 192.

INTERSTATE 480 (CLEVELAND)

E ↕ W

Exit #	Services
42	I-80, PA Tpk, I-480 begins/ends, **0-2 mi S gas:** BP, Marathon/Circle K, Sheetz/24hr, Shell, Speedway, **food:** Applebees, Arby's, Baskin Robbins/Dunkin Dounts, Big Boy, Bob Evans, Brown Derby Roadhouse, Buffalo Wild Wings, Burger King, CiCi's Pizza, Denny's, DQ, Eat'n Park, KFC, McDonald's, Mr Hero, New Peking Chinese, Pizza Hut, Quizno's, Rockney's Grill, Ruby Tuesday, Sonic, Steak'n Shake, Taco Bell, Wendy's, Zeppe's Pizza, **lodging:** Best Value Inn, Comfort Inn, Econolodge, Fairfield Inn, Hampton Inn, Holiday Inn Express, Microtel, TownePlace Suites, Wingate Inn, **other:** H, Aldi Foods, AutoZone, Buick/GMC, Curves, Defer Tire, $General, Giant Eagle, Home Depot, Honda, Hyundai, K-Mart, Lowes Whse, Midas, NAPA, NTB, Save-a-Lot Foods, Staples, Target, U-Haul, Van's Tires, Walgreens, Walmart SuperCtr, mall, USPO, Vet, to Kent St U
41	Frost Rd, Hudson-Aurora
37	OH 91, Solon, Twinsburg, **N food:** Arby's, Pizza Hut, Taco Bell, **other:** Comfort Suites, **other:** Giant Eagle, **S gas:** BP
36	OH 82, Aurora, Twinsburg, **N gas:** BP/dsl, Get'n Go, **food:** Burger King, **lodging:** Super 8, **S gas:** Marathon, Bob Evans, Cracker Barrel, Damon's, Donato's Pizza, McDonald's, Wendy's, **lodging:** Hilton Garden
26	I-271, to Erie, PA
25a b c	OH 8, OH 43, Northfield Rd, Bedford, **N other:** Harley-Davidson, **S food:** McDonald's, Rally's, White Castle
23	OH 14, Broadway Ave, **N gas:** Gulf/dsl, **food:** Burger King, KFC

INTERSTATE 480 (CLEVELAND)

Exit #	Services
22	OH 17, Garanger, Maple Hts, Garfield Hts
21	Transportation Blvd, to E 98th St, **S other:** Giant Eagle Foods, JoAnn Fabrics, Walmart
20b a	I-77, Cleveland
17	(eb only) OH 176, Cleveland
16	OH 94, to OH 176 S, State Rd, **S gas:** BP, Sunoco/dsl, **other:** Kia
15	10 US 42, Ridge Rd, **N gas:** BP, **food:** Applebee's, McDonald's, Ponderosa, Starbucks, **other:** Chevrolet, Lowe's Whse, Marc's Foods, TJMaxx, Top's Foods, **S gas:** Speedway, **food:** Arby's, Donato's, **other:** K-Mart, Best Buy
13	Teideman Rd, Brooklyn, **N gas:** Marathon, **S gas:** BP, Speedway, **food:** Carrabba's, Cracker Barrel, Don Pablo's, Max&Erma's, Panera Bread, Schlotsky's, Steak 'n Shake, TGIFriday's, **lodging:** Extended Stay America, Hampton Inn
12	W 150th, W 130th, Brookpark, **S gas:** Marathon, Shell, **food:** Arby's, Big Boy, Bob Evans, Thursday's Grill, **lodging:** Day's Inn, Best Value, **other:** Acura, Dodge, Lexus, Tire Kingdom, Toyota
11	I-71, Cleveland, Columbus
10	S rd 237, Airport Blvd, (wb only)
9	OH 17, Brookpark Rd, **N lodging:** Hilton Garden, **other:** [H], **S lodging:** Ramada Inn, ✈, 7 (wb only) Clague Rd, to WestLake
6	OH 252, to N Olmsted, **N gas:** BP, Shell, **food:** Applebee's, Bennigan's, Chick-fil-A, Chili's, Harry Buffalo, Lonestar Steaks, Macaroni Grill, Red Lobster, Red Robin, **lodging:** Candlewood Suites, Courtyard, Hampton Inn, Homestead Suites, Radisson, Studio+, **other:** Dillard's, Firestone, JC Penney, Michael's, Sears/auto, Walmart, mall
3	Stearns Rd, **2 mi S food:** Razzle's Cafe
2	OH 10, Lorain Rd, to OH Tpk, **N gas:** BP, Marathon, Sheetz/24hr, Speedway/dsl, **food:** Gourme Rest., McDonald's, **lodging:** Motel 6, Super 8, **other:** U-Haul
2	OH 10, Lorain Rd, to OH Tpk, **N gas:** BP, Marathon, Sheetz/24hr, Speedway/dsl, **food:** Gourme Rest., McDonald's, **lodging:** Motel 6, Super 8, **other:** U-Haul
0mm	OH 10, to Cleveland, **I-480 begins/ends on exit 151, OH Tpk**

INTERSTATE 680 (YOUNGSTOWN)

Exit #	Services
14	OH 164, to Western Reserve Rd, **N gas:** BP, **S gas:** Shell, Sheetz, **food:** McDonald's, Pizza Hut, Soffo's Café, Wendy's, **lodging:** Ramada Ltd., Holiday Inn Express, **other:** [H]
11a b	US 224, **S food:** LJ Silver, McDonald's, Olive Garden, Red Lobster, Starbucks, Springfield Grill, TGIFriday's, **lodging:** Fairfield Inn, Hampton Inn, Holiday Inn, Microtel, Red Roof Inn, Residence Inn, **other:** [H], Giant Eagle, Lowe's Whse, Marc's Foods, Sam's Club, Walmart
9a	OH 625, OH 170, Midlothian Blvd, **S food:** McDonald's
8	Shirley Rd, downtown
7	S Ave, downtown
6a	US 62, OH 7, Mkt St, downtown
5	Glenwood Ave, Mahoning, downtown
4a	OH 193, to US 422, New Castle, [H], museum
3b	Belle Vista Ave, Connecticut Ave
3a	OH 711 E
2	Meridian Rd, **S gas:** Marathon, **other:** Ford
1	OH 11

OHIO TURNPIKE

Exit #	Services
241mm	Ohio/Pennsylvania state line
239mm	toll plaza, ☎
237mm	**Mahoning Valley Travel Plaza eb, Glacier Hills Travel Plaza wb,** Valero/dsl/24hr, McDonald's, gifts, ☎
234	I-680 (from wb), to Youngstown
232	OH 7, to Boardman, Youngstown, **N gas:** Sheetz/24hr (1mi), **food:** DQ, Rita's Ice Cream, Steamer's Stonewall Tavern, **lodging:** Best Value Inn, Budget Inn, Holiday Inn Express, Quality Inn, **other:** [H], antiques, **S gas:** Pilot/McDonald's/dsl/scales/24hr, **lodging:** Davis Motel, Liberty Inn, **other:** truck repair
218	I-80 E, to Youngstown. **OH Tpk runs with I-76 eb, I-80 wb.,** Niles, **services S** on Mahoning
216	Lordstown (from wb), **N** GM Plant
215	Lordstown (from eb), **N** GM Plant
210mm	Mahoning River
209	OH 5, to Warren, **N lodging:** Rodeway Inn, **S gas:** Marathon/dsl, **lodging:** Econolodge, Holiday Inn Express
197mm	**Portage Service Plaza wb, Bradys Leap Service Plaza eb,** Valero/dsl/24hr, FoodCourt, McDonald's, gifts, ☎
193	OH 44, to Ravenna
192mm	Cuyahoga River
187	OH 14 S, I-480, to Streetsboro, **0-2mi S gas:** BP, Marathon/Circle K, Sheetz/24hr, Shell, Speedway, **food:** Applebees, Arby's, Baskin Robbins/Dunkin Dounts, Big Boy, Bob Evans, Brown Derby Roadhouse, Buffalo Wild Wings, Burger King, CiCi's Pizza, Denny's, DQ, Eat'n Park, KFC, McDonald's, Mr Hero, New Peking Chinese, Pizza Hut, Quizno's, Rockney's Grill, Ruby Tuesday, Sonic, Steak'n Shake, Taco Bell, Wendy's, Zeppe's Pizza, **lodging:** Best Value Inn, Comfort Inn, Econolodge, Fairfield Inn, Hampton Inn, Holiday Inn Express, Microtel, TownePlace Suites, Wingate Inn, **other:** [H], Aldi Foods, AutoZone, Buick/GMC, Curves, Defer Tire, $General, Giant Eagle, Home Depot, Honda, Hyundai, K-Mart, Lowes Whse, Midas, NAPA, NTB, Save-a-Lot Foods, Staples, Target, U-Haul, Van's Tires, Walgreens, Walmart SuperCtr, mall, USPO, Vet, to Kent St U
180	OH 8, to I-90 E, **N lodging:** Comfort Inn, Holiday Inn, **other:** Harley-Davidson, **S gas:** BP/dsl, **other:** to Cuyahoga Valley NRA
177mm	Cuyahoga River
173	OH 21, to I-77, **N gas:** Pilot/Wendy's/dsl/scales, **lodging:** Holiday Inn Express, Howard Johnson, **S food:** DQ, Memories Rest., Richfield Rest., Subway, **lodging:** Hampton Inn, Quality Inn, Super 8
170mm	**Towpath Service Plaza eb, Great Lakes Service Plaza wb, gas:** Valero/dsl/24hr, **food:** Burger King, FoodCourt, Panera Bread, Pizza Hut, **other:** gifts, phone
161	US 42, to I-71, Strongsville, **N on US 42...gas:** AP/

OHIO TURNPIKE CONT'D

E ↕ W

Exit #	Services
161	Continued dsl, **food:** Buffalo Wild Wings, Jennifer's Rest, Mad Cactus Mexican, **lodging:** Day's Inn, Kings Inn, La Siesta Motel, Metrick's Motel, Village Motel, **other:** Circle K, Home Depot, Lowes Whse, Walmart, Vet, **S on US 42...food:** Burger King, DQ, J-Bella Rest., KFC, La Volte Grill, Marco's Pizza, Olympia's Cafe, **lodging:** Elmhaven Motel, **other:** Dodge, NAPA, Staples
152	OH 10, to Oberlin, I-480, Cleveland, **N gas:** BP, Marathon, Sheetz/24hr, Speedway/dsl, **food:** Gourme Rest., McDonald's, **lodging:** Motel 6, Super 8, **other:** U-Haul **S other:** Moore's RV Ctr, drive-in theatre (seasonal)
151	I-480 E (from eb), to Cleveland, ✈
146mm	Black River
145	OH 57, to Lorain, to I-90, Elyria, **N food:** Burger King, KFC, George's Rest., **other:** U-Haul, Vet, **S gas:** BP/McDonald's/dsl, Shell, Speedway **food:** Applebee's, Arby's, Bennigan's, Bob Evans, Buffalo Wild Wings, Denny's, Eat'n Park, Fazoli's, Golden Corral, Harry Buffalo, Jumbo Buffet, Olive Garden, Qdoba Mexican, Red Lobster, Subway, TGIFriday's, Tokyo Steaks, Wendy's, **lodging:** Best Western, Comfort Inn, Country Inn&Suites, Econolodge, Holiday Inn, Howard Johnson, Red Roof Inn, Super 8, **other:** Best Buy, Curves,$Tree, Firestone/auto, Home Depot, Honda/Hyundai, JC Penney, Jo-Ann Fabrics, Marc's Foods, Michael's, Lowe's Whse, Macy's, NTB, PetsMart, Radio Shack, Sears/auto, Staples, Target, Walmart/auto
142	I-90 (from eb, exits left), OH 2, to W Cleveland
140	OH 58, Amherst, **0-2 mi N gas:** BP, Speedway, Sunoco/Subway/dsl, food Bob Evans, DQ, **lodging:** Days Inn, Motel 6, **other:** Chevrolet, Chrysler/Dodge, NAPA, Rite Aid, Suzuki, VW, repair, **S other:** Ford
139mm	**Service Plaza both lanes...gas:** Valero/dsl/24hr, **food:** Burger King, Great Steak, Panera Bread, Popeye's, Starbucks, TCBY, **other:** gifts, ☎, **RV parking**
135	rd 51, Baumhart Rd, to Vermilion
132mm	Vermilion River
118	US 250, to Norwalk, Sandusky, **N gas:** BP/Circle K/Dunkin Donuts, Marathon/dsl, **food:** 4Monks Italian, McDonald's, Subway, **lodging:** Comfort Inn, Day's Inn, Hampton Inn, Motel 6, Red Roof Inn, Super 8, **other:** RV Park, to Edison's Birthplace, **S food:** Maw's Place, **lodging:** Colonial Inn, **other:** Chevrolet/Hyundai
110	OH 4
100mm	**Service Plaza both lanes...gas:** Valero/dsl/24hr, **food:** Burger King, Cinnabon, Sbarro's, Starbucks, **other:** ☎
93mm	Sandusky River
91	OH 53, to Fremont, Port Clinton, **N lodging:** Day's Inn, **0-1 mi S gas:** BP/Subway/dsl/24hr, **food:** Applebees, Bob Evan's, Burger King, Fricker's, McDonald's, Pizza Hut, Ryan's, Subway, Taco Bell, **lodging:** Comfort Inn (2mi), Delux Inn, Fremont Inn, Hampton Inn, **other:** H, Aldi Foods, Ford/Lincoln/Mercury, Lowes Whse, Staples, Walmart SuperCtr/gas, Rutherford B. Hayes Library, USPO, Vet
81	OH 51, Elmore, Woodville, Gibsonburg
80.5mm	Portage River
77mm	**Service Plaza both lanes...gas:** Valero/dsl/24hr, **food:** Hardee's, Mancino's, ☎

LORAIN

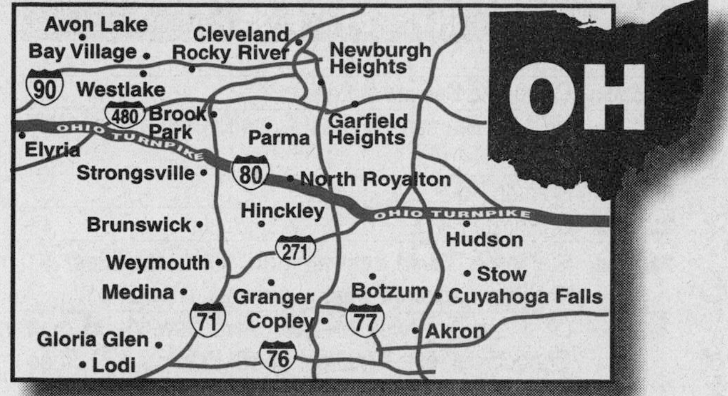

Exit #	Services
71	I-280, OH 420, to Stony Ridge, Toledo, **N gas:** Petro/Mobil/dsl/rest./scales/24hr/@, ***FLYING J***/dsl/rest./scales/24hr/LP, **lodging:** Budget Inn, Crown Inn, Howard Johnson, Super 8, Vista Inn, **other:** Blue Beacon, **S gas:** FuelMart/Subway/dsl/scales, Pilot/dsl/24hr/scales, TA/BP/Burger King/Taco Bell/dsl/scales/24hr/@, **food:** McDonald's, **other:** truckwash
64	I-75 N, to Toledo, Perrysburg, **S other:** BP/Subway/dsl, **lodging:** Country Inn&Suites, Courtyard, Hampton Inn
63mm	Maumee River
59	US 20, to I-475, Maumee, Toledo, **N gas:** BP/dsl, Shell, Speedway/dsl, **food:** Arby's, Bob Evans, McDonald's, Nick's Cafe, Olive Garden, Pizza Hut, Steak'n Shake, Subway, Waffle House, **lodging:** Clarion, Motel 6, **other:** Family$, Goodyear/auto, Jo-Ann Fabrics, K-Mart, Murray's Parts, NAPA, Radio Shack, Rite Aid, Savers, Walgreens, to Toledo Stadium, **S gas:** Speedway/dsl, **food:** Big Boy, Chipotle Mexican, Donato's Pizza, Fazoli's, Fricker's, Friendly's, Jed's BBQ, Red Lobster, Schlotsky's, Taco Bell, **lodging:** Comfort Inn, Day's Inn, Econolodge, Hampton Inn, Holiday Inn, Red Roof Inn, **other:** Chevrolet, Ford, Honda, Meijer, Toyota
52	OH 2, to Toledo, **S lodging:** Days Inn, **other:** RV/truck repair, ✈
49mm	**service plaza both lanes, gas:** Valero/dsl/24hr, **food:** Chicago Pizza, Nathan's, gifts/ice cream
39	OH 109, **S gas:** Country Corral/Valero/Winchesters/dsl/scales/wi-fi/24hr
34	OH 108, to Wauseon, **S gas:** Shell/Subway/dsl/24hr, **food:** Smith's Rest., **lodging:** Arrowhead Motel, Best Western, Holiday Inn Express, Super 8, **other:** H Woods Trucking/repair (1mi), **2 mi S on US 20A...gas:** BP/Circle K, Marathon, Valero, **food:** A&W/KFC, Arby's, Burger King, DQ, Grasshopper Rest., McDonald's, Pizza Hut, Subway, Taco Bell, Wendy's, **other:** Ace Hardware, AutoZone, Rite Aid, Walmart SuperCtr/gas
25	OH 66, Burlington, **N other:** Harrison Lake SP, **3 mi S other:** Sauder Village Museum
24.5mm	Tiffen River
13	OH 15, to Bryan, Montpelier, **S gas:** Marathon/dsl, Sunoco, **lodging:** Econolodge, Holiday Inn Express, Rainbow Motel, Ramada Inn, **other:** Hutch's dsl Repair
11.5mm	St Joseph River
3mm	toll plaza, ☎
2	OH 49, to US 20, **N food:** Burger King, Subway, **other:** info, truck tires
0mm	Ohio/Indiana state line

TOLEDO

INTERSTATE 35

Exit #	Services
236mm	Oklahoma/Kansas state line
231	US 177, Braman, **E gas:** Conoco/Grab'n Dash Deli/dsl
230	Braman Rd
229mm	Chikaskia River
225mm	**Welcome Ctr sb, rest area nb, full facilities, litter barrels, vending, petwalk, RV dump**
222	OK 11, to Blackwell, Medford, Alva, Newkirk, **E gas:** Conoco/dsl/rest., Shell/dsl, **food:** Braum's, KFC/Taco Bell, Los Potros Mexican, McDonald's, Plains Man Rest., Subway, **lodging:** Best Way Inn, Best Western, Comfort Inn, **other:** H
218	Hubbard Rd
216mm	**weigh sta both lanes**
214	US 60, to Tonkawa, Lamont, Ponca City, N OK Coll, **W gas:** Cenex/dsl, **lodging:** New Western Inn, **other:** Woodland RV Park, tires
213mm	Salt Fork of Arkansas River
211	Fountain Rd, **E gas:** Love's/Chester Fried/Subway/dsl/scales/24hr/RV Dump
209mm	**rest area, litter barrels, parking area**
203	OK 15, to Marland, Billings, **E gas:** Conoco/DQ/dsl/scales/24hr
199mm	Red Rock Creek
195mm	**parking area both lanes, litter barrels**
194b a	US 412, US 64 W, **E** Cimarron Tpk (eb), to Tulsa, **W** to Enid, Phillips U
193	Airport rd (from nb, no return)
191mm	Black Bear Creek
186	US 64 E, to Fir St, Perry, **E gas:** Mobil/Subway/dsl, **food:** Braum's, McDonald's, Taco Mayo, **lodging:** Super 8, **other:** H, museum, **W gas:** Exxon/dsl, **lodging:** Comfort Suites, Holiday Inn Express, Regency Inn
185	US 77, to Covington, Perry, **E lodging:** American Inn, **W gas:** Conoco/dsl/motel/rest./24hr, **other:** RV camping
180	Orlando Rd
174	OK 51, to Stillwater, Hennessey, **E gas:** Conoco/dsl, Phillips 66/dsl, **food:** Boondocks Cafe, **lodging:** Fairfield Inn (12mi), Hampton Inn (12mi), Motel 6 (12mi), **other:** Lake Carl Blackwell RV Park, to OSU
173mm	**parking area sb, litter barrels, parking only**
171mm	**parking area nb, litter barrels, parking only**
170	Mulhall Rd
166mm	Cimarron River
157	OK 33, to Cushing, Guthrie, **W gas:** K&L/dsl, Love's/Subway/dsl, Shell/dsl, Valero/dsl, **food:** Arby's, Braum's, El Rodeo Mexican, KFC (2mi), Mazzio's, McDonald's (3mi), Pizza Hut, Sonic, The Ribshack, **lodging:** Best Western, Holiday Inn Express, Interstate Motel, Sleep Inn, **other:** H, OK Terr Museum, Langston U, RV camping
153	US 77 N (exits left from nb), Guthrie, **W food:** McDonald's, Taco Bell, **other:** Buick/Pontiac, Chevrolet/Ford, Chrysler/Dodge/Jeep
151	Seward Rd, **E gas:** Shell/cafe/dsl, **other:** Lazy E Arena (4mi), Pioneer RV park
149mm	**weigh sta both lanes**
146	Waterloo Rd, **E gas:** Shell/dsl
143	Covell Rd
142	Danforth Rd (from nb)
141	US 77 S, OK 66E, to 2nd St, Edmond, Tulsa, **W gas:** Conoco, Phillips 66/dsl, **lodging:** Best Western, Comfort Inn, Fairfield Inn, Hampton Inn, Holiday Inn Express, **other:** H, Vet
140	SE 15th St, Spring Creek, Arcadia Lake, Edmond Park, **W gas:** Phillips 66/Circle K/Subway, **food:** Braum's, McDonald's, **other:** Walmart SuperCtr/24hr
139	SE 33 rd St, **3 mi W food:** Applebee's, **lodging:** Sleep Inn
138d	Memorial Rd, **W other:** Enterprise Square USA
138c	Sooner Rd (from sb)
138b	Kilpatrick Tpk
138a	I-44 Tpk E to Tulsa
	I-35 S and I-44 W run together 8 mi.
137	NE 122nd St, to OK City, **E gas:** Shamrock/dsl, Shell/dsl, **food:** Charly's Rest., IHOP, **lodging:** Knights Inn, Sleep Inn, **W gas:** FLYING J/Conoco/CountryMkt/dsl/scales/LP/24hr, Love's/Subway/Godfathers Pizza/dsl/24hr, **food:** Cracker Barrel, McDonald's, Sonic, Waffle House, **lodging:** Comfort Inn, Days Inn, Econolodge, Economy Inn, Motel 6, Red Carpet Inn, Super 8, **other:** Abe's RV Park, Frontier City Funpark, Oklahoma Visitors Ctr/info/restrooms
136	Hefner Rd, **W gas:** Conoco/dsl, same as 137
135	Britton Rd
134	Wilshire Blvd, **W lodging:** Executive Inn, **other:** Blue Beacon
	I-35 N and I-44 E run together 8 mi
133	I-44 W, to Amarillo, **W** St Capitol, Cowboy Hall of Fame
132b	NE 63rd St (from nb), **1/2 mi E gas:** Conoco/dsl, **food:** Braum's, **lodging:** Remington Inn
132a	NE 50th St, Remington Pk, **W other:** funpark, info, museum, zoo
131	NE 36th St, **W gas:** Phillips 66/dsl/24hr, **other:** 45th Inf Division Museum
130	US 62 E, NE 23rd St, **E** gas/dsl, **W** to St Capitol
129	NE 10th St, **E gas:** Conoco/McDonald's/dsl
128	I-40 E, to Ft Smith
127	Eastern Ave, OK City, **W gas:** Petro/dsl/rest./Blue Beacon/24hr/@, JR's Trvl Ctr/Wendy's/dsl/scales/24hr/@, Shamrock/dsl, **food:** Waffle House, **lodging:** Brick-Town Hotel, Best Western, Central Plaza Hotel, Econolodge, Quality Inn, **other:** Blue Beacon, Lewis RV Ctr
126a	I-40, W to Amarillo, I-235 N, to St Capitol
126b	I-35 S to Dallas
125d	SE 15th St, **E gas:** Conoco/dsl
125b	SE 22nd St (from nb)
125a	SE 25th, same as 124b
124b	SE 29th St, **E food:** China Queen, Denny's, McDonald's, Sonic, Taco Bell, **lodging:** Days Inn, Plaza Inn, Royal Inn, Super 8, **W gas:** Phillips 66, **food:** Mama Lou's Rest., same as 125a
124a	Grand Blvd, **E lodging:** Suburban Lodge
123b	SE 44th St, **E gas:** Shell, **food:** Dominos, Sonic, **lodging:** Best Value Inn, Courtesy Inn, **W food:** Pizza 44, Subway, Taco Mayo, **other:** Bi-4-Less Foods, $General, Family$, SavALot Foods, USPO
123a	SE 51st St, **E gas:** Conoco/dsl, **lodging:** Best Value Inn

N ↕ S

BLACKWELL

GUTHRIE

OKLAHOMA CITY

OK

INTERSTATE 35 CONT'D

N ↕ S

OKLAHOMA CITY

Exit #	Services
122b	SE 59th St, **E gas:** Phillips 66/dsl, **W gas:** Shell, Valero/dsl
122a	SE 66th St, **E food:** Luby's, McDonald's, Subway, Taco Bell, Texas Roadhouse, Zeke's Rest., **lodging:** Fairfield Inn, Ramada Inn, Residence Inn, **other:** Best Buy, Dillard's, Firestone, JC Penney, Macys, Tires+, mall, **W gas:** 7-11, **food:** Arby's
121b	US 62 W, I-240 E
121a	SE 82nd St, (from sb), **W lodging:** Baymont Inn
120	SE 89th St, **E gas:** Valero/dsl/scales, **lodging:** Ford, **W gas:** Love's/Subway/dsl/24hr, **other:** Classic Parts
119b	N 27th St, **E gas:** Shell/Circle K/dsl, **W food:** Pickles Rest., **other:** Harley-Davidson
119a	Shields Blvd (exits left from nb)
118	N 12th St, **E food:** Mazzio's, Peking Buffet, **lodging:** Super 8, **W gas:** 7-11, Shell, **food:** A&W/LJ Silver, Arby's, Braum's, DQ, Grandy's, Harry Bear's Grill, KFC, La Fajitas, Mamma Lou's, Mazzio's, McDonald's, Papa John's, Subway, Taco Bell, Wendy's, Western Sizzlin, **lodging:** Best Western, Candlewood Suites, Comfort Inn, SpringHill Suites, **other:** Ace Hardware, AutoZone, Family$
117	OK 37, S 4th St, **W gas:** Valero, **food:** China Wok, Van BBQ, **other:** USPO
116	S 19th St, **E gas:** Conoco, Shell, **food:** Braum's, Capt D's, Carl's Jr, DQ, McDonald's, Popeye's, Sara's Rest., Taco Bell, Waffle House, Whataburger, **lodging:** Microtel, **other:** Best Buy, Firestone/auto, Goodyear/auto, JC Penney, Office Depot, PetsMart, Ross, **W food:** Arby's, Alfredo's Mexican, Applebees, Arby's, Buffalo Wild Wings, Buffet King, Burger King, Chick-fil-A, Earl's Ribs, Freddy's Frozen Custard, Furr's Buffet, IHOP, Jimmy's Egg, Louie's Grill, McAlister's Deli, Panda Express, Quizno's, Sonic, Subway, **lodging:** La Quinta, **other:** Aldi Foods, Discount Tire, $Tree, Gordman's, Harley-Davidson, Home Depot, Kohl's, Lowe's Whse, Radio Shack, Russell Stover Candies, Tires+, Walmart SuperCtr/gas/24hr
114	Indian Hill Rd, **E food:** Bill's Fishhouse, Indian Hills Rest., **lodging:** ValuePlace Hotel, **other:** Guy RV Ctr
113	US 77 S (from sb, exits left), Norman
112	Tecumseh Rd, **E other:** Nissan, Toyota/Scion
110b a	Robinson St, **E food:** Carl's Jr, Cheddar's, Logan's Roadhouse, Sonic, Taco Bell, Teimei Asian Buistro, **lodging:** Days Inn, Embassy Suites, **other:** [H], Chrysler/Jeep, Ford, GMC/Pontiac, Homeland Foods/drug, Honda, Hyundai, Kohl's, Lincoln/Mercury/Mazda, PetCo, Subaru, Super Target, Tires+, TJ Maxx, **W gas:** Conoco/Subway, **food:** Arby's, Braum's, Cafe Escondido, Cracker Barrel, Golden Chef,

NORMAN

Exit #	Services
110b a	Continued Outback Steaks, Papa John's, Rib Crib, Saltgrass Steaks, Santa Fe Cattle Co, Waffle House, **lodging:** Comfort Inn, Courtyard, Hilton Garden, Holiday Inn, **other:** Kia/Isuzu
109	Main St, **E gas:** Phillips 66, Shell, **food:** Arby's, Braum's, CiCi's, Denny's, Golden Corral, JR's Rest., Krispy Kreme, LJ Silver, Panera Bread, Prairie Kitchen, Subway, Taco Cabana, Waffle House, Wendy's, **lodging:** Days Inn, Econolodge, Guest Inn, Quality Inn, Ramada Inn, Super 8, Thunderbird Lodge, Travelodge, **other:** AutoZone, Best Buy, Cadillac, Chevrolet, Dodge/Jeep, Hastings Books, Lowe's Whse, Nissan, Subaru, Tires+, Walmart SuperCtr/gas/24hr, **W gas:** Conoco/Circle K/dsl, **food:** Applebee's, BJ's Brewhouse, Burger King, Don Pablo, Charleston's Rest. Chili's, Escondido Mexican, Marie Callender's, McDonald's, Olive Garden, On the Border, Outback Steaks, Piccadilly's, Red Lobster, Red River Steaks, Rio Cafe, Village Inn Rest., **lodging:** Fairfield Inn, Hampton Inn, La Quinta, **other:** Barnes&Noble, Borders Books, Dillard's, IGA Foods, JC Penney, Kia, Michael's, Old Navy, Saab, Sam's Club, Sears/auto, SteinMart, mall
108b a	OK 9 E, Norman, **E gas:** Conoco, **food:** Arby's, Braum's, Del Rancho Steaks, Schlotzky's, Taco Bell, **lodging:** Residence Inn, Sooner Legends Inn, **other:** to U of OK, **W food:** Carino's Italian, IHOP, Jasons Deli, Othello's Italian, Red Robin, Souper Salad, **lodging:** Country Inn&Suites, La Quinta, **other:** Home Depot, Michaels, PetsMart, Ross
107mm	Canadian River
106	OK 9 W, to Chickasha, **E other:** Casino, **W gas:** Love's/Subway/dsl/24hr, Shell, **food:** McDonald's, Sonic, **lodging:** Sleep Inn, **other:** casino
104	OK 74 S, Goldsby, **E other:** Floyd's RV Ctr, **W gas:** Shamrock/dsl, Sinclair/dsl, **food:** Libby's Cafe
101	Ladd Rd
98	Johnson Rd, **E gas:** Shamrock/dsl
95	US 77 (exits left from sb), Purcell, **1-3 mi E gas:** Shell, **food:** Braum's, KFC, Mazzio's, Pizza Hut, Subway, **other:** [H], Ford

INTERSTATE 35 CONT'D

Exit #	Services
91	OK 74, to OK 39, Maysville, **E gas:** Conoco/dsl, Murphy USA/dsl, Phillips 66/dsl, **food:** Braum's, McDonald's, New China, Subway, Taco Mayo, **lodging:** EconoLodge, Executive Inn, Ruby's Inn/rest., **other:** Ace Hardware, American RV Park (1mi), Walmart SuperCtr, **W gas:** Shell/dsl, **food:** A&W/LJ Silver
86	OK 59, Wayne, Payne, **E other:** American RV Park
79	OK 145 E, Paoli, **E gas:** Phillips 66
76mm	Washita River
74	OK 19, Kimberlin Rd
72	OK 19, Paul's Valley, **E gas:** Conoco/dsl, Murphy USA/dsl, Valero/dsl/rest./24hr, **food:** Arby's, Baby D's Cafe&Creamery, Braum's, Chicken Express, Green Tea Chinese, Happy Days Diner, KFC/Taco Bell, Little Ben's Pizza, McDonald's, Sonic, Stevenson BBQ, Subway, Taco Mayo, **lodging:** American Inn, Comfort Inn, Days Inn, Garden Inn, Holiday Inn Express, Relax Inn, **other:** AT&T, Buick/Cadillac/GMC/Pontiac, Chrysler/Dodge/Jeep, Ford/Lincoln/Mercury, Walmart SuperCtr, **W gas:** Love's/Godfather's/dsl/24hr, Phillips 66/dsl/24hr, **other:** truckwash
70	Airport Rd, **E** H
66	OK 29, Wynnewood, **W gas:** Kent's Fuel/dsl, Shell/dsl
64	OK 17A E, to Wynnewood, **E** GW Exotic Animal Park
60	Ruppe Rd
59mm	**rest area both lanes, full facilities, phone, picnic, litter barrels, petwalk, RV dump**
55	OK 7, Davis, **E gas:** Conoco, Phillips 66/A&W/dsl/24hr, **other:** Microtel, **other:** casino, to Chickasaw NRA, **W other:** Oak Hill RV Park/gas/deli, to Arbuckle Ski Area
54.5mm	Honey Creek Pass
53mm	**weigh sta both lanes**
51	US 77, Turner Falls, **E lodging:** Arbuckle Mtn Motel, Mountainview Inn (3mi), **other:** to Arbuckle Wilderness, RV camping, **W gas:** Sinclair/grill, **other:** Botanic Gardens
49mm	scenic turnout both lanes
47	US 77, Turner Falls Area
46mm	scenic turnout both lanes
42	OK 53 W, Springer, Comanche, **W gas:** Exxon/dsl
40	OK 53 E, Gene Autry, **E gas:** Shell/dsl/café/24hr, **food:** Broaster Rest, **other:** Gene Autry Museum (8mi)
33	OK 142, Ardmore, **E gas:** Phillips 66/dsl/24hr, **food:** IHOP, Ponder's Rest., **lodging:** Guest Inn, La Quinta, SpringHill Suites, Super 8, **W gas:** FLYING J/Conoco/Country Mkt/dsl/scales/LP
32	12th St, Ardmore, **E gas:** Conoco/dsl, **food:** Braum's, Quizno's, Santa Fe Steaks, Whataburger, **lodging:** Candlewood Suites, La Quinta, **other:** $Tree, Lowe's Whse, PetCo, Toyota, **W gas:** Love's/Godfather's/Subway/dsl/24hr/@, **food:** McDonald's, **lodging:** Microtel
31b a	US 70 W, OK 199 E, Ardmore, **E gas:** Shell/dsl, Valero/dsl, **food:** Applebee's, Burger King, Cattle Rustlers, Denny's, El Chico, Jack-in-the-Box, KFC, Mazzio's, McDonald's, Pizza Hut, Polo's Mexican, Prairie Kitchen, 2Frogs Grill, **lodging:** Best Western, Days Inn, Hampton Inn, Holiday Inn, Motel 6,
31b a	Continued Rodeway Inn, **other:** AutoZone, Honda, O'Reilly Parts, **W gas:** Conoco/dsl, **other:** Ardmore RV Park, Chrysler/Dodge/Jeep, Ford/Lincoln/Mercury, Nissan, Vet
29	US 70 E, Ardmore, **E lodging:** Economy Inn (1mi), **other:** to Lake Texoma SP, **W other:** Hidden Lake RV Park
24	OK 77 S, **E other:** Red River Livestock Mkt, to Lake Murray SP
22.5mm	Hickory Creek
21	Oswalt Rd, **W gas:** Valero, **other:** KOA
15	OK 32, Marietta, **E gas:** Valero/dsl/24hr, **food:** Carl's Jr, McDonald's, Pizza Hut, Robertson's Sandwiches, Sonic, **other:** H, $General, to Lake Texoma SP, **W gas:** Phillips 66/24hr, **food:** Hickory House BBQ
5	OK 153, Thackerville, **W other:** Shorty's Foods/gas, Red River Ranch RV Park
3.5mm	**Welcome Ctr nb, full facilities, phone, picnic, litter barrels, vending, petwalk**
1	US 77 N, **E gas:** Phillips 66/dsl, **food:** River Ridge Rest., **lodging:** Best Western, Mictotel, **other:** Winstar Casino, **W other:** Red River RV Resort (3mi)
0mm	Oklahoma/Texas state line, Red River

INTERSTATE 40

Exit #	Services
331mm	Oklahoma/Arkansas state line
330	OK 64D S (from eb), Ft Smith
325	US 64, Roland, Ft Smith, **N gas:** Cherokee Trkstp/Valero/Subway/dsl/scales/24hr, **food:** Four Star Diner, **lodging:** Cherokee Inn, Travelodge, **other:** casino, **S gas:** Pilot/Wendy's/dsl/scales/24hr, Shell/dsl/scales, Valero/dsl, **food:** Arby's, El Celaya Mexican, McDonald's, Mazzio's, Sonic, Subway, Taco Bell, **lodging:** Interstate Inn, **other:** $General, Marvin's Foods
321	OK 64b N, Muldrow, **N food:** Sonic (1mi), **S gas:** Shell/dsl, **food:** Arena Rest, **lodging:** Best Value, **other:** auto/dsl repair
316mm	**rest area eb, full facilities, info, phone, picnic, litter barrels, vending, petwalk, RV dump**
313mm	**rest area wb, full facilities, info, phone, picnic, litter barrels, vending, petwalk, RV dump**
311	US 64, Sallisaw, **N gas:** Cox's/dsl, ED's Trkstp/Phillips 66/diner/dsl, **food:** Hardee's, KFC/Taco Bell, Pizza Hut, Simon's Pizza, Taco Mayo, **lodging:** Motel 6, Sallisaw Inn, **other:** H, AutoZone, Brushy Lake SP (10mi), $General, NAPA, Sequoyahâ€™s Home (12mi), USPO
308	US 59, Sallisaw, **N gas:** Murphy USA/dsl, Phillips 66/dsl, **food:** A&W/LJ Silver, Arby's, Braum's, China Panda, Mazzio's, McDonald's, Sonic, Subway, Taco Pronto, Western Sizzlin, **lodging:** Best Value, Blue Ribbon Inn, Days Inn, Golden Spur Motel, Super 8, **other:** H, $General, $Tree, Walmart SuperCtr, antiques, casino, to Blue Ribbon Downs, **S gas:** Shell/dsl, **food:** Ole South Pancakes, **other:** Chevrolet/Buick, Chrysler/Dodge/Jeep, Ford, KOA, Lakeside RV Park (6 mi), to Kerr Lake, truck/tire repair
303	Dwight Mission Rd, **3 mi N other:** Blue Ribbon Downs
297	OK 82 N, Vian, **N gas:** FL/dsl, **food:** Subway, **other:** Cherokee Landing SP (24 mi), IGA Foods, to Tenkiller Lake RA, USPO, **S other:** Sequoia NWR

N S ARDMORE E W SALLISAW

OK

E ↕ W

INTERSTATE 40 CONT'D

Exit #	Services
291	OK 10 N, to Gore, **N other:** Greenleaf SP (10mi), Tenkiller SP (21mi)
290mm	Arkansas River
287	OK 100 N, to Webbers Falls, **N gas:** Love's/Subway/dsl/24hr, **food:** Charlie's Chicken, Godfather's Pizza, **lodging:** Sleepy Traveler Motel, **other:** parts/tires/repair
286	Muskogee Tpk, to Muskogee
284	Ross Rd
283mm	**parking area both lanes, litter barrels**
278	US 266, OK 2, Warner, **N gas:** Conoco, Phillips 66/dsl, Sinclair/McDonald's/dsl, **food:** Big Rob's Grill, Simon's Pizza, Subway, **lodging:** Sleepy Traveler Motel, **other:** Auburn RV Park, $General, Parts+, TrueValue, LP
270	Texanna Rd, to Porum Landing, **S gas:** Sinclair
265	US 69 bus, Checotah, **N food:** Pizza Hut, Sonic, **S gas:** Shell/dsl **lodging:** Budget Inn, **other:** Chevrolet/Chrysler/Dodge/Jeep
264b a	US 69, to Eufaula, **1 mi N gas:** *FLYING J*/Country Mkt/dsl/LP/scales/RV dump/24hr, Phillips 66/dsl/24hr, **food:** Charlie's Chicken, McDonald's, Simon's Pizza, Subway, **lodging:** Best Value Inn, **other:** Ace Hardware, $General, O'Reilly Parts, True Value, Walmart SuperCtr, auto repair
262	to US 266, Lotawatah Rd, **N gas:** Sinclair
261mm	Lake Eufaula
259	OK 150, to Fountainhead Rd, **S gas:** Shell, **lodging:** Lake Eufaula Inn, **other:** to Lake Eufaula SP
255	Pierce Rd, **N** KOA
251mm	**rest area both lanes, no facilities**
247	Tiger Mtn Rd, **S other:** Quilt Barn/antiques
240b a	US 62 E, US 75 N, Henryetta, **N gas:** Love's/dsl, Phillips 66, Shell, Sinclair, **food:** Arby's, Braum's, KFC, Mazzio's, McDonald's, Sonic, Subway, **lodging:** Colonial Motel, Economy Inn, Henryetta Inn/rest., LeBaron Motel, Relax Inn, **other:** Chevrolet, Chrysler/Jeep, Ford, O'Reilly Parts, Walmart, tires, **S** Indian Nation Tpk
237	US 62, US 75, Henryetta, **N gas:** Shell/dsl/24hr, **food:** Pig Out Palace, **lodging:** Green Country Inn, **other:** H, Henryetta RV Park (2mi), **S food:** Hungry Traveler Rest., **lodging:** Super 8
231	US 75 S, to Weleetka, **N gas:** Phillips 66/dsl, **food:** Cowpoke's Cafe
227	Clearview Rd, **S** casino
221	US 62, OK 27, Okemah, **N gas:** Conoco/dsl, Shamrock, Valero/Subway/dsl/24hr, **food:** $General, Mazzio's, Sonic, **lodging:** Day's Inn, **other:** H, Chevrolet, $General, Homeland Foods, Parts+, TrueValue, **S gas:** Love's/Chester Fried/dsl/24hr, Shell/dsl, **food:** Kellogg's Rest, **other:** casino, truck repair
217	OK 48, to Bristow, Bearden, **S** gas
216mm	N Canadian River
212	OK 56, to Cromwell, Wewoka, **N other:** auto/tire repair, **S gas:** Shell/cafe/dsl, to Seminole Nation Museum
208mm	Gar Creek

HENRYETTA

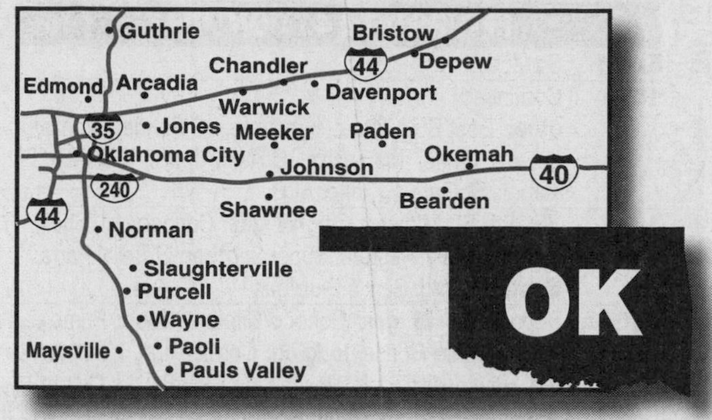

SHAWNEE

Exit #	Services
202mm	Turkey Creek
200	US 377, OK 99, to Little, Prague, **S gas:** Conoco/dsl/24hr, Love's/Subway/dsl/24hr, Sinclair/dsl, **food:** Robertson's Ham Sandwiches, Roundup Rest/RV Park
197mm	**rest area both lanes, full facilities, , , litter barrels, petwalk**
192	OK 9A, Earlsboro, **S gas:** Shell/dsl
189mm	N Canadian River
186	OK 18, to Shawnee, **N gas:** Phillips 66, Sinclair, **food:** Denny's, **lodging:** American Inn, Best Value, Comfort Inn, Day's Inn, La Quinta, Motel 6, Super 8, **S food:** Van's BBQ, **other:** Chevrolet/Cadillac, Chrysler/Jeep, Curves, Ford, Homeland Foods, Vet
185	185 OK 3E, Shawnee Mall Dr, to Shawnee, **N gas:** Murphy USA/dsl, **food:** Chili's, KFC, Red Lobster, Santa Fe Steaks, Taco Bueno, Wendy's, **lodging:** Holiday Inn Express, **other:** Dillard's, $Tree, JC Penney, Old Navy, Radio Shack, Ross, Sears/auto, Walgreens, Walmart SuperCtr, mall, **S gas:** Phillips 66/Circle K/Quizno's/dsl, **food:** Braum's, Buddy's BBQ, Burger King, Cracker Barrel, Garfield's Rest., IHOP, Mazzio's, McAlister's Deli, McDonald's, Popeye's, Sonic, Starbucks, Taco Bell, **lodging:** Hampton Inn, **other:** CVS Drug, Kwik Kar Lube, Lowe's Whse, Staples
181	US 177, US 270, to Tecumseh, **S lodging:** Budget Inn
180mm	N Canadian River
178	OK 102 S, Dale, **N gas:** Firelake/dsl, **other:** casino
176	OK 102 N, McLoud Rd, **S gas:** Love's/Subway/dsl/24hr, Sinclair, **food:** Curtis Watson Rest.
172	Newalla Rd, to Harrah
169	Peebly Rd
166	Choctaw Rd, to Woods, **N gas:** Love's/Subway/dsl/24hr, **other:** KOA, **S gas:** Phillips 66/dsl, **food:** Sonic, **other:** to Lake Thunderbird SP (11mi)
165	I-240 W (from wb), to Dallas
162	Anderson Rd, **N** Leisure Time RV Ctr, LP
159b	Douglas Blvd, **N gas:** Conoco, Shell, **food:** Denny's, LJ Silver, McDonald's, Sonic, Subway, Taco Bell, **other:** Eastland Hills RV Park, **S other:** Tinker AFB, H
159a	Hruskocy Gate, **N gas:** Shell, **food:** Denny's, McDonlad's, Taco Bell, **other:** Dodge, Family$, Nissan, U-Haul, same as 157, **S** Gate 7, Tinker AFB
157c	Eaker Gate, Tinker AFB, same as 159
157b	Air Depot Blvd, **N gas:** Shell/Circle K, **food:** Chick-fil-A, Chili's, Logans Roadhouse, Old Chicago Grill, Panda Express, Pizza Inn, Qdoba Grill, Santa Fe Steaks, Starbucks, Steak & Shake, **lodging:** Super 8,

OK

INTERSTATE 40 CONT'D

E ↕ W

Exit #	Services
157b	Continued **other:** Best Buy, Target, Firestone, JC Penney, Kohl's, Lowe's Whse, Marshall's, O'Reilly Parts, PetsMart, Target, **S** Gate 1, Tinker AFB
157a	SE 29th St, Midwest City, **N gas:** Conoco/dsl, Shell, **lodging:** Best Western, Super 8, **other:** O'Reilly Parts, **S other:** Ford, Sam's Club/gas
156b a	Sooner Rd, **N gas:** Conoco/Circle K, **food:** Primo's Rest., Waffle House, **lodging:** Comfort Inn, Hampton Inn, Hawthorn Suites, Holiday Inn Express, La Quinta, Sheraton, Studio 6, **other:** Home Depot, Nissan, Radio Shack, Walmart SuperCtr/Subway, **S food:** Buffalo Wild Wings, **lodging:** Motel 6, **other:** Chevrolet/Pontiac/GMC, Tires+, Toyota/Scion
155b	SE 15th St, Del City, **N gas:** Shell, **other:** Family$, **S food:** Madison's Kitchen
155a	Sunny Lane Rd, Del City, **N gas:** Conoco/dsl, **other:** Hyundai, U-Haul, **S gas:** Shell, Shamrock, **food:** Braum's, Dunkin Donuts, Sonic, **other:** Ace Hardware, $General
154	Reno Ave, Scott St, **N gas:** Sinclair, **lodging:** Value Place Motel, **S gas:** Phillips 66/dsl, 7-11/gas
152	(153 from wb) I-35 N, to Wichita
127	Eastern Ave (from eb), Okla City, **N gas:** Petro/Mobil/dsl/scales/rest./@, JR's Trvl Crt/Corky's Grill/dsl/24hr, Shamrock, **food:** Waffle House, **lodging:** Bricktown Hotel, Econolodge, Quality Inn, **other:** Blue Beacon, Lewis RV Ctr
151b c	I-35, S to Dallas, I-235 N, to downtown, st capitol
151a	Lincoln Blvd, **N gas:** Conoco/Subway/Circle K/dsl, **food:** Earl's Rib Palace, Falcon's Pizza, IHOP, Sonic, **lodging:** Residence Inn, Hampton Inn, **other:** Bass Pro Shop, Bricktown Stadium
150c	Robinson Ave (from wb), OK City, **N food:** Spaghetti Whse, Zio's Italian, **lodging:** Courtyard, Residence Inn, Westin Hotel, **other:** U-Haul, Ford Ctr
150b	Harvey Ave (from eb), downtown, **N lodging:** Courtyard, Renaissance Hotel, Sheraton, Westin Hotel, **other:** Ford
150a	Walker Ave (from eb), **N food:** La Luna Mexican, **other:** Ford/Lincoln/Mercury, **S** transmissions
149b	Classen Blvd (from wb), to downtown, same as 149a, to downtown
149a	Western Ave, Reno Ave, **N gas:** Valero/Subway/dsl, **food:** China Queen, McDonald's, Sonic, Taco Bell, **S gas:** Conoco/dsl, Shell, **food:** Sweis Gyros
148c	Virginia Ave (from wb), to downtown
148b	Penn Ave (from eb), **N gas:** Shamrock, **S other:** Isuzu Trucks
148a	Agnew Ave, Villa Ave, **N gas:** Phillips 66/dsl
147c	May Ave
147b a	I-44, E to Tulsa, W to Lawton
146	Portland Ave (from eb, no return), **N gas:** Conoco/Subway/dsl, **other:** water funpark
145	Meridian Ave, OK City, **N gas:** Conoco/Circle K/dsl, Shell/Circle K/dsl, **food:** Cimarron Steakhouse, Denny's, Earl's Ribs, Mango's, McDonald's, Jin Wei Aisan, On the Border, Shiki, Shorty Small's Rest., Trapper's Rest., **lodging:** Best Western, Biltmore Hotel, Day's Inn, Econolodge, Extended Stay America,
145	Continued Howard Johnson, Red Roof Inn, Residence Inn, Super 8, **other:** Chevrolet, USPO, **S gas:** Phillips 66/dsl, Sinclair, **food:** Arby's, Burger King, Charleston Rest., Chili's, Cracker Barrel, El Sombrero, Golden Palace Chinese, IHOP, Kona Ranch Steaks, Mazzio's, Mackie's Steaks, Panera Bread, Pearl's Fish House, Quizno's, Rib Crib, Riggin's Grill, Santa Fe Grill, Sonic, Subway, Taco Bell, Taco Bueno, Waffle House, Whataburger, Zapata's, Zio's Italian, **lodging:** Best Value Inn, Candlewood Suites, Clarion Hotel, Comfort Suites, Courtyard, Embassy Suites, Governor Suites, Hampton Inn, Hilton Garden, Holiday Inn Express, Hyatt Place, La Quinta, Meridian Inn, Motel 6, Oak Tree Inn, Ramada Ltd, Regency Inn, Sleep Inn, Staybridge Suites, Wingate Inn, Wyndham Garden, **other:** Celebration Sta., Shepler's
144	MacArthur Blvd, **N gas:** Shell/Circle K/dsl, **food:** Applebee's, Coldstone Creamery, Golden Corral, KFC, Lin's Buffet, McDonald's, Quizno's, Ryan's, Sonic, Starbucks, Taco Cabana, Texas Roadhouse, **lodging:** SpringHill Suites, **other:** $Tree, GNC, Hobby Lobby, Office Depot, PetsMart, Radio Shack, Ross, Walmart SuperCtr/24hr, **S lodging:** Green Carpet Inn, Microtel, Super 10 Motel, Travelodge, **other:** Kenworth, Sam's Club/gas, dsl repair
143	Rockwell Ave, **N gas:** Shell/dsl, **food:** Buffalo Wild Wings, **lodging:** Homewood Suites, Rodeway Inn, **other:** Best Buy, Camping World/McClain's RV Ctr, Harley Davidson, Home Depot, Tires+, **S lodging:** Sands Motel/RV Park/LP, **other:** Rockwell RV Park, A-OK RV Park
142	Council Rd, **N gas:** Shell, Sinclair, **food:** Braum's, McDonald's, Subway, Taco Bell, **lodging:** Best Budget Inn, **other:** Goodyear/auto, **S gas:** TA/Country Pride/dsl/scales/24hr/@, **lodging:** Econolodge, **other:** Council rd RV Park, IA-80 Truckwash, dsl repair
140	Morgan Rd, **N gas:** Pilot/McDonald's/dsl/24hr/@, TA/Phillips 66/Popeye's/dsl/24hr/@, **other:** Blue Beacon, **S gas:** ***FLYING J***/Conoco/cookery/dsl/LP/scales/24hr/@, Love's/Subway/dsl/scales/24hr/@, **food:** Ricky's Cafe, Sonic, **other:** Speedco
139	Kilpatrick Tpk
138	OK 4, to Yukon, Mustang, **N lodging:** Comfort Inn, Super 7, **other:** Chrysler/Dodge/Jeep, **S gas:** Conoco/Circle K/dsl, **food:** Braum's, Burger King, Hunan Express, IHOP, Interurban Grill, McDonald's, Sonic, Subway, **lodging:** Best Western, La Quinta, **other:** CVS Drug, Homeland Food/drug, Cottman Transmissions
137	Cornwell Dr, Czech Hall Rd, **N** Homeland Food/drug
136	OK 92, to Yukon, **N gas:** Murphy USA/dsl, Shell/Circle K, **food:** A&W/LJ Silver, Braum's, Harry's Rest., KFC, McDonald's, Primo's Italian, Subway, Taco Mayo, Waffle House, Wendy's, Yukon Buffet, **lodging:** Hampton Inn, **other:** AutoZone, Big Lots, Big O Tire, Chevrolet, $Tree, Hancock Fabrics, Hastings Books, Radio Shack, Tuesday Morning, Walmart SuperCtr, Walgreens, USPO, **S food:** Alfredo's, Carino's Italian, Chili's, Jimmy's Egg Café, Louie's Grill, Pizza Hut, Quizno's, Rib Crib, Santa Fe Steaks, Starbucks, Taco Bueno, **lodging:** Holiday Inn Express, **other:** [H], Ford, Kohl's, Kwik Kar, Lowe's Whse, PetsMart, Staples, Target, Tires+

OKLAHOMA CITY

OK

INTERSTATE 40 CONT'D

Exit #	Services
132	Cimarron Rd, **S** ✈
130	Banner Rd, **N gas:** Shell/dsl/rest.
129mm	**weigh st both lanes**
125	US 81, to El Reno, **N gas:** Conoco/dsl, Love's/Subway/dsl, **food:** China King, Serapio's Mexican, Taco Mayo, **lodging:** Deluxe Inn, Economy Express, Super 8, **other:** Chevrolet, Chrysler/Jeep/Dodge, $General, Ford/Lincoln/Mercury, Pontiac/GMC/Buick, **S** truck repair
123	Country Club Rd, to El Reno, **N gas:** Phillips 66, Murphy USA/dsl, Shell, Valero, **food:** Arby's, Braum's, Burger King, Greatwall Chinese, KFC, Little Caesar's, Mazzio's, McDonald's, Pizza Hut, Subway, Taco Bell, **lodging:** Motel 6, **other:** H, $Tree, Radio Shack, Walmart SuperCtr, Walgreens, **S gas: food:** Denny's, Mt Mikes Steaks, **lodging:** Best Western/RV Park, Comfort Inn, Day's Inn, Regency Motel
119	Lp 40, to El Reno
115	US 270, to Calumet
111mm	**picnic area eb, litter barrels**
108	US 281, to Geary, **N gas:** Shell/Subway/dsl/24hr, **other:** KOA/Indian Trading Post, to Roman Nose SP, **S gas:** Phillips 66/dsl
105mm	S Canadian River
104	Methodist Rd
101	US 281, OK 8, to Hinton, **N** to Roman Nose SP, **S gas:** Loves/Sonic/dsl/scales, **food:** Subway, **lodging:** Microtel, **other:** Chevrolet, picnic area, to Red Rock Canyon SP
95	Bethel Rd
94.5mm	**picnic area wb, litter barrels**
88	OK 58, to Hydro, Carnegie
84	Airport Rd, **N gas:** Phillips 66/dsl/scales/24hr, **food:** Lucille's Roadhouse, **lodging:** Holiday Inn Express, Travel Inn, **other:** H, Buick/Pontiac/GMC, Chevrolet/Cadillac, Chrysler/Dodge/Jeep
82	E Main St, Weatherford, **N gas:** Conoco/dsl, Phillips 66, Shell/Subway/dsl, Sinclair, Valero, **food:** Arby's, Braum's, Carl's Jr, Jerry's Rest., KFC/Taco Bell, Mark Rest., McDonald's, Pizza Hut, Quizno's, Sonic, Taco Mayo, T-Bonz Steaks, Vinicio's Mexican, **lodging:** Best Western, Comfort Inn, Scottish Inn, **other:** H GNC, O'Reilly Parts, Radio Shack, Walgreens, Stafford Aerospace Museum, to SW OSU, **S other:** Wal-Mart SuperCtr
80	(80a from eb) W Main St, **N gas:** Shell, **lodging:** Economy Inn
71	Custer City Rd, **N gas:** Love's/Subway/dsl/rest., **other:** Cherokee Trading Post
69	Lp 40 (from wb), to Clinton, **2 mi N food:** DQ, **lodging:** Travel Inn
67.5mm	Washita River
66	US 183, Clinton, **S gas:** Shell/dsl, **other:** Ford/Lincoln/Mercury, Chrysler/Dodge/Jeep
65a	10th St, Neptune Dr, Clinton, **N food:** Braum's, China King, Lupita's Mexican, Pizza Hut, **lodging:** Day's Inn, Relax Inn, Super 8, **other:** United Foods, Wink's Campground, **S lodging:** Econolodge

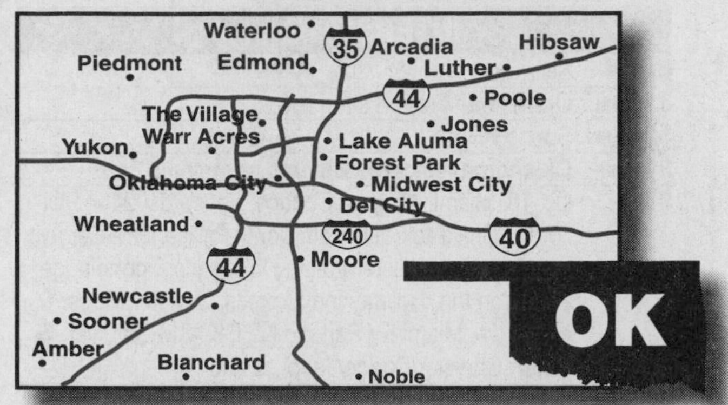

Exit #	Services
65	Gary Blvd, Clinton, **N gas:** Conoco, Shell/dsl, **food:** Braum's, Del Rancho, DQ, LJ Silver, McDonald's, Mtn Mike's, Taco Mayo, **lodging:** Budget Inn, Hampton Inn, Ramada Inn, Tradewinds Inn, **other:** H, $General, K-Mart, Rte 66 Museum
62	Parkersburg Rd, **S** Harg US RV Ctr
61	Haggard Rd
57	Stafford Rd
53	OK 44, Foss, **N** to Foss RA, **S** gas/dsl
50	Clinton Lake Rd, **N other:** KOA/LP/dsl
47	Canute, **S gas:** Shell, **lodging:** Sunset Inn
41	OK 34 (exits left from eb), Elk City, **N gas:** Love's/Subway/dsl, Shell, **food:** Home Cooking Rest., **lodging:** Ambassador Inn, Best Western (3mi), Economy Express, Motel 6, Red Carpet Inn, Travel Inn, Travelodge, Super 8, **other:** H, Elk Run RV Park, Rte 66 Museum
40	E 7th St, Elk City, **N food:** Portobello Grill, same as 41
38	OK 6, Elk City, **N gas:** Conoco/dsl, Phillips 66/dsl, **food:** Arby's, China Super Buffet, Denny's, LJ Silver, McDonald's, Quizno's, Western Sizzlin, **lodging:** Bedford Inn, Day's Inn, **other:** Ace Hardware, Elk Creek RV Park, Rolling Retreat RV Ctr, **S gas:** Phillips 66/dsl, **lodging:** Comfort Inn, Econolodge, Holiday Inn, Ramada Inn, **other:** to Quartz Mtn SP
34	Merritt Rd
32	OK 34 S (exits left from eb), Elk City
26	Cemetery Rd, **N** dsl repair, **S gas:** TA/Taco Bell/Subway/dsl/scales/24hr/@
25	Lp 40, Sayre, **1 mi N gas:** Shell/dsl, **lodging:** Western Motel, **other:** H, Chevrolet/Pontiac/GMC, $General, Ford
23	OK 152, Sayre, **S gas:** Shell/dsl
22.5mm	N Fork Red River
20	US 283, Sayre, **N gas:** *FLYING J*/CountryMkt/dsl/LP/RV dump/scales/24hr, **lodging:** AmericInn, **other:** truckwash, to Washita Bfd Site (25mi)
14	Hext Rd
13.5mm	**check sta both lanes, litter barrels**
11	Lp 40, to Erick,, Hext
10mm	**Welcome Ctr/rest area both lanes, full facilities, litter barrels, petwalk, RV dump**
7	OK 30, Erick, **N lodging:** Comfort Inn, **S gas:** Love's/Subway/dsl/scales, **food:** Simple Simon's Pizza, **lodging:** Days Inn
5	Lp 40, Honeyfarm Rd
1	Texola, **S gas:** gas/dsl/rest., **other:** RV camping
0mm	Oklahoma/Texas state line

E ↕ W

MIAMI

INTERSTATE 44

Exit #	Services
329mm	Oklahoma/Missouri state line
321mm	Spring River
314mm	**Oklahoma Welcome Ctr, info, restrooms**
313	OK 10, Miami, **N gas:** Conoco, Love's/dsl/24hr, Phillips 66, SnakAtak/dsl, **food:** Donut Palace, Okie Burger, **lodging:** Best Western/rest., Deluxe Inn, Econolodge, Hampton Inn, Holiday Inn Express, Microtel, Super 8, **other:** [H], Miami RV Park, to NE OK A&M Coll, Vet, **S other:** Chrysler/Dodge/Jeep, casino
312mm	Neosho River
302	US 59, US 69, Afton, **S gas:** Conoco/dsl, **food:** Subway, **3 mi S lodging:** OK 66 Motel
299mm	**rest area eb, rest rooms, [picnic], litter barrel**
289	US 60, Vinita, **N gas:** Murphy USA/dsl, **food:** Braum's, Clanton's Cafe, McDonald's, Pizza Hut, Sonic, Subway, Woodshed Deli, **lodging:** Holiday Inn Express, **other:** [H], Ace Hardware, AT&T, Chevrolet, O'Reilly Parts, Walmart SuperCtr/24hr, st patrol
288mm	**service plaza both lanes**, Phillips 66/dsl/24hr, McDonald's, [phone]
286mm	toll plaza
283	US 69, Big Cabin, **N gas:** Shell/Big Cabin/dsl/rest./scales/24hr/@/repair, **lodging:** Super 8, **other:** rv park, trk repair
271mm	**picnic eb, [picnic], litter barrel**
269	OK 28 (from eb, no re-entry), to Adair, Chelsea
269mm	**rest area eb, rest rooms, [picnic], litter barrel**
256mm	**rest area wb, rest rooms, [picnic], litter barrel, [phone]**
255	OK 20, to Pryor, Claremore, **0-2 mi N gas:** Kum&Go, Murphy USA/dsl, **food:** Carl's Jr, Chili's, Woody's Cafe, **lodging:** Best Western, Clairmore Inn, Super 8, Travel Inn, Will Rogers Inn, **other:** [H], Curves, Walgreens, Walmart SuperCtr/24hr, to Rogers U, Will Rogers Memorial, museum
248	to OK 266, Port of Catoosa, **N gas:** QT, **lodging:** Comfort Inn, Will Rogers Inn
244mm	Kerr-McClellan Navigation System
241mm	Will Rogers Tpk begins eb, ends wb, [phone]
241	OK 66 E, to Catoosa
240b	US 412 E, Choteau
240a	OK 167 N, 193rd E Ave, **N food:** KFC, McDonald's, Taco Bell, Taco Bueno, Waffle House, Wendy's, **lodging:** Cherokee Inn/Casino, Hardrock Hotel/Casino, **other:** KOA, Walgreens, **S gas:** QT, **food:** Mazzio's, PortCity Diner, Sonic, Subway, **lodging:** Holiday Inn Express, **other:** $General, O'Reilly Parts, tires/repair
238	161st E Ave, **N gas:** Sinclair/dsl/scales/rest./24hr, **other:** Goodyear Trk Tires, truckwash, **S gas:** QT/dsl/scales/24hr, **food:** Arby's, Burger King, **lodging:** Microtel, **other:** OK Welcome Ctr, Walker RV Ctr
236b	I-244 W, to downtown Tulsa, [airport]
236a	129th E Ave, **N gas:** ***FLYING J***/Conoco/dsl/LP/rest./24hr, **S food:** McDonald's
235	E 11th St, Tulsa, **N food:** Big Daddy's BBQ, Mazzio's, Rioberto's Mexican, Sonic, Subway, **lodging:** Executive Inn, Garnett Inn, Motel 6, Super 8, **other:** $General, Drug Whse, O'Reilly Parts, **S gas:** QT, **food:** Braum's, Denny's, Taco Bueno, **lodging:** Econolodge, **other:** Whse Foods
234b a	US 169, N to Owasso, to [airport], S to Broken Arrow, **N gas:** QT, **food:** Braum's, Mazzio's, **lodging:** Motel 6, **other:** $General, May's Drug, **S other:** Whse Mkt
233	E 21st St, **S food:** El Chico, **lodging:** Comfort Suites, **other:** K-Mart, Dean's RV Ctr, Vet
231	(232 from wb) US 64, OK 51, to Muskogee, E 31st St, Memorial Dr, **N food:** Whataburger, **lodging:** Days Inn, Georgetown Plaza Hotel, Regency Inn, Tulsa Inn, **S gas:** Shell, **food:** Cracker Barrel, IHOP, McDonald's, Pizza Hut, Ruby Tuesday, Village Inn, **lodging:** Best Western, Comfort Suites, Courtyard, Econolodge, Embassy Suites, Fairfield Inn, Hampton Inn, Holiday Inn Express, Quality Inn, Sleep Inn, Super 8, **other:** Cavender's Boots, Chevrolet, Harley-Davidson, Nissan
230	E 41st St, Sheridan Rd, **N food:** Carl's Jr, El Chico, On-the-Border, Panera Bread, Quizno's, Subway, TGIFriday, Whataburger/24hr, **other:** AT&T, Barnes&Noble, Curves, Dillard's, JC Penney, Jo-Ann Fabrics, Michael's, Old Navy, Petsmart, Robertson Tire, Ross, **S food:** Carino's Italian, **lodging:** La Quinta, **other:** Batteries+, Home Depot
229	Yale Ave, Tulsa, **N gas:** Shell, **food:** McDonald's, **other:** Firestone/auto, JC Penney, Macy's, Michael's, Old Navy, PetCo, Ross, mall, **S gas:** Phillips 66/dsl, QT/24hr, **food:** Applebee's, Arby's, Braum's, Delta Cafe, Outback Steaks, Qdoba, Red Lobster, Smoothie King, Sonic, Taco Bell, Village Inn, **lodging:** Baymont Inn, Days Inn, Red Roof Inn, Tulsa Select Hotel, **other:** [H], Best Buy, Kia, Vet
228	Harvard Ave, Tulsa, **N food:** El Tequila Mexican, NYC Pizza, **lodging:** Best Western, Tradewinds Motel, **S food:** A&W/LJ Silver, Chili's, Chimi's Mexican, Freckle's Frozen Custard, Jamil's Rest, LoneStar Steaks, Marie Callender's, Mario's Pizza, Osaka Steaks, Papa John's, Piccadilly Cafeteria, Starbucks, Subway, **other:** $Tree, Food Pyramid, Hobby Lobby, K-Mart, Stein-Mart
227	Lewis Ave, Tulsa, **S gas:** Phillips 66, **food:** El Chico, **other:** Walgreens
226b	Peoria Ave, Tulsa, **N gas:** Kum&Go, QT, **food:** Arby's, Biga Italian, Burger St., CiCi's, Egg Roll, La Hacienda Mexican, Mazzio's, KFC, Pizza Hut, Ron's Burgers/Chili, Subway, Taco Bell, Taco Buenco, Waffle House, **lodging:** Peoria Inn, **other:** Hancock Fabrics, Harley-Davidson, O'Reilly Parts, Radio Shack, Robertson Tire, Vet, Walmart Mkt, **S food:** Braum's, Golden Palace, **other:** AutoZone, $General, Family$, May's Drug
226a	Riverside Dr
225mm	Arkansas River
225	Elwood Ave, **N other:** Chevrolet, Ford, **S lodging:** Budget Inn
224b a	US 75, to Okmulgee, Bartlesville, **N gas:** QT/dsl, **food:** KFC, Mazzio's, Sonic, Subway, **other:** $General, Whse Mkt, **S lodging:** Royal Inn, **other:** RV park
223c33	rd W Ave, Tulsa, **N food:** Braum's, Domino's, **S gas:** Conoco, **food:** Rib Crib BBQ, **other:** U-Haul
223b	51st St (from wb)
223a	I-244 E, to Tulsa, downtown
222c	(from wb), **S lodging:** Value Inn
222b	55th Place, **N lodging:** Capri Motel, Crystal Motel, **S lodging:** Days Inn, Economy Inn

TULSA

INTERSTATE 44 CONT'D

E ↕ W

Exit #	Services
222a	49th W Ave, Tulsa, **N food:** Carl's Jr, Kelly's Country Cooking, Monterey Mexican, **lodging:** Gateway Motel, Interstate Inn, Motel 6, Rest Inn, **other:** BigLots, $General, **S gas:** QT/Wendy's/dsl/scales/24hr, **food:** Arby's, McDonald's, Taco Bueno, Village Inn, Waffle House, **lodging:** Super 8, **other:** Buick/GMC/Pontiac, Freightliner, Peterbilt, Volvo Trucks
221a	57th W Ave, (from wb), **S food:** Avalon Steaks, **other:** Buick/GMC/Pontiac
221mm	Turner Tkp begins wb, ends eb
218	Creek Tpk E (from eb)
215	OK 97, to Sand Sprgs, Sapulpa, **S gas:** Kum&Go, **food:** Arby's, Freddy's, Subway, Whataburger, **lodging:** Super 8, **other:** H, Hunter RV Ctr, Route 66 RV Park
211	OK 33, to Kellyville, Drumright, Heyburn SP, **S gas:** Shell/dsl
207mm	**service plaza wb, gas:** Phillips 66/dsl
204mm	**picnic area eb, litter barrels,**
197mm	**service plaza eb, food:** McDonald's
196	OK 48, Bristow, **S gas:** Conoco/dsl, Phillips 66, **food:** Mazzio's, Pizza Hut, Steak'nEgg Rest, Taco Mayo, **lodging:** Carolyn Inn, **other:** H, Buick/Chevrolet/Pontiac, Ford, Walmart SuperCtr
190mm	**picnic area eb, litter barrels,**
182mm	toll plaza
179	OK 99, to Drumright, Stroud, **N lodging:** Best Western/rest, **S gas:** Kids/dsl, Phillips 66/Subway/dsl, **food:** 5Star BBQ, Mazzio's, McDonald's, Mi Casa Mexican, Sonic, Vallarta's Rest, **lodging:** Sooner Motel, **other:** H, auto/tire repair
178mm	**Hoback Plaza both lanes** (exits left), **gas:** Phillips 66/dsl, **food:** McDonald's
171mm	**picnic area eb, litter barrels,**
167mm	**service plaza (from eb), S gas:** Phillips 66/dsl
166	OK 18, to Cushing, Chandler, **N other:** Chrysler/Dodge/Jeep, **S gas:** Phillips 66, **food:** Sonic, **lodging:** Econolodge, Lincoln Motel, **other:** Chandler Tire
166mm	**picnic area wb, , litter barrels,**
158	OK 66, to Wellston, **N gas:** Kum&Go/Subway/dsl/24hr
157	service plaza (from wb), **N food:** McDonald's**other:** museum info
138d	to Memorial Rd, to Enterprise Square
138a	I-35, I-44 E to Tulsa, Turner Tpk
I-44 and I-35 run together 8 mi. See Interstate 35 Exits 137-134.	
130	I-35 S, to Dallas, **access to facilities on I-35 S**
129	MLK Ave, Remington Park, **N food:** County Line BBQ, **lodging:** Garden Inn, **other:** Cowboy Museum, **S food:** McDonald's, **other:** Family$
128b	Kelley Ave, OK City, **N gas:** Conoco, Valero/Subway/dsl, **food:** Sonic
128a	Lincoln Blvd, st capitol, **S lodging:** Oxford Inn, Whitten Inn
127	I-235 S, US 77, City Ctr, Broadway St, **1 exit N gas:** Conoco, Phillips 66/dsl, Shell, **lodging:** Best Western, Holiday Inn
126	Western Ave, **N food:** Camille's Cafe, Deep Fork Rest., Sonic, Flip's Rest.

OKLAHOMA CITY

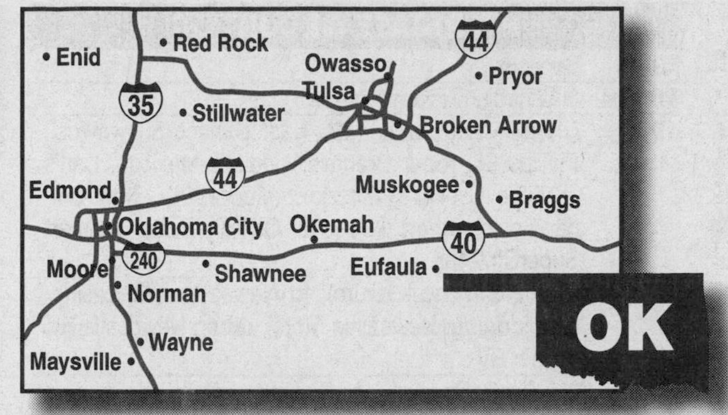

OKLAHOMA CITY

Exit #	Services
125c	NW Expressway (exits left from sb)
125	Classen Blvd, (exits left from wb), OK City, **N gas:** Shell, **food:** Cheesecake Factory, Chili's, Elephant Bar Rest., Moe's SW Grill, Olive Garden, **other:** Acura, Dillard's, JC Penney, Macy's, Old Navy, Radio Shack, Ross, Walmart SuperCtr/24hr, **S food:** IHOP, McDonald's, **lodging:** AmeriSuites, Courtyard, Hawthorn Suites
125a	OK 3A, Penn Ave, to NW Expswy, **N gas:** Conoco/dsl/24hr, **S gas:** Shell, **food:** Braum's, Coit's Cafe, **lodging:** Habana Inn, **other:** Homeland Foods,
124	N May, **W gas:** Shell/Subway, **food:** San Marco's Mexican, **lodging:** Comfort Inn, Day's Inn, Super 8, **other:** Dodge, O'Reilly Parts, **S other:** Aamco, Ford, Lowes Whse
123b	OK 66 W, NW 39th, to Warr Acres, **N gas:** Valero/McDonald's/dsl, **food:** Asian Palace, Carl's Jr, Chinese Buffet, Jimmy's Egg, Los Mariachi's, Quizno's, **lodging:** Carlyle Motel, Hospitality Inn, **other:** $General
123a	NW 36th St
122	NW 23rd St, **N gas:** Conoco/7-11, **food:** Church's, EggRoll King, Taco Mayo, **other:** Tires+, **S gas:** Conoco, **food:** Arby's, Sonic, **other:** Big O Tire, Family$
121b a	NW 10th St, **N gas:** Shell, **S gas:** 7-11/gas, Sinclair, **other:** $General, Family$, Whittaker's Foods/24hr, antiques, fairgrounds
120b a	I-40, W to Amarillo, E to Ft Smith
119	SW 15th St
118	OK 152 W, SW 29th St, OK City, **E gas:** 7-11/gas, **food:** A&W/LJ Silver, Burger King, KFC/Taco Bell, La Fiesta Mexican, McDonald's, Sonic, Subway, Taco Bueno, **other:** Advance Parts, AutoZone, $General, $Tree, Grider's Foods/gas, O'Reilly Parts, Walgreen, **W gas:** Shell, **other:** U-Haul, transmissions
117	SW 44th St, **W** auto repair
116b	Airport rd (exits left from nb), **W**
116a	SW 59th St, **E gas:** Conoco, **W** Will Rogers
115	I-240 E, US 62 E, to Ft Smith
114	SW 74th St, OK City, **E gas:** TK, Valero, **food:** Braum's, Burger King, Perry's Rest., **lodging:** Cambridge Inn, Ramada Ltd, **other:** $General
113	SW 89th St, **E gas:** Love's/Subway/dsl/24hr, OG, 7-11/gas, Valero/dsl, **food:** McDonald's, Sonic, Taco Mayo, **other:** H, CVS Drug
112	SW 104th St, **E gas:** Valero, **W gas:** Shell/rest./dsl
111	SW 119th St, **E food:** Sonic, **other:** Walker RV Ctr
110	OK 37 E, to Moore, **E gas:** Sinclair/dsl, **food:** Sonic
109	SW 149th St, **E food:** JR's Grill

INTERSTATE 44 CONT'D

E ↕ W — CHICKASHA — LAWTON

Exit #	Services
108mm	S Canadian River
108	OK 37 W, to Tuttle, **W gas:** Conoco/Subway/dsl, Phillips 66, **food:** Braum's, Carlito's Mexican, Carl's Jr, Little Caesar's, Mazzio's, McDonald's, New China, Sonic, **other:** $General, O'Reilly Parts, Walmart SuperCtr/24hr
107	US 62 S (no wb return), to Newcastle, **E** casino/gas, **lodging:** Newcastle Motel, **other:** Newcastle RV, Walker RV
99	H E Bailey Spur, rd 4, to Blanchard, Norman
97mm	toll booth, phone
95.5mm	**picnic area wb, ⛱, litter barrels**
85.5mm	**service plaza, both lanes exit left**, Phillips 66/dsl, McDonald's
83	US 62, Chickasha, **W gas:** Jay's/dsl, Valero/dsl, **other:** Indian Museum
80	US 81, Chickasha, **E gas:** Conoco/dsl, Phillips 66/dsl, Shell/dsl, **food:** Eduardo's Mexican, Western Sizzlin, **lodging:** Day's Inn, Holiday Inn Express, Royal American Inn, Super 8, **other:** [H], Buick/Chevrolet/Pontiac/Cadillac, Chrysler/Dodge/Jeep, $Tree, **W gas:** Conoco, Love's, Valero, **food:** Arby's, Braum's, China Moon, Denny's, Domino's, El Rancho Mexican, KFC, LJ Silver, Mazzio's Pizza, McDonald's, Napoli's Rest., New China, Pizza Hut, Quizno's, Sonic, Taco Bell, Taco Mayo, **lodging:** Best Western, Budget Motel, Ranch House Motel, **other:** AutoZone, CVS Drug, Family$, Ford/Lincoln/Mercury, O'Reilly Parts, Radio Shack, Staples, Walmart SuperCtr/Subway/gas
78mm	toll plaza, ☎
63mm	**picnic area wb, ⛱, litter barrels**
62	to Cyril (from wb)
60.5mm	**picnic area eb, ⛱, litter barrels**
53	US 277, Elgin, Lake Ellsworth, **E gas:** Shamrock, **food:** Goodcents Subs, Sonic, Taco Tico, **W gas:** Fina/dsl
46	US 62 E, US 277, US 281, to Elgin, Apache, Comanche Tribe, last free exit nb
45	OK 49, to Medicine Park, **W gas:** Love's/Subway/dsl/24hr, **food:** Burger King, Sonic, **other:** Whichita NWR
41	to Ft Sill, Key Gate, **W** Ft Sill Museum
40c	Gate 2, to Ft Sill
40a	US 62 W, to Cache, **E gas:** Fina/dsl, **W lodging:** Super 8
39b	US 281 (from sb), **W lodging:** Ramada Inn
39a	US 281, Cache rd (exits left from nb), Lawton, **1-3 mi W gas:** Phillips 66, Valero/dsl, **food:** Applebee's, Braum's, Chili's, Chick-fil-A, Fire Mtn Grill, Golden Corral, KFC, Ryan's, Subway, Wendy's, **lodging:** Baymont Inn, Holiday Inn, Super 8, Super 9 Motel, **other:** $General, U-Haul, transmissions
37	Gore Blvd, Lawton, **E gas:** Conoco, **food:** Braum's, Los Tres Amigos, Sonic, Taco Mayo, Woody's Mexican, **lodging:** Best Western, **other:** Curves, casino, **W food:** Arby's (3mi), Cracker Barrel, Mike's Grille, **lodging:** Fairfield Inn, Holiday Inn Express, Ramada Inn (2mi), SpringHill Suites, **other:** Harley-Davidson, Lincoln/Mercury
36a	OK 7, Lee Blvd, Lawton, **E gas:** Phillips 66, **W gas:** Fina/dsl/repair, Shamrock/dsl, Suncountry/dsl, Welch/dsl, **food:** Big Chef Rest., KFC/Taco Bell, Leo&Ken's Rest., Popeye's, Salas Mexican, Sonic, **lodging:** Motel 6, **other:** [H], $General, airport, Vet
33	US 281, 11th St, Lawton, **W other:** [H], gas, food, lodging, ✈, to Ft Sill
30	OK 36, Geronimo
20.5mm	**Elmer Graham Plaza**, both lanes exit left, Phillips 66/dsl, McDonald's, info
20	OK 5, to Walters, **E food:** BBQ
19.5mm	toll plaza
5	US 277 N, US 281, Randlett, last free exit nb, **E gas:** Shamrock/dsl
1	OK 36, to Grandfield
0mm	Oklahoma/Texas state line, Red River

OK

INTERSTATE 240 (OKLAHOMA CITY)

E ↕ W — OKLAHOMA CITY

Exit #	Services
16mm	I-240 begins/ends on I-40.
14	Anderson Rd, **S gas:** Conoco
11b a	Douglas Blvd, **N** Tinker AFB
9	Air Depot Blvd
8	OK 77, Sooner Rd, **N gas:** Shell/dsl, **S gas:** Phillips 66/Popeye's/dsl, Valero/McDonald's/dsl
7	Sunnylane Ave, **S gas:** Valero/Subway/dsl, **lodging:** Value Place Motel
6	Bryant Ave
5	S Eastern Ave
4c	Pole Rd, **N food:** Burger King, Luby's, Taco Bell, TX Roadhouse, **lodging:** Fairfield Inn, Ramada Inn, Residence Inn, **other:** Best Buy, Dillard's, JC Penney, Tires+, Maceys, mall
4b a	I-35, N to OK City, S to Dallas, US 77 S, US 62/77 N
3b	S Shields, **N gas:** Valero/dsl, **other:** Home Depot, **S food:** Chili's, **other:** Ford, Lowe's Whse, Nissan, Walmart SuperCtr/gas
3a	S Santa Fe, **S gas:** Shell, **food:** Chili's, IHOP, **other:** Buick, Dodge, Chrysler/Jeep, Staples, Lowe's Whse, Walmart SuperCtr/24hr
2b	S Walker Ave, **N gas:** Shell/7-11, **food:** Rib Crib, **S food:** Carino's, ChuckeCheese, Jimmy's Egg Grill, On-the-Border, Premo's Italian, **other:** Chevrolet, PepBoys
2a	S Western Ave, **N gas:** Conoco, **food:** Burger King, House of Szechwan, Nino's Mexican, Taste of China, **other:** Hyundai, Suzuki, Tires+, **S gas:** 7-11/gas, Valero, **food:** A&W/LJ Silver, Arby's, Ashley's Rest./24hr, Grandy's, HomeTown Buffet, KFC, Krispy Kreme, McDonald's, Red Lobster, Steak&Ale, **lodging:** Best Western, Holiday Inn Express, Quality Inn, **other:** Big O Tire, Chevrolet, Honda, Office Depot, Radio Shack
1c	S Penn Ave, **N gas:** Conoco, **food:** Carl's Jr, Denny's, Don Pablo, Golden Corral, Harrigan's Rest., Hooters, Olive Garden, Outback Steaks, Pioneer Pies, Santa Fe Grill, Schlotsky's, **other:** BigLots, GNC, Radio Shack, Michaels, **S gas:** Shell/Circle K, **food:** Hunan Buffet, Joe' s Crabshack, Mazzio's, Pancho's Mexican, Papa John's, Subway, Taco Bueno, Wendy's, Western Sizzlin, **other:** $Tree, Hancock Fabrics
1b	S May Ave, **N gas:** 7-11/gas, **food:** Capt D's, Outlaw's BBQ, Taco Bell, Waffle House, **other:** Albertson's, O'Reilly Parts, **S gas:** Valero, **food:** Braum's, Burger King, Perry's Rest., **lodging:** Cambridge Inn, Ramada Ltd
1a	I-44, US 62, I-240 begins ends on I-44.

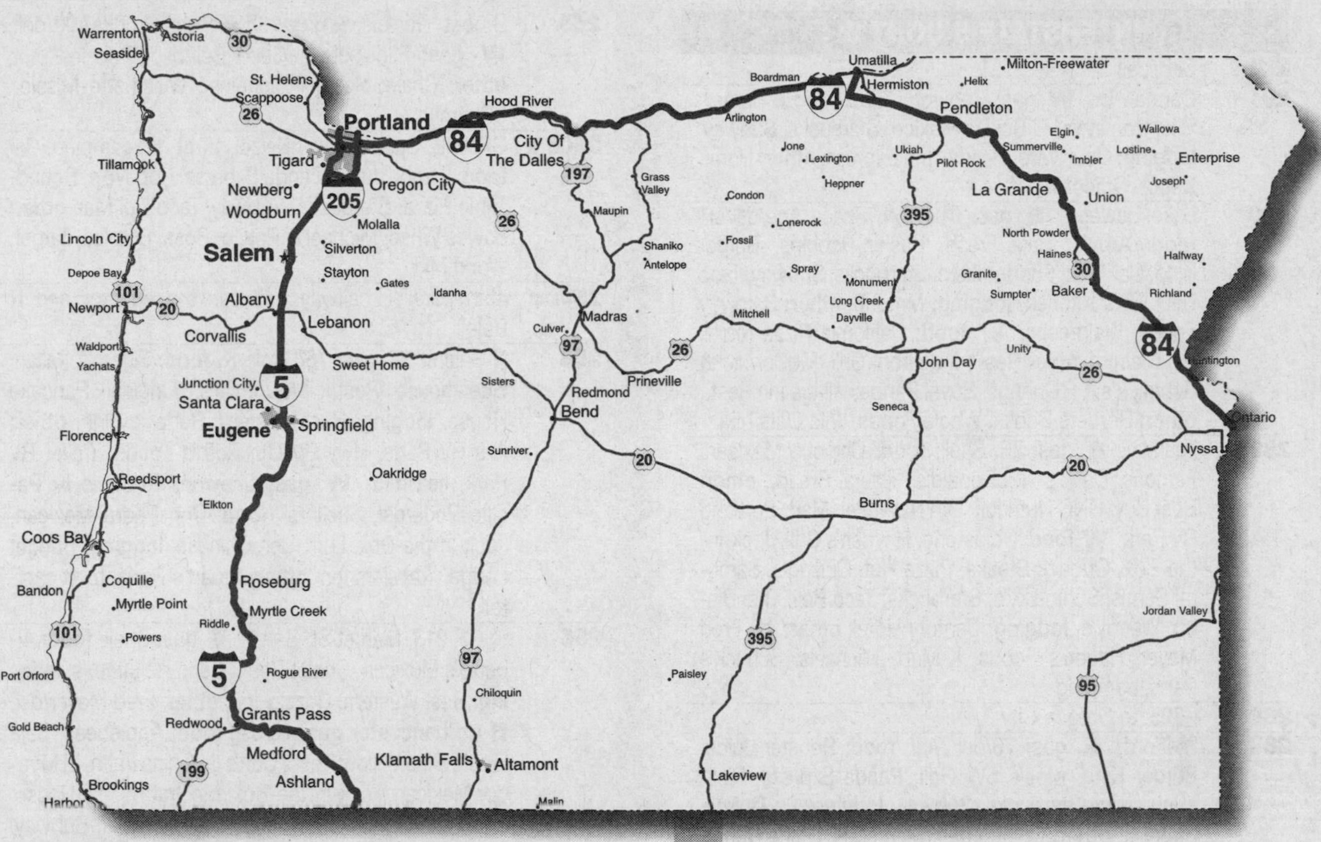

INTERSTATE 5

N ↕ S

PORTLAND

Exit #	Services
308.5mm	Oregon/Washington state line, Columbia River
308	Jansen Beach Dr, **E gas:** Chevron/24hr, **food:** Burger King, Starbucks, Taco Bell, **lodging:** Oxford Suites, Red Lion, **other:** Safeway, **W food:** BJ's Brewery, Bradley's Grill, Denny's, Chang's Mongolian, Hooters, McDonald's, Newport Bay Rest., Original Joe's, Stanford's Rest., Subway, **other:** Barnes&Noble, Best Buy, Home Depot, Jansen Beach RV Park, Office Depot, Old Navy, Ross, Michael's, Staples, Target, mall
307	OR 99E S, MLK Blvd, Union Ave, Marine Dr (sb only), **E gas:** Jubitz Trvl Ctr/rest/dsl/@, 76/dsl, **food:** Portland Cascade Grill, **lodging:** Courtyard, Fairfield Inn, Portlander Inn, Residence Inn, **other:** Blue Beacon, Expo Ctr, truck repair
306b	Interstate Ave, Delta Park, **E gas:** 76, **food:** Burger King, Elmer's Rest., Shari's, **lodging:** Best Western, Day's Inn, Motel 6, **other:** Lowe's Whse, Portland Meadows
306a	Columbia (from nb), same as 306b
305b a	US 30, Lombard St (from nb), **E food:** Little Caesars, **W gas:** Stro, Shell, **food:** Panda Express, Subway, Wendy's, **other:** Fred Meyer, Knecht's Parts
304	Portland Blvd, U of Portland, **W** Arco, 76/dsl, **food:** Nite Hawk Cafe, Taco Time, **lodging:** Super Value, Viking Motel
303	Alberta St, Swan Island, **W food:** Subway, Taco Bell, **lodging:** Budget Motel, Monticello Motel, **E** [H]
302b	I-405, US 30 W, **W** to ocean beaches, zoo
302a	Rose Qtr, City Ctr, **E gas:** 76/Circle K/dsl, Shell/dsl, **food:** Burger King, Chipotle Mexican, McDonald's, Starbucks, Taco Bell, Wendy's, **lodging:** Crowne Plaza, **other:** [H], Toyota/Scion, Schwab Tire, 7-11, Walgreens, **W other:** coliseum

PORTLAND

Exit #	Services
301	I-84 E, US 30 E, facilities E off I-84 exits
300	US 26 E (from sb), Milwaukie Ave, **W lodging:** Hilton, Marriott
299b	I-405
299a	US 26 E, OR 43 (from nb), City Ctr, to Lake Oswego
297	Terwilliger Blvd, **W food:** Burger King, KFC, **other:** [H] Fred Meyer, to Lewis and Clark Coll.
296b	Multnomah Blvd
296a	Barbur, **W gas:** Chevron/24hr, Shell, 76/dsl, **food:** Belagio's Pizza, Original Pancake House, Szechuan Chinese, Subway, Taco Del Mar, **lodging:** Budget Lodge, Capitol Hill Motel, **other:** 7-11, Schwab Tire, Vet
295	Capitol Hwy (from sb), Taylors Ferry Rd (from nb), **E gas:** Shell/dsl, **food:** Juan Colorado Mexican, Koji Japanese, McDonald's, RoundTable Pizza, Starbucks, **lodging:** Hospitality Motel, **E food:** Taco Time, Wendy's
294	OR 99W, to Tigard, **E** Comfort Suites, **W gas:** Chevron, 76, Shell, **food:** Arby's, Baja Fresh, Banning's Rest., Burger King, Gators Eatery, Hihat Chinese, KFC, Little Caesars, Mazatlan Mexican, McDonald's, Newport Bay Rest., Quizno's, Starbucks, Subway, Taco Bell, **lodging:** Quality Inn, **other:** Americas Tire, Baxter Parts, Costco, Fred Meyer, Petco, Radio Shack, Schwab Tire, U-Haul, Winco Foods, transmissions, Vet
293	Haines St, **W other:** Ford
292	OR 217, Kruse Way, Lake Oswego, **E gas:** Shell, **food:** Applebee's, Coldstone, Chevy's Mexican, Olive Garden, Quizno's, Stanford's Rest., Stanford's Rest., Starbucks, Taco Del Mar, **lodging:** Crowne Plaza, Hilton Garden, Phoenix Inn, Residence Inn, **other:** AAA, Curves, LDS Temple, **W lodging:** Homestead Suites, **other:** Lowe's Whse

INTERSTATE 5 CONT'D

N ↕ S

Exit #	Services
291	Carman Dr, **W** **gas:** Chevron, 76/dsl, **food:** Burgerville, Domino's, El Sol De Mexico, Starbucks, Subway, **lodging:** Courtyard, Holiday Inn Express, **other:** Home Depot, Office Depot
290	Lake Oswego, **E** **gas:** Chevron, Space Age/dsl/LP, **food:** Arby's, Baja Fresh, Baskin-Robbins, Burger King, Carl's Jr., Fuddruckers, Starbucks, Subway, Taco Bell, Wu's Kitchen, **lodging:** Motel 6, **other:** Safeway Foods, Walgreens, **W** **food:** California Pizza Kitchen, Claim Jumper Rest., Macaroni Grill, McCormick& Schmick's, PF Changs, Royal Panda, Village Inn Rest., **other:** Borders Books, Whole Foods, Wild Oats Mkt
289	Tualatin, **E** **gas:** 76, Shell, **food:** Chipotle Mexican, Famous Dave's, McDonald's, Paera Bread, **other:** Best Buy, GNC Nutrition, Old Navy, PetsMart, Portland RV Park, **W** **food:** Coldstone, Hayden's Grill, Jack-in-the-Box, Ouback Steaks, Pizza Hut, Quizno's, Samurai Sam's, Schlotzky's, Starbucks, Taco Bell, Thai Bistro, Wendy's, **lodging:** Century Hotel, **other:** H, Fred Meyer, Hagen's Foods, K-Mart, Michaels, Schuck's Parts, camping
288	I-205, to Oregon City
286	Stafford, **E** **gas:** 76/dsl/24hr, **food:** Booster Juice, Burger King, Moe's SW Grill, Panda Express, PizzaSchmizza, Starbucks, Subway, **lodging:** La Quinta, Super 8, **other:** Costco/gas, Mercedes, Office Depot, PetsMart, Pheasant Ridge RV Resort, Target, **W** **gas:** Chevron, **food:** Big Town Gyro, **lodging:** Holiday Inn/rest., **other:** Camping World RV Service/supplies, Chevrolet, Dodge, Nissan, Toyota/Scion
283	Wilsonville, **E** **gas:** 76/dsl, **food:** Abella Italian, Arby's, Country Grains Cafe., Denny's, Jamba Juice, Juan Colorado Mexican, McDonald's, Papa Murphy's, Quizno's, Red Robin, Shari's/24hr, Starbucks, Subway, Taco Bell, TCBY, Wanker's Café, Wendy's, Wong's Chinese, **lodging:** Best Western, SnoozInn, **other:** Fry's Electronics, GNC, Lamb's Foods, NAPA, Rite Aid, Schwab Tire, USPO, Vet, funpark, **W** **gas:** Baskin-Robbins, Chevron, **food:** Burger King/24hr, Deno's Pizzaria, Domino's, Hunan Kitchen, Sonic, Starbucks, **lodging:** Wilsonville Inn, **other:** Albertson's, 7-11, Walgreens
282.5mm	Willamette River
282	Charbonneau District, **E** **food:** Langdon Farms Rest., **other:** Langdon Farms Golf
281.5mm	**rest area both lanes, full ♿ facilities, ☎, info, picnic tables, litter barrels, petwalk, vending, coffee**
278	Donald, **E** **gas:** Conoco/Circle K/LP/dsl, **other:** Aurora Acres RV Park, **W** **gas:** Leather's/dsl/@, Shell/CFN/dsl, TA/Country Pride/Popeye's/dsl/scales/24hr/@, **other:** Papa Joe's BBQ, **other:** Speedco Lube, truckwash, to Champoeg SP
274mm	**weigh sta both lanes**
271	OR 214, Woodburn, **E** **gas:** Arco/24hr, Chevron/24hr, Conoco, 76/repair, **food:** Burger King, Country Cottage Rest., DQ, Denny's, KFC, McDonald's/playplace, Subway, Taco Bell, **lodging:** Best Western, Super 8, **other:** Fairway Drug, Walmart SuperCtr/24hr, Vet, **W** **gas:** Shell, **food:** Arby's, Elmer's Rest., Jack-in-the-Box, Quizno's, Starbucks, **lodging:** La Quinta, **other:** Chevrolet, Chrysler/Dodge/Jeep, Ford, Outlet/famous brands, Woodburn RV Park, Woodburn Outlets
263	Brooks, Gervais, **E** **gas:** 76/LP, **other:** Brooks Mkt/deli, **W** **gas:** Pilot/Subway/Taco Bell/dsl/LP/scales/24hr, **other:** Chalet Rest., Freightliner, Willamette Mission SP (4mi)
260b a	OR 99E, Salem Pkwy, Keizer, **2 mi** **E** camping, **W** **food:** Jamba Juice, Panda Express, Popeye's, RoundTable Pizza, Starbucks, Subway, Taco Del Mar, **other:** Lowes Whse, Michael's, PetCo, Ross, Staples, Target, World Mkt
259mm	45th parallel, halfway between the equator and N Pole
258	N Salem, **E** **gas:** 76/Circle K, **food:** Figaro's Italian, Guesthouse Rest., McDonald's, Original Pancake House, **lodging:** Best Western, Rodeway Inn, **other:** Al's RV Parts, Hwy RV Ctr, Roth's Foods, Trailer RV Park, flea mkt, **W** **gas:** Chevron, 76/Circle K, Pacific Pride/dsl, Shell/dsl, **food:** Don Pedro Mexican, Jack-in-the-Box, LumYuen Chinese, **lodging:** Budget Lodge, Travelers Inn, **other:** Stuart's Parts, to st capitol
256	to OR 213, Market St, Salem, **E** **gas:** Shell, **food:** Alberto's Mexican, Chalet Rest., Denny's, Elmer's, **lodging:** Best Western, Cozzzy Inn, **other:** Fred Meyer/dsl, **E on Lancaster gas:** 76/dsl, **food:** Applebees, Baja Fresh, Blue Willow Rest., Carl's Jr, China Faith, El Mirador Mexican, Jack-in-the-Box, McGrath's Fish House, Olice Garden, Outback, Quizno's, Skipper's, Subway, Taco Bell, **other:** American Tire, Best Buy, BigLots, Macy's, Sears, Schwab Tires, Target, Walgreens, **W** **gas:** Arco/24hr, Pacific Pride/dsl, Shell/dsl/24hr, Texaco/dsl, **food:** Almost Home Rest., Baskin-Robbins, DQ, McDonald's, Newport Bay Seafood, Pietro's Pizza, Subway, **lodging:** Comfort Inn, Holiday Lodge, Motel 6, Phoenix Inn, Red Lion Hotel, Shilo Inn, Super 8, **other:** Buick/GMC, Jack's IGA, Kia/Mazda/Suzuki, Nissan
253	OR 22, Salem, Stayton, **E** **gas:** Chevron/repair, Shell/dsl, 76, **food:** Arby's, Burger King, Carl's Jr, Las Polomas Mexican, McDonald's/playplace, Shari's, Subway, **other:** $Tree, Home Depot, ShopKO, Sportsman's Whse, WinCo Foods, Salem Camping, to Detroit RA, **W** **gas:** Shell/dsl, **food:** DQ, Denny's, Panda Express, Sybil's Omelette, **lodging:** Best Western, Comfort Suites, Holiday Inn Express, Phoenix Hotel, Residence Inn, Travelodge, **other:** H, AAA, Chevrolet/Cadillac/Subaru, Chrysler/Jeep, Costco/gas, K-Mart, Lowe's Whse, Schwab Tire, Toyota/Scion, Walmart SuperCtr, st police
252	Kuebler Blvd, **2 mi** **W** **on Commercial...gas:** Arco/24hr, 76/24hr, **food:** Applebee's, Arby's, Burger King, Jack-in-the-Box, McDonald's, Muchas Gracias, Papa Murphy's, Quizno's, Shari's, Subway, **lodging:** Phoenix Inn, **other:** H, Circle K, Curves, $Tree, Jo-Anne, Roberson RV Ctr, Schwab Tire, Walmart
249	to Salem (exits left from nb), **2 mi** **W** **food:** Arby's, Burger King, Carl's Jr., King's Buffet, **lodging:** Phoenix Inn
248	Sunnyside, **E** **other:** Enchanted Forest Themepark, KOA, Willamette Valley Vineyards, **W** **gas:** Pacific Pride/dsl
244	to Jefferson
243	Ankeny Hill

WILSONVILLE

SALEM

OR

INTERSTATE 5 CONT'D

N ↕ S

Exit #	Services
242	Talbot Rd
241mm	**rest area both lanes, full ♿ facilities, info, ☎, ⛺, litter barrels, petwalk**
240.5mm	Santiam River
240	Hoefer Rd
239	Dever-Conner
238	S Jefferson, Scio
237	Viewcrest (from sb)
235	(from nb), Millersburg
234	OR 99E, Albany, **E lodging:** Comfort Suites, Holiday Inn Express, **other:** Harley-Davidson, Knox Butte Camping, RV dump, ✈, **W gas:** Chevron, **food:** A&W, Burger King, Carl's Jr., China Buffet, DQ, KFC, McDonald's, Subway, Taco Bell, **lodging:** Best Western/rest., La Quinta, Motel 6, **other:** H, Costco/gas, K-Mart, Kohl's, Nissan, RV repair, to Albany Hist Dist
233	US 20, Albany, **E gas:** Chevron/dsl/LP/24hr, 76/dsl, **food:** Denny's, LumYuen Chinese, **lodging:** Econolodge, Phoenix Inn, Quality Inn, **other:** Chevrolet, Home Depot, Honda, Lassen RV Ctr, RV camping, Toyota/Scion, st police, **W gas:** 76/dsl, Shell, **food:** Abby's Pizza, Arby's, Baskin-Robbins, Burgerville, Carl's Jr., Elmer's, Figaro's, Fox Den Pizza, Jack-in-the-Box, Lee's Wok, Los Tequilos Mexican, Original Breakfast Cafe, Sizzler, Skipper's, Starbucks, Taco Time, **lodging:** Valu Inn, **other:** H, Albertson's, Bi-Mart, CarQuest, Chrysler/Dodge/Jeep/Subaru/Hyundai, Fred Meyer/gas/dsl, Jo-Ann Fabrics, Knecht's Parts, NAPA, PetCo, Rite Aid, Schwab Tires, Staples, Subaru, Target, Walgreens
228	OR 34, to Lebanon, Corvallis, **E gas:** Leather's/dsl, 76/dsl/24hr, **food:** Pine Cone Cafe, **other:** Mallard Creek RV Resort, **W gas:** Arco/24hr, Chevron/CFN/A&W/dsl, Shell/dsl, **other:** to OSU, KOA (5mi)
222mm	Butte Creek
216	OR 228, Halsey, Brownsville, **E gas:** Pioneer Villa TrkStp/76/Blimpie/dsl/24hr/@, **lodging:** Travelodge, **other:** parts/repair/towing, **W gas:** Shell/dsl
209	to Jct City, Harrisburg, **W other:** Diamond Hill RV Park
206mm	**rest area both lanes, full ♿ facilities, info, ☎, ⛺, litter barrels, petwalk**
199	Coburg, **E gas:** Fuel'n Go/dsl, **other:** Premier RV Park, RV Ctr, **W gas:** Shell/LP, TA/CFN/Country Pride/Truck'n'Travel Motel/dsl/rest./24hr/@, **other:** Corral RV Ctr, Eugene RV park, Freightliner/GMC, Guaranty RV Ctr, Paradise RV Ctr, Volvo, dsl repair, hist dist
197mm	McKenzie River
195b a	N Springfield, **E gas:** Arco/24hr, Chevron/24hr, 76/Circel K/dsl/24hr, **food:** Applebee's, Cabo Grill, Carl's Jr, China Sun, Ciao Pizza, ChuckeCheese, Denny's, Elmer's Rest., FarMan Chinese, Gateway Chinese, HomeTown Buffet, Howling Coyote, IHOP, Jack-in-the-Box, KFC, McDonald's, Outback Steaks, Quizno's, Roadhouse Grill, Shari's/24hr, Sizzler, Starbucks, Subway, Taco Bell, **lodging:** Best Western, Comfort Suites, Courtyard, Holiday Inn Express, Holiday Inn, Motel 6, Quality Inn, Shilo Inn/rest., Super 8, **other:** H, Best Buy, Kohl's, Michaels, Ross, Sears/auto, Staples, Target, USPO, mall, st police, **W food:** Taco Bell, **other:** Costco/gas, Office Depot, PetsMart, ShopKO, to ✈

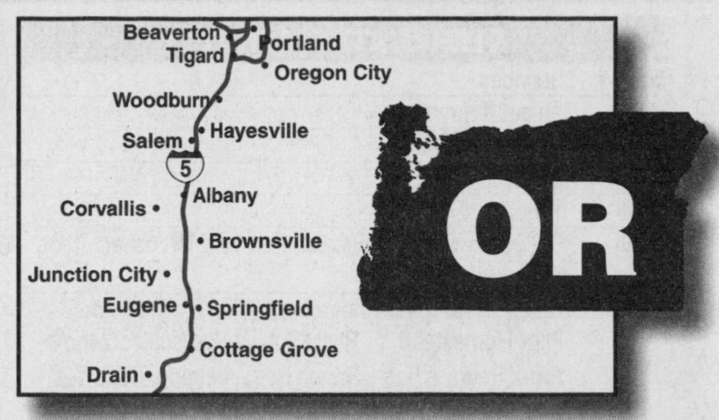

Exit #	Services
194b a	OR 126 E, I-105 W, Springfield, Eugene, **1 mi W gas:** Chevron, 76/repair, **food:** Carl's Jr., PF Chang's, Quizno's, Starbucks, **lodging:** Red Lion Inn, Residence Inn, **other:** Albertson's/gas, Borders Books, Old Navy, Subaru, TJ Maxx, U Of O, mall
193mm	Willamette River
192	OR 99 (from nb), to Eugene, **W gas:** 76, **food:** Boulevard Grill, House Of Chen, Wendy's, **lodging:** Days Inn, Best Western, Holiday Inn Express, Univeristy Inn, **other:** Mkt Of Choice
191	Glenwood, **W gas:** Shell/dsl/LP/24hr, **food:** Denny's, **lodging:** Comfort Suites, Motel 6
189	30th Ave S, Eugene, **E gas:** Shell/dsl/LP, **other:** Harley-Davidson, Shamrock RV Park, marine ctr, mobile village, **W gas:** 76/dsl
188b	rd 99 S (nb only), Goshen
188a	OR 58, to Oakridge, OR 99S, **E other:** Deerwood RV Camping, **W gas:** Pacific Pride/dsl/rest./24hr, **other:** Big Boy's RV Ctr, tires
186	to Goshen (from nb)
182	Creswell, **E food:** Subway, **other:** Bi-Mart Foods, Ray's Foods/drug, golf, **W gas:** Arco/24hr, 76/dsl, **food:** China Wok, Figaro's Pizza, Hawaiian BBQ, TJ's Rest., **lodging:** Super 8, **other:** Dari Mart, KOA, Knecht's Parts, NAPA, Tire Factory
180mm	Coast Fork of Willamette River
178mm	**rest area both lanes, full ♿ facilities, ☎, ⛺, litter barrels, petwalk, coffee**
176	Saginaw
175mm	Row River
174	Cottage Grove, **E gas:** Chevron/dsl/repair/24hr, Pacific Pride, Shell, **food:** El Paraiso Mexican, Subway, Taco Bell, **lodging:** Village Resort/RV park, **other:** H, Brad's RV Ctr, Chevrolet/Pontiac/Buick/GMC, Chrysler/Dodge/Jeep, Walmart/auto, **W gas:** Chevron/dsl/LP, 76/dsl, Shell/dsl, **food:** Arby's, Burger King, Carl's Jr, Figaro's Pizza, KFC, McDonald's/**RV parking**, Szechuan Chinese, Subway, Torero's Mexican, Vintage Rest./24hr, **lodging:** City Ctr Motel, Comfort Inn, Holiday Inn Express, Relax Inn, **other:** H, Chevrolet, $Tree, Mazda, Shopsmart Foods, Village Green Motel/RV Park
172	6th St (no EZ return nb), Cottage Grove Lake, **2 mi E** Cottage Grove RV Park
170	to OR 99, London Rd (nb only), Cottage Grove Lake, 6 mi **E** Cottage Grove RV Park
163	Curtin, Lorane, **E lodging:** Stardust Motel, **other:** Pass Creek RV Park, USPO, antiques, **W gas:** 76
162	162 OR 38, OR 99 to Drain, Elkton

INTERSTATE 5 CONT'D

Exit #	Services
161	Anlauf (from nb)
160	Salt Springs Rd
159	Elk Creek, Cox Rd
154	Yoncalla, Elkhead
150	OR 99, to OR 38, Yoncalla, Red Hill, **W other:** Trees of Oregon RV Park
148	Rice Hill, **E gas:** Chevron/LP/24hr, Pacific Pride/dsl, Pilot/Homestead Rest./Subway/dsl/scales/24hr/@, **food:** Peggy's Rest., Ranch Rest., **lodging:** Best Western, Ranch Motel, **other:** Rice Hill RV Park, towing/dsl repair, **W food:** K-R Drive-In
146	Rice Valley
144mm	**rest area sb, full ♿ facilities, ☎, ⛱, litter barrels, petwalk**
143mm	**rest area nb, full ♿ facilities, ☎, ⛱, litter barrels, petwalk**
142	Metz Hill
140	OR 99 (from sb), Oakland, **E food:** Tolly's Rest., **other:** Oakland Hist Dist
138	OR 99 (from nb), Oakland, **E food:** Tolly's Rest., **other:** Oakland Hist Dist
136	OR 138W, Sutherlin, **E gas:** Chevron/A&W/dsl/24hr, 76/Quizno's/dsl, **food:** Abby's Pizza, Apple Peddler Rest., Burger King, Hong Kong Chinese, McDonald's, Papa Murphy's, Pedotti's Italian, **lodging:** Relax Inn, Sutherlin Inn, Umpqua Regency Inn, **other:** CarQuest, I-5 RV Ctr, **W gas:** Shell, **food:** Dakota St Pizza, DQ, Si Casa Flores, Subway, Taco Bell, **other:** Hi-Way Haven RV Camp, Oak Hills RV Park
135	Wilbur, Sutherlin, **E gas:** CFN/dsl, Shell/dsl/LP, muffler repair
130mm	**weigh sta sb, ☎**
129	OR 99, Winchester, **E** gas, food, camping, dsl repair, RV Ctr (1mi)
129mm	N Umpqua River
127	Stewart Pkwy, Edenbower Rd, N Roseburg, **E gas:** Shell, **food:** Sheri's Rest., **lodging:** Motel 6, Super 8, **other:** Home Depot, Lowe's Whse, Mt Nebo RV Park, **W gas:** Texaco/Taco Maker/dsl, **food:** Applebee's, Coldstone Creamery, Jack-in-the-Box, McDonald's/playplace, Red Robin, Subway, **lodging:** Sleep Inn, **other:** [H], Albertson's/gas, Big O Tire, Harley-Davidson, K-Mart, Office Depot, Sherm's Foods, Walmart/auto/drugs, Vet
125	Garden Valley Blvd, Roseburg, **E gas:** Texaco, **food:** Brutke's Rest., Casey's Rest., Elmer's, Gilberto's Mexican, Jack-in-the-Box, KFC, Los Dos Amigo's Mexican, McDonald's, Papa Murphy's, Taco Bell, **lodging:** Comfort Inn, Quality Inn, Windmill Inn/rest., **other:** BigLots, GMC, NAPA, Safeway Foods/gas, Toyota, UHaul, Walgreens, transmissions, **W gas:** Chevron/dsl, Shell/LP/repair, **food:** Arby's, Burger King, Carl's Jr, Foxden Cafe, IHOP, Quizno's, Rodeo Steaks, RoundTable Pizza, Sizzler, Skippers, Taco Bell, Wendy's, **lodging:** Best Value Inn, Best Western, **other:** Bi-Mart, Fred Meyer, JC Penney, PetCo, Rite Aid, Ross, Sears/auto, Schuck's Parts, Staples, mall
124	OR 138, Roseburg, City Ctr, **E gas:** 76/dsl/24hr, Texaco/dsl, **food:** Chi's Chinese, Denny's, **lodging:**
124	Continued Douglas Co. Inn, Dunes Motel, Holiday Inn Express, Travelodge, **other:** Honda, Mazda, Rite Aid, **W gas:** 76/dsl, Shell/dsl, **food:** A&W, Charley's BBQ, Fox's Pizza, Gay 90's Deli, KFC/LJ Silver, Pete's Drive Inn, Subway, Taco Time, **other:** [H], Grocery Outlet, Harvard Ave Drug, Hometown Drug
123	Roseburg, **E other:** to Umpqua Park, camping, museum
121	McLain Ave
120.5mm	S Umpqua River
120	OR 99 N (no EZ nb return), Green District, Roseburg, **E lodging:** Shady Oaks Motel, **W other:** Do It Hardware, auto repair
119	OR 99 S, OR 42 W, Winston, **E other:** Ingraham Dist., **W gas:** Chevron/A&W/dsl/24hr, Love's/Arby's/dsl/scales/LP/24hr, Shell/dsl, **food:** Coyote Jack's Grill, Fox's Pizza, McDonald's, Papa Murphy's, Subway, **other:** Ray's Foods, UPS, Western Star RV Park
113	Clarks Branch Rd, Round Prairie, **W lodging:** Quikstop Motel, **other:** On the River RV Park (2mi), Quikstop Mkt, dsl repair
112.5mm	S Umpqua River, S Umpqua River
112	OR 99, OR 42, Dillard, **E other:** Rivers West RV park, **rest area nb, full ♿ facilities, ⛱, ☎, litter barrels, petwalk**
111mm	**rest area sb, full ♿ facilities, ☎, ⛱, litter barrels, petwalk, weigh sta nb**
110	Boomer Hill Rd
108	Myrtle Creek, **E food:** DQ, Golf Course Cafe, Myrtle Creek Cafe, **other:** Myrtle Creek RV Park
106	Weaver Rd
103	Tri City, Myrtle Creek, **E other:** Tri-City RV Park, **W gas:** Chevron/A&W/dsl/24hr, Pacific Pride, **food:** McDonald's
102	Gazley Rd, **E** Surprise Valley RV Park (1mi)
101.5mm	S Umpqua River, S Umpqua River
101	Riddle, Stanton Park, **W** camping
99	Canyonville, **E gas:** Penny Pincher, **food:** Burger King, El Paraiso, **lodging:** Riverside Motel, 7 Feathers Hotel/casino, Valley View Motel, **other:** Canyon Mkt, **W gas:** 7 Feathers Trkstp/dsl/24/café/@, **food:** Creekside Rest., **lodging:** Best Western, **other:** 7 Feathers RV Resort
98	OR 99, Canyonville, Days Creek, **E gas:** 76/dsl, Shell/dsl/24hr, **food:** Canyon Cafe, El Pariso Mexican, Feed-Lot Rest., Ken's Cafe, Sarafino's Italian, **lodging:** Leisure Inn, **other:** NAPA, Ray's Foods, **W other:** Bill's Tire/repair, museum
95	Canyon Creek
90mm	Canyon Creek Pass, Canyon Creek Pass, elev 2020
88	Azalea
86	Barton Rd, Quine's Creek, **E gas:** Spirit/dsl/LP, **other:** Heaven on Earth Rest./rest., Meadow Wood RV Park (3mi)
83	Barton Rd (from nb), **E other:** Meadow Wood RV Park
82mm	**rest area both lanes, full ♿ facilities, ☎, ⛱, litter barrels, petwalk**
80	Glendale, **W gas:** Country Jct./LP, **food:** Village Inn Rest.
79.5mm	Stage Road Pass, elev 1830

INTERSTATE 5 CONT'D

N ↕ S

GRANTS PASS

Exit #	Services
78	Speaker Rd
76	Wolf Creek, **W gas:** Pacific Pride/dsl, 76/deli/dsl, Texaco/dsl/24hr, **food:** Wolf Creek Inn Rest., **other:** Creekside RV park, auto repair
74mm	Smith Hill Summit, elev 1730
71	Sunny Valley, **E lodging:** Sunny Valley Motel, **other:** Covered Bridge Store/gas, **W other:** Sunny Valley RV Park
69mm	Sexton Mtn Pass, elev 1960
66	Hugo, **E other:** Joe Creek Waterfalls RV Camping
63mm	**rest area both lanes, full [handicapped] facilities, [phone], info, [picnic], litter barrels, vending, petwalk**
61	Merlin, **W gas:** Shell/dsl, **other:** Almeda RV Park, Beaver Creek RV Resort (2mi), OR RV Ctr, Ray's Foods, Rouge Valley RV Ctr, repair
58	OR 99, to US 199, Grants Pass, **W gas:** CFN/dsl, Chevron, 76/dsl/RV dump, Shell/dsl/repair, Texaco/dsl, TownePump Gas, **food:** Burger King, Carl's Jr, China Hut, Della's Rest., DQ, Denny's, Hart's Cafe, Jack-in-the-Box, McDonald's, Muchas Gracias Mexican, Papa Murphy's, Pizza Hut, Sizzler, Subway, Taco Bell, Tubby's Rest., Wendy's, **lodging:** Best Way Inn, Comfort Inn, La Quinta, Motel 6, Royal Vue Motel, Shilo Inn, Sunset Inn, Super 8, SweetBreeze Inn, Travelodge, **other:** [H], AutoZone, Chevrolet/Honda, Chrysler/Dodge/Jeep, Curves, $Tree, Jack's RV Resort, Radio Shack, Ray's Foods, Rouge Valley RV Park, Schwab Tire, st police, towing
55	US 199, Redwood Hwy, E Grants Pass, **W gas:** Arco/24hr, CFN/dsl, **food:** Applebee's, Abby's Pizza, Arby's, Elmer's, Iguana Grill, McDonald's, Quizno's, Shari's/24hr, Si Casa Flores Mexican, Subway, Taco Bell, **lodging:** Best Western, Holiday Inn Express, **other:** [H], Albertson's/gas, Big Lots, Big O Tire, $Tree, Fred Meyer/gas/dsl, Grocery Outlet, JC Penney, Moon Mnt. PetCo, RV Park, Rite Aid, RiverPark RV Park, Schuck's Parts, Siskiyou RV Ctr, Staples, Walmart SuperCtr
48	Rogue River, **E gas:** Chevron/dsl, **food:** Abby's Pizza, Aunt Betty's, Baci's Pizza, Homestead Rest., Tarasco Mexican, **other:** Ace Hardware, Curves, NAPA, Rogue River Drug, Rogue River RA, **W food:** Karen's Kitchen, Mkt Basket Deli, **lodging:** Best Western, **other:** Chinook Winds RV Park, Bridgeview RV Park, Whispering Pines RV Park, visitors ctr/info
45b	**W other: Valley of the Rogue SP/rest area both lanes, full [handicapped] facilities, [phone], [picnic], litter barrels, petwalk, camping**
45mm	Rogue River
45a	OR 99, Savage Rapids Dam, **E other:** Cypress Grove RV Park
43	OR 99, OR 234, to Crater Lake, Gold Hill, **E food:** Rhino's Grill, **lodging:** B&B, Lazy Acres Motel/RV Park
40	OR 99, OR 234, Gold Hill, **E food:** Gold Hill Auto Ctr/gas, Patti's Kitchen, **other:** to Shady Cove Trail, KOA, Lazy Acres Motel/RV Park, Running Salmon RV Park, **W** Dardanell's RV Ctr/gas, Dardanell's Trailer Park
35	OR 99, Blackwell Rd, Central Point, **2-4 mi W** gas, food, lodging, st police, Jacksonville Nat Hist Landmark

MEDFORD

Exit #	Services
33	Central Point, **E gas:** Chevron, Pilot/Subway/Taco Bell/dsl/scales/24hr, **food:** Burger King, KFC, Quizno's, Shari's, Sonic, **lodging:** Candlewood Suites (2mi), Courtyard (2mi), Fairfield Inn, Holiday Inn Express, Super 8, **other:** RV Ctr, funpark, **W gas:** 76/Circle K/dsl, Shell/dsl/24hr, **food:** Abby's Pizza, Mazatlan Grill, McDonald's, **other:** Albertson's, USPO
30	OR 62, to Crater Lake, Medford, **E gas:** Chevron, Witham Trkstp/76/rest./dsl/24hr/@, **food:** Burger King, Carl's Jr., Del Taco, Elmer's, IHOP, Marie Callender's, McDonald's, Olive Garden, Outback Steaks, Panda Express, Papa John's, Pizza Hut, Quizno's, Red Robin, Si Casa Mexican, Sizzler, Sonic, Starbucks, Subway, Taco Bell, Taco Delite, Thai Bistro, Wendy's, **lodging:** Comfort Inn, Hampton Inn, Motel 6, Quality Inn, Ramada, Rogue Regency Hotel, Shilo Inn, **other:** Ace Hardware, Barnes&Noble, BigLots, BiMart Foods, Costco/gas, $Tree, Ford/Lincoln/Mercury, Fred Meyer, Food-4Less, Jo-Ann, Lowe's Whse, Mercedes, Michael's, Old Navy, Radio Shack, Ross, Safeway, Sears/auto, Schwab Tire, Sportsman's Whse, Triple A RV, USPO, Walmart, st police, **W gas:** Chevron/dsl, 76/dsl, Shell/dsl, **food:** KFC, King Wah Chinese, Red Lobster, Wendy's, **other:** [H], CarQuest, JC Penney, Kohl's, Macy's, Target, Toyota/Scion, mall
27	Barnett Rd, Medford, **E food:** Blackbear Diner, DQ, **lodging:** Best Western, Day's Inn/rest., Homewood Suites, Motel 6, Travelodge, **other:** [H], AAA, **W gas:** Chevron/24hr, 76/Circle K, Shell/dsl/24hr, **food:** Abby's Pizza, Arby's, Burger King, Carl's Jr, HomeTown Buffet, Jack-in-the-Box, KFC, Kim's Chinese, McDonald's, McGrath's FishHouse, Pizza Hut, Quizno's, Rooster's Rest., Senor Sam's Mexican, Shari's, Starbucks, Subway, Taco Bell, Wendy's, lodging:Capri Motel, Comfort Inn, Holiday Inn Express, Residence Inn, Royal Crest Motel, Springhill Suites, TownePlace Suites, **other:** Ford/Mercury/Lincoln, Fred Meyer, Grocery Outlet, Harry&David's, Office Depot, Radio Shack, Schwab Tires, Shucks Parts, Staples, Toyota, Walgreens, WinCo Foods
24	Phoenix, **E gas:** Petro/Iron Skillet/dsl/rest./scales/RV dump/24hr/@, **lodging:** PearTree Motel/rest./RV park, Super 8, **other:** Home Depot, Peterbilt/GMC, **W gas:** 76/Circle K/dsl, **food:** Angelo's Pizza, Annie's Cafe, Jack-in-the-Box, McDonald's, Sicasa Flores Mexican, **lodging:** Bavarian Inn, **other:** Curves, Ray's Foods, Holiday RV Park, Vet
22mm	**rest area sb, full [handicapped] facilities, [phone], [picnic], litter barrels, vending, petwalk**

INTERSTATE 5 CONT'D

N ↕ S — ASHLAND

Exit #	Services
21	Talent, **W gas:** Chevron/dsl, **food:** Avalon Grill, Figaro's Italian, **lodging:** GoodNight Inn, **other:** American RV Resort, Walmart/auto, repair
19	Valley View Rd, Ashland, **W gas:** Pacific Pride/dsl, 76/dsl, Shell/dsl/LP, **food:** Burger King, El Tapatio Mexican, **lodging:** Econolodge, La Quinta, **other:** Chevrolet, Ford
18mm	**weigh sta both lanes**
14	OR 66, to Klamath Falls, Ashland, **E gas:** Chevron, 76/dsl/LP, Shell/dsl, **food:** Miguel's, OakTree Rest., **lodging:** Best Western, Holiday Inn Express, Relax Inn, Windmill Inn, **other:** Emigrant Lake Camping (3mi), Glenyan RV Park (3mi), KOA (3mi), Nat Hist Museum, **W gas:** Arco/24hr, Texaco, **food:** Apple Bakery, Arrieo Mexican, Subway, Taco Bell, Wendy's, Wild Goose Cafe, Yuan yuan Chinese, **lodging:** Knight's Inn/rest., Super 8, **other:** Albertson's, Bi-Mart, Radio Shack, Rite Aid, Schwab Tire
11.5mm	chainup area
11	OR 99, Siskiyou Blvd (nb only, no return), **services 2-4 mi W**
6	to Mt Ashland, **E lodging:** Callahan's Siskiyou Lodge/rest., **other:** phone, ski area
4mm	Siskiyou Summit, elev 4310, brake check both lanes
1	to Siskiyou Summit, (from nb, no return)
0mm	Oregon/California state line

INTERSTATE 84

E ↕ W — ONTARIO, BAKER, LA GRANDE

Exit #	Services
378mm	Oregon/Idaho state line, Snake River
377.5mm	**Welcome Ctr wb, full ♿ facilities, info, ☎, 🛆, litter barrels, vending, petwalk**
376b a	US 30, to US 20/26, Ontario, Payette, **N gas:** Chevron/dsl, **food:** A&W/KFC, Burger King, Carl's Jr, China Buffet, Country Kitchen, DQ, Denny's, Domino's, McDonald's, Primo's Pizza, Quizno's, Taco Del Mar, Wingers, **lodging:** Best Western, Colonial Inn, Holiday Inn, Motel 6, Sleep Inn, Super 8, **other:** Chrysler/Dodge/Jeep, Curves, $Tree, Home Depot, K-Mart, Radio Shack, Staples, Toyota/Scion, Walgreens, Walmart SuperCtr/24hr, st police, **S gas:** CFN, Pilot/Arby's/dsl/scales/24hr, Shell/dsl, **food:** DJ's, Far East Chinese, Ogawa's Japanese, Rusty's Steaks, Sizzler, Subway, Taco Bell, Wendy's, **lodging:** Economy Inn, Holiday Inn Express, OR Trail Motel, Rodeway Inn, Stockman's Motel, **other:** H, Commercial Tire, NAPA, Radio Shack, Schwab Tire, 4 Wheeler Museum
374	US 30, OR 201, to Ontario, **N** to Ontario SP, **S gas:** Loves/Subway/dsl/scales/24hr/@, Pacific Pride, **lodging:** Budget Inn, **other:** H
373.5mm	Malheur River
371	Stanton Blvd, **2 mi S** to correctional institution
362	Moores Hollow Rd
356	OR 201, to Weiser, ID, **3 mi N** Catfish Junction RV Park, Oasis RV Park
354.5mm	**weigh sta eb**
353	US 30, to Huntington, **N weigh sta wb, gas:** Joy Travel Plaza/Texaco/rest./dsl, **lodging:** Farewell Bend Motel, **other:** to Farewell Bend SP, truck repair, RV camping, info
351mm	Pacific/Mountain time zone
345	US 30, Lime, Huntington, **1 mi N** gas, food, lodging, to Snake River Area, Van Ornum BFD
342	Lime (from eb)
340	Rye Valley
338	Lookout Mountain
337mm	Burnt River
335	to Weatherby, **N rest area both lanes, full ♿ facilities, Oregon Trail Info, 🛆, litter barrels, vending, petwalk**
330	Plano Rd, to Cement Plant Rd, **S** cement plant
329mm	pulloff eb
327	Durkee, **N gas:** Co-op/dsl/LP/café
325mm	Pritchard Creek
321mm	Alder Creek
317	to Pleasant Valley (from wb)
315	to Pleasant Valley (from wb)
313	to Pleasant Valley (from eb)
306	US 30, Baker, **2-3 mi S gas:** Chevron/dsl, **food:** DQ, **lodging:** Baker City Motel/RV Park, Bridge Street Hotel, OR Trail Motel/rest., **other:** H, Schwab Tire, to st police, same as 304
304	OR 7, Baker, **N gas:** Chevron/dsl, **lodging:** Super 8, Welcome Inn, **S gas:** Shell/dsl/24hr, Sinclair/dsl/rest./scales/24hr, **food:** Arceo's Mexican, Domino's, DQ, Fong's Chinese, Golden Crown, McDonald's, Papa Murphy's, Starbucks, Subway, Sumpter Jct Rest., Taco Time, **lodging:** Best Western, Budget Inn, Eldorado Inn, Geyser Grand Motel, Rodeway Inn, Western Motel, **other:** H, Albertson's/gas, Bi-Mart, CarQuest, $Tree, Ford, Mtn View RV Park (3mi), Rite Aid, Safeway Foods, museum, transmissions, to hist dist
302	OR 86 E to Richland, **S other:** H, Or Tr RV Park/LP, st police
298	OR 203, to Medical Springs
297mm	Baldock Slough
295mm	**rest area both lanes, full ♿ facilities, info, ☎, 🛆, litter barrels, vending, petwalk**
289mm	Powder River
287.5mm	45th parallel halfway between the equator and north pole
286mm	N Powder River
285	US 30, OR 237, North Powder, **N lodging:** North Powder Motel/cafe, **S other:** to Anthony Lakes, ski area
284mm	Wolf Creek
283	Wolf Creek Lane
278	Clover Creek
273	Frontage Rd
270	Ladd Creek Rd (from eb, no return)
269mm	**rest area both lanes, full ♿ facilities, info, ☎, 🛆, litter barrels, vending, petwalk**
268	Foothill Rd
265	OR 203, LaGrande, **N other:** Eagles Hot Lake RV Park, ✈, **S gas:** *FLYING J*/Shell/dsl/rest./scales/24hr, **food:** SmokeHouse Rest. (2mi), **other:** Freightliner
261	OR 82, LaGrande, **N gas:** Chevron/dsl, Shell/dsl, **food:** Burger King, Denny's, Pizza Hut, Quizno's, Starbucks, Taco Bell, **lodging:** LaGrande Inn, **other:** Chrysler/Dodge/Jeep, Ford/Lincoln/Mercury, Grocery Outlet, Thunder RV Ctr, Walmart Super Ctr, st police, Vet, **S gas:** Chevron, 76/Subway/dsl, Texaco/dsl,

OR

INTERSTATE 84 CONT'D

E ↕ W

Exit #	Services
261	Continued **food:** Bear Mtn. Pizza, China Buffet, Cinco de Mayo Mexican, DQ, Dutch Bro's Coffee, KFC, La Fiesta Mexican, McDonald's, Moy's Dynasty, Nell's Steakburger, Papa Murphy's, Smokehouse Rest., Taco Time, **lodging:** Best Value Inn, Best Western, Moon Motel, Orchard Motel, Royal Motel, Sandman Inn, Super 8, Travelodge, **other:** H, Albertson's, $Tree, Parts+, Rite Aid, Safeway/gas, Schwab Tire, Vet, E OR U, Wallowa Lake
260mm	Grande Ronde River
259	US 30 E (from eb), to La Grande, **1-2 mi S gas:** Chevron, Shell, **food:** Burger King, **lodging:** All-American Motel, Greenwell Motel/rest., Royal Motel, **other:** Safeway/gas, same as 261
257	Perry (from wb)
256.5mm	**weigh sta eb**
256	Perry (from eb)
255mm	Grande Ronde River
254mm	scenic wayside
252	OR 244, to Starkey, Lehman Springs, **S other:** Hilgard SP, camping, chainup area
251mm	Wallowa-Whitman NF, eastern boundary
248	Spring Creek Rd, to Kamela, **3 mi N** Oregon Trail Visitors Park
246mm	Wallowa-Whitman NF, western boundary
243	Summit Rd, Mt Emily Rd, to Kamela, Oregon Trail info, **2 mi N other:** Emily Summit SP
241mm	Summit of the Blue Mtns, elev 4193
238	Meacham, **1 mi N** food, **other:** Oregon Trail info
234	Meacham, **S other:** Emigrant Sprs SP, RV camping
231.5mm	Umatilla Indian Reservation, eastern boundary
228mm	**Deadman Pass, Oregon Trail info, rest area both lanes, full ♿ facilities, ☎ (wb), picnic, litter barrel, petwalk, vending, RV Dump (wb)**
227mm	**weigh sta wb, brake check area**
224	Poverty Flats Rd, Old Emigrant Hill Rd, to Emigrant Springs SP
223mm	wb viewpoint, no restrooms
221.5mm	eb viewpoint, no restrooms
220mm	wb runaway truck ramp
216	Mission, McKay Creek, **N gas:** Arrowhead Trkstp/Pacific Pride/McDonald's/dsl/24hr, **other:** Wildhorse Casino/RV Park
213	US 30 (from wb), Pendleton, **3-5 mi N gas:** Chevron/dsl, Shell, **lodging:** Travelers Inn, **other:** H, Pendleton NHD
212mm	Umatilla Indian Reservation western boundary
210	OR 11, Pendleton, **N other:** H, museum, st police, **S gas:** Chevron/Circle K/dsl, Shell/dsl/LP, **food:** Shari's/24hr, **lodging:** Best Western, Hampton Inn, Holiday Inn Express, Motel 6, Red Lion Inn/rest., Super 8, **other:** KOA
209	US 395, Pendleton, **N gas:** Arco, **food:** A&W/Taco Bell, DQ, Jack-in-the-Box, KFC, **lodging:** Oxford Suites, Travelodge, **other:** Dean's Mkt, $Tree, Radio Shack, Rite Aid, Safeway/dsl, Schuck's Parts, Walmart SuperCtr/Subway, **S gas:** Astro Gas, 76/dsl, **food:** Abby's Pizza, Burger King, Denny's, McDonald's, Rooster's Rest, Starbucks, Subway, Wendy's, **lodging:** Econolodge, **other:** Buick/Chevrolet/Pontiac, Honda, Schwab Tire, Thompson RV Ctr

LA GRANDE

PENDLETON

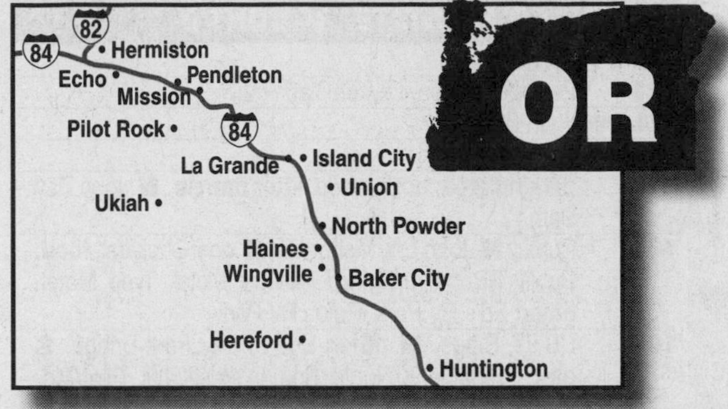

Exit #	Services
208mm	Umatilla River
207	US 30, W Pendleton, **N gas:** Shell/dsl/LP, **other:** Lookout RV Park, truck repair
202	Barnhart Rd, to Stage Gulch, **N** Woodpecker Truck Repair, **S lodging:** Rodeo Inn, **other:** Oregon Trail info
199	Stage Coach Rd, Yoakum Rd
198	Lorenzen Rd, McClintock Rd, **N other:** trailer/reefer repair
193	Echo Rd, to Echo, Oregon Trail Site
188	US 395 N, Hermiston, **N gas:** Chevron/dsl (1mi), Pilot/Subway/McDonald's/dsl/24hr/RV park, **5 mi N food:** Denny's/24hr, Jack-in-the-Box, McDonald's, Shari's/24hr, **lodging:** Best Western, Economy Inn, Oak Tree Inn, Oxford Suites, **other:** H, **S other:** Henrietta RV Park (1mi), Echo HS
187mm	**rest area both lanes, full ♿ facilities, ☎, info, picnic, litter barrels, petwalk**
182	OR 207, to Hermiston, **N other:** Space Age/A&W/dsl/LP/24hr, **food:** Macario's Mexican, **lodging:** Comfort Inn
180	Westland Rd, to Hermiston, McNary Dam, **N other:** Freightliner, trailer repair, **S gas:** Shell/Western Express/dsl/24hr
179	I-82 W, to Umatilla, Kennewick, WA
177	Umatilla Army Depot
171	Paterson Ferry Rd, to Paterson
168	US 730, to Irrigon, **8 mi N other:** Green Acres RV Park, Oasis RV Park, Oregon Trail info
165	Port of Morrow, **S gas:** Pacific Pride/dsl
164	Boardman, **N gas:** Chevron/Circle K/dsl, Shell/dsl, **food:** C&D Drive-In, Lynard's Cafe, **lodging:** Dodge City Motel, Riverview Motel, **other:** Boardman Drug, Boardman RV/Marina Park, USPO, **S gas:** Shell/dsl, **lodging:** Rodeway Inn, **lodging:** NAPA, Family Foods, Oregon Trail Library, tires
161mm	**rest area both lanes, full ♿ facilities, ☎, picnic, litter barrels, vending, petwalk**
159	Tower Rd
151	Threemile Canyon
147	OR 74, to Ione, Blue Mtn Scenic Byway, Heppner, Oregon Trail Site
137	OR 19, Arlington, **S gas:** Shell/dsl, **food:** Happy Canyon Cafe, Pheasant Grill, Village Inn, **other:** Ace Hardware, Arlington RV Park, Thrifty Foods, city park, USPO
136.5mm	view point wb, picnic, litter barrels
131	Woelpern Rd (from eb, no return)
129	Blalock Canyon, Lewis&Clark Trail

INTERSTATE 84 CONT'D

Exit #	Services
123	Philippi Canyon, Lewis&Clark Trail
114.5mm	John Day River
114	**S** LePage Park
112	**parking area, both lanes, litter barrels, N** John Day Dam
109	Rufus, **N** John Day Visitor Ctr, **S gas:** Shell/dsl, **food:** Bob's T-Bone, **lodging:** Hillview Motel, Tyee Motel, **other:** Ed's RV Park, Rufus RV Park
104	US 97, Biggs, **N other:** Des Chutes Park Bridge, **S gas:** 76/Circle K/Noble Roman's/dsl/24hr, Pilot/McDonald's/dsl/scales/24hr, Linda's/Shell/Subway/rest./dsl, **lodging:** Biggs Motel/café, Dinty's Motel, 3 Rivers Inn, **other:** Maryhill Museum, dsl repair
100mm	Deschutes River, Columbia River Gorge Scenic Area
97	OR 206, Celilo, **N other:** Celilo SP, restrooms, **S other:** Deschutes SP, Indian Village
92	pullout, eb
88	**N** to The Dalles Dam
87	US 30, US 197, to Dufur, **N gas:** Chevron, 76/dsl/24hr, **food:** McDonald's, Portage Grill, **lodging:** Comfort Inn, Shilo Inn/rest., **other:** Columbia Hills RV Park, Lone Pine RV Park, st police, **S food:** Big Jim's Drive-In, **lodging:** Riverview Inn, **other:** Schwab Tire
85	The Dalles, **N Riverfront Park, restrooms,** [phone], [picnic], **litter barrels, playground, marina, S gas:** Chevron, 76/dsl, Shell, **food:** Burgerville, Domino's, Taco Del Mar, **lodging:** Dalles Inn, Oregon Motel, **other:** [H], AJ's Radiators, Dalles Parts, NAPA, Toyota/Scion, TrueValue, camping, USPO, to Nat Hist Dist
83	(84 from wb) W The Dalles, **N food:** Casa El Mirador, Orient Café, **other:** Tire Factory, **S gas:** Shell/dsl, **food:** Arby's, Burger King, Denny's, DQ, Dutch Bro's Coffee, Ixtapa Mexican, KFC, McDonald's, Papa Murphy's, Quizno's, Shari's Rest., Skipper's, Starbucks, Subway, Taco Bell, Taco Time, Wendy's, **lodging:** Cousin's Inn/rest., Motel 6, Super 8, **other:** [H], Buick/GMC/Pontiac, Chevrolet, Chrysler/Dodge/Jeep, $Tree, Ford, Fred Meyer, Grocery Outlet, Jo-Ann Fabrics, K-Mart, Nissan, Oil Can Henry's, PetCo, Radio Shack, Rite Aid, Safeway, Schuck's Parts, Staples, Subaru, Walgreens
82	Chenowith Area, **S gas:** Astro/dsl/24hr, 76/dsl, **food:** Spooky's Café, **other:** Bi-Mart Foods, Columbia Discovery Ctr, Home Depot, museum, same as 83
76	Rowena, **N other:** Mayer SP, Lewis & Clark info, windsurfing
73mm	**Memaloose SP, rest area both lanes, full** [handicap] **facilities,** [picnic], **litter barrels,** [phone], **petwalk, RV dump, camping**
69	US 30, Mosier, **S food:** Goodriver Rest. 10 Speed East Rest., **other:** USPO
66mm	**N** Koberg Beach SP, **rest area wb, full facilities,** [picnic] **litter barrels**
64	US 30, OR 35, to White Salmon, Hood River, **N gas:** Chevron, Shell/24hr, **food:** McDonald's, Riverside Grill, Starbucks, **lodging:** Best Western, **other:** marina, museum, st police, **visitors info**
63	Hood River, City Ctr, **N gas:** 76/dsl, **S food:** Andrew's Pizza, Annz Cafe, Crazy Pepper Mexican, Horse Feathers Grill, Pietro's Pizza, Sage's Cafe, Taco Del Mar, 3 River's Grill, **lodging:** Hood River Hotel/rest., Oakstreet Hotel, **other:** [H], USPO, same as 64
62	US 30, Westcliff Dr, W Hood River, **N food:** Charburger, **lodging:** Columbia Gorge Hotel, Vagabond Lodge, **S gas:** Chevron/dsl/LP, 76/dsl, **food:** Domino's, DQ, Egg Harbor Cafe, HoHo Rest., Ixtapa Mexican, McDonald's, Pizzicato, Quizno's, Red Carpet Cafe, Starbucks, Subway, Taco Bell, **lodging:** Comfort Suites, Lone Pine Motel, Prater's Motel, Riverview Lodge, Sunset Motel, **other:** [H], Oil Can Henry's, Rite Aid, Safeway, Schwab Tire, Walmart
61mm	pulloff wb
60	service rd wb (no return)
58	Mitchell Point Overlook (from eb)
56	**N other:** Viento SP, RV camping, [phone]
55	Starvation Peak Tr Head (from eb), restrooms
54mm	**weigh sta wb**
51	Wyeth, **S** camping
49mm	pulloff eb
47	Forest Lane, Hermon Creek (from wb), camping
45mm	**weigh sta eb**
44	US 30, to Cascade Locks, **1-4 mi N gas:** CFN, Shell/dsl, **food:** Charburger, Pacific Crest Pub, **lodging:** Best Western, Bonneville Hot Spring Hotel, Bridge of the Gods Motel, Cascade Motel, Econolodge, Skamania Springs Hotel, **other:** to Bridge of the Gods, KOA, Stern Wheeler RV Park
41	Eagle Creek RA (from eb), to fish hatchery
40	**N other:** Bonneville Dam NHS, info, to fish hatchery
37	Warrendale (from wb)
35	Historic Hwy, Multnomah Falls, **S other:** Ainsworth SP, scenic loop highway, waterfall area, Fishery RV Park 31 Multnomah Falls (exits left from both lanes), **S lodging:** Multnomah Falls Lodge/Rest. (hist site), camping
31	Multnomah Falls (exits left from both lanes), **S** Multnomah Falls Lodge/Rest. (hist site), camping
30	**S** Benson SRA (from eb)
29	Dalton Point (from wb)
28	to Bridal Veil (7 mi return from eb), **S** USPO
25	**N** Rooster Rock SP
23mm	viewpoint wb, hist marker
22	Corbett, **2 mi S gas:** Corbett Mkt, **food:** View Point Rest., **other:** Crown Point RV Camping
19mm	Columbia River Gorge scenic area
18	Lewis&Clark SP, to Oxbow SP, lodging, food, RV camping
17.5mm	Sandy River
17	Marine Dr, Troutdale, **N food:** Wendy's, **lodging:** Holiday Inn Express, **S gas:** Chevron/24hr, ***FLYING J*** J/Roadside Diner/dsl/LP/scales/24hr, TA/Buckhorn Rest./Popeye's/Subway/dsl/scales/24hr/@, Shell/dsl, **food:** Arby's, McDonald's, Shari's/24hr, Subway, Taco Bell, Troutdale Diner, **lodging:** Comfort Inn, Motel 6, **other:** Premium Outlets/famous brands, Sandy Riverfront RV Resort
16	238th Dr, Fairview, **N gas:** Arco/dsl/24hr, **food:** Bronx Eatery, Burger King, Jack-in-the-Box, Quizno's, Taco Del Mar, **lodging:** Travelodge, **other:** Camping World, Walmart SuperCtr/24hr, **S gas:** 76, **lodging:** Best Western, **other:** [H]
14	207th Ave, Fairview, **N gas:** Shell/Taco Time/dsl, **food:** GinSun Chinese, **other:** American Dream RV Ctr, NAPA, Portland RV Park, Rolling Hills RV Park, auto repair

INTERSTATE 84 CONT'D

E ↔ W PORTLAND

Exit #	Services
13	181st Ave, Gresham, **N gas:** Chevron/dsl, **lodging:** Hampton Inn, **S gas:** Arco, Texaco, **food:** Burger King, Carl's Jr, Jung's Chinese, McDonald's, Plumtree Rest., Quizno's, RoundTable Pizza, Shari's/24hr, Starbucks, Tom's Pizza, Wendy's, Xavier's, **lodging:** Comfort Suites, Days Inn, Extended Stay America, Quality Inn, Sheraton, **other:** Albertson's, Candy Basket Chocolates, Curves, Rite Aid, Safeway, 7-11, 76, auto repair, Vet
10	122nd Ave (from eb)
9	I-205, S to Salem, N to Seattle, to ✈, (to 102nd Ave from eb)
8	I-205 N (from eb), **N** to ✈
7	Halsey St (from eb), Gateway Dist
6	I-205 S (from eb)
5	OR 213, to 82nd Ave (eb only), **N lodging:** Days Inn, **S food:** Eastern Cathay, **lodging:** Comfort Inn
4	68th Ave (from eb), to Halsey Ave
3	58th Ave (from eb), **S gas:** Shell, **other:** H, Fred Meyer
2	43rd Ave, 39th Ave, Halsey St, **N gas:** Chevron, 76, Shell, Texaco, **food:** Baja Fresh, Burger King, China Kitchen, McDonald's, Panera Bread, Quizno's, Poor Richard's Rest., Subway, **lodging:** Banfield Motel, Rodeway Inn, **other:** Radio Shack, Rite Aid, Trader Joe's, **S other:** H, Buick/Jeep/Pontiac, same as 1
1	33rd Ave, Lloyd Blvd (eb only), downtown, same as 2, **N food:** Applebee's, **lodging:** DoubleTree Inn, Residence Inn, **other:** $Tree, Macy's, Marshall's, JC Penney, Sears, **S food:** Pizza Hut, **other:** Cadillac
1	to downtown (wb only)
0mm	I-84 begins/ends on I-5, exit 301.

INTERSTATE 205 (PORTLAND)

N ↔ S PORTLAND AREA

Exit #	Services
37mm	I-205 begins/ends on I-5. Exits 36-27 are in Washington.
36	NE 134th St (from nb), **E gas:** Arco, 7-11, 76, TrailMart/dsl, **food:** Applebee's, Billygan's Roadhouse, Booster Juice, Burger King, Burgerville, Jack-in-the-Box, McDonald's, Muchas Gracias, Panda Express, Round Table Pizza, Starbucks, Subway, Taco Bell, Taco Del Mar, **lodging:** Comfort Inn, Holiday Inn Express, Olympia Motel, Red Lion, Salmon Creek Inn, Shilo Inn, **other:** H, Albertson's/gas, Long's Drugs, Safeway/gas, Zupan's Mkt, 99 RV Park, to Portland Airport, **W gas:** Shell, **food:** Baskin-Robbins, Coldstone, El Tapatio, Papa Murphy's, PizzaSchmitzza, Quizno's, Starbucks, The Great Impasta, **lodging:** La Quinta, **other:** Fred Meyer
32	NE 83rd St, Andreson Rd, Battle Ground, **W gas:** Shell/dsl/24hr, **food:** Burger King, Emporor Chinese, Krispy Kreme, Panda Express, Starbucks, Subway, Wendy's, Weinerschnitzel, **other:** Costco/gas, Home Depot
30c b a	WA 500, Orchards, Vancouver, **E gas:** 76, Shell/24hr, **food:** ABC Buffet, Applebee's, Burger King, Burgerville, DQ, Imperial Palace, McDonald's, Papa Murphy's, Starbucks, Subway, Wendy's, **other:** Jo-Ann Crafts, Office Depot, PetCo, Sportsman's Whse, Toyota, Tuesday Morning, Walgreens, **W gas:** Chevron/24hr,

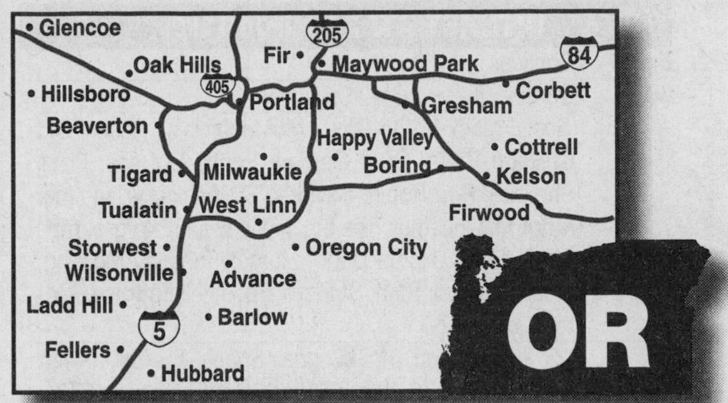

PORTLAND AREA

Exit #	Services
30c b a	Continued Shell/dsl, **food:** A&W, Azteca Mexican, Buffet City, Burgerville, Chevy's Mexican, ChuckeCheese, Elmer's Rest., Golden Tent BBQ, IHOP, Jamba Juice, Muchas Gracias, Newport Bay Seafood, Olive Garden, Outback Steaks, Red Lobster, Red Robin, RoundTable Pizza, Shari's/24hr, Starbucks, Subway, Taco Bell, TCBY, TGIFriday, **lodging:** Best Western, Comfort Suites, Ramada, Residence Inn, Rodeway Inn, Staybridge Inn, **other:** Americas Tire, Big Lots, $Tree, Ford, JC Penney, Lincoln/Mercury, Macy's, Old Navy, Ross, Sears/auto, Target, VW, mall, RV park
28	Mill Plain Rd, **E gas:** Chevron/24hr, 76/Circle K, Shell/dsl, **food:** Baskin-Robbins, Burger King, Burgerville, DQ, Elmer's Rest., Irishtown Grill, Kings Buffet, McDonald's, Muchas Gracias Mexican, Pizza Hut, Quizno's, Shari's, Starbucks, Taco Bell, **lodging:** Best Western, Extended Stay America, Motel 6, **other:** $Tree, Fred Meyer, PetCo, Schuck's Parts, Schwab Tire, 7-11, **W gas:** Arco/24hr, 76, 7-11, **food:** Arby's, Jack-in-the-Box, Subway, Taco Del Mar, **other:** H, Chevrolet, Walmart SuperCtr/24hr, Walgreens, auto/tire repair, Vet, transmissions
27	WA 14, Vancouver, Camas, Columbia River Gorge
25mm	Oregon/Washington state line. Columbia River. **Exits 27-36 are in Washington.**
24	122nd Ave, Airport Way, **E food:** Burger King, China Wok, CoffeeHouse, Jack-in-the-Box, McDonald's, Shari's, Subway, **lodging:** Clarion, Comfort Suites, Courtyard, Fairfield Inn, Hilton Garden, Holiday Inn Express, La Quinta, Residence Inn, Shilo Inn/rest., SpringHill Suites, Staybridge Suites, Super 8, **other:** Home Depot, **W lodging:** Embassy Suites, Hampton Inn, Loft Hotel, Sheraton/rest., **other:** Best Buy, PetsMart, Ross, Staples, ✈
23b a	US 30 byp, Columbia Blvd, **E gas:** Leather's Fuel/dsl, Shell/dsl, **food:** Bill's Steaks, Elmer's Rest., **lodging:** Best Western, Carolina Motel, Comfort Inn, Econolodge, Quality Inn, Rodeway Inn, **other:** H, **W gas:** Shell, **lodging:** Best Value Inn, Holiday Inn, Radisson, Ramada Inn, **other:** camping
22	I-84 E, US 30 E, to The Dalles
21b	I-84 W, US 30 W, to Portland
21a	Glisan St, **E on NE 102nd St...gas:** Arco, 76, **food:** Applebee's, Carl's Jr, Jamba Juice, Quizno's, McDonald's, **other:** Fred Meyer, Kohl's, Office Depot, Ross, WinCo Foods
20	Stark St, Washington St, **E gas:** Chevron/dsl, **food:** Arby's, Baja Fresh, Burger King, Denny's, Elmer's

INTERSTATE 205 (PORTLAND)

N ↕ S — PORTLAND AREA

Exit #	Services
20	Continued Rest., Jack-in-the-Box, McMenamin's Rest., Old Chicago Pizza, Olive Garden, Panda Express, Pizza Shmizza, Red Robin, Saylor's, Starbucks, Village Inn, **lodging:** Chestnut Tree Inn, Holiday Inn Express, **other:** Big Lots, Home Depot, Target, Tuesday Morning, mall, **W food:** Stark St Pizza, Taco Bell, **lodging:** Motel 6, **other:** 7-11
19	US 26, Division St, **E gas:** Space Age/dsl, **other:** H, **W gas:** 76, **food:** Burgerville, Campbell's BBQ, ChuckeCheese, McDonald's, Subway, **other:** Jo-Ann Fabrics, 7-11, Wal-Mart
17	Foster Rd, **1 mi W gas:** Chevron, 76, Shell, **food:** Arby's, Burger King, IHOP, McDonald's, Wendy's, **lodging:** Econolodge, Home Depot, **other:** U-Haul
16	Johnson Creek Blvd, **W gas:** 76, **food:** Applebee's, Arby's, Bajio, Burger King, Carl's Jr, Jack-in-the-Box, Krispy Kreme, McDonald's, Outback Steaks, Pizza Shmizza, Quizno's, Ron's Café, RoundTable Pizza, Starbucks, Subway, Taco Bell, WeiWei, **other:** Best Buy, Fred Meyer/gas, Home Depot, Knecht's Parts, PetsMart, RV Ctrs, Schuck's Parts, 7-11, Trader Joe's, Walgreens, Wal-Mart
14	Sunnyside Rd, **E gas:** 76, **food:** A&W/KFC, Baja Fresh, Chen's Kitchen, Domino's, Gustav's Grill, Izzy's Pizza, KFC, McMenamin's, Quizno's, Starbucks, Subway, TCBY, **lodging:** Best Western, Days Inn, **other:** H, Office Depot, **W gas:** Texaco/dsl/24hr, **food:** Burger King, CA Pizza Kitchen, Chevy's Mexican, Chili's, Claim Jumper, Denny's, DQ, Macaroni Grill, McDonald's, Noodles&Co, Old Spaghetti Factory, Olive Garden, Pizza Hut, Red Robin, Stanford's Rest., Taco Time, Wendy's, **lodging:** Courtyard, Monarch Hotel/rest., **other:** America's Tire, Barnes&Noble, JC Penney, Kohl's, Macy's, Nordstroms, Old Navy,
14	Continued PetCo, Sears/auto, Target, U-Haul, Walgreens, World Mkt, mall
13	OR 224, to Milwaukie, **W other:** K-Mart, Lowe's Whse
12	OR 213, to Milwaukie, **E gas:** Chevron/24hr, Pacific Pride, Shell, **food:** Denny's, Elmer's, KFC, McDonald's, Subway, Taco Bell/24hr, Wendy's, **lodging:** Clackamas Inn, Hampton Inn, **other:** Fred Meyer, 7-11, **W lodging:** Comfort Suites
11	82nd Dr, Gladstone, **W gas:** Arco/24hr, Chevron, **food:** McDonald's, **lodging:** Oxford Suites, **other:** Harley-Davidson, Safeway, Starbucks
100	R 213, Park Place, **E gas:** 76/Pacific Pride/dsl, **other:** H, Home Depot, to Oregon Trail Ctr
90	R 99E, Oregon City, **E gas:** Chevron, 76, **food:** KFC, **other:** H, NAPA, Subaru, **W food:** La Hacienda Mexican, McDonald's, Shari's, Starbucks, Subway, Thai Rest., **lodging:** Best Western Rivershore, **other:** Coastal Ranch Store, $Tree, Firestone/auto, Michael's, Rite Aid
8.5mm	Willamette River
80	R 43, W Linn, Lake Oswego, **E other:** museum, **W gas:** 76, Shell/dsl/24hr, **food:** Blue Sage Cafe, Centanni's Pizza, Coldstone Creamery, Starbucks, Taco Del Mar, **other:** Mkt of Choice, USPO
7mm	viewpoint nb, hist marker
6	10th St, W Linn St, **E gas:** Chevron/LP, 76, **food:** 5 Guys Burgers, Ixtapa Mexican, McDonald's, McMenamin's Rest., Papa Murphy's, Rose's Rest, Shari's/24hr, Wilamet Coffee House, **other:** Oil Can Henry's, Schwab Tire, **W food:** Jack-in-the-Box, Starbucks, Subway, **other:** Albertsons/Sav-On
4mm	Tualatin River
3	Stafford Rd, Lake Oswego, **W food:** Corner Saloon, **other:** H
0mm	I-205 begins/ends on I-5, exit 288.

OR / PA

PENNSYLVANIA

INTERSTATE 70

E ↕ W — BREEZEWOOD

Exit #	Services
171mm	Pennsylvania/Maryland state line, **Welcome Ctr wb, full ♿ facilities, info, ☎, vending, picnic, litter barrels, petwalk**
168	US 522 N, Warfordsburg, **N gas:** Exxon/dsl, **S** fireworks
163	PA 731 S, Amaranth
156	PA 643, Town Hill, **N lodging:** Day's Inn, **other:** NAPA
153mm	**rest area eb, full ♿ facilities, ☎, picnic, litter barrels, vending, petwalk**
151	PA 915, Crystal Spring, **N food:** CornerStone Family Rest., **other:** auto repair, **S other:** Country Store/USPO
149	US 30 W, to Everett, S Breezewooo immediate wb return), **3 mi S food:** McDonald's, **lodging:** Penn Aire Motel, Redwood Motel, Wildwood Motel
147	US 30, Breezewood, **Services on US 30...gas:** BP/dsl, Citgo, Exxon/dsl, Mobil/dsl/24hr, Sheetz/24hr, Shell, Sunoco/dsl/café, TA/dsl/rest./24hr/@,
147	Continued Texaco/Subway, **food:** Arby's, Big John's Buffet, Bob Evans, Burger King, DQ, Denny's, Domino's, Family House Rest., Hardee's, KFC, McDonald's, Perkins, Pizza Hut, Taco Bell, Wendy's, **lodging:** Best Western, Breezewood Motel, Comfort Inn/rest., Econolodge, Holiday Inn Express, Penn Aire Motel, Quality Inn, Ramada Inn, Wiltshire Motel, **other:** museum I-70 W and I-76/PA Turnpike W run together
I-70 and	**I-76/PA Turnpike run together 71 mi. For I-70 and I-76/PA TPK Exits 146-75 See Pennsylvania Interstate 76/PA TPK.**
142mm	**parking area wb**
57	I-70 W, US 119, PA 66 (toll), New Stanton, **N gas:** Exxon, Sheetz, **food:** Bob Evans, Eat'n Park, KFC, McDonald's, Pagano's Rest., Pizza Hut, Quizno's, Subway, Szechuan Wok, Wendy's, **lodging:** Budget Inn, Comfort Inn, Day's Inn, Fairfield Inn, Howard Johnson, Quality Inn, Super 8, **S gas:** BP/7-11/dsl, Sunoco/24hr, **food:** Cracker Barrel, La Tavola Risorante, TJ's Rest., **other:** USPO

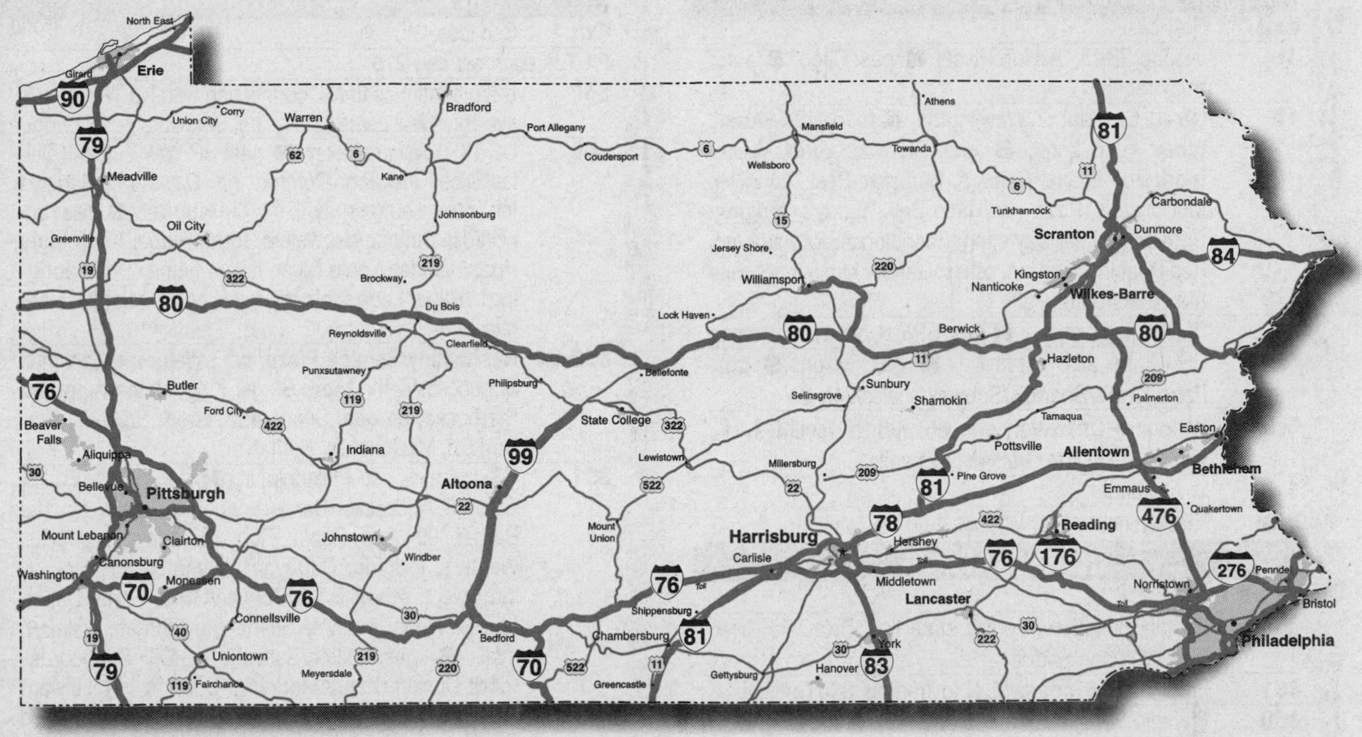

INTERSTATE 70 CONT'D

E ↕ W

Exit #	Services
54	Madison, **N** KOA, truck repair
53	Yukon
51b a	PA 31, West Newton
49	Smithton, **N** **gas:** Citgo/dsl/rest./scales/@, *FLYING J*/Country Mkt/dsl/scales/LP/24hr/@
46b a	PA 51, Pittsburgh, **N** **gas:** BP/dsl, **food:** Burger King, **lodging:** Comfort Inn, **other:** Buick/Cadillac/Chevrolet/Kia/Pontiac, Harley-Davidson, **S** **gas:** GetGo/dsl/24hr, **lodging:** Holiday Inn, Knotty Pine Motel, Relax Inn
44	Arnold City
43b a	(43 from eb)PA 201, Fayette City, **S** **gas:** Exxon/24hr, **food:** A&W/LJ Silver, Burger King, China 88 Buffet, Denny's, Eat'n Park, Hoss' Rest., KFC, Little Bamboo, McDonald's, Pizza Hut, Quizno's, Sonny's Grille, Starbucks, Subway, Wendy's, **lodging:** Hampton Inn, **other:** Advance Parts, Aldi Foods, Big Lots, Curves, CVS Drug, $General, $Tree, Giant Eagle Foods, GNC, Jo-Ann Fabrics, K-Mart, Lowes Whse, Radio Shack, Rite Aid, Staples, Walmart SuperCtr
42a	Monessen
42	N Belle Vernon, **S** **gas:** BP/7-11/McDonald's, Sunoco/dsl, **food:** DQ
41	PA 906, Belle Vernon
40mm	Monongahela River
40	PA 88, Charleroi, **N** **gas:** BP, Gulf, Sunoco, **food:** McDonald's, **other:** [H], Sav-a-Lot Foods, Valley Tire
39	Speers, **N** **food:** Loraine's Rest., **S** **gas:** Exxon
37b a	PA 43
36	Lover (from wb, no re-entry)
35	PA 481, Centerville
32b a	PA 917, Bentleyville, **S** **gas:** BP/dsl, Pilot/DQ/Sub

FAYETTE CITY

Exit #	Services
32b a	Continued way/dsl/scales/24hr, **food:** Burger King, CJ's Cafe, King Rest., McDonald's, **lodging:** Best Western, Holiday Inn Express, **other:** Advance Parts, Blue Beacon, $General, Ford, Giant Eagle Foods, Rite Aid
31	to PA 136, Kammerer, **N** **lodging:** Carlton Motel, **food:** Carlton Kitchen
27	Dunningsville, **S** **lodging:** Avalon Motel
25	PA 519, to Eighty Four, **S** **gas:** BP/7-11 Diner/dsl/24hr, Sunoco/dsl
21	I-79 S, to Waynesburg
I-70 W and I-79 N run together 3.5 mi.	
20	PA 136, Beau St, **S** to Washington & Jefferson Coll
19b a	US 19, Murtland Ave, **N** **food:** Applebee's, Arby's, Bruster's, Cracker Barrel, Krispy Kreme, Max&Erma's, McDonald's, Outback Steaks, Panera Bread, Ponderosa, Quizno's, Red Lobster, Red Robin, Starbucks, Subway, TX Roadhouse, TGIFriday, **lodging:** Springhill Suites, **other:** Aldi Foods, $Tree, Giant Eagle Foods, GNC, Honda, Hyundai, JC Penney, Kohl's, Lowes Whse, Mercedes, Michael's, Nissan, PetCo, PetsMart, Radio Shack, Sam's Club/gas, Sav-a-Lot Foods, Target, Toyota, Walmart SuperCtr/24hr, Vet, **S** **gas:** BP/dsl, Exxon, Sunoco, Valero, **food:** A&W/LJ Silver, Bob Evans, CiCi's Pizza, Eat'n Park/24hr, Evergreen Chinese, KFC, Old Mexico, Papa John's, Pizza Hut, **lodging:** Hampton Inn, Motel 6, **other:** [H], Big Lots, Buick/Cadillac/GMC, Firestone/auto, Home Depot, Jo-Ann Fabrics, Rite Aid, Staples, Subaru, mall
18	**I-79 N, to Pittsburgh. I-70 E & I-79 S run together 3.5 mi.**
17	PA 18, Jefferson Ave, Washington, **N** **gas:** GetGo, **food:** DQ, McDonald's, **other:** Family$, Rite Aid, **S** **gas:** CoGo's/dsl, Sunoco, **food:** Burger King, Domino's, 4Star Pizza, Little Caesars, Subway, **other:** Advance Parts

WASHINGTON

INTERSTATE 70 CONT'D

Exit #	Services
16	Jessop Place, Jessop Place, **N gas:** Citgo, **S** auto/truck repair
15	US 40, Chesnut St, Washington, **N food:** USA Steaks, **other:** Food Land, **S gas:** BP, Sunoco/dsl, Valero, **food:** Bob Evans, Denny's, Garfield's Rest., LJ Silver, McDonald's, Pizza Hut, Taco Bell, Wendy's, **lodging:** Comfort Suites, Day's Inn, Econolodge, Ramada Inn, Red Roof Inn, The Inn, **other:** Gander Mtn Macy's, Rite Aid, Sears/auto, mall
11	PA 221, Taylorstown, **N gas:** BP/dsl, **other:** truck repair
6to	US 40, PA 231, Claysville, **N gas:** Exxon, **S gas:** Petro/King's/Sbarro's/Subway/scales/24hr@
5mm	**Welcome Ctr/weigh sta. eb, full [♿] facilities, [☎], vending, [picnic], litter barrels, petwalk**
1	W Alexander
0mm	Pennsylvania/West Virginia state line

INTERSTATE 76

Exit #	Services
354mm	Pennsylvania/New Jersey state line, Delaware River, Walt Whitman Bridge
351	Front St, I-95 (from wb), N to Trenton, S to Chester
350	Packer Ave, 7th St, to I-95 (fromeb), **S lodging:** Holiday Inn, **other:** to sports complex
349	to I-95, PA 611, Broad St
348	PA 291, W to Chester, **S lodging:** Ramada Inn
347a	to I-95 S
347b	Passyunk Ave, Oregon Ave, **S other:** sports complex
346c	28th St, Vare Ave, Mifflin St (from wb)
346b	Grays Ferry Ave, University Ave, civic center, **N food:** McDonald's, PathMark Foods, **other:** Radio Shack, **S gas:** BP/24hr, Hess
346a	South St
345	30th St, Market St, downtown
344	I-676 E, US 30 E, to Philadelphia (no return from eb)
343	Spring Garden St, Haverford
342	US 13, US 30 W, Girard Ave, Philadelphia Zoo, E Fairmount Park
341	Montgomery Dr, W River Dr, W Fairmount Park, W Fairmount Park
340b	US 1 N, Roosevelt Blvd, to Philadelphia
339	US 1 S, **S lodging:** Adams Mark Hotel, Holiday Inn
340a	Lincoln Dr, Kelly Dr, to Germantown
338	Belmont Ave, Green Lane, **N other:** CVS Drug, **S gas:** Sunoco/24hr, **food:** WaWa
337	Hollow Rd (from wb), Gladwyne
332	PA 23 (from wb), Conshohocken, **N lodging:** Marriott
331b a	I-476, PA 28 (from eb), to Chester, Conshohocken
330	PA 320, Gulph Mills, **S** to Villanova U
328	US 202 N, to King of Prussia, **N gas:** Exxon/dsl, Mobil, WaWa, **food:** Charlie's Place Rest., Dunkin Donuts, Friendly's, Sizzler, TGIFriday, Uno Pizzaria, **lodging:** Econolodge, Holiday Inn, Howard Johnson, McIntosh Inn, **other:** JC Penney, Macy's, Sears/auto, Thrift Drug, mall, **S** George Washington Lodge
327	US 202 S, Goddard Blvd, to Valley Forge, Valley Forge Park, Valley Forge Park
326	I-76 wb becomes I-76/PA Tpk to Ohio

For I-76 westbound to Ohio, see I-76/PA Turnpike.

INTERSTATE 76 (TURNPIKE)

Exit #	Services
	PA Tpk runs wb as I-276.
359	I-276 continues to NJ, connecting with NJ TPK, Pennsylvania/New Jersey state line, Delaware River Bridge
358	US 13, Delaware Valley, **N gas:** BP, WaWa, **food:** Dallas Diner, **lodging:** Comfort Inn, Day's Inn, Ramada Inn, **other:** auto repair, 7-11, U-Haul, Vet, **S gas:** LukOil/dsl, Sunoco/dsl, Valero, **food:** Burger King, Gigi's Pizza, Golden Eagle Diner, Italian Family Pizza, **lodging:** Villager Lodge, **other:** Buick, $General, Mr. Transmission
352mm	**Neshaminy Service Plaza, wb...Welcome Ctr, gas:** Sunoco/dsl/24hr, **food:** Burger King, Nathan's, **other:** Starbucks, eb **gas:** Sunoco/dsl, **food:** Breyer's, Hot-Dog Co, McDonald's, Nathan's
351	US 1, to I-95, to Philadelphia, **N food:** Bob Evans, Chick-fil-A, Cracker Barrel, Longhorn Steaks, On The Border, 99, Red Robin, Ruby Tuesday, Starbucks, Wendy's, **lodging:** Courtyard, Hampton Inn, Holiday Inn Select, **other:** Buick/Pontiac/GMC, Home Depot, Lowes Whse, Macy's, Sears/auto, Target, Walmart, mall, **S gas:** Exxon/Subway, LukOil, Sunoco/dsl, **food:** Dunkin Donuts, **lodging:** Comfort Inn, Howard Johnson, Knight's Inn, Neshaminy Inn, Radisson, Red Roof Inn, Sunrise Inn, **other:** Toyota/Scion
343	PA 611, Willow Grove, **N gas:** Shell, **food:** Carrabba's, **lodging:** Candlewood Suites (5mi), Courtyard, **other:** [H], **S gas:** Hess/dsl, Shell, Sunoco, **food:** Bennigan's, Bonefish Grill, China Garden, Domino's, Dunkin Donuts, Friendly's, McDonald's, Nino's Pizza, Ooka Japanese, Starbucks, Williamson Rest., **lodging:** Hampton Inn, **other:** Audi/Infiniti, Best Buy, Pep-Boys, 7-11, Staples, repair, transmissions
340	VA Dr., EZ tagholder only, no trucks, no return eb (New Exit)
339	PA 309, Ft Washington, **N gas:** Gulf, LukOil/dsl, **food:** Dunkin Donuts, Friendly's, Subway, **lodging:** Best Western, Hilton Garden, Holiday Inn, **other:** BMW, Mercedes, Volvo, WaWa
334	PA Tpk NE Extension, I-476 S. to Philadelphia, N to Allentown
333	Germantown Pike, to Norristown, **N gas:** LukOil/dsl, Sunoco/Dunkin Donuts, **food:** California Pizza Kitchen, Houlihan's, PF Chang's, Red Stone Grill, Starbucks, **lodging:** Courtyard, DoubleTree, Extended Stay America, SpringHill Suites, **other:** [H], Boscov's, Macy's, **S gas:** LukOil
328mm	**King of Prussia Service Plaza wb** Sunoco/dsl/24hr, Breyer's, McDonald's
	PA Tpk runs eb as I-276, wb as I-76.
326	I-76 E, to US 202, I-476, Valley Forge, **N gas:** Shell, **food:** Burger King, Cracker Barrel, Hooters, Hoss' Rest., **lodging:** MainStay Suites, Radisson, Sleep Inn, **S gas:** Exxon, LukOil, Shell, Sunoco, WaWa, **food:** American Grill, Bennigan's, California Pizza Kitchen, Cheesecake Factory, Chili's, Denny's, Houlihan's, Lone Star Steaks, Maggiano's, McDonald's, Red Lobster, Ruth's Chriss Steaks, Sullivan Steaks, **lodging:** Best Western, Comfort Inn, Hampton Inn, Holiday Inn Express, McIntosh Inn, Motel 6, **other:** Borders Books, Best Buy, Costco, Crate&Barrel, Home Depot, JC Penney, Macy's, Neiman Marcus, Nordstrom, Sears/auto, Walmart SuperCtr, mall

INTERSTATE 76 CONT'D (TURNPIKE)

E ↕ W

Exit #	Services
325mm	**Valley Forge Service Plaza eb gas:** Sunoco/dsl/24hr, **food:** Burger King, Nathan's, Starbucks, TCBY, gifts
312	PA 100, to Downingtown, Pottstown, **N gas:** Valero, **other:** CarSense, Harley-Davidson, **S gas:** Sunoco/dsl/24hr, WaWa, **food:** Hoss' Rest, Isaac's Rest, Quizno's, Red Robin, Starbucks, Uno, **lodging:** Comfort Suites, Extended Stay America, Fairfield Inn, Hampton Inn, Holiday Inn Express, Inn at Chester Springs, Residence Inn, **other:** H
305mm	**Camiel Service Plaza wb**...Sunoco/dsl/24hr, Mrs Fields, Roy Rogers, Sbarro's, Starbucks, TCBY, gifts
298	I-176, PA 10, to Reading, Morgantown, **N lodging:** Economy Lodge, Heritage Motel/rest., **other:** H, Walmart SuperCtr, **S gas:** Exxon, Sheetz, **food:** McDonald's, **lodging:** Holiday Inn, **other:** Chevrolet, Rite Aid
290mm	**Bowmansville Service Plaza eb...gas:** Sunoco/dsl/24hr, **food:** Big Boy, Pizza Hut, Starbucks, Taco Bell, TCBY, **other:** gifts
286	US 322, PA 272, to Reading, Ephrata, **N gas:** Citgo/dsl, Turkey Hill, **food:** Bejing Chef, Park Place Diner, Subway, Zia Maria Italian, **lodging:** Black Horse Lodge/rest., Knights Inn, Penn Amish Motel, **other:** Antiques Galore, Dutch Cousins Camping, **S gas:** Turkey Hill, **food:** Dunkin Donuts, **lodging:** Econo Lodge, Holiday Inn, Red Carpet Inn
266	PA 72, to Lebanon, Lancaster, **N gas:** Hess/Blimpie/dsl, Sunoco, **food:** Farmer's Hope Inn Rest, **lodging:** Holiday Inn Express (17 mi), Red Carpet Inn, Rodeway Inn, **other:** Harley-Davidson, NAPA, **S food:** Hitz Mkt/deli, **lodging:** Hampton Inn, **other:** H, Mt Hope Winery, Pinch Pond Camping
259mm	**Lawn Service Plaza wb...gas:** Sunoco/dsl/24hr, **food:** Burger King, Hershey's Ice Cream, Starbucks, Uno, **other:** RV dump
250mm	**Highspire Service Plaza eb...gas:** Sunoco/dsl/24hr, **food:** Sbarro's
247	I-283, PA 283, to Harrisburg, Harrisburg East, Hershey, **N gas:** Exxon/dsl, Sunoco, **food:** Bob Evans, Capitol Diner, Eat'n Park, McDonald's, Taco Bell, Wendy's, **lodging:** Best Western, Courtyard, Day's Inn, EconoLodge, Holiday Inn Express, Howard Johnson, La Quinta, Red Roof Inn, Rodeway Inn, Sheraton, Super 8, Travelodge, Wingate Inn, Wyndham, **other:** Harrisburg East Camping, JC Penney, Kia, Target
246mm	Susquehannah River
242	I-83, Harrisburg West, **N gas:** BP, Hess/Dunkin Donuts, **food:** Bob Evans, Doc Holliday's Rest, Eat'n Park, McDonald's, Pizza Hut, **lodging:** Best Western, Comfort Inn, Holiday Inn, Motel 6, Quality Inn, Rodeway Inn, Travel Inn, **other:** Vet, **S lodging:** Days Inn, Keystone Inn
236	US 15, to Gettysburg, Gettysburg Pike, Harrisburg, **N gas:** BP/dsl, Exxon, **food:** Isaac's Rest, McDonald's, Papa John's, Peppermill Rest, Subway, **lodging:** Comort Inn, Country Inn&Suites, Courtyard, EconoLodge, Hampton Inn/rest., Holiday Inn, Homewood Suites, **other:** H, U-haul, Vet, **S gas:** Sheetz/24hr, **food:** Arby's, Burger King, Cracker Barrel, Quizno's, Wendy's, **lodging:** Best Western, Wingate Inn, **other:** Giant Food/gas/24hr, GNC, Rite Aid

HARRISBURG

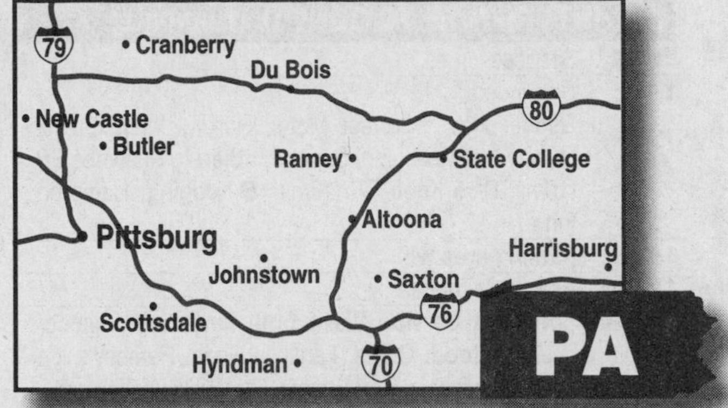

Exit #	Services
226	US 11, to I-81, to Harrisburg, Carlisle, **N gas:** BP, Petro/dsl/24hr/@, ***FLYING J***/dsl/LP/rest./24hr/scales, Pilot/Wendy's/dsl/24hr, Shell/dsl/scales, Sunoco, Universal/dsl, **food:** Arby's, Bob Evans, Carelli's Subs, Country Club Diner, Country Oven Rest, Dunkin Donuts, Ember's Steaks, McDonald's, Middlesex Diner/24hr, Waffle House, **lodging:** Best Inn, EconoLodge, Hampton Inn, Holiday Inn, Hotel Carlisle, Howard Johnson, Quality Inn, Ramada Ltd, Residence Inn, Rodeway Inn, Super 8, Travelodge, **other:** H, Blue Beacon, **S gas:** Rutter's, Sheetz/24hr, Turkey Hill, **food:** Hoss' Rest., **lodging:** Best Western, Motel 6, **other:** H, U-haul, Vet
219mm	**Plainfield Service Plaza eb...gas:** Sunoco/dsl/24hr, **food:** Hershey's Ice Cream, Roy Rogers, **other:** gifts
203mm	**Blue Mtn Service Plaza wb...gas:** Sunoco/dsl/24hr, **food:** Nathan's, Hershy's Ice Cream, Roy Rogers, Uno
201	PA 997, to Shippensburg, Blue Mountain, **S lodging:** Johnnie's Motel/rest., Kenmar Motel
199mm	Blue Mountain Tunnel
197mm	Kittatinny Tunnel
189	PA 75, Willow Hill, **S lodging:** Willow Hill Motel/rest.
187mm	Tuscarora Tunnel
180	US 522, Ft Littleton, **N gas:** BP/dsl, Noname/dsl, **food:** The Family Rest., **lodging:** Downes Motel, **other:** H, st police
172mm	**Sideling Hill Service Plaza both lane S gas:** Sunoco/dsl/24hr, **food:** Burger King, Famiglia Pizza, Hershey's Ice Cream, Popeye's, Starbucks, **other:** gifts
161	US 30, **Breezewood, Services on US 30...gas:** TA/Gateway Rest/dsl/rest./24hr/@, BP/dsl, Exxon/dsl, Petro/Blue Beacon, Sheetz/24hr, Shell/Blimpie, Sunoco/dsl/café, Valero/dsl, **food:** Bob Evans, DQ, Denny's, Domino's, Family House Rest., Hardee's, KFC, McDonald's, Perkins, Pizza Hut, Quizno's, Starbucks, Subway, Taco Bell, Wendy's, **lodging:** Best Western, Breezewood Motel, Holiday Inn Express, Howard Johnson, Penn Aire Motel, Quality Inn, Ramada Inn, Village Motel, Wiltshire Motel, **other:** Radio Shack, camping, museum, truck/tire repair
161mm	**I-70 W and I-76/PA Turnpike W run together**
150mm	roadside park wb
148mm	**Midway Service Plaza both lanes**, Sunoco/dsl/24hr, Hershey's Ice Cream, KFC, Quizno's, Sbarro's, Starbucks, gifts
146	US 220, to I-99, Bedford, **N gas:** BP/dsl, Pacific Pride, Sheetz/dsl, **food:** Arena Rest., Denny's, Ed's Steaks, Hoss' Rest., LJ Silver, McDonald's, Pizza Hut, Subway, Wendy's, **lodging:** Best Western,

BREEZEWOOD

INTERSTATE 76 CONT'D (TURNPIKE)

Exit # Services

146 Continued
Budget Host, Hillcrest Motel, Holiday Inn Express, Quality Inn, Relax Inn, Super 8, **other:** to Shawnee SP (10mi), Blue Knob SP (15mi), **S lodging:** Hampton Inn

142mm **parking area wb**

123mm Allegheny Tunnel

112mm **Somerset Service Plaza both lanes...eb** Sunoco/dsl/24hr, **food:** Chili's, Famiglia Pizza, Hershey's Ice Cream, Quizno's, Roy Rogers, Starbucks, **other:** gifts

110 PA 601, to US 219, Somerset, **N gas:** KwikFill/dsl, Sheetz/24hr, **food:** Hog Father's BBQ, Hoss' Rest., King's Rest., Pizza Hut, **lodging:** $ Inn, Economy Inn, **other:** Advance Parts, Chrysler/Jeep, Ford, tires, **S gas:** Somerset TravelCtr/dsl/@, Turkey Hill, **food:** Arby's, Bruster's Ice Cream, DQ, Donut Connection, Eat'n Park, KFC, LJ Silver, Maggie Mae's Café, McDonald's, Pine Grill, Ruby Tuesday, Starbucks, Subway, Summit Diner, Wendy's, **lodging:** Best Western, Budget Host, Budget Inn, Day's Inn, Hampton Inn, Holiday Inn, Knight's Inn, Quality Inn, Super 8, **other:** Dodge, Harley-Davidson

91 PA 711, Donegal, **N food:** Tall Cedars Rest., **S gas:** BP/McDonald's, Exxon/Subway/dsl, Sunoco/dsl, **food:** DQ, Ladle's Rest., **lodging:** Day's Inn, **other:** camping, golf

78mm **service plaza wb...gas:** Sunoco/dsl/24hr, **food:** Quizno's, Starbucks, Uno

I-70 E runs with I-76/PA Turnpike eb.

75 I-70 W, US 119, PA 66 (toll), New Stanton, **N gas:** Exxon, Sheetz, **food:** Bob Evans, Eat'n Park, KFC, McDonald's, Pagano's Rest., Pizza Hut, Quizno's, Subway, Szechuan Wok, Wendy's, **lodging:** Budget Inn, Comfort Inn, Day's Inn, Fairfield Inn, Howard Johnson, Quality Inn, Super 8, **S gas:** BP/7-11/dsl, Sunoco/24hr, **food:** Cracker Barrel, La Tavola Risorante, TJ's Rest., **other:** USPO

74.6mm **Hemphill Service Plaza eb...gas:** Sunoco/dsl/24hr, **food:** Breyer's, McDonald's, **other:** atm

67 US 30, to Greensburg, Irwin, **N gas:** BP/dsl, Sheetz/24hr, **other:** [H], Ford, tires, Vet, **S gas:** Marathon/7-11, Sunoco/24hr, **food:** Arby's, Bob Evans, Burger King, CiCi's Pizza, Denny's, DQ, Dunkin Donuts, Eat'n Park, KFC, LJ Silver, Los Campesinos Mexican, McDonald's, Panera Bread, Pizza Hut, Subway, Taco Bell, Teddy's Rest., Wendy's, **lodging:** Conley Inn, Holiday Inn Express, **other:** Advance Parts, Aldi Foods, CarQuest, $Tree, Giant Eagle Foods/24hr, GNC, Kohl's, Radio Shack, Rite Aid, Target

61mm **parking area eb**

57 I-376, US 22, to Pittsburgh, Monroeville, **S gas:** Citgo/dsl, Exxon, Sheetz, Sunoco, **food:** A&W/LJ Silver, Arby's, Baskin-Robbins, Bob Evan's, Chick-fil-A, China Palace, ChuckeCheese, CiCi's Pizza, Damon's, Denny's, Golden Corral, Honeybaked Ham, Max&Erma's, McDonald's, Olive Garden, Outback Steaks, Panera Bread, Park Diner, Pizza Hut, Primanti Bro's, Quizno's, Red Lobster, Starbucks, Taco Bell, TGIFridays, Wendy's, **lodging:** Comfort Suites, Courtyard, Day's Inn, Extended Stay America, Hampton Inn, Holiday Inn,

57 Continued
Radisson Inn, Red Roof Inn, Springhill Suites, **other:** [H], Aamco, Big Lots, Border's Books, Firestone/auto, Honda, Jaguar/Land Rover, Jo-Ann Fabrics, Marshall's, Michael's, Lowes Whse, NTB, Office Depot, Old Navy, PetCo, Pet Land, Radio Shack, Rite Aid, to Three Rivers Stadium

49mm **Oakmont Service Plaza eb** Sunoco/dsl/24hr, **Food-Court, [picnic], litter barrels, [phone]**

48.5mm Allegheny River

48 PA 28, to Pittsburgh, Allegheny Valley, New Kensington, **N gas:** Shell/24hr, Sunoco, **food:** Pizza Hut, Subway, **other:** CarQuest, Rite Aid, **S gas:** Exxon/dsl, GetGo, **food:** Bob Evans, Bruster's, Denny's, Gino Bro's Pizza, KFC, King's Rest., McDonald's, Ponderosa, Primanti Bro's, Subway, Taco Bell, Wendy's, **lodging:** Comfort Inn, Day's Inn, Holiday Inn Express, Super 8, Valley Motel, **other:** Advance Parts, Ford, Target

41mm **parking area/call box eb**

39 PA 8, to Pittsburgh, Butler Valley, **0-1 mi N gas:** Exxon/7-11/dsl, GetGo, Sheetz/24hr, Sunoco, **food:** Applebees, Atria's Rest., Bruno's Pizza, Buffalo Wild Wings, Eat'n Park, King's Rest., Max&Erma's, McDonald's, Sonic, Starbucks, Taco Bell, Wendy's, **lodging:** Comfort Inn, Pittsburgh N Motel/rest, **other:** Advance Parts, Curves, Dodge, $Tree, Giant Eagle Foods, GNC, Kohl's, Lowes Whse, Rite Aid, Shop'n Save Foods, Target, TJ Maxx, Walmart/auto/drugs, **S gas:** BP, Sunoco/dsl, **food:** Arby's, Brusters, Burger King, China Bistro, KFC, McDonald's, Pasquales Pizza, Panera Bread, Pizza Hut, Subway, Vocelli Pizza, Wendy's, **other:** [H], AutoZone, Firestone/auto, Goodyear/auto, Home Depot, Mr. Tire, Radio Shack, Rite Aid, USPO

31mm Toll Plaza wb

28 to I-79, to Cranberry, Pittsburgh, **N gas:** BP/dsl, Exxon/dsl/24hr, GetGo, Sheetz/24hr, Sunoco/24hr, **food:** A&W/LJ Silver, Alladin's Eatery, Arby's, Bob Evans, Boston Mkt, Box's Pizza, Bravo Italian, Burger King, CiCi's Pizza, Denny's, DQ, Dunkin Donuts, Eat'n Park, Hartner's Rest., HotDog Shoppe, Ichiban Steakhouse, King's Rest., Krispy Kreme, LoneStar Steaks, Max&Erma's, McDonald's, Montecello's Grill, Panera Bread, Papa John's, Perkins, Pizzaroma, Primanti Bro's, Subway, TCBY, Wendy's, **lodging:** Comfort Inn, Fairfield Inn, Hampton Inn, Holiday Inn Express, Hyatt Place, Motel 6, Oak Leaf Motel, Red Roof Inn, Residence Inn, Sheraton, Super 8, **other:** Barnes&Noble, Best Buy, CarQuest, Costco/gas, Curves, GNC, Giant Eagle, Goodyear/auto, Home Depot, Jo-Ann Fabrics, Kuhn's Foods, Michael's, Old Navy, PepBoys, PetCo, Radio Shack, Rite Aid, Toyota/Scion, Walgreens, Walmart SuperCtr, mall, transmissions, USPO, Vet

23.5mm pulloff eb

22mm **Zelienople Service Plaza eb Welcome Ctr...gas:** Sunoco/dsl/24hr, **food:** FoodCourt, **other:** crafts, gifts

17mm **parking area eb**

13.4mm **parking area eb**

13mm Beaver River

13 PA 8, to Ellwood City, Beaver Valley, **N gas:** Al's Corner, **food:** Subway, **lodging:** Alpine Inn, Beaver Falls Motel, HillTop Motel, Holiday Inn, Lark Motel, **other:** [H], **S lodging:** Super 8

INTERSTATE 76 CONT'D (TURNPIKE)

E ↕ W

Exit #	Services
10	PA 60 (toll), to New Castle, Pittsburgh, **S** services (6mi), to ✈
6mm	pulloff eb
2mm	pulloff eb
1mm	**toll plaza eb, ☎, call boxes located at 1 mi intervals**
0mm	Pennsylvania/Ohio state line

INTERSTATE 78

E ↕ W

Exit #	Services
77	Pennsylvania/New Jersey state line, Delaware River
76mm	**Welcome Ctr wb, full ♿ facilities, ☎, vending, picnic, litter barrels, petwalk, toll booth wb**
75	to PA 611, Easton, **N gas:** TurkeyHill/dsl, **food:** McDonald's (1mi), **lodging:** Quality Inn, **other:** Crayola Factory, **S gas:** Exxon
71	PA 33, to Stroudsburg, **1 mi N on Freemansburg Ave...food:** Frank's Pizza, JJ Wong's, Panera Bread, Ruby Tuesday, Texas Roadhouse, TGIFriday, **lodging:** Courtyard, **other:** Barnes&Noble, Lowes Whse, Michael's, Pet Supplies+, Staples
67	PA 412, Hellertown, **N gas:** TurkeyHill/gas, **lodging:** Comfort Suites (3mi), **food:** Wendy's, **other:** H, Chevrolet, **S gas:** Citgo, Exxon/dsl, Lukoil, Sunoco, **food:** McDonald's, Rocco's Pizza, Rita's Shakes, Vassi's Drive-In, Waffle House, **lodging:** Holiday Inn Express, **other:** CVS Drug, Firestone, 7-11, repair
60b a	PA 309 S, Quakertown
59	to PA 145 (from eb), Summit Lawn
58	Emaus St (from wb), **S gas:** Gulf, Sunoco
57	Lehigh St, **N gas:** Hess/dsl, WaWa, **food:** Arby's, Dragon Pond Chinese, IHOP, Palumbo Pizza, Queen City Diner, Subway, Willy Joe's Rest., **lodging:** Day's Inn, **other:** BigLots, CVS Drug, $Tree, Family$, Home Depot, Dodge/Kia/Isuzu, Lincoln/Mercury, Radio Shack, Redner's Whse, Shop Fair Foods, VW, Whse Mkt Foods, **S gas:** Lukoil, Pipeline/dsl, Sunoco, TurkeyHill/gas, **food:** Bennigan's, Bob Evans, Brass Rail Rest., Domino's, Dunkin Donuts, Dynasty Chinese, Friendly's, Japanese Steaks, McDonald's, Papa John's, Perkins, Pizza Hut/Taco Bell, Rossi's Pizza, Subway, Wendy's, **other:** Acura, Audi/Mercedes/Porsche, BonTon, Buick/GMC/Jeep, Chevrolet/Saab, Chrysler, Ford, Honda, Hyundai, Lehigh Tire, Mazda, Mitsubishi, PetCo, Staples, SteinMart, Volvo
55	PA 29, Cedar Crest Blvd, **S** H
54	US 222, Hamilton Blvd, **N gas:** Hess, **food:** Baskin-Robbins, Boston Mkt, Burger King, Cali Burrito, Carrabba's, Friendly's, Ice Cream World, King George Rest., Mango's Rest, McDonald's, Perkins, Subway, Teppan Steaks, TGIFriday, Wendy's, **lodging:** Comfort Suites/rest., Holiday Inn Express, Howard Johnson, **other:** Aamco, Dorney Funpark, Dorneyville Drug, King's Food/drug, Office Depot, Rite Aid, **S gas:** Sunoco, WaWa/gas, **food:** Dunkin Donuts, Pizza Hut, **lodging:** Wingate Inn, **other:** Queen City Tire, Subaru
53	PA 309 (wb only)
51	to I-476, US 22 E, PA 33 N (eb only), Whitehall
49b a	PA 100, Fogelsville, **N food:** Arby's, Cracker Barrel, LJ Silver, Panda&Fish Chinese, Pizza Hut,

ALLENTOWN

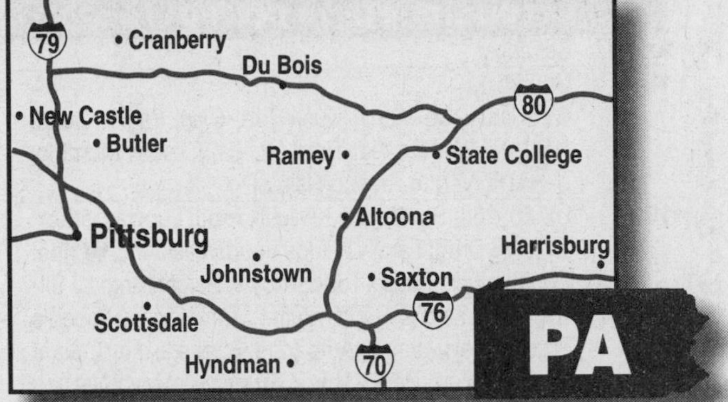

Exit #	Services
49b a	Continued **lodging:** Comfort Inn, Hawthorn Inn, **other:** Curves, KOA, Rite Aid, STS Tire/repair, **S gas:** Shell, Sunoco/24hr, WaWa, **food:** Boston's Grill, Burger King, Damon's, Starlite Diner, Taco Bell, Yocco's Hotdogs, **lodging:** Hampton Inn, Hilton Garden, Holiday Inn, Sleep Inn, Staybridge Suites, **other:** Clover Hill Winery, Toyota/Scion, st police
45	PA 863, to Lynnport, **N gas:** Exxon/Subway/dsl, Sunoco/dsl, **other:** New Smithfield Diner, **S lodging:** Super 8
40	PA 737, Krumsville, **N other:** Pine Hill Campground, Robin Hill RV Park (4mi), **S gas:** Shell/dsl, **lodging:** Skyview Rest.
35	PA 143, Lenhartsville, **3 mi S** Robin Hill Park
30	Hamburg, **S food:** Hamburg Mkt
29b a	PA 61, to Reading, Pottsville, **N gas:** Shell/dsl, **food:** Baskin Robbins/Dunkin Donuts, Burger King, Campfire Rest., Cracker Barrel, LJ Silver/Taco Bell, McDonald's, Pappy T's, Pizza Hut, Wendy's, **lodging:** Microtel, **other:** Cabela's Outdoor, Harley-Davidson (8mi), Toyota/Scion, st police, **S other:** Boat'n RV Ctr RV (4mi)
23	Shartlesville, **N gas:** Love's/McDonald's/Subway/dsl/scales/24hr, **other:** Appalachian Campsites, **S food:** Blue Mtn Family Rest., **lodging:** Haag's Motel/rest., **other:** Dutch Haus/gifts, antiques, camping, USPO
19	PA 183, Strausstown, **N gas:** Lukoil, **S gas:** Power/dsl, **food:** C&C Pizza
17	PA 419, Rehrersburg, **N gas:** Best/dsl, truck/tire repair
16	Midway, **N gas:** Exxon/dsl, Sunoco/dsl, **food:** Midway Diner, **lodging:** Comfort Inn, **S** auto/truck repair
15	Grimes
13	PA 501, Bethel, **N gas:** Shell/dsl/24hr, **S gas:** Exxon/dsl
10	PA 645, Frystown, **S gas:** All-American Trkstp/rest./dsl/24hr/@, Gulf/dsl/24hr
6	(8 from wb, US 22) PA 343, Fredricksburg, **1 mi S gas:** Pacific Pride/dsl, Redner's Whse/mkt, **food:** Esther's Rest., **other:** KOA (5mi)
1	I-81. I-78 begins/ends on I-81, exit 89.

INTERSTATE 79

N ↕ S

Exit #	Services
183b a	PA 5, 12th St, Erie, **E gas:** Shell, **other:** H, **W gas:** Country Fair, Sunoco, **food:** Applebee's, Backyard Burger, Bob Evans, Eat'n Park/24hr, Hibachi Japanese, KFC, McDonald's, Panera Bread, Serafini's Italian, Taco Bell, Tim Horton, Wendy's, **lodging:** Comfort Inn (2mi), **other:** Advance Parts, Aldi Foods, Big Lots,

PA

INTERSTATE 79 CONT'D

Exit #	Services
183b a	Continued CVS Drug, $General, Dunn Tire, Giant Eagle Foods, GNC, NAPA, Rite Aid, Tires-4-Less, Tuesday Morning, U-HAUL, Vet, to Presque Isle SP
182	US 20, 26th St, **E gas:** KwikFill, **food:** Subway, **other:** [H], CVS Drug, Family$, Tops Foods/gas/24hr, **W gas:** Country Fair, GetGo, **food:** Arby's, Burger King, LJ Silver, McDonald's, Super Buffet, Tim Horton, Vocelli's Pizza, **other:** Aamco, AutoZone, $General, Ford, Giant Eagle, K-Mart, Radio Shack, TrueValue, Volvo, Vet
180	US 19, to Kearsarge, **E food:** Arby's, Buffalo Wild Wings, Coldstone Cramery, Fox&Hound, KFC, Max&Erma's, Olive Garden, Outback Steaks, Ponderosa, Red Lobster, Roadhouse Grill, Smokey Bones BBQ, Starbucks, Subway, Wendy's, **lodging:** Fairfield Inn, Homewood Suites, SpringHill Suites, TownePlace Suites, **other:** [H], Audi/Cadillac, Barnes&Noble, Borders Books, Chrysler/Jeep, Gander Mtn, JC Penney, Macy's, Michael's, Office Depot, Old Navy, PetCo, Sears/auto, TJ Maxx, Toyota/Scion, mall, **W gas:** Country Fair, **other:** camping
178b a	I-90, E to Buffalo, W to Cleveland
174	to McKean, **E** access to gas/dsl, **W** camping
166	US 6N, to Edinboro, **E gas:** Citgo, Sheetz, **food:** Burger King (3mi), McDonald's (3mi), Perkins (2mi), Subway, Wendy's, **lodging:** Comfort Suites, Edinboro Inn, **other:** $Tree, Walmart SuperCtr, Vet, **W** camping
163mm	**rest area both lanes, full [handicapped] facilities, [phone], vending, [picnic], litter barrels, petwalk**
154	PA 198, to Saegertown, Conneautville
147b a	US 6, US 322, to Meadville, **E gas:** All American Gas/wash, Country Fair, GetGo, Sheetz/dsl/24hr, **food:** Applebee's, Chovy's Italian, Cracker Barrel, DQ, Hoss' Rest., KFC, Perkins, Pizza Hut, Steak&Shake, Super Buffet, **lodging:** Best Value, Day's Inn/rest., Holiday Inn Express, **other:** [H], Advance Parts, Giant Eagle/24hr, Home Depot, Radio Shack, **W gas:** Sheetz, **food:** King's Rest./24hr, McDonald's, Ponderosa, Red Lobster, Subway, Yuen's Garden, **lodging:** Quality Inn, **other:** Aldi Foods, AutoZone, Buick/Pontiac/Cadillac/GMC, Chevrolet, $Tree, K-Mart, Staples, Toyota/Scion, Walmart SuperCtr, to Pymatuning SP, st police
141	PA 285, to Geneva, **E** to Erie NWR (20mi), **W food:** Aunt Bee's Rest./dsl
135mm	**rest area/weigh sta both lanes, full [handicapped] facilities, [phone], vending, [picnic], litter barrels, petwalk**
130	PA 358, to Sandy Lake, **W other:** [H] (13mi), to Goddard SP
121	US 62, to Mercer, **E other:** Valley Tire, **W gas:** Sunoco/dsl, **other:** st police
116b a	I-80, E to Clarion, W to Sharon
113	PA 208, PA 258, to Grove City, **E gas:** BP, Country Fair/dsl/24hr, **other:** [H], **W gas:** KwikFill/Subway, Sheetz/24hr, **food:** Eat'n Park/24hr, Elephant&Castle Rest., Hoss's Rest., King's Rest., McDonald's, Wendy's, **lodging:** Best Western, Comfort Inn, Hampton Inn, Holiday Inn Express, Microtel, Super 8, **other:** KOA (3mi), Prime Outlets/famous brands, tires
110mm	**rest area sb, full [handicapped] facilities, [phone], vending, [picnic], litter barrels, petwalk**
107mm	**rest area nb, full [handicapped] facilities, [phone], vending, [picnic], litter barrels, petwalk**
105	PA 108, to Slippery Rock, **E gas:** QuickStop/dsl, **food:** DQ, **lodging:** Evening Star Motel/rest., **other:** Slippery Rock Camping, to Slippery Rock U
99	US 422, to New Castle, **E** to Moraine SP, **W** gas Pilot/Subway/McDonald's/dsl/scales/24hr, **other:** Coopers Lake Camping to Rose Point Camping
96	PA 488, Portersville, **E** Bear Run Camping, Moraine SP, **W food:** Brown's Country Kitchen, McConnell's Mill SP (3mi), gas/dsl
88	(87 from nb), to US 19, PA 68, (no ez return), Zelienople, **W gas:** Exxon, **food:** Bruster's, Thompson's Rest
85	(83 from nb), PA 528 (no quick return), to Evans City, **W other:** Buick/Pontiac
80mm	**parking area both lanes**
78	(76 from nb, exits left from nb), US 19, PA 228, to Mars, **access to I-76, PA TPK, E gas:** Citgo/7-11, **food:** Applebees, Chick-fil-A, DiBella's Subs, McDonald's, Moe's SW Grill, Olive Garden, On-the-Border, Quizno's, Red Robin, Smokey Bones BBQ, Subway, Taipei Chinese, **lodging:** Marriott, **other:** [H], Kohl's, Lowes Whse, PetsMart, Staples, Target, TJ Maxx, **W on US 19...gas:** BP/dsl, Exxon/dsl/24hr, GetGo, Sheetz/24hr, Sunoco/24hr, **food:** A&W/LJ Silver, Alladin's Eatery, Arby's, Bob Evans, Boston Mkt, Box's Pizza, Bravo Italian, Burger King, CiCi's Pizza, Denny's, DQ, Dunkin Donuts, Eat'n Park, Hartner's Rest., HotDog Shoppe, Ichiban Steakhouse, King's Rest., Krispy Kreme, LoneStar Steaks, Max&Erma's, McDonald's, Montecello's Grill, Panera Bread, Papa John's, Perkins, Pizzaroma, Primanti Bro's, Subway, TCBY, Wendy's, **lodging:** Comfort Inn, Fairfield Inn, Hampton Inn, Holiday Inn Express, Hyatt Place, Motel 6, Oak Leaf Motel, Red Roof Inn, Residence Inn, Sheraton, Super 8, **other:** Barnes&Noble, Best Buy, CarQuest, Costco/gas, Curves, GNC, Giant Eagle, Goodyear/auto, Home Depot, Jo-Ann Fabrics, Kuhn's Foods, Michael's, Old Navy, PepBoys, PetCo, Radio Shack, Rite Aid, Toyota/Scion, Walgreens, Walmart SuperCtr, mall, transmissions, USPO, Vet
77	I-76/Tpk, to Youngstown, **E food:** Quizno's
75	US 19 S (from nb), to Warrendale, **services along US 19**
73	PA 910, to Wexford, **E gas:** BP/24hr, **food:** Eat'n Park, King's Family Rest./24hr, Starbucks, **lodging:** Best Inn, **other:** **W gas:** Exxon/dsl/24hr, **food:** Carmody's Rest
72	I-279 S (from sb), to Pittsburgh
68	Mt Nebo Rd, **W** [H], gas
66	to PA 65, Emsworth
65	to PA 51, Coraopolis, Neville Island, **E gas:** Gulf, **lodging:** Fairfield Inn, **other:** Penske Trucks, **W food:** Subway
64.5mm	Ohio River
64	PA 51 (from nb), to Coraopolis, McKees Rocks
60b a	PA 60, Crafton, **E gas:** Exxon/dsl/24hr, **food:** King's Rest./24hr, Primanti Bros, **lodging:** Carefree Inn, Comfort Inn, Econolodge, Motel 6, Pittsburgh Motel, **other:** [H], **W gas:** BP/Subway/dsl (1mi), **food:** Juliano's Rest.

PA

N ↕ S

INTERSTATE 79 CONT'D

Exit #	Services
59b	US 22 W, US 30 (from nb), **W** ✈
59	al-279 N, to Pittsburgh
57	to Carnegie, **1-3 mi E gas:** BP, Exxon, **food:** LJ Silver, McDonald's, **lodging:** Ford, Lowes Whse, Radio Shack, Shop'n Save, Walgreens, Walmart, mall
55	PA 50, to Heidelberg, **E on PA 50...gas:** Sunoco, **food:** Arby's, Bob Evans, ChuckeCheese, CiCi's Pizza, Damon's, DQ, Eat'n Park, KFC, King's Rest., Pizza Hut, Firestone/auto, Starbucks, Taco Bell, Wendy's, **other:** Big Lots, $Discount, Giant Eagle Foods, GNC, Home Depot, Jo-Ann Fabrics, K-Mart/Little Caesar's, Mr Tire, TJ Maxx, Tuesday Morning
54	PA 50, to Bridgeville, **E gas:** BP/dsl, Exxon/dsl, **food:** Burger King, King's Rest./24hr, McDonald's, **lodging:** Holiday Inn Express, **other:** H, Chevrolet, Dodge, NAPA, Rite Aid, USPO, **W gas:** Sunoco, **lodging:** Knight's Inn
50mm	**rest area/weigh sta both lanes, full ♿ facilities, ☎, vending, 🅿, litter barrels, petwalk**
48	South Pointe, **W food:** Jackson's Rest., Subway, **lodging:** Hilton Garden
45	to PA 980, Canonsburg, **E gas:** Sheetz, **W gas:** BP/24hr, Citgo, **food:** KFC/Taco Bell, LJ Silver, McDonald's, Papa John's, Pizza Hut, Quizno's, Starbucks, Subway, Wendy's, **lodging:** Super 8, **other:** Advance Parts, Walgreens
43	PA 519, Houston, **E gas:** BP/dsl, **W gas:** Sunoco/24hr, **other:** Freightliner
41	Race Track Rd, **E gas:** Exxon, **food:** Brick Oven Pizza, Buger King, McDonald's, Waffle House, Wendy's, **lodging:** Comfort Inn, Hampton Inn, Holiday Inn, **W gas:** BP/dsl, **lodging:** Candlewood Suites, **other:** Trolley Museum
40	Meadow Lands (from nb, no re-entry), **W other:** Trolley Museum (3mi), golf, racetrack
38	I-70 W, to Wheeling
19b a	(I-77), US 19, Murtland Ave, **N food:** Applebee's, Arby's, Bruster's, Cracker Barrel, Krispy Kreme, Max&Erma's, McDonald's, Outback Steaks, Panera Bread, Ponderosa, Quizno's, Red Lobster, Red Robin, Starbucks, Subway, TX Roadhouse, TGIFriday, **lodging:** Springhill Suites, **other:** Aldi Foods, $Tree, Giant Eagle Foods, GNC, Honda, Hyundai, JC Penney, Kohl's, Lowes Whse, Mercedes, Michael's, Nissan, PetCo, PetsMart, Radio Shack, Sam's Club/gas, Sav-a-Lot Foods, Target, Toyota, Walmart SuperCtr/24hr, Vet, **S gas:** BP/dsl, Exxon, Sunoco, Valero, **food:** A&W/LJ Silver, Bob Evans, CiCi's Pizza, Eat'n Park/24hr, Evergreen Chinese, KFC, Old Mexico, Papa John's, Pizza Hut, **lodging:** Hampton Inn, Motel 6, **other:** H, Big Lots, Buick/Cadillac/GMC, Firestone/auto, Home Depot, Jo-Ann Fabrics, Rite Aid, Staples, Subaru, mall
20	(I-77) PA 136, to Beau St, **S** to Washington&Jefferson Coll
34	I-70 E, to Greensburg
33	US 40, to Laboratory, **W other:** KOA
31mm	**parking area/weigh sta sb**
30	US 19, to Amity, **W gas:** Exxon/Subway/dsl
23	to Marianna, Prosperity

WASHINGTON

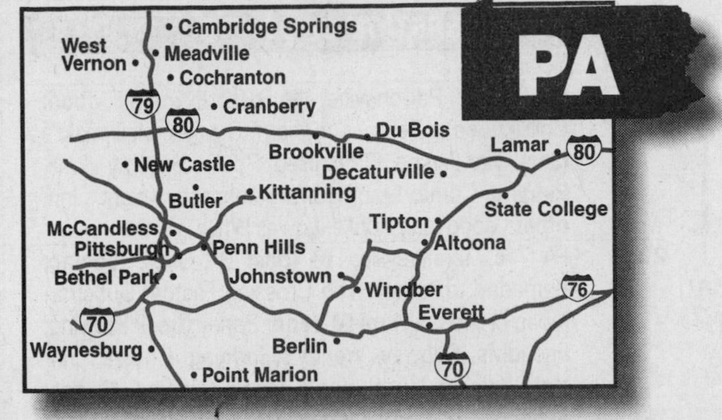

Exit #	Services
19	PA 221, to US 19, Ruff Creek, **W gas:** BP/dsl
14	PA 21, to Waynesburg, **E gas:** Sunoco, **food:** Bob Evans, **lodging:** Comfort Inn, **other:** Walmart SuperCtr, visitor info, **W gas:** BP/dsl/24hr, Exxon/dsl, GetGo, Marathon, 7-11, Sheetz, **food:** Burger King, DQ, Golden Wok, Hardee's, KFC, Little Caesar's, McDonald's, Scotty's Pizza, Subway, Vocelli Pizza, Wendy's, **lodging:** Econolodge, Super 8, **other:** H, Advance Parts, Aldi Foods, AutoZone, Big Lots, Buick/GMC/Pontiac, Cadillac/Chevrolet/Subaru, Chrysler/Dodge/Jeep, CVS Drug, $General, Giant Eagle Foods, Family$, Radio Shack, Rite Aid, Walgreens, st police
7	to Kirby
6mm	**Welcome Ctr/weigh sta nb, full ♿ facilities, ☎, 🅿, litter barrels, vending, petwalk**
1	Mount Morris, **E gas:** Citgo/dsl/rest./scales, **other:** Honda/Mazda, **W gas:** BP/dsl, Marathon, **other:** Mt Morris Campground
0mm	Pennsylvania/West Virginia state line

E ↕ W

INTERSTATE 80

Exit #	Services
311mm	Pennsylvania/New Jersey state line, Delaware River
310.5	toll booth wb, ☎
310	PA 611, Delaware Water Gap, **S Welcome Ctr/rest area, full services, info, gas:** BP, Gulf/repair, **food:** Doughboys Pizza, Water Gap Diner
309	US 209 N, PA 447, to Marshalls Creek, **N gas:** Exxon/dsl/24hr, Gulf, **food:** Blue Tequila Mexican, DQ, Wendy's (2mi), **lodging:** Shannon Motel, **other:** H
308	East Stroudsburg, **N gas:** Exxon, **other:** H, WaWa, Vet, **1 mi N food:** Arby's, Burger King, China King, Friendly's, McDonald's, **other:** Goodyear/auto, K-Mart, NAPA, Radio Shack, ShopRite Foods, Walmart SuperCtr/24hr, Weis Foods, **S food:** JR's Grill, **lodging:** Budget Motel, Super 8
307	PA 191, Broad St, **N lodging:** Hampton Inn, **other:** H **S gas:** Sunoco, **food:** Compton's, **lodging:** Budget Host
306	Dreher Ave (from wb, no EZ return), **N gas:** Wawa
305	US 209, Main St, **N gas:** Gulf, Shell, **food:** Perkins/24hr, **lodging:** Quality Inn, **S gas:** Exxon/24hr, **lodging:** Alpines Motel
304	US 209, to PA 33, 9th St (from wb), same as 303
303	9th st, (from eb), **N gas:** Lukoil, **food:** Arby's, Boston Mkt, Burger King, Dunkin Donuts, Fulay Chinese, Garfield's Rest., McDonald's, Panera Bread, Pizza Hut, Ruby Tuesday, Starbucks, TX Roadhouse, **other:** Best Buy, Border's Books, Cadillac, Chevrolet, CVS Drug, $Tree, JC Penney, Nissan, Old Navy, PetsMart

STROUDSBURG

PA

INTERSTATE 80 CONT'D

E ↕ W

Exit #	Services
302	PA 611, to Bartonsville, **N gas:** Exxon/dsl, **food:** Chili's, Lee's Rest., Longhorn Steaks, McDonald's (3mi), Ponderosa (3mi), Red Robin, Subway (2mi), **lodging:** Comfort Inn, Howard Johnson, Knight's Inn, **other:** Goodyear, Kohl's, Lowes Whse
299	PA 715, Tannersville, **N gas:** BP, Shell, **lodging:** Ramada Ltd, **other:** The Crossing Factory Outlet/famous brands, **1-4 mi N food:** Barley Creek Brewing, Friendly's, Subway, Wendy's, **lodging:** Chateau Inn/rest., Knight's Inn, Super 8, **other:** camping, **S gas:** Sunoco/24hr, **food:** Tannersville Diner, **lodging:** Day's Inn, Summit Resort, **other:** to Camelback Ski Area, to Big Pocono SP
298	PA 611 (from wb), to Scotrun, **N gas:** Shell, Sunoco/dsl, **food:** Anthony's Steaks, Plaza Deli, **lodging:** Scotrun Diner/motel, **other:** to Mt Pocono
295mm	**rest area eb, full ♿ facilities, ☎, picnic, litter barrels, vending, petwalk**
293	I-380 N, to Scranton, (exits left from eb)
284	PA 115, to Wilkes-Barre, Blakeslee, **N gas:** WaWa (1mi), **lodging:** Best Western, Blakeslee Inn (2mi), **other:** Fern Ridge Camping, st police, **S gas:** Exxon/dsl, **other:** to Pocono Raceway
277	PA 940, to PA Tpk (I-476), to Pocono, Lake Harmony, Allentown, **N gas:** WaWa, **food:** A&W/LJ Silver, Arby's, Denny's, Gino's Pizza, McDonald's, **lodging:** Comfort Inn, CountryPlace Inn, Day's Inn, Ramada Inn, Split Rock Resort
274	PA 534, **N gas:** Hickory Run/Valero/dsl/rest./scales/24hr, Sunoco/Subway/dsl/24hr, **other:** towing/repair, **S other:** to Hickory Run SP (6mi)
273mm	Lehigh River
273	PA 940, PA 437, to Freeland, White Haven, **N gas:** BP, Exxon, **S food:** Powerhouse Eatery, **other:** Sandy Valley Campground
270mm	**rest area eb, full ♿ facilities, info, ☎, picnic, litter barrels, vending, petwalk**
262	PA 309, to Hazleton, Mountain Top, **N gas:** BP, **food:** Mary's Rest., Stagecoach Rest., Wendy's, **lodging:** Econolodge, **other:** Hazelton Campground, **S lodging:** Holiday Inn Express, **other:** st police
260b a	I-81, N to Wilkes-Barre, S to Harrisburg
256	PA 93, to Nescopeck, Conyngham, **N gas:** Pilot/Subway/dsl/scales/24hr, Sunoco/repair, **lodging:** Lookout Motel, **S food:** Tom's Kitchen (2mi), **lodging:** Best Value Inn, Hampton Inn (4mi), **other:** H, towing/truck repair
251mm	Nescopeck River
246mm	**rest area/weigh sta both lanes, full ♿ facilities, weather info, ☎, picnic, litter barrels, vending, petwalk**
242	PA 339, to Mainville, Mifflinville, **N gas:** Loves/Arby's/dsl/24hr, **food:** McDonald's, **lodging:** Super 8/rest., **S gas:** Citgo/dsl/repair, **lodging:** Best Western
241mm	Susquehanna River
241b a	US 11, to Berwick, Lime Ridge, Bloomsburg, **N lodging:** Red Maple Inn (2mi), **other:** H, **S gas:** Exxon, **food:** Kemler's Rest., **lodging:** Budget Host, 2-5 mi **S gas:** Sheetz/dsl/24hr, **food:** Applebee's, Arby's, Bennigan's, Burger King, China Queen, Domino's,
241b a	Continued Dunkin Donuts, McDonald's, Morris Rest., New China Buffet, Pizza Hut, Playa Cancun, Subway, Taco Bell, Terrapins Cantina, Wendy's, **other:** Ace Hardware, Advance Parts, Bardo's Tires, BigLots, Bloomsburg RV Ctr, Buick/GMC/Pontiac, Cadillac/Chevrolet, CVS Drug, $Tree, Ford/Honda, Giant Foods/gas, Kost Tire, Rite Aid, Staples, U-Haul, Weis Foods/gas
236	PA 487, to Bloomsburg, Lightstreet, **S gas:** Sunoco/24hr, **food:** Denny's/24hr, **lodging:** Hampton Inn, Tennytown Motel (2mi), Turkey Hill Inn, **other:** H to Bloomsburg U
232	PA 42, Buckhorn, **N gas:** Exxon, TA/BP/Subway/dsl/scales/24hr/@, **food:** Burger King, Charlie Brown's Steaks, Cracker Barrel, KFC, Perkins, Quaker Steak&Lube, Ruby Tuesday, Wendy's, **lodging:** Econolodge, Holiday Inn Express, **other:** Home Depot, JC Penney, Sears, mall, **S food:** Gourmet Buffet, Panera Bread, **other:** $Tree, Indian Head camping (3mi), Lowes Whse, Office Depot, Walmart SuperCtr/24hr
224	PA 54, to Danville, **N gas:** Shell/Subway/dsl/24hr, Sunoco, **food:** Country Kitchen, **lodging:** Quality Inn, **S food:** Friendly's, McDonald's, Mom's Dutch Kitchen, **lodging:** Best Western, Day's Inn, Hampton Inn, Key Motel, Red Roof Inn, **other:** H
219mm	**rest area both lanes, full ♿ facilities, info, ☎, picnic, litter barrels, vending, petwalk**
215	PA 254, Limestonevill, **N gas:** Milton 32 Trkstp/dsl/rest./24hr, **S gas:** Petro/Shell/Iron Skillet/Subway/dsl/rest./24hr/@
212b a	I-180 W, PA 147 S, to Muncy, Williamsport, **S gas:** Sunoco/24hr (1mi)
210.5mm	Susquehanna River
210b a	US 15, to Williamsport, Lewisburg, **S gas:** Citgo, **food:** Bonanza, **lodging:** Comfort Inn, Holiday Inn Express, **other:** H, KOA (5mi)
199	Mile Run Rd
194mm	**rest area/weigh sta both lanes, full ♿ facilities, ☎, picnic, litter barrels, vending, petwalk**
192	PA 880, to Jersey Shore, **N gas:** Citgo/dsl/24hr, **food:** Pit-Stop Rest., **S gas:** BP/dsl, **other:** H, towing/truck repair
185	PA 477, Loganton, **N gas:** BP, **other:** camping, **S food:** Twilight Diner, RV Winter SP (12mi)
178	US 220, Lock Haven, 5 mi **N gas:** KwikFill/dsl, Sheetz, **food:** Ruby Tuesday, Subway, **other:** Advance Parts, K-Mart, Lowes Whse, Walmart SuperCtr/24hr
173	PA 64, Lamar, **N gas:** Pilot/Subway/dsl/scales/24hr, **food:** Cottage Rest., McDonald's, Perkins, **lodging:** Comfort Inn/rest., Hampton Inn, **S gas:** Citgo, ***FLYING J***/Shell/Country Mkt/dsl/LP/scales, TA/Country Pride/Subway/dsl/scales/24hr/@, **food:** DQ, **other:** auto repair
161	PA 26, US 220 S, to Bellafonte, **S other:** KOA, to PSU
158	US 220 S, PA 150, to Altoona, Milesburg, **N gas:** BP/Subway, Bestway/dsl/rest./motel/24hr/@, Citgo/dsl, TA/dsl/scales/24hr/@, **food:** Buckhorn Rest., McDonald's, **lodging:** Holiday Inn, **S** st police
147	PA 144, to Snow Shoe, **N gas:** Citgo/dsl/24hr, Exxon/dsl/repair/24hr, **food:** Snow Shoe Sandwich Shop, Subway, **other:** Hall's Foods, repair

LAMAR

PA

INTERSTATE 80 CONT'D

E ↕ W

Exit #	Services
146mm	**rest area both lanes, full ♿ facilities, ☎, picnic tables, litter barrels, vending, petwalk**
138mm	Moshanna River
133	PA 53, to Philipsburg, Kylertown, **N gas:** KwikFill/motel/dsl/scales, Sunoco/LP, **food:** Roadhouse Rest., **other:** USPO, dsl repair, Black Moshannon SP (9mi), **S other:** [H]
123	PA 970, to Shawville, Woodland, **S gas:** BP/dsl (1mi), Pacific Pride/dsl, **food:** Gio's BBQ (2mi), **other:** st police
120mm	Susquehanna River, W Branch
120	PA 879, Clearfield, **N gas:** Sapp Bros/dsl/rest./24hr/2, **lodging:** Econolodge, **S gas:** BP, Sheetz/24hr, Snappy's Gas, **food:** Arby's, Burger King, Dunkin Donuts, Dutch Pantry, KFC/Pizza Hut/Taco Bell, McDonald's, **lodging:** Comfort Inn, Day's Inn, Hampton Inn, Holiday Inn Express, Super 8, **other:** [H], Lowes Whse, Walmart SuperCtr/Subway/gas/24hr
111mm	highest point on I-80 east of Mississippi River, 2250 ft
111	PA 153, to Penfield, **N** to Parker Dam, to SB Elliot SP, **S** [H]

DU BOIS

Exit #	Services
101	PA 255, Du Bois, **N gas:** Snappy's/24hr, **other:** camping, **S other:** [H], st police, **1-2 mi S gas:** Sheetz/dsl/24hr, **food:** A&W/LJ Silver, Arby's, Bruster's, Burger King, Eat'n Park/24hr, Italian Oven, McDonald's, Maxwell St Rest., Perkins/24hr, Ponderosa, Red Lobster, Ruby Tuesday, Subway, Taco Bell, Valley Dairy Rest., Wendy's, **lodging:** Best Western, Hampton Inn, **other:** Big Lots, BiLo Foods, BonTon, $Tree, Goodyear/auto, JC Penney, Jo-Ann Fabrics, K-Mart, Lowes Whse, Old Navy, Rite Aid, Ross, Sears, Shop'n Save Foods, Staples, Walmart/drugs, mall
97	US 219, to Brockway, Du Bois, **S gas:** Pilot/Arby's/dsl/24hr, Sheetz/dsl/24hr, **food:** Dutch Pantry Rest., **lodging:** Clarion, Holiday Inn Express, **other:** [H], Freightliner, st police, **2 mi S food:** Hoss' Rest., Pizza Hut, **lodging:** Best Western, **other:** Advance Parts
90	**N gas:** Du Bois Regional ✈
87.5mm	**rest area both lanes, full ♿ facilities, ☎, picnic tables, litter barrels, vending, petwalk**
86	PA 830, to Reynoldsville

BROOKVILLE

Exit #	Services
81	PA 28, to Brookville, to Hazen, **S** to Brookville, hist dist (2mi)
78	PA 36, to Sigel, Brookville, **N gas:** ***FLYING J***/Country Mkt/dsl/scales/LP/24hr, TA/BP/Taco Bell/dsl/scales/24hr/@, **food:** DQ, KFC, McDonald's, Pizza Hut, **lodging:** Howard Johnson, Super 8, **other:** NAPA, to Cook Forest SP, **S gas:** Country Fair/24hr, Sheetz, Sunoco, **food:** Arby's, Burger King, Plyler's Buffet, Subway, **lodging:** Budget Host, Day's Inn, Holiday Inn Express, Quality Inn, **other:** Chrysler/Dodge/Jeep, Family$
73	PA 949, Corsica, **N other:** to Clear Creek SP, **S** USPO
70	US 322, to Strattanville
64	PA 66 S, to New Bethlehem, Clarion, **N** to Clarion U
62	PA 68, to Clarion, **N gas:** BP/24hr, KwikFill/dsl, **food:** A&W/LJ Silver, Arby's, Eat'n Park, Hunan King, McDonald's, Perkins/24hr, Pizza Hut, RRR Roadhouse,

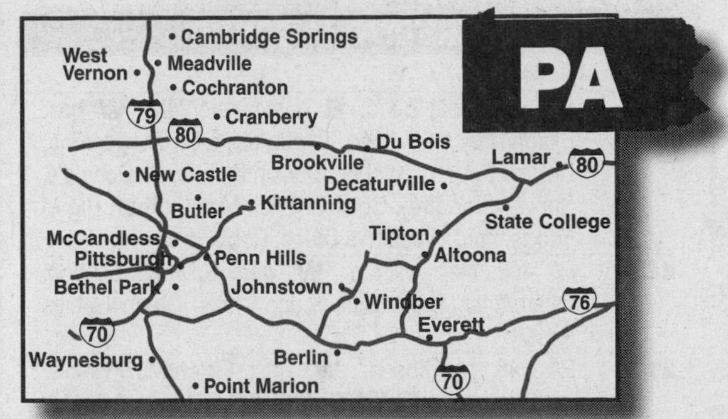

CLARION

Exit #	Services
62	Continued Subway, Taco Bell, **lodging:** Comfort Inn, Hampton Inn, Holiday Inn/rest., Microtel, Quality Inn, Super 8, **other:** [H], Advance Parts, Aldi Foods, $Tree, JC Penney, K-Mart, Radio Shack, Staples, Walmart SuperCtr/24hr, mall
61mm	Clarion River
60	PA 66 N, to Shippenville, **N gas:** Citgo, **other:** to Cook Forest SP, camping
56mm	**parking area/weigh sta both lanes**
53	to PA 338, to Knox, **N gas:** Satterlee Gas/dsl, **food:** BJ's Eatery, **other:** Countryside Crafts/Quilts, Wolf's Camping Resort, **S other:** Good Tire Service
45	PA 478, to St Petersburg, Emlenton, **4 mi S other:** Golf Hall of Fame
44.5mm	Allegheny River
42	PA 38, to Emlenton, **N gas:** Exxon/Subway/dsl/24hr, Roady's Trkstp/dsl/rest./scales/24hr, **lodging:** Deluxe Motel, **other:** Gaslight RV Park, truck/RV repair
35	PA 308, to Clintonville
30.5mm	**rest area both lanes, full ♿ facilities, ☎, picnic tables, litter barrels, vending, petwalk**
29	PA 8, to Franklin, Barkeyville, **N food:** Arby's, Burger King, King's Rest., **lodging:** Comfort Inn, Super 8, **other:** Freightliner, **S gas:** Citgo/dsl/24hr, KwikFill/dsl/scales//24hr, TA/BP/Subway/dsl/scales/24hr/@, **other:** to Slippery Rock U
24	PA 173, to Grove City, Sandy Lake, **S other:** [H], Grove City Coll, Wendell August Forge/gifts (3mi), truck repair
19b a	I-79, N to Erie, S to Pittsburgh
15	US 19, to Mercer, **N gas:** BP, PP/dsl, **food:** Charlie B's Rest., Burger King, McDonald's, **lodging:** Comfort Inn, **other:** st police, **2 mi S food:** Iron Bridge Rest., **other:** KOA (4mi)
4b a	PA 18, PA 60, to Sharon-Hermitage, New Castle, **N gas:** Sheetz, Sunoco/Subway/dsl/24hr, **lodging:** Comfort Inn, Holiday Inn Express, Quality Inn, Radisson, Super 8, **S food:** DQ, MiddleSex Diner/24hr, **other:** Auto Value Parts
2.5mm	Shenango River
1mm	**Welcome Ctr eb, full ♿ facilities, ☎, picnic tables, litter barrels, vending, petwalk**
0mm	Pennsylvania/Ohio state line

INTERSTATE 81

Exit #	Services
233mm	Pennsylvania/New York state line
232mm	**Welcome Ctr/weigh sta sb, full ♿ facilities, ☎, picnic tables, litter barrels, petwalk**

INTERSTATE 81 CONT'D

N ↕ S

Exit #	Services
230	PA 171, Great Bend, **E gas:** Valero/24hr, **W gas:** Exxon/Arby's/dsl/24hr, Sunoco/dsl, **food:** Burger King, Dobb's Country Kitchen, Dunkin Donuts, McDonald's, Subway, **lodging:** Colonial Brick Motel, **other:** Big M Foods, Ford, Reddon's Drugs, Rob's Mkt
223	PA 492, New Milford, **W gas:** Gulf/dsl, Sunoco, Valero/24hr, **food:** Blue Ridge Motel, Green Gables Rest.
219	PA 848, to Gibson, **W gas:** Exxon/McDonald's/dsl/24hr, ***FLYING J***/Shell/Country Mkt/dsl/scales/24hr, **lodging:** Holiday Inn Express, st police
217	PA 547, Harford, **E gas:** Exxon/Subway/dsl/24hr, Getty's/dsl/rest./24hr
211	PA 92, Lenox, **E** Elk Mtn Ski Area, Shady Rest Camping (3mi), **W gas:** Lukoil/dsl/24hr, Shell/dsl, **food:** Bingham's Rest., Mamasita's Mexican, **other:** Lenox Drug
209mm	**rest area sb, full ♿ facilities, ☎, 🛆, litter barrel, vending, petwalk**
206	PA 374, to Glenwood, Lenoxville, **E** to Elk Mountain Ski Resort
203mm	**rest area nb, full ♿ facilities, ☎, 🛆, litter barrels, vending, petwalk**
202	PA 107, to Fleetville, Tompkinsville
201	PA 438, East Benton, **W gas:** Duchniks/dsl/repair
199	PA 524, Scott, **E gas:** BP/dsl, **W gas:** Exxon/Subway, **lodging:** Motel 81, **other:** to Lackawanna SP
197	PA 632, Waverly, **E other:** Mr Z's Foods, Rite Aid, **W gas:** Sunoco/24hr, **food:** Doc's Deli/24hr
194	US 6, US 11, to I-476/PA Tpk, Clarks Summit, **W gas:** Shell/dsl, Sheetz/24hr, Sunoco/dsl, **food:** Bennigan's, Burger King, Damon's, Dino&Francesco's, Domino's, Dunkin Donuts, Euro Cafe, Friendly's, Krispy Kreme, Kyoto, McDonald's, New Century Chinese, Pizza Hut, Quizno's, Starbucks, Subway, Taco Bell, Waffle House, Wendy's, **lodging:** Comfort Inn, Econolodge, Hampton Inn, Nichols Village Inn, Ramada Inn, **other:** Advance Parts, $Bazaar, Kost Tire, Radio Shack, Rite Aid, Weis Foods
191b a	US 6, US 11, to Carbondale, **E gas:** Shell/dsl, Sheetz/dsl, **food:** A&W/LJ Silver, Applebees, Arby's, Burger King, Chicago Grill, China Wok, ChuckeCheese, Denny's, Don Pablo, Eastern Buffet, 5 Guys Cafe, Fresno's, La Tonalateca, McDonald's, Old Country Buffet, Olive Garden, Perkins, Pizza Hut, Red Lobster, Red Robin, Ruby Tuesday, Smokey Bones BBQ, Subway, TCBY, TX Roadhouse, TGIFriday, **lodging:** Days Inn, **other:** Aldi Foods, Borders Books, Firestone/auto, Harley-Davidson, Home Depot, Hyundai, JC Penney, Jo-Ann Crafts, K-Mart, Kohl's, Macy's, Marshall's, Michael's, PepBoys, PetsMart, Radio Shack, Sears/auto, Target, TJ Maxx, **Walmart SuperCtr/24hr**, William's Tires, mall, **W other:** to Anthracite Museum
190	Main Ave, Dickson City, **E food:** Charlie Brown's Steaks, Wendy's, **lodging:** Fairfield Inn, Residence Inn, **other:** Best Buy, Gander Mtn Lowes Whse, Sam's Club/gas, Staples, **W other:** Toyota/Scion
188	PA 347, Throop, **E gas:** Sheetz/24hr, Sunoco/dsl, **food:** China World Buffet, McDonald's, Quizno's, Wendy's, **lodging:** Day's Inn, Sleep Inn, Super 8,

SCRANTON

Exit #	Services
188	Continued **other:** Advance Parts, Big Lots, Kost Tire, PriceChopper Foods, st police, **W gas:** Exxon, **food:** Burger King, Dunkin Donuts, Friendly's, New China Star, Subway
187	to I-84, I-380, US 6 (no return from nb)
186	PA 435, Drinker St (from nb), **E gas:** Valero, **lodging:** Holiday Inn, **W gas:** Exxon
185	Central Scranton Expwy (exits left from nb), **W** H
184	to PA 307, River St, **W gas:** Citgo, Lukoil, Shell, USA/Subway/dsl, **food:** Dunkin Donuts, **lodging:** Clarion, **other:** H, Curves, CVS Drug, $Tree, Gerrity Foods
182	Davis St, Montage Mtn Rd, **E gas:** Exxon, **food:** Mugg's Rest., Ruby Tuesday, Stadium Club Rest., **lodging:** Comfort Suites, Courtyard, Hampton Inn, **W gas:** Sunoco, **food:** Dunkin Donuts, Waffle House, Wendy's, **other:** CVS Drug, USPO
180	to US 11, PA 502, to Moosic, (exits left from nb), **W gas:** BP/Subway/dsl/24hr
178b a	to US 11, Avoca, **E lodging:** Holiday Inn Express, **W gas:** Petro/Sunoco/dsl/rest./24hr/@
175b a	PA 315 S, to I-476, Dupont, **E gas:** Exxon, Sunoco/24hr, **food:** Arby's, McDonald's, Perkins, **lodging:** Knight's Inn, Super 8, **other:** Chevrolet, **W gas:** Getty/repair, Pilot/Wendy's/dsl/scales/24hr, **lodging:** Quality Inn, **other:** Walmart
170b a	PA 115, PA 309, Wilkes-Barre, **E gas:** Exxon/Subway/dsl, Sunoco/dsl, **lodging:** Best Western, **other:** to Pocono Downs, **W gas:** BP, Sunoco/24hr, **food:** Burger King, Denny's, Friendly's, LJ Silver, Lonestar Steaks, McDonald's, Pizza Hut, Ruby Tuesday, TGIFriday, **lodging:** Day's Inn, Extended Stay Deluxe, Holiday Inn, Red Roof Inn, **other:** H, BonTon, Chevrolet, Goodyear, Land Rover/Mercedes, Macy's, Sears/auto, mall
168	Highland Park Blvd, Wilkes-Barre, **W gas:** Sheetz/24hr, Sunoco, **food:** Applebees, Bennigan's, Bob Evans, Chili's, ChuckeCheese, Cracker Barrel, Grotto Pizza, Ground Round, King's Buffet, Logan's Roadhouse, McDonald's, Olive Garden, Outback Steaks, Panera Bread, Quizno's, Red Robin, Smokey Bones BBQ, Subway, Starbucks, Wendy's, **lodging:** Best Western, Days Inn, Hilton Garden, Ramada Inn, **other:** Barnes&Noble, Best Buy, BonTon, Firestone, JC Penney, Kohl's, Kost Tire, Lowes Whse, Macy's, Marshall's, Michael's, Office Depot, Old Navy, PetCo, Ross, Sam's Club/gas, Staples, Target, TJ Maxx, Walmart SuperCtr/24hr, Wegman's Foods
165b a	PA 309 S, Wilkes-Barre, **W gas:** BP/dsl, Gulf, **food:** Dunkin Donuts, Mark II Rest., McDonald's, Perkins, Taco Bell, **lodging:** Comfort Inn, Econolodge, **other:** Advance Parts, K-Mart, Rite Aid
164	PA 29, to Nanticoke, Ashley
159	Nuangola, **W gas:** BP/cafe/24hr
157mm	**rest area/weigh sta sb, full ♿ facilities, vending, ☎, 🛆, litter barrels, petwalk**
156mm	**rest area/weigh sta nb, full ♿ facilities, vending, ☎, 🛆, litter barrels, petwalk**
155	to Dorrance, **E gas:** Sunoco/dsl/24hr, **lodging:** Econolodge (2mi), **W gas:** Blue Ridge Plaza/dsl
151b a	I-80, E to Mountaintop, W to Bloomsburg

PA

INTERSTATE 81 CONT'D

N ↕ S

HAZLETON

Exit #	Services
145	PA 93, W Hazleton, **E gas:** Exxon, Sunoco/dsl/24hr, TurkeyHill, **food:** Bonanza, Damon's, Friendly's, Ground Round, McDonald's, Perkins, Pizza Hut, Taco Bell, Wendy's, **lodging:** Best Western (2mi), Comfort Inn, Fairfield Inn, Forest Hill Inn, Ramada Inn (2mi), **other:** [H], Aldi Foods, Buick/Cadillac/GMC/Pontiac, Chrysler/Dodge/Jeep, $Tree, JC Penney, K-Mart, Mazda, st police, **W food:** Top of the 80's, **lodging:** Candlewood Suites, Hampton Inn
143	PA 924, to Hazleton, **W gas:** Exxon/dsl, Shell, Turkey-Hill, **food:** Subway, **lodging:** Residence Inn
141	PA 424, S Hazleton Beltway
138	PA 309, to McAdoo, **2 mi E lodging:** Pines Motel
134	to Delano
132mm	**parking area/weigh sta both lanes**
131b a	PA 54, Mahanoy City, **E other:** to Tuscarora/Locust Lake SP, **W gas:** Exxon, Shell/dsl
124b a	PA 61, to Frackville, **E food:** China Palace, Cracker Barrel, McDonald's, **lodging:** Holiday Inn Express, **other:** Big Lots, BonTon, K-Mart, Sears/auto, mall, **W gas:** Exxon, Hess, **food:** Anthony's Pizza, Dutch Kitchen, Subway, **lodging:** Econolodge, Granny's Motel, Rodeway Inn, **other:** [H], Rite Aid, st police
119	High Ridge Park Rd, to Gordon, **E lodging:** Country Inn&Suites, **other:** [H]
116	PA 901, to Minersville, **E food:** 901 Rest.
112	PA 25, to Hegins, **W** camping
107	US 209, to Tremont
104	PA 125, Ravine, **E gas:** Exxon/Pizza Hut/Quizno's/dsl/24hr, **other:** Echo Valley Campgrd
100	PA 443, to Pine Grove, **E gas:** Exxon/dsl, **food:** Arby's, McDonald's, **lodging:** Comfort Inn, Econolodge, **W gas:** Shell/DQ/Subway/dsl/scales/24hr, Sunoco/dsl/24hr, **food:** Gooseberry Far MS Rest., **lodging:** Hampton Inn, **other:** KOA (5mi)
90	PA 72, to Lebanon, **E gas:** Exxon/Subway, Hess/Blimpie/dsl, Love's/McDonald's/dsl/scales/24hr, **food:** DQ/Sbarro's, Wendy's, **lodging:** Best Western, Day's Inn, **other:** KOA (5mi), Lickdale Camping, st police, **W lodging:** Quality Inn
89	I-78 E, to Allentown
85b a	PA 934, to Annville, **2 mi W gas:** LukOil/dsl/24hr, **food:** Funck's Rest., **other:** to IndianTown Gap Nat Cem
80	PA 743, Grantville, **E gas:** LukOil/dsl, **lodging:** Days Inn, Hampton Inn, **W gas:** Exxon/dsl, **food:** Winner's Circle, **lodging:** Comfort Suites, Holiday Inn, **other:** camping, racetrack
79mm	**rest area/weigh sta both lanes, full ♿ facilities, ☎, vending, picnic tables, litter barrels, petwalk**
77	PA 39, to Hershey, **E gas:** Exxon/dsl, Pilot/Pizza Hut/dsl/scales/24hr, Valero, **lodging:** Country Hearth Inn, Country Inn&Suites, Howard Johnson, Scottish Inn, **other:** to Hershey Attractions, st police, **W gas:** Citgo/Subway/dsl, TA/dsl/scales/24hr/@, Wilco/Hess/Perkins/Stuckey's/dsl/24hr/@, **food:** McDonald's, **lodging:** Comfort Inn, Daystop, **other:** Goodyear
72	to US 22, Linglestown, **E gas:** Hess/dsl, Sunoco/dsl, **food:** Burger King, McDonald's, **lodging:** Holiday Inn Express, Quality Inn, **other:** Advance Parts,

LEBANON

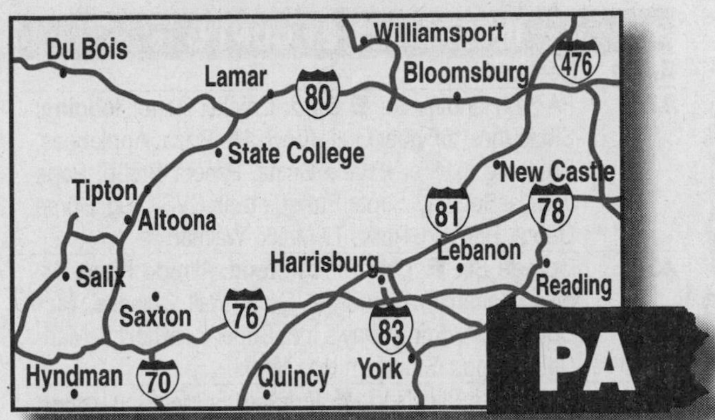

HARRISBURG

Exit #	Services
72	Continued CVS Drug, Harley-Davidson, Jo-Ann Fabrics, Karn's Foods, Toyota/Scion, U-haul, **W food:** Country Oven Rest., **lodging:** Best Western, MainStay Suites, **other:** Ace Hardware
70	I-83 S, to York, ✈
69	Progress Ave, **E gas:** 7-11, **food:** Cracker Barrel, Damon's, Macaroni Grill, Moe's SW Grill, Starbucks, **other:** Maggie Moo's, Susquehanna Shoppes, st police, **W gas:** Turkey Hill, **food:** Arby's, Steak House, YP Rest., **lodging:** Capital Plaza Inn, Red Roof Inn
67b a	US 22, US 322 W, PA 230, Cameron St, to Lewistown
66	Front St, **E** [H], **W gas:** Exxon, Sunoco, **food:** Jade Buffet, McDonald's, Pizza Hut, Taco Bell, Wendy's, **lodging:** Day's Inn, Super 8
65	US 11/15, to Enola, **1 mi E gas:** Sunoco/dsl/24hr, Tom's, **food:** Al's Pizza, China Taste, DQ, Dunkin Donuts, McDonald's, Subway, Summerdale Diner, Wendy's, **lodging:** Quality Inn, **other:** Advance Parts, $Tree, Fischer Parts, K-Mart, Radio Shack, Rite Aid
61	PA 944, to Wertzville
59	PA 581, to US 11, I-83, Harrisburg, **3 mi E food:** Bob Evans, Burger King, Friendly's, McDonald's, Wendy's, **lodging:** Comfort Inn, Hampton Inn, Holiday Inn
57	PA 114, to Mechanicsburg, **1-2 mi E food:** Arby's, Isaac's Rest., McDonald's, Pizza Hut, Red Robin, Taco Bell, **lodging:** Ramada Ltd
52b a	US 11, to I-76/PA Tpk, Middlesex, **E gas:** Exxon/Taco Bell/24hr, Sheetz/24hr, **food:** Hoss' Rest., **lodging:** Motel 6, **other:** [H], Chrysler/Jeep, U-Haul, **W gas:** BP, Petro/dsl/24hr/@, ***FLYING J***/dsl/LP/rest./24hr/@, Pilot/Wendy's/dsl/24hr, Shell/dsl/scales, Sunoco, Universal/dsl, **food:** Arby's, Bob Evans, Carelli's Subs, Country Club Diner, Country Oven Rest, McDonald's, Middlesex Diner/24hr, Waffle House, **lodging:** Best Western, Hampton Inn, Holiday Inn, Howard Johnson, Quality Inn, Ramada Ltd, Rodeway Inn, Super 8, Travelodge, **other:** [H], Blue Beacon
49	PA 74 (no EZ sb return), **E food:** Red Robin, Starbucks, **other:** Kohl's, Michael's, Old Navy, PetsMart, Target, **W gas:** Citgo, **food:** Burger King, McDonald's, same as 48
48	PA 74, York St (no EZ nb return), **E food:** Coldstone Creamery, Red Robin, Starbucks, **other:** Aldi Foods, $Tree, Kohl's, Michael's, Old Navy, PetsMart, Rite Aid, Target, **W gas:** Gulf, Hess, KwikFill, **other:** Ford, 1 mi **W food:** Burger King, McDonald's, Pizza Hut, Quizno's, Taco Bell, **other:** BonTon, CVS Drug, Lowes Whse, Radio Shack, Weis Foods

CARLISLE

INTERSTATE 81 CONT'D

N ↕ S — CHAMBERSBURG

Exit #	Services
47	PA 34, Hanover St, **E food:** Cracker Barrel, **lodging:** Sleep Inn, **W gas:** Gulf, **food:** Al's Pizza, Applebees, Bruster's, Chili's, Palace China, Panera Bread, Papa John's, Subway, Super Buffet, **other:** CVS Drug, Home Depot, Rite Aid, Ross, TJ Maxx, Walmart
45	College St, **E gas:** BP/dsl, **food:** Alfredo Pizza, Arby's, Bonanza, Friendly's, Great Wall Chinese, McDonald's, **lodging:** Day's Inn, Super 8, **other:** K-Mart, Nell's Foods, Staples, tires, **W** H
44	PA 465, to Plainfield, **E lodging:** Fairfield Inn, **other:** st police, **W gas:** Sheetz/24hr, **food:** Subway
38mm	**rest area both lanes, full facilities, litter barrels, petwalk**
37	PA 233, to Newville, **E** Pine Grove Furnace SP, **W** Col Denning SP
29	PA 174, King St, **E gas:** Shippensburg TP/dsl/scales/24hr, **lodging:** Budget Host, **W gas:** Rutter's/dsl, **food:** Burger King, China House, Little Caesar's, McDonald's (2mi), Subway, Wendy's, **lodging:** Best Western, **other:** Ford, K-Mart, Walmart SuperCtr
24	PA 696, Fayette St, **W gas:** Exxon/dsl, Pacific Pride
20	PA 997, Scotland, **E gas:** Exxon/dsl, **food:** McDonald's, **lodging:** Comfort Inn, Super 8, **other:** Gander Mtn JC Penney, Sears/auto, mall, **W gas:** BP/dsl, Sunoco/24hr, **lodging:** Sleep Inn
17	Walker Rd, **W gas:** Sheetz/24hr, **food:** Bruster's, Fox's Pizza, Fuddrucker's, Jerry's Subs, Moe's SW Grill, Panera Bread, Quizno's, Red Robin, TGIFriday, **lodging:** Country Inn&Suites, **other:** Ford, Giant Foods/gas, Kohl's, Michael's, PetsMart, Staples, Target
16	US 30, to Chambersburg, **E gas:** Exxon, Fuel Ctr, Sheetz/24hr, **food:** Arby's, Best Way Pizza, Bro's Pizza, Chris's Country Kitchen, Hoss's Rest., KFC, Meadow's Custard, Montezuma Mexican, Perkins, Popeye's, Quizno's, Rita's Ice Cream, Ryan's, Waffle House, Wendy's, **lodging:** Days Inn, **other:** Aldi Foods, Curves, $Tree, Harley-Davidson, Jo-Ann Fabrics, Lowes Whse, Nissan/Toyota/Scion, Radio Shack, Walmart SuperCtr/Subway, st police, Vet, **W gas:** Hess/dsl, **food:** Burger King, Copper Kettle, Hardee's, LJ Silver, McDonald's, Pizza Hut, Ponderosa, Ruby Tuesday, Starbucks, Taco Bell, **lodging:** Best Western, Country Inn&Suites, Sheraton, Travelodge, **other:** H, Advance Parts, AutoZone, Lincoln/Mercury, Walgreens
14	PA 316, Wayne Ave, **E food:** Bob Evans, Cracker Barrel, **lodging:** Fairfield Inn, Hampton Inn, Red Carpet Inn, **W gas:** BP, KwikFill, Sheetz, **food:** Applebee's, Arby's, China Wok, Dakota Steaks, Denny's, Mario's, Montezuma Mexican, New China, Papa John's, Pizza Hut, Quizno's, Red Lobster, Subway, Wendy's, **lodging:** Econolodge, Holiday Inn Express, Quality Inn, **other:** CVS Drug, $Tree, Giant Foods/gas, GNC, K-Mart, Staples, Weis Foods
12mm	**weigh sta sb**
10	PA 914, Marion
7mm	**weigh sta nb**
5	PA 16, Greencastle, **E gas:** TA/BP/dsl/rest./scales/24hr/@, Sunoco/grill/dsl, **food:** Arby's, McDonald's, Subway, **lodging:** Econolodge, Rodeway Inn, **other:** Whitetail Ski Resort, **W gas:** Exxon/dsl, **lodging:** Castle Green Motel/rest.
3	US 11, **E gas:** Exxon, **food:** Bro's Pizza, **lodging:** Comfort Inn
2mm	**Welcome Ctr nb, full facilities, litter barrels, vending, petwalk**
1	PA 163, Mason-Dixon Rd, **W lodging:** Knight's Inn, **other:** Keystone RV Ctr
0mm	Pennsylvania/Maryland state line, Mason-Dixon Line

INTERSTATE 83

N ↕ S — HARRISBURG

Exit #	Services
51b a	I-83 begins/ends on I-81, exit 70.
50b a	US 22, Jonestown Rd, Harrisburg, **E gas:** Hess/dsl, Sunoco/dsl, USA, **food:** Applebees, Arby's, Atlanta Bread, Chef Wong's, Cold Stone Creamery, Colonial Park Diner, Domino's, El Rodeo Mexican, Gander Mountain, Gilligan's Grill, Hong Kong City, LJ Silver, McDonald's, Old Country Buffet, Olive Garden, Pizza Hut, Red Lobster, Red Robin, Starbucks, Subway, Taco Bell, Tonino's Pizza, Vocelli's Pizza, Wendy's, **other:** Aamco, Advance Parts, Best Buy, BonTon, Borders Books, Boscov's, Chevrolet, Coscto/gas, CVS Drug, Ford, Giant Foods, Goodyear/auto, Home Depot, K-Mart, Kohl's, Marshall's, Michael's, NAPA, NTB, Old Navy, PepBoys, PetCo, Radio Shack, Ross, Sears/auto, Super Petz, Target, Tires+, U-haul, Weis Foods, William's Tires/repair, mall, **W gas:** Capital, **food:** Dairy Queen, Dunkin Donuts, Friendly's, Gabriella's Italian, KFC, Roberto's Pizza, **other:** Rite Aid
48	Union Deposit Rd, **E gas:** Sunoco, **food:** Arby's, Burger King, Dunkin Donuts, Evergreen Chinese, Panera Bread, **lodging:** Hampton Inn, Sheraton, **other:** H, Giant Foods, Rite Aid, Staples, mall, **W gas:** BP, **food:** Charlie Brown Steaks, ChuckeCheese, Great Wall Chinese, McDonald's, New China, OutBack Steaks, Rita's Ice Cream, Ruby Tuesday, Starbucks, Subway, Texas Roadhouse, TGIFriday, Waffle House, Wendy's, **lodging:** Country Inn&Suites, Fairfield Inn, Holiday Inn Express, **other:** Big Lots, Curves, $Tree, Hancock Fabrics, Lowes Whse, PriceRight Foods, Radio Shack, Tuesday Morning, Weis Foods
47	(46b from nb), US 322 E, to Hershey, Derry St, **E gas:** Hess Gas, **food:** Papa John's, **other:** Home Depot, PetsMart
46a b	I-283 S, to I-76/PA Tpk, **facilities E off I-283 S gas:** Exxon/dsl, Sunoco, **food:** Bob Evans, Capitol Diner, Doc Holliday's Steaks, Domino's, Eat'n Park, McDonald's, Waffle House, **lodging:** Courtyard, EconoLodge, Holiday Inn, Howard Johnson, La Quinta, Red Roof Inn, Sheraton, Super 8, Travelodge, Wyndham, **other:** Buick, JC Penney, LandRover, Target, VW/Audi, **W gas:** Sunoco, **food:** Taco Bell, Wendy's, **lodging:** Best Western, Day's Inn,
45	Paxton St, **E gas:** Sheetz/dsl, **food:** Applebees, Burger King, Dunkin Donuts, Fuddrucker's, Isaac's Rest., Pizza Hut, Ruby Tuesday, Starbucks, Wendy's, **lodging:** Hilton Garden, Homewood Suites, Towneplace Suites, **other:** Bass Pro Shops, Barnes&Noble, JC Penney, Macy's, Mazda/Subaru/Toyota, Nissan, mall
44b	17th St, 19th St, **E gas:** Sunoco, **food:** Bankok Thai Cuisine, Benihana Japanese, Dunkin Donuts, Hardee's, **other:** Advance Parts, AutoZone, Buick/GMC/Pontiac, Firestone/auto, Honda, Hyundai/Suzuki, Nissan, Pontiac, Tires+

PA

N ↕ S

INTERSTATE 83 CONT'D

Exit #	Services
44a	PA 230, 13th St, Harrisburg, downtown, **W other:** Chevrolet
43	2nd St, Harrisburg, downtown, St Capitol, **W lodging:** Crowne Plaza, Hilton, **other:** H
42.5mm	Susquehanna River
42	Lemoyne
41b	Highland Park, **E gas:** Hess, Turkey Hill, **food:** Burger King, KFC, **E gas:** Sunoco, **food:** Ciao Pizza, **other:** Ace Hardware, Family$, Weis Foods
41a	US 15, PA 581 W, to Gettysburg
40b	New Cumberland, **W gas:** BP/dsl, **food:** JoJo's Pizza, McDonald's, New China, Sidoti's Italian, Subway, **other:** CVS Drug, $General
40a	Limekiln Rd, to Lewisberry, **E gas:** BP, Tom's, **food:** Bob Evans, Doc Holliday's Rest, Eat'n Park, McDonald's, Pizza Hut, **lodging:** Comfort Inn, Holiday Inn, Quality Inn, Rodeway Inn, **W gas:** Hess, **lodging:** Best Western, Motel 6, Travel Inn, **other:** vet
39b	I-76/PA Tpk
39a	PA 114, Lewisberry Rd, **E lodging:** Day's Inn, Keystone Inn, Red Carpet Inn
38	Reesers Summit
36	PA 262, Fishing Creek, **E gas:** Hess, **food:** Bruster's, Culhane's Steaks, Mamma's Pizza, **other:** CVS Drug, **W gas:** Citgo/dsl
35	PA 177, Lewisberry, **E food:** Hillside Café, **W gas:** Exxon, **food:** Francescos, Summit Rest., **lodging:** Alpine Inn
34mm	**parking area/weigh sta sb**
34	Valley Green (from nb), same as 33
33	PA 392, Yocumtown, **E gas:** Hess/dsl, Rutter's, **food:** Alice's Rest., Burger King, Maple Donuts, McDonald's, NewBerry Diner, New China Buffet, 2 Bro's Pizza, **lodging:** Super 8, **other:** Family$, Radio Shack, Rite Aid, SuperFresh Food
33mm	**parking area/weigh sta nb**
32	PA 382, Newberrytown, **E gas:** Rutter's/Pizza Hut/dsl/24hr, **W gas:** Exxon/dsl
28	PA 295, Strinestown, **W gas:** Rutter's/24hr, **food:** 83 Diner, Wendy's
24	PA 238, Emigsville, **W gas:** Tom's, **food:** 4 Bro's Rest.
22	PA 181, N George St, **E gas:** Rutter's, **lodging:** Comfort Inn, Homewood Suites, **W** same as 21b
21b a	US 30, Arsenal Rd, to York, **E food:** Round-the-Clock, San Carlo's Rest., **lodging:** Day's Inn, Motel 6, Sheraton, **other:** Buick/GMC/Pontiac, **W gas:** Citgo, Rutter's/dsl, **food:** Arby's, Bob Evan's, Burger King, China Kitchen, Damon's, Denny's, DQ, El Rodeo Mexican, 5 Guys Burgers, Friendly's, Hardee's, Hooters, KFC, Logan's Roadhouse, LJ Silver, McDonald's, Nautilus Diner, Old Country Buffet, Olive Garden, Panera Bread, Pizza Hut, Popeye's, Quizno's, RipTide Seafood, Rita's Ice Cream, Ruby Tuesday, Smokey Bones BBQ, Subway, Taco Bell, TGIFriday, Wendy's, **lodging:** Best Western, Red Roof Inn, Super 8, Wingate Inn, **other:** Acura, Advance Parts, AutoZone, BJ's Whse, BMW, BonTon, Cadillac/Chevrolet, CVS Drug, Dodge, $General, Giant Foods/gas, Harley-Davidson,

LEWISBERRY

YORK

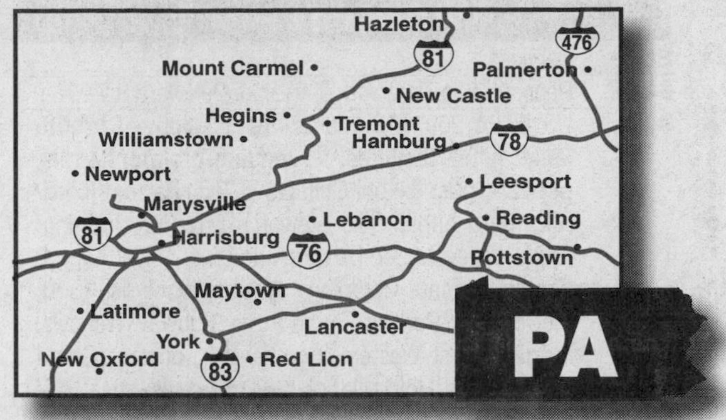

YORK

Exit #	Services
21b a	Continued Lowes Whse, Macy's, NTB, Office Depot, Old Navy, PepBoys, PetsMart, Radio Shack, Ross, Staples, Subaru, TJ Maxx, Walmart SuperCtr, Weis Foods/gas, transmissions
19	PA 462, Market St, **E gas:** Hess, **food:** Applebees, Arby's, ChuckeCheese, Coldstone Creamery, DQ, Fuddruckers, Outback Steaks, Papa John's, Perkins, Rita's Ice Cream, Taco Bell, Tokyo Diner, Wendy's, **lodging:** Quality Inn, **other:** H, Advance Parts, Aldi Foods, $General, $Tree, Giant Foods, Home Depot, Lowes Whse, Nissan, NTB, Sam's Club, Walgreens, Walmart SuperCtr, Weis Foods
18	PA 124, Mt Rose Ave, Prospect St, **E gas:** Pacific Pride, Rutters, **food:** Al Dente Italian, Burger King, 5 Guys, Nino's Pizza, Pizza Hut, Sweet House Chinese, Uncle Nick's Diner, **lodging:** Budget Host, **other:** Curves, K-Mart, Nello Tire
16b a	PA 74, Queen St, **E gas:** Tom's, **food:** Baskin-Robbins/Dunkin Donuts, Bella's Italian, China Buffet, Cracker Barrel, Isaac's Rest., Ruby Tuesday, **lodging:** Country Inn&Suites, **other:** Giant Foods/gas, Lincoln/Mercury, **W gas:** LukOil, Sheetz, **food:** Infinito's Pizza, McDonald's, Pizza Hut/Taco Bell, Quizno's, S Yorke Diner, Subway, **other:** BonTon, CVS Drug, $General, $Tree, Jo-Ann Fabrics, Price Rite Foods, Tuesday Morning, Walgreens
15	S George St, I-83 spur into York, **W** H
14	PA 182, Leader Heights, **E food:** Domino's, First Wok, Subway, **other:** vet, **W gas:** Rutter's/Pizza Hut, **food:** McDonald's, **lodging:** Holiday Inn Express, **other:** Rite Aid
10	PA 214, Loganville, **W food:** Elsie's Rest., Mamm a's Pizza, **lodging:** Midway Motel, **other:** TrueValue, st police
8	PA 216, Glen Rock, **E lodging:** Rocky Ridge Motel, **W other:** Amish Farmers Mkt (2mi)
4	PA 851, Shrewsbury, **E gas:** Tom's/dsl/24hr, **food:** Cracker Barrel, Ruby Tuesday, **lodging:** Hampton Inn, **other:** Home Depot, TrueValue, **W gas:** Exxon/dsl/24hr, **food:** Arby's, Chick-fil-A, Coachlight Rest., Emerald Garden Chinese, KFC/Taco Bell, McDonald's, Quizno's, Rita's Ice Cream, Starbucks, Subway, Szechuan Chinese, Wendy's, **other:** Advance Parts, Curves, $Tree, Giant Foods, GNC, Radio Shack, Sauble's Foods, Walmart SuperCtr/24hr
2mm	**Welcome Ctr nb, full ♿ facilities, ☎, vending, picnic tables, litter barrels, petwalk**
0mm	Pennsylvania/Maryland state line

INTERSTATE 84

Exit #	Services
54mm	Pennsylvania/New York state line, Delaware River
53	US 6, PA 209, Matamoras, **N Welcome Ctr/both lanes, full facilities, phone, vending, picnic, litter barrels, petwalk, gas:** Exxon, Gulf, Go24/Taco Palace, Turkey Hill, **food:** Apple Grill, Stewart's Drive-Inn, **lodging:** Apple Valley Motel, **other:** AutoZone, PriceChopper Foods, Tri-State Camping, **S gas:** Mobil/dsl, **food:** McDonald's, Perkins, Roma Pizza, Subway, Wendy's, **lodging:** Best Western, Scottish Inn, **other:** , Grand Union Foods, Home Depot, K-Mart, Lowes Whse, Staples, Walmart/SuperCtr/24hr, Riverbeach Camping
46	US 6, to Milford, **N gas:** Mobil/24hr, **2 mi S gas:** Citgo/dsl/24hr, Sunoco/dsl, **food:** Apple Valley Rest., **lodging:** Black Walnut B&B, Cliff Park Inn, Sherelyn Motel, Red Carpet Inn
34	PA 739, to Lords Valley, Dingmans Ferry, **S gas:** Mobil, Sunoco/Taco Xtra/dsl, **food:** Bruno's Pizza, China Dynasty, McDonald's, **other:** Curves, Family$, Mr Z's Foods, Rite Aid, USPO
30	PA 402, to Blooming Grove, **N** st police, to Lake Wallenpaupack
26	PA 390, to Tafton, **N** Exxon/dsl, to Lake Wallenpaupack, **S other:** to Promised Land SP
26mm	**rest area/weigh sta both lanes, full facilities, phone, vending, picnic, litter barrels, petwalk**
20	PA 507, Greentown, **N gas:** Exxon/dsl, Mobil/Sbway, **food:** John's Italian, **other:** Animal Park (5mi)
17	PA 191, to Newfoundland, Hamlin, **N gas:** Exxon/24hr, Howe's 84/dsl/24hr, **food:** Twin Rocks Rest., **lodging:** Comfort Inn/rest.
8	PA 247, PA 348, Mt Cobb, **N gas:** Gulf/dsl/24hr, **other:** golf, **S gas:** Mobil/dsl/24hr
4	I-380 S, to Mount Pocono
2	PA 435 S, to Elmhurst
1	Tigue St, **N lodging:** Holiday Inn, **S gas:** Mobil
0mm	I-84 begins/ends on I-81, exit 54.

INTERSTATE 90

Exit #	Services
46mm	Pennsylvania/New York state line, **Welcome Ctr/weigh sta wb, full facilities, phone, vending, picnic, litter barrels, petwalk**
45	US 20, to State Line, **N gas:** KwikFill/dsl/scales, **food:** McDonald's, **S gas:** BP/Subway/dsl, **lodging:** Red Carpet Inn, **other:** Niagara Falls Info, fireworks
41	PA 89, North East, **N gas:** Shell, **lodging:** Holiday Inn Express, Super 8, Vineyard B&B, **S** camping, winery
37	I-86 E, to Jamestown
35	PA 531, to Harborcreek, **N gas:** TA/BP/dsl/rest./scales/24hr/@, **food:** Pizza Hut, Subway, **lodging:** Rodeway Inn, **other:** Blue Beacon, dsl repair
32	PA 430, PA 290, to Wesleyville, **N gas:** Country Fair, st police, **S other:** camping
29	PA 8, to Hammett, **N gas:** Country Fair, **food:** Wendy's, **other:** H, **S lodging:** Travelodge, **other:** Peterbilt, dsl repair
27	PA 97, State St, Waterford, **N gas:** Country Fair/dsl/24hr, Kwikfill, **food:** Arby's, Barbato's Italian, Doc Holiday's Grill, McDonald's, **lodging:** Day's Inn, La Quinta, Red Roof Inn, Tallyho Inn, **other:** H,
27	Continued **S gas:** Pilot/Subway/dsl/scales/24hr, Shell/dsl, **lodging:** Quality Inn, Super 8, **other:** casino
24	US 19, Peach St, to Waterford, **N gas:** Country Fair, Delta Sonic, KwikFill, **food:** Applebee's, Bruster's, Burger King, Chick-fil-A, China Garden, ChuckeCheese, Cracker Barrel, Damon's, Eat'n Park, Golden Corral, Longhorn Steaks, McDonald's, Old Country Buffet, Panera Bread, Quaker Steak&Lube, Safari Grill, Steak'n Shake, Taco Bell, Texas Roadhouse, TGI Friday, Torero's Mexican, **lodging:** Courtyard, Hilton Garden, **other:** H, Advance Parts, Best Buy, Country Fair/deli, $Tree, Giant Eagle, Home Depot, Jo-Ann Fabrics, K-Mart, Kohl's, Lowes Whse, Marshall's, PetsMart, Sam's Club/gas, Staples, Target, VW, **Walmart/auto**, Wegman's Foods, **S gas:** BP, Country Fair, **Shell/dsl**, **food:** Bob Evans, Boston's Rest., **lodging:** Comfort Inn, Country Inn&Suites, Econolodge, Hampton Inn, Holiday Inn Express, Microtel, Residence Inn, **other:** waterpark
22b a	I-79, N to Erie, S to Pittsburgh, **3-5 mi N** services in Erie
18	PA 832, Sterrettania, **N gas:** Marathon/dsl/24hr, **food:** Burger King, **other:** Hill's Family Camping, to Presque Isle SP, **S lodging:** Quality Inn
16	PA 98, to Franklin Center, Fairview, **S other:** Follys Camping (2mi), Mar-Da-Jo-Dy Camping (5mi)
9	PA 18, to Girard, Platea, **N other:** Gulf/dsl repair, st police, **S lodging:** Green Roof Inn (2mi)
6	PA 215, to Albion, E Springfield, **N** lodging, **S gas:** Sunoco, lodging, repair
3	US 6N, to Cherry Hill, West Springfield, **N** lodging on US 20, **S gas:** BP/dsl/rest./scales/24hr
2.5mm	**Welcome Ctr/weigh sta eb, full facilities, info, phone, picnic, litter barrels, vending, petwalk**
0mm	Pennsylvania/Ohio state line

INTERSTATE 95

Exit #	Services
51mm	Pennsylvania/New Jersey state line, Delaware River
51	PA 32, to New Hope, **W** Washington Crossing Hist Park
49mm	**Welcome Ctr sb, full facilities, vending, phone, picnic, litter barrels, petwalk**
49	PA 332, to Yardley, Newtown, **W food:** Dunkin Donuts, **lodging:** Hampton Inn, **other:** H, to Tyler SP
46b a	US 1 to I-276, PA TPK, Langhorne, Oxford Valley, **E** H
44	US 1, PA 413, to Penndel, Levittown, **E gas:** Shell/dsl/24hr, **food:** Blue Fountain Diner, Cheeseburger Paradise, ChuckeCheese, Dunkin Donuts, Friendly's, Great American Diner, Hong Kong Pearl, Langhorn Ale House, Ming's Asian, Olive Garden, Panera Bread, Quizno's, Red Lobster, Ruby Tuesday, Subway, Tennessee BBQ, Wendy's, **other:** H, Acura, Border's Books, Chrysler, Dodge, $Tree, Firestone/auto, Ford, Goodyear/auto, Harley Davidson, Honda, Hyundai/Suzuki, Jeep, Kia, K-Mart, Lincoln/Mercury, Lowes Whse, Marshalls, Mazda/Subaru, NTB, Office Depot, Sam's Club, Staples, Subaru, Target, TJ Maxx, VW/Volvo, Redner's Whse Mkt, **W gas:** LukOil, **food:** Denny's, McDonald's, **other:** Toyota/Scion, U-Haul

ERIE

LEVITTOWN

PA

INTERSTATE 95

N ↕ S

Exit #	Services
40	PA 413, I-276, to Bristol Bridge, Burlington, **E gas:** Hess/dsl, **food:** Fish Factory Rest., Golden Eagle Diner/24hr, Pizza Hut, **other:** [H], Chevrolet, Walmart
37	PA 132, to Street Rd, **W gas:** BP/dsl/24hr, Shell, Sunoco/dsl, **food:** Burger King, China Sun Buffet, Golden Corral, IHOP, KFC, McDonald's, Sonic, Tx Roadhouse, Wendy's, **other:** $Tree, Firestone, GNC, K-Mart, PepBoys, Radio Shack, Sav-a-Lot, 7-11, U-haul, WaWa
35	PA 63, to US 13, Woodhaven Rd, Bristol Park, **W gas:** Liberty, **food:** Bob Evan's, Dunkin Donuts, Old Haven Pizza, Rita's Ice Cream, **lodging:** Hampton Inn, **other:** [H], Acme Foods, Hancock Fabrics, Home Depot, WaWa, **1 mi W gas:** BP, Exxon, LukOil, Sunoco/dsl, **food:** Arby's, Boston Mkt, Bugaboo Creek Steaks, Dave & Buster's, Dynasty Rest., International Buffet, KFC, McDonald's, Pizza Hut, Ruby Tuesday, Subway, Taco Bell, Uno, Wendy's, **other:** Big Lots, JC Penney, Marshall's, NTB, Sam's Club, Sears/auto, Steve&Barry's, SuperFresh Foods, Tires+, Walmart, mall
32	Academy Rd, **W other:** [H], K-Mart
30	PA 73, Cottman Ave, **W gas:** Sunoco
27	Bridge St, **W gas:** BP, Exxon, LukOil, 7-11, **food:** Dunkin Donuts, **other:** [H], Rite Aid
26	to NJ 90, Betsy Ross Brdg, **W gas:** BP, Hess, Sunoco/dsl, **food:** Applebees, Burger King, KFC, McDonald's, Wendy's, **other:** Home Depot, ShopRite Foods, Target
25	Allegheny Ave, **W gas:** Sunoco, **other:** [H], WaWa
23	Lehigh Ave, Girard Ave, **W gas:** Exxon, **food:** Applebees, Arby's, Cold Stone, Dunkin Donuts, Pizza Hut, Rita's Ice Cream, **other:** [H], AutoZone, CVS Drug, Family$, GNC, PepBoys, Radio Shack, Rite Aid, WaWa
22	I-676, US 30, to Central Philadelphia, Independence Hall
20	Columbus Blvd, Penns Landing, **E gas:** BP, LukOil, Sunoco, Xpress, **food:** Burger King, Boston Mkt, Dave&Buster's, ChartHouse Rest., ChuckeCheese, Enginehouse Rest, Grand King Buffet, Hooters, McDonald's, **lodging:** Comfort Inn, Hyatt Hotel (1mi), **other:** Best Buy, Home Depot, Lowes Whse, Marshall's, PepBoys, SavALot Foods, ShopRite Foods, Staples, Target, Walmart, WaWa
19	I-76 E, to Walt Whitman Bridge, **W on Oregon Ave... gas:** Shell, **food:** Burger King, Church's Chicken, McDonald's, Subway, Wendy's, **lodging:** Holiday Inn, **other:** Aldi, K-Mart, to stadium
17	PA 611, to Broad St, Pattison Ave, **W other:** [H], to Naval Shipyard, to stadium
15mm	Schuykill River
15	Enterprise Ave, Island Ave (from sb)
14	Bartram Ave, Essington Ave (from sb)
13	PA 291, to I-76 W (from nb), to Central Philadelphia, **E gas:** Exxon/dsl, **lodging:** Day's Inn, 4Points Sheraton, Guest Quarters, Hilton, Renaissance Inn, Residence Inn, Sheraton Suites, Westin Suites
12	**E** Philadelphia Intl ✈, services same as 10

PHILADELPHIA AREA

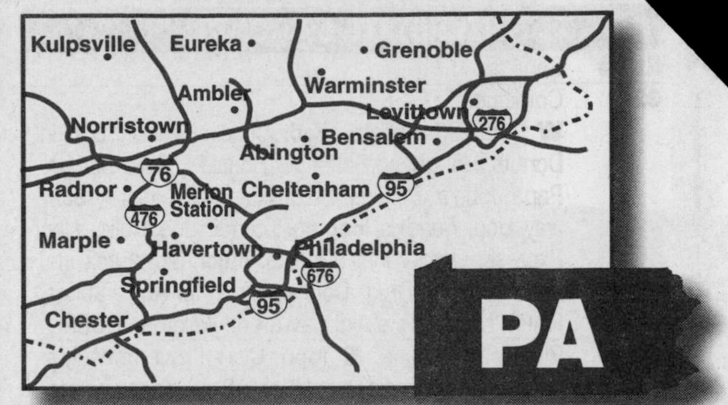

PHILADELPHIA AREA

Exit #	Services
10	PA 29, Bartrom Ave, (from nb), Cargo City, **E lodging:** Marriott, Renaissance Hotel, **W lodging:** Courtyard, Hampton Inn, Embassy Suites, Extended Stay America, Fairfield Inn, Microtel, Studio+
9b a	PA 420, to Essington, Prospect Park, **E gas:** Sunoco/dsl, Valero/dsl, **food:** Denny's, Lehmans Rest., Philly Diner, **lodging:** Comfort Inn, Holiday Inn, Motel 6, Ramada Inn, Red Roof Inn, **other:** USPO, WaWa
8	to Chester Waterfront, Ridley Park, **W on US13... food:** Stargate Diner
7	I-476 N, to Plymouth, Meeting
6	PA 352, PA 320, to Edgmont Ave, **1 mi E on US 13... food:** McDonald's, Popeye's, **other:** Radio Shack, Walmart/Subway, **W lodging:** Days Inn
5	Kerlin St (from nb), **E gas:** BP, Gulf
4	US 322 E, to NJ, to Barry Bridge, **W lodging:** Highland Motel
3	(3 from nb, no EZ return) US 322 W, Highland Ave, **E gas:** Sunoco/dsl/24hr, **other:** Ford/Lincoln/Mercury, Goodyear
2	PA 452, to US 322, Market St, **E gas:** LukOil, **W gas:** Exxon, **food:** McDonald's, Subway
1	Chichester Ave, **E gas:** Sunoco, **W gas:** BP
0mm	Pennsylvania/Delaware state line, **Welcome Ctr/weigh sta nb, full ♿ facilities, ☎, picnic, litter barrels, petwalk**

INTERSTATE 99

N ↕ S

Exit #	Services
67	PA 322 (I99 beings/ends on US 322 at st college), **E gas:** Exxon
61	US 322 W, Port Matilda, **E gas:** Best, **food:** Brother's Pizza, Subway, **lodging:** Port Matilda Hotel, **other:** USPO
52	PA 350, **E gas:** BP/Subway
48	PA 453, Tyrone, **W gas:** Choice, **food:** Burger King, **other:** [H], Rite Aid
45	Tipton, Grazierville, **W food:** Pizza Hut (2mi), Sammy's BBQ, **other:** [H], DelGrosso's Funpark
41	PA 865 N, Bellwood, **E** Ft Roberdeau HS, **W gas:** Martin Gen Store/dsl, Sheetz/dsl, **other:** DelGrosso's Funpark
39	PA 764 S, Pinecroft, **W** Oak Spring Winery
33	17th St, Altoona, **E** same as 32, **W gas:** Sheetz/24hr, **food:** Hoss' Rest., Subway (2mi), **other:** Lowes Whse, Railroader Museum, U-haul
32	PA 36, Frankstown Rd, Altoona, **E gas:** GetGo, **food:** Chili's, Panera Bread, **other:** Barnes&Noble, Best Buy, Boscov's, Giant Eagle Foods, GNC, Home Depot, Kohl's, Michael's, PetCo, Ross, Staples, Canoe Cr SP,

INTERSTATE 99 CONT'D

	rvices
	ntinued
	gas: BP, Sheetz, food: ChuckeCheese, Dunkin ...uts, HongKong Buffet, McDonald's, Olive Garden, ...pa John's, Perkins, Pizza Hut, Red Lobster, Subway, Uno, Wendy's, **lodging:** EconoLodge, Holiday Inn Express, Quality Inn, Super 8, **other:** H, AutoZone, Cadillac, CVS Drug, Dodge, $Tree, Jo-Ann Fabrics, NAPA, Nissan, Rite Aid, Sav-a-Lot, Walgreens, USPO
31	Plank Rd, Altoona, **E food:** Cici's Pizza, Friendly's, Hoss' Rest, Jethro's Rest., King's Rest., Krispy Kreme, Outback Steaks, Ruby Tuesday, TGIFriday, **lodging:** Comfort Inn, Ramada Inn, **other:** Firestone/auto, Radio Shack, Sam's Club/gas, Target, TJ Maxx, Walmart SuperCtr, st police, **W gas:** BP/Subway, **food:** Applebees, Arby's, Burger King, Cracker Barrel, Denny's, Eat'n Park, Hooters, KFC, Little Ceasars, LJ Silver, Ponderosa, Taco Bell, **lodging:** Hampton Inn, Motel 6, **other:** Advance Parts, BigLots, $General, Giant Eagle Foods, JC Penney, K-Mart, Macy's, PharMor, Sears/auto, Weis Foods
28	US 22, to Ebensburg, Holidaysburg
23	PA 36, PA 164, Roaring Spring, Portage, **E gas:** GetGo/dsl, Sheetz/24hr, Turkey Hill, **food:** Backyard Burger, **other:** H, Walmart SuperCtr, truck repair
15	Claysburg, King, **W food:** Subway, gas
10	to Imler, **W** gas, food, Blue Knob SP (8mi)
7	PA 869, Osterburg, St Clairsville, **W** gas, food, Blue Knob SP
3	PA 56, Johnstown, Cessna, **E other:** truck parts
1	I-70/76. I-99 begins/ends on US 220., **E gas:** BP/dsl, Pacific Pride, Sheetz/dsl, **food:** Arena Rest., Denny's, Ed's Steaks, Hoss' Rest, LJ Silver, McDonald's, Pizza Hut, Subway, Wendy's, **lodging:** Best Western, Budget Host, Hampton Inn, Hillcrest Motel, Holiday Inn Express, Quality Inn, Relax Inn, Super 8

INTERSTATE 476

Exit #	Services
131	US 11, US 6. I-476 begins/ends on I-81., services same as I-81, exit 194.
122	Keyser Ave, Old Forge, Taylor
121mm	**toll plaza**
115	I-81, PA 315, Wyoming Valley, Pittston, **W gas:** Mobil, Pilot/Wendy's/dsl/scales/24hr, Sunoco, **food:** Arby's, McDonald's, Perkins, **lodging:** Knight's Inn, Ramada Inn, **other:** Chevrolet
112mm	**toll plaza**
105	PA 115, Wilkes-Barre, Bear Creek, **E gas:** BP, Exxon, PSC
97mm	**parking areas both lanes**
95	I-80, PA 940, Pocono, Hazleton, **W gas:** BP/24hr, Texaco, WaWa, **food:** A&W/LJ Silver, Arby's, Denny's, Gino's Pizza, McDonald's, **lodging:** Comfort Inn, CountryPlace Inn, Day's Inn, Ramada Inn, Split Rock Resort
90mm	**parking area sb**
86mm	**Hickory Run Service Plaza both lanes, gas:** Sunoco/dsl, **food:** Breyer's, McDonald's, hot dogs
74	US 209, Mahoning Valley, Lehighton, Stroudsburg, **W gas:** Shell/Subway/dsl, **food:** Trainer's Inn Rest., **lodging:** Country Inn&Suites, Hampton Inn
71mm	Lehigh Tunnel
56	I-78, US 22, PA 309, Lehigh Valley, **E gas:** Gulf, **food:** Dunkin Donuts, Quizno's, Red Robin, Trivet Diner, Wendy's, **lodging:** Comfort Inn, Day's Inn, McIntosh Inn, **other:** BMW, CVS Drug, Infiniti, Jaguar, K-Mart, Land Rover, Staples, **W on US 22...gas:** Mobil, Sunoco, **food:** Chris Rest., Parma Pizza, **lodging:** Best Western, **other:** CVS Drug
56mm	**Allentown Service Plaza both lanes, gas:** Sunoco/dsl, **food:** Big Boy, Hershey's Ice Cream, Pizza Hut, Roy Rogers
44	PA 663, Quakertown, Pottstown, **E gas:** BP, Mobil/dsl, **food:** Avanti Grill, Faraco's Pizza, **lodging:** Best Western (3mi), Comfort Suites, Hampton Inn, Holiday Inn Express, Rodeway Inn, **other:** H
37mm	**parking area sb**
31	PA 63, Lansdale, **E gas:** Exxon, Lukoil, WaWa **food:** Bones Grill, **lodging:** Best Western, Courtyard, Lansdale Motel, Residence Inn, **other:** H
20	Germantown Pike W, to I-276 W, PA Tpk W
19	Germantown Pike E
18b a	(18 from sb), Conshohocken, Norristown, **E gas:** Lukoil, Sunoco, **food:** Baja Fresh, Burger King, Domino's, LoneStar Steaks, Maria's Pizza, McDonald's, Outback Steaks, Salad Works, Starbucks, **other:** , Genuradi's Foods, Marshall's, **E on Chemical rd food:** Cracker Barrel, Ruby Tuesday, **lodging:** Hampton Inn, **other:** Barnes&Noble, Best Buy, Giant Foods, Lowes Whse, Office Depot, PetsMart, Ross, Target, **W food:** Papa John's, Uno Pizzaria, Wendy's, **other:** BJ's Whse, Ford, Home Depot, Honda, Michael's, Nissan, Toyota
16b a	(16 from sb), I-76, PA 23, to Philadelpia, Valley Forge
13	US 30, **E gas:** Shell, **food:** Campus Pizza, Winger's, **other:** H, Fresh Grocer, Radnor Drugs, Staples, USPO, Villanova Hardware, to Villanova U
9	PA 3, Broomall, Upper Darby, **E food:** Barnaby's Rest, **other:** H, PathMark Foods, carwash
5	US 1, Lima, Springfield, **E food:** Mesa Mexican, Salad Central, **other:** Jo-Ann Fabrics, Marshall's, Old Navy
3	Baltimore Pike, Media, Swarthmore, **E** H, Swarthmore Coll
1	McDade Blvd, **E gas:** Exxon, **food:** Dunkin Donuts, KFC, McDonald's
0mm	I-476 begins/ends on I-95, exit 7.

RHODE ISLAND

INTERSTATE 95

Exit #	Services
43mm	Rhode Island/Massachusetts state line
30 (42)	East St, to Central Falls, **E food:** Dunkin Donuts, Subway
29 (41)	US 1, Cottage St, **W food:** d'Angelo's, **other:** Firestone
28 (40)	RI 114, School St, **E gas:** Sunoco, **other:** H, Tire Pro, to hist dist
27 (39)	US 1, RI 15, Pawtucket, **W gas:** Shell/repair, Sunoco/dsl/24hr, **food:** Burger King, Dunkin Donuts, Ground Round, **lodging:** Comfort Inn, **other:** H
26 (38)	RI 122, Lonsdale Ave (from nb), **E other:** U-Haul
25 (37)	US 1, RI 126, N Main St, Providence, **E gas:** Hess, Shell, **food:** Chili's, Dunkin Donuts, Gregg Rest., Subway, **other:** H, PepBoys, Rite Aid, Shaw's Foods,

INTERSTATE 95 CONT'D

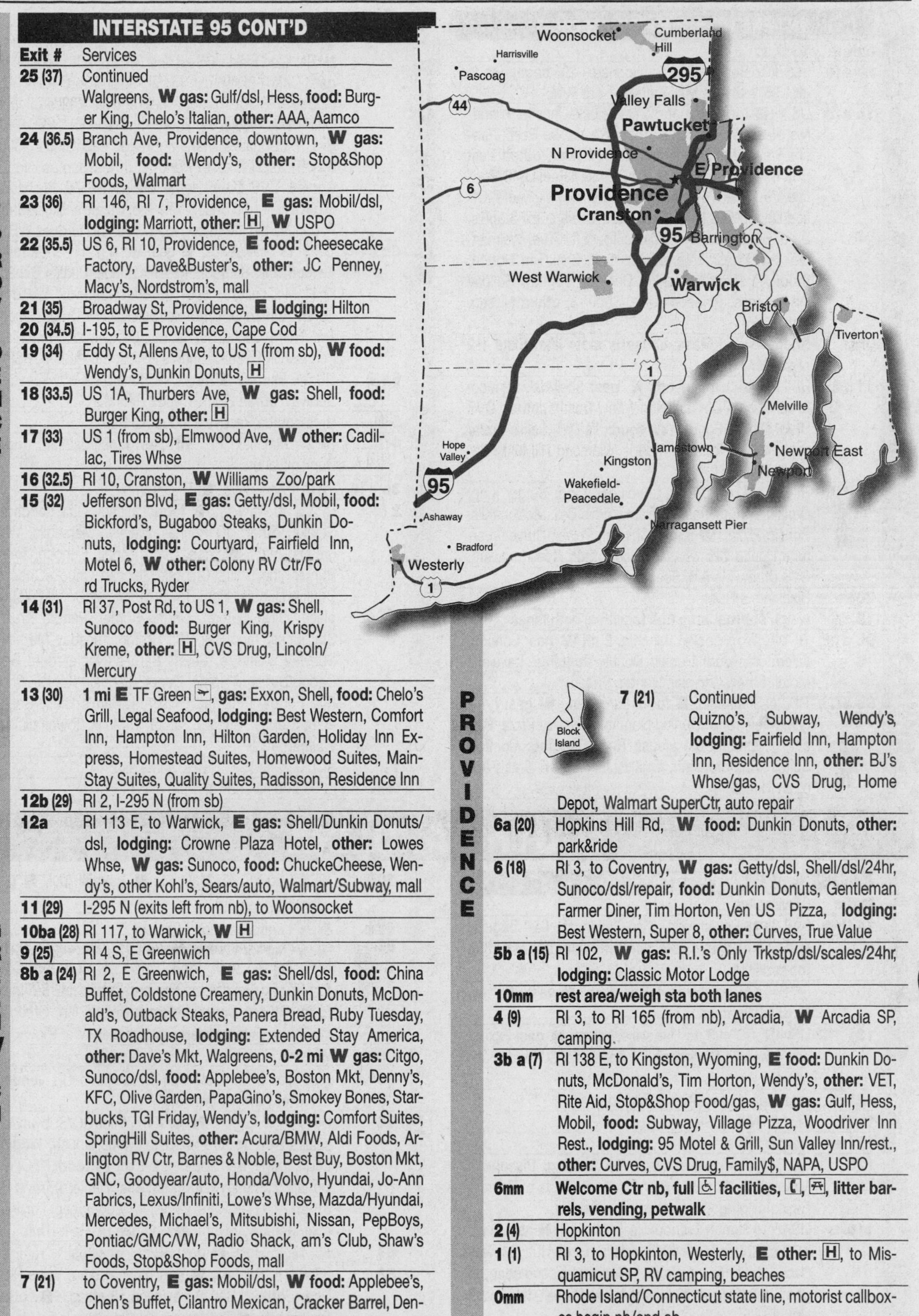

Exit #	Services
25 (37)	Continued Walgreens, **W gas:** Gulf/dsl, Hess, **food:** Burger King, Chelo's Italian, **other:** AAA, Aamco
24 (36.5)	Branch Ave, Providence, downtown, **W gas:** Mobil, **food:** Wendy's, **other:** Stop&Shop Foods, Walmart
23 (36)	RI 146, RI 7, Providence, **E gas:** Mobil/dsl, **lodging:** Marriott, **other:** [H], **W** USPO
22 (35.5)	US 6, RI 10, Providence, **E food:** Cheesecake Factory, Dave&Buster's, **other:** JC Penney, Macy's, Nordstrom's, mall
21 (35)	Broadway St, Providence, **E lodging:** Hilton
20 (34.5)	I-195, to E Providence, Cape Cod
19 (34)	Eddy St, Allens Ave, to US 1 (from sb), **W food:** Wendy's, Dunkin Donuts, [H]
18 (33.5)	US 1A, Thurbers Ave, **W gas:** Shell, **food:** Burger King, **other:** [H]
17 (33)	US 1 (from sb), Elmwood Ave, **W other:** Cadillac, Tires Whse
16 (32.5)	RI 10, Cranston, **W** Williams Zoo/park
15 (32)	Jefferson Blvd, **E gas:** Getty/dsl, Mobil, **food:** Bickford's, Bugaboo Steaks, Dunkin Donuts, **lodging:** Courtyard, Fairfield Inn, Motel 6, **W other:** Colony RV Ctr/Ford Trucks, Ryder
14 (31)	RI 37, Post Rd, to US 1, **W gas:** Shell, Sunoco **food:** Burger King, Krispy Kreme, **other:** [H], CVS Drug, Lincoln/Mercury
13 (30)	**1 mi E** TF Green [airport], **gas:** Exxon, Shell, **food:** Chelo's Grill, Legal Seafood, **lodging:** Best Western, Comfort Inn, Hampton Inn, Hilton Garden, Holiday Inn Express, Homestead Suites, Homewood Suites, MainStay Suites, Quality Suites, Radisson, Residence Inn
12b (29)	RI 2, I-295 N (from sb)
12a	RI 113 E, to Warwick, **E gas:** Shell/Dunkin Donuts/dsl, **lodging:** Crowne Plaza Hotel, **other:** Lowes Whse, **W gas:** Sunoco, **food:** ChuckeCheese, Wendy's, other Kohl's, Sears/auto, Walmart/Subway, mall
11 (29)	I-295 N (exits left from nb), to Woonsocket
10ba (28)	RI 117, to Warwick, **W** [H]
9 (25)	RI 4 S, E Greenwich
8b a (24)	RI 2, E Greenwich, **E gas:** Shell/dsl, **food:** China Buffet, Coldstone Creamery, Dunkin Donuts, McDonald's, Outback Steaks, Panera Bread, Ruby Tuesday, TX Roadhouse, **lodging:** Extended Stay America, **other:** Dave's Mkt, Walgreens, **0-2 mi W gas:** Citgo, Sunoco/dsl, **food:** Applebee's, Boston Mkt, Denny's, KFC, Olive Garden, PapaGino's, Smokey Bones, Starbucks, TGI Friday, Wendy's, **lodging:** Comfort Suites, SpringHill Suites, **other:** Acura/BMW, Aldi Foods, Arlington RV Ctr, Barnes & Noble, Best Buy, Boston Mkt, GNC, Goodyear/auto, Honda/Volvo, Hyundai, Jo-Ann Fabrics, Lexus/Infiniti, Lowe's Whse, Mazda/Hyundai, Mercedes, Michael's, Mitsubishi, Nissan, PepBoys, Pontiac/GMC/VW, Radio Shack, am's Club, Shaw's Foods, Stop&Shop Foods, mall
7 (21)	to Coventry, **E gas:** Mobil/dsl, **W food:** Applebee's, Chen's Buffet, Cilantro Mexican, Cracker Barrel, Denny's, Dunkin Donuts, Honeydew Doughnuts,
7 (21)	Continued Quizno's, Subway, Wendy's, **lodging:** Fairfield Inn, Hampton Inn, Residence Inn, **other:** BJ's Whse/gas, CVS Drug, Home Depot, Walmart SuperCtr, auto repair
6a (20)	Hopkins Hill Rd, **W food:** Dunkin Donuts, **other:** park&ride
6 (18)	RI 3, to Coventry, **W gas:** Getty/dsl, Shell/dsl/24hr, Sunoco/dsl/repair, **food:** Dunkin Donuts, Gentleman Farmer Diner, Tim Horton, Ven US Pizza, **lodging:** Best Western, Super 8, **other:** Curves, True Value
5b a (15)	RI 102, **W gas:** R.I.'s Only Trkstp/dsl/scales/24hr, **lodging:** Classic Motor Lodge
10mm	**rest area/weigh sta both lanes**
4 (9)	RI 3, to RI 165 (from nb), Arcadia, **W** Arcadia SP, camping
3b a (7)	RI 138 E, to Kingston, Wyoming, **E food:** Dunkin Donuts, McDonald's, Tim Horton, Wendy's, **other:** VET, Rite Aid, Stop&Shop Food/gas, **W gas:** Gulf, Hess, Mobil, **food:** Subway, Village Pizza, Woodriver Inn Rest., **lodging:** 95 Motel & Grill, Sun Valley Inn/rest., **other:** Curves, CVS Drug, Family$, NAPA, USPO
6mm	**Welcome Ctr nb, full [handicapped] facilities, [phone], [picnic], litter barrels, vending, petwalk**
2 (4)	Hopkinton
1 (1)	RI 3, to Hopkinton, Westerly, **E other:** [H], to Misquamicut SP, RV camping, beaches
0mm	Rhode Island/Connecticut state line, motorist callboxes begin nb/end sb

RI

INTERSTATE 295 (PROVIDENCE)

E ↕ W PROVIDENCE

Exit #	Services
2b a (4)	I-95, N to Boston, S to Providence. **I-295 begins/ends on I-95, exit 4 in MA. Exits 2-1 are in MA.**
1b a (2)	US 1, **E food:** Chicago Grill, ChuckeCheese, Friendly's, Hearth'n Kettle, Longhorn Steaks, 99 Rest., Panera Bread, Papagino's Italian, TGIFriday, **other:** Best Buy, BJ's Whse, Borders, CVS Drug, $Tree, GMC/Pontiac, Jo-Anne, Lowe's Whse, Marshalls, Michael's, Office Depot, Old Navy, PetsMart, Sears/auto, Staples, Stop&Shop, Target, TJMaxx, Town fair Tire, Walmart, mall, **W gas:** Emerald/dsl, Gulf, Shell/Tim Horton, **food:** Applebee's, Dunkin Donuts, **lodging:** Holiday Inn Express, Pineapple Inn, Super 8, **other:** Nissan, Toyota
0mm	**Rhode Island/Massachusetts state line. Exits 1-2 are in MA.**
11 (24)	RI 114, to Cumberland, **E gas:** Shell/dsl, Sunoco, **food:** Dunkin Donuts, Honeydew Donuts, **other:** CVS Drug, Dave's Foods, **W food:** J's Deli, Saki's Pizza/subs, **other:** Tedeschi Foods, Diamond Hill Mkt, Diamond Hill SP
10 (21)	RI 122, **E gas:** Gulf, Lukoil/dsl, **food:** Burger King, Dunkin Donuts, Jacky's Rest., Jim's Deli, McDonald's, Ronzio Pizza, **W food:** Chicken Power, Curves, Fortune House Chinese, Subway, **other:** Ace Hardware, CVS Drug, Rite Aid, Seabra Foods
20mm	Blackstone River
19.5mm	**weigh sta/rest area (full facilities) both lanes**
9b a (19)	RI 146, Woonsocket, Lincoln, **2 mi W gas:** Sunoco, Valero/dsl, **food:** Dunkin Donuts, **lodging:** Traveler's Motel, **other:** Chrysler, Honda, Subaru
8b a (16)	RI 7, N Smithfield, **E food:** Euro Rest., **W gas:** 7-11/gas, Shell, **food:** Dunkin Donuts, House of Pizza, Parentes Rest., Roost House Rest., **lodging:** Comfort Suites, Hampton Inn, Quality Inn, **other:** Smith-Appleby House
7b a (13)	US 44, Centerdale, **E gas:** Hess, Mobil, **food:** Isabella's Deli, Orlando Rest., **other:** [H], Advance Parts, NAPA, CarQuest, 4 Seasons RV Ctr, auto repair, **W gas:** Citgo, Exxon/dsl, Mobil, Shell, **food:** A&W, Applebee's, Burger King, Chelo's Grill, Chicago Grill, Chili's, D'angelo's, Dominos, Dunkin Donuts, KFC/Taco Bell, McDonald's, Panera Bread, PapaGino's, Subway, TinTsin Chinese, Wendy's, **other:** Barnes&Noble, Curves, CVS Drug, Home Depot, Kohl's, Michael's, Old Navy, Radio Shack, Rite Aid, Staple's, Stop&Shop Foods, Target, TJ Maxx, to Powder Mill Ledges WR
6b c (10)	US 6, to Providence, **E gas:** Mobil, 7-11, Shell, **food:** Atwood Grill, Burger King, China Jade, Dunkin Donuts, KFC, McDonald's, Ruby Tuesday, Subway, Wendy's, **other:** AutoZone, Chevrolet/Buick, CVS Drug, General Tire, Home Depot, Honda, Kia, Office Depot, PetsMart, Pontiac/GMC, Saab, Shaw's Foods, Stop&Shop, USPO
6a (9)	US 6 E Expswy, **E food:** McDonald's, Ruby Tuesday, Subway, **other:** Home Depot, PetsMart
5 (8)	RI Resource Recovery Industrial Park
4 (7)	RI 14, Plainfield Pk, **W gas:** Mobil/dsl/24hr, **food:** Dunkin Donuts
3b a (4)	rd 37, Phenix Ave, **E** TF Green ✈
2 (2)	RI 2 S, to Warwick, **E food:** Chicago Grill, Longhorn Steaks, **other:** JC Penney, Macy's, Marshalls, Walgreens, mall, **W gas:** Citgo, Mobil, Sunoco, **food:** Burger King, Chili's, Chipotle Mexican, ChuckeCheese, Dunkin Donuts, HomeTown Buffet, McDonald's/playplace, Olive Garden, On-the-Border, Panera Bread, Starbucks, Taco Bell, Tim Horton, Tuesday Morning, Subway, Wendy's, **other:** Barnes&Noble, Best Buy, Dodge/Subaru, Home Depot, Jaguar, Kohl's, Price Rite Foods, PetsMart, Rite Aid, Sam's Club, Sears/auto, Staples, Subaru, Target, TJMaxx, TownFair Tire, Walmart, mall
1 (1)	RI 113 W, to W Warwick, same as 2
0mm	I-295 begins/ends on I-95, exit 11.

SOUTH CAROLINA

INTERSTATE 20

E ↕ W

Exit #	Services
141b a	I-95, N to Fayetteville, S to Savannah. **I-20 begins/ends on I-95, exit 160. See Interstate 95, exit 160a for services.**
137	SC 340, to Timmonsville, Darlington, **N gas:** BP (1mi), **S gas:** Marathon
131	US 401, SC 403, to Hartsville, Lamar, **N gas:** Exxon/dsl, **other:** to Darlington Int Raceway, **S food:** Subway (3mi)
129mm	**rest area no facilities both lanes**
123	SC 22, **N** Lee SP
121mm	Lynches River
120	SC 341, Bishopville, Elliot, **N lodging:** Bishopville Motel (3mi), **S gas:** Exxon/dsl, **food:** Taste of Country Rest., **lodging:** Best Value Inn, **other:** [H]
116	US 15, to Sumter, Bishopville, Shaw AFB, **N gas:** Shell/KFC/dsl/24hr, **food:** McDonald's, Pizza Hut, Subway (1mi), Waffle House, Zaxby's, **lodging:** Econolodge, **S gas:** Wilco/Hess/DQ/Wendy's/dsl/scales/24hr, **food:** Huddle House
108	SC 34, to SC 31, Manville, **N gas:** BP/dsl, **S gas:** Citgo/dsl
101	rd 329
98	US 521, to Camden, **N gas:** BP/dsl, Citgo, Exxon/McDonald's, Shell, **food:** Fatz Cafe, **lodging:** Comfort Suites, Holiday Inn Express, **other:** [H], 3-5 mi **N food:** Golden Corral, **lodging:** Colony Inn, Greenleaf Inn, Knight's Inn, **other:** Revolutionary War Pk
96mm	Wateree River
93mm	**rest area both lanes, full [handicapped] facilities, [phone], vending, [picnic], litter barrels, petwalk**
92	US 601, to Lugoff, **N gas:** BP, Pilot/DQ/Subway/dsl/scales/24hr, **food:** Hardee's, Waffle House, **lodging:** Econolodge, Ramada Ltd, **2-3 mi N food:** KFC, McDonald's, Shoney's, **lodging:** Best Western, Travel Inn, **other:** Ace Hardware, Chrysler/Dodge/Jeep, Ford/Lincoln/Mercury, Toyota, **S** Camden RV Park (1mi)
87	SC 47, to Elgin, **N gas:** BP/dsl, Shell/dsl
82	SC 53, to Pontiac, **N gas:** Shell, loding: Value Place Hotel, **other:** Harley-Davidson, Pontiac, **S other:** Clothing World Outlet

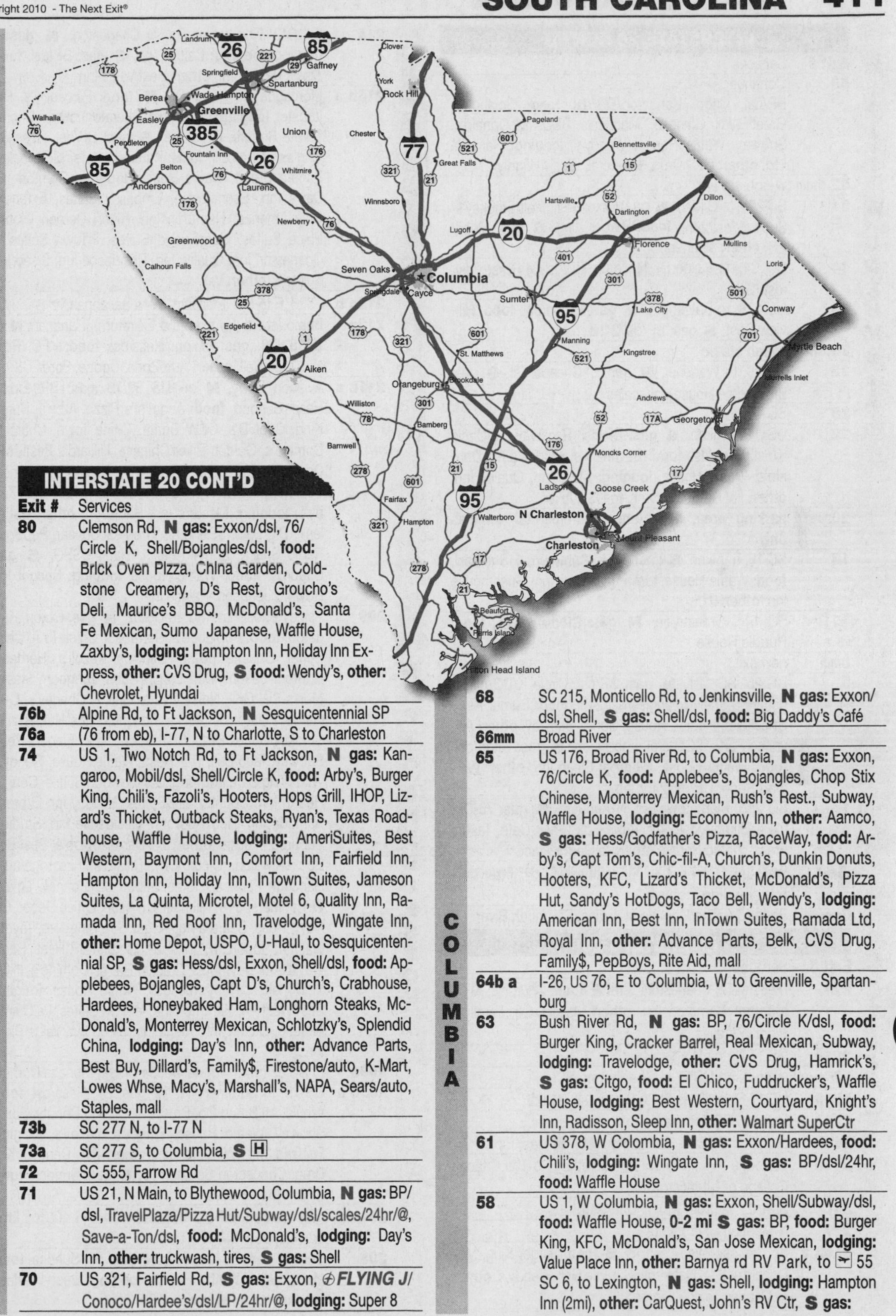

E ↕ W

INTERSTATE 20 CONT'D

Exit #	Services
80	Clemson Rd, **N gas:** Exxon/dsl, 76/ Circle K, Shell/Bojangles/dsl, **food:** Brick Oven Pizza, China Garden, Coldstone Creamery, D's Rest, Groucho's Deli, Maurice's BBQ, McDonald's, Santa Fe Mexican, Sumo Japanese, Waffle House, Zaxby's, **lodging:** Hampton Inn, Holiday Inn Express, **other:** CVS Drug, **S food:** Wendy's, **other:** Chevrolet, Hyundai
76b	Alpine Rd, to Ft Jackson, **N** Sesquicentennial SP
76a	(76 from eb), I-77, N to Charlotte, S to Charleston
74	US 1, Two Notch Rd, to Ft Jackson, **N gas:** Kangaroo, Mobil/dsl, Shell/Circle K, **food:** Arby's, Burger King, Chili's, Fazoli's, Hooters, Hops Grill, IHOP, Lizard's Thicket, Outback Steaks, Ryan's, Texas Roadhouse, Waffle House, **lodging:** AmeriSuites, Best Western, Baymont Inn, Comfort Inn, Fairfield Inn, Hampton Inn, Holiday Inn, InTown Suites, Jameson Suites, La Quinta, Microtel, Motel 6, Quality Inn, Ramada Inn, Red Roof Inn, Travelodge, Wingate Inn, **other:** Home Depot, USPO, U-Haul, to Sesquicentennial SP, **S gas:** Hess/dsl, Exxon, Shell/dsl, **food:** Applebees, Bojangles, Capt D's, Church's, Crabhouse, Hardees, Honeybaked Ham, Longhorn Steaks, McDonald's, Monterrey Mexican, Schlotzky's, Splendid China, **lodging:** Day's Inn, **other:** Advance Parts, Best Buy, Dillard's, Family$, Firestone/auto, K-Mart, Lowes Whse, Macy's, Marshall's, NAPA, Sears/auto, Staples, mall
73b	SC 277 N, to I-77 N
73a	SC 277 S, to Columbia, **S** [H]
72	SC 555, Farrow Rd
71	US 21, N Main, to Blythewood, Columbia, **N gas:** BP/ dsl, TravelPlaza/Pizza Hut/Subway/dsl/scales/24hr/@, Save-a-Ton/dsl, **food:** McDonald's, **lodging:** Day's Inn, **other:** truckwash, tires, **S gas:** Shell
70	US 321, Fairfield Rd, **S gas:** Exxon, ***FLYING J***/ Conoco/Hardee's/dsl/LP/24hr/@, **lodging:** Super 8

COLUMBIA

Exit #	Services
68	SC 215, Monticello Rd, to Jenkinsville, **N gas:** Exxon/ dsl, Shell, **S gas:** Shell/dsl, **food:** Big Daddy's Café
66mm	Broad River
65	US 176, Broad River Rd, to Columbia, **N gas:** Exxon, 76/Circle K, **food:** Applebee's, Bojangles, Chop Stix Chinese, Monterrey Mexican, Rush's Rest., Subway, Waffle House, **lodging:** Economy Inn, **other:** Aamco, **S gas:** Hess/Godfather's Pizza, RaceWay, **food:** Arby's, Capt Tom's, Chic-fil-A, Church's, Dunkin Donuts, Hooters, KFC, Lizard's Thicket, McDonald's, Pizza Hut, Sandy's HotDogs, Taco Bell, Wendy's, **lodging:** American Inn, Best Inn, InTown Suites, Ramada Ltd, Royal Inn, **other:** Advance Parts, Belk, CVS Drug, Family$, PepBoys, Rite Aid, mall
64b a	I-26, US 76, E to Columbia, W to Greenville, Spartanburg
63	Bush River Rd, **N gas:** BP, 76/Circle K/dsl, **food:** Burger King, Cracker Barrel, Real Mexican, Subway, **lodging:** Travelodge, **other:** CVS Drug, Hamrick's, **S gas:** Citgo, **food:** El Chico, Fuddrucker's, Waffle House, **lodging:** Best Western, Courtyard, Knight's Inn, Radisson, Sleep Inn, **other:** Walmart SuperCtr
61	US 378, W Colombia, **N gas:** Exxon/Hardees, **food:** Chili's, **lodging:** Wingate Inn, **S gas:** BP/dsl/24hr, **food:** Waffle House
58	US 1, W Columbia, **N gas:** Exxon, Shell/Subway/dsl, **food:** Waffle House, **0-2 mi S gas:** BP, **food:** Burger King, KFC, McDonald's, San Jose Mexican, **lodging:** Value Place Inn, **other:** Barnya rd RV Park, to ✈ 55 SC 6, to Lexington, **N gas:** Shell, **lodging:** Hampton Inn (2mi), **other:** CarQuest, John's RV Ctr, **S gas:**

INTERSTATE 20 CONT'D

E ↕ W — COLUMBIA

Exit #	Services
58	Continued BP/dsl, Citgo, Kangaroo/DQ/dsl, **food:** Bojangles, Great Wall Chinese, Maurice's BBQ, McDonald's, Subway, Waffle House, Wendy's, **lodging:** Ramada Ltd, **other:** CVS Drug, $General, Piggly Wiggly
52.5mm	**weigh sta wb**
51	SC 204, to Gilbert, **N gas:** Exxon/dsl, Shell/Stuckey's/Subway/dsl/24hr, **food:** Burger King, **S gas:** Mobil/dsl, **other:** $General
44	SC 34, to Gilbert, **N gas:** BP/dsl, 44Trkstp/dsl/rest./24hr
39	US 178, to Batesburg, **N gas:** Exxon/dsl, **food:** Hillview Rest. **S gas:** BP/dsl/24hr,
35.5mm	**weigh sta eb**
33	SC 39, to Wagener, **N gas:** El Cheapo/dsl, **S gas:** BP/Huddle House/dsl/scales
29	SC 49
22	US 1, to Aiken, **S gas:** BP/dsl, Raceway, 76/Circle K/dsl, Shell/dsl, **food:** Baynham's, Hardee's, McDonald's, Waffle House, **lodging:** Day's Inn, Quality Inn, **other:** RV Camping (5mi), to USC Aiken
20mm	**parking area, both lanes (commercial vehicles only)**
18	SC 19, to Aiken, **S gas:** Exxon/Subway/dsl, Shell/dsl, **food:** Waffle House, **lodging:** Deluxe Inn, Guesthouse Inn, **other:** [H]
11	SC 144, Graniteville, **N gas:** BP/dsl/scales, **food:** Huddle House
6mm	new exit
5	US 25, SC 121, **N gas:** BP/dsl, Circle K/DQ/pizza/dsl/24hr, Shell/Bojangles/dsl/24hr, **food:** Burger King, Checker's, Huddle House, Sonic, Subway, **other:** Advance Parts, $General, Food Lion, **S gas:** Citgo/dsl, **food:** Waffle House, **lodging:** Sleep Inn, **other:** Walmart Super Ctr/dsl/24hr (5mi)
1	SC 230, Martintown Rd, N Augusta, **S gas:** 76/Circle K/Blimpie/dsl/24hr, **food:** Fox Creek Cafe, Tastee Freez, Waffle House, **other:** to Garn's Place
.5mm	**Welcome Ctr eb, full [handicapped] facilities, [phone], [picnic], litter barrels, vending, petwalk**
0mm	South Carolina/Georgia state line, Savannah River

INTERSTATE 26

E ↕ W — CHARLESTON / NORTH CHARLESTON

Exit #	Services
221	Meeting St, Charleston, **2 mi E food:** Church's, KFC, **lodging:** Hampton Inn, **other:** Visitors Ctr, Family$, Piggly Wiggly
221b	US 17 N, to Georgetown
I-26 begins/ends on US 17 in Charleston, SC.	
221a	US 17 S, to Kings St, to Savannah, **N** [H]
220	Romney St (from wb)
219b	Morrison Dr, East Bay St (from eb), **N gas:** Exxon
219a	Rutledge Ave (from eb, no EZ return), to The Citadel, College of Charleston
218	Spruill Ave (from wb), N Charleston
217	N Meeting St (from eb)
216b a	SC 7, Cosgrove Ave, **1 mi S food:** Burger King, McDonald's, S&S Cafeteria, SunFire Grill, Wendy's, **other:** to Charles Towne Landing
215	SC 642, Dorchester Rd, N Charleston, **N gas:** El Cheapo, **lodging:** Deluxe Inn, **S gas:** BP/dsl, **food:** Alex's Rest./24hr, **other:** Best Value Inn
213b a	Montague Ave, Mall Dr, **N food:** Piccadilly's, Red Lobster, **lodging:** Courtyard, Sheraton, **other:** Charles Towne Square, Firestone, **S gas:** BP/dsl, Hess/Bojangles/dsl, Mobil, **food:** Kamille's Cafe, McDonald's, Panera Bread, Waffle House, **lodging:** Comfort Inn, Day's Inn, Econolodge, Embassy Suites, Extended Stay America, Hampton Inn, Hilton Garden, HomePlace Suites, Homewood Suites, InTown Suites, N Charleston Inn, Quality Inn, Residence Inn, Sleep Inn, Super 8, **other:** Vet
212c b	I-526, E to Mt Pleasant, W to Savannah, [airport]
212a	Remount Rd (from wb, no EZ return), Hanahan, **N on US 52/78...gas:** Exxon, Hess/dsl, **food:** KFC, Pizza Hut/Taco Bell, **other:** AutoZone, Dodge, Ford
211b a	Aviation Pkwy, **N on US 52/78...gas:** BP, Exxon, Hess, Sunoco, **food:** Andolini's Pizza, Arby's, Burger King, Capt D's, C&W Buffet, China Town, Church's, Domino's, Golden River Chinese, Hilliard's Rest., McDonald's, Pizza Hut, Pizza Inn, Popeye's, Quizno's, Schlotsky's, Shoney's, Sonic, Subway, Taco Bell, Zaxby's, **lodging:** Masters Inn, Radisson, **other:** Batteries+, Big Lots, $General, $Tree, Goodyear, PepBoys, Radio Shack, Super Pets, U-Haul, USPO, **S gas:** Citgo/dsl, **food:** Waffle House, **lodging:** Budget Inn, Howard Johnson, Palace Inn
209	Ashley Phosphate Rd, to US 52, **N gas:** Exxon, Kangaroo, **food:** Applebee's, Carraba's, Chick-fil-A, China Buffet, ChuckeCheese, Denny's, Fazoli's, Hardee's, Hooters, Jason's Deli, Larry's Subs, Longhorn Steaks, Moe's SW Grill, Noisy Oyster Grill, O'Charley's, Olive Garden, Outback Steaks, Perkins, Pizza Hut, Ryan's, Smokey Bones BBQ, Starbucks, Sticky Fingers Rest., Subway, Taco Bell, Thai Rest., Waffle House, Wendy's, Wild Wing Cafe, **lodging:** Candlewood Suites, Country Hearth Inn, Country Inn&Suites, Holiday Inn Express, Ramada Inn, Red Roof Inn, Residence Inn, Studio+, Suburban Lodge, **other:** [H], Barnes&Noble, Best Buy, BooksAMillion, Cicuit City, Dillard's, Firestone/auto, Hancock Fabrics, Home Depot, JC Penney, Lowe's Whse, Marshall's, Michael's, Nissan, Office Depot, Old Navy, Ross, Sears/auto, Target, Tire Kingdom, Toyota, Walmart SuperCtr/24hr, mall, **S gas:** BP, Hess, RaceWay, **food:** Bojangles, Cracker Barrel, Domino's, IHOP, McDonald's, Ruby Tuesday, Waffle House, **lodging:** Best Western, Hampton Inn, InTown Suites, La Quinta, Motel 6, Quality Inn, Relax Inn, Sleep Inn, Value Place Inn
209a	to US 52 (from wb), to Goose Creek, Moncks Corner
205b a	US 78, to Summerville, **N gas:** BP, Hess/dsl, **food:** Arby's, Atl Bread Co, Bruster's, Dunkin Donuts, Sonic, Subway, Waffle House, Wendy's, Zaxby's, **lodging:** Fairfield Inn, Wingate Inn, **other:** [H], Dentist, Kerr Drug, Charleston Southern U, **S gas:** Sunoco, **food:** KFC, **other:** KOA
204mm	**rest area eb, full [handicapped] facilities, vending, [phone], [picnic], litter barrels, petwalk**
203	College Park Rd, Ladson, **N gas:** BP, Sunoco, **food:** McDonald's, Waffle House, **lodging:** Best Western, Day's Inn, **2 mi S other:** KOA (2mi)

SC

INTERSTATE 26 CONT'D

E ↕ W

Exit #	Services
202mm	**rest area wb, full ♿ facilities, vending, ☎, ⛺, litter barrels, petwalk**
199b a	US 17 A, to Moncks Corner, Summerville, **N gas:** BP, Hess/dsl, Pilot/McDonald's/dsl/24hr, Shell, Texaco/dsl, **food:** KFC, Pizza Hut, Subway, **other:** Advance Parts, AutoZone, BiLo, Buick/GMC/Pontiac, $General, Family$, Vet, **S gas:** Shell, **food:** Applebee's, Atlanta Bread, Bojangles, Burger King, Coldstone Creamery, Domino's, Fazoli's, Hardee's, IHOP, La Hacienda, Logan's Roadhouse, McAlisters, Deli, Moe's SW Grill, O'Charleys, Papa John's, Perkins/24hr, Ryan's, Shoney's, Waffle House, Zaxby's, **lodging:** Comfort Suites, Country Inn&Suites, Econolodge, Hampton Inn, Holiday Inn Express, Sleep Inn, **other:** Best Buy, Belk, Chevrolet, Chrysler/Jeep, GNC, Home Depot, Kohl's, Lowe's Whse, PetsMart, Radio Shack, Staples, Superpetz, Target, Tire Kingdom, TJ Maxx, Walmart SuperCtr/24hr, Walgreens
194	SC 16, to Jedburg, access to Foreign Trade Zone 21
187	SC 27, to Ridgeville, St George, **N gas:** Shell, **S gas:** BP/dsl, 10 mi **S other:** Francis Beidler Forest
177	SC 453, to Holly Hill, Harleyville, **S gas:** Shell/dsl/LP
174mm	**weigh sta both lanes**
172b a	US 15, to Santee, St George, **S gas:** Horizon/Subway/dsl/scales/24hr
169b a	I-95, N to Florence, S to Savannah
165	SC 210, to Bowman, **N gas:** Exxon/dsl, **S gas:** BP/dsl/rest.
159	SC 36, to Bowman, **N gas:** Li'l Cricket/Stuckey's, Pilot/McDonald's/dsl/scales/@
154b a	US 301, to Santee, Orangeburg, **N lodging:** Days Inn, **S gas:** Exxon/dsl, Loves/Subway/dsl/scales/24hr, Shell, **food:** Waffle House
152mm	**rest area wb, full ♿ facilities, vending, ☎, ⛺, litter barrels, petwalk**
150mm	**rest area eb, full ♿ facilities, vending, ☎, ⛺, litter barrels, petwalk**
149	SC 33, to Cameron, to SC State Coll, Orangeburg, Claflin Coll
145b a	US 601, to Orangeburg, St Matthews, **S gas:** BP/24hr, Exxon, Shell, Sunoco/dsl, **food:** Burger King, Cracker Barrel, Fatz Café, Hardee's, KFC, McDonald's, Mediterranean Grill, Ruby Tuesday, Subway, Waffle House, Zaxby's, **lodging:** Best Western, Carolina Lodge, Comfort Inn, Country Inn&Suites, Fairfield Inn, Hampton Inn, Holiday Inn Express, Howard Johnson, Sleep Inn, Southern Lodge, Traveler's Inn, **other:** [H], **other:** Cadillac/Chevrolet, Chrysler/Dodge, Nissan, Toyota/Scion
139	SC 22, to St Matthews, **S gas:** Horizon, Li'l Cricket, Wilco/Hess/Arby's/dsl/scales/24hr, **other:** Sweetwater Lake Camping (2.5mi)
136	SC 6, to North, Swansea, **N gas:** Exxon/dsl/LP/rest./24hr
129	US 21, **N gas:** Shell/grill/dsl
125	SC 31, to Gaston, **N other:** Sandy Run Store/gas, Wolfe's Truck/trailer repair
123mm	**rest area both lanes, full ♿ facilities, vending, ☎, ⛺, litter barrels, petwalk**

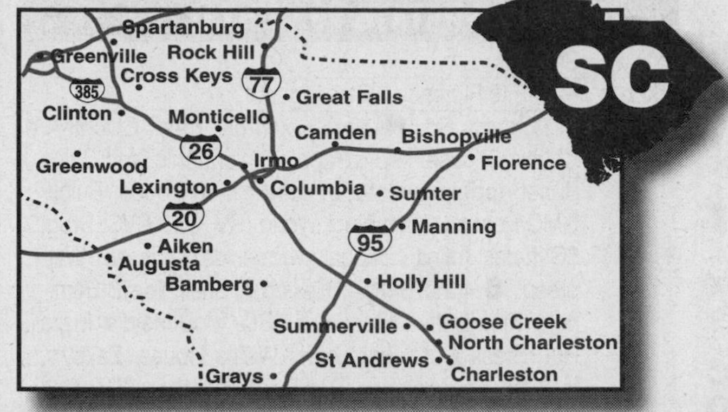

CAYCE

Exit #	Services
119	US 176, US 21, to Dixiana, **S gas:** BP/Subway/dsl, Exxon/Stuckey's/dsl
116	I-77 N, to Charlotte, US 76, US 378, to Ft Jackson
115	US 176, US 21, US 321, to Cayce, **N gas:** BP, Raceway/24hr, Texaco, **food:** Waffle House, **other:** Advance Parts, Bi-Lo, $General, Harley-Davidson, **S gas:** Pilot/DQ/Wendy's/dsl/scales/24hr, Shell, **food:** Bojangles, Great China, Hardee's, McDonald's, Subway, **lodging:** Country Hearth Inn, **other:** Firestone, Piggly Wiggly
113	SC 302, Cayce, **N gas:** Exxon, Mobil/Burger King, Sunoco, **food:** Waffle House, **lodging:** Airport Inn, Cambridge Plaza, Knight's Inn, Masters Inn, **other:** O'Reilly Parts, **S gas:** BP, Raceway, Shell/Circle K, **food:** Lizard's Thicket, Shoney's, Subway, Waffle House/24hr, **lodging:** Carolina Lodge, Comfort Inn, Country Inn& Suites, Sleep Inn, Travelers Inn, **other:** NAPA, ✈

COLUMBIA

Exit #	Services
111b a	US 1, to W Columbia, **N gas:** Raceway/dsl, Shell/Circle K, **food:** Domino's, Dragon City Chinese, Hardee's, Maurice's BBQ, Ruby Tuesday, Sonic, Subway, TCBY, Waffle House, Zaxby's, **lodging:** Holiday Inn, Quality Inn, **other:** BiLo Foods, $General, $Tree, GNC, Kroger, Pet Supplies+, Walgreens, Walmart SuperCtr/gas/24hr, to USC, **S gas:** Hess, **food:** Applebee's, Popeye's, Wendy's, **other:** Aldi Foods, Big Lots, Family$, Lowe's Whse, U-Haul
110	US 378, to W Columbia, Lexington, **N food:** Burger King, Grecian Garden, Lizard's Thicket, Maurice's BBQ, McDonald's, Rush's Rest., Subway, Waffle House, **lodging:** Best Value Inn, Day's Inn, Hampton Inn, Holiday Inn, **other:** CVS Drug, Food Lion, Rite Aid, U-Haul, **S gas:** Li'l Cricket/dsl, 76/Circle K, **food:** Atlanta Bread, Bojangles, Pizza Hut, **lodging:** Executive Inn, SpringHill Suites, **other:** [H]
108b a	I-126 to Columbia, Bush River Rd, **N gas:** Shell/dsl, **food:** Blimpie, Capt D's, Chick-fil-A, Hardee's, Peking Palace, Ruby Tuesday, Schlotsky's, Shoney's, Super China, Wendy's, Zaxby's, **lodging:** Day's Inn, Scottish Inn, Villager Lodge, Western Inn, **other:** Advance Parts, Belk, $General, Firestone/auto, K-Mart, Office Depot, Rite Aid, mall, **S gas:** City Gas, RaceWay, Sunoco/dsl, **food:** Cracker Barrel, Fuddrucker's, Villa Italian, Waffle House, **lodging:** Best Inn, Courtyard, Knight's Inn, Radisson, Sleep Inn, **other:** Walmart SuperCtr, **multiple services 1-3 mi N off I-126**, Greystone Blvd, **N gas:** BP, Exxon, **food:** Waffle House, **lodging:** Embassy Suites, Extended Stay America, Homewood Suites, Residence Inn, Studio+, **other:** Chrysler/Jeep, Dodge, Ford, Honda, Hyundai, KIA, Lincoln/Mercury, Mazda, **S** Riverbanks Zoo

INTERSTATE 26 CONT'D

E ↔ W

Exit #	Services
107b a	I-20, E to Florence, W to Augusta
106b a	St Andrews Rd, **N gas:** Exxon/dsl, **food:** Chic-fil-A, ChuckeCheese, IHOP, Papa John's, Sonic, Top China Buffet, **lodging:** Motel 6, **other:** BiLo Foods, Buick/GMC/Pontiac, Camping World RV Ctr, CVS Drug, $General, Infiniti, Jaguar, Kroger/deli, Nissan, Walgreen, **S gas:** BP/dsl, Hess/dsl, Shell, **food:** Domino's, King Buffet, Maurice's BBQ, McDonald's, Pizza Hut, Steak Out, Thai Lotus, Waffle House, Zaxby's, **lodging:** Ecocnolodge, Red Roof Inn, **other:** $General, Food Lion, Tire Kingdom
104	Piney Grove Rd, **N gas:** Sunoco/dsl, **food:** Hardee's, San Jose Mexican, Waffle House, **lodging:** Quiality Inn, **other:** Sportsman's Whse, RV/Marine Ctr, **S gas:** Exxon/dsl, Shell, **lodging:** Comfort Suites, Microtel, **other:** Carmax, Land Rover
103	Harbison Blvd, **N food:** Applebee's, Hooters, Hops Grill, Wendy's, **lodging:** Hampton Inn, **other:** Chevrolet, Home Depot, Hummer, Lowe's Whse, funpark, **S gas:** BP/24hr, Hess/dsl, Shell, **food:** Alehouse, Bailey's Grill, Blimpie, Bojangles, BoneFish Grill, Bruster's, Carrabba's, Chili's, Chick-fil-A, Coldstone, Copper River Grill, D's Rest., Denny's, Fazoli's, 5 Guys Pizza, Inyabi, LongHorn Steaks, Macaroni Grill, McAlister's, McDonald's, Monterrey Mexican, O'Charley's, Olive Garden, Outback Steaks, Panera Bread, Popeye's, Quizno's, Ruby Tuesday, Rush's Rest., Ryan's, Shoney's, Sonic, Sticky Fingers, Subway, Super Buffet, Texas Roadhouse, Tokyo Grill, Tsunami Steaks, Yamato Japanese, **lodging:** Comfort Suites, Country Inn&Suites, Fairfield Inn, Hilton Garden, Holiday Inn Express, InTown Suites, TownePlace Suites, Wingate Inn, **other:** Barnes& Noble, Belk, Best Buy, BooksAMillion, Dillard's, $Tree, Goodyear, Hancock Fabrics, Kohl's, Marshall's, Michael's, Midas, Old Navy, PetsMart, Publix, Rite Aid, Ross, Sam's Club/gas, Sears/auto, Target, Tire Kingdom, TJ Maxx, Walmart SuperCtr/24hr, mall
102	SC 60, Ballentine, Irmo, **N food:** Cracker Barrel, **lodging:** Extended Stay America, Hyatt Place, **S gas:** 76/Circle K, Shell, SKS, **food:** Arby's, Atlanta Bread, Bellacino's Pizza, Maurice's BBQ, Moe's SW Grill, New China, Papa John's, Quizno's, TCBY, Zaxby's, **other:** CVS Drug, Jiffy Lube, tires, same as 103
101b a	US 76, US 176, to N Columbia, **1/2 mi N gas:** Exxon/Subway/dsl, **food:** China House, Fatz Café, Zorba's, **other:** AutoZone, $General, Food Lion, Publix, Rite Aid, Walgreen, **S gas:** BP, Mobil, **food:** Burger King, Oyster House Grill, Waffle House, **other:** Toyota/Scion
97	US 176, to Ballentine, Peak, **N other:** Food Lion, Woodsmoke Camping, **S gas:** Exxon/dsl
94mm	**weigh sta wb,** [phone]
91	SC 48, to Chapin, **S gas:** BP/dsl, Exxon/Taco Bell/Blimpie/dsl, Shell/dsl, **food:** Hardee's (3mi), McDonald's, Subway (2mi), Waffle House, **other:** to Dreher Island SP
85	SC 202, Little Mountain, Pomaria, **S** to Dreher Island SP
82	SC 773, to Prosperity, Pomaria, **N gas:** BP/Subway/dsl/24hr/@, Wilco/Hess/Wendy's/dsl/scales, **other:** Flea Mkt Campground
81mm	**weigh sta eb**
76	SC 219, to Pomaria, Newberry, **2 mi S gas:** BP, Murphy USA, Loves/McDonald's/dsl/scales/24hr, **food:** Burger King, Wendy's, **lodging:** Hampton Inn, Holiday Inn Express, **other:** Walmart SuperCtr/24hr, to Newberry Opera House
74	SC 34, to Newberry, **N gas:** BP, Shell/dsl/24hr, **food:** Bill&Fran's Café, **lodging:** Best Western/rest., **S gas:** Citgo, **food:** Arby's, Capt D's, Hardee's (2mi), McDonald's (2mi), Waffle House, **lodging:** Comfort Inn (2mi), Days Inn, Economy Inn (2mi), Holiday Inn Express (2mi), **other:** [H], to NinetySix HS
72	SC 121, to Newberry, **S gas:** Citgo/dsl/@, **other:** [H], to Newberry Coll
66	SC 32, to Jalapa
63.5mm	**rest area both lanes, full [handicapped] facilities, [phone], vending, [picnic], litter barrels, petwalk**
60	SC 66, to Joanna, **S gas:** BP, **food:** Carolina Country Kitchen, **other:** Magnolia Camping
54	SC 72, to Clinton, **N gas:** BP, **S gas:** Citgo/dsl/24hr, **food:** Fatz Cafe, **lodging:** Hampton Inn, **other:** [H], to Presbyterian Coll, Thornwell Home
52	SC 56, to Clinton, **N gas:** Pilot/Subway/dsl/scales/24hr/@, **food:** Blue Ocean Rest., McDonald's, **lodging:** Comfort Suites, Quality Inn, **S gas:** Citgo/dsl, **food:** Hardee's, Waffle House, Wendy's, **lodging:** Clinton Hotel, Days Inn, Howard Johnson, **other:** [H]
51	I-385, to Greenville (from wb)
45.5mm	Enoree River
44	SC 49, to Cross Anchor, Union
41	SC 92, to Enoree, **N gas:** Valero
38	SC 146, to Woodruff, **N gas:** Hot Spot/Shell/Hardee's/dsl/24hr/@, **food:** Big Country Rest./lounge
35	SC 50, to Woodruff, **S gas:** BP/dsl/rest./24hr, **other:** [H]
33mm	S Tyger River
32mm	N Tyger River
28	US 221, to Spartanburg, **N gas:** Citgo/AuntM's/dsl/24hr, Shell/Subway/dsl/24hr, **food:** Burger King, Hardee's, Waffle House, Walnut Grove Seafood Rest., **other:** [H], Pine Ridge Camping (3mi), to Walnut Grove Plantation
22	SC 296, Reidville Rd, to Spartanburg, **N gas:** BP/dsl, Exxon, **food:** Arby's, BBQ, Capri's Italian, Fuddrucker's (1mi), Hong Kong Express, Little Caesar's, McDonald's, Outback Steaks, Ryan's, Waffle House, Zaxby's, **other:** Advance Parts, Rite Aid, to Croft SP, **S gas:** BP/dsl, **food:** Burger King, Denny's, Domino's, Hardee's, Subway, TCBY, Waffle House/24hr, **lodging:** Sleep Inn, Southern Suites, Super 8, **other:** Abbot Farms/fruit, BiLo, BMW, CVS Drug, Harris-Teeter, Toyota, Walgreen
21b a	US 29, to Spartanburg, **N gas:** BP, **food:** Bojangles, Burger King, Chick-fil-A, ChuckeCheese, CiCi's, City Range Grill, Corona Mexican, DQ, Fuji's, Golden Corral, Hardee's, Hooters, Jack-in-the-Box, Japanese Rest., LJ Silver/A&W, McAlister's Deli, Moe's SW Grill, O'Charley's, Olive Garden, Pizza Hut, Red Lobster, Ruby Tuesday, Ryan's, Schlotzsky's, Substation II, Subway, Wendy's, **lodging:** Hampton Inn, Holiday Inn Express, **other:** Barnes&Noble, Belk, Best Buy, Costco/gas, Dillard's, Discount Tire, $General, Firestone/auto, Goodyear, Home Depot, JC Penney, Lowe's

COLUMBIA — COLUMBIA — SPARTANBURG

E ↕ W SPARTANBURG

INTERSTATE 26 CONT'D

Exit #	Services
21b a	Continued Whse, Michael's, Office Depot, Old Navy, Rite Aid, Ross, Sears/auto, Walmart SuperCtr/24hr, mall, USPO, **S** gas: Citgo/dsl/cafe, Sphinx Gas, **food:** Applebee's, Blimpie, IHOP, McDonald's, Piccadilly's, Pizza Inn, Prime Sirloin, Shogun Japanese, Taco Bell, Taste of Thai, Waffle House, **other:** Advance Parts, CarQuest, $Tree, Ingles Foods/gas, Kohl's, Sam's Club/gas, Target, TrueValue
19b a	Lp I-85, Spartanburg, **N food:** Cracker Barrel, **lodging:** Country Hearth Inn, Radisson, Ramada Inn, Residence Inn, **S lodging:** Bradfo rd Inn, **other:** Lowes Whse, Walmart SuperCtr
18b a	I-85, N to Charlotte, S to Greenville
17	New Cut Rd, **S gas:** Chevron/dsl, Sunoco/dsl, **food:** Burger King, Fatz Café, McDonald's, Waffle House, **lodging:** Day's Inn, Econolodge, Howard Johnson Express, Quality Inn
16	John Dodd Rd, to Wellford, **N gas:** Citgo/Aunt M's/dsl, **other:** Camping World RV Ctr, **S** Cunningham RV Park (2mi)
15	US 176, to Inman, **N gas:** Breakers, Racetrac (2mi), 76/Circle K/dsl, **food:** Waffle House, **other:** [H] **S gas:** Mystik/dsl, **food:** Taco Bell (2mi)
10	SC 292, to Inman, **N gas:** Shell/Subway/dsl/24hr
7.5mm	Lake William C. Bowman
5	SC 11, Foothills Scenic Dr, Chesnee, Campobello, **N gas:** Kangaroo/Aunt M's Café/dsl/scales, **S gas:** Li'l Cricket
3mm	**Welcome Ctr eb, full [handicapped] facilities, info, [phone], [picnic], litter barrels, vending, petwalk**
1	SC 14, to Landrum, **S gas:** BP/Burger King/dsl, HotSpot/gas (2mi), **food:** Bojangles, China Cafe, Pizza Hut (1mi), Subway, **other:** BiLo Foods, $General, Ingles/café/gas/24hr, Vet
0mm	South Carolina/North Carolina state line

N ↕ S

INTERSTATE 77

Exit #	Services
91mm	South Carolina/North Carolina state line
90	US 21, Carowinds Blvd, **E gas:** Rocket Stop/fireworks, Texaco, **food:** Bojangles, **other:** [H], RV camping (4mi), **W gas:** Exxon/café, Shell/Circle K/Wendy's/dsl, Texaco/Subway, **food:** Cracker Barrel, El Cancun Mexican, KFC, Papa Pino's, Shoney's, **lodging:** Best Western, Comfort Inn, Holiday Inn Express, Motel 6, Plaza Motel, Sleep Inn, **other:** Carowinds Funpark, Carolina Pottery/outlet mall/famous brands
89.5mm	**Welcome Ctr sb, full [handicapped] facilities, info, [phone], vending, [picnic], litter barrels, petwalk/weigh sta nb**
88	Gold Hill Rd, to Pineville, **E other:** URGENT CARE, **W gas:** Exxon/dsl, Gate (2mi), Shell/dsl, **food:** Bojangles (2mi), **other:** Chrysler/Dodge/Jeep, Ford, Hyundai, KOA
85	SC 160, Ft Mill, Tega Cay, **E gas:** Exxon, **food:** Subway, **other:** Bi-Lo, Ft Mill Drug, **W gas:** BP/dsl, Circle K, **food:** Backyard Burger, Beef O'Brady's, Burger King, Chick-fil-A, Fratelli's Italian, Papa John's, Pizza Hut, Quizno's, Starbucks, Wendy's, **other:** CVS Drug, Goodyear/auto, Harris-Teeter, Lowe's Whse, Walgreens

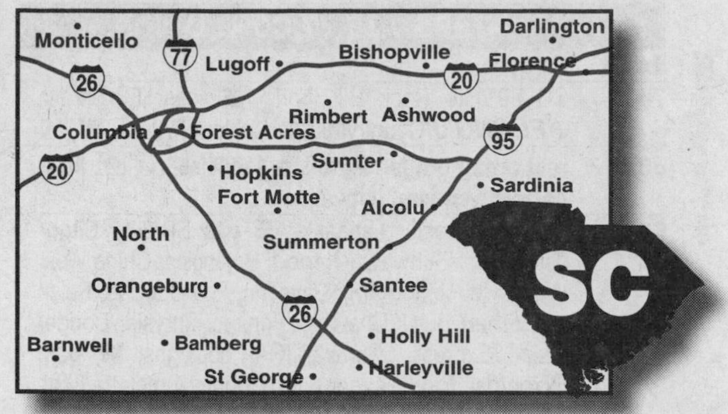

ROCK HILL

Exit #	Services
84.5mm	**weigh sta sb**
83	SC 49, Sutton Rd, **W gas:** Loves/Chester/Subway/dsl/scales/24hr
82.5mm	Catawba River
82c	US 21, SC 161, Rock Hill, Ft Mill, **E gas:** Exxon, **food:** IHOP, Sonny's BBQ, Steak'n Shake, Zaxby's, **other:** Home Depot, Petsmart, museum, **W gas:** Citgo, Shell, Texaco, **food:** Delicacy Chinese, Empire Sta Pizza, Hooters, Outback Steaks, Sonic, Starbucks, **lodging:** Courtyard, **other:** [H], Toyota, Tuffy Auto, U-Haul
82b a	**E gas:** Exxon, **lodging:** Motel 6, **W gas:** RaceWay, Sunoco/dsl, Texaco, **food:** Arby's, Bojangles, Burger King, Burk's BBQ, Capt's Galley, Chick-fil-A, CiCi's Pizza, Denny's, Firebonez, Golden Corral, Happy Garden, HoneyBaked Ham, Jack-in-the-Box, KFC, Little Caesar's, Marco's Pizza, McDonald's, Penn Sta., Pizza Hut, Sakura Japanese, Shoney's, Subway, Taco Bell, TCBY, Waffle House, Wendy's, **lodging:** Baymont Inn, Best Value Inn, Country Inn&Suites, Days Inn, EconoLodge, Microtel, Quality Inn, Regency Inn, Super 8, **other:** Aamco, Advance Parts, Aldi Foods, AutoZone, BigLots, Bi-Lo, Cadillac/Chevrolet, Compare Mkt, $General, Family$, Firestone/auto, Hancock Fabrics, K-Mart, NAPA, Nissan, Office Depot, O'Reilly Parts, PepBoys, Verizon, city park
79	SC 122, Dave Lyle Blvd, to Rock Hill, **E gas:** BP, Murphy USA/dsl, **food:** Applebee's, Chick-fil-A, Cracker Barrel, DQ, Hardee's, Longhorn Steaks, Maurice's BBQ, O'Charley's, Ryan's, Ruby Tuesday, **lodging:** Comfort Suites, Hampton Inn, Holiday Inn, TownePlace Suites, Wingate Inn, **other:** Belk, Discount Tire, $Tree, Food Lion, Harley-Davidson, Hobby Lobby, Honda, JC Penney, Kohl's, Lowe's Whse, Sears/auto, Staples, Tire Kingdom, Walmart SuperCtr/24hr, mall, **W gas:** Texaco/dsl, **food:** Baskin-Robbins/Dunkin Donuts, Bob Evans, Chili's, Jack-in-the-Box, McAlister's Deli, McDonald's, Moe's SW Grill, Olive Garden, Panera Bread, Quizno's, Stagebrush Steaks, Subway, Taco Bell, Wendy's, **lodging:** Hilton Garden, **other:** URGENT CARE, Best Buy, Books-a-Million, Ford/Lincoln/Mercury, Michael's, Ross, Target, TJ Maxx, visitor ctr
77	US 21, SC 5, to Rock Hill, **E gas:** BP/Subway/dsl, Cone/dsl/24hr, **other:** to Andrew Jackson SP (12mi), **W gas:** Exxon/dsl, Pride/dsl/scales, **food:** Bojangles, KFC (1mi), McDonald's (1mi), Subway (1mi), Waffle House, **other:** to Winthrop Coll
75	Porter Rd, **E gas:** Citgo, Texaco/fireworks

INTERSTATE 77 CONT'D

Exit #	Services
73	SC 901, to Rock Hill, York, **E gas:** Exxon/dsl, ***FLYING J***/CountryMkt/dsl/scales/LP/24hr, **W** H
66mm	**rest area both lanes, full facilities, phone, picnic, litter barrels, vending, petwalk**
65	SC 9, to Chester, Lancaster, **E gas:** BP/24hr, Citgo/dsl, Liberty/Subway/dsl, **food:** Bojangles, China Wok, Waffle House, **lodging:** Days Inn, EconoLodge, Relax Inn, **other:** Buick/Chevrolet/Ponitac, Chrysler/Dodge/Jeep, $Express, $General, IGA Foods/gas, **W gas:** Exxon/dsl, **food:** Burger King, Country Omelette/24hr, Front Porch Cafe, KFC, McDonald's, **lodging:** Comfort Inn, Rodeway Inn, Super 8, **other:** H
62	SC 56, to Fort Lawn, Richburg
55	SC 97, to Chester, Great Falls, **E gas:** Exxon/Noble Roman's/dsl, **W** H
48	SC 200, to Great Falls, **E gas:** Shell/Grand Central Rest./dsl/@, **W gas:** Wilco/Hess/DQ/Wendy's
46	SC 20, to White Oak
41	SC 41, to Winnsboro, **E** to Lake Wateree SP
34	SC 34, to Winnsboro, Ridgeway, **E lodging:** Ridgeway Motel (1mi), **other:** camping (1mi), **W gas:** Exxon/dsl, **food:** Waffle House, **lodging:** Ramada Ltd.
32	Peach Rd, Ridgeway
27	Blythewood Rd, **E gas:** BP/dsl, Exxon/Bojangles/dsl/24hr, **food:** Blythewood Pizza, Carolina Wings, Hardee's, KFC/Pizza Hut, McDonald's, San Jose Mexican, Southern Pig BBQ, Subway, Waffle House, Wendy's, **lodging:** Comfort Inn, Days Inn, Holiday Inn Express, **other:** Curves, $General, IGA Foods, repair/tires, **W food:** Lizard's Thicket, **other:** AT&T, Food Lion, Groucho's Deli
24	US 21, to Wilson Blvd., **E gas:** BP, Shell/Subway/dsl, **other:** auto repair, Vet
22	Killian Rd, **E food:** Zaxby's (2mi), **other:** Honda, Scion/Toyota, Walmart SuperCtr/McDonald's, **W food:** Monterrey's Mexican, **other:** Verizon
19	SC 555, Farrow Rd, **E gas:** BP, Exxon, Shell, **food:** Bojangles, Cracker Barrel, Wendy's, **lodging:** Courtyard, Residence Inn, **other:** H, Longs Drug, **W gas:** Shell/dsl, **food:** Waffle House, **other:** SC Archives
18	to SC 277, to I-20 W (from sb), Columbia
17	US 1, Two Notch Rd, **E gas:** BP, Citgo, Kangaroo, Shell/Circle K, **food:** Arby's, Burger King, TX Roadhouse, Waffle House, **lodging:** Holiday Inn, InTown Suites, Quality Inn, Wingate Inn, **other:** Rite Aid, U-Haul, USPO, to Sesquicentennial SP, **W gas:** Mobil, **food:** Chili's, Fazoli's, Hooters, IHOP, Lizard's Thicket, Outback Steaks, Waffle House, **lodging:** Comfort Inn, Fairfield Inn, Hampton Inn, Jameson Suites, La Quinta, Microtel, Motel 6, Ramada Ltd, Red Roof Inn, **other:** Home Depot, PepBoys, Walgreens, mall, Vet
16b a	I-20, W to Augusta, E to Florence, Alpine Rd
15b a	SC 12, to Percival Rd, **W gas:** El Cheapo/gas, Shell, 1/2 mi **W gas:** Exxon
13	Decker Blvd (from nb), **W gas:** El Cheapo
12	Forest Blvd, Thurmond Blvd, **E** to Ft Jackson, **W gas:** BP/dsl, 76/dsl, Shell/dsl/24hr, **food:** Bojangles, Chick-fil-A, Fatz Café, Golden Corral, Hardee's, McDonald's, RedBone Rest., Steak&Ale, Subway, Wendy's, **lodging:** Extended Stay America, Marlboro Inn, Super 8, **other:** H, $Tree, Sam's Club/gas, Walmart SuperCtr/24hr, museum
10	10 SC 760, Jackson Blvd, **E** to Ft Jackson, **2 mi W gas:** BP, **food:** Applebee's, Bojangles, Burger King, Maurices BBQ, Ruby Tuesday, Subway, **lodging:** Econolodge, Liberty Inn
9b a	US 76, US 378, to Sumter, Columbia, **E gas:** BP, Citgo, Hess/dsl, Sunoco/dsl, United, **food:** Arby's, Capt D's, Chick-fil-A, Domino's, KFC, Maurice's BBQ, McDonald's, Pizza Hut, Popeye's, Ruby Tuesday, Rush's Rest., Ryan's, Shoney's, Subway, Taco Bell, Waffle House, Zaxby's, **lodging:** Best Western, Candlewood Suites, Comfort Inn, Country Inn&Suites, Day's Inn, Hampton Inn, Holiday Inn Express, La Quinta, Quality Inn, Sleep Inn, **other:** Advance Parts, Aldi Foods, $Tree, Family$, Firestone/auto, Food Lion, Goodyear/auto, Interstate Batteries, Lowes Whse, NAPA, Piggly Wiggly, Pontiac/GMC, Radio Shack, Sears, Tire Kingdom, U-Haul, USPO, Walgreens, Walmart SuperCtr/gas/24hr/auto, **W gas:** Shell, **food:** CiCi's, Hardee's, Sonic, Wendy's, **lodging:** Best Value Inn, Economy Inn, **other:** H, BigLots, $General, Fred's Store, Jo-Ann Fabrics, Rite Aid, Sav-a-Lot Foods, Target
6b a	Shop Rd, **W** to USC Coliseum, fairgrounds
5	SC 48, Bluff Rd, **1 mi E gas:** 76, **W gas:** Shell/Burger King/dsl, **food:** Bojangles (2mi)
3mm	Congaree River
2	Saxe Gotha Rd
1	US 21, US 176, US 321 (from sb), Cayce, **W** accesses same as SC I-26, exit 115.
0mm	I-77 begins/ends on I-26, exit 116.

COLUMBIA

INTERSTATE 85

Exit #	Services
106.5mm	South Carolina/North Carolina state line
106	US 29, to Grover, **E gas:** BP/dsl, **W gas:** Exxon/dsl, Hickory Point/gas, Wilco/Hess/DQ/Wendy's/dsl/scales/24hr
104	SC 99
103mm	**Welcome Ctr sb, full facilities, info, phone, picnic, litter barrels, vending, petwalk**
102	SC 198, to Earl, **E gas:** BP/dsl, Shell/gas, **food:** Hardee's, **W gas:** Citgo/dsl, ***FLYING J***/Cookery/dsl/scales/LP/rest./24hr, **food:** McDonald's, Waffle House
100mm	Buffalo Creek
100	SC 5, to Blacksburg, Shelby, **W gas:** Sunoco/Subway/dsl/scales/24hr, Texaco/dsl
98	Frontage Rd (from nb), **E food:** Broad River Café
97mm	Broad River
96	SC 18, **W gas:** Kangaroo/Krystal/dsl, Sunoco/dsl
95	SC 18, to Gaffney, **E gas:** Kangaroo/Aunt M's Rest/dsl, **lodging:** Shamrock Inn, **food:** Mr Waffle, **other:** H, to Limestone Coll
92	SC 11, to Gaffney, **E gas:** Murphy USA, Texaco, **food:** Aegean Pizza, Applebee's, Bojangles, Burger King, Chick-fil-A, Daddy Joe's BBQ, Domino's, KFC, King Buffet, Little Ceasar's, McDonald's, New Century Buffet, Orca Bay Seafood, Pizza Hut, Sagebrush Steaks, Sonic, Subway, Taco Bell, Waffle House, Wendy's, Zaxby's, **lodging:** Jameson Inn, Super 8, **other:** Advance Parts, Belk, BigLots, BiLo, $General, $Tree, Ingles Foods, Lowe's Whse, Radio Shack, Rite Aid, Walgreens, Walmart SuperCtr, USPO, to Limestone Coll, **W gas:** BP, **food:** Fatz Cafe, **lodging:** Homestead Lodge, Quality Inn, **other:** Buick/GMC/Pontiac, Ford, to The Peach, Foothills Scenic Hwy

GAFFNEY

INTERSTATE 85 CONT'D

N ↕ S

Exit #	Services
90	SC 105, SC 42, to Gaffney, **E gas:** BP/DQ/dsl, Pilot/Arby's/dsl/scales/24hr, **food:** Bronco Mexican, Clock Rest., Starbucks, Subway, Waffle House, **lodging:** Red Roof Inn, Sleep Inn, **W gas:** Kangaroo/Burger King, Texaco, **food:** Cracker Barrel, FoodCourt, La Fogata Mexican, Outback Steaks, **lodging:** Hampton Inn, **other:** Hamrick's, Prime Outlets/famous brands, fruit stand
89mm	**rest area both lanes, full facilities, litter barrels, vending, petwalk**
87	SC 39, **E other:** camping, **W other:** Rug Outlet, fruit stand/peaches/fireworks
83	SC 110, **E gas:** Hot Spot/dsl, **other:** NAPA, fruit stand, truck repair, **W gas:** Auto Trkstp/Mr Waffle/dsl/24hr/@, **other:** to Cowpens Bfd, fruitstand
82	Frontage Rd (from nb)
80.5mm	Pacolet River
80	SC 57, to Gossett, **E gas:** Hot Spot/dsl
78	US 221, Chesnee, **E gas:** Citgo/dsl, **food:** Hardee's, **lodging:** Motel 6, **other:** fruit stand, **W gas:** BP, RaceWay/dsl, Sunoco/Burger King/dsl, **food:** Arby's, Bojangles, McDonald's, Subway, Waffle House, Wendy's, **lodging:** Hampton Inn, Holiday Inn Express, **other:** Advance Parts, $General, Harley-Davidson, Ingles Foods/cafe/dsl
77	Lp 85, Spartanburg, **facilities along Lp 85 exits E**
75	SC 9, Spartanburg, **E food:** Denny's, **lodging:** Best Western, **W gas:** BP/Burger King/dsl, Pure, RaceWay, **food:** Beef'O'Brady's, Bruster's, Capri's Italian, Copper River Grill, Del Taco, Fatz Café, Grapevine Rest, McDonald's, Pizza Hut, Pizza Inn, Ricky's Hotdogs, Smokin' Pig BBQ, Waffle House, Zaxby's, **lodging:** Days Inn, Comfort Inn, **other:** CVS Drug, Ingles/cafe/gas, USPO
72	US 176, to I-585, **E other:** to USC-S, Wofford/Converse Coll, **W gas:** BP, RaceWay, **food:** Subway, Waffle House, **other:** $General, Ingles Foods/cafe/gas, Masters RV Ctr
70b a	I-26, E to Columbia, W to Asheville
69	Lp 85, SC 41 (from nb), to Fairforest
68	SC 129, to Greer
67mm	N Tyger River
66	US 29, to Lyman, Wellford, **E gas:** Exxon/Subway/dsl, **food:** Waffle House
63	SC 290, to Duncan, **E gas:** Citgo/dsl, 76/Circle K, Spinx/Dunkin Donuts/dsl, **food:** A&W/KFC, Clock Rest., Cracker Barrel, Denny's, El Agave Mexican, Firehouse Subs, Jack-in-the-Box, Miami Subs, Paisanos Italian, Pizza Inn, Taco Bell, Thai Cuisine, Waffle House, Zaxby's, **lodging:** Hampton Inn, Jameson Inn, Microtel, **other:** Curves, **W gas:** BP, Marathon/dsl, Pilot/Wendy's/dsl/scales/24hr, TA/BP/DQ/rest./dsl/scales/24hr/@, **food:** Bojangles, Hardee's, La Molcajete Mexican, McDonald's, Waffle House, **lodging:** Days Inn, Holiday Inn Express, Quality Inn, ValuePlace Inn, **other:** Blue Beacon, Sonny's RV Ctr, Speedco
62.5mm	S Tyger River
60	SC 101, to Greer, **E gas:** Grand/dsl, Marathon, Sunoco/dsl, **food:** Senor Garcia's Mexican, Subway, Theo's Rest, **W gas:** Exxon/Burger King, **food:** Waffle House, **lodging:** Super 8, **other:** BMW Visitor Ctr

SPARTANBURG

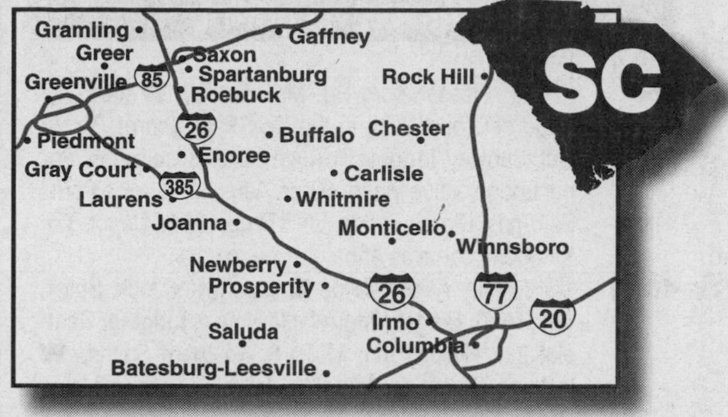

Exit #	Services
58	Brockman-McClimon Rd
57	**W other:** Greenville-Spartanburg
56	SC 14, to Greer, **E gas:** Citgo/dsl, **W gas:** Spinx/dsl, **other:** H, Goodyear, Outdoor World RV Ctr
55mm	Enoree River
54	Pelham Rd, **E gas:** BP/dsl, **food:** Burger King, Corona Mexican, Skin's Hotdogs, Waffle House, **lodging:** Best Western, **W gas:** BP/dsl, Spinx, **food:** Acropolis Rest, American Pie Factory, Atlanta Bread Co, Bojangles, Bertolos Pizza, California Dreaming Rest., Chick-fil-A, China Wok, Chophouse 47, Chops Cajun, Dunkin Donuts, 5 Guys Burgers, Hardee's, Jack-in-the-Box, Joe's Crabshack, Joy of Tokyo, Logan's Roadhouse, Macaroni Grill, McDonald's, MidTown Deli, Moes' SW Grill, On the Border, Rita's Custard, Ruby Tuesday, Schlotsky's, Starbucks, Subway, Wendy's, **lodging:** Courtyard, Extended Stay America, Fairfield Inn, Hampton Inn, Holiday Inn Express, Mainstay Suites, Marriott, Microtel, Wingate Inn, **other:** BiLo/24hr, CVS Drug, EarthFare Foods, Radio Shack, Walgreens, Walmart
52mm	**weigh sta nb**
51	I-385, SC 146, Woodruff Rd, **E gas:** Blue Jay/dsl, **food:** Bojangles, Chili's, Chipotle Mexican, Cold Stone Creamery, Cracker Barrel, Dochey's Asian, Fatz Café, Fuddrucker's, Hardee's, IHOP, Lieu's Bistro, Longhorn Steaks, Mimi's Cafe, Nihao Chinese, Panera Bread, PF Changs, Quizno's, Red Robin, Sticky Fingers, Wasibi Grill, **lodging:** Drury Inn, Hampton Inn, Hilton Garden, Homewood Suites, Staybridge Suites, **other:** Barnes&Noble, Best Buy, Goodyear/auto, Hamrick's Outlet, Koh's, Lowe's Whse, Marshall's, Petsmart, Ross, Sam's Club/gas, Whole Foods Mkt, Vet, **W gas:** BP, RaceWay/24hr, **food:** Atlanta Bread Co, Capri's Italian, Carraba's, Flatrock Grill, Jack-in-the-Box, Krystal, McDonald's, MidTown Deli, Ruby Tuesday, Ruth's Chris Steaks, TGIFriday, **lodging:** Crowne Plaza, Days Inn, Embassy Suites, Fairfield Inn, Holiday Inn Express, La Quinta, Marriott (3mi), Microtel, **other:** Costco/gas, Firestone/auto, Home Depot, Old Navy, Target, U-Haul
48b a	US 276, Greenville, **E food:** Waffle House, **lodging:** Red Roof Inn, **other:** CarMax, to Icar, **W gas:** Exxon/dsl, Murphy USA, Sunoco, **food:** Arby's, Bojangles, Burger King, Hooters, Jack-in-the-Box, McDonald's, Olive Garden, Pizza Hut/Taco Bell, Ryan's, **lodging:** Comfort Inn, Embassy Suites, Relax Inn, **other:** Acura, Advance Parts, Audi/Porsche/VW, AutoZone, Bi-Lo, BMW/Mini, BooksAMillion, Buick, Dodge, $Tree, Ford, GMC/Pontiac, Hancock Fabrics, Honda, Infiniti, Isuzu, Jaguar, Kia, Lexus, Marshall's, Mazda, Mercedes, Michael's, Nissan, Office Depot, Pepboys, Petsmart, Saab, Stein Mart, Subaru, Suzuki, Toyota, Volvo

GREENVILLE

INTERSTATE 85 CONT'D

N ↕ S

Exit #	Services
46c	rd 291, Pleasantburg Rd, Mauldin Rd, **W gas:** BP, Citgo/dsl, **food:** Jack-in-the-Box, Papa John's, Steak-Out, Subway, **lodging:** InTown Suites, Quality Inn, Super Lodge, Value Place, **other:** Aamco, Advance Parts, BiLo/gas, Bloom Foods, CVS Drug, Home Depot, Tire Kingdom, same as 46ba
46b a	US 25 bus, Augusta Rd, **E gas:** Mike&Jack, Spinx, Vgo, **food:** Burger King, Waffle House, **lodging:** Camelot Inn, Holiday Inn, Motel 6, Southern Suites, **W lodging:** Economy Inn, Traveler's Inn, **other:** Home Depot, same as 46c
44	US 25, White Horse Rd, **E gas:** Spinx/Subway/dsl, **W gas:** Citgo/McDonald's, RaceWay, **food:** Waffle House, **other:** H, Freightliner
44a	SC 20 (from sb), to Piedmont
42	I-185 toll, US 29, to Greenville, **W** H
40	SC 153, to Easley, **E gas:** Breakers/dsl, **food:** Waffle House, **W gas:** BP, Citgo/dsl, RaceWay, **food:** Arby's, Bojangles, Burger King, Cracker Barrel, El Sureno Mexican, Huddle House, KFC, McDonald's, Pizza House, Pizza Hut/Taco Bell, Sonny's BBQ, Subway, Zaxby's, **lodging:** Best Western, Executive Inn, Super 8, **other:** Advance Parts, BiLo, $General, GNC, Rite Aid
39	SC 143, to Piedmont, **E gas:** Vgo/dsl, **W gas:** Shell/dsl, **other:** antiques
35	SC 86, to Easley, Piedmont, **E gas:** Pilot/McDonald's/dsl/scales/24hr, **food:** Hardee's (1.5mi), Mozzerelli's Pizza, Subway (1.5mi), Sweet P's, **W gas:** BP/grill/dsl
34	US 29 (from sb), to Williamston
32	SC 8, to Pelzer, Easley, **E gas:** Hickory Point/dsl, Shell/dsl
27	SC 81, to Anderson, **E gas:** BP/dsl, Exxon, Shell/dsl, **food:** Arby's, KFC/Pizza Hut, McDonald's, Waffle House, **lodging:** Holiday Inn Express, **other:** H, **W food:** Charlie's Wings
23mm	**rest area sb, full ♿ facilities, ☎, vending, 🛆, litter barrels, petwalk**
21	US 178, to Anderson, **E gas:** Shell/dsl, **food:** Waffle House, **2 mi E food:** Applebee's, Chick-fil-a, Fazoli's, Longhorn Steaks, O'Charley's, Ruby Tuesday, **lodging:** Home-Towne Suites, Quality Inn, **other:** Publix/deli
19b a	US 76, SC 28, to Anderson, **E gas:** Exxon/dsl, **food:** Charlie T's Wings, Fuddruckers, Hardee's, **lodging:** Days Inn, Hilton Garden, Royal American Motel, **other:** Aldi Food, Buick/GMC, Chrysler, Publix, Russell Stover, **1 mi E gas:** BP/dsl, Shell, **food:** Chick-fil-A, Chili's, Grand China, Jack-in-the-Box, Longhorn Steaks, O'Charley's, Olive Garden, Panera Bread, Sonny BBQ, TX Roadhouse, Zaxby's, **lodging:** Best Value Inn, **other:** Aldi Foods, Best Buy, Curves, Ford, GNC, Harley-Davidson, Honda, KIA, K-Mart, Mazda, Old Navy, O'Reilley Parts, Ross, Sam's Club, Target, Walmart SuperCtr, Vet, **W gas:** HotSpot/McDonald's, RaceWay/dsl/24hr, **food:** Arby's, Cracker Barrel, Fatz Cafe, Hooters, Outback Steaks, Subway, Waffle House, Wendy's, Wild Wing Cafe, **lodging:** Comfort Suites, Country Inn&Suites, Fairfield Inn, Hampton Inn, Holiday Inn Express, Jameson Inn, Microtel, **other:** to Clemson U
18mm	**rest area nb, full ♿ facilities, ☎, vending, 🛆, litter barrels, petwalk**
15mm	Lake Hartwell
14	SC 187, to Clemson, Anderson, **E gas:** Shell/dsl, **food:** Huddle House/24hr, **other:** KOA (1mi), **W gas:** Hickory Point/dsl, **food:** Famous Pizza Grill, **lodging:** Budget Inn, **other:** to Clem Research Pk
12mm	Seneca River, Lake Hartwell
11	SC 24, SC 243, to Townville, **E gas:** Exxon/dsl, Sunoco/dsl/24hr, **food:** Subway, **other:** to Savannah River Scenic Hwy, **W gas:** Shell/dsl, **food:** Townville Cafe, **other:** RV camping
9mm	**weigh sta nb**
4	SC 243, to SC 24, **E gas:** Exxon, Mobil/dsl/LP/rest./scales/24hr, **W gas:** Marathon/Russell's Gen. Store
2	SC 59, to Fair Play, **W** fireworks
1	SC 11, to Walhalla, **W food:** Gazebo Rest., **other:** fireworks, to Lake Hartwell SP
.5mm	**Welcome Ctr nb, full ♿ facilities, info, ☎, 🛆, litter barrels, vending, petwalk**
0mm	South Carolina/Georgia state line, Lake Hartwell, Tagaloo River

ANDERSON

INTERSTATE 95

N ↕ S

Exit #	Services
198mm	South Carolina/North Carolina state line
196mm	**Welcome Ctr sb, full ♿ facilities, info, ☎, vending, 🛆, litter barrels, petwalk**
195mm	Little Pee Dee River
193	SC 9, SC 57, to N Myrtle Beach, Dillon, **E gas:** BP/24hr, Exxon, Mobil, Sunoco/dsl, **food:** Bojangles, Burger King, Fiesta Tapatia, Huddle House, Shoney's, Subway, Waffle House, Wendy's, Zaxby's, **lodging:** Best Value Inn, Comfort Inn, Deluxe Inn, Hampton Inn, Holiday Inn Express, Knights Inn, Ramada Ltd, **other:** H, Bi-Lo Foods, CVS Drug, $General, Food Lion, Walmart, **W gas:** BP/dsl, **lodging:** Econolodge, Super 8
190	SC 34, to Dillon, **E gas:** BP/Stuckey's/DQ, **other:** repair
181	SC 38, Oak Grove, **E gas:** BP/Subway/dsl/24hr, ***FLYING J***/Cookery/dsl/LP/scales/24hr/@, Shell/McDonald's/dsl/24hr, **W gas:** Wilco/Hess/DQ/Wendy's/dsl/scales/24hr, **lodging:** Best Western, **other:** auto/truck repair
175mm	Pee Dee River
172mm	**rest area both lanes, full ♿ facilities, ☎, 🛆, vending, litter barrels, petwalk**
170	SC 327, **E gas:** BP, Pilot/Wendy's/dsl/scales/24hr, **food:** McDonald's, **lodging:** Holiday Inn Express, **other:** to Myrtle Beach, Missile Museum, **W gas:** Citgo/dsl
169	TV Rd, to Florence, **E other:** KOA (1mi), Peterbilt, dsl repair, **W gas:** BP, Petro/Shell/Pizza Hut/dsl/rest./24hr/@, **lodging:** Best Value Inn, **other:** Blue Beacon
164	US 52, to Darlington, Florence, **E gas:** Exxon/Pizza Hut/dsl, RaceWay/24hr, Shell/Huddle House/dsl, **food:** Angelo's Seafood Rest., Cracker Barrel, Hardee's, McDonald's, Quincy's, Quizno's, Ruby Tuesday, Waffle House, Wendy's, **lodging:** Baymont Inn, Best Western, Comfort Inn, Holiday Inn, Motel 6, Suburban Lodge, Super 8, Travel Inn, **other:** H, Chrysler/Jeep,

DILLON

SC

INTERSTATE 95 CONT'D

Exit #	Services
164	Continued Hyundai, **W** **gas:** TA/BP/Popeye's/dsl/scales/@, Pilot/Subway/Taco Bell/dsl, **food:** Arby's, Bojangles, Burger King, Fatz Café, Shoney's, Zaxby's, **lodging:** Comfort Suites,Country Inn&Suites, Day's Inn, Hampton Inn, Knight's Inn, Microtel, Sleep Inn, Thunderbird Inn, Travel House Inn, Wingate Inn, **other:** to Darlington Raceway
160b	I-20 W, to Columbia
160a	Lp 20, to Florence, **E** **food:** Arby's, Bruster's Ice Cream, Burger King, Chick-fil-A, Chili's, Chucke-Cheese, IHOP, Indigo Joe's Rest., Longhorn Steaks, Olive Garden, Outback Steaks, Percy & Willy, Red Lobster, Ruby Tuesday, Shoney's, Waffle House, Western Sizzlin, **lodging:** Courtyard, Fairfield Inn, Hampton Inn, Hilton Garden, Holiday Inn Express, Quality Inn, Red Roof Inn, Residence Inn, SpringHill Suites, **other:** Barnes&Noble, Belk, Best Buy, $Tree, Hobby Lobby, Hamricks, Home Depot, JC Penney, Kohl's, Lowes Whse, Sam's Club, Sears/auto, Target, Walmart SuperCtr, mall
157	US 76, Timmtonsville, Florence, **E** **gas:** BP/dsl/repair, Exxon/McDonald's/dsl, Kangaroo/dsl, Marathon, **food:** La Palmas Mexican, Waffle House, **lodging:** Day's Inn, Howard Johnson Express, Swamp Fox Inn, Travelodge, **W** **gas:** Sunoco, **lodging:** Ramada/rest., Tree Top Inn, Swamp Fox Camping (1mi)
153	Honda Way, **W** **gas:** Exxon, **food:** Hardees (2mi), **other:** Honda Plant
150	SC 403, to Sardis, **E** **gas:** BP/scales/dsl, **food:** Hotplate Cafe, **lodging:** Econolodge, **W** **gas:** Exxon/dsl
147mm	Lynches River
146	SC 341, to Lynchburg, Olanta, **E** **gas:** Moneysaver/dsl, **lodging:** Relax Inn
141	SC 53, SC 58, to Shiloh, **E** **gas:** Exxon/dsl, **other:** DonMar RV Ctr, to Woods Bay SP, **W** **gas:** Shell
139mm	**rest area both lanes, full ♿ facilities, ☎, vending, [picnic], litter barrels, petwalk**
135	US 378, to Sumter, Turbeville, **E** **gas:** BP, Citgo/dsl/24hr, **food:** Compass Rest., **lodging:** America's Inn, Day's Inn, **W** **gas:** Exxon/Subway/dsl, **other:** Pineland Golf Course
132	SC 527, to Sardinia, Kingstree
130mm	Black River
122	US 521, to Alcolu, Manning, **W** **gas:** Exxon/dsl, **food:** Paradise Cafe
119	SC 261, to Paxville, Manning, **0-1 mi** **E** **gas:** Mobil, Murphy USA, Shell/24hr, **TA/BP/Popeye's/Pizza Hut/dsl/scales/24hr/@**, **food:** Arby's, Bojangles, Burger King, Huddle House, KFC, Mariachi Mexican, Shoney's, Sonic, Subway, Waffle House, Wendy's, Yucatan Mexican, Zaxby's, **lodging:** Best Western, Hampton Inn, Holiday Inn Express, Quality Inn, Ramada Inn, **other:** [H], AutoZone, Chrysler/Jeep/Dodge, Campers Paradise RV Park, CVS Drug, $General, Ford, Goodyear/auto, Radio Shack, **Walmart SuperCtr**, **W** **gas:** Horizon/dsl/E85, Paxville/24hr, **lodging:** Super 8, **other:** auto repair
115	US 301, to Summerton, Manning, **W** **gas:** Shell/dsl/24hr, **food:** Georgio's Greek, **lodging:** Executive Inn
108	SC 102, Summerton, **E** **gas:** BP/DQ/Stuckey's, TawCaw/dsl, **other:** TawCaw RV Park (6m), **W** **lodging:** Best Inn, Day's Inn, Deluxe Inn, Knight's Inn
102	US 15, US 301 N, to Santee, **E** **gas:** StopSpot/dsl, **food:** Arista Rest., **lodging:** Santee Resort/Motel, **other:** Bigwater RV Camping, Santee Lakes Camping, **W** **gas:** Horizon/dsl/E85, **other:** to Santee NWR
100mm	Lake Marion
99mm	**rest area both lanes, full ♿ facilities, ☎, info, vending, [picnic], litter barrels, petwalk**
98	SC 6, to Eutawville, Santee, **E** **gas:** BP/Bojangles, Chevron/LP, Citgo, Mobil, **food:** Captains Quarters Rest., Coaster's Seafood, Huddle House, KFC, La Fogata Mexican, LT's Rest., Pizza Hut, Shoney's, Subway, **lodging:** Best Western, Hampton Inn, Howard Johnson, Super 8, Travelodge, Whitten Inn, **other:** $General, Piggly Wiggly, Russell Stover Candy, Santee Outlets/famous brands, **W** **gas:** Citgo, Exxon, Hess/dsl, Horizon/Noble Roman's/dsl/24hr, **food:** Burger King, **Cracker Barrel**, Maurice's BBQ, McDonald's, Peking Chinese, Waffle House, Wendy's, **lodging:** Clark Inn/rest., Country Inn&Suites, Holiday Inn, Lake Marion Inn, Motel 6, Quality Inn, **other:** CarQuest, CVS Drug, Family$, Food Lion, USPO, to Santee SP (3mi)
97	US 301 S (from sb, no return), to Orangeburg
93	US 15, to Santee, Holly Hill
90	US 176, to Cameron, Holly Hill, **W** **gas:** Exxon/dsl
86b a	I-26, W to Columbia, E to Charleston
82	US 178, to Bowman, Harleyville, **E** **gas:** BP, Wilco/Hess/Stuckey's/Wendy's/DQ/dsl/scales/24hr, **lodging:** Peachtree Inn, **W** **gas:** Shell/dsl, **other:** tires/truck repair
77	US 78, to Bamberg, St George, **E** **gas:** Exxon/KFC, Monoco, Horizon/Subway/TCBY, Sunoco, **food:** Georgio's Rest., Hardee's, McDonald's, Mi Rancho Mexican, Pizza Hut, Skynyrd's Grill, Waffle House, **lodging:** Best Value Inn, Comfort Inn/RV Park, Econolodge, Quality Inn, **other:** Chevrolet/Pontiac/GMC, CVS Drug, $General, Family$, Ford, Jolly Acres RV Park, Radio Shack, Ried's Foods, USPO, **W** **gas:** BP, Shell/Taco Bell/dsl, **food:** Huddle House, **lodging:** Country Hearth Inn, Day's Inn, Southern Inn, Super 8
68	SC 61, Canadys, **E** **gas:** BP, El Cheapo/scales, Shell/Subway/dsl, **other:** truck lube/repair, to Colleton SP (3mi)
62	SC 34
57	SC 64, Walterboro, **E** **gas:** Horizon, Shell/DQ, Mobil/dsl, Sunoco/dsl, **food:** Arby's, Burger King, Capt D's, Dimitrio's Rest., Domino's, Huddle House, KFC,

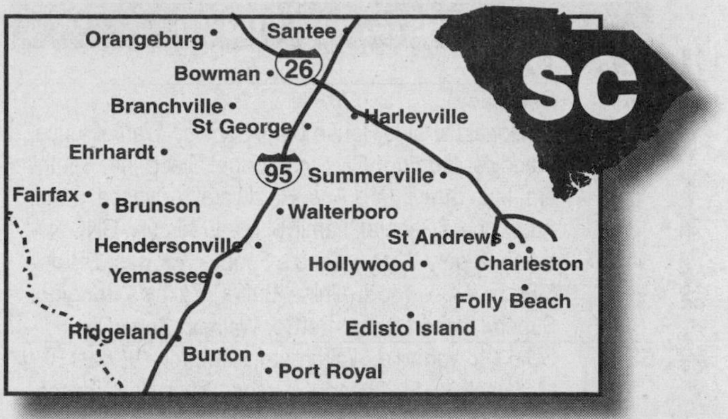

INTERSTATE 95 CONT'D

N ↕ S WALTERBORO

Exit #	Services
57	Continued McDonald's, Olde House Café, Subway, Waffle House, Wendy's, **lodging:** Carolina Lodge, Sleep Inn, Southern Inn, **other:** H, Ace Hardware, Advance Parts, AutoZone, $General, Family$, Ford/Mercury, GNC Nutrition, Piggly Wiggly, Reid's Foods, **W gas:** BP/dsl, Murphy USA, **food:** China Buffet, Zaxby's, **lodging:** Super 8, **other:** $Tree, PetCo, Walmart SuperCtr
53	SC 63, to Varnville, Walterboro, Hampton, **E gas:** BP/McDonald's, El Cheapo, Exxon, Shell/DQ, Texaco/dsl, **food:** Glasshouse Rest., KFC, Longhorn Steaks, Ruby Tuesday, Shoney's, Waffle House, **lodging:** Best Western, Comfort Inn/rest., Econo Inn, Motel 6, Quality Inn, Ramada Inn, Royal Inn, Rice Planter's Inn, **other:** fireworks, **W gas:** Horizon, **food:** Cracker Barrel, **lodging:** Country Hearth Inn, Day's Inn, Hampton Inn, Holiday Inn Express, Microtel, **other:** Green Acres Camping
47mm	**rest area both lanes, full ♿ facilities, ☎, vending, picnic, litter barrels, petwalk**
42	US 21, to Yemassee, Beaufort
40mm	Combahee River
38	SC 68, to Hampton, Yemassee, **E gas:** Horizon/dsl/E85, **other:** Family$, **W gas:** BP/Subway/TCBY, Exxon/dsl, Shell/dsl, **food:** Courtney Bay Seafood, J's Rest., **lodging:** Palmetto Lodge/rest., Super 8
33	US 17 N, to Beaufort, **E gas:** BP/dsl, Exxon/McDonald's, Shell, Texaco/TCBY/Subway, **food:** Denny's, Country Kitchen, Waffle House, Wendy's, **lodging:** Best Western, Budget Inn, Hampton Inn, Holiday Inn Express, Knight's Inn, **other:** Confederate Railroad Museum, KOA, Oaks RV Camping
30.5mm	Tullifinny River
29mm	Coosawhatchie River
28	SC 462, to Coosawhatchie, Hilton Head, Bluffton, **W gas:** Chevron/dsl, Citgo, Exxon/Chester Fried/dsl
22	US 17, Ridgeland, **W gas:** Sunoco, **lodging:** Ridgeland Inn, **other:** H
21	SC 336, to Hilton Head, Ridgeland, **E food:** Wendy's, **other:** Boat'n RV Whse, **W gas:** BP/DQ/dsl, Chevron/dsl/24hr, Exxon, Shell, **food:** Bella Pizza, Burger King, Hong Kong Chinese, Huddle House, Jasper's Porch, KFC, Subway, Waffle House, **lodging:** Carolina Lodge, Comfort Inn/rest., Days Inn, Quality Inn, **other:** H, Curves, $General, Harvey's Foods, Rite Aid
18	SC 13, to US 17, US 278, to Switzerland, Granville, Ridgeland
17mm	**parking area both lanes, commercial vehicles only**
8	US 278, to Bluffton, Hardeeville, **E gas:** BP/Wendy's/dsl/scales, Exxon, Kangaroo/McDonald's, **other:** H, **W gas:** Horizon/Subway/Dominos/dsl, Mobil/Kangaroo/dsl, **lodging:** Holiday Inn Express, Motel 6
5	US 17, US 321, to Savannah, Hardeeville, **E gas:** Chevron/dsl, Exxon/Blimpie, Shell/24hr, **food:** Mi Tierrita Mexican, Waffle House, **lodging:** Day's Inn, Economy Inn, Sleep Inn, **other:** fireworks, to Savannah NWR, **W gas:** BP/dsl, Citgo, Exxon, Sunoco/dsl, **food:** Burger King, Los 3 Garcia's, New China Rest., Shoney's, Smitty's Grill, Wendy's, **lodging:** Continued Clean Stay USA, Country Hearth Inn, Deluxe Inn, Econolodge, Knight's Inn, Quality Inn, Red Roof Inn, Super 8, **other:** $General, NAPA
4.5mm	**Welcome Ctr nb, full ♿ facilities, info, ☎, picnic, litter barrels, vending, petwalk**
4mm	**weigh sta both lanes**
0mm	South Carolina/Georgia state line, Savannah River

HARDEEVILLE

SC

INTERSTATE 385 (GREENVILLE)

N ↕ S GREENVILLE

Exit #	Services
42	US 276, Stone Ave, to Travelers Rest., to Greenville Zoo, **E other:** CarQuest, **W gas:** Spinx, **1-2 mi W multiple facilities on US 276, I-385 begins/ends on US 276.**
40b a	SC 291, Pleasantburg Dr, **E gas:** Sunoco, **food:** Jack-in-the-Box, Little Caesar's, Olive Tree, Pizza Hut, S&S Cafeteria, Sonic, Steak&Ale, Subway, Taco Casa, Wendy's, **other:** CVS Drug, Walgreens, to BJU, Furman U, **W gas:** Citg/dsl, **food:** Domino's, Krispy Kreme, **lodging:** Quality Inn, Sleep Inn, **other:** transmissions
39	Haywood Rd, **E gas:** BP, Exxon/dsl, **food:** Domino's, LongHorn Steaks, Outback Steaks, Tony's Pizzaria, **lodging:** AmeriSuites, Courtyard, GuestHouse Suites, Hawthorn Inn, Hilton, La Quinta, Quality Inn, Residence Inn, **other:** Firestone, TJ Maxx, **W gas:** Crown, Shell, Texaco, **food:** Arby's, Applebee's, Bennigan's, Blackeyed Pea, Buffalo's Café, Burger King, Chili's, ChuckeCheese, CityRange Steaks, Don Pablo, Hardee's, Italian Mkt/grill, Jack-in-the-Box, Jason's Deli, Kanpai Tokyo, O'Charley's, Ruby Tuesday, Senor Wrap's, Starbucks, Steak'n Shake, Waffle House, Wendy's, **lodging:** Hampton Inn, Studio+, **other:** Barnes&Noble, Belk, Dillard's, Discount Tire, Goodyear, Harley-Davidson, JC Penney, LensCrafters, Macy's, NTB, Sears/auto, mall
37	Roper Mtn Rd, **E other:** BiLo Foods, **W gas:** Amoco, BP/dsl, Exxon/Pantry, RaceTrac, **food:** Atl Bread Co, Backyard Burger, Burger King, Capri's Italian, Cracker Barrel, Fazoli's, LoneStar Steaks, McDonald's, Miyabi Japanese, Rafferty's, Remington's Rest., Waffle House, **lodging:** Day's Inn, Crowne Plaza, Embassy Suites, Fairfield Inn, Holiday Inn Select, La Quinta, Travelodge, **other:** BJ's Whse, Home Depot, Lowe's Whse, Old Navy, Target, mall
36b a	I-85, N to Charlotte, S to Atlanta
35	SC 146, Woodruff Rd, **E gas:** Spinx, **food:** Applebee's, AZ Steaks, Bojangles, Bone Fish Grill, Boston Pizzaria, Brewster's, Burger King, Chick-fil-A, Chili's, Fazoli's, Grand Buffet, Hardee's, Jersey Mike's Subs, KFC, King Buffet, McAlister's Deli, Moe's SW Grill, Perkins, Ryan's, Sonic, Starbucks, Subway, Taco Bell, Topper's Rest., Waffle House, Wendy's, Zaxby's, **other:** Ace Hardware, Aldi Foods, BiLo Foods, Discount Tire, $Tree, Kohl's, Publix, Radio Shack, Sam's Club/gas, Staples, Tire Kingdom, USPO, Walmart SuperCtr/24hr, **W gas:** Blue Jay/dsl, **food:** Bob Evan's, Burger King, Fatz Café, Fuddrucker's, IHOP, Lieus Bistro, Midori's Rest., Mimi's Cafe, Monterrey Mexican, Red Robin, Sticky Fingers, TCBY, Waffle House, **lodging:** Drury Inn, Hampton Inn, **other:** Barnes& Noble, Goodyear/auto, Hamrick's Outlet, Lowe's Whse, funpark

N ↕ S

SIMPSONVILLE

INTERSTATE 385 CONT'D (GREENVILLE)

Exit #	Services
34	Butler Rd, Mauldin, **E gas:** Exxon, **food:** Arby's, **other:** CVS Drug, **W gas:** Phillips 66, **lodging:** Super 8 (3mi)
33	Bridges Rd, Mauldin
31	I-185 toll, SC 417, to Laurens Rd, **E gas:** BP, **food:** Hardee's, Jack in the Box, **other:** [H], **S food:** A&W, LJSilver, **lodging:** Masters Inn
30	I-185 toll, US 276, Standing Springs Rd
29	Georgia Rd, to Simpsonville, **W lodging:** ValuePlace Inn
27	Fairview Rd, to Simpsonville, **E gas:** Shell, **food:** Carolina Rest., CoachHouse rest., Little Caesar's, McDonald's, Milano Pizzaria, New China Buffet, Subway, **lodging:** Palmetto Inn, **other:** [H], Advance Parts, AutoZone, $General, Tuesday Morning, **W gas:** Exxon, Murphy USA, Spinx, **food:** Anthony's Pizza, Applebee's, Arby's, AZ Steaks, Bellacino's, Bruster's, Burger King, Chick-fil-A, **Cracker Barrel**, Dragon Den Chinese, Hungry Howie's, Jack-in-the-Box, Jersey Mike's, KFC, La Fogata Mexican, McDonalds, Moe's SW Grill, O'Charley's, Panera Bread, Pizza Hut, Quizno's, Ruby Tuesday, Ryan's, Sonic, Starbucks, Subway, Taco Bell, Tequila's Mexican, Waffle House, Wendy's, Zaxby's, **lodging:** Comfort Suites, Days Inn, Hampton Inn, Holiday Inn Express, Quality Inn, **other:** AT&T, Belk, Bi-Lo, CVS Drug, $Tree, Ford, GNC, Goodyear/auto, Home Depot, Ingles Foods, Kohl's, Lowe's Whse, Publix, Radio Shack, Ross, Target, Tire Kingdom, TJ Maxx, Walgreens, **Walmart SuperCtr/24hr**, USPO
26	Harrison Bridge Rd (from sb)
24	Fairview St, **E gas:** Li'l Cricket, **food:** Hardee's, Waffle House, **other:** carwash
23	SC 418, to Fountain Inn, Fork Shoals, **E gas:** Exxon/pizza/subs/dsl/24hr
22	SC 14 W, Old Laurens Rd, to Fountain Inn
19	SC 14 E, to Gray Court, Owings
16	SC 101, to Woodruff, Gray Court
10	SC 23, Barksdale, Ora
9	US 221, to Laurens, Enoree, **E gas:** Gas/Pizza/Subs **food:** Waffle House, **lodging:** Budget Lodge, **W** Walmart Dist Ctr
6mm	**rest area both lanes (both lanes exit left), full [handicapped] facilities, [phone], vending, [picnic], litter barrels, petwalk**
5	SC 49, to Laurens, Union
2	SC 308, to Clinton, Ora, **W other:** [H], to Presbyterian Coll in Clinton
0mm	I-26 S to Columbia, **I-385 begins/ends on I-26 at 52mm**

E ↕ W

CHARLESTON

INTERSTATE 526 (CHARLESTON)

Exit #	Services
33mm	I-526 begins/ends.
32	US 17, **0-1 mi N gas:** Hess/dsl, Shell, **food:** Benito's Pizza, Burger King, Chili's, IHOP, LongHorn Steaks, Mama Fu's Asian, On The Border, Starbucks, TGIFriday, **lodging:** Courtyard, **other:** Advance Parts, Barnes&Noble, Belk, Chevrolet, CVS Drug, Firestone, Lowes Whse, Midas, Old Navy, Rite Aid, Tire Kingdom, TrueValue, Walgreens, **0-1 mi S gas:** Exxon/

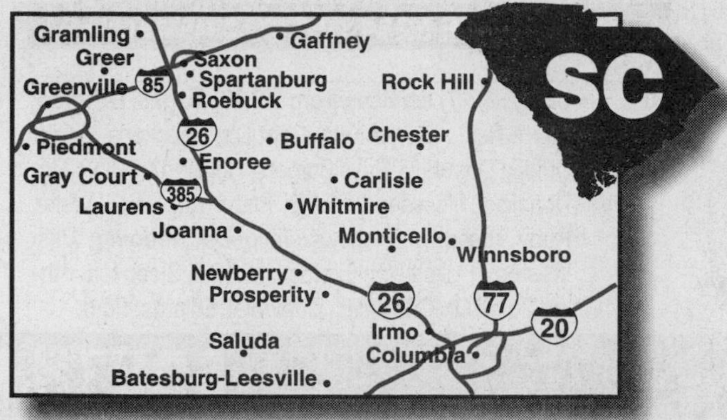

Exit #	Services
32	Continued Dunkin Donuts, Mobil, Shell/Circle K, Sunoco, **food:** Applebees, Arby's, Chick-fil-A, Cici's, Domino's, Hardee's, Huddle House, KFC, La Hacienda Mexicana, McDonald's, Outback Steaks, Papa John's, Sticky Fingers, Subway, Wendy's, Zeus Grill, **lodging:** Best Western, Day's Inn, Extended Stay America, Hampton Inn, Holiday Inn, Masters Inn, Quality Inn, Red Roof Inn, River Inn, **other:** Aamco, Bi-Lo, Cadillac, $General, Ford, Harris Teeter, Jiffy Lube, K-Mart, Marshall's, Office Depot, Radio Shack, Staples, TJ Maxx, USPO, VW, Walmart, Whole Foods Mkt, Vet
30	Long Point Rd, **N gas:** BP, Exxon, **food:** Bamboo Garden, Beef'o Brady's, McAlister's, Moe's SW Grill, Sonic, Starbucks, Subway, Waffle House, Wendy's, **other:** CVS Drug, Food Lion, Harris Teeter Foods, PetsMart, Ross, Steinmart, Charles Pinckney NHS
26mm	Wando River
24	Daniel Island, **S gas:** Texaco, **food:** Dragon Palace, Lana's Mexican, Queen Anne's Steaks/seafood, Subway, **lodging:** Hampton Inn, **other:** Publix
23b a	Clements Ferry Rd
21mm	Cooper River
20	Virginia Ave (from eb), **S gas:** Hess Depot
19	N Rhett Ave, **N gas:** Hess, Kangaroo/Subway/dsl, **food:** Hardee's, **other:** Family$, Food Lion, Rite Aid, **S gas:** BP
18b a	US 52, US 78, Rivers Ave, **N gas:** BP/dsl, Hess, Kangaroo/dsl, **food:** KFC, Peking Gourmet, Pizza Hut/Taco Bell, **other:** AutoZone, Dodge, Family$, Ford, H&L Foods, auto repair, **S gas:** Exxon
17b a	I-26, E to Charleston, W to Columbia
16	Montague Ave, Airport Rd, **S gas:** Sunoco, **food:** Chili's, La Hacienda, Panera Bread, Quizno's, Starbucks, Wendy's, **lodging:** Comfort Inn, Embassy Suites, Extended Stay America, Hilton Garden, Holiday Inn, Homewood Suites, Quality Inn, Residence Inn, Wingate Inn, **other:** Sam's Club, Staples, Tanger Outlet/famous brands, Walmart SuperCtr
15	SC 642, Dorchester Rd, Paramount Dr, **N gas:** BP, **food:** Pizza Roma (1mi), Wendy's (1mi), **S gas:** Citgo/dsl, Sunoco, **food:** Burger King, Checker's, Domino's, East Bay Deli, Huddle House, Pizza Hut, **lodging:** Airport Inn, **other:** Bi-Lo Foods, CVS Drug, Family$, Food Lion, Harley-Davidson, U-Haul
14	Leeds Ave, **S lodging:** Value Place Inn, **other:** [H], boat marina
13mm	Ashley River
11b a	SC 61, Ashley River Rd, **N food:** Chick-fil-A, McDonald's, O'Charley's, Subway, **other:** [H], Food Lion, Home Depot, Lowes Whse, Rite Aid

INTERSTATE 526 CONT'D (CHARLESTON)

E ↔ W

Exit #	Services
10	US 17, SC 7, **services from US 17, E gas:** BP, **food:** Alex's Rest., Burger King, Capt D's, Checker's, CiCi's, Dunkin Donuts, 5 Guys Burgers, Hopsing's, IHOP, McDonald's, Messengers BBQ, Pizza Hut, Red Lobster, Ruby Tuesday, Shoney's, Taco Bell, **lodging:** Best Western, Holiday Inn Express, Motel 6, Sleep Inn, **other:** Buick/GMC/Pontiac, Chevrolet, Dillards, Ford,
10	Continued Honda, Hyundai, Jaguar, Kerr Drug, K-Mart, Mazda, Mini, Mitsubishi, Nissan, Dodge, Pepboys, Piggly Wiggly, Sears/auto, Tire Kingdom, Vet, **W gas:** Exxon, Hess, Shell/Circle K, **food:** Halligan's Rest., Hardees, Subway, Waffle House, **lodging:** Econolodge, Hampton Inn, InTown Suites, **other:** Acura, Audi, Advance Parts, Carmax, Chrysler/Jeep, Costco/gas, CVS Drug, Family$, Food Lion, KIA, Subaru, Toyota
I-526 begins/ends on US 17	

SOUTH DAKOTA

INTERSTATE 29

N ↔ S

Exit #	Services
253mm	South Dakota/North Dakota state line
251mm	**Welcome Ctr sb, full ♿ facilities, info, ☎, [picnic], litter barrels, petwalk**
246	SD 127, to Rosholt, New Effington, **3 mi W** gas, food, RV camping, Sica Hollow SP (24mi)
242	no services
235mm	**weigh sta sb**
232	SD 10, Sisseton, **E gas:** Dakota Connection/dsl/casino/24hr, **food:** Crossroads Cafe, **1-3 mi W gas:** Amstar/dsl, FuelMax/dsl, Sinclair/dsl, Tesoro, **food:** Cottage Rest, DQ, Pizza Hut, Subway, Taco John's, West Inn Grille, **lodging:** Holiday Motel, I-29 Motel, Super 8, Viking Motel, **other:** Alco, Camp Dakotah, Buick/Chevrolet/Pontiac, Family$, NAPA, SuperValu Foods/gas, to Roy Lake SP (25mi), Ft Sisseton SP (35mi)
224	Peever, Sioux Tribal Hqtrs, **E gas:** Sunoco/dsl, **W** Pickerel Lake (16mi)
213	SD 15, to Wilmot, **rest area both lanes, full ♿ facilities, ☎, [picnic], litter barrels, petwalk, RV dump, st patrol, 7 mi E** gas, food, to Hartford Beach SP (17mi)
207	US 12, Summit, **E gas:** Sinclair/dsl/24hr, **food:** County Line Rest (1mi), **W** Blue Dog Fish Hatchery (15mi), Waubay NWR (19mi)
201	to Twin Brooks
193	SD 20, to South Shore, Stockholm
185	to Waverly, **4 mi W other:** Dakota Sioux Casino/rest.
180	US 81 S, to Watertown, **5 mi W gas:** Sinclair, **other:** Bramble Park Zoo, airport
177	US 212, Watertown, **E gas:** Tesoro/Grainery Cafe/dsl/24hr, **lodging:** Holiday Inn Express, **other:** Volvo, WW Tires, truck wash, **W gas:** Shell/dsl, **food:** Applebee's, Culver's, IHOP, JimmyJohn's, KFC/LJ Silver, Lonepine BBQ, McDonald's, Starbucks, **lodging:** Comfort Inn, Country Inn&Suites, Days Inn, Hampton Inn, **other:** [H], $Tree, Redlin Art Ctr, Walmart SuperCtr/Subway/24hr, **1-2 mi W gas:** Cenex/dsl, Clark/dsl, Freedom, Sinclair, Tesoro, **food:** Arby's, Burger King, Cici's Pizza, Domino's, DQ, Dragon Wall Chinese, Godfather's, Guadalajara Mexican, McDonald's, Papa Murphy's, Perkins, Pizza Hut, Quizno's, Senor Max's Mexican, Subway/TCBY, Taco John's, **lodging:** Drake Hotel, Travelers Inn, **other:** Advance Parts, Buick, Chrysler/Dodge/Jeep, EconoFoods, Ford, Goodyear/auto, Harley-Davidson, Herberger's, Hy-Vee Foods, JC Penney, Menard's, NAPA, O'Reilly Parts, Pronto Parts, ShopKO, Target, Tires+, Walgreens, mall, to Sandy Shore RA (10mi)
164	SD 22, to Castlewood, Clear Lake, **9 mi E gas:** Cenex/dsl, **other:** [H]
161mm	**rest area both lanes, full ♿ facilities, ☎, [picnic], litter barrels, vending, petwalk, RV dump**
157	to Brandt
150	SD 28, SD 15 N, to Toronto, **7 mi W** gas, food, lodging, 24 mi **W** Lake Poinsett RA, SD Amateur Baseball Hall of Fame
140	SD 30, to White, Bruce, **W** Oakwood Lakes SP (12mi)
133	US 14 byp, Brookings, **E other:** WW Tires, **W** to SD St U, museums, Laura Ingalls Wilder Home
132	US 14, Lp 29, Brookings, **E gas:** Cenex/Burger King/dsl, **food:** Applebee's, **lodging:** Fairfield Inn, Hampton Inn, Holiday Inn Express, Super 8, **W gas:** BP, Cenex, Shell, **food:** Arby's, Burger King, Culver's, DQ, JimmyJohn's, KFC, King's Wok, McDonald's, Papa John's, Papa Murphy's, Pavillion Grill, Perkins, Pizza Ranch, Qdoba Mexican, Quizno's, Subway, Z'Kota Grill, **lodging:** Comfort Inn, Days Inn, Staurolite Inn, **other:** [H], Advance Parts, CarQuest, Buick/Cadillac/Chevrolet/GMC/Pontiac, Lowe's Whse, Radio Shack, Walmart SuperCtr/24hr, city park
127	SD 324, to Elkton, Sinai
124mm	Big Sioux River
121	to Nunda, Ward, **E rest area both lanes, full ♿ facilities, ☎, [picnic], litter barrels, vending, petwalk, RV dump,** st patrol, **W** food, RV camping
114	SD 32, to Flandreau, **7 mi E gas:** Cenex, **food:** Subway, **lodging:** Sioux River Motel/RV park, **other:** Santee Tribal Hqtrs
109	SD 34, to Madison, Colman, **W gas:** BP/dsl/rest., Shell/dsl/rest., **20 mi W other:** to Lake Herman SP, Dakota St U, museum
104	to Trent, Chester
103mm	**parking area both lanes**
98	SD 115 S, Dell Rapids, **E** Chevrolet/Pontiac, **3 mi E gas:** Cenex, Shell, **food:** DQ, Pizza Ranch, **lodging:** Bilmar Inn, **other:** [H]
94	SD 114, to Baltic, **10 mi E other:** to EROS Data Ctr, US Geological Survey
86	to Renner, Crooks
84b a	I-90, W to Rapid City, E to Albert Lea
83	SD 38 W, 60th St, **E gas:** ***FLYING J***/Country Mkt/dsl/24hr/scales/@, **lodging:** Quality Suites, **other:** Freightliner Trucks, Harley-Davidson, Northview Campers, repair, **W other:** fireworks

WATERTOWN

BROOKINGS

SC

SD

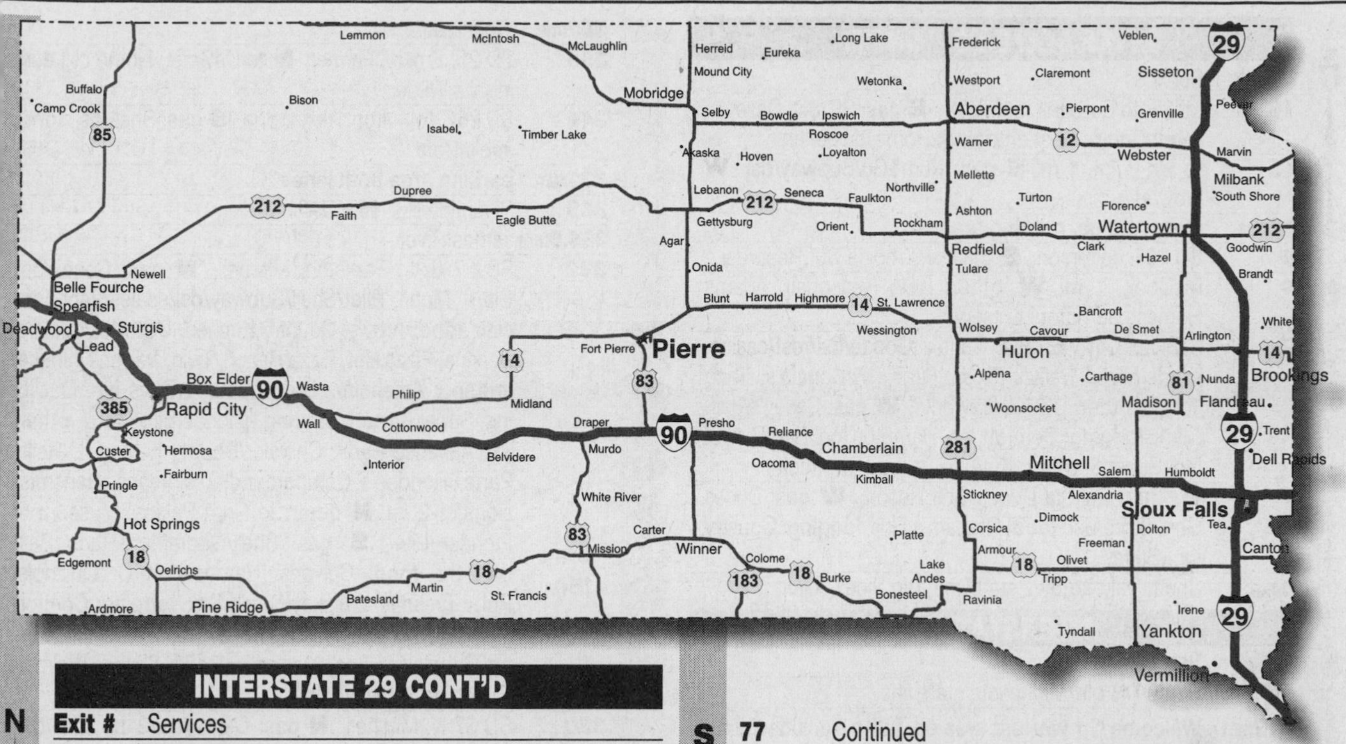

INTERSTATE 29 CONT'D

N ↕ S

SIOUX FALLS

Exit #	Services
82	Benson Rd
81	SD 38 E, Russell St, Sioux Falls, **E gas:** BP/24hr, Food'n Fuel, **food:** Michael's Steaks, Roll'n Pin Rest., **lodging:** Arena Motel, Best Western/Ramkota, Brimark Inn, Kelly Inn, Knight's Inn, Motel 6, Ramada Inn, Sheraton, Sleep Inn, **other:** Schaap's RV Ctr, st patrol, **W food:** Subway
80	Madison St, **E gas:** Sinclair/dsl, **other:** to fairgrounds
79	SD 42, 12th St, **E gas:** BP/24hr, Freedom, **food:** Burger King, Burger Time, Golden Harvest Chinese, KFC, McDonald's, Pizza Hut, Subway, Taco Bell, Taco John's, Tomacelli's Pizza, Wendy's, **lodging:** Ramada Ltd, ValuePlace Inn, **other:** H, Ace Hardware, Buick/Pontiac, Chevrolet, $General, K-Mart, Lewis Drug, NAPA, Scion/Toyota, Sunshine Foods, Walgreens, city park, USPO, to Great Plains Zoo/museum, **W gas:** BP/dsl, Cenex/dsl, Food'n Fuel, **other:** Tower RV Park
78	26th St, Empire St, **E gas:** BP, **food:** Carino's Italian, Carnival Brazillian Grill, Coldstone Creamery, Chevy's Mexican, ChuckeCheese, Cracker Barrel, Culver's, Domino's, Granite City Rest, Outback Steaks, Puerto Vallarta, Ruby Tuesday, **lodging:** Clubhouse Suites, Hampton Inn, Holiday Inn Express, StayBridge Suites, **other:** Home Depot, Petsmart, Sam's Club/gas, USPO, World Mkt, **W food:** Boss' Pizza, DQ, Dynasty Chinese, Oscar's Coffee, Papa John's, Quizno's, Referee Grill, Starbucks, **lodging:** TownePlace Suites, **other:** Curves, Hy-Vee Foods/gas, Lowe's Whse
77	41st St, Sioux Falls, **E gas:** BP/24hr, Sinclair/dsl, SA/dsl, **food:** Arby's, Burger King, Champp's Grill, Chili's, Fry'n Pan Rest., Fuddrucker's, HuHot Mongolian, KFC, McDonald's, Old Chicago Pizza, Olive Garden, Pancake House, Papa Murphy's, Perkins, Pizza Hut, Pizza Ranch, Qdoba Mexican, Quizno's, Red Lobster, Starbucks, Subway, Szechwan Chinese, Taco Bell, Taco John's, Texas Roadhouse, TimberLodge Steaks, Wendy's, **lodging:** Comfort Suites, Courtyard, Fairfield Inn, Microtel, Residence Inn, Rodeway Inn, SpringHill

SIOUX FALLS

Exit #	Services
77	Continued Suites, Super 8, **other:** Advance Parts, Barnes&Noble, Best Buy, Curves, Ford/Lincoln/Mercury, Goodyear/auto, Hancock Fabrics, Hy-Vee Foods, Hyundai/Nissan, JC Penney, Macy's, Mazda, Old Navy, PetCo, Radio Shack, Sears/auto, ShopKO, Target, Tires+, Walgreens, **Walmart SuperCtr**, Younkers, mall, **W gas:** Shell/dsl, **food:** Burger King, Denucci's Pizza, Godfather's, IHOP, Peking Chinese, Perkins/24hr, Subway, **lodging:** AmericInn, Baymont Inn, Days Inn, Red Roof Inn, **other:** Lewis Drug, USPO
75	I-229 E, to I-90 E
73	Tea, **E gas:** Sinclair/dsl, **food:** Marlin's Rest, **1.5mi W** Red Barn Camping
71	to Harrisburg, Lennox, **W** RV camping
68	to Lennox, Parker
64	SD 44, Worthing, **W other:** Buick/Chevrolet/Pontiac, Great Plains RV Ctr
62	US 18 E, to Canton, **E gas: Shell/pizza/dsl, lodging:** Countryside RV park/motel, **W** repair
59	US 18 W, to Davis, Hurley
56	to Fairview, **E** to Newton Hills SP (12mi)
53	to Viborg
50	to Centerville, Hudson
47	SD 46, to Irene, Beresford, **E gas:** BP/Burger King, Casey's, **Sinclair/dsl, food:** Emily's Café, Subway, **lodging:** Crossroads Motel, Super 8, **other:** Chevrolet, $General, Fiesta Foods, repair, **W gas:** Cenex/cafe/dsl/24hr
42	to Alcester, Wakonda
41mm	truck check (from sb)
38	to Volin, **E** to Union Grove SP (3mi)
31	SD 48, to Akron, Spink
26	SD 50, to Vermillion, **E Welcome Ctr/rest area both lanes, full (handicapped) facilities, info, (phone), (picnic), litter barrels, petwalk, RV dump, W gas:** BP/dsl, **6-7 mi W food:** Burger King, Godfather's Pizza, Subway, Taco John's, **lodging:** Comfort Inn, Holiday Inn Express, Super 8, Westside Inn, **other:** H, Hy-Vee Foods, **Walmart/deli**, to U of SD, to Lewis & Clark RA

INTERSTATE 29 CONT'D

N ↕ S

Exit #	Services
18	Lp 29, to Burbank, Elk Point, **E gas:** BP/dsl, Casey's, **food:** Cody's Rest., **lodging:** HomeTowne Inn
15	to Elk Point, **1 mi E gas:** Kum&Go/Subway/dsl, **W** fireworks
13mm	**weigh sta nb, parking area sb**
9	SD 105, Jefferson, **E gas:** BP/Choice Cut Rest./dsl
4	McCook, **1 mi W other:** KOA (seasonal), Adams Homestead/nature preserve
2	N Sioux City, **E gas:** Cenex, Goode/dsl/rest/casino, **food:** Glass Palace Rest. (1mi), McDonald's, Taco John's, **other:** USPO, fireworks, **W gas:** Casey's/gas, Clark, **lodging:** Comfort Inn, Hampton Inn, Red Carpet Inn, Super 8, **other:** KOA, to Sodrac Dogtrack
1	**E other:** Dakota Dunes Golf Resort, **W gas:** Dunes Gen. Store/dsl, **food:** Graham's Grill, **lodging:** Country Inn&Suites
0mm	South Dakota/Iowa state line, Big Sioux River

INTERSTATE 90

E ↕ W

SIOUX FALLS

Exit #	Services
412.5mm	South Dakota/Minnesota state line
412mm	**Welcome Ctr wb/rest area eb, full ♿ facilities, info, ☎, ⛱, litter barrels, petwalk, RV dump (wb), weigh sta (wb)**
410	Valley Springs, **N** Palisades SP (7mi), **S** Beaver Creek Nature Area, gas, food
406	SD 11, Brandon, Corson, **N** Palisades SP (10mi), **S gas:** BP/dsl, Shell, Sinclair/McDonald's/dsl, **food:** Brandon Steaks, DQ, Great Wall, Pizza Ranch, Subway, Taco John's, Tailgater's Grill, **lodging:** Comfort Inn, Holiday Inn Express, **other:** Curves, Lewis Drug, Sunshine Foods, TrueValue, to Big Sioux RA (4mi)
402	EROS Data Ctr, **N other:** Jellystone RV Park, tires
400	I-229 S
399	SD 115, Cliff Ave, Sioux Falls, **N gas:** TC's/BP/dsl, **other:** Spader RV Ctr, KOA, **S gas:** BP, Holiday/dsl, Pilot/Grandma Max's Rest./Subway/dsl/24hr/@, Shell/dsl, Sinclair, **food:** Arby's, Burger King, McDonald's/**truck parking**, Perkins, Taco Bell, Taco John's, **lodging:** Cloud Nine Motel, Days Inn, Econolodge, Super 8, **other:** [H], Blue Beacon, Graham Tire, Kenworth, Peterbilt, Volvo
398mm	Big Sioux River
396b a	I-29, N to Brookings, S to Sioux City
390	SD 38, Hartford, **N other:** Camp Dakota RV Park, Goos RV Ctr, **S gas:** Cowboy Town/dsl
387	rd 17, Hartford, **N gas:** BP/dsl, **food:** Pizza Ranch
379	SD 19, Humboldt, **N gas:** Mobil/dsl, Shell/Town&Country Store/dsl (1mi), **other:** USPO
375mm	E Vermillion River
374	to SD 38, Montrose, **5 mi S other:** Battle Creek Res., Lake Vermillion RA, RV camping
368	Canistota, 4 mi **S lodging:** Best Western
364	US 81, to Yankton, Salem, **4 mi N gas:** Cenex, Sinclair, **lodging:** Home Motel, **other:** Camp America
363.5mm	W Vermillion River
363mm	**rest area both lanes, full ♿ facilities, ☎, ⛱, litter barrels, vending, petwalk, RV dump, st patrol**
357	to Bridgewater, Canova
353	Spencer, Emery, **S gas:** FuelMart/Subway/dsl/casino/24hr

MITCHELL

CHAMBERLAIN

Exit #	Services
352mm	Wolf Creek
350	SD 25, Emery, Farmer, **N** to DeSmet, Home of Laura Ingalls Wilder
344	SD 262, to Fulton, Alexandria, **S gas:** Shell/dsl, **food:** Joe's Cafe
337mm	**parking area both lanes**
335	Riverside Rd, **N** KOA (1mi)
334.5mm	James River
332	SD 37 S, to Parkston, Mitchell, **N gas:** Cenex/dsl, Clark, Mobil, Pilot/Shell/Subway/dsl/scales/24hr, Sinclair, **food:** Arby's, Country Kitchen, DQ, McDonald's, Perkins, Pizza Hut, Pizza Ranch, Twin Dragon Chinese, **lodging:** AmericInn, Best Western, Days Inn, Quality Inn, Super 8/**truck parking**, Thunderbird Motel, **other:** [H], Advance Parts, Chrysler/Dodge, K-Mart, O'Reilly Parts, Rondee's Campground, Walgreens, transmissions, **1-2 mi N other:** to Corn Palace, Museum of Pioneer Life, **S gas:** Shell/Godfather's/Taco Bell/dsl/24hr, **food:** Culver's, Hardee's, KFC, Quizno's, Ruby Tuesday, Whiskey Creek Grill, **lodging:** Comfort Inn, Hampton Inn, Holiday Inn Express, Kelly Inn, **other:** Cabela's, $Tree, Menard's, Radio Shack, Walmart SuperCtr/Subway/24hr
330	SD 37 N, Mitchell, **N gas:** Cenex/dsl/24hr, Shell/dsl, Sinclair, **food:** DQ, **lodging:** Budget Inn, Econolodge, Motel 6, Ramada Inn, Siesta Motel, **other:** [H], County Fair Foods, Jack's Campers/RV ctr., Mr. Tire, to Corn Palace, museum, transmissions, **weigh sta**, **S other:** Dakota RV Park
325	Betts Rd, **S** Famil-e-Fun Camping
319	MT Vernon, **1 mi N gas:** Sinclair/dsl, Westey's One Stop
310	US 281, to Stickney, **S gas:** Sinclair/Deli Depot/dsl/24hr, **other:** to Ft Randall Dam
308	Lp 90, to Plankinton, **N gas:** Cenex, Sinclair/Al's Cafe/dsl, **food:** Commerce St Grille, **lodging:** Cabin Fever Motel/RV Park, Smart Choice Inn, **other:** Gordy's Camping, USPO, repair
301.5mm	**rest area both lanes, full ♿ facilities, ☎, ⛱, litter barrels, RV dump**
296	White Lake, **1 mi N gas:** A-Z Gas, Cenex/dsl, **lodging:** A-Z Motel, **other:** USPO, **S other:** Siding 36 Motel/RV Park
294mm	Platte Creek
293mm	**parking area both lanes**
289	SD 45 S, to Platte, **S other:** to Snake Cr/Platte Cr RA (25mi)
284	SD 45 N, Kimball, **N gas:** Clark, Ditty's/Diner/dsl, Phillips 66/dsl/24hr, **lodging:** Dakota Winds Motel, Super 8, **other:** Parkway Campground, repair/tires, **S other:** tractor museum
272	SD 50, Pukwana, **2 mi N** gas, food, lodging, **S other:** Snake/Platte Creek Rec Areas (25mi)
265	SD 50, Chamberlain, **N gas:** Cenex/DQ/dsl, **lodging:** AmericInn, **other:** [H], camping, **S gas:** SA/dsl, **other:** Happy Camper Campground
264mm	**rest area both lanes, full ♿ facilities, scenic view, info, ☎, ⛱, litter barrels**
263	Chamberlain, **N gas:** Sinclair/dsl, **food:** Casey's Café, McDonald's, Pizza Hut, Subway (1mi), Taco John's, **lodging:** Best Western (1mi), Bel Aire Motel (1mi), Riverview Inn, Super 8, **other:** Crow Creek Sioux Tribal Hqtrs, SD Hall of Fame

INTERSTATE 90

E ↕ W

	Exit #	Services
	262mm	Missouri River
	260	SD 50, Oacoma, **N gas:** Cenex/Arby's/dsl, Clark/dsl, Shell/dsl, **lodging:** Al's Oasis/Motel/Camping/cafe/mkt, Cedar Shore Motel/Camping (3mi), Days Inn, Holiday Inn Express, West River Inn, **other:** Buick/Chevrolet/Pontiac, Old West Museum, antiques
	251	SD 47, to Winner, Gregory
	248	SD 47, Reliance, **N gas:** Cenex (1mi), Farmer's Union/dsl (1mi), **other:** Sioux Tribal Hqtrs, to Big Bend RA
	241	to Lyman
	235	SD 273, Kennebec, **N gas:** Clark/dsl, **food:** Hot Rods Steaks, **lodging:** Budget Host, Kings Inn, **other:** KOA
	226	US 183 S, Presho, **N gas:** Cenex/dsl, Sinclair/dsl, **lodging:** Hutch's Motel/café/RV Park, **other:** New Frontier RV Park, museum, repair
	225	Lp 90, Presho, same as 226
	221mm	**rest area wb, full ♿ facilities, info, ☎, picnic, litter barrels, RV dump, petwalk**
	220	no services
	218mm	**rest area eb, full ♿ facilities, info, ☎, picnic, litter barrels, RV dump, petwalk**
	214	Vivian
	212	US 83 N, SD 53, to Pierre, **N gas:** Sinclair/dsl, **food:** Vivian Jct Rest., **other:** H (34mi)
	208	no services
	201	Draper, **N gas:** Farmer's Oil/Cafe
	194mm	**parking area both lanes**
MURDO	192	US 83 S, Murdo, **N gas:** HHH/Shell/dsl, Pioneer/dsl, Sinclair/dsl, **food:** Buffalo Rest., Murdo Drive-In, The Diner, Prairie Pizza, Rusty Spur Steaks, **lodging:** American Inn, Anchor Inn, Best Western, Day's Inn, Iversen Inn, Lee Motel, Sioux Motel, Super 8, **other:** American RV Park/camping, Murdo Foods, auto museum, USPO, **S lodging:** Country Inn, **other:** to Rosebud
	191	Murdo, **N** same as 192
	188mm	**parking area both lanes, litter barrels**
	183	Okaton, **S** gas, Ghost Town
	177	no services
	175mm	central/mountain timezone
	172	to Cedar Butte
	170	SD 63 N, to Midland, **N gas:** Shell/dsl, **other:** 1880's Town, KOA
	167mm	**rest area wb, full ♿ facilities, ☎, picnic, litter barrels, RV dump, petwalk**
	165mm	**rest area eb, full ♿ facilities, ☎, picnic, litter barrels, RV dump, petwalk**
	163	SD 63, Belvidere, **S gas:** Mobil/dsl
KADOKA	152	Lp 90, Kadoka, **N gas:** Conoco/dsl/rest./24hr, **S other:** Badlands Petrified Gardens, camping
	150	SD 73 S, Kadoka, **N lodging:** Dakota Inn/rest., **S gas:** Clark, Sinclair, **lodging:** Best Value Inn, Budget Host, Ponderosa Motel/RV Park, Rodeway Inn, Wagon Wheel Motel, **other:** Kadoka Kampground, to Buffalo Nat Grasslands, repair
	143	SD 73 N, to Philip, **15 mi N** H
	138mm	scenic overlook wb
	131	SD 240, **S gas:** Conoco, **lodging:** Badlands Inn (9mi), Cedar Pass Lodge/rest. (9mi), **other:** Circle 10 Camping, Prairie Home NHS, KOA (11mi), to Badlands NP

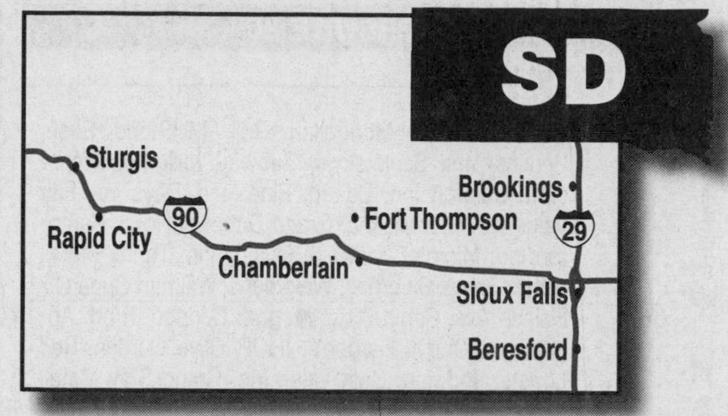

	Exit #	Services
	129.5mm	scenic overlook eb
	127	no services
	121	Bigfoot Rd
	116	239th St
	112	US 14 E, to Philip
WALL	110	SD 240, Wall, **N gas:** Conoco/dsl, Exxon, Phillips 66, **food:** DQ, Elkton House Rest., Red Rock Rest., Subway, Wall Drug Rest., **lodging:** Ann's Motel, Best Value Inn, Best Western, Days Inn, Econolodge, Fountain Hotel, Motel 6, Sunshine Inn, Super 8, The Wall Motel, Welsh Motel, **other:** Ace Hardware, Arrow Campground, NAPA, Wall Drug/gifts/rest., Wall Foods, Wounded Knee Museum, **S** to Badlands NP, RV camping
	109	W 4th Ave, Wall, **1-2 mi N** access to same as 110
	107	Cedar Butte Rd
	101	Jensen Rd, to Schell Ranch
	100mm	**rest area both lanes, full ♿ facilities, info, ☎, picnic, litter barrels, RV dump, vending, petwalk**
	99.5mm	Cheyenne River
	98	Wasta, **N gas:** Mobil/dsl, **lodging:** Redwood Motel, **other:** 24 Express RV Camping, USPO
	90	173rd Ave, to Owanka
	88	171st Ave (from eb, no re-entry)
	84	167th Ave, **N** Olde Glory Fireworks
	78	161st Ave, New Underwood, **1/2 mi S gas:** Sinclair, **other:** Boondocks Camping, Steve's General Store/gas/motel/rest.
	69mm	**parking area both lanes**
	67	to Box Elder, Ellsworth AFB, **N gas:** Loaf'n Jug, **other:** Air&Space Museum
	63	(eb only), to Box Elder, Ellsworth AFB
	61	Elk Vale Rd, **N gas:** ***FLYING J***/Conoco/CountryMkt/dsl/LP/RV dump/scales/24hr/@, **other:** Cabela's, Dakota RV Ctr, **S gas:** Conoco, Mobil/dsl, **food:** Arby's, McDonalds, **lodging:** Comfort Inn, Fairfield Inn, La Quinta, Sleep Inn, **other:** I-90 RV Ctr, KOA (2mi, seasonal), transmissions
RAPID CITY	60	Lp 90, to Mt Rushmore, Rapid City, **S other:** H, Gordman's, Menard's, Michael's, PetCo, Scheel's Sports, Target, TJ Maxx, Nat Coll of Mines/Geology
	59	La Crosse St, Rapid City, **N gas:** Mobil/24hr, Phillips 66, **food:** Boston's Rest, Burger King, Denny's, Fuddrucker's, Minerva's Rest., Outback Steaks, Starbucks, TGIFriday, **lodging:** Best Western, Country Inn&Suites, Econolodge, Hilton Garden, Holiday Inn Express, Super 8, **other:** Hobby Lobby, Old Navy, Sears/auto, mall, st patrol, **S gas:** Cenex/dsl, Exxon/24hr, **food:** Arnold's Diner, China Wok,

INTERSTATE 90

Exit #	Services
59	Continued Golden Corral, Mongolian Grill, MillStone Rest., Perkins/24hr, Schlotsky's, Subway, **lodging:** AmericInn, Comfort Inn, Dakota Pines Inn, Days Inn, Fair Value Inn, Foothills Inn, Grand Gateway Hotel, Hampton Inn, Microtel, Motel 6, Quality Inn, Thrifty Motel, **other:** Sam's Club/gas, Walgreens, Walmart SuperCtr
58	Haines Ave, Rapid City, **N gas:** Conoco, **food:** Applebee's, Chili's, Hardee's, IHOP, Olive Garden, Red Lobster, **lodging:** Best Value Inn, Grand Stay Motel, **other:** Best Buy, Borders, $Discount, Hancock Fabrics, Herbergers, JC Penney, Kohl's, Lowe's Whse, Petsmart, Tires+, to Rushmore Mall, **S gas:** Loaf'n Jug,, **food:** ChuckeCheese, Taco John's, Wendy's, **other:** H, ShopKO
57	I-190, US 16, to Rapid City, Mt Rushmore, **1 mi S on North St...gas:** Conoco, Exxon, **lodging:** Holiday Inn, Howard Johnson, Radisson, **other:** Ace Hardware, Family Thrift
55	Deadwood Ave, **N other:** Dakota RV Ctr, Harley-Davidson/cafe, **S gas:** Pilot/Sinclair/Subway/dsl/scales/24hr/@, **food:** Marlin's Rest., **other:** Black Hills Dogtrack, Chevrolet, dsl repair
52	Peaceful Pines Rd, Black Hawk, **N other:** Three Flags Camping (1mi), **S food:** Cenex, **food:** Longhorn Rest., **other:** Curves, Family$, USPO
48	Stagebarn Canyon Rd, **N other:** RV camping, **S gas:** C-Store/gas, Sinclair/Haggar's Mkt/food, **food:** Summerset Bistro, **lodging:** Ramada, **other:** Mid-States RV Ctr, auto repair
46	Piedmont Rd, Elk Creek Rd, **N** to Petrified Forest, camping, **S gas:** Conoco/Papa John's/dsl
44	Bethlehem Rd, **S other:** Jack's RV Ctr (2mi)
42mm	**rest area both lanes, full ♿ facilities, info, ☎, picnic, litter barrels, RV dump, petwalk, vending**
40	Tilford, **S** Tilford RV Park
39mm	**weigh sta eb**
37	Pleasant Valley Rd, **N other:** Elkview Camp, **S other:** Bulldog Camping, Rush-No-More Camping
34	**S other:** Black Hills Nat Cemetary, No Name City RV Park
32	SD 79, Jct Ave, Sturgis, **N gas:** Conoco, Exxon/dsl, **food:** Jambonz Rest., Phil-Town Rest., Taco John's, **lodging:** Best Western, StarLite Motel, **other:** H, Ford/Lincoln/Mercury, Grocery Mart, NAPA, Rodney RV Park, Vet, to Bear Butte SP
30	US 14A W, SD 34E, to Deadwood, Sturgis, **N gas:** Cenex/dsl, Fresh Start/dsl, **food:** McDonald's, Pizza Hut, Sturgis Doghouse, **other:** CarQuest, Famliy$, Mr Tire, O'Reilly Parts, Pamida/drug, Radio Shack, Day's End Camping, **S gas:** Conoco/dsl, RanchMart, **food:** Burger King, DQ, Pizza Ranch, Subway, **lodging:** Holiday Inn Express, Days Inn, Super 8/rest., **other:** Chevrolet
23	SD 34 W, to Belle Fourche, Whitewood, **N other:** Northern Hills RV Ctr, **S gas:** Howdy's/dsl, **food:** Whitewood Rest., **lodging:** Iron Horse Inn, Tony's Motel, **other:** USPO
17	US 85 S, to Deadwood, **9-12 mi S in Deadwood... food:** Silverado Café, **lodging:** AmericInn, Elkridge Motel, Franklin Motel, Holiday Inn Express, Mineral Palace Motel, Deadwood Gulch Resort, **other:** KOA, Whistler Gulch Camping
14	US 14A, Spearfish Canyon, **N food:** Applebee's, Culver's, Subway, **lodging:** Comfort Suites, Fairfield Inn, Holiday Inn/rest., Quality Inn, **other:** Walmart SuperCtr/24hr, **S gas:** Phillips 66/dsl, **food:** KFC/LJ Silver, Perkins, Pizza Ranch, **lodging:** Howard Johnson, Rodeway Inn, Super 8, **other:** Ace Hardware, Ford/Lincoln/Mercury, K-Mart, auto museum, camping
12	Jackson Blvd, Spearfish, **S gas:** Conoco/dsl, Exxon, Loaf'n Jug, Phillips 66, **food:** Arby's, Barbacoa's, Domino's, Millstone Rest., Papa Murphy's, Pizza Hut, Quizno's, Staduim Grill, Taco John's, **lodging:** Best Western, Travelodge, **other:** H, CarQuest, Chrysler/Dodge, Curves, Radio Shack, Black Hills St U, fish hatchery, same as 10
10	US 85 N, to Belle Fourche, **S food:** Burger King, Cedar House Rest., Golden Dragon Chinese, McDonald's, Subway, Taco Bell, **lodging:** Days Inn, **other:** H, Buick/Chevrolet/Pontiac, Cadillac/GMC, Jeep, Jo's Camping, KOA, Safeway/drug/gas, Walgreens, USPO, same as 12
8	McGuigan Rd, W Spearfish, **S** KOA (1mi)
2	**1 mi N** McNenny St Fish Hatchery
1mm	**Welcome Ctr eb, full ♿ facilities, info, ☎, picnic, litter barrels, RV dump, petwalk**
0mm	South Dakota/Wyoming state line

E ↔ W — RAPID CITY — STURGIS — SPEARFISH

INTERSTATE 229 (SIOUX FALLS)

Exit #	Services
10b a	I-90 E and W. I-229 begins/ends on I-90, exit 400.
9	Benson Rd, **W gas:** BP/pizza, **gas:** Marlin's Rest., **other:** Ford Trucks, Western Star
7.5mm	Big Sioux River
7	Rice St, **E** winter sports, **W** to stockyards
6	SD 38, 10th St, **E gas:** Mobil, Sinclair, **food:** A&W, Applebee's, Arby's, Boston's Rest., Denny's, DQ, Domino's, Fryn' Pan Rest., IHOP, KFC, Pizza Hut, Pizza Ranch, Quizno's, Sonic, Taco Bell, Tomacelli's Italian, **lodging:** Super 8, **other:** AutoZone, Family$, Hy-Vee Foods, K-Mart, ShopKO, Sunshine Foods, Sturdevant's Parts, Valvoline, USPO, Vet, **W gas:** BP, Corner, Shell, **food:** Burger King, BurgerTime, Godfather's, Little Caesar's, McDonald's, Pizza Inn, Puerto Vallarta, Steak-Out, Subway, Taco John's, **lodging:** Rushmore Motel, **other:** Lewis Drug, Vet
5.5mm	Big Sioux River
5	26th St, **E gas:** Shell/dsl, **food:** Burger King, Cherry Creek Grill, Dario's Pizza, McDonald's, SaiGon Panda, **other:** city park, **W other:** H
4	Cliff Ave, **E gas:** BP/dsl
3	SD 115, Lp 229, Minnesota Ave, **E** city park, **W gas:** BP, Sinclair, **food:** Burger King, Camilles Cafe, Culver's, DQ, Famous Dave's BBQ, Golden Bowl Chinese, Little Caesar's/TCBY, McDonald's, Subway, Z'kota Grille, **other:** Ace Hardware, Buick/GMC, $Tree, Hy-Vee Foods/gas, Kia, Lewis Drug, Staples, tire, USPO
2	Western Ave, **E gas:** Shell/dsl, **food:** Bracco Cafe, DQ, Joey's Grill, Nucci Italian, Scooters Coffee, Starbucks, **W gas:** Cenex/dsl, Shell, **food:** Buck's Roadhouse, Burger King, Champp's Café, China Buffet, Huhot Mongolian, Papa Murphy's, Qdoba Mexican, Quizno's, Redrossa Pizza, Scheell's, **other:** H, Advance Parts, Best Buy, Goodyear/auto, Hancock Fabrics, Radio Shack

N ↔ S — SIOUX FALLS

INTERSTATE 229 (SIOUX FALLS)

Exit #	Services
1.5mm	Big Sioux River
1c	Louise Ave, **E lodging:** Homewood Suites, **other:** [H], Dodge, **W gas:** BP, Phillips 66/dsl, **food:** Applebee's, Arby's, Burger King, Cici's Pizza, Jimmy John's,
1c	Continued McDonald's, Panera Bread, Qdoba Mexican, Red Lobster, Royal Palace, Spezia's Rest, Taco John's, Wendy's, **lodging:** Hilton Garden Inn, **other:** Barnes&Noble, Honda, Hy-Vee Foods/gas, JC Penney, Jo-Ann Fabrics, Kohl's, Target, Walgreens, mall
1b a	I-29 N and S. **I-229 begins/ends on I-29, exit 75.**

TENNESSEE

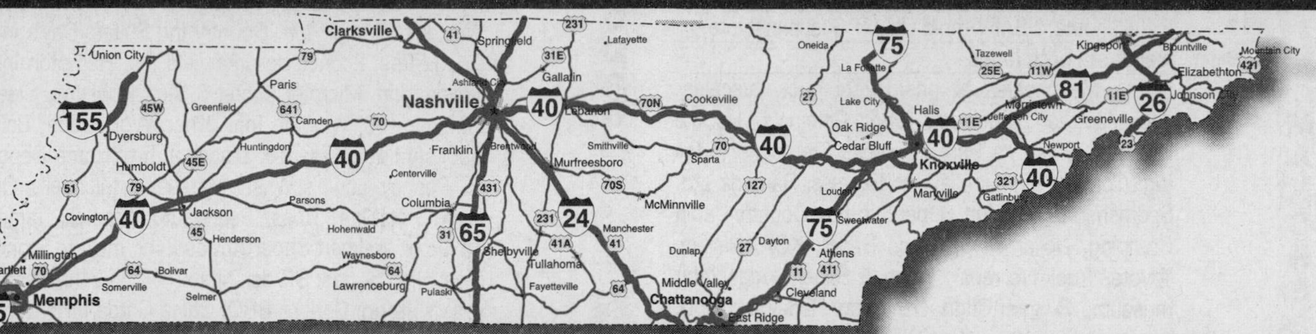

INTERSTATE 24

E ↕ W

CHATTANOOGA

Exit #	Services
185b a	I-75, N to Knoxville, S to Atlanta. I-24 begins/ends on I-75, exit 2 in Chattanooga.
184	Moore Rd, **S food:** Chef Lin Buffet, Provino's Italian, **other:** $Tree, Radio Shack, Sears Essentials/auto
183	(183a from wb), Belvoir Ave, Germantown Rd
181a	US 41 S, to East Ridge (from eb), **S food:** Westside Grill, King's Lodge, **other:** Ford Trucks
181	Fourth Ave, to TN Temple U, Chattanooga, **N gas:** Citgo/dsl, Exxon/dsl, Hi-Tech Fuel, Stop'n Save, **food:** Bojangles, Burger King, Capt D's, Central Park, Hardee's, Krystal/24hr, Subway, Waffle House, **lodging:** Villager Lodge, **other:** BiLo, $General, Family$, Goodyear, Mr Transmission, O'Reilly Parts, repair, Vet, **S gas:** Citgo
180b a	US 27 S, TN 8, Rossville Blvd, **N other:** U-Haul, to Chickamauga, UT Chatt, **S gas:** Exxon, RaceWay/dsl/24hr, **lodging:** Hamilton Inn, **other:** NTB
178	US 27 N, Market St, to Lookout Mtn Chattanooga, **N gas:** BP/dsl, Citgo, **lodging:** Day's Inn, La Quinta, Marriott, Ramada Inn, Staybridge Suites, **other:** Ford, Nissan, U-Haul, to Chattanooga ChooChoo, **S food:** KFC, **lodging:** Comfort Suites, Hampton Inn, Motel 6
175	Browns Ferry Rd, to Lookout Mtn **N gas:** BP, Exxon/dsl, **food:** China Gourmet, **lodging:** Best Value Inn, **other:** CVS Drug, $General, Food Lion, **S gas:** Market/dsl, Shell/dsl, **food:** Hardee's, McDonald's, **lodging:** Comfort Inn, Econolodge, Quality Inn
174	US 11, US 41, US 64, Lookout Valley, **N food:** Waffle House, **lodging:** Day's Inn, **other:** Racoon Mtn Camping (1mi), **S gas:** BP/dsl/24hr, Kangaroo, **food:** Cracker Barrel, New China, Taco Bell, Waffle House, Wendy's, **lodging:** Baymont Inn, Best Western, Budget Motel, Country Inn&Suites, Hampton Inn, Holiday Inn Express, Knight's Inn, Marriott, Ramada Ltd, Super 8, **other:** Ace Hardware, Lookout Valley Camping, Walmart SuperCtr, st patrol
172mm	**rest area eb, full [handicapped] facilities, [phone], [picnic], litter barrels, vending, petwalk**
171mm	Tennessee/Georgia state line
169	GA 299, to US 11, **N gas:** Exxon/dsl/24hr, **S gas,** BP/Momma's Chicken/dsl/24hr/@, Pilot/Subway/dsl/scales/24hr, RaceWay/24hr, **food:** Pappy's BBQ, **other:** repair
167	I-59 S, to Birmingham
167mm	Tennessee/Georgia state line, Central/Eastern time zone
161	TN 156, to Haletown, New Hope, **N gas:** BP/dsl (1mi), **other:** Hales RV Park, **S gas:** Chevron/fireworks, **other:** On The Lake Camping
160mm	Tennessee River/Nickajack Lake
159mm	**Welcome Ctr wb/rest area eb, full [handicapped] facilities, [phone], vending, [picnic], litter barrels, petwalk**
158	US 41, TN 27, Nickajack Dam, **S gas:** BP/dsl/fireworks, **other:** Shellmound Camping (2.5mi)
155	TN 28, Jasper, **N gas:** BP/dsl (1mi), Exxon/dsl, **food:** Dairy Queen (1mi), Hardee's, Western Sizzlin, **lodging:** Acuff Country Inn, **S gas:** BP/Quizno's/dsl, **other:** [H]
152	US 41, US 64, US 72, Kimball, S Pittsburg, **N gas:** BP/fireworks, RaceWay, Shell/dsl, **food:** A&W/LJ Silver, Arby's, China Buffet, Cracker Barrel, Domino's, KFC, Krystal, McDonald's, Mi Jacal Mexican, Pizza Hut, Shoney's, Subway, Taco Bell, Waffle House, Wendy's, **lodging:** Best Value, Comfort Inn, Country Hearth Inn, Holiday Inn Express, **other:** [H], Chevrolet/Pontiac/Buick, $Tree, Lowe's Whse, Radio Shack, Walmart SuperCtr/24hr, to Russell Cave NM, **3 mi S other:** Lodge Cast Iron
143	Martin Springs Rd, **N gas:** Chevron/dsl/fireworks
135	US 41 N, Monteagle, **N gas:** Citgo/dsl/rest./24hr, Mystik/dsl, **food:** Shan Chinese, Smok'n B's BBQ, **other:** S Cumberland RV Park, USPO, **S** Day's Inn
134	US 64, US 41A, to Sewanee, Monteagle, **N gas:** BP/McDonald's, Papa Ron's Grill, **lodging:** American Eagle Inn, **other:** Monteagle Winery, to S Cumberland SP, **S gas:** Citgo, Shell/dsl, **food:** Hardee's, Monteagle Diner, Pizza Hut, Smokehouse BBQ, Subway, Waffle House, **lodging:** Best Western, Regency Inn, **other:** $General, Fred's Drugs, iggly Wiggly, to U of The South

MONTEAGLE

INTERSTATE 24

E ↕ W

Exit #	Services
133mm	**rest area both lanes, full ♿ facilities, ☎, 🛒, litter barrels, vending, petwalk**
128mm	Elk River
127	US 64, TN 50, to Winchester, Pelham, **N gas:** BP, Phillips 66, Texaco/Stuckey's, **S gas:** Exxon/dsl, **other:** to Tims Ford SP/RV camping
119mm	**trucks only parking area both lanes**
117	to Tullahoma, USAF Arnold Ctr, UT Space Institute
116mm	**weigh sta both lanes**
114	US 41, Manchester, **N gas:** BP/24 Truckers/scales/dsl, Marathon, Shell/dsl, **food:** Domino's, Huddle House, O'Charley's, Panda Express, Starbucks, **lodging:** Comfort Inn, Holiday Inn Express, Ramada Ltd, Scottish Inn, Sleep Inn, Super 8, **other:** Country Cabin Camping, Dollar Stop, Home Depot, KOA, Nissan, Toyota, Truck/tire repair, Walmart SuperCtr/gas/24hr, museum, **S gas:** Citgo, Kangaroo, RaceWay, **food:** Arby's, Burger King, Capt D's, KFC, Krystal, McDonald's/playplace, Pizza Hut, Shoney's, Subway, Taco Bell, Waffle House, Wendy's, **lodging:** Country Inn Suites, Day's Inn, Royal Inn, **other:** Advance Parts, AutoZone, Chevrolet, Curves, Family$, Ford/Lincoln/Mercury, Fred's Drug, Goodyear, Napa, O'Reilly Parts, Russell Stover, USPO, carwash
111	TN 55, Manchester, **N gas:** BP/dsl, Citgo/dsl/24hr, Co-op gas/dsl, **other:** to Rock Island SP, **S gas:** BP, **food:** Hardee's, J&G Pizza/Steaks, Sonic, **other:** H, to Jack Daniels Dist HS, Old Stone Fort
110	TN 53, Manchester, **N gas:** BP, Kangaroo, Shell/dsl, **food:** Coconut Bay Cafe, Cracker Barrel, D Crockett's Roadhouse, Emma's Rest., Oak Rest., **lodging:** Ambassador Inn, Economy Inn, Hampton Inn, **S gas:** Shell/dsl/24hr, **food:** Los 3 Amigos Mexican, Waffle House, **other:** H, U-Haul
110mm	Duck River
105	US 41, **N gas:** BP/dsl/24hr, Shell/dsl, **food:** Ranch-House Rest., **S** tire/repair, to Normandy Dam, Dickle HS
97	TN 64, to Shelbyville, Beechgrove, **N other:** auto parts/repair, **S gas:** Citgo
89	Buchanan Rd, **N gas:** Love's/McDonald's/scales/dsl, Texaco/Outpost Rest/dsl, **S gas:** Shell/dsl/rest./24hr, **food:** Huddle House, **other:** A&L RV Ctr
84	Joe B. Jackson Pkwy
81	US 231, Murfreesboro, **N gas:** BP/dsl/24hr, Exxon, RaceWay/24hr, Shell, **food:** Cracker Barrel, King's Table Rest., Krystal, Parthenon Steaks, Shanghai Chinese, Shoney's, Waffle House/24hr, Wendy's, **lodging:** Best Value, Knight's Inn, Quality Inn, Ramada Ltd, Regal Inn, Scottish Inn, **other:** H, Dodge, Honda, Mazda, **S gas:** Citgo/24hr, Kangaroo, Mapco/dsl/24hr, Phillips 66/dsl/24hr/@, Pilot/Arbys/scales/dsl/24hr, **food:** La Siesta Mexican, McDonald's/playplace, Pizza Hut/Taco Bell, Quizno's, Sonic, Subway, Waffle House, Zaxby's, **lodging:** Howard Johnson, Safari Inn, Vista Inn, **other:** Gateway Tire, Rite Aid, Toyota/Scion
80	New Salem Hwy, rd 99, **S food:** Domino's
78	TN 96, to Franklin, Murfreesboro, **N gas:** BP, Citgo, Phillips 66/Church's/White Castle/dsl,
78	Continued Shell/Jack-in-the-Box, Texaco/24hr, **food:** Arby's, Applebee's, Bellacino's Pizza, Bonefish Grill, Buffalo Wild Wings, Chick-fil-A, ChuckeCheese, Coconut Bay Cafe, Cracker Barrel, Fazoli's, IHOP, Jason's Deli, Jim'n Nick's BBQ, KFC, McDonald's, Olive Garden, Outback Steaks, Panera Bread, Quizno's, Red Lobster, Red Robin, Ryan's, Santa Fe Steaks, Starbucks, Steak'n Shake, Subway, TGI Friday's, The Chophouse, Waffle House, Wendy's, Zaxby's, **lodging:** Baymont Inn, Best Western, Comfort Inn, Country Inn Suites, Day's Inn, DoubleTree, Econolodge, Fairfield Inn, Hampton Inn, Holiday Inn, Microtel, Motel 6, Red Roof Inn, Sleep Inn, Super 8, Wingate Inn, **other:** Aldi Foods, Belk, BooksAMillion, Dillard's, Discount Tire, Home Depot, JC Penney, Lowe's Whse, Marshall's, Michael's, Old Navy, PetsMart, Ross, Sears/auto, Staples, Target, TJ Maxx, Walmart SuperCtr/gas/24hr, mall, to Stones River Bfd, **S gas:** BP/dsl/24hr, Chevron/24hr, Kangaroo/dsl, **food:** Corky's BBQ, China Garden, Hardee's, Las Palmas, McDonald's, O'Charley's, Papa Murphy's, Pizza Hut, Sonic, Subway, Taco Bell, Waffle House, **other:** AutoZone, $General, Kohl's, Kroger, Old Time Pottery, Sam's Club/gas, Walgreen
76	Manson Pike, Medical Center Pkwy, **N other:** H, to Stones River Nat. Bfd
74b a	TN 840, to Lebanon, Franklin
70	TN 102, Lee Victory Pkwy, Almaville Rd, to Smyrna, **N gas:** Shell/dsl/scales, **S gas:** BP, Kangaroo/Quizno's/dsl, Mapco, **food:** McDonald's, Legends Steaks, Ringalino's, Sonic, **lodging:** Deerfield Inn, **other:** $General, Tennessee Expo
66	TN 266, Sam Ridley Pkwy, to Smyrna, **N gas:** Citgo/dsl/24hr, Shell/dsl, **food:** Arby's, A&W/LJ Silver, Blue Coast Burrito, Catfish House, Chili's, Famous Dave's, Hickory Falls Cafe, Jim'n Nick's BBQ, Logan's Roadhouse, Papa John's, Sonic, Starbucks, Subway, Wendy's, **other:** CVS Drug, Kohl's, Kroger/gas, PetsMart, Publix, Staples, Target, Nashville I-24 Camping (3mi), **S food:** Cracker Barrel, O'Charley's, Ruby Tuesday, **lodging:** Comfort Suites, Fairfield Inn, Hampton Inn, Hilton Garden, Holiday Inn Express, Sleep Inn, **other:** I-24 Expo
64	Waldron Rd, to La Vergne, **N gas:** Kangaroo, Kwik Sak, Pilot/Subway/dsl/24hr/scales, **food:** Arby's, Hardee's, Krystal/24hr, McDonald's, Waffle House, **lodging:** Comfort Inn, Holiday Inn Express, Super 8, **other:** Music City Camping (3mi), RV service, **S gas:** Mapco/dsl/24hr, **lodging:** Motel
62	TN 171, Old Hickory Blvd, **N gas:** Chevron, Citgo/Subway, Shell/dsl/24hr, TA/BP/Burger King/Popeye's/dsl/24hr/scales/@, **food:** El Arroyo Mexican, Waffle House, **lodging:** Best Western
60	Hickory Hollow Pkwy, **N gas:** BP, Mapco, Shell, **food:** Applebee's, Arby's, Bailey's Grill, Burger King, ChuckeCheese, Cracker Barrel, KFC, Logan's Roadhouse, McDonald's/Playplace, O'Charley's, Outback Steaks, Pizza Hut, Red Lobster, Starbucks, Subway, Taco Bell, TGIFriday, Wendy's, **lodging:** Country Inn Suites, Hampton Inn, Holiday Inn, **other:** Best Buy, Chevrolet, Dillard's, Dodge, $Tree, Firestone/auto, Kroger/gas, Macey's, Mazda, NTB, Office Depot,

MANCHESTER · MURFREESBORO · NASHVILLE

INTERSTATE 24 CONT'D

E ↕ W

Exit #	Services
60	Continued Rite Aid, Sears, mall, transmissions, **S gas:** BP/dsl, Shell, **food:** Camino Royale Mexican, Casa Fiesta Mexican, Evergreen Chinese, IHOP, Olive Garden, Shoney's, Steak'n Shake, Waffle House/24hr, **lodging:** Knight's Inn, Super 8, Vista Inn, **other:** Acura, Goodyear/auto, Home Depot, KIA, Target
59	TN 254, Bell Rd, same as 60
57	Haywood Lane, **N gas:** Kwik Sak, Marathon, **food:** Hardee's, Pizza Hut, **other:** CarQuest, $General, Food Lion, Walgreen, **S gas:** Kangaroo, Shell
56	TN 255, Harding Place, **N gas:** Chevron/dsl, Exxon, Mapco, Shell/dsl/24hr, **food:** Applebee's, KFC, McDonald's, Mikado Japanese, Pizza Hut/Taco Bell, Waffle House, Wendy's, **lodging:** Executive Inn, Knight's Inn, Motel 6, Stay Lodge, Thrifty Inn, **other:** Sam's Club/gas, **S gas:** Mapco, Shell, **food:** Burger King, Fiesta Mexican, Hooters, Jack-in-the-Box, **lodging:** Best Value Inn, Motel 6, **other:** H
54b a	TN 155, Briley Pkwy, to Opryland
53	I-440 W, to Memphis
52	US 41, Murfreesboro Rd, **N gas:** Shell, Texaco, **food:** Jack-in-the-Box, Piccadilly's, Pizza Hut, Taco Bell, Waffle House, **lodging:** Day's Inn, Economy Inn, Econolodge, Executive Inn, Holiday Inn Express, Howard Johnson, Quality Inn, Ramada Inn, Rodeway Inn, Scottish Inn, Sunrise Inn, **other:** CarQuest, Office Depot, **S other:** Chevrolet, Dodge
52b a	I-40, E to Knoxville, W to Memphis
I-24 & I-40 run together 2 mi. See Interstate 40 Exits 212-213.	
50b	I-40 W
48	James Robertson Pkwy, **N gas:** Citgo, Shell, **S gas:** Exxon, TA/Subway/dsl/24hr/@, **food:** Shoney's, **lodging:** Ramada Ltd, Stadium Inn, **other:** Titan Stadium, st capitol
47a	US 31E
47	N 1st St, Jefferson St, **N gas:** Express/dsl, **S gas:** Mystic Gas, **lodging:** Day's Inn, Knight's Inn, **other:** U-Haul
I-24 & I-65 run together. See Interstate 65 Exit 87 b a.	
87b a	US 431, Trinity Lane, **N gas:** Citgo, Pilot/Subway/scales/dsl, **food:** Krystal, White Castle, **lodging:** Cumberland Inn, Delux Inn, **S gas:** Chevron, Express, Exxon, **food:** Jack-in-the-Box, Jack's BBQ, McDonald's, Subway, Taco Bell, Waffle House, **lodging:** Best Value Inn, Comfort Inn, Day's Inn, Econolodge, Howard Johnson, Liberty Inn, Quality Inn, Travelodge, **other:** Family$, to American Bapt Coll
44b a	I-65, N to Louisville, S to Nashville
43	TN 155, Briley Pkwy, Brick Church Pike
40	TN 45, Old Hickory Blvd, **N gas:** BP/dsl, Shell/dsl, Phillips 66/dsl/24hr, **food:** Jack-in-the-Box (3mi), Subway, **lodging:** Super 8
35	US 431, to Joelton, Springfield, **S gas:** BP/Subway/dsl/24hr, Shell, **food:** Family Rest., Mazatlan Mexican, McDonald's, Nick's BBQ, **lodging:** Day's Inn, **other:** Curves, Family$, OK Camping
31	TN 249, New Hope Rd, **N gas:** Shell/dsl, **S gas:** BP/dsl, Shell/dsl/24hr

NASHVILLE

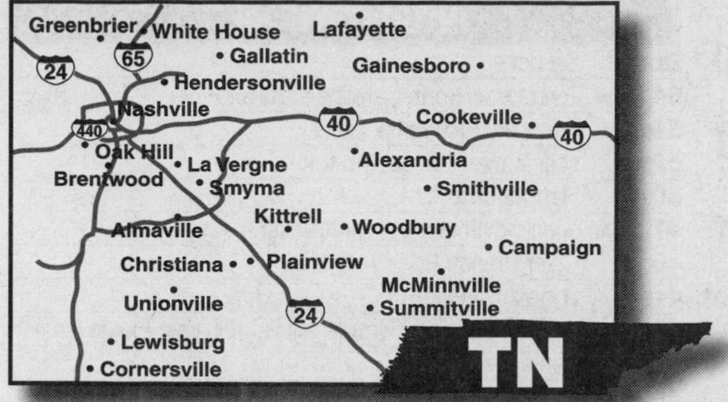

CLARKSVILLE

Exit #	Services
24	TN 49, to Springfield, Ashland City, **N gas:** BP/dsl, Mapco/dsl/24hr, Phillips 66/dsl/24hr, **other:** H, repair, **S gas:** Shell/dsl, SS/Wendy's, **food:** Dragon Buffet, KFC/Taco Bell, Sonic, Subway, **other:** $General, Hill Foods, USPO, Vet
19	TN 256, Maxey Rd, to Adams, **N gas:** BP/dsl, **S gas:** Shell
11	TN 76, to Adams, Clarksville, **N gas:** Shell/dsl/24hr, **S gas:** BP/dsl/24hr, **food:** McDonald's, Waffle House, **lodging:** Comfort Inn, Day's Inn, Holiday Inn Express, Quality Inn, Super 8, **other:** H
9mm	Red River
8	TN 237, Rossview Rd, **S** Dunbar Cave SP
4	US 79, to Clarksville, Ft Campbell, **N gas:** BP/dsl/24hr, **food:** Cracker Barrel, **lodging:** Hilton Garden, **other:** Sam's Club/gas, Spring Creek Camping (2mi), Clarksville RV Ctr, **S gas:** BP/dsl/24hr, Citgo/dsl, Shell/dsl, **food:** Applebee's, Arby's, Baskin-Robbins, Burger King, Capt D's, Chili's, ChuckeCheese, Church's/White Castle, DQ, Fazoli's, Golden Rule Buffet, Golden Corral, IHOP, KFC, Krystal, Logan's Roadhouse, LJ Silver, Longhorn Steaks, McDonald's, O'Charley's, Old Chicago Pizza, Olive Garden, Outback Steaks, Quizno's, Rafferty's, Red Lobster, Ryan's, Shogun Japanese, Shoney's, Starbucks, Steak'n Shake, Subway, Taco Bell, Waffle House, Wendy's, **lodging:** Best Value Inn, Best Western, Candlewood Suites, Comfort Inn, Country Inn&Suites, Courtyard, Day's Inn, Econolodge, Fairfield Inn, Guesthouse Inn, Hampton Inn, Hometowne Suites, Mainstay Suites, Microtel, Quality Inn, Ramada Ltd, Red Roof Inn, Super 8, ValuePlace Hotel, Wingate Inn, **other:** H, Advance Parts, Belk, Best Buy, BooksAMillion, Borders Books, Buick/GMC/Pontiac, $Tree, Goodyear/auto, Hancock Fabrics, Home Depot, Hyundai/Mazda, JC Penney, Kohl's, K-Mart, Lowe's Whse, Office Depot, Petsmart, Sears/auto, Subaru, Target, TJ Maxx, U-Haul, Walmart SuperCtr/gas/24hr, mall, winery, to Austin Peay St U, to Land Between the Lakes
1	TN 48, to Clarksville, Trenton, **N gas:** Shell/dsl, **other:** Clarksville RV Camping, **S gas:** BP, Mystik, **food:** Coldstone Creamery, El Tapatio Mexican, Gatti's Pizza, Sonic, **other:** $General, Walgreens
.5mm	**Welcome Ctr eb, full ♿ facilities, ☎, vending, picnic, litter barrels, petwalk**
0mm	Tennessee/Kentucky state line

INTERSTATE 26

Exit #	Services
54.5mm	Tennessee/North Carolina state line
54mm	runaway truck ramp wb
52mm	scenic overlook eb (no trucks)
50	Flagpond Rd
47.5mm	scenic overlook wb (no trucks)
46	Clear Branch Rd
44mm	S Indian Creek
43	US 19 W, rd 352, Temple Hill Rd, **N** **gas:** Exxon (2mi)
42mm	S Indian Creek
40	Jackson-Love Hwy, Erwin, Jonesborough, **N** **gas:** Appco Gas/A&W/LJ Silver, **lodging:** Holiday Inn Express, **other:** [H], Nolichucky Gorge Camping (2mi)
37	TN 81, rd 107, Erwin, Jonesborough, **N** **gas:** Shell/dsl/24hr, **food:** Huddle House/24hr, McDonald's, Sonic, **other:** [H], NAPA, Walgreens, **S** **lodging:** Super 8, **other:** River Park Camping (5mi)
36	Main St, Erwin, **N** **gas:** Appco/dsl, BP/24hr, **food:** Backwoods BBQ, El Azteca, Hardee's, KFC, Little Caesar's, Pizza Hut, Subway, Wendy's, **other:** Advance Parts, $General, Firestone, Rite Aid, White's Foods
34	Tinker Rd, **N** **other:** Walmart SuperCtr
32	rd 173, Unicoi Rd, to Cherokee NF, **N** **gas:** Volco Gas, **food:** Maple Grove Café, **S** Woodsmoke Camping
27	rd 359 N, Okolona Rd, **N** **gas:** BP, **food:** Kozy Kitchen, **lodging:** Budget Inn (3mi)
24	US 321, TN 67, Elizabethton, **N** **gas:** Shell/dsl, **food:** Schlotsky's, **S** **gas:** BP/dsl, **food:** Arby's, Burger King, Little Caesars, LJ Silver, Subway, **lodging:** Comfort Inn, Carnegie Hotel, **other:** Advance Parts, CVS Drug, Food City/gas, White's Foods, to ETSU, Roan Mtn SP
23	rd 91, Market St, **N** **food:** McDonald's, **S** **other:** museum
22	rd 400, Unaka Ave, Watauga Ave
20b a	US 11 E, US 19 N, to Roan St, **N** **gas:** Citgo, **food:** Arby's, DQ, El Chico, El Matador, Harbor House Seafood, Hardee's, Peerless Rest., Perkins, Pizza Hut, Sonic, **lodging:** Best Western, Holiday Inn, LJ Silver, Ramada Ltd, Super 8, **other:** Acura, Advance Parts, AutoZone, Big Lots, Ford, Honda, Mazda, Tuesday Morning, repair, **S** **food:** Applebees, Bailey's Grill, Carino's Italian, Fazoli's, Hooters, KFC, Lonestar Steaks, McDonald's, O'Charley's, Olive Garden, Red Lobster, Ruby Tuesday, Ryan's, Salsarito's, Shoney's, Smokey Bones BBQ, Starbucks, Subway, Taco Bell, TCBY, Texas Roadhouse, Zaxby's, **lodging:** Day's Inn, Econolodge, Quality Inn, Red Roof Inn, **other:** Books-a-Million, CVS Drug, $General, $Tree, Hancock Fabrics, Sears/auto, Target, TJ Maxx, Walgreens
19	TN 381, to St of Franklin Rd, to Bristol, **N** **gas:** Appco/McDonald's, **food:** El Chico Mexican, Golden Corral, Honeybaked Ham, Logan's Roadhouse, Quizno's, Outback Steaks, Subway, **lodging:** Comfort Suites, **other:** Big Lots, Radio Shack, VW, Walmart Super Ctr/gas, **S** **gas:** Exxon (2mi), **food:** Atlanta Bread, Barbarito's, Carrabba's, Cheddar's, Chick-fil-A, Chili's, China Chef, ChuckeCheese, CiCi's, Fuddruckers, IHOP, Panera Bread, Stir Fry Cafe, Wendy's, **lodging:** Hampton Inn (2mi), Sleep Inn, **other:** Barnes&Noble,
19	Continued Best Buy, Home Depot, K-Mart, Kohl's, Lowe's Whse, Natural Foods Mkt, Old Navy, Ross, Sam's Club/gas, Steinmart, Vet
17	Boone St, **N** **gas:** BP, **food:** Beef'o Brady's, Bob Evan's, Buck's Pizza, Burger King, Kemosabe's BBQ, **other:** Ingles Foods, **S** **gas:** Appco, Shell, **food:** Cracker Barrel, Domino's, El Matador Mexican, Waffle House, Wendy's, **lodging:** Jameson Inn, Value Place, **other:** Wilson Drugs
13	rd 77, Bobby Hicks Hwy, **N** **gas:** BP, Shell, **food:** China Luck, DQ, McDonald's, Papa John's, Pizza Hut, Subway, Taco Bell, Yong Asian, **other:** Advance Parts, General, Firestone, Food City/gas, Rite Aid, Walgreens, White's Foods, USPO, **S** **gas:** Appco
10	Eastern Star Rd
8b a	I-81, to Bristol, Knoxville
6	rd 37, Rock Springs Rd, **S** **gas:** Citgo
4	TN 93, Wilcox Dr, **N** **gas:** BP/Subway, Shell/dsl, **food:** Burger King, Damon's, Hardee's, La Carreta Mexican, McDonald's, Pizza Hut, Wendy's, **lodging:** Hampton Inn, Holiday Inn Express, Jameson Inn, **other:** Cave's Drug, $General, White's Foods, **S** **gas:** BP, Exxon/Arby's/dsl
3	Meadowview Pkwy, **N** **lodging:** Marriott
1	West Stone Dr, **N** **gas:** Shell, Valero/dsl, **food:** Little Caesar's, Molcajete's Mexican, **lodging:** Days Inn, Super 8, **other:** [H], Walgreens, **S** **gas:** BP, **food:** Bojangles, Fatz Cafe, Sonic, Subway, **other:** $Tree, Lowe's Whse, Walmart SuperCtr/gas
0mm	I-26 begins/ends on US 23.

INTERSTATE 40

Exit #	Services
451mm	Tennessee/North Carolina state line
451	Waterville Rd
447	Hartford Rd, **N** **gas:** Citgo/dsl, **S** **gas:** BP/dsl, **food:** Pigeon River Smokehouse, Smokey Mtn River Co Cafe, **other:** Foxfire Camping, Shauan's Riverside RV Park, whitewater rafting
446mm	**Welcome Ctr wb, full [handicapped] facilities, [phone], vending, [picnic], litter barrels, petwalk, NO TRUCKS**
443	Foothills Pkwy, to Gatlinburg, Great Smoky Mtns NP, **S** camping
443mm	Pigeon River
440	US 321, to Wilton Spgs Rd, Gatlinburg, **N** **gas:** Mtn View/dsl, **S** **gas:** BP, **other:** Arrow Creek Camping (14mi), CrazyHorse Camping (14mi)
439mm	Pigeon River
435	US 321, to Gatlinburg, Newport, **N** **gas:** Exxon/dsl, Shell/dsl/24hr, Stop'n Go, **food:** Arby's, Burger King, Hardee's, KFC, La Carreta Mexican, McDonald's, Pizza Hut, Pizza+, SageBrush Steaks, Shoney's, Subway, Taco Bell, **lodging:** Motel 6, Parkway Inn, **other:** [H], Town&Country Drug, **S** **gas:** BP, Muphy USA, **food:** Bojangles, Buddy's BBQ, Cracker Barrel, Monterrey Mexican, Papa John's, Quizno's, Ryan's, Ruby Tuesday, Waffle House/24hr, Wendy's, **lodging:** Best Western, Days Inn, Family Inn, Holiday Inn Express, Mountain Crest Inn, **other:** $General, $Tree, Lowe's Whse, Save-A-Lot, Walmart SuperCtr

E ↕ W ERWIN NEWPORT

INTERSTATE 40 CONT'D

E ↕ W

Exit #	Services
432b a	US 70, US 411, US 25W, to Newport, **N gas:** BP, Exxon/dsl/24hr, TimeOut Travel Ctr/Huddle House/dsl/scales/, Phillips 66, **food:** Bella's Country Kitchen, **lodging:** Comfort Inn, Relax Inn, **other:** Buick/Chevrolet/Pontiac, Chrysler/Dodge/Jeep, Ford/Mercury, KOA, TMC Camping, Westgate Tire, **S gas:** BP/Subway, Citgo/24hr, Texaco/dsl, Shell, **lodging:** Family Inn/rest.
426mm	**rest area wb, full facilities, phone, vending, picnic, litter barrels, petwalk**
425mm	French Broad River
424	TN 113, Dandridge, **N gas:** BP/dsl
421	I-81 N, to Bristol
420mm	**rest area eb, full facilities, phone, vending, picnic, litter barrels, petwalk**
417	TN 92, Dandridge, **N gas:** BP, Pilot/Subway/dsl/scales/24hr/@, **food:** Capt's Galley, Hardee's, McDonald's, Perkins, Ruby Tuesday, **lodging:** Econolodge, **S gas:** Shell/Wendy's/dsl, Texaco/KFC/dsl, Weigel's, **food:** LJ Silver/Taco Bell, Shoney's, Waffle House, **lodging:** Comfort Inn, Holiday Inn Express, Jefferson Inn, Super 8, **other:** Advance Parts
415	US 25W, US 70, to Dandridge, **S gas:** Dadu/dsl, **food:** Sonic (3mi)
412	Deep Sprgs Rd, to Douglas Dam, **N gas:** Love's/Chester Fried/Subway/dsl/scales/24hr, **S gas:** TR Trkstp/dsl/rest/scales/24hr/@/
407	TN 66, to Sevierville, Pigeon Forge, Gatlinburg, **N gas:** Citgo/Huddle House/dsl, **food:** Chophouse, Cracker Barrel, McDonald's, **lodging:** Fairfield Inn, Hampton Inn, Holiday Inn Express, Motel 6, **other:** Bass Pro Shops, RV Camping, **S gas:** BP/Buddy's BBQ, Exxon/Subway/dsl, Shell/Krystal/dsl, **food:** FlapJack's, Wendy's, **lodging:** Comfort Suites, Days Inn, Quality Inn, Smokie's Inn, **other:** Russell Stover, RV Camping, USPO, flea mkt, **3-10 mi S** multiple services/outlets
402	Midway Rd
398	Strawberry Plains Pk, **N gas:** BP/dsl, Exxon/dsl, Shell, **food:** McDonald's, Outback Steaks, Quality Inn, Ruby Tuesday, Waffle House, Wendy's, **lodging:** Baymont Inn, Country Inn&Suites, Econolodge, Hampton Inn, Holiday Inn Express, Quality Inn, Ramada Ltd, Super 8, **other:** Camping World/TN RV Ctr, **S gas:** Pilot/Subway/dsl/scales/24hr, Weigel's, **food:** Arby's, Burger King, Cracker Barrel, Golden Wok Chinese, KFC, Krystal, Puleo's Grille, Taco Bell, **lodging:** Best Western, Comfort Suites, Fairfield Inn, La Quinta, Motel 6
395mm	Holston River
394	US 70, US 11E, US 25W, Asheville Hwy, **N gas:** Mobil/dsl, Pilot, **food:** Subway, Wendy's, **lodging:** Gateway Inn, **other:** Advance Parts, AutoZone, $General, Food Lion, city park, **S gas:** Exxon, Shell/dsl, **food:** Waffle House/24hr, **lodging:** Days Inn, **other:** CVS Drug, Kroger/gas, Walgreens, Vet
393	I-640 W, to I-75 N
392	US 11W, Rutledge Pike, **N gas:** Shell/dsl, **other:** $General, U-Haul, repair, tires, **S gas:** BP, **food:** Buddy's BBQ, Hardee's, Shoney's, **lodging:** Family Inn, **other:** NAPA, Sav-a-Lot Foods, transmissions, to Knoxville Zoo

DANDRIDGE

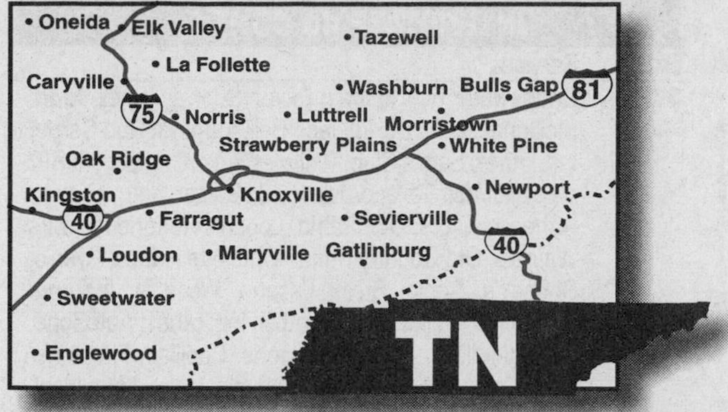

KNOXVILLE

Exit #	Services
390	Cherry St, Knoxville, **N gas:** Marathon/dsl, Top Fuel Mart, Weigel's/Subway, **food:** Happy Garden Chinese, **lodging:** Red Carpet Inn, **other:** tires, **1 mi S gas:** Exxon, **food:** Arby's, KFC, McDonald's, Subway, Taco Bell, WishBone's Wings, **lodging:** Regency Inn, **other:** Advance Parts, Family$, O'Reilly Parts, Walgreens
389	US 441 N, Broadway, 5th Ave, **1/2 mi N gas:** BP, Conoco, Star, **food:** Burger King, Capt D's, KFC, Krystal, SteakOut, Subway, Taco Bell, Wendy's, **other:** CVS Drug, $General, Family$, Firestone, Kroger/deli/24hr, Radio Shack, Tires+, USPO, Walgreens/24hr, transmissions
388	US 441 S (exits left from wb), downtown, **S lodging:** Hilton, Holiday Inn, Crowne Plaza, **other:** to Smokey Mtns, to U of TN
387b	TN 62, 17th St, **N gas:** Pilot/dsl, **lodging:** Best Inn, **other:** $General
387a	I-275 N, to Lexington
386b a	US 129, University Ave, to UT, **N** Food City/gas
385	I-75 N, I-640 E
I-40 W and I-75 S run together 17 mi.	
383	Papermill Rd, **N lodging:** Holiday Inn/rest., **S gas:** BP, Citgo, Spur Gas, **food:** Applebee's (1mi), Burger King, China Buffet, Darryl's, Dunkin Donuts, IHOP, Longhorn Steaks, McDonald's, Morrison's Cafeteria, Pizza Hut, Regas Café, Ruby Tuesday, Showbiz Pizza, Taco Bell, Taco Rancho Mexican, Waffle House, Western Sizzlin, **lodging:** Econolodge, Howard Johnson, Super 8, **other:** Buick/GMC, Firestone, same as 380
380	US 11, US 70, West Hills, **S gas:** BP, Citgo, Conoco, Pilot, Shell, Texaco/dsl, Weigel's, **food:** Amerigo's Italian, Applebee's, Arby's, Chick-fil-A, Chili's, China Buffet, Firehouse Subs, Hardee's, Honeybaked Ham, Hooters, IHOP, KFC, Macaroni Grill, Margarita's, Mr Gatti's, Mr Gatti's, O'Charley's, Olive Garden, Oscar's Rest., Papa John's, Petro's Chili, PF Chang's, Pizza Hut, Plumtree Chinese, Qdoba Mexican, Red Lobster, Schlotsky's, Sawyer's Chicken, Starbucks, Subway, Taco Bell, Texas Roadhouse, Wendy's, Wishbone Wings, Zaxby's, **lodging:** Comfort Hotel, Extended Stay America, Howard Johnson, Quality Inn, Super 8, **other:** Barnes&Noble, Belk, BiLo Foods, Borders Books, Dillard's, $General, Food Lion, JC Penney, K-Mart, Kohl's, NTB, Office Depot, Old Navy, O'Reilly Parts, Pet Supplies+, Ross, Sears, Staples, TJ Maxx, U-Haul, Walgreens, mall, st patrol, **1 mi S on Kingston Pike E gas:** Citgo/7-11, **food:** Morrison's Cafeteria, Central Park, Little Caesar's, **lodging:** Family Inn, **other:** Office Depot, Radio Shack

INTERSTATE 40 CONT'D

E ↕ W

Exit #	Services
379	Bridgewater Rd, **N gas:** Exxon/Subway, Shell, **food:** McDonald's, Pizza Hut/Taco Bell, **lodging:** Red Carpet Inn, **other:** Sam's Club, Walmart SuperCtr, **S gas:** BP/dsl, Pilot/dsl, Texaco/dsl, **food:** Burger King, Chuck-eCheese, Cici's, Don Pablo, Logan's Roadhouse, Mrs Winners, Old Country Buffet, Omelette House, Ryan's, Shoney's, Sonic, Steak Escape, Wendy's, **lodging:** Family Inn, Holiday Inn, Scottish Inn, **other:** AutoZone, BooksAMillion, Buy4Less Foods, Cadillac, Firestone/auto, Ford, Dodge, GMC, Goodyear, Isuzu, Mitsubishi, Nissan, Saab, SuperX Drug, transmissions
378	Cedar Bluff Rd, **N gas:** Pilot/Taco Bell, Shell, Texaco, Weigel's, **food:** Arby's, Burger King, Cracker Barrel, Dunkin Donuts, KFC, Little Caesar's, LJ Silver, McDonald's, Papa John's, Pizza Hut, Starbucks, Subway, Waffle House, Wendy's, **lodging:** Budget Inn, Econolodge, Hampton Inn, Holiday Inn, Ramada Inn, Sleep Inn, **other:** [H], Food Lion, Walgreen, **S gas:** Exxon, **food:** Applebee's, Bob Evans, Carrabba's, Corky's Ribs/BBQ, Denny's, Fazoli's, Famous Dave's BBQ, Firehouse Subs, Friendly's, Fuddrucker's, Grady's Grill, IHOP, Outback Steaks, Pulio's Grill, Rafferty's, Rubio's Grill, **lodging:** Best Western, Clubhouse Inn, Comfort Inn, Courtyard, Extended Stay America, Guesthouse Suites, Hilton Garden, Jameson Inn, La Quinta, Microtel, Red Roof Inn, Residence Inn, Signature Inn, **other:** Best Buy, Celebration Sta, Chevrolet, Chrysler, Ford, Jo-Ann Fabrics, Kia, Lowes Whse, Michael's, Staples, Walgreens
376	I-140 E, TN 162 N, to Maryville, **N** to Oak Ridge Museum
374	TN 131, Lovell Rd, **N gas:** BP, Shell/dsl, TA/dsl/rest./24hr/@, **food:** McDonald's, Taco Bell, Waffle House, **lodging:** Best Western, Knight's Inn, La Quinta, Travelodge, Vista Inn, **other:** Harley-Davidson, Passport RV Ctr, **S gas:** Citgo, Pilot/Wendy's/dsl/24hr/@, Speedway, **food:** Arby's, Carino's, Chick-fil-A, Chili's, Connor's, Krystal, McDonald's, Mimi's, Olive Garden, Ruby Tuesday, Shoney's, Steak&Shake, Texas Roadhouse, **lodging:** Candlewood Suites, Day's Inn/rest., Homewood Suites, Motel 6, Springhill Suites, **other:** Belk, CarMax, Honda, Land Rover, Lexus, Mercedes, Target, Toyota, Walmart SuperCtr
373	Campbell Sta Rd, **N gas:** Shell/dsl, Marathon/dsl **lodging:** Comfort Suites, Country Inn&Suites, Ramada Ltd, Super 8, **other:** Buddy Gregg RV Ctr, **S gas:** BP, Pilot, Weigel's, **food:** Cracker Barrel, Gridiron Burgers, Hardee's, Little Bangkok, Wild Wing Cafe, Yellow Mushroom, **lodging:** Baymont Inn, Holiday Inn Express, **other:** Gander Mtn
372mm	**weigh sta both lanes**
369	Watt Rd, **N gas:** *FLYING J*/Conoco/dsl/LP/scales/RV dump/24hr, Speedco, **S gas:** Exxon/dsl, Petro/Mobil/dsl/24hr/@, TA/BP/Burger King/Pizza Hut/dsl/24hr/@, **other:** Blue Beacon

I-40 E and I-75 N run together 17 mi.

Exit #	Services
368	I-75 and I-40
364	US 321, TN 95, Lenoir City, Oak Ridge, **N gas:** Melton Hill Mkt/gas, **other:** Crosseyed Cricket Camping (2mi), **4-5 mi S food:** KFC, Krystal, Ruby Tuesday, **lodging:** Comfort Inn, Days Inn, Econolodge, Hampton Inn, Holiday Inn Express, Ramada Ltd
363mm	**parking area wb, [phone], litter barrel**
362	Industrial Park Rd
360	Buttermilk Rd, **N** Soaring Eagle RV Park
356	TN 58 N, Gallaher Rd, to Oak Ridge, **N gas:** BP/dsl, Weigels/dsl, **food:** Huddle House, **lodging:** Budget Inn, Motel 6, **other:** 4 Seasons Camping
355	Lawnville Rd, **N gas:** Pilot/Subway/dsl
352	TN 58 S, Kingston, **N lodging:** Knight's Inn, **S gas:** Exxon/dsl, RaceWay, Shell, **food:** Buddy's BBQ, Hardee's, McDonald's, Pizza Hut, Sonic, Subway, Taco Bell, **lodging:** Comfort Inn, **other:** Family$, Marina RV Park, to Watts Bar Lake, Piggly Wiggly, USPO
351mm	Clinch River
350	US 70, Midtown, **S food:** Gondolier Italian, **other:** Caney Creek Camping (3mi), Kroger, Lowe's Whse, Patterson RV Supplies, Walgreens
347	US 27, Harriman, **N gas:** Phillips 66/Subway/dsl, **food:** Hardee's, KFC, Los Primos Mexican, LJ Silver, McDonald's, Pizza Hut, Ruby Tuesday, Taco Bell, Wendy's, **lodging:** Best Western, **other:** to Frozen Head SP, Big S Fork NRA, **S gas:** BP, Exxon, Shell/Krystal/dsl/24hr, **food:** Cancun Mexican, Cracker Barrel, Shoney's, **lodging:** Holiday Inn Express, Quality Inn, Super 8, **2-3 mi S gas:** Murphy USA, **food:** Capt D's, Domino's, Sonic, **other:** [H], Ace Hardware, Radio Shack, Walmart SuperCtr/Subway
340	TN 299 N, Airport Rd
339.5mm	eastern/central time zone line, eastern/central time zone line
338	TN 299 S, Westel Rd, **N gas:** BP/dsl, **S gas:** Shell/dsl, **other:** Boat-N-RV Ctr/Park
336mm	**parking area/weigh sta eb, litter barrel**
329	US 70, Crab Orchard, **N gas:** BP/dsl, Liberty/dsl, **other:** KOA (4mi), **S other:** Cumberland Trails SP, Wilson SP
327mm	**rest area wb, full [handicapped] facilities, [phone], [picnic], litter barrels, petwalk, vending**
324mm	**rest area eb, full [handicapped] facilities, [phone], [picnic], litter barrels, petwalk, vending**
322	TN 101, Peavine Rd, Crossville, **N gas:** BP/Bean Pot Rest., Exxon/dsl, Volunteer Gas/dsl, **food:** Hardee's, McDonald's, Quizno's, **lodging:** Holiday Inn Express, **other:** Deer Run Resort, KOA Camping, Roam-Roost RV Campground, to Fairfield Glade Resort, **S gas:** Texaco/dsl, **food:** Cancun Mexican, Taco Bell, **lodging:** Comfort Suites, Hampton Inn, Super 8, **other:** [H], Tennessee RV Ctr, Chestnut Hill Winery, Cumberland Mtn SP
320	TN 298, Crossville, **N gas:** Pilot/Wendy's/scales/dsl/24hr, **food:** Halcyon Rest., **other:** antiques, golf, winery, **S gas:** BP/DQ/Pizza Hut/dsl, Shell/dsl, **food:** Krystal (2mi), Wendy's (2mi), **other:** [H], Factory Outlet/famous brands, Save-A-Lot Foods, antiques, auto repair
318mm	Obed River
317	US 127, Crossville, **N gas:** BP/dsl, Exxon/Subway/dsl/24hr, Shell/dsl, Sunoco/Horizon/dsl, **food:** Shoneys, **lodging:** Best Western, Knight's Inn, La Quinta, **0-2 mi S gas:** Citgo, Jiffy Gas, Marathon, Murphy USA, Shell, **food:** America Rest., Arby's, Burger King, Cracker Barrel, McDonalds, Papa Johns, Peking Buffet, Ruby Tuesday, Ryan's, Sonic, Subway, Taco Bell,

KNOXVILLE

HARRIMAN

CROSSVILLE

TN

INTERSTATE 40 CONT'D

E ↕ W

Exit #	Services
317	Continued TCBY, Vegas Steaks, Waffle House, Vegas Steaks, Zaxby's, **lodging:** Best Value, Days Inn, Economy Inn, **other:** H, Chevrolet/Cadillac/Buick/Pontiac/GMC, Chrysler/Dodge/Jeep, $General, $Tree, GNC, Lowe's Whse, Rite Aid, Shadden Tires, Staples, Walmart SuperCtr, Walgreens, Vet, to Cumberland SP
311	Plateau Rd, **N gas:** Sunoco/dsl, **food:** Papa Lorenzo's Pizza, **S gas:** BP/dsl, Exxon
306mm	**parking area/weigh sta wb, litter barrels**
301	US 70 N, TN 84, Monterey, **N gas:** Phillips 66, Shell, **food:** Burger King, Cup N' Saucer Rest., DQ, Subway, **lodging:** Super 8
300	US 70, Monterey, **N gas:** Citgo/dsl, **food:** Hardee's
291mm	Falling Water River
290	US 70, Cookeville, **N gas:** BP (1mi), **S gas:** Citgo, **lodging:** Alpine Suites
288	TN 111, to Livingston, Cookeville, Sparta, **N** Cordell SP, **S gas:** Citgo/dsl, Mid Tenn Trkstp/Phillips 66/Gen. Lee's BBQ/Subway/dsl/24hr/@, **food:** Huddle House, **lodging:** Knight's Inn
287	TN 136, Cookeville, **N gas:** BP, Exxon, Murphy USA, **food:** Applebee's, Arby's, Baskin-Robbins, Bully's Rest., Burger King, Capt D's, Cheddars, Chick-fil-A, Chili's, Cracker Barrel, DQ, Fazoli's, Golden Corral, IHOP, Jack-in-the-Box, Jersey Mike's Subs, King Buffet, Krystal, LJ Silver, Logan's Roadhouse, Longhorn Steaks, McDonald's, Nick's Rest., O'Charley's, Olive Garden, Outback Steaks, Pizza Hut, Puleo's Grill, Quizno's, Red Lobster, Ruby Tuesday, Shoney's, Sonic, Starbucks, Steak'n Shake, Subway, Taco Bell, Waffle House, Wendy's, **lodging:** Best Value, Best Western, Clarion, Comfort Inn & Suites, Day's Inn, Hampton Inn, Super 8, **other:** Aldi Foods, BigLots, Firestone/auto, Harley-Davidson, JC Penney, K-Mart, Kroger/gas, Lowe's Whse, Middle TN RV/Airstream, Radio Shack, Walmart SuperCtr, st patrol, **S gas:** Exxon/dsl, Marathon/dsl, Pilot/dsl, **food:** KFC, Waffle House, **lodging:** Baymont Inn, Country Hearth Inn, Country Inn Suites, Fairfield Inn, Holiday Inn Express, **other:** Sam's Club/gas, URGENT CARE
286	TN 135, Burgess Falls Rd, **N gas:** BP, Exxon, RaceWay/dsl, Shell/dsl, **food:** Arby's, Beef'O'Brady's, Chick-fil-A, Christy's Cafe, El Milagro Mexican, Hardee's, Waffle House, **other:** H, Buick/Pontiac/GMC, Chrysler/Jeep/Dodge, GMC, Goodyear/auto, Kia, Mazda, Nissan, Toyota/Scion, USPO, to TTU, Vet, **S gas:** Citgo/dsl, **lodging:** Star Motor Inn, **other:** Burgess Falls SP
280	TN 56 N, Baxter, **N gas:** Loves/McDonalds/Subway/scales/dsl/24hr, **food:** Huddle House, **other:** Camp Discovery (2mi), Twin Lakes RV Park (2mi)
276	Old Baxter Rd
273	TN 56 S, to Smithville, **S gas:** BP/dsl, Phillips 66, **food:** Rose Garden Rest., **other:** USPO
268	TN 96, Buffalo Valley Rd, **S** to Edgar Evins SP/RV camping
267mm	Caney Fork River
267mm	**rest area both lanes, full ♿ facilities, info, ☎, picnic tables, litter barrels, petwalk, vending**

COOKEVILLE

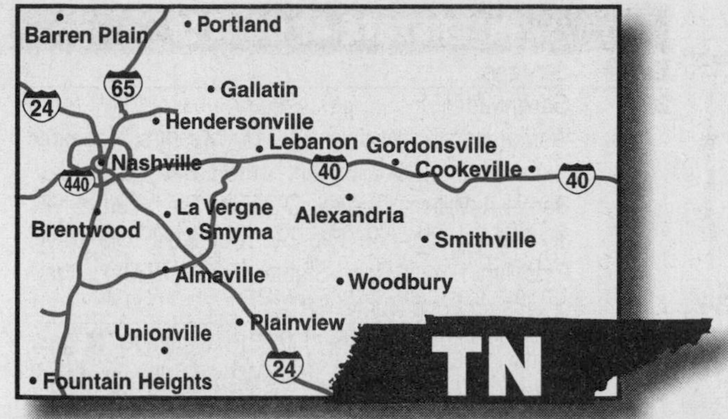

LEBANON

Exit #	Services
266mm	Caney Fork River
263mm	Caney Fork River
258	TN 53, Gordonsville, **N gas:** Exxon/KFC/Taco Bell, Shell/dsl, **food:** McDonald's, Timberloft Café, Waffle House, **lodging:** Comfort Inn, **other:** to Cordell Hull Dam, **S gas:** Chevron/dsl, **food:** Arby's, Cornerstone Cafe, **other:** $General
254	TN 141, to Alexandria
252mm	**parking area/weigh sta both lanes, picnic tables, litter barrels**
245	Linwood Rd, **N gas:** BP/dsl
239	US 70, Lebanon, **N gas:** Citgo/dsl, RaceWay, **S gas:** Phillips 66/Uncle Pete's/dsl/rest/scales
238	US 231, Lebanon, **N gas:** Exxon, Mapco, Shell, **food:** Applebee's, Arby's, Cici's Pizza, Cracker Barrel, Demo's Steaks, Gondola Rest., Hardee's, Jack-in-the-Box, KFC, King Buffet, La Loma Mexican, McDonald's, Mrs Winner's, Pizza Hut, Ponderosa, Ryan's, Shoney's, Sunset Rest., Subway, Taco Bell, Waffle House, Wendy's, White Castle, Whitt's BBQ, Zaxby's **lodging:** Best Value, Comfort Inn, Executive Inn, Holiday Inn Express, Quality Inn, Ramada, **other:** H, Aldi Foods, $Tree, Discount Tire, Lowe's Whse, Walgreens, Walmart SuperCtr, **S gas:** Pilot/Chester's/Subway/dsl/24hr/scales, Shell/dsl, **food:** O'Charley's, Sonic, **lodging:** Comfort Suites, Country Inn Suites, Day's Inn, Knight's Inn, Super 8, **other:** Prime Outlets/famous brands, Shady Acres, Timberline Campground, to Cedars of Lebanon SP, RV camping
236	S Hartmann Dr, **N gas:** Mapco, Shell, **food:** Chili's, Outback Steaks, Subway, **other:** Hampton Inn, **other:** H, Home Depot, Rose Tires, **2mi N food:** Ruby Tuesday
235	TN 840 W, to Murfreesboro
232	TN 109, to Gallatin, **N gas:** Citgo, Mapco/Quizno's, Shell/McDonald's/dsl/24hr, Thornton's/dsl, **food:** Bellacino's Pizza, Coach's Grill, NY Deli, Sonic, Subway, Waffle House, Wendy's, **lodging:** Sleep Inn, Value Place Inn, **2 mi S other:** Countryside Resort Camping
228mm	**truck sta, eb only**
229b a	Beckwitch Rd
226mm	**truck sta**
226	TN 171, Mt Juliet Rd, (226 c b a, from eb), **N gas:** BP/McDonald's/dsl, Citgo, Exxon/dsl, Mapco/dsl, Shell/dsl/24hr, **food:** Arby's, Capt D's, **other:** Lowe's Whse, Wal-Mart SuperCtr, **S gas:** Mapco/dsl, **food:** Chick-fil-A, Cracker Barrel, Fulins Asian, Logan's Roadhouse, O'Charly's, Olive Garden, Panera Bread, Red Lobster, Red Robin, Ruby Tuesday, Salsarita's Cantina, Smoothie King, Steak&Shake, Taco Bell,

INTERSTATE 40 CONT'D

E ↕ W

Exit #	Services
226	Continued Waffle House, Wasabi Steaks, Wendy's, **lodging:** Hampton Inn, Quality Inn, **other:** Belk, Best Buy, Books-A-Million, Curves, Discount Tire, Ford, GNC, JC Penney, JoAnne Fabrics, Kroger/dsl, Old Navy, PetsMart, Publix, Ross, Staples, Target, TJ Maxx, Walgreens, to Long Hunter SP
221	TN 45 N, Old Hickory Blvd, to The Hermitage, **N gas:** BP, Exxon, Mapco/dsl, RaceWay, Shell/24hr, **food:** Applebee's, Chick-fil-A, DQ, Hardees, IHOP, Jack-in-the-Box, O'Charley's, Outback, Panera Bread, Subway, Waffle House, **lodging:** Motel 6, Suburban Lodge, Super 8, Vista Hotel, **other:** [H], Kroger, PetCo, Walgreens, **S gas:** Phillips 66/White Castle, Shell/McDonald's, Texaco
219	Stewart's Ferry Pike, **N gas:** Mapco, **S gas:** Mapco/Subway, Shell/dsl, Thornton's/dsl, **food:** China King, Cracker Barrel, Hacienda Mexican, Sal's Pizza, Subway, Waffle House, **lodging:** Best Value Inn, Best Western, Comfort Suites, Country Inn Suites, Day's Inn, Family Inn, Sleep Inn, **other:** $General, FoodLion, Fred's Drug, Vet
216	(216 c from eb) TN 255, Donaldson Pk, **N gas:** BP/dsl, Mapco, RaceWay, Shell/Subway/dsl/24hr, **food:** Arby's, Backyard Burger, Darfon's, Domino's, Jalisco Mexican, KFC, McDonald's, New China, Pizza Hut/Taco Bell, Ruby Tuesday, Shoney's, Sonic, Waffle House, Wendy's, **lodging:** Country Inn Suites, Drury Inn, Fairfield Inn, Hampton Inn, Holiday Inn Express, Hyatt Place, La Quinta, Radisson, Red Roof Inn, Springhill Suites, Super 8, Wingate Inn, **other:** Advance Parts, Curves, K-Mart, Walgreens, USPO/24hr
216b a	(from eb), **S** Nashville Intn'l [airport]
215b a	TN 155, Briley Pkwy, to Opryland, **N on Elm Hill...gas:** Mapco, **food:** Casa Fiesta Mexican, Jack-in-the-Box, Waffle House, **lodging:** Alexis Inn, Comfort Suites, Courtyard, Embassy Suites, Extended Stay, Hampton Inn, Hilton Garden, Holiday Inn, Homestead Suites, La Quinta, Marriott, Ramada, Residence Inn, Studio+, **S gas:** Phillips 66/dsl, **food:** Mazatlan Mexican, Panda House, Subway, **lodging:** Hamilton Inn, Hotel Preston
213b	I-24 W
213a	I-24 E/I-440, E to Chattanooga
213	US 41 (from wb no return), to Spence Lane, **N other:** Kenworth, **S gas:** Shell, Texaco, **food:** Denny's, Waffle House, **lodging:** Day's Inn, Holiday Inn Express, Rodeway Inn, Sunrise Inn, Super 8, same as 212
212	Fessler's Lane (from eb, no return), **N other:** Freightliner, Harley-Davidson, **S gas:** Mapco/dsl, Shell/Dunkin Donuts, **food:** Burger King, Jack-in-the-Box, Krystal, McDonald's, Mrs Winners, Sonic, Wendy's, **lodging:** Best Value, same as 213
211mm	Cumberland River
211b	I-24 W
211a	I-24E, I-40 W
210c	US 31 S, US 41A, 2nd Ave, 4th Ave, **N lodging:** Hilton, Sheraton, Stouffer Hotel, **S** museum
210b a	I-65 S, to Birmingham
209b a	US 70 S, Charlotte Ave, Nashville, **N gas:** Exxon, **food:** McDonald's, **lodging:** Sheraton, **other:** Chrysler/Jeep, Nissan, Country Music Hall of Fame, Conv Ctr, transmissions, **S gas:** Exxon, **food:** Burger King, Krystal, Sonic, Subway, White Castle, **lodging:** Comfort Inn, Guesthouse Inn, **other:** Chevrolet, Lincoln/Mercury, Pontiac/GMC, Subaru, Toyota, Walgreens
208b a	I-65, N to Louisville, S to Birmingham
207	28th Ave, Jefferson St, Nashville, **N gas:** BP, Citgo, **food:** Subway, Wendy's, Wing Zone, **other:** [H], Family$, to TN St U
206	I-440 E, to Knoxville
205	46th Ave, W Nashville, **N other:** Harley-Davidson, **S gas:** Mapco, Shell, **food:** McDonald's, Mrs. Winners
204	TN 155, Briley Pkwy, **S gas:** BP/dsl, Citgo, **food:** Burger King, China Buffet, Church's/White Castle, Cinco De Mayo, Domino's, Jack-in-the-Box, KFC, Krystal, Las Palmas, Papa John's, Shoney's, Subway, Waffle House, **lodging:** Baymont Inn, Best Western, Comfort Inn, Days Inn, **other:** CarQuest, CVS Drug, Firestone/auto, Kroger/gas, NTB, O'Reilly Parts, PepBoys, Sav-a-lot Foods, Walgreens
201b a	US 70, Charlotte Pike, **N gas:** Exxon, Shell/dsl/24hr, **food:** Bojangles, China Buffet, Cracker Barrel, Jim 'N Nick's BBQ, Krystal, Subway, Waffle House, Wendy's, **lodging:** Super 8, **other:** $Tree, GNC, Kwik Kar, Lowe's Whse, Radio Shack, Walmart SuperCtr, **S gas:** BP, Mapco, Shell, **food:** Arby's, McDonald's, Pizza Hut, Red Robin, Taco Bell, **other:** Best Buy, Big Lots, Books-A-Million, BigLots, Costco/gas, Firestone/auto, Marshall's, Old Navy, PetsMart, Ross, Staples, Target, Uhaul, World Mkt
199	rd 251, Old Hickory Blvd, **N gas:** Shell, **S gas:** BP, Mapco, **food:** Sonic, Subway, **other:** Sam's Club/gas
196	US 70, to Bellevue, Newsom Sta, **N gas:** Mapco/dsl, **food:** Shoney's, **S gas:** BP, Mapco/dsl, Shell/dsl/24hr, **food:** Applebee's, Arby's, Baskin-Robbins, Jack-in-the-Box, O'Charley's, Pizza Hut, Sir Pizza, Sonic, Subway, Taco Bell, Waffle House, Wendy's, **lodging:** Hampton Inn, Microtel, **other:** $Tree, Firestone/auto, Home Depot, Michael's, Petco, Publix, Sears/auto, Staples, USPO, Walgreens
195mm	Harpeth River
192	McCrory Lane, to Pegram, **N gas:** Eddie's Mkt (1mi), **4 mi S food:** Loveless Cafe, **other:** Natchez Trace Pkwy
190mm	Harpeth River
188mm	Harpeth River
188	rd 249, Kingston Springs, **N gas:** BP, Mapco/dsl, Shell/Arby's/dsl, **food:** El Jardin Mexican, McDonald's/playplace, Sonic, Subway, **lodging:** Best Western, Mid-Town Inn, Relax Inn, **other:** USPO, **S gas:** Petro/Chevron/Quick Skillet/dsl/showers/scales/24hr/@, **other:** Vet
182	TN 96, to Dickson, Fairview, **N gas:** BP, Express Fuel, **lodging:** Fairview Inn, **other:** M Bell SP (16mi), **S gas:** ***FLYING J***/Conoco/Cookery/Country Mkt/dsl/LP/scales/24hr, Horizon/Backyard Burger/Dunkin Donuts/dsl, **lodging:** Deerfield Inn
176	TN 840

NASHVILLE

DICKSON

E ↕ W DICKSON

INTERSTATE 40 CONT'D

Exit #	Services
172	TN 46, to Dickson, **N gas:** Citgo/Subway, Exxon, Pilot/Wendy's/dsl/scales/24hr, Shell, **food:** Arby's, Cracker Barrel, Farmer's Rest., McDonald's, Ruby Tuesday, Waffle House/24hr, Wang's China, **lodging:** Best Western, Comfort Inn, Econolodge, Hampton Inn, Motel 6, Quality Inn, Super 8, **other:** H, Chappell's Foods, Chevrolet, Dickson RV Park, Ford/Lincold/Mercury, NAPACare, Nissan, truck repair, to M Bell SP, **S gas:** BP, Shell, **food:** O'Charley's, Sonic, **lodging:** Day's Inn, Holiday Inn Express, Ramada
170	**rest area both lanes, full ♿ facilities, ☎, 🛆, litter barrels, vending, petwalk**
166mm	Piney River
163	rd 48, to Dickson, **N gas:** Phillips 66/dsl, **other:** tire repair, **S gas:** Shell, **other:** Pinewood Camping (7mi), Tanbark Camping
152	rd 230, Bucksnort, **N gas:** Citgo, **food:** Rudy's Rest., **lodging:** Travel Inn
149mm	Duck River
148	rd 50, Barren Hollow Rd, to Turney Center
143	TN 13, to Linden, Waverly, **N gas:** BP, Pilot/Arby's/scales/dsl/24hr, Shell, **food:** Buffalo River Mexican, Loretta's Kitchen, McDonald's, Subway, **lodging:** Best Western, Day's Inn, Holiday Inn Express, Knight's Inn, **other:** KOA/LP, tires, **S gas:** Exxon/dsl, **food:** El Paso Mexican, **lodging:** Scottish Inn
141mm	Buffalo River
137	Cuba Landing, **N other:** TN River RV Park, **S food:** Cuba Landing Rest./gas
133mm	Tennessee River
133	rd 191, Birdsong Rd, **9 mi N lodging:** Birdsong RV Resort/marina, Good Sam RV Park
131mm	**rest area both lanes, full ♿ facilities, ☎, vending, 🛆, litter barrels, petwalk**
126	US 641, TN 69, to Camden, **N gas:** Marathon/Subway/dsl, Phillips 66/North 40/dsl/, Shell/dsl, **other:** Paris Landing SP, tire/truck repair, to NB Forrest SP, **S gas:** BP/dsl, Shell/dsl, **lodging:** Day's Inn, **other:** H, Mouse-tail Landing
116	rd 114, **S other:** to Natchez Trace SP, RV camping
110mm	Big Sandy River
108	TN 22, to Lexington, Parkers Crossroads, **N gas:** BP/McDonald's/24hr/dsl, Citgo/dsl/24hr, Phillips 66/dsl, **food:** Bailey's Rest., DQ, Subway, **lodging:** Knight's Inn, **other:** USPO, city park, **S gas:** Exxon, **lodging: lodging:** OJ's BBQ, Po' Boys Pizza, Country Hearth Inn, **other:** H, RV camping, Parkers Crossroads Bfd Visitors Ctr, to Shiloh Nat Bfd (51mi)
103mm	**parking area/truck sta eb, litter barrels**
102mm	**parking area/truck sta wb, litter barrels**
101	rd 104, **N gas:** 101 TP/rest/tires/dsl/24hr, **other:** golf (3mi)
93	rd 152, Law Rd, **N gas:** Phillips 66/dsl/deli/24hr, **S gas:** BP/dsl, Super Way/dsl
87	US 70, US 412, Huntingdon, McKenzie, **N gas:** Coastal/dsl, **S gas:** BP/dsl, Love's/Hardee's/scales/dsl/24hr
85	Christmasville Rd, to Jackson, **N gas:** BP/dsl, Exxon/dsl/24hr, Pilot/Denny's/dsl/scales/24hr, **lodging:** Howard Johnson Express, **other:** $General, **S gas:**

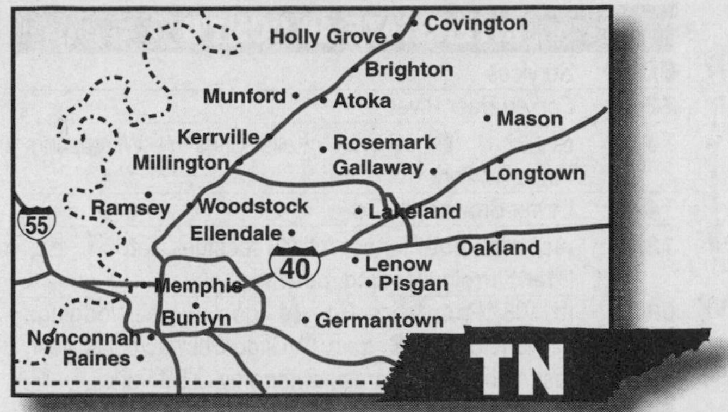

JACKSON

Exit #	Services
85	Continued Horizon/Baskin-Robbins, **food:** Lenny's Subs, Los Portales, McDonald's, Reggi's BBQ, Sonic, Sparky's
83	Campbell St, **N gas:** Exxon/Old Madina Mkt/dsl **S lodging:** Courtyard, Hampton Inn
82b a	US 45, Jackson, **N gas:** BP, Exxon, **food:** Cracker Barrel, **lodging:** Knight's Inn, Microtel, **other:** Batteries+, Curves, Smallwoods RV Ctr (4mi), **S gas:** BP, Clark Gas/dsl, Exxon, RaceWay, **food:** Barley's Cafe, Burger King, Capt D's, Catfish Galley, ChuckeCheese, DQ, KFC, Krystal, Little Caesars, LJ Silver, McDonald's/playplace, Papa John's, Pizza Hut, Popeye's, Shoney's, Sonic, Subway, Taco Bell, Waffle House, Wendy's, **lodging:** Executive Inn, La Quinta, Ramada Ltd, Super 8, Travellers Motel, **other:** Advance Parts, AutoZone, BigLots, $General, Firestone/auto, Fred's Drug, Goodyear/auto, Kroger/24hr, Office Depot, Radio Shack, Sears/auto, TJ Maxx, mall, Vet
80b a	US 45 Byp, Jackson, **N gas:** Murphy USA, **food:** Asahi Japanese, Baskin-Robbins, Buffalo Wild Wings, Chili's, Chick-fil-A, China Pan, Corky's BBQ, Fazoli's, Honey Baked Ham, IHOP, Jason's Deli, KFC, Lenny's Subs, Lonestar Steaks, Longhorn Steaks, Los Portales, McAlisters Deli, Moe's SW Grill, Olive Garden, Peking Chinese, Perkins, Popeye's, Red Robin, Ruby Tuesday, Schlotsky's, Starbucks, Steak'n Shake, TGIFriday's, Wendy's, Zaxby's, **lodging:** Baymont Inn, Jameson Inn, SigNature Hotel, **other:** Best Buy, Firestone/auto, Home Depot, Kohl's, Lowe's Whse, Marshalls, Nissan, PetsMart, Ross, Sam's Club/gas, Walmart SuperCtr/24hr, **1 mi N on 45 byp...food:** Arby's, Burger King, LJ Silver, McDonald's, Outback Steaks, Sonic, Subway, **other:** Books-A-Million, Cadillac/Chevrolet, Gateway Tires, Steinmart, Target, **S gas:** BP/Circle K, Goldline Gas, Phillips 66/dsl, **food:** Arby's, Barnhill's Buffet, Burger King, Dunkin Donuts, El Chico's, Logan's Roadhouse, Mazatlan Mexican, McDonald's, O'Charley's, Old Hickory Steakhouse, Old Town Spaghetti, Red Bones Rest., Subway, Taco Bell, Waffle House, **lodging:** Best Western, Casey Jones Motel, Comfort Suites, Day's Inn, DoubleTree, Econolodge, Guesthouse Inn, Holiday Inn, Motel 6, Old Hickory Inn, Quality Inn, **other:** H, $General, Hancock Fabrics, Harley-Davidson, King Tires, K-Mart, Toyota/Scion, Tuesday Morning, to Pinson Mounds SP, Chickasaw SP
79	US 412, Jackson, **N other:** Gander Mtn., **S gas:** BP/dsl, Exxon, **lodging:** Day's Inn, **other:** Jackson RV Park

INTERSTATE 40 CONT'D

E ↕ W

Exit #	Services
78mm	Forked Deer River
76	rd 223 S, **S other:** McKellar-Sites ✈, Whispering Pines RV Park
74	Lower Brownsville Rd
73mm	**rest area both lanes, full ♿ facilities, info, ☎, picnic, litter barrels, vending, petwalk**
68	rd 138, Providence Rd, **N gas:** BP/dsl, **lodging:** Ole South Inn, **S gas:** TA/Citgo/Subway/dsl/scales/rest./24hr/@, Valero/dsl, **other:** Joy-O RV Park
66	US 70, to Brownsville, **N other:** Ft Pillow SHP (51mi), **S gas:** Exxon/dsl, **lodging:** Motel 6
60	rd 19, Mercer Rd
56	TN 76, to Brownsville, **N gas:** BP, Shell/dsl/24hr, **food:** DQ, KFC, McDonald's/playplace, Pizza Hut/Taco Bell, **lodging:** Best Value, Comfort Inn, Day's Inn, Econolodge, **S gas:** Exxon/Huddle House/dsl/24hr
55mm	Hatchie River
52	TN 76, rd 179, Koko Rd, to Whiteville
50mm	**weigh sta both lanes, ☎**
47	TN 179, to Stanton, Dancyville, **S gas:** Exit 47 Trkstp/dsl
42	TN 222, to Stanton, **N lodging:** Best Value, **S gas:** Exxon/dsl, Pilot/Chester's/Subway/dsl/scales/24hr, **lodging:** Deerfield Inn
35	TN 59, to Somerville, **S gas:** BP/dsl/scales, **food:** Longtown Rest.
29.5mm	Loosahatchie River
25	TN 205, Airline Rd, to Arlington, **N gas:** Shell/dsl, **S gas:** Horizon/Backyard Burger/dsl, **other: vistor ctr**
24	TN 385, rd 204, to Arlington, Millington, Collierville
20	Canada Rd, Lakeland, **N gas:** BP/McDonald's, Shell, **food:** Cracker Barrel, Waffle House, **lodging:** Day's Inn, Relax Inn, Super 8, **S gas:** Exxon/Subway/dsl, **other:** Factory Outlet/famous brands/food court, Memphis East Camping, Old Time Pottery
18	US 64, to Bartlett, **N gas:** Shell/Burger King, **food:** Abuelo's, Bob Evans, Buffalo Wings, Dyer's Cafe, El Porton, Firebird's Grill, Hooters, McAlisters Deli, Longhorn Steaks, O'Charley's, Olive Garden, Steak'n Shake, TGI Friday's, TX Roadhouse, **lodging:** Best Western, Fairfield Inn, Holiday Inn, La Quinta, SpringHill Suites, **other:** Buick/Pontiac/GMC, Firestone, Goodyear/auto, Hummer, Lowe's Whse, Sam's Club/gas, Walmart SuperCtr, same as 16, **S gas:** BP/Circle K, Citgo/dsl, **food:** Backyard Burger, KFC, Lenny's Subs, Pizza Hut, Subway, **other:** Kroger, Schnuck's/gas, Walgreens, Zaxby's
16b a	TN 177, to Germantown, **N gas:** BP/Circle K, Shell/Circle K, **food:** Abuelo's, Arby's, Bahama Breeze, Baskin-Robbins, Burger King, Casa Mexicana, Chili's, Chick-fil-A, Colton's Steaks, Danver's, IHOP, J. Alexander's, Joe's Crabshack, Logan's Roadhouse, Macaroni Grill, McDonald's/playplace, Melting Pot Rest., On-the-Border, Red Lobster, Red Sun Buffet, Taco Bell, TCBY, Tellini's Italian, Waffle House, Wendy's, **lodging:** Extended Stay Deluxe, Hampton Inn, Hyatt Place, **other:** H, Barnes&Noble, Best Buy, Chevrolet, Chrysler/Dodge, Dillard's, $Tree, Ford, Home Depot, Honda, Infiniti, JC Penney, Macy's, Michael's, Nissan, Office Depot, Old Navy, Sears/auto, Target, TJ Maxx,
16b a	Continued Walgreens, mall, **S gas:** BP/Circle K, Shell/Circle K, **food:** Abbay's Rest., Backyard Burger, Burger King, ChuckeCheese, Corky's BBQ, Pei Wei Chinese, Qdoba Mexican, Shogun Japanese, Smoothie King, Newk's Cafe, Howard's Doughnut's, Jim'n Nick's BBQ, Jimmy John's, La Hacienda Mexican, Lenny's Subs, McDonald's, Newk's Cafe, Wendy's, Zaxby's, **lodging:** Comfort Suites, Microtel, Quality Inn, Studio+, Wingate Inn, **other:** AutoZone, Costco/gas, Gordman's, Kroger, Kohl's, Rite Aid, Ross, Toyota/Scion
15b a	Appling Rd, **N gas:** BP/Circle K/dsl, Shell/dsl
14	Whitten Rd, **N gas:** Citgo/dsl, Mapco, Shell/Burger King, **food:** Sidecar Café, **other:** Harley-Davidson, **S gas:** BP/Circle K, Shell/Backyard Burger/dsl, **food:** Dunkin Donuts, **lodging:** Travelers Inn, **other:** Walgreens
12	Sycamore View Rd, **N gas:** Citgo/dsl, Texaco/dsl, **food:** Cajun Catfish Co., Capt D's, Church's, Cracker Barrel, IHOP, Krystal, Lenny's Subs, McDonald's, Mrs Winner's, Perkins, Ruby Tuesday, Shoney's, Sonic, Taco Bell, Waffle House, **lodging:** Baymont Inn, Drury Inn, Econolodge, Extended Stay America, Memphis Plaza, Ramada Ltd, Red Roof Inn, Value Place Hotel, **other:** AutoZone, $General, Fred's Drug, Walgreens, Vet, **S gas:** BP/Circle K/dsl, Citgo, Exxon, Mapco, **food:** Beijing Chinese, Burger King, Popeye's, Subway, Tops BBQ, Wendy's, **lodging:** Best Western, Comfort Inn, Day's Inn, Fairfield Inn, La Quinta, Memphis Inn, Motel 6, Quality Inn, Super 8, **other:** Bass Pro Shop
10.5mm	Wolf River
10b a	(from wb) I-240 W around Memphis, I-40 E to Nashville
12c	(from eb) I-240 W, to Jackson, I-40 E to Nashville
12b	Sam Cooper Blvd (from eb)
12a	US 64/70/79, Summer Ave, **N gas:** Mapco/dsl, Shell, **food:** Waffle House, **lodging:** Guest Inn, **other:** Ford, U-Haul, mall, **S gas:** Exxon, **food:** Arby's, Great China, McDonald's, Wendy's, **other:** Curves, $Tree, Firestone/auto, Fred's Drug, Goodyear/auto, Piggly Wiggly, Sav-a-Lot Foods
10	TN 204, Covington Pike, **N gas:** BP, **food:** McDonald's, Wendy's, **other:** Audi/VW, Buick, Chevrolet, Chrysler/Jeep/Dodge, Honda, Hyundai, Isuzu/Mazda, Kia, Mazda, Mitsubishi, Nissan, Pontiac/GMC, Sam's Club, Subaru, Suzuki, SuperLo Food/gas, Volvo
8b a	TN 14, Jackson Ave, **N gas:** Citgo/dsl, Shell, **lodging:** Day's Inn, Sleep Inn, **other:** Raleigh Tire, Vet, **S gas:** Citgo/dsl, Mapco, **other:** AutoZone, Family$, O'Reilly Parts, transmissions
6	Warford Rd
5	Hollywood St, **N gas:** BP, Mapco, **food:** Burger King, Mother's Rest., **other:** Walgreens, **S other:** Memphis Zoo
3	Watkins St, **N gas:** BP, Chevron/dsl, Texaco/dsl, **other:** Family$, U-Haul
2a	rd 300, to US 51 N, Millington, **N other:** Meeman-Shelby SP
2	Smith Ave, Chelsea Ave, **N gas:** Citgo, **S gas:** BP
1g f	TN 14, Jackson Ave, **S gas:** Mapco
1e	I-240 E
1d c b	US 51, Danny Thomas Blvd, **N gas:** Exxon, **food:** KFC, Wendy's, **other:** Ronald McDonald House, St Jude Research Ctr

MEMPHIS

INTERSTATE 40 CONT'D

Exit #	Services
1a	2nd St (from wb), downtown, **S lodging:** Crowne Plaza, Holiday Inn, Marriott, Sheraton, Wyndham Garden, **other:** Conv Ctr
1	Riverside Dr, Front St (from eb), Memphis, **S lodging:** Comfort Inn, **other:** Conv Ctr, Riverfront, Welcome Ctr
0mm	Tennessee/Arkansas state line, Mississippi River

INTERSTATE 55

Exit #	Services
13mm	Tennessee/Arkansas state line, Mississippi River
12c	Delaware St, Memphis, **W lodging:** Super 8
12b	Riverside Dr, downtown Memphis, **E TN Welcome Ctr**
12a	E Crump Blvd (from nb), **E gas:** BP, **other:** museum
11	McLemore Ave, Presidents Island, industrial area
10	S Parkway, **1/2 mi E gas:** BP/dsl
9	Mallory Ave, industrial area
8	Horn Lake Rd (from sb)
7	US 61, 3rd St, **E gas:** BP, Exxon/mart, **food:** Church's, Interstate BBQ, Taco Bell, **other:** AutoZone, Family$, Walgreens, **W gas:** MapCo, PitStop, **food:** KFC, McDonald's, Subway, **lodging:** Rest Inn, **other:** Fuller SP, Indian Museum
6b a	I-240
5b	US 51 S, Elvis Presley Blvd, to Graceland, **W gas:** BP, Citgo/dsl, Exxon, Phillips 66, **food:** Capt D's, Checker's, China Buffet, Kettle Rest., KFC, Peking Chinese, Picadilly's, Taco Bell, **lodging:** American Inn, Day's Inn, Graceland Inn, Heartbreak Hotel, Scottish Inn, Value Place Inn, **other:** [H], Advance Parts, D&N RV Ctr, Dodge's Store, Harley-Davidson, Presley RV Ctr, Walgreens, transmissions, to Graceland
5a	Brooks Rd, **E gas:** BP, Exxon, MapCo, **food:** Popeye's, **lodging:** Airport Inn, Best Value Inn, Budget Lodge, Clarion, Quality Inn, **other:** Freightliner, Peterbilt, Toyota
3mm	**Welcome Ctr nb, full [handicapped] facilities, [phone], vending, [picnic], litter barrels, petwalk**
2b a	TN 175, Shelby Dr, Whitehaven, **E gas:** BP/dsl, Citgo/Subway, Exxon, Shell/dsl, Texaco, **lodging:** Colonial Inn, **W gas:** BP, Citgo, **food:** Burger King, CK's Coffee, Dixie Queen, IHOP, McDonald's, Picadilly, Popeye's, **other:** Family$, Goodyear/auto, Macy's, Sav-a-Lot FOods, Schnuck's Foods, Sears, U-Haul, Walgreens
0mm	Tennessee/Mississippi state line

INTERSTATE 65

Exit #	Services
121.5mm	Tennessee/Kentucky state line
121mm	**Welcome Ctr sb, full [handicapped] facilities, [phone], [picnic], litter barrels, vending, petwalk**
119mm	**weigh sta both lanes**
117	TN 52, Portland, **E gas:** BP/Quizno's/Godfather's/dsl, Shell/dsl/fireworks, **other:** [H], **W gas:** BP/dsl, **lodging:** Budget Host, **other:** fireworks
116mm	Red River
113mm	Red River
112	TN 25, Cross Plains, **E gas:** BP/dsl, **food:** Biggs Chicken, Sad Sam's Deli, **other:** Bledsoe SP, antiques, fireworks **W gas:** Mapco/dsl, Shell/dsl

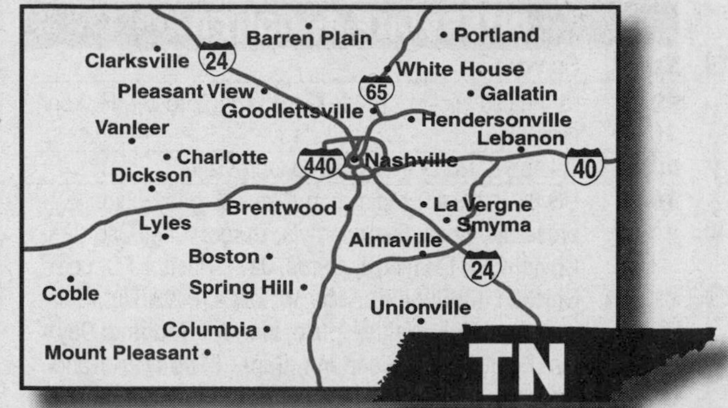

Exit #	Services
108	TN 76, White House, **E gas:** Nervous Charlie's/dsl, Shell, **food:** A&W/KFC, Cracker Barrel, DQ, Hardee's, McDonald's, Mr Wok, Sonic, Subway, Taco Bell, Waffle House, Wendy's, **lodging:** Comfort Inn, Hampton Inn, Holiday Inn Express, Quality Inn, **other:** Ace Hardware, Kroger/gas, O'Reilly Parts, Rite Aid, Walmart SuperCtr/Subway, Walgreens, USPO, park/playground, **W gas:** BP, **food:** Stop 30 BBQ, **lodging:** Day's Inn
104	rd 257, Bethel Rd, **E gas:** BP/rest./dsl, **W gas:** Shell, **other:** Owl's Roost Camping
98	US 31 W, Millersville, **E gas:** Citgo/dsl, RaceWay, Shell/dsl, **food:** Subway, Waffle House, **other:** $General, **W gas:** BP/dsl, **lodging:** Economy Inn, **other:** Nashville Country Camping
97	rd 174, Long Hollow Pike, **E gas:** BP/dsl, Exxon, Mapco, **food:** Arby's, Capt D's, Cracker Barrel, Domino's, Kabuto Japanese, KFC, McDonald's, Quizno's, Shoney's, Subway, Waffle House, Wendy's, **lodging:** Best Western, Days Inn, Executive Inn, Hampton Inn, Quality Inn, Red Roof Inn, **other:** K-Mart, Kroger, **W gas:** Shell/dsl, **food:** Hardee's, Jack-in-the-Box, Krystal/24hr, Poncho Villa Grill, Sonic, Stroud's BBQ, **lodging:** Holiday Inn Express, Motel 6, **other:** Rite Aid, Walgreens, Vet
96	Rivergate Pky, **E gas:** Citgo/dsl, Shell, **food:** Dougie Ray's Grill, El Chico, Hooters, Fuji Steaks, HoneyBaked Ham, Las Cibolas Mexican, Las Palmas Mexican, McDonald's, Mrs Winner's, O'Charley's, Pizza Hut, Subway, Waffle House, Wendy's, **lodging:** Best Value Inn, Comfort Suites, Rodeway Inn, Parkway Hotel, **other:** [H], Best One Tires, Cadillac, Dillard's, Goodyear, Macy's, NTB, JC Penney, Sears/auto, mall, E on Gallatin **N food:** Arby's, Bar-B-Cutie, Burger King, Calhoun's Cafe, Cici's Pizza, Checker's, Chick-fil-A, Chili's, ChuckeCheese, Fafari's Rest., Fazoli's, IHOP, Krispy Kreme, LJ Silver/A&W, Logan's Roadhouse, Longhorn Steaks, Hometown Buffet, Olive Garden, Outback Steaks, Panera Bread, Pizza Hut, Popeye's, Rafferty's, Red Lobster, Starbucks, Steak'n Shake, TGI Friday, Taco Bell, **other:** AAA, Best Buy, BooksA-Million, CarMax, Chevrolet, Chrysler/Jeep, CVS Drug, Discount Tire, Firestone, Goodyear/auto, Harley-Davidson, Home Depot, Honda, Jo-Ann's Etc., Lincoln/Mercury, Macy's, Marshall's, Michael's, Nissan, Office Depot, Old Navy, PepBoys, PetsMart, Sam's Club/gas, SuperPetz, Target, TJ Maxx, VW, Walgreens, Walmart/drugs, **W gas:** Chevron, Volunteer
95	TN 386, Vietnam Veterans Blvd (from nb)

INTERSTATE 65 CONT'D

N ↕ S

NASHVILLE

Exit #	Services
92	rd 45, Old Hickory Blvd, **E other:** H, to Old Hickory Dam
90b	TN 155 E, Briley Pkwy, **E** to Opreyland
90a	US 31W, US 41, Dickerson Pike, **E gas:** Exxon, Express/dsl, Shell, **food:** Arby's, Burger King, Capt D's, China King, Domino's, Gyros, Jay's Rest., KFC, Lee's Chicken, McDonald's, Mrs Winner's, Pizza Hut, Subway, Taco Bell, Waffle House, Wendy's, **lodging:** Day's Inn, Econolodge, Sleep Inn, Super 8, **other:** Advance Parts, AutoZone, Camping World RV Supply, CVS Drug, Family$, KOA, Kroger, Walgreens
88b a	I-24, W to Clarksville, E to Nashville
87b a	US 431, Trinity Lane, **E gas:** Citgo, Pilot/Subway/scales/dsl, **food:** Krystal, White Castle, **lodging:** Cumberland Inn, **W gas:** Chevron, Express, Exxon, **food:** Jack-in-the-Box, Jack's BBQ, McDonald's, Subway, Taco Bell, Waffle House, **lodging:** Best Value Inn, Comfort Inn, Day's Inn, Econolodge, Howard Johnson, Liberty Inn, Quality Inn, Travelodge, **other:** Family$, to American Bapt Coll
86	I-24 E, to I-40 E, to Memphis
86mm	Cumberland River
85	US 41A, 8th Ave, **E gas:** Citgo, **other:** tires, to st capitol, **W gas:** Exxon, **food:** Arby's, McDonald's, Pizza Hut, Starbucks, Subway, Taco Bell, Wendy's, **lodging:** Millennium Motel, Springhill Suites, **other:** Cadillac/Honda, Saab
84b a	I-40, E to Knoxville, W to Memphis
209 [I-40]	US 70, Charlotte Ave, Church St, **E food:** McDonald's, **other:** Nissan, **W gas:** Exxon, **food:** Burger King, Krystal, Subway, White Castle, **lodging:** Comfort Inn, **other:** Chevrolet/Pontiac/GMC, Chrysler/Jeep, Firestone, Isuzu/Subaru
82b a	I-40, W to Memphis, E to Nashville
81	Wedgewood Ave, **W gas:** BP, Exxon, Shell, **food:** Burger King, Krystal, McDonald's, Mrs Winner's, **other:** $General, $Tree, Kroger, U-Haul, Walgreens
80	I-440, to Memphis, Knoxville
79	Armory Dr, **E on Powell gas:** Citgo, Shell, **food:** Applebee's, Rafferty's, Subway, Wendy's, **other:** Chiropractor, CarMax, Home Depot, Michael's, Ross, Staples, mall
78b a	rd 255, Harding Place, **E gas:** Express, Marathon, Shell, **food:** Cracker Barrel, Mama Mia's Italian, Sub House, Waffle House, **lodging:** La Quinta, Red Roof Inn, Traveler's Rest Hist Home, **other:** CVS Drug
74	TN 254, Old Hickory Blvd, to Brentwood, **E food:** Capt D's, Coldstone, LongHorn Steaks, Panera Bread, Qdoba Mexican, Shoney's, Waffle House, **lodging:** Best Western, Holiday Inn, Hyatt Place, Steeplechase Inn, **other:** GNC, Target, **W gas:** BP, Exxon, Shell/dsl, **food:** Brentwood Grille, Chick-fil-A, Corky's BBQ, Mazatlan Mexican, McAlister's Deli, McDonald's, Mrs Winner's, O'Charley's, Papa John's, Pizza Hut, Ruby Tuesday, Starbucks, Wendy's, **lodging:** Courtyard, Extended Stay America, Hampton Inn, Hilton Suites, Homestead Suites, Studio+, **other:** Border Books, CVS Drug, Fresh Mkt Foods, Harris-Teeter, Kroger, Office Depot, Rite Aid, SteinMart, TJ Maxx, USPO, Walgreens
71	TN 253, Concord Rd, to Brentwood
69	rd 441, Moores Lane, Galleria Blvd, **E gas:** MapCo/dsl, Shell, **food:** Amerigo's Grill, Cozymel's, Domino's, Outback Steaks, Shogun Japanese, Saltgrass Steaks, Sonic, Starbucks, **lodging:** Hyatt Place, Red Roof Inn, Wingate Inn, **other:** Acura/Lexus, CVS Drug, Home Depot/gas, Michael's, PetsMart, Publix, Walgreens, Vet, **W gas:** BP, Shell/dsl, **food:** Backyard Burger, Buca Italian, Chili's, Famous Dave's, J Alexander's Rest., Logan's Roadhouse, Macaroni Grill, McDonald's, Pizza Hut/Taco Bell, Red Lobster, Schlotsky's, Stoney River Steaks, Subway, **lodging:** Sleep Inn, **other:** Barnes&Noble, Belk, Best Buy, Costco/gas, Dillard's, $Tree, JC Penney, Old Navy, Ross, Sears/auto, Target, Whole Foods Mkt, mall
68b a	Cool Springs Blvd, **E food:** Mexicani Grill, **lodging:** Embassy Suites, Marriott, **W gas:** Exxon, Shell, **food:** A&W, Atl Bread, Baja Fresh, BoneFish Grill, Carrabba's, Chicken Fingers, ChuckeCheese, Genghis Grill, Golden Corral, Jack-in-the-Box, Jason's Deli, KFC, McAlister's Deli, McDonald's, Ming Chinese, Moe's SW Grill, Omikoshi Japanese, Papa John's, PF Chang's, Ruby Tuesday, Starbucks, TGIFriday, Wendy's, **lodging:** Country Inn & Suites, Hampton Inn, **other:** Acura, Borders Books, Harley-Davidson, Harris-Teeter, Home Depot, Jo-Ann Fabrics, Kohl's, Kroger, Lowe's Whse, Marshall's, Office Depot, Sam's Club, Staples, Walgreens, Walmart SuperCtr/24hr, to Galleria Mall
67	McEwen Dr
65	TN 96, to Murfreesboro, Franklin, **E gas:** Mapco, Shell, **food:** Cracker Barrel, Steak'n Shake, **lodging:** Best Value Inn, Comfort Inn, Day's Inn, Holiday Inn Express, La Quinta, **other:** Buick/Pontiac/GMC/Kia, Chevrolet, Food Lion, Honda/Volvo, Walgreens, **W gas:** BP/dsl, Mapco/dsl, Shell/dsl, **food:** Arby's, Backyard Burger, CiCi's, Hardee's, Jack-in-the-Box, KFC, McDonald's, O'Charley's, Papa John's, Pizza Hut, Shoney's, Starbucks, Subway, Taco Bell, Waffle House, Wendy's, **lodging:** Best Western, Quality Inn, **other:** Big Lots, CVS Drug, $General, Ford/Mercury, Home Depot, Kroger, K-Mart, Rite Aid, SteinMart, Toyota, USPO, to Confederate Cem at Franklin, Vet
64mm	Harpeth River
61	TN 248, Peytonsville Rd, to Spring Hill, **E gas:** TA/BP/dsl/rest./scales/24hr/@, **W gas:** Mapco/24hr, Shell/dsl, **other:** Goose Creek Inn/rest.
59b a	TN 840
58mm	W Harpeth River
53	TN 396, Saturn Pkwy, Spring Hill, Columbia, TN Scenic Pkwy
48mm	**truck insp/weigh sta nb, litter barrels**
46	US 412, TN 99, to Columbia, Chapel Hill, **E gas:** Loves/Arbys/dsl/scales/24hr, Texaco/dsl, **W gas:** BP, Citgo/dsl, Horizon/dsl, TJ's/Burger King, **food:** Cracker Barrel, Waffle House, Wendy's, **lodging:** Best Value Inn, Comfort Inn, Hampton Inn, Holiday Inn Express, Relax Inn, **other:** H
40.5mm	Duck River
37	TN 50, to Columbia, Lewisburg, **E other:** H, TN Walking Horse HQ, **W gas:** Shell/dsl, **other:** to Polk Home
32	rd 373, to Lewisburg, Mooresville, **E gas:** Exxon/dsl

NASHVILLE

FRANKLIN

TN

INTERSTATE 65 CONT'D

Exit #	Services
27	rd 129, to Lynnville, Cornersville, **E other:** Texas T Camping
25mm	**parking area sb, litter barrels**
24mm	**parking area nb, litter barrels**
22	US 31A, to Pulaski, **E gas:** Tennesseean Trkst/BP/TN Rest./dsl/rest./scales/24hr/@, **food:** McDonald's, Subway, **lodging:** Econolodge, **W gas:** Pilot/dsl/scales, Shell/dsl/24hr
14	US 64, to Pulaski, **E gas:** BP/dsl, Shell/dsl, **food:** Sarge's Shack Rest., **lodging:** Super 8, **other:** TN Valley RV Park, to Jack Daniels Distillery, **W** [H], to David Crockett SP
6	rd 273, Bryson, **E gas:** Phillips 66/dsl/rest., **lodging:** Best Value Inn, **other:** dsl repair, **W gas:** Marathon (2mi)
4mm	Elk River
3mm	**Welcome Ctr nb, full [handicapped] facilities, info, [phone], [picnic], litter barrels, petwalk**
1	US 31, rd 7, Ardmore, **E gas:** Chevron/dsl/24hr, Exxon/Chicken Express/dsl, **1-2 mi E gas:** Shell/repair, **food:** DQ, Hardee's, McDonald's, Subway
0mm	Tennessee/Alabama state line

INTERSTATE 75

Exit #	Services
161.5mm	Tennessee/Kentucky state line
161mm	**Welcome Ctr sb, full [handicapped] facilities, [phone], vending, [picnic], litter barrels, petwalk**
160	US 25W, Jellico, **E gas:** BP, Exxon/dsl, Marathon/dsl, **lodging:** Jellico Motel, **W gas:** BP/Wendy's, Shell/Arby's/dsl, **food:** Hardee's, Heritage Pizza, Subway, **lodging:** Best Value Inn, Days Inn/rest., **other:** [H], camping, fireworks, to Indian Mtn SP
156	Rarity Mtn Rd
144	Stinking Creek Rd, **4 mi E gas:** Ride Royal Blue Camping
141	TN 63, to Royal Blue, Huntsville, **E gas:** Shell/Stuckey's/24hr, **W gas:** Pilot/Subway/dsl/scales/24hr, Shell/Stuckey's/dsl, **lodging:** Comfort Inn, **other:** fireworks, repair/truckwash, to Big South Fork NRA
134	US 25W, TN 63, Caryville, **E gas:** Exxon/dsl, Shell/24hr, **food:** Takumi Japanese, Waffle House/24hr, **lodging:** Econolodge, Hampton Inn, Super 8, **other:** [H], to Cove Lake SP, Cumberland Gap NHP, **W gas:** BP/dsl, **food:** Shoney's, Scotty's Hamburgers, **lodging:** Budget Host, **other:** USPO
129	US 25W S, Lake City, **W gas:** BP/Sonic, Exxon/Subway/dsl/24hr, Mobil, Shell/dsl, **food:** Cracker Barrel, KFC/Taco Bell, La Fiesta Mexican, McDonald's, **lodging:** Days Inn, Blue Haven Motel, Lamb's Inn/rest., Scottish Inn, **other:** $General, fireworks, same as 128
128	US 441, to Lake City, **E gas:** BP, Sunoco, **other:** Mountain Lake Marina (4mi), **W gas:** Exxon/dsl/24hr, Shell, **food:** Cottage Rest., **other:** Advance Parts, $General, antique cars, to Norris Dam SP, same as 129
126mm	Clinch River
122	TN 61, Bethel, Norris, **E gas:** Shell, Wiegel's, **food:** Shoney's, **other:** Fox Inn Camping, Suzuki, Toyota, antiques, museum, **W gas:** BP, Exxon/Burger King/

BETHEL

Exit #	Services
122	Continued Subway/dsl/24hr, Git'n Go, Phillips 66, Shell, **food:** Arby's, Golden Girls Rest., Hardee's, Harrison's Grill, Krystal/24hr, McDonald's, Starbucks, Waffle House, Wendy's, Zaxby's, **lodging:** Comfort Inn, Country Inn&Suites, Holiday Inn Express, Red Roof Inn, Super 8, Travelodge, **other:** Ford, Walgreens, Walmart SuperCtr, Big Pine Ridge SP
117	TN 170, Racoon Valley Rd, **E gas:** Pilot/dsl/scales/24hr, **other:** Quarterhorse RV Park, **W lodging:** Valley Inn/camping, **other:** Escapee's RV Park
112	TN 131, Emory Rd, to Powell, **E gas:** BP/Buddy's BBQ/dsl, Pilot/DQ/Taco Bell/dsl/24hr, **food:** Arby's, Aubrey's Rest., Firehouse Subs, 5 Guys Burgers, McDonald's, Krystal, Ruby Tuesday, Starbucks, Steak'n Shake, Subway, Wendy's, Zaxby's, **lodging:** Comfort Inn, Country Inn&Suites, Holiday Inn Express, **other:** [H], CVS Drug, Family$, Ingles/gas, O'Reilly Parts, **W gas:** Exxon/dsl/24hr, Shell/dsl/24hr, Weigel's/dsl, **food:** Hardee's, Shoney's, Waffle House/24hr, **lodging:** Super 8

KNOXVILLE

Exit #	Services
110	Callahan Dr, **E gas:** Weigel's, **lodging:** Knight's Inn, Quality Inn/rest., **other:** Honda, **W gas:** BP, **lodging:** Scottish Inn, **other:** GMC/Mack/Volvo
108	Merchants Dr, **E gas:** BP/dsl, Citgo/dsl, Pilot/dsl, Shell/dsl, **food:** Applebee's, Cracker Barrel, El Chico's, Hooters, Monterrey Mexican, O'Charley's, Pizza Hut, Starbucks, Sonic, Puelo's Grill, Ramsey's Rest., Sonic, Waffle House, Wok Hay Asian, **lodging:** Best Western, Comfort Suites, Days Inn, Hampton Inn, Highway Host, Mainstay Suites, Quality Inn, Red Roof Inn, Sleep Inn, **other:** Ingles, Valvoline, **W gas:** Conoco, Exxon/Godfather's/dsl, Pilot, **food:** Baskin-Robbins, Burger King, Capt D's, Great American Steaks, IHOP, Mandarin House, McDonald's, Outback Steaks, Quaker Steak, Red Lobster, Subway, **lodging:** Best Value Inn, Clarion Inn, Econolodge, Motel 6, Super 8, **other:** Walgreens
107	I-640 & I-75
3b [I-640]	US 25W, (from nb), **W other:** Chevrolet, Dodge, Ford, Nissan
1 [I-640]	TN 62, Western Ave, **E food:** Hardee's, Krystal, **other:** Advance Parts, O'Reilly Parts, **W gas:** Exxon/dsl, Marathon, Raceway, **food:** Central Park, KFC, Little Caesars, LJ Silver, McDonald's, Panda Chinese, Shoney's, Sonic, Subway, Taco Bell, Wendy's, **other:** CVS Drug, Kroger, Walgreens
	I-75 and I-40 run together 17 mi. See Interstate 40 exits 369 through 385.
84 b a [368]	I-40, W to Nashville, E to Knoxville

N ↕ S

SWEETWATER

ATHENS

INTERSTATE 75 CONT'D

Exit #	Services
81	US 321, TN 95, to Lenoir City, **E gas:** BP/Buddy's BBQ/TCBY/dsl, Exxon/Subway/dsl, Mobil, Murphy USA, Shell/dsl, Texaco/dsl, **food:** Angelo's Brick Oven, Aubrey's Rest., Bojangles, Burger King, Capt D's, Chili's, China Buffet, Cracker Barrel, Dinner Bell Rest., KFC, McDonald's, Monterrey Mexican, Panda Buffet, Quizno's, Shoney's, Tokyo Express, Waffle House, Zaxby's, **lodging:** Days Inn, Hampton Inn, Holiday Inn Express, King's Inn/rest., **other:** AutoZone, $Tree, Food City/gas, Home Depot, Lazy Acres RV Park (6mi), Radio Shack, Walmart SuperCtr/Subway/24hr, Great Smokies NP, Ft Loudon Dam, **W gas:** Citgo/dsl, Shell/dsl, **food:** Krystal, Ruby Tuesday, **lodging:** Comfort Inn, Econolodge, Ramada Ltd, **other:** Crosseyed Cricket Camping (6mi), Matlock Tires/Repair
76	rd 324, Sugar Limb Rd, **W** to TN Valley Winery
74mm	Tennessee River
72	TN 72, to Loudon, **E gas:** BP/McDonald's, Shell/Wendy's, **food:** KFC, Log Cabin BBQ, Taco Bell, **lodging:** Country Inn&Suites, Super 8, **other:** Weigel's, to Ft Loudon SP, **W gas:** Citgo, **lodging:** Best Value Inn, **other:** Express RV Park
68	rd 323, to Philadelphia, **E gas:** BP/dsl, Sunoco (2mi), **food:** cheese factory/store (2mi)
62	rd 322, Oakland Rd, to Sweetwater, **E food:** Dinner Bell Rest., **W other:** KOA
60	TN 68, Sweetwater, **E gas:** BP, RaceWay, Shell/dsl, **food:** A&W/LJ Silver, Bradley's BBQ, Burger King, Hardees, McDonald's, Subway, Taco Bell, **lodging:** Comfort Inn, Day's Inn, Economy Inn, Hilltop Motel, Knights Inn, **other:** [H], Advance Parts, O'Reilly Parts, $General, Ford, to Lost Sea Underground Lake, **W gas:** BP/dsl, Marathon, Kangaroo/dsl, **food:** Sweetwater Steaks, **lodging:** Magnuson Hotel, Quality Inn, **other:** flea mkt, to Watts Bar Dam, tires/repair
56	rd 309, Niota, **E gas:** BP/dsl/rest./scales/24hr/@, **other:** TN Country Camping, **W** tires
52	rd 305, Mt Verd Rd, to Athens, **E gas:** Marathon (2mi), **food:** Subway (2mi), **other:** Overniter RV Park, **W gas:** BP, **lodging:** Travelodge
49	TN 30, to Athens, **E gas:** BP, Marathon, Murphy USA, Kangaroo, RaceWay, Shell/dsl/24hr, **food:** Applebee's, Buddy's BBQ, Burger King, Capt. D's, China Wok, Hardee's, Hibachi Express, KFC, Krystal, Ruby Tuesday, Shoney's, Subway, Waffle House, Wendy's, Western Sizzlin, **lodging:** Day's Inn, Econolodge, Hampton Inn, Holiday Inn Express, Homestead Inn, Motel 6, Super 8, **other:** [H], Athens I-75 Camping, Russell Stover, Wal-Mart SuperCtr, to TN Wesleyan Coll, **W gas:** Shell, **food:** Cracker Barrel, **lodging:** Comfort Inn, Homestead Inn
45mm	**rest areas, both lanes, full [handicapped] facilities, [picnic], litter barrels, [phone]**
42	TN 39, Riceville RD, **E gas:** Citgo/dsl, **lodging:** Relax Inn, Rice Inn (2mi)
36	TN 163, to Calhoun, **E food:** Hardee's (3mi), **other:** Hiwassee/Ocoee River SP
35mm	Hiwassee River
33	rd 308, to Charleston, **E** 33 Camping, gas, **W gas:** Love's/McDonald's/Subway/dsl/scales/24hr, Shell/dsl/rest./24hr

CLEVELAND

Exit #	Services
27	Paul Huff Pkwy, **1 mi E gas:** Murphy USA, Phillips 66, **food:** Applebee's, Capt D's, Chick-fil-A, Chili's, CiCi's, DQ, Fazoli's, Five Guys Burgers, Golden Corral, IHOP, Logan's Roadhouse, McDonald's, O'Charley's, Outback Steaks, Panera Bread, Quizno's, Ryan's, Sonic, Steak'n Shake/24hr, Subway, Taco Bell, **lodging:** Jameson Inn, **other:** AutoZone, Belk, Buick/Pontiac/GMC, CVS Drug, $Tree, Food Lion, Goodyear/auto, Hobby Lobby, Home Depot, JC Penney, K-Mart, Lowe's Whse, PetCo, Rite Aid, Sears, Staples, TJ Maxx, Walgreens, Walmart SuperCtr, auto repair, mall, **W gas:** Exxon, Shell/Subway, Texaco/dsl, **food:** Denny's/24hr, Hardee's, Shane's Ribshack, Stevi B's Pizza, Waffle House, Wendy's, **lodging:** Classic Suites, Hampton Inn, Quality Inn, Ramada Ltd, Royal Inn, Super 8, **other:** BooksAmillion, Kohls, Ross, Target
25	TN 60, Cleveland, **E gas:** Chevron, RaceWay, Shell/dsl, Texaco, **food:** Bojangle's, Burger King, Capt. D's, Cracker Barrel, Hardee's, McDonald's, Old Fort Rest., Schlotsky's, Sonic, Waffle House, Zaxby's, **lodging:** Best Inn, Colonial Inn, Day's Inn, Douglas Inn, Fairfield Inn, Howard Johnson, Knight's Inn, Travel Inn, **other:** [H], Ace Hardware, Rite Aid, to Lee Coll, **W gas:** Shell, **lodging:** Baymont Inn, Holiday Inn, Wingate Inn
23mm	**truck/weigh sta nb**
20	US 64 byp, to Cleveland, **1-4 mi E gas:** FuelMart, **other:** Ford, Honda, **W gas:** Cruise-in/DQ/Pizza Hut/dsl/24hr, Exxon/dsl/24hr, **other:** KOA (1mi), Toyota/Scion, fireworks
16mm	scenic view sb
13mm	**truck/weigh sta, litter barrels sb**
11	US 11 N, US 64 E, Ooltewah, **E gas:** BP, RaceWay, Shell, **food:** Arby's, Bojangles, Burger King, Cracker Barrel, Capt D's, China Rose, El Matador Mexican, Hardee's, McDonald's, Subway, Taco Bell, Wendy's, Zaxby's, **lodging:** Hampton Inn Express, Holiday Inn, **other:** BiLo, Curves, O'Reilly Parts, Walgreens, Walmart SuperCtr/24hr, **W gas:** BP/Quizno's/dsl, **food:** Krystal, **lodging:** Super 8, **other:** Publix, to Harrison Bay SP
9	no services
7b a	US 11, US 64, Lee Hwy, **E gas:** Exxon/dls, **W gas:** Shell, **food:** City Cafe, Waffle House, **lodging:** Best Inn, Best Value Inn, Best Western, Comfort Inn, Econolodge, Motel 6, **other:** Harley-Davidson, Jaguar/Land Rover/Porsche, repair
5	Shallowford Rd, **E food:** Alexander's, Arby's, Capt. D's, Chili's, Chophouse Rest., CiCi's, Country Place Rest., DQ, Famous Dave's, J. Alexanders, Krystal, Logan's Roadhouse, Macaroni Grill, McAlister's Deli, McDonald's/playplace, Outback Steaks, Smokey Bones BBQ, Starbucks, Steak'n Shake/24hr, Souper Salad, Taco Bell, Zaxby's, **lodging:** Courtyard, Quality Inn, Wingate Inn, **other:** Barnes&Noble, Best Buy, BooksAMillion, Firestone/auto, Ford, FreshMkt Foods, Hobby Lobby, Home Depot, Lowe's Whse, Office Depot, Old Navy, PetsMart, SteinMart, Target, Walgreens, Walmart SuperCtr/24hr, World Mkt, **W gas:** BP, Citgo/dsl, Exxon, Shell, **food:** Applebee's, Blimpie, Cracker Barrel, Fazoli's, GlenGene Deli, O'Charley's, Papa John's, Shoney's, Sonic, Subway, TX Roadhouse, Waffle House, Wendy's, **lodging:** Clarion, Comfort Inn,

TN

INTERSTATE 75 CONT'D

N ↕ S CHATANOOGA

Exit #	Services
5	Continued Country Inn&Suites, Fairfield Inn, Guesthouse Inn, Hampton Inn, Hilton Garden, Homewood Suites, Knights Inn, La Quinta, MainStay Suites, Microtel, Ramada Ltd, Red Roof Inn, Residence Inn, Sleep Inn, Staybridge Suites, Super 8, **other:** H, Bi~Lo, CVS Drug, Goodyear/auto, U of TN/Chatt, same as 4a
4a	(from nb) Hamilton Place Blvd, **E food:** Abuelo's, Acropolis, Big River Grille, BoneFish Grill, Carraba's, DQ, El Mason, Firehouse Subs, Five Guys Burgers, Fox&Hound Grill, Golden Corral, Jason's Deli, Moe's SW Grill, Olive Garden, Outback Steaks, Panera Bread, PF Chang's, Piccadilly's, Red Lobster, Ruby Tuesday, Salsarita's Mexican, Shogun Japanese, Starbucks, Sticky Fingers BBQ, Kampai Of Tokyo, **lodging:** InTown Suites, **other:** AAA, Belk, Dillard's, Firestone, JC Penney, Kohl's, Marshall's, Michael's, Ross, Sears/auto, Staples, Target, TJ Maxx, mall, same as 5
4	TN 153, Chickamauga Dam Rd
3b a	TN 320, Brainerd Rd, **E gas:** BP, **food:** Baskin-Robbins, Subway, **W other:** BMW
2	I-24 W, to I-59, to Chattanooga, Lookout Mtn
1.5mm	**Welcome Ctr nb, full facilities, , vending, , litter barrels, petwalk**
1b a	US 41, Ringgold Rd, to Chattanooga, **E gas:** BP, Texaco/dsl, **food:** Wendy's, **lodging:** Best Value Inn, Comfort Inn, Country Hearth Inn, Crown Inn, Knights Inn, Motel 6, Ramada Ltd, **other:** Bi~Lo Foods, Camping World RV Ctr/park, Family$, **W gas:** Conoco/dsl, Mapco, **food:** A&W/LJ Silver, Arby's, Baskin-Robbins, Burger King, Central Park Burger, Cracker Barrel, Hardee's, Krystal, McDonald's, PortoFino Italian, Shoney's, Subway, Taco Bell, Teriyaki House, Uncle Bud's Catfish, Waffle House, Wally's Rest., **lodging:** Day's Inn, Fairfield Inn, Holiday Inn Express, Super 8, Superior Creek Lodge, Waverly Motel, **other:** Holiday Travel Park, O'Reilly Parts, U-Haul
0mm	Tennessee/Georgia state line

INTERSTATE 81

N ↕ S

Exit #	Services
75mm	Tennessee/Virginia state line, **Welcome Ctr sb, full facilities, info, , vending, , litter barrels, petwalk**
74b a	US 11W, to Bristol, Kingsport, **E lodging:** Day's Inn, Hampton Inn, **other:** H, **W gas:** Valero, **lodging:** Best Western, Bristol Inn
69	TN 394, to Blountville, **E gas:** BP/Subway/dsl, **food:** Arby's, Burger King (1mi), McDonald's, **other:** Advance Parts, Bristol Int Speedway, Lakeview RV Park (8mi)
66	TN 126, to Kingsport, Blountville, **E gas:** BP/dsl, **W gas:** Chevron/24hr, **food:** McDonald's, **other:** Carolina Pottery
63	rd 357, Tri-City ✈, **E gas:** BP/Taco Bell/Krystal/dsl, Shell/Subway/dsl/24hr, **food:** Cracker Barrel, Wendy's, **lodging:** La Quinta, Sleep Inn, **W gas:** Citgo/dsl, **lodging:** Red Carpet Inn, **other:** KOA, Rocky Top Camping
60mm	Holston River

JOHNSON CITY

Exit #	Services
59	rd 36, to Johnson City, Kingsport, **E gas:** Citgo/dsl, **lodging:** Super 8, **W gas:** BP/LP, Shell/dsl, Sunoco, Zoomerz, **food:** Arby's, Domino's, Hardee's, HotDog Hut, La Carreta Mexican, Little Caesar's, McDonald's, Pal's Drive-Thru, Perkins, Pizza Hut, Sonic, Steak House, Subway, The Shack BBQ, **lodging:** Best Western, Comfort Inn, **other:** Advance Parts, CVS Drug, $General, $Tree, Firestone/auto, Food City/gas, Ingles/deli, Walgreens, USPO, to Warrior's Path SP
57b a	I-26
56	Tri-Cities Crossing
50	TN 93, Fall Branch, **W other:** auto auction, st patrol
44	Jearoldstown Rd, **E gas:** Marathon
41mm	**rest area sb, full facilities, , vending, , litter barrels, petwalk**
38mm	**rest area nb, full facilities, , vending, , litter barrels, petwalk**
36	rd 172, to Baileyton, **E gas:** Pilot/Subway/dsl/scales, **W gas:** BP/dsl/24hr, Shell/Subway/dsl/24hr, TA/Country Pride/dsl/scales/24hr/@, **food:** Pizza+, **lodging:** 36 Motel, **other:** Baileyton Camp (2mi), Family$
30	TN 70, to Greeneville, **E gas:** Exxon/DQ/Stuckey's/dsl
23	US 11E, to Greeneville, **E gas:** BP/Wendy's, Mobil/Subway, **other:** to Andrew Johnson HS, Crockett SP, **W gas:** Exxon/dsl, Phillips 66/dsl/rest./scales, **food:** McDonald's, Taco Bell, Tony's BBQ, **lodging:** Best Western, Super 8
21mm	**weigh sta sb**
15	rd 340, Fish Hatchery Rd
12	TN 160, to Morristown, **E gas:** Phillips 66, **W gas:** Shell/dsl, **lodging:** Days Inn (6mi), Hampton Inn (12mi), Motel 6 (6mi), **other:** to Crockett Tavern HS
8	US 25E, to Morristown, **E gas:** Shell/dsl/repair, **food:** Sonic (2mi), **lodging:** Twin Pines Motel (3mi), **W gas:** BP/dsl, **food:** Cracker Barrel, Hardee's, **lodging:** Holiday Inn/rest., Parkway Inn, Super 8, **other:** to Cumberland Gap NHP
4	rd 341, White Pine, **E gas:** Pilot/McDonald's/dsl/scales/24hr/@, **lodging:** Crown Inn, **W gas:** Wilco/Hess/Wendy's/dsl/scales/24hr/@, **food:** Huddle House/24hr, **lodging:** Day's Inn, **other:** to Panther Cr SP
2.5mm	**rest area sb, full facilities, , , litter barrels, vending, petwalk**
1b a	I-40, E to Asheville, W to Knoxville. **I-81 begins/ends on I-40, exit 421.**

INTERSTATE 640 (KNOXVILLE)

E ↕ W

Exit #	Services
9mm	**I-640 begins/ends on I-40, exit 393.**
8	Millertown Pike, Mall rd N, **N gas:** Exxon/DQ/24hr, Shell, **food:** Applebee's, Burger King, Don Pablos, Gunthor's, KFC, Krystal, McDonald's, Pizza Hut, Taco Bell, TX Roadhouse, Wendy's, **other:** Belk, $General, Food City, JC Penney, Kohl's, Marshall's, NTB, Old Navy, Ross, Sam's Club, Sears/auto, Target, Walmart SuperCtr, mall, **S gas:** Shell, **food:** Cracker Barrel, Little Caesars, O'Charley's, Subway, **other:** Food Lion, Home Depot, Lowe's Whse, PepBoys
6	US 441, to Broadway, **N gas:** Citgo, Phillips 66, Pilot/dsl, Shell, **food:** Arby's, Austin's Steaks, Cancun Mexican, Chop House, CiCi's, Fazoli's, Hardee's, Krispy Kreme, Lenny's Subs, LJ Silver, Marble Slab,

KNOXVILLE

6	Continued McDonald's, Panera Bread, Papa John's, Ruby Tuesday, Sonic, Subway, Taco Bell, **other:** Advance Parts, AutoZone, BigLots, CVS Drug, $General, Firestone, Food City/gas, Kroger/24hr, Walgreens, repair/tires, **S food:** Buddy's BBQ, Little Caesars, Shoney's, **other:** $General, Food City, K-Mart, Office Depot
3a	I-75 N to Lexington, I-275 S to Knoxville
3b	US 25W, Clinton Hwy, (from eb), **N other:** Chevrolet, Dodge, Ford, Nissan, services on frontage rds
1	TN 62, Western Ave, **N gas:** Exxon/dsl, Marathon, Raceway, **food:** Central Park, KFC, Little Caesars, LJ Silver, McDonald's, Panda Chinese, Shoney's, Sonic, Subway, Taco Bell, Wendy's, **other:** CVS Drug, Kroger, Walgreens, **S food:** Hardee's, Krystal, **other:** Advance Parts, O'Reilly Parts,
0mm	I-640 begins/ends on I-40, exit 385.

TEXAS

INTERSTATE 10

E ↕ W

Exit #	Services
880.5mm	Texas/Louisiana state line, Sabine River
880	Sabine River Turnaround, RV camping
879mm	**Welcome Ctr wb, full [handicapped] facilities, [phone], [picnic], litter barrels, vending, petwalk**
878	US 90, Orange, **N gas:** Mobil/dsl, **other:** airboat rides, RV Park, **S other:** Western Store
877	TX 87, 16th St, Orange, **N gas:** Exxon/dsl, Shamrock/dsl, **food:** Pizza Hut, Subway, **lodging:** Hampton Inn, **other:** Ace Hardware, $General, Market Basket/deli, **S gas:** Exxon, Shell/dsl, Valero/dsl, **food:** Casa Ole, Church's, DQ, General Wok, Jack-in-the-Box, McDonald's, Popeye's, Senor Toro's, Sonic, Taco Bell, **other:** CVS Drug, HEB Foods, Kroger/gas, Modica Tires, O'Reilly Parts, Walgreens
876	Adams Bayou, frontage rd, Adams Bayou, **N food:** Gary's Café, Waffle House, **lodging:** Best Value Inn, Days Inn, Econolodge, Executive Inn, Motel 6, Ramada Inn, Super 8, **other:** Pontiac/Buick/GMC, Toyota, **S gas:** Chevron/dsl, **lodging:** Holiday Inn Express, same as 877
875	FM 3247, MLK Dr, **S other:** [H], Chrysler/Dodge/Jeep
874	US 90, Womack Rd, to Orange, **S** [H]
873	TX 62, TX 73, to Bridge City, **N gas:** Exxon/dsl/24hr, *FLYING J*/Conoco/Cookery/dsl/LP/scales/24hr, **other:** RV Park, **S gas:** Pilot/Subway/Wendy's/dsl/scales/24hr, Shell/Church's/dsl, Valero, **food:** Jack-in-the-Box, McDonald's, Sonic, Waffle House, Whataburger, lodging Comfort Inn, La Quinta, Sleep Inn
872	frontage rd, from wb
870	FM 1136
869	FM 1442, to Bridge City, **S gas:** Chevron, **other:** Lloyd's RV Ctr
868.5mm	**rest areas both lanes, full [handicapped] facilities, vending, [picnic], litter barrels**
867	frontage rd (from eb)
865	Doty Rd (from wb), frontage rd
864	FM 1132, FM 1135, **N lodging:** Budget Inn
862c	Timberlane Dr (from eb)

ORANGE

862b	Old Hwy (from wb)
862a	Railroad Ave
861d	TX 12, Deweyville
861c	Denver St, **N gas:** Conoco/dsl
861b	Lamar St (from wb), **N gas:** Conoco/dsl
861a	FM 105, Vidor, **N gas:** Chevron/dsl, Conoco/dsl, Shell, Valero, **food:** Casa Ole, Church's, DQ, Domino's, Jack-in-the-Box, McDonald's/playplace, Ming's Buffet, Navrozky's, Popeye's, Senor Toro, Waffle House, **other:** Ace Hardware, AutoZone, Brookshire Bro.s Foods, Curves, CVS Drug, $General, Mktbasket Foods, O'Reilly Parts, Radio Shack, Walgreens, Walmart, **S gas:** Exxon/dsl, Texaco, **food:** Burger King, Pizza Hut, Sonic, Subway, Taco Bell, Whataburger, **lodging:** Holiday Inn, La Quinta, **other:** Family$, auto repair, tires
860b a	Dewitt Rd, frontage rd, W Vidor
859	Bonner Turnaround (from eb), Asher Turnaround (from wb), **N other:** Boomtown RV Park, **S gas:** Chevron/dsl/24hr
858	Rose City
856	Old Hwy 90 (from eb), Rose City
855b	Magnolia St (from wb)
855a	US 90 bus, to downtown, Port of Beaumont
854	ML King Pkwy, Beaumont, **N gas:** Conoco, **food:** Texas Brotha's, **S gas:** Exxon, Shamrock/dsl, **food:** McDonald's
853b	11th St, **N food:** Cafe Del Rio, Red Lobster, Waffle House, **lodging:** Best Value Inn, Days Inn, Holiday Inn, Motel 6, Sleep Inn, Studio 6, Super 8, Travel Inn, **other:** MktBasket, **S gas:** Texaco/dsl, Fina/dsl, **food:** Checker's, Chula Vista Mexican, Dunkin Donuts, Luby's, **lodging:** Howard Johnson Express, Rodeway Inn, **other:** [H]
853a	US 69 N, to Lufkin
852	Harrison Ave, Calder Ave, Beaumont, **N gas:** Shell/dsl, Valero, **food:** Casa Ole Mexican, Chili's, Frankie's Italian, Olive Garden, Willie Ray's BBQ, **S food:** Church's, McDonald's, **lodging:** Econolodge, La Quinta, **other:** [H]
851	US 90, College St, **N gas:** Exxon/dsl, RaceWay, **food:** Acapulco Mexican, Carrabba's, Floyd's Cajun Cafe,

VIDOR

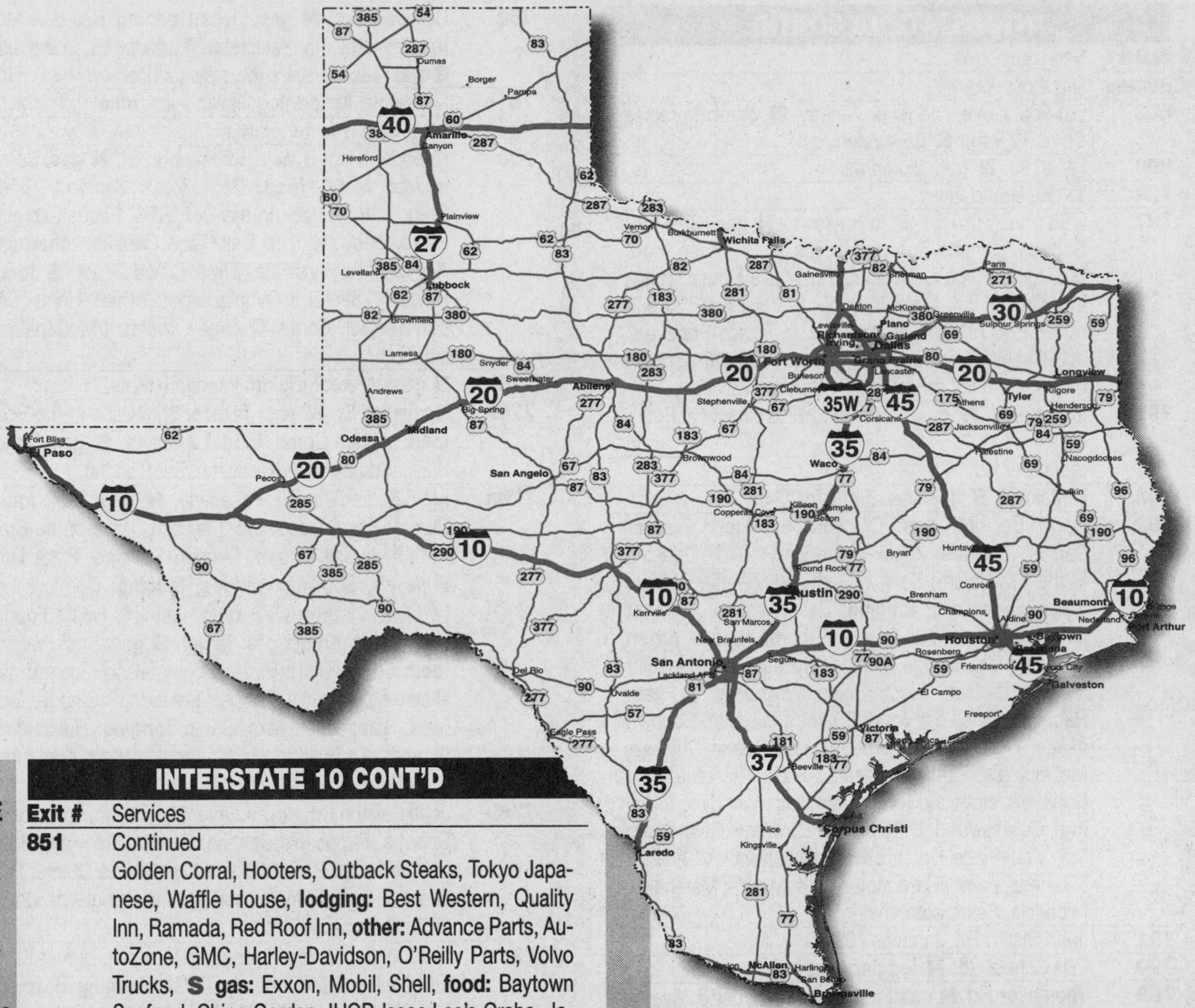

INTERSTATE 10 CONT'D

E ↕ W

BEAUMONT

Exit #	Services
851	Continued Golden Corral, Hooters, Outback Steaks, Tokyo Japanese, Waffle House, **lodging:** Best Western, Quality Inn, Ramada, Red Roof Inn, **other:** Advance Parts, AutoZone, GMC, Harley-Davidson, O'Reilly Parts, Volvo Trucks, **S gas:** Exxon, Mobil, Shell, **food:** Baytown Seafood, China Garden, IHOP, Issac Lee's Crabs, Jason's Deli, KFC, Pizza Hut, Quizno's, Sonic, Taco Bell, Wendy's, Whataburger, **lodging:** Courtyard, Economy Inn, Elegante Motel, Fairfield Inn, Motel 6, ValuePlace Hotel, **other:** [H], BMW, Chrysler/Jeep, CVS Drug, Discount Tire, Dodge, $Tree, Firestone/auto, GMC/Cadillac, HEB Foods, Honda, Jeep, Mercedes, Nissan, NTB, Office Depot, Radio Shack, Sam's Club/gas, U-Haul, Walgreens
850	wb only, same as 851
849	US 69 S, Washington Blvd, to Port Arthur, [airport]
848	Walden Rd, **N gas:** Shell, **food:** Pappadeaux Seafood, Sonic, **lodging:** Comfort Suites, Holiday Inn/rest., La Quinta, **other:** USPO, **S gas:** Petro/Mobil/dsl/scales/24hr/@, Shell, **food:** Carino's Italian, Cheddar's, Cracker Barrel, Jack-in-the-Box, Joe's Crabshack, Waffle House, **lodging:** Candlewood Suites, Courtyard, Hampton Inn, Homewood Suites, Hilton Garden, Knight's Inn, Residence Inn, Super 8, **other:** Blue Beacon
847	Brooks Rd (from wb), (845 from eb), **S other:** Gulf Coast RV Resort
843	Smith Rd
838	FM 365, Fannett, **N food:** Alligator Park/Rest., Bar-H BBQ, **other:** T&T RV Park
837.5mm	**[picnic] both lanes, litter barrels, [accessible] accessible**
833	Hamshire Rd

WINNIE

Exit #	Services
829	FM 1663, Winnie, **N gas:** Exxon/dsl, Shell/dsl/24hr, Texaco/Burger King/dsl, **food:** McDonald's, Taco Bell, Whataburger/24hr, **lodging:** Days Inn, **other:** RV Park, **S gas:** Chevron/Chester's/dsl, **food:** Al-T Seafood, Hunan Chinese, Jack-in-the-Box, Pizza Inn, Waffle House, **lodging:** Comfort Inn, Holiday Inn Express, La Quinta, Motel 6, Quality Inn, Winnie Inn/RV Park, **other:** [H], Chevrolet/Dodge, Ford
828	TX 73, TX 124 (from eb), to Winnie, **S** [H], same as 829
827	FM 1406
822	FM 1410
819	Jenkins Rd
817	FM 1724
815mm	**check sta both lanes**
813	TX 61 (from wb), Hankamer, **N gas:** Shell/dsl, **lodging:** Days Inn, **S gas:** Exxon/DJ's Diner/dsl, **food:** McDonald's, same as 812
812	TX 61, Hankamer
811	Turtle Bayou Turnaround, **S gas:** Gator Jct/dsl, **other:** Ford, Turtle Bayou RV Park
810	FM 563, to Anahuac, Liberty, **S gas:** Chevron/Blimpie/dsl, Shell/Jack-in-the-Box/dsl, **other:** Ford
807	to Wallisville, **S other:** Heritage Park
806	frontage rd (from eb), turnaround
805.5mm	Trinity River

INTERSTATE 10 CONT'D

E ↕ W

BAYTOWN

Exit #	Services
804mm	Old, Lost Rivers
803	FM 565, Cove, Old River-Winfrey, **N other:** Paradise Cove RV Park, **S gas:** Valero/dsl
800	FM 3180, **N gas:** Exxon/dsl
799	TX 99, Grand Pkwy
797	(798 from wb) TX 146, to Baytown, **N gas:** Chevron/Subway, Conoco/Subway/dsl/scales, Shell/dsl, **food:** DQ, Iguana Joe's, McDonald's, Waffle House, **lodging:** Crystal Inn, Motel 6, Super 8, Value Inn/RV Park, **other:** L&R RV Park, **S gas:** Exxon, Texaco/Popeye's/dsl, RaceWay/dsl, **food:** Baytown Seafood, Jack-in-the-Box, Sonic, **other:** H, RV Service, Vet
796	frontage rd, **N gas:** Chevron/Phillips/Chemical Refinery
795	Sjolander Rd
793	N Main St, **S gas:** Valero/KFC/dsl/24hr
792	Garth Rd, **N gas:** Chevron/24hr, **food:** Cracker Barrel, Denny's, Jack-in-the-Box, Red Lobster, Richard's Cajun, Sonic, Starbucks, Waffle House, Whataburger/24hr, **lodging:** Best Western, Comfort Inn, Hampton Inn, La Quinta, Suburban Lodge, **other:** Chrysler/Jeep/Dodge, Honda, Hyundai, Kia, Lincoln/Mercury, Nissan, Toyota/Scion, Walgreens, **S gas:** RaceWay, Shell/dsl, **food:** Bravos's Mexican, Carino's Italian, Chili's, Chinese Buffet, Lee Palace Chinese, McDonald's, Outback Steaks, Pizza Hut/Taco Bell, Popeye's, Subway, Tortuga Mexican, Wendy's, **lodging:** Candlewood Suites, HomeTowne Suites, Sleep Inn, ValuePlace Hotel, **other:** H, Chevrolet/Cadillac, $General, Ford, JC Penney, Kohl's, Macy's, Marshall's, Micheals, Sears/auto, mall
791	John Martin Rd, same as 792
790	Ellis School Rd, **N lodging:** Super 8
789	Thompson Rd, **N gas:** Pilot/McDonald's/dsl/@, Valero/dsl, **other:** Buick/Pontiac/GMC, **S gas:** ***FLYING J*** /CountryMkt/dsl/LP/scales/RV dump/24hr, TA/SpeedCo Lube/dsl/rest./24hr/scales/@, **other:** Blue Beacon, truck repair/lube
788.5mm	**rest area eb, full ♿ facilities, ☎, picnic, litter barrels, petwalk**
788	sp 330 (from eb), to Baytown
787	sp 330, Crosby-Lynchburg Rd, to Highlands, **N gas:** Texaco/Domino's/dsl, **food:** Jack-in-the-Box (2mi) Subway (1mi), Village Pizza (1mi), **other:** RV Camping (1mi), **S gas:** JR's/dsl, **food:** Four Corners BBQ, **other:** to San Jacinto SP, camping
786.5mm	San Jacinto River
786	Monmouth Dr
785	Magnolia Ave, to Channelview, **N gas:** Shell/dsl, **S gas:** Exxon/dsl, same as 784
784	Cedar Lane, Bayou Dr, **N gas:** Valero/dsl, **lodging:** Budget Lodge, Knight's Inn
783	Sheldon Rd, **N gas:** Shell, Texaco/dsl, Valero, **food:** Burger King, Church's, General Wok, Jack-in-the-Box, Pizza Hut, Pizza Inn, Popeye's, Subway, Taco Bell, Whataburger, **lodging:** Best Value, Day's Inn, Economy Inn, Leisure Inn, Travelers Inn, **other:** Advance Parts, AutoZone, Discount Tire, Family$, FoodFair, USPO, **S gas:** Chevron/Quizno's, **food:** Hilda's Mexican, McDonald's, Wendy's, **lodging:** Holiday Inn Express, Scottish Inn

HOUSTON

Exit #	Services
782	Dell-Dale Ave, **N gas:** Exxon, **lodging:** Dell-Dale Motel, Economy Inn, Palace Inn, Parkway Inn, **other:** H, **S gas:** Texaco/dsl, **other:** RV service
781b	Market St, **N lodging:** Holiday Inn, **other:** H
781a	TX 8, Sam Houston Pkwy
780	(779a from wb) Uvalde Rd, Freeport St, **N gas:** Chevron/dsl, Mobil, **food:** Capt Tom's Seafood, China Dragon, IHOP, Jack-in-the-Box, KFC, Panda Express, Sonic, Subway, Taco Bell, Taco Cabana, **other:** H, Aamco, Ace Hardware, $Tree, Office Depot, **S food:** Baytown Seafood, Whataburger, **other:** Home Depot, U-Haul, Sam's Club/gas, Walmart/McDonald's/auto/24hr
779b	**N gas:** Valero, **lodging:** Interstate Motel
778b	Normandy St, **N gas:** Texaco, Shell/Jack-in-the-Box, **food:** Golden Corral, **food:** La Quinta, **S gas:** Citgo, Shell, **lodging:** Normandy Inn, Scottish Inn
778a	FM 526, Federal Rd, Pasadena, **N gas:** Shell, **food:** Burger King, Casa Ole Mexican, Jack-in-the-Box, KFC/Taco Bell, Luby's, Mambo Seafood, Pizza Hut, Popeye's, Subway, Wendy's, **lodging:** Comfort Inn, La Quinta, **other:** CVS Drug, Family$, Fiesta Foods, HEB Foods, Kroger/gas, Target, **S gas:** Shell, Valero, **food:** Chili's, Cici's Pizza, Coney Island, Joe's Crabshack, McDonald's, Pappa's Seafood, Peking Bo Chinese, Saltgrass Steaks, Sonic, **lodging:** Holiday Inn Express, Lamplight Inn, Super 8, **other:** AutoZone, Discount Tire, O'Reilly Parts
776b	John Ralston Rd, Holland Ave, **N gas:** Chevron, **food:** Denny's, Papacito's Cantina, Rancho Del Viejo, Subway, **lodging:** Best Western, Day Inn, La Quinta, Palace Inn, Regency Inn, **other:** Family$, Kroger/deli/24hr, NTB, **S** same as 778
776a	Mercury Dr, **N food:** Aranda's Mexican, Burger King, E China Rest., McDonald's, TX Grill, **lodging:** Baymont Inn, Best Western, Day's Inn, Premier Inn, Quality Inn, **other:** Volvo Trucks, **S gas:** Shell/dsl, Valero
775b a	I-610
774	Gellhorn (from eb) Blvd, Anheuser-Busch Brewery
773b	McCarty St, **N gas:** Mobil/dsl, Shell
773a	US 90A, N Wayside Dr, **N gas:** Powerful, **food:** Jack-in-the-Box, Whataburger/24hr, **S gas:** Chevron/dsl, Shell, Texaco, **food:** Church's, **other:** NAPA, dsl repair
772	Kress St, Lathrop St, **N gas:** Conoco, Exxon, **food:** Popeye's, **S food:** Burger King, Seafood Rest.
771b	Lockwood Dr, **N gas:** Chevron/Subway/dsl, **food:** McDonald's, **other:** Family$, **S gas:** Shell/dsl, **lodging:** Palace Inn
771a	Waco St
770c	US 59 N
770b	Jenson St, Meadow St, Gregg St
770a	US 59 S, to Victoria
769c	McKee St, Hardy St, Nance St, downtown
769a	Smith St (from wb), to downtown
768b a	I-45, N to Dallas, S to Galveston
767b	Taylor St
767a	Studemont Dr, Yale St, Heights Blvd, **S gas:** Shell/dsl, **food:** Chili's, Subway, **other:** PetsMart, Target
766	(from wb), Heights Blvd, Yale St, same as 767a
765b	N Durham Dr, N Shepherd Dr, **N gas:** Shell/dsl, **food:** Wendy's, **lodging:** Howard Johnson, **other:** vet, **S gas:** Valero/dsl

HOUSTON

INTERSTATE 10 CONT'D

E ↕ W

HOUSTON

Exit #	Services
765a	TC Jester Blvd, **N food:** Wendy's, **S gas:** Exxon/dsl, Texaco/dsl
764	Westcott St, Washington Ave, Katy Rd, **N food:** Denny's, **lodging:** Comfort Inn, **S gas:** Chevron, **food:** IHOP, **lodging:** Scottish Inn
763	I-610
762	Silber Rd, Post Oak Rd, **N food:** Cafe Adobe, Panda Express, Quizno's, Red Robin, SteaKountry, Wings & More, **other:** Dodge, Firestone/auto, **S gas:** Shell, **food:** Jack-in-the-Box, **lodging:** Best Western, Holiday Inn Express, Plaza Hotel, Ramada Inn, **other:** Chevrolet, NTB, carwash
761b	Antoine Rd, **N food:** Hunan Chinese, **S gas:** Exxon, Shell, **food:** Blue Oyster Grill, McDonald's, Papa John's, Subway, Whataburger/24hr, **lodging:** Wellesley Inn, **other:** CVS Drug, NTB
761a	Wirt Rd, Chimney Rock Rd, **S gas:** Chevron, Exxon/TCBY, Shell, **food:** McDonald's
760	Bingle Rd, Voss Rd, **N food:** Starbucks, **other:** Home Depot, **S gas:** Citgo, Mobil, Shell, **food:** Goode Co BBQ, Marie Callender, Mason Jar Rest., Pappy's Café, Redwood Grill, SaltGrass Steaks, Sweet Tomatos, TX BBQ, **other:** H
759	Campbell Rd (from wb), same as 758b
758b	Blalock Rd, Campbell Rd, **N food:** Ciro's Italian, Sonic, **other:** Adam's Automotive, Lowe's Whse, LubeStop, Mail It, cleaners, **S gas:** Chevron/McDonald's/dsl, Exxon, Texaco, **other:** H, Kroger, Walgreens
758a	Bunker Hill Rd, **N gas:** Exxon, **food:** Arby's, Boudreaux's Cajun, CiCi's, Dennys, Five Guys Burgers, Olive Garden, Panda Express, Quizno's, **other:** Best Buy, Costco/gas, HEB Foods, Lowe's Whse, Michael's, PepBoys, Radio Shack, **S gas:** Texaco/dsl, Circle K, **food:** Charlie's Burgers, Guadalajara Mexican, Quizno's, Subway, **lodging:** Days Inn, Howard Johnson, Super 8, **other:** Ford, Goodyear/auto, Marshall's, Nissan, Ross, Target
757	Gessner Rd, **N food:** Bennigan's, Chili's, Cici's, DQ, McDonald's, Olive Garden, Schlotsky's, Taco Bell, SteaKountry, Wendy's, Whataburger/24hr, **other:** CVS Drug, Hobby Lobby, Home Depot, NAPA, PetsMart, Radio Shack, Sam's Club/gas, U-Haul, **S food:** 59 Diner, Fuddrucker's, Goode Co. Seafood, Jason's Deli, Pappasito's, Papadeaux Seafood, Perry's Steaks, Taste of TX Rest., **lodging:** Sheraton, **other:** H, Firestone/auto, Ford, Goodyear, Macy's, Office Depot, Target, mall
756	TX 8, Sam Houston Tollway
755	Willcrest Rd, **N other:** Buick, Discount Tire, Mazda, Lincoln/Mercury, NTB, U-Haul, **S gas:** Citgo/dsl, Exxon/McDonald's/24hr, Phillips 66, **food:** Carabbas, China View, Denny's, Dimassi Mediterranean, IHOP, McDonald's, Steak&Ale, Subway, Taco Cabana, **lodging:** Extended Stay America, Hampton Inn, La Quinta, Radisson, Sheraton
754	Kirkwood Rd, **N lodging:** Embassy Suites, **other:** Lexus, Lincoln/Mercury, Toyota/Scion, same as 753b, **S gas:** Chevron/dsl, Shell/24hr, **food:** Carrabba's, IHOP/24hr, Kingfish Mkt, Mesa Grill, Original Pasta Co, Subway, Taco Cabana, **lodging:** Extended Stay America, **other:** Chevrolet, Discount Tire, Subaru

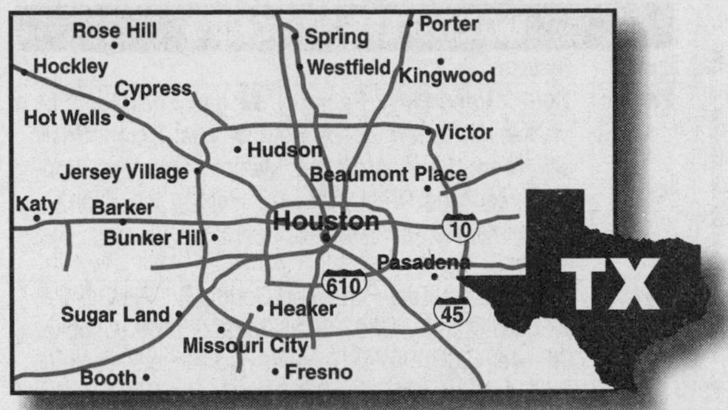

HOUSTON

Exit #	Services
753b	Dairy-Ashford Rd, **N other:** Buick, Chrysler/Dodge, Infiniti, Lexus, Nissan, Toyota, Volvo, **S gas:** Exxon/dsl, Shell, **food:** Beck's Prime Rest., Subway, TX Cattle Steaks, Whataburger, **lodging:** Courtyard, Hilton Garden, Holiday Inn Express, **other:** Cadillac, Chevrolet
753a	Eldridge Pkwy, **N gas:** Conoco/dsl, **lodging:** Omni Hotel, **S gas:** Valero
751	TX 6, to Addicks, **N gas:** Shell, **food:** Bro.'s Pizza, Cattlegard Rest., Waffle House, **lodging:** Crowne Plaza, Drury Inn, Homewood Suites, Red Roof Inn, Studio 6, **other:** Sam's Club/gas, **S lodging:** Extended Stay Deluxe, Fairfield Inn, Holiday Inn, Hyatt Suites, La Quinta, Motel 6, Summerfield Suites, Super 8, TownePlace Suites, **other:** Acura, BMW
750	Park Ten Blvd, eb only, **S other:** Hoover RV Ctr, Hyundai, Subaru
748	Barker-Cypress Rd, **N gas:** Texaco/Subway, **food:** Coaches Grill, Firehouse Subs, Panchero's Mexican, Ruby Tuesday, **other:** H, **S food:** Cracker Barrel, **other:** Dodge, GMC/Pontiac, Hyundai, Subaru, VW
747	Fry Rd, **N gas:** Mobil/dsl, Murphy USA, Shell/24hr, **food:** Applebee's, Arby's, Burger King, DQ, Denny's, McDonald's, Murphy's Deli, Panda Express, Pizza Hut, Sonic, Souper Salad, Subway, Taco Bell, TX Roadhouse, Waffle House, Whataburger, **other:** Best Buy, HEB Food/gas, Hobby Lobby, Home Depot, Kohl's, Kroger/gas, O'Reilly Parts, Ross, Sam's Club/gas, Walgreens, Walmart SuperCtr, **S gas:** Valero, **food:** Capt Tom's Seafood, Fazoli's, IHOP, McDonald's, Omar's Mexican, Outback Steaks, Quizno's, Wendy's, Willie's, **lodging:** ValuePlace Hotel, **other:** H, Ford, Lowe's Whse, PetsMart, Radio Shack, Target, U-Haul
746	W Green Blvd, wb only, **N food:** Chang's Chinese, Cheddar's, Coldstone Creamery, NY Pizza, Springcreek BBQ, Tequila Mexican, Wild Wings Cafe, **lodging:** Holiday Inn Express, **S other:** CVS Drug, Honda
745	Mason Rd, **S gas:** Chevron/dsl, Exxon/24hr, Shell/24hr, Valero, **food:** Babin's Seafood, Blackeyed Pea, Burger King, Carino's Italian, Chick-fil-A, Chili's, CiCi's, DQ, Fuzzy's Pizza, Hartz Chicken, Jack-in-the-Box, Jason's Deli, KFC, Landry's Seafood, Luby's, McDonald's, Panda Express, Papa John's, Pizza Hut, Popeye's, SaltGrass Steaks, Schlotsky's, Subway, Taco Bell, Taco Cabana, Whataburger/24hr, **lodging:** Comfort Inn, Hampton Inn, Holiday Inn Express, La Quinta, Super 8, **other:** Discount Tire, Dodge, $Tree, Fiesta Foods, Firestone/auto, Goodyear/auto, Hancock Fabrics, HEB Food/gas, Kroger, Randall's Food, Toyota/Scion, Walgreens, transmissions

INTERSTATE 10 CONT'D

E ↕ W

Exit #	Services
743	TX 99, Grand Pkwy, Peek Rd, **N gas:** Shell, **food:** La Madeleine, **other:** JC Penney, **S gas:** Exxon, Shell/dsl, **food:** A&W, Arrandas Mexican, Hooters, Popeye's, **lodging:** Best Western, Holiday Inn Express, La Quinta, Super 8, **other:** Chevrolet, CVS Drug, Kia, Kroger
741	(742 from wb)Katy-Fort Bend County Rd, Pin Oak Rd, **S gas:** Murphy USA, Shell, Texaco, **food:** Chucke-Cheese, Cici's Pizza, Dennys, Fuddruckers, Jack-in-the-Box, LJ Silver/Taco Bell, Los Cucos, Red Lobster, Subway, TGIFriday's, **lodging:** Residence Inn, SpringHill Suites, **other:** H, BassPro Shops, Discount Tire, Katy Mills Outlet/famous brands, Walgreens, Walmart SuperCtr/24hr
740	FM 1463, **N food:** McDonald's, Sonic, **other:** RV World of TX, Yamaha, **S gas:** Chevron, **food:** Rain-Forest Café, **other:** Books-A-Million
737	Pederson Rd, **N gas:** Loves/Arby's/dsl/scales/24hr, **S other:** Camping World RV Super Ctr, Holiday World RV Ctr
735	Igloo Rd, new exit
732	FM 359, to Brookshire, **N gas:** Exxon/dsl, ***FLYING J***/CountryMkt/dsl/LP/scales/24hr/@, Shell, **food:** Orlando's Pizza, **lodging:** Executive Inn, **other:** RV camping, **S gas:** Chevron/dsl, Citgo/dsl, Exxon/Burger King/dsl/24hr, **food:** Jack-in-the-Box, **lodging:** Super 8, **other:** truckwash
731	FM 1489, to Koomey Rd, **N gas:** Exxon/dsl, **food:** Ernesto's Mexican, **lodging:** Carefree Inn, **other:** RV Park, **S lodging:** La Quinta
729	Peach Ridge Rd, Donigan Rd (730 from wb)
726	Chew Rd (from eb), **S** golf
725	Mlcak Rd (from wb)
724mm	**check sta wb**
723	FM 1458, to San Felipe, **N gas:** Exxon/Subway/dsl/scales/24hr, **other:** to Stephen F Austin SP (3mi), **S other:** Riverside Tire
721	(from wb) US 90, **N gas:** Shell/dsl, **other:** Ford, **S other:** Sealy Mall
720a	Outlet Ctr Dr, **N gas:** Shell/dsl, **S** to Sealy Mall
720	TX 36, to Sealy, **N gas:** Shell/dsl, **food:** DQ, Hartz Chicken, McDonald's, Sonic, Tony's Rest., **other:** Chevrolet/Pontiac/Buick/GMC, Jones RV Ctr, Walgreens, **S gas:** Chevron/dsl/24hr, Mobil/dsl, Murphy USA/dsl, Shell/dsl/24hr, **food:** Cazadore's Mexican, Hinze's BBQ, Hunan Chinese, Jack-in-the-Box, KFC/Taco Bell, Mirabelli Italian, Pizza Hut, Subway, Whataburger/24hr, **lodging:** Best Western, Holiday Inn Express, Rodeway Inn, Super 8, **other:** Chrysler/Dodge/Jeep, Walmart SuperCtr
718	US 90 (from eb), to Sealy
716	Pyka Rd, **N gas:** Exxon/dsl/rest./showers/24hr/@
713	Beckendorff Rd
709	FM 2761, Bernardo Rd
704	FM 949, **N** Happy Oaks RV Park (3mi)
701mm	no services
699	FM 102, to Eagle Lake, **N other:** Happy Oaks RV Park, antiques, **S other:** Eagle Lake SP (14mi)
698	Alleyton Rd, **N food:** Mikeska's BBQ, **lodging:** Passport Inn, **S gas:** Shell/Taco Bell/dsl, **other:** Chrysler/Jeep/Dodge, Ford
697mm	Little Colorado River
696	TX 71, Columbus, **N gas:** Chevron/dsl/24hr, Shell/dsl, **food:** Denny's, Jack-in-the-Box, Nancy's Seafood, Pizza Hut, Schobel's Rest., Whataburger, **lodging:** Columbus Inn, Holiday Inn Express, **other:** H, AutoZone, HEB Foods, Walmart/drugs, **S gas:** Citgo/Church's/dsl, Valero/dsl, **food:** Los Cabos Mexican, McDonald's, Nancy's Steaks, Sonic, Subway, **lodging:** Country Hearth Inn, LaQuinta, **other:** Columb US RV Ctr
695	TX 71 (from wb), to La Grange
693	FM 2434, to Glidden
692mm	**rest areas both lanes, full ♿ facilities, vending, ☎, picnic, litter barrels, RV dump, petwalk**
689	US 90, to Hattermann Lane, **N** KOA
682	FM 155, to Wiemar, **N gas:** Exxon/dsl, Shell/BBQ/dsl, **food:** DQ, Subway/Texas Burger, **lodging:** Czech Inn, **other:** H, $General, Tire Pros, **S other:** Buick/Chevrolet
678mm	E Navidad River
677	US 90
674	US 77, Schulenburg, **N gas:** Chevron/Subway/dsl, Exxon/dsl, **food:** McDonald's, Oak Ridge Smokehouse, **lodging:** Executive Inn, Oak Ridge Motel, **other:** Ford, Potter Country Store, **S gas:** Citgo, Shell/dsl, Valero/Subway, **food:** DQ, Express BBQ Depot, Guadalajara Mexican, Whataburger, **lodging:** Best Western, Holiday Inn Express, **other:** $General, Schulenberg RV Park
672mm	W Navidad River
668	FM 2238, to Engle
661	TX 95, FM 609, to Flatonia, **N food:** Joel's, BBQ, San Jose Mexican, **S gas:** Shell/McDonald's/Grumpy's Rest./motel, Valero, **food:** DQ, **lodging:** Carefree Inn, **other:** $General, NAPA
658mm	**picnic both lanes, litter barrels**
653	US 90, Waelder, **N gas:** Shell/dsl/cafe
649	TX 97, to Waelder
642	TX 304, to Gonzales
637	FM 794, to Harwood
632	US 90/183, to Gonzales, **N gas:** Love's/Subway/dsl/scales/24hr, **lodging:** Coachway Inn (2mi), **S gas:** Shell/Buc-ee's/dsl, **other:** to Palmetto SP, camping
630mm	San Marcos River
628	TX 80, to Luling, **N gas:** Exxon (2mi), Valero/Church's/dsl/24hr, **food:** DQ (2mi), **other:** H, Riverbend RV Park
625	Darst Field Rd
624.5mm	Smith Creek
621mm	**weigh sta, both lanes**
620	FM 1104
619mm	**rest area both lanes, full ♿ facitlities, ☎, picnic, petwalk**
617	FM 2438, to Kingsbury
614.5mm	Mill Creek
612	US 90
611mm	Geronimo Creek
610	TX 123, to San Marcos, **N gas:** Exxon/dsl, Shell/Subway/dsl, **food:** Chili's, IHOP, Joe's Italian, Los Cucos Mexican, **lodging:** Comfort Inn, Hampton Inn, Holiday Inn Express, Quality Inn, **other:** tires, **S gas:** Valero/dsl, **food:** Taco Cabana, **other:** H, River Shade RV
609	TX 123, Austin St, **S gas:** Phillips 66/dsl, **other:** Chevrolet, Home Depot

SEALY

COLUMBUS

INTERSTATE 10 CONT'D

E ↕ W

Exit #	Services
607	TX 46, FM 78, to New Braunfels, **N gas:** Texaco/Jack-in-the-Box/dsl, **lodging:** Alamo Inn, **S gas:** Chevron/dsl, Exxon/DQ/dsl, Valero, **food:** Bill Miller BBQ, Dixie Grill, Kettle, McDonald's, Whataburger/24hr, **lodging:** La Quinta, Super 8, **other:** Chrysler/Dodge/Jeep
605	FM 464, **N other:** Twin Palms RV Park
605mm	Guadalupe River
604	FM 725, to Lake McQueeney, **N other:** Explore USA RV Ctr, Twin Palms RV Park
603	US 90 E, US 90A, to Seguin, **N other:** Explore USA RV Sales
601	FM 775, to New Berlin, **N gas:** Chevron/Subway/dsl/scales/24hr
600	Schwab Rd
599	FM 465, to Marion
599mm	Santa Clara Creek
597	Santa Clara Rd, **N** auto racetrack
595	Zuehl Rd
594mm	Cibolo Creek
593	FM 2538, Trainer Hale Rd, **N gas:** Texaco/Quizno's/dsl, **S gas:** Exxon/Lucille's Rest./dsl/rest./24hr
593mm	Woman Hollering Creek
591	FM 1518, to Schertz, **N** Alamo Trvl Ctr/Shell/dsl, **other:** repair
589	Pfeil Rd, Graytown Rd
589mm	Salatrillo Creek
587	LP 1604, Randolph AFB, to Universal City
585.5mm	Escondido Creek
585	FM 1516, to Converse, **N gas:** Shell/Church's/dsl/scales, **lodging:** Best Western, **S other:** Kenworth, Peterbilt/GMC/Freightliner
585mm	Martinez Creek
583	Foster Rd, **N gas:** *FLYING J*/Conoco/Cookery/dsl/LP/scales/24hr/@, Valero/Subway/dsl/24hr, **food:** Jack-in-the-Box/24hr, **lodging:** La Quinta, **other:** Charlie's Truckwash, Speedco Lube, T&W Tire, Tire Mart, **S gas:** TA/Chevron/Burger King/Pizza Hut/Popeye's/dsl/24hr/@
582.5mm	Rosillo Creek
582	Ackerman Rd, Kirby, **N gas:** Pilot/Subway/dsl/scales/24hr, **other:** Blue Beacon, **S gas:** Petro/Iron Skillet/dsl/scales/24hr/@, **lodging:** Rest Inn, **other:** Petrolube, Blue Beacon Truckwash
581	I-410
580	LP 13, WW White Rd, **N gas:** Chevron, Fina/dsl, **food:** Frijoles Rest., Wendy's, **lodging:** Motel 6, Red Roof Inn, Rodeway Inn, **other:** RV camping, tires, **S gas:** Exxon/dsl, **food:** Bill Miller BBQ, McDonald's, Popeye's, Pizza Hut, Sandrita's Mexican, Sonic, Subway, **lodging:** Econolodge, Quality Inn, Rodeway Inn, Rosepark Inn, Super 8, **other:** Ford/Volvo Trucks, tires/repair
579	Houston St, **N gas:** Valero/dsl, **lodging:** Travelodge, **S gas:** Chevron, **lodging:** Comfort Inn, Day's Inn, Passport Inn
578	Pecan Valley Dr, ML King Dr, **N** gas
577	US 87 S, to Roland Ave, **S food:** Whataburger/24hr, **lodging:** Super 8
576	New Braunfels Ave, Gevers St, **S gas:** Valero, **food:** McDonald's

KIRBY

SAN ANTONIO

Exit #	Services
575	Pine St, Hackberry St, **S food:** Little Red Barn Steaks, Pizza Hut
574	I-37, US 281
573	Probandt St, **N food:** Jack-in-the-Box, Miller's BBQ, **S gas:** Valero, **other:** to SA Missions HS, tires
572	**I-10 and I-35 run together 3 miles**
154a (I-35)	Nogalitos St
154b (I-35)	S Laredo St, Cevallos St, **E gas:** Exxon, Shell, **food:** April's Chinese, Church's, McDonald's, Piedra's Negras, Pizza Hut, Wendy's, **lodging:** Best Western, Day's Inn, Holiday Inn Express, Ramada Ltd, **other:** USPO, **W gas:** Conoco, **lodging:** Microtel
155a (I-35)	South Alamo St, same as 154b
155b (I-35)	Durango St, downtown, **E food:** Bill Miller BBQ, **lodging:** Best Western, Comfort Suites, Courtyard, Fairfield Inn, Holiday Inn, La Quinta, Residence Inn, **other:** H **W food:** McDonald's, **lodging:** Microtel, Motel 6, Radisson
156 (I-35)	I-10 E, US 90 W, US 87, to Kelly AFB, Lackland AFB
570	**I-10 and I-35 run together 3 miles**
569c	Santa Rosa St, downtown, to Our Lady of the Lake U
568	spur 421, Culebra Ave, Bandera Ave, **S** to St Marys U
567	Lp 345, Fredericksburg Rd (from eb upper level accesses I-35 S, I-10 E, US 87 S, lower level accesses I-35 N)
566b	Fresno Dr, **S gas:** Exxon
566a	West Ave, **N gas:** Exxon, **food:** CarCare, Whataburger
565c	(from wb), access to same as 565 a b, **S gas:** Shell, **food:** Guadalahara Mexican, Starbucks, **lodging:** La Quinta
565b	Vance Jackson Rd, **N gas:** Murphy USA, **food:** Bill Miller BBQ, IHOP, **lodging:** Comfort Inn, Days Inn, Econolodge, **other:** Walmart SuperCtr, **S gas:** Shell, **lodging:** La Quinta
565a	Crossroads Blvd, Balcone's Heights, **N gas:** Exxon, Shell/dsl, **food:** Denny's, Whataburger, **lodging:** Comfort Suites, Howard Johnson, Rodeway Inn, **S food:** Dave&Buster's, El Pollo Loco, McDonald's, **lodging:** SpringHill Suites, Super 8, **other:** Firestone/auto, Mazda, Office Depot, RV Ctr, Target, Toyota, mall, transmissions
564b a	I-410, **services off of I-410 W**, Fredericksburg Rd
563	Callaghan Rd, **N gas:** Valero, **food:** Las Palapas Mexican, Philly Connection, Subway, **lodging:** Embassy Suites, Marriott, **other:** $General, Ford, Lexus, Mazda, Sun Harvest Foods, Toyota, **S gas:** Exxon, **food:** Mamacita's Rest., **other:** Lowe's Whse

INTERSTATE 10 CONT'D

E ↕ W — SAN ANTONIO

Exit #	Services
561	Wurzbach Rd, **N gas:** Texaco/dsl, **food:** Bolo's Grille, County Line BBQ, Egg & I, Fuddrucker's, Honeybaked Ham, Jason's Deli, Pappasito's Cantina, Popeye's, Quizno's, Sea Island Shrimphouse, Taste Of China, TX Land&Cattle, Wasabi Grill, **lodging:** Homewood Suites, Hyatt Place, Knight's Inn, Omni Hotel, Staybridge Suites, Studio+, **other:** AutoZone, BigLots, Ford, HEB Food/gas, Office Depot, Toyota, **S gas:** Shell/dsl, **food:** Alamo Café, Arby's, Benihana, Chester's Burgers, China Sea, Church's, Denny's, El Taco Tote, IHOP, Jack-in-the-Box, Mamma Margie's Mexican, McDonald's, Pizza Hut, Taco Bell, Wendy's, **lodging:** Baymont Inn, Best Western, Candlewood Suites, Drury Inn, Holiday Inn Express, La Quinta, Motel 6, Residence Inn, Sleep Inn, **other:** H, CarMax
560b	frontage rd (from eb), **N food:** Water St Seafood
560a	Huebner Rd, **N food:** Carrabba's, Champp's, La Madeleine, Macaroni Grill, On the Border, Panera Bread, SaltGrass Steaks, **other:** Acura, Borders, Chrysler/Jeep/Dodge, Hummer/Cadillac, Old Navy, Ross, Smart Car, **S gas:** Chevron, Exxon, **food:** Burger King, Cracker Barrel, Jim's Rest., **lodging:** Day's Inn, Hampton Inn, Homestead Village
559	Lp 335, US 87, Fredericksburg Rd, **N food:** Brew Wok, La Madeleine, Macaroni Grill, On-the-Border, Outback Steaks, Panera Bread, Pearl Inn, Saltgrass Steaks, Starbucks, **other:** Acura, Ross Old Navy, **S gas:** Shell, Texaco, **food:** Cracker Barrel, Jack-in-the-Box, Krispy Kreme, **lodging:** Days Inn, Hampton Inn, HomeGate Studios, Motel 6, SpringHill Suttes, **other:** Infinity
558	De Zavala Rd, **N gas:** Chevron, Shell/Subway, **food:** Bill Miller BBQ, Burger King, Carrabba's, Chick-fil-A, Chili's, Joe's Crabshack, KFC/Taco Bell, Logan's Roadhouse, McDonald's, Outback Steaks, Papa Murphy's, Sonic, Taco Cabana, The Earl of Sandwich, Wendy's, **lodging:** Super 8, **other:** GNC, HEB Food/gas, Home Depot, Hyundai, Marshall's, PetCo, PetsMart, Steinmart, Target, **S food:** Cracker Barrel, IHOP, Schlotsky's, **lodging:** Hampton Inn, Sleep Inn, SpringHill Suites, Studio6, **other:** Buick, Discount Tire, Sam's Club, Walmart SuperCtr/24hr
557	Spur 53, Univ of TX at San Antonio, **N gas:** Exxon/dsl, **lodging:** Best Western, Econolodge, Howard Johnson, Super 8, **other:** Audi, Chevrolet, Hyundai, Jaguar/Mazerati/Ferrari, **S food:** A&W/LJ Silver, Cici's Pizza, Huhot Chinese, IHOP, Matamoro's Cantina, My Sam Chinese, Quizno's, TGIFriday's, Zio's Italian, Whataburger, **other:** Costco/gas, Land Rover, Sams Club/gas, Walmart SuperCtr
556b	frontage rd
556a	to Anderson Lp, **S lodging:** Comfort Inn, **other:** to Seaworld
555	La Quintera Pkwy, **N food:** Chick-fil-A, Little Italy, Mimi's Cafe, Red Robin, **lodging:** Courtyard, Residence Inn, **other:** Bass Pro Shops, Best Buy, JC Penney, Ross, Target, **S food:** Olive Garden, Red Lobster, **lodging:** Drury Inn, La Quinta, Motel 6, **other:** Honda, to La Cantera Pkwy
554	Camp Bullis Rd, **N gas:** Citgo, **food:** TGIFriday's, **other:** Lowe's Whse, Old Navy, Russell CP, TJ Maxx, **S gas:** Shell, **lodging:** Rodeway Inn
551	Boerne Stage Rd (from wb), to Leon Springs, **N gas:** Shamrock/dsl, **food:** Rudy's BBQ, Sonic, **S food:** Las Palapas Mexican, Longhorns Rest., Pappa Nacho's, Quizno's, Starbucks, **other:** GNC, HEB Foods/gas, Vet
550	FM 3351, Ralph Fair Rd, **N gas:** Exxon/McDonald's/dsl, Valero/dsl, **food:** Leon Creek Steaks, **lodging:** La Quinta, **S gas:** Shell/Domino's/dsl
546	Fair Oaks Pkwy, Tarpon Dr, **N food:** Papa John's, **other:** American Dream RV Ctr, Harley-Davidson, Vet, **S gas:** Chevron/dsl/café, Exxon/dsl/café, **other:** Goodyear/auto, Hoover RV Ctr
543	Boerne Stage Rd, to Scenic LP Rd, **N gas:** Valero/Subway/dsl, **lodging:** Caverns Inn/rest., Fairfield Inn, **other:** Ancira RV Ctr, Buick/Pontiac/GMC, Chevrolet, Chrysler/Dodge/Jeep, Ford, NAPA, Pontiac/Buick/GMC, W&W Tires, to Cascade Caverns, **S other:** Explore USA RV Ctr, Mercedes, Toyota/Scion
542	(from wb), **N gas:** Shamrock, **food:** Dominos, Pizza Hut, Wendy's, **other:** Alamo Fiesta RV Park, $Tree, same as 540
540	TX 46, to New Braunfels, **N gas:** Exxon/Taco Bell/dsl, Murphy USA, Shell/dsl/24hr, **food:** Baskin-Robbins, Burger King, Church's, DQ, Denny's, El Rio Mexican, Guadalajara Mexican, Little Caesar's, Marble Slab Creamery, Margarita's Café, Pizza Hut, Quizno's, Shanghai Chinese, Sonic, Taco Cabana, Wendy's, **lodging:** Best Value, Holiday Inn Express, Key to the Hills Motel, **other:** AutoZone, HEB Food/gas, Radio Shack, Walgreens, Walmart SuperCtr, **S food:** Chili's, Starbucks, Whataburger, **lodging:** Hampton Inn, **other:** Home Depot
539	Johns Rd, **N lodging:** La Quinta, **S gas:** Valero/dsl/LP
538mm	Cibolo Creek
538	Ranger Creek Rd
537	US 87, to Boerne
533	FM 289, Welfare, **N food:** Po-Po Family Rest., **other:** Top of the Hill RV Park (1mi)
532mm	Little Joshua Creek
531mm	**wb, litter barrels**
530mm	Big Joshua Creek
529.5mm	**wb, litter barrels**
527	FM 1621 (from wb), to Waring
526.5mm	Holiday Creek
524	TX 27, FM 1621, to Waring, **N** Vet, **S gas:** Chevron/dsl, Shell/24hr
523.5mm	Guadalupe River
523	US 87 N, to Comfort, **N gas:** Chevron/McDonald's/dsl, **S gas:** Exxon/dsl/24hr, Texaco, **food:** DQ, **lodging:** Executive Inn, **other:** $General, NAPACare, USA RV Park
521.5mm	Comfort Creek
520	FM 1341, to Cypress Creek Rd
515mm	Cypress Creek
514mm	**rest areas both lanes, full facilities, vending, , litter barrels, RV dump, petwalk, playground, wireless internet**

INTERSTATE 10 CONT'D

E ↕ W

KERRVILLE

Exit #	Services
508	TX 16, Kerrville, **N gas:** Exxon/dsl, **other:** Chevrolet/Pontiac/Buick/Cadillac, RV camping, **0-2 mi S gas:** Exxon, Shell/McDonald's/dsl/24hr, TC, Valero/dsl, **food:** Acapulco Mexican, Bamboo Asian, Cracker Barrel, DQ, IHOP, KFC, Jack-in-the-Box, Little Caesars, Luby's, McDonald's, Santo Coyote, Schlotsky's, Sonic, Taco Bell, Taco Casa, Wing King, **lodging:** Best Value Inn, Best Western, Big Texas Inn, Comfort Inn, Day's Inn, Hampton Inn, Holiday Inn Express, La Quinta, Motel 6, Whitten Inn, Yo Ranch Hotel, **other:** [H], Advance Parts, Big Lots, $Tree, Hastings Books, Home Depot, Kerrville RV Ctr, O'Reilly Parts, Walgreens, Vet
505	FM 783, to Kerrville, **S gas:** Exxon/dsl, **3 mi S on TX 27...gas:** Chevron, Phillips 66/dsl, Shell, TC/dsl, **food:** Chili's, CiCi's Pizza, Culver's, DQ, Mamcita's, McDonald's, Pizza Hut, Quizno's, Starbucks, Sonic, Subway, Taco Casa, Wendy's, Whataburger, **lodging:** Inn of the Hills, **other:** AutoZone, Curves, CVS Drug, Discount Tire, $General, HEB Foods/gas, Walmart SuperCtr
503.5mm	scenic views both lanes, litter barrels
501	FM 1338, **N other:** Buckhorn RV Resort, **S other:** KOA (2mi)
497mm	**[picnic] both lanes, litter barrels**
492	FM 479, **S other:** Lone Oak Store
490	TX 41
488	TX 27, to Ingram, Mountain Home
484	Midway Rd
477	US 290, to Fredericksburg
476.5mm	service rd eb
472	Old Segovia Rd
465	FM 2169, to Segovia, **S gas:** Phillips 66/dsl/rest., **lodging:** Econolodge/RV park
464.5mm	Johnson Fork Creek
462	US 83 S, to Uvalde
461mm	**[picnic] eb, litter barrels**
460	(from wb), to Junction
459mm	**[picnic] wb, litter barrels**

JUNCTION

Exit #	Services
457	FM 2169, to Junction, **N gas:** Shell/dsl, **S lodging:** Day's Inn/rest., **other:** RV camping, S. Llano River SP
456.5mm	Llano River
456	US 83/377, Junction, **N gas:** Chevron/dsl, Valero/McDonald's/dsl/24hr, **food:** Cooper's BBQ, JR's Rest., **lodging:** Motel 6, **S gas:** Big Star/dsl, Exxon/Church's, Shell/dsl, **food:** A&M Rest., DQ, Isaack Rest., La Familia Mexican, Lum's BBQ, Sonic, Subway, **lodging:** Best Western, Hills Motel, La Familia Rest., Lazy T, Legends Inn, Legends Inn, **other:** [H], CarQuest, Do it Hardware, $General, KOA (.5mi), Food Basket Foods, Plumley's Store, Radio Shack, Super S Foods, to S Llano River SP
452.5mm	Bear Creek
451	RM 2291, to Cleo Rd
448mm	North Creek
445	RM 1674, **S** camping
444.5mm	Stark Creek
442mm	Copperas Creek
442	RM 1674, to Ft McKavett, **N** to Ft McKavett SHS
439mm	N Llano River
438	Lp 291 (from wb), to Roosevelt, same as 437

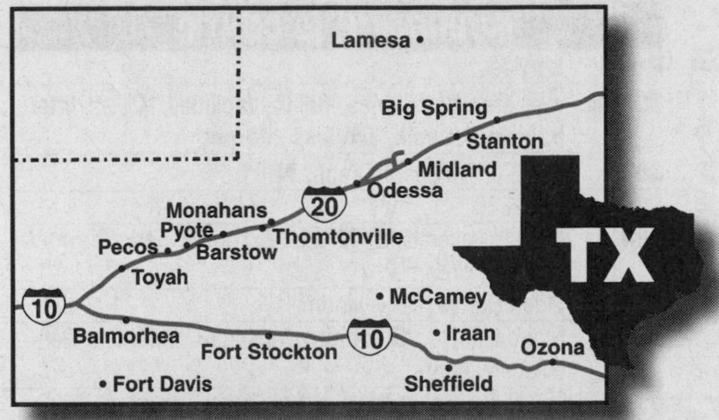

SONORA

Exit #	Services
437	Lp 291 (from eb, no EZ return), to Roosevelt, **1 mi N gas:** Simon Bros Mercantile/dsl, **other:** USPO
429	RM 3130, to Harrell
423mm	**parking area both lanes, litter barrels**
420	RM 3130, to Baker Rd
412	Allison Rd, RM 3130
404	RM 3130, RM 864, **N** to Ft McKavett St HS, **3 mi S gas:** TC/dsl, **lodging:** Best Value Inn, Holiday Host Motel, **other:** [H]
400	US 277, Sonora, **N gas:** Shell/dsl, **food:** Sutton Co Steaks, **lodging:** Day's Inn, **other:** vet, **S gas:** Alco, Chevron/dsl, Exxon/dsl/24hr, Fina/7-11/dsl, T&C/dsl, **food:** Country Cookin Café, DQ, La Mexicana Rest., Pizza Hut, Sonic, **lodging:** Best Western, Comfort Inn, **other:** Alco, Family$, NAPA, USPO
399	(from eb) LP 467, Sonora, **N lodging:** Days Inn, **S gas:** Chevron/dsl, Fina/24hr, Exxon/dsl/24hr, TC, **food:** DQ, Subway, **other:** [H], RV camping
394mm	**rest area both lanes, full [handicapped] facilities, [phone], [picnic], litter barrel, petwalk, RV dump**
392	RM 1989, Caverns of Sonora Rd, **8 mi S other:** Caverns of Sonora Camping, [phone]
388	RM 1312 (from wb)
381	RM 1312 (from eb)
372	Taylor Box Rd, **N gas:** Exxon/rest./dsl/scales/24hr, **lodging:** Super 8, **other:** Circle Bar RV Park, auto museum
368	LP 466, **N** same as 365 & 363

OZONA

Exit #	Services
365	TX 163, Ozona, **N gas:** Chevron/dsl, Exxon, T&C/Country Cookin Cafe/Godfather's/dsl, **food:** Café NextDoor, DQ, Sonic, Subway, **lodging:** Best Value, Best Western, Economy Inn/RV Park, Hillcrest Inn, Holiday Inn Express, **other:** [H], $General, NAPA, to David Crockett Mon, **S gas:** Chevron, **food:** El Chato
363	Lp 466, to Ozona
361	RM 2083, Pandale Rd
357mm	Eureka Draw
351mm	Howard Draw
350	FM 2398, to Howard Draw
349mm	**parking area wb, litter barrels**
346mm	**parking area eb, litter barrels**
343	TX 290 W, **S** Ft. Lancaster Historic Site
337	Live Oak Rd
336.5mm	Live Oak Creek
328	River Rd, Sheffield
327.5mm	Pecos River
325	TX 290, TX 349, to Iraan, Sheffield, **N** [H]
320	frontage rd
314	frontage rd

INTERSTATE 10 CONT'D

E ↕ W

Exit #	Services
309mm	**rest area both lanes, full [handicapped] facilities, [phone], [picnic], litter barrels, petwalk, wireless internet**
307	US 190, FM 305, to Iraan, **N** [H]
298	RM 2886
294	FM 11, Bakersfield, **N gas:** Exxon, **S gas:** Chevron/dsl/café, **other:** [phone]
288	Ligon Rd, **N** many windmills
285	McKenzie Rd, **S other:** Domaine Cordier Ste Genevieve Winery
279mm	**[picnic] eb, tables, litter barrels**
277	FM 2023
273	US 67/385, to McCamey, **[picnic] wb, tables, litter barrels**
272	University Rd
264	Warnock Rd, **N other:** Fort Stockton RV Park/BBQ/cafe
261	US 290 W, US 385 S, **N gas:** Exxon/dsl, **1-2 S gas:** T&C, **lodging:** Econolodge, **food:** DQ, Pizza Hut, Sonic, Subway, **other:** [H], RV camping, to Big Bend NP
259b a	(259 from eb) TX 18, FM 1053, Ft Stockton, **N gas:** Apache Fuel Ctr/dsl, Fina/dsl, Shell/Burger King/dsl, **other:** I-10 RV Park
257	US 285, to Pecos, Ft Stockton, **N other:** Comanche Land RV Park, golf, **S gas:** Chevron/TC/dsl, Exxon/dsl/rest., Shell, Texaco, Valero/dsl, **food:** DQ, IHOP, KFC/Taco Bell, McDonald's, Pizza Hut, Pizza Pro, Sonic, Steak House, Subway, Texan Inn, **lodging:** Day's Inn, Hampton Inn, Knight's Inn, La Quinta, Motel 6, Sands Motel, Town&Country Motel, **other:** Ace Hardware, AutoZone, Chevrolet/Pontiac/Buick, $General, Firestone/auto, Ford/Lincoln/Mercury, IGA Foods, McKissack Tires, O'Reilly Parts, Pizza Hut, Walmart, tires/repair
256	to US 385 S, Ft Stockton, **1 mi S gas:** Shell/dsl, Valero/dsl, **food:** DQ, K-Bob's Steaks, La Herradura Rest., Sonic, Subway, **lodging:** Best Western, Comfort Suites, Holiday Inn Express, Motel 6, Sleep Inn, Super 8, **other:** [H], Ford, O'Reilly Parts, to Ft Stockton Hist Dist, Big Bend NP, auto/RV repair
253	FM 2037, to Belding
248	US 67, FM 1776, to Alpine, **S** to Big Bend NP
246	Firestone
241	Kennedy Rd
235	Mendel Rd
233mm	**rest area both lanes, full [handicapped] facilities, [phone], [picnic], litter barrels, petwalk**
229	Hovey Rd
222	Hoefs Rd
214	(from wb), FM 2448
212	TX 17, FM 2448, to Pecos, **N [picnic], litter barrels, S gas:** Fina/café/dsl, Saddleback RV Camping
209	TX 17, **S other:** to Balmorhea SP, to Davis Mtn SP, Ft Davis NHS
206	FM 2903, to Balmorhea, **S other:** to Balmorhea SP
192	FM 3078, to Toyahvale, **S other:** to Balmorhea SP
188	Giffin Rd
187	I-20, to Ft Worth, Dallas
186	I-10, E to San Antonio (from wb)
185mm	**[picnic] both lanes, litter barrels**
184	Springhills
181	Cherry Creek Rd, **S gas:** Chevron/24hr
176	TX 118, FM 2424, to Kent, **N gas:** Chevron/dsl, **S other:** to McDonald Observatory, Davis Mtn SP, Ft Davis
173	Hurd's Draw Rd
166	Boracho Sta
159	Plateau, **N gas:** Exxon/dsl/rest./24hr
153	Michigan Flat
146	Wild Horse Rd
146mm	**weigh sta wb**
145mm	**rest area both lanes, full [handicapped] facilities, [picnic], litter barrels, petwalk, wireless internet**
140b	Ross Dr, Van Horn, **N gas:** Chevron/dsl, Exxon/dsl, Love's/Subway/dsl/24hr, **lodging:** Day's Inn, Desert Inn, Sands Motel/rest., **other:** El Campo RV Park, repair, **S other:** Mountain View RV Park/dump
140a	US 90, TX 54, Van Horn Dr, **N gas:** Phillips 66/dsl, **other:** [H], Ace Hardware, $General, NAPA, True Value, USPO, **S gas:** Exxon, Pilot/Wendy's/dsl/scales/24hr, **food:** Papa's Café, **other:** KOA, RV Dump
138	Lp 10, to Van Horn, **N food:** Chuy's Rest., DQ, **lodging:** Best Value, Budget Inn, Econolodge, Economy Inn, Knights Inn, Motel 6, Ramada Ltd, Value Inn, **other:** Eagles Nest RV Park, Pueblo Foods, auto/dsl repair, visitor info, **S gas:** Chevron/dsl/24hr, **food:** McDonald's, **lodging:** Hampton Inn, Holiday Inn Express, Super 8, **other:** tires/repair
137mm	**weigh sta eb**
136mm	**scenic overlook wb, [picnic], litter barrels**
135mm	Mountain/Central time zone line, Mountain/Central time zone line
133	(from wb) frontage rd
129	to Hot Wells, Allamore
108	to Sierra Blanca (from wb), same as 107
107	FM 1111, Sierra Blanca Ave, **N gas:** Exxon/dsl/24hr, **food:** Michael's Rest., Mario's Grill/RV Park, **other:** truck/tire repair, USPO, to Hueco Tanks SP, **S gas:** Chevron, **food:** La Familia, **other:** Stagecoach Trading Post
105	(106 from wb) Lp 10, Sierra Blanca, same as 107
102.5mm	**insp sta eb**
99	Lasca Rd, **N other: [picnic] both lanes, litter barrels, no restrooms**
98mm	**[picnic] eb, litter barrels, no restrooms**
95	frontage rd (from eb)
87	FM 34, **S gas:** Driver's Travel Mart/dsl/rest./24hr
85	Esperanza Rd
81	FM 2217
78	TX 20 W, to McNary
77mm	**truck parking area wb**
72	spur 148, to Ft Hancock, **S gas:** Shell/dsl, **food:** Angie's Rest., **lodging:** Ft Hancock Motel, **other:** USPO
68	Acala Rd
55	Tornillo
51mm	**rest area both lanes, full [handicapped] facilities, [picnic], litter tables, petwalk**
49	FM 793, Fabens, **S gas:** Exxon, Fast Trac/dsl, **lodging:** Fabens Inn/Cafe, **1 mi S food:** Church's, McDonald's, Subway, **other:** Curves, Family$, San Eli Foods
42	FM 1110, to Clint, **S gas:** Exxon/dsl, **food:** Boll Weevil, Cotton Eyed Joe's, **lodging:** Adobe Inn, Cotton Valley Motel/RV Park/rest./dump, Super 8

FORT STOCKTON · VAN HORN · EL PASO

INTERSTATE 10 CONT'D

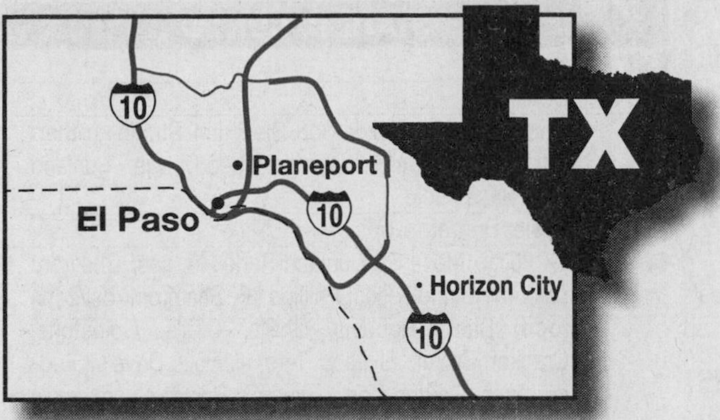

Exit #	Services
37	FM 1281, Horizon Blvd, **N gas:** *FLYING J*/ Cookery/scales/@, Love's/Chester Fried/Subway/dsl/ scales/24hr, **lodging:** Americana Inn, **other:** Freightliner, Speedco Lube, **S gas:** Petro/Mobil/Subway/dsl/ scales/24hr/@, **food:** McDonald's, **lodging:** Deluxe Inn, **other:** Blue Beacon
35	Eastlake Blvd.
34	TX 375, Americas Ave, **N gas:** Chevron/dsl/24hr, Exxon, Shamrock/dsl, **lodging:** Microtel, Value Place, **other:** GMC, Mission RV Camping, Peterbilt, **S other:** RV camping, El Paso Museum of Hist
32	FM 659, Zaragosa Rd, **N gas:** Fina/7-11, **food:** Arby's, Barrigos Mexican, BJ's Grill, Cheddar's, Chico's Tacos, Famous Daves, Furr's Buffet, Great American Steaks, IHOP, Krispy Kreme, LJ Silver/Taco Bell, Logan's Roadhouse, Macaroni Grill, Outback Steaks, Peiwei Asian, Peter Piper Pizza, San Francisco Oven, Sonic, Starbucks, Subway, Taco Bell, Village Inn, Whataburger/24hr, **lodging:** Holiday Inn Express, **other:** Chevrolet, Discount Tire, Kohl's, Lowe's Whse, Michael's, Nissan, Office Depot, Walgreens, World Mkt, **S gas:** Shamrock/dsl, **food:** Howah Chinese
30	Lee Trevino Dr, **N gas:** Circle K/gas, Exxon, **food:** Chili's, Jack-in-the-Box, Taco Cabana, Whataburger, **lodging:** La Quinta, Motel 6, Red Roof Inn, Studio 6, **other:** Discount Tire, Firestone, Ford, Isuzu, Home Depot, Lexus, NTB, Sears/auto, Toyota, mall, **S gas:** Fina/7-11/24hr, **lodging:** Ramada, **other:** Nissan
29	Lomaland Dr, **N food:** Denny's, **lodging:** Hyatt Place, **S gas:** Fina/7-11, **lodging:** Ramada, **other:** Chrysler/ Jeep/Dodge, Harley-Davidson
28b	Yarbrough Dr, El Paso, **N gas:** Murphy USA, Shell/ Coldstone, **food:** Beijing Lili, Bennigan's, Burger King, Grandy's, Dunkin Donuts, El Ciro's, Hong Kong Buffet, LJ Silver, McDonald's, Peter Piper Pizza, Quizno's, Sonic, Subway, Texas Roadhouse, Wendy's, Whataburger, Wienerschnitzel, **lodging:** Days Inn, **other:** Marshall's, PepBoys, PetsMart, Radio Shack, Ross, Walmart SuperCtr/24hr, **S gas:** Shamrock/24hr, **food:** Applebee's, Fuddrucker's, Julio's Cafe, Lin's Buffet, Pizza Hut, Rudy's BBQ/gas, Shangri-La, Villa Del Mar, **lodging:** Comfort Inn, InTown Suites, La Quinta, Suburban Lodge, **other:** [H]
28a	FM 2316, McRae Blvd, **N gas:** Texaco/dsl, **food:** ChuckeCheese, Grand China, Jack-in-the-Box, KFC, Pizza Hut, Red Barrel Grill, Taco Bell, Taco Campero, **lodging:** La Quinta, **other:** [H], Barnes&Noble, Best Buy, BigLots, $General, $Tree, Firestone/auto, Goodyear/auto, Jo-Ann Fabrics, K-Mart, Michael's, Office Depot, Walgreens, **S gas:** Circle K, Shamrock, **food:** Fuddrucker's, **lodging:** Comfort Inn, La Quinta
27	Hunter Dr, Viscount Blvd, **N gas:** Fina/7-11, Valero, **food:** Carrow's Rest., Grand China Buffet, K-Bob's, Red Lobster, Taco Bell, **lodging:** La Quinta, **other:** Barnes&Noble, Best Buy, Firestone, **S gas:** Exxon/ Subway/dsl, Shell, **food:** Whataburger/24hr, **other:** Family$, Food City
26	Hawkins Blvd, El Paso, **N gas:** Chevron, Murphy USA, Shamrock, Shell, **food:** Arby's, Burger King, Country Kitchen, DQ, Golden Corral, IHOP, Landry's Seafood, Luby's, Olive Garden, Red Lobster, Taco Cabana,
26	Continued Wyatt's Cafeteria, **lodging:** Howard Johnson, **other:** Dillard's, JC Penney, Macy's, Office Depot, Pennzoil, Sam's Club/gas, Sears/auto, Walmart SuperCtr, **S gas:** Shamrock/dsl, **food:** China King, Hooters, McDonald's, Village Inn Rest., **lodging:** Best Western, **other:** Tony Lama Boots
25	Airway Blvd, El Paso, **N gas:** Shell/dsl/24hr, **food:** Jack-in-the-Box, Landry's Seafood, Starbucks, Whataburger, **lodging:** Courtyard, Hampton Inn, Holiday Inn, Radisson, Residence Inn, **other:** VW/Volvo/ Mercedes, **S gas:** Chevron/rest./dsl/24hr, **lodging:** Homewood Suites, **other:** Goodyear/auto, Subaru
24b	Geronimo Dr, **N food:** Steak&Ale, Taco Cabana, **lodging:** Wingate Inn, **other:** Dillard's, Office Depot, Marshall's, Ross, Target, Walgreens, mall, **S gas:** Circle K/gas, Phillips 66, **food:** IHOP, Senses De Brazil, Bombay Bicycle Club, Denny's, **lodging:** Embassy Suites, Hyatt Place, La Quinta, **other:** 7-11
24a	Trowbridge Dr, **N gas:** Fina, Thunderbird Gas, **food:** Alexandrio's Mexican, Luby's, McDonald's, Steak&Ale, Whataburger, **lodging:** Budget Inn, **other:** Chiropractor, Ford, Nissan, Toyota
23b	US 62/180, to Paisano Dr, **N food:** Jack-in-the-Box, McDonald's, **lodging:** Budget Inn, Sleep Inn, **other:** Ford, U-Haul, to Carlsbad
23a	Raynolds St, **S food:** Arby's, **lodging:** Motel 6, Super 8, **other:** [H]
22b	US 54, Patriot Fwy
22a	Copia St, El Paso, **N gas:** Shamrock, **food:** KFC
21	Piedras St, El Paso, **N food:** Burger King, McDonald's, **other:** Family$
20	Dallas St, Cotton St, **N gas:** Shamrock, **food:** Church's, Subway
19	TX 20, El Paso, downtown, **N gas:** Chevron, **S lodging:** DoubleTree Inn, Holiday Inn Express
18b	Franklin Ave, Porfirio Diaz St
18a	Schuster Ave, **N** Sun Bowl, **S** to UTEP
16	Executive Ctr Blvd, **N gas:** Shamrock/24hr, **lodging:** Howard Johnson
13b a	US 85, Paisano Dr, to Sunland Park Dr, **N gas:** Shamrock/24hr, **food:** Barrigo's Café, Carino's Italian, ChuckeCheese, Grand China, IHOP, Olive Garden, PF Chang's, Quizno's, Red Lobster, Sonic, Whataburger/24hr, **other:** Barnes&Noble, Best Buy, Dillard's, JC Penney, K-Mart, Macy's, Office Depot, Old Navy, PetsMart, Sears/auto, Target, mall, **S gas:** Shamrock/dsl/24hr, Shell, **food:** La Malinche Mexican, McDonald's, Sonic, Subway, **lodging:** Best Western,

TX

INTERSTATE 10 CONT'D

E ↕ W — EL PASO

Exit #	Services
13b a	Continued Comfort Suites, Holiday Inn, Sleep Inn, Studio+, **other:** GMC/Pontiac/Buick, Chrysler/Jeep/Dodge, Sunland Park RaceTrack
12	Resler Dr (from wb)
11	TX 20, to Mesa St, Sunland Park, **N gas:** Chevron/dsl/24hr, Circle K/gas, Phillips 66, Shamrock/dsl/24hr, **food:** Baskin-Robbins, Chili's, CiCi's, Coldstone, Cracker Barrel, El Taco Tote, Famous Dave's, Fuddruckers, Golden Corral, Jaxon's Rest/brewery, Leo's Mexican, LJ Silver/A&W, Mi General Mexican, PacoWong's Chinese, Papa John's, Peiwei Asian, Popeye's, Rancher's Grill, Souper Salad, Starbucks, Subway, Taco Tote, TX Roadhouse, Wienerschnitzel, Wendy's, **lodging:** Comfort Suites, Econolodge, Hampton Inn, Holiday Inn Express, La Quinta, Red Roof Inn, **other:** Albertson's, BigLots, Curves, $General, Family$, Firestone/auto, GNC, Goodyear/auto, Home Depot, PepBoys, SteinMart, Walmart SuperCtr/24hr, USPO, **S gas:** Chevron/dsl/24hr, Valero/dsl/24hr, **food:** Ay Caramba Mexican, Burger King, Church's, Golden Buddha, Jack-in-the-Box, KFC, McDonald's, Peter Piper Pizza, Pizza Hut, Smoothie King, Starbucks, Taco Cabana, Village Inn Rest., **lodging:** Day's Inn, Super 8, Travelodge, **other:** AutoZone, Big 8 Foods, $Tree, Hobby Lobby, Martin Tires, Radio Shack, Sam's Club/gas, Walgreens
9	Redd Rd, **N gas:** Valero, **food:** Applebee's, Baskin-Robbins, Burger King, Double Dave's Pizza, Pizza Hut, Starbucks, Subway, **other:** Albertson's/gas, Ford, Kohl's, Lowe's Whse, O'Reilly Parts, **S gas:** Circle K/gas, Shamrock, **other:** Chevrolet, Honda
8	Artcraft Rd, **S gas:** Shell/dsl, **food:** Carl's Jr, Rudy's BBQ, **lodging:** Hampton Inn, Holiday Inn Express, Microtel
6	Lp 375, to Canutillo, **N gas:** Shell/DQ/dsl, **other:** to Trans Mountain Rd, Franklin Mtns SP, **S gas:** Chevron/McDonald's, Shorty's/Mama's Mexican/dsl, **other:** El Paso Shops/Famous Brands, RV camping
5mm	**truck check sta eb**
2	Westway, Vinton, **N gas:** Petro/Mobil/Subway/dsl/scales/24hr/@, **other:** American RV Park, Camping World (1mi), PetroLube/tires, **S gas:** gas/24hr, **other:** Mack, truck repair/tires
1mm	**Welcome Ctr eb, full ♿ facilities, info, ☎, ⛺, litter barrels, petwalk, weigh sta wb**
0	FM 1905, Anthony, **N gas:** *FLYING J*/Conoco/dsl/LP/RV dump/24hr, **lodging:** Super 8, **S gas:** Fina/7-11/dsl, Pilot/Subway/Wendy's/dsl/24hr/@, **food:** Great American Steaks, **lodging:** Best Western, Burger King, KFC, Taco Bell, **other:** Anthony RV Ctr, Big 8 Foods, $General, Walgreens, funpark, truckwash, tires
0mm	Texas/New Mexico state line

INTERSTATE 20

E ↕ W — MARSHALL

Exit #	Services
636mm	Texas/Louisiana state line
635.5mm	**Welcome Ctr wb/parking area eb, full ♿ facilities, ☎, ⛺, litter barrels, petwalk**
635	TX 9, TX 156, to Waskom, **N gas:** Chevron/Burger King/dsl, Exxon/dsl, **food:** DQ, Jim's BBQ, **other:** Family$, USPO
633	US 80, FM 9, FM 134, to Waskom, **N gas:** Texaco, **food:** Catfish Village Rest., **S other:** Miss Ellie's RV Park
628	to US 80, to frontage rd
624	FM 2199, to Scottsville
620	FM 31, to Elysian Fields
617	US 59, Marshall, **0-2 mi N gas:** Exxon/dsl, Texaco/24hr, **food:** Applebee's, Burger King, Cafe Italia, Catfish Express, Golden Corral, Gucci's Pizza, IHOP, LJ Silver, McDonald's, Pizza Hut, Sonic, Subway, Taco Bell, Waffle House, Wendy's, Whataburger, **lodging:** Best Western, Comfort Suites, Fairfield Inn, Hampton Inn, La Quinta, Quality Inn, **other:** Buick/GMC/Pontiac, Cadillac/Chevrolet, Chrysler/Dodge/Jeep, Ford/Lincoln/Mercury, Toyota/Scion, Country Pines RV Park (8mi), **S gas:** Chevron/dsl, Pony Express/rest./dsl, Valero/dsl, **food:** Hungri Maverick Rest., **lodging:** Econolodge, Guest Inn, Holiday Inn Express, Motel 6, Super 8
614	TX 43, to Marshall, **S** to Martin Creek Lake SP
610	FM 3251
608mm	**rest area both lanes, full ♿ facilities, ☎, vending, ⛺, litter barrels**
604	FM 450, Hallsville, **N gas:** Shamrock/dsl, **other:** 450 Hitchin' Post RV Park, to Lake O' the Pines
600mm	Mason Creek
599	FM 968, Longview, **N lodging:** Comfort Suites, Fairfield Inn (8mi), Wingate Inn (8mi), **other:** Kenworth Trucks, **S gas:** Chevron/Natl TrkStp/Quizno's/dsl/scales/@, Exxon/dsl, **other:** Goodyear, truck repair
596	US 259 N, TX 149, to Lake O' Pines, **N gas:** Exxon/Grandy's/dsl, **food:** Burger King, Whataburger, **lodging:** Comfort Suites, Microtel, Super 8, **other:** H, **S gas:** Valero/dsl, **lodging:** Holiday Inn Express, **other:** to Martin Lake SP
595b a	TX 322, Estes Pkwy, **N gas:** Exxon, EZ Mart, Texaco/dsl/24hr, **food:** Jack-in-the-Box, McDonald's, Pizza Hut, Waffle House, **lodging:** Best Value Inn, Day's Inn, Express Inn, Guest Inn, La Quinta, **S gas:** Fina/dsl, Mobil, **food:** KFC/Taco Bell, **lodging:** Baymont Inn, Hampton Inn, Motel 6, **other:** Walmart SuperCtr/gas
593mm	Sabine River
591	FM 2087, FM 2011
589b a	US 259, TX 31, Kilgore (exits left from both lanes), **1-3 mi S food:** Kilgore Café, **lodging:** Budget Inn, Comfort Inn, Day's Inn, Holiday Inn Express, Homewood Suites, Ramada Inn, **S other:** E Texas Oil Museum
587	TX 42, Kilgore, **N gas:** Valero, **food:** Bodacious BBQ, **S gas:** Exxon/dsl, **other:** E TX Oil Museum, **3 mi S other:** Walmart SuperCtr
583	TX 135, to Kilgore, Overton, **N gas:** Exxon/dsl, **other:** Shallow Creek RV Resort
582	FM 3053, Liberty City, **N gas:** Chevron/Whataburger/dsl, Exxon/Subway/dsl, **food:** Bob's BBQ, DQ, Java House, Soda Shoppe, Sonic
579	Joy-Wright Mtn Rd
575	Barber Rd
574mm	**picnic area both lanes, ⛺, litter barrels, ♿ accessible**

INTERSTATE 20

E ↕ W

Exit #	Services
571b	FM 757, Omen Rd, to Starrville
571a	US 271, to Gladewater, Tyler, **S** **gas:** Shell/Sonic/Texas Smokehouse/dsl/scales/24hr
567	TX 155, **N** **gas:** Valero/dsl/24hr, **S** **lodging:** Day's Inn, **other:** H
565	FM 2015, to Driskill-Lake Rd
562	FM 14, **N** **food:** Bodacious BBQ, **other:** Northgate RV Park, to Tyler SP
560	Lavender Rd
557	Jim Hogg Rd, **N** **gas:** Shell
556	US 69, to Tyler, **N** **gas:** RaceWay, Shamrock/dsl, **food:** Burger King, Chili's, Domino's, Eastern Buffet, KFC\LJ Silver, Juanita's Mexicans, McDonald's, Pizza Inn, Posado's Cafe, Sonic, Subway, Taco Bell, Texas BBQ, **lodging:** Best Western, Comfort Suites, Day's Inn, Hampton Inn, La Quinta, **other:** Ace Hardware, Curves, Lowes Whse, Walmart SuperCtr/gas, Vet, **S** **gas:** Chevron, Exxon, **food:** Cracker Barrel, DQ, Wendy's, **lodging:** Best Value Inn
554	Harvey Rd, **S** **other:** Yellow Rose RV Park
552	FM 849, **N** **gas:** Shell, **food:** La Valleta Italian
548	TX 110, to Grand Saline, **N** **gas:** Exxon/dsl, **S** **gas:** Valero/dsl
546mm	**check sta eb**
544	Willow Branch Rd, **N** **gas:** Conoco/dsl/rest., **other:** Willow Branch RV Park
540	FM 314, to Van, **N** **gas:** Love's/Carl's Jr/dsl/24hr, **food:** DQ, **lodging:** Van Inn
538mm	**rest area both lanes, full ♿ facilities, ☎, vending, picnic, litter barrels, petwalk**
537	FM 773, FM 16
536	Tank Farm Rd
533	Oakland Rd, to Colfax, **N** **gas:** Shamrock/dsl/rest.
530	FM 1255, **N** **other:** RV Camping
528	FM 17, to Grand Saline
527	TX 19, **N** **gas:** Texaco/dsl/24hr, **food:** Burger King, Whataburger/24hr, **lodging:** Comfort Inn, Luxury Suites, Super 8, **S** **gas:** Chevron/dsl/24hr, Circle K/dsl/24hr, Shell/Subway/dsl, **food:** DQ, Dairy Palace, Juanita's Mexican, KFC/Taco Bell, McDonald's, Senorita's Mexican, **lodging:** Best Western, Day's Inn, **other:** Chrysler/Dodge/Jeep, Ford/Mercury, Mule Creek Ranch RV Resort, to First Monday SP, LP
526	FM 859, to Edgewood
523	TX 64, to Canton
521	Myrtle Springs Rd, **N** trailer sales, **S** **other:** Marshall's RV Ctr, RV camp/dump, U-Haul
519	Turner-Hayden Rd, **S** Canton RV Park
516	FM 47, to Wills Point, **N** to Lake Tawakoni, **S** **gas:** Shamrock/24hr, **food:** Robertson's Café/gas, **lodging:** Interstate Motel
512	FM 2965, Hiram-Wills Point Rd
512mm	**weigh sta both lanes**
509	Hiram Rd, **S** **gas:** Phillips 66/dsl/café
506	FM 429, FM 2728, College Mound Rd, **S** Blue Bonnet Ridge RV Park
503	Wilson Rd, **S** **gas:** TA/Shell/Country Fair/Pizza Hut/Subway/dsl/LP/24hr/@

CANTON

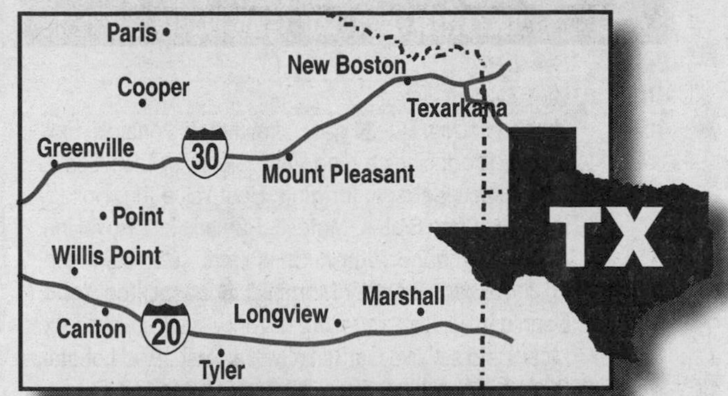

TERRELL

Exit #	Services
501	TX 34, to Terrell, **N** **gas:** Chevron/24hr, Exxon/dsl, **food:** Capt D's, Schlotsky's, Sonic, Starbucks, Waffle House, **lodging:** Best Value Inn, Best Western, Comfort Inn, Day's Inn, La Quinta, Motel 6, other: H, Home Depot, **S** gas: Circle K, Valero/dsl/24hr, **food:** Applebee's, Carmona's Cantina, IHOP, McDonald's, Wendy's, lodging: Holiday Inn Express, Super 8, **other:** Tanger Outlet/famous brands
499b	Rose Hill Rd, to Terrell
499a	to US 80, W to Dallas, same as 498
498	FM 148, to Terrell, **N** **gas:** Exxon/Denny's/Subway/dsl, Shell/dsl
493	FM 1641, **S** **gas:** Exxon/Pizza Inn/Sonic/dsl
491	FM 2932, Helms Tr, to Forney, **N** **gas:** Shell/Subway/dsl
490	FM 741, to Forney
487	FM 740, to Forney, **S** Forney RV park
483	Lawson Rd, Lasater Rd
482	Belt Line Rd, to Lasater, **S** **gas:** Shell/KFC/Pizza Hut/Subway, **other:** RV park
481	Seagoville Rd, **N** **gas:** Valero/dsl, Shell/Church's, **lodging:** La Quinta, **S** **food:** Lindy's Rest.
480	I-635, N to Mesquite
479b a	US 175, **S** **gas:** Shell/dsl
477	St Augustine Rd, **S** **gas:** Shell/dsl, **food:** Sonic
476	Dowdy Ferry Rd
474	TX 310 N, Central Expsy
473b a	JJ Lemmon Rd, I-45 N to Dallas, S to Houston
472	Bonnie View Rd, **N** **gas:** ***FLYING J***/Conoco/dsl/LP/rest./24hr/@, Shell, **food:** Jack-in-the-Box, **lodging:** Ramada Ltd, **other:** Blue Beacon, Speedco Lube, **S** **gas:** TA/Exxon/Burger King/Taco Bell/dsl/scales/24hr/@
470	TX 342, Lancaster Rd, **N** **gas:** Chevron, USA/Texaco/Popeye's/dsl/scales/24hr, **food:** Big Bruce's BBQ, **S** **gas:** Pilot/Wendy's/dsl/24hr, Shell, **food:** McDonald's, Sonic, Subway, Taco Bell/LJ Silver, Whataburger, William's Chicken, **lodging:** Day's Inn
468	Houston School Rd, **S** **gas:** Exxon/dsl, **food:** Whataburger
467b a	I-35E, N to Dallas, S to Waco, **1 mi N off of I-35E... gas:** Shell, **food:** McDonald's
466	S Polk St, **N** **gas:** Exxon, Texaco, **food:** DQ, Sonic, Subway, **S** **gas:** Love's/Carl's Jr/dsl/scales/24hr
465	Wheatland/S Hampton Rds, **N** **gas:** Shell/dsl, **S** **gas:** Chevron/McDonald's, RaceWay, **food:** Arby's, Cheddar's, Jack-in-the-Box, Popeye's, Sonic, Spring Creek BBQ, Taco Bell, Wendy's, **lodging:** Comfort Inn, Super 8, **other:** H, Buick/GMC/Pontiac, Home Depot, Honda, Hyundai, Lincoln/Mercury, Lowes Whse, Mazda, PetsMart, Sam's Club/gas, Walmart SuperCtr/24hr

DALLAS

INTERSTATE 20 CONT'D

E ↕ W

DALLAS

Exit #	Services
464b a	US 67, Love Fwy
463	Camp Wisdom Rd, **N gas:** Chevron/McDonald's, Exxon, TA, **food:** Catfish King Rest., Denny's, Taco Bell/LJ Silver, Taco Cabana, **lodging:** Best Value Inn, Holiday Inn, Lexington Suites, Motel 6, Ramada Inn, Royal Inn, Suburban Lodge, **other:** Chief Parts, Chrysler/Jeep, Ford, Nissan, Tuesday Morning, **S gas:** Citgo, **food:** Bennigan's, Blimpie, Burger King, Jack-in-the-Box, McDonald's, Olive Garden, Owens Rest., Red Lobster, Subway, Wendy's, **other:** Advance Parts, Best Buy, K-Mart, NTB, PepBoys, Pontiac, Target, Toyota
462b a	Duncanville Rd (no EZ wb return), **S gas:** Exxon, Shell/dsl, **food:** Arby's, KFC, Mr Gatti's, Whataburger, **lodging:** Hilton Garden, Motel 6, **other:** Goodyear, Kroger, Radio Shack
461	Cedar Ridge Rd
460	TX 408
458	MT Creek Pkwy
457	FM 1382, to Grand Prairie, **N gas:** Shell/dsl, Valero/dsl, **food:** Waffle House, **S gas:** RaceTrac, **food:** Jack-in-the-Box, **other:** to Joe Pool Lake
456	Carrier Pkwy, to Corn Valley Rd, **N food:** Chick-fil-A, Don Pablo, Taco Cabana, Whataburger, **other:** Home Depot, Kohl's, Radio Shack, Target, **S gas:** Shell, **food:** Boston Mkt, Chapp's Cafe, Cheddar's, Chili's, Denny's, IHOP, McDonald's, Spring Creek BBQ, Subway, **lodging:** Holiday Inn Express, **other:** Albertson's/gas, CVS Drug, Walgreens, Vet
454	Great Southwest Pkwy, **N gas:** Chevron/24hr, Conoco/dsl, **food:** Beto's, Carino's Italian, China Dragon, ChuckeCheese, KFC, McDonald's, Taco Bell, Taco Bueno, Texas Roadhouse, Waffle House, Wendy's, Wienerschnitzel, **lodging:** Heritage Inn, La Quinta, Quality Inn, **other:** H, Harley-Davidson, **S gas:** 7-11, Shell/Subway/dsl, Valero/dsl, **food:** Applebee's, Arby's, Buffalo Wild Wings, Burger King, Schlotsky's, Sonic, **lodging:** Comfort Inn, Super 8, **other:** Discount Tire, Dodge, $Tree, Kroger, Office Depot, PetsMart, Sam's Club, Walgreens, Walmart SuperCtr/24hr, to Joe Pool Lake
453b a	TX 360
452	Frontage Rd
451	Collins St, New York Ave, **N gas:** Mobil, RaceTrac, **food:** Jack-in-the-Box, Pizza Hut, **other:** Acura, Chrysler/Jeep, Kia/Mazda/VW, **S gas:** QT, Shamrock, Shell, **food:** Chicken Express, McDonald's, Sonic, Taco Bueno, **lodging:** Hampton Inn, **other:** Buick/GMC/Pontiac, Lincoln/Mercury, Nissan
450	Matlock Rd, **N gas:** Citgo/7-11, Fina/dsl, **food:** BJ's Brewhouse, Bravo Italian, Genghis Grill, IHOP, Mercado Juarez Café, PF Changs, Rio Bravo, Spaghetti Whse, Wendy's, **lodging:** Quality Inn, **other:** H, Border's, Jo-Ann Fabrics, Lowes Whse, Michael's, Old Navy, PetsMart, Staples, **S gas:** Citgo/7-11, Shamrock, Shell, **food:** Joe's Pizza, **other:** Fry's Electronics, NTB
449	FM 157, Cooper St, **N gas:** Mobil, Shell, 7-11, Texaco, **food:** Abuelo's Mexican, Atlanta Bread, Bennigan's, Blackeyed Pea, Cheesecake Factory, Chili's, China Café, CiCi's, Corner Bakery, Don Pablo,

DALLAS

Exit #	Services
449	Continued Golden Corral, Grandy's, Hong Kong Cafe, Jason's Deli, KFC, McDonald's, On-the-Border, Outback Steaks, Razzoo's Cajun Café, Red Lobster, Rock Fish Grill, Salt Grass Steaks, Schlotsky's, Souper Salad, Spaghetti Whse, Starbucks, Thai Cuisine, Wendy's, Whataburger, **lodging:** Best Western, Days Inn, Holiday Inn Express, Homestead Village, La Quinta, Studio 6, **other:** Barnes&Noble, Best Buy, Dillard's, Discount Tire, Hancock Fabrics, Hyundai, JC Penney, Office Depot, PetCo, Sears/auto, Subaru, Target, TJ Maxx, mall, **S gas:** Chevron, Conoco, Shell, **food:** Applebee's, Arby's, Boston Mkt, Burger King, Burger St, Chick-fil-A, Denny's, El Fenix Mexican, LJ Silver, Luby's, Macaroni Grill, McDonald's, Olive Garden, Panda Express, Popeye's, Ryan's, Sonic, Subway, Taco Bueno, TGIFriday, **lodging:** InTown Suites, **other:** Acura, Ford, GMC, Home Depot, Honda, Hyundai, Isuzu, Kia, K-Mart, Kroger, Pontiac, Ross, Walmart SuperCtr/24hr
448	Bowen Rd, **N gas:** QT, RaceTrac, Shell/24hr, **food:** Cracker Barrel, **S gas:** Shell
447	Kelly-Elliott Rd, Park Springs Blvd, **N gas:** Lonestar Express, 7-11, **S gas:** Exxon, Fina/Blimpie, **other:** camping
445	Green Oaks Blvd, **N gas:** Conoco, Shell, **food:** Arby's, Boston Mkt, Burger King, Grandy's, Hooters, Jack-in-the-Box, KFC, Koltr's BBQ, Mac's Grill, Pizza Hut, Pizza Inn, Schlotsky's, Taco Bell, Taco Cabana, Taipan Chinese, Whataburger, **other:** Albertson's, /24hr, Minyard/gas/food, Office Depot, **S gas:** Chevron/24hr, Citgo/7-11, Shamrock, **food:** Cheddar's, IHOP, Fazoli's, Khaki's, McDonald's, Pancho's Mexican, Panda Express, Sonic, Steak&Ale, Taco Bueno, Waffle House, **other:** AutoZone, Discount Tire, $General, O'Reilly Parts
444	US 287 S, to Waxahatchie
443	Bowman Springs Rd (from wb)
442b a	I-820 to Ft Worth, US 287 bus, **N gas:** Valero, **lodging:** Great Western Inn, Super 8, **S gas:** Chevron
441	Anglin Dr, Hartman Lane, **N gas:** Valero/dsl, **lodging:** Super 8, **S gas:** Conoco/dsl
440b	Forest Hill Dr, **N gas:** Value Place Inn, **S gas:** Chevron/24hr, Conoco, Shell/dsl, **food:** Braum's, Capt D's, CiCi's, DQ, Denny's, Domino's, Jack-in-the-Box, Luby's, McDonald's, Sonic, Starbucks, Subway, **lodging:** Comfort Inn, **other:** AutoZone, CVS Drug, Discount Tire, $General, $Tree, Super 1 Foods, Walgreens
440a	Wichita St, **N gas:** Chevron/dsl, **food:** #1 Chinese, Taco Casa, Wendy's, **S gas:** Texaco, Valero, **food:** Braum's, Chicken Express, Denny's, Domino's, McDonald's, Pizza Hut, Schlotzsky's, Taco Bueno, Whataburger, **lodging:** Comfort Inn
439	Camp US Dr, **N other:** Ford, Chrysler/Jeep, **S other:** Sam's Club/gas
438	Oak Grove Rd, **1 mi N gas:** Shell, **food:** Burger King, Denny's, Jack-in-the Box, McDonald's, Whataburger, **lodging:** Day's Inn, **S gas:** Valero
437	I-35W, N to Ft Worth, S to Waco
436b	Hemphill St, **N gas:** Shell/dsl, **S other:** Chevrolet
436a	FM 731 (from eb), to Crowley Ave, **N gas:** Valero, **other:** $General, Sav-a-Lot Foods, **S gas:** Conoco/dsl, **food:** DQ, Pizza Hut/Taco Bell, Subway

FT WORTH

INTERSTATE 20 CONT'D

E ↔ W

FT WORTH

Exit #	Services
435	McCart St, **N gas:** Shell, Shamrock, **S gas:** Mobil
434b	Trail Lakes Dr, **S gas:** Shell, **food:** Sonic, Starbucks, **other:** CVS Drug
434a	Granbury rd, **S food:** Pancho's Mexican, Wendy's, **other:** JoAnn Fabrics
433	Hulen St, **N gas:** Shell/dsl, **food:** ChuckeCheese, Grady's Grill, Hooters, Olive Garden, Souper Salad, Subway, TGIFriday, **lodging:** TownePlace Suites, **other:** Albertson's, Home Depot, Office Depot, PetsMart, TJ Maxx, **S gas:** Valero, **food:** Bennigan's, Denny's, Jack-in-the-Box, McDonald's, Red Lobster, Taco Bell, **lodging:** Hampton Inn, **other:** Borders, Dillards, Macy's, Ross, mall
431	(432 from wb), TX 183, Bryant-Irvin Rd, **N food:** Chipotle Mexican, Genghis Grill, Mimi's Café, On-the-Border, Taste of Asia, **other:** Best Buy, Kohls, Lowes Whse, Sam's Club/gas, **S gas:** Chevron/24hr, Exxon, QT, Shell, Texaco, **food:** Blackeyed Pea, Chicken Express, Chick-fil-A, Cousin's BBQ, Fuddruckers, IHOP, Outback Steaks, Quizno's, Razzoo's Cajun, Rio Mambo, SaltGrass Steaks, Schlotzsky's, Sonic, Starbucks, Subway, **lodging:** AmeriSuites, Extended Stay America, Holiday Inn Express, Hyatt Place, La Quinta, **other:** H, Buick, Costco/gas, Ford, Goodyear/auto, Lexus, Mazda, PetCo, Suzuki, Staples, Target, Tom Thumb/gas, Walgreens, transmissions/repair
430mm	Clear Fork Trinity River
429b	Winscott Rd, **N gas:** Circle K/dsl **food:** Cracker Barrel, **lodging:** Best Western, Comfort Suites
429a	US 377, to Granbury, **S gas:** RaceTrac/24hr, Valero, **food:** Arby's, Burger King, Chicken Express, Domino's, DQ, Jack-in-the-Box, KFC/Taco Bell, McDonald's, Sonic, Starbucks, Waffle House, Whataburger/24hr, **lodging:** Motel 6, **other:** Albertson's, AutoZone, $General, Walgreens
428	I-820, N around Ft Worth
426	RM 2871, Chapin School Rd
425	Markum Ranch Rd
421	I-30 E (from eb), to Ft Worth
420	FM 1187, Aledo, Farmer, **parking**
419mm	**weigh sta eb**
418	Ranch House Rd, Willow Park, Willow Park, **N gas:** Exxon, Shell/dsl, **food:** Los Vaqueros, Pizza Hut, Sonic, Subway, Taco Casa, Whataburger, **S gas:** Shell/ChickenExpress/dsl, **food:** Domino's, McDonald's, **lodging:** Ramada Inn, **other:** Cowtown RV Park, Brookshire Foods, Funtime RV Park (1mi)
417mm	**weigh sta wb**
415	FM 5, Mik US Rd, Annetta, **S gas:** Shell/dsl, **other:** 415 RV Ctr
413	(414 from wb), US 180 W, Lake Shore Dr, **N gas:** RaceTrac, Texaco/dsl, Valero, **food:** DQ, Sonic, **other:** Buick/GMC/Pontiac, Cadillac/Chevrolet, Ford, Jeep, Lincoln/Mercury, Nissan, Toyota/Scion, Walmart SuperCtr/Subway/dsl/24hr, **S gas:** Chevron/dsl, Valero
410	Bankhead Hwy, **S gas:** Loves/Subway/dsl/24hr
409	FM 2552 N, Clear Lake Rd, **N gas:** Petro/Mobil/dsl/rest./24hr/@, **food:** David Beard's Catfish, Jack-in-the-Box, **lodging:** Best Western, Sleepgo, **other:** H Blue Beacon, **S gas:** Shell/dsl

WEATHERFORD

Exit #	Services
408	TX 171, FM 1884, FM 51, Tin Top Rd, Weatherford, **N gas:** Exxon/Pizza Inn/24hr, Mobil, **food:** Applebee's, Baker's Ribs, Braum's, Chicken Express, China Garden, Cotton Patch Cafe, Dickey's BBQ, Golden Corral, IHOP, LJ Silver, Logan's Roadhouse, McDonald's, Mt Rest., Schlotsky's, Starbucks, Subway, Taco Bell, Taco Bueno, Wendy's, Whataburger, **lodging:** La Quinta, Sleep Inn, Super 8, **other:** AutoZone, Belk, Discount Tire, $Tree, Home Depot, JC Penney, Kroger, Walmart SuperCtr/gas/24hr, **S gas:** Exxon/Subway/dsl, Shell/Burger King/dsl/24hr, **food:** Chick-fil-A, Chili's, Coldstone Creamery, Cracker Barrel, On-the-Border, Waffle House, **lodging:** Comfort Suites, Hampton Inn, Holiday Inn Express, Motel 6, Super Value Inn, **other:** Best Buy, GNC, Kohls, Lowes Whse, NTB, Ross, Target
407	Tin Top Rd (from eb), **S other:** Serenity Ranch RV Park, same as 408
406	Old Dennis Rd, **N gas:** Conoco/dsl/24hr, **food:** Chuck Wagon Rest., **lodging:** Quest Inn, **S gas:** Pilot/Wendy's/dsl/scales/24hr, **lodging:** Econolodge, Quality 1 Motel, **other:** Rip Griffin Repair
402	(403 from wb), TX 312, to Weatherford
397	FM 1189, to Brock, **N gas:** Valero/dsl, **S** tires
394	FM 113, to Millsap, **N other:** Hillbilly Haven RV Park
393mm	Brazos River
391	Gilbert Pit Rd
390mm	**rest area both lanes, full facilities, vending, litter barrels, petwalk**
386	US 281, to Mineral Wells, **N gas:** Shell/Subway/dsl
380	FM 4, Santo, **S food:** Sunday Creek BBQ, **other:** Windmill Acres RV Park
376	Blue Flat Rd, Panama Rd
373	TX 193, Gordon
370	TX 108 S, FM 919, Gordon, **N gas:** Texaco/Bar-B/dsl/rest., **S gas:** Exxon/dsl, **other:** Cactus Rose RV Park, Longhorn Inn/Country Store
367	TX 108 N, Mingus, **N food:** Smoke Stack Café, **other:** Thurber Sta, **S food:** NY Hill Rest.
364mm	Palo Pinto Creek
363	Tudor Rd, **area, litter barrels**
362mm	**Bear Creek, area both lanes, litter barrels**
361	TX 16, to Strawn
358	(from wb), frontage rd
356mm	Russell Creek
354	Lp 254, Ranger
351	(352 from wb), College Blvd
349	FM 2461, Ranger, **N gas:** Love's/Godfather's/Subway/dsl/scales/24hr, **food:** DQ, **lodging:** Best Value Inn, Relax Inn (2mi), **other:** RL RV Park, **S gas:** Shell/dsl, repair

INTERSTATE 20 CONT'D

E ↕ W

Exit #	Services
347	FM 3363 (from wb), Olden, **S** **other:** TX Steak Exchange
345	FM 3363 (from eb), Olden, **S** **food:** Texas Steakhouse
343	TX 112, FM 570, Eastland, Lake Leon, **N** **gas:** Conoco/dsl, Fina/7-11/Subway, Shell, **food:** Chicken Express, DQ, McDonald's, Pizza Inn, Sonic, Starbucks, Taco Bell, **lodging:** La Quinta, Super 8/RV park, **other:** AutoZone, Buick/Cadillac/Chevrolet, Chrysler/Dodge/Jeep, Curves, $General, Ford/Mercury, GMC/Pontiac, O'Reilly Parts, Walmart/SuperCtr/dsl/24hr, **S** **gas:** Exxon/dsl/24hr, **food:** Pulido's Mexican, **lodging:** Budget Host, Ramada Inn
340	TX 6, Eastland, **N** **gas:** Chevron/dsl, **other:** H, **S** **gas:** Shell/dsl
337	spur 490, **N** **other:** The Wild Country RV Park
332	US 183, Cisco, **N** **gas:** Exxon, **food:** Cow Pokes, DQ, Pizza Heaven, Sonic, Subway, **lodging:** Executive Inn, Knight's Inn, **S** **gas:** Fina/dsl
330	TX 206, Cisco, **N** **lodging:** Best Value Inn, **other:** H
329mm	**area wb, litter barrels, accessible**
327mm	**area eb, litter barrels, accessible**
324	Scranton Rd
322	Cooper Creek Rd
320	FM 880 N, FM 2945 N, to Moran
319	FM 880 S, Putnam, **N** **gas:** gas/dsl/café, **other:** USPO
316	Brushy Creek Rd
313	FM 2228
310	Finley Rd
308	Lp 20, Baird
307	US 283, Clyde, **N** **food:** DQ, **lodging:** Baird Motel/RV park/dump, **S** **gas:** Conoco/dsl, **food:** Robertson's Café
306	FM 2047, Baird, **N** **other:** Chevrolet/GMC/Pontiac, Chrysler/Dodge/Jeep, Hanner RV Ctr
303	Union Hill Rd
301	FM 604, Cherry Lane, **N** **gas:** Exxon/Subway/dsl, **food:** Sonic, Whataburger/24hr, **S** **gas:** Fina/7-11/dsl/café, Shell/dsl/24hr, **food:** DQ, **other:** Family$
300	FM 604 N, Clyde, **N** **other:** Chrysler/Dodge/Jeep, **S** **gas:** Conoco/dsl, **other:** White's RV Park/dump
299	FM 1707, Hays Rd
297	FM 603, Eula Rd
296.5mm	**rest area both lanes, full facilities, , , litter barrels, petwalk**
294	Buck Creek Rd, **N** RV Dump, **S** West TX RV Ctr
292b	Elmdale Rd
292a	Lp 20 (exits left from wb)
290	TX 36, Lp 322, **S** , zoo
288	TX 351, **N** **gas:** Fina/7-11/Subway/dsl, **food:** Chili's, Cracker Barrel, DQ, Skillet's Café, **lodging:** Comfort Suites, Day's Inn, Executive Inn, Holiday Inn Express, Quality Inn, Whitten Inn, **other:** $Tree, Lowes Whse, Walmart SuperCtr/gas/24hr, **S** **lodging:** Super 8, **other:** H
286c	FM 600, Abilene, **N** **gas:** Exxon/dsl, Fina/dsl, **food:** Denny's/24hr, **lodging:** Best Western, Hampton Inn, La Quinta, **S** **gas:** Fina/7-11/dsl, **other:** Russell Stover's Candies
286	US 83, Pine St, Abilene, **S** **gas:** Fina, **lodging:** Budget Host, **other:** H
285	Old Anson Rd, **N** **gas:** Exxon/dsl, **lodging:** Travel Inn, **S** **gas:** Exxon/dsl
283a	US 277 S, US 83 (exits left from wb)
282	FM 3438, Shirley Rd, **S** **lodging:** Motel 6, **other:** KOA
280	Fulwiler Rd, to Dyess air force base
279	US 84 E, to Abilene, **1-3 mi S access to services**
278	Lp 20, **N** **gas:** Conoco/dsl/24hr, **other:** dsl repair, **S** **gas:** Conoco/dsl/rest./scales/@, **other:** Mac Trucks/Volvo
277	FM 707, Tye, **N** **gas:** ***FLYING J***/Shell/Country Mkt/dsl/LP/24hr/@, **other:** Tiey RV Park, **S** **gas:** Fina/7-11/dsl
274	Wells Lane
272	Wimberly Rd
270	FM 1235, Merkel, **N** **gas:** Conoco/dsl, Shell/dsl/café/24hr
269	FM 126, **N** **food:** Subway, **lodging:** Scottish Inn, **S** **gas:** Fina/dsl/rest./24hr, Shell, **food:** DQ, Skeet's BBQ
267	Lp 20, Merkel, **1 mi S** access to gas, food, lodging
266	Derstine Rd
264	Noodle Dome Rd
263	Lp 20, Trent
262	FM 1085, **S** **gas:** Fina/7-11/dsl/24hr
261	Lp 20, Trent
259	Sylvester Rd
258	White Flat Rd, oil wells
257mm	**rest area both lanes, full facilities, , vending, , litter barrels, petwalk**
256	Stink Creek Rd
255	Adrian Rd
251	Eskota Rd
249	FM 1856
247	TX 70 N, Sweetwater
246	Alabama Ave, Sweetwater
245	Arizona Ave (from wb), same as 244
244	TX 70 S, Sweetwater, **N** **gas:** Chevron/dsl, Fina/dsl/24hr, **food:** Domino's, DQ, McDonald's, Subway, Wendy's, **lodging:** Best Western, La Quinta, Motel 6, **other:** H, AutoZone, Ford/Mercury, Health Mart Drugs, Walmart SuperCtr/gas/24hr, **S** **gas:** Chevron, Shell, **food:** Buck's BBQ, Golden Chick, Great Wall, Schlotsky's, Taco Bell, **lodging:** Days Inn, Holiday Inn Express, Ranch House Motel/rest., Super 8, **other:** Buick/Cadillac/Chevrolet/Pontiac, K-Mart,
243	Hillsdale Rd, Robert Lee St, **N** **other:** Bewley's Service
242	Hopkins Rd, **S** **gas:** TA/Conoco/Pizza Hut/dsl/scales/24hr/@, **other:** Rolling Plains RV Park, truck/tire repair
241	Lp 20, Sweetwater, **N** gas, food, lodging, **S** RV camping
240	Lp 170, **N** , camping
239	May Rd
238b a	US 84 W, Blackland Rd
237	Cemetery Rd
236	FM 608, Roscoe, **N** **gas:** Shell, TC/Country Cookin/dsl, **other:** NAPA
235	to US 84, Roscoe, **S** **other:** Travel Stop/rest./truck repair/dsl

ABILENE

SWEETWATER

TX

INTERSTATE 20 CONT'D

E ↕ W

Exit #	Services
230	FM 1230, many wind turbines
229mm	**area wb, litter barrels, ♿ accessible**
228mm	**area eb, litter barrels, ♿ accessible**
227	Narrell Rd
226b	Lp 20 (from wb), Loraine
226a	FM 644 N, Wimberly Rd
225	FM 644 S, **1 mi S** access to gas, food
224	Lp 20, to Loraine, **1 mi S** gas, food
223	Lucas Rd, **S other:** 223 RV Park
221	Lasky Rd
220	FM 1899
219	Lp 20, Country Club Rd, Colorado City
217	TX 208 S
216	TX 208 N, **N gas:** Chevron/Subway/dsl, **food:** DQ, **lodging:** Day's Inn, **S gas:** TC/Country Cookin/dsl, **food:** China Star, Pizza Hut, Sonic, **lodging:** American Inn, **other:** [H], Alco, Health Mart Drugs, Parts+
215	FM 3525, Rogers Rd, **2 mi S** access to gas, food
214.5mm	Colorado River
213	Lp 20, Enderly Rd, Colorado City
212	FM 1229
211mm	FM 1229, Morgan Creek
210	FM 2836, **S gas:** Just Stop/dsl, **other:** to Lake Colorado City SP, area, camping
209	Dorn Rd
207	Lp 20, Westbrook
206	FM 670, to Westbrook
204mm	**rest area wb, full ♿ facilities, ☎, , litter barrels, petwalk**
200	Conaway Rd
199	Latan Rd
195	frontage rd (from eb)
194a	E Howard Field Rd
192	FM 821, many oil wells
191mm	**rest area eb, full ♿ facilities, ☎, , litter barrels, petwalk**
190	Snyder Field Rd
189	McGregor Rd
188	FM 820, Coahoma, **N gas:** TC/Country Cookin/dsl, **food:** DQ, **other:** USPO
186	Salem Rd, Sand Springs
184	Moss Lake Rd, Sand Springs, **N gas:** Fina/dsl, **S** RV camping
182	Midway Rd
181b	Refinery Rd, **N gas:** Fina Refinery
181a	FM 700, **N** ✈, RV camping, **2 mi S** [H]
179	US 80, Big Spring, **S gas:** Fina/7-11, **food:** Denny's, **lodging:** Camlot Inn, Comfort Inn, Quality Inn, **other:** $General, Buick/Cadillac/Chevrolet
178	TX 350, Big Spring, **N gas:** Shell/dsl, **S other:** truck repair
177	US 87, Big Spring, **N gas:** Exxon/dsl, TA/Popeye's/Subway/dsl/scales/24hr/@, **food:** Texas Cajan Cafe, **lodging:** Advantage Inn, Motel 6, Whitten Inn, **S gas:** Chevron/dsl, Fina/dsl, **food:** Casa Blanca Mexican, DQ, **lodging:** Best Western, Holiday Inn Express
176	TX 176, Andrews
174	Lp 20 E, Big Springs, **S gas:** Shell/dsl, **other:** [H], ✈
172	Cauble Rd

BIG SPRING

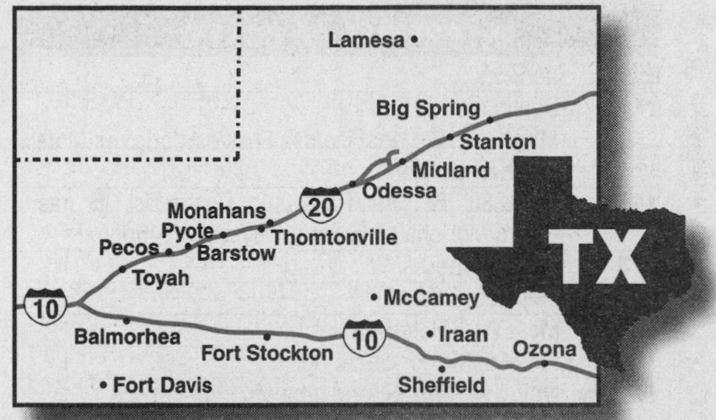

Exit #	Services
171	Moore Field Rd
169	FM 2599
168mm	**area both lanes, litter barrels**
165	FM 818
158	Lp 20 W, to Stanton, **N** RV camping
156	TX 137, Lamesa, **S gas:** Phillips 66/Country Cookin/Subway/dsl/24hr, **food:** Sonic
154	US 80, Stanton, **2 mi S** access to gas, food, lodging
151	FM 829 (from wb)
144	Loop 250, **2-3 mi N services in Midland**
143mm	frontage rd (from eb)
142mm	**area both lanes, litter barrels, hist marker**
140	FM 307 (from eb)
138	TX 158, FM 715, Greenwood, **N gas:** Shell/dsl, United/dsl, **food:** KD's BBQ, Whataburger/24hr, **S gas:** TC/Subway/dsl
137	Old Lamesa Rd
136	TX 349, Midland, **N gas:** Fina/dsl, **food:** Domino's, DQ, Gatty's Pizza, IHOP, Little Caesar's, McAlister's Deli, Sonic, Starbucks, **lodging:** Comfort Inn, West Texas Inn, **other:** Advance Parts, AutoZone, $Tree, Family$, McAllister's Deli, Petroleum Museum, Walmart SuperCtr/gas/24hr, tires, **S gas:** Exxon/Burger King/dsl, Daves Gas/NAPA, TC/Country Cookin
134	Midkiff Rd, **0-1 mi** (Wall St) **N gas:** Chevron/Subway/dsl, Fina/7-11, Exxon/dsl, **food:** Denny's, DQ, **lodging:** Best Value Inn, Clarion, Day's Inn, Executive Inn, La Quinta, Motel 6, Super 8, **other:** [H], Bo's RV Ctr, Casey's Camper, Chevrolet, Chrysler/Jeep, Honda, Ford, Mercedes/Volvo, Midland RV Park, Nissan, Toyota
131	TX 158, Midland, **N lodging:** Travelodge, **other:** Midland RV Park
126	FM 1788, **N gas:** Chevron/dsl, Pilot/McDonald's/dsl, Warfield/Texaco/Subway/dsl/scales/@, **other:** Western Auto, museum, ✈
121	Lp 338, Odessa, **0-3 mi** (**TX 191**) **N gas:** Chevron/dsl, Fina/7-11, **food:** Carino's, Chili's, Fazoli's, Logan's Roadhouse, McDonald's, Pizza Hut, Quizno's, Rosa's Cafe, Schlotzky's, Whataburger, **lodging:** Day's Inn, Elegante Hotel, Fairfield Inn, Grand Hotel, Hampton Inn, Holiday Inn, La Quinta, Marriott, Motel 6, **other:** Albertson's, Buick/GMC/Pontiac, Home Depot, Sears/auto, Sam's Club/gas, Staples, Target, Walmart SuperCtr/24hr, U of TX Permian Basin
120	JBS Pkwy, new exit
118	FM 3503, Grandview Ave, **N gas:** Fina/dsl, **other:** Freightliner/Peterbilt,
116	US 385, Craine, Andrews, **N gas:** Chevron, **food:** DQ, **lodging:** Best Western, Delux Inn, Villa West Inn,

MIDLAND

INTERSTATE 20 CONT'D

E ↔ W — MONAHANS — PECOS

Exit #	Services
116	Continued **other:** [H], **S gas:** Fina/dsl, Shell/dsl, **lodging:** Motel 6, **other:** city park
115	FM 1882, **N gas:** TC/Country Cookin/dsl, **S gas:** Love's/McDonald's/Subway/dsl/scales/24hr
113	TX 302, Odessa
112	FM 1936, Odessa
108	Moss Ave, Meteor Crater
104	FM 866, Meteor Crater Rd
103.5mm	**weigh sta wb/parking area eb, litter barrels**
101	FM 1601, Penwell
93	FM 1053
86	TX 41, **N** Monahans Sandhills SP, camping
83	US 80, Monahans, **2 mi N other:** [H], RV camping
80	TX 18, Monahans, **N gas:** Chevron/dsl/24hr, **food:** Bar-H Steaks, DQ, Great Wall Buffet, McDonald's, Pappy's BBQ, Pizza Hut, Sonic, **other:** [H], Alco Discount, CarQuest, $General, Family$, Kwik Lube, Lowe's Foods, RV Park, **S gas:** Fina/dsl/24hr, Kent Gas, TC/Subway/dsl, **lodging:** Best Value Inn, Best Western, Texan Inn, **other:** Buick/Chevrolet/GMC/Pontiac, Chrysler/Dodge/Jeep
79	Lp 464, Monahans
76	US 80, Monahans, **2 mi N other:** to Million Barrel Museum, RV camping
73	FM 1219, Wickett, **N gas:** Shell/Allsup's, **S gas:** Texaco/Subway/dsl/24hr
70	TX 65
69.5mm	**rest area both lanes, full [handicapped] facilities, [phone], [picnic], litter barrels, petwalk**
66	FM 1927, to Pyote
58	frontage rd, multiple oil wells
52	Lp 20 W, to Barstow
49	FM 516, to Barstow
48mm	Pecos River
44	Collie Rd
42	US 285, Pecos, **N gas:** Chevron/24hr, Fina, ***FLYING J***/Conoco/dsl/scales/24hr/@, Shell/dsl, Valero, **food:** DQ, El Rodeo Mexican, Panda House, Pizza Hut, **lodging:** Motel 6, Quality Inn, OakTree Inn, **other:** AutoZone, Walmart/24hr, museum, tire repair
40	Country Club Dr, **N** st patrol, **S gas:** Chevron/Subway, **lodging:** Best Western/rest., **other:** Chevrolet, RV camping, municipal park
39	TX 17, Pecos, **S other:** Chevrolet/Buick
37	Lp 20 E, **2 mi N food:** Sonic
33	FM 869
29	Shaw Rd, **S** to TX AM Ag Sta
25mm	**[picnic] area both lanes, litter barrels, [handicapped] accessible**
22	FM 2903, to Toyah
13	McAlpine Rd
7	Johnson Rd
3	Stocks Rd
0mm	**I-20 begins/ends on I-10, 187mm**

INTERSTATE 27

N ↔ S — AMARILLO

Exit #	Services
	I-27 begins/ends on I-40, exit 70 in Amarillo.
123b	I-40, W to Albuquerque, E to OK City
123a	26th Ave, **E gas:** Fina, **W food:** DJ Burgers, La Campana Mexican
122c	from sb only
122b	34th Ave, Tyler St, **E gas:** Conoco, Shell, Valero, **food:** Sonic
122a	FM 1541, Washington St, Parker St, Moss Lane, **W food:** Hungry Howie's
121b	Hawthorne Dr, Austin St, **E lodging:** Amarillo Motel, **other:** Honda Motorcycles, **W other:** Scottie's Transmissions
121a	Georgia St, **E gas:** Phillips 66/dsl, **food:** BBQ, Waffle House, **other:** Buick/Pontiac/GMC, Honda, Mazda, Nissan, Sizemore RV, Subaru, Toyota, Walmart SuperCtr/24hr/gas
120b	45th Ave, **E gas:** Fina, **food:** Waffle House, **other:** repair, **W gas:** Exxon, Valero, **food:** Abuelo's Mexican, Burger King (.5mi), Gatti's Pizza, Grand Burger, McDonald's, Whataburger, **other:** Advance Parts, BMW, Dodge, $General, Drug Emporium
120a	Republic Ave
119b	Western St, 58th Ave, **E gas:** Phillips 66, **food:** Sonic, **other:** $General, **W gas:** Shell/dsl, Valero, **food:** Arby's, Braum's, LJ Silver, Ming Palace Chinese, Pizza Hut, Wendy's, **other:** Aamco, Stout RV Ctr, U-Haul, USPO
119a	W Hillside
117	Bell St, Arden Rd, **E other:** transmissions, **W gas:** Shell/24hr, **food:** Burger Palace, LJ Silver, Popeye's, Sonic, **other:** $General
116	Lp 335, Hollywood Rd, **E gas:** Love's/Subway/dsl/24hr, Phillips 66/dsl, **food:** McDonald's, Waffle House, Whataburger, **lodging:** Comfort Suites, Day's Inn, **W other:** [H] (8mi)
115	Sundown Lane
113	McCormick Rd, **E other:** Ford, **W other:** Family Camping Ctr
112	FM 2219, **E other:** Stater's RV Ctr
111	Rockwell Rd, **E other:** Chevrolet, **W other:** Buick/GMC/Pontiac
110	(from sb) US 87 S, US 60 W, Canyon
109	Buffalo Stadium Rd, **W** stadium
108	FM 3331, Hunsley Rd
106	TX 217, to Palo Duro Cyn SP, Canyon, **E other:** Palo Duro RV Park, RV camping, **W lodging:** Holiday Inn Express (2mi), **other:** Plains Museum, to WTA&M
103	FM 1541 N, Cemetery Rd
99	Hungate Rd
98mm	**parking area both lanes, litter barrels**
96	Dowlen Rd
94	FM 285, to Wayside
92	Haley Rd
90	FM 1075, Happy, **W** gas/dsl
88b a	US 87 N, FM 1881, Happy, same as 90
83	FM 2698
82	FM 214
77	US 87, Tulia, **1-2 mi E gas:** Phillips 66, **food:** Pizza Hut, Sonic, **lodging:** Lasso Inn, **other:** [H], Ford, [airport]
75	NW 6th St, Tulia, **1 mi E gas:** Phillips 66, Shell, **food:** DQ, Pizza Hut, Sonic, **lodging:** Lasso Motel, **W** same as 74
74	TX 86, Tulia, **E lodging:** Lasso Motel, **other:** [H], **W gas:** Rip Griffin/Phillips 66/Subway/Chester's/dsl/scales/24hr/@, **lodging:** Select Inn

INTERSTATE 27

Exit #	Services
70mm	**parking area both lanes, litter barrels**
68	FM 928
63	FM 145, Kress, **1 mi E** gas/dsl, food, phone
61	US 87, County Rd
56	FM 788
54	FM 3183, to Plainview, **W** truck service
53	Lp 27, Plainview, **E other:** [H], access to gas, camping, food, lodging
51	Quincy St
50	TX 194, Plainview, **E gas:** Phillips 66, **other:** [H], to Wayland Bapt U
49	US 70, Plainview, **E gas:** Allstar Fuel/dsl, Conoco, Fina/dsl, Valero/dsl, Shell/dsl, **food:** Alfredo Italian, Carlito's Mexican, China Dragon, Cotton Patch Café, Domino's, Far East Chinese, Furr's Café, Kettle, Leal's Mexican, LJ Silver/A&W, Pizza Hut, Sonic, Thai Taste, Tokyo Steaks, **lodging:** Best Western, Comfort Suites, Day's Inn, **other:** Beall's, Buick/Pontiac/Cadillac/GMC, Chrysler/Jeep, $Tree, Ford/Lincoln/Mercury/Toyota, GNC, Hastings Books, NAPA, O'Reilly Parts, Pinnell Drug, Radio Shack, United Foods, **W gas:** Chevron, Phillips 66/dsl, 76, **food:** Burger King, Chicken Express, Chili's, IHOP, Little Mexico, McDonald's, New China, Quizno's, Sonic, Starbucks, Subway, Taco Bell, Wendy's, **lodging:** Best Value, Holiday Inn Express, **other:** JC Penney, Walmart SuperCtr/24hr/gas
45	Lp 27, to Plainview
43	FM 2337
41	County Rd
38	Main St
37	FM 1914, Cleveland St, **E gas:** Co-op, **food:** Sylvia's Cafe, **W** [H]
36	FM 1424, Hale Center
32	FM 37 W
31	FM 37 E
29mm	**rest area both lanes, full ♿ facilities, ☎, ⛱, litter barrels, petwalk, tornado shelter**
27	County Rd
24	FM 54, **W** RV park/dump
22	Lp 369, Abernathy, **W** Filling Sta Cafe/dsl
21	FM 597, Main St, Abernathy, **W gas:** Conoco/dsl, **food:** DQ, Shady's BBQ, **other:** $General, USPO
20	Abernathy (from nb)
17	County rd 53
15	Lp 461, to New Deal, same as 14
14	FM 1729, **E gas:** Fina/rest./dsl/scales/24hr
13	Lp 461, to New Deal
12	access rd (from nb)
11	FM 1294, Shallowater
10	Keuka St, **E other:** DHL, Fed Ex
9	Airport Rd, **E** ✈, **W other:** Lubbock RV Park/LP/dump
8	FM 2641, Regis St
7	Yucca Lane, **E** Pharr RV Ctr
6b a	Lp 289, Ave Q, Lubbock, **E other:** Pharr RV
5	B. Holly Ave, Municipal Dr, **E other:** Mackenzie Park
4	US 82, US 87, 4th St, to Crosbyton, **W gas:** ***FLYING J***/CountryMkt/dsl/24hr/@, **other:** to TTU

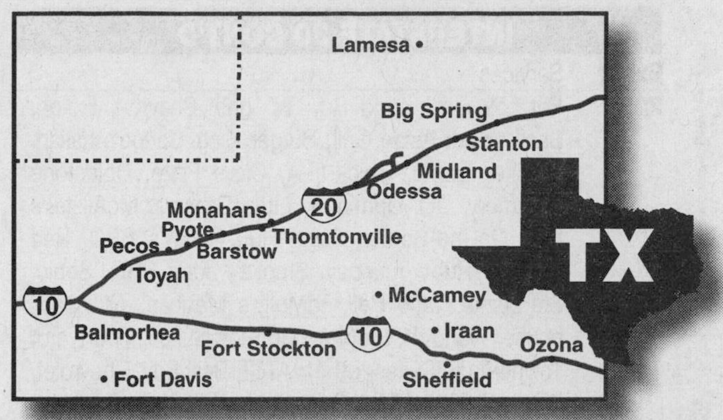

Exit #	Services
3	US 62, TX 114, 19th St
2	34th St, **E gas:** Phillips 66, **food:** Pete's Drive Inn, **W food:** Simple Simon's Pizza, **other:** AutoZone, Hall Drug, I-27 RV Ctr
1c	50th St, **E gas:** Fina, **food:** El Jalapeno Café, Prince Castle, **W gas:** Bolton Fuel, Conoco, Valero, **food:** Bryan's Steaks, Burger King, China Star, Church's, DQ, Domino's, Grand Buffet, KFC, LJ Silver/A&W, McDonald's, Pinocchio's Pizza, Pizza Hut/Taco Bell, Subway, Taco Villa, Whataburger, Wienerschnitzel, **lodging:** Howard Johnson, **other:** Chrysler/Jeep, $General, O'Reilly Parts, United Food/drug/gas, USPO, Walgreen, Woody Tire
1b	US 84, **E lodging:** Circus Inn, Day's Inn, **W lodging:** Best Western, Comfort Inn, Holiday Inn Express, Motel 6, Quality Inn, Ramada, Super 8, Value Place
1a	Lp 289
1	82nd St, **W gas:** Phillips 66

I-27 begins/ends on US 87 at 82nd St in S Lubbock.

INTERSTATE 30

Exit #	Services
223mm	Texas/Arkansas state line
223b a	US 59, US 71, State Line Ave, Texarkana, **N gas:** EZ Mart, Mobil, Shell, **food:** Denny's, IHOP, Pizza Inn, Waffle House, **lodging:** Baymont Inn, Best Western, Budget Host, Holiday Inn Express, Holiday Inn Express, LaCrosse Hotel, Quality Inn, Ramada Inn, Super 8, **other:** Cooper Tire, KOA, **S gas:** Exxon, EZ Mart, RaceWay/dsl, Shell, **food:** Bennigan's, Burger King, Cattleman's Steaks, China Inn, China King, Dixie Diner, Hooters, KFC, La Carreta Mexican, Little Caesars, LJ Silver, Marble Slab, McDonald's, Papa John's, Pizza Hut, Pizza Inn, Popeye's, Quizno's, Subway, Taco Bell, Taco Tico, Wendy's, Whataburger/24hr, **lodging:** Ambassador Inn, Best Value Inn, Best Western, Comfort Inn, Days Inn, Econolodge, Economy Inn, Executive Inn, La Quinta, Rodeway Inn, **other:** Albertson's/Sav-On, $General, Hancock Fabrics, KIA, O'Reilly Parts, Radio Shack, Walgreens, Walmart SuperCtr/24hr
223mm	**Welcome Ctr wb, full ♿ facilities, info, ☎, ⛱, litter barrels, vending, petwalk**
222	TX 93, FM 1397, Summerhill Rd, **N gas:** EZ Mart, Shell, Valero/Subway/dsl, **food:** Applebee's, McDonald's, Shogun Steaks, Waffle House, **lodging:** Motel 6, **other:** AT&T, Freightliner, Hyundai, **S gas:** Shell/24hr, **food:** Bryce's Rest., Catfish King, **other:** Chrysler/Dodge, Discount Tire, Ford, Gateway Tires, Lincoln/Mercury, Mercedes, Nissan, Toyota

INTERSTATE 30 CONT'D

E ↕ W

TEXARKANA

Exit #	Services
220b	FM 559, Richmond Rd, **N gas:** Chevron, Exxon, Shell, **food:** Asian Grill, Burger King, Carino's Italian, Cracker Barrel, Chick-fil-A, Cici's Pizza, Coldstone Creamery, DQ, Domino's, Little Caesars, McAlister's Deli, On-the-Border, Pizza Hut, Randy's BBQ, Red Lobster, Ruby Tuesday, Smokey Joe's BBQ, Sonic, Starbucks, Taco Bell, TaMolly's Mexican, TX Roadhouse, Wendy's, **lodging:** Comfort Suites, Courtyard, TownePlace Suites, **other:** AT&T, Best Buy, Chevrolet, Discount Tire, $Tree, Gander Mtn Home Depot, Honda, Kohls, Kwik Kar, Old Navy, PetsMart, Sam's Club/gas, Staples, Super 1 Food/gas, Target, TJ Maxx, **S gas:** Valero/dsl, **food:** Arby's, Chili's, ChuckeCheese, Golden Corral, Grandy's, McDonald's, Olive Garden, Outback Steaks, Quizno's, Subway, Taco Bueno, **lodging:** Candlewood Suites, Fairfield Inn, Hampton Inn, Holiday Inn Express, **other:** AT&T, Albertson's/Sav-On, Books-A-Million, Buick/GMC/Pontiac, Cadillac, Cavender's Boots, Dillard's, Hobby Lobby, JC Penney, Jeep, Mazda, Michael's, Office Depot, Ross, Sears/auto, Tuesday Morning, Walgreens, mall
220a	US 59 S, Texarkana, **S gas:** Exxon/Wendy's, Murphy USA, **food:** DQ, Subway, **other:** Lowe's Whse, Radio Shack, Walmart SuperCtr/24hr, mall
218	FM 989, Nash, **N gas:** Road Runner/dsl, **food:** Dixie Diner, **S gas:** Exxon/Burger King/dsl, **other:** GMC/Peterbilt, to Lake Patman
213	FM 2253, Leary, **N other:** Palma RV Ctr
212	spur 74, Lone Star Army Ammo Plant, **S gas:** Shell
208	FM 560, Hooks, **N food:** Old Farm Mkt/BBQ, **other:** Hooks Camper Ctr., **S gas:** Texaco/Subway/dsl/scales/24hr, **food:** DQ, Noble Roman's, Sonic, Tastee-House Rest., **other:** $General, Family$, Hooks Tire

NEW BOSTON

Exit #	Services
206	TX 86, **S other:** Red River Army Depot
201	TX 8, New Boston, **N gas:** Shell/dsl, Valero/dsl, **food:** Pitt Grill, **lodging:** Tex Inn, **other:** Chevrolet, Chrysler/Dodge/Jeep, **S gas:** Murphy USA/dsl, Shell/dsl, **food:** Catfish King, Church's, DQ, KFC/Taco Bell, McDonald's, Nana's Diner, Pizza Hut, Randy's BBQ, Sonic, **lodging:** Best Value Inn, Bostonian Inn, Holiday Inn Express, **other:** [H], Brookshire's Foods/gas, Curves, Ford/Mercury, O'Reilly Parts, Walmart SuperCtr/Subway/24hr, RV park
199	US 82, DeKalb, **1/2 mi N gas:** Shell
198	TX 98, **1/2 mi N gas:** Shell
193mm	Anderson Creek
192	FM 990, **N gas:** FuelStop/Culpeppers Rest/dsl
186	FM 561
181mm	Sulphur River
178	US 259, to DeKalb, Omaha
174mm	White Oak Creek
170	FM 1993
165	FM 1001, **S gas:** Exxon/dsl
162b a	US 271, FM 1402, FM 2152, Mt Pleasant, **N gas:** Exxon/dsl/24hr, **food:** Applebee's, Blalock BBQ, Pitt Grill, **lodging:** Holiday Inn Express, Super 8, **other:** KOA, **S gas:** Shell/dsl, Valero/Subway/dsl, **food:** Burger King, McDonald's, Pizza Inn, Sonic, **lodging:** Best Western, **other:** [H], Cadillac/Chevrolet, Family$, Ford, Vet
160	US 271, FM 1734, Mt Pleasant, **N gas:** Texaco/dsl, **food:** Senorita's Mexican, **lodging:** La Quinta, **other:** Buick/GMC/Pontiac (1mi), Lowe's Whse, Ramblin Fever RV Park, Toyota, Verizon, **S gas:** Exxon/dsl, Shell/dsl, **food:** El Chico, IHOP, Western Sizzlin, **lodging:** Comfort Inn, Days Inn, Executive Inn, Hampton Inn, **other:** Sandlin SP
158mm	**weigh sta both lanes**
156	frontage rd
153	spur 185, to Winfield, Millers Cove, **N gas:** I-30, Phillips 66, Winfield/dsl, **S gas:** Shamrock/dsl
150	Ripley Rd, **N other:** Lowe's Distribution
147	spur 423, **N gas:** Love's/Chester's/Subway/dsl/scales/24hr, **lodging:** American Inn, Economy Inn, **other:** tires/repair
146	TX 37, Mt Vernon, **N gas:** Shell/dsl, **food:** Sonic, **other:** Alco, **other:** [H], **S gas:** Exxon/dsl, Fina/dsl/24hr, **food:** Burger King, DQ, Mi Casita, Mt Vernon Cafe, **lodging:** Super 8, **other:** to Lake Bob Sandlin SP, auto repair, antiques
143	**rest area both lanes, full ♿ facilities, ☎, picnic, litter barrels, vending, petwalk**
142	County Line Rd (from eb)
141	FM 900, Saltillo Rd
136	FM 269, Weaver Rd
135	US 67 N
131	FM 69
127	US 67, Lp 301, **N lodging:** Comfort Suites, Quality 1 Inn, Super Hotel, **other:** [H], **S gas:** Shell, **food:** Burton's Rest./24hr, **lodging:** Best Western
126	FM 1870, College St, **S gas:** Exxon, **food:** Burton's Rest./24hr, **lodging:** Best Western, **other:** Firestone/auto, same as 127

SULPHUR SPRINGS

Exit #	Services
125	Bill Bradford Rd, same as 124
124	TX 11, TX 154, Sulphur Springs, **N gas:** Exxon, **food:** Bodacious BBQ, Chicken Express, Dominos, Juan Pablo's Mexican, Pitt Grill, Pizza Hut, San Remo Italian, Subway, **lodging:** Holiday Inn Express, La Quinta, Royal Inn, **other:** [H], AutoZone, Buick/Chevrolet/GMC, CVS Drug, $General, Family$, Ford, FSA Outlet/famous brands, O'Reilly Parts, Walgreens, USPO, **S gas:** Exxon/dsl, Murphy USA/dsl, Shell, **food:** Braum's, Burger King, Chili's, Dominos, Furr's Rest., Jack-in-the-Box, LJ Silver/Taco Bell, McDonald's, Pizza Inn, Sonic, Tierra Del Sol, Whataburger, **other:** Discount Tire, Lowe's Whse, Radio Shack, Verizon, Walmart SuperCtr/24hr
123	FM 2297, League St, **N gas:** Shamrock, Shell
122	TX 19, to Emory, **N gas:** Shamrock, **other:** [H] Chrysler/Dodge/Jeep, **S gas:** Pilot/Arby's/dsl/scales/24hr, **other:** RV Park, Vet, to Cooper Lake
120	US 67 bus
116	FM 2653, Brashear Rd
112	FM 499 (from wb)
110	FM 275, Cumby, **N gas:** Phillips 66, **S gas:** Shell/24hr
104	FM 513, FM 2649, Campbell, **S** to Lake Tawakoni
101	TX 24, TX 50, FM 1737, to Commerce, **N gas:** Valero/dsl, **other:** to E TX St U
97	Lamar St, **N gas:** Exxon/dsl, **lodging:** Budget Hotel, Dream Lodge Motel
96	Lp 302

INTERSTATE 30 CONT'D

E ↕ W

GREENVILLE

Exit #	Services
95	Division St, **S other:** [H], Puddin Hill Fruit Cakes
94b	US 69, US 380, Greenville, **N gas:** Valero/dsl, **food:** Ninja's Grill, Senorita's Mexican, **lodging:** Best Value Inn, Days Inn, Royal Inn, **S gas:** Exxon, Fina/dsl, **food:** Arby's, Catfish Cove Rest., McDonald's, **lodging:** Econolodge, Economy Inn, Motel 6, Quality Inn, Super 8
94a	US 69, US 380, Greenville, **S gas:** Valero, **other:** Chrysler/Dodge/Jeep, Hyundai, Nissan
93b a	US 67, TX 34 N, **N gas:** Chevron, Exxon, Texaco, **food:** Applebee's, Chick-fil-A, Chicken Express, CiCi's, DQ, Grandy's, IHOP, Jack-in-the-Box, KFC, Little Caesars, Pizza Hut, Schlotsky's, Sonic, Starbucks, Steak Angus, Subway, Taco Bell, Taco Bueno, Tony's Italian, Wendy's, Whataburger/24hr, **lodging:** Hampton Inn, **other:** [H], Ace Hardware, AT&T, Belk, BigLots, Brookshire's Foods, Buick/GMC/Pontiac, Cadillac, Discount Tire, JC Penney, Lowes Whse, O'Reilly Parts, Staples, Walgreens, USPO, mall, transmissions, **S gas:** Exxon/dsl/24hr, Valero/dsl, **food:** Chili's, Cracker Barrel, Eastrock Buffet, Paesano Italian, Papa Murphy's, Red Lobster, Subway, TaMolly's Mexican, **lodging:** Best Western, Holiday Inn Express, **other:** $Tree, Ford/Lincoln/Mercury, Home Depot, Mitsubishi, NTB, Radio Shack, RV Ctr, Walmart SuperCtr/24hr
90mm	Farber Creek
89	FM 1570, **S lodging:** Luxury Inn
89mm	E Caddo Creek
87	FM 1903, **N gas:** Chevron/Pizza Inn/dsl, **other:** fireworks, **S gas:** Pilot/McDonald's/dsl/scales/24hr, Texaco/Pancake House/dsl, **other:** tire repair
87mm	Elm Creek
85	FM 36, Caddo Mills, **N** KOA
85mm	W Caddo Creek
83	FM 1565 N, **N gas:** Exxon/dsl
79	FM 2642, **N** Budget RV Ctr, **S** Vet
77b	FM 35, Royse City, **N gas:** Exxon/dsl, Texaco/Subway/dsl/scales/24hr, **food:** Soulman's BBQ, **other:** Family$
77a	TX 548, Royse City, **N gas:** Shell/dsl, **food:** Jack-in-the-Box, McDonald's, **lodging:** Sun Royse Inn, **other:** AutoZone, tires, **S gas:** Exxon/KFC/Quizno's, **food:** Denny's, Sonic, Wingdingers, **lodging:** Holiday Inn Express
73	FM 551, Fate
70	FM 549, **N other:** Happy Trails RV Ctr, Hyundai, McLains RV Ctr, **S gas:** Love's/Carl's Jr./dsl/scales/24hr **other:** KIA
69	(from wb), frontage rd, **N lodging:** Super 8, **S other:** Toyota/Scion
68	TX 205, to Rock Wall, **N gas:** RaceWay, Shell, **food:** Braum's, DQ, Jowilly's Grill, KFC, Luigi's Italian, Pizza Hut, Pizza Inn, Subway, Taco Casa, Whataburger, **lodging:** Holiday Inn Express, Super 8, Value Place, **other:** Chevrolet, Dodge, Ford/Mercury, Hobby Lobby, **S gas:** TA/Burger King/Starbucks/dsl/rest./24hr/scales/@, Valero/dsl, **other:** Belk, Costco/gas
67	FM 740, Ridge Rd, **N gas:** Chevron, Murphy USA/dsl, **food:** Arby's, Burger King, Carabba's, Culver's, Dominos, Grandy's, IHOP, Logan's Roadhouse,

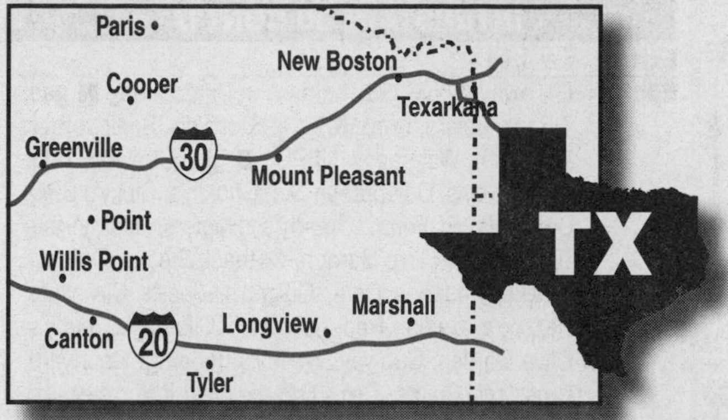

GARLAND

Exit #	Services
67	Continued McDonald's, Popeye's, Schlotsky's, Smoothie King, Starbucks, Steak'n Shake, Taco Bueno, Taco Cabana, Waffle House, Wendy's, **lodging:** Hampton Inn, **other:** Firestone/auto, Goodyear/auto, Kwik Kar, Walmart SuperCtr/24hr, **S gas:** Exxon, Shell, Valero, **food:** Applebee's, Bahama Buck's Ice Cream, Blackeyed Pea, Buffalo Wild Wings, Carino's Italian, Chick-fil-A, Chili's, Chipotle Mexican, ChuckeCheese, CiCi's, Cotton Patch Cafe, El Chico, Jack-in-the-Box, La Madelein, McDonald's, On-the-Border, Pizza Hut/Taco Bell, Quizno's, Shogun Steaks, Sonic, Soulman's BBQ, Starbucks, Subway, TGIFriday's, **lodging:** La Quinta, **other:** Albertson's, AT&T, Best Buy, CVS Drug, Discount Tire, $Tree, GNC, Home Depot, Kohl's, Lowe's Whse, Michael's, Office Depot, Old Navy, PetCo, PetsMart, Radio Shack, Ross, Staples, SteinMart, Target, Walgreens, to Lake Tawakoni, Vet
67a	Horizon Rd, Village Dr, **N gas:** Valero, **food:** Genghis Grill, Kyoto Japanese, Saltgrass Steaks, Starbucks, **lodging:** Hampton Inn, **S lodging:** Hilton
66mm	Ray Hubbard Reservoir
64	Dalrock Rd, Rowlett, **N gas:** Exxon, Valero/dsl, **lodging:** Comfort Suites, **other:** [H], Express Drug
63mm	Ray Hubbard Reservoir
62	Bass Pro Rd, **N lodging:** Best Western, **other:** to Hubbard RA, **S gas:** Shell, Texaco, Valero, **food:** CiCi's, Flying Saucer Grill, Primo's Grill, Sonic, TX Land&Cattle, Whataburger, **other:** Bass Pro Shops
61	Zion Rd (from wb), **N gas:** Exxon/dsl, **lodging:** Discovery Inn
60b	Bobtown Rd (eb only), **N gas:** Exxon, **food:** Jack-in-the-Box, **lodging:** La Quinta, **S gas:** Shell, **food:** Subway
60a	Rose Hill Dr
59	Beltline Rd, Garland, **N gas:** QT, 7-11, **food:** Chili's, China City, Denny's, India Garden, KFC, McDonald's, Papa John's, Pizza Hut/Taco Bell, Quizno's, Starbucks, Subway, Taco Casa, Taco Cabana, Whataburger, Wendy's, **other:** Albertson's, GNC, Radio Shack, Tuesday Morning, Walgreens, Walmart SuperCtr/24hr, **S food:** Buffet King, DQ, Sonic, Waffle House, Williams Chicken, **lodging:** Best Value Inn, Motel 6, Super 8, **other:** Kroger
58	Northwest Dr, **N gas:** Shell, Valero/dsl, **other:** Hyundai, Nissan, **S gas:** Fina, **food:** Jack-in-the-Box, **other:** Lowe's Whse
56c b	I-635 S-N

E ↕ W

DALLAS

INTERSTATE 30 CONT'D

Exit #	Services
56a	Galloway Ave, G US Thomasson Dr (from eb), **N gas:** Texaco, Valero, **food:** KFC, McDonald's, Sonic, **other:** AutoZone, Walgreens, USPO, **S gas:** Chevron, 7-11, **food:** Arby's, Celebration Sta, Church's, Dicky's BBQ, Domino's, El Fenix, Grandy's, Hooters, Jack-in-the-Box, Luby's, Olive Garden, Outback Steaks, Outback Steaks, Posades Cafe, Quizno's, Sports City Cafe, Razzoo's Cajun, Red Lobster, TGIFriday's, Luby's, Olive Garden, Subway, Wendy's, **lodging:** Courtyard, Crossland Suites, Delux Inn, Fairfield Inn, **other:** H, Aldi Foods, BigLots, Firestone/auto, Kroger, Nichols RV Ctr, NTB
55	Motley Dr, **N gas:** Shell/dsl, **lodging:** Astro Inn, Executive Inn, **S gas:** Chevron, **lodging:** Microtel, **other:** H, to Eastfield Coll
54	Big Town Blvd, **N gas:** Texaco, Valero/dsl, **lodging:** Mesquite Inn, **S other:** Explore RV Ctr, Holiday World RV Ctr, dsl repair
53b	US 80 E (from eb), to Terrell
53a	Lp 12, Buckner, **N gas:** RaceTrac, Texaco, **food:** Burger King, **lodging:** Lamplighter Inn, Luxury Inn, Super 8, **other:** Chevrolet, Toyota/Scion, **S gas:** 7-11, **food:** CiCi's, Enrique's Cafe, Taco Cabana, Whataburger, **lodging:** Holiday Inn Express, **other:** $Tree, Sam's Club, Staples, Walmart SuperCtr/gas/24hr
51	(52 a from wb), Highland Rd, Jim Miller Blvd, **N gas:** Exxon, **food:** Country China, Denny's, Luby's, McDonald's, **lodging:** Holiday Inn Express, La Quinta, **S gas:** RaceWay, Shell/dsl, **food:** Burger King, Capt D's, Furr's Cafe, Grandy's, KFC, Pizza Hut, Popeye's, Subway, Taco Bell, Wendy's, **lodging:** Howard Johnson, Super 7 Inn, **other:** AutoZone, CVS Drug, O'Reilly Parts
50b a	Ferguson Rd, **N gas:** Texaco, **S other:** Brake-O, U-Haul
49b	Dolphin Rd, Lawnview Ave, Samuell Ave, **N gas:** Shell, **lodging:** Best Value Inn
49a	Winslow St, **N gas:** Circle K/gas, Shell/dsl/repair, Texaco, **food:** McDonald's, **S gas:** Shell/24hr
48b	TX 78, E Grand, **S** fairpark, arboretum
48a	Carroll Ave, Central Ave, Peak St, Haskell Ave, **N gas:** 7-11, Shamrock, **other:** H, Hamm's Tires, **S gas:** Fina, **food:** Joe's Rest
47	2nd Ave, **S food:** McDonald's, **other:** Cotton Bowl, fairpark
46b	I-45, US 75, to Houston
46a	Central Expswy, downtown
45	I-35E, N to Denton, to Commerce St, Lamar St, Griffin St, **S gas:** Fuel City, **food:** McDonald's, **lodging:** Ambassador Inn
44b	I-35E S, Industrial Blvd
44a	I-35E N, Beckley Ave (from eb)
43b a	Sylvan Ave (from wb), **N gas:** Valero/Quizno's/dsl, **other:** H, Family$, USPO
42	Hampton Rd
41	Westmorland Ave
39	Cockrell Hill Rd, **N food:** KFC/Taco Bell, IHOP, Luckio's BBQ, Polo Cantero, Sonic, Wing Stop, **lodging:** Comfort Suites, Hampton Inn, **other:** Staples, **S gas:** Murphy USA, **food:** Chili's, Golden Corral, Lucky Rice, McDonald's, Panda Express, Starbucks, Subway, Taco Cabana, Wendy's, Whataburger, **lodging:** Holiday Inn Express, **other:** AT&T, Best Buy, $Tree, Lowe's Whse, Radio Shack, Ross, Walmart SuperCtr
38	Lp 12, **1 mi N gas:** Exxon, Fina, **food:** Burger King, Popeye's
36	MacArthur Blvd, **S other:** U-Haul
34	Belt Line Rd, **N gas:** Chevron, RaceTrac, **lodging:** Studio 6, Super 8, **other:** Ford, Ripley's Museum, **S gas:** RaceTrac/dsl, Shell/Subway, Valero, **food:** Burger King, Popeye's, Schlotzky's, Starbucks
32	NW 19th, **N gas:** Shamrock, **S gas:** Texaco, **food:** Church's, Denny's, Whataburger, **lodging:** La Quinta
30	TX 360, Six Flags Dr, Arlington Stadium, **N gas:** Mobil, Shell, **food:** China Sea, Cracker Barrel, Grand Buffet, Saltgrass Steaks, Steak'n Shake, TrailDust Steaks, Wendy's, **lodging:** Best Value Inn, Budget Suites, Crowne Plaza, Executive Inn, Fairfield Inn, Hilton, Hilton Garden, Homestead Suites, Studio+, **S gas:** Conoco/dsl, Shell/7-11/dsl, Valero, **food:** Bennigan's, Denny's, Jack-in-the-Box, McDonald's, Mariano's Mexican, Pancho's Mexican, Patomino's, **lodging:** Baymont Inn, Holiday Inn Express, Knight's Inn, La Quinta, Motel 6, **other:** Ford/Lincoln/Mercury, Office Depot, Six Flags Funpark
29	Ball Park Way, **N gas:** Chevron, QT, Valero, **food:** Dicky's BBQ, Sonic, **lodging:** Springhill Suites, Towneplace Suites, **other:** Toyota, **S gas:** Fina/dsl, **food:** On-the-Border, Texas Land&Cattle, **lodging:** Howard Johnson, Sheraton, **other:** Six Flags Funpark
28b	TX 157, Nolan Ryan Expswy, **N gas:** Chevron, **food:** Boston Mkt, Waffle House, **lodging:** Country Inn&Suites, **other:** Cadillac, Chrysler/Dodge/Jeep, **S lodging:** EconoLodge, Holiday Inn Express, **other:** Barnes&Noble, TX Stadium
28a	FM 157, Collins St, **N food:** Whataburger, **other:** H Dodge, **S food:** Blackeyed Pea, Chick-fil-A, Colter's BBQ, Jason's Deli, Marble Slab, Olen Jack's Grill, Panera Bread, Pappasito's Cantina, Souper Salad, Taco Bueno, TGIFriday's, Wendy's, **lodging:** Comfort Suites, **other:** Best Buy, Curves, $Tree, Home Depot, Pepboys, PetsMart, Ross, Sav-a-Lot Foods, Stein-Mart
27	Lamar Blvd, Cooper St, **N gas:** Texaco, **food:** Jack-in-the-Box, **other:** BigLots, Family$, Kroger/gas, Vet, **S gas:** 7-11, Shell, **food:** Burger King, Denny's, Tom's Burgers
26	Fielder Rd, **S other:** to Six Flags (from eb)
25mm	Village Creek
24	Eastchase Pkwy, **N food:** Jack-in-the-Box, Panda Express, **lodging:** La Quinta, **other:** CarMax, Lowe's Whse, Sam's Club/gas, Walmart SuperCtr/24hr, **S gas:** Chevron/dsl, RaceTrac, Shell/7-11/dsl, **food:** Asian Grill, Burger King, Chicken Express, IHOP, McDonald's, No Frills Grill, Schlotzky's, Subway, Taco Bell, Wendy's, Whataburger, **other:** GNC, Office Depot, Radio Shack, Ross, Target
23	Cooks Lane, **S gas:** Shell
21a	Bridgewood Dr, **N gas:** Chevron, **food:** Bennigan's, Church's, KFC, Jack-in-the-Box, Luby's, Subway, Wendy's, **other:** Albertson's, Braums Foods, Discount Tire, Home Depot, Kroger, U-Haul, **S gas:** Conoco, QT, Shamrock, **food:** Taco Bueno, Whataburger/24hr

DALLAS

INTERSTATE 30 CONT'D

E ↕ W — FT WORTH

Exit #	Services
21c b	I-820
19	Brentwood Stair Rd (from eb), **N gas:** Chevron, Shell/dsl, **S gas:** Shamrock
18	Oakland Blvd, **N gas:** Circle K, Shell/dsl, **food:** Taco Bell, Waffle House, **lodging:** Motel 6
16c	Beach St, **S gas:** 7-11, **lodging:** Quality Inn, Inn Suites
16b a	Riverside Dr (from wb), **S lodging:** Great Western Inn
15b a	I-35W N to Denton, S to Waco
14b	Jones St, Commerce St, Ft Worth, downtown
14a	TX 199, Henderson St, Ft Worth, downtown
13b	TX 199, Henderson St, **N lodging:** Omni, Sheraton
13a	8th Ave, **N lodging:** Holiday Inn Express
12d	Forest Park Blvd, **N food:** Pappa's Burgers, Pappadeaux Café, Pappasito's, **S other:** H
12b	Rosedale St
12a	University Dr, City Parks, **S lodging:** SpringHill Suites
11	Montgomery St, **S gas:** Shell/7-11/dsl, **food:** Whataburger, **other: visitor info**
10	Hulen St, Ft Worth, **S food:** Chick-fil-A, Coldstone, Republic Grill, Smoothie King, **other:** Borders Books, WorldMkt
9b	US 377, Camp Bowie Blvd, Horne St, **N food:** Uncle Julio's Mexican, **S gas:** Exxon, 7-11, Texaco/dsl, **food:** Jack-in-the-Box, Mexican Inn, Pizza Hut/Taco Bell, Qdoba, Subway, Taco Bueno, Wendy's, **other:** Batteries+, Radio Shack
9a	Bryant-Irvin Rd, **S gas:** Shell, same as 9b
8b	Ridgmar, Ridglea, **N gas:** Valero/dsl
8a	TX 183, Green Oaks Rd, **N food:** Applebee's, Arby's, Chili's, Don Pablo, Grand Buffet, Jack-in-the-Box, New Grand Buffet, Olive Garden, Quizno's, Subway, Starbucks, Taco Bueno, **lodging:** Courtyard, **other:** Albertson's, AT&T, Best Buy, $Tree, Dillard's, Firestone/auto, JC Penney, Jo-Ann Fabrics, Lowe's Whse, Macy's, Neiman Marcus, NTB, Office Depot, PetsMart, Radio Shack, Ross, Sam's Club/gas, Sears/auto, Target, U-Haul, Walmart SuperCtr, **S food:** Tommy's Burgers, **lodging:** Comfort Suites, Hampton Inn
7b a	Cherry Lane, TX 183, spur 341, to Green Oaks Rd, **N gas:** Shell/7-11, Texaco/dsl, Valero/dsl, **food:** Chuck-eCheese, IHOP/24hr, Popeye's, Ryan's, Subway, Taco Bell, Wendy's, **lodging:** La Quinta, Super 8, **other:** BigLots, O'Reilly Parts, Suzuki, U-Haul, **S lodging:** Holiday Inn Express, Quality Inn, **other:** Nissan
6	Las Vegas Trail, **N gas:** Chevron/McDonald's, **food:** Jack-in-the-Box, Waffle House, **lodging:** Days Inn, **other:** Hyundai, Lincoln/Mercury, Mitsubishi, **S gas:** Fina, Shell/7-11/dsl, Valero/dsl, **lodging:** Best Budget Suites, Best Value Inn, Motel 6, **other:** AutoZone, Kia
5b c	I-820 S and N
5a	Alemeda St (from eb, no EZ return)
3	RM 2871, Chapel Creek Blvd, **S gas:** Exxon/Church's/Subway, **food:** Sonic
2	spur 580 E
1b	Linkcrest Dr, **S gas:** Mobil/dsl
0mm	I-20 W. I-30 begins/ends on I-20, exit 421.

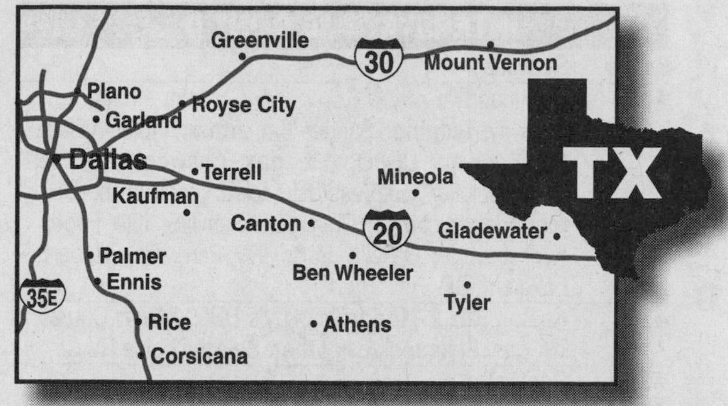

INTERSTATE 35

N ↕ S — GAINESVILLE

Exit #	Services
504mm	Texas/Oklahoma state line, Red River
504	frontage rd, access to Texas Welcome Ctr
503mm	**parking area both lanes**
502mm	**Welcome Ctr sb, full ♿ facilities, TX Tourist Bureau/info, ☎, picnic, litter barrels, wireless internet**
501	FM 1202, Prime Outlets Blvd, **E other:** Chrysler/Dodge/Jeep, Ford/Mercury, **W gas:** Conoco/dsl/café, **food:** Applebee's, Cracker Barrel, **lodging:** Hampton Inn, La Quinta, **other:** Prime Outlets/famous brands, Western Outfitter, RV camping
500	FM 372, Gainesville, **W gas:** Hitchin' Post/Shell/dsl
498b a	US 82, to Wichita Falls, Gainesville, Sherman, **E gas:** Exxon, Phillips 66/dsl, Shell/dsl, Valero/dsl, **food:** Catfish Louie's, CiCi's, Subway, Whatburger/24hr, **lodging:** Bed&Bath Inn, Budget Host, Comfort Inn, Delux Inn, Super 8, 12 Oaks Inn, **other:** H, Firestone, **W gas:** Exxon/dsl, **lodging:** Bed&Bath Inn, Comfort Suites, Days Inn, Fairfield Inn, Rodeway Inn
497	frontage rd, **W gas:** Valero/dsl
496b	TX 51, FM 51, California St, Gainesville, **E gas:** Chevron, Conoco/dsl, **food:** Arby's, Braum's, IHOP, McDonald's, Starbucks, Taco Bell, Taco Casa, Sonic, Starbucks, Wendy's, **lodging:** Holiday Inn Express, Quality Inn, **other:** Cadillac, Dodge, Goodyear/auto, Mkt Place Foods, N Central TX Coll, **W gas:** Valero, **food:** Chili's
496a	to Weaver St
496mm	Elm Fork of the Trinity River
495	frontage rd
494	FM 1306
492mm	**picnic area sb, litter barrels**
491	Spring Creek Rd
490mm	**picnic area nb, litter barrels**
489	(488 from nb) FM 1307, to Hockley Creek Rd
487	FM 922, Valley View, **W gas:** Chevron/dsl/24hr, **food:** Big Fatty's BBQ, DQ, **other:** USPO
486	FM 1307, **W gas:** Texaco/dsl, **lodging:** Valley View Inn, **other:** $General
485	frontage rd (from sb)
483	FM 3002, Lone Oak Rd, **E** Shell/Subway/dsl, **other:** Roberts Lake SP
482	Chisam Rd
481	View Rd, **W other:** TX Sundown Ranch RV Park
480	Lois Rd, **E other:** Walmart Dist Ctr
479	Belz Rd, Sanger, same as 478
478	FM 455, to Pilot Pt, Bolivar, **E gas:** QuikTrack, Shell, Valero, **food:** DQ, Migualito's Mexican, Sonic,

INTERSTATE 35 CONT'D

N ↕ S

DENTON

Exit #	Services
478	Continued Subway, **lodging:** Sanger Inn, **other:** Indian Village Campground, USPO, **W gas:** Chevron/24hr, Fuel 4 TX/Chicken Express/dsl, **food:** Jack-in-the-Box, McDonald's, **other:** Chevrolet, Family$, IGA Foods, Kwikar Lube, O'Reilly Parts, RV Park, Ray Roberts Lake and SP
477	Keaton Rd, **E food:** Smokey's BBQ, **other:** Curves, **W gas:** Shamrock/dsl, **other:** Select Choice RV Ctr
475b	Rector Rd
475a	FM 156, to Krum (from sb)
474	Cowling rd (from nb)
473	FM 3163, Milam Rd, **E gas:** Love's/Subway/dsl/24hr
472	Ganzer Rd, **W** RV sales
471	US 77, FM 1173, Lp 282, to Denton, Krum, **E gas:** TA/Pizza Hut/Taco Bell/dsl/scales/24hr/@, **food:** Good Eats Café, **other:** H, **W gas:** Fina/dsl/café/scales/24hr, Texaco/dsl/scales/24hr/@, **other:** Foster's Western Shop, to Camping World RV Supply
470	Lp 288, same services as 469 from sb
469	US 380, University Dr, to Decatur, McKinney, **E gas:** Chevron/Subway, RaceTrac, **food:** Braum's, Catfish King, ChinaTown Café, Cracker Barrel, Luigi's Pizza, McDonald's, **lodging:** Best Western, Fairfield Inn, **other:** Albertson's/Sav-On, **W gas:** Conoco/dsl, Shell/dsl, Valero, **food:** DQ, Denny's, Sonic, Waffle House, **lodging:** Comfort Inn, Holiday Inn Express, Howard Johnson, Motel 6, Travelodge, ValuePlace Inn, **other:** H, Camping World RV Supply, to TX Woman's U
468	FM 1515, Airport Rd, W Oak St, **E** H
467	I-35W, S to Ft Worth

I-35 divides into E and W sb, converges into I-35 nb. See Texas I-35 W.

Exit #	Services
466b	Ave D, **E gas:** Exxon/dsl, **food:** Central Grill, Chicken Express, IHOP, McDonald's, NY Sub Hub, Pancho's Mexican, Taco Cabana, **lodging:** Comfort Suites, **other:** $General, Sack'n Save Foods, to NTSU
466a	McCormick St, **E gas:** Phillips 66, Shell/dsl, **lodging:** Royal Inn, **W gas:** Fina/dsl/U-Haul
465b	US 377, Ft Worth Dr, **E gas:** RaceTrac, Valero, **food:** Michael's Kitchen, Taco Bueno, Whataburger/24hr, **lodging:** La Quinta, **W gas:** Conoco, QuickTrack, **food:** Outback Steaks, Sonic, **lodging:** Day's Inn
465a	FM 2181, Teasley Ln, **E gas:** 7-11, **food:** Applebee's, Braum's, Carino's, ChuckeCheese, Hooters, KFC, Little Caesar's, Pizza Hut, **lodging:** Hampton Inn, Holiday Inn, Quality Inn, **other:** Brookshires Foods, bank, **W gas:** Exxon, Shell, **food:** Rudy's BBQ/gas, **lodging:** Best Value Inn, Super 8
464	US 77, Pennsylvania Dr, Denton, same as 463
463	Lp 288, to McKinney, **E gas:** RaceTrac, **food:** Arby's, Burger King, Chick-fil-A, Colter's BBQ, Grandy's, Jason's Deli, KFC/Taco Bell, McAlister's Deli, Pizza Hut, On-the-Border, Sonic, Starbucks, Texas Roadhouse, Wendy's, Wienerschnitzel, **other:** Barnes&Noble, Big Lots, Burlington Coats, Dillards, Discount Tire, $Tree, Hastings Books, Home Depot, JC Penney, Kroger, Macy's, Office Depot, Old Navy, Ross, Sears/auto, Staples, PetCo, **W gas:** Chevron/dsl, **food:** Blackeyed Pea, Chili's, Jack-in-the-Box, Luby's, Red Lobster, Red Pepper's Rest., Schlotsky's, **other:** Albertson's, Vet, same as 464
462	State School Rd, Mayhill Rd, **E gas:** QT, Texaco/dsl, **food:** Dickey's BBQ, Olive Garden, **other:** H, Hyundai, **W gas:** Chevron, Exxon/café, **food:** Shogun Japanese, Sonic, **other:** Albertsons, Buick/Pontiac/GMC, Cadillac, Chevrolet, Dodge, Honda, Toyota/Scion
461	Sandy Shores Rd, Post Oak Dr, **E other:** Ford, McClain RV Ctr, **W other:** Chrysler/Jeep/Kia, Lincoln/Mercury/Mazda, Nissan
460	Corinth Pkwy, **E gas:** Chevron/dsl/repair, **other:** McClain RV Ctr, camping, **W other:** Harley-Davidson
459	frontage rd, **W other:** Destiny RV Resort
458	FM 2181, Swisher Rd, **E gas:** Circle K, **lodging:** Best Western, **other:** O'Reilly Parts, **W gas:** Chevron/McDonald's, Exxon, **food:** Burger King, Chick-fil-A, IHOP, Jack-in-the-Box, JC China, KFC/Pizza Hut/Taco Bell, McDonald's, Quizno's, Starbucks, Subway, Wendy's, Whataburger, **other:** Albertson's, AutoZone, Discount Tire, GNC, Radio Shack, Walmart SuperCtr/gas/24hr
457b	Denton Rd, Hundley Dr, Lake Dallas, **E gas:** Shell, **food:** Chili's, Hickory Creek BBQ, Subway, TX L&C Steaks, Vet
457a	Hundley Dr (from nb), Lake Dallas
456	Highland Village
456mm	Lewisville Lake
454b	Garden Ridge Blvd, **W gas:** Fuel 4 TX, **other:** city park
454a	FM 407, Justin, **E gas:** Valero, **food:** BBQ, **W gas:** QT, Texaco, **food:** McDonald's
453	Valley Ridge Blvd, **E other:** Ford, **W gas:** Chevron, **food:** Burger King, Subway, **other:** Home Depot, Kohl's, Lowes Whse, Staples
452	FM 1171, to Flower Mound, **E food:** IHOP, Taco Bueno, **lodging:** Days Inn, **other:** H, **W gas:** Chevron, Exxon/dsl, Shell, **food:** Burger King, Chick-fil-A, Chipotle Mexican, CiCi's Pizza, Golden Corral, Grandy's, Panda Express, Taco Bell, Whataburger/24hr, **other:** Sam's Club/gas, Staples, U-Haul, Walmart SuperCtr same as 451
451	Fox Ave, **E gas:** Shell/dsl, **food:** Braum's, **W gas:** Chevron/24hr, Conoco/dsl, QuickTrack Gas, **food:** Cracker Barrel, El Chico, **lodging:** Econolodge, Hampton Inn, **other:** transmissions, VW
450	TX 121, Lewisville, **E gas:** Citgo/7-11, RaceTrac, **food:** China Dragon, Owens Rest., Sugarbaby's BBQ, **lodging:** Ramada Ltd, Rodeway Inn, **other:** Chevrolet/Subaru, Dodge, **W gas:** Chevron, Conoco/dsl, 7-11, Texaco/dsl, **food:** Burger King, Chili's, Church's, IHOP, KFC, LJ Silver, McDonald's, Pancho's Mexican, Pizza Hut, Subway, Taco Bell, Waffle House, Whataburger/24hr, **lodging:** Best Value Inn, Crossroads Inn, Super 8, **other:** Chief Parts, Firestone/auto, Food Lion, KIA, Kroger, Mitsubishi, Nissan, Toyota, transmissions
449	Corporate Drive, **E gas:** Conoco, **food:** China Dragon, Hooters, On-the-Border, **lodging:** Extended Stay America, Hearthside Inn, Motel 6, **other:** Cavender's Boots, Honda, Ross, Target, **W gas:** Texaco, **food:** Chili's, **lodging:** Best Western, La Quinta, Sun Suites, **other:** Honda, Kia, NTB
448b a	FM 3040, Round Grove Rd, **E gas:** 7-11, **food:** Abuelo's Mexican, Bennigan's, Cane's, Jack-in-the-Box, Joe's Crabshack, Mimi's Cafe, Olive Garden, Peiwei

LEWISVILLE

TX

INTERSTATE 35 CONT'D

N ↕ S

Exit #	Services
448b a	Continued Chinese, **lodging:** Homewood Suites, **other:** Honda, Ross, Target, **W gas:** Exxon, **food:** Applebee's, BJ's Grill, Buffalo Wild Wings, Cantina Laredo, Carino's Italian, Chick-fil-A, Chipotle Mexican, Denny's, Don Pablo, Logan's Roadhouse, Macaroni Grill, McDonald's, Outback Steaks, Red Lobster, Schlotsky's, Sonic, Spring Creek BBQ, Steak'n Shake, Taco Bueno, Taco Cabana, TGIFriday, Tony Roma, Wendy's, **lodging:** Comfort Suites, Country Inn&Suites, Courtyard, Fairfield Inn, Hilton Garden, Holiday Inn Express, Old Country Inn, **other:** Barnes&Noble, Best Buy, Costco/gas, Dillard's, Discount Tire, JC Penney, Macy's, Marshall's, Michael's, Office Depot, Old Navy, Sears/auto, Target, mall
446	Frankford Rd, **E gas:** RaceTrac, **food:** La Hacienda Ranch Grill, **other:** Buick/GMC/Pontiac, Volvo
445b	Pres Geo Bush Tpk
444	Whitlock Lane, Sandy Lake Rd, **E gas:** Shell, **food:** Pizza Pasta, **lodging:** Rodeway Inn, **other:** RV camping, **W food:** McDonald's, Starbucks, **lodging:** Delux Inn, **other:** Harley-Davidson
443	Belt Line Rd, Crosby Rd, **E gas:** RaceTrac, **other:** Ford, Hyundai, NTB, **W gas:** Shell, **other:** U-Haul
442	Valwood Pkwy, **E gas:** Chevron/Subway, **food:** El Chico, Grandy's, Jack-in-the-Box, Redline Burgers, Taco Bueno, Waffle House, **lodging:** Comfort Inn, Guest Inn, LoneStar Inn, Royal Inn, **W gas:** Fina/dsl, **other:** transmissions
441	Valley View Lane, **W gas:** Mobil, Shell, **food:** Michael's Rest., **lodging:** Best Value Inn, Day's Inn, Econolodge, La Quinta
440b	I-635 E
440c	I-635 W, to DFW ✈
439	Royal Lane, **E gas:** Fina, Shell, **food:** McDonald's, Wendy's, Whataburger/24hr, **other:** Daewoo, **W gas:** Chevron, Conoco, **food:** Jack-in-the-Box
438	Walnut Hill Lane, **E gas:** Chevron, Shell, Valero, **food:** Burger King, Church's, Dave&Buster's, Denny's, Porter House Steaks, Trail Dust Steaks, Wild Turkey Grill, **lodging:** Comfort Inn, Hampton Inn, Quality Inn, **other:** Isuzu, **W gas:** Chevron, Shell/dsl, **other:** RV Ctr
437	Manana Rd (from nb), same as 438
436	TX 348, to DFW, Irving, **E gas:** Exxon/dsl, Shell, **food:** Bennigan's, IHOP, Luby's, Waffle House, **lodging:** Courtyard, Days Inn, Elegante Hotel, Holiday Inn Express, La Quinta, Springhill Suites, Studio 6, Suburban Lodge, **W gas:** Fina, Mobil, Shell, **food:** Bennigan's, Chili's, Don Pablo, Ghengis Grill, Jack-in-the-Box, Jason's Deli, Joe's Crabshack, McDonald's, Olive Garden, Outback Steaks, Papadeaux Seafood, Pappasito's Mexican, Red Lobster, Taco Bell/Pizza Hut, Tony Roma's, TX L&C, Wendy's, Wing House, **lodging:** Budget Lodge, Century Inn
435	Harry Hines Blvd (from nb), **E gas:** RaceTrac, **food:** Arby's, **other:** U-Haul, same as 436
434b	Regal Row, **E gas:** Texaco/Grandy's, **food:** Denny's, Whataburger/24hr, **lodging:** Econolodge, **W lodging:** Ramada Inn

DALLAS

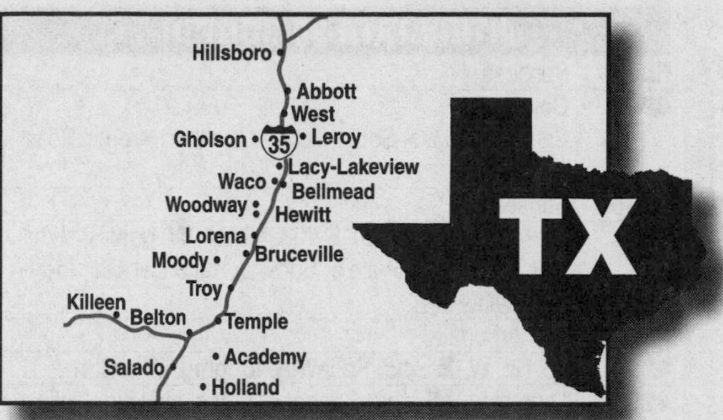

Exit #	Services
434a	Empire, Central, **E gas:** Chevron/McDonald's, **food:** Sonic, Tony's Grill, Wendy's, **lodging:** Budget Suites, Candlewood Suites, InTown Suites, Wingate Inn, **other:** Office Depot, **W gas:** Texaco, **food:** Burger King, Pizza Hut/Taco Bell, Schlotsky's
433b	Mockingbird Lane, Love Field ✈, **E gas:** Shell, **food:** Jack-in-the-Box, **lodging:** Budget Suites, Comfort Inn, Crowne Plaza, InTown Suites, Sheraton, Radisson, Residence Inn
433a	(432b from sb)TX 356, Commonwealth Dr, **W lodging:** Delux Inn
432a	Inwood Rd, **E gas:** Exxon, **other:** H, Chevrolet, **W gas:** Texaco/Subway/dsl, Shell, **food:** Whataburger/24hr, **lodging:** Embassy Suites, Homewood Suites
431	Motor St, **E gas:** Chevron, **food:** Denny's, **other:** H **W gas:** Shell, **food:** Pepe's Grill, **lodging:** Marriott Suites
430c	Wycliff Ave, **E food:** JoJo's Rest., **lodging:** Holiday Inn, Renaissance Hotel, **other:** Intn'l Apparel Mart, **W lodging:** Hilton Anatole, Hilton Garden
430b	Mkt Ctr Blvd, **E other:** World Trade Ctr, **W gas:** Shell, **food:** Denny's, **lodging:** Courtyard, Fairfield Inn, Ramada Inn, Sheraton, Wilson World Hotel, Wyndham Garden
430a	Oak Lawn Ave, **E lodging:** Holiday Inn, **W gas:** Shell, Texaco/dsl, **food:** Denny's, Medieval Times Rest., **other:** to Merchandise Mart
429c	HiLine Ave (from nb)
429b	Continental Ave, Commerce St W, downtown, **E food:** Hooters, **W gas:** Exxon, Shell, **food:** McDonald's
429a	to I-45, US 75, to Houston
428e	Commerce St E, Reunion Blvd, Dallas, downtown
428d	I-30 W, to Ft Worth
428a	I-30 E, to I-45 S
428b	Industrial Blvd, **E gas:** Chevron, **W gas:** Fina, Kwik-Stop/dsl, Shamrock
427b	I-30 E
427a	Colorado Blvd, **E** H
426c	Jefferson Ave, **E gas:** Shell/dsl
426b	TX 180 W, 8th St, **E gas:** Shell/dsl
426a	Ewing Ave, **E food:** McDonald's, Popeye's
425c	Marsalis Ave, **E lodging:** Dallas Inn, **W gas:** Chevron, Valero
425b	Beckley Ave, 12th St, sb only, **W gas:** Shell, Valero, **food:** Wendy's
425a	Zang Blvd, same as 425b
424	Illinois Ave, **E gas:** Chevron, **food:** William's Chicken, **other:** H, **W gas:** Exxon, **food:** Jack-in-the-Box,

DALLAS

INTERSTATE 35 CONT'D

N ↕ S

Exit #	Services
424	Continued Pancake House, Sonic, Taco Bell, **other:** Kroger, Ross, Walgreens
423b	Saner Ave
423a	(422b from nb) US 67 S, Kiest Blvd, **W gas:** Shell/repair, **food:** McDonald's, Subway, Taco Del Mar, **lodging:** Dallas Inn
421b	Ann Arbor St
421a	Lp 12E W, **E gas:** RaceWay, **lodging:** Delux Inn
420	Laureland, **W gas:** Conoco, Texaco, **lodging:** Linfield Inn
419	Camp Wisdom Rd, **E gas:** Exxon, **lodging:** Oak Cliff Inn, **W gas:** Chevron, Shell/24hr, **food:** McDonald's, **lodging:** Suncrest Inn, **other:** U-Haul
418c	Danieldale Rd (from sb)
418b	I-635/I-20 E, to Shreveport
418a	I-20 W, to Ft Worth
417	Wheatland Rd (from nb)
416	Wintergreen Rd, **E other:** repair, **W gas:** Citgo/7-11, **food:** Cracker Barrel, Golden Corral, Waffle House, **lodging:** Holiday Inn Express, Red Roof Inn
415	Pleasant Run Rd, **E gas:** Chevron/24hr, RaceTrac, Shell/Blimpie/dsl, **food:** Bienvenidos Mexican, Evergreen Buffet, Subway, Waffle House, **lodging:** Great Western Inn, Royal Inn, Spanish Trails Motel, Super 8, **other:** Chrysler/Jeep, PepBoys, transmissions, **W gas:** Chevron, Exxon, **food:** Burger King, El Chico, Golden Corral, KFC, LJ Silver, Luby's, McDonald's, On the Border, Outback Steaks, Pizza Inn, Taco Bueno, Wendy's, **lodging:** Best Western, **other:** H, Chevrolet, Discount Tire, Ford, Kroger, K-Mart, Office Depot, Ross
414	FM 1382, Desoto Rd, Belt Line Rd, **E food:** Chili's, Whataburger, **other:** Walmart SuperCtr/gas/24hr
413	Parkerville Rd, **W gas:** Exxon/Subway, **other:** U-Haul
412	Bear Creek Rd, **W gas:** Shell/dsl, **food:** Bubba's BBQ, Jack-in-the-Box, Whataburger, **other:** HiHo RV Park, transmissions
411	FM 664, Ovilla Rd, **E gas:** Exxon/TCBY/24hr, RaceTrac/24hr, **food:** LJ Silver/Taco Bell, McDonald's, Whataburger, **lodging:** Comfort Inn, **other:** Brookshire's Foods, CVS Drug, **W gas:** Exxon/Subway, Shamrock
410	Red Oak Rd, **E gas:** Citgo/dsl, Nock's/Shell/Pizza Inn/Subway/dsl, **food:** Denny's, Merryland Chinese, **lodging:** Day's Inn, **W other:** Hilltop Travel Trailers
408	US 77, TX 342, to Red Oak, **E** golf
406	Sterrett Rd, **E** fireworks
405	FM 387, **E gas:** Phillips 66/dsl
404	Lofland Rd, industrial area
403	US 287, to Ft Worth, **E food:** Jack-in-the-Box, McDonald's, Taco Bell, Waffle House, **lodging:** Hampton Inn, **other:** Chevrolet/Cadillac, Jeep, **W other:** Buick/Pontiac/GMC, Chrysler/Dodge, Ford/Mercury
401b	US 287 bus, Waxahatchie, **E lodging:** Best Western, Super 8
401a	Brookside Rd, **E lodging:** Best Value Inn, Days Inn
399b	FM 1446
399a	FM 66, FM 876, Maypearl, **E lodging:** Texas Inn, **W gas:** Chevron/dsl, StarMart/dsl/24hr
397	to US 77, to Waxahachie
393mm	**rest area both lanes, full ♿ facilities, ☎, 🛆, litter barrels, vending, petwalk**
391	FM 329, Forreston Rd
386	TX 34, Italy, **E** gas Shell/dsl, **food:** DQ, Smokehouse BBQ, Sonic, **other:** $General, **W gas:** Exxon/Grandy's/Mcdonald's/Subway/Pizza Inn/dsl, **lodging:** Italy Inn, **other:** truckwash
384	Derrs Chapel Rd
381	FM 566, Milford Rd
377	FM 934
374	FM 2959, Carl's Corner, **W gas:** Carl's Trkstp/dsl/rest.
371	**I-35 W. I-35 divides into E and W nb, converges sb, See Texas I-35 W.**
370	US 77 N, FM 579, Hillsboro
368b	FM 286, **E food:** LoneStar Café, Taco Bell, Wendy's, **lodging:** Hampton Inn, **other:** Prime Outlets/famous brands, **W gas:** Exxon/Domino's, Valero/dsl, **food:** Braum's, Domino's, DQ, El Conquistador Mexican, El Taco Jalisco, McDonald's, Pizza Hut, **lodging:** Best Western, Comfort Inn, La Quinta, **other:** H
368a	TX 22, TX 171, to Whitney, **E gas:** 7-11, Love's/Chester's/Subway/dsl/scales/24hr, **food:** Arby's, Blackeyed Pea, Harvest Buffet, IHOP, McDonald's, Starbucks, **lodging:** Comfort Suites, Days Inn, Holiday Inn Express, Motel 6, Super 8, **W gas:** Chevron, Mobil, Murphy USA/dsl, Shell/dsl, **food:** Chicken Express, Jack-in-the-Box, KFC, Schlotsky's, Whataburger/24hr, **lodging:** Thunderbird Motel/rest., **other:** Cadillac/Chevrolet, Ford/Mercury, Radio Shack, Walmart SuperCtr/Subway
367	Old Bynum Rd (from nb)
364b	TX 81 N, to Hillsboro (exits left from nb)
364a	FM 310
362	Chatt Rd
359	FM 1304, **W gas:** Mobil/dsl/24hr, **other:** truckwash
358	FM 1242 E, Abbott, **E gas:** Exxon/dsl, **food:** Up in Smoke BBQ
356	Cord 3102
355	County Line Rd, **E other:** KOA
354	Marable St, **E other:** KOA
353	FM 2114, West, **E gas:** Chevron, Fina/dsl, Shell/Czech Bakery, **food:** Bush's Chicken, Sonic, Subway, **other:** Ford, **W gas:** Exxon, Texaco, **lodging:** Czech Inn, **other:** Chevrolet
351	FM 1858, **E** tires/repair
349	Wiggins Rd
347	FM 3149, Tours Rd
346	Ross Rd, **E gas:** Shell/dsl/24hr, **W gas:** Exxon/Church's/dsl/24hr, **other:** I-35 RV Park/LP, antiques
345	Old Dallas Rd, **E other:** antiques, **W other:** I-35 RV Park/LP
345a	frontage rd, same as 345
343	FM 308, Elm Mott, **E gas:** Exxon/DQ, Shell/Jct Cafe/dsl/scales/24hr, **W gas:** Chevron/dsl/24hr, **food:** El Mezcal, Heitmiller Steaks
342b	US 77 bus, **W** North Crest RV Park
342a	FM 2417, Crest Dr, **W gas:** Valero/dsl, **food:** Bush's Chicken, DQ, **lodging:** Everyday Inn, **other:** Family$, auto repair
341	Craven Ave, Lacy Lakeview, **W gas:** Chevron, Shell
340	Myers Lane (from nb)

HILLSBORO

INTERSTATE 35 CONT'D

N ↕ S

Exit #	Services
339	to TX 6 S, FM 3051, Lake Waco, **E gas:** Valero/dsl, **food:** Casa Ole, Cici's, Domino's, El Conquistador, Jack-in-the-Box, Luby's, Pizza Hut, Popeye's, Sonic, Wendy's, Whataburger/24hr, **lodging:** Holiday Inn, **other:** Advance Parts, Discount Tire, $General, Home Depot, Radio Shack, Walmart SuperCtr/24hr/gas, **W gas:** Chevron, Citgo, **food:** Burger King, Cracker Barrel, KFC, McDonald's, Papa John's, Starbucks, Taco Bell, **lodging:** Fairfield Inn, Hampton Inn, **other:** to ✈
338b	Behrens Circle (from nb), **E food:** Jack-in-the-Box, Sonic, same as 339, **W gas:** Shell/dsl/LP, **food:** Cracker Barrel, **lodging:** Comfort Inn, Country Inn, Days Inn, Delta Inn, Hampton Inn, Knight's Inn, Motel 6
337	(338a from nb) US 84, to TX 31, Waco Dr, **E gas:** Phillips 66, **food:** ChopStix, **lodging:** Value Place Suites, **other:** AutoZone, Family$, HEB Food/gas, O'Reilly Parts, Sam's Club/gas, **W lodging:** Radisson, **other:** H
335c	Lake Brazos Dr, MLK Blvd, **E lodging:** Hotel Waco, **W food:** Buzzard Billy's, **lodging:** Scottish Inn, Victorian Inn, **other:** H
335mm	Brazos River
335b	FM 434, University Parks Dr, **E food:** China Grill, Jim's Rest., Quizno's, Thai Cuisine, **lodging:** Best Western, **other:** Baylor U, TX Ranger Museum, **W food:** Arby's, Jack-in-the-Box, Magic China, **lodging:** Best Value Inn, Residence Inn
335a	4th St, 5th St, **E gas:** Exxon/Subway/dsl, **food:** Denny's, IHOP, Lupito's Mexican, Pizza Hut, **lodging:** Best Western, La Quinta, **other:** Baylor U, **W gas:** Chevron, Valero, **food:** Fazoli's, LJ Silver, McDonald's, Taco Bell, Taco Bueno, Taco Cabana, Wendy's, Whataburger/24hr, **lodging:** Clarion
334b	US 77 S, 17th St, 18th St, **E gas:** Shell/dsl, **food:** Burger King, Popeye's, Schlotsky's, Vitek's BBQ, **lodging:** Budget Inn, EconoLodge, Super 8, **W gas:** Phillips 66/dsl, Shell, **food:** Arranda's Mexican, **other:** H
333a	Lp 396, Valley Mills Dr, **E food:** El Chico, Elite Café, Rudy's BBQ, TX Roadhouse, Trujillo's Mexican, **lodging:** Comfort Suites, La Quinta, Motel 6, **other:** Isuzu/Mazda, KIA, Suzuki, **W gas:** RaceWay, Valero, **food:** Bush's Chicken, Catfish King, Church's, Jack-in-the-Box, Little Caesars, Papa John's, Sonic, Subway, **other:** Aamco, Advance Parts, AutoZone, CVS Drug, Family$, Freightliner, HEB Foods, Lincoln/Mercury, Walgreens
331	New Rd, **E lodging:** New Road Inn, Relax Inn, Rodeway Inn, **W gas:** *FLYING J*/CountryMkt/dsl/scales/24hr, **food:** Hooters, IHOP, **lodging:** Quality Inn, **other:** Harley Davidson
330	Lp 340, TX 6, **0-2 mi W gas:** Chevron, **food:** Bush's Chicken, Camille's Cafe, Coldstone, Don Carlo's Mexican, Logan's Roadhouse, Outback Steaks, Panera Bread, TGIFridays, Subway, **lodging:** Extended Stay America, Fairfield Inn, Hampton Inn, Homewood Suites, **other:** Belk, Best Buy, Books-A-Million, Ford, Honda, Hyundai, Kohl's, Lowe's Whse, Marshall's, Nissan, Office Depot, Ross, Old Navy, Toyota/Scion, Verizon, Walmart SuperCtr/24hr

WACO

Exit #	Services
328	FM 2063, FM 2113, Moody, **E gas:** Pilot/Subway/Wendy's/dsl/scales/24hr/@, **food:** McDonald's, **lodging:** La Quinta, **other:** Kenworth, **W gas:** Shell/24hr, Valero/dsl, **lodging:** Sleep Inn
325	FM 3148, Moonlight Dr, **W gas:** Conoco/dsl, **other:** Walkabout RV Ctr
323	FM 2837 (from sb), Lorena, **W gas:** Brookshire Bros/Conoco, **food:** Pizza House, Sonic
322	Lorena, **E gas:** Phillips 66/dsl, **food:** Baytown Seafood, **W food:** Bush's Chicken, Ruthy's Mexican, **other:** $General
319	Woodlawn Rd
318b a	Bruceville, **E gas:** Conoco/dsl, **other:** picnic area both lanes, litter barrels
315	TX 7, FM 107, Eddy, **1 mi E** RV Park, **W gas:** Shell/Subway/dsl/24hr, Texaco, **other:** Family$, to Mother Neff SP
314	Old Blevins Rd
311	Big Elm Rd, **E** fireworks, **W** picnic
308	FM 935, Troy, **E gas:** Shell, **other:** Troy Foods, **W gas:** Exxon, **other:** dsl repair
306	FM 1237, Pendleton, **W gas:** Love's/Subway/dsl/24hr, **other:** Temple RV Park/LP
305	Berger Rd, **W gas:** Exxon/dsl/scales/24hr, **lodging:** Sharon Jean's Rest, **other:** Lucky's RV Park, Temple RV Park, repair
304	Lp 363, Dodgen Loop, **W gas:** Shell/Wendy's/dsl, Valero/dsl/24hr, **other:** Freightliner
303	spur 290, N 3rd St, Temple, **E gas:** S-2 Gas, **lodging:** Texas Inn, **W lodging:** Continental Inn
302	Nugent Ave, **E gas:** Exxon/dsl, Texaco, **lodging:** Comfort Suites, EconoLodge, Quality Inn, Red Roof Inn, **W gas:** Pay Less Gas, Shell, **food:** Denny's, **lodging:** Best Western, Days Inn, Knight's Inn, Motel 6, Stratford House Inn
301	TX 53, FM 2305, Adams Ave, **E gas:** Valero, **food:** Arby's, Chick-fil-A, KFC, LJ Silver, McDonald's, Pizza Hut, Starbucks, Subway, Taco Bell, Wendy's, Whataburger, **lodging:** La Quinta, **other:** H, Advance Parts, Ford/Lincoln/Mercury, HEB Foods, **W food:** TX Roadhouse, **lodging:** Best Western
300	Ave H, 49th–57th Sts, **E gas:** Shell, **food:** Clem Mikeskas BBQ, **W gas:** Shell
299	US 190 E, TX 36, **E gas:** Shell, **food:** Cracker Barrel, Jack-in-the-Box, Luby's, Olive Garden, **lodging:** Best Value Inn, Residence Inn, **other:** H, Ancira RV Ctr, Chrysler/Dodge/Jeep, **W food:** BJ's Rest, Chili's, IHOP, McDonald's, Taco Cabana, **other:** Batteries+, Best Buy, Home Depot, PetsMart, Target

TEMPLE

INTERSTATE 35 CONT'D

N ↕ S

Exit #	Services
298	nb only, to frontage rd, **E lodging:** Residence Inn
297	FM 817, Midway Dr, **E gas:** Phillips 66, **lodging:** Holiday Inn, Super 8/rest., **other:** Nissan, Suzuki, **W gas:** Valero, **other:** Buick/GMC/Pontiac, Fed Ex, VW
294b	FM 93, 6th Ave, **E gas:** Shell/dsl, **food:** McDonald's, **other:** Chevrolet, Toyota/Scion, **W food:** Subway, **lodging:** River Forest Inn, **other:** Harley-Davidson, U of Mary Hardin Baylor
294a	Central Ave, **W gas:** Shell/dsl, **food:** Burger King, Mexicano Grill, Pizza Hut, Schlotzky's, Sonic, Taco Bell, Whataburger, **lodging:** Knight's Inn, **other:** AutoZone, Goodyear, O'Reilly Parts, Parts+
293b	TX 317, FM 436, Main St
293a	US 190 W, to Killeen, Ft Hood
292	Lp 121 (same as 293a), **E gas:** Valero/dsl/rest./24hr, **lodging:** Budget Host, **W gas:** Mobil/dsl/24hr, **food:** Oxbow Steaks, **lodging:** La Quinta, **other:** Belton RV Park, Family$, Ford, Sunbelt RV Ctr, auto/tire repair
290	Shanklin Rd
289	Tahuaya Rd, **E other:** Hi-Way Parts
287	Amity Rd
286	FM 2484, **E lodging:** Best Western, Holiday Inn Express, **W other:** to Stillhouse Hollow Lake, Vet
285	FM 2268, Salado, **E gas:** Conoco/Brookshire Foods, **food:** Subway, **lodging:** Holiday Inn Express, **W gas:** Pay Less, **food:** Cowboys BBQ, Robertson's Rest., Sonic
284	Stagecoach Rd, **E gas:** Exxon/Arby's, **food:** Roy T's, **W gas:** Texaco/dsl, **food:** DQ, **lodging:** Super 8
283	FM 2268, FM 2843, to Holland, Salado, **E lodging:** Stagecoach Inn
282	FM 2115, **E gas:** Valero/dsl, **other:** RV camping, **rest area sb, full ♿ facilities, ☎, picnic, litter barrels, vending, petwalk, RV dump**
281mm	**rest area nb, full ♿ facilities, ☎, picnic, litter barrels, vending, petwalk, RV dump**
280	Prairie Dell
279	Hill Rd, **W other:** RV Park
277	Yankee Rd
275	FM 487, to Florence, Jarrell, **E gas:** Exxon/dsl, **W gas:** Shell, **other:** USPO
274	rd 312, **E gas:** Chevron/dsl, Exxon/Subway, ***FLYING J***dsl, **food:** Burger King, Denny's, McDonald's
271	Theon Rd, **E gas:** Explore USA RV Ctr, **W gas:** Shell/Subway/dsl/24hr
268	FM 972, Walburg, **E other:** Crestview RV Ctr
266	TX 195, **E gas:** Phillips 66/dsl
265	TX 130 S, to Austin
264	Lp 35, Georgetown
262	RM 2338, Lake Georgetown, **E gas:** Valero, **food:** Burger King, Chipotle Mexican, Keva Juice, KFC, McDonald's, Pizza Hut, Quizno's, Shangahi Express, Sonic, Starbucks, Subway, **other:** URGENT CARE, CVS Drug, $Tree, Parts+, Radio Shack, **W gas:** Shell, **food:** DQ, La Tapatia, Placa Greek, Whataburger, **lodging:** Georgetown Inn, Holiday Inn Express, La Quinta
261	TX 69, Georgetown, **E gas:** Shell/dsl, **food:** Applebee's, Chili's, Luby's, Schlotsky's, Taco Bell, **lodging:** Comfort Suites, Holiday Inn Express, **other:**

GEORGETOWN

Exit #	Services
261	Continued Albertson's, HEB Foods, Hobby Lobby, Tuesday Morning, same as 262, **W gas:** Murphy USA/dsl, **food:** Casa Ole, Chick-fil-A, CiCi's, Genghis Grill, Ichyban Buffet, IHOP, Mama Fu's, McAlister's Deli, Mt Mike's, Panda Express, Souper Salad, Taco Cabana, **other:** AT&T, Beall's, Best Buy, Home Depot, Kohl's, Office Depot, Old Navy, PetsMart, Target, TJ Maxx, Walgreens, Walmart SuperCtr/24hr, antiques
260	RM 2243, Leander, **E other:** [H], USPO, **W gas:** Chevron, Exxon, Texaco, **food:** Jack-in-the-Box, **lodging:** Quality Inn
259	Lp 35, **W other:** RV Outlet Ctr, to Interspace Caverns
257	Westinghouse Rd, **E other:** Buick/Chevrolet, Ford, Hummer Kia, Mazda, Mercedes, Mitsubishi, Volvo, VW
256	RM 1431, Chandler Rd, **E food:** Chili's, Jamba Juice, La Madeline, Mimi's Cafe, **other:** Round Rock Outlet, Hummer, Mazda, JC Penney, Jo-Ann Fabrics, PetsMart, Ross, Volvo
254	FM 3406, Round Rock, **E gas:** Chevron, **food:** Arby's, Garcia's Mexican, Gatti's Pizza, McDonald's, **lodging:** Best Western, **other:** CVS Drug, $General, Firestone, Harley-Davidson, Honda, Hyundai, Smart Car, Toyota, **W gas:** Phillips 66/dsl, Shell, **food:** Carino's Italian, Chuy's Mexican, Cracker Barrel, Dave's Pizza, Denny's, La Margarita Mexican, Mesa Rosa Mexican, Rudy's BBQ, SaltGrass Steaks, Summer Palace, **lodging:** Country Inn&Suites, Courtyard, Hilton Garden, Holiday Inn, La Quinta, Round Rock Inn, Red Roof Inn, SpringHill Suites, ValuePlace, **other:** GMC/Pontiac, Nissan
253b	US 79, to Taylor, **E gas:** Chevron, Shell, Texaco, **food:** Arby's, Baskin-Robbins, DQ, Famous Sam's Café, Fuddrucker's, KFC, LoneStar Café, LJ Silver, Que Pasa Mexican, Sirloin Stockade, **lodging:** Wingate Inn, **other:** [H], AutoZone, Beall's, Cottman Transmissions, HEB/deli, **W gas:** Exxon/dsl, Shell/dsl/24hr, **food:** Gatti's Pizza, Hunan Lion, IHOP, Popeye's, Starbucks, Taco Bell, **lodging:** Country Inn&Suites, La Quinta, Red Roof Inn, Sleep Inn, ValuePlace, **other:** CVS Drug, $Tree, Tuesday Morning, USPO
253a	Frontage Rd, same as 253 b
252b a	RM 620, **E gas:** Shell/dsl/24hr, **lodging:** Candlewood Suites, Extended Stay America, **other:** NAPA, **W gas:** Texaco/dsl, **food:** Little Caesar's, McDonald's, Quizno's, Starbucks, Wendy's, **lodging:** Comfort Suites, Staybridge Suites
251	Lp 35, Round Rock, **E gas:** Valero, **food:** CiCi's Pizza, Outback Steaks, Whataburger, **lodging:** Residence Inn, **other:** Aamco, BigLots, Brake Check, $General, **W gas:** Shell, **food:** Burger King, Jack-in-the-Box, Lucky Dog Grill, Luby's, Taco Cabana, **lodging:** Mariott, **other:** GNC, Hastings Books, NTB, Walgreens
250	FM 1325, **E food:** Chick-fil-A, Chili's, El Chico, Jason's Deli, Joe's Crabshack, Macaroni Grill, McDonald's, Panda Express, Subway, Twin Peaks Rest., **lodging:** Hampton Inn, Residence Inn, **other:** Best Buy, Discount Tire, Home Depot, PetsMart, Radio Shack, Target, Walmart SuperCtr/24hr, **W gas:** Shell, **food:** Applebee's, Fast Eddie's, Hooters, Jimmy John's,

ROUND ROCK

TX

INTERSTATE 35 CONT'D

N ↕ S

Exit #	Services
250	Continued Mongolian Grille, Olive Garden, Starbucks, **lodging:** Extended Stay America, La Quinta, **other:** AT&T, Barnes&Noble, Hobby Lobby, Kohl's, Lowe's Whse, Marshall's, Michael's, Office Depot, Old Navy, PetCo, Ross, Sam's Club/gas, Steinmart, World Mkt
248	Grand Ave Pkwy, **E gas:** Citgo, Shell, Texaco/Subway/dsl, **food:** Cheddar's, Chucho's Mexican, Fish Daddy's Grill, Jack-in-the-Box, Taco Cabana, Thundercloud Subs, TX Roadhouse, **lodging:** Comfort Suites, **other:** URGENT CARE, Firestone, **W gas:** Chevron/McDonald's
247	FM 1825, Pflugerville, **E gas:** RaceTrac, **food:** Jack-in-the-Box, Sonic, Taco Cabana, Wendy's, **other:** Firestone/auto, HEB Foods, cinema, **W gas:** Exxon, Shell/Church's, **food:** KFC, Miller's BBQ, Whataburger, **lodging:** Holiday Inn Express
246	Howard Lane, **E gas:** Citgo, Shell/dsl, **food:** Arby's, Baby Acapulco, Carino's, Chili's, McDonald's, Subway, Wings'n More, **other:** Home Depot, Kohl's, NTB, **W gas:** Valero/dsl, **food:** IHOP, Whataburger
245	FM 734, Parmer Lane, to Yager Lane (244 from nb), **E food:** Bennigan's, Carino's, Chick-fil-A, Chili's, Schlotzsky's, Subway, **lodging:** Courtyard, **other:** HEB Food/gas, JC Penney, Kohl's, PetsMart, Radio Shack, Ross, Sears Grand, Target, **W gas:** Conoco/dsl, Murphy USA, **food:** Hoho Chinese, Red Robin, Starbucks, **lodging:** Fairfield Inn, Hilton Garden, Residence Inn, SpringHill Suites, **other:** CarMax, Discount Tire, Lowe's Whse, Walmart SuperCtr/24hr
243	Braker Lane, **E gas:** Valero, **food:** Jack-in-the-Box, Whataburger/24hr, **other:** U-Haul, **W gas:** Citgo, Shell/dsl, **lodging:** Austin Motel, ValuePlace, **other:** $General
241	Rundberg Lane, **E gas:** Exxon, **food:** Grand China Buffet, Jack-in-the-Box, Mr Gatti's, Old San Francisco Steaks, **lodging:** Extended Stay Deluxe, Ramada Inn, **other:** Albertson's, Chevrolet, $General, U-Haul, Walmart SuperCtr/24hr, **W gas:** Chevron, Shell, **lodging:** Austin Suites, Austin Village, Budget Inn, Economy Inn, Holiday Inn Express, Motel 6, Red Roof Inn, Super 8, Wingate Inn
240a	US 183, Lockhart, **E gas:** Exxon, **food:** DQ, Jack-in-the-Box, Old San Francisco Steaks, **lodging:** Days Inn, Ramada Inn, **W gas:** Chevron/dsl/24hr, Texaco/dsl, **lodging:** Motel 6, Red Roof Inn, Super 8, Wingate Inn
239	St John's Ave, **E gas:** Shell, **food:** Burger King, Chili's, Fuddruckers, Japon Japanese, Jim's Rest., Pappadeaux, Pappasito's Mexican, Steak&Egg, **lodging:** Budget Host, Crowne Plaza, Days Inn, DoubleTree, Drury Inn, Hampton Inn, Red Lion Hotel, Studio 6, **other:** Dodge, Home Depot, KIA, Volvo, Walmart SuperCtr/24hr, USPO, **W gas:** Conoco, Exxon, Valero, **food:** Antonio's Texmex, Applebee's, Bennigan's, Carrabba's, Denny's, IHOP, Panda Express, Quizno's, Wendy's, **lodging:** Baymont Inn, Best Value Inn, Comfort Inn, Country Inn&Suites, Courtyard, Holiday Inn Express, Hyatt Place, La Quinta, Radisson, Ramada Inn, Sheraton, Sumner Suites, **other:** Office Depot

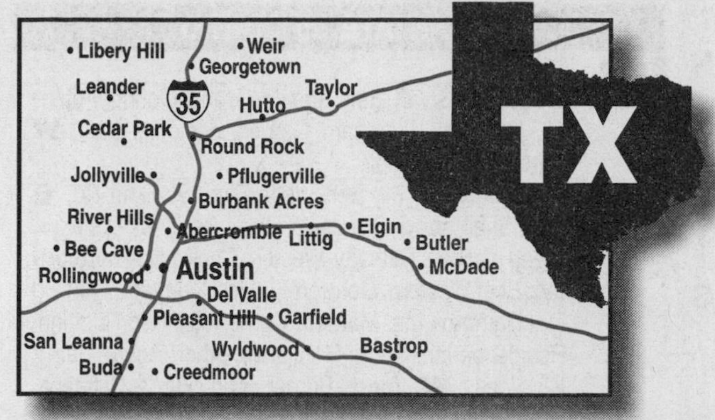

AUSTIN

Exit #	Services
238b	US 290 E, RM 222, same as 238a, frontage rds connect several exits
238a	51st St, **E gas:** Exxon, Chevron, Shell, **food:** Burger King, Chili's, Fuddrucker's, LJ Silver, McDonald's, Sonic, Subway, TX Steaks, Whataburger, **lodging:** Doubletree Hotel, Drury Inn, Econolodge, Embassy Suites, Holiday Inn, **other:** Advance Parts, Best Buy, $Tree, Firestone, FoodLand, Home Depot, Jo-Ann Crafts, Marshall's, Old Navy, PetsMart, Ross, Staples, Target, Volvo, Walgreens, **W gas:** Shell, **food:** Baby Acapulco, Capt Benny's Seafood, Carrabba's, IHOP, Outback Steaks, Quizno's, **lodging:** Capital Inn, Courtyard, Drury Inn, Fairfield Inn, Hilton, La Quinta, Motel 6, Quality Inn, Ramada Ltd, Super 8, **other:** Dillard's, Ford, Office Depot
237b	51st St, same as 238a
237a	Airport Blvd, **E food:** BBQ, **W food:** Jack-in-the-Box, Wendy's, **other:** GNC, Goodyear, HEB Foods, Old Navy, PetCo, Sears/auto
upper level is I-35 thru, lower level accesses downtown	
236b	39th St, **E gas:** Chevron/dsl, **food:** Short Stop Burgers, Subway, **other:** Fiesta Foods, HiLo Parts, O'Reilly Parts, U-Haul, **W gas:** Shell/dsl, **other:** Tune&Lube, tires, to U of TX
236a	26th-32nd Sts, **E food:** Los Altos Mexican, Subway, **lodging:** Days Inn, **W lodging:** Rodeway Inn, **other:** H
235b	Manor Rd, same as 236a, **E food:** Denny's, **lodging:** DoubleTree, **W lodging:** Rodeway Inn, **other:** U of TX, st capitol, Vet
235a	MLK, 15th St, **W** H
upper level is I-35 thru, lower level accesses downtown	
234c	11th St, 12th St, downtown, **E gas:** Chevron, Shell, **food:** Denny's, Wendy's, **lodging:** DoubleTree Hotel, Super 8, **other:** CVS Drug, **W gas:** Chevron, Shell, Texaco, **food:** Wendy's, **lodging:** Crowne Plaza, Marriott, Hilton Garden, Omni Motel, Radisson, Sheraton, **other:** H, museum, st capitol
234b	8th-3rd St, **W food:** IHOP
234a	Cesar Chavez St, Holly St, downtown
233	Riverside Dr, Town Lake, **E gas:** Citgo, **lodging:** Extended Stay America, **W gas:** Chevron/dsl, **lodging:** Holiday Inn
232mm	Little Colorado River
232b	Woodland Ave
232a	Oltorf St, **E gas:** Shell/dsl, **food:** Luby's, **lodging:** Best Value Inn, Country Garden Inn, Howard Johnson, La Quinta, Motel 6, Parkwest Inn, Suburban Lodge, **W gas:** Chevron, Exxon, **food:** Denny's, Mesa Ranch Grill, Starbucks, **lodging:** Clarion, Quality Inn

INTERSTATE 35 CONT'D

N ↕ S

Exit #	Services
231	Woodward St, **E gas:** Shell/dsl, **food:** Country Kitchen, **lodging:** Wyndham Garden, same as 232, **W other:** Home Depot
230b a	US 290 W, TX 71, Ben White Blvd, St Elmo Rd, **E gas:** Shell, **food:** Domino's, Jim's Rest., McDonald's, Sigon Kitchen, Subway, Western Choice Steaks, **lodging:** Best Western, Comfort Suites, Courtyard, Fairfield Inn, Hampton Inn, Marriott, Omni Hotel, Red Roof Inn, Residence Inn, SpringHill Suites, **other:** Acura, Sam's Club/gas, **W food:** Burger King, Furr's Cafeteria, IHOP, Pizza Hut, Taco Cabana, **lodging:** Candlewood Suites, Days Inn, Hawthorn Suites, La Quinta, **other:** H, BMW, Carmax, Chrysler/Dodge/Jeep, Ford, GMC, Honda, Hyundai, Kia, Lincoln/Mercury, Mazda, Nissan, NTB, Suzuki/Kia, Toyota/Scion
229	Stassney Lane, **W food:** Chili's, Krispy Kreme, Logan's Roadhouse, Macaroni Grill, Pizza Hut, Rockfish Grill, TX Cattle Co Steaks, Twin Peaks Rest., **other:** Albertson's/gas, Fiesta Foods, KIA, Lowe's Whse
228	Wm Cannon Drive, **E gas:** Exxon, Valero, **food:** Applebee's, McDonald's, Taco Bell, **other:** Brake Check, Chrysler, Discount Tire, HEB Foods, Hyundai/Subaru, Mitsubishi, Nissan, Radio Shack, Target, **W gas:** Texaco, Shell/dsl, **food:** Arby's, Burger King, China Harbor, Gatti's Pizza, Jack-in-the-Box, KFC, LJ Silver, Peter Piper Pizza, Taco Cabana, Wendy's, Whataburger/24hr, **other:** Advance Parts, BigLots, Chevrolet, CVS Drug, $General, Firestone
227	Slaughter Lane, Lp 275, S Congress, **E gas:** Shell/dsl, **food:** IHOP, **other:** Home Depot, Lone Star RV Resort, U-Haul, **W gas:** Murphy USA, Texaco, Valero/dsl, **food:** Carino's, Chili's, Chipotle Mexican, Miller BBQ, Sonic, Starbucks, Steak'n Shake, Subway, Jack-in-the-Box, TGIFriday's, TX Roadhouse, Whataburger, **other:** Border's Books, Hobby Lobby, JC Penney, Marshall's, PetsMart, Ross, Target, Walmart SuperCtr/24hr
226	Slaughter Creek Overpass
225	FM 1626, Onion Creek Pkwy, **E gas:** Shell, Texaco, **other:** Harley-Davidson
224	frontage rd (from nb)
223	FM 1327
221	Lp 4, Buda, **E gas:** Chevron/McDonald's, Shell/dsl, **food:** Starbucks, **lodging:** Best Value Inn, Comfort Suites, Holiday Inn Express, **other:** Ford, **W gas:** Chevron/24hr, Murphy USA, Shell, **food:** Arby's, Chili's, Cracker Barrel, Culver's, Dan's Hamburgers, Jack-in-the-Box, KFC/LJ Silver, Sonic, Subway, Taco Bell, lodging: Hampton Inn, **other:** AT&T, Cabela's, HEB Food/gas, Radio Shack, Walgreens, Walmart SuperCtr
220	FM 2001, Niederwald, **E gas:** Shell, **other:** Camper Clinic RV Ctr, Marshall's RV Park, **W other:** Crestview RV Ctr/Park, GMC/Peterbilt, auto repair
217	Lp 4, Buda, **E gas:** Conoco/dsl/24hr, **lodging:** La Quinta, **W gas:** Exxon/dsl, Valero/dsl, **food:** Burger King, **lodging:** Best Western, **other:** Home Depot
215	Bunton Overpass, **E gas:** Exxon/KFC/LJ Silver, **other:** H, Lowe's Whse, Walgreens, **W food:** Jack-in-the-Box, Papa Murphy's, Starbucks, Subway, Whataburger, **other:** Explore USA RV Ctr, HEB Foods/dsl, Kohl's, PetCo, Target

SAN MARCOS

Exit #	Services
213	FM 150, Kyle, **E gas:** Valero/dsl, **food:** DQ, **other:** AutoZone, Goodyear/auto, **W gas:** Conoco/dsl, **other:** CVS Drug, repair
210	Yarrington Rd, **E other:** Hyundai, **W other:** Plum Creek RV Park
208mm	Blanco River
208	**insp sta**
207	Frontage Rd, Blanco River Rd, **W other:** GM
206	Lp 82, Aquarena Springs Rd, **E gas:** Conoco, Valero, **other:** San Marcos RV Park, **W gas:** Citgo/dsl, Exxon/dsl, Shell, Texaco, **food:** Pancake House, Popeye's, Sonic, **lodging:** Best Value Inn, Comfort Inn, Howard Johnson, La Quinta, Motel 6, Ramada Ltd, River Inn, Rodeway Inn, Super 8, **other:** to SW TX U
205	TX 80, TX 142, Bastrop, **E gas:** Exxon, Quix, RaceWay, Shell/dsl, Valero, **food:** Arby's, DQ, Fazoli's, Jason's Deli, Subway, Wing Stop, **lodging:** Executive Inn, **other:** AutoZone, CVS Drug, $General, Hastings Books, Hobby Lobby, Walmart SuperCtr/24hr, Vet, **W gas:** Valero, **food:** A&W/LJ Silver, Burger King, Church's, CiCi's, Furr's Cafe, IHOP, KFC, Kobe Japanese, Logan's Roadhouse, McDonald's, Pizza Hut, Taco Cabana, Wendy's, **lodging:** Best Western, Budget Inn, Days Inn, Gateway Inn, Knight's Inn, Red Roof Inn, Rodeway Inn, **other:** Brake Check, GNC, JC Penney, Office Depot, Radio Shack
204mm	San Marcos River
204b	CM Allen Pkwy, **W gas:** Shell/dsl, Spirit, **food:** DQ, Mazatlan Mexican, Plucker's Grill, Sonic, **lodging:** Best Western, Econolodge, **other:** AutoZone, O'Reilly Parts
204a	Lp 82, TX 123, to Seguin, **E gas:** Conoco, Valero, **food:** Burger King, Carino's, Chili's, FasTaco, Golden Corral, Luby's, McDonald's, Red Lobster, Whataburger/24hr, **lodging:** Comfort Suites, Hampton Inn, Holiday Inn Express, **other:** H, Ford/Mercury, Jeep/Chrysler, transmissions
202	FM 3407, Wonder World Dr, **E gas:** Exxon, Shell/Church's, **food:** Fuschaks BBQ, Hardees, Jack-in-the-Box, Taco Bueno, Taste of China, Wienerschnitzel, **other:** H, Best Buy, Discount Tire, $Tree, Lowe's Whse, Marshalls, PetsMart, Ross, Sams Club/gas, **W gas:** Valero/dsl, **food:** TX Roadhouse, **lodging:** Country Inn&Suites, **other:** repair, transmissions
201	McCarty Lane, **E lodging:** Embassy Suites, **W other:** Beall's, Chrysler/Dodge, JC Penney, Nissan, Target
200	Centerpoint Rd, **E food:** Bennigan's, Cracker Barrel, Food Court, Outback Steaks, River City Grill, Subway, Taco Bell, Wendy's, **other:** Cavender's Boots, GNC, Old Navy, Prime Outlets/famous brands, Tanger Outlet/famous brands, **W gas:** Valero/dsl, **food:** Craig O's Pizza, McDonald's, Quizno's, Starbucks, Whataburger/24hr, **lodging:** Baymont Inn, **other:** Honda
199	Posey Rd, **E other:** Tanger Outlets/famous brands, Toyota/Scion, same as 200
196	FM 1106, York Creek Rd, **W other:** King&Trail RV Park
195	Watson Lane, Old Bastrop Rd
193	Conrads Rd, Kohlenberg Rd, **W gas:** TA/Country Fare Rest/Popeye's/Subway/dsl/scales/24hr/@, **other:** Camping World RV Ctr

N ↕ S

NEW BRAUNFELS

INTERSTATE 35 CONT'D

Exit #	Services
191	FM 306, FM 483, Canyon Lake, **E other:** AT&T, Best Buy, I-35 RV Camping, JC Penney, Ross, Target, Verizon, Walmart Dist Ctr, **W gas:** Chevron, Exxon/dsl, **food:** Burger King, **lodging:** Wingate Inn, **other:** transmissions
190c	Post Rd
190b	frontage rd
190a	frontage rd, same as 189
189	TX 46, Seguin, **E gas:** Shell/dsl, **food:** Chili's, Denny's, Olive Garden, Oma's Ha US Rest., Quizno's, Taco Bueno, **lodging:** Best Value Inn, Econolodge, Hampton Inn, La Quinta, Super 8, **other:** Discount Tire, Home Depot, K-Mart, Kohl's, Office Depot, Vet, **W gas:** Texaco, **food:** Applebee's, Garden Buffet, IHOP, McDonald's, Pizza Hut, Taco Bell, Taco Cabana, Wendy's, **lodging:** Days Inn, Edelweiss Inn, Fairfield Inn, Hilton Garden, Holiday Inn, Howard Johnson, Motel 6, Rodeway Inn, Quality Inn, Sleep Inn, **other:** H, Walgreens
188	Frontage Rd, **W food:** Mamacita's Rest., Ryan's, **lodging:** River Ranch Resort, **other:** Hastings Books
188mm	Guadalupe River
187	FM 725, Lake McQueeny Rd, **E food:** A&W/LJ Silver, Arby's, Burger King, CiCi's, Schobell's Rest., Subway, Whataburger/24hr, **other:** Aamco, BigLots, Family$, Ford/Lincoln/Mercury, Hobby Lobby, Jeep, **W gas:** Shell/dsl, **food:** Adobe Café, DQ, Jack-in-the-Box, Jason's Deli, Mesquite Pit BBQ, Steaks to Go, **lodging:** Budget Inn, **other:** H, CVS Drug, River Ranch RV Resort, transmissions
186	Walnut Ave, **E gas:** Exxon/Subway, Murphy USA/dsl, Valero, **food:** Chick-fil-A, McDonald's, Popeye's, Schlotsky's, Taco Bell, **lodging:** Red Roof Inn, **other:** Lowe's Whse, Walmart SuperCtr, **W gas:** Shell/dsl, **food:** Baskin-Robbins, KFC, Mr Gatti's, Panda Express, Papa John's, Starbucks, **other:** AT&T, AutoZone, Brake Check, $Tree, GNC, HEB Foods/gas, Radio Shack, U-Haul, Walgreens
185	FM 1044
184	FM 482, Lp 337, Ruekle Rd, **E gas:** Shell/dsl, **other:** Buick/GMC/Pontiac, Kia, Mazda, RV Camping, **W gas:** Pilot/McDonald's/dsl/scales, **other:** Suzuki
183	Solms Rd, **W gas:** Exxon
182	Engel Rd, **E other:** Stamann RV Ctr
180	Schwab Rd
179mm	**rest area both lanes, full ♿ facilities, ☎, picnic tables, litter barrels, vending, petwalk**
178	FM 1103, Cibolo Rd, Hubert US Rd, **E gas:** Shell/dsl, **other:** Walgreens
177	FM 482, FM 2252, **E other:** Stone Creek RV Park
176	Weiderstein Rd, same as 175
175	FM 3009, Natural Bridge, **E gas:** Valero, **food:** Chili's, IHOP, La Pasadita Mexican, McDonald's, Miller's BBQ, Schlotsky's, Sonic, Taco Cabana, **lodging:** Fairfield Inn, Hampton Inn, **other:** HEB Food/gas, Lowe's Whse, **W gas:** Chevron, Murphy USA/dsl, Shell/dsl, Valero/Subway/dsl, **food:** Abel's Diner, Arby's, Bellacino's, Denny's, Domino's, Jack-in-the-Box, KFC/Taco Bell/Pizza Hut, Marble Slab, McDonald's, Panda Express, Pazzo Italian, Quizno's, Wendy's, Whataburger, Wing Stop, **lodging:** La Quinta, **other:** AT&T, $Tree, Factory Shoestore, Walmart SuperCtr

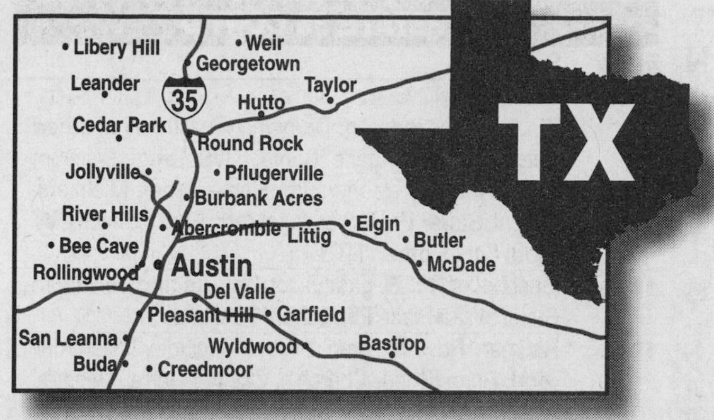

Exit #	Services
174b	Schertz Pkwy, **E gas:** Shell
174a	FM 1518, Selma, **E gas:** Phillips 66, **food:** Ruddy's BBQ, **other:** Honda/Mitsubishi, Subaru, **W lodging:** Comfort Inn, **other:** Tex-All RV Ctr
173	Old Austin Rd, Olympia Pkwy, **E food:** Baskin Robbins, Chick-fil-A, Chili's, Chipotle Mexican, Firehouse Subs, Freddy's Custard, Hooters, IHOP, Macaroni Grill, Outback Steaks, Panda Express, Peter Piper Pizza, Red Robin, Sea Island Srimp, Starbucks, Subway, TGIFriday's, Wendy's, **lodging:** Holiday Inn Express, **other:** AT&T, Beall's, Best Buy, Borders Books, Costco/gas, Discount Tire, GNC, Hobby Lobby, Home Depot, Kohl's, NTB, Old Navy, PetsMart, Ross, Verizon, Target, TJ Maxx, WorldMkt, **W food:** ChuckeCheese, Chuy's Mexican, Houlihan's, **other:** Retama Park RaceTrack
172	TX 218, Anderson Lp, P Booker Rd, **E food:** Buffalo Wild Wings, Coldstone Creamery, IHOP, Krystal, On-the-Border, Outback Steaks, TX Roadhouse, Zio's, **lodging:** Comfort Inn, ValuePlace, **other:** Ford, Nissan, Home Depot, Hyundai, Kohls, Target, to Randolph AFB, **W** to SeaWorld
171	Topperwein Rd, same as 170
170	Judson Rd, to Converse, **E food:** Denny's, Subway, Whataburger/24hr, **lodging:** Great Value Inn, La Quinta, **other:** H, Chevrolet, Chrysler, Ford, Hyundai, Nissan, Pontiac/GMC, Toyota, **W gas:** Exxon, **lodging:** Best Western, **other:** Kia, Mazda, Sam's Club/gas
169	O'Conner Rd, Wurzbach Pkwy, **E gas:** Exxon/dsl, **food:** McDonald's, Quizno's, Subway, Taco Cabana, **lodging:** Comfort Suites, **other:** Chrysler/Jeep, Lowe's Whse, Walgreens, **W gas:** Shell/dsl, Valero, **food:** Jack-in-the-Box, Jim's Rest., Mi Casa Mexican, Sonic, **other:** Mazda
168	Weidner Rd, **E gas:** Citgo/dsl, **lodging:** Days Inn, Comfort Suites, **W gas:** Chevron, **lodging:** Park Inn, Super 8, **other:** Harley-Davidson, Volvo Trucks
167b	Thousand Oaks Dr, Starlight Terrace, **E gas:** Valero/dsl
167a	Randolph Blvd, **E gas:** Valero, **W lodging:** Continental Inn, Days Inn, Motel 6, Rodeway Inn, Ruby Inn
166	I-410 W, Lp 368 S, **W other:** to Sea World
165	FM 1976, Walzem Rd, **E gas:** Shell, Valero/dsl, **food:** Applebee's, Bill Miller BBQ, Burger King, China Harbor, ChuckeCheese, Church's, Domino's, Firehouse Grill, IHOP, Jack-in-the-Box, KFC/Taco Bell, Las Palapas Mexican, LJ Silver, Luby's, McDonald's, Marie Callender's, Olive Garden, Pizza Hut, Red Lobster, Shoneys, Starbucks, Subway, Taco Cabana, Wendy's,

N ↕ S

SAN ANTONIO

INTERSTATE 35 CONT'D

Exit #	Services
165	Continued Whataburger, **lodging:** Drury Inn, PearTree Inn, **other:** AutoZone, Cavender's Boots, CVS Drug, Discount Tire, $World, Firestone/auto, Home Depot, Michael's, 99cent Store, PepBoys, PetsMart, Radio Shack, **W food:** Sonic, **other:** NTB
164b	Eisenhauer Rd, **E gas:** Exxon/dsl, **lodging:** Hawthorn Suites, ValuePlace Inn, **other:** $General
164a	Rittiman Rd, **E gas:** Exxon, Shell/dsl, Valero/dsl, **food:** Burger King, Church's, Cracker Barrel, Denny's, Guadalajara Mexican, Jack-in-the-Box, McDonald's, Taco Cabana, Whataburger/24hr, **lodging:** Best Western, Comfort Suites, La Quinta, Motel 6, Rittiman Inn, **other:** HEB Foods, dsl repair, **W gas:** Chevron/dsl, Valero, **food:** Bill Miller BBQ, Popeye's, Sonic
163	I-410 S (162 from nb, exits left from sb)
161	Binz-Engleman Rd (from nb), same as 160
160	Splashtown Dr, **E gas:** Valero/Subway/dsl/24hr, **lodging:** Delux Inn, **other:** funpark, **W food:** Grady's BBQ, **lodging:** Best Value Inn, Clarion, Days Inn, Howard Johnson, Microtel, Super 8, Travelodge
159b	Walters St, **E food:** McDonald's, **W lodging:** Econolodge, **other:** to Ft Sam Houston
159a	New Braunfels Ave, **E gas:** Shell/dsl, Texaco/Burger King, **W gas:** Chevron, Valero/dsl/24hr, **food:** Bill Miller BBQ, Sonic, **lodging:** Antonian Suites, **other:** to Ft Sam Houston
158c	N Alamo St, Broadway
158b	I-37 S, US 281 S, to Corpus Christi, to Alamo
158a	US 281 N (from sb), to Johnson City
157b a	Brooklyn Ave, Lexington Ave, N Flores, downtown, **E lodging:** Super 8, **other:** [H], **W food:** Luby's
156	I-10 W, US 87, to El Paso
155b	Durango Blvd, downtown, **E lodging:** Best Western, Courtyard, Fairfield Inn, Holiday Inn, La Quinta, Residence Inn, Woodfield Suites, **other:** v[H], **W food:** McDonald's, **lodging:** Motel 6, Radisson
155a	South Alamo St, **E gas:** Exxon, Shell, **food:** Church's, Denny's, McDonald's, Piedras Negras Mexican, Pizza Hut, Wendy's, **lodging:** Best Western, Comfort Inn, Days Inn, Holiday Inn, La Quinta, Ramada Ltd, Residence Inn, **other:** USPO, **W gas:** Conoco, **lodging:** Microtel
154b	S Laredo St, Ceballos St, same as 155b
154a	Nogalitos St
153	I-10 E, US 90 W, US 87, to Kelly AFB, Lackland AFB
152b	Malone Ave, Theo Ave, **E food:** Taco Cabana/24hr, **W gas:** Shamrock, Shell
152a	Division Ave, **E gas:** Chevron, **food:** Bill Miller BBQ, Las Cazuelas Mexican, Whataburger/24hr, **lodging:** Quality Inn, **W food:** Sonic, **other:** transmissions
151	Southcross Blvd, **E gas:** Exxon, Shell, **W gas:** Shell/dsl, **food:** Mazatlan Mexican
150b	Lp 13, Military Dr, **E gas:** Valero, **food:** Applebee's, Arby's, Denny's, Don Pedro Mexican, KFC, Pizza Hut, Sonic, Starbucks, Subway, Taco Cabana, **lodging:** La Quinta, **other:** AutoZone, Discount Tire, U-Haul, **W gas:** Exxon, **food:** Chili's, Coyote Canyon, Freddy's Custard, Hungry Farmer Rest, Jack-in-the-Box, KFC, LJ Silver, Luby's, Moma Margie's Mexican, McDonald's, Mr Gatti, Olive Garden, Panda Express,
150b	Continued Pizza Hut, Sea Island Shrimp House, Wendy's, Whataburger, **lodging:** La Quinta, **other:** Best Buy, $Tree, Firestone/auto, HEB Foods, Home Depot, JC Penney, Lowe's Whse, Macy's, Office Depot, Old Navy, Sears/auto, Walgreens, mall,
150a	Zarzamora St (149 fom sb), same as 150b
149	Hutchins Blvd (from sb), **E gas:** Valero/dsl, **lodging:** Motel 6, ValuePlace, **other:** [H], **W other:** Chevrolet, Ford, Honda, Hyundai, Kia
148b	Palo Alto Rd, **W gas:** Valero
148a	TX 16 S, spur 422 (from nb), Poteet, **E gas:** Chevron, **lodging:** Days Inn, **W gas:** Phillips 66, **other:** $General
147	Somerset Rd, **E gas:** Shell/dsl, **W other:** Dodge
146	Cassin Rd (from nb)
145b	Lp 353 N
145a	I-410, TX 16
144	Fischer Rd, **E gas:** Valero/Subway/dsl/scales/24hr, **lodging:** D&D Motel, **other:** lube, RV camping, **W gas:** Love's/Carl's Jr/dsl/scales/24hr, **other:** Scion/Toyota
142	Medina River Turnaround (from nb)
141	Benton City Rd, Von Ormy, **W gas:** Shell/dsl/Parador Café
140	Anderson Lp, 1604, **E gas:** Exxon/dsl/24hr, **food:** Burger King, **W gas:** Valero/Church's/dsl/scales/24hr, **other:** Alamo River RV Resort, to Sea World
139	Kinney Rd
137	Shepherd Rd, **E** truck repair, **W** gas/dsl, dsl repair
135	Luckey Rd
133	TX 132 S (from sb), Lytle, same as 131
131	FM 3175, FM 2790, Benton City Rd, **E other:** NAPA, **W gas:** Conoco/dsl/24hr, **food:** Bill Miller BBQ, DQ, McDonald's, Eatza Pizza, Sonic, Topis Mexican, **lodging:** Days Inn, **other:** AutoZone, Crawford Drug, $General, HEB Food/dsl
129mm	**rest area both lanes, full [♿] facilities, [phone], [picnic], litter barrels, vending, petwalk**
127	FM 471, Natalia
124	FM 463, Bigfoot Rd, **E** Ford
122	TX 173, Devine, **E gas:** Exxon/dsl, **other:** Chevrolet, Chrysler/Dodge/Jeep, **W gas:** Chevron/McDonald's/Subway/dsl, Exxon, Shamrock, Shell, **food:** CCC Steaks, Church's, Pizza Inn, Sonic, Viva Zapatas Mexican, **lodging:** Country Corner Inn/rest
121	TX 132 N, Devine
118.5mm	**weigh sta both lanes**
114	FM 462, Yancey, Bigfoot, **E gas:** Lucky/dsl
111	US 57, to Eagle Pass, **W gas:** Valero/dsl
104	Lp 35, **3 mi E gas:** Valero, **food:** McDonald's, **lodging:** Executive Inn, **other:** [H]
101	FM 140, Pearsall, **E gas:** Chevron/dsl, **food:** Cowpokes BBQ, **lodging:** Best Western, Rio Frio Motel, Royal Inn, **other:** [H], GMC, **W gas:** Exxon/Subway/dsl/24hr, Valero/Porter House Rest/dsl/scales/24hr
99	FM 1581, to Divot, Pearsall
93mm	**parking [picnic] both lanes, litter barrels, [♿] accessible**
91	FM 1583, Derby
90mm	Frio River
86	Lp 35, Dilley
85	FM 117, **E food:** Garcia Café, **lodging:** Relax Inn, **W gas:** Exxon, **food:** DQ, **lodging:** Budget Inn, Sona Inn, **other:** RV park

PEARSALL

INTERSTATE 35 CONT'D

N ↕ S

Exit #	Services
84	TX 85, Dilley, **E** **gas:** Conoco/Burger King/dsl, **food:** Millie's Mexican, **other:** H, Chevrolet/Pontiac, Super S Foods/dsl, **W** **gas:** Shell/Pollo Grande/dsl/24hr, Valero/Subway/dsl/24hr, **lodging:** Executive Inn
82	County Line Rd, to Dilley
77	FM 469, Millett
74	Gardendale
69	Lp 35, Cotulla, **E** Super S Food/gas
67	FM 468, to Big Wells, **E** **gas:** Exxon/Wendy's/dsl/24hr, JJ's/dsl, Valero/deli/dsl/24hr, **food:** DQ, **lodging:** Executive Inn, Village Inn, **other:** tire repair, **W** **gas:** Chevron/McDonald's/dsl/scales/24hr, **lodging:** Best Western, **other:** RV park
65	Lp 35, Cotulla
63	Elm Creek Interchange
59mm	**area both lanes, litter barrels**
56	FM 133, Artesia Wells
48	Caiman Creek Interchange
39	TX 44, Encinal, **E** **gas:** Love's/Chester Fried/Subway/dsl/scales/24hr, **W** **gas:** Exxon/dsl
38	TX 44 (from nb), Encinal
32	San Roman Interchange
29mm	**inspection sta nb**
27	Callaghan Interchange
24	255 toll, Camino Colombia toll rd, to Monterrey
22	Webb Interchange
18	US 83 N, to Carrizo Springs, **E** **TX Travel Info Ctr (8am-5pm) rest area, full facilities, , litter barrels, petwalk, wireless internet,** **W** RV Camping
14mm	**parking area, sb**
12b	(13 from sb)Uniroyal Interchange, **E** **gas:** Pilot/McDonald's/Subway/dsl/scales/24hr, **other:** Blue Beacon, **W** **gas:** *FLYING J*/CountryMkt/dsl/scales/24hr, TA/Burger King/Subway/Taco Bell/dsl/scales/24hr/@
12a	Port Loredo
10	Port Laredo Carriers Dr (from nb)
9	Industrial Blvd, to Bob Bullock Lp (from sb only)
9	Industrial Blvd, to Bob Bullock Lp (from sb only)
8b	Lp 20 W, to Solidarity Bridge
8a	Lp 20 W, to to World Trade Bridge, Milo
5	San Isidro Pkwy
7	Shilo Dr, Las Cruces Dr, **E** **gas:** Valero/dsl, **food:** El Pescador Mexican
4	FM 1472, Del Mar Blvd, **E** **gas:** Exxon/Burger King/dsl, Valero, **food:** Applebee's, Carino's Italian, CiCi's, IHOP, Jack-in-the-Box, McDonald's, Quizno's, Whataburger, **lodging:** Extended Stay America, Hampton Inn, Residence Inn, **other:** Best Buy, HEB Foods/gas, Honda, Lowe's Whse, Marshall's, Old Navy, Radio Shack, Target, **W** **gas:** Shell/dsl, **lodging:** Days Inn, **other:** Harley-Davidson
3b	Mann Rd, **E** **food:** Buffalo Wild Wings, Krispy Kreme, Lin's Chinese, **other:** URGENT CARE, Buick/GMC/Pontiac, Dillard's, Ford/Lincoln/Mercury, Honda, Lowe's Whse, Mazda, Toyota, mall, **W** **food:** Chili's, Danny's Rest, Golden Corral, Hayashi Japanese, Outback Steaks, Kettle Pancake House, Subway, Taco Palenque, Whataburger, **lodging:** Family Garden Inn, Gateway Inn, La Hacienda Motel, Monterey Inn, Motel 6, Red Roof Inn, SpringHill Suites, **other:** $Tree,

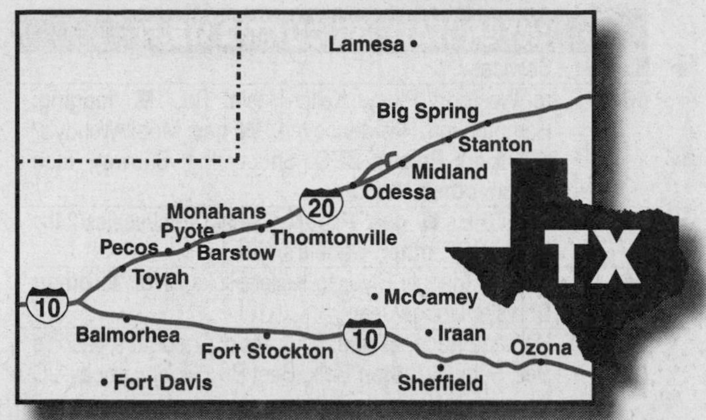

LAREDO

Exit #	Services
3b	Continued Home Depot, Kohl's, Michael's, Office Depot, PetCo, Ross, Verizon, Walmart/auto/24hr
3a	San Bernardo Ave, **E** **gas:** Shell/dsl, **food:** Chick-fil-A, El Taco Tote, Emperor Chinese, Fuddrucker's, LJ Silver, Logan's Roadhouse, Luby's, Olive Garden, Peter Piper Pizza, Red Lobster, Sirloin Stockade, Tony Roma's, **lodging:** Fairfield Inn, **other:** Advance Parts, HEB Foods/gas, K-Mart, Macy's, NAPA, PepBoys, Sears/auto, SteinMart, mall, **W** **gas:** Valero, **food:** Arby's, Burger King, Chick-fil-A, Logan's Roadhouse, McDonald's, Pizza Hut, Popeye's, Taco Bell, Taco Palenque, Tori Cafe, Wendy's, **other:** O'Reilly Parts, Radio Shack, Sam's Club
2	US 59, Saunders Rd, **E** **gas:** Conoco, Shell, **food:** Jack-in-the-Box, **other:** H, **W** **gas:** Exxon/Burger King/dsl, Shell, **food:** Church's, Denny's, **lodging:** Courtyard, Holiday Inn, La Quinta, Relax Inn, Super8, **other:** Advance Parts, AutoZone, Mexico Insurance
1b	Park St, to Sanchez St, **W** **gas:** Conoco/dsl, **food:** La Mexicana Rest., Popeye's
1a	Victoria St, Scott St, Washington St (from sb), **E** **gas:** Exxon, Shell, Valero, **W** **gas:** Chevron, Exxon/dsl, Shell, Valero, **food:** KFC, Mariachi Express, McDonald's, Wendy's, **other:** Firestone/auto, tires/auto repair, transmissions

I-35 begins/ends in Laredo at Victoria ST .access to multiple facilities

INTERSTATE 35 WEST

N ↕ S

Exit #	Services
I-35	W begins/ends on I-35, exit 467.
85b	W Oak St, **E** H
85a	I-35E S
84	FM 1515, Bonnie Brae St, **E** H
82	FM 2449, to Ponder
79	Crawford Rd
76	FM 407, to Justin, Argyle, **W** **gas:** Phillips 66/dsl/24hr, **other:** Corral City RV Park, Paradise Foods
76mm	**area both lanes, litter barrels**
74	FM 1171, to Lewisville
72	Dale Earnhardt Way, **E** same as 70, **W** TX Motor Speedway
70	TX 114, to Dallas, Bridgeport, **E** **gas:** 7-11, Shell/Subway/dsl, **food:** Waffle House/24hr, **lodging:** Motel 6, Sleep Inn, **other:** North Lake RV Park, to DFW Airport, **W** **other:** TX Motor Speedway
68	Eagle Pkwy, **W**
67	Alliance Blvd, **W** **other:** to Alliance , FedEx

TX

INTERSTATE 35 CONT'D WEST

N ↕ S

Exit #	Services
66	to Westport Pkwy, Keller-Haslet Rd, **E** **lodging:** Hampton Inn, Residence Inn, **W** **gas:** Mobil/Wendy's/dsl, **food:** Bryan's BBQ, Snooty Pig, Subway, Taco Bueno, **other:** USPO
65	TX 170 E, **E** **gas:** Pilot/McDonald's/dsl/scales/24hr, **food:** IHOP, **other:** Cabela's/cafe
64	Golden Triangle Blvd, to Keller-Hicks Blvd, **E** **other:** Chrysler/Dodge/Jeep
63	Heritage Trace, **E** **gas:** 7-11, **food:** Cheddar's, Jason's Deli, Subway, **other:** Belk, Best Buy, Hobby Lobby, JC Penney, PetsMart
62	North Tarrant Pkwy, **E** **food:** Pizza Inn
60	US 287 N, US 81 N, to Decatur
59	Basswood (sb only), **E** **gas:** Chevron/Jack-in-the-Box/dsl, **food:** Sonic, **other:** Home Depot
58	Western Ctr Blvd, **E** **gas:** 7-11, Shell/Church's, **food:** Braum's, Casa Rita, Chili's, Denny's, Dublin Square Rest., Flips Grill, Genghis Grill, Macaroni Grill, On-the-Border, Posados Cafe, Quizno's, SaltGrass Steaks, Shady Oak Grill, Wendy's, Wing Stop, Zio's Italian, **lodging:** Best Western, Residence Inn, **other:** AT&T, Kauffman Tire, **W** **food:** Bardo's Pizza, Boston's, Firehouse subs, Joe's Crabshack, Popeye's, Rosa's Cafe, Starbucks, Subway, Waffle House, Whataburger, **lodging:** Holiday Inn Express, **other:** URGENT CARE, repair
57b a	I-820 E&W
56b	Melody Hills
56a	Meacham Blvd, **E** **gas:** Shell, **lodging:** Hilton Garden, Howard Johnson, La Quinta, **W** **gas:** Texaco/dsl, **food:** Cracker Barrel, McDonald's, Subway, **lodging:** Baymont Inn, Holiday Inn, Radisson, Super 8, **other:** USPO
55	Pleasantdale Ave (from nb)
54c	33rd St, Long Ave (from nb), **W** **gas:** Conoco/dsl, Valero/dsl, **lodging:** Motel 6
54b a	TX 183 W, Papurt St, **W** **gas:** QuikStop/dsl, **food:** Chester's Chicken, **lodging:** Classic Inn
53	North Side Dr, Yucca Dr, **E** **gas:** Shell/dsl, **W** **food:** Mercado Juarez Café, **lodging:** Country Inn&Suites
53mm	Trinity River
52e	Carver St (from nb)
52d	Pharr St
52b	US 377N, Belknap
52a	US 377 N, TX 121, to DFW
51a	I-31 E, to Avalene (from nb), downtown Ft Worth
50c a	I-30 W, E to Dallas
50b	TX 180 E (from nb)
49b	Rosedale St, **W** [H]
49a	Allen Ave, **E** **gas:** Valero, **W** [H]
48b	Morningside Ave (from sb), same as 48a
48a	Berry St, **E** **gas:** Chevron/McDonald's, **food:** Texas Style Rest., **other:** Autozone, Sack'n Save Foods, **W** **gas:** RaceTrac, **other:** U-Haul, zoo
47	Ripy St, **E** **other:** transmissions, **W** **lodging:** Astro Inn
46b	Seminary Dr, **E** **gas:** RaceWay, **food:** Grandy's, Jack-in-the-Box, Rice Bowl, Subway, Taco Cabana, Whataburger, **lodging:** Days Inn, Delux Inn, Regency Inn, Super 7 Inn, **other:** NAPA, **W** **gas:** Shamrock, Shell, **food:** Denny's, Sonic, Wendy's, **other:** Fiesta Foods, Firestone/auto, Pepboys
46a	Felix St, **E** **gas:** Valero, **lodging:** Dalworth Inn, **W** **food:** McDonald's, **other:** Family$, Super Plaza Foods
45b a	I-20, E to Dallas, W to Abilene
44	Altamesa, **E** **lodging:** Radisson, **W** **gas:** Prism, **food:** Rig Steaks, Waffle House, **lodging:** Baymont Inn, Best Western, Comfort Suites, Motel 6, South Lp Inn
43	Sycamore School Rd, **W** gas Exxon, **food:** Chicken Express, Jack-in-the-Box, Sonic, Subway, Whataburger, **other:** $General, Home Depot, Radio Shack, repair
42	Everman Pkwy, **W** gas QT/dsl/scales, Shell
41	Risinger Rd, **W** **other:** Camping World RV Service/Supplies, McClain's RV Ctr
40	Garden Acres Dr, **E** **gas:** Love's/Subway/dsl/scales/24hr, **lodging:** Microtel, **other:** [H], **W** **food:** Taco Bell
39	FM 1187, McAlister Rd, **E** [H], **W** **gas:** Shamrock/dsl/24hr, Shell, **food:** Buffalo Wild Wings, Firehouse Subs, Logan's Roadhouse, Olive Garden, Panda Express, Red Lobster, TGIFriday's, Waffle House, **lodging:** Howard Johnson, **other:** Best Buy, Kohl's, Staples, Verizon
38	Alsbury Blvd, **E** **gas:** Chevron/24hr, Mobil/dsl, **food:** Chili's, Cracker Barrel, Hibachi Japanese, IHOP, McDonald's, Mexican Inn Cafe, On-the-Border, Outback Steaks, Over Time Grill, Spring Creek BBQ, **lodging:** Hampton Inn, Holiday Inn Express, La Quinta, Super 8, **other:** Discount Tire, Ford, Lowe's Whse, **W** **gas:** RaceTrac, Shamrock, Shell/24hr, **food:** Applebees, Arby's, Burger King, Chick-fil-A, Coldstone Creamery, Cotton Patch Cafe, Denny's, Pancho's Mexican, Sonic, Taco Cabana, Wendy's, **other:** Albertson's, Borders Books, Chevrolet, JC Penney, Kwik Kar, Michael's, PetsMart, Radio Shack, Ross, Vet
37	TX 174, Wilshire Blvd, to Cleburne, **W** Walmart Super Ctr/24hr (2mi), from sb, same as 36
36	FM 3391, TX 174S, Burleson, **E** **gas:** Chevron, Mobil, **food:** Miranda's Cantina, Sonic, Waffle House, **lodging:** Best Western, Comfort Suites, Days Inn, **W** **other:** Curves, $General, transmissions
35	Briaroaks Rd (from sb), **W** RV camping
33mm	**rest area sb, full ♿ facilities, ☎, picnic, litter barrels**
32	Bethesda Rd, **E** **gas:** Valero, **lodging:** Best Value Inn, **other:** RV Ranch Park, **W** **other:** Mockingbird Hill RV Park
31mm	**rest area nb, full ♿ facilities, ☎, picnic, litter barrels**
30	FM 917, Mansfield, **E** **gas:** Shell/Sonic/dsl, **W** **gas:** Shell/dsl, **food:** RanchHouse Rest.
27	rd 604, rd 707
26b a	US 67, Cleburne, **E** **gas:** Chevron/KFC/dsl, **food:** Chicken Express, DQ, McDonald's, Pizza Hut, Sonic, Waffle House, Whataburger, **lodging:** Best Western, Days Inn, La Quinta, Super 8, **other:** Ancira RV Ctr, AutoZone, Brookshire Foods, $General, Family$, Motor Home Specialist, Parts+, Walmart SuperCtr
24	FM 3136, FM 1706, Alvarado, **E** **gas:** Shell/Grandy's/dsl/scales/24hr, **food:** Longhorn Grill
21	rd 107, to Greenfield
17	FM 2258
16	TX 81 S, rd 201, Grandview
15	FM 916, Maypearl, **W** **gas:** Chevron/dsl, Mobil/dsl, **food:** Subway

INTERSTATE 35 CONT'D WEST

Exit #	Services
12	FM 67
8	FM 66, Itasca, **E gas:** Valero/dsl/café/24hr, **W food:** DQ, **other:** Ford, **picnic tables, litter barrels**
7	FM 934, **E** , **litter barrels, W gas:** Exxon/dsl, **food:** Golden Chick Cafe
3	FM 2959, **E** to Hillsboro
I-35	W begins/ends on I-35, 371mm .

INTERSTATE 37

Exit #	Services
142b a	I-35 S to Laredo, N to Austin. I-37 begins/ends on I-35 in San Antonio.
141c	Brooklyn Ave, Nolan St (from sb), downtown
141b	Houston St, **E lodging:** Red Roof Inn, **other:** tires, **W gas:** Citgo, **food:** Denny's, **lodging:** Crockett Hotel, Crowne Plaza, Days Inn, Drury Inn, Hampton Inn, Hyatt Hotel, Marriott, La Quinta, Residence Inn, **other:** Macy's, to The Alamo
141a	Commerce St, **E lodging:** Staybridge Suites, **W food:** Denny's, **lodging:** La Quinta, Marriott, **other:** Macy's
140b	Durango Blvd, downtown, **E food:** Bill Miller BBQ, **other:** to Alamo Dome
140a	Carolina St, Florida St, **E gas:** Citgo/dsl
139	I-10 W, US 87, US 90, to Houston, **W other:** to Sea World
138c	Fair Ave, Hackberry St, **E food:** DQ, Jack-in-the-Box, La Tapatia Mexian, Pimpilo Chicken, Popeye's, **other:** Brake Check, Family$, Home Depot, **W gas:** Exxon, Shell
138b	E New Braunfels Ave (from sb), **E food:** IHOP, Little Caesar's, McDonald's, Taco Cabana, Whataburger, Wendy's, **other:** HEB/dsl, Marshall's, **W gas:** Exxon, **food:** Sonic
138a	Southcross Blvd, W New Braunfels Ave, **E gas:** McDonald's, Taco Cabana, Wendy's, **W gas:** Exxon, **food:** Sonic
137	Hot Wells Blvd, **W food:** IHOP, **lodging:** Motel 6, Super 8
136	Pecan Valley Dr, **E gas:** Citgo/dsl, **food:** KFC/Taco Bell, Pizza Hut, **lodging:** Pecan Valley Inn, **other:** AutoZone, O'Reilly Parts, **W** H
135	Military Dr, Lp 13, **E gas:** Shell, Valero, **food:** Jack-in-the-Box, **lodging:** Best Western, **other:** Mission Trail RV park, **W gas:** Valero/Subway/dsl, **food:** A&W/LJ Silver, Buffalo Wild Wings, Burger King, Carino's Italian, Cherry's Buffet, Chick-fil-A, Chili's, IHOP, Little Caesar's, Longhorn Cafe, Panda Express, Panda Express, Peter Piper Pizza, Quizno's, Sonic, Starbucks, Subway, Whataburger/24hr, **lodging:** La Quinta, **other:** Advance Parts, AT&T, Best Buy, BigLots, Discount Tire, $Tree, Hancock Fabrics, HEB Food/gas, Home Depot, Lowe's Whse, Office Depot, PetCo, Radio Shack, Ross, Target, Walgreens, Walmart SuperCtr, to Brooks AFB
133	I-410, US 281 S
132	US 181 S, to Floresville (no SB return), **E gas:** Shell, **other:** $General
130	Donop Rd, Southton Rd, **E gas:** Valero/dsl, **food:** Tom's Burgers, **lodging:** Guest House Inn, **other:** Braunig Lake RV Resort, **W gas:** Shell/dsl, **other:** car/truckwash

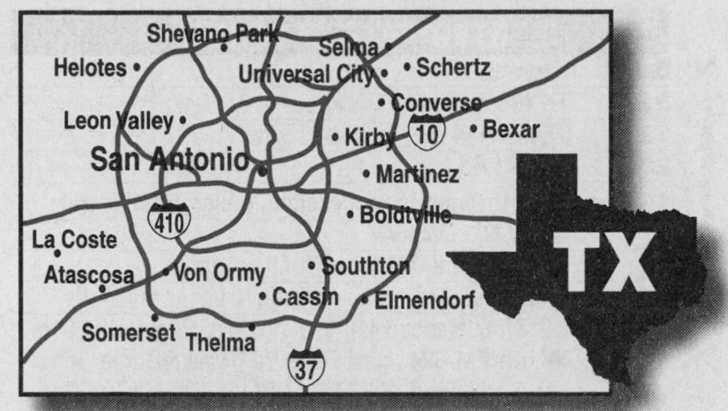

Exit #	Services
127	San Antonio River Turnaround (from nb), Braunig Lake
127mm	San Antonio River
125	FM 1604, Anderson Lp, **E gas:** Conoco/dsl/24hr, **food:** Burger King, **W gas:** Citgo/dsl, Exxon/dsl, **food:** Bill Miller BBQ, Whataburger, **other:** tires
122	Priest Rd, Mathis Rd
120	Hardy Rd
117	FM 536
113	FM 3006
112mm	**area both lanes, accessible, litter barrels**
109	TX 97, to Floresville, **E gas:** Chevron/dsl/rest., **food:** Selly's Mexican, **other:** Chrysler/Dodge/Jeep
106	Coughran Rd
104	spur 199, Leal Rd, to Pleasanton (no immediate sb return), same as 103
103	US 281 N, Leal Rd, to Pleasanton, **E gas:** Valero/dsl, **food:** DQ, K&K Cafe, **lodging:** Kuntry Inn
98	TX 541, McCoy
92	US 281A, Campbellton, **2 mi W gas:** Kuntry Korner gas, **food:** Stetson's Cafe
88	FM 1099, to FM 791, Campbellton
83	FM 99, Whitsett, Peggy, **E gas:** Shell/dsl/cafe, **W gas:** Chevron/dsl, Exxon/dsl
82mm	**rest area sb, full facilities, , , litter barrels**
78mm	**rest area nb, full facilities, , , litter barrels**
76	US 281A, FM 2049, Whitsett
75mm	**truck weigh sta sb**
74mm	**truck weigh sta nb**
72	US 281 S, Three Rivers, **4 mi W gas:** Valero, **food:** DQ, Staghorn Rest, Subway, **lodging:** Best Western, Econolodge, **other:** to Rio Grande Valley
69	TX 72, Three Rivers, **W gas:** Valero/dsl/café/24hr, **other:** tires, to Choke Canyon SP
65	FM 1358, Oakville, **E food:** Van's BBQ
59	FM 799
56	US 59, George West, **E gas:** Valero/dsl/24hr, **W gas:** Shell/Subway/24hr, Valero/Burger King/dsl/24hr
51	Hailey Ranch Rd
47	FM 3024, FM 534, Swinney Switch Rd, **W other:** Mike's Mkt/gas (1mi), to KOA (4mi)
44mm	**parking area sb**
42mm	**parking area nb**
40	FM 888
36	TX 359, to Skidmore, Mathis, **W gas:** Valero/dsl (1mi), Shell/McDonald's/dsl, Texaco/Subway/dsl, **food:** Pizza Hut, **lodging:** Best Western, **other:** Lake Corpus Christi SRA
34	TX 359 W, **E other:** Adventure TX RV Ctr/LP, **W gas:** Citgo, Shell, Valero/dsl, **lodging:** Church's, DQ, Pizza Hut, **other:** $General, O'Reilly Parts, to Lake Corpus Christi SP

INTERSTATE 37 CONT'D

N ↕ S — CORPUS CHRISTI

Exit #	Services
31	TX 188, to Sinton, Rockport
22	TX 234, FM 796, to Odem, Edroy
20b	Cooper Rd
19.5mm	**[picnic] both lanes, [handicap] accessible, tables, litter barrels**
17	US 77 N, to Victoria
16	LaBonte Park, **W info**, [picnic], **litter barrels**
15	Sharpsburg Rd (from sb), Redbird Ln
14	US 77 S, Redbird Ln, to Kingsville, Robstown, **1 mi W on FM 624...gas:** RaceWay, Valero/Burger King/dsl, Shell, **food:** Bill Miller BBQ, Chili's, CiCi's, Denny's, Good'n Crisp Chicken, Papa John's, Pizza Hut, Popeye's, Sonic, Subway, Whataburger/24hr, Wienerschnitzel, **lodging:** Comfort Inn, Holiday Inn Express, **other:** [H], Beall's, CVS Drug, Firestone/auto, GNC, Hobby Lobby, Home Depot, O'Reilly Parts, Radio Shack, Walmart SuperCtr/24hr
13b	Sharpsburg Rd (from nb)
13a	FM 1694, Callicoatte Rd, Leopard St
11b	FM 24, Violet Rd, Hart Rd, **E food:** Chicken Shack, **lodging:** La Quinta, **W gas:** Exxon/dsl, Valero/dsl, **food:** DQ, Domino's, Fliz Amancer Mexican, KFC/LJ Silver, Little Caesar's, McDonald's, Schlotzsky's, Sonic, Subway, Taco Bell, Whataburger/24hr, **lodging:** Best Western, Hampton Inn, **other:** AutoZone, Family$, HEB Food/gas, O'Reilly Parts, Walgreens, Vet
11a	McKinzie Rd, **E gas:** Shell, **food:** Jack-in-the-Box, **lodging:** La Quinta, **W gas:** Valero/dsl
10	Carbon Plant Rd
9	FM 2292, Up River Rd, Rand Morgan Rd, **W gas:** Valero/dsl, **food:** Whataburger/24hr
7	Suntide Rd, Tuloso Rd, Clarkwood Rd, **W other:** Freightliner
6	Southern Minerals Rd, **E gas:** refinery
5	Corn Products Rd, Valero Way, **E other:** Kenworth, **W gas:** PetroFleet, **food:** Jalisco Rest., **lodging:** Super 8, Travelodge, Val-u-Stay
4b	Lantana St, McBride Lane (from sb), **W lodging:** Airport Inn, Motel 6
4a	TX 358, to Padre Island, **W gas:** Shell/dsl, **lodging:** Holiday Inn, Plaza Inn, Quality Inn, **other:** Walmart SuperCtr/24hr (4mi)
3b	McBride Lane (from nb), **W other:** Gulf Coast Racing
3a	Navigation Blvd, **E gas:** Valero/dsl, **lodging:** Rodeway Inn, **W gas:** Exxon/dsl, **food:** BBQ Man, Denny's, **lodging:** Best Western, Days Inn, Hampton Inn, La Quinta, **other:** CarQuest
2	Up River Rd, **E** refinery
1e	Lawrence Dr, Nueces Bay Blvd, **E** refinery, **W gas:** Valero, **food:** Church's, **lodging:** Red Roof Inn, **other:** Aamco, AutoZone, HEB Foods, Firestone, USPO
1d	Port Ave (from sb), **W gas:** Coastal, Shell, **food:** Vick's Burgers, **lodging:** EconoLodge, **other:** Radio Shack, Port of Corp US Christi
1c	US 181, TX 286, Shoreline Blvd, Corpus Christi, **W** [H]
1b	Brownlee St (from nb), **W** Shell
1a	Buffalo St (from sb), **0-1mi W on Shoreline gas:** Valero/dsl, **food:** Burger King, Joe's Crabshack, Landry's Seafood, Subway, Whataburger, **lodging:** Bayfront Inn, Best Western, Omni Hotel, Super 8, **other:** Curves, U-Haul, USPO, I-37 begins/ends on US 181 in Corpus Christi.

INTERSTATE 40

E ↕ W — SHAMROCK

Exit #	Services
177mm	Texas/Oklahoma state line
176	spur 30 (from eb), to Texola
175mm	**[picnic] area wb, litter barrels**
169	FM 1802, Carbon Black Rd
167	FM 2168, Daberry Rd
165mm	**check sta wb**
164	Lp 40 (from wb), to Shamrock, **1 mi S lodging:** Econolodge, **other:** [H], museum, **weigh sta eb**
163	US 83, to Wheeler, Shamrock, **N gas:** Chevron/dsl, **food:** Mitchell's Rest., **lodging:** Best Western, Irish Inn, **other:** Ace Hardware, **S gas:** Phillips 66/Subway/24hr, Valero/dsl, **food:** DQ, McDonald's, **lodging:** Budget Host, Econolodge, Holiday Inn Express, Sleep Inn, Western Motel
161	Lp 40, Rte 66 (from eb), to Shamrock, **S gas:** Chevron
157	FM 1547, Lela, **1 mi S other:** West 40 RV Camping
152	FM 453, Pakan Rd, **S** gas, food
150mm	**[picnic] area wb, litter barrels**
149mm	**[picnic] area eb, litter barrels**
148	FM 1443, Kellerville Rd
146	County Line Rd
143	Lp 40 (from wb), to McLean, to gas
142	TX 273, FM 3143, to McLean, **N gas:** Shell, **lodging:** Cactus Inn, **other:** RV Camping/dump, USPO
141	Rte 66 (from eb), McLean, same as 142
135	FM 291, Rte 66, Alanreed, **S gas:** Conoco/motel/café/RV park/dump, **other:** USPO
132	Johnson Ranch Rd, ranch access
131mm	**rest area wb, full [handicap] facilities, [phone], [picnic], litter barrels, petwalk**
129mm	**rest area eb, [picnic] area wb, litter barrels, playground**
128	FM 2477, to Lake McClellan, **N other:** Lake McClellan RA/RV Dump
124	TX 70 S, to Clarendon, **S** RV camping/dump
121	TX 70 N, to Pampa
114	Lp 40, Groom
113	FM 2300, Groom, **S gas:** Texaco/dsl, **food:** DQ, **lodging:** Chalet Inn
112	FM 295, Groom, **S other:** Biggest Cross, **1 mi S** gas
110	Lp 40, Rte 66
109	FM 294
108mm	**parking area wb, litter barrels**
106mm	**parking area eb, [picnic], litter barrels**
105	FM 2880, grain silo
98	TX 207 S (from wb), to Claude
96	TX 207 N, to Panhandle, **N gas:** Love's/Subway/dsl/24hr, **S lodging:** Budget Host, Conway Inn/cafe
89	FM 2161, to Rte 66
87	FM 2373
87mm	**[picnic] areas both lanes, litter barrels**
85	Amarillo Blvd, Durrett Rd, access to camping
81	FM 1912, **N gas:** Phillips 66/dsl
80	FM 228, **N other:** AOK RV Park
78	US 287 S (from eb), FM 1258, Pullman Rd, same as 77
77	FM 1258, Pullman Rd, **N gas:** Travel Plaza/dsl/scales/24hr, **S other:** Custom RV Ctr
76	spur 468, **N gas:** ***FLYING J***/Conoco/dsl/LP/rest./LP/RV dump/scales/24hr, Shell/dsl, **lodging:** Holiday Inn Express, **other:** GMC/Volvo/Mac Trucks, tourist info, **S gas:** Speedco, **other:** Custom RV Ctr, TX info

INTERSTATE 40 CONT'D

E ↕ W

AMARILLO

Exit #	Services
75	Lp 335, Lakeside Rd, **N gas:** Pilot/McDonald's/dsl/rest./24hr/@, **food:** Waffle House, **lodging:** Best Value Inn, Quality Inn, Super 8, **other:** UPS, Peterbilt Trucks, KOA (2mi), **S gas:** Petro/dsl/rest./scales/@, **other:** Blue Beacon
74	Whitaker Rd, **N lodging:** Big Texan Inn/café, **other:** RV camping, **S gas:** Love's/Subway/dsl/scales/@, TA/Exxon/FoodCourt/dsl/24hr/@, **lodging:** Budget Inn, **other:** Blue Beacon
73	Eastern St, Bolton Ave, Amarillo, **N gas:** Shell/dsl, **food:** Stockman's Rest., **lodging:** Motel 6, Value Place, **S gas:** Chevron/dsl, **lodging:** Best Western, Motel 6, **other:** Ford Trucks
72b	Grand St, Amarillo, **N gas:** Shell, **food:** Henk's BBQ, **lodging:** Value Inn, **other:** Family$, O'Reilly Parts, **S gas:** Murphy USA, Phillips 66, Valero, **food:** Braum's, Chicken Express, McDonald's, Pizza Hut, Pizza Palm, Sonic, Starbucks, Subway, Taco Cabana, Taco Villa, Whataburger, **lodging:** Motel 6, **other:** Advance Parts, AutoZone, Big Lots, $General, Walmart SuperCtr, same as 73
72a	Nelson St, **N food:** Cracker Barrel, KFC, **lodging:** Ashmore Inn, Budget Host, Econolodge, La Kiva Hotel, Ramada Inn, Sleep Inn, Super 8, Travelodge, **other:** Qtrhorse Museum, **S gas:** Chevron, Shell/dsl, **lodging:** Camelot Inn, **other:** Chevrolet
71	Ross St, Osage St, Amarillo, **N gas:** Shell/dsl, **food:** Burger King, IHOP, LJ Silver/A&W, McDonald's, Schlotsky's, Subway, Wienerschnitzel, **lodging:** Comfort Inn, Day's Inn, Holiday Inn, Microtel, Quality Inn, Sleep Inn, **S food:** Arby's, Denny's, Fiesta Grande Mexican, Sonic, Taco Bell, Wendy's, **lodging:** Hampton Inn, Howard Johnson, La Quinta, **other:** Chevrolet, Ford Trucks, Sam's Club/gas, USPO
70	I-27 S, US 60 W, US 87, US 287, to Canyon, Lubbock, to downtown Amarillo
69b	Washington St, Amarillo, **S food:** DQ, Subway, **other:** CVS Drug
69a	Crockett St, access to same as 68b
68b	Georgia St, **N gas:** Shell/Subway, **food:** BBQ, Fast Eddy's, Schlotzky's, TGIFriday, **lodging:** Ambassador Hotel, **S gas:** Phillips 66, Valero, **food:** Baker Bro.s Deli, Bennigan's, Burger King, Church's Chicken, Coldstone Creamery, Denny's, Furr's Café, LJ Silver, Pizza Hut, Red Lobster, Roaster's, Sonic, Starbucks, Taco Bueno, Taco Villa, TX Roadhouse, Western Sizzlin, Whataburger, **lodging:** Baymont Inn, Comfort Suites, Econolodge, Holiday Inn Express, Motel 6, Quality Inn, Travelodge, **other:** H, Cadillac, Chrysler/Dodge, Discount Tire, Hastings Books, Home Depot, K-Mart, Mitsubishi, Office Depot, Radio Shack, Walgreens
68a	Julian Blvd, Paramount Blvd, **N gas:** Chevron, Shell, **food:** Arby's, Chili's, Macaroni Joe's, Nick's Rest., Pizza Hut, Schlotzsky's, Wendy's, **lodging:** Harley Hotel, same as 67, **S gas:** Valero, **food:** Caboose Diner, Cactus Grill, Cajun Magic, Calico Country Café, El Torrito, Fernando's Rest., Godfather's, New China, Orient Express, Peking Rest., Pizza Planet, Popeye's, Red Lobster, Ruby Tequila's Mexican, Steak&Ale, **lodging:** Best Value, Comfort Suites, Travelodge, **other:** Pennzoil

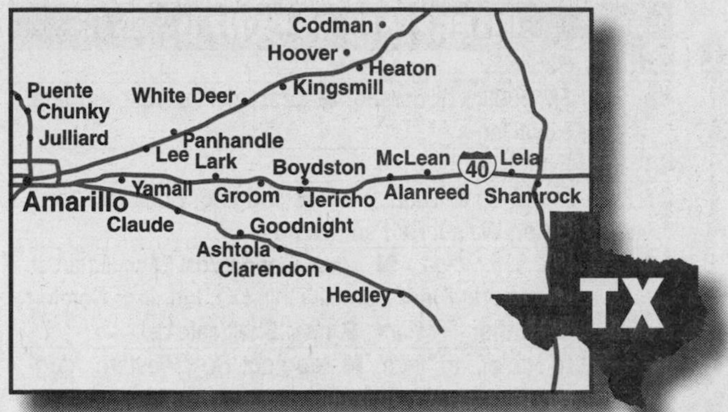

AMARILLO

Exit #	Services
67	Western St, Amarillo, **N gas:** Phillips 66, Shell, **food:** Beef Rigger Rest., Bourbon St. Cafe, Braum's, Burger King, Cadillac Joe's Grill, Chili's, Cty Line BBQ, Grill, Legends Grill, Marie Callender's, McDonald's, Pancho's Mexican, Rosa's Cafe, Sonic, Subway, Taco Bell, Wendy's, **S gas:** Rudy's/BBQ/dsl, Valero, **food:** Blue Sky Rest., Cheddar's, Olive Garden, Starbucks, Waffle House, Wienerschnitzel, **lodging:** Baymont Inn, Comfort Suites, **other:** Discount Tire, Firestone, Michael's, Petco, same 68
66	Bell St, Amarillo, **N gas:** Shell/dsl, Valero/dsl, **lodging:** Fairfield Inn, Motel 6, Quality Inn, Residence Inn, **other:** Harley-Davidson, **S food:** Doughnut Stop, King & I Chinese, Taco Bueno, **other:** Albertson's
65	Coulter Dr, Amarillo, **N gas:** Phillips 66/dsl, **food:** Arby's, Golden Corral, Luby's, My Thai Café, Subway, Taco Bell, Waffle House, **lodging:** Best Western, Comfort Inn, Courtyard, Day's Inn, Executive Inn, La Quinta, **other:** H, Chevrolet/Cadillac, Curves, Discount Tire, Dodge, Firestone/auto, Nissan, **S gas:** Chevron/Chicken Express/dsl, Shell, **food:** ChinaStar, ChuckeCheese, CiCi's, Hoffbrau Steaks, Jason's Deli, Outback Steaks, Pizza Hut, Wendy's, Whataburger, Wienerschnitzel, **lodging:** Hampton Inn, 5th Season Inn, **other:** Goodyear/auto, Sears/auto
64	Soncy Rd, to Pal Duro Cyn, **N food:** Carino's Italian, Furr's Buffet, Joe's Crabshack, Kabuki Japanese, Red Robin, Lin's Chinese, Logan's Roadhouse, **lodging:** Comfort Inn, Country Inn&Suites, Drury Inn, Extended Stay America, Hilton Garden, Homewood Suites, **other:** Cavender's Boots, Discount Tire, **S gas:** Valero/dsl/24hr, **food:** Applebee's, Baker Brothers Deli, DQ, Fazoli's, Hooters, Marble Slab Creamery, McDonald's, On-the-Border, Pei Wei, Ruby Tequila's Mexican, Starbucks, Subway, **other:** Barnes&Noble, Best Buy, Dillard's, $Tree, Ford, Home Depot, JC Penney, Jo-Ann, Kohl's, Lincoln/Mercury, Old Navy, PetsMart, Ross, Sears/auto, Target, World Mkt, mall
62b	Lp 40, Amarillo Blvd, **N** Gander Mtn.
62a	Hope Rd, Helium Rd, **S other:** RV camping, antiques
60	Arnot Rd, **S gas:** Love's/Subway/dsl, **other:** Oasis RV Resort/dump
57	RM 2381, to Bushland, **N** grain silos, **S gas:** Shell/dsl, **food:** Original Fried Pie Place, **other:** USPO, RV camping/dump (1mi)
55mm	**parking area wb, litter barrels**
54	Adkisson Rd
53.5mm	**parking area eb, litter barrels**

TX

INTERSTATE 40 CONT'D

Exit #	Services
49	FM 809, to Wildorado, **S gas:** Crist Fuel/dsl, **lodging:** Royal Inn
42	Everett Rd
37	Lp 40 W, to Vega, **1 mi N lodging:** Bonanza Motel, **other:** Walnut RV Park, same as 36
36	US 385, Vega, **N gas:** Conoco/dsl/24hr, Fina/dsl, Shamrock, **food:** Boothill Grill, DQ, **lodging:** Comfort Inn, **other:** RV Park, **S gas:** Shell/cafe/dsl
35	to Rte 66, to Vega, **N lodging:** Best Western, **lodging:** Bonanza Motel (1mi), **other:** Walnut RV Park (1mi), same as 36
32mm	**area both lanes, litter barrels**
28	to Rte 66, Landergin
23	to Adrian, Vega, same as 22
22	TX 214, to Adrian, **N food:** Midpoint Cafe, **other:** USPO, auto repair, **S gas:** Phillips 66/dsl/Tommy's Café
18	FM 2858, Gruhlkey Rd, **S gas:** Shell/Stuckey's/cafe/dsl
15	Ivy Rd
13mm	**area both lanes, litter barrels**
5.5mm	turnout
0	Lp 40, to Glenrio
0mm	Texas/New Mexico state line, Central/Mountain time zone

INTERSTATE 44

Exit #	Services
15mm	Texas/Oklahoma state line, Red River
14	Lp 267, E 3rd St, **W other:** Burk RV Park
13	Glendale St, **W food:** Subway, **other:** Beall's, Family$, Sav-A-Lot Foods, Walmart
12	Burkburnett, **E lodging:** Hampton Inn, **W gas:** Fina/7-11, **food:** Braum's, Feedlot Rest., Lite Pan Asian, Mazzio's, McDonald's, Whataburger/24hr, **other:** CarQuest, Chevrolet/Pontiac, Ford
11	FM 3429, Daniels Rd
9mm	**area both lanes, litter barrels, petwalk**
7	East Rd
6	Bacon Switch Rd
5a	FM 3492, Missile Rd, **E food:** El Mejicano Rest., Hunan Chinese, Pizza Hut, **other:** st patrol, **W gas:** Exxon/dsl
5	Access Rd
4	City Loop St
3c	FM 890, **W food:** Cracker Barrel, KFC/Taco Bell, Subway, **other:** Walmart SuperCtr/gas/24hr, Vet
3b	sp 325, Sheppard AFB
3a	US 287 N, to Amarillo, **W gas:** Shell, **food:** Carl's Jr, **lodging:** Ramada Ltd
2	Maurine St, **E gas:** Fina/7-11/dsl, Shell/dsl, **lodging:** Best Value Inn, Comfort Inn, Motel 6, Quality Inn, **other:** Chevrolet, Mazda, **W gas:** Fina/7-11, **food:** China Star, Denny's, El Chico, LJ Silver, Whataburger/24hr, **lodging:** Best Western, Candlewood Suites, La Quinta, Super 8, Travelers Inn
1d	US 287 bus, Lp 370, **W gas:** Conoco/dsl, **lodging:** Travelodge
1c	Texas Tourist Bureau, **E gas:** $Saver, **W lodging:** The Inn
1b	Scotland Park (from nb)
1a	US 277 S, to Abilene
0mm	I-44 begins/ends in Witchita Falls, **1-2 mi S in Wichita Falls S gas:** Valero, **food:** Arby's, Burger King, Carl's Jr, IHOP, McDonald's, Popeye's, Subway, **lodging:** Econolodge, Holiday Inn, Howard Johnson, Knights Inn, **other:** [H]

INTERSTATE 45

Exit #	Services
286	to I-35 E, to Denton. I-45 begins/ends in Dallas.
285	Bryan St E, US 75 N
284b a	I-30, W to Ft Worth, E to Texarkana, access to [H]
283b	Pennsylvania Ave, to MLK Blvd, **E gas:** Shamrock
283a	Lamar St
281	Overton St (from sb), **W gas:** Chevron
280	Illinois Ave, Linfield St, **E lodging:** Star Motel, **W gas:** Shell/dsl
279b a	Lp 12
277	Simpson Stuart Rd, **W other:** to Paul Quinn Coll
276b a	I-20, W to Ft Worth, E to Shreveport
275	TX 310 N (from nb, no re-entry)
274	Dowdy Ferry Rd, Hutchins, **E gas:** Exxon/Subway/dsl, Shell/McDonald's/dsl, **lodging:** Gold Inn, La Quinta, Super 8, **W food:** DQ, Jack-in-the-Box, Whataburger
273	Wintergreen Rd
272	Fulghum Rd, **E gas:** Love's/Carl's Jr/dsl/scales/24hr, **W weigh sta, both lanes**
271	Pleasant Run Rd
270	Belt Line Rd, to Wilmer, **E gas:** Texaco/Pizza Inn/dsl, **W gas:** Exxon/Sonic/dsl, Shell/Church's/Subway/dsl, **other:** $General
269	Mars Rd
268	Malloy Bridge Rd
267	Frontage Rd
266	FM 660, **E food:** Jack-in-the-Box, **W gas:** Shamrock/dsl, **food:** DQ
265	Lp 45, Ferris, nb only
263a b	Lp 561
262	frontage rd
260	Lp 45, **E food:** Trailer RV Park **W gas:** Shell/Sonic/dsl
259	FM 813, FM 878, Jefferson St, **W other:** Goodyear
258	Lp 45, Palmer, **E gas:** Exxon/Subway/dsl/scales/24hr, **other:** golf, **W lodging:** Palmer Motel
255	FM 879, Garrett, **E gas:** Exxon/dsl
253	Lp 45, **W gas:** Shell/Subway/dsl
251b	TX 34, Ennis, **E gas:** Fina/dsl, Shell/dsl, **food:** Bubba's BBQ, McDonald's, **lodging:** Baymont Inn, Comfort Suites, Days Inn, Holiday Inn Express, La Quinta, **other:** Ford, **W gas:** Chevron/dsl, Exxon/dsl/24hr, Murphy USA/dsl, **food:** Braum's, Broster Chicken, Burger King, Chili's, Denny's, DQ, Domino's, Grand Buffet, IHOP, Jack-in-the-Box, KFC, Sonic, Starbucks, Subway, Taco Cabana, Vero Pizza, Waffle House, Wall Chinese, Wendy's, Whataburger/24hr, **lodging:** Ennis Inn, Quality Inn, **other:** [H], AutoZone, Beall's, Chevrolet/Pontiac, Chrysler/Dodge/Jeep, $Tree, Ford/Mercury, Radio Shack, Walmart SuperCtr/24hr, RV camping
251a	Creechville Rd, FM 1181, **W** [H]
249	FM 85, Ennis, **E lodging:** Budget Inn, **W gas:** Exxon/Subway, **other:** Blue Beacon, **other:** repair

TX

INTERSTATE 45 CONT'D

N ↕ S

Exit #	Services
247	US 287 N, to Waxahatchie
246	FM 1183, Alma, **W gas:** Chevron
244	FM 1182
243	Frontage Rd
242	Calhoun St, Rice
239	FM 1126, **W gas:** 45 Kwik Stop
238	FM 1603, **E gas:** Exxon/dsl/rest/24hr, **other:** Casita RV Trailers
237	Frontage Rd
235b	Lp I-45 (from sb), to Corsicana
235a	Frontage Rd
232	Roane Rd, E 5th Ave
231	TX 31, Corsicana,, **E gas:** Phillips 66/dsl, **food:** Jack-in-the-Box, **lodging:** Best Western, Colonial Inn, La Quinta, **other:** Buick/Cadillac/Chevrolet/GMC/Pontiac, **W gas:** Chevron, Exxon/Subway/dsl, **food:** Bill's Fried Chicken, DQ, McDonald's, **lodging:** Comfort Inn, **other:** [H], Chrysler/Dodge/Jeep, Ford/Lincoln/Mercury, to Navarro Coll
229	US 287, Palestine, **E gas:** Exxon/Wendy's/dsl, Shell/dsl/24hr, **food:** Chili's, Collin St Bakery, Denny's, Russell Stover Candies, Sonic, Taco Bell, **lodging:** Hampton Inn, Holiday Inn Express, **other:** Gander Mtn Home Depot, Office Depot, VF Outlet/famous brands, **W food:** Waffle House, **lodging:** Corsicana Inn, Motel 6, Royal Inn
228b	Lp 45 (exits left from nb), Corsicana, **2 mi W** services in Corsicana
228a	15th St, Corsicana, **W other:** Scion/Toyota
225	FM 739, Angus, **E gas:** Conoco/dsl, **other:** to Chambers Reservoir, RV park, **W other:** Camper Depot
221	Frontage Rd
220	Frontage Rd
219b	Frontage Rd
219a	TX 14 (from sb), to Mexia, Richland, **W gas:** Shell
218	FM 1394 (from nb), Richland, **W gas:** Shell
217mm	**rest area both lanes, full [♿] facilities, [phone], [picnic], litter barrels, vending, petwalk**
213	TX 75 S, FM 246, to Wortham, **W gas:** Chevron, Exxon/dsl
211	FM 80, to Streetman, Kirvin
206	FM 833, **3 mi W on frntge rd:** I-45 RV Park
198	FM 27, to Wortham, **E gas:** Shell/Pitt BBQ, **food:** Gilberto's Mexican, **lodging:** La Quinta, **other:** [H], Cedar Grove RV Park (3mi), **W gas:** Exxon, Love's/Burger King/dsl/scales/24hr, **lodging:** Budget Inn, **other:** I-45 RV Park (4mi)
197	US 84, Fairfield, **E gas:** Chevron/dsl, Exxon/dsl, Shell/dsl, **food:** DQ, Jack-in-the-Box, McDonald's, Ponte's Diner, Sam's Rest., Sonic, Subway/Texas Burger, **lodging:** Days Inn, Holiday Inn Express, Super 8, **other:** Brookshire Foods/gas, Chevrolet, Chrysler/Dodge/Jeep, Fred's Store, Hyundai, **W gas:** Exxon/dsl, Shell/dsl, Texaco/dsl, **food:** Dalia's Mexican, I-45 Rest., KFC/Taco Bell, Pizza Hut, Sammy's Rest., **lodging:** Best Value Inn, Regency Inn, **other:** Ace Hardware, Ford
189	TX 179, to Teague, **E gas:** Exxon/Chester's/dsl/cafe, Citgo/Shirley's Cafe/dsl

FAIRFIELD

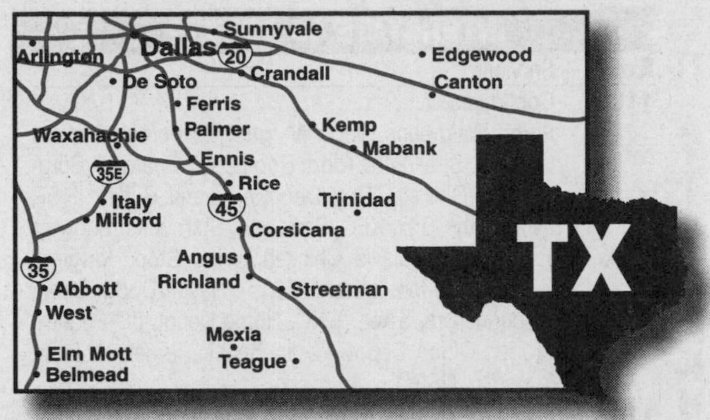

Exit #	Services
187mm	**[picnic] area both lanes, litter barrels**
180	TX 164, to Groesbeck
178	US 79, Buffalo, **E gas:** Gilliam's/dsl, Shell/dsl, **food:** Subway/Texas Burger, **other:** Brookshire Foods/gas, Family$, **W gas:** Exxon/Church's/Pizza Inn/dsl/scales, Mobil/dsl, Shamrock/dsl/24hr, **food:** Dickey's BBQ, DQ, Longhorn BBQ, Pitt Grill/24hr, Rancho Mexican, Sonic, **lodging:** Best Western, Comfort Inn, Economy Inn, Hampton Inn
175mm	Bliss Creek
166mm	**weigh sta sb**
164	TX 7, Centerville, **E gas:** Chevron, Shell/Woody's BBQ/dsl, **food:** Country Cousins BBQ, Subway/Texas Burger, **lodging:** Days Inn, **W gas:** Exxon/24hr, Shell/Woody's BBQ/dsl, **food:** DQ, Jack-in-the-Box, Roble's Mexican
160mm	**[picnic] area sb, tables, litter barrels, hist marker, [♿] accessible**
159mm	Boggy Creek
156	FM 977, to Leona, **W gas:** Exxon/dsl
155mm	**[picnic] area nb, tables, litter barrels, hist marker, [♿] accessible**
152	TX OSR, to Normangee, **W gas:** Chevron/dsl, **other:** Yellow Rose RV Park/café
146	TX 75
142	US 190, TX 21, Madisonville, **E gas:** Exxon/BBQ/dsl, Shell/Buc-ees, **lodging:** Best Western, Carefree Inn, **W gas:** Chevron/Church's, Shell/Subway/24hr, **food:** Jack-in-the-Box, McDonald's, Pizza Hut, Sonic, Taco Bell, Texas Burger, **lodging:** Budget Motel, Western Lodge, **other:** [H], Ford, Toyota
136	spur 67, **E** Home on the Range RV camping/LP (3mi)
132	FM 2989
124mm	**rest area both lanes, full [♿] facilities, [phone], [picnic], litter barrels, vending, petwalk**
123	FM 1696
118	TX 75, **E gas:** Shell/Hitchin Post/dsl/24hr/@, **other:** Texas Prison Museum, truckwash, **W gas:** Pilot/Wendy's/dsl/scales/24hr, **food:** Rodeo Mexican
116	US 190, TX 30, **E gas:** Phillips 66, Valero/dsl, **food:** Arby's, Bandera Grill, Church's, El Chico, Mr Gatti's, Golden Corral, Imperial Garden Chinese, Jct Steaks, McDonald's, Popeye's, Schlotzsky's, Sonic, Whataburger, **lodging:** Days Inn, EconoLodge, Holiday Inn Express, La Quinta, Motel 6, **other:** [H], AutoZone, Brookshire Foods/gas, Buick/Cadillac/Chevrolet/GMC/Pontiac, Cavander's Boots, CVS Drug, Family$, Firestone/auto, Hastings Books, NAPA, O'Reilly

HUNTSVILLE

N ↕ S HUNTSVILLE

INTERSTATE 45 CONT'D

Exit #	Services
116	Continued Parts, Walgreens, Vet, **W gas:** Exxon/dsl, Murphy USA/dsl, Shell/24hr, **food:** Bob Luby's Seafood, Burger King, Chili's, CiCi's, Denny's, Grand Buffet, IHOP, Jack-in-the-Box, KFC, Pizza Hut, Starbucks, Subway, Taco Bell, Tinsley's Chicken, Wing Stop, **lodging:** Guesthouse Inn, **other:** AT&T, Chrysler/Dodge/Jeep, Discount Tire, $Tree, GNC, Home Depot, JC Penney, Kroger, Office Depot, Radio Shack, Target, Walmart SuperCtr, USPO
114	FM 1374, **E gas:** Exxon/dsl, Shell, **food:** DQ, Margaritas Rest., **lodging:** Gateway Inn, Super 8, **W gas:** Citgo/dsl, Valero/dsl, **food:** Country Inn Steaks, **lodging:** Best Value Inn, Comfort Suites, **other:** H, Ford/Lincoln/Mercury, Hyundai
113	TX 19 (from nb), Huntsville
112	TX 75, **E gas:** Citgo, **lodging:** Baker Motel, **other:** Houston Statue, to Sam Houston St U, museum
109	Park 40, **W other:** to Huntsville SP
105mm	**area both lanes, litter barrels**
103	FM 1374/1375 (from sb), to New Waverly
102	FM 1374/1375, TX 150 (from nb), to New Waverly, **E gas:** Valero/dsl (1mi), **W food:** Waverly Rest.
101mm	**weigh sta nb**
98	TX 75, Danville Rd, Shepard Hill Rd, **E other:** Convenience RV Park/repair
95	(from nb, no return) Calvary, Longstreet Rd
94	FM 1097, Longstreet Rd, to Willis, **E food:** Jack-in-the-Box, Mr Gatti, Quizno's, Sonic, **other:** AutoZone, $General, Kroger/gas, **W gas:** Chevron/Popeye's, Shell/Taco Bell/dsl/24hr, **food:** McDonald's, Subway, **lodging:** Best Western
92	FM 830, Seven Coves Dr, **W other:** Omega Farms RV Park, RV Park on the Lake (3mi), Thousand Trails Resort
91	League Line Rd, **E gas:** Chevron/McDonald's, **food:** Mamma Juanita's Mexican, Subway, Waffle House, Wendy's, **lodging:** Comfort Inn, La Quinta, Supreme Inn, **other:** Conroe Outlets/famous brands, **W gas:** Citgo, Shell/Jack-in-the-Box, **food:** Cracker Barrel
90	FM 3083, Teas Nursery Rd, Montgomery Co Park, **E gas:** Exxon/dsl, **food:** Applebee's, Buck's Burgers, Buffalo Wild Wings, Popeye's, **lodging:** Fairfield Inn, **other:** AT&T, Kohl's, Old Navy, Petsmart, Ross, TJ Maxx, convention center (4mi), **W food:** Olive Garden, Subway, **lodging:** ValuePlace Inn, **other:** JC Penney
88	Lp 336, to Cleveland, Navasota, **E gas:** Mobil/Chester's/dsl, Valero/dsl, **food:** Arby's, A&W/LJ Silver, Burger King, Chili's, China Delight, Denny's, Domino's, Los Cucos Mexican, Marble Slab Creamery, Margarita's Mexican, McDonald's, Papa John's, Pizza Hut, Quizno's, Sonic, TX Roadhouse, Whataburger, Wing Stop, **lodging:** Hampton Inn, Holiday Inn Express, **other:** Advance Parts, Buick/Pontiac, CVS Drug, Discount Tire, $Tree, GNC, HEB Foods/gas, Hobby Lobby, Just Brakes, Kroger/gas, Michael's, Walgreens, Vet, **W gas:** Chevron/24hr, **food:** Blackeyed Pea, Casa Ole Mexican, El Bosque Mexican, KFC, Ryan's, Subway, **other:** Hancock Fabrics, Lowe's Whse, 99Cent Store, PetCo, Sam's Club/gas, Tuesday Morning, Walmart SuperCtr/24hr

CONROE

Exit #	Services
87	TX 105, Conroe, **E food:** Burger King, Jack-in-the-Box, Kettle, Luther's BBQ, McDonald's, Outback Steaks, Popeye's, Sonic, Saltgrass Steaks, Taco Bell, Tast of China, **lodging:** Super 8, **other:** H, CVS Drug, $General, Firestone/auto, Hyundai, Kia, NTB, **W gas:** Exxon, **food:** Bennigan's, Chick-fil-A, Coney Island, Luby's, Panda Express, Panera Bread, Quizno's, Schlotzsky's, Shogun Japanese, Smoothie King, Starbucks, Subway, Taco Bell, Taco Bueno, Whataburger, **other:** Best Buy, Buick/GMC/Pontiac, Hastings Books, Home Depot, Office Depot, Radio Shack, Target, Tiremaxx
85	FM 2854, Gladstell St, **E gas:** Citgo/dsl, **lodging:** Motel 6, **other:** H, Honda, Nissan, **W gas:** Shell/dsl, Valero, **food:** IHOP, **lodging:** Baymont Inn, Days Inn, **other:** Cadillac, Chrysler/Dodge/Jeep, Fun Country RV Ctr, Mazda, Scion/Toyota
84	TX 75 N, Frazier St, **E gas:** Chevron, **lodging:** Corporate Inn, Ramada Ltd, **other:** Ford/Mercury, U-Haul, **W gas:** Shell, **food:** China Buffet, Incredible Pizza, Subway, Taco Cabana, Waffle House, **other:** H, Albertson's, Discount Tire, K-Mart, Kroger
83	Crighton Rd, Camp Strake Rd
82	River Plantation Dr
82mm	San Jacinto River
81	FM 1488, to Hempstead, Magnolia, **E gas:** Citgo, **W gas:** Valero/Subway, **other:** CamperLand RV Ctr
80	Needham Rd (from sb)
79	TX 242, Needham, **E gas:** Shell/McDonald's, **food:** Mama Juanita's Mexican, Quizno's, **lodging:** Best Western, **other:** Batteries+, **W gas:** Chevron, Murphy USA/dsl, **food:** Adobe Cafe, Arby's, Burger King, ChuckeCheese, Domino's, Outback Steaks, Popeye's, Sonic, Subway, Taco Cabana, Wendy's, Whataburger, Willie's Grill, Wings'N More, **lodging:** Country Suites, Fairfield Inn, TownPlace Suites, **other:** H, BMW/Mini, Firestone/auto, Kohl's, Lowe's Whse, Walgreens, Walmart SuperCtr
78	Needham Rd (from sb), Tamina Rd, access to same as 77
77	Woodlands Pkwy, Robinson, Chateau Woods, **E gas:** Chevron, Conoco/dsl, **food:** Babin's Seafood, Buca Italian, Buffalo Wild Wings, Church's, Chuy's, Hooters, Lupe Tortilla, Melting Pot, Pancho's Mexican, Pappa's BBQ, Pappadeaux, PeiWei, Pizza Hut, Red Robin, Saltgrass Steaks, Subway, Tom's Steaks, **lodging:** Best Value Inn, Budget Inn, **other:** Discount Tire, Home Depot, Jo-Ann Fabrics, Michael's, NTB, Office Depot, Old Navy, Petsmart, Sam's Club/gas, SteinMart, Walgreens, funpark, Vet, **W gas:** Exxon, Shell, Texaco, Valero/dsl, **food:** A&W/KFC, Blackeyed Pea, Cane's, Chick-fil-A, Chili's, Chipotle Mexican, Culver's, Denny's, El Bosque Mexican, Guadalajara Mexican, Jack-in-the-Box, Jason's Deli, JimmyJohn's, Kabab House, Kirby's Steakhouse, La Madeliene, Landry's Seafood, Luby's, Macaroni Grill, Olive Garden, Red Lobster, Sweet Tomatos, TGIFriday's, **lodging:** Comfort Suites, Days Inn, Drury Inn, Hampton Inn, Homewood Suites, La Quinta, Marriott, Shenandoa Inn, **other:** H, Best Buy, Dillard's, HEB Foods, Macy's, Marshall's, Sears, Ross, Target, World Mkt, auto repair, mall

INTERSTATE 45 CONT'D

N ↕ S HOUSTON

Exit #	Services
76	Research Forest Dr, Tamina Rd, **E gas:** Chevron/dsl, **food:** LJ Silver, Pappa's BBQ, **other:** URGENT CARE, Firestone/auto, JustBrakes, Tiremaxx, Vet, **W gas:** Shell, **food:** Carrabba's, Denny's, El Chico, IHOP, Jack-in-the-Box, Kyoto Japanese, Macaroni Grill, Olive Garden, TGIFriday's, Tortuga Mexican, **lodging:** Crossland Suites, Courtyard, Residence Inn, **other:** Goodyear/auto, JC Penney, Sears/auto, Woodlands Mall
73	Rayford Rd, Sawdust Rd, **E gas:** Conoco, Shell, Valero, **food:** Hartz Chicken, Jack-in-the-Box, McDonald's, Popeye's, Sonic, Taqueria Arandas, Thomas BBQ, **lodging:** Holiday Inn Express, La Quinta, **other:** Aamco, AutoZone, O'Reilly Parts, U-Haul, **W gas:** Mobil/dsl, Shell, Texaco, **food:** Carrabba's, Cici's Pizza, Grand Buffet, IHOP, Subway, Taipei Chinese, Tortuga, **lodging:** Extended Stay America, Red Roof Inn, Super 8, **other:** Brake Check, Discount Tire, GNC, Goodyear/auto, Harley-Davidson, HEB Foods, Kroger, Walgreens
72a	Spring Crossing Dr, **W gas:** Texaco/dsl
72b	to Hardy Toll rd from sb
70b	Spring-Stuebner Rd, **E** Vaughn RV Ctr
70a	FM 2920, to Tomball, **E gas:** Exxon, Murphy USA/dsl, Rudy's BBQ/dsl, Shell, **food:** Arby's, Chick-fil-A, El Palenque Mexican, Godfather's Pizza, Golden Jade Chinese, Hartz Chicken, McDonald's, Pizza Hut, Subway, Quizno's, Taco Cabana, Wendy's, Whataburger, **other:** BigLots, $General, $Tree, Kohl's, Kroger, Lincoln/Mercury, Michael's, O'Reilly Parts, Radio Shack, Ross, Scion/Toyota, Vaughn's RV Ctr, Walmart SuperCtr/24hr, transmissions, **W gas:** Chevron, RaceTrac, Texaco, **food:** Burger King, Taco Bell, Tuscan Sun Coffee, Whataburger/24hr, **lodging:** Travelodge, **other:** Ford, U-Haul
68	Holzwarth Rd, Cypress Wood Dr, **E gas:** Texaco/dsl, **food:** Burger King, Pizza Hut/Taco Bell, Sonic, Wendy's, **other:** Albertson's, AT&T, Gander Mtn GNC, Tiremaxx, **W gas:** Chevron/dsl, **food:** Cheddar's, Denny's, Jack-in-the-Box, Lenny's Subs, Pizza Hut, Popeye's, Starbucks, **lodging:** Motel 6, Spring Lodge, **other:** Advance Parts, Best Buy, Chrysler/Dodge/Jeep, Firestone/auto, Ford, Home Depot, Lowe's Whse, Office Depot, PetCo, Target, Walgreens
66	FM 1960, to Addicks, **E gas:** Chevron, RaceTrac, Shell, **food:** Jack-in-the-Box, Sonic, Subway, TX Roadhouse, **other:** Acura, AT&T, BMW, Chevrolet, Honda, Mercedes, Mistubishi, Petsmart, Radio Shack, Subaru, **W gas:** Exxon, Shell/dsl/24hr, Texaco/dsl, Valero, **food:** Cici's Pizza, Hooters, Jack-in-the-Box, James Coney Island, McDonald's, Outback Steaks, Panda Express, Red Lobster, Subway, Taco Bell, Taquiera Arendas, **lodging:** Baymont Inn, Comfort Suites, Fairfield Inn, Hampton Inn, Studio 6, **other:** H, Audi, Infiniti, Jaguar/LandRover, Lexus, NTB, U-Haul, mall
64	Richey Rd, **E food:** Atchafalaya River Café, **lodging:** Best Value Inn, Holiday Inn, Lexington Suites, Ramada, **other:** Carmax, Discount Tire, Sam's Club/gas, **W gas:** *FLYING J*/Conoco/Country Mkt/dsl/24hr/scales, **food:** Cracker Barrel, House of Creole,

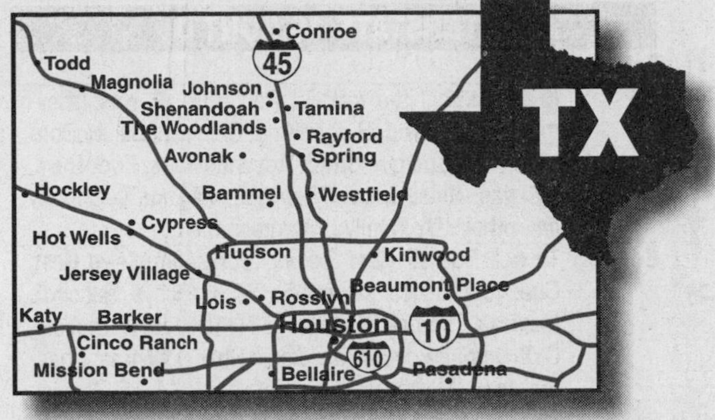

HOUSTON

Exit #	Services
64	Continued Jack-in-the-Box, Joe's Crabshack, Lupe Tortilla, Mamacita's Mexican, Michoacan Rest, SaltGrass Steaks, Tokyohana, Whataburger, Wings'N More, Zio's Italian, **other:** Jones RV Ctr
63	Airtex Dr, **E gas:** Texaco/Subway, Valero/Church's, **food:** China Bear, Pappasito's Cantina, **lodging:** ValuePlace Inn, **other:** Acura, Cadillac, LoneStar RV Ctr, Nissan, **W food:** Cracker Barrel, Jack-in-the-Box, Whataburger, **lodging:** Best Western, Guesthouse Suites
62	Rankin Rd, Kuykendahl, **E lodging:** Best Classic Inn, Scottish Inn, **W gas:** Chevron/McDonald's, RaceTrac, Shell, **food:** Luby's, Shiply Donuts, **lodging:** Palace Inn, Studio+, SunSuites, **other:** Buick/GMC/Pontiac, Demontrono RV Ctr, Hummer, Hyundai, Kia, Lamborghini, Mercedes, Volvo, VW
61	Greens Rd, **E gas:** Texaco, **food:** Brown Sugar's BBQ, IHOP, Imperial Dragon, Luna's, **lodging:** Knights Inn, **other:** Dillard's, JC Penney, Macy's, Sears/auto, mall, **W food:** Burger King, Luby's, Subway, **lodging:** Baymont Inn, Comfort Inn, **other:** Burlington Coat Factory, $General, Kroger
60c	Beltway E
60	(b a from nb) TX 525, **E gas:** Shell, **food:** Burger King, China Border, Denny's, Domino's, Mambo Seafood, Michoacan Rest, Moon Palace Chinese, Pizza Hut, Taco Cabana, **other:** Chrysler/Dodge/Jeep, Family$, Firestone/auto, Honda, Office Depot, **W food:** Pappas Seafood, **other:** U-Haul
59	FM 525, West Rd, **E food:** A&W, LJ Silver, McDonald's, **other:** CarQuest, Fiesta Foods, **W gas:** Exxon, Shell, **food:** Chili's, Jalisco's Mexican, Panda Express, Papa John's Pizza, Quizno's, Starbucks, Subway, Taco Bell, Taco Cabana, Wendy's, Whataburger, Wing Stop, **lodging:** Best Value Inn, Best Western, **other:** AT&T, Best Buy, Discount Tire, $Tree, Fry's Electronics, Home Depot, Office Depot, NTB, PepBoys, Radio Shack, Ross, Verizon, Walmart SuperCtr/24hr
57	(b a from nb) TX 249, Gulf Bank Rd, Tomball, **E gas:** Mobil/dsl, Texaco/Church's, **food:** Wings'N More, **other:** Discount Tire, **W gas:** Shell, **food:** Sonic, Tombico Seafood, **lodging:** Greenchase Motel, La Quinta, Quality Inn, **other:** CVS Drug, Family$, Giant$, Mas Club/dsl
56	Canino Rd, **E lodging:** Taj Inn Suites, **W gas:** Shell, Texaco, **food:** Capt D's, Denny's, Jack-in-the-Box, KFC, Luby's, **lodging:** Best Value Inn, EconoLodge, Gulfwind Motel, Passport Inn, **other:** Ford, Isuzu, USPO

INTERSTATE 45 CONT'D

N ↕ S

Exit #	Services
55	(b a from nb) Little York Rd, Parker Rd, **E gas:** Chevron, Texaco, **food:** Burger King, China Panda, McDonald's, Whataburger, **other:** Advance Parts, FoodTown, **W gas:** Shell, **food:** Popeye's, **lodging:** Symphony Inn, **other:** H, Family$, Walgreens
54	Tidwell Rd, **E gas:** Exxon, **food:** Aunt Bea's Rest, Chacho's Mexican, China Border, Frenchys, Pancho's Mexican, Thomas BBQ, Wings'N More, **other:** BigLots, CVS Drug, Discount Tire, Radio Shack, **W gas:** Chevron, **food:** McDonald's, **lodging:** Guest Motel, Scottish Inn, Southwind Motel, Town Inn, **other:** U-Haul
53	Airline Dr, **E gas:** Citgo, **food:** Popeye's, **other:** Fiesta Foods/drug, **W gas:** Citgo, Shell, **food:** Little Mexico, Wendy's, **lodging:** Luxury Inn, Palace Inn
52	**(b a from nb)** Crosstimbers Rd, **E gas:** Shell/dsl, **food:** Burger King, China Star, CiCi's, IHOP, Jack-in-the-Box, James Coney Island, KFC, Pappas BBQ, Pizza Hut, Sonic, Subway, Taco Bell, **other:** AT&T, Discount Tire, $Tree, Firestone, Marshall's, Ross, mall, **W gas:** Chevron/dsl, **food:** Whataburger/24hr, **lodging:** Texan Inn
51	I-610
50	**(b a from nb)** Patton St, Calvacade St, Link Rd, **E gas:** Citgo, Exxon, Pilot/Wendy's/dsl/scales, Shell, **lodging:** Best Value Inn, Luxury Inn, **W lodging:** Astro Inn, **other:** NAPA
49b	N Main St, Houston Ave, **E gas:** Citgo, **food:** Casa Grande Mexican, **lodging:** Best Value Inn, Luxury Inn, **W gas:** Exxon/dsl, **food:** Domino's, McDonald's, Subway, Whataburger/24hr, **lodging:** Sleep Inn, **other:** O'Reilly Parts
48b a	I-10, E to Beaumont, W to San Antonio
47d	Dallas St, Pierce St (from sb), **E other:** H
47c	McKinney St (from sb, exits left)
47b	Houston Ave, Memorial Dr, downtown, **W lodging:** Double Tree Hotel
47a	Allen Pkwy (exits left from sb)
46b a	US 59, N to Cleveland, S to Victoria, **E gas:** Chevron, **food:** BBQ, **W gas:** Texaco, **food:** McDonald's, Taco Bell, **other:** BMW
45b a	South St, Scott St, Houston, **E gas:** Shell, **other:** Firestone, to TSU
44	Cullen Blvd, Houston, **E gas:** Valero/dsl, to U of Houston
43b	Telephone Rd, Houston, **E food:** Luby's
43a	Tellepsen St, **E food:** Luby's, **lodging:** Day's Inn, **W other:** U of Houston
41b	US 90A, Broad St, S Wayside Dr, **E gas:** Phillips 66, **food:** La Terraza, **lodging:** Day's Inn, Red Carpet Inn, **W gas:** Chevron, Exxon, Mobil, **food:** Jack-in-the-Box, McDonald's, Monterrey Mexican, Subway, Taquiera Mexican, Wings and More, **other:** $Tree, K-Mart, Sellars Foods
41a	Woodridge Dr, **E gas:** Shell, **food:** Bennigan's, Bonnie's Seafood, Denny's, McDonald's, Pappa's Seafood House, Schlotsky's, **W gas:** Citgo, **food:** BoneBreak BBQ, IHOP, Pappas BBQ, Sonic, Subway, Whataburger, Wendy's, **other:** Chevrolet/Buick, Dillard's, HEB Food/gas, Home Depot, Lowe's Whse, Marshall's, Office Depot, Old Navy, Radio Shack, Ross, mall
40c	I-610 W
40b	I-610 E, to Pasadena, **E food:** Bennigan's
40a	Frontage Rd (from nb)
39	Park Place Blvd, Broadway Blvd, **E gas:** Shell, **W food:** Kelley's Rest., Los Campos, **other:** Chevrolet, Dodge, Family$
38b	Howard Dr, Bellfort Dr (from sb), **E gas:** Shell, **food:** Jack-in-the-Box, Wendy's, **W gas:** Citgo, **food:** Chilo's Seafood, **lodging:** Camelot Inn, Mustang Inn, Palace Inn, Passport Inn, **other:** HEB Food/gas, PepBoys
38	TX 3, Monroe Rd, **E gas:** Chevron, Shell, Valero, **food:** DQ, Jack-in-the-Box, Luther's BBQ, Ninfa, Wendy's, **other:** Firestone, NTB, U-Haul, **W gas:** Chevron/dsl, Texaco/dsl, **food:** Luby's, Manny's Seafood, Pappa's BBQ, **lodging:** Best Western, Holiday Inn Express, Quality Inn, Smile Inn, **other:** Firestone, Kottman Transmissions, Radio Shack, Suzuki, U-Haul
36	College Ave, Airport Blvd, **E gas:** Shamrock, Shell, **food:** DQ, Waffle House, **lodging:** Best Value, Day's Inn, Fairfield Inn, Rodeway Inn, **other:** RV Ctr, **W gas:** Exxon, Mobil, Shell, Valero, **food:** Church's Chicken, Denny's, Taco Cabana, **lodging:** AmeriSuites, Baymont Inn, Comfort Inn, Country Inn, Courtyard, Drury Inn, Hampton Inn, Holiday Inn Express, La Quinta, Marriott/Damon's, Motel 6, Red Roof Inn, Regency Inn, SpringHill Suites, Super 8, Travel Inn, **other:** Discount Tire
35	Edgebrook Dr, **E gas:** Chevron, Exxon, RaceTrac, **food:** Burger King, Aranda's Bakery, Jack-in-the-Box, KFC, Popeye's, Subway, Taco Bell, Taquiera Arrandas, Waffle House, **lodging:** Airport Inn, **other:** , Family$, Fiesta Foods, Firestone, Office Depot, Terry Vaugn's RV Ctr, Walgreens, **W gas:** Exxon, Shell, Circle K, **food:** James Coney Island, KFC, LJ Silver, McDonald's, Pizza Hut, Whataburger, **other:** Academy Sports, Honda, NTB
34	S Shaver Rd, **E gas:** Conoco, RaceWay, **food:** McDonald's, **lodging:** Island Suites, **other:** Acura, Honda, Kia, Pontiac/GMC, Toyota, Vaughn's RV Ctr, **W gas:** Chevron/24hr, Exxon, Mobil, **food:** Arby's, Burger King, Pancho's Mexican, Wendy's, **lodging:** Scottish Inn, **other:** Best Buy, Discount Tire, $Tree, Honda, Jo-Ann Fabrics, Macy's, Nissan, NTB, Target, Walmart SuperCtr/gas
33	Fuqua St, **E gas:** Shamrock, **food:** Chili's, Fuddrucker's, Las Haciendas, Luby's, Olive Garden, Schlotzky's, TGIFriday, **lodging:** Studio 6, Sun Suites, **other:** Chrysler/Jeep, Dodge, Ford, Honda, Hyundai, Isuzu, Lincoln/Mercury, **W food:** Bennigan's, Blackeyed Pea, Boston Mkt, Bouderaux's Cajun Kitchen, Casa Mexican, Casa Ole, CiCi's Pizza, Fox&Hound, Golden Corral, Gringo's Mexican, IHOP, Joe's Crabshack, Outback Steaks, Steak&Ale, Subway, Taco Cabana, Taco Bell, TX Cattle Steaks, Whataburger, **other:** BigLots, CarMax, Chevrolet, Firestone, JC Penney, Kroger, Macy's, Old Navy, Radio Shack, Ross, Sam's Club, Subaru, Tire Station, mall
32	Sam Houston Tollway
31	FM 2553, Scarsdale Blvd, **W gas:** Shell, **other:** Chevrolet, Mitsubishi
30	FM 1959, Dixie Farm Rd, Ellington Field, **E gas:** Shell/dsl, **food:** Subway, **lodging:** Howard Johnson, **other:** H, Dodge, Infiniti, **W gas:** RaceWay, Shell/dsl, **food:** McDonald's, Popeye's, **lodging:** Palace Inn, **other:** Lonestar RV, VW

INTERSTATE 45 CONT'D

Exit #	Services
29	FM 2351, Clear Lake City Blvd, to Clear Lake RA, Friendswood
27	El Dorado Blvd, **E gas:** Shell, **food:** DQ, **W food:** Sonic, Texas Roadhouse, Whataburger, **other:** Cadillac, Hummer, Kohl's, Lexus, Radio Shack, Sam's Club/gas, Walmart SuperCtr/24hr
26	Bay Area Blvd, **E food:** Red Lobster, TGI Friday's, **other:** H, Barnes&Noble, Lowe's Whse, Michael's, Old Navy, Oshman's Sports, Steinmart, to Houston Space Ctr, **W gas:** Shell, **food:** Chick-fil-A, Denny's/24hr, McDonald's, Olive Garden, **lodging:** Best Western, **other:** Dillard's, Macy's, Office Depot, Sears/auto, Target, U of Houston, mall
25	FM 528, NASA rd 1, **E gas:** Conoco, Shamrock, Texaco, **food:** Cheddar's, Chili's, Hooters, IHOP, Las Haciendas Mexican, Pappasito's Cantina, Saltgrass Steaks, Waffle House, Vito's, **lodging:** Best Western, Comfort Suites, La Quinta, Motel 6, **other:** H, Audi, Best Buy, Big Lots, Fry's Electronics, Home Depot, Honda, Mazda, Volvo, **W food:** Hot Wok Chinese, Pappa's, Subway, **other:** Fiesta Foods, Radio Shack, Tuesday Morning
23	FM 518, League City, **E gas:** RaceWay, Shell/dsl, **food:** Applebee's, Burger King, Jack in the Box, KFC, Little Caesar's, Pepper's Beef, Sonic, Subway, Sudie's Seafood, **other:** Academy Sports, BMW, Just Brakes, Kroger, Mercedes, Walgreens, **W gas:** Chevron, Exxon/24hr, Mobil, **food:** Cracker Barrel, Hartz Chicken, McDonald's, Taco Bell, Waffle House, Wendy's, **lodging:** Super 8, **other:** Discount Tire, Space Ctr RV Park, U-Haul
22	Calder Dr, Brittany Bay Blvd, **E other:** Nissan, Toyota, camping, **W other:** Holiday World RV Ctr
20	FM 646, Santa Fe, Bacliff, **E food:** Denny's, Panda Express, Whataburger, **other:** Best Buy, Home Depot, JC Penney, Lowes Whse, Radio Shack, Walmart Super Ctr, **W gas:** Valero/dsl, **food:** Chili's, Subway, Taco Cabana, **other:** HEB Foods/gas, Kohl's, PetCo
19	FM 517, Dickinson Rd, Hughes Rd, **E food:** Jack-in-the-Box, Monterey Mexico, Pizza Inn, **other:** Adventure Out RV Park, Buick/Pontiac/GMC/Subaru, CVS Drug, Family$, Food King, Radio Shack, **W gas:** Mobil, Shell/dsl, **food:** Burger King, Dickenson's Seafood, Heartbreak Grill, KFC, McDonald's, Pizza Hut, Sonic, Subway, Taco Bell, Wendy's, Whataburger/24hr, **lodging:** Day's Inn, El Rancho Motel, **other:** Ford, Kroger, Subaru, Target, Walgreens
17	Holland Rd, **W** to Gulf Greyhound Park
16	FM 1764 E (from sb), Texas City, same as 15
15	FM 2004, FM 1764, Hitchcock, **E gas:** Shell, **food:** Gringo's Cafe, Jack-in-the-Box, Olive Garden, Popeye's, Ryan's, Uncle Chan's, **lodging:** Best Western, Fairfield Inn, Hampton Inn, Holiday Inn Express, **other:** H, Chevrolet/Toyota/RV Ctr, Dillard's, JC Penney, Lowe's Whse, Macy's, Sam's Club/gas, Sears/auto, mall, **W gas:** Mobil/Subway, Shell, **food:** IHOP, Sonic, Waffle House, Wendy's, Whataburger, **lodging:** Super 8, **other:** Chevrolet/RV Ctr, Gulf Greyhound Park, Radio Shack, Toyota/Scion, Walmart SuperCtr/24hr/gas
13	Century Blvd, Delany Rd, **E gas:** Valero, **W food:** Acupulco Mexican, **lodging:** Super 8, Travelodge, **other:** VF Factory Outlet/famous brands
12	FM 1765, La Marque, **E gas:** Chevron/24hr, **food:** Domino's, Jack-in-the-Box, Kelley's Rest., Sonic
11	Vauthier Rd
10	**E gas:** Valero, **food:** McDonald's, **W gas:** Shell/dsl, **other:** Oasis RV Park
9	Frontage Rd (from sb)
8	Frontage Rd (from nb)
7c	Frontage Rd
7b	TX 146, TX 6 (exits left from nb), Texas City, **W gas:** EZ Mart
7a	TX 146, TX 3
6	Frontage Rd (from sb)
5	Frontage Rd
4	Frontage Rd, Village of Tiki Island, **W gas:** Valero **other:** public boat ramp
4mm	West Galveston Bay
1c	TX 275, FM 188 (from nb), Port Ind Blvd, Teichman Rd, Port of Galveston, **E gas:** Exxon, Mobil/dsl, Valero, **lodging:** Howard Johnson, Motel 6, **other:** Chevrolet, Chrysler/Dodge/Jeep, Ford, Honda, Mazda, Mitsubishi, Nissan, Toyota/Scion
1b	71st St (from sb), **E gas:** EZ Mart/gas, same as 1c
1a	TX 342, 61st St, to W Beach, **E gas:** Chevron, **other:** GNC, Home Depot, NTB, Target, **W gas:** RaceWay, **food:** Church's, McDonald's, Taco Bell, **lodging:** Day's Inn, **other:** Big Lots, Chevrolet/Pontiac/Buick/Cadillac, Chrysler/Jeep, Family$, Honda, O'Reilly Parts, U-Haul, USPO, **1-2 mi W gas:** Chevron/dsl, Exxon/dsl, Valero, **food:** China Island, CiCi's Pizza, Happy Buddah, Jack-in-the-Box, KFC, Little Caesar's, Luby's, Mario's Italian, McDonald's, Papa John's, Pizza Hut, Popeye's, Quizno's, Starbucks, Subway, Taco Cabana, Waffle House, Whataburger, **lodging:** Baymont Inn, Beachcomber Inn, Best Value Inn, Quality Inn, Super 8, **other:** Curves, CVS Drug, Firestone/auto, Hastings Books, HEB Foods, Office Depot, Randall's Food/gas, Ross, Walgreens

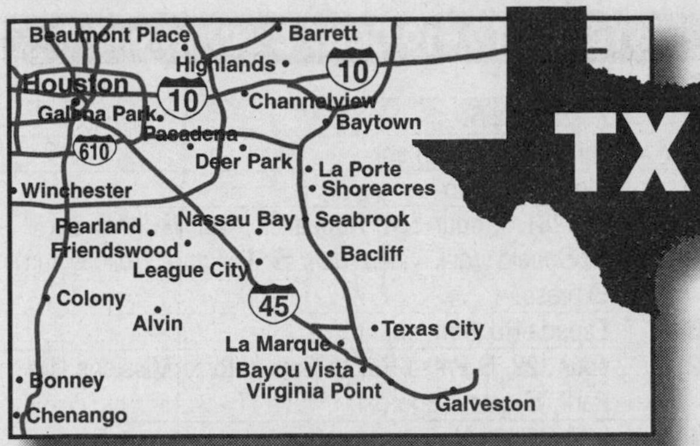

I-45 begins/ends on TX 87 in Galveston.

INTERSTATE 410 (SAN ANTONIO)

Exit #	Services
53	I-35, S to Laredo, N to San Antonio
51	FM 2790, Somerset Rd
49	TX 16 S, spur 422, **N gas:** Chevron, Texaco/dsl, **food:** Church's, Domino's, Sonic, Subway, Whataburger, **lodging:** Days Inn, **other:** H, to Palo Alto Coll, **S gas:** Valero/dsl, **food:** Jack-in-the-Box, **lodging:** Best Western

INTERSTATE 410 CONT'D (SAN ANTONIO)

Exit #	Services
48	Zarzamora St
47	Turnaround (from eb)
46	Moursund Blvd
44	US 281 S, spur 536, Roosevelt Ave, **N gas:** Shell/McDonald's/dsl, Valero/dsl, **S lodging:** Holiday Inn Express
43	Espada Rd (from eb)
42	spur 122, S Presa Rd, to San Antonio Missions Hist Park, **S gas:** Citgo/dsl
41	I-37, US 281 N
39	spur 117, WW White Rd
37	Southcross Blvd, Sinclair Rd, Sulphur Sprs Rd, **N gas:** Valero, **food:** Capparelli's Pizza, other: H
35	US 87, Rigsby Ave, **E gas:** Exxon, Murphy USA/dsl, Valero/dsl, **food:** A&W, BorderTown Mexican, Cici's Pizza, Denny's, Jack-in-the-Box, LJ Silver, McDonald's, Subway, Taco Bell, **other:** $Tree, Radio Shack, Walmart SuperCtr/24hr, **W gas:** Chevron, **food:** Barnacle Bill's Seafood, Bill Miller BBQ, Domino's, El Tapito Mexican, Luby's, Sonic, Taco Cabana, Whataburger, **lodging:** Days Inn, **other:** Aamco, Advance Parts, $General, O'Reilly Parts, U-Haul, Walgreens, auto/dsl repair, Vet
34	FM 1346, E Houston St, **W gas:** Valero/dsl
33	I-10 E, US 90 E, to Houston, I-10 W, US 90 W, to San Antonio
32	Dietrich Rd (from sb), FM 78 (from nb), to Kirby
31b	Lp 13, WW White Rd
31a	FM 78, Kirby, **E gas:** Citgo, Valero/dsl, **other:** Family$
30	Binz-Engleman, Space Center Dr (from nb)

I-410 and I-35 run together 7 mi, See Interstate 35, Exits 161 thru 165.

Exit #	Services
27	I-35, N to Austin, S to San Antonio
26	Lp 368 S, Alamo Heights
25b	FM 2252, Perrin-Beitel Rd, **N gas:** Chevron/dsl, Valero, **food:** Carl's Jr, KFC/Taco Bell, Quizno's, Schlotsky's, Tastee-Freez/Wienerschnitzel, Wendy's, **lodging:** Best Value Inn, **other:** Brake Check, **S food:** Jim's Rest.
25a	Starcrest Dr, **N gas:** Valero, **food:** Jack-in-the-Box, Los Patios Mexican, **other:** H, Toyota
24	Harry Wurzbach Hwy, **N food:** Taco Cabana, **S gas:** Chevron, **food:** BBQ Sta., **other:** VW
23	Nacogdoches Rd, **N gas:** Shell, **food:** Bill Miller BBQ, Church's, IHOP, Jack-in-the-Box, Luby's, Mamma's Cafe, Pizza Hut, Sonic, Wendy's, **lodging:** Crowne Plaza, **S gas:** Chevron
22	Broadway St, **N gas:** Shell/dsl, **food:** Chili's, Las Palapas, McDonald's, **lodging:** Cambria Suites, Courtyard, **other:** vet, **S gas:** Citgo, Valero, **food:** Chesters Hamburgers, Jim's Rest., Little Caesar's, Martha's Mexican, Quizno's, Taco Palenque, Whataburger, **lodging:** Residence Inn, TownHouse Motel
21	US 281 S, Airport Rd, Jones Maltsberger Rd, **N food:** Applebee's, Bubba's Rest, **lodging:** Best Western, Drury Suites, Hampton Inn, Holiday Inn, Holiday Inn Express, PearTree Inn, **S gas:** Murphy USA/dsl, **food:** Pappadeaux, Red Lobster, Texas Land&Cattle, Whataburger, **lodging:** Best Western, Courtyard, Days Inn, Fairfield Inn, La Quinta, Renaissance Hotel,
21	Continued Staybridge Suites, TownePlace Suites, **other:** Hyundai/Kia, Mitsubishi, Subaru, Target, TJ Maxx, Walmart/McDonald's/24hr
20	TX 537, **N gas:** Valero, **food:** Arby's, Chick-fil-A, Jack-in-the-Box, Jason's Deli, McDonald's, Subway, TGIFriday's, **lodging:** DoubleTree Hotel, Hilton, **other:** Barnes&Noble, Bealls, Best Buy, Brake Check, Cavender's Boots, Chevrolet, Honda, Jo-Ann Fabrics, Lexus, Lincoln/Mercury, Marshall's, Mazda, Office Depot, PetCo, Ross, WorldMkt, **S food:** Bennigan's, Cheesecake Factory, El Pollo Loco, Luby's, La Madeleine, Taco Cabana, **other:** AT&T, CVS Drug, Dillard's, Dodge, JC Penney, Macy's, Saks 5th, Sears/auto, Target, Verizon, mall
19b	FM 1535, FM 2696, Military Hwy, **N food:** Guajillos Mexican, Souper Salad, **S food:** Denny's, Jim's Rest.
19a	Honeysuckle Lane, Castle Hills
17b	(18 from wb), **S gas:** Shell, **food:** Bill Miller BBQ, Subway, **other:** Firestone/auto, HEB Foods/gas
17	Vance Jackson Rd, **N gas:** Valero/dsl, **food:** Jack-in-the-Box, McDonald's, Sonic, Taco Cabana, Whataburger, **lodging:** Embassy Suites, Marriott, **other:** Aamco, Discount Tire, **S gas:** Citgo, Shell, **food:** Church's, Subway, **other:** U-Haul
16b a	I-10 E, US 87 S, to San Antonio, I-10 W, to El Paso, US 87 N
15	Lp 345, Fredericksburg Rd, **E gas:** Citgo, **food:** Church's, Dave&Buster's, Denny's, El Pollo Loco, Jack-in-the-Box, Jim's Rest., Luby's, McDonald's, Taco Cabana, Wendy's, Whataburger, **lodging:** Best Value Inn, SpringHill Suites, **other:** AT&T, Family$, Firestone/auto, Hobby Lobby, Jo-Ann Fabrics, SteinMart, Target, transmissions, **W gas:** Chevron/dsl, **other:** CVS Drug
14	**(c b a from sb)** Callaghan Rd, Babcock Ln, **E gas:** Chevron/dsl, Valero, **food:** Marie Callender's, Popeye's, **lodging:** Comfort Inn, Hampton Inn, Travelodge Suites, **other:** AT&T, GMC/Pontiac, Hyundai, **W gas:** Shell, Valero, **food:** Burger King, Chili's, ChopSticks Chinese, DingHow Chinese, Golden Corral, Henry's Tacos, IHOP, Jack-in-the-Box, Jim's Rest, Joe's Crabshack, Las Palapas Mexican, McDonald's, Quizno's, Red Lobster, Taco Cabana, Wendy's, **other:** H, Cavander's Boots, Chevrolet, Home Depot, NTB, Petsmart, Sam's Club/gas, Walmart SuperCtr/Subway/24hr, Vet
13	**(b a from sb)** TX 16 N, Bandera Rd, Evers Rd, Leon Valley, **E food:** Outback Steaks, Panda Express, **other:** Audi, HEB Foods/dsl, Office Depot, Old Navy, Toyota, U-Haul, **W food:** Bill Miller BBQ, Henry's Tacos, Jim's Rest., Schlotzsky's, Sea Island Rest, Taco Cabana, **other:** BigLots, Chevrolet
12	**(from sb) W food:** Fortune Cookie Chinese, Jason's Deli, Sea Island Shrimp House, Starbucks, **other:** AT&T, Barnes&Noble, Best Buy, $Tree, Marshall's, Michael's, Ross
11	Ingram Rd, **E gas:** Shell/dsl, **food:** KFC/Taco Bell, Krystal, Panda Buffet, TX Roadhouse, **lodging:** Days Inn, Comfort Suites, Courtyard, EconoLodge, Holiday Inn Express, Red Roof Inn, Residence Inn, **other:** Aamco, BrakeCheck, Chrysler/Dodge/Jeep,

INTERSTATE 410 CONT'D (SAN ANTONIO)

Exit #	Services
11	Contintued Mazda, **W** **food:** Applebee's, Casa Real Mexican, Chick-fil-A, ChuckeCheese, Denny's, Fuddrucker's, Jack-in-the-Box, Whataburger, **lodging:** Best Western, **other:** Dillard's, Firestone/auto, JC Penney, Macy's, Sears/auto, mall
10	FM 3487, Culebra Rd, **E** **food:** Bill Miller BBQ, Denny's, J Anthony's Seafood, McDonald's, Wendy's, **lodging:** La Quinta, Ramada Ltd, **other:** Harley-Davidson, to St Mary's U, **W** **gas:** Phillips 66, **other:** Ford, Mitsubishi
9	(b a from sb)TX 151, **W** gas Murphy USA/dsl, **food:** Buffalo Wild Wings, Carino's Italian, Cheddar's, Chili's, Chipotle Mexican, IHOP, McAlister's Deli, Panda Express, Starbucks, Taco Bueno, TGIFriday's, Cracker Barrel, **lodging:** Alamo City Hotel, Quality Inn, Sleep Inn, **other:** Home Depot, Lowe's Whse, Office Depot, Petsmart, Ross, Target, Verizon, Walmart SuperCtr/24hr, to Sea World
7	(8 from sb)Marbach Dr, **E** **gas:** Exxon, **food:** Church's, IHOP, **other:** PepBoys, **W** **gas:** Chevron/dsl, Shell, **food:** Acadiena Café, Asia Kitchen, Burger King, Coyote Canyon, Golden Wok, Jack-in-the-Box, Jim's Rest., KFC, LJ Silver, McDonald's, Mr Gatti's, Pancho's Mexican, Peter Piper Pizza, Pizza Hut, Red Lobster, Sonic, Subway, Taco Bell, Taco Cabana, Whataburger/24hr, **lodging:** Motel 6, Super 8, **other:** Advance Parts, Bealls, BigLots, BrakeCheck, Discount Tire, $General, $Tree, Firestone/auto, HEB Foods/gas
6	US 90, to Lackland AFB, **E** **lodging:** Country Inn Motel, **W** **gas:** Shell/dsl, Valero/dsl, **food:** Andrea's Mexican, **lodging:** Best Western, **other:** Explore USA RV Ctr
4	Valley Hi Dr, to Del Rio, San Antonio, **E** **gas:** Valero, **food:** Burger King, Church's, McDonald's, Pizza Hut, Sonic, **other:** AutoZone, HEB Food/gas, Radio Shack, **W** **gas:** Valero, **food:** Jack-in-the-Box, **other:** Walgreens, to Lackland AFB
3	**(b a from sb)** Ray Ellison Dr, Medina Base, **E** **gas:** Chevron/dsl, **W** **gas:** Valero/Subway/dsl
2	FM 2536, Old Pearsall Rd, **E** **gas:** Shell/dsl, Valero/dsl, **food:** Bill Miller BBQ, Church's, Mexico Taqueria, McDonald's, Sonic, Subway, **other:** O'Reilly Parts
1	Frontage Rd, **S** Scion/Toyota

INTERSTATE 610 (HOUSTON)

Exit #	Services
38c a	TX 288 N, downtown, access to zoo
37	Scott St, **N** **gas:** Citgo, Valero
36	FM 865, Cullen Blvd, **N** **lodging:** Crystal Inn, **S** **gas:** Chevron/McDonald's, Mobil, Shell, Valero, **food:** Timmy Chan, **lodging:** Crown Inn, Cullen Inn
35	Calais Rd, Crestmont St, MLK Blvd, **N** **gas:** Exxon, Valero, **food:** Burger King
34S	Wayside Dr, Long Dr, **N** **gas:** Chevron, Phillips 66, Shell, **food:** Church's, Wendy's, **other:** Fiesta Foods, **S** **gas:** Valero, Shell
33	Woodridge Dr, Telephone Rd, **N** **gas:** Shell/dsl, **food:** IHOP, KFC/Taco Bell, McDonald's, Papa John's, Wendy's, **lodging:** South Lp Inn, **other:** Lowe's Whse, Old

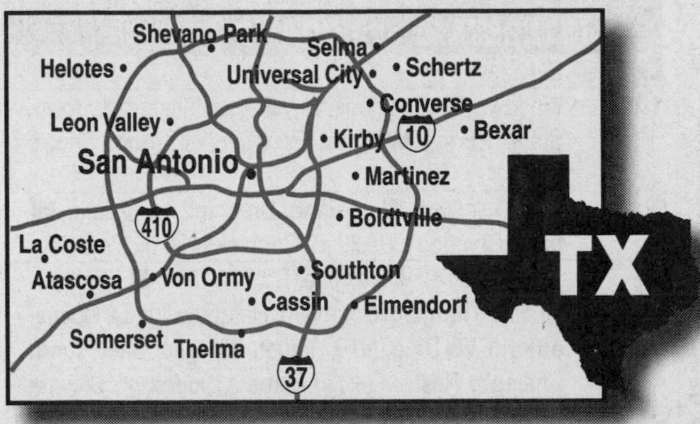

Shevano Park, Selma, Helotes, Universal City, Schertz, Converse, Leon Valley, Kirby, 10, Bexar, San Antonio, Martinez, 410, Boldtville, La Coste, Atascosa, Von Ormy, Southton, Cassin, Elmendorf, Somerset, Thelma, 37, TX

Exit #	Services
33	Continued Navy, **S** **gas:** Texaco, **food:** BBQ, Burger King, KFC, Piccadilly's Cafeteria, Spanky's Pizza, Whataburger, **other:** Dodge, Ford, mall
32b a	I-45, S to Galveston, N to Houston, to ✈
31	Broadway Blvd, **S** **gas:** Valero/dsl, Texaco/dsl
30c b	TX 225, to Pasadena, San Jacinto Mon
29	Port of Houston Main Entrance
28	Clinton Dr, to Galina Park
27	Turning Basin Dr, industrial area
26b	Market St
26a	I-10 E, to Beaumont, I-10 W, to downtown
24	**(b a from sb)** US 90 E, Wallisville Rd, **E** **gas:** Citgo/dsl, Love's/Arby's/dsl/scales/24hr, Pilot/McDonald's/dsl/scales, Texaco/dsl, Valero/Heart's Chicken/dsl/scales/24hr, **food:** Luby's, Wendy's, **other:** Blue Beacon, **W** **gas:** Citgo/dsl
23b	N Wayside, **N** **gas:** Valero
23a	Kirkpatrick Blvd
22	Homestead Rd, Kelley St, **N** **gas:** Shell/dsl, **food:** Whataburger, **lodging:** Super 8, **S** **gas:** Chevron/Subway/dsl/scales
21	Lockwood Dr, **N** **gas:** Chevron/McDonald's, Shell, **food:** Church's, Popeye's, Timmy Chan Chinese, **other:** H, Family$, Fiesta Foods
20a b	US 59, to downtown
19b	Hardy Toll Rd
19a	Hardy St, Jensen Dr (from eb)
18	Irvington Blvd, Fulton St, **N** **gas:** Chevron, **S** **gas:** Shell/dsl
17b c	I-45, N to Dallas, S to Houston
17a	**(eb only)** Airline Dr, **S** **gas:** Shell, **food:** Jack-in-the-Box, **lodging:** Western Inn
16	**(b a from eb)** Yale St, N Main St, Shamrock, **N** **gas:** Exxon, **other:** Harley-Davidson, **S** **gas:** Texaco, **food:** Burger King, Church's, KFC/Taco Bell, Starbucks
15	TX 261, N Shepherd Dr, **N** **food:** Sonic, Taco Cabana, **S** **gas:** Chevron, Shell, **food:** Wendy's, Whataburger, **other:** Home Depot, PepBoys
14	Ella Blvd, **N** **gas:** Exxon, Texaco, **food:** A&W, KFC, McDonald's, Popeye's, Taco Bell, **S** **gas:** Shell, **food:** Thomas BBQ, **other:** H, BrakeCheck, Lowe's Whse, Office Depot
13c	TC Jester Blvd, **N** **gas:** Mobil, Shell, **food:** Denny's, Juanita's Mexican, Po' Boys Sandwiches, **lodging:** Courtyard, SpringHill Suites, **S** **gas:** Phillips 66/dsl
13b a	US 290 (exits left from nb)
12	W 18th St, **E** **food:** Applebee's, Whataburger, **W** **gas:** Shell, **food:** Burger King, **lodging:** Sheraton
11	I-10, W to San Antonio, E to downtown Houston

INTERSTATE 610 CONT'D (HOUSTON)

N ↕ S — HOUSTON

Exit #	Services
10	Woodway Dr, Memorial Dr, **E gas:** Shamrock, **food:** Steak'n Egg, **W gas:** Exxon, Shell, **food:** Shug's Rest.
9b	Post Oak Blvd, **E lodging:** Drury Inn, La Quinta, **W food:** Champp's Rest., McCormick&Schmick's Café
9a	San Felipe Rd, Westheimer Rd, FM 1093, **E gas:** Mobil, Shell, **lodging:** Courtyard, Hampton Inn, La Quinta, **other:** CVS Drug, NTB, Target, **W gas:** Shell, **food:** Champ's Rest., Luke's Burgers, **lodging:** Crowne Plaza Hotel, HomeStead Suites, Marriott, Sheraton, **other:** Best Buy, Dillard's, Nieman-Marcus
8a	US 59, Richmond Ave, **E lodging:** Holiday Inn, Extended Stay America, **other:** CVS Drug, **W gas:** Shell, **other:** Dillards,
7	Bissonet St, West Park Dr, Fournace Place, **E food:** Beudreax's Kitchen, **lodging:** Candlewood Suites, **other:** Home Depot, **W gas:** Shell/dsl/repair
6	Bellaire Blvd
5b	Evergreen St
5a	Beechnut St, **E gas:** Chevron, **food:** Boston Mkt, IHOP, Lowe's Whse, McDonald's, Outback Steaks, **other:** bank, **W gas:** Citgo, Shell, **food:** Escalante Mexican Grill, James Coney Island, Saltgrass Steaks,
5a	Continued Smoothie King, **other:** Borders Books, GNC, Marshall's, mall
4a	S Post Oak Rd, Brasswood, **E gas:** Citgo, **food:** Outback Steaks, **lodging:** Days Inn, **W other:** Target, Walmart
3	Stella Link Rd, **N gas:** Chevron, **food:** Jack-in-the-Box, **other:** Discount Tire, Food City, Radio Shack, **S gas:** Exxon, Phillips 66/dsl, Shell
2	US 90A, **N gas:** Chevron, Conoco, Valero, **food:** Arby's, Bennigan's, Burger King, Church's, Denny's/24hr, KFC, McDonald's, Shoney's, Taco Bell, Wendy's, **lodging:** Grand Plaza Hotel, Howard Johnson, Villa Motel, **other:** CVS Drug, Discount Tire, Ford, Honda, Walgreen, **S gas:** Chevron, Shell, **food:** Golden Corral, Pizza Hut/Taco Bell, Whataburger/24hr, **lodging:** CareFree Inn, La Quinta, Motel 6, Super 8, **other:** Chevrolet, Firestone, Mazda, Nissan, Toyota, U-Haul, to Buffalo Speedway
1c	Kirby Dr (from eb), **N food:** Shell, **food:** Burger King, **lodging:** Radisson, **S food:** Joe's Crabshack, Pappadeaux Seafood, Pappasito's Cantina, **other:** Cavender's Boots, NTB, Pontiac/GMC, Sam's Club, Toyota
1b a	FM 521, Almeda St, Fannin St, **N gas:** Chevron, Shell, **food:** Burger King, **lodging:** Scottish Inn, **other:** Astro Arena, **S gas:** Shell, **food:** McDonald's, **other:** Aamco, to Six Flags

UTAH

INTERSTATE 15

N ↕ S — BRIGHAM CITY — OGDEN

Exit #	Services
400.5mm	Utah/Idaho state line
398	Portage
392	UT 13 S, Plymouth, **E gas:** Sinclair/Subway/dsl
385	UT 30 E, to Riverside, Fielding, **1 mi E gas:** Sinclair/Riverside Grill/dsl
381	Tremonton, Garland, **2 mi E other:** [H], gas, food, lodging
379	I-84 W, to Boise
376	UT 13, to Tremonton, **E gas:** Texaco/Arby's/dsl/24hr, **2-3 mi E food:** Arctic Circle, Crossroads Rest., El Parral Mexican, JC'S Diner, Subway, Taco Time, **lodging:** Marble Motel, Sandman Motel
372	UT 240, to UT 13, to rec area, Honeyville, **E other:** Crystal Hot Springs Camping
370mm	**rest area sb, full ♿ facilities, info, ☎, picnic, litter barrels, vending, petwalk**
365	UT 13, Brigham City, **W other:** to Golden Spike NHS
363	Forest St, Brigham City, **W other:** Bear River Bird Refuge
362	US 91, to US 89, Brigham City, Logan, **E gas:** Chevron/dsl, ***FLYING J***/dsl/rest./24hr, Mirastar, 7-11/gas, Sinclair, **food:** Arby's, Beto's Mexican, Burger King, Donna's Rest., Hunan Chinese, KFC/Taco Bell, Little Caesar's, McDonald's, Old Grist Mill Bread, Pizza Hut, Pizza Press, Sonic, Subway, Taco Time, Wendy's, Wingers, **lodging:** Bushnell Motel, Crystal Inn, Galaxie Motel, Howard Johnson Express, **other:** [H], AutoZone, Checker Parts, Chevrolet/Buick/Cadillac/Pontiac, Chrysler/Dodge/Jeep, $Tree, Golden
362	Continued Spike RV Park, KOA, Smith's, Radio Shack, ShopKO, Walmart SuperCtr, to Yellowstone NP via US 89, **W gas:** ***FLYING J***/Crt St Grill/dsl/24hr, **lodging:** Days Inn
361mm	**rest area nb, full ♿ facilities, ☎, picnic, litter barrels, vending, petwalk**
359	**Port of Entry both lanes**
357	UT 315, to Willard, Perry, **E gas:** ***FLYING J***/Country Mkt/Pepperoni's/dsl/LP, **other:** KOA (2mi)
351	UT 126, to US 89, to Utah's Fruit Way, Willard Bay, **W other:** Smith & Edwards hardware
349	UT 134, N Ogden, Farr West, **E gas:** Exxon/Wendy's, Maverik, 7-11, **food:** Arby's, Domino's, Jumbo Burger, McDonald's, Melina's Mexican, Subway, **lodging:** Comfort Inn, **other:** Kwik Lube, **W gas:** Conoco/dsl
346	to Harrisville, **W gas:** Chevron/dsl, Maverik, Cal Store, dsl repair
344	UT 39, 12th St, Ogden, **E gas:** Chevron, Phillips 66, Shell/dsl, **lodging:** Best Western/rest., **1-2 mi E gas:** Chevron, **food:** Denny's, KFC, McDonald's, Sizzler, Village Inn Rest., **lodging:** Motel 6, **other:** to Ogden Canyon RA, **W gas:** Pilot/DQ/Subway/Taco Bell/dsl/24hr, **food:** Iron Pan Bistro, **lodging:** Sleep Inn, Western Inn
343	UT 104, 21st St, Ogden, **E gas:** Chevron/Arby's/dsl, ***FLYING J***/Conoco/dsl/LP/24hr, Phillips 66/dsl, **food:** Cactus Red's Rest., McDonalds, Outlaw Rest., **lodging:** Best Western, Comfort Suites, Holiday Inn Express, ValuePlace Inn, **other:** Justus RV Ctr, RV Repair, **W gas:** Texaco, **lodging:** Super 8, **other:** Century RV Park

INTERSTATE 15 CONT'D

N–S

OGDEN

Exit #	Services
342	(from nb), UT 53, 24th St, Ogden, **E gas:** Sinclair/dsl
341b a	UT 79 W, 31st St, Ogden, **1-2 mi E on Wall St gas:** 7-11, **food:** Arby's, Golden Corral, JJ North's Buffet, Sizzler, **lodging:** Day's Inn, Hampton Inn, Marriott, **other:** [H], Dillard's, Chevrolet, Ford/Lincoln/Mercury, RV Ctr, mall, to Weber St U, **W** [airport]
340	I-84 E (from sb), to Cheyenne, Wyo
339	UT 26 (from nb), to I-84 E, Riverdale Rd, **E gas:** Conoco/dsl, Sinclair, **food:** Applebee's, Arby's, Boston Mkt, Carl's Jr, Chili's, La Salsa Mexican, McDonald's, **lodging:** Motel 6, **other:** Chrysler/Jeep, Harley-Davidson, Home Depot, Honda/Nissan, Isuzu, Jo-Ann Fabrics, Lincoln/Mercury/Toyota/Kia, Mazda, Mitsubishi, Pontiac/Buick/GMC, Sam's Club/gas, Target, Toyota, Walmart SuperCtr/24hr, Wilderness RV
338	UT 97, Roy, Sunset, **E other:** Air Force Museum, **W gas:** Exxon/dsl, Phillips 66, 7-11, Sinclair, **food:** Arby's, Arctic Circle, Blimpie, Burger King, Central Park, DQ, KFC, McDonald's, Panda Express, Pizza Hut, Ponderosa, Sonic, Subway, Taco Bell, Village Inn Rest., Wendy's, **lodging:** Quality Inn, Motel 6, **other:** AutoZone, BrakeWorks, Checker Parts, Citte RV Ctr, Discount Tire, Early Tires, Firestone, Goodyear, Radio Shack, RiteAid, Schwab Tires, Smith's/gas, Walgeen, transmissions
335	UT 103, Clearfield, **E** Hill AFB, **W gas:** Chevron, Conoco, PetroMart, 7-11, Texaco, Circle K, **food:** Arby's, Carl's Jr, KFC, McDonald's, Skipper's, Subway, Taco Bell, Winger's, **lodging:** Days Inn, The Cottage Inn, **other:** Big O Tire, Sierra RV Ctr
334	UT 193, Clearfield, to Hill AFB, **E gas:** Chevron, Maverik, **W gas:** Chevron/dsl, **food:** Wendy's
332	UT 108, Syracuse, **E gas:** Chevron, Phillips 66/dsl, Circle K, **food:** Applebee's, Carl's Jr., Cracker Barrel, Famous Dave's, Golden Corral, JB's, Marie Callender's, Outback Steaks, Quizno's, Red Robin, TimberLodge Steaks, **lodging:** Courtyard, Fairfield Inn, Hampton Inn, Hilton Garden, Holiday Inn Express, La Quinta, TownePlace Suites, **other:** Barnes&Noble, Lowe's Whse, Office Depot, Old Navy, Target, **W gas:** Conoco, 7-11, **food:** Arby's, McDonald's, **other:** [H], to Antelope Island
331	UT 232, UT 126, Layton, **E gas:** Mobil, Phillips 66, Texaco, **food:** Denny's, Garcia's, McDonald's, Olive Garden, Red Lobster, Sizzler, Training Table Rest.,

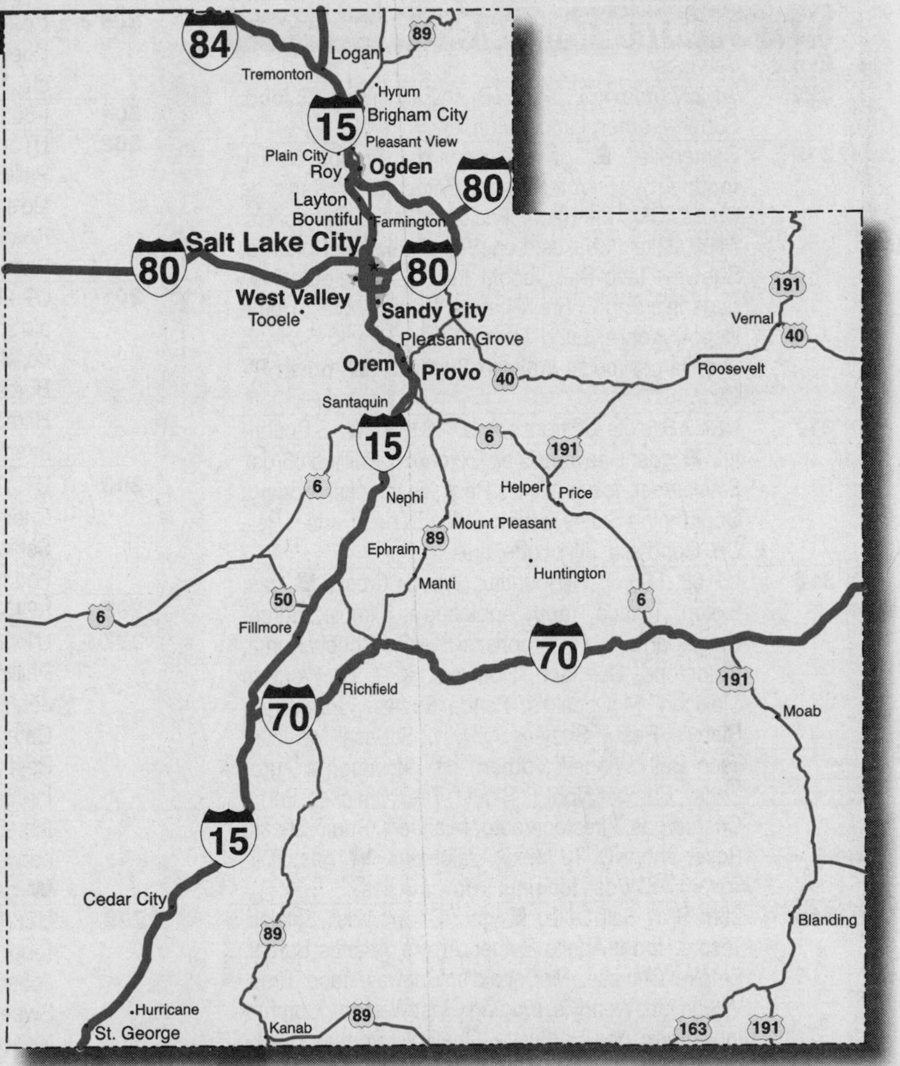

LAYTON

Exit #	Services
331	Continued Wendy's, **lodging:** Comfort Inn, Hilton Garden, **other:** JC Penney, mall, to Hill AFB S Gate, **W gas:** ***FLYING J***, **food:** Blimpie, Burger King, China Buffet, ChuckeCheese, IHOP, KFC, Krispy Kreme, LoneStar Steaks, McGrath's FishHouse, Taco Bell, **other:** Batteries+, Chevrolet, Discount Tire, Dodge, Home Depot, NTB, Jeep, Pontiac/Cadillac/GMC, Ream's Foods, Sam's Club/gas, ShopKO, Staples, Walmart SuperCtr
330	to UT 126 (from nb), Layton, **E food:** Little Orient Chinese, **other:** repair, **W gas:** Texaco, **other:** Jensen's RV
328	UT 273, Kaysville, **E gas:** Chevron/McDonald's, Citgo/7-11, Phillips 66/dsl, Sinclair, **food:** Arby's, Cutler's Sandwiches, DQ, Joanie's Rest., Gandolfo's, KFC, Subway, Taco Maker, Taco Time, Wendy's, Winger's, **other:** Albertson's, Checker Parts, Schwab Tire, Walgreens, **W other:** Camping World/Jensen RV Ctt
325mm	**parking area both lanes**
325	UT 225, Lagoon Dr, Farmington (from sb), **E food:** Subway, **other:** funpark, camping
324	US 89 N, UT 225, Legacy Pkwy (from sb), **1 mi E gas:** Conoco/Smith's Foods/dsl, Maverik/gas, **food:** Arby's, Burger King, Little Caesar's, Subway, **other:** Aunt Pam's, Goodyear/auto, RV Park, to I-84

N ↕ S

INTERSTATE 15 CONT'D

Exit #	Services
322	UT 227 (from nb), Lagoon Dr, to Farmington, **E food:** Subway, **other:** Lagoon Funpark/RV Park
319	Centerville, **E gas:** Chevron/dsl, Phillips 66/dsl, **food:** Arby's, Arctic Circle, Burger King, Carl's Jr, Chili's, DQ, Del Taco, Fusion of Asia, Gandolfo's, IHOP, Jake's Shakes, LoneStar Steaks, McDonald's, Subway, Taco Bell, TacoMaker, Wendy's, **other:** Albertson's, Big O Tire, Checker Parts, Curves, Home Depot, Kohl's, Land Rover, Radio Shack, Schwab Tire, Target/foods, Walmart SuperCtr, **W other:** RV Ctr
317	US 89 S (exits left from sb), UT 131, 500W,, S Bountiful, **E gas:** Chevron/24hr, Exxon/dsl, Phillips 66/dsl, Sinclair/dsl, **food:** Alicia's Rest., Starbucks, **lodging:** Country Inn Suites, **other:** Office Depot, Parts+, PetCo, Goodyear, Jiffy Lube, tires
316	UT 68, 500 S, W Bountiful, Woods Cross, **E gas:** Exxon, Texaco, **food:** Applebee's, Blimpie, Burger King, Carl's Jr, Christopher's Steaks, ChuckaRama, Coldstone, Del Taco, HogiYogi, KFC, La Frontera Mexican, McDonald's, Panda Express, Pizza Hut, Rinny's Rest., Sizzler, Subway, SuCasa Mexican, Taco Bell, Winger's, **other:** H, Albertson's, AutoZone, Barnes&Noble, Big O Tire, Checker Parts, Costco/gas, Firestone/auto, Michael's, Radio Shack, Ross, ShopKO, TJ Maxx, Walgreens, **W gas:** Phillips 66/A&W/dsl, **lodging:** InTown Suites
315	26th S, N Salt Lake, **E gas:** Chevron/dsl, Sinclair, Tesoro, **food:** Apollo Burger, Arby's, Atlantis Burger, Empire Chinese, McDonald's, Subway, Taco Time, Village Inn, Wendy's, **lodging:** Best Western, Comfort Inn, **other:** Ace Hardware, Chevrolet/Pontiac/Buick/Kia, Discount Tire, Dodge, Ford/Lincoln/Mercury, Honda, K-Mart, Mazda, Mitsubishi, Nissan, Schwab Tire, Smith's Foods, Toyota, Tunex, U-Haul, **W gas:** Conoco, **food:** Denny's, Lorena's Mexican, **lodging:** Hampton Inn, Motel 6, **other:** Goodyear
314	Center St, Cudahy Lane (from sb), N Salt Lake, **E** gas
313	I-215 W (from sb), to ✈
312	US 89 S, to Beck St, N Salt Lake
311	2300 N
310	900 W, **W food:** Tia Maria's Mexican, **lodging:** Regal Inn, Salt City Motel, **other:** 7-11, Self's conv/rest.
309	600 N, **E other:** H, LDS Temple, downtown, to UT State FairPark
308	I-80 W, to Reno, ✈
307	400 S, downtown
306	600 S, SLC City Ctr, **1 mi E gas:** Chevron, Phillips 66/dsl, Circle K, **food:** Burger King, DQ, Denny's, McDonald's, Wendy's, **lodging:** Embassy Suites, Hampton Inn, Little America, Motel 6, Quality Inn, Ramada Inn, Residence Inn, Super 8, **other:** Ford, Toyota, to Temple Square, LDS Church Offices
305c-a	1300 S, 2100 S UT 201 W, West Valley, **E gas:** Phillips 66, Texaco, **food:** Atlantis Burgers, Carl's Jr, McDonald's, Wienerschnitzel, **other:** Costco/gas, Home Depot, PetsMart, U-Haul, Walmart SuperCtr, **W gas:** ⊕ ***FLYING J***/Conoco/dsl/LP/rest./24hr, **food:** Wendy's, **other:** Best Buy, Blue Beacon, Cadillac,
305 c-a	Continued Chevrolet, $Tree, Ford, Goodyear, Hummer, Mitsubishi, Napa, Office Depot
304	I-80 E, to Denver, Cheyenne
303	UT 171, 3300 S, S Salt Lake, **E gas:** Citgo/7-11, Phillips 66, **food:** Apollo Diner, Burger King, McDonald's, Taco Bell, **lodging:** Bonneville Inn, Day's Inn, Roadrunner Motel, **W gas:** Maverik/gas, **other:** Sam's Club/gas, GMC
301	UT 266, 4500 S, Murray, Kearns, **E food:** McDonald's, **other:** UpTown Tire, **W gas:** Chevron, Conoco, Shell/dsl, Sinclair/Burger King/dsl, Texaco, **food:** Burger King, Denny's, Wendy's, **lodging:** Fairfield Inn, Hampton Inn, Holiday Inn Express, Quality Inn, **other:** InterMtn RV Ctr, Lowe's Whse
300	UT 173, 5300 S, Murray, Kearns, **E** H, **W gas:** Chevron, Conoco, Sinclair, 7-11, **food:** KFC, Schlotsky's, **lodging:** Reston Hotel, **other:** Smith's Foods, FunDome, Jenson's RV Ctr
298	I-215 E and W
297	UT 48, 7200 S, Midvale, **E gas:** Chevron, Conoco, Phillips 66, Sinclair, Texaco/LP, **food:** Chili's, Denny's, John's Place, KFC, McDonald's, Midvale Mining Café, Sizzler, South Seas Café, Taco Bell, Village Inn Rest., **lodging:** Best Western, Day's Inn, Discovery Inn/café, Executive Inn, La Quinta, Motel 6, Rodeway Inn, Sandman Inn, Super 8, **other:** Cadillac/Buick, carwash, to Brighton, Solitude Ski Areas, Walgreens, **W gas:** Sinclair/Subway/dsl
295	UT 209, 9000 S, Sandy, **E gas:** Chevron, Sinclair, **food:** Arby's, Burger King, Fuddrucker's, Hardee's, Johanna's Kitchen, Schlotzky's, Sconecutter's Rest., Sweet Tomato, **lodging:** Comfort Inn, Majestic Rockies Motel, **other:** Discount Tire, Early Tires, Firestone, Ford, NAPA, to Snowbird, Alta Ski Areas, **W gas:** Maverik, Tesoro, **food:** KFC, Village Inn **other:** H, Aamco
293	106th S, Sandy, S Jordan, **E gas:** Conoco, Phillips 66, Tesoro, **food:** Bennett's BBQ, Carver's Prime Rib, Chili's, Eat a Burger, HomeTown Buffet, Jim's Rest., Johanna's Rest., Subway, TGIFriday, Village Inn, Wendy's, **lodging:** Best Western, Courtyard, Extended Stay America, Hampton Inn, Hilton Garden, Hyatt Summerfield, Marriott, Residence Inn, TownePlace Suites, **other:** Best Buy, Chevrolet, Chrysler/Jeep, Costco/gas, Dillard's, Goodyear, Honda, JC Penney, Nissan, Target, Toyota, mall, **W food:** Denny's, **lodging:** Country Inn Suites, Sleep Inn, Super 8, **other:** Buick/GMC/Pontiac, CarMax, VW, Walmart SuperCtr
291	UT 71, 12300 S, Draper, Riverton, **E gas:** Chevron, ⊕ ***FLYING J***/dsl, **food:** Arby's, Arctic Circle, Café Rio Mexican, Carl's Jr, Del Taco, Fazoli's, Guadalahonky's Mexican, In-N-Out, Jamba Juice, KFC, McDonald's, Panda Express, Pizza Hut, Quizno's, Ruby Tuesday, Sonic, Teriyaki Express, Wendy's, Wienerschnitzel, Wingers Diner, **lodging:** Comfort Inn, Fairfield Inn, Ramada Ltd, **other:** Brown RV, Camping World RV Supplies (1mi), Discount Tire, Goodyear/auto, Greenbax, Kohl's, Mountain Shadows Camping, Smith's Foods, FSA Outlets/famous brands **W** gas Phillips 66, **other:** Walmart SuperCtr
289	Bangerter Hwy, **W** gas Exxon, 7-11, **food:** Quizno's

SALT LAKE · SANDY · DRAPER

N ↕ S

INTERSTATE 15 CONT'D

Exit #	Services
288	UT 140, Bluffdale, **E gas:** Chevron/dsl, **other:** Kohl's, Camping World RV Supplies (2mi), Quality RV Ctr, **W gas:** Common Sense/gas, 7-11, **other:** st prison
284	UT 92, to Alpine, Highland, **E other:** Cabela's, **W gas:** Chevron/Iceberg Café/dsl, Maverik/dsl, **food:** Del Taco, JCW Burgers, **lodging:** Hampton Inn, SpringHill Suites, **other:** Lone Peak RV Ctr, Thanksgiving Point/café, to Timpanogas Cave
282	US 89 S, 12th W, to UT 73, Lehi, **W gas:** Chevron
279	UT 73, to Lehi, **E gas:** Texaco/dsl, **food:** Applebee's, 1 Man Band Diner, Panda Express, TX Roadhouse, Wienershnitzel, **lodging:** Motel 6, **other:** Costco/gas, Lowe's Whse, Home Depot, Petsmart, Schwab Tire, Walgreens, Walmart Superctr, **W gas:** Chevron/dsl/24hr, Phillips 66/Wendy's/24hr, **food:** Arctic Circle, Dutch Oven Rest., KFC/Pizza Hut, McDonald's, Papa Murphy's, Subway, Tepenyki Japanese, Wingers, **lodging:** Best Western, Comfort Inn, Day's Inn, Super 8, **other:** Albertson's, Big O Tire, Checker Parts, GNC, Dave's Chiropractic, USPO, museum
278	Main St, American Fork, **E gas:** Phillips 66/dsl/24hr, Texaco, **food:** Chili's, Cobblestone Pizza, Del Taco, In-N-Out, Ottavio's Italian, Pier 49, Sonic, Wendy's, **other:** [H], Chevrolet, Chrysler/Dodge/Jeep, $Tree, Home Depot, K-Mart, Kohl's, Office Depot, Old Navy, Smith's Foods, Subaru/Suzuki, Target, Walmart SuperCtr, **W lodging:** Value Place
276	5th E, Pleasant Grove, **E gas:** Conoco/Blimpie, **food:** Carl's Jr, Denny's, McDonald's, Taco Bell, **lodging:** Quality Inn, **other:** Stewart's RV Ctr, **1-2 mi E gas:** Circle K, Phillips 66, Texaco, **food:** Arby's, Del Taco, Golden Corral, Hardee's, KFC, Subway, Wendy's, **other:** [H], American Camping, Chevrolet, **W other:** Buick/GMC/Pontiac, Ford, Land Rover
275	Pleasant Grove, **E food:** Bajio Grill, Panda Express, Sonic, Wienerschnitzel, **other:** BMW, Macey's Foods
273	Orem, Lindon, **E gas:** Exxon/dsl, Holiday, **food:** Costa Vida Mexican, Del Taco, **other:** Discount Tire, Home Depot, Lexus, Mercedes, Schwab Tire, **W other:** Harley-Davidson
272	UT 52, to US 189, 8th N, Orem, **E gas:** Maverik, Phillips 66, **lodging:** La Quinta, **1 mi E food:** Arby's, Cafe Rio, DQ, Denny's, Sonic, **other:** to Sundance RA
271	Center St, Orem, **E gas:** Conoco, 7-11, **other:** [H] funpark, **1-2 mi E food:** Burger King, Cafe Rio, KFC, Panda Express, Taco Bell, Wendy's, **W gas:** Tesoro, **food:** La Casita Blanca Mexican, **lodging:** Econolodge, **other:** LP
269	272 UT 265, 12th St S, University Pkwy, , **E gas:** Texaco/Wendy's/dsl/24hr, Sinclair, **food:** HoneyBaked Ham, IHOP, Krispy Kreme, McDonald's, McGrath's FishHouse, Subway, Thai Evergreen, **lodging:** Comfort Inn, Hampton Inn, La Quinta, **other:** Ford, JiffyLube, Mazda, Scion/Toyota, Walmart SuperCtr, **1-3 mi E gas:** Chevron, **food:** Applebee's, Arby's, Carrabba's, Chili's, Fuddrucker's, Golden Corral, Noodles & Co., Outback Steaks, Pizza Hut, Sakura Japanese, Sizzler, Starbucks, Village Inn, **lodging:** Best Western, Courtyard, **other:** Barnes&Noble, Best Buy, Honda, JC Penney, Jo-Ann Fabrics, Lowe's Whse,

OREM

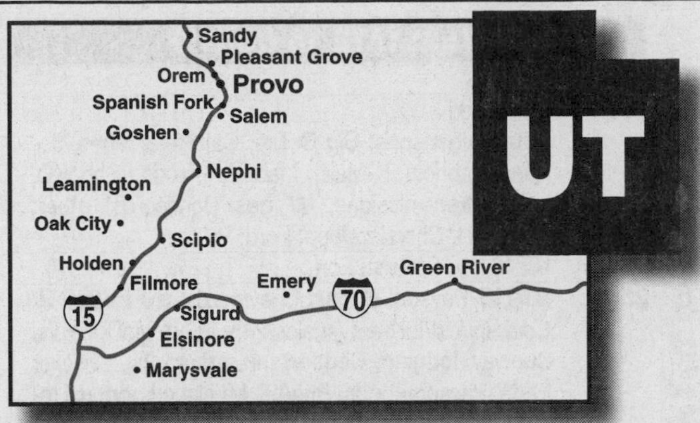

Exit #	Services
269	Continued Mazda, Michael's, Mitsubishi, Nissan, Office Depot, Old Navy, Petsmart, Ross, Subaru, TJ Maxx, mall, to BYU, VW, many services on US 89, **W gas:** Chevron
265b a	UT 114, Center St, Provo, **E gas:** Conoco, Phillips 66/Wendy's, Shell, Sinclair/dsl, 7-11, **other:** [H], Albertson's, Checker Parts, Firestone/auto, auto repair, **1 mi E lodging:** Marriott, Travelers Inn, Travelodge, **W gas:** Chevron, Shell/dsl, **food:** Great Steak Rest., Subway, **lodging:** Econolodge, **other:** KOA, Lakeside RV, to Utah Lake SP
263	US 189 N, University Ave, Provo, **E gas:** Chevron/24hr, Conoco/dsl, Maverik, Sinclair, **food:** A&W/KFC, Arby's, Burger King, ChuckaRama, Fazoli's, Hogi Yogi, McDonald's, Papa Murphy's, Ruby River Steaks, Sizzler, Taco Bell, Taco Time, Village Inn Rest., Wendy's, **lodging:** Best Western, Colony Inn, Fairfield Inn, Hampton Inn, La Quinta, Motel 6, National 9 Inn, Sleep Inn, Super 8, **other:** Curves, Dillard's, GoodEarth Foods, Home Depot, JC Penney, K-Mart, Les Schwab, NAPA, Sam's Club/gas, Sears/auto, Staples, Silver Fox RV Camping, mall, to BYU, **1 mi E food:** Los Three Amigos Mexican, **lodging:** Safari Motel, Western Inn, **other:** CarQuest, VW/Audi, auto repair
261	UT 75, Springville, **E gas:** *FLYING J*/dsl/rest./scales/24hr/scales, Maverik, **food:** McDonald's (1mi), **lodging:** Best Western, **other:** E Bay RV Park, RestStop
260	UT 77, Springville, Mapleton, **E gas:** Phillips 66/Quizno's/dsl, **food:** Del Taco, DQ, IHOP, Mongolian Grill, Pizza Hut, Quizno's, Wendy's, **other:** Big O Tire, JiffyLube, Walmart SuperCtr, **W gas:** Chevron/Arby's/dsl, **food:** Cracker Barrel, **lodging:** Days Inn, **other:** Quality RV Ctr
258	US 89 S, US 6 E (from sb), to Price, **E gas:** Chevron/dsl, Phillips 66, Texaco, **food:** Arby's, Burger King, Carl's Jr, KFC, McDonald's, Papa Murphy's, Subway, Taco Bell, Wendy's, Winger's, **lodging:** Holiday Inn Express, Western Inn, **other:** Albertson's/gas, AutoZone, Checker Parts, Fakler's Tire, K-Mart, Radio Shack, RV Ctr
257	US 6 E, UT 156, Spanish Fork, **E gas:** Chevron, Phillips 66, Sinclair, Tesoro, Texaco/dsl/LP, **food:** Amber Rest., Arby's, Bajio Grill, Burger King, China Wok, Hogi Yogi, Italian Place, KFC, Little Caesar's, McDonald's, One Man Band Diner, Pizza Factory, Sonic, Subway, Taco Bell, Taco Time, Wendy's,

PROVO

SPRINGVILLE

INTERSTATE 15 CONT'D

N ↕ S

Exit #	Services
257	Continued **other:** Albertsons, Big O Tire, Cal Store, $Tree, Jo-Anne Fabrics, K-Mart, Macey's Foods, ShopKO, USPO, transmissions, **W gas:** Conoco/dsl, **other:** Chevrolet, Chrysler/Jeep, Ford, RV Ctr
253	UT 164, to Spanish Fork
250	UT 115, Payson, **E gas:** Chevron/dsl, ***FLYING J***/Cookery/dsl/LP/rest./scales/24hr, **food:** McDonald's, Subway, **lodging:** Comfort Inn, **other:** H, Checker Parts, Payson Foods, RiteAid, Mt Nebo Loop, dsl repair
248	Payson, Salem, **E gas:** Chevron, Sinclair/Arby's/dsl, **food:** Tsing Tao Asian, Hunan City, Pizza Hut, Subway, **other:** $Tree, Walmart SuperCtr, **W gas:** Phillips 66/Wendy's/dsl
244	US 6 W, Santaquin, **E gas:** Maverik, **other:** Tire Factory, TrueValue, **W gas:** Conoco/dsl, Sinclair, **food:** Family Tree Rest., One Man Band Diner, Santa Queen Burgers, Subway, Taco Time, **other:** Family$, Ford, Main St Mkt, Nat Hist Area, USPO, auto/tire care
242	to S Santaquin, **W** Chevron/dsl
233	UT 54, Mona
228	UT 28, to Nephi, **2-4 mi W** services
225	UT 132, Nephi, **E gas:** Tesoro/dsl/LP, **food:** Quizno's, Salt Creek Steaks, Taco Time, One Man Band Rest., **other:** Burn's Bros RV Park (5mi), **W gas:** Chevron/Arby's/dsl, Phillips 66/Wendy's/dsl, **lodging:** Economy Inn, **other:** H, Big O Tire
222	UT 28, to I-70, Nephi, **E gas:** Chevron/dsl, Sinclair/Hogi Yogi/scales/dsl/24hr, Texaco/dsl/24hr, **food:** Burger King, Mickelson's Rest., Subway, **lodging:** Motel 6, Roberta's Cove Motel, Super 8, **other:** dsl repair, **W gas:** ***FLYING J***/Cookery/dsl/LP/scales/24hr, **food:** Lisa's Country Kitchen, **lodging:** Best Western, Safari Motel, **other:** H, Hi-Country RV Park
207	to US 89, Mills
202	Yuba Lake, [phone], access to boating, camping, rec services
188	US 50 E, to I-70, Scipio, **E gas:** Sinclair/Subway/dsl, Texaco, **lodging:** Super 8, **W gas:** ***FLYING J***/DQ/dsl/rest stop/24hr,
184	ranch exit
178	US 50, to Delta, **W** gas, [phone], to Great Basin NP
174	to US 50, Holden, to great Basin NP
167	Lp 15, Fillmore, **0-3 mi E gas:** Chevron/dsl, Shell, Sinclair/dsl, **food:** 5 Buck Pizza, Old Frontier Steaks, **lodging:** Best Western/rest., **other:** H, CarQuest, Goodyear, KOA, WagonsWest RV Park, **W gas:** Chevron/Subway/rest stop, Texaco/dsl, **food:** Carl's Jr
163	Lp 15, to UT 100, Fillmore, **E gas:** Chevron/Arby's/dsl/24hr, Maverik, **lodging:** Comfort Inn, **other:** H, KOA, **W gas:** Texaco/Burger King, **lodging:** motel
158	UT 133, Meadow, **E gas:** Chevron/dsl, Shell/dsl
153mm	view area sb
151mm	view area nb
146	Kanosh, **2 mi E** gas, chainup area
138	ranch exit
135	Cove Fort Hist Site, **E gas:** Chevron/Subway, **other:** rest stop
132	I-70 E, to Denver, Capitol Reef NP, Fremont Indian SP
129	Sulphurdale, chainup area
125	ranch exit
120	Manderfield, chainup area nb
112	to UT 21, Beaver, Manderfield, **E gas:** Chevron, Sinclair/dsl, Conoco/dsl, **food:** Arby's, Arshel's Café, Hunan Chinese, McDonald's, Paradise Canyon Grill, Subway, **lodging:** Best Western, Country Inn, Day's Inn, Rodeway Inn, **other:** H, Family$, KOA (1mi), auto repair, **W gas:** ***FLYING J***/cafe/dsl/24hr/scales, **food:** Wendy's, **lodging:** Eagle's Landing Hotel, Super 8, **other:** to Great Basin NP
109	to UT 21, Beaver, **E gas:** Phillips 66/dsl, Shell/Burger King/dsl/24hr, **lodging:** Best Western, Comfort Inn, **other:** H, Cache Valley Cheese, Camper Land RV Park, Mike's Foodtown, NAPA, auto repair, **W gas:** Chevron/DQ/dsl/24hr, **food:** KanKun Mexican, Timberline Rest., **lodging:** Quality Inn, **other:** RV park, truckwash, to Great Basin NP
100	ranch exit
95	UT 20, to US 89, to Panguitch, Bryce Canyon NP
88mm	**rest area both lanes, full [handicapped] facilities, [phone], picnic table, litter barrel, petwalk, hist site**
82	UT 271, Paragonah
78	UT 141, **1 mi E gas:** Chevron/dsl, Maverik, **lodging:** Day's Inn, **other:** ski areas, **W gas:** TA/Subway/Taco Bell/LP/dsl/scales/24hr/@
75	UT 143, **2 mi E lodging:** Day's Inn, **other:** to Brian Head/Cedar Breaks Ski Resorts
71	Summit
62	UT 130, Cedar City, **E gas:** Loves/Carl's Jr/Subway/dsl/scales/24hr, Phillips 66/dsl, **food:** Arctic Circle, Godfather's Pizza, **other:** Country Aire RV Park, KOA (2mi), st patrol, **W gas:** Maverik/dsl, Shell/dsl/24hr/dsl repair, **lodging:** Travelodge
59	UT 56, Cedar City, **0-2 mi E gas:** Chevron, ***FLYING J***/dsl/rest./24hr, FoodMart/dsl, Maverik, Phillip 66/LP/dsl, **food:** A&W/KFC, Arby's, Bajio, Burger King, Denny's, Godfather's, Great Harvest Bread Co., IHOP, Little Caesars, McDonald's/playplace, Papa Murphy's, Pizza Factory, Sizzler, Sonic, Taco Bell, Wendy's, **lodging:** Abbey Inn, Best Western, Econolodge, Quality Inn, Stratford Hotel, **other:** Buick/Chevrolet, $Tree, Goodyear/auto, Lin's Mkt, NAPA, Tire Co., USPO, **W gas:** Maverik, Sinclair/dsl, **food:** Bard's Cafe, Subway, **lodging:** Crystal Inn, Motel 6, Super 8
57	Lp 15, to UT 14, Cedar City, **0-2 mi E gas:** Chevron/repair/24hr, Phillips 66/dsl, Shell, Sinclair/dsl, **food:** DQ, Domino's, Hogi Yogi, Pizza Hut, Subway, **lodging:** Comfort Inn, Days Inn, Holiday Inn Express, Knights Inn, Rodeway Inn, SpringHill Suites, **other:** H, Albertson's, AutoZone, Beall's, Big O Tire, CAL Ranch, Checker Parts, Country Aire RV Park, Family$, KOA, Main 57 Tire, NAPA Auto Care, Smith's Food/gas/24hr, Staples, to Cedar Breaks, Navajo Lake, Bryce Cyn, Duck Crk, **W gas:** Chevron/dsl, **food:** Applebee's, Chili's, Costa Vida, Del Taco, Lupita's Mexican, Ninja Japanese, Panda Express, Quizno's, Starbucks, Subway, Winger's, **lodging:** Hampton Inn, **other:** GNC, Home Depot, Jiffy Lube, Radio Shack, Tunex, Walgreens, Walmart SuperCtr/gas/24hr

PAYSON · NEPHI · FILLMORE · BEAVER · CEDAR CITY

INTERSTATE 15 CONT'D

Exit #	Services
51	Kanarraville, Hamilton Ft
44mm	**rest area both lanes, full ♿ facilities, ☎, [picnic], litter barrels, petwalk, hist site**
42	New Harmony, Kanarraville, **W gas:** Texaco/dsl
40	to Kolob Canyon, **E other:** Zion's NP, tourist info/ phone, scenic drive
36	ranch exit
33	ranch exit
31	Pintura
30	Browse
27	UT 17, Toquerville, **E other:** to Zion NP, to Grand Cayon, to Lake Powell
23	Leeds, Silver Reef (from sb), **3 mi E other:** Leed's RV Park/gas, hist site, museum
22	Leeds, Silver Reef (from nb), same as 23
16	UT 9, to Hurricane, **E gas:** Shell/Arby's/dsl, **lodging:** Holiday Inn Express, **other:** Harley-Davidson, Walmart Dist Ctr, **10 mi E gas:** Chevron, Shell, **food:** Calydascope Cafe, Coral Canyon Grille, **lodging:** Comfort Inn, Motel 6, Travelodge, **other:** to Zion NP, Grand Canyon, Lake Powell, RV Camping
13	Washington Pkwy, **E gas:** Maverik/dsl
10	Middleton Dr, Washington, **E gas:** Phillips 66/dsl, Sinclair, **food:** Arby's, Arctic Circle, Bajio, Burger King, Del Taco, Honeybaked Ham, IHOP, In-N-Out, Jack-in-the-Box, Jimmy John's, Little Caesars, Lucky Buffet, Noble Romans, Pizza Factory, Ruby Tuesday, Sonic, Steak&Seafood, Subway, TX Roadhouse, Toro Moro Mexican, Wendy's, **lodging:** Country Inn&Suites, Red Cliffs Inn, **other:** AAA, Albertsons/Sav-On, AutoZone, Barnes&Noble, Best Buy, Big Lots, Checker Parts, Costco/gas, Dillard's, Discount Tire, Home Depot, Kohl's, JC Penney, Jiffy Lube, PetCo, Sears/auto, Sportsman's Whse, Tunex, Walmart SuperCtr/gas, mall, **W gas:** Chevron/dsl/LP, Texaco/24hr, **other:** auto repair
8	St George Blvd, St George, **E gas:** Chevron/Subway/dsl, Freddy's/dsl, Texaco/dsl, **food:** Applebee's, Arby's, Carl's Jr, Chili's, ChuckaRama, Coldstone Creamery, Don Jose Mexican, Fazoli's, Golden Corral, Mongolian BBQ, Olive Garden, Outback Steaks, Pachanga's, Panda Express, Papa John's, Quizno's, Red Lobster, Sharky's Mexican, Starbucks, Village Inn Rest., Winger's, **lodging:** Best Inn, Courtyard, Hampton Inn, Ramada Inn, TownePlace Suites, **other:** H, $Tree, Harmon's Foods, Lowe's Whse, Michael's, Old Navy, Ross, Staples, Sunrise Tire, Target, TJ Maxx, Zion Factory Stores/famous brands, same as 10, **W gas:** Conoco/dsl, Maverik/dsl, Shell, Sinclair/Domino's/LP/dsl, Texaco/dsl, **food:** A&W/KFC, Burger King, Cafe Rio, Denny's, Fairway Grill, Iceberg Drive-In, Jimmy John's, Larsen's Drive-In, Mandarin Buffet, McDonald's, Panda Garden, Roberto's, Taco Bell, Taco Time, Wendy's, **lodging:** Best Western, Coronada Inn, Days Inn, Econolodge, Economy Inn, Motel 6, Rodeway Inn, Sands Motel, SunTime Inn, Super 8, **other:** Aamco, Big O Tire, Checker Parts, Desert Coach RV Ctr, NAPA, Rite Aid, St Geo RV, to LDS Temple

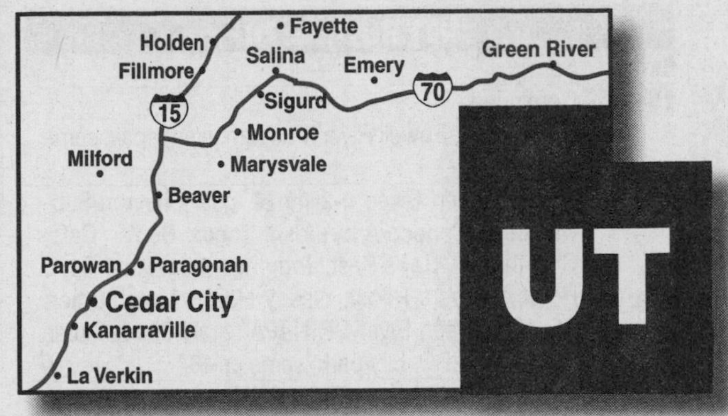

Exit #	Services
6	UT 18, Bluff St, St George, **E gas:** Chevron/dsl/24hr, Texaco/dsl/24hr, **food:** Cracker Barrel, Jack-in-the-Box, Player's Grill, Subway, **lodging:** Ambassador Inn, Comfort Inn, Fairfield Inn, Hilton Garden, **other:** Buick/GMC/Pontiac, Firestone/auto, Hyundai, U-Haul, **W gas:** Shell, Texaco, **food:** Arby's, Burger King, Claimjumper Steaks, DQ, Denny's, JB's, Jimmy John's, McDonald's, Pizza Hut, SF Pizza, **lodging:** Best Value Inn, Best Western, Budget Inn, Claridge Inn, Comfort Suites, Crystal Inn, Desert Palms, Holiday Inn, Howard Johnson, Knight's Inn, Quality Inn, **other:** H, Albertson's, AutoZone, Big O Tire, Cadillac/Chevrolet, Chrysler/Dodge/Jeep, Ford/Lincoln/ Mercury, Goodyear/auto, Honda, Jo-Ann Fabrics, K-Mart, Kwik Lube, Mazda, NAPA, Nissan, Parts+, Radio Shack, Staples, Subaru, TempleView RV Park, Toyota, Vacation World RV Ctr, funpark
4	Bloomington, **E gas:** ***FLYING J***/Burger King/dsl/ scales/24hr, **lodging:** La Quinta, **W gas:** Chevron/ Taco Bell, **food:** Hungry Howie's, Subway, Taco Time, Wendy's, **lodging:** Wingate Inn, **other:** Checker Parts, Walmart SuperCtr/dsl
2	Southern Pkwy
1	**Port of Entry/weigh sta both lanes**
0mm	Utah/Arizona state line

INTERSTATE 70

Exit #	Services
232mm	Utah/Colorado state line
228mm	**view area wb, litter barrels**
227	Westwater
221	ranch exit
214	to Cisco
204	UT 128, to Cisco
193	Yellowcat Ranch Exit
190mm	**Welcome Ctr wb, full ♿ facilities, vending, info, [picnic], litter barrels**
187	Thompson Springs, **N gas:** Shell/dsl, **other:** café, camping, lodging
182	US 191 S, Crescent Jct, to Moab, **N gas:** Papa Joe's, **S** to Arches/Canyonlands NP
181mm	**rest area eb, full ♿ facilities, scenic view, [picnic], litter barrels**
175	ranch exit
164	UT 19, Green River, **1-3 mi N gas:** Phillis 66/Burger King/dsl, Silver Eagle/Blimpie/dsl, Westwinds Trkstp/ Sinclair/rest/dsl/scales/24hr, **food:** Tamarisk Rest., **lodging:** Best Western, Comfort Inn, Holiday Inn Express, Motel 6, Super 8, Ramada Ltd, Rodeway Inn,

INTERSTATE 70

Exit #	Services
164	Continued other: KOA, Powell River Museum, tires/repair, same as 160
160	UT 19, Green River, **0-2 mi N gas:** Chevron/Subway/dsl, Conoco/Arby's/dsl, **food:** Ben's Cafe, Chowhound, Ray's Rest., **lodging:** Budget Inn, Ray's Hotel, Robbers Roost, Sleepy Hollow Motel, **other:** AG Mkt, Green River SP, NAPA/repair, Shady Acres RV Park, USPO, city park, same as 164
157	US 6 W, US 191 N, to Price, Salt Lake
147	UT 24 W, to Hanksville, to Capitol Reef, Lake Powell
144mm	**rest area wb, restrooms ♿, litter barrels**
141.5mm	runaway truck ramp eb
140mm	**rest area both lanes, view area, restrooms ♿, litter barrels**
139mm	runaway truck ramp eb
136mm	brake test area eb
129	ranch exit
120mm	**rest area both lanes, restrooms ♿, litter barrels**
114	to Moore, **N rest area both lanes, restrooms ♿, litter barrels**
105	ranch exit
102mm	**rest area both lanes, restrooms ♿, litter barrels**
91	ranch exit
89	UT 10 N, UT 72, to Emery, Price, **12 mi N** gas, **S** to Capitol Reef NP
84mm	**S rest area both lanes, full ♿ facilities, litter barrels, petwalk**
72	ranch exit
61	Gooseberry Rd
56	US 89 N, to Salina, US 50 W, to Delta, **0-1 mi N gas:** Conoco/dsl, Maverik, Phillips 66/dsl, Sinclair/Burger King/dsl, **food:** Denny's, El Mexicano Mexican, Losta Motsa Pizza, Mom's Cafe, Subway, **lodging:** Best Western, Rodeway Inn, Super 8, **other:** Barrett Foods, Butch Cassidy RV Camp, NAPA, auto repair, dsl repair, radiators, Next Services 108 ni eb
48	UT 24, to US 50, Sigurd, Aurora, **1-2 mi S** gas, food, to Fishlake NF, Capitol Reef NP
40	Lp 70, Richfield, **0-2 mi S gas:** Chevron, *FLYING J* /Pepperoni's/dsl/LP/rest./24hr, Maverik, Texaco/dsl, **food:** Arby's, Frontier Village Rest., JB's Rest., South China Rest., Subway, Taco Time, **lodging:** Best Western, Budget Host, Day's Inn/rest., Holiday Inn Express, Quality Inn, Super 8, Travelodge, **other:** H Albertson's/drug, Big O Tire, Chevrolet, Buick/Pontiac/Cadillac/GMC, Family$, Lin's Mkt, NAPA, USPO, RV/truck repair
37	Lp 70, Richfield, **S gas:** Phillips 66/Wendy's/dsl, **food:** KFC/Taco Bell, Wingers, **lodging:** Comfort Inn, Fairfield Inn, Hampton Inn, **other:** Home Depot, golf, **1-2 mi S gas:** Sinclair/Burger King/dsl, Texaco, **food:** Lotsa Motsa Pizza, McDonald's, Papa Murphy's, Pizza Hut, Rice King Chinese, **lodging:** Quality Inn, Royal Inn, Travelodge, **other:** Ace Hardware, AutoZone, K-mart, Checker Parts, $Tree, K-Mart, KOA, Walmart SuperCtr/Subway, to Fish Lake/Capitol Reef Parks, st patrol
31	Elsinore, Monroe, **S gas:** Silver Eagle/gas
25	UT 118, Joseph, Monroe, **S gas:** Diamond D Travel Plaza/dsl, Flying U Country Store/dsl, **other:** RV park
23	US 89 S, to Panguitch, Bryce Canyon
17	**N other:** Fremont Indian Museum, info, ☎, camping
13mm	brake test area eb
8	Ranch Exit
3mm	Western Boundary Fishlake NF
1	Historic Cove Fort, **N gas:** Chevron (2mi)
0mm	**I-15, N to SLC, S to St George. I-70 begins/ends on I-15, exit 132.**

GREEN RIVER · N ↕ S · RICHFIELD

INTERSTATE 80

Exit #	Services
197mm	Utah/Wyoming state line
193	Wahsatch
189	ranch exit
185	Castle Rock
182mm	**Port of Entry/weigh sta wb**
180	Emery (from wb)
170	**Welcome Ctr wb/rest area eb, full ♿ facilities, ☎, vending, picnic, litter barrels, petwalk, RV dump**
169	Echo, **1 mi N** gas/dsl, food, lodging
168	I-84 W, to Ogden, I-80 E, to Cheyenne
166	**view area both lanes, litter barrels**
164	164 Coalville, **N gas:** Phillips 66/dsl/mart, **lodging:** Best Western, **other:** Holiday Hills RV Camp/LP, CamperWorld RV Park, **S gas:** Chevron/dsl, Sinclair, **other:** Griffith's Foods, NAPA, USPO, to Echo Res RA
155	UT 32 S, Wanship, **N food:** Spring Chicken Café, **S gas:** Sinclair/dsl, **other:** to Rockport SP
150	**toll gate promontory**
146b a	US 40 E, to Heber, Provo, **N gas:** Sinclair/Blimpie/dsl, **S other:** Home Depot
145	UT 224, Kimball Jct, to Park City, **N other:** Chevrolet, Ford/Mercury, RV camping, **S gas:** Chevron, **food:** Arby's, Bajio Grill, Coldstone Creamery, Gandalfo's Deli, Ghidottis Italian, Loco Lizard Cantina, McDonald's, Panda Express, Quizno's, Starbucks, Subway, Ruby Tuesday, Taco Bell, Wendy's, Wild Oats Cafe, Wingers, **lodging:** Best Western, Hampton Inn, Holiday Inn Express, **other:** GNC, Smith's Foods, USPO, Walmart, Outlet Mall/famous brands, RV camping, to ski areas
144mm	view area eb
141	ranch exit, **N gas:** Phillips 66/Blimpie, **food:** Pizza Hut, **other:** to Jeremy Ranch, **S food:** Booster Juice, Cafe Sabor, Oh Shucks Grill, **other:** Albertson's, camping, ski area
140	Parley's Summit, **S gas:** Sinclair/dsl, **food:** No Worries Café
137	Lamb's Canyon
134	UT 65, Emigration Canyon, East Canyon, Mountaindale RA
133	utility exit (from eb)
132	ranch exit
131	(from eb) Quarry
130	I-215 S (from wb)
129	UT 186 W, Foothill Dr, Parley's Way, **N** H
128	I-215 S (from eb)

E ↕ W · KIMBALL JCT

INTERSTATE 80 CONT'D

E ↕ W — SALT LAKE

Exit #	Services
127	UT 195, 23rd E St, to Holladay
126	UT 181, 13th E St, to Sugar House, **N gas:** Chevron, Texaco, **food:** Olive Garden, Red Lobster, Sizzler, Training Table Rest., Wendy's, **other:** ShopKO
125	UT 71, 7th E St, **gas:** Texaco, **other:** Firestone, **N food:** McDonald's
124	US 89, S State St, **N gas:** Citgo/7-11, Chevron, Texaco/dsl, **food:** Burger King, Skipper's, Taco Bell, Uncle Sid's Rest., Wendy's, Woody's Drive-In, **other:** Buick, Chrysler/Jeep, Discount Tire, Dodge, Honda, Jeep, Suzuki, transmissions, **S food:** KFC, Pizza Hut, **lodging:** Ramada Inn
123mm	I-15, N to Ogden, S to Provo
I-80 and I-15 run together approx 4 mi. See Interstate 15 Exits 308-310.	
121	600 S, to City Ctr
120	I-15 N, to Ogden
118	UT 68, Redwood Rd, to N Temple, **1 mi N on N Temple E gas:** Chevron/Subway/dsl, Maverik, Pilot/Arby's/dsl/scales/24hr, Tesoro, **food:** A&W/KFC, Burger King, Carls Jr, Denny's, Taco Bell, Wendy's, **lodging:** Airport Inn, Candlewood Suites, Comfort Suites, Day's Inn, Holiday Inn Express, Motel 6, Quality Inn, Radisson, Utah St Fairpark, **S** [H]
117	I-215, N to Ogden, S to Provo
115b a	40th W, W Valley Fwy, **N** to Salt Lake [airport]
114	Wright Bros Dr (from wb), **N** same as 113
113	5600 W (from eb), **N gas:** Phillips 66/mart, **food:** Perkins, Pizza Hut, Subway, **lodging:** Best Western, Comfort Inn, Courtyard, Fairfield Inn, Hampton Inn, Hilton, Holiday Inn, Hyatt Place, La Quinta, Microtel, Residence Inn, SpringHill Suites, Super 8
111	7200 W, **N visitor ctr**
104	UT 202, Saltair Dr, to Magna, **N other:** Great Salt Lake SP, beaches
102	UT 201 (from eb), to Magna
101mm	view area wb
99	UT 36, to Tooele, **S gas:** Chevron/Subway, ***FLYING J***/Conoco/Country Mkt/dsl/scales/LP/24hr, TA/Burger King/Taco Bell/dsl/scales/24hr/@, Shell/dsl, Speedco, **food:** Del Taco, McDonald's, **lodging:** Oquirrh Motel/RV Park, **other:** [H], Blue Beacon, Mamie's Place
88	to Grantsville
84	UT 138, to Grantsville, Tooele
77	UT 196, to Rowley, Dugway
70	to Delle, **S gas:** Delle/Sinclair/dsl/café/24hr
62	to Lakeside, Eagle Range, military area
56	to Aragonite
55mm	**rest area both lanes, full [handicapped] facilities, [phone], [picnic], litter barrels, petwalk, vending**
49	to Clive
41	Knolls
26mm	architectural point of interest
10mm	**rest area both lanes, full [handicapped] facilities, [phone], [picnic], litter barrels, vending, petwalk, observation area**
4	Bonneville Speedway, **N gas:** Sinclair/dsl/café/24hr
3mm	**Port of Entry, weigh sta both lanes**
2	UT 58 (no EZ wb return), Wendover, **S gas:** Sinclair/dsl, Shell/dsl, **food:** Quizno's, Subway, Taco Poblano, **lodging:** Best Western, Bonneville Inn, Day's Inn, Econolodge, Knight's Inn, Motel 6, Nugget Hotel/casino, Western Ridge Motel, **other:** CarQuest, Family$, Fred's Foods, Bonneville Speedway Museum, Montego Bay, Stateline Inn/casino, RV park, USPO, auto repair
0mm	Utah/Nevada state line, Mountain/Pacific time zone

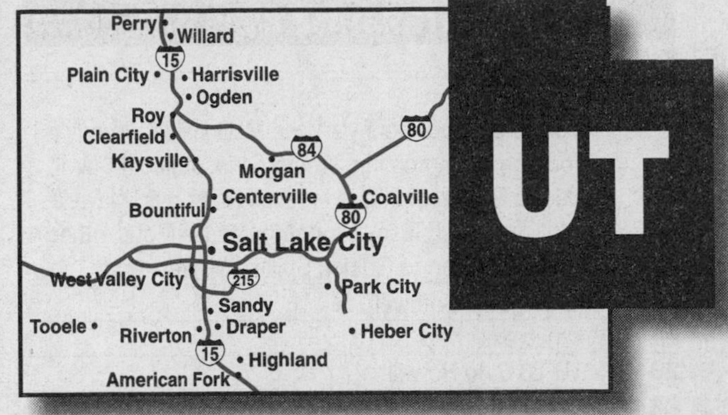

INTERSTATE 84

E ↕ W

Exit #	Services
120	I-84 begins/ends on I-80, exit 168 near Echo, Utah.
115	to Henefer, Echo, **1/2 mi S other:** USPO, to E Canyon RA, **1/2 mi S other:** USPO, to E Canyon RA
112	Henefer, **S** gas, food, lodging
111	Croydon
111mm	Devil's Slide Scenic View
108	Taggart, **N** gas, food, [phone]
106	ranch exit
103	UT 66, Morgan, E Canyon RA, **N** Ford, **S gas:** Chevron, Phillips 66, Shell, **food:** Chicken Hut, Spring Chicken Café, Steph's Drive-In, **other:** Jubilee Foods, USPO, city park
96	Peterson, **N gas:** Sinclair (3mi), **other:** to Snow Basin, Powder Mtn, Nordic Valley Ski Areas, **S gas:** Phillips 66/dsl
94mm	**rest area wb, full [handicapped] facilities, [picnic], litter barrels, petwalk**
92	UT 167 (from eb), to Huntsville, **N gas:** Sinclair/dsl (2mi), **other:** trout farm (1mi), to ski areas
91mm	**rest area eb, full [handicapped] facilities, [picnic], litter barrels, petwalk**
87b a	US 89, to Layton, Ogden, Hill AFB, **N food:** McDonald's (2mi), **1/2 mi S gas:** Shell
85	S Weber, Uintah
81	to I-15 S, UT 26, Riverdale Rd, **N gas:** Conoco/dsl, Sinclair, **food:** Applebee's, Boston Mkt, Carl's Jr, Chili's, La Salsa Mexican, McDonald's, **other:** Chrysler/Jeep, Harley-Davidson, Home Depot, Honda/Nissan, Isuzu, Lincoln/Mercury/Toyota/Kia, Lowe's Whse, Mazda, Mitsubishi, PepBoys, Pontiac/Buick/GMC, Sam's Club/gas, Target, Walmart SuperCtr/24hr, Wilderness RV, **S food:** McDonald's, **lodging:** Motel 6
I-84 and I-15 run together. See Interstate 15 Exits 341-346.	
41	I-15 N to Pocatello
40	UT 102, Tremonton, Bothwell, **N gas:** Chevron/Quizno's/dsl/wash/24hr, Sinclair/Burger King/dsl/

INTERSTATE 84

Exit #	Services
40	Continued scales/@, **food:** Denny's/24hr, McDonald's, Wendy's, **lodging:** Hampton Inn, Western Inn, **other:** H (4mi), Jack's RV Ctr, truck/tire repair, **1 mi N gas:** Maverik, Phillips 66/dsl, Tesoro, **lodging:** Marble Motel, **other:** Alco, **S other:** to Golden Spike NM, tires/repair
39	to Garland, Bothwell, **N** H
32	ranch exit
26	UT 83 S, to Howell
24	to Valley
20	to Blue Creek
17	ranch exit
16	to Hansel Valley
12	ranch exit
7	Snowville, **N gas:** Chevron/Subway/dsl, ***FLYING J***/Pepperoni's/dsl/LP/24hr, **food:** Mollie's Café, Ranch House Diner, **lodging:** Outsiders Inn, **other:** Lotti Dell RV camping
5	UT 30, to Park Valley
0mm	Utah/Idaho state line

INTERSTATE 215 (SALT LAKE)

SALT LAKE CITY

Exit #	Services
29	I-215 begins/ends on I-15.
28	UT 68, Redwood Rd, **W gas:** ***FLYING J***/dsl/rest./mart/24hr/@, Maverik/24hr, **food:** Subway, **other:** BMW (motorcycles)
26	Legacy Pkwy
25	22nd N
23	7th N, **E gas:** Exxon, Maverik, Pilot/Arbys/dsl/scales/24hr (1.5 mi), **food:** Arby's, KFC, McDonald's, Taco Bell, Wendy's, **lodging:** Motel 6, **W lodging:** Airport Inn, Baymont Inn, Candlewood Suites, Comfort Suites, Holiday Inn Express, Radisson
22b a	I-80, W to Wendover, E to Cheyenne
21	California Ave, **E gas:** Chevron/dsl, Sapp Bros/Sinclair/Burger King/dsl/@, **food:** Great American Diner, Subway, **other:** Goodyear
20b a	UT 201, W to Magna, 21st S, **W other:** Goodyear, Kenworth
18	UT 171, 3500 S, W Valley, **E gas:** Sinclair, **food:** Applebee's, Chili's, Costa Vida Mexican, Cowloon Moon, Cracker Barrel, Denny's, IHOP, Training Table, **lodging:** Baymont Inn, Country Inn Suites,
18	Continued Crystal Inn, Extended Stay America, La Quinta, Ruby Tuesday, Sleep Inn, **other:** H, PepBoys, **W food:** Olive Garden, Pizza Hut, Red Robin, Starbucks, TGIFriday's, Winger's, **other:** Big O Tire, Costco/gas, JC Penney, Jubilee Foods, Macy's, Staples, Verizon
15	UT 266, 47th S, **E gas:** Conoco/dsl, **food:** Dee's Rest., KFC, Pizza Hut, Taco Time, Taco Bell, Village Inn, Wendy's, **other:** Albertson's, Goodyear/auto, Marie Callender's, Rite Aid, Walgreens, **W gas:** Chevron, **food:** Arby's
13	UT 68, Redwood Rd, **E gas:** Chevron, Tesoro, **food:** Applebee's, Apollo Burger, Arby's, Bajio Grill, Burger King, Carl's Jr, Golden China, Great Harvest Bread, Honey Baked Ham, McDonald's/playplace, Old Spaghetti Factory, Panda Express, Papa John's, Souper Salad, Starbucks, Subway, TX Roadhouse, Tuesday Morning, **lodging:** Homestead Suites, **other:** $Tree, Harmon's, Jo-Ann Fabrics, PetsMart, Radio Shack, Ross, ShopKO, Walmart SuperCtr/auto
12	I-15, N to SLC, S to Provo
11	same as 10 (from eb), same as 10 (from eb)
10	UT 280 E, **E other:** Sam's Club, **W food:** Applebee's, Arby's, Hooters, Jason's Deli, La Salsa Mexican, Macaroni Grill, Olive Garden, Red Lobster, Taco Bell, Wendy's, Village Inn, **other:** H
9	Union Park Ave, **E food:** Black Angus, Carl's Jr, Chili's, Denny's, Famous Dave's BBQ, LaSalsa Mexican, Marie Callender's, Outback Steaks, Sweet Tomato, Tony Roma, **lodging:** Best Western, Crystal Inn, Extended Stay America, Homewood Suites, **other:** Albertson's, Barnes&Noble, Home Depot, Old Navy, Ross, Smith's Foods, Target, Walmart/auto, **W gas:** Tesoro, **lodging:** Crystal Inn, Motel 6, Super 8
8	UT 152, 2000 E, **E gas:** Chevron, **food:** KFC, Panda Express, Taco Bell, **W food:** Wendy's
6	6200 S, **E food:** Loco Lizards Café, Mikado Café, Quizno's, **other:** Alta, Brighton, Snowbird, Solitude/ski areas
5	UT 266, 45th S, Holladay, **W gas:** Tesoro
4	39thS, **E gas:** Chevron, Sinclair, **food:** Barbacoa Grill, Rocky Mtn Pizza, **other:** Ace Hardware, Dan's Foods, **W** H
3	33rd S, Wasatch, **W gas:** Tesoro, **food:** Burger King, KFC, McDonald's, Taco Bell, Wendy's
2	I-80 W

I-215 begins/ends on I-80, exit 130.

VERMONT

INTERSTATE 89

ST ALBANS

Exit #	Services
130mm	I-89 Begins/Ends, US/Canada Border, Vermont state line
129.5mm	**rest area sb, full facilities, litter barrels, petwalk**
22 (129)	US 7 S, Highgate Springs, **E other:** DutyFree, **3 mi E gas:** Mobil/dsl
129mm	Latitude 45 N, midway between N Pole and Equator
128mm	Rock River
21 (123)	US 7, VT 78, Swanton, **E gas:** Exxon/dsl/24hr, **W gas:** Mobil/dsl, Shell, Sunoco/dsl, **food:** Dunkin
21 (123)	Continued Donuts, Jacob's Rest., McDonald's, **other:** Grand Union Foods, NAPA
20 (118)	US 7, VT 207, St Albans, **W gas:** Mobil/dsl Shell/dsl, **food:** Burger King, Dunkin Donuts, KFC/Taco Bell, McDonald's, Oriental Kitchen, Panda China, Pizza Hut, Wendy's, **other:** H, Advance Parts, Aubuchon Hardware, Chevrolet, Ford, Hannaford Foods, Kinney Drug, PriceChopper Foods, Radio Shack, Sears, Staples
19 (114)	US 7, VT 36, VT 104, St Albans, **W gas:** Exxon/dsl, Mobil/dsl, **lodging:** La Quinta, **other:** H, st police, Vet

VT

INTERSTATE 89 CONT'D

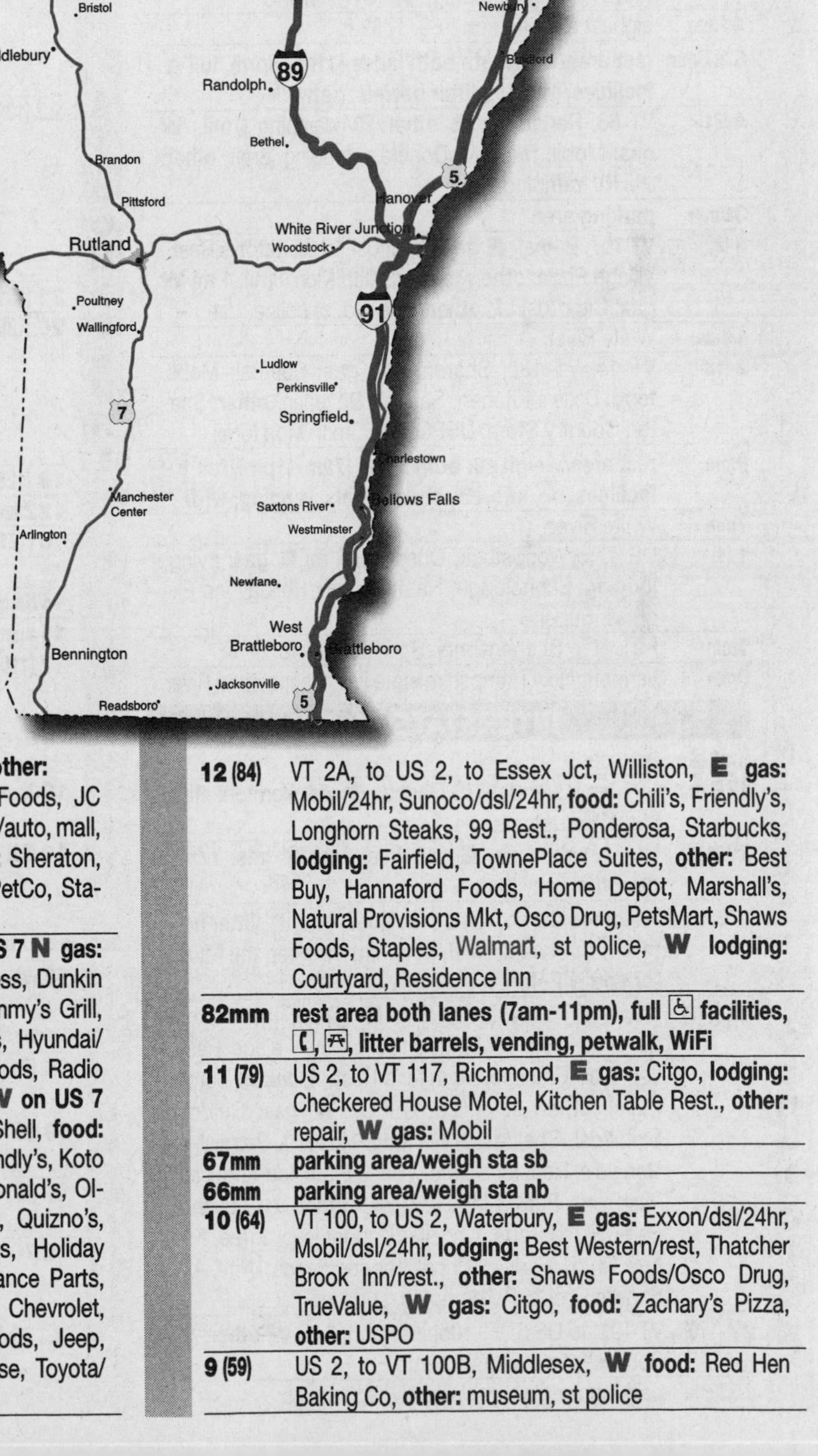

N ↑ ↓ S

Exit #	Services
111mm	**rest area both lanes, full ♿ facilities, info, 📞, picnic, litter barrels, vending, petwalk**
18 (107)	US 7, VT 104A, Georgia Ctr, **E gas:** Citgo, Mobil/dsl, Shell, **food:** GA Farmhouse Rest., **other:** GA Auto Parts, Homestead RV Park, USPO, repair
17 (98)	US 2, US 7, Lake Champlain Islands, **E gas:** Exxon, Mobil, **other:** camping (4mi), **W other:** to NY Ferry, camping (6mi)
96mm	**weigh sta both lanes**
16 (92)	US 7, US 2, Winooski, **E gas:** Mobil, **food:** Friendly's, T-Bones Rest., **lodging:** Hampton Inn, **other:** CostCo, Osco Drug, Shaw's Foods, **W gas:** Citgo, GoGo Gas, Shell/dsl, **food:** Burger King, Jr's Italian, Libby's Diner, McDonald's, Subway, **lodging:** Motel 6, Quality Inn
15 (91)	VT 15 (from nb no return), Winooski, **E lodging:** Day's Inn, Handys Extended Stay Suites, **W gas:** Exxon, Mobil, **other:** USPO
90mm	Winooski River
14 (89)	US 2, Burlington, **E gas:** Citgo/repair, Exxon, Gulf, Maverick, Mobil, Shell/dsl, **food:** Al's Cafe, Applebee's, Burger King, CheeseTraders, Dunkin Donuts, Friendly's, Kohl's, Leonardo's Pizza, Marco's Pizza, McDonald's, Moe's SW Grill, Nothing but Noodles, Outback Steaks, Quizno's, Starbucks, Zachary's Pizza, **lodging:** Anchorage Inn, Best Western, Comfort Inn, DoubleTree Hotel, Hawthorn Suites, Holiday Inn, La Quinta, SwissHost Motel, **other:** Barnes&Noble, BonTon, Grand Union Foods, JC Penney, Kohl's, Natural Foods Mkt, Sears/auto, mall, USPO, **W gas:** Exxon, Mobil, **lodging:** Sheraton, **other:** H, Advance Parts, Michael's, PetCo, Staples
13 (87)	I-189, to US 7, Burlington, **2 mi W on US 7 N gas:** Citgo, Shell, **food:** Blimpe, China Express, Dunkin Donuts, KFC, Starbucks, TGIFriday, Tommy's Grill, **lodging:** Liberty Inn, **other:** Bond Parts, Hyundai/Subaru, Kinney Drug, PriceChopper Foods, Radio Shack, Shaws Foods, TJ Maxx, **2 mi W on US 7 S gas:** Exxon, Gulf, Mobil, Sunoco, Shell, **food:** Burger King, Chicago Grill, Denny's, Friendly's, Koto Japanese, Lakeview House Rest., McDonald's, Olive Garden, Pauline's Cafe, Pizza Hut, Quizno's, Zen Garden, **lodging:** Comfort Suites, Holiday Inn Express, Rodeway Inn, **other:** Advance Parts, Audi/VW, Buick/Cadilac/GMC/Pontiac, Chevrolet, Chrysler, Dodge, Ford, Hannaford Foods, Jeep, K-Mart, Lowes Whse, Nissan, Tire Whse, Toyota/Scion, Vet
12 (84)	VT 2A, to US 2, to Essex Jct, Williston, **E gas:** Mobil/24hr, Sunoco/dsl/24hr, **food:** Chili's, Friendly's, Longhorn Steaks, 99 Rest., Ponderosa, Starbucks, **lodging:** Fairfield, TownePlace Suites, **other:** Best Buy, Hannaford Foods, Home Depot, Marshall's, Natural Provisions Mkt, Osco Drug, PetsMart, Shaws Foods, Staples, Walmart, st police, **W lodging:** Courtyard, Residence Inn
82mm	**rest area both lanes (7am-11pm), full ♿ facilities, 📞, picnic, litter barrels, vending, petwalk, WiFi**
11 (79)	US 2, to VT 117, Richmond, **E gas:** Citgo, **lodging:** Checkered House Motel, Kitchen Table Rest., **other:** repair, **W gas:** Mobil
67mm	**parking area/weigh sta sb**
66mm	**parking area/weigh sta nb**
10 (64)	VT 100, to US 2, Waterbury, **E gas:** Exxon/dsl/24hr, Mobil/dsl/24hr, **lodging:** Best Western/rest, Thatcher Brook Inn/rest., **other:** Shaws Foods/Osco Drug, TrueValue, **W gas:** Citgo, **food:** Zachary's Pizza, **other:** USPO
9 (59)	US 2, to VT 100B, Middlesex, **W food:** Red Hen Baking Co, **other:** museum, st police

WINOOSKI

BURLINGTON

INTERSTATE 89 CONT'D

N ↕ S

Exit #	Services
8 (53)	US 2, Montpelier, **1 mi E gas:** CF/gas, Citgo, Exxon/dsl, Gulf/dsl, Mobil, Sunoco/repair, **food:** La Pizzaria, Sarducci's Rest., Subway, **lodging:** Capitol Plaza Hotel, Montpelier Inn, **other:** Bond Parts, Shaw's Foods, camping (6mi), to VT Coll
7 (50)	VT 62, to US 302, Barre, **E gas:** Mobil/dsl/24hr, **food:** Applebee's, **lodging:** Comfort Suites, **other:** Honda, Shaw's Foods, Staples, **1 mi E lodging:** Hilltop Inn, **other:** H, Cadillac/GMC/Toyota, JC Penney, Jo-Ann Fabrics, camping (7mi)
6 (47)	VT 63, to VT 14, S Barre, **4 mi E** gas, food, lodging, camping, info
5 (43)	VT 64, to VT 12, VT 14, Williamstown, **6 mi E** gas/dsl, food, lodging, camping, **W** to Norwich U
41mm	highest elevation on I-89, 1752 ft
34.5mm	**rest area/weigh sta both lanes (11am-9pm), full facilities, info, phone, litter barrels, petwalk**
4 (31)	VT 66, Randolph, **E other:** RV camping (1mi), **W gas:** Mobil, **food:** McDonald's, lodging (3mi), **other:** H, RV camping (5mi)
30mm	**parking area**
3 (22)	VT 107, Bethel, **E gas:** Shell/dsl, **food:** Eaton's Rest., Village Pizza, **other:** to Jos Smith Mon (8mi), **1 mi W gas:** Citgo/dsl/LP, **other:** Rite Aid, st police, Vet
14mm	White River
2 (13)	VT 14, VT 132, Sharon, **W gas:** Gulf/dsl, Mobil, **food:** Dixie's Kitchen, Sandy's Drive Inn, **other:** Sharon Country Store, USPO, Jos Smith Mon (6mi)
9mm	**rest area/weigh sta both lanes (7am-11pm), full facilities, phone, info, picnic, litter barrels, vending, wi-fi**
7mm	White River
1 (4)	US 4, to Woodstock, Quechee, **3 mi E gas:** Irving, **lodging:** Econolodge, Hampton Inn, Holiday Inn Express, Super 8
1mm	I-91, N to St Johnsbury, S to Brattleboro
0mm	Vermont/New Hampshire state line, Connecticut River

INTERSTATE 91

N ↕ S

Exit #	Services
178mm	I-91 begins/ends., US/Canada Border, Vermont state line, US Customs
29 (177)	US 5, Derby Line, **E** Dutyfree, **1 mi W gas:** Irving/dsl, **other:** city park
176.5mm	**Welcome Ctr sb, full facilities, info, picnic, litter barrels, phone, petwalk, wi-fi, Midpoint between the Equator and N Pole**
28 (172)	US 5, VT 105, Derby Ctr, **E gas:** Citgo, Exxon/dsl/24hr, Gulf, Mobil/dsl, **food:** Cow Palace Rest., Lee Wah Chinese, Jennifer's Rest., **lodging:** Border Motel, **other:** st police, USPO, **W gas:** Gulf/dsl, Mobil/dsl, Shell/dsl/24hr, **food:** Hoagie's Pizza, McDonald's, Roaster's Cafe, Village Pizza, **lodging:** Lady Pearl's Inn, Pepin's Motel, Super 8, **other:** H, Advance Parts, Bond Parts, Chrysler/Dodge/Jeep, $Tree, Kinney Drug, Parts+, PriceChopper Foods, Rite Aid, Shaw's Foods, RV camping, st police
27 (170)	VT 191, to US 5, VT 105, Newport, **3 mi W other:** H Border Patrol, camping, info
167mm	**parking area nb, rest area/weigh sta sb**

DERBY CTR

Exit #	Services
26 (161)	US 5, VT 58, Orleans, **E gas:** Sunoco, **food:** Subway, **other:** Austin's Drugs, Cole's Mkt, Family $, Orleans Gen Store, TrueValue, camping (8mi), USPO
156.5mm	Barton River
25 (156)	VT 16, Barton, **1 mi E gas:** Gulf, Irving/dsl, **food:** Ming's Chinese, Parson's Corner Rest., **other:** Bond Parts, C&C Foods, Ford, USPO, camping (2mi), repair
154mm	**parking area nb**
150.5mm	highest elevation on I-91, 1856 ft
143mm	scenic overlook nb
141mm	**rest area sb, full facilities, info, picnic, litter barrels, phone**
24 (140)	VT 122, Wheelock, **2 mi E** gas, food, lodging
23 (137)	US 5, to VT 114, Lyndonville, **E gas:** Gulf/dsl, Mobil/Dunkin Donuts, **food:** Hoagie Pizza, McDonald's, **lodging:** Colonnade Inn, **other:** Ace Hardware, NAPA, Kinney Drug, Rite Aid, White Mkt Foods, **W lodging:** Lyndon Motel
22 (132)	to US 5, St Johnsbury, **1-2 mi E gas:** Citgo/dsl/LP, **food:** KFC/Taco Bell, Kham's Cuisine, Pizza Hut, **other:** H, Aubuchon Hardware, Bond Parts, Buick/GMC/Pontiac, Kinney Drug, PriceChopper Foods, repair, **3 mi E on US 5...gas:** Irving, **other:** Firestone, JC Penney, Radio Shack, Sears
21 (131)	US 2, to VT 15, St Johnsbury, **1-2 mi E** services
20 (129)	US 5, to US 2, St Johnsbury, **E gas:** Irving/dsl, Mobil, Shell/dsl, **food:** Anthony's Diner, Dunkin Donuts, East Garden Chinese, McDonald's, Subway, **other:** Family$, Kevin's Repair, Rite Aid, **W lodging:** Comfort Inn, **other:** st police
19 (128)	I-93 S to Littleton NH
122mm	scenic view nb
18 (121)	to US 5, Barnet, **E other:** camping (5mi), **W other:** camping (5mi)
115mm	**rest area sb**
114mm	**rest area nb**
17 (110)	US 302, to US 5, Wells River, NH, **E food:** Warner's Rest., **other:** camping (10mi), RV Ctr, **W gas:** P&H Trkstp/dsl/rest./scales/24hr, **other:** H (5mi), camping (9mi)
100mm	**nb rest area, full facilities, phone, info, picnic, litter barrels, petwalk, sb parking area/weigh sta**
16 (98)	VT 25, to US 5, Bradford, **E gas:** Mobil/dsl/LP/café, **food:** Hungry Bear Rest., **lodging:** Bradford Motel, **other:** Kinney Drug, NAPA, P&C Foods, Pierson Farm Mkt, **W** st police
15 (92)	Fairlee, **E gas:** Citgo/dsl, Gulf, Mobil/deli, Shell/dsl/LP, **food:** Subway, Your Place Rest., **other:** USPO, camping, golf
14 (84)	VT 113, to US 5, Thetford, **1 mi E other:** food, camping, **W other:** camping
13 (75)	US 5, VT 10a, Hanover, NH, **E other:** H, camping, to Dartmouth, **W** Subaru
12 (72)	US 5, White River Jct, Wilder, **E gas:** Gulf/dsl/24hr, Mobil
11 (71)	US 5, White River Jct, **E gas:** Exxon/Subway/dsl, Mobil, **food:** China Moon Cafe, Crossroads Café, McDonald's, **lodging:** Comfort Inn, Regency Inn, **other:** Ford/Lincoln/Mercury, Hyundai, Jct Mktplace, Toyota, USPO, **W gas:** Citgo, Irving/Dunkin Donuts, Lukoil, **lodging:** Comfort Suites, Econolodge,

ST JOHNSBURY

INTERSTATE 91 CONT'D

N ↕ S

Exit #	Services
11 (71)	Continued Hampton Inn, Holiday Inn Express, Super 8, **other:** [H], Nissan, Saab
10N	(70)I-89 N, to Montpelier
10S	I-89 S, to NH, ✈
68mm	**rest area/weigh sta both lanes (7am-11pm), full ♿ facilities, picnic tables, litter barrels, ☎, vending, petwalk**
9 (60)	US 5, VT 12, Hartland, **E** [H], **W gas:** Mobil (1mi), info
8 (51)	US 5, VT 12, VT 131, Ascutney, **E gas:** Citgo/dsl, Gulf/dsl, Irving, Sunoco/Dunkin Donuts/dsl, **food:** Mr. G's Rest., RedBarn Cafe, **lodging:** Yankee Village Motel, **other:** [H], USPO
7 (42)	US 5, VT 106, VT 11, Springfield, **W gas:** Irving/scales/dsl/24hr, **lodging:** Holiday Inn Express, **other:** [H] (5mi), camping
39mm	**parking area both lanes**
6 (34)	US 5, VT 103, to Bellows Falls, Rockingham, **E gas:** Shell/dsl, **food:** Leslie's Rest., **lodging:** Every Day Inn, **W gas:** Sunoco/dsl/24hr, **other:** st police (6mi)
5 (29)	VT 121, to US 5, to Bellows Falls, Westminster, **3 mi E** gas, food, ☎, lodging
24mm	**parking area both lanes**
22mm	**weigh sta sb**
20mm	parking area nb
4 (18)	US 5, Putney, **E lodging:** Putney Inn/rest., **W gas:** Sunoco/dsl/LP/24hr, **other:** camping (3mi)
3 (11)	US 5, VT 9 E, Brattleboro, **E gas:** Agway/dsl, Citgo, Mobil, Sunoco, **food:** Bickford's, China Buffet, Dunkin Donuts, Friendly's, KFC, McDonald's, 99 Rest., Pizza Hut, Steak-out Rest, Wendy's, **lodging:** Best Inn, Colonial Motel, Hampton Inn, Holiday Inn Express, Motel 6, Red Roof Inn, Super 8, **other:** Advance Parts, Chrysler/Dodge/Jeep, Consumer Parts, $Tree, Ford/Mercury, GNC, Hannaford Foods, NAPA, Pontiac/Buick/GMC, Radio Shack, Rite Aid, Staples, Subaru, True Value, U-Haul, USPO
2 (9)	VT 9 W, to rd 30, Brattleboro, **E gas:** Sunoco, **W gas:** Shell, **food:** Country Deli, VT Country Deli, **other:** to Marlboro Coll, st police
1 (7)	US 5, Brattleboro, **E gas:** Getty, Gulf/dsl, Irving/dsl, Planet/Dunkin Donuts, Shell/Subway/dsl, Sunoco, **food:** Burger King, Millenium Pizzaria, Quizno's, VT Inn Pizza, **lodging:** Econolodge, **other:** [H], PriceChopper Foods, Rite Aid, Walgreens, to Ft Dummer SP
6mm	**Welcome Ctr nb, full ♿ facilities, info, ☎, picnic tables, litter barrels, vending, petwalk, playground**
0mm	Vermont/Massachusetts state line

BRATTLEBORO

INTERSTATE 93

see New Hampshire Interstate 93.

VIRGINIA

INTERSTATE 64

E ↕ W

NORFOLK

Exit #	Services
299b a	I-264 E, to Portsmouth. **I-64 begins/ends on I-264.**
297	US 13, US 460, Military Hwy, **N gas:** 7-11/gas
296b a	US 17, to Portsmouth, **N gas:** 7-11/gas, **S gas:** BP
294mm	S Br Elizabeth River
292	VA 190, to VA 104 (from eb, no EZ return), Dominion Blvd, **S gas:** BP, Shell, **food:** Burger King, Hardee's, **other:** Family$, Food Lion, Rite Aid
291b a	I-464 N, VA 104 S, to Elizabeth City, Outer Banks, same services as 292
290b a	VA 168, Battlefield Blvd, to Nag's Head, Manteo, **N other:** K-mart, Merchant's Auto Ctr, **S gas:** BP/dsl/24hr, 7-11, Shell/Blimpie, **food:** Applebee's, Burger King, Carrabba's, Chick-fil-A, Chuck-eCheese, Dunkin Donuts, Firehouse Subs, Five Guys Burgers, Golden Corral, Grand China Buffet, Hardee's, Honey Glazed Ham, Silver Diner, Starbucks, Texas Steakhouse, TGIFriday's, Waffle House, Wendy's, Woodchick's BBQ, **lodging:** Day's Inn, Hampton Inn, Savannah Suites, Super 8, **other:** $Tree, Home Depot, Kohl's, Lowe's Whse, Sam's Club/gas,
290b a	Continued Walgreens, Walmart SuperCtr, USPO, Vet
289b a	Greenbrier Pkwy, **N gas:** BP, Citgo, 7-11/gas, Wawa, **food:** Burger King, Crazywing Cantina, Taco Bell, Subway, Wendy's, **lodging:** Cedar Tree Inn, Extended Stay, Hampton Inn, InTown Suites, Marriott, Red Roof Inn, Staybridge Suites, TownePlace Suites, Wingate Inn, **other:** Acura, BMW, Chevrolet, Cloth World, Dodge, Ford, Honda, Hyundai, Isuzu, Macy's, Mitsubishi, Pontiac, Subaru, Toyota/Acura, Volvo, U-Haul, auto repai/transmissions, Vet, **S food:**

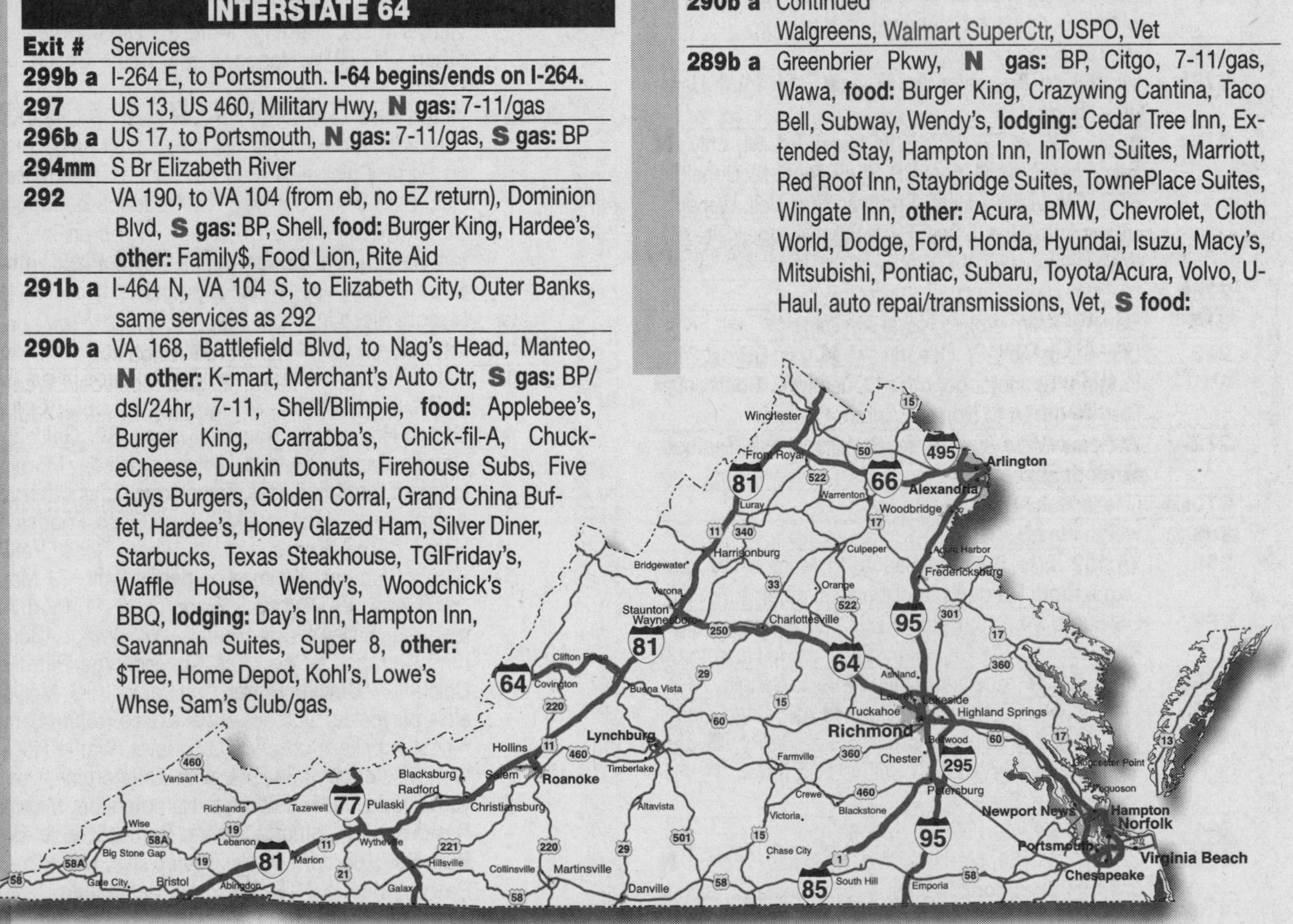

INTERSTATE 64

Exit #	Services
289b a	Continued Boston Mkt, Coldstone Creamery, Fazoli's, Fuddruckers, Jason's Deli, Joe's Crabshack, LoneStar Café, McDonald's, Old Country Buffet, Olive Garden, Panera Bread, Paradocks Grill, Ruby Tuesday, Smokey Bones BBQ, Starbucks, **lodging:** Aloha Hotel, Comfort Suites, Courtyard, Extended Stay America, Fairfield Inn, Hilton Garden, Homewood Suites, Residence Inn, Springhill Suites, Sun Suites, **other:** Barnes&Noble, Best Buy, Dillard's, $General, Food Lion, Harris Teeter, Macy's, Marshall's, Michael's, Office Depot, Old Navy, Ross, Sears/auto, Steinmart, Target, TJ Maxx, mall
286b a	Indian River Rd, **N gas:** BP/dsl, Hess/dsl, RaceCo/dsl, Shell, Texaco, **food:** Hardee's, **S gas:** Sunoco/dsl, **food:** Capt D's, Shoney's, Top's China, Waffle House, **lodging:** Founder's Inn, **other:** 7-11
285	E Branch Elizabeth River
284a	I-264, to Norfolk, to VA Beach (exits left from eb)
284b	Newtown Rd
282	US 13, Northampton Blvd, **N lodging:** Quality Inn, Sleep Inn, **other:** to Chesapeake Bay Br Tunnel
281	VA 165, Military Hwy (no EZ eb return), **N gas:** Shell/dsl/24hr, **lodging:** Econolodge, **other:** Aamco, **S food:** Max&Erma's, **lodging:** Hampton Inn, Hilton, Holiday Inn Select, Ramada, Residence Inn, **other:** Firestone/auto
279	Norview Ave, **N gas:** Shell, **food:** Golden Corral, Pizza Hut, Wendy's, **other:** $General, Food Lion, K-Mart/gas, to ✈ & botannical garden
278	VA 194 S (no EZ return)
277b a	VA 168, to Tidewater Dr, **N gas:** 7-11, **food:** Hardee's, **S gas:** BP
276c	to US 460 W, VA 165, Little Creek Rd, wb only, **N gas:** Flag Gas, **S gas:** BP, Shell, **food:** McDonald's, KFC, Old Virginia Ham, Subway, Taco Bell, Wendy's, **other:** AutoZone, $Tree, Farm Fresh, Kroger, Rite Aid, Walgreens
276b a	I-564 to Naval Base
274	Bay Ave (from wb), to Naval Air Sta
273	US 60, 4th View St, Oceanview, **N gas:** BP/dsl/24hr, **lodging:** Econolodge, **other:** Oceanview Boathouse/Pier, **S other:** to Norfolk Visitors Ctr, info
272	W Ocean View Ave, **N food:** Willoughby's Seafood, **S food:** Sunset Grill
270mm	Chesapeake Bay Tunnel
269mm	**weigh sta eb**
268	VA 169 E, to Buckroe Beach, Ft Monroe, **N gas:** Citgo, **food:** Hardee's, McDonald's, **other:** to VA Ctr
267	US 60, to VA 143, Settlers Ldg Rd, **S food:** Burger King, Golden City Chinese, **other:** [H], to Hampton U
265c	(from eb), **N other:** Armistead Ave, to Langley AFB
265b a	VA 134, VA 167, to La Salle Ave, **N gas:** Citgo, RaceWay, **lodging:** Super 8, **other:** Home Depot, **S gas:** BP, **food:** McDonald's, KFC/Taco Bell, **other:** [H], Advance Parts, Family$
264	I-664, to Newport News, Suffolk
263b a	US 258, VA 134, Mercury Blvd, to James River Br, **N gas:** BP, Shell, **food:** Applebee's, Bennigan's, Blimpie, Boston Mkt, Burger King, Chick-fil-A, Chili's,

HAMPTON

Exit #	Services
263b a	Continued Denny's, Dunkin Donuts, Golden Corral, Hooters, IHOP, KFC, McDonald's, New Garden Buffet, Olive Garden, Outback Steaks, Pizza Hut, Quizno's, Rally's, Red Lobster, Rockola Café, Schlotzky's, Steak&Ale, Taco Bell, Waffle House, Wendy's, **lodging:** Clarion, Comfort Inn, Courtyard, Day's Inn, Embassy Suites, Fairfield Inn, Holiday Inn, Quality Inn, Red Roof Inn, **other:** Chevrolet/Mazda, Chrysler/Jeep, $Tree, Ford, Goodyear/auto, JC Penney, Jo-Anne, Macy's, Mazda, NAPA, Office Depot, Target, U-Haul, Volvo, USPO, Walmart SuperCtr/24hr, **S gas:** BJ's Whse, Citgo/dsl, Miller's Gas, **food:** Cracker Barrel, Lone Star Steaks, Pizza Hut, Sonic, Texas Steaks, Waffle House, **lodging:** Best Western, Econolodge, Hampton Bay Suites, Hilton Garden, Interstate Inn, La Quinta, Savannah Suites, Springhill Suites, **other:** Advance Parts, BassPro Shop, BigLots, $General, Firestone/auto, Lowe's Whse, PepBoys, Radio Shack, Toyota
262	VA 134, Magruder Blvd (from wb, no EZ return), **N gas:** Exxon, 7-11/gas, **other:** Dodge/Acura
261b a	Center Pkwy, to Hampton Roads, **S gas:** Shell, Zooms, **food:** Azteca Mexican, ChuckeCheese, McDonald's, Peking Chinese, Pizza Hut/Taco Bell, Ruby Tuesday, Subway, **other:** BooksAMillion, $Tree, FarmFresh Foods, FoodLion, Rite Aid, TJMaxx
258b a	US 17, J Clyde Morris Blvd, **N gas:** BP, Shell/dsl, **food:** Chatfield's Grill, Domino's, New China, Waffle House, **lodging:** BudgetLodge, Country Inn & Suites, Holiday Inn, Host Inn, PointPlaza Hotel, Super 8, **other:** Advance Parts, Food Lion, 7-11/24hr, **S gas:** BP, Citgo/dsl/24hr, WaWa, **food:** Angelo's Steaks, Burger King, DQ, KFC, Starbucks, Subway, Taco Bell/KFC, Vinny's Pizza, **lodging:** Motel 6, Omni Hotel/rest., **other:** [H], BMW/Honda, $Tree, Radio Shack, museum
256b a	Victory Blvd, Oyster Point Rd, **N gas:** BP, Citgo/Kangaroo/dsl, **food:** Arby's, Blimpie, Burger King, Chicago Pizza, Chick-fil-A, Fuddrucker's, Hardee's, Pizza Hut, Starbucks, Subway, TX Roadhouse, **lodging:** CandleWood Suites, Courtyard, Hampton Inn, Hilton Garden, Staybridge Suites, TownePlace, **other:** $Tree, K-Mart, Kroger, **S lodging:** Crestwood Suites, Mariott, Sleep Inn
255b a	VA 143, to Jefferson Ave, **N gas:** Shell/dsl, **food:** Castle Italian, Chilli's, FarmFresh Foods, Red City Buffet, Red Lobster, Smokey Bones BBQ, Golden Corral, Hooters, McDonald's, Moe's SW Grill, Olive Garden, Panera Bread, Silver Diner, Tuesday Morning, **lodging:** Comfort Suites, Travelodge (2mi), **other:** [H] Acura, Buick/Cadillac/GMC, FarmFresh Foods/deli, Home Depot, Kohl's, Lowe's Whse, Ross, PetCo, Sam's Club/gas, Walmart SuperCtr/24hr, TJ Maxx, ✈, **S gas:** BP, Citgo/dsl, Exxon/dsl, 7-11, **food:** Applebee's, Bailey's Grill, Buffalo Wild Wings, Burger King, Carrabba's, Cheddar's, Cheeseburger Paradise, Chick-fil-A, Cracker Barrel, Don Pablo, KFC, McDonald's/playpalce, Outback Steaks, Red Robin, Samurai, Starbucks, Subway, TGIFriday's, Waffle House, Wendy's, **lodging:** Best Western, Comfort Inn, Courtyard, Day's Inn, Econolodge, Hampton Inn, Microtel, Residence Inn, Studio+, **other:** Barnes&Noble, Best Buy, Belk, Borders Book, Costco/gas, Dillard's, JC Penney, Macy's, NTB, PetsMart, Sears/auto, Target, World Mkt, mall

E ↕ W

INTERSTATE 64 CONT'D

Exit #	Services
250b a	to US Army Trans Museum, **N gas:** BP/dsl, Dodge's Gas, Exxon/dsl, 7-11/gas, Sunoco, **food:** China Dragon, Hardee's, **other:** B&L Auto Repair, $Green, Newport News Campground/Park (1mi), to Yorktown Victory Ctr, Vet, **S gas:** RaceTrac, **food:** McDonald's, Taco Bell, Wendy's, **lodging:** Ft Eustis Inn, Holiday Inn Express, Mulberry Inn, TDY Inn
247	VA 143, to VA 238 (no EZ return wb), **N gas:** Citgo, 7-11/gas, **other:** to Yorktown, **S other:** to Jamestown Settlement
243	VA 143, to Williamsburg, exits left from wb, **S** same as 242a
242b a	VA 199, to US 60, to Williamsburg, **N lodging:** Day's Hotel/rest., **other:** Best Buy, JC Penney, Kohl's, Target, water funpark, to Yorktown NHS, **1 mi S gas:** 7-11/gas, **food:** Starbucks, Subway, Wendy's, Burger King, LJ Silver, McDonald's, Wendy's, **lodging:** Country Inn & Suites, Courtyard, Marriott/rest., Quality Inn, Rodeway Inn, **other:** 1st Settlers Camping, to William&Mary Coll, Busch Gardens, to Jamestown NHS
238	VA 143, to Colonial Williamsburg, Camp Peary, **2-3 mi S on US 60...gas:** 7-11/gas, Shell, Texaco, Zooms, **food:** Chicago Grill, Cracker Barrel, DQ, Golden Corral, Hooter's, IHOP, McDonald's, Mirabella's Pizza, Pizza Hut, Sal's Rest., The Gazebo Pancakes, **lodging:** Comfort Inn, Country Inn & Suites, Day's Inn, Econolodge, Embassy Suites, Fairfield Inn, Hampton Inn, Holiday Inn/rest., Homewood Suites, La Quinta, Quality Inn/rest., Ramada, Sleep Inn, Travelodge, **other:** H, Anvil Camping (4mi), K-Mart
234	VA 646, to Lightfoot, **1-2 mi N other:** KOA, **2-3 mi S gas:** BP/dsl, Exxon/dsl, Shell/dsl, **food:** Burger King, Chick-fil-A, Hardee's, IHOP, KFC, McDonald's, Pierce's BBQ, Sonic, Starbucks, Subway, **lodging:** Day's Inn, Greatwolf Lodge, Quality Inn, **other:** Ford/Lincoln/Mercury, Go-Carts+, Home Depot, Lowe's Whse, PetCo, Pottery Camping (3mi), Radio Shack, Ross, Ukrops Foods, Walmart SuperCtr/24hr
231b a	VA 607, to Norge, Croaker, **N gas:** 7-11/gas, **other:** to York River SP, **1-2 mi S on US 60...gas:** Shell/dsl, **food:** FarmFresh Deli/gas, Candle Light Rest., Wendy's, **lodging:** Econolodge, **other:** American Heritage RV Park, Dodge, Doll Factory, Honda, Hyundai, Vet
227	VA 30, to US 60, to West Point, Toano, **S gas:** BP/dsl, Shell/Stuckey's/dsl, **food:** Big South Rest., McDonald's
220	VA 33 E, to West Point, **N gas:** Exxon/dsl
214	VA 155, to New Kent, Providence Forge, **S gas:** Exxon/DQ/dsl, **food:** Antonio's Pizza, Tops China, **other:** Colonial Downs Racetrack, Rockahock Camping (8mi)
213mm	**rest area both lanes, full ♿ facilities, ☎, vending, picnic, litter barrels, petwalk**
211	VA 106, to Talleysville, to James River Plantations, **S gas:** Pilot/Subway/dsl/scales/24hr
205	VA 33, VA 249, to US 60, Bottoms Bridge, Quinton, **N gas:** Exxon/dsl, Valero, **food:** Pearl City Chinese, Subway, **other:** Food Lion, Rite Aid, USPO, **S gas:**

WILLIAMSBURG

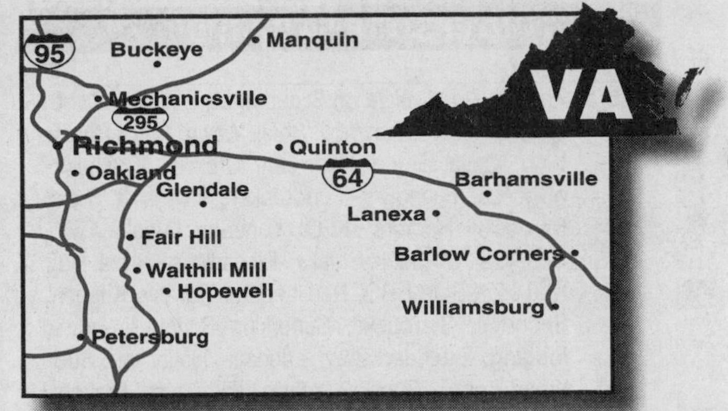

205	Continued FasMart, Shell/dsl, **food:** McDonald's, Prima Pizza, **lodging:** Star Motel (3mi)
204mm	Chickahominy River
203mm	**weigh sta both lanes**
200	I-295, N to Washington, S to Rocky Mount, to US 60
197b a	VA 156, Airport Dr, to Highland Springs, **N gas:** 7-11/gas, Shell/dsl, Valero, **food:** Domino's, Hardee's, Subway, Tops China, **other:** Advance Parts, CVS Drug, Farmers Foods, **S gas:** BP, Citgo/dsl, East Coast/dsl, 7-11/gas, Wawa, **food:** Arby's, Aunt Sarah's, Burger King, Chicago Pizza, Pizza Hut, Waffle House, **lodging:** Best Value, Clarion, Courtyard, Day's Inn, Econolodge, Hampton Inn, Hilton Garden, Holiday Inn, Homewood Suites, Microtel, Motel 6, Red Roof Inn, Super 8, Wingate Inn, **other:** to ✈
195	Laburnum Ave, **N gas:** Chevron, Shell, **other:** repair, **S gas:** BP/24hr, Exxon, 7-11/gas, **food:** Applebee's, Burger King, Capt D's, Chick-fil-A, Chinese Buffet, Cici's Pizza, Firehouse Subs, Hardee's, KFC, Longhorn Steaks, McDonald's, Papa John's, Qdoba Mexican, Red Lobster, Starbucks, Steak&Shake, Subway, Taco Bell, TGIFriday, Wendy's, **lodging:** Airport Inn, Hyatt, Wyndham Garden, **other:** Books-A-Million, CarQuest, CVS Drug, $Tree, Ford, JC Penney, Kroger, Lowe's, PetsMart, Radio Shack, Sam's Club/gas, Target, Ukrops Foods, Walgreens
193b a	VA 33, Nine Mile Rd, **N gas:** Exxon/Subway, **food:** McDonald's (2mi), **S** H
192	US 360, to Mechanicsville, **N gas:** Chevron, Citgo/dsl, **food:** McDonald's, **S gas:** BP, Citgo, **food:** Church's
190	I-95 S, to Petersburg, 5th St, **N other:** Richmond Nat Bfd Park, **S lodging:** Marriott, **other:** st capitol, coliseum.

I-64 W and I-95 N run together. See Virginia Interstate 95, exits 76-78.

187	I-95 N (exits left from eb), to Washington.
186	I-195, to Powhite Pkwy, from wb, Richmond
185b a	US 33, Staples Mill Rd, Dickens Rd
183c	from wb, US 250 W, Broad St, Glenside Dr N, same as exit 183
183	US 250, Broad St E, Glenside Dr S., **N gas:** Chevron, **food:** Bob Evans, Buffalo Wild Wings, Famous Dave's, Olive Garden, TGIFriday, Waffle House, **lodging:** Best Western, Embassy Suites, **other:** Dodge, Honda, Hyundai, K-Mart, Volvo, same as 181, **S other:** H, to U of Richmond

RICHMOND

E ↕ W RICHMOND

INTERSTATE 64 CONT'D

Exit #	Services
181b a	Parham Rd, **2 mi N on Broad...gas:** BP/24hr, Citgo, Exxon, Hess, Sheetz/dsl, Shell, Wawa, **food:** Burger King, Casa Grande Mexican, Chick-fil-A, Chuck-eCheese, Friendly's, Fuddruckers, Gyros & Subs, Hardee's, Hooters, KFC, LoneStar Steaks, Mc-Donald's, Outback Steaks, Piccadilly's, Pizza Hut, Red Hot&Blue BBQ, Red Lobster, Sarah's Kitchen, Shoney's, Starbucks, Superking Buffet, Wendy's, **lodging:** Extended Stay America, Quality Inn, Sub-urban Lodge, Super 8, **other:** H, Acura, BigLots, BooksAMillion, CVS Drug, $General, Ford/Lincoln/ Mercury, Hancock Fabrics, Honda/Mitsubishi, Infiniti, Lowe's, Lincoln/Mercury, Mazda/BMW, Mercedes, Napa, PepBoys, Subaru, Staples, TJ Maxx, Toyota, Walgreens, Ukrops Foods, transmissions, tires
180	Gaskins Rd, **N gas:** BP/24hr, East Coast, Shell/dsl, **food:** Cracker Barrel, Starbucks, **lodging:** Courtyard, Fairfield Inn, Holiday Inn Express, Residence Inn, Springhill Suites, Studio+, **other:** Goodyear, Kroger, **N on Broad...food:** Applebee's, Arby's, Boston Mkt, Burger King, Golden Corral, IHOP, KFC, McDonald's, O'Charley's, Pizza Hut, Qdoba Mexican, Ruby Tues-day's, Subway, Taco Bell, Tripp's Rest., Wendy's, **other:** BMW/Mini, Borders Books, Cadillac, Chrysler/ Jeep, Costso/gas, Costco, $Tree, Goodyear/auto, Lowe's Whse, Michael's, Office Depot, Sam's Club, VW, mall
178b a	US 250, Short Pump, **N gas:** Citgo, Exxon/dsl, 7-11, **food:** Capitol Ale House, Chipotle Mexican, DQ, Fire-house Subs, Five Guys Burgers, Leonardo's Pizza, Moe's SW Grill, Panera Bread, Starbucks, **lodging:** Comfort Suites, Courtyard, Hampton Inn, Hilton Gar-den, Hyatt Place, **other:** CarMax, Firestone/auto, Ford, Hagen Daaz, **1 mi S gas:** BP, Citgo, 7-11/gas, Shell, Valero, **food:** Arby's, Bertucci's, Burger King, Cheese-cake Factory, Chick-fil-A, Chilli's, Chipotle Mexican, Kanpai, KFC, Longhorn Steaks, McDonald's/play-place, Mexico Rest., Red Robin, Taco Bell, TGIFri-day, Wendy's, **lodging:** Candlewood Suites, **other:** Barnes&Noble, Best Buy, CarQuest, Chevrolet/Ponti-ac/GMC, Goodyear/auto, Home Depot, Kohl's, Krog-er, Lowe's Whse, Nissan, Nordstrom, PetCo, Target, Ukrop's Foods, Walmart SuperCtr/24hr, World Mkt
177	I-295, to I-95 N to Washington, to Norfolk, VA Beach, Williamsburg
175	VA 288
173	VA 623, to Rockville, Manakin, **S gas:** Citgo/dsl, Valero, **food:** Manakin Grill, **other:** $General, Food Lion
169mm	**rest area both lanes, full ♿ facilities, vending, ☎, ⛱, litter barrels, petwalk**
167	VA 617, to Goochland, Oilville, **N gas:** Exxon/dsl, **S gas:** BP/Bullets/dsl/24hr
159	US 522, to Goochland, Gum Spring, **N gas:** Exxon/ dsl, **S gas:** BP/DQ/dsl, Citgo
152	VA 629, Hadensville, **S gas:** BP (1mi)
148	VA 605, Shannon Hill
143	VA 208, to Louisa, Ferncliff, **7 mi N other:** Small Country Camping, **S gas:** Citgo/dsl, Exxon/dsl
136	US 15, to Gordonsville, Zion Crossroads, **S lodging:** Best Western, **other:** Lowe's, **S gas:** BP/McDon-ald's/dsl/24hr, Citgo/Blimpie/dsl, Exxon/Burger King/ dsl, **food:** Crescent Rest.
129	VA 616, Keswick, Boyd Tavern, **S gas:** Citgo
124	US 250, to Shadwell, **2 mi N gas:** BP, Exxon, Liberty, **food:** Applebees, Aunt Sarah's, Burger King, Guada-lajara Mexican, McDonald's, Ponderosa, Quizno's, Starbucks, Taco Bell, Topeka's Steaks, Wendy's, **lodging:** Hilton Garden, Town&Country Motel, White House Motel, **other:** H, Audi, CarMax, Ford, Giant Foods, Kia, Rite Aid, **S lodging:** Comfort Inn
123mm	Rivanna River
121	VA 20, to Charlottesville, Scottsville, **N gas:** BP/ Blimpie/dsl, **other:** H, **S other:** KOA (10mi), to Monticello
120	VA 631, 5th St, to Charlottesville, **N gas:** Exxon/dsl, Shell, **food:** Amigo's Mexican, Burger King, Domino's, Hardee's, Jade Garden, McDonald's, Pizza Hut/Taco Bell, Waffle House, Wendy's, **lodging:** Hampton Inn (2mi), Holiday Inn, Omni Hotel (2mi), Sleep Inn, **other:** CVS Drug, Family$, Food Lion
118b a	US 29, to Lynchburg, Charlottesville, **1-4 mi N gas:** BP, Citgo/dsl, Exxon, Shell, **food:** Blimpie, Hardee's, Subway, **lodging:** Best Western, Boar's Head Inn, Budget Inn, Comfort Inn, Econolodge, **other:** H, UVA
114	VA 637, to Ivy
113mm	**rest area wb, full ♿ facilities, ☎, vending, ⛱, litter barrels, petwalk**
111mm	Mechum River
108mm	Stockton Creek
107	US 250, Crozet, **1 mi N gas:** Exxon, Shell/dsl, 1 mi **S other:** Misty Mtn Camping
105mm	**rest area eb, full ♿ facilities, ☎, vending, ⛱, litter barrels, petwalk**
104mm	scenic area eb, litter barrels, no truck or buses
100mm	scenic area eb, litter barrels, hist marker, no trucks or buses
99	US 250, to Waynesboro, Afton, **N lodging:** Colony Motel, **other:** to Shenandoah NP, Skyline Drive, ski area, to Blue Ridge Pkwy, **S lodging:** Afton Inn
96	VA 622, to Lyndhurst, Waynesboro, **3 mi N gas:** Shell, **food:** Tastee Freez **lodging:** Quality Inn, **other:** Waynesboro Camping
95mm	South River
94	US 340, to Stuarts Draft, Waynesboro, **N gas:** Exx-on/dsl, 7-11/dsl, **food:** Applebee's, Arby's, Burger King, Cracker Barrel, Fosters Grille, Giovanni's Pizza, Jack's Rest., KFC, Quizno's, Ruby Tuesday, Shoney's, Sonic, South River Rest., Taco Bell (1mi), Starbucks, Wendy's, **lodging:** Best Western, Comfort Inn, Day's Inn, Holiday Inn Express, Residence Inn, Super 8, **other:** H, Home Depot, Lowe's, Martin's Food/Drug, Radio Shack, Waynesboro N 340 Camp-ing (9mi), Walmart SuperCtr, **S gas:** Shell/dsl, **other:** Kohl's, PetsMart, Ross, Target, Waynesboro Outlet Village, museum
91	Va 608, to Stuarts Draft, Fishersville, **N gas:** Shell/ Dunkin Donuts/dsl, **food:** Subway, **lodging:** Hampton Inn, **other:** H, **S gas:** Exxon/McDonald's, Sheetz/ dsl, **other:** Shenadoah Acres Camping (8mi), Walnut Hills Camping (9mi)

INTERSTATE 64 CONT'D

Exit #	Services
89mm	Christians Creek
87	I-81, N to Harrisonburg, S to Roanoke
I-64 and I-81 run together 20 miles. See Interstate 81 exits 220-195.	
220 {I-81}	VA 262, to US 11, Staunton, **1 mi S gas:** BP, Citgo, Exxon, Shell, **food:** Applebee's, Arby's, Burger King, Country Cookin', KFC, McDonald's, Red Lobster, **lodging:** Budget Inn, Hampton Inn, **other:** Advance Parts, Belk, Books A Million, Buick/Pontiac/GMC, Chrysler, CVS Drug, $Tree, Ford/Lincoln/Mercury, Harley-Davidson, Honda, Hyundai, JC Penney, Jeep/Dodge, Merchant's Tire/auto, Nissan, Rule RV Ctr, VW
217 {I-81}	VA 654, to Mint Spring, Stuarts Draft, **N gas:** BP/Subway/dsl, Exxon/dsl, **lodging:** Day's Inn, **S gas:** Citgo/Stuckey's/dsl/24hr, Liberty, **lodging:** Relax Inn, Walnut Hill Camping (3mi)
213ba {I-81}	US 11, US 340, Greenville, **N gas:** BP/Subway, Pilot/Arby's/scales/dsl/24hr, Shell, **food:** Edelweiss Rest., **lodging:** Budget Host
205 {I-81}	VA 606, Raphine, **N gas:** Exxon/Burger King, Smiley's/BBQ/dsl/24hr, Whites/dsl/24hr/motel/@, **S gas:** Wilco/Hess/Wendy's/dsl/scales/24hr, **lodging:** Day's Inn/rest. **other:** Koogler RV Ctr
200 {I-81}	VA 710, Fairfield, **N gas:** BP/McDonald's/dsl/24hr, Texaco, **S gas:** Exxon/Subway/dsl, Shell/dsl
199mm {I-81}	**rest area sb, full [handicapped] facilities, [phone], vending, [picnic], litter barrels, petwalk**
195 {I-81}	US 11, Lee Highway, **N lodging:** Maple Hall Lodging/dining, **S gas:** Citgo/dsl/24hr, Shell/dsl, **food:** Aunt Sarah's, **lodging:** Best Value, Days Inn, Howard Johnson/rest., **other:** Lee-Hi Camping
I-64 and I-81 run together 20 miles. See Interstate 81 exits 195-220.	
55	US 11, to VA 39, **N gas:** Exxon, **food:** Burger King, Crystal Chinese, Naples Pizza, Ruby Tuesday, Waffle House, **lodging:** Best Western, Sleep Inn, Super 8, Wingate Inn, **other:** $Tree, Radio Shack, Stonewall Jackson Museum, Lowe's, Walmart SuperCtr, **S gas:** BP/DQ, Texaco/Subway, **food:** Country Cookin', Redwood Rest., **lodging:** Country Inn & Suites, Econolodge, Holiday Inn Express
50	US 60, VA 623, to Lexington, **3 mi S lodging:** Day's Inn
43	VA 780, to Goshen
35	VA 269, VA 850, Longdale Furnace
33mm	**truck rest area eb**
29	VA 269, VA 850, **S gas:** Citgo/dsl/rest.
27	US 60 W, US 220 S, VA 629, Clifton Forge, **N other:** to Douthat SP, **S gas:** BP, Citgo/dsl, Exxon, **food:** Pizza Hut, **other:** Alleghany Highlands Arts/crafts
24	US 60, US 220, Clifton Forge, **1 mi S gas:** Shell/dsl, **food:** DQ, Hardee's
21	to VA 696, Low Moor, **S gas:** Exxon, **food:** Quizno's, **other:** [H]
16	US 60 W, US 220 N, to Hot Springs, Covington, **N gas:** BP, Exxon, Shell, Texaco, **food:** Belly-up Cafe, Cucci's, Starbucks, Western Sizzlin, **lodging:** Best Value Inn, Best Western, Holiday Inn Express, Pinhurst Hotel, **other:** to ski area, **S food:** McDonald's, **lodging:** Compare Inn, **other:** K-Mart
14	VA 154, to Hot Springs, Covington, **N gas:** Exxon/Arby's, Sunoco, **food:** Hong Kong Chinese, KFC, Little Caesar's, LJ Silver, Subway, Wendy's,

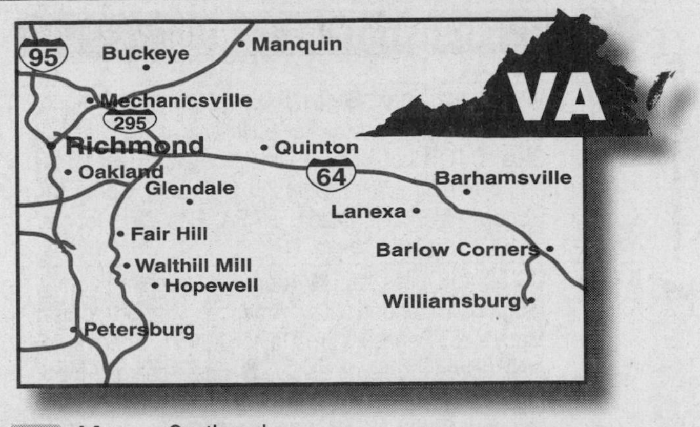

Exit #	Services
14	Continued **lodging:** Budget Motel, **other:** Advance Parts, AutoZone, CVS Drug, Family$, Food Lion, **S food:** Applebee's, China House, Mama Pizza, **other:** $Tree, Walmart SuperCtr/24hr
10	US 60 E, VA 159 S, Callaghan, **S gas:** Marathon/dsl/LP
7	VA 661
2.5mm	**Welcome Ctr eb, full [handicapped] facilities, [phone], [picnic], litter barrels, petwalk**
1	Jerry's Run Trail, **N** to Allegheny Trail
0mm	Virginia/West Virginia state line

INTERSTATE 66

Exit #	Services
77mm	Independence Ave, to Lincoln Mem. I-66 begins/ends in Washington, DC.
76mm	Potomac River, T Roosevelt Memorial Bridge
75	US 50 W (from eb), to Arlington Blvd, G Wash Pkwy, I-395, US 1, **S** Iwo Jima Mon
73	US 29, Lee Hwy, Key Bridge, to Rosslyn, **N lodging:** Marriott, **S lodging:** Holiday Inn
72	to US 29, Lee Hwy, Spout Run Pkwy (from eb, no EZ return), **N gas:** Shell, **lodging:** Virginia Inn, **S food:** Starbucks, Tarbouch Grill, **other:** CVS Drug, Starbucks, Giant Foods, Rite Aid
71	VA 120, Glebe Rd (no EZ return from wb), **N** [H], **S gas:** Sunoco, **food:** Booeymonger Grill, IHOP, Melting Pot, PF Chang's, **lodging:** Comfort Inn, Holiday Inn
69	US 29, Sycamore St, Falls Church, **N gas:** Exxon, **S lodging:** Econolodge
68	Westmoreland St (from eb), same as 69
67	to I-495 N (from wb), to Baltimore, Dulles [airport]
66	VA 7, Leesburg Pike, to Tysons Corner, Falls Church, **N gas:** Exxon, Sunoco, **food:** China King, Honeybaked Ham, Jason's Deli, Ledo's Pizza, Olive Garden (2mi), Starbucks, Tara Thai, **other:** Whole Foods Mkt, **S gas:** Citgo, **food:** Chicken Out, LJ Silver, McDonald's, Starbucks, Taco Bell, **other:** Giant Foods, GNC, Volvo, Vet
64b a	I-495 S, to Richmond
62	VA 243, Nutley St, to Vienna, **S gas:** Chevron, **other:** CVS Drug, Michael's, Safeway Foods, **1 mi S on Lee Hwy gas:** Citgo, Shell, Sunoco/dsl, **food:** Dunkin Donuts, IHOP/24hr, McDonald's, Up-Town Grill, **lodging:** Econolodge, **other:** Advance Parts, Harley-Davidson, Home Depot, Jeep, Radio Shack, 7-11, Subaru,

INTERSTATE 66 CONT'D

E ↕ W

Exit #	Services
60	VA 123, to Fairfax, **S gas:** Exxon, Shell/24hr, Sunoco, **food:** Denny's, Fuddrucker's, Hooters, KFC, Outback Steaks, Red Lobster, 29 Diner, **lodging:** Best Western, **other:** Chevrolet, Chrysler, CVS Drug, Goodyear, Honda, Hyundai, Mazda, NAPA, Rite Aid, Toyota/Scion, to George Mason U
57a b	US 50, to Dulles ✈, **N food:** Cheesecake Factory, **lodging:** Extended Stay America, Marriott, **other:** Macy's, JC Penney, Lord&Taylor, Macy's, Sears/auto, mall, access to same as 55, **S gas:** Shell/dsl, **food:** McDonald's, Ruby Tuesday, Wendy's, **lodging:** Candlewood Suites, Comfort Inn/rest., Courtyard, **other:** Goodyear/auto, K-Mart, Giant Foods, NRA Museum
55	Fairfax Co Pkwy, to US 29, **N** 4 Lakes Mall, **gas:** Exxon, Sunoco, **food:** Applebees, Blue Iguana Café, Burger King, Cantina Italiana, Cooker Rest., Joe's Crabshack, Logan's Roadhouse, Malibu Grill, Olive Garden, Pizza Hut/Taco Bell, Red Robin, Sakura Japanese, Starbucks, Wendy's, **lodging:** Hyatt Hotel, Residence Inn, **other:** H, Best Buy, BJ's Whse, Bloom's Foods, GNC, Kohl's, Michael's, PetsMart, Radio Shack, Target, Walmart, Whole Foods Mkt, World Mkt
53b a	VA 28, to Centreville, Dulles ✈, Manassas Museum, **S** same as 52
52	US 29, to Bull Run Park, Centreville, **N gas:** Mobil, **other:** Bull Run Park/RV Dump, Goodyear/auto, **S gas:** Exxon, Sunoco, **food:** Austin Grill, Carrabba's, Domino's, Panda Express, Quizno's, Red Rock King Grille, Ruby Tuesday, Wendy's, **other:** SpringHill Suites, **other:** CVS Drug, Giant Foods, Grand Mart, Jo-Ann Fabrics, Shoppers Foods, same as 53
49mm	**rest area both lanes, full ♿ facilities, ☎, ⛱, litter barrels, petwalk**
47b a	VA 234, to Manassas, **N gas:** Shell/dsl, **food:** Cracker Barrel, 5 Guys Burgers, Golden Corral, Jerry's Subs, Uno Pizzaria, Wendy's, **lodging:** Country Inn&Suites, Courtyard, Fairfield Inn, Sheraton, **other:** Borders, Kohl's, Old Navy, Manassas Nat Bfd, **S gas:** BP, Exxon, Hess, RaceWay/dsl/24hr, Shell/repair, 7-11, Sunoco/24hr, **food:** Arby's, Backyard Grill, Baja Fresh, Bob Evans, Burger King, Casa Chimayo, Checker's, Chili's, China Jade, Chipotle Mexican, Coldstone Creamery, Denny's, Domino's, Don Pablo's, El Tolteca, Foster's Grill, Great American Buffet, Hooters, KFC, Logan's Roadhouse, McDonald's, Olive Garden, Panera Bread, Papa John's, Pizza Hut, Popeye's, Potbelly's, Red Hot&Blue BBQ, Red Lobster, Ruby Tuesday, Shoney's, Starbucks, Subway, Taco Bell, TGIFriday, Wendy's, Wok'n Roll, **lodging:** Best Western, Comfort Suites, Hampton Inn, Holiday Inn, Quality Inn, Red Roof Inn, Residence Inn, Super 8, **other:** Aamco, Advance Parts, AutoZone, Barnes&Noble, Best Buy, Bottom$ Foods, Buick/GMC/Pontiac, Burlington Coats, Camping World RV Service/supples/Reines RV Ctr, Costco/gas, CVS Drug, Chevrolet, Family$, Giant Foods, Macy's, Home Depot, Honda, JC Penney, Jo-Ann Fabrics, K-Mart, Lowes Whse, Marshall's, Merchant Auto Ctr, Michael's, NTB, Office Depot, PepBoys, PetCo, Ross, Sears/auto, Shopper's Foods, Staples, Target, Toyota, Tuesday Morning, U-Haul, Walmart, Vet
44	VA 234, Manassas
43b a	US 29, to Warrenton, Gainesville, **N gas:** WaWa, **S gas:** 7-11, Sunoco, **food:** Burger King, Chick-fil-A, Chili's, Coldstone Creamery, Domino's, 5 Guys Burgers, Joe's Italian/pizza, KFC/Pizza Hut/Taco Bell, McDonald's, Mimi's Cafe, Papa Johns, PeiWei, Qdoba, Steakmaster's Grill, Subway, Wendy's, lodging Hampton Inn, **other:** Best Buy, Giant Foods/drug, GNC, Goodyear/auto, Lowes Whse, PetsMart, Target/foods, Walgreens, World Mkt
40	US 15, Haymarket, **N other:** Greenville Farm Camping, **S gas:** Sheetz/dsl/24hr, **food:** Guiseppe's Italian, McDonald's, Papa John's, Subway, **other:** Bloom Foods, Home Depot, Safeway Foods
31	VA 245, to Old Tavern, **1 mi N gas:** BP/dsl
28	US 17 S, Marshall, **N gas:** BP/McDonald's/dsl, 7-11, **food:** Anthony's Pizza, Foster's Grille, Great Wall Chinese, Subway, **other:** H, Bloom Foods, Radio Shack, Vet
27	VA 55 E, VA 647, Marshall, **1 mi N gas:** Chevron/dsl/LP, Citgo, **food:** Marshall Diner, **other:** IGA Foods
23	US 17 N, VA 55, Delaplane (no eb re-entry)
20mm	Goose Creek
18	VA 688, Markham
13	VA 79, to VA 55, Linden, Front Royal, **S gas:** Exxon/dsl/24hr, Shell, **food:** Applehouse Rest., **other:** to Shenandoah NP, Skyline Drive
11mm	Manassas Run
7mm	Shenandoah River
6	US 340, US 522, to Winchester, Front Royal, **N gas:** Quarle's/Bullet's/dsl, 7-11, **food:** Applebees, Checkers, Cracker Barrel, Ledo's Pizza, Los Potrollo's, Panda Express, Quizno's, Starbucks, TGIFriday, **other:** Buick/GMC/Pontiac, Ford, GNC, Lowes Whse, Staples, Target, Walmart SuperCtr, **S gas:** Exxon/Dunkin Donuts, 7-11, Shell, **food:** McDonald's, **lodging:** Hampton Inn, **other:** Southfork Camping (2mi)
1b a	I-81, N to Winchester, S to Roanoke
0mm	I-66 begins/ends on I-81, exit 300.

MANASSAS

INTERSTATE 77

N ↕ S

Exit #	Services
67mm	Virginia/West Virginia state line, East River Mtn
66	VA 598, to East River Mtn
64	US 52, VA 61, to Rocky Gap
62	VA 606, to South Gap
62mm	**Welcome Ctr sb, full ♿ facilities, info, ☎, vending, ⛱, litter barrels, petwalk**
60mm	**rest area nb, full ♿ facilities, ☎, vending, ⛱, litter barrels, petwalk**
58	US 52, to Bastian, **E gas:** BP/dsl, **food:** Front Porch Cafe, **W gas:** Citgo/dsl, Exxon/dsl
56mm	runaway ramp nb
52	US 52, VA 42, Bland, **E gas:** Citgo, **food:** Subway, **other:** $General, IGA Foods, **W gas:** Kangaroo/DQ/dsl, **lodging:** Big Walker Motel
51.5mm	**weigh sta both lanes**
48mm	Big Walker Mtn
47	VA 717, **6 mi W other:** to Deer Trail Park/NF Camping
41	VA 610, Peppers Ferry, Wytheville, **E food:** Sagebrush Steaks, **lodging:** Best Western, Sleep Inn,

INTERSTATE 77 CONT'D

N ↕ S

Exit #	Services
41	Continued Super 8, **W** **gas:** Kangaroo/dsl/scales/24hr, TA/BP/Country Pride/Popeye's/Subway/Taco Bell/dsl/scales/24hr/@, **food:** Southern Diner, **lodging:** Comfort Suites, Country Inn&Suites, Fairfield Inn, Hampton Inn, Ramada Inn
40	I-81 S, to Bristol, US 52 N

I-77 and I-81 run together 9 mi. See Interstate 81 exits 73-80.

WYTHEVILLE

73	US 11 S, Wytheville, **W** **gas:** BP, Go-Mart, Kangaroo, **food:** Applebee's, Bob Evans, Cracker Barrel, DQ, El Puerto Mexican, Hardee's, LJ Silver, Ocean Bay Rest., Shoney's, Sonic, Waffle House, Wendy's, **lodging:** Days Inn, Knight's Inn, La Quinta, Motel 6, Quality Inn, Red Carpet Inn, Red Rood Inn, Travelodge, **other:** H, AutoZone, Buick/Cadillac/Chevrolet/GMC/Pontiac, CVS Drug, $General, Food Lion, Ford, Goodyear/auto, Harley-Davidson, K-Mart, Nissan, Rite Aid, Subaru
32	I-81 N, to Roanoke
26mm	New River
24	VA 69, to Poplar Camp, **E** **gas:** Pure/gas, **other:** to Shot Tower SP, New River Trail Info Ctr, **W** **gas:** Citgo/dsl
19	VA 620, [airport]
14	US 58, US 221, to Hillsville, Galax, **E** **gas:** Citgo/Subway, **food:** Peking Palace, **lodging:** Red Carpet Inn, **other:** H, **W** **gas:** BP/24hr, Chevron/dsl/24hr, Exxon/DQ/dsl, Marathon, Shell, **food:** Countryside Rest., McDonald's, Pizza Inn/TCBY, Shoney's, Wendy's, **lodging:** Best Western, Comfort Inn, Hampton Inn, Holiday Inn Express, Quality Inn, Super 8, **other:** Carrollwood Camping (1mi)
8	VA 148, VA 775, to Fancy Gap, **E** **gas:** Chevron (2mi), Citgo/dsl, **food:** Fancy Gap Cafe (2mi), **lodging:** Lakeview Motel/rest., Mountaintop Motel/rest., **other:** Chance's Creek RV Ctr, to Blue Ridge Pkwy, **W** **gas:** BP, Citgo/dsl, **lodging:** Countryview Inn, Days Inn, **other:** KOA (2mi)
6.5mm	runaway truck ramp sb
4.5mm	runaway truck ramp sb
3mm	runaway truck ramp sb
1	VA 620
.5mm	**Welcome Ctr nb, full [handicapped] facilities, info, [phone], [picnic], litter barrels, petwalk**
0mm	Virginia/North Carolina state line

INTERSTATE 81

N ↕ S

Exit #	Services
324mm	Virginia/West Virginia state line
323	RD 669, to US 11, Whitehall, **E** **gas:** Exxon, **W** **gas:** ***FLYING J***/Country Mkt/dsl/LP/scales/24hr
321	RD 672, Clearbrook, **E** **gas:** Citgo/dsl, **food:** Olde Stone Rest.
320mm	**Welcome Ctr sb, full [handicapped] facilities, [phone], vending, [picnic], litter barrels, petwalk**
317	US 11, Stephenson, **E** **food:** Arby's, Daily Grind, Subway, **other:** Lowes Whse, Target, **W** **gas:** Exxon/dsl, Liberty/Blimpie/dsl, Sheetz/dsl/24hr, Sunoco/dsl, **food:** Burger King, Denny's, Godfather's Pizza,

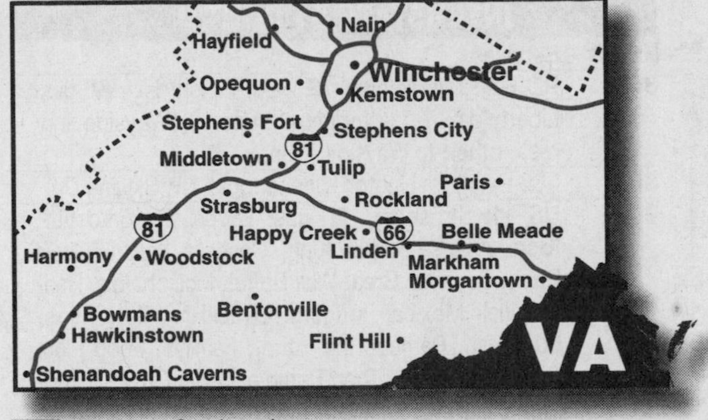

WINCHESTER

317	Continued McDonald's, Pizza Hut/Taco Bell, Tastee Freez, **lodging:** Comfort Inn, Econolodge, Holiday Inn Express (3mi), **other:** H, Candy Hill Camping
315	VA 7, Winchester, **E** **gas:** Exxon, Sheetz/24hr, **food:** Foster's Grille, Ledo's Pizza, Maggie Moo's, Quizno's, Sonic, Starbucks, **other:** Curves, Dodge, $Tree, Martin's Foods, PetCo, **W** **gas:** Chevron/dsl, Exxon/Subway, Liberty/dsl, Shell/dsl, **food:** Arby's, Baskin-Robbins/Dunkin Donuts, Camino Real Mexican, Chian Town, 5 Guys Burgers, George's Pizza, KFC, LJ Silver, McDonald's, Pizza Hut, Wendy's, **lodging:** Hampton Inn, Shoney's Inn/rest., **other:** AutoZone, CVS Drug, Food Lion, TrueValue
314mm	Abrams Creek
313	US 17/50/522, Winchester, **E** **gas:** BP/dsl, Citgo, Exxon/Subway, Shell/dsl, **food:** Cracker Barrel, Golden Corral, IHOP, Los Tolteco's Mexican, TX Steaks, Waffle House, **lodging:** Candlewood Suites, Holiday Inn, Fairfield Inn, Red Roof Inn, Sleep Inn, Super 8, Travelodge, **other:** Big Lots, Costco/gas, Food Lion, Jo-Ann Fabrics, Nissan, Vet, **W** **gas:** Sheetz/24hr, **food:** Bob Evans, Chick-fil-A, Chili's, China Jade, Chipotle Mexican, CiCi's, Glory Days Grill, KFC, McDonald's, Olive Garden, Panera Bread, Perkin's, Pizza Hut/Taco Bell, Quizno's, Rancho Mexican, Red Lobster, Ruby Tuesday, TGIFriday, Subway, Waffle House, Wendy's, **lodging:** Best Western, Hampton Inn, Hilton Garden, Wingate Inn, **other:** Belk, BooksAMillion, Border's, $Tree, Home Depot, Food Lion, JC Penney, K-Mart, Kohl's, Lowes Whse, Martin's Foods, Michael's, PepBoys, PetsMart, Old Navy, Ross, Sears/auto, Staples, Target, Walgreens, Walmart SuperCtr, mall, to Shenandoah U
310	VA 37, to US 50W, **W** **gas:** Sunoco, **food:** Bo's Express, Daily Grind, McDonald's, Outback Steaks, Popeye's, **lodging:** Best Value Inn, Country Inn&Suites, Days Inn, Royal Inn, **other:** H, Bloom Foods, Camping World, Carquest, CVS Drug, Gander Mtn, Honda, Suzuki, VW
307	VA 277, Stephens City, **E** **gas:** CB's, 7-11, Shell/Subway/dsl, **food:** Arby's, Burger King, Butcher Block Cafe, Daily Grind, KFC/Taco Bell, McDonald's, Pizza Hut, Roma Italian, Waffle House, Wendy's, **lodging:** Comfort Inn, Holiday Inn Express, **other:** Advance Parts, Curves, $General, Food Lion, Martin's Foods/gas, McCoy's Dairy Barn, Rite Aid, Vet, **W** **gas:** Exxon/Dunkin Donuts, Sheetz/24hr
304mm	**weigh sta both lanes**

VA

INTERSTATE 81 CONT'D

N ↕ S

Exit #	Services
302	RD 627, Middletown, **E** **gas:** Exxon/dsl, **W** **gas:** Liberty/dsl, 7-11, **lodging:** Super 8, Wayside Inn/rest., **other:** to Wayside Theatre
300	I-66 E, to Washington, Shenandoah NP, Skyline Dr
298	US 11, Strasburg, **E** **gas:** BP/dsl, Exxon/dsl/LP, **food:** Arby's, Burger King, Castiglia Italian, Ciro's Pizza, Denny's, Great Wall Buffet, McDonald's, Rancho Viejo Mexican, **lodging:** Fairfield Inn, Hotel Strasburg/rest., Ramada Inn, **other:** Family$, Food Lion, Rite Aid, Vet, **W** **other:** Battle of Cedar Grove Camping, to Belle Grove Plantation
296	US 48, VA 55, Strasburg, **E** **other:** to Hupp's Hill Bfd Museum
291	RD 651, Toms Brook, **E** **lodging:** Budget Inn, **W** **gas:** Love's/Arby's/dsl/scales/24hr/@, Wilco/Hess/DQ/dsl/scales/24hr, **food:** Milestone Rest., **other:** truckwash
283	VA 42, Woodstock, **E** **gas:** Liberty/7-11, Sheetz, Shell, **food:** Arby's, Dunkin Donuts, Hardee's, KFC, McDonald's, Pizza Hut, Ponderosa, Taco Bell, Wendy's, **lodging:** Budget Host, Comfort Inn, Holiday Inn Express, **other:** [H], CVS Drug, Food Lion, Radio Shack, Rite Aid, to Massanutten Military Academy, **W** **gas:** Exxon/dsl/24hr, Sunoco, **food:** China Wok, Cracker Barrel, Domino's, Subway, **other:** Curves, $Tree, Lowes Whse, Walmart SuperCtr
279	VA 185, RD 675, Edinburg, **E** **gas:** BP/dsl, Exxon/dsl, Shell/dsl/24hr, **food:** Subway, **other:** Ace Hardware, Creekside Camping (2mi)
277	VA 614, Bowmans Crossing
273	VA 292, RD 703, Mt Jackson, **E** **gas:** Exxon/dsl, Liberty/Blimpie/dsl/scales/24hr, 7-11, Sheetz/Wendy's/dsl/scales/24hr, **food:** Burger King, China King, Denny's, Godfather's, **lodging:** Super 8, **other:** Curves, $General, Food Lion/24hr, USPO, to Mt Jackson Hist Dist
269	rd 730, to Shenandoah Caverns, **E** **gas:** Chevron/dsl
269mm	N Fork Shenandoah River
264	US 211, New Market, **E** **gas:** BP/Blimpie/dsl, Chevron/dsl, Exxon/dsl, Shell/dsl, Texaco, **food:** Appleseed's Rest., Burger King, Godfather's, McDonald's, Publik House Rest., Southern Kitchen, **lodging:** Budget Inn, Quality Inn, Shenvalee Motel/rest., **other:** NAPA, Rancho Camping, to Shenandoah NP Skyline Dr, **W** **gas:** 7-11, **lodging:** Day's Inn, **other:** to New Market Bfd
262mm	**rest area both lanes, full [♿] facilities, [☎], vending, [picnic], litter barrels, petwalk**
257	US 11, VA 259, to Broadway, **E** **gas:** Liberty/Burger King/Blimpie/Godfather's/dsl, **3-5 mi** **E** **other:** KOA, Endless Caverns Camping
251	US 11, Harrisonburg, **W** **gas:** Exxon/dsl, **lodging:** Economy Inn
247b a	US 33, Harrisonburg, **E** **gas:** BP/Blimpie/dsl, Citgo/dsl, Royal, Sheetz, **food:** Applebees, Bob Evans, Bruster's, Chili's, CiCi's Pizza, Domino's, El Charro Mexican, 5 Buys Burgers, Golden Corral, Great Wok, Heavenly Ham, IHOP, Jess' Lunch, LJ Silver, O'Charley's, Outback Steaks, Panera Bread,

HARRISONBURG

Exit #	Services
247b a	Continued Quizno's, Red Lobster, Ruby Tuesday, Shoney's, Smokin Pig, Taco Bell, TX Steaks, Waffle House, Wendy's, **lodging:** Best Western, Candlewood Suites, Comfort Inn, Courtyard, Econolodge, Hampton Inn, Holiday Inn, Jameson Inn, Motel 6, Sleep Inn, **other:** Barnes&Noble, Belk, Books-a-Million, $Tree, Firestone/auto, Home Depot, JC Penney, K-Mart, Kohl's, Kroger, Lowes Whse, Martin's Foods/gas, Michael's, Nissan, Office Depot, Old Navy, PepBoys, PetsMart, Ross, Staples, Target, TJ Maxx, Walmart SuperCtr/gas/24hr, to Shenandoah NP, Skyline Dr, mall, **W** **gas:** Chevron/dsl, Exxon/dsl, Royal, Sheetz, Texaco, **food:** Arby's, China Inn, Ciro's Italian, Dragon Palace, Dunkin Donuts, Golden China, Hardee's, KFC, Kyoto, La Italia, Little Caesar's, McDonald's, Papa John's, Pizza Hut, Sam's Hotdogs, Subway, **other:** [H], Advance Parts, Big Lots, CVS Drug, Food Lion
245	VA 659, Port Republic Rd, **E** **gas:** Exxon/Subway/dsl, Liberty/dsl, Neighbor's, Texaco, **lodging:** Day's Inn, **W** **other:** [H], to James Madison U
243	US 11, to Harrisonburg, **W** **gas:** BP/dsl, Exxon/dsl, Harrisonburg Travel Ctr/diner/dsl/scales, Liberty, 7-11, Sheetz, **food:** Burger King, China Gourmet, Cracker Barrel, Dunkin Donuts, McDonald's, Pizza Hut, Subway, Taco Bell, Waffle House, **lodging:** Country Inn&Suites, Hampton Inn, Holiday Inn Express, Ramada Inn, Red Carpet Inn, Super 8, **other:** Advance Parts, AutoZone, BMW, Buick/GMC/Pontiac, Chrysler, Ford, Honda, Hyundai, Kia, Lincoln/Mercury, Subaru, Toyota
240	VA 257, RD 682, Mount Crawford, **1-3 mi** **W** **gas:** Exxon/dsl, **food:** Burger King, Mrs. Rowe's, **lodging:** Village Inn
235	VA 256, Weyers Cave, **E** **gas:** Texaco/dsl, **W** **gas:** BP/Subway/dsl, Exxon/dsl**other:** Freightliner, antiques, to Grand Caverns
232mm	**rest area both lanes, full [♿] facilities, [☎], vending, [picnic], litter barrels, petwalk**
227	RD 612, Verona, **E** **gas:** BP/Subway/dsl, **food:** Waffle Inn, **W** **gas:** Citgo/Wendy's/dsl, Exxon, Shell, **food:** Burger King, Ciro's Pizza, Dunkin Donuts, Hardee's, McDonald's, **lodging:** Knight's Inn, **other:** Food Lion, Good Sam RV Park (3mi), Rite Aid, antiques
225	VA 275, Woodrow Wilson Pkwy, **E** **lodging:** Quality Inn, **W** **lodging:** Day's Inn, Holiday Inn/rest.

STAUNTON

Exit #	Services
222	US 250, Staunton, **E** **gas:** BP, Texaco/dsl, **food:** Cracker Barrel, McDonald's, Mrs Rowe's Rest., Shoney's, TX Steaks, **lodging:** Best Western, Guesthouse Inn, Sleep Inn, **W** **gas:** Hess, Sheetz, **food:** Burger King, Chili's, Dunkin Donuts, 5 Guys Burgers, Quizno's, Starbucks, Waffle House, **lodging:** Comfort Inn, Econolodge, Microtel, Super 8, **other:** AutoZone, Lowes Whse, Martin's Foods/gas, TireMart, Toyota/sSion, Walmart SuperCtr, American Frontier Culture Museum
221	I-64 E, to Charlottesville, Skyline Dr, Shenandoah NP
220	VA 262, to US 11, Staunton, **1 mi** **W** **gas:** BP, Citgo, Exxon, Shell, **food:** Applebee's, Arby's, Burger King, Country Cookin', KFC, McDonald's, Red Lobster, **lodging:** Budget Inn, Hampton Inn, **other:** Advance Parts, Belk, Books A Million, Buick/Pontiac/GMC,

VA

INTERSTATE 81 CONT'D

N ↕ S

Exit #	Services
220	Continued Chrysler, CVS Drug, $Tree, Ford/Lincoln/Mercury, Harley-Davidson, Honda, Hyundai, JC Penney, Jeep/Dodge, Merchant's Tire/auto, Nissan, Rule RV Ctr, VW
217	RD 654, to Mint Spring, Stuarts Draft, **E gas:** BP/Subway/dsl, Exxon/dsl, **lodging:** Day's Inn, **W gas:** Citgo/Stuckey's/dsl/24hr, Liberty, **lodging:** Relax Inn, Walnut Hill Camping (3mi)
213b a	US 11, US 340, Greenville, **E gas:** BP/Subway, Pilot/Arby's/scales/dsl/24hr, Shell, **food:** Edelweiss Rest., **lodging:** Budget Host
205	RD 606, Raphine, **E gas:** Exxon/Burger King, Smiley's/BBQ/dsl/24hr, Whites/dsl/24hr/motel/@, **W gas:** Wilco/Hess/Wendy's/dsl/scales/24hr, **lodging:** Day's Inn/rest. **other:** Koogler RV Ctr
200	RD 710, Fairfield, **E gas:** BP/McDonald's/dsl/24hr, Texaco, **W gas:** Exxon/Subway/dsl, Shell/dsl
199mm	**rest area sb, full facilities, phone, vending, picnic, litter barrels, petwalk**
195	US 11, Lee Hwy, **E lodging:** Maple Hall Lodging/dining, **W gas:** Citgo/dsl/24hr, Shell/dsl, **food:** Aunt Sarah's, **lodging:** Best Value, Days Inn, Howard Johnson/rest., **other:** Lee-Hi Camping
191	I-64 W (exits left from nb), US 60, to Charleston
188b a	US 60, to Lexington, Buena Vista, **3-5 mi E gas:** BP, Exxon, **food:** Hardee's, KFC, LJ Silver, McDonald's, Pizza Hut, Taco Bell, Wendy's, **lodging:** Budget Inn, Buena Vista Inn, **other:** H, to Glen Maury Park, to Stonewall Jackson Home, Marshall Museum, to Blue Ridge Pkwy, **W gas:** Exxon/dsl/24hr, **lodging:** Day's Inn, Hampton Inn, **other:** to Washington&Lee U, VMI
180	US 11, Natural Bridge, **E gas:** Shell/dsl, **lodging:** Relax Inn, **other:** Cave Mtn NF, **W gas:** Shell/dsl, **food:** Pink Cadillac Diner, **lodging:** Budget Inn, **other:** KOA, (180a exits left from sb)
175	US 11 N, to Glasgow, Natural Bridge, **E gas:** Exxon, **lodging:** Natural Bridge Hotel/rest., **other:** to James River RA, Jellystone Camping
168	VA 614, US 11, Arcadia, **E gas:** Shell, **food:** Mtn View Rest., **lodging:** Wattstull Inn, **other:** Middle Creek Camping (6mi), **2 mi W gas:** Exxon, **food:** Burger King, Mtn View Rest
167	US 11 (from sb), Buchanan
162	US 11, Buchanan, **E gas:** Exxon/dsl, **other:** to BR Pkwy, **W gas:** Texaco/Subway/24hr
158mm	**rest area sb, full facilities, phone, vending, picnic, litter barrels, petwalk**
156	RD 640, to US 11, **E gas:** Exxon/Brugh's Mill/dsl
150	US 11/220, to Fincastle, **E gas:** Citgo/dsl/24hr, Dodge's/dsl, Pilot/Subway/dsl/24hr, TA/dsl/@, **food:** Country Cookin', Cracker Barrel, Hardee's, McDonald's, Shoney's, Taco Bell, Waffle House, **lodging:** Comfort Inn, Holiday Inn Express, Red Roof Inn, Travelodge, **other:** Berglund RV Ctr, CVS Drug, $General, truckwash, **W gas:** BP/dsl, Exxon/dsl/24hr, **food:** Bojangles, Pizza Hut, Rancho Viejo Mexican, Wendy's, **lodging:** Howard Johnson, Super 8, **other:** Curves, Kroger/gas, Vet

LEXINGTON

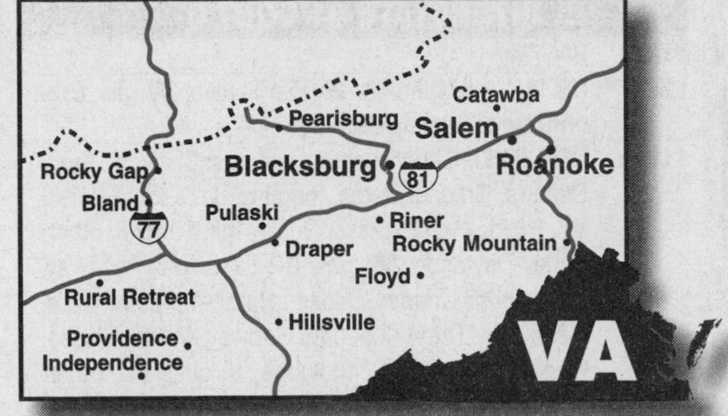

ROANOKE

Exit #	Services
149mm	**weigh sta both lanes**
146	VA 115, Cloverdale, **E gas:** Exxon, Shell/dsl, **food:** Anthony's Diner, Burger King, El Rodeo Mexican, Hardees, McDonald's, Subway, **lodging:** Country Inn&Suites, Day's Inn/rest., Fairfield Inn, Hampton Inn, **other:** Camping World, CVS Drug, Gander Mtn
143	I-581, US 220, to Roanoke, Blue Ridge Pkwy (exits left from sb), **1 mi E gas:** Sheetz, **food:** El Toreo, Subway, Waffle House, **lodging:** Hampton Inn, Holiday Inn, Knights Inn, Quality Inn, Super 8, **2-3 mi E on Hershberger...gas:** BP, Exxon, Shell, **food:** Abuelo's Mexican, Applebees, Buffalo Wild Wings, Carrabba's, Chick-fil-A, Flat Rock Grille, Hardee's, IHOP, Logan's Roadhouse, O'Charley's, Olive Garden, Panera Bread, Red Palace Chinese, Ruby Tuesday, Shaker's, Smokey Bones BBQ, Starbucks, Subway, TX Steaks, TGIFriday, **lodging:** Best Western, Comfort Inn, Courtyard, Extended Stay America, Holiday Inn, Howard Johnson, Hyatt Place, MainStay Suites, Residence Inn, **other:** Barnes&Noble, Belk, JC Penney, Macy's, Old Navy, Sears/auto, Target, U-Haul, Walmart SuperCtr/gas, mall
141	VA 419, Salem, **E gas:** BP, Liberty/Burger King, Valero, **food:** Hardee's, Country Cookin' Rest., McDonald's, **lodging:** Econolodge, Holiday Inn Express, La Quinta, Quality Inn, **other:** H, Chevrolet, Kroger/gas, **W gas:** BP/dsl, Citgo
140	VA 311, Salem, **1 mi E food:** Mac&Bob's Cafe, **1 mi W food:** Hanging Rock Grill/golf
137	VA 112, VA 619, Salem, **E gas:** BP, Chevron, Citgo, Exxon/dsl, Go-Mart, Liberty, Sheetz/24hr, **food:** Anthony's Cafe, Applebees, Arby's, Bojangles, Burger King, China Wok, Denny's, Dickey's BBQ, Dynasty Buffet, El Rodeo Mexican, Firehouse Subs, Hardee's, K&W Cafeteria, KFC, LJ Silver, Mamma Maria Italian, McDonald's, Omelette Shoppe, Pizza Hut, Quizno's, Shoney's, Sonic, Starbucks, Subway, Taco Bell, Tokyo Express, Wendy's, **lodging:** Comfort Inn, Econolodge, Super 8, **other:** Aamco, Advance Parts, AutoZone, BigLots, $General, Tree, Food Lion, Goodyear, K-Mart, Kroger, Merchant's Tire, Mitsubishi, Snyder's RV, Walgreens, Walmart SuperCtr/24hr, **W lodging:** Holiday Inn, Howard Johnson
132	VA 647, to Dixie Caverns, **E gas:** Citgo, Shell, **lodging:** Budget Host, **other:** Dixie Caverns Camping, st police
129mm	**rest area nb, full facilities, phone, vending, picnic, litter barrels, petwalk**

SALEM

VA

INTERSTATE 81 CONT'D

N ↕ S

Exit #	Services
128	US 11, VA 603, Ironto, **E gas:** Texaco, **W gas:** Exxon/Dixie's/Subway/dsl/24hr
118c b a	US 11/460, Christiansburg, **E gas:** Shell/dsl, **food:** Denny's, Cracker Barrel, **lodging:** Day's Inn, Fairfield Inn, Holiday Inn Express, Quality Inn, Super 8, **other:** Harley-Davidson, **W gas:** BP, Exxon/dsl, RaceWay, Shell, **food:** Country Cookin, Hardee's, McDonald's, Pizza Hut, Ruby Tuesday, Subway, Waffle House, Wendy's, **lodging:** Econolodge, Knight's Inn, **other:** H, Advance Parts, Chevrolet/Subaru, Chrysler/Dodge, Ford, Honda, Hyundai, KIA, Subaru, Toyota, to VA Tech
114	VA 8, Christiansburg, **0-1 mi W gas:** Citgo, Sunoco, **food:** Anthony's Cafe, Burger King, Macado's Rest., Pizza Inn, **lodging:** Budget Inn, **other:** $General, repair
109	VA 177, VA 600, **E other:** H, **0-2 mi W gas:** BP/dsl, Marathon, **lodging:** Best Western, Comfort Inn, La Quinta, Super 8
107mm	**rest area both lanes, full ♿ facilities, ☎, vending, picnic, litter barrels, petwalk**
105	VA 232, RD 605, to Radford, **W gas:** Citgo (2mi), **lodging:** Executive Motel (4mi), **other:** museum
101	RD 660, to Claytor Lake SP, **E lodging:** Claytor Lake Inn, Sleep Inn, **W gas:** Citgo/DQ/dsl, Shell/Omelette Shoppe/Taco Bell/dsl/scales/@
98	VA 100 N, to Dublin, **E gas:** Exxon/Subway/dsl, **food:** Bojangles, Shoney's, **lodging:** Comfort Inn, Hampton Inn, Holiday Inn Express, **W gas:** Liberty/Blimpie/dsl, Marathon, **food:** Arby's, Burger King, Fatz Cafe, McDonald's, Subway, Wendy's, **lodging:** Super 8, **other:** H, Walmart SuperCtr, to Wilderness Rd Museum
94b a	VA 99 N, to Pulaski, **E lodging:** Day's Inn, **0-2 mi W gas:** Exxon, **food:** Domino's, LJ Silver, Pizza Hut, **other:** H, $General, Sav-a-Lot Foods
92	RD 658, to Draper, **E gas:** BP, **other:** to New River Trail SP
89b a	US 11 N, VA 100, to Pulaski
86	RD 618, Service Rd, **W gas:** Sunoco/Appletree Rest./dsl, **other:** repair
84	RD 619, to Grahams Forge, **W gas:** Kangaroo/DQ/dsl/24hr, Love's/Chester Fried/Subway/dsl/scales/24hr, **lodging:** Fox Mtn Inn, Trail Motel
81	I-77 S, to Charlotte, to Blue Ridge Pkwy. **I-81 S and I-77 N run together 9 mi.**, Galax
80	US 52 S, VA 121 N, to Ft Chiswell, **E gas:** BP/Burger King/dsl, *FLYING J*/Cookery/dsl/scales/24hr/@, **food:** Wendy's, **lodging:** Hampton Inn, Super 8, **other:** Blue Beacon, Ft Chiswell Outlets/famous brands, Ft Chiswell RV Park, NAPA, **W gas:** BP, Citgo/Kangaroo/dsl, **food:** McDonald's, **lodging:** Comfort Inn, **other:** Speedco,
77	Service Rd, **E gas:** Citgo/Subway/dsl/24hr, *FLYING J* J/Cookery/dsl/LP/RV Dump/24hr, Wilco/Hess/dsl/LP, **food:** Burger King, **other:** KOA, **W gas:** Exxon/dsl, Wilco/Hess/Arby's/DQ/dsl/scales/24hr, **other:** Truck'o Mat, st police
73	US 11 S, Wytheville, **E gas:** BP, Go-Mart, Kangaroo, **food:** Applebee's, Bob Evans, Cracker Barrel, DQ, El Puerto Mexican, Hardee's, LJ Silver, Ocean Bay Rest., Shoney's, Sonic, Waffle House, Wendy's, **lodging:** Days Inn, Knight's Inn, La Quinta, Motel 6, Quality Inn, Red Carpet Inn, Red Rood Inn, Travelodge, **other:** H, AutoZone, Buick/Cadillac/Chevrolet/GMC/Pontiac, CVS Drug, $General, Food Lion, Ford, Goodyear/auto, Harley-Davidson, K-Mart, Nissan, Rite Aid, Subaru
I-81 N and I-77 S run together 9 mi	
72	I-77 N, to Bluefield, 1 mi N, I-77 exit 41 **E food:** Sagebrush Steaks, **lodging:** Best Western, Sleep Inn, Super 8, **W gas:** Kangaroo/dsl/24hr, TA/Country Pride/Popeye's/Subway/Taco Bell/dsl/scales/24hr/@, **food:** Southern Diner, **lodging:** Comfort Suites, Country Inn&Suites, Fairfield Inn, Hampton Inn, Ramada/rest.
70	US 21/52, Wytheville, **E gas:** BP/dsl, Exxon, Sheetz, **food:** Arby's, China Wok, KFC/Taco Bell, Little Caesar's, McDonald's, Ruby Tuesday, Starbucks, Subway, Wendy's, **other:** H, $Tree, Food Lion, IGA Foods, Lowes Whse, Old Navy, Radio Shack, Walmart SuperCtr/24hr, **W gas:** Kangaroo, **lodging:** Comfort Inn
67	US 11 (from nb, no re-entry), to Wytheville
61mm	**rest area nb, full ♿ facilities, ☎, vending, picnic, litter barrels, petwalk, NO TRUCKS**
60	VA 90, Rural Retreat, **E gas:** Chevron/dsl, **food:** El Ranchero, McDonald's, Subway, **other:** to Rural Retreat Lake, camping
54	rd 683, to Groseclose, **E gas:** Shell/dsl, **food:** The Barn Rest., **lodging:** Relax Inn, **other:** Settler's Museum
53.5mm	**rest area sb, full ♿ facilities, ☎, vending, picnic, litter barrels, petwalk**
50	US 11, Atkins, **W gas:** Citgo/Subway/dsl/24hr, Exxon/Pizza+, **food:** Atkins Diner, **lodging:** Comfort Inn
47	US 11, to Marion, **W gas:** BP/Subway, Chevron/dsl/24hr, **food:** Arby's, KFC/Taco Bell, Little Caesar's, LJ Silver, McDonald's, Pizza Hut, Puerto Mexican, Sonic, Wendy's, **lodging:** Best Western/rest., Econolodge, VA House Inn, **other:** H, Advance Parts, AutoZone, Buick/Chevrolet/GMC/Pontiac, Chrysler/Dodge/Jeep, CVS Drug, $General, Family$, Food City, Food Lion, Ford, Ingles, Marion Drug, O'Reilly Parts, Radio Shack, Rite Aid, Walgreens, Walmart, to Hungry Mother SP (4mi)
45	VA 16, Marion, **E gas:** Valero, **food:** AppleTree Rest., **other:** to Grayson Highlands SP, Mt Rogers NRA, **W gas:** BP, Chevron, **food:** Hardee's, **other:** NAPA, USPO
44	US 11, Marion, **W gas:** Marathon/dsl
39	US 11, RD 645, Seven Mile Ford, **E lodging:** Budget Inn/rest., **W other:** Interstate Camping/food
35	RD 107, Chilhowie, **E food:** Hardees, **lodging:** Knight's Inn, **W gas:** Chevron, Gas'n Go, Exxon/dsl, Rouse Fuel, **food:** McDonald's, Subway, TasteeFreez, **lodging:** Budget Inn (1mi), **other:** Curves, $General, Food City, NAPA
32	US 11, to Chilhowie, **E other:** Greenway Creek RV Park

WYTHEVILLE

MARION

INTERSTATE 81 CONT'D

N ↕ S

Exit #	Services
29	VA 91, to Damascus, Glade Spring, **E gas:** Marathon/Subway/dsl, Petro/dsl/rest./24hr/@, Valero, **food:** Giardino's Italian, Pizza+, Wendy's, **lodging:** Swiss Inn, Travel Inn, **other:** $General, Peterbilt, **W gas:** Chevron/dsl/24hr, Coastal, Exxon
26	VA 737, Emory, **W food:** Emory Crossing Deli, **other:** to Emory&Henry Coll
24	VA 80, Meadowview Rd, **W** auto repair
22	VA 704, Enterprise Rd
19	US 11/58, to Abingdon, **E gas:** Shell/Subway/dsl, **food:** Pizza+, **other:** Vet, to Mt Rogers NRA, **W gas:** Chevron/dsl/24hr, Exxon/dsl, **food:** Burger King, Cracker Barrel, DaVinci's Cafe, Harbor House Seafood, Huddle House, Wendy's, **lodging:** Alpine Motel, Days Inn, Holiday Inn Express, Quality Inn
17	US 58A, VA 75, Abingdon, **E food:** Domino's, LJ Silver, **lodging:** Hampton Inn, **other:** Mr Transmission, **W gas:** Chevron, Exxon, Gas'n Go, **food:** Arby's, China Wok, Hardee's, KFC, Los Arcos Mexican, McDonald's, Papa John's, Pizza Hut, Shoney's, Taco Bell, Tuscan Grill, Wendy's, **lodging:** Martha Washington Inn, Super 8, **other:** [H], Advance Parts, $General, Food City, GNC, Kroger, K-Mart, Medicine Shoppe, Radio Shack
14	US 19, VA 140, Abingdon, **W gas:** Chevron/dsl/24hr, Exxon, Shell/dsl, **food:** McDonald's, Milano's Italian, Pizza Inn, Subway, **lodging:** Comfort Inn, **other:** CarQuest, Ford/Lincoln/Mercury, Riverside Camping (10mi)
13.5mm	**TRUCKERS ONLY rest area nb, full ♿ facilities, ☎, vending, [picnic], litter barrels**
13	VA 611, to Lee Hwy, **W gas:** Shell/dsl, **other:** Kenworth, MACK
10	US 11/19, Lee Hwy, **W gas:** Appco, BP/dsl, Chevron, **lodging:** Beacon Inn, Deluxe Inn, Evergreen Inn, Red Carpet Inn, Skyland Inn
7	Old Airport Rd, **E gas:** Shell/dsl, **food:** Bojangles, Cracker Barrel, Sonic, **lodging:** La Quinta, **W gas:** BP/dsl, Conoco/dsl, Marathon, **food:** Chili's, Chop's Rest., Damon's, Domino's, El Patio Mexican, Fazoli's, Golden Corral, IHOP, Kobe Japanese, Logan's Roadhouse, Los Arco's, O'Charley's, Outback Steaks, Perkins, Pizza Hut, Red Lobster, Ruby Tuesday, Starbucks, Subway, Taco Bell, Wendy's, **lodging:** Courtyard, Holiday Inn, Microtel, Motel 6, **other:** Advance Parts, Best Buy, Curves, $Tree, $General, Home Depot, Lowes Whse, Office Depot, Old Navy, PetsMart, Ross, Sam's Club/gas, Target, Walmart SuperCtr/24hr, Sugar Hollow Camping
5	US 11/19, Lee Hwy, **E gas:** Shell, **food:** Arby's, Burger King, Hardee's, KFC, LJ Silver, McDonald's, Shoney's, **lodging:** Budget Inn, Super 8, **other:** Family$, Food Lion, Harley-Davidson, USPO, **W gas:** Exxon, **lodging:** Comfort Inn, **other:** Blevins Tire, Buick/Pontiac, Lee Hwy Camping
3	I-381 S, to Bristol, **1 mi E gas:** Chevron, Exxon/dsl, **food:** Arby's, Krystal, Ryan's
1b a	US 58/421, Bristol, **1 mi E gas:** Appco, Chevron, Citgo, Shell, **food:** Burger King, Capt D's, Chick-fil-A, KFC, Lighthouse Cafe, LJ Silver, McDonald's, Pizza Hut, Sonic, Subway, Taco Bell, Wendy's, **lodging:**

ABINGDON

BRISTOL

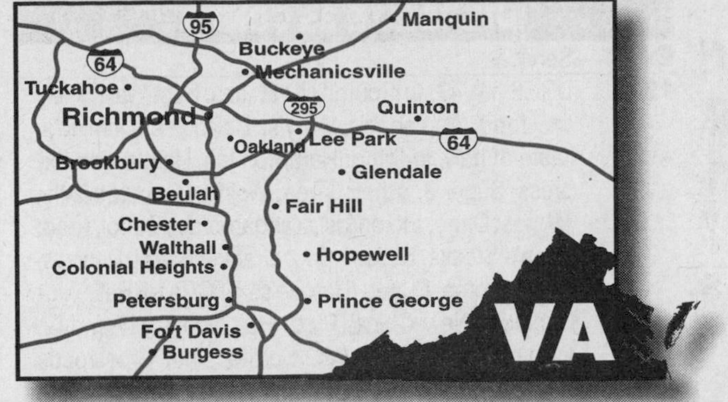

Exit #	Services
1b a	Continued Howard Johnson, Knight's Inn, **other:** [H], Belk, Chrysler/Jeep, CVS Drug, Dodge, Family$, K-Mart, Kroger, Sears/auto, Toyota/Scion, Walgreens, mall
0mm	Virginia/Tennessee state line, **Welcome Ctr nb, full ♿ facilities, info, ☎, vending, [picnic], litter barrels, petwalk, NO TRUCKS**

INTERSTATE 85

N ↕ S

Exit #	Services
69mm	I-85 begins/ends on I-95.
69	US 301, Wythe St, Washington St, Petersburg, **W lodging:** Regency Inn
68	I-95 S, US 460 E, to Norfolk, Crater Rd, **E** [H], 3/4 mi **E gas:** Exxon/dsl, RaceTrac/dsl, Shell, **food:** Hardee's, **lodging:** California Inn, **other:** to Petersburg Nat Bfd
65	Squirrel Level Rd, **E other:** to Richard Bland Coll, **W gas:** BP
63b a	US 1, to Petersburg, **E gas:** Chubby's, Exxon/dsl/24hr, Shell/Burger King, **food:** Hardee's, Waffle House, **lodging:** Holiday Inn Express, **W gas:** BP, **food:** McDonald's
61	US 460, to Blackstone, **E gas:** EastCoast/Subway/dsl/LP, **food:** Huddle House, **lodging:** Day's Inn (3mi), **W gas:** Shell/dsl, Valero (1mi), **other:** ✈
55mm	**rest area both lanes, full ♿ facilities, ☎, [picnic], litter barrels, vending, petwalk**
53	VA 703, Dinwiddie, **W gas:** Exxon/dsl, **food:** Home-Place Rest. (3mi), Rumorz Cafe, **other:** to 5 Forks Nat Bfd
52mm	Stony Creek
48	VA 650, DeWitt
42	VA 40, McKenney, **W gas:** Citgo, Exxon, **other:** auto repair, 1.5 mi **W lodging:** Economy Inn
40mm	Nottoway River
39	VA 712, to Rawlings, **E other:** VA Battlerama, **W gas:** Chevron/Davis/dsl/24hr, Citgo/dsl, **lodging:** Nottoway Motel/rest.
34	VA 630, Warfield, **W gas:** Exxon/dsl
32mm	**rest area both lanes, full ♿ facilities, ☎, [picnic], litter barrels, vending, petwalk**
28	US 1, Alberta, **W gas:** Exxon
27	VA 46, to Lawrenceville, **E other:** to St Paul's Coll
24	VA 644, to Meredithville
22mm	**weigh sta both lanes**
20mm	Meherrin River
15	US 1, to South Hill, **E gas:** Citgo/deli, **W gas:** Valero, **food:** Kahill's Diner, Rumorz

PETERSBURG

INTERSTATE 85 CONT'D

Exit #	Services
12	US 58, VA 47, to South Hill, **E gas:** RaceWay, Shell/dsl, **food:** Applebee's, Arby's, Bojangles, Domino's, Taste of Italy, **lodging:** Hampton Inn, Holiday Inn Express, Super 8, **other:** $Tree, Walmart Superctr/24hr, **W gas:** Citgo, Exxon/dsl, Kangaroo/dsl, Petrol, **food:** Brian's Steaks, Burger King, Cracker Barrel, Denny's, Down Home Buffet, Hardee's, KFC/Taco Bell, McDonald's, New China, Pizza Hut, Subway, Wendy's, **lodging:** Best Value Inn, Comfort Inn, Crossroads Inn, **other:** H, CVS Drug, $General, Food Lion, Goodyear/auto, Home Depot, Roses
4	VA 903, to Bracey, Lake Gaston, **E gas:** BP/DQ/Subway/dsl, Exxon/Simmon's/dsl/rest./scales/24hr/@, **other:** Americamps Camping (5mi), **W gas:** Shell/Pizza Hut/Quizno's, **food:** Memphis Grill, **lodging:** Lake Gaston Inn
3mm	Lake Gaston
1mm	**Welcome Ctr nb, full ♿ facilities, phone, picnic, phone, litter barrels, vending, petwalk**
0mm	Virginia/North Carolina state line

INTERSTATE 95

Exit #	Services
178mm	Virginia/Maryland state line, Potomac River, W Wilson Mem Br
177c b a	US 1, to Alexandria, Ft Belvoir, **E food:** Great American Steak Buffet, **lodging:** Budget Host, Hampton Inn, **other:** Chevrolet, Chrysler/Jeep, Dodge, **W gas:** Hess, Liberty/repair
176b a	VA 241, Telegraph Rd, **E gas:** Hess/dsl, **W lodging:** Courtyard, Holiday Inn
174	Eisenhower Ave Connector, to Alexandria
173	rd 613, Van Dorn St, to Franconia, **E lodging:** Comfort Inn, **1 mi W gas:** Exxon, Shell, **food:** Dunkin Donuts, Jerry's Subs, McDonald's, Papa John's, Quizno's, Red Lobster, **other:** Aamco, Giant Foods, NTB
170a	I-495 N, **I-495 & I-95 N run together to MD., to Rockville**
170b	I-395 N, to Washington
169b a	rd 644, Springfield, Franconia, **E food:** Family Diner, Starbucks, Subway, TGIFriday's, **lodging:** Best Western, Courtyard, Extended Stay America, Hampton Inn, Hilton, **other:** H, Barnes&Noble, Best Buy, CVS Drug, Firestone/auto, Ford, Home Depot, JC Penney, Macy's, Michael's, Old Navy, PetsMart, Staples, Target, mall, **W gas:** BP, Mobil, Shell, Sunoco, **food:** Chipotle Mexican, Deliah's Grill, Domino's, Dunkin Donuts, KFC, McDonald's, Outback Steaks, Quizno's, Starbucks, Subway, Tokyo Japanese, **lodging:** Holiday Inn Express, Red Roof Inn, **other:** CVS Drug, Diahatsu, Giant Foods, Goodyear/auto, K-Mart, Mr. Tire, Toyota/Scion, Vet
167	VA 617, Backlick Rd (from sb), **W gas:** InterFuel/dsl, **other:** Chevrolet
166b a	VA 7100, Newington, to Ft Belvoir, **E gas:** Exxon/dsl, **W gas:** Exxon, **food:** McDonald's
163	VA 642, Lorton, **E gas:** Shell/24hr, **W gas:** Shell, **food:** Antoneli's Pizza, Burger King, McDonald's, **lodging:** Comfort Inn
161	US 1 S (exits left from sb), to Ft Belvoir, Mt Vernon, Woodlawn Plantation, Gunston Hall, **1 mi E gas:** BP, Exxon, Shell, Sunoco, **food:** Denny's, DixieBones BBQ, Dunkin Donuts, McDonald's, Taco Bell, **lodging:** Econolodge, Hampton Inn, Quality Inn, Rodeway Inn, VA Inn, **other:** Aldi Foods
160.5mm	Occoquan River
160b a	VA 123 N, Woodbridge, Occoquan, **E** odging: Comfort Inn, Econolodge, Hampton Inn, Quality Inn, **other:** Aldi Foods, GNC, Radio Shack, **W gas:** BP, Exxon/dsl, Shell, **food:** KFC, McDonald's, VA Grill, Wendy's, **other:** 7-11, same as 161
158b a	VA 3000, Prince William Pkwy, Woodbridge, **W gas:** Exxon, Shell, 7-11, Sunoco, WaWa, **food:** Chick-fil-A, Chipotle Mexican, ChuckeCheese, Coldstone Creamery, Famous Dave's BBQ, Fuddrucker's, Hooter's, Macaroni Grill, Old Country Buffet, On-the-Border, Red Lobster, Smokey Bones BBQ, Taco Bell, TGIFriday, UNO, Wendy's, **lodging:** Country Inn&Suites, Courtyard, Fairfield Inn, Holiday Inn Express, Residence Inn, Sleep Inn, **other:** Best Buy, Border's Books, $Tree, Lowes Whse, Michael's, Office Depot, PetsMart, Sam's Club/gas, Shopper's Foods, Target, Walmart SuperCtr/Subway
156	VA 784, Potomac Mills, **E gas:** Exxon, Wawa/gas, **food:** Checkers, McDonald's, Taco Bell, **other:** H Hyundai, Kia, Lincoln/Mercury, Mazda, Mitsubishi, Nissan, Radio Shack, Safeway, Trak Auto, to Leesylvania SP, **W gas:** Chevron, Exxon, Shell, Sunoco, Texaco, **food:** Bamboo Buffet, Bob Evans, Burger King, Chili's, Denny's, Domino's, DQ, El Charro Mexican, Guapo's, Jerry's Subs, McDonald's, Olive Garden, Outback Steaks, Popeye's, Silver Diner, Subway, Wendy's, **lodging:** Best Western, Wytestone Suites, **other:** Book-a-Million, Costco/gas, Family$, Firestone/auto, Jo-Ann Fabrics, K-Mart, Marshall's, Michael's, NAPA, Nordstrom's, NTB, Potomic Mills Outlets/Famous Brands, Staples, TJ Maxx, U-Haul, **rest area both lanes, full ♿ facilities, phone, vending, picnic, litter barrels, petwalk, NO TRUCKS**
154mm	**truck rest area/weigh sta both lanes**
152	VA 234, Dumfries, to Manassas, **E gas:** BP/dsl/24hr, Chevron/service, Shell/dsl, **food:** Golden Corral, KFC, McDonald's, Subway, Taco Bell, **lodging:** Sleep Inn, Super 8, **other:** NAPA Autocare, Weems-Botts Museum, **W gas:** Exxon/Blimpie, 7-11, Shell, **food:** Cracker Barrel, MontClair Rest., Tiziano Italian, Waffle House, **lodging:** Comfort Inn, Day's Inn, Econolodge, Hampton Inn, Holiday Inn, Holiday Inn Express, **other:** Prince William Camping
150	VA 619, Quantico, to Triangle, **E gas:** Exxon, Shell/dsl, 7-11, **food:** Burger King, Dunkin Donuts, McDonald's, Wendy's, **lodging:** Best Value Inn, Ramada Inn, **other:** auto repair, to Marine Corps Base, **W** Prince William Forest Park
148	to Quantico, **2 mi E gas:** Texaco/dsl, **lodging:** Spring Lake Motel, **other:** to Marine Corps Base
143b a	to US 1, VA 610, Aquia, **E gas:** BP, Exxon, Shell/dsl/24hr, **food:** Carlos O'Kelly's, DQ, DaVanzo's Italian, KFC, Kingstreet BBQ, McDonald's, Pizza Hut, Ruby Tuesday, Shoney's, Vocelli's Pizza, Wendy's, **lodging:** Best Western, Day's Inn, Hampton Inn,

VA

N ↕ S

WASHINGTON DC AREA

DUMFRIES

N ↕ S

INTERSTATE 95 CONT'D

Exit #	Services
143b a	Continued **other:** Tires+, **W gas:** BP/dsl, Exxon, 7-11/dsl, WaWa, **food:** Applebees, Bob Evans, Burger King, Chick-fil-A, China Wok, Dunkin Donuts, 5 Guys Burgers, Golden Corral, Hardee's, IHOP, Jerry's Subs, Kobe Japanese, Maggie Moo's, Moe's SW Grill, Outback Steaks, Pancho Villa, Panera Bread, Popeye's, Ruby Tuesday, Starbucks, Taco Bell, Wendy's, **lodging:** Comfort Inn, Country Inn, Holiday Inn Express, Super 8, Wingate Inn, **other:** AutoZone, Best Buy, Border's Books, CVS Drug, $General, $Tree, Giant Foods, Home Depot, Kohl's, Lowes Whse, Michael's, PetsMart, Ross, Shopper's Foods, Staples, Target, TJ Maxx, Toyota, Walmart/auto, Aquia Pines Camping
140	VA 630, Stafford, **E gas:** 7-11, Sunoco, Valero, **food:** McDonald's, **lodging:** Bradshaw Motel (3mi), **W gas:** BP/dsl, Shell/dsl
137mm	Potomac Creek
136	rd 8900, Centreport, **W** ✈
133b a	US 17 N, to Warrenton, **E gas:** Exxon/dsl, Texaco, **food:** Arby's, **lodging:** Howard Johnson Express, Motel 6, **other:** CarQuest, 7-11, **W gas:** BP/dsl, EastCoast/Subway/dsl, Shell/dsl, **food:** Burger King, Foster's Grille, Hardee's, McDonald's, Perkin's, Pizza Hut, Ponderosa, Taco Bell, Waffle House, Wendy's, **lodging:** Best Inn, Comfort Inn, Country Inn&Suites, Day's Inn, Holiday Inn, Quality Inn, Sleep Inn, Super 8, Travelodge, Wingate Inn, **other:** Advance Parts, Blue Beacon, Honda, PetsMart, Target
132.5mm	Rappahannock River
132mm	**rest area sb, full ♿ facilities, ☎, 🏕, litter barrels, petwalk, vending**
130b a	VA 3, to Fredericksburg, **E gas:** BP/dsl/24hr, Shell, Texaco, Wawa/24hr, **food:** Arby's, Bob Evans, Carlos O'Kelly's, Chesapeake, Friendly's, KFC, King Buffet, Mexico Lindo, Mkt St Buffet, Popeye's, Shoney's, Starbucks, Subway, TCBY, Vinny's Pizza, Wendy's, **lodging:** Best Western, Quality Inn, **other:** H, Batteries+, BigLots, $King, Hancock Fabrics, Home Depot, PepBoys, Radio Shack, Staples, U-Haul, **W gas:** BP, Chevron, Exxon/dsl/24hr, Shell, Sheetz, Valero, Wawa/24hr, **food:** A&W/LJ Silver, Applebees, Arby's, Asia Bistro, Aunt Sarah's, Baja Fresh, BoneFish Grill, Boston Mkt, Buffalo Wild Wings, Burger King, Caribou Coffee, Carrabba's, Checker's, Cheeseburger Paradise, Chick-fil-A, Chili's, China Jade, ChuckeCheese, CiCi's Pizza, Cracker Barrel, Denny's, Dunkin Donuts, El Paso Mexican, 5 Guy's Burgers, Firehouse Subs, Fuddrucker's, Great Steak, IHOP, Joe's Crabshack, Krispy Kreme, Ledo Pizza, Logan's Roadhouse, McDonald's, Melting Pot, Noodles&Co, NY Diner, O'Charley's, Old Country Buffet, Olive Garden, Outback Steaks, Pancho Villa, Panda Express, Panera Bread, Piccadilly, Pizza Hut, Popeye's, Qdoba, Quizno's, Red Lobster, Red Hot&Blue BBQ, Ruby Tuesday, Ryan's, Santa Fe Grill, Smokey Bones BBQ, Starbucks, Subway, Taco Bell, TGIFriday, Tia's Tex-Mex, TX Steaks, Waffle House, **lodging:** Best

FREDERICKSBURG

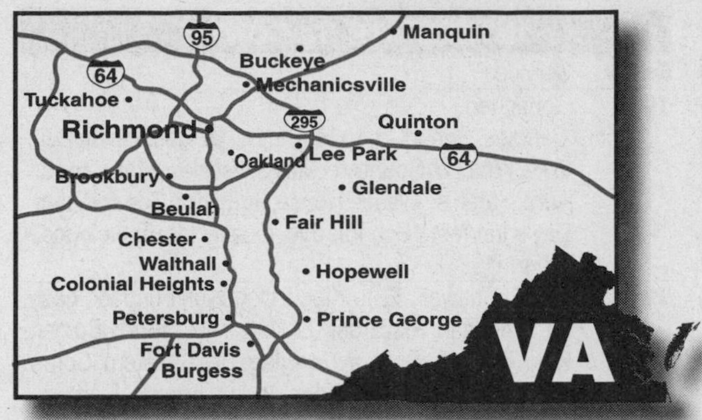

Exit #	Services
130b a	Continued Western, Hampton Inn, Hilton Garden, Homewood Suites, Ramada Inn, Super 8, **other:** Advance Parts, AutoZone, Belk, Best Buy, BJ's Whse, Borders Books, Costco, CVS Drug, $Tree, Gander Mtn, Giant Foods, GNC, Macy's, JC Penney, Kohl's, K-Mart, Lowes Whse, Macy's, Merchants Tire, Michaels, NTB, Office Depot, Old Navy, PetsMart, Ross, Sears/auto, Shopper's Foods, Target, Walmart SuperCtr/gas/24hr, mall
126	US 1, US 17 S, to Fredericksburg, **E gas:** BP, Chevron, Citgo, Exxon, Shell/dsl, **food:** Arby's, Bates Grill, Denny's, DQ, Friendly's, Hardee's, Hooters, McDonald's, Pizza Hut, Ruby Tuesday, Subway, Taco Bell, Waffle House, **lodging:** Country Inn&Suites, Day's Inn/rest., Econolodge, Fairfield Inn, Hampton Inn, Heritage Inn, Ramada Inn, Super 8, TownePlace Inn, **other:** Advance Parts, Aldi Foods, AutoZone, BMW, Buick/GMC/Pontiac, Cadillac, CVS Drug, Dodge, Goodyear/auto, Honda/Nissan, Little Tires, Rite Aid, Subaru, **W gas:** Exxon, Sunoco/dsl, WaWa, **food:** Applebees, Bob Evans, Burger King, Chick-fil-A, Chili's, China Jade, Chipotle Mexican, Coldstone Creamery, Cracker Barrel, El Charro Mexican, Famous Dave's BBQ, Firehouse Subs, 5 Guys Burgers, Foster's Grill, Golden China, KFC, Lenny's Subs, Longhorn Steaks, McDonald's, Mimi's Cafe, Moe's SW Grill, Noodles&Co, Panera Bread, Papa John's, Pollo Campero, Red Robin, UNO, Starbucks, Sonic, Subway, Wendy's, **lodging:** Comfort Inn, Sleep Inn, WyteStone Suites, **other:** Best Buy, Carmax, CVS Drug, $Plus, Kohl's, Lowes Whse, Marshall's, PetsMart, Rite Aid, Ross, Target, Walmart SuperCtr, World Mkt, USPO
118	VA 606, to Thornburg, **E gas:** Shell/dsl, **other:** Safford RV Ctr, to Stonewall Jackson Shrine, **W gas:** Citgo/dsl, Exxon, Shell/DQ, Valero, **food:** Angela's Rest., Burger King, McDonald's, Subway, **lodging:** Holiday Inn Express, Lamplighter Motel, Quality Inn, **other:** KOA (7mi), to Lake Anna SP
110	VA 639, to Ladysmith, **E gas:** Citgo, Shell/dsl, **W gas:** Citgo/dsl, Exxon/dsl, **food:** Domino's, Guiseppe's Rest., Subway, VA BBQ, **other:** Express Tire/repair, Family$, Food Lion
104	VA 207, to US 301, Bowling Green, **E gas:** Chevron, Exxon/dsl, Mr Fuel/dsl, Petro/dsl/rest./24hr/@, Pilot/Subway/DQ/dsl/24hr, Shell/dsl, Valero/dsl, **food:** McDonald's, Wendy's, **lodging:** Howard Johnson, Super 8, **other:** Blue Beacon, Russell Stover

FREDERICKSBURG

VA

INTERSTATE 95 CONT'D

N ↕ S

Exit #	Services
104	Continued Candies, SpeedCo, to Ft AP Hill, **W gas:** Exxon/dsl, *FLYING J*/Country Mkt/dsl/scales/24hr, **food:** Aunt Sarah's, Waffle House, **lodging:** Comfort Inn, Day's Inn/rest., Econolodge, Quality Inn, Travelodge, **other:** USPO
98	VA 30, Doswell, **E** to King's Dominion Funpark, **gas:** All American Plaza/dsl, Exxon, 7-11, **food:** Burger King, Denny's, Subway, **lodging:** Best Western, Comfort Suites, Day's Inn, Econolodge, **other:** All American Camping, King's Dominion Camping, truckwash
92	VA 54, Ashland, **E gas:** Sunoco, **W gas:** BP, TA/dsl/rest./@, Citgo/dsl, EastCoast/Blimpie/Krispy Kreme/dsl, Exxon/Subway, Shell/dsl, **food:** Applebees, Arby's, Burger King, Capt D's, Cracker Barrel, DQ, Hardee's, KFC/LJ Silver, McDonald's, New China Buffet, Perkin's, Pizza Hut, Ponderosa, Ruby Tuesday, Starbucks, Taco Bell, Waffle House, Wendy's, **lodging:** Day's Inn, Econolodge, Hampton Inn, Holiday Inn Express, Howard Johnson, Motel 6, Quality Inn, Ramada Inn, Sleep Inn, Super 8, Travelodge, **other:** Advance Parts, AutoZone, Buick/Pontiac, CarQuest, CVS Drug, Family$, Food Lion, Rite Aid, Tuesday Morning, Ukrop's Foods
89	VA 802, to Lewistown Rd, **E gas:** Shell, TA/Pizza Hut/Popeye's/dsl/café/24hr/@, **other:** Americamps RV Camp, **W lodging:** Cadillac Motel, **other:** Bass Pro Shops, Kosmo Village Camping, Rolling Hills RV Ctr
86b a	VA 656, Elmont, to Atlee, **E gas:** Sheetz, Valero, **food:** Burger King, McDonald's, Waffle House, **other:** CVS Drug, **W food:** CiCi'S Pizza, Jade Chinese, **other:** Gander Mtn, Home Depot, **W on US 1...gas:** 7-11, Shell/dsl, **food:** Applebees, Arby's, Buffalo Wild Wings, Burger King, Chick-fil-A, Chili's, Chipotle Mexican, Chophouse, Famous Dave's BBQ, McDonald's, O'Charley's, Panera Bread, Papa John's, Pizzaro, Quizno's, Red Robin, Ruby Tuesday, Shoney's, Subway, TX Roadhouse, Vinny's Grill, Wendy's, **lodging:** Candlewood Suites, Comfort Suites, Courtyard, Hampton Inn, SpringHill Suites, **other:** Barnes&Noble, Best Buy, Dillard's, Firestone/auto, Goodyear/auto, Home Depot, JC Penney, Macy's, Merchant's Tire, Michael's, Old Navy, PetsMart, Sears/auto, Target, Tire America, Ukrop's Foods, Walgreens, mall
84b a	I-295 W, to I-64, to Norfolk
83b a	VA 73, Parham Rd, **W gas:** EC/dsl, Exxon/DQ, 7-11, Shell/dsl, **food:** Aunt Sarah's, Burger King, El Paso Mexican, Hardee's, KFC, McDonald's, Papa Lou's, River City Diner, Starbucks, Subway, Waffle House, Wendy's, **lodging:** Econolodge, Holiday Inn, Knight's Inn, Sleep Inn, **other:** BigLots, CVS Drug, Family$, Food Lion, Kroger, Lowes Whse, Walmart SuperCtr
82	US 301, Chamberlayne Ave, **E gas:** Exxon/dsl, Sunoco, Texaco, WaWa, **food:** Friendly's, McDonald's, Subway, **lodging:** Days Inn, Super 8, **other:** Food Lion
81	US 1, Chamberlayne Ave (from nb), same as 82
80	Hermitage Rd, Lakeside Ave (from nb, no return), **W gas:** EC/Subway, **other:** Goodyear/auto, Ginter Botanical Gardens
79	I-64 W, to Charlottesville, I-195 S, to U of Richmond
78	Boulevard (no EZ nb return), **E gas:** BP, **lodging:** Holiday Inn, **W gas:** Citgo/dsl, **food:** Bill's BBQ, **other:** [H], to VA HS, stadium
76	Chamberlayne Ave, Belvidere, **E other:** [H], VA Union U
75	I-64 E, VA Beach, to Norfolk, [airport]
74c	US 33, US 250 W, to Broad St, **W other:** [H], st capitol, Museum of the Confederacy
74b	Franklin St, **E other:** Richmond Nat Bfd Park
74a	I-195 N, to Powhite Expswy, downtown
73.5mm	James River
73	Maury St, to US 60, US 360, industrial area
69	VA 161, Bells Rd, **E** Port of Richmond, **W gas:** Exxon/dsl/24hr, Shell/dsl, **food:** McDonald's, Subway, **lodging:** Candlewood Suites, Hampton Inn, Ramada Inn, Red Roof Inn
67b a	VA 895 (toll E), VA 150, to Chippenham Pkwy, Falling Creek, **W gas:** Raceway
64	VA 613, to Willis Rd, **E gas:** BP, Exxon, **lodging:** Best Value Inn, Econolodge, **other:** Drewry's Bluff Bfd, **W gas:** Chubby's, Citgo, 7-11, Shell/dsl, Sunoco, **food:** Burger King, Hank's BBQ, McDonald's, Subway, **lodging:** Country Inn&Suites, Economy House Motel, La Quinta, Sleep Inn, VIP Inn, **other:** flea mkt
62	VA 288 N, to Chesterfield, Powhite Pkwy, to [airport]
61b a	VA 10, Chester, **E gas:** Raceway, **food:** Don Jose Mexican, Hardee's, **lodging:** Comfort Inn, Courtyard, Hampton Inn, Holiday Inn Express, Homewood Suites, Quality Inn, **other:** [H], to James River Plantations, City Point NHS, Petersburg NBF, **W gas:** BP, EC/dsl, Exxon/dsl, 7-11, Texaco, **food:** Applebees, Burger King, Capt D's, Chili's, CiCi's, Cracker Barrel, Denny's, 5 Guys Burgers, Friendly's, Hardees, Hooter's, IHOP, KFC, McDonald's, O'Charley's, Panera Bread, Pizza Hut, Shoney's, Subway, Taco Bell, UNO, Waffle House, Wendy's, **lodging:** Clarion, Country Inn&Suites, Day's Inn, Fairfield Inn, Super 8, **other:** Aamco, Chevrolet, CVS Drug, $General, $Tree, Food Lion, Home Depot, K-Mart, Kohl's, Lowes Whse, NAPA, PetCo, Rite Aid, Target, Tuesday Morning, Ukrops Foods, to Pocahontas SP
58	VA 746, to Ruffinmill Rd, **E other:** Honda, Hyundai, Toyota/Scion, **W gas:** Exxon, **food:** Dunkin Donuts, Subway, **lodging:** Candlewood Suites
54	VA 144, Temple Ave, Hopewell, to Ft Lee, **E gas:** BP/24hr, Exxon, Sheetz, Shell, **food:** Applebees, Arby's, Buffalo Wild Wings, Burger King, CicC's Pizza, El Caporal Mexican, 5 Guys Burgers, Golden Corral, Great China, LoneStar Steaks, McDonald's, Olive Garden, Outback Steaks, Panera Bread, Picadilly's, Pizza Hut, Quizno's, Red Lobster, Ruby Tuesday, Starbucks, Subway, Taco Bell, Wendy's, **lodging:** Comfort Suites, Hampton Inn, Hilton Garden, Holiday Inn, **other:** Best Buy, Books-a-Million, Chevrolet/Cadillac/Buick/Nissan, Dillard's, $Tree, Macy's, Home Depot, JC Penney, Jo-Ann Fabrics, KIA, K-Mart, Macy's, Marshall's, Merchant's Tire, Michael's, Nissan, PetsMart, Sam's Club/gas, Sears/auto, Staples, Target, Walmart SuperCtr/24hr, mall, **W gas:** Kangaroo, **food:** DQ, Hardee's, Waffle House, **other:** U-Haul, to VSU

ELMONT

CHESTER

VA

N ↕ S

PETERSBURG

INTERSTATE 95 CONT'D

Exit #	Services
53	S Park Blvd (from nb), **E** same as 54
52.5mm	Appomattox River
52	Washington St, Wythe St, **E gas:** Exxon/dsl, Valero, **food:** Jade Garden, **lodging:** Best Value Inn, Knight's Inn, Red Carpet Inn, Royal Inn, Super 8, Travelodge, **other:** Petersburg Nat Bfd, **W gas:** Liberty, **lodging:** Ramada Inn, Rodeway Inn, **other:** H
51	I-85 S, to South Hill, US 460 W
50d	Wythe St, (from nb), same as 52
50b c	**E gas:** 7-11, **lodging:** Knight's Inn
50a	US 301, US 460 E, to Crater Rd, County Dr, **E gas:** BP, Citgo, RaceWay, **food:** Hardee's, McDonald's, **lodging:** Armada Inn, California Inn, Knight's Inn, Quality Inn, **other:** H
48b a	Wagner Rd, **W on Crater Rd...food:** Capt D's, KFC, Pizza Hut, Taste of China, Taco Bell, **other:** Curves, CVS Drug, $Tree, $General, Lincoln/Mercury, Pepboys, Radio Shack, Ukrops Foods, Walgreens, Walmart SuperCtr, Vet
47	VA 629, to Rives Rd, **W gas:** Citgo, Texaco/dsl, **lodging:** Heritage Motel, **1-2 mi W food:** Arby's, Burger King, Mad Italian, McDonald's, Pizza Hut, Subway, Taco Bell, **lodging:** Crater Inn, LaSalle Motel, **other:** Softball Hall of Fame Museum, same as 48 on US 301
46	I-295 N (exits left from sb), to Washington
45	US 301, **E gas:** Shell/dsl, **W gas:** Exxon, **food:** Lighthouse Rest., Nanny's BBQ, Steven-Kent Rest., **lodging:** Best Western, Comfort Inn, Day's Inn/rest., Hampton Inn, Holiday Inn Express, Quality Inn
41	US 301, VA 35, VA 156, **E gas:** Chevron/dsl, **lodging:** Econolodge, **other:** South 40 camp resort, **W lodging:** Knight's Inn, Traveler's Inn
40mm	**weigh sta both lanes**
37	US 301, Carson, **W gas:** BP/dsl, Shell/dsl
36mm	**rest area nb, full (handicapped) facilities, (phone), vending, (picnic), litter barrel, petwalk**
33	VA 602, **W gas:** Chevron/dsl, Davis/Exxon/Subway/Starbucks/dsl/scales/24hr, **food:** Burger King, Denny's/24hr, **lodging:** Hampton Inn, Sleep Inn
31	VA 40, Stony Creek, to Waverly, **W gas:** Shell/dsl/24hr, Sunoco, **food:** Tastee Hut
24	VA 645
20	VA 631, Jarratt, **W gas:** Exxon/Blimpie/Pizza Hut/dsl/24hr, Race-in/dsl, **other:** Ford
17	US 301, **1 mi E lodging:** Knight's Inn, Reste Motel, **other:** Jellystone Park Camping
13	VA 614, to Emporia, **E gas:** Shell/dsl
12	US 301 (from nb)
11b a	US 58, Emporia, to South Hill, **E gas:** BP/DQ/Subway/dsl, Citgo/Burger King, Exxon/LJ Silver/Stuckey's, Texaco, **food:** Applebee's, Arby's, Cracker Barrel, Hardee's, KFC, McDonald's, Pizza Hut, Wendy's, **lodging:** Country Inn & Suites, Fairfield Inn, Holiday Inn, US Inn, **other:** H, Advance Parts, CVS Drug, $Tree, Family$, Food Lion, NAPA, Radio Shack, Rite Aid, Walmart SuperCtr/24hr, **W gas:** Exxon, Petrol, Race-In/dsl, Shell/Sadler/dsl/rest./scales/24hr/@, **food:** Bojangles, Pueblo Viejo, Quizno's, Shoney's, Starbucks, **lodging:** Best Western, Day's Inn, Hampton Inn, Holiday Inn Express, Quality Inn, Sleep Inn

EMPORIA

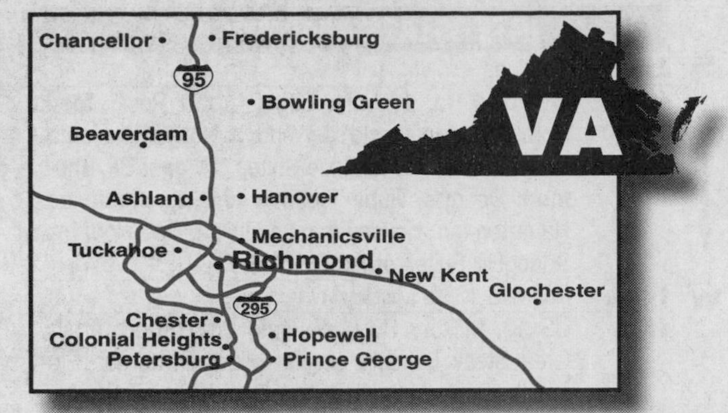

Exit #	Services
8	US 301, **E gas:** BP/Simmon's/dsl/rest./scales/24hr, Exxon, **lodging:** Red Carpet Inn, Super 8, **other:** truck repair
4	VA 629, to Skippers, **E gas:** Loves/McDonald's/dsl/scales/24hr, **W gas:** Shell/dsl, **lodging:** Econolodge, **other:** Cattail Creek Camping (2mi)
3.5mm	Fountain's Creek
.5mm	**Welcome Ctr nb, full (handicapped) facilities, (phone), vending, (picnic), litter barrels, petwalk**
0mm	Virginia/North Carolina state line

E ↕ W

INTERSTATE 264 (NORFOLK)

Exit #	Services
23mm	I-264 begins/ends, BP, Shell, convention ctr
22	Birdneck Rd, I-264 begins/ends, **S food:** McDonald's/playplace, **lodging:** DoubleTree Hotel, **other:** museum
21	VA Beach Blvd, First Colonial Rd, **N gas:** BP, Shell, **food:** Applebee's, Burger King, McDonald's, Outback Steaks, Taco Bell, Target, Wendy's, Virginian Steaks, **other:** Borders Books, K-Mart, **S other:** 7-11, NAPA
20	US 58 E, to VA Beach Blvd (eb only), **N food:** Capt. George's Seafood, China Moon, Hardee's, Ruby Tuesday, Tuesday Morning, **other:** Family$, Food Lion, Lincoln/Mercury, Lowe's Whse, 7-11, TJ Maxx
19	Lynnhaven Pkwy, **N gas:** 7-11, Wawa, **food:** Mauie Wowie, Moe's SW Grill, Quizno's, Subway, **other:** Audi, Ford, Jaguar, PepBoys, Porsche, VW, **S food:** McDonald's
18	Rosemont, **N gas:** BJ's Whse, Exxon, **food:** Bonefish Grill, Burger King, Denny's, Hardee's, KFC, LJ Silver, McDonald's, Mi Casita Mexican, Papa John's, Taco Bell, Wendy's, **lodging:** Econolodge, Nissan, Radio Shack, **other:** Food Lion, Harris Teeter, Home Depot, Honda, Kroger, Merchant's Tire/Auto, Rite Aid, Sam's Club/gas, Walgreens, **S gas:** Hess/dsl, Shell, Wawa, **food:** Four Seasons Chinese, **other:** Chrysler/Dodge
17.5mm	**wb only, inspection sta**
17a b	Independance Blvd, **N gas:** Exxon, **food:** Fuddruckers, Macaroni Grill, Max & Erma's, McDonald's, Smokey Bones BBQ, Starbucks, Taco Bell, Tripps Rest., Wendy's, Village Inn, **lodging:** Crowne Plaza, Extended Stay, Motel 6, **other:** Best Buy, Sears/auto, **S gas:** BP, Exxon, 7-11/gas, Wawa, **food:** Arby's, Azteca Mexican, Golden Corral, Hardee's, KFC, Quizno's, Starbucks, Wing Zone, **lodging:** InTown Suites, **other:** $General, Food Lion, Mazda, Rite Aid
16	Witchduck

VA

INTERSTATE 264 (NORFOLK)

E ↕ W

Exit #	Services
15a b	Newtown Rd, **N gas:** Citgo, Crown Royal, **food:** Domino's, McDonald's, Wendy's, **lodging:** Homewood Suites, TownePlace Suites, **S gas:** BP, Shell, **food:** Denny's, Ruby Tuesday, **lodging:** Courtyard, Hampton Inn, Holiday Inn, La Quinta, Red Roof Inn, SpringHill Suites **other:** Rite Aid, 7-11
14b a	I-64. US 13, to Military Hwy
13	US 13, Military Hwy, **N gas:** Shell, **food:** Arbys, Great Steak, Lonestar Steaks, Mihogar Mexican, Piccadilly, Schlotzky's, **lodging:** Best Value, Day's Inn, Econolodge, Motel 6, Ramada Ltd, **other:** Firestone/auto, JC Penney, Ross, Sears/auto,
12	Ballentine Blvd, **N other:** H, Norfolk SU
11b a	US 460, VA 166/168, Brambleton Ave, Campostello Rd, **N gas:** 7-11/gas, Shell
10	Tidewater Dr, City Hall Ave, downtown
9	St Paul's Blvd, Waterside Dr, to Harbor Park Stadium
8	I-464 S, to Chesapeake
7.5mm	tunnel
7b a	VA 141, Effingham St, Crawford St, **N gas:** 7-11, **food:** Hardees, **other:** Naval H, **S other:** Shipyard
6.5mm	**weigh sta eb**
6	Des Moines Ave (from eb)
5	US 17, Frederick Blvd, Midtown Tunnel, **N** H, **S gas:** BP, **other:** Harley-Davidson
4	VA 337, Portsmouth Blvd
3	Victory Blvd, **N gas:** Exxon, 7-11/gas, Wawa, **food:** Capt D's, DQ, Domino's, McDonald's, Pizza Hut, Ruby Tuesday, Wendy's, **other:** AutoZone, BigLots, $Tree, FarmFresh Food/drug, Ford, Lowe's Whse, PepBoys, Radio Shack, **S gas:** Valero/dsl
2b a	Greenwood Dr
0mm	I-264 begins/ends on I-64, exit 299.

INTERSTATE 295 (RICHMOND)

N ↕ S

Exit #	Services
53b a	I-64, W to Charlottesville, E to Richmond, to US 250, I-295 begins/ends.
51b a	Nuckols Rd, **1 mi N gas:** Miller's Gas/dsl, Valero, **food:** Bottoms Up Pizza, Bruster's, Cheeburger, Chen's Chinese, McDonald's, Nonna's Pizzaria, Salsarita's Cantina, Smoothie Cafe, Starbucks, Subway, **other:** CVS Drug, Food Lion, Walgreens, Vet, **S gas:** Exxon, **food:** Capital Alehouse, Mkt Cafe, **other:** USPO
49b a	US 33, Richmond, **1 mi S food:** Carbel's Ice Cream, Quizno's, **other:** Ukrop's Foods
45b a	Woodman Rd, **1-2 mi S gas:** 7-11, Valero, Little Caesar's, **other:** CVS Drug, $General, Meadow Farm Museum
43	I-95, US 1, N to Washington, S to Richmond (exits left from nb), **N on US 1...gas:** 7-11, Shell/dsl, **food:** Applebees, Arby's, Buffalo Wild Wings, Burger King, Chick-fil-A, Chili's, Chipotle Mexican, Chophouse, Famous Dave's BBQ, McDonald's, O'Charley's, Panera Bread, Papa John's, Pizzaro, Quizno's, Red Robin, Ruby Tuesday, Shoney's, Subway, TX Roadhouse, Vinny's Grill, Wendy's, **lodging:** Candlewood Suites, Comfort Suites, Courtyard, Hampton Inn,

MECHANICSVILLE

Exit #	Services
43	Continued SpringHill Suites, **other:** Barnes&Noble, Best Buy, Dillard's, Firestone/auto, Goodyear/auto, Home Depot, JC Penney, Macy's, Merchant's Tire, Michael's, Old Navy, PetsMart, Sears/auto, Target, Tire America, Ukrop's Foods, Walgreens, mall, **1-2 mi S gas:** Exxon, EC/dsl, 7-11, Shell, WaWa/dsl, **food:** Aunt Sarah's, Burger King, El Paso Mexican, Hardee's, McDonald's, Subway, Waffle House, Wendy's, **lodging:** Broadway Motel, Cavalier Motel, Econolodge, GuestHouse Inn, Howard Johnson, Knight's Inn, **other:** Aamco, Food Lion, Firestone, Lowes Whse, Rite Aid, Walmart SuperCtr
41b a	US 301, VA 2, **E gas:** BP/dsl, Valero, **food:** Burger King, McDonald's, Subway, **W gas:** Exxon/dsl, **food:** Friendly's, **lodging:** Holiday Inn, Super 8, Travelodge
38b a	VA 627, Pole Green Rd, **E gas:** BP/Miller's Mkt/dsl, Exxon (1mi), 7-11, **food:** Bruster's, Chen's Rest., Coffee Lane, Mimmo's Rest., Nacho Mamas, Subway, **other:** Curves, Food Lion, Vet, **W gas:** 7-11, Valero
37b a	US 360, **1 mi E gas:** Shell/dsl, Texaco, **food:** Applebees, Arby's, Buffalo Wild Wings, Chick-fil-A, Cracker Barrel, IHOP, KFC, McDonald's, Moe's SW Grill, Noodles&Co, Outback Steaks, Panera Bread, Ruby Tuesday, Starbucks, Super Buffet, Taco Bell, Waffle House, Wendy's, **lodging:** Hampton Inn, Holiday Inn Express, **other:** Best Buy, BJ's Whse/Gas, $General, $Tree, GNC, Home Depot, Kohl's, Marshall's, PetsMart, Radio Shack, Target, Ukrops Foods, Walmart SuperCtr, **W gas:** 7-11, Sunoco, Valero, **other:** to Mechanicsville
34b a	VA 615, Creighton Rd, **E gas:** 7-11, Valero
31b a	VA 156, **E gas:** Citgo/dsl, **other:** to Cold Harbor Bfd
28	I-64, to US 60, **W other:** museum
25	Rd 895 W (toll), to Richmond, **E gas:** Shell, Valero, **food:** Dunkin Donuts
22b a	VA 5, Charles City, **E gas:** Exxon/dsl, **food:** DQ, **other:** Shirley Plantation, **W gas:** Valero/dsl, **food:** Portabella's Cafe, **other:** Food Lion, Richmond Nat Bfd
18mm	James River
15b a	VA 10, Hopewell, **E gas:** BP/dsl, **food:** Burger King, **lodging:** Evergreen Motel (3mi), **other:** H, James River Plantations, **W gas:** EC/Subway/dsl, Exxon/dsl, Sheetz, WaWa, **food:** Chen's Rest., McDonald's, River's Bend Cafe, Wendy's, **lodging:** Hyatt Place, **other:** Curves, CVS Drug, Food Lion, 7-11, Vet
13mm	Appomattox River
9b a	VA 36, Hopewell, **E gas:** Chevron, Petrol, WaWa, **food:** Bojangles, El Nopal Mexican, Hardees, Hong Kong's Rest., Huddle House, KFC, Little Caesar's, Rosa's Italian, **lodging:** Best Western, Econolodge, Fairfield Inn, Stayover Suites, **other:** Advance Parts, AutoZone, Family$, Walgreens, Vet, **W gas:** BP/dsl/24hr, Shell, Valero, **food:** Burger King, Denny's, DQ, Dunkin Donuts, McDonald's, Papa John's, Pizza Hut, Ruby Tuesday, Shoney's, Subway, Taco Bell, Waffle House, Wendy's, **lodging:** Candlewood Suites, Comfort Inn, Hampton Inn, Quality Inn, **other:** Chevrolet, $General, Family$, Food Lion, Rite Aid, U-Haul, US Army Museum, to Petersburg NBF

HOPEWELL

N ↕ S

INTERSTATE 295 CONT'D (RICHMOND)

Exit #	Services
5.5mm	Blackwater Swamp
3b a	US 460, Petersburg, to Norfolk, **E gas:** EC/dsl, Hess, Texaco, **food:** Prince George BBQ, Subway, Wendy's, **1-2 mi W gas:** BP/dsl, **food:** Hardee's, McDonald's
1	I-95, N to Petersburg, S to Emporium, I-295 begins/ends.

N ↕ S

WASHINGTON DC AREA

INTERSTATE 495 (WASHINGTON DC)

Exit #	Services
27	I-95, N to Baltimore, S to Richmond. I-495 & I-95 S run together.
28b a	MD 650, New Hampshire Ave, **N gas:** Citgo, Exxon/dsl, Shell/repair, **food:** Domino's, Quizno's, Starbucks, Urban BBQ, **other:** CVS Drug, Radio Shack, Safeway, 7-11
29b a	MD 193, University Blvd
30b a	US 29, Colesville, **N gas:** BP, Getty, Shell, **food:** McDonald's, Subway, **other:** CVS Drug, Safeway, 7-11/Jerry's Subs
31b a	MD 97, Georgia Ave, Silver Springs, **N gas:** [H], **S gas:** CG Gas, Chevron, Exxon/dsl, Shell, **food:** Domino's, Mayflower Chinese, **other:** CVS Drug, Snider's Foods, Staples
33	MD 185, Connecticut Ave, **N other:** LDS Temple, **S gas:** Citgo/repair, Liberty, Sunoco, **food:** Chevy Chase Foods
34	MD 355, Wisconsin Ave, Bethesda
35	(from wb), I-270
36	MD 187, Old Georgetown Rd, **S other:** [H]
38	I-270, to Frederick
39	MD 190, River Rd, Washington, Potomac
40	Cabin John Pkwy, Glen Echo (from sb), no trucks
41	Clara Barton Pkwy, Carderock, Great Falls, no trucks
42mm	Potomac River, Virginia/Maryland state line. **Exits 41-27 are in Maryland.**
43	G Washington Mem Pkwy, no trucks
44	VA 193, Langley
45b a	VA 267 W (toll), to I-66 E, to Dulles ✈
46b a	VA 123, Chain Bridge Rd, **W lodging:** Hilton
47b a	VA 7, Leesburg Pike, Tysons Corner, Falls Church, **E lodging:** Westin, **W gas:** BP/dsl, Exxon, Shell, **food:** Chili's, McDonald's, NY Deli, Olive Garden, On-the-Border, Panera Bread, Pizza Hut, Starbucks, Wendy's, **lodging:** Best Western, Courtyard, Marriott, **other:** Best Buy, Borders Books, Chevrolet/Chrysler, Ford, Marshall's, Merchant's Tire, PetCo, Staples, Subaru, mall
49c b a	I-66 (exits left from both lanes), to Manassas, Front Royal
50b a	US 50, Arlington Blvd, Fairfax, Arlington, **E lodging:** Marriott, **E gas:** Shell, Sunoco, **food:** Chevy's Mexican, KFC, McDonald's, Panda Express, Panera Bread, Wendy's, **lodging:** Residence Inn, **other:** [H], CVS Drug
51	VA 657, Gallows Rd, **W gas:** Exxon, **other:** [H], 7-11
52b a	VA 236, Little River Tpk, Fairfax, **N gas:** Citgo, Sunoco/repair, **food:** La Fondita, McDonald's, Wendy's, **other:** 7-11

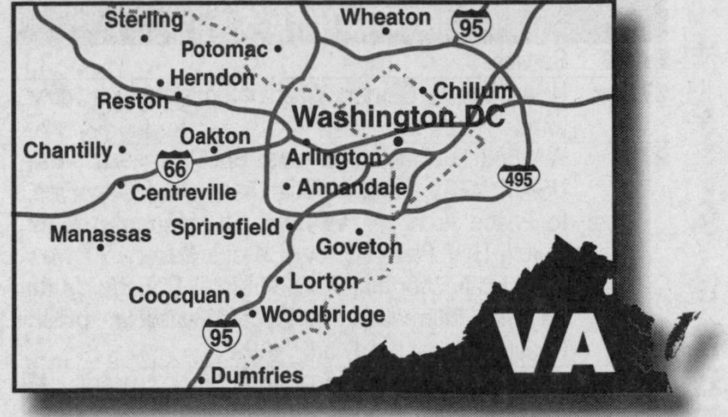

Exit #	Services
54b a	VA 620, Braddock Rd, Ctr for the Arts, Geo Mason U, **S gas:** Sunoco, **food:** DQ, **other:** NTB, Rite Aid, Safeway
56c b a	I-95 S, I-395 N, I-95 N. I-495 & I-95 N run together.

E ↕ W

PORTSMOUTH

INTERSTATE 664 (NORFOLK)

Exit #	Services
15b a	I-64 to Chesapeake, I-264 E to Portsmouth & Norfolk, I-664 begins/ends on I-64, exit 299.
13b a	US 13, US 58, US 460, Military Hwy, **E gas:** Shell/dsl, **lodging:** Econolodge
12	VA 663, Dock Landing Rd
11b a	VA 337, Portsmouth Blvd, **E gas:** BP, 7-11, Shell/dsl, **food:** Applebees, Arby's, Backyard Burger, Burger King, Chick-fil-A, ChuckeCheese, Fazoli's, KFC, McDonald's, Outback Steaks, Pizza Hut, Red Lobster, Red Robin, Taco Bell, **lodging:** Hampton Inn, Holiday Inn Express, Springhill Suites, **other:** AutoZone, Dodge, $Tree, Home Depot, JC Penney, K-Mart, Michael's, PetsMart, Sears/auto
10	10 VA 659, Pughsville Rd, **E gas:** 7-11, Shell, **food:** IHOP, McDonald's
9b a	US 17, US 164, **E gas:** Hess, 7-11, Wa Wa, **food:** Captain D's, DQ, Dunkin Donuts, Sonic, **lodging:** Budget Lodge, Hampton Inn, Sleep Inn, Super 8, **other:** [H], Chevrolet, Farm Fresh Foods, Honda, Nissan, tires, **W** to James River Br, museum
8b a	VA 135, College Dr, **E gas:** 7-11, Shell/Burger King, **food:** Applebees, Firehouse Subs, McDonald's, Panchero's Mexican, Ruby Tuesday, Subway, Wendy's, **other:** FoodLion, Kohl's, Radio Shack, Staples, Walmart SuperCtr/24hr, **W food:** Riverstone Chophouse, **lodging:** Courtyard, TownePlace Suites
11.5mm	**insp sta nb**
9mm	James River
8mm	tunnel
7	Terminal Ave
6	25th St, 26th St, **E gas:** 7-11, **food:** McDonald's
5	US 60 W, 35th St, Jefferson Ave, **E gas:** Citgo, **food:** Church's, Pizza Palace
4	Chesnut Ave, Roanoke Ave
3	Aberdeen Rd, **E gas:** Zooms/dsl, **W food:** Hardee's, McDonald's, Wendy's
2	Powhatan Pkwy, **E gas:** 7-11, **1-2 mi W gas:** BJ's Whse, **food:** Coldstone Creamery, Cracker Barrel, Joe's Crabshack, Lonstar Steaks, McFadden's Rest., **lodging:** Hilton Garden, **other:** Bass Pro Shop, Lowe's Whse
1b a	I-64, W to Richmond, E to Norfolk. **I-664 begins/ends on I-64.**

INTERSTATE 5

Exit #	Services
277mm	USA/Canada Border, Washington state line, customs
276	WA 548 S, Blaine, **E gas:** Shell/dsl, Texaco/dsl, USA/dsl/24hr, **food:** Big Al's Diner, **other:** Duty Free, to Peace Arch SP, **W gas:** Chevron/repair, **food:** Chada Thai, Pizza Factory, Seaside Bakery, Subway, **lodging:** Anchor Inn, Bayside Motel, Cottage by the Bay B&B, International Motel/cafe, Sunset Inn, **other:** Coast to Coast Hardware, NAPA
275	WA 543 N (from nb, no return), truck customs, **E gas:** Chevron/dsl, Exxon/dsl, Shell/dsl, **food:** Burger King, **other:** Ace Hardware, CostCutter Foods, $Tree, Rite Aid, Vet
274	Peace Portal Drive (from nb, no return), Blaine, **W gas:** Shell, **other:** Semi-ah-moo Resort, camping
270	Birch Bay, Lynden, **W gas:** Shell/Domino's/Subway/dsl/24hr, **food:** Bob's Burgers, Jack-in-the-Box, **lodging:** Semi-ah-moo Resort, **other:** Birch Bay Outlet/famous brands, Curves, Lighthouse RV Park (5mi), Mkt Foods, Vet
269mm	**Welcome Ctr sb, full [handicapped] facilities, info, [phone], [picnic], litter barrels, petwalk, vending**
267mm	**rest area nb, full [handicapped] facilities, info, [phone], [picnic], litter barrels, petwalk, vending**
266	WA 548 N, Grandview Rd, Custer, **W gas:** Arco/24hr, **other:** Birch Bay SP
263	Portal Way, **E gas:** Pacific Pride/dsl, Shell/dsl, **other:** AA RV Park, Cedars RV Park
263mm	Nooksack River
262	Main St, Ferndale, **E gas:** 76/dsl, Texaco/dsl, **food:** Denny's, McDonald's, Subway, **lodging:** Super 8, **other:** RV Park, TDS Tires, **W gas:** Gull/dsl, 76, Shell/Domino's/dsl, **food:** Asian Bistro, Bob's Burgers, DQ, Quizno's, Sonic, **lodging:** Scottish Lodge, **other:** Costcutter Foods, Haggen's Foods, NAPA, Schwab Tire, Walgreens, Vet
260	Slater Rd, Lummi Island, **E gas:** Arco/24hr, **other:** El Monte RV Ctr, antiques, **4 mi W gas:** 76, Shell/dsl, **lodging:** Silver Reef Hotel/Casino, **other:** Lummi Ind Res
258	Bakerview Rd, **E food:** Magic Dragon, Subway, **other:** Fred Meyer/gas, **W gas:** Arco/24hr, 76, **food:** Mykono's Greek Rest., **lodging:** Hampton Inn, Shamrock Motel, **other:** Bellingham RV Park, [airport], st patrol
257	Northwest Ave, **E other:** Cadillac/Chevrolet
256b	Bellis Fair Mall Pkwy, **E other:** Sears, Target, mall
256a	WA 539 N, Meridian St, **E gas:** Meridian, Shell/dsl, Super Gas, **food:** Arby's, Burger King, China Palace, Coldstone Creamery, Denny's, Kowloon Garden, Lorenzo's Italian, McHale's Rest., Olive Garden, Pad Thai, Quizno's, Red Robin, Shari's/24hr, Starbucks, Subway, Taco Bell, Taco Del Mar, Taco Time, Wendy's, **lodging:** Best Western, Comfort Inn, Holiday Inn Express La Quinta, Quality Inn, **other:** AAA, Barnes&Noble, Best Buy, Costco/gas, Costcutter Foods, $Tree, Home Depot, JC Penney, Macy's, Michael's, Nordstrom's, Office Depot, PetCo, Rite Aid, Ross, Safeway, Schuck's Parts, Schwab Tire, Sears, Target, TJ Maxx, U-haul, Walgreens, Walmart/auto, mall, st patrol, to Nooksack Ind Res, **W food:** Eleni's Rest., **lodging:** Econolodge, Rodeway Inn
255	WA 542 E, Sunset Dr, Bellingham, **E gas:** Chevron/dsl/24hr, 76, Shell/Subway/Domino's/dsl, **food:** A&W/KFC, Applebees, Domino's, Hawaii BBQ, Jack-in-the-Box, Panda Express, RoundTable Pizza, Taco Bell, **other:** Costcutter Foods, Jo-Ann Fabrics, K-Mart, Lowes Whse, Tuesday Morning, Walgreens, USPO, to Mt Baker, **W other:** [H]
254	Iowa St, State St, Bellingham, **E gas:** 76, Valero, **other:** Audi/VW, Honda, Hyundai, Mercedes, Kia, Nissan, Toyota/Scion, Vacation Land RV Ctr, Volvo, **W gas:** Chevron/24hr, Shell, **food:** DQ, McDonald's, Skipper's Rest., Subway, **other:** Chrysler/Dodge, Ford/Lincoln/Mercury, NAPA, Schuck's Parts, Subaru, repair
253	Lakeway Dr, Bellingham, **E food:** Burger Me, Lychee Buffet, Little Caesar's, Papa Murphy's, Port of Subs, Sol de Mexico, Subway, **lodging:** Best Western, Guesthouse Inn, **other:** Costcutter Foods, Discount Tire, Fred Meyer, Radio Shack, 7-11, **W** same as 252
252	Samish Way, Bellingham, **E lodging:** Evergreen Motel, **other:** same as 253, **W gas:** Chevron, Mobil, 76, Shell/dsl/24hr, **food:** Arby's, Diego's Mexican, 5 Columns Steaks, IHOP, McDonald's, Pizza Hut, Pizza Pipeline, Popeye's, Quizno's, Starbucks, Taco Time, Thai Cuisine, Wendy's, **lodging:** Bay City Motel, Cascade Inn, Coachman Inn, Days Inn, Mac's Motel, Motel 6, Travelodge, Villa Inn, **other:** Haggen Foods, Rite Aid
250	WA 11 S, Chuckanut Dr, Bellingham, Fairhaven Hist Dist, **W gas:** Arco, Chevron/repair, **other:** Food Pavilion, Larrabee SP, to Alaska Ferry, Vet
246	N Lake Samish, **W gas:** Shell/dsl, **other:** Lake Padden RA, RV camping
242	Nulle Rd, S Lake Samish
240	Alger, **E gas:** Shell/dsl/LP/RV dump, **food:** Alger Grille, **lodging:** Whispering Firs Motel/**RV Parking**
238mm	**rest area both lanes, full [handicapped] facilities, [phone], [picnic], litter barrels, vending, petwalk**
236	Bow Hill Rd, **E** Skagit Hotel Casino/rest./dsl/LP
235mm	**weigh sta sb**
234mm	Samish River
232	Cook Rd, Sedro-Woolley, **E gas:** 76/Subway/dsl, Shell/dsl, **food:** Bob's Burgers, Jack-in-the-Box, **lodging:** Fairfield Inn, **other:** [H], KOA
231	WA 11 N, Chuckanut Dr, **E other:** Camping World RV Ctr, Kia, st patrol, **W** to Larrabee SP (14mi)
230	WA 20, Burlington, **E gas:** Shell/dsl, **food:** Burger King, Cascade Brewery Rest., China Wok, El Cazador, Jack-in-the-Box, Krispy Kreme, Outback Steaks, Pizza Factory, Red Robin, Subway, **lodging:** Cocusa Motel, Sterling Motel, **other:** [H], Fred Meyer, Haggen Foods, JC Penney, Macy's, Schwab Tire, Sears/auto, 7-11, Target, mall, transmissions, to N Cascades NP, **W food:** McDonald's, **lodging:** Holiday Inn Express, Mark II Motel, **other:** Harley-Davidson, Hyundai, to San Juan Ferry
229	George Hopper Rd, **E gas:** Arco/24hr, USA/dsl, **food:** Jamba Juice, McDonald's, Olive Garden, Sakura Japenese, Shari's, Starbucks, Subway, Taco Del Mar, Wendy's, **lodging:** Hampton Inn, **other:** Best Buy, Costco/gas, Costcutter Foods, Discount

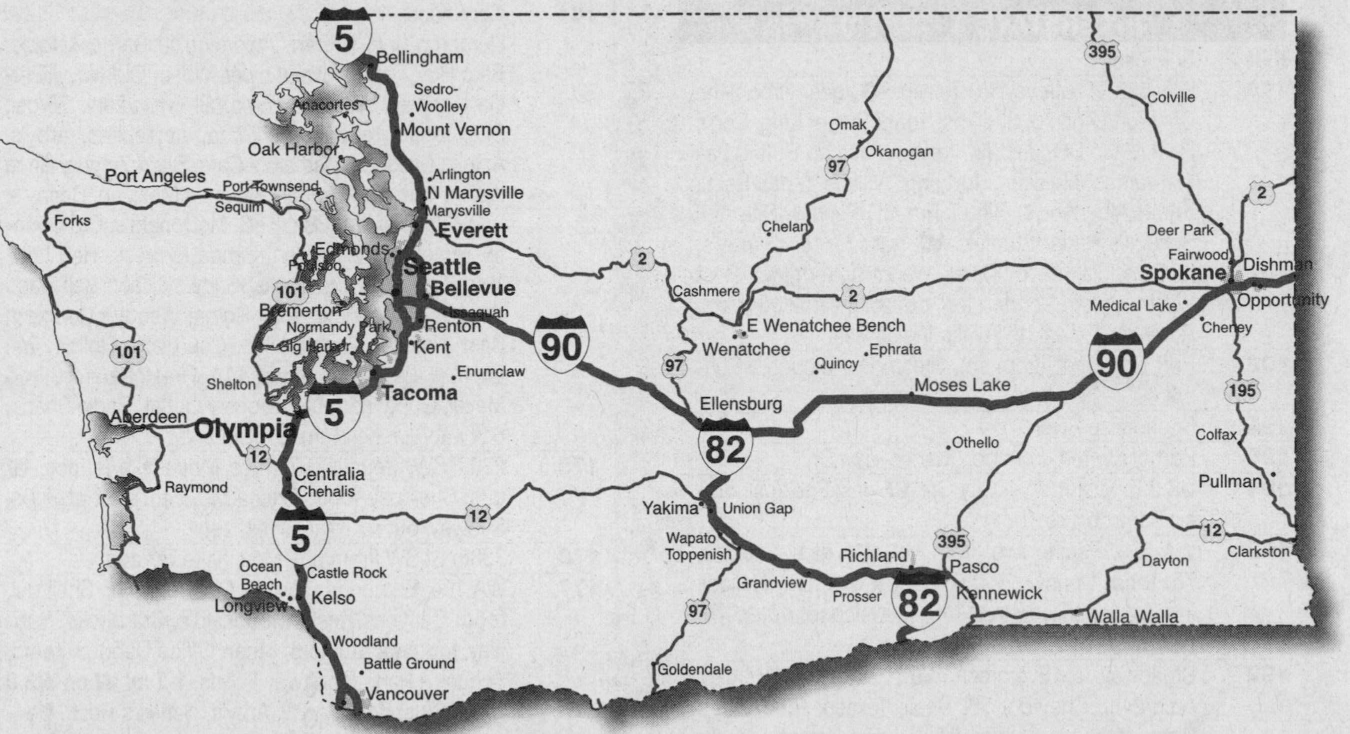

INTERSTATE 5 CONT'D

N ↕ S

Exit #	Services
229	Continued Tire, Home Depot, K-Mart, Kohl's, NAPA, Old Navy, PetsMart, Outlet Shops/famous brands, Ross, See's Candies, Sportsman's Whse, **W other:** Buick/Pontiac, Cadillac, Chrysler/Jeep/Dodge, Ford, Mazda/Honda, Nissan, Toyota/Scion, Subaru, VW, RV Ctr
228mm	Skagit River
227	WA 538 E, College Way, Mt Vernon, **E gas:** 76, **food:** A&W, Big Scoop Rest., Denny's, Jack-in-the Box, KFC, La Hacienda, Pizza Hut/Taco Bell, Quizno's, Round Table Pizza, Skipper's, Taco Time, **lodging:** Best Western, Day's Inn, West Winds Motel, **other:** Ace Hardware, AutoZone, Buick/Cadillac/GMC, $Plus, $Tree, Goodyear/auto, Jo-Ann Fabrics, Office Depot, PetCo, Rite Aid, Safeway/gas, Schuck's Parts, ValueVillage Foods, Walmart/auto, **W gas:** FuelExpress/24hr, Shell/dsl, **food:** Arby's, Burger King, Cranberry Tree Rest., DQ, Forks&Knives Steaks, Fortune Chinese, Royal Fork Buffet, **lodging:** Best Western, Quality Inn, Tulip Inn, **other:** Chevrolet, Lowes Whse
226	WA 536 W, Kincaid St, City Ctr, **E** [H], **W food:** Old Towne Grainery Rest., Skagit River Brewing Co, **other:** NAPA, Red Apple Foods, Valley RV Ctr, RV camping, antiques
225	Anderson Rd, **E gas:** Fuel Express, 76/dsl, **other:** Lifestyles RV Ctr, **other:** transmissions, **W gas:** Truck City Trkstp/dsl, Valero, **food:** Long Haul Cafe, **other:** Freightliner, Pulsbo RV Ctr, Valley RV Ctr
224	WA 99 S (from nb, no return), S Mt Vernon, **E** gas/dsl, food
221	WA 534 E, Conway, Lake McMurray, **E gas:** Shell/dsl/24hr, **W gas:** 76/dsl, Texaco/dsl, **food:** Conway Deli, **lodging:** Channel Lodge/Rest. (11mi), **other:** Blake's RV Park/marina (6mi)
218	Starbird Rd, **W lodging:** Hillside Motel
215	300th NW, **W gas:** Interstate/dsl
214mm	**weigh sta nb**
212	WA 532 W, Stanwood, Bryant, **W gas:** 76/dsl, Shell/dsl, **other:** Camano Island SP (19mi)
210	236th NE, **E other:** Casino
209mm	Stillaguamish River
208	WA 530, Silvana, Arlington, **E gas:** Chevron/24hr, 76/Circle K, Shell, Tesoro, **food:** Denny's, O'Brien Turkeyhouse, **lodging:** Arlington Motel, **other:** [H], to N Cascades Hwy, **W gas:** 76/dsl
207mm	**rest area both lanes, full [handicapped] facilities, [phone], [picnic], litter barrels, coffee, vending, RV dump, petwalk**
206	WA 531, Lakewood, **E gas:** Arco/24hr, Shell/24hr, 7-11, **food:** Alfy's Pizza, Baskin-Robbins, Buzz Inn Steaks, Domino's, Jack-in-the-Box, KFC, La Corona Mexican, McDonald's, Olympia Pizza, Quizno's, Starbucks, Subway, Taco Del Mar, Taco Time, Weinerschnitzel, Wendy's, **lodging:** Hawthorn Suites, Smokey Point Motel, **other:** Buick/GMC/Pontiac, Chrysler/Dodge/Jeep, $Plus, Harley Davidson, Lowes Whse, Rite Aid, Safeway/gas/24hr, Schuck's Parts, **W gas:** Chevron/24hr, **food:** Bajio, Boston's Rest., IHOP, Jamba Juice, Paradise Grill, Pizza Hut, Red Robin, Taco Bell, Village Rest., **other:** Best Buy, Costco/gas, Discount Tire, Marshall's, Michael's, Office Depot, PetCo, Target, to Wenburg SP
202	116th NE, **E gas:** 76/dsl, Shell/dsl, Texaco, **food:** Carl's Jr, Magic Dragon Chinese, Starbucks, Subway, Taco Bell, **other:** Albertson's, Kohl's, PetCo, Rite Aid, Ross, WinCo Foods, **W gas:** Donna's Trkstp/Gull/dsl/scales/24hr/@, **food:** McDonald's, **other:** Seattle Premium Outlets/famous brands, st patrol
200	88th St NE, Quil Ceda Way, **E gas:** 7-11, 76, Shell/dsl/LP, **food:** Applebees, Neapolis Rest., Quizno's, Starbucks, **lodging:** Holiday Inn Express, **other:** Haggen's Foods/24hr, **W food:** Bob's Burgers, Port of Subs, Taco Del Mar, **other:** Home Depot, Walmart/SuperCtr/gas, casino

N ↕ S

WA

INTERSTATE 5 CONT'D

Exit #	Services
199	WA 528 E, Marysville, Tulalip, **E** **gas:** Arco/24hr, Chevron/24hr, 76, Shell/dsl, **food:** Burger King, Don's Rest./24hr, DQ, Jack-in-the-Box, Jumbo Buffet, Las Margaritas Mexican, **lodging:** Village Motel/Rest., **other:** Albertson's, Big O Tire, JC Penney, Rite Aid, Schuck's Parts, Staples, **W** **gas:** 76, **food:** Arby's, McDonald's, Taco Time, Wendy's, **lodging:** Best Western/rest., Comfort Inn, **other:** Chevrolet/Subaru, Robinson RV Ctr, to Tulalip Indian Res
198	Port of Everett (from sb), Steamboat Slough, st patrol
195mm	Snohomish River
195	Port of Everett (from nb), Marine View Dr
194	US 2 E, Everett Ave, City Ctr, **W** **gas:** Shell/dsl, **other:** Schwab Tire
193	WA 529, Pacific Ave (from nb), **W** **gas:** Chevron, 76, **food:** Denny's, **lodging:** Best Western, Holiday Inn, Marina Village Inn (3mi), Travelodge, **other:** [H] Lowes Whse
192	Broadway, to Evergreen Way, City Ctr, **W** **gas:** Arco/24hr, Chevron, 76, Shell, Texaco, **food:** Alfy's Pizza, Buzz Inn Steaks, IHOP, Iver's Seafood, Jack-in-the-Box, McDonald's, O'Donnell's Café, Starbucks, Subway, Taco Bell, **lodging:** Days Inn, ravelodge, **other:** Ford
189	WA 526 W, WA 527, Everett Mall Way, Everett, **E** **gas:** Arco/24hr, Chevron, Shell/dsl, **food:** Alfy's Pizza, Burger King, Buzz Inn Steaks, McDonald's, Subway, Wendy's, **lodging:** Travelodge, **other:** Costco/gas, Vet, **W** **gas:** Shell, **lodging:** Days Inn, Extended Stay America, Motel 6, **other:** Goodyear/auto, Macy's, mall
188mm	**rest area/weigh sta sb, full [handicapped] facilities, info, [phone], [picnic] litter barrels, coffee, RV dump**
186	WA 96, 128th SW, **E** **gas:** 76, Shell/dsl/24hr, Texaco, **food:** O'Donnells Rest., **lodging:** Quality Inn, **other:** Lakeside RV Park, Silver Lake RV Park, **W** **gas:** Arco/24hr, Chevron/24hr, 7-11, Shell, **food:** A&W/KFC, Acropolis Pizza, DQ, Denny's, McDonald's, Ming Dynasty, Mitzel's Kitchen, Papa John's, Pizza Hut, Skipper's, Starbucks, Taco Bell, Taco Time, **lodging:** Holiday Inn Express, La Quinta, Motel 6, **other:** Albertson's/Sav-on, $Tree, Goodyear/auto, Maple RV Park, transmissions
183	164th SW, **E** **gas:** Arco, Shell/dsl/24hr, **food:** Jack-in-the-Box/24hr, Panda Express, Quizno's, Starbucks, Subway, Taco Del Mar, Taco Time, **other:** Curves, Radio Shack, Walgreens, Walmart, **W** **gas:** Shell/dsl
182	WA 525, Alderwood Mall Blvd, to Alderwood Mall, **E** I-405 S, to Bellevue, **W** **gas:** Arco/24hr, **food:** Keg Steaks/seafood, Panera Bread, PF Chang's, Red Robin, Subway, TCBY, **lodging:** Residence Inn, **other:** Border's Books, JC Penney, Kohl's, Macy's, Marshall's, Michael's, Nordstrom's, Sears/auto, Target, Evans Tire
181	44th Ave W, to WA 524, Lynnwood, **E** **gas:** Arco, 76, Shell, **food:** Little Caesar's, McDonald's, Old Spaghetti Factory, Papa Murphy's, Wok Inn, **lodging:** Embassy Suites, Extended Stay America,

EVERETT

SEATTLE

181	Continued Hampton Inn, **other:** Albertson's, Barnes&Noble, Best Buy, Land Rover, Lowes Whse, Old Navy, PetCo, Staples, **W** **gas:** Arco, Chevron/24hr, 76/dsl, Shell/repair, **food:** Alfy's Pizza, Applebees, Arby's, Azteca Mexican, Barbara's Cafe, Black Angus, Buca Italian, Chevy's Mexican, Chipotle Mexican, Denny's, IHOP, Jack-in-the-Box, KFC, McDonald's, Old Country Buffet, Olive Garden, Panda Express, Red Lobster, Rock Grill, Starbucks, Subway, Taco Bell, Taco Del Mar, Taco Time, Tony Roma, Wendy's, **lodging:** Best Western, Comfort Inn, Courtyard, Holiday Inn Express, La Quinta, **other:** AAA, Firestone/auto, Fred Meyer, Goodyear/auto, Grocery Outlet, Radio Shack, Schwab Tire, 7-11, mall, USPO, Vet
179	220th SW, Mountlake Terrace, Mountlake Terrace, **W** **gas:** Shell/dsl, **food:** Azteca Mexican, Port of Subs, Subway, **other:** [H], Curves, Vet
178	236th St SW (from nb), Mountlake Terrace
177	WA 104, Edmonds, **E** **gas:** Chevron/24hr, Shell/dsl, **food:** Canyons Rest., McDonald's, Starbucks, Subway, **lodging:** Studio 6, **other:** Office Depot, RiteAid, Schuck's Parts, Thriftway Foods, **1-2 mi W on WA 9** **gas:** 76/dsl, **food:** A&W, Arby's, Barlee's Rest., Denny's, KFC, Scott's Grill, Starbucks, **lodging:** Day's Inn, **other:** Costco, Discount Tire, GNC, Home Depot, Nissan, PetCo, Radio Shack, VW
176	NE 175th St, Aurora Ave N, to Shoreline
175	WA 523, NE 145th, 5th Ave NE
174	NE 130th, Roosevelt Way
173	1st Ave NE, Northgate Way, **E** **gas:** 76, **food:** Azteca Mexican, California Pizza Kitchen, Chipotle Mexican, Macaroni Grill, Marie Callender's, Panera Bread, Quizno's, Ram Rest., Stanford's Rest., Super Buffet, Taco Del Mar, **other:** Barnes&Noble, Best Buy, Curves, Discount Tire, JC Penney, Macys, Nordstrom's, Ross, Target, mall, **W** **gas:** 76, Shell/dsl, **food:** Arby's, McDonald's, Pizza Xpress, Saffron Grill, Starbucks, **lodging:** Hotel Nexus, **other:** 7-11
172	N 85th, Aurora Ave
171	WA 522, Lake City Way, Bothell
170	(nb only) Ravenna Blvd, **E** **gas:** Shell/dsl
169	NE 45th, NE 50th, **E** **gas:** 76, Shell, **food:** Subway, **other:** [H], PetCo, U of WA, **W** **other:** to Seattle Pacific U, zoo
168b	WA 520, to Bellevue
168a	Lakeview Blvd, downtown
167	Mercer St (exits left from nb), Fairview Ave, Seattle Ctr, **W** **gas:** Shell, **lodging:** Silver Cloud Inn
166	Olive Way, Stewart St, **E** **other:** [H], **W** **lodging:** SpringHill Suites, **other:** Honda
165a	Seneca St (exits left from nb), James St, **E** **other:** [H]
165b	Union St, **E** **lodging:** Homewood Suites, **W** **food:** Ruth's Chris Steaks, **lodging:** Renaissance Inn
164b	4th Ave S, to Kingdome, downtown
164a	I-90 E, to Spokane, downtown
163	6th Ave, S Spokane St, W Seattle Br, Columbian Way, **1 mi W on 4th Ave S** **gas:** Arco, **food:** Arby's, Burger King/24hr, Denny's, McDonald's, Subway, Taco Bell, **other:** Sears, auto repair, transmissions
162	Corson Ave, Michigan St (exits left from nb), same as 161

SEATTLE

N ↕ S SEATTLE

INTERSTATE 5 CONT'D

Exit #	Services
161	Swift Ave, Albro Place, **W gas:** Shell/dsl, **food:** Starbucks, Thai Rest., **lodging:** Georgetown Inn
158	Pacific Hwy S, E Marginal Way, **W gas:** Chevron, **other:** NAPA
157	ML King Way
156	WA 539 N, Interurban Ave (no EZ return to sb), Tukwila, **E gas:** Pacific Pride/dsl, **food:** Gordon's Rest., **W gas:** 76/dsl, Shell/dsl, **food:** Emerald Green, Jack-in-the-Box, Quizno's, Starbucks, **lodging:** Day's Inn, **other:** Harley-Davidson
154b	WA 518, Burien, **W lodging:** Extended Stay America
154a	I-405, N to Bellevue
153	S Center Pkwy, (from nb), **E gas:** Chevron/dsl, **food:** Applebees, Azteca Mexican, Bahama Breeze, Cheesecake Factory, Chipotle Mexican, Claim Jumper, Famous Dave's, IHOP, Jamba Juice, Johnny Rockets Cafe, Newport Bay Rest., Olive Garden, Outback Steaks, Panda Express, Rainforest Cafe, Red Robin, Sizzler, Starbucks, Stanford's Rest, Taco Del Mar, Thai Rest., Zoopa, **lodging:** Courtyard, DoubleTree Inn, **other:** Acura, Best Buy, Borders, Jo-Ann Fabrics, Kohl's, Macy's, Marshall's, Nordstrom, Old Navy, PetCo, Sears/auto, Schwab Tire, Ross, Target, World Mkt, mall
152	S 188th, Orillia Rd, **W gas:** 76/dsl, **lodging:** Motel 6, **other:** to ✈
151	S 200th, Military Rd, **E gas:** Shell/dsl, **lodging:** Motel 6, **W gas:** Chevron, 7-11, 76, **food:** Burger Teriyaki, Herfy's Burgers, IHOP, **lodging:** Best Value, Best Western, Days Inn, Comfort Inn, Econolodge, Fairfield Inn, Hampton Inn, Holiday Inn Express, Quality Inn, Skyway Inn, Sleep Inn, Super 8, **other:** NAPA, Uhaul
149	WA 516, to Kent, Des Moines, **E lodging:** Century Motel, **other:** Poulsbo RV Ctr, **W gas:** Shell/dsl/24hr, **food:** Burger King, McDonald's, Midway Doughnuts, Pizza Hut, Subway, Taco Bell, **lodging:** Garden Suites, Kings Arms Motel, New Best Inn, **other:** $Tree, Radio Shack, Walgreens, USPO, to Saltwater SP
147	S 272nd, **E gas:** 76/Circle K, **W on Pacific Hwy... gas:** Arco/24hr, Shell/dsl, **food:** Fox Hollow Coffee, Jack-in-the-Box, La Cabana Grill, McDonald's, Quizno's, Subway, Taco Bell, Thai 3, **other:** Ace Hardware, AutoZone, Bartell Drug, Rite Aid, Safeway/24hr
143	S 320th, Federal Way, **W gas:** Arco/24hr, 76/Circle K, Shell/dsl/24hr, **food:** Applebee's, Arby's, Azteca Mexican, Black Angus, Black Bear Diner, Blimpie, Chipotle Mexican, Church's, Denny's, Grand Buffet, Great Harvest Bread, Herfy's Burgers, Jasmine Mongolian, Marie Callender, McDonald's, McGrath's Fishouse, Mongolian Grill, Old Country Buffet, Outback Steaks, Panda Express, Panera Bread, Qdoba Mexican, Quizno's, Red Lobster, Red Robin, Starbucks, Subway, Taco Bell, Taco Del Mar, Taco Time, Torero's Mexican, Taco Bell, Tokyo Japanese Steaks, Tony Roma, Torero's Mexican, Village Inn, Wendy's, **lodging:** Best Western, Comfort Inn, Courtyard, Extended Stay America, **other:** Barnes & Noble, Best Buy, Big Lots, Borders Books, Discount Tire, Jo-Ann Fabrics, K-Mart, Long's Drugs, Macy's, Michaels,

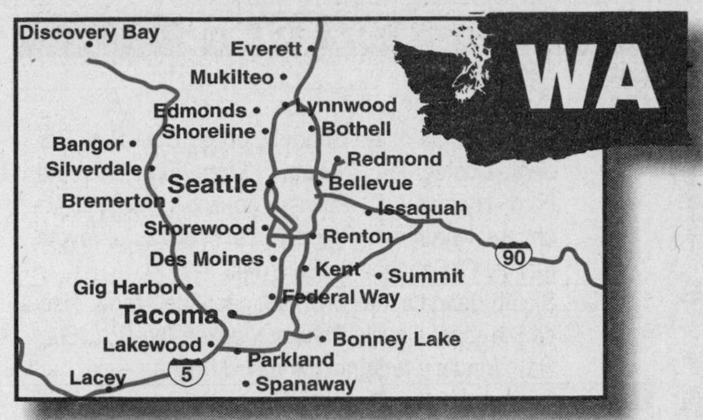

WA

TACOMA

Exit #	Services
143	Continued PetCo, PetsMart, Radio Shack, Rite Aid, Ross, Safeway/24hr, Sears/auto, Shuck's Parts, Target, TJ Maxx, Top Foods, mall, to Dash Point SP
142b a	WA 18 E, S 348th, Enchanted Pkwy, **E other:** funpark, **W gas:** Chevron, Shell/dsl, **food:** Arby's, Burger King, DQ, Del Taco, Denny's, Fatburger, Jack-in-the-Box, Jamba Juice, Jimmy Mac's Roadhouse, KFC, LJ Silver, McDonald's, Olive Garden, Panda Express, Popeye's, Puerta Vallarta, Quizno's, RoundTable Pizza, Shari's, Starbucks, Taco Bell, Taco Del Mar, Time Out Grill, **lodging:** Days Inn, Quality Inn, Super 8, **other:** H, Chevrolet Costco/gas, Home Depot, Lowe's Whse, NAPA, Office Depot, Schwab Tire, Walmart SuperCtr
140mm	**weigh sta, both lanes. Rest area, nb, full ♿ facilities, litter barrels, ☎, petwalk, RV dump**
137	WA 99, Fife, Milton, **E gas:** Arco/24hr, Chevron/dsl/24hr, 76/dsl, Shell/24hr, **food:** DQ, Johnny's Rest., **lodging:** Motel 6, **other:** Acura, Cadillac, Hummer, Infinity, Saab, **W gas:** 76/Circle K, **food:** Arby's, Baskin-Robbins, Denny's, Herfy Burgers, KFC/A&W, McDonald's, Mitzel's Kitchen, Pizza Hut/Taco Bell, Poodle Dog, Quizno's, Starbucks, Subway, Taco Del Mar, Taco Time, **lodging:** Emerald Guesthouse Inn, Queen Motel, EQC Motel/casino, Fife Motel, Kings Motel, Quality Inn, **other:** Camping World RV Ctr, Great American RV Ctr, Holiday RV Ctr, Infinity, NAPA, Schwab Tire, Shuck's Parts, Western Motorcoach RV Ctr, Volvo
136b a	Port of Tacoma, **E gas:** CFN/dsl, **other:** Costco, Great American RV Ctr, Honda, Mercedes, Mini/BMW, Peterbilt, Tacoma RV Ctr, **W gas:** Chevron, ***FLYING J***/dsl/LP/rest./24hr, Gull/dsl, Shell/dsl, **food:** Jack-in-the-Box, Subway, **lodging:** Best Inn, Day's Inn, Econolodge, Extended Stay America, Howard Johnson, Sunshine Motel, Travelodge, **other:** Goodyear/biodsl, Harley-Davidson, Land Rover/Jaguar/Lexus, Nissan, Volvo
135	Bay St, Puyallup, **E gas:** Shell, **other:** Majestic RV Park (4mi), **W gas:** Arco/24hr, **lodging:** La Quinta, **other:** to Tacoma Dome
134	Portland Ave (from nb), same as 135
133	WA 7, I-705, City Ctr, **W lodging:** Best Western, Courtyard, Hotel Murano, **other:** Tacoma Dome, museum
132	WA 16 W, S 38th, Gig Harbor, to Bremerton, **W gas:** Tesoro, **food:** Adriatic Grill, BJ's Rest., Jamba Juice, Jimmy John's, Krispy Kreme, Quizno's, Red Robin,

N ↕ S TACOMA

WA

INTERSTATE 5 CONT'D

Exit #	Services
132	Continued Subway, TGIFriday, Wendy's, **other:** Best Buy, Borders, Costco/gas, Diahatsu, $Tree, Firestone/auto, Ford, Hyundai, JC Penney, Jo-Ann's, Macy's, Michael's, Nordstrom, Petco, Ross, Sears/auto, Toyota, mall, to Pt Defiance Pk/Zoo, mall
130	S 56th, Tacoma Mall Blvd, **W gas:** Shell, **food:** Axteca Mexican, ChuckeCheese, Jack-in-the-Box, Subway, Wingers, **lodging:** Extended Stay America
129	S 72nd, S 84th, **E gas:** Chevron/24hr, Valero, **food:** Burger King, DQ, Denny's, Elmer's Rest., Famous Dave's, IHOP, Mongolian Grill, Olive Garden, Popeye's, Red Lobster, RoundTable Pizza, Shari's, Starbucks, **lodging:** Motel 6, Shilo Inn, **other:** Lowe's Whse, MegaFoods, **W food:** Hooters, **lodging:** Day's Inn, **other:** Home Depot, to Steilacoom Lake
128	(from nb) same as 129, **E gas:** 76, Shell/dsl, **food:** Denny's, Greatwall Chinese, Herman's Hamburgers, Subway, **lodging:** Comfort Inn, Crossland Suites, Econolodge, Hampton Inn, Holiday Inn Express, King Oscar Motel, Red Lion Inn, Rodeway Inn, Rothem Inn, Tacoma Inn, **W gas:** Shell, **food:** Ruby Tuesday, **other:** Discount Tire
127	WA 512, S Tacoma Way, Puyallup, Mt Ranier, **W gas:** 7-11, 76/Circle K, **food:** DQ, Mazatlan Mexican, McDonald's, Sizzler, Starbucks, Subway, Taco Guaynas, Taco Time, Wendy's, **lodging:** Budget Inn, Western Inn, Vagabond Motel, **other:** Schuck's Parts, transmissions
125	to McChord AFB, Lakewood, **W gas:** 76/Circle K/dsl, Shell/dsl, **food:** A&W/KFC, Black Angus, Church's, Denny's, Pizza Hut, Wendy's, **lodging:** La Quinta, **other:** [H], Aamco, Ford, 7-11, U-Haul, mall, Vet
124	Gravelly Lake Dr, **W gas:** Arco/repair, 76/24hr, **food:** El Toro Mexican, **other:** CarQuest, same as 125
123	Thorne Lane, Tillicum Lane
122	Camp Murray, **E other:** [H], **W gas:** Chevron/repair, **food:** Baskin-Robbins, Domino's, Gertie's Grill, Happy Wok, KFC, McDonald's, Papa John's, Subway, Taco Bell, Teriyaki House,**other:** AutoZone, 7-11
120	Ft Lewis, **E other:** Ft Lewis Military Museum
119	Du Pont Rd, Steilacoom, **E** to Ft Lewis, **W gas:** Chevron, 76, **food:** Jack-in-the-Box, Starbucks, Subway
118	Center Dr, **W food:** Bruceski's Pizza, Domino's, Farrelli's Pizza, Harbor Rock Grill, Jack-in-the-Box, Koko's Wok, Pegasus Cafe, Quizno's, Subway, Super Buffet, Viva Mexico, **lodging:** GuestHouse Inn, Liberty Inn
117mm	**weigh sta nb**
116	Mounts Rd, Old Nisqually, **E** Blue Camas Buffet (8mi)
115mm	Nisqually River
114	Nisqually, **E gas:** Chevron/repair, Exxon/dsl, Shell/dsl/LP, Texaco (1mi), **food:** Nisqually Grill, Norma's Burgers, Shipwreck Café, **other:** Nisqually RV Park, River Bend RV Park (3mi)
111	WA 510 E, Marvin Rd, to Yelm, **E gas:** Chevron/24hr, 76/Circle K, Shell/dsl, **food:** Burger King, Coldstone, Hawk's Prairie Rest./casino, Jamba Juice, McDonald's, Panda Express, Panera Bread, Papa Murphy's, Puerto Vallarta, Quizno's, RoundTable Pizza, Ruby Tuesday, Starbucks, Taco Del Mar, **lodging:** King Oscar Motel, **other:** Best Buy, Big Lots, Costco/gas, $Tree, Harley Davidson, Home Depot, Radio Shack, Rite Aid, Safeway/gas/24hr, Schuck's Parts, Schwab Tire, Sportsman's Whse, Walgreens, Walmart SuperCtr/Subway, **W gas:** Pacific Pride/dsl, **food:** Mayan Mexican, **other:** Cabela's, Tolmie SP (5mi), RV camping
109	Martin Way, Sleator-Kenny Rd, **E food:** Main Chinese Buffet, Pizza Hut/Taco Bell, The Rock Pizza, **other:** Discount Tire, ShopKO, Top Food/24hr, **W gas:** 76/Circle K, Shell/dsl/24hr, **food:** Casa Mia Rest., Denny's, El Serape Mexican, IHOP, Mandarin House, Red Lobster, Shari's Rest./24hr, Subway, **lodging:** AmeriTel, Comfort Inn, Quality Inn, La Quinta, Super 8, **other:** [H], Tire Factory, NAPA
108	Sleater-Kinney Rd, **E gas:** Shell/dsl, **food:** Applebee's, Arby's, McDonald's/playplace, Wendy's, **other:** $Tree, Firestone/auto, Fred Meyer, Kohl's, Marshall's, Michael's, Office Depot, PetsMart, Radio Shack, Rite Aid, Sears/auto, Target, **W gas:** Arco, Shell, **food:** Casa Mia, Coldstone, El Sarape Mexican, Jack-in-the-Box, Subway, Vietnamese Rest., **lodging:** AmeriTel Inn, **other:** [H], K-Mart, Lowes Whse, Safeway/gas, Tire Factory, same as 109
107	Pacific Ave, **E gas:** Shell/dsl, **food:** Izzy's Pizza, Shari's, Sizzler, Subway, Taco Time, **other:** Albertson's/Sav-on, Home Depot, Ross, mall, Vet, **W other:** Columbus RV Ctr, Ford
105	St Capitol, **W gas:** Chevron/24hr, Shell/Subway/dsl/24hr, **lodging:** Quality Inn, **other:** to St Capitol
104	US 101 N, W Olympia, to Aberdeen, **W gas:** Arco, Chevron, 7-11, Shell/dsl, **food:** Jack-in-the-Box, **lodging:** Extended Stay America, Red Lion Motel, **other:** [H], to Capitol Mall
103	2nd Ave
102	Trosper Rd, Black Lake, **E gas:** Shell/dsl/24hr, **food:** Arby's, Brewery City Pizza, Burger King, Cattin's Rest./24hr, El Sarape Mexican, Happy Teriyaki, Jack-in-the-Box, KFC, McDonald's, Starbucks, Subway, Taco Bell, Taco Time, **lodging:** Best Western, Motel 6, **other:** Ace Hardware, Curves, $Store, Goodyear/auto, Schuck's Parts, **W gas:** Chevron/24hr, 76/Circle K, **food:** Nickelby's Rest., Panda Express, Quizno's, Starbucks, The Brick Rest., **other:** Albertson's/gas, Alderbrook RV Park, AutoZone, Costco/gas, Fred Meyer, GNC, Home Depot, MegaFoods/24hr, Radio Shack
101	Airdustrial Way, **E gas:** Chevron, Shell, **food:** DQ (1mi), Inferno Pizza, Quizno's, Teriyaki Wok, **lodging:** Comfort Inn, GuestHouse Inn, Olympia Camping, USPO
99	WA 121 S, 93rd Ave, Scott Lake, **E gas:** Pilot/McDonald's/Subway/dsl/scales, **other:** American Heritage Camping, **W gas:** Shell/Deanna's Rest./rest/dsl/LP, **lodging:** Restover Motel
95	WA 121, Littlerock, **3 mi E other:** Millersylvania SP, RV camping, **W food:** Farmboy Drive-In

OLYMPIA

INTERSTATE 5 CONT'D

N ↕ S

CENTRALIA

Exit #	Services
93.5mm	**rest area sb, full ♿ facilities, info, ☎, picnic, litter barrels, vending, coffee, petwalk**
91mm	**rest area nb, full ♿ facilities, info, ☎, picnic, litter barrels, vending, coffee, petwalk**
88	US 12, Rochester, **E other:** RV Service, **W gas:** Arco/24hr, CFN, 76/dsl, Shell/dsl/LP/repair, **food:** DQ, Little Red Barn Rest., Lucky Eagle Casino/café, Quizno's, The Grill, **lodging:** Great Wolf Lodge, **other:** Curves, Outback RV Park (2mi)
82	Harrison Ave, Factory Outlet Way, Centralia, **E gas:** Arco/24hr, Shell/dsl, **food:** Burger King, Burgerville, Casa Ramos Mexican, DQ, Panda Chinese, Peking House Chinese, Pizza Hut, Quizno's, Thai Dish, Wendy's, **lodging:** Econolodge, Ferryman's Inn, King Oscar Motel **other:** H, VF/famous brands, **W gas:** Chevron, Shell, Texaco/Circle K, **food:** Arby's, Bill & Bea's, Country Cousin Rest., Denny's, Dominos, Jack-in-the-Box, McDonald's, Papa Murphy's, Starbucks, Subway, Taco Bell, **lodging:** Motel 6, **other:** Centralia Outlets, GNC, Midway RV Park, Outlet Mall/famous brands, Rite Aid, Safeway/gas, Schuck's Parts, Schwab Tire
82mm	Skookumchuck River
81	WA 507, Mellen St, **E gas:** Chevron, Shell, **food:** PJ's Rest., Subway, **lodging:** Empress Inn, Pepper Tree Motel/RV Park/dump, Travel Inn, **W** H
79	Chamber Way, **E gas:** Shell/dsl/24hr, **food:** Jalisco Mexican, **other:** Ford, Goodyear/auto, museum, vistor info, **W gas:** Texaco/Burger King/dsl/LP, **food:** Applebees, McDonald's, Roobucks Pizza, Starbucks, Subway, Taco Del Mar, Wendy's, **other:** $Tree, GNC, Grocery Outlet, Home Depot, K-Mart/Little Caesar's, Michael's, Quizno's, Radio Shack, Scion/Toyota, Walgreens, Walmart SuperCtr, st patrol
77	WA 6 W, Chehalis, **E gas:** Cenex/dsl, 76/dsl, **food:** Dairy Bar, **other:** NAPA, Schwab Tire, **W other:** Rainbow Falls SP (16mi), museum, truck parts
76	13th St, **E gas:** Arco/24hr, Chevron, Texaco, **food:** Denny's, Jack-in-the-Box, Kit Carson Rest., South Pacific Bistro, Subway, **lodging:** Best Western, Chehalis Inn, Relax Inn, **other:** Baydo's RV Ctr, I-5 RV Ctr, Safeway, Uhlmann RV Ctr/RV dump, **W** RV park/dump
73	new exit, **W** Poulsbo RV Ctr
72	Rush Rd, Napavine, **E gas:** Shell/dsl/scales, **food:** Burger King, McDonald's, Subway, **other:** Dave's RV Ctr, RV park, **W gas:** Chevron/FoodCourt/dsl/24hr, Shell/dsl
72mm	Newaukum River
71	WA 508 E, Onalaska, Napavine, **E gas:** 76/dsl/KC Truck Parts
68	US 12 E, Morton, **E gas:** Arco/24hr, **food:** Spiffy's Rest./24hr, **other:** to Lewis&Clark SP, Mt Ranier NP, **W gas:** 76/dsl/rest./24hr, **food:** Jammer's Rest.
63	WA 505, Winlock, **E other:** RV park (3mi), **W gas:** Shell/Cruisin' Cafe/dsl/LP
60	Vader Rd, Toledo
59	WA 506 W, Vader, **E gas:** Shell/dsl, **food:** Beesley's Cafe, **W gas:** Chevron/Subway/dsl/24hr, **food:** Country House Rest.

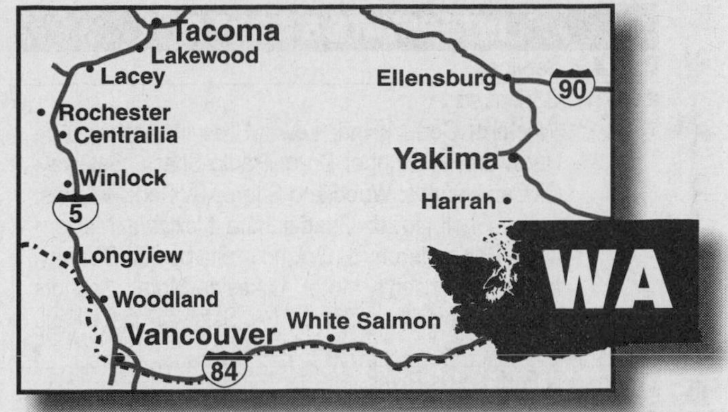

WA

KELSO

KALAMA

Exit #	Services
59mm	Cowlitz River
57	Barnes Dr, Jackson Hwy, **E other:** R&R Tires, **W gas:** GeeCee's/dsl/scales/café/24hr/@, **other:** repair, RV camping
55mm	**rest area both lanes, full ♿ facilities, ☎, picnic, litter barrels, vending, petwalk**
52	Toutle Park Rd, **E other:** Paradise Cove RV Park/general store
50mm	Toutle River
49	WA 504 E, Castle Rock, **E gas:** Shell/dsl, Texaco/dsl/LP, **food:** Burger King, C&L Burgers, El Compadre Mexican, 49er Diner, Papa Pete's Pizza, RoseTree Rest., Subway, **lodging:** Mt St Helens Motel, 7 West Motel, Silver Lake Motel/resort, Timberland Inn, **other:** Seaquest SP (5mi)
48	Huntington Ave, **W food:** Hattie's Rest., **other:** RV dump
46	Pleasant Hill Rd, **E other:** RV Park
44mm	**weigh sta sb,** ☎
42	Ostrander Rd
40	to WA 4, Kelso-Longview
39	WA 4, Kelso, to Longview, **E gas:** Arco/24hr, Shell, **food:** Denny's, Hilander Rest., McDonald's, Shari's/24hr, Subway, Taco Time, **other:** Brook Hollow RV Park, **lodging:** Motel 6, Red Lion Motel, Super 8, **other:** Rite Aid, **W food:** Azteca Mexican, Burger King, ChuckeCheese, DQ, Izzy's Pizza, Red Lobster, Starbucks, Taco Bell, **lodging:** Comfort Inn, GuestHouse Inn, **other:** JC Penney, Macys, Safeway/drug/gas, Sears/auto, Target, mall, museum
36	WA 432 W, to WA 433, US 30, Kelso, **E other:** U-Neek RV Ctr, **1-3 mi W other:** Toyota/Scion
32	Kalama River Rd, **E food:** Fireside Café, **other:** Camp Kalama RV Park/gifts
31mm	Kalama River
30	Kalama, **E gas:** Chevron, Texaco, **food:** Burger Bar, Columbia Rest., Lucky Dragon Chinese, Playa Azul Mexican, Subway, **lodging:** Columbia Motel, Kalama River Inn, **other:** USPO, antiques, **W gas:** Spirit/gas, **other:** RV camping
27	Todd Rd, Port of Kalama, **E gas:** Shell/dsl/café/24hr
22	Dike Access Rd, **E other:** Tire Factory, transmissions, **W gas:** CFN/dsl/24hr, **other:** Columbia Riverfront
21	WA 503 E, Woodland, **E gas:** Arco/24hr, Chevron, Pacific Pride, Shell/LP/dsl, **food:** Burgerville, Casa Tapatia, Figaro's, Gilliano's, Mali Thai, McDonald's, OakTree Rest., Rosie's Rest., Subway, **lodging:** Best

INTERSTATE 5 CONT'D

Exit #	Services
21	Continued Western, Cedar's Inn, Lewis River Inn, **other:** Ace Hardware, Hi-School Drug, Radio Shack, Safeway, Oil Can Henry's, Woodland Shores RV Park, **W gas:** Astro, Shell, **food:** Guadalahara Mexican, McDonald's, Papa Murphy's, Quizno's, Starbucks, Subway, **lodging:** Hansen's Motel, Lakeside Motel, Scandia Motel, **other:** Chevrolet, NAPA, Safeway/gas, Uhaul, repair
20mm	N Fork Lewis River
18mm	E Fork Lewis River
16	NW 319th St, La Center, **E gas:** Shell/dsl/24hr, **food:** Twin Dragons Rest., **other:** Paradise Point SP, Tri-Mountain Golf/rest.
15mm	**weigh sta nb**
14	WA 501 W, NW 269th St, **E gas:** Arco/24hr, 76/Circle K/dsl, **food:** Country Café, Papa Pete's Pizza, Subway, **other:** to Battleground Lake SP (14mi), Big Fir RV Park (4mi), Ridgefield WR, Tri-Mountain RV Park, **W gas:** Chevron/dsl
13mm	**rest area sb, full facilities, info, litter barrels, vending, petwalk, RV dump**
11	WA 502, Battleground, **rest area nb, full facilities, info, litter barrels, vending, petwalk, RV dump**
9	NE 179th St, **E food:** Jollie's Rest./24hr, **other:** Poulsbo RV, **W gas:** Chevron/dsl, **other:** RV Park
7	I-205 S (from sb), to I-84, WA 14, NE 134th St, **E gas:** Arco, 7-11, 76, TrailMart/dsl, **food:** Applebee's, Billygan's Roadhouse, Booster Juice, Burger King, Burgerville, Jack-in-the-Box, McDonald's, Muchas Gracias, Panda Express, Round Table Pizza, Starbucks, Subway, Taco Bell, Taco Del Mar, **lodging:** Comfort Inn, Holiday Inn Express, Olympia Motel, Red Lion, Salmon Creek Inn, Shilo Inn, **other:** H, Albertson's/gas, Long's Drugs, Safeway/gas, Zupan's Mkt, 99 RV Park, to Portland, **W gas:** Shell, **food:** Baskin-Robbins, Coldstone, El Tapatio, Papa Murphy's, PizzaSchmitzza, Quizno's, Starbucks, The Great Impasta, **lodging:** La Quinta, **other:** Fred Meyer
5	NE 99th St, **E gas:** 7-11, **food:** Burgerville, Carl's Jr, Del Taco, Domino's, Fat Dave's Rest., Quizno's, **other:** Harley-Davidson, Nissan/Kia, Walgreens, Walmart/Subway, Winco Foods/gas/24hr, **W gas:** Arco/24hr, Chevron/24hr, **food:** Applebee's, Bortolemi's Pizza, McDonald's, Papa John's, Primo's Subs, Subway, Taco Del Mar, **other:** $Tree, Kohl's, Office Depot, PetCo, Target
4	NE 78th St, Hazel Dell, **E gas:** 76, 7-11, **food:** Baja Fresh, Burger King, Don Pedro Mexican, Dragon Buffet, KFC, McDonald's, Pizza Hut, PeachTree Rest., Skipper's, Smokey's Pizza, Steakburger, Subway, Taco Bell, **lodging:** Quality Inn, **other:** Aamco, CarQuest, CostLess Parts, Firestone, Fred Meyer, Dodge, Ford, Mazda, Nissan, Radio Shack, Save A Lot Foods, Schuck's Parts, Tire Factory, U-Haul, **W gas:** Shell/dsl/LP, **food:** Jack-in-the-Box, Nick & Willy's Pizza, Panda Express, RoundTable Pizza, Starbucks, Tully's Coffee, Wendy's, **other:** PetsMart, Ross, Safeway, Tuesday Morning
3	NE Hwy 99, Main St, Hazel Dell, **E gas:** 7-11, **food:** Muchas Gracias Mexican, Pizza Hut, Skippers, **other:** H, Schwab Tire, **W gas:** 76/dsl, **other:** Safeway, transmissions
2	WA 500 E, 39th St, to Orchards
1d	E 4th, Plain Blvd W, to WA 501, Port of Vancouver
1c	Mill Plain Blvd, City Ctr, **W gas:** Chevron, **food:** Black Angus, Cattle Co Rest., Burgerville, Denny's, **lodging:** Shilo Inn, **other:** Ford, Lincoln/Mercury, Pontiac/Cadillac/GMC, Jeep, Mitsubishi, Suzuki, Clark Coll, st patrol
1b	6th St, **E food:** Joe's Crabshack, **W lodging:** Econolodge, Hilton, Red Lion
1a	WA 14 E, to Camas, **E** H, **W lodging:** Red Lion
0mm	Washington/Oregon state line, Columbia River

INTERSTATE 82

Exit #	Services
11mm	I-82 Oregon begins/ends on I-84, exit 179.
10	Westland Rd, **E other:** to Umatilla Army Depot, **other:** H
5	Power Line Rd
1.5mm	Umatilla River
1	US 395/730, Umatilla, **E food:** Jack-in-the-Box (5mi), **lodging:** Best Western (8mi), Desert Inn/rest. (2mi), Motel 6 (8mi), Oxford Inn (5mi), **other:** Hatrock Camping (8mi), to McNary Dam, **W gas:** Shell/Crossroads Trkstp/dsl/rest./24hr, Tesoro/Subway/dsl, Texaco, **lodging:** Tillicum Motel, Umatilla Inn, **other:** Harvest Foods, USPO, st police, Umatilla Marina/RV Park, **Welcome Ctr, weigh sta**
132mm	Washington/Oregon state line, Columbia River
131	WA 14 W, Plymouth, **N other:** RV camping, to McNary Dam
130mm	**weigh sta wb**
122	Coffin Rd
114	Locust Grove Rd
113	US 395 N, to I-182, Kennewick, Pasco, **2-4 mi N gas:** Chevron, Exxon, Tesoro/dsl, **food:** A&W/KFC, Azteca Mexican, Burger King, Carl's Jr, DQ, Denny's, Jack-in-the-Box, Little Ceasar's, McDonald's, Taco Bell, Panda Express, Papa Murphy's, Starbucks, Subway, Taco Del Mar, **lodging:** Best Western, Day's Inn, EconoLodge, La Quinta, Wingate Inn, **other:** $Tree, Fiesta Foods, Fred Meyer, GNC, Harley-Davidson, Hastings Books, Home Depot, PetCo, Radio Shack, Rite Aid, Safeway/food/gas, Traveland RV Ctr, Walgreens, Walmart SuperCtr/gas, st patrol
109	Badger Rd, W Kennewick, **N gas:** Shell/Subway/dsl/24hr, **food:** Chico's Tacos, **3 mi N lodging:** Guesthouse Suites, Quality Inn, Red Lion Inn, Super 8
104	Dallas Rd, **3 mi N gas:** Conoco/dsl/24hr
102	I-182, US 12 E, to US 395, Spokane, H, facilities in Richland, Pasco
96	WA 224, Benton City, **N gas:** Conoco/cafe/dsl/24hr, **other:** Beach RV Park
93	Yakitat Rd
88	Gibbon Rd
82	WA 22, WA 221, Mabton, **S gas:** Conoco, **2 mi S food:** Blue Goose Rest., **lodging:** Prosser Motel, **other:** H, to WA St U Research, to Wine Tasting Facilities, museum

INTERSTATE 82 CONT'D

E ↕ W

Exit #	Services
82mm	Yakima River
80	Gap Rd, **S gas:** Chevron, Pacific Pride, Shell/dsl/scales, **food:** Blue Goose Rest., Burger King, El Rancho Alegre, KFC/Taco Bell, McDonald's, Starbucks, Subway, **lodging:** Barn Motel/RV Park/rest., Best Western, Prosser Motel, **other:** H, Ford/Mercury, Wine Country RV Park, Vet, **rest area both lanes, full ♿ facilities, ☎, picnic, litter barrels, rv dump**
76mm	**weigh sta eb**
75	County Line Rd, Grandview, **S gas:** Cenex/dsl, Conoco/dsl/24hr (1mi), **1 mi S lodging: other:** Safeway Food & Drug/gas, same as 73
73	Stover Rd, Wine Country Rd, Grandview, **S gas:** Chevron/Subway/dsl, Conoco/dsl/24hr, **food:** DQ, Eli&Kathy's Breakfast, New Hong Kong, 10-4 Café, Subway, **lodging:** Apple Valley Motel, Grandview Motel, **other:** Chrystler/Jeep/Dodge, Grandview Market, RV park/dump, Safeway, Schwab Tire, auto repair
69	WA 241, to Sunnyside, **N gas:** Arco/dsl/24hr, Shell/TacoMaker/dsl/scales/24hr, **food:** A&W, Arby's, Burger King, China Buffet, China Grove, DQ, El Charrito Mexican, KFC, Little Ceasar's, McDonald's, Papa Murphy's, Pizza Hut, Subway, Taco Bell, **lodging:** Best Western, Rodeway Inn, **other:** Buick/Chevrolet/Nissan, $Tree, Fiesta Foods, GNC, JC Penney, Radio Shack, Rite Aid, Schuck's Parts, Walmart SuperCtr/gas
67	Sunnyside, Port of Sunnyside, **N gas:** Chevron/CFN/dsl, Conoco/dsl/E85, **food:** Jack-in-the-Box, **other:** H, BiMart Foods, **S other:** DariGold Cheese
63	Outlook, Sunnyside, **3 mi N food:** Burger Ranch, Snipe's Rest., **lodging:** Country Inn, Sunnyside B&B, Travel Inn, **other:** RV camping
58	WA 223 S, to Granger, **S gas:** Chevron/dsl, Conoco/dsl
54	Division Rd, Yakima Valley Hwy, to Zillah, **S other:** Teapot Dome NHS
52	Zillah, Toppenish, **N gas:** Chevron/dsl, 76/dsl, Shell/dsl/24hr, **food:** El Porton Mexican, McDonald's, Pizza Hut, Subway, **lodging:** Comfort Inn
50	WA 22 E, to US 97 S, Toppenish, **3-4 mi S food:** Legends Buffet/casino, McDonald's, **lodging:** Best Western Toppenish **other:** H, Murals Museum, RV Park, to Yakima Nation Cultural Ctr
44	Wapato, **N gas:** Shell/dsl
40	Thorp Rd, Parker Rd, Yakima Valley Hwy, **N other:** Sagelands Vineyard/Winery, **S other:** Windy Point Vineyard
39mm	Yakima River
38	Union Gap (from wb), **1 mi S food:** Peppermint Stick Drive-In, **other:** gas, lodging, museum
37	US 97 (from eb), **1 mi S gas:** Shell
36	Valley Mall Blvd, Yakima, **S gas:** Arco/dsl/24hr, Cenex/dsl, Shell/Gearjammer/dsl/Subway/scales/24hr/@, **food:** A&W/KFC, Cold Stone Creamery, Denny's/24hr, El Porton Mexican, IHOP, McDonald's, Miner's Drive-In, Old Country Buffet, Old Town Station Rest., Outback Steaks, SeaGalley Rest., Shari's, Skipper's, Starbucks, Taco Bell, **lodging:** Quality Inn, Super 8, **other:** Best Buy, Border's Books, Canopy

SUNNYSIDE

YAKIMA

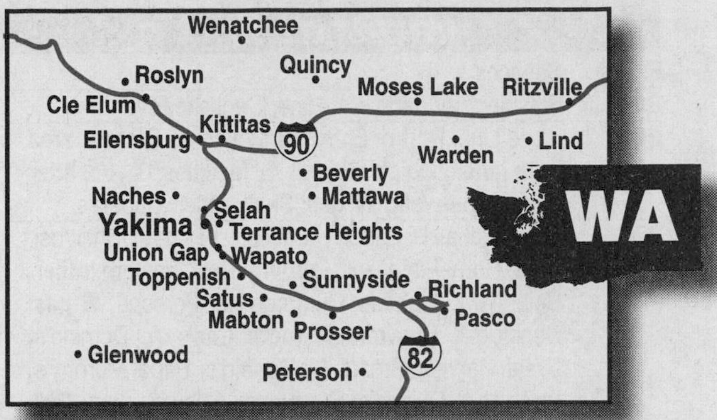

WA

Exit #	Services
36	Continued RV Ctr, Gap Autoparts, Lowes Whse, Office Depot, Old Navy, Macy's, Rite Aid, Ross, Sears/auto, ShopKO, Tire Factory, TJ Maxx, dsl/repair, mall, st patrol
34	WA 24 E, Nob Hill Blvd, Yakima, **N other:** K-Mart, Sportsman SP, KOA, dsl/repair, International, **S gas:** Arco/24hr, Chevron/dsl/24hr, CFN/dsl, 7-11, Time/dsl, **food:** Arby's, McDonald's, **other:** H, 19th Hole RV Park, Fiesta Foods, Freightliner, Peterbuilt, Shuck's Parts, GMC/Volvo/trucks, museum
33	Yakima Ave, Yakima, **N gas:** Chevron/dsl, Shell/Chester's/dsl, **food:** Burger King, El Mirador Mexican, **lodging:** Oxford Inn&Suites, **other:** Chevrolet, GMC/Honda, Hyundai, Mazda, Walmart SuperCtr/McDonald's/24hr, **S gas:** Arco/24hr, 7-11, **food:** Asian Express, DQ, Pizza Hut, Taco Bell, **lodging:** Cedars Motel, Fairfield Inn, Hilton Garden, Holiday Inn Express, Howard Johnson, Ledgestone Hotel, Red Lion Motel, **other:** Schwab Tire, Target, mall
31b a	US 12 W, N 1st St, to Naches, **S gas:** Arco/dsl/24hr, Shell, **food:** Arctic Circle, Black Angus Steaks, El Sieta Marie's Mexican, Golden Moon Chinese, Jack-in-the-Box, Peking Palace, Red Apple Rest., Red Lobster, Smokin' Bones BBQ, Subway, Waffle's Cafe, Wendy's, **lodging:** All Star Motel, Best Western, Day's Inn, Clarion, Econolodge, Economy Inn, Motel 6, Quality Inn, Ramada Inn, Red Apple Motel, Sun Country Inn, Tourist Motel, Yakima Inn, **other:** Harley-Davidson, Nendel's, Trailer Inns RV park
30	WA 823 N, Rest Haven Rd, to Selah
29	E Selah Rd, **N other:** fruits/antiques
26	WA 821 N, to WA 823, Canyon Rd, **N gas:** Shell/dsl/Noble Romans
24mm	**rest area eb, full ♿ facilities, picnic, litter barrels, RV dump**
23mm	Selah Creek
22mm	**rest area wb, full ♿ facilities, picnic, litter barrels, RV dump**
21mm	S Umptanum Ridge, 2265 elev
19mm	Burbank Creek
17mm	N Umptanum Ridge, 2315 elev
15mm	Lmuma Creek
11	Military Area, Military Area
8mm	view point both lanes, Manastash Ridge, 2672 elev
3	WA 821 S, Thrall Rd
0mm	**I-90, E to Spokane, W to Seattle. I-82 begins/ends on I-90, exit 110.**

YAKIMA

INTERSTATE 90

Exit #	Services
300mm	Washington/Idaho state line, Spokane River
299	State Line, Port of Entry, **N Welcome Ctr/rest area both lanes, weigh sta, full [handicapped] facilities, [phone], [picnic], litter barrels, petwalk, N gas:** Shell, **other:** Cabela's
296	Otis Orchards, Liberty Lakes, **N gas:** Shell/dsl, **food:** HomePlate Grill, **lodging:** Best Western, **other:** Buick/GMC/Pontiac, Hummer, Kia, Porsche, **S gas:** Cenex/dsl, Chevron/LP, **food:** Carl's Jr, Domino's, Great Harvest Bread, McDonald's, Papa Murphy's, Pizza Hut, Quizno's, Starbucks, Subway, Taco Bell, Taco Time, **lodging:** Cedar's Inn, **other:** Albertson's/Sav-On, Alton's Tire, Curves, GNC, Home Depot, RNR RV Ctr, Safeway/gas, Walgreens, Vet
294	Sprague Ave (from wb, no EZ return), **S other:** North Country RV/marine, Nut Factory, auto repair
293	Barker Rd, Greenacres, **N gas:** Conoco/dsl, **food:** Roadside Grill, Wendy's, **other:** Freedom RV Ctr, **S gas:** Exxon/Subway/dsl/24hr, Shell/dsl/24hr, **other:** NW RV Ctr, repair
291b	Sullivan Rd, Veradale, **N food:** Arby's, Hooters, Krispy Kreme, Outback Steaks, **lodging:** Oxford Suites, Residence Inn, **other:** Barnes&Noble, Best Buy, Staples, mall, **S gas:** Cenex, Chevron, 76, Shell/dsl, Tesoro, **food:** A&W, Bruchi's Rest., DQ, Jack-in-the Box, KFC, McDonald's, Mongolian BBQ, Noodle Express, Panda Express, Pizza Hut, Quizno's, Round Table Pizza, Schlotsky's, Shari's/24hr, Starbucks, Subway, Taco Bell, Wendy's, **lodging:** Mirabeau Park Hotel, Ramada Inn, **other:** Ace Hardware, $Tree, Fred Meyer/gas, Hancock Fabrics, Hastings Books, Kohl's, Lowes Whse, Michael's, NAPA, PetCo, PetsMart, Ross, Schwab Tires, Walgreens, Walmart SuperCtr/24hr/auto, Yoke's Foods, USPO
291a	Evergreen Rd, **N food:** Black Angus, Boston's Rest, Honey Baked Ham, IHOP, Red Robin, TGIFriday, Wingers, **other:** JC Penney, Macy's, Old Navy, Sportsman's Whse, Sears/auto, TJ Maxx, mall, **S gas:** Shell
289	WA 27 S, Pines Rd, Opportunity, **N gas:** 7-11, **food:** Old Matthews Rest., **S gas:** Cenex, Holiday, Shell/dsl, **food:** Applebees, DQ, Jack-in-the-Box, Old Country Buffet, Quizno's, **lodging:** Pheasant Hill Inn, **other:** [H], Jo-Ann Fabrics, Walgreens, repair
287	Argonne Rd, Millwood, **N gas:** Holiday/dsl, **food:** Burger King, Denny's, Domino's, DQ, Jack-in-the-Box, Longhorn BBQ, Marie Callender's, McDonald's, Panda Express, Papa Murphy's, Pizza Hut, Starbucks, Subway, Taco Time, Tasty House Chinese, Wendy's, **lodging:** Motel 6, Super 8, **other:** Albertson's/gas, Yoke's Foods, Savon, Schuck's Parts, Walgreens, $ Tree, **S gas:** Cenex/dsl, Shell, **food:** Casa de Oro Mexican, Perkins, Starbucks, **lodging:** Holiday Inn Express, Quality Inn, **other:** Curves, Rite Aid/24hr, Safeway
286	Broadway Ave, **N gas:** Chevron, *FLYING J*/Conoco/Rest./dsl/LP/scales/24hr/@, **food:** Zip's Burgers, Goodyear, **lodging:** Rodeway Inn, **Other:** International Trucks, Volvo, Kenworth, Peterbuilt, Schwab Tire, TDS Tires, **S Other:** 7-11
285	Sprague Ave, **N food:** Dragon Garden Rest, IHOP, Jack-in-the-Box, McDonald's, Subway, Wendy's, **lodging:** ParkLane Motel, **other:** Costco/gas, Grocery Outlet, Freightliner, Home Depot, K-Mart, Lowes Whse, Radio Shack, Schuck's Parts, **S gas:** Conoco, **food:** Puerta Vallarta Mexican, Starbucks, Taco Time, Zip's Burger, **other:** Alton's Tire, Chrysler, Dodge, Nissan/Saab, Trailer Inn RV Park, transmissions, Vet
284	Havana St (from eb, no EZ return), **N food:** Jack-in-the-Box, McDonald's
283b	Freya St, Thor St, **N gas:** Tesoro/dsl/24hr, **food:** Jack-in-the-Box, McDonald's, Wolf Lodge Steaks, **S gas:** Conoco/dsl, **Other:** Fred Myer
283a	Altamont St, **S gas:** Cenex
282b	2nd Ave, **N gas:** Shell, **lodging:** Comfort Inn, **other:** Office Depot
282a	WA 290 E, Trent Ave, Hamilton St, **N gas:** Shell/dsl, **lodging:** Comfort Inn, **other:** Office Depot
281	US 2, US 395, to Colville, **N gas:** 7-11, Shell/repair, Tesoro/dsl, **food:** Arby's, Dick's Hamburgers, Franky Doodles Rest., Jack-in-the-Box, Starbucks, Taco Time, **lodging:** Day's Inn, Howard Johnson, **other:** Firestone/auto, Ford, Schwab Tire, U-haul, **S lodging:** Quality Inn, **other:** [H]
280b	Lincoln St, **N gas:** Chevron, Conoco/dsl, Shell, **food:** Carl's Jr, Domino's, Jack-in-the-Box, McDonald's, Molly's Rest., Taco Bell, Taste of Asia, Zip's Burgers, **lodging:** Ramada Inn, Rodeway Inn, Tradewinds Motel, **other:** Honda, Scion/Toyota, Tire Factory, **S** [H]
280a	downtown, **N gas:** Chevron/McDonald's/dsl, Conoco/dsl, Fuel USA, **food:** Arctic Circle, Frank's Diner, Pizza Hut, Subway, **lodging:** Select Inn, **other:** AAA, Jaguar, Land Rover, Lexus
279	US 195 S, Pullman, to Colfax
277b a	US 2 W (no ez wb return), to Grand Coulee Dam, Fairchild AFB, **N lodging:** Econolodge, Hampton Inn, Motel 6, Ramada Inn, Spokanne House, Travelodge, West Wynn Motel
276	Geiger Blvd, **N gas:** *FLYING J*/dsl/LP/24hr, **food:** Denny's, Subway, **lodging:** Airway Express Inn, Best Western, **other:** USPO, st patrol, **S gas:** Shell/dsl/LP, **other:** Hideaway RV Park
272	WA 902, Medical Lake, **N gas:** Shell/dsl, **other:** Overland Sta/RV Park, **S gas:** Petro/dsl/rest./24hr/@, **food:** Iron Skillet, Subway, **lodging:** Super 8, **other:** Freightliner, Ponderosa Falls RV Resort, truck repair
270	WA 904, Cheney, Four Lakes, **S gas:** Exxon, **lodging:** Willow Springs Motel (6mi), **other:** Peaceful Pines RV Park, Ford, E WA U
264	WA 902, Salnave Rd, to Cheney, Medical Lake, **2 mi N** camping
257	WA 904, Tyler, to Cheney, **S other:** Tyler Store/RV Park, to Columbia Plateau Trail SP
254	Fishtrap, **S other:** Fishtrap RV camping/tents
245	WA 23, Sprague, **S gas:** Chevron/dsl, **food:** Viking Drive-In, lodging:, Sprague Motel, **other:** 4 Seasons RV Park (6mi), Sprague Lake Resort/RV Park
242mm	**rest area both lanes, full [handicapped] facilities, [phone], [picnic], litter barrels, tourist/weather info, petwalk, RV dump (eb)**
231	Tokio, **S weigh sta both lanes, gas:** Exxon/Templin's Café/dsl, **other:** RV Park

E ↕ W

VERDALE

SPOKANE

CHENEY

WA

INTERSTATE 90 CONT'D

E ↕ W

Exit #	Services
226	Schoessler Rd
221	WA 261 S, Ritzville, City Ctr, **N gas:** Conoco/dsl, Chevron/McDonald's, Shell/Subway/dsl, **food:** Circle T Rest., Killian's Kitchen, Perkins, Sharon's Drive-in, Starbucks, Whisperin Palms, Zip's Rest., **lodging:** Best Value Inn, Best Western, The Cottage/RV Park, Empire Motel, La Quinta/RV Park, Top Hat Motel, **other:** H, Cow Creek Merchantile, hist dist
220	to US 395 S, Ritzville, **N gas:** Pacific Pride, Texaco/Jake's Rest/dsl, **lodging:** Top Hat Motel, **other:** Chrysler/Dodge/Jeep, Harvest Foods, NAPA, Schwab Tires, st patrol
215	Paha, Packard
206	WA 21, Odessa, to Lind
199mm	**rest area both lanes, full ♿ facilities, ☎, ⛺, litter barrels, vending, RV dump, petwalk**
196	Deal Rd, to Schrag
188	U Rd, to Warden, Ruff
184	Q Rd
182	O Rd, to Wheeler
179	WA 17, Moses Lake, **N gas:** Conoco/dsl, Ernie's Trkstp/Chevron/dsl/café/24hr, Exxon/Subway, 76/dsl, Shell/dsl, **food:** Arby's, Burger King, DQ, Denny's, McDonald's, Shari's Rest./24hr, Starbucks, Taco Bell, **lodging:** Comfort Suites, Holiday Inn Express, Moses Lake Inn, Ramada Inn, Shilo Inn/rest./24hr, **other:** H, Buick/Chevrolet/Pontiac, Chrysler/Dodge/Jeep Lowes Whse, Toyota, Vet, **1 mi N food:** DQ, Subway, **lodging:** El Rancho Motel, **other:** $tree, Ford, Honda, Nissan, Sun Country RV Park, USPO, **S other:** I-90 RV, Mardon RV Park (15mi), Willows RV Park (2mi), Potholes SP (22mi)
177mm	Moses Lake
176	WA 171, Moses Lake, **1 mi N gas:** Cenex/dsl, Chevron/dsl, Conoco, Exxon/dsl, 76/dsl, Shell/dsl, **food:** El Rodeo Mexican, Paradise Rest., Perkins/24hr, Subway, Taco Del Mar, **lodging:** Best Western/rest., Interstate Inn, Motel 6, Oasis Motel, Super 8, **other:** H, AAA RV Park, Ace Hardware, Harvest Foods, Lake Front RV Park, OK Tires, auto repair, transmissions, Vet, **S lodging:** Lakeshore Motel
175	Westshore Dr (from wb), **N other:** Moses Lake SP, to Mae Valley, **S other:** st patrol
174	Mae Valley, **N other:** Suncrest Resort/RV, **S gas:** Conoco/dsl, **other:** Pier RV Park, st patrol
169	Hiawatha Rd
164	Dodson Rd, **N other:** Sunbasin RV park/camp (1mi)
162mm	**rest area wb, full ♿ facilities, ☎, ⛺, litter barrels, petwalk, RV dump**
161mm	**rest area eb, full ♿ facilities, ☎, ⛺, litter barrels, petwalk, RV dump**
154	Adams Rd
151	WA 281 N, to Quincy, **N gas:** Shell/dsl/pizza/subs, **other:** H (12mi), Shady Grove RV park
149	WA 281 S, George, **N** H (12mi), **S gas:** Cenex/dsl, 76/Subway/dsl, **other:** RV camp
143	Silica Rd, to The Gorge Ampitheatre
139mm	Wild Horses Mon, scenic view both lanes
137	WA 26 E, to WA 243, Othello, Richland

MOSES LAKE — SPOKANE

Tacoma
Lakewood
Lacey
Ellensburg
90
Rochester
Centrailia
Yakima
Winlock
Harrah
5
Longview
WA
Woodland
Vancouver
White Salmon
84

ELLENSBURG — CLE ELUM

Exit #	Services
137mm	Columbia River
136	Huntzinger Rd, Vantage, **N gas:** Shell, Texaco/dsl, **food:** Blustry's Burger Drive-in, Harvest Room Rest., **lodging:** Motel Vantage, **other:** Riverstone Resort RV park, Vantage Gen. Store, to Ginkgo/Wanapum SP (3mi), auto repair, **4 mi S other:** Gettys Cove RV Park
126mm	Ryegrass, elev 2535, **rest area both lanes, full ♿ facilities, ☎, ⛺, litter barrels, petwalk**
115	Kittitas, **N gas:** Shell/dsl/LP/24hr, **other:** Olmstead Place SP
110	I-82 E, US 97 S, to Yakima
109	Canyon Rd, Ellensburg, **N gas:** Astro/dsl, Chevron/24hr, Circle K, Eagle/dsl, 76, Shell/24hr, **food:** Arby's, Baskin Robbins, Burger King, Fiesta Mexican, Golden Dragon Chinese, KFC, Los Cabos Mexican, McDonald's, Papa Murphy's, Quizno's, RanchHouse Rest., Roadhouse Grill, Subway, Taco Bell, Taco Del Mar, Wendy's, Yuan Chinese, **lodging:** Best Western, Comfort Inn, Goose Creek Inn, Holiday Inn Express, Quality Inn, Super 8, **other:** H, AutoZone, CarQuest, Chevrolet, Fred Meyer, NAPA, Radio Shack, Rite Aid, Schwab Tire, Super 1 Food/24hr, TrueValue, Vet, **S gas:** *FLYING J*/Sak's/dsl/scales/LP/24hr, **food:** Buzz Inn Steaks, **lodging:** Days Inn/RV park
106	US 97 N, to Wenatchie, **N gas:** Chevron, Conoco/dsl, Pilot/Subway/dsl/24hr, 76/dsl, **food:** DQ, Perkins, **lodging:** Hampton Inn, Harold's Motel (2mi), I-90 Inn, **other:** Buick/Pontiac/GMC, Canopy Country RV Ctr, Chrystler/Jeep, Truck/RV Wash, **S other:** KOA, st patrol
101	Thorp Hwy, **N gas:** Arco, **other:** antiques/fruits/vegetables
93	Elk Heights Rd, Taneum Creek
92.5mm	Elk Heights, elev 2359
89mm	Indian John Hill, elev 2141, **rest area both lanes, full ♿ facilities, ☎, ⛺, litter barrels, RV dump, petwalk, vending**
85	WA 970, WA 903, to Wenatchie, **N gas:** Gas Save, 76/dsl, Shell/dsl/24hr, **food:** Cottage Café/24hr, DQ, Giant Burger, Home Stead Rest., McKean's Drive-In, **lodging:** Aster Inn, Cascade Mtn Inn, Chalet Motel, Cle Elum Motel, Traveler's Inn, **other:** Vet
84	Cle Elum (from eb, return at 85), **N gas:** Chevron/dsl, Pacific Pride/dsl, Shell/Subway/dsl, **food:** Burger King, Cle Elum Bakery, DQ, El Caporal Mexican, Mama Vallones, Quizno's, Sahara Pizza, Spaconi's Rest., Sunset Café, Taco Del Mar, **lodging:** Timber Lodge Motel, Stewart Lodge, **other:** H, Cle Elum

WA

INTERSTATE 90 CONT'D

Exit #	Services
84	Continued Drug, NAPA, Radio Shack, Safeway/gas, Trailer Corral RV Park, museum
81mm	Cle Elum River
80	Roslyn, Salmon la Sac
80mm	**weigh sta both lanes, [C]**
78	Golf Course Rd, **S other:** Sun Country Golf/RV Park
74	W Nelson Siding Rd
71	Easton, **S gas:** CB's Store/dsl/LP, **other:** USPO, John Wayne Tr, Iron Horse SP
71mm	Yakima River
70	Lake Easton SP, **N gas:** Shell/RV Town/dsl/café, **food:** Mtn High Burger, **other:** Silver Ridge Ranch RV Park, repair, **S other:** Lake Easton SP
63	Cabin Creek Rd
62	Stampede Pass, elev 3750, to Lake Kachess, camping both lanes
56mm	**parking area, eb (.5mi)**
54	Hyak, Gold Creek, **S** Ski Area
53	Snoqualmie Pass, elev 3022, info, **S gas:** Chevron, **food:** Family Pancake House, **lodging:** Summit Lodge, **other:** to rec areas
52	W Summit (from eb), same as 53
47	Tinkham Rd, Denny Creek, Asahel Curtis, **N other:** chain area, **S other:** RV camping/dump
45	USFS Rd 9030, **N other:** to Lookout Point Rd
42	Tinkham Rd
38	**N other:** fire training ctr
35mm	S Fork Snoqualmie River
34	468th Ave SE, Edgewick Rd, **N gas:** 76/BBQ/dsl, Shell/Subway/dsl/24hr, TA/dsl only/rest./@, **food:** Ken's Rest., **lodging:** Edgewick Inn, **other:** NW RV Park
32	436th Ave SE, North Bend Ranger Sta, **1 mi N** gas, food, lodging
31	WA 202 W, North Bend, Snoqualmie, **N gas:** Chevron/dsl, Shell/dsl, **food:** Arby's, Blimpie, Burger King, Los Cabos, McDonald's, Mongolian Grill, Papa Murphy's, Starbucks, Subway, Taco Time, **lodging:** North Bend Motel, Sallish Lodge, Sunset Motel, **other:** [H], NorthBend Stores/famous brands, Safeway/deli/24hr, Shuck's Parts, museum, st patrol
27	North Bend, Snoqualmie (from eb), **N gas:** Shell, **other:** [H]
25	WA 18 W, Snoqualmie Pkwy, Tacoma, to Auburn, **N food:** Mike's Grill, **other: weigh sta**
22	Preston, **N gas:** Shell/dsl/24hr, **food:** Burgers& Teriyaki, Sherm's BBQ, **other:** USPO, LP, NAPA, Snoqualmie River RV Park (4mi), **S other:** Blue Sky RV Park
20	High Point Way
18	E Sunset Way, Issaquah, **S gas:** Shell (1mi), **food:** Flying Pie Pizza, Front St Mkt, Issaquah Brewhouse, Jack's Grill, Korean Grill, Mandarin Garden, Shanghai Garden Chinese, Stan's BBQ
17	E Sammamish Rd, Front St, Issaquah, **N gas:** Chevron, 76, **food:** Coho Café, Coldstone Creamery, Fatburger, Jamba Juice, Krispy Kreme, McDonald's, Qdoba Mexican, Papa John's, Pallino Pasta,
17	Continued Starbucks, **other:** Fred Meyer, Home Depot, Walgreens, **S gas:** Chevron/24hr, Shell, **food:** Boehms Chocolates, Domino's, Extreme Pizza, La Costa Mexican, Las Margaritas, Pogacha Rest., **other:** Big O Tire, U-Haul, transmissions
15	WA 900, Issaquah, Renton, **N gas:** Arco/24hr, **food:** Cocina Cocina, IHOP, Ochar Thai, Red Robin, Tully's Coffee, **lodging:** Holiday Inn, Motel 6, **other:** Barnes&Noble, Costco/gas, Lowes Whse, Michael's, Office Depot, PetsMart, Trader Joe's, to Lk Sammamish SP, Vet, **S gas:** Shell, **food:** Baskin-Robbins, Burger King, Chipotle Mexican, Denny's, Georgio's Subs, Issaquah Cafe, Jack-in-the-Box, Jamba Juice, KFC/Taco Bell, Lombardi's Italian, McDonald's, O'Ginger Bistro, Papa Murphy's, RoundTable Pizza, Starbucks, Subway, Taco Time, **lodging:** Hilton Garden, **other:** Chevrolet, Firestone/auto, Ford, GNC, PetCo, QFC Foods, Rite Aid, Ross, Safeway Foods, Schuck's Parts, Target, USPO
13	SE Newport Way, W Lake Sammamish
11	SE 150th, 156th, 161st, Bellevue, **N** LDS Temple, **gas:** Shell, **food:** DQ, Greenwood Mandarin Chinese, Lil' Jon's Rest., McDonald's, Starbucks, Subway, Tulley's Coffee, **lodging:** Day's Inn, Embassy Suites, Silver Cloud Inn, **other:** Ford, 7-11, Subaru/VW, Safeway, Toyota, **S gas:** 76, Standard, Shell/dsl/24hr, **food:** Baskin-Robbins, Domino's, Outback Steaks, Pizza Hut, **lodging:** Homestead Suites, **other:** Albertson's, Honda, Larkspur Landing, Rite Aid, Schuck's Parts
10	I-405, N to Bellevue, S to Renton, facilities located off I-405 S, exit 10
9	Bellevue Way
8	E Mercer Way, Mercer Island
7c	80th Ave SE (exits left from wb)
7b a	SE 76th Ave, 77th Ave, Island Crest Way, Mercer Island, **S gas:** Chevron, 76/repair, Shell/dsl/repair, **food:** McDonald's, Starbucks, Subway, Thai Rest., Tully's Coffee, **lodging:** Travelodge, **other:** Island Foods, TrueValue, Walgreens
6	W Mercer Way (from eb), same as 7
5mm	Lake Washington
3b a	Ranier Ave, Seattle, downtown, **N gas:** Shell/dsl, **other:** Vet
2c b	I-5, N to Vancouver, S to Tacoma
2a	4th Ave S, to King Dome

I-90 begins/ends on I-5 at exit 164.

INTERSTATE 182 (RICHLAND)

Exit #	Services
14b a	US 395 N, WA 397 S, OR Ave, **N gas:** *FLYING J* /dsl/scales/24hr, King City/Shell/rest/dsl/@, **food:** Burger King, Subway, **lodging:** Knight's Inn, **other:** Goodyear, Peterbilt, **S lodging:** Motel 6, I-182 begins/ends on US 395 N.
13	N 4th Ave, Cty Ctr, **N gas:** CFN/dsl, **lodging:** Airport Motel, Starlite Motel, **S gas:** 76/dsl/24hr, **other:** [H], RV park, museum
12b	N 20th Ave, **N lodging:** Best Western, Red Lion Inn
12a	US 395 S, Court St, **S** on Court St. **gas:** Conoco, Exxon/Jack-in-the-Box, Shell, Tesoro, Texaco, **food:** A&W/KFC, Baskin Robbins, Burger King, DQ, Francisco's Rest., Little Ceasar's, McDonald's, Pizza Hut,

E ↕ W RICHLAND

INTERSTATE 182 (RICHLAND)

Exit #	Services
12a	Continued Quizno's, Round Table Pizza, Subway, Super China Buffet, Taco Bell, Wendy's, **other:** Albertson's/gas, AutoZone, Cadillac/Chevrolet/Pontiac, Chief RV Ctr, Ford, Nissan, Rite Aid, Sav-a-Lot Foods, Subaru, U-haul, Walgreens
9	rd 68, Trac, **N gas:** Shell, Tesoro, **food:** Antonio's Pizza, Applebees, Arby's, Bruchi's & Figaro's Pizza, Cousin's Rest., Eatza Pizza Buffet, Emperial Buffet, Fiesta Mexican, IHOP, King China Buffet, Jack-in-the-Box, McDonald's, Nick n Willy's Pizza, Panda Express, Pier 39 Seafood, Quizno's, Sonic, Starbucks, Subway, Taco Bell, Teryaki Grill, **lodging:** Holiday Inn Express, **other:** Lowes Whse, Walgreens, Walmart Super Ctr/24hr, Yokes Foods
7	Broadmoor Blvd, **N lodging:** Sleep Inn, **other:** Broadmoor Outlet Mall/famous brands, GNC, **S other:** Broadmoor RV Ctr, Sandy Heights RV Park
6.5mm	Columbia River
5b a	WA 240 E, Geo Washington Way, to Kennewick, **N food:** Applebees, Jack In the Box, Starbucks, **lodging:** Courtyard, Day's Inn, Economy Inn, Hampton Inn, Red Lion, Royal Hotel, Shilo Inn, **other:** $Tree, Winco Foods/gas
4	WA 240 W, **N gas:** Conoco/dsl, **food:** McDonald's, Rancho Boninto, **other:** Fred Meyer/gas
3.5mm	Yakima River
3	Keene Rd, Queensgate, **N gas:** Shell, **food:** A&W/KFC, Burger King, El Rancho Alegre, LJ Silver, McDonald's, Panda Express, Starbucks, Subway, Taco Bell, **other:** Home Depot, PetCo, Target, Walmart Super Ctr/auto/gas, **S other:** RV Park (3mi)
0mm	I-182 begins/ends on I-82, exit 102.

N ↕ S SEATTLE

INTERSTATE 405 (SEATTLE)

Exit #	Services
30	I-5, N to Canada, S to Seattle, **I-405 begins/ends on I-5, exit 182.**
26	WA 527, Bothell, Mill Creek, **E food:** Canyon's Rest., McDonald's, Thai-Rama, **other:** Lake Pleasant RV Park, **W gas:** Shell/dsl, **food:** Applebees, Arby's, Bamboo House, Bonefish Grill, Crystal Creek Cafe, Denny's, Fortune Cookie Chinese, Grazie Ristorante, Imperial Wok, Jack-in-the-Box, Mongolian Grill, Outback Steaks, Papa Murphy's, Qdoba Mexican, Quizno's, Subway, Taco Bell, Taco Time, Tully's Coffee, Wendy's, **lodging:** Comfort Inn, Extended Stay America, Holiday Inn Express, **other:** Albertson's, Bartell Drug, Curves, Goodyear/auto, QFC Foods, Radio Shack, Rite Aid, 7-11
24	NE 195th St, Beardslee Blvd, **E gas:** Shell/Quizno's/dsl, **food:** Teryaki Etc, **lodging:** Country Inn&Suites, Residence Inn
23b	WA 522 W, Bothell
23a	WA 522 E, to WA 202, Woodinville, Monroe
22	NE 160th St, **E gas:** Chevron, Shell/dsl/24hr, **food:** Denice's Cafe
20	NE 124th St, **E gas:** Shell/dsl/24hr, **food:** Denny's, Georgio's Subs, Pizza Hut, Santa Fe Mexican, Shari's, Zaburo's Grill, **lodging:** Baymont Inn, Comfort Inn,

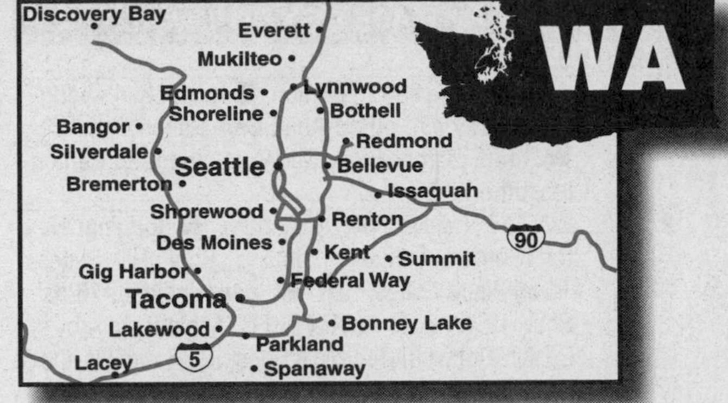

SEATTLE

Exit #	Services
20	Continued Motel 6, **other:** [H], Big O Tire, Chrysler/Dodge/Jeep, Discount Tire, Firestone, Infiniti, Radio Shack, Rite Aid, Ross, Schucks Parts, Schwab Tire, Toyota/Scion, mall, **W gas:** Arco/24hr, 76, **food:** Azteca Mexican, Burger King, Domino's, Hunan Wok, McDonald's, Romio's Pizza, Olive Garden, Starbucks, Subway, Taco Time, Wendy's, **lodging:** Courtyard, **other:** Buick/GMC/Pontiac, Fred Meyer, GNC, QFC Foods/24hr
18	WA 908, Kirkland, Redmond, **E gas:** Arco/dsl, Chevron/24hr, 7-11, 76/Circle K, Shell/dsl, **food:** Garlic Jim's, McDonald's, Outback Steaks, Starbucks, Subway, Valhalla Grill, **other:** Chevrolet, Costco, Hancock Fabrics, Honda, Mazda, Nissan, PetCo, Safeway Foods, Schuck's Parts, 7-11, Tuesday Morning, U-Haul, Walgreens, **W gas:** Chevron, Shell, **food:** Acropolis Pizza, Cafe Creek, Crab Cracker, Papa John's, Subway, TGIFriday, Wendy's, **other:** QFC Foods, Tire Factory, Vet
17	NE 70th Pl
14b a	WA 520, Seattle, Redmond
13b	NE 8th St, **E gas:** Chevron/dsl, Shell/dsl, **food:** Denny's, **lodging:** Coast Hotel, Extended Stay America, **other:** [H], Best Buy, Buick/Pontiac, Ford, Home Depot, Hummer, Larry's Mkt, Lincoln/Mercury, Mercedes, Whole Foods Mkt, **W food:** Starbucks, Subway, **lodging:** Courtyard, Hyatt
13a	NE 4th St, **E lodging:** Extended Stay America, **other:** Ford, Lexus, **W lodging:** Best Western, Doubletree Hotel, Hilton, Ramada Ltd., Red Lion/Bellevue Inn, Sheraton
12	SE 8th St, **W lodging:** Residence Inn
11	I-90, E to Spokane, W to Seattle
10	Cold Creek Pkwy, Factoria, **E on Factoria Blvd... gas:** Chevron, 76/Circle K, **food:** Applebees, Burger King, Coldstone Creamery, Jamba Juice, KFC, Keg Steaks, McDonald's, Old Country Buffet, Peking Wok, Quizno's, Red Robin, Romio's Pizza, Sideline Grill, Starbucks, Subway, Taco Bell, Taco Time, Torero's Mexican, **other:** Old Navy, PetCo, QFC Foods, Rite Aid, Safeway, Schuck's Parts, 7-11, Target, mall, Vet
9	112th Ave SE, Newcastle, [phone]
7	NE 44th St, **E food:** Denny's/24hr, McDonald's, Subway, **lodging:** Econolodge
6	NE 30th St, **E gas:** Arco/24hr, **W gas:** Chevron/24hr, Shell, **other:** 7-11
5	WA 900 E, Park Ave N, Sunset Blvd NE, **W other:** Fry's Electronics

INTERSTATE 405 CONT'D (SEATTLE)

N ↕ S

Exit #	Services
4	WA 169 S, Wa 900 W, Renton, **E food:** Shari's, **lodging:** Quality Inn, **other:** Aqua Barn Ranch Camping, **W food:** Burger King, Stir Rest., **lodging:** Renton Inn, **other:** 7-11,
2	WA 167, Rainier Ave, to Auburn, **E lodging:** Hilton Garden, Larkspur Landing, SpringHill Suites, TownePlace Suites, [H], **W gas:** Chevron, 76/dsl, Shell, USA/dsl, **food:** A&W/KFC, Applebees, Arby's, Baskin-Robbins, Georgio's Subs, IHOP, Jack-in-the-Box, Jimmy Mack's, King Buffet, Mazatlan Mexican, McDonald's, PanAsia, Panda Express, Papa Murphy's, Pizza Hut, Popeye's, Qdoba Mexican, Starbucks, Subway, Taco Bell, Taco Time, Torero's Mexican, Wendy's, Yankee Grill, **lodging:** Holiday Inn,

SEATTLE

Exit #	Services
2	Continued **other:** Aamco, Buick/Cadillac/GMC/Pontiac, Chevrolet, Chrysler/Jeep, Discount Tire, Dodge, Ford, Fred Meyer, Firestone/auto, Honda/Hyundai/Kia/Mazda, Isuzu, Radio Shack, Rite Aid, Safeway/gas, Sam's Club/gas, Schuck's Parts, Schwab Tire, Subaru, Toyota/Scion, Walgreens, Walmart/auto, Vet
1	WA 181 S, Tukwila, **E gas:** Chevron/dsl, 76/dsl, Shell/dsl, **food:** Barnaby's Rest., Jack-in-the-Box, McDonald's, Sushi & Grill, Taco Bell, Teriyaki Wok, Wendy's, **lodging:** Best Western, Courtyard, Embassy Suites, Hampton Inn, Homestead Suites, Residence Inn, **other:** 7-11, mall, **W gas:** Shell, **lodging:** Comfort Suites, Homewood Suites, **other:** fun center
0mm	I-5, N to Seattle, S to Tacoma, WA 518 W. I-405 begins/ends on I-5, exit 154.

WEST VIRGINIA

INTERSTATE 64

E ↕ W

LEWISBURG

Exit #	Services
184mm	West Virginia/Virginia state line
183	VA 311, Crows (from eb)
181	US 60, WV 92 (no ez wb return), White Sulphur Springs, **N gas:** BP/Godfather's, Exxon/Quizno's, Shell, **food:** April's Pizzaria, Hardee's, Legends Rest., Pizza Hut, Taco Bell, Wendy's (4mi), **lodging:** Budget Inn, Greenbrier Resort, Old White Motel, **other:** Family$, Food Lion, NAPA, Rite Aid, USPO, to Midland Trail, ski area, **S lodging:** Allstate Motel, **other:** Twilite Camping
179mm	**Welcome Ctr wb, info, full [handicapped] facilities, [phone], [picnic], litter barrels, petwalk**
175	US 60, WV 92, Caldwell, **N gas:** Chevron/dsl/24hr, Exxon, Shell/Subway/dsl, **food:** Granny's House Rest., Greenbrier's Mountainaire Rest., McDonald's, Wendy's, **lodging:** Village Motel, **other:** $General, **S other:** Greenbrier SF, camping
173mm	Greenbrier River
169	US 219, Lewisburg, Hist Dist, **N gas:** Shell, **food:** Blackwell's Rest., **lodging:** Relax Inn, **S gas:** Exxon/dsl, Gomart, Shell, **food:** Applebee's, Arby's, Bob Evans, Hardee's, Ruby Tuesday, Shoney's, Subway, Western Sizzlin, **lodging:** Brier Inn, Econolodge, Hampton Inn, Holiday Inn Express, Super 8, **other:** [H], Chevrolet, Ford, Lowe's Whse, Walmart SuperCtr/gas/24hr
161	WV 12, Alta, **S gas:** Alta Sta/cafe, Exxon, **other:** Greenbrier River Camping (14mi)
156	US 60, Midland Trail, Sam Black Church, **N gas:** Citgo, Exxon/dsl, Shell/dsl, **food:** Linda's Rest.
150	Dawson, **S gas:** Exxon, **food:** Cheddar's Cafe, **lodging:** Dawson Inn, **other:** RV camping
147mm	**runaway truck ramp wb**
143	WV 20, Green Sulphur Springs, **N gas:** Liberty/dsl
139	WV 20, Sandstone, Hinton, **S gas:** Citgo/dsl, **other:** Blue Stone SP (16mi), Richmond Store, to Pipestem Resort Park (25 mi), USPO
138mm	New River
133	WV 27, Bragg Rd, Sandstone Mtn (Elev. 2765), mandatory truck stop eb, **S** RV camping
129	WV 9, Shady Spring, **N other:** to Grandview SP, **S gas:** Exxon/dsl, Shell/dsl, **food:** Subway, **other:** Little Beaver SP
125	WV 307, Airport Rd, Beaver, **N gas:** Shell/dsl, **food:** Biscuit World, **lodging:** Sleep Inn, **S gas:** BP/dsl, Exxon, GoMart/gas, **food:** Hardee's, KFC, LJ Silver, McDonald's, Pizza Hut, **lodging:** Glade Spgs Resort, Patriot Motel
124	US 19, E Beckley, **0-2 mi N gas:** BP, Exxon, GoMart/gas, **food:** Capt D's, Huddle House, **lodging:** Microtel, **other:** last exit before toll rd wb
121	I-77 S, to Bluefield

I-64 and I-77 run together 61 mi. See Interstate 77 Exits 42 through 100.

Exit #	Services
59	I-77 N (from eb), to I-79
58c	US 60, Washington St, **N gas:** Exxon, GoMart/gas, **food:** Arby's, **other:** Lincoln/Mercury, **S food:** LJ Silver, Shoney's, **lodging:** Embassy Suites, Hampton Inn, Holiday Inn Express, Marriott, **other:** [H], civic ctr, mall
58b	US 119 N (from eb), Charleston, downtown
58a	US 119 S, WV 61, MacCorkle Ave, **S food:** Steak&Ale
56	Montrose Dr, **N gas:** Chevron, Exxon/dsl, Speedway, **food:** Hardee's, Los Agaves Mexican, **lodging:** Microtel, Ramada Inn, Wingate Inn, **other:** Advance Parts, Chevrolet, Chrysler, Dodge, Hyundai, Kia, NAPA, Rite Aid, Toyota, VW
55	Kanawha Tpk
54	US 60, MacCorkle Ave, **N food:** Burger King, Subway, **other:** Kroger/gas, **S gas:** Citgo, **food:** Bob Evans, KFC, LJ Silver, McDonald's, Pizza Hut, Schlotsky's, Taco Bell, Wendy's, **other:** [H], Aamco, Harley-Davidson, Honda, Mazda/Mitsubishi
53	Roxalana Rd, to Dunbar, **S gas:** GoMart/gas, **food:** BiscuitWorld, Capt D's, Gino's Pizza, McDonald's, Shoney's, Subway, Wendy's, **lodging:** Super 8, Travelodge, **other:** Advance Parts, Aldi, CarQuest, CVS Drug, Family$, Jo-Ann Fabrics, Kroger, NTB, Radio Shack
50	VW 25, Institute, **S gas:** GoMart/gas

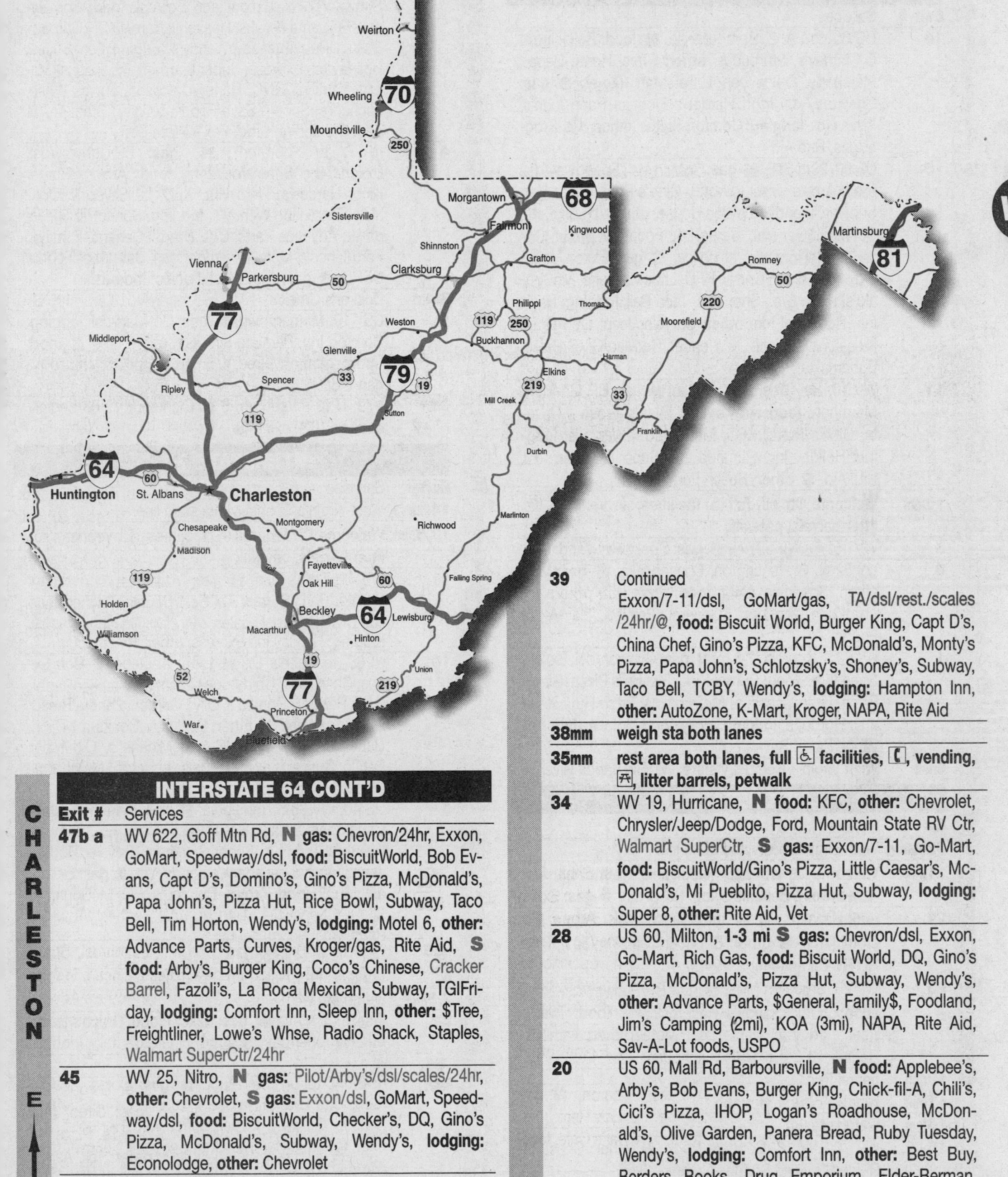

WV

INTERSTATE 64 CONT'D

CHARLESTON

E ↕ W

Exit #	Services
47b a	WV 622, Goff Mtn Rd, **N gas:** Chevron/24hr, Exxon, GoMart, Speedway/dsl, **food:** BiscuitWorld, Bob Evans, Capt D's, Domino's, Gino's Pizza, McDonald's, Papa John's, Pizza Hut, Rice Bowl, Subway, Taco Bell, Tim Horton, Wendy's, **lodging:** Motel 6, **other:** Advance Parts, Curves, Kroger/gas, Rite Aid, **S food:** Arby's, Burger King, Coco's Chinese, Cracker Barrel, Fazoli's, La Roca Mexican, Subway, TGIFriday, **lodging:** Comfort Inn, Sleep Inn, **other:** $Tree, Freightliner, Lowe's Whse, Radio Shack, Staples, Walmart SuperCtr/24hr
45	WV 25, Nitro, **N gas:** Pilot/Arby's/dsl/scales/24hr, **other:** Chevrolet, **S gas:** Exxon/dsl, GoMart, Speedway/dsl, **food:** BiscuitWorld, Checker's, DQ, Gino's Pizza, McDonald's, Subway, Wendy's, **lodging:** Econolodge, **other:** Chevrolet
44.3mm	Kanawha River
44	US 35, St Albans, **S gas:** Chevron/dsl, **other:** 7-11
41	Scott Depot, **S food:** DQ
39	WV 34, Winfield, **N gas:** BP/Arby's, GoMart/dsl, **food:** Applebee's, Bob Evans, Hardee's, Taste of Asia, **lodging:** Day's Inn, Holiday Inn Express, Red Roof Inn, **other:** Advance Parts, Big Lots, $General, GNC, Home Depot, Radio Shack, USPO, **S gas:**
39	Continued Exxon/7-11/dsl, GoMart/gas, TA/dsl/rest./scales/24hr/@, **food:** Biscuit World, Burger King, Capt D's, China Chef, Gino's Pizza, KFC, McDonald's, Monty's Pizza, Papa John's, Schlotzsky's, Shoney's, Subway, Taco Bell, TCBY, Wendy's, **lodging:** Hampton Inn, **other:** AutoZone, K-Mart, Kroger, NAPA, Rite Aid
38mm	**weigh sta both lanes**
35mm	**rest area both lanes, full ♿ facilities, ☎, vending, picnic, litter barrels, petwalk**
34	WV 19, Hurricane, **N food:** KFC, **other:** Chevrolet, Chrysler/Jeep/Dodge, Ford, Mountain State RV Ctr, Walmart SuperCtr, **S gas:** Exxon/7-11, Go-Mart, **food:** BiscuitWorld/Gino's Pizza, Little Caesar's, McDonald's, Mi Pueblito, Pizza Hut, Subway, **lodging:** Super 8, **other:** Rite Aid, Vet
28	US 60, Milton, **1-3 mi S gas:** Chevron/dsl, Exxon, Go-Mart, Rich Gas, **food:** Biscuit World, DQ, Gino's Pizza, McDonald's, Pizza Hut, Subway, Wendy's, **other:** Advance Parts, $General, Family$, Foodland, Jim's Camping (2mi), KOA (3mi), NAPA, Rite Aid, Sav-A-Lot foods, USPO
20	US 60, Mall Rd, Barboursville, **N food:** Applebee's, Arby's, Bob Evans, Burger King, Chick-fil-A, Chili's, Cici's Pizza, IHOP, Logan's Roadhouse, McDonald's, Olive Garden, Panera Bread, Ruby Tuesday, Wendy's, **lodging:** Comfort Inn, **other:** Best Buy, Borders Books, Drug Emporium, Elder-Berman, Firestone/auto, JC Penney, Jo-Ann Fabrics, Kohl's, Lowe's Whse, Macy's, Michael's, NTB, Sears/auto, mall, Walmart SuperCtr, **S gas:** BP, **food:** Cracker Barrel, Famous Dave's BBQ, Outback Steaks, Sam's Hotdogs, Sonic, Steak&Shake, Subway, Taco Bell, TCBY, **lodging:** Best Western, Comfort Inn, Hampton Inn, Holiday Inn, **other:** KOA, Toyota

INTERSTATE 64 CONT'D

Exit #	Services
18	US 60, to WV 2, Barboursville, **N food:** Bellacino's, O'Charley's, Starbucks, **other:** $Tree, Home Depot, Marshall's, Office Depot, PetsMart, Target, **S gas:** Chevron/7-11, **food:** Hardee's, Hooters, Papa John's, Pizza Hut, **lodging:** Comfort Suites, **other:** Kia, Kroger/gas, Rite Aid
15	US 60, 29th St E, **N gas:** GoMart/dsl, Speedway/dsl, **food:** Arby's, Biscuit World, Gino's Pizza, Pizza Hut, Subway, Wendy's, Waffle House, **other:** H, BigLots, Curves, $General, Sav-a-Lot Foods, Walmart SuperCtr/McDonald's, st police, **S gas:** Exxon, **food:** Fazoli's, Golden Corral, KFC, Little Caesar's, McDonald's, Penn Sta., Shoney's, Taco Bell, **lodging:** Day's Inn, Red Roof Inn, **other:** Chrysler/Jeep, CVS Drug, Nissan/Mitsubishi, Pontiac/Cadillac/GMC/Buick, Subaru
11	WV 10, Hal Greer Blvd, **0-2 mi N gas:** BP, Go-Mart, Marathon, **food:** Arby's, Bob Evan's, Frostop Drive-In, Gino's Pizza, KFC, McDonald's, Wendy's, **lodging:** Holiday Inn, Ramada Ltd, Super 8, **other:** H, Rite Aid, **S other:** Beech Fork SP (8mi)
10mm	**Welcome Ctr eb, full facilities, phone, vending, picnic, litter barrels, petwalk**
8	WV 152 S, WV 527 N, **S gas:** Speedway, **food:** DQ
6	US 52 N, W Huntington, Chesapeake, **N gas:** Marathon, Speedway/24hr, **food:** Pizza Hut, **other:** H AutoZone, BigLots, $General, Family$, Sav-A-Lot Foods
1	US 52 S, Kenova, **1-3 mi N gas:** Chevron/dsl, Exxon, Speedway, **food:** Burger King, Evaroni's Pizza, Gino's Pizza, Little Caesar's, McDonald's, Pizza Hut, Stewart's Hotdogs, **lodging:** Hollywood Motel, **other:** Advance Parts, Sav-A-Lot
0mm	West Virginia/Kentucky state line, Big Sandy River

INTERSTATE 68

Exit #	Services
32mm	West Virginia/Maryland state line
31mm	**Welcome Ctr wb, full facilities, picnic, litter barrels, phone, vending, petwalk**
29	rd 5, Hazelton Rd, **N gas:** Sunoco/dsl, **lodging:** Microtel (1mi), **S other:** Big Bear Camping (3mi), Pine Hill RV Camp (4mi)
23	WV 26, Bruceton Mills, **N gas:** BP/Subway/dsl/24hr, Sunoco/Little Sandy's Rest./dsl/24hr, **food:** Twila's Rest., **lodging:** Maple Leaf Motel, **other:** Family$, Hostetler's Store, USPO, antiques
18mm	Laurel Run
17mm	**runaway truck ramp eb**
16mm	**weigh sta wb**
15	WV 73, WV 12, Coopers Rock, **N other:** Chestnut Ridge SF, Sand Springs Camping (2mi)
12mm	**runaway truck ramp wb**
10	WV 857, Fairchance Rd, Cheat Lake, **N gas:** BP/Little Ceasar's/TCBY/dsl/24hr, Exxon/dsl, **food:** China Kitchen, Pizza'n Pasta, Subway, USPO, **lodging:** Lakeview Resort, **S food:** Burger King, Dimitri's Steaks
9mm	Cheat Lake
7	rd 705, Pierpont Rd, **N gas:** BP/Little Ceasar's/Subway/TCBY, Exxon/Taco Bell/dsl, **food:** Bob Evans, Fujiyama Steaks, Heavenly Ham, IHOP, Outback Steaks, Ruby Tuesday, Wendy's, **lodging:** Euro Suites, Holiday Inn Express, Super 8, **other:** H, BooksAMillion, Family$, GNC, Harley-Davidson, Lowes Whse, Michael's, Shop'n Save Foods, to WVU Stadium, **S gas:** Crestpoint, **food:** Fox's Pizza Den
4	rd 7, to Sabraton, **N gas:** BP/Subway/dsl, Exxon/24hr, Sheetz/dsl/24hr, **food:** Arby's, Burger King, Hardee's, Hero Hut, KFC, LJ Silver, McDonald's, Pizza Hut, Wendy's, **lodging:** SpringHill Suites, **other:** Advance Parts, CVS Drug, $General, Family$, Ford/Lincoln/Mercury, Kroger/gas, Sav-a-Lot Foods, USPO, **S gas:** Allstar/dsl, Pacific Pride/dsl
3mm	Decker's Creek
1	US 119, Morgantown, **N gas:** Go-Mart/dsl, **lodging:** Comfort Inn, Ramada Inn/rest., **other:** tires, **S food:** Subway, **other:** $Tree, Walmart SuperCtr/24hr, to Tygart L SP
0mm	I-79, N to Pittsburgh, S to Clarksburg. I-68 begins/ends on I-79, exit 148.

INTERSTATE 70

Exit #	Services
14mm	West Virginia/Pennsylvania state line
13.5mm	**Welcome Ctr wb, full facilities, phone, vending, picnic, litter barrels, petwalk**
11	WV 41, Dallas Pike, **N gas:** TA/dsl/rest./@, **lodging:** Comfort Inn, **S gas:** AM Best/Country Kitchen/Taco Joe/CK Burger/dsl/scales/24hr, Exxon, Mobil/DQ/dsl, **lodging:** Holiday Inn Express, **other:** RV camping
10	rd 65, to Cabela Dr, **N food:** Applebee's, Bob Evans, Cheddar's, Coldstone Creamery, Cracker Barrel, Eat'n Park, McDonald's, Olive Garden, Panera Bread, Quizno's, Wendy's, **other:** Best Buy, Books-a-Million, Cabela's, JC Penney, Kohl's, Michael's, Old Navy, PetCo, Russel Stover Candies, Target, TJ Maxx, Walmart SuperCtr
5	US 40, WV 88 S, Tridelphia, **N gas:** Marathon, **food:** Christopher's Café, Hoss' Rest., Pizza Hut, Subway, Wendy's, **lodging:** Super 8, **other:** Chrysler/Dodge/Jeep, Family$, Riesbeck's Foods, Vet, **S gas:** Exxon/dsl, Mobil, **food:** Arby's, Domino's, DQ, McDonald's, Silver Chopsticks, Undo's Rest., **other:** Advance Parts, Rite Aid, museum
5a	I-470 W, to Columbus
4	WV 88 N (from eb), Elm Grove, same as 5
3.5mm	**weigh sta wb**
2b	Washington Ave, **N gas:** Exxon, **food:** Greco's Rest., **other:** Kroger/gas, **S food:** Figaretti's Italian, **other:** H
2a	rd 88 N, to Oglebay Park, **N gas:** Exxon, Sheetz, **food:** Bob Evans, Hardee's, LJ Silver, Papa John's, Perkins, Subway, Super Buffet, Tim Horton's, TJ's Rest, **lodging:** Hampton Inn, Springhill Suites, **other:** Advance Parts, CVS Drug, Kroger/gas, NTB, Radio Shack
1b	US 250 S, WV 2 S, S Wheeling
1mm	tunnel
1a	US 40 E, WV 2 N, Main St, downtown, **S lodging:** Wheeling Inn
0	US 40 W, Zane St, Wheeling Island, **N gas:** Exxon/dsl, **food:** Burger King, KFC
0mm	West Virginia/Ohio state line, Ohio River

INTERSTATE 77

N ↕ S — PARKERSBURG

Exit #	Services
186mm	West Virginia/Ohio state line, Ohio River
185	WV 14, WV 31, Williamstown, **W gas:** GoMart, 7-11/ gas (1mi), **food:** Dutch Pantry, Subway (1mi), **lodging:** Day's Inn, **other:** Glass Factory Tours, WV **Welcome Ctr/rest area, full facilities, info, [picnic], litter barrels**
179	WV 2 N, WV 68 S, to Waverly, **E gas:** Exxon, **other:** [airport], **W gas:** BP, Chevron (3mi), **food:** Burger King, Hardee's (3mi), **lodging:** Red Carpet Inn, **other:** [H]
176	US 50, 7th St, Parkersburg, **E** to North Bend SP, **W gas:** BP, GoMart, 7-11, **food:** Bob Evans, Burger King, Domino's, DQ, LJ Silver, McDonald's, Mountaineer Rest./24hr, Omelette Shoppe, Wendy's, **lodging:** Econolodge, Knight's Inn, Red Roof Inn, Travelodge, **other:** Advance Parts, CVS Drug, Family$, Ford, Hyundai, Kroger/dsl, Lincoln/Mercury, Mercedes, NAPA, Rite Aid, Toyota, to Blennerhassett Hist Park, Vet
174	WV 47, Staunton Ave, **1 mi E gas:** FinishLine, **food:** Subway, **W gas:** 47 Carry Out
174mm	Little Kanawha River
173	WV 95, Camden Ave, **E gas:** Marathon/dsl, **1-4 mi W gas:** BP, **food:** Hardee's, **lodging:** Blennerhassett Hotel, **other:** [H]
170	WV 14, Mineral Wells, **E gas:** BP/dsl/repair/24hr, Chevron, FinishLine Gas, Parkersburg Trkstp/dsl/ scales/24hr, Liberty Trkstp/dsl/24hr, **food:** McDonald's, Subway, Taco Bell, Wendy's, **lodging:** Comfort Suites, Hampton Inn, **other:** USPO, **W food:** Cracker Barrel, **lodging:** AmeriHost, Holiday Inn Express, Microtel
169mm	**weigh sta both lanes, [phone]**
166mm	**rest area both lanes, full [handicapped] facilities, [phone], [picnic], litter barrels, vending, petwalk, RV dump**
161	WV 21, Rockport, **W gas:** Marathon
154	WV 1, Medina Rd
146	WV 2 S, Silverton, Ravenswood, **E other:** Ruby Lake Camping (4mi), **W gas:** BP/dsl, Exxon/24hr, Marathon/dsl/24hr, **food:** DQ, Gino's Pizza, McDonald's (3mi), Wendy's (3mi), Subway (4mi), **lodging:** Scottish Inn
138	US 33, Ripley, **E gas:** BP/dsl/24hr, Exxon/24hr, Marathon/dsl, **food:** Arby's, KFC, LJ Silver, McDonald's, Pizza Hut, Taco Bell, Wendy's, **lodging:** Fairfield Inn, McCoy's Inn, Super 8, **other:** Family$, Kroger, NAPA, Rite Aid, Sav-a-Lot Foods, Walmart SuperCtr/Subway, Vet, **W gas:** Exxon/dsl/24hr, **food:** Bob Evan's, Ponderosa, Shoney's, Subway, **lodging:** Holiday Inn Express, **other:** [H]
132	WV 21, Fairplain, **E gas:** BP/7-11/dsl, GoMart/dsl, **food:** Burger King, Fratello's Italian, Village Pizza, **other:** Curves, $General, Ford/Lincoln, Statts Mills RV Park (6mi), **W gas:** Loves/Subway/dsl/scales/24hr
124	WV 34, Kenna, **E gas:** Exxon
119	WV 21, Goldtown, same as 116
116	WV 21, Haines Branch Rd, Sissonville, **4 mi E other:** Rippling Waters Camping
114	WV 622, Pocatalico Rd, **E gas:** BP/dsl, **other:** Fas-Chek Foods/drug, Tom's Hardware
111	WV 29, Tuppers Creek Rd, **W gas:** BP/Subway/dsl, **food:** Gino's (2mi), Tudor's Biscuit World, Wendy's (2mi)

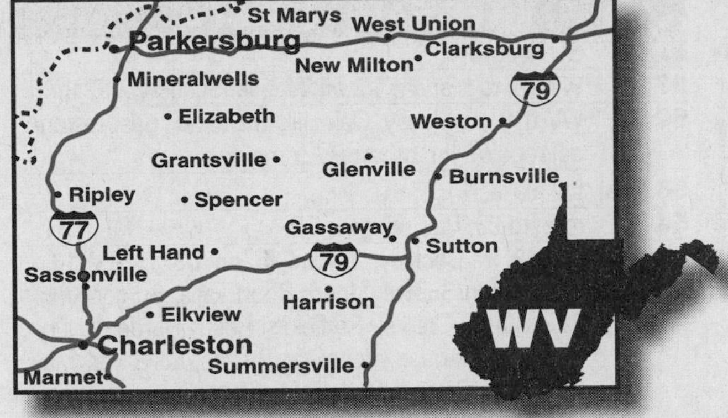

CHARLESTON

Exit #	Services
106	WV 27, Edens Fork Rd, **W gas:** Chevron/dsl/country store, **lodging:** Sunset Motel (3mi)
104	I-79 N, to Clarksburg
102	US 119 N, Westmoreland Rd, **E gas:** BP/7-11/24hr, GoMart/24hr, **food:** Hardee's/24hr, **lodging:** Parsley Motel
101	I-64, E to Beckley, W to Huntington
100	Broad St, Capitol St, **W food:** Charleston House Rest., **lodging:** Fairfield Inn, Holiday Inn, Marriott, Super 8, **other:** [H], CVS Drug, Family$, GMC, Honda Motorcycles, JC Penney, Kroger
99	WV 114, Capitol St, **E** [airport], **W gas:** Exxon, Domino's, **food:** KFC/Taco Bell, McDonald's, Wendy's, **other:** to museum, st capitol
98	35th St Bridge (from sb), **W food:** KFC/Taco Bell, McDonald's, Steak Escape, Shoney's, Subway, Taco Bell, Wendy's, **other:** [H], Rite Aid, to U of Charleston
97	US 60 W (from nb), Kanawha Blvd
96	US 60 E, Midland Trail, Belle, **W food:** Biscuit World, Gino's, **lodging:** Budget Host
96mm	W Va Turnpike begins/ends
95.5mm	Kanawha River
95	WV 61, to MacCorkle Ave, **E gas:** BP/Subway/ dsl, GoMart/dsl/24hr, **food:** Bob Evans, IHOP, Lonestar Steaks, McDonald's, TX Steaks, Wendy's, **lodging:** Comfort Suites, Country Inn&Suites, Day's Inn, Knight's Inn, Motel 6, Red Roof Inn, **other:** Advance Parts, AutoZone, K-Mart, **W gas:** Ashland/Blimpie/24hr, Chevron/7-11, Exxon/dsl/24hr, GoMart/24hr, **food:** Applebee's, Arby's, Burger King, Capt D's, Cracker Barrel, Hooters, La Carreta Mexican, Pizza Hut/Taco Bell, Southern Kitchen/24hr, **other:** Drug Emporium, Foodland, Kroger/gas, Lowe's Whse, mall
89	WV 61, WV 94, to Marmet, **E gas:** Exxon/Subway/ dsl/24hr, GoMart, Sunoco, **food:** BiscuitWorld, Gino's Pizza, Hardee's, LJ Silver, Sam's Hotdogs, Wendy's, **other:** Family$, Ford (1mi), Kroger/deli, NAPA, Rite Aid
85	US 60, WV 61, East Bank, **E gas:** GoMart/dsl/24hr, **food:** Gino's Pizza, McDonald's, Shoney's, **other:** Chevrolet, $General, Kroger, tire repair, USPO
82.5mm	toll booth
79	Cabin Creek Rd, Sharon
74	WV 83, Paint Creek Rd
72mm	**Morton Service Area eb, gas:** Exxon/dsl, **food:** Burger King, KFC, Pizza Hut, Starbucks, TCBY, atm
69mm	**rest area wb, full [handicapped] facilities, [phone], [picnic], litter barrels**

INTERSTATE 77 CONT'D

Exit #	Services
66	WV 15, to Mahan, **1/2 mi W gas:** Sunoco/dsl/24hr
60	WV 612, to Mossy, Oak Hill, **1/2 mi E gas:** Exxon/dsl/repair/24hr, **other:** RV camping
56.5mm	toll plaza, [phone]
54	rd 2, rd 23, Pax, **E gas:** BP
48	US 19, N Beckley, **1-4 mi E on US 19/WV 16... gas:** Exxon/Subway, **food:** Bob Evans, Burger King, Chick-fil-A, Chilli's, Garfield's Rest., Hardee's, Logan's Roadhouse, LoneStar Steaks, LJ Silver, McDonald's, Peking Buffet, Ryan's, Starbucks, Taco Bell, Wendy's, **lodging:** Days Inn, **other:** Advance Parts, Acura, AutoZone, Belk, Buick, Chevrolet/Cadillac, CVS Drug, $General, $Tree, Food Lion, JC Penney, Honda, Hyundai, Kohl's, Lowe's, Nissan, Radio Shack, Rite Aid, Sam's Club, Sears, Staples, Subaru/Kia, Toyota, Turning Wheel RV Ctr, U-Haul, Walmart SuperCtr/gas/24hr
45mm	**Tamarack Service Area both lanes, W gas:** Exxon/dsl, **food:** Burger King, Quizno's, Sbarro's, Starbucks, TCBY, **other:** gifts
44	WV 3, Beckley, **E gas:** Chevron/dsl, Exxon, Shell/Hardee's/24hr, **food:** Applebee's, Campestre Mexican, DQ, Hibachi Japanese, Hooters, IHOP, McDonald's, Omelette Shoppe, Outback Steaks, Pizza Hut, **lodging:** Econolodge, Best Western, Courtyard, Fairfield Inn, Howard Johnson, Quality Inn/rest., Super 8, **other:** CVS Drug, Kroger/gas, Outback Steaks, Rite Aid, Tires, **W gas:** BP/Subway/dsl, GoMart/dsl, **food:** Bob Evans, Cracker Barrel, Ruby Tuesday, Texas Roadhouse, Wendy's, **lodging:** Country Inn&Suites, Hampton Inn, Holiday Inn, Microtel, Park Inn
42	WV 16, WV 97, to Mabscott, **2 mi E food:** Biscuit-World, **lodging:** Budget Inn, **other:** [H], **W gas:** BP/dsl, GoMart, **food:** Godfather's, Subway, **other:** AutoValue Parts, Walmart/SuperCtr/24hr, USPO
40	I-64 E, to Lewisburg
30mm	toll booth, [phone]
28	WV 48, to Ghent, **E gas:** Exxon/dsl, Marathon/dsl, **food:** Subway, **lodging:** Glade Springs Resort (1mi), Appalachian Resort Inn (12mi), **other:** to ski area, **W lodging:** Knight's Inn
26.5mm	Flat Top Mtn, elevation 3252
20	US 19, to Camp Creek, **E gas:** Exxon/dsl, **W other:** Camp Creek SP/RV camping
18.5mm	scenic overlook/**parking area/weigh sta sb**, Bluestone River
17mm	**Bluestone Service Area/weigh sta nb, full [handicap] facilities, scenic view, [picnic]**, Exxon/dsl, Blimpie, Starbucks, TCBY, atm/fax
14	WV 20, Athens Rd, **E other:** Pipestem Resort SP, to Concord U
9mm	WV Turnpike begins/ends
9	US 460, Princeton, Pearisburg, **E food:** Kimono Japanese, Outback Steaks, Ryan's, **lodging:** Country Inn&Suites, **other: Welcome Ctr/Rest Area, pinic tables, little barrels, [phone], full facilities,** $Tree, Radio Shack, Walmart SuperCtr/24hr, **W gas:** BP/dsl, Chevron/dsl/24hr, Exxon/dsl/24hr, Marathon/Subway/dsl, **food:** Applebee's, Arby's, Bob Evans,
9	Continued Capt D's, Chili's, Cracker Barrel, DQ, Hardee's, McDonald's, Omelette Spot, Shoney's, Starbucks, TX Steaks, Wendy's, **lodging:** Comfort Inn, Days Inn, Hampton Inn, Holiday Inn Express, Microtel, Sleep Inn, Turnpike Motel, **other:** [H], Hyundai, Lowe's Whse, Suzuki
7	WV 27, Ingleside Rd (from nb, no re-entry)
5	WV 112 (from sb, no re-entry), to Ingleside
3mm	East River
1	US 52 N, to Bluefield, **4 mi W food:** KFC/LJ Silver, Wendy's, **lodging:** EconoLodge, Holiday Inn/rest., Knight's Inn, **other:** [H], to Bluefield St Coll
0mm	West Virginia/Virginia state line, East River Mtn

INTERSTATE 79

Exit #	Services
160mm	West Virginia/Pennsylvania state line
159	**Welcome Ctr sb, full [handicap] facilities, info, [picnic], litter barrels, [phone], vending, petwalk**
155	US 19, WV 7, **0-3 mi E gas:** GetGo, Sheetz, **food:** Burger King, Cheddars, Chili's, Cracker Barrel, Eat'n Park, EverGreen Buffet, Golden Corral, LJ Silver, Longhorn Steaks, McDonald's, Olive Garden, Shoney's, Wendy's, **lodging:** Fairfield Inn, Hampton Inn, Holiday Inn, **other:** [H], Barnes&Noble, Best Buy, CVS Drug, $Tree, Giant Eagle Foods, Old Navy, PetCo, Sam's Club, Target, TJ Maxx, Walmart SuperCtr, to WVU
152	US 19, to Morgantown, **E gas:** BP/dsl, Exxon, **food:** Arby's, China Wok, McDonald's, Pizza Hut, Subway, Taco Bell, **lodging:** Econolodge, **other:** Advance Parts, Big Lots, KIA, Shop'n Save Foods, **W food:** Bob Evans, Burger King, Garfield's Rest., **lodging:** Microtel, **other:** Belk, JC Penney, K-Mart, Lowes Whse, Sears/auto, mall
150mm	Monongahela River
148	I-68 E, to Cumberland, MD, **1 mi E gas:** Exxon/dsl/24hr, **lodging:** Regatta Grill, **lodging:** Comfort Inn, Morgantown Motel, Ramada Inn
146	WV 77, to Goshen Rd
141mm	**weigh sta both lanes**
139	WV 33, E Fairmont, **E gas:** Chevron, **W gas:** Exxon/24hr, K&T/BP/dsl, **other:** RV camping, tires, Vet, to Prickett's FT SP
137	WV 310, to Fairmont, **E gas:** BP, Exxon/dsl/24hr, **food:** Subway, **lodging:** Holiday Inn, **other:** to Valley Falls SP, Vet, **W gas:** Chevron, **food:** Domino's, KFC, McDonald's, Wendy's, **other:** [H]
136	new exit
135	WV 64, Pleasant Valley Rd
133	Kingmont Rd, **E gas:** BP/Subway/dsl, **food:** Cracker Barrel, **lodging:** Super 8, **W gas:** Chevron/dsl/24hr, King/dsl, **food:** DJ's Diner, **lodging:** Comfort Inn
132	US 250, S Fairmont, **E gas:** Chevron, **food:** Applebees, Arby's, Bob Evans, Colasessano's Italian, Dragon Buffet, Dutchman's Daughter, Hardee's, Hunan Rest., McDonald's, Subway, Taco Bell, **lodging:** Day's Inn, Fairfield Inn, Red Roof Inn, **other:** Ace Hardware, Advance Parts, Chrysler/Dodge/Jeep, $General, GNC, Sav-a-Lot Foods, Shop'n Save, Walmart SuperCtr, mall, to Tygart Lake SP, **W gas:**

INTERSTATE 79 CONT'D

N ↕ S

CLARKSBURG

Exit #	Services
132	Continued Exxon/dsl/24hr, GoMart/dsl/24hr, Sunoco, **lodging:** Country Club Motel (4mi), **other:** H, Buick/GMC/ Pontiac, Ford/Lincoln/Mercury, Toyota/Scion, Trailer City RV Ctr
125	WV 131, Saltwell Rd, to Shinnston, **E food:** Oliverio's Rest. (4mi), **W gas:** Exxon/Subway/dsl/24hr
124	rd 279, Jerry Dove Dr, **E gas:** Exxon, **food:** Buffalo Wild Wings, **lodging:** Microtel, Wingate Inn
123mm	**rest area both lanes, full ♿ facilities, info, ☎, ⛺, litter barrels, vending, petwalk, RV dump**
121	WV 24, Meadowbrook Rd, **E gas:** GoMart/24hr, Sheetz, **food:** Bob Evans, Gino's Pizza, Subway, **lodging:** Hampton Inn, **other:** Hyundai/Subaru, **W gas:** Exxon/dsl, **food:** Burger King, Garfield's Rest., Outback Steaks, **lodging:** Super 8, **other:** Honda, JC Penney, Jo-Ann Fabrics, NTB, Old Navy, Sears/auto, Target, mall
119	US 50, to Clarksburg, **E gas:** Exxon/dsl, GoMart/gas, **food:** A&W/LJ Silver, CiCi's Pizza, Denny's, Eat'n Park, Grand China, KFC, Las Trancas, Little Caesar's, Maxey's Rest., McDonald's, Panera Bread, Pizza Hut, Quizno's, Shogun Japanese, Starbucks, Taco Bell, TX Roadhouse, USA Steaks, Wendy's, **lodging:** Comfort Inn, Day's Inn, Holiday Inn, Knight's Inn, Sleep Inn, Sutton Inn, **other:** H, Advance Parts, Big Lots, Chevrolet, GNC, Home Depot, K-Mart, Kohl's, Kroger/gas/24hr, Lowes Whse, Nissan, Radio Shack, Sam's Club/gas, USPO
117	WV 58, to Anmoore, **E gas:** BP/dsl, **food:** Applebee's, Arby's, Ruby Tuesday, Ryan's, Subway, **other:** Hilton Garden, **other:** Aldi Foods, $Tree, , Walmart SuperCtr/24hr
115	WV 20, Nutter Fort, to Stonewood, **E gas:** BP/7-11/dsl, Chevron, Exxon/dsl, **food: other:** Stonewood Bulk Foods, **W lodging:** Greenbrier Motel (5mi)
110	Lost Creek, **E gas:** BP/dsl
105	WV 7, to Jane Lew, **E gas:** Chevron/dsl/rest., I-79 Trkstp/dsl/rest., **lodging:** Plantation Inn, **W gas:** GoMart, **other:** glass factory tours
99	US 33, US 119, to Weston, **E gas:** Fuel Ctr, Sheetz/24hr, **food:** Burger King, Gino's Pizza, McDonald's, Peking Buffet, Steer Steakhouse, Subway, **lodging:** Comfort Inn/rest., Hampton Inn (9mi), Holiday Inn Express, Super 8, **other:** Advance Parts, Family$, GNC, Kroger, Radio Shack, Walmart, **W gas:** Chevron, Rich Gas, **food:** Domino's, Fox's Den Pizza, Hardee's, KFC, LJ Silver, Pizza Hut, Wendy's, **other:** H, $General, Ford, NAPA, Sav-a-Lot, Twin Lakes Camper Sales, to Canaan Valley Resort, Blackwater Falls
96	WV 30, to S Weston, **E other:** Broken Wheel Camping, to S Jackson Lake SP
91	US 19, to Roanoke, **E gas:** Marathon, **food:** Stillwaters Rest, **other:** Whisper Mtn Camping, to S Jackson Lake SP
85mm	**rest area both lanes, full ♿ facilities, info, ⛺, litter barrels, ☎, vending, petwalk, RV dump**
79.5mm	Little Kanawha River

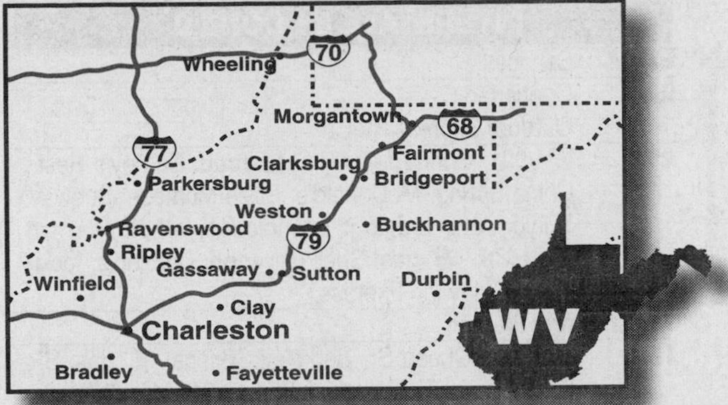

WV

CHARLESTON

Exit #	Services
79	WV 5, Burnsville, **E gas:** Exxon/24hr, **lodging:** 79 Motel/rest., **other:** NAPA, **W gas:** GoMart, **food:** Gino's Pizza, **other:** Cedar Cr SP
78mm	Saltlick Creek
67	WV 4, to Flatwoods, **E gas:** BP/Arby's//dsl, Chevron/dsl, Exxon/dsl, Go-Mart/dsl, **food:** KFC/Taco Bell, McDonald's, Subway, Waffle Hut, **lodging:** Day's Inn, Sutton Lake Motel, **other:** Buick/Chevrolet, to Sutton Lake RA, antiques, camping, **W gas:** Sunoco/motel/dsl, **food:** China Buffet, Shoney's, Wendy's, **other:** Bulk Foods, Flatwood Factory Stores
62	WV 4, Gassaway, to Sutton, **E food:** Century Rest. (2mi), **lodging:** Elk Motel, **W gas:** GoMart, **food:** Giovanni's Pizza, LJ Silver, Pizza Hut, **lodging:** Microtel, **other:** H, Chrysler/Dodge/Jeep, CVS Drug, Ford, Kroger/deli, Super$
57	US 19 S, to Beckley
52mm	Elk River
51	WV 4, to Frametown, **E** antiques
49mm	**rest area both lanes, full ♿ facilities, ⛺, ☎, litter barrels, vending, petwalk, RV dump**
46	WV 11, Servia Rd
40	WV 16, to Big Otter, **E gas:** GoMart/dsl, **W gas:** Exxon/dsl
34	WV 36, to Wallback, **10 mi E food:** Gino's Diner, BiscuitWorld
25	WV 29, to Amma, **E gas:** Exxon/dsl
19	US 119, VW 53, to Clendenin, **E gas:** BP/dsl/24hr, **food:** BiscuitWorld, Gino's Diner, **other:** Shafer's Superstop
9	WV 43, to Elkview, **E gas:** GoMart/dsl, **food:** Burger King, **W gas:** Exxon/Arby's/dsl, Speedway/dsl/24hr, **food:** Bob Evans, McDonald's, Pizza Hut, Ponderosa, Subway, **lodging:** Country Inn&Suites, **other:** Advance Parts, CVS Drug, $Tree, K-Mart, Kroger, Radio Shack
5	WV 114, to Big Chimney, **1 mi E gas:** Exxon, **food:** Hardee's/24hr, **other:** Rite Aid, Smith's Foods
1	US 119, Mink Shoals, **E food:** Harding's Family Rest., **lodging:** Sleep Inn
0	I-77, S to Charleston, N to Parkersburg. I-79 begins/ends on I-77, exit 104.

INTERSTATE 81

Exit #	Services
26mm	West Virginia/Maryland state line, Potomac River
25mm	**Welcome Ctr sb, full ♿ facilities, info, ☎, ⛺, litter barrels, petwalk**
23	US 11, Marlowe, Falling Waters, **1 mi E other:** Falling Waters Camping, **W gas:** BP/dsl, 7-11, **other:**

INTERSTATE 81 CONT'D

Exit #	Services
23	Continued Outdoor Express RV Ctr
20	WV 901, Spring Mills Rd, **E food:** Barney's Rest., China Spring, McDonald's, Pizza Montese, Subway, Tokyo Cafe, **lodging:** Econolodge, **other:** Walmart SuperCtr, **W gas:** Shell/dsl, **food:** Domino's, **lodging:** Holiday Inn Express
19mm	**rest area sb**
16	WV 9, N Queen St, Berkeley Springs, **E gas:** BP, Citgo, Exxon/Subway/dsl, Sheetz/24hr, **food:** Arby's, Casa Gonzales Mexican, China King, Domino's, Hoss's, KFC, LJ Silver, McDonald's, Popeye's, Thai Hut, Waffle House, **lodging:** Comfort Inn, Knight's Inn, Super 8, Rodeway Inn, **other:** Advance Parts, AutoZone, CVS Drug, Food Lion, **W gas:** Citgo, Shell/dsl
14	rd 13, Dry Run Rd, **E other:** H, **W other:** Butler's Farm Mkt (1mi)
13	rd 15, Kings St, Martinsburg, **E gas:** BP/Subway/dsl, Sheetz/24hr, **food:** Applebees, Arkena's Cafe, Buffalo Wild Wings, Burger King, Cracker Barrel, Jerry's Subs, Kobe Japanese, Las Trancas, Outback Steaks, Pizza Hut, Shoney's, Wendy's, **lodging:** Day's Inn, Holiday Inn/rest., **other:** H, Chevrolet/Toyota/Scion, Tanger/famous brands, Walmart SuperCtr/24hr, same as 12
12	WV 45, Winchester Ave, **E gas:** Citgo/dsl, Sheetz/24hr, Shell/dsl, **food:** Arby's, Bob Evans, Chick-fil-A, China City Buffet, McDonald's, Papa John's, Quizno's, Ryan's, Ruby Tuesday, Taco Bell, TX Steaks, Waffle House, Wendy's, **lodging:** Comfort Suites, Economy Inn, Hampton Inn, Kristalite Inn, Relax Inn, **other:** Advance Parts, AutoZone, BonTon, Food Lion, JC Penney, K-mart/Little Caesar's, Lowes Whse, Martin's Foods/gas, Sears/auto, mall, same as 13
8	RD 32, Tablers Sta Rd, **2 mi E lodging:** Pikeside Motel, **W other:** Orr's Farm Mkt
5	WV 51, Inwood, to Charles Town, **E gas:** Exxon, Liberty, 7-11, Sheetz, Shell/dsl, **food:** Burger King, DQ, KFC, McDonald's, Pizza Hut, Pizza Oven, Subway, Waffle House, **lodging:** Hampton Inn, **other:** CVS Drug, Family$, Food Lion, NAPA, **W other:** Lazy-A Camping (9mi)
2mm	**Welcome Ctr/weigh sta nb, full facilities, info, phone, vending, picnic, litter barrels, petwalk**
0mm	West Virginia/Virginia state line

WISCONSIN

INTERSTATE 39

Exit #	Services
211	US 51, rd K, Merrill, **2 mi W gas:** Cenex, **food:** Chip's Burgers, Hardee's, Pizza Hut, **other:** airport
210mm	Prairie River
208	WI 64, WI 70, Merrill, **W food:** Taco Bell, **W gas:** Mobil/dsl, Shell/dsl, **food:** Frazier's Grille, McDonald's, Subway, Taco Bell, Three's Company Rest., **lodging:** Americinn, Pine Ridge Inn, Super 8, **other:** H, Chrysler/Dodge/Jeep, $Tree, Piggly Wiggly, Walmart, to Council Grounds SP
206mm	Wisconsin River
205	US 51, rd Q, Merrill, **E gas:** BP/dsl/rest./24hr, Hwy 51 TrkStp, **other:** Buick/Cadillac/Chevrolet/Pontiac
197	rd WW, to Brokaw, **W gas:** Citgo/dsl
194	US 51, rd U, rd K, Wausau, **E gas:** F&F/dsl, KwikTrip/gas, **food:** McDonald's, Taco Bell, **other:** Toyota/Scion, **E food:** BP, **food:** Arby's, **other:** Ford/Mercedes, KIA
193	Bridge St, **E food:** Culvers, Quizno's, **lodging:** Plaza Hotel, **W** H
192	WI 29 W, WI 52 E, Wausau, to Chippewa Falls, same as 191
191	Sherman St, **E gas:** BP, **food:** Annie's Rest., Applebee's, Buffalo Wild Wings, Coldstone Creamery, Cousins Subs, Herford&Hops, Figaro's Pizza, Hong Kong Buffet, Hudson's Grill, Little Caesar's, McDonald's, Subway, **lodging:** Country Inn&Suites, Courtyard, Hampton Inn, La Quinta, Super 8, **other:** H **W food:** Burger King, Hardee's, 2510 Deli, **other:** Audi/Nissan/VW, County Mkt Foods, Home Depot, Honda, Menard's
190mm	Rib River
190	rd NN, **E gas:** Mobil/Burger King, **food:** Krumbee's Bakery, **lodging:** Howard Johnson, **W gas:** The Store/Subway/dsl, **lodging:** Best Western, **other:** Rib Mtn Ski Area, st patrol
188	rd N, **E gas:** BP/dsl/scales/24hr, Phillips 66/dsl, **food:** El Tapatio, Fazoli's, Hong Kong Buffet, McDonald's, Starbucks, Subway, Texas Roadhouse, Wendy's, **lodging:** Country Inn&Suites (1mi), Day's Inn, **other:** Aldi, Barnes&Noble, Best Buy, Chevrolet, GNC, Gordman's, Jo-Ann Fabrics, King's RV Ctr, Kohl's, Nissan, PetCo, Peterbilt, Radio Shack, Sam's Club, TJ Maxx, Tires+, Volvo, VW, Walmart SuperCtr/24hr, **W other:** Rib Mtn SP
187mm	I-39 begins/ends. Freeway continues N as US 51.
187	WI 29 E, to Green Bay
186mm	Wisconsin River
185	US 51, **E gas:** Cenex, **food:** Arby's, Culver's, Denny's, Green Mill Rest., Subway, Tony Roma's, **lodging:** Candlewood Suites, Cedar Creek Lodge, Comfort Inn, Holiday Inn, Rodeway Inn, Stoney Creek Inn, **other:** Cedar Creek Factory Stores/famous brands, Gander Mtn, Harley Davidson, Pick'n Save Foods, mall, visitor ctr
183mm	**sb, restroom facilities, drinking water, picnic**
181	Maple Ridge Rd, **W** Kenworth
179	WI 153, Mosinee, **W gas:** BP/Subway/dsl, KwikTrip, Shell/dsl/24hr, **food:** McDonald's, StageStop Rest., Subway, **lodging:** Super 8
178mm	**nb, restroom facilities, drinking water, picnic**
175	WI 34, Knowlton, to WI Rapids, **1 mi W other:** Mullins Cheese Factory
171	rd DB, Knowlton, **E** camping, **W other:** to gas, food, lodging

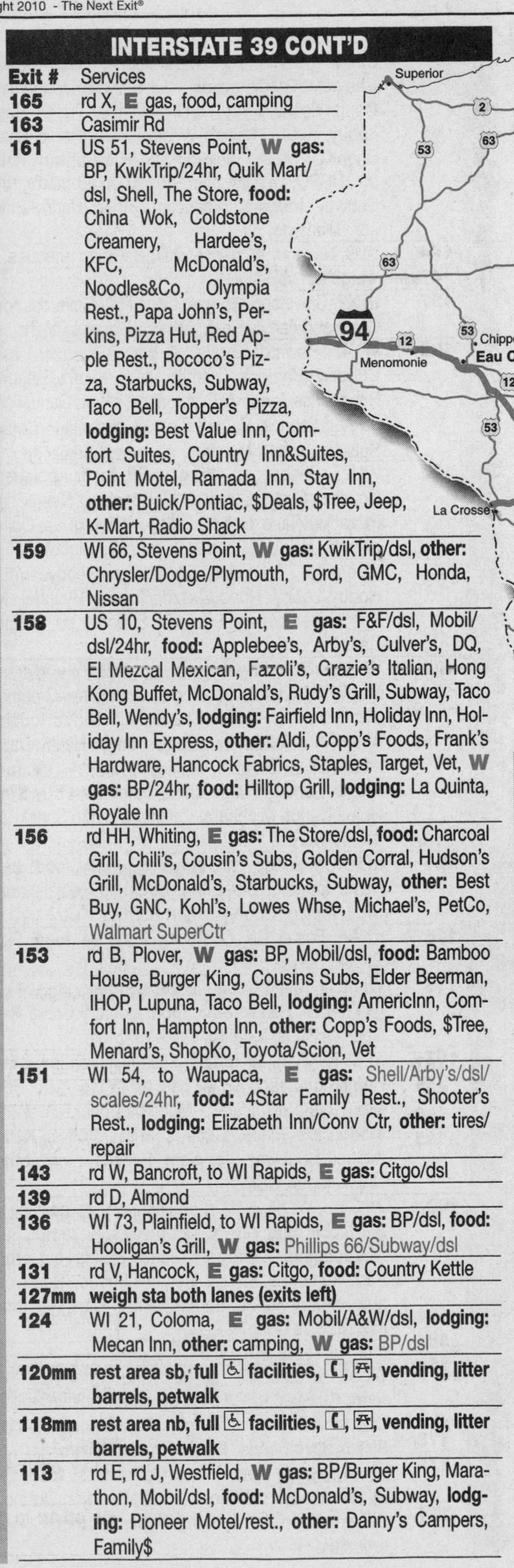

INTERSTATE 39 CONT'D

N ↕ S — STEVENS POINT

Exit #	Services
165	rd X, **E** gas, food, camping
163	Casimir Rd
161	US 51, Stevens Point, **W gas:** BP, KwikTrip/24hr, Quik Mart/dsl, Shell, The Store, **food:** China Wok, Coldstone Creamery, Hardee's, KFC, McDonald's, Noodles&Co, Olympia Rest., Papa John's, Perkins, Pizza Hut, Red Apple Rest., Rococo's Pizza, Starbucks, Subway, Taco Bell, Topper's Pizza, **lodging:** Best Value Inn, Comfort Suites, Country Inn&Suites, Point Motel, Ramada Inn, Stay Inn, **other:** Buick/Pontiac, $Deals, $Tree, Jeep, K-Mart, Radio Shack
159	WI 66, Stevens Point, **W gas:** KwikTrip/dsl, **other:** Chrysler/Dodge/Plymouth, Ford, GMC, Honda, Nissan
158	US 10, Stevens Point, **E gas:** F&F/dsl, Mobil/dsl/24hr, **food:** Applebee's, Arby's, Culver's, DQ, El Mezcal Mexican, Fazoli's, Grazie's Italian, Hong Kong Buffet, McDonald's, Rudy's Grill, Subway, Taco Bell, Wendy's, **lodging:** Fairfield Inn, Holiday Inn, Holiday Inn Express, **other:** Aldi, Copp's Foods, Frank's Hardware, Hancock Fabrics, Staples, Target, Vet, **W gas:** BP/24hr, **food:** Hilltop Grill, **lodging:** La Quinta, Royale Inn
156	rd HH, Whiting, **E gas:** The Store/dsl, **food:** Charcoal Grill, Chili's, Cousin's Subs, Golden Corral, Hudson's Grill, McDonald's, Starbucks, Subway, **other:** Best Buy, GNC, Kohl's, Lowes Whse, Michael's, PetCo, Walmart SuperCtr
153	rd B, Plover, **W gas:** BP, Mobil/dsl, **food:** Bamboo House, Burger King, Cousins Subs, Elder Beerman, IHOP, Lupuna, Taco Bell, **lodging:** AmericInn, Comfort Inn, Hampton Inn, **other:** Copp's Foods, $Tree, Menard's, ShopKo, Toyota/Scion, Vet
151	WI 54, to Waupaca, **E gas:** Shell/Arby's/dsl/scales/24hr, **food:** 4Star Family Rest., Shooter's Rest., **lodging:** Elizabeth Inn/Conv Ctr, **other:** tires/repair
143	rd W, Bancroft, to WI Rapids, **E gas:** Citgo/dsl
139	rd D, Almond
136	WI 73, Plainfield, to WI Rapids, **E gas:** BP/dsl, **food:** Hooligan's Grill, **W gas:** Phillips 66/Subway/dsl
131	rd V, Hancock, **E gas:** Citgo, **food:** Country Kettle
127mm	**weigh sta both lanes (exits left)**
124	WI 21, Coloma, **E gas:** Mobil/A&W/dsl, **lodging:** Mecan Inn, **other:** camping, **W gas:** BP/dsl
120mm	**rest area sb, full ♿ facilities, ☎, picnic, vending, litter barrels, petwalk**
118mm	**rest area nb, full ♿ facilities, ☎, picnic, vending, litter barrels, petwalk**
113	rd E, rd J, Westfield, **W gas:** BP/Burger King, Marathon, Mobil/dsl, **food:** McDonald's, Subway, **lodging:** Pioneer Motel/rest., **other:** Danny's Campers, Family$

PORTAGE

Exit #	Services
106	WI 82 W, WI 23 E, Oxford, **E lodging:** Crossroads Motel, **W gas:** Citgo/dsl
104	(from nb, no EZ return) rd D, Packwaukee
100	WI 23 W, rd P, Endeavor, **E gas:** BP/dsl
92	US 51 S, Portage, **E gas:** KwikTrip/dsl, Mobil, **food:** Culver's, Dino's Rest., Jimmy John's, KFC, La Tolteca Mexican, McDonald's, Subway, Taco Bell, Wendy's, World Buffet, **lodging:** Best Western, Ridge Motel, Super 8, **other:** H, Ace Hardware, AutoZone, Chrysler/Dodge/Jeep, Curves, $Tree, Ford/Lincoln/Mercury, GNC, K-Mart, Pierce's Foods, Radio Shack, Staples, Walgreens, Walmart SuperCtr/24hr
89b a	WI 16, to WI 127, Portage, **E food:** Hitching Post Eatery
88.5mm	Wisconsin River
87	WI 33, Portage, **W** ski area
86mm	Baraboo River
85	Cascade Mt Rd
84	**I-39, I-90 & I-94 run together sb.**

INTERSTATE 43

N ↕ S

Exit #	Services
192mm	I-43 begins/ends at Green Bay on US 41.
192b	US 41 S, US 141 S, to Appleton, services on Velp Ave, **1 mi S gas:** BP/A&W/dsl, Express, Mobil/Arby's, **food:** Black Forest Rest, Burger King, Kim's Grill, Rite View Diner, Riverside Coffee House, Riverstreet Rest, Taco Bell, Watering Hole Rest, **lodging:** AmericInn, **other:** Bumper Parts, Curves
192a	US 41 N, US 141 N
189	Atkinson Dr, to Velp Ave, Port of Green Bay
188mm	Fox River
187	East Shore Dr, Webster Ave, **W gas:** Shell/dsl/24hr,

WI

INTERSTATE 43 CONT'D

Exit #	Services
187	Continued food: Maria's Italian, McDonald's, Wendy's, other: H
185	WI 54, WI 57, University Ave, to Algoma, W gas: Citgo, Mobil, Shell/A&W, food: Green Bay Pizza, Harvest Cafe, Kahn's Mongolian, Lee's Cantonese Chinese, Pizza Hut, Subway, Taco Bell, other: NAPA, SuperValu Foods, Walgreens, U of WI GB
183	Mason St, rd V, E food: Culver's, Ground Round, Makinaw's Grill, Tim Horton, lodging: Country Inn&Suites, Super 8, other: H, 1 mi W gas: BP, Mobil/dsl, Shell, food: Applebee's, Arby's, Burger King, China Buffet, China Kitchen, Country Kitchen, DQ, Fazoli's, Grand Buffet, Great Lakes Sandwiches, KFC, Little Caesar's, LJ Silver, McDonald's, Papa John's, Papa Murphy's, Perkins, Pizza Hut, Starbucks, Taco Bell, other: Advance Parts, Aldi Foods, AT&T, AutoZone, Batteries+, Cadillac, Chevrolet, Chrysler/Dodge/Jeep, Copps Foods, Dodge, $General, Goodyear/auto, Hobby Lobby, Kohl's, Mazda, PetCo, ShopKO, Subaru, Tires+, Walgreens, Walmart/Subway
181	Eaton Rd, rd JJ, E gas: BP/McDonald's/dsl, food: Blimpie, Hardee's, Jimmy John's, K-2 Rest, Luigi's, Taco John's, other: Ford/Kia, Harley-Davidson, Home Depot, W gas: Mobil/Subway/dsl, Shell, food: A&W, Ravine Grill, lodging: AmericInn, other: Farm&Fleet/gas, Festival Foods, Menard's
180	WI 172 W, to US 41, 1 exit W gas: BP/Taco Bell/24hr, Citgo/Country Express/dsl/scales/24hr, Kwik Trip, Shell, food: Burger King, McDonald's, Subway, Tuscon's Rest., lodging: Guest House Inn, other: H, Copps Foods, Target, Walgreens, to stadium, 5 mi W multiple services
178	US 141, to WI 29, rd MM, Bellevue, E gas: Shell/Arby's/dsl, W repair
171	WI 96, rd KB, Denmark, E gas: BP/dsl, food: Lorrie's Café, McDonald's, Steve's Cheese, Subway, other: Shady Acres Camping
168mm	**rest area both lanes, full ♿ facilities, ☎, vending, picnic, litter barrels, petwalk**
166mm	Devils River
164	WI 147, rd Z, Maribel, W gas: BP/dsl, food: Ridge Rest
160	rd K, Kellnersville, 1 mi W gas: BP, food
157	rd V, Hillcrest Rd, Francis Creek, E gas: Citgo/Subway/dsl, Marathon/diner/dsl
154	US 10 W, WI 310, Two Rivers, to Appleton, E gas: Mobil, other: H, W gas: Cenex
153mm	Manitowoc River
152	US 10 E, WI 42 N, rd JJ, Manitowoc, E food: TimeOut Grill, other: H, antiques, maritime museum
149	US 151, WI 42 S, Manitowoc, E gas: BP, Exxon, KwikTrip/dsl, Mobil/dsl/24hr, Shell/dsl/24hr, food: A&W, Applebee's, Arby's, Burger King, Charcoal Grill, China Buffet, Country Kitchen, Cousins Subs, Culver's, DQ, 4 Seasons Rest., Jimmy John's, McDonald's, Papa Murphy's, Penguin Drive-In, Perkins, Ponderosa, Starbucks, Taco Bell, Wendy's, lodging: Birch Creek Inn, Comfort Inn, Holiday Inn, Super 8,
149	Continued other: H, Aldi Foods, AutoZone, Buick/Cadillac/Chevrolet/GMC/Pontiac, Chrysler/Dodge/Jeep, Copps Foods, $Tree, Family$, Festival Foods, Hobby Lobby, Kohl's, Lowe's Whse, PetCo, Radio Shack, ShopKO, Tires+, Walmart SuperCtr/Subway, museum, USPO, Vet, W gas: BP/McDonald's/24hr, food: Subway, lodging: AmericInn, other: Harley-Davidson, Menards
144	rd C, Newton, E gas: Mobil/dsl, other: antiques
142mm	**weigh sta sb, ☎**
137	rd XX, Cleveland, E gas: Citgo/PJ's Grille/dsl, food: Cleveland Family Rest., other: Wagner's RV Ctr
128	WI 42, Howards Grove, E gas: BP/dsl/24hr, food: Culver's, Hardee's, Harry's Diner, Shuff's Rest, TX Roadhouse, lodging: Comfort Inn, other: Gander Mtn, Jo-Ann Fabrics, Pomp's Tire, W gas: Citgo/Cousins Subs/dsl, other: Menards, Walmart SuperCtr
126	WI 23, Sheboygan, E gas: BP, food: Applebee's, Cousins Subs, Culver's, McDonald's, New China, Pizza Hut/Taco Bell, Quizno's, lodging: La Quinta, other: H, Aldi Foods, Batteries+, BigLots, Firestone/auto, Ford/Lincoln/Mercury, Goodyear/auto, Hobby Lobby, Honda/Mazda/Toyota, Hyundai, Kia, Kohl's, Sears/auto, ShopKO, Subaru, W lodging: Days Inn
123	WI 28, rd A, Sheboygan, E gas: Citgo/dsl/24hr, Mobil/McDonald's/dsl, food: Coldstone Creamery, Jimmy John's, Perkins, Starbucks, Wendy's, lodging: AmericInn, Holiday Inn Express, other: Harley-Davidson/Cruisers Burgers, Walmart SuperCtr, W food: Arby's, Century Buffet, Chili's, other: Best Buy, $Tree, Home Depot, Michael's, Petsmart, Radio Shack, Target, TJ Maxx
120	rds OK, V, Sheboygan, E gas: Citgo/dsl, food: Judi's Rest., lodging: Sleep Inn, other: to Kohler-Andrae SP, camping, 1 mi W other: Horn's RV Ctr
116	rd AA, Foster Rd, Oostburg, 1 mi W food: Pizza Ranch, Subway
113	WI 32 N, rd LL, Cedar Grove, W gas: Citgo/dsl/repair, Mobil, Renew/e-85, food: Country Grove Rest, Cousins Subs, lodging: Lakeview Motel
107	rd D, Belgium, E lodging: Lake Church Inn, other: Harrington Beach SP, W gas: BP/DQ/dsl/24hr, How-Dea Trkstp/dsl/scales, Mobil/McDonald's/dsl/24hr, food: Bic's Place, Curley's Rest., Hobo's Korner Kitchen, Subway, lodging: Regency Inn, other: NAPA, repair, USPO
100	WI 32 S, WI 84 W, Port Washington, E gas: Citgo/dsl, Mobil, food: Arby's, McDonald's, Pizza Hut, Subway, lodging: Country Inn&Suites, Holiday Inn, other: Allen-Edmonds Shoes, Century Foods, Goodyear/auto, Sentry Foods, ShopKO, True Value, W lodging: Nisleit's Country Rest.
97	(from nb, exits left), WI 57, Fredonia
96	WI 33, to Saukville, E gas: Citgo, Mobil/dsl/24hr, food: Culver's, KFC/LJ Silver, other: Buick/Cadillac/Chevrolet/Pontiac, Dodge, Ford/Lincoln/Mercury, Pick'n Save Foods, Piggly Wiggly, Walgreens, Walmart/drug, W gas: Exxon/McDonald's, food: DQ, Domino's, Lam's Chinese, Papa Murphy's, Quizno's, Subway, Taco Bell, lodging: Super 8, other: Curves, repair/tires

N ↕ S GREEN BAY · MANITOWAC · MILWAUKEE · WI

INTERSTATE 43 CONT'D

N ↕ S MILWAUKEE

Exit #	Services
93	WI 32 N, WI 57 S, Grafton, **1-2 mi E gas:** Citgo, **food:** Dairy House Rest., Mamma Mia's Cafe, Pied Piper Rest., Smith Bros Fish (4mi), **lodging:** Best Western, Holiday Inn, **W food:** Flannery's Cafe
92	WI 60, rd Q, Grafton, **E food:** GhostTown Rest., **lodging:** Hampton Inn, **W gas:** Citgo/DQ/dsl, **food:** Charcoal Grill, Noodles&Co, Qdoba, Quizno's, Starbucks, Subway, **lodging:** Baymont Inn, **other:** H, AT&T, Best Buy, Costco/gas, Home Depot, Kohl's, Michael's, Petsmart, Target, Vet
89	rd C, Cedarburg, **W gas:** Mobil/dsl, **food:** Cedar Crk Settlement Café (6mi), **lodging:** StageCoach Inn, Washington House Inn, **other:** H
85	WI 57 S, WI 167 W, Mequon Rd, **W gas:** Citgo/dsl, Mobil/24hr, **food:** Casa Grande Mexican, Caribou Coffee, Chancery Rest., Cousins Subs, Culver's, DQ, Hong Palace Chinese, Jimmy John's, McDonald's, Panera Bread, Papa Murphy's, Starbucks, Subway, **lodging:** Best Western, Chalet Motel, **other:** H, Ace Harware, Kohl's, Office Depot, Pick'n Save Foods, Sendik's Foods, Walgreens, Vet
83	rd W, Port Washington Rd (from nb only)
82b a	WI 32 S, WI 100, Brown Deer Rd, **E gas:** BP/24hr, Sendik's/dsl, **food:** Benji's Deli, Cold Stone, Jimmy John's, La Paisa Mexican, Max Field's Pancakes, McDonald's, Noodles&Co, Pizza Hut, Qdoba, Spring Garden Chinese, Starbucks, Subway, Toppers Pizza, **other:** Best Buy, Borders Books, CVS Drug, GNC, Land's Inlet, Walgreens
80	Good Hope Rd, **E gas:** BP, **food:** Jimmy John's, King's Wok, Nick-n-Willy's Pizza, Samurai Japanese, Stonecreek Coffee, **lodging:** Radisson, Residence Inn, **other:** Pick'n Save Foods, to Cardinal Stritch U
78	Silver Spring Dr, **E gas:** BP, Citgo, **food:** Applebee's, BD Mongolian, Boston Mkt, Bravo Italian, Burger King, CA Pizza Kitchen, Carabou Coffee, Cheesecake Factory, Cousins Subs, 5 Guys Burgers, Food Court, Gyro Palace, Kopps, McDonald's, Panera Bread, Perkins, Pizza Hut, Qdoba, Quizno's, Subway, Taco Bell, **lodging:** La Quinta, Super 8, **other:** AT&T, Barnes&Noble, Batteries+, Cadillac, Goodyear/auto, Kohl's, Radio Shack, Sears/auto, Trader Joe's, Walgreens, mall, USPO, **W** other H
77b a	(from nb), **E food:** Anchorage Rest., **food:** Solly's Grill, **lodging:** Hilton
76b a	WI 57, WI 190, Green Bay Ave, **E food:** Anchorage Rest, **lodging:** Hilton, **other:** Home Depot, **W gas:** Citgo, **food:** Burger King, **other:** Jaguar/Volvo
75	Atkinson Ave, Keefe Ave, **E gas:** Mobil, **W gas:** BP, Citgo/dsl
74	Locust St
73c	North Ave (rom sb), **E food:** Wendy's, **W food:** McDonald's
73a	WI 145 E, 4th St (exits left from sb), Broadway, downtown
72c	Wells St, **E lodging:** Hilton, **other:** H, Civic Ctr, museum
72b	(from sb), I-94 W, to madison
72a	(310c from nb, exits left from sb), I-794 E, I-94 W to Madison, to Lakefront, downtown

Exit #	Services
311	WI 59, National Ave, 6th St, downtown
312a	Lapham Blvd, Mitchell St, **W gas:** Shell
312b	(from nb), Becher St, Lincoln Ave
314a	Holt Ave, **E gas:** Andy's/dsl, **food:** Applebee's, Arby's, China King, Little Caesars, Quizno's, Starbucks, Subway, Wendy's, **other:** $General, Home Depot, Pick'n Save Foods, Sentry Foods, Target, Vet, **W** H, to Alverno Coll
314b	Howard Ave
10b	(316 from sb), I-94 S to Chicago, ✈
9b a	US 41, 27th St, **E gas:** BP, Citgo, Clark, **food:** Arby's, Burger King, Chancery Rest., Famous Dave's, Pizza Hut, Rusty Skillet Rest., Subway, **lodging:** Suburban Motel, **other:** AutoZone, Carquest, Curves, K-Mart, Subaru, Target, USPO, Walgreens, **W food:** Boston Mkt, DQ, Denny's, Los Burritos Tapatios, McDonald's, Rich's Cakes, Wong's Wok, Zebb's Rest, **lodging:** Hity Inn, Rodeway Inn, **other:** H, AAA, Advance Parts, Chevrolet, CVS Drug, $Tree, Firestone/auto, Ford, Goodyear/auto, GMC/Hyundai, Kohl's, Michael's, Pick'n Save Foods, Sav-a-Lot Foods
8a	WI 36, Loomis Rd, **E gas:** BP, Citgo, **food:** Los Mariachi's, **other:** Aldi Foods, Walgreens, **W food:** George Webb Rest, **other:** to Alverno Coll
7	60th St, **E gas:** Speedway/dsl, **food:** Subway, Wendt's Grille, **other:** Harley-Davidson, **W gas:** Speedway
5b	76th St (from sb, no EZ return), **E gas:** Speedway/dsl, **food:** Applebee's, Bakers Square, Burger King, Carrabba's Italian, Champ's Grill, Cousins Subs, George Webb Rest, Hooters, Jimmy John's, Kopp's Burgers, Kyoto Japanese, McDonald's, Noodles&Co, Old Country Buffet, Olive Garden, Outback Steaks, Qdoba, Red Lobster, Ruby Tuesday, TGIFriday's, Topper's Pizza, Wendy's, **other:** AT&T, Barnes&Noble, Best Buy, Borders Books, Breadsmith, $Tree, Firestone/auto, Isuzu, Jo-Ann Fabrics, Office Depot, PetCo, Sears/auto, Tuesday Morning, Valvoline, Verizon, Vitamin Shoppe, **W food:** Arby's, Pizza Hut, Ponderosa, Popeye's, **other:** Pick'n Save Foods, TJ Maxx, Walgreens, USPO
5a	WI 24 W, Forest Home Ave, **E gas:** Citgo, **other:** Boerner Botanical Gardens
61	(4 from sb), I-894/US 45 N, I-43/US 45 S
60	US 45 S, WI 100, 108th St (exits left from sb), **E gas:** BP, Citgo, Marathon, Mobil, **food:** A&W, Amore Italian, Baskin-Robbins, Cousins Subs, Fortune Chinese, George Webb Rest, McDonald's, Open Flame Grill, Pizza Hut, Taco Bell, **other:** AutoZone, $Tree,

NV

INTERSTATE 43 CONT'D

Exit #	Services
60	Continued K-Mart, Radio Shack, Sentry Foods, Vet, **W gas:** Phillips 66, **food:** Forum Rest., McDonald's, Omega Custard, Organ Piper Pizza, **other:** Aldi Foods, Badger Transmissions, Cabela's, $Daze, Goodyear, NAPA, Walgreens, Walmart/drug, Vet
59	WI 100, Layton Ave (from nb, exits left), Hales Corner, **W gas:** BP, same as 60
57	Moorland Rd, **E gas:** Mobil/dsl, **food:** Applebee's, Stonefire Pizza Co, TX Roadhouse, **lodging:** La Quinta, **W gas:** Speedway/dsl/24hr, **food:** Buffalo Wild Wings, Quizno's, Passport Grill, **lodging:** Holiday Inn Express, **other:** Michael's, Target
54	rd Y, Racine Ave, **1-2 mi E gas:** Citgo/dsl, KwikTrip, **other:** Culver's, Cousins Subs, McDonald's
50	WI 164, Big Bend, **W gas:** Citgo/dsl, **food:** Coach House Grill, Long Neck's Rest, McDonald's
44mm	Fox River
43	WI 83, Mukwonago, **E gas:** BP/dsl, **other:** Home Depot, Walmart SuperCtr/24 hr, **W gas:** Citgo, **food:** Antigua Real Cafe, Boneyard Grill, Chen's Kitchen, DQ, Dominos, Imperial House Chinese, Mario's, Pastime Grille, Taco Bell, **lodging:** Sleep Inn
38	WI 20, East Troy, **W gas:** BP, Pilot/Road Ranger/Subway/dsl/24hr, Shell/McDonald's, **food:** Burger King, Roma's Ristorante, **other:** Carquest, Chrysler/Dodge/Jeep, $General
36	WI 120, East Troy, **E lodging:** Alpine Valley Resort, **W lodging:** Country Inn&Suites
33	Bowers Rd, **E** to Alpine Valley Music Theatre
32mm	**rest area both lanes, full ♿ facilities, 📞, 🛒, litter barrels, vending, petwalk**
29	WI 11, Elkhorn, fairgrounds
27b a	US 12, to Lake Geneva, **E** [H]
25	WI 67, Elkhorn, **E gas:** BP/dsl, **lodging:** AmericInn, **other:** Buick/Chevrolet/GMC, Chrysler/Dodge/Jeep, Vet, **W gas:** Speedway/dsl/24hr, **food:** Burger King, Subway, **lodging:** Hampton Inn (2mi), **other:** Dehaan Auto/RV Ctr
21	WI 50, Delavan, **E gas:** Shell/dsl/24hr, **food:** Brodie's Beef, Chili's, China 1, Culvers, Domino's, Panera Bread, Papa Murphy's, Quizno's, Starbucks, Subway, Yoshi Japanese, **other:** Aldi Foods, AT&T, F&F Tires, Greyhound DogTrack, Kohl's, Lowe's Whse, Petsmart, Radio Shack, Staples, Walmart SuperCtr/24hr, **W gas:** Mobil/24hr, Speedway/dsl, **food:** Cousins Subs, KFC, McDonald's, Perkins, Pizza Hut, Taco Bell, Wendy's, **lodging:** Comfort Suites, Super 8, **other:** Ace Hardware, AutoZone, Cadillac/Chevrolet, $Tree, Ford/Lincoln/Mercury, GNC, NAPA, Piggly Wiggly, ShopKO, Walgreens
17	rd X, Delavan, Darien, **W gas:** BP
15	US 14, Darien, **E gas:** Mobil/dsl, **food:** West Wind Diner
6	WI 140, Clinton, **E gas:** Citgo/Subway/dsl, **other:** Ford
2	rd X, Hart Rd, **E food:** Butterfly Fine Dining
1b a	I-90, E to Chicago, W to Madison, **S gas:** BP, Mobil/McDonald's, Pilot/Road Ranger/DQ/Taco Bell/dsl/scales/24hr, Shell, Speedway/dsl, **food:** Applebee's,
1b a	Continued Arby's, Asia Buffet, Atlanta Bread, Burger King, Cousins Subs, Culver's, Jimmy John's, Papa Murphy's, Perkins, Road Dog Rest, Starbucks, Subway, Wendy's, **lodging:** Comfort Inn, Econolodge, Fairfield Inn, Hampton Inn, Holiday Inn Express, Rodeway Inn, **other:** Aldi Foods, Buick/GMC/Pontiac, Cadillac/Chevrolet, $Tree, GNC, Menards, Radio Shack, Staples, Tires +, Walmart SuperCtr/24hr

I-43 begins/ends on I-90, exit 185 in Beloit.

INTERSTATE 90

Exit #	Services
187mm	**I-90 & I-39 run together nb., Wisconsin/Illinois state line**
187mm	**Welcome Ctr wb, full ♿ facilities, info, 📞, 🛒, litter barrels, vending, petwalk**
185b	I-43 N, to Milwaukee
185a	WI 81, Beloit, **S gas:** BP, Mobil/McDonald's, Pilot/Road Ranger/DQ/Taco Bell/dsl/scales/24hr, Shell, Speedway/dsl, **food:** Applebee's, Arby's, Asia Buffet, Atlanta Bread, Burger King, Cousins Subs, Culver's, Jimmy John's, Papa Murphy's, Perkins, Road Dog Rest, Starbucks, Subway, Wendy's, **lodging:** Comfort Inn, Econolodge, Fairfield Inn, Hampton Inn, Holiday Inn Express, Rodeway Inn, **other:** Aldi Foods, Buick/GMC/Pontiac, Cadillac/Chevrolet, $Tree, GNC, Menards, Radio Shack, Staples, Tires +, Walmart SuperCtr/24hr
183	Shopiere Rd, rd S, to Shopiere, **S gas:** BP/Rollette/dsl/24hr, **other:** [H], camping, repair
181mm	**weigh sta, wb**
177	WI 11 W, Janesville, **2 mi S gas:** BP, KwikTrip, **food:** Bobble Heads Grill, El Jardin Mexican, **other:** to Blackhawk Tec Coll, Rock Co ✈
175b a	WI 11 E, Janesville, to Delavan, **N gas:** BP/Subway/dsl/24hr, **food:** Denny's, **lodging:** Baymont Inn, **S gas:** BP, **food:** DQ, Hardee's, **lodging:** Lannon Stone Motel
171c b	US 14, WI 26, Janesville, **N gas:** TA/Mobil/Wendy's/dsl/scales, **food:** Cold Stone Creamery, Cozumel Mexican, Damon's, Fuddruckers, IHOP, Old Country Buffet, Starbucks, Subway, TX Roadhouse, **lodging:** Holiday Inn Express, Microtel, **other:** Best Buy, Gander Mtn, GNC, Home Depot, Michael's, Old Navy, PetCo, Staples, Tires+, TJ Maxx, **S gas:** Citgo, Exxon, Kwik Trip/dsl/24hr, **food:** Applebee's, Arby's, Asia Buffet, Buffalo Wild Wings, Burger King, Chucke-Cheese, Culver's, Del Taco, Famous Dave's, Fazoli's, Ground Round, Hardee's, Hooters, KFC, La Tolteca Mexican, Little Caesars, McDonald's, Milwaukee Grill, Noodle's & Co., Olive Garden, Papa Murphy's, Peking Chinese, Perkins, Pizza Hut, Prime Quarter Steaks, Red Robin, Road Dawg, Subway, Taco Bell, Taco John's, **lodging:** Econolodge, Super 8, **other:** [H], Aldi Foods, CarQuest, $Tree, F&F, Ford/Lincoln/Mercury, Harley-Davidson, Hobby Lobby, Hyundai, JC Penney, Kohl's, K-Mart, Mazda, Menards, O'Reilly Parts, Sears/auto, ShopKO, Subaru, Target, Toyota, mall, USPO
171a	WI 26, **N gas:** Phillips 66/dsl, **food:** Cracker Barrel, **lodging:** Best Western/rest., Hampton Inn, Motel 6, **other:** Chrysler/Dodge/Jeep, Sam's Club, VW, Walmart SuperCtr, Walgreens, **S** same as 171c b

N ↕ S MILWAUKEE DELAVAN

E ↕ W BELOIT JANESVILLE

WI

INTERSTATE 90

E ↕ W

Exit #	Services
168mm	**rest area eb, full ♿ facilities, ☎, 🅿, litter barrels, vending, petwalk**
163.5mm	Rock River
163	WI 59, Edgerton, to Milton, **N gas:** Mobil/Subway/dsl, Shell/Taco John's, **food:** Culver's, McDonald's, Shore Thing Pizza, WI Cheese Store, **lodging:** Comfort Inn, **other:** marina
160	US 51S, WI 73, WI 106, Oaklawn Academy, to Deerfield, **N other:** Hickory Hills Camping, **S gas:** BP/dsl/scales/24hr/@, KwikTrip, **food:** Subway, Winchester Rest., **other:** H, Janesville RV Ctr
156	US 51N, to Stoughton, **S lodging:** Coachman's Inn/rest., H
148mm	**weigh sta wb**
147	rd N, Cottage Grove, to Stoughton, **S gas:** BP/Arby's/24hr, Road Ranger/Pilot/Subway/dsl, **other:** Lake Kegonsa SP, fireworks
146mm	**weigh sta eb**
142b a	(142a exits left from wb) US 12, US 18, Madison, to Cambridge, **N gas:** BP/dsl, **food:** Roadhouse Rest, **lodging:** Best Value Inn, Wingate Inn, **other:** Harley-Davidson, **S gas:** Cenex/dsl, Phillips 66/Arby's/dsl, **food:** Culver's, Denny's, Quizno's, Wendy's, **lodging:** AmericInn, Days Inn, Holiday Inn Express, Rodeway Inn, **other:** H, Menards, UWI
138a	I-94, E to Milwaukee, W to La Crosse, **I-90 W and I-94 W run together for 93 miles, (exits left from EB)**
138b	WI 30, Madison, **S** ✈
135c b	US 151, Madison, **N gas:** BP, **food:** Erin's Cafe, Happy Wok, Subway, Uno, **lodging:** Courtyard, Fairfield Inn, Holiday Inn, La Quinta, Staybridge Suites,**other:** Buick/GMC/Pontiac, Chrysler/Jeep, Ford/Kia Hyundai, Isuzu, Nissan, Scion/Toyota
135a	US 151, Madison, **S gas:** BP/24hr, Citgo, Mobil, Shell, **food:** Applebee's, Arby's, BD Mongolian, Buffalo Wild Wings, Chili's, Chipotle Mexican, Country Kitchen, Cracker Barrel, Culver's, Denny's, Fazoli's, Hardee's, IHOP, Imperial Garden, Jimmy John's, KFC, La Bamba, McDonald's, Noodles & Co., Old Country Buffet, Olive Garden, Outback Steaks, Panera Bread, Perkins, Potbelly's Rest, Pizza Hut, Qdoba, Red Lobster, Red Robin, Rocky's Pizza, Subway, TGIFriday, TX Roadhouse, Wendy's, **lodging:** Baymont Inn, Best Western, Comfort Inn, Crowne Plaza Hotel/rest., Econolodge, Hampton Inn, Howard Johnson, Microtel, Motel 6, Red Roof Inn, Residence Inn, Select Inn, Super 8, **other:** Aldi Foods, Barnes&Noble, Best Buy, Borders Books, $Tree, Firestone/auto, Home Depot, JC Penney, Jo-Ann Fabrics, Kohl's, Marshall's, Menards, Office Depot, Old Navy, Petsmart, Sears/auto, ShopKO, Tuesday Morning, mall, st patrol, Vet
132	US 51, Madison, De Forest, **N gas:** Shell/Pinecone Rest/dsl/scales/24hr, **other:** Camping World RV Ctr, Gander Mtn, **S gas:** TA/Mobil/Subway/Taco Bell/dsl/scales/24hr/@, **other:** Goodyear, Peterbilt, Freightliner/GMC/Volvo, WI RV World, camping
131	WI 19, Waunakee, **N gas:** Kwik Trip/dsl, Mobil, Speedway/dsl, **food:** A&W, McDonald's, Rodeside

MADISON

131	Continued Grill, **lodging:** Days Inn, Super 8, **other:** Cheese Mousehouse, Kenworth Trucks, truckwash, **S lodging:** Country Inn Suites (4mi)
126	rd V, De Forest, to Dane, **N gas:** BP, Phillips 66/Arby's/dsl, **food:** Burger King, Culver's, DeForest Rest., McDonald's, Subway, **lodging:** Holiday Inn Express, **other:** Cheese Chalet, KOA, **S gas:** Citgo, Exxon/dsl, **lodging:** Comfort Inn
119	WI 60, Arlington, to Lodi, **S gas:** Mobil/Cousins Subs/dsl, **food:** A&W, Rococo's Pizza, **lodging:** Best Western, **other:** Interstate RV Ctr
115	rd CS, Poynette, to Lake Wisconsin, **N gas:** BP/dsl, **food:** McDonald's, Subway, **other:** Smokey Hollow Camping, dsl truck/trailer repair, motel, trout fishing
113mm	**rest area both lanes, full ♿ facilities, ☎, 🅿, litter barrels, vending, petwalk**
111mm	Wisconsin River
108b a	I-39 N, WI 78, to US 51 N, Portage, **N other:** H, to WI Dells, **S gas:** BP, Petro/DQ/Subway/dsl/24hr/@, **lodging:** Comfort Suites, Days Inn, Devil's Head Resort/Conv Ctr, **other:** Blue Beacon
106mm	Baraboo River
106	WI 33, Portage, **N other:** H, **S gas:** BP, **other:** Kamp Dakota, SkyHigh Camping, to Cascade Mtn Ski Area, Devil's Lake SP, Circus World Museum, Wayside Park, motel
92	US 12, to Baraboo, **N gas:** BP/dsl, Mobil/dsl/24hr, Sinclair/Subway/dsl, **food:** Buffalo Phil's Grille, Burger King, Cracker Barrel, Cheese Factory Rest, Culver's, Damon's, Denny's, Domino's, Field's Steaks, Mark's Rest, McDonald's, Monk's Grill, Ponderosa, Sarento's Italian, Wintergreen Grill, Uno, **lodging:** Alakai Hotel, Country Squire Motel, Dell Creek Motel, Grand Marquis Inn, Great Wolf Lodge, Holiday Motel, Holiday Inn Express, Kalahari Resort, Lake Delton Motel, Ramada, Wilderness Hotel, Wintergreen Hotel, **other:** Broadway Theater, Kalahari Conv Ctr, Mkt Square Cheese, Tanger Outlets Famous Brands, WI Cheese, museum, **S lodging:** Motel 6, **other:** H, Scenic Traveler RV Ctr, Jellystone Camping, Red Oak Camping, Mirror Lake SP
89	WI 23, Lake Delton, **N gas:** Phillips 66, Shell/dsl, **food:** Brathouse Grill, Denny's Diner, Howie's Rest., KFC, Moosejaw Pizza, **lodging:** Econolodge, Hilton Garden, Kings Inn, Malibu Inn, Olympia Motel, **other:** Crystal Grand Music Theatre, Springbrook Camping, Jellystone Camping, USPO, **S food:** McDonald's, **other:** Home Depot, Kohl's, Walmart SuperCtr/

INTERSTATE 90 CONT'D

E ↕ W

Exit #	Services
89	Continued Subway/24hr, Country Roads RV Park, Wannabee Campground
87	WI 13, Wisconsin Dells, **N gas:** Citgo, Mobil/Arby's/dsl, Shell, **food:** Applebee's, Bunyan's Rest., Burger King, Cold Stone Creamery, Country Kitchen, Denny's, Grandma Honey's Rest, IHOP, McDonald's, Mexicaly Rose Rest., Perkins, Quizno's, Rococo Pizza, Starbucks, Taco Bell, Wendy's, **lodging:** AmeriсInn, Best Western, Comfort Inn, Days Inn, Polynesian Hotel, Super 8, **other:** Family$, KOA, Sherwood Forest Camping, Tepee Park Camping, Walgreens, golf, waterpark, info
85	US 12, WI 16, Wisconsin Dells, **0-3 mi N food:** Crabby's Seafood, Starbucks, **lodging:** Days Inn, Mayflower Motel, **other:** American World RV Park/Hotel, KOA, Sherwood Forest Camping, Standing Rock Camping, to Rocky Arbor SP, **S gas:** BP, **food:** Piccadilly's, **lodging:** Arrowhead Camping, Edge-O-the-Dell RV Camping, Summer Breeze Resort
79	rd HH, Lyndon Sta, **S gas:** BP/Subway/dsl/24hr
76mm	**rest area wb, full ♿ facilities, ☎, picnic, litter barrels, vending, petwalk**
74mm	**rest area eb, full ♿ facilities, ☎, picnic, litter barrels, vending, petwalk**
69	WI 82, Mauston, **N gas:** Mauston TP/Taco Bell/24hr, Pilot/Wendy's/dsl/scales/24hr, Shell/24hr, **food:** Country Kitchen, **lodging:** Best Western Oasis, Country Inn, Super 8, **other:** Car Valley Cheese, to Buckhorn SP, **S gas:** KwikTrip/rest/scales/dsl, Marathon, Mobil, **food:** CJ's Italian, Culver's, Garden Valley Rest., McDonald's, Pizza Hut, Roman Castle Rest., Subway, **lodging:** Alaskan Inn, Best Value Inn, **other:** H, Buckhorn SP, $General, Family$, Festival Foods, K-Mart, Walgreens, Vet
61	WI 80, New Lisbon, to Necedah, **N gas:** Mobil/A&W/Subway/dsl, New Lisbon Trkstp/dsl/24hr/@, **lodging:** Edge O' the Wood Motel, Travelers Inn, **other:** Buckhorn SP, Chrysler/Jeep, Ford, fireworks, **S gas:** KwikTrip/24hr, **other:** Barnes Foods, True Value, Elroy-Sparta ST Tr
55	rd C, Camp Douglas, **N other:** wayside, to Camp Williams, Volk Field, **S gas:** BP/dsl, Mobil/Subway/dsl, **food:** German Haus Rest., **lodging:** K&K Motel, **other:** to Mill Bluff SP
49mm	**weigh sta both lanes**
48	rd PP, Oakdale, **N gas:** Road Ranger/Pilot/Subway/dsl/scales/24hr, **other:** Granger's Camping, KOA, truck/car wash, antiques, **S gas:** Love's/Hardee's/dsl/scales/24hr, **other:** Mill Bluff SP, repair
45	I-94 W, to St Paul, **I-90 E and I-94 E run together for 93 miles**
43	US 12, WI 16, Tomah, **N gas:** BP, KwikTrip/dsl/24hr, **food:** Burnstadt's Café, DQ, Embers Rest., **lodging:** Daybreak Inn, **other:** H, Vet
41	WI 131, Tomah, to Wilton, **N gas:** Mobil/dsl, KwikTrip/dsl/24hr, **food:** Burnstadts Cafe, **lodging:** Daybreak Inn, **other:** VA MED CTR, **S** st patrol
28	WI 16, Sparta, Ft McCoy, **N gas:** BP/diner/dsl/scales, Kwiktrip/dsl, **lodging:** Best Western, **other:** H
25	WI 27, Sparta, to Melvina, **N gas:** Cenex/dsl, KwikTrip, Phillips 66/Taco Bell, Shell/dsl, **food:** Burger King, Country Kitchen, Culver's, DQ, KFC, McDonald's, Pizza Hut, Subway, **lodging:** Best Nights Inn, Country Inn, Super 8, **other:** H, Ace Hardware, Buick/Chevrolet/Pontiac, $General, Family$, Ford/Mercury, Piggly Wiggly, Walgreens, Walmart SuperCtr/24hr (2mi, WI 16), **S** camping
22mm	**rest area wb, full ♿ facilities, ☎, picnic, litter barrels, vending, petwalk**
20mm	**rest area eb, full ♿ facilities, ☎, picnic, litter barrels, vending, petwalk**
15	WI 162, Bangor, to Coon Valley, **N** gas, **S other:** Chevrolet
12	rd C, W Salem, **N gas:** Cenex/cafe/dsl/24hr, **other:** Coulee Region RV Ctr, NAPA, Neshonoc Camping, **S gas:** BP/Quizno's/dsl, **lodging:** AmericInn
10mm	**weigh sta eb**
5	WI 16, La Crosse, **N food:** Buffalo Wild Wings, Cold Stone Creamery, Manny's Mexican, Outback Steaks, Quizno's, **lodging:** Baymont Inn, Hampton Inn, Microtel, **other:** Aldi Foods, $Tree, Freightliner, Gander Mtn, Home Depot, Walmart SuprCtr/Subway, Woodman's Foods/gas/lube, **S gas:** Kwik Trip/dsl/24hr, **food:** Burracho's Mexican Grill, Carlos O'Kelly's, ChuckeCheese, Culver's, Fazoli's, Jimmy John's, McDonald's, Hong Kong Buffet, Old Country Buffet, Olive Garden, Perkins, Starbucks, TGIFriday, **lodging:** Holiday Inn Express, **other:** H, Barnes&Noble, Best Buy, F&F, Hobby Lobby, JC Penney, Kohl's, Lincoln/Mercury, Macy's, Michael's, Sears/auto, ShopKO, Target, mall
4	US 53 N, WI 16, to WI 157, La Crosse, **N other:** Harley-Davidson, **S gas:** Kwik Trip/gas, TO, **food:** Applebee's, Burger King, China Inn, Famous Dave's BBQ, Grizzly's Rest, Panera Bread, Papa Murphy's, Red Lobster, Rococo's Pizza, Subway, Taco Bell, Wendy's, **lodging:** Comfort Inn, **other:** H, Festival Food/24hr, GNC, Goodyear/auto, Office Depot, Old Navy, PetCo, Petsmart, Sam's Club, Super Lube, Tires+, TJ Maxx, SuperLube, La Crosse River St Trail
3	US 53 S, WI 35, to La Crosse, **S gas:** Citgo, Kwik Trip, **food:** Burger King, Coney Island, Edwardo's Pizza, Hardee's, KFC, La Crosse Rest., McDonald's, North Country Steaks, Perkins, Pizza Hut, Subway, **lodging:** Best Value Inn, Best Western, Brookstone Inn, Econolodge, Howard Johnson, Settle Inn, Super 8, **other:** ShopKo, U-Haul, Walgreens, to Great River St Trail, Viterbo Coll
2.5mm	Black River
2	rd B, French Island, **N other:** airport, **S gas:** BP/dsl, Kwik Trip, **lodging:** Days Hotel/rest
1mm	**Welcome Ctr eb, full ♿ facilities, info, ☎, picnic, litter barrels, vending, petwalk**
0mm	Wisconsin/Minnesota state line, Mississippi River

TOMAH

LA CROSSE

INTERSTATE 94

Exit #	Services
349mm	Wisconsin/Illinois state line, (from nb), **weigh sta nb**
347	WI 165, rd Q, Lakeview Pkwy, **E gas:** BP/dsl, **food:** Chancery Rest., Culver's, McDonald's, Quizno's,

WI

E ↕ W

KENOSHA

INTERSTATE 94 CONT'D

Exit #	Services
347	Continued **lodging:** Radisson/rest., **other:** Old Navy, Prime Outlets/famous brands, **Welcome Ctr, full facilities, W other:** GolfShack Whse
345	rd C, **E gas:** Phillips 66/dsl
345mm	Des Plaines River
344	WI 50, Lake Geneva, to Kenosha, **E food:** Citgo/dsl, Shell, Woodman's/gas, **food:** Buffalo Wild Wings, Nick&Willy's Pizza, Noodles&Co, Perkins, Pizza Hut, Quizno's, Starbucks, Texas Roadhouse, White Castle, **lodging:** La Quinta, Super 8, **other:** [H], Best Buy, Gander Mtn, Walgreens, **W gas:** BP/Subway, Speedway/dsl, **food:** Arby's, Birchwood Grill, Cracker Barrel, KFC, McDonald's, Pheonix Rest., Taco Bell, Wendy's, **lodging:** Best Western, Country Inn&Suites, Day's Inn, Value Inn, **other:** BMW, BratStop Cheese Store, Carmax, Chevrolet, Toyota/Scion
342	WI 158, to Kenosha, **E** Harley-Davidson, **W** antiques
340	WI 142, rd S, to Kenosha, **E gas:** Mobil/dsl, **other:** [H], **W food:** Mars Cheese Castle Rest., StarBar Rest., **lodging:** Oasis Inn, **other:** to Bong RA
339	rd E, **E gas:** Marathon/dsl/24hr
337	County Line Rd, rd KR, **E other:** to Great Lakes Dragaway, **W food:** Apple Holler Rest.
335	WI 11, Burlington, to Racine
333	US 20, Waterford, to Racine, **E gas:** KwikTrip/dsl/24hr, Shell/Cousins Subs/dsl, **food:** Burger King, McDonald's, **lodging:** Holiday Inn Express, Ramada Ltd, **other:** [H], **W gas:** Citgo/Wendy's/dsl/24hr, Petro/Mobil/Iron Skillet/dsl/scales/@, **food:** Culver's, Spokes Rest., Subway, **lodging:** Grandview Inn, **other:** Burlington RV Ctr
329	rd K, Thompsonville, to Racine, **E gas:** Pilot/Arby's/dsl/scales/24hr, **W gas:** Mobil/A&W
328mm	**weigh sta eb**
327	rd G, **W other:** Black Jack's Fireworks
326	7 Mile Rd, **E gas:** BP/24hr, **other:** Jellystone Park, **W gas:** Mobil/24hr, antiques
325	US 41 N (from wb), to 27th St
322	WI 100, to Ryan Rd, **E food:** McDonald's, Wendy's, Wild Wild Burgers, **other:** Goodyear/Cummins dsl, **W gas:** *FLYING J*/Country Mkt/dsl/scales/24hr, Mobil, Pilot/Subway/dsl/LP/scales/24hr, Shell/A&W/KFC/dsl, **food:** Arby's, Cousins Subs, Perkins, Starbucks, Yen Hwa Chinese, **other:** Blue Beacon, Freightliner/repair, Pick'n Save, Walgreens
320	rd BB, Rawson Ave, **E gas:** BP/24hr, Mobil, **food:** Applebee's, Burger King, **lodging:** La Quinta
319	rd ZZ, College Ave, **E gas:** Shell/Subway, Speedway/dsl, **food:** Branded Steer Rest., Houlihan's, McDonald's, **lodging:** Comfort Suites, Country Inn&Suites, Econolodge, Hampton Inn, Holiday Inn Express, MainStay Suites, Radisson, Red Roof Inn, **W gas:** BP/24hr, Citgo/dsl
318	WI 119
317	Layton Ave, **E gas:** Andy's/dsl, Clark, **food:** Burger King, Culver's, IHOP, J-Roberts Porterhouse Steaks, Martino's Rest., Prime Qtr Steaks, Wendy's, **other:** Checker Parts, **W food:** Spring Garden Rest., **lodging:** Howard Johnson

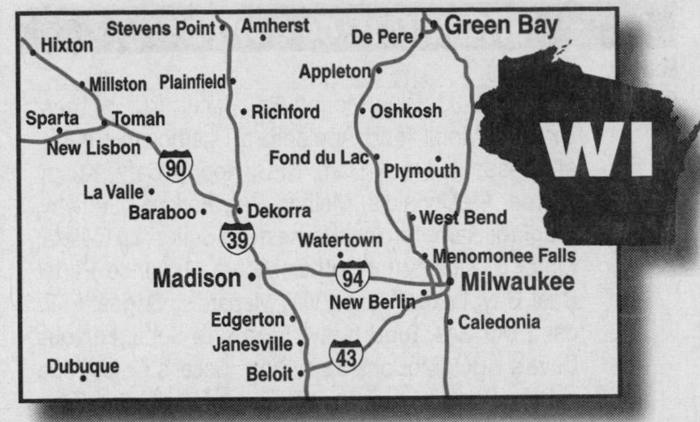

WI

Exit #	Services
316	I-43 S, I-894 W (I-94 exits left from eb), to Beloit
314b	Howard Ave, to Milwaukee, **W** to Alverno Coll
314a	Holt Ave, **E gas:** Andy's/dsl, **food:** Applebee's, Arby's, China King, Little Caesars, Quizno's, Starbucks, Subway, Wendy's, **other:** $General, Home Depot, Pick'n Save Foods, Sentry Foods, Target, Vet, **W** [H], to Alverno Coll
312b a	Becher St, Mitchell St, Lapham Blvd, **W gas:** Shell
311	WI 59, National Ave, 6th St, downtown
310a	13th St (from eb), **E** [H]
310b	I-43 N, to Green Bay
310c	I-794 E, **E lodging:** Hilton, Holiday Inn, **other:** to downtown and Lake Michigan Port of Entry
309b	26th St, 22nd St, Clybourn St, St Paul Ave, **N other:** [H], to Marquette U
309a	35th St, **N gas:** BP, Speedway, **other:** [H]
308c b	US 41
308a	VA Ctr, **N other:** Miller Brewing, **S other:** County Stadium
307b	68th-70th St, Hawley Rd
307a	**N**...68th St, **N other:** Valvoline
306	WI 181, to 84th St, **N** [H], **S other:** Olympic Training Facility
305b	US 45 N, to Fond du Lac, **N** [H]
305a	I-894 S, US 45 S, to Chicago, to [airport], to [airport]
304b a	WI 100, **N gas:** Mobil, OP, Shell/dsl, **food:** Cousins Subs, Edwardo's Pizza, Ghengis Khan Mongolian, Honeybaked Cafe, Jimmy John's, Moe's Irish Grill, Pony Rest., Qdoba Mexican, Starbucks, Taco Bell, **lodging:** 40 Winks Inn, Super 8, **other:** [H], zoo, **S gas:** MiniMart/dsl, Mobil, Speedway/dsl, **food:** DQ, Fazoli's, McDonald's, Wendy's, **other:** Checker Parts, U-Haul, Walgreens
301b a	Moorland Rd, **N gas:** BP, **food:** Bakers Square, Bravo Italiano, Chicago Grill, Claim Jumper Rest., Fleming's Rest., Houlihan's, McDonald's, Mitchell's Fish Mkt, **lodging:** Sheraton, **other:** Ace Hardware, Barnes&Noble, JC Penney, Office Depot, PetCo, Sears/auto, Walgreens, mall, Vet, N on US 18...**gas:** Mobil, **food:** Caribou Coffee, Chili's, Fuddrucker's, Noodles&Co, Old Country Buffet, Pedro's Mexican, Starbucks, TGI Fridays, **lodging:** Courtyard, Towneplace Suites, **other:** Fresh Mkt Foods, Goodyear/auto, Jo-Ann Fabrics, Michael's, Office Depot, PetCo, TJ Maxx, World Mkt, **S food:** Champp's Grill, Charcoal Grill, Maxwell's Rest., Panera Bread, Outback Steaks, **lodging:** Best Western Midway, Brookfield Suites, Country Inn&Suites, Midway Motel, Residence Inn, **other:** Pick'n Save Foods, Walgreens, golf

INTERSTATE 94 CONT'D

E ↕ W

Exit #	Services
297	US 18, rd JJ, Blue Mound Rd, Barker Rd, **N gas:** BP/24hr, Mobil, **food:** Applebee's, Charhouse, ChuckeCheese, Heavenly Ham, KFC, Kopp's Cafe, Krispy Kreme, McDonald's, Melting Pot, Perkins, Subway, **lodging:** Hampton Inn, Homestead Suites, La Quinta, Motel 6, Quality Inn, **other:** Acura, Advance Parts, Best Buy, Lexus/Mazda/VW, Menard's, **S gas:** F&F/dsl, PDQ Gas, **food:** Arby's, Cousin's Subs, Famous Dave's BBQ, McDonald's, Milio's, Oscar's Cafe, Papa John's, Starbucks, Taco Bell, Texas Roadhouse, Topper's Pizza, Wendy's, **lodging:** Extended Stay America Ramada Ltd, **other:** Cadillac/GMC, Carmax, Firestone, Ford/Lincoln/Mercury, Gander Mtn, Home Depot, Infiniti, KIA, Kohl's, Mercedes, Sam's Club, Target, Tires+, Walgreens, st patrol
295	WI 164, Waukesha, **N gas:** KwikTrip/gas, **food:** Jimmy John's, **lodging:** Marriott, **S other:** H, to Carroll Coll
294	rd J, to Waukesha, **N gas:** Mobil, **food:** Machine Shed Rest., Thunder Bay Grille, **lodging:** Comfort Suites, Radisson, **S other:** Expo Ctr, Peterbilt
293c	WI 16 W, Pewaukee (from wb), **N other:** GE Plant
293b a	rd T, Wausheka, Pewaukee, **S gas:** Mobil, KwikTrip, **food:** Canyon City Wood Grill, Cousins Subs, Culver's, Denny's, Fazoli's, Great Northern BBQ, McDonald's, Mr. Wok, Peking House, Qdoba Mexican, Quizno's, Rococo's Pizza, Spring City Rest., Subway, Taco Amigo, Weissgerber's Gasthaus Rest., **lodging:** Best Western, **other:** Central Mkt Foods, CVS Drug, $Tree, Firestone/auto, GNC, Jo-Ann Fabrics, Office Depot, Osco Drug, Pick'n Save Foods, Radio Shack, Walgreens
291	rd G, **N lodging:** Country Springs Inn
290	rd SS
287	WI 83, Hartland, to Wales, **N food:** Applebees, 5 Guys Burgers, Hardee's, McDonald's, Noodles&Co, Panera Bread, Perkins, Qdoba, Starbucks, Water St Brewery/rest., **lodging:** Holiday Inn Express, **other:** Amish Barn Gifts, Best Buy, GNC, Kohl's, Marshall's, Radio Shack, Sentry Foods, Walgreens, **S gas:** BP/dsl/24hr, PDQ/dsl/24hr, **food:** Burger King, Delafield Bewhaus, DQ, Rococo's Pizza, Subway, **lodging:** La Quinta, **other:** Ace Hardware, Home Depot, PetCo, Target, Walmart/drugs, Vet
285	rd C, Delafield, **N gas:** BP, Mobil/deli, **lodging:** Delafield Hotel, **other:** to St John's Military Academy, **S other:** to Kettle Moraine SF
283	rd P, to Sawyer Rd (from wb)
282	WI 67, Dousman, to Oconomowoc, **N gas:** BP, KwikTrip, **food:** Chili's, Culver's, Pizza Hut, Quizno's, Rococo's Pizza, Schlotsky's, Subway, **lodging:** Hilton Garden, Olympia Resort, **other:** H, Aldi Foods, K-Mart, Pick'n Save, **S other:** H, Harley-Davidson, Vet, to Kettle Morraine SF (8mi), Old World WI HS (13mi)
277	Willow Glen Rd (from eb, no return)
275	rd F, Ixonia, to Sullivan, **N gas:** BP/dsl, **other:** Concord Gen Store, **S** camping
267	WI 26, Johnson Creek, to Watertown, **N gas:** BP/McDonald's/dsl, Shell/dsl/rest./scales/24hr, **food:** Arby's, Hwy Harry's Cafe, **lodging:** Comfort Suites, Day's Inn, **other:** Goodyear/auto, Johnson Creek Outlet Ctr/famous brands, Old Navy, **S gas:** Kwik-Trip/dsl, **food:** Culver's, Subway, **other:** H, Kohl's, Menard's, to Aztalan SP
266mm	Rock River
264mm	**rest area wb, full ♿ facilities, ☎, picnic, litter barrels, vending, petwalk**
263mm	Crawfish River
261mm	**rest area eb, full ♿ facilities, ☎, picnic, litter barrels, vending, petwalk**
259	WI 89, Lake Mills, to Waterloo, **N gas:** Citgo/dsl/24hr, **lodging:** Best Value Inn, **other:** truck repair, **S gas:** BP/dsl/24hr, KwikTrip/dsl/24hr, **food:** McDonald's, Pizza Pit, Subway, **lodging:** Pyramid Motel/RV park, **other:** Buick/Cadillac/Chevrolet, Country Campers RV Ctr, Walgreens, urgent care, to Aztalan SP
250	WI 73, Deerfield, to Marshall
244	rd n, Sun Prairie, Cottage Grove, **N gas:** Citgo/dsl, **S gas:** Shell, **food:** Arby's, Subway
240	I-90 **E.**
I-94 and I-90 run together 93 miles.	
147	I-90 W, to La Crosse, **I-94 and I-90 run together 93 miles. See Interstate 90 exits 48-138.**
143	US 12, WI 21, Tomah, **N gas:** Mobil/dsl, **food:** A&W/LJ Silver, Four Star Rest., Perkins, **lodging:** AmericInn, Holiday Inn, Microtel, Super 8, **other:** Humbird Cheese/gifts, **S gas:** BP, KwikTrip/dsl/rest./scales/24hr, **food:** China Buffet, Culver's, Ground Round, KFC, McDonald's, Pizza Hut, Quizno's, Subway, Taco Bell, **lodging:** Comfort Inn, Cranberry Suites, Econolodge, **other:** H, Advance Parts, Aldi Foods, $Tree, U-Haul, Walmart SuperCtr/24hr, to Ft McCoy (9mi), **S on US 12...food:** Burger King, **other:** Ace Hardware, Buick/Chevrolet, Chrysler/Dodge/Jeep, Curves, Firestone/auto, Ford/Lincoln/Mercury, Radio Shack
135	rd EW, Warrens, **N gas:** BP, **lodging:** 3 Bears Resort, **other:** Jellystone Camping, **S food:** Bog Rest.
128	rd O, Millston, **N other:** Black River SF, camping, **S gas:** Cenex/dsl, **other:** USPO
123mm	**rest area/scenic view both lanes, full ♿ facilities, ☎, picnic, litter barrels, vending, petwalk**
116	WI 54, **N gas:** Cenex/Subway/Taco Johns/dsl/LP, **food:** Perkins, **lodging:** Best Western Arrowhead/rest., Holiday Inn Express, Super 8, **other:** Black River RA, Parkland Camp, casino, **S gas:** *FLYING J*/Cookery/dsl/24hr/@, KwikTrip/dsl/rest., **food:** Burger King, Culvers, McDonald's, Oriental Kitchen, Pizza Hut, **lodging:** Day's Inn, **other:** Buick/Chevrolet/GMC/Pontiac, $Tree, $General, Walmart SuperCtr
115mm	Black River
115	US 12, Black River Falls, to Merrillan, **S gas:** BP, Holiday/dsl, **food:** Hardee's, KFC, Subway, Sunrise Rest., **other:** H, Ace Hardware, Harley-Davidson, NAPA
105	to WI 95, Hixton, to Alma Center, **N lodging:** Motel 95/campground, **other:** KOA (3mi), **S gas:** Cenex/dsl, Clark/dsl/rest./24hr, **other:** city park
98	WI 121, Northfield, Pigeon Falls, to Alma Center, **S gas:** Cenex/dsl, **food:** DeeDee's Diner, Jackie's Café

INTERSTATE 94 CONT'D

E ↕ W

Exit #	Services
88	US 10, Osseo, to Fairchild, **N gas:** BP/DQ, Mobil/dsl, Shell/Elderberry's/dsl/scales, **food:** Hardee's, Moe's Diner, **lodging:** 10-7 Inn, Super 8, **other:** Chevrolet, Ford, Stony Cr RV Park, **S gas:** Speedway/dsl, **food:** McDonald's, Subway, Taco John's, **lodging:** Osseo Inn, **other:** H, Family$
81	rd HH, rd KK, Foster, **S gas:** BP/dsl/LP, **food:** Foster Cheesehaus
70	US 53, Eau Claire, **N off Golf Rd...gas:** Mobil/dsl, **food:** A&W, Applebee's, Bakers Square, Bear Creek Grille, Buffalo Wild Wings, Burracho's, Coldstone Creamery, Fazoli's, Jade Garden, McDonald's, Nanny's Grill, Noodles&Co, Olive Garden, Outback Steaks, Panera Bread, Texas Roadhouse, TGIFriday, **lodging:** Country Inn&Suites, Grandstay, Heartland Inn, **other:** Aldi Foods, Best Buy, Borders Books, Gander Mtn, JC Penney, Kohl's, Macy's, Menard's, Michael's, Office Depot, PetCo, Sam's Club, Scheel's Sports, Sears/auto, Target, TJ Maxx, Younker's, Walmart SuperCtr/24hr, mall, **S other:** Gander Mtn, st police
68	WI 93, to Eleva, **N gas:** BP, Holiday, KwikTrip, **food:** Burger King, DQ, Red Robin, **lodging:** Econolodge, **other:** Chrysler/Dodge, Family$, Firestone/auto, Goodyear/auto, Jeep, NAPA, Nissan, Subaru, USPO, transmission, same as 70, **S gas:** BP, **other:** Audi/VW, Buick/Cadillac/GMC/Hyundai/Pontiac, Ford/Lincoln/Mercury
65	WI 37, WI 85, Eau Claire, to Mondovi, **N gas:** BP, **food:** Arby's, Green Mill Rest., Hardee's, Mancino's Rest., McDonald's, Randy's Rest., Red Lobster, Starbucks, Subway, Taco Bell, Wendy's, **lodging:** Best Western, Comfort Inn, Day's Inn/rest., Hampton Inn, Highlander Inn, Holiday Inn/rest., Quality Inn, Super 8, **other:** H, Castle Foods, Mazda/Toyota, Radio Shack, ShopKo, Walgreens
64mm	Chippewa River
59	to US 12, rd EE, to Eau Claire, **N gas:** BP/Burger King/dsl/24hr, Holiday/Subway/dsl/24hr, **food:** Embers Rest., McDonald's, **lodging:** AmericInn, Day's Inn, Super 8, **other:** H, Freightliner, Mack/Volvo Trucks, Peterbilt, auto repair/towing, **S** US RV Ctr, trailer repair
52	US 12, WI 29, WI 40, Elk Mound, to Chippewa Falls, **S gas:** U-Fuel/pizza
49mm	**weigh sta wb**
45	rd B, Menomonie, **N gas:** Cenex/dsl/rest./scales, **S gas:** KwikTrip/Subway/dsl/scales/24hr, **food:** Country Kitchen, Culver's, **lodging:** Comfort Inn, **other:** H AOK RV Ctr, Kenworth, Walmart Dist Ctr
44mm	Red Cedar River
43mm	**rest areas both lanes, full ♿ facilities, ☎, picnic, litter barrels, vending, petwalk, weather info**
41	WI 25, Menomonie, **N gas:** Cenex, **food:** Applebee's, Burracho's, China Buffet, Pizza Hut, Quizno's, Subway, **other:** H, Aldi Foods, $Tree, Radio Shack, Walmart SuperCtr/24hr, Edgewater Camping, GS Camping, **S gas:** F&F/dsl, Holiday, SA/dsl, **food:** Arby's, Green Mill Rest., Kernel Rest., KFC, McDonald's, Perkins, Taco Bell, Taco John's, Wendy's, **lodging:** AmericInn, Country Inn&Suites, Motel 6,

EAU CLAIRE

MENOMONIE

WI WY

Exit #	Services
41	Continued Super 8, **other:** Advance Parts, Chevrolet, Chrysler/Jeep, Ford, K-Mart, NAPA, O'Reilly Parts, Walgreens, to Red Cedar St Tr
32	Rd Q, to Knapp
28	WI 128, Wilson, Elmwood, to Glenwood City, **N gas:** KwikTrip/dsl/rest./24hr, **S other:** Eau Galle RA, camping, dsl repair
24	rd B, to Baldwin, **N gas:** BP, **food:** Wild Wood Rest., **lodging:** Woodville Motel, **S other:** Eau Galle RA, camping
19	US 63, Baldwin, to Ellsworth, **N gas:** Freedom/dsl, KwikTrip/Subway/dsl, **food:** A&W, DQ, Hardee's, McDonald's, **lodging:** AmericInn, **other:** H, **S gas:** Mobil/rest./dsl, **lodging:** Super 8
16	rd T, Hammond
10	WI 65, Roberts, to New Richmond
8mm	**weigh sta eb**
4	US 12, rd U, Somerset, **N gas:** BP/dsl, TA/Country Pride/dsl/rest./24hr/@, **food:** Rich's Eatery, **lodging:** Best Value Inn, **other:** Vet, to Willow River SP, **S other:** Curves
3	WI 35, to River Falls, U of WI River Falls
2	rd F, Carmichael Rd, Hudson, **N gas:** BP/repair, Freedom/dsl, Holiday, **food:** Applebee's, Caribou Coffee, Cousin's Subs, Culver's, Domino's, KFC, Fiesta Mexicana, Papa Murphy's, Taco John's, **lodging:** Royal Inn, **other:** Family Fresh Foods, GNC, Radio Shack, Target, TrueValue, **S Welcome Ctr both lanes, full ♿ facilities, ☎, picnic table, litter barrel, info, petwalk, gas:** F&F/dsl, Holiday, KwikTrip/dsl, **food:** Arby's, Buffalo Wild Wings, Burger King, Chipotle Mexican, Coldstone Creamery, Country Kitchen, Denny's, Green Mill Rest., McDonald's, Pizza Hut, Perkins, Starbucks, Subway, Taco Bell, Wendy's, **lodging:** Best Western, Comfort Inn, Fairfield Inn, Holiday Inn Express, Super 8, **other:** H, Checker Parts, Chevrolet/GMC/Pontiac, Chrysler/Dodge/Jeep, County Mkt Foods, Ford/Mercury, Home Depot, Menard's, NAPA, Tires+, Walmart, USPO, to Kinnickinnic SP
1	WI 35 N, Hudson, **1 mi N gas:** Freedom/dsl, Holiday, **food:** DQ
0mm	Wisconsin/Minnesota state line, St Croix River

HUDSON

WYOMING

INTERSTATE 25

Exit #	Services
300	**I-90, E to Gillette, W to Billings. I-25 begins/ends on I-90, exit 56.**

N ↕ S

BUFFALO

WY

INTERSTATE 25 CONT'D

Exit #	Services
299	US 16, Buffalo, **E gas:** Exxon/dsl, Johnson Cty/dsl, Shell/dsl/24hr, **food:** Winchester Steaks, **lodging:** Comfort Inn, Holiday Inn Express, Motel 6, **other:** Deer Park Camping, NAPA, Vet, **W gas:** Bighorn/dsl/24hr, Cenex/dsl/rest./24hr, **food:** Bozeman Tr Steaks, Dash Inn Rest., Hardee's, Hoot'n Howl Rest., McDonald's, Pizza Hut, Sub Shop, Subway, Taco John's, **lodging:** Best Western Crossroads, Econolodge, WY Motel, Super 8, **other:** H, Ace Hardware, Family$, Indian RV Camp
298	US 87, Buffalo, **W** Nat Hist Dist Info
291	Trabing Rd
280	Middle Fork Rd
274mm	**parking area both lanes, litter barrels**
265	Reno Rd
254	Kaycee, **E gas:** Exxon/dsl, **food:** Country Inn Diner, **lodging:** Cassidy Inn Motel, Siesta Motel, **other:** Kaycee Gen. Store, NAPA Repair, Powder River RV Park, USPO, museum, **W rest area both lanes, full ♿ facilities, ☎, picnic, litter barrels, petwalk, gas:** Sinclair/dsl/LP/motel, **other:** KC RV Park
249	TTT Rd
246	Powder River Rd
235	Tisdale Mtn Rd
227	WY 387 N, Midwest, Edgerton
223	no services
219mm	**parking area both lanes, litter barrels**
216	Ranch Rd
210	Horse Ranch Creek Rd, Midwest, Edgerton
197	Ormsby Rd
191	Wardwell Rd, to Bar Nunn, **W gas:** Minimart/dsl, **other:** KOA
189	US 20, US 26 W, to Shoshone, Port of Entry, ✈
188b	WY 220, Poplar St, **E food:** El Jarro Mexican, JB's, Poor Boy's Steaks, Sideline BBQ, **lodging:** Best Western, Hampton Inn, Hilton Garden, Motel 6, Quality Inn, Ramada, **W gas:** Exxon, **food:** Burger King, Casper's Rest., DQ, **other:** Harley-Davidson, to Ft Casper HS
188a	Center St, Casper, **E gas:** Conoco/dsl, Shell/dsl, **food:** Taco John's, **lodging:** National 9 Inn, Ramada, **W food:** Platte River Rest., Subway, **lodging:** Day's Inn, Parkway Plaza Motel, **other:** USPO
187	McKinley St, Casper, **E gas:** Loaf'n Jug/dsl, **lodging:** Ranch House Motel, **other:** repair/transmissons
186	US 20, US 26, US 87, Yellowstone St, **E other:** Audi/VW, dsl repair, **W gas:** Exxon, **other:** H, Checker Parts, Chevrolet/Subaru, Toyota
185	WY 258, Wyoming Blvd, E Casper, **E gas:** Kum&Go/dsl, Loaf'n Jug/dsl, **food:** Applebee's, IHOP, Outback Steaks, **lodging:** C'mon Inn, Comfort Inn, Shilo Inn, Super 8, **other:** KOA (1mi), Smith RV Ctr, **W gas:** Exxon/dsl, ***FLYING J***/Conoco/Cookery/dsl/LP/scales/24hr, **food:** Arby's, Burger King, DQ, Hardee's, HomeTowne Buffet, KFC/LJ Silver, McDonald's/playplace, Mongolian Grill, Old Chicago Grill, Perkins, Pizza Hut, Red Lobster, South Sea Chinese Rest.,

CASPER

Exit #	Services
185	Continued Sanford's Cafe, Starbucks, Taco Bell, Taco John's, Village Inn Rest., Wendy's, **lodging:** Coutyard, 1st Interstate Motel, Holiday Inn Express, **other:** AutoZone, Home Depot, JC Penney, K-Mart, PetCo, Plains Tire, Red Lobster, Safeway Foods, Sam's Club/gas, Sears/auto, Sportsman's Warehouse, Staples, Target, Village Inn, Walgreens, Walmart SuperCtr/24hr, to Oregon Tr, mall
182	WY 253, Brooks Rd, Hat Six Rd, **E gas:** Sinclair/Chesterfried/dsl, **food:** Lou's Rest., **lodging:** Sleep Inn, **other:** to Wilkins SP, **W food:** Firerock Rest., **lodging:** Holiday Inn, Mainstay Suites, **other:** H Buick/Cadillac/Pontiac/GMC, Menard's, Rendezvous RV Ctr
171mm	**parking area both lanes, litter barrels**
165	Glenrock, **2 mi E gas:** Sinclair/dsl, **lodging:** Higgins Hotel, **other:** Deer Creek Village RV Camping (apr-nov)
160	US 87, US 20, US 26, E Glenrock, **E other:** to Johnston Power Plant
156	Bixby Rd
154	Barber Rd
153mm	**parking area both lanes, litter barrels**
151	Natural Bridge
150	Inez Rd
146	La Prele Rd
140	WY 59, Douglas, **E gas:** Conoco/Subway/dsl, Maverik/dsl, **food:** Arby's, La Costa Mexican, McDonald's, Taco John's, **lodging:** Best Western, Holiday Inn Express, Super 8, **other:** H, Buick/Chevrolet/GMC/Pontiac, KOA, Lone Tree RV Park, Pioneer Museum, WY St Fair,
135	US 20, US 26, US 87, Douglas, **E gas:** Sinclair/dsl/rest., **lodging:** Alpine Inn, 1st Interstate Inn, **other:** H, auto repair, **1-2 mi E gas:** Sinclair, **food:** Four Seasons Chinese, Hoggie's Rest., KFC/Taco Bell, Plains Trading Post Rest., Village Inn Rest., **lodging:** Plains Motel, **other:** Ace Hardware, Chrysler/Dodge/Jeep, Family$, Ford/Mercury, Pamida, Safeway
129mm	**parking area both lanes**
126	US 18, US 20 E, Orin, **E Orin Jct Rest Area both lanes, full ♿ facilities, ☎, picnic, litter barrels, petwalk, RV dump, gas:** Sinclair/Orin Jct Trkstp/dsl/café
125mm	N Platte River
111	Glendo, **E gas:** Sinclair/dsl, **food:** Glendo Marina Café, **lodging:** Howard's Motel, **other:** to Glendo SP, Glendo Lakeside RV camping
104	to Middle Bear
100	Cassa Rd
94	El Rancho Rd
92	US 26 E, Dwyer, **E rest area both lanes, full ♿ facilities, picnic, litter barrel, petwalk, RV dump to Guernsey SP**, Ft Laramie NHS
87	Johnson Rd
84	Laramie River Rd
84mm	Laramie River

DOUGLAS

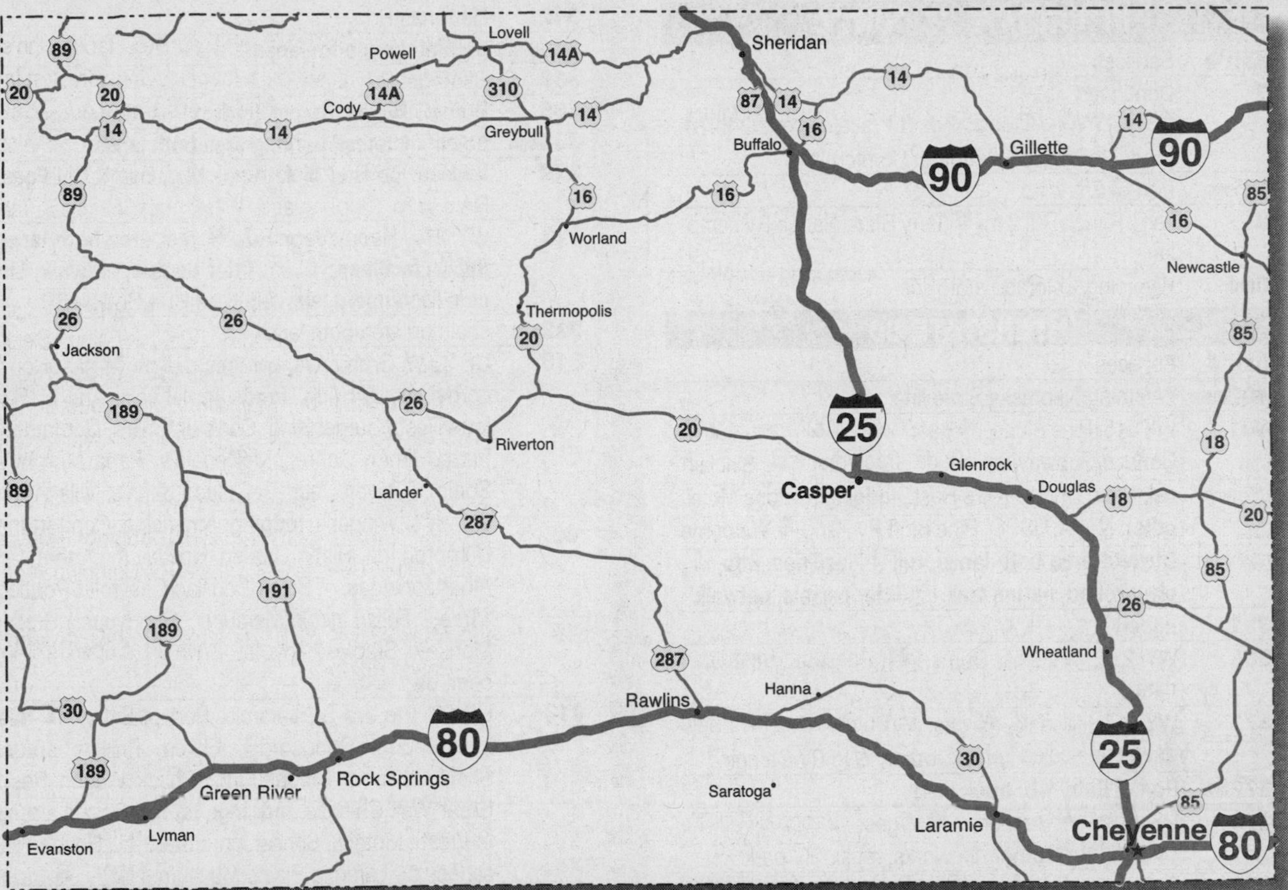

WY

INTERSTATE 25 CONT'D

N ↕ S

Exit #	Services
80	US 87, Laramie Power Sta, Wheatland, Laramie Power Sta, **E gas:** Sinclair/A&W/dsl/24hr, **food:** Pizza Hut, **lodging:** Best Western, Super 8, **other:** CarQuest, Chevrolet/Pontiac/Buick/Cadillac, Chrysler/Dodge/Jeep, Family$, Ford/Mercury, Pamida/drug, Safeway, Arrowhead RV Park, same as 78
78	US 87, Wheatland, **E gas:** Cenex/dsl, Loaf'n Jug/dsl, Maverik/dsl, Shell/dsl, **food:** Arby's, Burger King, Subway, Taco John's, Wheatland Rest., **lodging:** Motel 6, Vimbo's Motel/rest., Wyo Motel, **other:** H, **W gas:** Exxon/dsl, Pitstop/dsl, **other:** Radio Shack, Mtn. View RV Park
73	WY 34 W, to Laramie
70	Bordeaux Rd
68	Antelope Rd
66	Hunton Rd
65.5mm	**parking area both lanes, litter barrels**
65	Slater Rd
64mm	Richeau Creek
57	TY Basin Rd, Chugwater
54	Lp 25, Chugwater, **E gas:** Sinclair/dsl, **lodging:** Buffalo Lodge/Grill, **other:** RV camping, **rest area both lanes, full ♿ facilities, ☎, 🛆, litter barrels, petwalk, RV dump**
47	Bear Creek Rd
39	Little Bear Community
36mm	Little Bear Creek
34	Nimmo Rd
33mm	Horse Creek
29	Whitaker Rd
25	ranch exit
21	Ridley Rd
17	US 85 N, to Torrington, **W food:** Little Bear Rest. (2mi)
16	WY 211, Horse Creek Rd
13	Vandehei Ave, **E gas:** Loaf'n Jug/Subway, **food:** Silvermine Subs, **W gas:** Shamrock/dsl
12	Central Ave, Cheyenne, **E gas:** Exxon, **lodging:** Rodeway Inn, **other:** H, Frontier Days Park, museum, E on Dellrang **E food:** Applebee's, McDonald's, **lodging:** Fairfield Inn
11b	Warren AFB, Gate 1, Randall Ave, **E other:** to WY St Capitol, museum
10b d	Warren AFB, Gate 2, Missile Dr, WY 210, HappyJack Rd, **W other:** to Curt Gowdy SP
9	US 30, W Lincolnway, Cheyenne, **E gas:** Crossroads/Exxon/dsl, **food:** Comfort Inn, Country Kitchen, Denny's, Outback Steaks, Village Inn Rest., **lodging:** Candlewood Suites, Day's Inn, Express Inn, Hampton Inn, Holiday Inn Express, La Quinta, Microtel, Motel 6, Ramada Inn, Super 8, **other:** Cadillac, Chevrolet, Ford/Lincoln/Mercury, Home Depot, Honda, Hyundai, Nissan, Subaru, Toyota, **W gas:** Little America/Sinclair/dsl/rest./motel/@
8d b	I-80, E to Omaha, W to Laramie
7	WY 212, College Dr, **E gas:** Love's/Wendy's/dsl/scales/24hr/@, Shamrock/Subway/dsl/24hr, **food:** Arby's, **other:** A-B RV Park (2mi), Bailey Tire, Truck Repair, **W WY Info Ctr/rest area both lanes, full ♿ facilities, ☎, 🛆, litter barrels, petwalk, gas:**

CHEYENNE

INTERSTATE 25 CONT'D

Exit #	Services
7	Continued /FLYING J/Conoco/dsl/LP/scales/rest./24hr/@, **food:** McDonald's, **lodging:** Comfort Inn
6.5mm	Port of Entry, nb
2	Terry Ranch Rd, **2 mi E** Terry Bison Ranch RV camping
0mm	Wyoming/Colorado state line

INTERSTATE 80

Exit #	Services
402mm	Wyoming/Nebraska State line
401	WY 215, Pine Bluffs, **N gas:** Cenex/A&W/dsl/24hr/@, Conoco/Subway/dsl, Race Track/rest./dsl, Sinclair/dsl, **food:** Uncle Fred's Rest., **lodging:** Gator's Motel, **other:** NAPA, USPO, Pine Bluff RV Park, **S Welcome Ctr/rest area both lanes, full facilities, info, , playground, nature trail, , litter barrels, petwalk**
391	Egbert
386	WY 213, WY 214, Burns, **N** Antelope Trkstp/dsl/cafe
377	WY 217, Hillsdale, **N gas:** TA/Burger King/Taco Bell/dsl/motel/scales/24hr/@, **other:** Wyo RV Camping
372mm	Port of Entry wb, **truck insp**
370	US 30 W, Archer, **N gas:** Sapp/dsl/T-Joe's Rest./24hr/@, **other:** fireworks, repair, RV park
367	Campstool Rd, **N gas:** Pilot/Subway/dsl/scales/24hr, **lodging:** Sleep Inn, **other:** KOA (seasonal), **S other:** to Wyoming Hereford Ranch
364	WY 212, to E Lincolnway, Cheyenne, **1 mi N on Lincolnway...gas:** Loaf'n Jug/Subway, Valero, **food:** IHOP, McDonald's, Papa John's, Perkins, Pizza Hut, Shari's Rest., Taco Bell, Wendy's, **other:** H, AutoZone, BigLots, Checker Parts, $Tree, Econo Foods, Harley-Davidson, Sierra Trading Post, **S other:** AB Camping (4mi), Peterbilt
362	US 85, I-180, to Central Ave, Cheyenne, Greeley, **1 mi N on Dell Range Rd...gas:** Kum&Go/dsl, Sinclair/dsl, Spirit Gas, **food:** Arby's, Carls' Jr., Hacienda Mexican, **other:** CarQuest, dsl repair, museum, st capitol, **S gas:** Exxon/Domino's/dsl, Shamrock/dsl, **food:** Burger King, GoodTimes Grill/Taco John's, Little Caesar's, Sonic, Subway, **lodging:** Holiday Inn, Roundup Motel, SpringHill Suites, **other:** H, Family$, Safeway/gas, RV camping, transmissions
359c a	I-25, US 87, N to Casper, S to Denver
358	US 30, W Lincolnway, Cheyenne, **N gas:** Exxon/dsl/24hr, Little America/Sinclair/dsl/motel/@, **food:** Denny's, Outback Steaks, Pizza Inn, **lodging:** Village Inn, Day's Inn, Econolodge, Express Inn, Hampton Inn, Hitching Post Inn, Holiday Inn Express, La Quinta, Luxury Inn, Motel 6, Super 8, **other:** H, Chevrolet, Home Depot, Honda
357	Wy 222, Roundtop Rd
348	Otto Rd
345	Warren Rd, **N truck parking**
344mm	no services
343.5mm	no services
342	Harriman Rd
341mm	**parking area both lanes**
339	Remount Rd
335	Buford, **S gas:** Buford Trading Post/Cenex/dsl/24hr
333mm	point of interest, **parking area both lanes**
329	Vedeauwoo Rd, **S** to Ames Monument, Nat Forest RA
323	WY 210, Happy Jack Rd, **N rest area both lanes, full facilities, , , litter barrels, petwalk, Lincoln Monument**, elev. 8640, to Curt Gowdy SP
322mm	chain up area both lanes
316	US 30 W, Grand Ave, Laramie, **1-2 mi N gas:** Conoco/dsl, Loaf'N Jug, **food:** Applebee's, Arby's, Bailey's Rest., Burger King, Carl's Jr, Chili's, Godfather's Pizza, Jimmy John's, McDonald's, Papa Murphy's, Sonic, Subway, Taco Bell, Taco John's, Village Inn, Wendy's, Winger's, **lodging:** AmericInn, Comfort Inn, Hampton Inn, Hilton Garden, Holiday Inn, **other:** H Albertsons/gas, Buick/Cadillac/Chevrolet/Pontiac, $Tree, Ford/Lincoln/Mercury, Goodyear, Grease Monkey, Staples, Toyota, Walmart SuperCtr/24hr, conf. ctr
313	US 287, to 3rd St, Laramie, Port of Entry, **N gas:** Loaf'N Jug, Conoco/dsl, Exxon, Phillips 66/dsl, Shell/dsl, **food:** Burger King, Chuck Wagon Rest., Great Wall Chinese, **lodging:** 1st Inn Gold, Laramie Inn/rest., Motel 8, Sunset Inn, **other:** H, Honda/Nissan/Isuzu, Laramie Plains Museum, NAPA, **S lodging:** Motel 6, Ramada Inn
312mm	Laramie River
311	WY 130, WY 230, Snowy Range Rd, Laramie, **S gas:** Conoco/dsl, Phillips 66/dsl, Sinclair/dsl/LP, **food:** McDonald's, Subway, **lodging:** Best Value Inn, Howard Johnson, to Snowy Range Ski Area, WY Terr Park
310	Curtis St, Laramie, **N gas:** Pilot/Wendy's/dsl/24hr/@, Shamrock/café/dsl, **lodging:** Best Western, Days Inn, Econolodge, Super 8, **other:** H, Goodyear/service/towing, KOA, **1 mi N on 3rd...food:** Pizza Hut, Shari's Rest., **other:** Checker Parts, Family$, Hastings, Jeep/Subaru, K-Mart, Safeway Foods, **S gas:** Petro/Iron Skillet/dsl/scales/24hr/@, Blue Beacon, **lodging:** Fairfield Inn, Quality Inn
307mm	**parking area both lanes, litter barrels**
297	WY 12, Herrick Lane
290	Quealy Dome Rd, **S** gas/dsl
279	Cooper Cove Rd
272mm	Rock Creek
272	WY 13, to Arlington, **N** gas, RV camping
267	Wagonhound Rd, **S rest area both lanes, full facilities, , , litter barrels, petwalk**
262mm	**parking area both lanes**
260	CR 402
259mm	Medicine Bow River, E Fork
257mm	Medicine Bow River
255	WY 72, Elk Mtn, to Hanna, **N gas:** Conoco/dsl,
238	Peterson Rd
235	US 30/87, WY 130, **N gas:** Shell/dsl/café
229mm	N Platte River
228	Ft Steele HS, **N rest area both lanes, full facilities, , , litter barrels, petwalk**

N ↕ S

E ↕ W

WY

CHEYENNE

LARAMIE

INTERSTATE 80 CONT'D

E ↔ W

RAWLINS

Exit #	Services
221	E Sinclair, N gas: Phillips 66/dsl/rest./24hr, other: to Seminoe SP, camping
219	W Sinclair, N other: to Seminoe SP, camping
215	Cedar St, Rawlins, N gas: City Mkt, Conoco/dsl, Phillips 66/dsl, Shell/KFC/Taco Bell, Sinclair, food: McDonald's, Pizza Hut, Subway, Taco John's, lodging: Comfort Inn, Day's Inn, 1st Choice Inn, Hampton Inn, Holiday Inn Express, Quality Inn, OakTree Inn, The Key Motel, other: Alco, Buick/Chevrolet/Pontiac/GMC, CarQuest, Checker Parts, Chrysler/Dodge/Jeep, City Mkt Food/gas, Pamida, TDS Tire, museum, Frontier Prison NHS, to Yellowstone/Teton NP
214	Higley Blvd, Rawlins, N lodging: Microtel, other: KOA, S gas: TA/Shell/Subway/dsl/24hr/@, lodging: Best Value Inn
211	WY 789, to US 287 N, Spruce St, Rawlins, N gas: Conoco/dsl, Exxon/dsl, Phillips 66, Sinclair/dsl, food: Cappy's Rest., Golden 8 Chinese, lodging: Best Western, Budget Inn, Econolodge, Express Inn, Ideal Motel, La Bella, Super 8, Sunset Motel, Travelodge, other: H, Family$, RV World, V1/LP, Western Hills Camping, 1 mi N lodging: Economy Inn, other: Ford/Lincoln/Mercury
209	Johnson Rd, N gas: FLYING J/dsl/LP/rest./scales/24hr/@
206	Hadsell Rd (no return)
205.5mm	continental divide, elev 7000
204	Knobs Rd
201	Daley Rd
196	Riner Rd
190mm	parking area wb, litter barrels
189mm	parking area eb, picnic, litter barrels
187	WY 789, Creston, Baggs Rd
184	Continental Divide Rd
173	Wamsutter, N gas: Loves/Chester Fried/Subway/dsl/24hr/@, S gas: Conoco/dsl/repair/café/24hr, Phillips 66/dsl/@, food: Broadway Café, lodging: Wamsutter Motel
170	Rasmussen Rd
168	Frewen Rd
166	Booster Rd
165	Red Desert
158	Tipton Rd, continental divide, elev 6930
156	GL Rd
154	BLM Rd
152	Bar X Rd
150	Table Rock Rd
146	Patrick Draw Rd
144mm	rest area both lanes, full handicapped facilities, phone, picnic, litter barrels, petwalk
143mm	parking area both lanes, litter barrels
142	Bitter Creek Rd
139	Red Hill Rd
136	Black Butte Rd
133mm	parking area both lanes
130	Point of Rocks, N gas: Conoco/dsl
122	WY 371, to Superior

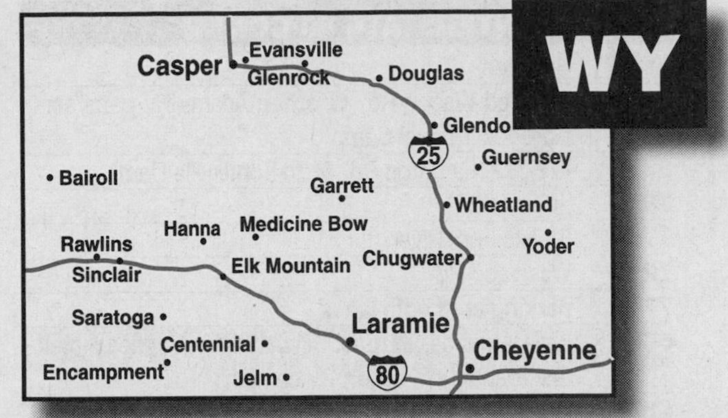

ROCK SPRINGS

Exit #	Services
111	Airport Rd, Baxter Rd, S airport
107	Pilot Butte Ave, Rock Springs, S gas: Mobil/dsl/lodging, Phillips 66/dsl, lodging: Sands Inn/cafe, Springs Motel
104	US 191 N, Elk St, Rock Springs, N gas: Exxon, FLYING J/Conoco/dsl/LP/rest./24hr, Kum&Go/gas, Phillips 66/dsl, Sinclair, Texaco/Burger King/dsl, food: Fiesta Guadalajara Mexican, McDonald's, Renegade Rest., Santa Fe Trail Rest., Taco Time, lodging: Best Western, Econolodge/rest., other: Buick/Pontiac/GMC, Great Western RV, Jeep, truck repair, to Teton/Yellowstone Nat Parks via US 191, S gas: Exxon/dsl, lodging: Day's Inn
103	College Dr, Rock Springs, S gas: Loaf'n Jug/dsl/24hr, food: Domino's other: H, W WY Coll
102	WY 430, Dewar Dr, Rock Springs, N gas: Exxon, Loaf'N Jug, Sinclair/dsl, food: Applebee's, China King, KFC/LJ Silver, Taco Time, lodging: Best Value Inn, Comfort Inn La Quinta, Motel 6, The Inn, other: Chevrolet/Cadillac, Chrysler/Dodge/Subaru, $Tree, Harley-Davidson, Home Depot, K-Mart, JC Penney, Smith's Foods, S gas: Kum&Go, Loaf'N Jug, Mirastar, Mobil, food: Arby's, Bonsai Chinese, Burger King, Golden Corral, IHOP, JB's, McDonald's, Pizza Hut, Quizno's, Sonic, Starbucks, Subway, Taco Bell, Village Inn Rest., Wendy's, Wingers, lodging: Hampton Inn, Holiday Inn, Homewood Suites, Motel 8, Quality Inn, Super 8, Wingate Inn, other: H, Albertson's, AutoZone, Big O Tire, Checker Parts, Curves, Hastings Books, NAPA, Radio Shack, Walgreens, Walmart SuperCtr/24hr
99	US 191 S, E Flaming Gorge Rd, N other: KOA (1mi), S gas: Sinclair/dsl/rest./24hr/@, food: Ted's Rest., other: fireworks, transmissions
94mm	Kissing Rock

GREEN RIVER

Exit #	Services
91	US 30, to WY 530, Green River, S gas: Gasamat, Loaf'N Jug/gas food: Arctic Circle, Buckaroo's Rest., China Garden, Don Pedro's Mexican, McDonald's, Pizza Hut, Subway, Taco John's, Taco Time, lodging: Coachman Inn, Mustang Inn, Super 8, Western Motel, other: Expedition NHS, to Flaming Gorge NRA, same as 89
89	US 30, Green River, N lodging: Hampton Inn, S gas: Exxon, Sinclair/dsl, food: Don Pedro's, McDonald's, Penny's Diner, Pizza Hut, Taco Time, lodging: OakTree Inn, Super 8, Western Inn, other: Adam's RV Service, NAPA, Tex's RV Camp, to Flaming Gorge NRA
87.5mm	Green River

INTERSTATE 80 CONT'D

Exit #	Services
85	Covered Wagon Rd, **S other:** Adams RV parts/service, Tex's Travel Camp
83	WY 372, La Barge Rd, **N** to Fontenelle Dam
78	(from wb)
77mm	Blacks Fork River
72	Westvaco Rd
71mm	**parking area both lanes**
68	Little America, **N gas:** Sinclair/Little America Hotel/rest./dsl/24hr@, **other:** RV camping
66	US 30 W, to Teton, Yellowstone, Fossil Butte NM, Kemmerer
61	Cedar Mt Rd, to Granger
60mm	**parking area both lanes, litter barrels**
54mm	**parking area eb, litter barrels**
53	Church Butte Rd
49mm	**parking area wb, litter barrels**
48	Lp 80, Lyman, Ft Bridger, Hist Ft Bridger
45mm	Blacks Fork River
41	WY 413, Lyman, **N gas:** Gas'n Go/dsl/cafe/@, **S rest area both lanes, full ♿ facilities, ☎, picnic, litter barrels, petwalk, food:** Taco Time, **other:** Gateway Inn (2mi), KOA (1mi)
39	WY 412, WY 414, to Carter, Mountain View
34	Lp 80, to Ft Bridger, **S gas:** Phillips 66, **lodging:** Wagon Wheel Motel, **other:** Ft Bridger RV Camp, Ft Bridger NHS, to Flaming Gorge NRA
33.5mm	**parking area eb, litter barrels**
33	Union Rd
30	Bigelow Rd, **N gas:** TA/Tesoro/Burger King/Taco Bell/Fork In the Road/dsl/scales/24hr/@, **S** fireworks
28	French Rd
28mm	French Rd, **parking area both lanes**
24	Leroy Rd
23	Bar Hat Rd
21	Coal Rd
18	US 189 N, to Kemmerer, to Nat Parks, Fossil Butte NM
15	Guild Rd (from eb)
14mm	**parking area both lanes**
13	Divide Rd
10	Painter Rd, to Eagle Rock Ski Area, to Eagle Rock Ski Area
6	US 189, Bear River Dr, Evanston, **N gas:** Pilot/Subway/dsl/scales/24hr, Sinclair/dsl, **food:** Bear Town Rest., Don Pedro Mexican, **lodging:** Best Value Inn, Holiday Inn Express, Motel 6, Prairie Inn, Vagabond Motel, **other:** Bear River RV Park, CarQuest, Freeway Tire, Ford/Mercury, Goodyear, KC's RV Ctr, Tire Factory, Wyo Downs Racetrack, **S Welcome Ctr both lanes, full ♿ facilities, ☎, picnic, litter barrels, petwalk, RV dump (seasonal), playground,** Bear River SP
5	WY 89, Evanston, **N gas:** Chevron/Taco Time/dsl, Maverik/dsl, Sinclair/LP, **food:** Arby's, DragonWall Chinese, McDonald's, Papa Murphy's, Shakey's Pizza, Starbucks, Subway, Wendy's, **lodging:** Best Value Inn, **other:** H, AutoZone, Chevrolet/Buick, Family$, Jiffy Lube, Jubilee foods/gas, Murdoch's, NAPA, Radio Shack, Walmart SuperCtr, **S** WY St H
3	US 189, Harrison Dr, Evanston, **N gas:** Chevron/dsl, *FLYING J*/dsl/rest./scales/24hr/@, Gasamat, Sinclair, **food:** JB's, Legal Tender, Lotty's Rest., Taco Time, Wally's Burgers, **lodging:** Best Western/rest., Comfort Inn, Days Inn, Economy Inn, Hampton Inn, HighCountry Inn, HillCrest Motel, Holiday Inn Express, Howard Johnson, The Lodge, Weston Inn, **other:** Automotive+, Chrysler/Jeep, GMC/Pontiac/Cadillac, USPO, **S food:** KFC/Taco Bell, **other:** H, fireworks
.5mm	**Port of Entry eb, weigh sta wb**
0mm	Wyoming/Utah state line

E ↕ W — EVANSTON

INTERSTATE 90

Exit #	Services
207mm	Wyoming/South Dakota state line
205	Beulah, **N gas:** Shell/dsl/LP, **food:** Buffalo Jump Rest., **lodging:** The Mill, **other:** Sand Creek Camping, USPO, **S** Ranch A NHP (5mi)
204.5mm	Sand Creek
199	WY 111, to Aladdin, Devil's Tower NM, Vore Buffalo Jump NHP
191	Moskee Rd
189	US 14 W, Sundance, **N gas:** Conoco/dsl/24hr, **other:** H, Mt View Camping, to Devil's Tower NM, museum, **S rest area both lanes, full ♿ facilities, info, ☎, picnic litter barrels, playground, petwalk, RV dump, port of entry/weigh sta**
187	WY 585, Sundance, **N gas:** Fresh Start/dsl, Sinclair/dsl, **food:** Aro Rest. (2mi), Subway (2mi), **lodging:** Bear Lodge, Best Western, Budget Host Arrowhead, Pineview Motel, Rodeway Inn, **other:** Decker's Foods, NAPA
185	to WY 116, to Sundance, **S gas:** Conoco/dsl/service, **food:** Aro Rest., Subway, **lodging:** Bear Lodge, Best Western, Budget Host, **other:** Mt View Camping, to Devil's Tower
178	Coal Divide Rd
177mm	**parking area both lanes**
172	Inyan Kara Rd
171mm	**parking area eb, litter barrels**
165	Pine Ridge Rd, to Pine Haven, **N** to Keyhole SP
163mm	**parking area both lanes**
160	Wind Creek Rd
154	US 14, US 16, **S gas:** Cenex/dsl, **food:** Donna's Diner, Subway, **lodging:** Cozy Motel, Moorcourt Motel, Rangerland Motel/RV Park, Wyo Motel, **other:** Diehl's Foods/gas, USPO, museum, city park
153	US 16 E, US 14, W Moorcroft, **N rest area both lanes, full ♿ facilities, ☎, picnic, litter barrels, petwalk**
152mm	Belle Fourche River
141	Rozet
138mm	**parking area both lanes**
132	Wyodak Rd
129	Garner Lake Rd, **S other:** Harley-Davidson, High Plains Camping, WY Marine/RV ctr, auto repair
128	US 14, US 16, Gillette, Port of Entry, **N gas:** Cenex, Conoco, Maverik/dsl, **food:** Mona's American/Mexican, Taco John's, Village Inn Rest., **lodging:** Howard

E ↕ W — SUNDANCE

E ↕ W

GILLETTE

INTERSTATE 90 CONT'D

Exit #	Services
128	Continued Johnson, National 9 Inn, Smart Choice Inn, **other:** Crazy Woman Camping (2mi), East Side RV Ctr., **S other:** High Plains Camping
126	WY 59, Gillette, **N gas:** Cenex/dsl, Conoco, **food:** Hardee's, Maria's Mexican, McDonald's, Papa John's, Pokey's BBQ, Prime Rib Rest., Starbucks, Subway, **lodging:** Best Value, Rolling Hills Motel, **other:** Radio Shack, Smith's Foods, Tire Factory, city park, **S gas:** Exxon, *FLYING J*/dsl/rest./24hr, Loaf'n Jug, **food:** A&W/LJ Silver, Applebee's, Arby's, Burger King, DQ, Goodtimes Grill/Taco John's, Golden Corral, KFC, Las Margaritas, Papa Murphy's, Perkins/24hr, Pizza Hut, Popeye's, Quizno's, Taco Bell, Wendy's, **lodging:** Clarion, Country Inn&Suites, Days Inn, Fairfield Inn, Holiday Inn Express, Wingate Inn, **other:** Ace Hardware, Albertson's, Chrysler/Dodge/Jeep, GNC, Goodyear/auto, Home Depot, K-Mart, Office Depot, O'Reilly Parts, Osco Drug, Tire-O-Rama, Walgreens, Walmart SuperCtr, city park, RV dump
124	WY 50, Gillette, **N gas:** Conoco/dsl/24hr, Shell/Burger King/dsl, **food:** Granny's Kitchen, Hong Kong Rest., Pizza Hut, Subway, **lodging:** Best Western/rest., Budget Inn, Comfort Inn, Hampton Inn, Motel 6, Super 8, **other:** H, Don's Foods, **S gas:** Cenex/dsl, **other:** Bighorn Tire, Buick/Cadillac/Chevrolet/GMC/Pontiac
116	Force Rd
113	Wild Horse Creek Rd
110mm	no services
106	Kingsbury Rd
102	Barber Creek Rd
91	Dead Horse Creek Rd
89mm	Powder River
88	Powder River Rd, **N gas:** Exit 88 Fuel/dsl/motel/camping, **rest area both lanes, full ♿ facilities, ☎, picnic, litter barrels, petwalk**
82	Indian Creek Rd
77	Schoonover Rd
73.5mm	Crazy Woman Creek
73	Crazy Woman Creek Rd
69	Dry Creek Rd
68.5mm	**parking area both lanes, litter barrels (wb only)**
65	Red Hills Rd, Tipperary Rd
60mm	**parking area both lanes, litter barrels**
58	US 16, to Ucross, Buffalo, **S gas:** Cenex/dsl/rest/24hr, Exxon/dsl, **other:** Bighorn Tire, **1-3 mi S gas:** Johnson Cty/dsl, Shell/dsl/24hr, **food:** Bozeman Tr Steaks, Dash Inn Rest., Hardee's, Hoot'n Howl Rest., McDonald's, Pizza Hut, Sub Shop, Subway, Taco John's, Winchester Steaks, **lodging:** Best Western Crossroads, Comfort Inn, Econolodge, Holiday Inn Express, Motel 6, Super 8, WY Motel, **other:** H, Ace Hardware, Deer Park Camping, Family$, Indian RV Camp, NAPA, Nat Hist Dist, Vet
56b	I-25 S, US 87 S, to Buffalo
56a	25 Bus, 90 Bus, to Buffalo, **services 2mi S** (from eb)
53	Rock Creek Rd

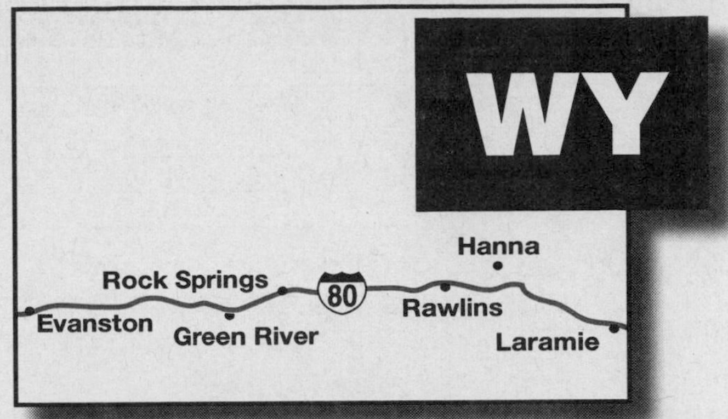

SHERIDAN

Exit #	Services
51	Lake DeSmet, **1 mi N** Lake Stop gas/motel/cafe, Lake De Smet RV park
47	Shell Creek Rd
44	US 87 N, Piney Creek Rd, to Story, Banner, **N other:** Ft Phil Kearney, museum, **5 mi S** Wagon Box Cabins/Rest.
39mm	scenic turnout wb
37	Prairie Dog Creek Rd, to Story
33	Meade Creek Rd, to Big Horn
31mm	**parking area eb**
25	US 14 E, Sheridan, **N lodging:** Quality Inn, **other:** Dalton's RV Ctr, **S gas:** Exxon/dsl, Holiday, Loaf'n Jug/dsl, Maverik/dsl, **food:** Arby's, Burger King, Goodtimes/Taco John's, JB's, Los Agaves, Ole's Pizza, Papa Murphy's, Perkins/24hr, Starbucks, Subway, Taco Bell, Wendy's, **lodging:** Candlewood Suites, Days Inn, Holiday Inn, Mill Inn, Parkway Motel, **other:** Ace Hardware, Albertson's/Osco Drug, Buick/Cadillac/GMC/Pontiac, $Tree, Firestone, Ford/Lincoln/Mercury, Goodyear, Home Depot, Jeep, NAPA, O'Reilly Parts, Tire-Rama, Toyota, Walgreens, Walmart SuperCtr/24hr, ✈, mall, to Hist Dist, Sheridan Coll, Vet
23	WY 336, 5th St, Sheridan, **N gas:** Rock Stop/Subway/dsl, **lodging:** Wingate Inn, **rest area both lanes, full ♿ facilities, info, ☎, picnic, litter barrels, petwalk, RV dump, 1-2 mi S gas:** Cenex, Holiday/dsl, **food:** DQ, Olivia's Kitchen, Pablo's Mexican, Quizno's, **lodging:** Alamo Motel, Best Value Inn, Best Western, Hampton Inn, Motel 6, Sheridan Inn, **other:** H, Honda, Peter D's RV Park, Sheridan Cty Museum, park, radiators
20	Main St, Sheridan, **S gas:** Exxon/dsl/scales/24hr, Gas A Mat/dsl, Maverik, Shell/dsl, **food:** Country Kitchen, Domino's, Little Ceasar's, McDonald's, Pizza Hut, **lodging:** Aspen Inn, Bramble Motel, Budget Host, Stage Stop Motel, Sundown Motel, Super 8, Super Saver Motel, Trails End Motel/rest., **other:** H, K-Mart, Peerless Tires
16	to Decker, Montana, port of entry
15mm	Tongue River
14	Acme Rd
9	US 14 W, Ranchester, **1mi S gas:** Big Country Oil/dsl, **other:** Western Motel, **other:** Foothills Campground, Lazy R Campground, to Yellowstone, Teton NPs, Conner Bfd NHS, Ski Area
1	Parkman
0mm	Wyoming/Montana state line

Assist A Fellow Traveler with...

Published annually,
the Next EXIT®
provides the best
USA Interstate Highway Information available.
Use this form to order another copy of the Next EXIT®
for yourself or someone special.

Please send ______ copies of the Next Exit® to the address below.
I've enclosed my check or money order for $20.95 US/$23.95 Canadian per copy.

Name: ____________________

Address: ____________________ Apt./Suite # ____________

City: ____________________ State: _____ Zip: ____________

THREE EASY ORDER OPTIONS:

1. ***MAIL ORDER FORM TO:***
   the Next EXIT®, Inc.
   PO Box 888
   Garden City, Utah 84028
2. ***ORDER ON THE WEB AT:***
   www.theNextExit.com
3. ***Give Us A Call & Use Your Charge Card***
   1-800-NEX-EXIT or 1-800-639-3948

the Next EXIT® is available online at: www.theNextExit.com
iPhone App FREE with your subscription.

the Next Exit Order Form